STAFF

Published by
Pokémon USA
1177 Avenue of the Americas
New York, NY 10036

Editor-in-Chief
Lawrence Neves

Editors
Kristina Naudus
Anthony Zumpano

Acknowledgements
Tony Davis
Colin Palmer
Yasuhiro Usui
Koji Kondo
Maya Nakamura
John Hershberger
Katherine Fang
Saiko Fujise-Kwee
Kaori Manabe
Ian Levenstein

Translation Services
Claire Samuels

Cover Design
Chris Brixey
Ray Yuen

Design & Production
Prima Games
Mario De Govia
Kate Abbott
Stephanie Sanchez
99 Lives Design, LLC
Emily Crowell
Oliver Crowell
Sonja Morris

ISBN: **978-0-7615-6208-5**
Library of Congress Catalog Card Number: **2009920742**
09 10 11 12 GG 10 9 8 7 6 5 4 3 2 1

Published in the United States using materials from *Pokémon Platinum Official Clear Guide*. Published in Japan 2008 by Media Factory, Inc.

Special Thanks to:
Editor: Shusuke Motomiya and ONEUP, Inc.
Design & Layout: RAGTIME CO., LTD. and SUZUKIKOUBOU, INC.

THE WORLD OF POKÉMON IS FILLED

The time has come for your first step into the world of Pokémon. What awaits you is an odyssey filled with heart-pounding adventure.

Piplup

Chimchar

Turtwig

You're joined on your quest by a Pokémon partner—only one at first, but as you keep throwing Poké Balls, you'll capture more and more new members to add to your entourage.

Dialga

Giratina
Origin Forme

Palkia

Your journey will expose you to unbelievable drama and the legendary VIPs of the Pokémon world. There will be challenges, but just gather up your courage and take them on. One day you can claim your seat as champion of the elite Pokémon League!

WITH DREAMS AND ADVENTURE

POKÉMON PLATINUM

Contents

Town and Route Locator

Special Sections

Recommended path

Here is the path we recommend to players in their grand adventure through the Sinnoh region. Check here when you want to see how you're doing, or you don't know what to do next.

1 Twinleaf Town — P.34
- Your rival comes up to 2F of your house
- Go to 2F of your rival's house

2 Route 201 — P.35
- Professor Rowan comes to meet you both
- Pick a starter Pokémon: Turtwig, Chimchar, or Piplup
- First battle with your rival

3 Twinleaf Town — P.34
- Mom gives you the Running Shoes

4 Route 201 — P.35
- Go with your rival to Lake Verity

5 Lake Verity — P.37
- Meet Cyrus

6 Sandgem Town — P.38
- Rowan's assistant brings you to the Pokémon lab
- Professor Rowan gives you the Pokédex
- Rowan's assistant shows you around town

7 Twinleaf Town — P.34
- Mom gives you the Journal
- Your rival's mom entrusts you with a Parcel for your rival

8 Route 202 — P.41
- Rowan's assistant gives you five Poké Balls

9 Jubilife City — P.42
- Meet International Police member Looker
- Looker gives you the Battle Recorder
- Find your rival at Trainer School and give him the Parcel
- Your rival gives you the Town Map
- Obtain three coupons by correctly answering the quizzes given by three clowns
- Trade the coupons for a Pokétch
- A fisherman gives you the Old Rod

10 Route 203 — P.45
- Second battle with your rival

11 Oreburgh Gate — P.46
- Man gives you HM06 Rock Smash

12 Oreburgh City — P.47
- The Wi-Fi Club and Wi-Fi Playroom open in the Pokémon Center basement
- Teala gives you the Pal Pad

13 Oreburgh Mine — P.50
- Talk to Oreburgh Gym Leader Roark

14 Oreburgh City — P.47

Gym Battle 1: Gym Leader Roark

15 Jubilife City — P.42
- The Global Terminal becomes accessible
- Meet Professor Rowan and Rowan's assistant again
- Team up with Rowan's assistant for a Tag Battle with Team Galactic
- A Jubilife TV employee gives you the Accessory Case
- You can now take photos of your Pokémon at Jubilife TV
- The Pokétch Company president gives you the Pokétch App Memo Pad

16 Route 204 — P.52

17 Ravaged Path — P.52

18 Route 204 — P.52
- First Double Trainer Battle

19 Floaroma Town — P.54
- The Pick a Peck of Colors Flower Shop employee gives you the Sprayduck Watering Can

20 Route 205 — P.56
- A little girl asks you to save her father

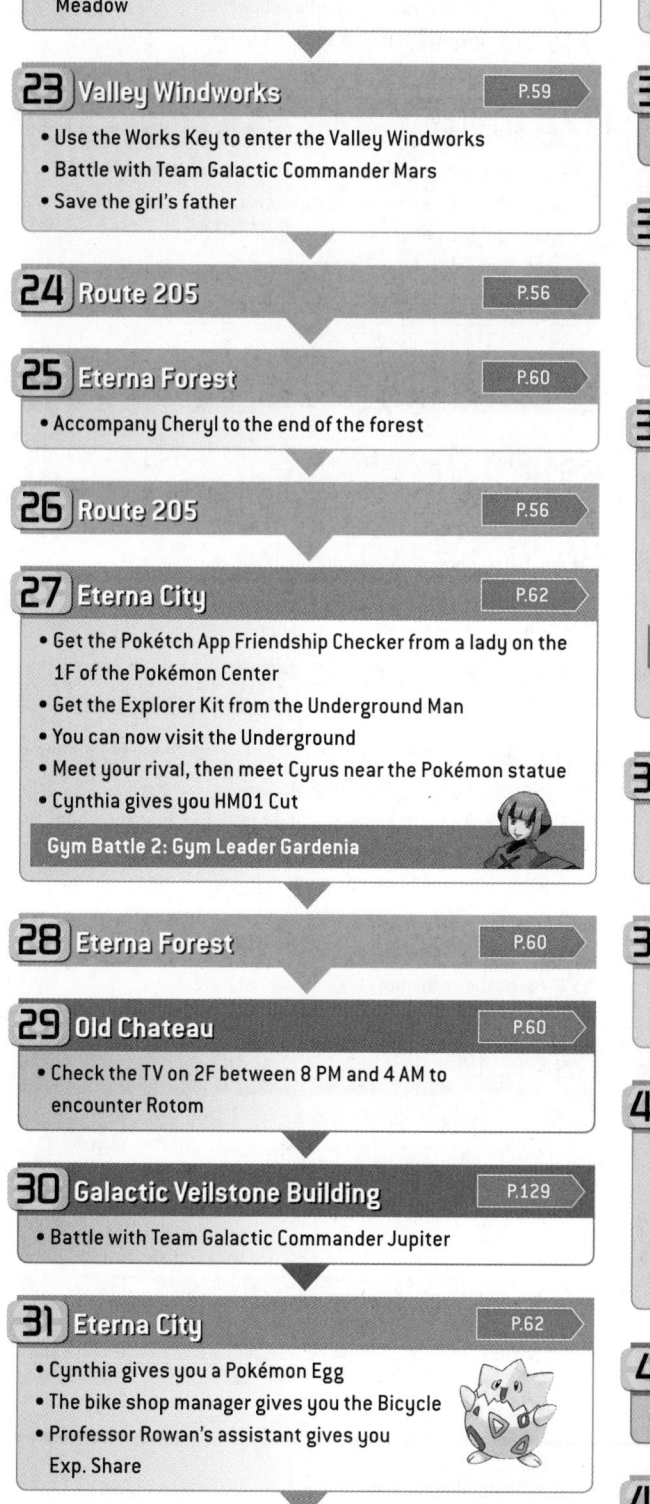

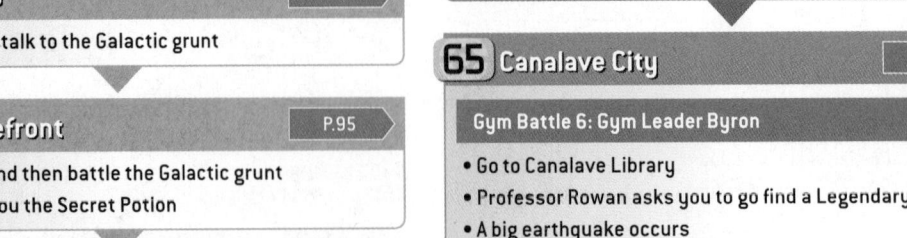

RECOMMENDED PATH

89 Sunyshore City P.146

- Elite Four member Flint tells you to challenge the Gym Leader to a match
- Talk to Gym Leader Volkner at the Vista Lighthouse
- Bring the boy in the house a Pokémon with a Serious Nature to get the Pokétch App Calendar
- Bring the boy a Pokémon with a Naive Nature to get the Pokétch App Dot Art
- Bring the boy a Pokémon with a Quirky Nature to get the Pokétch App Roulette

Gym Battle 8: Gym Leader Volkner

- Jasmine gives you HM07 Waterfall

90 Mt. Coronet (Middle) P.133

- Proceed to 4F(2) and get the Adamant Orb and the Lustrous Orb

91 Route 223 P.150

92 Victory Road P.151

93 Pokémon League P.153

- Sixth battle with your rival
- Battle the Elite Four and Pokémon League Champion Cynthia

After the Hall of Fame

1 Twinleaf Town P.34

- Check your Pokédex and get to 210 Pokémon seen

2 Sandgem Town P.38

- Professor Oak comes to the Pokémon lab
- Professor Oak upgrades your Sinnoh Pokédex to the National Pokédex
- Professor Rowan gives you the Poké Radar

3 Celestic Town P.108

- Talk to the elder, and she'll show you an antique book

4 Mt. Coronet (Middle) • Spear Pillar P.133

- Catch Dialga
- Catch Palkia

5 Pal Park P.40

- Professor Oak gives you the Pokétch App Poke Radar Counter
- Show Snorlax to the girl on 1F to get the Pokétch App Kitchen Timer
- Show Kecleon to the girl on 1F to get the Pokétch App Color Changer

6 Eterna City P.62

- Talk to Professor Oak in the house
- Catch the roving Zapdos
- Catch the roving Moltres
- Catch the roving Articuno

7 Canalave City P.112

- Go to the house of Eldritch the sailor and talk to the mom
- Talk to the sailor

8 Fullmoon Island P.163

- Approach Cresselia, and it starts to wander
- Get the Lunar Wing
- Catch the roving Cresselia

9 Canalave City P.112

- Go to Eldritch's house and talk to the boy

And the journey continues!

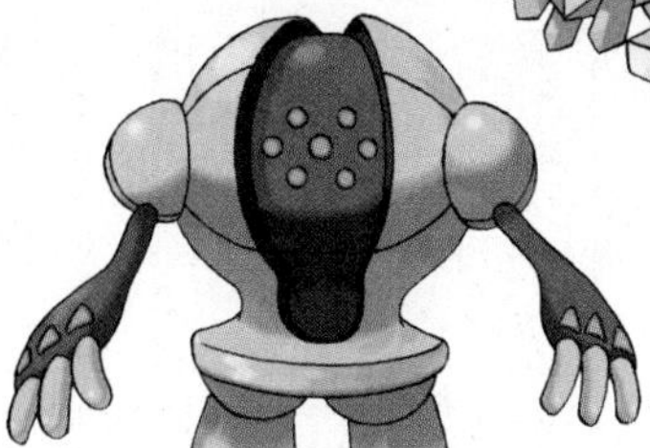

How to Use This Book

It's All Here!

Pokémon Trainer Primer
page 13

This section gathers all the basics concerning Pokémon and your Pokémon journey. Beginners to the Pokémon games should start here.

Sinnoh Walkthrough
page 33

Covers in detail everything from your departure from Twinleaf Town to your arrival at the Resort Area.

Pokémon Battle Seminar
page 185

Compiles information on how to win Pokémon battles, including how to raise strong Pokémon and how to use moves and Abilities.

Battle Frontier Walkthrough
page 199

Detailed information on the unique characteristics of each location, how to play there, how to progress through the Frontier Brains, and how to enjoy the Battle Frontier.

Pokémon Super Contest Guide
page 223

An easy-to-use guide that shows how to enjoy Pokémon Contests, which include competitions in Visual and Dance.

Underground Play Guide
page 239

A guide to the three components of underground play—Fossil Excavation, Secret Base, and Capture the Flag—along with handy examples.

Link Play Guide
page 251

Details the various modes of play available when you use the DS wireless connection or Nintendo Wi-Fi.

Sinnoh Pokédex Guide
page 259

Explains the best ways to find all 210 Pokémon that inhabit the Sinnoh region, so that you can complete your Sinnoh Pokédex.

National Pokédex Guide
page 369

An easy-to-use guide that shows how to catch the 482 Pokémon that hail from all around the world, so you can complete your National Pokédex.

Adventure Data List
page 521

A comprehensive list of key information in the game, from Pokémon moves and Abilities to item effects and locations.

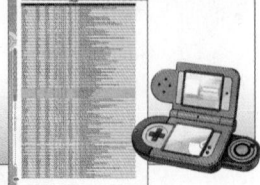

Pokémon Trainer Primer

RAISE YOUR POKÉMON WITH TLC

 ## There are many kinds of Pokémon

Pokémon are wondrous creatures. Much about their way of life is still a mystery to us. Wild Pokémon live in the fields and the seas, on grassy plains, and in dark, mysterious caves. Many Pokémon, however, live together in harmony with humans. New kinds of Pokémon are discovered every day; nobody knows how many there are in all.

 ## Acquire Pokémon

To reach the final goal of your adventure, you must catch Pokémon and use their powers. And for that, you must have a solid grasp on the different ways to get your own Pokémon.

• Primary ways of acquiring Pokémon

 Catch wild Pokémon

Wild Pokémon live in different areas, such as in the tall grasses along routes, inside caves, and in the ocean. Seek them out and catch them.

A wild STARLY appeared!

 Send a Pokémon into battle to evolve it

Some kinds of Pokémon can evolve into other kinds by building up their strength through battling. Many of a Pokémon's attributes can change upon evolving, including its name, appearance, and moves.

Max. HP	+ 3
Attack	+ 1
Defense	+ 1
Sp. Atk	+ 1
Sp. Def	+ 2
Speed	+ 1

PIPLUP grew to Lv. 8!

 Receive Pokémon at set events in the story

Search the towns for people in need. Help them and you might sometimes get a Pokémon Egg for your trouble. Make it a point to talk to townspeople!

I wanted you to have this Pokémon Egg. Will you accept it?

Trade Pokémon with a friend

Some elite Pokémon are nearly impossible to obtain through normal means. The best way to get one of these Pokémon is to trade with a friend.

 ## The more you battle, the stronger you get

If you send Pokémon out into battle, they get stronger and develop in amazing ways. They collect Exp. (experience) for every victory in battle. And when they have enough Exp., they level up, raising their stats. Raise your Pokémon with special care to make them strong.

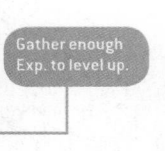

Gather enough Exp. to level up.

What will PSYDUCK do?

When the Exp. bar is full, it triggers a level-up.

14

Level up to evolve your Pokémon

Some Pokémon can evolve into other Pokémon. There are several different ways to evolve a Pokémon, but the most basic way is to battle and gain Exp.

GABITE is evolving!

• Evolution path: Gible

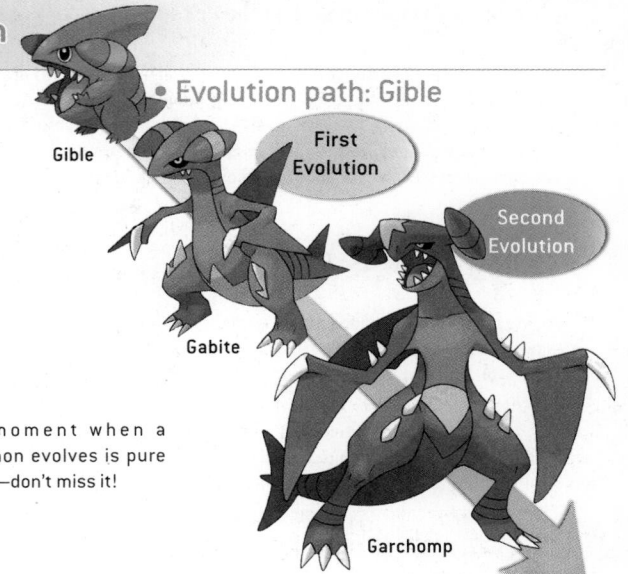

Gible

First Evolution

Second Evolution

Gabite

Garchomp

The moment when a Pokémon evolves is pure magic—don't miss it!

• Other primary ways of evolving Pokémon

Use a stone

Many stones, like the Moon Stone and the Thunderstone, contain hidden powers. Use one of these on a Pokémon to trigger an instantaneous Evolution.

Develop a friendship with the Pokémon

As you raise and care for a Pokémon, it can become more attached to you. Some Pokémon will evolve once their affection for you reaches a certain threshold.

It's quite friendly to you. It must be happy being with you.

Meet a certain condition

Some Pokémon will evolve if certain conditions are met, such as if you keep them in your party, or if they know a certain move while leveling up.

Trade with a friend

Some Pokémon evolve when they're traded. Some of them need an extra kick from items like Dragon Scale.

Catch wild Pokémon like a pro

Catching wild Pokémon definitely requires using a Poké Ball. But that won't be enough in most cases. Wild Pokémon are full of pep and can pop right out of a Poké Ball. There are three main ways to improve your chances.

• Primary ways of catching wild Pokémon

① Reduce the Pokémon's HP to the minimum

All wild Pokémon have HP, which is an indicator of the Pokémon's stamina. When its HP reaches 0, the Pokémon faints. To catch a Pokémon, you need to lower its HP by attacking it with battle moves. When the wild Pokémon's HP bar is red, that means it's weak. Use a Poké Ball then and your chances of a successful capture will be a lot higher.

Reduce its HP to the minimum.

2 Inflict a status ailment on the Pokémon

Pokémon can take on an abnormal status condition like Poison or Paralysis as a result of attacks used during battle (see page 23). Inflicting such a status condition on a Pokémon increases your chances of catching it. There are six kinds of status ailments. Sleep and Freeze will give the biggest assist to your capture. If you reduce the Pokémon's HP and give it a status ailment on top of that, you'll have the best chance of catching the Pokémon.

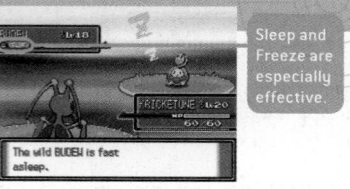

Sleep and Freeze are especially effective.

The wild BUDEW is fast asleep.

3 Pick the best Poké Ball for the job

There are many different kinds of Poké Balls. Each Poké Ball has unique characteristics that make it excel at catching different Pokémon. The Net Ball, for instance, has properties that allow it to catch Water- and Bug-type Pokémon with ease. Selecting the most effective Poké Ball for the Pokémon you want to catch is key.

Lucas used one Net Ball!

Use the best Poké Ball for each Pokémon

Fifteen different kinds of Poké Balls are featured in Pokémon Platinum. Each kind of ball has a particular effect depending on factors like the type of Pokémon it's used on or where it's used. Master them all and memorize them so that you can use the most effective Poké Ball in any given situation.

• 15 Types of Poké Balls

Poké Ball
Your standard-issue ball for catching Pokémon
• How to get
Sold from the beginning of the game

Great Ball
Better at catching Pokémon than the Poké Ball
• How to get
Sold once you have three Gym Badges

Ultra Ball
Better at catching Pokémon than the Great Ball
• How to get
Sold once you have five Gym Badges

Master Ball
The ultimate Poké Ball, capable of catching any Pokémon
• How to get
Receive from Team Galactic Boss Cyrus at Galactic Veilstone Building

Premier Ball
Same characteristics as a Poké Ball; received as a bonus
• How to get
Buy 10 Poké Balls at once
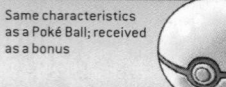

Heal Ball
A ball that restores the HP and status of the Pokémon caught inside it
• Sold at:
Jubilife City, Oreburgh City, etc.

Net Ball
A ball that excels at catching Bug- and Water-type Pokémon
• Sold at:
Oreburgh City, Solaceon Town, etc.

Dusk Ball
A ball that excels at catching Pokémon at night, in caves, and in similar low-light situations
• Sold at:
Solaceon Town, Pastoria City, etc.

Nest Ball
A ball that has a higher success rate on weaker Pokémon
• Sold at:
Eterna City, Hearthome City, etc.

Quick Ball
A ball that excels at catching Pokémon when thrown immediately at the start of battle
• Sold at:
Pastoria City, Celestic Town, etc.
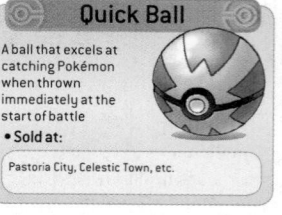

Timer Ball
A ball that is more effective the more turns have passed
• Sold at:
Celestic Town, Snowpoint City, etc.
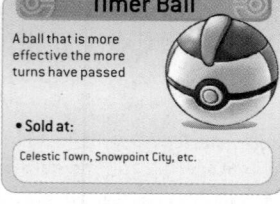

Repeat Ball
A ball with a higher success rate on Pokémon you've caught before
• Sold at:
Canalave City, Pokémon League
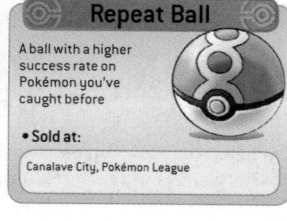

Dive Ball
A ball that excels at catching Pokémon underwater
• How to get
Working for the Pokémon News Press in Solaceon Town

Luxury Ball
A ball that endears you to the Pokémon you've just caught with it
• Sold at:
Pastoria City, Pokémon League

Safari Ball
A ball used only at the Great Marsh at Pastoria City
• How to get
Participate in the Safari Game at the Great Marsh at Pastoria City
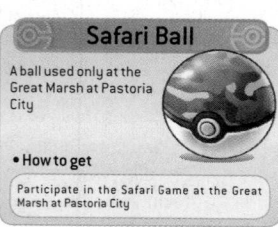

Pokémon can learn moves

Pokémon can learn a variety of moves that are useful in battle and on the field. There are over 380 moves in all; each has different effects and uses. It's through your choice of moves that your Pokémon's individual nature shines through.

Pokémon can learn up to four moves.

• Pokémon can use three different kinds of moves

Attack moves

These moves attack a foe in battle and inflict damage. But that's not all—there are many subcategories of moves that deal damage while also inflicting a status ailment like poison or burn, or that seize the initiative to attack first in a turn.

Defense moves

These moves can be useful when you're low on HP after a foe's attack. They can do many things, from recovering HP to healing your Pokémon's status. Some moves can even recover your Pokémon's HP while damaging the opponent, or recover a little bit of your Pokémon's HP each turn.

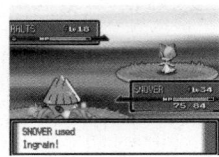

Assist moves

These moves can make your Pokémon stronger or your opponent weaker. They can do anything from increasing your Pokémon's stats to saddling the foe with a status ailment like poison or burn, or sapping HP from the foe over time. There are even moves that can force your opponent to switch Pokémon.

• Primary ways to teach a Pokémon a move

Level it up

Pokémon have moves tied to certain levels. When they reach those levels, they learn the move.

Use a TM

TMs (Technical Machines) are items that teach moves to Pokémon. Unfortunately, each one can be used only once.

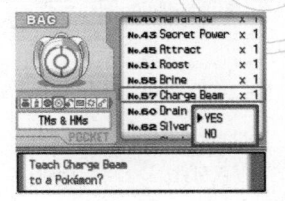

Use an HM

HMs (Hidden Machines) are items that contain special moves (see page 19). You can use a single HM to teach a move to as many Pokémon as you like.

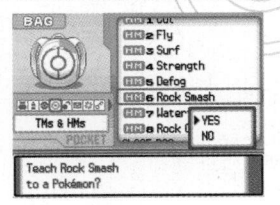

Have a person teach the move

You'll meet some people on your journey who can teach a move to a Pokémon. Be sure to learn all kinds of moves this way.

Different Pokémon have different Abilities

All Pokémon have different Abilities depending on which kind of Pokémon they are. For instance, Pikachu has the Ability Static. Some Abilities exert their effect in battle, and some are especially useful in catching wild Pokémon.

Some Pokémon can have one of two Abilities.

• Sample Abilities and their effects

Pickup

The Pokémon finds items during the battle. The items differ depending on the kind of battle (see page 561).

• Primary Pokémon with this Ability

Pachirisu, Munchlax, etc.

Insomnia

The Pokémon cannot fall asleep, even after being hit with moves like Sing, Grass Flute, or Sleep.

• Primary Pokémon with this Ability

Hoothoot, Noctowl, etc.

Sturdy

Makes the Pokémon immune to one-hit K.O. moves like Fissure, Sheer Cold, and Guillotine

• Primary Pokémon with this Ability

Geodude, Sudowoodo, etc.

Pokémon forge friendships with their Trainer

Pokémon have a bond of trust with their Trainer called Friendship. Make a Pokémon happy and it will increase its Friendship with you. Treat it poorly and it will decrease its Friendship.

• Primary ways to increase friendship

Travel with the Pokémon in your party

Add the Pokémon to your party to raise your Friendship with it. The longer you travel with it, the more attached to you it gets.

Catch the Pokémon using a Luxury Ball

Use a Luxury Ball to catch the Pokémon and it will be more friendly toward you than normal.

Give the Pokémon a Soothe Bell

Have the Pokémon hold a Soothe Bell to increase your Friendship with it. You can get the Soothe Bell from Cheryl in Eterna Forest.

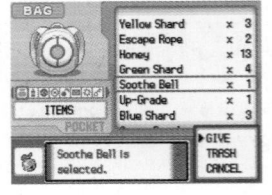

Give the Pokémon stat-boosting items

Give the Pokémon stat-boosting items like Protein or Zinc and you'll also boost its affection for you.

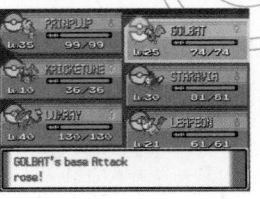

Pokémon have Natures

Each individual Pokémon has its own Nature. There are 25 different Natures in all. They affect different things, like which stats are raised upon leveling up.

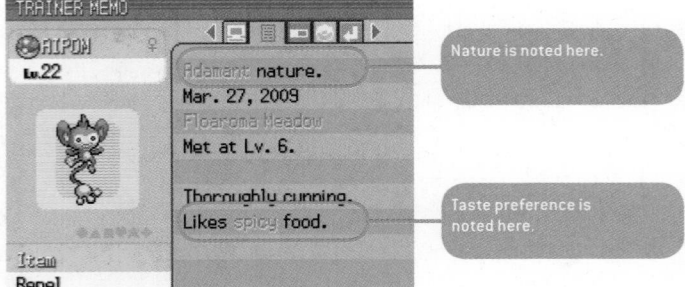

Nature is noted here.

Taste preference is noted here.

• Effects of different Natures

Stat increases are affected

When a Pokémon levels up, its HP and battle stats go up. The Pokémon's Nature affects the distribution of these stat increases.

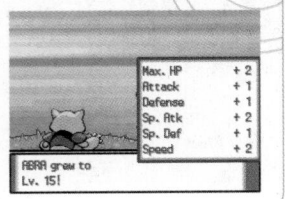

Effects of berries are altered

If you give a Pokémon a berry to hold, it can use the berry to heal itself. But if it doesn't care for the flavor, it will become confused.

The Pokémon's taste in Poffins is affected

Poffins are a kind of Pokémon food. Each Pokémon has its own particular taste in Poffins. Give a Pokémon a Poffin that it likes to make its condition easy to raise.

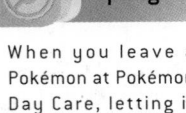

Offspring can inherit their parents' Natures

When you leave a Pokémon at Pokémon Day Care, letting it hold an Everstone will increase the chances of its offspring having the same Nature.

Everstone

See page 545 for more on Pokémon Natures.

Pokémon have unique personalities

Pokémon have personalities, just like you. These personalities are a clue as to which of the Pokémon's stats develops the highest. For instance, a Pokémon that has good endurance wil develop high Defense.

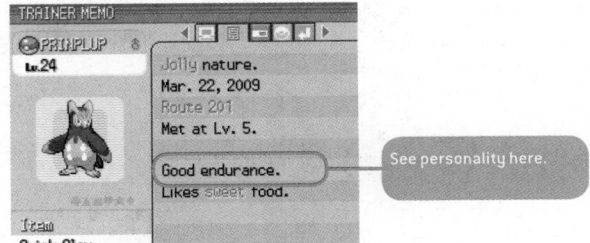

See personality here.

See page 545 for more on Pokémon personalities.

Pokémon can take their Trainers to all sorts of places

Some Pokémon moves are classified as HM moves. These moves capitalize on a Pokémon's particular powers to allow you access to areas on the field that you wouldn't be able to get to normally. You just need to have the right Gym Badge if you want to use a particular HM move.

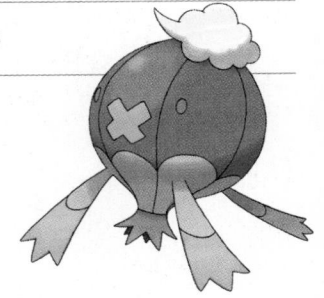

• HM moves that are useful on the field

⊙ HM 01 Cut

Cut chops down small trees that are blocking your path.

• How to get   From Cynthia in Eterna Forest

⊙ HM 02 Fly

Fly spirits you instantly to a town you've been to before, dropping you off in front of the Pokémon Center.

• How to get   Galactic Warehouse

POKÉMON TRAINER PRIMER

RAISE YOUR POKÉMON WITH TLC

HM 03 Surf

Surf allows you to move across bodies of water like oceans and lakes, ferrying you around freely.

- **How to get** — From the Celestic Town elder

HM 04 Strength

This move exerts incredible strength to move even the most heavily rooted rocks.

- **How to get** — From Riley at the Iron Island entrance

HM 05 Defog

Defog dispels mist blanketing an area, restoring visibility.

- **How to get** — Solaceon Ruins B4F 2

HM 06 Rock Smash

This move crushes troublesome rocks into gravel, clearing the path.

- **How to get** — From a man in Oreburgh City

HM 07 Waterfall

This move lets you scale waterfalls, allowing you access to the areas above.

- **How to get** — From Jasmine at Sunyshore City

HM 08 Rock Climb

With Rock Climb you can scale the rough walls of small mountains and hills.

- **How to get** — Route 217

Some regular moves can be used on the field as well

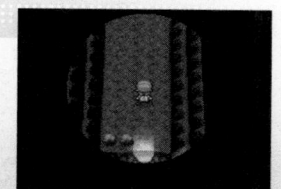

HMs can help you move around in routes and caves and other areas. But some regular moves perform similarly. For instance, Dig lets you escape from inside of a pit, and Flash illuminates the pitch-black cave below the Cycling Road. See page 534 for more such moves.

STRATEGY FOR WINNING BATTLES

Master the Pokémon types

Pokémon can be divided up into different types, such as Normal, Fire, Water, Grass, and many others. There are 17 types in all, and all Pokémon belong to at least one. Types play a huge part in determining the outcome of battles, so make sure they're working for you instead of against you.

• 17 Pokémon types in all

for example:

NORMAL	FIRE	WATER	GRASS	ELECTRIC	ICE	FIGHTING	POISON	GROUND
Bidoof	Chimchar	Piplup	Turtwig	Shinx	Snover	Riolu	Croagunk	Hippopotas

FLYING	PSYCHIC	BUG	ROCK	GHOST	DRAGON	DARK	STEEL
Chatot	Mr. Mime	Burmy (Plant Cloak)	Sudowoodo	Duskull	Gible	Houndour	Bronzor

Both Pokémon and moves have a type

Moves and Pokémon both have types. For instance, this Piplup is a Water-type Pokémon, but like most Pokémon, it can learn other types of moves as well.

• Example: Piplup

Pokémon type
WATER

Peck move type is
FLYING

• Move type affects attack

Piplup attacks the enemy Bidoof with a Flying-type move.

Attacks with Peck

• Pokémon type affects defense

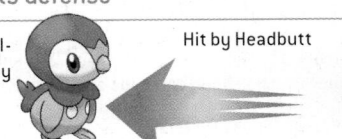

Piplup is hit by a Normal-type move from the enemy Bidoof.

Hit by Headbutt

Hit your enemy's weakness for an upset victory

All types are strong against some types and weak against other types. It's like a big game of rock-paper-scissors: Water is strong against Fire but weak against Grass. When you compare the type of the attacking Pokémon and the type of the defending Pokémon, it's called a type match-up. A good type match-up will deal twice as much damage as normal.

• Good type match-ups

Chimchar
FIRE

Turtwig
GRASS

Piplup
WATER

• A good match-up deals twice the damage!

Attacks with a Grass-type move

Turtwig
GRASS

Piplup
WATER

The attack deals double damage since it's a good match-up.

• A bad match-up deals half the damage.

Attacks with a Grass-type move

Turtwig
GRASS

Chimchar
FIRE

The damage is halved because it's a bad match-up.

Use multipliers to maximize damage

If everything works out right, your attack can deal more than 1.5 times as much damage as it normally would. And the more damage you deal, the closer you are to victory. Several factors can increase the damage you deal:

• Primary ways to increase damage

1 **Use a move with the same type as your Pokémon**

When your Pokémon and its move are of the same type, the move deals 1.5 times the regular amount of damage.

Damage
1.5x

2 **Attack with a move that your enemy is weak against**

When your move is a type that the enemy Pokémon is weak against, the move deals twice the normal amount of damage.

Damage
2x

3 **Score a critical hit**

Sometimes a move will score a critical hit, dealing twice the regular amount of damage.

Damage
2x

• Battle messages tell you how much damage is inflicted

Message	Match-up	Damage
It's super effective!	Good	2-4x
It's not very effective...	Bad	Half
(No message)	Normal	Normal
It doesn't affect....	Very bad	No damage
Critical hit	—	2x

The six stats that determine strength

Each Pokémon has a set of stats like Attack and Defense. There are six stats in all, and the numbers indicate how strong the Pokémon is in that area. Raising a powerful Pokémon demands careful attention to how these stats operate.

• The six Pokémon stats

HP

The Pokémon's stamina: If the Pokémon is attacked and its HP reaches 0, the Pokémon faints.

Speed

The speed of the Pokémon's attacks: The higher this number, the more likely the Pokémon is to attack before its opponent.

Physical stats

Attack

The higher this number, the greater the damage the Pokémon deals in physical attacks.

Defense

The higher this number, the less damage the Pokémon receives from physical attacks.

Special stats

Sp. Attack

The higher this number, the greater the damage the Pokémon deals in special attacks.

Sp. Defense

The higher this number, the less damage the Pokémon receives from special attacks.

Moves can affect stats

Moves can be classified as one of three types: physical, special, or status. All these types of moves are inextricably bound to the Pokémon's stats. For instance, if you have a Pokémon with a high Attack stat, teaching it physical moves is a sure way to inflict lots of damage.

• The three kinds of moves

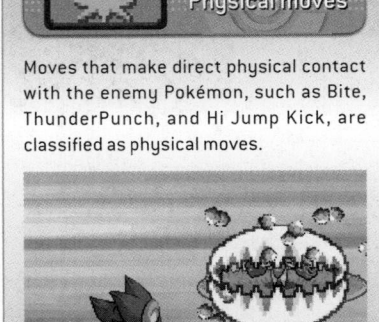

Physical moves

Moves that make direct physical contact with the enemy Pokémon, such as Bite, ThunderPunch, and Hi Jump Kick, are classified as physical moves.

LUXRAY used Crunch!

Special moves

Moves that don't make direct physical contact with the enemy, such as Discharge, Ember, and BubbleBeam, are considered special moves.

LUXRAY used Discharge!

Status moves

Status moves are moves, such as Swagger, that alter the stats or condition of your Pokémon or the enemy Pokémon.

LUXRAY used Swagger!

Inflicting status ailments can pave your way to victory

When a Pokémon has a special condition like poison or sleep, that's called a status condition or ailment. Status conditions can affect a Pokémon in various ways, from reducing its HP to making it unable to act. You can use moves to inflict status ailments on your opponent and turn the tide of battle in your favor.

The wild CHATOT is hurt by poison!

Status ailments can have dramatic effects

Make sure to try out these moves and see their effects for yourself.

• The six kinds of Pokémon status ailments

Poison

Drains HP on every turn. Does not heal automatically during battle.

Effect Lowers foe's HP.

Paralysis

Lowers the Pokémon's Speed and has a 25 percent chance of preventing it from attacking. Does not heal automatically during battle.

Effect Makes it harder for the foe to damage you, and makes it easier for you to strike first.

Burn

Lowers the Pokémon's Attack and then drains HP on each turn. Does not heal automatically during battle.

Effect Lowers the foe's HP and lowers its Attack slightly.

Sleep

Makes the Pokémon unable to attack. Goes away on its own after a few turns.

Effect Protects you from being attacked by the foe, letting you attack with impunity.*

Freeze

Makes the Pokémon unable to attack. Goes away on its own after a few turns.

Effect Protects you from being attacked by the foe, letting you attack with impunity.

Confuse

Makes the Pokémon prone to attacking itself. Goes away on its own after a few turns.

Effect Makes it difficult for the foe to attack you and lowers its HP.

*The moves Sleep Talk and Snore are exceptions.

Some useful afflictions that are similar to status ailments

Some moves inflict statuses that are similar to status conditions. These effects can be stacked with status ailments. In other words, a Pokémon can suffer from both poison and attract at the same time.

Curse
Affected Pokémon loses 25 percent of its max HP every turn.

Attract
Affected Pokémon finds it harder to attack a foe of the opposite gender.

Flinch
Affected Pokémon is unable to attack during that turn.

Leech Seed
Lowers HP every turn and transfers it to the enemy Pokémon.

Guidelines for stacking status conditions

1. Pokémon can suffer only one status ailment at a time, except for Confuse.
2. These other status afflictions can be combined.

Make the most of Pokémon Abilities

Abilities are special characteristics that are unique to each Pokémon. Many Abilities can turn the tide of battle in your favor. Master them and their various effects and you can combine them skillfully with moves.

The foe's GYARADOS's Intimidate cuts PRINPLUP's

Abilities have a significant effect on battles.

• Starter Pokémon Abilities

Overgrow
Makes Grass-type moves 1.5 times as powerful when Turtwig's HP is below 33 percent.

Turtwig

Blaze
Makes Fire-type moves 1.5 times as powerful when Chimchar's HP is below 33 percent.

Chimchar

Torrent
Makes Water-type moves 1.5 times as powerful when Piplup's HP is below 33 percent.

Piplup

• Some useful battle Abilities

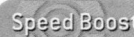

Speed Boost
Raises Speed by 1 each turn during battle.

• Held mainly by:
Yanma, Yanmega, etc.

Levitate
Makes Pokémon immune to Ground-type moves.

• Held mainly by:
Duskull, Chingling, etc.

Poison Point
If attacked directly, the user has a 30 percent chance of counterattacking with poison.

• Held mainly by:
Budew, Roselia, etc.

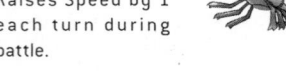

Give Pokémon items to hold

Pokémon can hold a single item at a time. Some items can be exceptionally useful and can be the cornerstone of your battle strategy. For instance, if your Pokémon holds the Shell Bell, it will recover 1/8 the HP that it inflicts on a foe.

MUNCHLAX restored a little HP using its Shell Bell!

• Some useful battle items

 Shell Bell
Recovers 1/8 the HP that the user inflicts.

 Leftovers
Restores a little bit of HP each turn.

 Quick Claw
Raises your chance of striking first.

 Lum Berry
Cures status conditions.

 Focus Band
Sometimes lets the Pokémon hang on with 1 HP remaining.

 Amulet Coin
Doubles the battle prize money, even if you call the Pokémon back.

USE YOUR TOOLS AND ITEMS

 **Bag**

Your bag is where you put all the items you acquire on your journey. To makes things easier to find, the bag has eight pockets into which all items are automatically sorted according to category—like Items, Key Items, TMs, and Poké Balls.

Boy's Bag

Girl's Bag

 ### Register commonly-used items

Some items you'll use over and over again, like the Bicycle or the Fishing Rod. Register such an item and you can use it with just a press of the Y button. This lets you breeze along on your journey without having to root through your bag.

How do I register an item?

Put the cursor over the item and press the A button, then select Register.

 ### Organize your items

The more items you accumulate, the harder it'll get to find the one you need. When you're overwhelmed by items, try organizing your bag. If you get your Potions, Super Potions, and Hyper Potions in a row, it'll be easy to find the right one for the task at hand.

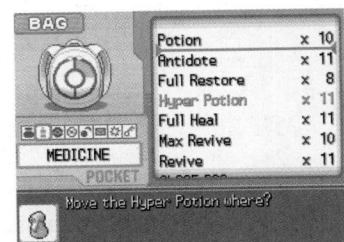

How do I organize my items?

Move the cursor over an item and press Select, and then you can change the item's position freely.

• Some useful travel items

 Poké Ball

An item for catching Pokémon. Look up the various kinds of Poké Balls on page 16 to be sure you use the right one for the right Pokémon.

 Potion

An item for healing your Pokémon. Go shopping and stock yourself with several different kinds of Potions so you'll have one to restore just the amount you need at any time.

 Status-healing items

An item that cures Pokémon of status conditions. Equip yourself with lots of different kinds so that you can address any ailment.

 PP-restoratives

PP is the indicator of how many times a Pokémon can use a move. There are several different PP-restoring items. They are critical items, so use them with care.

 Repel

This allows you to avoid encounters with Pokémon that are at a lower level than yours. Use it when you're in a hurry to get to your destination.

 Escape Rope

This item returns you instantly to the entrance of a cave. It's very useful when you're deep in a cave and your Pokémon are badly injured.

Pokédex

The Pokédex is an item that automatically records information about Pokémon. Whenever you encounter a Pokémon in the wild or in a Trainer Battle, an entry for that Pokémon is recorded under "Seen." The entry includes name, appearance, and habitat. When you acquire a Pokémon, a more detailed entry is made under "Obtained."

• The course of recording a Pokémon in the Pokédex

1 No pre-existing entry

An entry is left open for each Pokémon you haven't encountered yet. There's no name or picture; all you can see is the number.

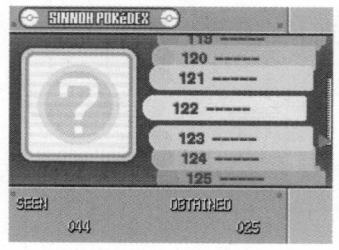

2 Appearance and habitat recorded

A Pokémon's name and appearance are recorded upon your meeting it in the wild or in a Trainer Battle. If it's a wild Pokémon, its habitat will be recorded too.

3 All attributes recorded

Only once you have acquired the Pokémon are its type, size, weight, and other attributes recorded. This is the complete entry for a Pokémon.

• Other basic functions.

Area

Shows the Pokémon's habitat. Move the sun on the Touch Screen to see morning, midday, and nighttime habitats.

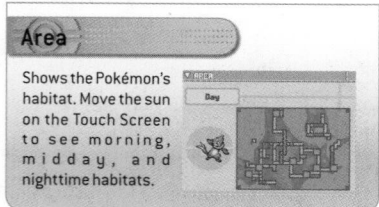

Cry

Listen to the Pokémon's cry. You can add aural effects like chorus and panning.

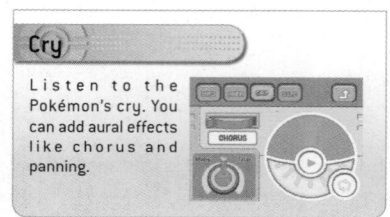

Size

Shows the size of the Pokémon's body as compared to the main character's.

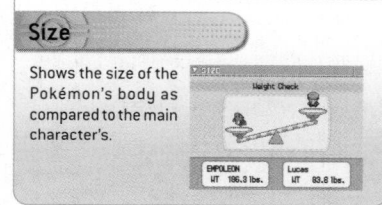

Forms

Lets you observe differences in appearance between gender or region.

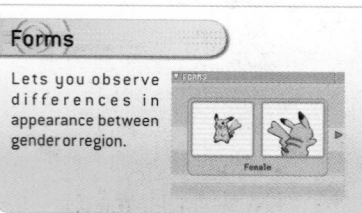

Sort Functions

Sort Pokédex entries by number, alphabetical order, weight, etc.

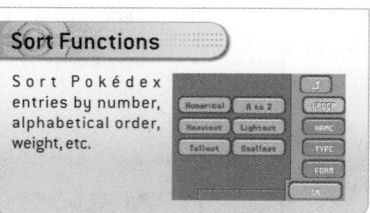

The Bicycle

The Bicycle is a highly useful item that lets you move around a lot faster than the Running Shoes. The newest feature on the Bicycle is a gearshift. Press B to shift between 3rd and 4th gear. It's easier to maneuver in 3rd gear, but 4th lets you cross things like flowing sand slopes.

• Terrain crossable only by Bicycle

Sandy Slopes

Your feet sink into the sand, making these hills impossible to climb on foot. But you can clear them by setting the Bicycle to 4th gear and getting a running start.

Jump Stand

If you stumble across annoying boulders sticking out of the ground in caves, shift to 4th gear and get a good running start, and you can sail over two units of terrain.

Narrow Bridge

Ribbon-thin bridges that connect two areas of land. They are just wide enough to allow passage by Bike, using either gear setting.

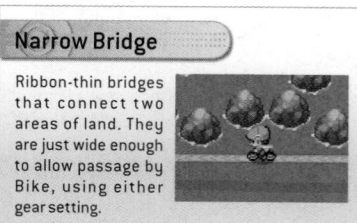

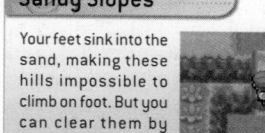

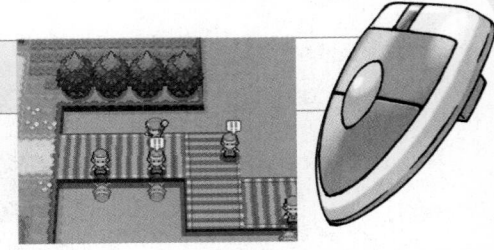

Vs. Seeker

Some Trainers will want a rematch after you've battled them once. The Vs. Seeker is an item that finds these Trainers for you. When you're wandering in the field, a cave, or anywhere else, the Vs. Seeker will mark these Trainers with a "!!" over their heads, so you can challenge them to the rematch.

Take 100 steps to recharge

The Vs. Seeker is rechargeable. Using it once depletes the charge, so you can't keep using it several times in a row. The charge builds up gradually as you walk around. After 100 steps, it's fully charged again.

Number of steps required to fully charge the battery: 30

Check your steps as you go

Use the Battle Searcher while it's recharging to see how many more steps you have to go in order to finish charging it.

Trainers get stronger

Pokémon Trainers get stronger each time you face them again, so do your homework on their strategy and their Pokémon. Make these rematches as beneficial to you as possible.

This karate man hasn't forgotten being pulverized by you!

Fun with battles

The Trainers' dialogue changes each time you re-challenge them, adding something else to look forward to.

Vs. Recorder

The Vs. Recorder is a completely new item that debuts in Pokémon Platinum. It can make one recording of a link battle or a Battle Frontier battle. You can then take that battle recording and post it at the Battle Video Corner on the third floor of the Global Terminal. Up to three battle recordings from other Trainers can also be saved there.

• The Vs. Recorder's three functions

Record battles

At the end of some battles, like link battles and Frontier Brain battles at the Battle Frontier, the Vs. Recorder will present you with the option of recording the preceding battle. Select "Yes" to save the battle data.

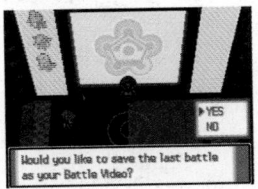

Would you like to save the last battle as your Battle Video?

Post the battle

At the Battle Video Corner on the third floor of the Global Terminal, you can post your own battle videos for other trainers to see. You can only save one of your own videos there at a time.

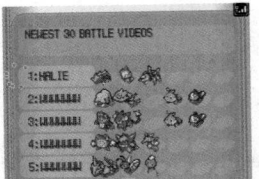

Watch battle videos

At the Battle Video Corner on the third floor of the Global Terminal, you can also watch videos posted by other Trainers. You can save up to three videos from other Trainers on your own Vs. Recorder.

The foe's ARBOK used Poison Fang!

Pokétch

The Pokémon Watch, or Pokétch for short, is a high-end miniaturized computer. You use it by wearing it on your wrist like a watch. You can add functions to the Pokétch by loading applications called Pokétch Apps. Starting with the Pokétch Company in Jubilife City, you can get Apps from all sorts of people, and keep evolving the functionality of your Pokétch as you travel.

Boy's Model

Girl's Model

• Pokétch Apps

1 Digital Watch

A digital watch featuring Pikachu. The watch is synched to the internal clock in your DS, and displays the time in a 24-hour format.

• How to obtain

Comes with the Pokétch

2 Calculator

A 10-digit calculator. Enter a Pokémon's National Pokédex number and press "=" to hear the Pokémon's cry.

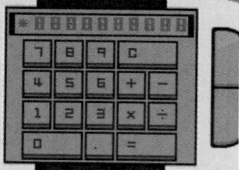

• How to obtain

Comes with the Pokétch

3 Memo Pad

Click on the pencil and eraser icons, and write and erase notes using the DS Stylus.

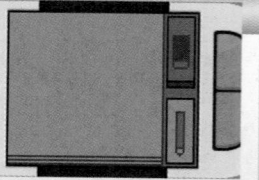

• How to obtain

Receive from the Pokétch Company president at the Pokétch Company in Jubilife City after winning the Oreburgh City Gym battle

4 Pedometer

Clocks how many steps you've taken, even including the amount of steps used by riding the Bicycle or surfing.

• How to obtain

Comes with the watch

5 Pokémon List

Displays at a glance the HP of the Pokémon in your party. Displays an icon to the right of the Pokémon if it's holding an item.

• How to obtain

Comes with the Pokétch

6 Friendship Checker

Check your Friendship with a Pokémon by seeing how it responds when you tap it with the stylus.

• How to obtain

Receive from a girl on the first floor of the Pokémon Center in Eterna City

7 Dowsing Machine

Uncovers items on the field that are invisible to the naked eye. Displays the location of found items on the screen.

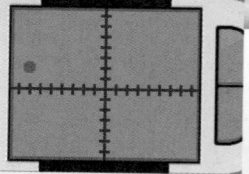

• How to obtain

Receive from Rowan's assistant on Route 207 after you acquire the Bicycle

8 Berry Searcher

Displays a berry marker to let you know when a berry plant has matured and borne fruit.

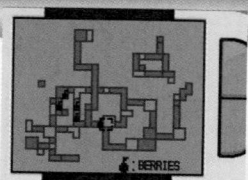

• How to obtain

Receive from the girl in the berry man's house along Route 208

9 Day Care Checker

Lets you see Pokémon you've left at the Pokémon Day Care. Also displays an Egg if one has been discovered.

• How to obtain

Receive from the boy at the Pokémon Day Care in Solaceon Town after checking in

10 Pokémon History

Displays your 12 most recent Pokémon in reverse chronological order. Tap a Pokémon to hear its cry.

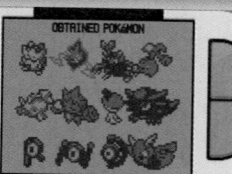

• How to obtain

Receive from a boy in Solaceon Town

11 Counter

Counts and displays the number of times you press the plus sign. Can be used for any variety of purposes.

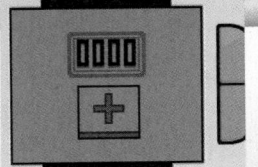

• How to obtain

Receive from the receptionist on the second floor of the Veilstone Department Store in Veilstone City

12 Analog Watch

Just like the Digital Watch, this analog clock is synched to your Nintendo DS's internal clock.

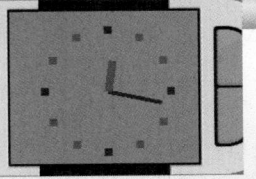

• How to obtain

Receive from a boy in a private house in Celestic Town

13 Marking Map

You can slide the six different symbols around this map to wherever you like. Use the symbols to mark locations.

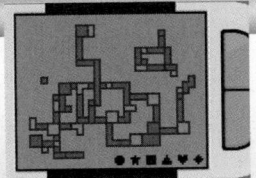

• How to obtain

Receive from the Pokétch Company president at the Pokétch Company in Jubilife City after winning the Hearthome Gym battle

14 Link Searcher

Finds players currently engaged in wireless play like the Union Room, Underground, and Colosseum.

• How to obtain

Receive from the Pokétch Company president at the Pokétch Company in Jubilife City after winning the Pastoria Gym battle

15 Coin Toss

Tap the screen to flip a Magikarp coin and see which side it lands on. Useful for a wide variety of purposes.

• How to obtain

Receive from a boy in the cottage along Route 213 after winning the Snowpoint City Gym battle

16 Move Tester

Enter the type of your move and of your opponent's move, and you can see if it's a good or bad type match-up.

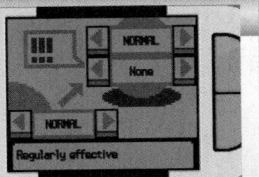

• How to obtain

Receive from the Pokétch Company president at the Pokétch Company in Jubilife City after winning the Snowpoint City Gym battle

17 Calendar

A one-month calendar. The current date is outlined. You can also mark a future date.

• How to obtain

Receive after showing a Pokémon with a Serious Nature to a boy in a private house in Sunyshore City

18 Dot Artist

Make your own dot art on this 24 x 20 grid—the amount of pressure you apply determines the dot thickness.

• How to obtain

Receive after showing a Pokémon with Naive Nature to a boy in a private house in Sunyshore City

19 Roulette

You can customize this roulette wheel by drawing or writing on it with the stylus.

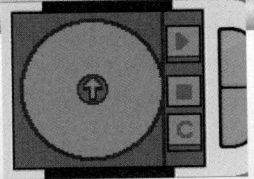

• How to obtain

Receive after showing a Pokémon with a Quirky Nature to a boy in a private house in Sunyshore City

20 Trainer Counter

Displays your top three most-often encountered, defeated, and captured Pokémon using the Poké Radar.

• How to obtain

Receive from Professor Oak at Pal Park along Route 221

MASTER ITEM USE

21 Kitchen Timer

This Snorlax-faced timer can count down from up to 99 minutes and 59 seconds. When it runs down, Snorlax alerts you by drumming on its stomach.

• How to obtain

Receive after showing Snorlax to a girl on the first floor of Pal Park, along Route 221

22 Color Changer

Use the touch slider to choose from among eight colors and change the color of the lower screen. The design is based on Kecleon.

• How to obtain

Receive after showing Kecleon to a girl on the first floor of Pal Park, along Route 221

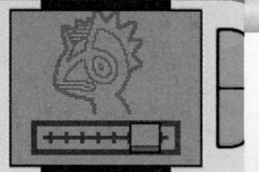

23 Match-up Checker

Before dropping off a pair of Pokémon at Pokémon Day Care, check the heart markers here to see how likely they are to produce a Pokémon Egg.

• How to obtain

Receive after you catch more than five Pokémon in one go at the Great Marsh at Pastoria City

USING TOWN SHOPS AND SERVICES

 Pokémart

The Pokémart is a shop that sells all kinds of items and goods that are essential to your progress in the game. The shop expands its offerings as you win Gym battles. There are two cashiers. The one on the right sells items that can be found in any town; the one on the left sells goods unique to that location. Talk to the other people in the Pokémart and you can sometimes gather valuable information.

• Items Sold at the Pokémart and How to Obtain Them

Items	Price	Condition	Explanation
Poké Ball	200P		Item for catching wild Pokémon
Great Ball	600P	▲	A more effective Poké Ball
Ultra Ball	1200P	■	More effective than the Great Ball
Potion	300P		Restores 20 HP to a Pokémon
Super Potion	700P	●	Restores 50 HP to a Pokémon
Hyper Potion	1200P	■	Restores 200 HP to a Pokémon
Max Potion	2500P	◆	Completely restores a Pokémon's HP
Full Restore	3000P	✳	Completely restores a Pokémon's HP and status

Items	Price	Condition	Explanation
Revive	1500P	▲	Revives a fainted Pokémon and restores half its HP
Antidote	100P		Heals Poison
Paralyz Heal	200P		Heals Paralysis
Awakening	250P	●	Heals Sleep
Burn Heal	250P	●	Heals Burn
Ice Heal	250P	●	Heals Frozen
Full Heal	600P	■	Heals all status ailments
Escape Rope	550P	●	Returns you instantly to the entrance of caves, etc.
Repel	350P	●	Shields you from encountering wild Pokémon for 100 paces
Super Repel	500P	▲	Shields you from encountering wild Pokémon for 200 paces
Max Repel	700P	■	Shields you from encountering wild Pokémon for 250 paces

Conditions for sale

None	Sold from the beginning of the game	■	After winning Pastoria Gym battle (5 badges)
●	After winning Oreburgh Gym battle (1 badge)	◆	After winning Snowpoint Gym battle (7 badges)
▲	After winning Hearthome Gym battle (3 badges)	✱	After winning Sunyshore Gym battle (8 badges)

 ## Pokémon Centers

Pokémon Centers are institutions set up to support Pokémon Trainers. Each center is three stories tall. The first floor is the main Pokémon Center, where you can heal your Pokémon. The second floor is where you can use the DS's wireless connection to trade or battle. The basement is where you can use the DS's Wi-Fi connection to trade or battle distant friends.

2F Pokémon Wireless Club

The Pokémon Wireless Club is where you can trade or battle wirelessly. The Pokémon Communication Club Colosseum is a place for you to participate in real Pokémon battles. In the Union Room, you and a group of friends can trade Pokémon or exchange records. At the desk on the far left, you can add your own signature to your Trainer Card.

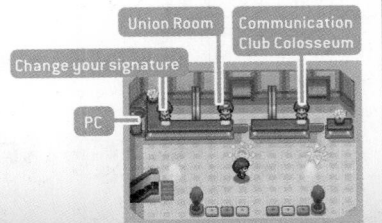

1F Pokémon Center

Hand over your Pokémon at the Pokémon Center, and their HP, PP, and status will be completely healed. You can also use the PC next to reception to store Pokémon or withdraw them from storage. The Pokémon Center is often full of other people you can talk to for helpful information or challenge to battle.

B1F Pokémon Wi-Fi Club

You can use the Nintendo DS's Wi-Fi connection to trade, battle, and more, with friends from all around the country. To use the Wi-Fi Club, first you need the Pal Pad. Tell your friends your Friend Code, and have them tell you theirs. If you use the Wi-Fi Playroom, though, you can join together without having to use any Friend Codes (p. 256).

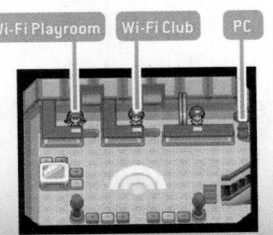

How to Read this Guide

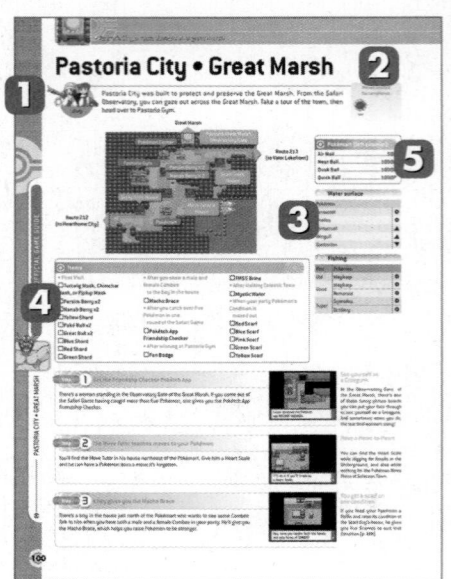

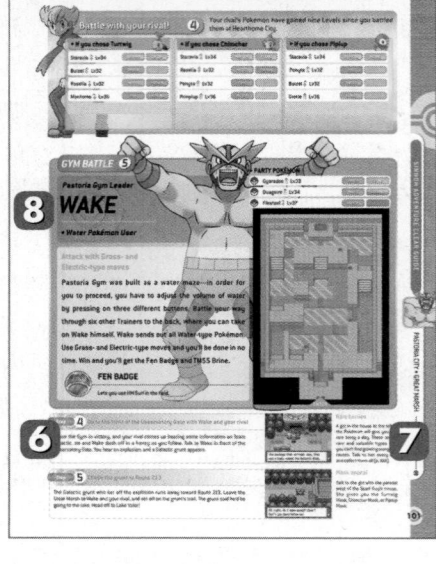

SINNOH WALKTHROUGH

HOW TO READ SINNOH ADVENTURE STRATEGY GUIDE

1 Story

A rundown of the features of the location, along with what you can expect to happen there.

2 Moves you need to get around

These icons show you which HMs you need to access the entire area and collect all the items available.

| Rock Smash | Cut | Defog | Surf | Strength | Rock Climb | Waterfall |

3 Wild Pokémon encounters

Shows which Pokémon appear in the area, when they appear, and other relevant information.

Appearance Probability

◎	Often	○	Normally
△	Rarely	▲	Hardly at all

Time of appearance

M	Morning (4 AM - 10 AM)
A	Afternoon (10 AM - 8 PM)
N	Night (8 PM - 4 AM)

Fishing rod types

Old	Old Rod
Good	Good Rod
Super	Super Rod

4 Items

Shows you the items you can find when exploring the area. Also explains if there are any conditions for finding them.

5 Pokémart

Shows you the items sold by the salesperson on the left side of the Pokémart in this town.

6 Steps to clear the area

A detailed rundown of the order of events and special conditions you'll need to know in order to experience everything there is to see in the area. Use this with the Basic Walkthrough on page 6, and you're good to go!

7 Other details

Any other information or special points that would be useful to this area.

8 Gym battles

Everything you need to know before you head into the Gym battle, from Gym specialties to the types of Pokémon the Gym Leader uses.

This book is written assuming you've picked a boy as your character, but everything applies to the girl character as well.

Sinnoh
Walkthrough

Twinleaf Town

Story

After watching the television special "Ask Professor Rowan!" you head downstairs to find that your mother has a message for you. Your friend and rival showed up earlier, so you should head over to his house to see what he wants.

Moves needed for completion

Surf

Route 201 (to Lake Verity)

Rival's House

Your House

Main character (boy)

🔘 Items

- Once you've been to Route 201
- ☐ **Running Shoes**
- After getting the Pokédex
- ☐ **Journal**
- ☐ **Parcel**

🔘 Water surface

Pokémon	
Psyduck	◎
Golduck	○

🔘 Fishing

Rod	Pokémon	
Old	Magikarp	◎
Good	Magikarp	◎
	Goldeen	◎
Great	Gyarados	◎
	Seaking	◎

Main character (girl)

Step 1 Your rival visits your house

Once you finish watching TV, your rival pops in, giddy with excitement. Professor Rowan has invited both of you to his lab to choose a Pokémon! After chatting a bit, your rival will head back home to get ready for his trip.

Oh, right, right! He're going to go see Prof. Rowan and get some Pokémon.

Television special "Ask Professor Rowan!"

Jubilife TV broadcasts this program nationwide. On your journey, you'll even get to visit Jubilife TV, an exciting opportunity for a dedicated fan like you!

Step 2 When Trainers collide

When you walk up to your rival's door, he bursts out, turns back for something he forgot, then takes off again! Just talk to his mother to find out where he's headed—Route 201.

Hey! I'm going to see Prof. Rowan! You should come, too! And quickly!

A Wii video game console

The video game console in the hero's room is a Nintendo Wii! Wonder what kind of games the hero likes to play?

Step 3 Head for Route 201

Hiya, Lucas. You're looking for John?

Route 201 is north of Twinleaf Town. It's a short walk to where your rival waits, wondering what took you so long to find him.

After you've been to Route 201 — Get the Running Shoes from your mom

Go home and tell your mom what happened on Route 201. If you've already received your Pokémon from Professor Rowan, Mom tells you to thank him. After you do that, she'll give you the Running Shoes. These stylish kicks let you dash when you press the B button.

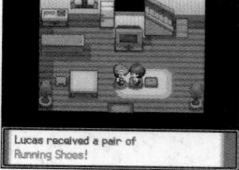

Lucas received a pair of Running Shoes!

SINNOH WALKTHROUGH

TWINLEAF TOWN

After you've been to Route 201

Follow your rival to Route 201

After you have the Running Shoes, head to your rival's house—except he's not there. His mom will tell you he headed back to Route 201. He never really stays in one place long, does he? Don't get left behind—head after him!

Focus on the flickering TV

Tune in to a blinking television to get the skinny on shops, institutions, and what other Trainers are up to. Talk to the reporter in Jubilife City and even you'll get some airtime.

After you get the Pokédex

Get the Journal from your mom

Once you get the Pokédex from Professor Rowan in Sandgem Town, go talk to your mom. She's thrilled you've been given such an important job, and in celebration she'll give you a special gift—the Journal, which records everything that happens on your journey.

Information everywhere

There are plenty of places to read about Pokémon basics—check out the PC on your desk, other PCs you encounter, and even posters on walls.

After you get the Pokédex

A Parcel for your rival

Once your mom gives you the Journal, your rival's mom shows up with a gift for her own kid. Unfortunately, he already left on his journey, so she's counting on you to bring it to him in Jubilife City.

Get schooled about Pokémon

Before you leave, check the PC on the desk in your rival's room for essential information like "The X Button opens the menu!" and "Record your progress with SAVE."

After you get the Pokédex

Follow your rival to Jubilife City

Jubilife City is north of Sandgem Town. On the way you'll run into a lot of wild Pokémon and Pokémon Trainers fixing for a battle. Prepare for the journey by talking to your mom at home to get your Pokémon's HP and PP replenished first.

• The road connecting Twinleaf Town, Lake Verity, and Sandgem Town

Route 201 • Verity Lakefront

Story

You and your rival start walking along Route 201 to see Professor Rowan in Sandgem Town, but just as you're about to enter the tall grass, the Professor himself appears behind you.

Lake Verity
• Route 201

Sandgem Town

• Verity Lakefront
Twinleaf Town

Items

• After Lake Verity

☐ Potion

Tall grass

Pokémon	M	A	N
Starly	◎	◎	◎
Bidoof	◎	◎	◎
Kricketot	○	X	○

Starly

NORMAL FLYING

Ability
• Keen Eye

Kricketot

BUG

Ability
• Shed Skin

Step 1 — Receive a Pokémon from Professor Rowan

Rowan will ask the two of you if you like Pokémon—answer yes, and his assistant Dawn/Lucas will open up his suitcase so you can pick your first Pokémon. Choose wisely!

Go on! Open the briefcase and choose a Pokémon!

The assistant's gender

If you choose the boy as your main character, Professor Rowan's assistant is a girl named Dawn. If you choose the girl, the assistant is a boy named Lucas.

• **You receive one of these Pokémon from Professor Rowan**

Turtwig Lv5

GRASS

Ability
• Overgrow

Chimchar Lv5

FIRE

Ability
• Blaze

Piplup Lv5

WATER

Ability
• Torrent

Step 2 — Your first Pokémon battle

Your rival is thrilled to receive his starter Pokémon, and he just can't wait to try it out! He challenges you to a battle—the first of many showdowns with him to come. It's possible to win this one, but don't break a sweat if you lose. It doesn't really affect the game.

Lucas! I challenge you to a battle!

Return home if you're injured

If your Pokémon are injured, go home and have your mom heal them. If every single one of the Pokémon in your party is fainted at the same time, you lose some of your money.

Battle with your rival! ①

Your rival is so excited about getting a Pokémon from Professor Rowan that he wants to battle you.

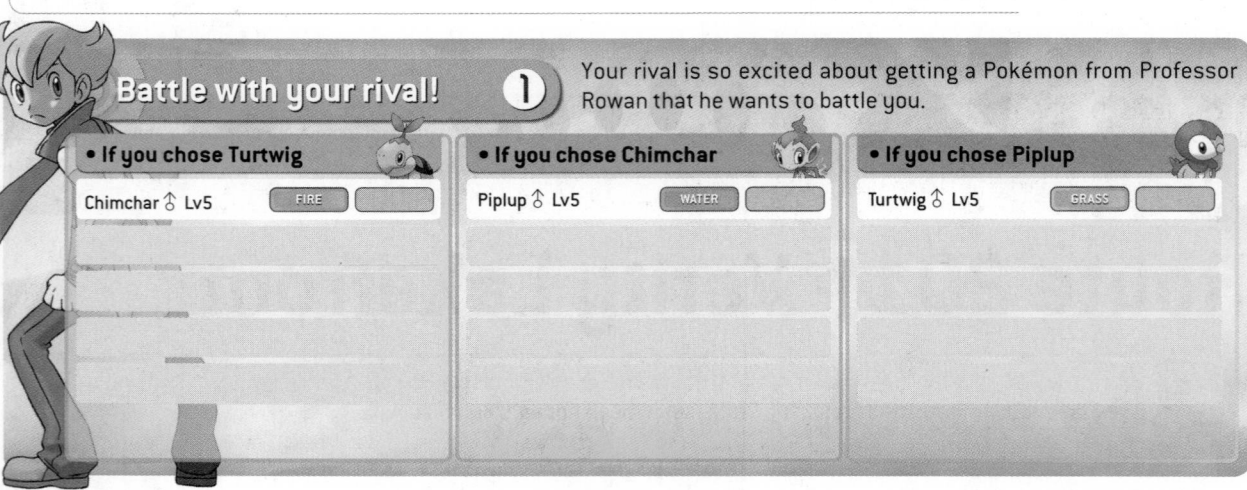

• **If you chose Turtwig**

Chimchar ♂ Lv5 — FIRE

• **If you chose Chimchar**

Piplup ♂ Lv5 — WATER

• **If you chose Piplup**

Turtwig ♂ Lv5 — GRASS

After getting the Running Shoes — Check out the Legend at Lake Verity

The two of you might hang out at Lake Verity often, but your rival says there's also a Legendary Pokémon hidden there! The two of you decide to catch it for Professor Rowan, so head left along Route 201 to get to Lake Verity.

Use items on Pokémon

Sometimes your Pokémon will be low on HP or affected by status changes when there's no Pokémon Center nearby. So always keep certain items in your Bag to use on your injured Pokémon in these situations.

After Lake Verity — Raise strong Pokémon

The Pokémon that Professor Rowan gave you is your first Pokémon, so you're going to depend on it a lot. Make it stronger by walking into the tall grass and battling wild Pokémon—each battle will earn Exp. and your Pokémon will eventually level up.

STARLY Lv2
PIPLUP Lv6
23 23
PIPLUP used Pound!

 **After Lake Verity** **Talk to the Pokémart employee**

Who's that lurking in the tall grass? It's a Pokémart employee, and if you go talk to him, he'll give you a Potion! A Potion heals up to 20 HP of one Pokémon. Use it right away if your Pokémon has been injured in battle.

Obtained the Potion!

Hop off ledges to get home

If your Pokémon is low on HP and you need to rush home to heal it, avoid the tall grass and the wild Pokémon living in it by stepping off the small ledges along the way! These ledges are a one-way trip, so they're only good for getting home in a hurry.

 **After Lake Verity** **Head for Sandgem Town**

After visiting Lake Verity, drop by the Pokémon lab in Sandgem Town to thank Professor Rowan for the Pokémon he gave you. Head right on Route 201 to reach Sandgem Town, just beyond the tall grass.

• A lake where a Legendary Pokémon sleeps

Lake Verity (First visit)

SINNOH WALKTHROUGH

Story — You and your rival start walking along Route 201 to see Professor Rowan in Sandgem Town, but just as you're about to enter the tall grass, the Professor himself appears behind you.

Verity Lakefront
(to Twinleaf Town)

Cyrus

ROUTE 201 • VERITY LAKEFRONT • LAKE VERITY (FIRST VISIT) –

 **Step 1** The mysterious man at the lake

You and your rival arrive at Lake Verity to look for the Legendary Pokémon, but what you find is a mysterious man named Cyrus talking to himself. It's unclear what he's muttering about, and he won't bother to tell you—instead, he shoves you and your rival aside and leaves.

...The flowing time...
...The expanding space...

Step 2 — The cry of a Pokémon

After Cyrus leaves, you finally hear what you think is the cry of a Legendary Pokémon from the bottom of the lake. But you don't have any Poké Balls, so you can't try to catch it right now.

Step 3 — Visit Professor Rowan

You and your rival decide to head to Sandgem Town to thank Professor Rowan for the Pokémon he gave you—well, that and to ask him about Poké Balls so you can catch more Pokémon. Your rival just can't wait on the latter, so he takes off ahead of you.

• A sandy town connected to the ocean

Sandgem Town

Story

You love Pokémon, and want to thank Professor Rowan for the starter Pokémon he gave you. He can tell you love Pokémon too, which is why he asks you to help fill the Pokédex.

Items
☐ Pokédex
☐ TM27 Return

Route 202
(to Jubilife City)

Pokémon Lab

Pokémon Center

Pokémart

Route 201
(to Twinleaf Town)

Dawn's/Lucas's House

Route 219
(to Pal Park)

Step 1 — Visit the Pokémon lab

When you enter Sandgem Town, Dawn/Lucas will be waiting there to take you to the lab. At the lab, Professor Rowan is leading your frustrated rival out the door. Wonder what happened?

Step 2 — Thank Professor Rowan

Professor Rowan asks to look at the Pokémon he gave you back on Route 201, and his response is quite positive—your starter Pokémon is happy to be with you, which makes Professor Rowan happy, and he's also quite happy to tell you so.

What's inside the fridge at the lab?

If you open it up, you'll find plenty of delicious treats. Does Professor Rowan have a bit of a sweet tooth?

Pokédex

Step 3 — Start to fill the Pokédex

Since you've grown so close to your first Pokémon, Professor Rowan wants you to travel throughout the Sinnoh region and meet many, many more Pokémon. He'll give you a Pokédex, which will help you (and him) keep track of what you've seen and caught.

Will you use it to record data on all the Pokémon in Sinnoh for me?

Nickname your Pokémon

You can give your Pokémon nicknames as long as 10 characters. Nicknames will bring you closer to your Pokémon, so be sure to come up with something special.

Step 4 — The professor gives you a TM

Before you leave, Professor Rowan has one parting gift to give you—TM27 Return. TMs are special move-teaching items that break after you use them on one Pokémon, so use them carefully.

Obtained the TM27!

Step 5 — Use the Pokémon Center

Pokémon Centers are great because they're located in almost every town, the people inside often have useful info, and at the desk you can heal your Pokémon's HP and PP. The first place you visit when you enter a new town should always be the Pokémon Center.

Would you like to rest your Pokémon?

The Underground Wi-Fi Club will open soon

The Pokémon Wi-Fi Club in the basement of the Pokémon Center is under renovation right now, but come back after you visit Oreburgh City and it will be open for business.

Step 6 — Sign the back of your Trainer Card

Visit the second floor of the Pokémon Center to access the Pokémon Wireless Club, where you can take part in link battles and trades. Talk to the girl at the far left reception desk to sign the back of your Trainer Card using your stylus.

Write your autograph!

DONE

Visit the assistant's house

The assistant's house is also in Sandgem Town, so drop by for a visit and meet Dawn's/Lucas's little sister and grandfather.

Step 7 — Stock up at the Pokémart

The Pokémart is the place to go for all kinds of items. If there are two cashiers, check the one on the right for a standard list of goods; the list gets longer after you beat a Gym Leader and earn a Gym Badge (p. 6). The cashier on the left sells goods unique to that town.

BUY
SELL
SEE YR!

Welcome!
What do you need?

Step 8 — Return to Twinleaf Town

Once Professor Rowan gives you the Pokédex, you're ready to start your Pokémon journey! Dawn/Lucas will remind you to visit your family first—you're not going to see them for a while.

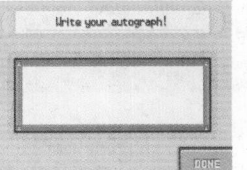

You may need to go far away, so I think you should let someone know.

Step 9 — Take a peek at Route 219

Just south of Sandgem Town a sandy shore leads to the ocean. You can't go out on the water yet—you'll need a Pokémon that knows Surf, and for that you need to have HM03 Surf and be able to use it on the field. Come back much later in the game to explore this watery route.

How do I use Surf?

You must beat Wake at the Pastoria Gym and earn the Fen Badge. Only then can your Pokémon use Surf outside of battle to travel on the water.

After getting the Journal — Go north to Route 202

Head north from Sandgem Town to reach Route 202, and beyond that is Jubilife City, where you must deliver the Parcel to your rival. You'll meet lots of wild Pokémon on the way, so come prepared with plenty of Poké Balls.

After visiting the Distortion World — Let Professor Rowan know you're safe

Once you're back from the Distortion World safe and sound, visit Professor Rowan to let him know you're okay. He'll be glad for the update, and will shower you with praise.

You've done it!
You really have done it!

After visiting the Distortion World — Capture Uxie, Azelf, and Mesprit

Professor Rowan has his own update for you—Uxie, Azelf, and Mesprit have returned from the Distortion World and headed back to their respective lakes. Visit Lake Acuity, Lake Valor, and Lake Verity to catch all three!

The three Pokémon of the lakes appear to have returned to their homes.

The final badge waits in Sunyshore City

Seeing that you have seven badges, Professor Rowan suggests you head to Sunyshore City to earn your eighth (and final) badge. Once you have that in hand, you can challenge the Pokémon League!

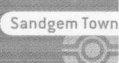

SINNOH WALKTHROUGH

SANDGEM TOWN

Route 219, Route 220, Route 221

South of Sandgem Town is a beautiful sandy beach bordering an ocean path. Cross this marine route and you'll run right into Pal Park, where you can meet (and catch) new Pokémon. But first you'll need HM Surf to travel the waves.

Moves needed for completion

Surf

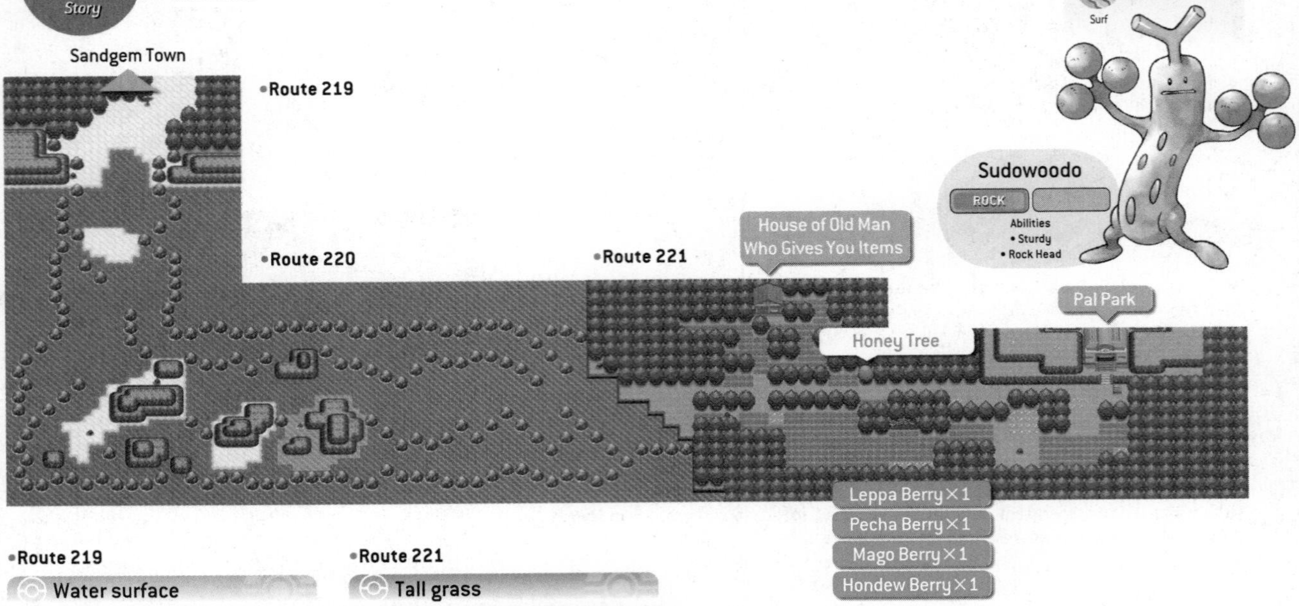

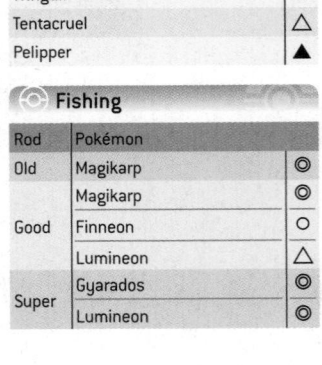

Sudowoodo

ROCK

Abilities
• Sturdy
• Rock Head

Sandgem Town
•Route 219
•Route 220
•Route 221

House of Old Man Who Gives You Items

Pal Park

Honey Tree

Leppa Berry ×1
Pecha Berry ×1
Mago Berry ×1
Hondew Berry ×1

•Route 219

Water surface

Pokémon	
Tentacool	◎
Wingull	◎
Tentacruel	△
Pelipper	▲

Fishing

Rod	Pokémon	
Old	Magikarp	◎
	Magikarp	◎
Good	Finneon	○
	Lumineon	△
Super	Gyarados	◎
	Lumineon	◎

•Route 220

Water surface

Pokémon	
Tentacool	◎
Wingull	◎
Tentacruel	△
Pelipper	▲

Fishing

Rod	Pokémon	
Old	Magikarp	◎
	Magikarp	◎
Good	Finneon	○
	Lumineon	△
	Gyarados	◎
Super	Lumineon	○
	Chinchou	○

•Route 221

Tall grass

Pokémon	M	A	N
Floatzel	○	○	◎
Girafarig	○	○	○
Roselia	○	○	○
Sudowoodo	○	○	○

Water surface

Pokémon	
Tentacool	◎
Wingull	◎
Tentacruel	△
Pelipper	▲

Fishing

Rod	Pokémon	
Old	Magikarp	◎
	Magikarp	◎
Good	Finneon	○
	Lumineon	△
Super	Gyarados	◎
	Lumineon	◎

Items

• First visit
☐ Antidote
• After winning at Pastoria Gym
☐ Max Repel
☐ Splash Plate
☐ Carbos
☐ Protein
☐ Ultra Ball
☐ Leppa Berry
☐ Pecha Berry
☐ Mago Berry
☐ Hondew Berry
☐ TM81 X-Scissor
☐ Pure Incense
• When you show the old man the Pokémon he asks for
☐ Black Belt
☐ Expert Belt
☐ Focus Sash

Step 1 To cross the ocean you need Surf

No matter how much you want to cross the ocean below Sandgem Town, you can't do it until you have HM Surf. And you can't use Surf until you've defeated the Pastoria Gym, so just let it go for now and come back later.

After winning at Pastoria Gym | **Use Surf to move on the water**

Once you've defeated the Pastoria Gym Leader, you'll be able to use Surf to travel on this route. The path is littered with battle-seeking Trainers, so make sure your Pokémon are in good health and your items are fully stocked before you make the trip.

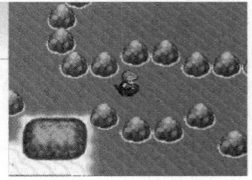

Get Surf at Celestic Town

Not sure where to find HM03 Surf? The elder in Celestic Town (p. 108) should have given it to you earlier in your adventure.

After winning at Pastoria Gym | **Show off the right Pokémon and get items**

The old man in the house on Route 221 will mention a number when you talk to him. Put a Pokémon at the head of your party with a level matching that number and voilà, he'll give you one of three items—a Black Belt, a Focus Sash, or an Expert Belt.

Show me a Pokémon that's Lv. 40. If you can, I'll reward you.

After winning at Pastoria Gym | **Pal Park is under construction**

You reach the end of Route 221 and see Pal Park, but unfortunately it's still under construction! You'll need to defeat the Pokémon League and obtain the National Pokédex first, and only then will enough time have passed for you to enter the park.

Pal Park isn't open yet. We're still setting up.

Take the return flight

Don't want to Surf all the way to Pal Park again? After you've visited once and obtained the National Pokédex, use HM Fly to zoom right to the front doorstep!

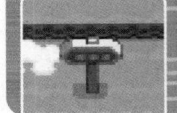

• The path connecting Sandgem Town and Jubilife City

Route 202

Story Head to Jubilife City to deliver the Parcel to your rival, and on the way, learn about catching wild Pokémon from Dawn/Lucas on Route 202.

Jubilife City

Sandgem Town

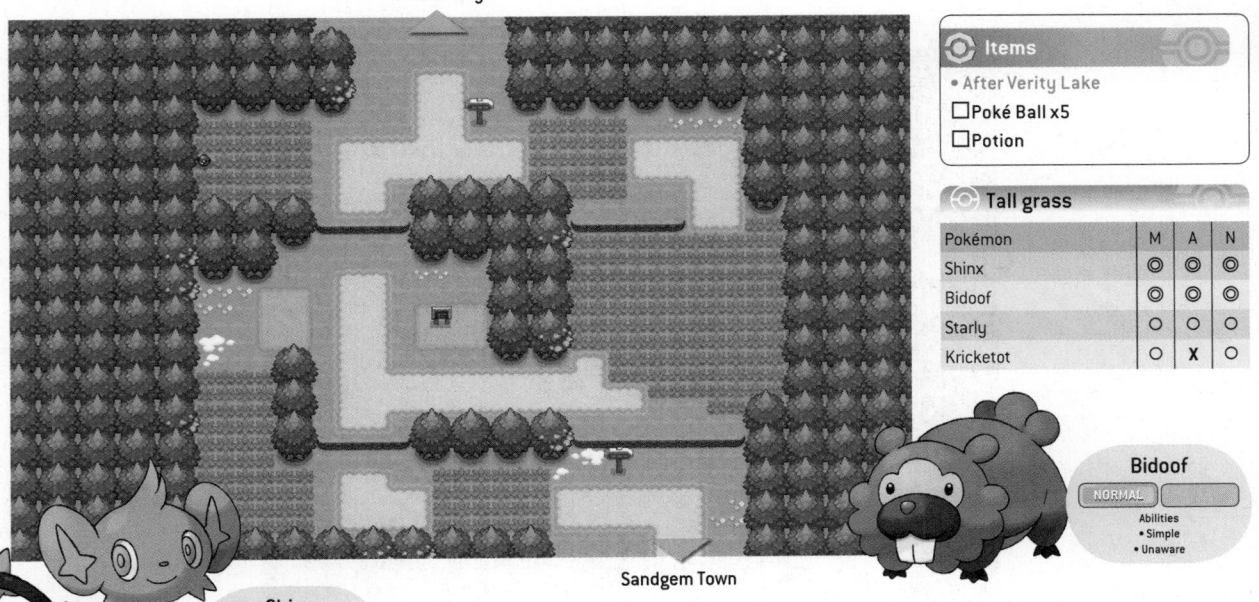

Items

• After Verity Lake
☐ Poké Ball x5
☐ Potion

Tall grass

Pokémon	M	A	N
Shinx	◎	◎	◎
Bidoof	◎	◎	◎
Starly	○	○	○
Kricketot	○	X	○

Shinx
ELECTRIC
Abilities
• Rivalry
• Intimidate

Bidoof
NORMAL
Abilities
• Simple
• Unaware

Step 1 How to catch Pokémon

When you enter the tall grass on Route 202, Dawn/Lucas will be waiting to show you how to catch wild Pokémon. It's fairly simple—pay attention to the way Dawn/Lucas lowers the Pokémon's HP first.

Step 2 Try catching a wild Pokémon

Dawn/Lucas will give you five Poké Balls to start with, so you might as well start building your Pokémon collection by catching some of the Pokémon that live on Route 202, like Shinx and Bidoof.

The right Poké Ball for the job

There's more than just one kind of Poké Ball—you'll encounter several varieties (p. 16), each suited to different situations or different Pokémon. Make sure to always use the right Poké Ball for the job.

Step 3 Battle Pokémon Trainers

Watch out for the Pokémon Trainers on the way—if they see you, they'll challenge you to a battle. This is actually a good thing, since if you win, your Pokémon gain Exp. and you get some prize money too.

Step 4 Head for Jubilife City

By heading up on Route 202 you'll reach Jubilife City, but you'll have to pass through the tall grasses first. If your Pokémon are injured from battle, either take them to the Pokémon Center or use a Potion on them before you go any further.

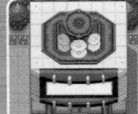

• This is Jubilife City, a joyful, bustling city

Jubilife City

Story

Jubilife City is a metropolis filled with attractions like the Global Terminal and Jubilife TV. Before you go sightseeing, make sure you deliver the Parcel to your rival first.

Route 204
(to Floaroma Town)

Pokétch Company

Jubilife TV

Jubilife Condominiums

Route 218
(to Canalave City)

Route 203
(to Oreburgh City)

Global Terminal

Pokémart

Trainers' School

Pokémon Center

Route 202
(to Sandgem Town)

Items

• First visit
- ☐ Battle Recorder
- ☐ X Attack
- ☐ Town Map
- ☐ Potion
- ☐ Coupon 1
- ☐ Coupon 2
- ☐ Coupon 3
- ☐ Pokétch
- ☐ Quick Claw
- ☐ Old Rod

• After winning at Oreburgh Gym
- ☐ Accessory: Ranch
- ☐ Fashion Case
- ☐ Turtwig Mask, Chimchar Mask, Piplup Mask (only one)
- ☐ Pokétch App: Memo Pad

• After winning at Hearthome Gym
- ☐ Pokétch App: Marking Map

• After winning at Pastoria Gym
- ☐ Pokétch App: Link Searcher

• After winning at Snowpoint Gym
- ☐ Pokétch App: Move Tester

Pokémart (left counter)

Air Mail 50
Heal Ball 300

• Jubilife TV Pokémon Loto

	Prize	Cond.
GP	Master Ball	Draw 5
1P	Max Revive	Draw 4
2P	Exp. Share	Draw 3
3P	PP Up	Draw 2
4P	Ultra Ball	Draw 1

Step 1 — International Policeman Looker

As soon as you stroll into town, Dawn/Lucas grabs and drags you to the Trainer's School. On the way, you discover a mysterious man lurking behind a lamppost! His code name is Looker, and he's a member of the International Police.

Looker

Step 2 — Looker gives you the Vs. Recorder

Looker is on the trail of some nefarious Pokénappers, so keep an eye open. When he finds out you're a Pokémon Trainer, he gives you a tool that you might find useful—the Vs. Recorder. The Vs. Recorder can record battles between friends or in the Battle Frontier.

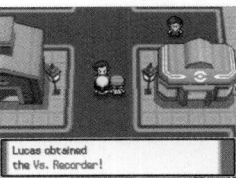

Study status conditions on the blackboard

Status conditions like poison and burn can really turn the tide of battle, so learn about their characteristics by reading all about them on the blackboard at the Trainer's School.

Step 3 — Receive the Town Map

Your rival is studying hard at the Trainer's School, so head there to give him the Parcel. Inside is a pair of Town Maps. He doesn't need two, so he hands you the extra. Make use of it on your journey.

Give an interview to be on TV

Interviewers from Jubilife TV are scattered throughout Jubilife City. Start a conversation with one of them now and later you might catch a glimpse of yourself on TV!

Step 4 — Answer the quiz for a Pokétch

A man near the Trainer's School will make you look for three clowns stationed around Jubilife City. Find them, answer their quizzes, and bring the three coupons back to the man—he'll give you a Pokétch!

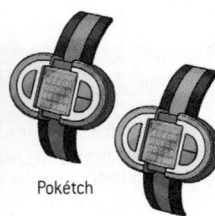

Pokétch

Step 5 — Get the Old Rod

Enter the gate to Route 218 and talk to the fisherman. He'll give you the Old Rod, which you can use to hook and capture Pokémon that inhabit oceans and lakes.

SINNOH WALKTHROUGH

JUBILIFE CITY

Step 6 — Start a group and share your records

Talk to the people near the fountain to join a group or even start your own. Lots of fun things can happen with a group—for example, if you pool the records of the people in the group, then the records from your friends' games will be broadcast on TV in your game.

If you join a group, you can compete or cooperate with fellow members.

Share records and get new photos

Spruce up the second floor of Jubilife TV by sharing records! Your friends' Dress-Up photos will be added to the wall; there are up to 10 slots for photos, so make sure you share with lots of different people to keep it exciting.

Step 7 — Have your Pokémon hold items

Talk to the girl on the first floor of the Jubilife Condominiums to obtain a Quick Claw—when a Pokémon holds it, its chance of attacking first is greatly increased. Give this to the Pokémon you battle with most.

Obtained the Quick Claw!

Recommended held items

There are plenty of other great held items besides the Quick Claw—keep an eye out for the Amulet Coin, which doubles the amount of prize money you receive when you defeat another Pokémon Trainer in battle.

Step 8 — Head for Oreburgh Gym

You've seen all there is to see in Jubilife City, so now it's time to hit up Oreburgh City and its Pokémon Gym. Exit to the east and travel along Route 203, and it will take you straight there. Prepare for the journey by stopping by the Pokémart first.

After winning at Oreburgh Gym — Go Global at the Global Terminal

Come back after winning a badge at Oreburgh Gym and you'll be granted entrance to the Global Terminal, where all sorts of Wi-Fi fun await you (p. 255).

The Global Terminal has three floors.

A new backdrop every day

Drop by the first floor of the Global Terminal once a day and talk to the girl to the right of the globe display. She'll give you a new backdrop Accessory every day, so collect as many as you can to take some fabulous photos on the second floor.

After winning at Oreburgh Gym — New Pokétch Apps

The Pokétch Company promises to improve the Pokétch by creating new Apps for it on a regular basis. When will these be available? Just come back when you have have an odd number of badges—1, 3, 5, and 7—and they'll happily add the new Apps to your Pokétch (p. 28).

Lucas obtained the Pokétch app MEMO PAD.

After winning at Oreburgh Gym — A Team Galactic Double Battle

Professor Rowan seems to be having a problem with Team Galactic over by the Jubilife Condominums! Head on over there to team up with Dawn/Lucas for a Double Battle. You each contribute one Pokémon to the fray, so work together and teach those grunts a lesson.

Dawn: Lucas!
Let's battle together!

Play Pokémon Lotto

Jubilife TV holds a daily Pokémon Lotto on the first floor. Drop by every day to see if the drawn number matches ID number of one of your Pokémon, because you'll win a lavish prize (p. 43).

After winning at Oreburgh Gym — Fashion flash at Jubilife TV

Once you've defeated the Team Galactic grunts, a Jubilife TV employee will gift you the Fashion Case, which allows you to play Dress-Up with your Pokémon on the second floor of the Jubilife TV building. Have the staff take a photo of your accessorized Pokémon to hang on the wall there.

Lucas
PURE POWER

Starter Pokémon mask

Chat with the man near the second floor stairway of Jubilife TV, and he'll give you a very special gift—a mask of Turtwig, Chimchar, or Piplup, whichever one you picked as your starter Pokémon.

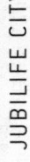

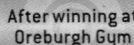

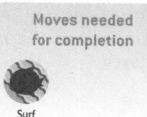

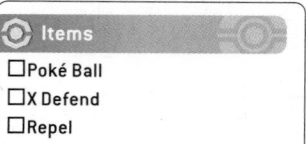

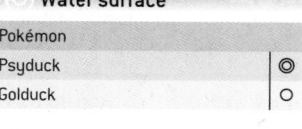

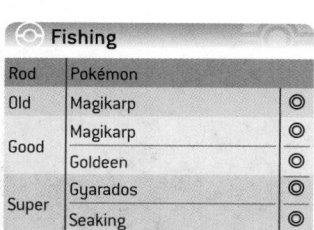

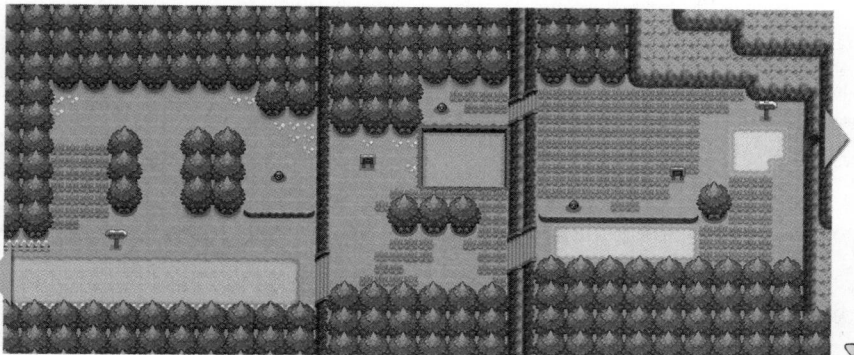

Route 203

Story

Your next destination is Oreburgh City, but first you'll have to travel along Route 203 and battle your rival. You aren't the only one who's been training hard—it should be quite a battle!

Moves needed for completion

Surf

Oreburgh Gate
(to Oreburgh City)

Jubilife City

Items

- ☐ Poké Ball
- ☐ X Defend
- ☐ Repel

Water surface

Pokémon	
Psyduck	◎
Golduck	○

Tall grass

Pokémon	M	A	N
Starly	◎	◎	○
Shinx	○	○	○
Kricketot	○	X	○
Bidoof	○	○	○
Abra	○	○	○
Zubat	X	X	○

Fishing

Rod	Pokémon	
Old	Magikarp	◎
Good	Magikarp	◎
	Goldeen	◎
Super	Gyarados	◎
	Seaking	◎

Abra

PSYCHIC

Abilities
- Synchronize
- Inner Focus

Psyduck

WATER

Abilities
- Damp
- Cloud Nine

Step 1 — A rival challenge!

Be careful as you exit east from Jubilife City and step onto Route 203—your rival was waiting for you, and now he wants to battle! He has a type advantage against you, but with a little effort and strategy, you can be victorious.

John: Hey! Lucas!
Tell me you got a little tougher!

Battle with your rival! ②

Your rival challenges you to battle on Route 203, and now he has a Starly.

• If you chose Turtwig

Starly ♂ Lv7	NORMAL	FLYING
Chimchar ♂ Lv9	FIRE	

• If you chose Chimchar

Starly ♂ Lv7	NORMAL	FLYING
Piplup ♂ Lv9	WATER	

• If you chose Piplup

Starly ♂ Lv7	NORMAL	FLYING
Turtwig ♂ Lv9	GRASS	

SINNOH WALKTHROUGH

ROUTE 203

Step 2 Try out the Old Rod

If you got the Old Rod in Jubilife City, give it a test run in the small pond on Route 203. Sure, all you can catch there is Magikarp, but it will be good practice for bigger catches later on.

Landed a Pokémon!

Fishing is all about timing

If you see "!!" appear over your head as you fish, that means only one thing—you've hooked a Pokémon! Start mashing the A button as fast as you can, and hopefully you'll reel it in.

Step 3 Right to Oreburgh City

At the end of Route 203 you'll run into Oreburgh Gate, a cave leading straight to Oreburgh City. Caves are risky places if you have injured Pokémon, so you should head back to a Pokémon Center to patch them up before going in.

• The road to Oreburgh City

Oreburgh Gate

Story

The tunnel leading to Oreburgh City is called Oreburgh Gate, and all you can do on your first visit is pass straight through. Once you've got some HMs on your side, you'll be able to explore B1F to your heart's content.

Moves needed for completion

Rock Smash   Surf   Strength

•1F

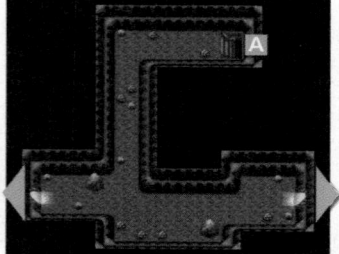

Route 203 (to Jubilife City)   Oreburgh City

•B1F

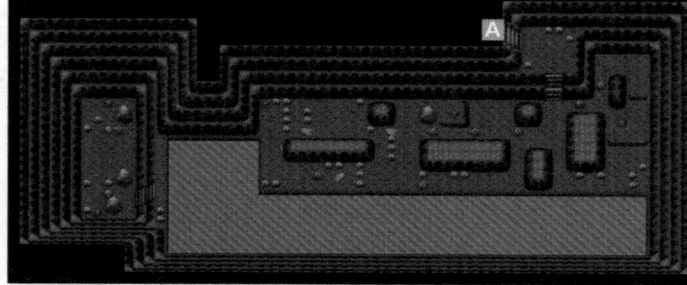

Items

• First visit
☐ HM 06 Rock Smash
• After winning at Oreburgh Gym
☐ TM 70 Flash
☐ Big Pearl
• After getting the Bicycle
☐ TM31 Brick Break
• After winning at Canalave Gym
☐ Earth Plate
☐ TM01 Focus Punch

•1F

Cave

Pokémon	M	A	N
Zubat	◎	◎	◎
Psyduck	◎	◎	◎
Geodude	○	○	○

•B1F

Cave

Pokémon	M	A	N
Zubat	◎	◎	◎
Psyduck	◎	◎	◎
Geodude	○	○	○
Golbat	△	△	△

Water surface

Pokémon	
Psyduck	◎
Zubat	◎
Golduck	△
Golbat	△

Fishing

Rod	Pokémon	
Old	Magikarp	◎
Good	Magikarp	◎
	Barboach	◎
Super	Gyarados	◎
	Whiscash	◎

Zubat
POISON FLYING
Ability
• Inner Focus

Step 1 Get HM06 Rock Smash

Just inside Oreburgh Gate is a man who gives you HM06 Rock Smash. This will let you break through rocks (like those in the cave), but you can't use it until you beat the Oreburgh Gym and earn the Coal Badge.

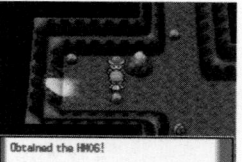
Obtained the HM06!

Straight on to Oreburgh City

On B1F of Oreburgh Gate is a huge lake that you can't reach until you know HM06 Rock Smash, so just pass on through the cave and come back after you defeat the Oreburgh Gym.

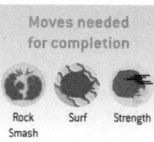

After winning at Oreburgh Gym — Get TM70 Flash

You'll have to come back this way after defeating the Oreburgh Gym Leader, but now you can use Rock Smash to break through the rocks and explore the lower level. Down in the depths you'll find TM70 Flash, which will provide illumination in deeper, darker caves than this one.

GEODUDE used Rock Smash!

Return to Jubilife City

You have your first badge, so head back to the Pokétch Company for a special reward—you'll receive the Memo Pad Pokétch App (p. 28), which lets you jot down things you might want to remember for your journey.

After getting the Bicycle — Bike tricks for Brick Break

Once you've gotten the Bicycle from Eterna City, come back to B1F and use it to hop over some rocks, letting you explore the cave even further. Your bike ride will eventually lead you to TM31 Brick Break.

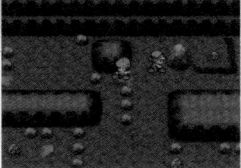

After winning at Canalave Gym — It takes Strength

After your victory at Canalave Gym, you'll finally be able to use HM Strength to reach the deepest part of the cave. Waiting for you at the very end will be the Earth Plate and TM01 Focus Punch.

Lucas found an Earth Plate!

What are plates used for?

These rectangular tiles are special items that, when held by Pokémon in battle, will strengthen certain types. For example, the Earth Plate boosts Ground-type moves.

• Oreburgh City, a place brimming with energy

Oreburgh City

Story

Oreburgh is known as the "City of Energy," probably because of the magnificent coal mine they have, or the entire museum dedicated to mining. You want to battle their Gym Leader, Roark, except there's one problem—he's not at the Gym!

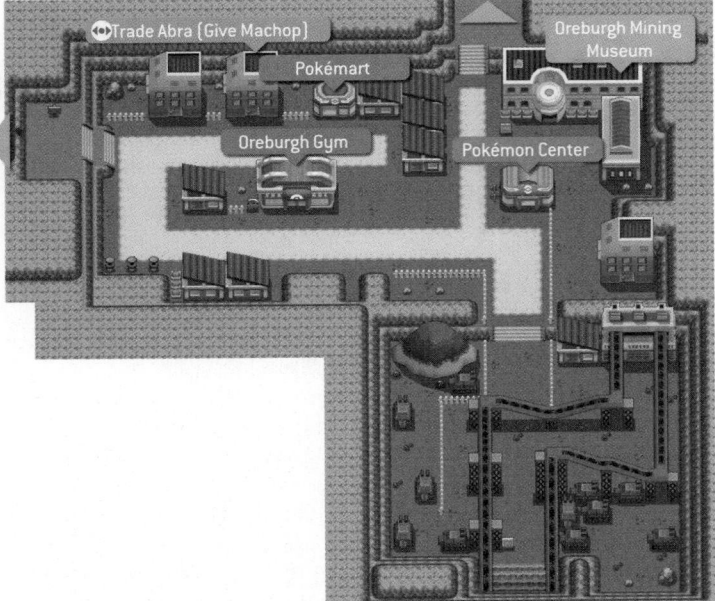

Route 207 (to Mt. Coronet base)
Trade Abra (Give Machop)
Pokémart
Oreburgh Mining Museum
Oreburgh Gym
Pokémon Center
Oreburgh Gate
Oreburgh Mine

Items

• First visit
- ☐ Pal Pad
- ☐ Dusk Ball
- ☐ Great Ball
- ☐ Dire Hit
- ☐ Yellow Shard
- ☐ Super Potion

• After winning at Oreburgh Gym
- ☐ Coal Badge
- ☐ TM76 Stealth Rock

• Showing Geodude to a townsperson
- ☐ Heal Ball

Pokémart (left counter)

Tunnel Mail	50P
Heal Ball	300P
Net Ball	1000P

Step 1 — Where's Gym Leader Roark?

Anyway, the Gym Leader's gone off to the coal mine.

You reach the Oreburgh Gym to find that your rival has already won the Gym Badge and you can't get one just yet—Roark isn't at the Gym! He's only gone to the mine, so after you take a look around, go the south side of town.

Like father, like son

Roark takes after his father—none other than Byron, the Canalave City Gym Leader! He's known as the steel-bodied man due to his expertise in Steel-type Pokémon.

Step 2 — The Wi-Fi Club is open for business!

Lucas obtained the Pal Pad!

The Wi-Fi Club at the Pokémon Center is up and running, so head into the basement and speak to Teala, the guide. She'll give you the Pal Pad, which helps you trade and battle with distant friends (p. 251).

You need a connection

To enjoy all the different features of the Wi-Fi Connection, first you need some way to connect. One way is to use the Nintendo Wi-Fi USB Connector; see Nintendo's website for more details.

Step 3 — Pick your avatar

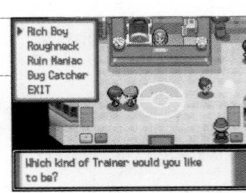

Which kind of Trainer would you like to be?

When you talk to the man on the first floor of the Pokémon Center, he'll ask you which Pokémon Trainer you like best. Be honest—the one you choose will determine your appearance to your friends in Union Room games (p.253).

Step 4 — A Pokémon town trade

Would you be willing to trade your MACHOP for my ABRA?

The girl in the apartment building really wants to make a trade. Give her a Machop, and she'll trade you an elusive Abra. If you've been having trouble catching Abra in the wild (because it always Teleports away), this is your best bet for obtaining one.

Four trades

You'll encounter four people in Sinnoh who wish to make a Pokémon trade with you. Give them a chance—it's fun, and it's a great way to help fill your Pokédex.

Step 5 — Show the kid a Geodude

If you don't mind, how about showing me a Pokémon called GEODUDE?

On the second floor of one of the apartment buildings is a boy who'd like to see a Geodude. When you put one at the head of your party and talk to him, he'll hand you a Heal Ball.

Geodude are all around you

Geodude are common in the area around Oreburgh City, so finding one isn't hard. They even inhabit the mine in the south of town, so try and catch one when you're there looking for Roark.

Step 6 — Tour the Mining Museum

On the verge of a breakthrough, I am, to achieve extraction from Fossils.

The Oreburgh Mining Museum keeps all sorts of fascinating data on the Oreburgh Mine—and admission is free of charge! If you dig up any Pokémon fossils in the Sinnoh Underground, bring them to the scientist at the counter to have them restored into living Pokémon (p. 242).

Step 7 — Searching for Roark

Your rival tells you that Roark went into the Oreburgh Mine at the south end of town. Too bad you don't have a hard hat—you could really use one when you head into the mine to ask Roark for a Gym battle.

After visiting the Oreburgh Mine — Get ready to rumble

Roark is waiting in the Gym to battle you, so don't dally and make sure you head to the Pokémart first. You'll want to stock up on Potions and other items, because they'll be a huge help when things get tough in the Gym.

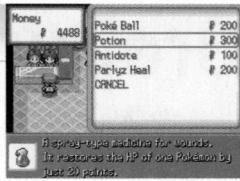

Money	4488
Poké Ball	₽ 200
Potion	₽ 300
Antidote	₽ 100
Parlyz Heal	₽ 200
CANCEL	

A spray-type medicine for wounds. It restores the HP of one Pokémon by just 20 points.

GYM BATTLE ①

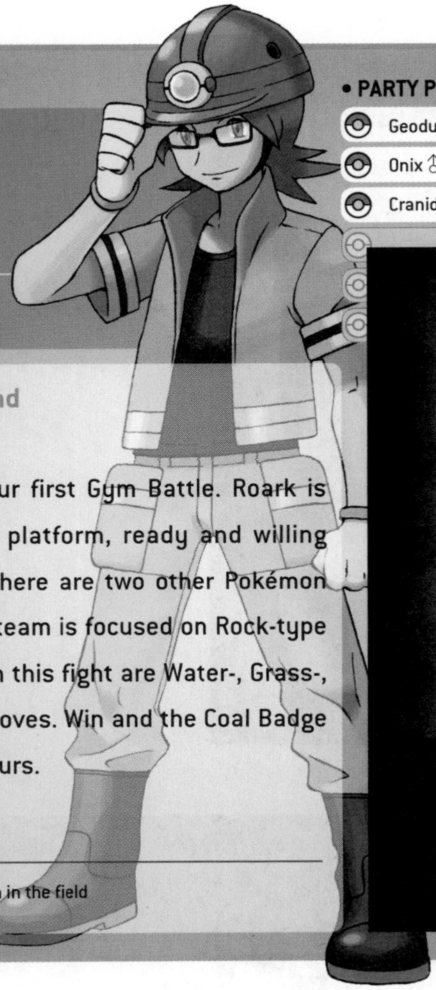

Oreburgh Gym Leader
ROARK

• Rock Pokémon user

• PARTY POKÉMON

Geodude ♂ Lv12	ROCK	GROUND
Onix ♂ Lv12	ROCK	GROUND
Cranidos ♂ Lv14	ROCK	

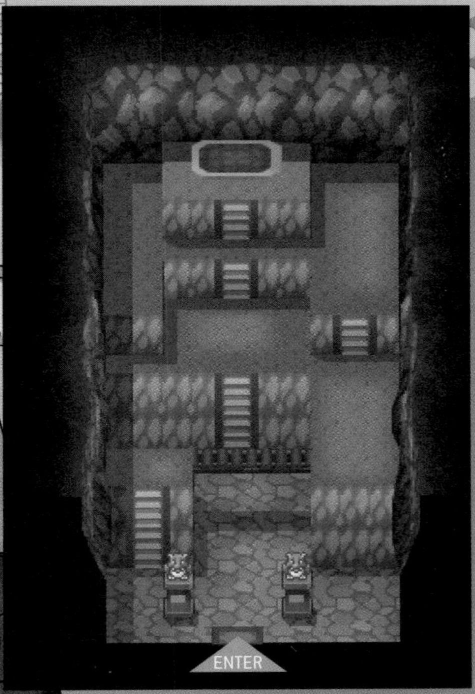

Attack Roark with Water- and Grass-type Moves

Oreburgh Gym is host to your first Gym Battle. Roark is standing on the uppermost platform, ready and willing to take up your challenge. There are two other Pokémon Trainers in the Gym. Roark's team is focused on Rock-type Pokémon. Your best assets in this fight are Water-, Grass-, Fighting-, and Ground-type moves. Win and the Coal Badge and TM76 Stealth Rock are yours.

COAL BADGE

Lets you use Rock Smash in the field

ENTER

After winning at Oreburgh Gym — Take a trip back to Jubilife City

Your next Gym Badge awaits in Eterna City. Route 207 is one way there, but you need a Bicycle to get through. Take your rival's advice and return to Jubilife City, then get to Eterna City via Floaroma Town.

So, I'm going back to Jubilife City. Next stop, the Eterna Gym Badge!

After obtaining the Explorer Kit — Have your fossils restored

Talk to the Underground Man in Eterna City to receive an Explorer Kit (p. 63). With the Explorer Kit, you can venture into the Sinnoh Underground and dig out fossils buried in the walls. If you find a Pokémon fossil, you can bring it to the Mining Museum and have them restore it for you.

I am in the process of extracting your Pokémon from a Fossil.

Buried treasure

Pokémon fossils aren't the only things buried in the walls of the Sinnoh Underground. There are also Spheres, items to assist in Evolution, battle items, and tons more. Time to get digging (p. 567)

Oreburgh Mine

Story

Oreburgh Mine is a cave that contains an enormous reserve of coal. Miners and their Machop work around the clock to dig through the cave. You must descend to B2F to find Oreburgh Gym Leader Roark.

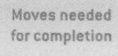

•B1F

Oreburgh City

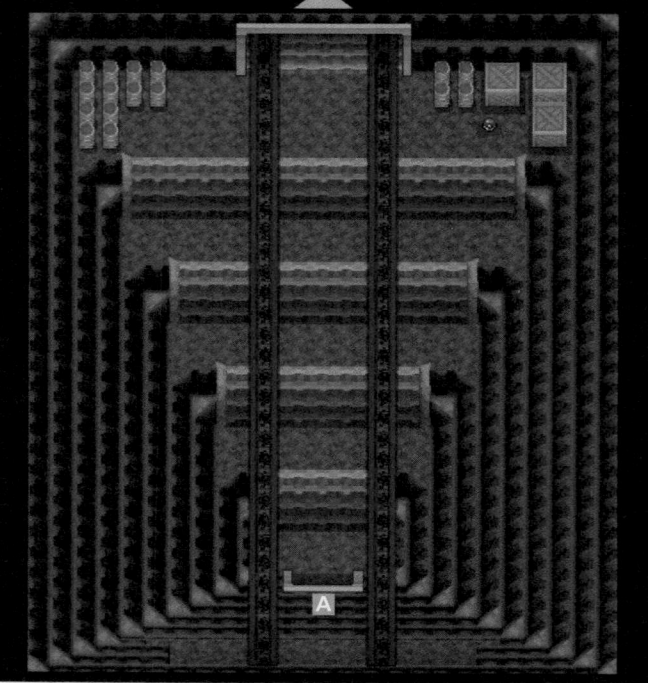

A

Onix

ROCK GROUND

Abilities
•Rock Head
• Sturdy

Geodude

ROCK GROUND

Abilities
•Rock Head
• Sturdy

Items

- ☐ Poké Ball
- ☐ Potion
- ☐ Escape Rope

•1F

B1F • B2F

Pokémon	M	A	N
Geodude	◎	◎	◎
Zubat	○	○	○
Onix	○	○	○

•B2F

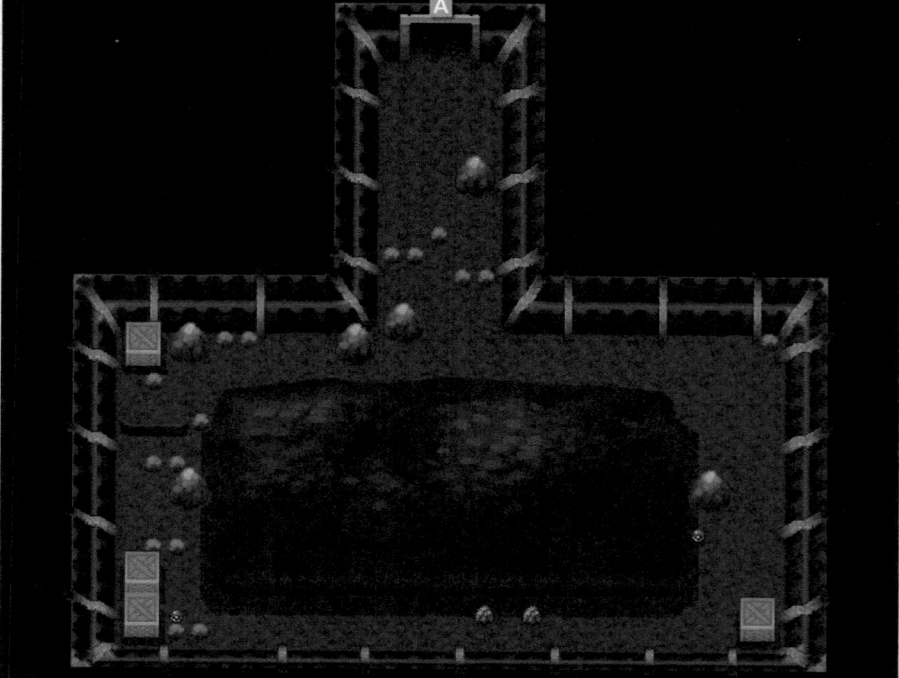

A

 **Step 1** Find Gym Leader Roark

Gym Leader Roark can be found on the second basement level, in front of the gigantic piece of coal. Talk to him and he'll explain how to use the HM Rock Smash before returning to his Gym. Head for the Gym yourself and take him on.

Step 2 Catch Geodude in the mine

You'll find wild Geodude appearing in Oreburgh Mine. Catch one for the boy in the Oreburgh apartment building who wanted to see it. If you show it to him, he'll give you a Heal Ball (p. 48).

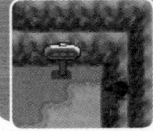

• The road linking Oreburgh City and Mt. Coronet

Route 207

 **Story** Route 207 is a road that runs to Mt. Coronet. Head to Eterna City for a Bicycle; you'll need it to get up Route 207's sandy slopes.

Moves needed for completion

Rock Climb

Oran Berry ×2
Cheri Berry ×1
Bluk Berry ×1

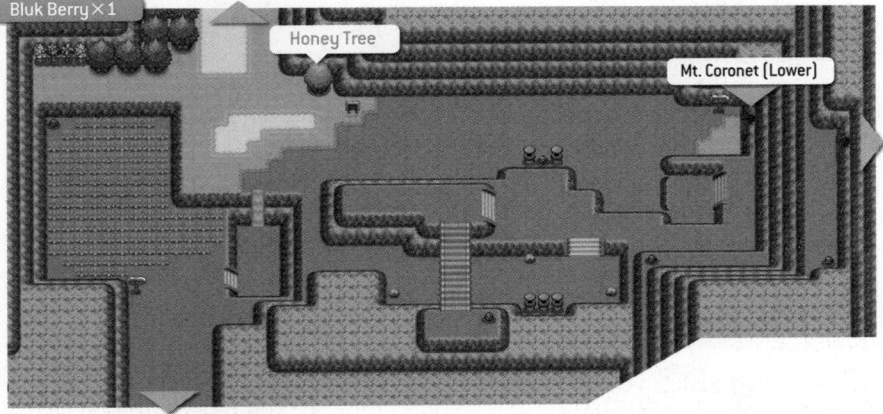

Route 206 (to Eterna City)

Honey Tree

Mt. Coronet (Lower)

Mt. Coronet (Middle)

Oreburgh City

Ponyta
FIRE
Abilities
• Run Away
• Flash Fire

Machop
FIGHTING
Abilities
• Guts
• No Guard

Items

• First visit
☐ Poké Ball
• After getting the Bicycle
☐ Oran Berry x2
☐ Cheri Berry
☐ Bluk Berry
☐ Revive
☐ Super Potion
☐ Vs. Seeker
☐ Pokétch App Dowsing Machine
• After winning at Snowpoint Gym
☐ Timer Ball
☐ Iron

Tall grass

Pokémon	M	A	N
Machop	◎	◎	◎
Geodude	◎	◎	◎
Ponyta	○	○	○
Kricketot	○	X	○
Zubat	X	X	○

Step 1 To catch a Machop

You don't have a bike the first time you visit Route 207, so you can't go any farther. But you can still find Machop in the tall grass there. A girl in Oreburgh City wants one, so catch it here.

After getting the Bicycle — Take a break in Oreburgh City

What lies ahead after you've gotten the Bicycle in Eterna City is a long trek through Route 206 and a blind fumble through a pitch-black cave. Your Pokémon are sure to sustain injuries. So first, return to Oreburgh City and rest up at the Pokémon Center.

After getting the Bicycle — Get Apps from Rowan's assistant

As you approach the entrance to Mt. Coronet, Rowan's assistant appears and gives you the Vs. Seeker (p. 29) and the Pokétch App Dowsing Machine. You're asked which you'd prefer, but don't sweat it—the assistant will give you both, whichever one you pick.

Use the Dowsing Machine to search for items

The Dowsing Machine is a useful Pokétch App that uncovers invisible items. Tap the touch screen when you're in an area that looks like it's hiding something.

After getting the Bicycle — On your way to Mt. Coronet

Proceed east along Route 207 to enter Mt. Coronet, the enormous mountain range bisecting the Sinnoh region. Before you enter, be sure to go to the Pokémart in Oreburgh City and load up on Potions and other items.

Use Rock Climb for those items on higher ledges

Rock Climb is an HM that lets you scale rough rock walls. You can use it as soon as you defeat Snowpoint Gym Leader Candice and earn your Icicle Badge. When that happens, be sure to give Mt. Coronet a return visit.

• The road and underground tunnel that connects Jubilife City to Floaroma Town

Route 204 • Ravaged Path

Story Route 204 is a road bristling with natural beauty, from its ponds to its stands of trees. There's a shortcut cut into one of the cliffs here. To pass, you'll need the HM Rock Smash.

Moves needed for completion

Rock Smash   Cut   Surf

Floaroma Town   • Route 204   • Ravaged Path

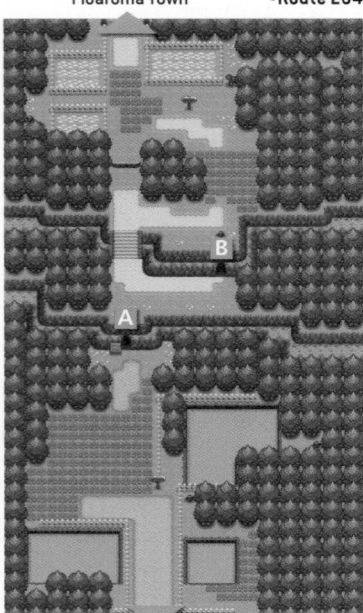

Jubilife City

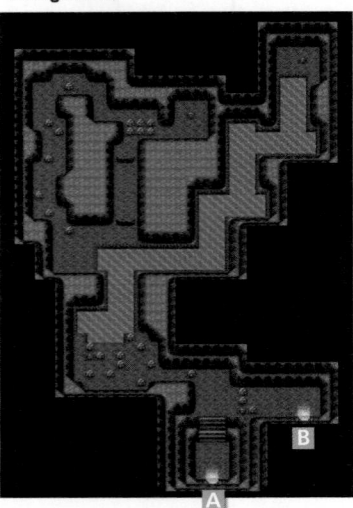

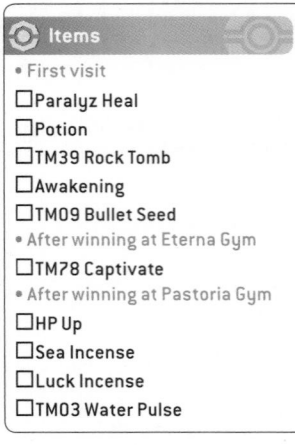

Items

• First visit
- ☐ Paralyz Heal
- ☐ Potion
- ☐ TM39 Rock Tomb
- ☐ Awakening
- ☐ TM09 Bullet Seed
• After winning at Eterna Gym
- ☐ TM78 Captivate
• After winning at Pastoria Gym
- ☐ HP Up
- ☐ Sea Incense
- ☐ Luck Incense
- ☐ TM03 Water Pulse

•Route 204

Tall grass

Pokémon	M	A	N
Starly	○	○	○
Bidoof	○	○	○
Wurmple	○	○	X
Kricketot	○	X	○
Budew	○	○	○
Shinx	○	○	○
Zubat	X	X	○

Water surface

Pokémon	
Psyduck	◎
Golduck	○

Fishing

Rod	Pokémon	
Old	Magikarp	◎
Good	Magikarp	◎
	Goldeen	◎
Super	Gyarados	◎
	Seaking	◎

•Ravaged Path

Cave

Pokémon	M	A	N
Zubat	◎	◎	◎
Psyduck	◎	◎	◎

Water surface

Pokémon	
Psyduck	◎
Zubat	◎
Golduck	△
Golbat	△

Fishing

Rod	Pokémon	
Old	Magikarp	◎
Good	Magikarp	◎
	Barboach	◎
Super	Gyarados	◎
	Whiscash	◎

Wurmple

BUG

Ability
•Shield Dust

Budew

GRASS POISON

Abilities
•Natural Cure
•Poison Point

Step 1 Take the cave into the Ravaged Path

To get to Floaroma Town, you'll be taking the Ravaged Path, found right in the middle of Route 204. You can enter through a hole cut into one of the cliffs here. Be sure to teach one of your Pokémon HM Rock Smash, since you'll need it if you want to get anywhere inside.

Step 2 Use Rock Smash to proceed

Make your way east once inside the cave, and you should emerge topside of the cliff on Route 204. You'll need to use HM Rock Smash to take down rocks blocking the way. Also make time to pick up all the items before you leave.

To Surf, man

You need HM Surf to reach the very back of the Ravaged Path. Come back once you've won at Pastoria Gym and gotten your Fen Badge.

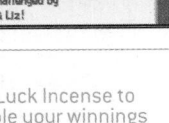

Step 3 Double Trouble in a Double Battle

Just before you make it out of the Ravaged Path, you're waylaid by a pair of twin Trainers. You send out two Pokémon at once for your first Double Battle. Remember that in Double Battles, the first Pokémon sent out are the two at the top of your party.

After winning at Eterna Gym Use HM Cut to gather items

Triumphing at Eterna Gym nets you the Forest Badge, which lets you use Cut to slice down trees. Use Cut to cut down a tree on Route 204 and snag the item hidden behind it.

Use Luck Incense to double your winnings

Send a Pokémon holding Luck Incense out into battle even once, and you'll double the amount of money you win for the battle. You can use HM Surf to find the Luck Incense. Once you have it, take advantage of it to fatten your wallet.

Floaroma Town

Story

Blossoming flowers carpet Floaroma Town and cloak it with their sweet perfume. The town contains a flower shop run by true flower lovers. Team Galactic is blocking passage to Floaroma Meadow north of town.

• Floaroma Meadow

Honey Tree

Fuego Ironworks

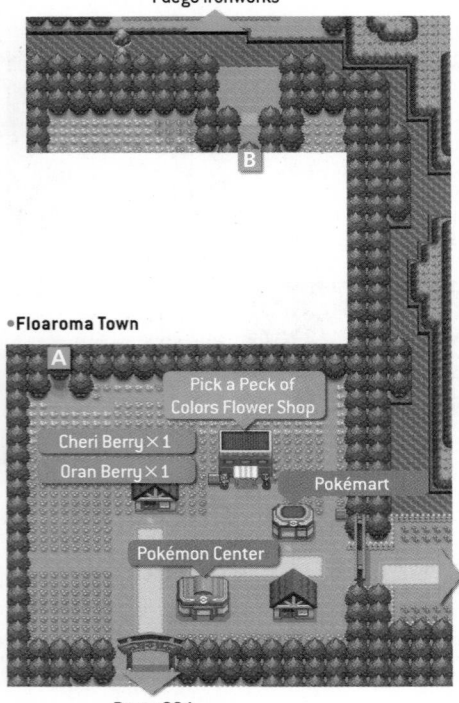

• Floaroma Town

Pick a Peck of Colors Flower Shop

Cheri Berry × 1

Oran Berry × 1

Pokémart

Pokémon Center

Route 205 (Valley Windworks)

Route 204 (to Jubilife City)

Items

• First visit
- ☐ Cheri Berry
- ☐ Oran Berry
- ☐ Sprayduck
- ☐ TM88 Pluck

• After visiting Valley Windworks
- ☐ Works Key
- ☐ Honey x10

• After winning at Pastoria Gym
- ☐ Leaf Stone
- ☐ Ultra Ball
- ☐ Miracle Seed
- ☐ Rare Candy

Pokémart (left counter)

Bloom Mail.................................50P
Heal Ball 300P
Net Ball..............................1000P

Floaroma Meadow man

Honey 100P

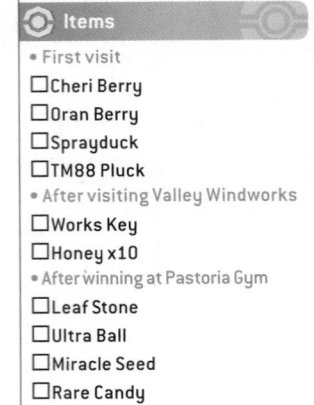

Cherubi

GRASS

Ability
• Chlorophyll

Combee

BUG   FLYING

Ability
• Honey Gather

Burmy
[Trash Cloak]

BUG

Ability
• Shed Skin

Burmy
[Plant Cloak]

BUG

Ability
• Shed Skin

Burmy
[Sandy Cloak]

BUG

Ability
• Shed Skin

 Step 1 Do your berry best

There's a flowering plant in front of the Flower Shop where you can pick some berries. Berries are highly useful items that you can use on Pokémon or just give them to hold. At Hearthome City, you can even use berries as an ingredient in making Poffins, the Pokémon snack.

There is an Oran Berry! Want to pick it?

 **Step 2 Go green and replant**

You can take berries you've acquired and plant them in areas of soft soil. You can help them grow, and they'll give you more berries in return. If you're short on any particular berry, hold off on using it until you've planted and reaped more of it.

What are Gracidea flowers?

The woman next to the sign will tell you about Gracidea flowers. She'll give you one if you talk to her with Shaymin in your party. Use the Gracidea flower on Shaymin to make it change into its Sky Forme. (p. 88)

Step 3 Trade for berry nice accessories

Berries can be traded for accessories at the Flower Shop. You can use accessories when taking photos at Jubilife TV (p. 44) and in Pokémon Super Contests at Hearthome City (p. 229).

• Accessories you can trade for at Pick a Peck of Colors Flower Shop

Accessory Received	Berries Needed	Accessory Received	Berries Needed
Red Flower	Cheri Berry x1	Colored Parasol	Wepear Berry x10
Pink Flower	Chesto Berry x1	Old Umbrella	Pinap Berry x10
White Flower	Pecha Berry x1	Spotlight	Cornn Berry x50
Blue Flower	Oran Berry x1	Cape	Pamtre Berry x100
Orange Flower	Rawst Berry x1	Standing Mike	Magost Berry x50
Yellow Flower	Aspear Berry x1	Surfboard	Watmel Berry x100
Googly Specs	Leppa Berry x1	Carpet	Rabuta Berry x50
Black Specs	Persim Berry x1	Retro Pipe	Nomel Berry x50
Gorgeous Specs	Razz Berry x10	Fluffy Bed	Durin Berry x100
Sweet Candy	Bluk Berry x10	Mirror Ball	Spelon Berry x100
Confetti	Nanab Berry x10	Photo Board	Belue Berry x100

Step 4 Water, water, everywhere

Talk to the girl in the Flower Shop and she'll give you the Sprayduck. The Sprayduck is an item for watering berries you've planted in areas of soft soil. Water your plants carefully and attentively if you want them to grow nice and big.

Get one berry a day from the store clerk

The girl at the Flower Shop gives you a new berry each day—either a Cheri Berry, a Chesto Berry, a Pecha Berry, a Rawst Berry, or an Aspear Berry.

Step 5 Think outside the block

There's an entrance to the Floaroma Meadow above the town. But you can't get in, because some Team Galactic grunts are blocking the way. Just what is Team Galactic up to in a flower meadow, anyway?

Step 6 Head for Eterna City

Eterna City is where your rival is headed for his next Gym challenge. It's after Route 205 and beyond Eterna Forest. Exit the town to the east and proceed along Route 205 on your way to Eterna City.

After visiting the Valley Windworks Obtain the Works Key

You enter Floaroma Meadow to find Team Galactic threatening a man in order to get their hands on some Honey. Save the man by driving off the two grunts. They'll drop the Works Key in their haste to escape.

After visiting the Valley Windworks Honey changes everything

After you chase off the Team Galactic grunts, you can buy Honey from the man in the Floaroma Meadow. Honey is a very handy item for luring out wild Pokémon. Buy lots, so you can fill out your Pokédex.

What happens if I use Honey in tall grass?

Use Honey while you're in tall grass to trigger a wild Pokémon encounter, just as if you'd used the Sweet Scent move.

After visiting the Valley Windworks — Lure Pokémon out with Honey

You can take the Honey you bought from the man in the Floaroma Meadow and spread it on sweet-smelling Honey Trees to lure out wild Pokémon (p. 77). After you've spread Honey on a tree, come back and check on it after about half a day.

Slather the bark with Honey?

Honey loses its effectiveness after one day

When you spread Honey on a Honey Tree, it loses its effectiveness after a day. Make sure you remember where you've spread your Honey and be sure to return in time, so you don't waste Honey.

After winning at Pastoria Gym — Meddle in the Meadow

After you've won at Pastoria Gym and gained the ability to use Surf, travel south from the Fuego Ironworks into Floaroma Town. Search the Meadow with a fine-toothed comb for fallen items that will help you on your journey.

Lucas found a Rare Candy!

• The road connecting Floaroma Town and Eterna City

Route 205 • Fuego Ironworks

Story

Route 205 is lined with gently flowing rivers and undulating terrain. To the east is the Windworks, to the west the Fuego Ironworks. And sprawling northward is Eterna Forest.

Moves needed for completion

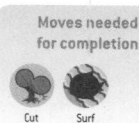

Cut   Surf

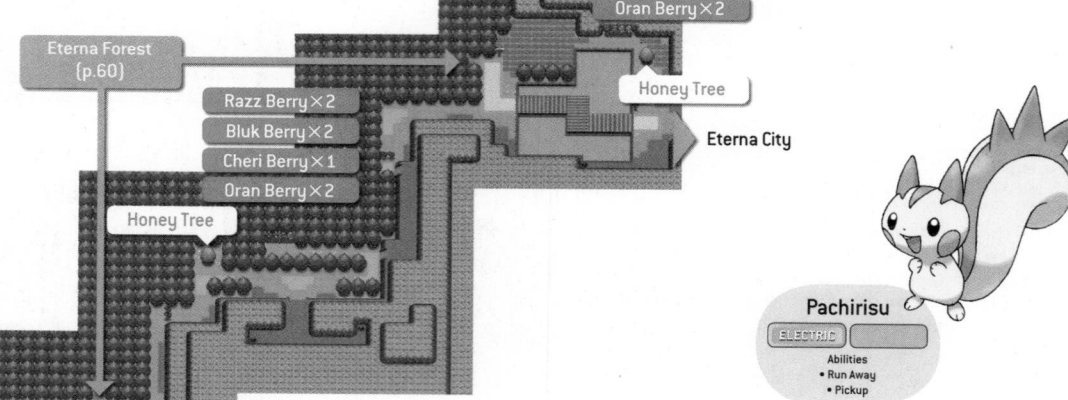

• Route 205

Cheri Berry × 1
Pecha Berry × 1
Oran Berry × 2

Eterna Forest (p.60)

Razz Berry × 2
Bluk Berry × 2
Cheri Berry × 1
Oran Berry × 2

Honey Tree

Honey Tree

Eterna City

Fuego Ironworks

Pecha Berry × 2
Oran Berry × 1

Honey Tree

Chesto Berry × 1
Pecha Berry × 1

Floaroma Town   Valley Windworks

Pachirisu

ELECTRIC

Abilities
• Run Away
• Pickup

Items

• First visit
☐ Chesto Berry
☐ Pecha Berry
• After visiting Valley Windworks
☐ X Sp. Def
☐ Pecha Berry
☐ Oran Berry
☐ Heal Ball
☐ Repel
☐ Super Potion
• After visiting Eterna Forest
☐ Cheri Berry
☐ Pecha Berry
☐ Oran Berry x2

☐ Guard Spec
• After winning at Pastoria Gym
☐ Sitrus Berry
☐ Wepear Berry x4
☐ Kelpsy Berry
☐ Calcium
☐ Star Piece
☐ Red Shard
☐ Blue Shard
☐ Yellow Shard
☐ Green Shard
☐ Fire Stone
☐ Rock Incense
☐ TM35 Flamethrower

56

•Fuego Ironworks exterior

Sitrus Berry × 1
Wepear Berry × 4
Kelpsy Berry × 1

Honey Tree

Route 205

Floaroma Town
(Floaroma Meadow)

•Fuego Ironworks interior

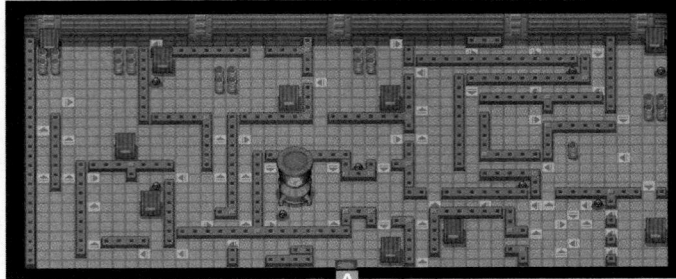

A

•Route 205 (Eterna City side)

Tall grass

Pokémon	M	A	N
Bidoof	◎	◎	◎
Budew	○	◎	○
Wurmple	○	○	✕
Kricketot	○	✕	○
Silcoon	○	○	○
Cascoon	○	○	○
Beautifly	▲	▲	▲
Dustox	▲	▲	▲
Hoothoot	✕	✕	○

Water surface

Pokémon	
Psyduck	◎
Golduck	○

Fishing

Rod	Pokémon	
Old	Magikarp	◎
Good	Magikarp	◎
	Barboach	◎
Super	Gyarados	◎
	Whiscash	◎

•Route 205 (Floaroma Town side)

Tall grass

Pokémon	M	A	N
Shellos	◎	◎	◎
Buizel	○	○	○
Bidoof	○	○	○
Pachirisu	○	○	○

Water surface

Pokémon	
Shellos	◎
Tentacool	◎
Gastrodon	△
Tentacruel	▲

Fishing

Rod	Pokémon	
Old	Magikarp	◎
Good	Magikarp	◎
	Finneon	◎
	Lumineon	◎
Super	Gyarados	○
	Shellder	○

•Fuego Ironworks exterior

Tall grass

Pokémon	M	A	N
Magnemite	◎	◎	◎
Magmar	◎	◎	○
Floatzel	○	○	○
Gastrodon	○	○	○

Water surface

Pokémon	
Tentacool	◎
Shellos	◎
Tentacruel	△
Gastrodon	▲

Fishing

Rod	Pokémon	
Old	Magikarp	◎
Good	Magikarp	◎
	Finneon	◎
	Lumineon	◎
Super	Gyarados	○
	Shellder	○

Magnemite
ELECTRIC STEEL
Abilities
• Magnet Pull
• Sturdy

Magmar
FIRE
Ability
• Flame Body

Shellder
WATER
Abilities
• Shell Armor
• Skill Link

ROUTE 205 • FUEGO IRONWORKS

SINNOH WALKTHROUGH

Step 1 — Help a Father Out

Head from Floaroma Town onto Route 205, and you see a little girl. Talk to her and she'll ask you to go bring her father, who works at the Valley Windworks. Hurry over to the Windworks (p. 59).

Please, Trainer!
I miss my papa!

Use Pickup to find items

Some of the Pachirisu appearing in the tall grass on Route 205 have the Pickup Ability. Put one of these Pachirisu in your party and go about your business, and this handy Ability scoops up items when you're not even looking (p. 561).

Step 2 — Find Another Way

Some Team Galactic grunts have blocked off the footbridge you need to cross in order to reach Eterna Forest. It seems they're conducting some kind of investigation in the forest. Forget the bridge for now and hurry on to the east, toward the Valley Windworks.

We, Team Galactic, are conducting research in the Eterna Forest!

After rescuing the girl's father | Hike into Eterna Forest

Once you rescue the little girl's father, who was being held at the Valley Windworks, the Galactic grunts at the bridge pull back, clearing passage over the bridge. Go on over and set out for Eterna Forest.

Heal your Pokémon at people's houses

There's a private house, near the entrance to Eterna Forest, where you can get your Pokémon's HP and PP restored. Take a breather there before heading into the forest.

After visiting Eterna Forest | Clear Eterna Forest and head for Eterna City

Clearing Eterna Forest, you'll find yourself back on Route 205. As soon as you cross the big bridge with all the fishermen on it, you'll find Eterna City straight ahead. Keep going, and remember your plan to challenge the Gym Leader here.

Take a shortcut using Cut

There's a tree near the entrance to Eterna Forest. Chop it down with Cut, and you can make an end run around the forest and proceed straight to Eterna City. Once you can use Cut, this is clearly the way to go.

After winning at Pastoria Gym | Head to Fuego Ironworks using Surf

There's a waterway right where you step onto Route 205 from Floaroma Town. Use HM Surf here to travel to the Fuego Ironworks. Once you reach a dead end, head up north to the Fuego Ironworks, or south to the Floaroma Meadow.

After winning at Pastoria Gym | Gather items inside the Fuego Ironworks

There are lots of arrow tiles inside the Fuego Ironworks, which send you traveling in the direction of the arrow. Study the directions and pick up all the items in the Ironworks. You'll find the manager, Fuego, standing near the blast furnace.

Evolve Pokémon with the Fire Stone

Inside the Fuego Ironworks, you'll acquire the Fire Stone, an item that can make certain Pokémon evolve. You can use it on the Eevee you get from Bebe in Hearthome City to evolve it into Flareon.

After winning at Pastoria Gym | It's a Shard Hock Life

Talk to Ironworks manager Mr. Fuego and he'll give you a Star Piece. Talk to him again later to hock other Star Pieces for a Red Shard, a Blue Shard, a Yellow Shard, or a Green Shard.

You can also find the Star Piece in the Underground

The Star Piece can also be found in the Sinnoh Underground as a treasure during fossil-digging. You can sell them at Pokémarts for 4900 Poké.

After winning at Pastoria Gym | Poke around the hidden part of the Meadow

Just south of the Fuego Ironworks you can access the northern area of the Floaroma Meadow, which you couldn't get to from Floaroma Town. Case the place and pick up the items. On your way back, there's a ledge you can jump down to take a shortcut to Floaroma Town.

58

Valley Windworks

Story

At the Valley Windworks, the winds that sweep the valley power windmills and generate energy. It's for that reason that Team Galactic takes command of the Valley Windworks plant.

Moves needed for completion

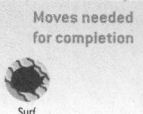

Surf

•Valley Windworks exterior

A Honey Tree

Route 205 (to Floaroma Town)

Items

• First visit
☐ Potion
• After winning at Pastoria Gym
☐ Electirizer
☐ TM24 Thunderbolt

Drifloon

GHOST   FLYING

Abilities
• Aftermath
• Unburden

•Valley Windworks interior

A

•Valley Windworks exterior

Tall grass

Pokémon	M	A	N
Shellos	◎	◎	◎
Shinx	○	○	○
Buizel	○	○	○
Pachirisu	○	○	○

Water surface

Pokémon	
Shellos	◎
Tentacool	◎
Gastrodon	△
Tentacruel	▲

Fishing

Rod	Pokémon	
Old	Magikarp	◎
Good	Magikarp	◎
	Finneon	◎
	Lumineon	◎
Super	Gyarados	○
	Shellder	○

Step 1 Locked Down!

You visit the Valley Windworks, only to find a Team Galactic grunt blocking the entrance. You defeat him in battle, but he just shuts himself inside and locks the door. Go to the Floaroma Meadow to find the Works Key to open the door.

It's locked from inside!

Use Surf to look for items

Once you have the ability to use Surf, come here and you can follow the nearby waterway to find an item. It's an Electirizer, which helps a certain Pokémon evolve (p. 388).

After getting the Works Key Bash your way through Team Galactic to the back

With the Works Key in hand, you can enter the Valley Windworks. Make your way through the Team Galactic-occupied interior, fighting Galactic grunts as you go. At last you'll find and battle the Commander, Mars. Win, and you can save the little girl's father, who's been held hostage.

Collecting electricity from the Valley Windworks... That's our mission.

Battle with Team Galactic Commander Mars! ①

Team Galactic Commander Mars sends out two Pokémon to battle, each of which is quite different type-wise from the other. Use Electric-, Psychic-, Rock-, and Ice-type moves on Zubat, and Fighting-type moves on Purugly, and fight your way to victory.

• PARTY POKÉMON

Zubat ♀ Lv15	POISON	FLYING
Purugly ♀ Lv17	NORMAL	

After getting the Works Key — Head for Eterna City and its Pokémon Gym

Defeat Team Galactic ringleader Mars, and fellow Commander Charon leads the rest of the team in retreat. This includes the grunts who were barricading Route 205. Now you can cross the bridge and head for Eterna City.

Drifloon appears every Friday

After you drive off Team Galactic, the little girl's father tells you how Pokémon show up every week in front of the Windworks. Visit on Friday and you're sure to see Drifloon. This is the perfect chance to catch one.

• A place where time flows eternal

Eterna Forest and Old Chateau

Story — Eterna Forest is a forest where rows of trees cluster together to form a natural maze. At its heart stands the abandoned, deserted Old Chateau. Go east from the area just in front of the chateau. It's not far to Eterna City.

Moves needed for completion

Cut

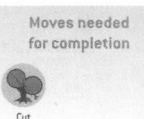

Hoothoot

NORMAL FLYING

Abilities
• Insomnia
• Keen Eye

Buneary

NORMAL

Abilities
• Run Away
• Klutz

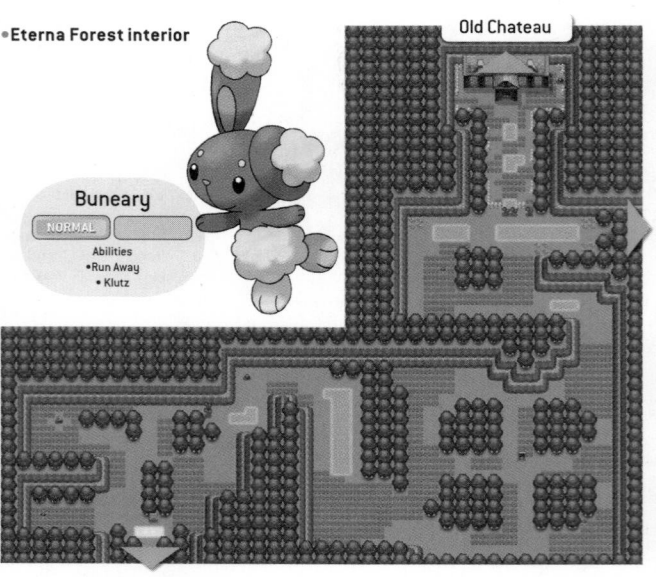

• Eterna Forest interior

Old Chateau

Route 205 (to Eterna City)

Route 205 (to Floaroma Town)

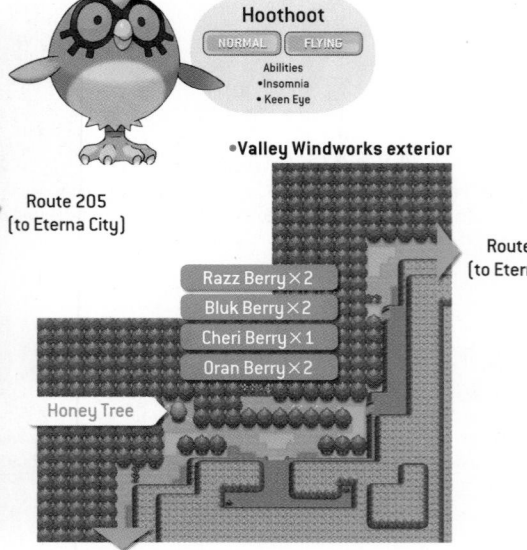

• Valley Windworks exterior

Route 205 (to Eterna City)

Razz Berry × 2
Bluk Berry × 2
Cheri Berry × 1
Oran Berry × 2

Honey Tree

Route 205 (to Floaroma Town)

SINNOH WALKTHROUGH

VALLEY WINDWORKS • ETERNA FOREST AND OLD CHATEAU

Items

• First visit
- ☐ Antidote
- ☐ Paralyz Heal
- ☐ Net Ball
- ☐ Potion
- ☐ Green Shard
- ☐ Soothe Bell

• After visiting Eterna Forest
- ☐ Ether
- ☐ Big Pearl
- ☐ Rare Candy
- ☐ Old Gateau
- ☐ TM90 Substitute
- ☐ Dread Plate

- ☐ Razz Berry x2
- ☐ Bluk Berry x2
- ☐ Cheri Berry
- ☐ Oran Berry x2
- ☐ Big Tree Accessory
- ☐ Silverpowder
- ☐ TM82 Sleep Talk

• Eterna Forest interior

Tall grass

Pokémon	M	A	N
Budew	◎	◎	◎
Buneary	○	○	○
Bidoof	○	○	○
Wurmple	○	○	✗
Kricketot	○	✗	○
Hoothoot	✗	✗	○
Silcoon	△	△	△
Cascoon	△	△	△
Gastly	△	△	△
Beautifly	▲	▲	▲
Dustox	▲	▲	▲

• Old Chateau

Interior

Pokémon	M	A	N
Gastly	◎	◎	◎

• Old Chateau 2F

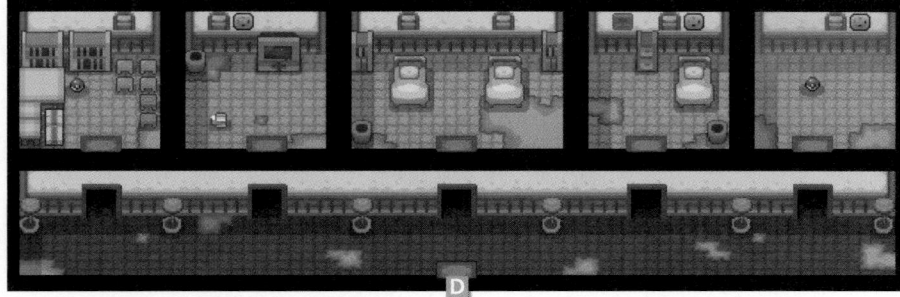

• Old Chateau 1F • Dining Area

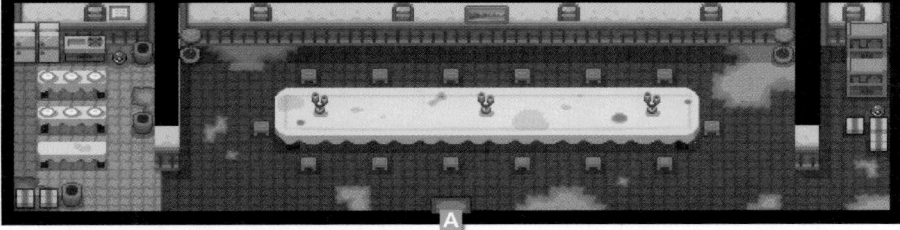

• 2F • Room 1

• Old Chateau 1F

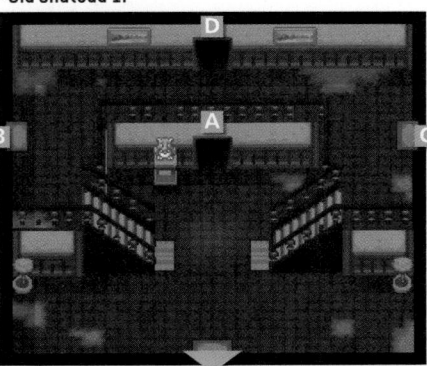

Eterna Forest

• 2F • Room 2

Cheryl

Gastly
GHOST POISON
Ability
•Levitate

Step 1 — Pass through the forest with Cheryl

Upon entering Eterna Forest, talk to the girl named Cheryl. She's feeling uneasy because of the reports of Team Galactic casing the area. Accept her request to travel with her until you reach the end of the forest.

I think there'd be safety in numbers. Please, may I go through with you?

Cheryl is a giver

When Cheryl is traveling with you through Eterna Forest, she heals your Pokémon's HP, PP, and status ailments after each battle. This is the perfect opportunity to level up any weak Pokémon you have.

 **Step 2** Wild Pokémon Double Up

As long as you're traveling with Cheryl, wild Pokémon attack two at a time. You're used to battling wild Pokémon one-on-one, but here your Pokémon get to fight alongside Cheryl's Chansey.

A wild CASCOON and DUSTOX appeared!

You can only catch "single" Pokémon

When you're up against a pair of wild Pokémon, you can't throw a Poké Ball at either one until you isolate one. If a Pokémon that you want to catch appears in a pair, knock out its partner first.

 **Step 3** Parting is Such Sweet Sorrow

As soon as you reach the exit to Eterna Forest, Cheryl parts ways with you. Before leaving, she gives you the Soothe Bell as thanks for accompanying her out of the forest. Continue to the east and on towards Eterna City.

Cheryl: Oh! There's the exit! I'm so relieved... We finally got here.

The mystery of the mossy rock

There's a moss-covered rock at the western edge of Eterna Forest. This rock is for Eevee Evolutions. Level up Eevee in Eterna Forest, and it evolves into Leafeon (p. 382).

After winning at Eterna Gym | **Catch Rotom at the Old Chateau**

Use Cut to slice down a tree so you can enter the Old Chateau. Examine the TV on the second floor at any time between 8 PM and 4 AM, and you'll encounter Rotom. Don't miss your chance to catch this hard-to-find Pokémon.

Inside the TV... There appears to be a Pokémon?...

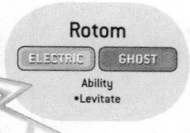

Rotom

ELECTRIC | GHOST

Ability
• Levitate

• Eterna City, a city with a rich, living history

Eterna City

Story

Eterna City is a city where modern buildings exist side-by-side with the shadows of the past. Currently, the townspeople are troubled by the advent of Team Galactic, which is erecting a mysterious and creepy building to serve as its home base.

Moves needed for completion

Cut | Surf

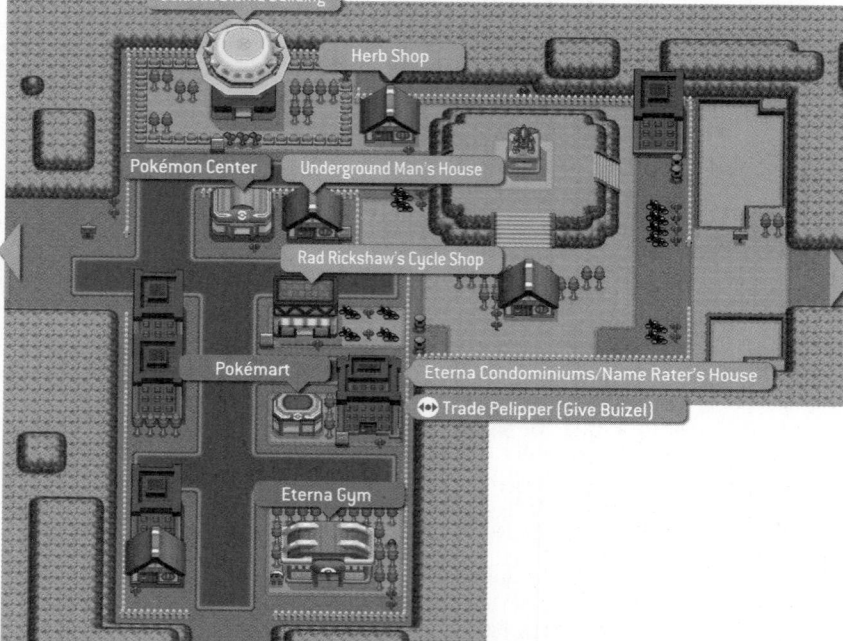

Galactic Eterna Building

Herb Shop

Pokémon Center

Underground Man's House

Route 205 (to Eterna Forest)

Rad Rickshaw's Cycle Shop

Route 211 (to Mt. Coronet peak)

Pokémart

Eterna Condominiums/Name Rater's House

Trade Pelipper (Give Buizel)

Eterna Gym

Route 206 (to Oreburgh City)

Items

- First visit
- ☐ Pokétch App
  Friendship Checker
- ☐ Explorer Kit
- ☐ Super Potion
- ☐ TM67 Recycle
- ☐ HM01 Cut
- After winning at Eterna Gym
- ☐ Forest Badge
- ☐ TM86 Grass Knot
- ☐ TM46 Thief
- After visiting Galactic
  Eterna Building
- ☐ Pokémon Egg
- ☐ Bicycle
- ☐ Exp. Share

Pokémart (left counter)

Air Mail	50P
Heal Ball	300P
Net Ball	1000P
Nest Ball	1000P

Herb Shop

Heal Powder	450P
EnergyPowder	500P
Energy Root	800P
Revival Herb	2800P

Water surface

Pokémon	
Psyduck	◎
Golduck	○

Fishing

Rod	Pokémon	
Old	Magikarp	◎
Good	Magikarp	◎
	Barboach	◎
Super	Gyarados	◎
	Whiscash	◎

Step 1 Get the Pokétch App Friendship Checker

A girl in the Pokémon Center gives you the Pokétch App Friendship Checker when you talk to her. Talk to her again and she'll tell you how well the lead Pokémon in your party likes you.

Lucas obtained the Pokétch app FRIENDSHIP CHECKER.

The name game

On the first floor of Eterna Condominiums is a name rater—a man who'll tell your Pokémon's fortune based on its name. You can also change the Pokémon's nickname an unlimited number of times.

Step 2 Get the Explorer Kit from the Underground Man

The Underground Man is the person who first dug out the tunnels that make up the Sinnoh Underground. Talk to him and he'll give you the Explorer Kit. Use it to complete the tasks he gives you. Clear all the areas and you can set out on a full-fledged underground adventure of your own.

Lucas obtained the Explorer Kit!

Explorer Kit

Learn what it said on the missing plate

At a private house south of the Pokémon statue, someone tells you about the writing on the plate that was removed from the statue. You learn there was information concerning space and time, and about one other matter.

Step 3 Go with your rival to see the Pokémon statue

Go east from the Pokémon Center and your rival will show you to the Pokémon statue. In front of the statue, you'll run into Cyrus, that same guy you first saw at Lake Verity. He's saying something about Pokémon of time and space, but leaves before he gets any more comprehensible.

Shaping our world are time and space in an intertwining spiral.

Cynthia gives you an HM—but who is she, really?

Cynthia tells you she's a Pokémon Trainer fond of exploring Pokémon legends. Seeing your Pokédex brings back memories for her, she says. But what's her deal, really?

Step 4 Acquire HM01 Cut

Talk to a girl named Cynthia in front of the Galactic Eterna Building. She gives you HM 01 Cut, suggesting that you use it. Unfortunately, you can't until you win at Eterna Gym.

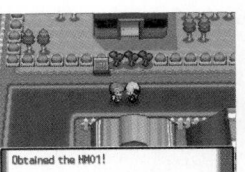

Obtained the HM01!

Herbal medicines lower a Pokémon's friendship rating

To the right of the Galactic Eterna Building is the medicine shop. Herbal medicines are tremendously effective, but their bitter taste lowers a Pokémon's Friendship with you. Make sure a Pokémon is well-disposed toward you before you give it herbal medicine.

Step 5 Look for the Cycle Shop manager

Rad Rickshaw's Cycle Shop is the only bike shop in the Sinnoh Region. But unfortunately, it seems the manager went to the Galactic Eterna Building and never came back. To get into the Galactic Eterna Building yourself, you need to use Cut, so your next step is to challenge the Eterna Gym Leader.

The manager's gone off to the Team Galactic building and hasn't returned.

GYM BATTLE ②

Eterna Gym Leader

GARDENIA

- *Grass Pokémon user*

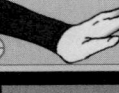

• PARTY POKÉMON

⊙ Turtwig ♂ Lv20	GRASS	
⊙ Cherrim ♀ Lv20	GRASS	
⊙ Roserade ♀ Lv22	GRASS	POISON

Fight using Fire- and Flying-type moves

The path inside Eterna Gym is barricaded by water fountains and a huge flower clock. Beat the three other Trainers in the Gym to be able to cross over these obstacles and challenge Gardenia. Gardenia's Pokémon are all Grass-types. Use Fire-, Ice-, and Flying-type moves. Win, and you receive the Forest Badge and TM 86 Grass Knot.

FOREST BADGE

Lets you use Cut in the field. Pokémon up to Lv. 30, even those received in trade, will obey your commands.

ENTER

After winning at Eterna Gym — Break into the Galactic Eterna Building

Once you defeat Gardenia and receive the Forest Badge, you can use HM Cut to cut down small trees. Then you can get into the Galactic Eterna Building, where the Cycle Shop manager was last seen, and check out the situation.

This tree looks like it can be cut down! Would you like to cut it?

Use HM Cut to find items

Once you have HM Cut, you'll be able to penetrate farther into the Galactic Eterna grounds. There, you'll find TM 46 Thief—rather fitting for a Team Galactic secret base.

After visiting the Galactic Eterna Building — Receive a Pokémon Egg from Cynthia

After you've driven Team Galactic out of the Galactic Eterna Building and made your way outside the building, you run into Cynthia on your way down through the city. Cynthia says she's been looking for you in order to give you something, which turns out to be a Pokémon Egg. The Egg will hatch into Togepi.

I wanted you to have this Pokémon Egg. Will you accept it?

After visiting the Galactic Eterna Building — Get your bike on

Make your way to the Cycle Shop and talk to the manager, whose Clefairy you've safely retrieved from Team Galactic. The manager gives you a Bicycle to express his gratitude. It's the very latest model, featuring the ability to change gears.

It's the latest model Bicycle! You must take it. I insist!

Mount your Bicycle at bike racks

Bike racks are set up next to Pokémon Centers and at town entrances. Just stand in front of a bike rack and press A to mount and dismount your Bicycle with ease.

After getting the Bicycle — Receive the Exp. Share from Rowan's lab assistant

Entering the gate on your way to Route 206, you find Rowan's lab assistant waiting for you. If you have more than 35 Pokémon sighted in your Pokédex, the assistant will reward you with the Exp. Share.

Obtained the Exp. Share!

Level up faster

The Exp. Share is a useful item that distributes Exp. to Pokémon even if you don't send them into a battle. Try giving it to a weaker Pokémon you want to develop more quickly.

After getting the Bicycle — Off to Cycling Road

Route 206, south of Eterna City, is also known as Cycling Road because of its suitability for bike travel. Take the Bicycle you got from the Bike Shop manager, saddle up, and coast down the road.

Gettin' Down in the Underground

Clear all five areas of the test to get ready for the real Underground

The Underground Man is the person who first dug out the tunnels underneath the Sinnoh region. He presents you with a test, comprising five areas in all, to make sure you're up to speed for a full-on underground expedition. You also get a prize for each section of the test you complete. Clear them all.

 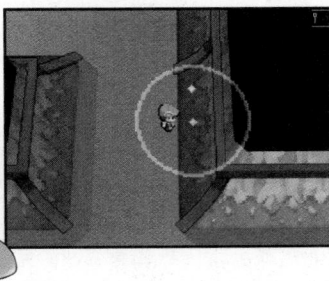

Dig This

Test **1** Go Underground

Use the Explorer Kit the Underground Man gave you to enter the Underground. Once you're under, select "Surface" and return above ground.

Prize Move Trap/Bubble Trap/Leaf Trap

Test **2** Excavate items

Go to a spot where the Radar blinks yellow, and tap the touch screen, to find a wall with buried treasure. Examine the wall and use the hammer and pick to dig out the items.

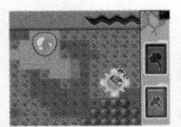

Prize Prism Sphere 1/Red Sphere 1/Red Sphere 1

Test **3** Bury a Sphere

Once you're back below ground, take the Sphere you got and bury it. Unearth it again after a short period and it will have grown. Tap the touch screen and confirm the spot where it was buried.

Prize Digger Drill

Test **4** Build a secret base

You can make your very own secret base in the walls of the Underground. Use the Digger Drill to make your base in any spot you like. Inside the base are where your personal PC and flag are kept.

Prize Plain Table/Wooden Chair/Small Bookshelf/Buneary Doll

Test **5** Decorate your base

Okay, so you've made a secret base. Now you can redecorate, and store items there. Try out the Plain Table, Wooden Chair, or Small Bookshelf you won for passing Test 4.

Prize Turtwig Doll, Chimchar Doll, Piplup Doll (one only)

Bonus Capture the flag

Use the Nintendo DS Wireless capability to go burrowing with your friends in the Underground. You gain victories by stealing the flags hidden in your friends' secret bases, and taking them back to your own base.

Prize Pretty Gem

Galactic Eterna Building

Story

There's lots of murmuring going on among the Eterna City townspeople about the suspicious and imposing Galactic Eterna Building. You sneak inside in search of the missing Cycle Shop manager.

• 4F

• 2F

• 3F

• 1F
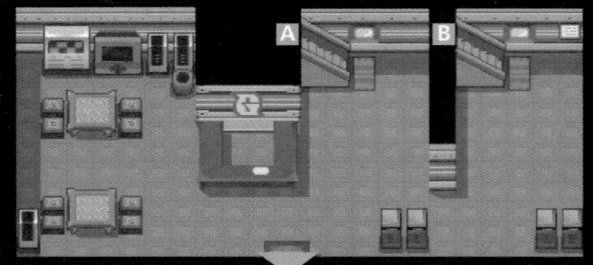

to Eterna City

 Items

☐ X Speed
☐ X Special
☐ Revive
☐ Blue Shard
☐ Up-Grade

Team Galactic grunts

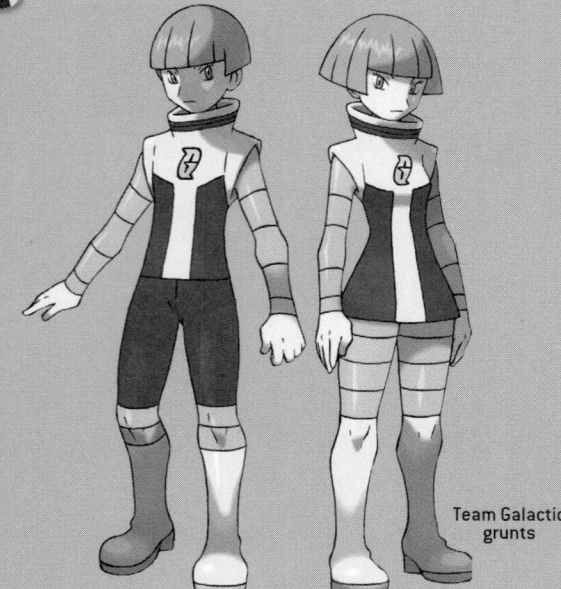

 Step 1 Run into Looker in Team Galactic guise

Upon sneaking into the Galactic Eterna Building, you're approached by Looker, who's now sporting Team Galactic duds. He says that there are two staircases on each floor, one of which is a trap. Before you take the stairs, check the wall nearby for a sign—that's how you know it's the real staircase.

Stairway to Heaven (y items)

If a staircase in the Galactic Eterna Building doesn't have a sign near it, it's a fake staircase. But it can still lead you to useful items, so make sure you check them out.

Looker: Hello! It is me! Me! Hahaha! I have startled you, yes?

Step 2 Fight to the fourth!

The Galactic Eterna Building contains four stories. And Looker's info is right on the money—there are two upward staircases on each floor. Take the staircases marked by those conspicuous signs on the wall, and make your way up to the 4th floor. That's where you'll find Galactic Commander Jupiter and the Cycle Shop manager.

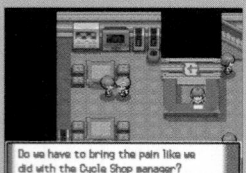

The manager came to get his Clefairy back

The Cycle Shop manager came to get back his Clefairy, which Team Galactic kidnapped. You can also see Buneary, which the boy at the Cycle Shop mentioned being stolen.

Do we have to bring the pain like we did with the Cycle Shop manager?

Battle with Team Galactic Commander Jupiter! ❶

Team Galactic Commander Jupiter sends out Zubat and Skuntank to battle. Your most effective moves against Zubat will be Electric-, Ice-, Psychic-, and Rock-types. Against Skuntank, Ground-type moves will lead you to victory.

•PARTY POKÉMON

| Zubat ♀ Lv21 | POISON | FLYING |
| Skuntank ♀ Lv23 | POISON | DARK |

Step 3 — Rescue the Cycle Shop manager

Defeat Team Galactic Commander Jupiter, and she splits, while dropping some new information: the Team Galactic boss is investigating myths and trying to employ Legendary Pokémon to take over the Sinnoh region. Rescue the Cycle Shop manager and put the Galactic Eterna Building behind you.

I can't thank you enough right now, but cruise by my Cycle Shop, OK?

Up-Grade is an Evolution Item

On the 4th floor of the Galactic Eterna Building, you get Up-Grade, an item involved with Porygon Evolution. You'll get a Porygon in Veilstone City, so tuck it away for now.

• The road joining Eterna City and Route 207

Route 206 • Wayward Cave

Route 206 is also known as Cycling Road. Its paved surface makes it optimal for biking. Under Cycling Road is the entrance to the Wayward Cave.

Moves needed for completion
Rock Smash | Cut

•Route 206
Items
• First Visit
- ☐ Flag Accessory
- ☐ Razz Berry x2
- ☐ PP Up
- ☐ Burn Heal
- ☐ Rawst Berry x2
- ☐ Super Repel
- ☐ Poison Barb
- ☐ Escape Rope
- ☐ Revive
- ☐ TM32 Double Team
- ☐ Max Ether
- ☐ Grip Claw
- ☐ Rare Candy
- ☐ TM26 Earthquake

•Route 206
Tall Grass

Pokémon	M	A	N
Geodude	◎	◎	◎
Ponyta	○	◎	○
Gligar	○	○	○
Machop	○	○	○
Kricketune	○	X	○
Zubat	X	X	○

Gligar
GROUND | FLYING
Abilities
•Hyper Cutter
•Sand Veil

Kricketune
BUG
Ability
• Swarm

ROUTE 206 • WAYWARD CAVE

•Route 206

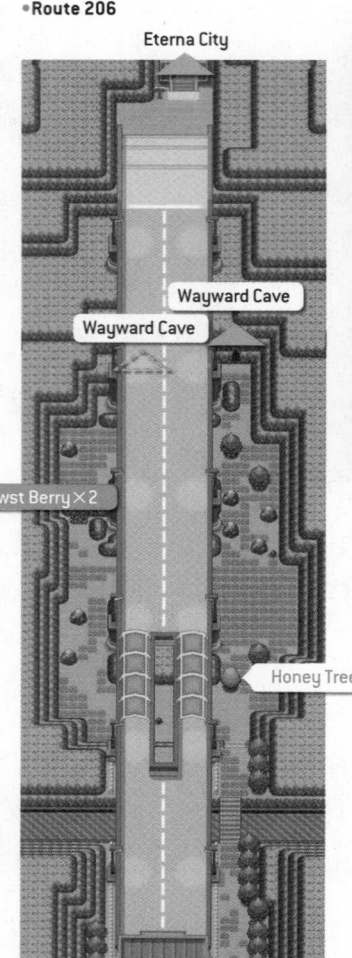

Eterna City

Wayward Cave

Wayward Cave

Rawst Berry×2

Honey Tree

Razz Berry×2

Route 207 (to Oreburgh City)

•Wayward Cave 1F

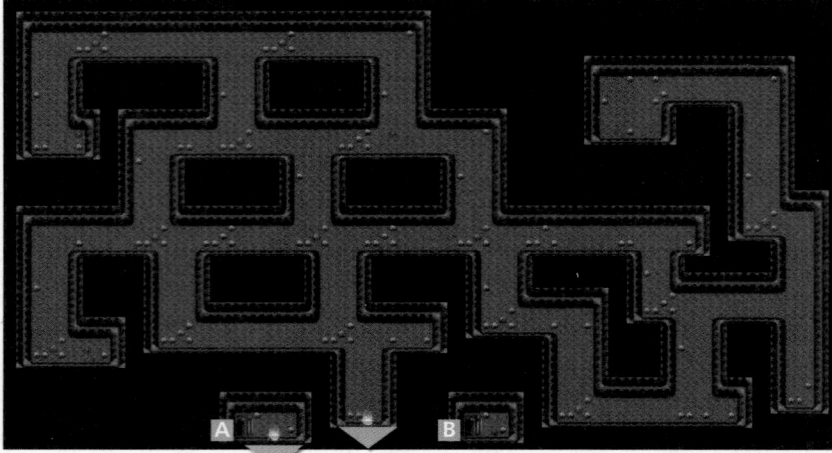

A   B

Route 206

Route 206

•Wayward Cave 1F

Pokémon	M	A	N
Bronzor	◎	◎	◎
Geodude	◎	◎	◎
Zubat	○	○	○
Onix	○	○	○

•Wayward Cave B1F

Pokémon	M	A	N
Bronzor	◎	◎	◎
Geodude	○	○	○
Zubat	○	○	○
Onix	○	○	○
Gible	○	○	○

•Wayward Cave B1F

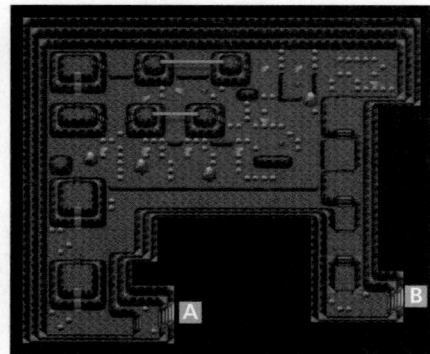

A   B

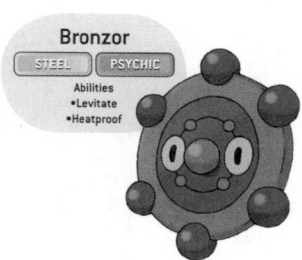

Bronzor

STEEL   PSYCHIC

Abilities
•Levitate
•Heatproof

Gible

DRAGON   GROUND

Ability
•Sand Veil

Mira

Step 1 Coast down Cycling Road

Step out onto Route 206—it's Cycling Road, full of bicyclers peddling around. The road slopes downward, so you can coast all the way from Eterna City to the gate at the southern end. Cross paths with other Trainers and battle your way through.

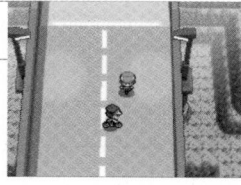

Saddle Up

Since Cycling Road is a dedicated bicycling road, you'll need to saddle up while you're at the gate that connects Eterna City to Route 206. If you don't, it'll just make the lady behind the counter mad, and you won't be allowed to go through.

Step 2 Enter the Wayward Cave

The entrance to the Wayward Cave is right underneath Cycling Road. First you have to ride your Bicycle to the bottom of the road, then you have to walk north to the cave entrance, using HM Cut to hack through the trees in your way.

Get the Flag accessory

Once you reach the bottom of Cycling Road, a girl inside the gate gives you the Flag Accessory. You can use the Flag in Pokémon Super Contests and when cosplaying at Jubilife TV.

Step 3 Use Flash to light up the cave

It's so dark inside the cave that you can only see a small distance away from yourself. Use the Pokémon move Flash to illuminate the inside of the cave. Now you can see far ahead, so you can walk around much more freely.

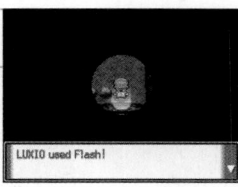

Get Flash at the Oreburgh Gate

You get TM70 Flash at Oreburgh Gate. You'll find it deep inside the cave, behind rocks that you need HM Rock Smash to eliminate.

Step 4 Keep Mira Nearer

A Pokémon Trainer named Mira has become lost in the Wayward Cave. You'll find her in the southeast corner of the ground level. Team up with her to find the cave exit. Mira restores your Pokémon's HP, PP, and status after every battle.

Mira sends Kadabra to battle

Wayward Mira will join you for battles as long as you're traveling together. All wild Pokémon battles will be Double Battles, with Mira pitching in with Kadabra.

Step 5 Enter the Wayward Cave via the hidden entrance

There's a second, hidden entrance to the Wayward Cave. Stand where your character is hidden by Cycling Road and walk up to find this entrance. Immediately to the left is a downward staircase. Take it down and explore the subterranean level.

Step 6 Practice your bike-riding skill

There are spots in the subterranean level of the Wayward Cave where you'll need your Bicycle to jump over rocks or ride a narrow rail. You're probably still learning how to use your Bicycle, so pedal around the open spaces a bit first to get some practice.

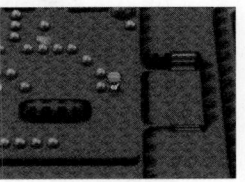

Step 7 Use the right gear for the bike jumps

When jumping over rocks with the Bicycle in the subterranean level of the Wayward Cave, what gear you're on will determine the distance of your jump. On 3rd gear, you'll leap over one square, and on 4th you'll leapfrog two squares. Adjust your gears accordingly as you go.

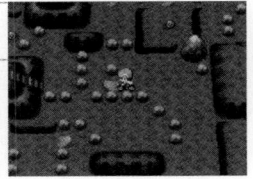

Step 8 Head from Route 207 to Mt. Coronet

Proceed south from Route 206 to reach Route 207, which leads to Mt. Coronet. On the Oreburgh City side, there's that flowing sand slope that you couldn't pass earlier. But now that you have the Bicycle, you can scale the slope easily.

Rest up at Oreburgh City

Before you head on to Mt. Coronet, hop on south to Oreburgh City, where you can rest your battle-weary Pokémon.

Mt. Coronet (Lower)

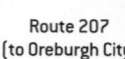
Story

Mt. Coronet is the biggest mountain in the entire Sinnoh region. There's an entrance down below and one up top. The lower entrance plays an important role, as it connects Oreburgh City and Hearthome City.

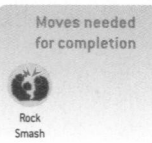
Moves needed for completion

Rock Smash

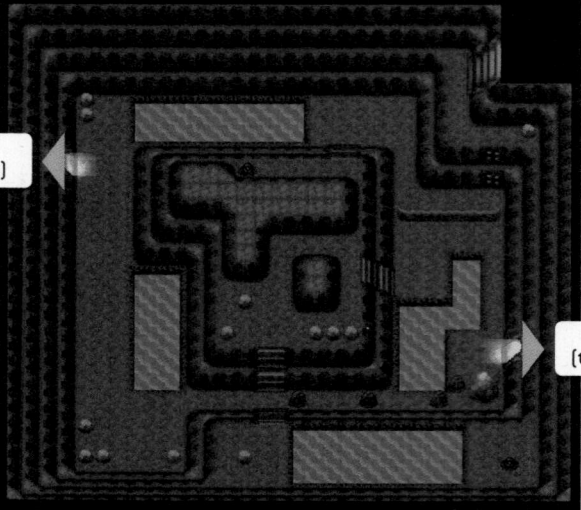

Route 207 (to Oreburgh City)

Route 208 (to Hearthome City)

Cave

Pokémon	M	A	N
Geodude	○	◎	○
Bronzor	○	○	○
Meditite	○	○	○
Machop	○	○	○
Chingling	○	○	○
Clefairy	○	X	○
Zubat	△	△	○
Nosepass	△	△	△

Water surface

Pokémon	
Zubat	◎
Golbat	○

Fishing

Rod	Pokémon	
Old	Magikarp	◎
Good	Magikarp	◎
	Barboach	◎
Super	Gyarados	◎
	Whiscash	◎

Nosepass

ROCK

Abilities
• Sturdy
• Magnet Pull

Step **1** Cyrus Again

Once you go from Route 207, near Oreburgh City, into Mt. Coronet, you run once again into Cyrus, whom you saw at Lake Verity and Eterna City. He leaves, saying something about how Mt. Coronet is where the Sinnoh region began. Just what is his deal?

According to one theory, Mt. Coronet is where the Sinnoh region began.

Pass through the mountain to the right

To go any deeper into Mt. Coronet, you need HM Surf or HM Rock Climb. You're stuck at this point in the game, so just keep east and pass through the mountain.

Trade Pokémon with townspeople

Thanks to the Nintendo DS's wireless link technology and Wi-Fi capability, your friends, your family, and other Pokémon fans from coast to coast are the bedrock of your Pokémon trading circle. But you can also trade with characters in the game. Help grant the characters' wishes, and you'll get some Pokémon trading practice as well.

A chance to acquire rare and important Pokémon

Some of the people you meet on your journey want to trade Pokémon. Be sure to respond to them if you're looking to trade. This isn't just an easy way to get your feet wet trading Pokémon. It's also a way to get semi-rare Pokémon like Abra and Gastly. Complete the trade and your Pokédex is one step closer to being complete.

Would you be willing to trade your MACHOP for my ABRA?

• In-game Pokémon trades

Trade 1 Girl in Oreburgh City

You can encounter Abra on Route 203 and Route 215, but it's elusive and hard to catch. If you're having trouble capturing it, you should jump right on this trade. The girl wants a Machop, which you can find on Route 207.

Receive — **Abra**
•Held item
Oran Berry

Give — **Machop**
•Primary Location
Route 207

Trade 2 Boy in Eterna City

Chatot inhabit Route 218, but only come out in the morning and afternoon. For the many players who play mainly at night, it's a hard Pokémon to catch. You can find the Buizel the boy wants at the Valley Windworks.

Receive — **Chatot**
•Held item
Leppa Berry

Give — **Buizel**
•Primary Location
Valley Windworks

Trade 3 Girl in Snowpoint City

Haunter don't appear in the wild at all before you receive the National Pokédex. To get one, you have to level up a Gastly to Level 25. Or, you can give this girl a Medicham—Medicham are common on the 2nd floor of Mt. Coronet (middle)—and she'll give you a Haunter.

Receive — **Haunter**
•Held item
Everstone

Give — **Medicham**
•Primary Location
Mt. Coronet (middle) 2F

Trade 4 Meister on Route 226

You can hook a Magikarp just about anywhere, but if you get Meister's Magikarp, you can read Magikarp's description in German. The Finneon Meister wants can be found on Route 218.

Receive — **Magikarp**
•Held item
Lum Berry

Give — **Finneon**
•Primary Location
Route 218

Route 208

Route 208 consists of dangerous, steep mountan roads and a grassy, tree-lined path. Once you're out of Mt. Coronet, proceed to the east and you'll reach Hearthome City. On the way you'll find the Berry Master's House, where you can receive a berry every day.

Moves needed for completion

Rock Smash · Surf · Rock Climb · Waterfall

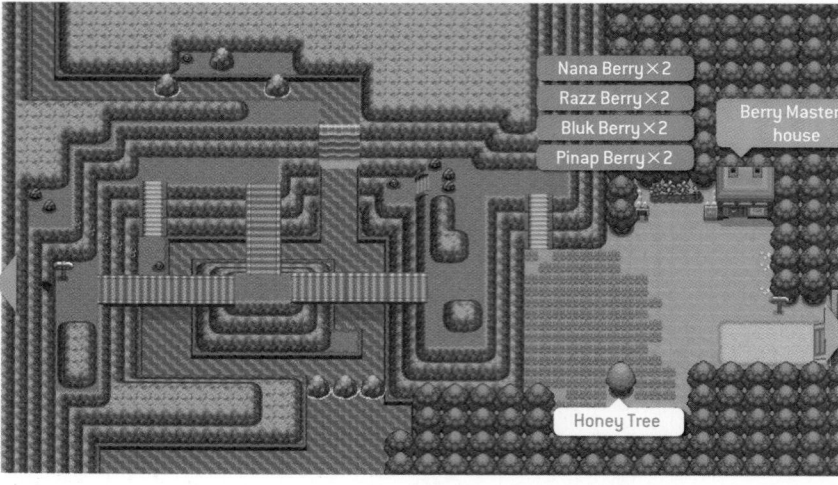

Nana Berry×2
Razz Berry×2
Bluk Berry×2
Pinap Berry×2

Berry Master's house

Mt. Coronet (Lower)

Hearthome City

Honey Tree

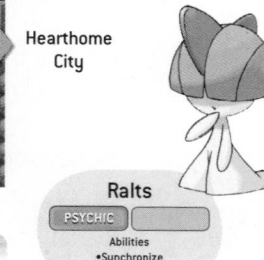

Ralts

PSYCHIC

Abilities
• Synchronize
• Trace

Roselia

GRASS POISON

Abilities
• Natural Cure
• Poison Point

Items

• First Visit
- ☐ Great Ball
- ☐ Ether
- ☐ Nanab Berry x2
- ☐ Razz Berry x2
- ☐ Bluk Berry x2
- ☐ Pinap Berry x2
- ☐ Pokétch App Berry Searcher
- ☐ Odd Keystone

• After winning at Sunyshore Gym
- ☐ Carbos

Berry Master's house

Growth Mulch	200P
Damp Mulch	200P
Stable Mulch	200P
Gooey Mulch	200P

Tall Grass

Pokémon	M	A	N
Budew	◎	◎	○
Bidoof	○	○	○
Ralts	○	○	○
Roselia	○	○	○
Bibarel	○	○	○
Zubat	X	X	○

Water surface

Pokémon	
Psyduck	◎
Golduck	○

Fishing

Rod	Pokémon	
Old	Magikarp	◎
Good	Magikarp	◎
	Goldeen	◎
Super	Gyarados	◎
	Seaking	◎

Step 1 Get the Berry Searcher Pokétch App

Talk to the girl at the Berry Master's house. She'll ask you if you're the type that forgets where you bury your berries. Answer yes and she'll give you the Pokétch App Berry Searcher. This Pokétch App can tell you at a glance where there's a berry-bearing plant.

Lucas obtained the Pokétch app BERRY SEARCHER.

The Berry Master is berry happy to share

The Berry Master hands out one berry each day. Berries have tons of uses. You can plant them in soft soil, give them to Pokémon to help out in battle, bake them into Poffins to raise a Pokémon's condition, and more.

Step 2 Mulch Ado About Mulching

There's a girl in the Berry Master's house who will sell you mulch, to help your berries grow. You use mulch by spreading it on soft soil. It lets you totally adjust the growth process to your own needs, from making the soil stay damp for longer to making it take longer for the berries to drop.

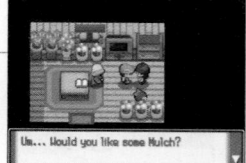

Um... Would you like some Mulch?

Step 3 Receive the Odd Keystone from a Hidden Man

There's a young man hidden underneath a tree below the Berry Master's house. Talk to the man and he gives you the Odd Keystone in exchange for your silence. The Odd Keystone fits into a slot on the broken stone tower on Route 209 (p. 79).

What happens when I complete the broken stone tower?

Slot the Odd Keystone into the broken stone tower to turn it the Hallowed Tower. Go Underground and check out all 32 people down there. Then come back and inspect the Hallowed Tower again, and you'll encounter Spiritomb (p. 377).

Step 4 Home is where the Heart is

Head east on Route 208 to reach Hearthome City. Hearthome City has a number of interesting sights, like the Pokémon Super Contest Hall and Amity Square. Bring your favorite Pokémon to enter with you.

Use an HM to find more items

Having the HM Surf or HM Waterfall will allow you to reach otherwise inaccessible areas in the mountain path portion of Route 208. Be sure to return once you're able to use these HMs.

• Hearthome City, where people's hearts touch one another

Hearthome City

Story

Hearthome City is a town of friendship, where people and Pokémon congregate at fun places like the Contest Hall and Amity Square. If you don't know where to find these facilities, just ask the friendly guide. He'll show you around.

Items

• **First Visit**
- [ ] Shell Bell
- [ ] Poffin Case
- [ ] TM43 Hidden Power
- [ ] TM45 Attract
- [ ] Amulet Coin
- [ ] Spooky Plate
- [ ] Glitter Powder accessory
- [ ] Tuxedo/Dress
- [ ] Mild Poffin

• **After winning at Hearthome Gym**
- [ ] Relic Badge
- [ ] TM65 Shadow Claw

•Amity Square

•**Hearthome City**

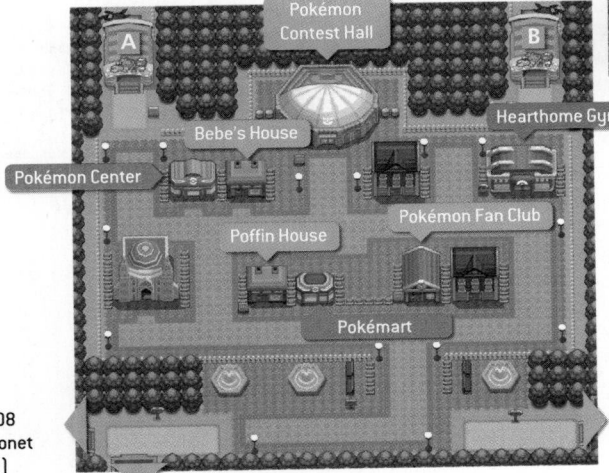

Route 208 (to Mt. Coronet (lower))

Route 212 (to Pastoria City)

Route 209 (to Solaceon Town)

Pokémart (left counter)

Heart Mail	50P
Heal Ball	300P
Net Ball	1000P
Nest Ball	1000P

SINNOH WALKTHROUGH

ROUTE 208 • HEARTHOME CITY

 **1** Catch Keira's Buneary

Enter the town from Route 208, and a Buneary comes running towards you—it probably escaped from its Poké Ball. Catch it and its grateful owner, Contest Judge Keira, tells you to come to the Contest Hall so she can properly thank you.

Oh, thank goodness that you happened to be there!

Rumors of a Pokémon Egg

Talk to the boy in front of the gate on the right side of town and he'll share with you a rumor about a Pokémon Egg found in Solaceon Town. You'll see what he's talking about when you get to Solaceon Town.

 **2** Will you stay, Berry Poffins?

Talk to the head of the Pokémon Fan Club to receive the Poffin Case. This case is where you put the Poffins you make out of berries. Head over to the Poffin house.

I declare this Poffin Case to be a gift from me to you!

That's what friends are for

Talk to the girl at the Pokémon Fan Club, and she'll tell you your Friendship rating with the lead Pokémon in your party. Some Pokémon evolve according to their Friendship rating, so check that rating here.

 **3** Lovin' from the oven

The Poffin House is where you can make Poffins, a snack that Pokémon love. Mix the berries into the dough and stir it, being careful not to spill it or burn it (p. 227).

Here you say cook Berries and turn them into Poffins.

Four friends can bake together wirelessly

Using the DS Wireless Connection, up to four friends can bake Poffins together. It uses more berries than for a single person, and makes a higher-level Poffin (p. 227).

 **4** Meet PC admin Bebe

Next to the Pokémon Center is the house of Bebe, the PC administrator. After talking to Bebe, what previously was called Someone's PC now appears as Bebe's PC.

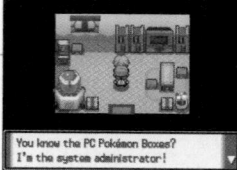

You know the PC Pokémon Boxes? I'm the system administrator!

 **5** Get an Eevee from Bebe

Talk to PC Administrator Bebe. When asked if you want an Eevee, answer yes, and you'll get one. Eevee is a highly unusual Pokémon that can evolve into one of seven different kinds depending on a number of conditions.

▸YES / NO

I know this is out of the blue, but do you want a Pokémon named EEVEE?

Eevee

NORMAL

Abilities
• Run Away
• Adaptability

 **6** Get the goods from Mr. Goods

The man standing just south of Bebe's house is Mr. Goods. He lives his life in search of mysterious and unusual items. Talk to him after meeting certain conditions, and he'll give you a rare item for your base (p. 114).

I dedicate myself to seeking rarities. It's what I live for.

The Shell Bell restores HP

A girl in the condominium next to the Pokémon Fan Club gives you the Shell Bell. This useful item, when held by a Pokémon, restores its HP a little bit each time it damages its opponent.

 **Step 7 Fantina is unavailable at the moment**

There's a man in dark glasses standing in front of the entrance to Hearthome Gym. He'll tell you that the Gym Leader is away, so you can't challenge her to battle. She's at the Contest Hall, he says. Put your Gym battle on the back burner and head for the Contest Hall.

 **Step 8 Mom gives you a Tuxedo/Dress**

Inside the Contest Hall, you run into Keira and your mother. To thank you for helping her with her Buneary before, Keira gives you Glitter Powder. And your mother gives you a tuxedo or dress to wear.

Your Mom Has a Secret

When you meet your mom in the Contest Hall, you get the feeling she comes here a lot. And going by what you hear from judge Keira, your mom seems to be quite a contender.

 **Step 9 Talk to Fantina in the Contest Hall**

You'll find Hearthome Gym Leader Fantina in the lower right corner of the Contest Hall. Talk to her, and she announces she'll be waiting at the Gym, before hustling off. Head straight back to Hearthome Gym to challenge Fantina for your third Gym Badge.

GYM BATTLE 3

Hearthome Gym Leader
FANTINA

• **Ghost Pokémon User**

• **PARTY POKÉMON**

Duskull ♀ Lv24	GHOST	
Haunter ♀ Lv24	GHOST	DARK
Mismagius ♀ Lv26	GHOST	

Make your move with Ghost- and Dark-type moves

Light up the darkness in Hearthome Gym while advancing through the door with a symbol matching the one on the floor. In the last room you battle Fantina. There are six other Pokémon Trainers; you fight them if your lights fall on each other. Fantina uses Ghost-type Pokémon. Use Ghost- and Dark-type moves to deal heavy damage. Win and you get the Relic Badge and TM65 Shadow Claw.

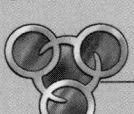 **RELIC BADGE**

Lets you use Defog in the field

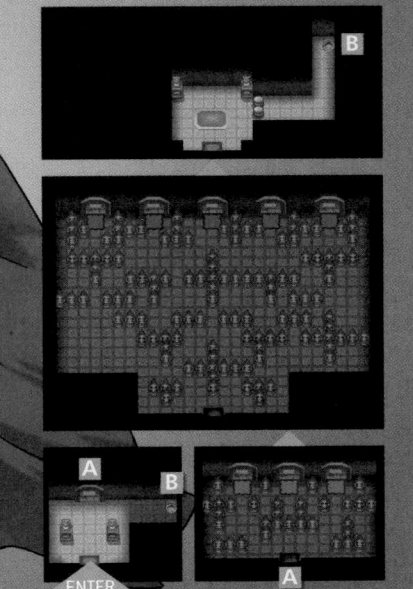

75

Step 10 — Take on Pokémon Super Contests

In the Contest Hall, you can enter Pokémon Super Contests using the Pokémon in your party. The Contests are judged on three skills: Visual, Dance, and Acting. You should put aside the pressure of battling for a moment and check it out.

I can help you with registering for a Super Contest.

Your mom's secret— she's awesome!

At the Pokémon Super Contest Master Rank, participants include Hearthome Gym Leader Fantina, your mom, and Johto region Gym Leader Jasmine. All three possess awesome skill.

Step 11 — Take a stroll through Amity Square

Go through either of the two gates at the northern part of the city and you'll find yourself in Amity Square. You can walk with your starter Pokémon, or with Pikachu, Clefairy, Psyduck, Pachirisu, Happiny, Buneary, or Drifloon. Enjoy the downtime wisely—there are tough battles ahead.

Pokémon make berry good companions

When you take a Pokémon for a walk at Amity Square, your Pokémon will sometimes pick up Accessories or Berries. The berries you'll find here are special ones that you can't find anywhere else (p. 564).

Step 12 — Take Route 209 to Solaceon Town

Pass through the gate on the east side of town and make your way along Route 209. There you'll find the Lost Tower and the broken stone tower that needs the Odd Keystone. At the end of the route is Solaceon Town, origin of the rumors of a Pokémon Egg. When you enter the gate, you'll find yourself challenged by your rival.

Get an accessory from the park man

There's a man standing just inside the eastern gate of Amity Square. Talk to him and he'll give you an accessory or berry he found, once each day.

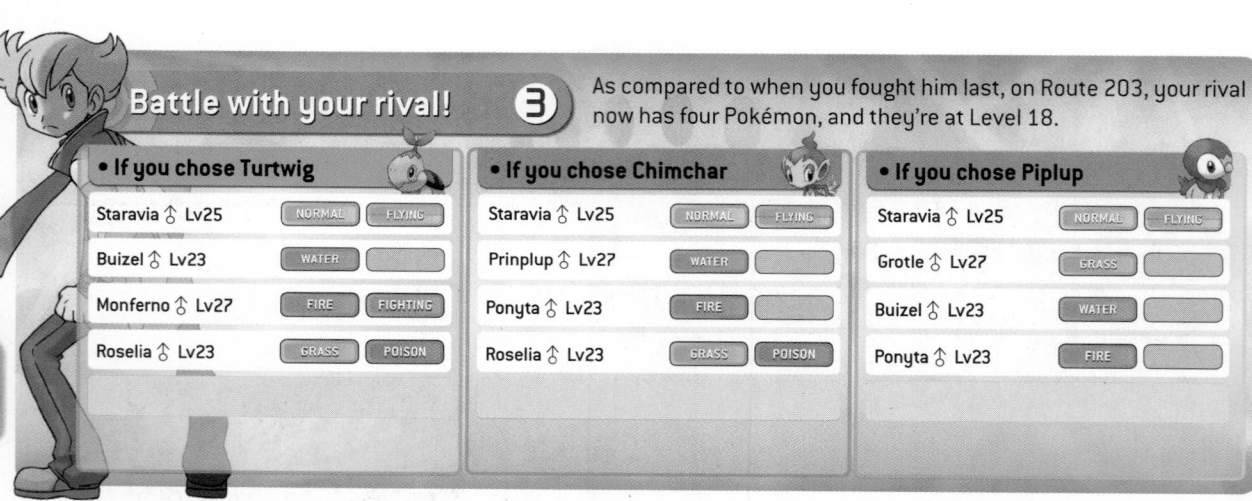

Battle with your rival! ③

As compared to when you fought him last, on Route 203, your rival now has four Pokémon, and they're at Level 18.

• If you chose Turtwig

Staravia ♂ Lv25	NORMAL	FLYING
Buizel ♂ Lv23	WATER	
Monferno ♂ Lv27	FIRE	FIGHTING
Roselia ♂ Lv23	GRASS	POISON

• If you chose Chimchar

Staravia ♂ Lv25	NORMAL	FLYING
Prinplup ♂ Lv27	WATER	
Ponyta ♂ Lv23	FIRE	
Roselia ♂ Lv23	GRASS	POISON

• If you chose Piplup

Staravia ♂ Lv25	NORMAL	FLYING
Grotle ♂ Lv27	GRASS	
Buizel ♂ Lv23	WATER	
Ponyta ♂ Lv23	FIRE	

Clefairy

NORMAL

Abilities
•Cute Charm
•Magic Guard

Buneary

NORMAL

Abilities
•Run Away
•Klutz

Happiny

NORMAL

Abilities
•Natural Cure
•Serene Grace

Tree's a Crowd

There are some trees growing in the Sinnoh region that give off a sweet scent. Spread Honey on these trees, and wild Pokémon may be lured out. Some of them are rare Pokémon, like Munchlax, which you'll definitely want to catch.

How to sweeten up your Pokémon

Spread Honey on a Honey Tree and wait. Eventually, a Pokémon will come out. Some trees are luckier than others, and have a chance of attracting Pokémon that are "lured occasionally" or "lured rarely." Spread Honey on lots of different trees, and you should be able to find which are the lucky ones. Also keep in mind that Honey loses its effectiveness one day after being spread.

Get Honey

A man in Floaroma Meadow sells it to you for 100 Poké a serving.

Give it some time

Pokémon won't appear immediately. Wait until about half a day has passed before you check the tree.

● Pokémon found at Honey Trees

Good Tree	Normal	Rare	Very Rare
Normal Tree	Rare	Normal	Never Lured
High	Burmy	Combee	
	Cherubi	Wurmple	
Probability	Combee	Burmy	Munchlax
	Aipom	Cherubi	
Low	Heracross	Aipom	

*All kinds of tree may occasionally fail to lure a Pokémon

Honey up as many trees as you can!

There are 20 Honey Trees in all of Sinnoh. Hit the easiest-to-access ones first. The tree will shake when a Pokémon has appeared. The more vigorously it's shaking, the higher the chance that it's a hard-to-find Pokémon.

● Locations of Honey Trees

Tree Location	Page	Tree Location	Page
Route 205 x2	P.56	Route 214	P.95
Route 206	P.67	Route 215	P.85
Route 207	P.51	Route 218	P.111
Route 208	P.72	Route 221	P.40
Route 209	P.78	Route 222	P.145
Route 210 x2	P.85	Floaroma Meadow	P.54
Route 211	P.121	Fuego Ironworks	P.56
Route 212 x2	P.105	Valley Windworks	P.59
Route 213	P.95	Eterna Forest	P.60

Route 209 • The Lost Tower

On Route 209, a river runs among meadows, forests, and a grassy field. You'll also find the Lost Tower here, which was dedicated to the spirits of Pokémon that have passed on. It has been rumored that Fantina has visited here often, probably to train.

Story

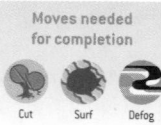

Moves needed for completion

Cut   Surf   Defog

Items

• First Visit
- ☐ Great Ball
- ☐ Good Rod
- ☐ Hyper Potion
- ☐ Leppa Berry
- ☐ Chesto Berry
- ☐ Ether
- ☐ Razz Berry x2
- ☐ Calcium
- ☐ TM47 Steel Wing

- ☐ Oval Stone
- ☐ Revive
- ☐ TM27 Return
• After winning at Hearthome Gym
- ☐ Cleanse Tag
- ☐ Spell Tag
• After winning at Pastoria Gym
- ☐ TM19 Giga Drain

• Route 209   Solaceon Town   The Lost Tower

Razz Berry × 2

Leppa Berry × 1   Honey Tree
Chesto Berry × 1

Broken Stone Tower

Hearthome City

Chansey

NORMAL

Ability
• Natural Cure
• Serene Grace

• Route 209

Tall Grass

Pokémon	M	A	N
Bibarel	◎	◎	◎
Roselia	○	○	○
Staravia	○	○	○
Ralts	○	○	○
Chansey	△	△	△
Zubat	X	X	○
Duskull	X	X	○

Water surface

Pokémon	
Psyduck	◎
Golduck	○

Fishing

Rod	Pokémon	
Old	Magikarp	◎
Good	Magikarp	◎
	Goldeen	◎
Super	Gyarados	◎
	Seaking	◎

• Lost Tower 4F   • Lost Tower 5F

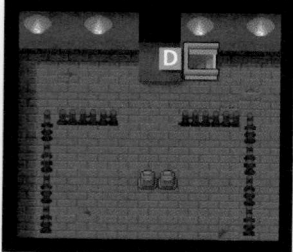

Duskull

GHOST

Ability
• Levitate

• Lost Tower 1F   • Lost Tower 2F   • Lost Tower 3F

Route 209

SINNOH WALKTHROUGH

ROUTE 209 • THE LOST TOWER

•Lost Tower 1F-2F
Interior

Pokémon	M	A	N
Gastly	◎	◎	◎
Zubat	◎	◎	◎
Duskull	X	X	○

•Lost Tower 3F
Interior

Pokémon	M	A	N
Gastly	◎	◎	◎
Zubat	◎	◎	◎
Golbat	▲	▲	▲
Duskull	X	X	○

•Lost Tower 4F
Interior

Pokémon	M	A	N
Gastly	◎	◎	◎
Zubat	◎	◎	◎
Golbat	△	△	△
Duskull	X	X	○

•Lost Tower 5F
Interior

Pokémon	M	A	N
Gastly	◎	◎	◎
Zubat	◎	◎	◎
Golbat	○	○	○
Duskull	X	X	○

Step 1 — Get the Good Rod from a Fisherman

There's a fisherman on a pier along Route 209 who'll give you the Good Rod. The Good Rod can catch more kinds of Pokémon than the Old Rod can. Give it a shot and try to bag a Goldeen.

Lucas obtained the Good Rod!

Pikachu, is that you?

There's a Pikachu standing at the end of a pier on Route 209. Talk to it, and you'll find that it's not a Pokémon but a Pokémon Trainer who's "becoming" a Pokémon. It looks so much like the real thing, there are bound to be a lot of surprised people.

Step 2 — Use the Odd Keystone

There's a broken stone tower on Route 209. Try fitting in the Odd Keystone you got from the man on Route 208. You'll restore the tower to its original state, turning it into the Hallowed Tower.

The stone tower has been restored! "Hallowed Tower" is written on it.

Another Odd Keystone?

The Odd Keystone needed to complete the broken stone tower can also be found in the Underground. You need to have the National Pokédex first, and then the odds are low—but you can sometimes find it while digging for fossils. Give it a try (p. 567).

Step 3 — Climb the Lost Tower

There are five stories in the Lost Tower. The third floor is cloaked in fog, making it hard to see any distance. Talk to the old ladies on the fifth floor. They ask you to dispel the fog. Come back and do so once you can use the HM Defog.

Step 4 — Leave and head for Solaceon Town

Go outside and proceed north to find Solaceon Town. You'll find facilities like the Pokémon Day Care, where you can find Pokémon Eggs. The Solaceon Ruins, inhabited by Unown, are another.

After winning at Hearthome City — Receive tags from the old ladies on the fifth floor

Use HM05 Defog, which you'll find at the Solaceon Ruins, and teach Defog to a Pokémon. Then return to the Lost Tower and dispel the fog. The ladies on the fifth floor will give you a Cleanse Tag and a Spell Tag in gratitude.

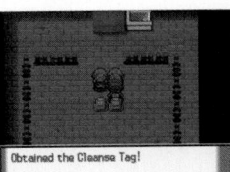
Obtained the Cleanse Tag!

Cleanse Tag helps you make a "clean" break

The Cleanse Tag lowers your rate of wild Pokémon encounters. If your Pokémon are injured or worn out, give it to your lead Pokémon and leave the tower.

SINNOH WALKTHROUGH

ROUTE 209 • THE LOST TOWER

Pokémon That Are Different Because of Battle Location or Habitat ①

The Sinnoh region is home to many different kinds of Pokémon. Some Pokémon are special, in that they take on different forms depending on where you catch them or where they're battling. Take Shellos and Burmy, for example.

Shellos — The Other Side of the Mountain

Shellos have different colors, depending on which side of Mt. Coronet they're from. The ones from the western side of Mt. Coronet are pink, and the ones from the eastern side are blue. Their heads and backs are shaped differently, too. And the differences continue into their evolved form, Gastrodon.

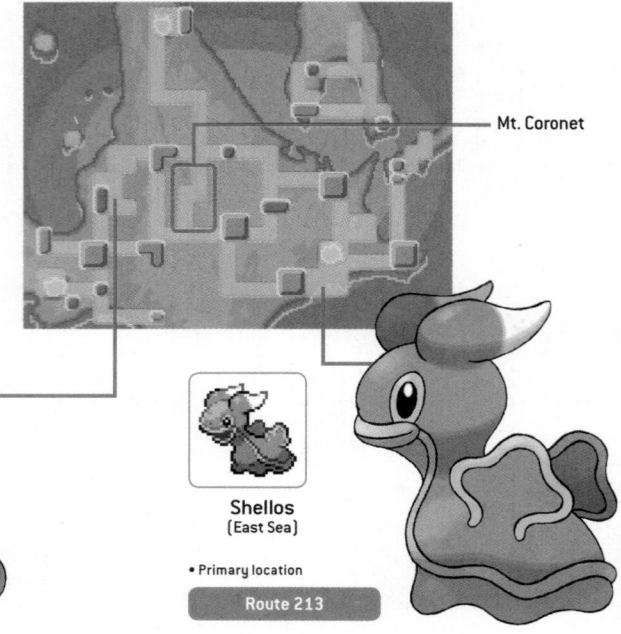

Mt. Coronet

Shellos
(West Sea)

• Primary location

Route 205

Shellos
(East Sea)

• Primary location

Route 213

Burmy — Cloak and Dagger

Burmy changes its cloak depending on the battle terrain. It wears a Plant Cloak when the battle takes place in tall grass, a Sandy Cloak when in it's caves or rocky areas, and a Trash Cloak when it's on hard, paved surfaces, like in buildings.

Evolves after battle

Burmy evolves after the battle is over. Check its cloak after battle.

Burmy
(Plant Cloak)

• Battle location

Tall grass

Burmy
(Sandy Cloak)

• Battle location

Caves, rocks

Burmy
(Trash Cloak)

• Battle location

Buildings

Solaceon Town • Solaceon Ruins

Story

Thanks to the temperate weather, the attitude among Solaceon Town's citizens and Pokémon is pretty peaceful. Here you can find the Pokémon Day Care, the Pokémon News Press, and, beyond the groves of trees, the Unown-inhabited Solaceon Ruins.

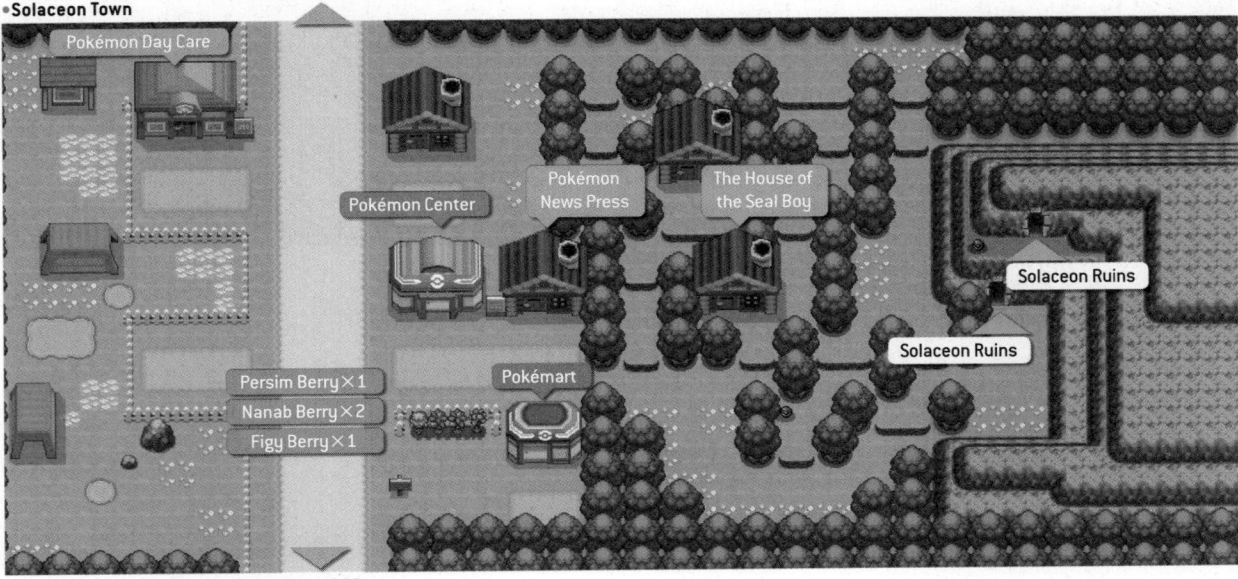

Route 210
(Celestic Town/Veilstone City)

• Solaceon Town

Pokémon Day Care

Pokémon Center

Pokémon News Press

The House of the Seal Boy

Solaceon Ruins

Solaceon Ruins

Persim Berry × 1
Nanab Berry × 2
Figy Berry × 1

Pokémart

Route 209
(to Hearthome City)

Items

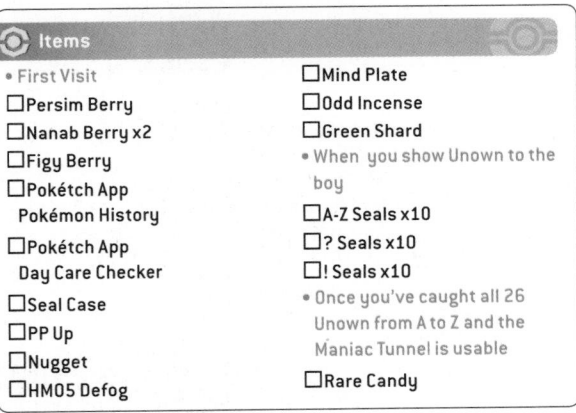

- First Visit
- ☐ Persim Berry
- ☐ Nanab Berry x2
- ☐ Figy Berry
- ☐ Pokétch App
  Pokémon History
- ☐ Pokétch App
  Day Care Checker
- ☐ Seal Case
- ☐ PP Up
- ☐ Nugget
- ☐ HM05 Defog

- ☐ Mind Plate
- ☐ Odd Incense
- ☐ Green Shard
- When you show Unown to the boy
- ☐ A-Z Seals x10
- ☐ ? Seals x10
- ☐ ! Seals x10
- Once you've caught all 26 Unown from A to Z and the Maniac Tunnel is usable
- ☐ Rare Candy

Pokémart (left counter)

Air Mail	50P
Net Ball	1000P
Nest Ball	1000P
Dusk Ball	1000P

• Solaceon Ruins
• 2F

Cave

Pokémon	M	A	N
Unown !	◎	◎	◎
Unown ?	◎	◎	◎

Unown
PSYCHIC
Ability
• Levitate

• B1F

Cave

Pokémon	M	A	N
Unown F	◎	◎	◎

• B2F

Cave

Pokémon	M	A	N
Unown R	◎	◎	◎

• B3F 1

Cave

Pokémon	M	A	N
Unown I	◎	◎	◎

• B3F 2

Cave

Pokémon	M	A	N
Unown N	◎	◎	◎

• B4F 1

Cave

Pokémon	M	A	N
Unown E	◎	◎	◎

• B4F 2

Cave

Pokémon	M	A	N
Unown D	◎	◎	◎

• Dead-end rooms on each floor

Cave

Pokémon	M	A	N
Unown A	◎	◎	◎
Unown B	◎	◎	◎
Unown C	◎	◎	◎
Unown G	◎	◎	◎
Unown H	◎	◎	◎
Unown J	◎	◎	◎
Unown K	◎	◎	◎
Unown L	◎	◎	◎
Unown M	◎	◎	◎
Unown O	◎	◎	◎
Unown P	◎	◎	◎
Unown Q	◎	◎	◎
Unown S	◎	◎	◎
Unown T	◎	◎	◎
Unown U	◎	◎	◎
Unown V	◎	◎	◎
Unown W	◎	◎	◎
Unown X	◎	◎	◎
Unown Y	◎	◎	◎
Unown Z	◎	◎	◎

•Solaceon Ruins

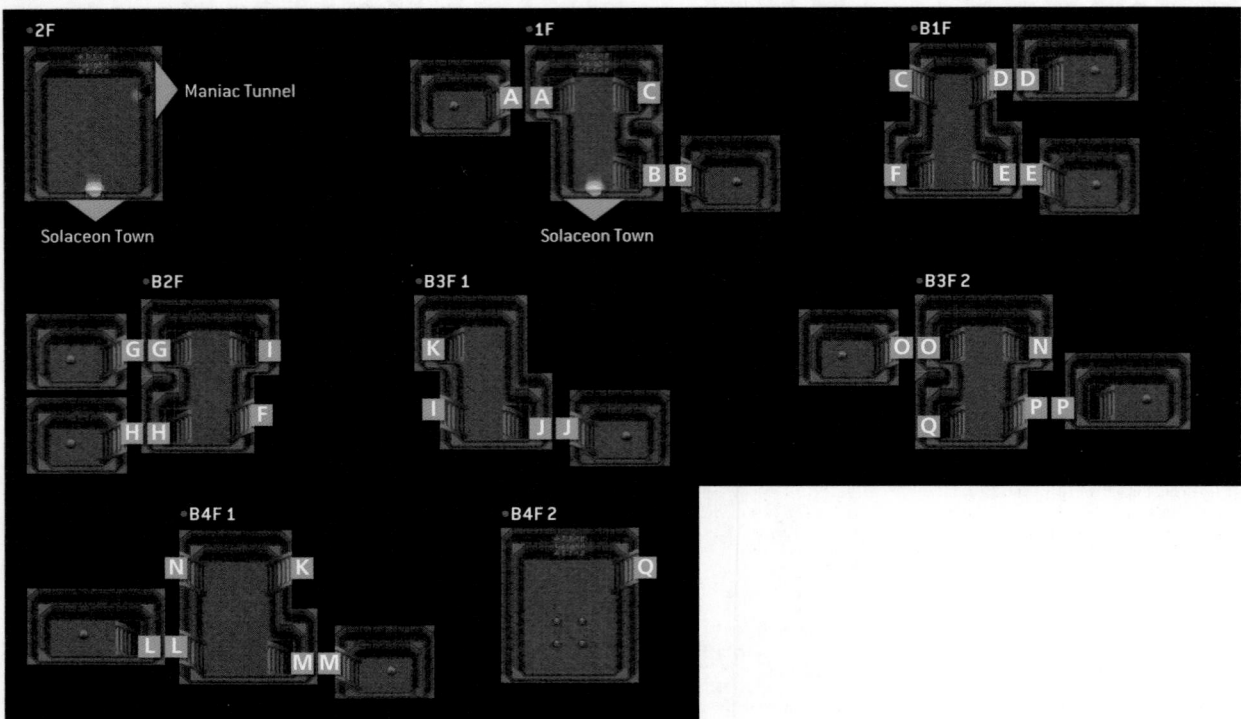

• 2F → Maniac Tunnel → Solaceon Town

• 1F → Solaceon Town

• B1F

• B2F

• B3F 1

• B3F 2

• B4F 1

• B4F 2

Step 1 Get the Pokétch App Pokémon History

A man to the west of the Pokémon Center gives you the Pokétch App Pokémon History. This App displays your 12 most recently caught Pokémon. Tap a Pokémon with the stylus to hear its cry.

Lucas obtained the Pokétch app POKéMON HISTORY.

Step 2 Leave Pokémon at Day Care

The Pokémon Day Care is a place where you can drop off Pokémon to have them raised for you. Use it for Pokémon you want to raise but don't want to keep around in your party. You can drop off two Pokémon at once. You're charged for the amount of time the Pokémon stays, and you pay when you pick the Pokémon up.

I'm the Day-Care Lady. We can raise Pokémon for you.

An Egg-citing surprise

When you leave a male and a female Pokémon at the Day Care, sometimes a Pokémon Egg will turn up, which will be left with the elderly man outside the Day Care (p. 383).

Step 3 Get the Pokétch App Day Care Checker

A man appears at the Day Care center when you drop off a Pokémon, and gives you the Pokétch App Day Care Checker. This App lets you check up on the condition of your Pokémon at Day Care remotely.

Lucas obtained the Pokétch app DAY-CARE CHECKER.

Step 4 Get the Seal Case

You can get the Seal Case from a girl in a house on the east side of town. This is a case for the stickers, or Seals, that you can put on Poké Balls. The case comes with five Seals already included. You can get more from this man and at Sunyshore Market (p. 146).

Oh, you don't have a Seal Case? Well, here you go!

Customize your Poké Balls using Seals

You can collect and organize your Poké Balls through your PC. Use the Seals in your Seal Case to craft your own original Poké Balls (p. 117).

Step 5 — Get Defog at the Solaceon Ruins

Go east in Solaceon Town and jump down off the ledge to reach the entrance to the Solaceon Ruins. Here you can find HM Defog. You'll need it to get rid of some fog, and to get it you'll need to go deep into the heart of the ruins.

The writing's on the wall

There are some mysterious words written in an ancient script on 1F and B4F(2) of the Solaceon Ruins. Look closely at the writing. Don't the letters look kind of like Unown? Try deciphering it to see what it says.

Step 6 — Catch Unown

You encounter wild Unown at the Solaceon Ruins. There are 28 different forms of Unown. In the Solaceon Ruins, accessible through Solaceon Town, you can catch forms A through Z—26 in all. Walk around the ruins so you can see them all.

Dusk to dusk

The best way to catch Unown is to use the Dusk Ball, which raises your Pokémon capture rate inside of caves. Buy a bunch of them at the Pokémart in Solaceon Town.

Step 7 — Show Unown to the boy in the Seal House

Remember the girl who gave you the Seal Case? There's a boy living in that house too. Once you've caught an Unown at the Solaceon Ruins, put it at the head of your party and go back to the house to talk to him. He'll give you 10 seals with the letter matching the Unown you showed him. Very useful for organizing your Poké Balls.

Lend a guy Defog

There's a man on B1F of the Solaceon Ruins. Go talk to him once you have HM Defog, and he'll give you a Green Shard in return.

Step 8 — Show Pokémon to the Pokémon News Press

To the east of the Pokémon Center you'll find the Pokémon News Press. Talk to the editor and he'll ask you to bring a Pokémon that's being featured in an article. Bring it to him before the day is out, and in return he'll give you a Heart Scale and three of one kind of Poké Ball.

Get any one kind of Poké Ball

At the Pokémon News Press, you can get three of any one type of Poké Ball—12 types in all, excepting the Premium Ball and the Master Ball. What a great chance to get Poké Balls for free!

Step 9 — Head for Veilstone City

Take the Defog you got at the Solaceon Ruins and use it to clear out the fog in the Lost Tower. Then, go through Routes 210 and 215, and you're on your way to Veilstone City. There are tons of fun attractions in Veilstone City apart from the Veilstone Gym, including the Veilstone Dept. Store and the Game Corner.

After the Maniac Tunnel is opened — Collect all 28 Unown

If you catch all the Unown, from A to Z, in the Ruin Maniac Cave on Route 214, it becomes the Maniac Tunnel and connects to 2F of the Solaceon Ruins. There you can catch the "!" and "?" Unown and complete your set of all 28 shapes.

Go outdoors on 2F to find an item

From 2F of the Solaceon Ruins, you can access an outdoor area you couldn't get to before. Go outside and you'll find a Rare Candy.

•The 28 shapes of Unown

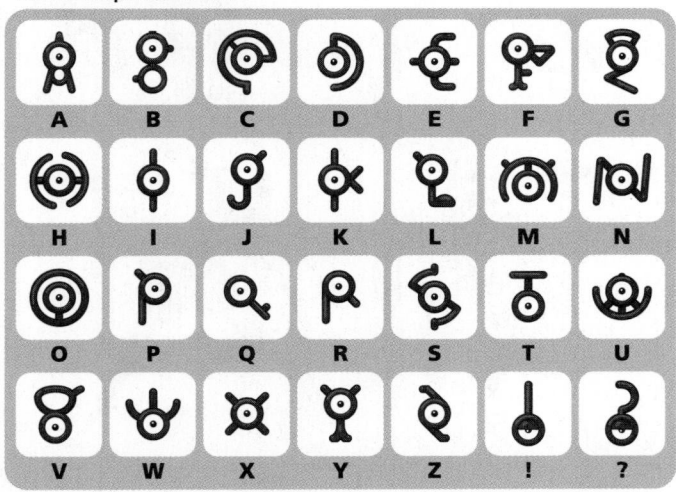

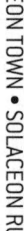

Pokémon That Are Different Because of Battle Location or Habitat ②

Among all the Pokémon in the National Pokédex, there are some that can alter their very form and type. Castform changes while on the battlefield, and Deoxys changes at a particular location. Check out the ways in which these Pokémon change form.

POKÉMON THAT ARE DIFFERENT BECAUSE OF BATTLE LOCATION OR HABITAT 2

Castform — Changes form according to the weather

When the weather is altered, as by a Pokémon's move or Ability, Castform's shape changes drastically. It changes to Sunny form in Sunny weather, Rainy form in Rainy weather, and Snowy form in Hail weather. It's a truly wondrous Pokémon.

The sunlight turned harsh!

Normal
NORMAL

Sunny form
FIRE

Rainy form
WATER

Snowy form
ICE

Deoxys — Forme changes by touching the meteorite in Veilstone City

When Deoxys is in your party, it changes into one of its four Formes when you touch the meteorite in Veilstone City. Uniquely among Pokémon, even Deoxys's stats and learned moves change greatly between Formes.

Touching the meteorite heightened the offensive capabilities of

Stand next to the meteorite and press A to Forme Change the Deoxys in your party.

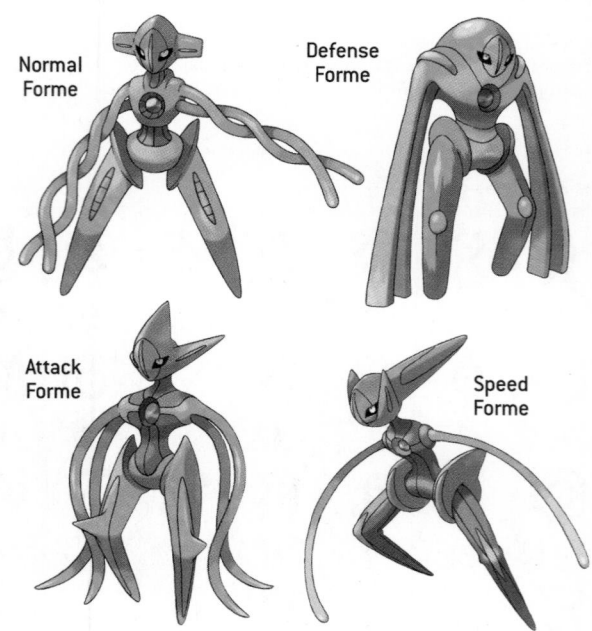

Normal Forme

Defense Forme

Attack Forme

Speed Forme

84

Route 210 • Route 215

Story

Proceed through Route 210, which is covered with tall grass, and venture past a deep ravine to get to Celestic Town. To get to the next Gym, you need to head east past the Café Cabin and along Route 215, and keep going until you reach Veilstone City.

Moves needed for completion

Rock Smash | Cut | Defog

Surf | Rock Climb | Waterfall

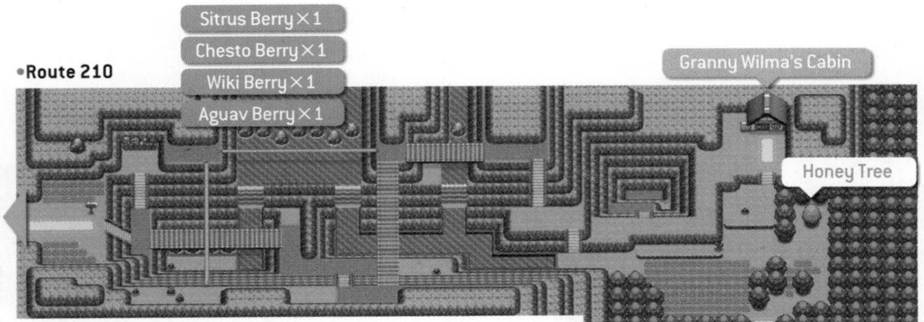

• Route 210

Sitrus Berry × 1
Chesto Berry × 1
Wiki Berry × 1
Aguav Berry × 1

Granny Wilma's Cabin

Honey Tree

Celestic Town

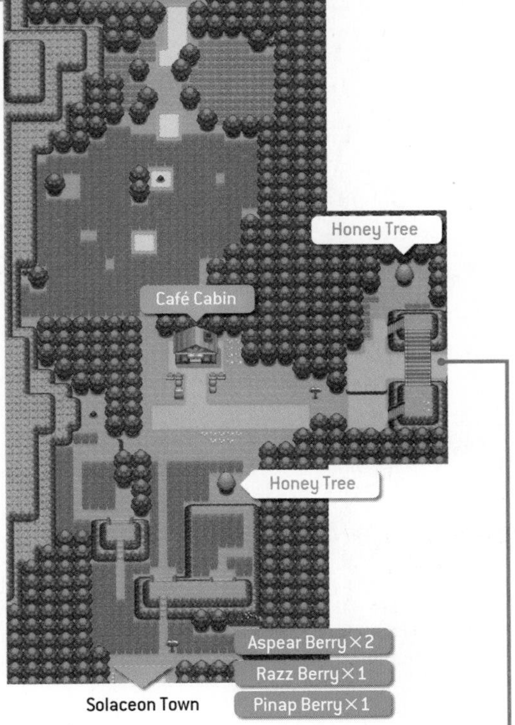

Honey Tree

Café Cabin

Honey Tree

Solaceon Town

Aspear Berry × 2
Razz Berry × 1
Pinap Berry × 1

Items

• First Visit
- ☐ Aspear Berry x2
- ☐ Razz Berry
- ☐ Pinap Berry
- ☐ Super Repel
- ☐ TM51 Roost
- ☐ Max Ether
- ☐ TM66 Payback
- ☐ Fist Plate
- ☐ Pecha Berry x2
- ☐ Bluk Berry x2
- ☐ Hyper Potion
- ☐ HP Up
- ☐ TM34 Shock Wave
- ☐ Full Heal
- ☐ Wiki Berry
- ☐ Mago Berry

• After you get the Secret Potion
- ☐ Old Charm
- ☐ Max Repel
- ☐ Hyper Potion
- ☐ Nest Ball
- ☐ Red Shard
- ☐ TM30 Shadow Ball
- ☐ Smoke Ball
- ☐ Sitrus Berry
- ☐ Chesto Berry
- ☐ Wiki Berry
- ☐ Aguav Berry

• After winning at Snowpoint Gym
- ☐ Zinc

• After winning at Sunyshore Gym
- ☐ Wave Incense

Café Cabin

Moomoo Milk............................500P

Pecha Berry × 2
Bluk Berry × 2

• Route 215

Wiki Berry × 1
Mago Berry × 1

Veilstone City

•Route 210 (Solaceon Town side)

Tall Grass

Pokémon	M	A	N
Ponyta	O	◎	O
Staravia	O	O	O
Geodude	O	O	O
Roselia	O	O	O
Scyther	O	△	△
Chansey	△	△	△
Noctowl	X	X	O
Hoothoot	X	X	O

•Route 210 (Celestic Town side)

Tall Grass

Pokémon	M	A	N
Swablu	O	◎	O
Bibarel	O	O	O
Meditite	O	O	O
Machop	O	O	O
Machoke	O	O	O
Scyther	O	△	△
Noctowl	X	X	O
Hoothoot	X	X	O

Water surface

Pokémon			
Psyduck			◎
Golduck			O

Fishing

Rod	Pokémon	
Old	Magikarp	◎
Good	Magikarp	◎
	Barboach	O
	Whiscash	△
Super	Gyarados	◎
	Whiscash	◎

•Route 215

Tall Grass

Pokémon	M	A	N
Staravia	◎	◎	O
Marill	O	O	◎
Lickitung	O	O	O
Abra	O	O	O
Kadabra	O	O	O
Scyther	O	△	△

Step 1 — Run through the really tall grass

Route 210 (on the Solaceon Town side) has some really tall grass growing there. It's so bad that you can't ride your Bicycle through it. Your best option is to run through these areas on foot.

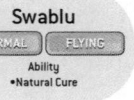

Swablu
NORMAL FLYING
Ability
•Natural Cure

Scyther
BUG FLYING
Abilities
•Swarm
•Technician

Lickitung
NORMAL
Abilities
•Own Tempo
•Oblivious

Step 2 — Buy Moomoo Milk at the Café Cabin

There's a café and rest house sitting right between Routes 210 and 215. You can enjoy some Pokémon battles with the customers there. You can also buy Moomoo Milk. One serving costs 500 Poké and restores 100 HP.

Money ₽ 66272
▶ 1 BOTTLE
1 DOZEN
NO THANKS

Would you like to add some to your traveling supplies?

You can buy 12 Moomoo Milks at a time

Moomoo Milk restores 100 HP to a Pokémon. You can buy a batch of one dozen of the drinks here. Not a bad idea to buy in bulk, since you'll definitely be needing to restore HP to injured Pokémon.

Step 3 — A Psyduck roadblock

There's a flock of four Psyduck outside the café. They seem to have paralyzing headaches, and are blocking the road. You can't get past for now, so just proceed to Route 215 to the east.

The PSYDUCK are standing fire.
They aren't inclined to move at all.

Step **4** **Take Route 215 to Veilstone City**

It always rains on Route 215, even during battles. The Rainy weather raises the power of Water-type moves, but lowers that of Fire-type moves. Pick your battles carefully. Veilstone City is just ahead.

Abilities rock!

Some Abilities can give you a big advantage in Rainy weather. Try bringing some Pokémon with Dry Skin or Swift Swim Abilities (p. 610).

After getting the Secret Potion **Use the SecretPotion on the Psyduck**

Take the SecretPotion you got from Cynthia at Valor Lakefront, and use it on the ailing Psyduck. It cures their headaches, and they take off, clearing the road. Now you can get to Celestic Town.

After getting the Secret Potion **Take the Old Charm from Cynthia**

Cynthia comes up to you after you've cured the Psyduck's headaches. She gives you an Old Charm to take to her grandmother. Head for Celestic Town to deliver it.

Three ninjas, no waiting

A group of three wannabe ninjas is hiding in the really tall grass north of the Café Cabin. Check every spot that seems suspicious, and find all of them.

After getting the Secret Potion **Use HM Defog to dispel the mist**

Further north along Route 210, it becomes very foggy, and you won't be able to see. Use HM Defog to clear the way. Proceed into the mountains and take the bridge to the west. You'll soon reach Celestic Town.

Thick fog = poor accuracy

If you proceed without using HM Defog, your battles with wild Pokémon will take place under Foggy conditions. This lowers move Accuracy, so you'll want to use Defog before continuing.

After winning at Snowpoint Gym **Learn the strongest Dragon-type move**

Use HM Rock Climb to take Route 210 north until you reach Granny Wilma's Cabin. Bring a Dragon-type Pokémon that you have a good Friendship rating with, and she'll teach it Draco Meteor, the strongest Dragon-type move available.

Come back with HM Waterfall

There are waterways on Route 210 that you need HM Surf and HM Waterfall to access. You'll be rewarded with items that will be quite useful on your journey, so don't forget to come back here once you've taught a Pokémon those HMs.

Gible
DRAGON GROUND
Ability
•Sand Veil

Gabite
DRAGON GROUND
Ability
•Sand Veil

Garchomp
DRAGON GROUND
Ability
•Sand Veil

Pokémon That Are Different Because of Battle Location or Habitat ③

Two Pokémon that have a dramatic Forme Change upon the fulfillment of certain conditions are Giratina and Shaymin. These changes are bold and breathtaking. Items are the trigger in this case. Let's uncover the mysteries of Giratina's and Shaymin's Forme Changes.

Giratina — Changes Forme from the normal world to the Distortion World.

Giratina appears in its Origin Forme in the Distortion World. Back in the normal world, it sports its Altered Forme. But there is a way to make it take its Origin Forme in the normal world. Have it hold the Griseous Orb, an item found in the Distortion World.

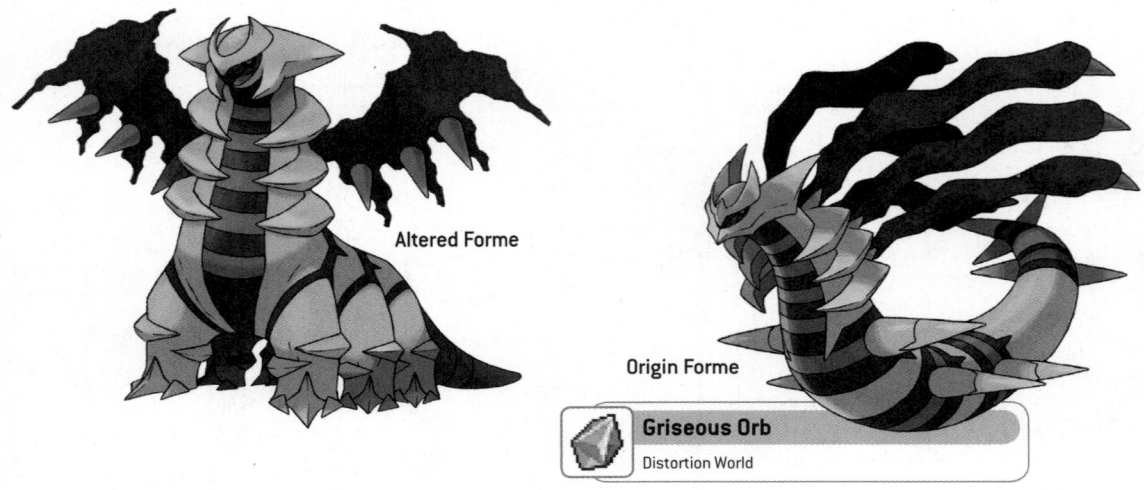

Altered Forme

Origin Forme

Griseous Orb
Distortion World

Shaymin — Bring Shaymin into *Pokémon Platinum* to get it to Forme Change

Shaymin was already distributed to players of *Pokémon Diamond* and *Pokémon Pearl*. But it's when you bring it into *Pokémon Platinum* and give it the Gracidea that it transforms from its Land Forme into its Sky Forme. This is quite a drastic change, as Shaymin doubles in length.

Land Forme

Sky Forme

Shaymin returns to its Land Forme and can't use the Gracidea between 8 PM and 4 AM. It also returns to Land Forme when frozen.

Veilstone City

Veilstone City was built into the face of a huge, steep mountain. The ever-popular Veilstone Dept. Store and Game Corner are here, as well as the sinister Team Galactic HQ. But first things first: it's Gym Battle time.

Moves needed for completion

Rock Climb

Galactic Veilstone Bldg.

Galactic Storage

Route 215
(to Celestic Town/
Solaceon Town)

Veilstone Dept. Store

Veilstone Gym

Pokémon Center

Massage Girl's House

Veilstone
Game Corner

Prize Exchange

Route 214
(to Pastoria City)

Items

- First Visit
- ☐ Star Piece
- ☐ Turtwig Mask, Chimchar Mask, or Piplup Mask
- ☐ Pokétch App Counter
- ☐ Sticky Barb
- ☐ TM63 Embargo
- ☐ Coin Case
- ☐ Rare Candy

- After a 10-win combo at the slots
- ☐ TM64 Explosion
- After winning at Veilstone Gym
- ☐ Cobble Badge
- ☐ TM60 Drain Punch
- ☐ HM02 Fly
- After winning at Snowpoint Gym
- ☐ Full Incense

Accessories received after a Pokémon massage

Pretty Dewdrop	Poison Extract
Snow Crystal	Wealthy Coin
Sparks	Eerie Thing
Shimmering Fire	Spring
Mystic Fire	Seashell
Determination	Humming Note
Peculiar Spoon	Shiny Powder
Puffy Smoke	Glitter Powder

Step 1 — A grunt is guarding the Galactic Warehouse

To the east of the town entrance stands the Galactic Warehouse. You try to enter, but a Galactic grunt stands in your way, telling you to go play at the Pokémon Gym. Try again after your Gym Battle.

This is Team Galactic's warehouse! It ain't no playground for kids!

Talk to a Trainer from overseas

Talk to the blond man on the hill near the southern part of Veilstone City. It seems he's asking you if you like Pokémon. Answer him yes or no.

Step 2 — Get the Coin Case from a clown

A clown in the house west of the Game Corner offers you a test. If you can correctly guess which hand he has a coin in, he gives you the Coin Case. Now you can play at the Game Corner!

Lucas obtained the Coin Case!

Daily massage gets you Accessories

There's a Massage Girl near the bottom of Veilstone City who will give a Pokémon a massage once a day. After it's over, she'll give you an Accessory, saying the Pokémon was holding it.

Step 3 — Obtain Porygon

Talk to a man in a house north of the Pokémon Center. He asks you to take a Pokémon he found near the Galactic Veilstone Building. It's the super-rare Porygon! Leave an open space in your party to take Porygon.

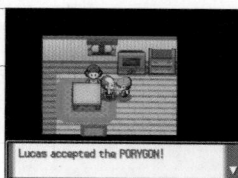

Lucas accepted the PORYGON!

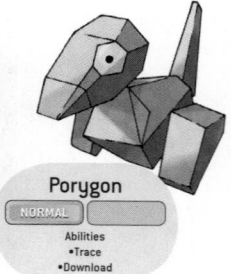

Porygon

NORMAL

Abilities
•Trace
•Download

Step 4 — Get the Pokétch App Counter

Talk to the girl at the counter on 2F of the Veilstone Dept. Store to receive the Pokétch App Counter. The Counter App can count up to 9999. Use it when you need to count stuff.

Lucas obtained the Pokétch app COUNTER.

Get a mask at 1F of the Dept. Store

Talk to the girl at 1F of the Veilstone Dept. Store to receive a Pokémon mask. What kind of mask depends on the Pokémon you chose at the start of the game.

Step 5 — Play the slots at the Game Corner

You can use special game coins to play the slot machines at the Game Corner. Pick a machine and insert a coin to begin. Stop the three tumblers, and if the images match up, you win more coins (p. 93).

During regular play, you should stop the reels from the left.

Get 70 coins

Talk to the people enjoying the slots at the Game Corner. Some will give you coins free of charge, just so they won't go to waste. You can get a total of 70 coins this way. Use them to take on the slot machines.

Step 6 — Find the key

The Galactic Veilstone Building north of the Pokémon Center is actually Team Galactic's headquarters. This is where they're conducting research into the creation of a new type of energy. Unfortunately for you, the door to everything above the first floor is locked and needs a special key to open it.

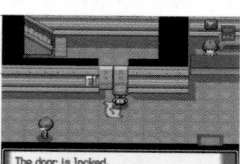

The door is locked. A special key is needed.

How to determine the type of Hidden Power

If a Pokémon in your party has the Hidden Power move, the man at the Prize Exchange will tell you what type it is. If you have a Pokémon with this move, and you want to know, this is where you ask.

GYM BATTLE ④

Veilstone Gym Leader
MAYLENE

• **Fighting Pokémon User**

• **PARTY POKÉMON**

Meditite ♀ Lv28	FIGHTING	PSYCHIC
Lucario ♂ Lv32	FIGHTING	STEEL
Machoke ♂ Lv29	FIGHTING	

Flying- and Psychic-type moves are the key

To reach Maylene at the back of Veilstone Gym, destroy the obstacles by sliding the sandbags around. There are four other Trainers here. You'll compete best against Maylene's Pokémon if you use Flying-, Psychic-, Fire-, and Ground-type moves. Win and you'll get the Cobble Badge and TM60 Drain Punch.

ENTER

COBBLE BADGE

Lets you use HM Fly in the field. Pokémon up to Lv. 50 will obey your commands—even Pokémon received from other people.

Step 7 — Help Rowan's assistant out of trouble

You leave the Gym in victory, only to find Rowan's assistant in trouble. The assistant claims that Team Galactic has stolen the Pokédex. You can help get it back by joining the assistant in a Tag Battle with the grunt in front of Galactic Storage.

Some Team Galactic goons took my Pokédex away from me.

Who is the man coming out of the Gym?

On your first time to Veilstone Gym, you see a man on his way out. He says he's been training with Maylene. It turns out that he is Pastoria Gym Leader Wake.

Step 8 — Looker helps you get HM Fly

Once you defeat the Galactic grunt in front of Galactic Warehouse, you can go inside. Looker approaches you, and the two of you do a joint investigation. There's a locked door inside that prevents you from going any farther, but you do at least acquire HM02 Fly.

Lucas found an HM02 Fly!

What's the deal with Galactic Warehouse?

The Team Galactic grunt standing guard at the Galactic Warehouse says something about a particular piece of cargo that was in the warehouse. Apparently it's already been transported to Pastoria City. Could it have something to do with the new kind of energy that was being researched in the Galactic Veilstone Building?

Step 9 — Head south to Pastoria City

After you're done checking out Galactic Warehouse, Looker passes along the fact that Team Galactic has moved something to Pastoria City. Take Route 214, south of Veilstone City, to Pastoria City in pursuit of Team Galactic.

After visiting Lake Acuity — Have Looker open the Galactic Warehouse

Follow Jupiter back to town from Lake Acuity. The Galactic grunt in front of the warehouse flees, saying that he doesn't know anything about the warehouse key. That's when Looker shows up with the key, and invites you along to check out the warehouse with him.

Well? Will you enter the hideout? You have your reasons, yes?

▶ YES
NO

Use Rock Climb to find an item

Once you can use HM Rock Climb, you'll be able to clamber up the rough stone wall in the middle of town. Use it to find the Full Incense.

Shop Till You Drop!

The Biggest Department Store in All of Sinnoh!

This five-story department store has everything, from battle items, TMs, and base decorations, to berries and Poffins. It's your one-stop shop when you want to buy a lot of items. Just board the elevator and you'll be whisked to exactly what you need. If you're overwhelmed by the selection, just ask the cashier on the right-hand side of the counter of each floor what she recommends.

A can of Fresh Water dropped down.

Sometimes one of the vending machines on 5F will give you a drink for free.

VEILSTONE
Veilstone Dept. Store Directory

5F Rooftop Plaza		
Vending Machine — Fresh Water........200P	Soda Pop........300P	Lemonade........350P

4F Goods and Dolls		
Yellow Cushion........500P	Pretty Sink........3000P	Mantyke Doll........3000P
Cupboard........1000P	Munchlax Doll........2000P	Buizel Doll........3000P
TV........4500P	Bonsly Doll........2000P	Chatot Doll........3000P
Refrigerator........1000P	Mime Jr. Doll........2000P	

3F TM Collection		
TM83 Natural Gift........2000P	TM16 Light Screen........2000P	TM22 Solar Beam........3000P
TM17 Protect........2000P	TM70 Flash........1000P	TM52 Focus Blast........5500P
TM54 False Swipe........2000P	TM38 Fire Blast........5500P	TM15 Hyper Beam........7500P
TM20 Safeguard........2000P	TM25 Thunder........5500P	
TM33 Reflect........2000P	TM14 Blizzard........5500P	

2F Stat Boosters		
X Speed........350P	X Accuracy........950P	Calcium........9800P
X Attack........500P	X Special........350P	Zinc........9800P
X Defend........550P	X Sp. Def........350P	Carbos........9800P
Guard Spec.........700P	Protein........9800P	HP Up........9800P
Dire Hit........650P	Iron........9800P	

1F Trainer Zone		
Potion........300P	Awakening........250P	Max Repel........700P
Super Potion........700P	Full Heal........600P	Grass Mail........50P
Hyper Potion........1200P	Poké Ball........200P	Flame Mail........50P
Max Potion........2500P	Great Ball........600P	Bubble Mail........50P
Revive........1500P	Ultra Ball........1200P	Space Mail........50P
Antidote........100P	Escape Rope........550P	
Paralyz Heal........200P	Poké Doll........1000P	
Burn Heal........250P	Repel........350P	
Ice Heal........250P	Super Repel........500P	

B1F Natural Foods		
Figy Berry........20P	Spicy-Sweet Poffin........6400P	Sweet-Bitter Poffin........6400P
Wiki Berry........20P	Spicy-Bitter Poffin........6400P	Sweet-Sour Poffin........6400P
Mago Berry........20P	Spicy-Sour Poffin........6400P	Bitter-Sour Poffin........6400P
Aguav Berry........20P	Dry-Sweet Poffin........6400P	Lava Cookie........200P
Iapapa Berry........20P	Dry-Bitter Poffin........6400P	
Spicy-Dry Poffin........6400P	Dry-Sour Poffin........6400P	

SINNOH WALKTHROUGH
VEILSTONE CITY

Challenge the slots at the Veilstone Game Corner

Win coins at the slot machines, get items and TMs

You use special coins to play the slot machines at the Veilstone Game Corner. Line up the pictures on all three tumblers of the slot machine to win more coins. Once you have enough coins, take them to the Prize Exchange and trade them for items and TMs.

⚙ Game Coins	
50	1000P
500	10000P

⚙ Items at Prize Exchange			
Silk Scarf	1000	TM10 Hidden Power	6000
Wide Lens	1000	TM27 Return	8000
Zoom Lens	1000	TM21 Frustration	8000
Metronome	1000	TM35 Flamethrower	10000
TM90 Substitute	2000	TM24 Thunderbolt	10000
TM58 Endure	2000	TM13 Ice Beam	10000
TM75 Swords Dance	4000	TM29 Psychic	10000
TM32 Double Team	4000	TM74 Gyro Ball	15000
TM44 Rest	6000	TM68 Giga Impact	20000
TM89 U-Turn	6000		

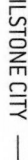

① Slot Machine Rule — Line up images to win coins

The premise of the slot machine is to stop the tumblers and line up the images. Different images win you different amounts of coins. If you get a row of "Replay" images, you get to go again without spending any coins.

Coin prizes for the different images

7 7 7	100	🐟🐟🐟 15
🔔🔔🔔	100	🐭🐭🐭 10
🦋	2	REPLAY REPLAY REPLAY Replay 15*

*If you get a row of Replays during Clefairy Bonus, you win 15 coins.

② Slot Machine Rule — Watch the tumblers carefully to line them up

There are three rotating tumblers—one on the left, one in the middle, and one on the right. You can halt them in any order, but Replay and Pikachu are easiest to get if you go in order from the left. Try to learn the pattern and predict which image is coming up next.

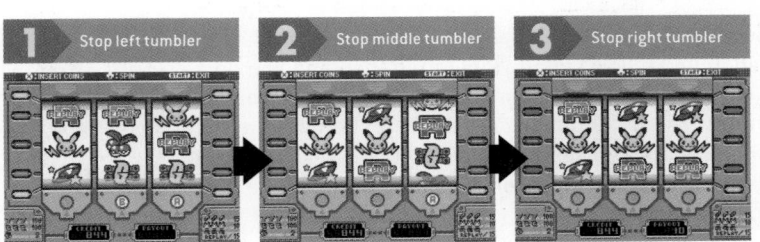

1 Stop left tumbler	2 Stop middle tumbler	3 Stop right tumbler

Slot Machine Rule

3 Changing the Modes

The slot machine advances through three different modes, depending on the images you line up on the tumblers: Normal Mode, Clefairy Mode, and Clefairy Bonus Mode. Each mode has different images that are the easiest to line up, and features a different little show on the Touch Screen. Master each mode to have the best chance at winning coins. The Clefairy Bonus, where Clefairy helps you line up the tumblers, is your chance to get a windfall of coins.

The three changing modes

Mode 1	Mode 2	Mode 3
Normal Mode	**Clefairy Mode**	**Clefairy Bonus**
It's easy to line up Replay and Pikachu from the left. Also try lining up a Poké Ball or a Moon Stone.	Clefairy appears, and it becomes easier to get 7's or G's by sight. If you get one of them, the machine goes into Clefairy Bonus.	Stop the tumblers in the order that Clefairy points to for a surefire win. You get 15 rounds before the mode changes.

Slot Machine Rule

4 The type of Clefairy makes it easier to combo bonuses

A combo is when the bonus continues after the tumblers have spun, for 15 times. How easy it is to get a combo depends on what kind of Clefairy comes out of the Poké Ball. Also, after the Bonus, if Pikachu comes out it's easy to get a combo, but if Clefairy comes out again it's hard to get one.

Ditto Clefairy	Clefairy	Shiny Clefairy
Hard to get combo	Easy to get combo	Very easy to get combo

 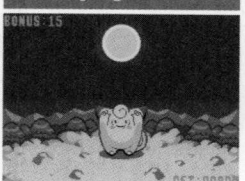 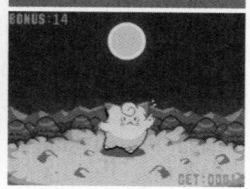

A Ditto transformed into a Clefairy means a combo will be hard to get.

If a regular Clefairy comes out, it'll be easy to combo into a Clefairy Bonus.

You have a very high chance of combo-ing with this Clefairy of a different color.

Slot Machine Rule

5 Avoid lining up Replays when the moon is glowing red

Sometimes, during a Clefairy Bonus, the moon will glow red. If you follow Clefairy's pointing then and line up a Replay, you'll reduce your chances of getting a combo. Instead, stop the tumblers in a different order from the one indicated by Clefairy, avoiding the Replays. On the other hand, when the moon is glowing white, you're sure to get a combo.

Don't line up the Replays when the moon is glowing red

If you line up the Replays with the moon glowing red, Clefairy will get exhausted, and you'll have a harder time getting a combo.

Route 214 • Valor Lakefront • Route 213

Story

You'll pass through several locations on your trip south from Veilstone City to Pastoria City. First is Route 214, a pastoral gem. Then is Valor Lakefront, right near the lake wherein slumbers a hidden legend. Lastly you'll pass Route 213, a peaceful beachfront path.

Moves needed for completion

Rock Smash | Surf | Rock Climb

Items

- **First Visit**
- ☐ Cheri Berry
- ☐ Sitrus Berry
- ☐ Chesto Berry
- ☐ Pomeg Berry
- ☐ Max Repel
- ☐ Big Root
- ☐ Red Shard
- ☐ Magmarizer
- ☐ Ultra Ball
- ☐ PP Up
- ☐ TM92 Trick Room
- ☐ Yellow Shard
- ☐ TM40 Aerial Ace
- ☐ Aguav Berry
- ☐ Rawst Berry x2
- ☐ Iapapa Berry

- **Prize for finding the Suite Key**
- ☐ White Flute
- **When your lead Pokémon likes you**
- ☐ Footstep Bow
- **After winning at Pastoria Gym**
- ☐ SecretPotion
- **After visiting Celestic Town**
- ☐ Rare Candy
- ☐ Water Stone
- ☐ Max Revive
- **After winning at Snowpoint Gym**
- ☐ TM05 Roar
- ☐ Pokétch App Coin Toss
- ☐ Protein
- ☐ Iron
- ☐ TM85 Dream Eater

Rhyhorn
GROUND | ROCK
Abilities
• Lightningrod
• Rock Head

Chatot
NORMAL | FLYING
Abilities
• Keen Eye
• Tangled Feet

Houndour
DARK | FIRE
Abilities
• Early Bird
• Flash Fire

• Route 213

Tall Grass

Pokémon	M	A	N
Shellos	◎	◎	◎
Buizel	○	○	○
Wingull	○	○	○
Chatot	○	○	X

Water surface

Pokémon	
Tentacool	◎
Wingull	◎
Tentacruel	△
Shellos	△
Gastrodon	▲

Fishing

Rod	Pokémon	
Old	Magikarp	◎
Good	Magikarp	◎
	Remoraid	◎
Super	Gyarados	◎
	Octillery	◎

• Route 214

Tall Grass

Pokémon	M	A	N
Graveler	◎	◎	◎
Rhyhorn	◎	◎	○
Geodude	○	○	○
Houndour	○	○	○
Zubat	X	X	○

Water surface

Pokémon	
Psyduck	◎
Golduck	○

Fishing

Rod	Pokémon	
Old	Magikarp	◎
Good	Magikarp	◎
	Goldeen	◎
Super	Gyarados	◎
	Seaking	◎

• Valor Lakefront

Tall Grass

Pokémon	M	A	N
Bibarel	◎	◎	◎
Staravia	○	○	○
Girafarig	○	○	○
Houndour	○	○	○
Kricketune	○	X	○

Graveler
ROCK | GROUND
Abilities
• Rock Head
• Sturdy

Girafarig
NORMAL | PSYCHIC
Abilities
• Inner Focus
• Early Bird

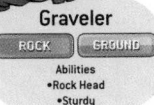

Shellos
[East Sea]
WATER
Abilities
• Sticky Hold
• Storm Drain

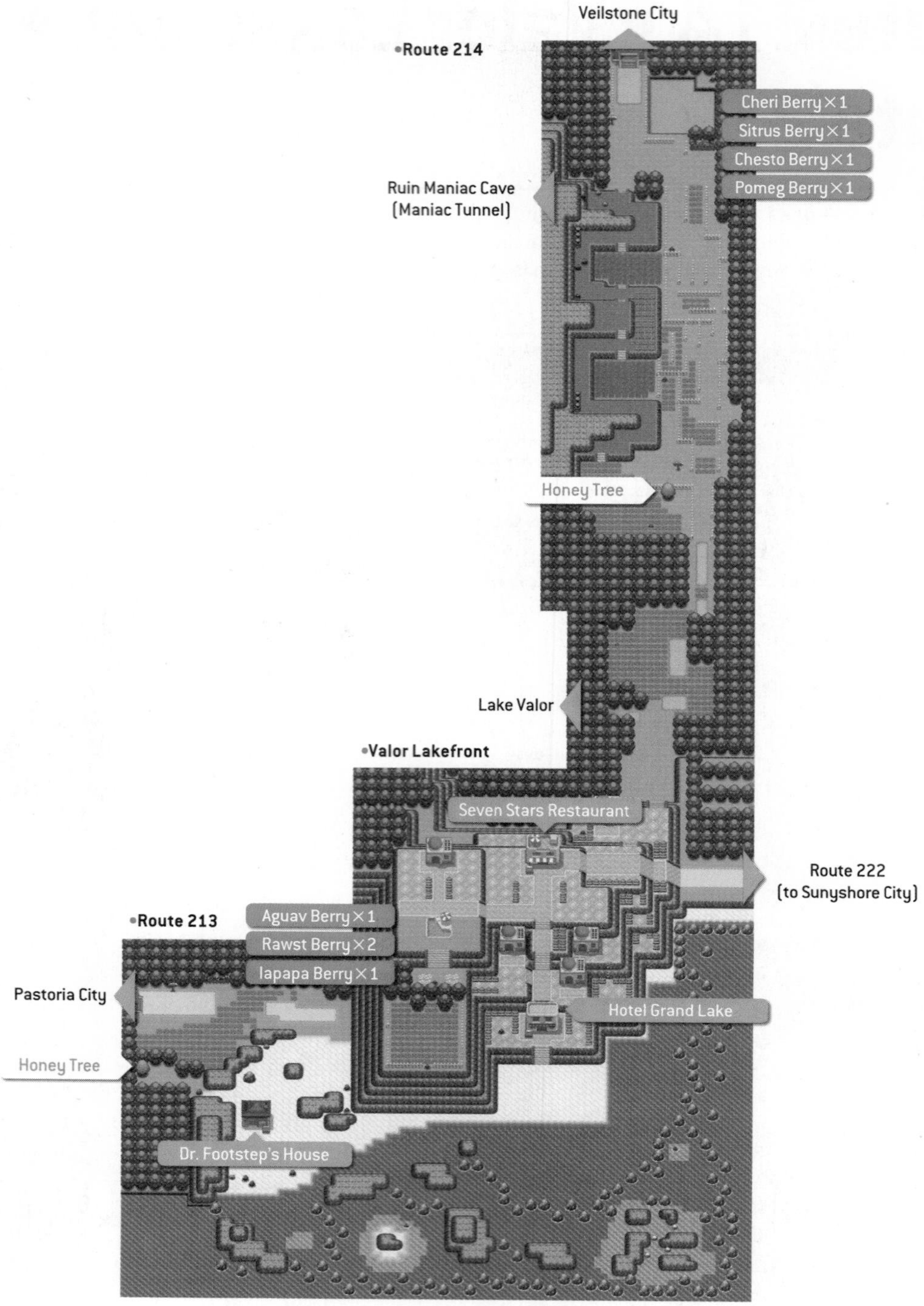

Veilstone City

•Route 214

Cheri Berry × 1
Sitrus Berry × 1
Chesto Berry × 1
Pomeg Berry × 1

Ruin Maniac Cave
(Maniac Tunnel)

Honey Tree

Lake Valor

•Valor Lakefront

Seven Stars Restaurant

Route 222
(to Sunyshore City)

•Route 213

Aguav Berry × 1
Rawst Berry × 2
Iapapa Berry × 1

Pastoria City

Hotel Grand Lake

Honey Tree

Dr. Footstep's House

Step 1 Travel south along Route 214

Team Galactic has transported something to Pastoria City. Pursue them south through Route 214. There's a cave along the way being dug by the Ruin Maniac. He'll be at a different point in his digging depending on how many kinds of Unown you've caught, and the cave will be different (p. 99).

The Magmarizer

You can find a Magmarizer on the ground on Route 214. This is the essential item needed to evolve Magmar into Magmortar.

Step 2 — The road to Lake Valor is closed

You pass through Route 214 and arrive at Valor Lakefront. But the entrance to Lake Valor is blocked by a cameraman who's waiting to snap the picture of a red Gyarados. Just leave for now, and follow the path southward.

Route 222 is impassable

You can pass through Valor Lakefront to Route 222. But Sunyshore City, on the other end of Route 222, is suffering a power outage. You can't go there right now. You'll be able to visit after you've been to the Distortion World.

Step 3 — Have fun battling at the Seven Stars Restaurant

You'll find the Seven Stars Restaurant on a plateau south of Lake Valor. It's a slightly unusual restaurant, in that, during its business hours from 9 AM to 11 PM, you can enjoy Pokémon battles with the other customers. You can also accept challenges from pairs looking for Double Battles.

Pick a fight and earn some cash

The Trainers enjoying a meal at the Seven Stars Restaurant can be challenged to battle every day. The lady and gentleman here are high rollers, too, so battling them will be especially remunerative.

Step 4 — Use the Dowsing Machine to find the Suite Key

The girl standing in front of the cottage is in quite a pickle—she's lost her Suite Key. She's sure she had it when she went to reception. Check all around the Hotel Grand Lake, using the Pokétch App Dowsing Machine to find the key.

Hoenn item makes an appearance

In return for finding the Suite Key, you get the White Flute. Use it to easily encounter wild Pokémon. The girl who gives it to you says that it's a rare glass flute from the Hoenn region.

Step 5 — Heal your Pokémon at the Hotel Grand Lake

You can heal the HP and PP of your party Pokémon at the Hotel Grand Lake, on Route 213. Talk to the receptionist to rest up, then once you're ready to rock, keep heading west along Route 213.

Kanto and Johto

A man in the upper-right cottage of the Hotel Grand Lake will tell you rumors about the Kanto and Johto regions. Lend an ear and get the lowdown on these other regions.

Step 6 — Get ribbons at Dr. Footstep's House

The guy at Footstep House on the beach along route 213 is called Dr. Footstep. Talk to him and he'll tell you the feelings of the lead Pokémon in your party, just from its footsteps. If the Pokémon likes you enough, Dr. Footstep gives you the Footstep Ribbon.

Feet don't fail me now

You'd think that Dr. Footstep would have a hard time reading the feelings of a Pokémon that makes no footsteps. However, he'll still give you the Footstep Ribbon if that Pokémon is fond enough of you.

Step 7 — Head for Pastoria City

Travel west along Route 213 and you'll arrive at Pastoria City, home of the Pastoria Great Marsh, where you can find some rare Pokémon, and the Move Maniac, who can teach your Pokémon moves.

After winning at Pastoria Gym — Pursue the escaped Galactic grunt

The Galactic grunt who escaped from Pastoria City is catching his breath on Route 213. Approach him and he'll take off for the beach. Catch up to him on the beach and he mumbles to himself about a Galactic bomb, and how powerful it is, before fleeing to Lake Valor.

After winning at Pastoria Gym — Chase the grunt and corner him into a battle

Chase the Galactic grunt near the Seven Stars Restaurant, and he'll keep fleeing toward Lake Valor. Catch up to him at the lake entrance, however, and he'll quit running and leap into battle. Defeat him, and he gives up and flees, telling you to give "this" to his leader.

After winning at Pastoria Gym — Get the SecretPotion from Cynthia

After you've defeated the Galactic grunt at the Lake Valor entrance, Cynthia comes up to talk to you. She's at the lake to find out more about its legends. She gives you the SecretPotion, saying it might be able to help the Psyduck. Take it to Route 210 to cure the Psyduck's headaches.

Cynthia and the Mystery Pokémon

Cynthia says she's here to investigate ancient tales of a Pokémon living on an island in the middle of the lake. Do you think there's a connection to the fact that the Galactic grunt was holding a bomb?

After winning at Pastoria Gym — Head for Route 212

To use the SecretPotion, you have to return to Route 210 via Route 212, which you haven't been on before. While you're on 212, stop by the Pokémon Mansion and visit the Trophy Garden, where many Pokémon are said to appear.

After visiting Celestic Town — Hang ten on 213

Once you can use HM Surf in the field, use it at the beach on Route 213 to explore the ocean. Not only can you find valuable items, you can also enjoy battles with other floating Pokémon Trainers.

After the earthquake at Canalave City — Investigate the Legendary Pokémon at Lake Valor

Go to Lake Valor in search of the Legendary Pokémon Professor Rowan asked you to find. He said that a sailor from Canalave City caused an explosion in Lake Valor. Does this have something to do with the Legendary Pokémon?

The bomb caused the boom!

Team Galactic set off an explosion at Verity Lake, and that's what caused the tremors felt in Canalave City. No question about it, Team Galactic has something nefarious in mind for the lake where the Legendary Pokémon lives.

After winning at Snowpoint Gym — Use HM Rock Climb to find items

Once you win your Icicle Badge at Snowpoint Gym, you'll be able to use HM Rock Climb in the field. Then you can scale the rough rock wall at Valor Lakefront and Route 213 to find all kinds of items.

After winning at Snowpoint Gym — Get the Pokétch App Coin Toss

Use the HM Rock Climb to visit the cottage below the Seven Stars Restaurant. There, you can get the Pokétch App Coin Toss from a man whose choice of room was actually determined by coin toss. Use it when you want to test your luck.

Check the trash!

In the cottage where you get the Pokétch App Coin Toss, you can find an item in the trash can. Just a reminder to leave no stone unturned in looking for items.

After completing the Sinnoh Pokédex — Speak to the Game Director

In the cottage just west of the Seven Stars Restaurant is a man who calls himself a Game Director. Pay him a call when you complete your Sinnoh Pokédex or National Pokédex. He might just have a fabulous prize for you!

The director is from GAME FREAK

The Game Director in the hotel cottage is actually a member of GAME FREAK, the company that creates the Pokémon games.

Ruin Maniac Cave • Maniac Tunnel

The Ruin Maniac Cave is a cave that the Ruin Maniac has dug into the face of the mountain on Route 214. His progress in excavating the cave is determined by how many Unown you've caught.

•First stage:
Ruin Maniac Cave

Route 214
(to Veilstone City)

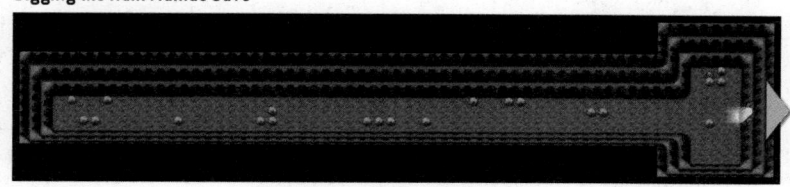

•Second stage:
Digging the Ruin Maniac Cave

Route 214
(to Veilstone City)

•Third stage: Maniac Tunnel

To Solaceon
Ruins

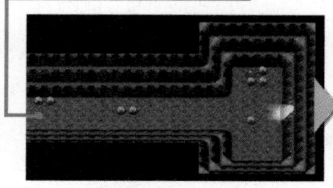

Route 214
(to Veilstone City)

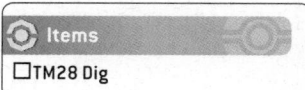

⊙ Items

☐ TM28 Dig

Geodude

| ROCK | GROUND |

Abilities
•Rock Head
•Sturdy

•First stage: Ruin Maniac Cave

⊙ Cave

Pokémon	M	A	N
Geodude	◎	◎	◎
Hippopotas	△	△	△

•Second stage: Digging
•Third stage: Maniac Tunnel

⊙ Cave

Pokémon	M	A	N
Geodude	◎	◎	◎
Hippopotas	○	○	○

Hippopotas

| GROUND | |

Ability
•Sand Stream

Step 1 — Compete with the Ruin Maniac

The Ruin Maniac who's digging the Ruin Maniac Cave is also a big Unown fan. He challenges you to a competition—the more Unown you catch, the farther he'll dig his cave. Catch lots of different Unown, and be sure to come back and let him know.

I know it's a little sudden, but how about you and me have a race?

The Unown are in the Solaceon Ruins

You'll find the Unown for your competition at the Solaceon Ruins. You can catch varieties A through Z there (p. 83).

Step 2 — Check in at ten

Go check up on the Ruin Maniac when you've caught ten kinds (or more) of Unown. The cave is a lot farther along than it used to be. The next step comes when you've caught 26 kinds of Unown. Go back to the Solaceon Ruins for the ones you're missing.

I'll just go on chipping away at the rock wall a little at a time.

Ruin Maniac becomes Digging Maniac

Once the Ruin Maniac is in the second stage of digging his cave, he picks up a new nickname: the Digging Maniac. Digging that far single-handedly is quite an accomplishment.

After getting 26 kinds of Unown — The tunnel connects to the Solaceon Ruins

Once you've caught 26 different Unown at the Solaceon Ruins, the cave is complete. It's now called the Maniac Tunnel, and its other end empties out into a hidden cave at the Solaceon Ruins. Here you can catch the "!" and "?" Unown to complete your set of 28.

Wow... My digging punched me through to this weird place.

Pastoria City • Pastoria Great Marsh

Story

Pastoria City was built to protect and preserve the Pastoria Great Marsh. From the Safari Observatory, you can gaze out across the Pastoria Great Marsh. Take a tour of the town, then head over to Pastoria Gym.

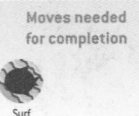

Moves needed for completion

Surf

Pastoria Great Marsh

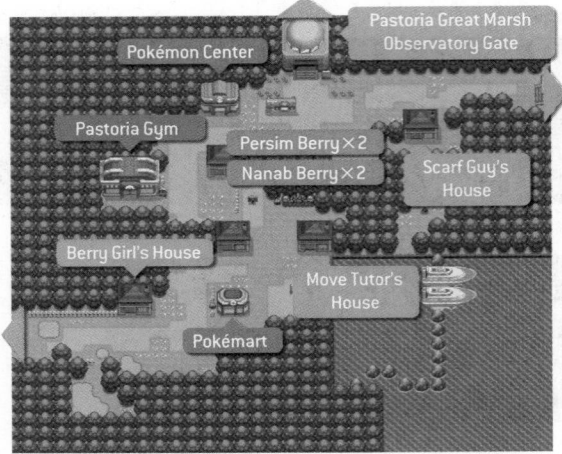

Pastoria Great Marsh Observatory Gate

Pokémon Center

Route 213 (to Valor Lakefront)

Pastoria Gym

Persim Berry×2
Nanab Berry×2

Scarf Guy's House

Berry Girl's House

Move Tutor's House

Route 212 (to Hearthome City)

Pokémart

Pokémart (left counter)

Air Mail	50P
Nest Ball	1000P
Dusk Ball	1000P
Quick Ball	1000P

Water surface

Pokémon	
Tentacool	◎
Shellos	◎
Tentacruel	△
Wingull	△
Gastrodon	▲

Fishing

Rod	Pokémon	
Old	Magikarp	◎
Good	Magikarp	◎
	Remoraid	◎
Super	Gyarados	◎
	Octillery	◎

Items

• First Visit
- ☐ Turtwig Mask, Chimchar Mask, or Piplup Mask
- ☐ Persim Berry x2
- ☐ Nanab Berry x2
- ☐ Yellow Shard
- ☐ Poké Ball x2
- ☐ Great Ball x2
- ☐ Blue Shard
- ☐ Red Shard
- ☐ Green Shard

• After you show a male and female Combee to the boy in the house
- ☐ Macho Brace

• After you catch over five Pokémon in one round of the Safari Game
- ☐ Pokétch App Matchup Checker

• After winning at Pastoria Gym
- ☐ Fen Badge

- ☐ TM55 Brine

• After visiting Celestic Town
- ☐ Mystic Water

• When your party Pokémon's Condition is maxed out
- ☐ Red Scarf
- ☐ Blue Scarf
- ☐ Pink Scarf
- ☐ Green Scarf
- ☐ Yellow Scarf

Step 1 Get the Matchup Checker Pokétch App

There's a woman standing in the Observatory Gate of the Pastoria Great Marsh. If you come out of the Safari Game having caught more than five Pokémon, she gives you the Pokétch App Matchup Checker.

Lucas obtained the Pokétch app MATCHUP CHECKER.

See yourself as a Croagunk

At the Observatory Gate of the Pastoria Great Marsh, there's one of those funny picture boards you can put your face through to see yourself as a Croagunk. And sometimes when you do, the real deal wanders along!

Step 2 The Move Tutor teaches moves to your Pokémon

You'll find the Move Tutor in his house northeast of the Pokémart. Give him a Heart Scale and he can have a Pokémon learn a move it's forgotten.

I'll do it if you'll trade me a Heart Scale.

Have a Heart-to-Heart

You can find the Heart Scale while digging for fossils in the Underground, and also while working for the Pokémon News Press at Solaceon Town.

Step 3 A boy gives you the Macho Brace

There's a boy in the house just north of the Pokémart who wants to see some Combee. Talk to him when you have both a male and a female Combee in your party. He'll give you the Macho Brace, which helps you raise Pokémon to be stronger.

Hey, have you caught both the female and male forms of COMBEE?

You get a scarf on one condition

If you feed your Pokémon a Poffin and raise its condition at the Scarf Guy's house, he gives you one of five Scarves that suit that condition (p. 229).

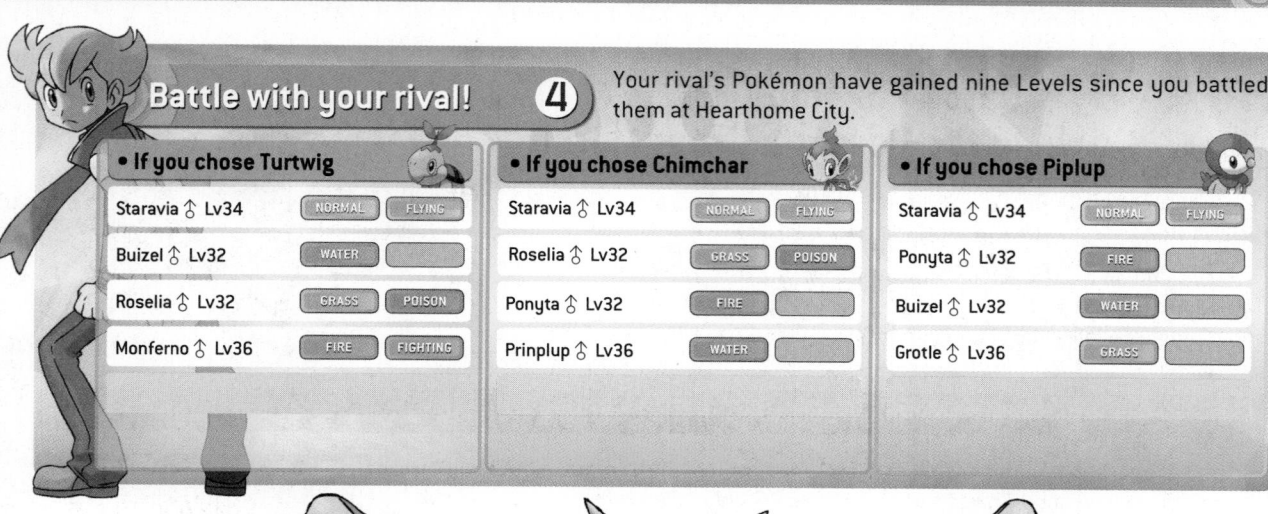

Battle with your rival! ④

Your rival's Pokémon have gained nine Levels since you battled them at Hearthome City.

• If you chose Turtwig
- Staravia ♂ Lv34 — NORMAL FLYING
- Buizel ♂ Lv32 — WATER
- Roselia ♂ Lv32 — GRASS POISON
- Monferno ♂ Lv36 — FIRE FIGHTING

• If you chose Chimchar
- Staravia ♂ Lv34 — NORMAL FLYING
- Roselia ♂ Lv32 — GRASS POISON
- Ponyta ♂ Lv32 — FIRE
- Prinplup ♂ Lv36 — WATER

• If you chose Piplup
- Staravia ♂ Lv34 — NORMAL FLYING
- Ponyta ♂ Lv32 — FIRE
- Buizel ♂ Lv32 — WATER
- Grotle ♂ Lv36 — GRASS

GYM BATTLE ⑤

Pastoria Gym Leader
WAKE

• *Water Pokémon User*

PARTY POKÉMON
- Gyarados ♂ Lv33 — WATER FLYING
- Quagsire ♂ Lv34 — WATER GROUND
- Floatzel ♂ Lv37 — WATER

Attack with Grass- and Electric-type moves

Pastoria Gym was built as a water maze—in order for you to proceed, you have to adjust the volume of water by pressing on three different buttons. Battle your way through six other Trainers to the back, where you can take on Wake himself. Wake sends out all Water-type Pokémon. Use Grass- and Electric-type moves and you'll be done in no time. Win and you'll get the Fen Badge and TM55 Brine.

FEN BADGE
Lets you use HM Surf in the field.

ENTER

SINNOH WALKTHROUGH

PASTORIA CITY • PASTORIA GREAT MARSH

Step 4 Go to the front of the Observatory Gate with Wake and your rival

Leave the Gym in victory, and your rival comes up bearing some information on Team Galactic. He and Wake dash off in a frenzy as you follow. Talk to Wake in front of the Observatory Gate. You hear an explosion, and a Galactic grunt appears.

The package that arrived, see, that was a bomb, named the Galactic Bomb.

Step 5 Chase the grunt to Route 213

The Galactic grunt who set off the explosion runs away toward Route 213. Leave the Pastoria Great Marsh to Wake and your rival, and set off on the grunt's trail. The grunt said he'd be going to the lake. Head off to Lake Valor!

All right, do I make myself clear? Don't you dare follow me!

Rare berries
A girl in the house to the left of the Pokémart will give you one rare berry a day. These are all rare and valuable types that you can't find growing along any routes. Talk to her every day and collect them all (p. 564).

Mask appeal
Talk to the girl with the parasol west of the Scarf Guy's house. She gives you the Turtwig Mask, Chimchar Mask, or Piplup Mask.

Catch Pokémon in the Pastoria Great Marsh

Grab your gear and run wild in the Pastoria Great Marsh!

You can go on a Safari Game in the Pastoria Great Marsh for 500 Poké per turn. You get 30 Safari Balls, and then it's a Pokémon-catching free-for-all until you either take 500 steps or run out of Safari Balls.

 Capture tip 1 Learn to move freely around the Pastoria Great Marsh

The Pastoria Great Marsh is split into six areas, which you can move between by riding the Quick Trams. The game is over once you've taken 500 steps, so conserve your steps by taking the train instead. This is especially helpful when you're trying to get to an area that's far away. Once you're at your area you can start walking, but stick to the paler patches of ground, to prevent you from sinking.

 Capture tip 2 Throw food or mud

In addition to Safari Balls, you can also throw food or mud. Food makes a hard-to-catch Pokémon easier to catch, and mud makes it harder for an antsy Pokémon to escape. Master the particulars of food and mud, and you should do well in the Safari Game.

Throw Food → Easier to catch, but also more likely to run away

Throw Mud → Harder to catch, but less likely to run away

 Capture tip 3 Observe the native Pokémon from the viewing area

Each area has one additional Pokémon that shows up depending on the day of the week. There are eight Pokémon whose appearance varies by day before you're enshrined in the Hall of Fame, and eight more that appear after. There are many Pokémon unique to this area, so don't neglect to catch them. You can use the telescope at the Observatory to find the Pokémon. Use it to make sure the Pokémon you want to capture is there today.

Pastoria Great Marsh

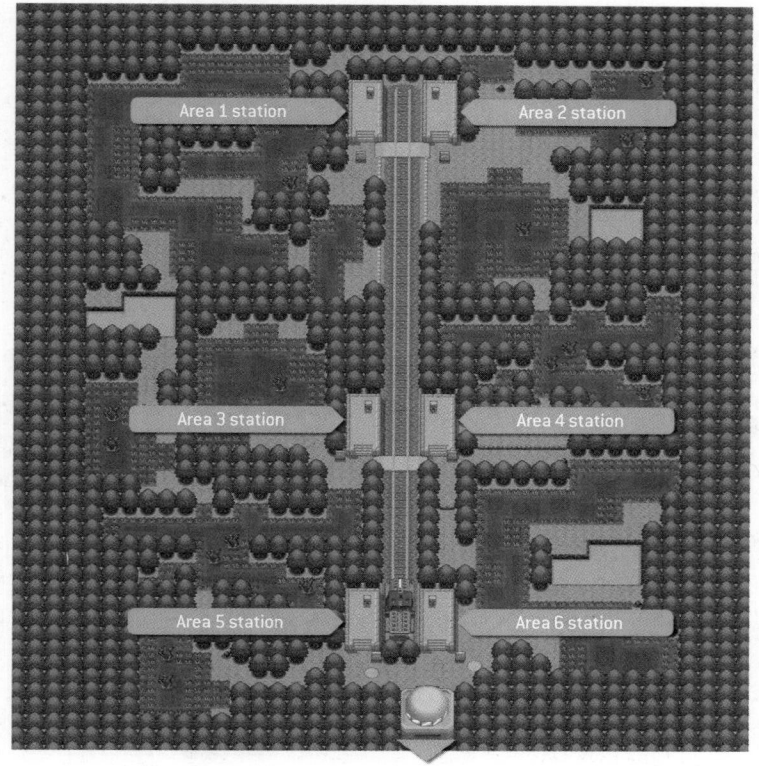

Area 1 station
Area 2 station
Area 3 station
Area 4 station
Area 5 station
Area 6 station

Pastoria City

Kecleon
NORMAL
Ability
•Color Change

Paras
BUG GRASS
Abilities
•Effect Spore
•Dry Skin

Exeggcute
GRASS PSYCHIC
Ability
•Chlorophyll

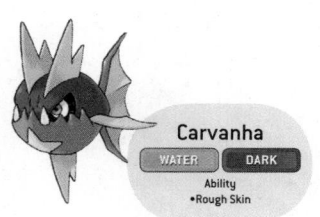

Carvanha
WATER DARK
Ability
•Rough Skin

Tropius
GRASS FLYING
Abilities
•Chlorophyll
•Solar Power

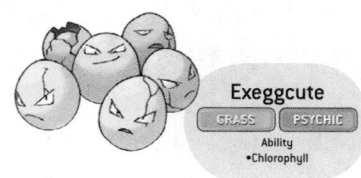

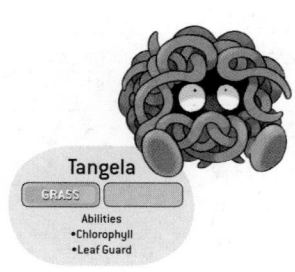

Tangela
GRASS
Abilities
•Chlorophyll
•Leaf Guard

Gulpin
POISON
Abilities
•Liquid Ooze
•Sticky Hold

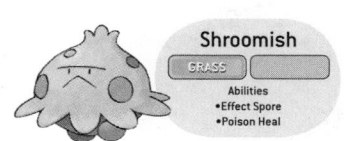

Shroomish
GRASS
Abilities
•Effect Spore
•Poison Heal

Pastoria Great Marsh (continued)

•Area Map

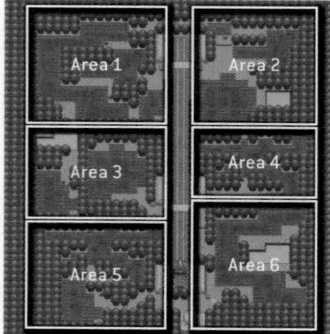

Area 1 | Area 2
Area 3 | Area 4
Area 5 | Area 6

•Area 1-2

Tall Grass

Pokémon	M	A	N
Wooper	◎	◎	◎
Bibarel	○	○	○
Tropius	○	○	X
Quagsire	○	○	○
Yanma	△	△	△
Tangela	△	△	△
Noctowl	X	X	○

•Area 3-4

Tall Grass

Pokémon	M	A	N
Wooper	◎	◎	◎
Bibarel	◎	◎	○
Quagsire	○	○	○
Yanma	△	△	△
Tangela	○	○	○
Noctowl	X	X	○
Hoothoot	X	X	○

•Area 5-6

Tall Grass

Pokémon	M	A	N
Wooper	◎	◎	◎
Bibarel	◎	◎	○
Yanma	○	○	○
Quagsire	○	○	○
Tangela	△	△	△
Hoothoot	X	X	○

•Common to all areas (Before getting the National Pokédex)

Change by day

Pokémon	M	A	N
Wooper	○	○	○
Carnivine	○	○	○
Skorupi	○	○	○
Croagunk	○	○	○
Quagsire	○	○	○
Yanma	○	○	○
Tropius	○	○	○
Tangela	○	○	○

•Common to all areas (After getting the National Pokédex)

Change by day

Pokémon	M	A	N
Toxicroak	○	○	○
Kecleon	○	○	○
Carnivine	○	○	○
Skorupi	○	○	○
Croagunk	○	○	○
Quagsire	○	○	○
Drapion	○	○	○
Kangaskhan	○	○	○
Paras	○	○	○
Exeggcute	○	○	○
Yanma	○	○	○
Shroomish	○	○	○
Gulpin	○	○	○
Tropius	○	○	○
Tangela	○	○	○

Water surface

Pokémon	
Wooper	◎
Quagsire	○

Fishing

Rod	Pokémon	
Old	Magikarp	◎
Good	Magikarp	◎
	Barboach	◎
	Carvanha	◎
Super	Gyarados	○
	Whiscash	○

Kangaskhan
NORMAL
Abilities
•Early Bird
•Scrappy

Drapion
POISON | DARK
Abilities
•Battle Armor
•Sniper

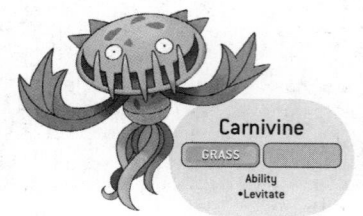

Carnivine
GRASS
Ability
•Levitate

Skorupi
POISON | BUG
Abilities
•Battle Armor
•Sniper

Toxicroak
POISON | FIGHTING
Abilities
•Anticipation
•Dry Skin

Yanma
BUG | FLYING
Abilities
•Speed Boost
•Compoundeyes

Wooper
WATER | GROUND
Abilities
•Damp
•Water Absorb

Quagsire
WATER | GROUND
Abilities
•Damp
•Water Absorb

Route 212 • Pokémon Mansion

Story

There are two main parts to Route 212. One part is deluged in a constant downpour and is cratered with bogs. The other part contains the mysterious Pokémon Mansion. You should check out the mansion's Trophy Garden.

Moves needed for completion

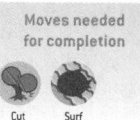

Cut   Surf

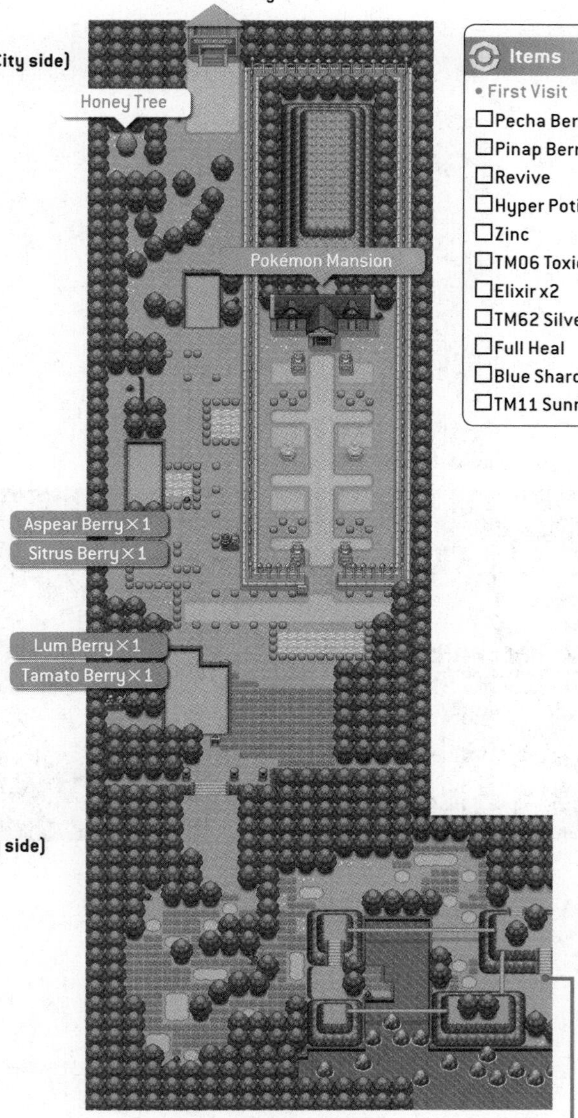

• **Route 212 (Hearthome City side)**

Hearthome City

Honey Tree

Pokémon Mansion

Aspear Berry × 1
Sitrus Berry × 1

Lum Berry × 1
Tamato Berry × 1

• **Route 212 (Pastoria City side)**

Move Tutor's House

Honey Tree

Pecha Berry × 1
Pinap Berry × 3

Pastoria City

Items

• First Visit
- ☐ Pecha Berry
- ☐ Pinap Berry x3
- ☐ Revive
- ☐ Hyper Potion
- ☐ Zinc
- ☐ TM06 Toxic
- ☐ Elixir x2
- ☐ TM62 Silver Wind
- ☐ Full Heal
- ☐ Blue Shard
- ☐ TM11 Sunny Day

- ☐ Green Shard
- ☐ TM87 Swagger
- ☐ Soothe Bell
- ☐ Luxury Ball
- ☐ Aspear Berry
- ☐ Sitrus Berry

• After winning at Pastoria Gym
- ☐ TM84 Poison Jab
- ☐ Lum Berry
- ☐ Tamato Berry
- ☐ Rose Incense
- ☐ Iron

• Route 212 (Hearthome City side)

Tall Grass

Pokémon	M	A	N
Roselia	◎	◎	◎
Marill	○	○	◎
Staravia	○	○	○
Kirlia	○	○	○
Ralts	X	○	X

Water surface

Pokémon		
Psyduck		◎
Golduck		○

Fishing

Rod	Pokémon	
Old	Magikarp	◎
Good	Magikarp	◎
	Goldeen	◎
Super	Gyarados	◎
	Seaking	◎

• Route 212 (Pastoria City side)

Tall Grass

Pokémon	M	A	N
Shellos	◎	◎	◎
Quagsire	◎	◎	◎
Buizel	○	○	○
Croagunk	○	○	○

Water surface

Pokémon	
Shellos	◎
Tentacool	◎
Gastrodon	△
Tentacruel	▲

Fishing

Rod	Pokémon	
Old	Magikarp	◎
Good	Magikarp	◎
	Remoraid	◎
Super	Gyarados	◎
	Octillery	◎

Kirlia
PSYCHIC
Abilities
•Synchronize
•Trace

Pichu
ELECTRIC
Ability
•Static

Pikachu
ELECTRIC
Ability
•Static

Mime Jr.
PSYCHIC
Abilities
•Soundproof
•Filter

Croagunk
POISON FIGHTING
Abilities
•Anticipation
•Dry Skin

•Pokémon Mansion Trophy Garden

Tall Grass

Pokémon	M	A	N
Pichu	◎	◎	◎
Roselia	◎	◎	◎
Staravia	○	◎	○
Kricketune	○	X	○
Pikachu	○	○	○

•Change each time you talk (After getting the National Pokédex)

Tall Grass

Pokémon	M	A	N
Eevee	○	○	○
Bonsly	○	○	○
Happiny	○	○	○
Meowth	○	○	○
Cleffa	○	○	○
Clefairy	○	○	○
Igglybuff	○	○	○
Plusle	○	○	○
Jigglypuff	○	○	○
Ditto	○	○	○
Castform	○	○	○
Minun	○	○	○
Mime Jr.	○	○	○
Marill	○	○	○
Chansey	○	○	○
Azurill	○	○	○

SINNOH WALKTHROUGH

ROUTE 212 • POKÉMON MANSION

•Pokémon Mansion Trophy Garden

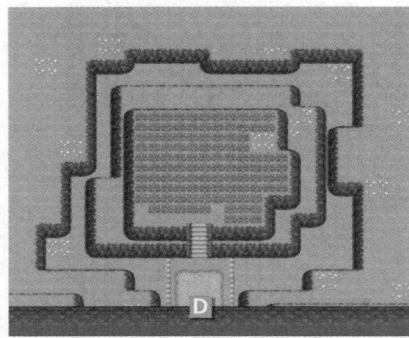

•Pokémon Mansion 1F (Maid's Room)

•Pokémon Mansion 1F (Mr. Backlot's Room)

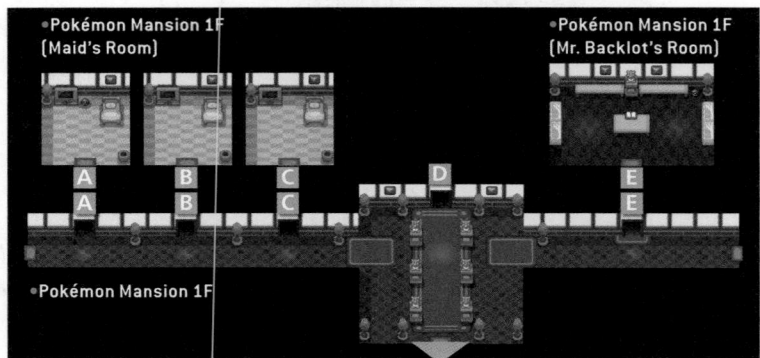

•Pokémon Mansion 1F

Route 212 (to Hearthome City/Pastoria City)

Step 1 Wiggle it, just a little bit

The deluge along the Pastoria City side of Route 212 has created lots of bogs. There are some spots where you can sink right in and not be able to move. If that happens, mash the D-pad around until you get loose.

Judge a bog by its color

If you look carefully at the bogs, you can tell which areas are deep and which are shallow. Keep to the lighter-colored areas and you won't sink in.

Step 2 Shard dressed man

Just as you've crossed the bogs coming from Pastoria City, you'll find a Move Tutor's house. He'll teach a move for each set of colored shards you give him (check the table on the next page). He has 13 moves in all to teach. There are three Move Tutors in Sinnoh.

If you'd share your shards with me, I can teach your Pokémon some moves.

Shard search

You can get tons of shards by digging for fossils in the Underground. Slowly dig at the sparkly walls, and you can collect all four types (p. 240).

• Moves taught according to the colored shards

Move	Type	Shards Required			
		Red	Blue	Yellow	Green
Dive	Water	2	4	2	0
Fury Cutter	Bug	0	8	0	0
Icy Wind	Ice	0	6	0	2
ThunderPunch	Electric	2	6	0	0
Fire Punch	Fire	2	6	0	0
Ice Punch	Ice	2	6	0	0
Ominous Wind	Ghost	0	6	0	2

Move	Type	Shards Required			
		Red	Blue	Yellow	Green
Air Cutter	Flying	2	4	0	2
Zen Headbutt	Psychic	0	4	4	0
Vacuum Wave	Fighting	2	4	0	2
Trick	Psychic	0	4	4	0
Knock Off	Dark	4	4	0	0
Sucker Punch	Dark	0	6	2	0

 **Step 3** Visit the Pokémon Mansion

The Pokémon Mansion on the Hearthome City end of the route belongs to a guy named Mr. Backlot. The mansion includes the Trophy Garden, where Pokémon appear. Take your time to find items, capture Pokémon, and battle.

But what makes me the most proud is my trophy garden in the back!

Touch the statue at night

Inside Mr. Backlot's room there's a copper statue guarded by a policeman The policeman is away between 2 AM and 6 AM, so you can go up and sneak a touch.

 **Step 4** Record Manaphy in your Sinnoh Pokédex

Mr. Backlot's room is decorated with display cases, a statue, and valuable books. Sitting on the desk in the back is a book with Manaphy's picture in it. Look at it to record Manaphy's appearance in the Pokédex and log it as "seen."

never been seen, let alone captured, in Sinnoh.

 **Step 5** Catch Pokémon in the Trophy Garden

Mr. Backlot, the owner of the Pokémon Mansion, keeps a luxurious Trophy Garden where rare Pokémon appear. At first, only five kinds of Pokémon appear, including Pichu and Pikachu. But after you get the National Pokédex, that number is increased to 21.

A wild PICHU appeared!

After obtaining the National Pokédex...

After you get the National Pokédex, you can have Mr. Backlot tell you about the Trophy Garden. When you do, one new Pokémon species will appear in the Trophy Garden. From that point on, that one additional species will change daily when you talk to Backlot.

 **Step 6** Maids to Order

Talk to the maid on the western end of the hallway in the Pokémon Mansion to enter a Pokémon battle against a gauntlet of five challengers. You have to beat each opponent within a set number of turns. Get through all five Trainers and you'll face either the young master or the young mistress of the house. The turn limit for the battles changes each day.

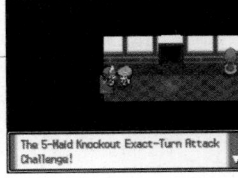
The 5-Maid Knockout Exact-Turn Attack Challenge!

Stealing candy from a Blissey

Beat all five maids, each within a set turn limit, and you face the young master or mistress. She or he sends out a Blissey that is holding a Rare Candy. Use Thief to snatch the candy.

 **Step 7** Fly for the Cure

Travel from Route 212 to Hearthome City. Your next stop should be Route 210, to cure the Psyduck's headaches using the Secret Potion you got from Cynthia. The shortest way to get there is by using HM Fly to go to Solaceon Town, then traveling north from there.

The Watchman

At the Pokémon Mansion, if the night watchman catches you on his rounds, he'll challenge you to battle. He must have mistaken you for a wrongdoer in the dark!

Celestic Town

Celestic Town maintains its revered past, while moving forward into an ever-changing present. There's a ruin in the center of town, with ancient Pokémon paintings on the wall. Chase away the Galactic grunt in front of it.

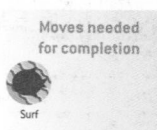

Moves needed for completion

Surf

Elder's House

Item Sellers

Ruins

Route 211 (to upper Mt. Coronet)

Route 210 (to Solaceon Town/Veilstone City)

Pokémon Center

Items

• **First Visit**

☐ Pokétch App Analog Watch
☐ Dragon Fang
☐ HM03 Surf

• When your lead Pokémon has a high friendship rating with you

☐ Great Ball

Item Sellers' House (old man)

Air Mail	50P
Dusk Ball	1000P
Quick Ball	1000P
Timer Ball	1000P

Item Sellers' House (Items given by the young man)

4 AM—10 AM	Choice Specs
10 AM—8 PM	BlackGlasses
8 PM—4 AM	Wise Glasses

Water surface

Pokémon	
Psyduck	◎
Golduck	○

Fishing

Rod	Pokémon			
Old	Magikarp	◎		
Good	Magikarp	◎		
	Goldeen	◎		
Super	Gyarados	○		
	Corphish	○		
	Crawdaunt	○		
	Seaking	△		

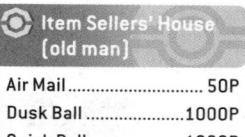

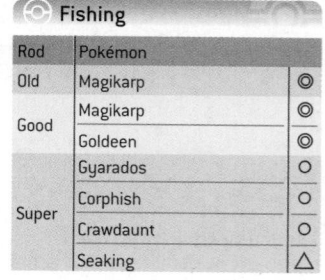

Step 1 Get the Pokétch App Analog Watch

A boy in the house to the left of the Pokémon Center gives you the Pokétch App Analog Watch. The Analog Watch shows the time in an analog format, with a big hand and a little hand. It's a nice change from the digital watch, and you'll dig it if you're old-fashioned.

Lucas obtained the Pokétch app ANALOG WATCH.

Step 2 Home shopping

There's no Pokémart in Celestic Town. Instead, items are bought and sold at a private house in the northwest corner of town. The lady on the right sells Poké Balls, Potions, and the like. The man on the left handles things like Mail.

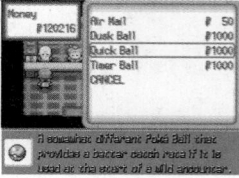

Who created Sinnoh?

According to a boy you meet in town, the entire Sinnoh region was created by Pokémon. The Pokémon depicted on the ruin wall look like they might have something to do with that.

Step 3 A vision plan

In the house where you can buy items, there's a boy who gives you Specs. His selection include the Choice Specs, the BlackGlasses, and the Wise Glasses. Depending on what time of day you talk to him, you'll get a different one out of the three. Go talk to him at different times to get all three.

Obtained the BlackGlasses!

Go ahead—have a Ball!

A man on 1F of the Pokémon Center will give you one Great Ball a day if your lead Pokémon is fond enough of you when you talk to him. Talk to him every day.

Step 4 Grapple with a grunt

There's a Galactic grunt standing in front of the ruin in the middle of town. He seems to be ticked off at the town for no real reason. He's threatening to blow stuff up with a Galactic bomb, though, so show him the error of his ways through battle, and chase him off.

If you try to mess with me, I'll shut you down with a Pokémon battle.

Three Legendaries

Deep inside the ruin, there's a triangle drawn around something sparkly on the wall. The elder says that it represents the forms of three Pokémon. Could it be related to the Legendary Pokémon that Cynthia was researching?

Step 5 Give the Old Charm to the elder

After battling the Galactic grunt, the town elder (and Cynthia's grandmother) comes to talk to you. Give her the Old Charm you've been keeping for her. She'll give you a tour of the ruins in exchange for the charm.

You say Cynthia entrusted you with it to deliver to me?

Study Sinnoh history

There's an old book on the desk at the elder's house that records the history of the Sinnoh region. It includes information about Pokémon that rule over reason, feeling, and thought.

Step 6 Cyrus suddenly appears

As you're listening to what the elder is telling you in the ruin, the blue-haired man you saw at Lake Verity and Mt. Coronet appears. It's Cyrus, the Team Galactic Boss. Answer "yes" to his questions and you're pulled into a battle. Fight with all your might—or, you could answer "no" and just write a report.

As the boss of Team Galactic, I will show you the error of your ways.

Battle with Team Galactic Boss Cyrus! ①

All of the Pokémon that Cyrus sends out are weak against Rock-type moves. You can also do well using Electric- and Ice-type moves against Murkrow and Golbat, and Fighting-, Fire-, Bug-, and Steel-type moves against Sneasel.

• Party Pokémon

Sneasel ♂ Lv34	DARK	ICE
Golbat ♂ Lv34	POISON	FLYING
Murkrow ♂ Lv36	DARK	FLYING

Step 7 Surf's you right!

After you defeat Cyrus, the elder gives you HM03 Surf. You find Cynthia waiting outside the ruin, recommending that you go to Canalave City. Pass west through Jubilife City to Route 218.

Obtained the HM03!

Hang ten in different areas

Using HM Surf in the field opens up all sorts of new avenues across lakes and oceans. Use it often and you could find lots of items on the other side of bodies of water.

Pokémon with unique moves and characteristics

Some Pokémon in the Sinnoh region have moves and characteristics that set them apart in the Pokémon world. Two such Pokémon are Chatot, which can speak like a human, and Cherrim, whose bud opens in Sunny weather to reveal its face. Here are some more details.

Chatot — Speaks human words with Chatter

Chatot learns the Chatter move upon reaching Level 21. You can make it speak human language with this move. Select the Chatter move and then speak into the Nintendo DS microphone. Chatot will remember the word, and will reproduce it when using Chatter in battle.

Chatot

● How to teach Chatot a word

Select "Moves"

Speak the word into the mic

Chatot speaks the word

Cherrim — Its flower blooms when it learns the Sunny Day move

Cherrim is normally seen in bud form, its face hidden. But when it uses Sunny Day and changes the weather to Sunny, the bud opens and Cherrim shows its face to the world. Cherubi learns Sunny Day at Level 22. Teach it Sunny Day, then raise it to Level 25 and let it evolve into Cherrim.

Cherrim
Sunshine form

● How to make Cherrim's flower bloom

Use Sunny Day

The sun becomes strong

Cherrim's form changes

Route 218

Route 218 is a short one, but it's popular as a hidden gem for fishermen. Teach HM Surf to a Pokémon and head for Canalave City and its library.

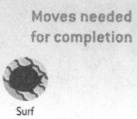

Moves needed for completion

Surf

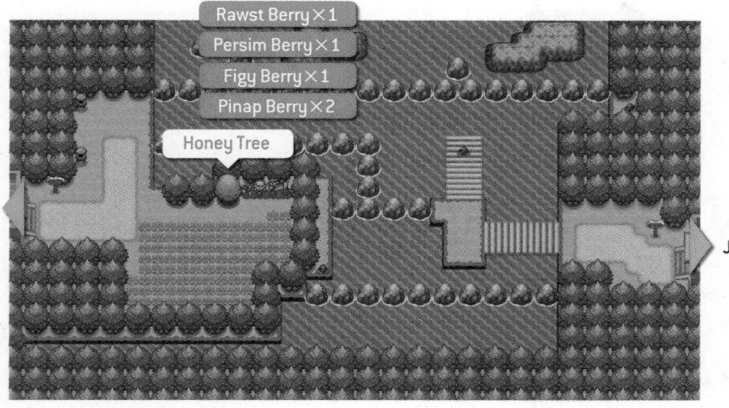

Rawst Berry×1
Persim Berry×1
Figy Berry×1
Pinap Berry×2

Honey Tree

Canalave City

Jubilife City

Items

- ☐ X Accuracy
- ☐ Hyper Potion
- ☐ Rare Candy
- ☐ Rawst Berry
- ☐ Persim Berry
- ☐ Figy Berry
- ☐ Pinap Berry x2

Tall Grass

Pokémon	M	A	N
Gastrodon	○	○	◎
Floatzel	◎	◎	◎
Chatot	○	○	X
Mr. Mime	○	○	○

Water surface

Pokémon	
Tentacool	◎
Shellos	◎
Tentacruel	△
Gastrodon	▲

Fishing

Rod	Pokémon	
Old	Magikarp	◎
Good	Magikarp	◎
	Finneon	◎
Super	Gyarados	◎
	Lumineon	◎

Shellos
(West Sea)

WATER

Abilities
•Sticky Hold
•Storm Drain

Gastrodon
(West Sea)

WATER   GROUND

Abilities
•Sticky Hold
•Storm Drain

Floatzel

WATER

Ability
•Swift Swim

Mr. Mime

PSYCHIC

Abilities
•Soundproof
•Filter

Step 1 — Use HM Surf as a Shortcut

Route 218 is the road that connects Jubilife City and Canalave City. The body of water at its center is divided by a stretch of land. But the land doesn't go all the way across. Stand on the edge and use HM Surf, and make your way west to the opposite shore, battling Pokémon Trainers as you go.

The water is a deep blue color...
Would you like to surf on it?
▶ YES
NO

Step 2 — Proceed left to Canalave City

As you cross the water to the west using HM Surf, the gate to Canalave City comes into view. Canalave City is a port town with attractions that include the Canalave Library and the harbor. The old books Cynthia mentioned can be read in the Canalave Library.

Step 3 — Gender ID

Professor Rowan's assistant comes to talk to you when you enter the gate to Canalave City. The assistant has been waiting here to power up your Pokédex. After the power-up, you'll be able to tell the visual difference between male and female Pokémon.

All done!
I've upgraded your Pokédex!

See the differences between male and female

With the powered-up Pokédex, select "Forms" on the Touch Screen to display the different male and female forms. Checking out Finneon, for instance, will let you see variations on the size of the lower part of its tail fin. Yep, sometimes, it's that subtle.

Canalave City

Story

Canalave City is a cosmopolitan port town, divided down the center by a canal. You're here on Cynthia's advice to check out the Canalave Library.

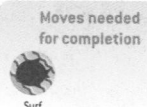

Moves needed for completion

Surf

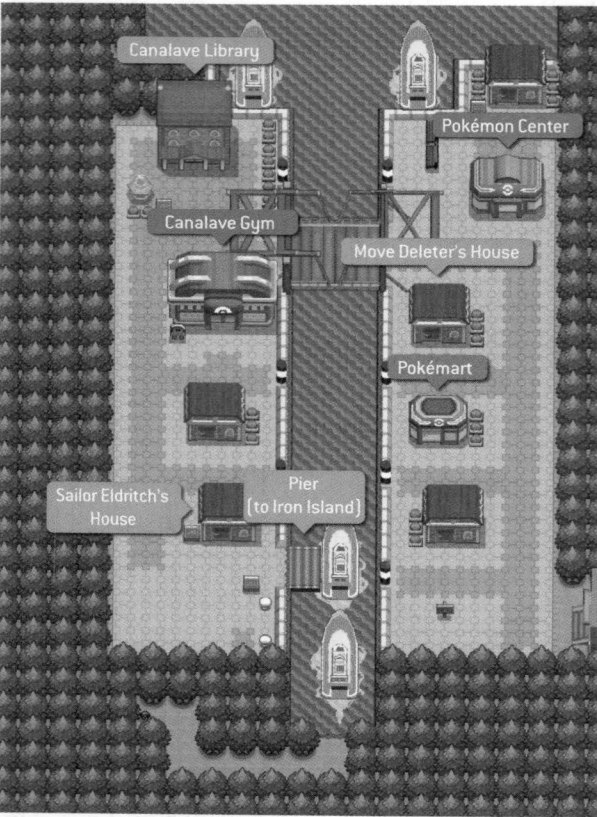

- Canalave Library
- Pokémon Center
- Canalave Gym
- Move Deleter's House
- Pokémart
- Sailor Eldritch's House
- Pier (to Iron Island)
- Route 218 (to Jubilife City)

Items

• First Visit

☐ TM48 Skill Swap

☐ TM89 U-turn

• After winning at Canalave Gym

☐ Mine Badge

☐ TM91 Flash Cannon

Pokémart (left counter)

Air Mail	50P
Quick Ball	1000P
Timer Ball	1000P
Repeat Ball	1000P

Water surface

Pokémon	
Tentacool	◎
Shellos	◎
Tentacruel	△
Gastrodon	▲

Fishing

Rod	Pokémon	
Old	Magikarp	◎
Good	Magikarp	◎
	Finneon	◎
	Lumineon	◎
Super	Gyarados	○
	Staryu	○

Lumineon

WATER

Abilities
• Swift Swim
• Storm Drain

Staryu

WATER

Abilities
• Illuminate
• Natural Cure

Step 1 Forget it

You can have the Move Deleter make a Pokémon forget a learned move. All you have to do is ask, and he can even delete HMs, which can't normally be forgotten by a Pokémon. Give him a call when you want to clear out an HM to make room for a new move.

Oh, yes, I remember now!
I'm the Move Deleter!

Get Ready to Rumble

When you start to cross the bridge in the middle of town, your rival comes running up and you get pulled into a battle. BEFORE that happens, take your Pokémon to the Pokémon Center in the northeast corner of town and heal them up.

Battle with your rival! 5

Your rival brings out a new Pokémon, Heracross. There are also some second-level Evolutions.

• If you chose Turtwig

Staravia ♂ Lv36	NORMAL	FLYING
Heracross ♂ Lv37	BUG	FIGHTING
Infernape ♂ Lv38	FIRE	FIGHTING
Roserade ♂ Lv35	GRASS	POISON
Floatzel ♂ Lv35	WATER	

• If you chose Chimchar

Staravia ♂ Lv36	NORMAL	FLYING
Heracross ♂ Lv37	BUG	FIGHTING
Empoleon ♂ Lv38	WATER	STEEL
Rapidash ♂ Lv35	FIRE	
Roserade ♂ Lv35	GRASS	POISON

• If you chose Piplup

Staravia ♂ Lv36	NORMAL	FLYING
Heracross ♂ Lv37	BUG	FIGHTING
Torterra ♂ Lv38	GRASS	GROUND
Rapidash ♂ Lv35	FIRE	
Floatzel ♂ Lv35	WATER	

Step 2 Secrets of the Local Library

The Canalave Library has lots of books containing myths and legends passed on throughout the Sinnoh region. Look at each of the bookshelves on 3F. There's information to be gleaned about mythical Sinnoh Pokémon, Legendary Pokémon, and other ancient tales.

This ancient book is titled "The Original Story." Want to read it?

Step 3 Take a boat to Iron Island

Talk to Eldritch, the sailor at the pier. He asks if you want a ride, and cheerfully ferries you to Iron Island. Go there and build up your Pokémon before taking on the Gym Leader here.

Do you wanna set sail?

You can't clock in at the Harbor Inn

The house above the Pokémon Center is the Harbor Inn. But the door is shut tight and you can't get in. What are they trying to hide?

Leave some Egg room

You'll get a Pokémon Egg at Iron Island. If you're there with a full party, you'll have to come back for the Egg later. So go with five or fewer Pokémon.

GYM BATTLE 6

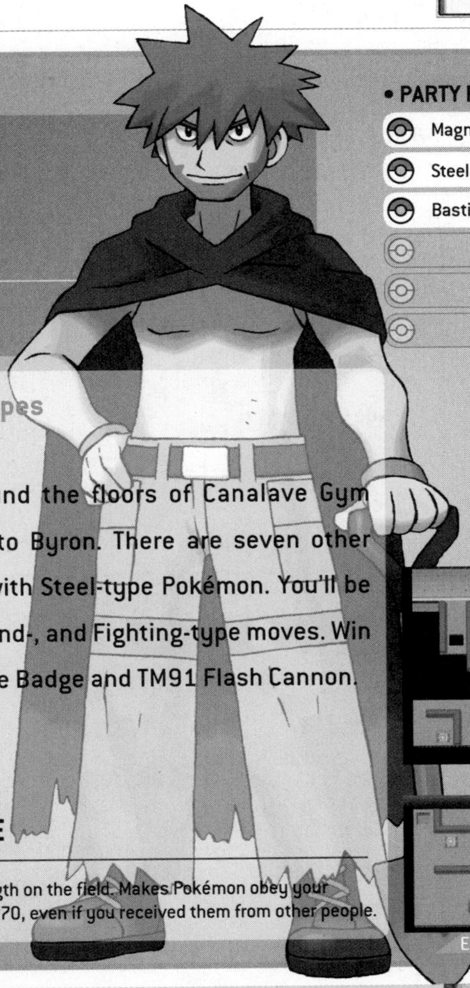

Canalave Gym Leader

BYRON

• **Steel Pokémon User**

Use Fire- and Ground-types for best results

The lifts carry you around the floors of Canalave Gym as you make your way to Byron. There are seven other Trainers. Byron attacks with Steel-type Pokémon. You'll be best served by Fire-, Ground-, and Fighting-type moves. Win and you'll receive the Mine Badge and TM91 Flash Cannon.

MINE BADGE

Lets you use Strength on the field. Makes Pokémon obey your commands up to Lv70, even if you received them from other people.

• PARTY POKÉMON

Magneton Lv37	ELECTRIC	STEEL
Steelix ♂ Lv38	STEEL	GROUND
Bastiodon ♂ Lv41	ROCK	STEEL

•4F
•2F
•3F
•1F
ENTER

After winning at Canalave Gym Go with your rival to the library

Your rival springs on you just as you leave the Gym in victory. He's champing at the bit to get to the Library, and speeds off ahead of you. Quick, follow him!

Anyway, Lucas, come with me to the library.

What's at sailor Eldritch's house?

Eldritch's wife and son live with him at his house. Some things happen here after you get the National Pokédex. Come visit again once that happens (p. 163).

After winning at Canalave Gym Earthquake! Quick, to Lake Valor!

Just as Professor Rowan asks you to find out about the legendary Pokémon at Lake Valor, there's a huge earthquake. Once outside, you discover that Team Galactic has detonated explosives at Lake Valor. Hustle over to Lake Valor to see what's going on.

Lucas, I don't like to demand, but I need you at Lake Valor.

Get rare items from Mr. Goods

Mr. Goods, in Hearthome City, gives you unique decorative goods as you reach certain milestones, like hitting a certain amount of progress in your journey or winning Pokémon Super Contests. Some of these goods are extremely hard to come by, and some can only be obtained here.

Decorate your base with items from Mr. Goods

Talk to Mr. Goods after accomplishing certain tasks, and he'll give you decorative goods. You can use these goods to decorate your secret base, so you can show it off to all your friends.

I dedicate myself to seeking rarities. It's what I live for.

Talk to Mr. Goods after meeting certain conditions

When you've fulfilled several conditions at a time, keep talking to Mr. Goods over and over again, until he's out of items to give you.

- ## Mr. Goods's Location

  Above the Poffin House in Hearthome City

- ## Mr. Goods's goods, and how to earn them

	Globe	Connect over Nintendo DS Wi-Fi
	Gym Statue	Get all 8 Gym Badges
	Cute Cup	Beat Master Rank of the Pokémon Super Contest Cute contest
	Cool Cup	Beat Master Rank of the Pokémon Super Contest Cool contest
	Beauty Cup	Beat Master Rank of the Pokémon Super Contest Beauty contest
	Tough Cup	Beat Master Rank of the Pokémon Super Contest Tough contest
	Smart Cup	Beat Master Rank of the Pokémon Super Contest Smart contest
	Blue Crystal	Greet 100 people in the Underground
	Pink Crystal	Give goods to people 100 times in the Underground
	Red Crystal	Unearth 100 fossils (Pokémon fossils or Rare Bones) in the Underground
	Yellow Crystal	Set 100 traps in the Underground

Iron Island

Story

Iron Island is a small island off the coast of Eterna City. It used to serve as a mine, but has recently enjoyed a renaissance as a training ground for Trainers in Sinnoh, and especially for Byron, the Gym Leader in Canalave City.

•**B3F 1**

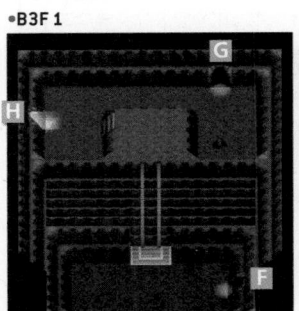

•**B3F 2**

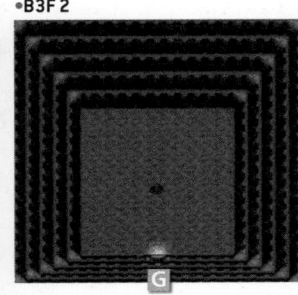

•**B2F 2**

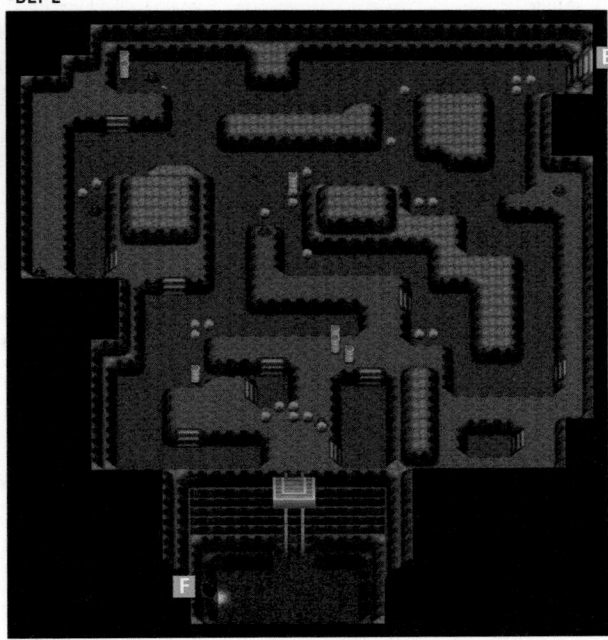

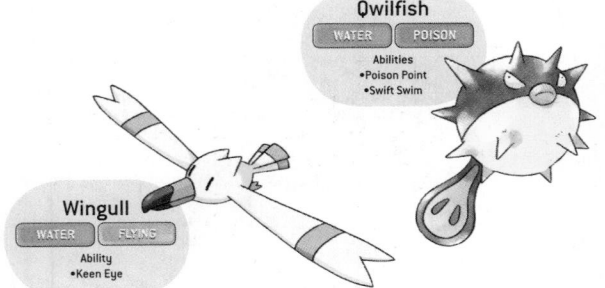

Qwilfish

WATER POISON

Abilities
•Poison Point
•Swift Swim

Wingull

WATER FLYING

Ability
•Keen Eye

•**B1F 1**

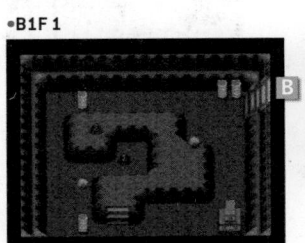

•**1F**

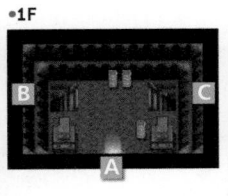

•**B1F 2**

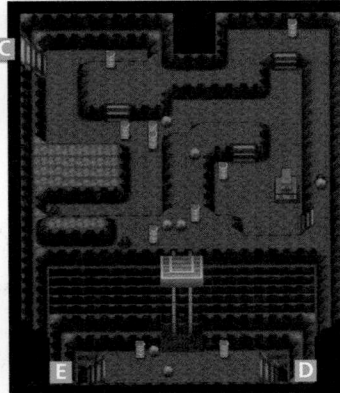

•**B2F 1**

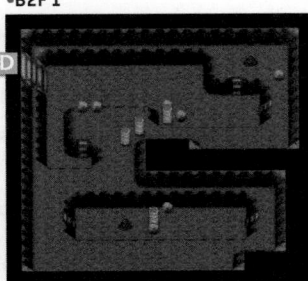

•**Exterior**

Canalave City

Riley

Items

- ☐ HM04 Strength
- ☐ Protector
- ☐ Yellow Shard
- ☐ Escape Rope
- ☐ Max Repel
- ☐ Revive
- ☐ Elixir
- ☐ TM23 Iron Tail
- ☐ Dusk Ball
- ☐ Magnet
- ☐ Ultra Ball
- ☐ Red Shard
- ☐ Max Potion
- ☐ HP Up
- ☐ Pokémon Egg
- ☐ Shiny Stone
- ☐ Metal Coat

•Exterior

Water surface

Pokémon	
Wingull	◎
Tentacool	◎
Pelipper	△
Tentacruel	▲

Fishing

Rod	Pokémon	
Old	Magikarp	◎
Good	Magikarp	◎
	Finneon	◎
	Gyarados	○
Super	Lumineon	◎
	Qwilfish	○

•1F

Cave

Pokémon	M	A	N
Geodude	◎	◎	◎
Graveler	◎	◎	◎
Zubat	○	○	○
Golbat	○	○	○
Onix	○	○	○

•B1F 1-2

Cave

Pokémon	M	A	N
Graveler	◎	◎	◎
Golbat	○	○	○
Onix	○	○	○

•B2F 1-2

Cave

Pokémon	M	A	N
Graveler	◎	◎	◎
Onix	○	○	○
Golbat	○	○	○
Steelix	○	○	○

•B3F 1

Cave

Pokémon	M	A	N
Steelix	◎	◎	◎
Graveler	◎	◎	◎
Golbat	○	○	○

Step 1 — You'll need your HM Strength

Disembark and head east and up the stairs. Riley, standing in front of the cave entrance, gives you HM04 Strength. You'll need to win the Mine Badge at Canalave City in order to use HM Strength in the field.

Obtained the HM04!

Empty nest?

There's a house at the top of the stairs near the pier, but no one's inside. However, once you get the National Pokédex, you can get Metal Coat here. Don't forget to make a return visit once you get the National Pokédex.

Step 2 — Explore the cave with Riley

You'll find Riley again when you descend to B2F(2). He's worried about the Pokémon's unrest. Explore the cave with him. Like Mira and Cynthia, Riley restores your Pokémon's HP and PP at the end of every battle.

If you don't mind, let's team up.
The Pokémon seem to be restless.

Step 3 — Grunt + grunt = Double Battle

Some Galactic grunts are blocking your way in front of the lift on B2F(2). Team up with Riley to defeat them. It's a Tag Battle, with you and Riley each sending out one Pokémon apiece. Riley's Pokémon is Lucario.

Come on, Lucas!
This is one battle we can't lose!

Step 4 — Get a Pokémon Egg from Riley

Once you defeat the Galactic grunts, Riley gifts you with a Pokémon Egg that will hatch into a Riolu. Unfortunately, it's a bittersweet present, as this is where you and this tailored Trainer will part.

►YES
 NO

Would you take it with you?

And baby makes six

Riley can't give you the Egg if your party is full. If that happens, return to Canalave City and clear out a space in your party. Then come back and talk to Riley.

Sticker It!

Ball Capsules are see-through containers for Poké Balls. Put a Seal on a Ball Capsule, and the images will appear when you send out any party Pokémon. Customize your Ball Capsule to make your very own dramatic entrance.

Edit the Ball Capsule via your PC

Access your PC to edit the Ball Capsule. Pick the capsule you want to edit, and decorate it with your favorite Seals. Apply them closer to the center of the capsule to make them appear more quickly, and farther outside to make them appear more slowly. Letter Seals will appear at the same rate no matter where you put them.

Put your favorite Seals on the capsule

You can cover a single capsule with eight Seals. Pay attention to the type and placement of the Seals.

● Ball Capsule decoration example

Display a message	Accentuate the Pokémon's type	Coordinate in a Double Battle

Collect lots of Seals

You can get Seals for your Ball Capsules from a boy in Solaceon Town, and at Sunyshore Market in Sunyshore City. The more Seals you collect, the more creative effects you can show off on your entrance into battle. Collect as many as you can and develop your own awesome style!

● Two ways to collect Seals

1 Show Unown at Solaceon Town

Show Unown to a boy in a house at Solaceon Town, and he gives you letter Seals with the same letter as the Unown.

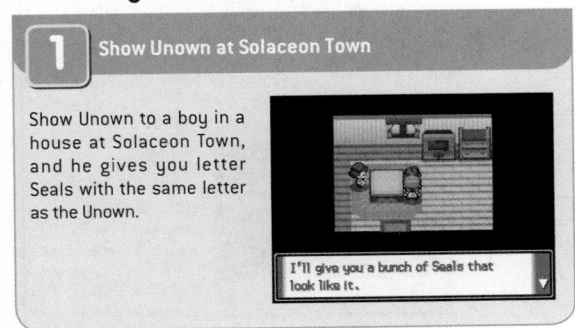

2 Buy them at Sunyshore Market in Sunyshore City

You can buy Seals from the boy at the upper-left counter in Sunyshore Market. The selection varies each day of the week.

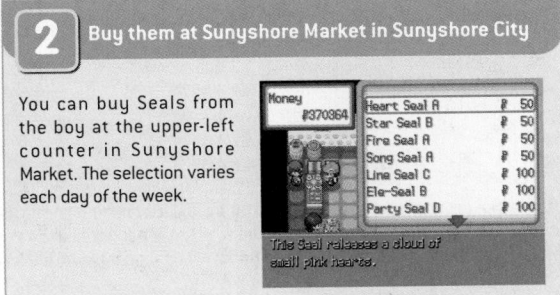

●●● See page 566 for a list of Seals ●●●

117

Lake Valor

Lake Valor is one of several lakes that are significant in the water-rich Sinnoh area, mainly because it is home to the Legendary Pokémon Azelf. Team Galactic has been causing some explosive trouble in the area so they can steal the Legendary Pokémon.

•Lake Valor

Valor Lakefront

Valor Cavern

•Valor Cavern

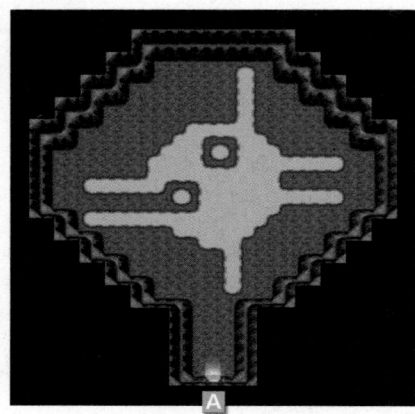

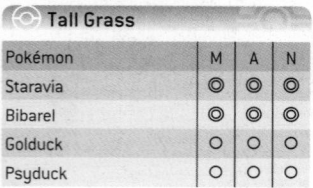

Items

• After visiting Distortion World

☐ TM25 Thunder

•Lake Valor
(after visiting Distortion World)

Tall Grass

Pokémon	M	A	N
Staravia	◎	◎	◎
Bibarel	◎	◎	◎
Golduck	○	○	○
Psyduck	○	○	○

Water surface

Pokémon	
Psyduck	◎
Golduck	○

Fishing

Rod	Pokémon	
Old	Magikarp	◎
Good	Magikarp	◎
	Goldeen	○
	Seaking	△
Super	Gyarados	◎
	Seaking	◎

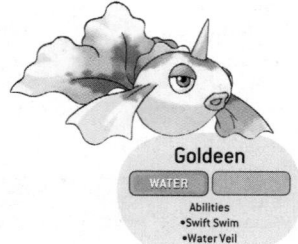

Goldeen
WATER
Abilities
•Swift Swim
•Water Veil

Bibarel
NORMAL WATER
Abilities
•Simple
•Unaware

Step 1 Global warning

The earthquake in Canalave City was caused by the Galactic bomb that Team Galactic set off. Another side effect of the bomb was to drain all the water from Lake Valor. When you arrive at the former lake, you find it already under occupation by Team Galactic forces.

Magikarp Can't Catch a Break

With the lake emptied out, you can see all the much-maligned Magikarp that lived in it flopping around on the ground. It looks like Team Galactic didn't want to steal Magikarp as well.

SINNOH WALKTHROUGH

LAKE VALOR

 **Step 2 Too late!**

Team Galactic says they've already stolen the Legendary Pokémon Azelf. You enter the cavern in the middle of the lake, only to run straight into the hands of Team Galactic Commander Saturn. Bring it!

And the Pokémon that lay in it? Well, what do you think?

Battle with Team Galactic Commander Saturn! ①

Saturn sends out Pokémon of several different types. Most effective would be to use Electric-, Ice-, or Rock-type moves against Golbat, Fire-type moves against Bronzor, and Ground-, Flying-, or Psychic-type moves against Toxicroak.

•PARTY POKÉMON

Golbat ♀ Lv38	POISON	FLYING
Bronzor Lv38	STEEL	PSYCHIC
Toxicroak ♀ Lv40	POISON	FIGHTING

 **Step 3 Verify at Verity**

When you defeat Saturn, he runs off saying that his colleague Mars should be stealing the next Pokémon at Lake Verity as he speaks. Professor Rowan sent his assistant to Lake Verity. You head for Lake Verity, hoping that Rowan's assistant is all right.

By now, Mars should have captured the Pokémon of Lake Verity...

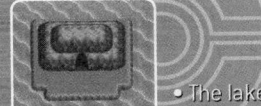
• The lake that's home to the Legendary Pokémon Mesprit

Lake Verity (Second Visit)

Story While you may be too late to stop Team Galactic from hunkering down at Lake Verity, you still have Professor Rowan and his assistant to worry about. Never give up!

Moves needed for completion: Surf

Items
☐ TM38 Fire Blast

Tall Grass
Pokémon	M	A	N
Starly	◎	◎	◎
Bidoof	◎	◎	◎

Water surface
Pokémon	
Psyduck	◎
Golduck	○

Fishing
Rod	Pokémon	
Old	Magikarp	◎
	Magikarp	◎
Good	Goldeen	○
	Seaking	△
Super	Gyarados	◎
	Seaking	◎

Golduck WATER — Abilities •Damp •Cloud Nine

Seaking WATER — Abilities •Swift Swim •Water Veil

Verity Lakefront (to Twinleaf Town)

 **Step 1** Lake Verity—too late?

You arrive at Lake Verity to find it under Team Galactic's thumb as well. Professor Rowan and Dawn/Lucas have been trying to fight back Team Galactic, but they seem to be over a barrel. Join them to defeat the Galactic grunts.

Those Team Galactic scoundrels are after the legendary Pokémon!

Come after battling Saturn at Lake Valor

If you haven't entered the cavern at Lake Valor and defeated Saturn, Team Galactic won't have appeared yet when you arrive at Lake Verity. So you have to follow the order of events.

 **Step 2** Assist the assistant

You head through the tall grass to find Rowan's assistant engaged in a showdown with Mars. It seems to be going badly for the good guys. Talk to Mars to jump into battle.

So, what is it? Are you some lovey-dovey couple to the rescue?

Battle with Team Galactic Commander Mars! ②

Most effective will be to use Electric-, Ice-, Psychic-, or Rock-type moves against Mars's Golbat, Fire-type moves against her Bronzor, and Fighting-type moves against her Purugly. If you have these moves, use them.

• PARTY POKÉMON

Golbat ♀ Lv38	POISON	FLYING
Bronzor Lv38	STEEL	PSYCHIC
Purugly ♀ Lv40	NORMAL	

 **Step 3** Showdown at Lake Acuity

Defeat Mars, and Team Galactic will retreat—but with the Legendary Pokémon Mesprit in their clutches. The last lake is Lake Acuity. Will the Pokémon there be all right? And the professor sent your rival there too—what happened to him? Better head there yourself to find out.

What is happening at Lake Acuity? Is John safe?

Route 211

Story

Route 211 is a mountain path that cuts east-west straight through Mt. Coronet, the largest mountain in Sinnoh. You'll need HM Rock Climb and HM Strength in order to pass through from Eterna City to Celestic Town.

Moves needed for completion

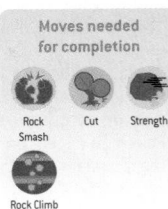

Rock Smash   Cut   Strength

Rock Climb

•Route 211 (Eterna City side)

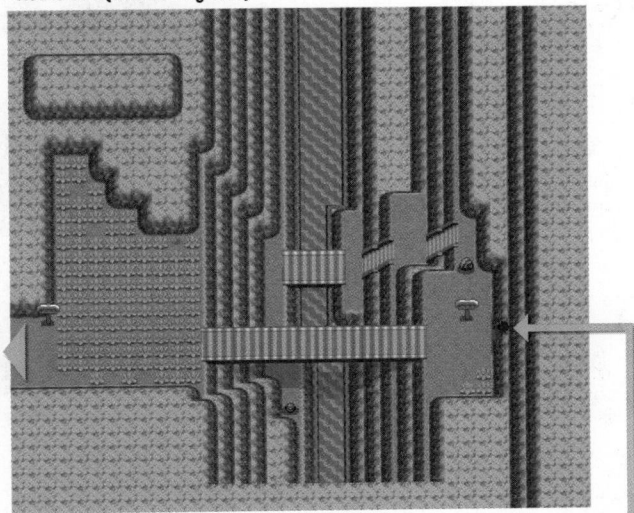

Eterna City →

Items

• First Visit
- ☐ TM12 Taunt
- ☐ Carbos
- ☐ Pecha Berry
- ☐ Aspear Berry
- ☐ Iapapa Berry
- ☐ Grepa Berry
- ☐ TM77 Psych Up

• After winning at Snowpoint Gym
- ☐ TM29 Psychic

•Route 211 (Eterna City side)

Tall Grass

Pokémon	M	A	N
Meditite	◎	◎	○
Bidoof	○	○	○
Chingling	○	○	○
Machop	○	○	○
Bronzor	○	○	○
Zubat	X	X	○
Hoothoot	X	X	○

•Route 211 (Celestic Town side)

Tall Grass

Pokémon	M	A	N
Meditite	◎	◎	○
Graveler	○	○	○
Chingling	○	○	○
Machoke	○	○	○
Bronzor	○	○	○
Zubat	X	X	○
Noctowl	X	X	○

Mt. Coronet (Upper) (P.122)

•Route 211 (Celestic Town side)

Pecha Berry × 1
Aspear Berry × 1
Iapapa Berry × 1
Grepa Berry × 1

Celestic Town →

Honey Tree

Step 1 — Proceed east from Eterna City

Proceed east from Eterna City onto Route 211, and the Mt. Coronet entrance comes into view. You remember Mt. Coronet—it's the enormous mountain that divides the Sinnoh region horizontally. Go ahead and cross through.

 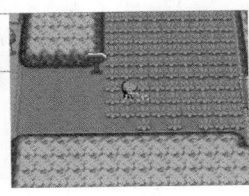

Peek-a-ninja

There's a patch of tall grass right where Eterna City leads into Route 211. Someone's hidden in the grass—search the grass to find his hiding place.

Step 2 — Cross through Mt. Coronet

Route 211 is bisected, with Mt. Coronet at its center. Go to the Celestic Town side to the east. There you'll encounter four Pokémon Trainers and a person who gives you a TM. Different Pokémon appear on each side of the mountain.

Step 3 — First stop—rest and relaxation

Across the upper part of Mt. Coronet, the far end of Route 211 leads into Celestic Town. The road to Lake Acuity is a long one, so take the chance to heal your Pokémon at the Celestic Town Pokémon Center. Once everything is in order, head back west and into the mountain.

After winning at Snowpoint Gym — Use an HM to find a TM

Pay a return visit to Route 211 once you're able to use HM Rock Climb in the field. Clamber up the rough rock face and you'll find TM29 Psychic. Don't pass up this powerful Psychic-type move, one of the most powerful in all of Sinnoh.

• The mountain that divides the Sinnoh region

Mt. Coronet (Upper)

The interior of Mt. Coronet is a huge cavern. This cavern and the one above it are critical thoroughfares connecting Eterna City, Celestic Town, and Snowpoint City.

Moves needed for completion: Rock Smash, Defog, Strength, Surf

• 1F 1

Route 211 (to Eterna City)
Route 211 (to Celestic Town)

• B1F

Items
• After visiting Lake Verity
- ☐ Escape Rope
- ☐ Ice Heal
- ☐ TM69 Rock Polish
- ☐ Rare Candy
- ☐ Ultra Ball
- ☐ Soft Sand
- ☐ Light Clay
- ☐ Max Elixir
- ☐ Revive
- ☐ Full Restore
- ☐ NeverMeltIce

• 1F 2
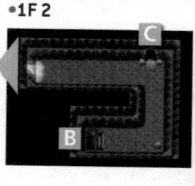
Route 216 (to Snowpoint City)

• 1F3
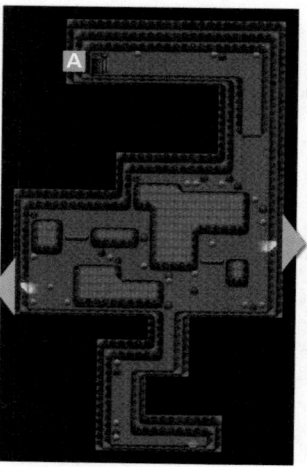

Meditite — FIGHTING / PSYCHIC — Ability • Pure Power

Cleffa — NORMAL — Abilities • Cute Charm • Magic Guard

Chingling — PSYCHIC — Ability • Levitate

•1F 1

Cave

Pokémon	M	A	N
Bronzor	○	○	○
Geodude	○	◎	○
Meditite	○	○	○
Cleffa	○	X	○
Machop	○	○	○
Chingling	○	○	○
Nosepass	△	△	△
Zubat	△	△	○

•1F 2 - B1F

Cave

Pokémon	M	A	N
Bronzor	○	○	○
Graveler	○	◎	○
Meditite	○	○	○
Clefairy	○	X	○
Machoke	○	○	○
Chingling	○	○	○
Nosepass	△	△	△
Golbat	△	△	○

Water surface

Pokémon		
Zubat		◎
Golbat		○

Fishing

Rod	Pokémon	
Old	Magikarp	◎
Good	Magikarp	◎
	Barboach	◎
Super	Gyarados	◎
	Whiscash	◎

*You can catch Feebas on B1F of Mt. Coronet (upper). See page 377 for more information.

Step 1 Use HM Strength to proceed into the cavern

You'll need HM Strength to get through the cavern and out onto Route 216. Entering from the Celestic Town side, use HM Strength to move the rocks and proceed north. At the end of the path there's a staircase to the subterranean level.

It's a big boulder, but a Pokémon may be able to push it aside.

Step 2 You can see clearly now

Down on B1F, you'll find the screen white with fog. Not only are you blind to your surroundings, but battles will take place in Foggy weather, lowering move Accuracy. Use the HM Defog to dispel the fog.

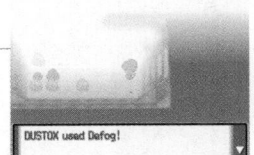

DUSTOX used Defog!

Collect Items

There are many major items, like Max Elixir and Light Clay, on B1F. Use HM Surf to case the floor from corner to corner.

Step 3 Rock blocker

Right below the Mt. Coronet entrance on the Celestic Town side, there's a rock that can be moved using HM Strength. The path beyond connects to the area leading to the Spear Pillar at the heart of the mountain (p. 133). But you can't get in from here. Just keep moving ahead.

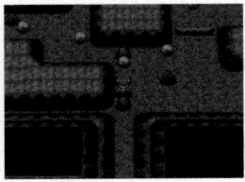

Step 4 A winter wonderland

Across the foggy subterranean level and up the stairs to 1F, you emerge into the open. You've arrived at Route 216, covered with a blanket of snow. Proceed through the snow to Lake Acuity.

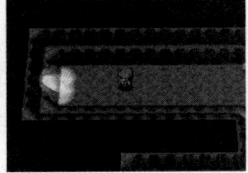

• The path connecting Mt. Coronet and Snowpoint City

Route 216 • Route 217 • Acuity Lakefront

Story

Routes 216 and 217 and Acuity Lakefront are the gusty, snow-covered areas beyond Mt. Coronet. The screen may be whited out by an occasional blizzard, but don't let that stop you!

Moves needed for completion

Rock Climb

Items

• First Visit
- ☐ Full Heal
- ☐ Revive
- ☐ Blue Shard
- ☐ Ultra Ball
- ☐ Iron
- ☐ Rare Candy
- ☐ TM07 Hail
- ☐ HM08 Rock Climb
- ☐ Icicle Plate
- ☐ Spell Tag

• After winning at Snowpoint Gym
- ☐ Mental Herb
- ☐ HP Up
- ☐ Max Potion
- ☐ TM13 Ice Beam
- ☐ Reaper Cloth

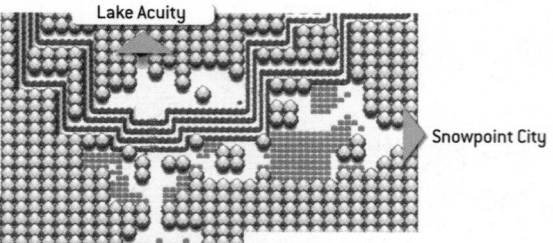

•Acuity Lakefront

Lake Acuity

Snowpoint City

•Route 217

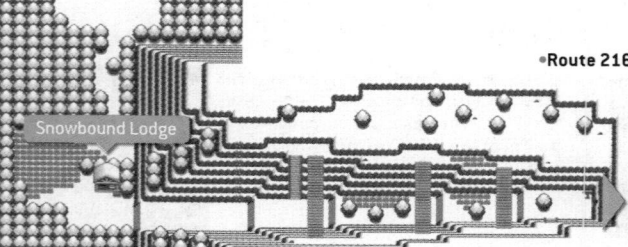

Snowbound Lodge

•Route 216

Mt. Coronet (Upper)

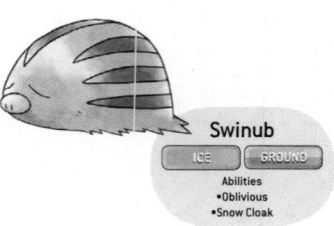

•Route 216

Tall Grass

Pokémon	M	A	N
Snover	◎	◎	◎
Sneasel	◎	◎	◎
Meditite	○	○	○
Graveler	△	△	△
Zubat	X	X	○
Snorunt	X	X	○

•Route 217 Acuity Lakefront

Tall Grass

Pokémon	M	A	N
Snover	◎	◎	◎
Swinub	◎	◎	◎
Sneasel	○	○	○
Snorunt	X	X	○

Swinub

ICE GROUND

Abilities
•Oblivious
•Snow Cloak

Snorunt

ICE

Abilities
•Inner Focus
•Ice Body

Step 1 The winter weather walk

It snows the whole way on Route 216 and Snowpoint City. Sometimes it builds up into snow piles that can snag your feet and stop you in place. If that happens, don't panic, just move forward slowly.

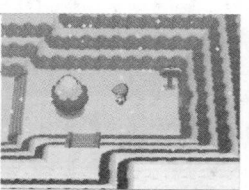

Hail drops keep fallin' on my head

The Hail weather will last in all the wild Pokémon battles from Route 216 to Snowpoint City. All Pokémon except for Ice-types take damage each turn.

Step 2 Snow place like home

The Snowbound Lodge is a cabin along Route 216. Stand in front of the bed inside and press A to restore your Pokémon's HP and PP. This is the last place to rest before Snowpoint City, so take full advantage of it.

Yahoo! This lodge's seen better days, but relax, make yourself at home!

Frozen fashion

The Elite Trainers appearing here wear heavy arctic clothes to keep out the cold and snow. Here, under the perpetually falling snow, is the only place to see them in these alternate outfits.

Step 3 Take it slow in the snow

Thanks to the blizzard, visibility is poor on Route 217. Snow is also thick on the ground, making it impossible to use your Running Shoes or Bicycle. Proceed slowly so you don't miss any items.

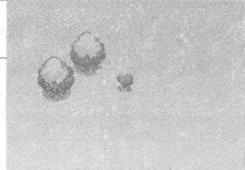

The mystery of the ice-encased rock

There's a rock encased in ice in the tall grass on Route 217. This has to do with Eevee Evolutions. If you level up Eevee on Route 217, it evolves into Glaceon (p. 382).

Step 4 Get HM Rock Climb

You can find HM Rock Climb outside of the house on the western end of Route 217. It's easy to overlook, given the poor visibility and the fact that the HM is buried in the snow. Make sure to find it.

Blue belle

On Route 217, you'll run into Veilstone Gym Leader Maylene, who's on her way to Snowpoint City for some training. She claims she's fine wearing only light clothes in the frigid weather, but her sneezing says differently.

Step 5 Visit houses, get items

Talk to the boy next to the house after you get HM Rock Climb, and he gives you the Icicle Plate. Then, talk to the girl at the house farther up Route 217 to receive a Spell Tag.

Get the most out of the Icicle Plate

The Icicle Plate raises the strength of Ice-type moves when held by a Pokémon. Give it to a Pokémon with the Ice Beam move for maximum effect.

Step 6 Lake Acuity—so close, and yet, so far

As you draw closer to Acuity Lakefront, a huge cliff looms before your eyes. Your rival is above, saying that you can climb it if you have a badge from Snowpoint Gym. Looks like your first order of business is going to Snowpoint City and defeating the Gym Leader there.

After winning at Snowpoint Gym Use Rock Climb to find an item

Once you can use HM Rock Climb in the field, head straight to Route 216 and use it to climb the rough rock face. On top, you'll find TM13 Ice Beam. This is a powerful TM you can't afford to miss.

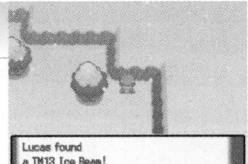

Don't fear the Reaper Cloth

The Reaper Cloth you get at Acuity Lakefront is essential if you want to complete the National Pokédex. Trade Dusclops while it's holding the Reaper Cloth to evolve it into Dusknoir.

After winning at Snowpoint Gym Use Rock Climb to head for Lake Acuity

Acuity Lakefront has two hills you can climb using HM Rock Climb. Climbing either one of them will lead you to Lake Acuity. You wonder how your rival is doing up ahead. Keep going and find out.

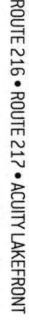

Snowpoint City

Blanketed under the falling snow, Snowpoint City is a world etched in gleaming silver. Your goal at this tranquil city of white is to obtain your seventh Gym Badge.

Items

- First visit
  - ☐ Ultra Ball
- After winning at Snowpoint City
  - ☐ Icicle Badge
  - ☐ TM72 Avalanche

Pokémart (left counter)

Snow Mail	50P
Dusk Ball	300P
Quick Ball	1000P
Timer Ball	1000P

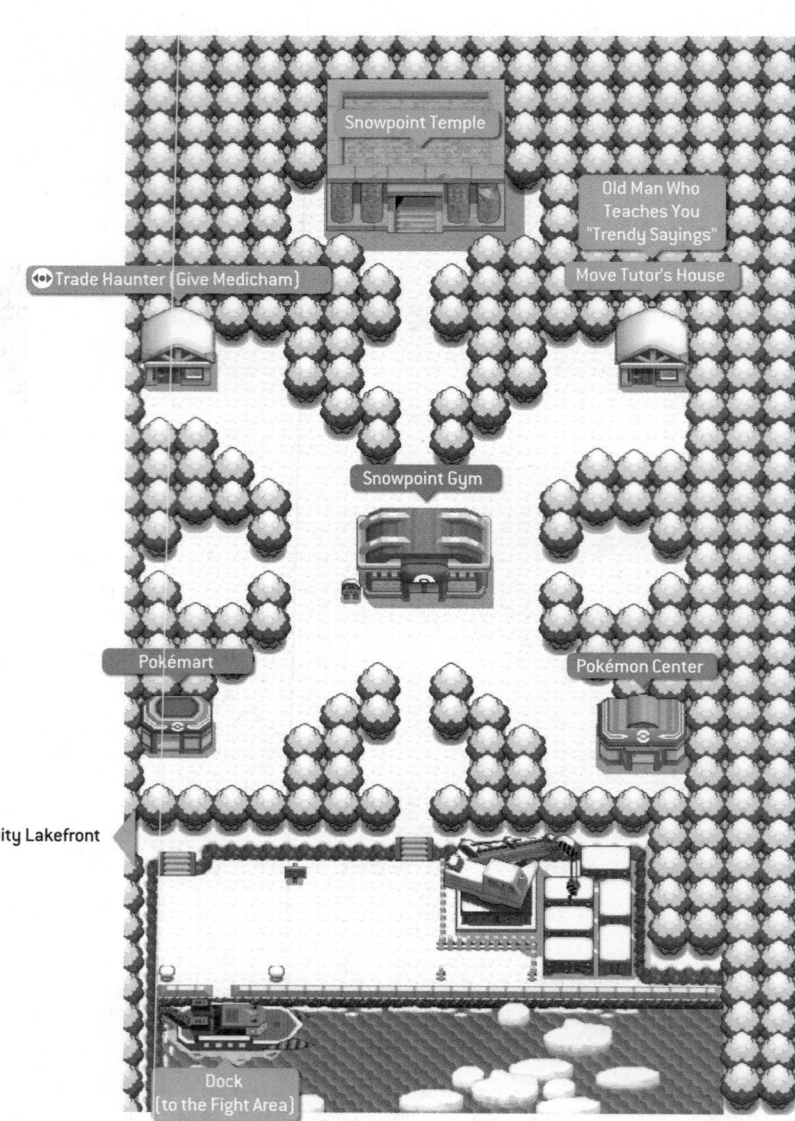

Step 1 Speaking of which

There's an old man in the upper-right house in Snowpoint City who'll teach you one Trendy Saying a day. He teaches you difficult words so that you can use them in interviews. Talk to him every day.

Hello, hello. Would you like to hear a trendy saying?

Good Will Haunter

There's a girl in the upper-left house in town. Give her a Medicham and she gives you a Haunter. This Haunter is holding an Everstone so that it doesn't evolve when traded (p. 71).

Step 2 Collect colored shards to learn moves

In the same house as the old man who teaches you Trendy Sayings is a Move Tutor. Collect colored shards, like the Green Shard, to learn a total of eight moves. There are three such men across the Sinnoh region.

Want me to teach a move?

Learnable moves and the number of shards to learn them

Move	Type	Shards Required				Move	Type	Shards Required			
		Red	Blue	Yellow	Green			Red	Blue	Yellow	Green
Snore	Normal	2	0	4	2	Magnet Rise	Electric	0	2	4	2
Spite	Ghost	0	0	8	0	Last Resort	Normal	0	0	0	8
Helping Hand	Normal	0	0	6	2	Swift	Normal	0	2	2	4
Synthesis	Grass	0	0	2	6	Uproar	Normal	0	0	6	2

 **Sorry, we're closed**

Above Snowpoint Gym is Snowpoint Temple. If you try to enter, you'll be stopped by the girl in front. You aren't allowed inside at this point. Come back after you've gotten the National Pokédex.

Are you cold now?

Inside the Pokémon Center, you'll find Maylene standing in a corner. She came to meet Candice, but she's warming her bones here first. Guess she's not immune to cold after all.

 **Only Hall of Fame players, sorry**

A sailor is standing near the town entrance. He tells you that he wants to give really strong Pokémon Trainers a ride on his boat. That doesn't include you yet. But come back after you've been enshrined in the Pokémon League Hall of Fame, and he'll ferry you to a new world of adventure.

I look forward to carrying someone like that on this ship!

GYM BATTLE 7

Snowpoint Gym Leader
CANDICE

- *Ice Pokémon User*

Attack using Fire- and Fighting-type moves

Make your way to Candice by sliding down from the upper levels to the lower levels, breaking apart the ice spheres you fall on. There are six other Trainers here. Use a combination of Fire- and Fighting-type moves and you should have success. Win and you get the Icicle Badge and TM72 Avalanche.

ICICLE BADGE

Lets you use HM Rock Climb in the field

• PARTY POKÉMON

Sneasel ♀ Lv40	DARK	ICE
Piloswine ♀ Lv40	ICE	GROUND
Abomasnow ♀ Lv42	GRASS	ICE
Froslass ♀ Lv44	ICE	GHOST

ENTER

 **Scale the cliff toward Lake Acuity**

Winning the Gym Battle at Snowpoint City enables you to use HM Rock Climb in the field. Scale the cliff your rival was standing on earlier to get to Lake Acuity so that you can check in on the Legendary Pokémon. Lake Acuity is just beyond the cliff.

Lake Acuity

Story

Lake Acuity is another of the three great lakes of the Sinnoh region. Just like Lake Valor and Lake Verity, this lake is home to a slumbering Legendary Pokémon. But this lake has also had its Pokémon stolen by Team Galactic.

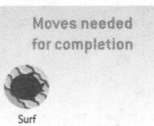
Moves needed for completion

Surf

Items

☐ TM14 Blizzard

Tall Grass

Pokémon	M	A	N
Snover	◎	◎	○
Bibarel	○	○	○
Golduck	○	○	○
Sneasel	○	○	○
Psyduck	△	△	△
Snorunt	X	X	○

Water surface

Pokémon	
Psyduck	◎
Golduck	○

Fishing

Rod	Pokémon	
Old	Magikarp	◎
Good	Magikarp	◎
	Goldeen	○
	Seaking	△
Super	Gyarados	◎
	Seaking	◎

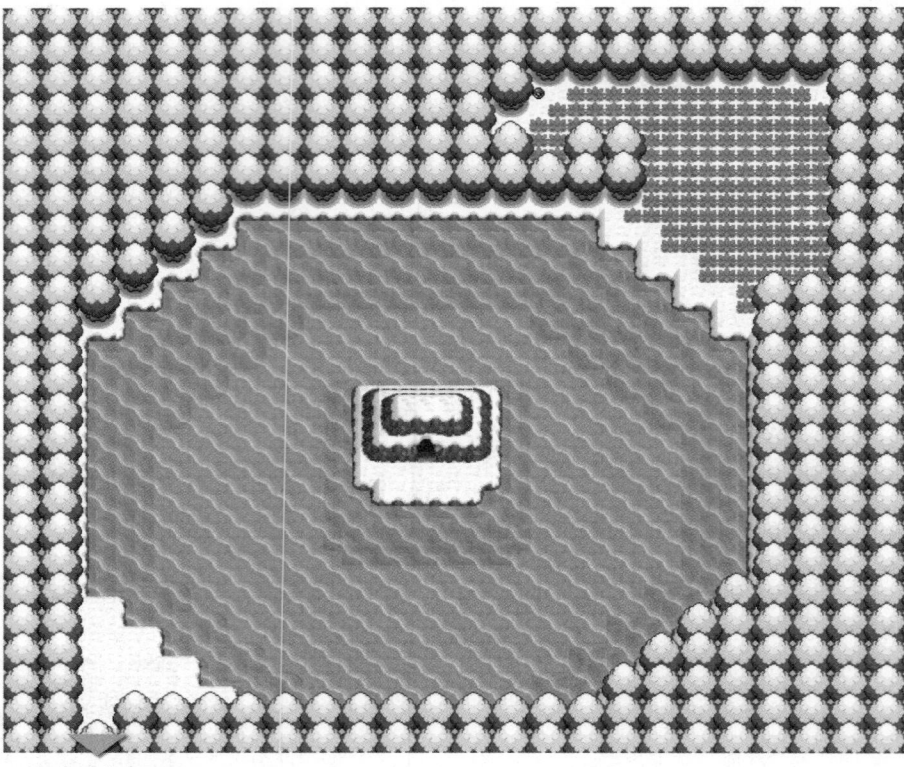

Acuity Lakefront
(to Snowpoint City)

Step **1** Jupiter puts the smack down

You arrive at Lake Acuity to find your rival spent after battling Team Galactic Commander Jupiter. It seems that the Legendary Pokémon has fallen into Jupiter's hands after all, and she's totally talking trash to him about it.

You're not getting away with this, Team Galactic!

Step **2** Jupiter returns to the Galactic HQ at Veilstone City

Jupiter leaves, returning to Galactic HQ at Veilstone City and announcing that from now on Team Galactic is going to be accomplishing some amazing things. Your defeated rival resolves to become stronger. Now that you know where Galactic Headquarters is, go!

But, aww, it's so cold here. Let's go back to the Veilstone HQ.

You need to pick it up

Team Galactic has now kidnapped three Legendary Pokémon, and spirited them back to their HQ at the Veilstone Galactic Building. It's a dark day. Hurry, go help the Pokémon!

Step 3 — Head for Veilstone City and Galactic HQ

What is Team Galactic planning to do with the Legendary Pokémon? Use HM Fly to jet over to Veilstone City and start turning Galactic HQ upside down. Descend the stairs in front of the Veilstone Pokémon Center and go up the path to the right to find yourself at the Galactic Veilstone Building.

Sneasel
DARK ICE
Abilities
•Inner Focus
•Keen Eye

Snover
GRASS ICE
Ability
•Snow Warning

• Team Galactic HQ in Veilstone City

Galactic Warehouse • Galactic Veilstone Building

Story

The Galactic Warehouse and Galactic Veilstone Building in Veilstone City make up Team Galactic's headquarters. A corridor connects the two locations. Steal inside the base to save the captured Legendary Pokémon.

•Galactic Warehouse

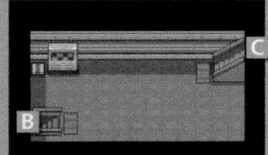

Veilstone City

•Building B1F

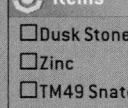

Items

- ☐ Dusk Stone
- ☐ Zinc
- ☐ TM49 Snatch
- ☐ Dubious Disc
- ☐ TM36 Sludge Bomb
- ☐ Galactic Key
- ☐ TM21 Frustration
- ☐ Green Shard
- ☐ Max Revive
- ☐ Protein
- ☐ Max Elixir
- ☐ Master Ball
- ☐ Full Restore

•Building B2F

•Hall

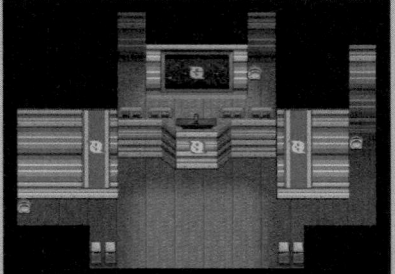

•Building 4F Back

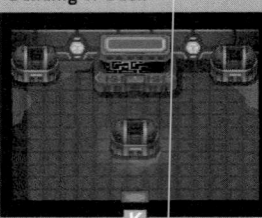

•Building 4F 1

•Building 4F 2

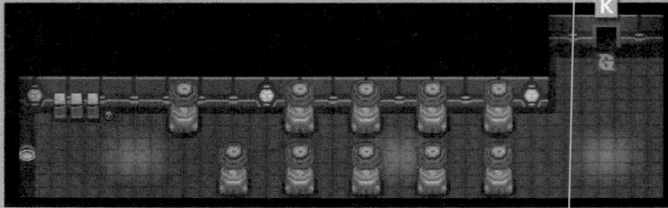

•Building 3F

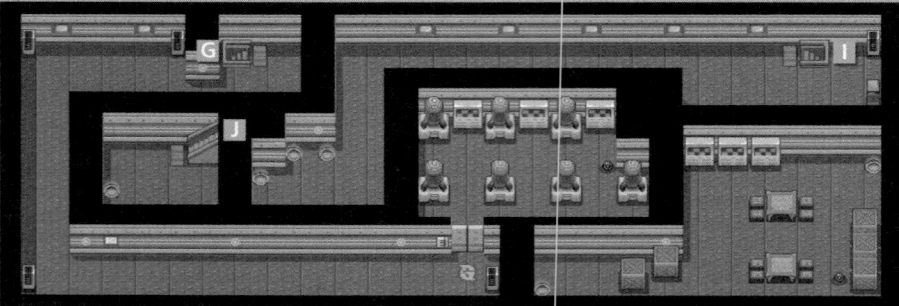

•Building 2F

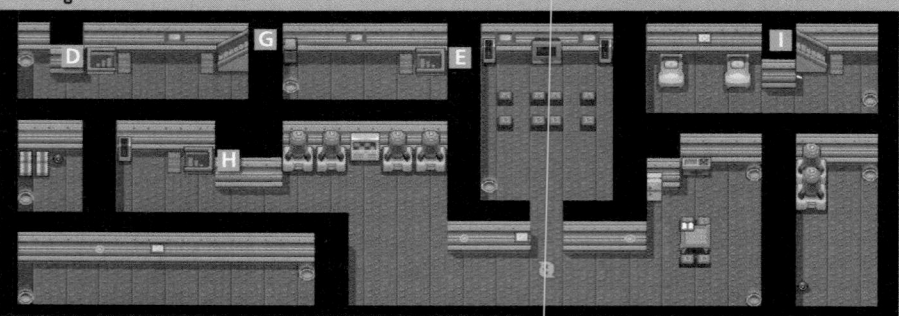

•Building 1F

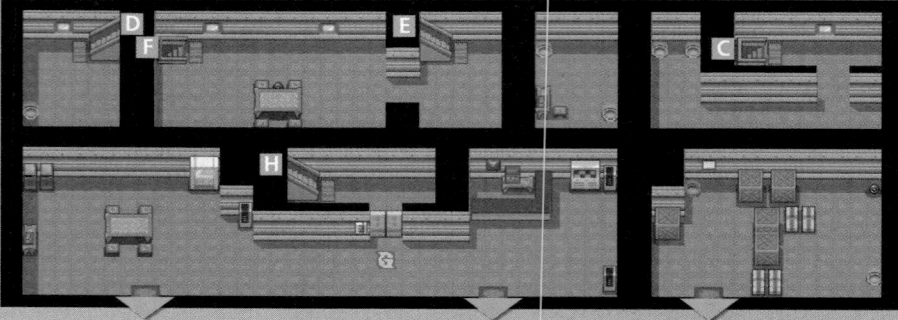

Veilstone City   Veilstone City   Veilstone City

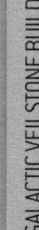

GALACTIC WAREHOUSE • GALACTIC VEILSTONE BUILDING

Step 1 Have Looker open the door for you

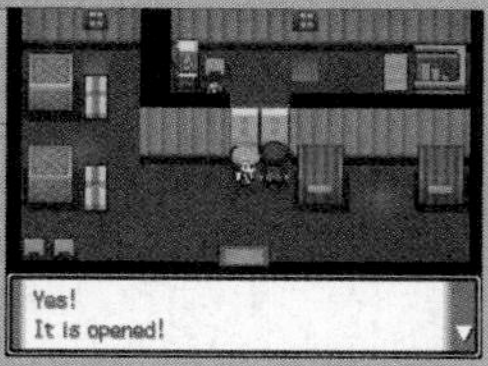

Talk to the Galactic grunt in front of the Galactic Veilstone Building. Agree to meet Looker at the warehouse, and then head on over there. As you enter and approach the front door, Looker comes up from behind and opens it for you. Descend the staircase and delve deep into the base.

Step 2 Get the Galactic Key

Use the warp tiles and go down the staircases as you sneak into the depths of the base. You find the Galactic Key upon reaching the center of B2F. This key is essential for opening doors in this base.

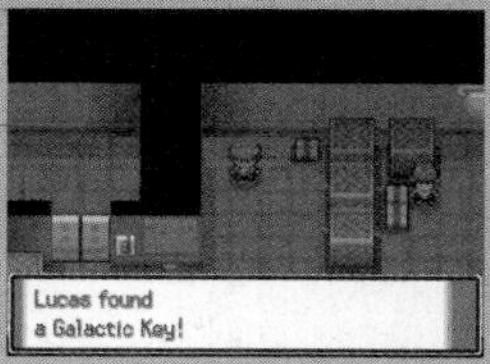

Workers of the galaxy, unite!

You'll find documents mounted on the wall in scattered locations throughout 2F and 3F. They can help you navigate the interior of the building, but can also provide clues about Team Galactic. Be sure to examine them when you see them.

Step 3 In through the front door

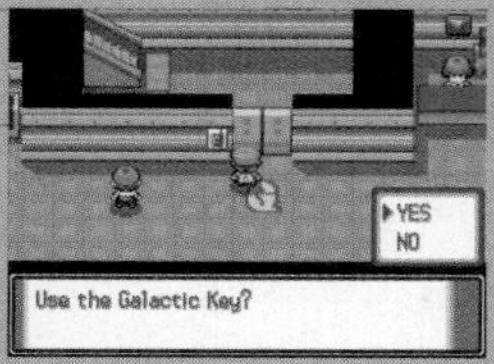

With the Galactic Key in hand, you step outside and sneak into the Galactic Veilstone Building via the center or left-hand door. The warehouse connects to the building via the basement. But the only way to get to Team Galactic Boss Cyrus on 4F is through the building entrance.

Step 4 Take a meeting

The warp on 2F will take you right to a large gathering of Galactic grunts. Looker has crept on ahead to eavesdrop. Finally Cyrus begins his presentation. Wait for it to finish, and then go left and up to 4F.

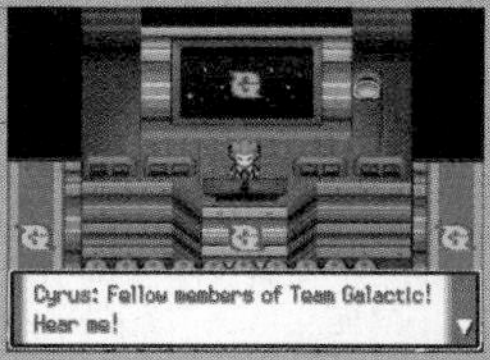

A little bed rest

After you've taken in the lecture, take the warp panel on the left side of the room to the Team Galactic break room. Stand in front of the bed and press A to restore your Pokémon. You'll need your rest when you head into battle with Cyrus and the other Team Galactic Commanders.

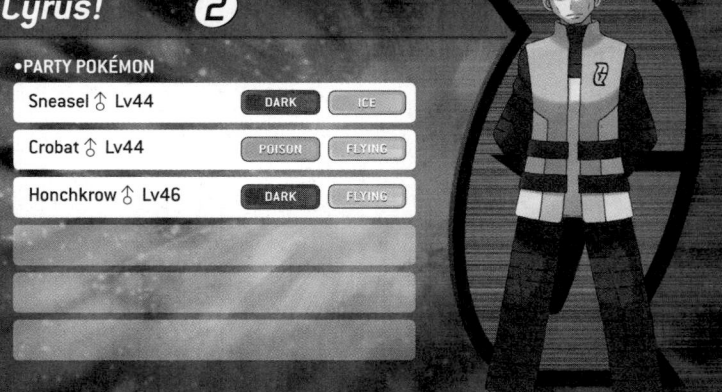

Battle with Team Galactic Boss Cyrus! 2

The Pokémon that Cyrus sends into battle are all weak against Rock-type moves. You'll fight most effectively using Electric- and Ice-type moves against Crobat and Honchkrow, and Fighting-, Fire-, Bug-, and Steel-type moves against Sneasel.

•PARTY POKÉMON

Pokémon	Type	Type
Sneasel ♂ Lv44	DARK	ICE
Crobat ♂ Lv44	POISON	FLYING
Honchkrow ♂ Lv46	DARK	FLYING

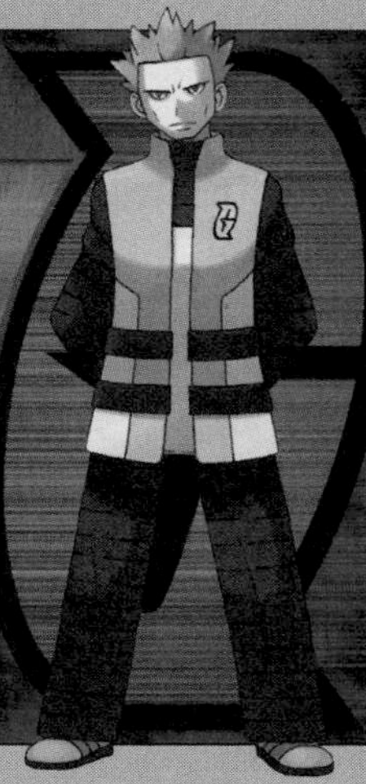

Step 5 Get the Master Ball from Cyrus

Defeat Cyrus, and he gives you a Master Ball. Then he tells you where the Legendary Pokémon are. Follow his directions, taking the warp panel to the back room of 4F, and free the Legendary Pokémon.

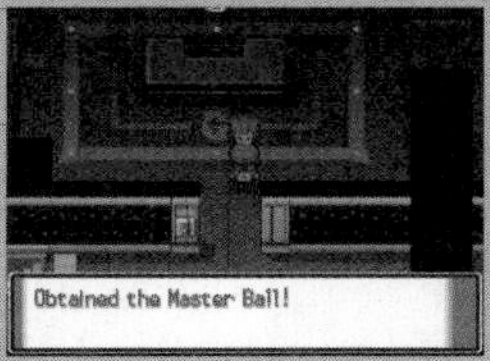

Read Team Galactic reports on the PC

The PC in the room with Cyrus has records of Team Galactic reports. Give them a read to enlighten yourself on things like the beginning of the universe and some of Team Galactic's evil plans.

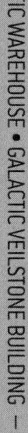

Battle with Team Galactic Commander Saturn! ❷

You battle Saturn inside 4F. Attack Golbat with Electric- and Ice-type moves, Bronzor with Fire-type moves, and Toxicroak with Ground-, Flying-, and Psychic-type moves.

• PARTY POKÉMON

Golbat ♀ Lv42	POISON FLYING
Bronzor Lv42	STEEL PSYCHIC
Toxicroak ♀ Lv44	POISON FIGHTING

Step 6 Pursue Cyrus to Mt. Coronet

Once you beat Saturn, he tells you how to free the Legendary Pokémon. Push the red button and set them loose. Then strike off for Mt. Coronet, where Cyrus said he would be going.

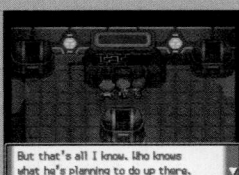

But that's all I know. Who knows what he's planning to do up there.

You don't fight Commander Charon

The person speaking to Saturn is Team Galactic Commander Charon. Charon won't attack you, but notes that he is coming up with new tactics for boss Cyrus. There's something unsettling about this guy.

• The mountain bisecting the Sinnoh region

Mt. Coronet (Middle) • Spear Pillar

Story Team Galactic Boss Cyrus has sapped the three Legendaries of their mysterious power, and is going to try something here. Pursue him to the heart of Mt. Coronet and proceed toward the Spear Pillar.

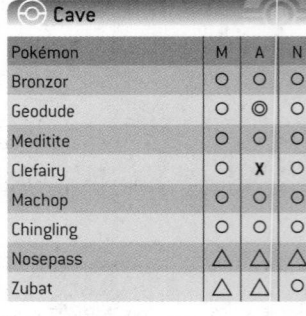

Moves needed for completion

Rock Smash / Surf / Strength / Rock Climb / Waterfall

Items

• First visit
- ☐ Dawn Stone
- ☐ Protein
- ☐ Max Repel
- ☐ Escape Rope
- ☐ Max Revive
- ☐ TM80 Rock Slide
- ☐ Black Flute

• After visiting Distortion World
- ☐ TM02 Dragon Claw

• After winning at Sunyshore Gym
- ☐ Lustrous Orb
- ☐ Adamant Orb

• 1F 1

Cave

Pokémon	M	A	N
Bronzor	○	○	○
Geodude	○	◎	○
Meditite	○	○	○
Clefairy	○	X	○
Machop	○	○	○
Chingling	○	○	○
Nosepass	△	△	△
Zubat	△	△	○

Water surface

Pokémon	
Zubat	◎
Golbat	○

Fishing

Rod	Pokémon	
Old	Magikarp	◎
Good	Magikarp	◎
	Barboach	◎
Super	Gyarados	◎
	Whiscash	◎

• 2F - 3F

Cave

Pokémon	M	A	N
Bronzong	○	○	○
Graveler	○	◎	○
Medicham	○	○	○
Clefairy	○	X	○
Machoke	○	○	○
Chingling	○	○	○
Nosepass	△	△	△
Golbat	△	△	○

Dratini

DRAGON

Ability
• Shed Skin

•3F

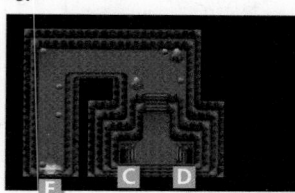

•2F

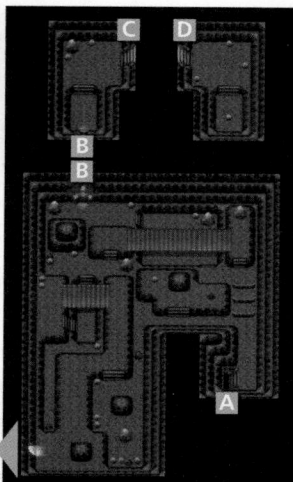

•1F 2

Cave

Pokémon	M	A	N
Graveler	◎	◎	◎
Medicham	○	○	○
Clefairy	○	X	○
Machoke	○	○	○
Chingling	○	○	○
Nosepass	△	△	△
Golbat	△	△	○

Dragonair

DRAGON

Ability
•Shed Skin

•1F 1

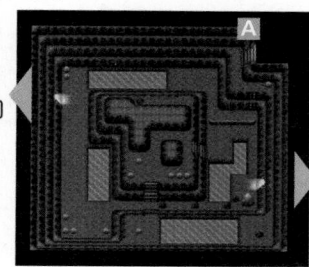

Route 207 →

Route 207
(to Oreburgh City) ◄

Route 208 ►
(to Hearthome City)

•Spear Pillar

•6F

•4F 3

•5F

•1F 2

•4F 1-2

Cave

Pokémon	M	A	N
Bronzong	○	○	○
Graveler	○	◎	○
Medicham	○	○	○
Clefairy	○	X	○
Machoke	○	○	○
Chingling	○	○	○
Nosepass	△	△	△
Golbat	△	△	○

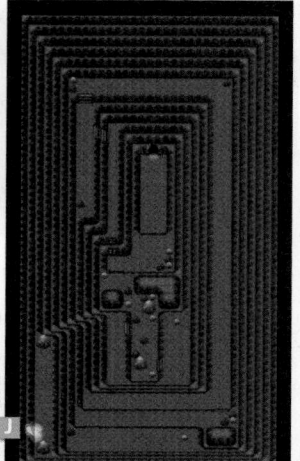

Water surface

Pokémon			
Zubat			◎
Golbat			○

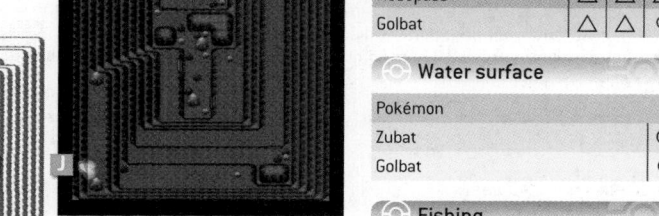

•4F 2

•Peak 2

Fishing

Rod	Pokémon	
Old	Magikarp	◎
Good	Magikarp	◎
	Barboach	◎
Super	Gyarados	○
	Dratini	○
	Whiscash	○
	Dragonair	△

•4F 1

•Peak 1

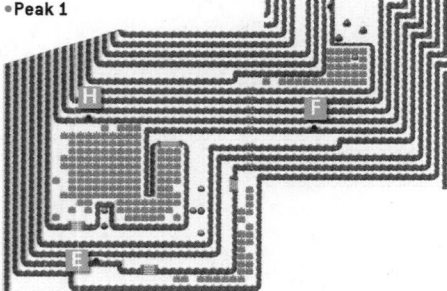

•Peak 1-2

Tall Grass

Pokémon	M	A	N
Snover	○	○	○
Abomasnow	◎	◎	○
Medicham	○	○	○
Machoke	○	○	○
Chingling	○	○	○
Nosepass	△	△	△
Absol	△	△	△
Golbat	X	X	○
Noctowl	X	X	○

Abomasnow

GRASS   ICE

Ability
•Snow Warning

•4F 3

Cave

Pokémon	M	A	N
Bronzong	O	O	O
Graveler	O	◎	O
Medicham	O	O	O
Clefairy	O	X	O
Machoke	O	O	O
Chingling	△	△	△
Nosepass	△	△	△
Golbat	△	△	O
Chimecho	▲	▲	▲

•5F - 6F

Cave

Pokémon	M	A	N
Bronzong	O	O	O
Graveler	O	◎	O
Medicham	O	O	O
Clefairy	O	X	O
Machoke	O	O	C
Nosepass	△	△	△
Golbat	△	△	O
Chimecho	O	O	O

Step 1 — Use HMs to proceed

You'll need the HMs Rock Smash, Surf, Strength, and Rock Climb to reach the Spear Pillar at the heart of Mt. Coronet. Make sure that the Pokémon in your party have all those moves covered.

It's a big boulder, but a Pokémon may be able to push it aside.

The Dowsing Machine

They're not visible to the naked eye, but there are some very useful items on the floor of Mt. Coronet. Use the Pokétch App Dowsing Machine to sweep them up.

Step 2 — Looker here! The Black Flute!

On 2F of Mt. Coronet, you bump into Looker, who's also after Team Galactic. He gives you the Black Flute, which lowers your encounter rate with wild Pokémon. Use it and you'll encounter wild Pokémon far less frequently, making the road ahead a cakewalk.

Obtained the Black Flute!

Step 3 — Climb every mountain

As you progress through Mt. Coronet, you'll suddenly find yourself outdoors. The snow is falling so heavily up here that visibility is close to zero. It's hard to find the rough handholds you need to use HM Rock Climb. Keep your eyes peeled, and search the whole area carefully as you proceed.

The wall is very rocky... Would you like to use Rock Climb?
► YES
NO

Let it snow

When you encounter wild Pokémon on the Mt. Coronet Peak, you'll be facing battles with Hail weather. All Pokémon except Ice-types take damage each turn. Keep an eye on everyone's HP.

Step 4 — No holes barred—except this one

The hole at the bottom of 1F(2) hooks up to the area on 1F of upper Mt. Coronet that connects to Eterna City and Celestic Town. But there's a Galactic grunt blocking the way. You can't get through here until after you've been to the Distortion World.

Yeah, right! You're absolutely right! I'm hopelessly lost!

Step 5 — Commander gauntlet

Team Galactic Boss Cyrus is gearing up to execute his dastardly scheme to use the Legendary Pokémon's power. As soon as you approach him, Commanders Mars and Jupiter, who have been standing by nearby, challenge you to battle. Your rival has just arrived on the scene. Team up with him to overthrow the two commanders.

Did you toughen up a bit? Sure, let's battle two-on-two!

Your first battle cooperating with your rival

You've faced your rival in battle five times already, but this is the first time you've stood beside him to face down Team Galactic. He sends out Munchlax to support you.

Battle with Team Galactic Commanders Mars and Jupiter!

Your best options are to use Fire-type moves against Bronzor and Electric-, Ice-, Rock-, and Psychic-type moves against Golbat. Attack Mars's Purugly with Fighting-type moves, and Jupiter's Skuntank with Ground-type moves.

• MARS'S PARTY POKÉMON

Bronzor Lv44	STEEL	PSYCHIC
Golbat ♀ Lv44	POISON	FLYING
Purugly ♀ Lv46	NORMAL	

• JUPITER'S PARTY POKÉMON

Bronzor Lv44	STEEL	PSYCHIC
Golbat ♀ Lv44	POISON	FLYING
Skuntank ♀ Lv46	POISON	DARK

 **6 Dialga and Palkia**

Just as you and your rival defeat Mars and Jupiter, Cyrus sets everything in place for his scheme. Using the power drawn from the three Legendary Pokémon, Cyrus successfully calls forth the fabled Pokémon Dialga and Palkia.

Step 7 Okay, that's impressive

As Dialga and Palkia appear, the trio of Uxie, Mesprit, and Azelf gathers at the Spear Pillar. Just then, a Pokémon as dark as night appears. This unknown Pokémon spreads its giant wings, and—yikes!—grabs Cyrus!

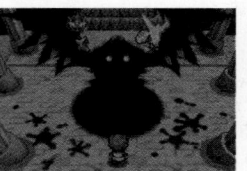

 **8 Dialga and Palkia disappear**

The unknown Pokémon disappears, dragging Cyrus along. Then Dialga and Palkia vanish too, leaving behind two spatial rifts. Where can the Pokémon have gone?

Come back later

You can meet Dialga and Palkia again, but only after you've made it into the Hall of Fame (p. 216). For now, you must join Cynthia and enter the vortex to another world.

 **9 The Distortion World**

A black vortex remains on the ground. Cynthia catches up to you and explains that the mystery Pokémon must have been Giratina. She says that the vortex is a connection to another world, and that the world is on a crash course toward destruction. Join her and leap into the void in pursuit of Cyrus.

After visiting the Distortion World Now no holes are barred

After you've been to the Distortion World, you can go through the corridor on 1F of upper Mt. Coronet. Don't pass up the chance to find TM02 Dragon Claw here.

After winning at Sunyshore Gym Find items related to Dialga and Palkia

Once you can use HM Waterfall, come back and scale the waterfall on 4F. There's a small cave above the waterfall containing an Adamant Orb and a Lustrous Orb. You'll need these to meet Dialga and Palkia after you've been added to the Hall of Fame (p. 159).

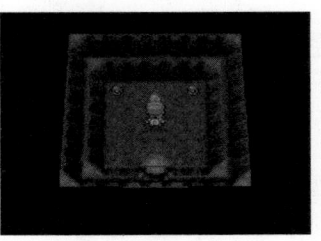

People Who Can Help You With Your Pokémon

There are lots of people in the Sinnoh region who can provide services for your Pokémon, from changing their nicknames to teaching them moves. Check this page for their locations when you can't remember where one is.

Check here for the people you're looking for

Change nicknames

Person | Eterna City's Name Rater

Can change a Pokémon's nickname for you. Unfortunately, you can't change the nickname of a Pokémon you've received in trade.

P.62

Learn Moves

Person | Pastoria City's Move Tutor

Give the Move Tutor a Heart Scale and he'll teach a move to a Pokémon. Forgotten moves are okay too.

P.100

Forget moves

Person | Canalave City's Move Deleter

Lets your Pokémon forget a move, even one that normally can't be forgotten, like an HM.

P.112

Learn moves in exchange for colored shards 1

Person | Route 212's Move Tutor

Can teach your Pokémon a total of 13 moves in trade for various combinations of colored shards. The taught moves differ according to the Pokémon.

P.105

Learn moves in exchange for colored shards 2

Person | Snowpoint City's Move Tutor

Can teach your Pokémon a total of 8 moves in trade for various combinations of colored shards. The taught moves differ according to the Pokémon.

P.126

Learn moves in exchange for colored shards 3

Person | The Survival Area's Move Tutor

Can teach your Pokémon a total of 17 moves in trade for various combinations of colored shards. The taught moves differ according to the Pokémon.

P.174

Learn the strongest Dragon-type move

Person | Route 210's Granny Wilma

Teaches Draco Meteor to a Dragon-type Pokémon with a high Friendship rating.

P.85

Learn the ultimate move

Person | Route 228's Move Tutor

Teaches the ultimate move to the final evolutionary form of your starter Pokémon (Infernape, Torterra, or Empoleon).

P.176

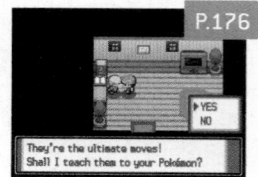

Distortion World

Story

Cynthia leads you into a bizarrely twisted world where time stands still. You must gather your courage and explore the Distortion World. Follow Giratina and Cyrus, and prevent your own world from being destroyed.

Moves needed for completion — Surf — Strength

• 1F

To B1F — 1 — 1 — To Spear Pillar

• B1F
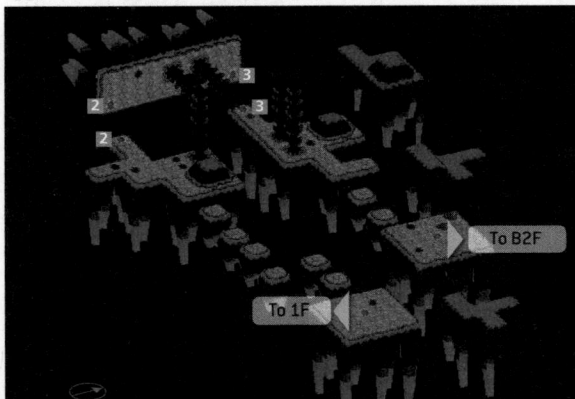
2 — 3 — 2 — 3 — 2 — To B2F — To 1F

• B4F

47 — 47 — 46 — 46 — To B5F

• B2F

12 — 12 — 13 — 7 — 8 — 11 — 5 — 11 — 7 — 13 — 6 — 8 — 5 — 6 — 14 — 9 — To B1F — 4 — 19 — 20 — 9 — 10 — 17 — 4 — 19 — 14 — 18 — 20 — 21 — 15 — 18 — 21 — To B3F — 10 — 17 — 16 — 15 — 16

• B3F
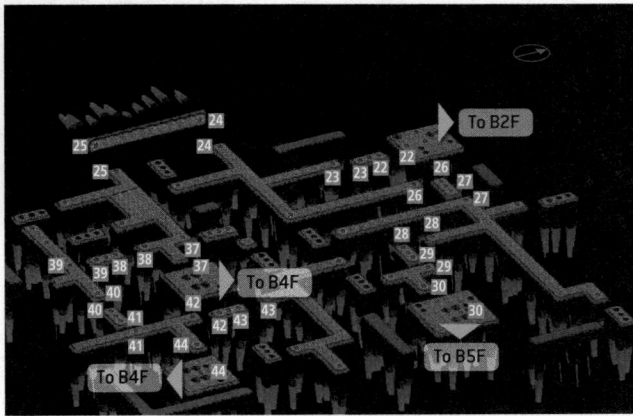
24 — To B2F — 25 — 24 — 25 — 23 — 23 — 22 — 26 — 27 — 25 — 23 — 22 — 26 — 27 — 28 — 39 — 37 — 28 — 39 — 38 — 37 — To B4F — 29 — 40 — 29 — 30 — 40 — 41 — 42 — 43 — 43 — 30 — 41 — 44 — 42 — To B5F — To B4F — 44

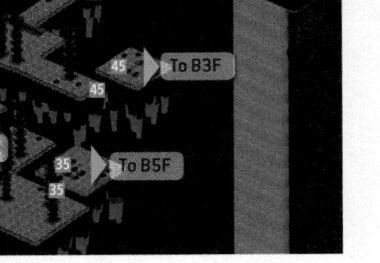
46 — 46 — 45 — To B3F — 36 — 36 — 45 — To B3F — 35 — To B5F — 35

137

•B5F

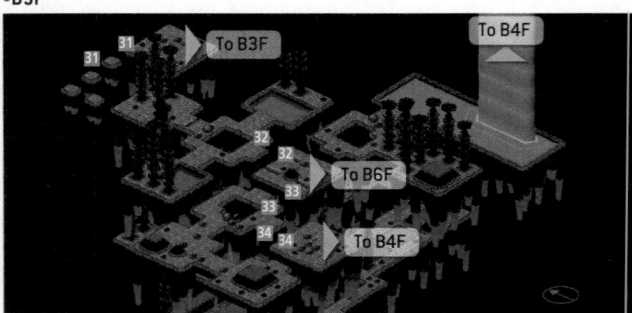

•B6F

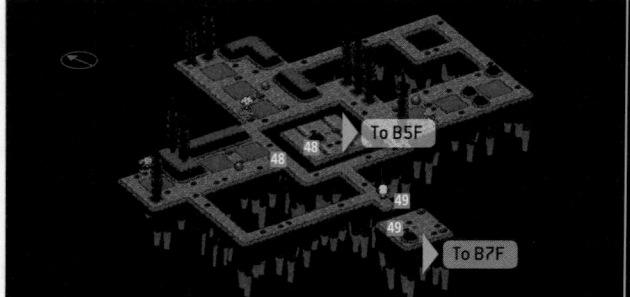

•B7F

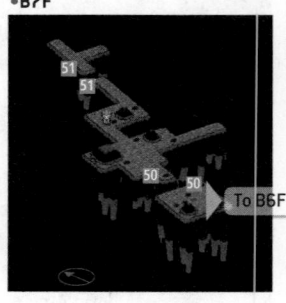

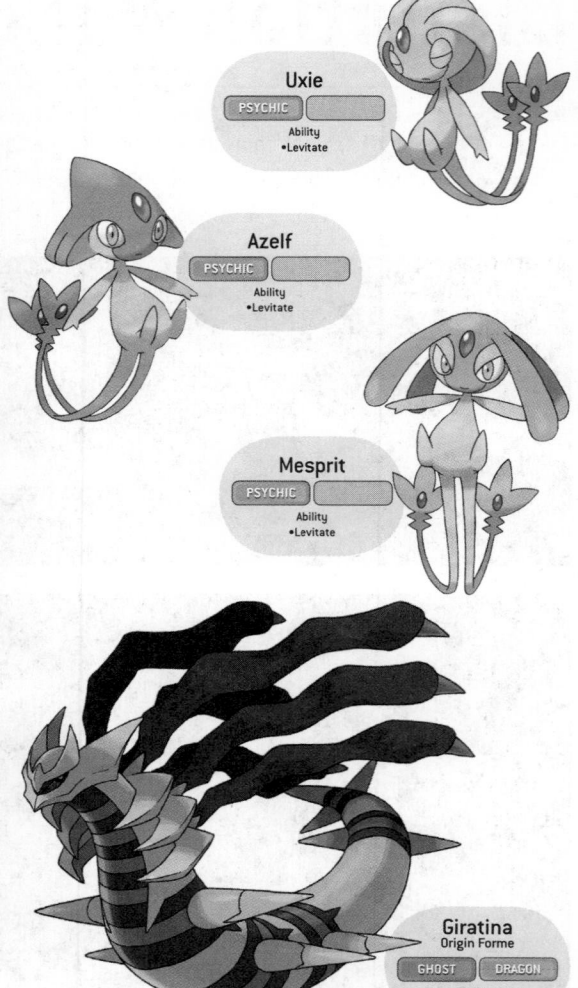

Uxie
PSYCHIC
Ability
•Levitate

Azelf
PSYCHIC
Ability
•Levitate

Mesprit
PSYCHIC
Ability
•Levitate

Giratina
Origin Forme
GHOST | DRAGON
Ability
•Levitate

| Step **1** | Things are Topsy-Turvy |

The black vortex left spinning at the Spear Pillar was the link to this never-before-seen dimension. Cynthia dubs it the Distortion World. Make your way across the floating rock platforms in your search for Giratina, who devoured Cyrus.

Return to the Spear Pillar

Press A while standing in front of the glowing hole from which you entered the Distortion World, and you'll return to the Spear Pillar at Mt. Coronet. Just be careful, because once you jump down the ledge on B5F, you can't go back.

| Step **2** | 30 Rocks |

The Distortion World contains eight floors. On each floor, you have to find the rock platform that will transport you to the next floor when you stand on the middle of it. The Legendary Pokémon trio will show up from time to time to guide you. Make your way to B5F with their help.

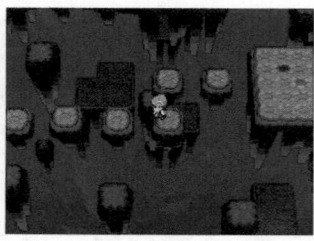

| Step **3** | Find the devoured Cyrus |

Once you reach B3F, Cyrus, whom Giratina dragged to the Distortion World, appears. Cyrus says that Giratina is to be found farther in. Cyrus tells you that your world and the Distortion World support each other.

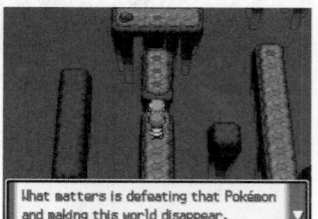

Step 4 — HM Strength comes in handy

Arriving on B5F, you cross the flying rocks and jump down to the ledge beyond. After that, there are some rocks that have to be moved by HM Strength. There are three rocks in all that you have to push off. To get to the last one, you have to make a big turn and cross over a waterfall.

It's a big boulder, but a Pokémon may be able to push it aside.

Trio of help

One of the Legendary Pokémon trio will appear when you have to push rocks off the platform. It's a sign that this is where you have to push the rocks off.

Step 5 — Use HM Surf to get around

As you cross from B3F to B4F and progress a little farther, you'll come to a lake that needs to be crossed with HM Surf. After crossing, walk along the wall until you reach the ceiling. You'll come to the base of a waterfall. Use HM Surf again. Scale the waterfall and you'll arrive at the third rock on B5F.

▶YES
NO

The water is a deep blue color... Would you like to surf on it?

Step 6 — Third rock and you're done

You'll find the last rock shortly beyond the waterfall. Get up next to the rock and Azelf appears, showing you where you should drop the rock. Use HM Strength and drop the rock into the hole in front of you. Then take the moving platform to B6F.

It's a big boulder, but a Pokémon may be able to push it aside.

Step 7 — Bye-bye trio

You find the Legendary Pokémon trio waiting for you on B6F. The rocks you pushed off of B5F have fallen down to this floor. Use HM Strength to carry the rocks over to the three Pokémon. Fit the rocks into the hollows to send the trio home.

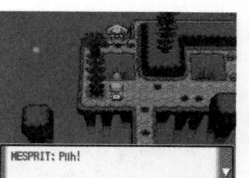

MESPRIT: Piih!

If a trio falls in the forest

After you've fitted the rocks into the hollows in the necessary spots, and the three Pokémon have started flying about, talk to Cynthia. A vertically moving platform appears. You can't move ahead as long as the three Pokémon are here.

Step 8 — Go to B7F with Cynthia

B7F is where Giratina lurks. Head there with Cynthia, and you find Team Galactic Boss Cyrus lying in wait. He takes you on in battle, in order to achieve his own selfish ambitions. It's your job to crush those ambitions!

Cynthia: ...So, you were already here.

Battle with Team Galactic Boss Cyrus! ❸

All of Cyrus's Pokémon are still weak against Rock-type moves. Other effective choices are to use Electric-type moves against Honchkrow and Crobat and Fighting-, Fire-, Bug-, and Steel-type moves against Weavile.

• PARTY POKÉMON

Houndoom ♂ Lv45	DARK	FIRE
Gyarados ♂ Lv46	WATER	FLYING
Weavile ♂ Lv48	DARK	ICE
Crobat ♂ Lv46	POISON	FLYING
Honchkrow ♂ Lv47	DARK	FLYING

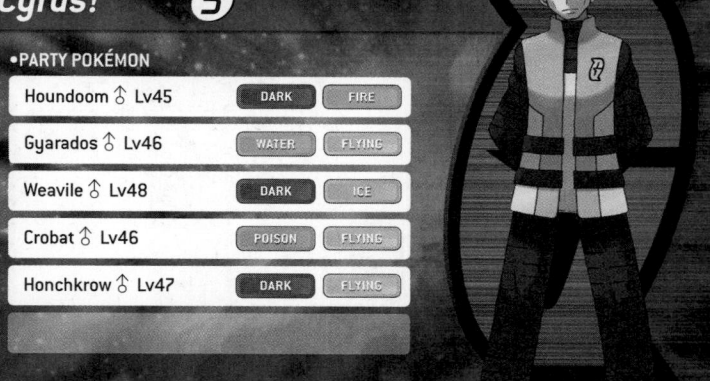

Step 9 — And now, Giratina

After you defeat Cyrus, Cynthia restores your Pokémon's HP and PP. She says that defeating or catching Giratina will halt the distortion of the world. Make your way back until you can't go any farther, and Giratina will appear.

Giygogagohgwooh!

Catch Giratina!

Take a big bite out of Giratina's HP right from the start with Ice-, Ghost-, Dragon-, and Dark-type moves, which deal double damage. After that, whittle down Giratina's HP bit by bit with Fire-, Water-, Grass,- Electric-, Poison,- and Bug-type moves, which deal only half damage.

Giratina Lv47
Origin Forme

| GHOST | DRAGON |

Ability • Levitate
Moves • Ominous Wind
AncientPower
Dragon Claw
Shadow Force

Step 10 Return with Cynthia to your home world

If you defeat or capture Giratina, or run away, its rage will finally be stilled (p. 560). Pass through the glowing white hole that appears, and return to your own world. On the other side of the hole, you find yourself at Sendoff Spring, near Route 214.

Let's go back home.

Cyrus Redux

After your battle with Giratina, Cyrus, his dreams crushed, leaves you with a few parting words. Just where has he gone?

• A hidden path along Route 214

Sendoff Spring • Spring Path

Story

Sendoff Spring is a strange and wonderful place that links your world and the Distortion World. From there you can take the Spring Path west until you reach Route 214.

Moves needed for completion

Surf   Rock Climb

• Sendoff Spring

to Turnback Cave (p. 164)

Dusclops

| GHOST | |

Ability
• Pressure

• Route 214

Veilstone City

• Spring Path

A

A

Tall Grass

Pokémon	M	A	N
Graveler	◎	◎	○
Bibarel	◎	◎	◎
Staravia	○	○	○
Chingling	○	○	○
Dusclops	△	△	○
Golbat	X	X	○

Water surface

Pokémon	
Golduck	◎

Fishing

Rod	Pokémon	
Old	Magikarp	◎
Good	Magikarp	◎
	Goldeen	◎
Super	Gyarados	◎
	Seaking	◎

Step 1 Spring is in the air

You return from the Distortion World with Cynthia to find yourself at Sendoff Spring, surrounded by groves of trees. Cynthia recommends that you let Professor Rowan know you've gotten back from the Distortion World in one piece. You head for Sandgem Town in order to do that.

Oh! That's right!
You have to go tell Prof. Rowan!

Come back when you're a Hall of Famer

There's an entrance into Sendoff Spring that you can't get into for now, since Cynthia is standing in front of it. Come back and try again after you've made it into the Hall of Fame. Cynthia will be gone, and you can go inside.

 • The lakes where the three Legendary Pokémon live

Lake Acuity • Lake Valor • Lake Verity

 The three Legendary Pokémon have returned once again to their majestic watery homes. Now is your chance to try and capture them and complete your Pokédex!

Moves needed for completion
Surf

Step 1 Uxie at Acuity

Use HM Fly to travel to Snowpoint City, then head west to Lake Acuity. Use HM Surf to proceed to the center of the lake and enter Acuity Cavern. Uxie is chilling inside the cave. Talk to it to go into battle.

Kyouuuun!

• Lake Acuity
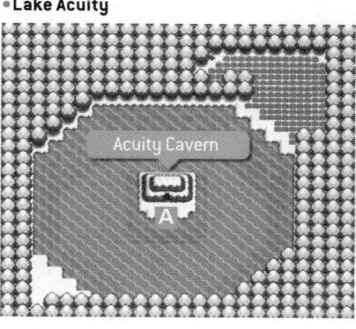
Acuity Cavern
A

• Acuity Cavern
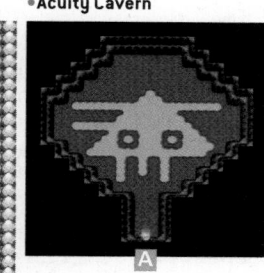
A

Catch Uxie!

Take a huge chunk out of of Uxie's HP using Bug-, Ghost-, and Dark-type moves, which cause Uxie a lot of damage. After that, slim its HP down using Fighting- and Psychic-type moves. Uxie uses the move Amnesia to raise its Sp. Defense, but it can still be easily damaged by physical moves.

Uxie Lv50
PSYCHIC
Ability • Levitate
Moves • Future Sight
Amnesia
Swift
Yawn

The Right Tools for the Easiest Capture

Just lowering its HP isn't likely to seal the deal in capturing a Pokémon that's unique in all the Sinnoh region. For maximum effect, you should also use the appropriate Poké Ball. Try a Dark Ball when at night or in caves, for instance, or a Timer Ball when a lot of turns have elapsed in the battle.

Lucas used one Dusk Ball!

Try throwing several Poké Balls

Try throwing not just one, but a variety of Poké Balls. One thing to try is a Quick Ball at the beginning of battle.

Step 2 Azelf at Valor

This time, use HM Fly to jet over to Pastoria City, and head east until you reach Lake Valor. Use HM Surf to head to the center of the lake, and enter Valor Cavern. Talk to Azelf inside the cavern to start battling it.

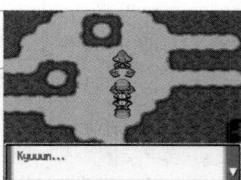

Kyuuun...

•**Lake Valor**

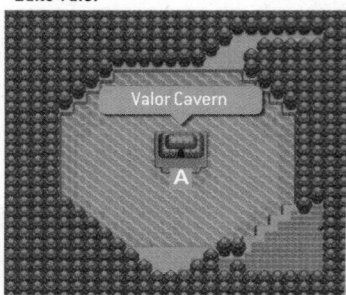

Valor Cavern

A

•**Valor Cavern**

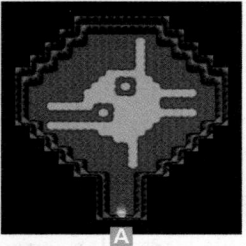

A

🔵 Catch Azelf!

Go to town using Bug-, Ghost-, and Dark-type moves. Then use Fighting- and Psychic-type moves to gradually wear down its HP. Azelf uses Nasty Plot to raise its Sp. Attack. Be careful to not succumb to its strengthened attacks.

Azelf Lv50

PSYCHIC

Ability • Levitate
Moves • Future Sight
Swift
Uproar
Nasty Plot

Step 3 Find Mesprit at Lake Verity

Now use HM Fly to go to Twinleaf Town, and take Route 201 west to Lake Verity. Use HM Surf to go out to the middle of the lake, where you can enter Verity Cavern and find Mesprit. Talk to it to record it in your Sinnoh Pokédex.

•**Lake Verity**

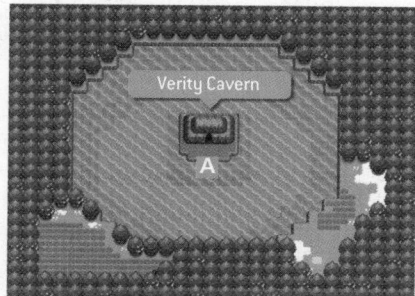

Verity Cavern

A

•**Verity Cavern**

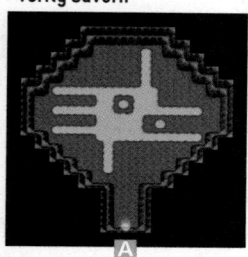

A

Step 4 The chase is on!

Once you approach Mesprit, it starts roaming all around the Sinnoh region. Use the Pokétch App Marking Map to check its location and head there yourself. Unfortunately, if you use HM Fly to get there, Mesprit will just take off for another location. You have to walk or use the Bicycle to get close (p. 393).

Get the Marking Map at Jubilife City

You can get the Pokétch App Marking Map at the Pokétch Company in Jubilife City after you've won your Hearthome Gym Battle. Head there now if you don't have it yet.

 Catch Mesprit!

Enter the tall grass or step onto the water's surface in an area indicated on the Pokétch App Marking Map. Mesprit will come flying out at you. Unfortunately, it flees right at the start of battle. Use the move Mean Look or Block to cut off its escape, then bring out your best to lower its HP.

Mesprit Lv50

PSYCHIC

Ability • Levitate
Moves • Swift
      Lucky Chant
      Future Sight
      Charm

SINNOH WALKTHROUGH

LAKE ACUITY • LAKE VALOR • LAKE VERITY

People who give you items, Ribbons, and Accessories ①

There are lots of people in the Sinnoh region who'll give you items, Accessories, Ribbons, and other goodies if you'll show them a Pokémon or meet certain other requirements. Here's an index of all of those people. Use this page to quickly locate a particular person.

Get prizes for meeting requirements or granting requests

Five Kinds of Scarves

Person   Pastoria City's Scarf Guy

Feed a Pokémon a Poffin to raise its condition. You'll get a Scarf coresponding to that condition.

P.100

Let me examine your Pokémon to see if it's worthy of a scarf!

Three Kinds of Items

Person   Man in house on Route 221

Show the man a Pokémon at the level he asks for, and he gives you a Black Belt, an Expert Belt, and/or a Focus Sash, all useful items in battle.

P.40

Show me a Pokémon that's Lv. 40. If you can, I'll reward you.

Macho Brace

Person   Boy in a house in Pastoria City

There's a boy in a house who'll give you the Macho Brace when you show him both a male and a female Combee.

P.100

Hey, have you caught both the female and male forms of COMBEE?

Three Kinds of Glasses

Person   Young man in a house in Celestic Town

Talk to the young man and receive the Choice Specs if it's morning, BlackGlasses if it's afternoon, and Wise Glasses if it's evening.

P.108

Putting on a pair of glasses changes how the world looks.

Accessories and Berries

Person   Guy in Amity Square in Hearthome City

The man inside the east gate of Amity Square gives you one Accessory or five Berries each day.

P.73

I don't mind the cleaning at all. I find all sorts of items doing so.

Exclusive Accessories

Person   Veilstone City masseuse

After giving a massage to a Pokémon in your party, the Massage Girl gives you an Accessory. You can get one massage a day.

P.89

▶ YES
  NO

If you'd like, I can give a massage to a Pokémon. Would you like that?

Route 222

Route 222 borders a beach bustling with fishing activity. This is the way to Sunyshore City, where you've got your eyes on your final Gym Badge.

Moves needed for completion

Rock Smash   Cut   Surf

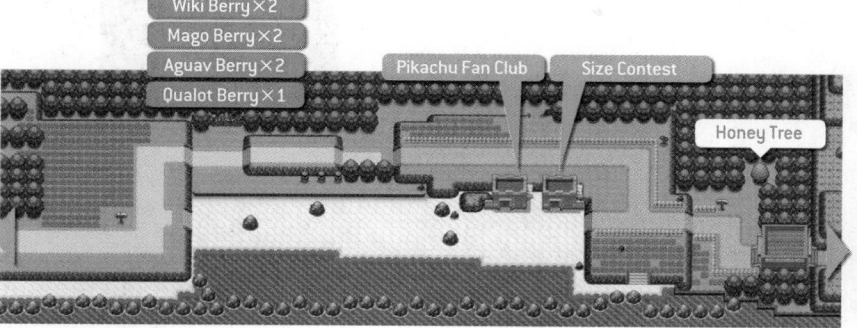

Wiki Berry × 2
Mago Berry × 2
Aguav Berry × 2
Qualot Berry × 1

Pikachu Fan Club   Size Contest

Honey Tree

Valor Lakefront

Sunyshore City

Items

• First Visit
- ☐ Wiki Berry x2
- ☐ Mago Berry x2
- ☐ Aguav Berry x2
- ☐ Qualot Berry
- ☐ Full Restore
- ☐ Carbos
- ☐ TM56 Fling
- ☐ PP Up
- ☐ Quick Ball

• On setting a new size record for Remoraid
- ☐ Net Ball

Tall Grass

Pokémon	M	A	N
Electabuzz	◎	◎	○
Floatzel	○	○	◎
Chatot	○	○	X
Wingull	○	○	○
Magnemite	○	○	○
Luxio	○	○	○
Pelipper	△	△	△
Magneton	△	△	△

Water surface

Pokémon	
Tentacool	◎
Wingull	◎
Tentacruel	△
Pelipper	▲

Fishing

Rod	Pokémon	
Old	Magikarp	◎
Good	Magikarp	◎
	Remoraid	◎
Super	Gyarados	◎
	Octillery	◎

Remoraid

WATER

Abilities
• Hustle
• Sniper

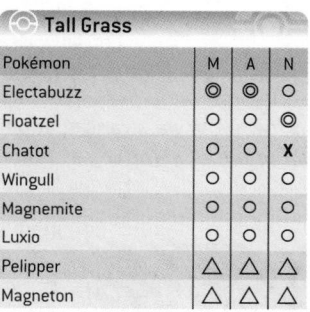

Electabuzz

ELECTRIC

Ability
• Static

Luxio

ELECTRIC

Abilities
• Rivalry
• Intimidate

Step 1 It's a shore thing

Take Route 213 or 214 to Valor Lakefront. Go east and enter Route 222. You couldn't get by here before, due to the blackout in Sunyshore City. But now everything's been safely restored, and the man who was blocking the path is gone.

Step 2 Head east toward Sunyshore City

Route 222 is pretty much a straight line from Valor Lakefront to Sunyshore City. All you have to do is travel east and you'll reach Sunyshore City. But there are a few things to do before you enter the town, like battle Trainers on the road and visit the houses.

Step 3 Pikachu, is that you?

The Pikachu Fan Club is the house of a man who adores Pikachu. Inside is a herd of Pikachu. But one of them is actually a Pokémon Trainer. It's impossible to pick him out by sight. Just talk to each and every Pikachu until you find the Trainer.

Bika bikabika!
Pigachu!

Step 4 Size Matters

In the house just to the right of the Pikachu Fan Club, you can take a Remoraid size-comparison challenge. If you've caught a Remoraid, add it to your party and talk to the boy in the house. If your Remoraid sets a new size record, you get a Net Ball.

25.2 inches...
This REMORAID is 25.2 inches...

Where to catch Remoraid

You can catch a Remoraid for the size contest right on Route 222. Leave some space in your party and catch a bunch of Remoraid, and then go straight to the boy in the house.

• Sunyshore City, a sun-drenched city

Sunyshore City

Story

Sunyshore City is an intricately designed port town. The walkways spanning the city also function as solar panels, supplying power to the city. You're here in order to get your eighth and final Gym Badge.

Moves needed for completion

Surf Rock Climb

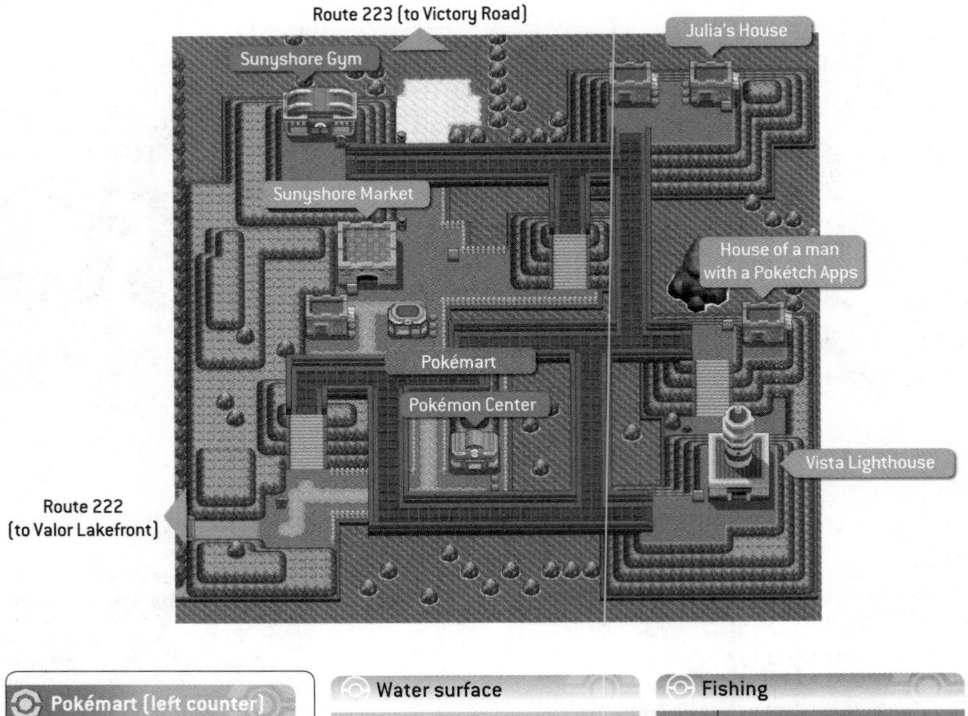

Route 223 (to Victory Road)

Julia's House

Sunyshore Gym

Sunyshore Market

House of a man with a Pokétch Apps

Pokémart

Pokémon Center

Vista Lighthouse

Route 222 (to Valor Lakefront)

Pokémart (left counter)	
Steel Mail	50P
Luxury Ball	1000P

Water surface

Pokémon	
Tentacool	◎
Wingull	◎
Tentacruel	△
Pelipper	▲

Fishing

Rod	Pokémon	
Old	Magikarp	◎
Good	Magikarp	◎
	Remoraid	◎
	Octillery	◎
Super	Gyarados	○
	Staryu	○

Items

- First Visit
- ☐ Thunderstone
- When your lead Pokémon is strong
- ☐ Effort Ribbon
- When you show the man a Serious Pokémon
- ☐ Pokétch App Calendar
- When you show the man a Naive Pokémon
- ☐ Pokétch App Dot Art
- When you show the man a Quirky Pokémon

- ☐ Pokétch App Roulette
- When you talk to Julia
- ☐ Alert Ribbon
- ☐ Shock Ribbon
- ☐ Downcast Ribbon
- ☐ Careless Ribbon
- ☐ Relax Ribbon
- ☐ Snooze Ribbon

- ☐ Smile Ribbon
- After winning at Sunyshore Gym
- ☐ Beacon Badge
- ☐ TM57 Charge Beam
- ☐ HM07 Waterfall

Step 1 In like Flint

As soon as you enter the town, you're approached by a young man with red hair. He introduces himself as Pokémon League Elite Four member Flint. He quickly tells you before taking off that he's here to restore some fighting spirit to the Sunyshore Gym Leader, who seems to have lost it.

The name's Flint! I'm one of the Pokémon League's Elite Four!

Volkner caused the blackout?

Remember that big power outage in Sunyshore City? Apparently it happened because Gym Leader Volkner used too much power when he was renovating the Gym. It seems all his passion for Pokémon battles was diverted into passion for his Gym renovations.

Step 2 Get the Effort Ribbon at Sunyshore Market

There's a girl at Sunyshore Market who gives you the Effort Ribbon when you talk to her with a strong Pokémon at the head of your party. Build your Pokémon in battle and get the Effort Ribbon from the girl.

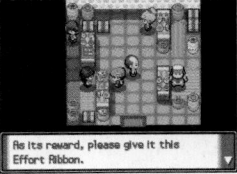

As its reward, please give it this Effort Ribbon.

A different Seal each day

The young man at the leftmost stall in Sunyshore Market sells Seals, which you can use on Ball Capsules. The selection changes according to the day of the week. Visit every day and collect all of the Seals (p. 566)!

Step 3 Get 7 different ribbons at Julia's house

Talk to Julia at her house and a little conversation will net you one ribbon every day. You'll get a different ribbon each day of the week, so come back every day to get all seven. Be sure to give each one to a Pokémon.

Lucas received the Smile Ribbon.

Underground authorities

You can get tips on how best to enjoy your time in the Sinnoh Underground at the house next to the Pokémart. Talk to everyone in the house and they'll tell you their tips.

Step 4 Add Some Apps

There's a house accessible only by using HM Rock Climb on the eastern side of town. There, you can get a total of three Pokétch Apps. Talk to the young man inside when you have a Pokémon with a Serious, Naive, or Quirky Nature, as he requests.

Yep! Your ELECTABUZZ has a Serious nature all right!

Step 5 Find the Gym Leader at Vista Lighthouse

You find Gym Leader Volkner inside Vista Lighthouse. Volkner senses your skill, and accepts your challenge. Follow him back to the Pokémon Gym and take him on.

...So, you're the latest challenger up against the Sunyshore Gym...

You can see for miles and miles

Looking through the binoculars at Vista Lighthouse, you can see some kind of castle-like building. It's actually the Pokémon League, out beyond Victory Road. It's your next stop after your Gym Battle here.

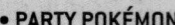

GYM BATTLE 8

Sunyshore Gym Leader
VOLKNER

- **Electric Pokémon User**

Ground-type moves will rock him!

Press a button inside the Gym to connect a route and try to find Volkner. There are eight other Trainers inside, too. Volkner's crew is made up entirely of Electric-type Pokémon. Use Ground-type moves and you'll ground Volkner out. Win and you get the Beacon Badge and TM57 Charge Beam.

BEACON BADGE
Lets you use Waterfall in the field. All Pokémon obey your commands.

• PARTY POKÉMON

⦿	Jolteon ♂ Lv46	ELECTRIC	
⦿	Raichu ♂ Lv46	ELECTRIC	
⦿	Electivire ♂ Lv50	ELECTRIC	
⦿	Luxray ♂ Lv48	ELECTRIC	

•1F 3

•1F 2

•1F 1

ENTER

Step 6 Get HM Waterfall

After you win your Gym Battle, go north of the city, to the beach. You'll exchange some words with your rival, then Johto region Gym Leader Jasmine gives you HM07 Waterfall. Teach it to a Pokémon right away.

...That Hidden Machine...
It contains Waterfall.

Mad props from your rival

With your Gym victory under your belt, head for the beach. Your rival calls out to you. This is the first time he gives you your due as a skilled Trainer. He seems pretty accomplished by this point as well.

148

People who give you items, Ribbons, and Accessories ②

There are people all throughout the Sinnoh region who give you items, ribbons, and Accessories. This page collects primarily those people who give you Accessories and ribbons. Use this page to find specific people if you're having trouble finding them.

Come by every day and fulfill the conditions to get items

Backdrops for Dress-Up

Person	Young woman at Global Terminal 1F

Talk to the young blonde woman on 1F of the Global Terminal in Jubilife City. She'll give you a new and different backdrop every day.

P.42

Whether you're an exhibitor or viewer, I have a Backdrop for you!

GBA cartridge Accessory

Person	Young woman at Pal Park 2F

Talk to the young woman with *Pokémon FireRed* in your GBA cart slot to receive the Crown. Have *Pokémon LeafGreen* in the GBA cart slot and you'll get the Tiara.

P.40

I feel compelled to give you this Tiara.

Seven Different Ribbons

Person	Julia of Sunyshore City

Julia is waiting for her sailor husband to come home. Answer her questions to get ribbons. She'll give up a different one depending on the day of the week.

P.146

I know! How about you visit me and tell me stories every so often?

The Effort Ribbon

Person	Girl at Sunyshore Market

If your lead Pokémon cannot raise its base points any higher, you get the Effort Ribbon.

P.146

As its reward, please give it this Effort Ribbon.

The Footprint Ribbon

Person	Route 213's Dr. Footstep

If your lead Pokémon and you share a good bond, and its Friendship rating is high enough, you'll get the Footprint Ribbon.

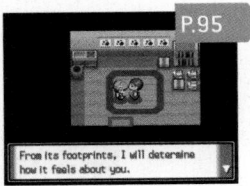
P.95

From its footprints, I will determine how it feels about you.

Heart Scale and Poké Balls

Person	Solaceon Town's Pokémon News Press

Bring the editor the Pokémon he requests within the day, and he'll give you a Heart Scale and three of one type of Poké Ball.

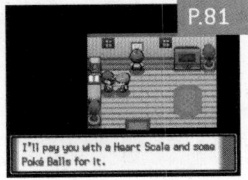
P.81

I'll pay you with a Heart Scale and some Poké Balls for it.

Route 223

Route 223 is filled with clear blue water, and plenty of rocks and shoals to navigate—along with tons of tough Trainers. But this will be nothing compared to the battle ahead.

Moves needed for completion

Surf   Waterfall

Victory Road

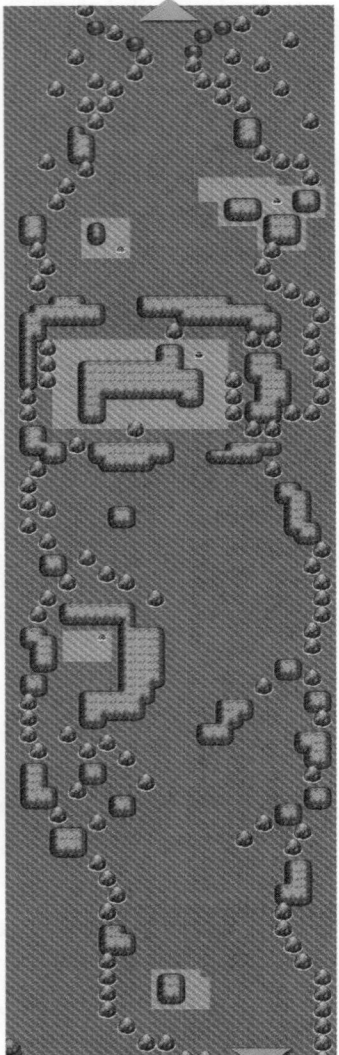

Sunyshore City

Items

☐ TM18 Rain Dance
☐ Ultra Ball
☐ Dive Ball
☐ Rare Candy

Water surface

Pokémon	
Tentacruel	◎
Pelipper	◎
Mantyke	○

Fishing

Rod	Pokémon	
Old	Magikarp	◎
Good	Magikarp	◎
	Remoraid	○
	Octillery	△
Super	Gyarados	○
	Wailmer	○
	Octillery	○
	Wailord	△

Mantyke
WATER FLYING
Abilities
•Water Absorb
•Swift Swim

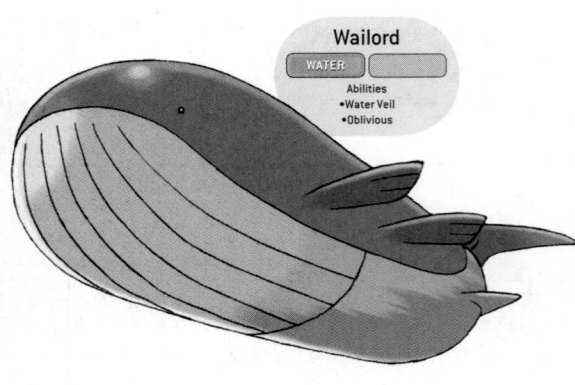

Wailord
WATER
Abilities
•Water Veil
•Oblivious

Step 1 Go north using HM Surf

Kick off from the beach at Sunyshore City and enter Route 223 using HM Surf. Keep going north across the water. Victory Road, your destination, lies ahead.

Step 2 Are you experienced?

Don't just Surf your way up to Victory Road—use the opportunity against the sea-hardened Trainers to battle some more and build up any weak Pokémon you need.

Don't think you're going to win easily!

Have a Pokémon hold Luck Incense

The Trainers you battle on the water aren't worth much by way of prize money. But have your lead Pokémon hold Luck Incense, and you'll double your winnings.

Step 3 No stone unturned

There are spots where you can squeeze between the rocks to find an item, and places where there are items sitting in the shallows. Search the route with a fine-toothed comb to find items like TM18 Sweet Scent and Rare Candy.

Lucas found
a TM18 Rain Dance!

Step 4 One waterfall to Go

As you reach the top of Route 223, you'll face a giant waterfall. Teach the HM Waterfall to a Pokémon and use it to climb up. Rest your Pokémon at the Pokémon Center just above. You'll need it before you hit Victory Road.

▶YES
　NO

It's a large waterfall.
Would you like to use Waterfall?

• A tunnel where Trainers who aspire to the Pokémon League gather

Victory Road

Story

Victory Road is where Pokémon Trainers make a pit stop and bulk up their Pokémon before taking on the League Champions. It's wise to take your time through here and really battle your heart out—because if you can make it through here, you definitely deserve to battle the Elite Four.

Moves needed for completion

Rock Smash | Surf | Strength
Rock Climb | Waterfall

•1F

Pokémon League

Pokémon League
(to Sunyshore City)

Items

- ☐ TM41 Torment
- ☐ Max Repel
- ☐ Max Elixir
- ☐ Full Restore
- ☐ TM71 Stone Edge
- ☐ Calcium
- ☐ Rare Candy
- ☐ Ultra Ball
- ☐ TM59 Dragon Pulse
- ☐ Razor Claw
- ☐ TM79 Dark Pulse
- ☐ Zinc

•1F

Cave

Pokémon	M	A	N
Graveler	◎	◎	○
Rhyhorn	○	○	○
Onix	○	○	○
Rhydon	○	○	○
Golbat	△	△	○
Steelix	△	△	△
Gabite	△	△	△

•2F

Cave

Pokémon	M	A	N
Magneton	◎	◎	◎
Steelix	◎	◎	◎
Graveler	○	○	△
Golbat	△	△	○
Onix	△	△	△
Gabite	△	△	△

•B1F

Cave

Pokémon	M	A	N
Floatzel	◎	◎	◎
Azumarill	◎	◎	◎
Graveler	○	○	△
Onix	○	○	○
Golbat	△	△	○
Steelix	△	△	△
Gabite	△	△	△

Water surface

Pokémon		
Floatzel		◎
Golbat		○

Fishing

Rod	Pokémon	
Old	Magikarp	◎
Good	Magikarp	◎
Super	Gyarados	◎

SINNOH WALKTHROUGH — VICTORY ROAD

•2F

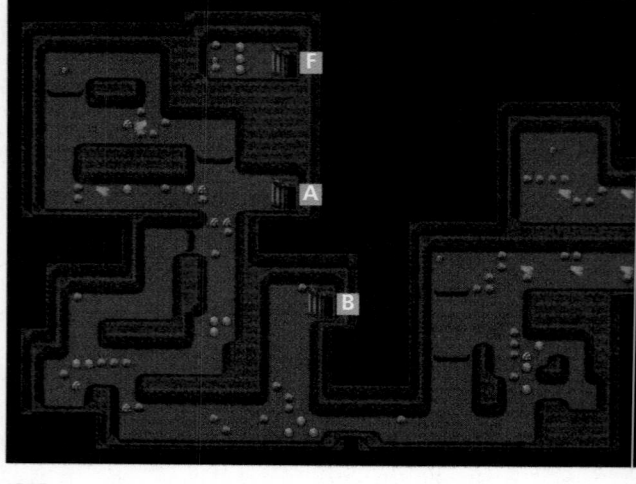

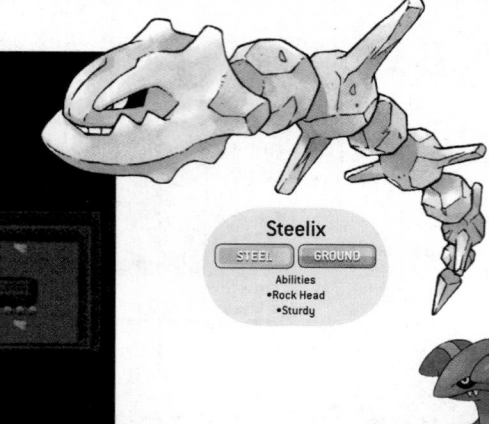

Steelix
STEEL GROUND
Abilities
•Rock Head
•Sturdy

•B1F

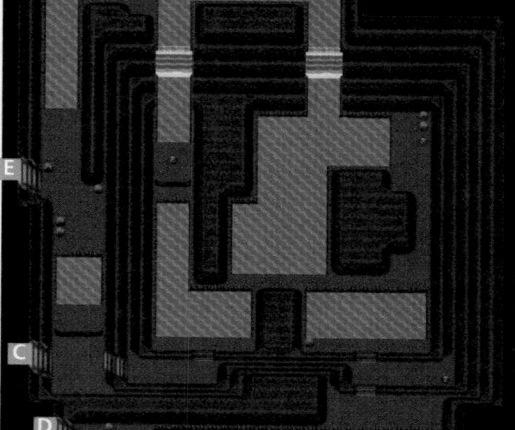

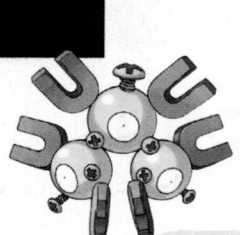

Gabite
DRAGON GROUND
Ability
•Sand Veil

Magneton
ELECTRIC STEEL
Abilities
•Magnet Pull
• Sturdy

Step 1 Round and round

Although the entrance and exit of Victory Road are on the same map, connecting the two is something of a challenge. You'll need to go down a few floors and up a few floors if you want to see daylight again.

I am a Psychic!
I can see your future!

Step 2 Item-palooza

Along with four TMs, you can also find valuable items like Max Elixir, Rare Candy, Razor Claw, Calcium, and Zinc on Victory Road. Explore the whole cave to make sure you don't miss any of these items.

Lucas found a Max Elixir!

Sniff out items using the Dowsing Machine

Lots of items are hidden out of sight on Victory Road. You can find them using the Pokétch App Dowsing Machine.

Step 3 Use HM Strength to clear the path

The path on 2F is blocked by scattered rocks. The rocks form a bit of a puzzle for you. Use HM Strength to move the rocks, solve the puzzle, and clear the path. If you mess up, go to another floor and come back, and you'll find the rocks reset.

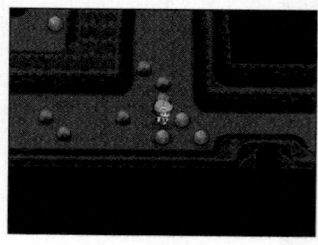

Step 4 You shall not pass!

Near the exit to the Pokémon League, there's another exit, but this one is blocked by a person standing in front of it. Unfortunately, you can't go through at this point. You have to come back once you have the National Pokédex. But make sure to come back—don't let anyone tell you you can't do something!

Aim for the Pokémon League!
That's all you should be thinking about.

Pokémon League

Story

After braving the trials of Victory Road, Trainers come at last to the end of their journey, the pinnacle of everything it means to be a Pokémon Trainer. One last trial awaits you—a string of grueling battles against the illustrious Elite Four and, finally, the Pokémon League Champion.

Moves needed for completion

Surf   Waterfall

• Entrance

Pokémon League

Victory Road

Pokémon Center

Victory Road

Route 223
(to Sunyshore City)

• Pokémon League

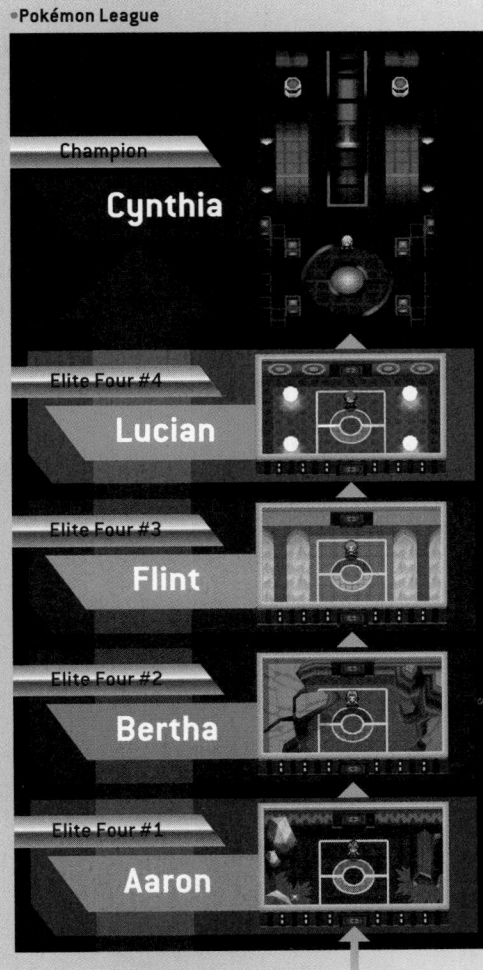

Champion
Cynthia

Elite Four #4
Lucian

Elite Four #3
Flint

Elite Four #2
Bertha

Elite Four #1
Aaron

• Pokémon League Lobby

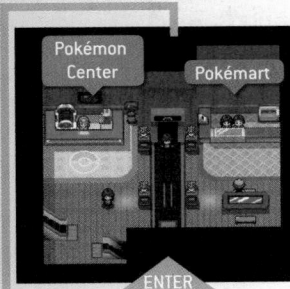

Pokémon Center   Pokémart

ENTER

🔘 Pokémart (right counter)	
Heal Ball	300P
Net Ball	1000P
Nest Ball	1000P
Dusk Ball	1000P
Quick Ball	1000P
Timer Ball	1000P
Repeat Ball	1000P
Luxury Ball	1000P

🔘 Water surface	
Pokémon	
Wingull	◎
Pelipper	◎
Tentacruel	△

🔘 Fishing		
Rod	Pokémon	
Old	Magikarp	◎
Good	Magikarp	◎
	Remoraid	◎
	Gyarados	○
Super	Octillery	◎
	Luvdisc	○

Step 1 — Take on your rival first

Just when you're ready to go through the door and face the Elite Four, your rival pops up behind you, looking for a battle. He wants to battle the Elite Four, but he doesn't mind taking you down first. Show him what you're made of.

Let's see who's more worthy of asking the challenge with a battle!

Battle with your rival! 6

Your rival now has six Pokémon since you last battled him in Canalave City, and his team has increased 12-13 levels.

• If you chose Turtwig

Staraptor ♂ Lv48	NORMAL	FLYING
Heracross ♂ Lv48	BUG	FIGHTING
Infernape ♂ Lv51	FIRE	FIGHTING
Roserade ♂ Lv47	GRASS	POISON
Floatzel ♂ Lv47	WATER	
Snorlax ♂ Lv49	NORMAL	

• If you chose Chimchar

Staraptor ♂ Lv48	NORMAL	FLYING
Heracross ♂ Lv48	BUG	FIGHTING
Empoleon ♂ Lv51	WATER	STEEL
Rapidash ♂ Lv47	FIRE	
Roserade ♂ Lv47	GRASS	POISON
Snorlax ♂ Lv49	NORMAL	

• If you chose Piplup

Staraptor ♂ Lv48	NORMAL	FLYING
Heracross ♂ Lv48	BUG	FIGHTING
Torterra ♂ Lv51	GRASS	GROUND
Rapidash ♂ Lv47	FIRE	
Floatzel ♂ Lv47	WATER	
Snorlax ♂ Lv49	NORMAL	

Step 2 — Prepare for victory

You've taken out your rival, but can you do the same for the Pokémon League? Go to the Pokémart and stock up items like Full Restore and Max Potion, as well as items that restore PP so your Pokémon don't get caught without their most powerful moves to use.

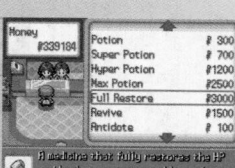

Money #339184	
Potion	₽ 300
Super Potion	₽ 700
Hyper Potion	₽1200
Max Potion	₽2500
Full Restore	₽3000
Revive	₽1500
Antidote	₽ 100

A medicine that fully restores the HP and heals any status problems of a single Pokémon.

The battle rages on

Your rival isn't the type to give up—losing to you only encourages him to do better, so you're sure to battle him again, especially once you enter the Hall of Fame and obtain the National Pokédex.

Step 3 — Step through the door

Once you're ready to go, approach the man guarding the inner entrance to the Pokémon League. He'll verify your badges and open the door for you—all you have to do now is step inside, and it's time for the toughest battles yet!

Demonstrate the power that brought you here and go for glory!

ELITE FOUR BATTLE ❶

AARON

• Bug Pokémon user

Seize victory with Fire- and Flying-type moves

Exploit the Bug-type weakness by using Fire-type moves against Yanmega, Heracross, Vespiquen, and Scizor. The odd one out is the Poison-and-Dark-type Drapion, which can be taken out with Ground-type moves. Focus on using powerful moves like Flamethrower, Drill Peck, and Earthquake.

• PARTY POKÉMON

Yanmega ♂ Lv49

BUG   FLYING

Effective move types: ROCK   FIRE   ELECTRIC   ICE   FLYING

Drapion ♂ Lv53

POISON   DARK

Effective move types: GROUND

Heracross ♂ Lv51

BUG   FIGHTING

Effective move types: FLYING   FIRE   PSYCHIC

Vespiquen ♀ Lv50

BUG   FLYING

Effective move types: ROCK   FIRE   ELECTRIC   ICE   FLYING

Scizor ♂ Lv49

BUG   STEEL

Effective move types: FIRE

ELITE FOUR BATTLE ❷

BERTHA

•Ground Pokémon user

Attack using Grass- and Ice-type moves

All of Bertha's Pokémon have pronounced weaknesses—use Grass-type moves against her Whiscash, Golem, and Rhyperior for 4x the damage; Ice-type moves will do the same against Gliscor. Hippowdon can be taken out by Grass-, Water-, or Ice-type moves. Use moves like Solar Beam, Ice Beam, and Surf for the upper hand in this battle.

• PARTY POKÉMON

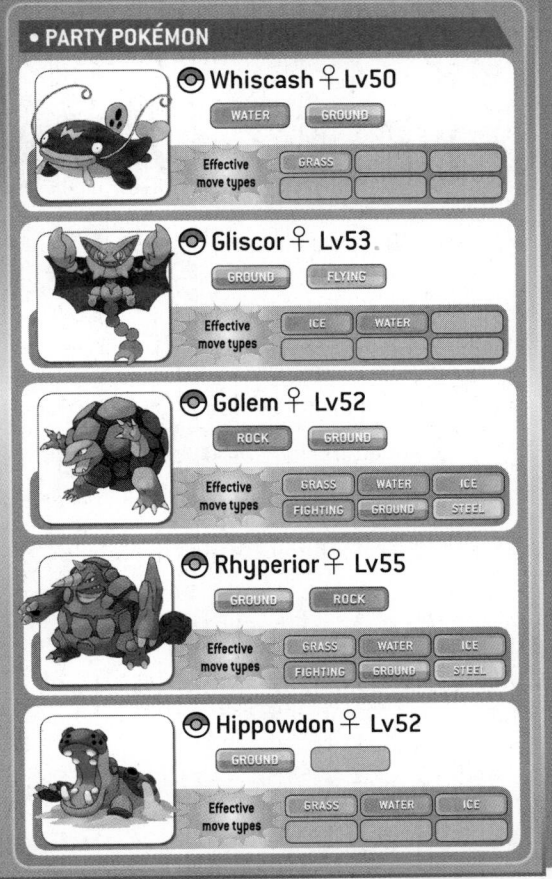

Whiscash ♀ Lv50

WATER   GROUND

Effective move types: GRASS

Gliscor ♀ Lv53

GROUND   FLYING

Effective move types: ICE   WATER

Golem ♀ Lv52

ROCK   GROUND

Effective move types: GRASS   WATER   ICE   FIGHTING   GROUND   STEEL

Rhyperior ♀ Lv55

GROUND   ROCK

Effective move types: GRASS   WATER   ICE   FIGHTING   GROUND   STEEL

Hippowdon ♀ Lv52

GROUND

Effective move types: GRASS   WATER   ICE

ELITE FOUR BATTLE ❸

FLINT

•Fire Pokémon user

Take him out with Water- and Ground-type moves

Flint has three pure Fire-type Pokémon and two dual types: one Dark-and-Fire and one Fire-and-Fighting. Lucky for you they're all weak to Water- and Ground-type moves, so use the powerful HM move Surf and/or Earthquake and victory will be yours.

• PARTY POKÉMON

⊚ Rapidash ♂ Lv53
FIRE

Effective move types: WATER | GROUND | ROCK

⊚ Houndoom ♂ Lv52
DARK | FIRE

Effective move types: WATER | FIGHTING | GROUND | ROCK

⊚ Flareon ♂ Lv55
FIRE

Effective move types: WATER | GROUND | ROCK

⊚ Magmortar ♂ Lv57
FIRE

Effective move types: WATER | GROUND | ROCK

⊚ Infernape ♂ Lv55
FIRE | FIGHTING

Effective move types: WATER | GROUND | FLYING | PSYCHIC

ELITE FOUR BATTLE ❹

LUCIAN

• Psychic Pokémon user

Come out swinging with Ghost- and Dark-type moves

Lucian's team might be loaded with Psychic-types, but they all have different weaknesses. Use Bug-, Ghost-, and Dark-type moves against Mr. Mime, Espeon, and Alakazam. Hit Gallade with Flying- and Ghost-type moves, while taking down Bronzong with Fire-type moves. For a sure victory, bring in Pokémon that know the moves Flamethrower and Shadow Ball.

• PARTY POKÉMON

⊚ Mr. Mime ♂ Lv53
PSYCHIC

Effective move types: BUG | GHOST | DARK

⊚ Espeon ♂ Lv55
PSYCHIC

Effective move types: BUG | GHOST | DARK

⊚ Bronzong Lv54
STEEL | PSYCHIC

Effective move types: FIRE

⊚ Alakazam ♂ Lv56
PSYCHIC

Effective move types: BUG | GHOST | DARK

⊚ Gallade ♂ Lv59
PSYCHIC | FIGHTING

Effective move types: FLYING | GHOST

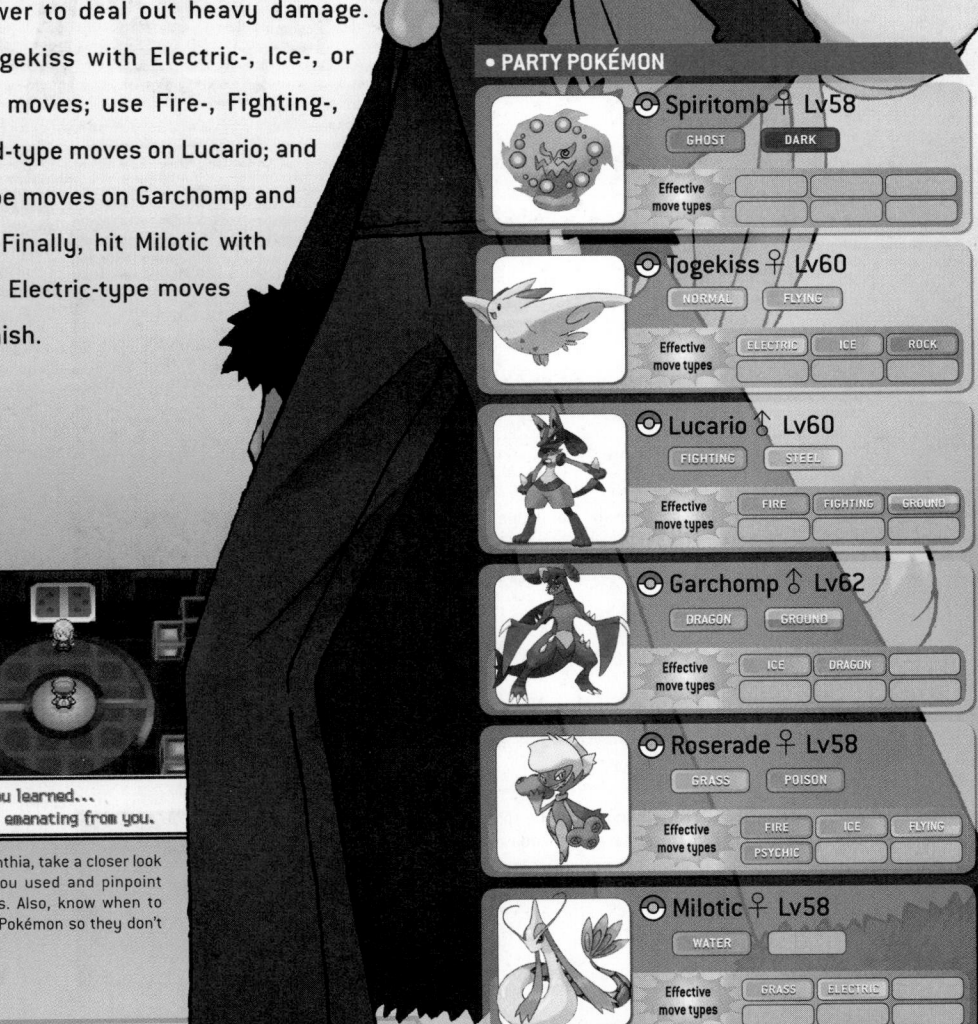

CHAMPION BATTLE

CYNTHIA

• *All-around Pokémon user*

Be flexible and come in with different move types

Cynthia's Spiritomb has no type weakness, so just hit it with moves that have high attack power to deal out heavy damage. Handle Togekiss with Electric-, Ice-, or Rock-type moves; use Fire-, Fighting-, and Ground-type moves on Lucario; and use Ice-type moves on Garchomp and Roserade. Finally, hit Milotic with Grass- and Electric-type moves for a big finish.

> The power you learned...
> I can feel it emanating from you.

If you lose to Cynthia, take a closer look at the moves you used and pinpoint your weak spots. Also, know when to switch out your Pokémon so they don't get knocked out.

• PARTY POKÉMON

Spiritomb ♀ Lv58
GHOST | DARK
Effective move types:

Togekiss ♀ Lv60
NORMAL | FLYING
Effective move types: ELECTRIC | ICE | ROCK

Lucario ♂ Lv60
FIGHTING | STEEL
Effective move types: FIRE | FIGHTING | GROUND

Garchomp ♂ Lv62
DRAGON | GROUND
Effective move types: ICE | DRAGON

Roserade ♀ Lv58
GRASS | POISON
Effective move types: FIRE | ICE | FLYING | PSYCHIC

Milotic ♀ Lv58
WATER
Effective move types: GRASS | ELECTRIC

Defeat the Champion and enter the Hall of Fame!

If you defeat Cynthia, you'll enter the Hall of Fame and all of your party Pokémon will receive Champion Ribbons. But that isn't the end of your adventure—there's so much more to see—just turn the page!

You are challenged by Champion Cynthia!

World Traveler

A bigger world waits for you

You may have become the new Pokémon League Champion, but your adventure is far from over! There are new places to explore, new Pokémon from other regions to meet, and lots of other cool new things to experience. So what are you waiting for? Your Pokémon journey continues!

Twinleaf Town — Record 210 Pokémon sightings

You'll wake up back in your room. First thing to do is check your Pokédex. If you've seen 210 Pokémon, that means your Pokédex is complete, so head over to Sandgem Town to show Professor Rowan.

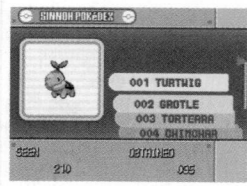

What if you haven't seen 210 Pokémon?

If the number of Pokémon seen isn't 210, you still have work to do. Check the Sinnoh Pokédex guide on page 259 to find out how to encounter the missing Pokémon.

Twinleaf Town — A message from your rival

Head downstairs, where your mother had a message for you from none other than your rival. He wants you to take the boat from Snowpoint City. This will take you to the Fight Area, where you can fight in as many Pokémon battles as you could ever crave.

he was shouting about you needing to get on a ship at Snowpoint City.

Get the National Pokédex first

Just beyond the Fight Area are the Survival Area and the Resort Area, but you aren't going anywhere until you have the National Pokédex. Take care of that, then board the boat from Snowpoint City.

Sandgem Town — Upgrade your Pokédex

When you go to talk to Professor Rowan about your Pokédex, you'll be approached by Professor Oak, the Kanto-region authority on Pokémon. Impressed by your hard work, he'll upgrade your Pokédex to the National version.

Lucas's Pokédex was upgraded with the National Mode!

Summons from the elder

Dawn/Lucas will meet you in front of the Pokémon lab with an important message from the elder of Celestic Town. You should go there to find out what's up.

Sandgem Town — Get the Poké Radar

For completing the Sinnoh Pokédex, Professor Rowan has something to give you too—the Poké Radar. This helps you find certain Pokémon in tall grass, a necessity if you want to complete the National Pokédex (p. 372).

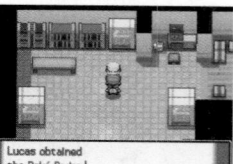

Lucas obtained the Poké Radar!

| Sandgem Town | Poké Radar lessons |

The Poké Radar is great, but how do you use it? Talk to Dawn/Lucas in front of the Pokémon lab and they'll show you how to use it to find Pokémon. For further tips, head out to Route 202.

Let me show you how the Poké Radar works.

Meet Pokémon from other regions

When you use the Poké Radar in tall grass, you might encounter Pokémon from other regions. The Pokémon vary from place to place, so make sure you use it in as many different locations as possible.

| Sandgem Town | Little sister has the scoop |

Once you have the National Pokédex, head over to Dawn's/Lucas's house. Her/his little sister has been hearing on the TV about mass outbreaks of Pokémon in locations throughout the region. Visit every day to find out where to go, and catch yourself a few (p. 373).

Route 228! They said there's a whole bunch of BELDUM there!

| Celestic Town | An old book |

When you visit Celestic Town, the elder will show you an old book. From there, head to the Spear Pillar at Mt. Coronet with the Adamant Orb and the Lustrous Orb. You'll encounter Dialga first, and once you defeat or capture it, Palkia will attack.

It seems the people of long ago met both DIALGA and PALKIA, the Pokémon

Be prepared

You'll need the Adamant Orb and the Lustrous Orb to see Dialga and Palkia, so pick them up on 4F(2) of Mt. Coronet (middle) (p. 133).

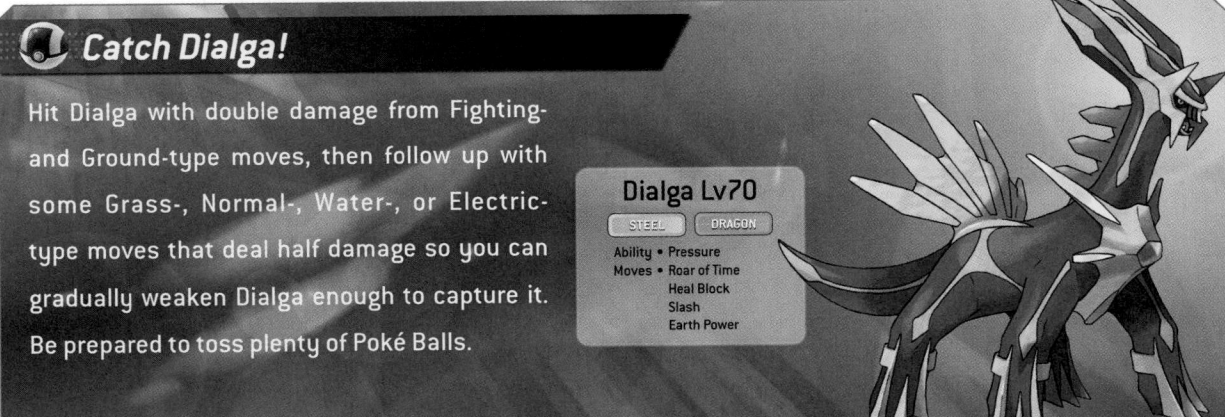

🔴 Catch Dialga!

Hit Dialga with double damage from Fighting- and Ground-type moves, then follow up with some Grass-, Normal-, Water-, or Electric-type moves that deal half damage so you can gradually weaken Dialga enough to capture it. Be prepared to toss plenty of Poké Balls.

Dialga Lv70

STEEL   DRAGON

Ability • Pressure
Moves • Roar of Time
        Heal Block
        Slash
        Earth Power

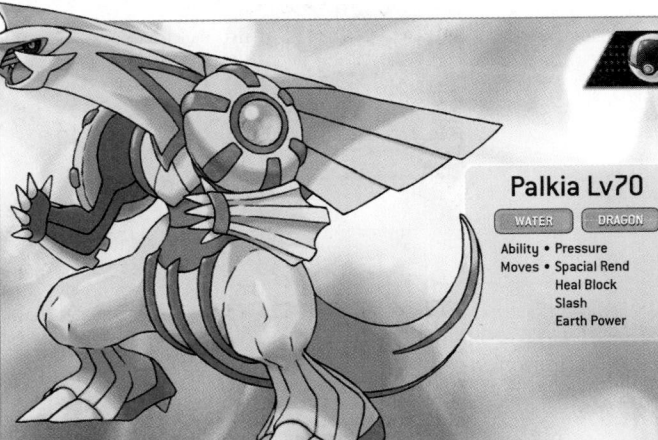

Palkia Lv70

WATER   DRAGON

Ability • Pressure
Moves • Spacial Rend
        Heal Block
        Slash
        Earth Power

🔴 Catch Palkia!

Start off with some strong Dragon-type moves, then whittle down Palkia's HP with Fire-, Water, or Steel-type moves. Then start tossing out the Poké Balls—Ultra Balls, Timer Balls, whatever—until one of them captures Palkia.

Pal Park — The Trainer Counter

Head to Pal Park along Route 221 and you'll run into Professor Oak. He'll give you the Trainer Counter for your Pokétch. This App records the number of times you meet the same Pokémon in a row, displaying the three Pokémon with the highest encounter rates.

Fly to Pal Park

On your first visit to Pal Park, you'll have to Surf on Routes 220 and 221 to get there, passing many Trainers and wild Pokémon on the way. But once you've been there, you can just use Fly to return.

Pal Park — Ported Pokémon at Pal Park

When you port Pokémon from a GBA game, you'll have to go to Pal Park to catch them. Many of these Pokémon cannot be found in *Pokémon Platinum*, so you'll definitely want to transfer them from your GBA games to complete your Pokédex (p. 389).

One way only

Once you transfer a Pokémon off a GBA cart into Pokémon Platinum, it cannot be sent back to the GBA game. Make sure you're absolutely sure before you bring Pokémon over.

Pal Park — Get the Kitchen Timer

There's a girl near the Pal Park entrance who would love nothing more than to see a Pokémon that just sleeps and eats all day. Why, she's talking about Snorlax! Put a Snorlax in your party and she'll happily give you the Kitchen Timer App for your Pokétch.

The Timer times

What else would the Kitchen Timer do but measure time—it can be set for up to 99:59, and when time is up, Snorlax will beat on its belly like a drum. Use the Kitchen Timer for cooking or anything else you can imagine.

Pal Park — Get the Color Changer

After you've gotten the Kitchen Timer, visit the girl again to find out that now, she wants to see a Pokémon that changes color. Put a Kecleon in your party and she'll give you the Color Changer App for your Pokétch.

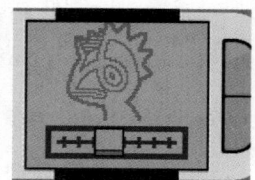

Shift the color of the screen using the Color Changer

The Color Changer is a Pokétch App that can shift the color of the Pokétch screen. If you don't like the standard green hue, you can choose from eight other colors. Set it to your favorite one.

Pal Park — The girl in the hat gives you headgear

Head upstairs to the back right corner and talk to the girl there. If you have *Pokémon FireRed* sitting in the GBA slot on your DS, she'll give you the Crown Accessory. If you have *Pokémon LeafGreen* in the slot, she'll give you the Tiara.

Byron on Iron Island

Drop by the empty house on Iron Island after getting the National Pokédex—it's not so empty now, because Byron's there. He'll give you the Metal Coat when you visit.

Eterna City — Professor Oak tells all

Once you've been to Pal Park, go visit Professor Oak in Eterna City. At that point, Zapdos, Moltres, and Articuno will start wandering throughout the Sinnoh region. Try to find them and catch them for your Pokédex (p. 393).

Get the Up-Grade

When you talk to Professor Oak in Eterna City, he'll give you the Up-Grade. Have Porygon hold the Up-Grade and then trade with a good friend (who will trade it back) to evolve Porygon into Porygon2.

Catch Zapdos!

Keep track of Zapdos' movements with the Marking Map Pokétch App. Use moves like Mean Look to keep it from running away and watch out for its Discharge—you'll need to keep healing your own Pokémon as you deal damage to Zapdos' HP.

Zapdos Lv60

ELECTRIC   FLYING

Ability • Pressure
Moves • Roost
         Discharge
         Agility
         Charge

Moltres Lv60

FIRE   FLYING

Ability • Pressure
Moves • Roost
         Flamethrower
         Safeguard
         Air Slash

Catch Moltres!

Find Moltres using the Marking Map and then use Mean Look to keep it from fleeing. Status conditions won't be much help against Moltres, which can be protected with its Safeguard move. Just lower its HP and be ready to throw a lot of Poké Balls.

Catch Articuno!

Use the Marking Map to track Articuno and then pin it down with Mean Look. Your biggest worry after that will be Articuno's Ice Beam, so watch the health of your own Pokémon carefully even as you chip away at Articuno's HP.

Articuno Lv60

ICE   FLYING

Ability • Pressure
Moves • Roost
         Ice Beam
         Agility
         Reflect

Once you've entered the Hall of Fame and traveled to Stark Mountain, you can revisit the Pokémon League for a rematch with a stronger Elite Four and Champion, all of whose Pokémon are the same but with a 15–16 level increase.

Lucian at Canalave City

Lucian of the Elite Four likes to hang out on 1F of the Canalave Library. Talk to him about all kinds of stuff—he even has different things to say before and after you enter the Hall of Fame.

I am Lucian.
I am a user of the Psychic type.

ELITE FOUR BATTLE 1
vs. AARON
• PARTY POKÉMON

Pokémon	Type 1	Type 2
Yanmega ♂ Lv65	BUG	FLYING
Drapion ♂ Lv69	POISON	DARK
Heracross ♂ Lv67	BUG	FIGHTING
Vespiquen ♀ Lv66	BUG	FLYING
Scizor ♂ Lv65	BUG	STEEL

ELITE FOUR BATTLE 2
vs. BERTHA
• PARTY POKÉMON

Pokémon	Type 1	Type 2
Whiscash ♀ Lv66	WATER	GROUND
Gliscor ♀ Lv69	GROUND	FLYING
Golem ♀ Lv68	ROCK	GROUND
Rhyperior ♀ Lv71	GROUND	ROCK
Hippowdon ♀ Lv68	GROUND	

ELITE FOUR BATTLE 3
vs. FLINT
• PARTY POKÉMON

Pokémon	Type 1	Type 2
Rapidash ♂ Lv69	FIRE	
Houndoom ♂ Lv68	DARK	FIRE
Flareon ♂ Lv71	FIRE	
Magmortar ♂ Lv73	FIRE	
Infernape ♂ Lv71	FIRE	FIGHTING

ELITE FOUR BATTLE 4
vs. LUCIAN
• PARTY POKÉMON

Pokémon	Type 1	Type 2
Mr. Mime ♂ Lv69	PSYCHIC	
Espeon ♂ Lv71	PSYCHIC	
Bronzong ♂ Lv70	STEEL	PSYCHIC
Alakazam ♂ Lv72	PSYCHIC	
Gallade ♂ Lv75	PSYCHIC	FIGHTING

CHAMPION
vs. CYNTHIA
• PARTY POKÉMON

Pokémon	Type 1	Type 2
Spiritomb ♀ Lv74	GHOST	DARK
Togekiss ♂ Lv76	NORMAL	FLYING
Lucario ♂ Lv76	FIGHTING	STEEL
Garchomp ♀ Lv78	DRAGON	GROUND
Roserade ♀ Lv74	GRASS	POISON
Milotic ♀ Lv74	WATER	

Fullmoon Island

In the center of the dense forest of Fullmoon Island is a single clearing with a crescent-shaped lake. You will see this lake and more when you visit to save a boy trapped within nightmares.

●Exterior

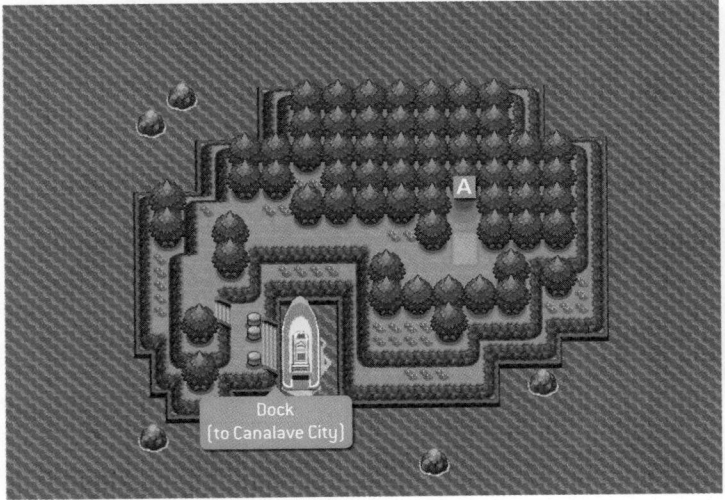

Dock
(to Canalave City)

●Interior

⊙ Items

☐ Lunar Wing

 **Trouble in Canalave City**

Eldritch's house isn't a happy place to be right now—his son is unable to wake up because he's trapped in a nightmare. Talk to Eldritch at the dock, and travel to Fullmoon Island to retrieve the Lunar Wing and save the boy.

I never thought our boy would fall into this endless nightmare...

No trips to Iron Island

Eldritch is too concerned about his son to take you anywhere but Fullmoon Island. Once the boy is saved, Eldritch will be only happy to take you to both Fullmoon and Iron Island.

 **Discover Cresselia**

Get off the boat and head into the forest to discover Cresselia near the lake. It flees when you approach it, but it leaves behind exactly what you need—the Lunar Wing. Pick it up and head back to Canalave City.

Save the boy!

Bring the Lunar Wing to Eldritch's house and approach the boy. The wing will dispel his nightmare and wake him up, setting things right in the Eldritch household.

 **Chasing Cresselia**

After it flees from Fullmoon Island, Cresselia will start to wander the Sinnoh region. Track it using the Marking Map, and approach on foot or by Bicycle to keep it from moving before you get to it (p. 393).

CRESSELIA Lv.50

A wild CRESSELIA appeared!

Catch Cresselia!

Cresselia always flees at the start of battle, so use Mean Look first to pin it down, then whittle down Cresselia's HP with Fighting- or Psychic-type moves.

Cresselia Lv50

PSYCHIC

Ability • Levitate
Moves • Mist
　　　　Aurora Beam
　　　　Future Sight
　　　　Slash

• A mysterious cave tucked behind Sendoff Spring

Turnback Cave • Distortion World

Story

Just behind Sendoff Spring is a large cave that twists and turns. At the end is the entrance to the Distortion World, where time and space themselves twist and turn.

Moves needed for completion

Rock Smash　　Defog

Items

• First Visit
☐ Griseous Orb
• When you arrive at Giratina's room on the 3rd room
☐ Reaper Cloth
• When you arrive at Giratina's room on the 4th-15th room
☐ Rare Bone
• When you arrive at Giratina's room on the 16th-30th room
☐ Stardust

• Entrance

to Sendoff Spring (p.140)

• Pillar room 1

• Pillar room 2

• Pillar room 3

• Giratina's room

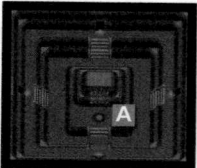

• Labyrinth 1

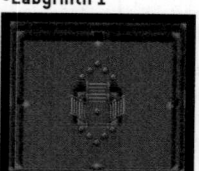

• Labyrinth 2

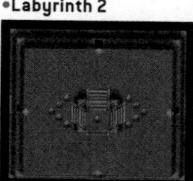

• Labyrinth 3

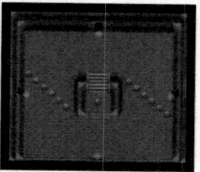

• Labyrinth 4

• Labyrinth 5

• Labyrinth 6

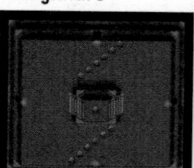

• Labyrinth 7

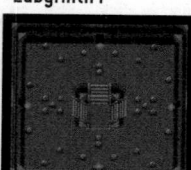

• Labyrinth 8

• Labyrinth 9

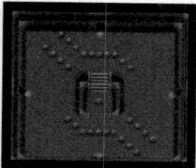

• Labyrinth 10

• Labyrinth 11

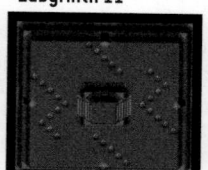

• Labyrinth 12

• Labyrinth 13

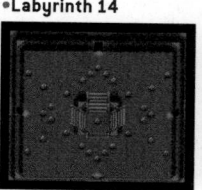

• Labyrinth 14

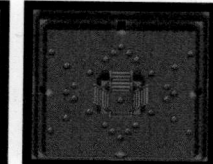

• Labyrinth 15

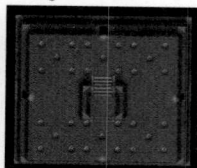

●Labyrinth 16

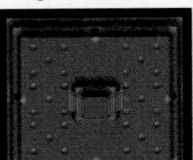

●Labyrinth 17

●Labyrinth 18

●Distortion World

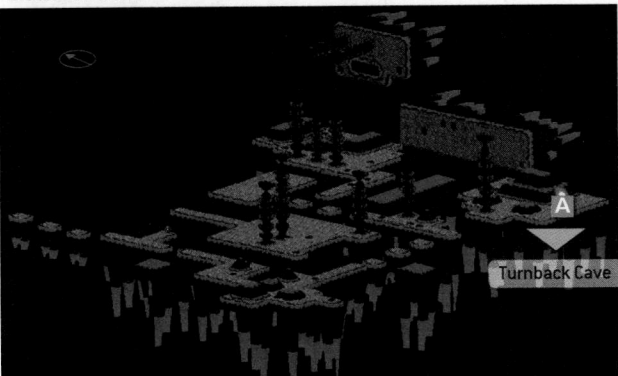

●Labyrinth up to pillar room 1

Cave			
Pokémon	M	A	N
Gastly	◎	◎	◎
Bronzor	○	○	○
Golbat	○	○	○
Chingling	○	○	○
Duskull	△	△	△
Dusclops	X	X	○

●Labyrinth up to pillar room 2

Cave			
Pokémon	M	A	N
Haunter	◎	◎	◎
Bronzor	○	○	○
Golbat	○	○	○
Chingling	△	△	△
Duskull	△	△	△
Dusclops	▲	▲	○
Chimecho	▲	▲	▲

●Labyrinth up to pillar room 3

Cave			
Pokémon	M	A	N
Haunter	◎	◎	◎
Bronzong	○	○	○
Golbat	○	○	○
Chimecho	○	○	○
Dusclops	△	△	

Step 1 Find the pillars

Inside Turnback Cave are three rooms with pillars, which you reach randomly through the four exits located in the other rooms. Once you've reached the third pillar, any of the exits in that room will take you to Giratina's room.

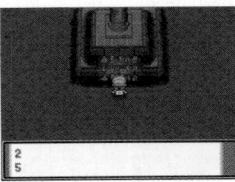

Right on Route 214

Head down the path to the right of Route 214 to reach Sendoff Spring, then use Rock Climb to reach the entrance of Turnback Cave (p. 140).

Step 2 In Giratina's room

If you caught Giratina on your first trip to the Distortion World, then all you'll find in the final room is a portal that leads to the Distortion World. However, if you knocked out Giratina or escaped from battle, then it will be waiting here for you to challenge it again.

Start over at 30

When you examine a pillar, two numbers will appear—the upper number indicates which pillar room you're in, while the lower number indicates how many rooms you've visited. If the lower number reaches 30, then the next door you enter will take you back to the entrance.

Step 3 Get the Griseous Orb

Examine the portal and select "yes" to travel to the Distortion World. Unlike your first trip there, the path is now pretty straightforward. At the very end you'll find the Griseous Orb.

Change forms with the Griseous Orb

The Griseous Orb is an item that allows Giratina to change Forme. If it holds the orb while in its Altered Forme, it will change to its Origin Forme.

Step 4 Find one of three items

Return to Giratina's room after you've caught it to find one of three items waiting for you. The exact item depends on how many rooms you've passed through—3 rooms is the Reaper Cloth, 4–15 rooms is the Rare Bone, and 16–30 leaves you Stardust.

SINNOH WALKTHROUGH (POST-HALL OF FAME)

TURNBACK CAVE • DISTORTION WORLD —

Days of the Week

Time passes in Sinnoh just like it does in your own life, and there are different things to do every day. Some events occur daily, while others are keyed to certain days of the week. Drop by every day to collect berries, purchase seals and more.

Daily events

Win items at the Pokémon lotto

Location	Jubilife TV 1F, Jubilife City

Check the reception desk at Jubilife TV for the Pokémon Lotto, where a new number is drawn every day. If the number matches the ID of one of your party Pokémon, you win a prize.

P.42

This is the Pokémon Lottery Corner. I'a Felicity, your attendant today.

Buy different seals at the market

Location	Sunyshore Market, Sunyshore City

The selection of seals available at the Sunyshore Market varies according to the day of the week.

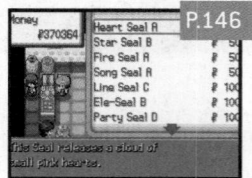
P.146

This Seal releases a cloud of small pink hearts.

Learn new trendy words

Location	Old man in house, Snowpoint City

Head to the house in the northeast corner and talk to the old man to learn trendy words like "cross-stitch" and "flambe."

P.126

Hello, hello. Would you like to hear a trendy saying?

Get one of 5 kinds of berry

Location	Flower Shop, Floaroma Town

Talk to the girl at the Pick a Peck of Colors Flower Shop to receive one of five kinds of berry.

P.54

I hope you will help us spread more Berries everywhere!

Get one of 17 kinds of berry

Location	Girl in house, Pastoria City

Talk to a girl in a home at the southwest of town to receive one of 17 kinds of rare berry.

P.100

I'll give you a Berry, too. Please plant it somewhere.

Get one of 26 kinds of berry

Location	Berry Master, Route 208

Talk to the Berry Master in his house and he'll give you one berry from a total selection of 26 kinds of berry.

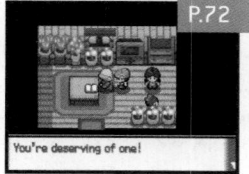
P.72

You're deserving of one!

Snowpoint Temple

Story

Snowpoint Temple is a protected shrine that only the chosen can enter. You're not allowed in at first, but after you win the Hall of Fame, Candice grants you permission to go inside.

Moves needed for completion

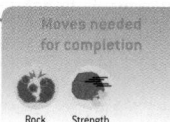

Rock Smash · Strength

•1F

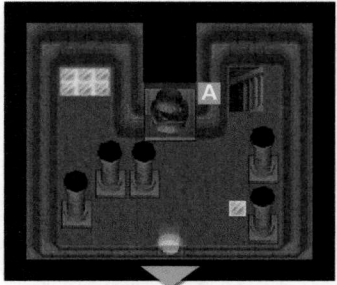

Snowpoint City

•B1F

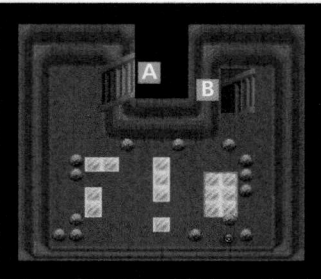

•B2F

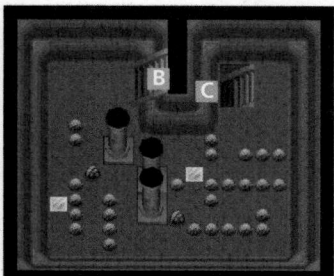

•B3F

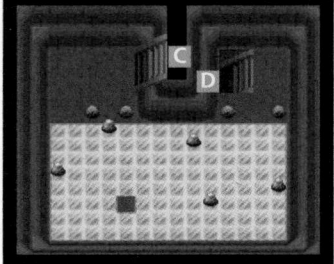

•B4F

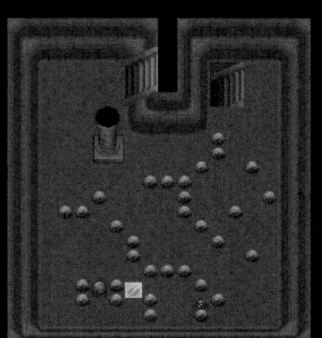

•B5F

Items

☐ Calcium
☐ Full Heal

•1F

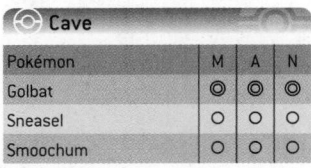

Cave

Pokémon	M	A	N
Golbat	◎	◎	◎
Sneasel	○	○	○
Smoochum	○	○	○

•B1F - B5F

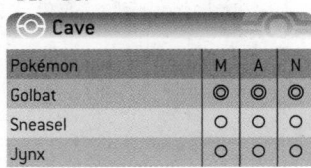

Cave

Pokémon	M	A	N
Golbat	◎	◎	◎
Sneasel	○	○	○
Jynx	○	○	○

Smoochum
ICE · PSYCHIC
Abilities
•Oblivious
•Forewarn

Jynx
ICE · PSYCHIC
Abilities
•Oblivious
•Forewarn

SINNOH WALKTHROUGH (POST-HALL OF FAME)

SNOWPOINT TEMPLE

Step 1 Bring Regirock, Regice, and Registeel

To catch Regigigas, you'll need to bring Regirock, Regice, and Registeel with you to the temple. These Pokémon are not available to catch in *Pokémon Platinum*—you must catch them in your GBA games instead and port them over to Pal Park.

Pokémon Ruby, Sapphire, or Emerald

The Regis appear in *Pokémon Ruby, Sapphire*, and *Emerald*. Go to Pal Park in *Pokémon Platinum* and transfer the Regis over from one of these GBA games.

Regirock

ROCK

Ability
•Clear Body

Regice

ICE

Ability
•Clear Body

Registeel

STEEL

Ability
•Clear Body

Step 2 Permission to enter

A young woman will stop you from entering Snowpoint Temple on your first visit to Snowpoint City. Come back once you've obtained the National Pokédex, and then Candice will run up and grant you access—you're one of the chosen now!

Candice: It's OK!
You can let that person in.

Step 3 The Regigigas statue

Slip and slide your way across the icy floors down to B5F, and examine the statue of Regigigas in the middle. If you have the other three Regis in your party, the statue will come to life and draw you into a battle!

...Zut zutt!

Catch Regigigas!

Despite its enormous size, this Regigigas is a very weak Lv1. Attack it only with Pokémon at Lv3–4, and inflict Confuse on Regigigas so it damages itself instead.

Regigigas Lv1

NORMAL

Ability • Slow Start
Moves • Dizzy Punch
        Knock Off
        Confuse Ray
        Foresight

Cover your Pokémon in Ribbons

Over the course of your adventure your Pokémon can earn up to 30 different kinds of Ribbons, by winning Super Contests, winning battles at the Battle Tower in the Battle Frontier, or just talking to the right people—see how many different ones you can collect!

Accomplished Pokémon are rewarded with Ribbons

Cool Ribbon

•How to get

Win the Cool Pokémon Super Contest at Normal Rank

Cool Ribbon Great

•How to get

Win the Cool Pokémon Super Contest at Great Rank

Cool Ribbon Ultra

•How to get

Win the Cool Pokémon Super Contest at Ultra Rank

Cool Ribbon Master

•How to get

Win the Cool Pokémon Super Contest at Master Rank

Beauty Ribbon

•How to get

Win the Beauty Pokémon Super Contest at Normal Rank

Beauty Ribbon Great

•How to get

Win the Beauty Pokémon Super Contest at Great Rank

Beauty Ribbon Ultra

•How to get

Win the Beauty Pokémon Super Contest at Ultra Rank

Beauty Ribbon Master

•How to get

Win the Beauty Pokémon Super Contest at Master Rank

Cute Ribbon

•How to get

Win the Cute Pokémon Super Contest at Normal Rank

Cute Ribbon Great

•How to get

Win the Cute Pokémon Super Contest at Great Rank

Cute Ribbon Ultra

•How to get

Win the Cute Pokémon Super Contest at Ultra Rank

Cute Ribbon Master

•How to get

Win the Cute Pokémon Super Contest at Master Rank

Smart Ribbon

•How to get

Win the Smart Pokémon Super Contest at Normal Rank

Smart Ribbon Great

•How to get

Win the Smart Pokémon Super Contest at Great Rank

Smart Ribbon Ultra

•How to get

Win the Smart Pokémon Super Contest at Ultra Rank

Smart Ribbon Master

•How to get

Win the Smart Pokémon Super Contest at Master Rank

Tough Ribbon

•How to get

Win the Tough Pokémon Super Contest at Normal Rank

Tough Ribbon Great

•How to get

Win the Tough Pokémon Super Contest at Great Rank

Tough Ribbon Ultra

•How to get

Win the Tough Pokémon Super Contest at Ultra Rank

Tough Ribbon Master

•How to get

Win the Tough Pokémon Super Contest at Master Rank

Footprint Ribbon

•How to get

Talk to Dr. Footstep on Route 213 when you have a good Friendship with your lead Pokémon

Effort Ribbon

•How to get

Talk to a girl at Sunyshore Market in Sunyshore City when your lead Pokémon is strong

Alert Ribbon

•How to get

Visit Julia in Sunyshore City on Monday and listen to her

Shock Ribbon

•How to get

Visit Julia in Sunyshore City on Tuesday and listen to her

Downcast Ribbon

•How to get

Visit Julia in Sunyshore City on Wednesday and listen to her

Careless Ribbon

•How to get

Visit Julia in Sunyshore City on Thursday and listen to her

Relax Ribbon

•How to get

Visit Julia in Sunyshore City on Friday and listen to her

Snooze Ribbon

•How to get

Visit Julia in Sunyshore City on Saturday and listen to her

Smile Ribbon

•How to get

Visit Julia in Sunyshore City on Sunday and listen to her

Sinnoh Champ Ribbon

•How to get

Defeat the Elite Four and the Pokémon League Champion, and get entered into the Hall of Fame

Ability Ribbon

•How to get

Defeat the Tower Tycoon who appears in single battle at the Battle Tower in the Battle Frontier (first battle)

Great Ability Ribbon

•How to get

Defeat the Tower Tycoon who appears in single battle at the Battle Tower in the Battle Frontier (second battle)

Double Ability Ribbon

•How to get

Win 50 Double Battles in a row at the Battle Tower in the Battle Frontier

Multi Ability Ribbon

•How to get

Win 50 Multi Battles in a row at the Battle Tower in the Battle Frontier

Pair Ability Ribbon

•How to get

Win 50 link Multi Battles in a row at the Battle Tower in the Battle Frontier

World Ability Ribbon

•How to get

Achieve Rank 5 in Wi-Fi Battles at the Battle Tower in the Battle Frontier

Luxury Ribbon

•How to get

Buy at the Ribbon Syndicate in the Resort Area (10,000P)

Royal Ribbon

•How to get

Buy at the Ribbon Syndicate in the Resort Area (100,000P)

Luxury Royal Ribbon

•How to get

Buy at the Ribbon Syndicate in the Resort Area (999,999P)

Victory Road • Route 224

As far as you venture into Victory Road, there are still parts you can't reach until you've gotten the National Pokédex. Beyond these you'll find Route 224, with its diverse landscape of tall grass, rocks, and ocean.

Moves needed for completion

Rock Smash · Defog · Surf · Strength · Rock Climb · Waterfall

• 1F

Pokémon League

Pokémon League (to Sunyshore City)

• 1F Back 1

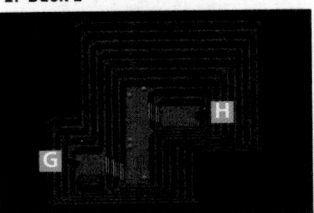

• 1F Back 2

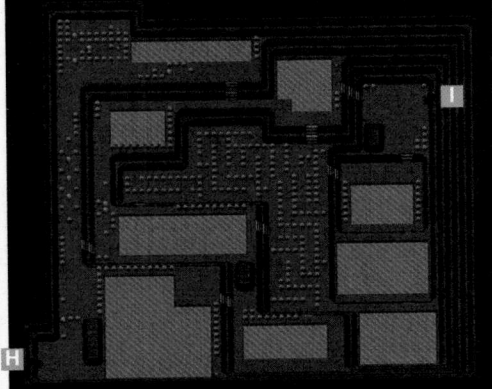

• 1F Back 3

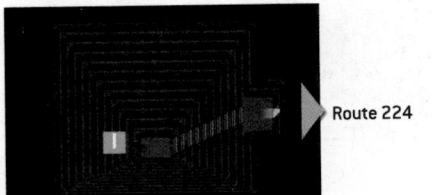

Route 224

• 2F

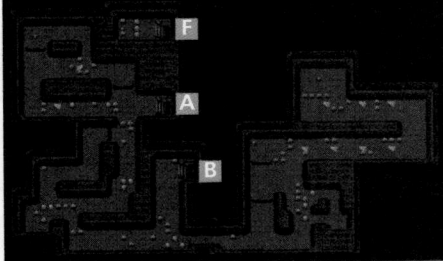

• B1F

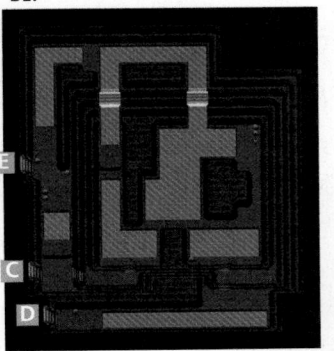

Marley

• Route 224

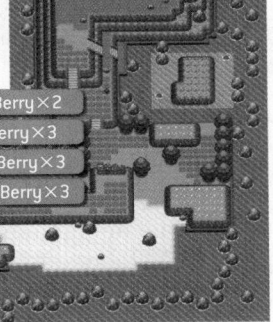

Sitrus Berry×2
Bluk Berry×3
Nanab Berry×3
Wepear Berry×3

Victory Road

• 1F

Cave

Pokémon	M	A	N
Graveler	◎	◎	○
Rhyhorn	○	○	○
Onix	○	○	○
Rhydon	○	○	○
Golbat	△	△	○
Steelix	△	△	△
Gabite	△	△	△

Items

- ☐ Dusk Stone
- ☐ Full Restore
- ☐ Nugget
- ☐ Leftovers
- ☐ Up-Grade
- ☐ Sitrus Berry x2
- ☐ Bluk Berry x3
- ☐ Nanab Berry x3
- ☐ Wepear Berry x3
- ☐ PP Max
- ☐ Razor Claw
- ☐ Repeat Ball
- ☐ Ultra Ball
- ☐ Destiny Knot

•1F Back 2

Cave

Pokémon	M	A	N
Floatzel	◎	◎	◎
Azumarill	◎	◎	◎
Graveler	○	○	△
Dewgong	○	○	○
Golbat	△	△	○
Gabite	△	△	△

Water surface

Pokémon	
Floatzel	◎
Dewgong	◎
Lapras	○

Fishing

Rod	Pokémon	
Old	Magikarp	◎
Good	Magikarp	◎
Super	Gyarados	◎

•Route 224

Tall Grass

Pokémon	M	A	N
Floatzel	○	○	○
Roselia	○	○	○
Bellsprout	○	○	X
Pelipper	○	○	○
Gastrodon	○	○	○
Gloom	△	△	△
Weepinbell	△	△	△
Beautifly	△	△	△
Dustox	△	△	△
Oddish	X	X	○

•1F Back 1 and 3

Cave

Pokémon	M	A	N
Graveler	◎	◎	○
Floatzel	◎	◎	◎
Onix	○	○	○
Golbat	△	△	○
Steelix	△	△	△
Gabite	△	△	△

•2F

Cave

Pokémon	M	A	N
Magneton	◎	◎	◎
Steelix	◎	◎	◎
Graveler	○	○	△
Golbat	△	△	○
Onix	△	△	△
Gabite	△	△	△

Water surface

Pokémon	
Pelipper	◎
Tentacruel	◎
Gastrodon	○

Fishing

Rod	Pokémon	
Old	Magikarp	◎
Good	Magikarp	◎
Good	Remoraid	◎
Good	Gyarados	○
Super	Octillery	◎
Super	Luvdisc	○

•B1F

Cave

Pokémon	M	A	N
Floatzel	◎	◎	◎
Azumarill	◎	◎	◎
Graveler	○	○	△
Onix	○	○	○
Golbat	△	△	○
Steelix	△	△	△
Gabite	△	△	△

Water surface

Pokémon	
Floatzel	◎
Golbat	○

Fishing

Rod	Pokémon	
Old	Magikarp	◎
Good	Magikarp	◎
Super	Gyarados	◎

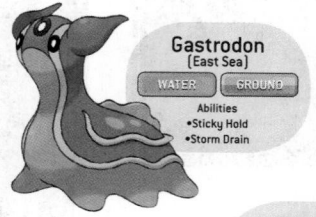

Gastrodon
(East Sea)
WATER GROUND
Abilities
•Sticky Hold
•Storm Drain

Bellsprout
GRASS POISON
Abilities
•Chlorophyll

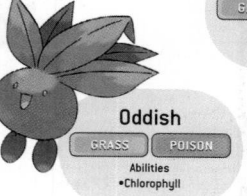

Oddish
GRASS POISON
Abilities
•Chlorophyll

Step 1 — The unblocked exit

When you first visited Victory Road, there was a door on the right blocked by a man. Now that you have the National Pokédex, the entrance is open, so enter Victory Road from the Pokémon League side and go through the door to explore further.

Step 2 — Meet Marley

You reach a dead end only to encounter a girl named Marley. She would appreciate your company—at least as far as the exit. While she's with you, your Pokémon will be healed after every battle.

I want to get through this tunnel. Will you let me go with you?

Double up with Marley

As long as you're with Marley, wild Pokémon will attack you in pairs, launching you into Double Battles. Marley will chip in with her Arcanine and the move Helping Hand.

Step 3 — Explore Route 224

Victory Road exits onto Route 224, a diverse route filled with Trainers to battle, items to collect, and Pokémon to catch. It's been a long trip, so take it all in.

For some reason I was drawn here, and it is here that I met you...

The mysterious white stone

To the upper right of Route 224 is a big white stone that shines like a mirror and has no writing on it. The only thing you know is that Marley said something about Pokémon appearing near the stone. Maybe there's something you should try?

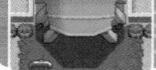

Fight Area

The Fight Area is a little port town that serves as a gathering place for battle-loving Pokémon Trainers. You're here at the request of your rival, who left a message at your house.

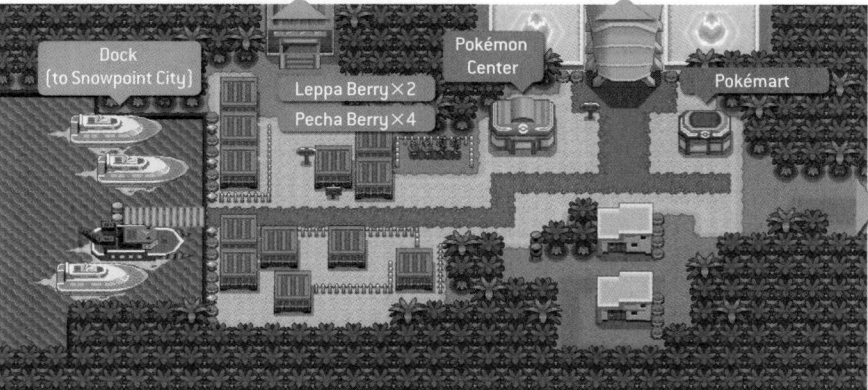

Route 225 (to Survival Area)

Battle Frontier

Dock (to Snowpoint City)

Pokémon Center

Leppa Berry×2
Pecha Berry×4

Pokémart

Route 230 (to Resort Area)

Items
- [ ] Super Rod
- [ ] Pomeg Berry x2
- [ ] Hondew Berry x4
- [ ] Scope Lens

 **Step 1** Your rival, your partner

Fresh off the boat and you're dragged by your rival into a battle! He takes you to the Battle Frontier, where Flint and Volkner happen to be standing in front. If you consent, you and your rival will face off against them in a Double Battle.

Like we did at the Spear Pillar. Let's show those guys how good we are!

Talk with Palmer and Buck

After you defeat Flint and Volkner, Palmer and Buck will come and talk to you. Buck will mention Stark Mountain—this is important, as you'll be visiting there later.

Tag Battle with Elite Four Flint and Gym Leader Volkner

All of Flint and Volkner's Pokémon are weak to Ground-type moves, so hit them hard with moves like Earthquake, which will damage both of their Pokémon at once. Be careful—it'll hit your Pokémon too. Water- and Rock-type moves are also greatly effective against Flint's Pokémon.

• FLINT'S PARTY POKÉMON
- Houndoom ♂ Lv56 — DARK FIRE
- Magmortar ♂ Lv58 — FIRE
- Flareon ♂ Lv56 — FIRE

• VOLKNER'S PARTY POKÉMON
- Luxray ♂ Lv56 — ELECTRIC
- Jolteon ♂ Lv56 — ELECTRIC
- Electivire ♂ Lv58 — ELECTRIC

 **Step 2** Receive the Super Rod

There's a fisherman standing near the gate to Route 225. When you talk to him, he'll give you the Super Rod. Better than the other rods, the Super Rod can hook Pokémon you had no chance of catching before.

Lucas obtained the Super Rod!

Get the Scope Lens

Talk to a young woman at the Pokémart to receive the Scope Lens, which grants any Pokémon holding this item in battle a higher rate of critical hits.

 **Step 3** Off to the Battle Frontier

You've defeated Flint and Volkner, so now it's off to the Battle Frontier, a theme park for Pokémon battles. There are five different battle facilities, each with its own unique features and challenges. Upgrade your Vs. Recorder as you enter.

Welcome to the Battle Frontier!

Step 4 Take Route 225

Route 225 is north of the Fight Area, while Route 230 lies to the east—while you could go either way, it's best to take Route 225 and head up to the Survival Area for now.

Route 225 • Survival Area

You'll travel up and down and all around as you walk up Route 225 to the Survival Area. As the Fight Area was for battling, the Survival Area is for training—people come here to work hard and become stronger Trainers.

Moves needed for completion: Cut, Surf, Rock Climb

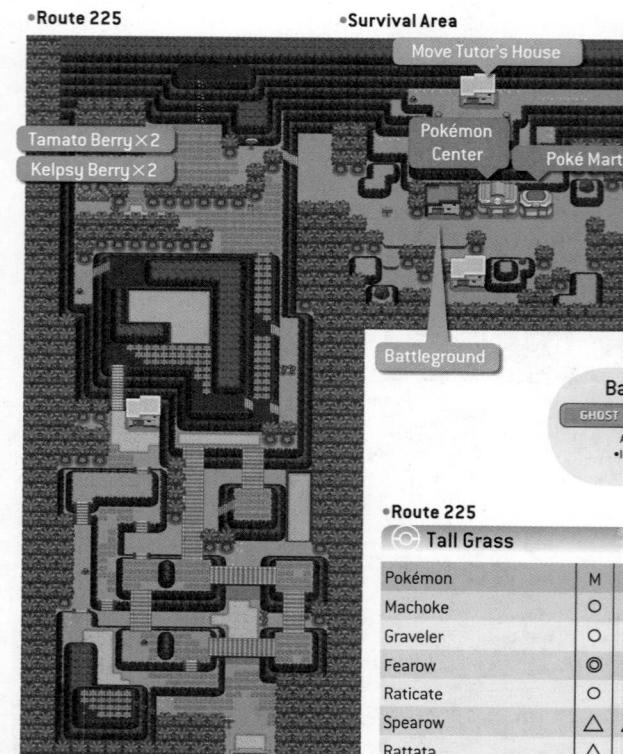

•Route 225 / •Survival Area

Move Tutor's House, Pokémon Center, Poké Mart, Tamato Berry×2, Kelpsy Berry×2, Battleground, Fight Area, Route 226 (to Stark Mountain)

Items

• First Visit
- ☐ Razor Fang
- ☐ Rare Candy
- ☐ HP Up
- ☐ Revive
- ☐ Lax Incense
- ☐ Fresh Water
- ☐ Dubious Disc
- ☐ Green Shard
- ☐ Tamato Berry x2
- ☐ Kelpsy Berry x2
- ☐ Dawn Stone
- ☐ TM42 Facade

• After visiting Route 226
- ☐ Red Shard

Banette
GHOST
Abilities
•Insomnia
•Frisk

•Route 225

Tall Grass

Pokémon	M	A	N
Machoke	○	○	○
Graveler	○	○	○
Fearow	◎	◎	○
Raticate	○	○	○
Spearow	△	△	△
Rattata	△	△	△
Banette	X	X	○

Water surface

Pokémon	
Golduck	◎
Psyduck	○

Fishing

Rod	Pokémon	
Old	Magikarp	◎
Good	Magikarp	◎
Good	Barboach	◎
Super	Gyarados	◎
Super	Whiscash	◎

Fearow
NORMAL FLYING
Abilities
•Keen Eye

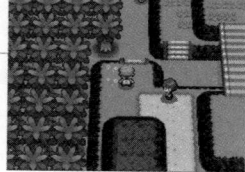 

Step 1 — Survive Route 225 first

Near the Fight Area port is the gate to Route 225, which stretches northward and is crawling with Trainers itching for a battle. Make your way along the twisting path and at the top, go down the stairs on the right to reach the Survival Area.

Get Fresh Water

Talk to a young man in a house along Route 225 to get some Fresh Water, an item that can restore 50 HP to a Pokémon.

Step 2 — Members Only?

Left of the Pokémon Center is a house with a locked door and a sign reading "Members Only." You're definitely not a member, so come back after you've visited Stark Mountain.

The door is shut tight. "Members Only" is painted on it.

After visiting Route 216 — **Collect colored shards to learn moves**

On the uppermost ledge of the Survival Area is a house where the Move Tutor lives. In exchange for 8 colored shards, he'll teach moves to your Pokémon. Which moves depends on the shards and the Pokémon. Talk to him to find out what moves he can teach your Pokémon (p. 568).

Would you like me to teach a move?

How do I get to his house?

You can't actually reach the Move Tutor's house from inside the Survival Area. Exit to the right, scale the wall using Rock Climb, then walk back to the left.

• Teachable moves and corresponding colored shards

Move	Type	Shards Required			
		Red	Blue	Yellow	Green
Iron Head	Steel	6	0	2	0
Aqua Trail	Water	6	0	0	2
Gastro Acid	Poison	4	0	2	2
Endeavor	Normal	4	0	4	0
Outrage	Dragon	6	0	2	0
AncientPower	Rock	6	0	0	2
Rollout	Rock	4	2	0	2
Signal Beam	Bug	2	2	2	2
Earth Power	Ground	6	0	0	2

Move	Type	Shards Required			
		Red	Blue	Yellow	Green
Gunk Shot	Poison	4	2	0	2
Twister	Dragon	6	0	0	2
Seed Bomb	Grass	4	0	0	4
Iron Defense	Steel	4	2	2	0
Bounce	Flying	4	0	2	2
Mud-Slap	Ground	4	4	4	0
Heat Wave	Fire	4	2	4	2
Super Power	Fighting	8	0	0	0

After visiting Stark Mountain — **The Battleground opens**

Once you visit Stark Mountain, return to the "Members Only" house to see Buck standing outside. It turns out that this is his house, so he invites you inside, where his grandfather welcomes you to the Battleground. Now you're free to come in whenever you please.

Welcome to the Battleground!

After visiting Stark Mountain — **New and improved Gym Leaders**

The Battleground is a busy spot visited by up to four Pokémon Trainers per day. Even Gym Leaders drop by from time-to-time, and they've really upped their game since the last time you saw them, so drop by daily for some good battling.

You'll get to see a different me than you saw at my Gym.

Battle your former companions

It's not just Gym Leaders who drop by for some action—you might encounter Cheryl, Mira, Riley, Marley, and, of course, Buck. Once they were your allies, now you can face them in battle.

After visiting Stark Mountain — **Accept your rival's call to battle**

Drop by the Battleground on Saturdays and Sundays to meet your rival outside and battle him. His Pokémon have gotten even more powerful since the last time you saw him, so it should be an exciting battle. You can battle him once per weekend day.

I'll prove it to you! Let's go!

Buck appears at the Battle Frontier

During your first visit to the Battleground, be sure to talk to Buck—from that point on he'll appear at the Battle Tower in the Battle Frontier. Keep winning battles, and you might battle him sometime.

Battle with your rival! ⑦

His Pokémon have gained 12–14 levels, and if you've entered the Hall of Fame more than 20 times, they'll be even stronger.

• If you chose Turtwig

Staraptor ♂ Lv61	NORMAL	FLYING
Heracross ♂ Lv61	BUG	FIGHTING
Infernape ♂ Lv65	FIRE	FIGHTING
Roserade ♂ Lv59	GRASS	POISON
Floatzel ♂ Lv59	WATER	
Snorlax ♂ Lv63	NORMAL	

• If you chose Chimchar

Staraptor ♂ Lv61	NORMAL	FLYING
Heracross ♂ Lv61	BUG	FIGHTING
Empoleon ♂ Lv65	WATER	STEEL
Rapidash ♂ Lv59	FIRE	
Roserade ♂ Lv59	GRASS	POISON
Snorlax ♂ Lv63	NORMAL	

• If you chose Piplup

Staraptor ♂ Lv61	NORMAL	FLYING
Heracross ♂ Lv61	BUG	FIGHTING
Torterra ♂ Lv65	GRASS	GROUND
Rapidash ♂ Lv59	FIRE	
Floatzel ♂ Lv59	WATER	
Snorlax ♂ Lv63	NORMAL	

Route 226 • Route 228
Route 229 • Route 230

Four different routes with four very different terrains, but all very beautiful—and challenging. Together they create a path that takes you between the Survival Area, the Fight Area, and the Resort Area.

Moves needed for completion

Cut · Strength · Surf · Rock Climb

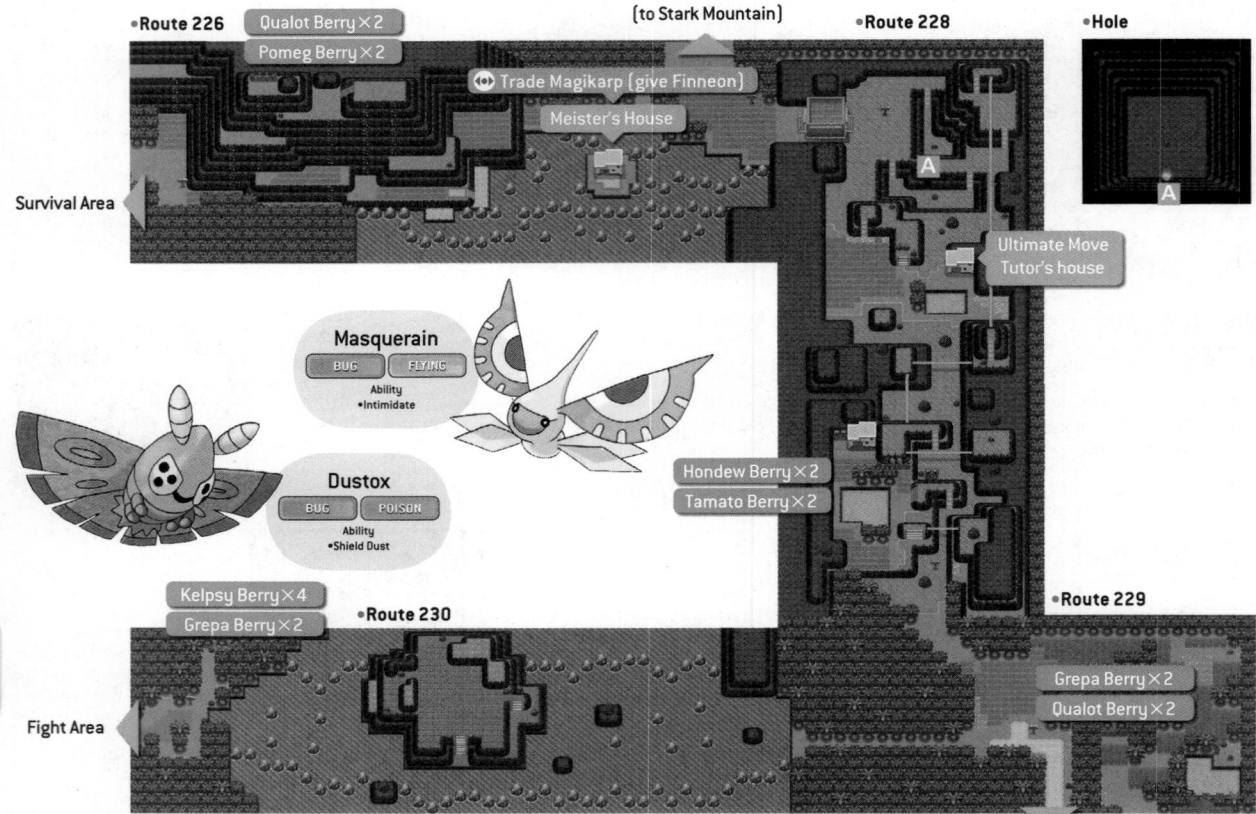

Route 227 (to Stark Mountain)

•Route 226 — Qualot Berry×2 / Pomeg Berry×2

Trade Magikarp (give Finneon) — Meister's House

•Route 228 · •Hole

Survival Area

A · A

Ultimate Move Tutor's house

Masquerain — BUG · FLYING — Ability •Intimidate

Dustox — BUG · POISON — Ability •Shield Dust

Hondew Berry×2 / Tamato Berry×2

Kelpsy Berry×4 / Grepa Berry×2 — •Route 230

•Route 229

Grepa Berry×2 / Qualot Berry×2

Fight Area

Resort Area

Items

- Qualot Berry x2
- Pomeg Berry x2
- Carbos
- Lagging Tail
- TM53 Energy Ball
- Protector
- Hard Stone
- Shiny Shell
- Shed Skin
- Iron
- TM37 Sandstorm
- Hondew Berry x2
- Tamato Berry x2
- Reaper Cloth
- Full Restore
- Nugget x2
- Protein
- Grepa Berry x2
- Qualot Berry x2
- Rare Candy
- Blue Shard
- Kelpsy Berry x4
- Grepa Berry x2

•Route 226

Tall Grass

Pokémon	M	A	N
Machoke	O	O	O
Graveler	O	O	O
Spearow	O	O	X
Wingull	O	O	O
Raticate	O	O	O
Rattata	△	△	△
Banette	X	X	O

Water surface

Pokémon	
Wingull	◎
Pelipper	◎
Tentacruel	O

Fishing

Rod	Pokémon	
Old	Magikarp	◎
Good	Magikarp	◎
	Horsea	◎
Super	Seadra	◎
	Gyarados	◎
	Relicanth	O

Relicanth — WATER · ROCK — Ability •Swift Swim •Rock Head

Route 228

Tall Grass

Pokémon	M	A	N
Dugtrio	◎	◎	◎
Cacturne	○	○	◎
Hippowdon	○	○	○
Rhydon	○	○	○
Diglett	△	△	△
Cacnea	△	△	△

Water surface

Pokémon	
Poliwhirl	◎
Poliwag	◎

Fishing

Rod	Pokémon	
Old	Magikarp	◎
Good	Magikarp	◎
	Barboach	○
	Whiscash	△
Super	Gyarados	◎
	Whiscash	◎

Route 229

Tall Grass

Pokémon	M	A	N
Roselia	◎	◎	◎
Ledian	○	X	X
Volbeat	○	○	○
Illumise	○	○	○
Pidgey	△	○	△
Beautifly	△	△	△
Dustox	△	△	△
Ariados	X	X	○

Water surface

Pokémon	
Surskit	◎
Masquerain	△

Fishing

Rod	Pokémon	
Old	Magikarp	◎
Good	Magikarp	◎
	Goldeen	◎
Super	Gyarados	◎
	Seaking	◎

Route 230

Tall Grass

Pokémon	M	A	N
Pelipper	◎	◎	◎
Floatzel	○	○	○
Bellsprout	○	○	X
Roselia	○	○	○
Gloom	△	△	△
Weepinbell	△	△	△
Wingull	△	△	△
Oddish	X	X	○

Water surface

Pokémon	
Sealeo	◎
Pelipper	◎
Tentacruel	○

Fishing

Rod	Pokémon	
Old	Magikarp	◎
Good	Magikarp	◎
	Remoraid	◎
Super	Gyarados	○
	Wailmer	○
	Octillery	○
	Wailord	△

Beautifly
BUG FLYING
Ability
•Swarm

Step 1 — Get a grip with Rock Climb

It's easy enough to exit from the Survival Area and enter Route 226, but you'll need to scramble over a few cliffs to go any further, so just use HM Rock Climb and in no time you'll be at the water where you can Surf instead.

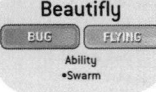

The wall is very rocky...
Would you like to use Rock Climb?
YES / NO

Step 2 — Visit Meister's house

In the middle of the water is Meister's house—pay this world traveler a visit, and he'll globalize your Pokédex, allowing you to read entries in French, Spanish, Italian, German and Japanese!

Now, you say read the descriptions of the Meister's Pokémon favorites

Trade Pokémon with Meister

Trade Meister a Finneon to get a Magikarp in return. Then check its Pokédex entry—the text is in German!

Step 3 — Stark Mountain is just ahead

Continue heading east until you reach a road sign, then turn and head up to Route 227. Just beyond that is Stark Mountain.

Crave some R-and-R?

If you're not feeling up to the Stark Mountain adventure just yet, feel free to continue right to Route 228. That will lead you down to the Resort Area.

Step 4 — Sandstorm on Route 228

You can hardly see a thing on Route 228, probably because of that endless sandstorm that rages there. Hop on the Bicycle to get through it quickly, but keep an eye out for items scattered throughout the route.

Sandstorm weather inflicts damage

All battles on Route 228 will take place in Sandstorm weather, meaning all Pokémon that aren't Rock-, Ground-, or Steel-types will take damage each turn. Keep an eye on their HP to avoid nasty surprises.

Step 5 Learn the ultimate moves

An old man on Route 228 is willing to teach your Pokémon the ultimate moves—Frenzy Plant, Blast Burn, and Hydro Cannon. These moves can only be taught to the final Evolution of starter Pokémon like Charizard or Empoleon.

Teach an unlimited number of Pokémon

There's no limit to how many Pokémon the old man will teach the moves to, so just bring him as many as you want.

Step 6 The old man's story

On the lower left of Route 228 is another old man who'd love for you to just give him a moment of your attention. Give him a listen to find out a sad story from Cyrus's childhood.

Step 7 Return to the Fight Area with Surf

Brave the sandstorms of Route 228 and eventually you'll reach Route 229. Go west to the water and Surf to reach Route 230, which takes you back around to the Fight Area.

Nuggets!

A guy standing beneath a tree on Route 229 loves to give out nuggets of wisdom—except he isn't very wise, so he'll just give you two Nuggets instead. These Nuggets can be sold for 5000 Poké.

Step 8 Take Route 229 to the Resort Area

Continue south down Route 229 to reach the Resort Area, but check out the tall grass to the right first—there's a few Trainers to battle and some items to collect.

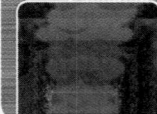
• Stark Mountain, an active volcano

Route 227 • Stark Mountain

As you travel further up Route 227, volcanic ash will fall all around you—that's how you know you're close to Stark Mountain, inside which lies an enormous cavern hollowed out by steam and magma.

Story

Moves needed for completion

Rock Smash   Strength   Surf

Rock Climb

Items

• First Visit
- ☐ Yellow Shard
- ☐ Zinc
- ☐ Charcoal
- ☐ Life Orb
- ☐ Max Elixir
- ☐ Escape Rope
- ☐ PP Up
- ☐ Full Heal
- ☐ Full Restore
- ☐ Iron Ball
- ☐ Max Revive
- ☐ Calcium
- ☐ TM50 Overheat
- ☐ Rare Candy

• After parting with Buck
- ☐ Ultra Ball
- ☐ Max Elixir
- ☐ Nugget

• Route 227
• Stark Mountain exterior

Tall Grass

Pokémon	M	A	N
Camerupt	O	O	O
Rhydon	O	O	O
Fearow	O	O	O
Graveler	O	O	O
Weezing	O	O	O
Skarmory	△	△	△
Numel	△	△	△
Rhyhorn	△	△	△
Golbat	X	X	O

Water surface

Pokémon	
Poliwhirl	◎
Poliwag	◎

Fishing

Rod	Pokémon	
Old	Magikarp	◎
Good	Magikarp	◎
Good	Barboach	◎
Super	Gyarados	◎
Super	Whiscash	◎

178

•Stark Mountain exterior

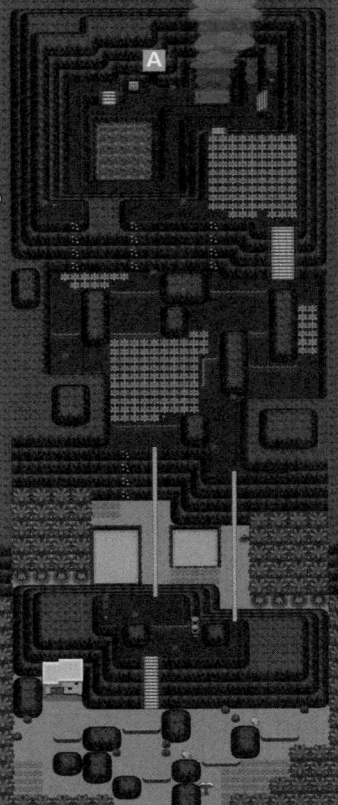

A

Buck

•Route 227

Route 226 (to Survival Area)

•Stark Mountain interior 3

•Stark Mountain interior 2

C
C

B

•Stark Mountain interior 1

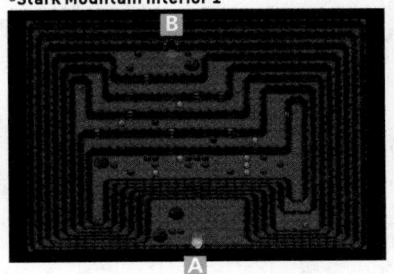

B

A

Koffing

POISON

Abilities
•Levitate

Rhydon

GROUND ROCK

Abilities
•Lightningrod
•Rock Head

SINNOH WALKTHROUGH (PRE-HALL OF FAME)

ROUTE 227 • STARK MOUNTAIN

•Stark Mountain interior 1 Cave				•Stark Mountain interior 2 Cave			
Pokémon	M	A	N	Pokémon	M	A	N
Magcargo	○	○	○	Magcargo	◎	◎	◎
Rhydon	○	○	○	Golbat	○	○	○
Golbat	○	○	○	Graveler	○	○	○
Graveler	○	○	○	Rhydon	○	○	○
Weezing	○	○	○	Weezing	○	○	○
Slugma	△	△	△	Slugma	△	△	△
Rhyhorn	△	△	△	Koffing	△	△	△

Step 1 Meet Wake and your Rival

At the top of Route 227 is a house, and in front of it is your rival and Wake, the Pastoria Gym Leader! Wake warns you about the strong Pokémon that inhabit Stark Mountain, and then the two of them depart, leaving you to face the mountain alone.

So, anyway, Lucas. You're going to Stark Mountain?

Heal your Pokémon first

The old lady inside the house will ask if your Pokémon need some rest. Say yes to heal up all their HP and PP, but be careful to say no when she asks again, otherwise you'll never leave.

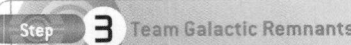

Step 2 — Go on patrol

Ride your Bicycle over a narrow bridge to encounter Buck at the other end of it. He's concerned about some strange goons in space suits seen mucking about, and he'd really appreciate it if you could go on patrol for him. Say yes and press on.

> ▶YES
> NO

> I'd like you to patrol Stark Mountain for me.

Step 3 — Team Galactic Remnants

The rumors turn out to be true—you see some Team Galactic grunts near the entrance to the mountain! Follow them inside to see what they're up to.

> That elder Charon is a Commander, but he can't replace Master Cyrus.

Step 4 — Showdown with Mars and Jupiter

Through the door you come face-to-face with Mars, Jupiter, and Charon. Mars and Jupiter would love to know where Cyrus went, so they question you about past events, then challenge you to a battle.

> Mars: Hey! You!
> Tell us where Master Cyrus went.

Discord between Mars and Jupiter?

They might both be looking for Cyrus, but it doesn't seem like Mars and Jupiter get along much otherwise—once you battle them, they withdraw their forces and go their separate ways.

Battle with Team Galactic Commander Mars! ❸

End it quickly and use Fire-type moves against Bronzong, hit Golbat with either Electric-, Ice-, Psychic-, or Rock-type moves, then finish off Purugly with Fighting-type moves.

• Party Pokémon

Bronzong Lv58	STEEL	PSYCHIC
Golbat ♀ Lv58	POISON	FLYING
Purugly ♀ Lv60	NORMAL	

Battle with Team Galactic Commander Jupiter! ❷

Deploy Fire-type moves against Bronzong and Electric-, Ice-, Psychic-, or Rock-type moves against Golbat. Take out her Skuntank with Ground-type moves for the win.

• Party Pokémon

Bronzong Lv58	STEEL	PSYCHIC
Golbat ♀ Lv58	POISON	FLYING
Skuntank ♀ Lv60	POISON	DARK

Step 5 · Chase Charon!

Charon has no interest in finding Cyrus—he's much rather steal the Magma Stone from within the cavern for the riches it could bring him. Go after him and prevent the theft!

Step 6 · Team up with Buck

You can't do this alone, so Buck arrives to help you nab those crooks. He uses a Claydol in battle, and heals your Pokémon when they're injured.

You can't use Rock Climb now

In Stark Mountain Interior (2) is a ledge that you could scale with Rock Climb, but not when Buck's with you. Just take the stairs for now and come back later when you're alone.

Step 7 · Looker to the rescue!

You get to the Interior (3) just a bit too late—Charon has the Magma Stone! Luckily, Looker is there in disguise, and he stops the theft before it goes any further. It's over for Team Galactic, and now it's time to part ways with Buck and Looker.

Master of disguise

Of all the things you would have expected, Looker disguised as a rock was not one of them. As silly as it seems, Looker has proven himself to be a highly skilled member of the International Police.

Step 8 · Use Rock Climb

Now that you don't have to worry about Buck, you can use Rock Climb to climb the walls of Stark Mountain Interior (2) and retrieve all the items you couldn't get to before.

After visiting the Battleground · Heatran appears

Return to Stark Mountain Interior (3) after visiting the Battleground—the cavern might have been empty before, but now Heatran waits for you to try and catch it.

Visit Buck at the Survival Area

Head back to the Survival Area to find Buck standing in front of the "Members Only" building. After you talk to him, he'll let you into the Battleground (p.175).

Catch Heatran!

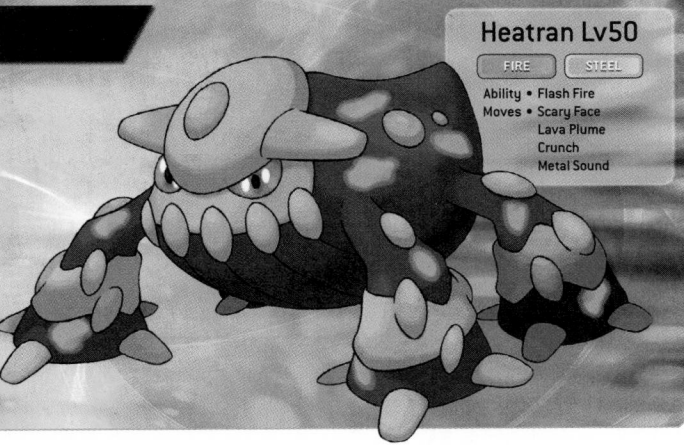

Hit it hard with Water- and Fighting-type moves, then chip away at its HP with Grass- and Ice-type moves that cause only 1/4 damage. Because of Heatran's Flash Fire Ability, you can't harm it with Fire-type moves.

Heatran Lv50 — FIRE STEEL
Ability • Flash Fire
Moves • Scary Face / Lava Plume / Crunch / Metal Sound

Different battles daily

Time passes in Sinnoh and each day is different—and so are the battles! These are the battles that vary based on the day of the week, so give them a try to strengthen up your Pokémon.

Battle every day to strengthen your Pokémon

Battle pairs of Trainers at the restaurant

Location	Seven Stars Restaurant, Valor Lakefront

Visit the restaurant during business hours (from 9am to 11pm) to battle different pairs of customers every day.

P.95

I'll have a battle with you if you keep your mouth shut.

Trainers await your challenge at the Pokémon Center

Location	Pokémon Center, various towns

Once you have the Vs. Seeker, Trainers will start appearing inside the Pokémon Center to battle. You can challenge them once a day, and they change often.

P.51

Want to battle and see for yourself?

Battle the 5 maids in a row at the Pokémon Mansion

Location	Pokémon Mansion, Route 212

Once a day you can battle five maids in a row. Finish in a certain number of turns to face the young master or mistress.

P.105

The challenge is to beat all five of us in a row without a break.

Enjoy a battle with a different Gym Leader

Location	Battleground, Survival Area

You can enjoy one battle a day with each of up to four Trainers, including Riley, Mira, and Gym Leaders. The available cast rotates every day.

P.174

I'm willing to beg. Let's battle!

The four Trainers you can battle comprise a random selection of Gym Leaders and the 5 Trainers above.

Battle your rival for fun on the weekends

Location	Your rival, Survival Area

Talk to your rival in the Survival Area on Saturday or Sunday to challenge him to battle. You can do this once a day.

P.174

I'll prove it to you! Let's go!

Resort Area

There's more to Pokémon than battling, and that's what the Resort Area is all about—people here like to just kick back and relax with their Pokémon. You can also try to get into the highly exclusive Ribbon Syndicate.

Route 229
(to Fight Area/Survival Area)

Ribbon Syndicate

Pokémon Center

Villa

Leppa Berry ×1
Qualot Berry ×2

Grepa Berry ×2
Lum Berry ×1

Items

- ☐ Nugget
- ☐ Leppa Berry
- ☐ Qualot Berry x2
- ☐ Grepa Berry x4
- ☐ Lum Berry

Water surface

Pokémon	
Golduck	◎
Psyduck	○

Fishing

Rod	Pokémon	
Old	Magikarp	◎
Good	Magikarp	◎
Super	Magikarp	◎

Magikarp

WATER

Abilities
•Swift Swim

Step 1 — Your very own villa

Head to the house in the lower right corner of the Resort Area, and before you know it, the owner has transferred ownership of his villa to you. There's a furniture catalog on the table, so save your money and decorate your new pad with the very best items available.

So don't say a word.
Just nod and this Villa is yours!

▶YES
NO

Receive guests at your villa

Lots of people will visit your new resort home, like your rival and Professor Rowan. Fancy up the place and you might even get a few celebrity guests like the Gym Leaders and Cynthia.

•**Furniture catalog**

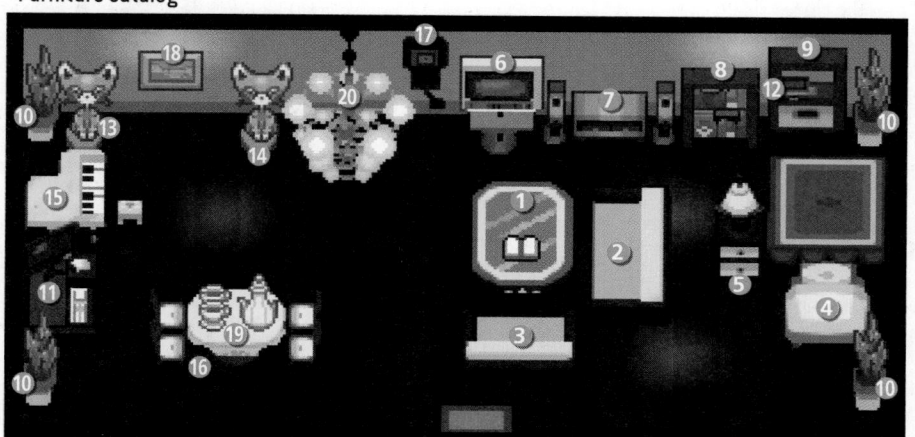

1	Table	0P	Receive when you get the villa
2	Big sofa	120,000P	Can order from the beginning
3	Small sofa	90,000P	Can order from the beginning
4	Bed	187,000P	Can order from the beginning
5	Night table	58,000P	Can order from the beginning
6	TV	220,000P	Can order from the beginning
7	Audio system	160,000P	Can order from the beginning
8	Bookshelf	150,000P	Can order from the beginning
9	Rack	127,000P	Can order from the beginning
10	Houseplant	120,000P	Can order from the beginning
11	PC desk	168,000P	Can order from the beginning
12	Music box	25,300P	Can order once you have the rack
13	Pokémon bust	150,000P	Can order once you battle each of the Battle Frontier facilities more than once
14	Pokémon bust	150,000P	Can order once you get any one type of Silver Print
15	Piano	146,700P	Can order once you've entered the Hall of Fame 10 times
16	Guest set	208,000P	Can order once you've had over 50 battles at the Battleground
17	Wall clock	52,000P	Can order once you've planted over 50 berries
18	Masterpiece	140,000P	Can order once you've hatched over 30 Eggs
19	Tea set	108,000P	Can order when you get the guest set
20	Chandelier	120,000P	Can order when you've taken over 300,000 steps since the beginning of the game

Step 2 — A highly selective club

To the upper right of the Resort Area is the Ribbon Syndicate, and they're very strict about who they let in. Unless you have 10 different Ribbons between your party Pokémon, the woman at the door will give you the brush-off.

If you wish to enter, I suggest you start by collecting lots of Ribbons.

Collect Ribbons from all across Sinnoh

There are many different Ribbons, so try to get as many as you can. You can win them in Super Contests, or you can always talk to Julia in Sunyshore City (p. 169).

Step 3 — An incredible Pokémon

You might want to try fishing in the lake on the left side of town—it's home to an incredible Pokémon that some call a great ruler of the pond, a Lv100 Magikarp!

After you've collected 10 different Ribbons — Enter the club and buy bows

Talk to the girl at the counter of the Ribbon Syndicate to buy even more Ribbons, like the Luxury Ribbon for 10,000 Poké. Even more lush is the Royal Ribbon, for 100,000 Poké. And finally, there's the Luxury Royal Ribbon, which will set you back 999,999 Poké.

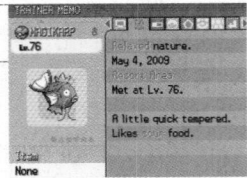

For a mere ₽10,000, you can be the proud owner of one.

Your membership is always good

The Ribbon Syndicate is exclusive, but once you're a member, you're always a member, so you don't have to have your Ribbon-laden Pokémon with you to enter after you join.

After you've collected 10 different Ribbons — The Pokémon Spa

Head to the second floor of the Ribbon Syndicate, where you can visit the Pokémon Spa. The attendants will pamper your Pokémon, which in turn raises its Friendship with you.

Would you care to have a spa treatment, Lucas?

Makeovers every day

Some Pokémon will only evolve once their Friendship with you is high, and a great way to achieve this is by taking them for a spa treatment every day (p. 380).

Pokémon
Battle
Seminar

Pokémon Battle Seminar

1

Raise Powerful Pokémon

Raise Pokémon you can depend on in battle

Work hard to make your Pokémon strong, and they'll be ready for any battle, whether it's casual matches with friends, or the tricky battles of the Battle Frontier.

Pokémon Raising Technique **1**

Choose Pokémon with high stats

The stats of individual Pokémon will vary from others of its kind, so you might want to catch several and compare their stats for the best results. For example, a Pokémon with high Speed will be faster than other Pokémon in battle. Stats are affected by Nature and personality, which are also listed in the Pokémon's summary.

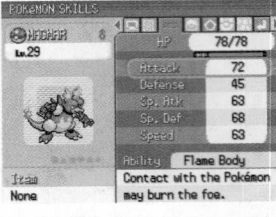

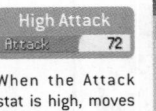

High Attack

Attack 72

When the Attack stat is high, moves like Fire Punch really pack a wallop.

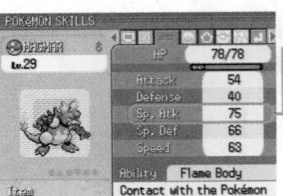

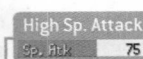

High Sp. Attack

Sp. Atk 75

When the Sp. Attack stat is high, moves like Flamethrower are highly dependable.

●●●See p. 545 for a detailed list of Pokémon Natures and personalities.●●●

Pokémon Raising Technique **2**

Use items to raise the EV of battle stats

Each of a Pokémon's 6 battle stats contain points called Effort Values, or EVs. The higher the EV, the more that stat will increase when the Pokémon levels up. If there's one particular stat you want to raise, you can encourage it with certain items. These items are most effective on a recently-caught Pokémon that has not yet been sent into battle.

● EV-raising Items

Item	Effect
HP Up	Raises HP EV
Protein	Raises Attack EV
Iron	Raises Defense EV
Calcium	Raises Sp. Attack EV
Zinc	Raises Sp. Defense EV
Carbos	Raises Speed EV

● EV-lowering Items

Berry	Effect
Pomeg Berry	Lowers HP EV
Kelpsy Berry	Lowers Attack EV
Qualot Berry	Lowers Defense EV
Hondew Berry	Lowers Sp. Attack EV
Grepa Berry	Lowers Sp. Defense EV
Tamato Berry	Lowers Speed EV

Pokémon Raising Technique **3**

Strengthen your Pokémon by battling

You need to raise a Pokémon's EVs to maximize its stat growth. You must enter battles to do this—the more foes you defeat, the more your Pokémon's EVs will grow. Seek out as many lower-level Pokémon as you can, and choose your opponents carefully—the stats that go up are determined by the Pokémon you battle.

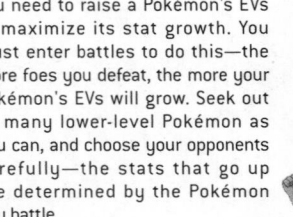

Bidoof
Raises HP EV

Primary Location
Route 201

Machop
Raises Attack EV

Primary Location
Route 207

Geodude
Raises Defense EV

Primary Location
Oreburgh Mine B1F

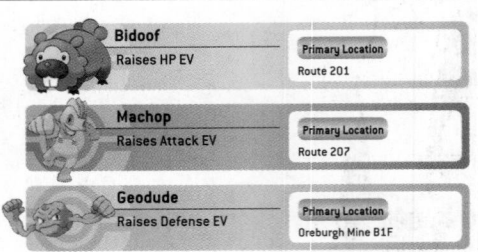

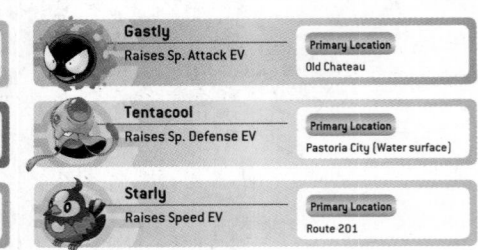

Gastly
Raises Sp. Attack EV

Primary Location
Old Chateau

Tentacool
Raises Sp. Defense EV

Primary Location
Pastoria City (Water surface)

Starly
Raises Speed EV

Primary Location
Route 201

Pokémon Raising Technique 4: Give your Pokémon items to hold in battle

Some items increase EV growth when held during battle. For example, holding the Macho Brace in battle lowers a Pokémon's Speed, but it will gain more EVs than usual.

• Items that greatly raise EVs

Item	Effect
Macho Brace	Gives you more stat EVs than usual
Power Weight	Gives you more HP EVs than usual
Power Bracer	Gives you more Attack EVs than usual
Power Belt	Gives you more Defense EVs than usual
Power Lens	Gives you more Sp. Attack EVs than usual
Power Band	Gives you more Sp. Defense EVs than usual
Power Anklet	Gives you more Speed EVs than usual

Pokémon Raising Technique 5: Choose the right moves for your battle style

Your Pokémon can only know four moves at a time, so you have to be picky about which moves it learns. It's best to have both physical and special attacks to keep your opponent off-balance, and to learn moves that work well against the types your Pokémon is weak against.

• Example learned moves

Physical and special moves

Have Lucario learn the physical move Force Palm and the special move Aura Sphere. Then select attacks based on your opponent.

Force Palm FIGHTING
Aura Sphere FIGHTING

Lucario

Target the weakness of an opponent that's strong against you

Prinplup is weak against Grass-type Pokémon, so have it learn Flying- or Ice-type moves, which are strong against Grass-type Pokémon.

Drill Peck FLYING
Ice Beam ICE

Prinplup

Auxiliary moves

Auxiliary moves can inflict status conditions or lower your foe's stats, assisting you in future turns.

Charm NORMAL
Sweet Kiss NORMAL

Pachirisu

Pokémon Battle Seminar 2: Pokémon Move Mastery

Be familiar with many kinds of moves

Moves that cause a lot of damage are great, but you should also get to know moves that inflict status conditions, alter stats, or help allied Pokémon—these all make the path to victory so much smoother.

Move Technique 1: Hit your foe with status conditions

Rather than cause direct damage, sometimes it's better to just inflict a status condition on your foe—being paralyzed or having its HP gradually lowered can be just as decisive in battle as hitting the foe hard with an attack move.

• Merits of status-altering moves

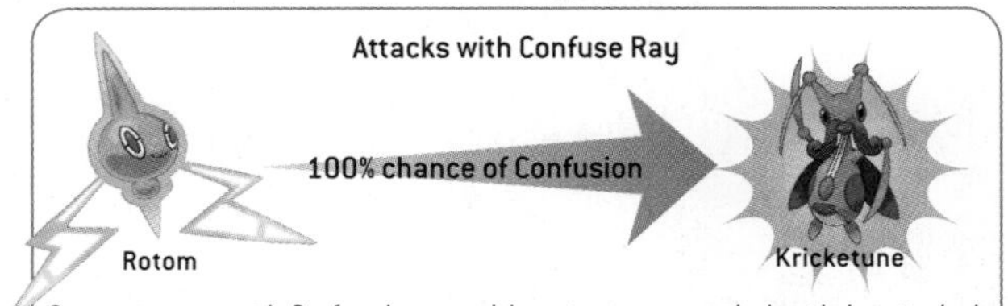
Attacks with Confuse Ray
100% chance of Confusion
Rotom
Kricketune
Once your opponent is Confused, you won't have to worry as much about being attacked.

•••See p. 23 for a full explanation of status conditions.•••

• Examples of status-altering moves

Move	Type	POW	ACC	Effect	Pokémon that can learn
Yawn	Normal	—	—	Puts opponent to sleep at the end of the next turn	Bibarel, Hippopotas, etc.
Lovely Kiss	Normal	—	75	Puts opponent to sleep	Jynx
Confuse Ray	Ghost	—	100	Confuses opponent	Mismagius, Spiritomb, etc.
Sing	Normal	—	55	Puts opponent to sleep	Jigglypuff, Kricketune, etc.

Move	Type	POW	ACC	Effect	Pokémon that can learn
Will-O-Wisp	Fire	—	75	Burns opponent	Vulpix, Duskull, etc.
Spore	Grass	—	100	Puts opponent to sleep	Paras, Shroomish, etc.
GrassWhistle	Grass	—	55	Puts opponent to sleep	Roselia, Leafeon, etc.
Psycho Shift	Psychic	—	90	Transfers status conditions to foe, cures self	Noctowl, Xatu, ec.
Hypnosis	Psychic	—	60	Puts opponent to sleep	Gastly, Gardevoir, etc.
Stun Spore	Grass	—	75	Paralyzes opponent	Bellsprout, Tangela, etc.
Supersonic	Normal	—	55	Confuses opponent	Zubat, Magnemite, etc.
Sweet Kiss	Normal	—	75	Confuses opponent	Smoochum, Luvdisc, etc.
Thunder Wave	Electric	—	100	Paralyzes opponent	Pichu, Jolteon, etc.
Poison Gas	Poison	—	55	Poisons opponent	Gulpin, Stunky, etc.
Toxic	Poison	—	85	Badly poisons opponent	Dustox, Vespiquen, etc.
PoisonPowder	Poison	—	75	Poisons opponent	Oddish, Venonat, etc.
Sleep Powder	Grass	—	75	Puts opponent to sleep	Exeggcute, Hoppip, etc.
Teeter Dance	Normal	—	100	Confuses opponent	Spinda, Mime Jr., etc.
Glare	Normal	—	75	Paralyzes opponent	Dunsparce, Seviper, etc.

Move Technique 2 — Strengthen your own Pokémon with auxiliary moves

Some moves can raise stats for the duration of a battle. Take Speed, which determines the order of attacks, or Attack and Sp. Attack, which determine the amount of damage inflicted (p. 22). Changing these stats can put the direction of battle in your control.

• Merits of auxiliary moves

Raises Speed by 2   Uses Agility

Floatzel

Raises user's Speed greatly, allowing it to attack before the foe.

• Examples of auxiliary moves

Move	Type	POW	ACC	Effect	Pokémon that can learn
Charm	Normal	—	100	Lowers foe's Attack by 2	Pachirisu, Glameow, etc.
Screech	Normal	—	85	Lowers foe's Defense by 2	Onix, Munchlax, etc.
Double Team	Normal	—	—	Raises user's Evasion by 1	Pikachu, Starly, etc.
Metal Sound	Steel	—	85	Lowers foe's Sp. Defense by 2	Magnemite, Skarmory, etc.
Agility	Psychic	—	—	Raises user's Speed by 2	Lopunny, Floatzel, etc.
Acupressure	Normal	—	—	Raises all of a random Pokémon's stats by 2	Doduo, Skorupi, etc.
Swords Dance	Normal	—	—	Raises user's Attack by 2	Ninjask, Lucario, etc.
FeatherDance	Flying	—	100	Raises user's Attack by 2	Pidgeotto, Charot, etc.
Flash	Normal	—	100	Lowers foe's Accuracy by 1	Volbeat, use TM70
Nasty Plot	Dark	—	—	Raises user's Sp. Attack by 2	Persian, Sableye, etc.

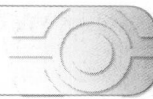

Move Technique 3 — Use moves with side effects

Some moves don't just cause damage, they also have side effects that include causing status conditions or lowering a foe's stats. For example, Poison Jab has a 30% chance of poisoning its target aside from the damage it inflicts.

Merits of moves with side effects

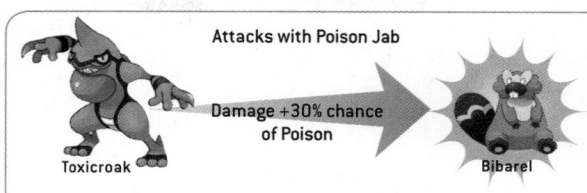

Attacks with Poison Jab

Toxicroak

Damage +30% chance of Poison

Bibarel

A poisoned foe loses HP on every turn

Examples of moves with side effects

Move	Type	POW	ACC	Effect	Pokémon that can learn
Rock Smash	Fighting	40	100	50% chance of lowering foe's Defense by 1	Use HM06
Rock Tomb	Rock	50	80	100% chance of lowering foe's Speed by 1	Onix, Sudowoodo, etc.
Icy Wind	Ice	55	95	100% chance of lowering foe's Speed by 1	Swinub, Snover, etc.
Smog	Poison	20	70	40% chance of poisoning foe	Koffing, Slugma, etc.
Charge Beam	Electric	50	90	70% chance of raising user's Sp. Attack by 1	Voltorb, Regirock, etc.
Poison Jab	Poison	80	100	30% chance of poisoning foe	Ariados, Toxicroak, etc.
Poison Fang	Poison	50	100	30% chance of badly poisoning foe	Crobat, Skorupi, etc.
Mud-Slap	Ground	20	100	100% chance of lowering foe's Accuracy by 1	Barboach, Shellos, etc.
Crush Claw	Normal	75	95	50% chance of lowering foe's Defense by 1	Kangaskhan, Armaldo, etc.
Mud Shot	Ground	55	95	100% chance of lowering foe's Speed by 1	Poliwhirl, Wooper, etc.

Move Technique 4 — Get the drop on your opponent

The order of attacks in battle is usually determined by the Pokémon's Speed. Sometimes the slower Pokémon can get the jump on their foe by using moves like Quick Attack and Mach Punch, which always attack first. Moves like these can be used to knock out a weak opponent before they even get a chance to attack.

Merits of initiative-seizing moves

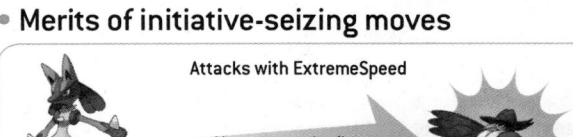

Attacks with ExtremeSpeed

Lucario — Always attacks first — Honchkrow

ExtremeSpeed has an Attack power of 80, as well as attacking first.

Initiative-seizing moves

Move	Type	POW	ACC	Effect	Pokémon that can learn
Aqua Jet	Water	40	100	Always attacks first	Carvanha, Buizel, etc.
Shadow Sneak	Ghost	40	100	Always attacks first	Duskull, Spiritomb, etc.
Ice Shard	Ice	40	100	Always attacks first	Sneasel, Snorunt, etc.
Vacuum Wave	Fighting	40	100	Always attacks first	Hitmonchan, Scyther, etc.
ExtremeSpeed	Normal	80	100	Always attacks first	Arcanine, Lucario, etc.
Quick Attack	Normal	40	100	Always attacks first	Starly, Pachirisu, etc.
Fake Out	Normal	40	100	Always goes first and makes foe flinch (first turn only)	Makuhita, Glameow, etc.
Bullet Punch	Steel	40	100	Always attacks first	Hitmonchan, Metang, etc.
Sucker Punch	Dark	80	100	Attacks first when the foe has chosen an attack move	Murkrow, Noctowl, etc.
Mach Punch	Fighting	40	100	Always attacks first	Ledyba, Monferno, etc.

*If the foe has also chosen one of these moves, the Pokémon with the highest Speed goes first.

POKÉMON BATTLE SEMINAR

POKÉMON MOVE MASTERY

5 Use sure-hit moves in low-accuracy situations

A move's Accuracy determines how likely it is to hit its target. Some moves like Sand-Attack lower Accuracy, while others like Double Team raise Evasion—both of these can make a high Accuracy less effective. When your opponent tries these tactics, counter by using a sure-hit move on them.

• Merits of sure-hit moves

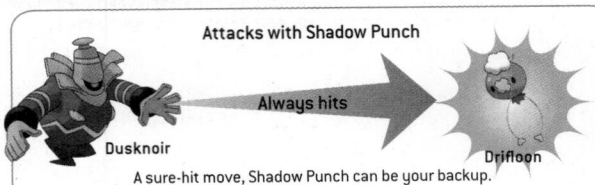

A sure-hit move, Shadow Punch can be your backup.
It's especially effective against Ghost-types.

• Sure-hit moves

Move	Type	POW	ACC	Effect	Pokémon that can learn
Vital Throw	Fighting	70	—	Always attacks last, but always hits its target	Pinsir, Makuhita, etc.
Trump Card	Normal	—	—	Always hits its target, has stronger Attack power the lower its PP is	Eevee, Minun, etc.
Shadow Punch	Ghost	60	—	Always hits its target	Gastly, Dusclops, etc.
Swift	Normal	60	—	Always hits its target	Voltorb, Espeon, etc.
Faint Attack	Dark	60	—	Always hits its target	Trapinch, Banette, etc.
Aerial Ace	Flying	60	—	Always hits its target	Heracross, Starly, etc.
Shock Wave	Electric	60	—	Always hits its target	Elekid, Rotom, etc.
Aura Sphere	Fighting	90	—	Always hits its target	Lucario, Togekiss, etc.
Magnet Bomb	Steel	60	—	Always hits its target	Magnemite, Probopass, etc.
Magical Leaf	Grass	60	—	Always hits its target	Tropius, Cherubi, etc.

6 Defeat tough opponents with set-damage moves

Having a high Attack or Sp. Attack raises the amount of damage you inflict—unless the foe has a high Defense or Sp. Defense, then the amount of damage is lowered. If your Pokémon has low Attack and the foe has high Defense, switch to moves that deliver a set amount of damage—in these cases, your opponent's Defense won't matter.

• Merits of set-damage moves

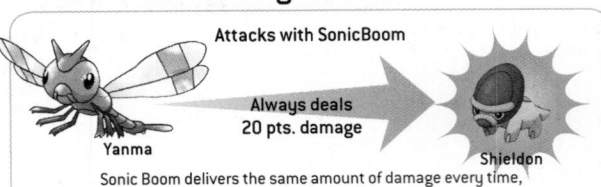

Sonic Boom delivers the same amount of damage every time,
no matter how high the foe's Defense is.

• Moves with set damage

Move	Type	POW	ACC	Effect	Pokémon that can learn
SonicBoom	Normal	—	90	Inflicts a set 20 points of damage	Electrode, Yanma, etc.
Seismic Toss	Fighting	—	100	Inflicts a set number of points of damage equal to user's HP	Machop, Pinsir, etc.
Night Shade	Ghost	—	100	Inflicts a set number of points of damage equal to user's level	Spinarak, Shuppet, etc.
Dragon Rage	Dragon	—	100	Inflicts a set 40 points of damage	Gyarados, Gible, etc.

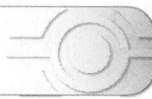

Move Technique 7 — Keep Pokémon healthy with recovery moves

Getting hit by attacks means a Pokémon is losing HP—and if they lose it all, they will faint. Having a Pokémon in your party that can heal HP is a huge lifesaver, as are any moves that can heal status conditions. Recovery moves can really make a long battle easier to endure.

• Example recovery move

Restores half of Chatot's HP

Use Roost

Chatot

Roost, which restores half of a Pokémon's HP, is a fitting move for a Flying-type Pokémon.

• Examples of recovery moves

Move	Type	POW	ACC	Effect	Pokémon that can learn
Aqua Ring	Water	—	—	Restores a bit of HP every turn	Goldeen, Finneon, etc.
Aromatherapy	Grass	—	—	Heals status conditions of all allied Pokémon	Chikorita, Roselia, etc.
Heal Bell	Normal	—	—	Heals status conditions of all allied Pokémon	Miltank, Chimecho, etc.
Giga Drain	Grass	60	100	Restores half as much HP to user as it causes to foe	Paras, Beautifly, etc.
Recover	Normal	—	—	Recovers half of max HP	Kadabra, Staryu, etc.
Softboiled	Normal	—	—	Recovers half of max HP	Chansey, Blissey
Drain Punch	Fighting	60	100	Restores half as much HP to user as it causes to foe	Use TM60
Wish	Normal	—	—	Restores half of max HP at the end of the next turn, even if the user switches out	Togepi, Natu, Illumise, etc.
Sleep	Psychic	—	—	Fully restores HP but puts user to sleep for 2 turns	Snorlax, Wailmer, etc.
Roost	Flying	—	—	Restores half of max HP and removes Flying-type for that turn	Pidgey, Spearow, Hoothoot, Chatot, etc.
Leech Seed	Grass	—	90	Steals HP from foe each turn	Exeggcute, Cherubi, Carnivine, etc.
Dream Eater	Psychic	100	100	Restores half as much HP to user as it causes to a sleeping foe	Gastly, Hoothoot, Ralts, Spiritomb, etc.
Refresh	Normal	—	—	Heals poison, paralysis, and burn	Lickitung, Happiny, etc.

Move Technique 8 — Strengthen your moves by controlling the weather

The weather can play a part in Pokémon battles, affecting move strength and Pokémon Abilities—for example, the move Synthesis will recover more HP in Sunny weather, while Pokémon with the Swift Swim Ability are faster when it rains. Some moves can control the weather, so take that into consideration when choosing your moveset.

• Merits of weather-based moves

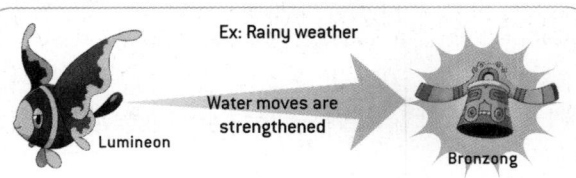

Ex: Rainy weather

Lumineon

Water moves are strengthened

Bronzong

Rainy weather will play to the advantage of Pokémon with Water-type moves

POKÉMON BATTLE SEMINAR

POKÉMON MOVE MASTERY

Sunny weather

The Sunny Day move creates Sunny weather for 5 turns. This strengthens Fire-type moves and weakens Water-type moves.

- Strengthens Fire-type moves
- Weakens Water-type moves
- Raises Attack and Sp. Attack of Pokémon with the Ability Flower Gift
- Raises Speed of Pokémon with the Ability Chlorophyll
- Pokémon with the Ability Leaf Guard are immune to status conditions
- Damages Pokémon with the Ability Dry Skin
- Raises Sp. Attack of Pokémon with the Ability Solar Power, but also damages them

Rainy weather

The Rain Dance move creates Rainy weather for 5 turns. This strengthens Water-type moves and weakens Fire-type moves.

- Strengthens Water-type moves
- Weakens Fire-type moves
- Gradually restores HP to Pokémon with the Ability Rain Dish
- Cures status conditions at the end of the turn for Pokémon with the Ability Hydration
- Gradually restores HP to Pokémon with the Ability Dry Skin
- Raises Speed of Pokémon with the Ability Swift Swim

Sandstorm weather

The Sandstorm move creates Sandstorm weather for 5 turns. Every turn, this weather deals damage to all Pokémon that aren't Ground-, Rock-, or Steel-type.

- Damages Pokémon that aren't Ground-, Rock-, or Steel-type
- Raises Evasion of Pokémon with the Ability Sand Veil
- Raises Sp. Attack of Rock-type Pokémon 1.5 times

Hail weather

The Hail move creates Hail weather for 5 turns, causing damage every turn to all Pokémon other than Ice-types.

- Damages all Pokémon aside from Ice-types
- Gradually restores HP to Pokémon with the Ability Ice Body
- Raises Evasion of Pokémon with the Ability Snow Cloak

• Weather-changing moves

Move	Type	POW	ACC	Effect	Pokémon that can learn
Rain Dance	Water	—	—	Makes Rainy weather	Marill, Finneon, etc.
Hail	Ice	—	—	Makes Hail weather	Spheal, Glaceon, etc.
Sandstorm	Rock	—	—	Makes Sandstorm weather	Onix, Gible, etc.
Sunny Day	Fire	—	—	Makes Sunny weather	Magby, Cherubi, etc.

• Moves affected by weather

Move	Type	POW	ACC	Effect	Pokémon that can learn
Morning Sun	Normal	—	—	Restores HP, effect changes with the weather	Espeon, Beautifly, etc.
Weather Ball	Normal	50	100	Move type changes with the weather, can become twice as powerful	Castform, Roserade
Thunder	Electric	120	70	Sure-hit move in rain weather	Pikachu, Elekid, etc.
Synthesis	Grass	—	—	Restores HP, effect changes with the weather	Turtwig, Leafeon, etc.
SolarBeam	Grass	120	100	Attacks on same turn in sunny weather	Venusaur, Chikorita, Tropius, Cherrim, etc.
Moonlight	Normal	—	—	Restores HP, effect changes with the weather	Umbreon, Dustox, etc.
Poison Fang	Poison	50	100	30% chance of badly poisoning foe	Crobat, Skorupi, etc.
Mud-Slap	Ground	20	100	100% chance of lowering foe's Accuracy by 1	Barboach, Shellos, etc.
Crush Claw	Normal	75	95	50% chance of lowering foe's Defense by 1	Kangaskhan, Armaldo, etc.
Mud Shot	Ground	55	95	100% chance of lowering foe's Speed by 1	Poliwhirl, Wooper, etc.

Pokémon Battle Seminar

3

Using Pokémon Abilities

Master the Pokémon's natural Abilities

Pokémon Abilities might be automatic, but they affect a lot of things, from giving and receiving attacks to switching your Pokémon out of battle. Be sure to incorporate them into your tactics.

1 ## Abilities can help your attacks

Take Pokémon Abilities into account when planning your attacks—some Abilities can raise Attack or change Accuracy. For example, the Ability Super Luck raises a Pokémon's critical hit rate, allowing it to deal double damage more often.

• Merits of attack Abilities

Swarm Ability is activated

Bug-type moves become 1.5 times stronger when Pokémon's HP is low

Mothim

Always pick Bug-type moves when your Pokémon's HP is low—they'll be stronger than normal.

• Examples of attack Abilities

Ability	Effect	Pokémon that can learn
Rock Head	No recoil damage from moves like Takedown and Tackle	Sudowoodo, Relicanth, etc.
Tinted Lens	Nullifies a move's type weakness	Illumise, Yanmega, etc.
Mold Breaker	Enables user to use moves regardless of the effects of the foe's Ability	Pinsir, Rampardos, etc.
Scrappy	Enables Normal-type moves to hit Ghost-type Pokémon	Kangaskhan, Miltank
Super Luck	Raises critical hit rate	Absol, Honchkrow, etc.
Torrent	Water-type moves become 1.5x stronger when user's HP is below 1/3 of max	Empoleon, Swampert, etc.
Guts	Attack becomes 1.5x stronger when user has a status condition	Raticate, Hariyama, etc.
Overgrow	Grass-type moves become 1.5x stronger when user's HP is below 1/3 of max	Torterra, Sceptile, etc.
Skill Link	Serial moves strike the maximum number of times (always 5 times for a move that strikes 2–5 times)	Shellder, Cloyster
Reckless	Strengthens moves with recoil damage	Hitmonlee
Huge Power	Raises Attack (Attack is halved if the Ability is nullified)	Azurill, Marill, Azumarill
Adaptability	Type match-up has a greater effect when an attack move has the same type as the user	Eevee, Porygon-Z
Technician	Moves that deal less than 60 points of damage become 1.5x more powerful	Scizor, Hitmontop, etc.
Iron Fist	Strengthens punching moves	Hitmonchan
Serene Grace	Moves become twice as likely to inflict side effects	Dunsparce, Togekiss, etc.
No Guard	Both user and foe's moves hit 100% of the time	Machoke, Machamp, etc.
Normalize	All of user's moves come out as Normal-type moves	Skitty, Delcatty
Compoundeyes	Increases Accuracy 1.3x	Butterfree, Yanma, etc.
Swarm	Bug-type moves become 1.5x stronger when user's HP is below 1/3 of max	Beautifly, Mothim, etc.
Blaze	Fire-type moves become 1.5x stronger when user's HP is below 1/3 of max	Infernape, Blaziken, etc.

2   Cushion the blow with defensive Abilities

Some Abilities come into play when the Pokémon is on the receiving end of an attack—like protecting against damage by a certain type, or preventing certain status conditions. For example, Quagsire's Ability Water Absorb restores Quagsire's HP when Quagsire is hit by a Water-type move. Take advantage of these types of Abilities and watch your opponent's attacks backfire on them!

Merits of defense Abilities

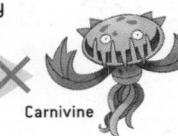

Levitate comes into play

Ground-type move Earthquake ✕ Carnivine

Hippowdon

Pokémon with Levitate are completely immune to Ground-type moves.

Examples of defensive Abilities

Ability	Effect	Pokémon that can learn
Battle Armor	Protects against critical hits	Kabutops, Drapion, etc.
Dry Skin	Recovers HP when user is hit by a Water-type move	Parasect, Toxicroak, etc.
Heatproof	Halves damage incurred from Fire-type moves and the burn condition	Bronzor, Bronzong
Volt Absorb	Electric-type moves restore user's HP rather than inflicting damage	Zapdos, Lanturn, etc.
Water Absorb	Water-type moves restore user's HP rather than inflicting damage	Vaporeon, Mantine, etc.
Motor Drive	Electric-type moves raise user's Speed by 1 rather than inflicting damage	Electivire
Solid Rock	Lessens damage received from a super effective move	Camerupt, Rhyperior
Filter	Lessens damage received from a super effective mov e	Mime Jr., Mr. Mime
Levitate	Makes user immune to Ground-type moves	Gengar, Rotom, etc.
Flash Fire	When user is hit by a Fire-type move, it receives no damage, but its own Fire-type moves become 1.5x stronger	Arcanine, Houndoom, etc.

3   Status condition Abilities

Some Abilities are useful for a counter-attack when a Pokémon is directly attacked—like Magcargo's Flame Body, which has a 30% chance of burning any Pokémon that attacks Magcargo directly. Other Abilities are more useful to their Pokémon, like Altaria's Natural Cure, which heals status conditions when the Pokémon is switched out of battle.

Merits of status condition Abilities

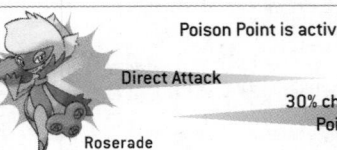 

Poison Point is activated

Direct Attack

Roserade

30% chance of Poison

Bibarel

Foes should hesitate to launch a direct attack on a Pokémon with the Ability Poison Point.

Examples of status-condition Abilities

Ability	Effect	Pokémon that can learn
Natural Cure	Heals status conditions when user is withdrawn from battle	Starmie, Happiny, etc.
Synchronize	If user gets poisoned, paralyzed, or burned, inflicts same status on foe	Alakazam, Gardevoir, etc.
Static	30% chance of counter-inflicting paralysis when attacked directly	Raichu, Ampharos, etc.
Shed Skin	33% chance every turn of healing status conditions	Arbok, Kricketot, etc.
Poison Point	30% chance of counter-inflicting paralysis when attacked directly	Qwilfish, Roserade, etc.
Early Bird	User awakens quickly from sleep	Dodrio, Girafarig, etc.
Poison Heal	Restores HP every turn when user is poisoned	Shroomish, Breloom
Effect Spore	30% chance of counter-inflicting poison, paralysis, or sleep when attacked directly	Parasect, Breloom, etc.
Flame Body	30% chance of counter-inflicting burn when attacked directly	Magcargo, Magmortar, etc.
Cute Charm	30% chance of counter-inflicting attraction when attacked directly	Wigglytuff, Lopunny, etc.

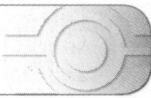

Ability Technique 4 — Use Abilities to alter stats

Some Abilities can raise the user's stats or lower those of the opponent. Some Abilities protect your stats from being lowered by one of the foe's moves or Abilities. A major advantage of these Abilities is that they can alter stats without using up any turns, unlike stat-altering moves.

Merits of stat-altering Abilities

Intimidate Ability activates

Staraptor → Intimidate → Bonsly — Lowers Attack

Intimidate lowers the foe's Attack by 1 when the user enters battle.

Examples of of stat-altering Abilities

Ability	Effect	Pokémon that can learn
Intimidate	Lowers foe's Attack by 1 when user enters battle	Staraptor, Gyarados, etc.
Anger Point	Raises user's Attack to maximum if hit by a critical hit	Primeape, Tauros, etc.
Hyper Cutter	Keeps Attack from being lowered	Kingler, Crawdaunt, etc.
Speed Boost	Raises Speed by 1 every turn	Yanmega, Ninjask, etc.
Unburden	Doubles Speed if user loses its held item	Drifloon, Drifblim
Clear Body	Keeps stats from being lowered by the foe's moves	Tentacruel, Metagross, etc.
White Smoke	Keeps stats from being lowered by the foe's moves	Torkoal
Keen Eye	Keeps Accuracy from being lowered	Noctowl, Chatot, etc.
Huge Power	Raises user's Attack (Attack is halved if the Ability becomes nullified)	Azurill, Marill, Azumarill
Unaware	Stats cannot be altered by foe	Bidoof, Bibarel
Rivalry	Raises Attack when facing a foe with the same Nature, lowers it when facing one with a different Nature	Nidoqueen, Luxray, etc.
Hustle	Attack is increased by 50%, Accuracy is decreased by 20%	Remoraid, Delibird, etc.
Plus	Sp. Attack is increased by 50% if there is a Pokémon on the battlefield with the Ability Minus	Plusle
Minus	Sp. Attack is increased by 50% if there is a Pokémon on the battlefield with the Ability Plus	Minun
Pure Power	Makes user's Attack high (Attack is halved if the Ability becomes nullified)	Meditite, Medicham

Ability Technique 5 — Abilities that activate when Pokémon are switched

Some Abilities come into effect only when Pokémon are switching in or out of battle. An example is Wobbuffet and Wynaut's Ability Shadow Tag, which prevents opponents from switching out. Switching Pokémon out of battle is a basic Pokémon strategy, so these Abilities can really throw a wrench into your foe's plans.

Merits of Pokémon-switching Abilities

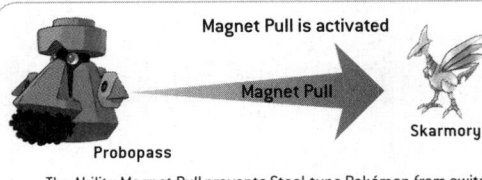

Magnet Pull is activated

Probopass → Magnet Pull → Skarmory ✕ Cannot switch out

The Ability Magnet Pull prevents Steel-type Pokémon from switching out.

Examples of Pokémon-switching Abilities

Ability	Effect	Pokémon that can learn
Arena Trap	Prevents foe from fleeing or switching out (no effect against Flying-type Pokémon or those with the Ability Levitate)	Diglett, Dugtrio, Trapinch
Shadow Tag	Prevents foe from fleeing or switching out (no effect if both Pokémon have Shadow Tag)	Wynaut, Wobbuffet
Suction Cups	Immune to Pokémon-switching moves like Whirlwind and Roar	Octillery, Cradily, etc.
Magnet Pull	Prevents Steel-type Pokémon from fleeing or switching out	Magnezone, Probopass, etc.

Pokémon Battle Seminar

4

Send Out Powerful Pokémon

Combine moves, Abilities, and items for a winning strategy

Succeed in battle by using Pokémon moves, Abilities, and items together in a way that enhances their overall effectiveness—also known as a combo.

Combo 1 — Choose Pokémon with high stats

Ability	+	Move	+	Item
Sniper		Cross Poison		Scope Lens

Try using this combo, which makes it easier for you to score critical hits on your enemies. Cross Poison is a move with a high critical hit rate, Scope Lens raises a Pokémon's critical hit rate, and Sniper raises the damage inflicted in a critical hit. Critical hits usually deal twice the normal amount of damage, but this combo is sure to do much more. There are other variations of this strategy, like using other moves with high critical hit rates like Farfetch'd's Slash.

Pokémon that can use this combo	Skorupi, Drapion

Drapion
POISON · DARK
Abilities
• Battle Armor
• Sniper

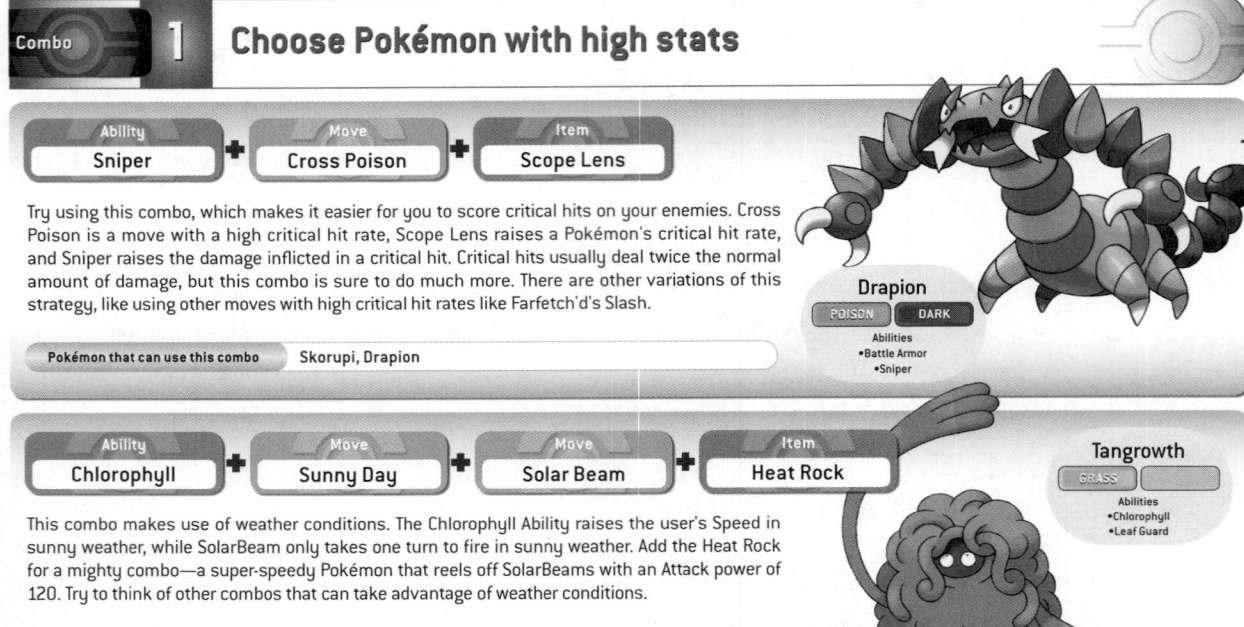

Ability	+	Move	+	Move	+	Item
Chlorophyll		Sunny Day		Solar Beam		Heat Rock

This combo makes use of weather conditions. The Chlorophyll Ability raises the user's Speed in sunny weather, while SolarBeam only takes one turn to fire in sunny weather. Add the Heat Rock for a mighty combo—a super-speedy Pokémon that reels off SolarBeams with an Attack power of 120. Try to think of other combos that can take advantage of weather conditions.

Pokémon that can use this combo	Exeggcutor, Bellossom, Tropius, Tangrowth, Cherubi, etc.

Tangrowth
GRASS
Abilities
• Chlorophyll
• Leaf Guard

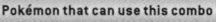

Move	+	Move
Endure		Reversal

Reversal is a move whose attack power is higher the lower the user's HP. Combine it with Endure, which stops HP loss at 1 HP, and it can deal a great amount of damage.

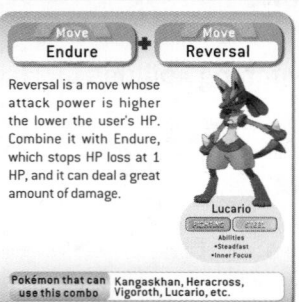

Lucario
FIGHTING · STEEL
Abilities
• Steadfast
• Inner Focus

Pokémon that can use this combo	Kangaskhan, Heracross, Vigoroth, Lucario, etc.

Move	+	Move
Defense Curl		Rollout

Rollout is a move that attacks over 5 turns, increasing in power with each strike. If you use Defense Curl first, it doubles Rollout's attack power. Rollout can also power up Ice Ball.

Lickilicky
NORMAL
Abilities
• Own Tempo
• Oblivious

Pokémon that can use this combo	Graveler, Bibarel, Munchlax, Lickilicky, etc.

Ability	+	Item
Guts		Flame Orb

The Flame Orb inflicts the burn condition on the Pokémon holding it, which usually lowers their Attack. However, the Ability Guts increases Attack 1.5x, so combining the two allows you to ignore the ill effects of the Flame Orb while enjoying its powerful attacks.

Heracross
BUG · FIGHTING
Abilities
• Swarm
• Guts

Pokémon that can use this combo	Raticate, Heracross, Ursaring, Swellow, etc.

Ability	+	Item
Poison Heal		Toxic Orb

The Poison Heal Ability restores HP every turn that its user is poisoned. Combine this with the Toxic Orb, which badly poisons the Pokémon holding it, to create a healing combo. What's really great is that you can heal your Pokémon without using berries or moves.

Breloom
GRASS · FIGHTING
Abilities
• Effect Spore
• Poison Heal

Pokémon that can use this combo	Shroomish, Breloom

Move	+	Item
Sleep		Chesto Berry

The Sleep move completely restores its user's HP, but the user falls asleep. So give your Pokémon a Chesto Berry to hold before battle. That way, when the Pokémon uses Sleep, it eats the berry at the end of its current turn, and is awake and ready to battle next turn.

Snorlax
NORMAL
Abilities
• Immunity
• Thick Fat

Pokémon that can use this combo	Snorlax, Ursaring, Wailmer, Walrein, etc.

Move	+	Move
Hypnosis		Dream Eater

Put your opponent to sleep with Hypnosis, then hit them with Dream Eater, which inflicts damage on sleeping opponents, all the while absorbing HP equal to half the damage dealt.

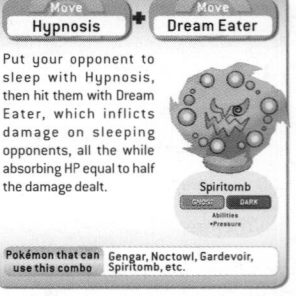

Spiritomb
GHOST · DARK
Abilities
• Pressure

Pokémon that can use this combo	Gengar, Noctowl, Gardevoir, Spiritomb, etc.

Ability	+	Move
Mold Breaker		Earthquake

Mold Breaker allows its user to act without being affected by the foe's Abilities. For example, if the foe has Levitate, Earthquake and Dig will still connect. Use Earthquake against an opponent that never counted on getting hit by it, slamming it hard with an attack power of 100.

Rampardos
ROCK
Abilities
• Mold Breaker

Pokémon that can use this combo	Pinsir, Cranidos, Rampardos

Ability	+	Move
Rock Head		Double-Edge

The move Double-Edge has an attack power of 120, but the user takes recoil damage. So it's best utilized by a Pokémon with the Ability Rock Head, which nullifies recoil damage. This lets you freely use Double-Edge without worry.

Marowak
GROUND
Abilities
• Rock Head
• Lightningrod

Pokémon that can use this combo	Marowak, Sudowoodo, Steelix, Aggron, etc.

Ability		Move
No Guard	+	**DynamicPunch**

With the Ability No Guard, all of your moves and your opponent's moves will strike their targets. The move DynamicPunch only has an Accuracy of 50%, but it also has an attack power of 100 and a 100% chance of confusing the foe. Don't hesitate to use it when No Guard is in play.

Machamp
FIGHTING
Abilities
•Guts
•No Guard

| Pokémon that can use this combo | Machop, Machoke, Machamp |

Move		Item
Air Strike	+	**King's Rock**

Air Strike is a move with a 30% chance of causing its target to flinch. Increase that chance by having your Pokémon hold the King's Rock, which can cause an opponent to flinch, and using a Pokémon like Togekiss is even better—its Ability, Serene Grace, makes it more likely that move side effects (like making a foe flinch) will activate.

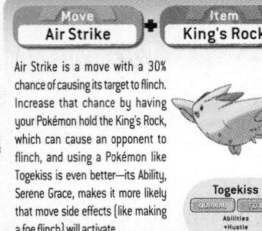

Togekiss
NORMAL FLYING
Abilities
•Hustle
•Serene Grace

| Pokémon that can use this combo | Scyther, Mothim, Togekiss, Yanmega, etc. |

Move		Item
Fury Cutter	+	**Metronome**

The Metronome is an item that raises the strength of a move used more than once in a row. Have your Pokémon hold it while using Fury Cutter—a move that doubles its strength with every hit. Using this combo, your power increases every turn.

Kricketune
BUG
Abilities
•Swarm

| Pokémon that can use this combo | Scyther, Kricketune, Vespiquen, Gallade, etc. |

Move		Move
Screech	+	**Confuse Ray**

Use Screech to lower the foe's Defense, and then confuse Ray to confuse it. This tactic maximizes the damage that the confused opponent will do to itself. You might not be attacking the foe directly, but it's just as effective at lowering their HP.

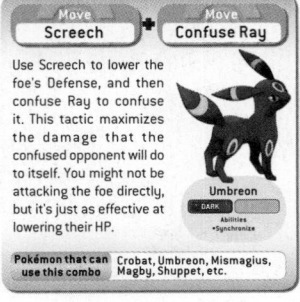

Umbreon
DARK
Abilities
•Synchronize

| Pokémon that can use this combo | Crobat, Umbreon, Mismagius, Magby, Shuppet, etc. |

Combo 2 — **Examples of Double Battle combos**

Type		Move
Ghost	+	**Explosion**

The move Explosion attacks all of the other Pokémon on the field, injuring your ally Pokémon in a Double Battle. Since it's a Normal-type move, Ghost-types won't be hurt by it, so try and play that into a combo.

Drifblim
GHOST FLYING
Abilities
•Aftermath
•Unburden

Skuntank
POISON DARK
Abilities
•Stench
•Aftermath

| Pokémon that can use this combo | Drifblim (Ghost-type) and Skuntank (Explosion), etc. |

Type		Move
Flying	+	**Earthquake**

The move Earthquake attacks all of the other Pokémon on the field, injuring your ally Pokémon in a Double Battle. Ground-type moves don't effect Flying-type Pokémon, so partner with a Flying-type, and you'll only hit foes with Earthquake.

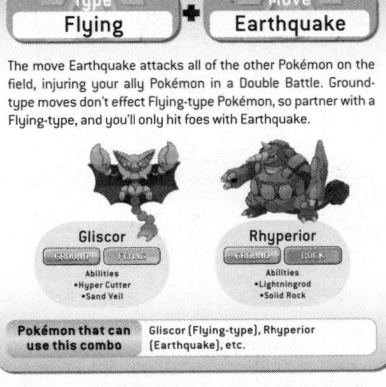

Gliscor
GROUND FLYING
Abilities
•Hyper Cutter
•Sand Veil

Rhyperior
GROUND ROCK
Abilities
•Lightningrod
•Solid Rock

| Pokémon that can use this combo | Gliscor (Flying-type), Rhyperior (Earthquake), etc. |

Ability		Move
Own Tempo	+	**Swagger**

A Pokémon with the Ability Own Tempo cannot become confused, so try using Swagger on an ally that has Own Tempo—this move confuses its target while raising their Attack by 2. Your partner will only benefit.

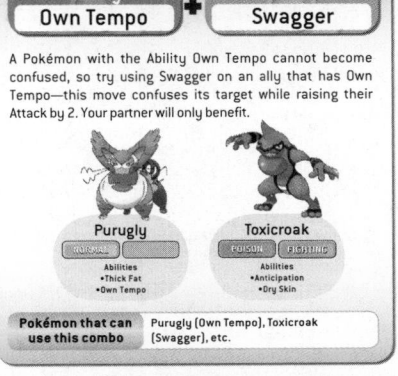

Purugly
NORMAL
Abilities
•Thick Fat
•Own Tempo

Toxicroak
POISON FIGHTING
Abilities
•Anticipation
•Dry Skin

| Pokémon that can use this combo | Purugly (Own Tempo), Toxicroak (Swagger), etc. |

Ability		Move
Volt Absorb	+	**Discharge**

Discharge will hit all of the other Pokémon on the field, injuring your ally in a Double Battle—unless they have Volt Absorb. Volt Absorb heals HP, so you'll be helping your ally while hurting your opponents.

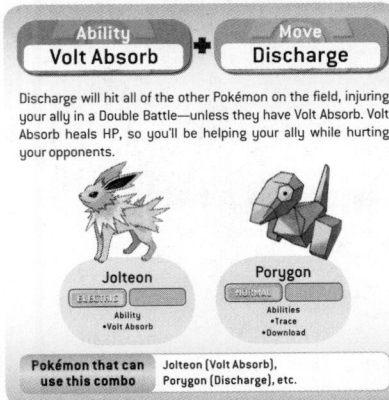

Jolteon
ELECTRIC
Ability
•Volt Absorb

Porygon
NORMAL
Abilities
•Trace
•Download

| Pokémon that can use this combo | Jolteon (Volt Absorb), Porygon (Discharge), etc. |

Ability		Move
Truant	+	**Skill Swap**

Slakoth and Slaking's Ability, Truant, makes it so that they can only act every other turn. Overcome this problem by using the Ability-switching move Skill Swap to let them escape Truant's harmful effects.

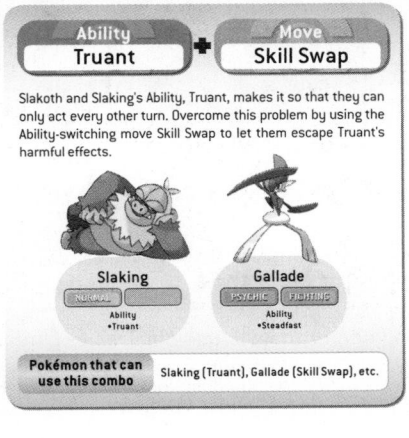

Slaking
NORMAL
Ability
•Truant

Gallade
PSYCHIC FIGHTING
Ability
•Steadfast

| Pokémon that can use this combo | Slaking (Truant), Gallade (Skill Swap), etc. |

Move		Move
Mean Look	+	**Perish Song**

The move Perish Song knocks out all of the Pokémon in battle after 3 turns. This effect is lost when Pokémon switch out of battle, so hit them with Mean Look to prevent them from fleeing.

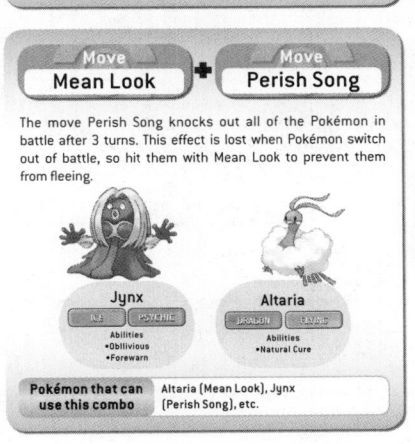

Jynx
ICE PSYCHIC
Abilities
•Oblivious
•Forewarn

Altaria
DRAGON FLYING
Abilities
•Natural Cure

| Pokémon that can use this combo | Altaria (Mean Look), Jynx (Perish Song), etc. |

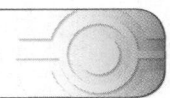

Level up your Trainer Card

Your Trainer Card levels up as you complete major goals, like defeating the Pokémon League, entering the Hall of Fame, and upgrading to the National Pokédex. When the card levels up, its color changes and another star is added to the upper right.

The 6 levels of your Trainer Card

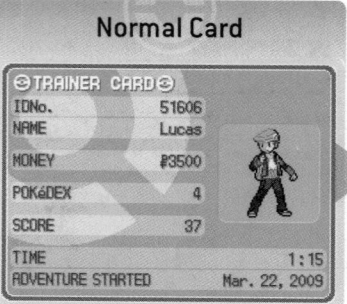

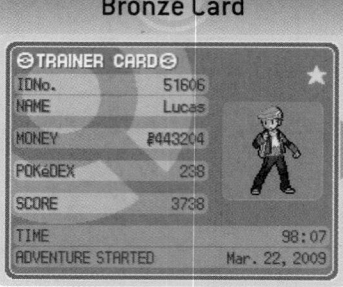

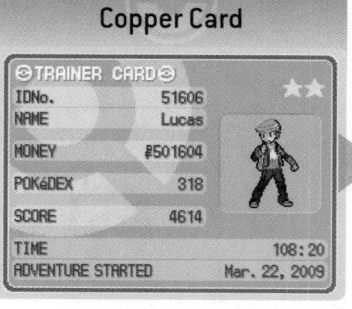

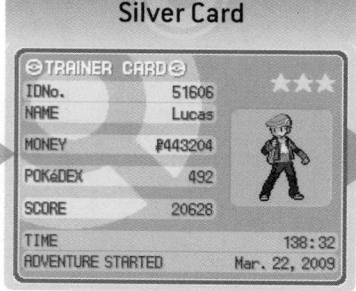

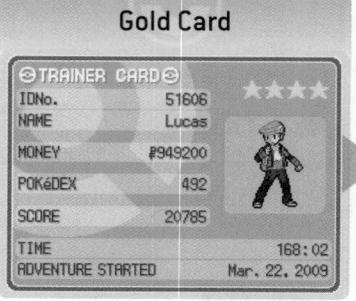

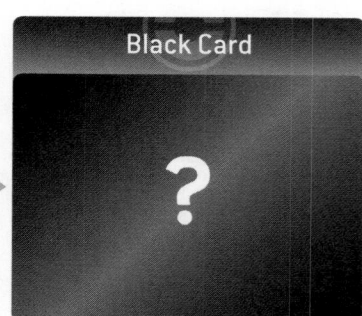

Achieve certain goals to level up your Trainer Card

Below are the 5 goals you have to fulfill in order to level up your Trainer Card. Complete them in any order you wish. When you achieve every last challenge in Pokémon Platinum, you will receive the Black Card.

• Conditions for leveling up your Trainer Card

1 Enter the Hall of Fame

2 Complete the National Pokédex

3 Earn the Platinum Flag in the Underground

4 Win one Contest at Master Rank

5 Win 100 battles at the Battle Tower

Take your Trainer Card through the colors as you achieve your biggest goals!

Battle Frontier Walkthrough

Welcome to the Battle Frontier

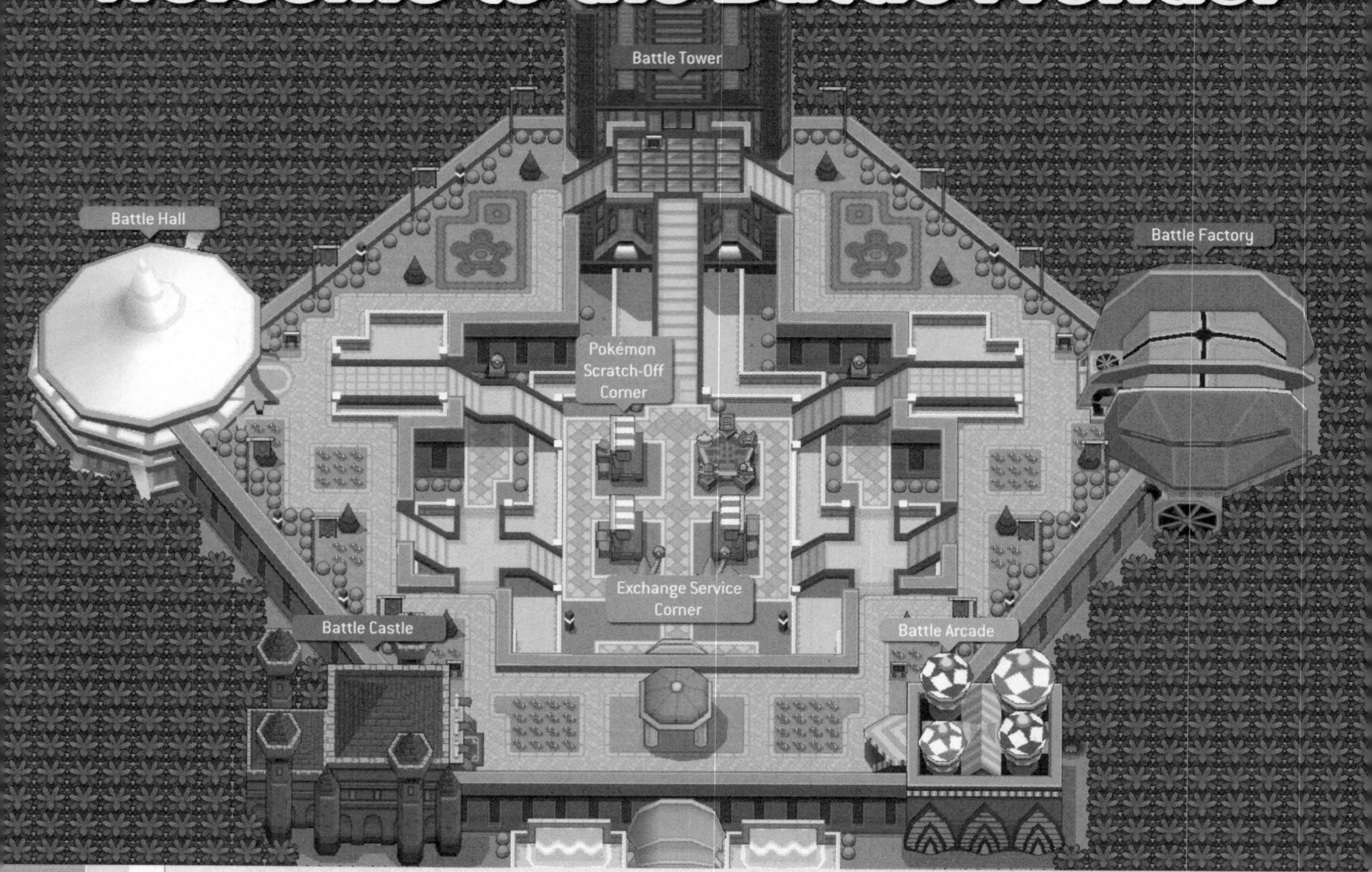

Battle Tower

Battle Hall

Battle Factory

Pokémon Scratch-Off Corner

Exchange Service Corner

Battle Castle

Battle Arcade

Have fun at five different battle facilities

Battle Frontier is home to five facilities devoted to the art of Pokémon battling—start at any one you like. Defeat the Frontier Brains to receive commemorative prints—a Silver Print for your first win, and a Gold Print for your second.

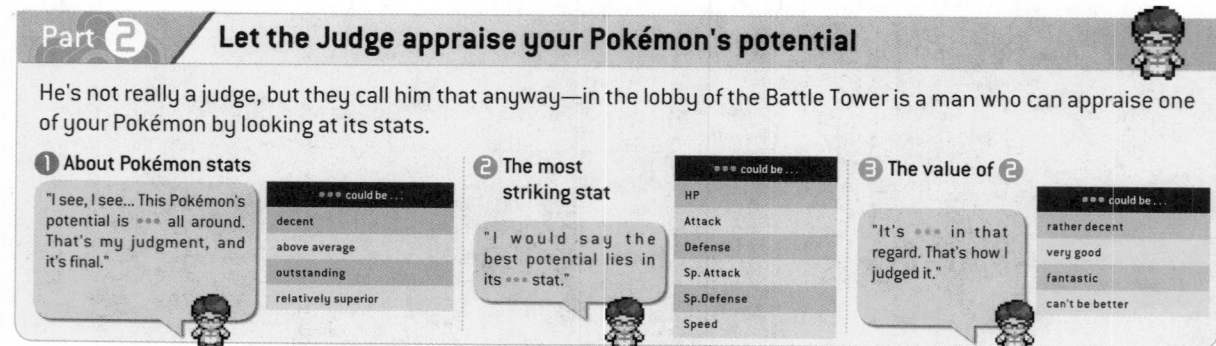

Part 2	Let the Judge appraise your Pokémon's potential

He's not really a judge, but they call him that anyway—in the lobby of the Battle Tower is a man who can appraise one of your Pokémon by looking at its stats.

1 About Pokémon stats

"I see, I see... This Pokémon's potential is ••• all around. That's my judgment, and it's final."

••• could be . . .
decent
above average
outstanding
relatively superior

2 The most striking stat

"I would say the best potential lies in its ••• stat."

••• could be . . .
HP
Attack
Defense
Sp. Attack
Sp.Defense
Speed

3 The value of 2

"It's ••• in that regard. That's how I judged it."

••• could be . . .
rather decent
very good
fantastic
can't be better

Part ① Save up BP to get items

Defeat the Pokémon Trainers and Frontier Brains at each facility to receive Battle Points (BP). You can use BP inside the Battle Frontier to pay for useful items and TMs. Use them to refine your Pokémon's skills and continue your trip through the Battle Frontier.

Prizes at the left counter	BP		Prizes at the left counter	BP		Prizes at the left counter	BP
Protein	1BP		White Herb	32BP		TM61 Will-O-Wisp	32BP
Calcium	1BP		Power Herb	32BP		TM45 Attract	32BP
Iron	1BP		Bright Powder	48BP		TM40 Aerial Ace	40BP
Zinc	1BP		Choice Band	48BP		TM31 Brick Break	40BP
Carbos	1BP		Focus Band	48BP		TM08 Bulk Up	48BP
HP Up	1BP		Scope Lens	48BP		TM04 Calm Mind	48BP
Power Wrist	16BP		Muscle Band	48BP		TM81 X-Scissor	64BP
Power Belt	16BP		Focus Sash	48BP		TM30 Shadow Ball	64BP
Power Lens	16BP		Choice Scarf	48BP		TM53 Energy Ball	64BP
Power Band	16BP		Razor Claw	48BP		TM36 Sludge Bomb	80BP
Power Anklet	16BP		Razor Fang	48BP		TM59 Dragon Pulse	80BP
Power Weight	16BP		Rare Candy	48BP		TM71 Stone Edge	80BP
Toxic Orb	16BP		TM06 Toxic	32BP		TM26 Earthquake	80BP
Flame Orb	16BP		TM73 Thunder Wave	32BP			

Part ③ Win rare berries with a Scratch-Off Card

Pokémon Scratch-Off is a game you can play for just 1 BP. You get 3 cards—scratch off 3 silver squares on each, and if you uncover 3 of the same Pokémon, you win! The prizes include rare berries and the high-priced Nugget.

Prizes			
Nugget ×1	Pomeg Berry ×3	Kelpsy Berry ×3	Charti Berry ×3
Qualot Berry ×3	Hondew Berry ×3	Grepa Berry ×3	Colbur Berry ×3
Tamato Berry ×3	Occa Berry ×3	Passho Berry ×3	Kasib Berry ×3
Wacan Berry ×3	Rindo Berry ×3	Yache Berry ×3	Babiri Berry ×3
Chople Berry ×3	Kebia Berry ×3	Shuca Berry ×3	Haban Berry ×3
Coba Berry ×3	Payapa Berry ×3	Tanga Berry ×3	Chilan Berry ×3

* Ditto acts as a wild card.

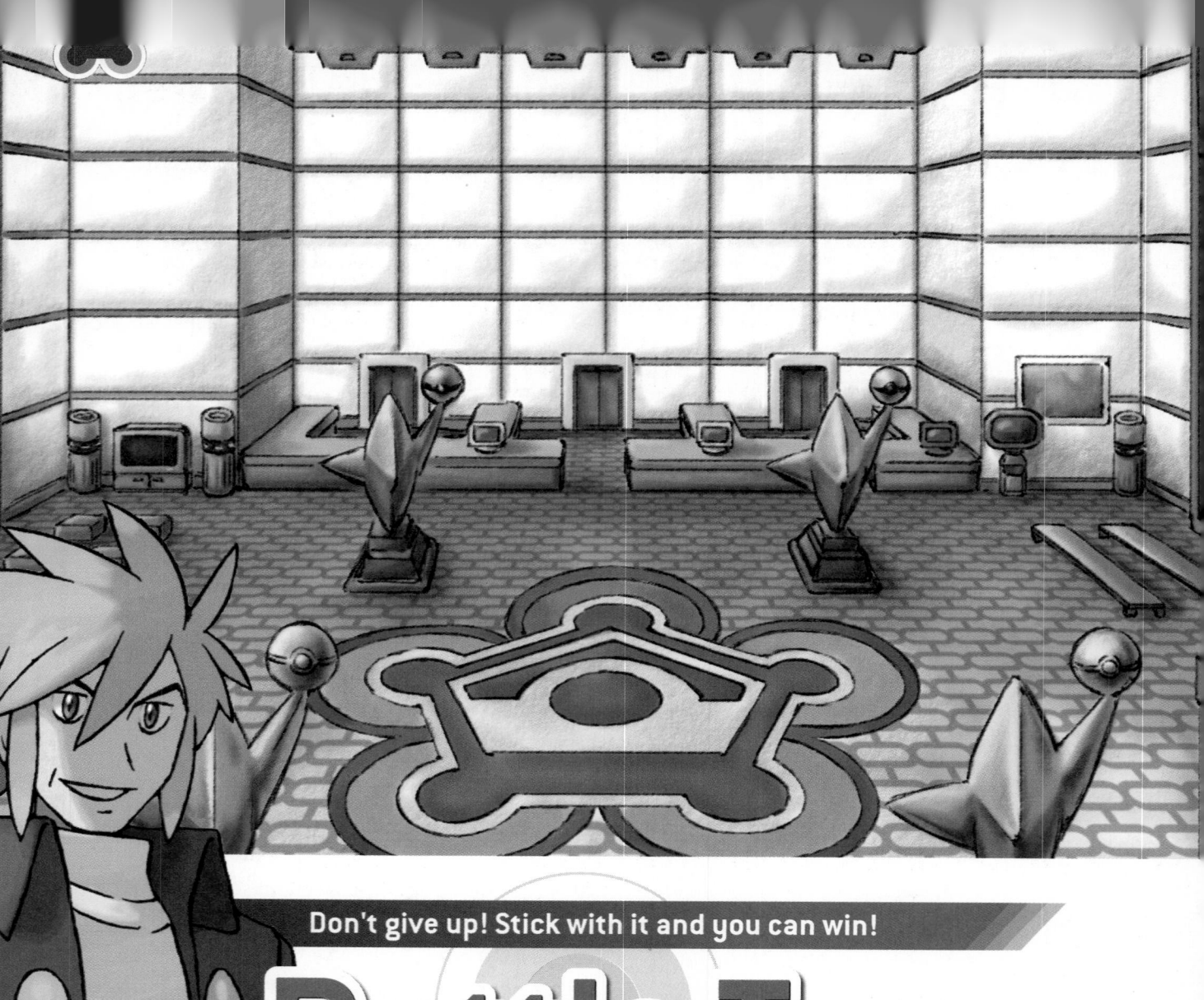

Don't give up! Stick with it and you can win!

Battle Tower

Battle Tower directory

• Forms of battle

Single Battle

Double Battle

Multi Battle (link)

Wi-Fi Battle Room

• Entry level cap

Lv 50

• BP obtainable

Normal

• No. battles in a round

7

• No. wins to get a commemorative print

Silver Print   21

Gold Print   49

• Participating Pokémon

Single Battle   3 (all different kinds)

Double Battle   4 (all different kinds)

Item   All different held items

• Pokémon that cannot participate

Mewtwo, Mew, Ho-Oh, Lugia, Celebi, Kyogre, Groudon, Rayquaza, Jirachi, Deoxys, Dialga, Palkia, Giratina, Phione, Manaphy, Darkrai, Shaymin, Pokémon Eggs

Build your consecutive win record

The most normal battles in the Battle Frontier are found in the Battle Tower, where you battle seven Trainers in a row, trying to increase your number of consecutive wins. Treat these as you would normal battles, with all your usual Pokémon and strategy, but being ever mindful of the increasing strength of your opponents.

I put this team together with my Internet buddies. It took us all day!

Battle Tower features 1 — Pokémon become stronger the more rounds you go

The difficulty of battles here is based on how many rounds you've endured—the first round features fast opponents, the second round has Pokémon holding items, and starting in the third round they begin to use clever combos. Figure out their methods and tricks now so you can keep up as the opponents become more difficult.

• Enemy Pokémon based on round number

Round 1

Small, fast Pokémon

Pachirisu — ELECTRIC
Buneary — NORMAL
Staryu — WATER
Elekid — ELECTRIC

Round 2

Holding items for a boost

Chansey — NORMAL — Sitrus Berry
Bellossom — GRASS — Petaya Berry
Swalot — POISON — Black Sludge
Swellow — NORMAL FLYING — Toxic Orb

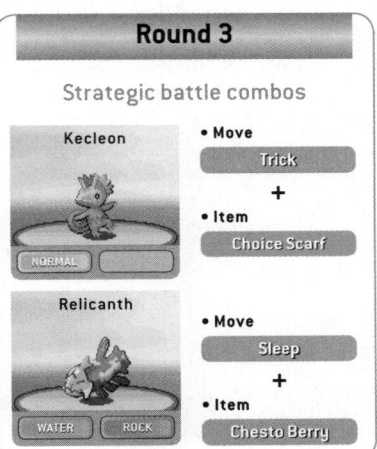

Round 3

Strategic battle combos

Kecleon — NORMAL
• Move: Trick
+
• Item: Choice Scarf

Relicanth — WATER ROCK
• Move: Sleep
+
• Item: Chesto Berry

Battle Tower features 2 — Win goods and ribbons with consecutive wins

Unlike the other facilities at the Battle Frontier, the Battle Tower awards you special goods and Ribbons for meeting certain conditions. Not only are there prizes for Single Battles, but also for winning consecutive Double Battles or Multi Battles in the Wi-Fi Battle Room (p. 169).

• Special goods

Goods	Conditions
Bronze Trophy	Win 20 consecutive Single Battles
Silver Trophy	Win 50 consecutive Single Battles
Gold Trophy	Win 100 consecutive Single Battles

• Commemorative Ribbons

Bows	Conditions
Ability Ribbon	Defeat the Tower Tycoon in Single Battle (1st time)
Great Ability Ribbon	Defeat the Tower Tycoon in Single Battle (2nd time)
Double Ability Ribbon	Win 50 consecutive Double Battles
Multi Ability Ribbon	Win 50 consecutive Multi Battles
Pair Ability Ribbon	Win 50 consecutive Multi Battles (over wireless)
World Ability Ribbon	Attain Rank 5 at the Wi-Fi Battle Room

Tips for winning at the Battle Tower | **Assemble your team**

Deciding which Pokémon to bring into the Battle Tower is extremely important, and also very difficult—you can only bring three Pokémon, and they have to be able to survive seven battles in a row. Here are four things to consider when selecting a team.

• Considerations for Pokémon to bring to the Battle Tower

Tip 1 High Speed to attack first

Select Pokémon that have a high Speed stat—if they attack first, they can inflict status conditions and lots of damage to foes before the opponent even has a chance to strike back. Having your Pokémon hold a Quick Claw is also good.

•**Examples of Pokémon with high Speed**

Xatu — PSYCHIC FLYING
Weavile — DARK ICE
Yanmega — BUG FLYING

Tip 2 A diverse set of move types

You need to be able to counter any move types that your opponents will throw at you, so make sure your Pokémon have a good variety of move types available.

•**Examples of Pokémon with a variety of move types**

Salamence — DRAGON FLYING
• Sample learned moves
Dragon Claw
Flamethrower
Earthquake
Aerial Ace

Lucario — FIGHTING STEEL
• Sample learned moves
Aura Sphere
Psychic
Dark Pulse
Shadow Ball

Tip 3 Few type weaknesses

Your opponent will try to benefit from your Pokémon's type weaknesses, so try to have as few as possible to reduce the amount of damage your team will take. You can also use the Magnet Rise move to make your Pokémon immune to Ground-type moves.

•**Examples of Pokémon with few type weaknesses**

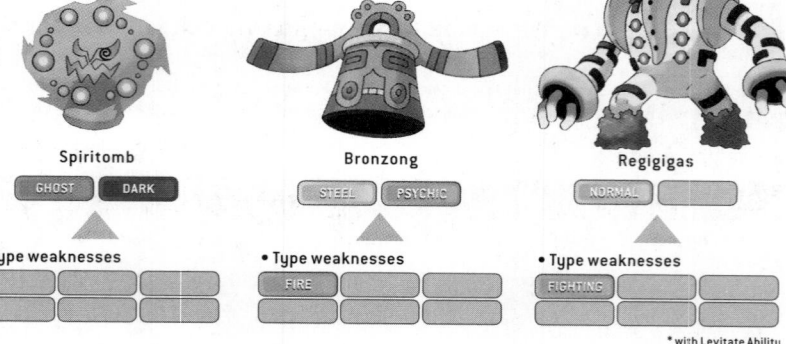

Spiritomb — GHOST DARK
Bronzong — STEEL PSYCHIC
Regigigas — NORMAL

• Type weaknesses
(Spiritomb: none)
• Type weaknesses
FIRE
• Type weaknesses
FIGHTING

* with Levitate Ability

Tip 4 Moves that inflict status conditions

Status conditions like confusion, attraction, and paralysis can easily take out the opponent and hand victory to you, so try to pick Pokémon with the appropriate moves and Abilities.

•**Examples of Pokémon with status-inflicting moves and Abilities**

Roserade — GRASS POISON
• Moves
Toxic
Swagger
• Abilities
Poison Point

Wigglytuff — NORMAL
• Moves
Sing
• Abilities
Cute Charm

Face off against Pokémon with high stats

In your 22nd battle you'll face off against Palmer and his super strong Pokémon. Not only do the Pokémon have high stats, but also great combos of items and moves. Have your Pokémon hold the Muscle Band or Choice Specs if you're having trouble with Palmer.

Charizard
FIRE / FLYING

Slowking
WATER / PSYCHIC

Flygon
GROUND / DRAGON

Abomasnow
GRASS / ICE

Mamoswine
ICE / GROUND

Probopass
ROCK / STEEL

PALMER
Tower Tycoon

Team 1 (Battle 21)

Use Grass- and Ice-type moves

Palmer's first lineup is filled with final Evolutions, with the high stats to match. Prey on their weaknesses with Grass- and Ice-type moves.

• PARTY POKÉMON

Milotic — WATER
- Surf
- ???
- Ice Beam
- Hypnosis

Effective move types: GRASS | ELECTRIC

Rhyperior — GROUND / ROCK
- ???
- Crunch
- Earthquake
- Roar

Effective move types: GRASS | WATER | ICE | FIGHTING | GROUND | STEEL

Dragonite — DRAGON / FLYING
- Dragon Claw
- Thunder Wave
- Aerial Ace
- ???

Effective move types: ICE | ROCK | DRAGON

Team 2 (Battle 49)

Fighting-type moves are key

Palmer's team is more impressive than the first, filled with some very rare and powerful Pokémon. Luckily, they're weak against Fighting-type moves, so just use moves like Close Combat and Brick Break to wipe the floor with him.

• PARTY POKÉMON

Heatran — FIRE / STEEL
- Magma Storm
- Earth Power
- Flash Cannon
- ???

Effective move types: GROUND | WATER | FIGHTING

Regigigas — NORMAL
- Crush Grip
- ???
- Earthquake
- Drain Punch

Effective move types: FIGHTING

???
- ???
- ???
- ???
- ???

Effective move types:

Fight with rental Pokémon

Battle Factory

Battle Factory directory

• Forms of battle	• Entry level limits	• No. battles in a round
Single Battle	Lv 50	7
Double Battle	Open level	• No. wins to get a commemorative print
Multi Battle (link)	• Battle Points acquired	Silver Print 21
	Lots	Gold Print 49

Swap rental Pokémon

In the Battle Factory, you're expected to rent Pokémon to battle with. To build a good team out of what's available, your extensive knowledge of types, moves, and Abilities will be prove useful. You'll only gain more knowledge as you work to win battles and advance in rank here.

Battle Factory Tip / **Choose your rental Pokémon based on your opponent**

The Battle Factory staff will hint about your opponents, feeding you information like that listed below. Use that data to decide which Pokémon you rent, and form a strategy—for example, pick a lead Pokémon with a distinct type advantage over your opponent.

• Staff hints about your opponents in Single Battle

Round	Information
1st round	Names of all 3 Pokémon
2nd round	Names of 2 of the 3 Pokémon
3rd round	Name of the lead Pokémon and one of its moves
4th round	One of the lead Pokémon's moves, but not the name of the Pokémon itself
5th round onward	The most common type on the team of 3 Pokémon.
	If no types are the same, you're told that there doesn't seem to be a type specialization.

• Staff hints about your opponent in Double and Multi Battles

Round	Information
1st round	Names of all 4 Pokémon
2nd round	Names of the 2 lead Pokémon out of the team of 4
3rd round	Names of the 2 lead Pokémon and one move from each
4th round	One of the moves from one of the 2 lead Pokémon, but not the names of the Pokémon themselves
5th round onward	The most common type on the team of 4 Pokémon.
	If it's a tie between 2 types, you're told only one of the 2 types.
	If no types are the same, you're told that there doesn't seem to be a type specialization.

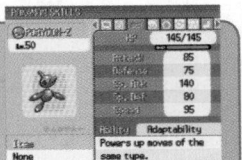

Trade often for access to strong Pokémon

To have strong Pokémon offered to you in trade at the start of a round, make sure you trade often the previous round—in rounds after that you'll be offered more powerful Pokémon.

| **Trade rental Pokémon often**

After each battle at the Battle Factory, you can trade one of your current Pokémon for one of the ones you just defeated—so pay attention to their moves, Abilities and items. Also be careful to keep your team diverse, not picking Pokémon of the same type—you might later run into an opponent they're all weak against.

• Choose Pokémon for the battles ahead

1 Note your opponent's features

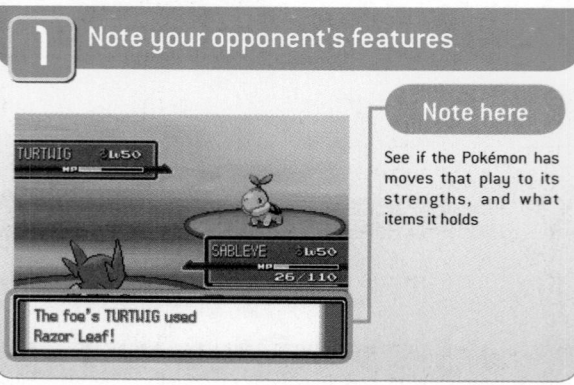

Note here

See if the Pokémon has moves that play to its strengths, and what items it holds

2 Get the scoop on your next opponent

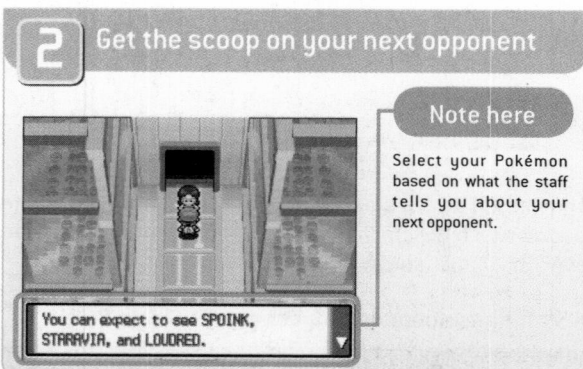

Note here

Select your Pokémon based on what the staff tells you about your next opponent.

• Examples of Pokémon choices and team roles

1 Lead Pokémon

A fast Pokémon with few weaknesses

Your Pokémon are sent out based on the order you picked them in, so your first Pokémon should be one with few type weaknesses. That way, you're less likely to have to switch the Pokémon out right away if you run into a troublesome type. It also helps to use a Pokémon with a high Speed stat, so that they get the first attack.

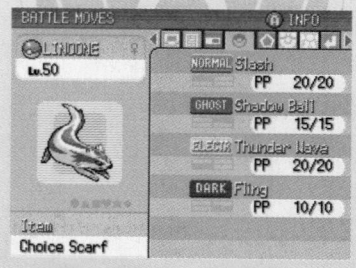

Normal-types are only weak against Fighting-type moves. Linoone has relatively high Speed.

2 Heart of the team

A Pokémon with a variety of move types

The middle Pokémon on your team should be one with a variety of move types, making it easier to exploit your opponent's weaknesses. Also try to get a Pokémon high in both Attack and Sp. Attack—if its Defense or Sp. Defense isn't up to spec, you can still chip away at the foe using auxiliary moves.

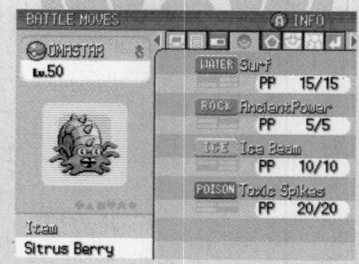

Omastar has high Sp. Attack. Have it use strong special Water- and Ice-type moves.

3 Defense Pokémon

A Pokémon that can endure a long battle

Hold down the fort using a Pokémon with high Defense or Sp. Defense. You can always switch in this Pokémon to take the brunt of attacks, chipping away at your opponent with status conditions and sure-hit moves instead of depending on high Attack power.

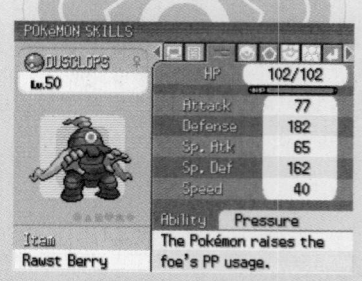

Dusclops has high Defense, and is immune to Normal- and Fighting-type moves.

Lots of powerful attacks

Once you beat Factory Head Thorton in the 21st battle, the Pokémon you face in the following battles will become even stronger—but keep in mind that also means stronger Pokémon to trade onto your team. In addition to anticipating attacks and exploiting weaknesses, making good Pokémon trades is key to increasing your win record.

Arcanine	Salamence	Dusknoir	Machamp	Starmie	Blaziken

FIRE	DRAGON · FLYING	GHOST	FIGHTING	WATER · PSYCHIC	FIRE · FIGHTING

 **Factory Head** # THORTON

1st time (21st battle)

**Trade for Pokémon
to face Thorton**

Thorton is subject to the same rules that you are—he has to use rental Pokémon too, so you don't know what Pokémon to expect. On the third round, try to trade for a team of mixed types that can stand against any opponent.

• **PARTY POKÉMON**

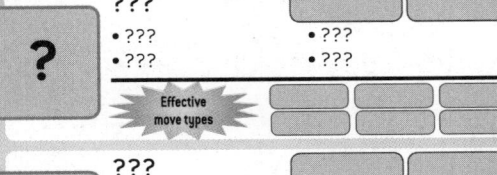

?	???		
	• ???	• ???	
	• ???	• ???	
	Effective move types		

?	???		
	• ???	• ???	
	• ???	• ???	
	Effective move types		

?	???		
	• ???	• ???	
	• ???	• ???	
	Effective move types		

2nd time (49th battle)

Trade for a winning team

You still have no idea what Pokémon Thorton will bring to the battle, so on each round just keep trading and trading—that way, by the 7th round, there should be some really strong Pokémon available for trade.

• **PARTY POKÉMON**

?	???		
	• ???	• ???	
	• ???	• ???	
	Effective move types		

?	???		
	• ???	• ???	
	• ???	• ???	
	Effective move types		

?	???		
	• ???	• ???	
	• ???	• ???	
	Effective move types		

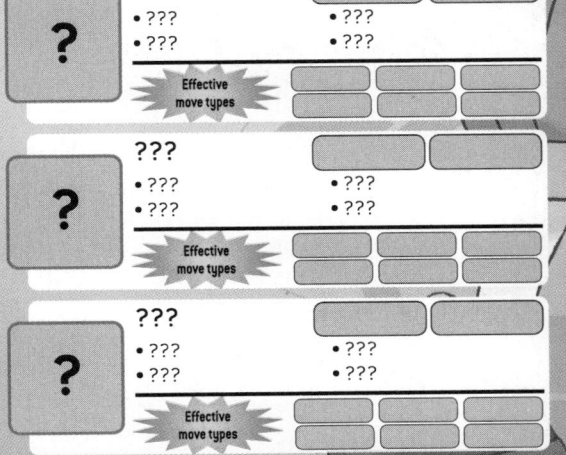

A thrilling mix of events waits for you

Battle Arcade

Battle Arcade directory

• Forms of battle	• Entry level limit	• No. battles in a round
Single Battle	Lv 50	7
Double Battle		• No. wins to get a commemorative print
Multi Battle (link)	• Battle Points to obtain	Silver Print 21
	Few	Gold Print 49

• Participating Pokémon		• Pokémon that cannot participate
Single Battle	3 (all different kinds)	Mewtwo, Mew, Ho-Oh, Lugia, Celebi, Kyogre, Groudon,
Double Battle	4 (all different kinds)	Rayquaza, Jirachi, Deoxys, Dialga, Palkia, Giratina,
Items	None	Phione, Manphy, Darkrai, Shaymin, Pokémon Eggs

The roulette affects the course of battle

Battles in the Battle Arcade are manipulated by a giant roulette that dishes out advantages and handicaps to both you and your opponent. The roulette also makes it possible for you to overcome a handicap by winning favorable Events, thus pulling off an upset victory.

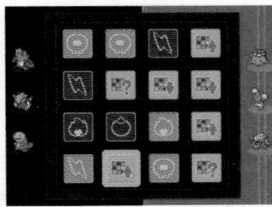

Events

Events		Target	Effect	Duration
	Lowers foe's HP	Foe	Lowers 3 Pokémon's HP by 20%*1	1 battle
	Poisons foe	Foe	Poisons 3 Pokémon*1	1 battle
	Paralyzes foe	Foe	Paralyzes 3 Pokémon*1	1 battle
	Burns foe	Foe	Burns 3 Pokémon*1	1 battle
	Puts foe to sleep	Foe	Puts one Pokémon to sleep	1 battle
	Freezes foe	Foe	Freezes one Pokémon	1 battle
	Foe gets berries	Foe	All 3 Pokémon hold the same berry*1	Entire round
	Foe gets items	Foe	All 3 Pokémon hold the same item*1	Entire round
	Foe level up	Foe	All 3 Pokémon get +3 levels*1	1 battle
	Lowers allies' HP	Ally	Lowers your 3 Pokémon's HP by 20% *1	1 battle
	Poisons allies	Ally	Poisons your 3 Pokémon*1	1 battle
	Paralyzes allies	Ally	Paralyzes your 3 Pokémon*1	1 battle
	Burns allies	Ally	Burns your 3 Pokémon*1	1 battle
	Puts ally to sleep	Ally	Puts one of your Pokémon to sleep	1 battle
	Freezes ally	Ally	Freezes one of your Pokémon	1 battle
	Allies get berries	Ally	All 3 of your Pokémon hold the same berry*1	Entire round
	Allies get items	Ally	All 3 of your Pokémon hold the same item*1	Entire round
	Ally level up	Ally	All 3 of your Pokémon get +3 levels *1	1 battle
	Sunny	—	Battle in Sunny weather	1 battle
	Rain	—	Battle in Rainy weather	1 battle
	Sandstorm	—	Battle in Sandstorm weather	1 battle
	Hail	—	Battle in Hail weather	1 battle
	Fog	—	Battle in thick fog	1 battle
	Trick Room	—	Battle in Trick Room conditions	1 battle
	Pokémon swap	—	Battle after swapping all 3 Pokémon with your foe	1 battle
	Speed Up	—	Increases the speed of subsequent roulette flashes by 1	Entire round
	Speed Down	—	Lowers the speed of subsequent roulette flashes by 1	Entire round
	Random	—	Makes subsequent roulette flashes move randomly*2	Entire round
	Get a few BP	—	Get a few BP, and move on to the next game without battling	1 battle
	No battle	—	Move on to the next game without battling	1 battle
	No Event	—	Battle with no Event	1 battle
	Get lots of BP	—	Get lots of BP, and move on to the next game without battling	1 battle

Abilities and types that nullify status condition Events

Ability/type to nullify Poison Event
Ability • Immunity
Types • Steel, Poison

Ability/type to nullify Freeze Event
Ability • Magma Armor
Types • Ice

Ability/type to nullify Burn Event
Ability • Water Veil
Types • Fire

Ability/type to nullify Sleep Event
Ability • Insomnia, Vital Spirit
Types • None

Ability/type to nullify Paralysis Event
Ability • Limber
Types • Ground

*1 Events described as affecting 3 Pokémon will affect all 4 Pokémon in the case of Wireless Multi Battles or Wi-Fi Multi Battles
*2 Speed Up and Speed Down effects are cumulative

 Tips for winning at Battle Roulette / **Control the roulette and control the battle**

If you can control the outcome of the roulette, you can control the outcome of the battle. No matter how strong your Pokémon are, bad luck at the roulette can still do you in. So learn how to control the outcome of the roulette, rather then leaving it all to chance.

• **Seven conditions for winning at roulette**

1 Know the Events

Knowing what all the possible Events are and what they look like is essential—so take a good look at the chart on page 211 before you take a spin.

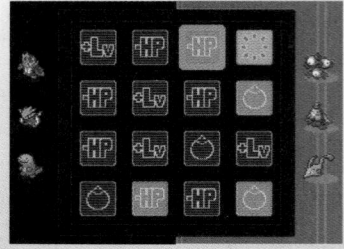

2 Develop your roulette hand

Learn how to push the button so that the roulette stops only on the Events you want it to.

3 Help your allies

Eventually you'll be able to stop the roulette on Events that benefit your entire team, really boosting your shot at victory.

Casimir's Pokémon will be loaned the Aspear Berry.

4 Handicap your foes

Play it crooked and try to handicap your opponents, hampering them with status conditions like burn or poison.

The match will commence with Jim's Pokémon paralyzed!

5 Use the weather

Some Events change the weather, which can really boost some moves and Pokémon or hurt others.

This match will be conducted under pelting hail.

6 Avoid status conditions

Use Abilities and moves to avoid status conditions brought on by Events. Try using the Pokémon mentioned on page 211.

What will EMPOLEON do?

7 Recruit Pokémon of varying types

No matter what facility you're battling at, always make sure to mix the types of Pokémon and moves on your team—too little diversity makes it easy for just one Pokémon or powerful move to take your entire team down.

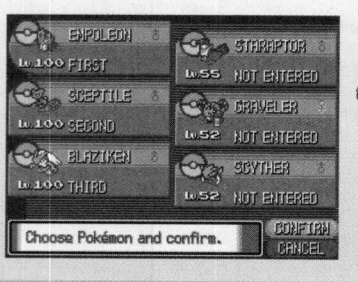

/ **Final Evolutions**

After your match with Arcade Star Dahlia, the Pokémon you face become much stronger—some of them are final evolutionary forms, with the powerful moves to match. Sometimes all you need to do to keep up is switch around your Pokémon, but if you're still having trouble beating them, you need to build up your team some more.

Feraligatr  WATER	Exploud  NORMAL	Vileplume 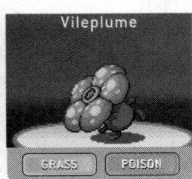 GRASS POISON	Meganium  GRASS	Gallade  PSYCHIC FIGHTING	Ursaring  NORMAL

Arcade Star

DAHLIA

1st match (21st battle)

Uniform type weakness

The Pokémon that Dahlia uses in her first match with you share common type weaknesses—Poison, Flying, and Ghost. So hit her hard with these types of moves, and you shouldn't have much difficulty—unless you get hit by the roulette, that is.

• **PARTY POKÉMON**

Ludicolo — WATER GRASS
• Waterfall
• Razor Leaf
• Drain Punch
• ???

Effective move types: POISON | FLYING | BUG

Dusknoir — GHOST
• Shadow Punch
• ???
• Will-O-Wisp
• Trick Room

Effective move types: GHOST | DARK

Medicham — FIGHTING PSYCHIC
• Zen Headbutt
• ???
• Endure
• Fake Out

Effective move types: FLYING | GHOST

2nd match (49th battle)

No uniform weakness

The second time you face Dahlia she's a little more diverse, with type weaknesses across the board and more powerful moves too. Try for an advantage on the roulette, and make you sure you come prepared with your strongest moves.

• PARTY POKÉMON

?

???
• ???
• ???
• ???
• ???

Effective move types:

Togekiss — NORMAL FLYING
• Hyper Beam
• Air Slash
• Aura Sphere
• ???

Effective move types: ELECTRIC | ICE | ROCK

Blaziken — FIRE FIGHTING
• Flare Blitz
• Superpower
• ???
• Night Slash

Effective move types: WATER | GROUND | FLYING | PSYCHIC

Battle Castle

Battle Castle directory

- **Forms of battle**

Single Battle
Double Battle
Multi Battle (link)

- **Entry level limit**

Lv 50

- **Battle Points to obtain**

Normal

- **No. battles in a round**

7

- **No. wins to get a commemorative print**

Silver Print	21
Gold Print	49

- **Participating Pokémon**

Single Battle	3 (all different kinds)
Double Battle	4 (all different kinds)
Items	None

- **Pokémon that cannot participate**

Mewtwo, Mew, Ho-Oh, Lugia, Celebi, Kyogre, Groudon, Rayquaza, Jirachi, Deoxys, Dialga, Palkia, Giratina, Phione, Manphy, Darkrai, Shaymin, Pokémon Eggs

Gain the upper hand with Castle Points

When you enter the Battle Castle, you receive 10 Castle Points (CP). Castle Points can be spent in ways that boost your team, like restoring HP or obtaining held items. You can earn more CP by accomplishing certain goals in battle—like finishing a match without taking damage or being affected by status conditions. Save up your CP, because you'll really need it in the battles to come.

Darach: Lucas, good show.
A hard-fought win, yes?

Battle Castle feature | **How to earn CP**

Check this chart to find out how you can earn CP in battle—there are certain conditions you can try to meet for more CP.

• Receiving CP

Feat	CP
# of Pokémon that have not fainted	No. x3CP
# of Pokémon with full HP	No. x3CP
# of Pokémon with more than half HP remaining	No. x2CP
# of Pokémon with less than half HP remaining	No. x1CP
# of Pokémon with no status ailments	No. x1CP

Feat	CP
You used under 5 PP total in battle	No. x8CP
You used under 10 PP total in battle	No. x6CP
You used under 15 PP total in battle	No. x4CP
# of foe's Pokémon that you gave +5 Lv	No. x7CP

• Use CP to your advantage

• CP needed to raise your rank

Kind	Rank	CP used	What you can do
Recovery	Level 1	—	Restore one Pokémon's HP
Recovery	Level 2	100CP	Restore one Pokémon's PP
Recovery	Level 3	100CP	Restore one Pokémon's HP and PP simultaneously
Item	Level 1	—	Can rent 8 kinds of berries
Item	Level 2	100CP	Can rent 8 kinds of berries and 12 kinds of items
Item	Level 3	150CP	Can rent 32 kinds of berries and 27 kinds of items
Info	Level 1	—	Can see the foe's stats, Abilities, etc.
Info	Level 2	50CP	Can see the foe's moves

• Info on foe

Action	Rank	CP used
Examine	Level 1	1CP
+5 Lv	Level 1	1CP
-5 Lv	Level 1	15CP
Strength	Level 1	2CP
Move	Level 2	5CP

• Party Recovery

Action	Rank	CP used
HP Recovery	Level 1	10CP
PP Recovery	Level 2	8CP
Full Recovery	Level 3	12CP

• Other

Action	Rounds	CP used
Pass	4 rounds	500CP

• Items you can borrow with CP

Items	Rank	CP used
Cheri Berry	Level 1	2CP
Chesto Berry	Level 1	2CP
Pecha Berry	Level 1	2CP
Rawst Berry	Level 1	2CP
Aspear Berry	Level 1	2CP
Persim Berry	Level 1	2CP
Lum Berry	Level 1	5CP
Sitrus Berry	Level 2	5CP
King's Rock	Level 2	10CP
Quick Claw	Level 2	15CP
Power Herb	Level 2	5CP
Shell Bell	Level 2	15CP
Metronome	Level 2	10CP
Light Clay	Level 2	10CP
Grip Claw	Level 3	10CP

Items	Rank	CP used
Big Root	Level 2	10CP
Toxic Orb	Level 2	10CP
Flame Orb	Level 2	10CP
Light Ball	Level 2	15CP
Thick Club	Level 2	15CP
Liechi Berry	Level 3	5CP
Ganlon Berry	Level 3	5CP
Salac Berry	Level 3	5CP
Petaya Berry	Level 3	5CP
Apicot Berry	Level 3	5CP
Lansat Berry	Level 3	5CP
Starf Berry	Level 3	5CP
Occa Berry	Level 3	5CP
Passho Berry	Level 3	5CP
Wacan Berry	Level 3	5CP

Items	Rank	CP used
Rindo Berry	Level 3	5CP
Yache Berry	Level 3	5CP
Chople Berry	Level 3	5CP
Kebia Berry	Level 3	5CP
Shuca Berry	Level 3	5CP
Coba Berry	Level 3	5CP
Papaya Berry	Level 3	5CP
Tanga Berry	Level 3	5CP
Charti Berry	Level 3	5CP
Kasib Berry	Level 3	5CP
Haban Berry	Level 3	5CP
Colbur Berry	Level 3	5CP
Babiri Berry	Level 3	5CP
Chilan Berry	Level 3	5CP
White Herb	Level 3	5CP

Items	Rank	CP used
Focus Band	Level 3	15CP
Focus Sash	Level 3	10CP
Leftovers	Level 3	20CP
Bright Powder	Level 3	20CP
Scope Lens	Level 3	20CP
Wide Lens	Level 3	20CP
Zoom Lens	Level 3	20CP
Choice Band	Level 3	20CP
Choice Specs	Level 3	20CP
Choice Scarf	Level 3	20CP
Muscle Band	Level 3	20CP
Wise Glasses	Level 3	20CP
Expert Belt	Level 3	20CP
Life Orb	Level 3	20CP

/ **Spend your CP wisely**

Castle Points lend you a huge advantage in battle by performing functions such as restoring HP and PP, giving you useful held items for your Pokémon, and even letting you know about future opponents. Spend your CP in all the right places for worry-free battling.

• How to use CP

1 Restore your Pokémon

You can restore your Pokémon's HP with CP. As you rise in rank, you'll be able to restore PP as well, or both at once.

2 Preview opponents

You can use CP to find out what Pokémon your next foe will use—and as you gain in rank, you can even see their moves.

• How to obtain CP

1 Win without taking damage

You earn lots of CP if you end the battle with lots of HP left, or unaffected by status conditions.

2 Strengthen your opponent

You can use CP to add or subtract 5 levels from your foe. Raising its level will earn you more CP after the battle.

3 Use the right moves

You don't earn as much CP if one of your Pokémon faints in battle, so choose moves that will wipe out the opponent while minimizing the damage to your own Pokémon.

Staraptor

NORMAL   FLYING

Move
•Quick Attack

4 Come in with the right moves

You can really rack up the CP if you end the battle with a lot of HP, so try to start with a diverse moveset that can handle any Pokémon. For example, if your foe has high Evasion, a sure-hit move like Shadow Punch is perfect.

Gengar

GHOST   POISON

Move
•Shadow Punch

Watch out for recovering foes

As if it isn't hard enough to damage your foe, some will use recovery moves in battle, drawing out the match and increasing the possibility of you taking damage. Enter with recovery moves and items of your own to lessen the blow.

| **Vexed by auxiliary moves**

This lineup is big on auxiliary moves—like Skuntank's Memento, which lowers your Attack and Sp. Attack, or Jynx's Lovely Kiss, which puts your Pokémon to sleep. Prepare yourself with recovery moves and held items.

Jynx	Skuntank	Kangaskhan	Nidoking	Muk	Girafarig
ICE PSYCHIC	POISON DARK	NORMAL	POISON GROUND	POISON	NORMAL PSYCHIC

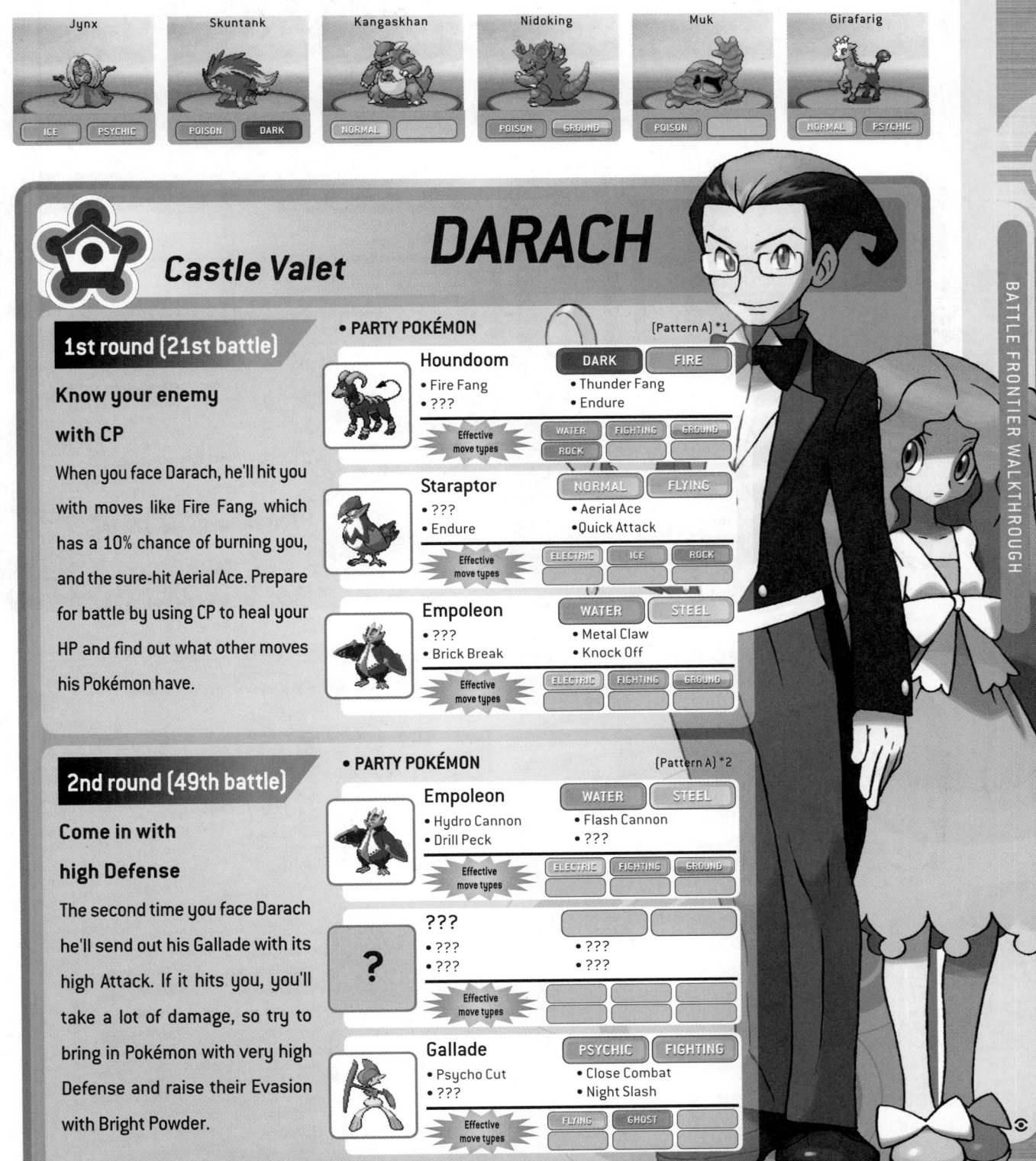

Castle Valet

DARACH

1st round (21st battle)

Know your enemy with CP

When you face Darach, he'll hit you with moves like Fire Fang, which has a 10% chance of burning you, and the sure-hit Aerial Ace. Prepare for battle by using CP to heal your HP and find out what other moves his Pokémon have.

• **PARTY POKÉMON**   [Pattern A] *1

Houndoom   DARK   FIRE
• Fire Fang   • Thunder Fang
• ???   • Endure

Effective move types: WATER FIGHTING GROUND ROCK

Staraptor   NORMAL   FLYING
• ???   • Aerial Ace
• Endure   • Quick Attack

Effective move types: ELECTRIC ICE ROCK

Empoleon   WATER   STEEL
• ???   • Metal Claw
• Brick Break   • Knock Off

Effective move types: ELECTRIC FIGHTING GROUND

2nd round (49th battle)

Come in with high Defense

The second time you face Darach he'll send out his Gallade with its high Attack. If it hits you, you'll take a lot of damage, so try to bring in Pokémon with very high Defense and raise their Evasion with Bright Powder.

• **PARTY POKÉMON**   [Pattern A] *2

Empoleon   WATER   STEEL
• Hydro Cannon   • Flash Cannon
• Drill Peck   • ???

Effective move types: ELECTRIC FIGHTING GROUND

???
• ???   • ???
• ???   • ???

Effective move types:

Gallade   PSYCHIC   FIGHTING
• Psycho Cut   • Close Combat
• ???   • Night Slash

Effective move types: FLYING GHOST

*1—In Pattern B, Houndoom has the moves Fire Fang, Crunch, Roar, and ???. Staraptor has Return, Aerial Ace, Double Team, and ???. Empoleon has ???, Aqua Jet, Shadow Claw, and Rock Slide.
*2—In Pattern B, Empoleon has the moves Surf, ???, Blizzard, and Signal Beam. Gallade has Psycho Cut, Aerial Ace, X-Scissor, and ???.

Each Pokémon tries for Number One!

Battle Hall

Battle Hall directory

- **Forms of battle**

| Single Battle |
| Double Battle |
| Multi Battle (link) |

- **Level limit**

| Lv 30—100 |

- **Obtainable BP**

| Few |

- **No. battles in a round**

| 10 |

- **No. wins to get a commemorative print**

| Silver Print | 50 |
| Gold Print | 170 |

- **Participating Pokémon**

Single Battle	1
Double Battle	2
Items	Yes

- **Pokémon that cannot participate**

Mewtwo, Mew, Ho-Oh, Lugia, Celebi, Kyogre, Groudon, Rayquaza, Jirachi, Deoxys, Dialga, Palkia, Giratina, Phione, Manaphy, Darkrai, Shaymin, Pokémon Eggs

Open to Pokémon over Lv 30

The Battle Hall is practically customized—pick the Pokémon type you want to face next, and bring in any Pokémon over Lv30 you like. So why not bring your favorite? Just keep in mind that you can't swap out Pokémon during the battle. Single Battles will be 1-on-1 while Double and Multi Battles are 2-on-2.

KINGDRA used Surf!

Battle Hall Features 1 **17 types with 10 ranks reach**

Your opponent can be chosen from any one of the 17 Pokémon types. Each type will start at Rank 1, and you can advance to Rank 2 if you win. The ranks go up to 10, with Ranks 8–10 having Pokémon of different types.

RANK 1 NORMAL	RANK 1 FIRE	RANK 1 WATER	RANK 1 ELECTRIC
RANK 1 GRASS	RANK 1 ICE	RANK 1 FIGHTING	RANK 1 POISON
RANK 1 GROUND	RANK 1 FLYING	RANK 1 PSYCHIC	RANK 1 BUG
RANK 1 ROCK	RANK 1 GHOST	RANK 1 DRAGON	RANK 1 DARK
RANK 1 STEEL	KINGDRA		RANK ???

Choose your next foe

When you win a battle, you return to the selection screen where you can choose your next opponent.

Battle Hall Features 2 **Raise your total record for more BP**

At the Battle Hall, they keep track of your total record—how many successive wins you've earned with all of your Pokémon. If your Infernape and Empoleon have both won 10 times, then your total record is 20. You earn BP based on your total record, so be sure to battle with as many Pokémon as possible.

Your total win-streak record has reached 10.

Talk to the person by the reception desk

Talk to the person with the green hat near the reception desk to learn about your total record.

• Total records to win BP

Total Record	BP received
10	1BP
30	3BP
50/100/150/200/250/300/350/400/450	5BP
500/600/700/800/900/1000	10BP
1200/1400/1600/1800	30BP
2000	50BP

* You continue to get BP in proportion to your total record even above 2000

Tips for winning at the Battle Hall / **Raising your consecutive win count**

You really need to come up with some good strategies for defeating Ranks 1–10 if you want to raise your consecutive win count. The opponent Pokémon's levels will rise accordingly with each rank, and you need to be mindful of types you're weak against, especially as the individual Pokémon are chosen randomly.

● **Tips for raising your consecutive win count**

1 Cover your weaknesses

If there's a type you're weak against, make sure your Pokémon knows moves that are super effective against that type.

2 Learn a variety of move types

Your Pokémon should have a mixture of move types with high Attack power.

3 Use held items

Every 10 wins you get to choose a held item for your Pokémon. Try to pick berries that lessen damage.

● **Recommended items**

Occa Berry	Passho Berry	Wacan Berry
Rindo Berry	Yache Berry	Chople Berry
Kebia Berry	Shuca Berry	Coba Berry
Payapa Berry	Tanga Berry	Charti Berry
Kasib Berry	Haban Berry	Colbur Berry
Babiri Berry	Chilan Berry	Lum Berry
Leftovers	Shell Bell	Bright Powder
Scope Lens	Quick Claw	King's Rock

4 Take out the tough types first

As your total record increases, the Pokémon you face increase in level. Battle the types you're weak against first, so at higher levels you have a type advantage.

RANK 1	RANK 1	RANK 1	RANK 1
NORMAL	FIRE	WATER	ELECTRIC
GRASS	ICE	FIGHTING	POISON
GROUND	FLYING	PSYCHIC	BUG
ROCK	GHOST	DRAGON	DARK
STEEL	KINGDRA		???

● **Recommended battle order**

1 Hardest type[s]

2 No type advantage on either side

3 Foe inflicts normal damage on you, and you have type-effective moves

4 Foe inflicts half damage on you, and you have no type-effective moves

5 Foe inflicts half damage on you, and you have type-effective moves

Gain fans as your total record increases

Serena

Winston

If your main character is a boy, your major fan is Serena; if you're a girl, it's Winston.

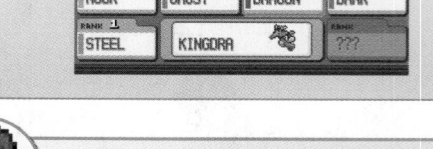

● **Fan Serena/Winston**

Found in the Hall lobby in various locations with varying dialogue.

● **Visiting fans**

You'll also get visitors cheering you on in the lobby. If your total record is over 500, you get Dawn/Lucas. Over 1000 you get Dawn/Lucas or your mother; and over 10,000 you get Dawn/Lucas, your mother, Professor Oak, or Jasmine.

Your foes rise in level

After you beat Argenta in your 50th match, opponents in Ranks 1–7 won't be that big of a deal anymore. However, Ranks 8–10 still have strong Pokémon, whose levels only increase as your total record goes up. Be sure to choose a held item every ten wins—you'll need it.

Raichu
ELECTRIC

Shiftry
GRASS | DARK

Drifblim
GHOST | FLYING

Dewgong
WATER | ICE

Primeape
FIGHTING

Sharpedo
WATER | DARK

Hall Matron

ARGENTA

1st round (50th battle)

Press your advantage

Argenta doesn't keep a set roster of Pokémon—instead, her Pokémon's type and level are based on the type and level of your own Pokémon. So try to choose a type that your moves are strong against.

• PARTY POKÉMON

2nd round (170th battle)

Save the easiest for the end

Like last time, Argenta's roster is determined by what Pokémon you bring to the battle. Save the type you're strongest against for last, because you should have super effective moves to use and your Pokémon will only take half damage or less.

• PARTY POKÉMON

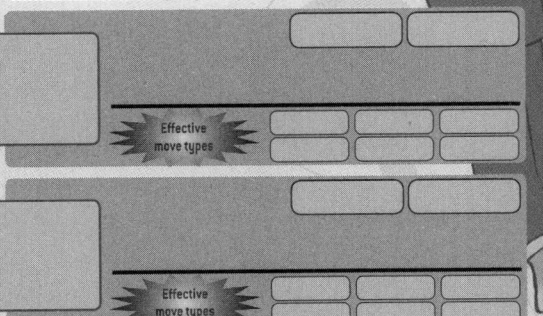

Pokémon Trainer Gallery ①

Here is part 1 of a gallery showcasing all of the different Trainers you met on your journey—seeing them must bring back memories.

Recall those Trainers who livened up your journey

 Pokemon Trainers

 Youngster	 Lass	 School Kid (boy)	 School Kid (girl)	 Camper	 Picnicker / Worker

 Reporter
 Cameraman
 Clown
 Interviewers
 Guitarist
 Pop Idol
 Poké Kid
 Aroma Lady

 Twins
 Hiker
 Battle Girl
 Bug Catcher
 Psychic (boy)
 Psychic (girl)
 PI
 Fisherman

 Beauty
 Ninja Boy
 Bird Keeper
 Biker (boy)
 Biker (girl)
 Scientist
 Collector
 Ruin Maniac

 Black Belt
 Artist
 Pokémon Breeder (male)
 Pokémon Breeder (female)
 Rancher
 Cowgirl
 Young Couple
 Roughneck

 Pokéfan (male)
 Pokéfan (female)
 Belle & Pa
 Waitress
 Watchman
 Gentleman
 Lady
 Veteran

Pokémon
Super
Contest
Guide

Take on Pokémon Contests

A test of Pokémon skills, talents, and appearance

In Hearthome City is another kind of Pokémon competition for you to take on—the Pokémon Super Contest. You will be judged over three rounds: Visual, Dance, and Acting. Four contestants compete, but only one can win the favor of the judges and crowd.

 **Contest basics 1** **Four ranks in five divisions**

There are five different Super Contest divisions—enter whichever one you want. Each division has four ranks. Any Pokémon can enter the Normal Rank Contests, but for the higher ranks a Pokémon must first win the previous rank to enter.

• Divisions and Ranks

Cool Contest	Show a Pokémon's "coolness"	Normal Rank / Great Rank / Ultra Rank / Master Rank
Beauty Contest	Show a Pokémon's "beauty"	Normal Rank / Great Rank / Ultra Rank / Master Rank
Cute Contest	Show a Pokémon's "cuteness"	Normal Rank / Great Rank / Ultra Rank / Master Rank

Smart Contest	Show a Pokémon's "smartness"	Normal Rank / Great Rank / Ultra Rank / Master Rank
Tough Contest	Show a Pokémon's "toughness"	Normal Rank / Great Rank / Ultra Rank / Master Rank

 **Contest basics 2** **Win fabulous prizes**

When you win a Contest, you also win an exclusive ribbon and Accessory according to the division and rank you won. How many will you add to your collection?

Our winner is awarded the Cool Ribbon!

• Prize Ribbons and Accessories

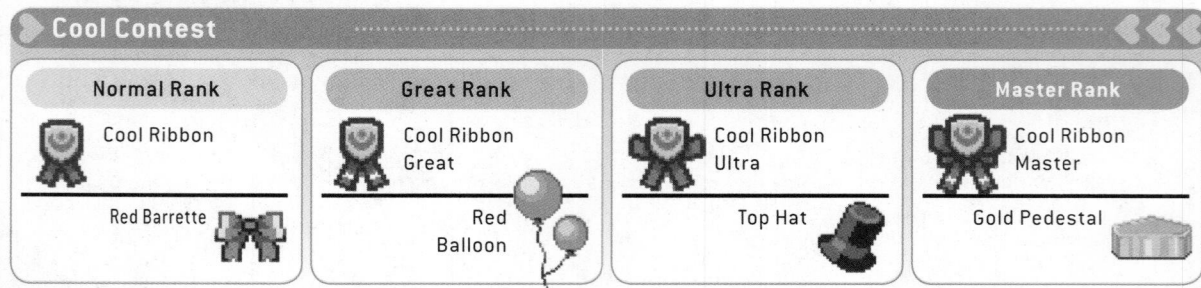

Cool Contest

Normal Rank	Great Rank	Ultra Rank	Master Rank
Cool Ribbon	Cool Ribbon Great	Cool Ribbon Ultra	Cool Ribbon Master
Red Barrette	Red Balloon	Top Hat	Gold Pedestal

Beauty Contest

Normal Rank	Great Rank	Ultra Rank	Master Rank
Beauty Ribbon	Beauty Ribbon Great	Beauty Ribbon Ultra	Beauty Ribbon Master
Blue Barrette	Blue Balloon 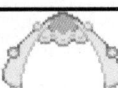	Silk Veil	Glass Stage

Cute Contest

Normal Rank	Great Rank	Ultra Rank	Master Rank
Cute Ribbon	Cute Ribbon Great	Cute Ribbon Ultra	Cute Ribbon Master
Pink Barrette	Pink Balloon	Lace Headdress 	Flower Stage

Smart Contest

Normal Rank	Great Rank	Ultra Rank	Master Rank
Genius Ribbon	Genius Ribbon Great	Genius Ribbon Ultra	Genius Ribbon Master
Green Barrette 	Green Balloon	Professor Hat 	Cube Stage

Tough Contest

Normal Rank	Great Rank	Ultra Rank	Master Rank
Power Ribbon	Power Ribbon Great	Power Ribbon Ultra	Power Ribbon Master
Yellow Barrette	Yellow Balloon 	Heroic Headband	Award Podium 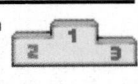

Contest basics 3 — Compete in three rounds

Super Contests take place over three rounds, each round using a different skill—Visual, Dance, and Acting. The scores from each round are combined at the end, and the highest score wins the Contest. Familiarize yourself with Contest procedures for a smooth and worry-free Contest experience.

• Pokémon Super Contest course of events

Step 1 — Choose your rank and division
Talk to the receptionist and choose the rank you want to enter, then the division.

Step 2 — Pick your contestant
Choose a qualifying Pokémon from your party to enter the Contest.

Step 3 — Round 1 - Visual

P. 226

Each of the four contestants appears before the audience, using their appearance to appeal to the crowd. Raise the Pokémon's condition before the Contest, and make sure to wear Accessories that correspond to that round's theme.

Step **4** **Round 2 - Dance**

All four contestants will line up and dance. One will take the lead while the others follow; all four Pokémon eventually have a turn as the lead dancer.

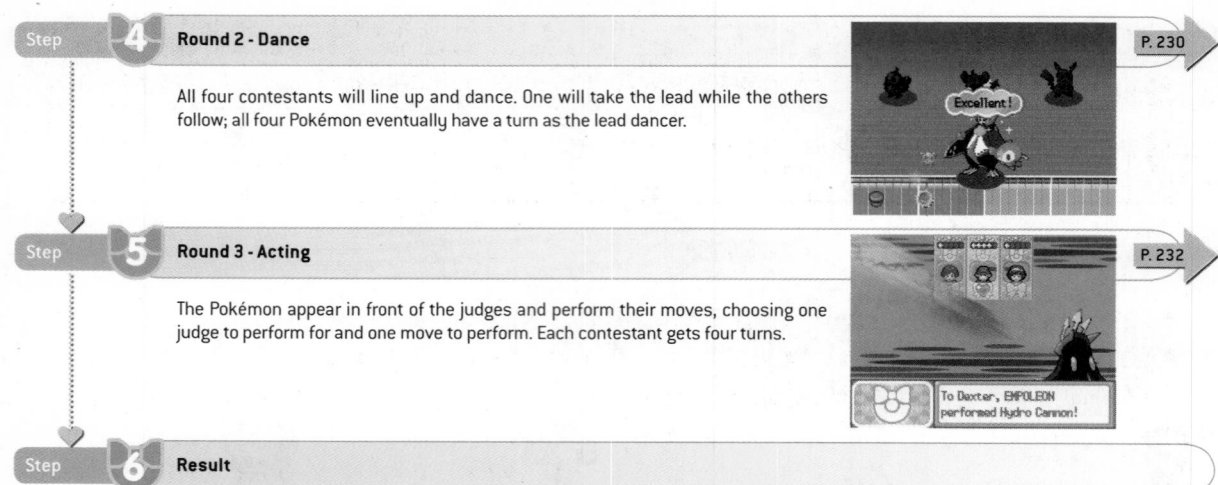

P. 230

Step **5** **Round 3 - Acting**

The Pokémon appear in front of the judges and perform their moves, choosing one judge to perform for and one move to perform. Each contestant gets four turns.

P. 232

Step **6** **Result**

At the conclusion of judging, the results are posted. The Pokémon with the highest point total is the winner.

Practice makes perfect

Talk to the receptionist on the upper right of the Contest Hall to get in a practice session. You can even practice each round separately to smooth out the rough spots before a real Contest.

Work on your weaknesses

For example, if you're having trouble with the Dance section, focus on it in practice.

First round: Visual

Get high marks in the Visual portion

Accessorize high-condition Pokémon

In the first round, the most important thing is your Pokémon's appearance. Increase its appeal by raising its condition and wearing Accessories that fit the Contest theme and dazzle the audience.

First Round Technique 1  ## Raise your Pokémon's condition with Poffin

A Pokémon's condition has five categories: Cool, Tough, Smart, Cute, and Beauty. These conditions can be raised with Poffin, but once the sheen meter at the bottom fills up, you cannot feed that Pokémon any more Poffin.

● **The link between Poffins and Condition**

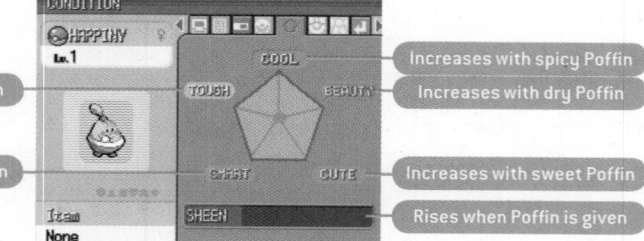

Increases with sour Poffin

Increases with bitter Poffin

Increases with spicy Poffin

Increases with dry Poffin

Increases with sweet Poffin

Rises when Poffin is given

First Round Technique 2  ## Pick Poffin flavors to suit the Contest category

Each contest division corresponds to one of the five Pokémon conditions, so focus on improving one particular condition in the Pokémon you wish to enter. If you compete in the Cool Contest, then you should be raising your Pokémon's coolness by feeding it spicy Poffin.

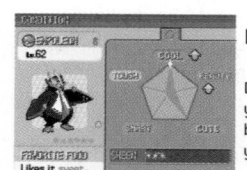

Plan ahead

Decide what division you want to enter before you start feeding your Pokémon Poffins.

• Conditions and how they affect each division

Category	Major effects	Minor effects	Effective Poffin
Cool Contest	Cool	Beauty/Tough/Sheen	Spicy
Beauty Contest	Beauty	Cuteness/Cool/Sheen	Dry
Cute Contest	Cute	Smart/Beauty/Sheen	Sweet
Smart Contest	Smart	Cuteness/Tough/Sheen	Bitter
Tough Contest	Tough	Smart/Cool/Sheen	Spicy

Learn Poffin particulars
First Round Technique 3

Poffins are snacks that raise a Pokémon's condition—how much it improves depends on how good the Poffin's flavor and richness are. Better Poffin means a better Pokémon.

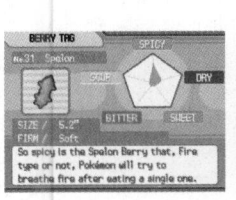 

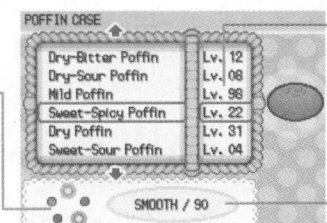

Poffin flavor

Flavors are determined by what berries are used to make the Poffin. Sometimes a Poffin has more than one flavor.

Level

Level is an indication of how rich the Poffin is—the higher the level, the richer the flavor.

Smoothness

The lower a Poffin's smoothness, the less it will fill the sheen meter, meaning you can feed your Pokémon more Poffin.

Create Poffin with berries
First Round Technique 4

Poffin is made by cooking berries. Using different berries will create different-flavored Poffin with varied richness and smoothness, so try to gather a wide variety of berries to create Poffin rich in flavor and low on smoothness.

Make Poffins at Hearthome City

You can make Poffins at the Hearthome City Poffiin House. It's bring-your-own-berries.

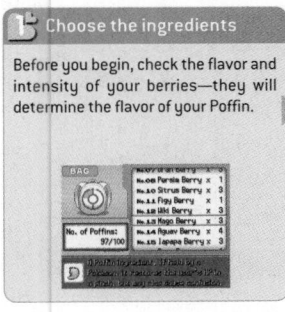

1 Choose the ingredients

Before you begin, check the flavor and intensity of your berries—they will determine the flavor of your Poffin.

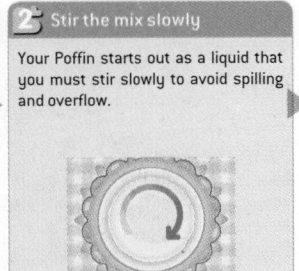

2 Stir the mix slowly

Your Poffin starts out as a liquid that you must stir slowly to avoid spilling and overflow.

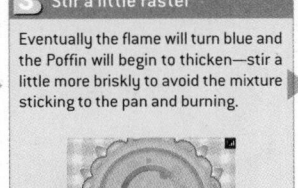 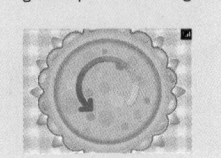

3 Stir a little faster

Eventually the flame will turn blue and the Poffin will begin to thicken—stir a little more briskly to avoid the mixture sticking to the pan and burning.

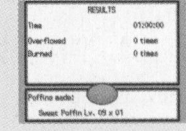

4 Ready to eat

Once finished, you will get a display with the cooking time, the kind of Poffin, its level, and the amount of times it overflowed or burned. Fewer mistakes means better Poffin.

Combine flavors to create superb Poffin
First Round Technique 5

Using the Nintendo DS Wireless Connection, you can make Poffin with friends! A variety of people means a variety of ingredients, allowing you to make higher-level Poffin. There are five different berry flavors, some of which cancel each other out. For example, Dry flavor can weaken Spicy flavor. You and your friends should coordinate with each other to avoid ruining your group Poffin.

• The flavor relationships

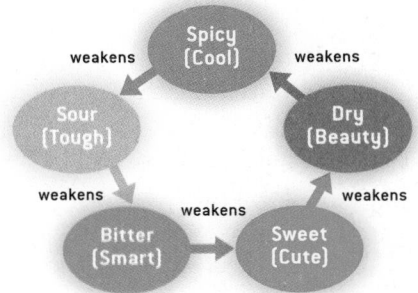

Spicy (Cool) — weakens → Sour (Tough)
Dry (Beauty) — weakens → Spicy (Cool)
Sour (Tough) — weakens → Bitter (Smart)
Bitter (Smart) — weakens → Sweet (Cute)
Sweet (Cute) — weakens → Dry (Beauty)

Make quality Poffins over the link connection

Four players can cook Poffins together, using the Nintendo DS wireless connection. Each player chooses a berry to contribute, making a high-level Poffin possible. As long as you don't mess up too much, the berry combinations below will result in a smooth level 70 Poffin. Give it a shot.

Choose "in a group" to begin

If you're using the wireless connection, select "in a group" at the Poffin House.

• Sample berry combinations for creating high-level Poffins

Strong spicy flavor

 Spelon Berry   Qualot Berry

 Figy Berry Pinap Berry

Strong dry flavor

 Pamtre Berry   Hondew Berry

 Wiki Berry   Razz Berry

Strong sweet flavor

 Watmel Berry   Grepa Berry

 Mago Berry   Bluk Berry

Strong bitter flavor

 Durin Berry   Pomeg Berry

 Aguav Berry   Nanab Berry

Strong sour flavor

 Belue Berry   Kelpsy Berry

 Iapapa Berry   Wepear Berry

Buy berries at the Veilstone Dept. Store

If you need more berries for Poffin-making, you can always buy Figy Berries, Wiki Berries, Mago Berries, Aguav Berries, and Iapapa Berries for 20 Poké each on B1F of the Veilstone Dept. Store.

First Round Technique 6 **Favorite flavors, better conditions**

Every Pokémon has their own personal preferences when it comes to Poffin, based on their Nature. Feed them what they like to make them happier and more content, which in turn raises the appropriate condition even higher.

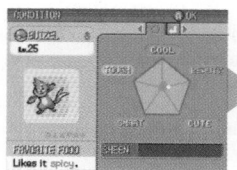
You can see a Pokémon's taste preferences on the Poffin-feeding screen or on the status screen.

Feed your Pokémon the Poffin they like so you can raise their condition higher than usual.

Nature and Poffin taste

Nature	Like	Dislike		Nature	Like	Dislike
Hardy	No preference	No preference		Naive	Sweet	Bitter
Adamant	Spicy	Dry		Hasty	Sweet	Sour
Brave	Spicy	Sweet		Calm	Bitter	Spicy
Naughty	Spicy	Bitter		Careful	Bitter	Dry
Lonely	Spicy	Sour		Sassy	Bitter	Sweet
Modest	Dry	Spicy		Quirky	No preference	No preference
Bashful	No preference	No preference		Gentle	Bitter	Sour
Quiet	Dry	Sweet		Bold	Sour	Spicy
Rash	Dry	Bitter		Impish	Sour	Dry
Mild	Dry	Sour		Relaxed	Sour	Sweet
Timid	Sweet	Spicy		Lax	Sour	Bitter
Jolly	Sweet	Dry		Docile	No preference	No preference
Serious	No preference	No preference				

Put a scarf on

There's a boy in Pastoria City giving out scarves to Pokémon with high conditions—just talk to him while you have a high condition Pokémon in the first slot on your team, and he'll hand you one of five different kinds of scarf, based on the highest condition of that Pokémon. Holding a scarf can help a Pokémon get a higher score during the Visual round of a Super Contest.

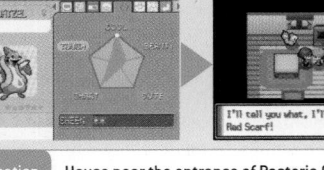
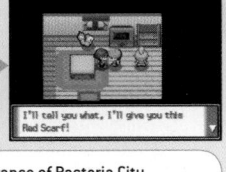

I'll tell you what, I'll give you this Red Scarf!

Location	House near the entrance of Pastoria City

Items received for high condition

Cool
• Red Scarf
Beauty
• Blue Scarf
Cute
• Pink Scarf

Smart
• Green Scarf
Tough
• Yellow Scarf

First Round Technique 7 — Dress your Pokémon in theme-appropriate Accessories

The first round is all about making your Pokémon look good, and part of that is using Accessories. There are 12 possible themes, so try to match the selected theme for a higher score from the audience.

Number of Accessories used

You can use 5 Accessories at Normal Rank, 10 at Great Rank, 15 at Ultra Rank, and 20 at Master Rank.

Accessory Case

Accessories you acquire are automatically sorted and stored here. Use your stylus to place them on your Pokémon.

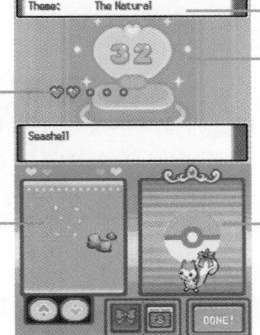

Theme

Time limit

The time limit for all ranks is 60 seconds. Place as many Accessories as you can before time is up.

Pokémon

Attach the Accessories securely to the Pokémon. If the Accessory is even a little off in its placement, it won't register as attached.

• Sample Accessories to match themes

The Colorful
• Yellow Fluff
• Pink Fluff
• Blue Scale
• Green Scale
• Red Flower
• Orange Flower
• Flag

Sharpness
• Narrow Scale
• Big Scale
• Blue Feather
• Red Feather
• Shed Horn
• Thin Mushroom
• Spring

The Natural
• White Fluff
• Brown Fluff
• Snaggy Pebble
• Shed Claw
• Thick Mushroom
• Pretty Dewdrop
• Snow Crystal

The Created
• Black Moustache
• White Moustache
• Spring
• Glitter Powder
• Googly Specs
• Black Specs
• Confetti

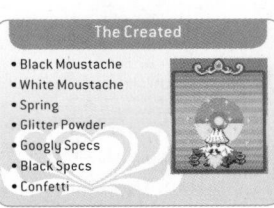

Shapely

- Round Pebble
- Jagged Boulder
- White Flower
- Pink Flower
- Turtwig Mask
- Chimchar Mask
- Piplup Mask

Intangible

- Glitter Powder
- Shimmering Fire
- Puffy Smoke
- Humming Note
- Confetti
- Spotlight
- Flag

Relaxation

- Brown Fluff
- Black Fluff
- Jagged Boulder
- Black Pebble
- Blue Scale
- Thin Scale
- Black Beard

Brightness

- Yellow Fluff
- White Fluff
- Glitter Boulder
- Big Scale
- Yellow Wing
- White Beard
- Shed Horn

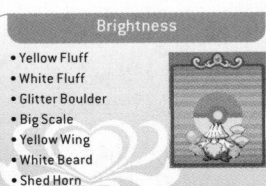

The Solid

- Jagged Boulder
- Mini Pebble
- Thin Scale
- Shed Horn
- Peculiar Spoon
- Black Specs
- Sweet Candy

Flexible

- Orange Fluff
- Black Moustache
- Small Leaf
- Pretty Dewdrop
- Sparks
- Poison Extract
- Confetti

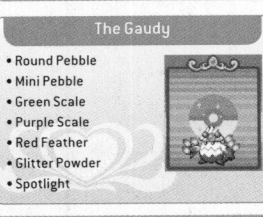

The Gaudy

- Round Pebble
- Mini Pebble
- Green Scale
- Purple Scale
- Red Feather
- Glitter Powder
- Spotlight

The Festive

- Glitter Boulder
- Pretty Dewdrop
- Snow Crystal
- Mystic Fire
- Glitter Powder
- Gorgeous Specs
- Colored Parasol

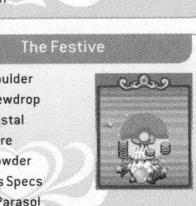

•••See p. 562 for a list of point values for themes and Accessories.•••

First Round Technique 8 — Load up on Accessories

How you do in Round 1 can depend on how many different Accessories you have on hand. Make sure you have a selection of each kind of Accessory so you are ready for any theme they select. Here are four ways to find Accessories.

• 4 ways to get Accessories

1 Amble in Amity Square

Amity Square is a lovely place in Hearthome City where you can take a walk with different kinds of Pokémon. Sometimes your Pokémon will pick up Accessories from the ground—and they all pick up a different Accessory, so take a walk with each of them to collect every possible one.

Talk to your Pokemon
Face your Pokemon and press A to accept an item that your Pokemon has picked up.

2 Keep the park clean

Head inside the ancient-looking building near the East Gate to warp to another spot in the park, where a man is busy keeping the place neat. He keeps finding items strewn about, and he doesn't mind giving them away—visit him every day for 5 berries or Accessories like the Black Pebble, Stump, and Thick Mushroom.

The man changes places every day
You'll find the man in a different spot every day, so warp around until you find him.

3 Get your Pokémon a massage

Head to the stairs north of the Game Corner of Veilstone City to find a lovely lady who will give your Pokémon one massage a day. When she does so, she gives you an Accessory that your Pokémon was holding. You can come by every day.

One massage a day
You get an Accessory no matter which Pokémon you put up for a massage.

4 Trade Berries for Accessories

At the Flower Shop in Floaroma Town, you can exchange your berries for their Accessories. But they won't just take a handful, so you'll need a lot! Bury your berries in soft soil and water them with the Sprayduck to grow a bounty of berries.

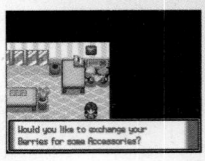

The Accessories available here are colorful flowers like the Red Flower and White Flower—what else would you expect from a flower shop?

Use mulch to increase your berries

Using some of the mulch for sale on Route 208 will make it a lot easier to grow berries.

There are 4 kinds of mulch. Pick the one with the growth property you want.

•••See p. 235 for a list of Accessories.•••

Second round: Dance — Dance for points

Move to the music

Round 2 is less about style and more about skill—you'll need to dance precisely and in rhythm with the music. As opposed to the other two rounds which rely more on preparation, this round is all about concentration. Use the castanets to tap a great performance out of your Pokémon!

Perform as a lead dancer and a backup dancer

All four contestant Pokémon will dance together, with one taking the role of lead while the other three follow along. All four Pokémon will get a shot at being the lead once in the round.

• Lead dancer vs. backup dancers

Click the castanets just like the lead dancer did

1 The lead dancer

The lead dancer steps up and starts to dance, which the other three Pokémon must imitate. As you progress in rank the lead Pokémon's dancing becomes harder and harder.

2 Backup dancers

In the role of backup dancer, you must click your castanets exactly as the lead dancer did. Their moves will be indicated on the blue bar at the lower left of the top screen. For higher points, click on the castanets at the exact same beat. To increase accuracy, memorize the location of the castanets.

Dance to the music according to your own rhythm

1 Your dancing

When dancing in the lead, your goal is to make the other Pokémon fail to follow you. To do so, you need to come up with more complicated steps that will be hard to imitate. Improvisation is your greatest ally.

2 Backup dancers

The backup dancers will dance the same dance that your lead Pokémon is doing. As you go up in rank, they will make fewer mistakes.

Be a tough act to follow

When you take the lead, you earn points when the other Pokémon screw up. You need to give them chances to make mistakes, so your dance should be as complex and difficult as possible.

Earn points for an advanced dance

You can try each of these patterns, but you should combine multiple ones for the best results.

• Sample advanced dances

 Use all four castanets

Just clicking on the same castanet over and over is too easy to follow. Use all 3 castanets—4 in the case of Ultra or Master Rank—for a more complex dance. Even if the rhythm is simple, the variation of the castanets can make things difficult for your opponents.

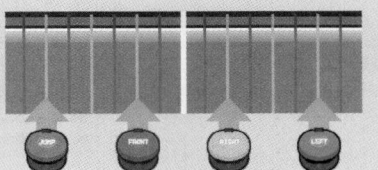

 Leave long gaps between castanet hits

At the start of your dance, click on your castanets, and then hold for a few seconds, clicking again toward the end of the music. During a long interval in clicks the other Pokémon's attention may waver, causing them to make mistakes.

Pattern 3 · Click the castanets on the dark lines

When you press the castanets on the beat, it makes a mark on the white lines and is easy to follow. Take a half step off of the beat, and place your marks on the dark lines—the other Pokémon will be likely to lose their place.

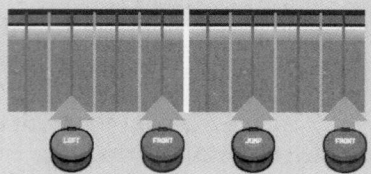

Pattern 4 · End with a blue castanet

At the start of the music, click on the blue castanets. Then click them again at the end of the music. Your Pokémon will step to the front, briefly obscuring the pink score. If the backup dancers have short memories, they will have trouble keeping up.

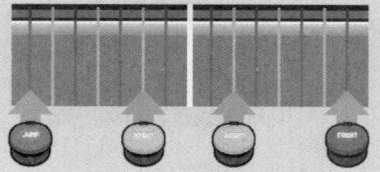

Third round: Performance · Put on a performance

Grab the judges' attention or a high score

The final round of the Super Contest is the Acting round, where your Pokémon perform battle moves for the judges. Points are indicated with hearts—the more hearts appear, the more impressed the judges are. Try to get as many as possible.

performed, Dexter's Voltage went up!

3rd Round Technique 1 · Go over the moves your Pokémon will use

Every Pokémon move has a specific effect in Contests. Before any Contest, check your Pokémon's move on the status screen to see what kind of performance it's going to give.

Four performances each! Let's see some enthusiasm!

Move effect (hearts earned)
Displays the number of hearts earned by using the move. Side effects can increase the heart count.

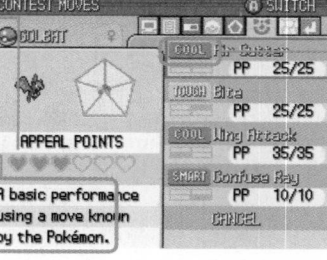

Move effects
Explains the move's side effects, if any.

Kind of move
There are 5 kinds, including Cool and Beauty.

You get 4 chances to perform

You have to perform 4 times, so make sure you have a good selection of moves available.

3rd Round Technique 2 · Choose your judge

There are three judges during the Acting round, and you have to choose one judge to perform for. If you don't choose the same judge as the other contestants, you'll have the entirety of their attention, earning you three additional hearts.

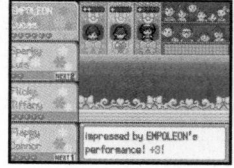

Make an impression for a big score

There's no way to know which judges the other contestants will pick, so you're lucky if you pick one the others don't.

3 Judges

Jordan

Dexter

Keira

Regular judge. Head judge. Regular judge.

Hearts awarded by the judges

Conditions	Hearts awarded
Sharing a judge with no one	Heart +3
Sharing a judge with 1 contestant	Heart +2 each
Sharing a judge with 2 contestants	Heart +1 each
Sharing a judge with 3 contestants	No hearts

3nd Round Technique 3 Raise your Voltage by matching division and move

Voltage measures the excitement in the Contest Hall, and using like-kind moves in a Contest—like Cool moves in the Cool Contest—will raise the Voltage of your judge by 1 and place a star above their head. Unfortunately, some moves can bring down the Voltage too.

Kinds of moves that raise or lower Voltage

Category	Voltage-raising moves	Voltage-lowering moves
Cool Contest	Cool	Cute/Smart
Beauty Contest	Beauty	Smart/Tough
Cute Contest	Cute	Tough/Cool
Smart Contest	Smart	Cool/Beauty
Tough Contest	Tough	Beauty/Cute

3nd Round Technique 4 Max out the Voltage for lots of hearts

If your selected judge reaches 5 Voltage during your turn, you get bonus hearts. Dexter will give you 8, while Jordan and Keira give you 5. Try to pick the judge whose Voltage is already high and get them to reach 5 Voltage as soon as possible.

Judge's Voltage reaches level 5

When the Voltage reaches level 5, the hall buzzes and stars line up above the judge's head.

Win bonus hearts

Win 8 or 5 extra hearts on top of what you earned for your performance.

Voltage bonuses

Judge	Hearts awarded
Dexter	+8
Jordan/Keira	+5

3nd Round Technique 5 Master performance moves

The moves you use in performance have many different effects. The ones with a high chance of success won't earn as many hearts, while the ones with a low chance of success earn a lot of hearts. Teach your Pokémon as many moves as possible for a diverse selection that can add up to a high score.

Sample moves and their effects

Moves that win a normal amount of hearts

These always win 3 hearts with no bonus effects.

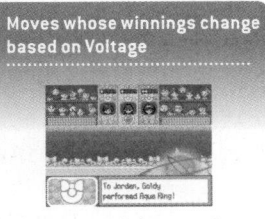

Moves whose winnings change based on Voltage

You win a different number of hearts depending on the Voltage.

Moves whose winnings vary based on order

You win a different number of hearts depending on when in the lineup you perform.

Moves whose winnings change based on special conditions

Winnings change based on things like how many Pokémon perform for a judge.

Aim for victory in all divisions

Select the best Pokémon for each division

When picking your Contest Pokémon, pay close attention to their movesets. Which moves will appeal to the judges the most? Here's a few Pokémon that have the moves to really shine in their division.

Lucas and PACHIRISU!
Congratulations!

Recommended Pokémon for the Cool Contest

Raise Chatot to Lv 33 and teach it Taunt and Roost. Taunt earns a lot of hearts when the Voltage is low, while Roost earns hearts when the Voltage is high. Choose your move based on the judge you perform for.

Chatot

- Recommended Nature

Adamant/Brave
Naughty/Lonely

- Recommended moves

| • Taunt | • Roost |
| • Peck | • Mimic |

Recommended Pokémon for the Beauty Contest

Bring Remoraid to Lv 36 without evolving it and teach it Signal Beam. This move will raise the judge's Voltage, earning you 2 additional hearts for a total of 4 during this performance.

Remoraid

- Recommended Nature

Modest/Quiet
Rash/Mild

- Recommended moves

| • Signal Beam | • Frustration |
| • BubbleBeam | • Water Gun |

Recommended Pokémon for the Cute Contest

Raise Kricketune to Lv 46 and teach it Bug Buzz. This move will earn additional hearts if you raise the Voltage. Unless your opponents use a move that prevents the Voltage from going up, you can earn 4 hearts.

Kricketune

- Recommended Nature

Timid/Jolly
Naive/Hasty

- Recommended moves

| • Bug Buzz | • Sleep Talk |
| • X-Scissor | • Sing |

Recommended Pokémon for the Smart Contest

Get Tentacool to Lv 33 without evolving it and teach it Poison Jab. Raise your judge's Voltage to earn 4 hearts—if you're the only one performing to that judge, you can get 7 hearts.

Tentacool

- Recommended Nature

Calm/Careful
Sassy/Gentle

- Recommended moves

| • Acid | • Poison Jab |
| • BubbleBeam | • Wrap |

Recommended Pokémon for the Tough Contest

Bring Geodude to Lv 39 without evolving it, and teach it Earthquake and Stone Edge. Stone Edge earns 4 hearts if the judge's Voltage goes up, while Earthquake wins 4 hearts if its the last performance in a turn.

Geodude

- Recommended Nature

Bold/Impish
Relaxed/Lax

- Recommended moves

| • Stone Edge | • Earthquake |
| • Rock Throw | • Rock Polish |

Accessory list

There are 99 kinds of Accessories

There are several ways to get Accessories. You can pick them up when walking with Pokémon in Amity Square, or exchange berries for them at Floaroma Town. Collect lots of Accessories and they'll help you advance in Contests.

Blue Scale

How to get
Walk through Amity Square with Chimchar, Monferno, Infernape, Psyduck, Buneary, or Drifloon

Blue Flower

How to get
Trade one Oran Berry at the Floaroma Flower Shop

Blue Feather

How to get
Walk through Amity Square with Psyduck, Buneary, or Drifloon

Blue Balloon

How to get
Win the Beauty Super Contest Great Rank

Red Flower

How to get
Trade one Cheri Berry at the Floaroma Flower Shop

Red Feather

How to get
Walk through Amity Square with Piplup, Prinplup, Empoleon, Pikachu, Clefairy, Pachirisu, or Happiny

Red Balloon

How to get
Win the Cool Super Contest Great Rank

Sweet Candy

How to get
Trade 10 Bluk Berries at the Floaroma Flower Shop

Big Scale

How to get
Walk through Amity Square with Chimchar, Monferno, Infernape, Pikachu, Clefairy, Pachirisu, or Happiny

Big Tree

How to get
Receive from the woman outside Eterna Forest

Big Leaf

How to get
Walk through Amity Square with Psyduck, Buneary, Drifloon, Jigglypuff, Torchic, Skitty, or Delcatty

Wealthy Coin

How to get
Trade one Cheri Berry at the Floaroma Flower Shop

Flower Stage

How to get
Win the Cute Super Contest Master Rank

Orange Flower

How to get
Trade one Rawst Berry at the Floaroma Flower Shop

Orange Fluff

How to get
Walk Chimchar, Monferno, Infernape, Pikachu, Clefairy, Pachirisu, or Happiny at Amity Square in Hearthome City

Carpet

How to get
Trade 50 Rabuta Berries at the Floaroma Flower Shop

Seashell

How to get
Get a Pokémon massage from the woman in Veilstone City

Photo Board

How to get
Trade 100 Belue Berries at the Floaroma Flower Shop

Confetti

How to get
Trade 10 Nanab Berries at the Floaroma Flower Shop

Old Umbrella

How to get
Trade 10 Pinap Berries at the Floaroma Flower Shop

Glass Stage

How to get
Win the Beauty Super Contest Master Rank

Colored Parasol

How to get
Trade 10 Wepear Berries at the Floaroma Flower Shop

Yellow Barrette

How to get
Win the Tough Super Contest Normal Rank

Yellow Flower

How to get
Trade 10 Apear Berries at the Floaroma Flower Shop

Yellow Flower

How to get
Walk through Amity Square with Piplup, Prinplup, Empoleon, Pikachu, Clefairy, Pachirisu, or Happiny

Yellow Balloon

How to get
Win the Tough Super Contest Great Rank

Yellow Fluff

How to get
Walk through Amity Square with Pikachu, Clefairy, Pachirisu, or Happiny

Silk Veil

How to get
Win the Beauty Super Contest Ultra Rank

Cube Stage

How to get
Win the Smart Super Contest Master Rank

Glitter Boulder

How to get
Walk through Amity Square with Turtwig, Grotle, Torterra, Psyduck, Buneary, or Drifloon

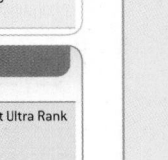

Glitter Powder

How to get ○○○
Get a Pokémon massage from the woman in Veilstone City

Stump

How to get ●●●
Walk through Amity Square with Chimchar, Monferno, or Infernape

Pretty Dewdrop

How to get ●●●
Get a Pokémon massage from the woman in Veilstone City

Gold Pedestal

How to get ●○○
Win the Cool Super Contest Master Rank

Crown

How to get ○○○
After getting the National Pokédex, insert *Pokémon FireRed* into your DS's GBA cartridge slot, and talk to the girl on 2F of Pal Park

Black Specs

How to get ●●●
Trade one Leppa Berry at the Floaroma Flower Shop

Black Moustache

How to get ●●●
Walk through Amity Square with Turtwig, Grotle, Torterra, Pikachu, Clefairy, Pachirisu, or Happiny

Black Beard

How to get ●●●
Walk through Amity Square with Piplup, Prinplup, Empoleon, Psyduck, Buneary, or Drifloon

Black Fluff

How to get ●●●
Walk through Amity Square with Jigglypuff, Torchic, Skitty, or Delcatty

Gorgeous Specs

How to get ●●●
Trade 10 Razz Berries at the Floaroma Flower Shop

Snaggy Pebble

How to get ●●●
Walk through Amity Square with Turtwig, Grotle, Torterra, Psyduck, Buneary, or Drifloon

Jagged Boulder

How to get ●●●
Walk through Amity Square with Turtwig, Grotle, Torterra, Jigglypuff, Torchic, Skitty, or Delcatty

Surfboard

How to get ●●●
Trade 10 Watmel Berries at the Floaroma Flower Shop

Top Hat

How to get ●●●
Win the Cool Super Contest Ultra Rank

White Moustache

How to get ●●●
Walk through Amity Square with Piplup, Prinplup, or Empoleon

White Flower

How to get ●●●
Trade one Pecha Berry at the Floaroma Flower Shop

White Feather

How to get ●●●
Walk through Amity Square with Chimchar, Monferno, Infernape, Psyduck, Buneary, or Drifloon

White Beard

How to get ●●●
Walk through Amity Square with Chimchar, Monferno, Infernape, Psyduck, Buneary, or Drifloon

White Fluff

How to get ●●●
Walk through Amity Square with Chimchar, Monferno, Infernape, Piplup, Prinplup, or Empoleon

Standing Mike

How to get ●○○
Trade 50 Magost Berries at the Floaroma Flower Shop

Spotlight

How to get ●○○
Trade 50 Cornn Berries at the Floaroma Flower Shop

Heroic Headband

How to get ●○○
Win the Tough Super Contest Ultra Rank

Small Leaf
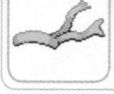
How to get ●●●
Walk through Amity Square with Chimchar, Monferno, Infernape, Pikachu, Clefairy, Pachirisu, or Happiny

Mini Pebble

How to get ●●●
Walk through Amity Square with Pikachu, Clefairy, Pachirisu, or Happiny

Brown Fluff

How to get ●●●
Walk through Amity Square with Turtwig, Grotle, Torterra, Pikachu, Clefairy, Pachirisu, or Happiny

Shed Horn

How to get ●●●
Walk through Amity Square with Turtwig, Grotle, Torterra, Jigglypuff, Torchic, Skitty, or Delcatty

Shed Claw

How to get ●●●
Walk through Amity Square with Turtwig, Grotle, Torterra, Jigglypuff, Torchic, Skitty, or Delcatty

Tiara

How to get ●●○
After getting the National Pokédex, insert *Pokémon LeafGreen* into your DS's GBA cartridge slot, and talk to the girl on 2F of Pal Park

Poison Extract

How to get ●●○
Get a Pokémon massage from the woman in Veilstone City

Turtwig Mask

How to get ●●○
Get from the young man on 2F of Jubilife TV in Jubilife City*

Retro Pipe

How to get ●●○
Trade 50 Nomel Berries at the Floaroma Flower Shop

Determination

How to get ●●○
Get a Pokémon massage from the woman in Veilstone City

Professor Hat

How to get ●●○
Win the Smart Super Contest Ultra Rank

Sparks

How to get ●●○
Get a Pokémon massage from the woman in Veilstone City

Humming Notes

How to get ●●○
Get a Pokémon massage from the woman in Veilstone City

Spring

How to get ●●○
Get a Pokémon massage from the woman in Veilstone City

*You get a mask of the Pokémon you got from Professor Rowan in the beginning of the game. After that, you can get the two remaining masks from a girl on 1F of the Veilstone Dept. Store and a girl in Pastoria City.

Shiny Powder
How to get ○○○

Get a Pokémon massage from the woman in Veilstone City

Chimchar Mask
How to get ○○○

Get from the young man on 2F of Jubilife TV in Jubilife City *

Award Podium
How to get ○○○

Win the Tough Super Contest Master Rank

Pink Scale
How to get ○○○

Walk through Amity Square with Psyduck, Buneary, Drifloon, Jigglypuff, Torchic, Skitty, or Delcatty

Pink Barrette
How to get ○○○

Win the Cute Super Contest Normal Rank

Pink Flower
How to get ○○○

Trade one Chesto Berry at the Floaroma Flower Shop

Pink Balloon
How to get ○○○

Win the Cute Super Contest Great Rank

Pink Fluff
How to get ○○○

Walk through Amity Square with Piplup, Prinplup, Empoleon, Jigglypuff, Torchic, Skitty, or Delcatty

Eerie Thing
How to get ○○○

Get a Pokémon massage from the woman in Veilstone City

Peculiar Spoon
How to get ○○○

Get a Pokémon massage from the woman in Veilstone City

Mystic Fire
How to get ○○○

Get a Pokémon massage from the woman in Veilstone City

Thick Mushroom
How to get ○○○

Walk through Amity Square with Turtwig, Grotle, or Torterra

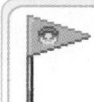
Flag
How to get ○○○

Get from the girl near the Gate on Cycling Road (Route 206)

Blue Barrette
How to get ○○○

Win the Beauty Super Contest Normal Rank

Fluffy Bed
How to get ○○○

Trade 100 Durin Berries at the Floaroma Flower Shop

Lace Headress
How to get ○○○

Win the Cute Super Contest Ultra Rank

Narrow Scale
How to get ○○○

Walk through Amity Square with Piplup, Prinplup, Empoleon, Turtwig, Grotle, or Torterra

Thin Mushroom
How to get ○○○

Walk through Amity Square with Chimchar, Monferno, Infernape, Psyduck, Buneary, or Drifloon

Narrow Leaf
How to get ○○○

Walk through Amity Square with Piplup, Prinplup, or Empoleon

Piplup Mask
How to get ○○○

Get from the young man on 2F of Jubilife TV in Jubilife City *

Red Barrette
How to get ○○○

Win the Cool Super Contest Normal Rank

Black Pebble
How to get ○○○

Walk through Amity Square with Jigglypuff, Torchic, Skitty, or Delcatty

Black Specs
How to get ○○○

Trade one Persim Berry at the Floaroma Flower Shop

Cape
How to get ○○○

Trade 100 Pamtre Berries at the Floaroma Flower Shop

Round Pebble
How to get ○○○

Walk through Amity Square with Chimchar, Monferno, Infernape, Turtwig, Grotle, or Torterra

Green Scale
How to get ○○○

Walk through Amity Square with Turtwig, Grotle, Torterra, Jigglypuff, Torchic, Skitty, or Delcatty

Green Barrette
How to get ○○○

Win the Smart Super Contest Normal Rank

Green Balloon
How to get ○○○

Win the Smart Super Contest Great Rank

Mirror Ball
How to get ○○○

Trade 100 Spelon Berries at the Floaroma Flower Shop

Purple Scale
How to get ○○○

Walk through Amity Square with Piplup, Prinplup, Empoleon, Pikachu, Clefairy, Pachirisu, or Happiny

Mystic Fire
How to get ○○○

Get a Pokémon massage from the woman in Veilstone City

Puffy Smoke
How to get ○○○

Get a Pokémon massage from the woman in Veilstone City

Snow Crystal
How to get ○○○

Get a Pokémon massage from the woman in Veilstone City

Pokémon Trainer Gallery ②

Part 2 of the Pokémon Trainer's gallery has most of the important Trainers you've met—your partners, the Gym Leaders, the Elite Four, even the Pokémon League Champion—as well as the nefarious Team Galactic.

Including your idols, the Gym Leaders and the Elite Four

Sailor

Jogger

Pokémon Ranger (male)

Pokémon Ranger (female)

Rich Boy

Lady

Ace Trainer (male)

Ace Trainer (female)

Double Team

Ace Trainer (male)

Ace Trainer (female)

Skier (male)

Skier (female)

Swimmer (male)

Swimmer (female)

Tuber (male)

Tuber (girl)

Parasol Lady

Dragon Tamer

Rival

**Gym Leaders
Elite Four
Champion**

Oreburgh Gym Leader
Roark

Eterna Gym Leader
Gardenia

Hearthome Gym Leader
Fantina

Veilstone Gym Leader
Maylene

Pastoria Gym Leader
Wake

Canalave Gym Leader
Byron

Snowpoint Gym Leader
Candice

Sunyshore Gym Leader
Volkner

Elite Four member
Aaron

Elite Four member
Bertha

Elite Four member
Flint

Elite Four member
Lucian

Pokémon League Champion
Cynthia

Partners

Cheryl

Mira

Riley

Marley

Buck

**Team
Galactic**

Team Galactic
Grunt (male)

Team Galactic
Grunt (female)

Galactic Commander
Mars

Galactic Commander
Jupiter

Galactic Commander
Saturn

Galactic Boss
Cyrus

Underground
Play Guide

Unearth fun in the Underground

A test of Pokémon skills, talents, and appearance

There's a sprawling system of tunnels underlying the Sinnoh region. You can go there and use your Nintendo DS wireless connection to participate in a plethora of games and fun activities with up to eight friends.

Three fun forms of Underground play

There are three main activities available in the Underground: fossil digging, building a secret base, and capturing an opponent's flag. Each activity can be as simple or as involved as you want it to be, and has aspects that you can play by yourself or with friends. Take a break from your main adventure to have some fun down under.

• Three Underground activities for you to experience

Dig for fossils	Make a secret base	Capture the flag
Swing your hammer and your pickaxe, and excavate treasure buried in the walls of the Underground. There's all kinds of stuff in them thar hills, including decorative goods, spheres, fossils that can be restored into Pokémon, shards you can trade to Move Tutors, and more. Dig out these treasures carefully, before the wall collapses!	Every player can make his or her own secret base in the Underground. Set out decorative goods to make your pad as rockin', or as adorable, as you like it. Collect your goods and arrange them nicely, and you'll have your own totally unique hideaway.	The object of this game is nab the flag from another player's secret base and spirit it back to your own base. If your flag is stolen, you'd better get on the heels of the one who snatched it. You can also lay traps in the passage floors to keep the thieves from getting too far.

Underground basics 1 Get the Explorer Kit from the spelunker

To travel between the Underground and the surface, you'll need the Explorer Kit. You can get it by talking to the Underground Man in Eterna City (p.65). You can use the Explorer Kit in any outdoor location in Sinnoh.

Pass the test

The Underground Man submits you to a six-part test. Pass the whole thing and you'll get a prize.

Underground basics ② The Underground underlies all of Sinnoh

The Underground is a huge, sprawling space beneath the entirety of the Sinnoh region. The radar on the top screen displays your location in the Underground, and that of any treasures. Rely on the radar and you won't get lost. Strike out and explore the Underground!

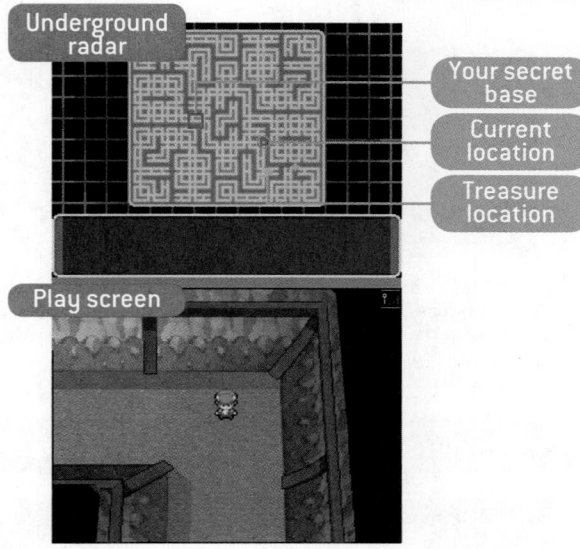

Underground radar

- Your secret base
- Current location
- Treasure location

Play screen

Underground basics ③ The touchscreen reacts when you tap it

Follow the Underground radar to the spot that was setting off the treasure reaction. Then tap the touchscreen once you're there. If there's treasure in the walls or traps in the floor, the spot will flash in response. Your radar and stylus will guide you through the fun of the Underground.

- Treasure
- Trap or buried sphere

Fossil excavation

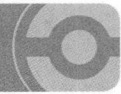

Walls of plenty

The bright spots on the walls hold a cornucopia of entombed goodies, including spheres, colored shards, and Pokémon fossils. Use your hammer and pickaxe judiciously to dig them out before the wall tumbles down.

Excercise caution while digging

The fissure meter grows as you dig at a wall. When it reaches all the way to the left, the wall crumbles. You can use your hammer as a blunt tool to excavate large areas, but it will make the fissure grow faster. The pickaxe is for more fine, precise digging, and will make the fissure grow more slowly.

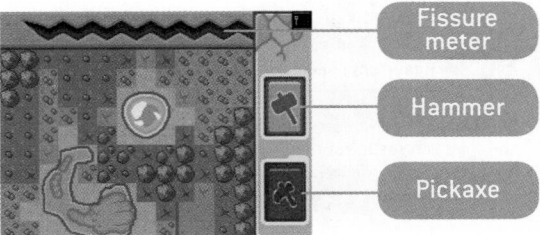

- Fissure meter
- Hammer
- Pickaxe

● Primary items found in the walls

Spheres
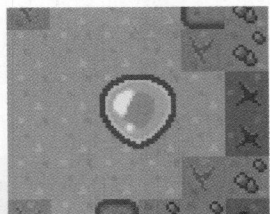
Can be traded for decorative goods. You can acquire some big ones if you dig them out before the wall crumbles.

Colored shards
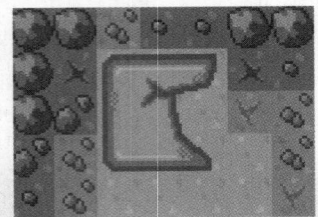
Collect a lot and trade them to any of the three Move Tutors to have them teach moves to your Pokémon.

Pokémon fossils
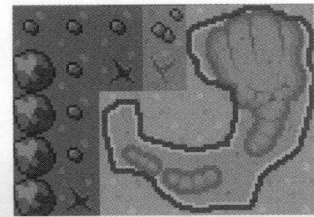
The fossil of a Pokémon that lived in ancient times. More types start appearing after you get the National Pokédex.

Evolution items
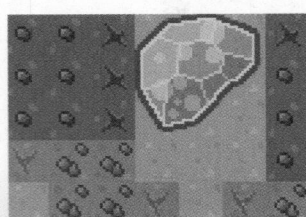
These stones, like the Water Stone, the Thunderstone, the Moon Stone, and others, can make Pokémon evolve.

Battle items
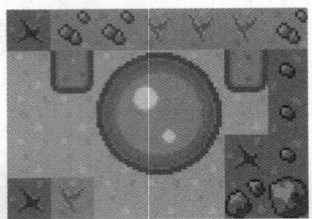
Some items you can find here, like the Iron Ball and Max Revive, can't be bought in stores.

Heart Scale

The Move Tutor in Pastoria City teaches you a move for each Heart Scale you bring him.

See p. 567 for a detailed list of buried items.

Trade excavated items for other items and Pokémon

There are certain people and places where you can bring your excavated items and get decorative goods in return, or have your fossils restored into Pokémon. Here's a representative sample.

● Places where you can trade excavated items

Spheres — **Trade spheres to guys in the Underground for traps or decorative goods**

You can bring your excavated spheres to traders in the Underground and trade them for other items. There are three kinds of these guys: one for goods, one for traps, and one for other types of loot. When you want decorative goods, find a goods guy; for traps, seek out a traps guy.

 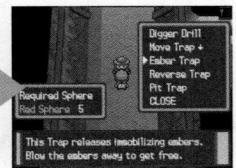

Fossils — **Resurrect Pokémon at the Oreburgh Mining Museum**

Bring fossils you've excavated to the receptionist at the Oreburgh Mining Museum, and they can resurrect the Pokémon inside for you. After you've handed over the fossil, resume your adventure for a while. Come back later and you'll receive the fully restored Pokémon.

Move Tutors across Sinnoh teach you moves

Unearthed shards can be brought to any of the three Move Tutors—one on Route 212, one in Snowpoint City, and one in the Survival Area. Each one will teach your Pokémon a move corresponding to the particular combination of shards you give him. When you've got a Pokémon that would be strengthened by learning a move, get cracking on collecting those shards (p. 533).

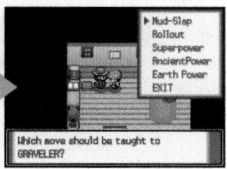

Put unearthed items in your bag when you return topside

You can't bring items like the Skull Fossil, Max Revive, or the Moon Stone to the surface with you straight away. First you have to select them on the Treasure menu and choose to put them in your bag. Then they can go topside with you. However, if the treasure pocket of your bag gets full, you can't carry any more treasures. Pay attention to what you put in your bag.

Make a secret base

Customize your secret base with the perfect arrangement of decorative goods

When you create a secret base in the Underground, you also get to remake it according to your own taste. Dig up spheres, swap them for decorative goods, and then arrange your favorite goods in any manner you wish to create a custom crib.

Your very own, one-of-a-kind secret base

Decorating your base is all controlled through the PC. The first thing you've got to do when you get some goods is put them on the PC. You can then place them anywhere, except on spots occupied by boulders. You'll be able to move boulders aside as you capture flags from your friends' secret bases (p. 244).

PC

Flag

Boulder

Trade spheres for goods

During your exploration of the Underground, you may bump into goods traders, trap traders, and loot traders. There are many people of each type. For instance, there are eight trap traders alone. You'll always find them in the same spot, so you can remember where they are and find them when there's something you need in a jiffy. Get to know them.

• **The three Underground guys**

Goods trader

Goods traders will give you goods in return for spheres of a particular size and color. The selection of goods varies from trader to trader, and then from day to day.

Trap trader

Trap traders will give you traps in exchange for orbs of particular colors and sizes. The selection of traps varies from trader to trader, and then from day to day.

Loot trader

Loot traders will give you Spheres in exchange for fossils, Evolution items, and battle items you've unearthed from the Underground walls. The color of the Spheres you get varies from trader to trader.

•••See the poster of this book for a map of the Underground.•••

UNDERGROUND PLAY GUIDE

UNEARTH FUN IN THE UNDERGROUND

Collect various decorative goods and deck out your base

There are over 80 decorative goods you can get pre-ending alone. There's a wide selection available from goods traders, and don't forget about the ones you can buy on 4F of the Veilstone Dept. Store, or the ones you can get from Mr. Goods in Hearthome City in return for fulfilling various conditions.

Brighten up your base

Here's one example of a base that's been decorated with goods. Use lots of goods to spruce up your own base.

• Primary base decorations

Tables	Chairs	Shelves	Dolls	Machines	Maze goods	Trophies	Flowers
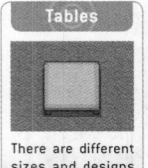	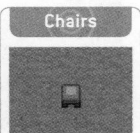						
There are different sizes and designs of tables, from the Big Table to the Small Table.	Chairs come in a wide variety of sizes and materials, including the Wood Chair and the Blue Chair.	There's a wide variety of shelves, like the Cupboard and the Bike Rack, to help you store your stuff.	There are lots of dolls of popular Pokémon, like the Piplup Doll and the Bonsly Doll.	The array of unique machines includes the Game Machine, Vending Machine, and Recovery Machine.	Use several Maze Blocks together to send intruders astray.	Cups and trophies, like the Cute Cup, give your base bragging rights.	Flowers of all different sizes and colors, including the Lush Flower, the Bonsai, and the Cute Flower, spruce up your space.

•••See page 246 for a list of decorative goods.•••

Bury spheres in the ground to make them grow

Not only can you dig up spheres in the Underground, you can also rebury them in the ground. Leave them in the ground and they get bigger by the day. Each kind of sphere grows at a different rate. See the sidebar to the right for a guide. You can also add more spheres of the same color to a spot where one is already buried. They'll merge underground and form a large sphere. This is a good way to get spheres to trade for decorative goods you've got your eye on.

• Spheres' growing tendencies

Prism Sphere	Hard to grow
Pale Sphere	Hard to grow
Red Sphere	Easy to grow
Blue Sphere	Easy to grow
Green Sphere	Easy to grow

Capture the Flag

A grand game of tag in the Sinnoh Underground: capture your friend's flag to win

Over the Nintendo DS wireless connection, you and your friends can descend to the Underground and play a game of capturing flags from one another's secret bases. It's fast-paced fun as flags get swiped back and forth.

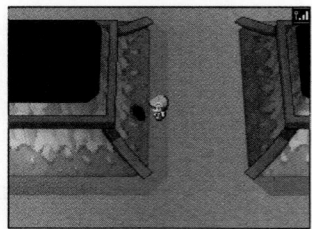

Abscond with the flags from your friends' secret bases

When you get a friend's flag all the way back to your own base, your flag gets upgraded. This gives you access to a wider range of decorative goods, and lets you move aside more boulders in your base, among other benefits. Capture the flags and spruce up your secret base.

You've obtained the Flag from Frank's Base!

Flag

• Flag upgrades

Normal Flag
- You haven't stolen any flags yet
- You can use up to 10 decorative items
- You cannot remove boulders

Bronze Flag
- You've captured one flag
- You can use up to 12 decorative items
- You can remove one boulder

Silver Flag
- You've captured 3 flags
- You can use up to 15 decorative items
- You can remove up to 5 boulders

Gold Flag
- You've captured 10 flags
- You can use up to 15 decorative items
- You can remove up to 10 boulders
- You can use the Fossil, Sphere, and Trap Radars

Platinum Flag
- You've captured 50 flags
- You can use up to 15 decorative items
- You can remove all boulders
- You can use the Fossil, Sphere, and Trap Radars

 Use the 3 Radars

The Fossil, Sphere, and Trap Radars are all controlled through the PC. The Fossil Radar shows where treasure is, the Sphere Radar shows buried spheres, and the Trap Radar shows where traps have been set.

Set traps to prevent friends from getting your flag home

Setting traps around your secret base is an effective way to keep your friends from making off with your flag. If a friend gets caught in your trap, he will be slowed, stalled, or flung far from your base. If he's holding your flag, just tap him before he gets back to his own base.

• Main traps

Move Trap
Flings the thief in any direction. There's also a Hurl Trap, which covers a larger distance.

Rock Trap
A rock falls from above. Tap it with the stylus to break it. There's also a Rockfall Trap, which is harder to break.

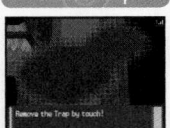
Smoke Trap
Smoke fills the screen. You can blow it away using the stylus. The Big Smoke Trap releases more smoke.

Foam Trap
Releases bubbles. Tap them with the stylus to burst them. The Bubble Trap releases a greater number of bubbles.

Leaf Trap
Leaves flutter around the screen. Blow into the microphone to blow them away. There's also a Flower Trap.

Ember Trap
Releases a flame. Blow into the mic to blow it out. The Fire Trap is harder to extinguish.

•••See page 567 for a list of Traps.•••

Combine traps for maximum effect

Setting traps to keep friends out of your secret base? It'll be more effective to set them in combination. Being blasted away from your secret base is sure to confuse a would-be thief. Below are some examples. Try to come up with your own combinations.

Move Trap →

Move Trap ↑

Rockfall Trap

Start off with a Move Trap →, blasting the thief to the right.

Follow up with a Move Trap ↑, carrying the thief up and farther afield.

Bury the thief under a Rockfall Trap for the coup de grâce.

Available decorative goods

Collect goods to decorate your base

With lots of decorative goods, you can make over your secret base in your own style. Get goods via trades for Spheres you've unearthed, or from Mr. Goods after completing certain tasks. Then make a lavishly decorated base you can show off with pride.

Goods you can get before getting the National Pokédex

Blue Crystal — Trophy
How to get
Talk to Mr. Goods in Hearthome City after greeting 100 people in the Underground
Trade goods ✕

Blue Tent — Maze Goods
How to get
Trade for 20–70 Pale Spheres in the Underground
Trade goods ○

Blue Cushion — Goods
How to get
Trade for 8–10 Red Spheres in the Underground
Trade goods ○

Red Bike — Goods
How to get
Trade for 33–40 Red Spheres in the Underground
Trade goods ○

Red Crystal — Trophy
How to get
Talk to Mr. Goods in Hearthome City after unearthing 100 fossils or Rare Bones in the Underground
Trade goods ✕

Red Tent — Maze Goods
How to get
Trade for 20–70 Pale Spheres in the Underground
Trade goods ○

Planted Tree — Goods
How to get
Trade for 20–25 Red Spheres in the Underground
Trade goods ○

Bonsly Doll — Plush Doll
How to get
Purchase at Veilstone Dept. Store 4F for 2000 Poké
Trade goods ✕

Beautiful Cup — Trophy
How to get
Talk to Mr. Goods in Hearthome City after winning the Beauty Super Contest, Master Rank
Trade goods ✕

Beautiful Flower — Goods
How to get
Trade for 8–10 Green Spheres in the Underground
Trade goods ○

Big Barrel — Goods
How to get
Trade for 10–40 Pale Spheres in the Underground
Trade goods ○

Big Bookshelf — Goods
How to get
Trade for 20–25 Green Spheres in the Underground
Trade goods ○

Big Table — Goods
How to get
Trade for 12–15 Blue Spheres in the Underground
Trade goods ○

Big TV — Goods
How to get
Trade for 9–10 Prism Spheres in the Underground. Purchase at Veilstone Dept. Store 4F for 4500 Poké
Trade goods ○

Recovery Machine — Goods
How to get
Trade for 90–99 Prism Spheres in the Underground
Trade goods ○

Glittering Gem — Trophy
How to get
Talk to the Underground Man in Eterna City after capturing 3 flags in the Underground and earning the Silver Flag
Trade goods ✕

Intelligence Cup — Trophy
How to get
Talk to Mr. Goods in Hearthome City after winning the intelligence Super Contest, Master Rank
Trade goods ✕

Coolness Cup — Trophy
How to get
Talk to Mr. Goods in Hearthome City after winning the coolness Super Contest, Master Rank
Trade goods ✕

Snorlax Doll — Plush Doll
How to get
Trade for 80–99 Red Spheres in the Underground
Trade goods ✕

Cute Cup — Trophy
How to get
Talk to Mr. Goods in Hearthome City after winning the cuteness Super Contest, Master Rank
Trade goods ✕

Cute Flower — Goods
How to get
Trade for 8–10 Green Spheres in the Underground
Trade goods ○

Yellow Cushion — Goods
How to get
Trade for 8–10 Red Spheres in the Underground. Purchase at Veilstone Dept. Store 4F for 500 Poké
Trade goods ○

Yellow Crystal — Trophy
How to get
Talk to Mr. Goods in Hearthome City after catching people in traps over 100 times in the Underground
Trade goods ✕

Wooden Chair — Goods
How to get
Trade for 8–10 Red Spheres in the Underground. Talk to the Underground Man in Eterna City after creating your secret base in the Underground
Trade goods ○

Wooden Dresser — Goods
How to get
Trade for 20–25 Green Spheres in the Underground
Trade goods ○

Crate — Goods
How to get
Trade for 33–40 Red Spheres in the Underground
Trade goods ○

UNDERGROUND PLAY GUIDE

— UNEARTH FUN IN THE UNDERGROUND

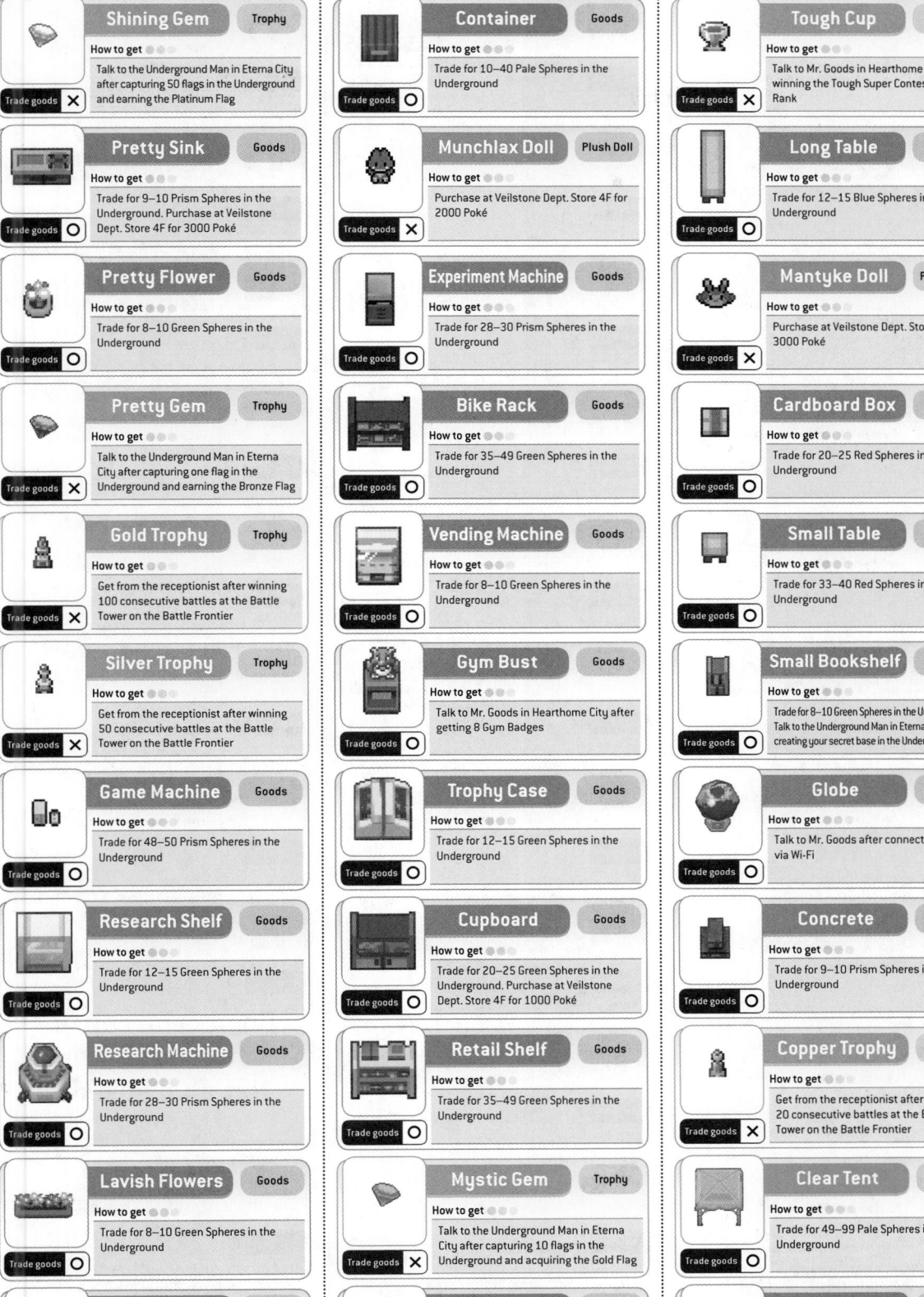

Shining Gem — Trophy
How to get ●●○
Talk to the Underground Man in Eterna City after capturing 50 flags in the Underground and earning the Platinum Flag
Trade goods ✕

Pretty Sink — Goods
How to get ●●○
Trade for 9–10 Prism Spheres in the Underground. Purchase at Veilstone Dept. Store 4F for 3000 Poké
Trade goods ○

Pretty Flower — Goods
How to get ●●○
Trade for 8–10 Green Spheres in the Underground
Trade goods ○

Pretty Gem — Trophy
How to get ●○○
Talk to the Underground Man in Eterna City after capturing one flag in the Underground and earning the Bronze Flag
Trade goods ✕

Gold Trophy — Trophy
How to get ●○○
Get from the receptionist after winning 100 consecutive battles at the Battle Tower on the Battle Frontier
Trade goods ✕

Silver Trophy — Trophy
How to get ●○○
Get from the receptionist after winning 50 consecutive battles at the Battle Tower on the Battle Frontier
Trade goods ✕

Game Machine — Goods
How to get ●●○
Trade for 48–50 Prism Spheres in the Underground
Trade goods ○

Research Shelf — Goods
How to get ●○○
Trade for 12–15 Green Spheres in the Underground
Trade goods ○

Research Machine — Goods
How to get ●○○
Trade for 28–30 Prism Spheres in the Underground
Trade goods ○

Lavish Flowers — Goods
How to get ●○○
Trade for 8–10 Green Spheres in the Underground
Trade goods ○

Wastebasket — Goods
How to get ●●○
Trade for 8–10 Red Spheres in the Underground
Trade goods ○

Container — Goods
How to get ●●○
Trade for 10–40 Pale Spheres in the Underground
Trade goods ○

Munchlax Doll — Plush Doll
How to get ●●○
Purchase at Veilstone Dept. Store 4F for 2000 Poké
Trade goods ✕

Experiment Machine — Goods
How to get ●●○
Trade for 28–30 Prism Spheres in the Underground
Trade goods ○

Bike Rack — Goods
How to get ●●○
Trade for 35–49 Green Spheres in the Underground
Trade goods ○

Vending Machine — Goods
How to get ●●○
Trade for 8–10 Green Spheres in the Underground
Trade goods ○

Gym Bust — Goods
How to get ●●○
Talk to Mr. Goods in Hearthome City after getting 8 Gym Badges
Trade goods ○

Trophy Case — Goods
How to get ●●○
Trade for 12–15 Green Spheres in the Underground
Trade goods ○

Cupboard — Goods
How to get ●●○
Trade for 20–25 Green Spheres in the Underground. Purchase at Veilstone Dept. Store 4F for 1000 Poké
Trade goods ○

Retail Shelf — Goods
How to get ●●○
Trade for 35–49 Green Spheres in the Underground
Trade goods ○

Mystic Gem — Trophy
How to get ●●○
Talk to the Underground Man in Eterna City after capturing 10 flags in the Underground and acquiring the Gold Flag
Trade goods ✕

Binoculars — Goods
How to get ●●○
Trade for 10–40 Prism Spheres in the Underground
Trade goods ○

Tough Cup — Trophy
How to get ●●○
Talk to Mr. Goods in Hearthome City after winning the Tough Super Contest, Master Rank
Trade goods ✕

Long Table — Goods
How to get ●●○
Trade for 12–15 Blue Spheres in the Underground
Trade goods ○

Mantyke Doll — Plush Doll
How to get ●●○
Purchase at Veilstone Dept. Store 4F for 3000 Poké
Trade goods ✕

Cardboard Box — Goods
How to get ●●○
Trade for 20–25 Red Spheres in the Underground
Trade goods ○

Small Table — Goods
How to get ●●○
Trade for 33–40 Red Spheres in the Underground
Trade goods ○

Small Bookshelf — Goods
How to get ●●○
Trade for 8–10 Green Spheres in the Underground. Talk to the Underground Man in Eterna City after creating your secret base in the Underground
Trade goods ○

Globe — Goods
How to get ●●○
Talk to Mr. Goods after connecting via Wi-Fi
Trade goods ○

Concrete — Goods
How to get ●●○
Trade for 9–10 Prism Spheres in the Underground
Trade goods ○

Copper Trophy — Trophy
How to get ●○○
Get from the receptionist after winning 20 consecutive battles at the Battle Tower on the Battle Frontier
Trade goods ✕

Clear Tent — Maze Goods
How to get ●○○
Trade for 49–99 Pale Spheres in the Underground
Trade goods ○

Barrel — Goods
How to get ●●○
Trade for 10–40 Pale Spheres in the Underground
Trade goods ○

UNEARTH FUN IN THE UNDERGROUND

Turtwig Doll — Plush Doll
How to get
Trade for 35–40 Green Spheres in the Underground. Talk to the Underground Man in Eterna City after placing goods in your secret base in the Underground*
Trade goods X

Glameow Doll — Plush Doll
How to get
Trade for 15–20 Blue Spheres in the Underground
Trade goods X

Pachirisu Doll — Plush Doll
How to get
Trade for 70–99 Pale Spheres in the Underground
Trade goods X

Pikachu Doll — Plush Doll
How to get
Trade for 70–99 Pale Spheres in the Underground
Trade goods X

Chimchar Doll — Plush Doll
How to get
Trade for 25–40 Red Spheres in the Underground. Talk to the Underground Man in Eterna City after placing goods in your secret base in the Underground*
Trade goods X

Clefairy Doll — Plush Doll
How to get
Trade for 40–70 Pale Spheres in the Underground
Trade goods X

Pink Crystal — Trophy
How to get
Talk to Mr. Goods in Hearthome City after catching people in traps 100 times in the Underground
Trade goods X

Pink Dresser — Goods
How to get
Trade for 50–60 Green Spheres in the Underground
Trade goods O

Happiny Doll — Plush Doll
How to get
Trade for 40–70 Pale Spheres in the Underground
Trade goods X

Buizel Doll — Plush Doll
How to get
Purchase at Veilstone Dept. Store 4F for 3000 Poké
Trade goods X

Fluffy Bed — Goods
How to get
Trade for 33–40 Blue Spheres in the Underground
Trade goods O

Normal Table — Goods
How to get
Trade for 8–10 Blue Spheres in the Underground. Talk to the Underground Man in Eterna City after creating your secret base in the Underground
Trade goods O

Drifblim Doll — Plush Doll
How to get
Trade for 33–40 Blue Spheres in the Underground
Trade goods X

Chatot Doll — Plush Doll
How to get
Purchase at Veilstone Dept. Store 4F for 3000 Poké
Trade goods X

Pokémon Center Table — Goods
How to get
Trade for 20–25 Blue Spheres in the Underground
Trade goods O

Pokémon Center Flowers — Goods
How to get
Trade for 10–40 Pale Spheres in the Underground
Trade goods O

Piplup Doll — Plush Doll
How to get
Trade for 35–40 Blue Spheres in the Underground. Talk to the Underground Man in Eterna City after placing goods in your secret base in the Underground*
Trade goods X

Bonsai — Goods
How to get
Trade for 8–10 Green Spheres in the Underground
Trade goods O

Weavile Doll — Plush Doll
How to get
Trade for 28–30 Prism Spheres in the Underground
Trade goods X

Mime Jr. Doll — Plush Doll
How to get
Purchase at Veilstone Dept. Store 4F for 2000 Poké
Trade goods X

Green Bike — Goods
How to get
Trade for 33–40 Green Spheres in the Underground
Trade goods O

Buneary Doll — Plush Doll
How to get
Trade for 15–30 Pale Spheres in the Underground. Talk to the Underground Man in Eterna City after creating your secret base in the Underground
Trade goods X

Maze Block 1 — Maze Goods
How to get
Trade for 48–50 Prism Spheres in the Underground
Trade goods O

Maze Block 2 — Maze Goods
How to get
Trade for 48–50 Prism Spheres in the Underground
Trade goods O

Maze Block 3 — Maze Goods
How to get
Trade for 48–50 Prism Spheres in the Underground
Trade goods O

Maze Block 4 — Maze Goods
How to get
Trade for 48–50 Prism Spheres in the Underground
Trade goods O

Maze Block 5 — Maze Goods
How to get
Trade for 48–50 Prism Spheres in the Underground
Trade goods O

Horizontal Sofa — Goods
How to get
Trade for 20–25 Blue Spheres in the Underground
Trade goods O

Horizontal Table — Goods
How to get
Trade for 12–15 Blue Spheres in the Underground
Trade goods O

Fridge — Goods
How to get
Trade for 12–15 Green Spheres in the Underground. Purchase at Veilstone Dept. Store 4F for 1000 Poké
Trade goods O

Goods you can get after getting the National Pokédex

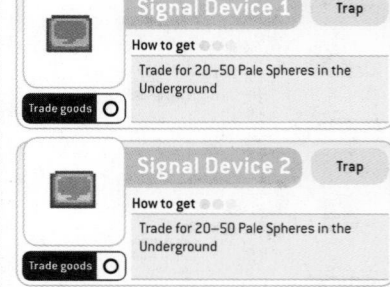

Signal Device 1 — Trap
How to get
Trade for 20–50 Pale Spheres in the Underground
Trade goods O

Signal Device 2 — Trap
How to get
Trade for 20–50 Pale Spheres in the Underground
Trade goods O

* Doll is of whichever Pokémon you got from Professor Rowan at the start of the game.

Signal Device 3 [Trap]
How to get ●○○
Trade for 20–50 Pale Spheres in the Underground
Trade goods O

Signal Device 4 [Trap]
How to get ●●○
Trade for 20–50 Pale Spheres in the Underground
Trade goods O

Torchic Doll [Plush Doll]
How to get ●○○
Trade for 25–30 Red Spheres in the Underground
Trade goods X

Hole Machine [Trap]
How to get ●○○
Trade for 10–12 Blue Spheres in the Underground
Trade goods O

Bubble Machine 1 [Trap]
How to get ●○○
Trade for 12–14 Blue Spheres in the Underground
Trade goods O

Rock Machine [Trap]
How to get ●○○
Trade for 10–12 Red Spheres in the Underground
Trade goods O

Skitty Doll [Plush Doll]
How to get ●○○
Trade for 15–20 Green Spheres in the Underground
Trade goods X

Smoke Machine 1 [Trap]
How to get ●●○
Trade for 28–32 Red Spheres in the Underground
Trade goods O

Pit Device [Trap]
How to get ●●○
Trade for 25–30 Blue Spheres in the Underground
Trade goods O

Treecko Doll [Plush Doll]
How to get ●○○
Trade for 25–30 Green Spheres in the Underground
Trade goods X

Smoke Machine 2 [Trap]
How to get ●●●
Trade for 12–14 Red Spheres in the Underground
Trade goods O

Leaf Machine [Trap]
How to get ●●●
Trade for 30–38 Green Spheres in the Underground
Trade goods O

Squirtle Doll [Plush Doll]
How to get ●●○
Trade for 25–30 Blue Spheres in the Underground
Trade goods X

Wobbuffet Doll [Plush Doll]
How to get ●●●
Trade for 80–99 Green Spheres in the Underground
Trade goods X

Chikorita Doll [Plush Doll]
How to get ●●○
Trade for 25–30 Green Spheres in the Underground
Trade goods X

Meowth Doll [Plush Doll]
How to get ●○○
Trade for 15–20 Red Spheres in the Underground
Trade goods X

Petal Machine [Trap]
How to get ●●●
Trade for 65–80 Green Spheres in the Underground
Trade goods O

Bubble Machine 2 [Trap]
How to get ●●●
Trade for 28–32 Blue Spheres in the Underground
Trade goods O

Charmander Doll [Plush Doll]
How to get ●●○
Trade for 25–30 Red Spheres in the Underground
Trade goods X

Cyndaquil Doll [Plush Doll]
How to get ●●○
Trade for 25–30 Red Spheres in the Underground
Trade goods X

Ember Machine [Trap]
How to get ●○○
Trade for 15–18 Red Spheres in the Underground
Trade goods O

Bulbasaur Doll [Plush Doll]
How to get ●●○
Trade for 25–30 Green Spheres in the Underground
Trade goods X

Plusle Doll [Plush Doll]
How to get ●●●
Trade for 60–70 Red Spheres in the Underground
Trade goods X

Jigglypuff Doll [Plush Doll]
How to get ●●●
Trade for 40–70 Pure Spheres in the Underground
Trade goods X

Wailmer Doll [Plush Doll]
How to get ●●●
Trade for 80–99 Blue Spheres in the Underground
Trade goods X

Fire Machine [Trap]
How to get ●●●
Trade for 33–40 Red Spheres in the Underground
Trade goods O

Minun Doll [Plush Doll]
How to get ●●●
Trade for 60–70 Blue Spheres in the Underground
Trade goods X

Mudkip Doll [Plush Doll]
How to get ●●○
Trade for 25–30 Blue Spheres in the Underground
Trade goods X

Rockfall Machine [Trap]
How to get ●●●
Trade for 25–30 Red Spheres in the Underground
Trade goods O

Totodile Doll [Plush Doll]
How to get ●●○
Trade for 25–30 Blue Spheres in the Underground
Trade goods X

Shiny Pokémon and the mysterious Pokérus

The world of Pokémon will always be full of secrets and mysteries. Two prime examples are Shiny Pokémon and the microscopic yet beneficial virus, Pokérus, that affects Pokémon. Let's try to solve the mysteries surrounding Pokémon biology.

SHINY POKÉMON AND THE MYSTERIOUS POKÉRUS

Pokémon color variants

Rare Pokémon with unusual coloration

Shiny Pokémon are so rarely seen by human eyes that some believe they don't even exist. Their stats are no different from those of ordinary Pokémon; what makes them special is their distinct coloration. You can tell when you're facing a Shiny Pokémon, because you'll hear a tinkling sound and see the Pokémon emit stars. Meeting one is pure luck, so value it if you manage to catch one.

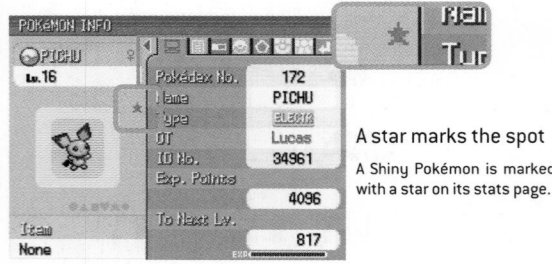

A star marks the spot

A Shiny Pokémon is marked with a star on its stats page.

It stays special even through Evolution

When a Shiny Pokémon evolves, it stays Shiny into its next form, too.

Mysterious Pokérus

A helpful virus that strengthens your Pokémon

Pokérus is a tiny virus that can sometimes attach itself to your Pokémon. You can't see it, but the receptionist at the Pokémon Center will tell you if your Pokémon have it when you bring them in to be healed. With Pokérus, a Pokémon's stats will grow more readily, so you can develop it to be stronger. The Pokérus will go away after a few days, but its effects remain. And if you put that Pokémon in your party while Pokérus is active, the other Pokémon will get it, too.

Stats grow more readily

A Pokérus infection is your chance to raise your Pokémon to be stronger.

Gone in 1 to 4 days

The Pokérus will go away, but it will leave behind a smiley face to show it was there.

Link Play
Guide

Link for Fun

Play with your friends using wireless and Wi-Fi Connections

Pokémon Platinum has a lot more to offer when you use the the DS's wireless connection capability, so don't miss out on all the fun!

Choose the mode of link play for your game version

The link play options available to you depend on which game version you're playing with. Some options are available in *Pokémon Diamond, Pearl*, and *Platinum*—and some are exclusive to Pokémon Platinum. Always check to see what versions you and your friends are using first so you don't end up disappointed.

● Link play modes

	Modes available in Diamond, Pearl, and Platinum	Modes exclusive to Platinum
Union Room	•Greeting •Drawing •Battle •Trade •Records •Chat	•Spin Trade
Wi-Fi Club	•Battle •Trade •Voice chat	•Cooking •Battle Frontier •Plaza Game
Colosseum	•Colosseum	————
Underground	•Underground	————
Pokemon Super Contest	•Pokémon Super Contest	————
Making Poffins	•Making Poffins	————
Global Terminal	•GTS •GeoNet	•Training Room •Battle Video •Battle Video Ranking •Voice Chat •Dress-Up Data
Wi-Fi Plaza	————	•Plaza Game •Plaza News •Survey •Footprint Stamp •Visitor Profiles
Battle Frontier	•Battle Tower	•Battle Hall •Battle Factory •Battle Castle •Battle Arcade

Playing over a wireless connection

Connecting to friends is easy and fun

You can use the Nintendo DS's wireless link feature to open up all sorts of link play modes for you and your nearby friends. Take on the Underground, Pokémon Super Contests, and more.

● What you can do over a wireless connection

- Pokémon Wireless Club Union Room
- Pokémon Link Club Colosseum
- Underground
- Pokémon Super Contest
- Make Poffins
- Battle Frontier (Multi Battles)

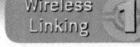 **Pokémon Wireless Club Union Room**

Check the second floor of any Pokémon Center to enter the Pokémon Wireless Club Union Room. Just talk to the receptionist at the middle desk, and you'll be able to see your nearby friends via wireless—together you can enjoy activities like trades, battles, mixing records, and spin trades.

• Playing in the Pokémon Wireless Club Union Room

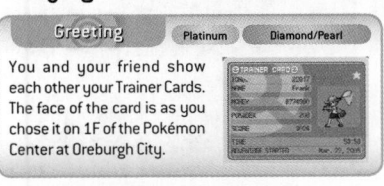

| Greeting | Platinum | Diamond/Pearl |

You and your friend show each other your Trainer Cards. The face of the card is as you chose it on 1F of the Pokémon Center at Oreburgh City.

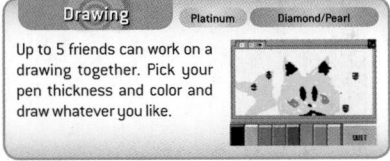

| Drawing | Platinum | Diamond/Pearl |

Up to 5 friends can work on a drawing together. Pick your pen thickness and color and draw whatever you like.

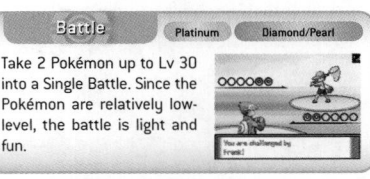

| Battle | Platinum | Diamond/Pearl |

Take 2 Pokémon up to Lv 30 into a Single Battle. Since the Pokémon are relatively low-level, the battle is light and fun.

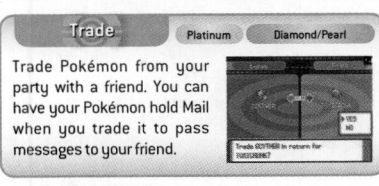

| Trade | Platinum | Diamond/Pearl |

Trade Pokémon from your party with a friend. You can have your Pokémon hold Mail when you trade it to pass messages to your friend.

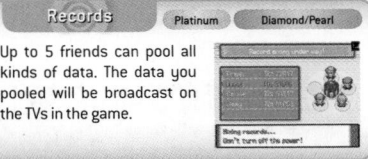

| Records | Platinum | Diamond/Pearl |

Up to 5 friends can pool all kinds of data. The data you pooled will be broadcast on the TVs in the game.

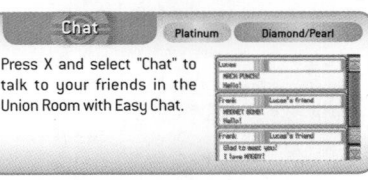

| Chat | Platinum | Diamond/Pearl |

Press X and select "Chat" to talk to your friends in the Union Room with Easy Chat.

Spin Trade | Platinum |

Up to 5 friends can bring Pokémon Eggs for a group trade. You won't know until it's over which Egg you're walking away with. Stop on the bonus area to get berries as well.

Tap the Touch Screen to switch Eggs around

Tap the Touch Screen during the trade, and the Eggs will bounce into different positions.

 Pokémon Link Club Colosseum | Platinum | Diamond/Pearl |

At the Pokémon Link Club Colosseum, real-life friends in groups of 2 or 4 can challenge each other to Pokémon battles of various styles. Just walk up to the right-hand counter on 2F of any Pokémon Center.

• Playing at the Pokémon Link Club Colosseum

2 players

• Single Battle

Each player sends out 1 Pokémon from his or her party at a time. This is the standard form of battle, and the one where individual differences in Pokémon development make the biggest difference.

Have your Pokémon learn moves of a wide variety of types, and you should do well against any foe.

• Double Battle

Both players send out 2 Pokémon at a time. Combine your Pokémon's moves strategically to defeat your opponent.

Double Battles let you use one Pokémon to cover for another's weaknesses.

• Mixed Battle

3 Pokémon are selected for the battle, and each player sends out one at a time. This style tests how well you can use Pokémon your opponent trained.

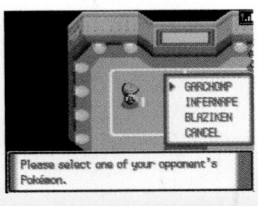

The key to this battle is choosing which Pokémon to swap in.

4 players

• Multi Battle

Players form two teams of two, and all participate in the battle. One player is chosen as the leader, and the others choose to join his or her group.

Have your Pokémon team up with a friend's to defeat your opponents' team.

Underground | Platinum | Diamond/Pearl |

Open up a whole new world for exploration when you receive the Explorer Kit from the Underground Man in Eterna City. Use the wireless function to have friends join you in the Underground for fossil digging and games of Capture the Flag.

- ### Playing in the Underground

Fossil digging

Examine the blinking areas on the radar to dig for fossils. When you dig together with a nearby friend, you combine the effects of your digging.

•••See p. 241 for info on how to dig for fossils•••

Secret Base

Using the Digger Drill, you can create a secret base of your own. Fill it up with decorative goods to impress your friends.

•••See p. 243 for info on how to use your secret base•••

Capture the Flag

Capture the Flag is a game where each player tries to steal the flag from the others' bases. Set traps and race your friends to see who gets their opponents' flags home first.

•••See p. 244 for info on how to play Capture the Flag•••

Wireless Linking 4 Pokémon Super Contest `Platinum` `Diamond/Pearl`

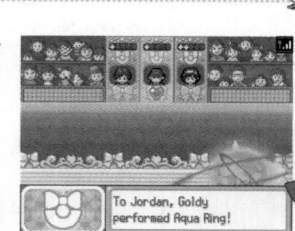

Up to 4 friends can face off in a Pokémon Super Contest, comparing their Pokémon's grace and beauty instead of battle prowess—just head to the left-hand counter inside the Hearthome Contest Hall.

•••See p. 224 for more on how to take part in Pokémon Super Contest.•••

Wireless Linking 5 Making Poffins `Platinum` `Diamond/Pearl`

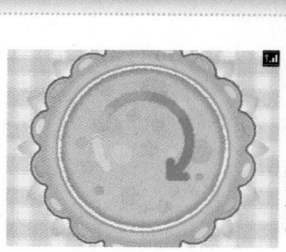

Join with up to 4 players to make Poffin at the Poffin House in Hearthome City, and do your best to make a high-level Poffin to feed your Pokémon.

Teamwork is key

Make sure you're all in synch so that you don't spill or burn the dough.

•••See p. 227 for more on how to make Poffins.•••

Wireless Linking 6 Battle Frontier (Multi Battle) `Platinum` `Diamond/Pearl`

Head to the Battle Frontier in the Fight Area, where each facility offers Multi Battles that you can participate in with friends. If you're having trouble in one of the facilities, working together with friends might give you just the boost you need to increase your record.

- ### Playing at the Battle Frontier (Multi Battles)

Battle Tower `Platinum` `Diamond/Pearl`

Battle 7 Trainers in a row using Lv 50 Pokémon—but you and your friends cannot use the same Pokémon or items.

Battle Hall `Platinum`

Pick a type and rank of Pokémon to challenge in battle. You and your friends must pick the same kind of Pokémon.

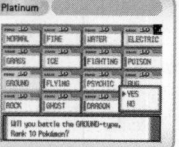

Battle Factory `Platinum`

Fight in a string of 7 battles using rental Pokémon—you can trade one of your Pokémon or your friend's in the middle.

Battle Castle `Platinum`

A challenge where you can use Castle Points (CP) for various purposes, including restoring your Pokémon. You and your friends can't choose the same item.

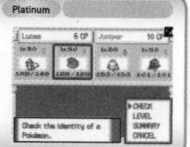

Battle Arcade `Platinum`

A battle with various conditions (Events) selected by roulette. You and your friends can't choose the same Pokémon or items as one another.

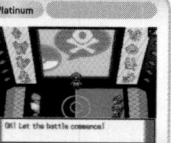

LINK PLAY GUIDE

LINK FOR FUN

Playing over the Wi-Fi Connection

Play with distant friends over the Internet

Your DS can connect to the Nintendo Wi-Fi Connection, allowing you to enjoy link play even with friends who are far away. Be sure to check out new features like the Global Terminal and the Wi-Fi Plaza.

• What you can do over Wi-Fi

- Global Terminal
- Wi-Fi Club
- Wi-Fi Plaza
- Battle Frontier (Wi-Fi Battle Room)

Enter Friend Codes in your Pal Pad before jumping on Wi-Fi

To play with your friends over Wi-Fi, you must first record their Friend Codes in your Pal Pad. That way, you only play with people you know and trust—up to 32 different players.

See your friend list

Here you can see detailed info on your recorded friends, as well as the results of battles you've shared and the number of Plaza games you've played.

Record a Friend Code

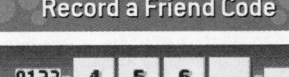

Here you manually record the Friend Code of a friend you're connecting with for the first time. Your friends' Friend Codes are added automatically if you play with them over the wireless connection.

Your Friend Code

Lucas's CODE

0001 8183 6804

By exchanging Friend Codes with other players, you may trade and battle with them over Nintendo WFC.

Here you can check your own Friend Code. You'll need to tell it to your friends, and get theirs in return, if you want to play with them over Wi-Fi.

• How to record Friend Codes in your Pal Pad

1 Get the Pal Pad
To play over Wi-Fi, you'll need the Pal Pad. Get it from Teala on B1F of the Pokémon Center.

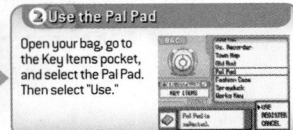

2 Use the Pal Pad
Open your bag, go to the Key Items pocket, and select the Pal Pad. Then select "Use."

3 Enter your friends' Friend Codes
In the Pal Pad, enter the Friend Codes of the friends you want to play with over Wi-Fi. Enter the 12-character code exactly.

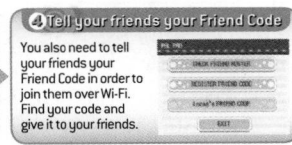

4 Tell your friends your Friend Code
You also need to tell your friends your Friend Code in order to join them over Wi-Fi. Find your code and give it to your friends.

 Wi-Fi Link ## Global Terminal

The Global Terminal is a place where you can make Pokémon trades, view many kinds of records, and share Battle Videos and Box Data with Trainers from all over the world via Wi-Fi. Just head to Jubilife City after winning your Oreburgh Gym battle.

The Global Terminal Your Gateway to the Whole World!

• Playing at the Global Terminal

Global Trade Station (GTS)

Platinum   Diamond/Pearl

The GTS lets you trade Pokémon with other Trainers from around the world. You can deposit Pokémon, and search Pokémon that other people have deposited.

• Deposit Pokémon

Deposit Pokémon you want to trade at the GTS. When a Pokémon is found that meets your requirements, the trade is carried out for the next time you log on.

• Search Pokémon

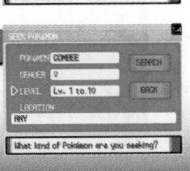

Here you can search though Pokémon that other Trainers have deposited on the GTS, to find one you want. If you meet the other Trainer's requirements, the trade takes place.

GeoNet

| Platinum | Diamond/Pearl |

Go to the globe on 1F to see a world map with the locations of the other Trainers you've had exchanges with over Wi-Fi.

Trainer Ranking

| Platinum | |

Ranks the results of Trainers from around the world, divided by team. Your own results are sent in automatically.

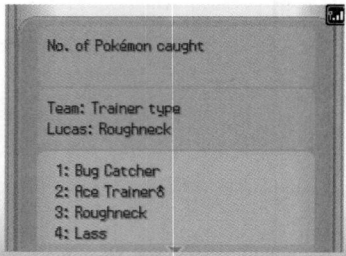

Battle Video

| Platinum | |

Upload a visual record of battles and Battle Frontier matches. You can also view videos from other Trainers.

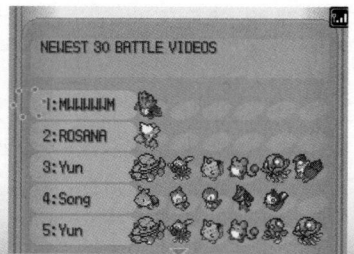

Battle Video Ranking

| Platinum | |

Ranks battle videos from around the world by popularity. You can even save your favorite video.

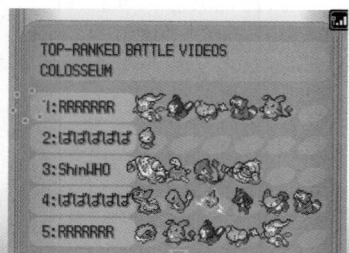

Box Data

| Platinum | |

Upload data about the boxes where your Pokémon are deposited, and see other Trainers' boxes.

Dress-Up Data

| Platinum | |

Upload your Pokémon Dress-Up photos and see other Trainers' photos. You can take these photos on 2F of Jubilife TV.

Wi-Fi Club

Head to the Wi-Fi Club on B1F of any Pokémon Center to battle, trade, cook, and play Plaza games with distant friends over Wi-Fi—you can even use voice chat to talk to them while you play!

Hang out with friends in the big lobby

Icons indicate your friends' conditions.

Friends' conditions at a glance

- Seeking battle/In battle
- Seeking trade/In trade
- Seeking cooks/Cooking
- Recruiting for Plaza Game/In Plaza Game
- Seeking Battle Frontier partners/At Battle Frontier
- In Voice Chat/Voice Chat off
- Standby
- Does not meet requirements for play

• Playing at the Wi-Fi Club

Voice Chat

| Platinum | Diamond/Pearl |

Press A near a person in standby to talk to them. You can then have a voice chat with them through your microphone. You can still voice chat even if engaged in battle, trading, or other Wi-Fi Club activities.

Recruit Friends

| Platinum | Diamond/Pearl |

Press A while standing in front of the PC at the Wi-Fi Club to recruit friends for battle, trades, and other group activities. Play begins once they accept your offer.

Join

| Platinum | Diamond/Pearl |

If you see people bouncing up and down in the Wi-Fi Club lobby, that's a sign that they're looking for partners for group activities. Press A and talk to them to join whatever activity they're recruiting for.

Cooking

Platinum

Up to 3 players can make Poffins together. Mix the dough without spilling or burning it to bake a perfect, high-level Poffin. You must have the Poffin Case to participate.

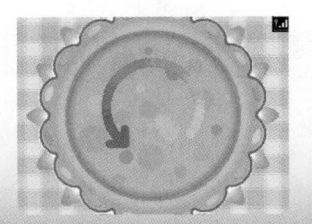

Battle Frontier

Platinum

You and a friend can take part in Multi Battles in any of the Battle Frontier facilities. However, both of you must have entered the Hall of Fame and visited the Battle Frontier at least once.

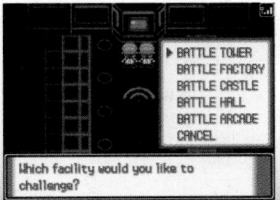

Plaza Games

Platinum

Up to 4 friends can play Plaza games. There are 3 games to choose from: Swalot Plop, Mime Jr. Top, and Wobbuffet Pop. Compete to see who can get the most points.

Wi-Fi Link 3 Wi-Fi Plaza **Platinum**

Head to B1F of any Pokémon Center to check out the Wi-Fi Plaza, where you can play a variety of games with Trainers from all over the world, up to 20 people—all without needing Friend Codes. Select messages for communicating with other Trainers, and try to make some new friends.

Pick messages for conversation

Reach out to other Trainers in the Plaza, which changes seasonally.

• Wi-Fi play stations

Information desk

Learn all about the features of the Wi-Fi Plaza. Look for the two girls in the middle of the Plaza.

Plaza News

Check up on your remaining play time at the Plaza, the number of participants, and the latest topics. Check out the electronic billboard behind the information desk.

Plaza Survey

Answer the machine's survey questions, and the results will be displayed during a Time Event. You can see results from the previous week at any time.

Footprint Board

Make a stamp of your party Pokémon's feet on the board. Up to 8 people can join in.

Visitor Profiles

Here you can see where all of the Plaza participants live, as well as the approximate local time there.

Plaza games

2 to 8 players can enjoy any of three simple games: Swalot Plop, Mime Jr. Top, and Wobbuffet Pop.

Sign up at the entrance. The game begins once you assemble 4 players or if you have at least 2 players when your time runs out.

•••See p. 258 for more on how to play Plaza games•••

Get Tap Toys from the door staff

Tap Toys are special toys that you can only play with in the Wi-Fi Plaza. You can get one of the nine toys from the staff at the door, and then share it with other people in the Plaza. When you do well in a Plaza game, it jazzes up your Tap Toy, making it more lively when you tap the Touch Screen.

• The 9 kinds of Tap Toys

Pop	Signal	Cymbal	Whirl	Sparkle	Drum	Balloon	Bell	Ripple
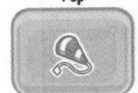		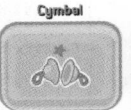		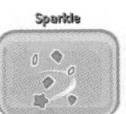				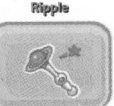

Plaza games

There are 3 Plaza games in all, and up to four players can play together. The player who scores the highest will have their Tap Toy powered up by 1.

● Plaza games

Swalot Plop	Mime Jr. Top	Wobbuffet Pop
Throw berries into the mouth of spinning Swalot. The player with the highest score gets their Tap Toy powered up by 1.	Roll the ball so that Mime Jr. doesn't fall off. The player whose Mime Jr. stays on top of the ball the longest gets their Tap Toy powered up by 1.	Push the pump to pop the balloons. Break more than 10, and everybody's Tap Toy gets powered up.

Flick the berries into Swalot's mouth with the stylus

Roll the ball with the stylus, and don't let Mime Jr. fall off

Use the pump to fill more than 10 balloons with air

Stay in the Wi-Fi Plaza a while to see a Time Event

When your time at the Wi-Fi Plaza starts to run out, it triggers a Time Event. The lighting changes, fireworks go off, and finally a parade appears—hop aboard and ride it out!

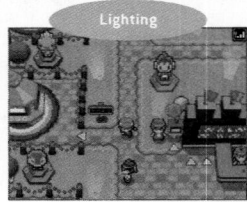
Lighting

Fireworks

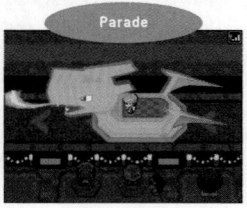
Parade

 Wi-Fi Link 4 Battle Frontier WIFI Battle Room (Battle Tower)   Platinum   Diamond/Pearl

At the Battle Tower in the Battle Frontier, you can download other Trainers' data over Wi-Fi and then battle the Trainers. You can upload your own data after finishing more battles.

After a string of Wi-Fi Battle victories, your rank goes up, and you can access more powerful opponents.

● Conditions for raising or lowering ranks in the Wi-Fi Battle Room

Rank	For Rank Up	For Rank Down		Rank	For Rank Up	For Rank Down
Rank 1	7 wins in a row	—		Rank 6	7 wins in a row	7 losses in a row, 3 times in a row
Rank 2	7 wins in a row	7 losses in a row, 5 times in a row		Rank 7	7 wins in a row	7 losses in a row, 2 times in a row
Rank 3	7 wins in a row	7 losses in a row, 4 times in a row		Rank 8	7 wins in a row	7 losses in a row, 2 times in a row
Rank 4	7 wins in a row	7 losses in a row, 4 times in a row		Rank 9	7 wins in a row	7 losses in a row
Rank 5	7 wins in a row	7 losses in a row, 3 times in a row		Rank 10	—	7 losses in a row

Sinnoh
Pokédex

Complete the Sinnoh Pokédex

The first goal of a Pokémon Trainer

At the very start of your adventure, Professor Rowan entrusts you with a Sinnoh Pokédex. You should be advancing that goal at the same time as you're working toward becoming Pokémon League Champion.

See all 210 Sinnoh-native Pokémon to complete

It's a simple business to record a Pokémon in the Sinnoh Pokédex. All you have to do is see it. If you see a Pokémon in the wild or on a rival Trainer's team, the Sinnoh Pokédex will automatically record it.

Bring up your "Seen" count to 210.

● Ways to complete your Sinnoh Pokédex in Platinum

1	Encounter Pokémon before the Hall of Fame, and bring your "Seen" count up to 210

What's the difference between the Sinnoh Pokédex and the National Pokédex?

The Sinnoh Pokédex can record Pokémon simply by you laying eyes on them. But the National Pokédex can't record a Pokémon until you catch it. So completing the National Pokédex is a much more lofty goal. It's the challenge that awaits you after the Sinnoh Pokédex.

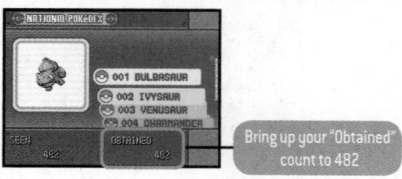

Bring up your "Obtained" count to 482.

Get a prize from the Game Director

After you've seen and recorded all 210 Sinnoh-native Pokémon in your Sinnoh Pokédex, go visit the Game Director at the cottage on Valor Lakefront. He should reward your skill with a lovely gift that should put a smile on your face.

The Game Director works for GAME FREAK

The Game Director works for GAME FREAK, the company that makes the Pokémon games.

How to Read the Pokédex

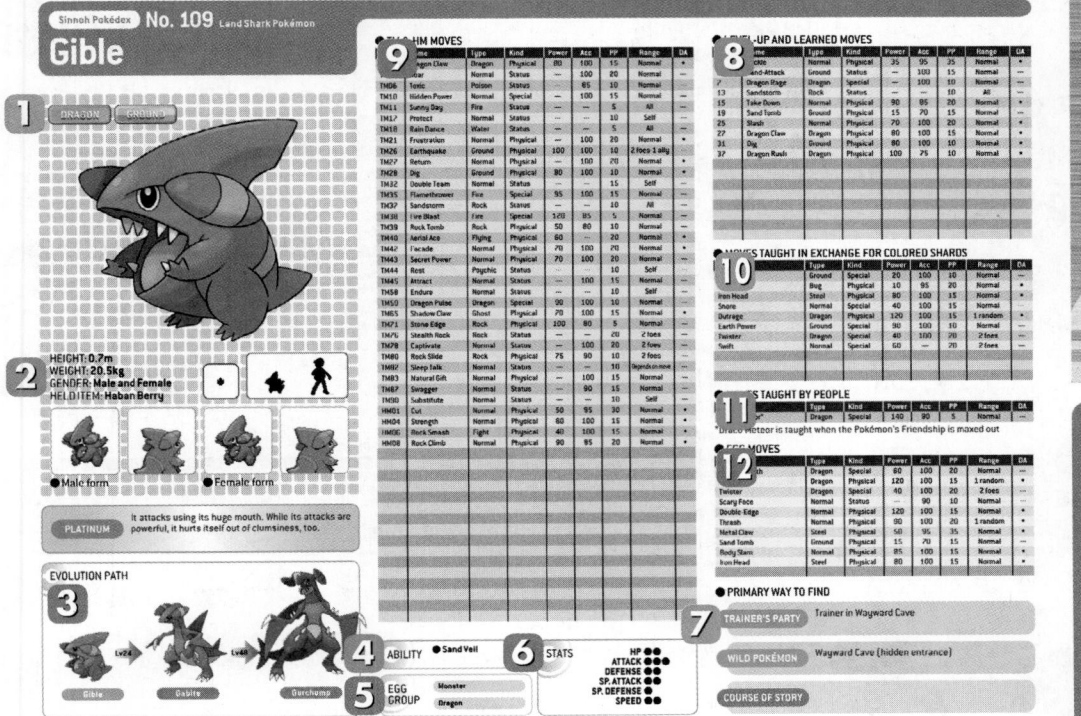

1 Pokémon type

The type of the Pokémon. Some Pokémon have two types.

2 Held item

The item that is sometimes held by the Pokémon when you encounter it in the wild.

3 Evolution path

The course of Evolution for the Pokémon, as well as any conditions governing its Evolution.

4 Abilities

The Pokémon's Ability. Sometimes a Pokémon is listed with two Abilities; in that case, the individual Pokémon will come with either one or the other.

5 Egg group

The Egg group the Pokémon belongs to. Some Pokémon belong to two groups.

6 Stats compiled by the editors

The value of the Pokémon's stats. The more dots shown, the easier that stat is to develop. The dot total is a relative measure across Pokémon from all regions, with a maximum of 5 dots.

7 Ways to record in the Sinnoh Pokédex

There are three ways to see and record a Pokémon in your Sinnoh Pokédex: see it in battle on a foe Trainer's team, see it in the wild, and see it in the course of the story.

8 Level-up moves

A list of the moves the Pokémon can learn by leveling up. Entries in blue are different from Pokémon Diamond and Pokémon Pearl.

9 TM and HM moves

A list of the moves the Pokémon can learn by using a TM or an HM.

10 Moves taught in exchange for colored shards

A list of the moves that the Pokémon can be taught by a Move Tutor in exchange for colored shards you dig up in the Underground.

11 Moves taught by people

A list of the moves that the Pokémon can be taught by people.

12 Egg moves

These moves are occasionally learned by the Pokémon upon hatching from an Egg, as long as they are known by the male Pokémon you leave at Pokémon Day Care.

Move legend

Lv	The level at which the move is learned
Type	Move type
Kind	Whether the move is a physical, special, or status move
Power	Attack power
Acc	Accuracy
PP	# of times you can use the move
Range	How many Pokémon the move affects at once
DA (Direct Attack)	Whether the user physically touches the target
DoM	Depends on move

Sinnoh Pokédex No. 001 Tiny Leaf Pokémon

Turtwig

GRASS

HEIGHT: 1'04"
WEIGHT: 22.5 lbs.
GENDER: Male and Female
HELD ITEM: None

● M/F have same form

PLATINUM — The shell on its back is made of soil. On a very healthy TURTWIG, the shell should feel moist.

EVOLUTION PATH

Turtwig — Lv18 → Grotle — Lv32 → Torterra

ABILITY ● Overgrow

EGG GROUP: Monster / Grass

STATS
HP ●●
ATTACK ●●
DEFENSE ●●
SP. ATTACK ●●
SP. DEFENSE ●●
SPEED ●

● TM & HM MOVES

No.	Name	Type	Kind	Power	Acc	PP	Range	DA
TM06	Toxic	Poison	Status	—	85	10	Normal	—
TM09	Bullet Seed	Grass	Physical	10	100	30	Normal	—
TM10	Hidden Power	Normal	Special	—	100	15	Normal	—
TM11	Sunny Day	Fire	Status	—	—	5	All	—
TM16	Light Screen	Psychic	Status	—	—	30	2 allies	—
TM17	Protect	Normal	Status	—	—	10	Self	—
TM19	Giga Drain	Grass	Special	60	100	10	Normal	—
TM20	Safeguard	Normal	Status	—	—	25	2 allies	—
TM21	Frustration	Normal	Physical	—	100	20	Normal	•
TM22	SolarBeam	Grass	Special	120	100	10	Normal	—
TM23	Iron Tail	Steel	Physical	100	75	15	Normal	•
TM27	Return	Normal	Physical	—	100	20	Normal	•
TM32	Double Team	Normal	Status	—	—	15	Self	—
TM33	Reflect	Psychic	Status	—	—	20	2 allies	—
TM42	Facade	Normal	Physical	70	100	20	Normal	•
TM43	Secret Power	Normal	Physical	70	100	20	Normal	•
TM44	Rest	Psychic	Status	—	—	10	Self	—
TM45	Attract	Normal	Status	—	100	15	Normal	—
TM53	Energy Ball	Grass	Special	80	100	10	Normal	—
TM58	Endure	Normal	Status	—	—	10	Self	—
TM70	Flash	Normal	Status	—	100	20	Normal	—
TM75	Swords Dance	Normal	Status	—	—	30	Self	—
TM76	Stealth Rock	Rock	Status	—	—	20	2 foes	—
TM78	Captivate	Normal	Status	—	100	20	2 foes	—
TM82	Sleep Talk	Normal	Status	—	—	10	DoM	—
TM83	Natural Gift	Normal	Physical	—	100	15	Normal	—
TM86	Grass Knot	Grass	Special	—	100	20	Normal	•
TM87	Swagger	Normal	Status	—	90	15	Normal	—
TM90	Substitute	Normal	Status	—	—	10	Self	—
HM01	Cut	Normal	Physical	50	95	30	Normal	•
HM04	Strength	Normal	Physical	80	100	15	Normal	•
HM06	Rock Smash	Fighting	Physical	40	100	15	Normal	•
HM08	Rock Climb	Normal	Physical	90	85	20	Normal	•

● LEVEL-UP AND LEARNED MOVES

Lv	Name	Type	Kind	Power	Acc	PP	Range	DA
Base	Tackle	Normal	Physical	35	95	35	Normal	•
5	Withdraw	Water	Status	—	—	40	Self	—
9	Absorb	Grass	Special	20	100	25	Normal	—
13	Razor Leaf	Grass	Physical	55	95	25	2 foes	•
17	Curse	???	Status	—	—	10	Normal•Self	—
21	Bite	Dark	Physical	60	100	25	Normal	•
25	Mega Drain	Grass	Special	40	100	15	Normal	—
29	Leech Seed	Grass	Status	—	90	10	Normal	—
33	Synthesis	Grass	Status	—	—	5	Self	—
37	Crunch	Dark	Physical	80	100	15	Normal	•
41	Giga Drain	Grass	Special	60	100	10	Normal	—
45	Leaf Storm	Grass	Special	140	90	5	Normal	—

● MOVES TAUGHT IN EXCHANGE FOR COLORED SHARDS

Name	Type	Kind	Power	Acc	PP	Range	DA
Mud-Slap	Ground	Special	20	100	10	Normal	•
Superpower	Fighting	Physical	120	100	5	Normal	•
Snore	Normal	Special	40	100	15	Normal	—
Synthesis	Grass	Status	—	—	5	Self	—
Earth Power	Ground	Special	90	100	10	Normal	—
Seed Bomb	Grass	Physical	80	100	15	Normal	—

● EGG MOVES

Name	Type	Category	Power	Acc	PP	Range	DA
Worry Seed	Grass	Status	—	100	10	Normal	—
Growth	Normal	Status	—	—	40	Self	—
Tickle	Normal	Status	—	100	20	Normal	—
Body Slam	Normal	Physical	85	100	15	Normal	•
Double-Edge	Normal	Physical	120	100	15	Normal	•
Sand Tomb	Ground	Physical	15	70	15	Normal	—
Seed Bomb	Grass	Physical	80	100	15	Normal	•
Thrash	Normal	Physical	90	100	20	1 random	•
Amnesia	Psychic	Status	—	—	20	Self	—
Superpower	Fighting	Physical	120	100	5	Normal	•

● PRIMARY WAY TO FIND

TRAINER'S PARTY — Eterna Gym Leader Gardenia

WILD POKÉMON

COURSE OF STORY — Receive from Professor Rowan on Route 201

Sinnoh Pokédex No. 002 Grove Pokémon

Grotle

GRASS

HEIGHT: 3'07"
WEIGHT: 213.8
GENDER: Male and Female
HELD ITEM: None

● M/F have same form

PLATINUM — It knows where pure water wells up. It carries fellow Pokémon there on its back.

EVOLUTION PATH

Turtwig — Lv18 → Grotle — Lv32 → Torterra

ABILITY ● Overgrow

EGG GROUP: Monster / Grass

STATS
HP ●●
ATTACK ●●●
DEFENSE ●●●
SP. ATTACK ●●
SP. DEFENSE ●●
SPEED ●

● TM & HM MOVES

No.	Name	Type	Kind	Power	Acc	PP	Range	DA
TM06	Toxic	Poison	Status	—	85	10	Normal	—
TM09	Bullet Seed	Grass	Physical	10	100	30	Normal	—
TM10	Hidden Power	Normal	Special	—	100	15	Normal	—
TM11	Sunny Day	Fire	Status	—	—	5	All	—
TM16	Light Screen	Psychic	Status	—	—	30	2 allies	—
TM17	Protect	Normal	Status	—	—	10	Self	—
TM19	Giga Drain	Grass	Special	60	100	10	Normal	—
TM20	Safeguard	Normal	Status	—	—	25	2 allies	—
TM21	Frustration	Normal	Physical	—	100	20	Normal	•
TM22	SolarBeam	Grass	Special	120	100	10	Normal	—
TM23	Iron Tail	Steel	Physical	100	75	15	Normal	•
TM27	Return	Normal	Physical	—	100	20	Normal	•
TM32	Double Team	Normal	Status	—	—	15	Self	—
TM33	Reflect	Psychic	Status	—	—	20	2 allies	—
TM42	Facade	Normal	Physical	70	100	20	Normal	•
TM43	Secret Power	Normal	Physical	70	100	20	Normal	•
TM44	Rest	Psychic	Status	—	—	10	Self	—
TM45	Attract	Normal	Status	—	100	15	Normal	—
TM53	Energy Ball	Grass	Special	80	100	10	Normal	—
TM58	Endure	Normal	Status	—	—	10	Self	—
TM70	Flash	Normal	Status	—	100	20	Normal	—
TM75	Swords Dance	Normal	Status	—	—	30	Self	—
TM76	Stealth Rock	Rock	Status	—	—	20	2 foes	—
TM78	Captivate	Normal	Status	—	100	20	2 foes	—
TM82	Sleep Talk	Normal	Status	—	—	10	DoM	—
TM83	Natural Gift	Normal	Physical	—	100	15	Normal	—
TM86	Grass Knot	Grass	Special	—	100	20	Normal	•
TM87	Swagger	Normal	Status	—	90	15	Normal	—
TM90	Substitute	Normal	Status	—	—	10	Self	—
HM01	Cut	Normal	Physical	50	95	30	Normal	•
HM04	Strength	Normal	Physical	80	100	15	Normal	•
HM06	Rock Smash	Fighting	Physical	40	100	15	Normal	•
HM08	Rock Climb	Normal	Physical	90	85	20	Normal	•

● LEVEL-UP AND LEARNED MOVES

Lv	Name	Type	Kind	Power	Acc	PP	Range	DA
Base	Tackle	Normal	Physical	35	95	35	Normal	•
Base	Withdraw	Water	Status	—	—	40	Self	—
5	Withdraw	Water	Status	—	—	40	Self	—
9	Absorb	Grass	Special	20	100	25	Normal	—
13	Razor Leaf	Grass	Physical	55	95	25	2 foes	•
17	Curse	???	Status	—	—	10	Normal•Self	—
22	Bite	Dark	Physical	60	100	25	Normal	•
27	Mega Drain	Grass	Special	40	100	15	Normal	—
32	Leech Seed	Grass	Status	—	90	10	Normal	—
37	Synthesis	Grass	Status	—	—	5	Self	—
42	Crunch	Dark	Physical	80	100	15	Normal	•
47	Giga Drain	Grass	Special	60	100	10	Normal	—
52	Leaf Storm	Grass	Special	140	90	5	Normal	—

● MOVES TAUGHT IN EXCHANGE FOR COLORED SHARDS

Name	Type	Kind	Power	Acc	PP	Range	DA
Mud-Slap	Ground	Special	20	100	10	Normal	•
Superpower	Fighting	Physical	120	100	5	Normal	•
Snore	Normal	Special	40	100	15	Normal	—
Synthesis	Grass	Status	—	—	5	Self	—
Earth Power	Ground	Special	90	100	10	Normal	—
Seed Bomb	Grass	Physical	80	100	15	Normal	—

● PRIMARY WAY TO FIND

TRAINER'S PARTY — Trainer on the Celestic Town side of Route 210

WILD POKÉMON

COURSE OF STORY — Level up Turtwig to Lv18

Sinnoh Pokédex **No. 003** Continent Pokémon

Torterra

GRASS GROUND

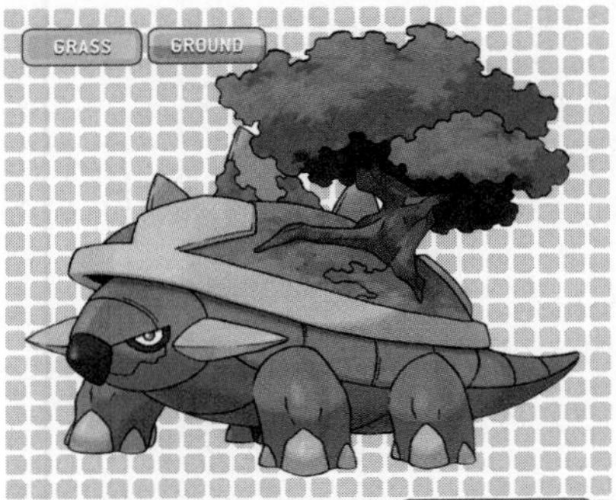

HEIGHT: 7'03"
WEIGHT: 683.4 lbs.
GENDER: Male and Female
HELD ITEM: None

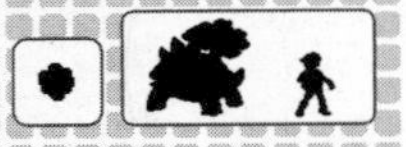

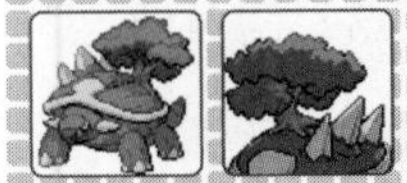

● M/F have same form

PLATINUM — Some Pokémon are born on a TORTERRA's back and spend their entire life there.

EVOLUTION PATH

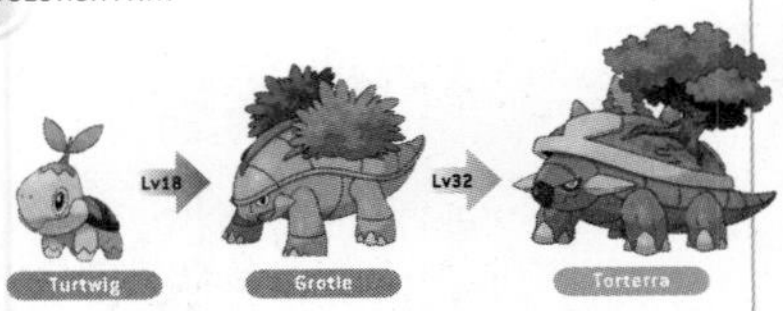

Turtwig
Lv18
Grotle
Lv32
Torterra

● TM & HM MOVES

No.	Name	Type	Kind	Power	Acc	PP	Range	DA
TM05	Roar	Normal	Status	—	—	20	Normal	—
TM06	Toxic	Poison	Status	—	85	10	Normal	—
TM09	Bullet Seed	Grass	Physical	10	100	30	Normal	—
TM10	Hidden Power	Normal	Special	—	100	15	Normal	—
TM11	Sunny Day	Fire	Status	—	—	5	All	—
TM15	Hyper Beam	Normal	Special	150	90	5	Normal	—
TM16	Light Screen	Psychic	Status	—	—	30	2 allies	—
TM17	Protect	Normal	Status	—	—	10	Self	—
TM19	Giga Drain	Grass	Special	60	100	10	Normal	—
TM20	Safeguard	Normal	Status	—	—	25	2 allies	—
TM21	Frustration	Normal	Physical	—	100	20	Normal	•
TM22	SolarBeam	Grass	Special	120	100	10	Normal	—
TM23	Iron Tail	Steel	Physical	100	75	15	Normal	•
TM26	Earthquake	Ground	Physical	100	100	10	2 foes • 1 ally	—
TM27	Return	Normal	Physical	—	100	20	Normal	•
TM32	Double Team	Normal	Status	—	—	15	Self	—
TM33	Reflect	Psychic	Status	—	—	20	2 allies	—
TM37	Sandstorm	Rock	Status	—	—	10	All	—
TM39	Rock Tomb	Rock	Physical	50	80	10	Normal	—
TM42	Facade	Normal	Physical	70	100	20	Normal	•
TM43	Secret Power	Normal	Physical	70	100	20	Normal	—
TM44	Rest	Psychic	Status	—	—	10	Self	—
TM45	Attract	Normal	Status	—	100	15	Normal	—
TM53	Energy Ball	Grass	Special	80	100	10	Normal	—
TM58	Endure	Normal	Status	—	—	10	Self	—
TM68	Giga Impact	Normal	Physical	150	90	5	Normal	•
TM69	Rock Polish	Rock	Status	—	—	20	Self	—
TM70	Flash	Normal	Status	—	100	20	Normal	—
TM71	Stone Edge	Rock	Physical	100	80	5	Normal	—
TM75	Swords Dance	Normal	Status	—	—	30	Self	—
TM76	Stealth Rock	Rock	Status	—	—	20	2 foes	—
TM78	Captivate	Normal	Status	—	100	20	2 foes	—
TM80	Rock Slide	Rock	Physical	75	90	10	2 foes	—
TM82	Sleep Talk	Normal	Status	—	—	10	DoM	—
TM83	Natural Gift	Normal	Physical	—	100	15	Normal	—
TM86	Grass Knot	Grass	Special	—	100	20	Normal	•
TM87	Swagger	Normal	Status	—	90	15	Normal	—
TM90	Substitute	Normal	Status	—	—	10	Self	—
HM01	Cut	Normal	Physical	50	95	30	Normal	•
HM04	Strength	Normal	Physical	80	100	15	Normal	•
HM06	Rock Smash	Fighting	Physical	40	100	15	Normal	•
HM08	Rock Climb	Normal	Physical	90	85	20	Normal	•

ABILITY ● Overgrow

EGG GROUP: Monster, Grass

STATS
HP ●●●
ATTACK ●●●●
DEFENSE ●●●●
SP. ATTACK ●●●
SP. DEFENSE ●●●
SPEED ●●

● LEVEL-UP AND LEARNED MOVES

Lv	Name	Type	Kind	Power	Acc	PP	Range	DA
Base	Wood Hammer	Grass	Physical	120	100	15	Normal	•
Base	Tackle	Normal	Physical	35	95	35	Normal	•
Base	Withdraw	Water	Status	—	—	40	Self	—
Base	Absorb	Grass	Special	20	100	25	Normal	—
Base	Razor Leaf	Grass	Physical	55	95	25	2 foes	—
5	Withdraw	Water	Status	—	—	40	Self	—
9	Absorb	Grass	Special	20	100	25	Normal	—
13	Razor Leaf	Grass	Physical	55	95	25	2 foes	—
17	Curse	???	Status	—	—	10	Normal•Self	—
22	Bite	Dark	Physical	60	100	25	Normal	•
27	Mega Drain	Grass	Special	40	100	15	Normal	—
32	Earthquake	Ground	Physical	100	100	10	2 foes • 1 ally	—
33	Leech Seed	Grass	Status	—	90	10	Normal	—
39	Synthesis	Grass	Status	—	—	5	Self	—
45	Crunch	Dark	Physical	80	100	15	Normal	•
51	Giga Drain	Grass	Special	60	100	10	Normal	—
57	Leaf Storm	Grass	Special	140	90	5	Normal	—

● MOVES TAUGHT IN EXCHANGE FOR COLORED SHARDS

Name	Type	Kind	Power	Acc	PP	Range	DA
Mud-Slap	Ground	Special	20	100	10	Normal	—
Superpower	Fighting	Physical	120	100	5	Normal	•
Iron Head	Steel	Physical	80	100	15	Normal	•
Snore	Normal	Special	40	100	15	Normal	—
Outrage	Dragon	Physical	120	100	15	1 random	•
Synthesis	Grass	Status	—	—	5	Self	—
Earth Power	Ground	Special	90	100	10	Normal	—
Seed Bomb	Grass	Physical	80	100	15	Normal	—

● MOVES TAUGHT BY PEOPLE

Name	Type	Kind	Power	Acc	PP	Range	DA
Frenzy Plant	Grass	Special	150	90	5	Normal	—

● PRIMARY WAY TO FIND

TRAINER'S PARTY: Trainer on Victory Road

WILD POKÉMON

COURSE OF STORY: Level up Grotle to Lv32

Sinnoh Pokédex **No. 004** Chimp Pokémon

Chimchar

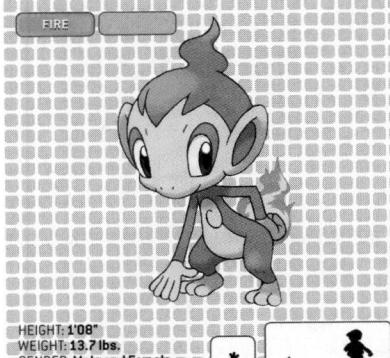

FIRE

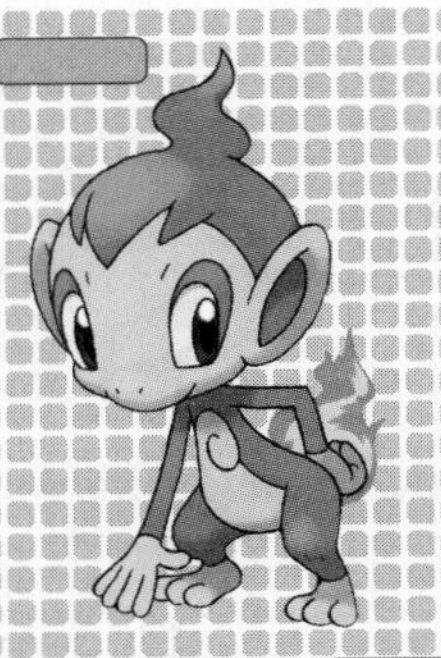

HEIGHT: 1'08"
WEIGHT: 13.7 lbs.
GENDER: Male and Female
HELD ITEM: None

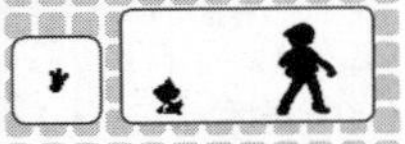

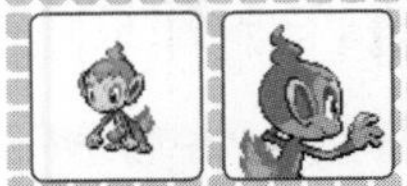

● M/F have same form

PLATINUM — It is very agile. Before going to sleep, it extinguishes the flame on its tail to prevent fires.

EVOLUTION PATH

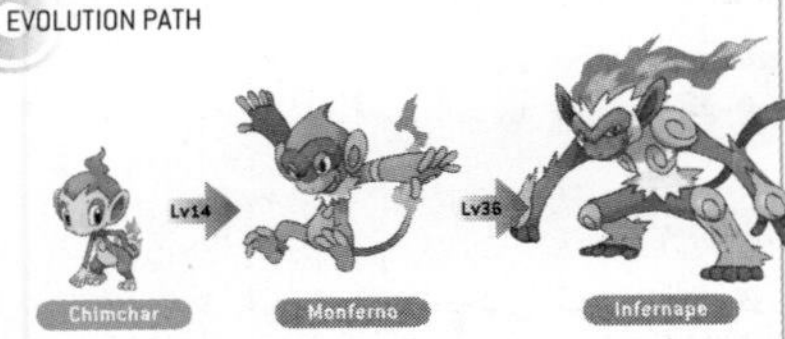

Chimchar
Lv14
Monferno
Lv36
Infernape

● TM & HM MOVES

No.	Name	Type	Kind	Power	Acc	PP	Range	DA
TM01	Focus Punch	Fighting	Physical	150	100	20	Normal	•
TM06	Toxic	Poison	Status	—	85	10	Normal	—
TM08	Bulk Up	Fighting	Status	—	—	20	Self	—
TM10	Hidden Power	Normal	Special	—	100	15	Normal	—
TM11	Sunny Day	Fire	Status	—	—	5	All	—
TM12	Taunt	Dark	Status	—	100	20	Normal	—
TM17	Protect	Normal	Status	—	—	10	Self	—
TM21	Frustration	Normal	Physical	—	100	20	Normal	•
TM23	Iron Tail	Steel	Physical	100	75	15	Normal	•
TM27	Return	Normal	Physical	—	100	20	Normal	•
TM28	Dig	Ground	Physical	80	100	10	Normal	•
TM31	Brick Break	Fighting	Physical	75	100	15	Normal	•
TM32	Double Team	Normal	Status	—	—	15	Self	—
TM35	Flamethrower	Fire	Special	95	100	15	Normal	—
TM38	Fire Blast	Fire	Special	120	85	5	Normal	—
TM40	Aerial Ace	Flying	Physical	60	—	20	Normal	•
TM41	Torment	Dark	Status	—	100	15	Normal	—
TM42	Facade	Normal	Physical	70	100	20	Normal	•
TM43	Secret Power	Normal	Physical	70	100	20	Normal	—
TM44	Rest	Psychic	Status	—	—	10	Self	—
TM45	Attract	Normal	Status	—	100	15	Normal	—
TM50	Overheat	Fire	Special	140	90	5	Normal	—
TM56	Fling	Dark	Physical	—	100	10	Normal	—
TM58	Endure	Normal	Status	—	—	10	Self	—
TM61	Will-O-Wisp	Fire	Status	—	75	15	Normal	—
TM65	Shadow Claw	Ghost	Physical	70	100	15	Normal	•
TM75	Swords Dance	Normal	Status	—	—	30	Self	—
TM76	Stealth Rock	Rock	Status	—	—	20	2 foes	—
TM78	Captivate	Normal	Status	—	100	20	2 foes	—
TM82	Sleep Talk	Normal	Status	—	—	10	DoM	—
TM83	Natural Gift	Normal	Physical	—	100	15	Normal	—
TM86	Grass Knot	Grass	Special	—	100	20	Normal	•
TM87	Swagger	Normal	Status	—	90	15	Normal	—
TM89	U-turn	Bug	Physical	70	100	20	Normal	•
TM90	Substitute	Normal	Status	—	—	10	Self	—
HM01	Cut	Normal	Physical	50	95	30	Normal	•
HM04	Strength	Normal	Physical	80	100	15	Normal	•
HM06	Rock Smash	Fighting	Physical	40	100	15	Normal	•
HM08	Rock Climb	Normal	Physical	90	85	20	Normal	•

ABILITY ● Blaze

EGG GROUP: Field, Human-Like

STATS
HP ●
ATTACK ●●
DEFENSE ●●
SP. ATTACK ●●
SP. DEFENSE ●●
SPEED ●●

● LEVEL-UP AND LEARNED MOVES

Lv	Name	Type	Kind	Power	Acc	PP	Range	DA
Base	Scratch	Normal	Physical	40	100	35	Normal	•
Base	Leer	Normal	Status	—	100	30	2 foes	—
7	Ember	Fire	Special	40	100	25	Normal	—
9	Taunt	Dark	Status	—	100	20	Normal	—
15	Fury Swipes	Normal	Physical	18	80	15	Normal	•
17	Flame Wheel	Fire	Physical	60	100	25	Normal	•
23	Nasty Plot	Dark	Status	—	—	20	Self	—
25	Torment	Dark	Status	—	100	15	Normal	—
31	Facade	Normal	Physical	70	100	20	Normal	•
33	Fire Spin	Fire	Special	15	70	15	Normal	—
39	Slack Off	Normal	Status	—	—	10	Self	—
41	Flamethrower	Fire	Special	95	100	15	Normal	—

● MOVES TAUGHT IN EXCHANGE FOR COLORED SHARDS

Name	Type	Kind	Power	Acc	PP	Range	DA
Mud-Slap	Ground	Special	20	100	10	Normal	—
Rollout	Rock	Physical	30	90	20	Normal	•
ThunderPunch	Electric	Physical	75	100	15	Normal	•
Fire Punch	Fire	Physical	75	100	15	Normal	•
Snore	Normal	Special	40	100	15	Normal	—
Helping Hand	Normal	Status	—	—	20	1 ally	—
Endeavor	Normal	Physical	—	100	5	Normal	•
Vacuum Wave	Fighting	Special	40	100	30	Normal	—
Gunk Shot	Poison	Physical	120	70	5	Normal	—
Heat Wave	Fire	Special	100	90	10	2 foes	—
Swift	Normal	Special	60	—	20	2 foes	—
Uproar	Normal	Special	50	100	10	1 random	—

● EGG MOVES

Name	Type	Kind	Power	Acc	PP	Range	DA
Fire Punch	Fire	Physical	75	100	15	Normal	•
ThunderPunch	Electric	Physical	75	100	15	Normal	•
Double Kick	Fighting	Physical	30	100	30	Normal	•
Encore	Normal	Status	—	100	5	Normal	—
Heat Wave	Fire	Special	100	90	10	2 foes	—
Focus Energy	Normal	Status	—	—	30	Self	—
Helping Hand	Normal	Status	—	—	20	1 ally	—
Fake Out	Normal	Physical	40	100	10	Normal	•
Blaze Kick	Fire	Physical	85	90	10	Normal	•
Counter	Fighting	Physical	—	100	20	Self	•

● PRIMARY WAY TO FIND

TRAINER'S PARTY: Trainer on Route 207

WILD POKÉMON

COURSE OF STORY: Receive from Professor Rowan on Route 201

Sinnoh Pokédex **No. 005** Playful Pokémon

Monferno

FIRE | Fighting

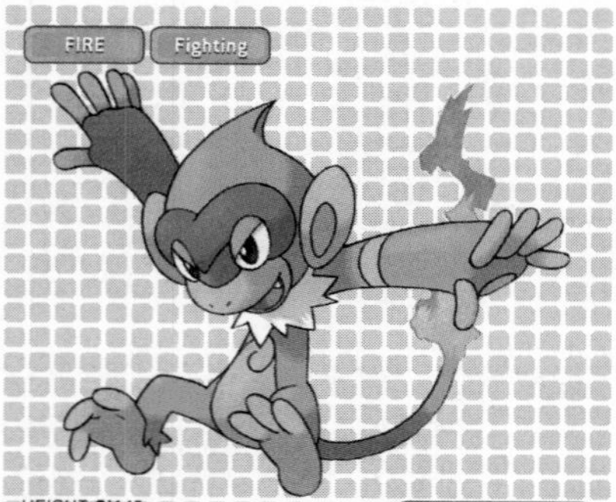

HEIGHT: **2'11"**
WEIGHT: **48.5 lbs.**
GENDER: **Male and Female**
HELD ITEM: **None**

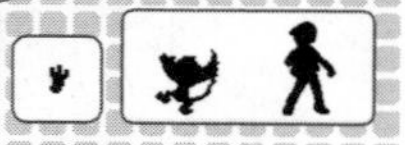

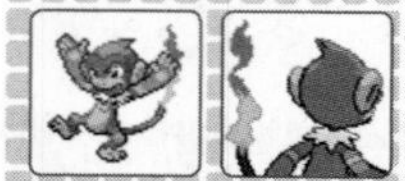

● M/F have same form

PLATINUM It skillfully controls the intensity of the fire on its tail to keep its foes at an ideal distance.

EVOLUTION PATH

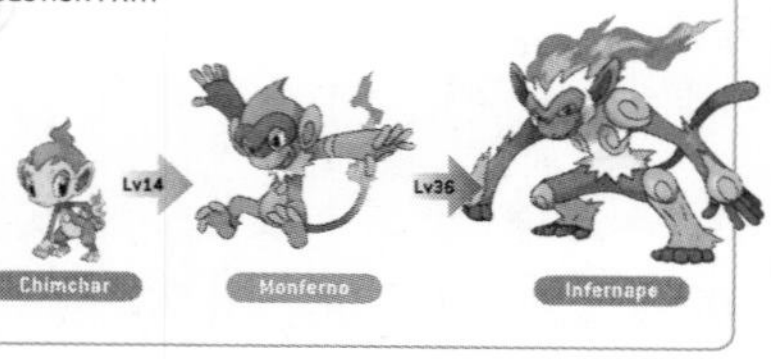

● TM & HM MOVES

No.	Name	Type	Kind	Power	Acc	PP	Range	DA
TM01	Focus Punch	Fighting	Physical	150	100	20	Normal	•
TM06	Toxic	Poison	Status	—	85	10	Normal	—
TM08	Bulk Up	Fighting	Status	—	—	20	Self	—
TM10	Hidden Power	Normal	Special	—	100	15	Normal	—
TM11	Sunny Day	Fire	Status	—	—	5	All	—
TM12	Taunt	Dark	Status	—	100	20	Normal	—
TM17	Protect	Normal	Status	—	—	10	Self	—
TM21	Frustration	Normal	Physical	—	100	20	Normal	•
TM23	Iron Tail	Steel	Physical	100	75	15	Normal	•
TM27	Return	Normal	Physical	—	100	20	Normal	•
TM28	Dig	Ground	Physical	80	100	10	Normal	•
TM31	Brick Break	Fighting	Physical	75	100	15	Normal	•
TM32	Double Team	Normal	Status	—	—	15	Self	—
TM35	Flamethrower	Fire	Special	95	100	15	Normal	—
TM38	Fire Blast	Fire	Special	120	85	5	Normal	—
TM39	Rock Tomb	Rock	Physical	50	80	10	Normal	—
TM40	Aerial Ace	Flying	Physical	60	—	20	Normal	•
TM41	Torment	Dark	Status	—	100	15	Normal	—
TM42	Facade	Normal	Physical	70	100	20	Normal	•
TM43	Secret Power	Normal	Physical	70	100	20	Normal	—
TM44	Rest	Psychic	Status	—	—	10	Self	—
TM45	Attract	Normal	Status	—	100	15	Normal	—
TM50	Overheat	Fire	Special	140	90	5	Normal	—
TM52	Focus Blast	Fighting	Special	120	70	5	Normal	—
TM56	Fling	Dark	Physical	—	100	10	Normal	—
TM58	Endure	Normal	Status	—	—	10	Self	—
TM61	Will-O-Wisp	Fire	Status	—	75	15	Normal	—
TM65	Shadow Claw	Ghost	Physical	70	100	15	Normal	•
TM75	Swords Dance	Normal	Status	—	—	30	Self	—
TM76	Stealth Rock	Rock	Status	—	—	20	2 foes	—
TM78	Captivate	Normal	Status	—	100	20	2 foes	—
TM80	Rock Slide	Rock	Physical	75	90	10	2 foes	—
TM82	Sleep Talk	Normal	Status	—	—	10	DoM	—
TM83	Natural Gift	Normal	Physical	—	100	15	Normal	—
TM84	Poison Jab	Poison	Physical	80	100	20	Normal	•
TM86	Grass Knot	Grass	Special	—	100	20	Normal	•
TM87	Swagger	Normal	Status	—	90	15	Normal	—
TM89	U-turn	Bug	Physical	70	100	20	Normal	•
TM90	Substitute	Normal	Status	—	—	10	Self	—
HM01	Cut	Normal	Physical	50	95	30	Normal	•
HM04	Strength	Normal	Physical	80	100	15	Normal	•
HM06	Rock Smash	Fighting	Physical	40	100	15	Normal	•
HM08	Rock Climb	Normal	Physical	90	85	20	Normal	•

ABILITY ● Blaze

EGG GROUP Field / Human-Like

STATS
HP ●●
ATTACK ●●●
DEFENSE ●●
SP. ATTACK ●●●
SP. DEFENSE ●
SPEED ●●●

● LEVEL-UP AND LEARNED MOVES

Lv	Name	Type	Kind	Power	Acc	PP	Range	DA
Base	Scratch	Normal	Physical	40	100	35	Normal	•
Base	Leer	Normal	Status	—	100	30	2 foes	—
Base	Ember	Fire	Special	40	100	25	Normal	—
7	Ember	Fire	Special	40	100	25	Normal	—
9	Taunt	Dark	Status	—	100	20	Normal	—
14	Mach Punch	Fighting	Physical	40	100	30	Normal	•
16	Fury Swipes	Normal	Physical	18	80	15	Normal	•
19	Flame Wheel	Fire	Physical	60	100	25	Normal	•
26	Feint	Normal	Physical	50	100	10	Normal	—
29	Torment	Dark	Status	—	100	15	Normal	—
36	Close Combat	Fighting	Physical	120	100	5	Normal	•
39	Fire Spin	Fire	Special	15	70	15	Normal	—
46	Slack Off	Normal	Status	—	—	10	Self	—
49	Flare Blitz	Fire	Physical	120	100	15	Normal	•

● MOVES TAUGHT IN EXCHANGE FOR COLORED SHARDS

Name	Type	Kind	Power	Acc	PP	Range	DA
Mud-Slap	Ground	Special	20	100	10	Normal	—
Rollout	Rock	Physical	30	90	20	Normal	•
ThunderPunch	Electric	Physical	75	100	15	Normal	•
Fire Punch	Fire	Physical	75	100	15	Normal	•
Snore	Normal	Special	40	100	15	Normal	—
Helping Hand	Normal	Status	—	—	20	1 ally	—
Endeavor	Normal	Physical	—	100	5	Normal	•
Vacuum Wave	Fighting	Special	40	100	30	Normal	—
Gunk Shot	Poison	Physical	120	70	5	Normal	—
Heat Wave	Fire	Special	100	90	10	2 foes	—
Swift	Normal	Special	60	—	20	2 foes	—

● PRIMARY WAY TO FIND

TRAINER'S PARTY Trainer on Route 212

WILD POKÉMON

COURSE OF STORY Level up Chimchar to Lv14

Sinnoh Pokédex **No. 006** Flame Pokémon

Infernape

FIRE | Fighting

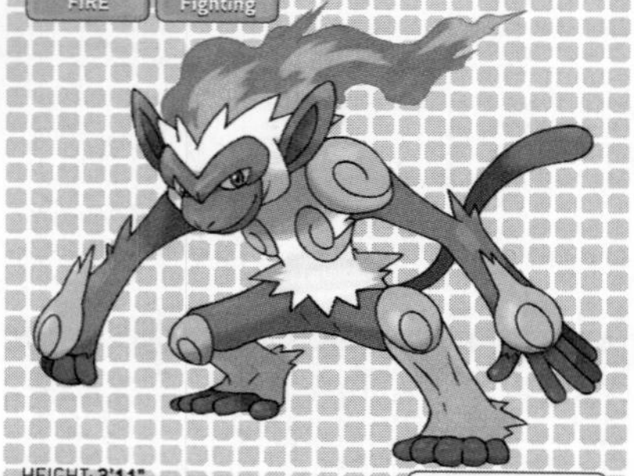

HEIGHT: **3'11"**
WEIGHT: **121.3 lbs.**
GENDER: **Male and Female**
HELD ITEM: **None**

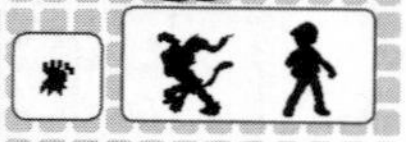

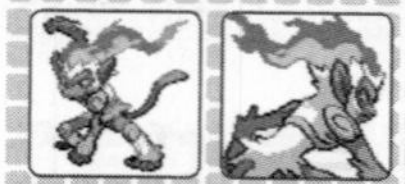

● M/F have same form

PLATINUM It uses unique Fighting moves with fire on its hands and feet. It will take on any opponent.

EVOLUTION PATH

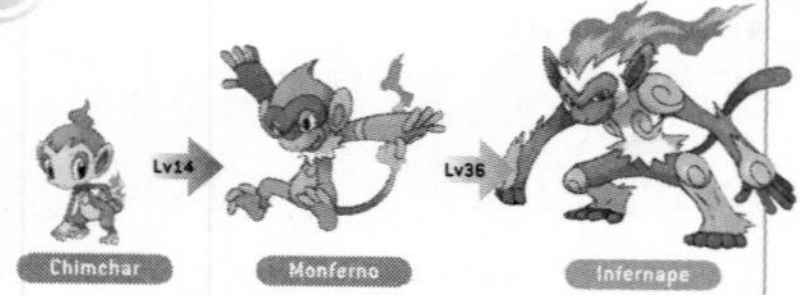

● TM & HM MOVES

No.	Name	Type	Kind	Power	Acc	PP	Range	DA
TM01	Focus Punch	Fighting	Physical	150	100	20	Normal	•
TM04	Calm Mind	Psychic	Status	—	—	20	Self	—
TM05	Roar	Normal	Status	—	100	20	Normal	—
TM06	Toxic	Poison	Status	—	85	10	Normal	—
TM08	Bulk Up	Fighting	Status	—	—	20	Self	—
TM10	Hidden Power	Normal	Special	—	100	15	Normal	—
TM11	Sunny Day	Fire	Status	—	—	5	All	—
TM12	Taunt	Dark	Status	—	100	20	Normal	—
TM15	Hyper Beam	Normal	Special	150	90	5	Normal	—
TM17	Protect	Normal	Status	—	—	10	Self	—
TM21	Frustration	Normal	Physical	—	100	20	Normal	•
TM22	SolarBeam	Grass	Special	120	100	10	Normal	—
TM23	Iron Tail	Steel	Physical	100	75	15	Normal	•
TM26	Earthquake	Ground	Physical	100	100	10	2 foes • 1 ally	—
TM27	Return	Normal	Physical	—	100	20	Normal	•
TM28	Dig	Ground	Physical	80	100	10	Normal	•
TM31	Brick Break	Fighting	Physical	75	100	15	Normal	•
TM32	Double Team	Normal	Status	—	—	15	Self	—
TM35	Flamethrower	Fire	Special	95	100	15	Normal	—
TM38	Fire Blast	Fire	Special	120	85	5	Normal	—
TM39	Rock Tomb	Rock	Physical	50	80	10	Normal	—
TM40	Aerial Ace	Flying	Physical	60	—	20	Normal	•
TM41	Torment	Dark	Status	—	100	15	Normal	—
TM42	Facade	Normal	Physical	70	100	20	Normal	•
TM43	Secret Power	Normal	Physical	70	100	20	Normal	—
TM44	Rest	Psychic	Status	—	—	10	Self	—
TM45	Attract	Normal	Status	—	100	15	Normal	—
TM50	Overheat	Fire	Special	140	90	5	Normal	—
TM52	Focus Blast	Fighting	Special	120	70	5	Normal	—
TM56	Fling	Dark	Physical	—	100	10	Normal	—
TM58	Endure	Normal	Status	—	—	10	Self	—
TM61	Will-O-Wisp	Fire	Status	—	75	15	Normal	—
TM65	Shadow Claw	Ghost	Physical	70	100	15	Normal	•
TM68	Giga Impact	Normal	Physical	150	90	5	Normal	•
TM71	Stone Edge	Rock	Physical	100	80	5	Normal	—
TM75	Swords Dance	Normal	Status	—	—	30	Self	—
TM76	Stealth Rock	Rock	Status	—	—	20	2 foes	—
TM78	Captivate	Normal	Status	—	100	20	2 foes	—
TM80	Rock Slide	Rock	Physical	75	90	10	2 foes	—
TM82	Sleep Talk	Normal	Status	—	—	10	DoM	—
TM83	Natural Gift	Normal	Physical	—	100	15	Normal	—
TM84	Poison Jab	Poison	Physical	80	100	20	Normal	•
TM86	Grass Knot	Grass	Special	—	100	20	Normal	•
TM87	Swagger	Normal	Status	—	90	15	Normal	—
TM89	U-turn	Bug	Physical	70	100	20	Normal	•
TM90	Substitute	Normal	Status	—	—	10	Self	—
HM01	Cut	Normal	Physical	50	95	30	Normal	•
HM04	Strength	Normal	Physical	80	100	15	Normal	•
HM06	Rock Smash	Fighting	Physical	40	100	15	Normal	•
HM08	Rock Climb	Normal	Physical	90	85	20	Normal	•

ABILITY ● Blaze

EGG GROUP Field / Human-Like

STATS
HP ●●
ATTACK ●●●●
DEFENSE ●●
SP. ATTACK ●●●●
SP. DEFENSE ●●
SPEED ●●●●

● LEVEL-UP AND LEARNED MOVES

Lv	Name	Type	Kind	Power	Acc	PP	Range	DA
Base	Scratch	Normal	Physical	40	100	35	Normal	•
Base	Leer	Normal	Status	—	100	30	2 foes	—
Base	Ember	Fire	Special	40	100	25	Normal	—
Base	Taunt	Dark	Status	—	100	20	Normal	—
7	Ember	Fire	Special	40	100	25	Normal	—
9	Taunt	Dark	Status	—	100	20	Normal	—
14	Mach Punch	Fighting	Physical	40	100	30	Normal	•
17	Fury Swipes	Normal	Physical	18	80	15	Normal	•
21	Flame Wheel	Fire	Physical	60	100	25	Normal	•
29	Feint	Normal	Physical	50	100	10	Normal	—
33	Punishment	Dark	Physical	—	100	5	Normal	•
41	Close Combat	Fighting	Physical	120	100	5	Normal	•
45	Fire Spin	Fire	Special	15	70	15	Normal	—
53	Calm Mind	Psychic	Status	—	—	20	Self	—
57	Flare Blitz	Fire	Physical	120	100	15	Normal	•

● MOVES TAUGHT IN EXCHANGE FOR COLORED SHARDS

Name	Type	Kind	Power	Acc	PP	Range	DA
Mud-Slap	Ground	Special	20	100	10	Normal	—
Rollout	Rock	Physical	30	90	20	Normal	•
ThunderPunch	Electric	Physical	75	100	15	Normal	•
Fire Punch	Fire	Physical	75	100	15	Normal	•
Snore	Normal	Special	40	100	15	Normal	—
Helping Hand	Normal	Status	—	—	20	1 ally	—
Endeavor	Normal	Physical	—	100	5	Normal	•
Vacuum Wave	Fighting	Special	40	100	30	Normal	—
Gunk Shot	Poison	Physical	120	70	5	Normal	—
Heat Wave	Fire	Special	100	90	10	2 foes	—
Swift	Normal	Special	60	—	20	2 foes	—

● MOVES TAUGHT BY PEOPLE

Name	Type	Kind	Power	Acc	PP	Range	DA
Blast Burn	Fire	Special	150	90	5	Normal	—

● PRIMARY WAY TO FIND

TRAINER'S PARTY Elite Four member Flint

WILD POKÉMON

COURSE OF STORY Level up Monferno to Lv36

Sinnoh Pokédex **No. 007** Penguin Pokémon

Piplup

WATER

HEIGHT: 1'04"
WEIGHT: 11.5 lbs.
GENDER: **Male and Female**
HELD ITEM: **None**

● M/F have same form

PLATINUM — A poor walker, it often falls down. However, its strong pride makes it puff up its chest without a care.

EVOLUTION PATH

Piplup — Lv16 → Prinplup — Lv36 → Empoleon

● TM & HM MOVES

No.	Name	Type	Kind	Power	Acc	PP	Range	DA
TM03	Water Pulse	Water	Special	60	100	20	Normal	—
TM06	Toxic	Poison	Status	—	85	10	Normal	—
TM07	Hail	Ice	Status	—	—	10	All	—
TM10	Hidden Power	Normal	Special	—	100	15	Normal	—
TM13	Ice Beam	Ice	Special	95	100	10	Normal	—
TM14	Blizzard	Ice	Special	120	70	5	2 foes	—
TM17	Protect	Normal	Status	—	—	10	Self	—
TM18	Rain Dance	Water	Status	—	—	5	All	—
TM21	Frustration	Normal	Physical	—	100	20	Normal	●
TM27	Return	Normal	Physical	—	100	20	Normal	●
TM28	Dig	Ground	Physical	80	100	10	Normal	●
TM31	Brick Break	Fighting	Physical	75	100	15	Normal	●
TM32	Double Team	Normal	Status	—	—	15	Self	—
TM39	Rock Tomb	Rock	Physical	50	80	10	Normal	●
TM40	Aerial Ace	Flying	Physical	60	—	20	Normal	●
TM42	Facade	Normal	Physical	70	100	20	Normal	●
TM43	Secret Power	Normal	Physical	70	100	20	Normal	●
TM44	Rest	Psychic	Status	—	—	10	Self	—
TM45	Attract	Normal	Status	—	100	15	Normal	—
TM55	Brine	Water	Special	65	100	10	Normal	—
TM56	Fling	Dark	Physical	—	100	10	Normal	●
TM58	Endure	Normal	Status	—	—	10	Self	—
TM76	Stealth Rock	Rock	Status	—	—	20	2 foes	—
TM78	Captivate	Normal	Status	—	100	20	2 foes	—
TM82	Sleep Talk	Normal	Status	—	—	10	DoM	—
TM83	Natural Gift	Normal	Physical	—	100	15	Normal	●
TM86	Grass Knot	Grass	Special	—	100	20	Normal	●
TM87	Swagger	Normal	Status	—	90	15	Normal	—
TM88	Pluck	Flying	Physical	60	100	20	Normal	●
TM90	Substitute	Normal	Status	—	—	10	Self	—
HM01	Cut	Normal	Physical	50	95	30	Normal	●
HM03	Surf	Water	Special	95	100	15	2 foes • 1 ally	—
HM05	Defog	Flying	Status	—	—	15	Normal	—
HM07	Waterfall	Water	Physical	80	100	15	Normal	●

● LEVEL-UP AND LEARNED MOVES

Lv	Name	Type	Kind	Power	Acc	PP	Range	DA
Base	Pound	Normal	Physical	40	100	35	Normal	●
4	Growl	Normal	Status	—	100	40	2 foes	—
8	Bubble	Water	Special	20	100	30	2 foes	—
11	Water Sport	Water	Status	—	—	15	All	—
15	Peck	Flying	Physical	35	100	35	Normal	●
18	BubbleBeam	Water	Special	65	100	20	Normal	—
22	Bide	Normal	Physical	—	—	10	Self	—
25	Fury Attack	Normal	Physical	15	85	20	Normal	●
29	Brine	Water	Special	65	100	10	Normal	—
32	Whirlpool	Water	Special	15	70	15	Normal	—
36	Mist	Ice	Status	—	—	30	2 allies	—
39	Drill Peck	Flying	Physical	80	100	20	Normal	●
43	Hydro Pump	Water	Special	120	80	5	Normal	—

● MOVES TAUGHT IN EXCHANGE FOR COLORED SHARDS

Name	Type	Kind	Power	Acc	PP	Range	DA
Dive	Water	Physical	80	100	10	Normal	●
Mud-Slap	Ground	Special	20	100	10	Normal	—
Icy Wind	Ice	Special	55	95	15	2 foes	—
Snore	Normal	Special	40	100	15	Normal	—
Signal Beam	Bug	Special	75	100	15	Normal	—

● EGG MOVES

Name	Type	Kind	Power	Acc	PP	Range	DA
Double Hit	Normal	Physical	35	90	10	Normal	●
Supersonic	Normal	Status	—	55	20	Normal	—
Yawn	Normal	Status	—	—	10	Normal	—
Mud Sport	Ground	Status	—	—	15	All	—
Mud-Slap	Ground	Special	20	100	10	Normal	—
Snore	Normal	Special	40	100	15	Normal	—
Flail	Normal	Physical	—	100	15	Normal	●
Agility	Psychic	Status	—	—	30	Self	—
Aqua Ring	Water	Status	—	—	20	Self	—
Hydro Pump	Water	Special	120	80	5	Normal	—

● PRIMARY WAY TO FIND

TRAINER'S PARTY	Trainer on Route 205
WILD POKÉMON	
COURSE OF STORY	Receive from Professor Rowan on Route 201

ABILITY ● Torrent

EGG GROUP: Water 1 / Field

STATS
HP ●●
ATTACK ●●
DEFENSE ●●
SP. ATTACK ●●
SP. DEFENSE ●●
SPEED ●●

Sinnoh Pokédex **No. 008** Penguin Pokémon

Prinplup

WATER

HEIGHT: 2'07"
WEIGHT: 50.7 lbs.
GENDER: **Male and Female**
HELD ITEM: **None**

● M/F have same form

PLATINUM — Because every PRINPLUP considers itself to be the most important, they can never form a group.

EVOLUTION PATH

Piplup — Lv16 → Prinplup — Lv36 → Empoleon

● TM & HM MOVES

No.	Name	Type	Kind	Power	Acc	PP	Range	DA
TM03	Water Pulse	Water	Special	60	100	20	Normal	—
TM06	Toxic	Poison	Status	—	85	10	Normal	—
TM07	Hail	Ice	Status	—	—	10	All	—
TM10	Hidden Power	Normal	Special	—	100	15	Normal	—
TM13	Ice Beam	Ice	Special	95	100	10	Normal	—
TM14	Blizzard	Ice	Special	120	70	5	2 foes	—
TM17	Protect	Normal	Status	—	—	10	Self	—
TM18	Rain Dance	Water	Status	—	—	5	All	—
TM21	Frustration	Normal	Physical	—	100	20	Normal	●
TM27	Return	Normal	Physical	—	100	20	Normal	●
TM28	Dig	Ground	Physical	80	100	10	Normal	●
TM31	Brick Break	Fighting	Physical	75	100	15	Normal	●
TM32	Double Team	Normal	Status	—	—	15	Self	—
TM39	Rock Tomb	Rock	Physical	50	80	10	Normal	●
TM40	Aerial Ace	Flying	Physical	60	—	20	Normal	●
TM42	Facade	Normal	Physical	70	100	20	Normal	●
TM43	Secret Power	Normal	Physical	70	100	20	Normal	●
TM44	Rest	Psychic	Status	—	—	10	Self	—
TM45	Attract	Normal	Status	—	100	15	Normal	—
TM55	Brine	Water	Special	65	100	10	Normal	—
TM56	Fling	Dark	Physical	—	100	10	Normal	●
TM58	Endure	Normal	Status	—	—	10	Self	—
TM65	Shadow Claw	Ghost	Physical	70	100	15	Normal	●
TM76	Stealth Rock	Rock	Status	—	—	20	2 foes	—
TM78	Captivate	Normal	Status	—	100	20	2 foes	—
TM82	Sleep Talk	Normal	Status	—	—	10	DoM	—
TM83	Natural Gift	Normal	Physical	—	100	15	Normal	●
TM86	Grass Knot	Grass	Special	—	100	20	Normal	●
TM87	Swagger	Normal	Status	—	90	15	Normal	—
TM88	Pluck	Flying	Physical	60	100	20	Normal	●
TM90	Substitute	Normal	Status	—	—	10	Self	—
HM01	Cut	Normal	Physical	50	95	30	Normal	●
HM03	Surf	Water	Special	95	100	15	2 foes • 1 ally	—
HM04	Strength	Normal	Physical	80	100	15	Normal	●
HM05	Defog	Flying	Status	—	—	15	Normal	—
HM06	Rock Smash	Fighting	Physical	40	100	15	Normal	●
HM07	Waterfall	Water	Physical	80	100	15	Normal	●

● LEVEL-UP AND LEARNED MOVES

Lv	Name	Type	Kind	Power	Acc	PP	Range	DA
Base	Tackle	Normal	Physical	35	95	35	Normal	●
Base	Growl	Normal	Status	—	100	40	2 foes	—
4	Growl	Normal	Status	—	100	40	2 foes	—
8	Bubble	Water	Special	20	100	30	2 foes	—
11	Water Sport	Water	Status	—	—	15	All	—
15	Peck	Flying	Physical	35	100	35	Normal	●
16	Metal Claw	Steel	Physical	50	95	35	Normal	●
19	BubbleBeam	Water	Special	65	100	20	Normal	—
24	Bide	Normal	Physical	—	—	10	Self	—
28	Fury Attack	Normal	Physical	15	85	20	Normal	●
33	Brine	Water	Special	65	100	10	Normal	—
37	Whirlpool	Water	Special	15	70	15	Normal	—
42	Mist	Ice	Status	—	—	30	2 allies	—
46	Drill Peck	Flying	Physical	80	100	20	Normal	●
51	Hydro Pump	Water	Special	120	80	5	Normal	—

● MOVES TAUGHT IN EXCHANGE FOR COLORED SHARDS

Name	Type	Kind	Power	Acc	PP	Range	DA
Dive	Water	Physical	80	100	10	Normal	●
Mud-Slap	Ground	Special	20	100	10	Normal	—
Icy Wind	Ice	Special	55	95	15	2 foes	—
Snore	Normal	Special	40	100	15	Normal	—
Signal Beam	Bug	Special	75	100	15	Normal	—

● PRIMARY WAY TO FIND

TRAINER'S PARTY	Trainer on Route 212
WILD POKÉMON	
COURSE OF STORY	Level up Piplup to Lv16

ABILITY ● Torrent

EGG GROUP: Water 1 / Field

STATS
HP ●●
ATTACK ●●
DEFENSE ●●
SP. ATTACK ●●●
SP. DEFENSE ●●
SPEED ●●

Sinnoh Pokédex **No. 009** Emperor Pokémon

Empoleon

WATER   STEEL

HEIGHT: 5'02"
WEIGHT: 186.3 lbs.
GENDER: Male and Female
HELD ITEM: None

● M/F have same form

PLATINUM   If anyone were to hurt its pride, it would slash them with wings that can cleave through an ice floe.

EVOLUTION PATH

Piplup → Lv16 → Prinplup → Lv36 → Empoleon

● TM & HM MOVES

No.	Name	Type	Kind	Power	Acc	PP	Range	DA
TM03	Water Pulse	Water	Special	60	100	20	Normal	—
TM05	Roar	Normal	Status	—	100	20	Normal	—
TM06	Toxic	Poison	Status	—	85	10	Normal	—
TM07	Hail	Ice	Status	—	—	10	All	—
TM10	Hidden Power	Normal	Special	—	100	15	Normal	—
TM13	Ice Beam	Ice	Special	95	100	10	Normal	—
TM14	Blizzard	Ice	Special	120	70	5	2 foes	—
TM15	Hyper Beam	Normal	Special	150	90	5	Normal	—
TM17	Protect	Normal	Status	—	—	10	Self	—
TM18	Rain Dance	Water	Status	—	—	5	All	—
TM21	Frustration	Normal	Physical	—	100	20	Normal	●
TM26	Earthquake	Ground	Physical	100	100	10	2 foes • 1 ally	—
TM27	Return	Normal	Physical	—	100	20	Normal	●
TM28	Dig	Ground	Physical	80	100	10	Normal	●
TM31	Brick Break	Fighting	Physical	75	100	15	Normal	●
TM32	Double Team	Normal	Status	—	—	15	Self	—
TM39	Rock Tomb	Rock	Physical	50	80	10	Normal	●
TM40	Aerial Ace	Flying	Physical	60	—	20	Normal	●
TM42	Facade	Normal	Physical	70	100	20	Normal	●
TM43	Secret Power	Normal	Physical	70	100	20	Normal	●
TM44	Rest	Psychic	Status	—	—	10	Self	—
TM45	Attract	Normal	Status	—	100	15	Normal	—
TM47	Steel Wing	Steel	Physical	70	90	25	Normal	●
TM55	Brine	Water	Special	65	100	10	Normal	●
TM56	Fling	Dark	Physical	—	100	10	Normal	●
TM58	Endure	Normal	Status	—	—	10	Self	—
TM65	Shadow Claw	Ghost	Physical	70	100	15	Normal	●
TM68	Giga Impact	Normal	Physical	150	90	5	Normal	●
TM72	Avalanche	Ice	Physical	60	100	10	Normal	●
TM75	Swords Dance	Normal	Status	—	—	30	Self	—
TM76	Stealth Rock	Rock	Status	—	—	20	2 foes	—
TM78	Captivate	Normal	Status	—	100	20	2 foes	—
TM80	Rock Slide	Rock	Physical	75	90	10	2 foes	—
TM82	Sleep Talk	Normal	Status	—	—	10	DoM	—
TM83	Natural Gift	Normal	Physical	—	100	15	Normal	—
TM86	Grass Knot	Grass	Special	—	100	20	Normal	—
TM87	Swagger	Normal	Status	—	90	15	Normal	—
TM88	Pluck	Flying	Physical	60	100	20	Normal	●
TM90	Substitute	Normal	Status	—	—	10	Self	—
TM91	Flash Cannon	Steel	Special	80	100	10	Normal	—
HM01	Cut	Normal	Physical	50	95	30	Normal	●
HM03	Surf	Water	Special	95	100	15	2 foes • 1 ally	●
HM04	Strength	Normal	Physical	80	100	15	Normal	●
HM05	Defog	Flying	Status	—	—	15	Normal	—
HM06	Rock Smash	Fighting	Physical	40	100	15	Normal	●
HM07	Waterfall	Water	Physical	80	100	15	Normal	●
HM08	Rock Climb	Normal	Physical	90	85	20	Normal	●

● LEVEL-UP AND LEARNED MOVES

Lv	Name	Type	Kind	Power	Acc	PP	Range	DA
Base	Tackle	Normal	Physical	35	95	35	Normal	●
Base	Growl	Normal	Status	—	100	40	2 foes	—
Base	Bubble	Water	Special	20	100	30	2 foes	—
4	Growl	Normal	Status	—	100	40	2 foes	—
8	Bubble	Water	Special	20	100	30	2 foes	—
11	Swords Dance	Normal	Status	—	—	30	Self	—
15	Peck	Flying	Physical	35	100	35	Normal	●
16	Metal Claw	Steel	Physical	50	95	35	Normal	●
19	BubbleBeam	Water	Special	65	100	20	Normal	—
24	Swagger	Normal	Status	—	90	15	Normal	—
28	Fury Attack	Normal	Physical	15	85	20	Normal	—
33	Brine	Water	Special	65	100	10	Normal	—
36	Aqua Jet	Water	Physical	40	100	20	Normal	●
39	Whirlpool	Water	Special	15	70	15	Normal	—
46	Mist	Ice	Status	—	—	30	2 allies	—
52	Drill Peck	Flying	Physical	80	100	20	Normal	●
59	Hydro Pump	Water	Special	120	80	5	Normal	—

● MOVES TAUGHT IN EXCHANGE FOR COLORED SHARDS

Name	Type	Kind	Power	Acc	PP	Range	DA
Dive	Water	Physical	80	100	10	Normal	●
Mud-Slap	Ground	Special	20	100	10	Normal	●
Fury Cutter	Bug	Physical	10	95	20	Normal	●
Icy Wind	Ice	Special	55	95	15	2 foes	—
Snore	Normal	Special	40	100	15	Normal	—
Signal Beam	Bug	Special	75	100	15	Normal	—
Iron Defense	Steel	Status	—	—	15	Self	—
Knock Off	Dark	Physical	20	100	20	Normal	●

● MOVES TAUGHT BY PEOPLE

Name	Type	Kind	Power	Acc	PP	Range	DA
Hydro Cannon	Water	Special	150	90	5	Normal	—

● PRIMARY WAY TO FIND

TRAINER'S PARTY	Trainer on Victory Road
WILD POKÉMON	
COURSE OF STORY	Level up Prinplup to Lv36

ABILITY ● Torrent

EGG GROUP Water 1 / Field

STATS
HP ●●●
ATTACK ●●●
DEFENSE ●●●
SP. ATTACK ●●●
SP. DEFENSE ●●●
SPEED ●●

Sinnoh Pokédex **No. 010** Starling Pokémon

Starly

NORMAL   FLYING

HEIGHT: 1'00"
WEIGHT: 4.4 lbs.
GENDER: Male and Female
HELD ITEM: Yache Berry

● Male form   ● Female form

PLATINUM   Because they are weak individually, they form groups. However, they bicker if the group grows too big.

EVOLUTION PATH

Starly → Lv14 → Staravia → Lv34 → Staraptor

● TM & HM MOVES

No.	Name	Type	Kind	Power	Acc	PP	Range	DA
TM06	Toxic	Poison	Status	—	85	10	Normal	—
TM10	Hidden Power	Normal	Special	—	100	15	Normal	—
TM11	Sunny Day	Fire	Status	—	—	5	All	—
TM17	Protect	Normal	Status	—	—	10	Self	—
TM18	Rain Dance	Water	Status	—	—	5	All	—
TM21	Frustration	Normal	Physical	—	100	20	Normal	●
TM27	Return	Normal	Physical	—	100	20	Normal	●
TM32	Double Team	Normal	Status	—	—	15	Self	—
TM40	Aerial Ace	Flying	Physical	60	—	20	Normal	●
TM42	Facade	Normal	Physical	70	100	20	Normal	●
TM43	Secret Power	Normal	Physical	70	100	20	Normal	—
TM44	Rest	Psychic	Status	—	—	10	Self	—
TM45	Attract	Normal	Status	—	100	15	Normal	—
TM46	Thief	Dark	Physical	40	100	10	Normal	—
TM47	Steel Wing	Steel	Physical	70	90	25	Normal	●
TM51	Roost	Flying	Status	—	—	10	Self	—
TM58	Endure	Normal	Status	—	—	10	Self	—
TM78	Captivate	Normal	Status	—	100	20	2 foes	—
TM82	Sleep Talk	Normal	Status	—	—	10	DoM	—
TM83	Natural Gift	Normal	Physical	—	100	15	Normal	—
TM87	Swagger	Normal	Status	—	90	15	Normal	—
TM88	Pluck	Flying	Physical	60	100	20	Normal	●
TM89	U-turn	Bug	Physical	70	100	20	Normal	●
TM90	Substitute	Normal	Status	—	—	10	Self	—
HM02	Fly	Flying	Physical	90	95	15	Normal	●
HM05	Defog	Flying	Status	—	—	15	Normal	—

● LEVEL-UP AND LEARNED MOVES

Lv	Name	Type	Kind	Power	Acc	PP	Range	DA
Base	Tackle	Normal	Physical	35	95	35	Normal	●
Base	Growl	Normal	Status	—	100	40	2 foes	—
5	Quick Attack	Normal	Physical	40	100	30	Normal	●
9	Wing Attack	Flying	Physical	60	100	35	Normal	●
13	Double Team	Normal	Status	—	—	15	Self	—
17	Endeavor	Normal	Physical	—	100	5	Normal	—
21	Whirlwind	Normal	Status	—	100	20	Normal	—
25	Aerial Ace	Flying	Physical	60	—	20	Normal	●
29	Take Down	Normal	Physical	90	85	20	Normal	●
33	Agility	Psychic	Status	—	—	30	Self	—
37	Brave Bird	Flying	Physical	120	100	15	Normal	●

● MOVES TAUGHT IN EXCHANGE FOR COLORED SHARDS

Name	Type	Kind	Power	Acc	PP	Range	DA
Mud-Slap	Ground	Special	20	100	10	Normal	—
Ominous Wind	Ghost	Special	60	100	5	Normal	—
Snore	Normal	Special	40	100	15	Normal	—
Air Cutter	Flying	Special	55	95	25	2 foes	—
Endeavor	Normal	Physical	—	100	5	Normal	—
Twister	Dragon	Special	40	100	20	2 foes	—
Heat Wave	Fire	Special	100	90	10	2 foes	—
Swift	Normal	Special	60	—	20	2 foes	—

● EGG MOVES

Name	Type	Kind	Power	Acc	PP	Range	DA
FeatherDance	Flying	Status	—	100	15	Normal	—
Fury Attack	Normal	Physical	15	85	20	Normal	●
Pursuit	Dark	Physical	40	100	20	Normal	●
Astonish	Ghost	Physical	30	100	15	Normal	●
Sand-Attack	Ground	Status	—	100	15	Normal	—
Foresight	Normal	Status	—	—	40	Normal	—
Double-Edge	Normal	Physical	120	100	15	Normal	●

● PRIMARY WAY TO FIND

TRAINER'S PARTY	Trainer on Route 202
WILD POKÉMON	Route 201
COURSE OF STORY	

ABILITY ● Keen Eye

EGG GROUP Flying

STATS
HP ●
ATTACK ●●
DEFENSE ●
SP. ATTACK ●
SP. DEFENSE ●
SPEED ●●

Staravia

Sinnoh Pokédex **No. 011** Starling Pokémon

NORMAL FLYING

HEIGHT: 2'00"
WEIGHT: 34.2 lbs.
GENDER: **Male and Female**
HELD ITEM: **Yache Berry**

● Male form ● Female form

PLATINUM Recognizing their own weakness, they always live in a group. When alone, a STARAVIA cries noisily.

EVOLUTION PATH

Starly → Lv14 → Staravia → Lv34 → Staraptor

● TM & HM MOVES

No.	Name	Type	Kind	Power	Acc	PP	Range	DA
TM06	Toxic	Poison	Status	—	85	10	Normal	•
TM10	Hidden Power	Normal	Special	—	100	15	Normal	—
TM11	Sunny Day	Fire	Status	—	—	5	All	—
TM17	Protect	Normal	Status	—	—	10	Self	—
TM18	Rain Dance	Water	Status	—	—	5	All	—
TM21	Frustration	Normal	Physical	—	100	20	Normal	•
TM27	Return	Normal	Physical	—	100	20	Normal	•
TM32	Double Team	Normal	Status	—	—	15	Self	—
TM40	Aerial Ace	Flying	Physical	60	—	20	Normal	•
TM42	Facade	Normal	Physical	70	100	20	Normal	•
TM43	Secret Power	Normal	Physical	70	100	20	Normal	•
TM44	Rest	Psychic	Status	—	—	10	Self	—
TM45	Attract	Normal	Status	—	100	15	Normal	•
TM46	Thief	Dark	Physical	40	100	10	Normal	•
TM47	Steel Wing	Steel	Physical	70	90	25	Normal	•
TM51	Roost	Flying	Status	—	—	10	Self	—
TM58	Endure	Normal	Status	—	—	10	Self	—
TM78	Captivate	Normal	Status	—	100	20	2 foes	—
TM82	Sleep Talk	Normal	Status	—	—	10	DoM	—
TM83	Natural Gift	Normal	Physical	—	100	15	Normal	•
TM87	Swagger	Normal	Status	—	90	15	Normal	—
TM88	Pluck	Flying	Physical	60	100	20	Normal	•
TM89	U-turn	Bug	Physical	70	100	20	Normal	•
TM90	Substitute	Normal	Status	—	—	10	Self	—
HM02	Fly	Flying	Physical	90	95	15	Normal	•
HM05	Defog	Flying	Status	—	—	15	Normal	—

● LEVEL-UP AND LEARNED MOVES

Lv	Name	Type	Kind	Power	Acc	PP	Range	DA
Base	Tackle	Normal	Physical	35	95	35	Normal	•
Base	Growl	Normal	Status	—	100	40	2 foes	—
Base	Quick Attack	Normal	Physical	40	100	30	Normal	•
5	Quick Attack	Normal	Physical	40	100	30	Normal	•
9	Wing Attack	Flying	Physical	60	100	35	Normal	•
13	Double Team	Normal	Status	—	—	15	Self	—
18	Endeavor	Normal	Physical	—	100	5	Normal	•
23	Whirlwind	Normal	Status	—	100	20	Normal	—
28	Aerial Ace	Flying	Physical	60	—	20	Normal	•
33	Take Down	Normal	Physical	90	85	20	Normal	•
38	Agility	Psychic	Status	—	—	30	Self	—
43	Brave Bird	Flying	Physical	120	100	15	Normal	•

● MOVES TAUGHT IN EXCHANGE FOR COLORED SHARDS

Name	Type	Kind	Power	Acc	PP	Range	DA
Mud-Slap	Ground	Special	20	100	10	Normal	—
Ominous Wind	Ghost	Special	60	100	5	Normal	—
Snore	Normal	Special	40	100	15	Normal	—
Air Cutter	Flying	Special	55	95	25	2 foes	—
Endeavor	Normal	Physical	—	100	5	Normal	•
Twister	Dragon	Special	40	100	20	2 foes	—
Heat Wave	Fire	Special	100	90	10	2 foes	—
Swift	Normal	Special	60	—	20	2 foes	—

ABILITY ● Intimidate

EGG GROUP Flying

STATS
HP ●●
ATTACK ●●●
DEFENSE ●●
SP. ATTACK ●●
SP. DEFENSE ●
SPEED ●●●

● PRIMARY WAY TO FIND

TRAINER'S PARTY Trainer on Route 206

WILD POKÉMON Route 209

COURSE OF STORY

Staraptor

Sinnoh Pokédex **No. 012** Predator Pokémon

NORMAL FLYING

HEIGHT: 3'11"
WEIGHT: 54.9 lbs.
GENDER: **Male and Female**
HELD ITEM: **None**

● Male form ● Female form

PLATINUM It never stops attacking even if it is injured. It fusses over the shape of its comb.

EVOLUTION PATH

Starly → Lv14 → Staravia → Lv34 → Staraptor

● TM & HM MOVES

No.	Name	Type	Kind	Power	Acc	PP	Range	DA
TM06	Toxic	Poison	Status	—	85	10	Normal	•
TM10	Hidden Power	Normal	Special	—	100	15	Normal	—
TM11	Sunny Day	Fire	Status	—	—	5	All	—
TM15	Hyper Beam	Normal	Special	150	90	5	Normal	—
TM17	Protect	Normal	Status	—	—	10	Self	—
TM18	Rain Dance	Water	Status	—	—	5	All	—
TM21	Frustration	Normal	Physical	—	100	20	Normal	•
TM27	Return	Normal	Physical	—	100	20	Normal	•
TM32	Double Team	Normal	Status	—	—	15	Self	—
TM40	Aerial Ace	Flying	Physical	60	—	20	Normal	•
TM42	Facade	Normal	Physical	70	100	20	Normal	•
TM43	Secret Power	Normal	Physical	70	100	20	Normal	•
TM44	Rest	Psychic	Status	—	—	10	Self	—
TM45	Attract	Normal	Status	—	100	15	Normal	•
TM46	Thief	Dark	Physical	40	100	10	Normal	•
TM47	Steel Wing	Steel	Physical	70	90	25	Normal	•
TM51	Roost	Flying	Status	—	—	10	Self	—
TM58	Endure	Normal	Status	—	—	10	Self	—
TM68	Giga Impact	Normal	Physical	150	90	5	Normal	•
TM78	Captivate	Normal	Status	—	100	20	2 foes	—
TM82	Sleep Talk	Normal	Status	—	—	10	DoM	—
TM83	Natural Gift	Normal	Physical	—	100	15	Normal	•
TM87	Swagger	Normal	Status	—	90	15	Normal	—
TM88	Pluck	Flying	Physical	60	100	20	Normal	•
TM89	U-turn	Bug	Physical	70	100	20	Normal	•
TM90	Substitute	Normal	Status	—	—	10	Self	—
HM02	Fly	Flying	Physical	90	95	15	Normal	•
HM05	Defog	Flying	Status	—	—	15	Normal	—

● LEVEL-UP AND LEARNED MOVES

Lv	Name	Type	Kind	Power	Acc	PP	Range	DA
Base	Tackle	Normal	Physical	35	95	35	Normal	•
Base	Growl	Normal	Status	—	100	40	2 foes	—
Base	Quick Attack	Normal	Physical	40	100	30	Normal	•
Base	Wing Attack	Flying	Physical	60	100	35	Normal	•
5	Quick Attack	Normal	Physical	40	100	30	Normal	•
9	Wing Attack	Flying	Physical	60	100	35	Normal	•
13	Double Team	Normal	Status	—	100	15	Self	—
18	Endeavor	Normal	Physical	—	100	5	Normal	•
23	Whirlwind	Normal	Status	—	100	20	Normal	—
28	Aerial Ace	Flying	Physical	60	—	20	Normal	•
33	Take Down	Normal	Physical	90	85	20	Normal	•
34	Close Combat	Fighting	Physical	120	100	5	Normal	•
41	Agility	Psychic	Status	—	—	30	Self	—
49	Brave Bird	Flying	Physical	120	100	15	Normal	•

● MOVES TAUGHT IN EXCHANGE FOR COLORED SHARDS

Name	Type	Kind	Power	Acc	PP	Range	DA
Mud-Slap	Ground	Special	20	100	10	Normal	—
Ominous Wind	Ghost	Special	60	100	5	Normal	—
Snore	Normal	Special	40	100	15	Normal	—
Air Cutter	Flying	Special	55	95	25	2 foes	—
Endeavor	Normal	Physical	—	100	5	Normal	•
Twister	Dragon	Special	40	100	20	2 foes	—
Heat Wave	Fire	Special	100	90	10	2 foes	—
Swift	Normal	Special	60	—	20	2 foes	—

ABILITY ● Intimidate

EGG GROUP Flying

STATS
HP ●●●
ATTACK ●●●●
DEFENSE ●●
SP. ATTACK ●●
SP. DEFENSE ●●
SPEED ●●●●

● PRIMARY WAY TO FIND

TRAINER'S PARTY Trainer on Victory Road

WILD POKÉMON

COURSE OF STORY

Bidoof

Sinnoh Pokédex No. 013 Plump Mouse Pokémon

NORMAL

HEIGHT: 1'08"
WEIGHT: 44.1 lbs.
GENDER: Male and Female
HELD ITEM: None

● Male form   ● Female form

PLATINUM: A comparison revealed that BIDOOF's front teeth grow at the same rate as RATTATA's.

EVOLUTION PATH

Bidoof → (Lv15) → Bibarel

● TM & HM MOVES

No.	Name	Type	Kind	Power	Acc	PP	Range	DA
TM06	Toxic	Poison	Status	—	85	10	Normal	—
TM10	Hidden Power	Normal	Special	—	100	15	Normal	—
TM11	Sunny Day	Fire	Status	—	—	5	All	—
TM12	Taunt	Dark	Status	—	100	20	Normal	—
TM13	Ice Beam	Ice	Special	95	100	10	Normal	—
TM14	Blizzard	Ice	Special	120	70	5	2 foes	—
TM17	Protect	Normal	Status	—	—	10	Self	—
TM18	Rain Dance	Water	Status	—	—	5	All	—
TM21	Frustration	Normal	Physical	—	100	20	Normal	•
TM23	Iron Tail	Steel	Physical	100	75	15	Normal	•
TM24	Thunderbolt	Electric	Special	95	100	15	Normal	—
TM25	Thunder	Electric	Special	120	70	10	Normal	—
TM27	Return	Normal	Physical	—	100	20	Normal	•
TM28	Dig	Ground	Physical	80	100	10	Normal	•
TM30	Shadow Ball	Ghost	Special	80	100	15	Normal	—
TM32	Double Team	Normal	Status	—	—	15	Self	—
TM34	Shock Wave	Electric	Special	60	—	20	Normal	—
TM42	Facade	Normal	Physical	70	100	20	Normal	•
TM43	Secret Power	Normal	Physical	70	100	20	Normal	•
TM44	Rest	Psychic	Status	—	—	10	Self	—
TM45	Attract	Normal	Status	—	100	15	Normal	•
TM46	Thief	Dark	Physical	40	100	10	Normal	•
TM57	Charge Beam	Electric	Special	50	90	10	Normal	—
TM58	Endure	Normal	Status	—	—	10	Self	—
TM73	Thunder Wave	Electric	Status	—	100	20	Normal	—
TM76	Stealth Rock	Rock	Status	—	—	20	2 foes	—
TM78	Captivate	Normal	Status	—	100	20	2 foes	—
TM82	Sleep Talk	Normal	Status	—	—	10	DoM	—
TM83	Natural Gift	Normal	Physical	—	100	15	Normal	•
TM86	Grass Knot	Grass	Special	—	100	20	Normal	•
TM87	Swagger	Normal	Status	—	90	15	Normal	—
TM88	Pluck	Flying	Physical	60	100	20	Normal	•
TM90	Substitute	Normal	Status	—	—	10	Self	—
HM01	Cut	Normal	Physical	50	95	30	Normal	•
HM06	Rock Smash	Fighting	Physical	40	100	15	Normal	•

● LEVEL-UP AND LEARNED MOVES

Lv	Name	Type	Kind	Power	Acc	PP	Range	DA
Base	Tackle	Normal	Physical	35	95	35	Normal	•
5	Growl	Normal	Status	—	100	40	2 foes	—
9	Defense Curl	Normal	Status	—	—	40	Self	—
13	Rollout	Rock	Physical	30	90	20	Normal	•
17	Headbutt	Normal	Physical	70	100	15	Normal	•
21	Hyper Fang	Normal	Physical	80	90	15	Normal	•
25	Yawn	Normal	Status	—	—	10	Normal	—
29	Amnesia	Psychic	Status	—	—	20	Self	—
33	Take Down	Normal	Physical	90	85	20	Normal	•
37	Super Fang	Normal	Physical	—	90	10	Normal	•
41	Superpower	Fighting	Physical	120	100	5	Normal	•
45	Curse	???	Status	—	—	10	Normal•Self	—

● MOVES TAUGHT IN EXCHANGE FOR COLORED SHARDS

Name	Type	Kind	Power	Acc	PP	Range	DA
Mud-Slap	Ground	Special	20	100	10	Normal	•
Fury Cutter	Bug	Physical	10	95	20	Normal	•
Icy Wind	Ice	Special	55	95	15	2 foes	—
Rollout	Rock	Physical	30	90	20	Normal	•
Superpower	Fighting	Physical	120	100	5	Normal	•
Aqua Tail	Water	Physical	90	90	10	Normal	•
Snore	Normal	Special	40	100	15	Normal	—
Last Resort	Normal	Physical	130	100	5	Normal	•
Swift	Normal	Special	60	—	20	2 foes	—

● EGG MOVES

Name	Type	Kind	Power	Acc	PP	Range	DA
Quick Attack	Normal	Physical	40	100	30	Normal	•
Water Sport	Water	Status	—	—	15	All	—
Double-Edge	Normal	Physical	120	100	15	Normal	•
Fury Swipes	Normal	Physical	18	80	15	Normal	•
Defense Curl	Normal	Status	—	—	40	Self	—
Rollout	Rock	Physical	30	90	20	Normal	•
Odor Sleuth	Normal	Status	—	—	40	Normal	—
Aqua Tail	Water	Physical	90	90	10	Normal	•

● PRIMARY WAY TO FIND

TRAINER'S PARTY: Trainer on Route 202
WILD POKÉMON: Route 201
COURSE OF STORY:

ABILITY: ● Simple ● Unaware
EGG GROUP: Water 1 / Field
STATS: HP ●● / ATTACK ● / DEFENSE ● / SP. ATTACK ● / SP. DEFENSE ● / SPEED ●

Bibarel

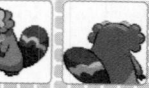

Sinnoh Pokédex No. 014 Beaver Pokémon

NORMAL   WATER

HEIGHT: 3'03"
WEIGHT: 69.4 lbs.
GENDER: Male and Female
HELD ITEM: Oran Berry/Sitrus Berry

● Male form   ● Female form

PLATINUM: A river dammed by BIBAREL will never overflow its banks, which is appreciated by people nearby.

EVOLUTION PATH

Bidoof → (Lv15) → Bibarel

● TM & HM MOVES

No.	Name	Type	Kind	Power	Acc	PP	Range	DA
TM01	Focus Punch	Fighting	Physical	150	100	20	Normal	—
TM03	Water Pulse	Water	Special	60	100	20	Normal	—
TM06	Toxic	Poison	Status	—	85	10	Normal	—
TM10	Hidden Power	Normal	Special	—	100	15	Normal	—
TM11	Sunny Day	Fire	Status	—	—	5	All	—
TM12	Taunt	Dark	Status	—	100	20	Normal	—
TM13	Ice Beam	Ice	Special	95	100	10	Normal	—
TM14	Blizzard	Ice	Special	120	70	5	2 foes	—
TM15	Hyper Beam	Normal	Special	150	90	5	Normal	—
TM17	Protect	Normal	Status	—	—	10	Self	—
TM18	Rain Dance	Water	Status	—	—	5	All	—
TM21	Frustration	Normal	Physical	—	100	20	Normal	•
TM23	Iron Tail	Steel	Physical	100	75	15	Normal	•
TM24	Thunderbolt	Electric	Special	95	100	15	Normal	—
TM25	Thunder	Electric	Special	120	70	10	Normal	—
TM27	Return	Normal	Physical	—	100	20	Normal	•
TM28	Dig	Ground	Physical	80	100	10	Normal	•
TM30	Shadow Ball	Ghost	Special	80	100	15	Normal	—
TM32	Double Team	Normal	Status	—	—	15	Self	—
TM34	Shock Wave	Electric	Special	60	—	20	Normal	—
TM42	Facade	Normal	Physical	70	100	20	Normal	•
TM43	Secret Power	Normal	Physical	70	100	20	Normal	•
TM44	Rest	Psychic	Status	—	—	10	Self	—
TM45	Attract	Normal	Status	—	100	15	Normal	•
TM46	Thief	Dark	Physical	40	100	10	Normal	•
TM56	Fling	Dark	Physical	—	100	10	Normal	•
TM57	Charge Beam	Electric	Special	50	90	10	Normal	—
TM58	Endure	Normal	Status	—	—	10	Self	—
TM68	Giga Impact	Normal	Physical	150	90	5	Normal	—
TM73	Thunder Wave	Electric	Status	—	100	20	Normal	—
TM76	Stealth Rock	Rock	Status	—	—	20	2 foes	—
TM78	Captivate	Normal	Status	—	100	20	2 foes	—
TM82	Sleep Talk	Normal	Status	—	—	10	DoM	—
TM83	Natural Gift	Normal	Physical	—	100	15	Normal	•
TM86	Grass Knot	Grass	Special	—	100	20	Normal	•
TM87	Swagger	Normal	Status	—	90	15	Normal	—
TM88	Pluck	Flying	Physical	60	100	20	Normal	•
TM90	Substitute	Normal	Status	—	—	10	Self	—
HM01	Cut	Normal	Physical	50	95	30	Normal	•
HM03	Surf	Water	Special	95	100	15	2 foes + 1 ally	—
HM04	Strength	Normal	Physical	80	100	15	Normal	•
HM06	Rock Smash	Fighting	Physical	40	100	15	Normal	•
HM07	Waterfall	Water	Physical	80	100	15	Normal	•
HM08	Rock Climb	Normal	Physical	90	85	20	Normal	•

● LEVEL-UP AND LEARNED MOVES

Lv	Name	Type	Kind	Power	Acc	PP	Range	DA
Base	Tackle	Normal	Physical	35	95	35	Normal	•
Base	Growl	Normal	Status	—	100	40	2 foes	—
5	Growl	Normal	Status	—	100	40	2 foes	—
9	Defense Curl	Normal	Status	—	—	40	Self	—
13	Rollout	Rock	Physical	30	90	20	Normal	•
15	Water Gun	Water	Special	40	100	25	Normal	—
18	Headbutt	Normal	Physical	70	100	15	Normal	•
23	Hyper Fang	Normal	Physical	80	90	15	Normal	•
28	Yawn	Normal	Status	—	—	10	Normal	—
33	Amnesia	Psychic	Status	—	—	20	Self	—
38	Take Down	Normal	Physical	90	85	20	Normal	•
43	Super Fang	Normal	Physical	—	90	10	Normal	•
48	Superpower	Fighting	Physical	120	100	5	Normal	•
53	Curse	???	Status	—	—	10	Normal•Self	—

● MOVES TAUGHT IN EXCHANGE FOR COLORED SHARDS

Name	Type	Kind	Power	Acc	PP	Range	DA
Dive	Water	Physical	80	100	10	Normal	•
Mud-Slap	Ground	Special	20	100	10	Normal	•
Fury Cutter	Bug	Physical	10	95	20	Normal	•
Icy Wind	Ice	Special	55	95	15	2 foes	—
Rollout	Rock	Physical	30	90	20	Normal	•
Superpower	Fighting	Physical	120	100	5	Normal	•
Aqua Tail	Water	Physical	90	90	10	Normal	•
Snore	Normal	Special	40	100	15	Normal	—
Last Resort	Normal	Physical	130	100	5	Normal	•
Swift	Normal	Special	60	—	20	2 foes	—

● PRIMARY WAY TO FIND

TRAINER'S PARTY: Trainer on Route 212
WILD POKÉMON: Route 208
COURSE OF STORY:

ABILITY: ● Simple ● Unaware
EGG GROUP: Water 1 / Field
STATS: HP ●● / ATTACK ●●● / DEFENSE ● / SP. ATTACK ● / SP. DEFENSE ● / SPEED ●●●

Kricketot

Sinnoh Pokédex No. 015 Cricket Pokémon

BUG

HEIGHT: 1'00"
WEIGHT: 4.9 lbs.
GENDER: Male and Female
HELD ITEM: Metronome

● Male form   ● Female form

PLATINUM — Its legs are short. Whenever it stumbles, its stiff antennae clack with a xylophone-like sound.

EVOLUTION PATH

Kricketot — Lv10 → Kricketune

● TM & HM MOVES

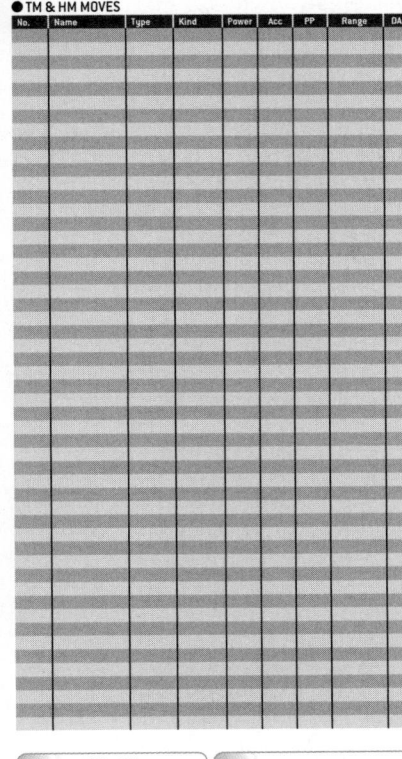

No.	Name	Type	Kind	Power	Acc	PP	Range	DA

● LEVEL-UP AND LEARNED MOVES

Lv	Name	Type	Kind	Power	Acc	PP	Range	DA
Base	Growl	Normal	Status	—	100	40	2 foes	—
Base	Bide	Normal	Physical	—	—	10	Self	●
16	Bug Bite	Bug	Physical	60	100	20	Normal	—

● MOVES TAUGHT IN EXCHANGE FOR COLORED SHARDS

Name	Type	Kind	Power	Acc	PP	Range	DA
Mud-Slap	Ground	Special	20	100	10	Normal	—
Snore	Normal	Special	40	100	15	Normal	—
Endeavor	Normal	Physical	—	100	5	Normal	●
Uproar	Normal	Special	50	100	10	1 random	—

● EGG MOVES

Name	Type	Kind	Power	Acc	PP	Range	DA

● PRIMARY WAY TO FIND

TRAINER'S PARTY — Trainer on Route 203

WILD POKÉMON — Route 201 (morning and night only)

COURSE OF STORY

ABILITY ● Shed Skin

EGG GROUP — Bug

STATS — HP ● / ATTACK ● / DEFENSE ● / SP. ATTACK ● / SP. DEFENSE ● / SPEED ●

Kricketune

Sinnoh Pokédex No. 016 Cricket Pokémon

BUG

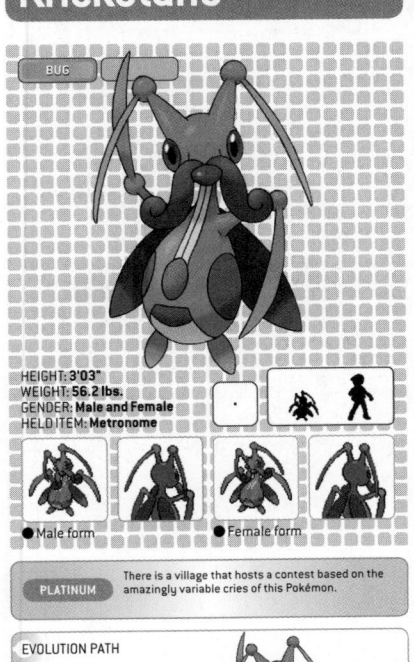

HEIGHT: 3'03"
WEIGHT: 56.2 lbs.
GENDER: Male and Female
HELD ITEM: Metronome

● Male form   ● Female form

PLATINUM — There is a village that hosts a contest based on the amazingly variable cries of this Pokémon.

EVOLUTION PATH

Kricketot — Lv10 → Kricketune

● TM & HM MOVES

No.	Name	Type	Kind	Power	Acc	PP	Range	DA
TM06	Toxic	Poison	Status	—	85	10	Normal	—
TM10	Hidden Power	Normal	Special	—	100	15	Normal	—
TM11	Sunny Day	Fire	Status	—	—	5	All	—
TM15	Hyper Beam	Normal	Special	150	90	5	Normal	—
TM17	Protect	Normal	Status	—	—	10	Self	—
TM18	Rain Dance	Water	Status	—	—	5	All	—
TM21	Frustration	Normal	Physical	—	100	20	Normal	●
TM27	Return	Normal	Physical	—	100	20	Normal	●
TM31	Brick Break	Fighting	Physical	75	100	15	Normal	●
TM32	Double Team	Normal	Status	—	—	15	Self	—
TM40	Aerial Ace	Flying	Physical	60	—	20	Normal	●
TM42	Facade	Normal	Physical	70	100	20	Normal	—
TM43	Secret Power	Normal	Physical	70	100	20	Normal	●
TM44	Rest	Psychic	Status	—	—	10	Self	—
TM45	Attract	Normal	Status	—	100	15	Normal	—
TM54	False Swipe	Normal	Physical	40	100	40	Normal	●
TM58	Endure	Normal	Status	—	—	10	Self	—
TM62	Silver Wind	Bug	Special	60	100	5	Normal	—
TM68	Giga Impact	Normal	Physical	150	90	5	Normal	●
TM70	Flash	Normal	Status	—	100	20	Normal	—
TM75	Swords Dance	Normal	Status	—	—	30	Self	—
TM78	Captivate	Normal	Status	—	100	20	2 foes	—
TM81	X-Scissor	Bug	Physical	80	100	15	Normal	●
TM82	Sleep Talk	Normal	Status	—	—	10	DoM	—
TM83	Natural Gift	Normal	Physical	—	100	15	Normal	●
TM87	Swagger	Normal	Status	—	90	15	Normal	—
TM90	Substitute	Normal	Status	—	—	10	Self	—
HM01	Cut	Normal	Physical	50	95	30	Normal	●
HM04	Strength	Normal	Physical	80	100	15	Normal	●
HM06	Rock Smash	Fighting	Physical	40	100	15	Normal	●

● LEVEL-UP AND LEARNED MOVES

Lv	Name	Type	Kind	Power	Acc	PP	Range	DA
Base	Growl	Normal	Status	—	100	40	2 foes	—
Base	Bide	Normal	Physical	—	—	10	Self	●
10	Fury Cutter	Bug	Physical	10	95	20	Normal	●
14	Leech Life	Bug	Physical	20	100	15	Normal	●
18	Sing	Normal	Status	—	55	15	Normal	—
22	Focus Energy	Normal	Status	—	—	30	Self	—
26	Slash	Normal	Physical	70	100	20	Normal	●
30	X-Scissor	Bug	Physical	80	100	15	Normal	●
34	Screech	Normal	Status	—	85	40	Normal	—
38	Taunt	Dark	Status	—	100	20	Normal	—
42	Night Slash	Dark	Physical	70	100	15	Normal	●
46	Bug Buzz	Bug	Special	90	100	10	Normal	—
50	Perish Song	Normal	Status	—	—	5	All	—

● MOVES TAUGHT IN EXCHANGE FOR COLORED SHARDS

Name	Type	Kind	Power	Acc	PP	Range	DA
Mud-Slap	Ground	Special	20	100	10	Normal	—
Fury Cutter	Bug	Physical	10	95	20	Normal	●
Snore	Normal	Special	40	100	15	Normal	—
Endeavor	Normal	Physical	—	100	5	Normal	●
Knock Off	Dark	Physical	20	100	20	Normal	●
Uproar	Normal	Special	50	100	10	1 random	—

● PRIMARY WAY TO FIND

TRAINER'S PARTY — Trainer on Route 218

WILD POKÉMON — Route 206 (morning and night only)

COURSE OF STORY

ABILITY ● Swarm

EGG GROUP — Bug

STATS — HP ●● / ATTACK ●●● / DEFENSE ●● / SP. ATTACK ●● / SP. DEFENSE ●● / SPEED ●●

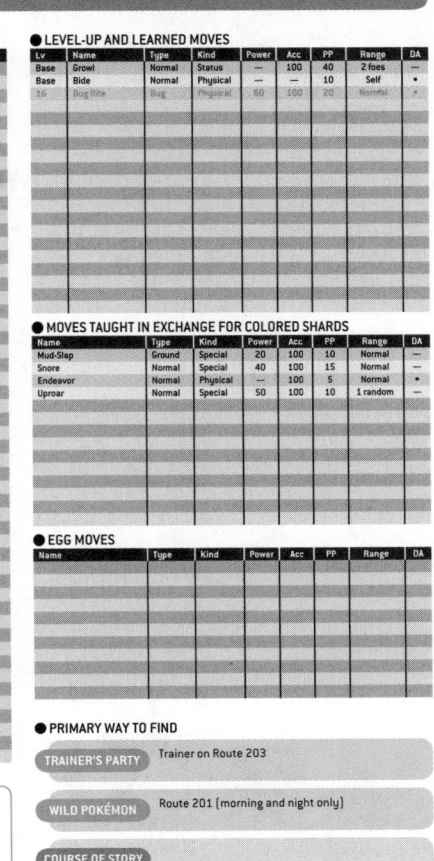

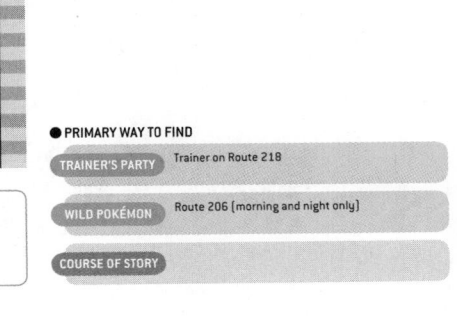

Sinnoh Pokédex No. 017 Flash Pokémon

Shinx

ELECTRIC

HEIGHT: 1'08"
WEIGHT: 20.9 lbs.
GENDER: Male and Female
HELD ITEM: None

● Male form ● Female form

PLATINUM The extension and contraction of its muscles generates electricity. It glows when in trouble.

EVOLUTION PATH

Shinx → Lv15 → Luxio → Lv30 → Luxray

ABILITY ● Rivalry ● Intimidate

EGG GROUP Field

STATS
HP ●●
ATTACK ●●●
DEFENSE ●●
SP. ATTACK ●●
SP. DEFENSE ●●
SPEED ●●

● TM & HM MOVES

No.	Name	Type	Kind	Power	Acc	PP	Range	DA
TM05	Roar	Normal	Status	—	100	20	Normal	—
TM06	Toxic	Poison	Status	—	85	10	Normal	—
TM10	Hidden Power	Normal	Special	—	100	15	Normal	—
TM16	Light Screen	Psychic	Status	—	—	30	2 allies	—
TM17	Protect	Normal	Status	—	—	10	Self	—
TM18	Rain Dance	Water	Status	—	—	5	All	—
TM21	Frustration	Normal	Physical	—	100	20	Normal	•
TM23	Iron Tail	Steel	Physical	100	75	15	Normal	•
TM24	Thunderbolt	Electric	Special	95	100	15	Normal	—
TM25	Thunder	Electric	Special	120	70	10	Normal	—
TM27	Return	Normal	Physical	—	100	20	Normal	•
TM32	Double Team	Normal	Status	—	—	15	Self	—
TM34	Shock Wave	Electric	Special	60	—	20	Normal	—
TM42	Facade	Normal	Physical	70	100	20	Normal	•
TM43	Secret Power	Normal	Physical	70	100	20	Normal	•
TM44	Rest	Psychic	Status	—	—	10	Self	—
TM45	Attract	Normal	Status	—	100	15	Normal	—
TM46	Thief	Dark	Physical	40	100	10	Normal	•
TM57	Charge Beam	Electric	Special	50	90	10	Normal	—
TM58	Endure	Normal	Status	—	—	10	Self	—
TM70	Flash	Normal	Status	—	100	20	Normal	—
TM73	Thunder Wave	Electric	Status	—	100	20	Normal	—
TM78	Captivate	Normal	Status	—	100	20	2 foes	•
TM82	Sleep Talk	Normal	Status	—	—	10	Depends on move	—
TM83	Natural Gift	Normal	Physical	—	100	15	Normal	—
TM87	Swagger	Normal	Status	—	90	15	Normal	—
TM90	Substitute	Normal	Status	—	—	10	Self	—
HM04	Strength	Normal	Physical	80	100	15	Normal	—

● LEVEL-UP AND LEARNED MOVES

Lv	Name	Type	Kind	Power	Acc	PP	Range	DA
Base	Tackle	Normal	Physical	35	95	35	Normal	•
5	Leer	Normal	Status	—	100	30	2 foes	—
9	Charge	Electric	Status	—	—	20	Self	—
13	Spark	Electric	Physical	65	100	20	Normal	•
17	Bite	Dark	Physical	60	100	25	Normal	•
21	Roar	Normal	Status	—	100	20	Normal	—
25	Swagger	Normal	Status	—	90	15	Normal	—
29	Thunder Fang	Electric	Physical	65	95	15	Normal	•
33	Crunch	Dark	Physical	80	100	15	Normal	•
37	Scary Face	Normal	Status	—	90	10	Normal	—
41	Discharge	Electric	Special	80	100	15	2 foes + 1 ally	—

● MOVES TAUGHT IN EXCHANGE FOR COLORED SHARDS

Name	Type	Kind	Power	Acc	PP	Range	DA
Mud-Slap	Ground	Special	20	100	10	Normal	—
Fury Cutter	Bug	Physical	10	95	20	Normal	•
Snore	Normal	Special	40	100	15	Normal	—
Signal Beam	Bug	Special	75	100	15	Normal	—
Magnet Rise	Electric	Status	—	—	10	Self	—
Swift	Normal	Special	60	—	20	2 foes	—

● EGG MOVES

Name	Type	Kind	Power	Acc	PP	Range	DA
Ice Fang	Ice	Physical	65	95	15	Normal	•
Fire Fang	Fire	Physical	65	95	15	Normal	•
Thunder Fang	Electric	Physical	65	95	15	Normal	•
Quick Attack	Normal	Physical	40	100	30	Normal	•
Howl	Normal	Status	—	—	40	Self	—
Take Down	Normal	Physical	90	85	20	Normal	•

● PRIMARY WAY TO FIND

TRAINER'S PARTY — Trainer on Route 203

WILD POKÉMON — Route 202

COURSE OF STORY

Sinnoh Pokédex No. 018 Spark Pokémon

Luxio

ELECTRIC

HEIGHT: 2'11"
WEIGHT: 67.2 lbs.
GENDER: Male and Female
HELD ITEM: None

● Male form ● Female form

PLATINUM Strong electricity courses through the tips of its sharp claws. A light scratch causes fainting in foes.

EVOLUTION PATH

Shinx → Lv15 → Luxio → Lv30 → Luxray

ABILITY ● Rivalry ● Intimidate

EGG GROUP Field

STATS
HP ●●
ATTACK ●●●
DEFENSE ●●
SP. ATTACK ●●
SP. DEFENSE ●●
SPEED ●●

● TM & HM MOVES

No.	Name	Type	Kind	Power	Acc	PP	Range	DA
TM05	Roar	Normal	Status	—	100	20	Normal	—
TM06	Toxic	Poison	Status	—	85	10	Normal	—
TM10	Hidden Power	Normal	Special	—	100	15	Normal	—
TM16	Light Screen	Psychic	Status	—	—	30	2 allies	—
TM17	Protect	Normal	Status	—	—	10	Self	—
TM18	Rain Dance	Water	Status	—	—	5	All	—
TM21	Frustration	Normal	Physical	—	100	20	Normal	•
TM23	Iron Tail	Steel	Physical	100	75	15	Normal	•
TM24	Thunderbolt	Electric	Special	95	100	15	Normal	—
TM25	Thunder	Electric	Special	120	70	10	Normal	—
TM27	Return	Normal	Physical	—	100	20	Normal	•
TM32	Double Team	Normal	Status	—	—	15	Self	—
TM34	Shock Wave	Electric	Special	60	—	20	Normal	—
TM42	Facade	Normal	Physical	70	100	20	Normal	•
TM43	Secret Power	Normal	Physical	70	100	20	Normal	•
TM44	Rest	Psychic	Status	—	—	10	Self	—
TM45	Attract	Normal	Status	—	100	15	Normal	—
TM46	Thief	Dark	Physical	40	100	10	Normal	•
TM57	Charge Beam	Electric	Special	50	90	10	Normal	—
TM58	Endure	Normal	Status	—	—	10	Self	—
TM70	Flash	Normal	Status	—	100	20	Normal	—
TM73	Thunder Wave	Electric	Status	—	100	20	Normal	—
TM78	Captivate	Normal	Status	—	100	20	2 foes	•
TM82	Sleep Talk	Normal	Status	—	—	10	Depends on move	—
TM83	Natural Gift	Normal	Physical	—	100	15	Normal	—
TM87	Swagger	Normal	Status	—	90	15	Normal	—
TM90	Substitute	Normal	Status	—	—	10	Self	—
HM04	Strength	Normal	Physical	80	100	15	Normal	—

● LEVEL-UP AND LEARNED MOVES

Lv	Name	Type	Kind	Power	Acc	PP	Range	DA
Base	Tackle	Normal	Physical	35	95	35	Normal	•
Base	Leer	Normal	Status	—	100	30	2 foes	•
5	Leer	Normal	Status	—	100	30	2 foes	—
9	Charge	Electric	Status	—	—	20	Self	—
13	Spark	Electric	Physical	65	100	20	Normal	•
18	Bite	Dark	Physical	60	100	25	Normal	•
23	Roar	Normal	Status	—	100	20	Normal	—
28	Swagger	Normal	Status	—	90	15	Normal	—
33	Thunder Fang	Electric	Physical	65	95	15	Normal	•
38	Crunch	Dark	Physical	80	100	15	Normal	•
43	Scary Face	Normal	Status	—	90	10	Normal	—
48	Discharge	Electric	Special	80	100	15	2 foes + 1 ally	—

● MOVES TAUGHT IN EXCHANGE FOR COLORED SHARDS

Name	Type	Kind	Power	Acc	PP	Range	DA
Mud-Slap	Ground	Special	20	100	10	Normal	—
Fury Cutter	Bug	Physical	10	95	20	Normal	•
Snore	Normal	Special	40	100	15	Normal	—
Signal Beam	Bug	Special	75	100	15	Normal	—
Magnet Rise	Electric	Status	—	—	10	Self	—
Swift	Normal	Special	60	—	20	2 foes	—

● PRIMARY WAY TO FIND

TRAINER'S PARTY — Trainer on Route 207

WILD POKÉMON — Route 222

COURSE OF STORY

017
SHINX

Luxray

ELECTRIC

HEIGHT: **4'07"**
WEIGHT: **92.6 lbs.**
GENDER: **Male and Female**
HELD ITEM: **None**

● Male form   ● Female form

| PLATINUM | It can see clearly through walls to track down its prey and seek its lost young. |

EVOLUTION PATH

Shinx — Lv15 → Luxio — Lv30 → Luxray

● TM & HM MOVES

No.	Name	Type	Kind	Power	Acc	PP	Range	DA
TM05	Roar	Normal	Status	—	100	20	Normal	—
TM06	Toxic	Poison	Status	—	85	10	Normal	—
TM10	Hidden Power	Normal	Special	—	100	15	Normal	—
TM15	Hyper Beam	Normal	Special	150	90	5	Normal	—
TM16	Light Screen	Psychic	Status	—	—	30	2 allies	—
TM17	Protect	Normal	Status	—	—	10	Self	—
TM18	Rain Dance	Water	Status	—	—	5	All	—
TM21	Frustration	Normal	Physical	—	100	20	Normal	●
TM23	Iron Tail	Steel	Physical	100	75	15	Normal	●
TM24	Thunderbolt	Electric	Special	95	100	15	Normal	—
TM25	Thunder	Electric	Special	120	70	10	Normal	—
TM27	Return	Normal	Physical	—	100	20	Normal	●
TM32	Double Team	Normal	Status	—	—	15	Self	—
TM34	Shock Wave	Electric	Special	60	—	20	Normal	—
TM42	Facade	Normal	Physical	70	100	20	Normal	●
TM43	Secret Power	Normal	Physical	70	100	20	Normal	●
TM44	Rest	Psychic	Status	—	—	10	Self	—
TM45	Attract	Normal	Status	—	100	15	Normal	—
TM46	Thief	Dark	Physical	40	100	10	Normal	●
TM57	Charge Beam	Electric	Special	50	90	10	Normal	—
TM58	Endure	Normal	Status	—	—	10	Self	—
TM68	Giga Impact	Normal	Physical	150	90	5	Normal	●
TM70	Flash	Normal	Status	—	100	20	Normal	—
TM73	Thunder Wave	Electric	Status	—	100	20	Normal	—
TM78	Captivate	Normal	Status	—	100	20	2 foes	—
TM82	Sleep Talk	Normal	Status	—	—	10	Depends on move	—
TM83	Natural Gift	Normal	Physical	—	100	15	Normal	●
TM87	Swagger	Normal	Status	—	90	15	Normal	—
TM90	Substitute	Normal	Status	—	—	10	Self	—
HM04	Strength	Normal	Physical	80	100	15	Normal	●

● LEVEL-UP AND LEARNED MOVES

Lv	Name	Type	Kind	Power	Acc	PP	Range	DA
Base	Tackle	Normal	Physical	35	95	35	Normal	●
Base	Leer	Normal	Status	—	100	30	2 foes	—
Base	Charge	Electric	Status	—	—	20	Self	—
5	Leer	Normal	Status	—	100	30	2 foes	—
9	Charge	Electric	Status	—	—	20	Self	—
13	Spark	Electric	Physical	65	100	20	Normal	●
18	Bite	Dark	Physical	60	100	25	Normal	●
23	Roar	Normal	Status	—	100	20	Normal	—
28	Swagger	Normal	Status	—	90	15	Normal	—
35	Thunder Fang	Electric	Physical	65	95	15	Normal	●
42	Crunch	Dark	Physical	80	100	15	Normal	●
49	Scary Face	Normal	Status	—	90	10	Normal	—
56	Discharge	Electric	Special	80	100	15	2 foes • 1 ally	—

● MOVES TAUGHT IN EXCHANGE FOR COLORED SHARDS

Name	Type	Kind	Power	Acc	PP	Range	DA
Mud-Slap	Ground	Special	20	100	10	Normal	—
Fury Cutter	Bug	Physical	10	95	20	Normal	●
Superpower	Fighting	Physical	120	100	5	Normal	●
Snore	Normal	Special	40	100	15	Normal	—
Signal Beam	Bug	Special	75	100	15	Normal	—
Magnet Rise	Electric	Status	—	—	10	Self	—
Swift	Normal	Special	60	—	20	2 foes	—

● PRIMARY WAY TO FIND

TRAINER'S PARTY	Trainer on Route 222
WILD POKÉMON	
COURSE OF STORY	

| ABILITY | ● Rivalry ● Intimidate |

| EGG GROUP | Field |

STATS	HP ●●
	ATTACK ●●●●
	DEFENSE ●●●●
	SP. ATTACK ●●●●
	SP. DEFENSE ●●●
	SPEED ●●●

Abra

PSYCHIC

HEIGHT: **2'11"**
WEIGHT: **43.0 lbs.**
GENDER: **Male and Female**
HELD ITEM: **TwistedSpoon**

● M/F have same form

| PLATINUM | Using its psychic power is such a strain on its brain that it needs to sleep for 18 hours a day. |

EVOLUTION PATH

Abra — Lv16 → Kadabra — Link trade → Alakazam

● TM & HM MOVES

No.	Name	Type	Kind	Power	Acc	PP	Range	DA
TM01	Focus Punch	Fighting	Physical	150	100	20	Normal	●
TM04	Calm Mind	Psychic	Status	—	—	20	Self	—
TM06	Toxic	Poison	Status	—	85	10	Normal	—
TM10	Hidden Power	Normal	Special	—	100	15	Normal	—
TM11	Sunny Day	Fire	Status	—	—	5	All	—
TM12	Taunt	Dark	Status	—	100	20	Normal	—
TM16	Light Screen	Psychic	Status	—	—	30	2 allies	—
TM17	Protect	Normal	Status	—	—	10	Self	—
TM18	Rain Dance	Water	Status	—	—	5	All	—
TM20	Safeguard	Normal	Status	—	—	25	2 allies	—
TM21	Frustration	Normal	Physical	—	100	20	Normal	●
TM23	Iron Tail	Steel	Physical	100	75	15	Normal	●
TM27	Return	Normal	Physical	—	100	20	Normal	●
TM29	Psychic	Psychic	Special	90	100	10	Normal	—
TM30	Shadow Ball	Ghost	Special	80	100	15	Normal	—
TM32	Double Team	Normal	Status	—	—	15	Self	—
TM33	Reflect	Psychic	Status	—	—	20	2 allies	—
TM34	Shock Wave	Electric	Special	60	—	20	Normal	—
TM41	Torment	Dark	Status	—	100	15	Normal	—
TM42	Facade	Normal	Physical	70	100	20	Normal	●
TM43	Secret Power	Normal	Physical	70	100	20	Normal	●
TM44	Rest	Psychic	Status	—	—	10	Self	—
TM45	Attract	Normal	Status	—	100	15	Normal	—
TM46	Thief	Dark	Physical	40	100	10	Normal	●
TM48	Skill Swap	Psychic	Status	—	—	10	Normal	—
TM49	Snatch	Dark	Status	—	—	10	Depends on move	—
TM53	Energy Ball	Grass	Special	80	100	10	Normal	—
TM56	Fling	Dark	Physical	—	100	10	Normal	●
TM57	Charge Beam	Electric	Special	50	90	10	Normal	—
TM58	Endure	Normal	Status	—	—	10	Self	—
TM60	Drain Punch	Fighting	Physical	60	100	5	Normal	●
TM63	Embargo	Dark	Status	—	100	15	Normal	—
TM67	Recycle	Normal	Status	—	—	10	Self	—
TM70	Flash	Normal	Status	—	100	20	Normal	—
TM73	Thunder Wave	Electric	Status	—	100	20	Normal	—
TM77	Psych Up	Normal	Status	—	—	10	Normal	—
TM78	Captivate	Normal	Status	—	100	20	2 foes	—
TM82	Sleep Talk	Normal	Status	—	—	10	Depends on move	—
TM83	Natural Gift	Normal	Physical	—	100	15	Normal	●
TM85	Dream Eater	Psychic	Special	100	100	15	Normal	—
TM86	Grass Knot	Grass	Special	—	100	20	Normal	●
TM87	Swagger	Normal	Status	—	90	15	Normal	—
TM90	Substitute	Normal	Status	—	—	10	Self	—
TM92	Trick Room	Psychic	Status	—	—	5	All	—

● LEVEL-UP AND LEARNED MOVES

Lv	Name	Type	Kind	Power	Acc	PP	Range	DA
Base	Teleport	Psychic	Status	—	—	20	Self	—

● MOVES TAUGHT IN EXCHANGE FOR COLORED SHARDS

Name	Type	Kind	Power	Acc	PP	Range	DA
ThunderPunch	Electric	Physical	75	100	15	Normal	●
Fire Punch	Fire	Physical	75	100	15	Normal	●
Ice Punch	Ice	Physical	75	100	15	Normal	●
Snore	Normal	Special	40	100	15	Normal	—
Signal Beam	Bug	Special	75	100	15	Normal	—
Zen Headbutt	Psychic	Physical	80	90	15	Normal	●
Trick	Psychic	Status	—	100	10	Normal	—
Knock Off	Dark	Physical	20	100	20	Normal	●

● EGG MOVES

Name	Type	Kind	Power	Acc	PP	Range	DA
Encore	Normal	Status	—	100	5	Normal	—
Barrier	Psychic	Status	—	—	30	Self	—
Knock Off	Dark	Physical	20	100	20	Normal	●
Fire Punch	Fire	Physical	75	100	15	Normal	●
ThunderPunch	Electric	Physical	75	100	15	Normal	●
Ice Punch	Ice	Physical	75	100	15	Normal	●
Power Trick	Psychic	Status	—	—	10	Self	—
Guard Swap	Psychic	Status	—	—	10	Normal	—

● PRIMARY WAY TO FIND

TRAINER'S PARTY	Trainer on Route 203
WILD POKÉMON	Route 203
COURSE OF STORY	

| ABILITY | ● Synchronize ● Inner Focus |

| EGG GROUP | Human-Like |

STATS	HP ●
	ATTACK ●
	DEFENSE ●●
	SP. ATTACK ●●●●
	SP. DEFENSE ●●
	SPEED ●●●

Sinnoh Pokédex No. 021 Psi Pokémon

Kadabra

PSYCHIC

HEIGHT: 4'03"
WEIGHT: 124.6 lbs.
GENDER: Male and Female
HELD ITEM: TwistedSpoon

● Male form   ● Female form

PLATINUM It stares at its silver spoon to focus its mind. It emits more alpha waves while doing so.

EVOLUTION PATH

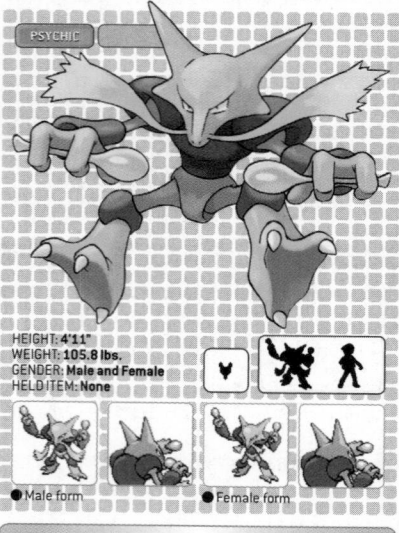

Abra → (Lv16) → Kadabra → (Link Trade) → Alakazam

● TM & HM MOVES

No.	Name	Type	Kind	Power	Acc	PP	Range	DA
TM01	Focus Punch	Fighting	Physical	150	100	20	Normal	●
TM04	Calm Mind	Psychic	Status	—	—	20	Self	—
TM06	Toxic	Poison	Status	—	85	10	Normal	—
TM10	Hidden Power	Normal	Special	—	100	15	Normal	—
TM11	Sunny Day	Fire	Status	—	—	5	All	—
TM12	Taunt	Dark	Status	—	100	20	Normal	—
TM16	Light Screen	Psychic	Status	—	—	30	2 allies	—
TM17	Protect	Normal	Status	—	—	10	Self	—
TM18	Rain Dance	Water	Status	—	—	5	All	—
TM20	Safeguard	Normal	Status	—	—	25	2 allies	—
TM21	Frustration	Normal	Physical	—	100	20	Normal	●
TM23	Iron Tail	Steel	Physical	100	75	15	Normal	●
TM27	Return	Normal	Physical	—	100	20	Normal	●
TM29	Psychic	Psychic	Special	90	100	10	Normal	—
TM30	Shadow Ball	Ghost	Special	80	100	15	Normal	—
TM32	Double Team	Normal	Status	—	—	15	Self	—
TM33	Reflect	Psychic	Status	—	—	20	2 allies	—
TM34	Shock Wave	Electric	Special	60	—	20	Normal	—
TM41	Torment	Dark	Status	—	100	15	Normal	—
TM42	Facade	Normal	Physical	70	100	20	Normal	●
TM43	Secret Power	Normal	Physical	70	100	20	Normal	●
TM44	Rest	Psychic	Status	—	—	10	Self	—
TM45	Attract	Normal	Status	—	100	15	Normal	—
TM46	Thief	Dark	Physical	40	100	10	Normal	●
TM48	Skill Swap	Psychic	Status	—	—	10	Normal	—
TM49	Snatch	Dark	Status	—	—	10	Depends on move	—
TM53	Energy Ball	Grass	Special	80	100	10	Normal	—
TM56	Fling	Dark	Physical	—	100	10	Normal	●
TM57	Charge Beam	Electric	Special	50	90	10	Normal	—
TM58	Endure	Normal	Status	—	—	10	Self	—
TM60	Drain Punch	Fighting	Physical	60	100	5	Normal	●
TM63	Embargo	Dark	Status	—	100	15	Normal	—
TM67	Recycle	Normal	Status	—	—	10	Self	—
TM70	Flash	Normal	Status	—	100	20	Normal	—
TM73	Thunder Wave	Electric	Status	—	100	20	Normal	—
TM77	Psych Up	Normal	Status	—	—	10	Normal	—
TM78	Captivate	Normal	Status	—	100	20	2 foes	—
TM82	Sleep Talk	Normal	Status	—	—	10	Depends on move	—
TM83	Natural Gift	Normal	Physical	—	100	15	Normal	—
TM85	Dream Eater	Psychic	Special	100	100	15	Normal	—
TM86	Grass Knot	Grass	Special	—	100	20	Normal	●
TM87	Swagger	Normal	Status	—	90	15	Normal	—
TM90	Substitute	Normal	Status	—	—	10	Self	—
TM92	Trick Room	Psychic	Status	—	—	5	All	—

● LEVEL-UP AND LEARNED MOVES

Lv	Name	Type	Kind	Power	Acc	PP	Range	DA
Base	Teleport	Psychic	Status	—	—	20	Self	—
Base	Kinesis	Psychic	Status	—	80	15	Normal	—
Base	Confusion	Psychic	Special	50	100	25	Normal	—
16	Confusion	Psychic	Special	50	100	25	Normal	—
18	Disable	Normal	Status	—	80	20	Normal	—
22	Miracle Eye	Psychic	Status	—	—	40	Normal	—
24	Psybeam	Psychic	Special	65	100	20	Normal	—
28	Reflect	Psychic	Status	—	—	20	2 allies	—
30	Recover	Normal	Status	—	—	10	Self	—
34	Psycho Cut	Psychic	Physical	70	100	20	Normal	—
36	Role Play	Psychic	Status	—	—	10	Normal	—
40	Psychic	Psychic	Special	90	100	10	Normal	—
42	Future Sight	Psychic	Special	80	90	15	Normal	—
46	Trick	Psychic	Status	—	100	10	Normal	—

● MOVES TAUGHT IN EXCHANGE FOR COLORED SHARDS

Name	Type	Kind	Power	Acc	PP	Range	DA
ThunderPunch	Electric	Physical	75	100	15	Normal	●
Fire Punch	Fire	Physical	75	100	15	Normal	●
Ice Punch	Ice	Physical	75	100	15	Normal	●
Snore	Normal	Special	40	100	15	Normal	—
Signal Beam	Bug	Special	75	100	15	Normal	—
Zen Headbutt	Psychic	Physical	80	90	15	Normal	●
Trick	Psychic	Status	—	100	10	Normal	—
Knock Off	Dark	Physical	20	100	20	Normal	●

ABILITY ● Synchronize ● Inner Focus

EGG GROUP Human-Like

STATS
HP ●
ATTACK ●
DEFENSE ●
SP. ATTACK ●●●●
SP. DEFENSE ●●●
SPEED ●●●●

● PRIMARY WAY TO FIND

TRAINER'S PARTY Trainer on 1F of the Galactic Veilstone Bldg.

WILD POKÉMON Route 215

COURSE OF STORY

Sinnoh Pokédex No. 022 Psi Pokémon

Alakazam

PSYCHIC

HEIGHT: 4'11"
WEIGHT: 105.8 lbs.
GENDER: Male and Female
HELD ITEM: None

● Male form   ● Female form

PLATINUM The spoons clutched in its hands are said to have been created by its psychic powers.

EVOLUTION PATH

Abra → (Lv16) → Kadabra → (Link Trade) → Alakazam

● TM & HM MOVES

No.	Name	Type	Kind	Power	Acc	PP	Range	DA
TM01	Focus Punch	Fighting	Physical	150	100	20	Normal	●
TM04	Calm Mind	Psychic	Status	—	—	20	Self	—
TM06	Toxic	Poison	Status	—	85	10	Normal	—
TM10	Hidden Power	Normal	Special	—	100	15	Normal	—
TM11	Sunny Day	Fire	Status	—	—	5	All	—
TM12	Taunt	Dark	Status	—	100	20	Normal	—
TM15	Hyper Beam	Normal	Special	150	90	5	Normal	—
TM16	Light Screen	Psychic	Status	—	—	30	2 allies	—
TM17	Protect	Normal	Status	—	—	10	Self	—
TM18	Rain Dance	Water	Status	—	—	5	All	—
TM20	Safeguard	Normal	Status	—	—	25	2 allies	—
TM21	Frustration	Normal	Physical	—	100	20	Normal	●
TM23	Iron Tail	Steel	Physical	100	75	15	Normal	●
TM27	Return	Normal	Physical	—	100	20	Normal	●
TM29	Psychic	Psychic	Special	90	100	10	Normal	—
TM30	Shadow Ball	Ghost	Special	80	100	15	Normal	—
TM32	Double Team	Normal	Status	—	—	15	Self	—
TM33	Reflect	Psychic	Status	—	—	20	2 allies	—
TM34	Shock Wave	Electric	Special	60	—	20	Normal	—
TM41	Torment	Dark	Status	—	100	15	Normal	—
TM42	Facade	Normal	Physical	70	100	20	Normal	●
TM43	Secret Power	Normal	Physical	70	100	20	Normal	●
TM44	Rest	Psychic	Status	—	—	10	Self	—
TM45	Attract	Normal	Status	—	100	15	Normal	—
TM46	Thief	Dark	Physical	40	100	10	Normal	●
TM48	Skill Swap	Psychic	Status	—	—	10	Normal	—
TM49	Snatch	Dark	Status	—	—	10	Depends on move	—
TM52	Focus Blast	Fighting	Special	120	70	5	Normal	—
TM53	Energy Ball	Grass	Special	80	100	10	Normal	—
TM56	Fling	Dark	Physical	—	100	10	Normal	●
TM57	Charge Beam	Electric	Special	50	90	10	Normal	—
TM58	Endure	Normal	Status	—	—	10	Self	—
TM60	Drain Punch	Fighting	Physical	60	100	5	Normal	●
TM63	Embargo	Dark	Status	—	100	15	Normal	—
TM67	Recycle	Normal	Status	—	—	10	Self	—
TM68	Giga Impact	Normal	Physical	150	90	5	Normal	●
TM70	Flash	Normal	Status	—	100	20	Normal	—
TM73	Thunder Wave	Electric	Status	—	100	20	Normal	—
TM77	Psych Up	Normal	Status	—	—	10	Normal	—
TM78	Captivate	Normal	Status	—	100	20	2 foes	—
TM82	Sleep Talk	Normal	Status	—	—	10	Depends on move	—
TM83	Natural Gift	Normal	Physical	—	100	15	Normal	—
TM85	Dream Eater	Psychic	Special	100	100	15	Normal	—
TM86	Grass Knot	Grass	Special	—	100	20	Normal	●
TM87	Swagger	Normal	Status	—	90	15	Normal	—
TM90	Substitute	Normal	Status	—	—	10	Self	—
TM92	Trick Room	Psychic	Status	—	—	5	All	—

● LEVEL-UP AND LEARNED MOVES

Lv	Name	Type	Kind	Power	Acc	PP	Range	DA
Base	Teleport	Psychic	Status	—	—	20	Self	—
Base	Kinesis	Psychic	Status	—	80	15	Normal	—
Base	Confusion	Psychic	Special	50	100	25	Normal	—
16	Confusion	Psychic	Special	50	100	25	Normal	—
18	Disable	Normal	Status	—	80	20	Normal	—
22	Miracle Eye	Psychic	Status	—	—	40	Normal	—
24	Psybeam	Psychic	Special	65	100	20	Normal	—
28	Reflect	Psychic	Status	—	—	20	2 allies	—
30	Recover	Normal	Status	—	—	10	Self	—
34	Psycho Cut	Psychic	Physical	70	100	20	Normal	—
36	Calm Mind	Psychic	Status	—	—	20	Self	—
40	Psychic	Psychic	Special	90	100	10	Normal	—
42	Future Sight	Psychic	Special	80	90	15	Normal	—
46	Trick	Psychic	Status	—	100	10	Normal	—

● MOVES TAUGHT IN EXCHANGE FOR COLORED SHARDS

Name	Type	Kind	Power	Acc	PP	Range	DA
ThunderPunch	Electric	Physical	75	100	15	Normal	●
Fire Punch	Fire	Physical	75	100	15	Normal	●
Ice Punch	Ice	Physical	75	100	15	Normal	●
Snore	Normal	Special	40	100	15	Normal	—
Signal Beam	Bug	Special	75	100	15	Normal	—
Zen Headbutt	Psychic	Physical	80	90	15	Normal	●
Trick	Psychic	Status	—	100	10	Normal	—
Knock Off	Dark	Physical	20	100	20	Normal	●

ABILITY ● Synchronize ● Inner Focus

EGG GROUP Human-Like

STATS
HP ●●
ATTACK ●●
DEFENSE ●●
SP. ATTACK ●●●●●
SP. DEFENSE ●●●
SPEED ●●●●

● PRIMARY WAY TO FIND

TRAINER'S PARTY Elite Four member Lucian

WILD POKÉMON

COURSE OF STORY

Magikarp

WATER

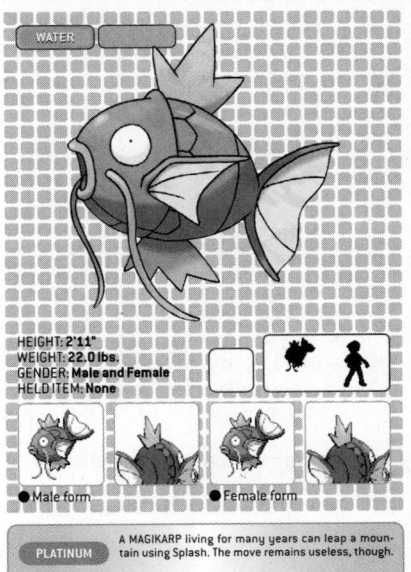

HEIGHT: 2'11"
WEIGHT: 22.0 lbs.
GENDER: Male and Female
HELD ITEM: None

● Male form ● Female form

PLATINUM A MAGIKARP living for many years can leap a mountain using Splash. The move remains useless, though.

EVOLUTION PATH

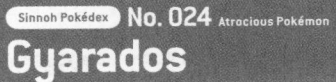

Magikarp — Lv20 → Gyarados

● TM & HM MOVES

No.	Name	Type	Kind	Power	Acc	PP	Range	DA

● LEVEL-UP AND LEARNED MOVES

Lv	Name	Type	Kind	Power	Acc	PP	Range	DA
Base	Splash	Normal	Status	—	—	40	Self	—
15	Tackle	Normal	Physical	35	95	35	Normal	•
30	Flail	Normal	Physical	—	100	15	Normal	•

● MOVES TAUGHT IN EXCHANGE FOR COLORED SHARDS

Name	Type	Kind	Power	Acc	PP	Range	DA
Bounce	Flying	Physical	85	85	5	Normal	—

● EGG MOVES

Name	Type	Kind	Power	Acc	PP	Range	DA

ABILITY ● Swift Swim

EGG GROUP Water 2 / Dragon

STATS
HP ●
ATTACK ●
DEFENSE ●●
SP.ATTACK ●
SP.DEFENSE ●●
SPEED ●●●

● PRIMARY WAY TO FIND

TRAINER'S PARTY Trainer on Route 204

WILD POKÉMON Route 203 [Old Rod]

COURSE OF STORY

Gyarados

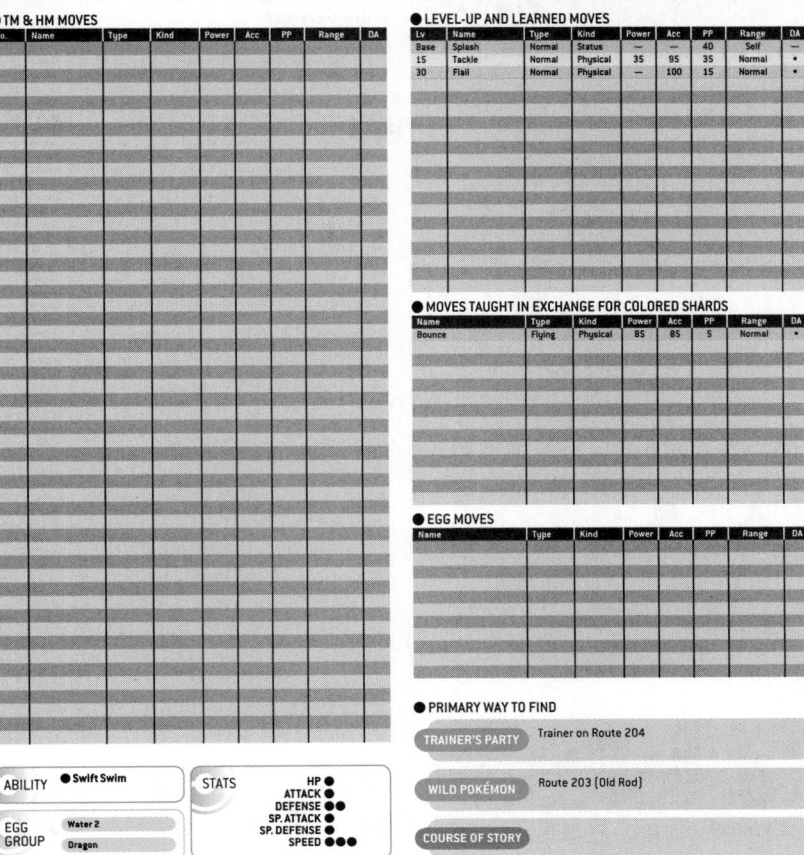

WATER FLYING

HEIGHT: 21'04"
WEIGHT: 518.1 lbs.
GENDER: Male and Female
HELD ITEM: None

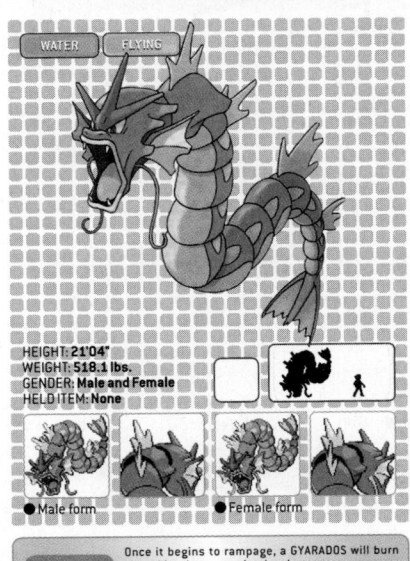

● Male form ● Female form

PLATINUM Once it begins to rampage, a GYARADOS will burn everything down, even in a harsh storm.

EVOLUTION PATH

Magikarp — Lv20 → Gyarados

● TM & HM MOVES

No.	Name	Type	Kind	Power	Acc	PP	Range	DA
TM03	Water Pulse	Water	Special	60	100	20	Normal	—
TM05	Roar	Normal	Status	—	100	20	Normal	—
TM06	Toxic	Poison	Status	—	85	10	Normal	—
TM07	Hail	Ice	Status	—	—	10	All	—
TM10	Hidden Power	Normal	Special	—	100	15	Normal	—
TM12	Taunt	Dark	Status	—	100	20	Normal	—
TM13	Ice Beam	Ice	Special	95	100	10	Normal	—
TM14	Blizzard	Ice	Special	120	70	5	2 foes	—
TM15	Hyper Beam	Normal	Special	150	90	5	Normal	—
TM17	Protect	Normal	Status	—	—	10	Self	—
TM18	Rain Dance	Water	Status	—	—	5	All	—
TM21	Frustration	Normal	Physical	—	100	20	Normal	•
TM24	Thunderbolt	Electric	Special	95	100	15	Normal	—
TM25	Thunder	Electric	Special	120	70	10	Normal	—
TM26	Earthquake	Ground	Physical	100	100	10	2 foes + 1 ally	•
TM27	Return	Normal	Physical	—	100	20	Normal	•
TM32	Double Team	Normal	Status	—	—	15	Self	—
TM35	Flamethrower	Fire	Special	95	100	15	Normal	—
TM37	Sandstorm	Rock	Status	—	—	10	All	—
TM38	Fire Blast	Fire	Special	120	85	5	Normal	—
TM41	Torment	Dark	Status	—	100	15	Normal	—
TM42	Facade	Normal	Physical	70	100	20	Normal	•
TM43	Secret Power	Normal	Physical	70	100	20	Normal	—
TM44	Rest	Psychic	Status	—	—	10	Self	—
TM45	Attract	Normal	Status	—	100	15	Normal	—
TM55	Brine	Water	Special	65	100	10	Normal	—
TM58	Endure	Normal	Status	—	—	10	Self	—
TM59	Dragon Pulse	Dragon	Special	90	100	10	Normal	—
TM66	Payback	Dark	Physical	50	100	10	Normal	•
TM68	Giga Impact	Normal	Physical	150	90	5	Normal	•
TM71	Stone Edge	Rock	Physical	100	80	5	Normal	—
TM72	Avalanche	Ice	Physical	60	100	10	Normal	•
TM73	Thunder Wave	Electric	Status	—	100	20	Normal	—
TM78	Captivate	Normal	Status	—	100	20	2 foes	—
TM79	Dark Pulse	Dark	Special	80	100	15	Normal	—
TM82	Sleep Talk	Normal	Status	—	—	10	DsM	—
TM83	Natural Gift	Normal	Physical	—	100	15	Normal	•
TM87	Swagger	Normal	Status	—	90	15	Normal	—
TM90	Substitute	Normal	Status	—	—	10	Self	—
HM03	Surf	Water	Special	95	100	15	2 foes + 1 ally	—
HM04	Strength	Normal	Physical	80	100	15	Normal	•
HM06	Rock Smash	Fighting	Physical	40	100	15	Normal	•
HM07	Waterfall	Water	Physical	80	100	15	Normal	•

● LEVEL-UP AND LEARNED MOVES

Lv	Name	Type	Kind	Power	Acc	PP	Range	DA
Base	Thrash	Normal	Physical	90	100	20	1 random	•
20	Bite	Dark	Physical	60	100	25	Normal	•
23	Dragon Rage	Dragon	Special	—	100	10	Normal	—
26	Leer	Normal	Status	—	100	30	2 foes	—
29	Twister	Dragon	Special	40	100	20	2 foes	—
32	Ice Fang	Ice	Physical	65	95	15	Normal	•
35	Aqua Tail	Water	Physical	90	90	10	Normal	•
38	Rain Dance	Water	Status	—	—	5	All	—
41	Hydro Pump	Water	Special	120	80	5	Normal	—
44	Dragon Dance	Dragon	Status	—	—	20	Self	—
47	Hyper Beam	Normal	Special	150	90	5	Normal	—

● MOVES TAUGHT IN EXCHANGE FOR COLORED SHARDS

Name	Type	Kind	Power	Acc	PP	Range	DA
Dive	Water	Physical	80	100	10	Normal	•
Icy Wind	Ice	Special	55	95	15	2 foes	—
Iron Head	Steel	Physical	80	100	15	Normal	•
Aqua Tail	Water	Physical	90	90	10	Normal	•
Snore	Normal	Special	40	100	15	Normal	—
Spite	Ghost	Status	—	100	10	Normal	—
Outrage	Dragon	Physical	120	100	15	1 random	•
Twister	Dragon	Special	40	100	20	2 foes	—
Bounce	Flying	Physical	85	85	5	Normal	—
Uproar	Normal	Special	50	100	10	1 random	—

ABILITY ● Intimidate

EGG GROUP Water 2 / Dragon

STATS
HP ●●●
ATTACK ●●●●
DEFENSE ●●●●
SP.ATTACK ●●
SP.DEFENSE ●●●
SPEED ●●●

● PRIMARY WAY TO FIND

TRAINER'S PARTY Pastoria Gym Leader Wake

WILD POKÉMON Route 203 [Super Rod]

COURSE OF STORY

Budew

GRASS   POISON

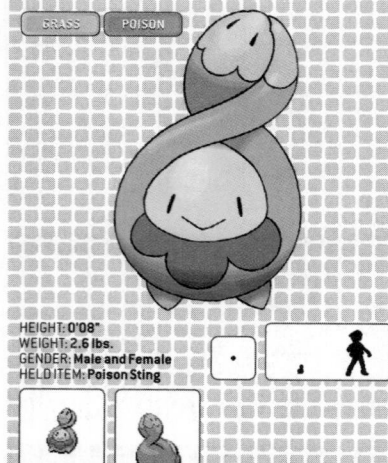

HEIGHT: 0'08"
WEIGHT: 2.6 lbs.
GENDER: Male and Female
HELD ITEM: Poison Sting

● M/F have same form

PLATINUM — Sensitive to changing temperature, the bud is said to bloom when it feels the sun's warm touch.

EVOLUTION PATH

Budew → (Level up between 4 AM and 8 PM when Friendship is high enough) Roselia → (Shining Stone) Roserade

ABILITY: ● Natural Cure ● Poison Point

EGG GROUP: No Eggs

STATS:
HP ●
ATTACK ●
DEFENSE ●
SP. ATTACK ●
SP. DEFENSE ●●
SPEED ●●

● TM & HM MOVES

No.	Name	Type	Kind	Power	Acc	PP	Range	DA
TM06	Toxic	Poison	Status	—	85	10	Normal	—
TM09	Bullet Seed	Grass	Physical	10	100	30	Normal	—
TM10	Hidden Power	Normal	Special	—	100	15	Normal	—
TM11	Sunny Day	Fire	Status	—	—	5	All	—
TM17	Protect	Normal	Status	—	—	10	Self	—
TM18	Rain Dance	Water	Status	—	—	5	All	—
TM19	Giga Drain	Grass	Special	60	100	10	Normal	—
TM21	Frustration	Normal	Physical	—	100	20	Normal	•
TM22	SolarBeam	Grass	Special	120	100	10	Normal	•
TM27	Return	Normal	Physical	—	100	20	Normal	•
TM30	Shadow Ball	Ghost	Special	80	100	15	Normal	—
TM32	Double Team	Normal	Status	—	—	15	Self	—
TM36	Sludge Bomb	Poison	Special	90	100	10	Normal	—
TM42	Facade	Normal	Physical	70	100	20	Normal	—
TM43	Secret Power	Normal	Physical	70	100	20	Normal	—
TM44	Rest	Psychic	Status	—	—	10	Self	—
TM45	Attract	Normal	Status	—	100	15	Normal	—
TM53	Energy Ball	Grass	Special	80	100	10	Normal	—
TM58	Endure	Normal	Status	—	—	10	Self	—
TM70	Flash	Normal	Status	—	100	20	Normal	—
TM75	Swords Dance	Normal	Status	—	—	30	Self	—
TM77	Psych Up	Normal	Status	—	—	10	Self	—
TM78	Captivate	Normal	Status	—	100	20	2 foes	—
TM82	Sleep Talk	Normal	Status	—	—	10	DoM	—
TM83	Natural Gift	Normal	Physical	—	100	15	Normal	•
TM86	Grass Knot	Grass	Special	—	100	20	Normal	•
TM87	Swagger	Normal	Status	—	90	15	Normal	—
TM90	Substitute	Normal	Status	—	—	10	Self	—
HM01	Cut	Normal	Physical	50	95	30	Normal	—

● LEVEL-UP AND LEARNED MOVES

Lv	Name	Type	Kind	Power	Acc	PP	Range	DA
Base	Absorb	Grass	Special	20	100	25	Normal	—
4	Growth	Normal	Status	—	—	40	Self	—
7	Water Sport	Water	Status	—	—	15	All	—
10	Stun Spore	Grass	Status	—	75	30	Normal	—
13	Mega Drain	Grass	Special	40	100	15	Normal	—
16	Worry Seed	Grass	Status	—	100	10	Normal	—

● MOVES TAUGHT IN EXCHANGE FOR COLORED SHARDS

Name	Type	Kind	Power	Acc	PP	Range	DA
Mud-Slap	Ground	Special	20	100	10	Normal	—
Snore	Normal	Special	40	100	15	Normal	—
Synthesis	Grass	Status	—	—	5	Self	—
Seed Bomb	Grass	Physical	80	100	15	Normal	—
Swift	Normal	Special	60	—	20	2 foes	—
Uproar	Normal	Special	50	100	10	1 random	—

● EGG MOVES

Name	Type	Kind	Power	Acc	PP	Range	DA
Spikes	Ground	Status	—	—	20	2 foes	—
Synthesis	Grass	Status	—	—	5	Self	—
Pin Missile	Bug	Physical	14	85	20	Normal	—
Cotton Spore	Grass	Status	—	85	40	Normal	—
Sleep Powder	Grass	Status	—	75	15	Normal	—
Razor Leaf	Grass	Physical	55	95	25	2 foes	—
Mind Reader	Normal	Status	—	—	5	Normal	—
Leaf Storm	Grass	Special	140	90	5	Normal	—
Extrasensory	Psychic	Special	80	100	30	Normal	—

● PRIMARY WAY TO FIND

TRAINER'S PARTY — Trainer on Route 203

WILD POKÉMON — Route 204

COURSE OF STORY

Roselia

GRASS   POISON

HEIGHT: 1'00"
WEIGHT: 4.4 lbs.
GENDER: Male and Female
HELD ITEM: Poison Sting

● Male form   ● Female form

PLATINUM — The more healthy the ROSELIA, the more pleasant its flowers' aroma. Its scent deeply relaxes people.

EVOLUTION PATH

Budew → (Level up between 4 AM and 8 PM when Friendship is high enough) Roselia → (Shining Stone) Roserade

ABILITY: ● Natural Cure ● Poison Point

EGG GROUP: Fairy / Grass

STATS:
HP ●●
ATTACK ●●
DEFENSE ●●
SP. ATTACK ●●●
SP. DEFENSE ●●●
SPEED ●●

● TM & HM MOVES

No.	Name	Type	Kind	Power	Acc	PP	Range	DA
TM06	Toxic	Poison	Status	—	85	10	Normal	—
TM09	Bullet Seed	Grass	Physical	10	100	30	Normal	—
TM10	Hidden Power	Normal	Special	—	100	15	Normal	—
TM11	Sunny Day	Fire	Status	—	—	5	All	—
TM17	Protect	Normal	Status	—	—	10	Self	—
TM18	Rain Dance	Water	Status	—	—	5	All	—
TM19	Giga Drain	Grass	Special	60	100	10	Normal	—
TM21	Frustration	Normal	Physical	—	100	20	Normal	•
TM22	SolarBeam	Grass	Special	120	100	10	Normal	•
TM27	Return	Normal	Physical	—	100	20	Normal	•
TM30	Shadow Ball	Ghost	Special	80	100	15	Normal	—
TM32	Double Team	Normal	Status	—	—	15	Self	—
TM36	Sludge Bomb	Poison	Special	90	100	10	Normal	—
TM42	Facade	Normal	Physical	70	100	20	Normal	•
TM43	Secret Power	Normal	Physical	70	100	20	Normal	•
TM44	Rest	Psychic	Status	—	—	10	Self	—
TM45	Attract	Normal	Status	—	100	15	Normal	—
TM53	Energy Ball	Grass	Special	80	100	10	Normal	—
TM58	Endure	Normal	Status	—	—	10	Self	—
TM70	Flash	Normal	Status	—	100	20	Normal	—
TM75	Swords Dance	Normal	Status	—	—	30	Self	—
TM77	Psych Up	Normal	Status	—	—	10	Self	—
TM78	Captivate	Normal	Status	—	100	20	2 foes	—
TM82	Sleep Talk	Normal	Status	—	—	10	DoM	—
TM83	Natural Gift	Normal	Physical	—	100	15	Normal	—
TM84	Poison Jab	Poison	Physical	80	100	20	Normal	•
TM86	Grass Knot	Grass	Special	—	100	20	Normal	•
TM87	Swagger	Normal	Status	—	90	15	Normal	—
TM90	Substitute	Normal	Status	—	—	10	Self	—
HM01	Cut	Normal	Physical	50	95	30	Normal	•

● LEVEL-UP AND LEARNED MOVES

Lv	Name	Type	Kind	Power	Acc	PP	Range	DA
Base	Absorb	Grass	Special	20	100	25	Normal	—
4	Growth	Normal	Status	—	—	40	Self	—
7	Poison Sting	Poison	Physical	15	100	35	Normal	—
10	Stun Spore	Grass	Status	—	75	30	Normal	—
13	Mega Drain	Grass	Special	40	100	15	Normal	—
16	Leech Seed	Grass	Status	—	90	10	Normal	—
19	Magical Leaf	Grass	Special	60	—	20	Normal	—
22	GrassWhistle	Grass	Status	—	55	15	Normal	—
25	Giga Drain	Grass	Special	60	100	10	Normal	—
28	Toxic Spikes	Poison	Status	—	—	20	2 foes	—
31	Sweet Scent	Normal	Status	—	100	20	2 foes	—
34	Ingrain	Grass	Status	—	—	20	Self	—
37	Toxic	Poison	Status	—	85	10	Normal	—
40	Petal Dance	Grass	Special	90	100	20	1 random	—
43	Aromatherapy	Grass	Status	—	—	5	All allies	—
46	Synthesis	Grass	Status	—	—	5	Self	—

● MOVES TAUGHT IN EXCHANGE FOR COLORED SHARDS

Name	Type	Kind	Power	Acc	PP	Range	DA
Mud-Slap	Ground	Special	20	100	10	Normal	—
Fury Cutter	Bug	Physical	10	95	20	Normal	•
Snore	Normal	Special	40	100	15	Normal	—
Synthesis	Grass	Status	—	—	5	Self	—
Seed Bomb	Grass	Physical	80	100	15	Normal	—
Swift	Normal	Special	60	—	20	2 foes	—

● EGG MOVES

Name	Type	Kind	Power	Acc	PP	Range	DA
Spikes	Ground	Status	—	—	20	2 foes	—
Synthesis	Grass	Status	—	—	5	Self	—
Pin Missile	Bug	Physical	14	85	20	Normal	—
Cotton Spore	Grass	Status	—	85	40	Normal	—
Sleep Powder	Grass	Status	—	75	15	Normal	—
Razor Leaf	Grass	Physical	55	95	25	2 foes	—
Mind Reader	Normal	Status	—	—	5	Normal	—
Leaf Storm	Grass	Special	140	90	5	Normal	—

● PRIMARY WAY TO FIND

TRAINER'S PARTY — Trainer on Route 205

WILD POKÉMON — Route 208

COURSE OF STORY

No. 027 Bouquet Pokémon

Roserade

GRASS | POISON

HEIGHT: 2'11"
WEIGHT: 32.0 lbs.
GENDER: Male and Female
HELD ITEM: None

● Male form   ● Female form

PLATINUM | Each of its hands contains different toxins, but both hands can jab with near-fatal power.

EVOLUTION PATH

Budew → (Level up between 4 AM and 8 PM if friendship is high enough) Roselia → (Shiny Stone) Roserade

● TM & HM MOVES

No.	Name	Type	Kind	Power	Acc	PP	Range	DA
TM06	Toxic	Poison	Status	—	85	10	Normal	—
TM09	Bullet Seed	Grass	Physical	10	100	30	Normal	—
TM10	Hidden Power	Normal	Special	—	100	15	Normal	—
TM11	Sunny Day	Fire	Status	—	—	5	All	—
TM15	Hyper Beam	Normal	Special	150	90	5	Normal	—
TM17	Protect	Normal	Status	—	—	10	Self	—
TM18	Rain Dance	Water	Status	—	—	5	All	—
TM19	Giga Drain	Grass	Special	60	100	10	Normal	—
TM21	Frustration	Normal	Physical	—	100	20	Normal	●
TM22	SolarBeam	Grass	Special	120	100	10	Normal	—
TM27	Return	Normal	Physical	—	100	20	Normal	●
TM30	Shadow Ball	Ghost	Special	80	100	15	Normal	—
TM32	Double Team	Normal	Status	—	—	15	Self	—
TM36	Sludge Bomb	Poison	Special	90	100	10	Normal	—
TM42	Facade	Normal	Physical	70	100	20	Normal	●
TM43	Secret Power	Normal	Physical	70	100	20	Normal	●
TM44	Rest	Psychic	Status	—	—	10	Self	—
TM45	Attract	Normal	Status	—	100	15	Normal	—
TM53	Energy Ball	Grass	Special	80	100	10	Normal	—
TM58	Endure	Normal	Status	—	—	10	Self	—
TM68	Giga Impact	Normal	Physical	150	90	5	Normal	●
TM70	Flash	Normal	Status	—	100	20	Normal	—
TM75	Swords Dance	Normal	Status	—	—	30	Self	—
TM77	Psych Up	Normal	Status	—	—	10	Normal	—
TM78	Captivate	Normal	Status	—	100	20	2 foes	—
TM82	Sleep Talk	Normal	Status	—	—	10	DoM	—
TM83	Natural Gift	Normal	Physical	—	100	15	Normal	—
TM84	Poison Jab	Poison	Physical	80	100	20	Normal	●
TM86	Grass Knot	Grass	Special	—	100	20	Normal	—
TM87	Swagger	Normal	Status	—	90	15	Normal	—
TM90	Substitute	Normal	Status	—	—	10	Self	—
HM01	Cut	Normal	Physical	50	95	30	Normal	—

● LEVEL-UP AND LEARNED MOVES

Lv	Name	Type	Kind	Power	Acc	PP	Range	DA
Base	Weather Ball	Normal	Special	50	100	10	Normal	—
Base	Poison Sting	Poison	Physical	15	100	35	Normal	—
Base	Mega Drain	Grass	Special	40	100	15	Normal	—
Base	Magical Leaf	Grass	Special	60	—	20	Normal	—
Base	Sweet Scent	Normal	Status	—	100	20	2 foes	—

● MOVES TAUGHT IN EXCHANGE FOR COLORED SHARDS

Name	Type	Kind	Power	Acc	PP	Range	DA
Mud-Slap	Ground	Special	20	100	10	Normal	—
Fury Cutter	Bug	Physical	10	95	20	Normal	●
Snore	Normal	Special	40	100	15	Normal	—
Synthesis	Grass	Status	—	—	5	Self	—
Seed Bomb	Grass	Physical	80	100	15	Normal	—
Swift	Normal	Special	60	—	20	2 foes	—

● PRIMARY WAY TO FIND

TRAINER'S PARTY | Eterna Gym Leader Gardenia

WILD POKÉMON

COURSE OF STORY

ABILITY | ● Natural Cure ● Poison Point

EGG GROUP | Fairy / Grass

STATS | HP ●● / ATTACK ●●● / DEFENSE ●● / SP. ATTACK ●●●● / SP. DEFENSE ●●●● / SPEED ●●●

No. 028 Bat Pokémon

Zubat

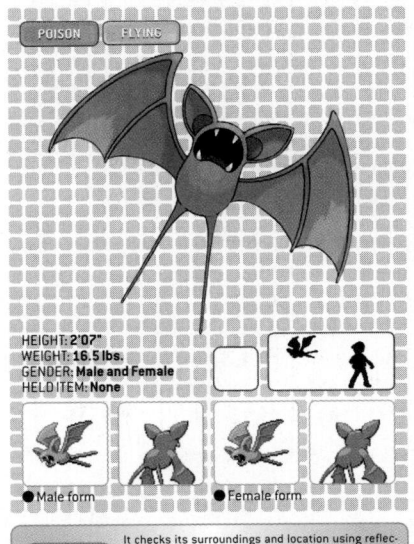

POISON | FLYING

HEIGHT: 2'07"
WEIGHT: 16.5 lbs.
GENDER: Male and Female
HELD ITEM: None

● Male form   ● Female form

PLATINUM | It checks its surroundings and location using reflections of the ultrasonic waves from its mouth.

EVOLUTION PATH

Zubat → (Lv22) Golbat → (Level up once friendship is high enough) Crobat

● TM & HM MOVES

No.	Name	Type	Kind	Power	Acc	PP	Range	DA
TM06	Toxic	Poison	Status	—	85	10	Normal	—
TM10	Hidden Power	Normal	Special	—	100	15	Normal	—
TM11	Sunny Day	Fire	Status	—	—	5	All	—
TM12	Taunt	Dark	Status	—	100	20	Normal	—
TM17	Protect	Normal	Status	—	—	10	Self	—
TM18	Rain Dance	Water	Status	—	—	5	All	—
TM19	Giga Drain	Grass	Special	60	100	10	Normal	—
TM21	Frustration	Normal	Physical	—	100	20	Normal	●
TM27	Return	Normal	Physical	—	100	20	Normal	●
TM30	Shadow Ball	Ghost	Special	80	100	15	Normal	—
TM32	Double Team	Normal	Status	—	—	15	Self	—
TM36	Sludge Bomb	Poison	Special	90	100	10	Normal	—
TM40	Aerial Ace	Flying	Physical	60	—	20	Normal	●
TM41	Torment	Dark	Status	—	100	15	Normal	—
TM42	Facade	Normal	Physical	70	100	20	Normal	●
TM43	Secret Power	Normal	Physical	70	100	20	Normal	●
TM44	Rest	Psychic	Status	—	—	10	Self	—
TM45	Attract	Normal	Status	—	100	15	Normal	—
TM46	Thief	Dark	Physical	40	100	10	Normal	—
TM47	Steel Wing	Steel	Physical	70	90	25	Normal	—
TM49	Snatch	Dark	Status	—	—	10	DoM	—
TM51	Roost	Flying	Status	—	—	10	Self	—
TM58	Endure	Normal	Status	—	—	10	Self	—
TM66	Payback	Dark	Physical	50	100	10	Normal	●
TM78	Captivate	Normal	Status	—	100	20	2 foes	—
TM82	Sleep Talk	Normal	Status	—	—	10	DoM	—
TM83	Natural Gift	Normal	Physical	—	100	15	Normal	—
TM87	Swagger	Normal	Status	—	90	15	Normal	—
TM88	Pluck	Flying	Physical	60	100	20	Normal	●
TM89	U-turn	Bug	Physical	70	100	20	Normal	●
TM90	Substitute	Normal	Status	—	—	10	Self	—
HM02	Fly	Flying	Physical	90	95	15	Normal	●
HM05	Defog	Flying	Status	—	—	15	Normal	—

● LEVEL-UP AND LEARNED MOVES

Lv	Name	Type	Kind	Power	Acc	PP	Range	DA
Base	Leech Life	Bug	Physical	20	100	15	Normal	●
5	Supersonic	Normal	Status	—	55	20	Normal	—
9	Astonish	Ghost	Physical	30	100	15	Normal	●
13	Bite	Dark	Physical	60	100	25	Normal	●
17	Wing Attack	Flying	Physical	60	100	35	Normal	●
21	Confuse Ray	Ghost	Status	—	100	10	Normal	—
25	Air Cutter	Flying	Special	55	95	25	2 foes	—
29	Mean Look	Normal	Status	—	—	5	Normal	—
33	Poison Fang	Poison	Physical	50	100	15	Normal	●
37	Haze	Ice	Status	—	—	30	All	—
41	Air Slash	Flying	Special	75	95	20	Normal	—

● MOVES TAUGHT IN EXCHANGE FOR COLORED SHARDS

Name	Type	Kind	Power	Acc	PP	Range	DA
Ominous Wind	Ghost	Special	60	100	5	Normal	—
Snore	Normal	Special	40	100	15	Normal	—
Air Cutter	Flying	Special	55	95	25	2 foes	—
Zen Headbutt	Psychic	Physical	80	90	15	Normal	●
Twister	Dragon	Special	40	100	20	2 foes	—
Heat Wave	Fire	Special	100	90	10	2 foes	—
Swift	Normal	Special	60	—	20	2 foes	—
Uproar	Normal	Special	50	100	10	1 random	—

● EGG MOVES

Name	Type	Kind	Power	Acc	PP	Range	DA
Quick Attack	Normal	Physical	40	100	30	Normal	●
Pursuit	Dark	Physical	40	100	20	Normal	●
Faint Attack	Dark	Physical	60	—	20	Normal	●
Gust	Flying	Special	40	100	35	Normal	—
Whirlwind	Normal	Status	—	100	20	Normal	—
Curse	???	Status	—	—	10	Normal ● Self	—
Nasty Plot	Dark	Status	—	—	20	Self	—
Hypnosis	Psychic	Status	—	60	20	Normal	—
Zen Headbutt	Psychic	Physical	80	90	15	Normal	●
Brave Bird	Flying	Physical	120	100	15	Normal	●

● PRIMARY WAY TO FIND

TRAINER'S PARTY | Trainer on Route 203

WILD POKÉMON | Oreburgh Gate 1F

COURSE OF STORY

ABILITY | ● Inner Focus

EGG GROUP | Flying

STATS | HP ● / ATTACK ●● / DEFENSE ●● / SP. ATTACK ● / SP. DEFENSE ●● / SPEED ●●

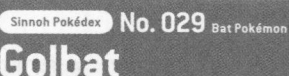

Golbat

Sinnoh Pokédex No. 029 Bat Pokémon

POISON FLYING

HEIGHT: 5'03"
WEIGHT: 121.3 lbs.
GENDER: Male and Female
HELD ITEM: None

● Male form   ● Female form

PLATINUM — Its sharp fangs puncture the toughest of hides and have small holes for greedily sucking blood.

EVOLUTION PATH

Zubat → Golbat (Lv22) → Crobat (Level up once Friendship is high enough)

● TM & HM MOVES

No.	Name	Type	Kind	Power	Acc	PP	Range	DA
TM06	Toxic	Poison	Status	—	85	10	Normal	—
TM10	Hidden Power	Normal	Special	—	100	15	Normal	—
TM11	Sunny Day	Fire	Status	—	—	5	All	—
TM12	Taunt	Dark	Status	—	100	20	Normal	—
TM15	Hyper Beam	Normal	Special	150	90	5	Normal	—
TM17	Protect	Normal	Status	—	—	10	Self	—
TM18	Rain Dance	Water	Status	—	—	5	All	—
TM19	Giga Drain	Grass	Special	60	100	10	Normal	—
TM21	Frustration	Normal	Physical	—	100	20	Normal	•
TM27	Return	Normal	Physical	—	100	20	Normal	•
TM30	Shadow Ball	Ghost	Special	80	100	15	Normal	•
TM32	Double Team	Normal	Status	—	—	15	Self	—
TM36	Sludge Bomb	Poison	Special	90	100	10	Normal	•
TM40	Aerial Ace	Flying	Physical	60	—	20	Normal	•
TM41	Torment	Dark	Status	—	100	15	Normal	—
TM42	Facade	Normal	Physical	70	100	20	Normal	•
TM43	Secret Power	Normal	Physical	70	100	20	Normal	•
TM44	Rest	Psychic	Status	—	—	10	Self	—
TM45	Attract	Normal	Status	—	100	15	Normal	—
TM46	Thief	Dark	Physical	40	100	10	Normal	•
TM47	Steel Wing	Steel	Physical	70	90	25	Normal	•
TM49	Snatch	Dark	Status	—	—	10	DoM	—
TM51	Roost	Flying	Status	—	—	10	Self	—
TM58	Endure	Normal	Status	—	—	10	Self	—
TM66	Payback	Dark	Physical	50	100	10	Normal	•
TM68	Giga Impact	Normal	Physical	150	90	5	Normal	•
TM78	Captivate	Normal	Status	—	100	20	2 foes	—
TM82	Sleep Talk	Normal	Status	—	—	10	DoM	—
TM83	Natural Gift	Normal	Physical	—	100	15	Normal	•
TM87	Swagger	Normal	Status	—	90	15	Normal	—
TM88	Pluck	Flying	Physical	60	100	20	Normal	•
TM89	U-turn	Bug	Physical	70	100	20	Normal	•
TM90	Substitute	Normal	Status	—	—	10	Self	—
HM02	Fly	Flying	Physical	90	95	15	Normal	—
HM05	Defog	Flying	Status	—	—	15	Normal	—

● LEVEL-UP AND LEARNED MOVES

Lv	Name	Type	Kind	Power	Acc	PP	Range	DA
Base	Screech	Normal	Status	—	85	40	Normal	—
Base	Leech Life	Bug	Physical	20	100	15	Normal	•
Base	Supersonic	Normal	Status	—	55	20	Normal	•
Base	Astonish	Ghost	Physical	30	100	15	Normal	•
5	Supersonic	Normal	Status	—	55	20	Normal	—
9	Astonish	Ghost	Physical	30	100	15	Normal	—
13	Bite	Dark	Physical	60	100	25	Normal	—
17	Wing Attack	Flying	Physical	60	100	35	Normal	—
21	Confuse Ray	Ghost	Status	—	100	10	Normal	—
27	Air Cutter	Flying	Special	55	95	25	2 foes	—
33	Mean Look	Normal	Status	—	—	5	Normal	—
39	Poison Fang	Poison	Physical	50	100	15	Normal	—
45	Haze	Ice	Status	—	—	30	All	—
51	Air Slash	Flying	Special	75	95	20	Normal	—

● MOVES TAUGHT IN EXCHANGE FOR COLORED SHARDS

Name	Type	Kind	Power	Acc	PP	Range	DA
Ominous Wind	Ghost	Special	60	100	5	Normal	—
Snore	Normal	Special	40	100	15	Normal	—
Air Cutter	Flying	Special	55	95	25	2 foes	—
Zen Headbutt	Psychic	Physical	80	90	15	Normal	•
Twister	Dragon	Special	40	100	20	2 foes	—
Heat Wave	Fire	Special	100	90	10	2 foes	—
Swift	Normal	Special	60	—	20	Normal	—
Uproar	Normal	Special	50	100	10	1 random	—

ABILITY ● Inner Focus
EGG GROUP: Flying
STATS: HP ●● ATTACK ●●● DEFENSE ●● SP.ATTACK ●● SP.DEFENSE ●● SPEED ●●●

● PRIMARY WAY TO FIND

TRAINER'S PARTY — Trainer on the Celestic Town side of Route 210
WILD POKÉMON — Lost Tower 5F
COURSE OF STORY

Crobat

Sinnoh Pokédex No. 030 Bat Pokémon

POISON FLYING

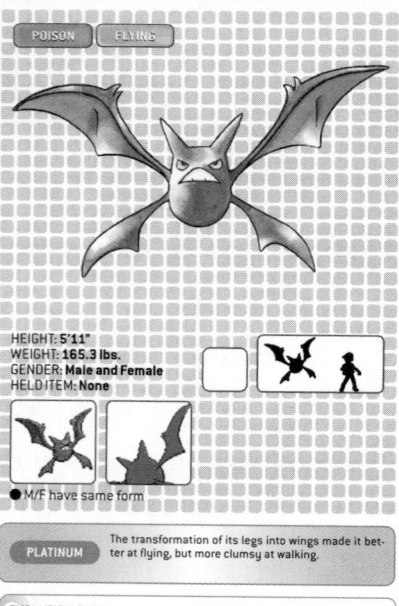

HEIGHT: 5'11"
WEIGHT: 165.3 lbs.
GENDER: Male and Female
HELD ITEM: None

● M/F have same form

PLATINUM — The transformation of its legs into wings made it better at flying, but more clumsy at walking.

EVOLUTION PATH

Zubat → Golbat (Lv22) → Crobat (Level up once Friendship is high enough)

● TM & HM MOVES

No.	Name	Type	Kind	Power	Acc	PP	Range	DA
TM06	Toxic	Poison	Status	—	85	10	Normal	—
TM10	Hidden Power	Normal	Special	—	100	15	Normal	—
TM11	Sunny Day	Fire	Status	—	—	5	All	—
TM12	Taunt	Dark	Status	—	100	20	Normal	—
TM15	Hyper Beam	Normal	Special	150	90	5	Normal	—
TM17	Protect	Normal	Status	—	—	10	Self	—
TM18	Rain Dance	Water	Status	—	—	5	All	—
TM19	Giga Drain	Grass	Special	60	100	10	Normal	—
TM21	Frustration	Normal	Physical	—	100	20	Normal	•
TM27	Return	Normal	Physical	—	100	20	Normal	•
TM30	Shadow Ball	Ghost	Special	80	100	15	Normal	•
TM32	Double Team	Normal	Status	—	—	15	Self	—
TM36	Sludge Bomb	Poison	Special	90	100	10	Normal	•
TM40	Aerial Ace	Flying	Physical	60	—	20	Normal	•
TM41	Torment	Dark	Status	—	100	15	Normal	—
TM42	Facade	Normal	Physical	70	100	20	Normal	•
TM43	Secret Power	Normal	Physical	70	100	20	Normal	•
TM44	Rest	Psychic	Status	—	—	10	Self	—
TM45	Attract	Normal	Status	—	100	15	Normal	—
TM46	Thief	Dark	Physical	40	100	10	Normal	•
TM47	Steel Wing	Steel	Physical	70	90	25	Normal	•
TM49	Snatch	Dark	Status	—	—	10	DoM	—
TM51	Roost	Flying	Status	—	—	10	Self	—
TM58	Endure	Normal	Status	—	—	10	Self	—
TM66	Payback	Dark	Physical	50	100	10	Normal	•
TM68	Giga Impact	Normal	Physical	150	90	5	Normal	•
TM78	Captivate	Normal	Status	—	100	20	2 foes	—
TM79	Dark Pulse	Dark	Special	80	100	15	Normal	•
TM81	X-Scissor	Bug	Physical	80	100	15	Normal	•
TM82	Sleep Talk	Normal	Status	—	—	10	DoM	—
TM83	Natural Gift	Normal	Physical	—	100	15	Normal	•
TM87	Swagger	Normal	Status	—	90	15	Normal	—
TM88	Pluck	Flying	Physical	60	100	20	Normal	•
TM89	U-turn	Bug	Physical	70	100	20	Normal	•
TM90	Substitute	Normal	Status	—	—	10	Self	—
HM02	Fly	Flying	Physical	90	95	15	Normal	—
HM05	Defog	Flying	Status	—	—	15	Normal	—

● LEVEL-UP AND LEARNED MOVES

Lv	Name	Type	Kind	Power	Acc	PP	Range	DA
Base	Cross Poison	Poison	Physical	70	100	20	Normal	•
Base	Screech	Normal	Status	—	85	40	Normal	—
Base	Leech Life	Bug	Physical	20	100	15	Normal	•
Base	Supersonic	Normal	Status	—	55	20	Normal	•
Base	Astonish	Ghost	Physical	30	100	15	Normal	•
5	Supersonic	Normal	Status	—	55	20	Normal	—
9	Astonish	Ghost	Physical	30	100	15	Normal	—
13	Bite	Dark	Physical	60	100	25	Normal	—
17	Wing Attack	Flying	Physical	60	100	35	Normal	—
21	Confuse Ray	Ghost	Status	—	100	10	Normal	—
27	Air Cutter	Flying	Special	55	95	25	2 foes	—
33	Mean Look	Normal	Status	—	—	5	Normal	—
39	Poison Fang	Poison	Physical	50	100	15	Normal	—
45	Haze	Ice	Status	—	—	30	All	—
51	Air Slash	Flying	Special	75	95	20	Normal	—

● MOVES TAUGHT IN EXCHANGE FOR COLORED SHARDS

Name	Type	Kind	Power	Acc	PP	Range	DA
Ominous Wind	Ghost	Special	60	100	5	Normal	—
Snore	Normal	Special	40	100	15	Normal	—
Air Cutter	Flying	Special	55	95	25	2 foes	—
Zen Headbutt	Psychic	Physical	80	90	15	Normal	•
Twister	Dragon	Special	40	100	20	2 foes	—
Heat Wave	Fire	Special	100	90	10	2 foes	—
Swift	Normal	Special	60	—	20	2 foes	—
Uproar	Normal	Special	50	100	10	1 random	—

ABILITY ● Inner Focus
EGG GROUP: Flying
STATS: HP ●●● ATTACK ●●● DEFENSE ●● SP.ATTACK ●● SP.DEFENSE ●●● SPEED ●●●●●

● PRIMARY WAY TO FIND

TRAINER'S PARTY — Team Galactic Boss Cyrus, when you Fight him at the Galactic Veilstone Bldg.
WILD POKÉMON
COURSE OF STORY

No. 031 Rock Pokémon

Geodude

ROCK GROUND

HEIGHT: 1'04"
WEIGHT: 44.1 lbs.
GENDER: Male and Female
HELD ITEM: Everstone

● M/F have same form

PLATINUM At rest, it looks just like a rock. Carelessly stepping on it will make it swing its fists angrily.

EVOLUTION PATH

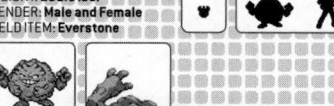

Geodude — Lv25 — Graveler — Link Trade — Golem

ABILITY ● Rock Head ● Sturdy

EGG GROUP Mineral

STATS HP ●
ATTACK ●●
DEFENSE ●●●
SP. ATTACK ●
SP. DEFENSE ●
SPEED ●

● TM & HM MOVES

No.	Name	Type	Kind	Power	Acc	PP	Range	DA
TM01	Focus Punch	Fighting	Physical	150	100	20	Normal	●
TM06	Toxic	Poison	Status	—	85	10	Normal	—
TM10	Hidden Power	Normal	Special	—	100	15	Normal	—
TM11	Sunny Day	Fire	Status	—	—	5	All	—
TM17	Protect	Normal	Status	—	—	10	Self	—
TM21	Frustration	Normal	Physical	—	100	20	Normal	●
TM26	Earthquake	Ground	Physical	100	100	10	2 foes • 1 ally	—
TM27	Return	Normal	Physical	—	100	20	Normal	●
TM28	Dig	Ground	Physical	80	100	10	Normal	●
TM31	Brick Break	Fighting	Physical	75	100	15	Normal	●
TM32	Double Team	Normal	Status	—	—	15	Self	—
TM35	Flamethrower	Fire	Special	95	100	15	Normal	—
TM37	Sandstorm	Rock	Status	—	—	10	All	—
TM38	Fire Blast	Fire	Special	120	85	5	Normal	—
TM39	Rock Tomb	Rock	Physical	50	80	10	Normal	●
TM42	Facade	Normal	Physical	70	100	20	Normal	●
TM43	Secret Power	Normal	Physical	70	100	20	Normal	●
TM44	Rest	Psychic	Status	—	—	10	Self	—
TM45	Attract	Normal	Status	—	100	15	Normal	—
TM56	Fling	Dark	Physical	—	100	10	Normal	●
TM58	Endure	Normal	Status	—	—	10	Self	—
TM64	Explosion	Normal	Physical	250	100	5	2 foes • 1 ally	—
TM69	Rock Polish	Rock	Status	—	—	20	Self	—
TM71	Stone Edge	Rock	Physical	100	80	5	Normal	●
TM74	Gyro Ball	Steel	Physical	—	100	5	Normal	●
TM76	Stealth Rock	Rock	Status	—	—	20	2 foes	—
TM78	Captivate	Normal	Status	—	100	20	2 foes	—
TM80	Rock Slide	Rock	Physical	75	90	10	2 foes	—
TM82	Sleep Talk	Normal	Status	—	—	10	Self	—
TM83	Natural Gift	Normal	Physical	—	100	15	Normal	—
TM87	Swagger	Normal	Status	—	90	15	Normal	—
TM90	Substitute	Normal	Status	—	—	10	Self	—
HM04	Strength	Normal	Physical	80	100	15	Normal	●
HM06	Rock Smash	Fighting	Physical	40	100	15	Normal	●
HM08	Rock Climb	Normal	Physical	90	85	20	Normal	●

● LEVEL-UP AND LEARNED MOVES

Lv	Name	Type	Kind	Power	Acc	PP	Range	DA
Base	Tackle	Normal	Physical	35	95	35	Normal	●
Base	Defense Curl	Normal	Status	—	—	40	Self	—
4	Mud Sport	Ground	Status	—	—	15	All	—
8	Rock Polish	Rock	Status	—	—	20	Self	—
11	Rock Throw	Rock	Physical	50	90	15	Normal	—
15	Magnitude	Ground	Physical	—	100	30	2 foes • 1 ally	—
18	Selfdestruct	Normal	Physical	200	100	5	2 foes • 1 ally	—
22	Rollout	Rock	Physical	30	90	20	Normal	●
25	Rock Blast	Rock	Physical	25	80	10	Normal	—
29	Earthquake	Ground	Physical	100	100	10	2 foes • 1 ally	—
32	Explosion	Normal	Physical	250	100	5	2 foes • 1 ally	—
36	Double-Edge	Normal	Physical	120	100	15	Normal	●
39	Stone Edge	Rock	Physical	100	80	5	Normal	●

● MOVES TAUGHT IN EXCHANGE FOR COLORED SHARDS

Name	Type	Kind	Power	Acc	PP	Range	DA
Mud-Slap	Ground	Special	20	100	10	Normal	—
Rollout	Rock	Physical	30	90	20	Normal	●
ThunderPunch	Electric	Physical	75	100	15	Normal	●
Fire Punch	Fire	Physical	75	100	15	Normal	●
Superpower	Fighting	Physical	120	100	5	Normal	●
Snore	Normal	Special	40	100	15	Normal	—
AncientPower	Rock	Special	60	100	5	Normal	—
Earth Power	Ground	Special	90	100	10	Normal	—
Sucker Punch	Dark	Physical	80	100	5	Normal	●

● EGG MOVES

Name	Type	Kind	Power	Acc	PP	Range	DA
Mega Punch	Normal	Physical	80	85	20	Normal	●
Rock Slide	Rock	Physical	75	90	10	2 foes	—
Block	Normal	Status	—	—	5	Normal	—
Hammer Arm	Fighting	Physical	100	90	10	Normal	●
Flail	Normal	Physical	—	100	15	Normal	●

● PRIMARY WAY TO FIND

TRAINER'S PARTY Trainer in the Oreburgh Mine

WILD POKÉMON Oreburgh Gate 1F

COURSE OF STORY

No. 032 Rock Pokémon

Graveler

ROCK GROUND

HEIGHT: 3'03"
WEIGHT: 231.5 lbs.
GENDER: Male and Female
HELD ITEM: Everstone

● M/F have same form

PLATINUM It rolls on mountain paths to move. Once it builds momentum, no Pokémon can stop it without difficulty.

EVOLUTION PATH

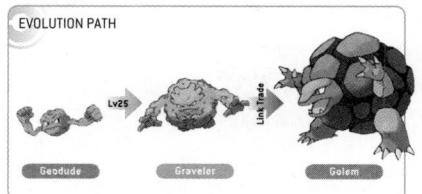

Geodude — Lv25 — Graveler — Link Trade — Golem

ABILITY ● Rock Head ● Sturdy

EGG GROUP Mineral

STATS HP ●●
ATTACK ●●●
DEFENSE ●●●●
SP. ATTACK ●
SP. DEFENSE ●
SPEED ●

● TM & HM MOVES

No.	Name	Type	Kind	Power	Acc	PP	Range	DA
TM01	Focus Punch	Fighting	Physical	150	100	20	Normal	●
TM06	Toxic	Poison	Status	—	85	10	Normal	—
TM10	Hidden Power	Normal	Special	—	100	15	Normal	—
TM11	Sunny Day	Fire	Status	—	—	5	All	—
TM17	Protect	Normal	Status	—	—	10	Self	—
TM21	Frustration	Normal	Physical	—	100	20	Normal	●
TM26	Earthquake	Ground	Physical	100	100	10	2 foes • 1 ally	—
TM27	Return	Normal	Physical	—	100	20	Normal	●
TM28	Dig	Ground	Physical	80	100	10	Normal	●
TM31	Brick Break	Fighting	Physical	75	100	15	Normal	●
TM32	Double Team	Normal	Status	—	—	15	Self	—
TM35	Flamethrower	Fire	Special	95	100	15	Normal	—
TM37	Sandstorm	Rock	Status	—	—	10	All	—
TM38	Fire Blast	Fire	Special	120	85	5	Normal	—
TM39	Rock Tomb	Rock	Physical	50	80	10	Normal	●
TM42	Facade	Normal	Physical	70	100	20	Normal	●
TM43	Secret Power	Normal	Physical	70	100	20	Normal	●
TM44	Rest	Psychic	Status	—	—	10	Self	—
TM45	Attract	Normal	Status	—	100	15	Normal	—
TM56	Fling	Dark	Physical	—	100	10	Normal	●
TM58	Endure	Normal	Status	—	—	10	Self	—
TM64	Explosion	Normal	Physical	250	100	5	2 foes • 1 ally	—
TM69	Rock Polish	Rock	Status	—	—	20	Self	—
TM71	Stone Edge	Rock	Physical	100	80	5	Normal	●
TM74	Gyro Ball	Steel	Physical	—	100	5	Normal	●
TM76	Stealth Rock	Rock	Status	—	—	20	2 foes	—
TM78	Captivate	Normal	Status	—	100	20	2 foes	—
TM80	Rock Slide	Rock	Physical	75	90	10	2 foes	—
TM82	Sleep Talk	Normal	Status	—	—	10	Self	—
TM83	Natural Gift	Normal	Physical	—	100	15	Normal	—
TM87	Swagger	Normal	Status	—	90	15	Normal	—
TM90	Substitute	Normal	Status	—	—	10	Self	—
HM04	Strength	Normal	Physical	80	100	15	Normal	●
HM06	Rock Smash	Fighting	Physical	40	100	15	Normal	●
HM08	Rock Climb	Normal	Physical	90	85	20	Normal	●

● LEVEL-UP AND LEARNED MOVES

Lv	Name	Type	Kind	Power	Acc	PP	Range	DA
Base	Tackle	Normal	Physical	35	95	35	Normal	●
Base	Defense Curl	Normal	Status	—	—	40	Self	—
Base	Mud Sport	Ground	Status	—	—	15	All	—
Base	Rock Polish	Rock	Status	—	—	20	Self	—
4	Mud Sport	Ground	Status	—	—	15	All	—
8	Rock Polish	Rock	Status	—	—	20	Self	—
11	Rock Throw	Rock	Physical	50	90	15	Normal	—
15	Magnitude	Ground	Physical	—	100	30	2 foes • 1 ally	—
19	Selfdestruct	Normal	Physical	200	100	5	2 foes • 1 ally	—
22	Rollout	Rock	Physical	30	90	20	Normal	●
27	Rock Blast	Rock	Physical	25	80	10	Normal	—
33	Earthquake	Ground	Physical	100	100	10	2 foes • 1 ally	—
38	Explosion	Normal	Physical	250	100	5	2 foes • 1 ally	—
44	Double-Edge	Normal	Physical	120	100	15	Normal	●
49	Stone Edge	Rock	Physical	100	80	5	Normal	●

● MOVES TAUGHT IN EXCHANGE FOR COLORED SHARDS

Name	Type	Kind	Power	Acc	PP	Range	DA
Mud-Slap	Ground	Special	20	100	10	Normal	—
Rollout	Rock	Physical	30	90	20	Normal	●
ThunderPunch	Electric	Physical	75	100	15	Normal	●
Fire Punch	Fire	Physical	75	100	15	Normal	●
Superpower	Fighting	Physical	120	100	5	Normal	●
Snore	Normal	Special	40	100	15	Normal	—
AncientPower	Rock	Special	60	100	5	Normal	—
Earth Power	Ground	Special	90	100	10	Normal	—
Sucker Punch	Dark	Physical	80	100	5	Normal	●

● PRIMARY WAY TO FIND

TRAINER'S PARTY Trainer on B2F of Iron Island

WILD POKÉMON Route 214

COURSE OF STORY

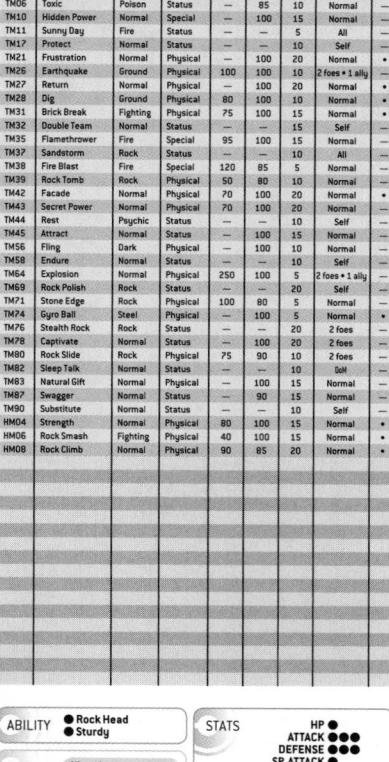

Sinnoh Pokédex **No. 033** Megaton Pokémon

Golem

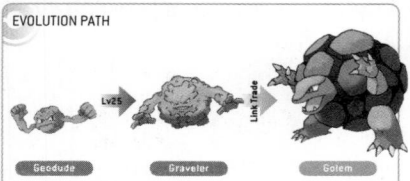

ROCK GROUND

HEIGHT: 4'07"
WEIGHT: 661.4 lbs.
GENDER: Male and Female
HELD ITEM: None

● M/F have same form

PLATINUM Even dynamite can't harm its hard, boulderlike body. It sheds its hide just once a year.

EVOLUTION PATH

Geodude — Lv25 → Graveler — Link Trade → Golem

● **TM & HM MOVES**

No.	Name	Type	Kind	Power	Acc	PP	Range	DA
TM01	Focus Punch	Fighting	Physical	150	100	20	Normal	•
TM05	Roar	Normal	Status	—	100	20	Normal	—
TM06	Toxic	Poison	Status	—	85	10	Normal	—
TM10	Hidden Power	Normal	Special	—	100	15	Normal	—
TM11	Sunny Day	Fire	Status	—	—	5	All	—
TM15	Hyper Beam	Normal	Special	150	90	5	Normal	—
TM17	Protect	Normal	Status	—	—	10	Self	—
TM21	Frustration	Normal	Physical	—	100	20	Normal	•
TM26	Earthquake	Ground	Physical	100	100	10	2 foes + 1 ally	•
TM27	Return	Normal	Physical	—	100	20	Normal	•
TM28	Dig	Ground	Physical	80	100	10	Normal	•
TM31	Brick Break	Fighting	Physical	75	100	15	Normal	•
TM32	Double Team	Normal	Status	—	—	15	Self	—
TM35	Flamethrower	Fire	Special	95	100	15	Normal	—
TM37	Sandstorm	Rock	Status	—	—	10	All	—
TM38	Fire Blast	Fire	Special	120	85	5	Normal	—
TM39	Rock Tomb	Rock	Physical	50	80	10	Normal	•
TM42	Facade	Normal	Physical	70	100	20	Normal	•
TM43	Secret Power	Normal	Physical	70	100	20	Normal	•
TM44	Rest	Psychic	Status	—	—	10	Self	—
TM45	Attract	Normal	Status	—	100	15	Normal	—
TM52	Focus Blast	Fighting	Special	120	70	5	Normal	—
TM56	Fling	Dark	Physical	—	100	10	Normal	•
TM58	Endure	Normal	Status	—	—	10	Self	—
TM64	Explosion	Normal	Physical	250	100	5	2 foes + 1 ally	•
TM68	Giga Impact	Normal	Physical	150	90	5	Normal	•
TM69	Rock Polish	Rock	Status	—	—	20	Self	—
TM71	Stone Edge	Rock	Physical	100	80	5	Normal	•
TM76	Stealth Rock	Rock	Status	—	—	20	2 foes	—
TM78	Captivate	Normal	Status	—	100	20	2 foes	—
TM80	Rock Slide	Rock	Physical	75	90	10	2 foes	•
TM82	Sleep Talk	Normal	Status	—	—	10	DoM	—
TM83	Natural Gift	Normal	Physical	—	100	15	Normal	•
TM87	Swagger	Normal	Status	—	90	15	Normal	—
TM90	Substitute	Normal	Status	—	—	10	Self	—
HM04	Strength	Normal	Physical	80	100	15	Normal	•
HM06	Rock Smash	Fighting	Physical	40	100	15	Normal	•
HM08	Rock Climb	Normal	Physical	90	85	20	Normal	•

● **LEVEL-UP AND LEARNED MOVES**

Lv	Name	Type	Kind	Power	Acc	PP	Range	DA
Base	Tackle	Normal	Physical	35	95	35	Normal	•
Base	Defense Curl	Normal	Status	—	—	40	Self	—
Base	Mud Sport	Ground	Status	—	—	15	All	—
Base	Rock Polish	Rock	Status	—	—	20	Self	—
4	Mud Sport	Ground	Status	—	—	15	All	—
8	Rock Polish	Rock	Status	—	—	20	Self	—
11	Rock Throw	Rock	Physical	50	90	15	Normal	—
15	Magnitude	Ground	Physical	—	100	30	2 foes + 1 ally	—
18	Selfdestruct	Normal	Physical	200	100	5	2 foes + 1 ally	•
22	Rollout	Rock	Physical	30	90	20	Normal	•
27	Rock Blast	Rock	Physical	25	80	10	Normal	—
33	Earthquake	Ground	Physical	100	100	10	2 foes + 1 ally	•
38	Explosion	Normal	Physical	250	100	5	2 foes + 1 ally	•
44	Double-Edge	Normal	Physical	120	100	15	Normal	•
49	Stone Edge	Rock	Physical	100	80	5	Normal	•

● **MOVES TAUGHT IN EXCHANGE FOR COLORED SHARDS**

Name	Type	Kind	Power	Acc	PP	Range	DA
Mud-Slap	Ground	Special	20	100	10	Normal	—
Fury Cutter	Bug	Physical	10	95	20	Normal	•
Rollout	Rock	Physical	30	90	20	Normal	•
ThunderPunch	Electric	Physical	75	100	15	Normal	•
Fire Punch	Fire	Physical	75	100	15	Normal	•
Superpower	Fighting	Physical	120	100	5	Normal	•
Iron Head	Steel	Physical	80	100	15	Normal	•
Snore	Normal	Special	40	100	15	Normal	•
AncientPower	Rock	Special	60	100	5	Normal	•
Earth Power	Ground	Special	90	100	10	Normal	—
Sucker Punch	Dark	Physical	80	100	5	Normal	•

ABILITY ● Rock Head ● Sturdy

EGG GROUP Mineral

STATS
HP ●●
ATTACK ●●●●
DEFENSE ●●●●
SP. ATTACK ●●
SP. DEFENSE ●●
SPEED ●●

● **PRIMARY WAY TO FIND**

TRAINER'S PARTY — Elite Four member Bertha

WILD POKÉMON

COURSE OF STORY

---

033 GOLEM

Sinnoh Pokédex **No. 034** Rock Snake Pokémon

Onix

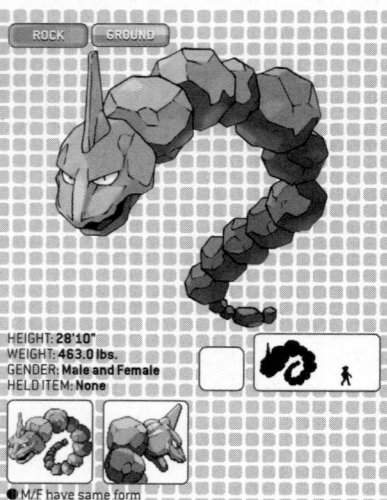

ROCK GROUND

HEIGHT: 28'10"
WEIGHT: 463.0 lbs.
GENDER: Male and Female
HELD ITEM: None

● M/F have same form

PLATINUM It burrows through the ground at a speed of 50 mph while feeding on large boulders.

EVOLUTION PATH

Onix — Trade while holding Metal Coat → Steelix

● **TM & HM MOVES**

No.	Name	Type	Kind	Power	Acc	PP	Range	DA
TM05	Roar	Normal	Status	—	100	20	Normal	—
TM06	Toxic	Poison	Status	—	85	10	Normal	—
TM10	Hidden Power	Normal	Special	—	100	15	Normal	—
TM11	Sunny Day	Fire	Status	—	—	5	All	—
TM12	Taunt	Dark	Status	—	100	20	Normal	—
TM17	Protect	Normal	Status	—	—	10	Self	—
TM21	Frustration	Normal	Physical	—	100	20	Normal	•
TM23	Iron Tail	Steel	Physical	100	75	15	Normal	•
TM26	Earthquake	Ground	Physical	100	100	10	2 foes + 1 ally	•
TM27	Return	Normal	Physical	—	100	20	Normal	•
TM28	Dig	Ground	Physical	80	100	10	Normal	•
TM32	Double Team	Normal	Status	—	—	15	Self	—
TM37	Sandstorm	Rock	Status	—	—	10	All	—
TM39	Rock Tomb	Rock	Physical	50	80	10	Normal	•
TM41	Torment	Dark	Status	—	100	15	Normal	—
TM42	Facade	Normal	Physical	70	100	20	Normal	•
TM43	Secret Power	Normal	Physical	70	100	20	Normal	•
TM44	Rest	Psychic	Status	—	—	10	Self	—
TM45	Attract	Normal	Status	—	100	15	Normal	—
TM58	Endure	Normal	Status	—	—	10	Self	—
TM59	Dragon Pulse	Dragon	Special	90	100	10	Normal	—
TM64	Explosion	Normal	Physical	250	100	5	2 foes + 1 ally	•
TM66	Payback	Dark	Physical	50	100	10	Normal	•
TM69	Rock Polish	Rock	Status	—	—	20	Self	—
TM71	Stone Edge	Rock	Physical	100	80	5	Normal	•
TM74	Gyro Ball	Steel	Physical	—	100	5	Normal	•
TM76	Stealth Rock	Rock	Status	—	—	20	2 foes	—
TM77	Psych Up	Normal	Status	—	—	10	Normal	—
TM78	Captivate	Normal	Status	—	100	20	2 foes	—
TM80	Rock Slide	Rock	Physical	75	90	10	2 foes	•
TM82	Sleep Talk	Normal	Status	—	—	10	DoM	—
TM83	Natural Gift	Normal	Physical	—	100	15	Normal	•
TM87	Swagger	Normal	Status	—	90	15	Normal	—
TM90	Substitute	Normal	Status	—	—	10	Self	—
TM91	Flash Cannon	Steel	Special	80	100	10	Normal	—
HM04	Strength	Normal	Physical	80	100	15	Normal	•
HM06	Rock Smash	Fighting	Physical	40	100	15	Normal	•
HM08	Rock Climb	Normal	Physical	90	85	20	Normal	•

● **LEVEL-UP AND LEARNED MOVES**

Lv	Name	Type	Kind	Power	Acc	PP	Range	DA
Base	Mud Sport	Ground	Status	—	—	15	All	—
Base	Tackle	Normal	Physical	35	95	35	Normal	•
Base	Harden	Normal	Status	—	—	30	Self	—
Base	Bind	Normal	Physical	15	75	20	Normal	•
6	Screech	Normal	Status	—	85	40	Normal	—
9	Rock Throw	Rock	Physical	50	90	15	Normal	—
14	Rage	Normal	Physical	20	100	20	Normal	•
17	Rock Tomb	Rock	Physical	50	80	10	Normal	•
22	Sandstorm	Rock	Status	—	—	10	All	—
25	Slam	Normal	Physical	80	75	20	Normal	•
30	Rock Polish	Rock	Status	—	—	20	Self	—
33	DragonBreath	Dragon	Special	60	100	20	Normal	—
38	Curse	???	Status	—	—	10	Normal + Self	—
41	Iron Tail	Steel	Physical	100	75	15	Normal	•
46	Sand Tomb	Ground	Physical	15	70	15	Normal	—
49	Double-Edge	Normal	Physical	120	100	15	Normal	•
54	Stone Edge	Rock	Physical	100	80	5	Normal	•

● **MOVES TAUGHT IN EXCHANGE FOR COLORED SHARDS**

Name	Type	Kind	Power	Acc	PP	Range	DA
Mud-Slap	Ground	Special	20	100	10	Normal	—
Rollout	Rock	Physical	30	90	20	Normal	•
Iron Head	Steel	Physical	80	100	15	Normal	•
Snore	Normal	Special	40	100	15	Normal	•
AncientPower	Rock	Special	60	100	5	Normal	•
Earth Power	Ground	Special	90	100	10	Normal	—
Twister	Dragon	Special	40	100	20	2 foes	—

● **EGG MOVES**

Name	Type	Kind	Power	Acc	PP	Range	DA
Rock Slide	Rock	Physical	75	90	10	2 foes	•
Flail	Normal	Physical	—	100	15	Normal	•
Explosion	Normal	Physical	250	100	5	2 foes + 1 ally	•
Block	Normal	Status	—	—	5	Normal	—
Defense Curl	Normal	Status	—	—	40	Self	—
Rollout	Rock	Physical	30	90	20	Normal	•
Rock Blast	Rock	Physical	25	80	10	Normal	—

ABILITY ● Rock Head ● Sturdy

EGG GROUP Mineral

STATS
HP ●
ATTACK ●●
DEFENSE ●●●●
SP. ATTACK ●
SP. DEFENSE ●
SPEED ●●●

● **PRIMARY WAY TO FIND**

TRAINER'S PARTY — Trainer on Route 205

WILD POKÉMON — Throughout Oreburgh Mine

COURSE OF STORY

Sinnoh Pokédex No. 035 Iron Snake Pokémon
Steelix

STEEL · GROUND

HEIGHT: 30'02"
WEIGHT: 881.8 lbs.
GENDER: Male and Female
HELD ITEM: Metal Coat

● Male form ● Female form

PLATINUM It is thought its body transformed as a result of iron accumulating internally from swallowing soil.

EVOLUTION PATH

Onix — Trade while holding Metal Coat → Steelix

● TM & HM MOVES

No.	Name	Type	Kind	Power	Acc	PP	Range	DA
TM05	Roar	Normal	Status	—	100	20	Normal	
TM06	Toxic	Poison	Status	—	85	10	Normal	
TM10	Hidden Power	Normal	Special	—	100	15	Normal	
TM11	Sunny Day	Fire	Status	—	—	5	All	
TM12	Taunt	Dark	Status	—	100	20	Normal	
TM15	Hyper Beam	Normal	Special	150	90	5	Normal	
TM17	Protect	Normal	Status	—	—	10	Self	
TM21	Frustration	Normal	Physical	—	100	20	Normal	•
TM23	Iron Tail	Steel	Physical	100	75	15	Normal	
TM26	Earthquake	Ground	Physical	100	100	10	2 foes • 1 ally	
TM27	Return	Normal	Physical	—	100	20	Normal	•
TM28	Dig	Ground	Physical	80	100	10	Normal	
TM32	Double Team	Normal	Status	—	—	15	Self	
TM37	Sandstorm	Rock	Status	—	—	10	All	
TM39	Rock Tomb	Rock	Physical	50	80	10	Normal	
TM41	Torment	Dark	Status	—	100	15	Normal	
TM42	Facade	Normal	Physical	70	100	20	Normal	
TM43	Secret Power	Normal	Physical	70	100	20	Normal	
TM44	Rest	Psychic	Status	—	—	10	Self	
TM45	Attract	Normal	Status	—	100	15	Normal	
TM58	Endure	Normal	Status	—	—	10	Self	
TM59	Dragon Pulse	Dragon	Special	90	100	10	Normal	
TM64	Explosion	Normal	Physical	250	100	5	2 foes • 1 ally	
TM66	Payback	Dark	Physical	50	100	10	Normal	
TM68	Giga Impact	Normal	Physical	150	90	5	Normal	
TM69	Rock Polish	Rock	Status	—	—	20	Self	
TM71	Stone Edge	Rock	Physical	100	80	5	Normal	
TM76	Stealth Rock	Rock	Status	—	—	20	2 foes	
TM77	Psych Up	Normal	Status	—	—	10	Normal	
TM78	Captivate	Normal	Status	—	100	20	2 foes	
TM79	Dark Pulse	Dark	Special	80	100	15	Normal	
TM80	Rock Slide	Rock	Physical	75	90	10	2 foes	
TM82	Sleep Talk	Normal	Status	—	—	10	DoM	
TM83	Natural Gift	Normal	Physical	—	100	15	Normal	
TM87	Swagger	Normal	Status	—	90	15	Normal	
TM90	Substitute	Normal	Status	—	—	10	Self	
TM91	Flash Cannon	Steel	Special	80	100	10	Normal	
HM01	Cut	Normal	Physical	50	95	30	Normal	
HM04	Strength	Normal	Physical	80	100	15	Normal	•
HM06	Rock Smash	Fighting	Physical	40	100	15	Normal	•
HM08	Rock Climb	Normal	Physical	90	85	20	Normal	

● LEVEL-UP AND LEARNED MOVES

Lv	Name	Type	Kind	Power	Acc	PP	Range	DA
Base	Thunder Fang	Electric	Physical	65	95	15	Normal	
Base	Ice Fang	Ice	Physical	65	95	15	Normal	
Base	Fire Fang	Fire	Physical	65	95	15	Normal	
Base	Mud Sport	Ground	Status	—	—	15	All	
Base	Tackle	Normal	Physical	35	95	35	Normal	
Base	Harden	Normal	Status	—	—	30	Self	
Base	Bind	Normal	Physical	15	75	20	Normal	
6	Screech	Normal	Status	—	85	40	Normal	
9	Rock Throw	Rock	Physical	50	90	15	Normal	
14	Rage	Normal	Physical	20	100	20	Normal	
17	Rock Tomb	Rock	Physical	50	80	10	Normal	
22	Sandstorm	Rock	Status	—	—	10	All	
25	Slam	Normal	Physical	80	75	20	Normal	
30	Rock Polish	Rock	Status	—	—	20	Self	
33	DragonBreath	Dragon	Special	60	100	20	Normal	
38	Curse	???	Status	—	—	10	Normal • Self	
41	Iron Tail	Steel	Physical	100	75	15	Normal	
46	Crunch	Dark	Physical	80	100	15	Normal	
49	Double-Edge	Normal	Physical	120	100	15	Normal	
54	Stone Edge	Rock	Physical	100	80	5	Normal	

● MOVES TAUGHT IN EXCHANGE FOR COLORED SHARDS

Name	Type	Kind	Power	Acc	PP	Range	DA
Mud-Slap	Ground	Special	20	100	10	Normal	
Rollout	Rock	Physical	30	90	20	Normal	
Iron Head	Steel	Physical	80	100	15	Normal	
Aqua Tail	Water	Physical	90	90	10	Normal	
Snore	Normal	Special	40	100	15	Normal	
AncientPower	Rock	Special	60	100	5	Normal	
Earth Power	Ground	Special	90	100	10	Normal	
Twister	Dragon	Special	40	100	20	2 foes	
Magnet Rise	Electric	Status	—	—	10	Self	

ABILITY ● Rock Head ● Sturdy
EGG GROUP Mineral

STATS
HP ●●
ATTACK ●●●●
DEFENSE ●●●●●
SP.ATTACK ●
SP.DEFENSE ●●
SPEED ●

● PRIMARY WAY TO FIND

TRAINER'S PARTY	Trainer on B2F of Iron Island
WILD POKÉMON	Iron Island, B2F and B3F
COURSE OF STORY	

Sinnoh Pokédex No. 036 Head Butt Pokémon
Cranidos

ROCK

HEIGHT: 2'11"
WEIGHT: 69.4 lbs.
GENDER: Male and Female
HELD ITEM: None

● M/F have same form

PLATINUM A lifelong jungle dweller from 100 million years ago, it would snap obstructing trees with head butts.

EVOLUTION PATH

Cranidos — Lv30 → Rampardos

● TM & HM MOVES

No.	Name	Type	Kind	Power	Acc	PP	Range	DA
TM05	Roar	Normal	Status	—	100	20	Normal	
TM06	Toxic	Poison	Status	—	85	10	Normal	
TM10	Hidden Power	Normal	Special	—	100	15	Normal	
TM11	Sunny Day	Fire	Status	—	—	5	All	
TM13	Ice Beam	Ice	Special	95	100	10	Normal	
TM14	Blizzard	Ice	Special	120	70	5	2 foes	
TM17	Protect	Normal	Status	—	—	10	Self	
TM18	Rain Dance	Water	Status	—	—	5	All	
TM21	Frustration	Normal	Physical	—	100	20	Normal	•
TM23	Iron Tail	Steel	Physical	100	75	15	Normal	
TM24	Thunderbolt	Electric	Special	95	100	15	Normal	
TM25	Thunder	Electric	Special	120	70	10	Normal	
TM26	Earthquake	Ground	Physical	100	100	10	2 foes • 1 ally	
TM27	Return	Normal	Physical	—	100	20	Normal	•
TM28	Dig	Ground	Physical	80	100	10	Normal	
TM32	Double Team	Normal	Status	—	—	15	Self	
TM34	Shock Wave	Electric	Special	60	—	20	Normal	
TM35	Flamethrower	Fire	Special	95	100	15	Normal	
TM37	Sandstorm	Rock	Status	—	—	10	All	
TM38	Fire Blast	Fire	Special	120	85	5	Normal	
TM39	Rock Tomb	Rock	Physical	50	80	10	Normal	
TM42	Facade	Normal	Physical	70	100	20	Normal	
TM43	Secret Power	Normal	Physical	70	100	20	Normal	
TM44	Rest	Psychic	Status	—	—	10	Self	
TM45	Attract	Normal	Status	—	100	15	Normal	
TM46	Thief	Dark	Physical	40	100	10	Normal	
TM56	Fling	Dark	Physical	—	100	10	Normal	
TM58	Endure	Normal	Status	—	—	10	Self	
TM59	Dragon Pulse	Dragon	Special	90	100	10	Normal	
TM66	Payback	Dark	Physical	50	100	10	Normal	
TM69	Rock Polish	Rock	Status	—	—	20	Self	
TM71	Stone Edge	Rock	Physical	100	80	5	Normal	
TM75	Swords Dance	Normal	Status	—	—	30	Self	
TM76	Stealth Rock	Rock	Status	—	—	20	2 foes	
TM78	Captivate	Normal	Status	—	100	20	2 foes	
TM80	Rock Slide	Rock	Physical	75	90	10	2 foes	
TM82	Sleep Talk	Normal	Status	—	—	10	DoM	
TM83	Natural Gift	Normal	Physical	—	100	15	Normal	
TM87	Swagger	Normal	Status	—	90	15	Normal	
TM90	Substitute	Normal	Status	—	—	10	Self	
HM04	Strength	Normal	Physical	80	100	15	Normal	
HM06	Rock Smash	Fighting	Physical	40	100	15	Normal	
HM08	Rock Climb	Normal	Physical	90	85	20	Normal	

● LEVEL-UP AND LEARNED MOVES

Lv	Name	Type	Kind	Power	Acc	PP	Range	DA
Base	Headbutt	Normal	Physical	70	100	15	Normal	•
Base	Leer	Normal	Status	—	100	30	2 foes	
6	Focus Energy	Normal	Status	—	—	30	Self	
10	Pursuit	Dark	Physical	40	100	20	Normal	
15	Take Down	Normal	Physical	90	85	20	Normal	
19	Scary Face	Normal	Status	—	90	10	Normal	
24	Assurance	Dark	Physical	50	100	10	Normal	
28	AncientPower	Rock	Special	60	100	5	Normal	
33	Zen Headbutt	Psychic	Physical	80	90	15	Normal	
37	Screech	Normal	Status	—	85	40	Normal	
43	Head Smash	Rock	Physical	150	80	5	Normal	

● MOVES TAUGHT IN EXCHANGE FOR COLORED SHARDS

Name	Type	Kind	Power	Acc	PP	Range	DA
Mud-Slap	Ground	Special	20	100	10	Normal	
ThunderPunch	Electric	Physical	75	100	15	Normal	
Fire Punch	Fire	Physical	75	100	15	Normal	
Superpower	Fighting	Physical	120	100	5	Normal	
Iron Head	Steel	Physical	80	100	15	Normal	
Snore	Normal	Special	40	100	15	Normal	
Spite	Ghost	Status	—	100	10	Normal	
Endeavor	Normal	Physical	—	100	5	Normal	
AncientPower	Rock	Special	60	100	5	Normal	
Zen Headbutt	Psychic	Physical	80	90	15	Normal	
Earth Power	Ground	Special	90	100	10	Normal	
Uproar	Normal	Special	50	100	10	1 random	

● EGG MOVES

Name	Type	Kind	Power	Acc	PP	Range	DA
Crunch	Dark	Physical	80	100	15	Normal	
Thrash	Normal	Physical	90	100	20	1 random	
Double-Edge	Normal	Physical	120	100	15	Normal	
Leer	Normal	Status	—	100	30	2 foes	
Slam	Normal	Physical	80	75	20	Normal	
Stomp	Normal	Physical	65	100	20	Normal	
Whirlwind	Normal	Status	—	100	20	Normal	
Hammer Arm	Fighting	Physical	100	90	10	Normal	

ABILITY ● Mold Breaker
EGG GROUP Monster

STATS
HP ●●
ATTACK ●●●●
DEFENSE ●
SP.ATTACK ●
SP.DEFENSE ●
SPEED ●●

● PRIMARY WAY TO FIND

TRAINER'S PARTY	Oreburgh Gym Leader Roark
WILD POKÉMON	
COURSE OF STORY	Get the Skull Fossil in the Underground and have it restored at the Oreburgh Mining Museum

Rampardos

Sinnoh Pokédex **No. 037** Head Butt Pokémon

ROCK

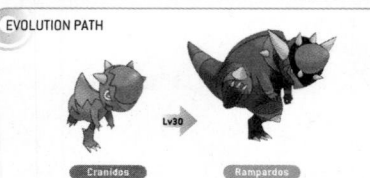

HEIGHT: 5'03"
WEIGHT: 226.0 lbs.
GENDER: Male and Female
HELD ITEM: None

● M/F have same form

PLATINUM — If two were to smash their heads together, their foot-thick skulls would keep them from fainting.

EVOLUTION PATH

Cranidos — Lv30 → Rampardos

● TM & HM MOVES

No.	Name	Type	Kind	Power	Acc	PP	Range	DA
TM01	Focus Punch	Fighting	Physical	150	100	20	Normal	—
TM05	Roar	Normal	Status	—	100	20	Normal	—
TM06	Toxic	Poison	Status	—	85	10	Normal	—
TM10	Hidden Power	Normal	Special	—	100	15	Normal	—
TM11	Sunny Day	Fire	Status	—	—	5	All	—
TM13	Ice Beam	Ice	Special	95	100	10	Normal	—
TM14	Blizzard	Ice	Special	120	70	5	2 foes	—
TM15	Hyper Beam	Normal	Special	150	90	5	Normal	—
TM17	Protect	Normal	Status	—	—	10	Self	—
TM18	Rain Dance	Water	Status	—	—	5	All	—
TM21	Frustration	Normal	Physical	—	100	20	Normal	●
TM23	Iron Tail	Steel	Physical	100	75	15	Normal	●
TM24	Thunderbolt	Electric	Special	95	100	15	Normal	—
TM25	Thunder	Electric	Special	120	70	10	Normal	—
TM26	Earthquake	Ground	Physical	100	100	10	2 foes + 1 ally	—
TM27	Return	Normal	Physical	—	100	20	Normal	●
TM28	Dig	Ground	Physical	80	100	10	Normal	●
TM31	Brick Break	Fighting	Physical	75	100	15	Normal	●
TM32	Double Team	Normal	Status	—	—	15	Self	—
TM34	Shock Wave	Electric	Special	60	—	20	Normal	—
TM35	Flamethrower	Fire	Special	95	100	15	Normal	—
TM37	Sandstorm	Rock	Status	—	—	10	All	—
TM38	Fire Blast	Fire	Special	120	85	5	Normal	—
TM39	Rock Tomb	Rock	Physical	50	80	10	Normal	●
TM42	Facade	Normal	Physical	70	100	20	Normal	●
TM43	Secret Power	Normal	Physical	70	100	20	Normal	●
TM44	Rest	Psychic	Status	—	—	10	Self	—
TM45	Attract	Normal	Status	—	100	15	Normal	—
TM46	Thief	Dark	Physical	40	100	10	Normal	●
TM52	Focus Blast	Fighting	Special	120	70	5	Normal	—
TM56	Fling	Dark	Physical	—	100	10	Normal	●
TM58	Endure	Normal	Status	—	—	10	Self	—
TM59	Dragon Pulse	Dragon	Special	90	100	10	Normal	—
TM66	Payback	Dark	Physical	50	100	10	Normal	●
TM68	Giga Impact	Normal	Physical	150	90	5	Normal	●
TM69	Rock Polish	Rock	Status	—	—	20	Self	—
TM71	Stone Edge	Rock	Physical	100	80	5	Normal	●
TM72	Avalanche	Ice	Physical	60	100	10	Normal	●
TM75	Swords Dance	Normal	Status	—	—	30	Self	—
TM76	Stealth Rock	Rock	Status	—	—	20	2 foes	—
TM78	Captivate	Normal	Status	—	100	20	2 foes	—
TM80	Rock Slide	Rock	Physical	75	90	10	2 foes	●
TM82	Sleep Talk	Normal	Status	—	—	10	DoM	—
TM83	Natural Gift	Normal	Physical	—	100	15	Normal	●
TM87	Swagger	Normal	Status	—	90	15	Normal	—
TM90	Substitute	Normal	Status	—	—	10	Self	—
HM01	Cut	Normal	Physical	50	95	30	Normal	●
HM03	Surf	Water	Special	95	100	15	2 foes + 1 ally	—
HM04	Strength	Normal	Physical	80	100	15	Normal	●
HM06	Rock Smash	Fighting	Physical	40	100	15	Normal	●
HM08	Rock Climb	Normal	Physical	90	85	20	Normal	●

● LEVEL-UP AND LEARNED MOVES

Lv	Name	Type	Kind	Power	Acc	PP	Range	DA
Base	Headbutt	Normal	Physical	70	100	15	Normal	●
Base	Leer	Normal	Status	—	100	30	2 foes	—
6	Focus Energy	Normal	Status	—	—	30	Self	—
10	Pursuit	Dark	Physical	40	100	20	Normal	●
15	Take Down	Normal	Physical	90	85	20	Normal	●
19	Scary Face	Normal	Status	—	90	10	Normal	—
24	Assurance	Dark	Physical	50	100	10	Normal	●
28	AncientPower	Rock	Special	60	100	5	Normal	—
30	Endeavor	Normal	Physical	—	100	5	Normal	●
36	Zen Headbutt	Psychic	Physical	80	90	15	Normal	●
43	Screech	Normal	Status	—	85	40	Normal	—
52	Head Smash	Rock	Physical	150	80	5	Normal	●

● MOVES TAUGHT IN EXCHANGE FOR COLORED SHARDS

Name	Type	Kind	Power	Acc	PP	Range	DA
Mud-Slap	Ground	Special	20	100	10	Normal	—
ThunderPunch	Electric	Physical	75	100	15	Normal	●
Fire Punch	Fire	Physical	75	100	15	Normal	●
Superpower	Fighting	Physical	120	100	5	Normal	●
Iron Head	Steel	Physical	80	100	15	Normal	●
Snore	Normal	Special	40	100	15	Normal	—
Spite	Ghost	Status	—	100	10	Normal	—
Endeavor	Normal	Physical	—	100	5	Normal	●
Outrage	Dragon	Physical	120	100	15	1 random	●
AncientPower	Rock	Special	60	100	5	Normal	—
Zen Headbutt	Psychic	Physical	80	90	15	Normal	●
Earth Power	Ground	Special	90	100	10	Normal	—
Uproar	Normal	Special	50	100	10	1 random	—

● PRIMARY WAY TO FIND

TRAINER'S PARTY — Trainer on Victory Road

WILD POKÉMON

COURSE OF STORY

ABILITY ● Mold Breaker

EGG GROUP — Monster

STATS
HP ●●●
ATTACK ●●●●●
DEFENSE ●●●
SP. ATTACK ●●●
SP. DEFENSE ●
SPEED ●●

Shieldon

Sinnoh Pokédex **No. 038** Shield Pokémon

ROCK   STEEL

HEIGHT: 1'08"
WEIGHT: 125.7 lbs.
GENDER: Male and Female
HELD ITEM: None

❶ M/F have same form

PLATINUM — It is outstandingly armored. As a result, it can eat grass and berries without having to fight.

EVOLUTION PATH

Shieldon — Lv30 → Bastiodon

● TM & HM MOVES

No.	Name	Type	Kind	Power	Acc	PP	Range	DA
TM05	Roar	Normal	Status	—	100	20	Normal	—
TM06	Toxic	Poison	Status	—	85	10	Normal	—
TM10	Hidden Power	Normal	Special	—	100	15	Normal	—
TM11	Sunny Day	Fire	Status	—	—	5	All	—
TM12	Taunt	Dark	Status	—	100	20	Normal	—
TM13	Ice Beam	Ice	Special	95	100	10	Normal	—
TM14	Blizzard	Ice	Special	120	70	5	2 foes	—
TM17	Protect	Normal	Status	—	—	10	Self	—
TM18	Rain Dance	Water	Status	—	—	5	All	—
TM21	Frustration	Normal	Physical	—	100	20	Normal	●
TM23	Iron Tail	Steel	Physical	100	75	15	Normal	●
TM24	Thunderbolt	Electric	Special	95	100	15	Normal	—
TM25	Thunder	Electric	Special	120	70	10	Normal	—
TM26	Earthquake	Ground	Physical	100	100	10	2 foes + 1 ally	—
TM27	Return	Normal	Physical	—	100	20	Normal	●
TM28	Dig	Ground	Physical	80	100	10	Normal	●
TM32	Double Team	Normal	Status	—	—	15	Self	—
TM34	Shock Wave	Electric	Special	60	—	20	Normal	—
TM35	Flamethrower	Fire	Special	95	100	15	Normal	—
TM37	Sandstorm	Rock	Status	—	—	10	All	—
TM38	Fire Blast	Fire	Special	120	85	5	Normal	—
TM39	Rock Tomb	Rock	Physical	50	80	10	Normal	●
TM41	Torment	Dark	Status	—	100	15	Normal	—
TM42	Facade	Normal	Physical	70	100	20	Normal	●
TM43	Secret Power	Normal	Physical	70	100	20	Normal	●
TM44	Rest	Psychic	Status	—	—	10	Self	—
TM45	Attract	Normal	Status	—	100	15	Normal	—
TM58	Endure	Normal	Status	—	—	10	Self	—
TM69	Rock Polish	Rock	Status	—	—	20	Self	—
TM71	Stone Edge	Rock	Physical	100	80	5	Normal	●
TM76	Stealth Rock	Rock	Status	—	—	20	2 foes	—
TM78	Captivate	Normal	Status	—	100	20	2 foes	—
TM80	Rock Slide	Rock	Physical	75	90	10	2 foes	●
TM82	Sleep Talk	Normal	Status	—	—	10	DoM	—
TM83	Natural Gift	Normal	Physical	—	100	15	Normal	●
TM87	Swagger	Normal	Status	—	90	15	Normal	—
TM90	Substitute	Normal	Status	—	—	10	Self	—
TM91	Flash Cannon	Steel	Special	80	100	10	Normal	—
HM04	Strength	Normal	Physical	80	100	15	Normal	●
HM06	Rock Smash	Fighting	Physical	40	100	15	Normal	●

● LEVEL-UP AND LEARNED MOVES

Lv	Name	Type	Kind	Power	Acc	PP	Range	DA
Base	Tackle	Normal	Physical	35	95	35	Normal	●
Base	Protect	Normal	Status	—	—	10	Self	—
6	Taunt	Dark	Status	—	100	20	Normal	—
10	Metal Sound	Steel	Status	—	85	40	Normal	—
15	Take Down	Normal	Physical	90	85	20	Normal	●
19	Iron Defense	Steel	Status	—	—	15	Self	—
24	Swagger	Normal	Status	—	90	15	Normal	—
33	AncientPower	Rock	Special	60	100	5	Normal	—
33	Endure	Normal	Status	—	—	10	Self	—
37	Metal Burst	Steel	Physical	—	100	10	Normal	●
43	Iron Head	Steel	Physical	80	100	15	Normal	●

● MOVES IN EXCHANGE FOR COLORED SHARDS

Name	Type	Kind	Power	Acc	PP	Range	DA
Mud-Slap	Ground	Special	20	100	10	Normal	—
Iron Head	Steel	Physical	80	100	15	Normal	●
Snore	Normal	Special	40	100	15	Normal	—
AncientPower	Rock	Special	60	100	5	Normal	—
Earth Power	Ground	Special	90	100	10	Normal	—
Iron Defense	Steel	Status	—	—	15	Self	—
Magnet Rise	Electric	Status	—	—	10	Self	—

● EGG MOVES

Name	Type	Kind	Power	Acc	PP	Range	DA
Headbutt	Normal	Physical	70	100	15	Normal	●
Scary Face	Normal	Status	—	90	10	Normal	—
Focus Energy	Normal	Status	—	—	30	Self	—
Double-Edge	Normal	Physical	120	100	15	Normal	●
Rock Blast	Rock	Physical	25	80	10	Normal	—
Body Slam	Normal	Physical	85	100	15	Normal	●
Screech	Normal	Status	—	85	40	Normal	—
Curse	???	Status	—	—	10	Normal + Self	—
Fissure	Ground	Physical	—	30	5	Normal	—

● PRIMARY WAY TO FIND

TRAINER'S PARTY — Trainer on Route 215

WILD POKÉMON

COURSE OF STORY — Get the Armor Fossil in the Underground and have it restored at the Oreburgh Mining Museum

ABILITY ● Sturdy

EGG GROUP — Monster

STATS
HP ●
ATTACK ●●
DEFENSE ●●●
SP. ATTACK ●●
SP. DEFENSE ●●
SPEED ●

Bastiodon

ROCK STEEL

HEIGHT: 4'03"
WEIGHT: 329.6 lbs.
GENDER: Male and Female
HELD ITEM: None

● M/F have same form

PLATINUM When they lined up side by side, no foe could break through. They shielded their young in that way.

EVOLUTION PATH

Shieldon → Lv30 → Bastiodon

● TM & HM MOVES

No.	Name	Type	Kind	Power	Acc	PP	Range	DA
TM05	Roar	Normal	Status	—	100	20	Normal	—
TM06	Toxic	Poison	Status	—	85	10	Normal	—
TM10	Hidden Power	Normal	Special	—	100	15	Normal	—
TM11	Sunny Day	Fire	Status	—	—	5	All	—
TM12	Taunt	Dark	Status	—	100	20	Normal	—
TM13	Ice Beam	Ice	Special	95	100	10	Normal	—
TM14	Blizzard	Ice	Special	120	70	5	2 foes	—
TM15	Hyper Beam	Normal	Special	150	90	5	Normal	—
TM17	Protect	Normal	Status	—	—	10	Self	—
TM18	Rain Dance	Water	Status	—	—	5	All	—
TM21	Frustration	Normal	Physical	—	100	20	Normal	●
TM23	Iron Tail	Steel	Physical	100	75	15	Normal	●
TM24	Thunderbolt	Electric	Special	95	100	15	Normal	—
TM25	Thunder	Electric	Special	120	70	10	Normal	—
TM26	Earthquake	Ground	Physical	100	100	10	2 foes + 1 ally	—
TM27	Return	Normal	Physical	—	100	20	Normal	●
TM28	Dig	Ground	Physical	80	100	10	Normal	●
TM32	Double Team	Normal	Status	—	—	15	Self	—
TM34	Shock Wave	Electric	Special	60	—	20	Normal	—
TM35	Flamethrower	Fire	Special	95	100	15	Normal	—
TM37	Sandstorm	Rock	Status	—	—	10	All	—
TM38	Fire Blast	Fire	Special	120	85	5	Normal	—
TM39	Rock Tomb	Rock	Physical	50	80	10	Normal	●
TM41	Torment	Dark	Status	—	100	15	Normal	—
TM42	Facade	Normal	Physical	70	100	20	Normal	●
TM43	Secret Power	Normal	Physical	70	100	20	Normal	●
TM44	Rest	Psychic	Status	—	—	10	Self	—
TM45	Attract	Normal	Status	—	100	15	Normal	—
TM58	Endure	Normal	Status	—	—	10	Self	—
TM68	Giga Impact	Normal	Physical	150	90	5	Normal	●
TM69	Rock Polish	Rock	Status	—	—	20	Self	—
TM71	Stone Edge	Rock	Physical	100	80	5	Normal	●
TM72	Avalanche	Ice	Physical	60	100	10	Normal	●
TM76	Stealth Rock	Rock	Status	—	—	20	2 foes	—
TM78	Captivate	Normal	Status	—	100	20	2 foes	—
TM80	Rock Slide	Rock	Physical	75	90	10	2 foes	—
TM82	Sleep Talk	Normal	Status	—	—	10	DoM	—
TM83	Natural Gift	Normal	Physical	—	100	15	Normal	●
TM87	Swagger	Normal	Status	—	90	15	Normal	—
TM90	Substitute	Normal	Status	—	—	10	Self	—
TM91	Flash Cannon	Steel	Special	80	100	10	Normal	—
HM04	Strength	Normal	Physical	80	100	15	Normal	●
HM06	Rock Smash	Fighting	Physical	40	100	15	Normal	●

● LEVEL-UP AND LEARNED MOVES

Lv	Name	Type	Kind	Power	Acc	PP	Range	DA
Base	Tackle	Normal	Physical	35	95	35	Normal	●
Base	Protect	Normal	Status	—	—	10	Self	—
Base	Taunt	Dark	Status	—	100	20	Normal	—
Base	Metal Sound	Steel	Status	—	85	40	Normal	—
6	Taunt	Dark	Status	—	100	20	Normal	—
10	Metal Sound	Steel	Status	—	85	40	Normal	—
15	Take Down	Normal	Physical	90	85	20	Normal	●
19	Iron Defense	Steel	Status	—	—	15	Self	—
24	Swagger	Normal	Status	—	90	15	Normal	—
28	AncientPower	Rock	Special	60	100	5	Normal	—
30	Block	Normal	Status	—	—	5	Normal	—
36	Endure	Normal	Status	—	—	10	Self	—
43	Metal Burst	Steel	Physical	—	100	10	Self	—
52	Iron Head	Steel	Physical	80	100	15	Normal	—

● MOVES TAUGHT IN EXCHANGE FOR COLORED SHARDS

Name	Type	Kind	Power	Acc	PP	Range	DA
Mud-Slap	Ground	Special	20	100	10	Normal	—
Iron Head	Steel	Physical	80	100	15	Normal	—
Snore	Normal	Special	40	100	15	Normal	—
Outrage	Dragon	Physical	120	100	15	1 random	—
AncientPower	Rock	Special	60	100	5	Normal	—
Earth Power	Ground	Special	90	100	10	Normal	—
Iron Defense	Steel	Status	—	—	15	Self	—
Magnet Rise	Electric	Status	—	—	10	Self	—

● PRIMARY WAY TO FIND

TRAINER'S PARTY	Canalave Gym Leader Byron
WILD POKÉMON	
COURSE OF STORY	

ABILITY ● Sturdy

EGG GROUP Monster

STATS
HP ●●
ATTACK ●●●
DEFENSE ●●●●●
SP. ATTACK ●●●
SP. DEFENSE ●●●●
SPEED ●

Machop

Fighting

HEIGHT: 2'07"
WEIGHT: 43.0 lbs.
GENDER: Male and Female
HELD ITEM: None

● M/F have same form

PLATINUM Though small in stature, it is powerful enough to easily heft and throw a number of GEODUDE at once.

EVOLUTION PATH

Machop → Lv28 → Machoke → Link Trade → Machamp

● TM & HM MOVES

No.	Name	Type	Kind	Power	Acc	PP	Range	DA
TM01	Focus Punch	Fighting	Physical	150	100	20	Normal	●
TM06	Toxic	Poison	Status	—	85	10	Normal	—
TM08	Bulk Up	Fighting	Status	—	—	20	Self	—
TM10	Hidden Power	Normal	Special	—	100	15	Normal	—
TM11	Sunny Day	Fire	Status	—	—	5	All	—
TM17	Protect	Normal	Status	—	—	10	Self	—
TM18	Rain Dance	Water	Status	—	—	5	All	—
TM21	Frustration	Normal	Physical	—	100	20	Normal	●
TM26	Earthquake	Ground	Physical	100	100	10	2 foes + 1 ally	●
TM27	Return	Normal	Physical	—	100	20	Normal	●
TM28	Dig	Ground	Physical	80	100	10	Normal	●
TM31	Brick Break	Fighting	Physical	75	100	15	Normal	●
TM32	Double Team	Normal	Status	—	—	15	Self	—
TM35	Flamethrower	Fire	Special	95	100	15	Normal	—
TM38	Fire Blast	Fire	Special	120	85	5	Normal	—
TM39	Rock Tomb	Rock	Physical	50	80	10	Normal	●
TM42	Facade	Normal	Physical	70	100	20	Normal	●
TM43	Secret Power	Normal	Physical	70	100	20	Normal	●
TM44	Rest	Psychic	Status	—	—	10	Self	—
TM45	Attract	Normal	Status	—	100	15	Normal	—
TM46	Thief	Dark	Physical	40	100	10	Normal	●
TM52	Focus Blast	Fighting	Special	120	70	5	Normal	—
TM56	Fling	Dark	Physical	—	100	10	Normal	●
TM58	Endure	Normal	Status	—	—	10	Self	—
TM66	Payback	Dark	Physical	50	100	10	Normal	●
TM78	Captivate	Normal	Status	—	100	20	2 foes	—
TM80	Rock Slide	Rock	Physical	75	90	10	2 foes	—
TM82	Sleep Talk	Normal	Status	—	—	10	DoM	—
TM83	Natural Gift	Normal	Physical	—	100	15	Normal	●
TM84	Poison Jab	Poison	Physical	80	100	20	Normal	●
TM87	Swagger	Normal	Status	—	90	15	Normal	—
TM90	Substitute	Normal	Status	—	—	10	Self	—
HM04	Strength	Normal	Physical	80	100	15	Normal	●
HM06	Rock Smash	Fighting	Physical	40	100	15	Normal	●
HM08	Rock Climb	Normal	Physical	90	85	20	Normal	●

● LEVEL-UP AND LEARNED MOVES

Lv	Name	Type	Kind	Power	Acc	PP	Range	DA
Base	Low Kick	Fighting	Physical	—	100	20	Normal	●
Base	Leer	Normal	Status	—	100	30	2 foes	—
7	Focus Energy	Normal	Status	—	—	30	Self	—
13	Karate Chop	Fighting	Physical	50	100	25	Normal	●
16	Foresight	Normal	Status	—	—	40	Normal	—
19	Seismic Toss	Fighting	Physical	—	100	20	Normal	●
22	Revenge	Fighting	Physical	60	100	10	Normal	●
25	Vital Throw	Fighting	Physical	70	—	10	Normal	●
31	Submission	Fighting	Physical	80	80	25	Normal	●
34	Wake-Up Slap	Fighting	Physical	60	100	10	Normal	●
37	Cross Chop	Fighting	Physical	100	80	5	Normal	●
43	Scary Face	Normal	Status	—	90	10	Normal	—
46	DynamicPunch	Fighting	Physical	100	50	5	Normal	●

● MOVES TAUGHT IN EXCHANGE FOR COLORED SHARDS

Name	Type	Kind	Power	Acc	PP	Range	DA
Mud-Slap	Ground	Special	20	100	10	Normal	—
ThunderPunch	Electric	Physical	75	100	15	Normal	●
Fire Punch	Fire	Physical	75	100	15	Normal	●
Superpower	Fighting	Physical	120	100	5	Normal	●
Ice Punch	Ice	Physical	75	100	15	Normal	●
Snore	Normal	Special	40	100	15	Normal	—
Helping Hand	Normal	Status	—	—	20	1 ally	—
Vacuum Wave	Fighting	Special	40	100	30	Normal	—

● EGG MOVES

Name	Type	Kind	Power	Acc	PP	Range	DA
Light Screen	Psychic	Status	—	—	30	2 allies	—
Meditate	Psychic	Status	—	—	40	Self	—
Rolling Kick	Fighting	Physical	60	85	15	Normal	●
Encore	Normal	Status	—	100	5	Normal	—
SmellingSalt	Normal	Physical	60	100	10	Normal	●
Counter	Fighting	Physical	—	100	20	Self	●
Rock Slide	Rock	Physical	75	90	10	2 foes	—
Close Combat	Fighting	Physical	120	100	5	Normal	●
Fire Punch	Fire	Physical	75	100	15	Normal	●
ThunderPunch	Electric	Physical	75	100	15	Normal	●
Ice Punch	Ice	Physical	75	100	15	Normal	●
Bullet Punch	Steel	Physical	40	100	30	Normal	●

● PRIMARY WAY TO FIND

TRAINER'S PARTY	Trainer on Route 203
WILD POKÉMON	Route 207
COURSE OF STORY	

ABILITY ● Guts ● No Guard

EGG GROUP Human-Like

STATS
HP ●●
ATTACK ●●●
DEFENSE ●●
SP. ATTACK ●
SP. DEFENSE ●
SPEED ●

040
MACHOP

Machoke

Fighting

HEIGHT: 4'11"
WEIGHT: 155.4 lbs.
GENDER: **Male and Female**
HELD ITEM: **None**

● M/F have same form

PLATINUM — It happily carries heavy cargo to toughen up. It willingly does hard work for people.

EVOLUTION PATH

Machop — Lv28 → Machoke — Link Trade → Machamp

● TM & HM MOVES

No.	Name	Type	Kind	Power	Acc	PP	Range	DA
TM01	Focus Punch	Fighting	Physical	150	100	20	Normal	•
TM06	Toxic	Poison	Status	—	85	10	Normal	—
TM08	Bulk Up	Fighting	Status	—	—	20	Self	—
TM10	Hidden Power	Normal	Special	—	100	15	Normal	•
TM11	Sunny Day	Fire	Status	—	—	5	All	—
TM17	Protect	Normal	Status	—	—	10	Self	—
TM18	Rain Dance	Water	Status	—	—	5	All	—
TM21	Frustration	Normal	Physical	—	100	20	Normal	•
TM26	Earthquake	Ground	Physical	100	100	10	2 foes • 1 ally	•
TM27	Return	Normal	Physical	—	100	20	Normal	•
TM28	Dig	Ground	Physical	80	100	10	Normal	•
TM31	Brick Break	Fighting	Physical	75	100	15	Normal	•
TM32	Double Team	Normal	Status	—	—	15	Self	—
TM35	Flamethrower	Fire	Special	95	100	15	Normal	•
TM38	Fire Blast	Fire	Special	120	85	5	Normal	•
TM39	Rock Tomb	Rock	Physical	50	80	10	Normal	•
TM42	Facade	Normal	Physical	70	100	20	Normal	•
TM43	Secret Power	Normal	Physical	70	100	20	Normal	•
TM44	Rest	Psychic	Status	—	—	10	Self	—
TM45	Attract	Normal	Status	—	100	15	Normal	—
TM46	Thief	Dark	Physical	40	100	10	Normal	•
TM52	Focus Blast	Fighting	Special	120	70	5	Normal	•
TM56	Fling	Dark	Physical	—	100	10	Normal	•
TM58	Endure	Normal	Status	—	—	10	Self	—
TM66	Payback	Dark	Physical	50	100	10	Normal	•
TM78	Captivate	Normal	Status	—	100	20	2 foes	—
TM80	Rock Slide	Rock	Physical	75	90	10	2 foes	•
TM82	Sleep Talk	Normal	Status	—	—	10	DoM	—
TM83	Natural Gift	Normal	Physical	—	100	15	Normal	•
TM84	Poison Jab	Poison	Physical	80	100	20	Normal	•
TM87	Swagger	Normal	Status	—	90	15	Normal	—
TM90	Substitute	Normal	Status	—	—	10	Self	—
HM04	Strength	Normal	Physical	80	100	15	Normal	•
HM06	Rock Smash	Fighting	Physical	40	100	15	Normal	•
HM08	Rock Climb	Normal	Physical	90	85	20	Normal	•

● LEVEL-UP AND LEARNED MOVES

Lv	Name	Type	Kind	Power	Acc	PP	Range	DA
Base	Low Kick	Fighting	Physical	—	100	20	Normal	•
Base	Leer	Normal	Status	—	100	30	2 foes	—
Base	Focus Energy	Normal	Status	—	—	30	Self	—
7	Focus Energy	Normal	Status	—	—	30	Self	—
10	Karate Chop	Fighting	Physical	50	100	25	Normal	•
13	Foresight	Normal	Status	—	—	40	Normal	—
19	Seismic Toss	Fighting	Physical	—	100	20	Normal	•
22	Revenge	Fighting	Physical	60	100	10	Normal	•
25	Vital Throw	Fighting	Physical	70	—	10	Normal	•
32	Submission	Fighting	Physical	80	80	25	Normal	•
36	Wake-Up Slap	Fighting	Physical	60	100	10	Normal	•
40	Cross Chop	Fighting	Physical	100	80	5	Normal	•
44	Scary Face	Normal	Status	—	90	10	Normal	—
51	DynamicPunch	Fighting	Physical	100	50	5	Normal	•

● MOVES LEARNED IN EXCHANGE FOR COLORED SHARDS

Name	Type	Kind	Power	Acc	PP	Range	DA
Mud-Slap	Ground	Special	20	100	15	Normal	—
ThunderPunch	Electric	Physical	75	100	15	Normal	•
Fire Punch	Fire	Physical	75	100	15	Normal	•
Superpower	Fighting	Physical	120	100	5	Normal	•
Ice Punch	Ice	Physical	75	100	15	Normal	•
Snore	Normal	Special	40	100	15	Normal	•
Helping Hand	Normal	Status	—	—	20	1 ally	—
Vacuum Wave	Fighting	Special	40	100	30	Normal	•

ABILITY
● Guts
● No Guard

EGG GROUP Human-Like

STATS
HP ●●
ATTACK ●●●
DEFENSE ●●●
SP. ATTACK ●●
SP. DEFENSE ●●
SPEED ●●

● PRIMARY WAY TO FIND

TRAINER'S PARTY — Trainer at Veilstone Gym

WILD POKÉMON — Celestic Town side of Route 210

COURSE OF STORY

Machamp

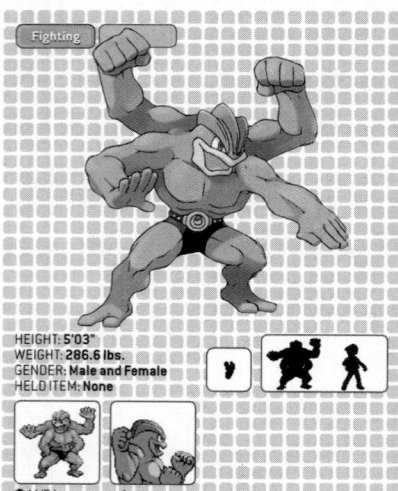

Fighting

HEIGHT: 5'03"
WEIGHT: 286.6 lbs.
GENDER: **Male and Female**
HELD ITEM: **None**

● M/F have same form

PLATINUM — Its four muscled arms slam foes with powerful punches and chops at blinding speed.

EVOLUTION PATH

Machop — Lv28 → Machoke — Link Trade → Machamp

● TM & HM MOVES

No.	Name	Type	Kind	Power	Acc	PP	Range	DA
TM01	Focus Punch	Fighting	Physical	150	100	20	Normal	•
TM06	Toxic	Poison	Status	—	85	10	Normal	—
TM08	Bulk Up	Fighting	Status	—	—	20	Self	—
TM10	Hidden Power	Normal	Special	—	100	15	Normal	•
TM11	Sunny Day	Fire	Status	—	—	5	All	—
TM15	Hyper Beam	Normal	Special	150	90	5	Normal	•
TM17	Protect	Normal	Status	—	—	5	Self	—
TM18	Rain Dance	Water	Status	—	—	5	All	—
TM21	Frustration	Normal	Physical	—	100	20	Normal	•
TM26	Earthquake	Ground	Physical	100	100	10	2 foes • 1 ally	•
TM27	Return	Normal	Physical	—	100	20	Normal	•
TM28	Dig	Ground	Physical	80	100	10	Normal	•
TM31	Brick Break	Fighting	Physical	75	100	15	Normal	•
TM32	Double Team	Normal	Status	—	—	15	Self	—
TM35	Flamethrower	Fire	Special	95	100	15	Normal	•
TM38	Fire Blast	Fire	Special	120	85	5	Normal	•
TM39	Rock Tomb	Rock	Physical	50	80	10	Normal	•
TM42	Facade	Normal	Physical	70	100	20	Normal	•
TM43	Secret Power	Normal	Physical	70	100	20	Normal	•
TM44	Rest	Psychic	Status	—	—	10	Self	—
TM45	Attract	Normal	Status	—	100	15	Normal	—
TM46	Thief	Dark	Physical	40	100	10	Normal	•
TM52	Focus Blast	Fighting	Special	120	70	5	Normal	•
TM56	Fling	Dark	Physical	—	100	10	Normal	•
TM58	Endure	Normal	Status	—	—	10	Self	—
TM66	Payback	Dark	Physical	50	100	10	Normal	•
TM68	Giga Impact	Normal	Physical	150	90	5	Normal	•
TM71	Stone Edge	Rock	Physical	100	80	5	Normal	•
TM78	Captivate	Normal	Status	—	100	20	2 foes	—
TM80	Rock Slide	Rock	Physical	75	90	10	2 foes	•
TM82	Sleep Talk	Normal	Status	—	—	10	DoM	—
TM83	Natural Gift	Normal	Physical	—	100	15	Normal	•
TM84	Poison Jab	Poison	Physical	80	100	20	Normal	•
TM87	Swagger	Normal	Status	—	90	15	Normal	—
TM90	Substitute	Normal	Status	—	—	10	Self	—
HM04	Strength	Normal	Physical	80	100	15	Normal	•
HM06	Rock Smash	Fighting	Physical	40	100	15	Normal	•
HM08	Rock Climb	Normal	Physical	90	85	20	Normal	•

● LEVEL-UP AND LEARNED MOVES

Lv	Name	Type	Kind	Power	Acc	PP	Range	DA
Base	Low Kick	Fighting	Physical	—	100	20	Normal	•
Base	Leer	Normal	Status	—	100	30	2 foes	—
Base	Focus Energy	Normal	Status	—	—	30	Self	—
7	Focus Energy	Normal	Status	—	—	30	Self	—
10	Karate Chop	Fighting	Physical	50	100	25	Normal	•
13	Foresight	Normal	Status	—	—	40	Normal	—
19	Seismic Toss	Fighting	Physical	—	100	20	Normal	•
22	Revenge	Fighting	Physical	60	100	10	Normal	•
25	Vital Throw	Fighting	Physical	70	—	10	Normal	•
32	Submission	Fighting	Physical	80	80	25	Normal	•
36	Wake-Up Slap	Fighting	Physical	60	100	10	Normal	•
40	Cross Chop	Fighting	Physical	100	80	5	Normal	•
44	Scary Face	Normal	Status	—	90	10	Normal	—
51	DynamicPunch	Fighting	Physical	100	50	5	Normal	•

● MOVES TAUGHT IN EXCHANGE FOR COLORED SHARDS

Name	Type	Kind	Power	Acc	PP	Range	DA
Mud-Slap	Ground	Special	20	100	10	Normal	—
ThunderPunch	Electric	Physical	75	100	15	Normal	•
Fire Punch	Fire	Physical	75	100	15	Normal	•
Superpower	Fighting	Physical	120	100	5	Normal	•
Ice Punch	Ice	Physical	75	100	15	Normal	•
Snore	Normal	Special	40	100	15	Normal	•
Helping Hand	Normal	Status	—	—	20	1 ally	—
Vacuum Wave	Fighting	Special	40	100	30	Normal	•

ABILITY
● Guts
● No Guard

EGG GROUP Human-Like

STATS
HP ●●●
ATTACK ●●●●
DEFENSE ●●●
SP. ATTACK ●●
SP. DEFENSE ●●
SPEED ●●

● PRIMARY WAY TO FIND

TRAINER'S PARTY — Trainer on Victory Road

WILD POKÉMON

COURSE OF STORY

No. 043 Duck Pokémon

Psyduck

WATER

HEIGHT: 2'07"
WEIGHT: 43.2 lbs.
GENDER: Male and Female
HELD ITEM: None

● M/F have same form

PLATINUM	Overwhelmed by enigmatic abilities, it suffers a constant headache. It sometimes uses mysterious powers.

EVOLUTION PATH

Psyduck — Lv33 — Golduck

● TM & HM MOVES

No.	Name	Type	Kind	Power	Acc	PP	Range	DA
TM01	Focus Punch	Fighting	Physical	150	100	20	Normal	●
TM03	Water Pulse	Water	Special	60	100	20	Normal	●
TM04	Calm Mind	Psychic	Status	—	—	20	Self	—
TM06	Toxic	Poison	Status	—	85	10	Normal	—
TM07	Hail	Ice	Status	—	—	10	All	—
TM10	Hidden Power	Normal	Special	—	100	15	Normal	—
TM13	Ice Beam	Ice	Special	95	100	10	Normal	—
TM14	Blizzard	Ice	Special	120	70	5	2 foes	—
TM17	Protect	Normal	Status	—	—	10	Self	—
TM18	Rain Dance	Water	Status	—	—	5	All	—
TM21	Frustration	Normal	Physical	—	100	20	Normal	●
TM23	Iron Tail	Steel	Physical	100	75	15	Normal	●
TM27	Return	Normal	Physical	—	100	20	Normal	●
TM28	Dig	Ground	Physical	80	100	10	Normal	●
TM29	Psychic	Psychic	Special	90	100	10	Normal	—
TM31	Brick Break	Fighting	Physical	75	100	15	Normal	●
TM32	Double Team	Normal	Status	—	—	15	Self	—
TM40	Aerial Ace	Flying	Physical	60	—	20	Normal	●
TM42	Facade	Normal	Physical	70	100	20	Normal	●
TM43	Secret Power	Normal	Physical	70	100	20	Normal	—
TM44	Rest	Psychic	Status	—	—	10	Self	—
TM45	Attract	Normal	Status	—	100	15	Normal	—
TM55	Brine	Water	Special	65	100	10	Normal	—
TM56	Fling	Dark	Physical	—	100	10	Normal	—
TM58	Endure	Normal	Status	—	—	10	Self	—
TM65	Shadow Claw	Ghost	Physical	70	100	15	Normal	●
TM70	Flash	Normal	Status	—	100	20	Normal	—
TM77	Psych Up	Normal	Status	—	—	10	Normal	—
TM78	Captivate	Normal	Status	—	100	20	2 foes	—
TM82	Sleep Talk	Normal	Status	—	—	10	DoM	—
TM83	Natural Gift	Normal	Physical	—	100	15	Normal	—
TM87	Swagger	Normal	Status	—	90	15	Normal	—
TM90	Substitute	Normal	Status	—	—	10	Self	—
HM03	Surf	Water	Special	95	100	15	2 foes ● 1 ally	●
HM04	Strength	Normal	Physical	80	100	15	Normal	●
HM06	Rock Smash	Fighting	Physical	40	100	15	Normal	●
HM07	Waterfall	Water	Physical	80	100	15	Normal	●

● LEVEL-UP AND LEARNED MOVES

Lv	Name	Type	Kind	Power	Acc	PP	Range	DA
Base	Water Sport	Water	Status	—	—	15	All	—
Base	Scratch	Normal	Physical	40	100	35	Normal	●
5	Tail Whip	Normal	Status	—	100	30	2 foes	—
9	Water Gun	Water	Special	40	100	25	Normal	—
14	Disable	Normal	Status	—	80	20	Normal	—
18	Confusion	Psychic	Special	50	100	25	Normal	—
22	Water Pulse	Water	Special	60	100	20	Normal	—
27	Fury Swipes	Normal	Physical	18	80	15	Normal	●
31	Screech	Normal	Status	—	85	40	Normal	—
35	Psych Up	Normal	Status	—	—	10	Normal	—
40	Zen Headbutt	Psychic	Physical	80	90	15	Normal	●
44	Amnesia	Psychic	Status	—	—	20	Self	—
48	Hydro Pump	Water	Special	120	80	5	Normal	—

● MOVES TAUGHT IN EXCHANGE FOR COLORED SHARDS

Name	Type	Kind	Power	Acc	PP	Range	DA
Dive	Water	Physical	80	100	10	Normal	●
Mud-Slap	Ground	Special	20	100	10	Normal	—
Icy Wind	Ice	Special	55	95	15	2 foes	—
Ice Punch	Ice	Physical	75	100	15	Normal	—
Aqua Tail	Water	Physical	90	90	10	Normal	●
Snore	Normal	Special	40	100	15	Normal	—
Signal Beam	Bug	Special	75	100	15	Normal	—
Zen Headbutt	Psychic	Physical	80	90	15	Normal	●
Swift	Normal	Special	60	—	20	2 foes	—

● EGG MOVES

Name	Type	Kind	Power	Acc	PP	Range	DA
Hypnosis	Psychic	Status	—	60	20	Normal	—
Psybeam	Psychic	Special	65	100	20	Normal	—
Foresight	Normal	Status	—	—	40	Normal	—
Light Screen	Psychic	Status	—	—	30	2 allies	—
Future Sight	Psychic	Special	80	90	15	Normal	—
Psychic	Psychic	Special	90	100	10	Normal	—
Cross Chop	Fighting	Physical	100	80	5	Normal	●
Refresh	Normal	Status	—	—	20	Self	—
Confuse Ray	Ghost	Status	—	100	10	Normal	—
Yawn	Normal	Status	—	—	10	Normal	—
Mud Bomb	Ground	Special	65	85	10	Normal	—

● PRIMARY WAY TO FIND

TRAINER'S PARTY	Trainer on Route 203
WILD POKÉMON	Oreburgh Gate 1F
COURSE OF STORY	

ABILITY	● Damp ● Cloud Nine

EGG GROUP	Water 1 / Field

STATS
HP ●●
ATTACK ●●
DEFENSE ●●
SP. ATTACK ●●
SP. DEFENSE ●●
SPEED ●●

No. 044 Duck Pokémon

Golduck

WATER

HEIGHT: 5'07"
WEIGHT: 168.9 lbs.
GENDER: Male and Female
HELD ITEM: None

● M/F have same form

PLATINUM	It is seen swimming dynamically and elegantly using its well-developed limbs and flippers.

EVOLUTION PATH

Psyduck — Lv33 — Golduck

● TM & HM MOVES

No.	Name	Type	Kind	Power	Acc	PP	Range	DA
TM01	Focus Punch	Fighting	Physical	150	100	20	Normal	●
TM03	Water Pulse	Water	Special	60	100	20	Normal	●
TM04	Calm Mind	Psychic	Status	—	—	20	Self	—
TM06	Toxic	Poison	Status	—	85	10	Normal	—
TM07	Hail	Ice	Status	—	—	10	All	—
TM10	Hidden Power	Normal	Special	—	100	15	Normal	—
TM13	Ice Beam	Ice	Special	95	100	10	Normal	—
TM14	Blizzard	Ice	Special	120	70	5	2 foes	—
TM15	Hyper Beam	Normal	Special	150	90	5	Normal	—
TM17	Protect	Normal	Status	—	—	10	Self	—
TM18	Rain Dance	Water	Status	—	—	5	All	—
TM21	Frustration	Normal	Physical	—	100	20	Normal	●
TM23	Iron Tail	Steel	Physical	100	75	15	Normal	●
TM27	Return	Normal	Physical	—	100	20	Normal	●
TM28	Dig	Ground	Physical	80	100	10	Normal	●
TM29	Psychic	Psychic	Special	90	100	10	Normal	—
TM31	Brick Break	Fighting	Physical	75	100	15	Normal	●
TM32	Double Team	Normal	Status	—	—	15	Self	—
TM40	Aerial Ace	Flying	Physical	60	—	20	Normal	●
TM42	Facade	Normal	Physical	70	100	20	Normal	●
TM43	Secret Power	Normal	Physical	70	100	20	Normal	—
TM44	Rest	Psychic	Status	—	—	10	Self	—
TM45	Attract	Normal	Status	—	100	15	Normal	—
TM52	Focus Blast	Fighting	Special	120	70	5	Normal	—
TM55	Brine	Water	Special	65	100	10	Normal	—
TM56	Fling	Dark	Physical	—	100	10	Normal	—
TM58	Endure	Normal	Status	—	—	10	Self	—
TM65	Shadow Claw	Ghost	Physical	70	100	15	Normal	●
TM68	Giga Impact	Normal	Physical	150	90	5	Normal	●
TM70	Flash	Normal	Status	—	100	20	Normal	—
TM77	Psych Up	Normal	Status	—	—	10	Normal	—
TM78	Captivate	Normal	Status	—	100	20	2 foes	—
TM82	Sleep Talk	Normal	Status	—	—	10	DoM	—
TM83	Natural Gift	Normal	Physical	—	100	15	Normal	—
TM87	Swagger	Normal	Status	—	90	15	Normal	—
TM90	Substitute	Normal	Status	—	—	10	Self	—
HM03	Surf	Water	Special	95	100	15	2 foes ● 1 ally	●
HM04	Strength	Normal	Physical	80	100	15	Normal	●
HM06	Rock Smash	Fighting	Physical	40	100	15	Normal	●
HM07	Waterfall	Water	Physical	80	100	15	Normal	●
HM08	Rock Climb	Normal	Physical	90	85	20	Normal	●

● LEVEL-UP AND LEARNED MOVES

Lv	Name	Type	Kind	Power	Acc	PP	Range	DA
Base	Aqua Jet	Water	Physical	40	100	20	Normal	●
Base	Water Sport	Water	Status	—	—	15	All	—
Base	Scratch	Normal	Physical	40	100	35	Normal	●
Base	Tail Whip	Normal	Status	—	100	30	2 foes	—
Base	Water Gun	Water	Special	40	100	25	Normal	—
5	Tail Whip	Normal	Status	—	100	30	2 foes	—
9	Water Gun	Water	Special	40	100	25	Normal	—
14	Disable	Normal	Status	—	80	20	Normal	—
18	Confusion	Psychic	Special	50	100	25	Normal	—
22	Water Pulse	Water	Special	60	100	20	Normal	—
27	Fury Swipes	Normal	Physical	18	80	15	Normal	●
31	Screech	Normal	Status	—	85	40	Normal	—
37	Psych Up	Normal	Status	—	—	10	Normal	—
44	Zen Headbutt	Psychic	Physical	80	90	15	Normal	●
50	Amnesia	Psychic	Status	—	—	20	Self	—
56	Hydro Pump	Water	Special	120	80	5	Normal	—

● MOVES TAUGHT IN EXCHANGE FOR COLORED SHARDS

Name	Type	Kind	Power	Acc	PP	Range	DA
Dive	Water	Physical	80	100	10	Normal	●
Mud-Slap	Ground	Special	20	100	10	Normal	—
Fury Cutter	Bug	Physical	10	95	20	Normal	—
Icy Wind	Ice	Special	55	95	15	2 foes	—
Ice Punch	Ice	Physical	75	100	15	Normal	—
Aqua Tail	Water	Physical	90	90	10	Normal	●
Snore	Normal	Special	40	100	15	Normal	—
Signal Beam	Bug	Special	75	100	15	Normal	—
Zen Headbutt	Psychic	Physical	80	90	15	Normal	●
Swift	Normal	Special	60	—	20	2 foes	—

● PRIMARY WAY TO FIND

TRAINER'S PARTY	Trainer at Pastoria Gym
WILD POKÉMON	Celestic Town (water surface)
COURSE OF STORY	

ABILITY	● Damp ● Cloud Nine

EGG GROUP	Water 1 / Field

STATS
HP ●●
ATTACK ●●●
DEFENSE ●●
SP. ATTACK ●●●
SP. DEFENSE ●●●
SPEED ●●●

044 GOLDUCK

Burmy

BUG

Plant Cloak   Sandy Cloak   Trash Cloak

HEIGHT: 0'08"
WEIGHT: 7.5 lbs.
GENDER: Male and Female
HELD ITEM: None

● Plant Cloak   ● Sandy Cloak   ● Trash Cloak

PLATINUM Even if it is born where there are no cocooning materials, it somehow always ends up with a cloak.

EVOLUTION PATH

Burmy (Plant Cloak) ♀ → Lv20 → Wormadam (Plant Cloak)
Burmy (Sandy Cloak) ♀ → Lv20 → Wormadam (Sandy Cloak)
Burmy (Trash Cloak) ♀ → Lv20 → Wormadam (Trash Cloak)
Burmy ♂ → Lv20 → Mothim

ABILITY ● Shed Skin

EGG GROUP Bug

STATS
HP ●
ATTACK ●
DEFENSE ●●
SP. ATTACK ●
SP. DEFENSE ●
SPEED ●

● TM & HM MOVES

No.	Name	Type	Kind	Power	Acc	PP	Range	DA

● LEVEL-UP AND LEARNED MOVES

Lv	Name	Type	Kind	Power	Acc	PP	Range	DA
Base	Protect	Normal	Status	—	—	10	Self	
10	Tackle	Normal	Physical	35	95	35	Normal	•
15	Bug Bite	Bug	Physical	60	100	20	Normal	•
20	Hidden Power	Normal	Special	—	100	15	Normal	

● MOVES TAUGHT IN EXCHANGE FOR COLORED SHARDS

Name	Type	Kind	Power	Acc	PP	Range	DA
Snore	Normal	Special	40	100	15	Normal	—

● EGG MOVES

Name	Type	Kind	Power	Acc	PP	Range	DA

● PRIMARY WAY TO FIND

TRAINER'S PARTY Trainer on Route 202

WILD POKÉMON Spread Honey on a Honey Tree

COURSE OF STORY

Wormadam [Plant Cloak]

BUG   **GRASS**

HEIGHT: 1'08"
WEIGHT: 14.3 lbs.
GENDER: Female only
HELD ITEM: None

● Female form

PLATINUM When evolving, its body takes in surrounding materials. As a result, there are many body variations.

EVOLUTION PATH

Burmy (Plant Cloak) ♀ → Lv20 → Wormadam (Plant Cloak)
Burmy (Sandy Cloak) ♀ → Lv20 → Wormadam (Sandy Cloak)
Burmy (Trash Cloak) ♀ → Lv20 → Wormadam (Trash Cloak)
Burmy ♂ → Lv20 → Mothim

ABILITY ● Anticipation

EGG GROUP Bug

STATS
HP ●●
ATTACK ●●
DEFENSE ●●●
SP. ATTACK ●●●
SP. DEFENSE ●●●
SPEED ●

● TM & HM MOVES

No.	Name	Type	Kind	Power	Acc	PP	Range	DA
TM06	Toxic	Poison	Status	—	85	10	Normal	—
TM09	Bullet Seed	Grass	Physical	10	100	30	Normal	—
TM10	Hidden Power	Normal	Special	—	100	15	Normal	—
TM11	Sunny Day	Fire	Status	—	—	5	All	—
TM15	Hyper Beam	Normal	Special	150	90	5	Normal	—
TM17	Protect	Normal	Status	—	—	10	Self	—
TM18	Rain Dance	Water	Status	—	—	5	All	—
TM19	Giga Drain	Grass	Special	60	100	10	Normal	—
TM20	Safeguard	Normal	Status	—	—	25	2 allies	—
TM21	Frustration	Normal	Physical	—	100	20	Normal	•
TM22	SolarBeam	Grass	Special	120	100	10	Normal	—
TM27	Return	Normal	Physical	—	100	20	Normal	•
TM29	Psychic	Psychic	Special	90	100	10	Normal	—
TM30	Shadow Ball	Ghost	Special	80	100	15	Normal	—
TM32	Double Team	Normal	Status	—	—	15	Self	—
TM42	Facade	Normal	Physical	70	100	20	Normal	•
TM43	Secret Power	Normal	Physical	70	100	20	Normal	•
TM44	Rest	Psychic	Status	—	—	10	Self	—
TM45	Attract	Normal	Status	—	100	15	Normal	—
TM46	Thief	Dark	Physical	40	100	10	Normal	•
TM48	Skill Swap	Psychic	Status	—	—	10	Normal	—
TM53	Energy Ball	Grass	Special	80	100	10	Normal	—
TM58	Endure	Normal	Status	—	—	10	Self	—
TM68	Giga Impact	Normal	Physical	150	90	5	Normal	•
TM70	Flash	Normal	Status	—	100	20	Normal	—
TM77	Psych Up	Normal	Status	—	—	10	Normal	—
TM78	Captivate	Normal	Status	—	100	20	2 foes	—
TM82	Sleep Talk	Normal	Status	—	—	10	DoM	—
TM83	Natural Gift	Normal	Physical	—	100	15	Normal	—
TM85	Dream Eater	Psychic	Special	100	100	15	Normal	—
TM86	Grass Knot	Grass	Special	—	100	20	Normal	•
TM87	Swagger	Normal	Status	—	90	15	Normal	—
TM90	Substitute	Normal	Status	—	—	10	Self	—

● LEVEL-UP AND LEARNED MOVES

Lv	Name	Type	Kind	Power	Acc	PP	Range	DA
Base	Tackle	Normal	Physical	35	95	35	Normal	•
10	Protect	Normal	Status	—	—	10	Self	•
15	Bug Bite	Bug	Physical	60	100	20	Normal	•
20	Hidden Power	Normal	Special	—	100	15	Normal	
23	Confusion	Psychic	Special	50	100	25	Normal	
26	Razor Leaf	Grass	Physical	55	95	25	2 foes	
29	Growth	Normal	Status	—	—	40	Self	
32	Psybeam	Psychic	Special	65	100	20	Normal	
35	Captivate	Normal	Status	—	100	20	2 foes	
38	Flail	Normal	Physical	—	100	15	Normal	
41	Attract	Normal	Status	—	100	15	Normal	
44	Psychic	Psychic	Special	90	100	10	Normal	
47	Leaf Storm	Grass	Special	140	90	5	Normal	

● MOVES TAUGHT IN EXCHANGE FOR COLORED SHARDS

Name	Type	Kind	Power	Acc	PP	Range	DA
Snore	Normal	Special	40	100	15	Normal	—
Endeavor	Normal	Physical	—	100	5	Normal	—
Synthesis	Grass	Status	—	—	5	Self	—
Signal Beam	Bug	Special	75	100	15	Normal	—
Seed Bomb	Grass	Physical	80	100	15	Normal	•
Sucker Punch	Dark	Physical	80	100	5	Normal	•
Uproar	Normal	Special	50	100	10	1 random	—

● PRIMARY WAY TO FIND

TRAINER'S PARTY Trainer on Route 214

WILD POKÉMON

COURSE OF STORY

Wormadam (Sandy Cloak)

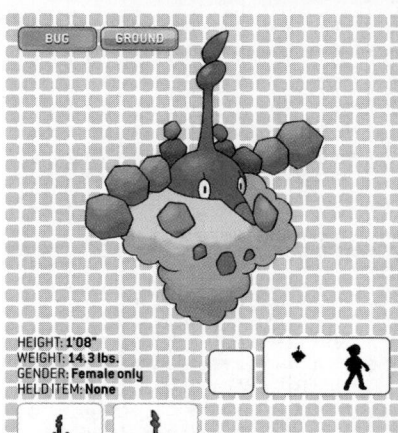

BUG GROUND

HEIGHT: 1'08"
WEIGHT: 14.3 lbs.
GENDER: Female only
HELD ITEM: None

● Female form

PLATINUM — When evolving, its body takes in surrounding materials. As a result, there are many body variations.

EVOLUTION PATH

Burmy (Plant Cloak) ♀	Lv20	Wormadam (Plant Cloak)
Burmy (Sandy Cloak) ♀	Lv20	Wormadam (Sandy Cloak)
Burmy (Trash Cloak) ♀	Lv20	Wormadam (Trash Cloak)
Burmy ♂	Lv20	Mothim

● TM & HM MOVES

No.	Name	Type	Kind	Power	Acc	PP	Range	DA
TM06	Toxic	Poison	Status	—	85	10	Normal	—
TM10	Hidden Power	Normal	Special	—	100	15	Normal	—
TM11	Sunny Day	Fire	Status	—	—	5	All	—
TM15	Hyper Beam	Normal	Special	150	90	5	Normal	—
TM17	Protect	Normal	Status	—	—	10	Self	—
TM18	Rain Dance	Water	Status	—	—	5	All	—
TM20	Safeguard	Normal	Status	—	—	25	2 allies	—
TM21	Frustration	Normal	Physical	—	100	20	Normal	•
TM26	Earthquake	Ground	Physical	100	100	10	2 foes + 1 ally	•
TM27	Return	Normal	Physical	—	100	20	Normal	•
TM28	Dig	Ground	Physical	80	100	10	Normal	•
TM29	Psychic	Psychic	Special	90	100	10	Normal	—
TM30	Shadow Ball	Ghost	Special	80	100	15	Normal	—
TM32	Double Team	Normal	Status	—	—	15	Self	—
TM37	Sandstorm	Rock	Status	—	—	10	All	—
TM39	Rock Tomb	Rock	Physical	50	80	10	Normal	•
TM42	Facade	Normal	Physical	70	100	20	Normal	•
TM43	Secret Power	Normal	Physical	70	100	20	Normal	•
TM44	Rest	Psychic	Status	—	—	10	Self	—
TM45	Attract	Normal	Status	—	100	15	Normal	—
TM46	Thief	Dark	Physical	40	100	10	Normal	•
TM48	Skill Swap	Psychic	Status	—	—	10	Normal	—
TM58	Endure	Normal	Status	—	—	10	Self	—
TM68	Giga Impact	Normal	Physical	150	90	5	Normal	•
TM70	Flash	Normal	Status	—	100	20	Normal	—
TM77	Psych Up	Normal	Status	—	—	10	Normal	—
TM78	Captivate	Normal	Status	—	100	20	2 foes	—
TM82	Sleep Talk	Normal	Status	—	—	10	DoM	—
TM83	Natural Gift	Normal	Physical	—	100	15	Normal	—
TM85	Dream Eater	Psychic	Special	100	100	15	Normal	—
TM87	Swagger	Normal	Status	—	90	15	Normal	—
TM90	Substitute	Normal	Status	—	—	10	Self	—

● LEVEL-UP AND LEARNED MOVES

Lv	Name	Type	Kind	Power	Acc	PP	Range	DA
Base	Tackle	Normal	Physical	35	95	35	Normal	•
10	Protect	Normal	Status	—	—	10	Self	—
15	Bug Bite	Bug	Physical	60	100	20	Normal	•
20	Hidden Power	Normal	Special	—	100	15	Normal	—
23	Confusion	Psychic	Special	50	100	25	Normal	—
26	Rock Blast	Rock	Physical	25	80	10	Normal	—
29	Harden	Normal	Status	—	—	30	Self	—
32	Psybeam	Psychic	Special	65	100	20	Normal	—
35	Captivate	Normal	Status	—	100	20	2 foes	—
38	Flail	Normal	Physical	—	100	15	Normal	•
41	Attract	Normal	Status	—	100	15	Normal	—
44	Psychic	Psychic	Special	90	100	10	Normal	—
47	Fissure	Ground	Physical	—	30	5	Normal	•

● MOVES TAUGHT IN EXCHANGE FOR COLORED SHARDS

Name	Type	Kind	Power	Acc	PP	Range	DA
Snore	Normal	Special	40	100	15	Normal	•
Endeavor	Normal	Physical	—	100	5	Normal	•
Signal Beam	Bug	Special	75	100	15	Normal	—
Sucker Punch	Dark	Physical	80	100	5	Normal	•
Uproar	Normal	Special	50	100	10	1 random	—
Mud-Slap	Ground	Special	20	100	10	Normal	—
Rollout	Rock	Physical	30	90	20	Normal	•
Earth Power	Ground	Special	90	100	10	Normal	—

ABILITY ● Anticipation
EGG GROUP Bug

STATS
HP ●●
ATTACK ●●●
DEFENSE ●●●
SP. ATTACK ●●●
SP. DEFENSE ●●●
SPEED ●

● PRIMARY WAY TO FIND

TRAINER'S PARTY — Trainer on Route 214
WILD POKÉMON
COURSE OF STORY

Wormadam (Trash Cloak)

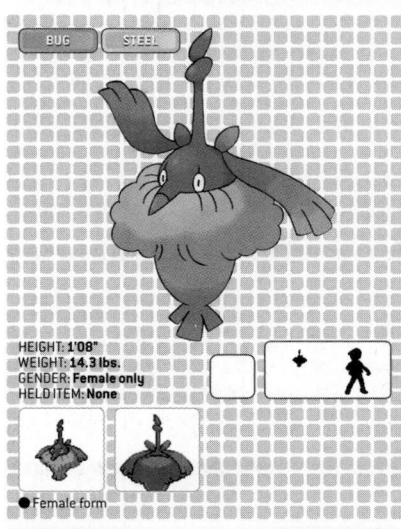

BUG STEEL

HEIGHT: 1'08"
WEIGHT: 14.3 lbs.
GENDER: Female only
HELD ITEM: None

● Female form

PLATINUM — When evolving, its body takes in surrounding materials. As a result, there are many body variations.

EVOLUTION PATH

Burmy (Plant Cloak) ♀	Lv20	Wormadam (Plant Cloak)
Burmy (Sandy Cloak) ♀	Lv20	Wormadam (Sandy Cloak)
Burmy (Trash Cloak) ♀	Lv20	Wormadam (Trash Cloak)
Burmy ♂	Lv20	Mothim

● TM & HM MOVES

No.	Name	Type	Kind	Power	Acc	PP	Range	DA
TM06	Toxic	Poison	Status	—	85	10	Normal	—
TM10	Hidden Power	Normal	Special	—	100	15	Normal	—
TM11	Sunny Day	Fire	Status	—	—	5	All	—
TM15	Hyper Beam	Normal	Special	150	90	5	Normal	—
TM17	Protect	Normal	Status	—	—	10	Self	—
TM18	Rain Dance	Water	Status	—	—	5	All	—
TM20	Safeguard	Normal	Status	—	—	25	2 allies	—
TM21	Frustration	Normal	Physical	—	100	20	Normal	•
TM27	Return	Normal	Physical	—	100	20	Normal	•
TM29	Psychic	Psychic	Special	90	100	10	Normal	—
TM30	Shadow Ball	Ghost	Special	80	100	15	Normal	—
TM32	Double Team	Normal	Status	—	—	15	Self	—
TM42	Facade	Normal	Physical	70	100	20	Normal	•
TM43	Secret Power	Normal	Physical	70	100	20	Normal	•
TM44	Rest	Psychic	Status	—	—	10	Self	—
TM45	Attract	Normal	Status	—	100	15	Normal	—
TM46	Thief	Dark	Physical	40	100	10	Normal	•
TM48	Skill Swap	Psychic	Status	—	—	10	Normal	—
TM58	Endure	Normal	Status	—	—	10	Self	—
TM68	Giga Impact	Normal	Physical	150	90	5	Normal	•
TM70	Flash	Normal	Status	—	100	20	Normal	—
TM74	Gyro Ball	Steel	Physical	—	100	5	Normal	•
TM76	Stealth Rock	Rock	Status	—	—	20	2 foes	—
TM77	Psych Up	Normal	Status	—	—	10	Normal	—
TM78	Captivate	Normal	Status	—	100	20	2 foes	—
TM82	Sleep Talk	Normal	Status	—	—	10	DoM	—
TM83	Natural Gift	Normal	Physical	—	100	15	Normal	—
TM85	Dream Eater	Psychic	Special	100	100	15	Normal	—
TM87	Swagger	Normal	Status	—	90	15	Normal	—
TM90	Substitute	Normal	Status	—	—	10	Self	—
TM91	Flash Cannon	Steel	Special	80	100	10	Normal	—

● LEVEL-UP AND LEARNED MOVES

Lv	Name	Type	Kind	Power	Acc	PP	Range	DA
Base	Tackle	Normal	Physical	35	95	35	Normal	•
10	Protect	Normal	Status	—	—	10	Self	—
15	Bug Bite	Bug	Physical	60	100	20	Normal	•
20	Hidden Power	Normal	Special	—	100	15	Normal	—
23	Confusion	Psychic	Special	50	100	25	Normal	—
26	Mirror Shot	Steel	Special	65	85	10	Normal	—
29	Metal Sound	Steel	Status	—	85	40	Normal	—
32	Psybeam	Psychic	Special	65	100	20	Normal	—
35	Captivate	Normal	Status	—	100	20	2 foes	—
38	Flail	Normal	Physical	—	100	15	Normal	•
41	Attract	Normal	Status	—	100	15	Normal	—
44	Psychic	Psychic	Special	90	100	10	Normal	—
47	Iron Head	Steel	Physical	80	100	15	Normal	•

● MOVES TAUGHT IN EXCHANGE FOR COLORED SHARDS

Name	Type	Kind	Power	Acc	PP	Range	DA
Snore	Normal	Special	40	100	15	Normal	•
Endeavor	Normal	Physical	—	100	5	Normal	•
Signal Beam	Bug	Special	75	100	15	Normal	—
Sucker Punch	Dark	Physical	80	100	5	Normal	•
Uproar	Normal	Special	50	100	10	1 random	—
Magnet Rise	Electric	Status	—	—	10	Self	—
Iron Head	Steel	Physical	80	100	15	Normal	•
Gunk Shot	Poison	Physical	120	70	5	Normal	•
Iron Defense	Steel	Status	—	—	15	Self	—

ABILITY ● Anticipation
EGG GROUP Bug

STATS
HP ●●
ATTACK ●●●
DEFENSE ●●●●
SP. ATTACK ●●●
SP. DEFENSE ●●●●
SPEED ●

● PRIMARY WAY TO FIND

TRAINER'S PARTY — Trainer on Route 214
WILD POKÉMON
COURSE OF STORY

Sinnoh Pokédex No. 047 Moth Pokémon

Mothim

BUG FLYING

HEIGHT: 2'11"
WEIGHT: 51.4 lbs.
GENDER: Male only
HELD ITEM: None

● Male form

PLATINUM While it loves floral honey, it won't gather any itself. Instead, it plots to steal some from COMBEE.

EVOLUTION PATH

Burmy (Plant Cloak) ♀	Lv20	Wormadam (Plant Cloak)
Burmy (Sandy Cloak) ♀	Lv20	Wormadam (Sandy Cloak)
Burmy (Trash Cloak) ♀	Lv20	Wormadam (Trash Cloak)
Burmy ♂	Lv20	Mothim

● TM & HM MOVES

No.	Name	Type	Kind	Power	Acc	PP	Range	DA
TM06	Toxic	Poison	Status	—	85	10	Normal	—
TM10	Hidden Power	Normal	Special	—	100	15	Normal	—
TM11	Sunny Day	Fire	Status	—	—	5	All	—
TM15	Hyper Beam	Normal	Special	150	90	5	Normal	—
TM17	Protect	Normal	Status	—	—	10	Self	—
TM18	Rain Dance	Water	Status	—	—	5	All	—
TM19	Giga Drain	Grass	Special	60	100	10	Normal	—
TM20	Safeguard	Normal	Status	—	—	25	2 allies	—
TM21	Frustration	Normal	Physical	—	100	20	Normal	•
TM22	SolarBeam	Grass	Special	120	100	10	Normal	—
TM27	Return	Normal	Physical	—	100	20	Normal	•
TM29	Psychic	Psychic	Special	90	100	10	Normal	—
TM30	Shadow Ball	Ghost	Special	80	100	15	Normal	—
TM32	Double Team	Normal	Status	—	—	15	Self	—
TM40	Aerial Ace	Flying	Physical	60	—	20	Normal	•
TM42	Facade	Normal	Physical	70	100	20	Normal	•
TM43	Secret Power	Normal	Physical	70	100	20	Normal	•
TM44	Rest	Psychic	Status	—	—	10	Self	—
TM45	Attract	Normal	Status	—	100	15	Normal	—
TM46	Thief	Dark	Physical	40	100	10	Normal	•
TM48	Skill Swap	Psychic	Status	—	—	10	Normal	—
TM51	Roost	Flying	Status	—	—	10	Self	—
TM53	Energy Ball	Grass	Special	80	100	10	Normal	—
TM58	Endure	Normal	Status	—	—	10	Self	—
TM62	Silver Wind	Bug	Special	60	100	5	Normal	—
TM68	Giga Impact	Normal	Physical	150	90	5	Normal	•
TM70	Flash	Normal	Status	—	100	20	Normal	—
TM77	Psych Up	Normal	Status	—	—	10	Normal	—
TM78	Captivate	Normal	Status	—	100	20	2 foes	—
TM82	Sleep Talk	Normal	Status	—	—	10	DoM	—
TM83	Natural Gift	Normal	Physical	—	100	15	Normal	—
TM85	Dream Eater	Psychic	Special	100	100	15	Normal	—
TM87	Swagger	Normal	Status	—	90	15	Normal	—
TM89	U-turn	Bug	Physical	70	100	20	Normal	•
TM90	Substitute	Normal	Status	—	—	10	Self	—
HM05	Defog	Flying	Status	—	—	15	Normal	—

● LEVEL-UP AND LEARNED MOVES

Lv	Name	Type	Kind	Power	Acc	PP	Range	DA
Base	Tackle	Normal	Physical	35	95	35	Normal	•
10	Protect	Normal	Status	—	—	10	Self	—
15	Bug Bite	Bug	Physical	60	100	20	Normal	•
20	Hidden Power	Normal	Special	100	100	15	Normal	—
23	Confusion	Psychic	Special	50	100	25	Normal	—
26	Gust	Flying	Special	40	100	35	Normal	—
29	PoisonPowder	Poison	Status	—	75	35	Normal	—
32	Psybeam	Psychic	Special	65	100	20	Normal	—
35	Camouflage	Normal	Status	—	—	20	Self	—
38	Silver Wind	Bug	Special	60	100	5	Normal	—
41	Air Slash	Flying	Special	75	95	20	Normal	—
44	Psychic	Psychic	Special	90	100	10	Normal	—
47	Bug Buzz	Bug	Special	90	100	10	Normal	—

● MOVES TAUGHT IN EXCHANGE FOR COLORED SHARDS

Name	Type	Kind	Power	Acc	PP	Range	DA
Mud-Slap	Ground	Special	20	100	10	Normal	—
Ominous Wind	Ghost	Special	60	100	5	Normal	—
Snore	Normal	Special	40	100	15	Normal	—
Air Cutter	Flying	Special	55	95	25	2 foes	—
Signal Beam	Bug	Special	75	100	15	Normal	—
Twister	Dragon	Special	40	100	20	2 foes	—
Swift	Normal	Special	60	—	20	2 foes	—

● PRIMARY WAY TO FIND

TRAINER'S PARTY	Trainer on 2F of the Lost Tower
WILD POKÉMON	
COURSE OF STORY	

ABILITY ● Swarm

EGG GROUP Bug

STATS
HP ●●
ATTACK ●●●
DEFENSE ●●●
SP. ATTACK ●●●
SP. DEFENSE ●●
SPEED ●●

Sinnoh Pokédex No. 048 Worm Pokémon

Wurmple

BUG

HEIGHT: 1'00"
WEIGHT: 7.9 lbs.
GENDER: Male and Female
HELD ITEM: None

● M/F have same form

PLATINUM Often targeted by bird Pokémon, it desperately resists by releasing poison from its tail spikes.

EVOLUTION PATH

Wurmple	Lv7	Silcoon	Lv10	Beautifly
	Lv7	Cascoon	Lv10	Dustox

● TM & HM MOVES

No.	Name	Type	Kind	Power	Acc	PP	Range	DA

● LEVEL-UP AND LEARNED MOVES

Lv	Name	Type	Kind	Power	Acc	PP	Range	DA
Base	Tackle	Normal	Physical	35	95	35	Normal	•
Base	String Shot	Bug	Status	—	95	40	2 foes	—
5	Poison Sting	Poison	Physical	15	100	35	Normal	—
15	Bug Bite	Bug	Physical	60	100	20	Normal	•

● MOVES TAUGHT IN EXCHANGE FOR COLORED SHARDS

Name	Type	Kind	Power	Acc	PP	Range	DA
Snore	Normal	Special	40	100	15	Normal	—

● EGG MOVES

Name	Type	Kind	Power	Acc	PP	Range	DA

● PRIMARY WAY TO FIND

TRAINER'S PARTY	Trainer on Route 204
WILD POKÉMON	Route 204 (morning and afternoon only)
COURSE OF STORY	

ABILITY ● Shield Dust

EGG GROUP Bug

STATS
HP ●●
ATTACK ●●
DEFENSE ●
SP. ATTACK ●
SP. DEFENSE ●
SPEED ●

047
● ● ● ● ●

MOTHIM

No. 049 Cocoon Pokémon
Silcoon

BUG

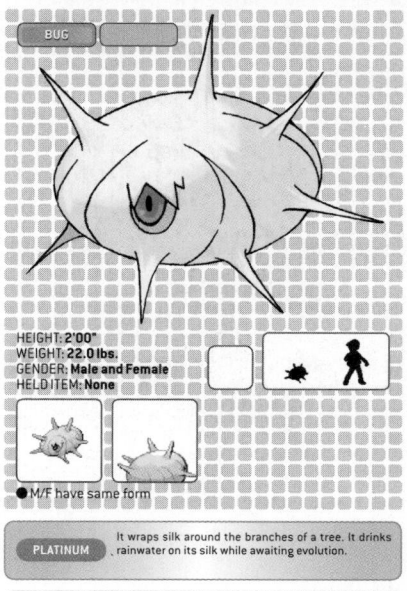

HEIGHT: 2'00"
WEIGHT: 22.0 lbs.
GENDER: Male and Female
HELD ITEM: None

● M/F have same form

PLATINUM — It wraps silk around the branches of a tree. It drinks rainwater on its silk while awaiting evolution.

EVOLUTION PATH

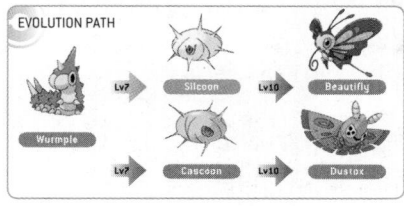

Wurmple — Lv7 → Silcoon — Lv10 → Beautifly
Wurmple — Lv7 → Cascoon — Lv10 → Dustox

● TM & HM MOVES

No.	Name	Type	Kind	Power	Acc	PP	Range	DA

● LEVEL-UP AND LEARNED MOVES

Lv	Name	Type	Kind	Power	Acc	PP	Range	DA
Base	Harden	Normal	Status	—	—	30	Self	—
7	Harden	Normal	Status	—	—	30	Self	—

● MOVES TAUGHT IN EXCHANGE FOR COLORED SHARDS

Name	Type	Kind	Power	Acc	PP	Range	DA
Iron Defense	Steel	Status	—	—	15	Self	—

● PRIMARY WAY TO FIND

TRAINER'S PARTY	Trainer in Eterna Forest
WILD POKÉMON	Eterna City side of Route 205
COURSE OF STORY	

ABILITY ● Shed Skin

EGG GROUP — Bug

STATS
HP ●●
ATTACK ●
DEFENSE ●●
SP. ATTACK ●
SP. DEFENSE ●
SPEED ●

No. 050 Butterfly Pokémon
Beautifly

BUG FLYING

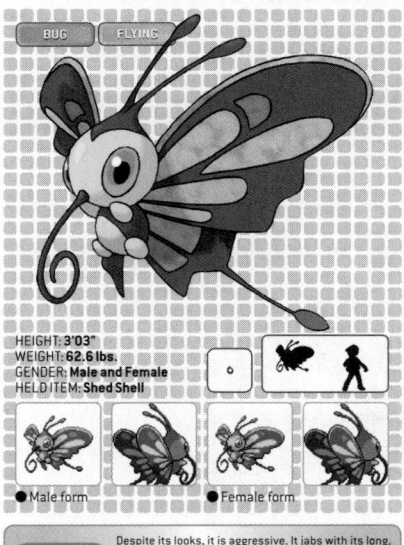

HEIGHT: 3'03"
WEIGHT: 62.6 lbs.
GENDER: Male and Female
HELD ITEM: Shed Shell

● Male form   ● Female form

PLATINUM — Despite its looks, it is aggressive. It jabs with its long, thin mouth if disturbed while collecting pollen.

EVOLUTION PATH

Wurmple — Lv7 → Silcoon — Lv10 → Beautifly
Wurmple — Lv7 → Cascoon — Lv10 → Dustox

● TM & HM MOVES

No.	Name	Type	Kind	Power	Acc	PP	Range	DA
TM06	Toxic	Poison	Status	—	85	10	Normal	—
TM10	Hidden Power	Normal	Special	—	100	15	Normal	—
TM11	Sunny Day	Fire	Status	—	—	5	All	—
TM15	Hyper Beam	Normal	Special	150	90	5	Normal	—
TM17	Protect	Normal	Status	—	—	10	Self	—
TM19	Giga Drain	Grass	Special	60	100	10	Normal	—
TM20	Safeguard	Normal	Status	—	—	25	2 allies	—
TM21	Frustration	Normal	Physical	—	100	20	Normal	●
TM22	SolarBeam	Grass	Special	120	100	10	Normal	—
TM27	Return	Normal	Physical	—	100	20	Normal	●
TM29	Psychic	Psychic	Special	90	100	10	Normal	—
TM30	Shadow Ball	Ghost	Special	80	100	15	Normal	—
TM32	Double Team	Normal	Status	—	—	15	Self	—
TM40	Aerial Ace	Flying	Physical	60	—	20	Normal	—
TM42	Facade	Normal	Physical	70	100	20	Normal	—
TM43	Secret Power	Normal	Physical	70	100	20	Normal	—
TM44	Rest	Psychic	Status	—	—	10	Self	—
TM45	Attract	Normal	Status	—	100	15	Normal	—
TM46	Thief	Dark	Physical	40	100	10	Normal	●
TM51	Roost	Flying	Status	—	—	10	Self	—
TM53	Energy Ball	Grass	Special	80	100	10	Normal	—
TM58	Endure	Normal	Status	—	—	10	Self	—
TM62	Silver Wind	Bug	Special	60	100	5	Normal	—
TM68	Giga Impact	Normal	Physical	150	90	5	Normal	●
TM70	Flash	Normal	Status	—	100	20	Normal	—
TM78	Captivate	Normal	Status	—	100	20	2 foes	—
TM82	Sleep Talk	Normal	Status	—	—	10	DoM	—
TM83	Natural Gift	Normal	Physical	—	100	15	Normal	—
TM87	Swagger	Normal	Status	—	90	15	Normal	—
TM89	U-turn	Bug	Physical	70	100	20	Normal	●
TM90	Substitute	Normal	Status	—	—	10	Self	—
HM05	Defog	Flying	Status	—	—	15	Normal	—

● LEVEL-UP AND LEARNED MOVES

Lv	Name	Type	Kind	Power	Acc	PP	Range	DA
Base	Absorb	Grass	Special	20	100	25	Normal	—
10	Absorb	Grass	Special	20	100	25	Normal	—
13	Gust	Flying	Special	40	100	35	Normal	—
17	Stun Spore	Grass	Status	—	75	30	Normal	—
20	Morning Sun	Normal	Status	—	—	5	Self	—
24	Mega Drain	Grass	Special	40	100	15	Normal	—
27	Whirlwind	Normal	Status	—	100	20	Normal	—
31	Attract	Normal	Status	—	100	15	Normal	—
34	Silver Wind	Bug	Special	60	100	5	Normal	—
38	Giga Drain	Grass	Special	60	100	10	Normal	—
41	Bug Buzz	Bug	Special	90	100	10	Normal	—

● MOVES TAUGHT IN EXCHANGE FOR COLORED SHARDS

Name	Type	Kind	Power	Acc	PP	Range	DA
Ominous Wind	Ghost	Special	60	100	5	Normal	—
Snore	Normal	Special	40	100	15	Normal	—
Air Cutter	Flying	Special	55	95	25	2 foes	—
Signal Beam	Bug	Special	75	100	15	Normal	—
Twister	Dragon	Special	40	100	20	2 foes	—
Swift	Normal	Special	60	—	20	2 foes	—

● PRIMARY WAY TO FIND

TRAINER'S PARTY	Trainer in Eterna Forest
WILD POKÉMON	Eterna Forest
COURSE OF STORY	

ABILITY ● Swarm

EGG GROUP — Bug

STATS
HP ●●
ATTACK ●●●
DEFENSE ●●
SP. ATTACK ●●●
SP. DEFENSE ●●
SPEED ●●

050

Sinnoh Pokédex No. 051 Cocoon Pokémon

Cascoon

BUG

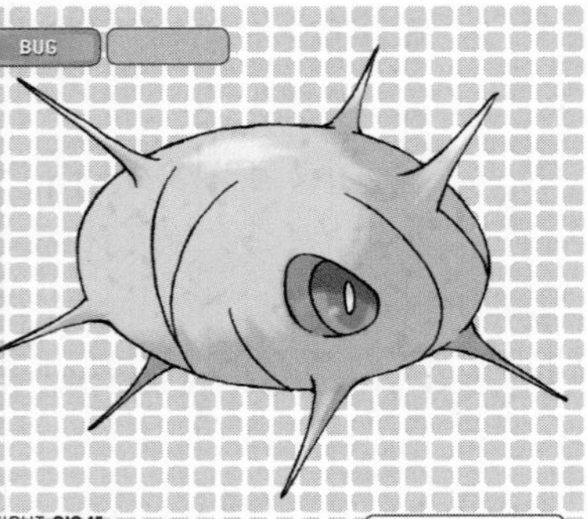

HEIGHT: 2'04"
WEIGHT: 25.4 lbs.
GENDER: Male and Female
HELD ITEM: None

● M/F have same form

PLATINUM It never forgets any attack it endured while in the cocoon. After evolution, it seeks payback.

EVOLUTION PATH

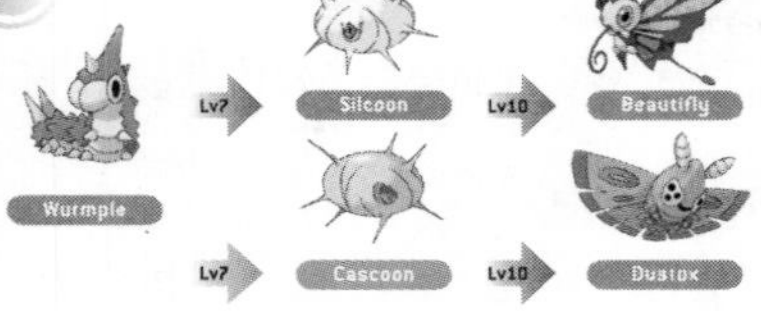

Wurmple — Lv7 → Silcoon — Lv10 → Beautifly
Wurmple — Lv7 → Cascoon — Lv10 → Dustox

● TM & HM MOVES

No.	Name	Type	Kind	Power	Acc	PP	Range	DA

● LEVEL-UP AND LEARNED MOVES

Lv	Name	Type	Kind	Power	Acc	PP	Range	DA
Base	Harden	Normal	Status	—	—	30	Self	—
7	Harden	Normal	Status	—	—	30	Self	—

● MOVES TAUGHT IN EXCHANGE FOR COLORED SHARDS

Name	Type	Kind	Power	Acc	PP	Range	DA
Iron Defense	Steel	Status	—	—	15	Self	—

ABILITY ● Shed Skin

EGG GROUP Bug

STATS
HP ●●
ATTACK ●
DEFENSE ●●
SP. ATTACK ●
SP. DEFENSE ●
SPEED ●

● PRIMARY WAY TO FIND

TRAINER'S PARTY Trainer in Eterna Forest

WILD POKÉMON Eterna City side of Route 205

COURSE OF STORY

051
CASCOON

Sinnoh Pokédex No. 052 Poison Moth Pokémon

Dustox

BUG   POISON

HEIGHT: 3'11"
WEIGHT: 69.7 lbs.
GENDER: Male and Female
HELD ITEM: Shed Shell

● Male form   ● Female form

PLATINUM Toxic powder is scattered with each flap. At night, it is known to strip leaves off trees lining boulevards.

EVOLUTION PATH

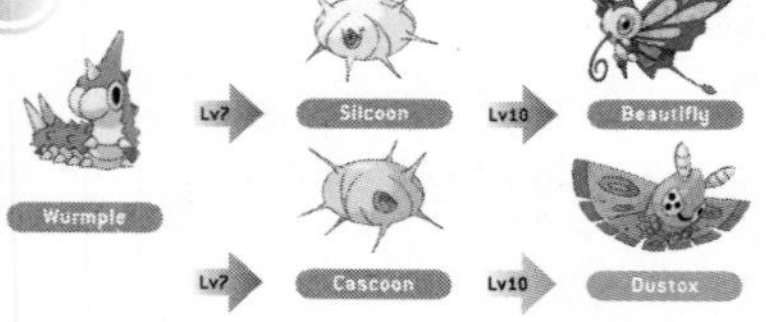

Wurmple — Lv7 → Silcoon — Lv10 → Beautifly
Wurmple — Lv7 → Cascoon — Lv10 → Dustox

● TM & HM MOVES

No.	Name	Type	Kind	Power	Acc	PP	Range	DA
TM06	Toxic	Poison	Status	—	85	10	Normal	—
TM10	Hidden Power	Normal	Special	—	100	15	Normal	—
TM11	Sunny Day	Fire	Status	—	—	5	All	—
TM15	Hyper Beam	Normal	Special	150	90	5	Normal	—
TM16	Light Screen	Psychic	Status	—	—	30	2 allies	—
TM17	Protect	Normal	Status	—	—	10	Self	—
TM19	Giga Drain	Grass	Special	60	100	10	Normal	—
TM21	Frustration	Normal	Physical	—	100	20	Normal	—
TM22	SolarBeam	Grass	Special	120	100	10	Normal	—
TM27	Return	Normal	Physical	—	100	20	Normal	—
TM29	Psychic	Psychic	Special	90	100	10	Normal	—
TM30	Shadow Ball	Ghost	Special	80	100	15	Normal	—
TM32	Double Team	Normal	Status	—	—	15	Self	—
TM36	Sludge Bomb	Poison	Special	90	100	10	Normal	—
TM40	Aerial Ace	Flying	Physical	60	—	20	Normal	●
TM42	Facade	Normal	Physical	70	100	20	Normal	—
TM43	Secret Power	Normal	Physical	70	100	20	Normal	●
TM44	Rest	Psychic	Status	—	—	10	Self	—
TM45	Attract	Normal	Status	—	100	15	Normal	—
TM46	Thief	Dark	Physical	40	100	10	Normal	—
TM51	Roost	Flying	Status	—	—	10	Self	—
TM53	Energy Ball	Grass	Special	80	100	10	Normal	—
TM58	Endure	Normal	Status	—	—	10	Self	—
TM62	Silver Wind	Bug	Special	60	100	5	Normal	—
TM68	Giga Impact	Normal	Physical	150	90	5	Normal	●
TM70	Flash	Normal	Status	—	100	20	Normal	—
TM78	Captivate	Normal	Status	—	100	20	2 foes	—
TM82	Sleep Talk	Normal	Status	—	—	10	DoM	—
TM83	Natural Gift	Normal	Physical	—	100	15	Normal	—
TM87	Swagger	Normal	Status	—	90	15	Normal	—
TM89	U-turn	Bug	Physical	70	100	20	Normal	●
TM90	Substitute	Normal	Status	—	—	10	Self	—
HM05	Defog	Flying	Status	—	—	15	Normal	—

● LEVEL-UP AND LEARNED MOVES

Lv	Name	Type	Kind	Power	Acc	PP	Range	DA
Base	Confusion	Psychic	Special	50	100	25	Normal	—
10	Confusion	Psychic	Special	50	100	25	Normal	—
13	Gust	Flying	Special	40	100	35	Normal	—
17	Protect	Normal	Status	—	—	10	Self	—
20	Moonlight	Normal	Status	—	—	5	Self	—
24	Psybeam	Psychic	Special	65	100	20	Normal	—
27	Whirlwind	Normal	Status	—	100	20	Normal	—
31	Light Screen	Psychic	Status	—	—	30	2 allies	—
34	Silver Wind	Bug	Special	60	100	5	Normal	—
38	Toxic	Poison	Status	—	85	10	Normal	—
41	Bug Buzz	Bug	Special	90	100	10	Normal	—

● MOVES TAUGHT IN EXCHANGE FOR COLORED SHARDS

Name	Type	Kind	Power	Acc	PP	Range	DA
Ominous Wind	Ghost	Special	60	100	5	Normal	—
Snore	Normal	Special	40	100	15	Normal	—
Air Cutter	Flying	Special	55	95	25	2 foes	—
Signal Beam	Bug	Special	75	100	15	Normal	—
Twister	Dragon	Special	40	100	20	2 foes	—
Swift	Normal	Special	60	—	20	2 foes	—

ABILITY ● Shield Dust

EGG GROUP Bug

STATS
HP ●●
ATTACK ●●
DEFENSE ●●
SP. ATTACK ●●
SP. DEFENSE ●●
SPEED ●●

● PRIMARY WAY TO FIND

TRAINER'S PARTY Trainer in Eterna Forest

WILD POKÉMON Eterna Forest

COURSE OF STORY

Combee

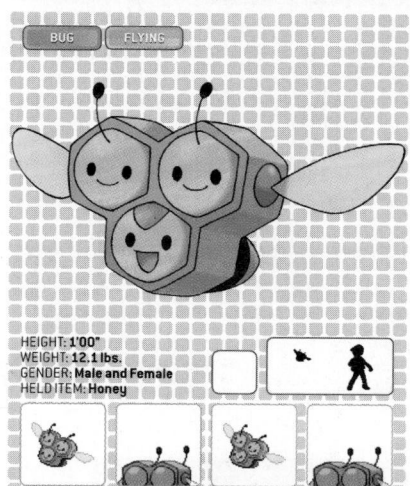

BUG | FLYING

HEIGHT: 1'00"
WEIGHT: 12.1 lbs.
GENDER: Male and Female
HELD ITEM: Honey

● Male form   ● Female form

PLATINUM The trio is together from birth. It constantly gathers honey from flowers to please VESPIQUEN.

EVOLUTION PATH

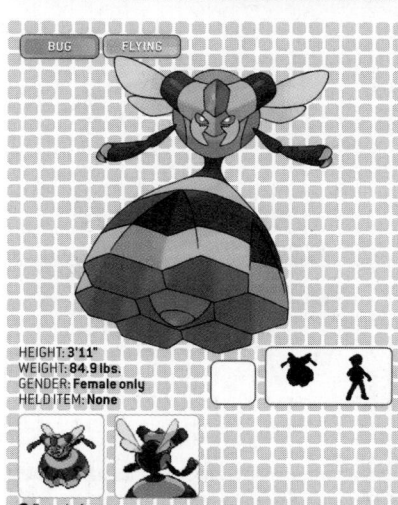

Combee ♀ — Lv21 → Vespiquen

● TM & HM MOVES

No.	Name	Type	Kind	Power	Acc	PP	Range	DA

● LEVEL-UP AND LEARNED MOVES

Lv	Name	Type	Kind	Power	Acc	PP	Range	DA
Base	Sweet Scent	Normal	Status	—	100	20	2 foes	—
Base	Gust	Flying	Special	40	100	35	Normal	—
13	Bug Bite	Bug	Physical	60	100	20	Normal	•

● MOVES TAUGHT IN EXCHANGE FOR COLORED SHARDS

Name	Type	Kind	Power	Acc	PP	Range	DA
Mud-Slap	Ground	Special	20	100	10	Normal	—
Ominous Wind	Ghost	Special	60	100	5	Normal	—
Snore	Normal	Special	40	100	15	Normal	—
Air Cutter	Flying	Special	55	95	25	2 foes	—
Endeavor	Normal	Physical	—	100	5	Normal	•
Swift	Normal	Special	60	—	20	2 foes	—

● EGG MOVES

Name	Type	Kind	Power	Acc	PP	Range	DA

● PRIMARY WAY TO FIND

TRAINER'S PARTY — Trainer on Route 208

WILD POKÉMON — Spread Honey on a Honey Tree

COURSE OF STORY

ABILITY ● Honey Gather

EGG GROUP — Bug

STATS
HP ●
ATTACK ●
DEFENSE ●
SP. ATTACK ●
SP. DEFENSE ●
SPEED ●●●

Vespiquen

BUG | FLYING

HEIGHT: 3'11"
WEIGHT: 84.9 lbs.
GENDER: Female only
HELD ITEM: None

● Female form

PLATINUM It releases various pheromones to make the grubs in its body do its bidding while fighting foes.

EVOLUTION PATH

Combee ♀ — Lv21 → Vespiquen

● TM & HM MOVES

No.	Name	Type	Kind	Power	Acc	PP	Range	DA
TM06	Toxic	Poison	Status	—	85	10	Normal	—
TM10	Hidden Power	Normal	Special	—	100	15	Normal	—
TM11	Sunny Day	Fire	Status	—	—	5	All	—
TM15	Hyper Beam	Normal	Special	150	90	5	Normal	—
TM17	Protect	Normal	Status	—	—	10	Self	—
TM18	Rain Dance	Water	Status	—	—	5	All	—
TM21	Frustration	Normal	Physical	—	100	20	Normal	•
TM27	Return	Normal	Physical	—	100	20	Normal	•
TM32	Double Team	Normal	Status	—	—	15	Self	—
TM36	Sludge Bomb	Poison	Special	90	100	10	Normal	—
TM40	Aerial Ace	Flying	Physical	60	—	20	Normal	•
TM42	Facade	Normal	Physical	70	100	20	Normal	—
TM43	Secret Power	Normal	Physical	70	100	20	Normal	•
TM44	Rest	Psychic	Status	—	—	10	Self	—
TM45	Attract	Normal	Status	—	100	15	Normal	—
TM46	Thief	Dark	Physical	40	100	10	Normal	•
TM51	Roost	Flying	Status	—	—	10	Self	—
TM56	Fling	Dark	Physical	—	100	10	Normal	•
TM58	Endure	Normal	Status	—	—	10	Self	—
TM62	Silver Wind	Bug	Special	60	100	5	Normal	—
TM68	Giga Impact	Normal	Physical	150	90	5	Normal	•
TM70	Flash	Normal	Status	—	100	20	Normal	—
TM78	Captivate	Normal	Status	—	100	20	2 foes	—
TM81	X-Scissor	Bug	Physical	80	100	15	Normal	•
TM82	Sleep Talk	Normal	Status	—	—	10	DoM	—
TM83	Natural Gift	Normal	Physical	—	100	15	Normal	•
TM87	Swagger	Normal	Status	—	90	15	Normal	—
TM89	U-turn	Bug	Physical	70	100	20	Normal	•
TM90	Substitute	Normal	Status	—	—	10	Self	—
HM01	Cut	Normal	Physical	50	95	30	Normal	•
HM05	Defog	Flying	Status	—	—	15	Normal	—

● LEVEL-UP AND LEARNED MOVES

Lv	Name	Type	Kind	Power	Acc	PP	Range	DA
Base	Sweet Scent	Normal	Status	—	100	20	2 foes	—
Base	Gust	Flying	Special	40	100	35	Normal	—
3	Poison Sting	Poison	Physical	15	100	35	Normal	—
7	Confuse Ray	Ghost	Status	—	100	10	Normal	—
9	Fury Cutter	Bug	Physical	10	95	20	Normal	•
13	Defend Order	Bug	Status	—	—	10	Self	—
15	Pursuit	Dark	Physical	40	100	20	Normal	•
19	Fury Swipes	Normal	Physical	18	80	15	Normal	•
21	Power Gem	Rock	Special	70	100	20	Normal	—
25	Heal Order	Bug	Status	—	—	10	Self	—
27	Toxic	Poison	Status	—	85	10	Normal	—
31	Slash	Normal	Physical	70	100	20	Normal	•
33	Captivate	Normal	Status	—	100	20	2 foes	—
37	Attack Order	Bug	Physical	90	100	15	Normal	—
39	Swagger	Normal	Status	—	90	15	Normal	—
43	Destiny Bond	Ghost	Status	—	—	5	Self	—

● MOVES TAUGHT IN EXCHANGE FOR COLORED SHARDS

Name	Type	Kind	Power	Acc	PP	Range	DA
Mud-Slap	Ground	Special	20	100	10	Normal	—
Fury Cutter	Bug	Physical	10	95	20	Normal	•
Ominous Wind	Ghost	Special	60	100	5	Normal	—
Snore	Normal	Special	40	100	15	Normal	—
Air Cutter	Flying	Special	55	95	25	2 foes	—
Endeavor	Normal	Physical	—	100	5	Normal	•
Signal Beam	Bug	Special	75	100	15	Normal	—
Swift	Normal	Special	60	—	20	2 foes	—

● PRIMARY WAY TO FIND

TRAINER'S PARTY — Elite Four member Aaron

WILD POKÉMON

COURSE OF STORY

ABILITY ● Pressure

EGG GROUP — Bug

STATS
HP ●●
ATTACK ●●●
DEFENSE ●●●
SP. ATTACK ●●●
SP. DEFENSE ●●●
SPEED ●●

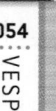

054 VESPIQUEN

Pachirisu

Sinnoh Pokédex **No. 055** Elesquirrel Pokémon

ELECTRIC

HEIGHT: 1'04"
WEIGHT: 8.6 lbs.
GENDER: Male and Female
HELD ITEM: None

● Male form   ● Female form

PLATINUM A pair may be seen rubbing their cheek pouches together in an effort to share stored electricity.

EVOLUTION PATH

Does not evolve

ABILITY ● Run Away
         ● Pickup

EGG GROUP Field
           Fairy

STATS
HP ●●
ATTACK ●●
DEFENSE ●●
SP. ATTACK ●●
SP. DEFENSE ●●
SPEED ●●●

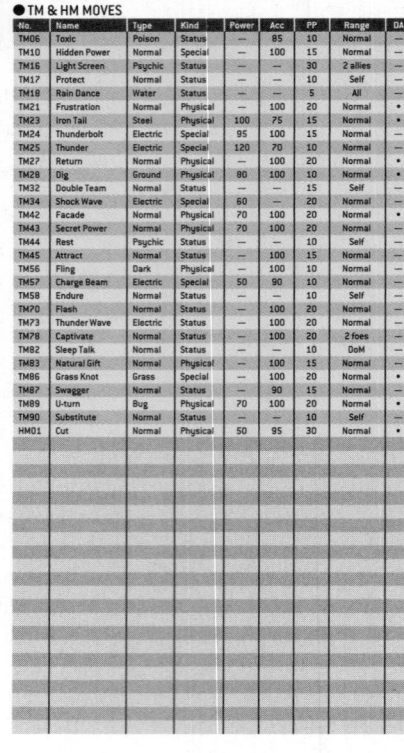

● TM & HM MOVES

No.	Name	Type	Kind	Power	Acc	PP	Range	DA
TM06	Toxic	Poison	Status	—	85	10	Normal	—
TM10	Hidden Power	Normal	Special	—	100	15	Normal	—
TM16	Light Screen	Psychic	Status	—	—	30	2 allies	—
TM17	Protect	Normal	Status	—	—	10	Self	—
TM18	Rain Dance	Water	Status	—	—	5	All	—
TM21	Frustration	Normal	Physical	—	100	20	Normal	●
TM23	Iron Tail	Steel	Physical	100	75	15	Normal	●
TM24	Thunderbolt	Electric	Special	95	100	15	Normal	—
TM25	Thunder	Electric	Special	120	70	10	Normal	—
TM27	Return	Normal	Physical	—	100	20	Normal	●
TM28	Dig	Ground	Physical	80	100	10	Normal	●
TM32	Double Team	Normal	Status	—	—	15	Self	—
TM34	Shock Wave	Electric	Special	60	—	20	Normal	—
TM42	Facade	Normal	Physical	70	100	20	Normal	●
TM43	Secret Power	Normal	Physical	70	100	20	Normal	●
TM44	Rest	Psychic	Status	—	—	10	Self	—
TM45	Attract	Normal	Status	—	100	15	Normal	—
TM56	Fling	Dark	Physical	—	100	10	Normal	●
TM57	Charge Beam	Electric	Special	50	90	10	Normal	—
TM58	Endure	Normal	Status	—	—	10	Self	—
TM70	Flash	Normal	Status	—	100	20	Normal	—
TM73	Thunder Wave	Electric	Status	—	100	20	Normal	—
TM78	Captivate	Normal	Status	—	100	20	2 foes	—
TM82	Sleep Talk	Normal	Status	—	—	10	DoM	—
TM83	Natural Gift	Normal	Physical	—	100	15	Normal	●
TM86	Grass Knot	Grass	Special	—	100	20	Normal	●
TM87	Swagger	Normal	Status	—	90	15	Normal	—
TM89	U-turn	Bug	Physical	70	100	20	Normal	●
TM90	Substitute	Normal	Status	—	—	10	Self	—
HM01	Cut	Normal	Physical	50	95	30	Normal	●

● LEVEL-UP AND LEARNED MOVES

Lv	Name	Type	Kind	Power	Acc	PP	Range	DA
Base	Growl	Normal	Status	—	100	40	2 foes	—
Base	Bide	Normal	Physical	—	—	10	Self	●
5	Quick Attack	Normal	Physical	40	100	30	Normal	●
9	Charm	Normal	Status	—	100	20	Normal	—
13	Spark	Electric	Physical	65	100	20	Normal	●
17	Endure	Normal	Status	—	—	10	Self	—
21	Swift	Normal	Special	60	—	20	2 foes	—
25	Sweet Kiss	Normal	Status	—	75	10	Normal	—
29	Discharge	Electric	Special	80	100	15	2 foes • 1 ally	—
33	Super Fang	Normal	Physical	—	90	10	Normal	—
37	Last Resort	Normal	Physical	130	100	5	Normal	●

● MOVES TAUGHT IN EXCHANGE FOR COLORED SHARDS

Name	Type	Kind	Power	Acc	PP	Range	DA
Mud-Slap	Ground	Special	20	100	10	Normal	—
Rollout	Rock	Physical	30	90	20	Normal	●
ThunderPunch	Electric	Physical	75	100	15	Normal	●
Snore	Normal	Special	40	100	15	Normal	—
Helping Hand	Normal	Status	—	—	20	1 ally	—
Gunk Shot	Poison	Physical	120	70	5	Normal	●
Seed Bomb	Grass	Physical	80	100	15	Normal	●
Magnet Rise	Electric	Status	—	—	10	Self	—
Last Resort	Normal	Physical	130	100	5	Normal	●
Swift	Normal	Special	60	—	20	2 foes	—
Uproar	Normal	Special	50	100	10	1 random	—

● EGG MOVES

Name	Type	Kind	Power	Acc	PP	Range	DA
Covet	Normal	Physical	40	100	40	Normal	—
Bite	Dark	Physical	60	100	25	Normal	●
Fake Tears	Dark	Status	—	100	20	Normal	—
Defense Curl	Normal	Status	—	—	40	Self	—
Rollout	Rock	Physical	30	90	20	Normal	●
Flatter	Dark	Status	—	100	15	Normal	—
Flail	Normal	Physical	—	100	15	Normal	●

● PRIMARY WAY TO FIND

TRAINER'S PARTY	Trainer on Route 204
WILD POKÉMON	Valley Windworks
COURSE OF STORY	

Buizel

Sinnoh Pokédex **No. 056** Sea Weasel Pokémon

WATER

HEIGHT: 2'04"
WEIGHT: 65.0 lbs.
GENDER: Male and Female
HELD ITEM: Wacan Berry

● Male form   ● Female form

PLATINUM It spins its two tails like a screw to propel itself through water. The tails also slice clinging seaweed.

EVOLUTION PATH

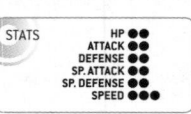

Lv26

Buizel   Floatzel

ABILITY ● Swift Swim

EGG GROUP Water 1
           Field

STATS
HP ●●
ATTACK ●●
DEFENSE ●●
SP. ATTACK ●●
SP. DEFENSE ●●
SPEED ●●●

● TM & HM MOVES

No.	Name	Type	Kind	Power	Acc	PP	Range	DA
TM01	Focus Punch	Fighting	Physical	150	100	20	Normal	●
TM03	Water Pulse	Water	Special	60	100	20	Normal	—
TM06	Toxic	Poison	Status	—	85	10	Normal	—
TM07	Hail	Ice	Status	—	—	10	All	—
TM08	Bulk Up	Fighting	Status	—	—	20	Self	—
TM10	Hidden Power	Normal	Special	—	100	15	Normal	—
TM13	Ice Beam	Ice	Special	95	100	10	Normal	—
TM14	Blizzard	Ice	Special	120	70	5	2 foes	—
TM17	Protect	Normal	Status	—	—	10	Self	—
TM18	Rain Dance	Water	Status	—	—	5	All	—
TM21	Frustration	Normal	Physical	—	100	20	Normal	●
TM23	Iron Tail	Steel	Physical	100	75	15	Normal	●
TM27	Return	Normal	Physical	—	100	20	Normal	●
TM28	Dig	Ground	Physical	80	100	10	Normal	●
TM31	Brick Break	Fighting	Physical	75	100	15	Normal	●
TM32	Double Team	Normal	Status	—	—	15	Self	—
TM39	Rock Tomb	Rock	Physical	50	80	10	Normal	●
TM42	Facade	Normal	Physical	70	100	20	Normal	●
TM43	Secret Power	Normal	Physical	70	100	20	Normal	●
TM44	Rest	Psychic	Status	—	—	10	Self	—
TM45	Attract	Normal	Status	—	100	15	Normal	—
TM55	Brine	Water	Special	65	100	10	Normal	—
TM58	Endure	Normal	Status	—	—	10	Self	—
TM78	Captivate	Normal	Status	—	100	20	2 foes	—
TM82	Sleep Talk	Normal	Status	—	—	10	DoM	—
TM83	Natural Gift	Normal	Physical	—	100	15	Normal	●
TM87	Swagger	Normal	Status	—	90	15	Normal	—
TM90	Substitute	Normal	Status	—	—	10	Self	—
HM03	Surf	Water	Special	95	100	15	2 foes • 1 ally	—
HM04	Strength	Normal	Physical	80	100	15	Normal	●
HM06	Rock Smash	Fighting	Physical	40	100	15	Normal	●
HM07	Waterfall	Water	Physical	80	100	15	Normal	●

● LEVEL-UP AND LEARNED MOVES

Lv	Name	Type	Kind	Power	Acc	PP	Range	DA
Base	SonicBoom	Normal	Special	—	90	20	Normal	—
Base	Growl	Normal	Status	—	100	40	2 foes	—
Base	Water Sport	Water	Status	—	—	15	All	—
3	Quick Attack	Normal	Physical	40	100	30	Normal	●
6	Water Gun	Water	Special	40	100	25	Normal	—
10	Pursuit	Dark	Physical	40	100	20	Normal	●
15	Swift	Normal	Special	60	—	20	2 foes	—
21	Aqua Jet	Water	Physical	40	100	20	Normal	●
28	Agility	Psychic	Status	—	—	30	Self	—
36	Whirlpool	Water	Special	15	70	15	Normal	—
45	Razor Wind	Normal	Special	80	100	10	2 foes	—

● MOVES TAUGHT IN EXCHANGE FOR COLORED SHARDS

Name	Type	Kind	Power	Acc	PP	Range	DA
Dive	Water	Physical	80	100	10	Normal	●
Mud-Slap	Ground	Special	20	100	10	Normal	—
Icy Wind	Ice	Special	55	95	15	2 foes	—
Ice Punch	Ice	Physical	75	100	15	Normal	●
Snore	Normal	Special	40	100	15	Normal	—
Swift	Normal	Special	60	—	20	2 foes	—

● EGG MOVES

Name	Type	Kind	Power	Acc	PP	Range	DA
Mud-Slap	Ground	Special	20	100	10	Normal	—
Headbutt	Normal	Physical	70	100	15	Normal	●
Fury Swipes	Normal	Physical	18	80	15	Normal	●
Slash	Normal	Physical	70	100	20	Normal	●
Odor Sleuth	Normal	Status	—	—	40	Normal	—
DoubleSlap	Normal	Physical	15	85	10	Normal	●
Fury Cutter	Bug	Physical	10	95	20	Normal	●
Baton Pass	Normal	Status	—	—	40	Self	—

● PRIMARY WAY TO FIND

TRAINER'S PARTY	Trainer in Wayward Cave
WILD POKÉMON	Valley Windworks
COURSE OF STORY	

Floatzel

Sinnoh Pokédex No. 057 Sea Weasel Pokémon

WATER

● Male form
● Female form

HEIGHT: 3'07"
WEIGHT: 73.9 lbs.
GENDER: Male and Female
HELD ITEM: Wacan Berry

PLATINUM It is a common sight around fishing ports. It is known to rescue people and carry off prey.

EVOLUTION PATH

Buizel → Lv26 → Floatzel

● TM & HM MOVES

No.	Name	Type	Kind	Power	Acc	PP	Range	DA
TM01	Focus Punch	Fighting	Physical	150	100	20	Normal	•
TM03	Water Pulse	Water	Special	60	100	20	Normal	—
TM05	Roar	Normal	Status	—	100	20	Normal	—
TM06	Toxic	Poison	Status	—	85	10	Normal	—
TM07	Hail	Ice	Status	—	—	10	All	—
TM08	Bulk Up	Fighting	Status	—	—	20	Self	—
TM10	Hidden Power	Normal	Special	—	100	15	Normal	•
TM12	Taunt	Dark	Status	—	100	20	Normal	—
TM13	Ice Beam	Ice	Special	95	100	10	Normal	—
TM14	Blizzard	Ice	Special	120	70	5	Normal	—
TM15	Hyper Beam	Normal	Special	150	90	5	Normal	—
TM17	Protect	Normal	Status	—	—	10	Self	—
TM18	Rain Dance	Water	Status	—	—	5	All	—
TM21	Frustration	Normal	Physical	—	100	20	Normal	•
TM23	Iron Tail	Steel	Physical	100	75	15	Normal	•
TM27	Return	Normal	Physical	—	100	20	Normal	•
TM28	Dig	Ground	Physical	80	100	10	Normal	—
TM31	Brick Break	Fighting	Physical	75	100	15	Normal	—
TM32	Double Team	Normal	Status	—	—	15	Self	—
TM39	Rock Tomb	Rock	Physical	50	80	10	Normal	•
TM41	Torment	Dark	Status	—	100	15	Normal	—
TM42	Facade	Normal	Physical	70	100	20	Normal	•
TM43	Secret Power	Normal	Physical	70	100	20	Normal	•
TM44	Rest	Psychic	Status	—	—	10	Self	—
TM45	Attract	Normal	Status	—	100	15	Normal	—
TM52	Focus Blast	Fighting	Special	120	70	5	Normal	—
TM55	Brine	Water	Special	65	100	10	Normal	—
TM58	Endure	Normal	Status	—	—	10	Self	—
TM66	Payback	Dark	Physical	50	100	10	Normal	•
TM68	Giga Impact	Normal	Physical	150	90	5	Normal	•
TM78	Captivate	Normal	Status	—	100	20	2 foes	—
TM82	Sleep Talk	Normal	Status	—	—	10	DoM	—
TM83	Natural Gift	Normal	Physical	—	100	15	Normal	—
TM87	Swagger	Normal	Status	—	90	15	Normal	—
TM90	Substitute	Normal	Status	—	—	10	Self	—
HM03	Surf	Water	Special	95	100	15	2 foes • 1 ally	
HM04	Strength	Normal	Physical	80	100	15	Normal	•
HM06	Rock Smash	Fighting	Physical	40	100	15	Normal	—
HM07	Waterfall	Water	Physical	80	100	15	Normal	—

● LEVEL-UP AND LEARNED MOVES

Lv	Name	Type	Kind	Power	Acc	PP	Range	DA
Base	Ice Fang	Ice	Physical	65	95	15	Normal	•
Base	SonicBoom	Normal	Special	—	90	20	Normal	—
Base	Growl	Normal	Status	—	100	40	2 foes	—
Base	Water Sport	Water	Status	—	—	15	All	—
Base	Quick Attack	Normal	Physical	40	100	30	Normal	•
3	Quick Attack	Normal	Physical	40	100	30	Normal	•
6	Water Gun	Water	Special	40	100	25	Normal	—
10	Pursuit	Dark	Physical	40	100	20	Normal	•
15	Swift	Normal	Special	60	—	20	2 foes	—
21	Aqua Jet	Water	Physical	40	100	20	Normal	•
26	Crunch	Dark	Physical	80	100	15	Normal	•
29	Agility	Psychic	Status	—	—	30	Self	—
39	Whirlpool	Water	Special	15	70	15	Normal	—
50	Razor Wind	Normal	Special	80	100	10	2 foes	—

● MOVES TAUGHT IN EXCHANGE FOR COLORED SHARDS

Name	Type	Kind	Power	Acc	PP	Range	DA
Dive	Water	Physical	80	100	10	Normal	•
Mud-Slap	Ground	Special	20	100	10	Normal	—
Icy Wind	Ice	Special	55	95	15	2 foes	—
Ice Punch	Ice	Physical	75	100	15	Normal	•
Aqua Tail	Water	Physical	90	90	10	Normal	•
Snore	Normal	Special	40	100	15	Normal	—
Swift	Normal	Special	60	—	20	2 foes	—

● PRIMARY WAY TO FIND

TRAINER'S PARTY	Pastoria Gym Leader Wake
WILD POKÉMON	Route 218
COURSE OF STORY	

ABILITY ● Swift Swim

EGG GROUP: Water 1 / Field

STATS
HP ●●●
ATTACK ●●●●
DEFENSE ●●
SP.ATTACK ●●●
SP.DEFENSE ●●●
SPEED ●●●●

Cherubi

Sinnoh Pokédex No. 058 Cherry Pokémon

GRASS

● M/F have same form

HEIGHT: 1'04"
WEIGHT: 7.3 lbs.
GENDER: Male and Female
HELD ITEM: Miracle Seed

PLATINUM The small ball is not only filled with nutrients, it is also tasty. STARLY try to peck it off.

EVOLUTION PATH

Cherubi → Lv25 → Cherrim

● TM & HM MOVES

No.	Name	Type	Kind	Power	Acc	PP	Range	DA
TM06	Toxic	Poison	Status	—	85	10	Normal	—
TM09	Bullet Seed	Grass	Physical	10	100	30	Normal	—
TM10	Hidden Power	Normal	Special	—	100	15	Normal	•
TM11	Sunny Day	Fire	Status	—	—	5	All	—
TM17	Protect	Normal	Status	—	—	10	Self	—
TM19	Giga Drain	Grass	Special	60	100	10	Normal	—
TM20	Safeguard	Normal	Status	—	—	25	2 allies	—
TM21	Frustration	Normal	Physical	—	100	20	Normal	•
TM22	SolarBeam	Grass	Special	120	100	10	Normal	—
TM27	Return	Normal	Physical	—	100	20	Normal	•
TM32	Double Team	Normal	Status	—	—	15	Self	—
TM42	Facade	Normal	Physical	70	100	20	Normal	•
TM43	Secret Power	Normal	Physical	70	100	20	Normal	•
TM44	Rest	Psychic	Status	—	—	10	Self	—
TM45	Attract	Normal	Status	—	100	15	Normal	—
TM53	Energy Ball	Grass	Special	80	100	10	Normal	—
TM58	Endure	Normal	Status	—	—	10	Self	—
TM70	Flash	Normal	Status	—	100	20	Normal	—
TM75	Swords Dance	Normal	Status	—	—	30	Self	—
TM78	Captivate	Normal	Status	—	100	20	2 foes	—
TM82	Sleep Talk	Normal	Status	—	—	10	DoM	—
TM83	Natural Gift	Normal	Physical	—	100	15	Normal	—
TM86	Grass Knot	Grass	Special	—	100	20	Normal	•
TM87	Swagger	Normal	Status	—	90	15	Normal	—
TM90	Substitute	Normal	Status	—	—	10	Self	—

● LEVEL-UP AND LEARNED MOVES

Lv	Name	Type	Kind	Power	Acc	PP	Range	DA
Base	Tackle	Normal	Physical	35	95	35	Normal	•
7	Growth	Normal	Status	—	—	40	Self	—
10	Leech Seed	Grass	Status	—	90	10	Normal	—
13	Helping Hand	Normal	Status	—	—	20	1 ally	—
19	Magical Leaf	Grass	Special	60	—	20	Normal	—
22	Sunny Day	Fire	Status	—	—	5	All	—
28	Worry Seed	Grass	Status	—	100	10	Normal	—
31	Take Down	Normal	Physical	90	85	20	Normal	•
37	SolarBeam	Grass	Special	120	100	10	Normal	—
40	Lucky Chant	Normal	Status	—	—	30	2 allies	—

● MOVES TAUGHT IN EXCHANGE FOR COLORED SHARDS

Name	Type	Kind	Power	Acc	PP	Range	DA
Rollout	Rock	Physical	30	90	20	Normal	•
Snore	Normal	Special	40	100	15	Normal	—
Helping Hand	Normal	Status	—	—	20	1 ally	—
Synthesis	Grass	Status	—	—	5	Self	—
Seed Bomb	Grass	Physical	80	100	15	Normal	—

● EGG MOVES

Name	Type	Kind	Power	Acc	PP	Range	DA
Razor Leaf	Grass	Physical	55	95	25	2 foes	—
Sweet Scent	Normal	Status	—	100	20	2 foes	—
Tickle	Normal	Status	—	100	20	Normal	—
Nature Power	Normal	Status	—	—	20	DoM	—
GrassWhistle	Grass	Status	—	55	15	Normal	—
Aromatherapy	Grass	Status	—	—	5	All allies	—

● PRIMARY WAY TO FIND

TRAINER'S PARTY	Trainer on Route 204
WILD POKÉMON	Spread Honey on a Honey Tree
COURSE OF STORY	

ABILITY ● Chlorophyll

EGG GROUP: Fairy / Grass

STATS
HP ●
ATTACK ●●
DEFENSE ●●
SP.ATTACK ●●
SP.DEFENSE ●●
SPEED ●

Cherrim

GRASS

Overcast form

Sunshine form

● Overcast form ● Sunshine form

HEIGHT: 1'08"
WEIGHT: 20.5 lbs.
GENDER: Male and Female
HELD ITEM: None

PLATINUM If it senses strong sunlight, it opens its folded petals to absorb the sun's rays with its whole body.

EVOLUTION PATH

Cherubi → (Lv25) → Cherrim

● TM & HM MOVES

No.	Name	Type	Kind	Power	Acc	PP	Range	DA
TM06	Toxic	Poison	Status	—	85	10	Normal	—
TM09	Bullet Seed	Grass	Physical	10	100	30	Normal	—
TM10	Hidden Power	Normal	Special	—	100	15	Normal	—
TM11	Sunny Day	Fire	Status	—	—	5	All	—
TM15	Hyper Beam	Normal	Special	150	90	5	Normal	—
TM17	Protect	Normal	Status	—	—	10	Self	—
TM19	Giga Drain	Grass	Special	60	100	10	Normal	—
TM20	Safeguard	Normal	Status	—	—	25	2 allies	—
TM21	Frustration	Normal	Physical	—	100	20	Normal	●
TM22	SolarBeam	Grass	Special	120	100	10	Normal	—
TM27	Return	Normal	Physical	—	100	20	Normal	●
TM32	Double Team	Normal	Status	—	—	15	Self	—
TM42	Facade	Normal	Physical	70	100	20	Normal	●
TM43	Secret Power	Normal	Physical	70	100	20	Normal	—
TM44	Rest	Psychic	Status	—	—	10	Self	—
TM45	Attract	Normal	Status	—	100	15	Normal	—
TM53	Energy Ball	Grass	Special	80	100	10	Normal	—
TM58	Endure	Normal	Status	—	—	10	Self	—
TM68	Giga Impact	Normal	Physical	150	90	5	Normal	●
TM70	Flash	Normal	Status	—	100	20	Normal	—
TM75	Swords Dance	Normal	Status	—	—	30	Self	—
TM78	Captivate	Normal	Status	—	100	20	2 foes	—
TM82	Sleep Talk	Normal	Status	—	—	10	DoM	—
TM83	Natural Gift	Normal	Physical	—	100	15	Normal	—
TM86	Grass Knot	Grass	Special	—	100	20	Normal	●
TM87	Swagger	Normal	Status	—	90	15	Normal	—
TM90	Substitute	Normal	Status	—	—	10	Self	—

● LEVEL-UP AND LEARNED MOVES

Lv	Name	Type	Kind	Power	Acc	PP	Range	DA
Base	Tackle	Normal	Physical	35	95	35	Normal	●
Base	Growth	Normal	Status	—	—	40	Self	—
7	Growth	Normal	Status	—	—	40	Self	—
10	Leech Seed	Grass	Status	—	90	10	Normal	—
13	Helping Hand	Normal	Status	—	—	20	1 ally	—
19	Magical Leaf	Grass	Special	60	—	20	Normal	—
22	Sunny Day	Fire	Status	—	—	5	All	—
25	Petal Dance	Grass	Special	90	100	20	1 random	—
30	Worry Seed	Grass	Status	—	100	10	Normal	—
35	Take Down	Normal	Physical	90	85	20	Normal	●
43	SolarBeam	Grass	Special	120	100	10	Normal	—
48	Lucky Chant	Normal	Status	—	—	30	2 allies	—

● MOVES TAUGHT IN EXCHANGE FOR COLORED SHARDS

Name	Type	Kind	Power	Acc	PP	Range	DA
Rollout	Rock	Physical	30	90	20	Normal	—
Snore	Normal	Special	40	100	15	Normal	—
Helping Hand	Normal	Status	—	—	20	1 ally	—
Synthesis	Grass	Status	—	—	5	Self	—
Seed Bomb	Grass	Physical	80	100	15	Normal	—

ABILITY ● Flower Gift

EGG GROUP Fairy / Grass

STATS HP ●● / ATTACK ●● / DEFENSE ●● / SP. ATTACK ●● / SP. DEFENSE ●●● / SPEED ●●●

● PRIMARY WAY TO FIND

TRAINER'S PARTY Eterna Gym Leader Gardenia

WILD POKÉMON

COURSE OF STORY

Shellos

WATER

West Sea

East Sea

● West Sea ● East Sea

HEIGHT: 1'00"
WEIGHT: 13.9 lbs.
GENDER: Male and Female
HELD ITEM: None

PLATINUM Beware of pushing strongly on its squishy body, as it makes a mysterious purple fluid ooze out.

EVOLUTION PATH

Shellos → (Lv30) → Gastrodon

(Lv30)

● TM & HM MOVES

No.	Name	Type	Kind	Power	Acc	PP	Range	DA
TM03	Water Pulse	Water	Special	60	100	20	Normal	—
TM06	Toxic	Poison	Status	—	85	10	Normal	—
TM07	Hail	Ice	Status	—	—	10	All	—
TM10	Hidden Power	Normal	Special	—	100	15	Normal	—
TM13	Ice Beam	Ice	Special	95	100	10	Normal	—
TM14	Blizzard	Ice	Special	120	70	5	2 foes	—
TM17	Protect	Normal	Status	—	—	10	Self	—
TM18	Rain Dance	Water	Status	—	—	5	All	—
TM21	Frustration	Normal	Physical	—	100	20	Normal	●
TM27	Return	Normal	Physical	—	100	20	Normal	●
TM32	Double Team	Normal	Status	—	—	15	Self	—
TM42	Facade	Normal	Physical	70	100	20	Normal	●
TM43	Secret Power	Normal	Physical	70	100	20	Normal	—
TM44	Rest	Psychic	Status	—	—	10	Self	—
TM45	Attract	Normal	Status	—	100	15	Normal	—
TM55	Brine	Water	Special	65	100	10	Normal	—
TM58	Endure	Normal	Status	—	—	10	Self	—
TM78	Captivate	Normal	Status	—	100	20	2 foes	—
TM82	Sleep Talk	Normal	Status	—	—	10	DoM	—
TM83	Natural Gift	Normal	Physical	—	100	15	Normal	—
TM87	Swagger	Normal	Status	—	90	15	Normal	—
TM90	Substitute	Normal	Status	—	—	10	Self	—
HM03	Surf	Water	Special	95	100	15	2 foes • 1 ally	—

● LEVEL-UP AND LEARNED MOVES

Lv	Name	Type	Kind	Power	Acc	PP	Range	DA
Base	Mud-slap	Ground	Special	20	100	10	Normal	—
2	Mud Sport	Ground	Status	—	—	15	All	—
4	Harden	Normal	Status	—	—	30	Self	—
7	Water Pulse	Water	Special	60	100	20	Normal	—
11	Mud Bomb	Ground	Special	65	85	10	Normal	—
16	Hidden Power	Normal	Special	—	100	15	Normal	—
22	Rain Dance	Water	Status	—	—	5	All	—
29	Body Slam	Normal	Physical	85	100	15	Normal	●
37	Muddy Water	Water	Special	95	85	10	2 foes	—
46	Recover	Normal	Status	—	—	10	Self	—

● MOVES TAUGHT IN EXCHANGE FOR COLORED SHARDS

Name	Type	Kind	Power	Acc	PP	Range	DA
Dive	Water	Physical	80	100	10	Normal	●
Mud-Slap	Ground	Special	20	100	10	Normal	—
Icy Wind	Ice	Special	55	95	15	2 foes	—
Snore	Normal	Special	40	100	15	Normal	—
AncientPower	Rock	Special	60	100	5	Normal	—
Earth Power	Ground	Special	90	100	10	Normal	—

● EGG MOVES

Name	Type	Kind	Power	Acc	PP	Range	DA
Counter	Fighting	Physical	—	100	20	Self	●
Mirror Coat	Psychic	Special	—	100	20	Self	—
Stockpile	Normal	Status	—	—	20	Self	—
Swallow	Normal	Status	—	—	10	Self	—
Spit Up	Normal	Special	—	100	10	Normal	—
Yawn	Normal	Status	—	—	10	Normal	—
Memento	Dark	Status	—	100	10	Normal	—
Curse	???	Status	—	—	10	Normal • Self	—
Amnesia	Psychic	Status	—	—	20	Self	—
Fissure	Ground	Physical	—	30	5	Normal	—

ABILITY ● Sticky Hold / ● Storm Drain

EGG GROUP Water 1 / Amorphous

STATS HP ●● / ATTACK ●● / DEFENSE ●● / SP. ATTACK ●● / SP. DEFENSE ●● / SPEED ●●

● PRIMARY WAY TO FIND

TRAINER'S PARTY Trainer in Wayward Cave

WILD POKÉMON Valley Windworks

COURSE OF STORY

Sinnoh Pokédex No. 061 Sea Slug Pokémon

Gastrodon

WATER GROUND

West Sea   East Sea

HEIGHT: 2'11"
WEIGHT: 65.9 lbs.
GENDER: Male and Female
HELD ITEM: None

● West Sea   ● East Sea

PLATINUM Long ago, its entire back was shielded with a sturdy shell. There are traces it left in its cells.

EVOLUTION PATH

Shellos   Lv30   Lv30   Gastrodon

ABILITY ● Sticky Hold ● Storm Drain

EGG GROUP Water 1 / Amorphous

STATS
HP ●●●
ATTACK ●●●
DEFENSE ●●●
SP. ATTACK ●●●
SP. DEFENSE ●●
SPEED ●●

● TM & HM MOVES

No.	Name	Type	Kind	Power	Acc	PP	Range	DA
TM03	Water Pulse	Water	Special	60	100	20	Normal	
TM06	Toxic	Poison	Status	—	85	10	Normal	
TM07	Hail	Ice	Status	—	—	10	All	
TM10	Hidden Power	Normal	Special	—	100	15	Normal	
TM13	Ice Beam	Ice	Special	95	100	10	Normal	
TM14	Blizzard	Ice	Special	120	70	5	2 foes	
TM15	Hyper Beam	Normal	Special	150	90	5	Normal	
TM17	Protect	Normal	Status	—	—	10	Self	
TM18	Rain Dance	Water	Status	—	—	5	All	
TM21	Frustration	Normal	Physical	—	100	20	Normal	•
TM26	Earthquake	Ground	Physical	100	100	10	2 foes • 1 ally	
TM27	Return	Normal	Physical	—	100	20	Normal	•
TM28	Dig	Ground	Physical	80	100	10	Normal	•
TM32	Double Team	Normal	Status	—	—	15	Self	
TM36	Sludge Bomb	Poison	Special	90	100	10	Normal	
TM37	Sandstorm	Rock	Status	—	—	10	All	
TM39	Rock Tomb	Rock	Physical	50	80	10	Normal	•
TM42	Facade	Normal	Physical	70	100	20	Normal	•
TM43	Secret Power	Normal	Physical	70	100	20	Normal	•
TM44	Rest	Psychic	Status	—	—	10	Self	
TM45	Attract	Normal	Status	—	100	15	Normal	
TM55	Brine	Water	Special	65	100	10	Normal	
TM58	Endure	Normal	Status	—	—	10	Self	
TM68	Giga Impact	Normal	Physical	150	90	5	Normal	•
TM70	Flash	Normal	Status	—	100	20	Normal	
TM71	Stone Edge	Rock	Physical	100	80	5	Normal	•
TM78	Captivate	Normal	Status	—	100	15	2 foes	
TM80	Rock Slide	Rock	Physical	75	90	10	2 foes	•
TM82	Sleep Talk	Normal	Status	—	—	10	DoM	
TM83	Natural Gift	Normal	Physical	—	100	15	Normal	•
TM87	Swagger	Normal	Status	—	90	15	Normal	
TM90	Substitute	Normal	Status	—	—	10	Self	
HM03	Surf	Water	Special	95	100	15	2 foes • 1 ally	
HM04	Strength	Normal	Physical	80	100	15	Normal	•
HM06	Rock Smash	Fighting	Physical	40	100	15	Normal	•
HM07	Waterfall	Water	Physical	80	100	15	Normal	•

● LEVEL-UP AND LEARNED MOVES

Lv	Name	Type	Kind	Power	Acc	PP	Range	DA
Base	Mud-Slap	Ground	Special	20	100	10	Normal	
Base	Mud Sport	Ground	Status	—	—	15	All	
Base	Harden	Normal	Status	—	—	30	Self	
Base	Water Pulse	Water	Special	60	100	20	Normal	
2	Mud Sport	Ground	Status	—	—	15	All	
4	Harden	Normal	Status	—	—	30	Self	
7	Water Pulse	Water	Special	60	100	20	Normal	
11	Mud Bomb	Ground	Special	65	85	10	Normal	
16	Hidden Power	Normal	Special	—	100	15	Normal	
22	Rain Dance	Water	Status	—	—	5	All	
29	Body Slam	Normal	Physical	85	100	15	Normal	•
41	Muddy Water	Water	Special	95	85	10	2 foes	
54	Recover	Normal	Status	—	—	10	Self	

● MOVES TAUGHT IN EXCHANGE FOR COLORED SHARDS

Name	Type	Kind	Power	Acc	PP	Range	DA
Dive	Water	Physical	80	100	10	Normal	•
Mud-Slap	Ground	Special	20	100	10	Normal	—
Icy Wind	Ice	Special	55	95	15	2 foes	—
Snore	Normal	Special	40	100	15	Normal	—
AncientPower	Rock	Special	60	100	5	Normal	—
Earth Power	Ground	Special	90	100	10	Normal	—

● PRIMARY WAY TO FIND

TRAINER'S PARTY Trainer on Route 220

WILD POKÉMON Route 218

COURSE OF STORY

Sinnoh Pokédex No. 062 Single Horn Pokémon

Heracross

BUG Fighting

HEIGHT: 4'11"
WEIGHT: 119.0 lbs.
GENDER: Male and Female
HELD ITEM: None

● Male form   ● Female form

PLATINUM It loves sweet honey. To keep all the honey to itself, it hurls rivals away with its prized horn.

EVOLUTION PATH

Does not evolve

ABILITY ● Swarm ● Guts

EGG GROUP Bug

STATS
HP ●●
ATTACK ●●●●
DEFENSE ●●●
SP. ATTACK ●●
SP. DEFENSE ●●
SPEED ●●●

● TM & HM MOVES

No.	Name	Type	Kind	Power	Acc	PP	Range	DA
TM01	Focus Punch	Fighting	Physical	150	100	20	Normal	•
TM06	Toxic	Poison	Status	—	85	10	Normal	
TM08	Bulk Up	Fighting	Status	—	—	20	Self	—
TM10	Hidden Power	Normal	Special	—	100	15	Normal	
TM11	Sunny Day	Fire	Status	—	—	5	All	
TM15	Hyper Beam	Normal	Special	150	90	5	Normal	•
TM17	Protect	Normal	Status	—	—	10	Self	
TM18	Rain Dance	Water	Status	—	—	5	All	
TM21	Frustration	Normal	Physical	—	100	20	Normal	•
TM26	Earthquake	Ground	Physical	100	100	10	2 foes • 1 ally	
TM27	Return	Normal	Physical	—	100	20	Normal	•
TM28	Dig	Ground	Physical	80	100	10	Normal	•
TM31	Brick Break	Fighting	Physical	75	100	15	Normal	•
TM32	Double Team	Normal	Status	—	—	15	Self	
TM39	Rock Tomb	Rock	Physical	50	80	10	Normal	•
TM40	Aerial Ace	Flying	Physical	60	—	20	Normal	•
TM42	Facade	Normal	Physical	70	100	20	Normal	•
TM43	Secret Power	Normal	Physical	70	100	20	Normal	•
TM44	Rest	Psychic	Status	—	—	10	Self	
TM45	Attract	Normal	Status	—	100	15	Normal	•
TM46	Thief	Dark	Physical	40	100	10	Normal	•
TM52	Focus Blast	Fighting	Special	120	70	5	Normal	•
TM56	Fling	Dark	Physical	—	100	10	Normal	•
TM58	Endure	Normal	Status	—	—	10	Self	
TM65	Shadow Claw	Ghost	Physical	70	100	15	Normal	•
TM68	Giga Impact	Normal	Physical	150	90	5	Normal	•
TM71	Stone Edge	Rock	Physical	100	80	5	Normal	•
TM75	Swords Dance	Normal	Status	—	—	30	Self	
TM78	Captivate	Normal	Status	—	100	20	2 foes	
TM80	Rock Slide	Rock	Physical	75	90	10	2 foes	•
TM82	Sleep Talk	Normal	Status	—	—	10	DoM	
TM83	Natural Gift	Normal	Physical	—	100	15	Normal	•
TM87	Swagger	Normal	Status	—	90	15	Normal	
TM90	Substitute	Normal	Status	—	—	10	Self	
HM01	Cut	Normal	Physical	50	95	30	Normal	•
HM04	Strength	Normal	Physical	80	100	15	Normal	•
HM06	Rock Smash	Fighting	Physical	40	100	15	Normal	•

● LEVEL-UP AND LEARNED MOVES

Lv	Name	Type	Kind	Power	Acc	PP	Range	DA
Base	Night Slash	Dark	Physical	70	100	15	Normal	•
Base	Tackle	Normal	Physical	35	95	35	Normal	•
Base	Leer	Normal	Status	—	100	30	2 foes	•
Base	Horn Attack	Normal	Physical	65	100	25	Normal	•
Base	Endure	Normal	Status	—	—	10	Self	—
7	Fury Attack	Normal	Physical	15	85	20	Normal	•
13	Aerial Ace	Flying	Physical	60	—	20	Normal	•
19	Brick Break	Fighting	Physical	75	100	15	Normal	•
25	Counter	Fighting	Physical	—	100	20	Self	•
31	Take Down	Normal	Physical	90	85	20	Normal	•
37	Close Combat	Fighting	Physical	120	100	5	Normal	•
43	Reversal	Fighting	Physical	—	100	15	Normal	•
49	Feint	Normal	Physical	50	100	10	Normal	•
55	Megahorn	Bug	Physical	120	85	10	Normal	•

● MOVES TAUGHT IN EXCHANGE FOR COLORED SHARDS

Name	Type	Kind	Power	Acc	PP	Range	DA
Fury Cutter	Bug	Physical	10	95	20	Normal	•
Snore	Normal	Special	40	100	15	Normal	•
Helping Hand	Normal	Status	—	—	20	1 ally	•
Vacuum Wave	Fighting	Special	40	100	30	Normal	•
Iron Defense	Steel	Status	—	—	15	Self	•
Knock Off	Dark	Physical	20	100	20	Normal	•

● EGG MOVES

Name	Type	Kind	Power	Acc	PP	Range	DA
Harden	Normal	Status	—	—	30	Self	•
Bide	Normal	Physical	—	—	10	Self	•
Flail	Normal	Physical	—	100	15	Normal	•
False Swipe	Normal	Physical	40	100	40	Normal	•
Revenge	Fighting	Physical	60	100	10	Normal	•
Pursuit	Dark	Physical	40	100	20	Normal	•
Double-Edge	Normal	Physical	120	100	15	Normal	•

● PRIMARY WAY TO FIND

TRAINER'S PARTY Trainer at the Café Cabin on the Solaceon Town side of Route 210

WILD POKÉMON Spread Honey on a Honey Tree

COURSE OF STORY

Sinnoh Pokédex **No. 063** Long Tail Pokémon

Aipom

NORMAL

HEIGHT: 2'07"
WEIGHT: 25.4 lbs.
GENDER: Male and Female
HELD ITEM: None

● Male form ● Female form

PLATINUM It lives high among the treetops. It can use its tail as freely and cleverly as its hands.

EVOLUTION PATH

Raise to Lv32 and teach it Double Hit. Or, level it up while it knows Double Hit.
Aipom
Ambipom

● TM & HM MOVES

No.	Name	Type	Kind	Power	Acc	PP	Range	DA
TM01	Focus Punch	Fight	Physical	150	100	20	Normal	•
TM03	Water Pulse	Water	Special	60	100	20	Normal	—
TM06	Toxic	Poison	Status	—	85	10	Normal	—
TM10	Hidden Power	Normal	Special	—	100	15	Normal	—
TM11	Sunny Day	Fire	Status	—	—	5	All	—
TM12	Taunt	Dark	Status	—	100	20	Normal	—
TM17	Protect	Normal	Status	—	—	10	Self	—
TM18	Rain Dance	Water	Status	—	—	5	All	—
TM21	Frustration	Normal	Physical	—	100	20	Normal	•
TM22	SolarBeam	Grass	Special	120	100	10	Normal	—
TM23	Iron Tail	Steel	Physical	100	75	15	Normal	•
TM24	Thunderbolt	Electric	Special	95	100	15	Normal	—
TM25	Thunder	Electric	Special	120	70	10	Normal	—
TM27	Return	Normal	Physical	—	100	20	Normal	•
TM28	Dig	Ground	Physical	80	100	10	Normal	•
TM30	Shadow Ball	Ghost	Special	80	100	15	Normal	—
TM31	Brick Break	Fight	Physical	75	100	15	Normal	•
TM32	Double Team	Normal	Status	—	—	15	Self	—
TM34	Shock Wave	Electric	Special	60	—	20	Normal	—
TM40	Aerial Ace	Flying	Physical	60	—	20	Normal	•
TM42	Facade	Normal	Physical	70	100	20	Normal	•
TM43	Secret Power	Normal	Physical	70	100	20	Normal	—
TM44	Rest	Psychic	Status	—	—	10	Self	—
TM45	Attract	Normal	Status	—	100	15	Normal	—
TM46	Thief	Dark	Physical	40	100	10	Normal	•
TM49	Snatch	Dark	Status	—	—	10	DoM	—
TM56	Fling	Dark	Physical	—	100	10	Normal	—
TM58	Endure	Normal	Status	—	—	10	Self	—
TM65	Shadow Claw	Ghost	Physical	70	100	15	Normal	•
TM66	Payback	Dark	Physical	50	100	10	Normal	•
TM73	Thunder Wave	Electric	Status	—	100	20	Normal	—
TM78	Captivate	Normal	Status	—	100	20	2 foes	—
TM82	Sleep Talk	Normal	Status	—	—	10	DoM	—
TM83	Natural Gift	Normal	Physical	—	100	15	Normal	—
TM85	Dream Eater	Psychic	Special	100	100	15	Normal	—
TM86	Grass Knot	Grass	Special	—	100	20	Normal	•
TM87	Swagger	Normal	Status	—	90	15	Normal	—
TM89	U-turn	Bug	Physical	70	100	20	Normal	•
TM90	Substitute	Normal	Status	—	—	10	Self	—
HM01	Cut	Normal	Physical	50	95	30	Normal	•
HM04	Strength	Normal	Physical	80	100	15	Normal	•
HM06	Rock Smash	Fight	Physical	40	100	15	Normal	•

ABILITY ● Run Away ● Pickup

EGG GROUP Field

STATS
HP ●●
ATTACK ●●●
DEFENSE ●●
SP. ATTACK ●●
SP. DEFENSE ●
SPEED ●●●

● LEVEL-UP AND LEARNED MOVES

Lv	Name	Type	Kind	Power	Acc	PP	Range	DA
Base	Scratch	Normal	Physical	40	100	35	Normal	•
Base	Tail Whip	Normal	Status	—	100	30	2 foes	—
4	Sand-Attack	Ground	Status	—	100	15	Normal	—
8	Astonish	Ghost	Physical	30	100	15	Normal	•
11	Baton Pass	Normal	Status	—	—	40	Self	—
15	Tickle	Normal	Status	—	100	20	Normal	—
18	Fury Swipes	Normal	Physical	18	80	15	Normal	•
22	Swift	Normal	Special	60	—	20	2 foes	—
25	Screech	Normal	Status	—	85	40	Normal	—
29	Agility	Psychic	Status	—	—	30	Self	—
32	Double Hit	Normal	Physical	35	90	10	Normal	•
36	Fling	Dark	Physical	—	100	10	Normal	—
39	Nasty Plot	Dark	Status	—	—	20	Self	—
43	Last Resort	Normal	Physical	130	100	5	Normal	•

● MOVES TAUGHT IN EXCHANGE FOR COLORED SHARDS

Name	Type	Kind	Power	Acc	PP	Range	DA
Mud-Slap	Ground	Special	20	100	10	Normal	—
Fury Cutter	Bug	Physical	10	95	20	Normal	•
ThunderPunch	Electric	Physical	75	100	15	Normal	•
Fire Punch	Fire	Physical	75	100	15	Normal	•
Ice Punch	Ice	Physical	75	100	15	Normal	•
Snore	Normal	Special	40	100	15	Normal	—
Spite	Ghost	Status	—	100	10	Normal	—
Gunk Shot	Poison	Physical	120	70	5	Normal	—
Seed Bomb	Grass	Physical	80	100	15	Normal	—
Last Resort	Normal	Physical	130	100	5	Normal	•
Bounce	Flying	Physical	85	85	5	Normal	•
Knock Off	Dark	Physical	20	100	20	Normal	•
Swift	Normal	Special	60	—	20	2 foes	—
Uproar	Normal	Special	50	100	10	1 random	—

● EGG MOVES

Name	Type	Kind	Power	Acc	PP	Range	DA
Counter	Fight	Physical	—	100	20	Self	•
Screech	Normal	Status	—	85	40	Normal	—
Pursuit	Dark	Physical	40	100	20	Normal	•
Agility	Psychic	Status	—	—	30	Self	—
Spite	Ghost	Status	—	100	10	Normal	—
Slam	Normal	Physical	80	75	20	Normal	•
DoubleSlap	Normal	Physical	15	85	10	Normal	•
Beat Up	Dark	Physical	10	100	10	Normal	—
Fake Out	Normal	Physical	40	100	10	Normal	•
Covet	Normal	Physical	40	100	40	Normal	•
Bounce	Flying	Physical	85	85	5	Normal	•

● PRIMARY WAY TO FIND

TRAINER'S PARTY Trainer on Route 205

WILD POKÉMON Spread Honey on a Honey Tree

COURSE OF STORY

Sinnoh Pokédex **No. 064** Long Tail Pokémon

Ambipom

NORMAL

HEIGHT: 3'11"
WEIGHT: 44.8 lbs.
GENDER: Male and Female
HELD ITEM: None

● Male form ● Female form

PLATINUM Split into two, the tails are so adept at handling and doing things, AMBIPOM rarely uses its hands.

EVOLUTION PATH

Raise to Lv32 and teach it Double Hit. Or, level it up while it knows Double Hit.
Aipom
Ambipom

● TM & HM MOVES

No.	Name	Type	Kind	Power	Acc	PP	Range	DA
TM01	Focus Punch	Fight	Physical	150	100	20	Normal	•
TM03	Water Pulse	Water	Special	60	100	20	Normal	—
TM06	Toxic	Poison	Status	—	85	10	Normal	—
TM10	Hidden Power	Normal	Special	—	100	15	Normal	—
TM11	Sunny Day	Fire	Status	—	—	5	All	—
TM12	Taunt	Dark	Status	—	100	20	Normal	—
TM15	Hyper Beam	Normal	Special	150	90	5	Normal	—
TM17	Protect	Normal	Status	—	—	10	Self	—
TM18	Rain Dance	Water	Status	—	—	5	All	—
TM21	Frustration	Normal	Physical	—	100	20	Normal	•
TM22	SolarBeam	Grass	Special	120	100	10	Normal	—
TM23	Iron Tail	Steel	Physical	100	75	15	Normal	•
TM24	Thunderbolt	Electric	Special	95	100	15	Normal	—
TM25	Thunder	Electric	Special	120	70	10	Normal	—
TM27	Return	Normal	Physical	—	100	20	Normal	•
TM28	Dig	Ground	Physical	80	100	10	Normal	•
TM30	Shadow Ball	Ghost	Special	80	100	15	Normal	—
TM31	Brick Break	Fight	Physical	75	100	15	Normal	•
TM32	Double Team	Normal	Status	—	—	15	Self	—
TM34	Shock Wave	Electric	Special	60	—	20	Normal	—
TM40	Aerial Ace	Flying	Physical	60	—	20	Normal	•
TM42	Facade	Normal	Physical	70	100	20	Normal	•
TM43	Secret Power	Normal	Physical	70	100	20	Normal	—
TM44	Rest	Psychic	Status	—	—	10	Self	—
TM45	Attract	Normal	Status	—	100	15	Normal	—
TM46	Thief	Dark	Physical	40	100	10	Normal	•
TM49	Snatch	Dark	Status	—	—	10	DoM	—
TM56	Fling	Dark	Physical	—	100	10	Normal	—
TM58	Endure	Normal	Status	—	—	10	Self	—
TM65	Shadow Claw	Ghost	Physical	70	100	15	Normal	•
TM66	Payback	Dark	Physical	50	100	10	Normal	•
TM68	Giga Impact	Normal	Physical	150	90	5	Normal	•
TM73	Thunder Wave	Electric	Status	—	100	20	Normal	—
TM78	Captivate	Normal	Status	—	100	20	2 foes	—
TM82	Sleep Talk	Normal	Status	—	—	10	DoM	—
TM83	Natural Gift	Normal	Physical	—	100	15	Normal	—
TM85	Dream Eater	Psychic	Special	100	100	15	Normal	—
TM86	Grass Knot	Grass	Special	—	100	20	Normal	•
TM87	Swagger	Normal	Status	—	90	15	Normal	—
TM89	U-turn	Bug	Physical	70	100	20	Normal	•
TM90	Substitute	Normal	Status	—	—	10	Self	—
HM01	Cut	Normal	Physical	50	95	30	Normal	•
HM04	Strength	Normal	Physical	80	100	15	Normal	•
HM06	Rock Smash	Fight	Physical	40	100	15	Normal	•

ABILITY ● Technician ● Pickup

EGG GROUP Field

STATS
HP ●●
ATTACK ●●●
DEFENSE ●●
SP. ATTACK ●●
SP. DEFENSE ●●
SPEED ●●●●

● LEVEL-UP AND LEARNED MOVES

Lv	Name	Type	Kind	Power	Acc	PP	Range	DA
Base	Scratch	Normal	Physical	40	100	35	Normal	•
Base	Tail Whip	Normal	Status	—	100	30	2 foes	—
Base	Sand-Attack	Ground	Status	—	100	15	Normal	—
Base	Astonish	Ghost	Physical	30	100	15	Normal	•
4	Sand-Attack	Ground	Status	—	100	15	Normal	—
8	Astonish	Ghost	Physical	30	100	15	Normal	•
11	Baton Pass	Normal	Status	—	—	40	Self	—
15	Tickle	Normal	Status	—	100	20	Normal	—
18	Fury Swipes	Normal	Physical	18	80	15	Normal	•
22	Swift	Normal	Special	60	—	20	2 foes	—
25	Screech	Normal	Status	—	85	40	Normal	—
29	Agility	Psychic	Status	—	—	30	Self	—
32	Double Hit	Normal	Physical	35	90	10	Normal	•
36	Fling	Dark	Physical	—	100	10	Normal	—
39	Nasty Plot	Dark	Status	—	—	20	Self	—
43	Last Resort	Normal	Physical	130	100	5	Normal	•

● MOVES TAUGHT IN EXCHANGE FOR COLORED SHARDS

Name	Type	Kind	Power	Acc	PP	Range	DA
Mud-Slap	Ground	Special	20	100	10	Normal	—
Fury Cutter	Bug	Physical	10	95	20	Normal	•
ThunderPunch	Electric	Physical	75	100	15	Normal	•
Fire Punch	Fire	Physical	75	100	15	Normal	•
Ice Punch	Ice	Physical	75	100	15	Normal	•
Snore	Normal	Special	40	100	15	Normal	—
Spite	Ghost	Status	—	100	10	Normal	—
Gunk Shot	Poison	Physical	120	70	5	Normal	—
Seed Bomb	Grass	Physical	80	100	15	Normal	—
Last Resort	Normal	Physical	130	100	5	Normal	•
Bounce	Flying	Physical	85	85	5	Normal	•
Knock Off	Dark	Physical	20	100	20	Normal	•
Swift	Normal	Special	60	—	20	2 foes	—
Uproar	Normal	Special	50	100	10	1 random	—

● PRIMARY WAY TO FIND

TRAINER'S PARTY Trainer on Route 216

WILD POKÉMON

COURSE OF STORY

Drifloon

Sinnoh Pokédex — No. 065 — Balloon Pokémon

GHOST | FLYING

HEIGHT: 1'04"
WEIGHT: 2.6 lbs.
GENDER: Male and Female
HELD ITEM: None

● M/F have same form

PLATINUM: Because of the way it floats aimlessly, an old folktale calls it a "Signpost for Wandering Spirits".

EVOLUTION PATH

Drifloon — Lv28 → Drifblim

● TM & HM MOVES

No.	Name	Type	Kind	Power	Acc	PP	Range	DA
TM04	Calm Mind	Psychic	Status	—	—	20	Self	
TM06	Toxic	Poison	Status	—	85	10	Normal	
TM10	Hidden Power	Normal	Special	—	100	15	Normal	
TM11	Sunny Day	Fire	Status	—	—	5	All	
TM17	Protect	Normal	Status	—	—	10	Self	
TM18	Rain Dance	Water	Status	—	—	5	All	
TM21	Frustration	Normal	Physical	—	100	20	Normal	●
TM24	Thunderbolt	Electric	Special	95	100	15	Normal	
TM25	Thunder	Electric	Special	120	70	10	Normal	
TM27	Return	Normal	Physical	—	100	20	Normal	●
TM29	Psychic	Psychic	Special	90	100	10	Normal	
TM30	Shadow Ball	Ghost	Special	80	100	15	Normal	
TM32	Double Team	Normal	Status	—	—	15	Self	
TM34	Shock Wave	Electric	Special	60	—	20	Normal	
TM42	Facade	Normal	Physical	70	100	20	Normal	
TM43	Secret Power	Normal	Physical	70	100	20	Normal	
TM44	Rest	Psychic	Status	—	—	10	Self	
TM45	Attract	Normal	Status	—	100	15	Normal	
TM46	Thief	Dark	Physical	40	100	10	Normal	●
TM48	Skill Swap	Psychic	Status	—	—	10	Normal	
TM57	Charge Beam	Electric	Special	50	90	10	Normal	
TM58	Endure	Normal	Status	—	—	10	Self	
TM61	Will-O-Wisp	Fire	Status	—	75	15	Normal	
TM62	Silver Wind	Bug	Special	60	100	5	Normal	
TM63	Embargo	Dark	Status	—	100	15	Normal	
TM64	Explosion	Normal	Physical	250	100	5	2 foes ● 1 ally	
TM66	Payback	Dark	Physical	50	100	10	Normal	
TM67	Recycle	Normal	Status	—	—	10	Self	
TM70	Flash	Normal	Status	—	100	20	Normal	
TM73	Thunder Wave	Electric	Status	—	100	20	Normal	
TM74	Gyro Ball	Steel	Physical	—	100	5	Normal	●
TM77	Psych Up	Normal	Status	—	—	10	Normal	
TM79	Captivate	Normal	Status	—	100	20	2 foes	
TM82	Sleep Talk	Normal	Status	—	—	10	DoM	
TM83	Natural Gift	Normal	Physical	—	100	15	Normal	
TM85	Dream Eater	Psychic	Special	100	100	15	Normal	
TM87	Swagger	Normal	Status	—	90	15	Normal	
TM90	Substitute	Normal	Status	—	—	10	Self	
HM01	Cut	Normal	Physical	50	95	30	Normal	●
HM05	Defog	Flying	Status	—	—	15	Normal	

● LEVEL-UP AND LEARNED MOVES

Lv	Name	Type	Kind	Power	Acc	PP	Range	DA
Base	Constrict	Normal	Physical	10	100	35	Normal	●
Base	Minimize	Normal	Status	—	—	20	Self	
6	Astonish	Ghost	Physical	30	100	15	Normal	●
11	Gust	Flying	Special	40	100	35	Normal	
14	Focus Energy	Normal	Status	—	—	30	Self	
17	Payback	Dark	Physical	50	100	10	Normal	
22	Stockpile	Normal	Status	—	—	20	Self	
27	Swallow	Normal	Status	—	—	10	Self	
27	Spit Up	Normal	Special	—	100	10	Normal	
30	Ominous Wind	Ghost	Special	60	100	5	Normal	
33	Baton Pass	Normal	Status	—	—	40	Self	
38	Shadow Ball	Ghost	Special	80	100	15	Normal	
43	Explosion	Normal	Physical	250	100	5	2 foes ● 1 ally	

● MOVES TAUGHT IN EXCHANGE FOR COLORED SHARDS

Name	Type	Kind	Power	Acc	PP	Range	DA
Mud-Slap	Ground	Special	20	100	10	Normal	—
Icy Wind	Ice	Special	55	95	15	2 foes	—
Rollout	Rock	Physical	30	90	20	Normal	—
Ominous Wind	Ghost	Special	60	100	5	Normal	—
Snore	Normal	Special	40	100	15	Normal	—
Spite	Ghost	Status	—	100	10	Normal	—
Air Cutter	Flying	Special	55	95	25	2 foes	—
Trick	Psychic	Status	—	100	10	Normal	—
Knock Off	Dark	Physical	20	100	20	Normal	—
Sucker Punch	Dark	Physical	80	100	5	Normal	—
Swift	Normal	Special	60	—	20	2 foes	—

● EGG MOVES

Name	Type	Kind	Power	Acc	PP	Range	DA
Memento	Dark	Status	—	100	10	Normal	—
Body Slam	Normal	Physical	85	100	15	Normal	●
Destiny Bond	Ghost	Status	—	—	5	Self	—
Disable	Normal	Status	—	80	20	Normal	—
Haze	Ice	Status	—	—	30	All	—
Hypnosis	Psychic	Status	—	60	20	Normal	—

● PRIMARY WAY TO FIND

TRAINER'S PARTY: Trainer on Route 214

WILD POKÉMON: Valley Windworks (Fridays only)

COURSE OF STORY:

ABILITY: ● Aftermath ● Unburden

EGG GROUP: Amorphous

STATS:
HP ●●●
ATTACK ●●
DEFENSE ●●
SP. ATTACK ●●
SP. DEFENSE ●●
SPEED ●●●

Drifblim

Sinnoh Pokédex — No. 066 — Blimp Pokémon

GHOST | FLYING

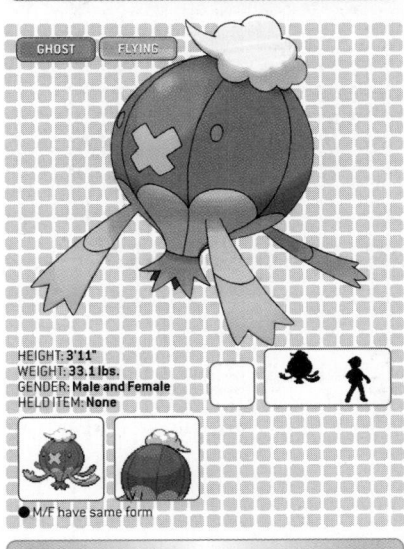

HEIGHT: 3'11"
WEIGHT: 33.1 lbs.
GENDER: Male and Female
HELD ITEM: None

● M/F have same form

PLATINUM: At dusk, swarms of them are carried aloft on winds. When noticed, they suddenly vanish.

EVOLUTION PATH

Drifloon — Lv28 → Drifblim

● TM & HM MOVES

No.	Name	Type	Kind	Power	Acc	PP	Range	DA
TM04	Calm Mind	Psychic	Status	—	—	20	Self	
TM06	Toxic	Poison	Status	—	85	10	Normal	
TM10	Hidden Power	Normal	Special	—	100	15	Normal	
TM11	Sunny Day	Fire	Status	—	—	5	All	
TM15	Hyper Beam	Normal	Special	150	90	5	Normal	
TM17	Protect	Normal	Status	—	—	10	Self	
TM18	Rain Dance	Water	Status	—	—	5	All	
TM21	Frustration	Normal	Physical	—	100	20	Normal	●
TM24	Thunderbolt	Electric	Special	95	100	15	Normal	
TM25	Thunder	Electric	Special	120	70	10	Normal	
TM27	Return	Normal	Physical	—	100	20	Normal	●
TM29	Psychic	Psychic	Special	90	100	10	Normal	
TM30	Shadow Ball	Ghost	Special	80	100	15	Normal	
TM32	Double Team	Normal	Status	—	—	15	Self	
TM34	Shock Wave	Electric	Special	60	—	20	Normal	
TM42	Facade	Normal	Physical	70	100	20	Normal	●
TM43	Secret Power	Normal	Physical	70	100	20	Normal	●
TM44	Rest	Psychic	Status	—	—	10	Self	
TM45	Attract	Normal	Status	—	100	15	Normal	
TM46	Thief	Dark	Physical	40	100	10	Normal	●
TM48	Skill Swap	Psychic	Status	—	—	10	Normal	
TM57	Charge Beam	Electric	Special	50	90	10	Normal	
TM58	Endure	Normal	Status	—	—	10	Self	
TM61	Will-O-Wisp	Fire	Status	—	75	15	Normal	
TM62	Silver Wind	Bug	Special	60	100	5	Normal	
TM63	Embargo	Dark	Status	—	100	15	Normal	
TM64	Explosion	Normal	Physical	250	100	5	2 foes ● 1 ally	
TM66	Payback	Dark	Physical	50	100	10	Normal	
TM67	Recycle	Normal	Status	—	—	10	Self	
TM68	Giga Impact	Normal	Physical	150	90	5	Normal	●
TM70	Flash	Normal	Status	—	100	20	Normal	
TM73	Thunder Wave	Electric	Status	—	100	20	Normal	
TM74	Gyro Ball	Steel	Physical	—	100	5	Normal	●
TM77	Psych Up	Normal	Status	—	—	10	Normal	
TM78	Captivate	Normal	Status	—	100	20	2 foes	
TM82	Sleep Talk	Normal	Status	—	—	10	DoM	
TM83	Natural Gift	Normal	Physical	—	100	15	Normal	
TM85	Dream Eater	Psychic	Special	100	100	15	Normal	
TM87	Swagger	Normal	Status	—	90	15	Normal	
TM90	Substitute	Normal	Status	—	—	10	Self	
HM01	Cut	Normal	Physical	50	95	30	Normal	●
HM02	Fly	Flying	Physical	90	95	15	Normal	●
HM05	Defog	Flying	Status	—	—	15	Normal	

● LEVEL-UP AND LEARNED MOVES

Lv	Name	Type	Kind	Power	Acc	PP	Range	DA
Base	Constrict	Normal	Physical	10	100	35	Normal	●
Base	Minimize	Normal	Status	—	—	20	Self	
Base	Astonish	Ghost	Physical	30	100	15	Normal	●
Base	Gust	Flying	Special	40	100	35	Normal	
6	Astonish	Ghost	Physical	30	100	15	Normal	●
11	Gust	Flying	Special	40	100	35	Normal	
14	Focus Energy	Normal	Status	—	—	30	Self	
17	Payback	Dark	Physical	50	100	10	Normal	
22	Stockpile	Normal	Status	—	—	20	Self	
27	Swallow	Normal	Status	—	—	10	Self	
27	Spit Up	Normal	Special	—	100	10	Normal	
32	Ominous Wind	Ghost	Special	60	100	5	Normal	
37	Baton Pass	Normal	Status	—	—	40	Self	
44	Shadow Ball	Ghost	Special	80	100	15	Normal	
51	Explosion	Normal	Physical	250	100	5	2 foes ● 1 ally	

● MOVES TAUGHT IN EXCHANGE FOR COLORED SHARDS

Name	Type	Kind	Power	Acc	PP	Range	DA
Mud-Slap	Ground	Special	20	100	10	Normal	—
Icy Wind	Ice	Special	55	95	15	2 foes	—
Rollout	Rock	Physical	30	90	20	Normal	—
Ominous Wind	Ghost	Special	60	100	5	Normal	—
Snore	Normal	Special	40	100	15	Normal	—
Spite	Ghost	Status	—	100	10	Normal	—
Air Cutter	Flying	Special	55	95	25	2 foes	—
Trick	Psychic	Status	—	100	10	Normal	—
Knock Off	Dark	Physical	20	100	20	Normal	—
Sucker Punch	Dark	Physical	80	100	5	Normal	—
Swift	Normal	Special	60	—	20	2 foes	—

● PRIMARY WAY TO FIND

TRAINER'S PARTY: Trainer on Route 215

WILD POKÉMON:

COURSE OF STORY:

ABILITY: ● Aftermath ● Unburden

EGG GROUP: Amorphous

STATS:
HP ●●●●
ATTACK ●●●
DEFENSE ●●
SP. ATTACK ●●●
SP. DEFENSE ●●
SPEED ●●●

Buneary

NORMAL

HEIGHT: 1'04"
WEIGHT: 12.1 lbs.
GENDER: Male and Female
HELD ITEM: Chople Berry

● M/F have same form

PLATINUM: Its ears are always rolled up. They can be forcefully extended to shatter even a large boulder.

EVOLUTION PATH

Buneary → (Level up when its Friendship level is high enough) → Lopunny

ABILITY: ● Run Away ● Klutz

EGG GROUP: Field / Human-Like

STATS: HP ●● | ATTACK ●● | DEFENSE ● | SP. ATTACK ● | SP. DEFENSE ● | SPEED ●●●

● TM & HM MOVES

No.	Name	Type	Kind	Power	Acc	PP	Range	DA
TM01	Focus Punch	Fight	Physical	150	100	20	Normal	—
TM03	Water Pulse	Water	Special	60	100	20	Normal	—
TM06	Toxic	Poison	Status	—	85	10	Normal	—
TM10	Hidden Power	Normal	Special	—	100	15	Normal	—
TM11	Sunny Day	Fire	Status	—	—	5	All	—
TM13	Ice Beam	Ice	Special	95	100	10	Normal	—
TM17	Protect	Normal	Status	—	—	10	Self	—
TM18	Rain Dance	Water	Status	—	—	5	All	—
TM21	Frustration	Normal	Physical	—	100	20	Normal	•
TM22	SolarBeam	Grass	Special	120	100	10	Normal	—
TM23	Iron Tail	Steel	Physical	100	75	15	Normal	•
TM24	Thunderbolt	Electric	Special	95	100	15	Normal	—
TM27	Return	Normal	Physical	—	100	20	Normal	•
TM28	Dig	Ground	Physical	80	100	10	Normal	•
TM30	Shadow Ball	Ghost	Special	80	100	15	Normal	—
TM32	Double Team	Normal	Status	—	—	15	Self	—
TM34	Shock Wave	Electric	Special	60	—	20	Normal	—
TM42	Facade	Normal	Physical	70	100	20	Normal	•
TM43	Secret Power	Normal	Physical	70	100	20	Normal	•
TM44	Rest	Psychic	Status	—	—	10	Self	—
TM45	Attract	Normal	Status	—	100	15	Normal	—
TM56	Fling	Dark	Physical	—	100	10	Normal	•
TM57	Charge Beam	Electric	Special	50	90	10	Normal	—
TM58	Endure	Normal	Status	—	—	10	Self	—
TM60	Drain Punch	Fight	Physical	60	100	5	Normal	•
TM73	Thunder Wave	Electric	Status	—	100	20	Normal	—
TM78	Captivate	Normal	Status	—	100	20	2 foes	—
TM82	Sleep Talk	Normal	Status	—	—	10	DoM	—
TM83	Natural Gift	Normal	Physical	—	100	15	Normal	•
TM86	Grass Knot	Grass	Special	—	100	20	Normal	•
TM87	Swagger	Normal	Status	—	90	15	Normal	—
TM90	Substitute	Normal	Status	—	—	10	Self	—
HM01	Cut	Normal	Physical	50	95	30	Normal	•
HM06	Rock Smash	Fight	Physical	40	100	15	Normal	•

● LEVEL-UP AND LEARNED MOVES

Lv	Name	Type	Kind	Power	Acc	PP	Range	DA
Base	Splash	Normal	Status	—	—	40	Self	—
Base	Pound	Normal	Physical	40	100	35	Normal	•
Base	Defense Curl	Normal	Status	—	—	40	Self	—
Base	Foresight	Normal	Status	—	—	40	Normal	—
6	Endure	Normal	Status	—	—	10	Self	—
13	Frustration	Normal	Physical	—	100	20	Normal	•
16	Quick Attack	Normal	Physical	40	100	30	Normal	•
23	Jump Kick	Fight	Physical	85	95	25	Normal	•
26	Baton Pass	Normal	Status	—	—	40	Self	—
33	Agility	Psychic	Status	—	—	30	Self	—
36	Dizzy Punch	Normal	Physical	70	100	10	Normal	•
43	Charm	Normal	Status	—	100	20	Normal	—
46	Bounce	Flying	Physical	85	85	5	Normal	•
53	Healing Wish	Psychic	Status	—	—	10	Self	—

● MOVES TAUGHT IN EXCHANGE FOR COLORED SHARDS

Name	Type	Kind	Power	Acc	PP	Range	DA
Mud-Slap	Ground	Special	20	100	10	Normal	—
Snore	Normal	Special	40	100	15	Normal	—
Helping Hand	Normal	Status	—	—	20	1 ally	—
Endeavor	Normal	Physical	—	100	5	Normal	•
Last Resort	Normal	Physical	130	100	5	Normal	•
Bounce	Flying	Physical	85	85	5	Normal	•
Swift	Normal	Special	60	—	20	2 foes	—
Uproar	Normal	Special	50	100	10	1 random	—

● EGG MOVES

Name	Type	Kind	Power	Acc	PP	Range	DA
Fake Tears	Dark	Status	—	100	20	Normal	—
Fake Out	Normal	Physical	40	100	10	Normal	•
Encore	Normal	Status	—	100	5	Normal	—
Sweet Kiss	Normal	Status	—	75	10	Normal	—
Double Hit	Normal	Physical	35	90	10	Normal	•
Attract	Normal	Status	—	100	15	Normal	—
Low Kick	Fight	Physical	—	100	20	Normal	•
Sky Uppercut	Fight	Physical	85	90	15	Normal	•
Switcheroo	Dark	Status	—	100	10	Normal	—
ThunderPunch	Electric	Physical	75	100	15	Normal	•
Ice Punch	Ice	Physical	75	100	15	Normal	•
Fire Punch	Fire	Physical	75	100	15	Normal	•

● PRIMARY WAY TO FIND

TRAINER'S PARTY: Trainer in Wayward Cave

WILD POKÉMON: Eterna Forest

COURSE OF STORY:

Lopunny

NORMAL

HEIGHT: 3'11"
WEIGHT: 73.4 lbs.
GENDER: Male and Female
HELD ITEM: None

● M/F have same form

PLATINUM: The ears appear to be delicate. If they are touched roughly, it kicks with its graceful legs.

EVOLUTION PATH

Buneary → (Level up when its Friendship level is high enough) → Lopunny

ABILITY: ● Cute Charm ● Klutz

EGG GROUP: Field / Human-Like

STATS: HP ●● | ATTACK ●● | DEFENSE ●● | SP. ATTACK ●● | SP. DEFENSE ●● | SPEED ●●●●

● TM & HM MOVES

No.	Name	Type	Kind	Power	Acc	PP	Range	DA
TM01	Focus Punch	Fight	Physical	150	100	20	Normal	•
TM03	Water Pulse	Water	Special	60	100	20	Normal	•
TM06	Toxic	Poison	Status	—	85	10	Normal	—
TM10	Hidden Power	Normal	Special	—	100	15	Normal	—
TM11	Sunny Day	Fire	Status	—	—	5	All	—
TM13	Ice Beam	Ice	Special	95	100	10	Normal	—
TM14	Blizzard	Ice	Special	120	70	5	2 foes	—
TM15	Hyper Beam	Normal	Special	150	90	5	Normal	—
TM17	Protect	Normal	Status	—	—	10	Self	—
TM18	Rain Dance	Water	Status	—	—	5	All	—
TM21	Frustration	Normal	Physical	—	100	20	Normal	•
TM22	SolarBeam	Grass	Special	120	100	10	Normal	—
TM23	Iron Tail	Steel	Physical	100	75	15	Normal	•
TM24	Thunderbolt	Electric	Special	95	100	15	Normal	—
TM25	Thunder	Electric	Special	120	70	10	Normal	—
TM27	Return	Normal	Physical	—	100	20	Normal	•
TM28	Dig	Ground	Physical	80	100	10	Normal	•
TM30	Shadow Ball	Ghost	Special	80	100	15	Normal	—
TM32	Double Team	Normal	Status	—	—	15	Self	—
TM34	Shock Wave	Electric	Special	60	—	20	Normal	—
TM42	Facade	Normal	Physical	70	100	20	Normal	•
TM43	Secret Power	Normal	Physical	70	100	20	Normal	•
TM44	Rest	Psychic	Status	—	—	10	Self	—
TM45	Attract	Normal	Status	—	100	15	Normal	—
TM52	Focus Blast	Fight	Special	120	70	5	Normal	—
TM56	Fling	Dark	Physical	—	100	10	Normal	•
TM57	Charge Beam	Electric	Special	50	90	10	Normal	—
TM58	Endure	Normal	Status	—	—	10	Self	—
TM60	Drain Punch	Fight	Physical	60	100	5	Normal	•
TM68	Giga Impact	Normal	Physical	150	90	5	Normal	•
TM73	Thunder Wave	Electric	Status	—	100	20	Normal	—
TM78	Captivate	Normal	Status	—	100	20	2 foes	—
TM82	Sleep Talk	Normal	Status	—	—	10	DoM	—
TM83	Natural Gift	Normal	Physical	—	100	15	Normal	•
TM86	Grass Knot	Grass	Special	—	100	20	Normal	•
TM87	Swagger	Normal	Status	—	90	15	Normal	—
TM90	Substitute	Normal	Status	—	—	10	Self	—
HM01	Cut	Normal	Physical	50	95	30	Normal	•
HM04	Strength	Normal	Physical	80	100	15	Normal	•
HM06	Rock Smash	Fight	Physical	40	100	15	Normal	•

● LEVEL-UP AND LEARNED MOVES

Lv	Name	Type	Kind	Power	Acc	PP	Range	DA
Base	Mirror Coat	Psychic	Special	—	100	20	Self	—
Base	Magic Coat	Psychic	Status	—	—	15	Self	—
Base	Splash	Normal	Status	—	—	40	Self	—
Base	Pound	Normal	Physical	40	100	35	Normal	•
Base	Defense Curl	Normal	Status	—	—	40	Self	—
Base	Foresight	Normal	Status	—	—	40	Normal	—
6	Endure	Normal	Status	—	—	10	Self	—
13	Return	Normal	Physical	—	100	20	Normal	•
16	Quick Attack	Normal	Physical	40	100	30	Normal	•
23	Jump Kick	Fight	Physical	85	95	25	Normal	•
26	Baton Pass	Normal	Status	—	—	40	Self	—
33	Agility	Psychic	Status	—	—	30	Self	—
36	Dizzy Punch	Normal	Physical	70	100	10	Normal	•
43	Charm	Normal	Status	—	100	20	Normal	—
46	Bounce	Flying	Physical	85	85	5	Normal	•
53	Healing Wish	Psychic	Status	—	—	10	Self	—

● MOVES TAUGHT IN EXCHANGE FOR COLORED SHARDS

Name	Type	Kind	Power	Acc	PP	Range	DA
Mud-Slap	Ground	Special	20	100	10	Normal	—
Fury Cutter	Bug	Physical	10	95	20	Normal	•
ThunderPunch	Electric	Physical	75	100	15	Normal	•
Fire Punch	Fire	Physical	75	100	15	Normal	•
Ice Punch	Ice	Physical	75	100	15	Normal	•
Snore	Normal	Special	40	100	15	Normal	—
Helping Hand	Normal	Status	—	—	20	1 ally	—
Endeavor	Normal	Physical	—	100	5	Normal	•
Last Resort	Normal	Physical	130	100	5	Normal	•
Bounce	Flying	Physical	85	85	5	Normal	•
Swift	Normal	Special	60	—	20	2 foes	—
Uproar	Normal	Special	50	100	10	1 random	—

● PRIMARY WAY TO FIND

TRAINER'S PARTY: Trainer on Route 221

WILD POKÉMON:

COURSE OF STORY:

Gastly

GHOST   POISON

HEIGHT: 4'03"
WEIGHT: 0.2 lbs.
GENDER: Male and Female
HELD ITEM: None

● M/F have same form

PLATINUM: Born from gases, anyone would faint if engulfed by its gaseous body, which contains poison.

EVOLUTION PATH

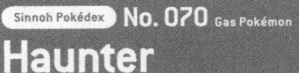

Gastly —Lv25→ Haunter —Link Trade→ Gengar

ABILITY ● Levitate

EGG GROUP Amorphous

STATS
HP ●
ATTACK ●
DEFENSE ●
SP. ATTACK ●●●●
SP. DEFENSE ●●
SPEED ●●●

● TM & HM MOVES

No.	Name	Type	Kind	Power	Acc	PP	Range	DA
TM06	Toxic	Poison	Status	—	85	10	Normal	—
TM10	Hidden Power	Normal	Special	—	100	15	Normal	—
TM11	Sunny Day	Fire	Status	—	—	5	All	—
TM12	Taunt	Dark	Status	—	100	20	Normal	—
TM17	Protect	Normal	Status	—	—	10	Self	—
TM18	Rain Dance	Water	Status	—	—	5	All	—
TM19	Giga Drain	Grass	Special	60	100	10	Normal	—
TM21	Frustration	Normal	Physical	—	100	20	Normal	●
TM24	Thunderbolt	Electric	Special	95	100	15	Normal	—
TM27	Return	Normal	Physical	—	100	20	Normal	●
TM29	Psychic	Psychic	Special	90	100	10	Normal	—
TM30	Shadow Ball	Ghost	Special	80	100	15	Normal	—
TM32	Double Team	Normal	Status	—	—	15	Self	—
TM36	Sludge Bomb	Poison	Special	90	100	10	Normal	—
TM41	Torment	Dark	Status	—	100	15	Normal	—
TM42	Facade	Normal	Physical	70	100	20	Normal	—
TM43	Secret Power	Normal	Physical	70	100	20	Normal	—
TM44	Rest	Psychic	Status	—	—	10	Self	—
TM45	Attract	Normal	Status	—	100	15	Normal	—
TM46	Thief	Dark	Physical	40	100	10	Normal	●
TM48	Skill Swap	Psychic	Status	—	—	10	Normal	—
TM49	Snatch	Dark	Status	—	—	10	DoM	—
TM53	Energy Ball	Grass	Special	80	100	10	Normal	—
TM58	Endure	Normal	Status	—	—	10	Self	—
TM61	Will-O-Wisp	Fire	Status	—	75	15	Normal	—
TM63	Embargo	Dark	Status	—	100	15	Normal	—
TM64	Explosion	Normal	Physical	250	100	5	2 foes • 1 ally	—
TM66	Payback	Dark	Physical	50	100	10	Normal	●
TM77	Psych Up	Normal	Status	—	—	10	Normal	—
TM78	Captivate	Normal	Status	—	100	20	2 foes	—
TM79	Dark Pulse	Dark	Special	80	100	15	Normal	—
TM82	Sleep Talk	Normal	Status	—	—	10	DoM	—
TM83	Natural Gift	Normal	Physical	—	100	15	Normal	—
TM85	Dream Eater	Psychic	Special	100	100	15	Normal	—
TM87	Swagger	Normal	Status	—	90	15	Normal	—
TM90	Substitute	Normal	Status	—	—	10	Self	—
TM92	Trick Room	Psychic	Status	—	—	5	All	—

● LEVEL-UP AND LEARNED MOVES

Lv	Name	Type	Kind	Power	Acc	PP	Range	DA
Base	Hypnosis	Psychic	Status	—	60	20	Normal	—
Base	Lick	Ghost	Physical	20	100	30	Normal	●
5	Spite	Ghost	Status	—	100	10	Normal	—
8	Mean Look	Normal	Status	—	—	5	Normal	—
12	Curse	???	Status	—	—	10	Normal • Self	—
15	Night Shade	Ghost	Special	—	100	15	Normal	—
19	Confuse Ray	Ghost	Status	—	100	10	Normal	—
22	Sucker Punch	Dark	Physical	80	100	5	Normal	●
26	Payback	Dark	Physical	50	100	10	Normal	●
29	Shadow Ball	Ghost	Special	80	100	15	Normal	—
33	Dream Eater	Psychic	Special	100	100	15	Normal	—
36	Dark Pulse	Dark	Special	80	100	15	Normal	—
40	Destiny Bond	Ghost	Status	—	—	5	Self	—
43	Nightmare	Ghost	Status	—	100	15	Normal	—

● MOVES TAUGHT IN EXCHANGE FOR COLORED SHARDS

Name	Type	Kind	Power	Acc	PP	Range	DA
Icy Wind	Ice	Special	55	95	15	2 foes	●
ThunderPunch	Electric	Physical	75	100	15	Normal	●
Fire Punch	Fire	Physical	75	100	15	Normal	●
Ice Punch	Ice	Physical	75	100	15	Normal	●
Ominous Wind	Ghost	Special	60	100	5	Normal	●
Snore	Normal	Special	40	100	15	Normal	—
Spite	Ghost	Status	—	100	10	Normal	—
Trick	Psychic	Status	—	100	10	Normal	—
Knock Off	Dark	Physical	20	100	20	Normal	●
Sucker Punch	Dark	Physical	80	100	5	Normal	●
Uproar	Normal	Special	50	100	10	1 random	—

● EGG MOVES

Name	Type	Kind	Power	Acc	PP	Range	DA
Psywave	Psychic	Special	—	80	15	Normal	—
Perish Song	Normal	Status	—	—	5	All	—
Haze	Ice	Status	—	—	30	All	—
Astonish	Ghost	Physical	30	100	15	Normal	●
Will-O-Wisp	Fire	Status	—	75	15	Normal	—
Grudge	Ghost	Status	—	—	5	Self	—
Explosion	Normal	Physical	250	100	5	2 foes • 1 ally	—
Fire Punch	Fire	Physical	75	100	15	Normal	●
Ice Punch	Ice	Physical	75	100	15	Normal	●
ThunderPunch	Electric	Physical	75	100	15	Normal	●

● PRIMARY WAY TO FIND

TRAINER'S PARTY: Trainer at Hearthome Gym
WILD POKÉMON: Old Chateau
COURSE OF STORY:

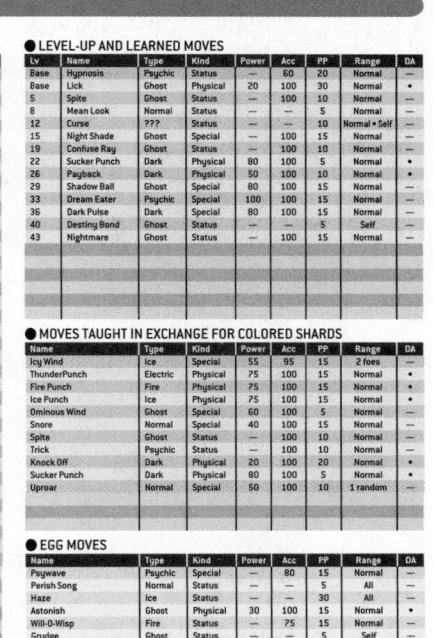

Haunter

GHOST   POISON

HEIGHT: 5'03"
WEIGHT: 0.2 lbs.
GENDER: Male and Female
HELD ITEM: None

● M/F have same form

PLATINUM: It likes to lurk in the dark and tap shoulders with a gaseous hand. Its touch causes endless shuddering.

EVOLUTION PATH

Gastly —Lv25→ Haunter —Link Trade→ Gengar

ABILITY ● Levitate

EGG GROUP Amorphous

STATS
HP ●
ATTACK ●●
DEFENSE ●●
SP. ATTACK ●●●●
SP. DEFENSE ●●
SPEED ●●●

● TM & HM MOVES

No.	Name	Type	Kind	Power	Acc	PP	Range	DA
TM06	Toxic	Poison	Status	—	85	10	Normal	—
TM10	Hidden Power	Normal	Special	—	100	15	Normal	—
TM11	Sunny Day	Fire	Status	—	—	5	All	—
TM12	Taunt	Dark	Status	—	100	20	Normal	—
TM17	Protect	Normal	Status	—	—	10	Self	—
TM18	Rain Dance	Water	Status	—	—	5	All	—
TM19	Giga Drain	Grass	Special	60	100	10	Normal	—
TM21	Frustration	Normal	Physical	—	100	20	Normal	●
TM24	Thunderbolt	Electric	Special	95	100	15	Normal	—
TM27	Return	Normal	Physical	—	100	20	Normal	●
TM29	Psychic	Psychic	Special	90	100	10	Normal	—
TM30	Shadow Ball	Ghost	Special	80	100	15	Normal	—
TM32	Double Team	Normal	Status	—	—	15	Self	—
TM36	Sludge Bomb	Poison	Special	90	100	10	Normal	—
TM41	Torment	Dark	Status	—	100	15	Normal	—
TM42	Facade	Normal	Physical	70	100	20	Normal	—
TM43	Secret Power	Normal	Physical	70	100	20	Normal	—
TM44	Rest	Psychic	Status	—	—	10	Self	—
TM45	Attract	Normal	Status	—	100	15	Normal	—
TM46	Thief	Dark	Physical	40	100	10	Normal	●
TM48	Skill Swap	Psychic	Status	—	—	10	Normal	—
TM49	Snatch	Dark	Status	—	—	10	DoM	—
TM53	Energy Ball	Grass	Special	80	100	10	Normal	—
TM56	Fling	Dark	Physical	—	100	10	Normal	—
TM58	Endure	Normal	Status	—	—	10	Self	—
TM61	Will-O-Wisp	Fire	Status	—	75	15	Normal	—
TM63	Embargo	Dark	Status	—	100	15	Normal	—
TM64	Explosion	Normal	Physical	250	100	5	2 foes • 1 ally	—
TM65	Shadow Claw	Ghost	Physical	70	100	15	Normal	●
TM66	Payback	Dark	Physical	50	100	10	Normal	●
TM77	Psych Up	Normal	Status	—	—	10	Normal	—
TM78	Captivate	Normal	Status	—	100	20	2 foes	—
TM79	Dark Pulse	Dark	Special	80	100	15	Normal	—
TM82	Sleep Talk	Normal	Status	—	—	10	DoM	—
TM83	Natural Gift	Normal	Physical	—	100	15	Normal	—
TM84	Poison Jab	Poison	Physical	80	100	20	Normal	●
TM85	Dream Eater	Psychic	Special	100	100	15	Normal	—
TM87	Swagger	Normal	Status	—	90	15	Normal	—
TM90	Substitute	Normal	Status	—	—	10	Self	—
TM92	Trick Room	Psychic	Status	—	—	5	All	—

● LEVEL-UP AND LEARNED MOVES

Lv	Name	Type	Kind	Power	Acc	PP	Range	DA
Base	Hypnosis	Psychic	Status	—	60	20	Normal	—
Base	Lick	Ghost	Physical	20	100	30	Normal	●
Base	Spite	Ghost	Status	—	100	10	Normal	—
5	Spite	Ghost	Status	—	100	10	Normal	—
8	Mean Look	Normal	Status	—	—	5	Normal	—
12	Curse	???	Status	—	—	10	Normal • Self	—
15	Night Shade	Ghost	Special	—	100	15	Normal	—
19	Confuse Ray	Ghost	Status	—	100	10	Normal	—
22	Sucker Punch	Dark	Physical	80	100	5	Normal	●
25	Shadow Punch	Ghost	Physical	60	—	20	Normal	●
28	Payback	Dark	Physical	50	100	10	Normal	●
33	Shadow Ball	Ghost	Special	80	100	15	Normal	—
39	Dream Eater	Psychic	Special	100	100	15	Normal	—
44	Dark Pulse	Dark	Special	80	100	15	Normal	—
50	Destiny Bond	Ghost	Status	—	—	5	Self	—
55	Nightmare	Ghost	Status	—	100	15	Normal	—

● MOVES TAUGHT IN EXCHANGE FOR COLORED SHARDS

Name	Type	Kind	Power	Acc	PP	Range	DA
Icy Wind	Ice	Special	55	95	15	2 foes	●
ThunderPunch	Electric	Physical	75	100	15	Normal	●
Fire Punch	Fire	Physical	75	100	15	Normal	●
Ice Punch	Ice	Physical	75	100	15	Normal	●
Ominous Wind	Ghost	Special	60	100	5	Normal	●
Snore	Normal	Special	40	100	15	Normal	—
Spite	Ghost	Status	—	100	10	Normal	—
Trick	Psychic	Status	—	100	10	Normal	—
Knock Off	Dark	Physical	20	100	20	Normal	●
Sucker Punch	Dark	Physical	80	100	5	Normal	●
Uproar	Normal	Special	50	100	10	1 random	—

● PRIMARY WAY TO FIND

TRAINER'S PARTY: Hearthome Gym Leader Fantina
WILD POKÉMON: Turnback Cave
COURSE OF STORY:

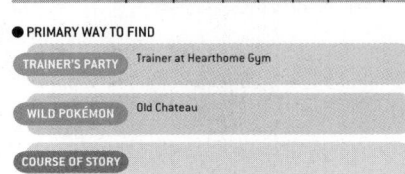

Sinnoh Pokédex **No. 071** Shadow Pokémon

Gengar

GHOST | POISON

HEIGHT: **4'11"**
WEIGHT: **89.3 lbs.**
GENDER: **Male and Female**
HELD ITEM: **None**

● M/F have same form

PLATINUM The leer that floats in darkness belongs to a GENGAR delighting in casting curses on people.

EVOLUTION PATH

Lv25
Link Trade
Gastly
Haunter
Gengar

● TM & HM MOVES

No.	Name	Type	Kind	Power	Acc	PP	Range	DA
TM01	Focus Punch	Fight	Physical	150	100	20	Normal	•
TM06	Toxic	Poison	Status	—	85	10	Normal	—
TM10	Hidden Power	Normal	Special	—	100	15	Normal	—
TM11	Sunny Day	Fire	Status	—	—	5	All	—
TM12	Taunt	Dark	Status	—	100	20	Normal	—
TM15	Hyper Beam	Normal	Special	150	90	5	Normal	—
TM17	Protect	Normal	Status	—	—	10	Self	—
TM18	Rain Dance	Water	Status	—	—	5	All	—
TM19	Giga Drain	Grass	Special	60	100	10	Normal	—
TM21	Frustration	Normal	Physical	—	100	20	Normal	•
TM24	Thunderbolt	Electric	Special	95	100	15	Normal	—
TM25	Thunder	Electric	Special	120	70	10	Normal	—
TM27	Return	Normal	Physical	—	100	20	Normal	•
TM29	Psychic	Psychic	Special	90	100	10	Normal	—
TM30	Shadow Ball	Ghost	Special	80	100	15	Normal	—
TM31	Brick Break	Fight	Physical	75	100	15	Normal	•
TM32	Double Team	Normal	Status	—	—	15	Self	—
TM36	Sludge Bomb	Poison	Special	90	100	10	Normal	—
TM41	Torment	Dark	Status	—	100	15	Normal	—
TM42	Facade	Normal	Physical	70	100	20	Normal	•
TM43	Secret Power	Normal	Physical	70	100	20	Normal	—
TM44	Rest	Psychic	Status	—	—	10	Self	—
TM45	Attract	Normal	Status	—	100	15	Normal	—
TM46	Thief	Dark	Physical	40	100	10	Normal	•
TM48	Skill Swap	Psychic	Status	—	—	10	Normal	—
TM49	Snatch	Dark	Status	—	—	10	DoM	—
TM52	Focus Blast	Fight	Special	120	70	5	Normal	—
TM53	Energy Ball	Grass	Special	80	100	10	Normal	—
TM56	Fling	Dark	Physical	—	100	10	Normal	—
TM58	Endure	Normal	Status	—	—	10	Self	—
TM60	Drain Punch	Fight	Physical	60	100	5	Normal	•
TM61	Will-O-Wisp	Fire	Status	—	75	15	Normal	—
TM63	Embargo	Dark	Status	—	100	15	Normal	—
TM64	Explosion	Normal	Physical	250	100	5	2 foes • 1 ally	—
TM65	Shadow Claw	Ghost	Physical	70	100	15	Normal	•
TM66	Payback	Dark	Physical	50	100	10	Normal	•
TM68	Giga Impact	Normal	Physical	150	90	5	Normal	•
TM77	Psych Up	Normal	Status	—	—	10	Normal	—
TM78	Captivate	Normal	Status	—	100	20	2 foes	—
TM79	Dark Pulse	Dark	Special	80	100	15	Normal	—
TM82	Sleep Talk	Normal	Status	—	—	10	DoM	—
TM83	Natural Gift	Normal	Physical	—	100	15	Normal	—
TM84	Poison Jab	Poison	Physical	80	100	20	Normal	•
TM85	Dream Eater	Psychic	Special	100	100	15	Normal	—
TM87	Swagger	Normal	Status	—	90	15	Normal	—
TM90	Substitute	Normal	Status	—	—	10	Self	—
TM92	Trick Room	Psychic	Status	—	—	5	All	—
HM04	Strength	Normal	Physical	80	100	15	Normal	•
HM06	Rock Smash	Fight	Physical	40	100	15	Normal	•

ABILITY ● **Levitate**

EGG GROUP **Amorphous**

STATS
HP ●●
ATTACK ●●
DEFENSE ●●
SP. ATTACK ●●●●●
SP. DEFENSE ●●
SPEED ●●●●

● LEVEL-UP AND LEARNED MOVES

Lv	Name	Type	Kind	Power	Acc	PP	Range	DA
Base	Hypnosis	Psychic	Status	—	60	20	Normal	—
Base	Lick	Ghost	Physical	20	100	30	Normal	•
Base	Spite	Ghost	Status	—	100	10	Normal	—
5	Spite	Ghost	Status	—	100	10	Normal	—
8	Mean Look	Normal	Status	—	—	5	Normal	—
12	Curse	???	Status	—	—	10	Normal • Self	—
15	Night Shade	Ghost	Special	—	100	15	Normal	—
19	Confuse Ray	Ghost	Status	—	100	10	Normal	—
22	Sucker Punch	Dark	Physical	80	100	5	Normal	•
25	Shadow Punch	Ghost	Physical	60	—	20	Normal	•
28	Payback	Dark	Physical	50	100	10	Normal	•
33	Shadow Ball	Ghost	Special	80	100	15	Normal	—
39	Dream Eater	Psychic	Special	100	100	15	Normal	—
44	Dark Pulse	Dark	Special	80	100	15	Normal	—
50	Destiny Bond	Ghost	Status	—	—	5	Self	—
55	Nightmare	Ghost	Status	—	100	15	Normal	—

● MOVES TAUGHT IN EXCHANGE FOR COLORED SHARDS

Name	Type	Kind	Power	Acc	PP	Range	DA
Icy Wind	Ice	Special	55	95	15	2 foes	—
ThunderPunch	Electric	Physical	75	100	15	Normal	•
Fire Punch	Fire	Physical	75	100	15	Normal	•
Ice Punch	Ice	Physical	75	100	15	Normal	•
Ominous Wind	Ghost	Special	60	100	5	Normal	—
Snore	Normal	Special	40	100	15	Normal	—
Spite	Ghost	Status	—	100	10	Normal	—
Trick	Psychic	Status	—	100	10	Normal	—
Knock Off	Dark	Physical	20	100	20	Normal	•
Sucker Punch	Dark	Physical	80	100	5	Normal	•
Uproar	Normal	Special	50	100	10	1 random	—

● PRIMARY WAY TO FIND

TRAINER'S PARTY Trainer on Victory Road

WILD POKÉMON

COURSE OF STORY

Sinnoh Pokédex **No. 072** Screech Pokémon

Misdreavus

GHOST

HEIGHT: **2'04"**
WEIGHT: **2.2 lbs.**
GENDER: **Male and Female**
HELD ITEM: **None**

● M/F have same form

PLATINUM A Pokémon that startles people in the middle of the night. It gathers fear as its energy.

EVOLUTION PATH

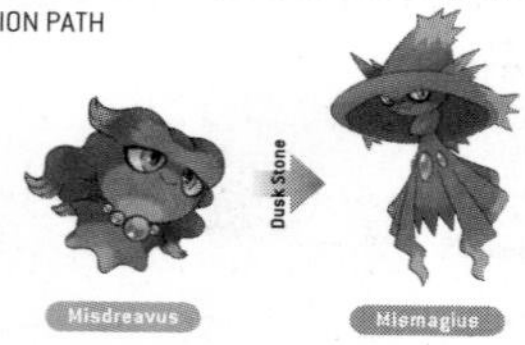

Dusk Stone
Misdreavus
Mismagius

● TM & HM MOVES

No.	Name	Type	Kind	Power	Acc	PP	Range	DA
TM04	Calm Mind	Psychic	Status	—	—	20	Self	—
TM06	Toxic	Poison	Status	—	85	10	Normal	—
TM10	Hidden Power	Normal	Special	—	100	15	Normal	—
TM11	Sunny Day	Fire	Status	—	—	5	All	—
TM12	Taunt	Dark	Status	—	100	20	Normal	—
TM17	Protect	Normal	Status	—	—	10	Self	—
TM18	Rain Dance	Water	Status	—	—	5	All	—
TM21	Frustration	Normal	Physical	—	100	20	Normal	•
TM24	Thunderbolt	Electric	Special	95	100	15	Normal	—
TM25	Thunder	Electric	Special	120	70	10	Normal	—
TM27	Return	Normal	Physical	—	100	20	Normal	•
TM29	Psychic	Psychic	Special	90	100	10	Normal	—
TM30	Shadow Ball	Ghost	Special	80	100	15	Normal	—
TM32	Double Team	Normal	Status	—	—	15	Self	—
TM34	Shock Wave	Electric	Special	60	—	20	Normal	—
TM40	Aerial Ace	Flying	Physical	60	—	20	Normal	•
TM41	Torment	Dark	Status	—	100	15	Normal	—
TM42	Facade	Normal	Physical	70	100	20	Normal	•
TM43	Secret Power	Normal	Physical	70	100	20	Normal	—
TM44	Rest	Psychic	Status	—	—	10	Self	—
TM45	Attract	Normal	Status	—	100	15	Normal	—
TM46	Thief	Dark	Physical	40	100	10	Normal	•
TM48	Skill Swap	Psychic	Status	—	—	10	Normal	—
TM49	Snatch	Dark	Status	—	—	10	DoM	—
TM57	Charge Beam	Electric	Special	50	90	10	Normal	—
TM58	Endure	Normal	Status	—	—	10	Self	—
TM61	Will-O-Wisp	Fire	Status	—	75	15	Normal	—
TM63	Embargo	Dark	Status	—	100	15	Normal	—
TM66	Payback	Dark	Physical	50	100	10	Normal	•
TM70	Flash	Normal	Status	—	100	20	Normal	—
TM73	Thunder Wave	Electric	Status	—	100	20	Normal	—
TM77	Psych Up	Normal	Status	—	—	10	Normal	—
TM78	Captivate	Normal	Status	—	100	20	2 foes	—
TM79	Dark Pulse	Dark	Special	80	100	15	Normal	—
TM82	Sleep Talk	Normal	Status	—	—	10	DoM	—
TM83	Natural Gift	Normal	Physical	—	100	15	Normal	—
TM85	Dream Eater	Psychic	Special	100	100	15	Normal	—
TM87	Swagger	Normal	Status	—	90	15	Normal	—
TM90	Substitute	Normal	Status	—	—	10	Self	—
TM92	Trick Room	Psychic	Status	—	—	5	All	—

ABILITY ● **Levitate**

EGG GROUP **Amorphous**

STATS
HP ●●
ATTACK ●●
DEFENSE ●●
SP. ATTACK ●●●
SP. DEFENSE ●●
SPEED ●●●●●

● LEVEL-UP AND LEARNED MOVES

Lv	Name	Type	Kind	Power	Acc	PP	Range	DA
Base	Growl	Normal	Status	—	100	40	2 foes	—
Base	Psywave	Psychic	Special	—	80	15	Normal	—
5	Spite	Ghost	Status	—	100	10	Normal	—
10	Astonish	Ghost	Physical	30	100	15	Normal	•
14	Confuse Ray	Ghost	Status	—	100	10	Normal	—
19	Mean Look	Normal	Status	—	—	5	Normal	—
23	Psybeam	Psychic	Special	65	100	20	Normal	—
28	Pain Split	Normal	Status	—	—	20	Normal	—
32	Payback	Dark	Physical	50	100	10	Normal	•
37	Shadow Ball	Ghost	Special	80	100	15	Normal	—
41	Perish Song	Normal	Status	—	—	5	All	—
46	Grudge	Ghost	Status	—	—	5	Self	—
50	Power Gem	Rock	Special	70	100	20	Normal	—

● MOVES TAUGHT IN EXCHANGE FOR COLORED SHARDS

Name	Type	Kind	Power	Acc	PP	Range	DA
Icy Wind	Ice	Special	55	95	15	2 foes	—
Ominous Wind	Ghost	Special	60	100	5	Normal	—
Snore	Normal	Special	40	100	15	Normal	—
Spite	Ghost	Status	—	100	10	Normal	—
Trick	Psychic	Status	—	100	10	Normal	—
Sucker Punch	Dark	Physical	80	100	5	Normal	•
Swift	Normal	Special	60	—	20	2 foes	—
Uproar	Normal	Special	50	100	10	1 random	—

● EGG MOVES

Name	Type	Kind	Power	Acc	PP	Range	DA
Screech	Normal	Status	—	85	40	Normal	—
Destiny Bond	Ghost	Status	—	—	5	Self	—
Psych Up	Normal	Status	—	—	10	Normal	—
Imprison	Psychic	Status	—	—	10	Self	—
Memento	Dark	Status	—	100	10	Normal	—
Sucker Punch	Dark	Physical	80	100	5	Normal	•
Shadow Sneak	Ghost	Physical	40	100	30	Normal	•
Curse	???	Status	—	—	10	Normal • Self	—
Spite	Ghost	Status	—	100	10	Normal	—
Ominous Wind	Ghost	Special	60	100	5	Normal	—

● PRIMARY WAY TO FIND

TRAINER'S PARTY Trainer on 4F of the Lost Tower

WILD POKÉMON

COURSE OF STORY

Mismagius

GHOST

HEIGHT: 2'11"
WEIGHT: 9.7 lbs.
GENDER: Male and Female
HELD ITEM: None

● M/F have same form

PLATINUM Its cry sounds like an incantation. It is said the cry may rarely be imbued with happiness-giving power.

EVOLUTION PATH

Misdreavus → (Dusk Stone) → Mismagius

ABILITY ● Levitate

EGG GROUP Amorphous

STATS
HP ●●
ATTACK ●●
DEFENSE ●●
SP. ATTACK ●●●
SP. DEFENSE ●●●●
SPEED ●●●●

● TM & HM MOVES

No.	Name	Type	Kind	Power	Acc	PP	Range	DA
TM04	Calm Mind	Psychic	Status	—	—	20	Self	—
TM06	Toxic	Poison	Status	—	85	10	Normal	—
TM10	Hidden Power	Normal	Special	—	100	15	Normal	—
TM11	Sunny Day	Fire	Status	—	—	5	All	—
TM12	Taunt	Dark	Status	—	100	20	Normal	—
TM15	Hyper Beam	Normal	Special	150	90	5	Normal	—
TM17	Protect	Normal	Status	—	—	10	Self	—
TM18	Rain Dance	Water	Status	—	—	5	All	—
TM21	Frustration	Normal	Physical	—	100	20	Normal	●
TM24	Thunderbolt	Electric	Special	95	100	15	Normal	—
TM25	Thunder	Electric	Special	120	70	10	Normal	—
TM27	Return	Normal	Physical	—	100	20	Normal	●
TM29	Psychic	Psychic	Special	90	100	10	Normal	—
TM30	Shadow Ball	Ghost	Special	80	100	15	Normal	—
TM32	Double Team	Normal	Status	—	—	15	Self	—
TM34	Shock Wave	Electric	Special	60	—	20	Normal	—
TM40	Aerial Ace	Flying	Physical	60	—	20	Normal	●
TM41	Torment	Dark	Status	—	100	15	Normal	—
TM42	Facade	Normal	Physical	70	100	20	Normal	●
TM43	Secret Power	Normal	Physical	70	100	20	Normal	●
TM44	Rest	Psychic	Status	—	—	10	Self	—
TM45	Attract	Normal	Status	—	100	15	Normal	—
TM46	Thief	Dark	Physical	40	100	10	Normal	●
TM48	Skill Swap	Psychic	Status	—	—	10	Normal	—
TM49	Snatch	Dark	Status	—	—	10	DoM	—
TM53	Energy Ball	Grass	Special	80	100	10	Normal	—
TM57	Charge Beam	Electric	Special	50	90	10	Normal	—
TM58	Endure	Normal	Status	—	—	10	Self	—
TM61	Will-O-Wisp	Fire	Status	—	75	15	Normal	—
TM63	Embargo	Dark	Status	—	100	15	Normal	—
TM66	Payback	Dark	Physical	50	100	10	Normal	●
TM68	Giga Impact	Normal	Physical	150	90	5	Normal	●
TM70	Flash	Normal	Status	—	100	20	Normal	—
TM73	Thunder Wave	Electric	Status	—	100	20	Normal	—
TM77	Psych Up	Normal	Status	—	—	10	Normal	—
TM78	Captivate	Normal	Status	—	100	20	2 foes	—
TM79	Dark Pulse	Dark	Special	80	100	15	Normal	●
TM82	Sleep Talk	Normal	Status	—	—	10	DoM	—
TM83	Natural Gift	Normal	Physical	—	100	15	Normal	●
TM85	Dream Eater	Psychic	Special	100	100	15	Normal	—
TM87	Swagger	Normal	Status	—	90	15	Normal	—
TM90	Substitute	Normal	Status	—	—	10	Self	—
TM92	Trick Room	Psychic	Status	—	—	5	All	—

● LEVEL-UP AND LEARNED MOVES

Lv	Name	Type	Kind	Power	Acc	PP	Range	DA
Base	Lucky Chant	Normal	Status	—	—	30	2 allies	—
Base	Magical Leaf	Grass	Special	60	—	20	Normal	—
Base	Growl	Normal	Status	—	100	40	2 foes	—
Base	Psywave	Psychic	Special	—	80	15	Normal	—
Base	Spite	Ghost	Status	—	100	10	Normal	—
Base	Astonish	Ghost	Physical	30	100	15	Normal	●

● MOVES TAUGHT IN EXCHANGE FOR COLORED SHARDS

Name	Type	Kind	Power	Acc	PP	Range	DA
Icy Wind	Ice	Special	55	95	15	2 foes	—
Ominous Wind	Ghost	Special	60	100	5	Normal	—
Snore	Normal	Special	40	100	15	Normal	—
Spite	Ghost	Status	—	100	10	Normal	—
Trick	Psychic	Status	—	100	10	Normal	—
Sucker Punch	Dark	Physical	80	100	5	Normal	●
Swift	Normal	Special	60	—	20	2 foes	—
Uproar	Normal	Special	50	100	10	1 random	—

● PRIMARY WAY TO FIND

TRAINER'S PARTY Hearthome Gym Leader Fantina

WILD POKÉMON

COURSE OF STORY

Murkrow

DARK FLYING

HEIGHT: 1'08"
WEIGHT: 4.6 lbs.
GENDER: Male and Female
HELD ITEM: None

● Male form ● Female form

PLATINUM If spotted, it will lure an unwary person into chasing it, then lose the pursuer on mountain trails.

EVOLUTION PATH

Murkrow → (Dusk Stone) → Honchkrow

ABILITY ● Insomnia ● Super Luck

EGG GROUP Flying

STATS
HP ●●
ATTACK ●●●
DEFENSE ●●
SP. ATTACK ●●●
SP. DEFENSE ●●
SPEED ●●●

● TM & HM MOVES

No.	Name	Type	Kind	Power	Acc	PP	Range	DA
TM04	Calm Mind	Psychic	Status	—	—	20	Self	—
TM06	Toxic	Poison	Status	—	85	10	Normal	—
TM10	Hidden Power	Normal	Special	—	100	15	Normal	—
TM11	Sunny Day	Fire	Status	—	—	5	All	—
TM12	Taunt	Dark	Status	—	100	20	Normal	—
TM17	Protect	Normal	Status	—	—	10	Self	—
TM18	Rain Dance	Water	Status	—	—	5	All	—
TM21	Frustration	Normal	Physical	—	100	20	Normal	●
TM27	Return	Normal	Physical	—	100	20	Normal	●
TM29	Psychic	Psychic	Special	90	100	10	Normal	—
TM30	Shadow Ball	Ghost	Special	80	100	15	Normal	—
TM32	Double Team	Normal	Status	—	—	15	Self	—
TM40	Aerial Ace	Flying	Physical	60	—	20	Normal	●
TM41	Torment	Dark	Status	—	100	15	Normal	—
TM42	Facade	Normal	Physical	70	100	20	Normal	●
TM43	Secret Power	Normal	Physical	70	100	20	Normal	●
TM44	Rest	Psychic	Status	—	—	10	Self	—
TM45	Attract	Normal	Status	—	100	15	Normal	—
TM46	Thief	Dark	Physical	40	100	10	Normal	●
TM47	Steel Wing	Steel	Physical	70	90	25	Normal	●
TM49	Snatch	Dark	Status	—	—	10	DoM	—
TM51	Roost	Flying	Status	—	—	10	Self	—
TM58	Endure	Normal	Status	—	—	10	Self	—
TM63	Embargo	Dark	Status	—	100	15	Normal	—
TM66	Payback	Dark	Physical	50	100	10	Normal	●
TM73	Thunder Wave	Electric	Status	—	100	20	Normal	—
TM77	Psych Up	Normal	Status	—	—	10	Normal	—
TM78	Captivate	Normal	Status	—	100	20	2 foes	—
TM79	Dark Pulse	Dark	Special	80	100	15	Normal	●
TM82	Sleep Talk	Normal	Status	—	—	10	DoM	—
TM83	Natural Gift	Normal	Physical	—	100	15	Normal	●
TM85	Dream Eater	Psychic	Special	100	100	15	Normal	—
TM87	Swagger	Normal	Status	—	90	15	Normal	—
TM88	Pluck	Flying	Physical	60	100	20	Normal	●
TM90	Substitute	Normal	Status	—	—	10	Self	—
HM02	Fly	Flying	Physical	90	95	15	Normal	●
HM05	Defog	Flying	Status	—	—	15	Normal	—

● LEVEL-UP AND LEARNED MOVES

Lv	Name	Type	Kind	Power	Acc	PP	Range	DA
Base	Peck	Flying	Physical	35	100	35	Normal	●
Base	Astonish	Ghost	Physical	30	100	15	Normal	●
5	Pursuit	Dark	Physical	40	100	20	Normal	●
11	Haze	Ice	Status	—	—	30	All	—
15	Wing Attack	Flying	Physical	60	100	35	Normal	●
21	Night Shade	Ghost	Special	—	100	15	Normal	—
25	Assurance	Dark	Physical	50	100	10	Normal	●
31	Taunt	Dark	Status	—	100	20	Normal	—
35	Faint Attack	Dark	Physical	60	—	20	Normal	—
41	Mean Look	Normal	Status	—	—	5	Normal	—
45	Sucker Punch	Dark	Physical	80	100	5	Normal	●

● MOVES TAUGHT IN EXCHANGE FOR COLORED SHARDS

Name	Type	Kind	Power	Acc	PP	Range	DA
Mud-Slap	Ground	Special	20	100	10	Normal	—
Icy Wind	Ice	Special	55	95	15	2 foes	—
Ominous Wind	Ghost	Special	60	100	5	Normal	—
Spite	Ghost	Status	—	100	10	Normal	—
Air Cutter	Flying	Special	55	95	25	2 foes	—
Twister	Dragon	Special	40	100	20	2 foes	—
Heat Wave	Fire	Special	100	90	10	2 foes	—
Sucker Punch	Dark	Physical	80	100	5	Normal	●
Swift	Normal	Special	60	—	20	2 foes	—
Uproar	Normal	Special	50	100	10	1 random	—

● EGG MOVES

Name	Type	Kind	Power	Acc	PP	Range	DA
Whirlwind	Normal	Status	—	100	20	Normal	—
Drill Peck	Flying	Physical	80	100	20	Normal	●
Mirror Move	Flying	Status	—	—	20	DoM	—
Wing Attack	Flying	Physical	60	100	35	Normal	●
Sky Attack	Flying	Physical	140	90	5	Normal	●
Confuse Ray	Ghost	Status	—	100	10	Normal	—
FeatherDance	Flying	Status	—	100	15	Normal	—
Perish Song	Normal	Status	—	—	5	All	—
Psycho Shift	Psychic	Status	—	90	10	Normal	—
Screech	Normal	Status	—	85	40	Normal	—
Faint Attack	Dark	Physical	60	—	20	Normal	—

● PRIMARY WAY TO FIND

TRAINER'S PARTY Trainer on 4F of the Lost Tower

WILD POKÉMON

COURSE OF STORY

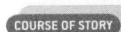

Sinnoh Pokédex No. 075 Big Boss Pokémon
Honchkrow

DARK | FLYING

HEIGHT: 2'11"
WEIGHT: 60.2 lbs.
GENDER: Male and Female
HELD ITEM: None

● M/F have same form

PLATINUM If one utters a deep cry, many MURKROW gather quickly. For this, it is called "Summoner of Night".

EVOLUTION PATH

Murkrow → (Dusk Stone) → Honchkrow

ABILITY
● Insomnia
● Super Luck

EGG GROUP Flying

STATS
HP ●●●
ATTACK ●●●●
DEFENSE ●●
SP. ATTACK ●●●●
SP. DEFENSE ●●
SPEED ●●●

● TM & HM MOVES

No.	Name	Type	Kind	Power	Acc	PP	Range	DA
TM04	Calm Mind	Psychic	Status	—	—	20	Self	—
TM06	Toxic	Poison	Status	—	85	10	Normal	—
TM10	Hidden Power	Normal	Special	—	100	15	Normal	—
TM11	Sunny Day	Fire	Status	—	—	5	All	—
TM12	Taunt	Dark	Status	—	100	20	Normal	—
TM15	Hyper Beam	Normal	Special	150	90	5	Normal	—
TM17	Protect	Normal	Status	—	—	10	Self	—
TM18	Rain Dance	Water	Status	—	—	5	All	—
TM21	Frustration	Normal	Physical	—	100	20	Normal	●
TM27	Return	Normal	Physical	—	100	20	Normal	●
TM29	Psychic	Psychic	Special	90	100	10	Normal	●
TM30	Shadow Ball	Ghost	Special	80	100	15	Normal	—
TM32	Double Team	Normal	Status	—	—	15	Self	—
TM40	Aerial Ace	Flying	Physical	60	—	20	Normal	—
TM41	Torment	Dark	Status	—	100	15	Normal	—
TM42	Facade	Normal	Physical	70	100	20	Normal	●
TM43	Secret Power	Normal	Physical	70	100	20	Normal	●
TM44	Rest	Psychic	Status	—	—	10	Self	—
TM45	Attract	Normal	Status	—	100	15	Normal	—
TM46	Thief	Dark	Physical	40	100	10	Normal	●
TM47	Steel Wing	Steel	Physical	70	90	25	Normal	●
TM49	Snatch	Dark	Status	—	—	10	DoM	—
TM51	Roost	Flying	Status	—	—	10	Self	—
TM58	Endure	Normal	Status	—	—	10	Self	—
TM63	Embargo	Dark	Status	—	100	15	Normal	—
TM66	Payback	Dark	Physical	50	100	10	Normal	●
TM68	Giga Impact	Normal	Physical	150	90	5	Normal	●
TM73	Thunder Wave	Electric	Status	—	100	20	Normal	—
TM77	Psych Up	Normal	Status	—	—	10	Normal	—
TM78	Captivate	Normal	Status	—	100	20	2 foes	—
TM79	Dark Pulse	Dark	Special	80	100	15	Normal	●
TM82	Sleep Talk	Normal	Status	—	—	10	DoM	—
TM83	Natural Gift	Normal	Physical	—	100	15	Normal	●
TM85	Dream Eater	Psychic	Special	100	100	15	Normal	—
TM87	Swagger	Normal	Status	—	90	15	Normal	—
TM88	Pluck	Flying	Physical	60	100	20	Normal	●
TM90	Substitute	Normal	Status	—	—	10	Self	—
HM02	Fly	Flying	Physical	90	95	15	Normal	●
HM05	Defog	Flying	Status	—	—	15	Normal	—

● LEVEL-UP AND LEARNED MOVES

Lv	Name	Type	Kind	Power	Acc	PP	Range	DA
Base	Astonish	Ghost	Physical	30	100	15	Normal	●
Base	Pursuit	Dark	Physical	40	100	20	Normal	●
Base	Haze	Ice	Status	—	—	30	All	—
Base	Wing Attack	Flying	Physical	60	100	35	Normal	●
25	Swagger	Normal	Status	—	90	15	Normal	—
35	Nasty Plot	Dark	Status	—	—	20	Self	—
45	Night Slash	Dark	Physical	70	100	15	Normal	●
55	Dark Pulse	Dark	Special	80	100	15	Normal	●

● MOVES TAUGHT IN EXCHANGE FOR COLORED SHARDS

Name	Type	Kind	Power	Acc	PP	Range	DA
Mud-Slap	Ground	Special	20	100	10	Normal	—
Superpower	Fight	Physical	120	100	5	Normal	—
Ominous Wind	Ghost	Special	60	100	5	Normal	—
Spite	Ghost	Status	—	100	10	Normal	—
Air Cutter	Flying	Special	55	95	25	2 foes	—
Twister	Dragon	Special	40	100	20	2 foes	—
Heat Wave	Fire	Special	100	90	10	2 foes	—
Sucker Punch	Dark	Physical	80	100	5	Normal	—
Swift	Normal	Special	60	—	20	2 foes	—
Uproar	Normal	Special	50	100	10	1 random	—

● PRIMARY WAY TO FIND

TRAINER'S PARTY Team Galactic Boss Cyrus, when you fight him at the Galactic Veilstone Building

WILD POKÉMON

COURSE OF STORY

Sinnoh Pokédex No. 076 Catty Pokémon
Glameow

NORMAL

HEIGHT: 1'08"
WEIGHT: 8.6 lbs.
GENDER: Male and Female
HELD ITEM: None

● M/F have same form

PLATINUM It hides its spiteful tendency of hooking its claws into the nose of its Trainer if it isn't fed.

EVOLUTION PATH

Glameow → (Lv38) → Purugly

ABILITY
● Limber
● Own Tempo

EGG GROUP Field

STATS
HP ●●
ATTACK ●●
DEFENSE ●
SP. ATTACK ●●
SP. DEFENSE ●●
SPEED ●●●

● TM & HM MOVES

No.	Name	Type	Kind	Power	Acc	PP	Range	DA
TM03	Water Pulse	Water	Special	60	100	20	Normal	—
TM06	Toxic	Poison	Status	—	85	10	Normal	—
TM10	Hidden Power	Normal	Special	—	100	15	Normal	—
TM11	Sunny Day	Fire	Status	—	—	5	All	—
TM12	Taunt	Dark	Status	—	100	20	Normal	—
TM17	Protect	Normal	Status	—	—	10	Self	—
TM18	Rain Dance	Water	Status	—	—	5	All	—
TM21	Frustration	Normal	Physical	—	100	20	Normal	●
TM23	Iron Tail	Steel	Physical	100	75	15	Normal	●
TM24	Thunderbolt	Electric	Special	95	100	15	Normal	—
TM25	Thunder	Electric	Special	120	70	10	Normal	—
TM27	Return	Normal	Physical	—	100	20	Normal	●
TM28	Dig	Ground	Physical	80	100	10	Normal	●
TM30	Shadow Ball	Ghost	Special	80	100	15	Normal	—
TM32	Double Team	Normal	Status	—	—	15	Self	—
TM34	Shock Wave	Electric	Special	60	—	20	Normal	—
TM40	Aerial Ace	Flying	Physical	60	—	20	Normal	—
TM41	Torment	Dark	Status	—	100	15	Normal	—
TM42	Facade	Normal	Physical	70	100	20	Normal	●
TM43	Secret Power	Normal	Physical	70	100	20	Normal	●
TM44	Rest	Psychic	Status	—	—	10	Self	—
TM45	Attract	Normal	Status	—	100	15	Normal	—
TM46	Thief	Dark	Physical	40	100	10	Normal	●
TM49	Snatch	Dark	Status	—	—	10	DoM	—
TM58	Endure	Normal	Status	—	—	10	Self	—
TM65	Shadow Claw	Ghost	Physical	70	100	15	Normal	●
TM66	Payback	Dark	Physical	50	100	10	Normal	●
TM70	Flash	Normal	Status	—	100	20	Normal	—
TM77	Psych Up	Normal	Status	—	—	10	Normal	—
TM78	Captivate	Normal	Status	—	100	20	2 foes	—
TM82	Sleep Talk	Normal	Status	—	—	10	DoM	—
TM83	Natural Gift	Normal	Physical	—	100	15	Normal	●
TM85	Dream Eater	Psychic	Special	100	100	15	Normal	—
TM87	Swagger	Normal	Status	—	90	15	Normal	—
TM89	U-turn	Bug	Physical	70	100	20	Normal	●
TM90	Substitute	Normal	Status	—	—	10	Self	—
HM01	Cut	Normal	Physical	50	95	30	Normal	●

● LEVEL-UP AND LEARNED MOVES

Lv	Name	Type	Kind	Power	Acc	PP	Range	DA
Base	Fake Out	Normal	Physical	40	100	25	Normal	●
5	Scratch	Normal	Physical	40	100	35	Normal	●
8	Growl	Normal	Status	—	100	40	2 foes	—
13	Hypnosis	Psychic	Status	—	60	20	Normal	—
17	Faint Attack	Dark	Physical	60	—	20	Normal	●
20	Fury Swipes	Normal	Physical	18	80	15	Normal	●
25	Charm	Normal	Status	—	100	20	Normal	—
29	Assist	Normal	Status	—	—	20	DoM	—
32	Captivate	Normal	Status	—	100	20	2 foes	—
37	Slash	Normal	Physical	70	100	20	Normal	●
41	Sucker Punch	Dark	Physical	80	100	5	Normal	●
45	Attract	Normal	Status	—	100	15	Normal	—

● MOVES TAUGHT IN EXCHANGE FOR COLORED SHARDS

Name	Type	Kind	Power	Acc	PP	Range	DA
Mud-Slap	Ground	Special	20	100	10	Normal	—
Fury Cutter	Bug	Physical	10	95	20	Normal	—
Snore	Normal	Special	40	100	15	Normal	—
Last Resort	Normal	Physical	130	100	5	Normal	—
Knock Off	Dark	Physical	20	100	20	Normal	—
Sucker Punch	Dark	Physical	80	100	5	Normal	—
Swift	Normal	Special	60	—	20	2 foes	—

● EGG MOVES

Name	Type	Kind	Power	Acc	PP	Range	DA
Bite	Dark	Physical	60	100	25	Normal	●
Tail Whip	Normal	Status	—	100	30	2 foes	—
Quick Attack	Normal	Physical	40	100	30	Normal	●
Sand-Attack	Ground	Status	—	100	15	Normal	—
Fake Tears	Dark	Status	—	100	20	Normal	—
Assurance	Dark	Physical	50	100	10	Normal	●

● PRIMARY WAY TO FIND

TRAINER'S PARTY Galactic grunt you battle in Jubilife City

WILD POKÉMON

COURSE OF STORY

Sinnoh Pokédex No. 077 Tiger Cat Pokémon
Purugly

NORMAL

HEIGHT: 3'03"
WEIGHT: 96.6 lbs.
GENDER: Male and Female
HELD ITEM: None

● M/F have same form

PLATINUM It binds its body with its tails to make itself look bigger. If it locks eyes, it will glare ceaselessly.

EVOLUTION PATH

Glameow — Lv38 — Purugly

● TM & HM MOVES

No.	Name	Type	Kind	Power	Acc	PP	Range	DA
TM03	Water Pulse	Water	Special	60	100	20	Normal	—
TM05	Roar	Normal	Status	—	100	20	Normal	—
TM06	Toxic	Poison	Status	—	85	10	Normal	—
TM10	Hidden Power	Normal	Special	—	100	15	Normal	—
TM11	Sunny Day	Fire	Status	—	—	5	All	—
TM12	Taunt	Dark	Status	—	100	20	Normal	—
TM15	Hyper Beam	Normal	Special	150	90	5	Normal	—
TM17	Protect	Normal	Status	—	—	10	Self	—
TM18	Rain Dance	Water	Status	—	—	5	All	—
TM21	Frustration	Normal	Physical	—	100	20	Normal	•
TM23	Iron Tail	Steel	Physical	100	75	15	Normal	•
TM24	Thunderbolt	Electric	Special	95	100	15	Normal	—
TM25	Thunder	Electric	Special	120	70	10	Normal	—
TM27	Return	Normal	Physical	—	100	20	Normal	•
TM28	Dig	Ground	Physical	80	100	10	Normal	•
TM30	Shadow Ball	Ghost	Special	80	100	15	Normal	—
TM32	Double Team	Normal	Status	—	—	15	Self	—
TM34	Shock Wave	Electric	Special	60	—	20	Normal	—
TM40	Aerial Ace	Flying	Physical	60	—	20	Normal	•
TM41	Torment	Dark	Status	—	100	15	Normal	—
TM42	Facade	Normal	Physical	70	100	20	Normal	•
TM43	Secret Power	Normal	Physical	70	100	20	Normal	•
TM44	Rest	Psychic	Status	—	—	10	Self	—
TM45	Attract	Normal	Status	—	100	15	Normal	—
TM46	Thief	Dark	Physical	40	100	10	Normal	•
TM49	Snatch	Dark	Status	—	—	10	DoM	—
TM58	Endure	Normal	Status	—	—	10	Self	—
TM65	Shadow Claw	Ghost	Physical	70	100	15	Normal	•
TM66	Payback	Dark	Physical	50	100	10	Normal	•
TM68	Giga Impact	Normal	Physical	150	90	5	Normal	•
TM70	Flash	Normal	Status	—	100	20	Normal	—
TM77	Psych Up	Normal	Status	—	—	10	Normal	—
TM78	Captivate	Normal	Status	—	100	20	2 foes	—
TM82	Sleep Talk	Normal	Status	—	—	10	DoM	—
TM83	Natural Gift	Normal	Physical	—	100	15	Normal	•
TM85	Dream Eater	Psychic	Special	100	100	15	Normal	—
TM87	Swagger	Normal	Status	—	90	15	Normal	—
TM89	U-turn	Bug	Physical	70	100	20	Normal	•
TM90	Substitute	Normal	Status	—	—	10	Self	—
HM01	Cut	Normal	Physical	50	95	30	Normal	•

● LEVEL-UP AND LEARNED MOVES

Lv	Name	Type	Kind	Power	Acc	PP	Range	DA
Base	Fake Out	Normal	Physical	40	100	10	Normal	•
Base	Scratch	Normal	Physical	40	100	35	Normal	•
Base	Growl	Normal	Status	—	100	40	2 foes	—
5	Scratch	Normal	Physical	40	100	35	Normal	•
8	Growl	Normal	Status	—	100	40	2 foes	—
13	Hypnosis	Psychic	Status	—	60	20	Normal	—
17	Faint Attack	Dark	Physical	60	—	20	Normal	•
20	Fury Swipes	Normal	Physical	18	80	15	Normal	•
25	Charm	Normal	Status	—	100	20	Normal	—
29	Assist	Normal	Status	—	—	20	DoM	—
32	Captivate	Normal	Status	—	100	20	2 foes	—
37	Slash	Normal	Physical	70	100	20	Normal	•
38	Swagger	Normal	Status	—	90	15	Normal	—
45	Body Slam	Normal	Physical	85	100	15	Normal	•
53	Attract	Normal	Status	—	100	15	Normal	—

● MOVES TAUGHT IN EXCHANGE FOR COLORED SHARDS

Name	Type	Kind	Power	Acc	PP	Range	DA
Mud-Slap	Ground	Special	20	100	10	Normal	—
Fury Cutter	Bug	Physical	10	95	20	Normal	•
Rollout	Rock	Physical	30	90	20	Normal	•
Snore	Normal	Special	40	100	15	Normal	—
Last Resort	Normal	Physical	130	100	5	Normal	•
Knock Off	Dark	Physical	20	100	20	Normal	•
Sucker Punch	Dark	Physical	80	100	5	Normal	•
Swift	Normal	Special	60	—	20	2 foes	—

● PRIMARY WAY TO FIND

TRAINER'S PARTY Team Galactic Commander Mars, when you battle her at Lake Verity

WILD POKÉMON

COURSE OF STORY

ABILITY
● Thick Fat
● Own Tempo

EGG GROUP — Field

STATS
HP ●●
ATTACK ●●●●
DEFENSE ●●●
SP. ATTACK ●●
SP. DEFENSE ●●
SPEED ●●●●

Sinnoh Pokédex No. 078 Goldfish Pokémon
Goldeen

WATER

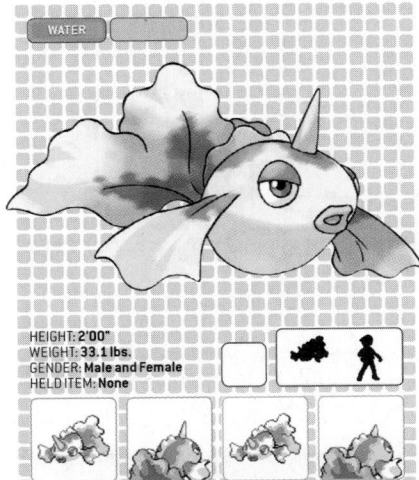

HEIGHT: 2'00"
WEIGHT: 33.1 lbs.
GENDER: Male and Female
HELD ITEM: None

● Male form ● Female form

PLATINUM Though it appears very elegant when swimming with fins unfurled, it can jab powerfully with its horn.

EVOLUTION PATH

Goldeen — Lv33 — Seaking

● TM & HM MOVES

No.	Name	Type	Kind	Power	Acc	PP	Range	DA
TM03	Water Pulse	Water	Special	60	100	20	Normal	—
TM06	Toxic	Poison	Status	—	85	10	Normal	—
TM07	Hail	Ice	Status	—	—	10	All	—
TM10	Hidden Power	Normal	Special	—	100	15	Normal	—
TM13	Ice Beam	Ice	Special	95	100	10	Normal	—
TM14	Blizzard	Ice	Special	120	70	5	2 foes	—
TM17	Protect	Normal	Status	—	—	10	Self	—
TM18	Rain Dance	Water	Status	—	—	5	All	—
TM21	Frustration	Normal	Physical	—	100	20	Normal	•
TM27	Return	Normal	Physical	—	100	20	Normal	•
TM32	Double Team	Normal	Status	—	—	15	Self	—
TM42	Facade	Normal	Physical	70	100	20	Normal	•
TM43	Secret Power	Normal	Physical	70	100	20	Normal	•
TM44	Rest	Psychic	Status	—	—	10	Self	—
TM45	Attract	Normal	Status	—	100	15	Normal	—
TM58	Endure	Normal	Status	—	—	10	Self	—
TM78	Captivate	Normal	Status	—	100	20	2 foes	—
TM82	Sleep Talk	Normal	Status	—	—	10	DoM	—
TM83	Natural Gift	Normal	Physical	—	100	15	Normal	•
TM84	Poison Jab	Poison	Physical	80	100	20	Normal	•
TM87	Swagger	Normal	Status	—	90	15	Normal	—
TM90	Substitute	Normal	Status	—	—	10	Self	—
HM03	Surf	Water	Special	95	100	15	2 foes + 1 ally	—
HM07	Waterfall	Water	Physical	80	100	15	Normal	•

● LEVEL-UP AND LEARNED MOVES

Lv	Name	Type	Kind	Power	Acc	PP	Range	DA
Base	Peck	Flying	Physical	35	100	35	Normal	•
Base	Tail Whip	Normal	Status	—	100	30	2 foes	—
Base	Water Sport	Water	Status	—	—	15	All	—
7	Supersonic	Normal	Status	—	55	20	Normal	—
11	Horn Attack	Normal	Physical	65	100	25	Normal	•
17	Water Pulse	Water	Special	60	100	20	Normal	—
21	Flail	Normal	Physical	—	100	15	Normal	•
27	Aqua Ring	Water	Status	—	—	20	Self	—
31	Fury Attack	Normal	Physical	15	85	20	Normal	•
37	Waterfall	Water	Physical	80	100	15	Normal	•
41	Horn Drill	Normal	Physical	—	30	5	Normal	•
47	Agility	Psychic	Status	—	—	30	Self	—
51	Megahorn	Bug	Physical	120	85	10	Normal	•

● MOVES TAUGHT IN EXCHANGE FOR COLORED SHARDS

Name	Type	Kind	Power	Acc	PP	Range	DA
Dive	Water	Physical	80	100	10	Normal	•
Mud-Slap	Ground	Special	20	100	10	Normal	—
Fury Cutter	Bug	Physical	10	95	20	Normal	•
Icy Wind	Ice	Special	55	95	15	2 foes	—
Aqua Tail	Water	Physical	90	90	10	Normal	•
Snore	Normal	Special	40	100	15	Normal	—
Bounce	Flying	Physical	85	85	5	Normal	•
Knock Off	Dark	Physical	20	100	20	Normal	•
Swift	Normal	Special	60	—	20	2 foes	—

● EGG MOVES

Name	Type	Kind	Power	Acc	PP	Range	DA
Psybeam	Psychic	Special	65	100	20	Normal	—
Haze	Ice	Status	—	—	30	All	—
Hydro Pump	Water	Special	120	80	5	Normal	—
Sleep Talk	Normal	Status	—	—	10	DoM	—
Mud Sport	Ground	Status	—	—	15	All	—
Mud-Slap	Ground	Special	20	100	10	Normal	—
Aqua Tail	Water	Physical	90	90	10	Normal	•

● PRIMARY WAY TO FIND

TRAINER'S PARTY Trainer on Route 205

WILD POKÉMON Route 209 (Good Rod)

COURSE OF STORY

ABILITY
● Swift Swim
● Water Veil

EGG GROUP — Water 2

STATS
HP ●
ATTACK ●●●
DEFENSE ●●
SP. ATTACK ●●
SP. DEFENSE ●●
SPEED ●●

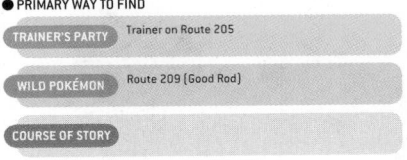

Seaking

WATER

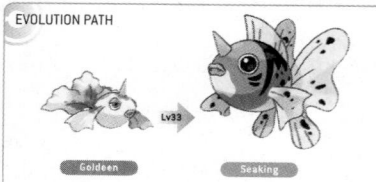

HEIGHT: 4'03"
WEIGHT: 86.0 lbs.
GENDER: Male and Female
HELD ITEM: None

● Male form   ● Female form

PLATINUM — In autumn, its body becomes more fatty in preparing to propose to a mate. It takes on beautiful colors.

EVOLUTION PATH

Goldeen → Lv33 → Seaking

ABILITY: ● Swift Swim ● Water Veil

EGG GROUP: Water 2

STATS: HP ●● ATTACK ●●● DEFENSE ●● SP. ATTACK ●● SP. DEFENSE ●● SPEED ●●●

● TM & HM MOVES

No.	Name	Type	Kind	Power	Acc	PP	Range	DA
TM03	Water Pulse	Water	Special	60	100	20	Normal	—
TM06	Toxic	Poison	Status	—	85	10	Normal	—
TM07	Hail	Ice	Status	—	—	10	All	—
TM10	Hidden Power	Normal	Special	—	100	15	Normal	—
TM13	Ice Beam	Ice	Special	95	100	10	Normal	—
TM14	Blizzard	Ice	Special	120	70	5	2 foes	—
TM15	Hyper Beam	Normal	Special	150	90	5	Normal	—
TM17	Protect	Normal	Status	—	—	10	Self	—
TM18	Rain Dance	Water	Status	—	—	5	All	—
TM21	Frustration	Normal	Physical	—	100	20	Normal	•
TM27	Return	Normal	Physical	—	100	20	Normal	•
TM32	Double Team	Normal	Status	—	—	15	Self	—
TM42	Facade	Normal	Physical	70	100	20	Normal	•
TM43	Secret Power	Normal	Physical	70	100	20	Normal	•
TM44	Rest	Psychic	Status	—	—	10	Self	—
TM45	Attract	Normal	Status	—	100	15	Normal	—
TM58	Endure	Normal	Status	—	—	10	Self	—
TM68	Giga Impact	Normal	Physical	150	90	5	Normal	•
TM78	Captivate	Normal	Status	—	100	20	2 foes	—
TM82	Sleep Talk	Normal	Status	—	—	10	DoM	—
TM83	Natural Gift	Normal	Physical	—	100	15	Normal	—
TM84	Poison Jab	Poison	Physical	80	100	20	Normal	•
TM87	Swagger	Normal	Status	—	90	15	Normal	—
TM90	Substitute	Normal	Status	—	—	10	Self	—
HM03	Surf	Water	Special	95	100	15	2 foes • 1 ally	—
HM07	Waterfall	Water	Physical	80	100	15	Normal	—

● LEVEL-UP AND LEARNED MOVES

Lv	Name	Type	Kind	Power	Acc	PP	Range	DA
Base	Poison Jab	Poison	Physical	80	100	20	Normal	•
Base	Peck	Flying	Physical	35	100	35	Normal	•
Base	Tail Whip	Normal	Status	—	100	30	2 foes	—
Base	Water Sport	Water	Status	—	—	15	All	—
Base	Supersonic	Normal	Status	—	55	20	Normal	—
?	Supersonic	Normal	Status	—	55	20	Normal	—
11	Horn Attack	Normal	Physical	65	100	25	Normal	•
17	Water Pulse	Water	Special	60	100	20	Normal	—
21	Flail	Normal	Physical	—	100	15	Normal	•
27	Aqua Ring	Water	Status	—	—	20	Self	—
31	Fury Attack	Normal	Physical	15	85	20	Normal	•
40	Waterfall	Water	Physical	80	100	15	Normal	•
47	Horn Drill	Normal	Physical	—	30	5	Normal	•
56	Agility	Psychic	Status	—	—	30	Self	—
63	Megahorn	Bug	Physical	120	85	10	Normal	•

● MOVES TAUGHT IN EXCHANGE FOR COLORED SHARDS

Name	Type	Kind	Power	Acc	PP	Range	DA
Dive	Water	Physical	80	100	10	Normal	•
Mud-Slap	Ground	Special	20	100	10	Normal	•
Fury Cutter	Bug	Physical	10	95	20	Normal	•
Icy Wind	Ice	Special	55	95	15	2 foes	—
Aqua Tail	Water	Physical	90	90	10	Normal	•
Snore	Normal	Special	40	100	15	Normal	—
Bounce	Flying	Physical	85	85	5	Normal	•
Knock Off	Dark	Physical	20	100	20	Normal	•
Swift	Normal	Special	60	—	20	2 foes	—

● PRIMARY WAY TO FIND

TRAINER'S PARTY — Trainer on Route 220

WILD POKÉMON

COURSE OF STORY

Barboach

WATER GROUND

HEIGHT: 1'04"
WEIGHT: 4.2 lbs.
GENDER: Male and Female
HELD ITEM: None

● M/F have same form

PLATINUM — Its slimy body is hard to grasp. In one region, it is said to have been born from hardened mud.

EVOLUTION PATH

Barboach → Lv30 → Whiscash

ABILITY: ● Oblivious ● Anticipation

EGG GROUP: Water 2

STATS: HP ● ATTACK ● DEFENSE ● SP. ATTACK ● SP. DEFENSE ●● SPEED ●●

● TM & HM MOVES

No.	Name	Type	Kind	Power	Acc	PP	Range	DA
TM03	Water Pulse	Water	Special	60	100	20	Normal	—
TM06	Toxic	Poison	Status	—	85	10	Normal	—
TM07	Hail	Ice	Status	—	—	10	All	—
TM10	Hidden Power	Normal	Special	—	100	15	Normal	—
TM13	Ice Beam	Ice	Special	95	100	10	Normal	—
TM14	Blizzard	Ice	Special	120	70	5	2 foes	—
TM17	Protect	Normal	Status	—	—	10	Self	—
TM18	Rain Dance	Water	Status	—	—	5	All	—
TM21	Frustration	Normal	Physical	—	100	20	Normal	•
TM26	Earthquake	Ground	Physical	100	100	10	2 foes • 1 ally	•
TM27	Return	Normal	Physical	—	100	20	Normal	•
TM32	Double Team	Normal	Status	—	—	15	Self	—
TM37	Sandstorm	Rock	Status	—	—	10	All	—
TM39	Rock Tomb	Rock	Physical	50	80	10	Normal	•
TM42	Facade	Normal	Physical	70	100	20	Normal	•
TM43	Secret Power	Normal	Physical	70	100	20	Normal	•
TM44	Rest	Psychic	Status	—	—	10	Self	—
TM45	Attract	Normal	Status	—	100	15	Normal	—
TM58	Endure	Normal	Status	—	—	10	Self	—
TM78	Captivate	Normal	Status	—	100	20	2 foes	—
TM82	Sleep Talk	Normal	Status	—	—	10	DoM	—
TM83	Natural Gift	Normal	Physical	—	100	15	Normal	—
TM87	Swagger	Normal	Status	—	90	15	Normal	—
TM90	Substitute	Normal	Status	—	—	10	Self	—
HM03	Surf	Water	Special	95	100	15	2 foes • 1 ally	—
HM07	Waterfall	Water	Physical	80	100	15	Normal	—

● LEVEL-UP AND LEARNED MOVES

Lv	Name	Type	Kind	Power	Acc	PP	Range	DA
Base	Mud-Slap	Ground	Special	20	100	10	Normal	—
6	Mud Sport	Ground	Status	—	—	15	All	—
6	Water Sport	Water	Status	—	—	15	All	—
10	Water Gun	Water	Special	40	100	25	Normal	—
14	Mud Bomb	Ground	Special	65	85	10	Normal	—
18	Amnesia	Psychic	Status	—	—	20	Self	—
22	Water Pulse	Water	Special	60	100	20	Normal	—
26	Magnitude	Ground	Physical	—	100	30	2 foes • 1 ally	—
31	Rest	Psychic	Status	—	—	10	Self	—
31	Snore	Normal	Special	40	100	15	Normal	—
35	Aqua Tail	Water	Physical	90	90	10	Normal	—
39	Earthquake	Ground	Physical	100	100	10	2 foes • 1 ally	—
43	Future Sight	Psychic	Special	80	90	15	Normal	—
47	Fissure	Ground	Physical	—	30	5	Normal	—

● MOVES TAUGHT IN EXCHANGE FOR COLORED SHARDS

Name	Type	Kind	Power	Acc	PP	Range	DA
Dive	Water	Physical	80	100	10	Normal	•
Mud-Slap	Ground	Special	20	100	10	Normal	•
Icy Wind	Ice	Special	55	95	15	2 foes	—
Aqua Tail	Water	Physical	90	90	10	Normal	•
Snore	Normal	Special	40	100	15	Normal	—
Earth Power	Ground	Special	90	100	10	Normal	—
Bounce	Flying	Physical	85	85	5	Normal	•

● EGG MOVES

Name	Type	Kind	Power	Acc	PP	Range	DA
Thrash	Normal	Physical	90	100	20	1 random	•
Whirlpool	Water	Special	15	70	15	Normal	•
Spark	Electric	Physical	65	100	20	Normal	•
Hydro Pump	Water	Special	120	80	5	Normal	—
Flail	Normal	Physical	—	100	15	Normal	•
Take Down	Normal	Physical	90	85	20	Normal	•

● PRIMARY WAY TO FIND

TRAINER'S PARTY — Trainer on 2F of the Lost Tower

WILD POKÉMON — Pastoria Great Marsh (Good Rod)

COURSE OF STORY

Sinnoh Pokédex No. 081 Whiskers Pokémon
Whiscash

WATER · GROUND

HEIGHT: 2'11"
WEIGHT: 52.0 lbs.
GENDER: Male and Female
HELD ITEM: None

● M/F have same form

PLATINUM — It is extremely protective of its territory. If any foe approaches, it attacks using vicious tremors.

EVOLUTION PATH

Barboach → Lv30 → Whiscash

● TM & HM MOVES

No.	Name	Type	Kind	Power	Acc	PP	Range	DA
TM03	Water Pulse	Water	Special	60	100	20	Normal	—
TM06	Toxic	Poison	Status	—	85	10	Normal	—
TM07	Hail	Ice	Status	—	—	10	All	—
TM10	Hidden Power	Normal	Special	—	100	15	Normal	—
TM13	Ice Beam	Ice	Special	95	100	10	Normal	—
TM14	Blizzard	Ice	Special	120	70	5	2 foes	—
TM15	Hyper Beam	Normal	Special	150	90	5	Normal	—
TM17	Protect	Normal	Status	—	—	10	Self	—
TM18	Rain Dance	Water	Status	—	—	5	All	—
TM21	Frustration	Normal	Physical	—	100	20	Normal	●
TM26	Earthquake	Ground	Physical	100	100	10	2 foes + 1 ally	—
TM27	Return	Normal	Physical	—	100	20	Normal	●
TM32	Double Team	Normal	Status	—	—	15	Self	—
TM37	Sandstorm	Rock	Status	—	—	10	All	—
TM39	Rock Tomb	Rock	Physical	50	80	10	Normal	—
TM42	Facade	Normal	Physical	70	100	20	Normal	●
TM43	Secret Power	Normal	Physical	70	100	20	Normal	●
TM44	Rest	Psychic	Status	—	—	10	Self	—
TM45	Attract	Normal	Status	—	100	15	Normal	—
TM58	Endure	Normal	Status	—	—	10	Self	—
TM68	Giga Impact	Normal	Physical	150	90	5	Normal	●
TM71	Stone Edge	Rock	Physical	100	80	5	Normal	●
TM78	Captivate	Normal	Status	—	100	20	2 foes	—
TM80	Rock Slide	Rock	Physical	75	90	10	2 foes	—
TM82	Sleep Talk	Normal	Status	—	—	10	DoM	—
TM83	Natural Gift	Normal	Physical	—	100	15	Normal	—
TM87	Swagger	Normal	Status	—	90	15	Normal	—
TM90	Substitute	Normal	Status	—	—	10	Self	—
HM03	Surf	Water	Special	95	100	15	2 foes + 1 ally	●
HM04	Strength	Normal	Physical	80	100	15	Normal	●
HM06	Rock Smash	Fighting	Physical	40	100	15	Normal	●
HM07	Waterfall	Water	Physical	80	100	15	Normal	●

● LEVEL-UP AND LEARNED MOVES

Lv	Name	Type	Kind	Power	Acc	PP	Range	DA
Base	Zen Headbutt	Psychic	Physical	80	90	15	Normal	●
Base	Tickle	Normal	Status	—	100	20	Normal	—
Base	Mud-Slap	Ground	Special	20	100	10	Normal	—
Base	Mud Sport	Ground	Status	—	—	15	All	—
Base	Water Sport	Water	Status	—	—	15	All	—
6	Mud Sport	Ground	Status	—	—	15	All	—
6	Water Sport	Water	Status	—	—	15	All	—
10	Water Gun	Water	Special	40	100	25	Normal	—
14	Mud Bomb	Ground	Special	65	85	10	Normal	—
18	Amnesia	Psychic	Status	—	—	20	Self	—
22	Water Pulse	Water	Special	60	100	20	Normal	—
26	Magnitude	Ground	Physical	—	100	30	2 foes + 1 ally	—
33	Rest	Psychic	Status	—	—	10	Self	—
33	Snore	Normal	Special	40	100	15	Normal	—
39	Aqua Tail	Water	Physical	90	90	10	Normal	—
45	Earthquake	Ground	Physical	100	100	10	2 foes + 1 ally	—
51	Future Sight	Psychic	Special	80	90	15	Normal	—
57	Fissure	Ground	Physical	—	30	5	Normal	—

● MOVES TAUGHT IN EXCHANGE FOR COLORED SHARDS

Name	Type	Kind	Power	Acc	PP	Range	DA
Dive	Water	Physical	80	100	10	Normal	●
Mud-Slap	Ground	Special	20	100	10	Normal	—
Icy Wind	Ice	Special	55	95	15	2 foes	—
Aqua Tail	Water	Physical	90	90	10	Normal	●
Snore	Normal	Special	40	100	15	Normal	—
Zen Headbutt	Psychic	Physical	80	90	15	Normal	●
Earth Power	Ground	Special	90	100	10	Normal	—
Bounce	Flying	Physical	85	85	5	Normal	●

● PRIMARY WAY TO FIND

TRAINER'S PARTY — Elite Four member Bertha

WILD POKÉMON — Pastoria Great Marsh [Super Rod]

COURSE OF STORY

ABILITY — ● Oblivious ● Anticipation

EGG GROUP — Water 2

STATS —
HP ●●●
ATTACK ●●
DEFENSE ●●
SP. ATTACK ●●
SP. DEFENSE ●●●
SPEED ●●

Sinnoh Pokédex No. 082 Bell Pokémon
Chingling

PSYCHIC

HEIGHT: 0'08"
WEIGHT: 1.3 lbs.
GENDER: Male and Female
HELD ITEM: Colbur Berry

● M/F have same form

PLATINUM — There is an orb inside its mouth. When it hops, the orb bounces all over and makes a ringing sound.

EVOLUTION PATH

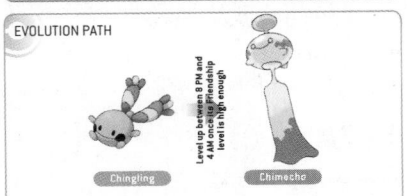

Chingling → Level up between 8 PM and 4 AM and its Friendship level is high enough → Chimecho

● TM & HM MOVES

No.	Name	Type	Kind	Power	Acc	PP	Range	DA
TM04	Calm Mind	Psychic	Status	—	—	20	Self	—
TM06	Toxic	Poison	Status	—	85	10	Normal	—
TM10	Hidden Power	Normal	Special	—	100	15	Normal	—
TM11	Sunny Day	Fire	Status	—	—	5	All	—
TM12	Taunt	Dark	Status	—	100	20	Normal	—
TM16	Light Screen	Psychic	Status	—	—	30	2 allies	—
TM17	Protect	Normal	Status	—	—	10	Self	—
TM18	Rain Dance	Water	Status	—	—	5	All	—
TM20	Safeguard	Normal	Status	—	—	25	2 allies	—
TM21	Frustration	Normal	Physical	—	100	20	Normal	●
TM27	Return	Normal	Physical	—	100	20	Normal	●
TM29	Psychic	Psychic	Special	90	100	10	Normal	—
TM30	Shadow Ball	Ghost	Special	80	100	15	Normal	—
TM32	Double Team	Normal	Status	—	—	15	Self	—
TM33	Reflect	Psychic	Status	—	—	20	2 allies	—
TM34	Shock Wave	Electric	Special	60	—	20	Normal	—
TM41	Torment	Dark	Status	—	100	15	Normal	—
TM42	Facade	Normal	Physical	70	100	20	Normal	●
TM43	Secret Power	Normal	Physical	70	100	20	Normal	●
TM44	Rest	Psychic	Status	—	—	10	Self	—
TM45	Attract	Normal	Status	—	100	15	Normal	—
TM48	Skill Swap	Psychic	Status	—	—	10	Normal	—
TM49	Snatch	Dark	Status	—	—	10	DoM	—
TM57	Charge Beam	Electric	Special	50	90	10	Normal	—
TM58	Endure	Normal	Status	—	—	10	Self	—
TM67	Recycle	Normal	Status	—	—	10	Self	—
TM70	Flash	Normal	Status	—	100	20	Normal	—
TM73	Thunder Wave	Electric	Status	—	100	20	Normal	—
TM77	Psych Up	Normal	Status	—	—	10	Normal	—
TM78	Captivate	Normal	Status	—	100	20	2 foes	—
TM82	Sleep Talk	Normal	Status	—	—	10	DoM	—
TM83	Natural Gift	Normal	Physical	—	100	15	Normal	—
TM85	Dream Eater	Psychic	Special	100	100	15	Normal	—
TM86	Grass Knot	Grass	Special	—	100	20	Normal	●
TM87	Swagger	Normal	Status	—	90	15	Normal	—
TM90	Substitute	Normal	Status	—	—	10	Self	—
TM92	Trick Room	Psychic	Status	—	—	5	All	—

● LEVEL-UP AND LEARNED MOVES

Lv	Name	Type	Kind	Power	Acc	PP	Range	DA
Base	Wrap	Normal	Physical	15	85	20	Normal	●
6	Growl	Normal	Status	—	100	40	2 foes	—
9	Astonish	Ghost	Physical	30	100	15	Normal	●
14	Confusion	Psychic	Special	50	100	25	Normal	—
17	Uproar	Normal	Special	50	100	10	1 random	—
22	Last Resort	Normal	Physical	130	100	5	Normal	—

● MOVES TAUGHT IN EXCHANGE FOR COLORED SHARDS

Name	Type	Kind	Power	Acc	PP	Range	DA
Icy Wind	Ice	Special	55	95	15	2 foes	—
Rollout	Rock	Physical	30	90	20	Normal	●
Snore	Normal	Special	40	100	15	Normal	—
Helping Hand	Normal	Status	—	—	20	1 ally	—
Signal Beam	Bug	Special	75	100	15	Normal	—
Zen Headbutt	Psychic	Physical	80	90	15	Normal	●
Last Resort	Normal	Physical	130	100	5	Normal	—
Trick	Psychic	Status	—	100	10	Normal	—
Knock Off	Dark	Physical	20	100	20	Normal	●
Swift	Normal	Special	60	—	20	2 foes	—
Uproar	Normal	Special	50	100	10	1 random	—

● EGG MOVES

Name	Type	Kind	Power	Acc	PP	Range	DA
Disable	Normal	Status	—	80	20	Normal	—
Curse	???	Status	—	—	10	Normal + Self	—
Hypnosis	Psychic	Status	—	60	20	Normal	—
Dream Eater	Psychic	Special	100	100	15	Normal	—
Wish	Normal	Status	—	—	10	Self	—
Future Sight	Psychic	Special	80	90	15	Normal	—
Recover	Normal	Status	—	—	10	Self	—

● PRIMARY WAY TO FIND

TRAINER'S PARTY — Trainer on Route 214

WILD POKÉMON — Route 211

COURSE OF STORY

ABILITY — ● Levitate

EGG GROUP — No Eggs

STATS —
HP ●
ATTACK ●
DEFENSE ●
SP. ATTACK ●●
SP. DEFENSE ●●
SPEED ●●

Sinnoh Pokédex No. 083 Wind Chime Pokémon

Chimecho

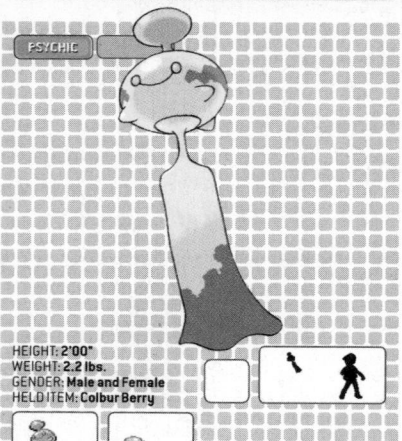

PSYCHIC

HEIGHT: 2'00"
WEIGHT: 2.2 lbs.
GENDER: Male and Female
HELD ITEM: Colbur Berry

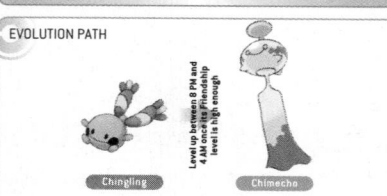

● M/F have same form

PLATINUM — Its cries echo inside its hollow body to emerge as beautiful notes for startling and repelling foes.

EVOLUTION PATH

Chingling → Level up between 8 PM and 4 AM on icts Friendship level is high enough → Chimecho

● TM & HM MOVES

No.	Name	Type	Kind	Power	Acc	PP	Range	DA
TM04	Calm Mind	Psychic	Status	—	—	20	Self	—
TM06	Toxic	Poison	Status	—	85	10	Normal	—
TM10	Hidden Power	Normal	Special	—	100	15	Normal	—
TM11	Sunny Day	Fire	Status	—	—	5	All	—
TM12	Taunt	Dark	Status	—	100	20	Normal	—
TM16	Light Screen	Psychic	Status	—	—	30	2 allies	—
TM17	Protect	Normal	Status	—	—	10	Self	—
TM18	Rain Dance	Water	Status	—	—	5	All	—
TM20	Safeguard	Normal	Status	—	—	25	2 allies	—
TM21	Frustration	Normal	Physical	—	100	20	Normal	•
TM27	Return	Normal	Physical	—	100	20	Normal	•
TM29	Psychic	Psychic	Special	90	100	10	Normal	—
TM30	Shadow Ball	Ghost	Special	80	100	15	Normal	—
TM32	Double Team	Normal	Status	—	—	15	Self	—
TM33	Reflect	Psychic	Status	—	—	20	2 allies	—
TM34	Shock Wave	Electric	Special	60	—	20	Normal	—
TM41	Torment	Dark	Status	—	100	15	Normal	—
TM42	Facade	Normal	Physical	70	100	20	Normal	•
TM43	Secret Power	Normal	Physical	70	100	20	Normal	•
TM44	Rest	Psychic	Status	—	—	10	Self	—
TM45	Attract	Normal	Status	—	100	15	Normal	—
TM48	Skill Swap	Psychic	Status	—	—	10	Normal	—
TM49	Snatch	Dark	Status	—	—	10	DoM	—
TM53	Energy Ball	Grass	Special	80	100	10	Normal	—
TM57	Charge Beam	Electric	Special	50	90	10	Normal	—
TM58	Endure	Normal	Status	—	—	10	Self	—
TM67	Recycle	Normal	Status	—	—	10	Self	—
TM70	Flash	Normal	Status	—	100	20	Normal	—
TM73	Thunder Wave	Electric	Status	—	100	20	Normal	—
TM77	Psych Up	Normal	Status	—	—	10	Normal	—
TM78	Captivate	Normal	Status	—	100	20	2 foes	—
TM82	Sleep Talk	Normal	Status	—	—	10	DoM	—
TM83	Natural Gift	Normal	Physical	—	100	15	Normal	•
TM85	Dream Eater	Psychic	Special	100	100	15	Normal	—
TM86	Grass Knot	Grass	Special	—	100	20	Normal	•
TM87	Swagger	Normal	Status	—	90	15	Normal	—
TM90	Substitute	Normal	Status	—	—	10	Self	—
TM92	Trick Room	Psychic	Status	—	—	5	All	—

● LEVEL-UP AND LEARNED MOVES

Lv	Name	Type	Kind	Power	Acc	PP	Range	DA
Base	Wrap	Normal	Physical	15	85	20	Normal	•
6	Growl	Normal	Status	—	100	40	2 foes	—
9	Astonish	Ghost	Physical	30	100	15	Normal	•
14	Confusion	Psychic	Special	50	100	25	Normal	—
17	Uproar	Normal	Special	50	100	10	1 random	—
22	Take Down	Normal	Physical	90	85	20	Normal	•
25	Yawn	Normal	Status	—	—	10	Normal	—
30	Psywave	Psychic	Special	—	80	15	Normal	—
33	Double-Edge	Normal	Physical	120	100	15	Normal	•
38	Heal Bell	Normal	Status	—	—	5	All allies	—
41	Safeguard	Normal	Status	—	—	25	2 allies	—
46	Extrasensory	Psychic	Special	80	100	30	Normal	—
49	Healing Wish	Psychic	Status	—	—	10	Self	—

● MOVES TAUGHT IN EXCHANGE FOR COLORED SHARDS

Name	Type	Kind	Power	Acc	PP	Range	DA
Icy Wind	Ice	Special	55	95	15	2 foes	—
Rollout	Rock	Physical	30	90	20	Normal	•
Snore	Normal	Special	40	100	15	Normal	—
Helping Hand	Normal	Status	—	—	20	1 ally	—
Signal Beam	Bug	Special	75	100	15	Normal	—
Zen Headbutt	Psychic	Physical	80	90	15	Normal	•
Last Resort	Normal	Physical	130	100	5	Normal	•
Trick	Psychic	Status	—	100	10	Normal	—
Knock Off	Dark	Physical	20	100	20	Normal	•
Uproar	Normal	Special	50	100	10	1 random	—

● EGG MOVES

Name	Type	Kind	Power	Acc	PP	Range	DA
Disable	Normal	Status	—	80	20	Normal	—
Curse	???	Status	—	—	10	Normal • Self	—
Hypnosis	Psychic	Status	—	60	20	Normal	—
Dream Eater	Psychic	Special	100	100	15	Normal	—
Wish	Normal	Status	—	—	10	Self	—
Future Sight	Psychic	Special	80	90	15	Normal	—

● PRIMARY WAY TO FIND

TRAINER'S PARTY	Trainer on Victory Road
WILD POKÉMON	Mt. Coronet (middle) 5F
COURSE OF STORY	

ABILITY ● Levitate

EGG GROUP Amorphous

STATS
HP ●●
ATTACK ●●
DEFENSE ●●
SP. ATTACK ●●●
SP. DEFENSE ●●●
SPEED ●●

Sinnoh Pokédex No. 084 Skunk Pokémon

Stunky

POISON DARK

HEIGHT: 1'04"
WEIGHT: 42.3 lbs.
GENDER: Male and Female
HELD ITEM: None

● M/F have same form

PLATINUM — It sprays a foul fluid from its rear. Its stench spreads over a mile radius, driving Pokémon away.

EVOLUTION PATH

Stunky → Lv.34 → Skuntank

● TM & HM MOVES

No.	Name	Type	Kind	Power	Acc	PP	Range	DA
TM05	Roar	Normal	Status	—	100	20	Normal	—
TM06	Toxic	Poison	Status	—	85	10	Normal	—
TM10	Hidden Power	Normal	Special	—	100	15	Normal	—
TM11	Sunny Day	Fire	Status	—	—	5	All	—
TM12	Taunt	Dark	Status	—	100	20	Normal	—
TM17	Protect	Normal	Status	—	—	10	Self	—
TM18	Rain Dance	Water	Status	—	—	5	All	—
TM21	Frustration	Normal	Physical	—	100	20	Normal	•
TM23	Iron Tail	Steel	Physical	100	75	15	Normal	•
TM27	Return	Normal	Physical	—	100	20	Normal	•
TM28	Dig	Ground	Physical	80	100	10	Normal	•
TM30	Shadow Ball	Ghost	Special	80	100	15	Normal	—
TM32	Double Team	Normal	Status	—	—	15	Self	—
TM35	Flamethrower	Fire	Special	95	100	15	Normal	—
TM36	Sludge Bomb	Poison	Special	90	100	10	Normal	—
TM38	Fire Blast	Fire	Special	120	85	5	Normal	—
TM41	Torment	Dark	Status	—	100	15	Normal	—
TM42	Facade	Normal	Physical	70	100	20	Normal	•
TM43	Secret Power	Normal	Physical	70	100	20	Normal	•
TM44	Rest	Psychic	Status	—	—	10	Self	—
TM45	Attract	Normal	Status	—	100	15	Normal	—
TM46	Thief	Dark	Physical	40	100	10	Normal	•
TM49	Snatch	Dark	Status	—	—	10	DoM	—
TM58	Endure	Normal	Status	—	—	10	Self	—
TM64	Explosion	Normal	Physical	250	100	5	2 foes • 1 ally	—
TM65	Shadow Claw	Ghost	Physical	70	100	15	Normal	•
TM66	Payback	Dark	Physical	50	100	10	Normal	—
TM78	Captivate	Normal	Status	—	100	20	2 foes	—
TM79	Dark Pulse	Dark	Special	80	100	15	Normal	—
TM82	Sleep Talk	Normal	Status	—	—	10	DoM	—
TM83	Natural Gift	Normal	Physical	—	100	15	Normal	•
TM87	Swagger	Normal	Status	—	90	15	Normal	—
TM90	Substitute	Normal	Status	—	—	10	Self	—
HM01	Cut	Normal	Physical	50	95	30	Normal	•
HM05	Defog	Flying	Status	—	—	15	Normal	—
HM06	Rock Smash	Fighting	Physical	40	100	15	Normal	•

● LEVEL-UP AND LEARNED MOVES

Lv	Name	Type	Kind	Power	Acc	PP	Range	DA
Base	Scratch	Normal	Physical	40	100	35	Normal	•
Base	Focus Energy	Normal	Status	—	—	30	Self	—
4	Poison Gas	Poison	Status	—	55	40	Normal	—
7	Screech	Normal	Status	—	85	40	Normal	—
10	Fury Swipes	Normal	Physical	18	80	15	Normal	•
14	SmokeScreen	Normal	Status	—	100	20	Normal	—
18	Feint	Normal	Physical	50	100	10	Normal	—
22	Slash	Normal	Physical	70	100	20	Normal	•
27	Toxic	Poison	Status	—	85	10	Normal	—
32	Night Slash	Dark	Physical	70	100	15	Normal	•
38	Memento	Dark	Status	—	100	10	Normal	—
44	Explosion	Normal	Physical	250	100	5	2 foes • 1 ally	—

● MOVES TAUGHT IN EXCHANGE FOR COLORED SHARDS

Name	Type	Kind	Power	Acc	PP	Range	DA
Mud-Slap	Ground	Special	20	100	10	Normal	—
Fury Cutter	Bug	Physical	10	95	20	Normal	•
Snore	Normal	Special	40	100	15	Normal	—
Sucker Punch	Dark	Physical	80	100	5	Normal	•
Swift	Normal	Special	60	—	20	2 foes	—

● EGG MOVES

Name	Type	Kind	Power	Acc	PP	Range	DA
Pursuit	Dark	Physical	40	100	20	Normal	—
Leer	Normal	Status	—	100	30	2 foes	—
Smog	Poison	Special	20	70	20	Normal	—
Double-Edge	Normal	Physical	120	100	15	Normal	•
Crunch	Dark	Physical	80	100	15	Normal	•
Scary Face	Normal	Status	—	90	10	Normal	—
Astonish	Ghost	Physical	30	100	15	Normal	•
Punishment	Dark	Physical	—	100	5	Normal	•

● PRIMARY WAY TO FIND

TRAINER'S PARTY	Galactic grunt you battle at Jubilife City
WILD POKÉMON	
COURSE OF STORY	

ABILITY ● Stench ● Aftermath

EGG GROUP Field

STATS
HP ●●
ATTACK ●●●
DEFENSE ●●
SP. ATTACK ●●
SP. DEFENSE ●●●
SPEED ●●●

Skuntank

Sinnoh Pokédex No. 085 Skunk Pokémon

POISON DARK

HEIGHT: 3'03"
WEIGHT: 83.8 lbs.
GENDER: Male and Female
HELD ITEM: None

● M/F have same form

PLATINUM: It attacks by spraying a horribly smelly fluid from the tip of its tail. Attacks from above confound it.

EVOLUTION PATH

Stunky → Lv34 → Skuntank

● TM & HM MOVES

No.	Name	Type	Kind	Power	Acc	PP	Range	DA
TM05	Roar	Normal	Status	—	100	20	Normal	
TM06	Toxic	Poison	Status	—	85	10	Normal	
TM10	Hidden Power	Normal	Special	—	100	15	Normal	
TM11	Sunny Day	Fire	Status	—	—	5	All	
TM12	Taunt	Dark	Status	—	100	20	Normal	
TM15	Hyper Beam	Normal	Special	150	90	5	Normal	
TM17	Protect	Normal	Status	—	—	10	Self	
TM18	Rain Dance	Water	Status	—	—	5	All	
TM21	Frustration	Normal	Physical	—	100	20	Normal	●
TM23	Iron Tail	Steel	Physical	100	75	15	Normal	●
TM27	Return	Normal	Physical	—	100	20	Normal	●
TM28	Dig	Ground	Physical	80	100	10	Normal	●
TM30	Shadow Ball	Ghost	Special	80	100	15	Normal	●
TM32	Double Team	Normal	Status	—	—	15	Self	
TM35	Flamethrower	Fire	Special	95	100	15	Normal	
TM36	Sludge Bomb	Poison	Special	90	100	10	Normal	
TM38	Fire Blast	Fire	Special	120	85	5	Normal	
TM41	Torment	Dark	Status	—	100	15	Normal	
TM42	Facade	Normal	Physical	70	100	20	Normal	●
TM43	Secret Power	Normal	Physical	70	100	20	Normal	●
TM44	Rest	Psychic	Status	—	—	10	Self	
TM45	Attract	Normal	Status	—	100	15	Normal	
TM46	Thief	Dark	Physical	40	100	10	Normal	●
TM49	Snatch	Dark	Status	—	—	10	DoM	
TM58	Endure	Normal	Status	—	—	10	Self	
TM64	Explosion	Normal	Physical	250	100	5	2 foes + 1 ally	
TM65	Shadow Claw	Ghost	Physical	70	100	15	Normal	●
TM66	Payback	Dark	Physical	50	100	10	Normal	●
TM68	Giga Impact	Normal	Physical	150	90	5	Normal	●
TM78	Captivate	Normal	Status	—	100	20	2 foes	
TM79	Dark Pulse	Dark	Special	80	100	15	Normal	
TM82	Sleep Talk	Normal	Status	—	—	10	DoM	
TM83	Natural Gift	Normal	Physical	—	100	15	Normal	●
TM84	Poison Jab	Poison	Physical	80	100	20	Normal	●
TM87	Swagger	Normal	Status	—	90	15	Normal	
TM90	Substitute	Normal	Status	—	—	10	Self	
HM01	Cut	Normal	Physical	50	95	30	Normal	●
HM04	Strength	Normal	Physical	80	100	15	Normal	●
HM05	Defog	Flying	Status	—	—	15	Normal	
HM06	Rock Smash	Fighting	Physical	40	100	15	Normal	●

● LEVEL-UP AND LEARNED MOVES

Lv	Name	Type	Kind	Power	Acc	PP	Range	DA
Base	Scratch	Normal	Physical	40	100	35	Normal	●
Base	Focus Energy	Normal	Status	—	—	30	Self	—
Base	Poison Gas	Poison	Status	—	55	40	Normal	—
4	Poison Gas	Poison	Status	—	55	40	Normal	—
7	Screech	Normal	Status	—	85	40	Normal	—
10	Fury Swipes	Normal	Physical	18	80	15	Normal	●
14	SmokeScreen	Normal	Status	—	100	20	Normal	—
18	Feint	Normal	Physical	50	100	10	Normal	●
22	Slash	Normal	Physical	70	100	20	Normal	●
27	Toxic	Poison	Status	—	85	10	Normal	—
32	Night Slash	Dark	Physical	70	100	15	Normal	●
34	Flamethrower	Fire	Special	95	100	15	Normal	—
42	Memento	Dark	Status	—	100	10	Normal	—
52	Explosion	Normal	Physical	250	100	5	2 foes + 1 ally	—

● MOVES TAUGHT IN EXCHANGE FOR COLORED SHARDS

Name	Type	Kind	Power	Acc	PP	Range	DA
Mud-Slap	Ground	Special	20	100	10	Normal	—
Fury Cutter	Bug	Physical	10	95	20	Normal	●
Snore	Normal	Special	40	100	15	Normal	—
Sucker Punch	Dark	Physical	80	100	5	Normal	●
Swift	Normal	Special	60	—	20	2 foes	—

● PRIMARY WAY TO FIND

TRAINER'S PARTY: Team Galactic Commander Jupiter, when you battle her at the Galactic Eterna Building

WILD POKÉMON

COURSE OF STORY

ABILITY: ● Stench ● Aftermath

EGG GROUP: Field

STATS: HP ●●● / ATTACK ●● / DEFENSE ●● / SP. ATTACK ●● / SP. DEFENSE ●● / SPEED ●●●

Meditite

Sinnoh Pokédex No. 086 Meditate Pokémon

Fighting PSYCHIC

HEIGHT: 2'00"
WEIGHT: 24.7 lbs.
GENDER: Male and Female
HELD ITEM: None

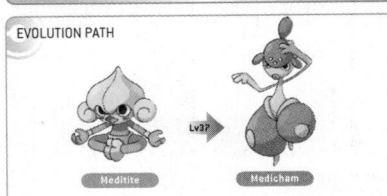

● Male form ● Female form

PLATINUM: It always trains deep in mountains. It levitates when it heightens its spiritual power through meditation.

EVOLUTION PATH

Meditite → Lv37 → Medicham

● TM & HM MOVES

No.	Name	Type	Kind	Power	Acc	PP	Range	DA
TM01	Focus Punch	Fighting	Physical	150	100	20	Normal	●
TM04	Calm Mind	Psychic	Status	—	—	20	Self	—
TM06	Toxic	Poison	Status	—	85	10	Normal	—
TM08	Bulk Up	Fighting	Status	—	—	20	Self	—
TM10	Hidden Power	Normal	Special	—	100	15	Normal	—
TM11	Sunny Day	Fire	Status	—	—	5	All	—
TM16	Light Screen	Psychic	Status	—	—	30	2 allies	—
TM17	Protect	Normal	Status	—	—	10	Self	—
TM18	Rain Dance	Water	Status	—	—	5	All	—
TM21	Frustration	Normal	Physical	—	100	20	Normal	●
TM27	Return	Normal	Physical	—	100	20	Normal	●
TM29	Psychic	Psychic	Special	90	100	10	Normal	—
TM30	Shadow Ball	Ghost	Special	80	100	15	Normal	—
TM31	Brick Break	Fighting	Physical	75	100	15	Normal	●
TM32	Double Team	Normal	Status	—	—	15	Self	—
TM33	Reflect	Psychic	Status	—	—	20	2 allies	—
TM39	Rock Tomb	Rock	Physical	50	80	10	Normal	●
TM42	Facade	Normal	Physical	70	100	20	Normal	●
TM43	Secret Power	Normal	Physical	70	100	20	Normal	●
TM44	Rest	Psychic	Status	—	—	10	Self	—
TM45	Attract	Normal	Status	—	100	15	Normal	—
TM52	Focus Blast	Fighting	Special	120	70	5	Normal	—
TM56	Fling	Dark	Physical	—	100	10	Normal	—
TM58	Endure	Normal	Status	—	—	10	Self	—
TM60	Drain Punch	Fighting	Physical	60	100	5	Normal	●
TM67	Recycle	Normal	Status	—	—	10	Self	—
TM70	Flash	Normal	Status	—	100	20	Normal	—
TM77	Psych Up	Normal	Status	—	—	10	Self	—
TM78	Captivate	Normal	Status	—	100	20	2 foes	—
TM80	Rock Slide	Rock	Physical	75	90	10	2 foes	—
TM82	Sleep Talk	Normal	Status	—	—	10	DoM	—
TM83	Natural Gift	Normal	Physical	—	100	15	Normal	—
TM84	Poison Jab	Poison	Physical	80	100	20	Normal	●
TM85	Dream Eater	Psychic	Special	100	100	15	Normal	—
TM86	Grass Knot	Grass	Special	—	100	20	Normal	—
TM87	Swagger	Normal	Status	—	90	15	Normal	—
TM90	Substitute	Normal	Status	—	—	10	Self	—
HM04	Strength	Normal	Physical	80	100	15	Normal	●
HM06	Rock Smash	Fighting	Physical	40	100	15	Normal	●

● LEVEL-UP AND LEARNED MOVES

Lv	Name	Type	Kind	Power	Acc	PP	Range	DA
Base	Bide	Normal	Physical	—	—	10	Self	—
4	Meditate	Psychic	Status	—	—	40	Self	—
8	Confusion	Psychic	Special	50	100	25	Normal	—
11	Detect	Fighting	Status	—	—	5	Self	—
15	Hidden Power	Normal	Special	—	100	15	Normal	—
18	Mind Reader	Normal	Status	—	—	5	Normal	—
22	Feint	Normal	Physical	50	100	10	Normal	●
25	Calm Mind	Psychic	Status	—	—	20	Self	—
29	Force Palm	Fighting	Physical	60	100	10	Normal	●
32	Hi Jump Kick	Fighting	Physical	100	90	20	Normal	●
36	Psych Up	Normal	Status	—	—	10	Self	—
39	Power Trick	Psychic	Status	—	—	10	Self	—
43	Reversal	Fighting	Physical	—	100	15	Normal	●
46	Recover	Normal	Status	—	—	10	Self	—

● MOVES TAUGHT IN EXCHANGE FOR COLORED SHARDS

Name	Type	Kind	Power	Acc	PP	Range	DA
Mud-Slap	Ground	Special	20	100	10	Normal	—
ThunderPunch	Electric	Physical	75	100	15	Normal	●
Fire Punch	Fire	Physical	75	100	15	Normal	●
Ice Punch	Ice	Physical	75	100	15	Normal	●
Snore	Normal	Special	40	100	15	Normal	—
Helping Hand	Normal	Status	—	—	20	1 ally	—
Signal Beam	Bug	Special	75	100	15	Normal	—
Zen Headbutt	Psychic	Physical	80	90	15	Normal	●
Vacuum Wave	Fighting	Special	40	100	30	Normal	—
Trick	Psychic	Status	—	100	10	Normal	—
Swift	Normal	Special	60	—	20	2 foes	—

● EGG MOVES

Name	Type	Kind	Power	Acc	PP	Range	DA
Fire Punch	Fire	Physical	75	100	15	Normal	●
ThunderPunch	Electric	Physical	75	100	15	Normal	●
Ice Punch	Ice	Physical	75	100	15	Normal	●
Foresight	Normal	Status	—	—	40	Normal	—
Fake Out	Normal	Physical	40	100	10	Normal	●
Baton Pass	Normal	Status	—	—	40	Self	—
DynamicPunch	Fighting	Physical	100	50	5	Normal	●
Power Swap	Psychic	Status	—	—	10	Normal	—
Guard Swap	Psychic	Status	—	—	10	Normal	—
Psycho Cut	Psychic	Physical	70	100	20	Normal	●
Bullet Punch	Steel	Physical	40	100	30	Normal	●

● PRIMARY WAY TO FIND

TRAINER'S PARTY: Trainer in Eterna Forest

WILD POKÉMON: Celestic Town side of Route 210

COURSE OF STORY

ABILITY: ● Pure Power

EGG GROUP: Human-Like

STATS: HP ● / ATTACK ●● / DEFENSE ●● / SP. ATTACK ●● / SP. DEFENSE ●● / SPEED ●●

Medicham

Fighting PSYCHIC

● TM & HM MOVES

No.	Name	Type	Kind	Power	Acc	PP	Range	DA
TM01	Focus Punch	Fighting	Physical	150	100	20	Normal	•
TM04	Calm Mind	Psychic	Status	—	—	20	Self	—
TM06	Toxic	Poison	Status	—	85	10	Normal	—
TM08	Bulk Up	Fighting	Status	—	—	20	Self	—
TM10	Hidden Power	Normal	Special	—	100	15	Normal	—
TM11	Sunny Day	Fire	Status	—	—	5	All	—
TM15	Hyper Beam	Normal	Special	150	90	5	Normal	—
TM16	Light Screen	Psychic	Status	—	—	30	2 allies	—
TM17	Protect	Normal	Status	—	—	10	Self	—
TM18	Rain Dance	Water	Status	—	—	5	All	—
TM21	Frustration	Normal	Physical	—	100	20	Normal	•
TM27	Return	Normal	Physical	—	100	20	Normal	•
TM29	Psychic	Psychic	Special	90	100	10	Normal	—
TM30	Shadow Ball	Ghost	Special	80	100	15	Normal	—
TM31	Brick Break	Fighting	Physical	75	100	15	Normal	•
TM32	Double Team	Normal	Status	—	—	15	Self	—
TM33	Reflect	Psychic	Status	—	—	20	2 allies	—
TM39	Rock Tomb	Rock	Physical	50	80	10	Normal	•
TM42	Facade	Normal	Physical	70	100	20	Normal	•
TM43	Secret Power	Normal	Physical	70	100	20	Normal	•
TM44	Rest	Psychic	Status	—	—	10	Self	—
TM45	Attract	Normal	Status	—	100	15	Normal	—
TM52	Focus Blast	Fighting	Special	120	70	5	Normal	—
TM53	Energy Ball	Grass	Special	80	100	10	Normal	—
TM56	Fling	Dark	Physical	—	100	10	Normal	•
TM58	Endure	Normal	Status	—	—	10	Self	—
TM60	Drain Punch	Fighting	Physical	60	100	5	Normal	•
TM67	Recycle	Normal	Status	—	—	10	Self	—
TM68	Giga Impact	Normal	Physical	150	90	5	Normal	•
TM70	Flash	Normal	Status	—	100	20	Normal	—
TM77	Psych Up	Normal	Status	—	—	10	Self	—
TM78	Captivate	Normal	Status	—	100	20	2 foes	—
TM80	Rock Slide	Rock	Physical	75	90	10	2 foes	•
TM82	Sleep Talk	Normal	Status	—	—	10	DoM	—
TM83	Natural Gift	Normal	Physical	—	100	15	Normal	•
TM84	Poison Jab	Poison	Physical	80	100	20	Normal	•
TM85	Dream Eater	Psychic	Special	100	100	15	Normal	—
TM86	Grass Knot	Grass	Special	—	100	20	Normal	•
TM87	Swagger	Normal	Status	—	90	15	Normal	—
TM90	Substitute	Normal	Status	—	—	10	Self	—
HM04	Strength	Normal	Physical	80	100	15	Normal	•
HM06	Rock Smash	Fighting	Physical	40	100	15	Normal	•

● LEVEL-UP AND LEARNED MOVES

Lv	Name	Type	Kind	Power	Acc	PP	Range	DA
Base	Fire Punch	Fire	Physical	75	100	15	Normal	•
Base	ThunderPunch	Electric	Physical	75	100	15	Normal	•
Base	Ice Punch	Ice	Physical	75	100	15	Normal	•
Base	Bide	Normal	Physical	—	—	10	Self	—
Base	Meditate	Psychic	Status	—	—	40	Self	—
Base	Confusion	Psychic	Special	50	100	25	Normal	—
Base	Detect	Fighting	Status	—	—	5	Self	—
4	Meditate	Psychic	Status	—	—	40	Self	—
11	Confusion	Psychic	Special	50	100	25	Normal	—
11	Detect	Fighting	Status	—	—	5	Self	—
15	Hidden Power	Normal	Special	—	100	15	Normal	—
18	Mind Reader	Normal	Status	—	—	5	Normal	—
22	Feint	Normal	Physical	50	100	10	Normal	—
25	Calm Mind	Psychic	Status	—	—	20	Self	—
29	Force Palm	Fighting	Physical	60	100	10	Normal	•
32	Hi Jump Kick	Fighting	Physical	100	90	20	Normal	•
36	Psych Up	Normal	Status	—	—	10	Self	—
42	Power Trick	Psychic	Status	—	—	10	Self	—
49	Reversal	Fighting	Physical	—	100	15	Normal	•
55	Recover	Normal	Status	—	—	10	Self	—

● MOVES TAUGHT IN EXCHANGE FOR COLORED SHARDS

Name	Type	Kind	Power	Acc	PP	Range	DA
Mud-Slap	Ground	Special	20	100	10	Normal	•
ThunderPunch	Electric	Physical	75	100	15	Normal	•
Fire Punch	Fire	Physical	75	100	15	Normal	•
Ice Punch	Ice	Physical	75	100	15	Normal	•
Snore	Normal	Special	40	100	15	Normal	—
Helping Hand	Normal	Status	—	—	20	1 ally	—
Signal Beam	Bug	Special	75	100	15	Normal	—
Zen Headbutt	Psychic	Physical	80	90	15	Normal	•
Vacuum Wave	Fighting	Special	40	100	30	Normal	—
Trick	Psychic	Status	—	100	10	Normal	—
Swift	Normal	Special	60	—	20	2 foes	—

HEIGHT: 4'03"
WEIGHT: 69.4 lbs.
GENDER: Male and Female
HELD ITEM: None

● Male form ● Female form

PLATINUM It gains the ability to see the aura of its opponents by honing its mind through starvation.

EVOLUTION PATH: Meditite — Lv37 — Medicham

ABILITY ● Pure Power
EGG GROUP Human-Like
STATS: HP ●● ATTACK ●●● DEFENSE ●● SP.ATTACK ●● SP.DEFENSE ●● SPEED ●●●

● PRIMARY WAY TO FIND
TRAINER'S PARTY Trainer on Route 220
WILD POKÉMON Mt. Coronet (middle) 2F
COURSE OF STORY

Bronzor

STEEL PSYCHIC

● TM & HM MOVES

No.	Name	Type	Kind	Power	Acc	PP	Range	DA
TM04	Calm Mind	Psychic	Status	—	—	20	Self	—
TM06	Toxic	Poison	Status	—	85	10	Normal	—
TM10	Hidden Power	Normal	Special	—	100	15	Normal	—
TM11	Sunny Day	Fire	Status	—	—	5	All	—
TM16	Light Screen	Psychic	Status	—	—	30	2 allies	—
TM17	Protect	Normal	Status	—	—	10	Self	—
TM18	Rain Dance	Water	Status	—	—	5	All	—
TM20	Safeguard	Normal	Status	—	—	25	2 allies	—
TM21	Frustration	Normal	Physical	—	100	20	Normal	•
TM22	SolarBeam	Grass	Special	120	100	10	Normal	—
TM26	Earthquake	Ground	Physical	100	100	10	2 foes • 1 ally	•
TM27	Return	Normal	Physical	—	100	20	Normal	•
TM29	Psychic	Psychic	Special	90	100	10	Normal	—
TM30	Shadow Ball	Ghost	Special	80	100	15	Normal	—
TM32	Double Team	Normal	Status	—	—	15	Self	—
TM33	Reflect	Psychic	Status	—	—	20	2 allies	—
TM37	Sandstorm	Rock	Status	—	—	10	All	—
TM39	Rock Tomb	Rock	Physical	50	80	10	Normal	•
TM42	Facade	Normal	Physical	70	100	20	Normal	•
TM43	Secret Power	Normal	Physical	70	100	20	Normal	•
TM44	Rest	Psychic	Status	—	—	10	Self	—
TM48	Skill Swap	Psychic	Status	—	—	10	Normal	—
TM57	Charge Beam	Electric	Special	50	90	10	Normal	—
TM58	Endure	Normal	Status	—	—	10	Self	—
TM66	Payback	Dark	Physical	50	100	10	Normal	•
TM67	Recycle	Normal	Status	—	—	10	Self	—
TM69	Rock Polish	Rock	Status	—	—	20	Self	—
TM70	Flash	Normal	Status	—	100	20	Normal	—
TM74	Gyro Ball	Steel	Physical	—	100	5	Normal	•
TM76	Stealth Rock	Rock	Status	—	—	20	2 foes	—
TM77	Psych Up	Normal	Status	—	—	10	Normal	—
TM80	Rock Slide	Rock	Physical	75	90	10	2 foes	•
TM82	Sleep Talk	Normal	Status	—	—	10	DoM	—
TM83	Natural Gift	Normal	Physical	—	100	15	Normal	•
TM85	Dream Eater	Psychic	Special	100	100	15	Normal	—
TM86	Grass Knot	Grass	Special	—	100	20	Normal	•
TM87	Swagger	Normal	Status	—	90	15	Normal	—
TM90	Substitute	Normal	Status	—	—	10	Self	—
TM91	Flash Cannon	Steel	Special	80	100	10	Normal	—
TM92	Trick Room	Psychic	Status	—	—	5	All	—

● LEVEL-UP AND LEARNED MOVES

Lv	Name	Type	Kind	Power	Acc	PP	Range	DA
Base	Tackle	Normal	Physical	35	95	35	Normal	•
Base	Confusion	Psychic	Special	50	100	25	Normal	—
7	Hypnosis	Psychic	Status	—	60	20	Normal	—
12	Imprison	Psychic	Status	—	—	10	Self	—
14	Confuse Ray	Ghost	Status	—	100	10	Normal	—
19	Extrasensory	Psychic	Special	80	100	30	Normal	—
26	Iron Defense	Steel	Status	—	—	15	Self	—
30	Safeguard	Normal	Status	—	—	25	2 allies	—
35	Gyro Ball	Steel	Physical	—	100	5	Normal	•
37	Future Sight	Psychic	Special	80	90	15	Normal	—
41	Faint Attack	Dark	Physical	60	—	20	Normal	—
49	Payback	Dark	Physical	50	100	10	Normal	•
52	Heal Block	Psychic	Status	—	100	15	2 foes	—

● MOVES TAUGHT IN EXCHANGE FOR COLORED SHARDS

Name	Type	Kind	Power	Acc	PP	Range	DA
Rollout	Rock	Physical	30	90	20	Normal	•
Snore	Normal	Special	40	100	15	Normal	—
AncientPower	Rock	Special	60	100	5	Normal	—
Signal Beam	Bug	Special	75	100	15	Normal	—
Trick	Psychic	Status	—	100	10	Normal	—

● EGG MOVES

Name	Type	Kind	Power	Acc	PP	Range	DA

HEIGHT: 1'08"
WEIGHT: 133.4 lbs.
GENDER: Unknown
HELD ITEM: Metal Coat

● Gender unknown

PLATINUM There are researchers who believe this Pokémon reflected like a mirror in the distant past.

EVOLUTION PATH: Bronzor — Lv33 — Bronzong

ABILITY ● Levitate ● Heatproof
EGG GROUP Mineral
STATS: HP ●● ATTACK ● DEFENSE ●●● SP.ATTACK ● SP.DEFENSE ●●● SPEED ●

● PRIMARY WAY TO FIND
TRAINER'S PARTY Trainer in the Wayward Cave
WILD POKÉMON Wayward Cave
COURSE OF STORY

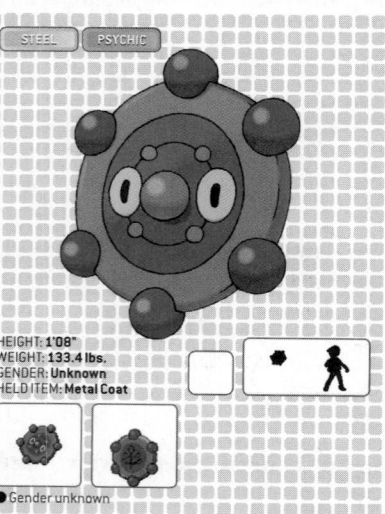

Bronzong

STEEL | PSYCHIC

HEIGHT: 4'03"
WEIGHT: 412.3 lbs.
GENDER: Unknown
HELD ITEM: Metal Coat

● Gender unknown

PLATINUM — It brought rains by opening portals to another world. It was revered as a bringer of plentiful harvests.

EVOLUTION PATH

Bronzor → Lv33 → Bronzong

| ABILITY | ● Levitate ● Heatproof |
| EGG GROUP | Mineral |

STATS
HP ●●
ATTACK ●●●
DEFENSE ●●●●
SP. ATTACK ●●●
SP. DEFENSE ●●●
SPEED ●

● TM & HM MOVES

No.	Name	Type	Kind	Power	Acc	PP	Range	DA
TM04	Calm Mind	Psychic	Status	—	—	20	Self	—
TM06	Toxic	Poison	Status	—	85	10	Normal	—
TM10	Hidden Power	Normal	Special	—	100	15	Normal	—
TM11	Sunny Day	Fire	Status	—	—	5	All	—
TM15	Hyper Beam	Normal	Special	150	90	5	Normal	—
TM16	Light Screen	Psychic	Status	—	—	30	2 allies	—
TM17	Protect	Normal	Status	—	—	10	Self	—
TM18	Rain Dance	Water	Status	—	—	5	All	—
TM20	Safeguard	Normal	Status	—	—	25	2 allies	—
TM21	Frustration	Normal	Physical	—	100	20	Normal	●
TM22	SolarBeam	Grass	Special	120	100	10	Normal	—
TM26	Earthquake	Ground	Physical	100	100	10	2 foes • 1 ally	—
TM27	Return	Normal	Physical	—	100	20	Normal	●
TM29	Psychic	Psychic	Special	90	100	10	Normal	—
TM30	Shadow Ball	Ghost	Special	80	100	15	Normal	—
TM32	Double Team	Normal	Status	—	—	15	Self	—
TM33	Reflect	Psychic	Status	—	—	20	2 allies	—
TM37	Sandstorm	Rock	Status	—	—	10	All	—
TM39	Rock Tomb	Rock	Physical	50	80	10	Normal	—
TM42	Facade	Normal	Physical	70	100	20	Normal	●
TM43	Secret Power	Normal	Physical	70	100	20	Normal	●
TM44	Rest	Psychic	Status	—	—	10	Self	—
TM48	Skill Swap	Psychic	Status	—	—	10	Normal	—
TM57	Charge Beam	Electric	Special	50	90	10	Normal	—
TM58	Endure	Normal	Status	—	—	10	Self	—
TM64	Explosion	Normal	Physical	250	100	5	2 foes • 1 ally	—
TM66	Payback	Dark	Physical	50	100	10	Normal	●
TM67	Recycle	Normal	Status	—	—	10	Self	—
TM68	Giga Impact	Normal	Physical	150	90	5	Normal	●
TM69	Rock Polish	Rock	Status	—	—	20	Self	—
TM70	Flash	Normal	Status	—	100	20	Normal	—
TM74	Gyro Ball	Steel	Physical	—	100	5	Normal	●
TM76	Stealth Rock	Rock	Status	—	—	20	2 foes	—
TM77	Psych Up	Normal	Status	—	—	10	Normal	—
TM80	Rock Slide	Rock	Physical	75	90	10	2 foes	—
TM82	Sleep Talk	Normal	Status	—	—	10	DoM	—
TM83	Natural Gift	Normal	Physical	—	100	15	Normal	●
TM85	Dream Eater	Psychic	Special	100	100	15	Normal	—
TM86	Grass Knot	Grass	Special	—	100	20	Normal	●
TM87	Swagger	Normal	Status	—	90	15	Normal	—
TM90	Substitute	Normal	Status	—	—	10	Self	—
TM91	Flash Cannon	Steel	Special	80	100	10	Normal	—
TM92	Trick Room	Psychic	Status	—	—	5	All	—
HM04	Strength	Normal	Physical	80	100	15	Normal	●
HM06	Rock Smash	Fighting	Physical	40	100	15	Normal	●

● LEVEL-UP AND LEARNED MOVES

Lv	Name	Type	Kind	Power	Acc	PP	Range	DA
Base	Sunny Day	Fire	Status	—	—	5	All	—
Base	Rain Dance	Water	Status	—	—	5	All	—
Base	Tackle	Normal	Physical	35	95	35	Normal	●
Base	Confusion	Psychic	Special	50	100	25	Normal	—
Base	Hypnosis	Psychic	Status	—	60	20	Normal	—
Base	Imprison	Psychic	Status	—	—	10	Self	—
7	Hypnosis	Psychic	Status	—	60	20	Normal	—
12	Imprison	Psychic	Status	—	—	10	Self	—
14	Confuse Ray	Ghost	Status	—	100	10	Normal	—
19	Extrasensory	Psychic	Special	80	100	30	Normal	—
26	Iron Defense	Steel	Status	—	—	15	Self	—
30	Safeguard	Normal	Status	—	—	25	2 allies	—
33	Block	Normal	Status	—	—	5	Normal	—
38	Gyro Ball	Steel	Physical	—	100	5	Normal	●
43	Future Sight	Psychic	Special	80	90	15	Normal	—
50	Faint Attack	Dark	Physical	60	—	20	Normal	—
61	Payback	Dark	Physical	50	100	10	Normal	●
67	Heal Block	Psychic	Status	—	100	15	2 foes	—

● MOVES TAUGHT IN EXCHANGE FOR COLORED SHARDS

Name	Type	Kind	Power	Acc	PP	Range	DA
Rollout	Rock	Physical	30	90	20	Normal	●
Iron Head	Steel	Physical	80	100	15	Normal	●
Snore	Normal	Special	40	100	15	Normal	—
AncientPower	Rock	Special	60	100	5	Normal	—
Signal Beam	Bug	Special	75	100	15	Normal	—
Zen Headbutt	Psychic	Physical	80	90	15	Normal	●
Trick	Psychic	Status	—	100	10	Normal	—

● PRIMARY WAY TO FIND

TRAINER'S PARTY	Elite Four member Lucian
WILD POKÉMON	Mt. Coronet (middle) 2F
COURSE OF STORY	

Ponyta

FIRE

HEIGHT: 3'03"
WEIGHT: 66.1 lbs.
GENDER: Male and Female
HELD ITEM: Shuca Berry

● M/F have same form

PLATINUM — As a newborn, it can barely stand. However, through galloping, its legs are made tougher and faster.

EVOLUTION PATH

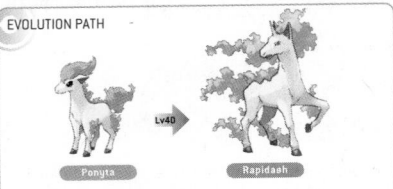

Ponyta → Lv40 → Rapidaah

| ABILITY | ● Run Away ● Flash Fire |
| EGG GROUP | Field |

STATS
HP ●●
ATTACK ●●●
DEFENSE ●●
SP. ATTACK ●●
SP. DEFENSE ●●●
SPEED ●●●

● TM & HM MOVES

No.	Name	Type	Kind	Power	Acc	PP	Range	DA
TM06	Toxic	Poison	Status	—	85	10	Normal	—
TM10	Hidden Power	Normal	Special	—	100	15	Normal	—
TM11	Sunny Day	Fire	Status	—	—	5	All	—
TM17	Protect	Normal	Status	—	—	10	Self	—
TM21	Frustration	Normal	Physical	—	100	20	Normal	●
TM22	SolarBeam	Grass	Special	120	100	10	Normal	—
TM23	Iron Tail	Steel	Physical	100	75	15	Normal	●
TM27	Return	Normal	Physical	—	100	20	Normal	●
TM32	Double Team	Normal	Status	—	—	15	Self	—
TM35	Flamethrower	Fire	Special	95	100	15	Normal	—
TM38	Fire Blast	Fire	Special	120	85	5	Normal	—
TM42	Facade	Normal	Physical	70	100	20	Normal	●
TM43	Secret Power	Normal	Physical	70	100	20	Normal	●
TM44	Rest	Psychic	Status	—	—	10	Self	—
TM45	Attract	Normal	Status	—	100	15	Normal	—
TM50	Overheat	Fire	Special	140	90	5	Normal	—
TM58	Endure	Normal	Status	—	—	10	Self	—
TM61	Will-O-Wisp	Fire	Status	—	75	15	Normal	—
TM78	Captivate	Normal	Status	—	100	20	2 foes	—
TM82	Sleep Talk	Normal	Status	—	—	10	DoM	—
TM83	Natural Gift	Normal	Physical	—	100	15	Normal	●
TM87	Swagger	Normal	Status	—	90	15	Normal	—
TM90	Substitute	Normal	Status	—	—	10	Self	—
HM04	Strength	Normal	Physical	80	100	15	Normal	●

● LEVEL-UP AND LEARNED MOVES

Lv	Name	Type	Kind	Power	Acc	PP	Range	DA
Base	Growl	Normal	Status	—	100	40	2 foes	—
Base	Tackle	Normal	Physical	35	95	35	Normal	●
8	Tail Whip	Normal	Status	—	100	30	2 foes	—
10	Ember	Fire	Special	40	100	25	Normal	—
15	Flame Wheel	Fire	Physical	60	100	25	Normal	●
19	Stomp	Normal	Physical	65	100	20	Normal	●
24	Fire Spin	Fire	Special	15	70	15	Normal	—
28	Take Down	Normal	Physical	90	85	20	Normal	●
33	Agility	Psychic	Status	—	—	30	Self	—
37	Fire Blast	Fire	Special	120	85	5	Normal	—
42	Bounce	Flying	Physical	85	85	5	Normal	●
46	Flare Blitz	Fire	Physical	120	100	15	Normal	●

● MOVES TAUGHT IN EXCHANGE FOR COLORED SHARDS

Name	Type	Kind	Power	Acc	PP	Range	DA
Snore	Normal	Special	40	100	15	Normal	—
Bounce	Flying	Physical	85	85	5	Normal	●
Heat Wave	Fire	Special	100	90	10	2 foes	—
Swift	Normal	Special	60	—	20	2 foes	—

● EGG MOVES

Name	Type	Kind	Power	Acc	PP	Range	DA
Flame Wheel	Fire	Physical	60	100	25	Normal	●
Thrash	Normal	Physical	90	100	20	1 random	●
Double Kick	Fighting	Physical	30	100	30	Normal	●
Hypnosis	Psychic	Status	—	60	20	Normal	—
Charm	Normal	Status	—	100	20	Normal	—
Double-Edge	Normal	Physical	120	100	15	Normal	●
Horn Drill	Normal	Physical	—	30	5	Normal	—

● PRIMARY WAY TO FIND

TRAINER'S PARTY	Trainer on Route 205
WILD POKÉMON	Route 206
COURSE OF STORY	

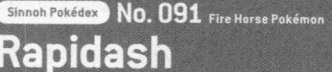

Rapidash

FIRE

HEIGHT: 5'07"
WEIGHT: 209.4 lbs.
GENDER: Male and Female
HELD ITEM: None

● M/F have same form

PLATINUM When at an all-out gallop, its blazing mane sparkles, enhancing its beautiful appearance.

EVOLUTION PATH

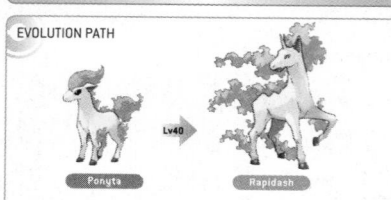

Ponyta — Lv40 → Rapidash

● TM & HM MOVES

No.	Name	Type	Kind	Power	Acc	PP	Range	DA
TM06	Toxic	Poison	Status	—	85	10	Normal	—
TM10	Hidden Power	Normal	Special	—	100	15	Normal	—
TM11	Sunny Day	Fire	Status	—	—	5	All	—
TM15	Hyper Beam	Normal	Special	150	90	5	Normal	—
TM17	Protect	Normal	Status	—	—	10	Self	—
TM21	Frustration	Normal	Physical	—	100	20	Normal	●
TM22	SolarBeam	Grass	Special	120	100	10	Normal	—
TM23	Iron Tail	Steel	Physical	100	75	15	Normal	●
TM27	Return	Normal	Physical	—	100	20	Normal	●
TM32	Double Team	Normal	Status	—	—	15	Self	—
TM35	Flamethrower	Fire	Special	95	100	15	Normal	—
TM38	Fire Blast	Fire	Special	120	85	5	Normal	—
TM42	Facade	Normal	Physical	70	100	20	Normal	●
TM43	Secret Power	Normal	Physical	70	100	20	Normal	●
TM44	Rest	Psychic	Status	—	—	10	Self	—
TM45	Attract	Normal	Status	—	100	15	Normal	—
TM50	Overheat	Fire	Special	140	90	5	Normal	—
TM58	Endure	Normal	Status	—	—	10	Self	—
TM61	Will-O-Wisp	Fire	Status	—	75	15	Normal	—
TM68	Giga Impact	Normal	Physical	150	90	5	Normal	●
TM78	Captivate	Normal	Status	—	100	20	2 foes	—
TM82	Sleep Talk	Normal	Status	—	—	10	DoM	—
TM83	Natural Gift	Normal	Physical	—	100	15	Normal	●
TM84	Poison Jab	Poison	Physical	80	100	20	Normal	●
TM87	Swagger	Normal	Status	—	90	15	Normal	—
TM90	Substitute	Normal	Status	—	—	10	Self	—
HM04	Strength	Normal	Physical	80	100	15	Normal	●

● LEVEL-UP AND LEARNED MOVES

Lv	Name	Type	Kind	Power	Acc	PP	Range	DA
Base	Poison Jab	Poison	Physical	80	100	20	Normal	●
Base	Megahorn	Bug	Physical	120	85	10	Normal	●
Base	Growl	Normal	Status	—	100	40	2 foes	—
Base	Quick Attack	Normal	Physical	40	100	30	Normal	●
Base	Tail Whip	Normal	Status	—	100	30	2 foes	—
Base	Ember	Fire	Special	40	100	25	Normal	—
6	Tail Whip	Normal	Status	—	100	30	2 foes	—
10	Ember	Fire	Special	40	100	25	Normal	—
15	Flame Wheel	Fire	Physical	60	100	25	Normal	—
19	Stomp	Normal	Physical	65	100	20	Normal	●
24	Fire Spin	Fire	Special	15	70	15	Normal	—
28	Take Down	Normal	Physical	90	85	20	Normal	●
33	Agility	Psychic	Status	—	—	30	Self	—
37	Fire Blast	Fire	Special	120	85	5	Normal	—
40	Fury Attack	Normal	Physical	15	85	20	Normal	●
47	Bounce	Flying	Physical	85	85	5	Normal	●
50	Flare Blitz	Fire	Physical	120	100	15	Normal	●

● MOVES TAUGHT IN EXCHANGE FOR COLORED SHARDS

Name	Type	Kind	Power	Acc	PP	Range	DA
Snore	Normal	Special	40	100	15	Normal	—
Bounce	Flying	Physical	85	85	5	Normal	●
Heat Wave	Fire	Special	100	90	10	2 foes	—
Swift	Normal	Special	60	—	20	2 foes	—

ABILITY ● Run Away ● Flash Fire

EGG GROUP Field

STATS
HP ●●
ATTACK ●●●
DEFENSE ●●●
SP. ATTACK ●●●
SP. DEFENSE ●●●
SPEED ●●●●

● PRIMARY WAY TO FIND

TRAINER'S PARTY Trainer on the Solaceon Town side of Route 210

WILD POKÉMON

COURSE OF STORY

Bonsly

ROCK

HEIGHT: 1'08"
WEIGHT: 33.1 lbs.
GENDER: Male and Female
HELD ITEM: None

● M/F have same form

PLATINUM It prefers an arid atmosphere. It leaks water that looks like tears when adjusting its moisture level.

EVOLUTION PATH

Bonsly — Raise to Lv.? and teach it Mimic. D/P: level it up while it knows Mimic. → Sudowoodo

● TM & HM MOVES

No.	Name	Type	Kind	Power	Acc	PP	Range	DA
TM04	Calm Mind	Psychic	Status	—	—	20	Self	—
TM06	Toxic	Poison	Status	—	85	10	Normal	—
TM10	Hidden Power	Normal	Special	—	100	15	Normal	—
TM11	Sunny Day	Fire	Status	—	—	5	All	—
TM17	Protect	Normal	Status	—	—	10	Self	—
TM21	Frustration	Normal	Physical	—	100	20	Normal	●
TM27	Return	Normal	Physical	—	100	20	Normal	●
TM28	Dig	Ground	Physical	80	100	10	Normal	●
TM31	Brick Break	Fighting	Physical	75	100	15	Normal	●
TM32	Double Team	Normal	Status	—	—	15	Self	—
TM37	Sandstorm	Rock	Status	—	—	10	All	—
TM39	Rock Tomb	Rock	Physical	50	80	10	Normal	●
TM42	Facade	Normal	Physical	70	100	20	Normal	●
TM43	Secret Power	Normal	Physical	70	100	20	Normal	●
TM44	Rest	Psychic	Status	—	—	10	Self	—
TM45	Attract	Normal	Status	—	100	15	Normal	—
TM46	Thief	Dark	Physical	40	100	10	Normal	●
TM58	Endure	Normal	Status	—	—	10	Self	—
TM64	Explosion	Normal	Physical	250	100	5	2 foes + 1 ally	—
TM69	Rock Polish	Rock	Status	—	—	20	Self	—
TM76	Stealth Rock	Rock	Status	—	—	20	2 foes	—
TM77	Psych Up	Normal	Status	—	—	10	Normal	—
TM78	Captivate	Normal	Status	—	100	20	2 foes	—
TM80	Rock Slide	Rock	Physical	75	90	10	2 foes	—
TM82	Sleep Talk	Normal	Status	—	—	10	DoM	—
TM83	Natural Gift	Normal	Physical	—	100	15	Normal	●
TM87	Swagger	Normal	Status	—	90	15	Normal	—
TM90	Substitute	Normal	Status	—	—	10	Self	—

● LEVEL-UP AND LEARNED MOVES

Lv	Name	Type	Kind	Power	Acc	PP	Range	DA
Base	Fake Tears	Dark	Status	—	100	20	Normal	—
Base	Copycat	Normal	Status	—	—	20	DoM	—
6	Flail	Normal	Physical	—	100	15	Normal	●
9	Low Kick	Fighting	Physical	—	100	20	Normal	●
14	Rock Throw	Rock	Physical	50	90	15	Normal	●
17	Mimic	Normal	Status	—	—	10	Normal	—
22	Block	Normal	Status	—	—	5	Normal	—
25	Faint Attack	Dark	Physical	60	—	20	Normal	●
30	Rock Tomb	Rock	Physical	50	80	10	Normal	●
33	Rock Slide	Rock	Physical	75	90	10	2 foes	—
38	Slam	Normal	Physical	80	75	20	Normal	●
41	Sucker Punch	Dark	Physical	80	100	5	Normal	●
46	Double-Edge	Normal	Physical	120	100	15	Normal	●

● MOVES TAUGHT IN EXCHANGE FOR COLORED SHARDS

Name	Type	Kind	Power	Acc	PP	Range	DA
Rollout	Rock	Physical	30	90	20	Normal	●
Snore	Normal	Special	40	100	15	Normal	—
Helping Hand	Normal	Status	—	—	20	1 ally	—
Earth Power	Ground	Special	90	100	10	Normal	—
Sucker Punch	Dark	Physical	80	100	5	Normal	●
Uproar	Normal	Special	50	100	10	1 random	—

● EGG MOVES

Name	Type	Kind	Power	Acc	PP	Range	DA
Selfdestruct	Normal	Physical	200	100	5	2 foes + 1 ally	—
Headbutt	Normal	Physical	70	100	15	Normal	●
Harden	Normal	Status	—	—	30	Self	—
Defense Curl	Normal	Status	—	—	40	Self	—
Rollout	Rock	Physical	30	90	20	Normal	●
Sand Tomb	Ground	Physical	15	70	15	Normal	—

ABILITY ● Sturdy ● Rock Head

EGG GROUP No Eggs

STATS
HP ●●
ATTACK ●●●
DEFENSE ●●●●
SP. ATTACK ●
SP. DEFENSE ●
SPEED ●

● PRIMARY WAY TO FIND

TRAINER'S PARTY Trainer on Route 209

WILD POKÉMON

COURSE OF STORY

Sinnoh Pokédex **No. 093** Imitation Pokémon

Sudowoodo

ROCK

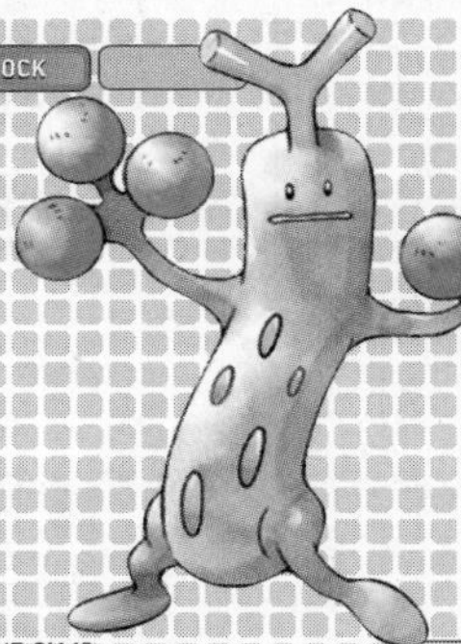

HEIGHT: **3'11"**
WEIGHT: **83.8 lbs.**
GENDER: **Male and Female**
HELD ITEM: **None**

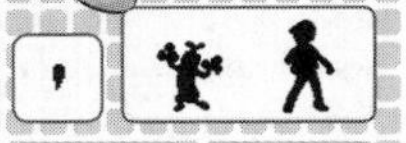

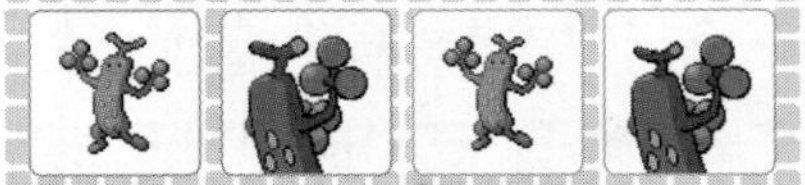

● Male form ● Female form

PLATINUM To avoid being attacked, it does nothing but mimic a tree. It hates water and flees from rain.

EVOLUTION PATH

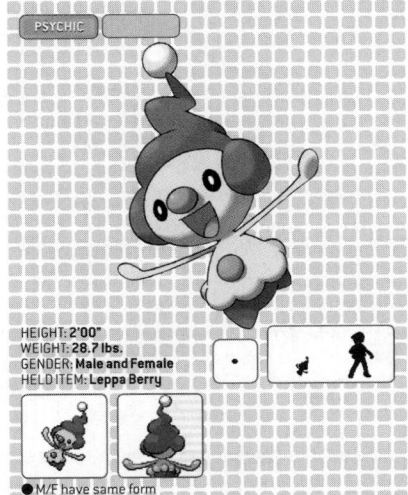

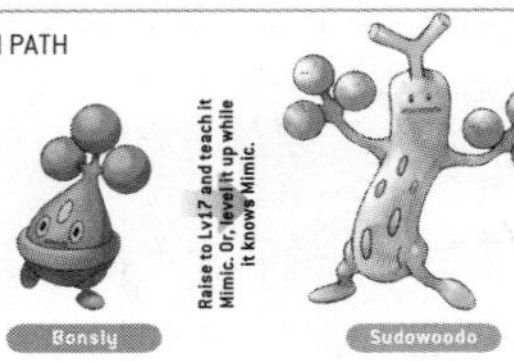
Raise to Lv17 and teach it Mimic. Or, level it up while it knows Mimic.
Bonsly
Sudowoodo

● TM & HM MOVES

No.	Name	Type	Kind	Power	Acc	PP	Range	DA
TM01	Focus Punch	Fighting	Physical	150	100	20	Normal	•
TM04	Calm Mind	Psychic	Status	—	—	20	Self	—
TM06	Toxic	Poison	Status	—	85	10	Normal	—
TM10	Hidden Power	Normal	Special	—	100	15	Normal	—
TM11	Sunny Day	Fire	Status	—	—	5	All	—
TM12	Taunt	Dark	Status	—	100	20	Normal	—
TM17	Protect	Normal	Status	—	—	10	Self	—
TM21	Frustration	Normal	Physical	—	100	20	Normal	•
TM26	Earthquake	Ground	Physical	100	100	10	2 foes • 1 ally	—
TM27	Return	Normal	Physical	—	100	20	Normal	•
TM28	Dig	Ground	Physical	80	100	10	Normal	•
TM31	Brick Break	Fighting	Physical	75	100	15	Normal	•
TM32	Double Team	Normal	Status	—	—	15	Self	—
TM37	Sandstorm	Rock	Status	—	—	10	All	—
TM39	Rock Tomb	Rock	Physical	50	80	10	Normal	—
TM41	Torment	Dark	Status	—	100	15	Normal	—
TM42	Facade	Normal	Physical	70	100	20	Normal	•
TM43	Secret Power	Normal	Physical	70	100	20	Normal	—
TM44	Rest	Psychic	Status	—	—	10	Self	—
TM45	Attract	Normal	Status	—	100	15	Normal	—
TM46	Thief	Dark	Physical	40	100	10	Normal	•
TM56	Fling	Dark	Physical	—	100	10	Normal	—
TM58	Endure	Normal	Status	—	—	10	Self	—
TM64	Explosion	Normal	Physical	250	100	5	2 foes • 1 ally	—
TM69	Rock Polish	Rock	Status	—	—	20	Self	—
TM71	Stone Edge	Rock	Physical	100	80	5	Normal	—
TM76	Stealth Rock	Rock	Status	—	—	20	2 foes	—
TM77	Psych Up	Normal	Status	—	—	10	Normal	—
TM78	Captivate	Normal	Status	—	100	20	2 foes	—
TM80	Rock Slide	Rock	Physical	75	90	10	2 foes	—
TM82	Sleep Talk	Normal	Status	—	—	10	DoM	—
TM83	Natural Gift	Normal	Physical	—	100	15	Normal	—
TM87	Swagger	Normal	Status	—	90	15	Normal	—
TM90	Substitute	Normal	Status	—	—	10	Self	—
HM04	Strength	Normal	Physical	80	100	15	Normal	•
HM06	Rock Smash	Fighting	Physical	40	100	15	Normal	•

ABILITY ● Sturdy ● Rock Head

EGG GROUP Mineral

STATS
HP ●●
ATTACK ●●●
DEFENSE ●●●
SP. ATTACK ●
SP. DEFENSE ●●
SPEED ●

● LEVEL-UP AND LEARNED MOVES

Lv	Name	Type	Kind	Power	Acc	PP	Range	DA
Base	Wood Hammer	Grass	Physical	120	100	15	Normal	•
Base	Copycat	Normal	Status	—	—	20	DoM	—
Base	Flail	Normal	Physical	—	100	15	Normal	•
Base	Low Kick	Fighting	Physical	—	100	20	Normal	•
Base	Rock Throw	Rock	Physical	50	90	15	Normal	—
6	Flail	Normal	Physical	—	100	15	Normal	•
9	Low Kick	Fighting	Physical	—	100	20	Normal	•
14	Rock Throw	Rock	Physical	50	90	15	Normal	—
17	Mimic	Normal	Status	—	—	10	Normal	—
22	Block	Normal	Status	—	—	5	Normal	—
25	Faint Attack	Dark	Physical	60	—	20	Normal	•
30	Rock Tomb	Rock	Physical	50	80	10	Normal	—
33	Rock Slide	Rock	Physical	75	90	10	2 foes	—
38	Slam	Normal	Physical	80	75	20	Normal	•
41	Sucker Punch	Dark	Physical	80	100	5	Normal	•
46	Double-Edge	Normal	Physical	120	100	15	Normal	•
49	Hammer Arm	Fighting	Physical	100	90	10	Normal	•

● MOVES TAUGHT IN EXCHANGE FOR COLORED SHARDS

Name	Type	Kind	Power	Acc	PP	Range	DA
Mud-Slap	Ground	Special	20	100	10	Normal	—
Rollout	Rock	Physical	30	90	20	Normal	•
ThunderPunch	Electric	Physical	75	100	15	Normal	•
Fire Punch	Fire	Physical	75	100	15	Normal	•
Ice Punch	Ice	Physical	75	100	15	Normal	•
Snore	Normal	Special	40	100	15	Normal	—
Helping Hand	Normal	Status	—	—	20	1 ally	—
Earth Power	Ground	Special	90	100	10	Normal	—
Sucker Punch	Dark	Physical	80	100	5	Normal	•

● EGG MOVES

Name	Type	Kind	Power	Acc	PP	Range	DA
Selfdestruct	Normal	Physical	200	100	5	2 foes • 1 ally	—
Headbutt	Normal	Physical	70	100	15	Normal	•
Harden	Normal	Status	—	—	30	Self	—
Defense Curl	Normal	Status	—	—	40	Self	—
Rollout	Rock	Physical	30	90	20	Normal	•
Sand Tomb	Ground	Physical	15	70	15	Normal	—

● PRIMARY WAY TO FIND

TRAINER'S PARTY Trainer on Route 216

WILD POKÉMON Route 221

COURSE OF STORY

Sinnoh Pokédex **No. 094** Mime Pokémon

Mime Jr.

PSYCHIC

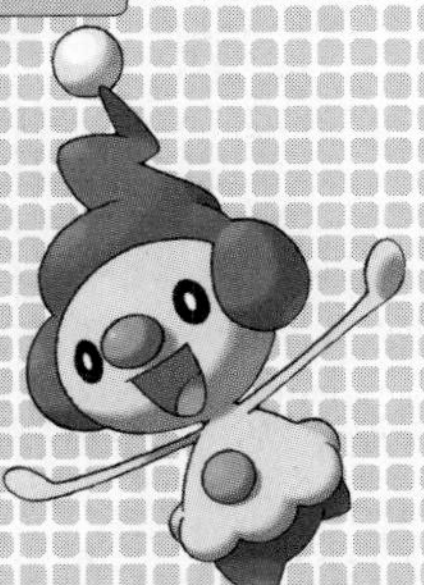

HEIGHT: **2'00"**
WEIGHT: **28.7 lbs.**
GENDER: **Male and Female**
HELD ITEM: **Leppa Berry**

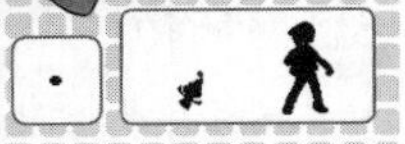

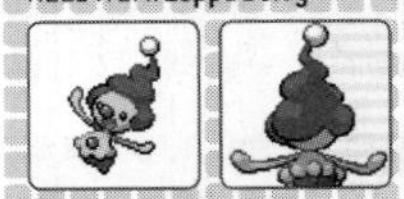

● M/F have same form

PLATINUM It mimics the expressions and motions of those it sees to understand the feelings of others.

EVOLUTION PATH

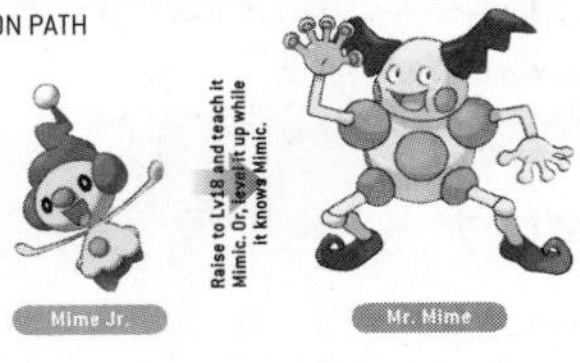
Raise to Lv18 and teach it Mimic. Or, level it up while it knows Mimic.
Mime Jr.
Mr. Mime

● TM & HM MOVES

No.	Name	Type	Kind	Power	Acc	PP	Range	DA
TM01	Focus Punch	Fighting	Physical	150	100	20	Normal	•
TM04	Calm Mind	Psychic	Status	—	—	20	Self	—
TM06	Toxic	Poison	Status	—	85	10	Normal	—
TM10	Hidden Power	Normal	Special	—	100	15	Normal	—
TM11	Sunny Day	Fire	Status	—	—	5	All	—
TM12	Taunt	Dark	Status	—	100	20	Normal	—
TM16	Light Screen	Psychic	Status	—	—	30	2 allies	—
TM17	Protect	Normal	Status	—	—	10	Self	—
TM18	Rain Dance	Water	Status	—	—	5	All	—
TM20	Safeguard	Normal	Status	—	—	25	2 allies	—
TM21	Frustration	Normal	Physical	—	100	20	Normal	•
TM22	SolarBeam	Grass	Special	120	100	10	Normal	—
TM24	Thunderbolt	Electric	Special	95	100	15	Normal	—
TM25	Thunder	Electric	Special	120	70	10	Normal	—
TM27	Return	Normal	Physical	—	100	20	Normal	•
TM29	Psychic	Psychic	Special	90	100	10	Normal	—
TM30	Shadow Ball	Ghost	Special	80	100	15	Normal	—
TM31	Brick Break	Fighting	Physical	75	100	15	Normal	•
TM32	Double Team	Normal	Status	—	—	15	Self	—
TM33	Reflect	Psychic	Status	—	—	20	2 allies	—
TM34	Shock Wave	Electric	Special	60	—	20	Normal	—
TM41	Torment	Dark	Status	—	100	15	Normal	—
TM42	Facade	Normal	Physical	70	100	20	Normal	•
TM43	Secret Power	Normal	Physical	70	100	20	Normal	—
TM44	Rest	Psychic	Status	—	—	10	Self	—
TM45	Attract	Normal	Status	—	100	15	Normal	—
TM46	Thief	Dark	Physical	40	100	10	Normal	•
TM48	Skill Swap	Psychic	Status	—	—	10	Normal	—
TM49	Snatch	Dark	Status	—	—	10	DoM	—
TM56	Fling	Dark	Physical	—	100	10	Normal	—
TM57	Charge Beam	Electric	Special	50	90	10	Normal	—
TM58	Endure	Normal	Status	—	—	10	Self	—
TM60	Drain Punch	Fighting	Physical	60	100	5	Normal	•
TM67	Recycle	Normal	Status	—	—	10	Self	—
TM70	Flash	Normal	Status	—	100	20	Normal	—
TM73	Thunder Wave	Electric	Status	—	100	20	Normal	—
TM77	Psych Up	Normal	Status	—	—	10	Normal	—
TM78	Captivate	Normal	Status	—	100	20	2 foes	—
TM82	Sleep Talk	Normal	Status	—	—	10	DoM	—
TM83	Natural Gift	Normal	Physical	—	100	15	Normal	—
TM85	Dream Eater	Psychic	Special	100	100	15	Normal	—
TM86	Grass Knot	Grass	Special	—	100	20	Normal	•
TM87	Swagger	Normal	Status	—	90	15	Normal	—
TM90	Substitute	Normal	Status	—	—	10	Self	—
TM92	Trick Room	Psychic	Status	—	—	5	All	—

ABILITY ● Soundproof ● Filter

EGG GROUP No Eggs

STATS
HP ●
ATTACK ●
DEFENSE ●●
SP. ATTACK ●●●
SP. DEFENSE ●●●
SPEED ●●

● LEVEL-UP AND LEARNED MOVES

Lv	Name	Type	Kind	Power	Acc	PP	Range	DA
Base	Tickle	Normal	Status	—	100	20	Normal	—
Base	Barrier	Psychic	Status	—	—	30	Self	—
Base	Confusion	Psychic	Special	50	100	25	Normal	—
4	Copycat	Normal	Status	—	—	20	DoM	—
8	Meditate	Psychic	Status	—	—	40	Self	—
11	Encore	Normal	Status	—	100	5	Normal	—
15	DoubleSlap	Normal	Physical	15	85	10	Normal	•
18	Mimic	Normal	Status	—	—	10	Normal	—
22	Light Screen	Psychic	Status	—	—	30	2 allies	—
22	Reflect	Psychic	Status	—	—	20	2 allies	—
25	Psybeam	Psychic	Special	65	100	20	Normal	—
29	Substitute	Normal	Status	—	—	10	Self	—
32	Recycle	Normal	Status	—	—	10	Self	—
36	Trick	Psychic	Status	—	100	10	Normal	—
39	Psychic	Psychic	Special	90	100	10	Normal	—
43	Role Play	Psychic	Status	—	—	10	Normal	—
46	Baton Pass	Normal	Status	—	—	40	Self	—
50	Safeguard	Normal	Status	—	—	25	2 allies	—

● MOVES TAUGHT IN EXCHANGE FOR COLORED SHARDS

Name	Type	Kind	Power	Acc	PP	Range	DA
Mud-Slap	Ground	Special	20	100	10	Normal	—
Snore	Normal	Special	40	100	15	Normal	—
Helping Hand	Normal	Status	—	—	20	1 ally	—
Signal Beam	Bug	Special	75	100	15	Normal	—
Trick	Psychic	Status	—	100	10	Normal	—
Uproar	Normal	Special	50	100	10	1 random	—

● EGG MOVES

Name	Type	Kind	Power	Acc	PP	Range	DA
Future Sight	Psychic	Special	80	90	15	Normal	—
Hypnosis	Psychic	Status	—	70	20	Normal	—
Mimic	Normal	Status	—	—	10	Normal	—
Psych Up	Normal	Status	—	—	10	Normal	—
Fake Out	Normal	Physical	40	100	10	Normal	•
Trick	Psychic	Status	—	100	10	Normal	—
Confuse Ray	Ghost	Status	—	100	10	Normal	—
Wake-Up Slap	Fighting	Physical	60	100	10	Normal	•
Teeter Dance	Normal	Status	—	100	20	2 foes • 1 ally	—
Healing Wish	Psychic	Status	—	—	10	Self	—
Charm	Normal	Status	—	100	20	Normal	—

● PRIMARY WAY TO FIND

TRAINER'S PARTY Trainer on Route 209

WILD POKÉMON

COURSE OF STORY

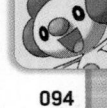

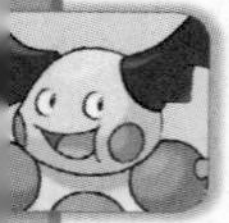

Sinnoh Pokédex **No. 095** Barrier Pokémon

Mr. Mime

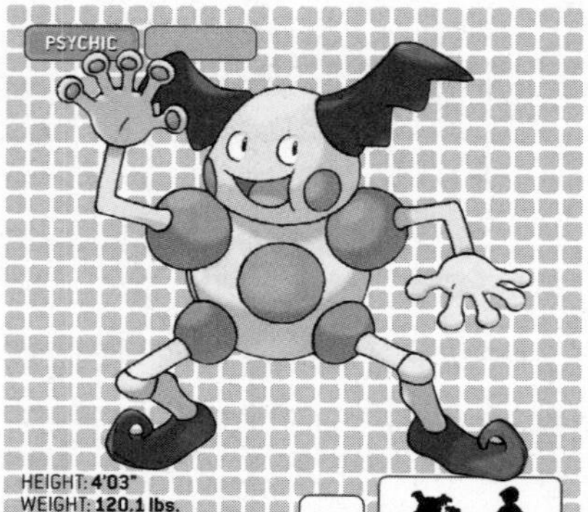
PSYCHIC

HEIGHT: 4'03"
WEIGHT: 120.1 lbs.
GENDER: Male and Female
HELD ITEM: Leppa Berry

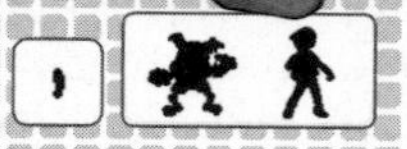

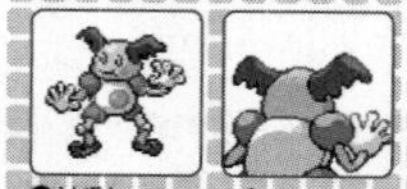

● M/F have same form

PLATINUM — It shapes an invisible wall in midair by minutely vibrating its fingertips to stop molecules in the air.

EVOLUTION PATH

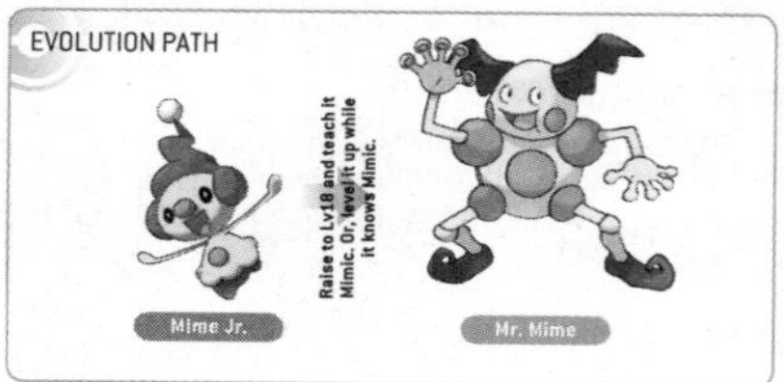
Raise to Lv18 and teach it Mimic. Or, level it up while it knows Mimic.
Mime Jr.
Mr. Mime

● TM & HM MOVES

No.	Name	Type	Kind	Power	Acc	PP	Range	DA
TM01	Focus Punch	Fighting	Physical	150	100	20	Normal	•
TM04	Calm Mind	Psychic	Status	—	—	20	Self	—
TM06	Toxic	Poison	Status	—	85	10	Normal	—
TM10	Hidden Power	Normal	Special	—	100	15	Normal	—
TM11	Sunny Day	Fire	Status	—	—	5	All	—
TM12	Taunt	Dark	Status	—	100	20	Normal	—
TM15	Hyper Beam	Normal	Special	150	90	5	Normal	—
TM16	Light Screen	Psychic	Status	—	—	30	2 allies	—
TM17	Protect	Normal	Status	—	—	10	Self	—
TM18	Rain Dance	Water	Status	—	—	5	All	—
TM20	Safeguard	Normal	Status	—	—	25	2 allies	—
TM21	Frustration	Normal	Physical	—	100	20	Normal	•
TM22	SolarBeam	Grass	Special	120	100	10	Normal	—
TM24	Thunderbolt	Electric	Special	95	100	15	Normal	—
TM25	Thunder	Electric	Special	120	70	10	Normal	—
TM27	Return	Normal	Physical	—	100	20	Normal	•
TM29	Psychic	Psychic	Special	90	100	10	Normal	—
TM30	Shadow Ball	Ghost	Special	80	100	15	Normal	—
TM31	Brick Break	Fighting	Physical	75	100	15	Normal	•
TM32	Double Team	Normal	Status	—	—	15	Self	—
TM33	Reflect	Psychic	Status	—	—	20	2 allies	—
TM34	Shock Wave	Electric	Special	60	—	20	Normal	—
TM40	Aerial Ace	Flying	Physical	60	—	20	Normal	•
TM41	Torment	Dark	Status	—	100	15	Normal	—
TM42	Facade	Normal	Physical	70	100	20	Normal	•
TM43	Secret Power	Normal	Physical	70	100	20	Normal	—
TM44	Rest	Psychic	Status	—	—	10	Self	—
TM45	Attract	Normal	Status	—	100	15	Normal	—
TM46	Thief	Dark	Physical	40	100	10	Normal	•
TM48	Skill Swap	Psychic	Status	—	—	10	Normal	—
TM49	Snatch	Dark	Status	—	—	10	DoM	—
TM52	Focus Blast	Fighting	Special	120	70	5	Normal	—
TM53	Energy Ball	Grass	Special	80	100	10	Normal	—
TM56	Fling	Dark	Physical	—	100	10	Normal	—
TM57	Charge Beam	Electric	Special	50	90	10	Normal	—
TM58	Endure	Normal	Status	—	—	10	Self	—
TM60	Drain Punch	Fighting	Physical	60	100	5	Normal	•
TM66	Payback	Dark	Physical	50	100	10	Normal	•
TM67	Recycle	Normal	Status	—	—	10	Self	—
TM68	Giga Impact	Normal	Physical	150	90	5	Normal	•
TM70	Flash	Normal	Status	—	100	20	Normal	—
TM73	Thunder Wave	Electric	Status	—	100	20	Normal	—
TM77	Psych Up	Normal	Status	—	—	10	Normal	—
TM78	Captivate	Normal	Status	—	100	20	2 foes	—
TM82	Sleep Talk	Normal	Status	—	—	10	DoM	—
TM83	Natural Gift	Normal	Physical	—	100	15	Normal	—
TM85	Dream Eater	Psychic	Special	100	100	15	Normal	—
TM86	Grass Knot	Grass	Special	—	100	20	Normal	•
TM87	Swagger	Normal	Status	—	90	15	Normal	—
TM90	Substitute	Normal	Status	—	—	10	Self	—
TM92	Trick Room	Psychic	Status	—	—	5	All	—

ABILITY ● Soundproof ● Filter

EGG GROUP: Human-Like

STATS
HP ●
ATTACK ●●
DEFENSE ●●
SP. ATTACK ●●●●
SP. DEFENSE ●●●
SPEED ●●●

● LEVEL-UP AND LEARNED MOVES

Lv	Name	Type	Kind	Power	Acc	PP	Range	DA
Base	Magical Leaf	Grass	Special	60	—	20	Normal	—
Base	Power Swap	Psychic	Status	—	—	10	Normal	—
Base	Guard Swap	Psychic	Status	—	—	10	Normal	—
Base	Barrier	Psychic	Status	—	—	30	Self	—
Base	Confusion	Psychic	Special	50	100	25	Normal	—
4	Copycat	Normal	Status	—	—	20	DoM	—
8	Meditate	Psychic	Status	—	—	40	Self	—
11	Encore	Normal	Status	—	100	5	Normal	—
15	DoubleSlap	Normal	Physical	15	85	10	Normal	•
18	Mimic	Normal	Status	—	—	10	Normal	—
22	Light Screen	Psychic	Status	—	—	30	2 allies	—
22	Reflect	Psychic	Status	—	—	20	2 allies	—
25	Psybeam	Psychic	Special	65	100	20	Normal	—
29	Substitute	Normal	Status	—	—	10	Self	—
32	Recycle	Normal	Status	—	—	10	Self	—
36	Trick	Psychic	Status	—	100	10	Normal	—
39	Psychic	Psychic	Special	90	100	10	Normal	—
43	Role Play	Psychic	Status	—	—	10	Normal	—
46	Baton Pass	Normal	Status	—	—	40	Self	—
50	Safeguard	Normal	Status	—	—	25	2 allies	—

● MOVES TAUGHT IN EXCHANGE FOR COLORED SHARDS

Name	Type	Kind	Power	Acc	PP	Range	DA
Mud-Slap	Ground	Special	20	100	10	Normal	—
ThunderPunch	Electric	Physical	75	100	15	Normal	•
Fire Punch	Fire	Physical	75	100	15	Normal	•
Ice Punch	Ice	Physical	75	100	15	Normal	•
Snore	Normal	Special	40	100	15	Normal	—
Helping Hand	Normal	Status	—	—	20	1 ally	—
Signal Beam	Bug	Special	75	100	15	Normal	—
Zen Headbutt	Psychic	Physical	80	90	15	Normal	•
Iron Defense	Steel	Status	—	—	15	Self	—
Trick	Psychic	Status	—	100	10	Normal	—

● EGG MOVES

Name	Type	Kind	Power	Acc	PP	Range	DA
Future Sight	Psychic	Special	80	90	15	Normal	—
Hypnosis	Psychic	Status	—	60	20	Normal	—
Mimic	Normal	Status	—	—	10	Normal	—
Psych Up	Normal	Status	—	—	10	Normal	—
Fake Out	Normal	Physical	40	100	10	Normal	•
Trick	Psychic	Status	—	100	10	Normal	—
Confuse Ray	Ghost	Status	—	100	10	Normal	—
Wake-Up Slap	Fighting	Physical	60	100	10	Normal	•
Teeter Dance	Normal	Status	—	100	20	2 foes • 1 ally	—

● PRIMARY WAY TO FIND

TRAINER'S PARTY — Trainer on Route 216

WILD POKÉMON — Route 218

COURSE OF STORY

Sinnoh Pokédex **No. 096** Playhouse Pokémon

Happiny

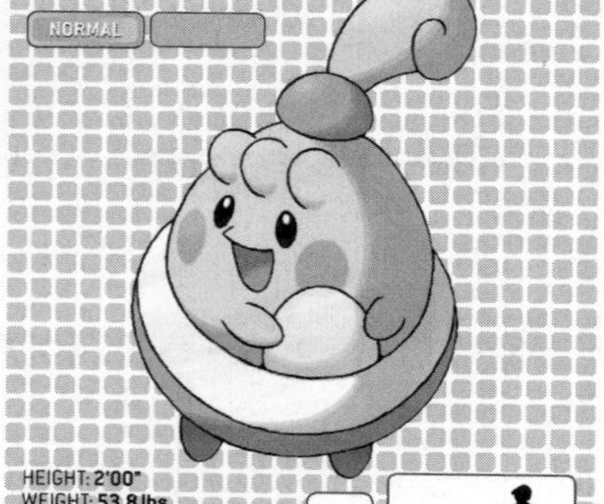
NORMAL

HEIGHT: 2'00"
WEIGHT: 53.8 lbs.
GENDER: Female only
HELD ITEM: Oval Stone/Lucky Punch

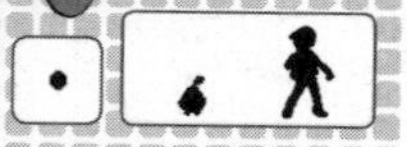

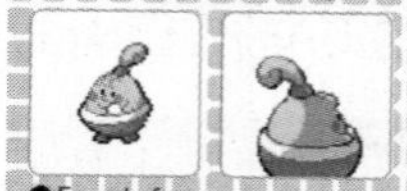

● Female form

PLATINUM — It likes to carry around a small rock. It may wander around others' feet and cause them to stumble.

EVOLUTION PATH

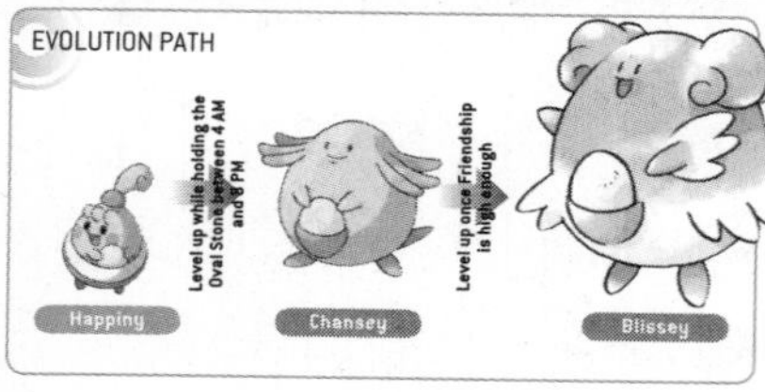
Level up while holding the Oval Stone between 4 AM and 8 PM
Level up once Friendship is high enough
Happiny
Chansey
Blissey

● TM & HM MOVES

No.	Name	Type	Kind	Power	Acc	PP	Range	DA
TM03	Water Pulse	Water	Special	60	100	20	Normal	—
TM06	Toxic	Poison	Status	—	85	10	Normal	—
TM07	Hail	Ice	Status	—	—	10	All	—
TM10	Hidden Power	Normal	Special	—	100	15	Normal	—
TM11	Sunny Day	Fire	Status	—	—	5	All	—
TM16	Light Screen	Psychic	Status	—	—	30	2 allies	—
TM17	Protect	Normal	Status	—	—	10	Self	—
TM18	Rain Dance	Water	Status	—	—	5	All	—
TM20	Safeguard	Normal	Status	—	—	25	2 allies	—
TM21	Frustration	Normal	Physical	—	100	20	Normal	•
TM22	SolarBeam	Grass	Special	120	100	10	Normal	—
TM27	Return	Normal	Physical	—	100	20	Normal	•
TM29	Psychic	Psychic	Special	90	100	10	Normal	—
TM30	Shadow Ball	Ghost	Special	80	100	15	Normal	—
TM32	Double Team	Normal	Status	—	—	15	Self	—
TM34	Shock Wave	Electric	Special	60	—	20	Normal	—
TM35	Flamethrower	Fire	Special	95	100	15	Normal	—
TM38	Fire Blast	Fire	Special	120	85	5	Normal	—
TM42	Facade	Normal	Physical	70	100	20	Normal	•
TM43	Secret Power	Normal	Physical	70	100	20	Normal	—
TM44	Rest	Psychic	Status	—	—	10	Self	—
TM45	Attract	Normal	Status	—	100	15	Normal	—
TM56	Fling	Dark	Physical	—	100	10	Normal	—
TM58	Endure	Normal	Status	—	—	10	Self	—
TM60	Drain Punch	Fighting	Physical	60	100	5	Normal	•
TM67	Recycle	Normal	Status	—	—	10	Self	—
TM70	Flash	Normal	Status	—	100	20	Normal	—
TM73	Thunder Wave	Electric	Status	—	100	20	Normal	—
TM77	Psych Up	Normal	Status	—	—	10	Normal	—
TM78	Captivate	Normal	Status	—	100	20	2 foes	—
TM82	Sleep Talk	Normal	Status	—	—	10	DoM	—
TM83	Natural Gift	Normal	Physical	—	100	15	Normal	—
TM85	Dream Eater	Psychic	Special	100	100	15	Normal	—
TM86	Grass Knot	Grass	Special	—	100	20	Normal	•
TM87	Swagger	Normal	Status	—	90	15	Normal	—
TM90	Substitute	Normal	Status	—	—	10	Self	—

ABILITY ● Natural Cure ● Serene Grace

EGG GROUP: No Eggs

STATS
HP ●●●
ATTACK ●
DEFENSE ●
SP. ATTACK ●
SP. DEFENSE ●●
SPEED ●●

● LEVEL-UP AND LEARNED MOVES

Lv	Name	Type	Kind	Power	Acc	PP	Range	DA
Base	Pound	Normal	Physical	40	100	35	Normal	•
Base	Charm	Normal	Status	—	100	20	Normal	—
5	Copycat	Normal	Status	—	—	20	DoM	—
9	Refresh	Normal	Status	—	—	20	Self	—
12	Sweet Kiss	Normal	Status	—	75	10	Normal	—

● MOVES TAUGHT IN EXCHANGE FOR COLORED SHARDS

Name	Type	Kind	Power	Acc	PP	Range	DA
Mud-Slap	Ground	Special	20	100	10	Normal	—
Icy Wind	Ice	Special	55	95	15	2 foes	—
Rollout	Rock	Physical	30	90	20	Normal	•
Snore	Normal	Special	40	100	15	Normal	—
Helping Hand	Normal	Status	—	—	20	1 ally	—
Endeavor	Normal	Physical	—	100	5	Normal	•
Zen Headbutt	Psychic	Physical	80	90	15	Normal	•
Last Resort	Normal	Physical	130	100	5	Normal	•
Uproar	Normal	Special	50	100	10	1 random	—

● EGG MOVES

Name	Type	Kind	Power	Acc	PP	Range	DA
Present	Normal	Physical	—	90	15	Normal	—
Metronome	Normal	Status	—	—	10	DoM	—
Heal Bell	Normal	Status	—	—	5	All allies	—
Aromatherapy	Grass	Status	—	—	5	All allies	—
Substitute	Normal	Status	—	—	10	Self	—
Counter	Fighting	Physical	—	100	20	Self	•
Helping Hand	Normal	Status	—	—	20	1 ally	—
Gravity	Psychic	Status	—	—	5	All	—
Last Resort	Normal	Physical	130	100	5	Normal	•

● PRIMARY WAY TO FIND

TRAINER'S PARTY — Trainer on Route 210

WILD POKÉMON — Trophy Garden at the Pokémon Mansion on Route 212 (talk to Mr. Backlot after getting the National Pokédex)

COURSE OF STORY

Chansey

NORMAL

HEIGHT: 3'07"
WEIGHT: 76.3 lbs.
GENDER: Female only
HELD ITEM: Oval Stone/Lucky Egg

● Female form

PLATINUM — A kindly Pokémon that lays highly nutritious eggs and shares them with injured Pokémon or people.

EVOLUTION PATH

Happiny → (Level up while holding the Oval Stone between 4 AM and 8 PM) → Chansey → (Level up once Friendship is high enough) → Blissey

ABILITY: ● Natural Cure ● Serene Grace
EGG GROUP: Fairy
STATS: HP ●●●●● / ATTACK ● / DEFENSE ● / SP. ATTACK ●● / SP. DEFENSE ●●● / SPEED ●●

● TM & HM MOVES

No.	Name	Type	Kind	Power	Acc	PP	Range	DA
TM01	Focus Punch	Fighting	Physical	150	100	20	Normal	•
TM03	Water Pulse	Water	Special	60	100	20	Normal	—
TM04	Calm Mind	Psychic	Status	—	—	20	Self	—
TM06	Toxic	Poison	Status	—	85	10	Normal	—
TM07	Hail	Ice	Status	—	—	10	All	—
TM10	Hidden Power	Normal	Special	—	100	15	Normal	—
TM11	Sunny Day	Fire	Status	—	—	5	All	—
TM13	Ice Beam	Ice	Special	95	100	10	Normal	—
TM14	Blizzard	Ice	Special	120	70	5	2 foes	—
TM15	Hyper Beam	Normal	Special	150	90	5	Normal	—
TM16	Light Screen	Psychic	Status	—	—	30	2 allies	—
TM17	Protect	Normal	Status	—	—	10	Self	—
TM18	Rain Dance	Water	Status	—	—	5	All	—
TM20	Safeguard	Normal	Status	—	—	25	2 allies	—
TM21	Frustration	Normal	Physical	—	100	20	Normal	•
TM22	SolarBeam	Grass	Special	120	100	10	Normal	—
TM23	Iron Tail	Steel	Physical	100	75	15	Normal	•
TM24	Thunderbolt	Electric	Special	95	100	15	Normal	—
TM25	Thunder	Electric	Special	120	70	10	Normal	—
TM26	Earthquake	Ground	Physical	100	100	10	2 foes + 1 ally	•
TM27	Return	Normal	Physical	—	100	20	Normal	•
TM29	Psychic	Psychic	Special	90	100	10	Normal	—
TM30	Shadow Ball	Ghost	Special	80	100	15	Normal	—
TM31	Brick Break	Fighting	Physical	75	100	15	Normal	•
TM32	Double Team	Normal	Status	—	—	15	Self	—
TM34	Shock Wave	Electric	Special	60	—	20	Normal	—
TM35	Flamethrower	Fire	Special	95	100	15	Normal	—
TM37	Sandstorm	Rock	Status	—	—	10	All	—
TM38	Fire Blast	Fire	Special	120	85	5	Normal	—
TM39	Rock Tomb	Rock	Physical	50	80	10	Normal	•
TM42	Facade	Normal	Physical	70	100	20	Normal	•
TM43	Secret Power	Normal	Physical	70	100	20	Normal	•
TM44	Rest	Psychic	Status	—	—	10	Self	—
TM45	Attract	Normal	Status	—	100	15	Normal	—
TM48	Skill Swap	Psychic	Status	—	—	10	Normal	—
TM49	Snatch	Dark	Status	—	—	10	DoM	—
TM56	Fling	Dark	Physical	—	100	10	Normal	•
TM57	Charge Beam	Electric	Special	50	90	10	Normal	—
TM58	Endure	Normal	Status	—	—	10	Self	—
TM60	Drain Punch	Fighting	Physical	60	100	5	Normal	•
TM67	Recycle	Normal	Status	—	—	10	Self	—
TM68	Giga Impact	Normal	Physical	150	90	5	Normal	•
TM70	Flash	Normal	Status	—	100	20	Normal	—
TM73	Thunder Wave	Electric	Status	—	100	20	Normal	—
TM76	Stealth Rock	Rock	Status	—	—	20	2 foes	—
TM77	Psych Up	Normal	Status	—	—	10	Normal	—
TM78	Captivate	Normal	Status	—	100	20	2 foes	—
TM80	Rock Slide	Rock	Physical	75	90	10	2 foes	•
TM82	Sleep Talk	Normal	Status	—	—	10	DoM	—
TM83	Natural Gift	Normal	Physical	—	100	15	Normal	•
TM85	Dream Eater	Psychic	Special	100	100	15	Normal	—
TM86	Grass Knot	Grass	Special	—	100	20	Normal	—
TM87	Swagger	Normal	Status	—	90	15	Normal	—
TM90	Substitute	Normal	Status	—	—	10	Self	—
HM04	Strength	Normal	Physical	80	100	15	Normal	•
HM06	Rock Smash	Fighting	Physical	40	100	15	Normal	•
HM08	Rock Climb	Normal	Physical	90	85	20	Normal	•

● LEVEL-UP AND LEARNED MOVES

Lv	Name	Type	Kind	Power	Acc	PP	Range	DA
Base	Pound	Normal	Physical	40	100	35	Normal	•
Base	Growl	Normal	Status	—	100	40	2 foes	—
5	Tail Whip	Normal	Status	—	100	30	2 foes	—
9	Refresh	Normal	Status	—	—	20	Self	—
12	Softboiled	Normal	Status	—	—	10	Self	—
16	DoubleSlap	Normal	Physical	15	85	10	Normal	•
20	Minimize	Normal	Status	—	—	20	Self	—
23	Sing	Normal	Status	—	55	15	Normal	—
27	Fling	Dark	Physical	—	100	10	Normal	•
31	Defense Curl	Normal	Status	—	—	40	Self	—
34	Light Screen	Psychic	Status	—	—	30	2 allies	—
38	Egg Bomb	Normal	Physical	100	75	10	Normal	•
42	Healing Wish	Psychic	Status	—	—	10	Self	—
46	Double-Edge	Normal	Physical	120	100	15	Normal	•

● MOVES TAUGHT IN EXCHANGE FOR COLORED SHARDS

Name	Type	Kind	Power	Acc	PP	Range	DA
Mud-Slap	Ground	Special	20	100	10	Normal	•
Icy Wind	Ice	Special	55	95	15	2 foes	—
Rollout	Rock	Physical	30	90	20	Normal	•
ThunderPunch	Electric	Physical	75	100	15	Normal	•
Fire Punch	Fire	Physical	75	100	15	Normal	•
Ice Punch	Ice	Physical	75	100	15	Normal	•
Snore	Normal	Special	40	100	15	Normal	—
Helping Hand	Normal	Status	—	—	20	1 ally	—
Endeavor	Normal	Physical	—	100	5	Normal	—
Zen Headbutt	Psychic	Physical	80	90	15	Normal	•
Last Resort	Normal	Physical	130	100	5	Normal	•

● EGG MOVES

Name	Type	Kind	Power	Acc	PP	Range	DA
Present	Normal	Physical	—	90	15	Normal	•
Metronome	Normal	Status	—	—	10	DoM	—
Heal Bell	Normal	Status	—	—	5	All allies	—
Aromatherapy	Grass	Status	—	—	5	All allies	—
Substitute	Normal	Status	—	—	10	Self	—
Counter	Fighting	Physical	—	100	20	Self	•
Helping Hand	Normal	Status	—	—	20	1 ally	—
Gravity	Psychic	Status	—	—	5	All	—

● PRIMARY WAY TO FIND

TRAINER'S PARTY — Cheryl, who goes through Eterna Forest with you
WILD POKÉMON — Route 209
COURSE OF STORY

Blissey

NORMAL

HEIGHT: 4'11"
WEIGHT: 103.2 lbs.
GENDER: Female only
HELD ITEM: None

● Female form

PLATINUM — The eggs it lays are filled with happiness. Eating even one bite will bring a smile to anyone.

EVOLUTION PATH

Happiny → (Level up while holding the Oval Stone between 4 AM and 8 PM) → Chansey → (Level up once Friendship is high enough) → Blissey

ABILITY: ● Natural Cure ● Serene Grace
EGG GROUP: Fairy
STATS: HP ●●●●● / ATTACK ● / DEFENSE ● / SP. ATTACK ●●● / SP. DEFENSE ●●●●● / SPEED ●●

● TM & HM MOVES

No.	Name	Type	Kind	Power	Acc	PP	Range	DA
TM01	Focus Punch	Fighting	Physical	150	100	20	Normal	•
TM03	Water Pulse	Water	Special	60	100	20	Normal	—
TM04	Calm Mind	Psychic	Status	—	—	20	Self	—
TM06	Toxic	Poison	Status	—	85	10	Normal	—
TM07	Hail	Ice	Status	—	—	10	All	—
TM10	Hidden Power	Normal	Special	—	100	15	Normal	—
TM11	Sunny Day	Fire	Status	—	—	5	All	—
TM13	Ice Beam	Ice	Special	95	100	10	Normal	—
TM14	Blizzard	Ice	Special	120	70	5	2 foes	—
TM15	Hyper Beam	Normal	Special	150	90	5	Normal	—
TM16	Light Screen	Psychic	Status	—	—	30	2 allies	—
TM17	Protect	Normal	Status	—	—	10	Self	—
TM18	Rain Dance	Water	Status	—	—	5	All	—
TM20	Safeguard	Normal	Status	—	—	25	2 allies	—
TM21	Frustration	Normal	Physical	—	100	20	Normal	•
TM22	SolarBeam	Grass	Special	120	100	10	Normal	—
TM23	Iron Tail	Steel	Physical	100	75	15	Normal	•
TM24	Thunderbolt	Electric	Special	95	100	15	Normal	—
TM25	Thunder	Electric	Special	120	70	10	Normal	—
TM26	Earthquake	Ground	Physical	100	100	10	2 foes • 1 ally	•
TM27	Return	Normal	Physical	—	100	20	Normal	•
TM29	Psychic	Psychic	Special	90	100	10	Normal	—
TM30	Shadow Ball	Ghost	Special	80	100	15	Normal	—
TM31	Brick Break	Fighting	Physical	75	100	15	Normal	•
TM32	Double Team	Normal	Status	—	—	15	Self	—
TM34	Shock Wave	Electric	Special	60	—	20	Normal	—
TM35	Flamethrower	Fire	Special	95	100	15	Normal	—
TM37	Sandstorm	Rock	Status	—	—	10	All	—
TM38	Fire Blast	Fire	Special	120	85	5	Normal	—
TM39	Rock Tomb	Rock	Physical	50	80	10	Normal	•
TM42	Facade	Normal	Physical	70	100	20	Normal	•
TM43	Secret Power	Normal	Physical	70	100	20	Normal	•
TM44	Rest	Psychic	Status	—	—	10	Self	—
TM45	Attract	Normal	Status	—	100	15	Normal	—
TM48	Skill Swap	Psychic	Status	—	—	10	Normal	—
TM49	Snatch	Dark	Status	—	—	10	DoM	—
TM52	Focus Blast	Fighting	Special	120	70	5	Normal	—
TM56	Fling	Dark	Physical	—	100	10	Normal	•
TM57	Charge Beam	Electric	Special	50	90	10	Normal	—
TM58	Endure	Normal	Status	—	—	10	Self	—
TM60	Drain Punch	Fighting	Physical	60	100	5	Normal	•
TM67	Recycle	Normal	Status	—	—	10	Self	—
TM68	Giga Impact	Normal	Physical	150	90	5	Normal	•
TM70	Flash	Normal	Status	—	100	20	Normal	—
TM72	Avalanche	Ice	Physical	60	100	10	Normal	•
TM73	Thunder Wave	Electric	Status	—	100	20	Normal	—
TM76	Stealth Rock	Rock	Status	—	—	20	2 foes	—
TM77	Psych Up	Normal	Status	—	—	10	Normal	—
TM78	Captivate	Normal	Status	—	100	20	2 foes	—
TM80	Rock Slide	Rock	Physical	75	90	10	2 foes	•
TM82	Sleep Talk	Normal	Status	—	—	10	DoM	—
TM83	Natural Gift	Normal	Physical	—	100	15	Normal	•
TM85	Dream Eater	Psychic	Special	100	100	15	Normal	—
TM86	Grass Knot	Grass	Special	—	100	20	Normal	—
TM87	Swagger	Normal	Status	—	90	15	Normal	—
TM90	Substitute	Normal	Status	—	—	10	Self	—
HM04	Strength	Normal	Physical	80	100	15	Normal	•
HM06	Rock Smash	Fighting	Physical	40	100	15	Normal	•
HM08	Rock Climb	Normal	Physical	90	85	20	Normal	•

● LEVEL-UP AND LEARNED MOVES

Lv	Name	Type	Kind	Power	Acc	PP	Range	DA
Base	Pound	Normal	Physical	40	100	35	Normal	•
Base	Growl	Normal	Status	—	100	40	2 foes	—
5	Tail Whip	Normal	Status	—	100	30	2 foes	—
9	Refresh	Normal	Status	—	—	20	Self	—
12	Softboiled	Normal	Status	—	—	10	Self	—
16	DoubleSlap	Normal	Physical	15	85	10	Normal	•
20	Minimize	Normal	Status	—	—	20	Self	—
23	Sing	Normal	Status	—	55	15	Normal	—
27	Fling	Dark	Physical	—	100	10	Normal	•
31	Defense Curl	Normal	Status	—	—	40	Self	—
34	Light Screen	Psychic	Status	—	—	30	2 allies	—
38	Egg Bomb	Normal	Physical	100	75	10	Normal	•
42	Healing Wish	Psychic	Status	—	—	10	Self	—
46	Double-Edge	Normal	Physical	120	100	15	Normal	•

● MOVES TAUGHT IN EXCHANGE FOR COLORED SHARDS

Name	Type	Kind	Power	Acc	PP	Range	DA
Mud-Slap	Ground	Special	20	100	10	Normal	•
Icy Wind	Ice	Special	55	95	15	2 foes	—
Rollout	Rock	Physical	30	90	20	Normal	•
ThunderPunch	Electric	Physical	75	100	15	Normal	•
Fire Punch	Fire	Physical	75	100	15	Normal	•
Ice Punch	Ice	Physical	75	100	15	Normal	•
Snore	Normal	Special	40	100	15	Normal	—
Helping Hand	Normal	Status	—	—	20	1 ally	—
Endeavor	Normal	Physical	—	100	5	Normal	—
Zen Headbutt	Psychic	Physical	80	90	15	Normal	•
Last Resort	Normal	Physical	130	100	5	Normal	•

● PRIMARY WAY TO FIND

TRAINER'S PARTY — Trainer on Victory Road
WILD POKÉMON
COURSE OF STORY

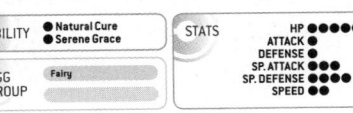

Cleffa

NORMAL

HEIGHT: 1'00"
WEIGHT: 6.6 lbs.
GENDER: Male and Female
HELD ITEM: Leppa Berry/Moon Stone

● M/F have same form

PLATINUM — It is often seen when shooting stars fill the night skies. It's said to arrive riding on a shooting star.

EVOLUTION PATH

Cleffa → Level up once Friendship level is high enough → Clefairy → Moon Stone → Clefable

ABILITY ● Cute Charm ● Magic Guard

EGG GROUP — No Eggs

STATS
HP ●●
ATTACK ●
DEFENSE ●
SP. ATTACK ●●
SP. DEFENSE ●●
SPEED ●

● TM & HM MOVES

No.	Name	Type	Kind	Power	Acc	PP	Range	DA
TM03	Water Pulse	Water	Special	60	100	20	Normal	—
TM06	Toxic	Poison	Status	—	85	10	Normal	—
TM10	Hidden Power	Normal	Special	—	100	15	Normal	—
TM11	Sunny Day	Fire	Status	—	—	5	All	—
TM16	Light Screen	Psychic	Status	—	—	30	2 allies	—
TM17	Protect	Normal	Status	—	—	10	Self	—
TM18	Rain Dance	Water	Status	—	—	5	All	—
TM20	Safeguard	Normal	Status	—	—	25	2 allies	—
TM21	Frustration	Normal	Physical	—	100	20	Normal	•
TM22	SolarBeam	Grass	Special	120	100	10	Normal	—
TM23	Iron Tail	Steel	Physical	100	75	15	Normal	—
TM27	Return	Normal	Physical	—	100	20	Normal	•
TM28	Dig	Ground	Physical	80	100	10	Normal	•
TM29	Psychic	Psychic	Special	90	100	10	Normal	—
TM30	Shadow Ball	Ghost	Special	80	100	15	Normal	—
TM32	Double Team	Normal	Status	—	—	15	Self	—
TM33	Reflect	Psychic	Status	—	—	20	2 allies	—
TM34	Shock Wave	Electric	Special	60	—	20	Normal	—
TM35	Flamethrower	Fire	Special	95	100	15	Normal	—
TM38	Fire Blast	Fire	Special	120	85	5	Normal	—
TM42	Facade	Normal	Physical	70	100	20	Normal	•
TM43	Secret Power	Normal	Physical	70	100	20	Normal	•
TM44	Rest	Psychic	Status	—	—	10	Self	—
TM45	Attract	Normal	Status	—	100	15	Normal	—
TM56	Fling	Dark	Physical	—	100	10	Normal	•
TM58	Endure	Normal	Status	—	—	10	Self	—
TM67	Recycle	Normal	Status	—	—	10	Self	—
TM70	Flash	Normal	Status	—	100	20	Normal	—
TM73	Thunder Wave	Electric	Status	—	100	20	Normal	—
TM77	Psych Up	Normal	Status	—	—	10	Normal	—
TM78	Captivate	Normal	Status	—	100	20	2 foes	—
TM82	Sleep Talk	Normal	Status	—	—	10	DoM	—
TM83	Natural Gift	Normal	Physical	—	100	15	Normal	—
TM85	Dream Eater	Psychic	Special	100	100	15	Normal	—
TM86	Grass Knot	Grass	Special	—	100	20	Normal	•
TM87	Swagger	Normal	Status	—	90	15	Normal	—
TM90	Substitute	Normal	Status	—	—	10	Self	—

● LEVEL-UP AND LEARNED MOVES

Lv	Name	Type	Kind	Power	Acc	PP	Range	DA
Base	Pound	Normal	Physical	40	100	35	Normal	•
Base	Charm	Normal	Status	—	100	20	Normal	—
4	Encore	Normal	Status	—	100	5	Normal	—
7	Sing	Normal	Status	—	55	15	Normal	—
10	Sweet Kiss	Normal	Status	—	75	10	Normal	—
13	Copycat	Normal	Status	—	—	20	Normal	—
16	Magical Leaf	Grass	Special	60	—	20	Normal	—

● MOVES TAUGHT IN EXCHANGE FOR COLORED SHARDS

Name	Type	Kind	Power	Acc	PP	Range	DA
Mud-Slap	Ground	Special	20	100	10	Normal	—
Icy Wind	Ice	Special	55	95	15	2 foes	—
Rollout	Rock	Physical	30	90	20	Normal	•
Snore	Normal	Special	40	100	15	Normal	—
Helping Hand	Normal	Status	—	—	20	1 ally	—
Endeavor	Normal	Physical	—	100	5	Normal	•
Signal Beam	Bug	Special	75	100	15	Normal	—
Zen Headbutt	Psychic	Physical	80	90	15	Normal	•
Last Resort	Normal	Physical	130	100	5	Normal	•
Trick	Psychic	Status	—	100	10	Normal	—
Uproar	Normal	Special	50	100	10	1 random	—

● EGG MOVES

Name	Type	Kind	Power	Acc	PP	Range	DA
Present	Normal	Physical	—	90	15	Normal	—
Metronome	Normal	Status	—	—	10	DoM	—
Amnesia	Psychic	Status	—	—	20	Self	—
Belly Drum	Normal	Status	—	—	10	Self	—
Splash	Normal	Status	—	—	40	Self	—
Mimic	Normal	Status	—	100	10	Normal	—
Wish	Normal	Status	—	—	10	Self	—
Substitute	Normal	Status	—	—	10	Self	—
Fake Tears	Dark	Status	—	100	20	Normal	—
Covet	Normal	Physical	40	100	40	Normal	•

● PRIMARY WAY TO FIND

TRAINER'S PARTY — Trainer on Route 209

WILD POKÉMON — Mt. Coronet (upper) 1F

COURSE OF STORY

Clefairy

NORMAL

HEIGHT: 2'00"
WEIGHT: 16.5 lbs.
GENDER: Male and Female
HELD ITEM: Leppa Berry/Moon Stone

● M/F have same form

PLATINUM — It is said that happiness will come to those who see a gathering of CLEFAIRY dancing under a full moon.

EVOLUTION PATH

Cleffa → Level up once Friendship level is high enough → Clefairy → Moon Stone → Clefable

ABILITY ● Cute Charm ● Magic Guard

EGG GROUP — Fairy

STATS
HP ●●
ATTACK ●●
DEFENSE ●●
SP. ATTACK ●●●
SP. DEFENSE ●●●
SPEED ●

● TM & HM MOVES

No.	Name	Type	Kind	Power	Acc	PP	Range	DA
TM01	Focus Punch	Fighting	Physical	150	100	20	Normal	•
TM03	Water Pulse	Water	Special	60	100	20	Normal	•
TM04	Calm Mind	Psychic	Status	—	—	20	Self	—
TM06	Toxic	Poison	Status	—	85	10	Normal	•
TM10	Hidden Power	Normal	Special	—	100	15	Normal	•
TM11	Sunny Day	Fire	Status	—	—	5	All	—
TM13	Ice Beam	Ice	Special	95	100	10	Normal	•
TM14	Blizzard	Ice	Special	120	70	5	2 foes	•
TM16	Light Screen	Psychic	Status	—	—	30	2 allies	—
TM17	Protect	Normal	Status	—	—	10	Self	—
TM18	Rain Dance	Water	Status	—	—	5	All	—
TM20	Safeguard	Normal	Status	—	—	25	2 allies	—
TM21	Frustration	Normal	Physical	—	100	20	Normal	•
TM22	SolarBeam	Grass	Special	120	100	10	Normal	•
TM23	Iron Tail	Steel	Physical	100	75	15	Normal	•
TM24	Thunderbolt	Electric	Special	95	100	15	Normal	•
TM25	Thunder	Electric	Special	120	70	10	Normal	•
TM27	Return	Normal	Physical	—	100	20	Normal	•
TM28	Dig	Ground	Physical	80	100	10	Normal	•
TM29	Psychic	Psychic	Special	90	100	10	Normal	•
TM30	Shadow Ball	Ghost	Special	80	100	15	Normal	•
TM31	Brick Break	Fighting	Physical	75	100	15	Normal	•
TM32	Double Team	Normal	Status	—	—	15	Self	—
TM33	Reflect	Psychic	Status	—	—	20	2 allies	—
TM34	Shock Wave	Electric	Special	60	—	20	Normal	•
TM35	Flamethrower	Fire	Special	95	100	15	Normal	•
TM38	Fire Blast	Fire	Special	120	85	5	Normal	•
TM42	Facade	Normal	Physical	70	100	20	Normal	•
TM43	Secret Power	Normal	Physical	70	100	20	Normal	•
TM44	Rest	Psychic	Status	—	—	10	Self	—
TM45	Attract	Normal	Status	—	100	15	Normal	•
TM49	Snatch	Dark	Status	—	—	10	DoM	—
TM56	Fling	Dark	Physical	—	100	10	Normal	•
TM57	Charge Beam	Electric	Special	50	90	10	Normal	•
TM58	Endure	Normal	Status	—	—	10	Self	—
TM60	Drain Punch	Fighting	Physical	60	100	5	Normal	•
TM67	Recycle	Normal	Status	—	—	10	Self	—
TM70	Flash	Normal	Status	—	100	20	Normal	—
TM73	Thunder Wave	Electric	Status	—	100	20	Normal	—
TM76	Stealth Rock	Rock	Status	—	—	20	2 foes	—
TM77	Psych Up	Normal	Status	—	—	10	Normal	—
TM78	Captivate	Normal	Status	—	100	20	2 foes	—
TM82	Sleep Talk	Normal	Status	—	—	10	DoM	—
TM83	Natural Gift	Normal	Physical	—	100	15	Normal	—
TM85	Dream Eater	Psychic	Special	100	100	15	Normal	—
TM86	Grass Knot	Grass	Special	—	100	20	Normal	•
TM87	Swagger	Normal	Status	—	90	15	Normal	—
TM90	Substitute	Normal	Status	—	—	10	Self	—
HM04	Strength	Normal	Physical	80	100	15	Normal	•
HM06	Rock Smash	Fighting	Physical	40	100	15	Normal	•

● LEVEL-UP AND LEARNED MOVES

Lv	Name	Type	Kind	Power	Acc	PP	Range	DA
Base	Pound	Normal	Physical	40	100	35	Normal	•
Base	Growl	Normal	Status	—	100	40	2 foes	—
4	Encore	Normal	Status	—	100	5	Normal	—
7	Sing	Normal	Status	—	55	15	Normal	—
10	DoubleSlap	Normal	Physical	15	85	10	Normal	•
13	Defense Curl	Normal	Status	—	—	40	Self	—
16	Follow Me	Normal	Status	—	—	20	Self	—
19	Minimize	Normal	Status	—	—	20	Self	—
22	Wake-Up Slap	Fighting	Physical	60	100	10	Normal	•
25	Cosmic Power	Psychic	Status	—	—	20	Self	—
28	Lucky Chant	Normal	Status	—	—	30	2 allies	—
31	Metronome	Normal	Status	—	—	10	DoM	—
34	Gravity	Psychic	Status	—	—	5	All	—
37	Moonlight	Normal	Status	—	—	5	Self	—
40	Light Screen	Psychic	Status	—	—	30	2 allies	—
43	Meteor Mash	Steel	Physical	100	85	10	Normal	•
46	Healing Wish	Psychic	Status	—	—	10	Self	—

● MOVES TAUGHT IN EXCHANGE FOR COLORED SHARDS

Name	Type	Kind	Power	Acc	PP	Range	DA
Mud-Slap	Ground	Special	20	100	10	Normal	—
Icy Wind	Ice	Special	55	95	15	2 foes	—
Rollout	Rock	Physical	30	90	20	Normal	•
ThunderPunch	Electric	Physical	75	100	15	Normal	•
Fire Punch	Fire	Physical	75	100	15	Normal	•
Ice Punch	Ice	Physical	75	100	15	Normal	•
Snore	Normal	Special	40	100	15	Normal	—
Helping Hand	Normal	Status	—	—	20	1 ally	—
Endeavor	Normal	Physical	—	100	5	Normal	•
Signal Beam	Bug	Special	75	100	15	Normal	—
Zen Headbutt	Psychic	Physical	80	90	15	Normal	•
Last Resort	Normal	Physical	130	100	5	Normal	•
Bounce	Flying	Physical	85	85	5	Normal	•
Trick	Psychic	Status	—	100	10	Normal	—
Knock Off	Dark	Physical	20	100	20	Normal	•

● PRIMARY WAY TO FIND

TRAINER'S PARTY — Trainer on the Solaceon Town side of Route 210

WILD POKÉMON — Mt. Coronet (lower) (morning and night only)

COURSE OF STORY

Sinnoh Pokédex No. 101 Fairy Pokémon
Clefable

NORMAL

HEIGHT: 4'03"
WEIGHT: 88.2 lbs.
GENDER: Male and Female
HELD ITEM: None

● M/F have same form

PLATINUM It is very wary and rarely shows itself to people. Its ears can hear a pin drop over half a mile away.

EVOLUTION PATH

Cleffa → Level up once (Friendship level high enough) → Clefairy → Moon Stone → Clefable

● TM & HM MOVES

No.	Name	Type	Kind	Power	Acc	PP	Range	DA
TM01	Focus Punch	Fighting	Physical	150	100	20	Normal	•
TM03	Water Pulse	Water	Special	60	100	20	Normal	—
TM04	Calm Mind	Psychic	Status	—	—	20	Self	—
TM06	Toxic	Poison	Status	—	85	10	Normal	—
TM10	Hidden Power	Normal	Special	—	100	15	Normal	—
TM11	Sunny Day	Fire	Status	—	—	5	All	—
TM13	Ice Beam	Ice	Special	95	100	10	Normal	—
TM14	Blizzard	Ice	Special	120	70	5	2 foes	—
TM15	Hyper Beam	Normal	Special	150	90	5	Normal	—
TM16	Light Screen	Psychic	Status	—	—	30	2 allies	—
TM17	Protect	Normal	Status	—	—	10	Self	—
TM18	Rain Dance	Water	Status	—	—	5	All	—
TM20	Safeguard	Normal	Status	—	—	25	2 allies	—
TM21	Frustration	Normal	Physical	—	100	20	Normal	•
TM22	SolarBeam	Grass	Special	120	100	10	Normal	—
TM23	Iron Tail	Steel	Physical	100	75	15	Normal	•
TM24	Thunderbolt	Electric	Special	95	100	15	Normal	—
TM25	Thunder	Electric	Special	120	70	10	Normal	—
TM27	Return	Normal	Physical	—	100	20	Normal	•
TM28	Dig	Ground	Physical	80	100	10	Normal	—
TM29	Psychic	Psychic	Special	90	100	10	Normal	—
TM30	Shadow Ball	Ghost	Special	80	100	15	Normal	—
TM31	Brick Break	Fighting	Physical	75	100	15	Normal	•
TM32	Double Team	Normal	Status	—	—	15	Self	—
TM33	Reflect	Psychic	Status	—	—	20	2 allies	—
TM34	Shock Wave	Electric	Special	60	—	20	Normal	—
TM35	Flamethrower	Fire	Special	95	100	15	Normal	—
TM38	Fire Blast	Fire	Special	120	85	5	Normal	—
TM42	Facade	Normal	Physical	70	100	20	Normal	•
TM43	Secret Power	Normal	Physical	70	100	20	Normal	•
TM44	Rest	Psychic	Status	—	—	10	Self	—
TM45	Attract	Normal	Status	—	100	15	Normal	—
TM49	Snatch	Dark	Status	—	—	10	DoM	—
TM52	Focus Blast	Fighting	Special	120	70	5	Normal	—
TM56	Fling	Dark	Physical	—	100	10	Normal	•
TM57	Charge Beam	Electric	Special	50	90	10	Normal	—
TM58	Endure	Normal	Status	—	—	10	Self	—
TM60	Drain Punch	Fighting	Physical	60	100	5	Normal	•
TM67	Recycle	Normal	Status	—	—	10	Self	—
TM68	Giga Impact	Normal	Physical	150	90	5	Normal	•
TM70	Flash	Normal	Status	—	100	20	Normal	—
TM73	Thunder Wave	Electric	Status	—	100	20	Normal	—
TM76	Stealth Rock	Rock	Status	—	—	20	2 foes	—
TM77	Psych Up	Normal	Status	—	—	10	Normal	—
TM78	Captivate	Normal	Status	—	100	20	2 foes	—
TM82	Sleep Talk	Normal	Status	—	—	10	DoM	—
TM83	Natural Gift	Normal	Physical	—	100	15	Normal	•
TM85	Dream Eater	Psychic	Special	100	100	15	Normal	—
TM86	Grass Knot	Grass	Special	—	100	20	Normal	•
TM87	Swagger	Normal	Status	—	90	15	Normal	—
TM90	Substitute	Normal	Status	—	—	10	Self	—
HM04	Strength	Normal	Physical	80	100	15	Normal	•
HM06	Rock Smash	Fighting	Physical	40	100	15	Normal	•

● LEVEL-UP AND LEARNED MOVES

Lv	Name	Type	Kind	Power	Acc	PP	Range	DA
Base	Sing	Normal	Status	—	55	15	Normal	—
Base	DoubleSlap	Normal	Physical	15	85	10	Normal	•
Base	Minimize	Normal	Status	—	—	20	Self	—
Base	Metronome	Normal	Status	—	—	10	DoM	—

● MOVES TAUGHT IN EXCHANGE FOR COLORED SHARDS

Name	Type	Kind	Power	Acc	PP	Range	DA
Mud-Slap	Ground	Special	20	100	10	Normal	—
Icy Wind	Ice	Special	55	95	15	2 foes	—
Rollout	Rock	Physical	30	90	20	Normal	•
ThunderPunch	Electric	Physical	75	100	15	Normal	•
Fire Punch	Fire	Physical	75	100	15	Normal	•
Ice Punch	Ice	Physical	75	100	15	Normal	•
Snore	Normal	Special	40	100	15	Normal	—
Helping Hand	Normal	Status	—	—	20	1 ally	—
Endeavor	Normal	Physical	—	100	5	Normal	•
Signal Beam	Bug	Special	75	100	15	Normal	—
Zen Headbutt	Psychic	Physical	80	90	15	Normal	•
Last Resort	Normal	Physical	130	100	5	Normal	•
Bounce	Flying	Physical	85	85	5	Normal	•
Trick	Psychic	Status	—	100	10	Normal	—
Knock Off	Dark	Physical	20	100	20	Normal	•

ABILITY ● Cute Charm ● Magic Guard

EGG GROUP Fairy

STATS HP ●●● / ATTACK ●● / DEFENSE ●● / SP. ATTACK ●●● / SP. DEFENSE ●●● / SPEED ●●

● PRIMARY WAY TO FIND

TRAINER'S PARTY Trainer on Victory Road

WILD POKÉMON

COURSE OF STORY

Sinnoh Pokédex No. 102 Music Note Pokémon
Chatot

NORMAL / FLYING

HEIGHT: 1'08"
WEIGHT: 4.2 lbs.
GENDER: Male and Female
HELD ITEM: Metronome

● M/F have same form

PLATINUM Its tongue is just like a human's. As a result, it can cleverly mimic human speech.

EVOLUTION PATH

Does Not evolve

● TM & HM MOVES

No.	Name	Type	Kind	Power	Acc	PP	Range	DA
TM06	Toxic	Poison	Status	—	85	10	Normal	—
TM10	Hidden Power	Normal	Special	—	100	15	Normal	—
TM11	Sunny Day	Fire	Status	—	—	5	All	—
TM12	Taunt	Dark	Status	—	100	20	Normal	—
TM17	Protect	Normal	Status	—	—	10	Self	—
TM18	Rain Dance	Water	Status	—	—	5	All	—
TM21	Frustration	Normal	Physical	—	100	20	Normal	•
TM27	Return	Normal	Physical	—	100	20	Normal	•
TM32	Double Team	Normal	Status	—	—	15	Self	—
TM40	Aerial Ace	Flying	Physical	60	—	20	Normal	•
TM41	Torment	Dark	Status	—	100	15	Normal	—
TM42	Facade	Normal	Physical	70	100	20	Normal	•
TM43	Secret Power	Normal	Physical	70	100	20	Normal	•
TM44	Rest	Psychic	Status	—	—	10	Self	—
TM45	Attract	Normal	Status	—	100	15	Normal	—
TM46	Thief	Dark	Physical	40	100	10	Normal	•
TM47	Steel Wing	Steel	Physical	70	90	25	Normal	•
TM51	Roost	Flying	Status	—	—	10	Self	—
TM58	Endure	Normal	Status	—	—	10	Self	—
TM78	Captivate	Normal	Status	—	100	20	2 foes	—
TM82	Sleep Talk	Normal	Status	—	—	10	DoM	—
TM83	Natural Gift	Normal	Physical	—	100	15	Normal	•
TM97	Swagger	Normal	Status	—	90	15	Normal	—
TM88	Pluck	Flying	Physical	60	100	20	Normal	•
TM89	U-turn	Bug	Physical	70	100	20	Normal	•
TM90	Substitute	Normal	Status	—	—	10	Self	—
HM02	Fly	Flying	Physical	90	95	15	Normal	•
HM05	Defog	Flying	Status	—	—	15	Normal	—

● LEVEL-UP AND LEARNED MOVES

Lv	Name	Type	Kind	Power	Acc	PP	Range	DA
Base	Peck	Flying	Physical	35	100	35	Normal	•
5	Growl	Normal	Status	—	100	40	2 foes	—
9	Mirror Move	Flying	Status	—	—	20	DoM	—
13	Sing	Normal	Status	—	55	15	Normal	—
17	Fury Attack	Normal	Physical	15	85	20	Normal	•
21	Chatter	Flying	Special	60	100	20	Normal	—
25	Taunt	Dark	Status	—	100	20	Normal	—
29	Mimic	Normal	Status	—	—	10	Normal	—
33	Roost	Flying	Status	—	—	10	Self	—
37	Uproar	Normal	Special	50	100	10	1 random	—
41	FeatherDance	Flying	Status	—	100	15	Normal	—
45	Hyper Voice	Normal	Special	90	100	10	2 foes	—

● MOVES TAUGHT IN EXCHANGE FOR COLORED SHARDS

Name	Type	Kind	Power	Acc	PP	Range	DA
Mud-Slap	Ground	Special	20	100	10	Normal	—
Ominous Wind	Ghost	Special	60	100	5	Normal	—
Snore	Normal	Special	40	100	15	Normal	—
Air Cutter	Flying	Special	55	95	25	2 foes	—
Twister	Dragon	Special	40	100	20	2 foes	—
Heat Wave	Fire	Special	100	90	10	2 foes	—
Swift	Normal	Special	60	—	20	2 foes	—
Uproar	Normal	Special	50	100	10	1 random	—

● EGG MOVES

Name	Type	Kind	Power	Acc	PP	Range	DA
Encore	Normal	Status	—	100	5	Normal	—
Night Shade	Ghost	Special	—	100	15	Normal	—
Agility	Psychic	Status	—	—	30	Self	—
Nasty Plot	Dark	Status	—	—	20	Self	—
Supersonic	Normal	Status	—	55	20	Normal	—

ABILITY ● Keen Eye ● Tangled Feet

EGG GROUP Flying

STATS HP ●● / ATTACK ●● / DEFENSE ●● / SP. ATTACK ●●● / SP. DEFENSE ●● / SPEED ●●●

● PRIMARY WAY TO FIND

TRAINER'S PARTY Trainer on 2F of the Lost Tower

WILD POKÉMON Route 218 (morning and afternoon only)

COURSE OF STORY

Sinnoh Pokédex No. 103 Tiny Mouse Pokémon

Pichu

ELECTRIC

HEIGHT: 1'00"
WEIGHT: 4.4 lbs.
GENDER: Male and Female
HELD ITEM: Oran Berry

● M/F have same form

| PLATINUM | The electric sacs in its cheeks are small. If even a little electricity leaks, it becomes shocked. |

EVOLUTION PATH

Pichu → (Level up once friendship level is high enough) → Pikachu → (Thunderstone) → Raichu

| ABILITY | ● Static |

| EGG GROUP | No Eggs |

STATS
- HP ●
- ATTACK ●●
- DEFENSE ●●
- SP. ATTACK ●●
- SP. DEFENSE ●●
- SPEED ●●

● TM & HM MOVES

No.	Name	Type	Kind	Power	Acc	PP	Range	DA
TM06	Toxic	Poison	Status	—	85	10	Normal	
TM10	Hidden Power	Normal	Special	—	100	15	Normal	
TM16	Light Screen	Psychic	Status	—	—	30	2 allies	
TM17	Protect	Normal	Status	—	—	10	Self	
TM18	Rain Dance	Water	Status	—	—	5	All	
TM21	Frustration	Normal	Physical	—	100	20	Normal	●
TM23	Iron Tail	Steel	Physical	100	75	15	Normal	●
TM24	Thunderbolt	Electric	Special	95	100	15	Normal	
TM25	Thunder	Electric	Special	120	70	10	Normal	
TM27	Return	Normal	Physical	—	100	20	Normal	●
TM32	Double Team	Normal	Status	—	—	15	Self	
TM34	Shock Wave	Electric	Special	60	—	20	Normal	
TM42	Facade	Normal	Physical	70	100	20	Normal	●
TM43	Secret Power	Normal	Physical	70	100	20	Normal	●
TM44	Rest	Psychic	Status	—	—	10	Self	
TM45	Attract	Normal	Status	—	100	15	Normal	
TM56	Fling	Dark	Physical	—	100	10	Normal	●
TM57	Charge Beam	Electric	Special	50	90	10	Normal	
TM58	Endure	Normal	Status	—	—	10	Self	
TM70	Flash	Normal	Status	—	100	20	Normal	
TM73	Thunder Wave	Electric	Status	—	100	20	Normal	
TM78	Captivate	Normal	Status	—	100	20	2 foes	
TM82	Sleep Talk	Normal	Status	—	—	10	DoM	
TM83	Natural Gift	Normal	Physical	—	100	15	Normal	●
TM86	Grass Knot	Grass	Special	—	100	20	Normal	●
TM87	Swagger	Normal	Status	—	90	15	Normal	
TM90	Substitute	Normal	Status	—	—	10	Self	

● LEVEL-UP AND LEARNED MOVES

Lv	Name	Type	Kind	Power	Acc	PP	Range	DA
Base	ThunderShock	Electric	Special	40	100	30	Normal	—
Base	Charm	Normal	Status	—	100	20	Normal	—
5	Tail Whip	Normal	Status	—	100	30	2 foes	—
10	Thunder Wave	Electric	Status	—	100	20	Normal	—
13	Sweet Kiss	Normal	Status	—	75	10	Normal	—
18	Nasty Plot	Dark	Status	—	—	20	Self	—

● MOVES TAUGHT IN EXCHANGE FOR COLORED SHARDS

Name	Type	Kind	Power	Acc	PP	Range	DA
Mud-Slap	Ground	Special	20	100	10	Normal	●
Rollout	Rock	Physical	30	90	20	Normal	●
Snore	Normal	Special	40	100	15	Normal	●
Helping Hand	Normal	Status	—	—	20	1 ally	—
Signal Beam	Bug	Special	75	100	15	Normal	—
Magnet Rise	Electric	Status	—	—	10	Self	—
Swift	Normal	Special	60	—	20	2 foes	—
Uproar	Normal	Special	50	100	10	1 random	—

● EGG MOVES

Name	Type	Kind	Power	Acc	PP	Range	DA
Reversal	Fighting	Physical	—	100	15	Normal	●
Bide	Normal	Physical	—	—	10	Self	●
Present	Normal	Physical	—	90	15	Normal	●
Encore	Normal	Status	—	100	5	Normal	—
DoubleSlap	Normal	Physical	15	85	10	Normal	●
Wish	Normal	Status	—	—	10	Self	—
Charge	Electric	Status	—	—	20	Self	—
Fake Out	Normal	Physical	40	100	10	Normal	●
ThunderPunch	Electric	Physical	75	100	15	Normal	●
Tickle	Normal	Status	—	100	20	Normal	—
Volt Tackle*	Electric	Physical	120	100	15	Normal	●

*To teach Volt Tackle, have either of the Pokémon you leave at the Pokémon Day Care hold the Light Ball. You'll sometimes find Light Balls held by wild Pikachu.

● PRIMARY WAY TO FIND

TRAINER'S PARTY	Trainer on Route 209
WILD POKÉMON	Trophy Garden at the Pokémon Mansion on Route 212
COURSE OF STORY	

Sinnoh Pokédex No. 104 Mouse Pokémon

Pikachu

ELECTRIC

HEIGHT: 1'04"
WEIGHT: 13.2 lbs.
GENDER: Male and Female
HELD ITEM: Oran Berry/Light Ball

● Male form ● Female form

| PLATINUM | It occasionally uses an electric shock to recharge a fellow PIKACHU that is in a weakened state. |

EVOLUTION PATH

Pichu → (Level up once friendship level is high enough) → Pikachu → (Thunderstone) → Raichu

| ABILITY | ● Static |

| EGG GROUP | Field / Fairy |

STATS
- HP ●
- ATTACK ●●
- DEFENSE ●●
- SP. ATTACK ●●
- SP. DEFENSE ●●
- SPEED ●●●

● TM & HM MOVES

No.	Name	Type	Kind	Power	Acc	PP	Range	DA
TM01	Focus Punch	Fighting	Physical	150	100	20	Normal	●
TM06	Toxic	Poison	Status	—	85	10	Normal	
TM10	Hidden Power	Normal	Special	—	100	15	Normal	
TM16	Light Screen	Psychic	Status	—	—	30	2 allies	
TM17	Protect	Normal	Status	—	—	10	Self	
TM18	Rain Dance	Water	Status	—	—	5	All	
TM21	Frustration	Normal	Physical	—	100	20	Normal	●
TM23	Iron Tail	Steel	Physical	100	75	15	Normal	●
TM24	Thunderbolt	Electric	Special	95	100	15	Normal	
TM25	Thunder	Electric	Special	120	70	10	Normal	
TM27	Return	Normal	Physical	—	100	20	Normal	●
TM28	Dig	Ground	Physical	80	100	10	Normal	●
TM31	Brick Break	Fighting	Physical	75	100	15	Normal	●
TM32	Double Team	Normal	Status	—	—	15	Self	
TM34	Shock Wave	Electric	Special	60	—	20	Normal	
TM42	Facade	Normal	Physical	70	100	20	Normal	●
TM43	Secret Power	Normal	Physical	70	100	20	Normal	●
TM44	Rest	Psychic	Status	—	—	10	Self	
TM45	Attract	Normal	Status	—	100	15	Normal	
TM56	Fling	Dark	Physical	—	100	10	Normal	●
TM57	Charge Beam	Electric	Special	50	90	10	Normal	
TM58	Endure	Normal	Status	—	—	10	Self	
TM70	Flash	Normal	Status	—	100	20	Normal	
TM73	Thunder Wave	Electric	Status	—	100	20	Normal	
TM78	Captivate	Normal	Status	—	100	20	2 foes	
TM82	Sleep Talk	Normal	Status	—	—	10	DoM	
TM83	Natural Gift	Normal	Physical	—	100	15	Normal	●
TM86	Grass Knot	Grass	Special	—	100	20	Normal	●
TM87	Swagger	Normal	Status	—	90	15	Normal	
TM90	Substitute	Normal	Status	—	—	10	Self	
HM04	Strength	Normal	Physical	80	100	15	Normal	●
HM06	Rock Smash	Fighting	Physical	40	100	15	Normal	●

● LEVEL-UP AND LEARNED MOVES

Lv	Name	Type	Kind	Power	Acc	PP	Range	DA
Base	ThunderShock	Electric	Special	40	100	30	Normal	—
Base	Growl	Normal	Status	—	100	40	2 foes	—
5	Tail Whip	Normal	Status	—	100	30	2 foes	—
10	Thunder Wave	Electric	Status	—	100	20	Normal	—
13	Quick Attack	Normal	Physical	40	100	30	Normal	●
18	Double Team	Normal	Status	—	—	15	Self	—
21	Slam	Normal	Physical	80	75	20	Normal	●
26	Thunderbolt	Electric	Special	95	100	15	Normal	—
29	Feint	Normal	Physical	50	100	10	Normal	●
34	Agility	Psychic	Status	—	—	30	Self	—
37	Discharge	Electric	Special	80	100	15	2 foes • 1 ally	—
42	Light Screen	Psychic	Status	—	—	30	2 allies	—
45	Thunder	Electric	Special	120	70	10	Normal	—

● MOVES TAUGHT IN EXCHANGE FOR COLORED SHARDS

Name	Type	Kind	Power	Acc	PP	Range	DA
Mud-Slap	Ground	Special	20	100	10	Normal	●
Rollout	Rock	Physical	30	90	20	Normal	●
ThunderPunch	Electric	Physical	75	100	15	Normal	●
Snore	Normal	Special	40	100	15	Normal	●
Helping Hand	Normal	Status	—	—	20	1 ally	—
Signal Beam	Bug	Special	75	100	15	Normal	—
Magnet Rise	Electric	Status	—	—	10	Self	—
Knock Off	Dark	Physical	20	100	20	Normal	●
Swift	Normal	Special	60	—	20	2 foes	—

● PRIMARY WAY TO FIND

TRAINER'S PARTY	Trainer on Route 206
WILD POKÉMON	Trophy Garden at the Pokémon Mansion on Route 212
COURSE OF STORY	

Sinnoh Pokédex No. 105 Mouse Pokémon
Raichu

ELECTRIC

HEIGHT: 2'07"
WEIGHT: 66.1 lbs.
GENDER: Male and Female
HELD ITEM: None

● Male form ● Female form

PLATINUM Its tail discharges electricity into the ground, protecting it from getting shocked.

EVOLUTION PATH

Pichu — Level up once friendship level is high enough → Pikachu — Thunderstone → Raichu

ABILITY ● Static

EGG GROUP — Field / Fairy

STATS
HP ●●●
ATTACK ●●●
DEFENSE ●●●
SP. ATTACK ●●●
SP. DEFENSE ●●●
SPEED ●●●●

● TM & HM MOVES

No.	Name	Type	Kind	Power	Acc	PP	Range	DA
TM01	Focus Punch	Fighting	Physical	150	100	20	Normal	●
TM06	Toxic	Poison	Status	—	85	10	Normal	—
TM10	Hidden Power	Normal	Special	—	100	15	Normal	●
TM15	Hyper Beam	Normal	Special	150	90	5	Normal	—
TM16	Light Screen	Psychic	Status	—	—	30	2 allies	—
TM17	Protect	Normal	Status	—	—	10	Self	—
TM18	Rain Dance	Water	Status	—	—	5	All	—
TM21	Frustration	Normal	Physical	—	100	20	Normal	●
TM23	Iron Tail	Steel	Physical	100	75	15	Normal	●
TM24	Thunderbolt	Electric	Special	95	100	15	Normal	—
TM25	Thunder	Electric	Special	120	70	10	Normal	—
TM27	Return	Normal	Physical	—	100	20	Normal	●
TM28	Dig	Ground	Physical	80	100	10	Normal	●
TM31	Brick Break	Fighting	Physical	75	100	15	Normal	●
TM32	Double Team	Normal	Status	—	—	15	Self	—
TM34	Shock Wave	Electric	Special	60	—	20	Normal	—
TM42	Facade	Normal	Physical	70	100	20	Normal	●
TM43	Secret Power	Normal	Physical	70	100	20	Normal	●
TM44	Rest	Psychic	Status	—	—	10	Self	—
TM45	Attract	Normal	Status	—	100	15	Normal	—
TM46	Thief	Dark	Physical	40	100	10	Normal	●
TM52	Focus Blast	Fighting	Special	120	70	5	Normal	—
TM56	Fling	Dark	Physical	—	100	10	Normal	●
TM57	Charge Beam	Electric	Special	50	90	10	Normal	—
TM58	Endure	Normal	Status	—	—	10	Self	—
TM68	Giga Impact	Normal	Physical	150	90	5	Normal	●
TM70	Flash	Normal	Status	—	100	20	Normal	—
TM73	Thunder Wave	Electric	Status	—	100	20	Normal	—
TM78	Captivate	Normal	Status	—	100	20	2 foes	—
TM82	Sleep Talk	Normal	Status	—	—	10	DoM	—
TM83	Natural Gift	Normal	Physical	—	100	15	Normal	—
TM86	Grass Knot	Grass	Special	—	100	20	Normal	●
TM87	Swagger	Normal	Status	—	90	15	Normal	—
TM90	Substitute	Normal	Status	—	—	10	Self	—
HM04	Strength	Normal	Physical	80	100	15	Normal	●
HM06	Rock Smash	Fighting	Physical	40	100	15	Normal	●

● LEVEL-UP AND LEARNED MOVES

Lv	Name	Type	Kind	Power	Acc	PP	Range	DA
Base	ThunderShock	Electric	Special	40	100	30	Normal	—
Base	Tail Whip	Normal	Status	—	100	30	2 foes	—
Base	Quick Attack	Normal	Physical	40	100	30	Normal	—
Base	Thunderbolt	Electric	Special	95	100	15	Normal	—

● MOVES TAUGHT IN EXCHANGE FOR COLORED SHARDS

Name	Type	Kind	Power	Acc	PP	Range	DA
Mud-Slap	Ground	Special	20	100	10	Normal	—
Rollout	Rock	Physical	30	90	20	Normal	●
ThunderPunch	Electric	Physical	75	100	15	Normal	●
Snore	Normal	Special	40	100	15	Normal	—
Helping Hand	Normal	Status	—	—	20	1 ally	—
Signal Beam	Bug	Special	75	100	15	Normal	—
Magnet Rise	Electric	Status	—	—	10	Self	—
Knock Off	Dark	Physical	20	100	20	Normal	●
Swift	Normal	Special	60	—	20	2 foes	—

● PRIMARY WAY TO FIND

TRAINER'S PARTY Trainer on Route 210

WILD POKÉMON

COURSE OF STORY

Sinnoh Pokédex No. 106 Owl Pokémon
Hoothoot

NORMAL FLYING

HEIGHT: 2'04"
WEIGHT: 46.7 lbs.
GENDER: Male and Female
HELD ITEM: None

● M/F have same form

PLATINUM It marks time precisely. Some countries consider it to be a wise friend, versed in the world's ways.

EVOLUTION PATH

Hoothoot — Lv20 → Noctowl

ABILITY ● Insomnia / ● Keen Eye

EGG GROUP — Flying

STATS
HP ●●
ATTACK ●
DEFENSE ●
SP. ATTACK ●
SP. DEFENSE ●
SPEED ●●

● TM & HM MOVES

No.	Name	Type	Kind	Power	Acc	PP	Range	DA
TM06	Toxic	Poison	Status	—	85	10	Normal	—
TM10	Hidden Power	Normal	Special	—	100	15	Normal	—
TM11	Sunny Day	Fire	Status	—	—	5	All	—
TM17	Protect	Normal	Status	—	—	10	Self	—
TM18	Rain Dance	Water	Status	—	—	5	All	—
TM21	Frustration	Normal	Physical	—	100	20	Normal	●
TM27	Return	Normal	Physical	—	100	20	Normal	●
TM29	Psychic	Psychic	Special	90	100	10	Normal	—
TM30	Shadow Ball	Ghost	Special	80	100	15	Normal	—
TM32	Double Team	Normal	Status	—	—	15	Self	—
TM33	Reflect	Psychic	Status	—	—	20	2 allies	—
TM40	Aerial Ace	Flying	Physical	60	—	20	Normal	●
TM42	Facade	Normal	Physical	70	100	20	Normal	●
TM43	Secret Power	Normal	Physical	70	100	20	Normal	●
TM44	Rest	Psychic	Status	—	—	10	Self	—
TM45	Attract	Normal	Status	—	100	15	Normal	—
TM46	Thief	Dark	Physical	40	100	10	Normal	●
TM47	Steel Wing	Steel	Physical	70	90	25	Normal	●
TM51	Roost	Flying	Status	—	—	10	Self	—
TM58	Endure	Normal	Status	—	—	10	Self	—
TM62	Silver Wind	Bug	Special	60	100	5	Normal	—
TM67	Recycle	Normal	Status	—	—	10	Self	—
TM77	Psych Up	Normal	Status	—	—	10	Normal	—
TM78	Captivate	Normal	Status	—	100	20	2 foes	—
TM82	Sleep Talk	Normal	Status	—	—	10	DoM	—
TM83	Natural Gift	Normal	Physical	—	100	15	Normal	—
TM85	Dream Eater	Psychic	Special	100	100	15	Normal	—
TM87	Swagger	Normal	Status	—	90	15	Normal	—
TM88	Pluck	Flying	Physical	60	100	20	Normal	●
TM90	Substitute	Normal	Status	—	—	10	Self	—
HM02	Fly	Flying	Physical	90	95	15	Normal	●
HM05	Defog	Flying	Status	—	—	15	Normal	—

● LEVEL-UP AND LEARNED MOVES

Lv	Name	Type	Kind	Power	Acc	PP	Range	DA
Base	Tackle	Normal	Physical	35	95	35	Normal	●
Base	Growl	Normal	Status	—	100	40	2 foes	—
Base	Foresight	Normal	Status	—	—	40	Normal	—
5	Hypnosis	Psychic	Status	—	60	20	Normal	—
9	Peck	Flying	Physical	35	100	35	Normal	●
13	Uproar	Normal	Special	50	100	10	1 random	—
17	Reflect	Psychic	Status	—	—	20	2 allies	—
21	Confusion	Psychic	Special	50	100	25	Normal	—
25	Take Down	Normal	Physical	90	85	20	Normal	●
29	Air Slash	Flying	Special	75	95	20	Normal	—
33	Zen Headbutt	Psychic	Physical	80	90	15	Normal	●
37	Extrasensory	Psychic	Special	80	100	30	Normal	—
41	Psycho Shift	Psychic	Status	—	90	10	Normal	—
45	Roost	Flying	Status	—	—	10	Self	—
49	Dream Eater	Psychic	Special	100	100	15	Normal	—

● MOVES TAUGHT IN EXCHANGE FOR COLORED SHARDS

Name	Type	Kind	Power	Acc	PP	Range	DA
Mud-Slap	Ground	Special	20	100	10	Normal	—
Ominous Wind	Ghost	Special	60	100	5	Normal	—
Air Cutter	Flying	Special	55	95	25	2 foes	—
Zen Headbutt	Psychic	Physical	80	90	15	Normal	●
Twister	Dragon	Special	40	100	20	2 foes	—
Heat Wave	Fire	Special	100	90	10	2 foes	—
Swift	Normal	Special	60	—	20	2 foes	—
Uproar	Normal	Special	50	100	10	1 random	—

● EGG MOVES

Name	Type	Kind	Power	Acc	PP	Range	DA
Mirror Move	Flying	Status	—	—	20	DoM	—
Supersonic	Normal	Status	—	55	20	Normal	—
Faint Attack	Dark	Physical	60	—	20	Normal	—
Wing Attack	Flying	Physical	60	100	35	Normal	●
Whirlwind	Normal	Status	—	100	20	Normal	—
Sky Attack	Flying	Physical	140	90	5	Normal	●
FeatherDance	Flying	Status	—	100	15	Normal	—
Agility	Psychic	Status	—	—	30	Self	—
Night Shade	Ghost	Special	—	100	15	Normal	—

● PRIMARY WAY TO FIND

TRAINER'S PARTY Trainer in Wayward Cave

WILD POKÉMON Eterna Forest (night only)

COURSE OF STORY

Noctowl

NORMAL FLYING

HEIGHT: 5'03"
WEIGHT: 89.9 lbs.
GENDER: **Male and Female**
HELD ITEM: **None**

● M/F have same form

PLATINUM — Its eyes are specially developed to enable it to see clearly even in murky darkness and minimal light.

EVOLUTION PATH

Hoothoot → (Lv20) → Noctowl

ABILITY ● Insomnia ● Keen Eye

EGG GROUP Flying

STATS
HP ●●●
ATTACK ●●
DEFENSE ●●
SP. ATTACK ●●●
SP. DEFENSE ●●●
SPEED ●●●

● TM & HM MOVES

No.	Name	Type	Kind	Power	Acc	PP	Range	DA
TM06	Toxic	Poison	Status	—	85	10	Normal	—
TM10	Hidden Power	Normal	Special	—	100	15	Normal	—
TM11	Sunny Day	Fire	Status	—	—	5	All	—
TM15	Hyper Beam	Normal	Special	150	90	5	Normal	—
TM17	Protect	Normal	Status	—	—	10	Self	—
TM18	Rain Dance	Water	Status	—	—	5	All	•
TM21	Frustration	Normal	Physical	—	100	20	Normal	•
TM27	Return	Normal	Physical	—	100	20	Normal	•
TM29	Psychic	Psychic	Special	90	100	10	Normal	—
TM30	Shadow Ball	Ghost	Special	80	100	15	Normal	—
TM32	Double Team	Normal	Status	—	—	15	Self	—
TM33	Reflect	Psychic	Status	—	—	20	2 allies	•
TM40	Aerial Ace	Flying	Physical	60	—	20	Normal	•
TM42	Facade	Normal	Physical	70	100	20	Normal	—
TM43	Secret Power	Normal	Physical	70	100	20	Normal	—
TM44	Rest	Psychic	Status	—	—	10	Self	—
TM45	Attract	Normal	Status	—	100	15	Normal	—
TM46	Thief	Dark	Physical	40	100	10	Normal	—
TM47	Steel Wing	Steel	Physical	70	90	25	Normal	•
TM51	Roost	Flying	Status	—	—	10	Self	—
TM58	Endure	Normal	Status	—	—	10	Self	—
TM62	Silver Wind	Bug	Special	60	100	5	Normal	•
TM67	Recycle	Normal	Status	—	—	10	Self	—
TM68	Giga Impact	Normal	Physical	150	90	5	Normal	—
TM77	Psych Up	Normal	Status	—	—	10	Normal	—
TM78	Captivate	Normal	Status	—	100	20	2 foes	—
TM82	Sleep Talk	Normal	Status	—	—	10	DoM	—
TM83	Natural Gift	Normal	Physical	—	100	15	Normal	—
TM85	Dream Eater	Psychic	Special	100	100	15	Normal	—
TM87	Swagger	Normal	Status	—	90	15	Normal	—
TM88	Pluck	Flying	Physical	60	100	20	Normal	•
TM90	Substitute	Normal	Status	—	—	10	Self	—
HM02	Fly	Flying	Physical	90	95	15	Normal	—
HM05	Defog	Flying	Status	—	—	15	Normal	—

● LEVEL-UP AND LEARNED MOVES

Lv	Name	Type	Kind	Power	Acc	PP	Range	DA
Base	Sky Attack	Flying	Physical	140	90	5	Normal	—
Base	Tackle	Normal	Physical	35	95	35	Normal	—
Base	Growl	Normal	Status	—	100	40	2 foes	—
Base	Foresight	Normal	Status	—	—	40	Normal	—
Base	Hypnosis	Psychic	Status	—	60	20	Normal	—
5	Hypnosis	Psychic	Status	—	60	20	Normal	—
9	Peck	Flying	Physical	35	100	35	Normal	•
13	Uproar	Normal	Special	50	100	10	1 random	—
17	Reflect	Psychic	Status	—	—	20	2 allies	•
22	Confusion	Psychic	Special	50	100	25	Normal	—
27	Take Down	Normal	Physical	90	85	20	Normal	•
32	Air Slash	Flying	Special	75	95	20	Normal	—
37	Zen Headbutt	Psychic	Physical	80	90	15	Normal	•
42	Extrasensory	Psychic	Special	80	100	30	Normal	—
47	Psycho Shift	Psychic	Status	—	90	10	Normal	—
52	Roost	Flying	Status	—	—	10	Self	—
57	Dream Eater	Psychic	Special	100	100	15	Normal	—

● MOVES TAUGHT IN EXCHANGE FOR COLORED SHARDS

Name	Type	Kind	Power	Acc	PP	Range	DA
Mud-Slap	Ground	Special	20	100	10	Normal	—
Ominous Wind	Ghost	Special	60	100	5	Normal	—
Air Cutter	Flying	Special	55	95	25	2 foes	—
Zen Headbutt	Psychic	Physical	80	90	15	Normal	•
Twister	Dragon	Special	40	100	20	2 foes	—
Heat Wave	Fire	Special	100	90	10	2 foes	—
Swift	Normal	Special	60	—	20	2 foes	—
Uproar	Normal	Special	50	100	10	1 random	—

● PRIMARY WAY TO FIND

TRAINER'S PARTY — Trainer on the Celestic Town side of Route 210

WILD POKÉMON — Route 210 (night only)

COURSE OF STORY

Spiritomb

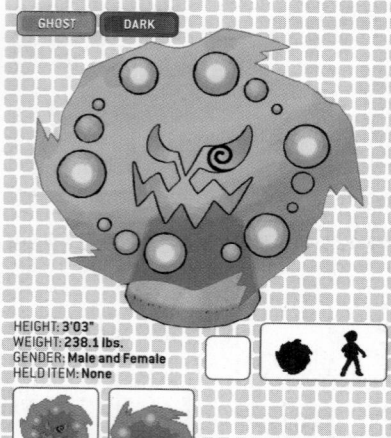

GHOST DARK

HEIGHT: 3'03"
WEIGHT: 238.1 lbs.
GENDER: **Male and Female**
HELD ITEM: **None**

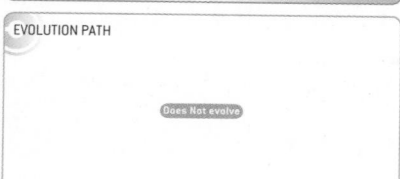

● M/F have same form

PLATINUM — Its constant mischief and misdeeds resulted in it being bound to an Odd Keystone by a mysterious spell.

EVOLUTION PATH

Does Not evolve

ABILITY ● Pressure

EGG GROUP Amorphous

STATS
HP ●●
ATTACK ●●●
DEFENSE ●●●●
SP. ATTACK ●●●
SP. DEFENSE ●●●●
SPEED ●

● TM & HM MOVES

No.	Name	Type	Kind	Power	Acc	PP	Range	DA
TM03	Water Pulse	Water	Special	60	100	20	Normal	—
TM04	Calm Mind	Psychic	Status	—	—	20	Self	—
TM06	Toxic	Poison	Status	—	85	10	Normal	—
TM10	Hidden Power	Normal	Special	—	100	15	Normal	—
TM11	Sunny Day	Fire	Status	—	—	5	All	—
TM12	Taunt	Dark	Status	—	100	20	Normal	—
TM15	Hyper Beam	Normal	Special	150	90	5	Normal	—
TM17	Protect	Normal	Status	—	—	10	Self	—
TM18	Rain Dance	Water	Status	—	—	5	All	—
TM21	Frustration	Normal	Physical	—	100	20	Normal	•
TM27	Return	Normal	Physical	—	100	20	Normal	•
TM29	Psychic	Psychic	Special	90	100	10	Normal	—
TM30	Shadow Ball	Ghost	Special	80	100	15	Normal	—
TM32	Double Team	Normal	Status	—	—	15	Self	—
TM34	Shock Wave	Electric	Special	60	—	20	Normal	—
TM39	Rock Tomb	Rock	Physical	50	80	10	Normal	—
TM41	Torment	Dark	Status	—	100	15	Normal	—
TM42	Facade	Normal	Physical	70	100	20	Normal	—
TM43	Secret Power	Normal	Physical	70	100	20	Normal	—
TM44	Rest	Psychic	Status	—	—	10	Self	—
TM45	Attract	Normal	Status	—	100	15	Normal	—
TM46	Thief	Dark	Physical	40	100	10	Normal	—
TM49	Snatch	Dark	Status	—	—	10	DoM	—
TM58	Endure	Normal	Status	—	—	10	Self	—
TM61	Will-O-Wisp	Fire	Status	—	75	15	Normal	—
TM62	Silver Wind	Bug	Special	60	100	5	Normal	—
TM63	Embargo	Dark	Status	—	100	15	Normal	—
TM68	Giga Impact	Normal	Physical	150	90	5	Normal	—
TM70	Flash	Normal	Status	—	100	20	Normal	—
TM77	Psych Up	Normal	Status	—	—	10	Normal	—
TM78	Captivate	Normal	Status	—	100	20	2 foes	—
TM79	Dark Pulse	Dark	Special	80	100	15	Normal	—
TM82	Sleep Talk	Normal	Status	—	—	10	DoM	—
TM83	Natural Gift	Normal	Physical	—	100	15	Normal	—
TM85	Dream Eater	Psychic	Special	100	100	15	Normal	—
TM87	Swagger	Normal	Status	—	90	15	Normal	—
TM90	Substitute	Normal	Status	—	—	10	Self	—

● LEVEL-UP AND LEARNED MOVES

Lv	Name	Type	Kind	Power	Acc	PP	Range	DA
Base	Curse	???	Status	—	—	10	Normal • Self	—
Base	Pursuit	Dark	Physical	40	100	20	Normal	—
Base	Confuse Ray	Ghost	Status	—	100	10	Normal	—
Base	Spite	Ghost	Status	—	100	10	Normal	—
Base	Shadow Sneak	Ghost	Physical	40	100	30	Normal	•
7	Faint Attack	Dark	Physical	60	—	20	Normal	—
13	Hypnosis	Psychic	Status	—	60	20	Normal	—
19	Dream Eater	Psychic	Special	100	100	15	Normal	—
25	Ominous Wind	Ghost	Special	60	100	5	Normal	—
31	Sucker Punch	Dark	Physical	80	100	5	Normal	•
37	Nasty Plot	Dark	Status	—	—	20	Self	—
43	Memento	Dark	Status	—	100	10	Normal	—
49	Dark Pulse	Dark	Special	80	100	15	Normal	—

● MOVES TAUGHT IN EXCHANGE FOR COLORED SHARDS

Name	Type	Kind	Power	Acc	PP	Range	DA
Icy Wind	Ice	Special	55	95	15	2 foes	—
Ominous Wind	Ghost	Special	60	100	5	Normal	—
Snore	Normal	Special	40	100	15	Normal	—
Spite	Ghost	Status	—	100	10	Normal	—
Trick	Psychic	Status	—	100	10	Normal	—
Sucker Punch	Dark	Physical	80	100	5	Normal	•
Uproar	Normal	Special	50	100	10	1 random	—

● EGG MOVES

Name	Type	Kind	Power	Acc	PP	Range	DA
Destiny Bond	Ghost	Status	—	—	5	Self	—
Pain Split	Normal	Status	—	—	20	Normal	—
SmokeScreen	Normal	Status	—	100	20	Normal	—
Imprison	Psychic	Status	—	—	10	Self	—
Grudge	Ghost	Status	—	—	5	Self	—
Shadow Sneak	Ghost	Physical	40	100	30	Normal	•

● PRIMARY WAY TO FIND

TRAINER'S PARTY — Pokémon League Champion Cynthia

WILD POKÉMON — Broken stone tower on Route 209*

COURSE OF STORY

*After you place the Odd Keystone in the broken stone tower, making it into the Hallowed Tower, greet 32 people in the Underground. Afterward, touch the Hallowed Tower and press A to encounter Spiritomb.

No. 109 Land Shark Pokémon

Gible

`DRAGON` `GROUND`

HEIGHT: 2'04"
WEIGHT: 45.2 lbs.
GENDER: **Male and Female**
HELD ITEM: **Haban Berry**

● Male form ● Female form

`PLATINUM` It attacks using its huge mouth. While its attacks are powerful, it hurts itself out of clumsiness, too.

EVOLUTION PATH

Gible — Lv24 → Gabite — Lv48 → Garchomp

● TM & HM MOVES

No.	Name	Type	Kind	Power	Acc	PP	Range	DA
TM02	Dragon Claw	Dragon	Physical	80	100	15	Normal	●
TM05	Roar	Normal	Status	—	100	20	Normal	—
TM06	Toxic	Poison	Status	—	85	10	Normal	—
TM10	Hidden Power	Normal	Special	—	100	15	Normal	●
TM11	Sunny Day	Fire	Status	—	—	5	All	—
TM17	Protect	Normal	Status	—	—	10	Self	—
TM18	Rain Dance	Water	Status	—	—	5	All	—
TM21	Frustration	Normal	Physical	—	100	20	Normal	●
TM26	Earthquake	Ground	Physical	100	100	10	2 foes • 1 ally	●
TM27	Return	Normal	Physical	—	100	20	Normal	●
TM28	Dig	Ground	Physical	80	100	10	Normal	●
TM32	Double Team	Normal	Status	—	—	15	Self	—
TM35	Flamethrower	Fire	Special	95	100	15	Normal	●
TM37	Sandstorm	Rock	Status	—	—	10	All	—
TM38	Fire Blast	Fire	Special	120	85	5	Normal	●
TM39	Rock Tomb	Rock	Physical	50	80	10	Normal	●
TM40	Aerial Ace	Flying	Physical	60	—	20	Normal	●
TM42	Facade	Normal	Physical	70	100	20	Normal	●
TM43	Secret Power	Normal	Physical	70	100	20	Normal	●
TM44	Rest	Psychic	Status	—	—	10	Self	—
TM45	Attract	Normal	Status	—	100	15	Normal	—
TM58	Endure	Normal	Status	—	—	10	Self	—
TM59	Dragon Pulse	Dragon	Special	90	100	10	Normal	●
TM65	Shadow Claw	Ghost	Physical	70	100	15	Normal	●
TM71	Stone Edge	Rock	Physical	100	80	5	Normal	●
TM76	Stealth Rock	Rock	Status	—	—	20	2 foes	—
TM78	Captivate	Normal	Status	—	100	20	2 foes	—
TM80	Rock Slide	Rock	Physical	75	90	10	2 foes	●
TM82	Sleep Talk	Normal	Status	—	—	10	DoM	—
TM83	Natural Gift	Normal	Physical	—	100	15	Normal	●
TM87	Swagger	Normal	Status	—	90	15	Normal	—
TM90	Substitute	Normal	Status	—	—	10	Self	—
HM01	Cut	Normal	Physical	50	95	30	Normal	●
HM04	Strength	Normal	Physical	80	100	15	Normal	●
HM06	Rock Smash	Fighting	Physical	40	100	15	Normal	●
HM08	Rock Climb	Normal	Physical	90	85	20	Normal	●

ABILITY ● Sand Veil

STATS
HP ●●
ATTACK ●●●
DEFENSE ●●●
SP. ATTACK ●●●
SP. DEFENSE ●●●
SPEED ●●

EGG GROUP Monster / Dragon

● LEVEL-UP AND LEARNED MOVES

Lv	Name	Type	Kind	Power	Acc	PP	Range	DA
Base	Tackle	Normal	Physical	35	95	35	Normal	●
3	Sand-Attack	Ground	Status	—	100	15	Normal	—
7	Dragon Rage	Dragon	Special	—	100	10	Normal	—
13	Sandstorm	Rock	Status	—	—	10	All	—
15	Take Down	Normal	Physical	90	85	20	Normal	●
19	Sand Tomb	Ground	Physical	15	70	15	Normal	●
25	Slash	Normal	Physical	70	100	20	Normal	●
27	Dragon Claw	Dragon	Physical	80	100	15	Normal	●
31	Dig	Ground	Physical	80	100	10	Normal	●
37	Dragon Rush	Dragon	Physical	100	75	10	Normal	●

● MOVES TAUGHT IN EXCHANGE FOR COLORED SHARDS

Name	Type	Kind	Power	Acc	PP	Range	DA
Mud-Slap	Ground	Special	20	100	10	Normal	—
Fury Cutter	Bug	Physical	10	95	20	Normal	—
Iron Head	Steel	Physical	80	100	15	Normal	●
Snore	Normal	Special	40	100	15	Normal	●
Outrage	Dragon	Physical	120	100	10	1 random	●
Earth Power	Ground	Special	90	100	10	Normal	●
Twister	Dragon	Special	40	100	20	2 foes	●
Swift	Normal	Special	60	—	20	2 foes	—

● MOVES TAUGHT BY PEOPLE

Name	Type	Kind	Power	Acc	PP	Range	DA
Draco Meteor*	Dragon	Special	140	90	5	Normal	●

*Draco Meteor is taught when the Pokémon's Friendship is maxed out

● EGG MOVES

Name	Type	Kind	Power	Acc	PP	Range	DA
DragonBreath	Dragon	Special	60	100	20	Normal	—
Outrage	Dragon	Physical	120	100	15	1 random	●
Twister	Dragon	Special	40	100	20	2 foes	●
Scary Face	Normal	Status	—	90	10	Normal	—
Double-Edge	Normal	Physical	120	100	15	Normal	●
Thrash	Normal	Physical	90	100	20	1 random	●
Metal Claw	Steel	Physical	50	95	35	Normal	●
Sand Tomb	Ground	Physical	15	70	15	Normal	●
Body Slam	Normal	Physical	85	100	15	Normal	●
Iron Head	Steel	Physical	80	100	15	Normal	●

● PRIMARY WAY TO FIND

`TRAINER'S PARTY` Trainer in Wayward Cave

`WILD POKÉMON` Wayward Cave (hidden entrance)

`COURSE OF STORY`

No. 110 Cave Pokémon

Gabite

`DRAGON` `GROUND`

HEIGHT: 4'07"
WEIGHT: 123.5 lbs.
GENDER: **Male and Female**
HELD ITEM: **Haban Berry**

● Male form ● Female form

`PLATINUM` It loves sparkly things. It seeks treasures in caves and hoards the loot in its nest.

EVOLUTION PATH

Gible — Lv24 → Gabite — Lv48 → Garchomp

● TM & HM MOVES

No.	Name	Type	Kind	Power	Acc	PP	Range	DA
TM02	Dragon Claw	Dragon	Physical	80	100	15	Normal	●
TM05	Roar	Normal	Status	—	100	20	Normal	—
TM06	Toxic	Poison	Status	—	85	10	Normal	—
TM10	Hidden Power	Normal	Special	—	100	15	Normal	●
TM11	Sunny Day	Fire	Status	—	—	5	All	—
TM17	Protect	Normal	Status	—	—	10	Self	—
TM18	Rain Dance	Water	Status	—	—	5	All	—
TM21	Frustration	Normal	Physical	—	100	20	Normal	●
TM23	Iron Tail	Steel	Physical	100	75	15	Normal	●
TM26	Earthquake	Ground	Physical	100	100	10	2 foes • 1 ally	●
TM27	Return	Normal	Physical	—	100	20	Normal	●
TM28	Dig	Ground	Physical	80	100	10	Normal	●
TM32	Double Team	Normal	Status	—	—	15	Self	—
TM35	Flamethrower	Fire	Special	95	100	15	Normal	●
TM37	Sandstorm	Rock	Status	—	—	10	All	—
TM38	Fire Blast	Fire	Special	120	85	5	Normal	●
TM39	Rock Tomb	Rock	Physical	50	80	10	Normal	●
TM40	Aerial Ace	Flying	Physical	60	—	20	Normal	●
TM42	Facade	Normal	Physical	70	100	20	Normal	●
TM43	Secret Power	Normal	Physical	70	100	20	Normal	●
TM44	Rest	Psychic	Status	—	—	10	Self	—
TM45	Attract	Normal	Status	—	100	15	Normal	—
TM58	Endure	Normal	Status	—	—	10	Self	—
TM59	Dragon Pulse	Dragon	Special	90	100	10	Normal	●
TM65	Shadow Claw	Ghost	Physical	70	100	15	Normal	●
TM71	Stone Edge	Rock	Physical	100	80	5	Normal	●
TM76	Stealth Rock	Rock	Status	—	—	20	2 foes	—
TM78	Captivate	Normal	Status	—	100	20	2 foes	—
TM80	Rock Slide	Rock	Physical	75	90	10	2 foes	●
TM82	Sleep Talk	Normal	Status	—	—	10	DoM	—
TM83	Natural Gift	Normal	Physical	—	100	15	Normal	●
TM87	Swagger	Normal	Status	—	90	15	Normal	—
TM90	Substitute	Normal	Status	—	—	10	Self	—
HM01	Cut	Normal	Physical	50	95	30	Normal	●
HM04	Strength	Normal	Physical	80	100	15	Normal	●
HM06	Rock Smash	Fighting	Physical	40	100	15	Normal	●
HM08	Rock Climb	Normal	Physical	90	85	20	Normal	●

ABILITY ● Sand Veil

STATS
HP ●●
ATTACK ●●●
DEFENSE ●●●
SP. ATTACK ●●
SP. DEFENSE ●●●
SPEED ●●●

EGG GROUP Monster / Dragon

● LEVEL-UP AND LEARNED MOVES

Lv	Name	Type	Kind	Power	Acc	PP	Range	DA
Base	Tackle	Normal	Physical	35	95	35	Normal	●
Base	Sand-Attack	Ground	Status	—	100	15	Normal	—
3	Sand-Attack	Ground	Status	—	100	15	Normal	—
7	Dragon Rage	Dragon	Special	—	100	10	Normal	—
13	Sandstorm	Rock	Status	—	—	10	All	—
15	Take Down	Normal	Physical	90	85	20	Normal	●
19	Sand Tomb	Ground	Physical	15	70	15	Normal	●
28	Slash	Normal	Physical	70	100	20	Normal	●
33	Dragon Claw	Dragon	Physical	80	100	15	Normal	●
40	Dig	Ground	Physical	80	100	10	Normal	●
49	Dragon Rush	Dragon	Physical	100	75	10	Normal	●

● MOVES TAUGHT IN EXCHANGE FOR COLORED SHARDS

Name	Type	Kind	Power	Acc	PP	Range	DA
Mud-Slap	Ground	Special	20	100	10	Normal	—
Fury Cutter	Bug	Physical	10	95	20	Normal	—
Iron Head	Steel	Physical	80	100	15	Normal	●
Snore	Normal	Special	40	100	15	Normal	●
Outrage	Dragon	Physical	120	100	10	1 random	●
Earth Power	Ground	Special	90	100	10	Normal	●
Twister	Dragon	Special	40	100	20	2 foes	●
Swift	Normal	Special	60	—	20	2 foes	—

● MOVES TAUGHT BY PEOPLE

Name	Type	Kind	Power	Acc	PP	Range	DA
Draco Meteor*	Dragon	Special	140	90	5	Normal	●

*Draco Meteor is taught when the Pokémon's Friendship level is maxed out

● PRIMARY WAY TO FIND

`TRAINER'S PARTY` Trainer on Victory Road

`WILD POKÉMON` Throughout Victory Road

`COURSE OF STORY`

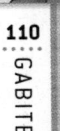

Sinnoh Pokédex **No. 111** Mach Pokémon

Garchomp

DRAGON GROUND

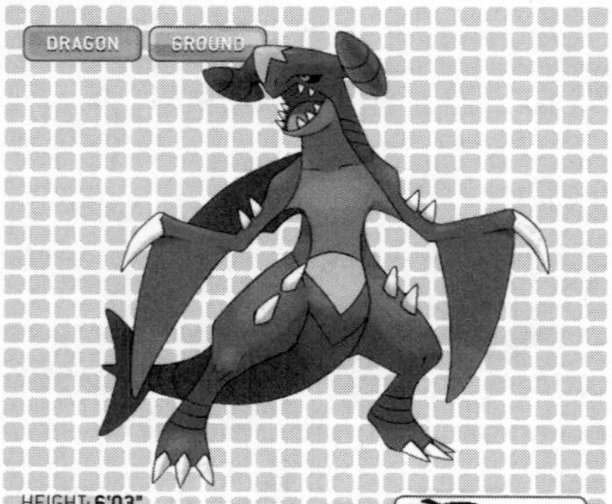

HEIGHT: **6'03"**
WEIGHT: **209.4 lbs.**
GENDER: **Male and Female**
HELD ITEM: **None**

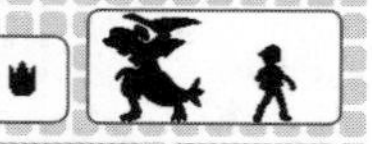

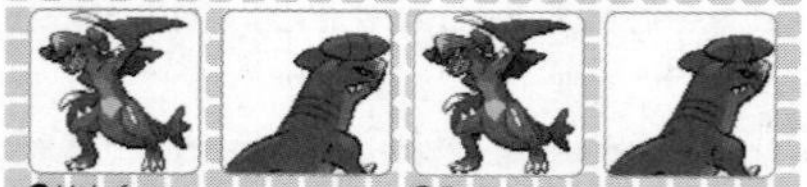

● Male form ● Female form

PLATINUM It is said that when one runs at high speed, its wings create blades of wind that can fell nearby trees.

EVOLUTION PATH

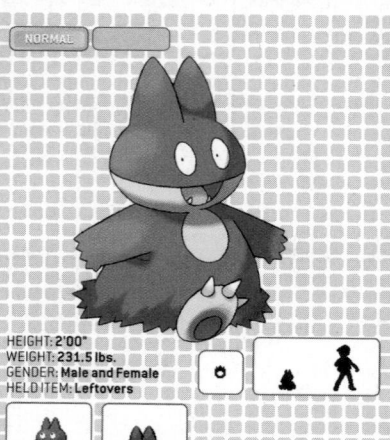

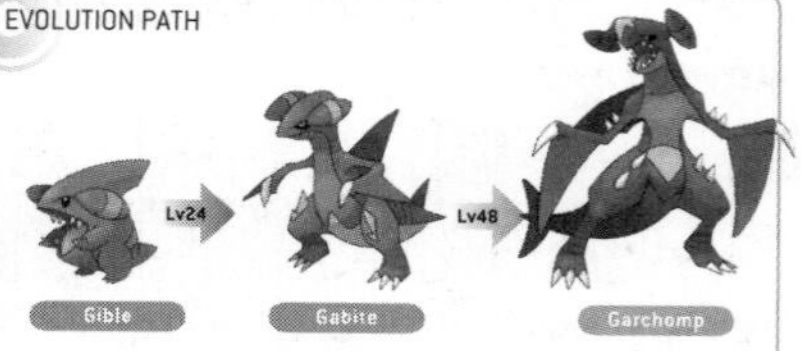
Lv24
Lv48
Gible
Gabite
Garchomp

● TM & HM MOVES

No.	Name	Type	Kind	Power	Acc	PP	Range	DA
TM02	Dragon Claw	Dragon	Physical	80	100	15	Normal	•
TM05	Roar	Normal	Status	—	100	20	Normal	—
TM06	Toxic	Poison	Status	—	85	10	Normal	—
TM10	Hidden Power	Normal	Special	—	100	15	Normal	—
TM11	Sunny Day	Fire	Status	—	—	5	All	—
TM15	Hyper Beam	Normal	Special	150	90	5	Normal	—
TM17	Protect	Normal	Status	—	—	10	Self	—
TM18	Rain Dance	Water	Status	—	—	5	All	—
TM21	Frustration	Normal	Physical	—	100	20	Normal	•
TM23	Iron Tail	Steel	Physical	100	75	15	Normal	•
TM26	Earthquake	Ground	Physical	100	100	10	2 foes • 1 ally	—
TM27	Return	Normal	Physical	—	100	20	Normal	•
TM28	Dig	Ground	Physical	80	100	10	Normal	•
TM31	Brick Break	Fighting	Physical	75	100	15	Normal	•
TM32	Double Team	Normal	Status	—	—	15	Self	—
TM35	Flamethrower	Fire	Special	95	100	15	Normal	—
TM37	Sandstorm	Rock	Status	—	—	10	All	—
TM38	Fire Blast	Fire	Special	120	85	5	Normal	—
TM39	Rock Tomb	Rock	Physical	50	80	10	Normal	—
TM40	Aerial Ace	Flying	Physical	60	—	20	Normal	•
TM42	Facade	Normal	Physical	70	100	20	Normal	•
TM43	Secret Power	Normal	Physical	70	100	20	Normal	—
TM44	Rest	Psychic	Status	—	—	10	Self	—
TM45	Attract	Normal	Status	—	100	15	Normal	—
TM54	False Swipe	Normal	Physical	40	100	40	Normal	•
TM56	Fling	Dark	Physical	—	100	10	Normal	—
TM58	Endure	Normal	Status	—	—	10	Self	—
TM59	Dragon Pulse	Dragon	Special	90	100	10	Normal	—
TM65	Shadow Claw	Ghost	Physical	70	100	15	Normal	•
TM68	Giga Impact	Normal	Physical	150	90	5	Normal	•
TM71	Stone Edge	Rock	Physical	100	80	5	Normal	—
TM75	Swords Dance	Normal	Status	—	—	30	Self	—
TM76	Stealth Rock	Rock	Status	—	—	20	2 foes	—
TM78	Captivate	Normal	Status	—	100	20	2 foes	—
TM80	Rock Slide	Rock	Physical	75	90	10	2 foes	—
TM82	Sleep Talk	Normal	Status	—	—	10	DoM	—
TM83	Natural Gift	Normal	Physical	—	100	15	Normal	—
TM84	Poison Jab	Poison	Physical	80	100	20	Normal	•
TM87	Swagger	Normal	Status	—	90	15	Normal	—
TM90	Substitute	Normal	Status	—	—	10	Self	—
HM01	Cut	Normal	Physical	50	95	30	Normal	•
HM03	Surf	Water	Special	95	100	15	2 foes • 1 ally	—
HM04	Strength	Normal	Physical	80	100	15	Normal	•
HM06	Rock Smash	Fighting	Physical	40	100	15	Normal	•
HM08	Rock Climb	Normal	Physical	90	85	20	Normal	•

ABILITY ● Sand Veil

EGG GROUP Monster / Dragon

STATS
HP ●●●
ATTACK ●●●●
DEFENSE ●●●
SP. ATTACK ●●●
SP. DEFENSE ●●
SPEED ●●●●

● LEVEL-UP AND LEARNED MOVES

Lv	Name	Type	Kind	Power	Acc	PP	Range	DA
Base	Fire Fang	Fire	Physical	65	95	15	Normal	•
Base	Tackle	Normal	Physical	35	95	35	Normal	•
Base	Sand-Attack	Ground	Status	—	100	15	Normal	—
Base	Dragon Rage	Dragon	Special	—	100	10	Normal	—
Base	Sandstorm	Rock	Status	—	—	10	All	—
3	Sand-Attack	Ground	Status	—	100	15	Normal	—
7	Dragon Rage	Dragon	Special	—	100	10	Normal	—
13	Sandstorm	Rock	Status	—	—	10	All	—
15	Take Down	Normal	Physical	90	85	20	Normal	•
19	Sand Tomb	Ground	Physical	15	70	15	Normal	—
28	Slash	Normal	Physical	70	100	20	Normal	•
33	Dragon Claw	Dragon	Physical	80	100	15	Normal	•
40	Dig	Ground	Physical	80	100	10	Normal	•
48	Crunch	Dark	Physical	80	100	15	Normal	•
55	Dragon Rush	Dragon	Physical	100	75	10	Normal	•

● MOVES TAUGHT IN EXCHANGE FOR COLORED SHARDS

Name	Type	Kind	Power	Acc	PP	Range	DA
Mud-Slap	Ground	Special	20	100	10	Normal	—
Fury Cutter	Bug	Physical	10	95	20	Normal	•
Iron Head	Steel	Physical	80	100	15	Normal	•
Aqua Tail	Water	Physical	90	90	10	Normal	•
Snore	Normal	Special	40	100	15	Normal	—
Outrage	Dragon	Physical	120	100	15	1 random	•
Earth Power	Ground	Special	90	100	10	Normal	—
Twister	Dragon	Special	40	100	20	2 foes	—
Swift	Normal	Special	60	—	20	2 foes	—

● MOVES TAUGHT BY PEOPLE

Name	Type	Kind	Power	Acc	PP	Range	DA
Draco Meteor*	Dragon	Special	140	90	5	Normal	—

*Draco Meteor is taught when the Pokémon's Friendship level is maxed out

● PRIMARY WAY TO FIND

TRAINER'S PARTY Pokémon League Champion Cynthia

WILD POKÉMON

COURSE OF STORY

Sinnoh Pokédex **No. 112** Big Eater Pokémon

Munchlax

NORMAL

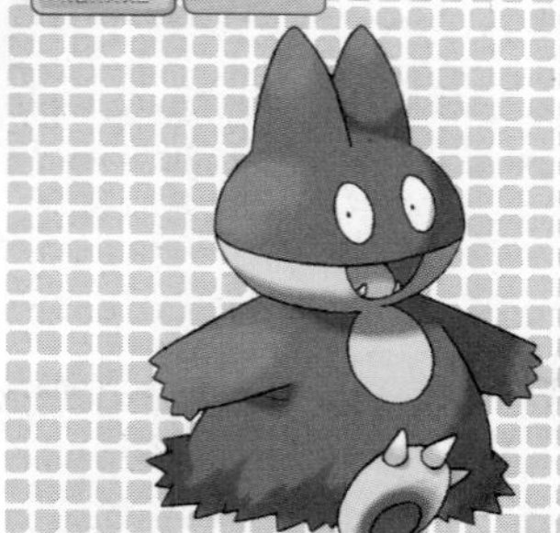

HEIGHT: **2'00"**
WEIGHT: **231.5 lbs.**
GENDER: **Male and Female**
HELD ITEM: **Leftovers**

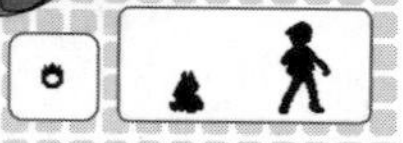

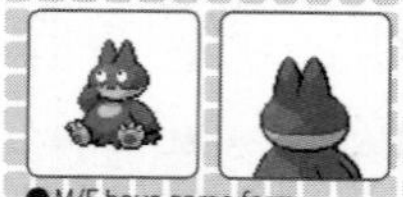

● M/F have same form

PLATINUM In its desperation to gulp down food, it forgets about the food it has hidden under its fur.

EVOLUTION PATH

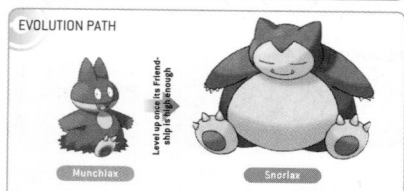

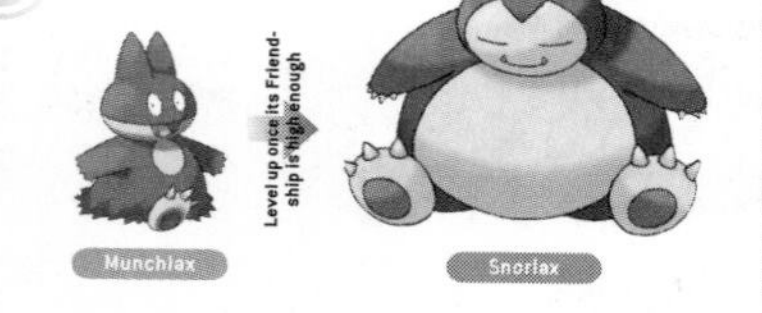
Level up once its Friendship is high enough
Munchlax
Snorlax

● TM & HM MOVES

No.	Name	Type	Kind	Power	Acc	PP	Range	DA
TM01	Focus Punch	Fighting	Physical	150	100	20	Normal	•
TM03	Water Pulse	Water	Special	60	100	20	Normal	—
TM06	Toxic	Poison	Status	—	85	10	Normal	—
TM10	Hidden Power	Normal	Special	—	100	15	Normal	—
TM11	Sunny Day	Fire	Status	—	—	5	All	—
TM13	Ice Beam	Ice	Special	95	100	10	Normal	—
TM14	Blizzard	Ice	Special	120	70	5	2 foes	—
TM17	Protect	Normal	Status	—	—	10	Self	—
TM18	Rain Dance	Water	Status	—	—	5	All	—
TM21	Frustration	Normal	Physical	—	100	20	Normal	•
TM22	SolarBeam	Grass	Special	120	100	10	Normal	—
TM24	Thunderbolt	Electric	Special	95	100	15	Normal	—
TM25	Thunder	Electric	Special	120	70	10	Normal	—
TM26	Earthquake	Ground	Physical	100	100	10	2 foes • 1 ally	—
TM27	Return	Normal	Physical	—	100	20	Normal	•
TM29	Psychic	Psychic	Special	90	100	10	Normal	—
TM30	Shadow Ball	Ghost	Special	80	100	15	Normal	—
TM31	Brick Break	Fighting	Physical	75	100	15	Normal	•
TM32	Double Team	Normal	Status	—	—	15	Self	—
TM34	Shock Wave	Electric	Special	60	—	20	Normal	—
TM35	Flamethrower	Fire	Special	95	100	15	Normal	—
TM37	Sandstorm	Rock	Status	—	—	10	All	—
TM38	Fire Blast	Fire	Special	120	85	5	Normal	—
TM39	Rock Tomb	Rock	Physical	50	80	10	Normal	—
TM42	Facade	Normal	Physical	70	100	20	Normal	•
TM43	Secret Power	Normal	Physical	70	100	20	Normal	—
TM44	Rest	Psychic	Status	—	—	10	Self	—
TM45	Attract	Normal	Status	—	100	15	Normal	—
TM56	Fling	Dark	Physical	—	100	10	Normal	—
TM58	Endure	Normal	Status	—	—	10	Self	—
TM67	Recycle	Normal	Status	—	—	10	Self	—
TM78	Captivate	Normal	Status	—	100	20	2 foes	—
TM80	Rock Slide	Rock	Physical	75	90	10	2 foes	—
TM82	Sleep Talk	Normal	Status	—	—	10	DoM	—
TM83	Natural Gift	Normal	Physical	—	100	15	Normal	—
TM87	Swagger	Normal	Status	—	90	15	Normal	—
TM90	Substitute	Normal	Status	—	—	10	Self	—
HM03	Surf	Water	Special	95	100	15	2 foes • 1 ally	—
HM04	Strength	Normal	Physical	80	100	15	Normal	•
HM06	Rock Smash	Fighting	Physical	40	100	15	Normal	•
HM08	Rock Climb	Normal	Physical	90	85	20	Normal	•

ABILITY ● Pickup ● Thick Fat

EGG GROUP No Eggs

STATS
HP ●●●●
ATTACK ●●●
DEFENSE ●●
SP. ATTACK ●●
SP. DEFENSE ●●
SPEED ●

● LEVEL-UP AND LEARNED MOVES

Lv	Name	Type	Kind	Power	Acc	PP	Range	DA
Base	Metronome	Normal	Status	—	—	10	DoM	—
Base	Odor Sleuth	Normal	Status	—	—	40	Normal	—
Base	Tackle	Normal	Physical	35	95	35	Normal	•
4	Defense Curl	Normal	Status	—	—	40	Self	—
9	Amnesia	Psychic	Status	—	—	20	Self	—
12	Lick	Ghost	Physical	20	100	30	Normal	•
17	Recycle	Normal	Status	—	—	10	Self	—
20	Screech	Normal	Status	—	85	40	Normal	—
25	Stockpile	Normal	Status	—	—	20	Self	—
28	Swallow	Normal	Status	—	—	10	Self	—
33	Body Slam	Normal	Physical	85	100	15	Normal	•
36	Fling	Dark	Physical	—	100	10	Normal	—
41	Rollout	Rock	Physical	30	90	20	Normal	•
44	Natural Gift	Normal	Physical	—	100	15	Normal	—
49	Last Resort	Normal	Physical	130	100	5	Normal	•

● MOVES TAUGHT IN EXCHANGE FOR COLORED SHARDS

Name	Type	Kind	Power	Acc	PP	Range	DA
Mud-Slap	Ground	Special	20	100	10	Normal	—
Icy Wind	Ice	Special	55	95	15	2 foes	—
Rollout	Rock	Physical	30	90	20	Normal	•
ThunderPunch	Electric	Physical	75	100	15	Normal	•
Fire Punch	Fire	Physical	75	100	15	Normal	•
Superpower	Fighting	Physical	120	100	5	Normal	•
Ice Punch	Ice	Physical	75	100	15	Normal	•
Snore	Normal	Special	40	100	15	Normal	—
Zen Headbutt	Psychic	Physical	80	90	15	Normal	•
Gunk Shot	Poison	Physical	120	70	5	Normal	—
Seed Bomb	Grass	Physical	80	100	15	Normal	—
Last Resort	Normal	Physical	130	100	5	Normal	•
Uproar	Normal	Special	50	100	10	1 random	—

● EGG MOVES

Name	Type	Kind	Power	Acc	PP	Range	DA
Lick	Ghost	Physical	20	100	30	Normal	•
Charm	Normal	Status	—	100	20	Normal	—
Double-Edge	Normal	Physical	120	100	15	Normal	•
Curse	???	Status	—	—	10	Normal • Self	—
Substitute	Normal	Status	—	—	10	Self	—
Whirlwind	Normal	Status	—	100	20	Normal	—
Pursuit	Dark	Physical	40	100	20	Normal	•
Zen Headbutt	Psychic	Physical	80	90	15	Normal	•

● PRIMARY WAY TO FIND

TRAINER'S PARTY Trainer at the Café Cabin on the Solaceon Town side of Route 210

WILD POKÉMON Spread Honey on a Honey Tree

COURSE OF STORY

Snorlax

NORMAL

HEIGHT: 6'11"
WEIGHT: 1014.1 lbs.
GENDER: Male and Female
HELD ITEM: None

● M/F have same form

PLATINUM
When its belly is full, it becomes too lethargic to even lift a finger, so it is safe to bounce on its belly.

EVOLUTION PATH

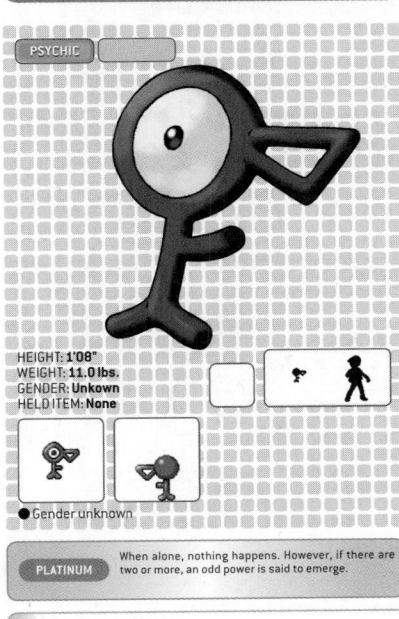

Munchlax → Level up once its Friend-ship level is high enough → Snorlax

● TM & HM MOVES

No.	Name	Type	Kind	Power	Acc	PP	Range	DA
TM01	Focus Punch	Fighting	Physical	150	100	20	Normal	●
TM03	Water Pulse	Water	Special	60	100	20	Normal	—
TM06	Toxic	Poison	Status	—	85	10	Normal	—
TM10	Hidden Power	Normal	Special	—	100	15	Normal	●
TM11	Sunny Day	Fire	Status	—	—	5	All	—
TM13	Ice Beam	Ice	Special	95	100	10	Normal	—
TM14	Blizzard	Ice	Special	120	70	5	2 foes	—
TM15	Hyper Beam	Normal	Special	150	90	5	Normal	—
TM17	Protect	Normal	Status	—	—	10	Self	—
TM18	Rain Dance	Water	Status	—	—	5	All	—
TM21	Frustration	Normal	Physical	—	100	20	Normal	●
TM22	SolarBeam	Grass	Special	120	100	10	Normal	—
TM24	Thunderbolt	Electric	Special	95	100	15	Normal	—
TM25	Thunder	Electric	Special	120	70	10	Normal	—
TM26	Earthquake	Ground	Physical	100	100	10	2 foes + 1 ally	—
TM27	Return	Normal	Physical	—	100	20	Normal	●
TM29	Psychic	Psychic	Special	90	100	10	Normal	—
TM30	Shadow Ball	Ghost	Special	80	100	15	Normal	—
TM31	Brick Break	Fighting	Physical	75	100	15	Normal	●
TM32	Double Team	Normal	Status	—	—	15	Self	—
TM34	Shock Wave	Electric	Special	60	—	20	Normal	—
TM35	Flamethrower	Fire	Special	95	100	15	Normal	—
TM37	Sandstorm	Rock	Status	—	—	10	All	—
TM38	Fire Blast	Fire	Special	120	85	5	Normal	—
TM39	Rock Tomb	Rock	Physical	50	80	10	Normal	—
TM42	Facade	Normal	Physical	70	100	20	Normal	●
TM43	Secret Power	Normal	Physical	70	100	20	Normal	●
TM44	Rest	Psychic	Status	—	—	10	Self	—
TM45	Attract	Normal	Status	—	100	15	Normal	—
TM52	Focus Blast	Fighting	Special	120	70	5	Normal	—
TM56	Fling	Dark	Physical	—	100	10	Normal	●
TM58	Endure	Normal	Status	—	—	10	Self	—
TM67	Recycle	Normal	Status	—	—	10	Self	—
TM68	Giga Impact	Normal	Physical	150	90	5	Normal	●
TM78	Captivate	Normal	Status	—	100	20	2 foes	—
TM80	Rock Slide	Rock	Physical	75	90	10	2 foes	—
TM82	Sleep Talk	Normal	Status	—	—	10	DoM	—
TM83	Natural Gift	Normal	Physical	—	100	15	Normal	—
TM87	Swagger	Normal	Status	—	90	15	Normal	—
TM90	Substitute	Normal	Status	—	—	10	Self	—
HM03	Surf	Water	Special	95	100	15	2 foes + 1 ally	—
HM04	Strength	Normal	Physical	80	100	15	Normal	●
HM06	Rock Smash	Fighting	Physical	40	100	15	Normal	●
HM08	Rock Climb	Normal	Physical	90	85	20	Normal	●

● LEVEL-UP AND LEARNED MOVES

Lv	Name	Type	Kind	Power	Acc	PP	Range	DA
Base	Tackle	Normal	Physical	35	95	35	Normal	●
4	Defense Curl	Normal	Status	—	—	40	Self	—
9	Amnesia	Psychic	Status	—	—	20	Self	—
12	Lick	Ghost	Physical	20	100	30	Normal	●
17	Belly Drum	Normal	Status	—	—	10	Self	—
20	Yawn	Normal	Status	—	—	10	Normal	—
25	Rest	Psychic	Status	—	—	10	Self	—
28	Snore	Normal	Special	40	100	15	Normal	—
28	Sleep Talk	Normal	Status	—	—	10	DoM	—
33	Body Slam	Normal	Physical	85	100	15	Normal	●
36	Block	Normal	Status	—	—	5	Normal	—
41	Rollout	Rock	Physical	30	90	20	Normal	●
44	Crunch	Dark	Physical	80	100	15	Normal	●
49	Giga Impact	Normal	Physical	150	90	5	Normal	●

● MOVES TAUGHT IN EXCHANGE FOR COLORED SHARDS

Name	Type	Kind	Power	Acc	PP	Range	DA
Mud-Slap	Ground	Special	20	100	10	Normal	●
Icy Wind	Ice	Special	55	95	15	2 foes	—
Rollout	Rock	Physical	30	90	20	Normal	●
ThunderPunch	Electric	Physical	75	100	15	Normal	●
Fire Punch	Fire	Physical	75	100	15	Normal	●
Superpower	Fighting	Physical	120	100	5	Normal	●
Ice Punch	Ice	Physical	75	100	15	Normal	●
Iron Head	Steel	Physical	80	100	15	Normal	●
Snore	Normal	Special	40	100	15	Normal	—
Outrage	Dragon	Physical	120	100	15	1 random	●
Zen Headbutt	Psychic	Physical	80	90	15	Normal	●
Gunk Shot	Poison	Physical	120	70	5	Normal	—
Seed Bomb	Grass	Physical	80	100	15	Normal	●
Last Resort	Normal	Physical	130	100	5	Normal	●

● EGG MOVES

Name	Type	Kind	Power	Acc	PP	Range	DA
Lick	Ghost	Physical	20	100	30	Normal	●
Charm	Normal	Status	—	100	20	Normal	—
Double-Edge	Normal	Physical	120	100	15	Normal	●
Curse	???	Status	—	—	10	Normal + Self	—
Fissure	Ground	Physical	—	30	5	Normal	—
Substitute	Normal	Status	—	—	10	Self	—
Whirlwind	Normal	Status	—	100	20	Normal	—
Pursuit	Dark	Physical	40	100	20	Normal	●

● PRIMARY WAY TO FIND

TRAINER'S PARTY Your rival, when you battle him at the Pokémon League

WILD POKÉMON

COURSE OF STORY

ABILITY ● Immunity ● Thick Fat

EGG GROUP Monster

STATS
HP ●●●●●
ATTACK ●●●●●
DEFENSE ●●
SP. ATTACK ●●
SP. DEFENSE ●●●
SPEED ●

Unown

PSYCHIC

HEIGHT: 1'08"
WEIGHT: 11.0 lbs.
GENDER: Unkown
HELD ITEM: None

● Gender unknown

PLATINUM
When alone, nothing happens. However, if there are two or more, an odd power is said to emerge.

EVOLUTION PATH

Does Not evolve

● UNOWN SHAPES

A B C D
E F G H
I J K L
M N O P
Q R S T
U V W X
Y Z ! ?

● LEVEL-UP AND LEARNED MOVES

Lv	Name	Type	Kind	Power	Acc	PP	Range	DA
Base	Hidden Power	Normal	Special	—	100	15	Normal	—

● TM & HM MOVES

No.	Name	Type	Kind	Power	Acc	PP	Range	DA

● PRIMARY WAY TO FIND

TRAINER'S PARTY

WILD POKÉMON Solaceon Ruins

COURSE OF STORY

ABILITY ● Levitate

EGG GROUP No Eggs

STATS
HP ●●
ATTACK ●●●
DEFENSE ●●
SP. ATTACK ●●●
SP. DEFENSE ●●
SPEED ●●

No. 115 — Riolu

Sinnoh Pokédex **No. 115** Emanation Pokémon

Riolu

Fighting

HEIGHT: 2'04"
WEIGHT: 44.5 lbs.
GENDER: Male and Female
HELD ITEM: None

● M/F have same form

PLATINUM: It has the peculiar power of being able to see emotions such as joy and rage in the form of waves.

EVOLUTION PATH

Riolu → Lucario (Level up between 4 AM and 8 PM once Friendship is high enough)

● TM & HM MOVES

No.	Name	Type	Kind	Power	Acc	PP	Range	DA
TM01	Focus Punch	Fighting	Physical	150	100	20	Normal	—
TM05	Roar	Normal	Status	—	100	20	Normal	—
TM06	Toxic	Poison	Status	—	85	10	Normal	—
TM08	Bulk Up	Fighting	Status	—	—	20	Self	—
TM10	Hidden Power	Normal	Special	—	100	15	Normal	—
TM11	Sunny Day	Fire	Status	—	—	5	All	—
TM17	Protect	Normal	Status	—	—	10	Self	—
TM18	Rain Dance	Water	Status	—	—	5	All	—
TM21	Frustration	Normal	Physical	—	100	20	Normal	•
TM23	Iron Tail	Steel	Physical	100	75	15	Normal	•
TM26	Earthquake	Ground	Physical	100	100	10	2 foes • 1 ally	•
TM27	Return	Normal	Physical	—	100	20	Normal	•
TM28	Dig	Ground	Physical	80	100	10	Normal	•
TM31	Brick Break	Fighting	Physical	75	100	15	Normal	•
TM32	Double Team	Normal	Status	—	—	15	Self	—
TM39	Rock Tomb	Rock	Physical	50	80	10	Normal	•
TM42	Facade	Normal	Physical	70	100	20	Normal	•
TM43	Secret Power	Normal	Physical	70	100	20	Normal	•
TM44	Rest	Psychic	Status	—	—	10	Self	—
TM45	Attract	Normal	Status	—	100	15	Normal	—
TM52	Focus Blast	Fighting	Special	120	70	5	Normal	•
TM56	Fling	Dark	Physical	—	100	10	Normal	•
TM58	Endure	Normal	Status	—	—	10	Self	—
TM60	Drain Punch	Fighting	Physical	60	100	5	Normal	•
TM65	Shadow Claw	Ghost	Physical	70	100	15	Normal	•
TM66	Payback	Dark	Physical	50	100	10	Normal	•
TM75	Swords Dance	Normal	Status	—	—	30	Self	—
TM78	Captivate	Normal	Status	—	100	20	2 foes	—
TM80	Rock Slide	Rock	Physical	75	90	10	2 foes	•
TM82	Sleep Talk	Normal	Status	—	—	10	DoM	—
TM83	Natural Gift	Normal	Physical	—	100	15	Normal	•
TM84	Poison Jab	Poison	Physical	80	100	20	Normal	•
TM87	Swagger	Normal	Status	—	90	15	Normal	—
TM90	Substitute	Normal	Status	—	—	10	Self	—
HM04	Strength	Normal	Physical	80	100	15	Normal	•
HM06	Rock Smash	Fighting	Physical	40	100	15	Normal	•

● LEVEL-UP AND LEARNED MOVES

Lv	Name	Type	Kind	Power	Acc	PP	Range	DA
Base	Quick Attack	Normal	Physical	40	100	30	Normal	•
Base	Foresight	Normal	Status	—	—	40	Normal	—
Base	Endure	Normal	Status	—	—	10	Self	—
6	Counter	Fighting	Physical	—	100	20	Self	•
11	Force Palm	Fighting	Physical	60	100	10	Normal	•
15	Feint	Normal	Physical	50	100	10	Normal	—
19	Reversal	Fighting	Physical	—	100	15	Normal	•
24	Screech	Normal	Status	—	85	40	Normal	—
29	Copycat	Normal	Status	—	—	20	DoM	—

● MOVES TAUGHT IN EXCHANGE FOR COLORED SHARDS

Name	Type	Kind	Power	Acc	PP	Range	DA
Mud-Slap	Ground	Special	20	100	10	Normal	•
Fury Cutter	Bug	Physical	10	95	20	Normal	•
ThunderPunch	Electric	Physical	75	100	15	Normal	•
Ice Punch	Ice	Physical	75	100	15	Normal	•
Snore	Normal	Special	40	100	15	Normal	•
Helping Hand	Normal	Status	—	—	20	1 ally	•
Zen Headbutt	Psychic	Physical	80	90	15	Normal	•
Vacuum Wave	Fighting	Special	40	100	30	Normal	•
Iron Defense	Steel	Status	—	—	15	Self	•
Magnet Rise	Electric	Status	—	—	10	Self	•
Swift	Normal	Special	60	—	20	2 foes	•

● EGG MOVES

Name	Type	Kind	Power	Acc	PP	Range	DA
Cross Chop	Fighting	Physical	100	80	5	Normal	•
Detect	Fighting	Status	—	—	5	Self	•
Bite	Dark	Physical	60	100	25	Normal	•
Mind Reader	Normal	Status	—	—	5	Normal	•
Sky Uppercut	Fighting	Physical	85	90	15	Normal	•
Hi Jump Kick	Fighting	Physical	100	90	20	Normal	•
Agility	Psychic	Status	—	—	30	Self	—
Vacuum Wave	Fighting	Special	40	100	30	Normal	•
Crunch	Dark	Physical	80	100	15	Normal	•
Low Kick	Fighting	Physical	—	100	20	Normal	•
Iron Defense	Steel	Status	—	—	15	Self	•
Blaze Kick	Fire	Physical	85	90	10	Normal	•
Bullet Punch	Steel	Physical	40	100	30	Normal	•

ABILITY: ● Steadfast ● Inner Focus
EGG GROUP: No Eggs

STATS:
HP ●
ATTACK ●●●
DEFENSE ●●
SP.ATTACK ●●
SP.DEFENSE ●●
SPEED ●●

● PRIMARY WAY TO FIND

TRAINER'S PARTY: Trainer on Route 217
WILD POKÉMON:
COURSE OF STORY: Hatch the Egg received from Riley at Iron Island

---

No. 116 — Lucario

Sinnoh Pokédex **No. 116** Aura Pokémon

Lucario

Fighting STEEL

HEIGHT: 3'11"
WEIGHT: 119.0 lbs.
GENDER: Male and Female
HELD ITEM: None

● M/F have same form

PLATINUM: A well-trained one can sense auras to identify and take in the feelings of creatures over half a mile away.

EVOLUTION PATH

Riolu → Lucario (Level up between 4 AM and 8 PM once Friendship is high enough)

● TM & HM MOVES

No.	Name	Type	Kind	Power	Acc	PP	Range	DA
TM01	Focus Punch	Fighting	Physical	150	100	20	Normal	•
TM03	Water Pulse	Water	Special	60	100	20	Normal	•
TM04	Calm Mind	Psychic	Status	—	—	20	Self	—
TM05	Roar	Normal	Status	—	100	20	Normal	—
TM06	Toxic	Poison	Status	—	85	10	Normal	—
TM08	Bulk Up	Fighting	Status	—	—	20	Self	—
TM10	Hidden Power	Normal	Special	—	100	15	Normal	•
TM11	Sunny Day	Fire	Status	—	—	5	All	—
TM15	Hyper Beam	Normal	Special	150	90	5	Normal	•
TM17	Protect	Normal	Status	—	—	10	Self	—
TM18	Rain Dance	Water	Status	—	—	5	All	—
TM21	Frustration	Normal	Physical	—	100	20	Normal	•
TM23	Iron Tail	Steel	Physical	100	75	15	Normal	•
TM26	Earthquake	Ground	Physical	100	100	10	2 foes • 1 ally	•
TM27	Return	Normal	Physical	—	100	20	Normal	•
TM28	Dig	Ground	Physical	80	100	10	Normal	•
TM29	Psychic	Psychic	Special	90	100	10	Normal	•
TM30	Shadow Ball	Ghost	Special	80	100	15	Normal	•
TM31	Brick Break	Fighting	Physical	75	100	15	Normal	•
TM32	Double Team	Normal	Status	—	—	15	Self	—
TM39	Rock Tomb	Rock	Physical	50	80	10	Normal	•
TM42	Facade	Normal	Physical	70	100	20	Normal	•
TM43	Secret Power	Normal	Physical	70	100	20	Normal	•
TM44	Rest	Psychic	Status	—	—	10	Self	—
TM45	Attract	Normal	Status	—	100	15	Normal	—
TM52	Focus Blast	Fighting	Special	120	70	5	Normal	•
TM56	Fling	Dark	Physical	—	100	10	Normal	•
TM58	Endure	Normal	Status	—	—	10	Self	—
TM59	Dragon Pulse	Dragon	Special	90	100	10	Normal	•
TM60	Drain Punch	Fighting	Physical	60	100	5	Normal	•
TM65	Shadow Claw	Ghost	Physical	70	100	15	Normal	•
TM66	Payback	Dark	Physical	50	100	10	Normal	•
TM68	Giga Impact	Normal	Physical	150	90	5	Normal	•
TM71	Stone Edge	Rock	Physical	100	80	5	Normal	•
TM75	Swords Dance	Normal	Status	—	—	30	Self	—
TM78	Captivate	Normal	Status	—	100	20	2 foes	—
TM79	Dark Pulse	Dark	Special	80	100	15	Normal	•
TM80	Rock Slide	Rock	Physical	75	90	10	2 foes	•
TM82	Sleep Talk	Normal	Status	—	—	10	DoM	—
TM83	Natural Gift	Normal	Physical	—	100	15	Normal	•
TM84	Poison Jab	Poison	Physical	80	100	20	Normal	•
TM87	Swagger	Normal	Status	—	90	15	Normal	—
TM90	Substitute	Normal	Status	—	—	10	Self	—
TM91	Flash Cannon	Steel	Special	80	100	10	Normal	•
HM04	Strength	Normal	Physical	80	100	15	Normal	•
HM06	Rock Smash	Fighting	Physical	40	100	15	Normal	•
HM08	Rock Climb	Normal	Physical	90	85	20	Normal	•

● LEVEL-UP AND LEARNED MOVES

Lv	Name	Type	Kind	Power	Acc	PP	Range	DA
Base	Dark Pulse	Dark	Special	80	100	15	Normal	•
Base	Quick Attack	Normal	Physical	40	100	30	Normal	•
Base	Foresight	Normal	Status	—	—	40	Normal	—
Base	Detect	Fighting	Status	—	—	5	Self	—
Base	Metal Claw	Steel	Physical	50	95	35	Normal	•
6	Counter	Fighting	Physical	—	100	20	Self	•
11	Force Palm	Fighting	Physical	60	100	10	Normal	•
15	Feint	Normal	Physical	50	100	10	Normal	—
19	Bone Rush	Ground	Physical	25	80	10	Normal	•
24	Metal Sound	Steel	Status	—	85	40	Normal	—
29	Me First	Normal	Status	—	—	20	DoM	—
33	Swords Dance	Normal	Status	—	—	30	Self	—
37	Aura Sphere	Fighting	Special	90	—	20	Normal	•
42	Close Combat	Fighting	Physical	120	100	5	Normal	•
47	Dragon Pulse	Dragon	Special	90	100	10	Normal	•
51	ExtremeSpeed	Normal	Physical	80	100	5	Normal	•

● MOVES TAUGHT IN EXCHANGE FOR COLORED SHARDS

Name	Type	Kind	Power	Acc	PP	Range	DA
Mud-Slap	Ground	Special	20	100	10	Normal	•
Fury Cutter	Bug	Physical	10	95	20	Normal	•
ThunderPunch	Electric	Physical	75	100	15	Normal	•
Ice Punch	Ice	Physical	75	100	15	Normal	•
Snore	Normal	Special	40	100	15	Normal	•
Helping Hand	Normal	Status	—	—	20	1 ally	•
Zen Headbutt	Psychic	Physical	80	90	15	Normal	•
Vacuum Wave	Fighting	Special	40	100	30	Normal	•
Iron Defense	Steel	Status	—	—	15	Self	•
Magnet Rise	Electric	Status	—	—	10	Self	•
Swift	Normal	Special	60	—	20	2 foes	•

ABILITY: ● Steadfast ● Inner Focus
EGG GROUP: Field / Human-Like

STATS:
HP ●●
ATTACK ●●●
DEFENSE ●●●
SP.ATTACK ●●●
SP.DEFENSE ●●●
SPEED ●●●

● PRIMARY WAY TO FIND

TRAINER'S PARTY: Veilstone Gym Leader Maylene
WILD POKÉMON:
COURSE OF STORY:

Wooper

WATER **GROUND**

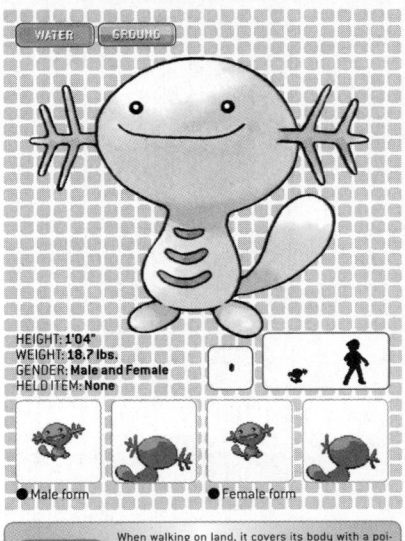

● Male form ● Female form

HEIGHT: 1'04"
WEIGHT: 18.7 lbs.
GENDER: **Male and Female**
HELD ITEM: **None**

PLATINUM When walking on land, it covers its body with a poisonous film that keeps its skin from dehydrating.

EVOLUTION PATH

Wooper → Lv20 → Quagsire

● TM & HM MOVES

No.	Name	Type	Kind	Power	Acc	PP	Range	DA
TM03	Water Pulse	Water	Special	60	100	20	Normal	
TM06	Toxic	Poison	Status	—	85	10	Normal	
TM07	Hail	Ice	Status	—	—	10	All	
TM10	Hidden Power	Normal	Special	—	100	15	Normal	
TM13	Ice Beam	Ice	Special	95	100	10	Normal	
TM14	Blizzard	Ice	Special	120	70	5	2 foes	
TM17	Protect	Normal	Status	—	—	10	Self	
TM18	Rain Dance	Water	Status	—	—	5	All	
TM21	Frustration	Normal	Physical	—	100	20	Normal	•
TM23	Iron Tail	Steel	Physical	100	75	15	Normal	•
TM26	Earthquake	Ground	Physical	100	100	10	2 foes • 1 ally	•
TM27	Return	Normal	Physical	—	100	20	Normal	•
TM28	Dig	Ground	Physical	80	100	10	Normal	•
TM32	Double Team	Normal	Status	—	—	15	Self	
TM36	Sludge Bomb	Poison	Special	90	100	10	Normal	
TM37	Sandstorm	Rock	Status	—	—	10	All	
TM42	Facade	Normal	Physical	70	100	20	Normal	•
TM43	Secret Power	Normal	Physical	70	100	20	Normal	•
TM44	Rest	Psychic	Status	—	—	10	Self	
TM45	Attract	Normal	Status	—	100	15	Normal	
TM58	Endure	Normal	Status	—	—	10	Self	
TM70	Flash	Normal	Status	—	100	20	Normal	
TM78	Captivate	Normal	Status	—	100	20	2 foes	
TM82	Sleep Talk	Normal	Status	—	—	10	DoM	
TM83	Natural Gift	Normal	Physical	—	100	15	Normal	•
TM87	Swagger	Normal	Status	—	90	15	Normal	
TM90	Substitute	Normal	Status	—	—	10	Self	
HM03	Surf	Water	Special	95	100	15	2 foes • 1 ally	•
HM06	Rock Smash	Fighting	Physical	40	100	15	Normal	•
HM07	Waterfall	Water	Physical	80	100	15	Normal	•

● LEVEL-UP AND LEARNED MOVES

Lv	Name	Type	Kind	Power	Acc	PP	Range	DA
Base	Water Gun	Water	Special	40	100	25	Normal	
Base	Tail Whip	Normal	Status	—	100	30	2 foes	
5	Mud Sport	Ground	Status	—	—	15	All	
9	Mud Shot	Ground	Special	55	95	15	Normal	•
15	Slam	Normal	Physical	80	75	20	Normal	•
19	Mud Bomb	Ground	Special	65	85	10	Normal	
23	Amnesia	Psychic	Status	—	—	20	Self	
29	Yawn	Normal	Status	—	—	10	Normal	
33	Earthquake	Ground	Physical	100	100	10	2 foes • 1 ally	•
37	Rain Dance	Water	Status	—	—	5	All	
43	Mist	Ice	Status	—	—	30	2 allies	
43	Haze	Ice	Status	—	—	30	All	
47	Muddy Water	Water	Special	95	85	10	2 foes	

● MOVES TAUGHT IN EXCHANGE FOR COLORED SHARDS

Name	Type	Kind	Power	Acc	PP	Range	DA
Dive	Water	Physical	80	100	10	Normal	•
Mud-Slap	Ground	Special	20	100	10	Normal	•
Icy Wind	Ice	Special	55	95	15	2 foes	•
Rollout	Rock	Physical	30	90	20	Normal	•
Ice Punch	Ice	Physical	75	100	15	Normal	•
Aqua Tail	Water	Physical	90	90	10	Normal	•
Snore	Normal	Special	40	100	15	Normal	•
AncientPower	Rock	Special	60	100	5	Normal	•
Earth Power	Ground	Special	90	100	10	Normal	

● EGG MOVES

Name	Type	Kind	Power	Acc	PP	Range	DA
Body Slam	Normal	Physical	85	100	15	Normal	•
AncientPower	Rock	Special	60	100	5	Normal	•
Safeguard	Normal	Status	—	—	25	2 allies	—
Curse	???	Status	—	—	10	Normal • Self	—
Mud Sport	Ground	Status	—	—	15	All	—
Stockpile	Normal	Status	—	—	20	Self	—
Swallow	Normal	Status	—	—	10	Self	—
Spit Up	Normal	Special	—	100	10	Normal	—
Counter	Fighting	Physical	—	100	20	Self	•
Encore	Normal	Status	—	—	5	Normal	—
Double Kick	Fighting	Physical	30	100	30	Normal	•

● PRIMARY WAY TO FIND

TRAINER'S PARTY	Trainer on Route 212
WILD POKÉMON	Pastoria Great Marsh
COURSE OF STORY	

ABILITY: ● Damp ● Water Absorb

STATS: HP ●● · ATTACK ●● · DEFENSE ●● · SP.ATTACK ●● · SP.DEFENSE ●● · SPEED ●

EGG GROUP: Water 1 / Field

Quagsire

WATER **GROUND**

● Male form ● Female form

HEIGHT: 4'07"
WEIGHT: 165.3 lbs.
GENDER: **Male and Female**
HELD ITEM: **None**

PLATINUM It has an easygoing nature. It doesn't care if it bumps its head on boats and boulders while swimming.

EVOLUTION PATH

Wooper → Lv20 → Quagsire

● TM & HM MOVES

No.	Name	Type	Kind	Power	Acc	PP	Range	DA
TM01	Focus Punch	Fighting	Physical	150	100	20	Normal	•
TM03	Water Pulse	Water	Special	60	100	20	Normal	
TM06	Toxic	Poison	Status	—	85	10	Normal	
TM07	Hail	Ice	Status	—	—	10	All	
TM10	Hidden Power	Normal	Special	—	100	15	Normal	
TM13	Ice Beam	Ice	Special	95	100	10	Normal	
TM14	Blizzard	Ice	Special	120	70	5	2 foes	
TM15	Hyper Beam	Normal	Special	150	90	5	Normal	
TM17	Protect	Normal	Status	—	—	10	Self	
TM18	Rain Dance	Water	Status	—	—	5	All	
TM21	Frustration	Normal	Physical	—	100	20	Normal	•
TM23	Iron Tail	Steel	Physical	100	75	15	Normal	•
TM26	Earthquake	Ground	Physical	100	100	10	2 foes • 1 ally	•
TM27	Return	Normal	Physical	—	100	20	Normal	•
TM28	Dig	Ground	Physical	80	100	10	Normal	•
TM31	Brick Break	Fighting	Physical	75	100	15	Normal	•
TM32	Double Team	Normal	Status	—	—	15	Self	
TM36	Sludge Bomb	Poison	Special	90	100	10	Normal	
TM37	Sandstorm	Rock	Status	—	—	10	All	
TM39	Rock Tomb	Rock	Physical	50	80	10	Normal	•
TM42	Facade	Normal	Physical	70	100	20	Normal	•
TM43	Secret Power	Normal	Physical	70	100	20	Normal	•
TM44	Rest	Psychic	Status	—	—	10	Self	
TM45	Attract	Normal	Status	—	100	15	Normal	
TM52	Focus Blast	Fighting	Special	120	70	5	Normal	
TM56	Fling	Dark	Physical	—	100	10	Normal	•
TM58	Endure	Normal	Status	—	—	10	Self	
TM68	Giga Impact	Normal	Physical	150	90	5	Normal	•
TM70	Flash	Normal	Status	—	100	20	Normal	
TM71	Stone Edge	Rock	Physical	100	80	5	Normal	•
TM78	Captivate	Normal	Status	—	100	20	2 foes	
TM80	Rock Slide	Rock	Physical	75	90	10	2 foes	•
TM82	Sleep Talk	Normal	Status	—	—	10	DoM	
TM83	Natural Gift	Normal	Physical	—	100	15	Normal	•
TM87	Swagger	Normal	Status	—	90	15	Normal	
TM90	Substitute	Normal	Status	—	—	10	Self	
HM03	Surf	Water	Special	95	100	15	2 foes • 1 ally	•
HM04	Strength	Normal	Physical	80	100	15	Normal	•
HM06	Rock Smash	Fighting	Physical	40	100	15	Normal	•
HM07	Waterfall	Water	Physical	80	100	15	Normal	•

● LEVEL-UP AND LEARNED MOVES

Lv	Name	Type	Kind	Power	Acc	PP	Range	DA
Base	Water Gun	Water	Special	40	100	25	Normal	
Base	Tail Whip	Normal	Status	—	100	30	2 foes	
Base	Mud Sport	Ground	Status	—	—	15	All	
5	Mud Sport	Ground	Status	—	—	15	All	
9	Mud Shot	Ground	Special	55	95	15	Normal	•
15	Slam	Normal	Physical	80	75	20	Normal	•
19	Mud Bomb	Ground	Special	65	85	10	Normal	
24	Amnesia	Psychic	Status	—	—	20	Self	
31	Yawn	Normal	Status	—	—	10	Normal	
36	Earthquake	Ground	Physical	100	100	10	2 foes • 1 ally	•
41	Rain Dance	Water	Status	—	—	5	All	
48	Mist	Ice	Status	—	—	30	2 allies	
48	Haze	Ice	Status	—	—	30	All	
53	Muddy Water	Water	Special	95	85	10	2 foes	

● MOVES TAUGHT IN EXCHANGE FOR COLORED SHARDS

Name	Type	Kind	Power	Acc	PP	Range	DA
Dive	Water	Physical	80	100	10	Normal	•
Mud-Slap	Ground	Special	20	100	10	Normal	•
Icy Wind	Ice	Special	55	95	15	2 foes	•
Rollout	Rock	Physical	30	90	20	Normal	•
Ice Punch	Ice	Physical	75	100	15	Normal	•
Aqua Tail	Water	Physical	90	90	10	Normal	•
Snore	Normal	Special	40	100	15	Normal	•
AncientPower	Rock	Special	60	100	5	Normal	•
Earth Power	Ground	Special	90	100	10	Normal	

● PRIMARY WAY TO FIND

TRAINER'S PARTY	Pastoria Gym Leader Wake
WILD POKÉMON	Pastoria City side of Route 212
COURSE OF STORY	

ABILITY: ● Damp ● Water Absorb

STATS: HP ●●● · ATTACK ●●● · DEFENSE ●●● · SP.ATTACK ●● · SP.DEFENSE ●● · SPEED ●

EGG GROUP: Water 1 / Field

Wingull

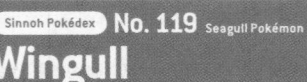

WATER FLYING

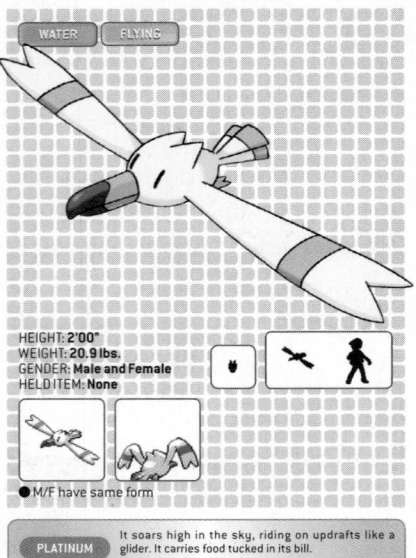

HEIGHT: 2'00"
WEIGHT: 20.9 lbs.
GENDER: Male and Female
HELD ITEM: None

● M/F have same form

PLATINUM | It soars high in the sky, riding on updrafts like a glider. It carries food tucked in its bill.

EVOLUTION PATH

Wingull → Lv25 → Pelipper

ABILITY ● Keen Eye

EGG GROUP: Water 1 / Flying

STATS
HP ●
ATTACK ●
DEFENSE ●
SP. ATTACK ●●
SP. DEFENSE ●
SPEED ●●●

● TM & HM MOVES

No.	Name	Type	Kind	Power	Acc	PP	Range	DA
TM03	Water Pulse	Water	Special	60	100	20	Normal	
TM06	Toxic	Poison	Status	—	85	10	Normal	
TM07	Hail	Ice	Status	—	—	10	All	
TM10	Hidden Power	Normal	Special	—	100	15	Normal	
TM13	Ice Beam	Ice	Special	95	100	10	Normal	
TM14	Blizzard	Ice	Special	120	70	5	2 foes	
TM17	Protect	Normal	Status	—	—	10	Self	
TM18	Rain Dance	Water	Status	—	—	5	All	
TM21	Frustration	Normal	Physical	—	100	20	Normal	●
TM27	Return	Normal	Physical	—	100	20	Normal	●
TM32	Double Team	Normal	Status	—	—	15	Self	
TM34	Shock Wave	Electric	Special	60	—	20	Normal	
TM40	Aerial Ace	Flying	Physical	60	—	20	Normal	●
TM42	Facade	Normal	Physical	70	100	20	Normal	●
TM43	Secret Power	Normal	Physical	70	100	20	Normal	●
TM44	Rest	Psychic	Status	—	—	10	Self	
TM45	Attract	Normal	Status	—	100	15	Normal	
TM46	Thief	Dark	Physical	40	100	10	Normal	●
TM47	Steel Wing	Steel	Physical	70	90	25	Normal	●
TM51	Roost	Flying	Status	—	—	10	Self	
TM55	Brine	Water	Special	65	100	10	Normal	
TM58	Endure	Normal	Status	—	—	10	Self	
TM78	Captivate	Normal	Status	—	100	20	2 foes	
TM82	Sleep Talk	Normal	Status	—	—	10	DoM	
TM83	Natural Gift	Normal	Physical	—	100	15	Normal	●
TM87	Swagger	Normal	Status	—	90	15	Normal	
TM88	Pluck	Flying	Physical	60	100	20	Normal	●
TM89	U-turn	Bug	Physical	70	100	20	Normal	●
TM90	Substitute	Normal	Status	—	—	10	Self	
HM02	Fly	Flying	Physical	90	95	15	Normal	●
HM05	Defog	Flying	Status	—	—	15	Normal	

● LEVEL-UP AND LEARNED MOVES

Lv	Name	Type	Kind	Power	Acc	PP	Range	DA
Base	Growl	Normal	Status	—	100	40	2 foes	
Base	Water Gun	Water	Special	40	100	25	Normal	
6	Supersonic	Normal	Status	—	55	20	Normal	
11	Wing Attack	Flying	Physical	60	100	35	Normal	●
16	Mist	Ice	Status	—	—	30	2 allies	
19	Water Pulse	Water	Special	60	100	20	Normal	
24	Quick Attack	Normal	Physical	40	100	30	Normal	●
29	Roost	Flying	Status	—	—	10	Self	
34	Pursuit	Dark	Physical	40	100	20	Normal	●
37	Agility	Psychic	Status	—	—	30	Self	
42	Aerial Ace	Flying	Physical	60	—	20	Normal	●
47	Air Slash	Flying	Special	75	95	20	Normal	

● MOVES TAUGHT IN EXCHANGE FOR COLORED SHARDS

Name	Type	Kind	Power	Acc	PP	Range	DA
Mud-Slap	Ground	Special	20	100	10	Normal	—
Icy Wind	Ice	Special	55	95	15	2 foes	—
Ominous Wind	Ghost	Special	60	100	5	Normal	—
Snore	Normal	Special	40	100	15	Normal	—
Air Cutter	Flying	Special	55	95	25	2 foes	—
Twister	Dragon	Special	40	100	20	2 foes	—
Knock Off	Dark	Physical	20	100	20	Normal	●
Swift	Normal	Special	60	—	20	2 foes	—
Uproar	Normal	Special	50	100	10	1 random	—

● EGG MOVES

Name	Type	Kind	Power	Acc	PP	Range	DA
Mist	Ice	Status	—	—	30	2 allies	—
Twister	Dragon	Special	40	100	20	2 foes	—
Agility	Psychic	Status	—	—	30	Self	—
Gust	Flying	Special	40	100	35	All	—
Water Sport	Water	Status	—	—	15	All	—
Aqua Ring	Water	Status	—	—	20	Self	—
Knock Off	Dark	Physical	20	100	20	Normal	●

● PRIMARY WAY TO FIND

TRAINER'S PARTY | Trainer at Pastoria Gym

WILD POKÉMON | Route 213

COURSE OF STORY

Pelipper

WATER FLYING

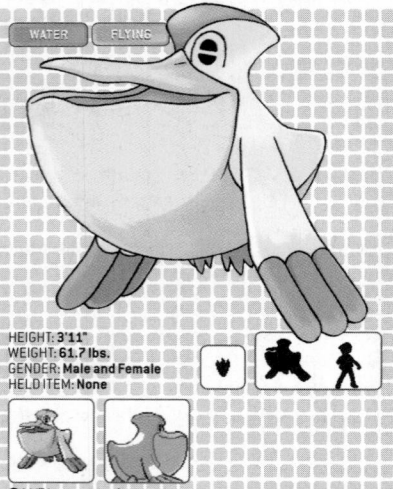

HEIGHT: 3'11"
WEIGHT: 61.7 lbs.
GENDER: Male and Female
HELD ITEM: None

● M/F have same form

PLATINUM | It is a messenger of the skies, carrying small Pokémon and eggs to safety in its bill.

EVOLUTION PATH

Wingull → Lv25 → Pelipper

ABILITY ● Keen Eye

EGG GROUP: Water 1 / Flying

STATS
HP ●●
ATTACK ●●
DEFENSE ●●●
SP. ATTACK ●●●
SP. DEFENSE ●●
SPEED ●●

● TM & HM MOVES

No.	Name	Type	Kind	Power	Acc	PP	Range	DA
TM03	Water Pulse	Water	Special	60	100	20	Normal	—
TM06	Toxic	Poison	Status	—	85	10	Normal	—
TM07	Hail	Ice	Status	—	—	10	All	—
TM10	Hidden Power	Normal	Special	—	100	15	Normal	—
TM13	Ice Beam	Ice	Special	95	100	10	Normal	—
TM14	Blizzard	Ice	Special	120	70	5	2 foes	—
TM15	Hyper Beam	Normal	Special	150	90	5	Normal	—
TM17	Protect	Normal	Status	—	—	10	Self	—
TM18	Rain Dance	Water	Status	—	—	5	All	—
TM21	Frustration	Normal	Physical	—	100	20	Normal	●
TM27	Return	Normal	Physical	—	100	20	Normal	●
TM32	Double Team	Normal	Status	—	—	15	Self	—
TM34	Shock Wave	Electric	Special	60	—	20	Normal	—
TM40	Aerial Ace	Flying	Physical	60	—	20	Normal	●
TM42	Facade	Normal	Physical	70	100	20	Normal	●
TM43	Secret Power	Normal	Physical	70	100	20	Normal	●
TM44	Rest	Psychic	Status	—	—	10	Self	—
TM45	Attract	Normal	Status	—	100	15	Normal	—
TM46	Thief	Dark	Physical	40	100	10	Normal	●
TM47	Steel Wing	Steel	Physical	70	90	25	Normal	●
TM51	Roost	Flying	Status	—	—	10	Self	—
TM55	Brine	Water	Special	65	100	10	Normal	—
TM56	Fling	Dark	Physical	—	100	10	Normal	●
TM58	Endure	Normal	Status	—	—	10	Self	—
TM66	Payback	Dark	Physical	50	100	10	Normal	●
TM68	Giga Impact	Normal	Physical	150	90	5	Normal	●
TM78	Captivate	Normal	Status	—	100	20	2 foes	—
TM82	Sleep Talk	Normal	Status	—	—	10	DoM	—
TM83	Natural Gift	Normal	Physical	—	100	15	Normal	●
TM87	Swagger	Normal	Status	—	90	15	Normal	—
TM88	Pluck	Flying	Physical	60	100	20	Normal	●
TM89	U-turn	Bug	Physical	70	100	20	Normal	●
TM90	Substitute	Normal	Status	—	—	10	Self	—
HM02	Fly	Flying	Physical	90	95	15	Normal	●
HM03	Surf	Water	Special	95	100	15	2 foes + 1 ally	●
HM05	Defog	Flying	Status	—	—	15	Normal	—

● LEVEL-UP AND LEARNED MOVES

Lv	Name	Type	Kind	Power	Acc	PP	Range	DA
Base	Growl	Normal	Status	—	100	40	2 foes	—
Base	Water Gun	Water	Special	40	100	25	Normal	—
Base	Water Sport	Water	Status	—	—	15	All	—
Base	Wing Attack	Flying	Physical	60	100	35	Normal	●
6	Supersonic	Normal	Status	—	55	20	Normal	—
11	Wing Attack	Flying	Physical	60	100	35	Normal	●
16	Mist	Ice	Status	—	—	30	2 allies	—
19	Water Pulse	Water	Special	60	100	20	Normal	—
24	Payback	Dark	Physical	50	100	10	Normal	●
25	Protect	Normal	Status	—	—	10	Self	—
31	Roost	Flying	Status	—	—	10	Self	—
38	Stockpile	Normal	Status	—	—	20	Self	—
38	Swallow	Normal	Status	—	—	10	Self	—
38	Spit Up	Normal	Special	—	100	10	Normal	—
43	Fling	Dark	Physical	—	100	10	Normal	●
50	Tailwind	Flying	Status	—	—	30	2 allies	—
57	Hydro Pump	Water	Special	120	80	5	Normal	—

● MOVES TAUGHT IN EXCHANGE FOR COLORED SHARDS

Name	Type	Kind	Power	Acc	PP	Range	DA
Mud-Slap	Ground	Special	20	100	10	Normal	—
Icy Wind	Ice	Special	55	95	15	2 foes	—
Ominous Wind	Ghost	Special	60	100	5	Normal	—
Snore	Normal	Special	40	100	15	Normal	—
Air Cutter	Flying	Special	55	95	25	2 foes	—
Gunk Shot	Poison	Physical	120	70	5	Normal	—
Twister	Dragon	Special	40	100	20	2 foes	—
Seed Bomb	Grass	Physical	80	100	15	Normal	—
Knock Off	Dark	Physical	20	100	20	Normal	●
Swift	Normal	Special	60	—	20	2 foes	—
Uproar	Normal	Special	50	100	10	1 random	—

● PRIMARY WAY TO FIND

TRAINER'S PARTY | Trainer at Pastoria Gym

WILD POKÉMON | Route 223 (water surface)

COURSE OF STORY

Girafarig

NORMAL   PSYCHIC

HEIGHT: 4'11"
WEIGHT: 91.5 lbs.
GENDER: Male and Female
HELD ITEM: Persim Berry

● Male form   ● Female form

PLATINUM The head on its tail contains a small brain. It can instinctively Fighting even while facing backward.

EVOLUTION PATH

Does Not evolve

● TM & HM MOVES

No.	Name	Type	Kind	Power	Acc	PP	Range	DA
TM04	Calm Mind	Psychic	Status	—	—	20	Self	—
TM06	Toxic	Poison	Status	—	85	10	Normal	—
TM10	Hidden Power	Normal	Special	—	100	15	Normal	—
TM11	Sunny Day	Fire	Status	—	—	5	All	—
TM16	Light Screen	Psychic	Status	—	—	30	2 allies	—
TM17	Protect	Normal	Status	—	—	10	Self	—
TM18	Rain Dance	Water	Status	—	—	5	All	—
TM21	Frustration	Normal	Physical	—	100	20	Normal	●
TM23	Iron Tail	Steel	Physical	100	75	15	Normal	●
TM24	Thunderbolt	Electric	Special	95	100	15	Normal	—
TM25	Thunder	Electric	Special	120	70	10	Normal	—
TM26	Earthquake	Ground	Physical	100	100	10	2 foes • 1 ally	—
TM27	Return	Normal	Physical	—	100	20	Normal	●
TM29	Psychic	Psychic	Special	90	100	10	Normal	—
TM30	Shadow Ball	Ghost	Special	80	100	15	Normal	—
TM32	Double Team	Normal	Status	—	—	15	Self	—
TM33	Reflect	Psychic	Status	—	—	20	2 allies	—
TM34	Shock Wave	Electric	Special	60	—	20	Normal	—
TM42	Facade	Normal	Physical	70	100	20	Normal	●
TM43	Secret Power	Normal	Physical	70	100	20	Normal	●
TM44	Rest	Psychic	Status	—	—	10	Self	—
TM45	Attract	Normal	Status	—	100	15	Normal	—
TM46	Thief	Dark	Physical	40	100	10	Normal	●
TM48	Skill Swap	Psychic	Status	—	—	10	Normal	—
TM53	Energy Ball	Grass	Special	80	100	10	Normal	—
TM57	Charge Beam	Electric	Special	50	90	10	Normal	—
TM58	Endure	Normal	Status	—	—	10	Self	—
TM67	Recycle	Normal	Status	—	—	10	Self	—
TM70	Flash	Normal	Status	—	100	20	Normal	—
TM73	Thunder Wave	Electric	Status	—	100	20	Normal	—
TM77	Psych Up	Normal	Status	—	—	10	Self	—
TM78	Captivate	Normal	Status	—	100	20	2 foes	—
TM82	Sleep Talk	Normal	Status	—	—	10	DoM	—
TM83	Natural Gift	Normal	Physical	—	100	15	Normal	●
TM85	Dream Eater	Psychic	Special	100	100	15	Normal	—
TM86	Grass Knot	Grass	Special	—	100	20	Normal	—
TM87	Swagger	Normal	Status	—	90	15	Normal	—
TM90	Substitute	Normal	Status	—	—	10	Self	—
TM92	Trick Room	Psychic	Status	—	—	5	All	—
HM04	Strength	Normal	Physical	80	100	15	Normal	●
HM06	Rock Smash	Fighting	Physical	40	100	15	Normal	●

● LEVEL-UP AND LEARNED MOVES

Lv	Name	Type	Kind	Power	Acc	PP	Range	DA
Base	Power Swap	Psychic	Status	—	—	10	Normal	—
Base	Guard Swap	Psychic	Status	—	—	10	Normal	—
Base	Astonish	Ghost	Physical	30	100	15	Normal	●
Base	Tackle	Normal	Physical	35	95	35	Normal	●
Base	Growl	Normal	Status	—	100	40	2 foes	—
Base	Confusion	Psychic	Special	50	100	25	Normal	—
5	Odor Sleuth	Normal	Status	—	—	40	Normal	—
10	Stomp	Normal	Physical	65	100	20	Normal	●
14	Agility	Psychic	Status	—	—	30	Self	—
19	Psybeam	Psychic	Special	65	100	20	Normal	—
23	Baton Pass	Normal	Status	—	—	40	Self	—
28	Assurance	Dark	Physical	50	100	10	Normal	●
32	Double Hit	Normal	Physical	35	90	10	Normal	●
37	Psychic	Psychic	Special	90	100	10	Normal	—
41	Zen Headbutt	Psychic	Physical	80	90	15	Normal	●
46	Crunch	Dark	Physical	80	100	15	Normal	●

● MOVES TAUGHT IN EXCHANGE FOR COLORED SHARDS

Name	Type	Kind	Power	Acc	PP	Range	DA
Mud-Slap	Ground	Special	20	100	10	Normal	—
Snore	Normal	Special	40	100	15	Normal	—
Signal Beam	Bug	Special	75	100	15	Normal	—
Zen Headbutt	Psychic	Physical	80	90	15	Normal	●
Trick	Psychic	Status	—	100	10	Normal	—
Sucker Punch	Dark	Physical	80	100	5	Normal	●
Swift	Normal	Special	60	—	20	2 foes	—
Uproar	Normal	Special	50	100	10	1 random	—

● EGG MOVES

Name	Type	Kind	Power	Acc	PP	Range	DA
Take Down	Normal	Physical	90	85	20	Normal	●
Amnesia	Psychic	Status	—	—	20	Self	—
Foresight	Normal	Status	—	—	40	Normal	—
Future Sight	Psychic	Special	80	90	15	Normal	—
Beat Up	Dark	Physical	10	100	10	Normal	●
Psych Up	Normal	Status	—	—	10	Normal	—
Wish	Normal	Status	—	—	10	Self	—
Magic Coat	Psychic	Status	—	—	15	Self	—
Double Kick	Fighting	Physical	30	100	30	Normal	●
Mirror Coat	Psychic	Special	—	100	20	Self	—

● PRIMARY WAY TO FIND

TRAINER'S PARTY Trainer on the Celestic Town side of Route 210

WILD POKÉMON Valor Lakefront

COURSE OF STORY

ABILITY ● Inner Focus ● Early Bird

EGG GROUP Field

STATS
HP ●●
ATTACK ●●●
DEFENSE ●●●
SP. ATTACK ●●●
SP. DEFENSE ●●●
SPEED ●●●

Hippopotas

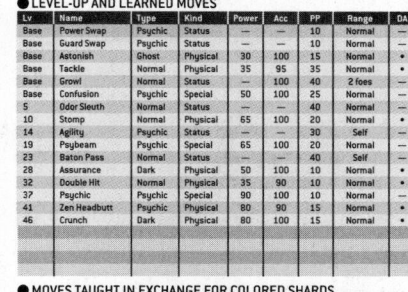

GROUND

HEIGHT: 2'07"
WEIGHT: 109.1 lbs.
GENDER: Male and Female
HELD ITEM: None

● Male form   ● Female form

PLATINUM It shuts its nostrils tight then travels through sand as if walking. They form colonies of around ten.

EVOLUTION PATH

Hippopotas →Lv34→ Hippowdon

● TM & HM MOVES

No.	Name	Type	Kind	Power	Acc	PP	Range	DA
TM03	Water Pulse	Water	Special	60	100	20	Normal	—
TM05	Roar	Normal	Status	—	100	20	Normal	—
TM06	Toxic	Poison	Status	—	85	10	Normal	—
TM10	Hidden Power	Normal	Special	—	100	15	Normal	—
TM11	Sunny Day	Fire	Status	—	—	5	All	—
TM17	Protect	Normal	Status	—	—	10	Self	—
TM21	Frustration	Normal	Physical	—	100	20	Normal	●
TM23	Iron Tail	Steel	Physical	100	75	15	Normal	●
TM26	Earthquake	Ground	Physical	100	100	10	2 foes • 1 ally	—
TM27	Return	Normal	Physical	—	100	20	Normal	●
TM32	Double Team	Normal	Status	—	—	15	Self	—
TM37	Sandstorm	Rock	Status	—	—	10	All	—
TM39	Rock Tomb	Rock	Physical	50	80	10	Normal	●
TM42	Facade	Normal	Physical	70	100	20	Normal	●
TM43	Secret Power	Normal	Physical	70	100	20	Normal	●
TM44	Rest	Psychic	Status	—	—	10	Self	—
TM45	Attract	Normal	Status	—	100	15	Normal	—
TM58	Endure	Normal	Status	—	—	10	Self	—
TM76	Stealth Rock	Rock	Status	—	—	20	2 foes	—
TM78	Captivate	Normal	Status	—	100	20	2 foes	—
TM80	Rock Slide	Rock	Physical	75	90	10	2 foes	—
TM82	Sleep Talk	Normal	Status	—	—	10	DoM	—
TM83	Natural Gift	Normal	Physical	—	100	15	Normal	●
TM87	Swagger	Normal	Status	—	90	15	Normal	—
TM90	Substitute	Normal	Status	—	—	10	Self	—
HM04	Strength	Normal	Physical	80	100	15	Normal	●
HM06	Rock Smash	Fighting	Physical	40	100	15	Normal	●

● LEVEL-UP AND LEARNES MOVES

Lv	Name	Type	Kind	Power	Acc	PP	Range	DA
Base	Tackle	Normal	Physical	35	95	35	Normal	●
Base	Sand-Attack	Ground	Status	—	100	15	Normal	—
7	Bite	Dark	Physical	60	100	25	Normal	●
13	Yawn	Normal	Status	—	—	10	Normal	—
19	Take Down	Normal	Physical	90	85	20	Normal	●
25	Sand Tomb	Ground	Physical	15	70	15	Normal	—
31	Crunch	Dark	Physical	80	100	15	Normal	●
37	Earthquake	Ground	Physical	100	100	10	2 foes • 1 ally	—
44	Double-Edge	Normal	Physical	120	100	15	Normal	●
50	Fissure	Ground	Physical	—	30	5	Normal	—

● MOVES TAUGHT IN EXCHANGE FOR COLORED SHARDS

Name	Type	Kind	Power	Acc	PP	Range	DA
Mud-Slap	Ground	Special	20	100	10	Normal	—
Superpower	Fighting	Physical	120	100	5	Normal	●
Snore	Normal	Special	40	100	15	Normal	—
Earth Power	Ground	Special	90	100	10	Normal	—

● EGG MOVES

Name	Type	Kind	Power	Acc	PP	Range	DA
Stockpile	Normal	Status	—	—	20	Self	—
Swallow	Normal	Status	—	—	10	Self	—
Spit Up	Normal	Special	—	100	10	Normal	—
Curse	???	Status	—	—	10	Normal • Self	—
Slack Off	Normal	Status	—	—	10	Self	—
Body Slam	Normal	Physical	85	100	15	Normal	●
Sand Tomb	Ground	Physical	15	70	15	Normal	—

● PRIMARY WAY TO FIND

TRAINER'S PARTY Trainer on B2F of Iron Island

WILD POKÉMON Maniac Tunnel

COURSE OF STORY

ABILITY ● Sand Stream

EGG GROUP Field

STATS
HP ●●
ATTACK ●●●
DEFENSE ●●●
SP. ATTACK ●
SP. DEFENSE ●
SPEED ●

Sinnoh Pokédex No. 123 Heavyweight Pokémon

Hippowdon

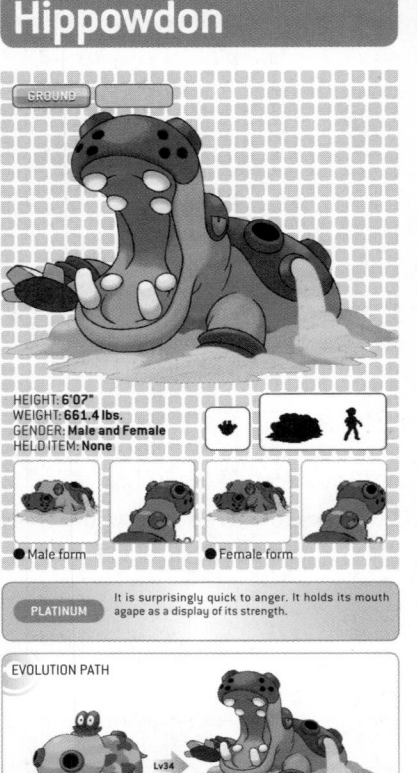

GROUND

HEIGHT: 6'07"
WEIGHT: 661.4 lbs.
GENDER: Male and Female
HELD ITEM: None

● Male form ● Female form

PLATINUM It is surprisingly quick to anger. It holds its mouth agape as a display of its strength.

EVOLUTION PATH

Hippopotas → Lv34 → Hippowdon

● TM & HM MOVES

No.	Name	Type	Kind	Power	Acc	PP	Range	DA
TM03	Water Pulse	Water	Special	60	100	20	Normal	—
TM05	Roar	Normal	Status	—	100	20	Normal	—
TM06	Toxic	Poison	Status	—	85	10	Normal	—
TM10	Hidden Power	Normal	Special	—	100	15	Normal	—
TM11	Sunny Day	Fire	Status	—	—	5	All	—
TM15	Hyper Beam	Normal	Special	150	90	5	Normal	—
TM17	Protect	Normal	Status	—	—	10	Self	—
TM21	Frustration	Normal	Physical	—	100	20	Normal	•
TM23	Iron Tail	Steel	Physical	100	75	15	Normal	•
TM26	Earthquake	Ground	Physical	100	100	10	2 foes • 1 ally	•
TM27	Return	Normal	Physical	—	100	20	Normal	•
TM32	Double Team	Normal	Status	—	—	15	Self	—
TM37	Sandstorm	Rock	Status	—	—	10	All	—
TM39	Rock Tomb	Rock	Physical	50	80	10	Normal	•
TM42	Facade	Normal	Physical	70	100	20	Normal	•
TM43	Secret Power	Normal	Physical	70	100	20	Normal	•
TM44	Rest	Psychic	Status	—	—	10	Self	—
TM45	Attract	Normal	Status	—	100	15	Normal	—
TM58	Endure	Normal	Status	—	—	10	Self	—
TM68	Giga Impact	Normal	Physical	150	90	5	Normal	•
TM71	Stone Edge	Rock	Physical	100	80	5	Normal	•
TM76	Stealth Rock	Rock	Status	—	—	20	2 foes	—
TM78	Captivate	Normal	Status	—	100	20	2 foes	—
TM80	Rock Slide	Rock	Physical	75	90	10	2 foes	•
TM82	Sleep Talk	Normal	Status	—	—	10	DoM	—
TM83	Natural Gift	Normal	Physical	—	100	15	Normal	•
TM87	Swagger	Normal	Status	—	90	15	Normal	—
TM90	Substitute	Normal	Status	—	—	10	Self	—
HM04	Strength	Normal	Physical	80	100	15	Normal	•
HM06	Rock Smash	Fighting	Physical	40	100	15	Normal	•

● LEVEL-UP AND LEARNED MOVES

Lv	Name	Type	Kind	Power	Acc	PP	Range	DA
Base	Ice Fang	Ice	Physical	65	95	15	Normal	•
Base	Fire Fang	Fire	Physical	65	95	15	Normal	•
Base	Thunder Fang	Electric	Physical	65	95	15	Normal	•
Base	Tackle	Normal	Physical	35	95	35	Normal	•
Base	Sand-Attack	Ground	Status	—	100	15	Normal	—
Base	Bite	Dark	Physical	60	100	25	Normal	•
Base	Yawn	Normal	Status	—	—	10	Normal	—
7	Bite	Dark	Physical	60	100	25	Normal	•
13	Yawn	Normal	Status	—	—	10	Normal	—
19	Take Down	Normal	Physical	90	85	20	Normal	•
25	Sand Tomb	Ground	Physical	15	70	15	Normal	•
31	Crunch	Dark	Physical	80	100	15	Normal	•
40	Earthquake	Ground	Physical	100	100	10	2 foes • 1 ally	•
50	Double-Edge	Normal	Physical	120	100	15	Normal	•
60	Fissure	Ground	Physical	—	30	5	Normal	—

● MOVES TAUGHT IN EXCHANGE FOR COLORED SHARDS

Name	Type	Kind	Power	Acc	PP	Range	DA
Mud-Slap	Ground	Special	20	100	10	Normal	—
Superpower	Fighting	Physical	120	100	5	Normal	•
Iron Head	Steel	Physical	80	100	15	Normal	•
Snore	Normal	Special	40	100	15	Normal	—
Earth Power	Ground	Special	90	100	10	Normal	—

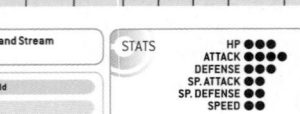

ABILITY ● Sand Stream

EGG GROUP Field

STATS
HP ●●●
ATTACK ●●●●
DEFENSE ●●●●
SP. ATTACK ●●
SP. DEFENSE ●●●
SPEED ●●

● PRIMARY WAY TO FIND

TRAINER'S PARTY Elite Four member Bertha

WILD POKÉMON Route 228

COURSE OF STORY

Sinnoh Pokédex No. 124 Polka Dot Pokémon

Azurill

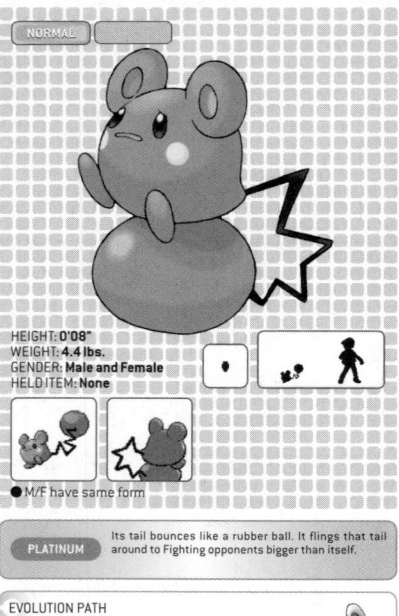

NORMAL

HEIGHT: 0'08"
WEIGHT: 4.4 lbs.
GENDER: Male and Female
HELD ITEM: None

● M/F have same form

PLATINUM Its tail bounces like a rubber ball. It flings that tail around to Fighting opponents bigger than itself.

EVOLUTION PATH

Azurill → (Level up once Friendship is high enough) → Marill → Lv18 → Azumarill

● TM & HM MOVES

No.	Name	Type	Kind	Power	Acc	PP	Range	DA
TM03	Water Pulse	Water	Special	60	100	20	Normal	—
TM06	Toxic	Poison	Status	—	85	10	Normal	—
TM07	Hail	Ice	Status	—	—	10	All	—
TM10	Hidden Power	Normal	Special	—	100	15	Normal	—
TM13	Ice Beam	Ice	Special	95	100	10	Normal	—
TM14	Blizzard	Ice	Special	120	70	5	2 foes	—
TM17	Protect	Normal	Status	—	—	10	Self	—
TM18	Rain Dance	Water	Status	—	—	5	All	—
TM21	Frustration	Normal	Physical	—	100	20	Normal	•
TM23	Iron Tail	Steel	Physical	100	75	15	Normal	•
TM27	Return	Normal	Physical	—	100	20	Normal	•
TM32	Double Team	Normal	Status	—	—	15	Self	—
TM42	Facade	Normal	Physical	70	100	20	Normal	•
TM43	Secret Power	Normal	Physical	70	100	20	Normal	•
TM44	Rest	Psychic	Status	—	—	10	Self	—
TM45	Attract	Normal	Status	—	100	15	Normal	—
TM58	Endure	Normal	Status	—	—	10	Self	—
TM78	Captivate	Normal	Status	—	100	20	2 foes	—
TM82	Sleep Talk	Normal	Status	—	—	10	DoM	—
TM83	Natural Gift	Normal	Physical	—	100	15	Normal	•
TM87	Swagger	Normal	Status	—	90	15	Normal	—
TM90	Substitute	Normal	Status	—	—	10	Self	—
HM03	Surf	Water	Special	95	100	15	2 foes • 1 ally	—
HM07	Waterfall	Water	Physical	80	100	15	Normal	•

● LEVEL-UP AND LEARNED MOVES

Lv	Name	Type	Kind	Power	Acc	PP	Range	DA
Base	Splash	Normal	Status	—	—	40	Self	—
2	Charm	Normal	Status	—	100	20	Normal	—
7	Tail Whip	Normal	Status	—	100	30	2 foes	—
10	Bubble	Water	Special	20	100	30	2 foes	—
15	Slam	Normal	Physical	80	75	20	Normal	•
18	Water Gun	Water	Special	40	100	25	Normal	—

● MOVES TAUGHT IN EXCHANGE FOR COLORED SHARDS

Name	Type	Kind	Power	Acc	PP	Range	DA
Mud-Slap	Ground	Special	20	100	10	Normal	—
Icy Wind	Ice	Special	55	95	15	2 foes	—
Rollout	Rock	Physical	30	90	20	Normal	•
Snore	Normal	Special	40	100	15	Normal	—
Helping Hand	Normal	Status	—	—	20	1 ally	—
Knock Off	Dark	Physical	20	100	20	Normal	•
Swift	Normal	Special	60	—	20	2 foes	—
Uproar	Normal	Special	50	100	10	1 random	—

● EGG MOVES

Name	Type	Kind	Power	Acc	PP	Range	DA
Encore	Normal	Status	—	100	5	Normal	—
Sing	Normal	Status	—	55	15	Normal	—
Refresh	Normal	Status	—	—	20	Self	—
Slam	Normal	Physical	80	75	20	Normal	•
Tickle	Normal	Status	—	100	20	Normal	—
Fake Tears	Dark	Status	—	100	20	Normal	—

ABILITY ● Thick Fat ● Huge Power

EGG GROUP No Eggs

STATS
HP ●●
ATTACK ●
DEFENSE ●
SP. ATTACK ●
SP. DEFENSE ●
SPEED ●

● PRIMARY WAY TO FIND

TRAINER'S PARTY Trainer at Pastoria Gym

WILD POKÉMON Trophy Garden at the Pokémon Mansion on Route 212 (talk to Mr. Backlot after you get the National Pokédex)

COURSE OF STORY

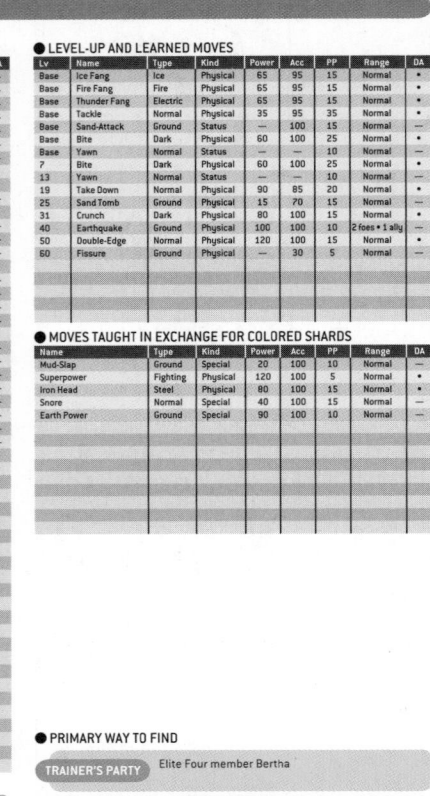

Sinnoh Pokédex No. 125 Aqua Mouse Pokémon

Marill

WATER

HEIGHT: 1'04"
WEIGHT: 18.7 lbs.
GENDER: Male and Female
HELD ITEM: None

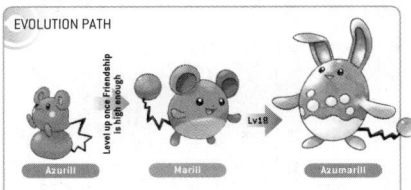

● M/F have same form

PLATINUM The oil-filled end of its tail floats on water. It keeps MARILL from drowning even in a strong current.

EVOLUTION PATH

Azurill → (Level up once Friendship is high enough) → Marill → Lv18 → Azumarill

ABILITY ● Thick Fat ● Huge Power

EGG GROUP Water 1 / Fairy

STATS
HP ●●
ATTACK ●●
DEFENSE ●●
SP. ATTACK ●●
SP. DEFENSE ●●
SPEED ●●

● TM & HM MOVES

No.	Name	Type	Kind	Power	Acc	PP	Range	DA
TM01	Focus Punch	Fighting	Physical	150	100	20	Normal	●
TM03	Water Pulse	Water	Special	60	100	20	Normal	—
TM06	Toxic	Poison	Status	—	85	10	Normal	—
TM07	Hail	Ice	Status	—	—	10	All	—
TM10	Hidden Power	Normal	Special	—	100	15	Normal	—
TM13	Ice Beam	Ice	Special	95	100	10	Normal	—
TM14	Blizzard	Ice	Special	120	70	5	2 foes	—
TM17	Protect	Normal	Status	—	—	10	Self	—
TM18	Rain Dance	Water	Status	—	—	5	All	—
TM21	Frustration	Normal	Physical	—	100	20	Normal	●
TM23	Iron Tail	Steel	Physical	100	75	15	Normal	●
TM27	Return	Normal	Physical	—	100	20	Normal	●
TM28	Dig	Ground	Physical	80	100	10	Normal	●
TM31	Brick Break	Fighting	Physical	75	100	15	Normal	●
TM32	Double Team	Normal	Status	—	—	15	Self	—
TM42	Facade	Normal	Physical	70	100	20	Normal	●
TM43	Secret Power	Normal	Physical	70	100	20	Normal	—
TM44	Rest	Psychic	Status	—	—	10	Self	—
TM45	Attract	Normal	Status	—	100	15	Normal	—
TM56	Fling	Dark	Physical	—	100	10	Normal	●
TM58	Endure	Normal	Status	—	—	10	Self	—
TM78	Captivate	Normal	Status	—	100	20	2 foes	—
TM82	Sleep Talk	Normal	Status	—	—	10	DoM	—
TM83	Natural Gift	Normal	Physical	—	100	15	Normal	●
TM86	Grass Knot	Grass	Special	—	100	20	Normal	●
TM87	Swagger	Normal	Status	—	90	15	Normal	—
TM90	Substitute	Normal	Status	—	—	10	Self	—
HM03	Surf	Water	Special	95	100	15	2 foes • 1 ally	—
HM04	Strength	Normal	Physical	80	100	15	Normal	●
HM06	Rock Smash	Fighting	Physical	40	100	15	Normal	●
HM07	Waterfall	Water	Physical	80	100	15	Normal	●

● LEVEL-UP AND LEARNED MOVES

Lv	Name	Type	Kind	Power	Acc	PP	Range	DA
Base	Tackle	Normal	Physical	35	95	35	Normal	●
2	Defense Curl	Normal	Status	—	—	40	Self	—
7	Tail Whip	Normal	Status	—	100	30	2 foes	—
10	Water Gun	Water	Special	40	100	25	Normal	—
15	Rollout	Rock	Physical	30	90	20	Normal	●
18	BubbleBeam	Water	Special	65	100	20	Normal	—
23	Aqua Ring	Water	Status	—	—	20	Self	—
27	Double-Edge	Normal	Physical	120	100	15	Normal	●
32	Rain Dance	Water	Status	—	—	5	All	—
37	Aqua Tail	Water	Physical	90	90	10	Normal	●
42	Hydro Pump	Water	Special	120	80	5	Normal	—

● MOVES TAUGHT IN EXCHANGE FOR COLORED SHARDS

Name	Type	Kind	Power	Acc	PP	Range	DA
Dive	Water	Physical	80	100	10	Normal	●
Mud-Slap	Ground	Special	20	100	10	Normal	—
Icy Wind	Ice	Special	55	95	15	2 foes	—
Rollout	Rock	Physical	30	90	20	Normal	●
Superpower	Fighting	Physical	120	100	5	Normal	●
Ice Punch	Ice	Physical	75	100	15	Normal	●
Aqua Tail	Water	Physical	90	90	10	Normal	●
Snore	Normal	Special	40	100	15	Normal	—
Helping Hand	Normal	Status	—	—	20	1 ally	—
Knock Off	Dark	Physical	20	100	20	Normal	●
Swift	Normal	Special	60	—	20	2 foes	—

● EGG MOVES

Name	Type	Kind	Power	Acc	PP	Range	DA
Light Screen	Psychic	Status	—	—	30	2 allies	—
Present	Normal	Physical	—	90	15	Normal	—
Amnesia	Psychic	Status	—	—	20	Self	—
Future Sight	Psychic	Special	80	90	15	Normal	—
Belly Drum	Normal	Status	—	—	10	Self	—
Perish Song	Normal	Status	—	—	5	All	—
Supersonic	Normal	Status	—	55	20	Normal	—
Substitute	Normal	Status	—	—	10	Self	—
Aqua Jet	Water	Physical	40	100	20	Normal	●
Superpower	Fighting	Physical	120	100	5	Normal	●
Refresh	Normal	Status	—	—	20	Self	—

● PRIMARY WAY TO FIND

TRAINER'S PARTY	Trainer on Route 213
WILD POKÉMON	Route 215
COURSE OF STORY	

Sinnoh Pokédex No. 126 Aqua Rabbit Pokémon

Azumarill

WATER

HEIGHT: 2'07"
WEIGHT: 62.8 lbs.
GENDER: Male and Female
HELD ITEM: None

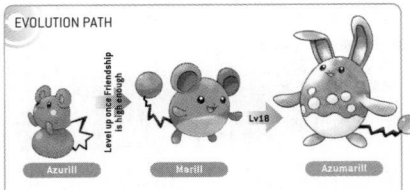

● M/F have same form

PLATINUM It can spend all day in water, since it can inhale and store a large volume of air.

EVOLUTION PATH

Azurill → (Level up once Friendship is high enough) → Marill → Lv18 → Azumarill

ABILITY ● Thick Fat ● Huge Power

EGG GROUP Water 1 / Fairy

STATS
HP ●●●
ATTACK ●●●
DEFENSE ●●
SP. ATTACK ●●
SP. DEFENSE ●●●
SPEED ●●

● TM & HM MOVES

No.	Name	Type	Kind	Power	Acc	PP	Range	DA
TM01	Focus Punch	Fighting	Physical	150	100	20	Normal	●
TM03	Water Pulse	Water	Special	60	100	20	Normal	—
TM06	Toxic	Poison	Status	—	85	10	Normal	—
TM07	Hail	Ice	Status	—	—	10	All	—
TM10	Hidden Power	Normal	Special	—	100	15	Normal	—
TM13	Ice Beam	Ice	Special	95	100	10	Normal	—
TM14	Blizzard	Ice	Special	120	70	5	2 foes	—
TM15	Hyper Beam	Normal	Special	150	90	5	Normal	—
TM17	Protect	Normal	Status	—	—	10	Self	—
TM18	Rain Dance	Water	Status	—	—	5	All	—
TM21	Frustration	Normal	Physical	—	100	20	Normal	●
TM23	Iron Tail	Steel	Physical	100	75	15	Normal	●
TM27	Return	Normal	Physical	—	100	20	Normal	●
TM28	Dig	Ground	Physical	80	100	10	Normal	●
TM31	Brick Break	Fighting	Physical	75	100	15	Normal	●
TM32	Double Team	Normal	Status	—	—	15	Self	—
TM42	Facade	Normal	Physical	70	100	20	Normal	●
TM43	Secret Power	Normal	Physical	70	100	20	Normal	—
TM44	Rest	Psychic	Status	—	—	10	Self	—
TM45	Attract	Normal	Status	—	100	15	Normal	—
TM52	Focus Blast	Fighting	Special	120	70	5	Normal	—
TM56	Fling	Dark	Physical	—	100	10	Normal	●
TM58	Endure	Normal	Status	—	—	10	Self	—
TM68	Giga Impact	Normal	Physical	150	90	5	Normal	●
TM78	Captivate	Normal	Status	—	100	20	2 foes	—
TM82	Sleep Talk	Normal	Status	—	—	10	DoM	—
TM83	Natural Gift	Normal	Physical	—	100	15	Normal	●
TM86	Grass Knot	Grass	Special	—	100	20	Normal	●
TM87	Swagger	Normal	Status	—	90	15	Normal	—
TM90	Substitute	Normal	Status	—	—	10	Self	—
HM03	Surf	Water	Special	95	100	15	2 foes • 1 ally	—
HM04	Strength	Normal	Physical	80	100	15	Normal	●
HM06	Rock Smash	Fighting	Physical	40	100	15	Normal	●
HM07	Waterfall	Water	Physical	80	100	15	Normal	●

● LEVEL-UP AND LEARNED MOVES

Lv	Name	Type	Kind	Power	Acc	PP	Range	DA
Base	Tackle	Normal	Physical	35	95	35	Normal	●
Base	Defense Curl	Normal	Status	—	—	40	Self	—
Base	Tail Whip	Normal	Status	—	100	30	2 foes	—
Base	Water Gun	Water	Special	40	100	25	Normal	—
2	Defense Curl	Normal	Status	—	—	40	Self	—
7	Tail Whip	Normal	Status	—	100	30	2 foes	—
10	Water Gun	Water	Special	40	100	25	Normal	—
15	Rollout	Rock	Physical	30	90	20	Normal	●
20	BubbleBeam	Water	Special	65	100	20	Normal	—
27	Aqua Ring	Water	Status	—	—	20	Self	—
33	Double-Edge	Normal	Physical	120	100	15	Normal	●
40	Rain Dance	Water	Status	—	—	5	All	—
47	Aqua Tail	Water	Physical	90	90	10	Normal	●
54	Hydro Pump	Water	Special	120	80	5	Normal	—

● MOVES TAUGHT IN EXCHANGE FOR COLORED SHARDS

Name	Type	Kind	Power	Acc	PP	Range	DA
Dive	Water	Physical	80	100	10	Normal	●
Mud-Slap	Ground	Special	20	100	10	Normal	—
Icy Wind	Ice	Special	55	95	15	2 foes	—
Rollout	Rock	Physical	30	90	20	Normal	●
Superpower	Fighting	Physical	120	100	5	Normal	●
Ice Punch	Ice	Physical	75	100	15	Normal	●
Aqua Tail	Water	Physical	90	90	10	Normal	●
Snore	Normal	Special	40	100	15	Normal	—
Helping Hand	Normal	Status	—	—	20	1 ally	—
Knock Off	Dark	Physical	20	100	20	Normal	●
Swift	Normal	Special	60	—	20	2 foes	—

● PRIMARY WAY TO FIND

TRAINER'S PARTY	Trainer at Pastoria Gym
WILD POKÉMON	Victory Road B1F
COURSE OF STORY	

126
AZUMARILL

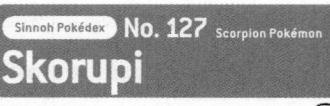

Skorupi
Sinnoh Pokédex No. 127 Scorpion Pokémon

POISON · BUG

HEIGHT: 2'07"
WEIGHT: 26.5 lbs.
GENDER: Male and Female
HELD ITEM: Poison Sting

● M/F have same form

PLATINUM As soon as the tail claws close, its needle tips secrete poison. It can survive a year without food.

EVOLUTION PATH
Skorupi → Lv40 → Drapion

TM & HM MOVES

No.	Name	Type	Kind	Power	Acc	PP	Range	DA
TM06	Toxic	Poison	Status	—	85	10	Normal	
TM10	Hidden Power	Normal	Special	—	100	15	Normal	
TM11	Sunny Day	Fire	Status	—	—	5	All	
TM12	Taunt	Dark	Status	—	100	20	Normal	
TM17	Protect	Normal	Status	—	—	10	Self	
TM18	Rain Dance	Water	Status	—	—	5	All	
TM21	Frustration	Normal	Physical	—	100	20	Normal	●
TM23	Iron Tail	Steel	Physical	100	75	15	Normal	●
TM27	Return	Normal	Physical	—	100	20	Normal	●
TM28	Dig	Ground	Physical	80	100	10	Normal	●
TM30	Shadow Ball	Ghost	Special	80	100	15	Normal	
TM31	Brick Break	Fighting	Physical	75	100	15	Normal	●
TM32	Double Team	Normal	Status	—	—	15	Self	
TM36	Sludge Bomb	Poison	Special	90	100	10	Normal	
TM39	Rock Tomb	Rock	Physical	50	80	10	Normal	●
TM40	Aerial Ace	Flying	Physical	60	—	20	Normal	●
TM41	Torment	Dark	Status	—	100	15	Normal	
TM42	Facade	Normal	Physical	70	100	20	Normal	●
TM43	Secret Power	Normal	Physical	70	100	20	Normal	●
TM44	Rest	Psychic	Status	—	—	10	Self	
TM45	Attract	Normal	Status	—	100	15	Normal	
TM46	Thief	Dark	Physical	40	100	10	Normal	●
TM54	False Swipe	Normal	Physical	40	100	40	Normal	●
TM56	Fling	Dark	Physical	—	100	10	Normal	●
TM58	Endure	Normal	Status	—	—	10	Self	
TM66	Payback	Dark	Physical	50	100	10	Normal	●
TM70	Flash	Normal	Status	—	100	20	Normal	
TM75	Swords Dance	Normal	Status	—	—	30	Self	
TM78	Captivate	Normal	Status	—	100	20	2 foes	
TM79	Dark Pulse	Dark	Special	80	100	15	Normal	
TM81	X-Scissor	Bug	Physical	80	100	15	Normal	●
TM82	Sleep Talk	Normal	Status	—	—	10	DoM	
TM83	Natural Gift	Normal	Physical	—	100	15	Normal	●
TM84	Poison Jab	Poison	Physical	80	100	20	Normal	●
TM87	Swagger	Normal	Status	—	90	15	Normal	
TM90	Substitute	Normal	Status	—	—	10	Self	
HM01	Cut	Normal	Physical	50	95	30	Normal	●
HM04	Strength	Normal	Physical	80	100	15	Normal	●
HM06	Rock Smash	Fighting	Physical	40	100	15	Normal	●

LEVEL-UP AND LEARNED MOVES

Lv	Name	Type	Kind	Power	Acc	PP	Range	DA
Base	Bite	Dark	Physical	60	100	25	Normal	●
Base	Poison Sting	Poison	Physical	15	100	35	Normal	●
Base	Leer	Normal	Status	—	100	30	2 foes	—
6	Knock Off	Dark	Physical	20	100	20	Normal	●
12	Pin Missile	Bug	Physical	14	85	20	Normal	●
17	Acupressure	Normal	Status	—	—	30	1 ally	●
23	Scary Face	Normal	Status	—	90	10	Normal	
28	Toxic Spikes	Poison	Status	—	—	20	2 foes	—
34	Bug Bite	Bug	Physical	60	100	20	Normal	●
39	Poison Fang	Poison	Physical	50	100	15	Normal	●
45	Crunch	Dark	Physical	80	100	15	Normal	●
50	Cross Poison	Poison	Physical	70	100	20	Normal	●

MOVES TAUGHT IN EXCHANGE FOR COLORED SHARDS

Name	Type	Kind	Power	Acc	PP	Range	DA
Mud-Slap	Ground	Special	20	100	10	Normal	—
Fury Cutter	Bug	Physical	10	95	20	Normal	—
Aqua Tail	Water	Physical	90	90	10	Normal	—
Snore	Normal	Special	40	100	15	Normal	—
Knock Off	Dark	Physical	20	100	20	Normal	—

EGG MOVES

Name	Type	Kind	Power	Acc	PP	Range	DA
Faint Attack	Dark	Physical	60	—	20	Normal	●
Screech	Normal	Status	—	85	40	Normal	
Sand-Attack	Ground	Status	—	100	15	Normal	
Slash	Normal	Physical	70	100	20	Normal	●
Confuse Ray	Ghost	Status	—	100	10	Normal	
Whirlwind	Normal	Status	—	100	20	Normal	—
Agility	Psychic	Status	—	—	30	Self	
Pursuit	Dark	Physical	40	100	20	Normal	●
Night Slash	Dark	Physical	70	100	15	Normal	●

PRIMARY WAY TO FIND
TRAINER'S PARTY Trainer on the Solaceon Town side of Route 210
WILD POKÉMON Pastoria Great Marsh (varies by day)
COURSE OF STORY

ABILITY ● Battle Armor ● Sniper
EGG GROUP Bug / Water 3
STATS HP ● / ATTACK ● / DEFENSE ●●● / SP.ATTACK ● / SP.DEFENSE ● / SPEED ●●

Drapion
Sinnoh Pokémon No. 128 Ogre Scorp Pokémon

POISON · DARK

HEIGHT: 4'03"
WEIGHT: 135.6 lbs.
GENDER: Male and Female
HELD ITEM: Poison Sting

● M/F have same form

PLATINUM Possessing a sturdy build, it takes pride in its strength, taking down foes without using toxins.

EVOLUTION PATH
Skorupi → Lv40 → Drapion

TM & HM MOVES

No.	Name	Type	Kind	Power	Acc	PP	Range	DA
TM05	Roar	Normal	Status	—	100	20	Normal	—
TM06	Toxic	Poison	Status	—	85	10	Normal	
TM10	Hidden Power	Normal	Special	—	100	15	Normal	
TM11	Sunny Day	Fire	Status	—	—	5	All	
TM12	Taunt	Dark	Status	—	100	20	Normal	
TM15	Hyper Beam	Normal	Special	150	90	5	Normal	
TM17	Protect	Normal	Status	—	—	10	Self	
TM18	Rain Dance	Water	Status	—	—	5	All	
TM21	Frustration	Normal	Physical	—	100	20	Normal	●
TM23	Iron Tail	Steel	Physical	100	75	15	Normal	●
TM26	Earthquake	Ground	Physical	100	100	10	2 foes + 1 ally	●
TM27	Return	Normal	Physical	—	100	20	Normal	●
TM28	Dig	Ground	Physical	80	100	10	Normal	●
TM30	Shadow Ball	Ghost	Special	80	100	15	Normal	
TM31	Brick Break	Fighting	Physical	75	100	15	Normal	●
TM32	Double Team	Normal	Status	—	—	15	Self	
TM36	Sludge Bomb	Poison	Special	90	100	10	Normal	
TM39	Rock Tomb	Rock	Physical	50	80	10	Normal	●
TM40	Aerial Ace	Flying	Physical	60	—	20	Normal	●
TM41	Torment	Dark	Status	—	100	15	Normal	
TM42	Facade	Normal	Physical	70	100	20	Normal	●
TM43	Secret Power	Normal	Physical	70	100	20	Normal	●
TM44	Rest	Psychic	Status	—	—	10	Self	
TM45	Attract	Normal	Status	—	100	15	Normal	
TM46	Thief	Dark	Physical	40	100	10	Normal	●
TM54	False Swipe	Normal	Physical	40	100	40	Normal	●
TM56	Fling	Dark	Physical	—	100	10	Normal	●
TM58	Endure	Normal	Status	—	—	10	Self	
TM66	Payback	Dark	Physical	50	100	10	Normal	●
TM68	Giga Impact	Normal	Physical	150	90	5	Normal	●
TM70	Flash	Normal	Status	—	100	20	Normal	
TM75	Swords Dance	Normal	Status	—	—	30	Self	
TM78	Captivate	Normal	Status	—	100	20	2 foes	
TM79	Dark Pulse	Dark	Special	80	100	15	Normal	
TM80	Rock Slide	Rock	Physical	75	90	10	2 foes	●
TM81	X-Scissor	Bug	Physical	80	100	15	Normal	●
TM82	Sleep Talk	Normal	Status	—	—	10	DoM	
TM83	Natural Gift	Normal	Physical	—	100	15	Normal	●
TM84	Poison Jab	Poison	Physical	80	100	20	Normal	●
TM87	Swagger	Normal	Status	—	90	15	Normal	
TM90	Substitute	Normal	Status	—	—	10	Self	
HM01	Cut	Normal	Physical	50	95	30	Normal	●
HM04	Strength	Normal	Physical	80	100	15	Normal	●
HM06	Rock Smash	Fighting	Physical	40	100	15	Normal	●
HM08	Rock Climb	Normal	Physical	90	85	20	Normal	●

LEVEL-UP AND LEARNED MOVES

Lv	Name	Type	Kind	Power	Acc	PP	Range	DA
Base	Thunder Fang	Electric	Physical	65	95	15	Normal	●
Base	Ice Fang	Ice	Physical	65	95	15	Normal	●
Base	Fire Fang	Fire	Physical	65	95	15	Normal	●
Base	Bite	Dark	Physical	60	100	25	Normal	●
Base	Poison Sting	Poison	Physical	15	100	35	Normal	●
Base	Leer	Normal	Status	—	100	30	2 foes	—
Base	Knock Off	Dark	Physical	20	100	20	Normal	●
15	Knock Off	Dark	Physical	20	100	20	Normal	●
12	Pin Missile	Bug	Physical	14	85	20	Normal	●
17	Acupressure	Normal	Status	—	—	30	1 ally	●
23	Scary Face	Normal	Status	—	90	10	Normal	
28	Toxic Spikes	Poison	Status	—	—	20	2 foes	—
34	Bug Bite	Bug	Physical	60	100	20	Normal	●
39	Poison Fang	Poison	Physical	50	100	15	Normal	●
49	Crunch	Dark	Physical	80	100	15	Normal	●
58	Cross Poison	Poison	Physical	70	100	20	Normal	●

MOVES TAUGHT IN EXCHANGE FOR COLORED SHARDS

Name	Type	Kind	Power	Acc	PP	Range	DA
Mud-Slap	Ground	Special	20	100	10	Normal	—
Fury Cutter	Bug	Physical	10	95	20	Normal	—
Aqua Tail	Water	Physical	90	90	10	Normal	—
Snore	Normal	Special	40	100	15	Normal	—
Knock Off	Dark	Physical	20	100	20	Normal	—

PRIMARY WAY TO FIND
TRAINER'S PARTY Elite Four member Aaron
WILD POKÉMON Pastoria Great Marsh (after getting the National Pokédex/varies by day)
COURSE OF STORY

ABILITY ● Battle Armor ● Sniper
EGG GROUP Bug / Water 3
STATS HP ●● / ATTACK ●●● / DEFENSE ●●● / SP.ATTACK ●● / SP.DEFENSE ●●● / SPEED ●●●

Sinnoh Pokédex **No. 129** Toxic Mouth Pokémon

Croagunk

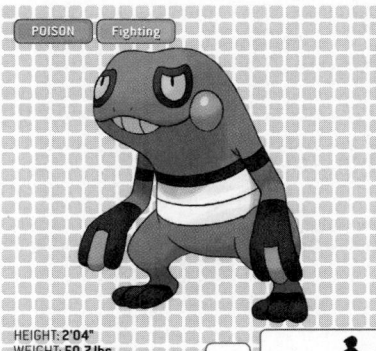

POISON | Fighting

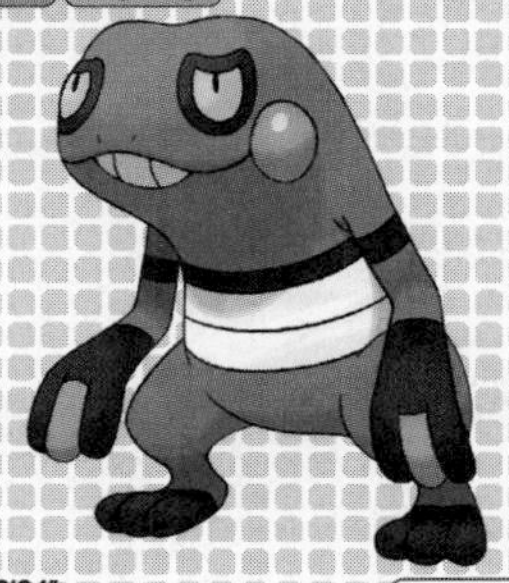

HEIGHT: **2'04"**
WEIGHT: **50.7 lbs.**
GENDER: **Male and Female**
HELD ITEM: **Black Sludge**

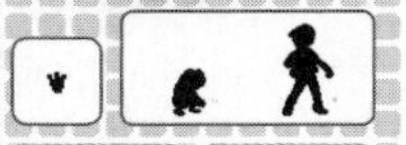

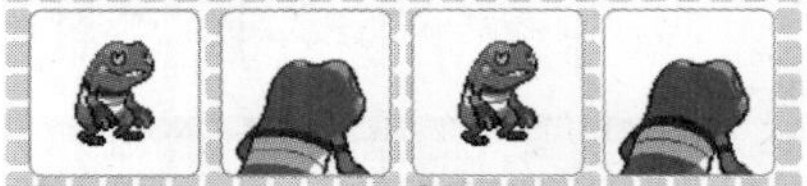

● Male form ● Female form

PLATINUM It rarely Fightings fairly, but that is strictly to ensure survival. It is popular as a mascot.

EVOLUTION PATH

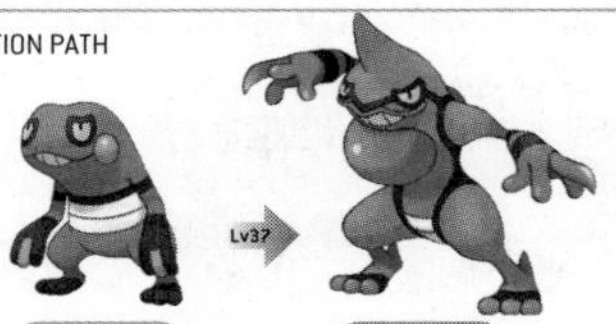

● TM & HM MOVES

No.	Name	Type	Kind	Power	Acc	PP	Range	DA
TM01	Focus Punch	Fighting	Physical	150	100	20	Normal	•
TM06	Toxic	Poison	Status	—	85	10	Normal	—
TM08	Bulk Up	Fighting	Status	—	—	20	Self	—
TM10	Hidden Power	Normal	Special	—	100	15	Normal	—
TM11	Sunny Day	Fire	Status	—	—	5	All	—
TM12	Taunt	Dark	Status	—	100	20	Normal	—
TM17	Protect	Normal	Status	—	—	10	Self	—
TM18	Rain Dance	Water	Status	—	—	5	All	—
TM21	Frustration	Normal	Physical	—	100	20	Normal	•
TM26	Earthquake	Ground	Physical	100	100	10	2 foes • 1 ally	—
TM27	Return	Normal	Physical	—	100	20	Normal	•
TM28	Dig	Ground	Physical	80	100	10	Normal	•
TM30	Shadow Ball	Ghost	Special	80	100	15	Normal	—
TM31	Brick Break	Fighting	Physical	75	100	15	Normal	•
TM32	Double Team	Normal	Status	—	—	15	Self	—
TM36	Sludge Bomb	Poison	Special	90	100	10	Normal	—
TM39	Rock Tomb	Rock	Physical	50	80	10	Normal	—
TM41	Torment	Dark	Status	—	100	15	Normal	—
TM42	Facade	Normal	Physical	70	100	20	Normal	•
TM43	Secret Power	Normal	Physical	70	100	20	Normal	—
TM44	Rest	Psychic	Status	—	—	10	Self	—
TM45	Attract	Normal	Status	—	100	15	Normal	—
TM46	Thief	Dark	Physical	40	100	10	Normal	•
TM49	Snatch	Dark	Status	—	—	10	DoM	—
TM52	Focus Blast	Fighting	Special	120	70	5	Normal	—
TM56	Fling	Dark	Physical	—	100	10	Normal	—
TM58	Endure	Normal	Status	—	—	10	Self	—
TM63	Embargo	Dark	Status	—	100	15	Normal	—
TM66	Payback	Dark	Physical	50	100	10	Normal	•
TM78	Captivate	Normal	Status	—	100	20	2 foes	—
TM79	Dark Pulse	Dark	Special	80	100	15	Normal	—
TM80	Rock Slide	Rock	Physical	75	90	10	2 foes	—
TM81	X-Scissor	Bug	Physical	80	100	15	Normal	•
TM82	Sleep Talk	Normal	Status	—	—	10	DoM	—
TM83	Natural Gift	Normal	Physical	—	100	15	Normal	—
TM84	Poison Jab	Poison	Physical	80	100	20	Normal	•
TM87	Swagger	Normal	Status	—	90	15	Normal	—
TM90	Substitute	Normal	Status	—	—	10	Self	—
HM04	Strength	Normal	Physical	80	100	15	Normal	•
HM06	Rock Smash	Fighting	Physical	40	100	15	Normal	•
HM08	Rock Climb	Normal	Physical	90	85	20	Normal	•

ABILITY ● Anticipation ● Dry Skin

EGG GROUP Human-Like

STATS
HP ●●
ATTACK ●●
DEFENSE ●
SP. ATTACK ●●
SP. DEFENSE ●
SPEED ●●

● LEVEL-UP AND LEARNED MOVES

Lv	Name	Type	Kind	Power	Acc	PP	Range	DA
Base	Astonish	Ghost	Physical	30	100	15	Normal	•
3	Mud-Slap	Ground	Special	20	100	10	Normal	—
8	Poison Sting	Poison	Physical	15	100	35	Normal	—
10	Taunt	Dark	Status	—	100	20	Normal	—
15	Pursuit	Dark	Physical	40	100	20	Normal	•
17	Faint Attack	Dark	Physical	60	—	20	Normal	•
22	Revenge	Fighting	Physical	60	100	10	Normal	•
24	Swagger	Normal	Status	—	90	15	Normal	—
29	Mud Bomb	Ground	Special	65	85	10	Normal	—
31	Sucker Punch	Dark	Physical	80	100	5	Normal	•
36	Nasty Plot	Dark	Status	—	—	20	Self	—
38	Poison Jab	Poison	Physical	80	100	20	Normal	•
43	Sludge Bomb	Poison	Special	90	100	10	Normal	—
45	Flatter	Dark	Status	—	100	15	Normal	—

● MOVES TAUGHT IN EXCHANGE FOR COLORED SHARDS

Name	Type	Kind	Power	Acc	PP	Range	DA
Mud-Slap	Ground	Special	20	100	10	Normal	—
Fury Cutter	Bug	Physical	10	95	20	Normal	•
Icy Wind	Ice	Special	55	95	15	2 foes	—
ThunderPunch	Electric	Physical	75	100	15	Normal	•
Ice Punch	Ice	Physical	75	100	15	Normal	•
Snore	Normal	Special	40	100	15	Normal	—
Spite	Ghost	Status	—	100	10	Normal	—
Helping Hand	Normal	Status	—	—	20	1 ally	—
Vacuum Wave	Fighting	Special	40	100	30	Normal	—
Gunk Shot	Poison	Physical	120	70	5	Normal	—
Bounce	Flying	Physical	85	85	5	Normal	•
Knock Off	Dark	Physical	20	100	20	Normal	•
Sucker Punch	Dark	Physical	80	100	5	Normal	•

● EGG MOVES

Name	Type	Kind	Power	Acc	PP	Range	DA
Me First	Normal	Status	—	—	20	DoM	—
Feint	Normal	Physical	50	100	10	Normal	—
DynamicPunch	Fighting	Physical	100	50	5	Normal	•
Headbutt	Normal	Physical	70	100	15	Normal	•
Vacuum Wave	Fighting	Special	40	100	30	Normal	—
Meditate	Psychic	Status	—	—	40	Self	—
Fake Out	Normal	Physical	40	100	10	Normal	•
Wake-Up Slap	Fighting	Physical	60	100	10	Normal	•
SmellingSalt	Normal	Physical	60	100	10	Normal	•
Cross Chop	Fighting	Physical	100	80	5	Normal	•
Bullet Punch	Steel	Physical	40	100	30	Normal	•

● PRIMARY WAY TO FIND

TRAINER'S PARTY Trainer on 1F of the Galactic Eterna Building

WILD POKÉMON Pastoria City side of Route 212

COURSE OF STORY

Sinnoh Pokédex **No. 130** Toxic Mouth Pokémon

Toxicroak

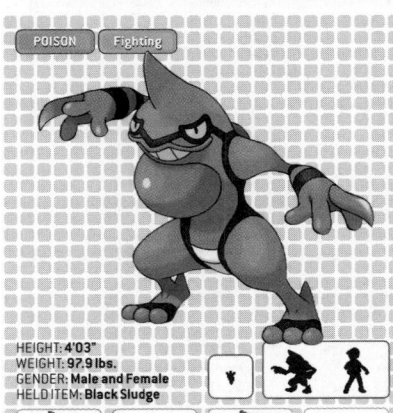

POISON | Fighting

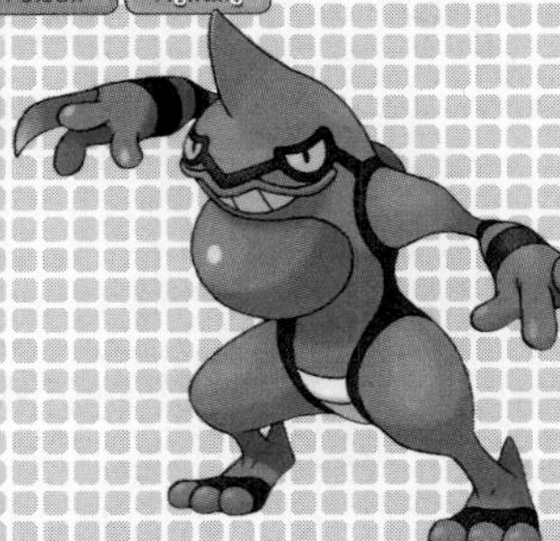

HEIGHT: **4'03"**
WEIGHT: **97.9 lbs.**
GENDER: **Male and Female**
HELD ITEM: **Black Sludge**

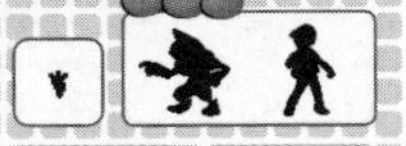

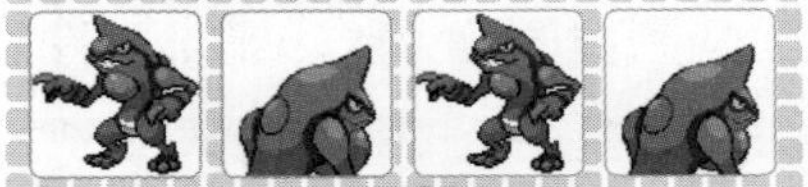

● Male form ● Female form

PLATINUM It has a poison sac at its throat. When it croaks, the stored poison is churned for greater potency.

EVOLUTION PATH

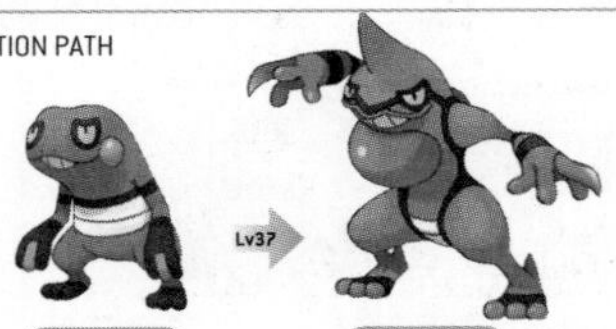

● TM & HM MOVES

No.	Name	Type	Kind	Power	Acc	PP	Range	DA
TM01	Focus Punch	Fighting	Physical	150	100	20	Normal	•
TM06	Toxic	Poison	Status	—	85	10	Normal	—
TM08	Bulk Up	Fighting	Status	—	—	20	Self	—
TM10	Hidden Power	Normal	Special	—	100	15	Normal	—
TM11	Sunny Day	Fire	Status	—	—	5	All	—
TM12	Taunt	Dark	Status	—	100	20	Normal	—
TM15	Hyper Beam	Normal	Special	150	90	5	Normal	—
TM17	Protect	Normal	Status	—	—	10	Self	—
TM18	Rain Dance	Water	Status	—	—	5	All	—
TM21	Frustration	Normal	Physical	—	100	20	Normal	•
TM26	Earthquake	Ground	Physical	100	100	10	2 foes • 1 ally	—
TM27	Return	Normal	Physical	—	100	20	Normal	•
TM28	Dig	Ground	Physical	80	100	10	Normal	•
TM30	Shadow Ball	Ghost	Special	80	100	15	Normal	—
TM31	Brick Break	Fighting	Physical	75	100	15	Normal	•
TM32	Double Team	Normal	Status	—	—	15	Self	—
TM36	Sludge Bomb	Poison	Special	90	100	10	Normal	—
TM39	Rock Tomb	Rock	Physical	50	80	10	Normal	—
TM41	Torment	Dark	Status	—	100	15	Normal	—
TM42	Facade	Normal	Physical	70	100	20	Normal	•
TM43	Secret Power	Normal	Physical	70	100	20	Normal	—
TM44	Rest	Psychic	Status	—	—	10	Self	—
TM45	Attract	Normal	Status	—	100	15	Normal	—
TM46	Thief	Dark	Physical	40	100	10	Normal	•
TM49	Snatch	Dark	Status	—	—	10	DoM	—
TM52	Focus Blast	Fighting	Special	120	70	5	Normal	—
TM56	Fling	Dark	Physical	—	100	10	Normal	—
TM58	Endure	Normal	Status	—	—	10	Self	—
TM63	Embargo	Dark	Status	—	100	15	Normal	—
TM66	Payback	Dark	Physical	50	100	10	Normal	•
TM68	Giga Impact	Normal	Physical	150	90	5	Normal	•
TM71	Stone Edge	Rock	Physical	100	80	5	Normal	—
TM75	Swords Dance	Normal	Status	—	—	30	Self	—
TM78	Captivate	Normal	Status	—	100	20	2 foes	—
TM79	Dark Pulse	Dark	Special	80	100	15	Normal	—
TM80	Rock Slide	Rock	Physical	75	90	10	2 foes	—
TM81	X-Scissor	Bug	Physical	80	100	15	Normal	•
TM82	Sleep Talk	Normal	Status	—	—	10	DoM	—
TM83	Natural Gift	Normal	Physical	—	100	15	Normal	—
TM84	Poison Jab	Poison	Physical	80	100	20	Normal	•
TM87	Swagger	Normal	Status	—	90	15	Normal	—
TM90	Substitute	Normal	Status	—	—	10	Self	—
HM01	Cut	Normal	Physical	50	95	30	Normal	•
HM04	Strength	Normal	Physical	80	100	15	Normal	•
HM06	Rock Smash	Fighting	Physical	40	100	15	Normal	•
HM08	Rock Climb	Normal	Physical	90	85	20	Normal	•

ABILITY ● Anticipation ● Dry Skin

EGG GROUP Human-Like

STATS
HP ●●●
ATTACK ●●●●
DEFENSE ●●●
SP. ATTACK ●●●
SP. DEFENSE ●●●
SPEED ●●●

● LEVEL-UP AND LEARNED MOVES

Lv	Name	Type	Kind	Power	Acc	PP	Range	DA
Base	Astonish	Ghost	Physical	30	100	15	Normal	•
Base	Mud-Slap	Ground	Special	20	100	10	Normal	—
Base	Poison Sting	Poison	Physical	15	100	35	Normal	—
3	Mud-Slap	Ground	Special	20	100	10	Normal	—
8	Poison Sting	Poison	Physical	15	100	35	Normal	—
10	Taunt	Dark	Status	—	100	20	Normal	—
15	Pursuit	Dark	Physical	40	100	20	Normal	•
17	Faint Attack	Dark	Physical	60	—	20	Normal	•
22	Revenge	Fighting	Physical	60	100	10	Normal	•
24	Swagger	Normal	Status	—	90	15	Normal	—
29	Mud Bomb	Ground	Special	65	85	10	Normal	—
31	Sucker Punch	Dark	Physical	80	100	5	Normal	•
36	Nasty Plot	Dark	Status	—	—	20	Self	—
41	Poison Jab	Poison	Physical	80	100	20	Normal	•
49	Sludge Bomb	Poison	Special	90	100	10	Normal	—
54	Flatter	Dark	Status	—	100	15	Normal	—

● MOVES TAUGHT IN EXCHANGE FOR COLORED SHARDS

Name	Type	Kind	Power	Acc	PP	Range	DA
Mud-Slap	Ground	Special	20	100	10	Normal	—
Fury Cutter	Bug	Physical	10	95	20	Normal	•
Icy Wind	Ice	Special	55	95	15	2 foes	—
ThunderPunch	Electric	Physical	75	100	15	Normal	•
Ice Punch	Ice	Physical	75	100	15	Normal	•
Snore	Normal	Special	40	100	15	Normal	—
Spite	Ghost	Status	—	100	10	Normal	—
Helping Hand	Normal	Status	—	—	20	1 ally	—
Vacuum Wave	Fighting	Special	40	100	30	Normal	—
Gunk Shot	Poison	Physical	120	70	5	Normal	—
Bounce	Flying	Physical	85	85	5	Normal	•
Knock Off	Dark	Physical	20	100	20	Normal	•
Sucker Punch	Dark	Physical	80	100	5	Normal	•

● PRIMARY WAY TO FIND

TRAINER'S PARTY Trainer on B2F of Iron Island

WILD POKÉMON Pastoria Great Marsh (after getting the National Pokédex/varies by day)

COURSE OF STORY

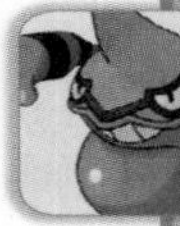

Carnivine

GRASS

HEIGHT: 4'07"
WEIGHT: 59.5 lbs.
GENDER: Male and Female
HELD ITEM: None

● M/F have same form

PLATINUM — It binds itself to trees in marshes. It attracts prey with its sweet-smelling drool and gulps them down.

EVOLUTION PATH

Does Not evolve

● TM & HM MOVES

No.	Name	Type	Kind	Power	Acc	PP	Range	DA
TM06	Toxic	Poison	Status	—	85	10	Normal	•
TM09	Bullet Seed	Grass	Physical	10	100	30	Normal	—
TM10	Hidden Power	Normal	Special	—	100	15	Normal	—
TM11	Sunny Day	Fire	Status	—	—	5	All	—
TM15	Hyper Beam	Normal	Special	150	90	5	Normal	—
TM17	Protect	Normal	Status	—	—	10	Self	—
TM19	Giga Drain	Grass	Special	60	100	10	Normal	—
TM21	Frustration	Normal	Physical	—	100	20	Normal	•
TM22	SolarBeam	Grass	Special	120	100	10	Normal	—
TM27	Return	Normal	Physical	—	100	20	Normal	•
TM32	Double Team	Normal	Status	—	—	15	Self	—
TM36	Sludge Bomb	Poison	Special	90	100	10	Normal	—
TM42	Facade	Normal	Physical	70	100	20	Normal	•
TM43	Secret Power	Normal	Physical	70	100	20	Normal	•
TM44	Rest	Psychic	Status	—	—	10	Self	—
TM45	Attract	Normal	Status	—	100	15	Normal	—
TM46	Thief	Dark	Physical	40	100	10	Normal	•
TM53	Energy Ball	Grass	Special	80	100	10	Normal	—
TM56	Fling	Dark	Physical	—	100	10	Normal	—
TM58	Endure	Normal	Status	—	—	10	Self	—
TM66	Payback	Dark	Physical	50	100	10	Normal	•
TM68	Giga Impact	Normal	Physical	150	90	5	Normal	•
TM70	Flash	Normal	Status	—	100	20	Normal	—
TM75	Swords Dance	Normal	Status	—	—	30	Self	—
TM78	Captivate	Normal	Status	—	100	20	2 foes	—
TM82	Sleep Talk	Normal	Status	—	—	10	DoM	—
TM83	Natural Gift	Normal	Physical	—	100	15	Normal	•
TM86	Grass Knot	Grass	Special	—	100	20	Normal	•
TM87	Swagger	Normal	Status	—	90	15	Normal	—
TM90	Substitute	Normal	Status	—	—	10	Self	—
HM01	Cut	Normal	Physical	50	95	30	Normal	•

● LEVEL-UP AND LEARNED MOVES

Lv	Name	Type	Kind	Power	Acc	PP	Range	DA
Base	Bind	Normal	Physical	15	75	20	Normal	•
Base	Growth	Normal	Status	—	—	40	Self	—
7	Bite	Dark	Physical	60	100	25	Normal	—
11	Vine Whip	Grass	Physical	35	100	15	Normal	—
17	Sweet Scent	Normal	Status	—	100	20	2 foes	—
21	Ingrain	Grass	Status	—	—	20	Self	—
27	Faint Attack	Dark	Physical	60	—	20	Normal	—
31	Stockpile	Normal	Status	—	—	20	Self	—
31	Spit Up	Normal	Special	—	100	10	Normal	—
31	Swallow	Normal	Status	—	—	10	Self	—
37	Crunch	Dark	Physical	80	100	15	Normal	—
41	Wring Out	Normal	Special	—	100	5	Normal	—
47	Power Whip	Grass	Physical	120	85	10	Normal	—

● MOVES TAUGHT IN EXCHANGE FOR COLORED SHARDS

Name	Type	Kind	Power	Acc	PP	Range	DA
Mud-Slap	Ground	Special	20	100	10	Normal	•
Fury Cutter	Bug	Physical	10	95	20	Normal	•
Gastro Acid	Poison	Status	—	100	10	Normal	—
Snore	Normal	Special	40	100	15	Normal	—
Synthesis	Grass	Status	—	—	5	Self	—
Seed Bomb	Grass	Physical	80	100	15	Normal	—
Knock Off	Dark	Physical	20	100	20	Normal	—

● EGG MOVES

Name	Type	Kind	Power	Acc	PP	Range	DA
Sleep Powder	Grass	Status	—	75	15	Normal	—
Stun Spore	Grass	Status	—	75	30	Normal	—
Razor Leaf	Grass	Physical	55	95	25	2 foes	—
Slam	Normal	Physical	80	75	20	Normal	—
Synthesis	Grass	Status	—	—	5	Self	—
Magical Leaf	Grass	Special	60	—	20	Normal	—
Leech Seed	Grass	Status	—	90	10	Normal	—
Worry Seed	Grass	Status	—	100	10	Normal	—

● PRIMARY WAY TO FIND

TRAINER'S PARTY — Trainer on Route 214

WILD POKÉMON — Pastoria Great Marsh (varies by day)

COURSE OF STORY

ABILITY ● Levitate

EGG GROUP — Grass

STATS
HP ●●
ATTACK ●●●
DEFENSE ●●●
SP. ATTACK ●●●
SP. DEFENSE ●●●
SPEED ●●

Remoraid

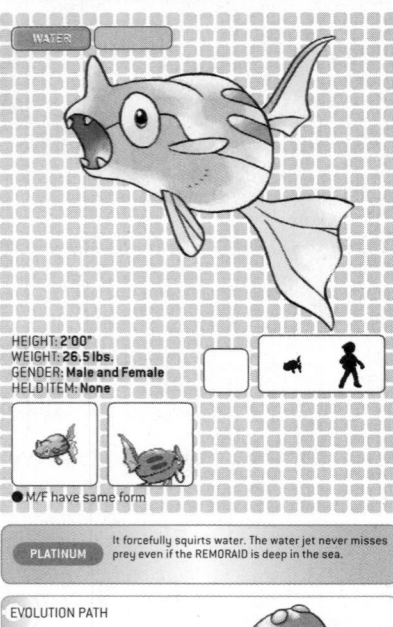

WATER

HEIGHT: 2'00"
WEIGHT: 26.5 lbs.
GENDER: Male and Female
HELD ITEM: None

● M/F have same form

PLATINUM — It forcefully squirts water. The water jet never misses prey even if the REMORAID is deep in the sea.

EVOLUTION PATH

Remoraid → Lv25 → Octillery

● TM & HM MOVES

No.	Name	Type	Kind	Power	Acc	PP	Range	DA
TM03	Water Pulse	Water	Special	60	100	20	Normal	—
TM06	Toxic	Poison	Status	—	85	10	Normal	—
TM09	Bullet Seed	Grass	Physical	10	100	30	Normal	—
TM10	Hidden Power	Normal	Special	—	100	15	Normal	—
TM11	Sunny Day	Fire	Status	—	—	5	All	—
TM13	Ice Beam	Ice	Special	95	100	10	Normal	—
TM14	Blizzard	Ice	Special	120	70	5	2 foes	—
TM15	Hyper Beam	Normal	Special	150	90	5	Normal	—
TM17	Protect	Normal	Status	—	—	10	Self	—
TM18	Rain Dance	Water	Status	—	—	5	All	—
TM21	Frustration	Normal	Physical	—	100	20	Normal	•
TM27	Return	Normal	Physical	—	100	20	Normal	•
TM29	Psychic	Psychic	Special	90	100	10	Normal	—
TM32	Double Team	Normal	Status	—	—	15	Self	—
TM35	Flamethrower	Fire	Special	95	100	15	Normal	—
TM38	Fire Blast	Fire	Special	120	85	5	Normal	—
TM42	Facade	Normal	Physical	70	100	20	Normal	•
TM43	Secret Power	Normal	Physical	70	100	20	Normal	•
TM44	Rest	Psychic	Status	—	—	10	Self	—
TM45	Attract	Normal	Status	—	100	15	Normal	—
TM46	Thief	Dark	Physical	40	100	10	Normal	•
TM55	Brine	Water	Special	65	100	10	Normal	—
TM57	Charge Beam	Electric	Special	50	90	10	Normal	—
TM58	Endure	Normal	Status	—	—	10	Self	—
TM73	Thunder Wave	Electric	Status	—	100	20	Normal	—
TM78	Captivate	Normal	Status	—	100	20	2 foes	—
TM82	Sleep Talk	Normal	Status	—	—	10	DoM	—
TM83	Natural Gift	Normal	Physical	—	100	15	Normal	•
TM87	Swagger	Normal	Status	—	90	15	Normal	—
TM90	Substitute	Normal	Status	—	—	10	Self	—
HM03	Surf	Water	Special	95	100	15	2 foes • 1 ally	—
HM07	Waterfall	Water	Physical	80	100	15	Normal	•

● LEVEL-UP AND LEARNED MOVES

Lv	Name	Type	Kind	Power	Acc	PP	Range	DA
Base	Water Gun	Water	Special	40	100	25	Normal	—
6	Lock-On	Normal	Status	—	—	5	Normal	—
10	Psybeam	Psychic	Special	65	100	20	Normal	—
14	Aurora Beam	Ice	Special	65	100	20	Normal	—
19	BubbleBeam	Water	Special	65	100	20	Normal	—
23	Focus Energy	Normal	Status	—	—	30	Self	—
27	Bullet Seed	Grass	Physical	10	100	30	Normal	—
32	Water Pulse	Water	Special	60	100	20	Normal	—
36	Signal Beam	Bug	Special	75	100	15	Normal	—
40	Ice Beam	Ice	Special	95	100	10	Normal	—
45	Hyper Beam	Normal	Special	150	90	5	Normal	—

● MOVES TAUGHT IN EXCHANGE FOR COLORED SHARDS

Name	Type	Kind	Power	Acc	PP	Range	DA
Dive	Water	Physical	80	100	10	Normal	—
Mud-Slap	Ground	Special	20	100	10	Normal	•
Icy Wind	Ice	Special	55	95	15	2 foes	—
Snore	Normal	Special	40	100	15	Normal	—
Signal Beam	Bug	Special	75	100	15	Normal	—
Gunk Shot	Poison	Physical	120	70	5	Normal	—
Seed Bomb	Grass	Physical	80	100	15	Normal	—
Bounce	Flying	Physical	85	85	5	Normal	—
Swift	Normal	Special	60	—	20	2 foes	—

● EGG MOVES

Name	Type	Kind	Power	Acc	PP	Range	DA
Aurora Beam	Ice	Special	65	100	20	Normal	—
Octazooka	Water	Special	65	85	10	Normal	—
Supersonic	Normal	Status	—	55	20	Normal	—
Haze	Ice	Status	—	—	30	All	—
Screech	Normal	Status	—	85	40	Normal	—
Thunder Wave	Electric	Status	—	100	20	Normal	—
Rock Blast	Rock	Physical	25	80	10	Normal	—
Snore	Normal	Special	40	100	15	Normal	—
Flail	Normal	Physical	—	100	15	Normal	—

● PRIMARY WAY TO FIND

TRAINER'S PARTY — Trainer on Route 213

WILD POKÉMON — Route 222 [Good Rod]

COURSE OF STORY

ABILITY ● Hustle ● Sniper

EGG GROUP — Water 1 / Water 2

STATS
HP ●●
ATTACK ●●
DEFENSE ●●
SP. ATTACK ●●
SP. DEFENSE ●●
SPEED ●●

Sinnoh Pokédex No. 133 Jet Pokémon

Octillery

WATER

● Male form   ● Female form

HEIGHT: 2'11"
WEIGHT: 62.8 lbs.
GENDER: Male and Female
HELD ITEM: None

PLATINUM It loves to lurk inside holes in rocks. It sometimes sprays ink on prey by sticking out only its mouth.

EVOLUTION PATH

Remoraid — Lv25 → Octillery

ABILITY ● Suction Cups ● Sniper

EGG GROUP Water 1 / Water 2

STATS
HP ●●
ATTACK ●●●
DEFENSE ●●●
SP.ATTACK ●●●●
SP.DEFENSE ●●●●
SPEED ●●

● TM & HM MOVES

No.	Name	Type	Kind	Power	Acc	PP	Range	DA
TM03	Water Pulse	Water	Special	60	100	20	Normal	
TM06	Toxic	Poison	Status	—	85	10	Normal	
TM09	Bullet Seed	Grass	Physical	10	100	30	Normal	
TM10	Hidden Power	Normal	Special	—	100	15	Normal	
TM11	Sunny Day	Fire	Status	—	—	5	All	
TM13	Ice Beam	Ice	Special	95	100	10	Normal	
TM14	Blizzard	Ice	Special	120	70	5	2 foes	
TM15	Hyper Beam	Normal	Special	150	90	5	Normal	
TM17	Protect	Normal	Status	—	—	10	Self	
TM18	Rain Dance	Water	Status	—	—	5	All	
TM21	Frustration	Normal	Physical	—	100	20	Normal	•
TM27	Return	Normal	Physical	—	100	20	Normal	•
TM29	Psychic	Psychic	Special	90	100	10	Normal	
TM32	Double Team	Normal	Status	—	—	15	Self	
TM35	Flamethrower	Fire	Special	95	100	15	Normal	
TM36	Sludge Bomb	Poison	Special	90	100	10	Normal	
TM38	Fire Blast	Fire	Special	120	85	5	Normal	
TM42	Facade	Normal	Physical	70	100	20	Normal	•
TM43	Secret Power	Normal	Physical	70	100	20	Normal	•
TM44	Rest	Psychic	Status	—	—	10	Self	
TM45	Attract	Normal	Status	—	100	15	Normal	
TM46	Thief	Dark	Physical	40	100	10	Normal	•
TM53	Energy Ball	Grass	Special	80	100	10	Normal	
TM55	Brine	Water	Special	65	100	10	Normal	
TM57	Charge Beam	Electric	Special	50	90	10	Normal	•
TM58	Endure	Normal	Status	—	—	10	Self	
TM66	Payback	Dark	Physical	50	100	10	Normal	•
TM68	Giga Impact	Normal	Physical	150	90	5	Normal	•
TM73	Thunder Wave	Electric	Status	—	100	20	Normal	
TM78	Captivate	Normal	Status	—	100	20	2 foes	
TM82	Sleep Talk	Normal	Status	—	—	10	DoM	
TM83	Natural Gift	Normal	Physical	—	100	15	Normal	
TM87	Swagger	Normal	Status	—	90	15	Normal	•
TM90	Substitute	Normal	Status	—	—	10	Self	
TM91	Flash Cannon	Steel	Special	80	100	10	Normal	
HM03	Surf	Water	Special	95	100	15	2 foes + 1 ally	
HM07	Waterfall	Water	Physical	80	100	15	Normal	•

● LEVEL-UP AND LEARNED MOVES

Lv	Name	Type	Kind	Power	Acc	PP	Range	DA
Base	Gunk Shot	Poison	Physical	120	70	5	Normal	—
Base	Rock Blast	Rock	Physical	25	80	10	Normal	—
Base	Water Gun	Water	Special	40	100	25	Normal	—
Base	Constrict	Normal	Physical	10	100	35	Normal	—
Base	Psybeam	Psychic	Special	65	100	20	Normal	—
Base	Aurora Beam	Ice	Special	65	100	20	Normal	—
6	Constrict	Normal	Physical	10	100	35	Normal	—
10	Psybeam	Psychic	Special	65	100	20	Normal	—
14	Aurora Beam	Ice	Special	65	100	20	Normal	—
19	BubbleBeam	Water	Special	65	100	20	Normal	—
23	Focus Energy	Normal	Status	—	—	30	Self	—
25	Octazooka	Water	Special	65	85	10	Normal	•
29	Bullet Seed	Grass	Physical	10	100	30	Normal	—
36	Wring Out	Normal	Special	—	100	5	Normal	•
42	Signal Beam	Bug	Special	75	100	15	Normal	—
48	Ice Beam	Ice	Special	95	100	10	Normal	—
55	Hyper Beam	Normal	Special	150	90	5	Normal	—

● MOVES TAUGHT IN EXCHANGE FOR COLORED SHARDS

Name	Type	Kind	Power	Acc	PP	Range	DA
Dive	Water	Physical	80	100	10	Normal	•
Mud-Slap	Ground	Special	20	100	10	Normal	—
Icy Wind	Ice	Special	55	95	15	2 foes	—
Snore	Normal	Special	40	100	15	Normal	—
Signal Beam	Bug	Special	75	100	15	Normal	—
Gunk Shot	Poison	Physical	120	70	5	Normal	—
Seed Bomb	Grass	Physical	80	100	15	Normal	•
Bounce	Flying	Physical	85	85	5	Normal	•
Swift	Normal	Special	60	—	20	2 foes	—

● PRIMARY WAY TO FIND

TRAINER'S PARTY Trainer on Route 220

WILD POKÉMON Route 223 (Good Rod)

COURSE OF STORY

Sinnoh Pokédex No. 134 Wing Fish Pokémon

Finneon

WATER

● Male form   ● Female form

HEIGHT: 1'04"
WEIGHT: 15.4 lbs.
GENDER: Male and Female
HELD ITEM: Rindo Berry

PLATINUM The line running down its side can store sunlight. It shines vividly at night.

EVOLUTION PATH

Finneon — Lv31 → Lumineon

ABILITY ● Swift Swim ● Storm Drain

EGG GROUP Water 2

STATS
HP ●●
ATTACK ●●
DEFENSE ●●
SP.ATTACK ●●●
SP.DEFENSE ●●
SPEED ●●

● TM & HM MOVES

No.	Name	Type	Kind	Power	Acc	PP	Range	DA
TM03	Water Pulse	Water	Special	60	100	20	Normal	•
TM06	Toxic	Poison	Status	—	85	10	Normal	—
TM07	Hail	Ice	Status	—	—	10	All	—
TM10	Hidden Power	Normal	Special	—	100	15	Normal	—
TM13	Ice Beam	Ice	Special	95	100	10	Normal	—
TM14	Blizzard	Ice	Special	120	70	5	2 foes	—
TM17	Protect	Normal	Status	—	—	10	Self	—
TM18	Rain Dance	Water	Status	—	—	5	All	—
TM20	Safeguard	Normal	Status	—	—	25	2 allies	—
TM21	Frustration	Normal	Physical	—	100	20	Normal	•
TM27	Return	Normal	Physical	—	100	20	Normal	•
TM32	Double Team	Normal	Status	—	—	15	Self	—
TM42	Facade	Normal	Physical	70	100	20	Normal	•
TM43	Secret Power	Normal	Physical	70	100	20	Normal	•
TM44	Rest	Psychic	Status	—	—	10	Self	—
TM45	Attract	Normal	Status	—	100	15	Normal	—
TM55	Brine	Water	Special	65	100	10	Normal	—
TM58	Endure	Normal	Status	—	—	10	Self	—
TM62	Silver Wind	Bug	Special	60	100	5	Normal	—
TM66	Payback	Dark	Physical	50	100	10	Normal	•
TM70	Flash	Normal	Status	—	100	20	Normal	—
TM77	Psych Up	Normal	Status	—	—	10	Normal	—
TM78	Captivate	Normal	Status	—	100	20	2 foes	—
TM82	Sleep Talk	Normal	Status	—	—	10	DoM	—
TM83	Natural Gift	Normal	Physical	—	100	15	Normal	—
TM87	Swagger	Normal	Status	—	90	15	Normal	•
TM89	U-turn	Bug	Physical	70	100	20	Normal	•
TM90	Substitute	Normal	Status	—	—	10	Self	—
HM03	Surf	Water	Special	95	100	15	2 foes + 1 ally	•
HM05	Defog	Flying	Status	—	—	15	Normal	•
HM07	Waterfall	Water	Physical	80	100	15	Normal	•

● LEVEL-UP AND LEARNED MOVES

Lv	Name	Type	Kind	Power	Acc	PP	Range	DA
Base	Pound	Normal	Physical	40	100	35	Normal	•
6	Water Gun	Water	Special	40	100	25	Normal	—
10	Attract	Normal	Status	—	100	15	Normal	—
13	Rain Dance	Water	Status	—	—	5	All	—
17	Gust	Flying	Special	40	100	35	Normal	—
22	Water Pulse	Water	Special	60	100	20	Normal	•
26	Captivate	Normal	Status	—	100	20	2 foes	—
29	Safeguard	Normal	Status	—	—	25	2 allies	—
33	Aqua Ring	Water	Status	—	—	20	Self	—
38	Whirlpool	Water	Special	15	70	15	Normal	—
42	U-turn	Bug	Physical	70	100	20	Normal	•
45	Bounce	Flying	Physical	85	85	5	Normal	•
49	Silver Wind	Bug	Special	60	100	5	Normal	—

● MOVES TAUGHT IN EXCHANGE FOR COLORED SHARDS

Name	Type	Kind	Power	Acc	PP	Range	DA
Dive	Water	Physical	80	100	10	Normal	•
Icy Wind	Ice	Special	55	95	15	2 foes	—
Aqua Tail	Water	Physical	90	90	10	Normal	•
Ominous Wind	Ghost	Special	60	100	5	Normal	—
Snore	Normal	Special	40	100	15	Normal	—
Air Cutter	Flying	Special	55	95	25	2 foes	—
Twister	Dragon	Special	40	100	20	2 foes	•
Bounce	Flying	Physical	85	85	5	Normal	•
Swift	Normal	Special	60	—	20	2 foes	—

● EGG MOVES

Name	Type	Kind	Power	Acc	PP	Range	DA
Sweet Kiss	Normal	Status	—	75	10	Normal	—
Charm	Normal	Status	—	100	20	Normal	—
Flail	Normal	Physical	—	100	15	Normal	•
Aqua Tail	Water	Physical	90	90	10	Normal	•
Splash	Normal	Status	—	—	40	Self	—
Psybeam	Psychic	Special	65	100	20	Normal	—
Tickle	Normal	Status	—	100	20	Normal	—
Agility	Psychic	Status	—	—	30	Self	—

● PRIMARY WAY TO FIND

TRAINER'S PARTY Trainer on Route 220

WILD POKÉMON Route 218 (Good Rod)

COURSE OF STORY

Sinnoh Pokédex No. 135 Neon Pokémon

Lumineon

WATER

● TM & HM MOVES

No.	Name	Type	Kind	Power	Acc	PP	Range	DA
TM03	Water Pulse	Water	Special	60	100	20	Normal	—
TM06	Toxic	Poison	Status	—	85	10	Normal	—
TM07	Hail	Ice	Status	—	—	10	All	—
TM10	Hidden Power	Normal	Special	—	100	15	Normal	—
TM13	Ice Beam	Ice	Special	95	100	10	Normal	—
TM14	Blizzard	Ice	Special	120	70	5	2 foes	—
TM15	Hyper Beam	Normal	Special	150	90	5	Normal	—
TM17	Protect	Normal	Status	—	—	10	Self	—
TM18	Rain Dance	Water	Status	—	—	5	All	—
TM20	Safeguard	Normal	Status	—	—	25	2 allies	—
TM21	Frustration	Normal	Physical	—	100	20	Normal	•
TM27	Return	Normal	Physical	—	100	20	Normal	•
TM32	Double Team	Normal	Status	—	—	15	Self	—
TM42	Facade	Normal	Physical	70	100	20	Normal	•
TM43	Secret Power	Normal	Physical	70	100	20	Normal	•
TM44	Rest	Psychic	Status	—	—	10	Self	—
TM45	Attract	Normal	Status	—	100	15	Normal	—
TM55	Brine	Water	Special	65	100	10	Normal	—
TM58	Endure	Normal	Status	—	—	10	Self	—
TM62	Silver Wind	Bug	Special	60	100	5	Normal	•
TM66	Payback	Dark	Physical	50	100	10	Normal	•
TM68	Giga Impact	Normal	Physical	150	90	5	Normal	•
TM70	Flash	Normal	Status	—	100	20	Normal	—
TM77	Psych Up	Normal	Status	—	—	10	Normal	—
TM78	Captivate	Normal	Status	—	100	20	2 foes	—
TM82	Sleep Talk	Normal	Status	—	—	10	DoM	—
TM83	Natural Gift	Normal	Physical	—	100	15	Normal	•
TM87	Swagger	Normal	Status	—	90	15	Normal	—
TM89	U-turn	Bug	Physical	70	100	20	Normal	•
TM90	Substitute	Normal	Status	—	—	10	Self	—
HM03	Surf	Water	Special	95	100	15	2 foes • 1 ally	—
HM05	Defog	Flying	Status	—	—	15	All	—
HM07	Waterfall	Water	Physical	80	100	15	Normal	•

● LEVEL-UP AND LEARNED MOVES

Lv	Name	Type	Kind	Power	Acc	PP	Range	DA
Base	Pound	Normal	Physical	40	100	35	Normal	•
Base	Water Gun	Water	Special	40	100	25	Normal	—
Base	Attract	Normal	Status	—	100	15	Normal	—
6	Water Gun	Water	Special	40	100	25	Normal	—
10	Attract	Normal	Status	—	100	15	Normal	—
13	Rain Dance	Water	Status	—	—	5	All	—
17	Gust	Flying	Special	40	100	35	Normal	—
22	Water Pulse	Water	Special	60	100	20	Normal	—
26	Captivate	Normal	Status	—	100	20	2 foes	—
29	Safeguard	Normal	Status	—	—	25	2 allies	—
35	Aqua Ring	Water	Status	—	—	20	Self	—
42	Whirlpool	Water	Special	15	70	15	Normal	—
48	U-turn	Bug	Physical	70	100	20	Normal	•
53	Bounce	Flying	Physical	85	85	5	Normal	—
59	Silver Wind	Bug	Special	60	100	5	Normal	•

● MOVES TAUGHT IN EXCHANGE FOR COLORED SHARDS

Name	Type	Kind	Power	Acc	PP	Range	DA
Dive	Water	Physical	80	100	10	Normal	•
Icy Wind	Ice	Special	55	95	15	2 foes	—
Aqua Tail	Water	Physical	90	90	10	Normal	•
Ominous Wind	Ghost	Special	60	100	5	Normal	—
Snore	Normal	Special	40	100	15	Normal	—
Air Cutter	Flying	Special	55	95	25	2 foes	—
Twister	Dragon	Special	40	100	20	2 foes	—
Bounce	Flying	Physical	85	85	5	Normal	—
Swift	Normal	Special	60	—	20	2 foes	—

HEIGHT: 3'11"
WEIGHT: 52.9 lbs.
GENDER: Male and Female
HELD ITEM: Rindo Berry

● Male form.　● Female form.

PLATINUM: It crawls along the seafloor using its long front fins like legs. It competes for food with LANTURN.

EVOLUTION PATH

Finneon → Lv31 → Lumineon

ABILITY: ● Swift Swim ● Storm Drain
EGG GROUP: Water 2

STATS: HP ●● ATTACK ●● DEFENSE ●● SP. ATTACK ●● SP. DEFENSE ●● SPEED ●●●

● PRIMARY WAY TO FIND

TRAINER'S PARTY: Trainer on Route 223
WILD POKÉMON: Route 219 (Good Rod)
COURSE OF STORY:

Sinnoh Pokédex No. 136 Jellyfish Pokémon

Tentacool

WATER　POISON

● TM & HM MOVES

No.	Name	Type	Kind	Power	Acc	PP	Range	DA
TM03	Water Pulse	Water	Special	60	100	20	Normal	—
TM06	Toxic	Poison	Status	—	85	10	Normal	—
TM07	Hail	Ice	Status	—	—	10	All	—
TM10	Hidden Power	Normal	Special	—	100	15	Normal	—
TM13	Ice Beam	Ice	Special	95	100	10	Normal	—
TM14	Blizzard	Ice	Special	120	70	5	2 foes	—
TM17	Protect	Normal	Status	—	—	10	Self	—
TM18	Rain Dance	Water	Status	—	—	5	All	—
TM19	Giga Drain	Grass	Special	60	100	10	Normal	—
TM21	Frustration	Normal	Physical	—	100	20	Normal	•
TM27	Return	Normal	Physical	—	100	20	Normal	•
TM32	Double Team	Normal	Status	—	—	15	Self	—
TM36	Sludge Bomb	Poison	Special	90	100	10	Normal	—
TM42	Facade	Normal	Physical	70	100	20	Normal	•
TM43	Secret Power	Normal	Physical	70	100	20	Normal	•
TM44	Rest	Psychic	Status	—	—	10	Self	—
TM45	Attract	Normal	Status	—	100	15	Normal	—
TM46	Thief	Dark	Physical	40	100	10	Normal	—
TM55	Brine	Water	Special	65	100	10	Normal	—
TM58	Endure	Normal	Status	—	—	10	Self	—
TM66	Payback	Dark	Physical	50	100	10	Normal	•
TM75	Swords Dance	Normal	Status	—	—	30	Self	—
TM78	Captivate	Normal	Status	—	100	20	2 foes	—
TM82	Sleep Talk	Normal	Status	—	—	10	DoM	—
TM83	Natural Gift	Normal	Physical	—	100	15	Normal	•
TM84	Poison Jab	Poison	Physical	80	100	20	Normal	•
TM87	Swagger	Normal	Status	—	90	15	Normal	—
TM90	Substitute	Normal	Status	—	—	10	Self	—
HM01	Cut	Normal	Physical	50	95	30	Normal	—
HM03	Surf	Water	Special	95	100	15	2 foes • 1 ally	—
HM07	Waterfall	Water	Physical	80	100	15	Normal	•

● LEVEL-UP AND LEARNED MOVES

Lv	Name	Type	Kind	Power	Acc	PP	Range	DA
Base	Poison Sting	Poison	Physical	15	100	35	Normal	—
5	Supersonic	Normal	Status	—	55	20	Normal	—
8	Constrict	Normal	Physical	10	100	35	Normal	•
12	Acid	Poison	Special	40	100	30	2 foes	—
15	Toxic Spikes	Poison	Status	—	—	20	2 foes	—
19	BubbleBeam	Water	Special	65	100	20	Normal	—
22	Wrap	Normal	Physical	15	85	20	Normal	•
26	Barrier	Psychic	Status	—	—	30	Self	—
29	Water Pulse	Water	Special	60	100	20	Normal	—
33	Poison Jab	Poison	Physical	80	100	20	Normal	•
36	Screech	Normal	Status	—	85	40	Normal	—
40	Hydro Pump	Water	Special	120	80	5	Normal	—
43	Wring Out	Normal	Special	—	100	5	Normal	•

● MOVES TAUGHT IN EXCHANGE FOR COLORED SHARDS

Name	Type	Kind	Power	Acc	PP	Range	DA
Dive	Water	Physical	80	100	10	Normal	•
Icy Wind	Ice	Special	55	95	15	2 foes	—
Snore	Normal	Special	40	100	15	Normal	—
Knock Off	Dark	Physical	20	100	20	Normal	•

● EGG MOVES

Name	Type	Kind	Power	Acc	PP	Range	DA
Aurora Beam	Ice	Special	65	100	20	Normal	—
Mirror Coat	Psychic	Special	—	100	20	Self	—
Rapid Spin	Normal	Physical	20	100	40	Normal	—
Haze	Ice	Status	—	—	30	All	—
Safeguard	Normal	Status	—	—	25	2 allies	—
Confuse Ray	Ghost	Status	—	100	10	Normal	—
Knock Off	Dark	Physical	20	100	20	Normal	•
Acupressure	Normal	Status	—	—	30	1 ally	—

HEIGHT: 2'11"
WEIGHT: 100.3 lbs.
GENDER: Male and Female
HELD ITEM: Poison Sting

● M/F have same form

PLATINUM: Because its body is almost entirely composed of water, it shrivels up if it is washed ashore.

EVOLUTION PATH

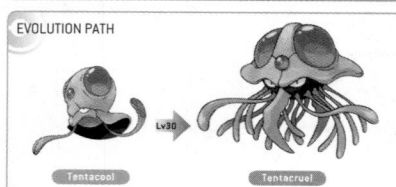

Tentacool → Lv30 → Tentacruel

ABILITY: ● Clear Body ● Liquid Ooze
EGG GROUP: Water 3

STATS: HP ●● ATTACK ●● DEFENSE ●● SP. ATTACK ●● SP. DEFENSE ●●● SPEED ●●●

● PRIMARY WAY TO FIND

TRAINER'S PARTY: Trainer on Route 220
WILD POKÉMON: Route 218 (water surface)
COURSE OF STORY:

Tentacruel

Sinnoh Pokédex No. 137 Jellyfish Pokémon

WATER | POISON

● TM & HM MOVES

No.	Name	Type	Kind	Power	Acc	PP	Range	DA
TM03	Water Pulse	Water	Special	60	100	20	Normal	—
TM06	Toxic	Poison	Status	—	85	10	Normal	—
TM07	Hail	Ice	Status	—	—	10	All	—
TM10	Hidden Power	Normal	Special	—	100	15	Normal	—
TM13	Ice Beam	Ice	Special	95	100	10	Normal	—
TM14	Blizzard	Ice	Special	120	70	5	2 foes	—
TM15	Hyper Beam	Normal	Special	150	90	5	Normal	—
TM17	Protect	Normal	Status	—	—	10	Self	—
TM18	Rain Dance	Water	Status	—	—	5	All	—
TM19	Giga Drain	Grass	Special	60	100	10	Normal	—
TM21	Frustration	Normal	Physical	—	100	20	Normal	•
TM27	Return	Normal	Physical	—	100	20	Normal	•
TM32	Double Team	Normal	Status	—	—	15	Self	—
TM36	Sludge Bomb	Poison	Special	90	100	10	Normal	—
TM42	Facade	Normal	Physical	70	100	20	Normal	•
TM43	Secret Power	Normal	Physical	70	100	20	Normal	•
TM44	Rest	Psychic	Status	—	—	10	Self	—
TM45	Attract	Normal	Status	—	100	15	Normal	—
TM46	Thief	Dark	Physical	40	100	10	Normal	•
TM55	Brine	Water	Special	65	100	10	Normal	—
TM58	Endure	Normal	Status	—	—	10	Self	—
TM66	Payback	Dark	Physical	50	100	10	Normal	•
TM68	Giga Impact	Normal	Physical	150	90	5	Normal	•
TM75	Swords Dance	Normal	Status	—	—	30	Self	—
TM78	Captivate	Normal	Status	—	100	20	2 foes	—
TM82	Sleep Talk	Normal	Status	—	—	10	DoM	—
TM83	Natural Gift	Normal	Physical	—	100	15	Normal	—
TM84	Poison Jab	Poison	Physical	80	100	20	Normal	•
TM87	Swagger	Normal	Status	—	90	15	Normal	—
TM90	Substitute	Normal	Status	—	—	10	Self	—
HM01	Cut	Normal	Physical	50	95	30	Normal	•
HM03	Surf	Water	Special	95	100	15	2 foes • 1 ally	—
HM07	Waterfall	Water	Physical	80	100	15	Normal	•

● LEVEL-UP AND LEARNED MOVES

Lv	Name	Type	Kind	Power	Acc	PP	Range	DA
Base	Poison Sting	Poison	Physical	15	100	35	Normal	—
Base	Supersonic	Normal	Status	—	55	20	Normal	—
Base	Constrict	Normal	Physical	10	100	35	Normal	•
5	Supersonic	Normal	Status	—	55	20	Normal	—
8	Constrict	Normal	Physical	10	100	35	Normal	•
12	Acid	Poison	Special	40	100	30	2 foes	—
15	Toxic Spikes	Poison	Status	—	—	20	2 foes	—
19	BubbleBeam	Water	Special	65	100	20	Normal	—
22	Wrap	Normal	Physical	15	85	20	Normal	—
26	Barrier	Psychic	Status	—	—	30	Self	—
29	Water Pulse	Water	Special	60	100	20	Normal	—
35	Poison Jab	Poison	Physical	80	100	20	Normal	—
42	Screech	Normal	Status	—	85	40	Normal	—
49	Hydro Pump	Water	Special	120	80	5	Normal	—
55	Wring Out	Normal	Special	—	100	5	Normal	—

● MOVES TAUGHT IN EXCHANGE FOR COLORED SHARDS

Name	Type	Kind	Power	Acc	PP	Range	DA
Dive	Water	Physical	80	100	10	Normal	—
Icy Wind	Ice	Special	55	95	15	2 foes	—
Snore	Normal	Special	40	100	15	Normal	—
Knock Off	Dark	Physical	20	100	20	Normal	—

HEIGHT: 5'03"
WEIGHT: 121.3 lbs.
GENDER: Male and Female
HELD ITEM: Poison Sting

● M/F have same form

PLATINUM: It extends its 80 tentacles to form an encircling poisonous net that is difficult to escape.

EVOLUTION PATH

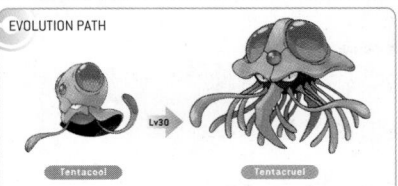

Tentacool — Lv30 — Tentacruel

ABILITY: ● Clear Body ● Liquid Ooze

EGG GROUP: Water 3

STATS:
HP ●●
ATTACK ●●●
DEFENSE ●●●
SP. ATTACK ●●●
SP. DEFENSE ●●●●
SPEED ●●●●

● PRIMARY WAY TO FIND

TRAINER'S PARTY: Trainer on Route 220

WILD POKÉMON: Route 218 (water surface)

COURSE OF STORY

Feebas

Sinnoh Pokédex No. 138 Fish Pokémon

WATER

● TM & HM MOVES

No.	Name	Type	Kind	Power	Acc	PP	Range	DA
TM03	Water Pulse	Water	Special	60	100	20	Normal	—
TM06	Toxic	Poison	Status	—	85	10	Normal	—
TM07	Hail	Ice	Status	—	—	10	All	—
TM10	Hidden Power	Normal	Special	—	100	15	Normal	—
TM13	Ice Beam	Ice	Special	95	100	10	Normal	—
TM14	Blizzard	Ice	Special	120	70	5	2 foes	—
TM17	Protect	Normal	Status	—	—	10	Self	—
TM18	Rain Dance	Water	Status	—	—	5	All	—
TM21	Frustration	Normal	Physical	—	100	20	Normal	•
TM27	Return	Normal	Physical	—	100	20	Normal	•
TM32	Double Team	Normal	Status	—	—	15	Self	—
TM42	Facade	Normal	Physical	70	100	20	Normal	•
TM43	Secret Power	Normal	Physical	70	100	20	Normal	•
TM44	Rest	Psychic	Status	—	—	10	Self	—
TM45	Attract	Normal	Status	—	100	15	Normal	—
TM58	Endure	Normal	Status	—	—	10	Self	—
TM78	Captivate	Normal	Status	—	100	20	2 foes	—
TM82	Sleep Talk	Normal	Status	—	—	10	DoM	—
TM83	Natural Gift	Normal	Physical	—	100	15	Normal	—
TM87	Swagger	Normal	Status	—	90	15	Normal	—
TM90	Substitute	Normal	Status	—	—	10	Self	—
HM03	Surf	Water	Special	95	100	15	2 foes • 1 ally	—
HM07	Waterfall	Water	Physical	80	100	15	Normal	•

● LEVEL-UP AND LEARNED MOVES

Lv	Name	Type	Kind	Power	Acc	PP	Range	DA
Base	Splash	Normal	Status	—	—	40	Self	—
15	Tackle	Normal	Physical	35	95	35	Normal	•
30	Flail	Normal	Physical	—	100	15	Normal	•

● MOVES TAUGHT IN EXCHANGE FOR COLORED SHARDS

Name	Type	Kind	Power	Acc	PP	Range	DA
Dive	Water	Physical	80	100	10	Normal	•
Icy Wind	Ice	Special	55	95	15	2 foes	—
Snore	Normal	Special	40	100	15	Normal	—
Swift	Normal	Special	60	—	20	2 foes	—

● EGG MOVES

Name	Type	Kind	Power	Acc	PP	Range	DA
Mirror Coat	Psychic	Special	—	100	20	Self	—
DragonBreath	Dragon	Special	60	100	20	Normal	—
Mud Sport	Ground	Status	—	—	15	All	—
Hypnosis	Psychic	Status	—	60	20	Normal	—
Light Screen	Psychic	Status	—	—	30	2 allies	—
Confuse Ray	Ghost	Status	—	100	10	Normal	—
Mist	Ice	Status	—	—	30	2 allies	—
Haze	Ice	Status	—	—	30	All	—
Tickle	Normal	Status	—	100	20	Normal	—

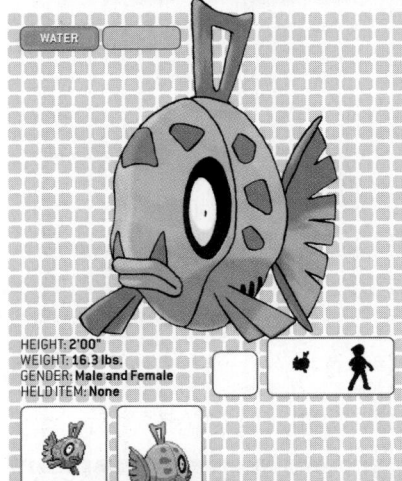

HEIGHT: 2'00"
WEIGHT: 16.3 lbs.
GENDER: Male and Female
HELD ITEM: None

● M/F have same form

PLATINUM: It is a shabby and ugly Pokémon. However, it is very hardy and can survive on little water.

EVOLUTION PATH

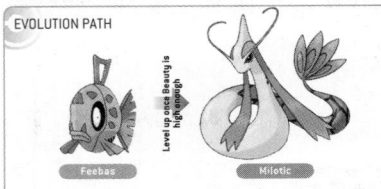

Feebas — Level up while Beauty is high enough — Milotic

ABILITY: ● Swift Swim

EGG GROUP: Water 1, Dragon

STATS:
HP ●
ATTACK ●
DEFENSE ●
SP. ATTACK ●
SP. DEFENSE ●
SPEED ●●●

● PRIMARY WAY TO FIND

TRAINER'S PARTY: Trainer on Route 222

WILD POKÉMON: Mt. Coronet (upper) B1F

COURSE OF STORY

Sinnoh Pokédex No. 139 Tender Pokémon
Milotic

WATER

● TM & HM MOVES

No.	Name	Type	Kind	Power	Acc	PP	Range	DA
TM03	Water Pulse	Water	Special	60	100	20	Normal	—
TM06	Toxic	Poison	Status	—	85	10	Normal	—
TM07	Hail	Ice	Status	—	—	10	All	—
TM10	Hidden Power	Normal	Special	—	100	15	Normal	—
TM13	Ice Beam	Ice	Special	95	100	10	Normal	—
TM14	Blizzard	Ice	Special	120	70	5	2 foes	—
TM15	Hyper Beam	Normal	Special	150	90	5	Normal	—
TM17	Protect	Normal	Status	—	—	10	Self	—
TM18	Rain Dance	Water	Status	—	—	5	All	—
TM20	Safeguard	Normal	Status	—	—	25	2 allies	—
TM21	Frustration	Normal	Physical	—	100	20	Normal	—
TM23	Iron Tail	Steel	Physical	100	75	15	Normal	•
TM27	Return	Normal	Physical	—	100	20	Normal	—
TM32	Double Team	Normal	Status	—	—	15	Self	—
TM42	Facade	Normal	Physical	70	100	20	Normal	—
TM43	Secret Power	Normal	Physical	70	100	20	Normal	•
TM44	Rest	Psychic	Status	—	—	10	Self	—
TM45	Attract	Normal	Status	—	100	15	Normal	—
TM58	Endure	Normal	Status	—	—	10	Self	—
TM59	Dragon Pulse	Dragon	Special	90	100	10	Normal	—
TM68	Giga Impact	Normal	Physical	150	90	5	Normal	•
TM72	Avalanche	Ice	Physical	60	100	10	Normal	—
TM77	Psych Up	Normal	Status	—	—	10	Normal	—
TM78	Captivate	Normal	Status	—	100	20	2 foes	—
TM82	Sleep Talk	Normal	Status	—	—	10	DoM	—
TM83	Natural Gift	Normal	Physical	—	100	15	Normal	—
TM87	Swagger	Normal	Status	—	90	15	Normal	—
TM90	Substitute	Normal	Status	—	—	10	Self	—
HM03	Surf	Water	Special	95	100	15	2 foes • 1 ally	—
HM07	Waterfall	Water	Physical	80	100	15	Normal	•

● LEVEL-UP AND LEARNED MOVES

Lv	Name	Type	Kind	Power	Acc	PP	Range	DA
Base	Water Gun	Water	Special	40	100	25	Normal	—
Base	Wrap	Normal	Physical	15	85	20	Normal	•
5	Water Sport	Water	Status	—	—	15	All	—
9	Refresh	Normal	Status	—	—	20	Self	—
13	Water Pulse	Water	Special	60	100	20	Normal	—
17	Twister	Dragon	Special	40	100	20	2 foes	—
21	Recover	Normal	Status	—	—	10	Self	—
25	Captivate	Normal	Status	—	100	20	2 foes	—
29	Aqua Tail	Water	Physical	90	90	10	Normal	—
33	Rain Dance	Water	Status	—	—	5	All	—
37	Hydro Pump	Water	Special	120	80	5	Normal	—
41	Attract	Normal	Status	—	100	15	Normal	—
45	Safeguard	Normal	Status	—	—	25	2 allies	—
49	Aqua Ring	Water	Status	—	—	20	Self	—

● MOVES TAUGHT IN EXCHANGE FOR COLORED SHARDS

Name	Type	Kind	Power	Acc	PP	Range	DA
Dive	Water	Physical	80	100	10	Normal	•
Mud-Slap	Ground	Special	20	100	10	Normal	—
Icy Wind	Ice	Special	55	95	15	2 foes	—
Iron Head	Steel	Physical	80	100	15	Normal	•
Aqua Tail	Water	Physical	90	90	10	Normal	—
Snore	Normal	Special	40	100	15	Normal	—
Twister	Dragon	Special	40	100	20	2 foes	—
Swift	Normal	Special	60	—	20	2 foes	—

HEIGHT: 20'04"
WEIGHT: 357.1 lbs.
GENDER: Male and Female
HELD ITEM: None

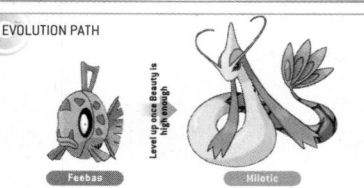

● Male form   ● Female form

PLATINUM — Its lovely scales are described as rainbow colored. They change color depending on the viewing angle.

EVOLUTION PATH

Level up once Beauty is high enough

Feebas → Milotic

ABILITY: ● Marvel Scale

EGG GROUP: Water 1 / Dragon

STATS:
HP ●●●
ATTACK ●●
DEFENSE ●●
SP.ATTACK ●●●
SP.DEFENSE ●●●●
SPEED ●●●

● PRIMARY WAY TO FIND

TRAINER'S PARTY — Pokémon League Champion Cynthia

WILD POKÉMON —

COURSE OF STORY —

Sinnoh Pokédex No. 140 Kite Pokémon
Mantyke

WATER   FLYING

● TM & HM MOVES

No.	Name	Type	Kind	Power	Acc	PP	Range	DA
TM03	Water Pulse	Water	Special	60	100	20	Normal	—
TM06	Toxic	Poison	Status	—	85	10	Normal	—
TM07	Hail	Ice	Status	—	—	10	All	—
TM10	Hidden Power	Normal	Special	—	100	15	Normal	—
TM13	Ice Beam	Ice	Special	95	100	10	Normal	—
TM14	Blizzard	Ice	Special	120	70	5	2 foes	—
TM17	Protect	Normal	Status	—	—	10	Self	—
TM18	Rain Dance	Water	Status	—	—	5	All	—
TM21	Frustration	Normal	Physical	—	100	20	Normal	—
TM26	Earthquake	Ground	Physical	100	100	10	2 foes • 1 ally	—
TM27	Return	Normal	Physical	—	100	20	Normal	—
TM32	Double Team	Normal	Status	—	—	15	Self	—
TM40	Aerial Ace	Flying	Physical	60	—	20	Normal	•
TM42	Facade	Normal	Physical	70	100	20	Normal	—
TM43	Secret Power	Normal	Physical	70	100	20	Normal	•
TM44	Rest	Psychic	Status	—	—	10	Self	—
TM45	Attract	Normal	Status	—	100	15	Normal	—
TM58	Endure	Normal	Status	—	—	10	Self	—
TM78	Captivate	Normal	Status	—	100	20	2 foes	—
TM82	Sleep Talk	Normal	Status	—	—	10	DoM	—
TM83	Natural Gift	Normal	Physical	—	100	15	Normal	—
TM87	Swagger	Normal	Status	—	90	15	Normal	—
TM90	Substitute	Normal	Status	—	—	10	Self	—
HM03	Surf	Water	Special	95	100	15	2 foes • 1 ally	—
HM07	Waterfall	Water	Physical	80	100	15	Normal	•

● LEVEL-UP AND LEARNED MOVES

Lv	Name	Type	Kind	Power	Acc	PP	Range	DA
Base	Tackle	Normal	Physical	35	95	35	Normal	•
Base	Bubble	Water	Special	20	100	30	2 foes	—
4	Supersonic	Normal	Status	—	55	20	Normal	—
10	BubbleBeam	Water	Special	65	100	20	Normal	—
13	Headbutt	Normal	Physical	70	100	15	Normal	•
19	Agility	Psychic	Status	—	—	30	Self	—
22	Wing Attack	Flying	Physical	60	100	20	Normal	—
28	Water Pulse	Water	Special	60	100	20	Normal	—
31	Take Down	Normal	Physical	90	85	20	Normal	—
37	Confuse Ray	Ghost	Status	—	100	10	Normal	—
40	Bounce	Flying	Physical	85	85	5	Normal	•
46	Aqua Ring	Water	Status	—	—	20	Self	—
49	Hydro Pump	Water	Special	120	80	5	Normal	—

● MOVES TAUGHT IN EXCHANGE FOR COLORED SHARDS

Name	Type	Kind	Power	Acc	PP	Range	DA
Dive	Water	Physical	80	100	10	Normal	•
Mud-Slap	Ground	Special	20	100	10	Normal	—
Icy Wind	Ice	Special	55	95	15	2 foes	—
Snore	Normal	Special	40	100	15	Normal	—
Air Cutter	Flying	Special	55	95	25	2 foes	—
Helping Hand	Normal	Status	—	—	20	1 ally	—
Bounce	Flying	Physical	85	85	5	Normal	•
Swift	Normal	Special	60	—	20	2 foes	—

● EGG MOVES

Name	Type	Kind	Power	Acc	PP	Range	DA
Twister	Dragon	Special	40	100	20	2 foes	—
Hydro Pump	Water	Special	120	80	5	Normal	—
Haze	Ice	Status	—	—	30	All	—
Slam	Normal	Physical	80	75	20	Normal	•
Mud Sport	Ground	Status	—	—	15	All	—
Rock Slide	Rock	Physical	75	90	10	2 foes	—
Mirror Coat	Psychic	Special	—	100	20	Self	—
Water Sport	Water	Status	—	—	15	All	—
Splash	Normal	Status	—	—	40	Self	—
Signal Beam	Bug	Special	75	100	15	Normal	—

HEIGHT: 3'03"
WEIGHT: 143.3 lbs.
GENDER: Male and Female
HELD ITEM: None

● M/F have same form

PLATINUM — People organize tours to see this Pokémon frolic and skim the tops of waves with REMORAID.

EVOLUTION PATH

Level up with Remoraid in party

Mantyke → Mantine

ABILITY: ● Swift Swim   ● Water Absorb

EGG GROUP: No Eggs

STATS:
HP ●
ATTACK ●
DEFENSE ●●
SP.ATTACK ●●
SP.DEFENSE ●●●
SPEED ●●

● PRIMARY WAY TO FIND

TRAINER'S PARTY — Trainer on Route 218

WILD POKÉMON — Route 223 (water surface)

COURSE OF STORY —

139
MILOTIC

Mantine

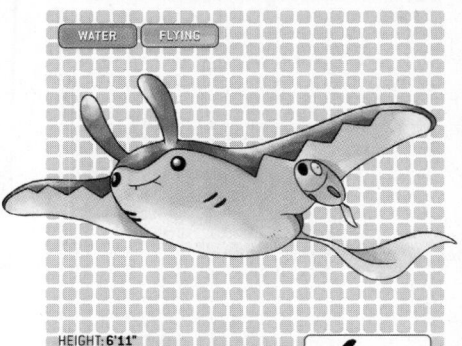

WATER | FLYING

HEIGHT: 6'11"
WEIGHT: 485.0 lbs.
GENDER: Male and Female
HELD ITEM: None

● M/F have same form

PLATINUM — While elegantly swimming in the sea, it ignores REMORAID that cling to its fins seeking food scraps.

EVOLUTION PATH

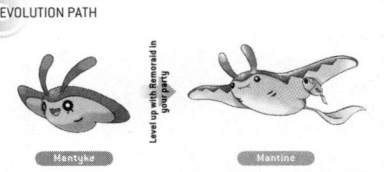

Mantyke → Level up with Remoraid in your party → Mantine

● TM & HM MOVES

No.	Name	Type	Kind	Power	Acc	PP	Range	DA
TM03	Water Pulse	Water	Special	60	100	20	Normal	—
TM06	Toxic	Poison	Status	—	85	10	Normal	—
TM07	Hail	Ice	Status	—	—	10	All	—
TM09	Bullet Seed	Grass	Physical	10	100	30	Normal	—
TM10	Hidden Power	Normal	Special	—	100	15	Normal	—
TM13	Ice Beam	Ice	Special	95	100	10	Normal	—
TM14	Blizzard	Ice	Special	120	70	5	2 foes	—
TM15	Hyper Beam	Normal	Special	150	90	5	Normal	—
TM17	Protect	Normal	Status	—	—	10	Self	—
TM18	Rain Dance	Water	Status	—	—	5	All	—
TM21	Frustration	Normal	Physical	—	100	20	Normal	•
TM26	Earthquake	Ground	Physical	100	100	10	2 foes • 1 ally	—
TM27	Return	Normal	Physical	—	100	20	Normal	•
TM32	Double Team	Normal	Status	—	—	15	Self	—
TM39	Rock Tomb	Rock	Physical	50	80	10	Normal	—
TM40	Aerial Ace	Flying	Physical	60	—	20	Normal	•
TM42	Facade	Normal	Physical	70	100	20	Normal	•
TM43	Secret Power	Normal	Physical	70	100	20	Normal	•
TM44	Rest	Psychic	Status	—	—	10	Self	—
TM45	Attract	Normal	Status	—	100	15	Normal	—
TM55	Brine	Water	Special	65	100	10	Normal	—
TM58	Endure	Normal	Status	—	—	10	Self	—
TM68	Giga Impact	Normal	Physical	150	90	5	Normal	•
TM78	Captivate	Normal	Status	—	100	20	2 foes	—
TM80	Rock Slide	Rock	Physical	75	90	10	2 foes	—
TM82	Sleep Talk	Normal	Status	—	—	10	DoM	—
TM83	Natural Gift	Normal	Physical	—	100	15	Normal	—
TM87	Swagger	Normal	Status	—	90	15	Normal	—
TM90	Substitute	Normal	Status	—	—	10	Self	—
HM03	Surf	Water	Special	95	100	15	2 foes • 1 ally	—
HM05	Defog	Flying	Status	—	—	15	Normal	—
HM07	Waterfall	Water	Physical	80	100	15	Normal	•

● LEVEL-UP AND LEARNED MOVES

Lv	Name	Type	Kind	Power	Acc	PP	Range	DA
Base	Psybeam	Psychic	Special	65	100	20	Normal	—
Base	Bullet Seed	Grass	Physical	10	100	30	Normal	—
Base	Signal Beam	Bug	Special	75	100	15	Normal	—
Base	Tackle	Normal	Physical	35	95	35	Normal	•
Base	Bubble	Water	Special	20	100	30	2 foes	—
Base	Supersonic	Normal	Status	—	55	20	Normal	—
Base	BubbleBeam	Water	Special	65	100	20	Normal	—
4	Supersonic	Normal	Status	—	55	20	Normal	—
10	BubbleBeam	Water	Special	65	100	20	Normal	—
13	Headbutt	Normal	Physical	70	100	15	Normal	•
19	Agility	Psychic	Status	—	—	30	Self	—
22	Wing Attack	Flying	Physical	60	100	35	Normal	•
28	Water Pulse	Water	Special	60	100	20	Normal	—
31	Take Down	Normal	Physical	90	85	20	Normal	•
37	Confuse Ray	Ghost	Status	—	100	10	Normal	—
40	Bounce	Flying	Physical	85	85	5	Normal	•
46	Aqua Ring	Water	Status	—	—	20	Self	—
49	Hydro Pump	Water	Special	120	80	5	Normal	—

● MOVES TAUGHT IN EXCHANGE FOR COLORED SHARDS

Name	Type	Kind	Power	Acc	PP	Range	DA
Dive	Water	Physical	80	100	10	Normal	•
Mud-Slap	Ground	Special	20	100	10	Normal	—
Icy Wind	Ice	Special	55	95	15	2 foes	—
Iron Head	Steel	Physical	80	100	15	Normal	•
Aqua Tail	Water	Physical	90	90	10	Normal	•
Snore	Normal	Special	40	100	15	Normal	—
Air Cutter	Flying	Special	55	95	25	2 foes	—
Helping Hand	Normal	Status	—	—	20	1 ally	—
Signal Beam	Bug	Special	75	100	15	Normal	—
Gunk Shot	Poison	Physical	120	70	5	Normal	•
Seed Bomb	Grass	Physical	80	100	15	Normal	—
Bounce	Flying	Physical	85	85	5	Normal	•
Swift	Normal	Special	60	—	20	2 foes	—

● EGG MOVES

Name	Type	Kind	Power	Acc	PP	Range	DA
Twister	Dragon	Special	40	100	20	2 foes	—
Hydro Pump	Water	Special	120	80	5	Normal	—
Haze	Ice	Status	—	—	30	All	—
Slam	Normal	Physical	80	75	20	Normal	•
Mud Sport	Ground	Status	—	—	15	All	—
Rock Slide	Rock	Physical	75	90	10	2 foes	—
Mirror Coat	Psychic	Special	—	100	20	Self	—
Water Sport	Water	Status	—	—	15	All	—
Splash	Normal	Status	—	—	40	Self	—

ABILITY — ● Swift Swim ● Water Absorb

EGG GROUP — Water 1

STATS
HP ●●
ATTACK ●●●
DEFENSE ●●
SP. ATTACK ●●●
SP. DEFENSE ●●●●
SPEED ●●●

● PRIMARY WAY TO FIND

TRAINER'S PARTY — Trainer on Route 223

WILD POKÉMON

COURSE OF STORY

Snover

GRASS | ICE

HEIGHT: 3'03"
WEIGHT: 111.3 lbs.
GENDER: Male and Female
HELD ITEM: NeverMeltIce

● Male form   ● Female form

PLATINUM — Seemingly curious about people, they gather around footsteps they find on snowy mountains.

EVOLUTION PATH

Snover → Lv40 → Abomasnow

● TM & HM MOVES

No.	Name	Type	Kind	Power	Acc	PP	Range	DA
TM03	Water Pulse	Water	Special	60	100	20	Normal	—
TM06	Toxic	Poison	Status	—	85	10	Normal	—
TM07	Hail	Ice	Status	—	—	10	All	—
TM09	Bullet Seed	Grass	Physical	10	100	30	Normal	—
TM10	Hidden Power	Normal	Special	—	100	15	Normal	—
TM13	Ice Beam	Ice	Special	95	100	10	Normal	—
TM14	Blizzard	Ice	Special	120	70	5	2 foes	—
TM16	Light Screen	Psychic	Status	—	—	30	2 allies	—
TM17	Protect	Normal	Status	—	—	10	Self	—
TM18	Rain Dance	Water	Status	—	—	5	All	—
TM19	Giga Drain	Grass	Special	60	100	10	Normal	—
TM20	Safeguard	Normal	Status	—	—	25	2 allies	—
TM21	Frustration	Normal	Physical	—	100	20	Normal	•
TM22	SolarBeam	Grass	Special	120	100	10	Normal	—
TM23	Iron Tail	Steel	Physical	100	75	15	Normal	•
TM27	Return	Normal	Physical	—	100	20	Normal	•
TM30	Shadow Ball	Ghost	Special	80	100	15	Normal	—
TM32	Double Team	Normal	Status	—	—	15	Self	—
TM42	Facade	Normal	Physical	70	100	20	Normal	•
TM43	Secret Power	Normal	Physical	70	100	20	Normal	•
TM44	Rest	Psychic	Status	—	—	10	Self	—
TM45	Attract	Normal	Status	—	100	15	Normal	—
TM53	Energy Ball	Grass	Special	80	100	10	Normal	—
TM58	Endure	Normal	Status	—	—	10	Self	—
TM70	Flash	Normal	Status	—	100	20	Normal	—
TM72	Avalanche	Ice	Physical	60	100	10	Normal	•
TM75	Swords Dance	Normal	Status	—	—	30	Self	—
TM78	Captivate	Normal	Status	—	100	20	2 foes	—
TM82	Sleep Talk	Normal	Status	—	—	10	DoM	—
TM83	Natural Gift	Normal	Physical	—	100	15	Normal	—
TM86	Grass Knot	Grass	Special	—	100	20	Normal	•
TM87	Swagger	Normal	Status	—	90	15	Normal	—
TM90	Substitute	Normal	Status	—	—	10	Self	—

● LEVEL-UP AND LEARNED MOVES

Lv	Name	Type	Kind	Power	Acc	PP	Range	DA
Base	Powder Snow	Ice	Special	40	100	25	2 foes	—
Base	Leer	Normal	Status	—	100	30	2 foes	—
5	Razor Leaf	Grass	Physical	55	95	25	2 foes	—
9	Icy Wind	Ice	Special	55	95	15	2 foes	—
13	GrassWhistle	Grass	Status	—	55	15	Normal	—
17	Swagger	Normal	Status	—	90	15	Normal	—
21	Mist	Ice	Status	—	—	30	2 allies	—
26	Ice Shard	Ice	Physical	40	100	30	Normal	—
31	Ingrain	Grass	Status	—	—	20	Self	—
36	Wood Hammer	Grass	Physical	120	100	15	Normal	•
41	Blizzard	Ice	Special	120	70	5	2 foes	—
46	Sheer Cold	Ice	Special	—	30	5	Normal	—

● MOVES TAUGHT IN EXCHANGE FOR COLORED SHARDS

Name	Type	Kind	Power	Acc	PP	Range	DA
Mud-Slap	Ground	Special	20	100	10	Normal	—
Icy Wind	Ice	Special	55	95	15	2 foes	—
Ice Punch	Ice	Physical	75	100	15	Normal	•
Snore	Normal	Special	40	100	15	Normal	—
Synthesis	Grass	Status	—	—	5	Self	—
Seed Bomb	Grass	Physical	80	100	15	Normal	—

● EGG MOVES

Name	Type	Kind	Power	Acc	PP	Range	DA
Leech Seed	Grass	Status	—	90	10	Normal	—
Magical Leaf	Grass	Special	60	—	20	Normal	—
Seed Bomb	Grass	Physical	80	100	15	Normal	—
Growth	Normal	Status	—	—	40	Self	—
Double-Edge	Normal	Physical	120	100	15	Normal	•
Mist	Ice	Status	—	—	30	2 allies	—
Stomp	Normal	Physical	65	100	20	Normal	•

ABILITY — ● Snow Warning

EGG GROUP — Monster / Grass

STATS
HP ●●
ATTACK ●●●
DEFENSE ●●
SP. ATTACK ●●●
SP. DEFENSE ●●●
SPEED ●●

● PRIMARY WAY TO FIND

TRAINER'S PARTY — Trainer on Route 217

WILD POKÉMON — Route 216

COURSE OF STORY

Sinnoh Pokédex **No. 143** Frost Tree Pokémon

Abomasnow

GRASS ICE

HEIGHT: 7'03"
WEIGHT: **298.7 lbs.**
GENDER: **Male and Female**
HELD ITEM: **NeverMeltIce**

● Male form ● Female form

PLATINUM They appear when the snow flowers bloom. When the petals fall, they retreat to places unknown again.

EVOLUTION PATH

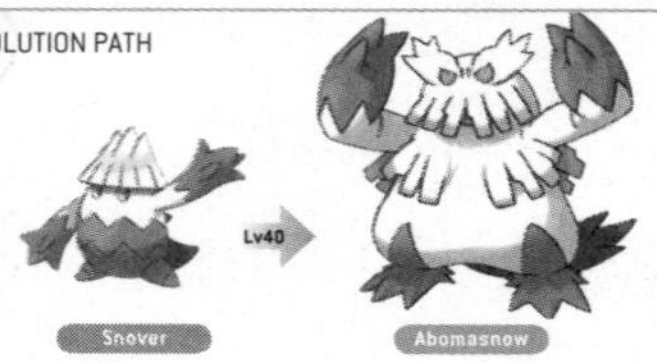
Lv40
Snover
Abomasnow

● TM & HM MOVES

No.	Name	Type	Kind	Power	Acc	PP	Range	DA
TM01	Focus Punch	Fighting	Physical	150	100	20	Normal	•
TM03	Water Pulse	Water	Special	60	100	20	Normal	—
TM06	Toxic	Poison	Status	—	85	10	Normal	—
TM07	Hail	Ice	Status	—	—	10	All	—
TM09	Bullet Seed	Grass	Physical	10	100	30	Normal	—
TM10	Hidden Power	Normal	Special	—	100	15	Normal	—
TM13	Ice Beam	Ice	Special	95	100	10	Normal	—
TM14	Blizzard	Ice	Special	120	70	5	2 foes	—
TM15	Hyper Beam	Normal	Special	150	90	5	Normal	—
TM16	Light Screen	Psychic	Status	—	—	30	2 allies	—
TM17	Protect	Normal	Status	—	—	10	Self	—
TM18	Rain Dance	Water	Status	—	—	5	All	—
TM19	Giga Drain	Grass	Special	60	100	10	Normal	—
TM20	Safeguard	Normal	Status	—	—	25	2 allies	—
TM21	Frustration	Normal	Physical	—	100	20	Normal	•
TM22	SolarBeam	Grass	Special	120	100	10	Normal	—
TM23	Iron Tail	Steel	Physical	100	75	15	Normal	•
TM26	Earthquake	Ground	Physical	100	100	10	2 foes • 1 ally	—
TM27	Return	Normal	Physical	—	100	20	Normal	•
TM30	Shadow Ball	Ghost	Special	80	100	15	Normal	—
TM31	Brick Break	Fighting	Physical	75	100	15	Normal	•
TM32	Double Team	Normal	Status	—	—	15	Self	—
TM39	Rock Tomb	Rock	Physical	50	80	10	Normal	—
TM42	Facade	Normal	Physical	70	100	20	Normal	•
TM43	Secret Power	Normal	Physical	70	100	20	Normal	—
TM44	Rest	Psychic	Status	—	—	10	Self	—
TM45	Attract	Normal	Status	—	100	15	Normal	—
TM52	Focus Blast	Fighting	Special	120	70	5	Normal	—
TM53	Energy Ball	Grass	Special	80	100	10	Normal	—
TM56	Fling	Dark	Physical	—	100	10	Normal	—
TM58	Endure	Normal	Status	—	—	10	Self	—
TM68	Giga Impact	Normal	Physical	150	90	5	Normal	•
TM70	Flash	Normal	Status	—	100	20	Normal	—
TM72	Avalanche	Ice	Physical	60	100	10	Normal	•
TM75	Swords Dance	Normal	Status	—	—	30	Self	—
TM78	Captivate	Normal	Status	—	100	20	2 foes	—
TM80	Rock Slide	Rock	Physical	75	90	10	2 foes	—
TM82	Sleep Talk	Normal	Status	—	—	10	DoM	—
TM83	Natural Gift	Normal	Physical	—	100	15	Normal	—
TM86	Grass Knot	Grass	Special	—	100	20	Normal	•
TM87	Swagger	Normal	Status	—	90	15	Normal	—
TM90	Substitute	Normal	Status	—	—	10	Self	—
HM04	Strength	Normal	Physical	80	100	15	Normal	•
HM06	Rock Smash	Fighting	Physical	40	100	15	Normal	•
HM08	Rock Climb	Normal	Physical	90	85	20	Normal	•

ABILITY ● Snow Warning

EGG GROUP Monster / Grass

STATS
HP ●●●
ATTACK ●●●
DEFENSE ●●
SP. ATTACK ●●●
SP. DEFENSE ●●
SPEED ●●

● LEVEL-UP AND LEARNED MOVES

Lv	Name	Type	Kind	Power	Acc	PP	Range	DA
Base	Ice Punch	Ice	Physical	75	100	15	Normal	•
Base	Powder Snow	Ice	Special	40	100	25	2 foes	—
Base	Leer	Normal	Status	—	100	30	2 foes	—
Base	Razor Leaf	Grass	Physical	55	95	25	2 foes	—
Base	Icy Wind	Ice	Special	55	95	15	2 foes	—
5	Razor Leaf	Grass	Physical	55	95	25	2 foes	—
9	Icy Wind	Ice	Special	55	95	15	2 foes	—
13	GrassWhistle	Grass	Status	—	55	15	Normal	—
17	Swagger	Normal	Status	—	90	15	Normal	—
21	Mist	Ice	Status	—	—	30	2 allies	—
26	Ice Shard	Ice	Physical	40	100	30	Normal	—
31	Ingrain	Grass	Status	—	—	20	Self	—
36	Wood Hammer	Grass	Physical	120	100	15	Normal	•
47	Blizzard	Ice	Special	120	70	5	2 foes	—
58	Sheer Cold	Ice	Special	—	30	5	Normal	—

● MOVES TAUGHT IN EXCHANGE FOR COLORED SHARDS

Name	Type	Kind	Power	Acc	PP	Range	DA
Mud-Slap	Ground	Special	20	100	10	Normal	—
Icy Wind	Ice	Special	55	95	15	2 foes	—
Ice Punch	Ice	Physical	75	100	15	Normal	•
Snore	Normal	Special	40	100	15	Normal	—
Outrage	Dragon	Physical	120	100	15	1 random	•
Synthesis	Grass	Status	—	—	5	Self	—
Seed Bomb	Grass	Physical	80	100	15	Normal	—

● PRIMARY WAY TO FIND

TRAINER'S PARTY Snowpoint Gym Leader Candice

WILD POKÉMON Mt. Coronet (middle) peak

COURSE OF STORY

Sinnoh Pokédex **No. 144** Sharp Claw Pokémon

Sneasel

DARK ICE

HEIGHT: 2'11"
WEIGHT: **61.7 lbs.**
GENDER: **Male and Female**
HELD ITEM: **Grip Claw/Quick Claw**

● Male form ● Female form

PLATINUM A smart and sneaky Pokémon. A pair may work together to steal eggs by having one lure the parents away.

EVOLUTION PATH

Level up between 8 PM and 4 AM while holding the Razor Claw
Sneasel
Weavile

● TM & HM MOVES

No.	Name	Type	Kind	Power	Acc	PP	Range	DA
TM01	Focus Punch	Fighting	Physical	150	100	20	Normal	•
TM04	Calm Mind	Psychic	Status	—	—	20	Self	—
TM06	Toxic	Poison	Status	—	85	10	Normal	—
TM07	Hail	Ice	Status	—	—	10	All	—
TM10	Hidden Power	Normal	Special	—	100	15	Normal	—
TM11	Sunny Day	Fire	Status	—	—	5	All	—
TM12	Taunt	Dark	Status	—	100	20	Normal	—
TM13	Ice Beam	Ice	Special	95	100	10	Normal	—
TM14	Blizzard	Ice	Special	120	70	5	2 foes	—
TM17	Protect	Normal	Status	—	—	10	Self	—
TM18	Rain Dance	Water	Status	—	—	5	All	—
TM21	Frustration	Normal	Physical	—	100	20	Normal	•
TM23	Iron Tail	Steel	Physical	100	75	15	Normal	•
TM27	Return	Normal	Physical	—	100	20	Normal	•
TM28	Dig	Ground	Physical	80	100	10	Normal	•
TM30	Shadow Ball	Ghost	Special	80	100	15	Normal	—
TM31	Brick Break	Fighting	Physical	75	100	15	Normal	•
TM32	Double Team	Normal	Status	—	—	15	Self	—
TM40	Aerial Ace	Flying	Physical	60	—	20	Normal	•
TM41	Torment	Dark	Status	—	100	15	Normal	—
TM42	Facade	Normal	Physical	70	100	20	Normal	•
TM43	Secret Power	Normal	Physical	70	100	20	Normal	—
TM44	Rest	Psychic	Status	—	—	10	Self	—
TM45	Attract	Normal	Status	—	100	15	Normal	—
TM46	Thief	Dark	Physical	40	100	10	Normal	•
TM49	Snatch	Dark	Status	—	—	10	DoM	—
TM54	False Swipe	Normal	Physical	40	100	40	Normal	•
TM56	Fling	Dark	Physical	—	100	10	Normal	—
TM58	Endure	Normal	Status	—	—	10	Self	—
TM63	Embargo	Dark	Status	—	100	15	Normal	—
TM65	Shadow Claw	Ghost	Physical	70	100	15	Normal	•
TM66	Payback	Dark	Physical	50	100	10	Normal	•
TM72	Avalanche	Ice	Physical	60	100	10	Normal	•
TM75	Swords Dance	Normal	Status	—	—	30	Self	—
TM77	Psych Up	Normal	Status	—	—	10	Normal	—
TM78	Captivate	Normal	Status	—	100	20	2 foes	—
TM79	Dark Pulse	Dark	Special	80	100	15	Normal	—
TM81	X-Scissor	Bug	Physical	80	100	15	Normal	•
TM82	Sleep Talk	Normal	Status	—	—	10	DoM	—
TM83	Natural Gift	Normal	Physical	—	100	15	Normal	—
TM84	Poison Jab	Poison	Physical	80	100	20	Normal	•
TM85	Dream Eater	Psychic	Special	100	100	15	Normal	—
TM87	Swagger	Normal	Status	—	90	15	Normal	—
TM90	Substitute	Normal	Status	—	—	10	Self	—
HM01	Cut	Normal	Physical	50	95	30	Normal	•
HM03	Surf	Water	Special	95	100	15	2 foes • 1 ally	—
HM04	Strength	Normal	Physical	80	100	15	Normal	•
HM06	Rock Smash	Fighting	Physical	40	100	15	Normal	•

ABILITY ● Inner Focus ● Keen Eye

EGG GROUP Field

STATS
HP ●●
ATTACK ●●●
DEFENSE ●
SP. ATTACK ●
SP. DEFENSE ●●
SPEED ●●●●

● LEVEL-UP AND LEARNED MOVES

Lv	Name	Type	Kind	Power	Acc	PP	Range	DA
Base	Scratch	Normal	Physical	40	100	35	Normal	•
Base	Leer	Normal	Status	—	100	30	2 foes	—
Base	Taunt	Dark	Status	—	100	20	Normal	—
8	Quick Attack	Normal	Physical	40	100	30	Normal	•
10	Screech	Normal	Status	—	85	40	Normal	—
14	Faint Attack	Dark	Physical	60	—	20	Normal	•
21	Fury Swipes	Normal	Physical	18	80	15	Normal	•
24	Agility	Psychic	Status	—	—	30	Self	—
28	Icy Wind	Ice	Special	55	95	15	2 foes	—
35	Slash	Normal	Physical	70	100	20	Normal	•
38	Beat Up	Dark	Physical	10	100	10	Normal	—
42	Metal Claw	Steel	Physical	50	95	35	Normal	•
49	Ice Shard	Ice	Physical	40	100	30	Normal	—

● MOVES TAUGHT IN EXCHANGE FOR COLORED SHARDS

Name	Type	Kind	Power	Acc	PP	Range	DA
Mud-Slap	Ground	Special	20	100	10	Normal	—
Fury Cutter	Bug	Physical	10	95	20	Normal	•
Icy Wind	Ice	Special	55	95	15	2 foes	—
Ice Punch	Ice	Physical	75	100	15	Normal	•
Snore	Normal	Special	40	100	15	Normal	—
Spite	Ghost	Status	—	100	10	Normal	—
Knock Off	Dark	Physical	20	100	20	Normal	•
Swift	Normal	Special	60	—	20	2 foes	—

● EGG MOVES

Name	Type	Kind	Power	Acc	PP	Range	DA
Counter	Fighting	Physical	—	100	20	Self	•
Spite	Ghost	Status	—	100	10	Normal	—
Foresight	Normal	Status	—	—	40	Normal	—
Reflect	Psychic	Status	—	—	20	2 allies	—
Bite	Dark	Physical	60	100	25	Normal	•
Crush Claw	Normal	Physical	75	95	10	Normal	•
Fake Out	Normal	Physical	40	100	10	Normal	•
Double Hit	Normal	Physical	35	90	10	Normal	•
Punishment	Dark	Physical	—	100	5	Normal	•
Pursuit	Dark	Physical	40	100	20	Normal	•
Ice Shard	Ice	Physical	40	100	30	Normal	—
Ice Punch	Ice	Physical	75	100	15	Normal	•

● PRIMARY WAY TO FIND

TRAINER'S PARTY Team Galactic Boss Cyrus, when you battle him in Celestic Town

WILD POKÉMON Route 216

COURSE OF STORY

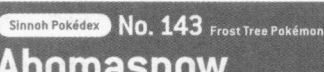

Sinnoh Pokédex No. 145 Sharp Claw Pokémon

Weavile

DARK | ICE

HEIGHT: 3'07"
WEIGHT: 75.0 lbs.
GENDER: Male and Female
HELD ITEM: None

● Male form ● Female form

PLATINUM Evolution made it even more devious. It communicates by clawing signs in boulders.

EVOLUTION PATH

Sneasel → Weavile
Level up between 8 PM and 4 AM while holding the Razor Claw

ABILITY ● Pressure

EGG GROUP: Field

STATS
HP ●●
ATTACK ●●●●
DEFENSE ●●●
SP. ATTACK ●●●
SP. DEFENSE ●●●
SPEED ●●●●

● TM & HM MOVES

No.	Name	Type	Kind	Power	Acc	PP	Range	DA
TM01	Focus Punch	Fighting	Physical	150	100	20	Normal	●
TM04	Calm Mind	Psychic	Status	—	—	20	Self	
TM06	Toxic	Poison	Status	—	85	10	Normal	
TM07	Hail	Ice	Status	—	—	10	All	
TM10	Hidden Power	Normal	Special	—	100	15	Normal	
TM11	Sunny Day	Fire	Status	—	—	5	All	
TM12	Taunt	Dark	Status	—	100	20	Normal	
TM13	Ice Beam	Ice	Special	95	100	10	Normal	
TM14	Blizzard	Ice	Special	120	70	5	2 foes	
TM15	Hyper Beam	Normal	Special	150	90	5	Normal	
TM17	Protect	Normal	Status	—	—	10	Self	
TM18	Rain Dance	Water	Status	—	—	5	All	
TM21	Frustration	Normal	Physical	—	100	20	Normal	●
TM23	Iron Tail	Steel	Physical	100	75	15	Normal	
TM27	Return	Normal	Physical	—	100	20	Normal	●
TM28	Dig	Ground	Physical	80	100	10	Normal	
TM30	Shadow Ball	Ghost	Special	80	100	15	Normal	
TM31	Brick Break	Fighting	Physical	75	100	15	Normal	
TM32	Double Team	Normal	Status	—	—	15	Self	
TM40	Aerial Ace	Flying	Physical	60	—	20	Normal	
TM41	Torment	Dark	Status	—	100	15	Normal	
TM42	Facade	Normal	Physical	70	100	20	Normal	
TM43	Secret Power	Normal	Physical	70	100	20	Normal	●
TM44	Rest	Psychic	Status	—	—	10	Self	
TM45	Attract	Normal	Status	—	100	15	Normal	
TM46	Thief	Dark	Physical	40	100	10	Normal	●
TM49	Snatch	Dark	Status	—	—	10	DoM	
TM52	Focus Blast	Fighting	Special	120	70	5	Normal	
TM54	False Swipe	Normal	Physical	40	100	40	Normal	
TM56	Fling	Dark	Physical	—	100	10	Normal	
TM58	Endure	Normal	Status	—	—	10	Self	
TM63	Embargo	Dark	Status	—	100	15	Normal	
TM65	Shadow Claw	Ghost	Physical	70	100	15	Normal	
TM66	Payback	Dark	Physical	50	100	10	Normal	
TM68	Giga Impact	Normal	Physical	150	90	5	Normal	
TM72	Avalanche	Ice	Physical	60	100	10	Normal	
TM75	Swords Dance	Normal	Status	—	—	30	Self	
TM77	Psych Up	Normal	Status	—	—	10	Normal	
TM78	Captivate	Normal	Status	—	100	20	2 foes	
TM79	Dark Pulse	Dark	Special	80	100	15	Normal	
TM81	X-Scissor	Bug	Physical	80	100	15	Normal	
TM82	Sleep Talk	Normal	Status	—	—	10	DoM	
TM83	Natural Gift	Normal	Physical	—	100	15	Normal	
TM84	Poison Jab	Poison	Physical	80	100	20	Normal	
TM85	Dream Eater	Psychic	Special	100	100	15	Normal	
TM87	Swagger	Normal	Status	—	90	15	Normal	
TM90	Substitute	Normal	Status	—	—	10	Self	
HM01	Cut	Normal	Physical	50	95	30	Normal	
HM03	Surf	Water	Special	95	100	15	2 foes • 1 ally	
HM04	Strength	Normal	Physical	80	100	15	Normal	
HM06	Rock Smash	Fighting	Physical	40	100	15	Normal	

● LEVEL-UP AND LEARNED MOVES

Lv	Name	Type	Kind	Power	Acc	PP	Range	DA
Base	Embargo	Dark	Status	—	100	15	Normal	
Base	Revenge	Fighting	Physical	60	100	10	Normal	
Base	Assurance	Dark	Physical	50	100	10	Normal	
Base	Scratch	Normal	Physical	40	100	35	Normal	
Base	Leer	Normal	Status	—	100	30	2 foes	
Base	Taunt	Dark	Status	—	100	20	Normal	
Base	Quick Attack	Normal	Physical	40	100	30	Normal	
8	Quick Attack	Normal	Physical	40	100	30	Normal	
10	Screech	Normal	Status	—	85	40	Normal	
14	Faint Attack	Dark	Physical	60	—	20	Normal	
21	Fury Swipes	Normal	Physical	18	80	15	Normal	
24	Nasty Plot	Dark	Status	—	—	20	Self	
28	Icy Wind	Ice	Special	55	95	15	2 foes	
35	Night Slash	Dark	Physical	70	100	15	Normal	
38	Fling	Dark	Physical	—	100	10	Normal	
42	Metal Claw	Steel	Physical	50	95	35	Normal	
49	Dark Pulse	Dark	Special	80	100	15	Normal	

● MOVES TAUGHT IN EXCHANGE FOR COLORED SHARDS

Name	Type	Kind	Power	Acc	PP	Range	DA
Mud-Slap	Ground	Special	20	100	10	Normal	—
Fury Cutter	Bug	Physical	10	95	20	Normal	
Icy Wind	Ice	Special	55	95	15	2 foes	
Ice Punch	Ice	Physical	75	100	15	Normal	
Snore	Normal	Special	40	100	15	Normal	
Spite	Ghost	Status	—	100	10	Normal	
Knock Off	Dark	Physical	20	100	20	Normal	
Swift	Normal	Special	60	—	20	2 foes	

● PRIMARY WAY TO FIND

TRAINER'S PARTY Team Galactic Boss Cyrus, when you battle him in the Distortion World

WILD POKÉMON

COURSE OF STORY

Sinnoh Pokédex No. 146 Knowledge Pokémon

Uxie

PSYCHIC

HEIGHT: 1'00"
WEIGHT: 0.7 lbs.
GENDER: Unknown
HELD ITEM: None

● Gender Unknown

PLATINUM When UXIE flew, people gained the ability to solve problems. It was the birth of knowledge.

EVOLUTION PATH

Does Not evolve

ABILITY ● Levitate

EGG GROUP: No Eggs

STATS
HP ●●
ATTACK ●●●
DEFENSE ●●●●
SP. ATTACK ●●●●
SP. DEFENSE ●●●●
SPEED ●●●

● TM & HM MOVES

No.	Name	Type	Kind	Power	Acc	PP	Range	DA
TM03	Water Pulse	Water	Special	60	100	20	Normal	
TM04	Calm Mind	Psychic	Status	—	—	20	Self	
TM06	Toxic	Poison	Status	—	85	10	Normal	
TM10	Hidden Power	Normal	Special	—	100	15	Normal	
TM11	Sunny Day	Fire	Status	—	—	5	All	
TM15	Hyper Beam	Normal	Special	150	90	5	Normal	
TM16	Light Screen	Psychic	Status	—	—	30	2 allies	
TM17	Protect	Normal	Status	—	—	10	Self	
TM18	Rain Dance	Water	Status	—	—	5	All	
TM19	Giga Drain	Grass	Special	60	100	10	Normal	
TM20	Safeguard	Normal	Status	—	—	25	2 allies	
TM21	Frustration	Normal	Physical	—	100	20	Normal	
TM22	SolarBeam	Grass	Special	120	100	10	Normal	
TM23	Iron Tail	Steel	Physical	100	75	15	Normal	
TM24	Thunderbolt	Electric	Special	95	100	15	Normal	
TM25	Thunder	Electric	Special	120	70	10	Normal	
TM27	Return	Normal	Physical	—	100	20	Normal	●
TM29	Psychic	Psychic	Special	90	100	10	Normal	
TM30	Shadow Ball	Ghost	Special	80	100	15	Normal	
TM32	Double Team	Normal	Status	—	—	15	Self	
TM33	Reflect	Psychic	Status	—	—	20	2 allies	
TM34	Shock Wave	Electric	Special	60	—	20	Normal	
TM37	Sandstorm	Rock	Status	—	—	10	All	
TM42	Facade	Normal	Physical	70	100	20	Normal	●
TM43	Secret Power	Normal	Physical	70	100	20	Normal	
TM44	Rest	Psychic	Status	—	—	10	Self	
TM48	Skill Swap	Psychic	Status	—	—	10	Normal	
TM53	Energy Ball	Grass	Special	80	100	10	Normal	
TM56	Fling	Dark	Physical	—	100	10	Normal	
TM57	Charge Beam	Electric	Special	50	90	10	Normal	
TM58	Endure	Normal	Status	—	—	10	Self	
TM67	Recycle	Normal	Status	—	—	10	Self	
TM68	Giga Impact	Normal	Physical	150	90	5	Normal	
TM70	Flash	Normal	Status	—	100	20	Normal	
TM73	Thunder Wave	Electric	Status	—	100	20	Normal	
TM76	Stealth Rock	Rock	Status	—	—	20	2 foes	
TM77	Psych Up	Normal	Status	—	—	10	Normal	
TM82	Sleep Talk	Normal	Status	—	—	10	DoM	
TM83	Natural Gift	Normal	Physical	—	100	15	Normal	
TM85	Dream Eater	Psychic	Special	100	100	15	Normal	
TM86	Grass Knot	Grass	Special	—	100	20	Normal	●
TM87	Swagger	Normal	Status	—	90	15	Normal	
TM89	U-turn	Bug	Physical	70	100	20	Normal	●
TM90	Substitute	Normal	Status	—	—	10	Self	
TM92	Trick Room	Psychic	Status	—	—	5	All	

● LEVEL-UP AND LEARNED MOVES

Lv	Name	Type	Kind	Power	Acc	PP	Range	DA
Base	Rest	Psychic	Status	—	—	10	Self	—
Base	Confusion	Psychic	Special	50	100	25	Normal	—
6	Imprison	Psychic	Status	—	—	10	Self	—
16	Endure	Normal	Status	—	—	10	Self	—
21	Swift	Normal	Special	60	—	20	2 foes	—
31	Yawn	Normal	Status	—	—	10	Normal	—
36	Future Sight	Psychic	Special	80	90	15	Normal	—
46	Amnesia	Psychic	Status	—	—	20	Self	—
51	Extrasensory	Psychic	Special	80	100	30	Normal	●
61	Flail	Normal	Physical	—	100	15	Normal	—
66	Natural Gift	Normal	Physical	—	100	15	Normal	—
76	Memento	Dark	Status	—	100	10	Normal	—

● MOVES TAUGHT IN EXCHANGE FOR COLORED SHARDS

Name	Type	Kind	Power	Acc	PP	Range	DA
Mud-Slap	Ground	Special	20	100	10	Normal	—
ThunderPunch	Electric	Physical	75	100	15	Normal	
Fire Punch	Fire	Physical	75	100	15	Normal	●
Ice Punch	Ice	Physical	75	100	15	Normal	●
Snore	Normal	Special	40	100	15	Normal	
Helping Hand	Normal	Status	—	—	20	1 ally	
Signal Beam	Bug	Special	75	100	15	Normal	
Zen Headbutt	Psychic	Physical	80	90	15	Normal	
Trick	Psychic	Status	—	100	10	Normal	
Knock Off	Dark	Physical	20	100	20	Normal	
Swift	Normal	Special	60	—	20	2 foes	

● PRIMARY WAY TO FIND

TRAINER'S PARTY

WILD POKÉMON

COURSE OF STORY Encounter at Lake Acuity (after visiting the Distortion World)

146 UXIE

Sinnoh Pokédex No. 147 Emotion Pokémon

Mesprit

PSYCHIC

HEIGHT: 1'00"
WEIGHT: 0.7 lbs.
GENDER: Unknown
HELD ITEM: None

● Gender Unknown

PLATINUM When MESPRIT flew, people learned the joy and sadness of living. It was the birth of emotions.

EVOLUTION PATH

Does Not evolve

● TM & HM MOVES

No.	Name	Type	Kind	Power	Acc	PP	Range	DA
TM03	Water Pulse	Water	Special	60	100	20	Normal	—
TM04	Calm Mind	Psychic	Status	—	—	20	Self	—
TM06	Toxic	Poison	Status	—	85	10	Normal	—
TM10	Hidden Power	Normal	Special	—	100	15	Normal	—
TM11	Sunny Day	Fire	Status	—	—	5	All	—
TM13	Ice Beam	Ice	Special	95	100	10	Normal	—
TM14	Blizzard	Ice	Special	120	70	5	2 foes	—
TM15	Hyper Beam	Normal	Special	150	90	5	Normal	—
TM16	Light Screen	Psychic	Status	—	—	30	2 allies	—
TM17	Protect	Normal	Status	—	—	10	Self	—
TM18	Rain Dance	Water	Status	—	—	5	All	—
TM20	Safeguard	Normal	Status	—	—	25	2 allies	—
TM21	Frustration	Normal	Physical	—	100	20	Normal	●
TM23	Iron Tail	Steel	Physical	100	75	15	Normal	●
TM24	Thunderbolt	Electric	Special	95	100	15	Normal	—
TM25	Thunder	Electric	Special	120	70	10	Normal	—
TM27	Return	Normal	Physical	—	100	20	Normal	●
TM29	Psychic	Psychic	Special	90	100	10	Normal	—
TM30	Shadow Ball	Ghost	Special	80	100	15	Normal	—
TM32	Double Team	Normal	Status	—	—	15	Self	—
TM33	Reflect	Psychic	Status	—	—	20	2 allies	—
TM34	Shock Wave	Electric	Special	60	—	20	Normal	—
TM37	Sandstorm	Rock	Status	—	—	10	All	—
TM42	Facade	Normal	Physical	70	100	20	Normal	●
TM43	Secret Power	Normal	Physical	70	100	20	Normal	●
TM44	Rest	Psychic	Status	—	—	10	Self	—
TM48	Skill Swap	Psychic	Status	—	—	10	Normal	—
TM53	Energy Ball	Grass	Special	80	100	10	Normal	—
TM56	Fling	Dark	Physical	—	100	10	Normal	●
TM57	Charge Beam	Electric	Special	50	90	10	Normal	—
TM58	Endure	Normal	Status	—	—	10	Self	—
TM67	Recycle	Normal	Status	—	—	10	Self	—
TM68	Giga Impact	Normal	Physical	150	90	5	Normal	●
TM70	Flash	Normal	Status	—	100	20	Normal	—
TM73	Thunder Wave	Electric	Status	—	100	20	Normal	—
TM76	Stealth Rock	Rock	Status	—	—	20	2 foes	—
TM77	Psych Up	Normal	Status	—	—	10	Normal	—
TM82	Sleep Talk	Normal	Status	—	—	10	DoM	—
TM83	Natural Gift	Normal	Physical	—	100	15	Normal	—
TM85	Dream Eater	Psychic	Special	100	100	15	Normal	—
TM86	Grass Knot	Grass	Special	—	100	20	Normal	●
TM87	Swagger	Normal	Status	—	90	15	Normal	—
TM89	U-turn	Bug	Physical	70	100	20	Normal	●
TM90	Substitute	Normal	Status	—	—	10	Self	—
TM92	Trick Room	Psychic	Status	—	—	5	All	—

● LEVEL-UP AND LEARNED MOVES

Lv	Name	Type	Kind	Power	Acc	PP	Range	DA
Base	Rest	Psychic	Status	—	—	10	Self	—
Base	Confusion	Psychic	Special	50	100	25	Normal	—
6	Imprison	Psychic	Status	—	—	10	Self	—
16	Protect	Normal	Status	—	—	10	Self	—
21	Swift	Normal	Special	60	—	20	2 foes	—
31	Lucky Chant	Normal	Status	—	—	30	2 allies	—
36	Future Sight	Psychic	Special	80	90	15	Normal	—
46	Charm	Normal	Status	—	100	20	Normal	—
51	Extrasensory	Psychic	Special	80	100	30	Normal	—
61	Copycat	Normal	Status	—	—	20	DoM	—
66	Natural Gift	Normal	Physical	—	100	15	Normal	—
76	Healing Wish	Psychic	Status	—	—	10	Self	—

● MOVES TAUGHT IN EXCHANGE FOR COLORED SHARDS

Name	Type	Kind	Power	Acc	PP	Range	DA
Mud-Slap	Ground	Special	20	100	10	Normal	●
ThunderPunch	Electric	Physical	75	100	15	Normal	●
Fire Punch	Fire	Physical	75	100	15	Normal	●
Ice Punch	Ice	Physical	75	100	15	Normal	●
Snore	Normal	Special	40	100	15	Normal	—
Helping Hand	Normal	Status	—	—	20	1 ally	—
Signal Beam	Bug	Special	75	100	15	Normal	—
Zen Headbutt	Psychic	Physical	80	90	15	Normal	●
Trick	Psychic	Status	—	100	10	Normal	—
Knock Off	Dark	Physical	20	100	20	Normal	●
Swift	Normal	Special	60	—	20	2 foes	—

ABILITY ● Levitate

EGG GROUP No Eggs

STATS
HP ●●
ATTACK ●●●●
DEFENSE ●●●●
SP. ATTACK ●●●●
SP. DEFENSE ●●●●
SPEED ●●●

● PRIMARY WAY TO FIND

TRAINER'S PARTY

WILD POKÉMON

COURSE OF STORY — Encounter at Lake Verity (after visiting the Distortion World)

Sinnoh Pokédex No. 148 Willpower Pokémon

Azelf

PSYCHIC

HEIGHT: 1'00"
WEIGHT: 0.7 lbs.
GENDER: Unknown
HELD ITEM: None

● Gender unknown

PLATINUM When AZELF flew, people gained the determination to do things. It was the birth of willpower.

EVOLUTION PATH

Does Not evolve

● TM & HM MOVES

No.	Name	Type	Kind	Power	Acc	PP	Range	DA
TM03	Water Pulse	Water	Special	60	100	20	Normal	—
TM04	Calm Mind	Psychic	Status	—	—	20	Self	—
TM06	Toxic	Poison	Status	—	85	10	Normal	—
TM10	Hidden Power	Normal	Special	—	100	15	Normal	—
TM11	Sunny Day	Fire	Status	—	—	5	All	—
TM12	Taunt	Dark	Status	—	100	20	Normal	—
TM15	Hyper Beam	Normal	Special	150	90	5	Normal	—
TM16	Light Screen	Psychic	Status	—	—	30	2 allies	—
TM17	Protect	Normal	Status	—	—	10	Self	—
TM18	Rain Dance	Water	Status	—	—	5	All	—
TM20	Safeguard	Normal	Status	—	—	25	2 allies	—
TM21	Frustration	Normal	Physical	—	100	20	Normal	●
TM23	Iron Tail	Steel	Physical	100	75	15	Normal	●
TM24	Thunderbolt	Electric	Special	95	100	15	Normal	—
TM25	Thunder	Electric	Special	120	70	10	Normal	—
TM27	Return	Normal	Physical	—	100	20	Normal	●
TM29	Psychic	Psychic	Special	90	100	10	Normal	—
TM30	Shadow Ball	Ghost	Special	80	100	15	Normal	—
TM32	Double Team	Normal	Status	—	—	15	Self	—
TM33	Reflect	Psychic	Status	—	—	20	2 allies	—
TM34	Shock Wave	Electric	Special	60	—	20	Normal	—
TM35	Flamethrower	Fire	Special	95	100	15	Normal	—
TM37	Sandstorm	Rock	Status	—	—	10	All	—
TM38	Fire Blast	Fire	Special	120	85	5	Normal	—
TM41	Torment	Dark	Status	—	100	15	Normal	—
TM42	Facade	Normal	Physical	70	100	20	Normal	●
TM43	Secret Power	Normal	Physical	70	100	20	Normal	●
TM44	Rest	Psychic	Status	—	—	10	Self	—
TM48	Skill Swap	Psychic	Status	—	—	10	Normal	—
TM53	Energy Ball	Grass	Special	80	100	10	Normal	—
TM56	Fling	Dark	Physical	—	100	10	Normal	●
TM57	Charge Beam	Electric	Special	50	90	10	Normal	—
TM58	Endure	Normal	Status	—	—	10	Self	—
TM64	Explosion	Normal	Physical	250	100	5	2 foes • 1 ally	●
TM66	Payback	Dark	Physical	50	100	10	Normal	●
TM67	Recycle	Normal	Status	—	—	10	Self	—
TM68	Giga Impact	Normal	Physical	150	90	5	Normal	●
TM70	Flash	Normal	Status	—	100	20	Normal	—
TM73	Thunder Wave	Electric	Status	—	100	20	Normal	—
TM76	Stealth Rock	Rock	Status	—	—	20	2 foes	—
TM77	Psych Up	Normal	Status	—	—	10	Normal	—
TM82	Sleep Talk	Normal	Status	—	—	10	DoM	—
TM83	Natural Gift	Normal	Physical	—	100	15	Normal	—
TM85	Dream Eater	Psychic	Special	100	100	15	Normal	—
TM86	Grass Knot	Grass	Special	—	100	20	Normal	●
TM87	Swagger	Normal	Status	—	90	15	Normal	—
TM89	U-turn	Bug	Physical	70	100	20	Normal	●
TM90	Substitute	Normal	Status	—	—	10	Self	—
TM92	Trick Room	Psychic	Status	—	—	5	All	—

● LEVEL-UP AND LEARNED MOVES

Lv	Name	Type	Kind	Power	Acc	PP	Range	DA
Base	Rest	Psychic	Status	—	—	10	Self	—
Base	Confusion	Psychic	Special	50	100	25	Normal	—
6	Imprison	Psychic	Status	—	—	10	Self	—
16	Detect	Fighting	Status	—	—	5	Self	—
21	Swift	Normal	Special	60	—	20	2 foes	—
31	Uproar	Normal	Special	50	100	10	1 random	—
36	Future Sight	Psychic	Special	80	90	15	Normal	—
46	Nasty Plot	Dark	Status	—	—	20	Self	—
51	Extrasensory	Psychic	Special	80	100	30	Normal	—
61	Last Resort	Normal	Physical	130	100	5	Normal	●
66	Natural Gift	Normal	Physical	—	100	15	Normal	—
76	Explosion	Normal	Physical	250	100	5	2 foes • 1 ally	●

● MOVES TAUGHT IN EXCHANGE FOR COLORED SHARDS

Name	Type	Kind	Power	Acc	PP	Range	DA
Mud-Slap	Ground	Special	20	100	10	Normal	●
ThunderPunch	Electric	Physical	75	100	15	Normal	●
Fire Punch	Fire	Physical	75	100	15	Normal	●
Ice Punch	Ice	Physical	75	100	15	Normal	●
Snore	Normal	Special	40	100	15	Normal	—
Helping Hand	Normal	Status	—	—	20	1 ally	—
Signal Beam	Bug	Special	75	100	15	Normal	—
Zen Headbutt	Psychic	Physical	80	90	15	Normal	●
Last Resort	Normal	Physical	130	100	5	Normal	●
Trick	Psychic	Status	—	100	10	Normal	—
Knock Off	Dark	Physical	20	100	20	Normal	●
Swift	Normal	Special	60	—	20	2 foes	—
Uproar	Normal	Special	50	100	10	1 random	—

ABILITY ● Levitate

EGG GROUP No Eggs

STATS
HP ●●●
ATTACK ●●●
DEFENSE ●●●
SP. ATTACK ●●●●
SP. DEFENSE ●●●
SPEED ●●●●

● PRIMARY WAY TO FIND

TRAINER'S PARTY

WILD POKÉMON

COURSE OF STORY — Encounter at Lake Valor (after visiting the Distortion World)

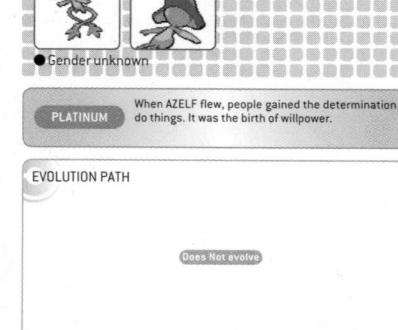

Sinnoh Pokédex **No. 149** Temporal Pokémon

Dialga

STEEL DRAGON

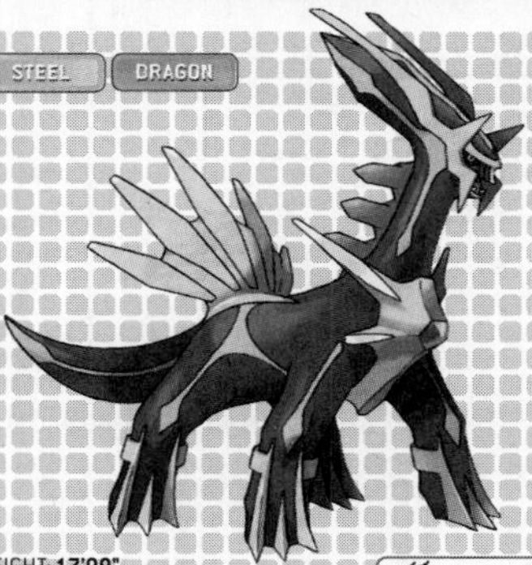

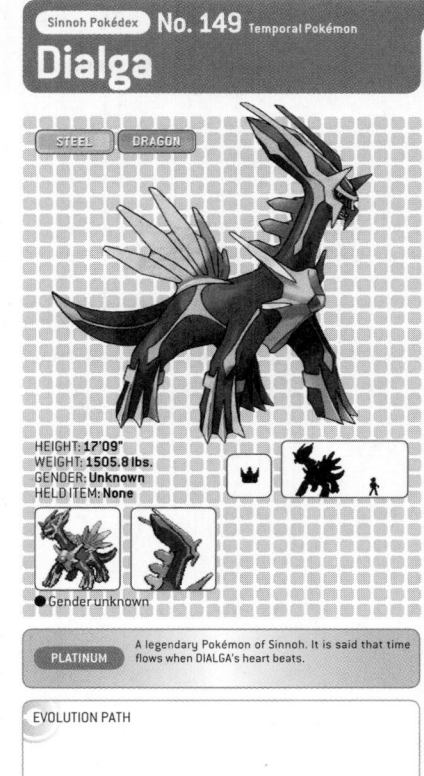

HEIGHT: **17'09"**
WEIGHT: **1505.8 lbs.**
GENDER: **Unknown**
HELD ITEM: **None**

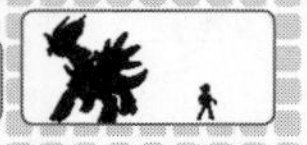

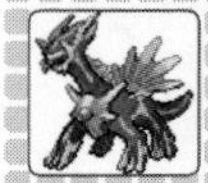

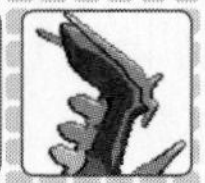

● Gender unknown

PLATINUM — A legendary Pokémon of Sinnoh. It is said that time flows when DIALGA's heart beats.

EVOLUTION PATH

Does Not evolve

● TM & HM MOVES

No.	Name	Type	Kind	Power	Acc	PP	Range	DA
TM02	Dragon Claw	Dragon	Physical	80	100	15	Normal	•
TM05	Roar	Normal	Status	—	100	20	Normal	—
TM06	Toxic	Poison	Status	—	85	10	Normal	—
TM08	Bulk Up	Fighting	Status	—	—	20	Self	—
TM10	Hidden Power	Normal	Special	—	100	15	Normal	—
TM11	Sunny Day	Fire	Status	—	—	5	All	—
TM13	Ice Beam	Ice	Special	95	100	10	Normal	—
TM14	Blizzard	Ice	Special	120	70	5	2 foes	—
TM15	Hyper Beam	Normal	Special	150	90	5	Normal	—
TM17	Protect	Normal	Status	—	—	10	Self	—
TM18	Rain Dance	Water	Status	—	—	5	All	—
TM20	Safeguard	Normal	Status	—	—	25	2 allies	—
TM21	Frustration	Normal	Physical	—	100	20	Normal	•
TM23	Iron Tail	Steel	Physical	100	75	15	Normal	•
TM24	Thunderbolt	Electric	Special	95	100	15	Normal	—
TM25	Thunder	Electric	Special	120	70	10	Normal	—
TM26	Earthquake	Ground	Physical	100	100	10	2 foes • 1 ally	—
TM27	Return	Normal	Physical	—	100	20	Normal	•
TM31	Brick Break	Fighting	Physical	75	100	15	Normal	•
TM32	Double Team	Normal	Status	—	—	15	Self	—
TM34	Shock Wave	Electric	Special	60	—	20	Normal	—
TM35	Flamethrower	Fire	Special	95	100	15	Normal	—
TM37	Sandstorm	Rock	Status	—	—	10	All	—
TM38	Fire Blast	Fire	Special	120	85	5	Normal	—
TM39	Rock Tomb	Rock	Physical	50	80	10	Normal	—
TM40	Aerial Ace	Flying	Physical	60	—	20	Normal	•
TM42	Facade	Normal	Physical	70	100	20	Normal	•
TM43	Secret Power	Normal	Physical	70	100	20	Normal	—
TM44	Rest	Psychic	Status	—	—	10	Self	—
TM50	Overheat	Fire	Special	140	90	5	Normal	—
TM58	Endure	Normal	Status	—	—	10	Self	—
TM59	Dragon Pulse	Dragon	Special	90	100	10	Normal	—
TM65	Shadow Claw	Ghost	Physical	70	100	15	Normal	•
TM68	Giga Impact	Normal	Physical	150	90	5	Normal	•
TM70	Flash	Normal	Status	—	100	20	Normal	—
TM71	Stone Edge	Rock	Physical	100	80	5	Normal	—
TM73	Thunder Wave	Electric	Status	—	100	20	Normal	—
TM76	Stealth Rock	Rock	Status	—	—	20	2 foes	—
TM77	Psych Up	Normal	Status	—	—	10	Normal	—
TM80	Rock Slide	Rock	Physical	75	90	10	2 foes	—
TM82	Sleep Talk	Normal	Status	—	—	10	DoM	—
TM83	Natural Gift	Normal	Physical	—	100	15	Normal	—
TM87	Swagger	Normal	Status	—	90	15	Normal	—
TM90	Substitute	Normal	Status	—	—	10	Self	—
TM91	Flash Cannon	Steel	Special	80	100	10	Normal	—
TM92	Trick Room	Psychic	Status	—	—	5	All	—
HM01	Cut	Normal	Physical	50	95	30	Normal	•
HM04	Strength	Normal	Physical	80	100	15	Normal	•
HM06	Rock Smash	Fighting	Physical	40	100	15	Normal	•

ABILITY ● Pressure

EGG GROUP No Eggs

STATS
HP ●●●
ATTACK ●●●●
DEFENSE ●●●
SP. ATTACK ●●●●●
SP. DEFENSE ●●●
SPEED ●●●

● LEVEL-UP AND LEARNED MOVES

Lv	Name	Type	Kind	Power	Acc	PP	Range	DA
Base	DragonBreath	Dragon	Special	60	100	20	Normal	—
Base	Scary Face	Normal	Status	—	90	10	Normal	—
10	Metal Claw	Steel	Physical	50	95	35	Normal	•
20	AncientPower	Rock	Special	60	100	5	Normal	—
30	Dragon Claw	Dragon	Physical	80	100	15	Normal	•
40	Roar of Time	Dragon	Special	150	90	5	Normal	—
50	Heal Block	Psychic	Status	—	100	15	2 foes	—
60	Earth Power	Ground	Special	90	100	10	Normal	—
70	Slash	Normal	Physical	70	100	20	Normal	•
80	Flash Cannon	Steel	Special	80	100	10	Normal	—
90	Aura Sphere	Fighting	Special	90	—	20	Normal	—

● MOVES TAUGHT IN EXCHANGE FOR COLORED SHARDS

Name	Type	Kind	Power	Acc	PP	Range	DA
Mud-Slap	Ground	Special	20	100	10	Normal	—
Fury Cutter	Bug	Physical	10	95	20	Normal	•
Iron Head	Steel	Physical	80	100	15	Normal	•
Snore	Normal	Special	40	100	15	Normal	—
Outrage	Dragon	Physical	120	100	15	1 random	•
AncientPower	Rock	Special	60	100	5	Normal	—
Earth Power	Ground	Special	90	100	10	Normal	—
Twister	Dragon	Special	40	100	20	2 foes	—
Iron Defense	Steel	Status	—	—	15	Self	—
Magnet Rise	Electric	Status	—	—	10	Self	—
Swift	Normal	Special	60	—	20	2 foes	—

● MOVES TAUGHT BY PEOPLE

Name	Type	Kind	Power	Acc	PP	Range	DA
Draco Meteor*	Dragon	Special	140	90	5	Normal	—

*Draco Meteor is taught when the Pokémon's Friendship is maxed out

● PRIMARY WAY TO FIND

TRAINER'S PARTY

WILD POKÉMON

COURSE OF STORY — Encounter at the Spear Pillar at Mt. Coronet (middle)

Sinnoh Pokédex **No. 150** Spatial Pokémon

Palkia

WATER DRAGON

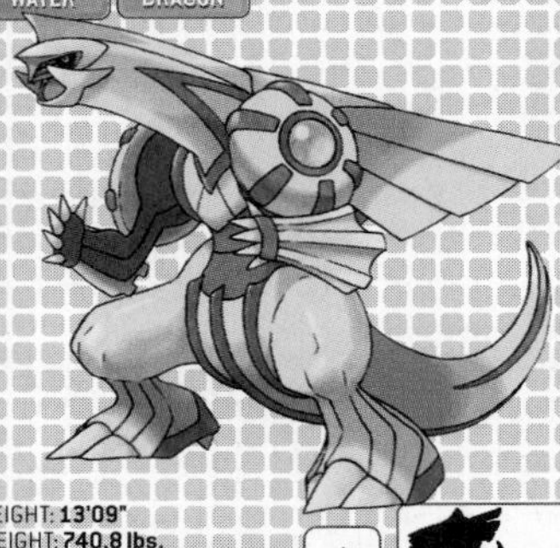

HEIGHT: **13'09"**
WEIGHT: **740.8 lbs.**
GENDER: **Unknown**
HELD ITEM: **None**

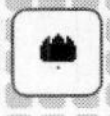

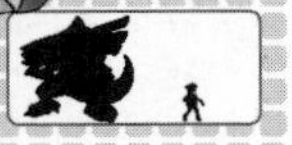

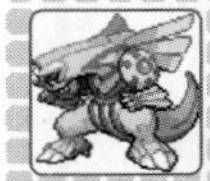

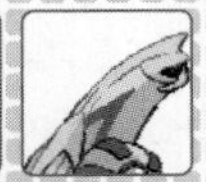

● Gender unknown

PLATINUM — A legendary Pokémon of Sinnoh. It is said that space becomes more stable with PALKIA's every breath.

EVOLUTION PATH

Does Not evolve

● TM & HM MOVES

No.	Name	Type	Kind	Power	Acc	PP	Range	DA
TM01	Focus Punch	Fighting	Physical	150	100	20	Normal	•
TM02	Dragon Claw	Dragon	Physical	80	100	15	Normal	•
TM03	Water Pulse	Water	Special	60	100	20	Normal	—
TM05	Roar	Normal	Status	—	100	20	Normal	—
TM06	Toxic	Poison	Status	—	85	10	Normal	—
TM07	Hail	Ice	Status	—	—	10	All	—
TM08	Bulk Up	Fighting	Status	—	—	20	Self	—
TM10	Hidden Power	Normal	Special	—	100	15	Normal	—
TM11	Sunny Day	Fire	Status	—	—	5	All	—
TM13	Ice Beam	Ice	Special	95	100	10	Normal	—
TM14	Blizzard	Ice	Special	120	70	5	2 foes	—
TM15	Hyper Beam	Normal	Special	150	90	5	Normal	—
TM17	Protect	Normal	Status	—	—	10	Self	—
TM18	Rain Dance	Water	Status	—	—	5	All	—
TM20	Safeguard	Normal	Status	—	—	25	2 allies	—
TM21	Frustration	Normal	Physical	—	100	20	Normal	•
TM24	Thunderbolt	Electric	Special	95	100	15	Normal	—
TM25	Thunder	Electric	Special	120	70	10	Normal	—
TM26	Earthquake	Ground	Physical	100	100	10	2 foes•1 ally	—
TM27	Return	Normal	Physical	—	100	20	Normal	•
TM31	Brick Break	Fighting	Physical	75	100	15	Normal	•
TM32	Double Team	Normal	Status	—	—	15	Self	—
TM34	Shock Wave	Electric	Special	60	—	20	Normal	—
TM35	Flamethrower	Fire	Special	95	100	15	Normal	—
TM37	Sandstorm	Rock	Status	—	—	10	All	—
TM38	Fire Blast	Fire	Special	120	85	5	Normal	—
TM39	Rock Tomb	Rock	Physical	50	80	10	Normal	—
TM40	Aerial Ace	Flying	Physical	60	—	20	Normal	•
TM42	Facade	Normal	Physical	70	100	20	Normal	•
TM43	Secret Power	Normal	Physical	70	100	20	Normal	—
TM44	Rest	Psychic	Status	—	—	10	Self	—
TM52	Focus Blast	Fighting	Special	120	70	5	Normal	—
TM55	Brine	Water	Special	65	100	10	Normal	—
TM56	Fling	Dark	Physical	—	100	10	Normal	—
TM58	Endure	Normal	Status	—	—	10	Self	—
TM59	Dragon Pulse	Dragon	Special	90	100	10	Normal	—
TM65	Shadow Claw	Ghost	Physical	70	100	15	Normal	•
TM68	Giga Impact	Normal	Physical	150	90	5	Normal	•
TM71	Stone Edge	Rock	Physical	100	80	5	Normal	—
TM72	Avalanche	Ice	Physical	60	100	10	Normal	•
TM73	Thunder Wave	Electric	Status	—	100	20	Normal	—
TM77	Psych Up	Normal	Status	—	—	10	Normal	—
TM80	Rock Slide	Rock	Physical	75	90	10	2 foes	—
TM82	Sleep Talk	Normal	Status	—	—	10	DoM	—
TM83	Natural Gift	Normal	Physical	—	100	15	Normal	—
TM87	Swagger	Normal	Status	—	90	15	Normal	—
TM90	Substitute	Normal	Status	—	—	10	Self	—
TM92	Trick Room	Psychic	Status	—	—	5	All	—
HM01	Cut	Normal	Physical	50	95	30	Normal	•
HM03	Surf	Water	Special	95	100	15	2 foes • 1 ally	—
HM04	Strength	Normal	Physical	80	100	15	Normal	•
HM06	Rock Smash	Fighting	Physical	40	100	15	Normal	•

ABILITY ● Pressure

EGG GROUP No Eggs

STATS
HP ●●●
ATTACK ●●●●
DEFENSE ●●●
SP. ATTACK ●●●●●
SP. DEFENSE ●●●
SPEED ●●●●

● LEVEL-UP AND LEARNED MOVES

Lv	Name	Type	Kind	Power	Acc	PP	Range	DA
Base	DragonBreath	Dragon	Special	60	100	20	Normal	—
Base	Scary Face	Normal	Status	—	90	10	Normal	—
10	Water Pulse	Water	Special	60	100	20	Normal	—
20	AncientPower	Rock	Special	60	100	5	Normal	—
30	Dragon Claw	Dragon	Physical	80	100	15	Normal	•
40	Spacial Rend	Dragon	Special	100	95	5	Normal	—
50	Heal Block	Psychic	Status	—	100	15	2 foes	—
60	Earth Power	Ground	Special	90	100	10	Normal	—
70	Slash	Normal	Physical	70	100	20	Normal	•
80	Aqua Tail	Water	Physical	90	90	10	Normal	•
90	Aura Sphere	Fighting	Special	90	—	20	Normal	—

● MOVES TAUGHT IN EXCHANGE FOR COLORED SHARDS

Name	Type	Kind	Power	Acc	PP	Range	DA
Dive	Water	Physical	80	100	10	Normal	•
Mud-Slap	Ground	Special	20	100	10	Normal	—
Fury Cutter	Bug	Physical	10	95	20	Normal	•
Aqua Tail	Water	Physical	90	90	10	Normal	•
Snore	Normal	Special	40	100	15	Normal	—
Outrage	Dragon	Physical	120	100	15	1 random	•
AncientPower	Rock	Special	60	100	5	Normal	—
Earth Power	Ground	Special	90	100	10	Normal	—
Twister	Dragon	Special	40	100	20	2 foes	—
Swift	Normal	Special	60	—	20	2 foes	—

● MOVES TAUGHT BY PEOPLE

Name	Type	Kind	Power	Acc	PP	Range	DA
Draco Meteor*	Dragon	Special	140	90	5	Normal	—

*Draco Meteor is taught when the Pokémon's Friendship is maxed out

● PRIMARY WAY TO FIND

TRAINER'S PARTY

WILD POKÉMON

COURSE OF STORY — Encounter at the Spear Pillar at Mt. Coronet (middle)

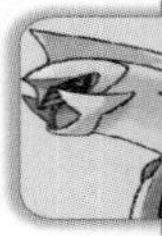

Sinnoh Pokédex No. 151 Seafaring Pokémon
Manaphy

WATER

HEIGHT: 1'00"
WEIGHT: 3.1 lbs.
GENDER: Unknown
HELD ITEM: None

● Gender unknown

PLATINUM It is born with a wondrous power that lets it bond with any kind of Pokémon.

EVOLUTION PATH

Does Not evolve

● TM & HM MOVES

No.	Name	Type	Kind	Power	Acc	PP	Range	DA
TM03	Water Pulse	Water	Special	60	100	20	Normal	—
TM04	Calm Mind	Psychic	Status	—	—	20	Self	—
TM06	Toxic	Poison	Status	—	85	10	Normal	—
TM07	Hail	Ice	Status	—	—	10	All	—
TM10	Hidden Power	Normal	Special	—	100	15	Normal	—
TM13	Ice Beam	Ice	Special	95	100	10	Normal	—
TM14	Blizzard	Ice	Special	120	70	5	2 foes	—
TM15	Hyper Beam	Normal	Special	150	90	5	Normal	—
TM16	Light Screen	Psychic	Status	—	—	30	2 allies	—
TM17	Protect	Normal	Status	—	—	10	Self	—
TM18	Rain Dance	Water	Status	—	—	5	All	—
TM20	Safeguard	Normal	Status	—	—	25	2 allies	—
TM21	Frustration	Normal	Physical	—	100	20	Normal	•
TM27	Return	Normal	Physical	—	100	20	Normal	•
TM29	Psychic	Psychic	Special	90	100	10	Normal	—
TM30	Shadow Ball	Ghost	Special	80	100	15	Normal	—
TM32	Double Team	Normal	Status	—	—	15	Self	—
TM33	Reflect	Psychic	Status	—	—	20	2 allies	—
TM42	Facade	Normal	Physical	70	100	20	Normal	•
TM43	Secret Power	Normal	Physical	70	100	20	Normal	•
TM44	Rest	Psychic	Status	—	—	10	Self	—
TM48	Skill Swap	Psychic	Status	—	—	10	Normal	—
TM53	Energy Ball	Grass	Special	80	100	10	Normal	—
TM55	Brine	Water	Special	65	100	10	Normal	—
TM56	Fling	Dark	Physical	—	100	10	Normal	•
TM58	Endure	Normal	Status	—	—	10	Self	—
TM68	Giga Impact	Normal	Physical	150	90	5	Normal	•
TM70	Flash	Normal	Status	—	100	20	Normal	—
TM77	Psych Up	Normal	Status	—	—	10	Self	—
TM82	Sleep Talk	Normal	Status	—	—	10	DoM	—
TM83	Natural Gift	Normal	Physical	—	100	15	Normal	•
TM86	Grass Knot	Grass	Special	—	100	20	Normal	—
TM87	Swagger	Normal	Status	—	90	15	Normal	—
TM89	U-turn	Bug	Physical	70	100	20	Normal	•
TM90	Substitute	Normal	Status	—	—	10	Self	—
HM03	Surf	Water	Special	95	100	15	2 foes + 1 ally	—
HM07	Waterfall	Water	Physical	80	100	15	Normal	•

● LEVEL-UP AND LEARNED MOVES

Lv	Name	Type	Kind	Power	Acc	PP	Range	DA
Base	Tail Glow	Bug	Status	—	—	20	Self	—
Base	Bubble	Water	Special	20	100	30	2 foes	—
Base	Water Sport	Water	Status	—	—	15	All	—
9	Charm	Normal	Status	—	100	20	Normal	—
16	Supersonic	Normal	Status	—	55	20	Normal	—
24	BubbleBeam	Water	Special	65	100	20	Normal	—
31	Acid Armor	Poison	Status	—	—	40	Self	—
39	Whirlpool	Water	Special	15	70	15	Normal	—
46	Water Pulse	Water	Special	60	100	20	Normal	—
54	Aqua Ring	Water	Status	—	—	20	Self	—
61	Dive	Water	Physical	80	100	10	Normal	•
69	Rain Dance	Water	Status	—	—	5	All	—
76	Heart Swap	Psychic	Status	—	—	10	Normal	—

● MOVES TAUGHT IN EXCHANGE FOR COLORED SHARDS

Name	Type	Kind	Power	Acc	PP	Range	DA
Dive	Water	Physical	80	100	10	Normal	•
Mud-Slap	Ground	Special	20	100	10	Normal	—
Icy Wind	Ice	Special	55	95	15	2 foes	—
Snore	Normal	Special	40	100	15	Normal	—
Helping Hand	Normal	Status	—	—	20	1 ally	—
AncientPower	Rock	Special	60	100	5	Normal	—
Signal Beam	Bug	Special	75	100	15	Normal	—
Last Resort	Normal	Special	130	100	5	Normal	—
Bounce	Flying	Physical	85	85	5	Normal	•
Knock Off	Dark	Physical	20	100	20	Normal	•
Swift	Normal	Special	60	—	20	2 foes	—
Uproar	Normal	Special	50	100	10	1 random	—

ABILITY ● Hydration

EGG GROUP Water 1 / Fairy

STATS
HP ●●●
ATTACK ●●●
DEFENSE ●●●●
SP. ATTACK ●●●●
SP. DEFENSE ●●●●
SPEED ●●●●

● PRIMARY WAY TO FIND

TRAINER'S PARTY

WILD POKÉMON

COURSE OF STORY — Look at the book in Mr. Backlot's room at the Poké-mon Mansion on Route 212

Sinnoh Pokédex No. 152 Plasma Pokémon
Rotom

ELECTRIC GHOST

● Normal

● Heat Rotom move: Overheat

● Wash Rotom move: Hydro Pump

● Frost Rotom move: Blizzard

● Fan Rotom move: Air Slash

● Mow Rotom move: Leaf Storm

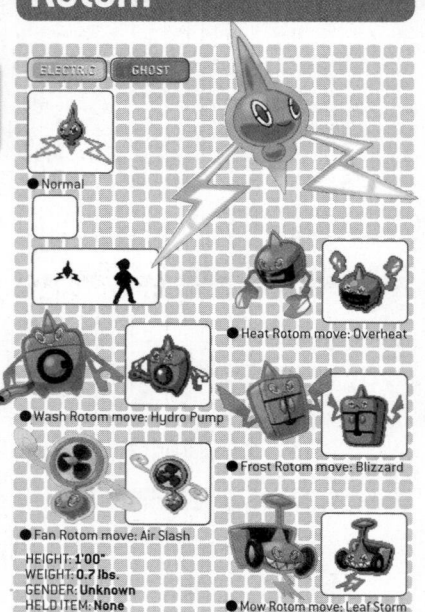

HEIGHT: 1'00"
WEIGHT: 0.7 lbs.
GENDER: Unknown
HELD ITEM: None

PLATINUM Its electric-like body can enter some kinds of ma-chines and take control in order to make mischief.

EVOLUTION PATH

Does Not evolve

● TM & HM MOVES

No.	Name	Type	Kind	Power	Acc	PP	Range	DA
TM06	Toxic	Poison	Status	—	85	10	Normal	—
TM10	Hidden Power	Normal	Special	—	100	15	Normal	—
TM11	Sunny Day	Fire	Status	—	—	5	All	—
TM16	Light Screen	Psychic	Status	—	—	30	2 allies	—
TM17	Protect	Normal	Status	—	—	10	Self	—
TM18	Rain Dance	Water	Status	—	—	5	All	—
TM21	Frustration	Normal	Physical	—	100	20	Normal	•
TM24	Thunderbolt	Electric	Special	95	100	15	Normal	—
TM25	Thunder	Electric	Special	120	70	10	Normal	—
TM27	Return	Normal	Physical	—	100	20	Normal	•
TM30	Shadow Ball	Ghost	Special	80	100	15	Normal	—
TM32	Double Team	Normal	Status	—	—	15	Self	—
TM33	Reflect	Psychic	Status	—	—	20	2 allies	—
TM34	Shock Wave	Electric	Special	60	—	20	Normal	—
TM42	Facade	Normal	Physical	70	100	20	Normal	•
TM43	Secret Power	Normal	Physical	70	100	20	Normal	•
TM44	Rest	Psychic	Status	—	—	10	Self	—
TM46	Thief	Dark	Physical	40	100	10	Normal	•
TM49	Snatch	Dark	Status	—	—	10	DoM	—
TM57	Charge Beam	Electric	Special	50	90	10	Normal	—
TM58	Endure	Normal	Status	—	—	10	Self	—
TM61	Will-O-Wisp	Fire	Status	—	75	15	Normal	—
TM70	Flash	Normal	Status	—	100	20	Normal	—
TM73	Thunder Wave	Electric	Status	—	100	20	Normal	—
TM77	Psych Up	Normal	Status	—	—	10	Self	—
TM79	Dark Pulse	Dark	Special	80	100	15	Normal	—
TM82	Sleep Talk	Normal	Status	—	—	10	DoM	—
TM83	Natural Gift	Normal	Status	—	100	15	Normal	—
TM85	Dream Eater	Psychic	Special	100	100	15	Normal	—
TM87	Swagger	Normal	Status	—	90	15	Normal	—
TM90	Substitute	Normal	Status	—	—	10	Self	—

● LEVEL-UP AND LEARNED MOVES

Lv	Name	Type	Kind	Power	Acc	PP	Range	DA
Base	Trick	Psychic	Status	—	100	10	Normal	—
Base	Astonish	Ghost	Physical	30	100	15	Normal	•
Base	ThunderShock	Electric	Special	40	100	30	Normal	—
Base	Confuse Ray	Ghost	Status	—	100	10	Normal	—
8	Uproar	Normal	Special	50	100	10	1 random	—
15	Double Team	Normal	Status	—	—	15	Self	—
22	Shock Wave	Electric	Special	60	—	20	Normal	—
29	Ominous Wind	Ghost	Special	60	100	5	Normal	—
36	Substitute	Normal	Status	—	—	10	Self	—
43	Charge	Electric	Status	—	—	20	Self	—
50	Discharge	Electric	Special	80	100	15	2 foes + 1 ally	—

● MOVES TAUGHT IN EXCHANGE FOR COLORED SHARDS

Name	Type	Kind	Power	Acc	PP	Range	DA
Mud-Slap	Ground	Special	20	100	10	Normal	—
Ominous Wind	Ghost	Special	60	100	5	Normal	—
Snore	Normal	Special	40	100	15	Normal	—
Spite	Ghost	Status	—	100	10	Normal	—
Signal Beam	Bug	Special	75	100	15	Normal	—
Trick	Psychic	Status	—	100	10	Normal	—
Sucker Punch	Dark	Physical	80	100	5	Normal	•
Swift	Normal	Special	60	—	20	2 foes	—
Uproar	Normal	Special	50	100	10	1 random	—

● EGG MOVES

Name	Type	Kind	Power	Acc	PP	Range	DA

ABILITY ● Levitate

EGG GROUP Amorphous

STATS
HP ●●
ATTACK ●●
DEFENSE ●●●
SP. ATTACK ●●●
SP. DEFENSE ●●●
SPEED ●●●

STATS (other Rotom)
HP ●●
ATTACK ●●●
DEFENSE ●●●●
SP. ATTACK ●●●●
SP. DEFENSE ●●●
SPEED ●●●

● PRIMARY WAY TO FIND

TRAINER'S PARTY

WILD POKÉMON

COURSE OF STORY — Examine the TV in the Old Cha-teau between 8 PM and 4 AM

*For Rotom to change form, you must have the Secret Key. The Secret Key is only available through distribution via Wi-Fi or special events and not through regular gameplay. Check Pokémon.com for the latest news on how to obtain this item.

**Rotom learns a move upon changing form, and forgets it upon changing back into Rotom.

Sinnoh Pokédex **No. 153** Flyscorpion Pokémon

Gligar

GROUND FLYING

HEIGHT: 3'07"
WEIGHT: 142.9 lbs.
GENDER: Male and Female
HELD ITEM: None

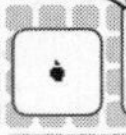

● Male form ● Female form

PLATINUM — It glides as if sliding. It startles foes by clamping on to their faces, then jabs with its poison stinger.

EVOLUTION PATH

Gligar

Level up between 8 PM and 4 AM while holding the Razor Fang

Gliscor

● TM & HM MOVES

No.	Name	Type	Kind	Power	Acc	PP	Range	DA
TM06	Toxic	Poison	Status	—	85	10	Normal	—
TM10	Hidden Power	Normal	Special	—	100	15	Normal	—
TM11	Sunny Day	Fire	Status	—	—	5	All	—
TM12	Taunt	Dark	Status	—	100	20	Normal	—
TM17	Protect	Normal	Status	—	—	10	Self	—
TM18	Rain Dance	Water	Status	—	—	5	All	—
TM21	Frustration	Normal	Physical	—	100	20	Normal	•
TM23	Iron Tail	Steel	Physical	100	75	15	Normal	•
TM26	Earthquake	Ground	Physical	100	100	10	2 foes • 1 ally	—
TM27	Return	Normal	Physical	—	100	20	Normal	•
TM28	Dig	Ground	Physical	80	100	10	Normal	•
TM31	Brick Break	Fighting	Physical	75	100	15	Normal	•
TM32	Double Team	Normal	Status	—	—	15	Self	—
TM36	Sludge Bomb	Poison	Special	90	100	10	Normal	—
TM37	Sandstorm	Rock	Status	—	—	10	All	—
TM39	Rock Tomb	Rock	Physical	50	80	10	Normal	—
TM40	Aerial Ace	Flying	Physical	60	—	20	Normal	•
TM41	Torment	Dark	Status	—	100	15	Normal	—
TM42	Facade	Normal	Physical	70	100	20	Normal	•
TM43	Secret Power	Normal	Physical	70	100	20	Normal	—
TM44	Rest	Psychic	Status	—	—	10	Self	—
TM45	Attract	Normal	Status	—	100	15	Normal	—
TM46	Thief	Dark	Physical	40	100	10	Normal	•
TM47	Steel Wing	Steel	Physical	70	90	25	Normal	•
TM51	Roost	Flying	Status	—	—	10	Self	—
TM54	False Swipe	Normal	Physical	40	100	40	Normal	•
TM56	Fling	Dark	Physical	—	100	10	Normal	—
TM58	Endure	Normal	Status	—	—	10	Self	—
TM66	Payback	Dark	Physical	50	100	10	Normal	•
TM69	Rock Polish	Rock	Status	—	—	20	Self	—
TM71	Stone Edge	Rock	Physical	100	80	5	Normal	—
TM75	Swords Dance	Normal	Status	—	—	30	Self	—
TM76	Stealth Rock	Rock	Status	—	—	20	2 foes	—
TM78	Captivate	Normal	Status	—	100	20	2 foes	—
TM79	Dark Pulse	Dark	Special	80	100	15	Normal	—
TM80	Rock Slide	Rock	Physical	75	90	10	2 foes	—
TM81	X-Scissor	Bug	Physical	80	100	15	Normal	•
TM82	Sleep Talk	Normal	Status	—	—	10	DoM	—
TM83	Natural Gift	Normal	Physical	—	100	15	Normal	—
TM84	Poison Jab	Poison	Physical	80	100	20	Normal	•
TM87	Swagger	Normal	Status	—	90	15	Normal	—
TM89	U-turn	Bug	Physical	70	100	20	Normal	•
TM90	Substitute	Normal	Status	—	—	10	Self	—
HM01	Cut	Normal	Physical	50	95	30	Normal	•
HM04	Strength	Normal	Physical	80	100	15	Normal	•
HM05	Defog	Flying	Status	—	—	15	Normal	—
HM06	Rock Smash	Fighting	Physical	40	100	15	Normal	•

ABILITY
● Hyper Cutter
● Sand Veil

EGG GROUP: Bug

STATS
HP ●●
ATTACK ●●●
DEFENSE ●●●
SP. ATTACK ●
SP. DEFENSE ●●
SPEED ●●●

● LEVEL-UP AND LEARNED MOVES

Lv	Name	Type	Kind	Power	Acc	PP	Range	DA
Base	Poison Sting	Poison	Physical	15	100	35	Normal	—
5	Sand-Attack	Ground	Status	—	100	15	Normal	—
9	Harden	Normal	Status	—	—	30	Self	—
12	Knock Off	Dark	Physical	20	100	20	Normal	•
16	Quick Attack	Normal	Physical	40	100	30	Normal	•
20	Fury Cutter	Bug	Physical	10	95	20	Normal	•
23	Faint Attack	Dark	Physical	60	—	20	Normal	•
27	Screech	Normal	Status	—	85	40	Normal	—
31	Slash	Normal	Physical	70	100	20	Normal	•
34	Swords Dance	Normal	Status	—	—	30	Self	—
38	U-turn	Bug	Physical	70	100	20	Normal	•
42	X-Scissor	Bug	Physical	80	100	15	Normal	•
45	Guillotine	Normal	Physical	—	30	5	Normal	•

● MOVES TAUGHT IN EXCHANGE FOR COLORED SHARDS

Name	Type	Kind	Power	Acc	PP	Range	DA
Fury Cutter	Bug	Physical	10	95	20	Normal	•
Aqua Tail	Water	Physical	90	90	10	Normal	•
Snore	Normal	Special	40	100	15	Normal	—
Earth Power	Ground	Special	90	100	10	Normal	—
Knock Off	Dark	Physical	20	100	20	Normal	•
Swift	Normal	Special	60	—	20	2 foes	—

● EGG MOVES

Name	Type	Kind	Power	Acc	PP	Range	DA
Metal Claw	Steel	Physical	50	95	35	Normal	•
Wing Attack	Flying	Physical	60	100	35	Normal	•
Razor Wind	Normal	Special	80	100	10	2 foes	—
Counter	Fighting	Physical	—	100	20	Self	•
Sand Tomb	Ground	Physical	15	70	15	Normal	—
Agility	Psychic	Status	—	—	30	Self	—
Baton Pass	Normal	Status	—	—	40	Self	—
Double-Edge	Normal	Physical	120	100	15	Normal	•
Feint	Normal	Physical	50	100	10	Normal	—
Night Slash	Dark	Physical	70	100	15	Normal	•
Cross Poison	Poison	Physical	70	100	20	Normal	•

● PRIMARY WAY TO FIND

TRAINER'S PARTY: Trainer on Route 207

WILD POKÉMON: Route 206

COURSE OF STORY

Sinnoh Pokédex **No. 154** Fang Scorp Pokémon

Gliscor

GROUND FLYING

HEIGHT: 6'07"
WEIGHT: 93.7 lbs.
GENDER: Male and Female
HELD ITEM: None

● M/F have same form

PLATINUM — If it succeeds in catching even a faint breeze properly, it can circle the globe without flapping once.

EVOLUTION PATH

Gligar

Level up between 8 PM and 4 AM while holding the Razor Fang

Gliscor

● TM & HM MOVES

No.	Name	Type	Kind	Power	Acc	PP	Range	DA
TM06	Toxic	Poison	Status	—	85	10	Normal	—
TM10	Hidden Power	Normal	Special	—	100	15	Normal	—
TM11	Sunny Day	Fire	Status	—	—	5	All	—
TM12	Taunt	Dark	Status	—	100	20	Normal	—
TM15	Hyper Beam	Normal	Special	150	90	5	Normal	—
TM17	Protect	Normal	Status	—	—	10	Self	—
TM18	Rain Dance	Water	Status	—	—	5	All	—
TM21	Frustration	Normal	Physical	—	100	20	Normal	•
TM23	Iron Tail	Steel	Physical	100	75	15	Normal	•
TM26	Earthquake	Ground	Physical	100	100	10	2 foes • 1 ally	—
TM27	Return	Normal	Physical	—	100	20	Normal	•
TM28	Dig	Ground	Physical	80	100	10	Normal	•
TM31	Brick Break	Fighting	Physical	75	100	15	Normal	•
TM32	Double Team	Normal	Status	—	—	15	Self	—
TM36	Sludge Bomb	Poison	Special	90	100	10	Normal	—
TM37	Sandstorm	Rock	Status	—	—	10	All	—
TM39	Rock Tomb	Rock	Physical	50	80	10	Normal	—
TM40	Aerial Ace	Flying	Physical	60	—	20	Normal	•
TM41	Torment	Dark	Status	—	100	15	Normal	—
TM42	Facade	Normal	Physical	70	100	20	Normal	•
TM43	Secret Power	Normal	Physical	70	100	20	Normal	—
TM44	Rest	Psychic	Status	—	—	10	Self	—
TM45	Attract	Normal	Status	—	100	15	Normal	—
TM46	Thief	Dark	Physical	40	100	10	Normal	•
TM47	Steel Wing	Steel	Physical	70	90	25	Normal	•
TM51	Roost	Flying	Status	—	—	10	Self	—
TM54	False Swipe	Normal	Physical	40	100	40	Normal	•
TM56	Fling	Dark	Physical	—	100	10	Normal	—
TM58	Endure	Normal	Status	—	—	10	Self	—
TM66	Payback	Dark	Physical	50	100	10	Normal	•
TM68	Giga Impact	Normal	Physical	150	90	5	Normal	•
TM69	Rock Polish	Rock	Status	—	—	20	Self	—
TM71	Stone Edge	Rock	Physical	100	80	5	Normal	—
TM75	Swords Dance	Normal	Status	—	—	30	Self	—
TM76	Stealth Rock	Rock	Status	—	—	20	2 foes	—
TM78	Captivate	Normal	Status	—	100	20	2 foes	—
TM79	Dark Pulse	Dark	Special	80	100	15	Normal	—
TM80	Rock Slide	Rock	Physical	75	90	10	2 foes	—
TM81	X-Scissor	Bug	Physical	80	100	15	Normal	•
TM82	Sleep Talk	Normal	Status	—	—	10	DoM	—
TM83	Natural Gift	Normal	Physical	—	100	15	Normal	—
TM84	Poison Jab	Poison	Physical	80	100	20	Normal	•
TM87	Swagger	Normal	Status	—	90	15	Normal	—
TM89	U-turn	Bug	Physical	70	100	20	Normal	•
TM90	Substitute	Normal	Status	—	—	10	Self	—
HM01	Cut	Normal	Physical	50	95	30	Normal	•
HM04	Strength	Normal	Physical	80	100	15	Normal	•
HM05	Defog	Flying	Status	—	—	15	Normal	—
HM06	Rock Smash	Fighting	Physical	40	100	15	Normal	•

ABILITY
● Hyper Cutter
● Sand Veil

EGG GROUP: Bug

STATS
HP ●●
ATTACK ●●●
DEFENSE ●●●●
SP. ATTACK ●●
SP. DEFENSE ●●
SPEED ●●●

● LEVEL-UP AND LEARNED MOVES

Lv	Name	Type	Kind	Power	Acc	PP	Range	DA
Base	Thunder Fang	Electric	Physical	65	95	15	Normal	•
Base	Ice Fang	Ice	Physical	65	95	15	Normal	•
Base	Fire Fang	Fire	Physical	65	95	15	Normal	•
Base	Poison Jab	Poison	Physical	80	100	20	Normal	•
Base	Sand-Attack	Ground	Status	—	100	15	Normal	—
Base	Harden	Normal	Status	—	—	30	Self	—
Base	Knock Off	Dark	Physical	20	100	20	Normal	•
5	Sand-Attack	Ground	Status	—	100	15	Normal	—
9	Harden	Normal	Status	—	—	30	Self	—
12	Knock Off	Dark	Physical	20	100	20	Normal	•
16	Quick Attack	Normal	Physical	40	100	30	Normal	•
20	Fury Cutter	Bug	Physical	10	95	20	Normal	•
23	Faint Attack	Dark	Physical	60	—	20	Normal	•
27	Screech	Normal	Status	—	85	40	Normal	—
31	Night Slash	Dark	Physical	70	100	15	Normal	•
34	Swords Dance	Normal	Status	—	—	30	Self	—
38	U-turn	Bug	Physical	70	100	20	Normal	•
42	X-Scissor	Bug	Physical	80	100	15	Normal	•
45	Guillotine	Normal	Physical	—	30	5	Normal	•

● MOVES TAUGHT IN EXCHANGE FOR COLORED SHARDS

Name	Type	Kind	Power	Acc	PP	Range	DA
Mud-Slap	Ground	Special	20	100	10	Normal	—
Fury Cutter	Bug	Physical	10	95	20	Normal	•
Aqua Tail	Water	Physical	90	90	10	Normal	•
Snore	Normal	Special	40	100	15	Normal	—
Earth Power	Ground	Special	90	100	10	Normal	—
Knock Off	Dark	Physical	20	100	20	Normal	•
Swift	Normal	Special	60	—	20	2 foes	—

● PRIMARY WAY TO FIND

TRAINER'S PARTY: Elite Four member Bertha

WILD POKÉMON

COURSE OF STORY

Sinnoh Pokédex No. 155 Compass Pokémon
Nosepass

ROCK

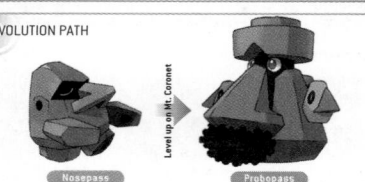

HEIGHT: 3'03"
WEIGHT: 213.8 lbs.
GENDER: Male and Female
HELD ITEM: Hard Stone

● M/F have same form

PLATINUM When endangered, it may protect itself by raising its magnetism and drawing iron objects to its body.

EVOLUTION PATH

Nosepass — Level up on Mt. Coronet → Probopass

ABILITY ● Sturdy ● Magnet Pull

EGG GROUP Mineral

STATS
HP ●●
ATTACK ●●
DEFENSE ●●●●
SP. ATTACK ●●
SP. DEFENSE ●●
SPEED ●

● TM & HM MOVES

No.	Name	Type	Kind	Power	Acc	PP	Range	DA
TM06	Toxic	Poison	Status	—	85	10	Normal	—
TM10	Hidden Power	Normal	Special	—	100	15	Normal	—
TM11	Sunny Day	Fire	Status	—	—	5	All	—
TM12	Taunt	Dark	Status	—	100	20	Normal	—
TM17	Protect	Normal	Status	—	—	10	Self	—
TM21	Frustration	Normal	Physical	—	100	20	Normal	●
TM24	Thunderbolt	Electric	Special	95	100	15	Normal	—
TM25	Thunder	Electric	Special	120	70	10	Normal	—
TM26	Earthquake	Ground	Physical	100	100	10	2 foes + 1 ally	—
TM27	Return	Normal	Physical	—	100	20	Normal	●
TM32	Double Team	Normal	Status	—	—	15	Self	—
TM34	Shock Wave	Electric	Special	60	—	20	Normal	—
TM37	Sandstorm	Rock	Status	—	—	10	All	—
TM39	Rock Tomb	Rock	Physical	50	80	10	Normal	—
TM41	Torment	Dark	Status	—	100	15	Normal	—
TM42	Facade	Normal	Physical	70	100	20	Normal	●
TM43	Secret Power	Normal	Physical	70	100	20	Normal	●
TM44	Rest	Psychic	Status	—	—	10	Self	—
TM45	Attract	Normal	Status	—	100	15	Normal	—
TM58	Endure	Normal	Status	—	—	10	Self	—
TM64	Explosion	Normal	Physical	250	100	5	2 foes + 1 ally	—
TM69	Rock Polish	Rock	Status	—	—	20	Self	—
TM71	Stone Edge	Rock	Physical	100	80	5	Normal	—
TM73	Thunder Wave	Electric	Status	—	100	20	Normal	—
TM76	Stealth Rock	Rock	Status	—	—	20	2 foes	—
TM78	Captivate	Normal	Status	—	100	20	2 foes	—
TM80	Rock Slide	Rock	Physical	75	90	10	2 foes	—
TM82	Sleep Talk	Normal	Status	—	—	10	DoM	—
TM83	Natural Gift	Normal	Physical	—	100	15	Normal	—
TM87	Swagger	Normal	Status	—	90	15	Normal	—
TM90	Substitute	Normal	Status	—	—	10	Self	—
HM04	Strength	Normal	Physical	80	100	15	Normal	●
HM06	Rock Smash	Fighting	Physical	40	100	15	Normal	●

● LEVEL-UP AND LEARNED MOVES

Lv	Name	Type	Kind	Power	Acc	PP	Range	DA
Base	Tackle	Normal	Physical	35	95	35	Normal	●
7	Harden	Normal	Status	—	—	30	Self	—
13	Rock Throw	Rock	Physical	50	90	15	Normal	—
19	Block	Normal	Status	—	—	5	Normal	—
25	Thunder Wave	Electric	Status	—	100	20	Normal	—
31	Rock Slide	Rock	Physical	75	90	10	2 foes	—
37	Sandstorm	Rock	Status	—	—	10	All	—
43	Rest	Psychic	Status	—	—	10	Self	—
49	Power Gem	Rock	Special	70	100	20	Normal	—
55	Discharge	Electric	Special	80	100	15	2 foes + 1 ally	—
61	Stone Edge	Rock	Physical	100	80	5	Normal	—
67	Zap Cannon	Electric	Special	120	50	5	Normal	—
73	Lock-On	Normal	Status	—	—	5	Normal	—
79	Earth Power	Ground	Special	90	100	10	Normal	—

● MOVES TAUGHT IN EXCHANGE FOR COLORED SHARDS

Name	Type	Kind	Power	Acc	PP	Range	DA
Mud-Slap	Ground	Special	20	100	10	Normal	—
Rollout	Rock	Physical	30	90	20	Normal	●
ThunderPunch	Electric	Physical	75	100	15	Normal	●
Fire Punch	Fire	Physical	75	100	15	Normal	●
Ice Punch	Ice	Physical	75	100	15	Normal	●
Snore	Normal	Special	40	100	15	Normal	—
AncientPower	Rock	Special	60	100	5	Normal	—
Earth Power	Ground	Special	90	100	10	Normal	—
Iron Defense	Steel	Status	—	—	15	Self	—
Magnet Rise	Electric	Status	—	—	10	Self	—

● EGG MOVES

Name	Type	Kind	Power	Acc	PP	Range	DA
Magnitude	Ground	Physical	—	100	30	2 foes + 1 ally	—
Rollout	Rock	Physical	30	90	20	Normal	●
Explosion	Normal	Physical	250	100	5	2 foes + 1 ally	—
Double-Edge	Normal	Physical	120	100	15	Normal	●
Block	Normal	Status	—	—	5	Normal	—

● PRIMARY WAY TO FIND

TRAINER'S PARTY — Trainer on Route 207

WILD POKÉMON — Mt. Coronet (lower)

COURSE OF STORY

Sinnoh Pokédex No. 156 Compass Pokémon
Probopass

ROCK STEEL

HEIGHT: 4'07"
WEIGHT: 749.6 lbs.
GENDER: Male and Female
HELD ITEM: None

● M/F have same form

PLATINUM It freely controls three small units called Mini-Noses using magnetic force.

EVOLUTION PATH

Nosepass — Level up on Mt. Coronet → Probopass

ABILITY ● Sturdy ● Magnet Pull

EGG GROUP Mineral

STATS
HP ●●
ATTACK ●●
DEFENSE ●●●●●
SP. ATTACK ●●●
SP. DEFENSE ●●●●●
SPEED ●●

● TM & HM MOVES

No.	Name	Type	Kind	Power	Acc	PP	Range	DA
TM06	Toxic	Poison	Status	—	85	10	Normal	—
TM10	Hidden Power	Normal	Special	—	100	15	Normal	—
TM11	Sunny Day	Fire	Status	—	—	5	All	—
TM12	Taunt	Dark	Status	—	100	20	Normal	—
TM15	Hyper Beam	Normal	Special	150	90	5	Normal	—
TM17	Protect	Normal	Status	—	—	10	Self	—
TM21	Frustration	Normal	Physical	—	100	20	Normal	●
TM24	Thunderbolt	Electric	Special	95	100	15	Normal	—
TM25	Thunder	Electric	Special	120	70	10	Normal	—
TM26	Earthquake	Ground	Physical	100	100	10	2 foes + 1 ally	—
TM27	Return	Normal	Physical	—	100	20	Normal	●
TM32	Double Team	Normal	Status	—	—	15	Self	—
TM34	Shock Wave	Electric	Special	60	—	20	Normal	—
TM37	Sandstorm	Rock	Status	—	—	10	All	—
TM39	Rock Tomb	Rock	Physical	50	80	10	Normal	—
TM41	Torment	Dark	Status	—	100	15	Normal	—
TM42	Facade	Normal	Physical	70	100	20	Normal	●
TM43	Secret Power	Normal	Physical	70	100	20	Normal	●
TM44	Rest	Psychic	Status	—	—	10	Self	—
TM45	Attract	Normal	Status	—	100	15	Normal	—
TM58	Endure	Normal	Status	—	—	10	Self	—
TM64	Explosion	Normal	Physical	250	100	5	2 foes + 1 ally	—
TM68	Giga Impact	Normal	Physical	150	90	5	Normal	●
TM69	Rock Polish	Rock	Status	—	—	20	Self	—
TM71	Stone Edge	Rock	Physical	100	80	5	Normal	—
TM73	Thunder Wave	Electric	Status	—	100	20	Normal	—
TM76	Stealth Rock	Rock	Status	—	—	20	2 foes	—
TM78	Captivate	Normal	Status	—	100	20	2 foes	—
TM80	Rock Slide	Rock	Physical	75	90	10	2 foes	—
TM82	Sleep Talk	Normal	Status	—	—	10	DoM	—
TM83	Natural Gift	Normal	Physical	—	100	15	Normal	—
TM87	Swagger	Normal	Status	—	90	15	Normal	—
TM90	Substitute	Normal	Status	—	—	10	Self	—
TM91	Flash Cannon	Steel	Special	80	100	10	Normal	—
HM04	Strength	Normal	Physical	80	100	15	Normal	●
HM06	Rock Smash	Fighting	Physical	40	100	15	Normal	●

● LEVEL-UP AND LEARNED MOVES

Lv	Name	Type	Kind	Power	Acc	PP	Range	DA
Base	Magnet Rise	Electric	Status	—	—	10	Self	—
Base	Gravity	Psychic	Status	—	—	5	All	—
Base	Tackle	Normal	Physical	35	95	35	Normal	●
Base	Iron Defense	Steel	Status	—	—	15	Self	—
Base	Magnet Bomb	Steel	Physical	60	—	20	Normal	—
Base	Block	Normal	Status	—	—	5	Normal	—
7	Iron Defense	Steel	Status	—	—	15	Self	—
13	Magnet Bomb	Steel	Physical	60	—	20	Normal	—
19	Block	Normal	Status	—	—	5	Normal	—
25	Thunder Wave	Electric	Status	—	100	20	Normal	—
31	Rock Slide	Rock	Physical	75	90	10	2 foes	—
37	Sandstorm	Rock	Status	—	—	10	All	—
43	Rest	Psychic	Status	—	—	10	Self	—
49	Power Gem	Rock	Special	70	100	20	Normal	—
55	Discharge	Electric	Special	80	100	15	2 foes + 1 ally	—
61	Stone Edge	Rock	Physical	100	80	5	Normal	—
67	Zap Cannon	Electric	Special	120	50	5	Normal	—
73	Lock-On	Normal	Status	—	—	5	Normal	—
79	Earth Power	Ground	Special	90	100	10	Normal	—

● MOVES TAUGHT IN EXCHANGE FOR COLORED SHARDS

Name	Type	Kind	Power	Acc	PP	Range	DA
Mud-Slap	Ground	Special	20	100	10	Normal	—
Rollout	Rock	Physical	30	90	20	Normal	●
ThunderPunch	Electric	Physical	75	100	15	Normal	●
Fire Punch	Fire	Physical	75	100	15	Normal	●
Ice Punch	Ice	Physical	75	100	15	Normal	●
Iron Head	Steel	Physical	80	100	15	Normal	●
Snore	Normal	Special	40	100	15	Normal	—
AncientPower	Rock	Special	60	100	5	Normal	—
Earth Power	Ground	Special	90	100	10	Normal	—
Iron Defense	Steel	Status	—	—	15	Self	—
Magnet Rise	Electric	Status	—	—	10	Self	—

● PRIMARY WAY TO FIND

TRAINER'S PARTY — Trainer on the Celestic Town side of Route 210

WILD POKÉMON

COURSE OF STORY

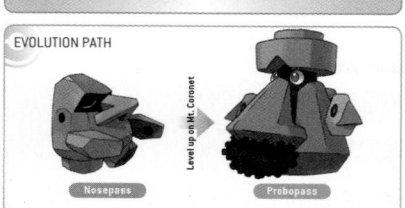

155
NOSEPASS

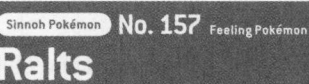

Sinnoh Pokémon **No. 157** Feeling Pokémon

Ralts

PSYCHIC

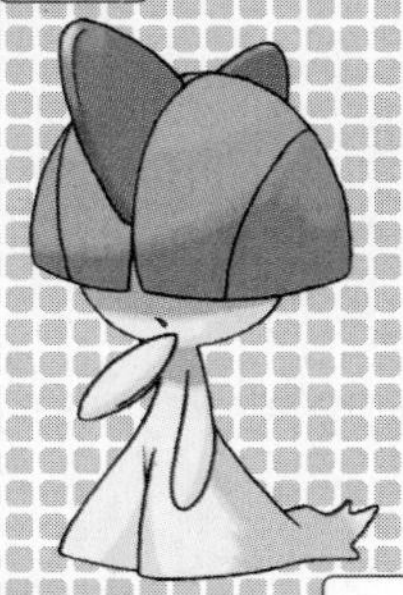

HEIGHT: **1'04"**
WEIGHT: **14.6 lbs.**
GENDER: **Male and Female**
HELD ITEM: **None**

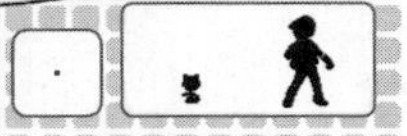

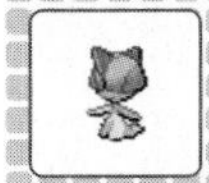

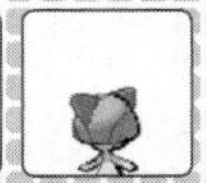

● M/F have same form

PLATINUM If its horns capture the warm feelings of people or Pokémon, its body warms up slightly.

EVOLUTION PATH

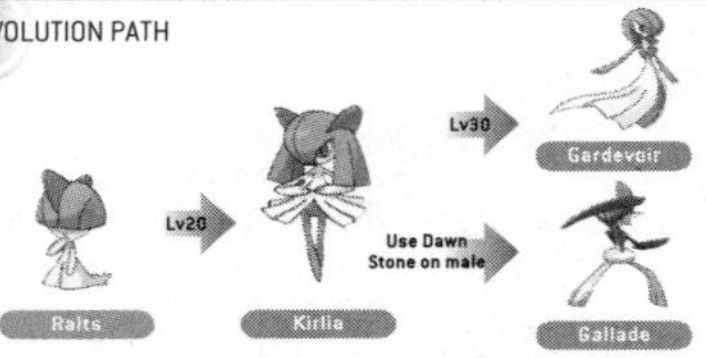

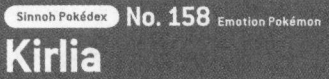

Lv30
Gardevoir
Lv20
Use Dawn Stone on male
Ralts
Kirlia
Gallade

● TM & HM MOVES

No.	Name	Type	Kind	Power	Acc	PP	Range	DA
TM04	Calm Mind	Psychic	Status	—	—	20	Self	—
TM06	Toxic	Poison	Status	—	85	10	Normal	—
TM10	Hidden Power	Normal	Special	—	100	15	Normal	—
TM11	Sunny Day	Fire	Status	—	—	5	All	—
TM12	Taunt	Dark	Status	—	100	20	Normal	—
TM16	Light Screen	Psychic	Status	—	—	30	2 allies	—
TM17	Protect	Normal	Status	—	—	10	Self	—
TM18	Rain Dance	Water	Status	—	—	5	All	—
TM20	Safeguard	Normal	Status	—	—	25	2 allies	—
TM21	Frustration	Normal	Physical	—	100	20	Normal	•
TM24	Thunderbolt	Electric	Special	95	100	15	Normal	—
TM27	Return	Normal	Physical	—	100	20	Normal	•
TM29	Psychic	Psychic	Special	90	100	10	Normal	—
TM30	Shadow Ball	Ghost	Special	80	100	15	Normal	—
TM32	Double Team	Normal	Status	—	—	15	Self	—
TM33	Reflect	Psychic	Status	—	—	20	2 allies	—
TM34	Shock Wave	Electric	Special	60	—	20	Normal	—
TM41	Torment	Dark	Status	—	100	15	Normal	—
TM42	Facade	Normal	Physical	70	100	20	Normal	•
TM43	Secret Power	Normal	Physical	70	100	20	Normal	—
TM44	Rest	Psychic	Status	—	—	10	Self	—
TM45	Attract	Normal	Status	—	100	15	Normal	—
TM46	Thief	Dark	Physical	40	100	10	Normal	•
TM48	Skill Swap	Psychic	Status	—	—	10	Normal	—
TM49	Snatch	Dark	Status	—	—	10	DoM	—
TM56	Fling	Dark	Physical	—	100	10	Normal	—
TM57	Charge Beam	Electric	Special	50	90	10	Normal	—
TM58	Endure	Normal	Status	—	—	10	Self	—
TM67	Recycle	Normal	Status	—	—	10	Self	—
TM70	Flash	Normal	Status	—	100	20	Normal	—
TM73	Thunder Wave	Electric	Status	—	100	20	Normal	—
TM77	Psych Up	Normal	Status	—	—	10	Normal	—
TM78	Captivate	Normal	Status	—	100	20	2 foes	—
TM82	Sleep Talk	Normal	Status	—	—	10	DoM	—
TM83	Natural Gift	Normal	Physical	—	100	15	Normal	—
TM85	Dream Eater	Psychic	Special	100	100	15	Normal	—
TM86	Grass Knot	Grass	Special	—	100	20	Normal	•
TM87	Swagger	Normal	Status	—	90	15	Normal	—
TM90	Substitute	Normal	Status	—	—	10	Self	—
TM92	Trick Room	Psychic	Status	—	—	5	All	—

ABILITY ● Synchronize ● Trace

EGG GROUP Amorphous

STATS
HP ●
ATTACK ●
DEFENSE ●
SP. ATTACK ●●
SP. DEFENSE ●●
SPEED ●●

● LEVEL-UP AND LEARNED MOVES

Lv	Name	Type	Kind	Power	Acc	PP	Range	DA
Base	Growl	Normal	Status	—	100	40	2 foes	—
6	Confusion	Psychic	Special	50	100	25	Normal	—
10	Double Team	Normal	Status	—	—	15	Self	—
12	Teleport	Psychic	Status	—	—	20	Self	—
17	Lucky Chant	Normal	Status	—	—	30	2 allies	—
21	Magical Leaf	Grass	Special	60	—	20	Normal	—
23	Calm Mind	Psychic	Status	—	—	20	Self	—
28	Psychic	Psychic	Special	90	100	10	Normal	—
32	Imprison	Psychic	Status	—	—	10	Self	—
34	Future Sight	Psychic	Special	80	90	15	Normal	—
39	Charm	Normal	Status	—	100	20	Normal	—
43	Hypnosis	Psychic	Status	—	60	20	Normal	—
45	Dream Eater	Psychic	Special	100	100	15	Normal	—

● MOVES TAUGHT IN EXCHANGE FOR COLORED SHARDS

Name	Type	Kind	Power	Acc	PP	Range	DA
Mud-Slap	Ground	Special	20	100	10	Normal	—
Icy Wind	Ice	Special	55	95	15	2 foes	—
ThunderPunch	Electric	Physical	75	100	15	Normal	•
Fire Punch	Fire	Physical	75	100	15	Normal	•
Ice Punch	Ice	Physical	75	100	15	Normal	•
Snore	Normal	Special	40	100	15	Normal	—
Helping Hand	Normal	Status	—	—	20	1 ally	—
Signal Beam	Bug	Special	75	100	15	Normal	—
Zen Headbutt	Psychic	Physical	80	90	15	Normal	•
Trick	Psychic	Status	—	100	10	Normal	—
Swift	Normal	Special	60	—	20	2 foes	—

● EGG MOVES

Name	Type	Kind	Power	Acc	PP	Range	DA
Disable	Normal	Status	—	80	20	Normal	—
Will-O-Wisp	Fire	Status	—	75	15	Normal	—
Mean Look	Normal	Status	—	—	5	Normal	—
Memento	Dark	Status	—	100	10	Normal	—
Destiny Bond	Ghost	Status	—	—	5	Self	—
Grudge	Ghost	Status	—	—	5	Self	—
Shadow Sneak	Ghost	Physical	40	100	30	Normal	•
Confuse Ray	Ghost	Status	—	100	10	Normal	—

● PRIMARY WAY TO FIND

TRAINER'S PARTY Trainer on Route 215

WILD POKÉMON Route 208

COURSE OF STORY

Sinnoh Pokédex **No. 158** Emotion Pokémon

Kirlia

PSYCHIC

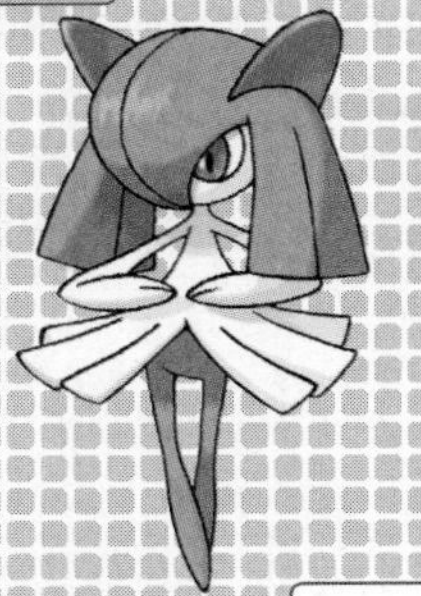

HEIGHT: **2'07"**
WEIGHT: **44.5 lbs.**
GENDER: **Male and Female**
HELD ITEM: **None**

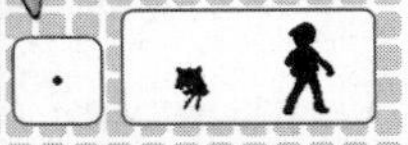

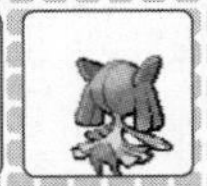

● M/F have same form

PLATINUM If its Trainer becomes happy, it overflows with energy, dancing joyously while spinning about.

EVOLUTION PATH

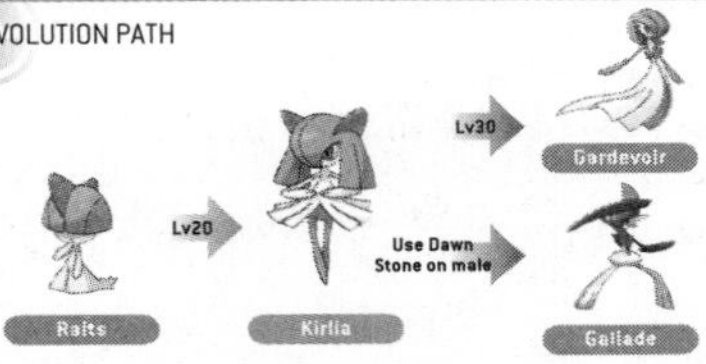

Lv30
Gardevoir
Lv20
Use Dawn Stone on male
Ralts
Kirlia
Gallade

● TM & HM MOVES

No.	Name	Type	Kind	Power	Acc	PP	Range	DA
TM04	Calm Mind	Psychic	Status	—	—	20	Self	—
TM06	Toxic	Poison	Status	—	85	10	Normal	—
TM10	Hidden Power	Normal	Special	—	100	15	Normal	—
TM11	Sunny Day	Fire	Status	—	—	5	All	—
TM12	Taunt	Dark	Status	—	100	20	Normal	—
TM16	Light Screen	Psychic	Status	—	—	30	2 allies	—
TM17	Protect	Normal	Status	—	—	10	Self	—
TM18	Rain Dance	Water	Status	—	—	5	All	—
TM20	Safeguard	Normal	Status	—	—	25	2 allies	—
TM21	Frustration	Normal	Physical	—	100	20	Normal	•
TM24	Thunderbolt	Electric	Special	95	100	15	Normal	—
TM27	Return	Normal	Physical	—	100	20	Normal	•
TM29	Psychic	Psychic	Special	90	100	10	Normal	—
TM30	Shadow Ball	Ghost	Special	80	100	15	Normal	—
TM32	Double Team	Normal	Status	—	—	15	Self	—
TM33	Reflect	Psychic	Status	—	—	20	2 allies	—
TM34	Shock Wave	Electric	Special	60	—	20	Normal	—
TM41	Torment	Dark	Status	—	100	15	Normal	—
TM42	Facade	Normal	Physical	70	100	20	Normal	•
TM43	Secret Power	Normal	Physical	70	100	20	Normal	—
TM44	Rest	Psychic	Status	—	—	10	Self	—
TM45	Attract	Normal	Status	—	100	15	Normal	—
TM46	Thief	Dark	Physical	40	100	10	Normal	•
TM48	Skill Swap	Psychic	Status	—	—	10	Normal	—
TM49	Snatch	Dark	Status	—	—	10	DoM	—
TM56	Fling	Dark	Physical	—	100	10	Normal	—
TM57	Charge Beam	Electric	Special	50	90	10	Normal	—
TM58	Endure	Normal	Status	—	—	10	Self	—
TM67	Recycle	Normal	Status	—	—	10	Self	—
TM70	Flash	Normal	Status	—	100	20	Normal	—
TM73	Thunder Wave	Electric	Status	—	100	20	Normal	—
TM77	Psych Up	Normal	Status	—	—	10	Normal	—
TM78	Captivate	Normal	Status	—	100	20	2 foes	—
TM82	Sleep Talk	Normal	Status	—	—	10	DoM	—
TM83	Natural Gift	Normal	Physical	—	100	15	Normal	—
TM85	Dream Eater	Psychic	Special	100	100	15	Normal	—
TM86	Grass Knot	Grass	Special	—	100	20	Normal	•
TM87	Swagger	Normal	Status	—	90	15	Normal	—
TM90	Substitute	Normal	Status	—	—	10	Self	—
TM92	Trick Room	Psychic	Status	—	—	5	All	—

ABILITY ● Synchronize ● Trace

EGG GROUP Amorphous

STATS
HP ●
ATTACK ●
DEFENSE ●
SP. ATTACK ●●
SP. DEFENSE ●●
SPEED ●●

● LEVEL-UP AND LEARNED MOVES

Lv	Name	Type	Kind	Power	Acc	PP	Range	DA
Base	Growl	Normal	Status	—	100	40	2 foes	—
Base	Confusion	Psychic	Special	50	100	25	Normal	—
Base	Double Team	Normal	Status	—	—	15	Self	—
Base	Teleport	Psychic	Status	—	—	20	Self	—
6	Confusion	Psychic	Special	50	100	25	Normal	—
10	Double Team	Normal	Status	—	—	15	Self	—
12	Teleport	Psychic	Status	—	—	20	Self	—
17	Lucky Chant	Normal	Status	—	—	30	2 allies	—
22	Magical Leaf	Grass	Special	60	—	20	Normal	—
25	Calm Mind	Psychic	Status	—	—	20	Self	—
31	Psychic	Psychic	Special	90	100	10	Normal	—
36	Imprison	Psychic	Status	—	—	10	Self	—
39	Future Sight	Psychic	Special	80	90	15	Normal	—
45	Charm	Normal	Status	—	100	20	Normal	—
50	Hypnosis	Psychic	Status	—	60	20	Normal	—
53	Dream Eater	Psychic	Special	100	100	15	Normal	—

● MOVES TAUGHT IN EXCHANGE FOR COLORED SHARDS

Name	Type	Kind	Power	Acc	PP	Range	DA
Mud-Slap	Ground	Special	20	100	10	Normal	—
Icy Wind	Ice	Special	55	95	15	2 foes	—
ThunderPunch	Electric	Physical	75	100	15	Normal	•
Fire Punch	Fire	Physical	75	100	15	Normal	•
Ice Punch	Ice	Physical	75	100	15	Normal	•
Snore	Normal	Special	40	100	15	Normal	—
Helping Hand	Normal	Status	—	—	20	1 ally	—
Signal Beam	Bug	Special	75	100	15	Normal	—
Zen Headbutt	Psychic	Physical	80	90	15	Normal	•
Trick	Psychic	Status	—	100	10	Normal	—
Swift	Normal	Special	60	—	20	2 foes	—

● PRIMARY WAY TO FIND

TRAINER'S PARTY Trainer on Route 214

WILD POKÉMON Hearthome City side of Route 212

COURSE OF STORY

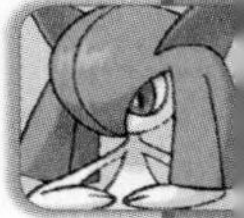

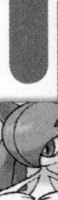

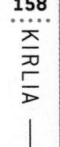

Sinnoh Pokédex **No. 159** Embrace Pokémon

Gardevoir

PSYCHIC

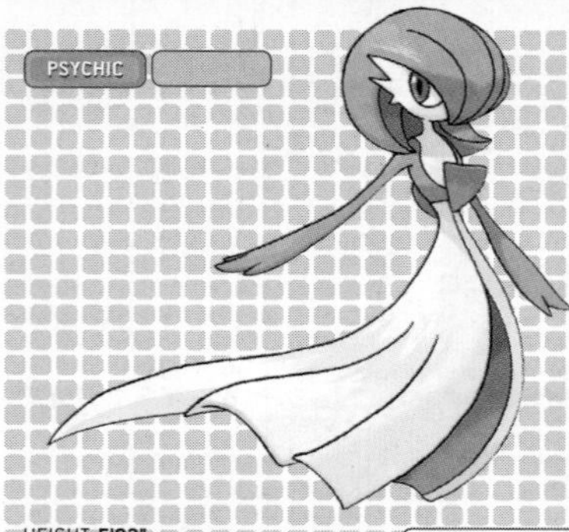

HEIGHT: **5'03"**
WEIGHT: **106.7 lbs.**
GENDER: **Male and Female**
HELD ITEM: **None**

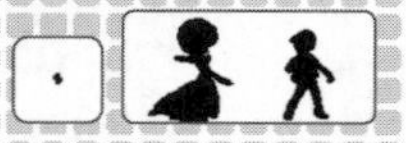

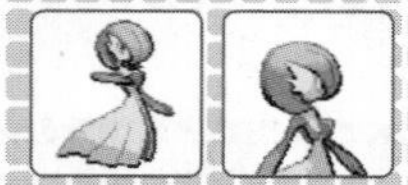

● M/F have same form

PLATINUM To protect its Trainer, it will expend all its psychic power to create a small black hole.

EVOLUTION PATH

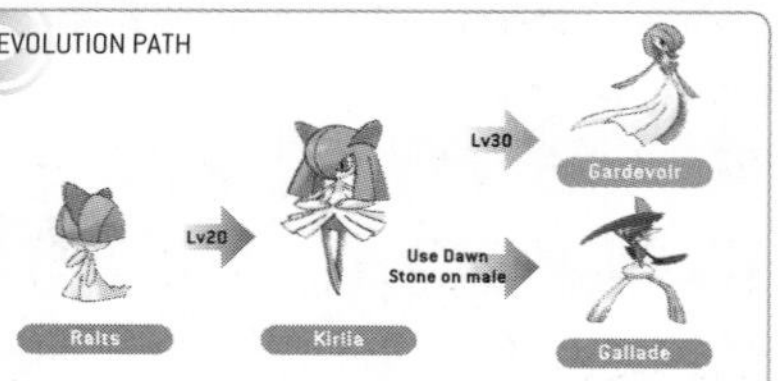
Ralts
Lv20
Kirlia
Lv30
Gardevoir
Use Dawn Stone on male
Gallade

● TM & HM MOVES

No.	Name	Type	Kind	Power	Acc	PP	Range	DA
TM04	Calm Mind	Psychic	Status	—	—	20	Self	—
TM06	Toxic	Poison	Status	—	85	10	Normal	—
TM10	Hidden Power	Normal	Special	—	100	15	Normal	—
TM11	Sunny Day	Fire	Status	—	—	5	All	—
TM12	Taunt	Dark	Status	—	100	20	Normal	—
TM15	Hyper Beam	Normal	Special	150	90	5	Normal	—
TM16	Light Screen	Psychic	Status	—	—	30	2 allies	—
TM17	Protect	Normal	Status	—	—	10	Self	—
TM18	Rain Dance	Water	Status	—	—	5	All	—
TM20	Safeguard	Normal	Status	—	—	25	2 allies	—
TM21	Frustration	Normal	Physical	—	100	20	Normal	•
TM24	Thunderbolt	Electric	Special	95	100	15	Normal	—
TM27	Return	Normal	Physical	—	100	20	Normal	•
TM29	Psychic	Psychic	Special	90	100	10	Normal	—
TM30	Shadow Ball	Ghost	Special	80	100	15	Normal	—
TM32	Double Team	Normal	Status	—	—	15	Self	—
TM33	Reflect	Psychic	Status	—	—	20	2 allies	—
TM34	Shock Wave	Electric	Special	60	—	20	Normal	—
TM41	Torment	Dark	Status	—	100	15	Normal	—
TM42	Facade	Normal	Physical	70	100	20	Normal	•
TM43	Secret Power	Normal	Physical	70	100	20	Normal	—
TM44	Rest	Psychic	Status	—	—	10	Self	—
TM45	Attract	Normal	Status	—	100	15	Normal	—
TM46	Thief	Dark	Physical	40	100	10	Normal	•
TM48	Skill Swap	Psychic	Status	—	—	10	Normal	—
TM49	Snatch	Dark	Status	—	—	10	DoM	—
TM52	Focus Blast	Fighting	Special	120	70	5	Normal	—
TM53	Energy Ball	Grass	Special	80	100	10	Normal	—
TM56	Fling	Dark	Physical	—	100	10	Normal	—
TM57	Charge Beam	Electric	Special	50	90	10	Normal	—
TM58	Endure	Normal	Status	—	—	10	Self	—
TM67	Recycle	Normal	Status	—	—	10	Self	—
TM68	Giga Impact	Normal	Physical	150	90	5	Normal	•
TM70	Flash	Normal	Status	—	100	20	Normal	—
TM73	Thunder Wave	Electric	Status	—	100	20	Normal	—
TM77	Psych Up	Normal	Status	—	—	10	Normal	—
TM78	Captivate	Normal	Status	—	100	20	2 foes	—
TM82	Sleep Talk	Normal	Status	—	—	10	DoM	—
TM83	Natural Gift	Normal	Physical	—	100	15	Normal	—
TM85	Dream Eater	Psychic	Special	100	100	15	Normal	—
TM86	Grass Knot	Grass	Special	—	100	20	Normal	•
TM87	Swagger	Normal	Status	—	90	15	Normal	—
TM90	Substitute	Normal	Status	—	—	10	Self	—
TM92	Trick Room	Psychic	Status	—	—	5	All	—

ABILITY
- Synchronize
- Trace

EGG GROUP: Amorphous

STATS
- HP ●●
- ATTACK ●●
- DEFENSE ●●
- SP. ATTACK ●●●●
- SP. DEFENSE ●●●●
- SPEED ●●●

● LEVEL-UP AND LEARNED MOVES

Lv	Name	Type	Kind	Power	Acc	PP	Range	DA
Base	Healing Wish	Psychic	Status	—	—	10	Self	—
Base	Growl	Normal	Status	—	100	40	2 foes	—
Base	Confusion	Psychic	Special	50	100	25	Normal	—
Base	Double Team	Normal	Status	—	—	15	Self	—
Base	Teleport	Psychic	Status	—	—	20	Self	—
6	Confusion	Psychic	Special	50	100	25	Normal	—
10	Double Team	Normal	Status	—	—	15	Self	—
12	Teleport	Psychic	Status	—	—	20	Self	—
17	Wish	Normal	Status	—	—	10	Self	—
22	Magical Leaf	Grass	Special	60	—	20	Normal	—
25	Calm Mind	Psychic	Status	—	—	20	Self	—
33	Psychic	Psychic	Special	90	100	10	Normal	—
40	Imprison	Psychic	Status	—	—	10	Self	—
45	Future Sight	Psychic	Special	80	90	15	Normal	—
53	Captivate	Normal	Status	—	100	20	2 foes	—
60	Hypnosis	Psychic	Status	—	60	20	Normal	—
65	Dream Eater	Psychic	Special	100	100	15	Normal	—

● MOVES TAUGHT IN EXCHANGE FOR COLORED SHARDS

Name	Type	Kind	Power	Acc	PP	Range	DA
Mud-Slap	Ground	Special	20	100	10	Normal	—
Icy Wind	Ice	Special	55	95	15	2 foes	—
ThunderPunch	Electric	Physical	75	100	15	Normal	•
Fire Punch	Fire	Physical	75	100	15	Normal	•
Ice Punch	Ice	Physical	75	100	15	Normal	•
Snore	Normal	Special	40	100	15	Normal	—
Helping Hand	Normal	Status	—	—	20	1 ally	—
Signal Beam	Bug	Special	75	100	15	Normal	—
Zen Headbutt	Psychic	Physical	80	90	15	Normal	•
Trick	Psychic	Status	—	100	10	Normal	—
Swift	Normal	Special	60	—	20	2 foes	—

● PRIMARY WAY TO FIND

TRAINER'S PARTY Trainer on Victory Road

WILD POKÉMON

COURSE OF STORY

Sinnoh Pokédex **No. 160** Blade Pokémon

Gallade

PSYCHIC | FIGHTING

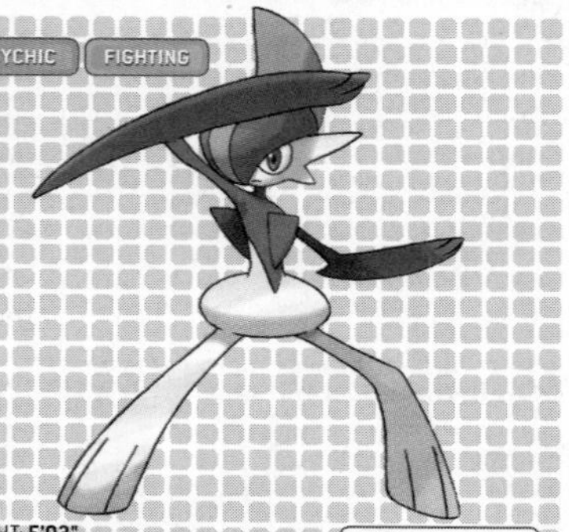

HEIGHT: **5'03"**
WEIGHT: **114.6 lbs.**
GENDER: **Male only**
HELD ITEM: **None**

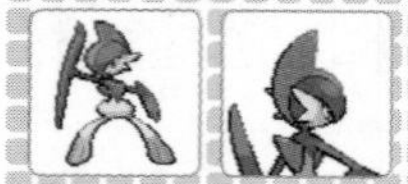

● Male form

PLATINUM When trying to protect someone, it extends its elbows as if they were swords and fights savagely.

EVOLUTION PATH

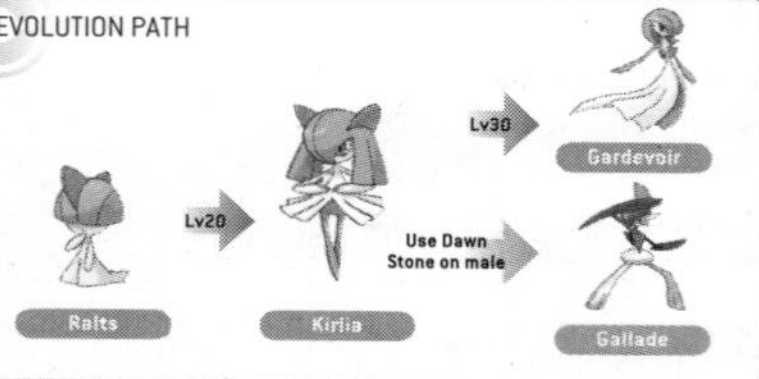
Ralts
Lv20
Kirlia
Lv30
Gardevoir
Use Dawn Stone on male
Gallade

● TM & HM MOVES

No.	Name	Type	Kind	Power	Acc	PP	Range	DA
TM01	Focus Punch	Fighting	Physical	150	100	20	Normal	•
TM04	Calm Mind	Psychic	Status	—	—	20	Self	—
TM06	Toxic	Poison	Status	—	85	10	Normal	—
TM08	Bulk Up	Fighting	Status	—	—	20	Self	—
TM10	Hidden Power	Normal	Special	—	100	15	Normal	—
TM11	Sunny Day	Fire	Status	—	—	5	All	—
TM12	Taunt	Dark	Status	—	100	20	Normal	—
TM15	Hyper Beam	Normal	Special	150	90	5	Normal	—
TM16	Light Screen	Psychic	Status	—	—	30	2 allies	—
TM17	Protect	Normal	Status	—	—	10	Self	—
TM18	Rain Dance	Water	Status	—	—	5	All	—
TM20	Safeguard	Normal	Status	—	—	25	2 allies	—
TM21	Frustration	Normal	Physical	—	100	20	Normal	•
TM24	Thunderbolt	Electric	Special	95	100	15	Normal	—
TM26	Earthquake	Ground	Physical	100	100	10	2 foes • 1 ally	—
TM27	Return	Normal	Physical	—	100	20	Normal	•
TM29	Psychic	Psychic	Special	90	100	10	Normal	—
TM30	Shadow Ball	Ghost	Special	80	100	15	Normal	—
TM31	Brick Break	Fighting	Physical	75	100	15	Normal	•
TM32	Double Team	Normal	Status	—	—	15	Self	—
TM33	Reflect	Psychic	Status	—	—	20	2 allies	—
TM34	Shock Wave	Electric	Special	60	—	20	Normal	—
TM39	Rock Tomb	Rock	Physical	50	80	10	Normal	—
TM40	Aerial Ace	Flying	Physical	60	—	20	Normal	•
TM41	Torment	Dark	Status	—	100	15	Normal	—
TM42	Facade	Normal	Physical	70	100	20	Normal	•
TM43	Secret Power	Normal	Physical	70	100	20	Normal	—
TM44	Rest	Psychic	Status	—	—	10	Self	—
TM45	Attract	Normal	Status	—	100	15	Normal	—
TM46	Thief	Dark	Physical	40	100	10	Normal	•
TM48	Skill Swap	Psychic	Status	—	—	10	Normal	—
TM49	Snatch	Dark	Status	—	—	10	DoM	—
TM52	Focus Blast	Fighting	Special	120	70	5	Normal	—
TM54	False Swipe	Normal	Physical	40	100	40	Normal	•
TM56	Fling	Dark	Physical	—	100	10	Normal	—
TM57	Charge Beam	Electric	Special	50	90	10	Normal	—
TM58	Endure	Normal	Status	—	—	10	Self	—
TM60	Drain Punch	Fighting	Physical	60	100	5	Normal	•
TM67	Recycle	Normal	Status	—	—	10	Self	—
TM68	Giga Impact	Normal	Physical	150	90	5	Normal	•
TM70	Flash	Normal	Status	—	100	20	Normal	—
TM71	Stone Edge	Rock	Physical	100	80	5	Normal	—
TM73	Thunder Wave	Electric	Status	—	100	20	Normal	—
TM75	Swords Dance	Normal	Status	—	—	30	Self	—
TM77	Psych Up	Normal	Status	—	—	10	Normal	—
TM78	Captivate	Normal	Status	—	100	20	2 foes	—
TM80	Rock Slide	Rock	Physical	75	90	10	2 foes	—
TM81	X-Scissor	Bug	Physical	80	100	15	Normal	•
TM82	Sleep Talk	Normal	Status	—	—	10	DoM	—
TM83	Natural Gift	Normal	Physical	—	100	15	Normal	—
TM84	Poison Jab	Poison	Physical	80	100	20	Normal	•
TM85	Dream Eater	Psychic	Special	100	100	15	Normal	—
TM86	Grass Knot	Grass	Special	—	100	20	Normal	•
TM87	Swagger	Normal	Status	—	90	15	Normal	—
TM90	Substitute	Normal	Status	—	—	10	Self	—
TM92	Trick Room	Psychic	Status	—	—	5	All	—
HM01	Cut	Normal	Physical	50	95	30	Normal	•
HM04	Strength	Normal	Physical	80	100	15	Normal	•
HM06	Rock Smash	Fighting	Physical	40	100	15	Normal	•

ABILITY
- Steadfast

EGG GROUP: Amorphous

STATS
- HP ●●
- ATTACK ●●●●
- DEFENSE ●●
- SP. ATTACK ●●
- SP. DEFENSE ●●●
- SPEED ●●●

● LEVEL-UP AND LEARNED MOVES

Lv	Name	Type	Kind	Power	Acc	PP	Range	DA
Base	Leaf Blade	Grass	Physical	90	100	15	Normal	•
Base	Night Slash	Dark	Physical	70	100	15	Normal	•
Base	Leer	Normal	Status	—	100	30	2 foes	—
Base	Confusion	Psychic	Special	50	100	25	Normal	—
Base	Double Team	Normal	Status	—	—	15	Self	—
Base	Teleport	Psychic	Status	—	—	20	Self	—
6	Confusion	Psychic	Special	50	100	25	Normal	—
10	Double Team	Normal	Status	—	—	15	Self	—
12	Teleport	Psychic	Status	—	—	20	Self	—
17	Fury Cutter	Bug	Physical	10	95	20	Normal	•
22	Slash	Normal	Physical	70	100	20	Normal	•
25	Swords Dance	Normal	Status	—	—	30	Self	—
31	Psycho Cut	Psychic	Physical	70	100	20	Normal	—
36	Helping Hand	Normal	Status	—	—	20	1 ally	—
39	Feint	Normal	Physical	50	100	10	Normal	—
45	False Swipe	Normal	Physical	40	100	40	Normal	•
50	Protect	Normal	Status	—	—	10	Self	—
53	Close Combat	Fighting	Physical	120	100	5	Normal	•

● MOVES TAUGHT IN EXCHANGE FOR COLORED SHARDS

Name	Type	Kind	Power	Acc	PP	Range	DA
Mud-Slap	Ground	Special	20	100	10	Normal	—
Fury Cutter	Bug	Physical	10	95	20	Normal	•
ThunderPunch	Electric	Physical	75	100	15	Normal	•
Fire Punch	Fire	Physical	75	100	15	Normal	•
Ice Punch	Ice	Physical	75	100	15	Normal	•
Snore	Normal	Special	40	100	15	Normal	—
Helping Hand	Normal	Status	—	—	20	1 ally	—
Signal Beam	Bug	Special	75	100	15	Normal	—
Zen Headbutt	Psychic	Physical	80	90	15	Normal	•
Vacuum Wave	Fighting	Special	40	100	30	Normal	—
Trick	Psychic	Status	—	100	10	Normal	—
Knock Off	Dark	Physical	20	100	20	Normal	•
Swift	Normal	Special	60	—	20	2 foes	—

● PRIMARY WAY TO FIND

TRAINER'S PARTY Elite Four member Lucian

WILD POKÉMON

COURSE OF STORY

Sinnoh Pokédex **No. 161** Licking Pokémon

Lickitung

NORMAL

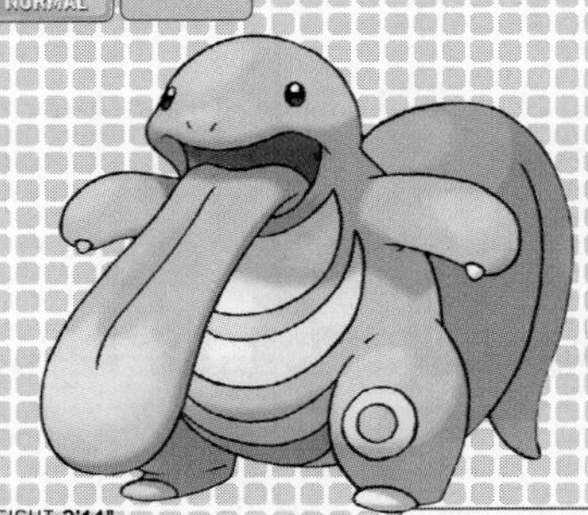

HEIGHT: **3'11"**
WEIGHT: **144.4 lbs.**
GENDER: **Male and Female**
HELD ITEM: **Lagging Tail**

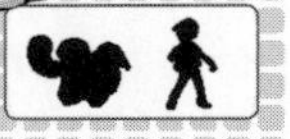

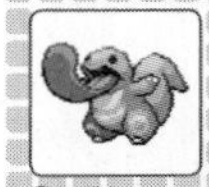

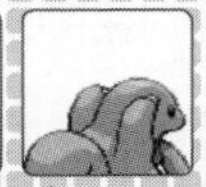

● M/F have same form

PLATINUM When it extends its over-six-foot-long tongue, its tail quivers. There is a possibility they are connected.

EVOLUTION PATH

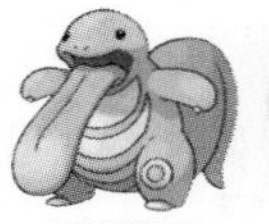

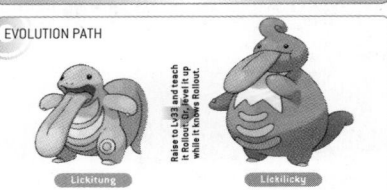

Lickitung

Raise to Lv33 and teach it Rollout. Or, level it up while it knows Rollout.

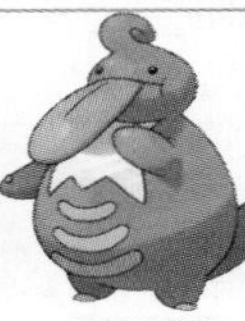

Lickilicky

● TM & HM MOVES

No.	Name	Type	Kind	Power	Acc	PP	Range	DA
TM01	Focus Punch	Fighting	Physical	150	100	20	Normal	•
TM03	Water Pulse	Water	Special	60	100	20	Normal	—
TM06	Toxic	Poison	Status	—	85	10	Normal	—
TM10	Hidden Power	Normal	Special	—	100	15	Normal	—
TM11	Sunny Day	Fire	Status	—	—	5	All	—
TM13	Ice Beam	Ice	Special	95	100	10	Normal	—
TM14	Blizzard	Ice	Special	120	70	5	2 foes	—
TM15	Hyper Beam	Normal	Special	150	90	5	Normal	—
TM17	Protect	Normal	Status	—	—	10	Self	—
TM18	Rain Dance	Water	Status	—	—	5	All	—
TM21	Frustration	Normal	Physical	—	100	20	Normal	•
TM22	SolarBeam	Grass	Special	120	100	10	Normal	—
TM23	Iron Tail	Steel	Physical	100	75	15	Normal	•
TM24	Thunderbolt	Electric	Special	95	100	15	Normal	—
TM25	Thunder	Electric	Special	120	70	10	Normal	—
TM26	Earthquake	Ground	Physical	100	100	10	2 foes • 1 ally	—
TM27	Return	Normal	Physical	—	100	20	Normal	•
TM28	Dig	Ground	Physical	80	100	10	Normal	•
TM30	Shadow Ball	Ghost	Special	80	100	15	Normal	—
TM31	Brick Break	Fighting	Physical	75	100	15	Normal	•
TM32	Double Team	Normal	Status	—	—	15	Self	—
TM34	Shock Wave	Electric	Special	60	—	20	Normal	—
TM35	Flamethrower	Fire	Special	95	100	15	Normal	—
TM37	Sandstorm	Rock	Status	—	—	10	All	—
TM38	Fire Blast	Fire	Special	120	85	5	Normal	—
TM39	Rock Tomb	Rock	Physical	50	80	10	Normal	—
TM42	Facade	Normal	Physical	70	100	20	Normal	•
TM43	Secret Power	Normal	Physical	70	100	20	Normal	—
TM44	Rest	Psychic	Status	—	—	10	Self	—
TM45	Attract	Normal	Status	—	100	15	Normal	—
TM46	Thief	Dark	Physical	40	100	10	Normal	•
TM56	Fling	Dark	Physical	—	100	10	Normal	—
TM58	Endure	Normal	Status	—	—	10	Self	—
TM68	Giga Impact	Normal	Physical	150	90	5	Normal	•
TM75	Swords Dance	Normal	Status	—	—	30	Self	—
TM77	Psych Up	Normal	Status	—	—	10	Normal	—
TM78	Captivate	Normal	Status	—	100	20	2 foes	—
TM80	Rock Slide	Rock	Physical	75	90	10	2 foes	—
TM82	Sleep Talk	Normal	Status	—	—	10	DoM	—
TM83	Natural Gift	Normal	Physical	—	100	15	Normal	—
TM85	Dream Eater	Psychic	Special	100	100	15	Normal	—
TM87	Swagger	Normal	Status	—	90	15	Normal	—
TM90	Substitute	Normal	Status	—	—	10	Self	—
HM01	Cut	Normal	Physical	50	95	30	Normal	•
HM03	Surf	Water	Special	95	100	15	2 foes • 1 ally	—
HM04	Strength	Normal	Physical	80	100	15	Normal	•
HM06	Rock Smash	Fighting	Physical	40	100	15	Normal	•
HM08	Rock Climb	Normal	Physical	90	85	20	Normal	•

ABILITY ● Own Tempo ● Oblivious

EGG GROUP Monster

STATS
HP ●●●
ATTACK ●●
DEFENSE ●●
SP. ATTACK ●●
SP. DEFENSE ●●
SPEED ●

● LEVEL-UP AND LEARNED MOVES

Lv	Name	Type	Kind	Power	Acc	PP	Range	DA
Base	Lick	Ghost	Physical	20	100	30	Normal	•
5	Supersonic	Normal	Status	—	55	20	Normal	—
9	Defense Curl	Normal	Status	—	—	40	Self	—
13	Knock Off	Dark	Physical	20	100	20	Normal	•
17	Wrap	Normal	Physical	15	85	20	Normal	•
21	Stomp	Normal	Physical	65	100	20	Normal	•
25	Disable	Normal	Status	—	80	20	Normal	—
29	Slam	Normal	Physical	80	75	20	Normal	•
33	Rollout	Rock	Physical	30	90	20	Normal	•
37	Me First	Normal	Status	—	—	20	DoM	—
41	Refresh	Normal	Status	—	—	20	Self	—
45	Screech	Normal	Status	—	85	40	Normal	—
49	Power Whip	Grass	Physical	120	85	10	Normal	•
53	Wring Out	Normal	Special	—	100	5	Normal	•

● MOVES TAUGHT IN EXCHANGE FOR COLORED SHARDS

Name	Type	Kind	Power	Acc	PP	Range	DA
Mud-Slap	Ground	Special	20	100	10	Normal	—
Icy Wind	Ice	Special	55	95	15	2 foes	—
Rollout	Rock	Physical	30	90	20	Normal	•
ThunderPunch	Electric	Physical	75	100	15	Normal	•
Fire Punch	Fire	Physical	75	100	15	Normal	•
Ice Punch	Ice	Physical	75	100	15	Normal	•
Aqua Tail	Water	Physical	90	90	10	Normal	•
Snore	Normal	Special	40	100	15	Normal	—
Zen Headbutt	Psychic	Physical	80	90	15	Normal	•
Knock Off	Dark	Physical	20	100	20	Normal	•

● EGG MOVES

Name	Type	Kind	Power	Acc	PP	Range	DA
Belly Drum	Normal	Status	—	—	10	Self	—
Magnitude	Ground	Physical	—	100	30	2 foes • 1 ally	—
Body Slam	Normal	Physical	85	100	15	Normal	•
Curse	???	Status	—	—	10	Normal•Self	—
SmellingSalt	Normal	Physical	60	100	10	Normal	•
Sleep Talk	Normal	Status	—	—	10	DoM	—
Snore	Normal	Special	40	100	15	Normal	—
Substitute	Normal	Status	—	—	10	Self	—
Amnesia	Psychic	Status	—	—	20	Self	—
Hammer Arm	Fighting	Physical	100	90	10	Normal	•

● PRIMARY WAY TO FIND

TRAINER'S PARTY Trainer on Route 215

WILD POKÉMON Route 215

COURSE OF STORY

Sinnoh Pokédex **No. 162** Licking Pokémon

Lickilicky

NORMAL

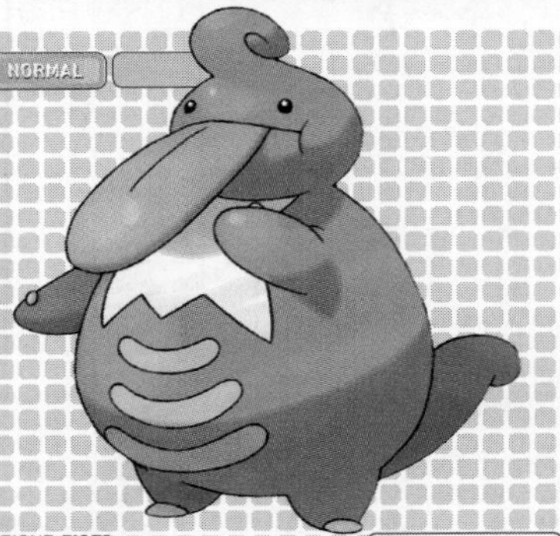

HEIGHT: **5'07"**
WEIGHT: **308.6 lbs.**
GENDER: **Male and Female**
HELD ITEM: **None**

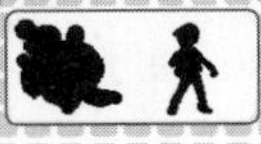

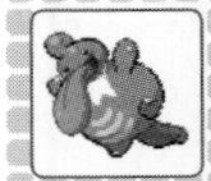

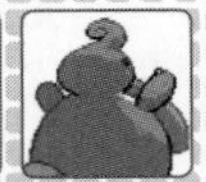

● M/F have same form

PLATINUM The long tongue is always soggy with slobber. The saliva contains a solvent that causes numbness.

EVOLUTION PATH

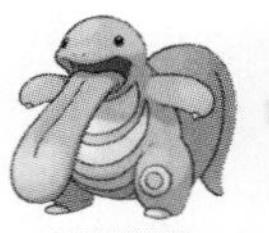

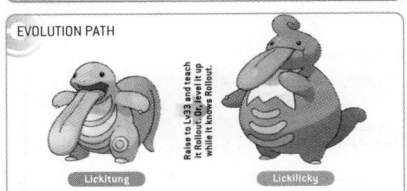

Lickitung

Raise to Lv33 and teach it Rollout. Or, level it up while it knows Rollout.

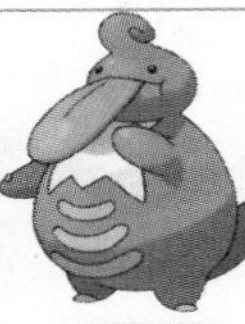

Lickilicky

● TM & HM MOVES

No.	Name	Type	Kind	Power	Acc	PP	Range	DA
TM01	Focus Punch	Fighting	Physical	150	100	20	Normal	•
TM03	Water Pulse	Water	Special	60	100	20	Normal	—
TM06	Toxic	Poison	Status	—	85	10	Normal	—
TM10	Hidden Power	Normal	Special	—	100	15	Normal	—
TM11	Sunny Day	Fire	Status	—	—	5	All	—
TM13	Ice Beam	Ice	Special	95	100	10	Normal	—
TM14	Blizzard	Ice	Special	120	70	5	2 foes	—
TM15	Hyper Beam	Normal	Special	150	90	5	Normal	—
TM17	Protect	Normal	Status	—	—	10	Self	—
TM18	Rain Dance	Water	Status	—	—	5	All	—
TM21	Frustration	Normal	Physical	—	100	20	Normal	•
TM22	SolarBeam	Grass	Special	120	100	10	Normal	—
TM23	Iron Tail	Steel	Physical	100	75	15	Normal	•
TM24	Thunderbolt	Electric	Special	95	100	15	Normal	—
TM25	Thunder	Electric	Special	120	70	10	Normal	—
TM26	Earthquake	Ground	Physical	100	100	10	2 foes • 1 ally	—
TM27	Return	Normal	Physical	—	100	20	Normal	•
TM28	Dig	Ground	Physical	80	100	10	Normal	•
TM30	Shadow Ball	Ghost	Special	80	100	15	Normal	—
TM31	Brick Break	Fighting	Physical	75	100	15	Normal	•
TM32	Double Team	Normal	Status	—	—	15	Self	—
TM34	Shock Wave	Electric	Special	60	—	20	Normal	—
TM35	Flamethrower	Fire	Special	95	100	15	Normal	—
TM37	Sandstorm	Rock	Status	—	—	10	All	—
TM38	Fire Blast	Fire	Special	120	85	5	Normal	—
TM39	Rock Tomb	Rock	Physical	50	80	10	Normal	—
TM42	Facade	Normal	Physical	70	100	20	Normal	•
TM43	Secret Power	Normal	Physical	70	100	20	Normal	—
TM44	Rest	Psychic	Status	—	—	10	Self	—
TM45	Attract	Normal	Status	—	100	15	Normal	—
TM46	Thief	Dark	Physical	40	100	10	Normal	•
TM52	Focus Blast	Fighting	Special	120	70	5	Normal	—
TM56	Fling	Dark	Physical	—	100	10	Normal	—
TM58	Endure	Normal	Status	—	—	10	Self	—
TM64	Explosion	Normal	Physical	250	100	5	2 foes • 1 ally	—
TM68	Giga Impact	Normal	Physical	150	90	5	Normal	•
TM74	Gyro Ball	Steel	Physical	—	100	5	Normal	•
TM75	Swords Dance	Normal	Status	—	—	30	Self	—
TM77	Psych Up	Normal	Status	—	—	10	Normal	—
TM78	Captivate	Normal	Status	—	100	20	2 foes	—
TM80	Rock Slide	Rock	Physical	75	90	10	2 foes	—
TM82	Sleep Talk	Normal	Status	—	—	10	DoM	—
TM83	Natural Gift	Normal	Physical	—	100	15	Normal	—
TM85	Dream Eater	Psychic	Special	100	100	15	Normal	—
TM87	Swagger	Normal	Status	—	90	15	Normal	—
TM90	Substitute	Normal	Status	—	—	10	Self	—
HM01	Cut	Normal	Physical	50	95	30	Normal	•
HM03	Surf	Water	Special	95	100	15	2 foes • 1 ally	—
HM04	Strength	Normal	Physical	80	100	15	Normal	•
HM06	Rock Smash	Fighting	Physical	40	100	15	Normal	•
HM08	Rock Climb	Normal	Physical	90	85	20	Normal	•

ABILITY ● Own Tempo ● Oblivious

EGG GROUP Monster

STATS
HP ●●●
ATTACK ●●●
DEFENSE ●●●
SP. ATTACK ●●●
SP. DEFENSE ●●●
SPEED ●●

● LEVEL-UP AND LEARNED MOVES

Lv	Name	Type	Kind	Power	Acc	PP	Range	DA
Base	Lick	Ghost	Physical	20	100	30	Normal	•
5	Supersonic	Normal	Status	—	55	20	Normal	—
9	Defense Curl	Normal	Status	—	—	40	Self	—
13	Knock Off	Dark	Physical	20	100	20	Normal	•
17	Wrap	Normal	Physical	15	85	20	Normal	•
21	Stomp	Normal	Physical	65	100	20	Normal	•
25	Disable	Normal	Status	—	80	20	Normal	—
29	Slam	Normal	Physical	80	75	20	Normal	•
33	Rollout	Rock	Physical	30	90	20	Normal	•
37	Me First	Normal	Status	—	—	20	DoM	—
41	Refresh	Normal	Status	—	—	20	Self	—
45	Screech	Normal	Status	—	85	40	Normal	—
49	Power Whip	Grass	Physical	120	85	10	Normal	•
53	Wring Out	Normal	Special	—	100	5	Normal	•
57	Gyro Ball	Steel	Physical	—	100	5	Normal	•

● MOVES TAUGHT IN EXCHANGE FOR COLORED SHARDS

Name	Type	Kind	Power	Acc	PP	Range	DA
Mud-Slap	Ground	Special	20	100	10	Normal	—
Icy Wind	Ice	Special	55	95	15	2 foes	—
Rollout	Rock	Physical	30	90	20	Normal	•
ThunderPunch	Electric	Physical	75	100	15	Normal	•
Fire Punch	Fire	Physical	75	100	15	Normal	•
Ice Punch	Ice	Physical	75	100	15	Normal	•
Aqua Tail	Water	Physical	90	90	10	Normal	•
Snore	Normal	Special	40	100	15	Normal	—
Zen Headbutt	Psychic	Physical	80	90	15	Normal	•
Knock Off	Dark	Physical	20	100	20	Normal	•

● PRIMARY WAY TO FIND

TRAINER'S PARTY Trainer on Victory Road

WILD POKÉMON

COURSE OF STORY

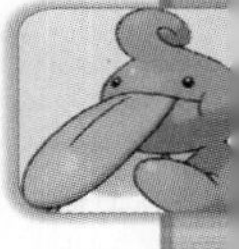

Sinnoh Pokédex No. 163 Evolution Pokémon

Eevee

NORMAL

HEIGHT: 1'00"
WEIGHT: 14.3 lbs.
GENDER: Male and Female
HELD ITEM: None

● M/F have same form

PLATINUM Because its genetic makeup is irregular, it quickly changes its form due to a variety of causes.

EVOLUTION PATH

Eevee
Vaporeon — Use Water Stone on Eevee
Jolteon — Use Thunderstone on Eevee
Flareon — Use Fire Stone on Eevee
Espeon — Level up Eevee in the morning or afternoon once its Friendship is high enough
Umbreon — Level up Eevee at night once its Friendship is high enough
Leafeon — Level up Eevee in Eterna Forest
Glaceon — Level up Eevee on Route 217

ABILITY ● Run Away ● Adaptability

EGG GROUP Field

STATS
HP ●●
ATTACK ●●
DEFENSE ●●
SP. ATTACK ●●
SP. DEFENSE ●●●
SPEED ●●

● TM & HM MOVES

No.	Name	Type	Kind	Power	Acc	PP	Range	DA
TM06	Toxic	Poison	Status	—	85	10	Normal	—
TM10	Hidden Power	Normal	Special	—	100	15	Normal	—
TM11	Sunny Day	Fire	Status	—	—	5	All	—
TM17	Protect	Normal	Status	—	—	10	Self	—
TM18	Rain Dance	Water	Status	—	—	5	All	—
TM21	Frustration	Normal	Physical	—	100	20	Normal	•
TM23	Iron Tail	Steel	Physical	100	75	15	Normal	•
TM27	Return	Normal	Physical	—	100	20	Normal	•
TM28	Dig	Ground	Physical	80	100	10	Normal	•
TM30	Shadow Ball	Ghost	Special	80	100	15	Normal	•
TM32	Double Team	Normal	Status	—	—	15	Self	—
TM42	Facade	Normal	Physical	70	100	20	Normal	•
TM43	Secret Power	Normal	Physical	70	100	20	Normal	—
TM44	Rest	Psychic	Status	—	—	10	Self	—
TM45	Attract	Normal	Status	—	100	15	Normal	—
TM58	Endure	Normal	Status	—	—	10	Self	—
TM78	Captivate	Normal	Status	—	100	20	2 foes	—
TM82	Sleep Talk	Normal	Status	—	—	10	DoM	—
TM83	Natural Gift	Normal	Physical	—	100	15	Normal	—
TM87	Swagger	Normal	Status	—	90	15	Normal	—
TM90	Substitute	Normal	Status	—	—	10	Self	—

● LEVEL-UP AND LEARNED MOVES

Lv	Name	Type	Kind	Power	Acc	PP	Range	DA
Base	Tail Whip	Normal	Status	—	100	30	2 foes	—
Base	Tackle	Normal	Physical	35	95	35	Normal	•
Base	Helping Hand	Normal	Status	—	—	20	1 ally	—
8	Sand-Attack	Ground	Status	—	100	15	Normal	—
15	Growl	Normal	Status	—	100	40	2 foes	—
22	Quick Attack	Normal	Physical	40	100	30	Normal	•
29	Bite	Dark	Physical	60	100	25	Normal	•
36	Baton Pass	Normal	Status	—	—	40	Self	—
43	Take Down	Normal	Physical	90	85	20	Normal	•
50	Last Resort	Normal	Physical	130	100	5	Normal	•
57	Trump Card	Normal	Special	—	—	5	Normal	—

● MOVES TAUGHT IN EXCHANGE FOR COLORED SHARDS

Name	Type	Kind	Power	Acc	PP	Range	DA
Mud-Slap	Ground	Special	20	100	10	Normal	—
Snore	Normal	Special	40	100	15	Normal	—
Helping Hand	Normal	Status	—	—	20	1 ally	—
Last Resort	Normal	Physical	130	100	5	Normal	•
Swift	Normal	Special	60	—	20	2 foes	—

● EGG MOVES

Name	Type	Kind	Power	Acc	PP	Range	DA
Charm	Normal	Status	—	100	20	Normal	—
Flail	Normal	Physical	—	100	15	Normal	•
Endure	Normal	Status	—	—	10	Self	—
Curse	???	Status	—	—	10	Normal • Self	—
Tickle	Normal	Status	—	100	20	Normal	—
Wish	Normal	Status	—	—	10	Self	—
Yawn	Normal	Status	—	—	10	Normal	—
Fake Tears	Dark	Status	—	100	20	Normal	—
Covet	Normal	Physical	40	100	40	Normal	•

● PRIMARY WAY TO FIND

TRAINER'S PARTY Trainer on Route 209

WILD POKÉMON Trophy Garden at Pokémon Mansion on Route 212 (Talk to Mr. Backlot after getting the National Pokédex)

COURSE OF STORY Receive from Bebe in Hearthome City

Sinnoh Pokédex No. 164 Bubble Jet Pokémon

Vaporeon

WATER

HEIGHT: 3'03"
WEIGHT: 63.9 lbs.
GENDER: Male and Female
HELD ITEM: None

● M/F have same form

PLATINUM Its cell composition is similar to water molecules. As a result, it can melt away into water.

EVOLUTION PATH

Eevee
Vaporeon — Use Water Stone on Eevee
Jolteon — Use Thunderstone on Eevee
Flareon — Use Fire Stone on Eevee
Espeon — Level up Eevee in the morning or afternoon once its Friendship is high enough
Umbreon — Level up Eevee at night once its Friendship is high enough
Leafeon — Level up Eevee in Eterna Forest
Glaceon — Level up Eevee on Route 217

ABILITY ● Water Absorb

EGG GROUP Field

STATS
HP ●●●●
ATTACK ●●●
DEFENSE ●●
SP. ATTACK ●●●●
SP. DEFENSE ●●●
SPEED ●●

● TM & HM MOVES

No.	Name	Type	Kind	Power	Acc	PP	Range	DA
TM03	Water Pulse	Water	Special	60	100	20	Normal	—
TM05	Roar	Normal	Status	—	100	20	Normal	—
TM06	Toxic	Poison	Status	—	85	10	Normal	—
TM07	Hail	Ice	Status	—	—	10	All	—
TM10	Hidden Power	Normal	Special	—	100	15	Normal	—
TM11	Sunny Day	Fire	Status	—	—	5	All	—
TM13	Ice Beam	Ice	Special	95	100	10	Normal	—
TM14	Blizzard	Ice	Special	120	70	5	2 foes	—
TM15	Hyper Beam	Normal	Special	150	90	5	Normal	—
TM17	Protect	Normal	Status	—	—	10	Self	—
TM18	Rain Dance	Water	Status	—	—	5	All	—
TM21	Frustration	Normal	Physical	—	100	20	Normal	•
TM23	Iron Tail	Steel	Physical	100	75	15	Normal	•
TM27	Return	Normal	Physical	—	100	20	Normal	•
TM28	Dig	Ground	Physical	80	100	10	Normal	•
TM30	Shadow Ball	Ghost	Special	80	100	15	Normal	—
TM32	Double Team	Normal	Status	—	—	15	Self	—
TM42	Facade	Normal	Physical	70	100	20	Normal	•
TM43	Secret Power	Normal	Physical	70	100	20	Normal	—
TM44	Rest	Psychic	Status	—	—	10	Self	—
TM45	Attract	Normal	Status	—	100	15	Normal	—
TM55	Brine	Water	Special	65	100	10	Normal	—
TM58	Endure	Normal	Status	—	—	10	Self	—
TM68	Giga Impact	Normal	Physical	150	90	5	Normal	•
TM78	Captivate	Normal	Status	—	100	20	2 foes	—
TM82	Sleep Talk	Normal	Status	—	—	10	DoM	—
TM83	Natural Gift	Normal	Physical	—	100	15	Normal	—
TM87	Swagger	Normal	Status	—	90	15	Normal	—
TM90	Substitute	Normal	Status	—	—	10	Self	—
HM03	Surf	Water	Special	95	100	15	2 foes + 1 ally	—
HM04	Strength	Normal	Physical	80	100	15	Normal	•
HM06	Rock Smash	Fighting	Physical	40	100	15	Normal	•
HM07	Waterfall	Water	Physical	80	100	15	Normal	•

● LEVEL-UP AND LEARNED MOVES

Lv	Name	Type	Kind	Power	Acc	PP	Range	DA
Base	Tail Whip	Normal	Status	—	100	30	2 foes	—
Base	Tackle	Normal	Physical	35	95	35	Normal	•
Base	Helping Hand	Normal	Status	—	—	20	1 ally	•
8	Sand-Attack	Ground	Status	—	100	15	Normal	—
15	Water Gun	Water	Special	40	100	25	Normal	—
22	Quick Attack	Normal	Physical	40	100	30	Normal	•
29	Bite	Dark	Physical	60	100	25	Normal	•
36	Aurora Beam	Ice	Special	65	100	20	Normal	—
43	Aqua Ring	Water	Status	—	—	20	Self	—
50	Last Resort	Normal	Physical	130	100	5	Normal	•
57	Haze	Ice	Status	—	—	30	All	—
64	Acid Armor	Poison	Status	—	—	40	Self	—
71	Hydro Pump	Water	Special	120	80	5	Normal	—
78	Muddy Water	Water	Special	95	85	10	2 foes	—

● MOVES TAUGHT IN EXCHANGE FOR COLORED SHARDS

Name	Type	Kind	Power	Acc	PP	Range	DA
Dive	Water	Physical	80	100	10	Normal	•
Mud-Slap	Ground	Special	20	100	10	Normal	—
Icy Wind	Ice	Special	55	95	15	2 foes	—
Aqua Tail	Water	Physical	90	90	10	Normal	•
Snore	Normal	Special	40	100	15	Normal	—
Helping Hand	Normal	Status	—	—	20	1 ally	—
Signal Beam	Bug	Special	75	100	15	Normal	—
Last Resort	Normal	Physical	130	100	5	Normal	•
Swift	Normal	Special	60	—	20	2 foes	—

● PRIMARY WAY TO FIND

TRAINER'S PARTY Trainer on Route 214

WILD POKÉMON

COURSE OF STORY

Jolteon

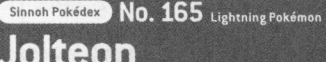

ELECTRIC

HEIGHT: 2'07"
WEIGHT: 54.0 lbs.
GENDER: **Male and Female**
HELD ITEM: **None**

● M/F have same form

PLATINUM — If agitated, it uses electricity to straighten out its fur and launch it in small bunches.

EVOLUTION PATH

Eevee	
Vaporeon — Use Water Stone on Eevee	Espeon — Level up Eevee in the morning or afternoon once its Friendship is high enough
Jolteon — Use Thunderstone on Eevee	Umbreon — Level up Eevee at night once its Friendship is high enough
Flareon — Use Fire Stone on Eevee	Leafeon — Level up Eevee in Eterna Forest
	Glaceon — Level up Eevee on Route 217

ABILITY ● Volt Absorb

EGG GROUP Field

STATS
HP ●●
ATTACK ●●●
DEFENSE ●●●
SP. ATTACK ●●●●
SP. DEFENSE ●●●●
SPEED ●●●●●

● TM & HM MOVES

No.	Name	Type	Kind	Power	Acc	PP	Range	DA
TM05	Roar	Normal	Status	—	100	20	Normal	—
TM06	Toxic	Poison	Status	—	85	10	Normal	—
TM10	Hidden Power	Normal	Special	—	100	15	Normal	—
TM11	Sunny Day	Fire	Status	—	—	5	All	—
TM15	Hyper Beam	Normal	Special	150	90	5	Normal	—
TM16	Light Screen	Psychic	Status	—	—	30	2 allies	—
TM17	Protect	Normal	Status	—	—	10	Self	—
TM18	Rain Dance	Water	Status	—	—	5	All	—
TM21	Frustration	Normal	Physical	—	100	20	Normal	●
TM23	Iron Tail	Steel	Physical	100	75	15	Normal	●
TM24	Thunderbolt	Electric	Special	95	100	15	Normal	—
TM25	Thunder	Electric	Special	120	70	10	Normal	—
TM27	Return	Normal	Physical	—	100	20	Normal	●
TM28	Dig	Ground	Physical	80	100	10	Normal	●
TM30	Shadow Ball	Ghost	Special	80	100	15	Normal	—
TM32	Double Team	Normal	Status	—	—	15	Self	—
TM34	Shock Wave	Electric	Special	60	—	20	Normal	—
TM42	Facade	Normal	Physical	70	100	20	Normal	●
TM43	Secret Power	Normal	Physical	70	100	20	Normal	●
TM44	Rest	Psychic	Status	—	—	10	Self	—
TM45	Attract	Normal	Status	—	100	15	Normal	—
TM57	Charge Beam	Electric	Special	50	90	10	Normal	—
TM58	Endure	Normal	Status	—	—	10	Self	—
TM68	Giga Impact	Normal	Physical	150	90	5	Normal	●
TM70	Flash	Normal	Status	—	100	20	Normal	—
TM73	Thunder Wave	Electric	Status	—	100	20	Normal	—
TM78	Captivate	Normal	Status	—	100	20	2 foes	—
TM82	Sleep Talk	Normal	Status	—	—	10	DoM	—
TM83	Natural Gift	Normal	Physical	—	100	15	Normal	●
TM87	Swagger	Normal	Status	—	90	15	Normal	—
TM90	Substitute	Normal	Status	—	—	10	Self	—
HM04	Strength	Normal	Physical	80	100	15	Normal	●
HM06	Rock Smash	Fighting	Physical	40	100	15	Normal	●

● LEVEL-UP AND LEARNED MOVES

Lv	Name	Type	Kind	Power	Acc	PP	Range	DA
Base	Tail Whip	Normal	Status	—	100	30	2 foes	—
Base	Tackle	Normal	Physical	35	95	35	Normal	●
Base	Helping Hand	Normal	Status	—	—	20	1 ally	—
8	Sand-Attack	Ground	Status	—	100	15	Normal	—
15	ThunderShock	Electric	Special	40	100	30	Normal	—
22	Quick Attack	Normal	Physical	40	100	30	Normal	●
29	Double Kick	Fighting	Physical	30	100	30	Normal	●
36	Pin Missile	Bug	Physical	14	85	20	Normal	●
43	Thunder Fang	Electric	Physical	65	95	15	Normal	●
50	Last Resort	Normal	Physical	130	100	5	Normal	●
57	Thunder Wave	Electric	Status	—	100	20	Normal	—
64	Agility	Psychic	Status	—	—	30	Self	—
71	Thunder	Electric	Special	120	70	10	Normal	—
78	Discharge	Electric	Special	80	100	15	2 foes+1 ally	—

● MOVES TAUGHT IN EXCHANGE FOR COLORED SHARDS

Name	Type	Kind	Power	Acc	PP	Range	DA
Mud-Slap	Ground	Special	20	100	10	Normal	—
Snore	Normal	Special	40	100	15	Normal	—
Helping Hand	Normal	Status	—	—	20	1 ally	—
Signal Beam	Bug	Special	75	100	15	Normal	—
Magnet Rise	Electric	Status	—	—	10	Self	—
Last Resort	Normal	Physical	130	100	5	Normal	●
Swift	Normal	Special	60	—	20	2 foes	—

● PRIMARY WAY TO FIND

TRAINER'S PARTY — Trainer on Route 214

WILD POKÉMON

COURSE OF STORY

Flareon

FIRE

HEIGHT: 2'11"
WEIGHT: 55.1 lbs.
GENDER: **Male and Female**
HELD ITEM: **None**

● M/F have same form

PLATINUM — Inhaled air is heated in the flame sac in its body to an intense fire over 3,000 degrees Fahrenheit.

EVOLUTION PATH

Eevee	
Vaporeon — Use Water Stone on Eevee	Espeon — Level up Eevee in the morning or afternoon once its Friendship is high enough
Jolteon — Use Thunderstone on Eevee	Umbreon — Level up Eevee at night once its Friendship is high enough
Flareon — Use Fire Stone on Eevee	Leafeon — Level up Eevee in Eterna Forest
	Glaceon — Level up Eevee on Route 217

ABILITY ● Flash Fire

EGG GROUP Field

STATS
HP ●●
ATTACK ●●●●
DEFENSE ●●●
SP. ATTACK ●●●
SP. DEFENSE ●●●●
SPEED ●●

● TM & HM MOVES

No.	Name	Type	Kind	Power	Acc	PP	Range	DA
TM05	Roar	Normal	Status	—	100	20	Normal	—
TM06	Toxic	Poison	Status	—	85	10	Normal	—
TM10	Hidden Power	Normal	Special	—	100	15	Normal	—
TM11	Sunny Day	Fire	Status	—	—	5	All	—
TM15	Hyper Beam	Normal	Special	150	90	5	Normal	—
TM17	Protect	Normal	Status	—	—	10	Self	—
TM18	Rain Dance	Water	Status	—	—	5	All	—
TM21	Frustration	Normal	Physical	—	100	20	Normal	●
TM23	Iron Tail	Steel	Physical	100	75	15	Normal	●
TM27	Return	Normal	Physical	—	100	20	Normal	●
TM28	Dig	Ground	Physical	80	100	10	Normal	●
TM30	Shadow Ball	Ghost	Special	80	100	15	Normal	—
TM32	Double Team	Normal	Status	—	—	15	Self	—
TM35	Flamethrower	Fire	Special	95	100	15	Normal	—
TM38	Fire Blast	Fire	Special	120	85	5	Normal	—
TM42	Facade	Normal	Physical	70	100	20	Normal	●
TM43	Secret Power	Normal	Physical	70	100	20	Normal	●
TM44	Rest	Psychic	Status	—	—	10	Self	—
TM45	Attract	Normal	Status	—	100	15	Normal	—
TM50	Overheat	Fire	Special	140	90	5	Normal	—
TM58	Endure	Normal	Status	—	—	10	Self	—
TM61	Will-O-Wisp	Fire	Status	—	75	15	Normal	—
TM68	Giga Impact	Normal	Physical	150	90	5	Normal	●
TM78	Captivate	Normal	Status	—	100	20	2 foes	—
TM82	Sleep Talk	Normal	Status	—	—	10	DoM	—
TM83	Natural Gift	Normal	Physical	—	100	15	Normal	●
TM87	Swagger	Normal	Status	—	90	15	Normal	—
TM90	Substitute	Normal	Status	—	—	10	Self	—
HM04	Strength	Normal	Physical	80	100	15	Normal	●
HM06	Rock Smash	Fighting	Physical	40	100	15	Normal	●

● LEVEL-UP AND LEARNED MOVES

Lv	Name	Type	Kind	Power	Acc	PP	Range	DA
Base	Tail Whip	Normal	Status	—	100	30	2 foes	—
Base	Tackle	Normal	Physical	35	95	35	Normal	●
Base	Helping Hand	Normal	Status	—	—	20	1 ally	—
8	Sand-Attack	Ground	Status	—	100	15	Normal	—
15	Ember	Fire	Special	40	100	25	Normal	—
22	Quick Attack	Normal	Physical	40	100	30	Normal	●
29	Bite	Dark	Physical	60	100	25	Normal	●
36	Fire Spin	Fire	Special	15	70	15	Normal	—
43	Fire Fang	Fire	Physical	65	95	15	Normal	●
50	Last Resort	Normal	Physical	130	100	5	Normal	●
57	Smog	Poison	Special	20	70	20	Normal	—
64	Scary Face	Normal	Status	—	90	10	Normal	—
71	Fire Blast	Fire	Special	120	85	5	Normal	—
78	Lava Plume	Fire	Special	80	100	15	2 foes+1 ally	—

● MOVES TAUGHT IN EXCHANGE FOR COLORED SHARDS

Name	Type	Kind	Power	Acc	PP	Range	DA
Mud-Slap	Ground	Special	20	100	10	Normal	—
Superpower	Fighting	Physical	120	100	5	Normal	●
Snore	Normal	Special	40	100	15	Normal	—
Helping Hand	Normal	Status	—	—	20	1 ally	—
Last Resort	Normal	Physical	130	100	5	Normal	●
Heat Wave	Fire	Special	100	90	10	2 foes	—
Swift	Normal	Special	60	—	20	2 foes	—

● PRIMARY WAY TO FIND

TRAINER'S PARTY — Trainer on Route 214

WILD POKÉMON

COURSE OF STORY

Espeon

Sinnoh Pokédex **No. 167** Sun Pokémon

PSYCHIC

HEIGHT: 2'11"
WEIGHT: 58.4 lbs.
GENDER: Male and Female
HELD ITEM: None

● M/F have same form

PLATINUM Its fur is so sensitive, it can sense minute shifts in the air and predict the weather.

EVOLUTION PATH

Eevee

Vaporeon — Use Water Stone on Eevee

Jolteon — Use Thunderstone on Eevee

Flareon — Use Fire Stone on Eevee

Espeon — Level up Eevee in the morning or afternoon once its Friendship is high enough

Umbreon — Level up Eevee at night once its Friendship is high enough

Leafeon — Level up Eevee in Eterna Forest

Glaceon — Level up Eevee on Route 217

● TM & HM MOVES

No.	Name	Type	Kind	Power	Acc	PP	Range	DA
TM04	Calm Mind	Psychic	Status	—	—	20	Self	—
TM06	Toxic	Poison	Status	—	85	10	Normal	—
TM10	Hidden Power	Normal	Special	—	100	15	Normal	—
TM11	Sunny Day	Fire	Status	—	—	5	All	—
TM15	Hyper Beam	Normal	Special	150	90	5	Normal	—
TM16	Light Screen	Psychic	Status	—	—	30	2 allies	—
TM17	Protect	Normal	Status	—	—	10	Self	—
TM18	Rain Dance	Water	Status	—	—	5	All	—
TM21	Frustration	Normal	Physical	—	100	20	Normal	•
TM23	Iron Tail	Steel	Physical	100	75	15	Normal	•
TM27	Return	Normal	Physical	—	100	20	Normal	•
TM28	Dig	Ground	Physical	80	100	10	Normal	•
TM29	Psychic	Psychic	Special	90	100	10	Normal	—
TM30	Shadow Ball	Ghost	Special	80	100	15	Normal	—
TM32	Double Team	Normal	Status	—	—	15	Self	—
TM33	Reflect	Psychic	Status	—	—	20	2 allies	—
TM42	Facade	Normal	Physical	70	100	20	Normal	•
TM43	Secret Power	Normal	Physical	70	100	20	Normal	•
TM44	Rest	Psychic	Status	—	—	10	Self	—
TM45	Attract	Normal	Status	—	100	15	Normal	—
TM48	Skill Swap	Psychic	Status	—	—	10	Normal	—
TM58	Endure	Normal	Status	—	—	10	Self	—
TM68	Giga Impact	Normal	Physical	150	90	5	Normal	•
TM70	Flash	Normal	Status	—	100	20	Normal	—
TM77	Psych Up	Normal	Status	—	—	10	Normal	—
TM78	Captivate	Normal	Status	—	100	20	2 foes	—
TM82	Sleep Talk	Normal	Status	—	—	10	DoM	—
TM83	Natural Gift	Normal	Physical	—	100	15	Normal	—
TM85	Dream Eater	Psychic	Special	100	100	15	Normal	—
TM86	Grass Knot	Grass	Special	—	100	20	Normal	—
TM87	Swagger	Normal	Status	—	90	15	Normal	—
TM90	Substitute	Normal	Status	—	—	10	Self	—
TM92	Trick Room	Psychic	Status	—	—	5	All	—
HM01	Cut	Normal	Physical	50	95	30	Normal	•

● LEVEL-UP AND LEARNED MOVES

Lv	Name	Type	Kind	Power	Acc	PP	Range	DA
Base	Tail Whip	Normal	Status	—	100	30	2 foes	—
Base	Tackle	Normal	Physical	35	95	35	Normal	•
Base	Helping Hand	Normal	Status	—	—	20	1 ally	—
8	Sand-Attack	Ground	Status	—	100	15	Normal	—
15	Confusion	Psychic	Special	50	100	25	Normal	—
22	Quick Attack	Normal	Physical	40	100	30	Normal	•
29	Swift	Normal	Special	60	—	20	2 foes	—
36	Psybeam	Psychic	Special	65	100	20	Normal	—
43	Future Sight	Psychic	Special	80	90	15	Normal	—
50	Last Resort	Normal	Physical	130	100	5	Normal	•
57	Psych Up	Normal	Status	—	—	10	Normal	—
64	Psychic	Psychic	Special	90	100	10	Normal	—
71	Morning Sun	Normal	Status	—	—	5	Self	—
78	Power Swap	Psychic	Status	—	—	10	Normal	—

● MOVES TAUGHT IN EXCHANGE FOR COLORED SHARDS

Name	Type	Kind	Power	Acc	PP	Range	DA
Mud-Slap	Ground	Special	20	100	10	Normal	—
Snore	Normal	Special	40	100	15	Normal	—
Helping Hand	Normal	Status	—	—	20	1 ally	—
Signal Beam	Bug	Special	75	100	15	Normal	—
Zen Headbutt	Psychic	Physical	80	90	15	Normal	•
Last Resort	Normal	Physical	130	100	5	Normal	•
Trick	Psychic	Status	—	100	10	Normal	—
Swift	Normal	Special	60	—	20	2 foes	—

ABILITY ● Synchronize

EGG GROUP — Field

STATS
HP ●●
ATTACK ●●
DEFENSE ●●
SP. ATTACK ●●●●●
SP. DEFENSE ●●●●
SPEED ●●●●●

● PRIMARY WAY TO FIND

TRAINER'S PARTY — Trainer on Route 212

WILD POKÉMON

COURSE OF STORY

Umbreon

Sinnoh Pokédex **No. 168** Moonlight Pokémon

DARK

HEIGHT: 3'03"
WEIGHT: 59.5 lbs.
GENDER: Male and Female
HELD ITEM: None

● M/F have same form

PLATINUM When exposed to the moon's aura, the rings on its body glow faintly and it gains a mysterious power.

EVOLUTION PATH

Eevee

Vaporeon — Use Water Stone on Eevee

Jolteon — Use Thunderstone on Eevee

Flareon — Use Fire Stone on Eevee

Espeon — Level up Eevee in the morning or afternoon once its Friendship is high enough

Umbreon — Level up Eevee at night once its Friendship is high enough

Leafeon — Level up Eevee in Eterna Forest

Glaceon — Level up Eevee on Route 217

● TM & HM MOVES

No.	Name	Type	Kind	Power	Acc	PP	Range	DA
TM06	Toxic	Poison	Status	—	85	10	Normal	—
TM10	Hidden Power	Normal	Special	—	100	15	Normal	—
TM11	Sunny Day	Fire	Status	—	—	5	All	—
TM12	Taunt	Dark	Status	—	100	20	Normal	—
TM15	Hyper Beam	Normal	Special	150	90	5	Normal	—
TM17	Protect	Normal	Status	—	—	10	Self	—
TM18	Rain Dance	Water	Status	—	—	5	All	—
TM21	Frustration	Normal	Physical	—	100	20	Normal	•
TM23	Iron Tail	Steel	Physical	100	75	15	Normal	•
TM27	Return	Normal	Physical	—	100	20	Normal	•
TM28	Dig	Ground	Physical	80	100	10	Normal	•
TM29	Psychic	Psychic	Special	90	100	10	Normal	—
TM30	Shadow Ball	Ghost	Special	80	100	15	Normal	—
TM32	Double Team	Normal	Status	—	—	15	Self	—
TM41	Torment	Dark	Status	—	100	15	Normal	—
TM42	Facade	Normal	Physical	70	100	20	Normal	•
TM43	Secret Power	Normal	Physical	70	100	20	Normal	•
TM44	Rest	Psychic	Status	—	—	10	Self	—
TM45	Attract	Normal	Status	—	100	15	Normal	—
TM49	Snatch	Dark	Status	—	—	10	DoM	—
TM58	Endure	Normal	Status	—	—	10	Self	—
TM66	Payback	Dark	Physical	50	100	10	Normal	•
TM68	Giga Impact	Normal	Physical	150	90	5	Normal	•
TM70	Flash	Normal	Status	—	100	20	Normal	—
TM77	Psych Up	Normal	Status	—	—	10	Normal	—
TM78	Captivate	Normal	Status	—	100	20	2 foes	—
TM79	Dark Pulse	Dark	Special	80	100	15	Normal	—
TM82	Sleep Talk	Normal	Status	—	—	10	DoM	—
TM83	Natural Gift	Normal	Physical	—	100	15	Normal	—
TM85	Dream Eater	Psychic	Special	100	100	15	Normal	—
TM87	Swagger	Normal	Status	—	90	15	Normal	—
TM90	Substitute	Normal	Status	—	—	10	Self	—
HM01	Cut	Normal	Physical	50	95	30	Normal	•

● LEVEL-UP AND LEARNED MOVES

Lv	Name	Type	Kind	Power	Acc	PP	Range	DA
Base	Tail Whip	Normal	Status	—	100	30	2 foes	—
Base	Tackle	Normal	Physical	35	95	35	Normal	•
Base	Helping Hand	Normal	Status	—	—	20	1 ally	•
8	Sand-Attack	Ground	Status	—	100	15	Normal	—
15	Pursuit	Dark	Physical	40	100	20	Normal	•
22	Quick Attack	Normal	Physical	40	100	30	Normal	•
29	Confuse Ray	Ghost	Status	—	100	10	Normal	—
36	Faint Attack	Dark	Physical	60	—	20	Normal	•
43	Assurance	Dark	Physical	50	100	10	Normal	•
50	Last Resort	Normal	Physical	130	100	5	Normal	•
57	Mean Look	Normal	Status	—	—	5	Normal	—
64	Screech	Normal	Status	—	85	40	Normal	—
71	Moonlight	Normal	Status	—	—	5	Self	—
78	Guard Swap	Psychic	Status	—	—	10	Normal	—

● MOVES TAUGHT IN EXCHANGE FOR COLORED SHARDS

Name	Type	Kind	Power	Acc	PP	Range	DA
Mud-Slap	Ground	Special	20	100	10	Normal	—
Snore	Normal	Special	40	100	15	Normal	—
Spite	Ghost	Status	—	100	10	Normal	—
Helping Hand	Normal	Status	—	—	20	1 ally	—
Last Resort	Normal	Physical	130	100	5	Normal	•
Sucker Punch	Dark	Physical	80	100	5	Normal	•
Swift	Normal	Special	60	—	20	2 foes	—

ABILITY ● Synchronize

EGG GROUP — Field

STATS
HP ●●●
ATTACK ●●
DEFENSE ●●●
SP. ATTACK ●●
SP. DEFENSE ●●●●
SPEED ●●

● PRIMARY WAY TO FIND

TRAINER'S PARTY — Trainer on Route 212

WILD POKÉMON

COURSE OF STORY

Leafeon

Sinnoh Pokédex **No. 169** Verdant Pokémon

GRASS

HEIGHT: 3'03"
WEIGHT: 56.2 lbs.
GENDER: **Male and Female**
HELD ITEM: **None**

● M/F have same form

PLATINUM It basically does not fight. With cells similar to those of plants, it can perform photosynthesis.

EVOLUTION PATH

- Eevee
- Vaporeon — Use Water Stone on Eevee
- Jolteon — Use Thunderstone on Eevee
- Flareon — Use Fire Stone on Eevee
- Espeon — Level up Eevee in the morning or afternoon once its Friendship is high enough
- Umbreon — Level up Eevee at night once its Friendship is high enough
- Leafeon — Level up Eevee in Eterna Forest
- Glaceon — Level up Eevee on Route 217

ABILITY ● Leaf Guard

EGG GROUP Field

STATS
HP ●●
ATTACK ●●●●
DEFENSE ●●●●
SP. ATTACK ●●●
SP. DEFENSE ●●●
SPEED ●●●

● TM & HM MOVES

No.	Name	Type	Kind	Power	Acc	PP	Range	DA
TM05	Roar	Normal	Status	—	100	20	Normal	—
TM06	Toxic	Poison	Status	—	85	10	Normal	—
TM09	Bullet Seed	Grass	Physical	10	100	30	Normal	—
TM10	Hidden Power	Normal	Special	—	100	15	Normal	—
TM11	Sunny Day	Fire	Status	—	—	5	All	—
TM15	Hyper Beam	Normal	Special	150	90	5	Normal	—
TM17	Protect	Normal	Status	—	—	10	Self	—
TM18	Rain Dance	Water	Status	—	—	5	All	—
TM19	Giga Drain	Grass	Special	60	100	10	Normal	—
TM21	Frustration	Normal	Physical	—	100	20	Normal	●
TM22	SolarBeam	Grass	Special	120	100	10	Normal	—
TM23	Iron Tail	Steel	Physical	100	75	15	Normal	●
TM27	Return	Normal	Physical	—	100	20	Normal	●
TM28	Dig	Ground	Physical	80	100	10	Normal	—
TM30	Shadow Ball	Ghost	Special	80	100	15	Normal	—
TM32	Double Team	Normal	Status	—	—	15	Self	—
TM40	Aerial Ace	Flying	Physical	60	—	20	Normal	●
TM42	Facade	Normal	Physical	70	100	20	Normal	—
TM43	Secret Power	Normal	Physical	70	100	20	Normal	●
TM44	Rest	Psychic	Status	—	—	10	Self	—
TM45	Attract	Normal	Status	—	100	15	Normal	—
TM53	Energy Ball	Grass	Special	80	100	10	Normal	—
TM58	Endure	Normal	Status	—	—	10	Self	—
TM68	Giga Impact	Normal	Physical	150	90	5	Normal	●
TM70	Flash	Normal	Status	—	100	20	Normal	—
TM75	Swords Dance	Normal	Status	—	—	30	Self	—
TM78	Captivate	Normal	Status	—	100	20	2 foes	—
TM81	X-Scissor	Bug	Physical	80	100	15	Normal	—
TM82	Sleep Talk	Normal	Status	—	—	10	DoM	—
TM83	Natural Gift	Normal	Physical	—	100	15	Normal	●
TM86	Grass Knot	Grass	Special	—	100	20	Normal	—
TM87	Swagger	Normal	Status	—	90	15	Normal	—
TM90	Substitute	Normal	Status	—	—	10	Self	—
HM04	Strength	Normal	Physical	80	100	15	Normal	●
HM06	Rock Smash	Fighting	Physical	40	100	15	Normal	●

● LEVEL-UP AND LEARNED MOVES

Lv	Name	Type	Kind	Power	Acc	PP	Range	DA
Base	Tail Whip	Normal	Status	—	100	30	2 foes	—
Base	Tackle	Normal	Physical	35	95	35	Normal	●
Base	Helping Hand	Normal	Status	—	—	20	1 ally	—
8	Sand-Attack	Ground	Status	—	100	15	Normal	—
15	Razor Leaf	Grass	Physical	55	95	25	2 foes	—
22	Quick Attack	Normal	Physical	40	100	30	Normal	●
29	Synthesis	Grass	Status	—	—	5	Self	—
36	Magical Leaf	Grass	Special	60	—	20	Normal	—
43	Giga Drain	Grass	Special	60	100	10	Normal	—
50	Last Resort	Normal	Physical	130	100	5	Normal	●
57	GrassWhistle	Grass	Status	—	55	15	Normal	—
64	Sunny Day	Fire	Status	—	—	5	All	—
71	Leaf Blade	Grass	Physical	90	100	15	Normal	●
78	Swords Dance	Normal	Status	—	—	30	Self	—

● MOVES TAUGHT IN EXCHANGE FOR COLORED SHARDS

Name	Type	Kind	Power	Acc	PP	Range	DA
Mud-Slap	Ground	Special	20	100	10	Normal	—
Fury Cutter	Bug	Physical	10	95	20	Normal	—
Snore	Normal	Special	40	100	15	Normal	—
Helping Hand	Normal	Status	—	—	20	1 ally	—
Synthesis	Grass	Status	—	—	5	Self	—
Seed Bomb	Grass	Physical	80	100	15	Normal	—
Last Resort	Normal	Physical	130	100	5	Normal	●
Knock Off	Dark	Physical	20	100	20	Normal	—
Swift	Normal	Special	60	—	20	2 foes	—

● PRIMARY WAY TO FIND

TRAINER'S PARTY Trainer on Route 212

WILD POKÉMON

COURSE OF STORY

Glaceon

Sinnoh Pokédex **No. 170** Fresh Snow Pokémon

ICE

HEIGHT: 2'07"
WEIGHT: 57.1 lbs.
GENDER: **Male and Female**
HELD ITEM: **None**

● M/F have same form

PLATINUM By controlling its body heat, it can freeze the atmosphere around it to make a diamond-dust flurry.

EVOLUTION PATH

- Eevee
- Vaporeon — Use Water Stone on Eevee
- Jolteon — Use Thunderstone on Eevee
- Flareon — Use Fire Stone on Eevee
- Espeon — Level up Eevee in the morning or afternoon once its Friendship is high enough
- Umbreon — Level up Eevee at night once its Friendship is high enough
- Leafeon — Level up Eevee in Eterna Forest
- Glaceon — Level up Eevee on Route 217

ABILITY ● Snow Cloak

EGG GROUP Field

STATS
HP ●●
ATTACK ●●
DEFENSE ●●●
SP. ATTACK ●●●●●
SP. DEFENSE ●●●●
SPEED ●●

● TM & HM MOVES

No.	Name	Type	Kind	Power	Acc	PP	Range	DA
TM03	Water Pulse	Water	Special	60	100	20	Normal	—
TM05	Roar	Normal	Status	—	100	20	Normal	—
TM06	Toxic	Poison	Status	—	85	10	Normal	—
TM07	Hail	Ice	Status	—	—	10	All	—
TM10	Hidden Power	Normal	Special	—	100	15	Normal	—
TM11	Sunny Day	Fire	Status	—	—	5	All	—
TM13	Ice Beam	Ice	Special	95	100	10	Normal	—
TM14	Blizzard	Ice	Special	120	70	5	2 foes	—
TM15	Hyper Beam	Normal	Special	150	90	5	Normal	—
TM17	Protect	Normal	Status	—	—	10	Self	—
TM18	Rain Dance	Water	Status	—	—	5	All	—
TM21	Frustration	Normal	Physical	—	100	20	Normal	●
TM23	Iron Tail	Steel	Physical	100	75	15	Normal	●
TM27	Return	Normal	Physical	—	100	20	Normal	●
TM28	Dig	Ground	Physical	80	100	10	Normal	—
TM30	Shadow Ball	Ghost	Special	80	100	15	Normal	—
TM32	Double Team	Normal	Status	—	—	15	Self	—
TM42	Facade	Normal	Physical	70	100	20	Normal	—
TM43	Secret Power	Normal	Physical	70	100	20	Normal	●
TM44	Rest	Psychic	Status	—	—	10	Self	—
TM45	Attract	Normal	Status	—	100	15	Normal	—
TM58	Endure	Normal	Status	—	—	10	Self	—
TM68	Giga Impact	Normal	Physical	150	90	5	Normal	●
TM72	Avalanche	Ice	Physical	60	100	10	Normal	●
TM78	Captivate	Normal	Status	—	100	20	2 foes	—
TM82	Sleep Talk	Normal	Status	—	—	10	DoM	—
TM83	Natural Gift	Normal	Physical	—	100	15	Normal	●
TM87	Swagger	Normal	Status	—	90	15	Normal	—
TM90	Substitute	Normal	Status	—	—	10	Self	—
HM04	Strength	Normal	Physical	80	100	15	Normal	●
HM06	Rock Smash	Fighting	Physical	40	100	15	Normal	●

● LEVEL-UP AND LEARNED MOVES

Lv	Name	Type	Kind	Power	Acc	PP	Range	DA
Base	Tail Whip	Normal	Status	—	100	30	2 foes	—
Base	Tackle	Normal	Physical	35	95	35	Normal	●
Base	Helping Hand	Normal	Status	—	—	20	1 ally	—
8	Sand-Attack	Ground	Status	—	100	15	Normal	—
15	Icy Wind	Ice	Special	55	95	15	2 foes	—
22	Quick Attack	Normal	Physical	40	100	30	Normal	●
29	Bite	Dark	Physical	60	100	25	Normal	●
36	Ice Shard	Ice	Physical	40	100	30	Normal	●
43	Ice Fang	Ice	Physical	65	95	15	Normal	●
50	Last Resort	Normal	Physical	130	100	5	Normal	●
57	Mirror Coat	Psychic	Special	—	100	20	Self	—
64	Hail	Ice	Status	—	—	10	All	—
71	Blizzard	Ice	Special	120	70	5	2 foes	—
78	Barrier	Psychic	Status	—	—	30	Self	—

● MOVES TAUGHT IN EXCHANGE FOR COLORED SHARDS

Name	Type	Kind	Power	Acc	PP	Range	DA
Mud-Slap	Ground	Special	20	100	10	Normal	—
Icy Wind	Ice	Special	55	95	15	2 foes	—
Aqua Tail	Water	Physical	90	90	10	Normal	●
Snore	Normal	Special	40	100	15	Normal	—
Helping Hand	Normal	Status	—	—	20	1 ally	—
Signal Beam	Bug	Special	75	100	15	Normal	—
Last Resort	Normal	Physical	130	100	5	Normal	●
Swift	Normal	Special	60	—	20	2 foes	—

● PRIMARY WAY TO FIND

TRAINER'S PARTY Trainer on Route 217

WILD POKÉMON

COURSE OF STORY

170
GLACEON

Swablu

NORMAL | FLYING

HEIGHT: 1'04"
WEIGHT: 2.6 lbs.
GENDER: Male and Female
HELD ITEM: None

● M/F have same form

PLATINUM
It can't relax if it or its surroundings are not clean. It wipes off dirt with its wings.

EVOLUTION PATH

Swablu —Lv35→ Altaria

ABILITY ● Natural Cure

EGG GROUP Flying / Dragon

STATS
HP ●
ATTACK ●
DEFENSE ●●
SP. ATTACK ●
SP. DEFENSE ●●●
SPEED ●●

● TM & HM MOVES

No.	Name	Type	Kind	Power	Acc	PP	Range	DA
TM06	Toxic	Poison	Status	—	85	10	Normal	—
TM10	Hidden Power	Normal	Special	—	100	15	Normal	—
TM11	Sunny Day	Fire	Status	—	—	5	All	—
TM13	Ice Beam	Ice	Special	95	100	10	Normal	—
TM17	Protect	Normal	Status	—	—	10	Self	—
TM18	Rain Dance	Water	Status	—	—	5	All	—
TM20	Safeguard	Normal	Status	—	—	25	2 allies	—
TM21	Frustration	Normal	Physical	—	100	20	Normal	●
TM22	SolarBeam	Grass	Special	120	100	10	Normal	—
TM27	Return	Normal	Physical	—	100	20	Normal	●
TM32	Double Team	Normal	Status	—	—	15	Self	—
TM40	Aerial Ace	Flying	Physical	60	—	20	Normal	●
TM42	Facade	Normal	Physical	70	100	20	Normal	●
TM43	Secret Power	Normal	Physical	70	100	20	Normal	●
TM44	Rest	Psychic	Status	—	—	10	Self	—
TM45	Attract	Normal	Status	—	100	15	Normal	—
TM46	Thief	Dark	Physical	40	100	10	Normal	●
TM47	Steel Wing	Steel	Physical	70	90	25	Normal	●
TM51	Roost	Flying	Status	—	—	10	Self	—
TM58	Endure	Normal	Status	—	—	10	Self	—
TM59	Dragon Pulse	Dragon	Special	90	100	10	Normal	—
TM77	Psych Up	Normal	Status	—	—	10	Normal	—
TM78	Captivate	Normal	Status	—	100	20	2 foes	—
TM82	Sleep Talk	Normal	Status	—	—	10	DoM	—
TM83	Natural Gift	Normal	Physical	—	100	15	Normal	●
TM85	Dream Eater	Psychic	Special	100	100	15	Normal	—
TM87	Swagger	Normal	Status	—	90	15	Normal	—
TM88	Pluck	Flying	Physical	60	100	20	Normal	●
TM90	Substitute	Normal	Status	—	—	10	Self	—
HM02	Fly	Flying	Physical	90	95	15	Normal	●

● LEVEL-UP AND LEARNED MOVES

Lv	Name	Type	Kind	Power	Acc	PP	Range	DA
Base	Peck	Flying	Physical	35	100	35	Normal	●
Base	Growl	Normal	Status	—	100	40	2 foes	—
5	Astonish	Ghost	Physical	30	100	15	Normal	●
9	Sing	Normal	Status	—	55	15	Normal	—
13	Fury Attack	Normal	Physical	15	85	20	Normal	●
18	Safeguard	Normal	Status	—	—	25	2 allies	—
23	Mist	Ice	Status	—	—	30	2 allies	—
28	Take Down	Normal	Physical	90	85	20	Normal	●
32	Natural Gift	Normal	Physical	—	100	15	Normal	●
36	Mirror Move	Flying	Status	—	—	20	DoM	—
40	Refresh	Normal	Status	—	—	20	Self	—
45	Dragon Pulse	Dragon	Special	90	100	10	Normal	—
50	Perish Song	Normal	Status	—	—	5	All	—

● MOVES TAUGHT IN EXCHANGE FOR COLORED SHARDS

Name	Type	Kind	Power	Acc	PP	Range	DA
Mud-Slap	Ground	Special	20	100	10	Normal	—
Ominous Wind	Ghost	Special	60	100	5	Normal	—
Snore	Normal	Special	40	100	15	Normal	—
Air Cutter	Flying	Special	55	95	25	2 foes	—
Outrage	Dragon	Physical	120	100	15	1 random	●
Twister	Dragon	Special	40	100	20	2 foes	—
Heat Wave	Fire	Special	100	90	10	2 foes	—
Swift	Normal	Special	60	—	20	2 foes	—
Uproar	Normal	Special	50	100	10	1 random	—

● EGG MOVES

Name	Type	Kind	Power	Acc	PP	Range	DA
Agility	Psychic	Status	—	—	30	Self	—
Haze	Ice	Status	—	—	30	All	—
Pursuit	Dark	Physical	40	100	20	Normal	●
Rage	Normal	Physical	20	100	20	Normal	●
FeatherDance	Flying	Status	—	100	15	Normal	—
Dragon Rush	Dragon	Physical	100	75	10	Normal	●

● PRIMARY WAY TO FIND

TRAINER'S PARTY Trainer on Victory Road

WILD POKÉMON Celestic Town side of Route 210

COURSE OF STORY

Altaria

DRAGON | FLYING

HEIGHT: 3'07"
WEIGHT: 45.4 lbs.
GENDER: Male and Female
HELD ITEM: None

● M/F have same form

PLATINUM
If it bonds with a person, it will gently envelop the friend with its soft wings, then hum.

EVOLUTION PATH

Swablu —Lv35→ Altaria

ABILITY ● Natural Cure

EGG GROUP Flying / Dragon

STATS
HP ●●
ATTACK ●●
DEFENSE ●●
SP. ATTACK ●●
SP. DEFENSE ●●●
SPEED ●●

● TM & HM MOVES

No.	Name	Type	Kind	Power	Acc	PP	Range	DA
TM02	Dragon Claw	Dragon	Physical	80	100	15	Normal	●
TM05	Roar	Normal	Status	—	100	20	Normal	—
TM06	Toxic	Poison	Status	—	85	10	Normal	—
TM10	Hidden Power	Normal	Special	—	100	15	Normal	—
TM11	Sunny Day	Fire	Status	—	—	5	All	—
TM13	Ice Beam	Ice	Special	95	100	10	Normal	—
TM15	Hyper Beam	Normal	Special	150	90	5	Normal	—
TM17	Protect	Normal	Status	—	—	10	Self	—
TM18	Rain Dance	Water	Status	—	—	5	All	—
TM20	Safeguard	Normal	Status	—	—	25	2 allies	—
TM21	Frustration	Normal	Physical	—	100	20	Normal	●
TM22	SolarBeam	Grass	Special	120	100	10	Normal	—
TM23	Iron Tail	Steel	Physical	100	75	15	Normal	●
TM26	Earthquake	Ground	Physical	100	100	10	2 foes • 1 ally	●
TM27	Return	Normal	Physical	—	100	20	Normal	●
TM32	Double Team	Normal	Status	—	—	15	Self	—
TM35	Flamethrower	Fire	Special	95	100	15	Normal	—
TM38	Fire Blast	Fire	Special	120	85	5	Normal	—
TM40	Aerial Ace	Flying	Physical	60	—	20	Normal	●
TM42	Facade	Normal	Physical	70	100	20	Normal	●
TM43	Secret Power	Normal	Physical	70	100	20	Normal	●
TM44	Rest	Psychic	Status	—	—	10	Self	—
TM45	Attract	Normal	Status	—	100	15	Normal	—
TM46	Thief	Dark	Physical	40	100	10	Normal	●
TM47	Steel Wing	Steel	Physical	70	90	25	Normal	●
TM51	Roost	Flying	Status	—	—	10	Self	—
TM58	Endure	Normal	Status	—	—	10	Self	—
TM59	Dragon Pulse	Dragon	Special	90	100	10	Normal	—
TM68	Giga Impact	Normal	Physical	150	90	5	Normal	●
TM77	Psych Up	Normal	Status	—	—	10	Normal	—
TM78	Captivate	Normal	Status	—	100	20	2 foes	—
TM82	Sleep Talk	Normal	Status	—	—	10	DoM	—
TM83	Natural Gift	Normal	Physical	—	100	15	Normal	●
TM85	Dream Eater	Psychic	Special	100	100	15	Normal	—
TM87	Swagger	Normal	Status	—	90	15	Normal	—
TM88	Pluck	Flying	Physical	60	100	20	Normal	●
TM90	Substitute	Normal	Status	—	—	10	Self	—
HM02	Fly	Flying	Physical	90	95	15	Normal	●
HM06	Rock Smash	Fighting	Physical	40	100	15	Normal	●

● LEVEL-UP AND LEARNED MOVES

Lv	Name	Type	Kind	Power	Acc	PP	Range	DA
Base	Pluck	Flying	Physical	60	100	20	Normal	●
Base	Peck	Flying	Physical	35	100	35	Normal	●
Base	Growl	Normal	Status	—	100	40	2 foes	—
Base	Astonish	Ghost	Physical	30	100	15	Normal	●
Base	Sing	Normal	Status	—	55	15	Normal	—
5	Astonish	Ghost	Physical	30	100	15	Normal	●
9	Sing	Normal	Status	—	55	15	Normal	—
13	Fury Attack	Normal	Physical	15	85	20	Normal	●
18	Safeguard	Normal	Status	—	—	25	2 allies	—
23	Mist	Ice	Status	—	—	30	2 allies	—
28	Take Down	Normal	Physical	90	85	20	Normal	●
32	Natural Gift	Normal	Physical	—	100	15	Normal	●
35	DragonBreath	Dragon	Special	60	100	20	Normal	—
39	Dragon Dance	Dragon	Status	—	—	20	Self	—
46	Refresh	Normal	Status	—	—	20	Self	—
54	Dragon Pulse	Dragon	Special	90	100	10	Normal	—
62	Perish Song	Normal	Status	—	—	5	All	—
70	Sky Attack	Flying	Physical	140	90	5	Normal	—

● MOVES TAUGHT IN EXCHANGE FOR COLORED SHARDS

Name	Type	Kind	Power	Acc	PP	Range	DA
Mud-Slap	Ground	Special	20	100	10	Normal	—
Ominous Wind	Ghost	Special	60	100	5	Normal	—
Snore	Normal	Special	40	100	15	Normal	—
Air Cutter	Flying	Special	55	95	25	2 foes	—
Outrage	Dragon	Physical	120	100	15	1 random	●
Twister	Dragon	Special	40	100	20	2 foes	—
Heat Wave	Fire	Special	100	90	10	2 foes	—
Swift	Normal	Special	60	—	20	2 foes	—
Uproar	Normal	Special	50	100	10	1 random	—

● MOVES TAUGHT BY PEOPLE

Name	Type	Kind	Power	Acc	PP	Range	DA
Draco Meteor*	Dragon	Special	140	90	5	Normal	—

*Draco Meteor is taught when the Pokémon's Friendship is maxed out

● PRIMARY WAY TO FIND

TRAINER'S PARTY Trainer on Victory Road

WILD POKÉMON

COURSE OF STORY

Sinnoh Pokédex **No. 173** Spike Ball Pokémon

Togepi

NORMAL

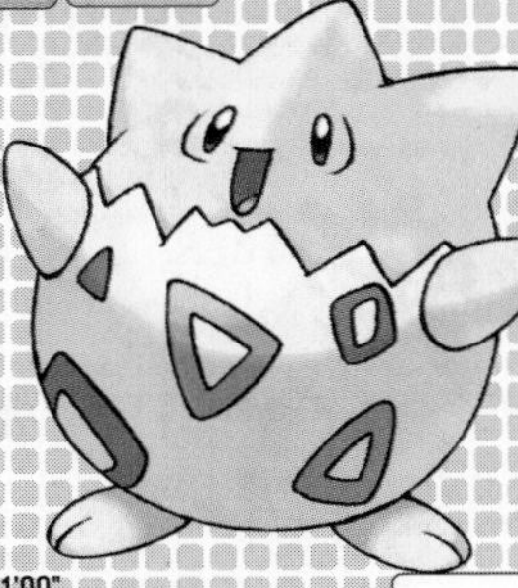

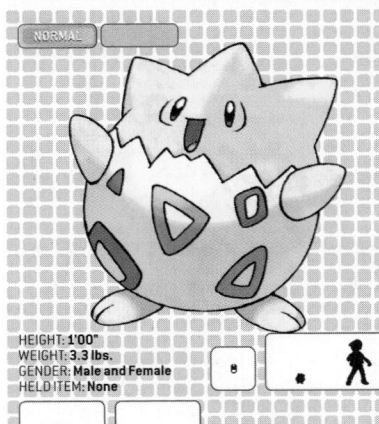

HEIGHT: **1'00"**
WEIGHT: **3.3 lbs.**
GENDER: **Male and Female**
HELD ITEM: **None**

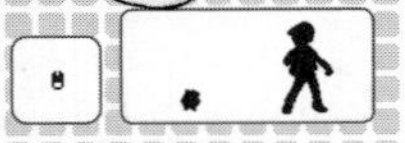

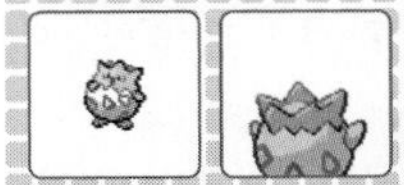

● M/F have same form

PLATINUM It transforms the kindness and joy of others into happiness, which it stores in its shell.

EVOLUTION PATH

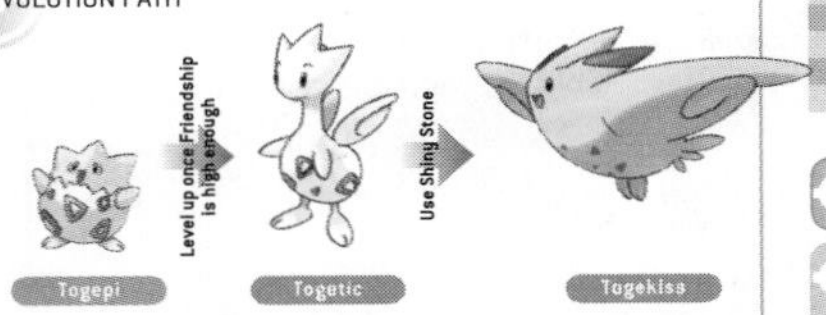
Level up once Friendship is high enough
Use Shiny Stone
Togepi
Togetic
Togekiss

● TM & HM MOVES

No.	Name	Type	Kind	Power	Acc	PP	Range	DA
TM03	Water Pulse	Water	Special	60	100	20	Normal	—
TM06	Toxic	Poison	Status	—	85	10	Normal	—
TM10	Hidden Power	Normal	Special	—	100	15	Normal	—
TM11	Sunny Day	Fire	Status	—	—	5	All	—
TM16	Light Screen	Psychic	Status	—	—	30	2 allies	—
TM17	Protect	Normal	Status	—	—	10	Self	—
TM18	Rain Dance	Water	Status	—	—	5	All	—
TM20	Safeguard	Normal	Status	—	—	25	2 allies	—
TM21	Frustration	Normal	Physical	—	100	20	Normal	•
TM22	SolarBeam	Grass	Special	120	100	10	Normal	—
TM27	Return	Normal	Physical	—	100	20	Normal	•
TM29	Psychic	Psychic	Special	90	100	10	Normal	—
TM30	Shadow Ball	Ghost	Special	80	100	15	Normal	—
TM32	Double Team	Normal	Status	—	—	15	Self	—
TM33	Reflect	Psychic	Status	—	—	20	2 allies	—
TM34	Shock Wave	Electric	Special	60	—	20	Normal	—
TM35	Flamethrower	Fire	Special	95	100	15	Normal	—
TM38	Fire Blast	Fire	Special	120	85	5	Normal	—
TM42	Facade	Normal	Physical	70	100	20	Normal	•
TM43	Secret Power	Normal	Physical	70	100	20	Normal	—
TM44	Rest	Psychic	Status	—	—	10	Self	—
TM45	Attract	Normal	Status	—	100	15	Normal	—
TM56	Fling	Dark	Physical	—	100	10	Normal	—
TM58	Endure	Normal	Status	—	—	10	Self	—
TM70	Flash	Normal	Status	—	100	20	Normal	—
TM73	Thunder Wave	Electric	Status	—	100	20	Normal	—
TM77	Psych Up	Normal	Status	—	—	10	Normal	—
TM78	Captivate	Normal	Status	—	100	20	2 foes	—
TM82	Sleep Talk	Normal	Status	—	—	10	DoM	—
TM83	Natural Gift	Normal	Physical	—	100	15	Normal	—
TM85	Dream Eater	Psychic	Special	100	100	15	Normal	—
TM86	Grass Knot	Grass	Special	—	100	20	Normal	•
TM87	Swagger	Normal	Status	—	90	15	Normal	—
TM90	Substitute	Normal	Status	—	—	10	Self	—
HM06	Rock Smash	Fighting	Physical	40	100	15	Normal	•

ABILITY ● Hustle ● Serene Grace

EGG GROUP: No Eggs

STATS: HP ●; ATTACK ●; DEFENSE ●●; SP. ATTACK ●●; SP. DEFENSE ●●; SPEED ●

● LEVEL-UP AND LEARNED MOVES

Lv	Name	Type	Kind	Power	Acc	PP	Range	DA
Base	Growl	Normal	Status	—	100	40	2 foes	—
Base	Charm	Normal	Status	—	100	20	Normal	—
6	Metronome	Normal	Status	—	—	10	DoM	—
10	Sweet Kiss	Normal	Status	—	75	10	Normal	—
15	Yawn	Normal	Status	—	—	10	Normal	—
19	Encore	Normal	Status	—	100	5	Normal	—
24	Follow Me	Normal	Status	—	—	20	Self	—
28	Wish	Normal	Status	—	—	10	Self	—
33	AncientPower	Rock	Special	60	100	5	Normal	—
37	Safeguard	Normal	Status	—	—	25	2 allies	—
42	Baton Pass	Normal	Status	—	—	40	Self	—
46	Double-Edge	Normal	Physical	120	100	15	Normal	•
51	Last Resort	Normal	Physical	130	100	5	Normal	•

● MOVES TAUGHT IN EXCHANGE FOR COLORED SHARDS

Name	Type	Kind	Power	Acc	PP	Range	DA
Mud-Slap	Ground	Special	20	100	10	Normal	—
Rollout	Rock	Physical	30	90	20	Normal	•
Snore	Normal	Special	40	100	15	Normal	—
Endeavor	Normal	Physical	—	100	5	Normal	•
AncientPower	Rock	Special	60	100	5	Normal	—
Signal Beam	Bug	Special	75	100	15	Normal	—
Zen Headbutt	Psychic	Physical	80	90	15	Normal	•
Last Resort	Normal	Physical	130	100	5	Normal	•
Trick	Psychic	Status	—	100	10	Normal	—
Swift	Normal	Special	60	—	20	2 foes	—
Uproar	Normal	Special	50	100	10	1 random	—

● EGG MOVES

Name	Type	Kind	Power	Acc	PP	Range	DA
Present	Normal	Physical	-	90	15	Normal	-
Mirror Move	Flying	Status	-	-	20	DoM	-
Peck	Flying	Physical	35	100	35	Normal	-
Foresight	Normal	Status	-	-	40	Normal	-
Future Sight	Psychic	Special	80	90	15	Normal	-
Substitute	Normal	Status	-	-	10	Self	-
Psych Up	Normal	Status	-	-	10	Normal	-
Nasty Plot	Dark	Status	-	-	20	Self	-
Psycho Shift	Psychic	Status	-	90	10	Normal	-
Lucky Chant	Normal	Status	-	-	30	2 allies	-

● PRIMARY WAY TO FIND

TRAINER'S PARTY Trainer on the Solaceon Town side of Route 210

WILD POKÉMON

COURSE OF STORY Hatch from the Egg received from Cynthia in Eterna City

Sinnoh Pokédex **No. 174** Happiness Pokémon

Togetic

NORMAL FLYING

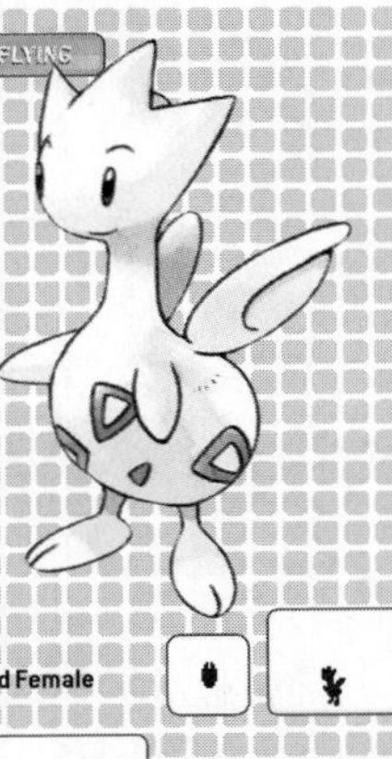

HEIGHT: **2'00"**
WEIGHT: **7.1 lbs.**
GENDER: **Male and Female**
HELD ITEM: **None**

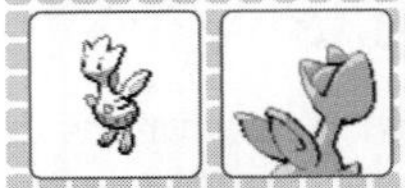

● M/F have same form

PLATINUM To share its happiness, it flies around the world seeking kind-hearted people.

EVOLUTION PATH

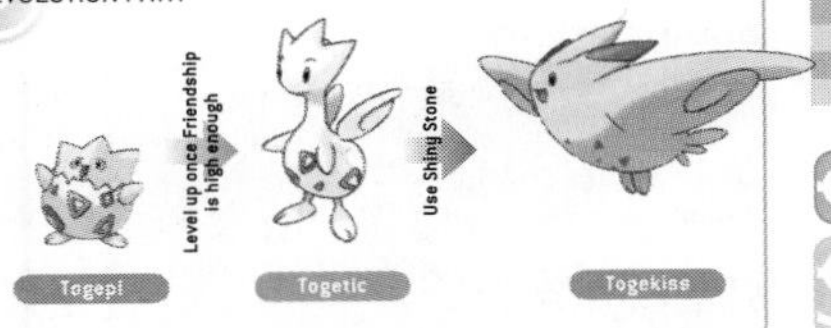
Level up once Friendship is high enough
Use Shiny Stone
Togepi
Togetic
Togekiss

● TM & HM MOVES

No.	Name	Type	Kind	Power	Acc	PP	Range	DA
TM01	Focus Punch	Fighting	Physical	150	100	20	Normal	•
TM03	Water Pulse	Water	Special	60	100	20	Normal	—
TM06	Toxic	Poison	Status	—	85	10	Normal	—
TM10	Hidden Power	Normal	Special	—	100	15	Normal	—
TM11	Sunny Day	Fire	Status	—	—	5	All	—
TM15	Hyper Beam	Normal	Special	150	90	5	Normal	—
TM16	Light Screen	Psychic	Status	—	—	30	2 allies	—
TM17	Protect	Normal	Status	—	—	10	Self	—
TM18	Rain Dance	Water	Status	—	—	5	All	—
TM20	Safeguard	Normal	Status	—	—	25	2 allies	—
TM21	Frustration	Normal	Physical	—	100	20	Normal	•
TM22	SolarBeam	Grass	Special	120	100	10	Normal	—
TM27	Return	Normal	Physical	—	100	20	Normal	•
TM29	Psychic	Psychic	Special	90	100	10	Normal	—
TM30	Shadow Ball	Ghost	Special	80	100	15	Normal	—
TM31	Brick Break	Fighting	Physical	75	100	15	Normal	•
TM32	Double Team	Normal	Status	—	—	15	Self	—
TM33	Reflect	Psychic	Status	—	—	20	2 allies	—
TM34	Shock Wave	Electric	Special	60	—	20	Normal	—
TM35	Flamethrower	Fire	Special	95	100	15	Normal	—
TM38	Fire Blast	Fire	Special	120	85	5	Normal	—
TM40	Aerial Ace	Flying	Physical	60	—	20	Normal	•
TM42	Facade	Normal	Physical	70	100	20	Normal	•
TM43	Secret Power	Normal	Physical	70	100	20	Normal	—
TM44	Rest	Psychic	Status	—	—	10	Self	—
TM45	Attract	Normal	Status	—	100	15	Normal	—
TM47	Steel Wing	Steel	Physical	70	90	25	Normal	•
TM51	Roost	Flying	Status	—	—	10	Self	—
TM56	Fling	Dark	Physical	—	100	10	Normal	—
TM58	Endure	Normal	Status	—	—	10	Self	—
TM60	Drain Punch	Fighting	Physical	60	100	5	Normal	•
TM62	Silver Wind	Bug	Special	60	100	5	Normal	—
TM68	Giga Impact	Normal	Physical	150	90	5	Normal	•
TM70	Flash	Normal	Status	—	100	20	Normal	—
TM73	Thunder Wave	Electric	Status	—	100	20	Normal	—
TM77	Psych Up	Normal	Status	—	—	10	Normal	—
TM78	Captivate	Normal	Status	—	100	20	2 foes	—
TM82	Sleep Talk	Normal	Status	—	—	10	DoM	—
TM83	Natural Gift	Normal	Physical	—	100	15	Normal	—
TM85	Dream Eater	Psychic	Special	100	100	15	Normal	—
TM86	Grass Knot	Grass	Special	—	100	20	Normal	•
TM87	Swagger	Normal	Status	—	90	15	Normal	—
TM90	Substitute	Normal	Status	—	—	10	Self	—
HM02	Fly	Flying	Physical	90	95	15	Normal	•
HM05	Defog	Flying	Status	—	—	15	Normal	—
HM06	Rock Smash	Fighting	Physical	40	100	15	Normal	•

ABILITY ● Hustle ● Serene Grace

EGG GROUP: Flying; Fairy

STATS: HP ●●; ATTACK ●●; DEFENSE ●●●; SP. ATTACK ●●●; SP. DEFENSE ●●●; SPEED ●●

● LEVEL-UP AND LEARNED MOVES

Lv	Name	Type	Kind	Power	Acc	PP	Range	DA
Base	Magical Leaf	Grass	Special	60	—	20	Normal	—
Base	Growl	Normal	Status	—	100	40	2 foes	—
Base	Charm	Normal	Status	—	100	20	Normal	—
Base	Metronome	Normal	Status	—	—	10	DoM	—
Base	Sweet Kiss	Normal	Status	—	75	10	Normal	—
6	Metronome	Normal	Status	—	—	10	DoM	—
10	Sweet Kiss	Normal	Status	—	75	10	Normal	—
15	Yawn	Normal	Status	—	—	10	Normal	—
19	Encore	Normal	Status	—	100	5	Normal	—
24	Follow Me	Normal	Status	—	—	20	Self	—
28	Wish	Normal	Status	—	—	10	Self	—
33	AncientPower	Rock	Special	60	100	5	Normal	—
37	Safeguard	Normal	Status	—	—	25	2 allies	—
42	Baton Pass	Normal	Status	—	—	40	Self	—
46	Double-Edge	Normal	Physical	120	100	15	Normal	•
51	Last Resort	Normal	Physical	130	100	5	Normal	•

● MOVES TAUGHT IN EXCHANGE FOR COLORED SHARDS

Name	Type	Kind	Power	Acc	PP	Range	DA
Mud-Slap	Ground	Special	20	100	10	Normal	—
Rollout	Rock	Physical	30	90	20	Normal	•
Ominous Wind	Ghost	Special	60	100	5	Normal	—
Snore	Normal	Special	40	100	15	Normal	—
Air Cutter	Flying	Special	55	95	25	2 foes	—
Endeavor	Normal	Physical	—	100	5	Normal	•
AncientPower	Rock	Special	60	100	5	Normal	—
Signal Beam	Bug	Special	75	100	15	Normal	—
Zen Headbutt	Psychic	Physical	80	90	15	Normal	•
Twister	Dragon	Special	40	100	20	2 foes	—
Last Resort	Normal	Physical	130	100	5	Normal	•
Trick	Psychic	Status	—	100	10	Normal	—
Heat Wave	Fire	Special	100	90	10	2 foes	—
Swift	Normal	Special	60	—	20	2 foes	—

● PRIMARY WAY TO FIND

TRAINER'S PARTY Trainer on Route 221

WILD POKÉMON

COURSE OF STORY

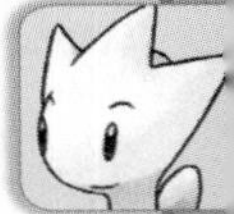

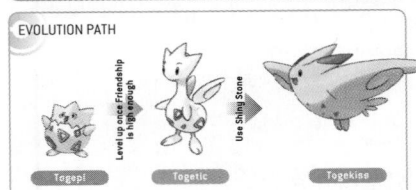

Togekiss

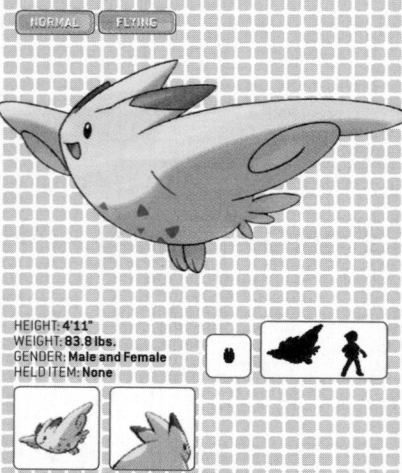

NORMAL | FLYING

HEIGHT: 4'11"
WEIGHT: 83.8 lbs.
GENDER: Male and Female
HELD ITEM: None

● M/F have same form

PLATINUM It shares many blessings with people who respect one another's rights and avoid needless strife.

EVOLUTION PATH

Togepi → (Level up once Friendship is high enough) Togetic → (Use Shiny Stone) Togekiss

| ABILITY | ● Hustle ● Serene Grace |
| EGG GROUP | Flying / Fairy |

STATS
HP ●●●
ATTACK ●●
DEFENSE ●●●
SP. ATTACK ●●●●
SP. DEFENSE ●●●●●
SPEED ●●●

● TM & HM MOVES

No.	Name	Type	Kind	Power	Acc	PP	Range	DA
TM01	Focus Punch	Fighting	Physical	150	100	20	Normal	●
TM03	Water Pulse	Water	Special	60	100	20	Normal	—
TM06	Toxic	Poison	Status	—	85	10	Normal	—
TM10	Hidden Power	Normal	Special	—	100	15	Normal	—
TM11	Sunny Day	Fire	Status	—	—	5	All	—
TM15	Hyper Beam	Normal	Special	150	90	5	Normal	—
TM16	Light Screen	Psychic	Status	—	—	30	2 allies	—
TM17	Protect	Normal	Status	—	—	10	Self	—
TM18	Rain Dance	Water	Status	—	—	5	All	—
TM20	Safeguard	Normal	Status	—	—	25	2 allies	—
TM21	Frustration	Normal	Physical	—	100	20	Normal	●
TM22	SolarBeam	Grass	Special	120	100	10	Normal	—
TM27	Return	Normal	Physical	—	100	20	Normal	●
TM29	Psychic	Psychic	Special	90	100	10	Normal	—
TM30	Shadow Ball	Ghost	Special	80	100	15	Normal	—
TM31	Brick Break	Fighting	Physical	75	100	15	Normal	●
TM32	Double Team	Normal	Status	—	—	15	Self	—
TM33	Reflect	Psychic	Status	—	—	20	2 allies	—
TM34	Shock Wave	Electric	Special	60	—	20	Normal	—
TM35	Flamethrower	Fire	Special	95	100	15	Normal	—
TM38	Fire Blast	Fire	Special	120	85	5	Normal	—
TM40	Aerial Ace	Flying	Physical	60	—	20	Normal	●
TM42	Facade	Normal	Physical	70	100	20	Normal	●
TM43	Secret Power	Normal	Physical	70	100	20	Normal	●
TM44	Rest	Psychic	Status	—	—	10	Self	—
TM45	Attract	Normal	Status	—	100	15	Normal	—
TM47	Steel Wing	Steel	Physical	70	90	25	Normal	●
TM51	Roost	Flying	Status	—	—	10	Self	—
TM56	Fling	Dark	Physical	—	100	10	Normal	●
TM58	Endure	Normal	Status	—	—	10	Self	—
TM60	Drain Punch	Fighting	Physical	60	100	5	Normal	●
TM62	Silver Wind	Bug	Special	60	100	5	Normal	—
TM68	Giga Impact	Normal	Physical	150	90	5	Normal	●
TM70	Flash	Normal	Status	—	100	20	Normal	—
TM73	Thunder Wave	Electric	Status	—	100	20	Normal	—
TM77	Psych Up	Normal	Status	—	—	10	Normal	—
TM78	Captivate	Normal	Status	—	100	20	2 foes	—
TM82	Sleep Talk	Normal	Status	—	—	10	DoM	—
TM83	Natural Gift	Normal	Physical	—	100	15	Normal	●
TM85	Dream Eater	Psychic	Special	100	100	15	Normal	—
TM86	Grass Knot	Grass	Special	—	100	20	Normal	●
TM87	Swagger	Normal	Status	—	90	15	Normal	—
TM88	Pluck	Flying	Physical	60	100	20	Normal	●
TM90	Substitute	Normal	Status	—	—	10	Self	—
HM02	Fly	Flying	Physical	90	95	15	Normal	●
HM05	Defog	Flying	Status	—	—	15	Normal	—
HM06	Rock Smash	Fighting	Physical	40	100	15	Normal	●

● LEVEL-UP AND LEARNED MOVES

Lv	Name	Type	Kind	Power	Acc	PP	Range	DA
Base	Sky Attack	Flying	Physical	140	90	5	Normal	—
Base	ExtremeSpeed	Normal	Physical	80	100	5	Normal	●
Base	Aura Sphere	Fighting	Special	90	—	20	Normal	—
Base	Air Slash	Flying	Special	75	95	15	Normal	—

● MOVES TAUGHT IN EXCHANGE FOR COLORED SHARDS

Name	Type	Kind	Power	Acc	PP	Range	DA
Mud-Slap	Ground	Special	20	100	10	Normal	●
Rollout	Rock	Physical	30	90	20	Normal	●
Ominous Wind	Ghost	Special	60	100	5	Normal	—
Snore	Normal	Special	40	100	15	Normal	—
Air Cutter	Flying	Special	55	95	25	2 foes	—
Endeavor	Normal	Physical	—	100	5	Normal	●
AncientPower	Rock	Special	60	100	5	Normal	—
Signal Beam	Bug	Special	75	100	15	Normal	—
Zen Headbutt	Psychic	Physical	80	90	15	Normal	●
Twister	Dragon	Special	40	100	20	2 foes	—
Last Resort	Normal	Physical	130	100	5	Normal	●
Trick	Psychic	Status	—	100	10	Normal	—
Heat Wave	Fire	Special	100	90	10	2 foes	—
Swift	Normal	Special	60	—	20	2 foes	—

● PRIMARY WAY TO FIND

TRAINER'S PARTY Pokémon League Champion Cynthia

WILD POKÉMON

COURSE OF STORY

Houndour

DARK | FIRE

HEIGHT: 2'00"
WEIGHT: 23.8 lbs.
GENDER: Male and Female
HELD ITEM: None

● M/F have same form

PLATINUM It is smart enough to hunt in packs. It uses a variety of cries for communicating with others.

EVOLUTION PATH

Houndour → (Lv 24) Houndoom

| ABILITY | ● Early Bird ● Flash Fire |
| EGG GROUP | Field |

STATS
HP ●●
ATTACK ●●
DEFENSE ●●
SP. ATTACK ●●●
SP. DEFENSE ●●
SPEED ●●●

● TM & HM MOVES

No.	Name	Type	Kind	Power	Acc	PP	Range	DA
TM05	Roar	Normal	Status	—	100	20	Normal	—
TM06	Toxic	Poison	Status	—	85	10	Normal	—
TM10	Hidden Power	Normal	Special	—	100	15	Normal	—
TM11	Sunny Day	Fire	Status	—	—	5	All	—
TM12	Taunt	Dark	Status	—	100	20	Normal	—
TM17	Protect	Normal	Status	—	—	10	Self	—
TM21	Frustration	Normal	Physical	—	100	20	Normal	●
TM22	SolarBeam	Grass	Special	120	100	10	Normal	—
TM23	Iron Tail	Steel	Physical	100	75	15	Normal	●
TM27	Return	Normal	Physical	—	100	20	Normal	●
TM30	Shadow Ball	Ghost	Special	80	100	15	Normal	—
TM32	Double Team	Normal	Status	—	—	15	Self	—
TM35	Flamethrower	Fire	Special	95	100	15	Normal	—
TM36	Sludge Bomb	Poison	Special	90	100	10	Normal	—
TM38	Fire Blast	Fire	Special	120	85	5	Normal	—
TM41	Torment	Dark	Status	—	100	15	Normal	—
TM42	Facade	Normal	Physical	70	100	20	Normal	●
TM43	Secret Power	Normal	Physical	70	100	20	Normal	●
TM44	Rest	Psychic	Status	—	—	10	Self	—
TM45	Attract	Normal	Status	—	100	15	Normal	—
TM46	Thief	Dark	Physical	40	100	10	Normal	●
TM49	Snatch	Dark	Status	—	—	10	DoM	—
TM50	Overheat	Fire	Special	140	90	5	Normal	—
TM58	Endure	Normal	Status	—	—	10	Self	—
TM61	Will-O-Wisp	Fire	Status	—	75	15	Normal	—
TM63	Embargo	Dark	Status	—	100	15	Normal	—
TM66	Payback	Dark	Physical	50	100	10	Normal	●
TM78	Captivate	Normal	Status	—	100	20	2 foes	—
TM79	Dark Pulse	Dark	Special	80	100	15	Normal	—
TM82	Sleep Talk	Normal	Status	—	—	10	DoM	—
TM83	Natural Gift	Normal	Physical	—	100	15	Normal	●
TM85	Dream Eater	Psychic	Special	100	100	15	Normal	—
TM87	Swagger	Normal	Status	—	90	15	Normal	—
TM90	Substitute	Normal	Status	—	—	10	Self	—
HM06	Rock Smash	Fighting	Physical	40	100	15	Normal	●

● LEVEL-UP AND LEARNED MOVES

Lv	Name	Type	Kind	Power	Acc	PP	Range	DA
Base	Leer	Normal	Status	—	100	30	2 foes	—
Base	Ember	Fire	Special	40	100	25	Normal	—
4	Howl	Normal	Status	—	—	40	Self	—
9	Smog	Poison	Special	20	70	20	Normal	—
14	Roar	Normal	Status	—	100	20	Normal	—
17	Bite	Dark	Physical	60	100	25	Normal	●
22	Odor Sleuth	Normal	Status	—	—	40	Normal	—
27	Beat Up	Dark	Physical	10	100	10	Normal	●
30	Fire Fang	Fire	Physical	65	95	15	Normal	●
35	Faint Attack	Dark	Physical	60	—	20	Normal	●
40	Embargo	Dark	Status	—	100	15	Normal	—
43	Flamethrower	Fire	Special	95	100	15	Normal	—
48	Crunch	Dark	Physical	80	100	15	Normal	●
53	Nasty Plot	Dark	Status	—	—	20	Self	—

● MOVES TAUGHT IN EXCHANGE FOR COLORED SHARDS

Name	Type	Kind	Power	Acc	PP	Range	DA
Mud-Slap	Ground	Special	20	100	10	Normal	—
Snore	Normal	Special	40	100	15	Normal	—
Spite	Ghost	Status	—	100	10	Normal	—
Heat Wave	Fire	Special	100	90	10	2 foes	—
Sucker Punch	Dark	Physical	80	100	5	Normal	●
Swift	Normal	Special	60	—	20	2 foes	—
Uproar	Normal	Special	50	100	10	1 random	—

● EGG MOVES

Name	Type	Kind	Power	Acc	PP	Range	DA
Fire Spin	Fire	Special	15	70	15	Normal	—
Rage	Normal	Physical	20	100	20	Normal	●
Pursuit	Dark	Physical	40	100	20	Normal	●
Counter	Fighting	Physical	—	100	20	Self	●
Spite	Ghost	Status	—	100	10	Normal	—
Reversal	Fighting	Physical	—	100	15	Normal	●
Beat Up	Dark	Physical	10	100	10	Normal	●
Will-O-Wisp	Fire	Status	—	75	15	Normal	—
Fire Fang	Fire	Physical	65	95	15	Normal	●
Thunder Fang	Electric	Physical	65	95	15	Normal	●
Nasty Plot	Dark	Status	—	—	20	Self	—
Punishment	Dark	Physical	—	100	5	Normal	●

● PRIMARY WAY TO FIND

TRAINER'S PARTY Team Galactic grunt you battle in Celestic Town

WILD POKÉMON Route 214

COURSE OF STORY

Houndoom

DARK   FIRE

HEIGHT: 4'07"
WEIGHT: 77.2 lbs.
GENDER: Male and Female
HELD ITEM: None

● Male form   ● Female form

PLATINUM | The flames it breathes when angry contain toxins. If they cause a burn, it will hurt forever.

EVOLUTION PATH

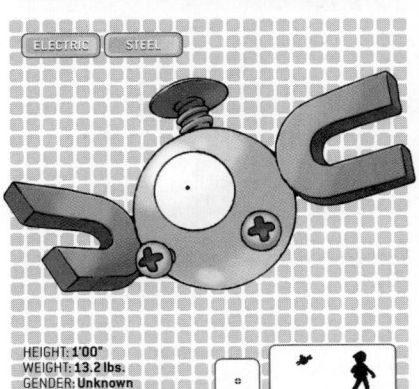

Houndour → Lv24 → Houndoom

● ABILITY: ● Early Bird ● Flash Fire

EGG GROUP: Field

● STATS
HP ●●
ATTACK ●●●
DEFENSE ●●●
SP. ATTACK ●●●●
SP. DEFENSE ●●●●
SPEED ●●●

● TM & HM MOVES

No.	Name	Type	Kind	Power	Acc	PP	Range	DA
TM05	Roar	Normal	Status	—	100	20	Normal	—
TM06	Toxic	Poison	Status	—	85	10	Normal	—
TM10	Hidden Power	Normal	Special	—	100	15	Normal	—
TM11	Sunny Day	Fire	Status	—	—	5	All	—
TM12	Taunt	Dark	Status	—	100	20	Normal	—
TM15	Hyper Beam	Normal	Special	150	90	5	Normal	—
TM17	Protect	Normal	Status	—	—	10	Self	—
TM21	Frustration	Normal	Physical	—	100	20	Normal	•
TM22	SolarBeam	Grass	Special	120	100	10	Normal	—
TM23	Iron Tail	Steel	Physical	100	75	15	Normal	—
TM27	Return	Normal	Physical	—	100	20	Normal	•
TM30	Shadow Ball	Ghost	Special	80	100	15	Normal	—
TM32	Double Team	Normal	Status	—	—	15	Self	—
TM35	Flamethrower	Fire	Special	95	100	15	Normal	—
TM36	Sludge Bomb	Poison	Special	90	100	10	Normal	—
TM38	Fire Blast	Fire	Special	120	85	5	Normal	—
TM41	Torment	Dark	Status	—	100	15	Normal	—
TM42	Facade	Normal	Physical	70	100	20	Normal	•
TM43	Secret Power	Normal	Physical	70	100	20	Normal	•
TM44	Rest	Psychic	Status	—	—	10	Self	—
TM45	Attract	Normal	Status	—	100	15	Normal	—
TM46	Thief	Dark	Physical	40	100	10	Normal	•
TM49	Snatch	Dark	Status	—	—	10	DoM	—
TM50	Overheat	Fire	Special	140	90	5	Normal	—
TM58	Endure	Normal	Status	—	—	10	Self	—
TM61	Will-O-Wisp	Fire	Status	—	75	15	Normal	—
TM63	Embargo	Dark	Status	—	100	15	Normal	—
TM66	Payback	Dark	Physical	50	100	10	Normal	•
TM68	Giga Impact	Normal	Physical	150	90	5	Normal	—
TM78	Captivate	Normal	Status	—	100	20	2 foes	—
TM79	Dark Pulse	Dark	Special	80	100	15	Normal	—
TM82	Sleep Talk	Normal	Status	—	—	10	DoM	—
TM83	Natural Gift	Normal	Physical	—	100	15	Normal	—
TM85	Dream Eater	Psychic	Special	100	100	15	Normal	—
TM87	Swagger	Normal	Status	—	90	15	Normal	—
TM90	Substitute	Normal	Status	—	—	10	Self	—
HM04	Strength	Normal	Physical	80	100	15	Normal	•
HM06	Rock Smash	Fighting	Physical	40	100	15	Normal	•

● LEVEL-UP AND LEARNED MOVES

Lv	Name	Type	Kind	Power	Acc	PP	Range	DA
Base	Thunder Fang	Electric	Physical	65	95	15	Normal	•
Base	Leer	Normal	Status	—	100	30	2 foes	—
Base	Ember	Fire	Special	40	100	25	Normal	—
Base	Howl	Normal	Status	—	—	40	Self	—
Base	Smog	Poison	Special	20	70	20	Normal	—
4	Howl	Normal	Status	—	—	40	Self	—
9	Smog	Poison	Special	20	70	20	Normal	—
14	Roar	Normal	Status	—	100	20	Normal	—
17	Bite	Dark	Physical	60	100	25	Normal	—
22	Odor Sleuth	Normal	Status	—	—	40	Normal	—
28	Beat Up	Dark	Physical	10	100	10	Normal	—
32	Fire Fang	Fire	Physical	65	95	15	Normal	•
38	Faint Attack	Dark	Physical	60	—	20	Normal	—
44	Embargo	Dark	Status	—	100	15	Normal	—
48	Flamethrower	Fire	Special	95	100	15	Normal	—
54	Crunch	Dark	Physical	80	100	15	Normal	—
60	Nasty Plot	Dark	Status	—	—	20	Self	—

● MOVES TAUGHT IN EXCHANGE FOR COLORED SHARDS

Name	Type	Kind	Power	Acc	PP	Range	DA
Mud-Slap	Ground	Special	20	100	10	Normal	—
Snore	Normal	Special	40	100	15	Normal	—
Spite	Ghost	Status	—	100	10	Normal	—
Heat Wave	Fire	Special	100	90	10	2 foes	—
Sucker Punch	Dark	Physical	80	100	5	Normal	•
Swift	Normal	Special	60	—	20	2 foes	—
Uproar	Normal	Special	50	100	10	1 random	—

● PRIMARY WAY TO FIND

TRAINER'S PARTY | Elite Four member Flint

WILD POKÉMON

COURSE OF STORY

Magnemite

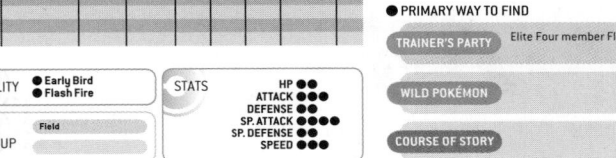

ELECTRIC   STEEL

HEIGHT: 1'00"
WEIGHT: 13.2 lbs.
GENDER: Unknown
HELD ITEM: Metal Coat

● Gender unknown

PLATINUM | The faster the units at its sides rotate, the greater the magnetic force they generate.

EVOLUTION PATH

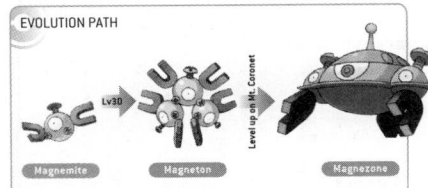

Magnemite → Lv30 → Magneton → Level up on Mt. Coronet → Magnezone

● ABILITY: ● Magnet Pull ● Sturdy

EGG GROUP: Mineral

● STATS
HP ●
ATTACK ●
DEFENSE ●●●
SP. ATTACK ●●●
SP. DEFENSE ●●
SPEED ●●

● TM & HM MOVES

No.	Name	Type	Kind	Power	Acc	PP	Range	DA
TM06	Toxic	Poison	Status	—	85	10	Normal	—
TM10	Hidden Power	Normal	Special	—	100	15	Normal	—
TM11	Sunny Day	Fire	Status	—	—	5	All	—
TM16	Light Screen	Psychic	Status	—	—	30	2 allies	—
TM17	Protect	Normal	Status	—	—	10	Self	—
TM18	Rain Dance	Water	Status	—	—	5	All	—
TM21	Frustration	Normal	Physical	—	100	20	Normal	•
TM24	Thunderbolt	Electric	Special	95	100	15	Normal	—
TM25	Thunder	Electric	Special	120	70	10	Normal	—
TM27	Return	Normal	Physical	—	100	20	Normal	•
TM32	Double Team	Normal	Status	—	—	15	Self	—
TM33	Reflect	Psychic	Status	—	—	20	2 allies	—
TM34	Shock Wave	Electric	Special	60	—	20	Normal	—
TM42	Facade	Normal	Physical	70	100	20	Normal	•
TM43	Secret Power	Normal	Physical	70	100	20	Normal	•
TM44	Rest	Psychic	Status	—	—	10	Self	—
TM57	Charge Beam	Electric	Special	50	90	10	Normal	—
TM58	Endure	Normal	Status	—	—	10	Self	—
TM64	Explosion	Normal	Physical	250	100	5	2 foes • 1 ally	—
TM67	Recycle	Normal	Status	—	—	10	Self	—
TM70	Flash	Normal	Status	—	100	20	Normal	—
TM73	Thunder Wave	Electric	Status	—	100	20	Normal	—
TM74	Gyro Ball	Steel	Physical	—	100	5	Normal	•
TM77	Psych Up	Normal	Status	—	—	10	Normal	—
TM82	Sleep Talk	Normal	Status	—	—	10	DoM	—
TM83	Natural Gift	Normal	Physical	—	100	15	Normal	—
TM87	Swagger	Normal	Status	—	90	15	Normal	—
TM90	Substitute	Normal	Status	—	—	10	Self	—
TM91	Flash Cannon	Steel	Special	80	100	10	Normal	—

● LEVEL-UP AND LEARNED MOVES

Lv	Name	Type	Kind	Power	Acc	PP	Range	DA
Base	Metal Sound	Steel	Status	—	85	40	Normal	•
Base	Tackle	Normal	Physical	35	95	35	Normal	—
6	ThunderShock	Electric	Special	40	100	30	Normal	—
11	Supersonic	Normal	Status	—	55	20	Normal	—
14	SonicBoom	Normal	Special	—	90	20	Normal	—
17	Thunder Wave	Electric	Status	—	100	20	Normal	—
22	Spark	Electric	Physical	65	100	20	Normal	•
27	Lock-On	Normal	Status	—	—	5	Normal	—
30	Magnet Bomb	Steel	Physical	60	—	20	Normal	—
33	Screech	Normal	Status	—	85	40	Normal	—
38	Discharge	Electric	Special	80	100	15	2 foes • 1 ally	—
43	Mirror Shot	Steel	Special	65	85	10	Normal	—
46	Magnet Rise	Electric	Status	—	—	10	Self	—
49	Gyro Ball	Steel	Physical	—	100	5	Normal	•
54	Zap Cannon	Electric	Special	120	50	5	Normal	—

● MOVES TAUGHT IN EXCHANGE FOR COLORED SHARDS

Name	Type	Kind	Power	Acc	PP	Range	DA
Rollout	Rock	Physical	30	90	20	Normal	•
Snore	Normal	Special	40	100	15	Normal	—
Signal Beam	Bug	Special	75	100	15	Normal	—
Iron Defense	Steel	Status	—	—	15	Self	—
Magnet Rise	Electric	Status	—	—	10	Self	—
Swift	Normal	Special	60	—	20	2 foes	—

● EGG MOVES

Name	Type	Kind	Power	Acc	PP	Range	DA

● PRIMARY WAY TO FIND

TRAINER'S PARTY | Trainer on Route 218

WILD POKÉMON | Fuego Ironworks

COURSE OF STORY

Sinnoh Pokédex No. 179 Magnet Pokémon

Magneton

ELECTRIC · **STEEL**

HEIGHT: 3'03"
WEIGHT: 132.3 lbs.
GENDER: Unknown
HELD ITEM: Metal Coat

● Gender unknown.

PLATINUM — Many mysteriously appear when more sunspots dot the sun. They stop TV sets from displaying properly.

EVOLUTION PATH

Magnemite → (Lv30) Magneton → (Level up on Mt. Coronet) Magnezone

ABILITY
● Magnet Pull
● Sturdy

EGG GROUP — Mineral

STATS
HP ●●
ATTACK ●●
DEFENSE ●●●
SP. ATTACK ●●●●
SP. DEFENSE ●●●
SPEED ●●●

● TM & HM MOVES

No.	Name	Type	Kind	Power	Acc	PP	Range	DA
TM06	Toxic	Poison	Status	—	85	10	Normal	—
TM10	Hidden Power	Normal	Special	—	100	15	Normal	—
TM11	Sunny Day	Fire	Status	—	—	5	All	—
TM15	Hyper Beam	Normal	Special	150	90	5	Normal	—
TM16	Light Screen	Psychic	Status	—	—	30	2 allies	—
TM17	Protect	Normal	Status	—	—	10	Self	—
TM18	Rain Dance	Water	Status	—	—	5	All	—
TM21	Frustration	Normal	Physical	—	100	20	Normal	•
TM24	Thunderbolt	Electric	Special	95	100	15	Normal	—
TM25	Thunder	Electric	Special	120	70	10	Normal	—
TM27	Return	Normal	Physical	—	100	20	Normal	•
TM32	Double Team	Normal	Status	—	—	15	Self	—
TM33	Reflect	Psychic	Status	—	—	20	2 allies	—
TM34	Shock Wave	Electric	Special	60	—	20	Normal	—
TM42	Facade	Normal	Physical	70	100	20	Normal	•
TM43	Secret Power	Normal	Physical	70	100	20	Normal	•
TM44	Rest	Psychic	Status	—	—	10	Self	—
TM57	Charge Beam	Electric	Special	50	90	10	Normal	—
TM58	Endure	Normal	Status	—	—	10	Self	—
TM64	Explosion	Normal	Physical	250	100	5	2 foes + 1 ally	—
TM67	Recycle	Normal	Status	—	—	10	Self	—
TM68	Giga Impact	Normal	Physical	150	90	5	Normal	•
TM70	Flash	Normal	Status	—	100	20	Normal	—
TM73	Thunder Wave	Electric	Status	—	100	20	Normal	—
TM74	Gyro Ball	Steel	Physical	—	100	5	Normal	•
TM77	Psych Up	Normal	Status	—	—	10	Normal	—
TM82	Sleep Talk	Normal	Status	—	—	10	DoM	—
TM83	Natural Gift	Normal	Physical	—	100	15	Normal	—
TM87	Swagger	Normal	Status	—	90	15	Normal	—
TM90	Substitute	Normal	Status	—	—	10	Self	—
TM91	Flash Cannon	Steel	Special	80	100	10	Normal	—

● LEVEL-UP AND LEARNED MOVES

Lv	Name	Type	Kind	Power	Acc	PP	Range	DA
Base	Tri Attack	Normal	Special	80	100	10	Normal	—
Base	Metal Sound	Normal	Status	—	85	40	Normal	—
Base	Tackle	Normal	Physical	35	95	35	Normal	•
Base	ThunderShock	Electric	Special	40	100	30	Normal	—
Base	Supersonic	Normal	Status	—	55	20	Normal	—
6	ThunderShock	Electric	Special	40	100	30	Normal	—
11	Supersonic	Normal	Status	—	55	20	Normal	—
14	SonicBoom	Normal	Special	—	90	20	Normal	—
17	Thunder Wave	Electric	Status	—	100	20	Normal	—
22	Spark	Electric	Physical	65	100	20	Normal	•
27	Lock-On	Normal	Status	—	—	5	Normal	—
30	Magnet Bomb	Steel	Physical	60	—	20	Normal	•
34	Screech	Normal	Status	—	85	40	Normal	—
40	Discharge	Electric	Special	80	100	15	2 foes + 1 ally	—
46	Mirror Shot	Steel	Special	65	85	10	Normal	—
50	Magnet Rise	Electric	Status	—	—	10	Self	—
54	Gyro Ball	Steel	Physical	—	100	5	Normal	•
60	Zap Cannon	Electric	Special	120	50	5	Normal	—

● MOVES TAUGHT IN EXCHANGE FOR COLORED SHARDS

Name	Type	Kind	Power	Acc	PP	Range	DA
Rollout	Rock	Physical	30	90	20	Normal	•
Snore	Normal	Special	40	100	15	Normal	—
Signal Beam	Bug	Special	75	100	15	Normal	—
Iron Defense	Steel	Status	—	—	15	Self	—
Magnet Rise	Electric	Status	—	—	10	Self	—
Swift	Normal	Special	60	—	20	2 foes	—

● PRIMARY WAY TO FIND

TRAINER'S PARTY — Canalave Gym Leader Byron
WILD POKÉMON — Victory Road 2F
COURSE OF STORY

---

179 ★★★★★
MAGNETON

Sinnoh Pokédex No. 180 Magnet Area Pokémon

Magnezone

ELECTRIC · **STEEL**

HEIGHT: 3'11"
WEIGHT: 396.8 lbs.
GENDER: Unknown
HELD ITEM: None

● Gender unknown

PLATINUM — A group tried to use scientific means to make MAGNEZONE evolve, but their efforts ended in failure.

EVOLUTION PATH

Magnemite → (Lv30) Magneton → (Level up on Mt. Coronet) Magnezone

ABILITY
● Magnet Pull
● Sturdy

EGG GROUP — Mineral

STATS
HP ●●
ATTACK ●●●
DEFENSE ●●●
SP. ATTACK ●●●●
SP. DEFENSE ●●●●
SPEED ●●

● TM & HM MOVES

No.	Name	Type	Kind	Power	Acc	PP	Range	DA
TM06	Toxic	Poison	Status	—	85	10	Normal	—
TM10	Hidden Power	Normal	Special	—	100	15	Normal	—
TM11	Sunny Day	Fire	Status	—	—	5	All	—
TM15	Hyper Beam	Normal	Special	150	90	5	Normal	—
TM16	Light Screen	Psychic	Status	—	—	30	2 allies	—
TM17	Protect	Normal	Status	—	—	10	Self	—
TM18	Rain Dance	Water	Status	—	—	5	All	—
TM21	Frustration	Normal	Physical	—	100	20	Normal	•
TM24	Thunderbolt	Electric	Special	95	100	15	Normal	—
TM25	Thunder	Electric	Special	120	70	10	Normal	—
TM27	Return	Normal	Physical	—	100	20	Normal	•
TM32	Double Team	Normal	Status	—	—	15	Self	—
TM33	Reflect	Psychic	Status	—	—	20	2 allies	—
TM34	Shock Wave	Electric	Special	60	—	20	Normal	—
TM42	Facade	Normal	Physical	70	100	20	Normal	•
TM43	Secret Power	Normal	Physical	70	100	20	Normal	•
TM44	Rest	Psychic	Status	—	—	10	Self	—
TM57	Charge Beam	Electric	Special	50	90	10	Normal	—
TM58	Endure	Normal	Status	—	—	10	Self	—
TM64	Explosion	Normal	Physical	250	100	5	2 foes + 1 ally	—
TM67	Recycle	Normal	Status	—	—	10	Self	—
TM68	Giga Impact	Normal	Physical	150	90	5	Normal	•
TM70	Flash	Normal	Status	—	100	20	Normal	—
TM73	Thunder Wave	Electric	Status	—	100	20	Normal	—
TM74	Gyro Ball	Steel	Physical	—	100	5	Normal	•
TM77	Psych Up	Normal	Status	—	—	10	Normal	—
TM82	Sleep Talk	Normal	Status	—	—	10	DoM	—
TM83	Natural Gift	Normal	Physical	—	100	15	Normal	—
TM87	Swagger	Normal	Status	—	90	15	Normal	—
TM90	Substitute	Normal	Status	—	—	10	Self	—
TM91	Flash Cannon	Steel	Special	80	100	10	Normal	—

● LEVEL-UP AND LEARNED MOVES

Lv	Name	Type	Kind	Power	Acc	PP	Range	DA
Base	Mirror Coat	Psychic	Special	—	100	20	Self	—
Base	Barrier	Psychic	Status	—	—	30	Self	—
Base	Metal Sound	Normal	Status	—	85	40	Normal	—
Base	Tackle	Normal	Physical	35	95	35	Normal	•
Base	ThunderShock	Electric	Special	40	100	30	Normal	—
Base	Supersonic	Normal	Status	—	55	20	Normal	—
6	ThunderShock	Electric	Special	40	100	30	Normal	—
11	Supersonic	Normal	Status	—	55	20	Normal	—
14	SonicBoom	Normal	Special	—	90	20	Normal	—
17	Thunder Wave	Electric	Status	—	100	20	Normal	—
22	Spark	Electric	Physical	65	100	20	Normal	•
27	Lock-On	Normal	Status	—	—	5	Normal	—
30	Magnet Bomb	Steel	Physical	60	—	20	Normal	•
34	Screech	Normal	Status	—	85	40	Normal	—
40	Discharge	Electric	Special	80	100	15	2 foes + 1 ally	—
46	Mirror Shot	Steel	Special	65	85	10	Normal	—
50	Magnet Rise	Electric	Status	—	—	10	Self	—
54	Gyro Ball	Steel	Physical	—	100	5	Normal	•
60	Zap Cannon	Electric	Special	120	50	5	Normal	—

● MOVES TAUGHT IN EXCHANGE FOR COLORED SHARDS

Name	Type	Kind	Power	Acc	PP	Range	DA
Rollout	Rock	Physical	30	90	20	Normal	•
Iron Head	Steel	Physical	80	100	15	Normal	•
Snore	Normal	Special	40	100	15	Normal	—
Signal Beam	Bug	Special	75	100	15	Normal	—
Iron Defense	Steel	Status	—	—	15	Self	—
Magnet Rise	Electric	Status	—	—	10	Self	—
Swift	Normal	Special	60	—	20	2 foes	—

● PRIMARY WAY TO FIND

TRAINER'S PARTY — Trainer on Victory Road
WILD POKÉMON
COURSE OF STORY

Tangela

GRASS

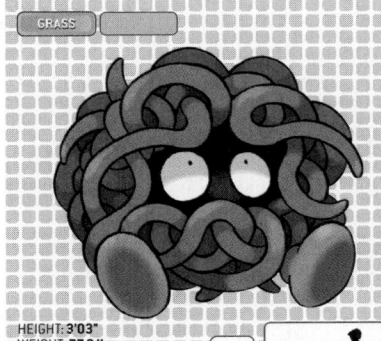

HEIGHT: 3'03"
WEIGHT: 77.2 lbs.
GENDER: Male and Female
HELD ITEM: None

● M/F have same form

PLATINUM — The blue vines shrouding its body are covered in a growth of fine hair. It is known to be ticklish.

EVOLUTION PATH

Tangela → (Raise to LV.33 and teach it AncientPower. Or, level it up while it knows AncientPower.) → Tangrowth

● TM & HM MOVES

No.	Name	Type	Kind	Power	Acc	PP	Range	DA
TM06	Toxic	Poison	Status	—	85	10	Normal	—
TM09	Bullet Seed	Grass	Physical	10	100	30	Normal	—
TM10	Hidden Power	Normal	Special	—	100	15	Normal	—
TM11	Sunny Day	Fire	Status	—	—	5	All	—
TM15	Hyper Beam	Normal	Special	150	90	5	Normal	—
TM17	Protect	Normal	Status	—	—	10	Self	—
TM19	Giga Drain	Grass	Special	60	100	10	Normal	—
TM21	Frustration	Normal	Physical	—	100	20	Normal	●
TM22	SolarBeam	Grass	Special	120	100	10	Normal	—
TM27	Return	Normal	Physical	—	100	20	Normal	●
TM32	Double Team	Normal	Status	—	—	15	Self	—
TM33	Reflect	Psychic	Status	—	—	20	2 allies	—
TM34	Shock Wave	Electric	Special	60	—	20	Normal	—
TM36	Sludge Bomb	Poison	Special	90	100	10	Normal	—
TM42	Facade	Normal	Physical	70	100	20	Normal	●
TM43	Secret Power	Normal	Physical	70	100	20	Normal	—
TM44	Rest	Psychic	Status	—	—	10	Self	—
TM45	Attract	Normal	Status	—	100	15	Normal	—
TM46	Thief	Dark	Physical	40	100	10	Normal	●
TM53	Energy Ball	Grass	Special	80	100	10	Normal	—
TM58	Endure	Normal	Status	—	—	10	Self	—
TM68	Giga Impact	Normal	Physical	150	90	5	Normal	●
TM70	Flash	Normal	Status	—	100	20	Normal	—
TM75	Swords Dance	Normal	Status	—	—	30	Self	—
TM77	Psych Up	Normal	Status	—	—	10	Normal	—
TM78	Captivate	Normal	Status	—	100	20	2 foes	—
TM82	Sleep Talk	Normal	Status	—	—	10	DoM	—
TM83	Natural Gift	Normal	Physical	—	100	15	Normal	—
TM86	Grass Knot	Grass	Special	—	100	20	Normal	—
TM87	Swagger	Normal	Status	—	90	15	Normal	—
TM90	Substitute	Normal	Status	—	—	10	Self	—
HM01	Cut	Normal	Physical	50	95	30	Normal	●
HM06	Rock Smash	Fighting	Physical	40	100	15	Normal	—

● LEVEL-UP AND LEARNED MOVES

Lv	Name	Type	Kind	Power	Acc	PP	Range	DA
Base	Ingrain	Grass	Status	—	—	20	Self	—
Base	Constrict	Normal	Physical	10	100	35	Normal	●
5	Sleep Powder	Grass	Status	—	75	15	Normal	—
8	Absorb	Grass	Special	20	100	25	Normal	—
12	Growth	Normal	Status	—	—	40	Self	—
15	PoisonPowder	Poison	Status	—	75	35	Normal	—
19	Vine Whip	Grass	Physical	35	100	15	Normal	●
22	Bind	Normal	Physical	15	75	20	Normal	●
26	Mega Drain	Grass	Special	40	100	15	Normal	—
29	Stun Spore	Grass	Status	—	75	30	Normal	—
33	AncientPower	Rock	Special	60	100	5	Normal	—
36	Knock Off	Dark	Physical	20	100	20	Normal	●
40	Natural Gift	Normal	Physical	—	100	15	Normal	—
43	Slam	Normal	Physical	80	75	20	Normal	●
47	Tickle	Normal	Status	—	100	20	Normal	—
50	Wring Out	Normal	Special	—	100	5	Normal	—
54	Power Whip	Grass	Physical	120	85	10	Normal	—

● MOVES TAUGHT IN EXCHANGE FOR COLORED SHARDS

Name	Type	Kind	Power	Acc	PP	Range	DA
Snore	Normal	Special	40	100	15	Normal	—
AncientPower	Rock	Special	60	100	5	Normal	—
Synthesis	Grass	Status	—	—	5	Self	—
Seed Bomb	Grass	Physical	80	100	15	Normal	—
Knock Off	Dark	Physical	20	100	20	Normal	●

● EGG MOVES

Name	Type	Kind	Power	Acc	PP	Range	DA
Flail	Normal	Physical	—	100	15	Normal	●
Confusion	Psychic	Special	50	100	25	Normal	—
Mega Drain	Grass	Special	40	100	15	Normal	—
Reflect	Psychic	Status	—	—	20	2 allies	—
Amnesia	Psychic	Status	—	—	20	Self	—
Leech Seed	Grass	Status	—	90	10	Normal	—
Nature Power	Normal	Status	—	—	20	DoM	—
Endeavor	Normal	Physical	—	100	5	Normal	—
Leaf Storm	Grass	Special	140	90	5	Normal	—

● PRIMARY WAY TO FIND

TRAINER'S PARTY — Trainer on Route 214

WILD POKÉMON — Pastoria Great Marsh

COURSE OF STORY

ABILITY — ● Chlorophyll ● Leaf Guard

EGG GROUP — Grass

STATS —
HP ●●
ATTACK ●●
DEFENSE ●●●
SP. ATTACK ●●●
SP. DEFENSE ●●●●●
SPEED ●●

Tangrowth

GRASS

HEIGHT: 6'07"
WEIGHT: 283.5 lbs.
GENDER: Male and Female
HELD ITEM: None

● Male form   ● Female form

PLATINUM — Its arms are made of plants that bind themselves to things. They grow back right away if cut.

EVOLUTION PATH

Tangela → (Raise to LV.33 and teach it AncientPower. Or, level it up while it knows AncientPower.) → Tangrowth

● TM & HM MOVES

No.	Name	Type	Kind	Power	Acc	PP	Range	DA
TM06	Toxic	Poison	Status	—	85	10	Normal	—
TM09	Bullet Seed	Grass	Physical	10	100	30	Normal	—
TM10	Hidden Power	Normal	Special	—	100	15	Normal	—
TM11	Sunny Day	Fire	Status	—	—	5	All	—
TM15	Hyper Beam	Normal	Special	150	90	5	Normal	—
TM17	Protect	Normal	Status	—	—	10	Self	—
TM19	Giga Drain	Grass	Special	60	100	10	Normal	—
TM21	Frustration	Normal	Physical	—	100	20	Normal	●
TM22	SolarBeam	Grass	Special	120	100	10	Normal	—
TM26	Earthquake	Ground	Physical	100	100	10	2 foes • 1 ally	—
TM27	Return	Normal	Physical	—	100	20	Normal	●
TM31	Brick Break	Fighting	Physical	75	100	15	Normal	—
TM32	Double Team	Normal	Status	—	—	15	Self	—
TM33	Reflect	Psychic	Status	—	—	20	2 allies	—
TM34	Shock Wave	Electric	Special	60	—	20	Normal	—
TM36	Sludge Bomb	Poison	Special	90	100	10	Normal	—
TM39	Rock Tomb	Rock	Physical	50	80	10	Normal	—
TM40	Aerial Ace	Flying	Physical	60	—	20	Normal	—
TM42	Facade	Normal	Physical	70	100	20	Normal	●
TM43	Secret Power	Normal	Physical	70	100	20	Normal	—
TM44	Rest	Psychic	Status	—	—	10	Self	—
TM45	Attract	Normal	Status	—	100	15	Normal	—
TM46	Thief	Dark	Physical	40	100	10	Normal	●
TM52	Focus Blast	Fighting	Special	120	70	5	Normal	—
TM53	Energy Ball	Grass	Special	80	100	10	Normal	—
TM56	Fling	Dark	Physical	—	100	10	Normal	●
TM58	Endure	Normal	Status	—	—	10	Self	—
TM66	Payback	Dark	Physical	50	100	10	Normal	●
TM68	Giga Impact	Normal	Physical	150	90	5	Normal	●
TM70	Flash	Normal	Status	—	100	20	Normal	—
TM75	Swords Dance	Normal	Status	—	—	30	Self	—
TM77	Psych Up	Normal	Status	—	—	10	Normal	—
TM78	Captivate	Normal	Status	—	100	20	2 foes	—
TM80	Rock Slide	Rock	Physical	75	90	10	2 foes	—
TM82	Sleep Talk	Normal	Status	—	—	10	DoM	—
TM83	Natural Gift	Normal	Physical	—	100	15	Normal	—
TM84	Poison Jab	Poison	Physical	80	100	20	Normal	—
TM86	Grass Knot	Grass	Special	—	100	20	Normal	—
TM87	Swagger	Normal	Status	—	90	15	Normal	—
TM90	Substitute	Normal	Status	—	—	10	Self	—
HM01	Cut	Normal	Physical	50	95	30	Normal	●
HM04	Strength	Normal	Physical	80	100	15	Normal	—
HM06	Rock Smash	Fighting	Physical	40	100	15	Normal	—

● LEVEL-UP AND LEARNED MOVES

Lv	Name	Type	Kind	Power	Acc	PP	Range	DA
Base	Ingrain	Grass	Status	—	—	20	Self	—
Base	Constrict	Normal	Physical	10	100	35	Normal	●
5	Sleep Powder	Grass	Status	—	75	15	Normal	—
8	Absorb	Grass	Special	20	100	25	Normal	—
12	Growth	Normal	Status	—	—	40	Self	—
15	PoisonPowder	Poison	Status	—	75	35	Normal	—
19	Vine Whip	Grass	Physical	35	100	15	Normal	●
22	Bind	Normal	Physical	15	75	20	Normal	●
26	Mega Drain	Grass	Special	40	100	15	Normal	—
29	Stun Spore	Grass	Status	—	75	30	Normal	—
33	AncientPower	Rock	Special	60	100	5	Normal	—
36	Knock Off	Dark	Physical	20	100	20	Normal	●
40	Natural Gift	Normal	Physical	—	100	15	Normal	—
43	Slam	Normal	Physical	80	75	20	Normal	●
47	Tickle	Normal	Status	—	100	20	Normal	—
50	Wring Out	Normal	Special	—	100	5	Normal	—
54	Power Whip	Grass	Physical	120	85	10	Normal	—
57	Block	Normal	Status	—	—	5	Normal	—

● MOVES TAUGHT IN EXCHANGE FOR COLORED SHARDS

Name	Type	Kind	Power	Acc	PP	Range	DA
Mud-Slap	Ground	Special	20	100	10	Normal	—
Snore	Normal	Special	40	100	15	Normal	—
AncientPower	Rock	Special	60	100	5	Normal	—
Synthesis	Grass	Status	—	—	5	Self	—
Seed Bomb	Grass	Physical	80	100	15	Normal	—
Knock Off	Dark	Physical	20	100	20	Normal	●

● PRIMARY WAY TO FIND

TRAINER'S PARTY — Trainer on Victory Road

WILD POKÉMON

COURSE OF STORY

ABILITY — ● Chlorophyll ● Leaf Guard

EGG GROUP — Grass

STATS —
HP ●●●
ATTACK ●●●●
DEFENSE ●●●
SP. ATTACK ●●●●
SP. DEFENSE ●●●
SPEED ●●

Yanma

Sinnoh Pokédex No. 183 Clear Wing Pokémon

BUG | FLYING

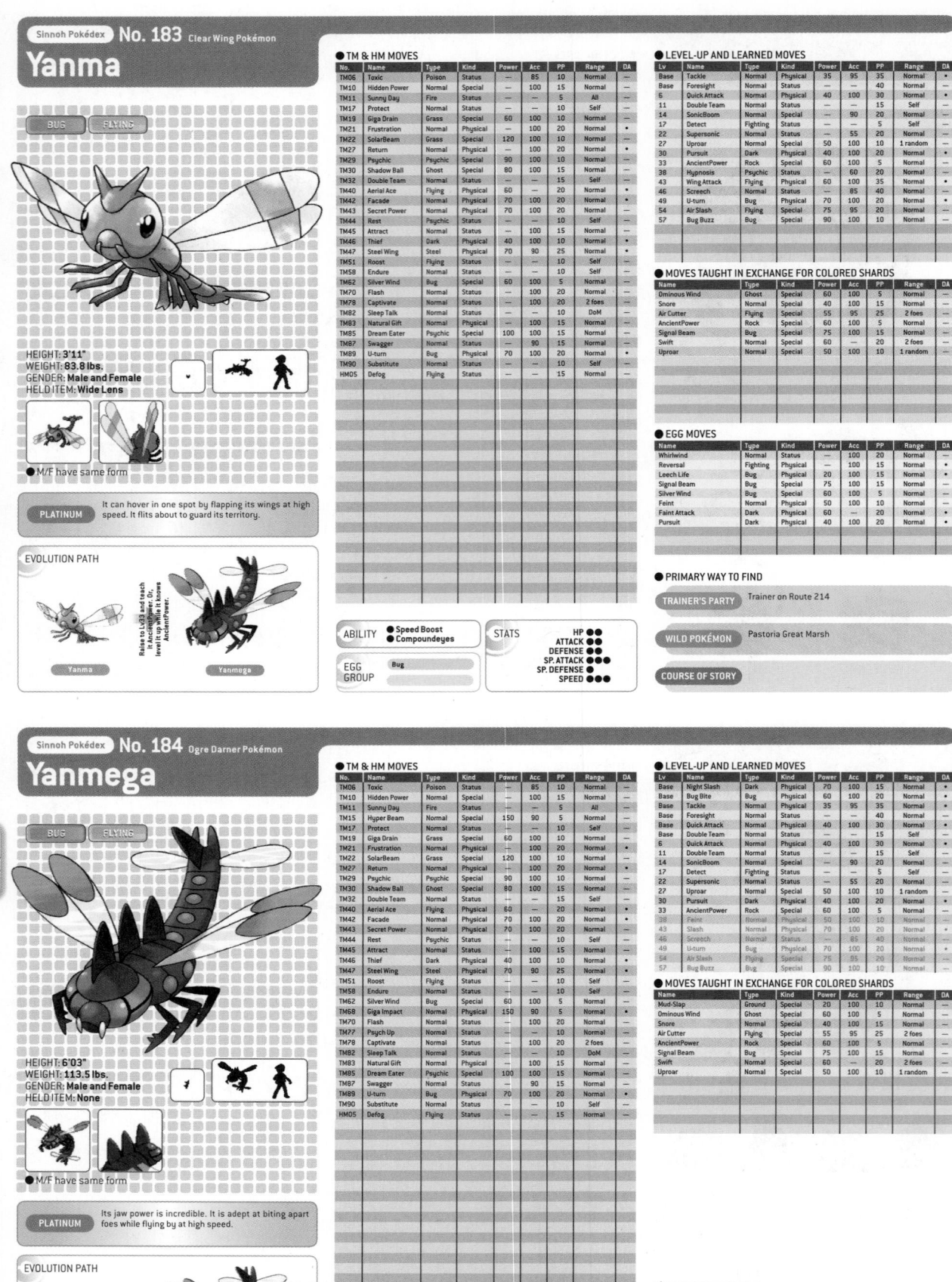

TM & HM MOVES

No.	Name	Type	Kind	Power	Acc	PP	Range	DA
TM06	Toxic	Poison	Status	—	85	10	Normal	—
TM10	Hidden Power	Normal	Special	—	100	15	Normal	—
TM11	Sunny Day	Fire	Status	—	—	5	All	—
TM17	Protect	Normal	Status	—	—	10	Self	—
TM19	Giga Drain	Grass	Special	60	100	10	Normal	—
TM21	Frustration	Normal	Physical	—	100	20	Normal	•
TM22	SolarBeam	Grass	Special	120	100	10	Normal	—
TM27	Return	Normal	Physical	—	100	20	Normal	•
TM29	Psychic	Psychic	Special	90	100	10	Normal	—
TM30	Shadow Ball	Ghost	Special	80	100	15	Normal	—
TM32	Double Team	Normal	Status	—	—	15	Self	—
TM40	Aerial Ace	Flying	Physical	60	—	20	Normal	•
TM42	Facade	Normal	Physical	70	100	20	Normal	•
TM43	Secret Power	Normal	Physical	70	100	20	Normal	•
TM44	Rest	Psychic	Status	—	—	10	Self	—
TM45	Attract	Normal	Status	—	100	15	Normal	—
TM46	Thief	Dark	Physical	40	100	10	Normal	•
TM47	Steel Wing	Steel	Physical	70	90	25	Normal	•
TM51	Roost	Flying	Status	—	—	10	Self	—
TM58	Endure	Normal	Status	—	—	10	Self	—
TM62	Silver Wind	Bug	Special	60	100	5	Normal	—
TM70	Flash	Normal	Status	—	100	20	Normal	—
TM78	Captivate	Normal	Status	—	100	20	2 foes	—
TM82	Sleep Talk	Normal	Status	—	—	10	DoM	—
TM83	Natural Gift	Normal	Physical	—	100	15	Normal	•
TM85	Dream Eater	Psychic	Special	100	100	15	Normal	—
TM87	Swagger	Normal	Status	—	90	15	Normal	—
TM89	U-turn	Bug	Physical	70	100	20	Normal	•
TM90	Substitute	Normal	Status	—	—	10	Self	—
HM05	Defog	Flying	Status	—	—	15	Normal	—

LEVEL-UP AND LEARNED MOVES

Lv	Name	Type	Kind	Power	Acc	PP	Range	DA
Base	Tackle	Normal	Physical	35	95	35	Normal	•
Base	Foresight	Normal	Status	—	—	40	Normal	—
6	Quick Attack	Normal	Physical	40	100	30	Normal	•
11	Double Team	Normal	Status	—	—	15	Self	—
14	SonicBoom	Normal	Special	—	90	20	Normal	—
17	Detect	Fighting	Status	—	—	5	Self	—
22	Supersonic	Normal	Status	—	55	20	Normal	—
27	Uproar	Normal	Special	50	100	10	1 random	—
30	Pursuit	Dark	Physical	40	100	20	Normal	•
33	AncientPower	Rock	Special	60	100	5	Normal	—
38	Hypnosis	Psychic	Status	—	60	20	Normal	—
43	Wing Attack	Flying	Physical	60	100	35	Normal	•
46	Screech	Normal	Status	—	85	40	Normal	—
49	U-turn	Bug	Physical	70	100	20	Normal	•
54	Air Slash	Flying	Special	75	95	20	Normal	—
57	Bug Buzz	Bug	Special	90	100	10	Normal	—

MOVES TAUGHT IN EXCHANGE FOR COLORED SHARDS

Name	Type	Kind	Power	Acc	PP	Range	DA
Ominous Wind	Ghost	Special	60	100	5	Normal	—
Snore	Normal	Special	40	100	15	Normal	—
Air Cutter	Flying	Special	55	95	25	2 foes	—
AncientPower	Rock	Special	60	100	5	Normal	—
Signal Beam	Bug	Special	75	100	15	Normal	—
Swift	Normal	Special	60	—	20	2 foes	—
Uproar	Normal	Special	50	100	10	1 random	—

EGG MOVES

Name	Type	Kind	Power	Acc	PP	Range	DA
Whirlwind	Normal	Status	—	100	20	Normal	—
Reversal	Fighting	Physical	—	100	15	Normal	•
Leech Life	Bug	Physical	20	100	15	Normal	•
Signal Beam	Bug	Special	75	100	15	Normal	—
Silver Wind	Bug	Special	60	100	5	Normal	—
Feint	Normal	Physical	50	100	10	Normal	—
Faint Attack	Dark	Physical	60	—	20	Normal	•
Pursuit	Dark	Physical	40	100	20	Normal	•

HEIGHT: 3'11"
WEIGHT: 83.8 lbs.
GENDER: Male and Female
HELD ITEM: Wide Lens

● M/F have same form

PLATINUM: It can hover in one spot by flapping its wings at high speed. It flits about to guard its territory.

EVOLUTION PATH

Yanma → Yanmega

Raise to Lv.33 and teach it AncientPower. Or, level it up while it knows AncientPower.

ABILITY: ● Speed Boost ● Compoundeyes
EGG GROUP: Bug

STATS:
HP ●●
ATTACK ●●
DEFENSE ●●
SP. ATTACK ●●
SP. DEFENSE ●●
SPEED ●●●

PRIMARY WAY TO FIND

TRAINER'S PARTY: Trainer on Route 214
WILD POKÉMON: Pastoria Great Marsh
COURSE OF STORY:

Yanmega

Sinnoh Pokédex No. 184 Ogre Darner Pokémon

BUG | FLYING

TM & HM MOVES

No.	Name	Type	Kind	Power	Acc	PP	Range	DA
TM06	Toxic	Poison	Status	—	85	10	Normal	—
TM10	Hidden Power	Normal	Special	—	100	15	Normal	—
TM11	Sunny Day	Fire	Status	—	—	5	All	—
TM15	Hyper Beam	Normal	Special	150	90	5	Normal	—
TM17	Protect	Normal	Status	—	—	10	Self	—
TM19	Giga Drain	Grass	Special	60	100	10	Normal	—
TM21	Frustration	Normal	Physical	—	100	20	Normal	•
TM22	SolarBeam	Grass	Special	120	100	10	Normal	—
TM27	Return	Normal	Physical	—	100	20	Normal	•
TM29	Psychic	Psychic	Special	90	100	10	Normal	—
TM30	Shadow Ball	Ghost	Special	80	100	15	Normal	—
TM32	Double Team	Normal	Status	—	—	15	Self	—
TM40	Aerial Ace	Flying	Physical	60	—	20	Normal	—
TM42	Facade	Normal	Physical	70	100	20	Normal	—
TM43	Secret Power	Normal	Physical	70	100	20	Normal	—
TM44	Rest	Psychic	Status	—	—	10	Self	—
TM45	Attract	Normal	Status	—	100	15	Normal	—
TM46	Thief	Dark	Physical	40	100	10	Normal	•
TM47	Steel Wing	Steel	Physical	70	90	25	Normal	•
TM51	Roost	Flying	Status	—	—	10	Self	—
TM58	Endure	Normal	Status	—	—	10	Self	—
TM62	Silver Wind	Bug	Special	60	100	5	Normal	—
TM68	Giga Impact	Normal	Physical	150	90	5	Normal	•
TM70	Flash	Normal	Status	—	100	20	Normal	—
TM77	Psych Up	Normal	Status	—	—	10	Normal	—
TM78	Captivate	Normal	Status	—	100	20	2 foes	—
TM82	Sleep Talk	Normal	Status	—	—	10	DoM	—
TM83	Natural Gift	Normal	Physical	—	100	15	Normal	•
TM85	Dream Eater	Psychic	Special	100	100	15	Normal	—
TM87	Swagger	Normal	Status	—	90	15	Normal	—
TM89	U-turn	Bug	Physical	70	100	20	Normal	•
TM90	Substitute	Normal	Status	—	—	10	Self	—
HM05	Defog	Flying	Status	—	—	15	Normal	—

LEVEL-UP AND LEARNED MOVES

Lv	Name	Type	Kind	Power	Acc	PP	Range	DA
Base	Night Slash	Dark	Physical	70	100	15	Normal	•
Base	Bug Bite	Bug	Physical	60	100	20	Normal	•
Base	Tackle	Normal	Physical	35	95	35	Normal	•
Base	Foresight	Normal	Status	—	—	40	Normal	—
Base	Quick Attack	Normal	Physical	40	100	30	Normal	•
Base	Double Team	Normal	Status	—	—	15	Self	—
6	Quick Attack	Normal	Physical	40	100	30	Normal	•
11	Double Team	Normal	Status	—	—	15	Self	—
14	SonicBoom	Normal	Special	—	90	20	Normal	—
17	Detect	Fighting	Status	—	—	5	Self	—
22	Supersonic	Normal	Status	—	55	20	Normal	—
27	Uproar	Normal	Special	50	100	10	1 random	—
30	Pursuit	Dark	Physical	40	100	20	Normal	•
33	AncientPower	Rock	Special	60	100	5	Normal	—
38	Feint	Normal	Physical	50	100	10	Normal	—
43	Slash	Normal	Physical	70	100	20	Normal	•
46	Screech	Normal	Status	—	85	40	Normal	—
49	U-turn	Bug	Physical	70	100	20	Normal	•
54	Air Slash	Flying	Special	75	95	20	Normal	—
57	Bug Buzz	Bug	Special	90	100	10	Normal	—

MOVES TAUGHT IN EXCHANGE FOR COLORED SHARDS

Name	Type	Kind	Power	Acc	PP	Range	DA
Mud-Slap	Ground	Special	20	100	10	Normal	—
Ominous Wind	Ghost	Special	60	100	5	Normal	—
Snore	Normal	Special	40	100	15	Normal	—
Air Cutter	Flying	Special	55	95	25	2 foes	—
AncientPower	Rock	Special	60	100	5	Normal	—
Signal Beam	Bug	Special	75	100	15	Normal	—
Swift	Normal	Special	60	—	20	2 foes	—
Uproar	Normal	Special	50	100	10	1 random	—

HEIGHT: 6'03"
WEIGHT: 113.5 lbs.
GENDER: Male and Female
HELD ITEM: None

● M/F have same form

PLATINUM: Its jaw power is incredible. It is adept at biting apart foes while flying by at high speed.

EVOLUTION PATH

Yanma → Yanmega

Raise to Lv.33 and teach it AncientPower. Or, level it up while it knows AncientPower.

ABILITY: ● Speed Boost ● Tinted Lens
EGG GROUP: Bug

STATS:
HP ●●●
ATTACK ●●●
DEFENSE ●●●●
SP. ATTACK ●●●●
SP. DEFENSE ●●●●
SPEED ●●●

PRIMARY WAY TO FIND

TRAINER'S PARTY: Eilte Four member Aaron
WILD POKÉMON:
COURSE OF STORY:

Sinnoh Pokédex **No. 185** Fruit Pokémon

Tropius

GRASS FLYING

HEIGHT: 6'07"
WEIGHT: 220.5 lbs.
GENDER: Male and Female
HELD ITEM: None

● M/F have same form

PLATINUM — Delicious fruits grew out from around its neck because it always ate the same kind of fruit.

EVOLUTION PATH

Does Not evolve

● TM & HM MOVES

No.	Name	Type	Kind	Power	Acc	PP	Range	DA
TM05	Roar	Normal	Status	—	100	20	Normal	—
TM06	Toxic	Poison	Status	—	85	10	Normal	—
TM09	Bullet Seed	Grass	Physical	10	100	30	Normal	—
TM10	Hidden Power	Normal	Special	—	100	15	Normal	—
TM11	Sunny Day	Fire	Status	—	—	5	All	—
TM15	Hyper Beam	Normal	Special	150	90	5	Normal	—
TM17	Protect	Normal	Status	—	—	10	Self	—
TM19	Giga Drain	Grass	Special	60	100	10	Normal	—
TM20	Safeguard	Normal	Status	—	—	25	2 allies	—
TM21	Frustration	Normal	Physical	—	100	20	Normal	•
TM22	SolarBeam	Grass	Special	120	100	10	Normal	—
TM26	Earthquake	Ground	Physical	100	100	10	2 foes • 1 ally	—
TM27	Return	Normal	Physical	—	100	20	Normal	•
TM32	Double Team	Normal	Status	—	—	15	Self	—
TM40	Aerial Ace	Flying	Physical	60	—	20	Normal	•
TM42	Facade	Normal	Physical	70	100	20	Normal	•
TM43	Secret Power	Normal	Physical	70	100	20	Normal	—
TM44	Rest	Psychic	Status	—	—	10	Self	—
TM45	Attract	Normal	Status	—	100	15	Normal	—
TM47	Steel Wing	Steel	Physical	70	90	25	Normal	•
TM51	Roost	Flying	Status	—	—	10	Self	—
TM53	Energy Ball	Grass	Special	80	100	10	Normal	—
TM58	Endure	Normal	Status	—	—	10	Self	—
TM62	Silver Wind	Bug	Special	60	100	5	Normal	—
TM68	Giga Impact	Normal	Physical	150	90	5	Normal	•
TM70	Flash	Normal	Status	—	100	20	Normal	—
TM75	Swords Dance	Normal	Status	—	—	30	Self	—
TM78	Captivate	Normal	Status	—	100	20	2 foes	—
TM82	Sleep Talk	Normal	Status	—	—	10	DoM	—
TM83	Natural Gift	Normal	Physical	—	100	15	Normal	—
TM86	Grass Knot	Grass	Special	—	100	20	Normal	•
TM87	Swagger	Normal	Status	—	90	15	Normal	—
TM90	Substitute	Normal	Status	—	—	10	Self	—
HM01	Cut	Normal	Physical	50	95	30	Normal	•
HM02	Fly	Flying	Physical	90	95	15	Normal	•
HM04	Strength	Normal	Physical	80	100	15	Normal	•
HM05	Defog	Flying	Status	—	—	15	Normal	—
HM06	Rock Smash	Fighting	Physical	40	100	15	Normal	•

ABILITY
● Chlorophyll
● Solar Power

EGG GROUP
Monster
Grass

STATS
HP ●●●
ATTACK ●●
DEFENSE ●●
SP. ATTACK ●●●
SP. DEFENSE ●●
SPEED ●●

● LEVEL-UP AND LEARNED MOVES

Lv	Name	Type	Kind	Power	Acc	PP	Range	DA
Base	Leer	Normal	Status	—	100	30	2 foes	—
Base	Gust	Flying	Special	40	100	35	Normal	—
7	Growth	Normal	Status	—	—	40	Self	—
11	Razor Leaf	Grass	Physical	55	95	25	2 foes	—
17	Stomp	Normal	Physical	65	100	20	Normal	•
21	Sweet Scent	Normal	Status	—	100	20	2 foes	—
27	Whirlwind	Normal	Status	—	100	20	Normal	—
31	Magical Leaf	Grass	Special	60	—	20	Normal	—
37	Body Slam	Normal	Physical	85	100	15	Normal	•
41	Synthesis	Grass	Status	—	—	5	Self	—
47	Air Slash	Flying	Special	75	95	20	Normal	—
51	SolarBeam	Grass	Special	120	100	10	Normal	—
57	Natural Gift	Normal	Physical	—	100	15	Normal	—
61	Leaf Storm	Grass	Special	140	90	5	Normal	—

● MOVES TAUGHT IN EXCHANGE FOR COLORED SHARDS

Name	Type	Kind	Power	Acc	PP	Range	DA
Mud-Slap	Ground	Special	20	100	10	Normal	—
Fury Cutter	Bug	Physical	10	95	20	Normal	•
Ominous Wind	Ghost	Special	60	100	5	Normal	—
Snore	Normal	Special	40	100	15	Normal	—
Air Cutter	Flying	Special	55	95	25	2 foes	—
Outrage	Dragon	Physical	120	100	15	1 random	•
Synthesis	Grass	Status	—	—	5	Self	—
Twister	Dragon	Special	40	100	20	2 foes	—

● EGG MOVES

Name	Type	Kind	Power	Acc	PP	Range	DA
Headbutt	Normal	Physical	70	100	15	Normal	•
Slam	Normal	Physical	80	75	20	Normal	•
Razor Wind	Normal	Special	80	100	10	2 foes	—
Leech Seed	Grass	Status	—	90	10	Normal	—
Nature Power	Normal	Status	—	—	20	DoM	—
Leaf Storm	Grass	Special	140	90	5	Normal	—
Synthesis	Grass	Status	—	—	5	Self	—
Curse	???	Status	—	—	10	Normal • Self	—
Leaf Blade	Grass	Physical	90	100	15	Normal	•

● PRIMARY WAY TO FIND

TRAINER'S PARTY — Trainer on Route 214

WILD POKÉMON — Pastoria Great Marsh Area 1 (morning and afternoon only)

COURSE OF STORY

Sinnoh Pokédex **No. 186** Spikes Pokémon

Rhyhorn

GROUND ROCK

HEIGHT: 3'03"
WEIGHT: 253.5 lbs.
GENDER: Male and Female
HELD ITEM: None

● Male form ● Female form

PLATINUM — Its powerful tackles can destroy anything. However, it is too slow witted to help people work.

EVOLUTION PATH

Lv42
Link trade while holding Protector
Rhyhorn
Rhydon
Rhyperior

● TM & HM MOVES

No.	Name	Type	Kind	Power	Acc	PP	Range	DA
TM05	Roar	Normal	Status	—	100	20	Normal	—
TM06	Toxic	Poison	Status	—	85	10	Normal	—
TM10	Hidden Power	Normal	Special	—	100	15	Normal	—
TM11	Sunny Day	Fire	Status	—	—	5	All	—
TM13	Ice Beam	Ice	Special	95	100	10	Normal	—
TM14	Blizzard	Ice	Special	120	70	5	2 foes	—
TM17	Protect	Normal	Status	—	—	10	Self	—
TM18	Rain Dance	Water	Status	—	—	5	All	—
TM21	Frustration	Normal	Physical	—	100	20	Normal	•
TM23	Iron Tail	Steel	Physical	100	75	15	Normal	•
TM24	Thunderbolt	Electric	Special	95	100	15	Normal	—
TM25	Thunder	Electric	Special	120	70	10	Normal	—
TM26	Earthquake	Ground	Physical	100	100	10	2 foes • 1 ally	—
TM27	Return	Normal	Physical	—	100	20	Normal	•
TM28	Dig	Ground	Physical	80	100	10	Normal	•
TM32	Double Team	Normal	Status	—	—	15	Self	—
TM34	Shock Wave	Electric	Special	60	—	20	Normal	—
TM35	Flamethrower	Fire	Special	95	100	15	Normal	—
TM37	Sandstorm	Rock	Status	—	—	10	All	—
TM38	Fire Blast	Fire	Special	120	85	5	Normal	—
TM39	Rock Tomb	Rock	Physical	50	80	10	Normal	—
TM42	Facade	Normal	Physical	70	100	20	Normal	•
TM43	Secret Power	Normal	Physical	70	100	20	Normal	—
TM44	Rest	Psychic	Status	—	—	10	Self	—
TM45	Attract	Normal	Status	—	100	15	Normal	—
TM46	Thief	Dark	Physical	40	100	10	Normal	•
TM58	Endure	Normal	Status	—	—	10	Self	—
TM59	Dragon Pulse	Dragon	Special	90	100	10	Normal	—
TM66	Payback	Dark	Physical	50	100	10	Normal	•
TM69	Rock Polish	Rock	Status	—	—	20	Self	—
TM71	Stone Edge	Rock	Physical	100	80	5	Normal	—
TM75	Swords Dance	Normal	Status	—	—	30	Self	—
TM76	Stealth Rock	Rock	Status	—	—	20	2 foes	—
TM78	Captivate	Normal	Status	—	100	20	2 foes	—
TM80	Rock Slide	Rock	Physical	75	90	10	2 foes	—
TM82	Sleep Talk	Normal	Status	—	—	10	DoM	—
TM83	Natural Gift	Normal	Physical	—	100	15	Normal	—
TM84	Poison Jab	Poison	Physical	80	100	20	Normal	•
TM87	Swagger	Normal	Status	—	90	15	Normal	—
TM90	Substitute	Normal	Status	—	—	10	Self	—
HM04	Strength	Normal	Physical	80	100	15	Normal	•
HM06	Rock Smash	Fighting	Physical	40	100	15	Normal	•
HM08	Rock Climb	Normal	Physical	90	85	20	Normal	•

ABILITY
● Lightningrod
● Rock Head

EGG GROUP
Monster
Field

STATS
HP ●●
ATTACK ●●●
DEFENSE ●●●
SP. ATTACK ●
SP. DEFENSE ●
SPEED ●

● LEVEL-UP AND LEARNED MOVES

Lv	Name	Type	Kind	Power	Acc	PP	Range	DA
Base	Horn Attack	Normal	Physical	65	100	25	Normal	•
Base	Tail Whip	Normal	Status	—	100	30	2 foes	—
9	Stomp	Normal	Physical	65	100	20	Normal	•
13	Fury Attack	Normal	Physical	15	85	20	Normal	•
21	Scary Face	Normal	Status	—	90	10	Normal	—
25	Rock Blast	Rock	Physical	25	80	10	Normal	—
33	Take Down	Normal	Physical	90	85	20	Normal	•
37	Horn Drill	Normal	Physical	—	30	5	Normal	•
45	Stone Edge	Rock	Physical	100	80	5	Normal	—
49	Earthquake	Ground	Physical	100	100	10	2 foes • 1 ally	—
57	Megahorn	Bug	Physical	120	85	10	Normal	•

● MOVES TAUGHT IN EXCHANGE FOR COLORED SHARDS

Name	Type	Kind	Power	Acc	PP	Range	DA
Mud-Slap	Ground	Special	20	100	10	Normal	—
Icy Wind	Ice	Special	55	95	15	2 foes	—
Rollout	Rock	Physical	30	90	20	Normal	•
Superpower	Fighting	Physical	120	100	5	Normal	•
Aqua Tail	Water	Physical	90	90	10	Normal	•
Snore	Normal	Special	40	100	15	Normal	—
Spite	Ghost	Status	—	100	10	Normal	—
Endeavor	Normal	Physical	—	100	5	Normal	•
AncientPower	Rock	Special	60	100	5	Normal	—
Earth Power	Ground	Special	90	100	10	Normal	—
Uproar	Normal	Special	50	100	10	1 random	—

● EGG MOVES

Name	Type	Kind	Power	Acc	PP	Range	DA
Crunch	Dark	Physical	80	100	15	Normal	•
Reversal	Fighting	Physical	—	100	15	Normal	•
Rock Slide	Rock	Physical	75	90	10	2 foes	—
Counter	Fighting	Physical	—	100	20	Self	•
Magnitude	Ground	Physical	—	100	30	2 foes • 1 ally	—
Swords Dance	Normal	Status	—	—	30	Self	—
Curse	???	Status	—	—	10	Normal • Self	—
Crush Claw	Normal	Physical	75	95	10	Normal	•
Dragon Rush	Dragon	Physical	100	75	10	Normal	•
Ice Fang	Ice	Physical	65	95	15	Normal	•
Fire Fang	Fire	Physical	65	95	15	Normal	•
Thunder Fang	Electric	Physical	65	95	15	Normal	•

● PRIMARY WAY TO FIND

TRAINER'S PARTY — Trainer on B2F of Iron Island

WILD POKÉMON — Route 214

COURSE OF STORY

Sinnoh Pokédex **No. 187** Drill Pokémon

Rhydon

GROUND ROCK

HEIGHT: 6'03"
WEIGHT: 264.6 lbs.
GENDER: Male and Female
HELD ITEM: None

● Male form ● Female form

PLATINUM — Standing on its hind legs freed its forelegs and made it smarter. It is very forgetful, however.

EVOLUTION PATH

Lv42
Link trade while holding Protector
Rhyhorn
Rhydon
Rhyperior

● TM & HM MOVES

No.	Name	Type	Kind	Power	Acc	PP	Range	DA
TM01	Focus Punch	Fighting	Physical	150	100	20	Normal	•
TM05	Roar	Normal	Status	—	100	20	Normal	—
TM06	Toxic	Poison	Status	—	85	10	Normal	—
TM10	Hidden Power	Normal	Special	—	100	15	Normal	—
TM11	Sunny Day	Fire	Status	—	—	5	All	—
TM13	Ice Beam	Ice	Special	95	100	10	Normal	—
TM14	Blizzard	Ice	Special	120	70	5	2 foes	—
TM15	Hyper Beam	Normal	Special	150	90	5	Normal	—
TM17	Protect	Normal	Status	—	—	10	Self	—
TM18	Rain Dance	Water	Status	—	—	5	All	—
TM21	Frustration	Normal	Physical	—	100	20	Normal	•
TM23	Iron Tail	Steel	Physical	100	75	15	Normal	•
TM24	Thunderbolt	Electric	Special	95	100	15	Normal	—
TM25	Thunder	Electric	Special	120	70	10	Normal	—
TM26	Earthquake	Ground	Physical	100	100	10	2 foes • 1 ally	—
TM27	Return	Normal	Physical	—	100	20	Normal	•
TM28	Dig	Ground	Physical	80	100	10	Normal	•
TM31	Brick Break	Fighting	Physical	75	100	15	Normal	•
TM32	Double Team	Normal	Status	—	—	15	Self	—
TM34	Shock Wave	Electric	Special	60	—	20	Normal	—
TM35	Flamethrower	Fire	Special	95	100	15	Normal	—
TM37	Sandstorm	Rock	Status	—	—	10	All	—
TM38	Fire Blast	Fire	Special	120	85	5	Normal	—
TM39	Rock Tomb	Rock	Physical	50	80	10	Normal	—
TM42	Facade	Normal	Physical	70	100	20	Normal	•
TM43	Secret Power	Normal	Physical	70	100	20	Normal	—
TM44	Rest	Psychic	Status	—	—	10	Self	—
TM45	Attract	Normal	Status	—	100	15	Normal	—
TM46	Thief	Dark	Physical	40	100	10	Normal	•
TM52	Focus Blast	Fighting	Special	120	70	5	Normal	—
TM56	Fling	Dark	Physical	—	100	10	Normal	—
TM58	Endure	Normal	Status	—	—	10	Self	—
TM59	Dragon Pulse	Dragon	Special	90	100	10	Normal	—
TM65	Shadow Claw	Ghost	Physical	70	100	15	Normal	•
TM66	Payback	Dark	Physical	50	100	10	Normal	•
TM68	Giga Impact	Normal	Physical	150	90	5	Normal	•
TM69	Rock Polish	Rock	Status	—	—	20	Self	—
TM71	Stone Edge	Rock	Physical	100	80	5	Normal	—
TM72	Avalanche	Ice	Physical	60	100	10	Normal	•
TM75	Swords Dance	Normal	Status	—	—	30	Self	—
TM76	Stealth Rock	Rock	Status	—	—	20	2 foes	—
TM78	Captivate	Normal	Status	—	100	20	2 foes	—
TM80	Rock Slide	Rock	Physical	75	90	10	2 foes	—
TM82	Sleep Talk	Normal	Status	—	—	10	DoM	—
TM83	Natural Gift	Normal	Physical	—	100	15	Normal	—
TM84	Poison Jab	Poison	Physical	80	100	20	Normal	•
TM87	Swagger	Normal	Status	—	90	15	Normal	—
TM90	Substitute	Normal	Status	—	—	10	Self	—
HM01	Cut	Normal	Physical	50	95	30	Normal	•
HM03	Surf	Water	Special	95	100	15	2 foes • 1 ally	—
HM04	Strength	Normal	Physical	80	100	15	Normal	•
HM06	Rock Smash	Fighting	Physical	40	100	15	Normal	•
HM08	Rock Climb	Normal	Physical	90	85	20	Normal	•

ABILITY ● Lightningrod ● Rock Head

EGG GROUP Monster, Field

STATS
HP ●●●
ATTACK ●●●●
DEFENSE ●●●
SP. ATTACK ●●
SP. DEFENSE ●
SPEED ●●

● LEVEL-UP AND LEARNED MOVES

Lv	Name	Type	Kind	Power	Acc	PP	Range	DA
Base	Horn Attack	Normal	Physical	65	100	25	Normal	•
Base	Tail Whip	Normal	Status	—	100	30	2 foes	—
Base	Stomp	Normal	Physical	65	100	20	Normal	•
Base	Fury Attack	Normal	Physical	15	85	20	Normal	•
9	Stomp	Normal	Physical	65	100	20	Normal	•
13	Fury Attack	Normal	Physical	15	85	20	Normal	•
21	Scary Face	Normal	Status	—	90	10	Normal	—
25	Rock Blast	Rock	Physical	25	80	10	Normal	—
33	Take Down	Normal	Physical	90	85	20	Normal	•
37	Horn Drill	Normal	Physical	—	30	5	Normal	•
42	Hammer Arm	Fighting	Physical	100	90	10	Normal	•
45	Stone Edge	Rock	Physical	100	80	5	Normal	—
49	Earthquake	Ground	Physical	100	100	10	2 foes • 1 ally	—
57	Megahorn	Bug	Physical	120	85	10	Normal	•

● MOVES TAUGHT IN EXCHANGE FOR COLORED SHARDS

Name	Type	Kind	Power	Acc	PP	Range	DA
Mud-Slap	Ground	Special	20	100	10	Normal	—
Fury Cutter	Bug	Physical	10	95	20	Normal	•
Icy Wind	Ice	Special	55	95	15	2 foes	—
Rollout	Rock	Physical	30	90	20	Normal	•
ThunderPunch	Electric	Physical	75	100	15	Normal	•
Fire Punch	Fire	Physical	75	100	15	Normal	•
Superpower	Fighting	Physical	120	100	5	Normal	•
Ice Punch	Ice	Physical	75	100	15	Normal	•
Aqua Tail	Water	Physical	90	90	10	Normal	•
Snore	Normal	Special	40	100	15	Normal	—
Spite	Ghost	Status	—	100	10	Normal	—
Endeavor	Normal	Physical	—	100	5	Normal	•
Outrage	Dragon	Physical	120	100	15	1 random	•
AncientPower	Rock	Special	60	100	5	Normal	—
Earth Power	Ground	Special	90	100	10	Normal	—
Uproar	Normal	Special	50	100	10	1 random	—

● PRIMARY WAY TO FIND

TRAINER'S PARTY — Trainer on Victory Road

WILD POKÉMON — Victory Road 1F

COURSE OF STORY

Sinnoh Pokédex **No. 188** Drill Pokémon

Rhyperior

GROUND ROCK

HEIGHT: 7'10"
WEIGHT: 623.5 lbs.
GENDER: Male and Female
HELD ITEM: None

● Male form ● Female form

PLATINUM — It can launch a rock held in its hand like a missile by tightening then expanding muscles instantly.

EVOLUTION PATH

Lv42
Link trade while holding Protector
Rhyhorn
Rhydon
Rhyperior

● TM & HM MOVES

No.	Name	Type	Kind	Power	Acc	PP	Range	DA
TM01	Focus Punch	Fighting	Physical	150	100	20	Normal	•
TM05	Roar	Normal	Status	—	100	20	Normal	—
TM06	Toxic	Poison	Status	—	85	10	Normal	—
TM10	Hidden Power	Normal	Special	—	100	15	Normal	—
TM11	Sunny Day	Fire	Status	—	—	5	All	—
TM13	Ice Beam	Ice	Special	95	100	10	Normal	—
TM14	Blizzard	Ice	Special	120	70	5	2 foes	—
TM15	Hyper Beam	Normal	Special	150	90	5	Normal	—
TM17	Protect	Normal	Status	—	—	10	Self	—
TM18	Rain Dance	Water	Status	—	—	5	All	—
TM21	Frustration	Normal	Physical	—	100	20	Normal	•
TM23	Iron Tail	Steel	Physical	100	75	15	Normal	•
TM24	Thunderbolt	Electric	Special	95	100	15	Normal	—
TM25	Thunder	Electric	Special	120	70	10	Normal	—
TM26	Earthquake	Ground	Physical	100	100	10	2 foes • 1 ally	—
TM27	Return	Normal	Physical	—	100	20	Normal	•
TM28	Dig	Ground	Physical	80	100	10	Normal	•
TM31	Brick Break	Fighting	Physical	75	100	15	Normal	•
TM32	Double Team	Normal	Status	—	—	15	Self	—
TM34	Shock Wave	Electric	Special	60	—	20	Normal	—
TM35	Flamethrower	Fire	Special	95	100	15	Normal	—
TM37	Sandstorm	Rock	Status	—	—	10	All	—
TM38	Fire Blast	Fire	Special	120	85	5	Normal	—
TM39	Rock Tomb	Rock	Physical	50	80	10	Normal	—
TM42	Facade	Normal	Physical	70	100	20	Normal	•
TM43	Secret Power	Normal	Physical	70	100	20	Normal	—
TM44	Rest	Psychic	Status	—	—	10	Self	—
TM45	Attract	Normal	Status	—	100	15	Normal	—
TM46	Thief	Dark	Physical	40	100	10	Normal	•
TM52	Focus Blast	Fighting	Special	120	70	5	Normal	—
TM56	Fling	Dark	Physical	—	100	10	Normal	—
TM58	Endure	Normal	Status	—	—	10	Self	—
TM59	Dragon Pulse	Dragon	Special	90	100	10	Normal	—
TM65	Shadow Claw	Ghost	Physical	70	100	15	Normal	•
TM66	Payback	Dark	Physical	50	100	10	Normal	•
TM68	Giga Impact	Normal	Physical	150	90	5	Normal	•
TM69	Rock Polish	Rock	Status	—	—	20	Self	—
TM71	Stone Edge	Rock	Physical	100	80	5	Normal	—
TM72	Avalanche	Ice	Physical	60	100	10	Normal	•
TM75	Swords Dance	Normal	Status	—	—	30	Self	—
TM76	Stealth Rock	Rock	Status	—	—	20	2 foes	—
TM78	Captivate	Normal	Status	—	100	20	2 foes	—
TM80	Rock Slide	Rock	Physical	75	90	10	2 foes	—
TM82	Sleep Talk	Normal	Status	—	—	10	DoM	—
TM83	Natural Gift	Normal	Physical	—	100	15	Normal	—
TM84	Poison Jab	Poison	Physical	80	100	20	Normal	•
TM87	Swagger	Normal	Status	—	90	15	Normal	—
TM90	Substitute	Normal	Status	—	—	10	Self	—
TM91	Flash Cannon	Steel	Special	80	100	10	Normal	—
HM01	Cut	Normal	Physical	50	95	30	Normal	•
HM03	Surf	Water	Special	95	100	15	2 foes • 1 ally	—
HM04	Strength	Normal	Physical	80	100	15	Normal	•

ABILITY ● Lightningrod ● Solid Rock

EGG GROUP Monster, Field

STATS
HP ●●●
ATTACK ●●●●●
DEFENSE ●●●●
SP. ATTACK ●●
SP. DEFENSE ●
SPEED ●●

● TM & HM MOVES

No.	Name	Type	Kind	Power	Acc	PP	Range	DA
HM06	Rock Smash	Fighting	Physical	40	100	15	Normal	•
HM08	Rock Climb	Normal	Physical	90	85	20	Normal	•

● LEVEL-UP AND LEARNED MOVES

Lv	Name	Type	Kind	Power	Acc	PP	Range	DA
Base	Poison Jab	Poison	Physical	80	100	20	Normal	•
Base	Horn Attack	Normal	Physical	65	100	25	Normal	•
Base	Tail Whip	Normal	Status	—	100	30	2 foes	—
Base	Stomp	Normal	Physical	65	100	20	Normal	•
Base	Fury Attack	Normal	Physical	15	85	20	Normal	•
9	Stomp	Normal	Physical	65	100	20	Normal	•
13	Fury Attack	Normal	Physical	15	85	20	Normal	•
21	Scary Face	Normal	Status	—	90	10	Normal	—
25	Rock Blast	Rock	Physical	25	80	10	Normal	—
33	Take Down	Normal	Physical	90	85	20	Normal	•
37	Horn Drill	Normal	Physical	—	30	5	Normal	•
42	Hammer Arm	Fighting	Physical	100	90	10	Normal	•
45	Stone Edge	Rock	Physical	100	80	5	Normal	—
49	Earthquake	Ground	Physical	100	100	10	2 foes • 1 ally	—
57	Megahorn	Bug	Physical	120	85	10	Normal	•
61	Rock Wrecker	Rock	Physical	150	90	5	Normal	—

● MOVES TAUGHT IN EXCHANGE FOR COLORED SHARDS

Name	Type	Kind	Power	Acc	PP	Range	DA
Mud-Slap	Ground	Special	20	100	10	Normal	—
Fury Cutter	Bug	Physical	10	95	20	Normal	•
Icy Wind	Ice	Special	55	95	15	2 foes	—
Rollout	Rock	Physical	30	90	20	Normal	•
ThunderPunch	Electric	Physical	75	100	15	Normal	•
Fire Punch	Fire	Physical	75	100	15	Normal	•
Superpower	Fighting	Physical	120	100	5	Normal	•
Ice Punch	Ice	Physical	75	100	15	Normal	•
Iron Head	Steel	Physical	80	100	15	Normal	•
Aqua Tail	Water	Physical	90	90	10	Normal	•
Snore	Normal	Special	40	100	15	Normal	—
Spite	Ghost	Status	—	100	10	Normal	—
Endeavor	Normal	Physical	—	100	5	Normal	•
Outrage	Dragon	Physical	120	100	15	1 random	•
AncientPower	Rock	Special	60	100	5	Normal	—
Earth Power	Ground	Special	90	100	10	Normal	—
Uproar	Normal	Special	50	100	10	1 random	—

● PRIMARY WAY TO FIND

TRAINER'S PARTY — Eilte Four member Bertha

WILD POKÉMON

COURSE OF STORY

Duskull

GHOST

HEIGHT: 2'07"
WEIGHT: 33.1 lbs.
GENDER: Male and Female
HELD ITEM: Kasib Berry

● M/F have same form

PLATINUM It loves the crying of children. It startles bad kids by passing through walls and making them cry.

EVOLUTION PATH

Duskull → Dusclops (Lv37) → Dusknoir (Link trade while holding Reaper Cloth)

ABILITY ● Levitate

EGG GROUP — Amorphous

STATS
HP ●
ATTACK ●
DEFENSE ●●●
SP. ATTACK ●●
SP. DEFENSE ●●
SPEED ●

● TM & HM MOVES

No.	Name	Type	Kind	Power	Acc	PP	Range	DA
TM04	Calm Mind	Psychic	Status	—	—	20	Self	—
TM06	Toxic	Poison	Status	—	85	10	Normal	—
TM10	Hidden Power	Normal	Special	—	100	15	Normal	—
TM11	Sunny Day	Fire	Status	—	—	5	All	—
TM12	Taunt	Dark	Status	—	100	20	Normal	—
TM13	Ice Beam	Ice	Special	95	100	10	Normal	—
TM14	Blizzard	Ice	Special	120	70	5	2 foes	—
TM17	Protect	Normal	Status	—	—	10	Self	—
TM18	Rain Dance	Water	Status	—	—	5	All	—
TM21	Frustration	Normal	Physical	—	100	20	Normal	●
TM27	Return	Normal	Physical	—	100	20	Normal	●
TM29	Psychic	Psychic	Special	90	100	10	Normal	—
TM30	Shadow Ball	Ghost	Special	80	100	15	Normal	—
TM32	Double Team	Normal	Status	—	—	15	Self	—
TM41	Torment	Dark	Status	—	100	15	Normal	—
TM42	Facade	Normal	Physical	70	100	20	Normal	●
TM43	Secret Power	Normal	Physical	70	100	20	Normal	—
TM44	Rest	Psychic	Status	—	—	10	Self	—
TM45	Attract	Normal	Status	—	100	15	Normal	—
TM46	Thief	Dark	Physical	40	100	10	Normal	●
TM48	Skill Swap	Psychic	Status	—	—	10	Normal	—
TM49	Snatch	Dark	Status	—	—	10	DoM	—
TM56	Fling	Dark	Physical	—	100	10	Normal	●
TM57	Charge Beam	Electric	Special	50	90	10	Normal	—
TM58	Endure	Normal	Status	—	—	10	Self	—
TM61	Will-O-Wisp	Fire	Status	—	75	15	Normal	—
TM63	Embargo	Dark	Status	—	100	15	Normal	—
TM66	Payback	Dark	Physical	50	100	10	Normal	●
TM70	Flash	Normal	Status	—	100	20	Normal	—
TM77	Psych Up	Normal	Status	—	—	10	Normal	—
TM78	Captivate	Normal	Status	—	100	20	2 foes	—
TM79	Dark Pulse	Dark	Special	80	100	15	Normal	—
TM82	Sleep Talk	Normal	Status	—	—	10	DoM	—
TM83	Natural Gift	Normal	Physical	—	100	15	Normal	—
TM85	Dream Eater	Psychic	Special	100	100	15	Normal	—
TM87	Swagger	Normal	Status	—	90	15	Normal	—
TM90	Substitute	Normal	Status	—	—	10	Self	—
TM92	Trick Room	Psychic	Status	—	—	5	All	—

● LEVEL-UP AND LEARNED MOVES

Lv	Name	Type	Kind	Power	Acc	PP	Range	DA
Base	Leer	Normal	Status	—	100	30	2 foes	—
Base	Night Shade	Ghost	Special	—	100	15	Normal	—
6	Disable	Normal	Status	—	80	20	Normal	—
9	Foresight	Normal	Status	—	—	40	Normal	—
14	Astonish	Ghost	Physical	30	100	15	Normal	●
17	Confuse Ray	Ghost	Status	—	100	10	Normal	—
22	Shadow Sneak	Ghost	Physical	40	100	30	Normal	●
25	Pursuit	Dark	Physical	40	100	20	Normal	●
30	Curse	???	—	—	—	10	Normal • Self	—
33	Will-O-Wisp	Fire	Status	—	75	15	Normal	—
38	Mean Look	Normal	Status	—	—	5	Normal	—
41	Payback	Dark	Physical	50	100	10	Normal	●
46	Future Sight	Psychic	Special	80	90	15	Normal	—

● MOVES TAUGHT IN EXCHANGE FOR COLORED SHARDS

Name	Type	Kind	Power	Acc	PP	Range	DA
Icy Wind	Ice	Special	55	95	15	2 foes	—
Ominous Wind	Ghost	Special	60	100	5	Normal	—
Snore	Normal	Special	40	100	15	Normal	—
Spite	Ghost	Status	—	100	10	Normal	—
Trick	Psychic	Status	—	100	10	Normal	—
Sucker Punch	Dark	Physical	80	100	5	Normal	●

● EGG MOVES

Name	Type	Kind	Power	Acc	PP	Range	DA
Imprison	Psychic	Status	—	—	10	Self	—
Destiny Bond	Ghost	Status	—	—	5	Self	—
Pain Split	Normal	Status	—	—	20	Normal	—
Grudge	Ghost	Status	—	—	5	Self	—
Memento	Dark	Status	—	100	10	Normal	—
Faint Attack	Dark	Physical	60	—	20	Normal	●
Ominous Wind	Ghost	Special	60	100	5	Normal	—

● PRIMARY WAY TO FIND

TRAINER'S PARTY Hearthome Gym Leader Fantina

WILD POKÉMON Lost Tower 3F (night only)

COURSE OF STORY

Dusclops

GHOST

HEIGHT: 5'03"
WEIGHT: 67.5 lbs.
GENDER: Male and Female
HELD ITEM: None

● M/F have same form

PLATINUM It seeks drifting will-o'-the-wisps and sucks them into its empty body. What happens inside is a mystery.

EVOLUTION PATH

Duskull → Dusclops (Lv37) → Dusknoir (Link trade while holding Reaper Cloth)

ABILITY ● Pressure

EGG GROUP — Amorphous

STATS
HP ●
ATTACK ●●●
DEFENSE ●●●●●
SP. ATTACK ●●●
SP. DEFENSE ●●●●●
SPEED ●

● TM & HM MOVES

No.	Name	Type	Kind	Power	Acc	PP	Range	DA
TM01	Focus Punch	Fighting	Physical	150	100	20	Normal	●
TM04	Calm Mind	Psychic	Status	—	—	20	Self	—
TM06	Toxic	Poison	Status	—	85	10	Normal	—
TM10	Hidden Power	Normal	Special	—	100	15	Normal	—
TM11	Sunny Day	Fire	Status	—	—	5	All	—
TM12	Taunt	Dark	Status	—	100	20	Normal	—
TM13	Ice Beam	Ice	Special	95	100	10	Normal	—
TM14	Blizzard	Ice	Special	120	70	5	2 foes	—
TM15	Hyper Beam	Normal	Special	150	90	5	Normal	—
TM17	Protect	Normal	Status	—	—	10	Self	—
TM18	Rain Dance	Water	Status	—	—	5	All	—
TM21	Frustration	Normal	Physical	—	100	20	Normal	●
TM26	Earthquake	Ground	Physical	100	100	10	2 foes • 1 ally	—
TM27	Return	Normal	Physical	—	100	20	Normal	●
TM29	Psychic	Psychic	Special	90	100	10	Normal	—
TM30	Shadow Ball	Ghost	Special	80	100	15	Normal	—
TM31	Brick Break	Fighting	Physical	75	100	15	Normal	—
TM32	Double Team	Normal	Status	—	—	15	Self	—
TM39	Rock Tomb	Rock	Physical	50	80	10	Normal	—
TM41	Torment	Dark	Status	—	100	15	Normal	—
TM42	Facade	Normal	Physical	70	100	20	Normal	●
TM43	Secret Power	Normal	Physical	70	100	20	Normal	—
TM44	Rest	Psychic	Status	—	—	10	Self	—
TM45	Attract	Normal	Status	—	100	15	Normal	—
TM46	Thief	Dark	Physical	40	100	10	Normal	●
TM48	Skill Swap	Psychic	Status	—	—	10	Normal	—
TM49	Snatch	Dark	Status	—	—	10	DoM	—
TM56	Fling	Dark	Physical	—	100	10	Normal	●
TM57	Charge Beam	Electric	Special	50	90	10	Normal	—
TM58	Endure	Normal	Status	—	—	10	Self	—
TM61	Will-O-Wisp	Fire	Status	—	75	15	Normal	—
TM63	Embargo	Dark	Status	—	100	15	Normal	—
TM66	Payback	Dark	Physical	50	100	10	Normal	●
TM68	Giga Impact	Normal	Physical	150	90	5	Normal	●
TM70	Flash	Normal	Status	—	100	20	Normal	—
TM77	Psych Up	Normal	Status	—	—	10	Normal	—
TM78	Captivate	Normal	Status	—	100	20	2 foes	—
TM79	Dark Pulse	Dark	Special	80	100	15	Normal	—
TM80	Rock Slide	Rock	Physical	75	90	10	2 foes	—
TM82	Sleep Talk	Normal	Status	—	—	10	DoM	—
TM83	Natural Gift	Normal	Physical	—	100	15	Normal	—
TM85	Dream Eater	Psychic	Special	100	100	15	Normal	—
TM87	Swagger	Normal	Status	—	90	15	Normal	—
TM90	Substitute	Normal	Status	—	—	10	Self	—
TM92	Trick Room	Psychic	Status	—	—	5	All	—
HM04	Strength	Normal	Physical	80	100	15	Normal	●
HM06	Rock Smash	Fighting	Physical	40	100	15	Normal	●

● LEVEL-UP AND LEARNED MOVES

Lv	Name	Type	Kind	Power	Acc	PP	Range	DA
Base	Fire Punch	Fire	Physical	75	100	15	Normal	●
Base	Ice Punch	Ice	Physical	75	100	15	Normal	●
Base	ThunderPunch	Electric	Physical	75	100	15	Normal	●
Base	Gravity	Psychic	Status	—	—	5	All	—
Base	Bind	Normal	Physical	15	75	20	Normal	●
Base	Leer	Normal	Status	—	100	30	2 foes	—
Base	Night Shade	Ghost	Special	—	100	15	Normal	—
Base	Disable	Normal	Status	—	80	20	Normal	—
6	Disable	Normal	Status	—	80	20	Normal	—
9	Foresight	Normal	Status	—	—	40	Normal	—
14	Astonish	Ghost	Physical	30	100	15	Normal	●
17	Confuse Ray	Ghost	Status	—	100	10	Normal	—
22	Shadow Sneak	Ghost	Physical	40	100	30	Normal	●
25	Pursuit	Dark	Physical	40	100	20	Normal	●
30	Curse	???	—	—	—	10	Normal • Self	—
33	Will-O-Wisp	Fire	Status	—	75	15	Normal	—
37	Shadow Punch	Ghost	Physical	60	—	20	Normal	●
43	Mean Look	Normal	Status	—	—	5	Normal	—
51	Payback	Dark	Physical	50	100	10	Normal	●
61	Future Sight	Psychic	Special	80	90	15	Normal	—

● MOVES TAUGHT IN EXCHANGE FOR COLORED SHARDS

Name	Type	Kind	Power	Acc	PP	Range	DA
Mud-Slap	Ground	Special	20	100	10	Normal	—
Icy Wind	Ice	Special	55	95	15	2 foes	—
ThunderPunch	Electric	Physical	75	100	15	Normal	●
Fire Punch	Fire	Physical	75	100	15	Normal	●
Ice Punch	Ice	Physical	75	100	15	Normal	●
Ominous Wind	Ghost	Special	60	100	5	Normal	—
Snore	Normal	Special	40	100	15	Normal	—
Spite	Ghost	Status	—	100	10	Normal	—
Trick	Psychic	Status	—	100	10	Normal	—
Sucker Punch	Dark	Physical	80	100	5	Normal	●

● PRIMARY WAY TO FIND

TRAINER'S PARTY Trainer on Route 216

WILD POKÉMON Sendoff Spring

COURSE OF STORY

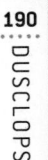

Sinnoh Pokédex No. 191 Gripper Pokémon
Dusknoir

GHOST

HEIGHT: 7'03"
WEIGHT: 235.0 lbs.
GENDER: Male and Female
HELD ITEM: None

● M/F have same form

PLATINUM — It is said to take lost spirits into its pliant body and guide them home.

EVOLUTION PATH

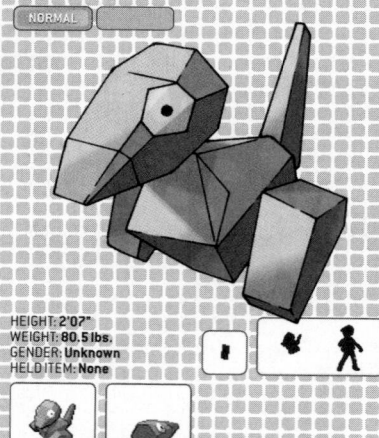

Duskull → Lv37 → Dusclops → Link trade while holding Reaper Cloth → Dusknoir

ABILITY ● Pressure

EGG GROUP — Amorphous

STATS
HP ●
ATTACK ●●●
DEFENSE ●●●●
SP. ATTACK ●●●
SP. DEFENSE ●●●●
SPEED ●●

● TM & HM MOVES

No.	Name	Type	Kind	Power	Acc	PP	Range	DA
TM01	Focus Punch	Fighting	Physical	150	100	20	Normal	●
TM04	Calm Mind	Psychic	Status	—	—	20	Self	—
TM06	Toxic	Poison	Status	—	85	10	Normal	—
TM10	Hidden Power	Normal	Special	—	100	15	Normal	—
TM11	Sunny Day	Fire	Status	—	—	5	All	—
TM12	Taunt	Dark	Status	—	100	20	Normal	—
TM13	Ice Beam	Ice	Special	95	100	10	Normal	—
TM14	Blizzard	Ice	Special	120	70	5	2 foes	—
TM15	Hyper Beam	Normal	Special	150	90	5	Normal	—
TM17	Protect	Normal	Status	—	—	10	Self	—
TM18	Rain Dance	Water	Status	—	—	5	All	—
TM21	Frustration	Normal	Physical	—	100	20	Normal	●
TM26	Earthquake	Ground	Physical	100	100	10	2 foes + 1 ally	●
TM27	Return	Normal	Physical	—	100	20	Normal	●
TM29	Psychic	Psychic	Special	90	100	10	Normal	—
TM30	Shadow Ball	Ghost	Special	80	100	15	Normal	●
TM31	Brick Break	Fighting	Physical	75	100	15	Normal	●
TM32	Double Team	Normal	Status	—	—	15	Self	—
TM39	Rock Tomb	Rock	Physical	50	80	10	Normal	●
TM41	Torment	Dark	Status	—	100	15	Normal	—
TM42	Facade	Normal	Physical	70	100	20	Normal	●
TM43	Secret Power	Normal	Physical	70	100	20	Normal	●
TM44	Rest	Psychic	Status	—	—	10	Self	—
TM45	Attract	Normal	Status	—	100	15	Normal	—
TM46	Thief	Dark	Physical	40	100	10	Normal	●
TM48	Skill Swap	Psychic	Status	—	—	10	Normal	—
TM49	Snatch	Dark	Status	—	—	10	DoM	—
TM52	Focus Blast	Fighting	Special	120	70	5	Normal	—
TM56	Fling	Dark	Physical	—	100	10	Normal	●
TM57	Charge Beam	Electric	Special	50	90	10	Normal	—
TM58	Endure	Normal	Status	—	—	10	Self	—
TM61	Will-O-Wisp	Fire	Status	—	75	15	Normal	—
TM63	Embargo	Dark	Status	—	100	15	Normal	—
TM66	Payback	Dark	Physical	50	100	10	Normal	●
TM68	Giga Impact	Normal	Physical	150	90	5	Normal	●
TM70	Flash	Normal	Status	—	100	20	Normal	—
TM77	Psych Up	Normal	Status	—	—	10	Normal	—
TM78	Captivate	Normal	Status	—	100	20	2 foes	—
TM79	Dark Pulse	Dark	Special	80	100	15	Normal	—
TM80	Rock Slide	Rock	Physical	75	90	10	2 foes	●
TM82	Sleep Talk	Normal	Status	—	—	10	DoM	—
TM83	Natural Gift	Normal	Physical	—	100	15	Normal	●
TM85	Dream Eater	Psychic	Special	100	100	15	Normal	—
TM87	Swagger	Normal	Status	—	90	15	Normal	—
TM90	Substitute	Normal	Status	—	—	10	Self	—
TM92	Trick Room	Psychic	Status	—	—	5	All	—
HM04	Strength	Normal	Physical	80	100	15	Normal	●
HM06	Rock Smash	Fighting	Physical	40	100	15	Normal	●

● LEVEL-UP AND LEARNED MOVES

Lv	Name	Type	Kind	Power	Acc	PP	Range	DA
Base	Fire Punch	Fire	Physical	75	100	15	Normal	●
Base	Ice Punch	Ice	Physical	75	100	15	Normal	●
Base	ThunderPunch	Electric	Physical	75	100	15	Normal	●
Base	Gravity	Psychic	Status	—	—	5	All	—
Base	Bind	Normal	Physical	15	75	20	Normal	●
Base	Leer	Normal	Status	—	100	30	2 foes	—
Base	Night Shade	Ghost	Special	—	100	15	Normal	—
Base	Disable	Normal	Status	—	80	20	Normal	—
6	Disable	Normal	Status	—	80	20	Normal	—
9	Foresight	Normal	Status	—	—	40	Normal	—
14	Astonish	Ghost	Physical	30	100	15	Normal	●
17	Confuse Ray	Ghost	Status	—	100	10	Normal	—
22	Shadow Sneak	Ghost	Physical	40	100	30	Normal	●
25	Pursuit	Dark	Physical	40	100	20	Normal	●
30	Curse	???	Status	—	—	10	Normal + Self	—
33	Will-O-Wisp	Fire	Status	—	75	15	Normal	—
37	Shadow Punch	Ghost	Physical	60	—	20	Normal	●
43	Mean Look	Normal	Status	—	—	5	Normal	—
51	Payback	Dark	Physical	50	100	10	Normal	●
61	Future Sight	Psychic	Special	—	90	15	Normal	—

● MOVES TAUGHT IN EXCHANGE FOR COLORED SHARDS

Name	Type	Kind	Power	Acc	PP	Range	DA
Mud-Slap	Ground	Special	20	100	10	Normal	●
Icy Wind	Ice	Special	55	95	15	2 foes	—
ThunderPunch	Electric	Physical	75	100	15	Normal	●
Fire Punch	Fire	Physical	75	100	15	Normal	●
Ice Punch	Ice	Physical	75	100	15	Normal	●
Ominous Wind	Ghost	Special	60	100	5	Normal	—
Snore	Normal	Special	40	100	15	Normal	—
Spite	Ghost	Status	—	100	10	Normal	—
Trick	Psychic	Status	—	100	10	Normal	—
Sucker Punch	Dark	Physical	80	100	5	Normal	—

● PRIMARY WAY TO FIND

TRAINER'S PARTY — Trainer on Victory Road

WILD POKÉMON

COURSE OF STORY

Sinnoh Pokédex No. 192 Virtual Pokémon
Porygon

NORMAL

HEIGHT: 2'07"
WEIGHT: 80.5 lbs.
GENDER: Unknown
HELD ITEM: None

● Gender unknown

PLATINUM — A man-made Pokémon created using advanced scientific means. It can move freely in cyberspace.

EVOLUTION PATH

Porygon → Link trade while holding Up-Grade → Porygon2 → Link trade while holding Dubious Disc → Porygon-Z

ABILITY ● Trace / ● Download

EGG GROUP — Mineral

STATS
HP ●●
ATTACK ●●
DEFENSE ●●
SP. ATTACK ●●●
SP. DEFENSE ●●
SPEED ●●

● TM & HM MOVES

No.	Name	Type	Kind	Power	Acc	PP	Range	DA
TM06	Toxic	Poison	Status	—	85	10	Normal	—
TM10	Hidden Power	Normal	Special	—	100	15	Normal	—
TM11	Sunny Day	Fire	Status	—	—	5	All	—
TM13	Ice Beam	Ice	Special	95	100	10	Normal	—
TM14	Blizzard	Ice	Special	120	70	5	2 foes	—
TM15	Hyper Beam	Normal	Special	150	90	5	Normal	—
TM17	Protect	Normal	Status	—	—	10	Self	—
TM18	Rain Dance	Water	Status	—	—	5	All	—
TM21	Frustration	Normal	Physical	—	100	20	Normal	●
TM22	SolarBeam	Grass	Special	120	100	10	Normal	—
TM23	Iron Tail	Steel	Physical	100	75	15	Normal	●
TM24	Thunderbolt	Electric	Special	95	100	15	Normal	—
TM25	Thunder	Electric	Special	120	70	10	Normal	—
TM27	Return	Normal	Physical	—	100	20	Normal	●
TM29	Psychic	Psychic	Special	90	100	10	Normal	—
TM30	Shadow Ball	Ghost	Special	80	100	15	Normal	—
TM32	Double Team	Normal	Status	—	—	15	Self	—
TM34	Shock Wave	Electric	Special	60	—	20	Normal	—
TM40	Aerial Ace	Flying	Physical	60	—	20	Normal	●
TM42	Facade	Normal	Physical	70	100	20	Normal	●
TM43	Secret Power	Normal	Physical	70	100	20	Normal	●
TM44	Rest	Psychic	Status	—	—	10	Self	—
TM46	Thief	Dark	Physical	40	100	10	Normal	●
TM57	Charge Beam	Electric	Special	50	90	10	Normal	—
TM58	Endure	Normal	Status	—	—	10	Self	—
TM67	Recycle	Normal	Status	—	—	10	Self	—
TM68	Giga Impact	Normal	Physical	150	90	5	Normal	●
TM70	Flash	Normal	Status	—	100	20	Normal	—
TM73	Thunder Wave	Electric	Status	—	100	20	Normal	—
TM77	Psych Up	Normal	Status	—	—	10	Normal	—
TM82	Sleep Talk	Normal	Status	—	—	10	DoM	—
TM83	Natural Gift	Normal	Physical	—	100	15	Normal	●
TM85	Dream Eater	Psychic	Special	100	100	15	Normal	—
TM87	Swagger	Normal	Status	—	90	15	Normal	—
TM90	Substitute	Normal	Status	—	—	10	Self	—
TM92	Trick Room	Psychic	Status	—	—	5	All	—

● LEVEL-UP AND LEARNED MOVES

Lv	Name	Type	Kind	Power	Acc	PP	Range	DA
Base	Conversion 2	Normal	Status	—	—	30	Self	—
Base	Tackle	Normal	Physical	35	95	35	Normal	●
Base	Conversion	Normal	Status	—	—	30	Self	—
Base	Sharpen	Normal	Status	—	—	30	Self	—
7	Psybeam	Psychic	Special	65	100	20	Normal	—
12	Agility	Psychic	Status	—	—	30	Self	—
18	Recover	Normal	Status	—	—	10	Self	—
23	Magnet Rise	Electric	Status	—	—	10	Self	—
29	Signal Beam	Bug	Special	75	100	15	Normal	—
34	Recycle	Normal	Status	—	—	10	Self	—
40	Discharge	Electric	Special	80	100	15	2 foes + 1 ally	—
45	Lock-On	Normal	Status	—	—	5	Normal	—
51	Tri Attack	Normal	Special	80	100	10	Normal	—
56	Magic Coat	Psychic	Status	—	—	15	Self	—
62	Zap Cannon	Electric	Special	120	50	5	Normal	—

● MOVES TAUGHT IN EXCHANGE FOR COLORED SHARDS

Name	Type	Kind	Power	Acc	PP	Range	DA
Icy Wind	Ice	Special	55	95	15	2 foes	—
Snore	Normal	Special	40	100	15	Normal	—
Signal Beam	Bug	Special	75	100	15	Normal	—
Zen Headbutt	Psychic	Physical	80	90	15	Normal	—
Last Resort	Normal	Physical	130	100	5	Normal	●
Trick	Psychic	Status	—	100	10	Normal	—
Swift	Normal	Special	60	—	20	2 foes	—

● EGG MOVES

Name	Type	Kind	Power	Acc	PP	Range	DA

● PRIMARY WAY TO FIND

TRAINER'S PARTY — Trainer on Route 214

WILD POKÉMON

COURSE OF STORY — Receive from a boy in a Veilstone City residence

Sinnoh Pokédex No. 193 Virtual Pokémon

Porygon2

NORMAL

HEIGHT: 2'00"
WEIGHT: 71.6 lbs.
GENDER: Unknown
HELD ITEM: None

● Gender unknown

| PLATINUM | It was upgraded to enable the exploration of other planets. However, it failed to measure up. |

● TM & HM MOVES

No.	Name	Type	Kind	Power	Acc	PP	Range	DA
TM06	Toxic	Poison	Status	—	85	10	Normal	—
TM10	Hidden Power	Normal	Special	—	100	15	Normal	—
TM11	Sunny Day	Fire	Status	—	—	5	All	—
TM13	Ice Beam	Ice	Special	95	100	10	Normal	—
TM14	Blizzard	Ice	Special	120	70	5	2 foes	—
TM15	Hyper Beam	Normal	Special	150	90	5	Normal	—
TM17	Protect	Normal	Status	—	—	10	Self	—
TM18	Rain Dance	Water	Status	—	—	5	All	—
TM21	Frustration	Normal	Physical	—	100	20	Normal	●
TM22	SolarBeam	Grass	Special	120	100	10	Normal	—
TM23	Iron Tail	Steel	Physical	100	75	15	Normal	●
TM24	Thunderbolt	Electric	Special	95	100	15	Normal	—
TM25	Thunder	Electric	Special	120	70	10	Normal	—
TM27	Return	Normal	Physical	—	100	20	Normal	●
TM29	Psychic	Psychic	Special	90	100	10	Normal	—
TM30	Shadow Ball	Ghost	Special	80	100	15	Normal	—
TM32	Double Team	Normal	Status	—	—	15	Self	—
TM34	Shock Wave	Electric	Special	60	—	20	Normal	—
TM40	Aerial Ace	Flying	Physical	60	—	20	Normal	—
TM42	Facade	Normal	Physical	70	100	20	Normal	●
TM43	Secret Power	Normal	Physical	70	100	20	Normal	●
TM44	Rest	Psychic	Status	—	—	10	Self	—
TM46	Thief	Dark	Physical	40	100	10	Normal	●
TM57	Charge Beam	Electric	Special	50	90	10	Normal	—
TM58	Endure	Normal	Status	—	—	10	Self	—
TM67	Recycle	Normal	Status	—	—	10	Self	—
TM68	Giga Impact	Normal	Physical	150	90	5	Normal	●
TM70	Flash	Normal	Status	—	100	20	Normal	—
TM73	Thunder Wave	Electric	Status	—	100	20	Normal	—
TM77	Psych Up	Normal	Status	—	—	10	Normal	—
TM82	Sleep Talk	Normal	Status	—	—	10	DoM	—
TM83	Natural Gift	Normal	Physical	—	100	15	Normal	—
TM85	Dream Eater	Psychic	Special	100	100	15	Normal	—
TM87	Swagger	Normal	Status	—	90	15	Normal	—
TM90	Substitute	Normal	Status	—	—	10	Self	—
TM92	Trick Room	Psychic	Status	—	—	5	All	—

● LEVEL-UP AND LEARNED MOVES

Lv	Name	Type	Kind	Power	Acc	PP	Range	DA
Base	Conversion 2	Normal	Status	—	—	30	Self	—
Base	Tackle	Normal	Physical	35	95	35	Normal	●
Base	Conversion	Normal	Status	—	—	30	Self	—
Base	Defense Curl	Normal	Status	—	—	40	Self	—
7	Psybeam	Psychic	Special	65	100	20	Normal	—
12	Agility	Psychic	Status	—	—	30	Self	—
18	Recover	Normal	Status	—	—	10	Self	—
23	Magnet Rise	Electric	Status	—	—	10	Self	—
29	Signal Beam	Bug	Special	75	100	15	Normal	—
34	Recycle	Normal	Status	—	—	10	Self	—
40	Discharge	Electric	Special	80	100	15	2 foes ● 1 ally	—
45	Lock-On	Normal	Status	—	—	5	Normal	—
51	Tri Attack	Normal	Special	80	100	10	Normal	—
56	Magic Coat	Psychic	Status	—	—	15	Self	—
62	Zap Cannon	Electric	Special	120	50	5	Normal	—
67	Hyper Beam	Normal	Special	150	90	5	Normal	—

● MOVES TAUGHT IN EXCHANGE FOR COLORED SHARDS

Name	Type	Kind	Power	Acc	PP	Range	DA
Icy Wind	Ice	Special	55	95	15	2 foes	—
Snore	Normal	Special	40	100	15	Normal	—
Signal Beam	Bug	Special	75	100	15	Normal	—
Zen Headbutt	Psychic	Physical	80	90	15	Normal	●
Last Resort	Normal	Physical	130	100	5	Normal	●
Trick	Psychic	Status	—	100	10	Normal	—
Swift	Normal	Special	60	—	20	2 foes	—

EVOLUTION PATH

Porygon — Link trade while holding Up-Grade — Porygon2 — Link trade while holding Dubious Disc — Porygon-Z

| ABILITY | ● Trace ● Download |
| EGG GROUP | Mineral |

STATS	HP ●●●
	ATTACK ●●●
	DEFENSE ●●●●
	SP. ATTACK ●●●●
	SP. DEFENSE ●●●●
	SPEED ●●

● PRIMARY WAY TO FIND

TRAINER'S PARTY	Trainer on Route 216
WILD POKÉMON	
COURSE OF STORY	

Sinnoh Pokédex No. 194 Virtual Pokémon

Porygon-Z

NORMAL

HEIGHT: 2'11"
WEIGHT: 75.0 lbs.
GENDER: Unknown
HELD ITEM: None

● Gender unknown

| PLATINUM | Its programming was modified to enable work in alien dimensions. It did not work as planned. |

● TM & HM MOVES

No.	Name	Type	Kind	Power	Acc	PP	Range	DA
TM06	Toxic	Poison	Status	—	85	10	Normal	—
TM10	Hidden Power	Normal	Special	—	100	15	Normal	—
TM11	Sunny Day	Fire	Status	—	—	5	All	—
TM13	Ice Beam	Ice	Special	95	100	10	Normal	—
TM14	Blizzard	Ice	Special	120	70	5	2 foes	—
TM15	Hyper Beam	Normal	Special	150	90	5	Normal	—
TM17	Protect	Normal	Status	—	—	10	Self	—
TM18	Rain Dance	Water	Status	—	—	5	All	—
TM21	Frustration	Normal	Physical	—	100	20	Normal	●
TM22	SolarBeam	Grass	Special	120	100	10	Normal	—
TM23	Iron Tail	Steel	Physical	100	75	15	Normal	●
TM24	Thunderbolt	Electric	Special	95	100	15	Normal	—
TM25	Thunder	Electric	Special	120	70	10	Normal	—
TM27	Return	Normal	Physical	—	100	20	Normal	●
TM29	Psychic	Psychic	Special	90	100	10	Normal	—
TM30	Shadow Ball	Ghost	Special	80	100	15	Normal	—
TM32	Double Team	Normal	Status	—	—	15	Self	—
TM34	Shock Wave	Electric	Special	60	—	20	Normal	—
TM40	Aerial Ace	Flying	Physical	60	—	20	Normal	—
TM42	Facade	Normal	Physical	70	100	20	Normal	●
TM43	Secret Power	Normal	Physical	70	100	20	Normal	●
TM44	Rest	Psychic	Status	—	—	10	Self	—
TM46	Thief	Dark	Physical	40	100	10	Normal	●
TM57	Charge Beam	Electric	Special	50	90	10	Normal	—
TM58	Endure	Normal	Status	—	—	10	Self	—
TM63	Embargo	Dark	Status	—	100	15	Normal	—
TM67	Recycle	Normal	Status	—	—	10	Self	—
TM68	Giga Impact	Normal	Physical	150	90	5	Normal	●
TM70	Flash	Normal	Status	—	100	20	Normal	—
TM73	Thunder Wave	Electric	Status	—	100	20	Normal	—
TM77	Psych Up	Normal	Status	—	—	10	Normal	—
TM79	Dark Pulse	Dark	Special	80	100	15	Normal	—
TM82	Sleep Talk	Normal	Status	—	—	10	DoM	—
TM83	Natural Gift	Normal	Physical	—	100	15	Normal	—
TM85	Dream Eater	Psychic	Special	100	100	15	Normal	—
TM87	Swagger	Normal	Status	—	90	15	Normal	—
TM90	Substitute	Normal	Status	—	—	10	Self	—
TM92	Trick Room	Psychic	Status	—	—	5	All	—

● LEVEL-UP AND LEARNED MOVES

Lv	Name	Type	Kind	Power	Acc	PP	Range	DA
Base	Trick Room	Psychic	Status	—	—	5	All	—
Base	Conversion 2	Normal	Status	—	—	30	Self	—
Base	Tackle	Normal	Physical	35	95	35	Normal	●
Base	Conversion	Normal	Status	—	—	30	Self	—
Base	Nasty Plot	Dark	Status	—	—	20	Self	—
7	Psybeam	Psychic	Special	65	100	20	Normal	—
12	Agility	Psychic	Status	—	—	30	Self	—
18	Recover	Normal	Status	—	—	10	Self	—
23	Magnet Rise	Electric	Status	—	—	10	Self	—
29	Signal Beam	Bug	Special	75	100	15	Normal	—
34	Embargo	Dark	Status	—	100	15	Normal	—
40	Discharge	Electric	Special	80	100	15	2 foes ● 1 ally	—
45	Lock-On	Normal	Status	—	—	5	Normal	—
51	Tri Attack	Normal	Special	80	100	10	Normal	—
56	Magic Coat	Psychic	Status	—	—	15	Self	—
62	Zap Cannon	Electric	Special	120	50	5	Normal	—
67	Hyper Beam	Normal	Special	150	90	5	Normal	—

● MOVES TAUGHT IN EXCHANGE FOR COLORED SHARDS

Name	Type	Kind	Power	Acc	PP	Range	DA
Icy Wind	Ice	Special	55	95	15	2 foes	—
Snore	Normal	Special	40	100	15	Normal	—
Signal Beam	Bug	Special	75	100	15	Normal	—
Zen Headbutt	Psychic	Physical	80	90	15	Normal	●
Last Resort	Normal	Physical	130	100	10	Normal	●
Trick	Psychic	Status	—	100	10	Normal	—
Swift	Normal	Special	60	—	20	2 foes	—
Uproar	Normal	Special	50	100	10	1 random	—

EVOLUTION PATH

Porygon — Link trade while holding Up-Grade — Porygon2 — Link trade while holding Dubious Disc — Porygon-Z

| ABILITY | ● Adaptability ● Download |
| EGG GROUP | Mineral |

STATS	HP ●●●
	ATTACK ●●●
	DEFENSE ●●●
	SP. ATTACK ●●●●●
	SP. DEFENSE ●●●
	SPEED ●●●

● PRIMARY WAY TO FIND

TRAINER'S PARTY	Trainer on Victory Road
WILD POKÉMON	
COURSE OF STORY	

194
PORYGON-Z

Scyther

BUG   FLYING

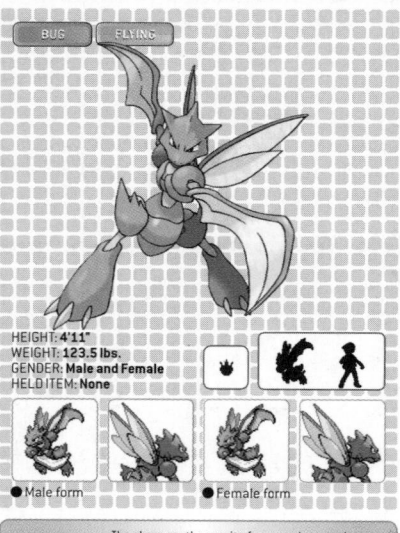

● Male form   ● Female form

HEIGHT: 4'11"
WEIGHT: 123.5 lbs.
GENDER: Male and Female
HELD ITEM: None

PLATINUM The sharp scythes on its forearms become increasingly sharp by cutting through hard objects.

EVOLUTION PATH

Scyther — Link trade while holding Metal Coat → Scizor

● TM & HM MOVES

No.	Name	Type	Kind	Power	Acc	PP	Range	DA
TM06	Toxic	Poison	Status	—	85	10	Normal	—
TM10	Hidden Power	Normal	Special	—	100	15	Normal	—
TM11	Sunny Day	Fire	Status	—	—	5	All	—
TM15	Hyper Beam	Normal	Special	150	90	5	Normal	•
TM17	Protect	Normal	Status	—	—	10	Self	—
TM18	Rain Dance	Water	Status	—	—	5	All	—
TM21	Frustration	Normal	Physical	—	100	20	Normal	•
TM27	Return	Normal	Physical	—	100	20	Normal	•
TM31	Brick Break	Fighting	Physical	75	100	15	Normal	•
TM32	Double Team	Normal	Status	—	—	15	Self	—
TM40	Aerial Ace	Flying	Physical	60	—	20	Normal	•
TM42	Facade	Normal	Physical	70	100	20	Normal	•
TM43	Secret Power	Normal	Physical	70	100	20	Normal	•
TM44	Rest	Psychic	Status	—	—	10	Self	—
TM45	Attract	Normal	Status	—	100	15	Normal	—
TM46	Thief	Dark	Physical	40	100	10	Normal	•
TM47	Steel Wing	Steel	Physical	70	90	25	Normal	•
TM51	Roost	Flying	Status	—	—	10	Self	—
TM54	False Swipe	Normal	Physical	40	100	40	Normal	•
TM58	Endure	Normal	Status	—	—	10	Self	—
TM62	Silver Wind	Bug	Special	60	100	5	Normal	—
TM68	Giga Impact	Normal	Physical	150	90	5	Normal	•
TM75	Swords Dance	Normal	Status	—	—	30	Self	—
TM78	Captivate	Normal	Status	—	100	20	2 foes	—
TM81	X-Scissor	Bug	Physical	80	100	15	Normal	•
TM82	Sleep Talk	Normal	Status	—	—	10	DoM	—
TM83	Natural Gift	Normal	Physical	—	100	15	Normal	•
TM87	Swagger	Normal	Status	—	90	15	Normal	—
TM89	U-turn	Bug	Physical	70	100	20	Normal	•
TM90	Substitute	Normal	Status	—	—	10	Self	—
HM01	Cut	Normal	Physical	50	95	30	Normal	•
HM05	Defog	Flying	Status	—	—	15	Normal	—
HM06	Rock Smash	Fighting	Physical	40	100	15	Normal	•

● LEVEL-UP AND LEARNED MOVES

Lv	Name	Type	Kind	Power	Acc	PP	Range	DA
Base	Vacuum Wave	Fighting	Special	40	100	30	Normal	•
Base	Quick Attack	Normal	Physical	40	100	30	Normal	•
Base	Leer	Normal	Status	—	100	30	2 foes	—
5	Focus Energy	Normal	Status	—	—	30	Self	—
9	Pursuit	Dark	Physical	40	100	20	Normal	•
13	False Swipe	Normal	Physical	40	100	40	Normal	•
17	Agility	Psychic	Status	—	—	30	Self	—
21	Wing Attack	Flying	Physical	60	100	35	Normal	•
25	Fury Cutter	Bug	Physical	10	95	20	Normal	•
29	Slash	Normal	Physical	70	100	20	Normal	•
33	Razor Wind	Normal	Special	80	100	10	2 foes	—
37	Double Team	Normal	Status	—	—	15	Self	—
41	X-Scissor	Bug	Physical	80	100	15	Normal	•
45	Night Slash	Dark	Physical	70	100	15	Normal	•
49	Double Hit	Normal	Physical	35	90	10	Normal	•
53	Air Slash	Flying	Special	75	95	20	Normal	—
57	Swords Dance	Normal	Status	—	—	30	Self	—
61	Feint	Normal	Physical	50	100	10	Normal	•

● MOVES TAUGHT IN EXCHANGE FOR COLORED SHARDS

Name	Type	Kind	Power	Acc	PP	Range	DA
Fury Cutter	Bug	Physical	10	95	20	Normal	•
Ominous Wind	Ghost	Special	60	100	5	Normal	—
Snore	Normal	Special	40	100	15	Normal	—
Knock Off	Dark	Physical	20	100	20	Normal	•
Swift	Normal	Special	60	—	20	2 foes	—

● EGG MOVES

Name	Type	Kind	Power	Acc	PP	Range	DA
Counter	Fighting	Physical	—	100	20	Self	•
Safeguard	Normal	Status	—	—	25	2 allies	—
Baton Pass	Normal	Status	—	—	40	Self	—
Razor Wind	Normal	Special	80	100	10	2 foes	—
Reversal	Fighting	Physical	—	100	15	Normal	•
Light Screen	Psychic	Status	—	—	30	2 allies	—
Endure	Normal	Status	—	—	10	Self	—
Silver Wind	Bug	Special	60	100	5	Normal	—
Bug Buzz	Bug	Special	90	100	10	Normal	—
Night Slash	Dark	Physical	70	100	15	Normal	•

● PRIMARY WAY TO FIND

TRAINER'S PARTY Trainer on Celestic Town side of Route 210

WILD POKÉMON Route 210

COURSE OF STORY

ABILITY ● Swarm ● Technician

EGG GROUP Bug

STATS
HP ●●
ATTACK ●●●
DEFENSE ●●●
SP. ATTACK ●●
SP. DEFENSE ●●
SPEED ●●●●

Scizor

BUG   STEEL

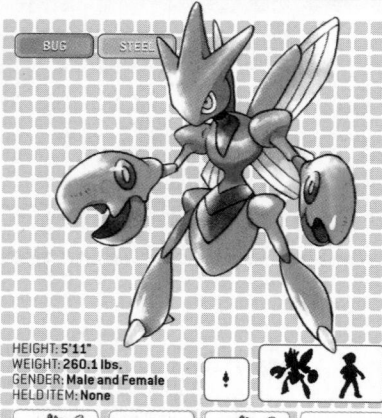

● Male form   ● Female form

HEIGHT: 5'11"
WEIGHT: 260.1 lbs.
GENDER: Male and Female
HELD ITEM: None

PLATINUM It raises its pincers with eyelike markings for intimidation. It also swings them down dangerously.

EVOLUTION PATH

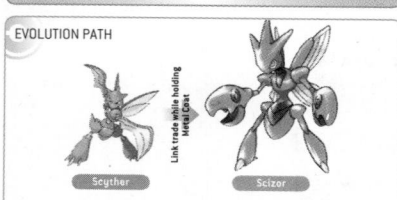

Scyther — Link trade while holding Metal Coat → Scizor

● TM & HM MOVES

No.	Name	Type	Kind	Power	Acc	PP	Range	DA
TM06	Toxic	Poison	Status	—	85	10	Normal	—
TM10	Hidden Power	Normal	Special	—	100	15	Normal	—
TM11	Sunny Day	Fire	Status	—	—	5	All	—
TM15	Hyper Beam	Normal	Special	150	90	5	Normal	•
TM17	Protect	Normal	Status	—	—	10	Self	—
TM18	Rain Dance	Water	Status	—	—	5	All	—
TM21	Frustration	Normal	Physical	—	100	20	Normal	•
TM27	Return	Normal	Physical	—	100	20	Normal	•
TM31	Brick Break	Fighting	Physical	75	100	15	Normal	•
TM32	Double Team	Normal	Status	—	—	15	Self	—
TM37	Sandstorm	Rock	Status	—	—	10	All	—
TM40	Aerial Ace	Flying	Physical	60	—	20	Normal	•
TM42	Facade	Normal	Physical	70	100	20	Normal	•
TM43	Secret Power	Normal	Physical	70	100	20	Normal	•
TM44	Rest	Psychic	Status	—	—	10	Self	—
TM45	Attract	Normal	Status	—	100	15	Normal	—
TM46	Thief	Dark	Physical	40	100	10	Normal	•
TM47	Steel Wing	Steel	Physical	70	90	25	Normal	•
TM51	Roost	Flying	Status	—	—	10	Self	—
TM54	False Swipe	Normal	Physical	40	100	40	Normal	•
TM56	Fling	Dark	Physical	—	100	10	Normal	•
TM58	Endure	Normal	Status	—	—	10	Self	—
TM62	Silver Wind	Bug	Special	60	100	5	Normal	—
TM68	Giga Impact	Normal	Physical	150	90	5	Normal	•
TM75	Swords Dance	Normal	Status	—	—	30	Self	—
TM78	Captivate	Normal	Status	—	100	20	2 foes	—
TM81	X-Scissor	Bug	Physical	80	100	15	Normal	•
TM82	Sleep Talk	Normal	Status	—	—	10	DoM	—
TM83	Natural Gift	Normal	Physical	—	100	15	Normal	•
TM87	Swagger	Normal	Status	—	90	15	Normal	—
TM89	U-turn	Bug	Physical	70	100	20	Normal	•
TM90	Substitute	Normal	Status	—	—	10	Self	—
TM91	Flash Cannon	Steel	Special	80	100	10	Normal	—
HM01	Cut	Normal	Physical	50	95	30	Normal	•
HM04	Strength	Normal	Physical	80	100	15	Normal	•
HM05	Defog	Flying	Status	—	—	15	Normal	—
HM06	Rock Smash	Fighting	Physical	40	100	15	Normal	•

● LEVEL-UP AND LEARNED MOVES

Lv	Name	Type	Kind	Power	Acc	PP	Range	DA
Base	Bullet Punch	Steel	Physical	40	100	30	Normal	•
Base	Quick Attack	Normal	Physical	40	100	30	Normal	•
Base	Leer	Normal	Status	—	100	30	2 foes	—
5	Focus Energy	Normal	Status	—	—	30	Self	—
9	Pursuit	Dark	Physical	40	100	20	Normal	•
13	False Swipe	Normal	Physical	40	100	40	Normal	•
17	Agility	Psychic	Status	—	—	30	Self	—
21	Metal Claw	Steel	Physical	50	95	35	Normal	•
25	Fury Cutter	Bug	Physical	10	95	20	Normal	•
29	Slash	Normal	Physical	70	100	20	Normal	•
33	Razor Wind	Normal	Special	80	100	10	2 foes	—
37	Iron Defense	Steel	Status	—	—	15	Self	—
41	X-Scissor	Bug	Physical	80	100	15	Normal	•
45	Night Slash	Dark	Physical	70	100	15	Normal	•
49	Double Hit	Normal	Physical	35	90	10	Normal	•
53	Iron Head	Steel	Physical	80	100	15	Normal	•
57	Swords Dance	Normal	Status	—	—	30	Self	—
61	Feint	Normal	Physical	50	100	10	Normal	•

● MOVES TAUGHT IN EXCHANGE FOR COLORED SHARDS

Name	Type	Kind	Power	Acc	PP	Range	DA
Fury Cutter	Bug	Physical	10	95	20	Normal	•
Superpower	Fighting	Physical	120	100	5	Normal	•
Iron Head	Steel	Physical	80	100	15	Normal	•
Ominous Wind	Ghost	Special	60	100	5	Normal	—
Snore	Normal	Special	40	100	15	Normal	—
Iron Defense	Steel	Status	—	—	15	Self	—
Knock Off	Dark	Physical	20	100	20	Normal	•
Swift	Normal	Special	60	—	20	2 foes	—

● PRIMARY WAY TO FIND

TRAINER'S PARTY Elite Four member Aaron

WILD POKÉMON

COURSE OF STORY

ABILITY ● Swarm ● Technician

EGG GROUP Bug

STATS
HP ●●
ATTACK ●●●●
DEFENSE ●●●
SP. ATTACK ●●
SP. DEFENSE ●●
SPEED ●●

Elekid

ELECTRIC

HEIGHT: 2'00"
WEIGHT: 51.8 lbs.
GENDER: **Male and Female**
HELD ITEM: **None**

● M/F have same form

PLATINUM A weak electric current flows between its horns. Sticking a hand there shocks the unwary.

EVOLUTION PATH

Elekid — Lv30 → Electabuzz — Link trade while holding Electirizer → Electivire

ABILITY ● Static

EGG GROUP: No Eggs

STATS: HP ●● / ATTACK ●● / DEFENSE ●● / SP. ATTACK ●● / SP. DEFENSE ● / SPEED ●●●

● TM & HM MOVES

No.	Name	Type	Kind	Power	Acc	PP	Range	DA
TM01	Focus Punch	Fighting	Physical	150	100	20	Normal	•
TM06	Toxic	Poison	Status	—	85	10	Normal	—
TM10	Hidden Power	Normal	Special	—	100	15	Normal	—
TM16	Light Screen	Psychic	Status	—	—	30	2 allies	—
TM17	Protect	Normal	Status	—	—	10	Self	—
TM18	Rain Dance	Water	Status	—	—	5	All	—
TM21	Frustration	Normal	Physical	—	100	20	Normal	•
TM24	Thunderbolt	Electric	Special	95	100	15	Normal	—
TM25	Thunder	Electric	Special	120	70	10	Normal	—
TM27	Return	Normal	Physical	—	100	20	Normal	•
TM29	Psychic	Psychic	Special	90	100	10	Normal	—
TM31	Brick Break	Fighting	Physical	75	100	15	Normal	•
TM32	Double Team	Normal	Status	—	—	15	Self	—
TM34	Shock Wave	Electric	Special	60	—	20	Normal	—
TM42	Facade	Normal	Physical	70	100	20	Normal	•
TM43	Secret Power	Normal	Physical	70	100	20	Normal	•
TM44	Rest	Psychic	Status	—	—	10	Self	—
TM45	Attract	Normal	Status	—	100	15	Normal	—
TM46	Thief	Dark	Physical	40	100	10	Normal	•
TM56	Fling	Dark	Physical	—	100	10	Normal	•
TM57	Charge Beam	Electric	Special	50	90	10	Normal	—
TM58	Endure	Normal	Status	—	—	10	Self	—
TM70	Flash	Normal	Status	—	100	20	Normal	—
TM73	Thunder Wave	Electric	Status	—	100	20	Normal	—
TM78	Captivate	Normal	Status	—	100	20	2 foes	—
TM82	Sleep Talk	Normal	Status	—	—	10	DoM	—
TM83	Natural Gift	Normal	Physical	—	100	15	Normal	—
TM87	Swagger	Normal	Status	—	90	15	Normal	—
TM90	Substitute	Normal	Status	—	—	10	Self	—
HM06	Rock Smash	Fighting	Physical	40	100	15	Normal	•

● LEVEL-UP AND LEARNED MOVES

Lv	Name	Type	Kind	Power	Acc	PP	Range	DA
Base	Quick Attack	Normal	Physical	40	100	30	Normal	•
Base	Leer	Normal	Status	—	100	30	2 foes	—
7	ThunderShock	Electric	Special	40	100	30	Normal	—
10	Low Kick	Fighting	Physical	—	100	20	Normal	•
16	Swift	Normal	Special	60	—	20	2 foes	—
19	Shock Wave	Electric	Special	60	—	20	Normal	—
25	Light Screen	Psychic	Status	—	—	30	2 allies	—
28	ThunderPunch	Electric	Physical	75	100	15	Normal	•
34	Discharge	Electric	Special	80	100	15	2 foes + 1 ally	—
37	Thunderbolt	Electric	Special	95	100	15	Normal	—
43	Screech	Normal	Status	—	85	40	Normal	—
46	Thunder	Electric	Special	120	70	10	Normal	—

● MOVES TAUGHT IN EXCHANGE FOR COLORED SHARDS

Name	Type	Kind	Power	Acc	PP	Range	DA
Mud-Slap	Ground	Special	20	100	10	Normal	—
ThunderPunch	Electric	Physical	75	100	15	Normal	•
Fire Punch	Fire	Physical	75	100	15	Normal	•
Ice Punch	Ice	Physical	75	100	15	Normal	•
Snore	Normal	Special	40	100	15	Normal	—
Helping Hand	Normal	Status	—	—	20	1 ally	—
Signal Beam	Bug	Special	75	100	15	Normal	—
Magnet Rise	Electric	Status	—	—	10	Self	—
Swift	Normal	Special	60	—	20	2 foes	—
Uproar	Normal	Special	50	100	10	1 random	—

● EGG MOVES

Name	Type	Kind	Power	Acc	PP	Range	DA
Karate Chop	Fighting	Physical	50	100	25	Normal	•
Barrier	Psychic	Status	—	—	30	Self	—
Rolling Kick	Fighting	Physical	60	85	15	Normal	•
Meditate	Psychic	Status	—	—	40	Self	—
Cross Chop	Fighting	Physical	100	80	5	Normal	•
Fire Punch	Fire	Physical	75	100	15	Normal	•
Ice Punch	Ice	Physical	75	100	15	Normal	•
DynamicPunch	Fighting	Physical	100	50	5	Normal	•

● PRIMARY WAY TO FIND

TRAINER'S PARTY — Trainer on Solaceon Town side of Route 210

WILD POKÉMON

COURSE OF STORY

Electabuzz

ELECTRIC

HEIGHT: 3'07"
WEIGHT: 66.1 lbs.
GENDER: **Male and Female**
HELD ITEM: **Electirizer**

● M/F have same form

PLATINUM It windmills its arms to slightly boost its punches. Foes have been known to escape in the meantime.

EVOLUTION PATH

Elekid — Lv30 → Electabuzz — Link trade while holding Electirizer → Electivire

ABILITY ● Static

EGG GROUP: Human-Like

STATS: HP ●● / ATTACK ●●● / DEFENSE ●● / SP. ATTACK ●●● / SP. DEFENSE ●● / SPEED ●●●●

● TM & HM MOVES

No.	Name	Type	Kind	Power	Acc	PP	Range	DA
TM01	Focus Punch	Fighting	Physical	150	100	20	Normal	•
TM06	Toxic	Poison	Status	—	85	10	Normal	—
TM10	Hidden Power	Normal	Special	—	100	15	Normal	—
TM15	Hyper Beam	Normal	Special	150	90	5	Normal	—
TM16	Light Screen	Psychic	Status	—	—	30	2 allies	—
TM17	Protect	Normal	Status	—	—	10	Self	—
TM18	Rain Dance	Water	Status	—	—	5	All	—
TM21	Frustration	Normal	Physical	—	100	20	Normal	•
TM23	Iron Tail	Steel	Physical	100	75	15	Normal	•
TM24	Thunderbolt	Electric	Special	95	100	15	Normal	—
TM25	Thunder	Electric	Special	120	70	10	Normal	—
TM27	Return	Normal	Physical	—	100	20	Normal	•
TM29	Psychic	Psychic	Special	90	100	10	Normal	—
TM31	Brick Break	Fighting	Physical	75	100	15	Normal	•
TM32	Double Team	Normal	Status	—	—	15	Self	—
TM34	Shock Wave	Electric	Special	60	—	20	Normal	—
TM42	Facade	Normal	Physical	70	100	20	Normal	•
TM43	Secret Power	Normal	Physical	70	100	20	Normal	•
TM44	Rest	Psychic	Status	—	—	10	Self	—
TM45	Attract	Normal	Status	—	100	15	Normal	—
TM46	Thief	Dark	Physical	40	100	10	Normal	•
TM52	Focus Blast	Fighting	Special	120	70	5	Normal	—
TM56	Fling	Dark	Physical	—	100	10	Normal	•
TM57	Charge Beam	Electric	Special	50	90	10	Normal	—
TM58	Endure	Normal	Status	—	—	10	Self	—
TM68	Giga Impact	Normal	Physical	150	90	5	Normal	•
TM70	Flash	Normal	Status	—	100	20	Normal	—
TM73	Thunder Wave	Electric	Status	—	100	20	Normal	—
TM78	Captivate	Normal	Status	—	100	20	2 foes	—
TM82	Sleep Talk	Normal	Status	—	—	10	DoM	—
TM83	Natural Gift	Normal	Physical	—	100	15	Normal	—
TM87	Swagger	Normal	Status	—	90	15	Normal	—
TM90	Substitute	Normal	Status	—	—	10	Self	—
HM04	Strength	Normal	Physical	80	100	15	Normal	•
HM06	Rock Smash	Fighting	Physical	40	100	15	Normal	•
HM08	Rock Climb	Normal	Physical	90	85	20	Normal	•

● LEVEL-UP AND LEARNED MOVES

Lv	Name	Type	Kind	Power	Acc	PP	Range	DA
Base	Quick Attack	Normal	Physical	40	100	30	Normal	•
Base	Leer	Normal	Status	—	100	30	2 foes	—
Base	ThunderShock	Electric	Special	40	100	30	Normal	—
7	ThunderShock	Electric	Special	40	100	30	Normal	—
10	Low Kick	Fighting	Physical	—	100	20	Normal	•
16	Swift	Normal	Special	60	—	20	2 foes	—
19	Shock Wave	Electric	Special	60	—	20	Normal	—
25	Light Screen	Psychic	Status	—	—	30	2 allies	—
28	ThunderPunch	Electric	Physical	75	100	15	Normal	•
37	Discharge	Electric	Special	80	100	15	2 foes + 1 ally	—
43	Thunderbolt	Electric	Special	95	100	15	Normal	—
52	Screech	Normal	Status	—	85	40	Normal	—
58	Thunder	Electric	Special	120	70	10	Normal	—

● MOVES TAUGHT IN EXCHANGE FOR COLORED SHARDS

Name	Type	Kind	Power	Acc	PP	Range	DA
Mud-Slap	Ground	Special	20	100	10	Normal	—
ThunderPunch	Electric	Physical	75	100	15	Normal	•
Fire Punch	Fire	Physical	75	100	15	Normal	•
Ice Punch	Ice	Physical	75	100	15	Normal	•
Snore	Normal	Special	40	100	15	Normal	—
Helping Hand	Normal	Status	—	—	20	1 ally	—
Signal Beam	Bug	Special	75	100	15	Normal	—
Magnet Rise	Electric	Status	—	—	10	Self	—
Swift	Normal	Special	60	—	20	2 foes	—

● PRIMARY WAY TO FIND

TRAINER'S PARTY — Trainer on Route 217

WILD POKÉMON — Route 222

COURSE OF STORY

Electivire

ELECTRIC

HEIGHT: 5'11"
WEIGHT: 305.6 lbs.
GENDER: Male and Female
HELD ITEM: None

● M/F have same form

PLATINUM Heedless of enemy attacks, it closes in, shoves its tails onto the foe, then looses high voltage.

EVOLUTION PATH

Elekid → (Lv30) Electabuzz → (Link trade while holding Electirizer) Electivire

ABILITY ● Motor Drive

EGG GROUP Human-Like

STATS
HP ●●
ATTACK ●●●●
DEFENSE ●●●
SP. ATTACK ●●●
SP. DEFENSE ●●●
SPEED ●●●

● TM & HM MOVES

No.	Name	Type	Kind	Power	Acc	PP	Range	DA
TM01	Focus Punch	Fighting	Physical	150	100	20	Normal	•
TM06	Toxic	Poison	Status	—	85	10	Normal	—
TM10	Hidden Power	Normal	Special	—	100	15	Normal	—
TM12	Taunt	Dark	Status	—	100	20	Normal	—
TM15	Hyper Beam	Normal	Special	150	90	5	Normal	•
TM16	Light Screen	Psychic	Status	—	—	30	2 allies	—
TM17	Protect	Normal	Status	—	—	10	Self	—
TM18	Rain Dance	Water	Status	—	—	5	All	—
TM21	Frustration	Normal	Physical	—	100	20	Normal	•
TM23	Iron Tail	Steel	Physical	100	75	15	Normal	•
TM24	Thunderbolt	Electric	Special	95	100	15	Normal	—
TM25	Thunder	Electric	Special	120	70	10	Normal	—
TM26	Earthquake	Ground	Physical	100	100	10	2 foes • 1 ally	•
TM27	Return	Normal	Physical	—	100	20	Normal	•
TM28	Dig	Ground	Physical	80	100	10	Normal	•
TM29	Psychic	Psychic	Special	90	100	10	Normal	—
TM31	Brick Break	Fighting	Physical	75	100	15	Normal	•
TM32	Double Team	Normal	Status	—	—	15	Self	—
TM34	Shock Wave	Electric	Special	60	—	20	Normal	—
TM35	Flamethrower	Fire	Special	95	100	15	Normal	—
TM39	Rock Tomb	Rock	Physical	50	80	10	Normal	•
TM41	Torment	Dark	Status	—	100	15	Normal	—
TM42	Facade	Normal	Physical	70	100	20	Normal	•
TM43	Secret Power	Normal	Physical	70	100	20	Normal	•
TM44	Rest	Psychic	Status	—	—	10	Self	—
TM45	Attract	Normal	Status	—	100	15	Normal	—
TM46	Thief	Dark	Physical	40	100	10	Normal	•
TM52	Focus Blast	Fighting	Special	120	70	5	Normal	—
TM56	Fling	Dark	Physical	—	100	10	Normal	•
TM57	Charge Beam	Electric	Special	50	90	10	Normal	—
TM58	Endure	Normal	Status	—	—	10	Self	—
TM68	Giga Impact	Normal	Physical	150	90	5	Normal	•
TM70	Flash	Normal	Status	—	100	20	Normal	—
TM73	Thunder Wave	Electric	Status	—	100	20	Normal	—
TM78	Captivate	Normal	Status	—	100	20	2 foes	—
TM80	Rock Slide	Rock	Physical	75	90	10	2 foes	•
TM82	Sleep Talk	Normal	Status	—	—	10	DoM	—
TM83	Natural Gift	Normal	Physical	—	100	15	Normal	•
TM87	Swagger	Normal	Status	—	90	15	Normal	—
TM90	Substitute	Normal	Status	—	—	10	Self	—
HM04	Strength	Normal	Physical	80	100	15	Normal	•
HM06	Rock Smash	Fighting	Physical	40	100	15	Normal	•
HM08	Rock Climb	Normal	Physical	90	85	20	Normal	•

● LEVEL-UP AND LEARNED MOVES

Lv	Name	Type	Kind	Power	Acc	PP	Range	DA
Base	Fire Punch	Fire	Physical	75	100	15	Normal	•
Base	Quick Attack	Normal	Physical	40	100	30	Normal	•
Base	Leer	Normal	Status	—	100	30	2 foes	—
Base	ThunderShock	Electric	Special	40	100	30	Normal	—
Base	Low Kick	Fighting	Physical	—	100	20	Normal	•
7	ThunderShock	Electric	Special	40	100	30	Normal	—
10	Low Kick	Fighting	Physical	—	100	20	Normal	•
16	Swift	Normal	Special	60	—	20	2 foes	—
19	Shock Wave	Electric	Special	60	—	20	Normal	—
25	Light Screen	Psychic	Status	—	—	30	2 allies	—
28	ThunderPunch	Electric	Physical	75	100	15	Normal	•
37	Discharge	Electric	Special	80	100	15	2 foes • 1 ally	—
43	Thunderbolt	Electric	Special	95	100	15	Normal	—
52	Screech	Normal	Status	—	85	40	Normal	—
58	Thunder	Electric	Special	120	70	10	Normal	—
67	Giga Impact	Normal	Physical	150	90	5	Normal	•

● MOVES TAUGHT IN EXCHANGE FOR COLORED SHARDS

Name	Type	Kind	Power	Acc	PP	Range	DA
Mud-Slap	Ground	Special	20	100	10	Normal	•
ThunderPunch	Electric	Physical	75	100	15	Normal	•
Fire Punch	Fire	Physical	75	100	15	Normal	•
Ice Punch	Ice	Physical	75	100	15	Normal	•
Snore	Normal	Special	40	100	15	Normal	•
Helping Hand	Normal	Status	—	—	20	1 ally	—
Signal Beam	Bug	Special	75	100	15	Normal	—
Magnet Rise	Electric	Status	—	—	10	Self	—
Swift	Normal	Special	60	—	20	2 foes	—

● PRIMARY WAY TO FIND

TRAINER'S PARTY — Sunyshore Gym Leader Volkner

WILD POKÉMON

COURSE OF STORY

Magby

FIRE

HEIGHT: 2'04"
WEIGHT: 47.2 lbs.
GENDER: Male and Female
HELD ITEM: None

● M/F have same form

PLATINUM Its magma-like blood circulates throughout its body. Its body's heat can top 1,100 degrees F.

EVOLUTION PATH

Magby → (Lv30) Magmar → (Link trade while holding Magmarizer) Magmortar

ABILITY ● Flame Body

EGG GROUP No Eggs

STATS
HP ●
ATTACK ●●●
DEFENSE ●●
SP. ATTACK ●●●
SP. DEFENSE ●●
SPEED ●●●

● TM & HM MOVES

No.	Name	Type	Kind	Power	Acc	PP	Range	DA
TM01	Focus Punch	Fighting	Physical	150	100	20	Normal	•
TM06	Toxic	Poison	Status	—	85	10	Normal	—
TM10	Hidden Power	Normal	Special	—	100	15	Normal	—
TM11	Sunny Day	Fire	Status	—	—	5	All	—
TM17	Protect	Normal	Status	—	—	10	Self	—
TM21	Frustration	Normal	Physical	—	100	20	Normal	•
TM23	Iron Tail	Steel	Physical	100	75	15	Normal	•
TM27	Return	Normal	Physical	—	100	20	Normal	•
TM29	Psychic	Psychic	Special	90	100	10	Normal	—
TM31	Brick Break	Fighting	Physical	75	100	15	Normal	•
TM32	Double Team	Normal	Status	—	—	15	Self	—
TM35	Flamethrower	Fire	Special	95	100	15	Normal	—
TM38	Fire Blast	Fire	Special	120	85	5	Normal	—
TM42	Facade	Normal	Physical	70	100	20	Normal	•
TM43	Secret Power	Normal	Physical	70	100	20	Normal	•
TM44	Rest	Psychic	Status	—	—	10	Self	—
TM45	Attract	Normal	Status	—	100	15	Normal	—
TM46	Thief	Dark	Physical	40	100	10	Normal	•
TM50	Overheat	Fire	Special	140	90	5	Normal	—
TM56	Fling	Dark	Physical	—	100	10	Normal	•
TM58	Endure	Normal	Status	—	—	10	Self	—
TM61	Will-O-Wisp	Fire	Status	—	75	15	Normal	—
TM78	Captivate	Normal	Status	—	100	20	2 foes	—
TM82	Sleep Talk	Normal	Status	—	—	10	DoM	—
TM83	Natural Gift	Normal	Physical	—	100	15	Normal	•
TM87	Swagger	Normal	Status	—	90	15	Normal	—
TM90	Substitute	Normal	Status	—	—	10	Self	—
HM06	Rock Smash	Fighting	Physical	40	100	15	Normal	•

● LEVEL-UP AND LEARNED MOVES

Lv	Name	Type	Kind	Power	Acc	PP	Range	DA
Base	Smog	Poison	Special	20	70	20	Normal	—
Base	Leer	Normal	Status	—	100	30	2 foes	—
7	Ember	Fire	Special	40	100	25	Normal	—
10	SmokeScreen	Normal	Status	—	100	20	Normal	—
16	Faint Attack	Dark	Physical	60	—	20	Normal	•
19	Fire Spin	Fire	Special	15	70	15	Normal	—
25	Confuse Ray	Ghost	Status	—	100	10	Normal	—
28	Fire Punch	Fire	Physical	75	100	15	Normal	•
34	Lava Plume	Fire	Special	80	100	15	2 foes • 1 ally	—
37	Flamethrower	Fire	Special	95	100	15	Normal	—
43	Sunny Day	Fire	Status	—	—	5	All	—
46	Fire Blast	Fire	Special	120	85	5	Normal	—

● MOVES TAUGHT IN EXCHANGE FOR COLORED SHARDS

Name	Type	Kind	Power	Acc	PP	Range	DA
Mud-Slap	Ground	Special	20	100	10	Normal	—
ThunderPunch	Electric	Physical	75	100	15	Normal	•
Fire Punch	Fire	Physical	75	100	15	Normal	•
Snore	Normal	Special	40	100	15	Normal	•
Helping Hand	Normal	Status	—	—	20	1 ally	—
Heat Wave	Fire	Special	100	90	10	2 foes	—
Uproar	Normal	Special	50	100	10	1 random	—

● EGG MOVES

Name	Type	Kind	Power	Acc	PP	Range	DA
Karate Chop	Fighting	Physical	50	100	25	Normal	•
Mega Punch	Normal	Physical	80	85	20	Normal	•
Barrier	Psychic	Status	—	—	30	Self	—
Screech	Normal	Status	—	85	40	Normal	—
Cross Chop	Fighting	Physical	100	80	5	Normal	•
ThunderPunch	Electric	Physical	75	100	15	Normal	•
Mach Punch	Fighting	Physical	40	100	30	Normal	•
DynamicPunch	Fighting	Physical	100	50	5	Normal	•
Flare Blitz	Fire	Physical	120	100	15	Normal	•

● PRIMARY WAY TO FIND

TRAINER'S PARTY — Trainer on Solaceon Town side of Route 210

WILD POKÉMON

COURSE OF STORY

Magmar

FIRE

HEIGHT: **4'03"**
WEIGHT: **98.1 lbs.**
GENDER: **Male and Female**
HELD ITEM: **Magmarizer**

● M/F have same form

PLATINUM — When it breathes deeply, heat waves form around its body, making it hard to see clearly.

EVOLUTION PATH

Magby → Magmar (Lv30) → Magmortar (Link trade while holding Magmarizer)

● TM & HM MOVES

No.	Name	Type	Kind	Power	Acc.	PP	Range	DA
TM01	Focus Punch	Fighting	Physical	150	100	20	Normal	●
TM06	Toxic	Poison	Status	—	85	10	Normal	—
TM10	Hidden Power	Normal	Special	—	100	15	Normal	—
TM11	Sunny Day	Fire	Status	—	—	5	All	—
TM15	Hyper Beam	Normal	Special	150	90	5	Normal	—
TM17	Protect	Normal	Status	—	—	10	Self	—
TM21	Frustration	Normal	Physical	—	100	20	Normal	●
TM23	Iron Tail	Steel	Physical	100	75	15	Normal	●
TM27	Return	Normal	Physical	—	100	20	Normal	●
TM29	Psychic	Psychic	Special	90	100	10	Normal	—
TM31	Brick Break	Fighting	Physical	75	100	15	Normal	●
TM32	Double Team	Normal	Status	—	—	15	Self	—
TM35	Flamethrower	Fire	Special	95	100	15	Normal	—
TM38	Fire Blast	Fire	Special	120	85	5	Normal	—
TM42	Facade	Normal	Physical	70	100	20	Normal	●
TM43	Secret Power	Normal	Physical	70	100	20	Normal	●
TM44	Rest	Psychic	Status	—	—	10	Self	—
TM45	Attract	Normal	Status	—	100	15	Normal	—
TM46	Thief	Dark	Physical	40	100	10	Normal	●
TM50	Overheat	Fire	Special	140	90	5	Normal	—
TM52	Focus Blast	Fighting	Special	120	70	5	Normal	—
TM56	Fling	Dark	Physical	—	100	10	Normal	●
TM58	Endure	Normal	Status	—	—	10	Self	—
TM61	Will-O-Wisp	Fire	Status	—	75	15	Normal	—
TM68	Giga Impact	Normal	Physical	150	90	5	Normal	●
TM78	Captivate	Normal	Status	—	100	20	2 foes	—
TM82	Sleep Talk	Normal	Status	—	—	10	DoM	—
TM83	Natural Gift	Normal	Physical	—	100	15	Normal	●
TM87	Swagger	Normal	Status	—	90	15	Normal	—
TM90	Substitute	Normal	Status	—	—	10	Self	—
HM04	Strength	Normal	Physical	80	100	15	Normal	●
HM06	Rock Smash	Fighting	Physical	40	100	15	Normal	●
HM08	Rock Climb	Normal	Physical	90	85	20	Normal	●

● LEVEL-UP AND LEARNED MOVES

Lv	Name	Type	Kind	Power	Acc	PP	Range	DA
Base	Smog	Poison	Special	20	70	20	Normal	
Base	Leer	Normal	Status	—	100	30	2 foes	
Base	Ember	Fire	Special	40	100	25	Normal	
7	Ember	Fire	Special	40	100	25	Normal	
10	SmokeScreen	Normal	Status	—	100	20	Normal	
16	Faint Attack	Dark	Physical	60	—	20	Normal	
19	Fire Spin	Fire	Special	15	70	15	Normal	
25	Confuse Ray	Ghost	Status	—	100	10	Normal	
28	Fire Punch	Fire	Physical	75	100	15	Normal	
36	Lava Plume	Fire	Special	80	100	15	2 foes + 1 ally	
41	Flamethrower	Fire	Special	95	100	15	Normal	
49	Sunny Day	Fire	Status	—	—	5	All	
54	Fire Blast	Fire	Special	120	85	5	Normal	

● MOVES TAUGHT IN EXCHANGE FOR COLORED SHARDS

Name	Type	Kind	Power	Acc	PP	Range	DA
Mud-Slap	Ground	Special	20	100	10	Normal	—
ThunderPunch	Electric	Physical	75	100	15	Normal	●
Fire Punch	Fire	Physical	75	100	15	Normal	●
Snore	Normal	Special	40	100	15	Normal	—
Helping Hand	Normal	Status	—	—	20	1 ally	—
Heat Wave	Fire	Special	100	90	10	2 foes	—

ABILITY ● Flame Body

EGG GROUP Human-Like

STATS
HP ●●
ATTACK ●●
DEFENSE ●●
SP. ATTACK ●●●
SP. DEFENSE ●●
SPEED ●●●

● PRIMARY WAY TO FIND

TRAINER'S PARTY Trainer at Fuego Ironworks

WILD POKÉMON Fuego Ironworks

COURSE OF STORY

Magmortar

FIRE

HEIGHT: **5'03"**
WEIGHT: **149.9 lbs.**
GENDER: **Male and Female**
HELD ITEM: **None**

● M/F have same form

PLATINUM — When launching 3,600 degrees F fireballs, its body takes on a whitish hue from the intense heat.

EVOLUTION PATH

Magby → Magmar (Lv30) → Magmortar (Link trade while holding Magmarizer)

● TM & HM MOVES

No.	Name	Type	Kind	Power	Acc	PP	Range	DA
TM01	Focus Punch	Fighting	Physical	150	100	20	Normal	●
TM06	Toxic	Poison	Status	—	85	10	Normal	—
TM10	Hidden Power	Normal	Special	—	100	15	Normal	—
TM11	Sunny Day	Fire	Status	—	—	5	All	—
TM12	Taunt	Dark	Status	—	100	20	Normal	—
TM15	Hyper Beam	Normal	Special	150	90	5	Normal	—
TM17	Protect	Normal	Status	—	—	10	Self	—
TM21	Frustration	Normal	Physical	—	100	20	Normal	●
TM22	SolarBeam	Grass	Special	120	100	10	Normal	—
TM23	Iron Tail	Steel	Physical	100	75	15	Normal	●
TM24	Thunderbolt	Electric	Special	95	100	15	Normal	—
TM26	Earthquake	Ground	Physical	100	100	10	2 foes + 1 ally	●
TM27	Return	Normal	Physical	—	100	20	Normal	●
TM29	Psychic	Psychic	Special	90	100	10	Normal	—
TM31	Brick Break	Fighting	Physical	75	100	15	Normal	●
TM32	Double Team	Normal	Status	—	—	15	Self	—
TM35	Flamethrower	Fire	Special	95	100	15	Normal	—
TM38	Fire Blast	Fire	Special	120	85	5	Normal	—
TM39	Rock Tomb	Rock	Physical	50	80	10	Normal	●
TM41	Torment	Dark	Status	—	100	15	Normal	—
TM42	Facade	Normal	Physical	70	100	20	Normal	●
TM43	Secret Power	Normal	Physical	70	100	20	Normal	●
TM44	Rest	Psychic	Status	—	—	10	Self	—
TM45	Attract	Normal	Status	—	100	15	Normal	—
TM46	Thief	Dark	Physical	40	100	10	Normal	●
TM50	Overheat	Fire	Special	140	90	5	Normal	—
TM52	Focus Blast	Fighting	Special	120	70	5	Normal	—
TM56	Fling	Dark	Physical	—	100	10	Normal	●
TM58	Endure	Normal	Status	—	—	10	Self	—
TM61	Will-O-Wisp	Fire	Status	—	75	15	Normal	—
TM68	Giga Impact	Normal	Physical	150	90	5	Normal	●
TM78	Captivate	Normal	Status	—	100	20	2 foes	—
TM80	Rock Slide	Rock	Physical	75	90	10	2 foes	●
TM82	Sleep Talk	Normal	Status	—	—	10	DoM	—
TM83	Natural Gift	Normal	Physical	—	100	15	Normal	●
TM87	Swagger	Normal	Status	—	90	15	Normal	—
TM90	Substitute	Normal	Status	—	—	10	Self	—
HM04	Strength	Normal	Physical	80	100	15	Normal	●
HM06	Rock Smash	Fighting	Physical	40	100	15	Normal	●
HM08	Rock Climb	Normal	Physical	90	85	20	Normal	●

● LEVEL-UP AND LEARNED MOVES

Lv	Name	Type	Kind	Power	Acc	PP	Range	DA
Base	ThunderPunch	Electric	Physical	75	100	15	Normal	●
Base	Smog	Poison	Special	20	70	20	Normal	—
Base	Leer	Normal	Status	—	100	30	2 foes	—
Base	Ember	Fire	Special	40	100	25	Normal	—
Base	SmokeScreen	Normal	Status	—	100	20	Normal	—
7	Ember	Fire	Special	40	100	25	Normal	—
10	SmokeScreen	Normal	Status	—	100	20	Normal	—
16	Faint Attack	Dark	Physical	60	—	20	Normal	●
19	Fire Spin	Fire	Special	15	70	15	Normal	—
25	Confuse Ray	Ghost	Status	—	100	10	Normal	—
28	Fire Punch	Fire	Physical	75	100	15	Normal	●
37	Lava Plume	Fire	Special	80	100	15	2 foes + 1 ally	—
43	Flamethrower	Fire	Special	95	100	15	Normal	—
52	Sunny Day	Fire	Status	—	—	5	All	—
58	Fire Blast	Fire	Special	120	85	5	Normal	—
67	Hyper Beam	Normal	Special	150	90	5	Normal	—

● MOVES TAUGHT IN EXCHANGE FOR COLORED SHARDS

Name	Type	Kind	Power	Acc	PP	Range	DA
Mud-Slap	Ground	Special	20	100	10	Normal	—
ThunderPunch	Electric	Physical	75	100	15	Normal	●
Fire Punch	Fire	Physical	75	100	15	Normal	●
Snore	Normal	Special	40	100	15	Normal	—
Helping Hand	Normal	Status	—	—	20	1 ally	—
Heat Wave	Fire	Special	100	90	10	2 foes	—

ABILITY ● Flame Body

EGG GROUP Human-Like

STATS
HP ●●
ATTACK ●●●
DEFENSE ●●
SP. ATTACK ●●●●
SP. DEFENSE ●●●
SPEED ●●●

● PRIMARY WAY TO FIND

TRAINER'S PARTY Elite Four member Flint

WILD POKÉMON

COURSE OF STORY

Swinub

ICE | GROUND

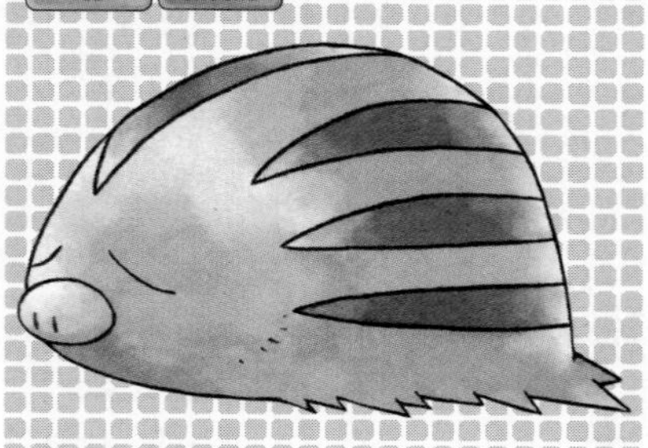

HEIGHT: 1'04"
WEIGHT: 14.3 lbs.
GENDER: Male and Female
HELD ITEM: None

● M/F have same form

PLATINUM It has a very sensitive nose. It can locate mushrooms, berries, and even hot springs buried under ice.

EVOLUTION PATH

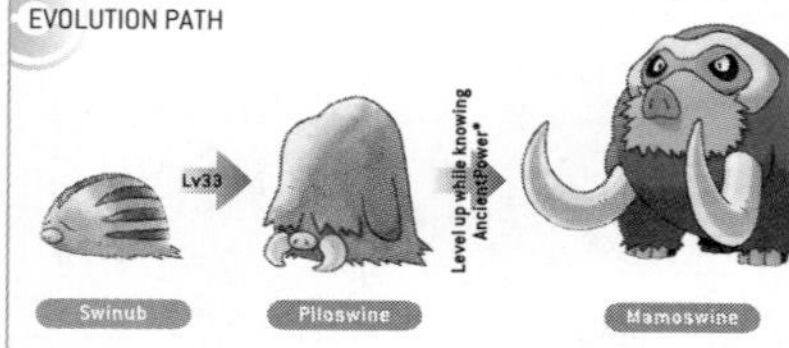

Swinub — Lv33 → Piloswine — Level up while knowing AncientPower* → Mamoswine

ABILITY ● Oblivious ● Snow Cloak
EGG GROUP Field

STATS
HP ●●
ATTACK ●
DEFENSE ●
SP. ATTACK ●
SP. DEFENSE ●
SPEED ●●

● TM & HM MOVES

No.	Name	Type	Kind	Power	Acc	PP	Range	DA
TM05	Roar	Normal	Status	—	100	20	Normal	—
TM06	Toxic	Poison	Status	—	85	10	Normal	—
TM07	Hail	Ice	Status	—	—	10	All	—
TM10	Hidden Power	Normal	Special	—	100	15	Normal	—
TM13	Ice Beam	Ice	Special	95	100	10	Normal	—
TM14	Blizzard	Ice	Special	120	70	5	2 foes	—
TM16	Light Screen	Psychic	Status	—	—	30	2 allies	—
TM17	Protect	Normal	Status	—	—	10	Self	—
TM18	Rain Dance	Water	Status	—	—	5	All	—
TM21	Frustration	Normal	Physical	—	100	20	Normal	•
TM26	Earthquake	Ground	Physical	100	100	10	2 foes • 1 ally	•
TM27	Return	Normal	Physical	—	100	20	Normal	•
TM28	Dig	Ground	Physical	80	100	10	Normal	•
TM32	Double Team	Normal	Status	—	—	15	Self	—
TM33	Reflect	Psychic	Status	—	—	20	2 allies	—
TM37	Sandstorm	Rock	Status	—	—	10	All	—
TM39	Rock Tomb	Rock	Physical	50	80	10	Normal	•
TM42	Facade	Normal	Physical	70	100	20	Normal	•
TM43	Secret Power	Normal	Physical	70	100	20	Normal	•
TM44	Rest	Psychic	Status	—	—	10	Self	—
TM45	Attract	Normal	Status	—	100	15	Normal	—
TM58	Endure	Normal	Status	—	—	10	Self	—
TM76	Stealth Rock	Rock	Status	—	—	20	2 foes	—
TM78	Captivate	Normal	Status	—	100	20	2 foes	—
TM80	Rock Slide	Rock	Physical	75	90	10	2 foes	•
TM82	Sleep Talk	Normal	Status	—	—	10	DoM	—
TM83	Natural Gift	Normal	Physical	—	100	15	Normal	•
TM87	Swagger	Normal	Status	—	90	15	Normal	—
TM90	Substitute	Normal	Status	—	—	10	Self	—
HM04	Strength	Normal	Physical	80	100	15	Normal	•
HM06	Rock Smash	Fighting	Physical	40	100	15	Normal	•

● LEVEL-UP AND LEARNED MOVES

Lv	Name	Type	Kind	Power	Acc	PP	Range	DA
Base	Tackle	Normal	Physical	35	95	35	Normal	•
Base	Odor Sleuth	Normal	Status	—	—	40	Normal	—
4	Mud Sport	Ground	Status	—	—	15	All	—
8	Powder Snow	Ice	Special	40	100	25	2 foes	—
13	Mud-Slap	Ground	Special	20	100	10	Normal	•
16	Endure	Normal	Status	—	—	10	Self	—
20	Mud Bomb	Ground	Special	65	85	10	Normal	—
25	Icy Wind	Ice	Special	55	95	15	2 foes	—
28	Ice Shard	Ice	Physical	40	100	30	Normal	—
32	Take Down	Normal	Physical	90	85	20	Normal	•
37	Earthquake	Ground	Physical	100	100	10	2 foes • 1 ally	•
40	Mist	Ice	Status	—	—	30	2 allies	—
44	Blizzard	Ice	Special	120	70	5	2 foes	—
49	Amnesia	Psychic	Status	—	—	20	Self	—

● MOVES TAUGHT IN EXCHANGE FOR COLORED SHARDS

Name	Type	Kind	Power	Acc	PP	Range	DA
Mud-Slap	Ground	Special	20	100	10	Normal	•
Icy Wind	Ice	Special	55	95	15	2 foes	—
Superpower	Fighting	Physical	120	100	5	Normal	•
Snore	Normal	Special	40	100	15	Normal	—
Endeavor	Normal	Physical	—	100	5	Normal	•
AncientPower	Rock	Special	60	100	5	Normal	—
Earth Power	Ground	Special	90	100	10	Normal	—

● EGG MOVES

Name	Type	Kind	Power	Acc	PP	Range	DA
Take Down	Normal	Physical	90	85	20	Normal	•
Bite	Dark	Physical	60	100	25	Normal	•
Body Slam	Normal	Physical	85	100	15	Normal	•
Rock Slide	Rock	Physical	75	90	10	2 foes	•
AncientPower	Rock	Special	60	100	5	Normal	—
Mud Shot	Ground	Special	55	95	15	Normal	—
Icicle Spear	Ice	Physical	10	100	30	Normal	—
Double-Edge	Normal	Physical	120	100	15	Normal	•
Fissure	Ground	Physical	—	30	5	Normal	—
Curse	???	Status	—	—	10	Normal • Self	—

● PRIMARY WAY TO FIND

TRAINER'S PARTY	Trainer on Route 217
WILD POKÉMON	Route 217
COURSE OF STORY	

*To teach AncientPower to Piloswine, give one Heart Scale to the Move Tutor in Pastoria City

---

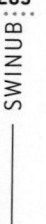

Piloswine

ICE | GROUND

HEIGHT: 3'07"
WEIGHT: 123.0 lbs.
GENDER: Male and Female
HELD ITEM: None

● Male form ● Female form

PLATINUM Covered by a shaggy coat, it is strong against the cold. Its tusks of ice thicken when it snows.

EVOLUTION PATH

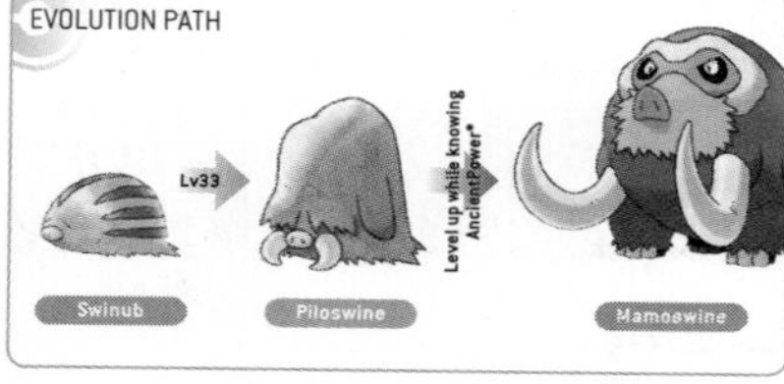

Swinub — Lv33 → Piloswine — Level up while knowing AncientPower* → Mamoswine

ABILITY ● Oblivious ● Snow Cloak
EGG GROUP Field

STATS
HP ●●●
ATTACK ●●●
DEFENSE ●●
SP. ATTACK ●●
SP. DEFENSE ●●
SPEED ●●

● TM & HM MOVES

No.	Name	Type	Kind	Power	Acc	PP	Range	DA
TM05	Roar	Normal	Status	—	100	20	Normal	—
TM06	Toxic	Poison	Status	—	85	10	Normal	—
TM07	Hail	Ice	Status	—	—	10	All	—
TM10	Hidden Power	Normal	Special	—	100	15	Normal	—
TM13	Ice Beam	Ice	Special	95	100	10	Normal	—
TM14	Blizzard	Ice	Special	120	70	5	2 foes	—
TM15	Hyper Beam	Normal	Special	150	90	5	Normal	—
TM16	Light Screen	Psychic	Status	—	—	30	2 allies	—
TM17	Protect	Normal	Status	—	—	10	Self	—
TM18	Rain Dance	Water	Status	—	—	5	All	—
TM21	Frustration	Normal	Physical	—	100	20	Normal	•
TM26	Earthquake	Ground	Physical	100	100	10	2 foes • 1 ally	•
TM27	Return	Normal	Physical	—	100	20	Normal	•
TM28	Dig	Ground	Physical	80	100	10	Normal	•
TM32	Double Team	Normal	Status	—	—	15	Self	—
TM33	Reflect	Psychic	Status	—	—	20	2 allies	—
TM37	Sandstorm	Rock	Status	—	—	10	All	—
TM39	Rock Tomb	Rock	Physical	50	80	10	Normal	•
TM42	Facade	Normal	Physical	70	100	20	Normal	•
TM43	Secret Power	Normal	Physical	70	100	20	Normal	•
TM44	Rest	Psychic	Status	—	—	10	Self	—
TM45	Attract	Normal	Status	—	100	15	Normal	—
TM58	Endure	Normal	Status	—	—	10	Self	—
TM68	Giga Impact	Normal	Physical	150	90	5	Normal	•
TM71	Stone Edge	Rock	Physical	100	80	5	Normal	•
TM72	Avalanche	Ice	Physical	60	100	10	Normal	•
TM76	Stealth Rock	Rock	Status	—	—	20	2 foes	—
TM78	Captivate	Normal	Status	—	100	20	2 foes	—
TM80	Rock Slide	Rock	Physical	75	90	10	2 foes	•
TM82	Sleep Talk	Normal	Status	—	—	10	DoM	—
TM83	Natural Gift	Normal	Physical	—	100	15	Normal	•
TM87	Swagger	Normal	Status	—	90	15	Normal	—
TM90	Substitute	Normal	Status	—	—	10	Self	—
HM04	Strength	Normal	Physical	80	100	15	Normal	•
HM06	Rock Smash	Fighting	Physical	40	100	15	Normal	•

● LEVEL-UP AND LEARNED MOVES

Lv	Name	Type	Kind	Power	Acc	PP	Range	DA
Base	AncientPower	Rock	Special	60	100	5	Normal	—
Base	Peck	Flying	Physical	35	100	35	Normal	•
Base	Odor Sleuth	Normal	Status	—	—	40	Normal	—
Base	Mud Sport	Ground	Status	—	—	15	All	—
Base	Powder Snow	Ice	Special	40	100	25	2 foes	—
4	Mud Sport	Ground	Status	—	—	15	All	—
8	Powder Snow	Ice	Special	40	100	25	2 foes	—
13	Mud-Slap	Ground	Special	20	100	10	Normal	•
16	Endure	Normal	Status	—	—	10	Self	—
20	Mud Bomb	Ground	Special	65	85	10	Normal	—
25	Icy Wind	Ice	Special	55	95	15	2 foes	—
28	Ice Fang	Ice	Physical	65	95	15	Normal	•
32	Take Down	Normal	Physical	90	85	20	Normal	•
33	Fury Attack	Normal	Physical	15	85	20	Normal	•
40	Earthquake	Ground	Physical	100	100	10	2 foes • 1 ally	•
48	Mist	Ice	Status	—	—	30	2 allies	—
56	Blizzard	Ice	Special	120	70	5	2 foes	—
65	Amnesia	Psychic	Status	—	—	20	Self	—

● MOVES TAUGHT IN EXCHANGE FOR COLORED SHARDS

Name	Type	Kind	Power	Acc	PP	Range	DA
Mud-Slap	Ground	Special	20	100	10	Normal	•
Icy Wind	Ice	Special	55	95	15	2 foes	—
Superpower	Fighting	Physical	120	100	5	Normal	•
Snore	Normal	Special	40	100	15	Normal	—
Endeavor	Normal	Physical	—	100	5	Normal	•
AncientPower	Rock	Special	60	100	5	Normal	—
Earth Power	Ground	Special	90	100	10	Normal	—

● PRIMARY WAY TO FIND

TRAINER'S PARTY	Trainer on Route 217
WILD POKÉMON	Route 217 (use Poké Radar)
COURSE OF STORY	

*To teach AncientPower to Piloswine, give one Heart Scale to the Move Tutor in Pastoria City

Sinnoh Pokédex No. 205 Twin Tusk Pokémon
Mamoswine

ICE · GROUND

HEIGHT: 8'02"
WEIGHT: 641.5 lbs.
GENDER: Male and Female
HELD ITEM: None

● Male form ● Female form

PLATINUM: A frozen one was dug up from soil dating back 10,000 years. It woke up to much amazement.

EVOLUTION PATH

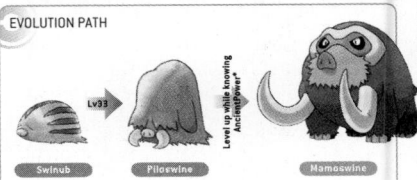

Swinub → Lv33 → Piloswine → Level up while knowing AncientPower* → Mamoswine

ABILITY: ● Oblivious ● Snow Cloak

EGG GROUP: Field

STATS:
HP ●●●
ATTACK ●●●●
DEFENSE ●●●
SP.ATTACK ●●●
SP.DEFENSE ●●●
SPEED ●●●

● TM & HM MOVES

No.	Name	Type	Kind	Power	Acc	PP	Range	DA
TM05	Roar	Normal	Status	—	100	20	Normal	—
TM06	Toxic	Poison	Status	—	85	10	Normal	—
TM07	Hail	Ice	Status	—	—	10	All	—
TM10	Hidden Power	Normal	Special	—	100	15	Normal	—
TM13	Ice Beam	Ice	Special	95	100	10	Normal	—
TM14	Blizzard	Ice	Special	120	70	5	2 foes	—
TM15	Hyper Beam	Normal	Special	150	90	5	Normal	—
TM16	Light Screen	Psychic	Status	—	—	30	2 allies	—
TM17	Protect	Normal	Status	—	—	10	Self	—
TM18	Rain Dance	Water	Status	—	—	5	All	—
TM21	Frustration	Normal	Physical	100	100	10	2 foes + 1 ally	●
TM26	Earthquake	Ground	Physical	100	100	10	2 foes + 1 ally	—
TM27	Return	Normal	Physical	—	100	20	Normal	●
TM28	Dig	Ground	Physical	80	100	10	Normal	●
TM32	Double Team	Normal	Status	—	—	15	Self	—
TM33	Reflect	Psychic	Status	—	—	20	2 allies	—
TM37	Sandstorm	Rock	Status	—	—	10	All	—
TM39	Rock Tomb	Rock	Physical	50	80	10	Normal	●
TM42	Facade	Normal	Physical	70	100	20	Normal	●
TM43	Secret Power	Normal	Physical	70	100	20	Normal	●
TM44	Rest	Psychic	Status	—	—	10	Self	—
TM45	Attract	Normal	Status	—	100	15	Normal	—
TM58	Endure	Normal	Status	—	—	10	Self	—
TM68	Giga Impact	Normal	Physical	150	90	5	Normal	●
TM71	Stone Edge	Rock	Physical	100	80	5	Normal	●
TM72	Avalanche	Ice	Physical	60	100	10	Normal	●
TM76	Stealth Rock	Rock	Status	—	—	20	2 foes	—
TM78	Captivate	Normal	Status	—	100	20	2 foes	—
TM80	Rock Slide	Rock	Physical	75	90	10	2 foes	●
TM82	Sleep Talk	Normal	Status	—	—	10	DoM	—
TM83	Natural Gift	Normal	Physical	—	100	15	Normal	●
TM87	Swagger	Normal	Status	—	90	15	Normal	—
TM90	Substitute	Normal	Status	—	—	10	Self	—
HM04	Strength	Normal	Physical	80	100	15	Normal	●
HM06	Rock Smash	Fighting	Physical	40	100	15	Normal	●
HM08	Rock Climb	Normal	Physical	90	85	20	Normal	●

● LEVEL-UP AND LEARNED MOVES

Lv	Name	Type	Kind	Power	Acc	PP	Range	DA
Base	AncientPower	Rock	Special	60	100	5	Normal	—
Base	Peck	Flying	Physical	35	100	35	Normal	●
Base	Odor Sleuth	Normal	Status	—	—	40	Normal	●
Base	Mud Sport	Ground	Status	—	—	15	All	—
Base	Powder Snow	Ice	Special	40	100	25	2 foes	—
4	Mud Sport	Ground	Status	—	—	15	All	—
8	Powder Snow	Ice	Special	40	100	25	2 foes	—
13	Mud-Slap	Ground	Special	20	100	10	Normal	—
16	Endure	Normal	Status	—	—	10	Self	—
20	Mud Bomb	Ground	Special	65	85	10	Normal	—
25	Hail	Ice	Status	—	—	10	All	—
28	Ice Fang	Ice	Physical	65	95	15	Normal	●
32	Take Down	Normal	Physical	90	85	20	Normal	●
33	Double Hit	Normal	Physical	35	90	10	Normal	●
40	Earthquake	Ground	Physical	100	100	10	2 foes + 1 ally	—
48	Mist	Ice	Status	—	—	30	2 allies	—
56	Blizzard	Ice	Special	120	70	5	2 foes	—
65	Scary Face	Normal	Status	—	90	10	Normal	—

● MOVES TAUGHT IN EXCHANGE FOR COLORED SHARDS

Name	Type	Kind	Power	Acc	PP	Range	DA
Mud-Slap	Ground	Special	20	100	10	Normal	—
Fury Cutter	Bug	Physical	10	95	20	Normal	●
Icy Wind	Ice	Special	55	95	15	2 foes	—
Superpower	Fighting	Physical	120	100	5	Normal	●
Iron Head	Steel	Physical	80	100	15	Normal	●
Snore	Normal	Special	40	100	15	Normal	—
Endeavor	Normal	Physical	—	100	5	Normal	●
AncientPower	Rock	Special	60	100	5	Normal	—
Earth Power	Ground	Special	90	100	10	Normal	—
Knock Off	Dark	Physical	20	100	20	Normal	●

● PRIMARY WAY TO FIND

TRAINER'S PARTY: Trainer on Victory Road

WILD POKÉMON

COURSE OF STORY

*To teach AncientPower to Piloswine, give one Heart Scale to the Move Tutor in Pastoria City

---

Sinnoh Pokédex No. 206 Snow Hat Pokémon
Snorunt

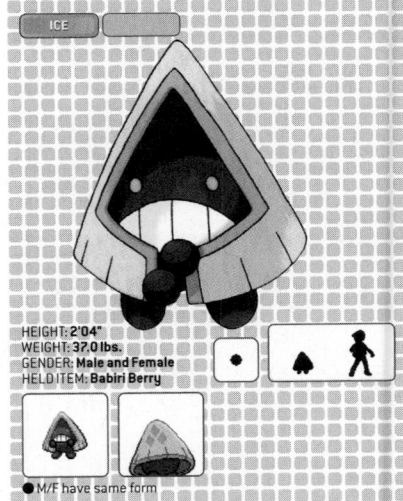

ICE

HEIGHT: 2'04"
WEIGHT: 37.0 lbs.
GENDER: Male and Female
HELD ITEM: Babiri Berry

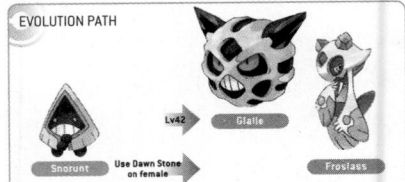

● M/F have same form

PLATINUM: It is said that several SNORUNT gather under giant leaves and live together in harmony.

EVOLUTION PATH

Snorunt → Lv42 → Glalie
Snorunt → Use Dawn Stone on female → Froslass

ABILITY: ● Inner Focus ● Ice Body

EGG GROUP: Fairy / Mineral

STATS:
HP ●●
ATTACK ●●
DEFENSE ●●
SP.ATTACK ●●
SP.DEFENSE ●●
SPEED ●●

● TM & HM MOVES

No.	Name	Type	Kind	Power	Acc	PP	Range	DA
TM03	Water Pulse	Water	Special	60	100	20	Normal	—
TM06	Toxic	Poison	Status	—	85	10	Normal	—
TM07	Hail	Ice	Status	—	—	10	All	—
TM10	Hidden Power	Normal	Special	—	100	15	Normal	—
TM13	Ice Beam	Ice	Special	95	100	10	Normal	—
TM14	Blizzard	Ice	Special	120	70	5	2 foes	—
TM16	Light Screen	Psychic	Status	—	—	30	2 allies	—
TM17	Protect	Normal	Status	—	—	10	Self	—
TM18	Rain Dance	Water	Status	—	—	25	2 allies	—
TM20	Safeguard	Normal	Status	—	—	25	2 allies	—
TM21	Frustration	Normal	Physical	—	100	20	Normal	●
TM27	Return	Normal	Physical	—	100	20	Normal	●
TM30	Shadow Ball	Ghost	Special	80	100	15	Normal	—
TM32	Double Team	Normal	Status	—	—	15	Self	—
TM42	Facade	Normal	Physical	70	100	20	Normal	●
TM43	Secret Power	Normal	Physical	70	100	20	Normal	●
TM44	Rest	Psychic	Status	—	—	10	Self	—
TM45	Attract	Normal	Status	—	100	15	Normal	—
TM58	Endure	Normal	Status	—	—	10	Self	—
TM70	Flash	Normal	Status	—	100	20	Normal	—
TM72	Avalanche	Ice	Physical	60	100	10	Normal	●
TM78	Captivate	Normal	Status	—	100	20	2 foes	—
TM82	Sleep Talk	Normal	Status	—	—	10	DoM	—
TM83	Natural Gift	Normal	Physical	—	100	15	Normal	●
TM87	Swagger	Normal	Status	—	90	15	Normal	—
TM90	Substitute	Normal	Status	—	—	10	Self	—

● LEVEL-UP AND LEARNED MOVES

Lv	Name	Type	Kind	Power	Acc	PP	Range	DA
Base	Powder Snow	Ice	Special	40	100	25	2 foes	—
Base	Leer	Normal	Status	—	100	30	2 foes	—
4	Double Team	Normal	Status	—	—	15	Self	—
10	Bite	Dark	Physical	60	100	25	Normal	●
13	Icy Wind	Ice	Special	55	95	15	2 foes	—
19	Headbutt	Normal	Physical	70	100	15	Normal	●
22	Protect	Normal	Status	—	—	10	Self	—
28	Ice Fang	Ice	Physical	65	95	15	Normal	●
31	Crunch	Dark	Physical	80	100	15	Normal	●
37	Ice Shard	Ice	Physical	40	100	30	Normal	—
40	Hail	Ice	Status	—	—	10	All	—
46	Blizzard	Ice	Special	120	70	5	2 foes	—

● MOVES TAUGHT IN EXCHANGE FOR COLORED SHARDS

Name	Type	Kind	Power	Acc	PP	Range	DA
Icy Wind	Ice	Special	55	95	15	2 foes	—
Rollout	Rock	Physical	30	90	20	Normal	●
Snore	Normal	Special	40	100	15	Normal	—
Spite	Ghost	Status	—	100	10	Normal	—

● EGG MOVES

Name	Type	Kind	Power	Acc	PP	Range	DA
Block	Normal	Status	—	—	5	Normal	—
Spikes	Ground	Status	—	—	20	2 foes	—
Rollout	Rock	Physical	30	90	20	Normal	●
Disable	Normal	Status	—	80	20	Normal	—
Bide	Normal	Physical	—	—	10	Self	●

● PRIMARY WAY TO FIND

TRAINER'S PARTY: Trainer on Route 217

WILD POKÉMON: Route 216 (night only)

COURSE OF STORY

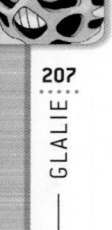

Glalie

ICE

HEIGHT: 4'11"
WEIGHT: 565.5 lbs.
GENDER: Male and Female
HELD ITEM: None

● M/F have same form

PLATINUM It prevents prey from escaping by instantaneously freezing moisture in the air.

EVOLUTION PATH

Snorunt → Lv42 → Glalie
Use Dawn Stone on female → Froslass

ABILITY ● Inner Focus ● Ice Body

EGG GROUP Fairy / Mineral

STATS HP ●● ATTACK ●●● DEFENSE ●●● SP. ATTACK ●●● SP. DEFENSE ●●● SPEED ●●●

● TM & HM MOVES

No.	Name	Type	Kind	Power	Acc	PP	Range	DA
TM03	Water Pulse	Water	Special	60	100	20	Normal	—
TM06	Toxic	Poison	Status	—	85	10	Normal	—
TM07	Hail	Ice	Status	—	—	10	All	—
TM10	Hidden Power	Normal	Special	—	100	15	Normal	—
TM12	Taunt	Dark	Status	—	100	20	Normal	—
TM13	Ice Beam	Ice	Special	95	100	10	Normal	—
TM14	Blizzard	Ice	Special	120	70	5	2 foes	—
TM15	Hyper Beam	Normal	Special	150	90	5	Normal	—
TM16	Light Screen	Psychic	Status	—	—	30	2 allies	—
TM17	Protect	Normal	Status	—	—	10	Self	—
TM18	Rain Dance	Water	Status	—	—	5	All	—
TM20	Safeguard	Normal	Status	—	—	25	2 allies	—
TM21	Frustration	Normal	Physical	—	100	20	Normal	•
TM26	Earthquake	Ground	Physical	100	100	10	2 foes + 1 ally	—
TM27	Return	Normal	Physical	—	100	20	Normal	•
TM30	Shadow Ball	Ghost	Special	80	100	15	Normal	—
TM32	Double Team	Normal	Status	—	—	15	Self	—
TM41	Torment	Dark	Status	—	100	15	Normal	—
TM42	Facade	Normal	Physical	70	100	20	Normal	•
TM43	Secret Power	Normal	Physical	70	100	20	Normal	•
TM44	Rest	Psychic	Status	—	—	10	Self	—
TM45	Attract	Normal	Status	—	100	15	Normal	—
TM58	Endure	Normal	Status	—	—	10	Self	—
TM64	Explosion	Normal	Physical	250	100	5	2 foes + 1 ally	—
TM66	Payback	Dark	Physical	50	100	10	Normal	•
TM68	Giga Impact	Normal	Physical	150	90	5	Normal	•
TM70	Flash	Normal	Status	—	100	20	Normal	—
TM72	Avalanche	Ice	Physical	60	100	10	Normal	•
TM74	Gyro Ball	Steel	Physical	—	100	5	Normal	•
TM78	Captivate	Normal	Status	—	100	20	2 foes	—
TM79	Dark Pulse	Dark	Special	80	100	15	Normal	—
TM82	Sleep Talk	Normal	Status	—	—	10	DoM	—
TM83	Natural Gift	Normal	Physical	—	100	15	Normal	•
TM87	Swagger	Normal	Status	—	90	15	Normal	—
TM90	Substitute	Normal	Status	—	—	10	Self	—

● LEVEL-UP AND LEARNED MOVES

Lv	Name	Type	Kind	Power	Acc	PP	Range	DA
Base	Powder Snow	Ice	Special	40	100	25	2 foes	—
Base	Leer	Normal	Status	—	100	30	2 foes	—
Base	Double Team	Normal	Status	—	—	15	Self	—
Base	Bite	Dark	Physical	60	100	25	Normal	•
4	Double Team	Normal	Status	—	—	15	Self	—
10	Bite	Dark	Physical	60	100	25	Normal	•
13	Icy Wind	Ice	Special	55	95	15	2 foes	—
19	Headbutt	Normal	Physical	70	100	15	Normal	•
22	Protect	Normal	Status	—	—	10	Self	—
28	Ice Fang	Ice	Physical	65	95	15	Normal	•
31	Crunch	Dark	Physical	80	100	15	Normal	•
37	Ice Beam	Ice	Special	95	100	10	Normal	—
40	Hail	Ice	Status	—	—	10	All	—
51	Blizzard	Ice	Special	120	70	5	2 foes	—
59	Sheer Cold	Ice	Special	—	30	5	Normal	—

● MOVES TAUGHT IN EXCHANGE FOR COLORED SHARDS

Name	Type	Kind	Power	Acc	PP	Range	DA
Icy Wind	Ice	Special	55	95	15	2 foes	—
Rollout	Rock	Physical	30	90	20	Normal	•
Iron Head	Steel	Physical	80	100	15	Normal	•
Snore	Normal	Special	40	100	15	Normal	—
Spite	Ghost	Status	—	100	10	Normal	—
Signal Beam	Bug	Special	75	100	15	Normal	—

● PRIMARY WAY TO FIND

TRAINER'S PARTY Trainer at Snowpoint Gym

WILD POKÉMON

COURSE OF STORY

Froslass

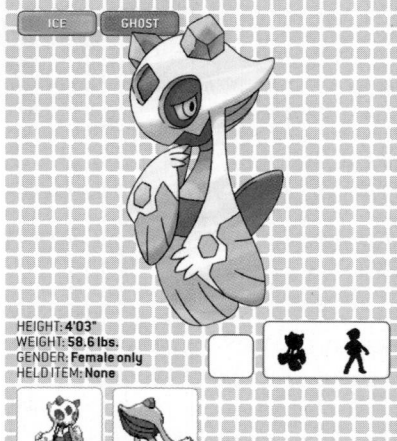
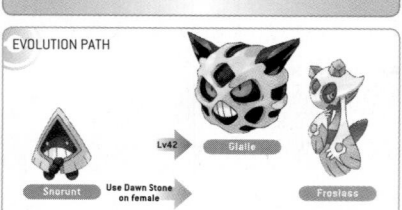

ICE   GHOST

HEIGHT: 4'03"
WEIGHT: 58.6 lbs.
GENDER: Female only
HELD ITEM: None

● Female form

PLATINUM It freezes prey by blowing its -58 degrees F breath. It is said to then secretly display its prey.

EVOLUTION PATH

Snorunt → Lv42 → Glalie
Use Dawn Stone on female → Froslass

ABILITY ● Snow Cloak

EGG GROUP Fairy / Mineral

STATS HP ●● ATTACK ●●● DEFENSE ●●● SP. ATTACK ●●● SP. DEFENSE ●●● SPEED ●●●●

● TM & HM MOVES

No.	Name	Type	Kind	Power	Acc	PP	Range	DA
TM03	Water Pulse	Water	Special	60	100	20	Normal	—
TM06	Toxic	Poison	Status	—	85	10	Normal	—
TM07	Hail	Ice	Status	—	—	10	All	—
TM10	Hidden Power	Normal	Special	—	100	15	Normal	—
TM12	Taunt	Dark	Status	—	100	20	Normal	—
TM13	Ice Beam	Ice	Special	95	100	10	Normal	—
TM14	Blizzard	Ice	Special	120	70	5	2 foes	—
TM15	Hyper Beam	Normal	Special	150	90	5	Normal	—
TM16	Light Screen	Psychic	Status	—	—	30	2 allies	—
TM17	Protect	Normal	Status	—	—	10	Self	—
TM18	Rain Dance	Water	Status	—	—	5	All	—
TM20	Safeguard	Normal	Status	—	—	25	2 allies	—
TM21	Frustration	Normal	Physical	—	100	20	Normal	•
TM24	Thunderbolt	Electric	Special	95	100	15	Normal	—
TM25	Thunder	Electric	Special	120	70	10	Normal	—
TM27	Return	Normal	Physical	—	100	20	Normal	•
TM29	Psychic	Psychic	Special	90	100	10	Normal	—
TM30	Shadow Ball	Ghost	Special	80	100	15	Normal	—
TM32	Double Team	Normal	Status	—	—	15	Self	—
TM34	Shock Wave	Electric	Special	60	—	20	Normal	—
TM41	Torment	Dark	Status	—	100	15	Normal	—
TM42	Facade	Normal	Physical	70	100	20	Normal	•
TM43	Secret Power	Normal	Physical	70	100	20	Normal	•
TM44	Rest	Psychic	Status	—	—	10	Self	—
TM45	Attract	Normal	Status	—	100	15	Normal	—
TM49	Snatch	Dark	Status	—	—	10	DoM	—
TM56	Fling	Dark	Physical	—	100	10	Normal	•
TM58	Endure	Normal	Status	—	—	10	Self	—
TM63	Embargo	Dark	Status	—	100	15	Normal	—
TM66	Payback	Dark	Physical	50	100	10	Normal	•
TM68	Giga Impact	Normal	Physical	150	90	5	Normal	•
TM70	Flash	Normal	Status	—	100	20	Normal	—
TM72	Avalanche	Ice	Physical	60	100	10	Normal	•
TM73	Thunder Wave	Electric	Status	—	100	20	Normal	—
TM77	Psych Up	Normal	Status	—	—	10	Normal	—
TM78	Captivate	Normal	Status	—	100	20	2 foes	—
TM82	Sleep Talk	Normal	Status	—	—	10	DoM	—
TM83	Natural Gift	Normal	Physical	—	100	15	Normal	•
TM85	Dream Eater	Psychic	Special	100	100	15	Normal	—
TM87	Swagger	Normal	Status	—	90	15	Normal	—
TM90	Substitute	Normal	Status	—	—	10	Self	—

● LEVEL-UP AND LEARNED MOVES

Lv	Name	Type	Kind	Power	Acc	PP	Range	DA
Base	Powder Snow	Ice	Special	40	100	25	2 foes	—
Base	Leer	Normal	Status	—	100	30	2 foes	—
Base	Double Team	Normal	Status	—	—	15	Self	—
Base	Astonish	Ghost	Physical	30	100	15	Normal	•
4	Double Team	Normal	Status	—	—	15	Self	—
10	Astonish	Ghost	Physical	30	100	15	Normal	•
13	Icy Wind	Ice	Special	55	95	15	2 foes	—
19	Confuse Ray	Ghost	Status	—	100	10	Normal	—
22	Ominous Wind	Ghost	Special	60	100	5	Normal	—
28	Wake-Up Slap	Fighting	Physical	60	100	10	Normal	•
31	Captivate	Normal	Status	—	100	20	2 foes	—
37	Ice Shard	Ice	Physical	40	100	30	Normal	—
40	Hail	Ice	Status	—	—	10	All	—
51	Blizzard	Ice	Special	120	70	5	2 foes	—
59	Destiny Bond	Ghost	Status	—	—	5	Self	—

● MOVES TAUGHT IN EXCHANGE FOR COLORED SHARDS

Name	Type	Kind	Power	Acc	PP	Range	DA
Mud-Slap	Ground	Special	20	100	10	Normal	—
Icy Wind	Ice	Special	55	95	15	2 foes	—
Rollout	Rock	Physical	30	90	20	Normal	•
Ice Punch	Ice	Physical	75	100	15	Normal	•
Ominous Wind	Ghost	Special	60	100	5	Normal	—
Snore	Normal	Special	40	100	15	Normal	—
Spite	Ghost	Status	—	100	10	Normal	—
Signal Beam	Bug	Special	75	100	15	Normal	—
Trick	Psychic	Status	—	100	10	Normal	—
Sucker Punch	Dark	Physical	80	100	5	Normal	•

● PRIMARY WAY TO FIND

TRAINER'S PARTY Snowpoint Gym Leader Candice

WILD POKÉMON

COURSE OF STORY

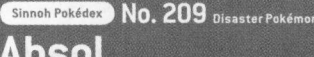

Sinnoh Pokédex No. 209 Disaster Pokémon

Absol

DARK

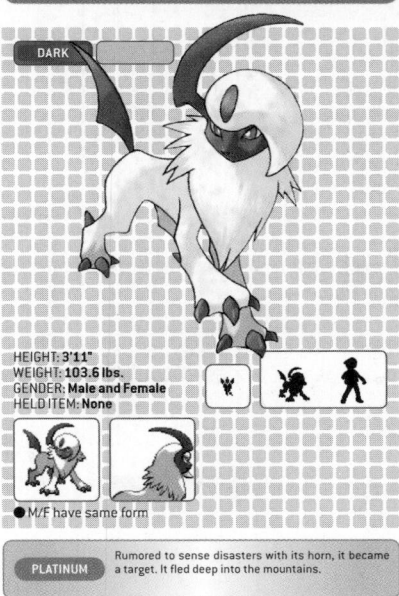

HEIGHT: 3'11"
WEIGHT: 103.6 lbs.
GENDER: Male and Female
HELD ITEM: None

● M/F have same form

PLATINUM Rumored to sense disasters with its horn, it became a target. It fled deep into the mountains.

EVOLUTION PATH

Does Not evolve

● TM & HM MOVES

No.	Name	Type	Kind	Power	Acc	PP	Range	DA
TM03	Water Pulse	Water	Special	60	100	20	Normal	
TM04	Calm Mind	Psychic	Status	—	—	20	Self	
TM06	Toxic	Poison	Status	—	85	10	Normal	
TM07	Hail	Ice	Status	—	—	10	All	
TM10	Hidden Power	Normal	Special	—	100	15	Normal	
TM11	Sunny Day	Fire	Status	—	—	5	All	
TM12	Taunt	Dark	Status	—	100	20	Normal	
TM13	Ice Beam	Ice	Special	95	100	10	Normal	
TM14	Blizzard	Ice	Special	120	70	5	2 foes	
TM15	Hyper Beam	Normal	Special	150	90	5	Normal	
TM17	Protect	Normal	Status	—	—	10	Self	
TM18	Rain Dance	Water	Status	—	—	5	All	
TM21	Frustration	Normal	Physical	—	100	20	Normal	
TM23	Iron Tail	Steel	Physical	100	75	15	Normal	
TM24	Thunderbolt	Electric	Special	95	100	15	Normal	
TM25	Thunder	Electric	Special	120	70	10	Normal	
TM27	Return	Normal	Physical	—	100	20	Normal	
TM30	Shadow Ball	Ghost	Special	80	100	15	Normal	
TM32	Double Team	Normal	Status	—	—	15	Self	
TM34	Shock Wave	Electric	Special	60	—	20	Normal	
TM35	Flamethrower	Fire	Special	95	100	15	Normal	
TM37	Sandstorm	Rock	Status	—	—	10	All	
TM38	Fire Blast	Fire	Special	120	85	5	Normal	
TM39	Rock Tomb	Rock	Physical	50	80	10	Normal	
TM40	Aerial Ace	Flying	Physical	60	—	20	Normal	•
TM41	Torment	Dark	Status	—	100	15	Normal	
TM42	Facade	Normal	Physical	70	100	20	Normal	
TM43	Secret Power	Normal	Physical	70	100	20	Normal	
TM44	Rest	Psychic	Status	—	—	10	Self	
TM45	Attract	Normal	Status	—	100	15	Normal	
TM46	Thief	Dark	Physical	40	100	10	Normal	
TM49	Snatch	Dark	Status	—	—	10	DoM	
TM54	False Swipe	Normal	Physical	40	100	40	Normal	•
TM57	Charge Beam	Electric	Special	50	90	10	Normal	
TM58	Endure	Normal	Status	—	—	10	Self	
TM61	Will-O-Wisp	Fire	Status	—	75	15	Normal	
TM65	Shadow Claw	Ghost	Physical	70	100	15	Normal	•
TM66	Payback	Dark	Physical	50	100	10	Normal	
TM68	Giga Impact	Normal	Physical	150	90	5	Normal	
TM70	Flash	Normal	Status	—	100	20	Normal	
TM71	Stone Edge	Rock	Physical	100	80	5	Normal	
TM73	Thunder Wave	Electric	Status	—	100	20	Normal	
TM75	Swords Dance	Normal	Status	—	—	30	Self	
TM77	Psych Up	Normal	Status	—	—	10	Self	
TM78	Captivate	Normal	Status	—	100	20	2 foes	
TM79	Dark Pulse	Dark	Special	80	100	15	Normal	
TM80	Rock Slide	Rock	Physical	75	90	10	2 foes	
TM81	X-Scissor	Bug	Physical	80	100	15	Normal	•
TM82	Sleep Talk	Normal	Status	—	—	10	DoM	
TM83	Natural Gift	Normal	Physical	—	100	15	Normal	
TM85	Dream Eater	Psychic	Special	100	100	15	Normal	
TM87	Swagger	Normal	Status	—	90	15	Normal	

● TM & HM MOVES

No.	Name	Type	Kind	Power	Acc	PP	Range	DA
TM90	Substitute	Normal	Status	—	—	10	Self	
HM01	Cut	Normal	Physical	50	95	30	Normal	•
HM04	Strength	Normal	Physical	80	100	15	Normal	•
HM06	Rock Smash	Fighting	Physical	40	100	15	Normal	•

● LEVEL-UP AND LEARNED MOVES

Lv	Name	Type	Kind	Power	Acc	PP	Range	DA
Base	Scratch	Normal	Physical	40	100	35	Normal	•
Base	Feint	Normal	Physical	50	100	10	Normal	•
4	Leer	Normal	Status	—	100	30	2 foes	
9	Taunt	Dark	Status	—	100	20	Normal	
12	Quick Attack	Normal	Physical	40	100	30	Normal	•
17	Razor Wind	Normal	Special	80	100	10	2 foes	
20	Pursuit	Dark	Physical	40	100	20	Normal	•
25	Swords Dance	Normal	Status	—	—	30	Self	
28	Bite	Dark	Physical	60	100	25	Normal	•
33	Double Team	Normal	Status	—	—	15	Self	
36	Slash	Normal	Physical	70	100	20	Normal	•
41	Future Sight	Psychic	Special	80	90	15	Normal	
44	Sucker Punch	Dark	Physical	80	100	5	Normal	•
49	Detect	Fighting	Status	—	—	5	Self	
52	Night Slash	Dark	Physical	70	100	15	Normal	•
57	Me First	Normal	Status	—	—	20	DoM	
60	Psycho Cut	Psychic	Physical	70	100	20	Normal	•
65	Perish Song	Normal	Status	—	—	5	All	

● MOVES TAUGHT IN EXCHANGE FOR COLORED SHARDS

Name	Type	Kind	Power	Acc	PP	Range	DA
Mud-Slap	Ground	Special	20	100	10	Normal	
Fury Cutter	Bug	Physical	10	95	20	Normal	•
Icy Wind	Ice	Special	55	95	15	2 foes	
Superpower	Fighting	Physical	120	100	5	Normal	•
Snore	Normal	Special	40	100	15	Normal	
Spite	Ghost	Status	—	100	10	Normal	
Zen Headbutt	Psychic	Physical	80	90	15	Normal	•
Bounce	Flying	Physical	85	85	5	Normal	•
Knock Off	Dark	Physical	20	100	20	Normal	•
Sucker Punch	Dark	Physical	80	100	5	Normal	•
Swift	Normal	Special	60	—	20	2 foes	

● EGG MOVES

Name	Type	Kind	Power	Acc	PP	Range	DA
Baton Pass	Normal	Status	—	—	40	Self	
Faint Attack	Dark	Physical	60	—	20	Normal	
Double-Edge	Normal	Physical	120	100	15	Normal	•
Magic Coat	Psychic	Status	—	—	15	Self	
Curse	???	Status	—	—	10	Normal • Self	
Substitute	Normal	Status	—	—	10	Self	
Mean Look	Normal	Status	—	—	5	Normal	
Zen Headbutt	Psychic	Physical	80	90	15	Normal	•
Punishment	Dark	Physical	—	100	5	Normal	•
Sucker Punch	Dark	Physical	80	100	5	Normal	•
Assurance	Dark	Physical	50	100	10	Normal	•
Me First	Normal	Status	—	—	20	DoM	

● PRIMARY WAY TO FIND

TRAINER'S PARTY	Trainer on Victory Road
WILD POKÉMON	Mt. Coronet (middle) peak
COURSE OF STORY	

ABILITY ● Pressure ● Super Luck

EGG GROUP Field

STATS
HP ●●
ATTACK ●●●●
DEFENSE ●●●
SP. ATTACK ●●●
SP. DEFENSE ●●●
SPEED ●●●

Sinnoh Pokédex No. 210 Renegade Pokémon

Giratina (Altered Forme)

GHOST DRAGON

HEIGHT: 14'09"
WEIGHT: 1653.5 lbs.
GENDER: Unknown
HELD ITEM: None

● Gender unknown

PLATINUM It was banished for its violence. It silently gazed upon the old world from the Distortion World.

EVOLUTION PATH

Does Not evolve

● TM & HM MOVES

No.	Name	Type	Kind	Power	Acc	PP	Range	DA
TM02	Dragon Claw	Dragon	Physical	80	100	15	Normal	•
TM04	Calm Mind	Psychic	Status	—	—	20	Self	
TM05	Roar	Normal	Status	—	100	20	Normal	
TM06	Toxic	Poison	Status	—	85	10	Normal	
TM10	Hidden Power	Normal	Special	—	100	15	Normal	
TM11	Sunny Day	Fire	Status	—	—	5	All	
TM15	Hyper Beam	Normal	Special	150	90	5	Normal	
TM17	Protect	Normal	Status	—	—	10	Self	
TM18	Rain Dance	Water	Status	—	—	5	All	
TM20	Safeguard	Normal	Status	—	—	25	2 allies	
TM21	Frustration	Normal	Physical	—	100	20	Normal	
TM23	Iron Tail	Steel	Physical	100	75	15	Normal	•
TM24	Thunderbolt	Electric	Special	95	100	15	Normal	
TM25	Thunder	Electric	Special	120	70	10	Normal	
TM26	Earthquake	Ground	Physical	100	100	10	2 foes • 1 ally	
TM27	Return	Normal	Physical	—	100	20	Normal	
TM29	Psychic	Psychic	Special	90	100	10	Normal	
TM30	Shadow Ball	Ghost	Special	80	100	15	Normal	
TM32	Double Team	Normal	Status	—	—	15	Self	
TM34	Shock Wave	Electric	Special	60	—	20	Normal	
TM40	Aerial Ace	Flying	Physical	60	—	20	Normal	•
TM42	Facade	Normal	Physical	70	100	20	Normal	
TM43	Secret Power	Normal	Physical	70	100	20	Normal	
TM44	Rest	Psychic	Status	—	—	10	Self	
TM47	Steel Wing	Steel	Physical	70	90	25	Normal	•
TM53	Energy Ball	Grass	Special	80	100	10	Normal	
TM57	Charge Beam	Electric	Special	50	90	10	Normal	
TM58	Endure	Normal	Status	—	—	10	Self	
TM59	Dragon Pulse	Dragon	Special	90	100	10	Normal	
TM61	Will-O-Wisp	Fire	Status	—	75	15	Normal	
TM62	Silver Wind	Bug	Special	60	100	5	Normal	
TM65	Shadow Claw	Ghost	Physical	70	100	15	Normal	•
TM66	Payback	Dark	Physical	50	100	10	Normal	
TM68	Giga Impact	Normal	Physical	150	90	5	Normal	
TM71	Stone Edge	Rock	Physical	100	80	5	Normal	
TM73	Thunder Wave	Electric	Status	—	100	20	Normal	
TM77	Psych Up	Normal	Status	—	—	10	Self	
TM79	Dark Pulse	Dark	Special	80	100	15	Normal	
TM82	Sleep Talk	Normal	Status	—	—	10	DoM	
TM83	Natural Gift	Normal	Physical	—	100	15	Normal	
TM85	Dream Eater	Psychic	Special	100	100	15	Normal	
TM87	Swagger	Normal	Status	—	90	15	Normal	
TM90	Substitute	Normal	Status	—	—	10	Self	
HM01	Cut	Normal	Physical	50	95	30	Normal	•
HM02	Fly	Flying	Physical	90	95	15	Normal	•
HM04	Strength	Normal	Physical	80	100	15	Normal	•
HM05	Defog	Flying	Status	—	—	15	Normal	
HM06	Rock Smash	Fighting	Physical	40	100	15	Normal	•
HM08	Rock Climb	Normal	Physical	90	85	20	Normal	•

● LEVEL-UP AND LEARNED MOVES

Lv	Name	Type	Kind	Power	Acc	PP	Range	DA
Base	DragonBreath	Dragon	Special	60	100	20	Normal	—
Base	Scary Face	Normal	Status	—	90	10	Normal	—
10	Ominous Wind	Ghost	Special	60	100	5	Normal	—
20	AncientPower	Rock	Special	60	100	5	Normal	—
30	Dragon Claw	Dragon	Physical	80	100	15	Normal	•
40	Shadow Force	Ghost	Physical	120	100	5	Normal	•
50	Heal Block	Psychic	Status	—	100	15	2 foes	—
60	Earth Power	Ground	Special	90	100	10	Normal	—
70	Slash	Normal	Physical	70	100	20	Normal	•
80	Shadow Claw	Ghost	Physical	70	100	15	Normal	•
90	Aura Sphere	Fighting	Special	90	—	20	Normal	—

● MOVES TAUGHT IN EXCHANGE FOR COLORED SHARDS

Name	Type	Kind	Power	Acc	PP	Range	DA
Mud-Slap	Ground	Special	20	100	10	Normal	—
Fury Cutter	Bug	Physical	10	95	20	Normal	•
Icy Wind	Ice	Special	55	95	15	2 foes	—
Iron Head	Steel	Physical	80	100	15	Normal	•
Aqua Tail	Water	Physical	90	90	10	Normal	•
Ominous Wind	Ghost	Special	60	100	5	Normal	—
Snore	Normal	Special	40	100	15	Normal	—
Spite	Ghost	Status	—	100	10	Normal	—
Air Cutter	Flying	Special	55	95	25	2 foes	—
Outrage	Dragon	Physical	120	100	15	1 random	•
AncientPower	Rock	Special	60	100	5	Normal	—
Earth Power	Ground	Special	90	100	10	Normal	—
Twister	Dragon	Special	40	100	20	2 foes	—
Swift	Normal	Special	60	—	20	2 foes	—

● MOVES TAUGHT BY PEOPLE

Name	Type	Kind	Power	Acc	PP	Range	DA
Draco Meteor*	Dragon	Special	140	90	5	Normal	—

*Draco Meteor is taught when the Pokémon's Friendship is maxed out

● PRIMARY WAY TO FIND

TRAINER'S PARTY	
WILD POKÉMON	
COURSE OF STORY	Encounter in the Distortion World

*Your Pokédex will record a different Forme and set of information for Giratina, depending on when in Pokémon Platinum you obtain it.

Giratina's Formes:
• Received in link trade: Altered Forme
• Caught in Distortion World: Origin Forme
• Caught in Turnback Cave (appears if you did not catch it in the Distortion World): Giratina appears in Altered Forme, but will be recorded as Origin Forme, since you first encountered it in the Distortion World

Info that changes:
• Comment, habitat, cry, size, artwork, footprint, height/weight

ABILITY ● Pressure

EGG GROUP No Eggs

STATS
HP ●●●●
ATTACK ●●●●
DEFENSE ●●●
SP. ATTACK ●●●●
SP. DEFENSE ●●●
SPEED ●●●

Giratina (Origin Forme)

GHOST | DRAGON

HEIGHT: 22'08
WEIGHT: 1433.0 lbs
GENDER: Unknown
HELD ITEM: None

● Gender unknown

PLATINUM It was banished for its violence. It silently gazed upon the old world from the Distortion World.

EVOLUTION PATH

Does Not evolve

● TM & HM MOVES

No.	Name	Type	Kind	Power	Acc	PP	Range	DA
TM02	Dragon Claw	Dragon	Physical	80	100	15	Normal	●
TM04	Calm Mind	Psychic	Status	—	—	20	Self	—
TM05	Roar	Normal	Status	—	100	20	Normal	—
TM06	Toxic	Poison	Status	—	85	10	Normal	—
TM10	Hidden Power	Normal	Special	—	100	15	Normal	—
TM11	Sunny Day	Fire	Status	—	—	5	All	—
TM15	Hyper Beam	Normal	Special	150	90	5	Normal	—
TM17	Protect	Normal	Status	—	—	10	Self	—
TM18	Rain Dance	Water	Status	—	—	5	All	—
TM20	Safeguard	Normal	Status	—	—	25	2 allies	—
TM21	Frustration	Normal	Physical	—	100	20	Normal	●
TM23	Iron Tail	Steel	Physical	100	75	15	Normal	●
TM24	Thunderbolt	Electric	Special	95	100	15	Normal	—
TM25	Thunder	Electric	Special	120	70	10	Normal	—
TM26	Earthquake	Ground	Physical	100	100	10	2 foes • 1 ally	●
TM27	Return	Normal	Physical	—	100	20	Normal	●
TM29	Psychic	Psychic	Special	90	100	10	Normal	—
TM30	Shadow Ball	Ghost	Special	80	100	15	Normal	—
TM32	Double Team	Normal	Status	—	—	15	Self	—
TM34	Shock Wave	Electric	Special	60	—	20	Normal	—
TM40	Aerial Ace	Flying	Physical	60	—	20	Normal	●
TM42	Facade	Normal	Physical	70	100	20	Normal	●
TM43	Secret Power	Normal	Physical	70	100	20	Normal	●
TM44	Rest	Psychic	Status	—	—	10	Self	—
TM47	Steel Wing	Steel	Physical	70	90	25	Normal	●
TM53	Energy Ball	Grass	Special	80	100	10	Normal	—
TM57	Charge Beam	Electric	Special	50	90	10	Normal	—
TM58	Endure	Normal	Status	—	—	10	Self	—
TM59	Dragon Pulse	Dragon	Special	90	100	10	Normal	—
TM61	Will-O-Wisp	Fire	Status	—	75	15	Normal	—
TM62	Silver Wind	Bug	Special	60	100	5	Normal	—
TM65	Shadow Claw	Ghost	Physical	70	100	15	Normal	●
TM66	Payback	Dark	Physical	50	100	10	Normal	●
TM68	Giga Impact	Normal	Physical	150	90	5	Normal	●
TM71	Stone Edge	Rock	Physical	100	80	5	Normal	●
TM73	Thunder Wave	Electric	Status	—	100	20	Normal	—
TM77	Psych Up	Normal	Status	—	—	10	Normal	—
TM79	Dark Pulse	Dark	Special	80	100	15	Normal	—
TM82	Sleep Talk	Normal	Status	—	—	10	DoM	—
TM83	Natural Gift	Normal	Physical	—	100	15	Normal	●
TM85	Dream Eater	Psychic	Special	100	100	15	Normal	—
TM87	Swagger	Normal	Status	—	90	15	Normal	—
TM90	Substitute	Normal	Status	—	—	10	Self	—
HM01	Cut	Normal	Physical	50	95	30	Normal	●
HM02	Fly	Flying	Physical	90	95	15	Normal	●
HM04	Strength	Normal	Physical	80	100	15	Normal	●
HM05	Defog	Flying	Status	—	—	15	Normal	—
HM06	Rock Smash	Fighting	Physical	40	100	15	Normal	●
HM08	Rock Climb	Normal	Physical	90	85	20	Normal	●

● LEVEL-UP AND LEARNED MOVES

Lv	Name	Type	Kind	Power	Acc	PP	Range	DA
Base	DragonBreath	Dragon	Special	60	100	20	Normal	—
Base	Scary Face	Normal	Status	—	90	10	Normal	—
10	Ominous Wind	Ghost	Special	60	100	5	Normal	—
20	AncientPower	Rock	Special	60	100	5	Normal	—
30	Dragon Claw	Dragon	Physical	80	100	15	Normal	●
40	Shadow Force	Ghost	Physical	120	100	5	Normal	●
50	Heal Block	Psychic	Status	—	100	15	2 foes	—
60	Earth Power	Ground	Special	90	100	10	Normal	—
70	Slash	Normal	Physical	70	100	20	Normal	●
80	Shadow Claw	Ghost	Physical	70	100	15	Normal	●
90	Aura Sphere	Fighting	Special	90	—	20	Normal	—

● MOVES TAUGHT IN EXCHANGE FOR COLORED SHARDS

Name	Type	Kind	Power	Acc	PP	Range	DA
Mud-Slap	Ground	Special	20	100	10	Normal	—
Fury Cutter	Bug	Physical	10	95	20	Normal	●
Icy Wind	Ice	Special	55	95	15	2 foes	—
Iron Head	Steel	Physical	80	100	15	Normal	●
Aqua Tail	Water	Physical	90	90	10	Normal	●
Ominous Wind	Ghost	Special	60	100	5	Normal	—
Snore	Normal	Special	40	100	15	Normal	—
Spite	Ghost	Status	—	100	10	Normal	—
Air Cutter	Flying	Special	55	95	25	2 foes	—
Outrage	Dragon	Physical	120	100	10	1 random	●
AncientPower	Rock	Special	60	100	5	Normal	—
Earth Power	Ground	Special	90	100	10	Normal	—
Twister	Dragon	Special	40	100	20	2 foes	—
Swift	Normal	Special	60	—	20	2 foes	—

● MOVES TAUGHT BY PEOPLE

Name	Type	Kind	Power	Acc	PP	Range	DA
Draco Meteor*	Dragon	Special	140	90	5	Normal	—

*Draco Meteor is taught when the Pokémon's Friendship is maxed out

ABILITY ● Levitate

EGG GROUP No Eggs

STATS
HP ●●●●
ATTACK ●●●●
DEFENSE ●●●●
SP. ATTACK ●●●●
SP. DEFENSE ●●●
SPEED ●●●

● PRIMARY WAY TO FIND

TRAINER'S PARTY

WILD POKÉMON

COURSE OF STORY   Encounter in the Distortion World

National Pokédex

Complete the National Pokédex

Realize the Pokémon Trainer's ultimate dream

The National Pokédex is the ultimate Pokédex, capable of recording Pokémon from all regions, including the Sinnoh, Kanto, and Hoenn regions. Obtain each and every Pokémon, and fill out this dream Pokédex.

Collect 482 Pokémon to complete

Your National Pokédex in *Pokémon Platinum* will be complete once you've collected, through capture or trade, all 482 Pokémon. (This total does not include Mew, Lugia, Ho-Oh, Celebi, Jirachi, Deoxys, Phione, Manaphy, Darkrai, and Shaymin.)

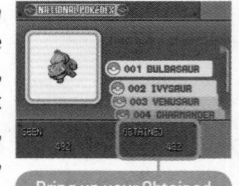

Bring up your Obtained count to 482.

● Ways to complete your National Pokédex in Platinum

1 Record Pokémon in your Pokédex, and bring your obtained count up to 482

Get your Pokédex upgraded to the National Pokédex

Want to complete the National Pokédex? First things first: have Professor Oak upgrade your Pokédex into the National Pokédex. With that accomplished, an all-new Pokémon journey lays ahead of you.

Lucas's Pokédex was upgraded with the National Mode!

● Conditions for upgrading your Pokédex to the National Pokédex

1 Win at the Pokémon League and make it into the Hall of Fame

2 Achieve 210 Pokémon seen in your Sinnoh Pokédex

3 Show your filled-out Pokédex to Professors Rowan and Oak

Synch with other Pokémon games

Synching with the GBA Pokémon games is critical to completing your Pokédex. Insert a Pokémon GBA cart into the Nintendo DS's GBA cartridge slot, and you can transfer Pokémon from the GBA cart to *Pokémon Platinum* by way of Pal Park.

● Ways to synch with *Pokémon Platinum*

1 Insert a Pokémon GBA game into the Nintendo DS's dual slot to make new wild Pokémon appear

2 Send Pokémon from your Pokémon GBA game to Pal Park in your *Pokémon Platinum* game, and catch them there

● Games that can synch with *Pokémon Platinum*

Get a prize from the Game Director when you complete your game

Once you complete the National Pokédex, you can go meet the Game Director at a cottage at the Hotel Grand Lake at Valor Lakefront. He'll celebrate your accomplishment, just like when you completed the Sinnoh Pokédex.

Your Pokédex is completed! That's outstanding work!

Awaiting your arrival
The Game Director is waiting day and night for you to complete your National Pokédex.

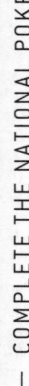

National Pokédex completion point

Techniques for catching wild Pokémon

Master these techniques to raise your capture rate

Wild Pokémon can be caught with Poké Balls. This is the most fundamental way to fill out your Pokédex. Master these techniques and bag any Pokémon you set your mind to.

A wild PACHIRISU appeared!

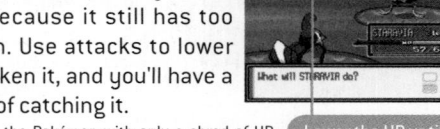

Capture technique 1 — Lower the Pokémon's HP to critical

Even if you use a Poké Ball on a wild Pokémon, the Pokémon may break free. This is because it still has too much strength. Use attacks to lower its HP and weaken it, and you'll have a better chance of catching it.

Leave the Pokémon with only a shred of HP, and you'll stand a better chance of catching it.

Lower the HP until the bar is red

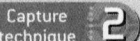

Capture technique 2 — Inflict status ailments

Some Pokémon moves can inflict status ailments like paralysis or poison. If you use these moves to inflict such status ailments on your target, it'll improve your capture odds. Lower the Pokémon's HP and inflict a status ailment, and the Pokémon is as good as yours.

● Status ailments that aid capture

Sleep — **Helps a lot**	Frozen — **Helps a lot**
The target becomes unable to attack. Status goes away on its own after a few turns.	Target becomes unable to attack. Status goes away on its own after a few turns.
● Main moves that cause Sleep Sing, Hypnosis	● Main moves that Freeze Ice Beam, Ice Punch

The wild DUSTOX is fast asleep.

Paralysis	Poison	Burn
Lowers target's Speed and has a 1 in 4 chance every turn of preventing the target from attacking. Status does not go away on its own during battle.	Lowers target's HP a little bit each turn. Does not go away on its own during battle.	Lowers target's Attack, and lowers its HP turn by turn. Does not go away on its own during battle.
● Main moves that Paralyze Thunder Wave, Stun Spore	● Main moves that cause Poison PoisonPowder, Poison Gas	● Main moves that cause Burn Will-O-Wisp, Flamethrower

National Pokédex completion point 2

Use Pokémon moves and Abilities

Flush out your target Pokémon and prevent it from fleeing

Some Pokémon moves can be very useful in flushing out wild Pokémon. Use them wisely to aid your chances of catching the Pokémon you seek.

┊Some useful moves for catching Pokémon

Sweet Scent

Use in tall grass, caves, and other places where Pokémon appear, to guarantee a Pokémon encounter.

● Pokémon that can use
Roselia, Combee, etc.

False Swipe

May deal great damage, but will always leave 1 HP remaining. Great for reducing the target's HP so you can catch it.

SCYTHER used False Swipe!

● Pokémon that can use
Scyther, Gallade, etc.

Mean Look

Prevents the wild Pokémon from escaping. Try it on Pokémon that always run away at the start of battle.

ZUBAT used Mean Look!

● Pokémon that can use
Zubat, Gastly, etc.

NATIONAL POKÉDEX

COMPLETE THE NATIONAL POKÉDEX

Some useful Abilities for catching Pokémon

Shadow Tag

Prevents the wild Pokémon from escaping—very useful against Pokémon that flee at the start of battle.

● **Pokémon that can use**
Wynaut, Wobbuffet

Arena Trap

When held by the leader of your party, raises your wild Pokémon encounter rate and makes those wild Pokémon unable to escape.

● **Pokémon that can use**
Diglett, Trapinch, etc.

Suction Cups

When held by the leader of your party, raises your rate of hooking aquatic Pokémon when you go fishing.

● **Pokémon that can use**
Octillery, Cradily, etc.

National Pokédex completion point

3

Use the Poké Radar to catch Pokémon

Detect Pokémon hiding in tall grass

Professor Rowan gives you the Poké Radar once you complete your Sinnoh Pokédex. Use it to find Pokémon hiding in the tall grass. Many Pokémon can only be found when you use the Poké Radar.

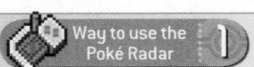 **Way to use the Poké Radar** 1 Use and encounter Pokémon in the rustling grass

You have to be standing in tall grass to use the Poké Radar. Use it and some of the grass around you will start to rustle. Move to a patch of rustling grass, and you're sure to encounter a Pokémon. If the grass is rustling violently, or glittering, then you've got a good chance of encountering one of the rare Pokémon on the facing page.

The Poké Radar is rechargable. After one use, just walk 50 paces to recharge it.

 **Way to use the Poké Radar** 2 More likely to encounter the same Pokémon after the first use

You can use the Poké Radar several times in succession. Sometimes, after you use it once, the grass will rustle again. If you move then to that spot, you'll have a greater chance of encountering the same kind of Pokémon. Use the Poké Radar successively this way, and keep encountering the same Pokémon over and over again, and you'll run a good chance of finding a shiny Pokémon.

Shiny Pokémon are exceedingly rare. Consider yourself extremely lucky if you find one. (p. 250)

 **Way to use the Poké Radar** 3 The effect runs out if you flee or leave the grass

The effects of the Poké Radar continue after you defeat or catch the Pokémon. But it runs out if you run from battle, encounter any Pokémon outside of the rustling grass, or encounter a different Pokémon from the one you ran into earlier.

 **Gotta get it!** The Pokémon made available by the Poké Radar (see the list to the right) are all Pokémon that you can't get by any other means. Keep at it; luck plays a big part in determining if you'll find a Pokémon.

NATIONAL POKÉDEX

COMPLETE THE NATIONAL POKÉDEX

Pokémon that appear when you use the Poké Radar

Location	Appears commonly	Appears rarely
Valley Windworks	Mareep	—
Eterna Forest	Nincada	—
Fuego Ironworks	Aron	—
Mt. Coronet (middle) peak	Loudred	—
Stark Mountain exterior	Torkoal	—
Lake Verity	Wobbuffet	—
Lake Valor	Wobbuffet	—
Valor Lakefront	Nidorino/Nidorina	—
Route 201	Nidoran ♀/Nidoran ♂	—
Route 202	Sentret	—
Route 204	Sunkern	—
Route 205 (Floaroma Town side)	Hoppip	—
Route 205 (Eterna City side)	Slowpoke	—
Route 206	Baltoy	—
Route 207	Stantler	—
Route 208	Smeargle	—

Location	Appears commonly	Appears rarely
Route 209	Kirlia	—
Route 210 (Solaceon Town side)	Miltank/Tauros	—
Route 210 (Celestic Town side)	Bagon	—
Route 211 (Eterna City side)	Tyrogue	—
Route 212 (Hearthome City side)	Smeargle	—
Route 212 (Pastoria City side)	Grimer	—
Route 213	Swellow	—
Route 214	Poochyena	—
Route 217	Piloswine	—
Route 221	Nidorino/Nidorina	—
Route 222	Flaaffy	—
Route 225	Primeape	Mankey
Route 226	Primeape	Mankey
Route 227	Torkoal	—
Route 229	Venomoth	Venonat
Route 230	Togepi	—

National Pokédex completion point 4

Take advantage of mass outbreaks

Rare and valuable Pokémon appear in mass outbreaks

A mass outbreak is a mysterious phenomenon where large numbers of a particular Pokémon appear suddenly in a particular place. Pokémon that appear in mass outbreaks are all rare and valuable kinds, so keep your ear to the ground about mass outbreaks and be ready to rush to take advantage.

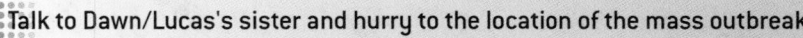

Talk to Dawn/Lucas's sister and hurry to the location of the mass outbreak

You can find out about mass outbreaks by talking to Dawn/Lucas's sister in Sandgem Town. The information changes at midnight, so be ready to hurry once you get it.

Route 226! They said there's a whole bunch of KRABBY there!

A wild KRABBY appeared!

Gotta get it!

Information about mass outbreaks changes every day. You never know when the Pokémon you want will be appearing. Talk to Dawn/Lucas's sister every day in Sandgem Town to be sure you don't miss a vital tipoff.

Pokémon that appear in mass outbreaks

Location	Pokémon
Valley Windworks	Electrike
Eterna Forest	Slakoth
Route 201	Doduo
Route 202	Zigzagoon
Route 203	Cubone
Route 206	Larvitar
Route 207	Phanpy
Route 208	Dunsparce
Route 209	Snubbull
Route 214	Spoink
Route 215	Drowzee
Route 217	Delibird
Route 218	Voltorb
Route 221	Farfetch'd
Route 222	Skitty
Route 224	Natu
Route 225	Makuhita
Route 226	Krabby
Route 227	Spinda
Route 228	Beldum
Route 229	Pinsir
Route 230	Corsola

5

Get Pokémon by restoring fossils

Restore ancient Pokémon to their original forms

Sometimes you can acquire a Pokémon fossil when you dig in the walls of the Underground. This is the fossil of a Pokémon that lived in ancient times. You can restore it into its original form. Dig out lots of fossils to restore, and collect, ancient Pokémon.

⋮ Have fossils restored at the Oreburgh Mining Museum

Bring fossils you've unearthed from the Underground walls to the Mining Museum at Oreburgh City. Leave them for a while with the receptionist, and the workers will restore them to life. Now you can add those Pokémon to your Pokédex.

● Pokémon that can be restored from fossils

Pokémon	Condition to get
Aerodactyl	Get Old Amber in the Underground
Anorith	Get Claw Fossil in the Underground
Cranidos	Get Skull Fossil in the Underground
Kabuto	Get Dome Fossil in the Underground
Lileep	Get Root Fossil in the Underground
Omanyte	Get Helix Fossil in the Underground
Shieldon	Get Armor Fossil in the Underground

*Depending on your Trainer ID, you may not be able to acquire the Skull Fossil or the Armor Fossil. See page 567 for more information.

This is your SHIELDON! You be good to it, OK!

Gotta get it! The Pokémon you get from restoring fossils are Pokémon you can't get any other way. Before you get the National Pokédex, you can only get Cranidos and Shieldon this way. Many more kinds will become available once you get the National Pokédex.

6

Get Pokémon from Honey Trees

Lure Pokémon with sweet scents

Spread Honey on any of the Honey Trees that grow in the Sinnoh region. Then check on the tree after about half a day, and a Pokémon will appear, lured out by the scent of the Honey. Some trees are more lucky than others. Lucky trees are more likely to house a rare and valuable Pokémon like Munchlax. (p. 77)

⋮ Spread Honey, and a Pokémon appears after about half a day

Once you get some Honey from the Honey man in Floaroma Meadow, start spreading it on trees. Start with the ones that are easiest to get to. Pokémon will appear half a day after you spread the Honey. The effect will wear off after a full day.

Slather the bark with Honey?

A wild CHERUBI appeared from the tree you slathered with Honey!

● Pokémon you can get by spreading Honey on Honey Trees

Pokémon	Conditions to encounter
Aipom	Spread Honey on a Honey Tree
Burmy	Spread Honey on a Honey Tree
Cherubi	Spread Honey on a Honey Tree
Combee	Spread Honey on a Honey Tree
Heracross	Spread Honey on a Honey Tree
Munchlax	Spread Honey on a Honey Tree

● Main way to get Honey

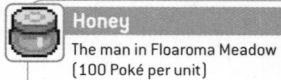

Honey
The man in Floaroma Meadow (100 Poké per unit)

Gotta get it! Aipom, Heracross, Burmy, Combee, and Cherubi can only be acquired with the Honey Tree method. If you want them, spread Honey on as many trees as you can get to.

Get Pokémon during story events

Get one-of-a-kind Pokémon

You acquire some Pokémon in accordance with the course of the story. Your starter Pokémon, for instance, you get from Professor Rowan. And you meet Giratina as part of the game's story. Pokémon like these are very rare and valuable.

Meet Pokémon even after you get the National Pokédex

There are several rare and valuable Pokémon you can meet after you get the National Pokédex, such as Regigigas and Heatran. Check the Sinnoh walkthrough in this book for more information on how to catch these Pokémon.

Lucas used one Dusk Ball!

● Pokémon acquired over the course of the story

Pokémon	Conditions to get
Turtwig	Receive from Professor Rowan on Route 201
Chimchar	Receive from Professor Rowan on Route 201
Piplup	Receive from Professor Rowan on Route 201
Togepi	Hatch an Egg received from Cynthia in Eterna City
Rotom	Examine the TV in the Old Chateau between 8 PM and 4 AM
Eevee	Receive from Bebe at Hearthome City
Porygon	Receive from a man in a residence in Veilstone City
Riolu	Hatch from an Egg received from Riley on Iron Island
Giratina (Origin Forme)	Distortion World
Uxie	Lake Acuity (after you've been to the Distortion World)
Azelf	Lake Valor (after you've been to the Distortion World)
Mesprit	Roams Sinnoh after you meet it at Lake Verity (after you've been to the Distortion World)
Dialga	Mt. Coronet (middle) • Spear Pillar (post-Hall-of-Fame)
Palkia	Mt. Coronet (middle) • Spear Pillar (post-Hall-of-Fame)
Cresselia	Roams the Sinnoh region after you meet it at Fullmoon Island
Giratina (Altered Forme)	Giratina's room in Turnback Cave (if you didn't catch it in the Distortion World)
Regigigas	Snowpoint Temple B5F (with Regirock, Regice, and Registeel in your party)
Heatran	Stark Mountain interior 3 (after Stark Mountain and after talking to Buck in the Survival Area)

Gotta get it!

You can only acquire one Pokémon out of the trio of Turtwig, Chimchar, and Piplup. So trade these Pokémon with your friends or family so you can record the remaining ones in your Pokédex. Another good way is to discover an Egg.

Evolve Pokémon to acquire new ones

Some Pokémon evolve by participating in battle

Many Pokémon aren't found in the wild; to acquire these, you have to level up and evolve other Pokémon. Refer to page 376 for information on how to raise these Pokémon.

SHELGON is evolving!

● Pokémon acquired by evolving

Pokémon	Conditions for evolving	Pokémon	Conditions for evolving
Aggron	Level up Lairon to Lv42	Linoone	Level up Zigzagoon to Lv20
Altaria	Level up Swablu to Lv35	Luxray	Level up Luxio to Lv30
Ampharos	Level up Flaaffy to Lv30	Manectric	Level up Electrike to Lv26
Armaldo	Level up Anorith to Lv40	Marowak	Level up Cubone to Lv28
Bastiodon	Level up Shieldon to Lv30	Metagross	Level up Metang to Lv45
Beedrill	Level up Kakuna to Lv10	Metang	Level up Beldum to Lv20
Breloom	Level up Shroomish to Lv23	Mightyena	Level up Poochyena to Lv18
Butterfree	Level up Metapod to Lv10	Monferno	Level up Chimchar to Lv14
Cherrim	Level up Cherubi to Lv25	Mothim	Level up Burmy ♂ to Lv20
Claydol	Level up Baltoy to Lv36	Muk	Level up Grimer to Lv38
Cradily	Level up Lileep to Lv40	Ninjask	Level up Nincada to Lv20
Dodrio	Level up Doduo to Lv31	Omastar	Level up Omanyte to Lv40
Donphan	Level up Phanpy to Lv25	Parasect	Level up Paras to Lv24
Dragonite	Level up Dragonair to Lv55	Persian	Level up Meowth to Lv28
Drifblim	Level up Drifloon to Lv28	Pidgeotto	Level up Pidgey to Lv18
Electrode	Level up Voltorb to Lv30	Pidgeot	Level up Pidgotto to Lv36
Empoleon	Level up Prinplup to Lv36	Piloswine	Level up Swinub to Lv33
Exploud	Level up Loudred to Lv40	Prinplup	Level up Piplup to Lv16
Forretress	Level up Pineco to Lv31	Pupitar	Level up Larvitar to Lv30
Furret	Level up Sentret to Lv15	Rampardos	Level up Cranidos to Lv30
Garchomp	Level up Gabite to Lv48	Rapidash	Level up Ponyta to Lv40
Gardevoir	Level up Kirlia to Lv30	Salamence	Level up Shelgon to Lv50
Glalie	Level up Snorunt to Lv42	Sharpedo	Level up Carvanha to Lv30
Granbull	Level up Snubbull to Lv23	Shelgon	Level up Bagon to Lv30
Grotle	Level up Turtwig to Lv18	Skiploom	Level up Hoppip to Lv18
Grumpig	Level up Spoink to Lv32	Slaking	Level up Vigoroth to Lv36
Hariyama	Level up Makuhita to Lv24	Slowbro	Level up Slowpoke to Lv37
Houndoom	Level up Houndour to Lv24	Staraptor	Level up Staravia to Lv34
Hypno	Level up Drowzee to Lv26	Swalot	Level up Gulpin to Lv26
Infernape	Level up Monferno to Lv36	Torterra	Level up Grotle to Lv32
Jumpluff	Level up Skiploom to Lv27	Tyranitar	Level up Pupitar to Lv55
Kabutops	Level up Kabuto to Lv40	Vespiquen	Level up Combee ♀ to Lv21
Kingler	Level up Krabby to Lv28	Vigoroth	Level up Slakoth to Lv18
Lairon	Level up Aron to Lv32	Walrein	Level up Sealeo to Lv44
Lanturn	Level up Chinchou to Lv27	Xatu	Level up Natu to Lv25

Gotta get it! Dragonite and Tyranitar stand out among Pokémon that are acquired by Evolution. These two have to reach Lv55 before they evolve into these forms. You'll have to use some elbow grease to get them.

Evolution technique 1 Have the Pokémon hold the Exp. Share

The Exp. Share is a supremely useful item that gives its holder a cut of the Exp. from a battle, even if the Pokémon did not participate. Give it to a Pokémon that's too low-level to safely participate in battles. It's a stress-free way to raise your Pokémon.

How to get the Exp. Share — Receive at the Gate on the west side of Eterna City (when your Sinnoh Pokédex "Pokémon seen" count is over 35)

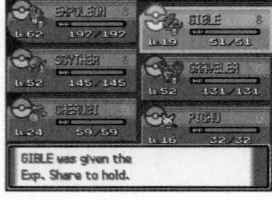
Let your more battle-hardy Pokémon go into battle.

The Pokémon holding the Exp. Share will receive half the Exp. from the battle.

Evolution technique 2 Have your Pokémon raised at Day Care

Pokémon Day Care is a shop where you can leave a Pokémon to have it leveled up for you. It costs money, but since you don't need to take the Pokémon into battles, it's a relatively painless way of raising a Pokémon.

Pokémon Day Care Location — Solaceon Town

Day Care takes on your Pokémon for a while, raising its level.

The Pokémon does not evolve while in Day Care—only by leveling up in battle.

Evolution technique 3 — Use Rare Candy on the Pokémon

Rare Candy is an item that can raise a Pokémon by 1 level. It's not sold in Pokémarts, but you can find several on your journey. Keep around a Pokémon with the Pickup Ability, and it will sometimes find a Rare Candy while you travel.

PACHIRISU was elevated to Lv. 49.

A Pokémon with Pickup is a useful member of your party.

Places where you can find Rare Candy
Floaroma Town, Old Chateau 1F/dining hall, Route 206, Mt. Coronet (upper) 1F (1), Solaceon Town, Veilstone City, Route 218, etc.

Pokémon with the Pickup Ability

National Pokédex completion point 9

Catch wild Pokémon with special preconditions

Fulfill special conditions to catch rare and valuable Pokémon

There are some wild Pokémon that only appear after you've met certain special conditions. Take Spiritomb and Feebas, for example. You'll need a helping hand from friends or family to catch Spiritomb. Everyone pitches in so you can record Pokémon in your Pokédex.

Spiritomb — Greet 32 people in the Underground

To make Spiritomb appear, you need to fit the Odd Keystone into the broken stone tower on Route 209, completing it and making it into the Hallowed Tower. Next, you need to go to the Underground and greet 32 people. When you do, Spiritomb will appear at the Hallowed Tower.

The stone tower has been restored! "Hallowed Tower" is written on it.

You can get the Odd Keystone from a young man on Route 208.

GREET
QUESTION
GIVE GOODS
EXIT

Hey, there!
What's up?

Pick "Greet" and bring up your "People met" count to 32.

Feebas — Only appears in 4 spots in the big lake in Mt. Coronet (upper) B1F

Feebas is a Pokémon that lives in Mt. Coronet (upper) B1F (p. 122), accessible from either Eterna City or Celestic Town. Feebas only appears in 4 small areas. Use Surf, and poke ahead gradually until you find a spot where you can hook Feebas with your fishing rod. The best way is to use the Old Rod. The spots where you can catch Feebas change each day.

FEEBAS   Lv 18

A wild FEEBAS appeared!

When you pool records with friends from your Group, Feebas's location will become the same across all of your games. Cooperate with your friends to find those locations.

Mt. Coronet (upper) B1F

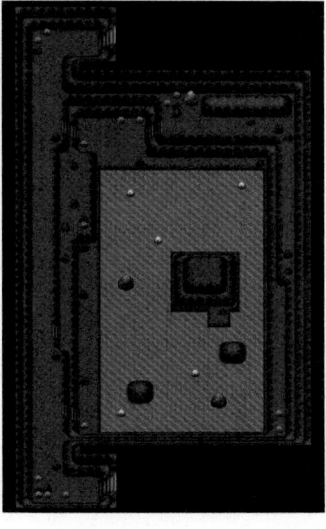

National Pokédex
completion point

10

Use stones to evolve Pokémon

Some Pokémon evolve with the power of stones

Some Pokémon can achieve Evolution by using special stones. Collect enough stones for all of the Pokémon you want to evolve, and use the necessary ones on your Pokémon.

Use a stone for instant Evolution

Pokémon that can evolve using stones will do so instantly the moment you use the stone. It's a relatively easy way to evolve, avoiding the need for the Pokémon to enter battles. Use Evolution Stones and fill out your Pokédex.

Congratulations! Your VULPIX evolved into NINETALES!

● Pokémon you can get by using stones

Pokémon	Pokémon and stone for evolving
Arcanine	Use Fire Stone on Growlithe
Bellossom	Use Sun Stone on Gloom
Clefable	Use Moon Stone on Clefairy
Cloyster	Use Water Stone on Shellder
Delcatty	Use Moon Stone on Skitty
Exeggutor	Use Leaf Stone on Exeggcute
Flareon	Use Fire Stone on Eevee
Froslass	Use Dawn Stone on Snorunt ♀
Gallade	Use Dawn Stone on Kirlia ♂
Jolteon	Use Thunderstone on Eevee
Ludicolo	Use Water Stone on Lombre
Nidoking	Use Moon Stone on Nidorino
Nidoqueen	Use Moon Stone on Nidorina

Pokémon	Pokémon and sone for evolving
Ninetales	Use Fire Stone on Vulpix
Poliwrath	Use Water Stone on Poliwhirl
Raichu	Use Thunderstone on Pikachu
Roserade	Use Shiny Stone on Roselia
Shiftry	Use Leaf Stone on Nuzleaf
Starmie	Use Water Stone on Staryu
Sunflora	Use Sun Stone on Sunkern
Togekiss	Use Shiny Stone on Togetic
Vaporeon	Use Water Stone on Eevee
Victreebel	Use Leaf Stone on Weepinbell
Vileplume	Use Leaf Stone on Gloom
Wigglytuff	Use Moon Stone on Jigglypuff

Gotta get it! You'll need all kinds of stones. Except for the Shiny Stone and the Dawn Stone, you can find them while digging for fossils in the walls of the Underground. Keep digging until you have as many as you need of the stone you're looking for. (p. 241)

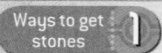

Ways to get stones **1** Pick them up on the field and in caves

The most basic way to get stones is to find them on the ground in places like fields and caves. Many are invisible but can be found when you use the Dowsing Machine. You can't find the Shiny Stone or the Dawn Stone through fossil digging, so be extra sure to pick them up on the field.

Lucas found a Leaf Stone!

Ways to get stones **2** Fossil digging

You'll need multiples of the Thunderstone, Fire Stone, Water Stone, Leaf Stone, Sun Stone, and Moon Stone. Luckily, you can dig up as many as you need from the walls of the Underground. Keep your nose to the grindstone until you've got all the stones you need.

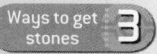 **Ways to get stones** **3** **Get from wild Pokémon**

Some wild Pokémon will be holding stones. Some wild Solrock are holding Sun Stones, just as some wild Cleffa, Clefairy, and Lunatone are holding Moon Stones. If you're having trouble finding all the stones you need in the Underground, try catching these Pokémon.

A wild LUNATONE appeared!

● **Where to get stones**

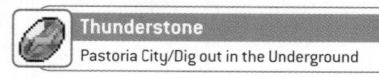
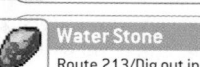
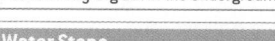

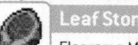

Thunderstone
Pastoria City/Dig out in the Underground

Fire Stone
Fuego Ironworks/Dig out in the Underground

Water Stone
Route 213/Dig out in the Underground

Leaf Stone
Floaroma Meadow/Dig out in the Underground

Sun Stone
Dig out in the Underground/Wild Solrock

Moon Stone
Underground/Held by wild Cleffa, Clefairy, etc.

Shiny Stone
Iron Island B3F/Route 228

Dusk Stone
Galactic Warehouse/Back of Victory Road 1F

Dawn Stone
Mt. Coronet (middle) 1F/Route 225

National Pokédex completion point **11**

Evolve Pokémon by earning their Friendship

Some Pokémon evolve when they feel love

There's a bond of trust that exists between a Pokémon and its Trainer, called Friendship. The happier you make your Pokémon, the more fond of you it will be. Some Pokémon will evolve if they level up when that Friendship is high enough.

Give your Pokémon lots of joy

A young woman in Hearthome City can tell you how fond of you a Pokémon is. Talk to her with that Pokémon at the head of your party and she'll evaluate its Friendship with you.

It's very friendly toward you. I can tell you treat it kindly.

What? RIOLU is evolving!

● **Pokémon you can get through Friendship Evolutions**

Pokémon	Conditions to encounter
Blissey	Level up Chansey with high enough Friendship
Crobat	Level up Golbat with high enough Friendship
Espeon	Level up Eevee with high enough Friendship between 4 AM and 8 PM
Lopunny	Level up Buneary with high enough Friendship
Lucario	Level up Lucario with high enough Friendship between 4 AM and 8 PM
Snorlax	Level up Munchlax with high enough Friendship
Togetic	Level up Togepi with high enough Friendship
Umbreon	Level up Eevee with high enough Friendship between 8 PM and 4 AM

Gotta get it! It's essential to raise all your Pokémon with loving care, so they grow attached to you. Don't let them faint too often. Pay careful attention in the case of Espeon, Umbreon, and Lucario. Not only do these Pokémon need high Friendship to evolve, it also needs to occur within a certain time period.

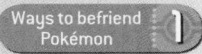 **Ways to befriend Pokémon** **1** **Keep it in your party as you travel**

The most basic way to bond with your Pokémon is to keep it in your party as you travel around. Its Friendship rises the longer it's in your party. But be careful, because its Friendship will fall if you send it into battle and it faints.

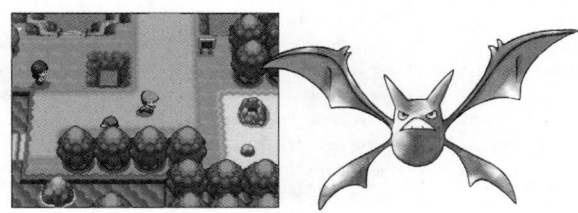

Ways to befriend Pokémon 2 — Use stat-raising items

Using EV-raising items like Protein, Iron, and Zinc also raises a Pokémon's Friendship. These items are for sale on 2F of the Veilstone Dept. Store in Veilstone City. At 9,800 Poké apiece, they're pricey, but they go a long way.

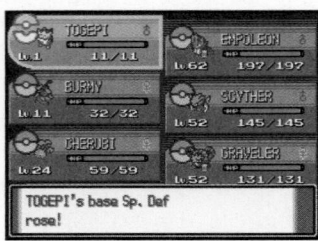

Ways to befriend Pokémon 3 — Have it hold the Soothe Bell

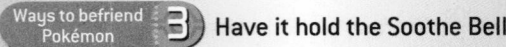

The Soothe Bell is an item that makes it easier for you to bond with the Pokémon that holds it. Put the Pokémon you want to bond with in your party and have it hold the Soothe Bell for higher-than-average results as you travel.

How to get the Soothe Bell

Receive from Cheryl in Eterna Forest

Ways to befriend Pokémon 4 — Get a spa treatment at the Ribbon Syndicate in the Resort Area

Once you become a member of the Ribbon Syndicate in the Resort Area, you can get a Pokémon spa treatment on the second floor. This will raise the Pokémon's Friendship too. You can join the Ribbon Syndicate when you bring a Pokémon with over 10 different ribbons. (p. 184)

National Pokédex completion point 12

Get Pokémon through special Evolutions

Evolve Pokémon by meeting special conditions

There are many Pokémon that only evolve once you meet certain special conditions. Here's a list of those Pokémon. These Pokémon are essential to completing your Pokédex, so put your mind to it and collect them all.

● Specially evolving Pokémon

Pokémon	Conditions for evolving
Ambipom	Level up Aipom to Lv32 and teach it Double Hit. Or, level it up while it knows Double Hit.
Glaceon	Level up Eevee near the ice-covered rock on Route 217
Gliscor	Level up Gligar while it holds the Razor Fang between 8 PM and 4 AM
Hitmonchan	Make Tyrogue's Defense higher than its Attack, then level it up to Lv20
Hitmonlee	Make Tyrogue's Attack higher than its Defense, then level it up to Lv20
Hitmontop	Make Tyrogue's Attack and Defense the same, then level it up to Lv20
Leafeon	Level up Eevee near the moss-covered rock in Eterna Forest
Lickilicky	Level up Lickitung to Lv33 and teach it Rollout. Or, level it up while it knows Rollout.
Magnezone	Level up Magneton on Mt. Coronet
Mamoswine	Level up Piloswine once it knows AncientPower
Mantine	Level up Mantyke with Remoraid in your party
Milotic	Level up Feebas with high enough Beauty
Mothim	Level up Burmy ♂ to Lv20
Probopass	Level up Nosepass on Mt. Coronet
Shedinja	Level up Nincada to Lv20 with an empty slot in your party and an empty Poké Ball
Tangrowth	Level up Tangela to Lv33 and teach it AncientPower. Or, level it up while it knows AncientPower.
Weavile	Level up Sneasel while it holds the Razor Claw between 8 PM and 4 AM
Wormadam (Plant Cloak)	Level up Burmy (Plant Cloak) ♀ to Lv20
Wormadam (Sandy Cloak)	Level up Burmy (Sandy Cloak) ♀ to Lv20
Wormadam (Trash Cloak)	Level up Burmy (Trash Cloak) ♀ to Lv20
Yanmega	Level up Yanma to Lv33 and teach it AncientPower. Or, level it up while it knows AncientPower.

Specially-evolving Pokémon 1 — A Pokémon with 3 different Evolutions corresponding to stats

When Tyrogue evolves at Lv20, it takes a different evolutionary branch depending on its Attack and Defense stats. You can adjust Tyrogue's Attack and Defense with stat-raising items. Before it levels up, use Protein to raise its Attack or Iron to raise its Defense.

● Stat-raising items

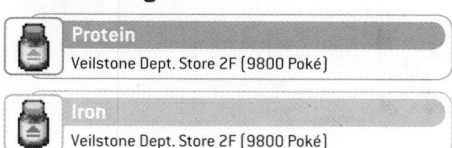

Protein
Veilstone Dept. Store 2F (9800 Poké)

Iron
Veilstone Dept. Store 2F (9800 Poké)

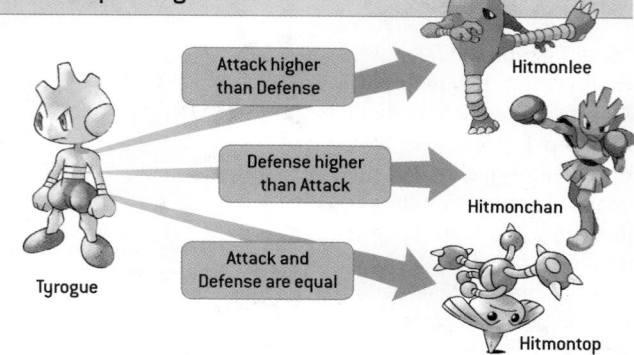

Attack higher than Defense → Hitmonlee

Defense higher than Attack → Hitmonchan

Attack and Defense are equal → Hitmontop

Tyrogue

Specially-evolving Pokémon 2 — Pokémon that evolve depending on your other party Pokémon

There are two Pokémon that evolve when you fulfill certain conditions having to do with your party. The first is Mantyke, which evolves into Mantine. Level up Mantyke while Remoraid is in your party to evolve Mantyke into Mantine. The second such Pokémon is Nincada, which evolves into Shedinja. Leave an empty slot in your party and have a Poké Ball on hand, and level up Nincada to Lv20. Nincada evolves into Ninjask, and Shedinja is added to your party.

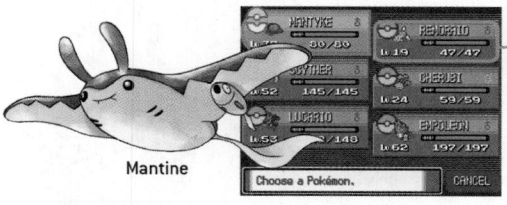

Mantine

Have Remoraid in your party

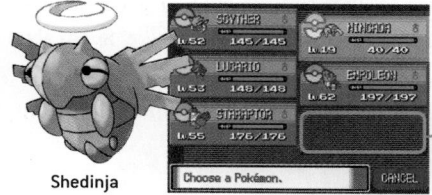

Shedinja

Leave a space in your party

Specially-evolving Pokémon 3 — A Pokémon that evolves through having high Beauty

When Feebas levels up with its Beauty condition high enough, it evolves into Milotic. You can raise Feebas's Beauty condition by making and feeding it dry-flavored Poffins.

● Ingredients for a Beauty-raising Poffin

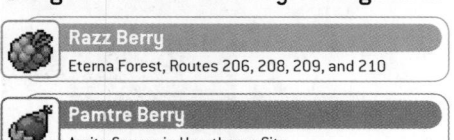

Razz Berry
Eterna Forest, Routes 206, 208, 209, and 210

Pamtre Berry
Amity Square in Hearthome City

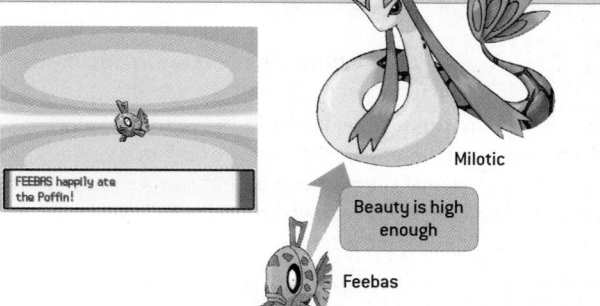

FEEBAS happily ate the Poffin!

Milotic

Beauty is high enough

Feebas

Specially-evolving Pokémon 4 — A Pokémon that evolves according to the cloak it wears

Burmy is a Pokémon that dons a Plant Cloak, a Sandy Cloak, or a Trash Cloak, depending on the location of the battle. Raise a female Burmy to Lv20 and it evolves into a Wormadam with the same cloak it had at the time of Evolution. The male Burmy evolves into Mothim.

Wormadam (Plant Cloak)

Wormadam (Sandy Cloak)

Wormadam (Trash Cloak)

Mothim

Burmy ♀ (Plant Cloak)
Wears the Plant Cloak in battles in tall grass and forests, on the water's surface, and on snowy ground.

Burmy ♀ (Sandy Cloak)
Wears the Sandy Cloak when it battles on mountains, in caves, and in sandy areas.

Burmy ♀ (Trash Cloak)
Wears the Trash Cloak when it battles in buildings.

Burmy ♂
The male Burmy evolves into Mothim, regardless of which cloak it's wearing.

Specially-evolving Pokémon 5 — Pokémon that evolve when they learn a certain move

Some Pokémon evolve when they level up while knowing a certain move that they've learned by leveling up or through other means. Piloswine doesn't learn AncientPower by leveling up, but can learn it if you bring a Heart Scale to the Move Maniac in Pastoria City. You can get Heart Scales in the Underground.

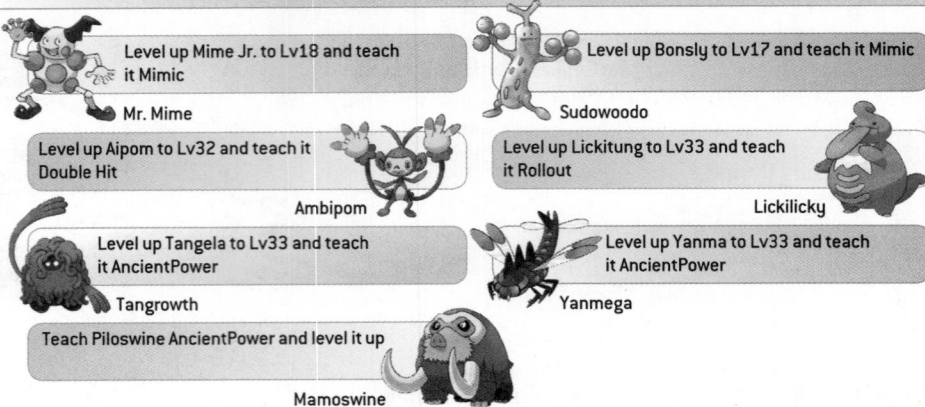

Level up Mime Jr. to Lv18 and teach it Mimic

Mr. Mime

Level up Bonsly to Lv17 and teach it Mimic

Sudowoodo

Level up Aipom to Lv32 and teach it Double Hit

Ambipom

Level up Lickitung to Lv33 and teach it Rollout

Lickilicky

Level up Tangela to Lv33 and teach it AncientPower

Tangrowth

Level up Yanma to Lv33 and teach it AncientPower

Yanmega

Teach Piloswine AncientPower and level it up

Mamoswine

Specially-evolving Pokémon 6 — Pokémon that evolve at night and holding items

The Sinnoh region experiences the passage of real time, and some Pokémon evolve in rhythm to it. Sneasel and Gligar only achieve Evolution when you level them up in deepest night, between 8 PM and 4 AM. Furthermore, Sneasel must be holding the Razor Claw, Gligar the Razor Fang.

● **Items needed for Sneasel and Gligar's Evolution**

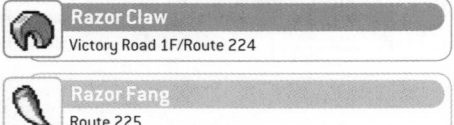

Razor Claw
Victory Road 1F/Route 224

Razor Fang
Route 225

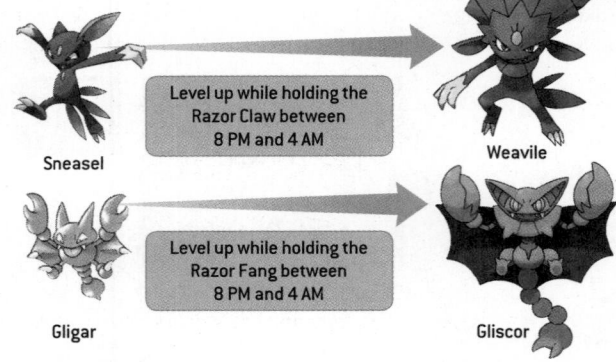

Sneasel

Level up while holding the Razor Claw between 8 PM and 4 AM

Weavile

Gligar

Level up while holding the Razor Fang between 8 PM and 4 AM

Gliscor

Specially-evolving Pokémon 7 — Pokémon that evolve in proximity to special rocks

There are two mysterious rocks in the Sinnoh region, and a Pokémon that uses them both in order to evolve. That Pokémon is Eevee. Level Eevee up in Eterna Forest and it evolves into Leafeon. Level it up on Route 217 and it evolves into Glaceon. Eevee has a total of 7 possible evolved forms. Leave it at Pokémon Day Care so you can get 7 Pokémon Eggs. (p. 383)

Eevee

Leafeon

Eterna Forest
The rock is covered in moss. It feels pleasantly cool.

Glaceon

Route 217
The boulder is encrusted with ice. It is bone chilling to touch.

Specially-evolving Pokémon 8 — Pokémon that evolve on Mt. Coronet

Some Pokémon evolve when leveled up in the caverns of Mt. Coronet, the mountain that divides the east side of Sinnoh from its west. Nosepass evolves into Probopass, Magneton into Magnezone. If either Nosepass or Magneton comes into your possession, hurry it to Mt. Coronet.

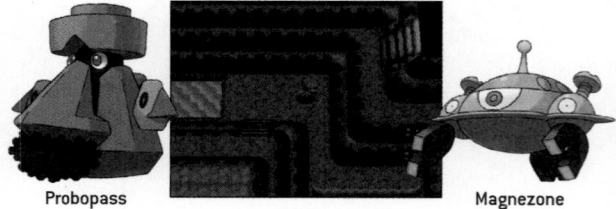

Probopass

Magnezone

13 Discover Eggs to get Pokémon

Eggs are discovered at Pokémon Day Care

If you leave two Pokémon together at Pokémon Day Care in Solaceon Town, sometimes you'll discover a Pokémon Egg. Depending on the pairing, the Egg could be that of a rare and valuable Pokémon.

Path from Egg discovery to Pokémon birth

1 Drop off Pokémon

Leave two Pokémon at Day Care and come back later.

2 Accept the Egg

If an Egg is discovered, it's given to you. Add it to your party as you journey.

3 The Egg hatches

Once you've traveled for long enough, the Egg hatches and a Pokémon is born.

● Pokémon obtained through discovering Eggs

Pokémon	Pairing of Pokémon for the Egg to occur
Bonsly	Mineral Group male + female Sudowoodo
Elekid	Human-like Group male + female Electabuzz or Electivire
Ledyba	Bug Group male + female Ledian
Magby	Human-like Group male + female Magmar or Magmortar
Mime Jr.	Human-like Group male + female Mr. Mime
Phione	Manaphy* + Ditto
Seel	Water Group 1 or Field Group male + female Dewgong
Shuppet	Amorphous Group male + female Banette
Spheal	Water Group 1 or Field Group male + female Sealeo or Walrein
Spinarak	Bug Group male + female Ariados
Taillow	Flying Group male + female Swellow
Whismur	Monster Group or Field Group male + female Loudred
Wynaut	Amorphous Group male + female Wobbuffet

*Only available via distribution at special events and not through regular gameplay. Check Pokémon.com for the latest news on how to catch this Pokémon.

Gotta get it! None of these Pokémon appear in the wild in Sinnoh. To record them in your Pokédex, you either need to discover their Eggs or import them through Pal Park.

Rules for discovering Eggs 1 Master the right pairings to discover certain Eggs

Leave a male and a female of the same kind of Pokémon at Day Care. That's the most basic Egg pairing. However, since all Pokémon belong to Egg Groups, you can even leave different species of Pokémon together at Day Care and as long as they're of the same Egg Group, an Egg will be found.

● Main Egg guidelines

1 If a male and a female Pokémon of the same Egg Group are left at Day Care together, an Egg will be found.

2 The Pokémon that hatches from the Egg will be the same as the female, or will be a pre-Evolution of it.

3 The Pokémon that hatches from the Egg is the initial form on the Evolution chain of that Pokémon.

*Some Pokémon have two Abilities. Luxray, for instance, can have either Rivalry or Intimidate. Even if you leave a Luxray with Rivalry at Day Care, the offspring may still have Intimidate instead.

● Male Chatot and female Swellow

Chatot ♂ — **Flying Group**

Swellow ♀ — **Flying Group**

Taillow

If you leave a male Chatot with a female Swellow, a Taillow Egg will be found.

▶▶▶ See page 385 for a list of Egg Groups. ◀◀◀

Rules for discovering Eggs **2** A pairing with Ditto can lead to all kinds of Eggs being found

Some Pokémon are of unknown gender. And some are all males. Normally such Pokémon couldn't lead to Eggs being discovered. But if you leave one with a Ditto, you can find an Egg. You can find Ditto in the Trophy Garden of the Pokémon Mansion on Route 212, after you get the National Pokédex.

● **Ditto and Metagross**

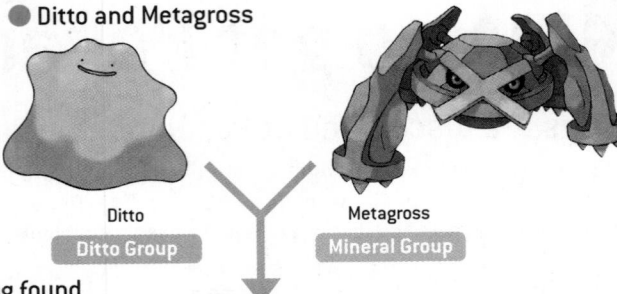

Ditto — Ditto Group

Metagross — Mineral Group

● **Location of wild Ditto**

Trophy Garden at the Pokémon Mansion (after you get the National Pokédex)

● **Pokémon of unknown gender that can lead to Eggs being found**

Baltoy	Magnemite	Porygon-Z
Beldum	Magneton	Rotom
Bronzong	Magnezone	Shedinja
Bronzor	Metagross	Solrock
Claydol	Metang	Starmie
Electrode	Porygon	Staryu
Lunatone	Porygon2	Voltorb

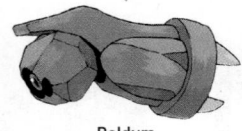

Beldum

Metagross is of indeterminate gender, but if you leave it in Day Care with a Ditto, you'll find an Egg of its pre-evolved form, Beldum.

Rules for discovering Eggs **3** Some Pokémon lead to Eggs being found when they hold items

Some Pokémon Eggs are found when a pair of Pokémon is left at Day Care with one of them holding a particular item. Take Munchlax, for instance, which can appear at Honey Trees, but is extremely rare. Employing this method, you can get a Munchlax Egg.

● **Pokémon whose Eggs can be found when Pokémon hold items**

Pokémon	Combination of Pokémon to find the Egg	Items needed
Azurill	Fairy Group or Water Group 1 male + female Marill or Azumarill	Sea Incense
Wynaut	Amorphous Group male + female Wobbuffet	Lax Incense
Mime Jr.	Human-like Group male + female Mr. Mime	Odd Incense
Bonsly	Mineral Group male + female Sudowoodo	Rock Incense
Munchlax	Monster Group male + female Snorlax	Full Incense
Mantyke	Water Group 1 male + female Mantine	Wave Incense
Budew	Fairy Group or Mineral Group male + female Roselia or Roserade	Rose Incense
Happiny	Fairy Group male + female Chansey or Blissey	Luck Incense
Chingling	Amorphous Group male + female Chimecho	Pure Incense

Rules for discovering Eggs **4** Leave Manaphy and Ditto to find a Phione Egg

When you leave Manaphy and Ditto at Day Care, you'll find a Phione Egg. This is the only way to get Phione, which doesn't appear at all in the wild. You can't find a Manaphy Egg, but Phione is rare and valuable enough to make up for it. You can also find Phione Eggs when you leave Phione and Ditto together at Day Care. Phione won't become Manaphy through leveling up or anything. If you don't have Manaphy and Phione, link trade for them so you can record them in your Pokédex, or go the Phione Egg route.

● **Ditto and Manaphy**

Ditto

Manaphy

Phione

 Use Abilities to hatch Eggs more quickly

When you want to hatch a Pokémon Egg more quickly, there are some Pokémon Abilities you can use. Put a Pokémon with Flame Body or Magma Armor in your party together with the Egg, and it will speed up the time it takes to hatch.

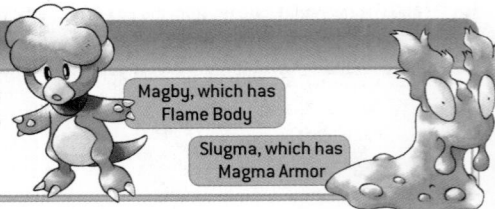

Magby, which has Flame Body

Slugma, which has Magma Armor

Rules for discovering Eggs 5 — The moves a Pokémon knows from birth can differ

All Pokémon hatch at Lv1, but sometimes they know moves that they normally would never have learned at that point in their development. Some of these moves are special moves called Egg Moves, which are learned specifically through the breeding process. Master the rules governing these moves, and you can breed Pokémon that are better in battle than you could ever have imagined.

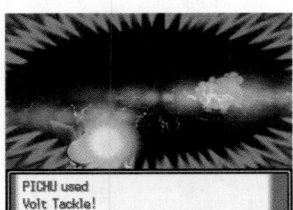

This Lickitung is Lv1. It has the Egg moves Snore and Belly Drum from birth.

● Guidelines of moves that Pokémon know upon hatching

1 That Pokémon's learned move for Lv1

2 A move that the Pokémon can learn by leveling up, that the male and female Pokémon at Day Care both know

3 A move that the Pokémon can learn from a TM, that the male Pokémon at Day Care knows

4 An Egg move for that Pokémon, that the male Pokémon at Day Care knows

Rules for discovering Eggs 6 — Pichu learns the special move Volt Tackle

You can find Pichu in the Trophy Garden at the Pokémon Mansion on Route 212, but if you hatch it from an Egg, it may emerge knowing Volt Tackle. For it to know Volt Tackle, have one of the Pokémon you leave at Pokémon Day Care hold a Light Ball. You can sometimes find Light Balls held by wild Pikachu.

● Sample pairing to get a Pichu that knows Volt Tackle

Cherrim ♂ Fairy Group
Pikachu ♀ Fairy Group
Light Ball
Pichu

Knows Volt Tackle!

Have the female Pikachu hold the Light Ball, and leave it with a male Cherrim, which is also from the Fairy Egg group.

PICHU used Volt Tackle!

Volt Tackle inflicts 1/3 of its damage back on the user, but it's massively powerful, with an attack power of 120.

Light Ball
Held by wild Pikachu

Pokémon Egg groups

1 Grass group			
No001	Bulbasaur	No270	Lotad
No002	Ivysaur	No271	Lombre
No003	Venusaur	No272	Ludicolo
No043	Oddish	No273	Seedot
No044	Gloom	No274	Nuzleaf
No045	Vileplume	No275	Shiftry
No046	Paras	No285	Shroomish
No047	Parasect	No286	Breloom
No069	Bellsprout	No315	Roselia
No070	Weepinbell	No331	Cacnea
No071	Victreebel	No332	Cacturne
No102	Exeggcute	No357	Tropius
No103	Exeggutor	No387	Turtwig
No114	Tangela	No388	Grotle
No152	Chikorita	No389	Torterra
No153	Bayleef	No407	Roserade
No154	Meganium	No420	Cherubi
No182	Bellossom	No421	Cherrim
No187	Hoppip	No455	Carnivine
No188	Skiploom	No459	Snover
No189	Jumpluff	No460	Abomasnow
No191	Sunkern	No465	Tangrowth
No192	Sunflora		

2 Bug group			
No010	Caterpie	No266	Silcoon
No011	Metapod	No267	Beautifly
No012	Butterfree	No268	Cascoon
No013	Weedle	No269	Dustox
No014	Kakuna	No283	Surskit
No015	Beedrill	No284	Masquerain
No046	Paras	No290	Nincada
No047	Parasect	No291	Ninjask
No048	Venonat	No313	Volbeat
No049	Venomoth	No314	Illumise
No123	Scyther	No328	Trapinch
No127	Pinsir	No329	Vibrava
No165	Ledyba	No330	Flygon
No166	Ledian	No401	Kricketot
No167	Spinarak	No402	Kricketune
No168	Ariados	No412	Burmy
No193	Yanma	No413	Wormadam
No204	Pineco	No414	Mothim
No205	Forretress	No415	Combee
No207	Gligar	No416	Vespiquen
No212	Scizor	No451	Skorupi
No213	Shuckle	No452	Drapion
No214	Heracross	No469	Yanmega
No265	Wurmple	No472	Gliscor

3 Flying group			
No016	Pidgey	No178	Xatu
No017	Pidgeotto	No198	Murkrow
No018	Pidgeot	No227	Skarmory
No021	Spearow	No276	Taillow
No022	Fearow	No277	Swellow
No041	Zubat	No278	Wingull
No042	Golbat	No279	Pelipper
No083	Farfetch'd	No333	Swablu
No084	Doduo	No334	Altaria
No085	Dodrio	No396	Starly
No142	Aerodactyl	No397	Staravia
No163	Hoothoot	No398	Staraptor
No164	Noctowl	No430	Honchkrow
No169	Crobat	No441	Chatot
No176	Togetic	No468	Togekiss
No177	Natu		

● Pokémon in green belong to two Egg groups

4 Human-like group

No063	Abra	No307	Meditite
No064	Kadabra	No308	Medicham
No065	Alakazam	No313	Volbeat
No066	Machop	No314	Illumise
No067	Machoke	No327	Spinda
No068	Machamp	No331	Cacnea
No096	Drowzee	No332	Cacturne
No097	Hypno	No390	Chimchar
No106	Hitmonlee	No391	Monferno
No107	Hitmonchan	No392	Infernape
No122	Mr. Mime	No427	Buneary
No124	Jynx	No428	Lopunny
No125	Electabuzz	No448	Lucario
No126	Magmar	No453	Croagunk
No237	Hitmontop	No454	Toxicroak
No296	Makuhita	No466	Electivire
No297	Hariyama	No467	Magmortar
No302	Sableye		

5 Monster group

No001	Bulbasaur	No199	Slowking
No002	Ivysaur	No246	Larvitar
No003	Venusaur	No247	Pupitar
No004	Charmander	No248	Tyranitar
No005	Charmeleon	No252	Treecko
No006	Charizard	No253	Grovyle
No007	Squirtle	No254	Sceptile
No008	Wartortle	No258	Mudkip
No009	Blastoise	No259	Marshtomp
No029	Nidoran♀	No260	Swampert
No032	Nidoran♂	No294	Loudred
No033	Nidorino	No295	Exploud
No034	Nidoking	No304	Aron
No079	Slowpoke	No305	Lairon
No080	Slowbro	No306	Aggron
No104	Cubone	No357	Tropius
No105	Marowak	No387	Turtwig
No108	Lickitung	No388	Grotle
No111	Rhyhorn	No389	Torterra
No112	Rhydon	No408	Cranidos
No115	Kangaskhan	No409	Rampardos
No131	Lapras	No410	Shieldon
No143	Snorlax	No411	Bastiodon
No152	Chikorita	No443	Gible
No153	Bayleef	No444	Gabite
No154	Meganium	No445	Garchomp
No158	Totodile	No459	Snover
No159	Croconaw	No460	Abomasnow
No160	Feraligatr	No463	Lickilicky
No179	Mareep	No464	Rhyperior
No180	Flaaffy		
No181	Ampharos		

6 Fairy group

No025	Pikachu	No300	Skitty
No026	Raichu	No301	Delcatty
No035	Clefairy	No303	Mawile
No036	Clefable	No311	Plusle
No039	Jigglypuff	No312	Minun
No040	Wigglytuff	No315	Roselia
No113	Chansey	No351	Castform
No176	Togetic	No361	Snorunt
No183	Marill	No362	Glalie
No184	Azumarill	No407	Roserade
No187	Hoppip	No417	Pachirisu
No188	Skiploom	No420	Cherubi
No189	Jumpluff	No421	Cherrim
No209	Snubbull	No468	Togekiss
No210	Granbull	No478	Froslass
No242	Blissey	No489	Phione
No285	Shroomish	No490	Manaphy
No286	Breloom		

7 Dragon group

No004	Charmander	No253	Grovyle
No005	Charmeleon	No254	Sceptile
No006	Charizard	No333	Swablu
No023	Ekans	No334	Altaria
No024	Arbok	No336	Seviper
No116	Horsea	No349	Feebas
No117	Seadra	No350	Milotic
No129	Magikarp	No371	Bagon
No130	Gyarados	No372	Shelgon
No147	Dratini	No373	Salamence
No148	Dragonair	No443	Gible
No149	Dragonite	No444	Gabite
No230	Kingdra	No445	Garchomp
No252	Treecko		

8 Mineral group

No074	Geodude	No338	Solrock
No075	Graveler	No343	Baltoy
No076	Golem	No344	Claydol
No081	Magnemite	No361	Snorunt
No082	Magneton	No362	Glalie
No095	Onix	No374	Beldum
No100	Voltorb	No375	Metang
No101	Electrode	No376	Metagross
No137	Porygon	No436	Bronzor
No185	Sudowoodo	No437	Bronzong
No208	Steelix	No462	Magnezone
No233	Porygon2	No474	Porygon-Z
No292	Shedinja	No476	Probopass
No299	Nosepass	No478	Froslass
No337	Lunatone		

9 Field group

No019	Rattata	No134	Vaporeon
No020	Raticate	No135	Jolteon
No023	Ekans	No136	Flareon
No024	Arbok	No155	Cyndaquil
No025	Pikachu	No156	Quilava
No026	Raichu	No157	Typhlosion
No027	Sandshrew	No161	Sentret
No028	Sandslash	No162	Furret
No029	Nidoran♀	No179	Mareep
No032	Nidoran♂	No180	Flaaffy
No033	Nidorino	No181	Ampharos
No034	Nidoking	No190	Aipom
No037	Vulpix	No194	Wooper
No038	Ninetales	No195	Quagsire
No050	Diglett	No196	Espeon
No051	Dugtrio	No197	Umbreon
No052	Meowth	No203	Girafarig
No053	Persian	No206	Dunsparce
No054	Psyduck	No209	Snubbull
No055	Golduck	No210	Granbull
No056	Mankey	No215	Sneasel
No057	Primeape	No216	Teddiursa
No058	Growlithe	No217	Ursaring
No059	Arcanine	No220	Swinub
No077	Ponyta	No221	Piloswine
No078	Rapidash	No225	Delibird
No083	Farfetch'd	No228	Houndour
No086	Seel	No229	Houndoom
No087	Dewgong	No231	Phanpy
No111	Rhyhorn	No232	Donphan
No112	Rhydon	No234	Stantler
No128	Tauros	No235	Smeargle
No133	Eevee	No241	Miltank

9 Field group

No255	Torchic	No363	Spheal
No256	Combusken	No364	Sealeo
No257	Blaziken	No365	Walrein
No261	Poochyena	No390	Chimchar
No262	Mightyena	No391	Monferno
No263	Zigzagoon	No392	Infernape
No264	Linoone	No393	Piplup
No273	Seedot	No394	Prinplup
No274	Nuzleaf	No395	Empoleon
No275	Shiftry	No399	Bidoof
No287	Slakoth	No400	Bibarel
No288	Vigoroth	No403	Shinx
No289	Slaking	No404	Luxio
No293	Whismur	No405	Luxray
No294	Loudred	No417	Pachirisu
No295	Exploud	No418	Buizel
No300	Skitty	No419	Floatzel
No301	Delcatty	No424	Ambipom
No303	Mawile	No427	Buneary
No309	Electrike	No428	Lopunny
No310	Manectric	No431	Glameow
No320	Wailmer	No432	Purugly
No321	Wailord	No434	Stunky
No322	Numel	No435	Skuntank
No323	Camerupt	No448	Lucario
No324	Torkoal	No449	Hippopotas
No325	Spoink	No450	Hippowdon
No326	Grumpig	No461	Weavile
No327	Spinda	No464	Rhyperior
No335	Zangoose	No470	Leafeon
No336	Seviper	No471	Glaceon
No352	Kecleon	No473	Mamoswine
No359	Absol		

10 Amorphous group

No088	Grimer	No351	Castform
No089	Muk	No353	Shuppet
No092	Gastly	No354	Banette
No093	Haunter	No355	Duskull
No094	Gengar	No356	Dusclops
No109	Koffing	No358	Chimecho
No110	Weezing	No422	Shellos
No200	Misdreavus	No423	Gastrodon
No202	Wobbuffet	No425	Drifloon
No218	Slugma	No426	Drifblim
No219	Magcargo	No429	Mismagius
No280	Ralts	No442	Spiritomb
No281	Kirlia	No475	Gallade
No282	Gardevoir	No477	Dusknoir
No316	Gulpin	No479	Rotom
No317	Swalot		

11 Water group 1

No007	Squirtle	No117	Seadra
No008	Wartortle	No131	Lapras
No009	Blastoise	No138	Omanyte
No054	Psyduck	No139	Omastar
No055	Golduck	No140	Kabuto
No060	Poliwag	No141	Kabutops
No061	Poliwhirl	No147	Dratini
No062	Poliwrath	No148	Dragonair
No079	Slowpoke	No149	Dragonite
No080	Slowbro	No158	Totodile
No086	Seel	No159	Croconaw
No087	Dewgong	No160	Feraligatr
No116	Horsea	No183	Marill

Cont'd above ↗   Cont'd above ↗

11 Water group 1

No184	Azumarill	No342	Crawdaunt
No186	Politoed	No349	Feebas
No194	Wooper	No350	Milotic
No195	Quagsire	No363	Spheal
No199	Slowking	No364	Sealeo
No222	Corsola	No365	Walrein
No223	Remoraid	No366	Clamperl
No224	Octillery	No367	Huntail
No225	Delibird	No368	Gorebyss
No226	Mantine	No369	Relicanth
No230	Kingdra	No393	Piplup
No258	Mudkip	No394	Prinplup
No259	Marshtomp	No395	Empoleon
No260	Swampert	No399	Bidoof
No270	Lotad	No400	Bibarel
No271	Lombre	No418	Buizel
No272	Ludicolo	No419	Floatzel
No278	Wingull	No422	Shellos
No279	Pelipper	No423	Gastrodon
No283	Surskit	No489	Phione
No284	Masquerain	No490	Manaphy
No341	Corphish		

12 Water group 2

No118	Goldeen	No319	Sharpedo
No119	Seaking	No320	Wailmer
No129	Magikarp	No321	Wailord
No130	Gyarados	No339	Barboach
No170	Chinchou	No340	Whiscash
No171	Lanturn	No369	Relicanth
No211	Qwilfish	No370	Luvdisc
No223	Remoraid	No456	Finneon
No224	Octillery	No457	Lumineon
No318	Carvanha		

13 Water group 3

No072	Tentacool	No141	Kabutops
No073	Tentacruel	No222	Corsola
No090	Shellder	No341	Corphish
No091	Cloyster	No342	Crawdaunt
No098	Krabby	No345	Lileep
No099	Kingler	No346	Cradily
No120	Staryu	No347	Anorith
No121	Starmie	No348	Armaldo
No138	Omanyte	No451	Skorupi
No139	Omastar	No452	Drapion
No140	Kabuto		

14 Ditto group

No132	Ditto

15 No Egg found group

No030	Nidorina	No380	Latias
No031	Nidoqueen	No381	Latios
No144	Articuno	No382	Kyogre
No145	Zapdos	No383	Groudon
No146	Moltres	No384	Rayquaza
No150	Mewtwo	No385	Jirachi
No151	Mew	No386	Deoxys
No172	Pichu	No406	Budew
No173	Cleffa	No433	Chingling
No174	Igglybuff	No438	Bonsly
No175	Togepi	No439	Mime Jr.
No201	Unown	No440	Happiny
No236	Tyrogue	No446	Munchlax
No238	Smoochum	No447	Riolu
No239	Elekid	No458	Mantyke
No240	Magby	No480	Uxie
No243	Raikou	No481	Mesprit
No244	Entei	No482	Azelf
No245	Suicune	No483	Dialga
No249	Lugia	No484	Palkia
No250	Ho-Oh	No485	Heatran
No251	Celebi	No486	Regigigas
No298	Azurill	No487	Giratina
No360	Wynaut	No488	Cresselia
No377	Regirock	No491	Darkrai
No378	Regice	No492	Shaymin
No379	Registeel		

National Pokédex completion point

14 Acquire Pokémon through link trades

Use the link function to trade for Pokémon you're short on

There are some Pokémon that appear in *Pokémon Diamond* and *Pearl* but not in *Pokémon Platinum*. To get these, you can enlist the cooperation of your friends and family, and trade for them.

● Pokémon that appear only in *Diamond* and *Pearl*

Pokémon	Location
Clamperl	Fish on Route 219 in *Diamond/Pearl* (Super Rod)
Flygon	Level up Vibrava to Lv45 in *Diamond/Pearl*
Glameow	Catch on Route 218 in *Pearl*
Honchkrow	Use the Dusk Stone on Murkrow in *Diamond*
Misdreavus	Catch in Eterna Forest in *Pearl*
Mismagius	Use the Dusk Stone on Misdreavus in *Pearl*
Murkrow	Catch in Eterna Forest in *Diamond*
Purugly	Catch on Route 222 in *Pearl*
Skuntank	Catch on Route 221 in *Diamond*
Stunky	Catch on Route 206 in *Diamond*
Trapinch	Catch on Route 228 in *Diamond/Pearl* (Poké Radar)
Vibrava	Catch on Route 228 in *Diamond/Pearl* (Poké Radar)

Gotta get it!

You can trade for Legendary Pokémon too

Some Pokémon were distributed or given away to players of *Pokémon Diamond* and *Pokémon Pearl*; you can bring these over to *Pokémon Platinum* by link trading. There's no other way to acquire them through regular gameplay. Check the official Pokémon website for possible further announcements on how to acquire these Pokémon.

Mew
Receive in trade from Hayley in *My Pokémon Ranch* when you meet certain conditions.

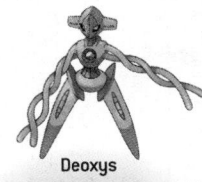

Deoxys
May be distributed via Mystery Gift at special events or selected retail locations.

Darkrai
Available for a limited time via a Special Mission in *Pokémon Ranger: Shadows of Almia*.

Shaymin
May be distributed via Mystery Gift at special events or selected retail locations.

Some Pokémon evolve when link traded

Some Pokémon evolve when you link trade them. Collect their pre-evolved forms and trade them with friends or family. Some among these need to be holding a certain item in order to evolve. They lose the item when they evolve.

● Pokémon that evolve when link traded

Pokémon	Conditions for evolving
Alakazam	Link trade Kadabra
Machamp	Link trade Machoke
Golem	Link trade Graveler
Gengar	Link trade Haunter
Politoed	Link trade Poliwhirl while it holds King's Rock
Slowking	Link trade Slowpoke while it holds King's Rock
Scizor	Link trade Scyther while it holds Metal Coat
Kingdra	Link trade Seadra while it holds Dragon Scale
Porygon2	Link trade Porygon while it holds Up-Grade
Huntail	Link trade Clamperl while it holds DeepSeaTooth
Gorebyss	Link trade Clamperl while it holds DeepSeaScale
Rhyperior	Link trade Rhydon while it holds Protector
Electivire	Link trade Electabuzz while it holds Electirizer
Magmortar	Link trade Magmar while it holds Magmarizer
Porygon-Z	Link trade Porygon2 while it holds Dubious Disc
Dusknoir	Link trade Dusclops while it holds Reaper Cloth

● Items that cause Pokémon link Evolution

King's Rock
Sometimes held by wild Poliwhirl

Metal Coat
Iron Ruins on Iron Island B3F

Dragon Scale
Sometimes held by wild Horsea and Seadra

Up-Grade
Galactic Eterna Bldg. 4F/Route 224

DeepSeaTooth
Sometimes held by wild Carvanha

DeepSeaScale
Sometimes held by wild Chinchou, Relicanth, etc.

Protector
Iron Island B1 (1)/Route 228

Electirizer
Sometimes held by wild Electabuzz

Magmarizer
Sometimes held by wild Magmar

Dubious Disc
Galactic Veilstone Bldg. 1F/Route 225

Reaper Cloth
Acuity Lakefront/Route 229

National Pokédex completion point

15 Use the dual slot to get Pokémon

Synch with a GBA Pokémon game to gain access to more Pokémon

After you get the National Pokédex, you can insert a GBA Pokémon cart into the Nintendo DS's GBA cartridge slot to introduce lots of Pokémon to *Pokémon Platinum* that didn't appear before. Catch them all and complete your National Pokédex.

Insert a GBA cart into your Nintendo DS

The five carts that work for this are *Pokémon Ruby, Sapphire, Emerald, FireRed*, and *LeafGreen*. Just insert the cart into the slot and the additional Pokémon will start to appear. If you don't have a cart, you can borrow one from a friend.

A wild SOLROCK appeared!

Insert *Pokémon Ruby*, for example, and you can encounter Solrock in the tall grass at Lake Verity, Lake Valor, and elsewhere.

● Cartridges to use in the dual slot

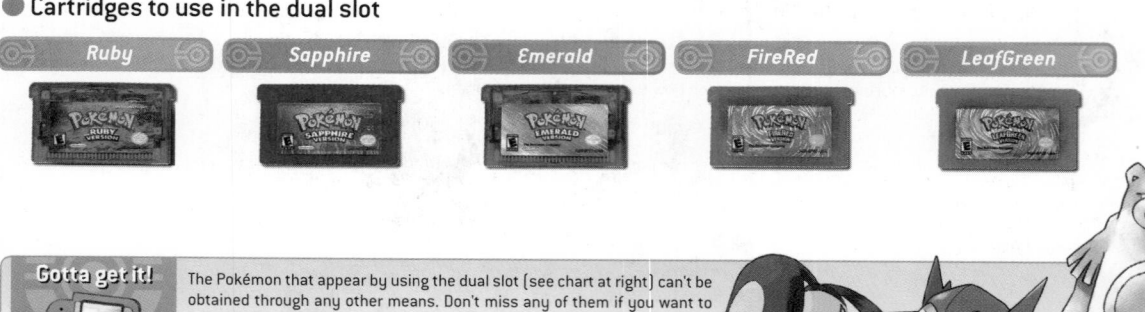

Ruby	Sapphire	Emerald	FireRed	LeafGreen

Gotta get it! The Pokémon that appear by using the dual slot (see chart at right) can't be obtained through any other means. Don't miss any of them if you want to complete your Pokédex.

● Pokémon that appear when you use the dual slot

Location	Ruby	Sapphire	Emerald	FireRed	LeafGreen
Eterna Forest	Seedot	—	Pineco	Caterpie Metapod	Weedle Kakuna
Mt. Coronet (middle)	Solrock	Lunatone	—	—	—
Great Marsh (throughout)	—	—	—	Arbok	—
Sendoff Spring	Solrock	Lunatone	—	—	—
Turnback Cave	Solrock	Lunatone	—	—	—
Wayward Cave	—	—	—	—	Sandshrew
Iron Island	Mawile	Sableye	—	—	—
Old Chateau (2F, 2nd room from the right)	Gengar	Gengar	Gengar	Gengar	Gengar
Lake Verity	Solrock	Lunatone	—	—	—
Lake Valor	Solrock	Lunatone	—	—	—
Lake Acuity	Solrock	Lunatone	Teddiursa	—	—
Acuity Lakefront	—	—	Ursaring	—	—
Route 201	—	—	—	Growlithe	—
Route 202	—	—	—	Growlithe	—
Route 203	Seedot	Lotad	Pineco	—	—
Route 204	Seedot	Lotad	Pineco	Caterpie	Weedle
Rotue 205 (Eterna City side)	—	Lotad	—	—	—
Route 208	Zangoose	Seviper	—	—	—
Route 209	—	—	—	—	Vulpix
Route 210 (Solaceon Town side)	Seedot Nuzleaf	—	Pineco	—	—
Route 210 (Celestic Town side)	Zangoose	Seviper	—	—	—
Route 211 (Eterna City side)	—	—	Teddiursa	—	—
Route 212 (Pastoria City side)	—	Lotad Lombre	—	Ekans	—
Route 214	—	—	—	—	Vulpix
Route 216	—	—	Ursaring	—	—
Route 217	—	—	Ursaring	—	—
Route 224	—	—	Shuckle	—	—
Route 228	—	—	—	—	Sandslash
Route 229	Nuzleaf	Lombre	Pineco	—	—

National Pokédex completion point 16

Get Pokémon at Pal Park

Transfer Pokémon from your GBA Pokémon games

Pal Park is a place set up so that you can transfer Pokémon you've caught in GBA Pokémon games to *Pokémon Platinum*. There are many rare and valuable Pokémon that you can only get by using this method, making it critical to completing your National Pokédex.

● Pokémon you can get by transferring to Pal Park

Pokémon	Version to transfer from		Pokémon	Version to transfer from
Bayleef	*Pokémon Emerald*		Lugia	*Pokémon FireRed/LeafGreen* *1
Blastoise	*Pokémon FireRed/LeafGreen*		Marshtomp	*Pokémon Ruby/Sapphire/Emerald*
Blaziken	*Pokémon Ruby/Sapphire/Emerald*		Meganium	*Pokémon Emerald*
Bulbasaur	*Pokémon FireRed/LeafGreen*		Mewtwo	*Pokémon FireRed/LeafGreen*
Celebi	*Any GBA Pokémon game* *2		Mudkip	*Pokémon Ruby/Sapphire/Emerald*
Charizard	*Pokémon FireRed/LeafGreen*		Quilava	*Pokémon Emerald*
Charmander	*Pokémon FireRed/LeafGreen*		Raikou	*Pokémon FireRed/LeafGreen*
Charmeleon	*Pokémon FireRed/LeafGreen*		Rayquaza	*Pokémon Ruby/Sapphire/Emerald*
Chikorita	*Pokémon Emerald*		Regice	*Pokémon Ruby/Sapphire/Emerald*
Combusken	*Pokémon Ruby/Sapphire/Emerald*		Regirock	*Pokémon Ruby/Sapphire/Emerald*
Croconaw	*Pokémon Emerald*		Registeel	*Pokémon Ruby/Sapphire/Emerald*
Cyndaquil	*Pokémon Emerald*		Sceptile	*Pokémon Ruby/Sapphire/Emerald*
Entei	*Pokémon FireRed/LeafGreen*		Squirtle	*Pokémon FireRed/LeafGreen*
Feraligatr	*Pokémon Emerald*		Suicune	*Pokémon FireRed/LeafGreen*
Groudon	*Pokémon Ruby/Emerald*		Swampert	*Pokémon Ruby/Sapphire/Emerald*
Grovyle	*Pokémon Ruby/Sapphire/Emerald*		Torchic	*Pokémon Ruby/Sapphire/Emerald*
Ho-Oh	*Pokémon FireRed/LeafGreen* *1		Totodile	*Pokémon Emerald*
Ivysaur	*Pokémon FireRed/LeafGreen*		Treecko	*Pokémon Ruby/Sapphire/Emerald*
Jirachi	*Pokémon Ruby/Sapphire* *2		Typhlosion	*Pokémon Emerald*
Kyogre	*Pokémon Sapphire/Emerald*		Venusaur	*Pokémon FireRed/LeafGreen*
Latias	*Pokémon Sapphire/Emerald*		Wartortle	*Pokémon FireRed/LeafGreen*
Latios	*Pokémon Ruby/Emerald*			

*1 Only available through distribution at special events, or by playing *Pokémon Colosseum* (Ho-Oh) and *Pokémon XD: Gale of Darkness* (Lugia) for the Nintendo GameCube and then transferring them to your GBA game.

*2 Only available through distribution at special events and not through regular gameplay. Check Pokémon.com for the latest news on how to catch these Pokémon.

 **Pal Park rules** **1** **Transfer 6 Pokémon at once from your GBA game**

You can use Pal Park once you get the National Pokédex upgrade from Professor Oak. The way it works is that you can transfer 6 Pokémon a day from any one cartridge. So if you have 5 carts, you can transfer 30 Pokémon a day to your *Pokémon Platinum* game. But you can't transfer the next 6 until you've caught all of the last 6 you transferred.

● **Main rules of Pal Park**

1	You can transfer 6 Pokémon a day (24 hours) from each cartridge
2	You can't transfer the next 6 Pokémon until you've caught all of the last batch you transferred
3	You cannot transfer Pokémon that know HMs or that are holding Mail
4	You cannot transfer Eggs
5	Once transferred to Pal Park, the Pokémon will cease to exist in the GBA game
6	Deoxys appears in the Forme it was in on the cartridge prior to transfer

 **Pal Park rules** **2** **Try for points as you catch your Pokémon**

When you sign up for the Capture Show, you're given 6 Park Balls. Park Balls capture Pokémon without fail. Pal Park is split into 5 main areas: forest, mountain, lake, tall grass, and sea. Each Pokémon appears in the area most appropriate to it. You get awarded more points in the Capture Show for catching rare Pokémon or completing your captures in a short period of time. Aim for a high score as you catch your Pokémon.

● **Point rules**

1	More points for rarer and more valuable Pokémon
2	Get points if all 6 Pokémon are different types
3	Get points when you catch a Pokémon of a different type from that of the last Pokémon you caught
4	More points for quicker captures

Pal Park Map

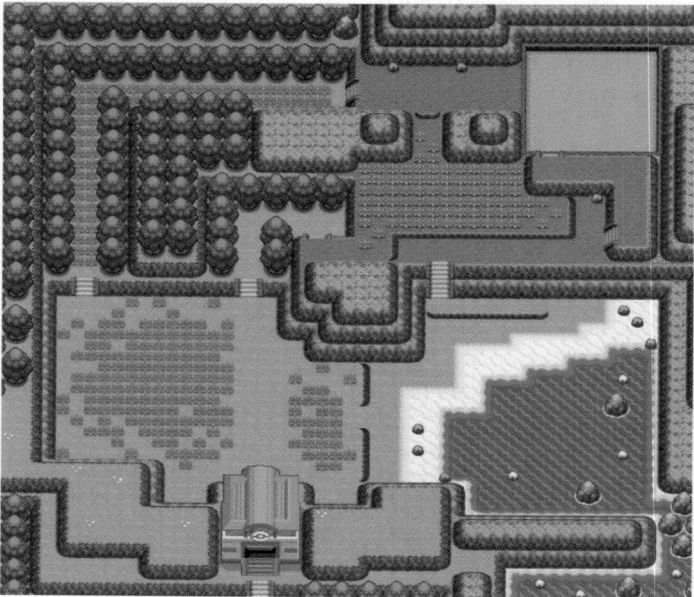

Get berries for points

You can get berries for the points you earn in the Pal Park Capture Show. The berries are as shown below.

~3000 points			3300~3499 points		
Cheri Berry	Chesto Berry	Pecha Berry	Razz Berry	Bluk Berry	Nanab Berry
Rawst Berry	Aspear Berry	Leppa Berry	Wepear Berry	Pinap Berry	Lum Berry
Oran Berry	Persim Berry	—	Sitrus Berry	—	—
3000~3299 points			**3500 points~**		
Figy Berry	Wiki Berry	Mago Berry	Pomeg Berry	Kelpsy Berry	Qualot Berry
Aguav Berry	Iapapa Berry	—	Hondew Berry	Grepa Berry	Tamato Berry

● **Area map**

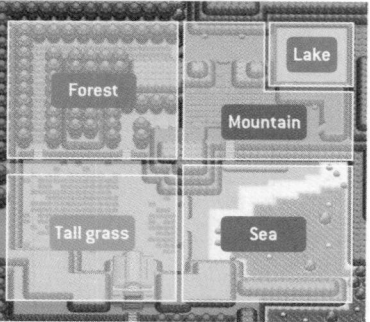

● Pokémon appearance patterns in Pal Park

No.	Pokémon	Location	Point Value	Freq.
1	Bulbasaur	Grass	Fairly low	O
2	Ivysaur	Grass	Fairly high	△
3	Venusaur	Grass	High	▲
4	Charmander	Grass	Fairly low	O
5	Charmeleon	Grass	Fairly high	△
6	Charizard	Grass	High	▲
7	Squirtle	Lake	Fairly low	O
8	Wartortle	Lake	Fairly high	△
9	Blastoise	Lake	High	▲
10	Caterpie	Forest	Low	◉
11	Metapod	Forest	Fairly low	O
12	Butterfree	Forest	Average	□
13	Weedle	Forest	Low	◉
14	Kakuna	Forest	Fairly low	O
15	Beedrill	Forest	Average	□
16	Pidgey	Grass	Low	◉
17	Pidgeotto	Grass	Fairly low	O
18	Pidgeot	Grass	Average	□
19	Rattata	Grass	Low	◉
20	Raticate	Grass	Fairly low	O
21	Spearow	Grass	Low	◉
22	Fearow	Grass	Fairly low	O
23	Ekans	Forest	Low	◉
24	Arbok	Forest	Fairly low	O
25	Pikachu	Forest	Fairly high	△
26	Raichu	Forest	High	▲
27	Sandshrew	Mountain	Fairly low	O
28	Sandslash	Mountain	Average	□
29	Nidoran♀	Grass	Low	◉
30	Nidorina	Grass	Fairly low	O
31	Nidoqueen	Grass	Average	□
32	Nidoran♂	Grass	Low	◉
33	Nidorino	Grass	Fairly low	O
34	Nidoking	Grass	Average	□
35	Clefairy	Mountain	Fairly high	△
36	Clefable	Mountain	High	▲
37	Vulpix	Grass	Average	□
38	Ninetales	Grass	Fairly high	△
39	Jigglypuff	Grass	Fairly high	△
40	Wigglytuff	Grass	High	▲
41	Zubat	Mountain	Low	◉
42	Golbat	Mountain	Fairly low	O
43	Oddish	Forest	Low	◉
44	Gloom	Forest	Fairly low	O
45	Vileplume	Forest	Average	□
46	Paras	Forest	Low	◉
47	Parasect	Forest	Fairly low	O
48	Venonat	Forest	Low	◉
49	Venomoth	Forest	Fairly low	O
50	Diglett	Mountain	Low	◉
51	Dugtrio	Mountain	Fairly low	O
52	Meowth	Grass	Fairly low	O
53	Persian	Grass	Average	□
54	Psyduck	Lake	Fairly low	O
55	Golduck	Lake	Average	□
56	Mankey	Mountain	Fairly low	O
57	Primeape	Mountain	Average	□
58	Growlithe	Grass	Average	□
59	Arcanine	Grass	Fairly high	△
60	Poliwag	Lake	Fairly low	O
61	Poliwhirl	Lake	Fairly high	△
62	Poliwrath	Lake	High	▲
63	Abra	Grass	Fairly low	O
64	Kadabra	Grass	Fairly high	△
65	Alakazam	Grass	High	▲
66	Machop	Mountain	Fairly low	O
67	Machoke	Mountain	Fairly high	△
68	Machamp	Mountain	High	▲
69	Bellsprout	Forest	Low	◉
70	Weepinbell	Forest	Fairly low	O
71	Victreebel	Forest	Average	□
72	Tentacool	Sea	Low	◉
73	Tentacruel	Sea	Fairly low	O
74	Geodude	Mountain	Low	◉
75	Graveler	Mountain	Fairly low	O
76	Golem	Mountain	Average	□
77	Ponyta	Grass	Fairly low	O
78	Rapidash	Grass	Average	□
79	Slowpoke	Lake	Fairly low	O
80	Slowbro	Lake	Average	□
81	Magnemite	Mountain	Fairly low	O
82	Magneton	Mountain	Average	□
83	Farfetch'd	Grass	Average	□
84	Doduo	Grass	Fairly low	O
85	Dodrio	Grass	Average	□
86	Seel	Sea	Fairly low	O
87	Dewgong	Sea	Average	□
88	Grimer	Grass	Fairly low	O
89	Muk	Grass	Average	□
90	Shellder	Sea	Fairly low	O
91	Cloyster	Sea	Average	□
92	Gastly	Forest	Fairly low	O
93	Haunter	Forest	Fairly high	△
94	Gengar	Forest	High	▲
95	Onix	Mountain	Fairly high	△
96	Drowzee	Forest	Fairly low	O
97	Hypno	Forest	Average	□
98	Krabby	Sea	Fairly low	O
99	Kingler	Sea	Average	□
100	Voltorb	Grass	Fairly low	O
101	Electrode	Grass	Average	□
102	Exeggcute	Forest	Fairly low	O
103	Exeggutor	Forest	Average	□
104	Cubone	Mountain	Fairly low	O
105	Marowak	Mountain	Average	□
106	Hitmonlee	Mountain	Fairly high	△
107	Hitmonchan	Mountain	Fairly high	△
108	Lickitung	Grass	Average	□
109	Koffing	Mountain	Fairly low	O
110	Weezing	Mountain	Average	□
111	Rhyhorn	Mountain	Fairly low	O
112	Rhydon	Mountain	Average	□
113	Chansey	Grass	High	▲
114	Tangela	Forest	Fairly low	O
115	Kangaskhan	Grass	Average	□
116	Horsea	Sea	Fairly low	O
117	Seadra	Sea	Average	□
118	Goldeen	Lake	Fairly low	O
119	Seaking	Lake	Average	□
120	Staryu	Sea	Fairly low	O
121	Starmie	Sea	Average	□
122	Mr. Mime	Grass	Average	□
123	Scyther	Grass	Average	□
124	Jynx	Grass	Average	□
125	Electabuzz	Mountain	Average	□
126	Magmar	Mountain	Average	□
127	Pinsir	Forest	Average	□
128	Tauros	Grass	Average	□
129	Magikarp	Lake	Low	◉
130	Gyarados	Lake	High	▲
131	Lapras	Sea	High	▲
132	Ditto	Grass	Average	□
133	Eevee	Grass	High	▲
134	Vaporeon	Grass	High	▲
135	Jolteon	Grass	High	▲
136	Flareon	Grass	High	▲
137	Porygon	Grass	Fairly high	△
138	Omanyte	Sea	Fairly low	O
139	Omastar	Sea	Average	□
140	Kabuto	Sea	Fairly low	O
141	Kabutops	Sea	Average	□
142	Aerodactyl	Mountain	Average	□
143	Snorlax	Grass	Fairly high	△
144	Articuno	Mountain	High	▲
145	Zapdos	Mountain	High	▲
146	Moltres	Mountain	High	▲
147	Dratini	Lake	Average	□
148	Dragonair	Lake	Fairly high	△
149	Dragonite	Mountain	High	▲
150	Mewtwo	Grass	High	▲
151	Mew	Forest	Very high	★
152	Chikorita	Grass	Fairly low	O
153	Bayleef	Grass	Fairly high	△
154	Meganium	Grass	High	▲
155	Cyndaquil	Grass	Fairly low	O
156	Quilava	Grass	Fairly high	△
157	Typhlosion	Grass	High	▲
158	Totodile	Lake	Fairly low	O
159	Croconaw	Lake	Fairly high	△
160	Feraligatr	Mountain	High	▲
161	Sentret	Grass	Low	◉
162	Furret	Grass	Fairly low	O
163	Hoothoot	Forest	Low	◉
164	Noctowl	Forest	Fairly low	O
165	Ledyba	Grass	Low	◉
166	Ledian	Grass	Fairly low	O
167	Spinarak	Grass	Low	◉
168	Ariados	Grass	Fairly low	O
169	Crobat	Mountain	High	▲
170	Chinchou	Sea	Fairly low	O
171	Lanturn	Sea	Average	□
172	Pichu	Grass	Fairly high	△
173	Cleffa	Grass	Fairly high	△
174	Igglybuff	Grass	Fairly high	△
175	Togepi	Grass	Fairly high	△
176	Togetic	Grass	High	▲
177	Natu	Forest	Fairly low	O
178	Xatu	Forest	Average	□
179	Mareep	Grass	Fairly low	O
180	Flaaffy	Grass	Average	□
181	Ampharos	Grass	Fairly high	△
182	Bellossom	Forest	Fairly high	△
183	Marill	Lake	Fairly low	O
184	Azumarill	Lake	Average	□
185	Sudowoodo	Mountain	Average	□
186	Politoed	Lake	Fairly high	△
187	Hoppip	Grass	Fairly low	O
188	Skiploom	Grass	Average	□

◉ ...Extremely common　O ...Common　□ ...Average　△ ...Uncommon　▲ ...Rare　★ ...Extremely rare

NATIONAL POKÉDEX

COMPLETE THE NATIONAL POKÉDEX

391

No.	Pokémon	Location	Point Value	Freq.	No.	Pokémon	Location	Point Value	Freq.
189	Jumpluff	Grass	Fairly high	△	288	Vigoroth	Forest	Average	□
190	Aipom	Forest	Average	□	289	Slaking	Forest	Fairly high	△
191	Sunkern	Grass	Fairly low	○	290	Nincada	Forest	Fairly low	○
192	Sunflora	Grass	Average	□	291	Ninjask	Forest	Average	□
193	Yanma	Grass	Fairly high	△	292	Shedinja	Forest	Fairly high	△
194	Wooper	Lake	Fairly low	○	293	Whismur	Mountain	Fairly low	○
195	Quagsire	Lake	Average	□	294	Loudred	Mountain	Average	□
196	Espeon	Grass	High	▲	295	Exploud	Mountain	Fairly high	△
197	Umbreon	Grass	High	▲	296	Makuhita	Mountain	Fairly low	○
198	Murkrow	Forest	Average	□	297	Hariyama	Mountain	Average	□
199	Slowking	Lake	Fairly high	△	298	Azurill	Mountain/Lake	Fairly high	△
200	Misdreavus	Forest	Average	□	299	Nosepass	Mountain	Average	□
201	Unown	Forest	Average	□	300	Skitty	Grass	Fairly low	○
202	Wobbuffet	Grass	Fairly high	△	301	Delcatty	Grass	Average	□
203	Girafarig	Grass	Average	□	302	Sableye	Mountain	Average	□
204	Pineco	Forest	Fairly low	○	303	Mawile	Mountain	Average	□
205	Forretress	Forest	Average	□	304	Aron	Mountain	Average	□
206	Dunsparce	Forest	High	▲	305	Lairon	Mountain	Average	□
207	Gligar	Mountain	Fairly low	○	306	Aggron	Mountain	Fairly high	△
208	Steelix	Mountain	High	▲	307	Meditite	Mountain	Fairly low	○
209	Snubbull	Grass	Fairly low	○	308	Medicham	Mountain	Average	□
210	Granbull	Grass	Average	□	309	Electrike	Grass	Fairly low	○
211	Qwilfish	Sea	Fairly high	△	310	Manectric	Grass	Average	□
212	Scizor	Grass	High	▲	311	Plusle	Grass	High	▲
213	Shuckle	Sea	Fairly high	△	312	Minun	Grass	High	▲
214	Heracross	Forest	Fairly high	△	313	Volbeat	Mountain	Average	□
215	Sneasel	Mountain	Fairly low	○	314	Illumise	Mountain	Average	□
216	Teddiursa	Forest	Fairly low	○	315	Roselia	Grass	Average	□
217	Ursaring	Forest	Average	□	316	Gulpin	Forest	Fairly low	○
218	Slugma	Mountain	Fairly low	○	317	Swalot	Forest	Average	□
219	Magcargo	Mountain	Average	□	318	Carvanha	Sea	Fairly low	○
220	Swinub	Mountain	Fairly low	○	319	Sharpedo	Sea	Average	□
221	Piloswine	Mountain	Average	□	320	Wailmer	Sea	Fairly low	○
222	Corsola	Sea	Average	□	321	Wailord	Sea	Fairly high	△
223	Remoraid	Sea	Fairly low	○	322	Numel	Mountain	Fairly low	○
224	Octillery	Sea	Average	□	323	Camerupt	Mountain	Average	□
225	Delibird	Mountain	Average	□	324	Torkoal	Mountain	Average	□
226	Mantine	Sea	Average	□	325	Spoink	Grass	Fairly low	○
227	Skarmory	Mountain	Average	□	326	Grumpig	Grass	Average	□
228	Houndour	Mountain	Fairly low	○	327	Spinda	Grass	Fairly low	○
229	Houndoom	Mountain	Average	□	328	Trapinch	Mountain	Fairly low	○
230	Kingdra	Sea	Fairly high	△	329	Vibrava	Mountain	Average	□
231	Phanpy	Mountain	Fairly low	○	330	Flygon	Mountain	Fairly high	△
232	Donphan	Mountain	Average	□	331	Cacnea	Mountain	Fairly low	○
233	Porygon2	Grass	Fairly high	△	332	Cacturne	Mountain	Average	□
234	Stantler	Grass	Fairly low	○	333	Swablu	Grass	Fairly low	○
235	Smeargle	Grass	Fairly high	△	334	Altaria	Grass	Fairly high	△
236	Tyrogue	Mountain	Fairly high	△	335	Zangoose	Grass	Average	□
237	Hitmontop	Mountain	Fairly high	△	336	Seviper	Forest	Average	□
238	Smoochum	Grass	Fairly high	△	337	Lunatone	Mountain	Average	□
239	Elekid	Mountain	Fairly high	△	338	Solrock	Mountain	Average	□
240	Magby	Mountain	Fairly high	△	339	Barboach	Mountain/Lake	Fairly low	○
241	Miltank	Grass	Average	□	340	Whiscash	Mountain/Lake	Average	□
242	Blissey	Grass	High	▲	341	Corphish	Mountain/Lake	Fairly low	○
243	Raikou	Mountain	High	▲	342	Crawdaunt	Mountain/Lake	Average	□
244	Entei	Mountain	High	▲	343	Baltoy	Mountain	Fairly low	○
245	Suicune	Mountain	High	▲	344	Claydol	Mountain	Average	□
246	Larvitar	Mountain	Average	□	345	Lileep	Sea	Average	□
247	Pupitar	Mountain	Fairly high	△	346	Cradily	Sea	Fairly high	△
248	Tyranitar	Mountain	High	▲	347	Anorith	Sea	Average	□
249	Lugia	Mountain	High	▲	348	Armaldo	Sea	Fairly high	△
250	Ho-Oh	Mountain	High	▲	349	Feebas	Sea	Average	□
251	Celebi	Forest	Very high	★	350	Milotic	Sea	High	▲
252	Treecko	Forest	Fairly low	○	351	Castform	Grass	Fairly high	△
253	Grovyle	Forest	Fairly high	△	352	Kecleon	Forest	Average	□
254	Sceptile	Forest	High	▲	353	Shuppet	Forest	Fairly low	○
255	Torchic	Grass	Fairly low	○	354	Banette	Forest	Average	□
256	Combusken	Grass	Fairly high	△	355	Duskull	Forest	Fairly low	○
257	Blaziken	Grass	High	▲	356	Dusclops	Forest	Average	□
258	Mudkip	Lake	Fairly low	○	357	Tropius	Forest	Average	□
259	Marshtomp	Lake	Fairly high	△	358	Chimecho	Mountain	Fairly high	△
260	Swampert	Lake	High	▲	359	Absol	Mountain	Fairly high	△
261	Poochyena	Grass	Low	◉	360	Wynaut	Grass	Fairly high	△
262	Mightyena	Grass	Fairly low	○	361	Snorunt	Mountain	Fairly low	○
263	Zigzagoon	Grass	Low	◉	362	Glalie	Mountain	Average	□
264	Linoone	Grass	Fairly low	○	363	Spheal	Sea	Fairly low	○
265	Wurmple	Forest	Low	◉	364	Sealeo	Sea	Average	□
266	Silcoon	Forest	Fairly low	○	365	Walrein	Sea	Fairly high	△
267	Beautifly	Forest	Average	□	366	Clamperl	Sea	Fairly low	○
268	Cascoon	Forest	Fairly low	○	367	Huntail	Sea	Fairly high	△
269	Dustox	Forest	Average	□	368	Gorebyss	Sea	Fairly high	△
270	Lotad	Lake	Low	◉	369	Relicanth	Sea	Fairly high	△
271	Lombre	Lake	Fairly low	○	370	Luvdisc	Sea	Fairly low	○
272	Ludicolo	Lake	Fairly high	△	371	Bagon	Mountain	Fairly low	○
273	Seedot	Forest	Low	◉	372	Shelgon	Mountain	Average	□
274	Nuzleaf	Forest	Fairly low	○	373	Salamence	Mountain	Fairly high	△
275	Shiftry	Forest	Fairly high	△	374	Beldum	Mountain	Average	□
276	Taillow	Grass	Low	◉	375	Metang	Mountain	Fairly high	△
277	Swellow	Grass	Fairly low	○	376	Metagross	Mountain	High	▲
278	Wingull	Sea	Low	◉	377	Regirock	Mountain	High	▲
279	Pelipper	Sea	Fairly low	○	378	Regice	Mountain	High	▲
280	Ralts	Grass	Fairly low	○	379	Registeel	Mountain	High	▲
281	Kirlia	Grass	Average	□	380	Latias	Grass	High	▲
282	Gardevoir	Grass	Fairly high	△	381	Latios	Grass	High	▲
283	Surskit	Lake	Fairly low	○	382	Kyogre	Sea	High	▲
284	Masquerain	Lake	Average	□	383	Groudon	Mountain	High	▲
285	Shroomish	Forest	Fairly low	○	384	Rayquaza	Grass	High	▲
286	Breloom	Forest	Average	□	385	Jirachi	Mountain	Very high	★
287	Slakoth	Forest	Fairly low	○	386	Deoxys	Mountain	Very high	★

◉...Extremely common ○....Common □...Average △...Uncommon ▲...Rare ★...Extremely rare

17

Catch wandering Pokémon

Seek out Pokémon flying around the routes and waterways

Zapdos, Moltres, Articuno, Mesprit, and Cresselia never stick around in one spot. Rather, they're in constant flight around the Sinnoh routes and waterways. You can see their locations displayed on the Marking Map. Approach carefully and catch them.

They flee instantly when discovered

Use moves like Mean Look and Block, or Abilities like Shadow Tag, to prevent them from fleeing.

The Marking Map shows their locations

The Marking Map shows the up-to-the-minute locations of these 5 Pokémon. Always check it when you're looking for them.

● Traits of wandering Pokémon

1 Current location is displayed on the Marking Map

2 Each Pokémon may appear in the grass or on the water's surface (but not in caves)

3 They fly away if you approach them using Fly

4 They move slightly when you enter a different town or cave

5 Each Pokémon may abruptly fly a great distance

6 Each Pokémon tries to flee as soon as you encounter it

How to read the National Pokédex

Pokémon Platinum Official Strategy Guide

Basic data

1 Pokémon type

The Pokémon's type. Some Pokémon have two types.

2 Evolution path

The conditions and results of a Pokémon's Evolution.

3 Ability

The Pokémon's Ability. Sometimes two Abilities are listed; an individual Pokémon in your game may have either one.

4 Stats compiled by the editors

The Pokémon's stats. More dots in any one stat means that the Pokémon builds up that stat more readily. The dots are a relative measurement across all the Pokémon in the National Pokédex. The maximum is 5 dots.

5 Moves learned by leveling up

A list of the moves the Pokémon learns upon leveling up. Moves listed in blue differ from those in *Diamond/Pearl*.

6 Main way to get

Main way to get the Pokémon in each Pokémon game version. If the Pokémon appears in the GBA Pokémon games and can be transferred to *Pokémon Platinum* through Pal Park, shows which GBA game the Pokémon can be acquired in.

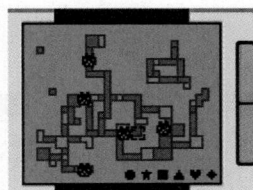
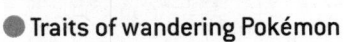

Move legend

Lv	The level at which the move is learned
Type	Move type
Kind	Whether the move is a physical, special, or status move
Power	Attack power
Acc	Accuracy
PP	# of times you can use the move
Range	How many Pokémon the move affects at once
DA (Direct Attack)	Whether the user physically touches the target
DoM	Depends on move

Bulbasaur

National Pokédex No. 001 Seed Pokémon

GRASS　POISON

STATS
HP ●
ATTACK ●●
DEFENSE ●●
SP.ATTACK ●●●
SP.DEFENSE ●●●
SPEED ●●

● M/F have same form

EVOLUTION PATH

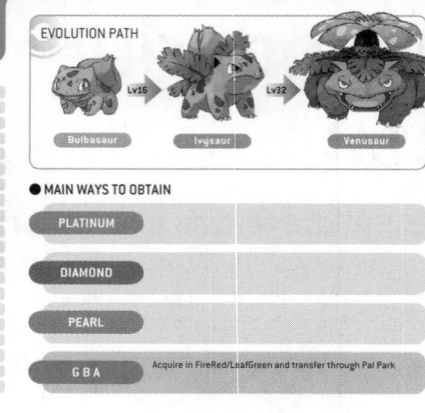

Bulbasaur → Lv16 → Ivysaur → Lv32 → Venusaur

MAIN WAYS TO OBTAIN

PLATINUM

DIAMOND

PEARL

GBA — Acquire in FireRed/LeafGreen and transfer through Pal Park

ABILITY ● Overgrow

● LEVEL-UP AND LEARNED MOVES

Lv	Name	Type	Kind	Power	Acc	PP	Range	DA
Base	Tackle	Normal	Physical	35	95	35	Normal	●
3	Growl	Normal	Status	—	100	40	2 foes	—
7	Leech Seed	Grass	Status	—	90	10	Normal	—
9	Vine Whip	Grass	Physical	35	100	15	Normal	●
13	PoisonPowder	Poison	Status	—	75	35	Normal	—
13	Sleep Powder	Grass	Status	—	75	15	Normal	—
15	Take Down	Normal	Physical	90	85	20	Normal	●
19	Razor Leaf	Grass	Physical	55	95	25	2 foes	—
21	Sweet Scent	Normal	Status	—	100	20	2 foes	—
25	Growth	Normal	Status	—	—	40	Self	—
27	Double-Edge	Normal	Physical	120	100	15	Normal	●
31	Worry Seed	Grass	Status	—	100	10	Normal	—
33	Synthesis	Grass	Status	—	—	5	Self	—
37	Seed Bomb	Grass	Physical	80	100	15	Normal	—

Ivysaur

National Pokédex No. 002 Seed Pokémon

GRASS　POISON

STATS
HP ●●
ATTACK ●●●
DEFENSE ●●●
SP.ATTACK ●●●
SP.DEFENSE ●●●
SPEED ●●

● M/F have same form

EVOLUTION PATH

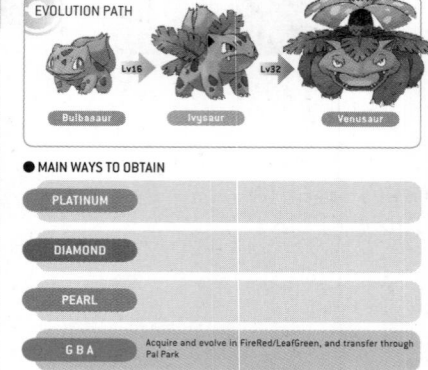

Bulbasaur → Lv16 → Ivysaur → Lv32 → Venusaur

MAIN WAYS TO OBTAIN

PLATINUM

DIAMOND

PEARL

GBA — Acquire and evolve in FireRed/LeafGreen, and transfer through Pal Park

ABILITY ● Overgrow

● LEVEL-UP AND LEARNED MOVES

Lv	Name	Type	Kind	Power	Acc	PP	Range	DA
Base	Tackle	Normal	Physical	35	95	35	Normal	●
Base	Growl	Normal	Status	—	100	40	2 foes	—
Base	Leech Seed	Grass	Status	—	90	10	Normal	—
3	Growl	Normal	Status	—	100	40	2 foes	—
7	Leech Seed	Grass	Status	—	90	10	Normal	—
9	Vine Whip	Grass	Physical	35	100	15	Normal	—
13	PoisonPowder	Poison	Status	—	75	35	Normal	—
13	Sleep Powder	Grass	Status	—	75	15	Normal	—
15	Take Down	Normal	Physical	90	85	20	Normal	—
20	Razor Leaf	Grass	Physical	55	95	25	2 foes	—
23	Sweet Scent	Normal	Status	—	100	20	2 foes	—
28	Growth	Normal	Status	—	—	40	Self	—
31	Double-Edge	Normal	Physical	120	100	15	Normal	—
36	Worry Seed	Grass	Status	—	100	10	Normal	—
39	Synthesis	Grass	Status	—	—	5	Self	—
44	SolarBeam	Grass	Special	120	100	10	Normal	—

Venusaur

National Pokédex No. 003 Seed Pokémon

GRASS　POISON

STATS
HP ●●●
ATTACK ●●●
DEFENSE ●●●
SP.ATTACK ●●●●
SP.DEFENSE ●●●●
SPEED ●●●

● Male form　　● Female form

EVOLUTION PATH

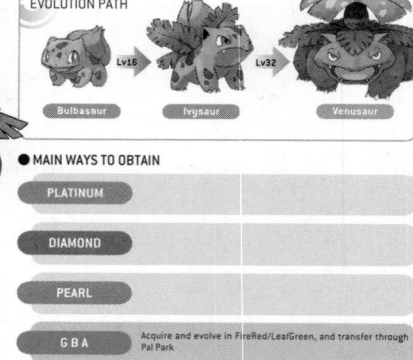

Bulbasaur → Lv16 → Ivysaur → Lv32 → Venusaur

MAIN WAYS TO OBTAIN

PLATINUM

DIAMOND

PEARL

GBA — Acquire and evolve in FireRed/LeafGreen, and transfer through Pal Park

ABILITY ● Overgrow

● LEVEL-UP AND LEARNED MOVES

Lv	Name	Type	Kind	Power	Acc	PP	Range	DA
Base	Tackle	Normal	Physical	35	95	35	Normal	●
Base	Growl	Normal	Status	—	100	40	2 foes	—
Base	Leech Seed	Grass	Status	—	90	10	Normal	—
Base	Vine Whip	Grass	Physical	35	100	15	Normal	●
3	Growl	Normal	Status	—	100	40	2 foes	—
7	Leech Seed	Grass	Status	—	90	10	Normal	—
9	Vine Whip	Grass	Physical	35	100	15	Normal	—
13	PoisonPowder	Poison	Status	—	75	35	Normal	—
13	Sleep Powder	Grass	Status	—	75	15	Normal	—
15	Take Down	Normal	Physical	90	85	20	Normal	—
20	Razor Leaf	Grass	Physical	55	95	25	2 foes	—
23	Sweet Scent	Normal	Status	—	100	20	2 foes	—
28	Growth	Normal	Status	—	—	40	Self	—
31	Double-Edge	Normal	Physical	120	100	15	Normal	—
32	Petal Dance	Grass	Special	90	100	20	1 Random	—
39	Worry Seed	Grass	Status	—	100	10	Normal	—
45	Synthesis	Grass	Status	—	—	5	Self	—
53	SolarBeam	Grass	Special	120	100	10	Normal	—

Charmander

National Pokédex No. 004 Lizard Pokémon

FIRE

STATS
HP ●
ATTACK ●●
DEFENSE ●●
SP.ATTACK ●●
SP.DEFENSE ●●
SPEED ●●●

● M/F have same form

EVOLUTION PATH

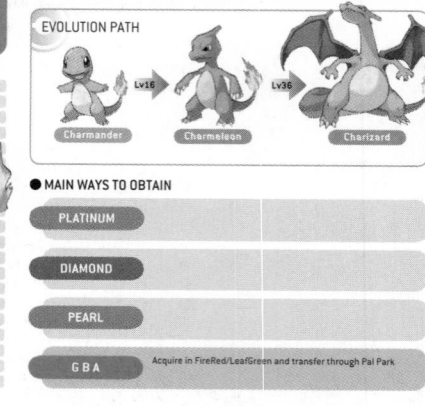

Charmander → Lv16 → Charmeleon → Lv36 → Charizard

MAIN WAYS TO OBTAIN

PLATINUM

DIAMOND

PEARL

GBA — Acquire in FireRed/LeafGreen and transfer through Pal Park

ABILITY ● Blaze

● LEVEL-UP AND LEARNED MOVES

Lv	Name	Type	Kind	Power	Acc	PP	Range	DA
Base	Scratch	Normal	Physical	40	100	35	Normal	●
Base	Growl	Normal	Status	—	100	40	2 foes	—
7	Ember	Fire	Special	40	100	25	Normal	—
10	SmokeScreen	Normal	Status	—	100	20	Normal	—
16	Dragon Rage	Dragon	Special	—	100	10	Normal	—
19	Scary Face	Normal	Status	—	90	10	Normal	—
25	Fire Fang	Fire	Physical	65	95	15	Normal	—
28	Slash	Normal	Physical	70	100	20	Normal	—
34	Flamethrower	Fire	Special	95	100	15	Normal	—
37	Fire Spin	Fire	Special	15	70	15	Normal	—

National Pokédex No. 005 Flame Pokémon
Charmeleon

FIRE

STATS
- HP ●●
- ATTACK ●●●
- DEFENSE ●●●
- SP. ATTACK ●●●
- SP. DEFENSE ●●●
- SPEED ●●●

● M/F have same form

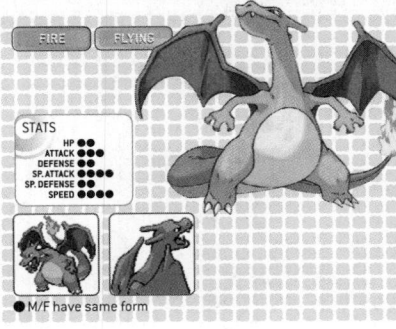

EVOLUTION PATH

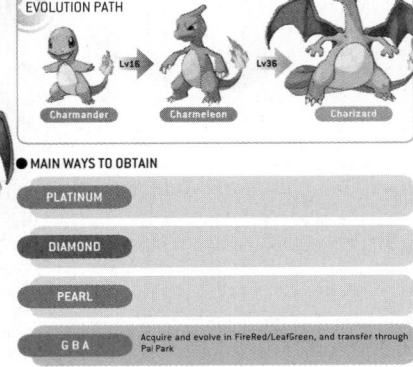

Charmander → Lv16 → Charmeleon → Lv36 → Charizard

● MAIN WAYS TO OBTAIN

PLATINUM

DIAMOND

PEARL

GBA — Acquire and evolve in FireRed/LeafGreen, and transfer through Pal Park

ABILITY ● Blaze

● LEVEL-UP AND LEARNED MOVES

Lv	Name	Type	Kind	Power	Acc	PP	Range	DA
Base	Scratch	Normal	Physical	40	100	35	Normal	●
Base	Growl	Normal	Status	—	100	40	2 foes	—
Base	Ember	Fire	Special	40	100	25	Normal	—
7	Ember	Fire	Special	40	100	25	Normal	—
10	SmokeScreen	Normal	Status	—	100	20	Normal	—
17	Dragon Rage	Dragon	Special	—	100	10	Normal	—
21	Scary Face	Normal	Status	—	90	10	Normal	—
28	Fire Fang	Fire	Physical	65	95	15	Normal	●
32	Slash	Normal	Physical	70	100	20	Normal	●
39	Flamethrower	Fire	Special	95	100	15	Normal	—
43	Fire Spin	Fire	Special	15	70	15	Normal	—

National Pokédex No. 006 Flame Pokémon
Charizard

FIRE FLYING

STATS
- HP ●●
- ATTACK ●●●
- DEFENSE ●●●
- SP. ATTACK ●●●●
- SP. DEFENSE ●●●
- SPEED ●●●●

● M/F have same form

EVOLUTION PATH

Charmander → Lv16 → Charmeleon → Lv36 → Charizard

● MAIN WAYS TO OBTAIN

PLATINUM

DIAMOND

PEARL

GBA — Acquire and evolve in FireRed/LeafGreen, and transfer through Pal Park

ABILITY ● Blaze

● LEVEL-UP AND LEARNED MOVES

Lv	Name	Type	Kind	Power	Acc	PP	Range	DA
Base	Dragon Claw	Dragon	Physical	80	100	15	Normal	●
Base	Shadow Claw	Ghost	Physical	70	100	15	Normal	●
Base	Air Slash	Flying	Special	75	95	20	Normal	—
Base	Scratch	Normal	Physical	40	100	35	Normal	●
Base	Growl	Normal	Status	—	100	40	2 foes	—
Base	Ember	Fire	Special	40	100	25	Normal	—
Base	SmokeScreen	Normal	Status	—	100	20	Normal	—
7	Ember	Fire	Special	40	100	25	Normal	—
10	SmokeScreen	Normal	Status	—	100	20	Normal	—
17	Dragon Rage	Dragon	Special	—	100	10	Normal	—
21	Scary Face	Normal	Status	—	90	10	Normal	—
28	Fire Fang	Fire	Physical	65	95	15	Normal	●
32	Slash	Normal	Physical	70	100	20	Normal	●
36	Wing Attack	Flying	Physical	60	100	35	Normal	●
42	Flamethrower	Fire	Special	95	100	15	Normal	—
49	Fire Spin	Fire	Special	15	70	15	Normal	—
59	Heat Wave	Fire	Special	100	90	10	2 foes	—
66	Flare Blitz	Fire	Physical	120	100	15	Normal	●

National Pokédex No. 007 Tiny Turtle Pokémon
Squirtle

WATER

STATS
- HP ●●
- ATTACK ●●
- DEFENSE ●●●
- SP. ATTACK ●●
- SP. DEFENSE ●●
- SPEED ●●

● M/F have same form

EVOLUTION PATH

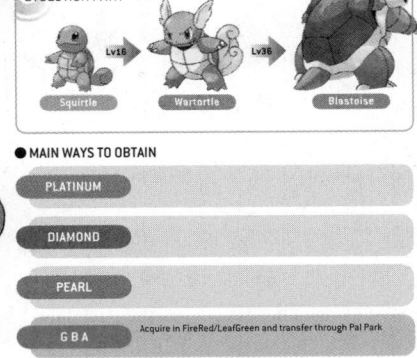

Squirtle → Lv16 → Wartortle → Lv36 → Blastoise

● MAIN WAYS TO OBTAIN

PLATINUM

DIAMOND

PEARL

GBA — Acquire in FireRed/LeafGreen and transfer through Pal Park

ABILITY ● Torrent

● LEVEL-UP AND LEARNED MOVES

Lv	Name	Type	Kind	Power	Acc	PP	Range	DA
Base	Tackle	Normal	Physical	35	95	35	Normal	●
4	Tail Whip	Normal	Status	—	100	30	2 foes	—
7	Bubble	Water	Special	20	100	30	2 foes	—
10	Withdraw	Water	Status	—	—	40	Self	—
13	Water Gun	Water	Special	40	100	25	Normal	—
16	Bite	Dark	Physical	60	100	25	Normal	●
19	Rapid Spin	Normal	Physical	20	100	40	Normal	●
22	Protect	Normal	Status	—	—	10	Self	—
25	Water Pulse	Water	Special	60	100	20	Normal	—
28	Aqua Tail	Water	Physical	90	90	10	Normal	●
31	Skull Bash	Normal	Physical	100	100	15	Normal	●
34	Iron Defense	Steel	Status	—	—	15	Self	—
37	Rain Dance	Water	Status	—	—	5	All	—
40	Hydro Pump	Water	Special	120	80	5	Normal	—

National Pokédex No. 008 Turtle Pokémon
Wartortle

WATER

STATS
- HP ●●
- ATTACK ●●●
- DEFENSE ●●●
- SP. ATTACK ●●●
- SP. DEFENSE ●●●
- SPEED ●●

● M/F have same form

EVOLUTION PATH

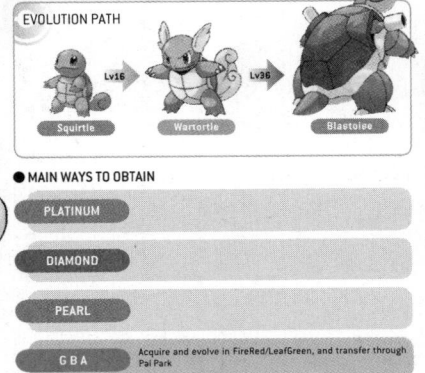

Squirtle → Lv16 → Wartortle → Lv36 → Blastoise

● MAIN WAYS TO OBTAIN

PLATINUM

DIAMOND

PEARL

GBA — Acquire and evolve in FireRed/LeafGreen, and transfer through Pal Park

ABILITY ● Torrent

● LEVEL-UP AND LEARNED MOVES

Lv	Name	Type	Kind	Power	Acc	PP	Range	DA
Base	Tackle	Normal	Physical	35	95	35	Normal	●
Base	Tail Whip	Normal	Status	—	100	30	2 foes	—
Base	Bubble	Water	Special	20	100	30	2 foes	—
4	Tail Whip	Normal	Status	—	100	30	2 foes	—
7	Bubble	Water	Special	20	100	30	2 foes	—
10	Withdraw	Water	Status	—	—	40	Self	—
13	Water Gun	Water	Special	40	100	25	Normal	—
16	Bite	Dark	Physical	60	100	25	Normal	●
20	Rapid Spin	Normal	Physical	20	100	40	Normal	●
24	Protect	Normal	Status	—	—	10	Self	—
28	Water Pulse	Water	Special	60	100	20	Normal	—
32	Aqua Tail	Water	Physical	90	90	10	Normal	●
36	Skull Bash	Normal	Physical	100	100	15	Normal	●
40	Iron Defense	Steel	Status	—	—	15	Self	—
44	Rain Dance	Water	Status	—	—	5	All	—
48	Hydro Pump	Water	Special	120	80	5	Normal	—

008
WARTORTLE

Blastoise

National Pokédex No. 009 — Shellfish Pokémon

WATER

STATS
- HP ●●
- ATTACK ●●●
- DEFENSE ●●●
- SP.ATTACK ●●●●
- SP.DEFENSE ●●●●
- SPEED ●●●

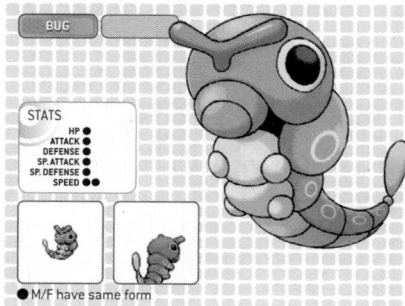

● M/F have same form

EVOLUTION PATH

Squirtle → Lv16 → Wartortle → Lv36 → Blastoise

● MAIN WAYS TO OBTAIN

PLATINUM	
DIAMOND	
PEARL	
GBA	Acquire and evolve in FireRed/LeafGreen, and transfer through Pal Park

ABILITY ● Torrent

● LEVEL-UP AND LEARNED MOVES

Lv	Name	Type	Kind	Power	Acc	PP	Range	DA
Base	Flash Cannon	Steel	Special	80	100	10	Normal	
Base	Tackle	Normal	Physical	35	95	35	Normal	
Base	Tail Whip	Normal	Status	—	100	30	2 foes	
Base	Bubble	Water	Special	20	100	30	2 foes	
Base	Withdraw	Water	Status	—	—	40	Self	
4	Tail Whip	Normal	Status	—	100	30	2 foes	
7	Bubble	Water	Special	20	100	30	2 foes	
10	Withdraw	Water	Status	—	—	40	Self	
13	Water Gun	Water	Special	40	100	25	Normal	
16	Bite	Dark	Physical	60	100	25	Normal	•
20	Rapid Spin	Normal	Physical	20	100	40	Normal	•
24	Protect	Normal	Status	—	—	10	Self	
28	Water Pulse	Water	Special	60	100	20	Normal	•
32	Aqua Tail	Water	Physical	90	90	10	Normal	•
39	Skull Bash	Normal	Physical	100	100	15	Normal	•
46	Iron Defense	Steel	Status	—	—	15	Self	
53	Rain Dance	Water	Status	—	—	5	All	
60	Hydro Pump	Water	Special	120	80	5	Normal	

Caterpie

National Pokédex No. 010 — Worm Pokémon

BUG

STATS
- HP ●●
- ATTACK ●
- DEFENSE ●
- SP.ATTACK ●
- SP.DEFENSE ●
- SPEED ●●

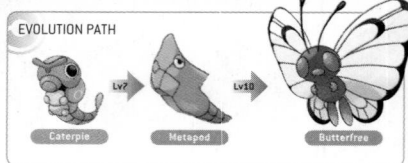

● M/F have same form

EVOLUTION PATH

Caterpie → Lv7 → Metapod → Lv10 → Butterfree

● MAIN WAYS TO OBTAIN

PLATINUM	Route 204(after you get the National Pokédex, insert a Pokémon FireRed cartridge into the Nintendo DS's GBA cartridge slot)
DIAMOND	Jubilife City side of Route 204 (after you get the National Pokédex, insert a Pokémon FireRed cartridge into the Nintendo DS's GBA cartridge slot)
PEARL	Jubilife City side of Route 204 (after you get the National Pokédex, insert a Pokémon FireRed cartridge into the Nintendo DS's GBA cartridge slot)
GBA	Catch in FireRed/LeafGreen and transfer through Pal Park

ABILITY ● Shield Dust

● LEVEL-UP AND LEARNED MOVES

Lv	Name	Type	Kind	Power	Acc	PP	Range	DA
Base	Tackle	Normal	Physical	35	95	35	Normal	•
Base	String Shot	Bug	Status	—	95	40	2 foes	
15	Bug Bite	Bug	Physical	60	100	20	Normal	•

Metapod

National Pokédex No. 011 — Cocoon Pokémon

BUG

STATS
- HP ●●
- ATTACK ●
- DEFENSE ●●
- SP.ATTACK ●
- SP.DEFENSE ●
- SPEED ●

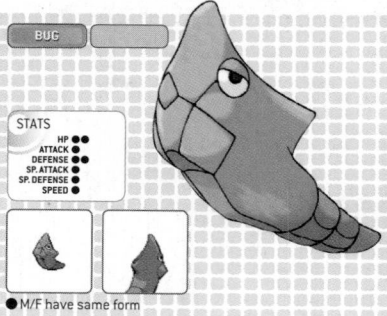

● M/F have same form

EVOLUTION PATH

Caterpie → Lv7 → Metapod → Lv10 → Butterfree

● MAIN WAYS TO OBTAIN

PLATINUM	Eterna Forest(after you get the National Pokédex, insert a Pokémon FireRed cartridge into the Nintendo DS's GBA cartridge slot)
DIAMOND	Eterna Forest(after you get the National Pokédex, insert a Pokémon FireRed cartridge into the Nintendo DS's GBA cartridge slot)
PEARL	Eterna Forest(after you get the National Pokédex, insert a Pokémon FireRed cartridge into the Nintendo DS's GBA cartridge slot)
GBA	Catch in FireRed/LeafGreen and transfer through Pal Park

ABILITY ● Shed Skin

● LEVEL-UP AND LEARNED MOVES

Lv	Name	Type	Kind	Power	Acc	PP	Range	DA
Base	Harden	Normal	Status	—	—	30	Self	—
7	Harden	Normal	Status	—	—	30	Self	—

Butterfree

National Pokédex No. 012 — Butterfly Pokémon

BUG **FLYING**

STATS
- HP ●●
- ATTACK ●●
- DEFENSE ●●
- SP.ATTACK ●●●
- SP.DEFENSE ●●●
- SPEED ●●●

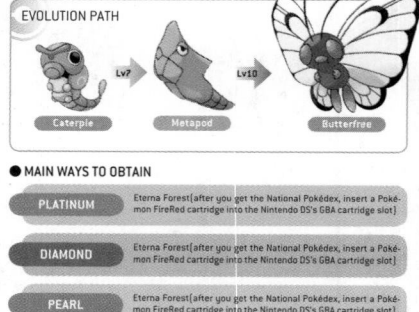

● Male form   ● Female form

EVOLUTION PATH

Caterpie → Lv7 → Metapod → Lv10 → Butterfree

● MAIN WAYS TO OBTAIN

PLATINUM	Level up Metapod to Lv10
DIAMOND	Level up Metapod to Lv10
PEARL	Level up Metapod to Lv10
GBA	Catch and evolve in FireRed/LeafGreen, and transfer through Pal Park

ABILITY ● Compoundeyes

● LEVEL-UP AND LEARNED MOVES

Lv	Name	Type	Kind	Power	Acc	PP	Range	DA
Base	Confusion	Psychic	Special	50	100	25	Normal	—
10	Confusion	Psychic	Special	50	100	25	Normal	—
12	PoisonPowder	Poison	Status	—	75	35	Normal	—
12	Stun Spore	Grass	Status	—	75	30	Normal	—
12	Sleep Powder	Grass	Status	—	75	15	Normal	—
16	Gust	Flying	Special	40	100	35	Normal	—
18	Supersonic	Normal	Status	—	55	20	Normal	—
22	Whirlwind	Normal	Status	—	100	20	Normal	—
24	Psybeam	Psychic	Special	65	100	20	Normal	—
28	Silver Wind	Bug	Special	60	100	5	Normal	—
30	Tailwind	Flying	Status	—	—	30	2 allies	—
34	Safeguard	Normal	Status	—	—	25	2 allies	—
36	Captivate	Normal	Status	—	100	20	2 foes	—
40	Bug Buzz	Bug	Special	90	100	10	Normal	—

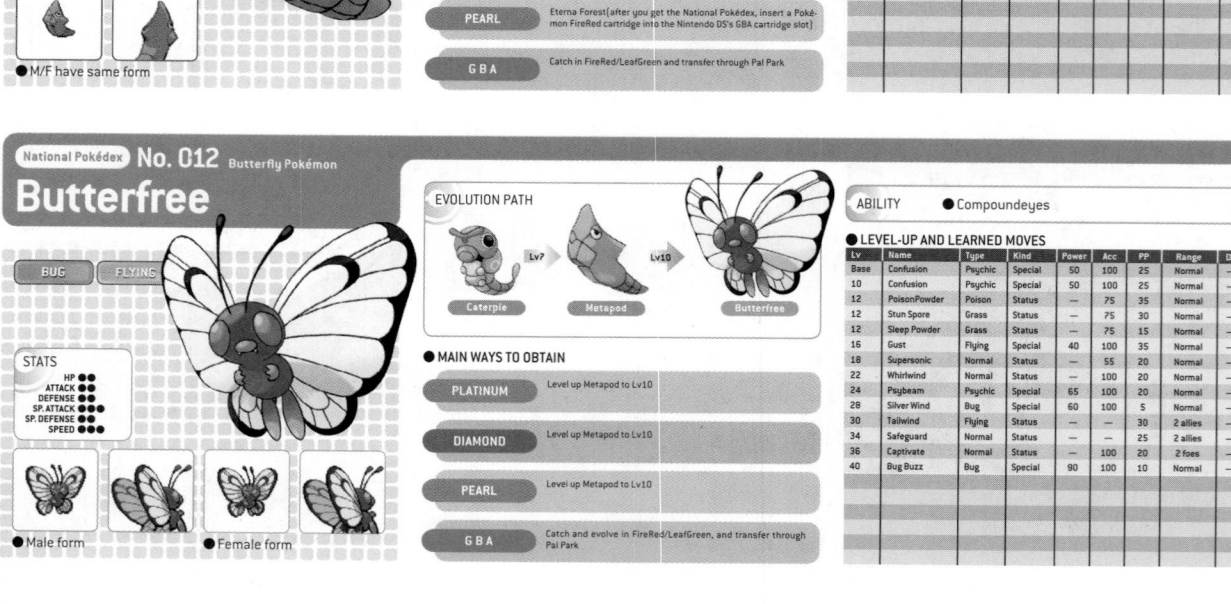

Weedle

National Pokédex No. 013 · Hairy Bug Pokémon

Weedle

BUG · POISON

STATS
- HP ●
- ATTACK ●
- DEFENSE ●
- SP. ATTACK ●
- SP. DEFENSE ●
- SPEED ●●

● M/F have same form

EVOLUTION PATH

Weedle → Lv7 → Kakuna → Lv10 → Beedrill

● MAIN WAYS TO OBTAIN

PLATINUM	Route 204 [after you get the National Pokédex, insert a Pokémon LeafGreen cartridge into the Nintendo DS's GBA cartridge slot]
DIAMOND	Jubilife City side of Route 204 [after you get the National Pokédex, insert a Pokémon LeafGreen cartridge into the Nintendo DS's GBA cartridge slot]
PEARL	Jubilife City side of Route 204 [after you get the National Pokédex, insert a Pokémon LeafGreen cartridge into the Nintendo DS's GBA cartridge slot]
G B A	Catch in FireRed/LeafGreen and transfer through Pal Park

ABILITY ● Shield Dust

● LEVEL-UP AND LEARNED MOVES

Lv	Name	Type	Kind	Power	Acc	PP	Range	DA
Base	Poison Sting	Poison	Physical	15	100	35	Normal	
Base	String Shot	Bug	Status	—	95	40	2 foes	
15	Bug Bite	Bug	Physical	60	100	20	Normal	●

Kakuna

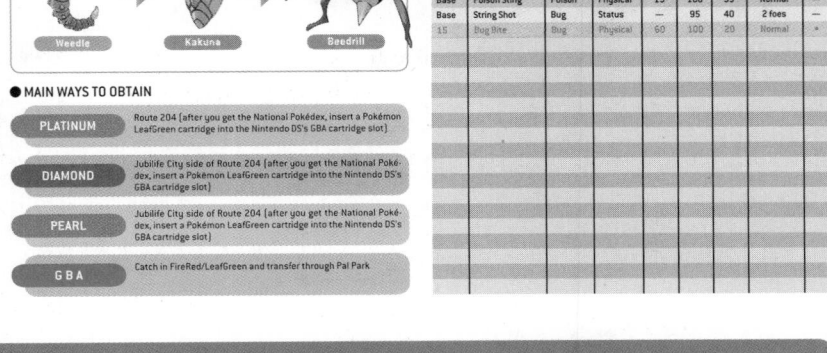

National Pokédex No. 014 · Cocoon Pokémon

Kakuna

BUG · POISON

STATS
- HP ●
- ATTACK ●
- DEFENSE ●●
- SP. ATTACK ●
- SP. DEFENSE ●
- SPEED ●

● M/F have same form

EVOLUTION PATH

Weedle → Lv7 → Kakuna → Lv10 → Beedrill

● MAIN WAYS TO OBTAIN

PLATINUM	Eterna Forest[after you get the National Pokédex, insert a Pokémon LeafGreen cartridge into the Nintendo DS's GBA cartridge slot]
DIAMOND	Eterna Forest[after you get the National Pokédex, insert a Pokémon LeafGreen cartridge into the Nintendo DS's GBA cartridge slot]
PEARL	Eterna Forest[after you get the National Pokédex, insert a Pokémon LeafGreen cartridge into the Nintendo DS's GBA cartridge slot]
G B A	Catch in FireRed/LeafGreen and transfer through Pal Park

ABILITY ● Shed Skin

● LEVEL-UP AND LEARNED MOVES

Lv	Name	Type	Kind	Power	Acc	PP	Range	DA
Base	Harden	Normal	Status	—		30	Self	—
7	Harden	Normal	Status	—		30	Self	—

Beedrill

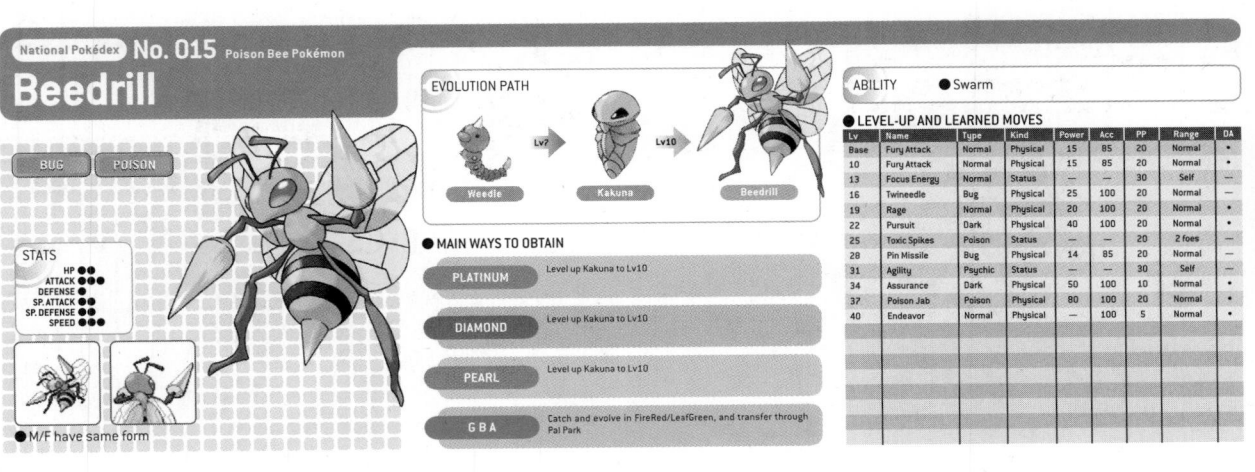

National Pokédex No. 015 · Poison Bee Pokémon

Beedrill

BUG · POISON

STATS
- HP ●●
- ATTACK ●●●
- DEFENSE ●●
- SP. ATTACK ●
- SP. DEFENSE ●●
- SPEED ●●●

● M/F have same form

EVOLUTION PATH

Weedle → Lv2 → Kakuna → Lv10 → Beedrill

● MAIN WAYS TO OBTAIN

PLATINUM	Level up Kakuna to Lv10
DIAMOND	Level up Kakuna to Lv10
PEARL	Level up Kakuna to Lv10
G B A	Catch and evolve in FireRed/LesfGreen, and transfer through Pal Park

ABILITY ● Swarm

● LEVEL-UP AND LEARNED MOVES

Lv	Name	Type	Kind	Power	Acc	PP	Range	DA
Base	Fury Attack	Normal	Physical	15	85	20	Normal	●
10	Fury Attack	Normal	Physical	15	85	20	Normal	●
13	Focus Energy	Normal	Status	—		30	Self	—
16	Twineedle	Bug	Physical	25	100	20	Normal	●
19	Rage	Normal	Physical	20	100	20	Normal	●
22	Pursuit	Dark	Physical	40	100	20	Normal	●
25	Toxic Spikes	Poison	Status	—		20	2 foes	—
28	Pin Missile	Bug	Physical	14	85	20	Normal	●
31	Agility	Psychic	Status	—		30	Self	—
34	Assurance	Dark	Physical	50	100	10	Normal	●
37	Poison Jab	Poison	Physical	80	100	20	Normal	●
40	Endeavor	Normal	Physical		100	5	Normal	●

016
● ● ● ● ●
PIDGEY

Pidgey

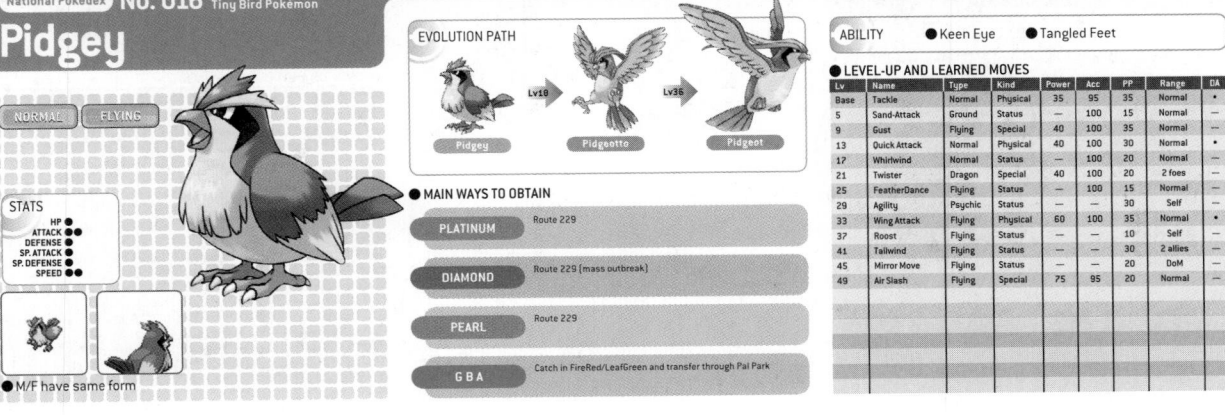

National Pokédex No. 016 · Tiny Bird Pokémon

Pidgey

NORMAL · FLYING

STATS
- HP ●
- ATTACK ●●
- DEFENSE ●●
- SP. ATTACK ●
- SP. DEFENSE ●
- SPEED ●●

● M/F have same form

EVOLUTION PATH

Pidgey → Lv10 → Pidgeotto → Lv36 → Pidgeot

● MAIN WAYS TO OBTAIN

PLATINUM	Route 229
DIAMOND	Route 229 [mass outbreak]
PEARL	Route 229
G B A	Catch in FireRed/LeafGreen and transfer through Pal Park

ABILITY ● Keen Eye ● Tangled Feet

● LEVEL-UP AND LEARNED MOVES

Lv	Name	Type	Kind	Power	Acc	PP	Range	DA
Base	Tackle	Normal	Physical	35	95	35	Normal	—
5	Sand-Attack	Ground	Status	—	100	15	Normal	—
9	Gust	Flying	Special	40	100	35	Normal	—
13	Quick Attack	Normal	Physical	40	100	30	Normal	●
17	Whirlwind	Normal	Status	—	100	20	Normal	—
21	Twister	Dragon	Special	40	100	20	2 foes	—
25	FeatherDance	Flying	Status	—	100	15	Normal	—
29	Agility	Psychic	Status	—		30	Self	—
33	Wing Attack	Flying	Physical	60	100	35	Normal	●
37	Roost	Flying	Status	—		10	Self	—
41	Tailwind	Flying	Status	—		30	2 allies	—
45	Mirror Move	Flying	Status	—		20	DoM	—
49	Air Slash	Flying	Special	75	95	20	Normal	—

National Pokédex No. 017 Bird Pokémon

Pidgeotto

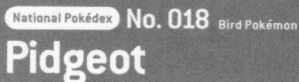

NORMAL FLYING

STATS
- HP ●●
- ATTACK ●●●
- DEFENSE ●●●
- SP. ATTACK ●●
- SP. DEFENSE ●●
- SPEED ●●●

● M/F have same form

EVOLUTION PATH

Pidgey → Lv18 → Pidgeotto → Lv36 → Pidgeot

● MAIN WAYS TO OBTAIN

PLATINUM	Level up Pidgey to Lv18
DIAMOND	Level up Pidgey to Lv18
PEARL	Level up Pidgey to Lv18
GBA	Catch in FireRed/LeafGreen and transfer through Pal Park

ABILITY ● Keen Eye ● Tangled Feet

● LEVEL-UP AND LEARNED MOVES

Lv	Name	Type	Kind	Power	Acc	PP	Range	DA
Base	Tackle	Normal	Physical	35	95	35	Normal	•
Base	Sand-Attack	Ground	Status	—	100	15	Normal	—
Base	Gust	Flying	Special	40	100	35	Normal	—
5	Sand-Attack	Ground	Status	—	100	15	Normal	—
9	Gust	Flying	Special	40	100	35	Normal	—
13	Quick Attack	Normal	Physical	40	100	30	Normal	•
17	Whirlwind	Normal	Status	—	100	20	Normal	—
22	Twister	Dragon	Special	40	100	20	2 foes	•
27	FeatherDance	Flying	Status	—	100	15	Normal	—
32	Agility	Psychic	Status	—	—	30	Self	—
37	Wing Attack	Flying	Physical	60	100	35	Normal	•
42	Roost	Flying	Status	—	—	10	Self	—
47	Tailwind	Flying	Status	—	—	20	2 allies	—
52	Mirror Move	Flying	Status	—	—	20	DoM	—
57	Air Slash	Flying	Special	75	95	20	Normal	—

National Pokédex No. 018 Bird Pokémon

Pidgeot

NORMAL FLYING

STATS
- HP ●●●
- ATTACK ●●●
- DEFENSE ●●
- SP. ATTACK ●●●
- SP. DEFENSE ●●
- SPEED ●●●

● M/F have same form

EVOLUTION PATH

Pidgey → Lv18 → Pidgeotto → Lv36 → Pidgeot

● MAIN WAYS TO OBTAIN

PLATINUM	Level up Pidgeotto to Lv36
DIAMOND	Level up Pidgeotto to Lv36
PEARL	Level up Pidgeotto to Lv36
GBA	Catch and evolve in FireRed/LeafGreen, and transfer through Pal Park

ABILITY ● Keen Eye ● Tangled Feet

● LEVEL-UP AND LEARNED MOVES

Lv	Name	Type	Kind	Power	Acc	PP	Range	DA
Base	Tackle	Normal	Physical	35	95	35	Normal	•
Base	Sand-Attack	Ground	Status	—	100	15	Normal	—
Base	Gust	Flying	Special	40	100	35	Normal	—
Base	Quick Attack	Normal	Physical	40	100	30	Normal	•
5	Sand-Attack	Ground	Status	—	100	15	Normal	—
9	Gust	Flying	Special	40	100	35	Normal	—
13	Quick Attack	Normal	Physical	40	100	30	Normal	•
17	Whirlwind	Normal	Status	—	100	20	Normal	—
22	Twister	Dragon	Special	40	100	20	2 foes	•
27	FeatherDance	Flying	Status	—	100	15	Normal	—
32	Agility	Psychic	Status	—	—	30	Self	—
38	Wing Attack	Flying	Physical	60	100	35	Normal	•
44	Roost	Flying	Status	—	—	10	Self	—
50	Tailwind	Flying	Status	—	—	30	2 allies	—
56	Mirror Move	Flying	Status	—	—	20	DoM	—
62	Air Slash	Flying	Special	75	95	20	Normal	—

National Pokédex No. 019 Mouse Pokémon

Rattata

NORMAL

STATS
- HP ●
- ATTACK ●●
- DEFENSE ●●
- SP. ATTACK ●●
- SP. DEFENSE ●●
- SPEED ●●●

● Male form ● Female form

EVOLUTION PATH

Rattata → Lv20 → Raticate

● MAIN WAYS TO OBTAIN

PLATINUM	Route 225
DIAMOND	Route 225
PEARL	Route 225
GBA	Catch in FireRed/LeafGreen and transfer through Pal Park

ABILITY ● Run Away ● Guts

● LEVEL-UP AND LEARNED MOVES

Lv	Name	Type	Kind	Power	Acc	PP	Range	DA
Base	Tackle	Normal	Physical	35	95	35	Normal	•
Base	Tail Whip	Normal	Status	—	100	30	2 foes	—
4	Quick Attack	Normal	Physical	40	100	30	Normal	•
7	Focus Energy	Normal	Status	—	—	30	Self	—
10	Bite	Dark	Physical	60	100	25	Normal	•
13	Pursuit	Dark	Physical	40	100	20	Normal	•
16	Hyper Fang	Normal	Physical	80	90	15	Normal	•
19	Sucker Punch	Dark	Physical	80	100	5	Normal	•
22	Crunch	Dark	Physical	80	100	15	Normal	•
25	Assurance	Dark	Physical	50	100	10	Normal	•
28	Super Fang	Normal	Physical	—	90	10	Normal	•
31	Double-Edge	Normal	Physical	120	100	15	Normal	•
34	Endeavor	Normal	Physical	—	100	5	Normal	•

National Pokédex No. 020 Mouse Pokémon

Raticate

NORMAL

STATS
- HP ●●
- ATTACK ●●●
- DEFENSE ●●
- SP. ATTACK ●●
- SP. DEFENSE ●●
- SPEED ●●●

● Male form ● Female form

EVOLUTION PATH

Rattata → Lv20 → Raticate

● MAIN WAYS TO OBTAIN

PLATINUM	Route 225
DIAMOND	Route 225
PEARL	Route 225
GBA	Catch in FireRed/LeafGreen and transfer through Pal Park

ABILITY ● Run Away ● Guts

● LEVEL-UP AND LEARNED MOVES

Lv	Name	Type	Kind	Power	Acc	PP	Range	DA
Base	Swords Dance	Normal	Status	—	—	30	Self	—
Base	Tackle	Normal	Physical	35	95	35	Normal	•
Base	Tail Whip	Normal	Status	—	100	30	2 foes	—
Base	Quick Attack	Normal	Physical	40	100	30	Normal	•
Base	Focus Energy	Normal	Status	—	—	30	Self	—
4	Quick Attack	Normal	Physical	40	100	30	Normal	•
7	Focus Energy	Normal	Status	—	—	30	Self	—
10	Bite	Dark	Physical	60	100	25	Normal	•
13	Pursuit	Dark	Physical	40	100	20	Normal	•
16	Hyper Fang	Normal	Physical	80	90	15	Normal	•
19	Sucker Punch	Dark	Physical	80	100	5	Normal	•
20	Scary Face	Normal	Status	—	90	10	Normal	—
24	Crunch	Dark	Physical	80	100	15	Normal	•
29	Assurance	Dark	Physical	50	100	10	Normal	•
34	Super Fang	Normal	Physical	—	90	10	Normal	•
39	Double-Edge	Normal	Physical	120	100	15	Normal	•
44	Endeavor	Normal	Physical	—	100	5	Normal	•

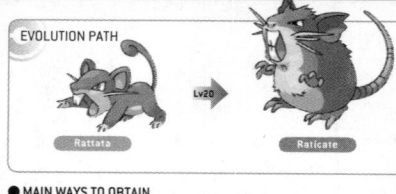
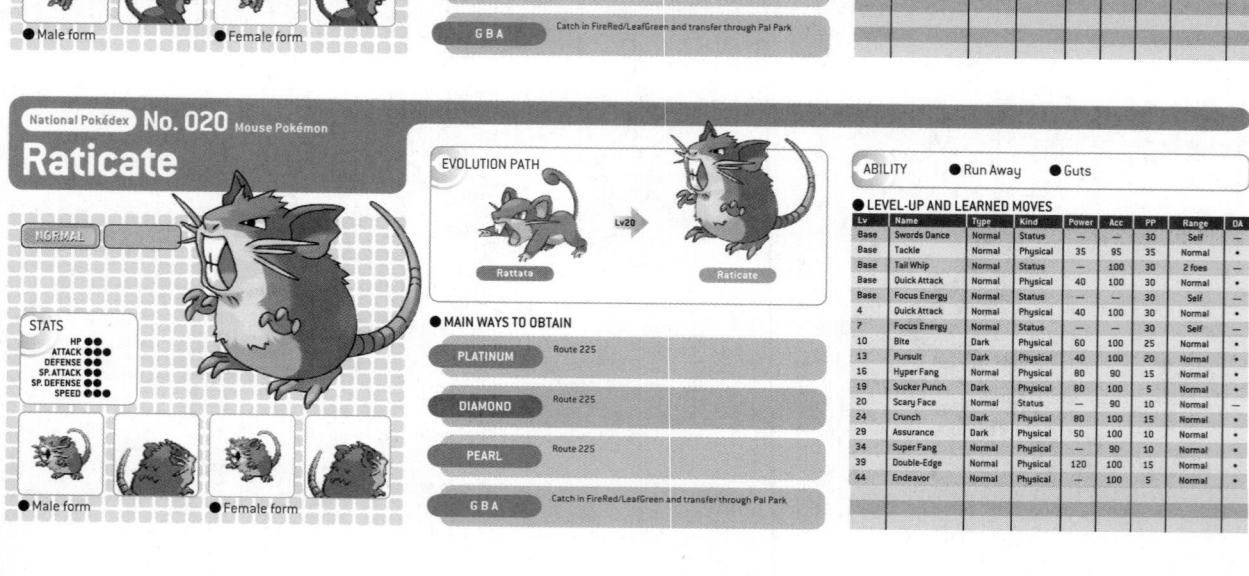

Spearow

National Pokédex No. 021 Tiny Bird Pokémon

NORMAL FLYING

STATS
HP ●
ATTACK ●●
DEFENSE ●
SP. ATTACK ●
SP. DEFENSE ●
SPEED ●●●

● M/F have same form

EVOLUTION PATH

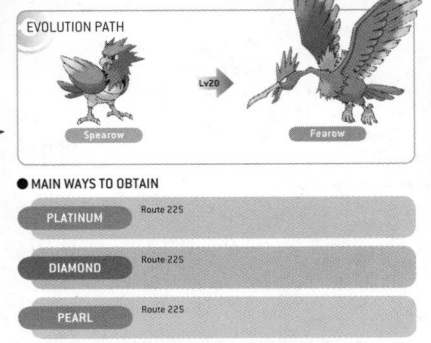

Spearow → Lv20 → Fearow

● **MAIN WAYS TO OBTAIN**

PLATINUM	Route 225
DIAMOND	Route 225
PEARL	Route 225
G B A	Catch in FireRed/LeafGreen and transfer through Pal Park

ABILITY   ● Keen Eye

● **LEVEL-UP AND LEARNED MOVES**

Lv	Name	Type	Kind	Power	Acc	PP	Range	DA
Base	Peck	Flying	Physical	35	100	35	Normal	•
Base	Growl	Normal	Status	—	100	40	2 foes	—
5	Leer	Normal	Status	—	100	30	2 foes	
9	Fury Attack	Normal	Physical	15	85	20	Normal	•
13	Pursuit	Dark	Physical	40	100	20	Normal	•
17	Aerial Ace	Flying	Physical	60	—	20	Normal	—
21	Mirror Move	Flying	Status	—	—	20	DoM	—
25	Agility	Psychic	Status	—	—	30	Self	—
29	Assurance	Dark	Physical	50	100	10	Normal	•
33	Roost	Flying	Status	—	—	10	Self	—
37	Drill Peck	Flying	Physical	80	100	20	Normal	•

Fearow

National Pokédex No. 022 Beak Pokémon

NORMAL FLYING

STATS
HP ●●
ATTACK ●●●
DEFENSE ●●
SP. ATTACK ●●
SP. DEFENSE ●●
SPEED ●●●●

● M/F have same form

EVOLUTION PATH

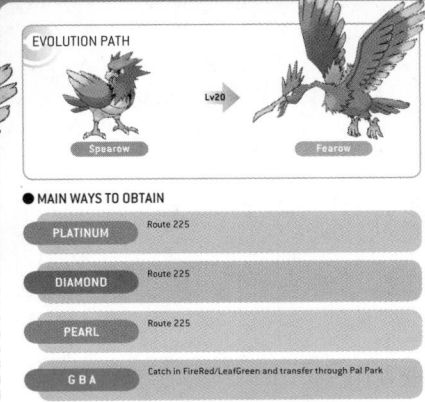

Spearow → Lv20 → Fearow

● **MAIN WAYS TO OBTAIN**

PLATINUM	Route 225
DIAMOND	Route 225
PEARL	Route 225
G B A	Catch in FireRed/LeafGreen and transfer through Pal Park

ABILITY   ● Keen Eye

● **LEVEL-UP AND LEARNED MOVES**

Lv	Name	Type	Kind	Power	Acc	PP	Range	DA
Base	Pluck	Flying	Physical	60	100	20	Normal	•
Base	Peck	Flying	Physical	35	100	35	Normal	•
Base	Growl	Normal	Status	—	100	40	2 foes	—
Base	Leer	Normal	Status	—	100	30	2 foes	
Base	Fury Attack	Normal	Physical	15	85	20	Normal	•
5	Leer	Normal	Status	—	100	30	2 foes	
9	Fury Attack	Normal	Physical	15	85	20	Normal	•
13	Pursuit	Dark	Physical	40	100	20	Normal	•
17	Aerial Ace	Flying	Physical	60	—	20	Normal	•
23	Mirror Move	Flying	Status	—	—	20	DoM	—
29	Agility	Psychic	Status	—	—	30	Self	—
35	Assurance	Dark	Physical	50	100	10	Normal	•
41	Roost	Flying	Status	—	—	10	Self	—
47	Drill Peck	Flying	Physical	80	100	20	Normal	•

Ekans

National Pokédex No. 023 Snake Pokémon

POISON

STATS
HP ●
ATTACK ●●
DEFENSE ●
SP. ATTACK ●
SP. DEFENSE ●
SPEED ●

● M/F have same form

EVOLUTION PATH

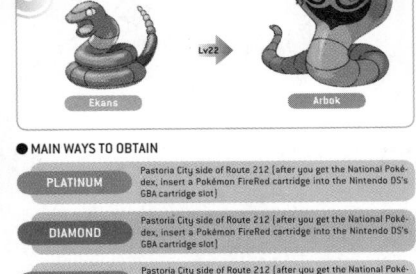

Ekans → Lv22 → Arbok

● **MAIN WAYS TO OBTAIN**

PLATINUM	Pastoria City side of Route 212 (after you get the National Pokédex, insert a Pokémon FireRed cartridge into the Nintendo DS's GBA cartridge slot)
DIAMOND	Pastoria City side of Route 212 (after you get the National Pokédex, insert a Pokémon FireRed cartridge into the Nintendo DS's GBA cartridge slot)
PEARL	Pastoria City side of Route 212 (after you get the National Pokédex, insert a Pokémon FireRed cartridge into the Nintendo DS's GBA cartridge slot)
G B A	Catch in FireRed and transfer through Pal Park

ABILITY   ● Intimidate   ● Shed Skin

● **LEVEL-UP AND LEARNED MOVES**

Lv	Name	Type	Kind	Power	Acc	PP	Range	DA
Base	Wrap	Normal	Physical	15	85	20	Normal	•
Base	Leer	Normal	Status	—	100	30	2 foes	—
4	Poison Sting	Poison	Physical	15	100	35	Normal	•
9	Bite	Dark	Physical	60	100	25	Normal	•
12	Glare	Normal	Status	—	75	30	Normal	—
17	Screech	Normal	Status	—	85	40	Normal	—
20	Acid	Poison	Special	40	100	30	2 foes	•
25	Stockpile	Normal	Status	—	—	20	Self	—
25	Swallow	Normal	Status	—	—	10	Self	—
25	Spit Up	Normal	Special	—	100	10	Normal	—
28	Mud Bomb	Ground	Special	65	85	10	Normal	•
33	Gastro Acid	Poison	Status	—	100	10	Normal	—
36	Haze	Ice	Status	—	—	30	All	—
41	Gunk Shot	Poison	Physical	120	70	5	Normal	•

024 ★★★★★ ARBOK

Arbok

National Pokédex No. 024 Cobra Pokémon

POISON

STATS
HP ●●
ATTACK ●●●
DEFENSE ●●
SP. ATTACK ●●
SP. DEFENSE ●●
SPEED ●●

● M/F have same form

EVOLUTION PATH

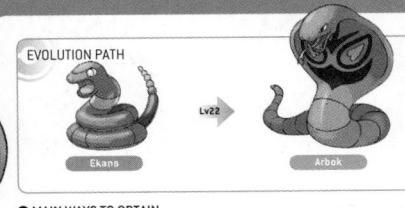

Ekans → Lv22 → Arbok

● **MAIN WAYS TO OBTAIN**

PLATINUM	Pastoria Great Marsh (after you get the National Pokédex, insert a Pokémon FireRed cartridge into the Nintendo DS's GBA cartridge slot)
DIAMOND	Pastoria Great Marsh (after you get the National Pokédex, insert a Pokémon FireRed cartridge into the Nintendo DS's GBA cartridge slot)
PEARL	Pastoria Great Marsh (after you get the National Pokédex, insert a Pokémon FireRed cartridge into the Nintendo DS's GBA cartridge slot)
G B A	Catch in FireRed and transfer through Pal Park

ABILITY   ● Intimidate   ● Shed Skin

● **LEVEL-UP AND LEARNED MOVES**

Lv	Name	Type	Kind	Power	Acc	PP	Range	DA
Base	Ice Fang	Ice	Physical	65	95	15	Normal	•
Base	Thunder Fang	Electric	Physical	65	95	15	Normal	•
Base	Fire Fang	Fire	Physical	65	95	15	Normal	•
Base	Wrap	Normal	Physical	15	85	20	Normal	•
Base	Leer	Normal	Status	—	100	30	2 foes	—
Base	Poison Sting	Poison	Physical	15	100	35	Normal	—
Base	Bite	Dark	Physical	60	100	25	Normal	•
4	Poison Sting	Poison	Physical	15	100	35	Normal	•
9	Bite	Dark	Physical	60	100	25	Normal	•
12	Glare	Normal	Status	—	75	30	Normal	—
17	Screech	Normal	Status	—	85	40	Normal	—
20	Acid	Poison	Special	40	100	30	2 foes	•
22	Crunch	Dark	Physical	80	100	15	Normal	•
28	Stockpile	Normal	Status	—	—	20	Self	—
28	Swallow	Normal	Status	—	—	10	Self	—
28	Spit Up	Normal	Special	—	100	10	Normal	—
34	Mud Bomb	Ground	Special	65	85	10	Normal	•
42	Gastro Acid	Poison	Status	—	100	10	Normal	—
48	Haze	Ice	Status	—	—	30	All	—
56	Gunk Shot	Poison	Physical	120	70	5	Normal	•

Pikachu

ELECTRIC

STATS
HP ●●
ATTACK ●●
DEFENSE ●
SP. ATTACK ●●
SP. DEFENSE ●●
SPEED ●●●

● Male form ● Female form

EVOLUTION PATH
Pichu → Pikachu → Raichu

Level up with high enough Friendship

Use Thunderstone

pg. 436

● MAIN WAYS TO OBTAIN

PLATINUM	Trophy Garden at the Pokémon Mansion on Route 212
DIAMOND	Trophy Garden at the Pokémon Mansion on Route 212
PEARL	Trophy Garden at the Pokémon Mansion on Route 212
GBA	Catch in any GBA-series Pokémon game and transfer through Pal Park

ABILITY ● Static

● LEVEL-UP AND LEARNED MOVES

Lv	Name	Type	Kind	Power	Acc	PP	Range	DA
Base	ThunderShock	Electric	Special	40	100	30	Normal	—
Base	Growl	Normal	Status	—	100	40	2 foes	—
5	Tail Whip	Normal	Status	—	100	30	2 foes	—
10	Thunder Wave	Electric	Status	—	100	20	Normal	—
13	Quick Attack	Normal	Physical	40	100	30	Normal	•
18	Double Team	Normal	Status	—	—	15	Self	—
21	Slam	Normal	Physical	80	75	20	Normal	—
26	Thunderbolt	Electric	Special	95	100	15	Normal	—
29	Feint	Normal	Physical	50	100	10	Normal	—
34	Agility	Psychic	Status	—	—	30	Self	—
37	Discharge	Electric	Special	80	100	15	2 foes+1 ally	—
42	Light Screen	Psychic	Status	—	—	30	2 allies	—
45	Thunder	Electric	Special	120	70	10	Normal	—

Raichu

ELECTRIC

STATS
HP ●●
ATTACK ●●●
DEFENSE ●●
SP. ATTACK ●●
SP. DEFENSE ●●
SPEED ●●●●

● Male form ● Female form

EVOLUTION PATH
Pichu → Pikachu → Raichu

Level up with high enough Friendship

Use Thunderstone

pg. 436

● MAIN WAYS TO OBTAIN

PLATINUM	Use the Thunderstone on Pikachu
DIAMOND	Use the Thunderstone on Pikachu
PEARL	Use the Thunderstone on Pikachu
GBA	Catch and evolve in any GBA-series Pokémon game and transfer through Pal Park

ABILITY ● Static

● LEVEL-UP AND LEARNED MOVES

Lv	Name	Type	Kind	Power	Acc	PP	Range	DA
Base	ThunderShock	Electric	Special	40	100	30	Normal	—
Base	Tail Whip	Normal	Status	—	100	30	2 foes	—
Base	Quick Attack	Normal	Physical	40	100	30	Normal	•
Base	Thunderbolt	Electric	Special	95	100	15	Normal	—

Sandshrew

GROUND

STATS
HP ●●
ATTACK ●●●
DEFENSE ●●●●
SP. ATTACK ●●
SP. DEFENSE ●●
SPEED ●●

● M/F have same form

EVOLUTION PATH
Sandshrew → Lv22 → Sandslash

● MAIN WAYS TO OBTAIN

PLATINUM	Wayward Cave (after you get the National Pokédex, insert a Pokémon LeafGreen cartridge into the Nintendo DS's GBA cartridge slot)
DIAMOND	Wayward Cave (after you get the National Pokédex, insert a Pokémon LeafGreen cartridge into the Nintendo DS's GBA cartridge slot)
PEARL	Wayward Cave (after you get the National Pokédex, insert a Pokémon LeafGreen cartridge into the Nintendo DS's GBA cartridge slot)
GBA	Catch in LeafGreen or Ruby/Sapphire/Emerald, and transfer through Pal Park

ABILITY ● Sand Veil

● LEVEL-UP AND LEARNED MOVES

Lv	Name	Type	Kind	Power	Acc	PP	Range	DA
Base	Scratch	Normal	Physical	40	100	35	Normal	•
3	Defense Curl	Normal	Status	—	—	40	Self	—
?	Sand-Attack	Ground	Status	—	100	15	Normal	—
9	Poison Sting	Poison	Physical	15	100	35	Normal	—
13	Rapid Spin	Normal	Physical	20	100	40	Normal	—
15	Swift	Normal	Special	60	—	20	2 foes	—
19	Fury Swipes	Normal	Physical	18	80	15	Normal	—
21	Rollout	Rock	Physical	30	90	20	Normal	—
25	Fury Cutter	Bug	Physical	10	95	20	Normal	—
27	Sand Tomb	Ground	Physical	15	70	15	Normal	—
31	Slash	Normal	Physical	70	100	20	Normal	—
33	Gyro Ball	Steel	Physical	—	100	5	Normal	—
37	Sandstorm	Rock	Status	—	—	10	All	—

Sandslash

GROUND

STATS
HP ●●●
ATTACK ●●●●
DEFENSE ●●●●●
SP. ATTACK ●●
SP. DEFENSE ●●
SPEED ●●

● M/F have same form

EVOLUTION PATH
Sandshrew → Lv22 → Sandslash

● MAIN WAYS TO OBTAIN

PLATINUM	Route 228 (after you get the National Pokédex, insert a Pokémon LeafGreen cartridge into the Nintendo DS's GBA cartridge slot)
DIAMOND	Route 228 (after you get the National Pokédex, insert a Pokémon LeafGreen cartridge into the Nintendo DS's GBA cartridge slot)
PEARL	Route 228 (after you get the National Pokédex, insert a Pokémon LeafGreen cartridge into the Nintendo DS's GBA cartridge slot)
GBA	Catch and evolve in LeafGreen or Ruby/Sapphire/Emerald, and transfer through Pal Park

ABILITY ● Sand Veil

● LEVEL-UP AND LEARNED MOVES

Lv	Name	Type	Kind	Power	Acc	PP	Range	DA
Base	Scratch	Normal	Physical	40	100	35	Normal	•
Base	Defense Curl	Normal	Status	—	—	40	Self	—
Base	Sand-Attack	Ground	Status	—	100	15	Normal	—
3	Defense Curl	Normal	Status	—	—	40	Self	—
?	Sand-Attack	Ground	Status	—	100	15	Normal	—
9	Poison Sting	Poison	Physical	15	100	35	Normal	—
13	Rapid Spin	Normal	Physical	20	100	40	Normal	—
15	Swift	Normal	Special	60	—	20	2 foes	—
19	Fury Swipes	Normal	Physical	18	80	15	Normal	—
21	Rollout	Rock	Physical	30	90	20	Normal	—
22	Crush Claw	Normal	Physical	75	95	10	Normal	—
28	Fury Cutter	Bug	Physical	10	95	20	Normal	—
33	Sand Tomb	Ground	Physical	15	70	15	Normal	—
40	Slash	Normal	Physical	70	100	20	Normal	—
45	Gyro Ball	Steel	Physical	—	100	5	Normal	—
52	Sandstorm	Rock	Status	—	—	10	All	—

National Pokédex No. 029 Poison Pin Pokémon

Nidoran ♀

POISON

STATS
HP ●●
ATTACK ●●
DEFENSE ●●●
SP. ATTACK ●●
SP. DEFENSE ●●
SPEED ●●

● Female form

EVOLUTION PATH

Nidoran ♀ —Lv16→ Nidorina —Use Moon Stone→ Nidoqueen

● MAIN WAYS TO OBTAIN
PLATINUM	Route 201 (Use the Poké Radar)
DIAMOND	Route 201 (Use the Poké Radar)
PEARL	Route 201 (Use the Poké Radar)
GBA	Catch in FireRed/LeafGreen and transfer through Pal Park

ABILITY ● Poison Point ● Rivalry

● LEVEL-UP AND LEARNED MOVES
Lv	Name	Type	Kind	Power	Acc	PP	Range	DA
Base	Growl	Normal	Status	—	100	40	2 foes	—
Base	Scratch	Normal	Physical	40	100	35	Normal	●
7	Tail Whip	Normal	Status	—	100	30	2 foes	●
9	Double Kick	Fighting	Physical	30	100	30	Normal	●
13	Poison Sting	Poison	Physical	15	100	35	Normal	●
19	Fury Swipes	Normal	Physical	18	80	15	Normal	●
21	Bite	Dark	Physical	60	100	25	Normal	●
25	Helping Hand	Normal	Status	—	—	20	1 ally	●
31	Toxic Spikes	Poison	Status	—	—	20	2 foes	—
33	Flatter	Dark	Status	—	100	15	Normal	—
37	Crunch	Dark	Physical	80	100	15	Normal	●
43	Captivate	Normal	Status	—	100	20	2 foes	—
45	Poison Fang	Poison	Physical	50	100	15	Normal	●

National Pokédex No. 030 Poison Pin Pokémon

Nidorina

POISON

STATS
HP ●●●
ATTACK ●●
DEFENSE ●●●
SP. ATTACK ●●
SP. DEFENSE ●●
SPEED ●●

● Female form

EVOLUTION PATH
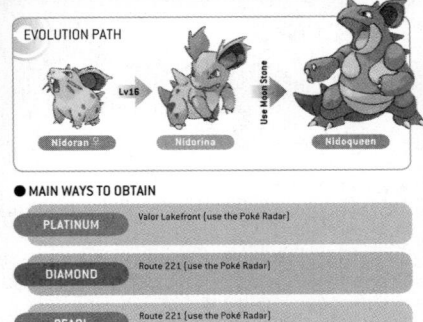
Nidoran ♀ —Lv16→ Nidorina —Use Moon Stone→ Nidoqueen

● MAIN WAYS TO OBTAIN
PLATINUM	Valor Lakefront (use the Poké Radar)
DIAMOND	Route 221 (use the Poké Radar)
PEARL	Route 221 (use the Poké Radar)
GBA	Catch in FireRed/LeafGreen and transfer through Pal Park

ABILITY ● Poison Point ● Rivalry

● LEVEL-UP AND LEARNED MOVES
Lv	Name	Type	Kind	Power	Acc	PP	Range	DA
Base	Growl	Normal	Status	—	100	40	2 foes	—
Base	Scratch	Normal	Physical	40	100	35	Normal	●
7	Tail Whip	Normal	Status	—	100	30	2 foes	●
9	Double Kick	Fighting	Physical	30	100	30	Normal	●
13	Poison Sting	Poison	Physical	15	100	35	Normal	●
20	Fury Swipes	Normal	Physical	18	80	15	Normal	●
23	Bite	Dark	Physical	60	100	25	Normal	●
28	Helping Hand	Normal	Status	—	—	20	1 ally	●
35	Toxic Spikes	Poison	Status	—	—	20	2 foes	—
38	Flatter	Dark	Status	—	100	15	Normal	—
43	Crunch	Dark	Physical	80	100	15	Normal	●
50	Captivate	Normal	Status	—	100	20	2 foes	—
58	Poison Fang	Poison	Physical	50	100	15	Normal	●

National Pokédex No. 031 Drill Pokémon

Nidoqueen

POISON GROUND

STATS
HP ●●●●
ATTACK ●●●
DEFENSE ●●●●
SP. ATTACK ●●●
SP. DEFENSE ●●●
SPEED ●●●

● Female form

EVOLUTION PATH
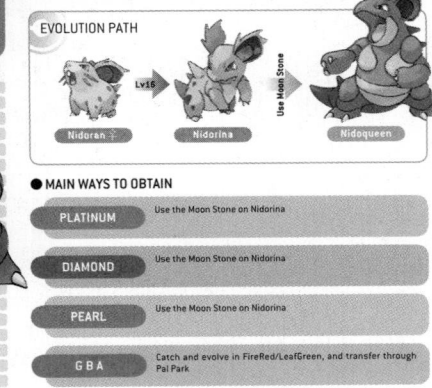
Nidoran ♀ —Lv16→ Nidorina —Use Moon Stone→ Nidoqueen

● MAIN WAYS TO OBTAIN
PLATINUM	Use the Moon Stone on Nidorina
DIAMOND	Use the Moon Stone on Nidorina
PEARL	Use the Moon Stone on Nidorina
GBA	Catch and evolve in FireRed/LeafGreen, and transfer through Pal Park

ABILITY ● Poison Point ● Rivalry

● LEVEL-UP AND LEARNED MOVES
Lv	Name	Type	Kind	Power	Acc	PP	Range	DA
Base	Scratch	Normal	Physical	40	100	35	Normal	●
Base	Tail Whip	Normal	Status	—	100	30	2 foes	●
Base	Double Kick	Fighting	Physical	30	100	30	Normal	●
Base	Poison Sting	Poison	Physical	15	100	35	Normal	●
23	Body Slam	Normal	Physical	85	100	15	Normal	●
43	Earth Power	Ground	Special	90	100	10	Normal	—
58	Superpower	Fighting	Physical	120	100	5	Normal	●

National Pokédex No. 032 Poison Pin Pokémon

Nidoran ♂

POISON

STATS
HP ●●
ATTACK ●●
DEFENSE ●●
SP. ATTACK ●●
SP. DEFENSE ●●
SPEED ●●

● Male form

EVOLUTION PATH
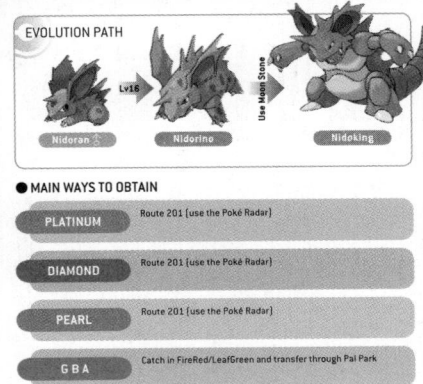
Nidoran ♂ —Lv16→ Nidorino —Use Moon Stone→ Nidoking

● MAIN WAYS TO OBTAIN
PLATINUM	Route 201 (use the Poké Radar)
DIAMOND	Route 201 (use the Poké Radar)
PEARL	Route 201 (use the Poké Radar)
GBA	Catch in FireRed/LeafGreen and transfer through Pal Park

ABILITY ● Poison Point ● Rivalry

● LEVEL-UP AND LEARNED MOVES
Lv	Name	Type	Kind	Power	Acc	PP	Range	DA
Base	Leer	Normal	Status	—	100	30	2 foes	—
Base	Peck	Flying	Physical	35	100	35	Normal	●
7	Focus Energy	Normal	Status	—	—	30	Self	—
9	Double Kick	Fighting	Physical	30	100	30	Normal	●
13	Poison Sting	Poison	Physical	15	100	35	Normal	●
19	Fury Attack	Normal	Physical	15	85	20	Normal	●
21	Horn Attack	Normal	Physical	65	100	25	Normal	●
25	Helping Hand	Normal	Status	—	—	20	1 ally	●
31	Toxic Spikes	Poison	Status	—	—	20	2 foes	—
33	Flatter	Dark	Status	—	100	15	Normal	—
37	Poison Jab	Poison	Physical	80	100	20	Normal	●
43	Captivate	Normal	Status	—	100	20	2 foes	—
45	Horn Drill	Normal	Physical	—	30	5	Normal	●

National Pokédex No. 033 Poison Pin Pokémon
Nidorino

POISON

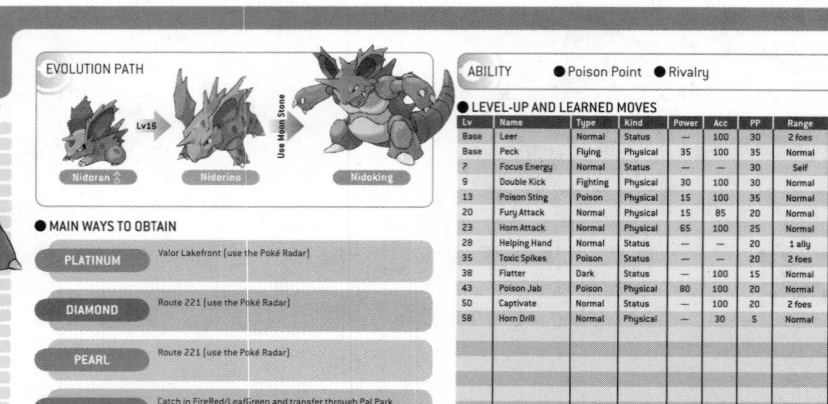

EVOLUTION PATH

Nidoran ♂ — Lv16 → Nidorino — Use Moon Stone → Nidoking

ABILITY ● Poison Point ● Rivalry

STATS
- HP ●●
- ATTACK ●●●
- DEFENSE ●●
- SP. ATTACK ●●
- SP. DEFENSE ●●
- SPEED ●●

● Male form

● MAIN WAYS TO OBTAIN

PLATINUM	Valor Lakefront (use the Poké Radar)
DIAMOND	Route 221 (use the Poké Radar)
PEARL	Route 221 (use the Poké Radar)
GBA	Catch in FireRed/LeafGreen and transfer through Pal Park

● LEVEL-UP AND LEARNED MOVES

Lv	Name	Type	Kind	Power	Acc	PP	Range	DA
Base	Leer	Normal	Status	—	100	30	2 foes	
Base	Peck	Flying	Physical	35	100	35	Normal	●
7	Focus Energy	Normal	Status	—	—	30	Self	—
9	Double Kick	Fighting	Physical	30	100	30	Normal	●
13	Poison Sting	Poison	Physical	15	100	35	Normal	●
20	Fury Attack	Normal	Physical	15	85	20	Normal	●
23	Horn Attack	Normal	Physical	65	100	25	Normal	●
28	Helping Hand	Normal	Status	—	—	20	1 ally	—
35	Toxic Spikes	Poison	Status	—	—	20	2 foes	—
38	Flatter	Dark	Status	—	100	15	Normal	—
43	Poison Jab	Poison	Physical	80	100	20	Normal	●
50	Captivate	Normal	Status	—	100	20	2 foes	—
58	Horn Drill	Normal	Physical	—	30	5	Normal	—

National Pokédex No. 034 Drill Pokémon
Nidoking

POISON GROUND

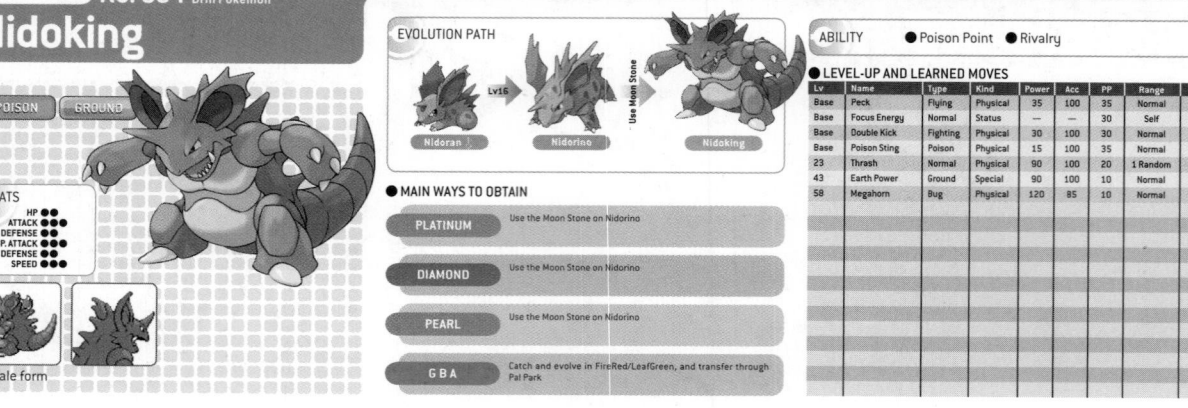

EVOLUTION PATH

Nidoran ♂ — Lv16 → Nidorino — Use Moon Stone → Nidoking

ABILITY ● Poison Point ● Rivalry

STATS
- HP ●●
- ATTACK ●●●
- DEFENSE ●●
- SP. ATTACK ●●●
- SP. DEFENSE ●●
- SPEED ●●●

● Male form

● MAIN WAYS TO OBTAIN

PLATINUM	Use the Moon Stone on Nidorino
DIAMOND	Use the Moon Stone on Nidorino
PEARL	Use the Moon Stone on Nidorino
GBA	Catch and evolve in FireRed/LeafGreen, and transfer through Pal Park

● LEVEL-UP AND LEARNED MOVES

Lv	Name	Type	Kind	Power	Acc	PP	Range	DA
Base	Peck	Flying	Physical	35	100	35	Normal	●
Base	Focus Energy	Normal	Status	—	—	30	Self	—
Base	Double Kick	Fighting	Physical	30	100	30	Normal	●
Base	Poison Sting	Poison	Physical	15	100	35	Normal	●
23	Thrash	Normal	Physical	90	100	20	1 Random	●
43	Earth Power	Ground	Special	90	100	10	Normal	—
58	Megahorn	Bug	Physical	120	85	10	Normal	●

National Pokédex No. 035 Fairy Pokémon
Clefairy

NORMAL

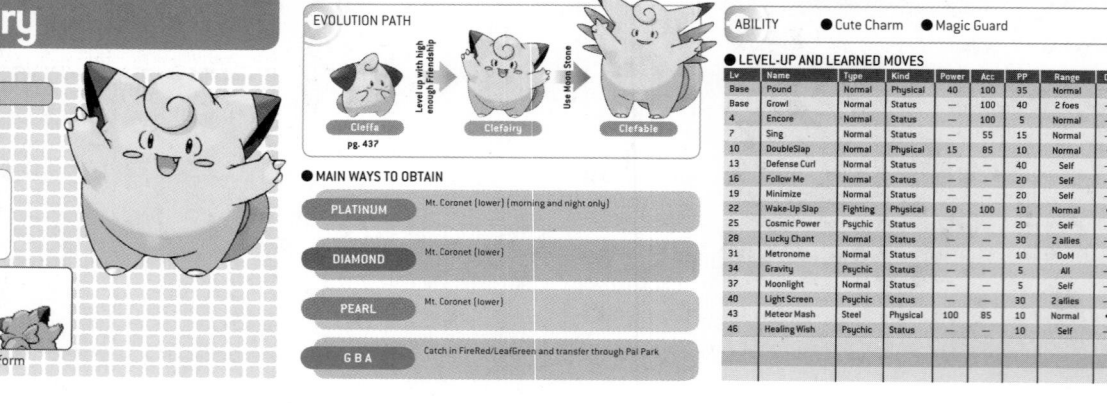

EVOLUTION PATH

Cleffa pg. 437 — Level up with high enough Friendship → Clefairy — Use Moon Stone → Clefable

ABILITY ● Cute Charm ● Magic Guard

STATS
- HP ●●
- ATTACK ●●
- DEFENSE ●●
- SP. ATTACK ●●
- SP. DEFENSE ●●
- SPEED ●

● M/F have same form

● MAIN WAYS TO OBTAIN

PLATINUM	Mt. Coronet (lower) (morning and night only)
DIAMOND	Mt. Coronet (lower)
PEARL	Mt. Coronet (lower)
GBA	Catch in FireRed/LeafGreen and transfer through Pal Park

● LEVEL-UP AND LEARNED MOVES

Lv	Name	Type	Kind	Power	Acc	PP	Range	DA
Base	Pound	Normal	Physical	40	100	35	Normal	●
Base	Growl	Normal	Status	—	100	40	2 foes	—
4	Encore	Normal	Status	—	100	5	Normal	—
7	Sing	Normal	Status	—	55	15	Normal	—
10	DoubleSlap	Normal	Physical	15	85	10	Normal	●
13	Defense Curl	Normal	Status	—	—	40	Self	—
16	Follow Me	Normal	Status	—	—	20	Self	—
19	Minimize	Normal	Status	—	—	20	Self	—
22	Wake-Up Slap	Fighting	Physical	60	100	10	Normal	●
25	Cosmic Power	Psychic	Status	—	—	20	Self	—
28	Lucky Chant	Normal	Status	—	—	30	2 allies	—
31	Metronome	Normal	Status	—	—	10	DoM	—
34	Gravity	Psychic	Status	—	—	5	All	—
37	Moonlight	Normal	Status	—	—	5	Self	—
40	Light Screen	Psychic	Status	—	—	30	2 allies	—
43	Meteor Mash	Steel	Physical	100	85	10	Normal	●
46	Healing Wish	Psychic	Status	—	—	10	Self	—

National Pokédex No. 036 Fairy Pokémon
Clefable

NORMAL

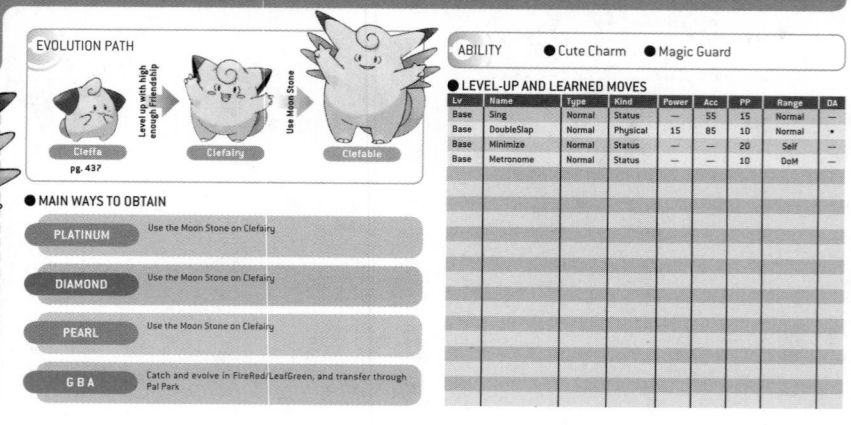

EVOLUTION PATH

Cleffa pg. 437 — Level up with high enough Friendship → Clefairy — Use Moon Stone → Clefable

ABILITY ● Cute Charm ● Magic Guard

STATS
- HP ●●●
- ATTACK ●●
- DEFENSE ●●
- SP. ATTACK ●●●
- SP. DEFENSE ●●
- SPEED ●●

● M/F have same form

● MAIN WAYS TO OBTAIN

PLATINUM	Use the Moon Stone on Clefairy
DIAMOND	Use the Moon Stone on Clefairy
PEARL	Use the Moon Stone on Clefairy
GBA	Catch and evolve in FireRed/LeafGreen, and transfer through Pal Park

● LEVEL-UP AND LEARNED MOVES

Lv	Name	Type	Kind	Power	Acc	PP	Range	DA
Base	Sing	Normal	Status	—	55	15	Normal	—
Base	DoubleSlap	Normal	Physical	15	85	10	Normal	●
Base	Minimize	Normal	Status	—	—	20	Self	—
Base	Metronome	Normal	Status	—	—	10	DoM	—

National Pokédex No. 037 Fox Pokémon
Vulpix

FIRE

STATS
HP ●
ATTACK ●●
DEFENSE ●
SP. ATTACK ●●●
SP. DEFENSE ●●●
SPEED ●●

● M/F have same form

EVOLUTION PATH

Vulpix — Use Fire Stone → Ninetales

MAIN WAYS TO OBTAIN

PLATINUM	Route 209 (after you get the National Pokédex, insert a Pokémon LeafGreen cartridge into the Nintendo DS's GBA cartridge slot)
DIAMOND	Route 209 (after you get the National Pokédex, insert a Pokémon LeafGreen cartridge into the Nintendo DS's GBA cartridge Slot)
PEARL	Route 209 (after you get the National Pokédex, insert a Pokémon LeafGreen cartridge into the Nintendo DS's GBA cartridge Slot)
GBA	Catch in LeafGreen or Ruby/Sapphire/Emerald, and transfer through Pal Park

ABILITY ● Flash Fire

● LEVEL-UP AND LEARNED MOVES

Lv	Name	Type	Kind	Power	Acc	PP	Range	DA
Base	Ember	Fire	Special	40	100	25	Normal	—
4	Tail Whip	Normal	Status	—	100	30	2 foes	—
7	Roar	Normal	Status	—	100	20	Normal	—
11	Quick Attack	Normal	Physical	40	100	30	Normal	●
14	Will-O-Wisp	Fire	Status	—	75	15	Normal	—
17	Confuse Ray	Ghost	Status	—	100	10	Normal	—
21	Imprison	Psychic	Status	—	—	10	Self	—
24	Flamethrower	Fire	Special	95	100	15	Normal	—
27	Safeguard	Normal	Status	—	—	25	2 allies	—
31	Payback	Dark	Physical	50	100	10	Normal	●
34	Fire Spin	Fire	Special	15	70	15	Normal	—
37	Captivate	Normal	Status	—	100	20	2 foes	—
41	Grudge	Ghost	Status	—	—	5	Self	—
44	Extrasensory	Psychic	Special	80	100	30	Normal	—
47	Fire Blast	Fire	Special	120	85	5	Normal	—

National Pokédex No. 038 Fox Pokémon
Ninetales

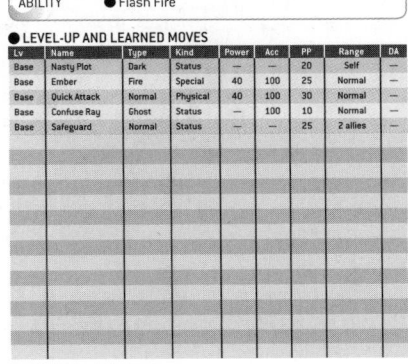

FIRE

STATS
HP ●●
ATTACK ●●●
DEFENSE ●●●
SP. ATTACK ●●●●
SP. DEFENSE ●●●●
SPEED ●●●●

● M/F have same form

EVOLUTION PATH

Vulpix — Use Fire Stone → Ninetales

MAIN WAYS TO OBTAIN

PLATINUM	Use the Fire Stone on Vulpix
DIAMOND	Use the Fire Stone on Vulpix
PEARL	Use the Fire Stone on Vulpix
GBA	Catch and evolve in LeafGreen or Ruby/Sapphire/Emerald, and transfer through Pal Park

ABILITY ● Flash Fire

● LEVEL-UP AND LEARNED MOVES

Lv	Name	Type	Kind	Power	Acc	PP	Range	DA
Base	Nasty Plot	Dark	Status	—	—	20	Self	—
Base	Ember	Fire	Special	40	100	25	Normal	—
Base	Quick Attack	Normal	Physical	40	100	30	Normal	●
Base	Confuse Ray	Ghost	Status	—	100	10	Normal	—
Base	Safeguard	Normal	Status	—	—	25	2 allies	—

National Pokédex No. 039 Balloon Pokémon
Jigglypuff

NORMAL

STATS
HP ●●●
ATTACK ●●
DEFENSE ●
SP. ATTACK ●●
SP. DEFENSE ●
SPEED ●●

● M/F have same form

EVOLUTION PATH

Igglybuff (pg. 437) — Level up with high enough Friendship → Jigglypuff — Use Moon Stone → Wigglytuff

MAIN WAYS TO OBTAIN

PLATINUM	Trophy Garden in the Pokémon Mansion on Route 212 (talk to Mr. Backlot after you get the National Pokédex)
DIAMOND	Trophy Garden in the Pokémon Mansion on Route 212 (talk to Mr. Backlot after you get the National Pokédex)
PEARL	Trophy Garden in the Pokémon Mansion on Route 212 (talk to Mr. Backlot after you get the National Pokédex)
GBA	Catch in any GBA-series Pokémon game and transfer through Pal Park

ABILITY ● Cute Charm

● LEVEL-UP AND LEARNED MOVES

Lv	Name	Type	Kind	Power	Acc	PP	Range	DA
Base	Sing	Normal	Status	—	55	15	Normal	—
5	Defense Curl	Normal	Status	—	—	40	Self	—
9	Pound	Normal	Physical	40	100	35	Normal	●
13	Disable	Normal	Status	—	80	20	Normal	—
17	Rollout	Rock	Physical	30	90	20	Normal	●
21	DoubleSlap	Normal	Physical	15	85	10	Normal	●
25	Rest	Psychic	Status	—	—	10	Self	—
29	Body Slam	Normal	Physical	85	100	15	Normal	●
33	Gyro Ball	Steel	Physical	—	100	5	Normal	●
37	Wake-Up Slap	Fighting	Physical	60	100	10	Normal	●
41	Mimic	Normal	Status	—	—	10	Normal	—
45	Hyper Voice	Normal	Special	90	100	10	2 foes	—
49	Double-Edge	Normal	Physical	120	100	15	Normal	●

National Pokédex No. 040 Balloon Pokémon
Wigglytuff

NORMAL

STATS
HP ●●●●
ATTACK ●●●
DEFENSE ●●
SP. ATTACK ●●●
SP. DEFENSE ●●
SPEED ●●

● M/F have same form

EVOLUTION PATH

Igglybuff (pg. 437) — Level up with high enough Friendship → Jigglypuff — Use Moon Stone → Wigglytuff

MAIN WAYS TO OBTAIN

PLATINUM	Use the Moon Stone on Jigglypuff
DIAMOND	Use the Moon Stone on Jigglypuff
PEARLS	Use the Moon Stone on Jigglypuff
GBA	Catch and evolve in any GBA-series Pokémon game and transfer through Pal Park

ABILITY ● Cute Charm

● LEVEL-UP AND LEARNED MOVES

Lv	Name	Type	Kind	Power	Acc	PP	Range	DA
Base	Sing	Normal	Status	—	55	15	Normal	—
Base	Disable	Normal	Status	—	80	20	Normal	—
Base	Defense Curl	Normal	Status	—	—	40	Self	—
Base	DoubleSlap	Normal	Physical	15	85	10	Normal	●

040
WIGGLYTUFF

041
ZUBAT

No. 041 Bat Pokémon
Zubat

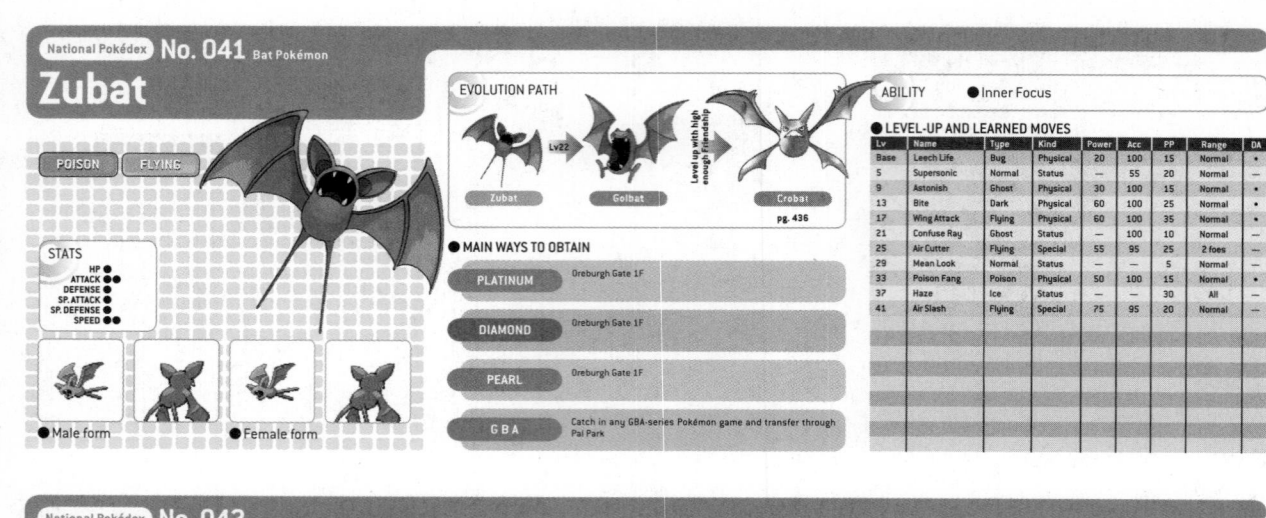

POISON | FLYING

STATS
HP ●
ATTACK ●●
DEFENSE ●●
SP. ATTACK ●
SP. DEFENSE ●●
SPEED ●●

● Male form   ● Female form

EVOLUTION PATH

Zubat → (Lv22) Golbat → (Level up with high enough friendship) Crobat pg. 436

ABILITY ● Inner Focus

● **MAIN WAYS TO OBTAIN**

PLATINUM	Oreburgh Gate 1F
DIAMOND	Oreburgh Gate 1F
PEARL	Oreburgh Gate 1F
GBA	Catch in any GBA-series Pokémon game and transfer through Pal Park

● **LEVEL-UP AND LEARNED MOVES**

Lv	Name	Type	Kind	Power	Acc	PP	Range	DA
Base	Leech Life	Bug	Physical	20	100	15	Normal	●
5	Supersonic	Normal	Status	—	55	20	Normal	—
9	Astonish	Ghost	Physical	30	100	15	Normal	●
13	Bite	Dark	Physical	60	100	25	Normal	●
17	Wing Attack	Flying	Physical	60	100	35	Normal	●
21	Confuse Ray	Ghost	Status	—	100	10	Normal	—
25	Air Cutter	Flying	Special	55	95	25	2 foes	—
29	Mean Look	Normal	Status	—	—	5	Normal	—
33	Poison Fang	Poison	Physical	50	100	15	Normal	—
37	Haze	Ice	Status	—	—	30	All	—
41	Air Slash	Flying	Special	75	95	20	Normal	●

No. 042 Bat Pokémon
Golbat

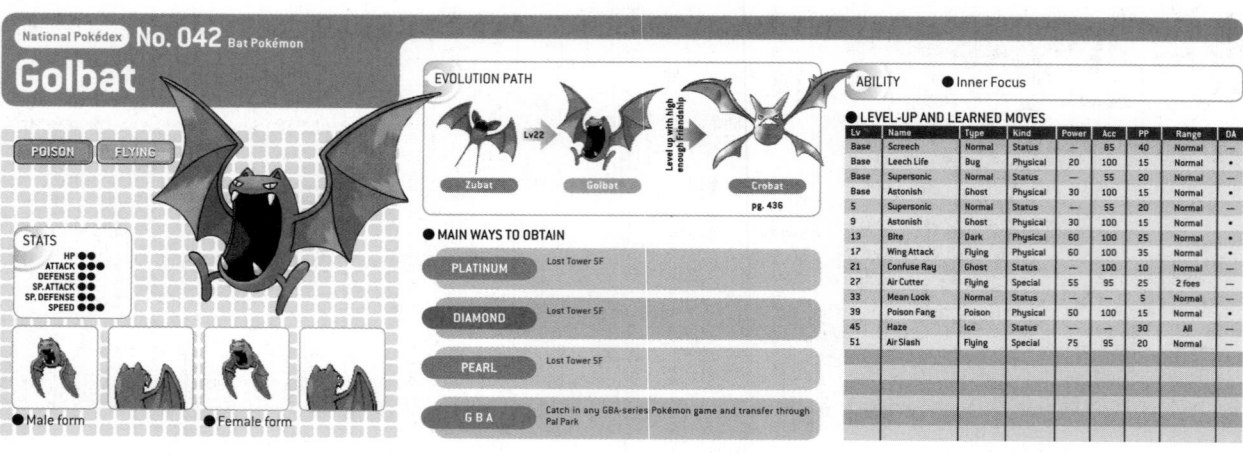

POISON | FLYING

STATS
HP ●●
ATTACK ●●●
DEFENSE ●●
SP. ATTACK ●●
SP. DEFENSE ●●
SPEED ●●●

● Male form   ● Female form

EVOLUTION PATH

Zubat → (Lv22) Golbat → (Level up with high enough friendship) Crobat pg. 436

ABILITY ● Inner Focus

● **MAIN WAYS TO OBTAIN**

PLATINUM	Lost Tower 5F
DIAMOND	Lost Tower 5F
PEARL	Lost Tower 5F
GBA	Catch in any GBA-series Pokémon game and transfer through Pal Park

● **LEVEL-UP AND LEARNED MOVES**

Lv	Name	Type	Kind	Power	Acc	PP	Range	DA
Base	Screech	Normal	Status	—	85	40	Normal	—
Base	Leech Life	Bug	Physical	20	100	15	Normal	●
Base	Supersonic	Normal	Status	—	55	20	Normal	—
Base	Astonish	Ghost	Physical	30	100	15	Normal	●
5	Supersonic	Normal	Status	—	55	20	Normal	—
9	Astonish	Ghost	Physical	30	100	15	Normal	●
13	Bite	Dark	Physical	60	100	25	Normal	●
17	Wing Attack	Flying	Physical	60	100	35	Normal	●
21	Confuse Ray	Ghost	Status	—	100	10	Normal	—
27	Air Cutter	Flying	Special	55	95	25	2 foes	—
33	Mean Look	Normal	Status	—	—	5	Normal	—
39	Poison Fang	Poison	Physical	50	100	15	Normal	—
45	Haze	Ice	Status	—	—	30	All	—
51	Air Slash	Flying	Special	75	95	20	Normal	●

No. 043 Weed Pokémon
Oddish

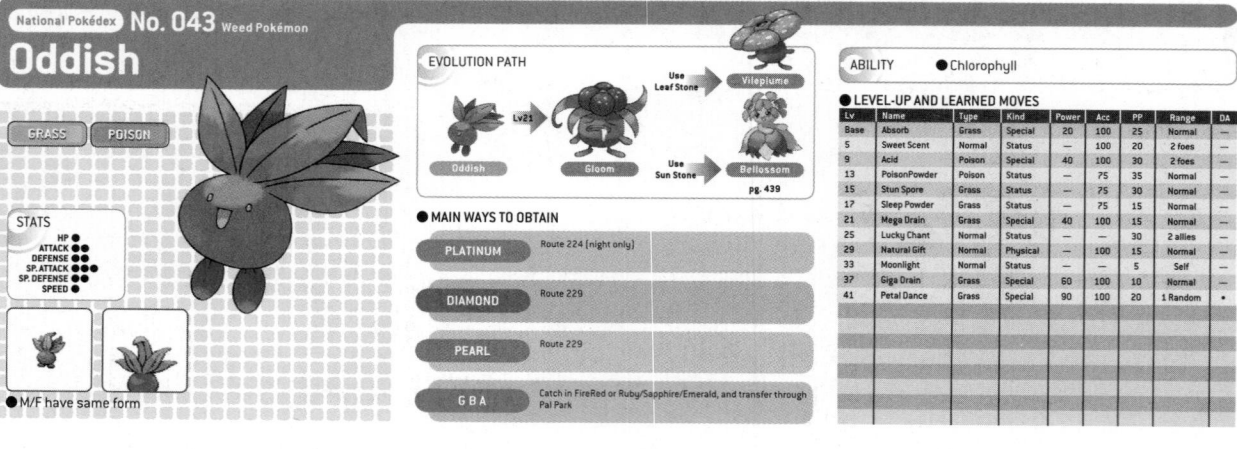

GRASS | POISON

STATS
HP ●
ATTACK ●●
DEFENSE ●●
SP. ATTACK ●●●
SP. DEFENSE ●●●
SPEED ●

● M/F have same form

EVOLUTION PATH

Oddish → (Lv21) Gloom → (Use Leaf Stone) Vileplume / (Use Sun Stone) Bellossom pg. 439

ABILITY ● Chlorophyll

● **MAIN WAYS TO OBTAIN**

PLATINUM	Route 224 (night only)
DIAMOND	Route 229
PEARL	Route 229
GBA	Catch in FireRed or Ruby/Sapphire/Emerald, and transfer through Pal Park

● **LEVEL-UP AND LEARNED MOVES**

Lv	Name	Type	Kind	Power	Acc	PP	Range	DA
Base	Absorb	Grass	Special	20	100	25	Normal	—
5	Sweet Scent	Normal	Status	—	100	20	2 foes	—
9	Acid	Poison	Special	40	100	30	2 foes	—
13	PoisonPowder	Poison	Status	—	75	35	Normal	—
15	Stun Spore	Grass	Status	—	75	30	Normal	—
17	Sleep Powder	Grass	Status	—	75	15	Normal	—
21	Mega Drain	Grass	Special	40	100	15	Normal	—
25	Lucky Chant	Normal	Status	—	—	30	2 allies	—
29	Natural Gift	Normal	Physical	—	100	15	Normal	—
33	Moonlight	Normal	Status	—	—	5	Self	—
37	Giga Drain	Grass	Special	60	100	10	Normal	—
41	Petal Dance	Grass	Special	90	100	20	1 Random	●

No. 044 Weed Pokémon
Gloom

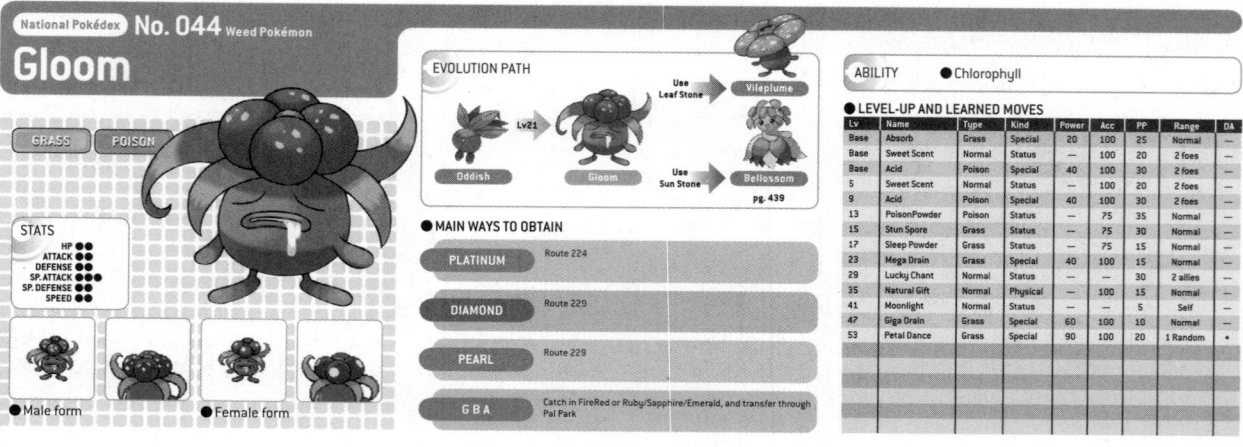

GRASS | POISON

STATS
HP ●●
ATTACK ●●●
DEFENSE ●●●
SP. ATTACK ●●●
SP. DEFENSE ●●●
SPEED ●●

● Male form   ● Female form

EVOLUTION PATH

Oddish → (Lv21) Gloom → (Use Leaf Stone) Vileplume / (Use Sun Stone) Bellossom pg. 439

ABILITY ● Chlorophyll

● **MAIN WAYS TO OBTAIN**

PLATINUM	Route 224
DIAMOND	Route 229
PEARL	Route 229
GBA	Catch in FireRed or Ruby/Sapphire/Emerald, and transfer through Pal Park

● **LEVEL-UP AND LEARNED MOVES**

Lv	Name	Type	Kind	Power	Acc	PP	Range	DA
Base	Absorb	Grass	Special	20	100	25	Normal	—
Base	Sweet Scent	Normal	Status	—	100	20	2 foes	—
Base	Acid	Poison	Special	40	100	30	2 foes	—
5	Sweet Scent	Normal	Status	—	100	20	2 foes	—
9	Acid	Poison	Special	40	100	30	2 foes	—
13	PoisonPowder	Poison	Status	—	75	35	Normal	—
15	Stun Spore	Grass	Status	—	75	30	Normal	—
17	Sleep Powder	Grass	Status	—	75	15	Normal	—
23	Mega Drain	Grass	Special	40	100	15	Normal	—
29	Lucky Chant	Normal	Status	—	—	30	2 allies	—
35	Natural Gift	Normal	Physical	—	100	15	Normal	—
41	Moonlight	Normal	Status	—	—	5	Self	—
47	Giga Drain	Grass	Special	60	100	10	Normal	—
53	Petal Dance	Grass	Special	90	100	20	1 Random	●

National Pokédex No. 045 — Flower Pokémon
Vileplume

GRASS | POISON

STATS
- HP ●●
- ATTACK ●●●
- DEFENSE ●●●
- SP. ATTACK ●●●●●
- SP. DEFENSE ●●●●
- SP. SPEED ●●

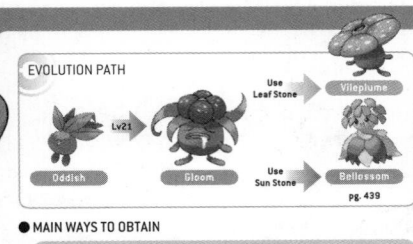

- ● Male form
- ● Female form

EVOLUTION PATH

Oddish → (Lv21) → Gloom → Use Leaf Stone → Vileplume
Gloom → Use Sun Stone → Bellossom (pg. 439)

● MAIN WAYS TO OBTAIN

PLATINUM	Use the Leaf Stone on Gloom
DIAMOND	Use the Leaf Stone on Gloom
PEARL	Use the Leaf Stone on Gloom
G B A	Catch and evolve in FireRed or Ruby/Sapphire/Emerald, and transfer through Pal Park

ABILITY ● Chlorophyll

● LEVEL-UP AND LEARNED MOVES

Lv	Name	Type	Kind	Power	Acc	PP	Range	DA
Base	Mega Drain	Grass	Special	40	100	15	Normal	—
Base	Aromatherapy	Grass	Status	—	—	5	All Allies	—
Base	Stun Spore	Grass	Status	—	75	30	Normal	—
Base	PoisonPowder	Poison	Status	—	75	35	Normal	—
53	Petal Dance	Grass	Special	90	100	20	1 Random	●
65	SolarBeam	Grass	Special	120	100	10	Normal	●

National Pokédex No. 046 — Mushroom Pokémon
Paras

BUG | GRASS

STATS
- HP ●
- ATTACK ●●●●
- DEFENSE ●●●
- SP. ATTACK ●●
- SP. DEFENSE ●●
- SPEED ●

- ● M/F have same form

EVOLUTION PATH

Paras → (Lv24) → Parasect

● MAIN WAYS TO OBTAIN

PLATINUM	Pastoria Great Marsh (after you get the National Pokédex/changes by day)
DIAMOND	Pastoria Great Marsh (after you get the National Pokédex/changes by day)
PEARL	Pastoria Great Marsh (after you get the National Pokédex/changes by day)
G B A	Catch in FireRed/LeafGreen and transfer through Pal Park

ABILITY ● Effect Spore ● Dry Skin

● LEVEL-UP AND LEARNED MOVES

Lv	Name	Type	Kind	Power	Acc	PP	Range	DA
Base	Scratch	Normal	Physical	40	100	35	Normal	—
6	Stun Spore	Grass	Status	—	75	30	Normal	—
6	PoisonPowder	Poison	Status	—	75	35	Normal	—
11	Leech Life	Bug	Physical	20	100	15	Normal	●
17	Spore	Grass	Status	—	100	15	Normal	—
22	Slash	Normal	Physical	70	100	20	Normal	●
27	Growth	Normal	Status	—	—	40	Self	—
33	Giga Drain	Grass	Special	60	100	10	Normal	●
38	Aromatherapy	Grass	Status	—	—	5	All Allies	—
43	X-Scissor	Bug	Physical	80	100	15	Normal	●

National Pokédex No. 047 — Mushroom Pokémon
Parasect

BUG | GRASS

STATS
- HP ●●
- ATTACK ●●●●
- DEFENSE ●●●●
- SP. ATTACK ●●
- SP. DEFENSE ●●●
- SPEED ●

- ● M/F have same form

EVOLUTION PATH

Paras → (Lv24) → Parasect

● MAIN WAYS TO OBTAIN

PLATINUM	Level up Paras to Lv24
DIAMOND	Level up Paras to Lv24
PEARL	Level up Paras to Lv24
G B A	Catch in FireRed/LeafGreen and transfer through Pal Park

ABILITY ● Effect Spore ● Dry Skin

● LEVEL-UP AND LEARNED MOVES

Lv	Name	Type	Kind	Power	Acc	PP	Range	DA
Base	Cross Poison	Poison	Physical	70	100	20	Normal	●
Base	Scratch	Normal	Physical	40	100	35	Normal	—
Base	Stun Spore	Grass	Status	—	75	30	Normal	—
Base	PoisonPowder	Poison	Status	—	75	35	Normal	—
Base	Leech Life	Bug	Physical	20	100	15	Normal	●
6	Stun Spore	Grass	Status	—	75	30	Normal	—
6	PoisonPowder	Poison	Status	—	75	35	Normal	—
11	Leech Life	Bug	Physical	20	100	15	Normal	●
17	Spore	Grass	Status	—	100	15	Normal	—
22	Slash	Normal	Physical	70	100	20	Normal	●
30	Growth	Normal	Status	—	—	40	Self	—
39	Giga Drain	Grass	Special	60	100	10	Normal	●
47	Aromatherapy	Grass	Status	—	—	5	All Allies	—
55	X-Scissor	Bug	Physical	80	100	15	Normal	●

National Pokédex No. 048 — Insect Pokémon
Venonat

BUG | POISON

STATS
- HP ●●●
- ATTACK ●●●
- DEFENSE ●●
- SP. ATTACK ●●
- SP. DEFENSE ●●●
- SPEED ●●

- ● M/F have same form

EVOLUTION PATH

Venonat → (Lv31) → Venomoth

● MAIN WAYS TO OBTAIN

PLATINUM	Route 229 (use the Poké Radar)
DIAMOND	Route 229 (use the Poké Radar)
PEARL	Route 229 (use the Poké Radar)
G B A	Catch in FireRed/LeafGreen and transfer through Pal Park

ABILITY ● Compoundeyes ● Tinted Lens

● LEVEL-UP AND LEARNED MOVES

Lv	Name	Type	Kind	Power	Acc	PP	Range	DA
Base	Tackle	Normal	Physical	35	95	35	Normal	●
Base	Disable	Normal	Status	—	80	20	Normal	—
Base	Foresight	Normal	Status	—	—	40	Normal	—
5	Supersonic	Normal	Status	—	55	20	Normal	—
11	Confusion	Psychic	Special	50	100	25	Normal	—
13	PoisonPowder	Poison	Status	—	75	35	Normal	—
17	Leech Life	Bug	Physical	20	100	15	Normal	●
23	Stun Spore	Grass	Status	—	75	30	Normal	—
25	Psybeam	Psychic	Special	65	100	20	Normal	—
29	Sleep Powder	Grass	Status	—	75	15	Normal	—
35	Signal Beam	Bug	Special	75	100	15	Normal	—
37	Zen Headbutt	Psychic	Physical	80	90	15	Normal	●
41	Poison Fang	Poison	Physical	50	100	15	Normal	●
47	Psychic	Psychic	Special	90	100	10	Normal	—

048
VENONAT

National Pokédex No. 049 — Poison Moth Pokémon

Venomoth

BUG   POISON

STATS
HP ●●
ATTACK ●●
DEFENSE ●●
SP. ATTACK ●●●
SP. DEFENSE ●●
SPEED ●●●

● M/F have same form

● EVOLUTION PATH

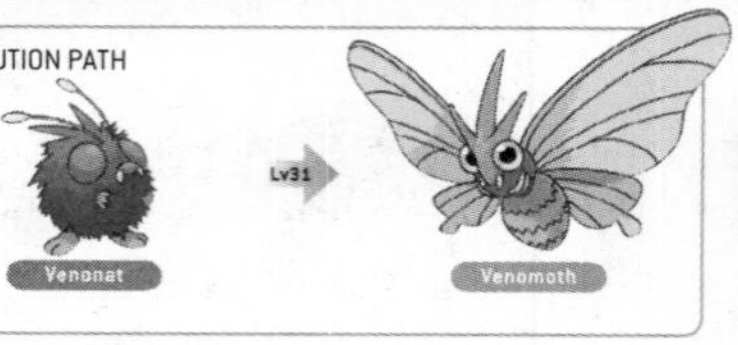

Venonat → Lv31 → Venomoth

● MAIN WAYS TO OBTAIN

PLATINUM	Route 229 (use the Poké Radar)
DIAMOND	Route 229 (use the Poké Radar)
PEARL	Route 229 (use the Poké Radar)
GBA	Catch in FireRed/LeafGreen and transfer through Pal Park

● ABILITY   ● Shield Dust   ● Tinted Lens

● LEVEL-UP AND LEARNED MOVES

Lv	Name	Type	Kind	Power	Acc	PP	Range	DA
Base	Silver Wind	Bug	Special	60	100	5	Normal	—
Base	Tackle	Normal	Physical	35	95	35	Normal	●
Base	Disable	Normal	Status	—	80	20	Normal	●
Base	Foresight	Normal	Status	—	—	40	Normal	—
Base	Supersonic	Normal	Status	—	55	20	Normal	—
5	Supersonic	Normal	Status	—	55	20	Normal	—
11	Confusion	Psychic	Special	50	100	25	Normal	—
13	PoisonPowder	Poison	Status	—	75	35	Normal	—
17	Leech Life	Bug	Physical	20	100	15	Normal	—
23	Stun Spore	Grass	Status	—	75	30	Normal	—
25	Psybeam	Psychic	Special	65	100	20	Normal	—
29	Sleep Powder	Grass	Status	—	75	15	Normal	—
31	Gust	Flying	Special	40	100	35	Normal	—
37	Signal Beam	Bug	Special	75	100	15	Normal	—
41	Zen Headbutt	Psychic	Physical	80	90	15	Normal	—
47	Poison Fang	Poison	Physical	50	100	15	Normal	—
55	Psychic	Psychic	Special	90	100	10	Normal	—
59	Bug Buzz	Bug	Special	90	100	10	Normal	—

National Pokédex No. 050 — Mole Pokémon

Diglett

GROUND

STATS
HP ●
ATTACK ●●
DEFENSE ●
SP. ATTACK ●●
SP. DEFENSE ●●
SPEED ●●●

● M/F have same form

● EVOLUTION PATH

Diglett → Lv26 → Dugtrio

● MAIN WAYS TO OBTAIN

PLATINUM	Route 228
DIAMOND	Route 228
PEARL	Route 228
GBA	Catch in FireRed/LeafGreen and transfer through Pal Park

● ABILITY   ● Sand Veil   ● Arena Trap

● LEVEL-UP AND LEARNED MOVES

Lv	Name	Type	Kind	Power	Acc	PP	Range	DA
Base	Scratch	Normal	Physical	40	100	35	Normal	●
Base	Sand-Attack	Ground	Status	—	100	15	Normal	●
4	Growl	Normal	Status	—	100	40	2 foes	●
7	Astonish	Ghost	Physical	30	100	15	Normal	●
12	Magnitude	Ground	Physical	—	100	30	2 foes + 1 ally	●
15	Mud-Slap	Ground	Special	20	100	10	Normal	—
18	Dig	Ground	Physical	80	100	10	Normal	—
23	Sucker Punch	Dark	Physical	80	100	5	Normal	—
26	Earth Power	Ground	Special	90	100	10	Normal	—
29	Mud Bomb	Ground	Special	65	85	10	Normal	—
34	Slash	Normal	Physical	70	100	20	Normal	—
37	Earthquake	Ground	Physical	100	100	10	2 foes + 1 ally	—
40	Fissure	Ground	Physical	—	30	5	Normal	—

National Pokédex No. 051 — Mole Pokémon

Dugtrio

GROUND

STATS
HP ●
ATTACK ●●
DEFENSE ●●
SP. ATTACK ●●
SP. DEFENSE ●●●
SPEED ●●●●

● M/F have same form

● EVOLUTION PATH

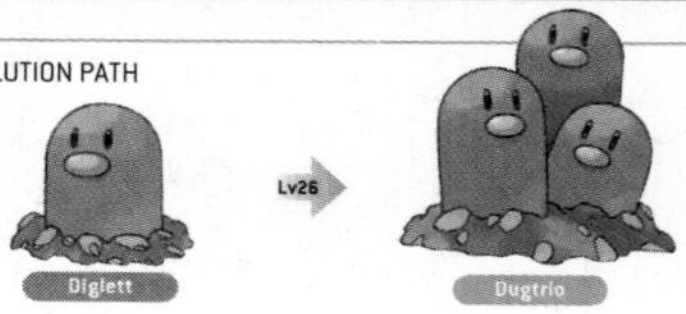

Diglett → Lv26 → Dugtrio

● MAIN WAYS TO OBTAIN

PLATINUM	Route 228
DIAMOND	Route 228
PEARL	Route 228
GBA	Catch in FireRed/LeafGreen and transfer through Pal Park

● ABILITY   ● Sand Veil   ● Arena Trap

● LEVEL-UP AND LEARNED MOVES

Lv	Name	Type	Kind	Power	Acc	PP	Range	DA
Base	Night Slash	Dark	Physical	70	100	15	Normal	—
Base	Tri Attack	Normal	Special	80	100	10	Normal	—
Base	Scratch	Normal	Physical	40	100	35	Normal	●
Base	Sand-Attack	Ground	Status	—	100	15	Normal	●
Base	Growl	Normal	Status	—	100	40	2 foes	●
4	Growl	Normal	Status	—	100	40	2 foes	●
7	Astonish	Ghost	Physical	30	100	15	Normal	●
12	Magnitude	Ground	Physical	—	100	30	2 foes + 1 ally	●
15	Mud-Slap	Ground	Special	20	100	10	Normal	—
18	Dig	Ground	Physical	80	100	10	Normal	—
23	Sucker Punch	Dark	Physical	80	100	5	Normal	—
26	Sand Tomb	Ground	Physical	15	70	15	Normal	—
28	Earth Power	Ground	Special	90	100	10	Normal	—
33	Mud Bomb	Ground	Special	65	85	10	Normal	—
40	Slash	Normal	Physical	70	100	20	Normal	—
45	Earthquake	Ground	Physical	100	100	10	2 foes + 1 ally	—
50	Fissure	Ground	Physical	—	30	5	Normal	—

National Pokédex No. 052 — Scratch Cat Pokémon

Meowth

NORMAL

STATS
HP ●●
ATTACK ●●
DEFENSE ●●
SP. ATTACK ●●
SP. DEFENSE ●●
SPEED ●●●

● M/F have same form

● EVOLUTION PATH

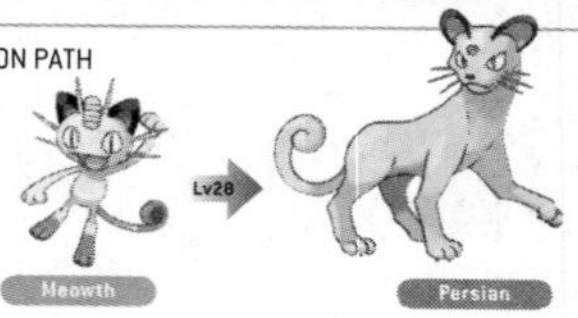

Meowth → Lv28 → Persian

● MAIN WAYS TO OBTAIN

PLATINUM	Trophy Garden in the Pokémon Mansion on Route 212 (talk to Mr. Backlot after you get the National Pokédex)
DIAMOND	Trophy Garden in the Pokémon Mansion on Route 212 (talk to Mr. Backlot after you get the National Pokédex)
PEARL	Trophy Garden in the Pokémon Mansion on Route 212 (talk to Mr. Backlot after you get the National Pokédex)
GBA	Catch in FireRed/LeafGreen and transfer through Pal Park

● ABILITY   ● Pickup   ● Technician

● LEVEL-UP AND LEARNED MOVES

Lv	Name	Type	Kind	Power	Acc	PP	Range	DA
Base	Scratch	Normal	Physical	40	100	35	Normal	●
Base	Growl	Normal	Status	—	100	40	2 foes	●
6	Bite	Dark	Physical	60	100	25	Normal	●
9	Fake Out	Normal	Physical	40	100	10	Normal	●
14	Fury Swipes	Normal	Physical	18	80	15	Normal	—
17	Screech	Normal	Status	—	85	40	Normal	—
22	Faint Attack	Dark	Physical	60	—	20	Normal	—
25	Taunt	Dark	Status	—	100	20	Normal	—
30	Pay Day	Normal	Physical	40	100	20	Normal	—
33	Slash	Normal	Physical	70	100	20	Normal	—
38	Nasty Plot	Dark	Status	—	—	20	Self	—
41	Assurance	Dark	Physical	50	100	10	Normal	—
46	Captivate	Normal	Status	—	100	20	2 foes	—
49	Night Slash	Dark	Physical	70	100	15	Normal	—
54	Feint	Normal	Physical	50	100	10	Normal	—

National Pokédex No. 053 Classy Cat Pokémon
Persian

NORMAL

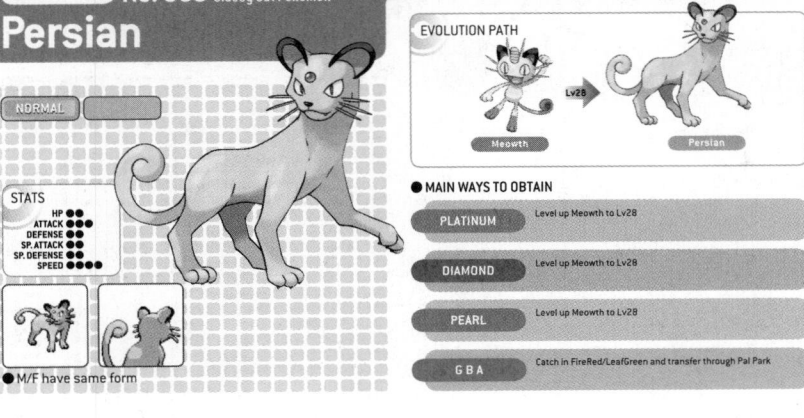

● M/F have same form

STATS
- HP ●●
- ATTACK ●●●
- DEFENSE ●●●
- SP. ATTACK ●●●
- SP. DEFENSE ●●●
- SPEED ●●●●

● EVOLUTION PATH

Meowth → Lv28 → Persian

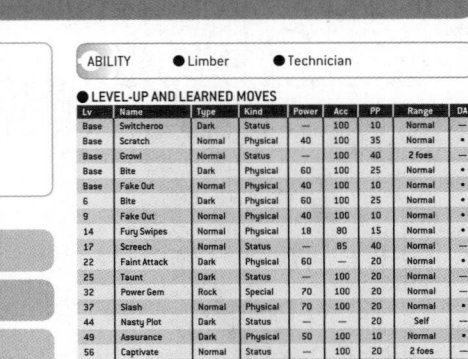

● MAIN WAYS TO OBTAIN

PLATINUM	Level up Meowth to Lv28
DIAMOND	Level up Meowth to Lv28
PEARL	Level up Meowth to Lv28
GBA	Catch in FireRed/LeafGreen and transfer through Pal Park

ABILITY ● Limber ● Technician

● LEVEL-UP AND LEARNED MOVES

Lv	Name	Type	Kind	Power	Acc	PP	Range	DA
Base	Switcheroo	Dark	Status	—	100	10	Normal	—
Base	Scratch	Normal	Physical	40	100	35	Normal	•
Base	Growl	Normal	Status	—	100	40	2 foes	•
Base	Bite	Dark	Physical	60	100	25	Normal	•
Base	Fake Out	Normal	Physical	40	100	10	Normal	•
6	Bite	Dark	Physical	60	100	25	Normal	•
9	Fake Out	Normal	Physical	40	100	10	Normal	•
14	Fury Swipes	Normal	Physical	18	80	15	Normal	•
17	Screech	Normal	Status	—	85	40	Normal	•
22	Faint Attack	Dark	Physical	60	—	20	Normal	—
25	Taunt	Dark	Status	—	100	20	Normal	—
32	Power Gem	Rock	Special	70	100	20	Normal	—
37	Slash	Normal	Physical	70	100	20	Normal	•
44	Nasty Plot	Dark	Status	—	—	20	Self	—
49	Assurance	Dark	Physical	50	100	10	Normal	•
56	Captivate	Normal	Status	—	100	20	2 foes	—
61	Night Slash	Dark	Physical	70	100	15	Normal	•
68	Feint	Normal	Physical	50	100	10	Normal	—

National Pokédex No. 054 Duck Pokémon
Psyduck

WATER

● M/F have same form

STATS
- HP ●●
- ATTACK ●●
- DEFENSE ●●
- SP. ATTACK ●●●
- SP. DEFENSE ●●
- SPEED ●●

● EVOLUTION PATH

Psyduck → Lv33 → Golduck

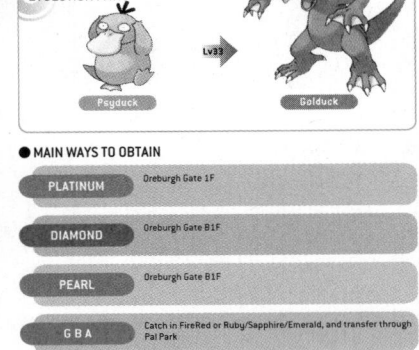

● MAIN WAYS TO OBTAIN

PLATINUM	Oreburgh Gate 1F
DIAMOND	Oreburgh Gate B1F
PEARL	Oreburgh Gate B1F
GBA	Catch in FireRed or Ruby/Sapphire/Emerald, and transfer through Pal Park

ABILITY ● Damp ● Cloud Nine

● LEVEL-UP AND LEARNED MOVES

Lv	Name	Type	Kind	Power	Acc	PP	Range	DA
Base	Water Sport	Water	Status	—	—	15	All	—
Base	Scratch	Normal	Physical	40	100	35	Normal	—
5	Tail Whip	Normal	Status	—	100	30	2 foes	—
9	Water Gun	Water	Special	40	100	25	Normal	—
14	Disable	Normal	Status	—	80	20	Normal	—
18	Confusion	Psychic	Special	50	100	25	Normal	—
22	Water Pulse	Water	Special	60	100	20	Normal	—
27	Fury Swipes	Normal	Physical	18	80	15	Normal	•
31	Screech	Normal	Status	—	85	40	Normal	—
35	Psych Up	Normal	Status	—	—	10	Normal	—
40	Zen Headbutt	Psychic	Physical	80	90	15	Normal	•
44	Amnesia	Psychic	Status	—	—	20	Self	—
48	Hydro Pump	Water	Special	120	80	5	Normal	—

National Pokédex No. 055 Duck Pokémon
Golduck

WATER

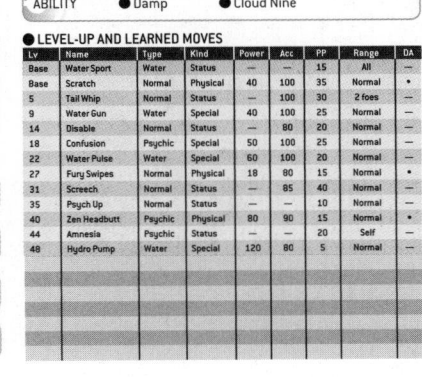

● M/F have same form

STATS
- HP ●●●
- ATTACK ●●●
- DEFENSE ●●●
- SP. ATTACK ●●●
- SP. DEFENSE ●●●
- SPEED ●●●

● EVOLUTION PATH

Psyduck → Lv33 → Golduck

● MAIN WAYS TO OBTAIN

PLATINUM	Celestic Town (water surface)
DIAMOND	Route 208 (water surface)
PEARL	Route 208 (water surface)
GBA	Catch in FireRed or Ruby/Sapphire/Emerald, and transfer through Pal Park

ABILITY ● Damp ● Cloud Nine

● LEVEL-UP AND LEARNED MOVES

Lv	Name	Type	Kind	Power	Acc	PP	Range	DA
Base	Aqua Jet	Water	Physical	40	100	20	Normal	—
Base	Water Sport	Water	Status	—	—	15	All	—
Base	Scratch	Normal	Physical	40	100	35	Normal	—
Base	Tail Whip	Normal	Status	—	100	30	2 foes	—
Base	Water Gun	Water	Special	40	100	25	Normal	—
5	Tail Whip	Normal	Status	—	100	30	2 foes	—
9	Water Gun	Water	Special	40	100	25	Normal	—
14	Disable	Normal	Status	—	80	20	Normal	—
18	Confusion	Psychic	Special	50	100	25	Normal	—
22	Water Pulse	Water	Special	60	100	20	Normal	—
27	Fury Swipes	Normal	Physical	18	80	15	Normal	•
31	Screech	Normal	Status	—	85	40	Normal	—
37	Psych Up	Normal	Status	—	—	10	Normal	—
44	Zen Headbutt	Psychic	Physical	80	90	15	Normal	•
50	Amnesia	Psychic	Status	—	—	20	Self	—
56	Hydro Pump	Water	Special	120	80	5	Normal	—

National Pokédex No. 056 Pig Monkey Pokémon
Mankey

FIGHTING

● M/F have same form

STATS
- HP ●
- ATTACK ●●
- DEFENSE ●●
- SP. ATTACK ●
- SP. DEFENSE ●●
- SPEED ●●●

● EVOLUTION PATH

Mankey → Lv28 → Primeape

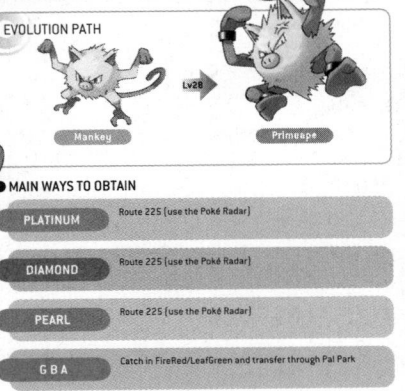

● MAIN WAYS TO OBTAIN

PLATINUM	Route 225 (use the Poké Radar)
DIAMOND	Route 225 (use the Poké Radar)
PEARL	Route 225 (use the Poké Radar)
GBA	Catch in FireRed/LeafGreen and transfer through Pal Park

ABILITY ● Vital Spirit ● Anger Point

● LEVEL-UP AND LEARNED MOVES

Lv	Name	Type	Kind	Power	Acc	PP	Range	DA
Base	Covet	Normal	Physical	40	100	40	Normal	•
Base	Scratch	Normal	Physical	40	100	35	Normal	•
Base	Low Kick	Fighting	Physical	—	100	20	Normal	•
Base	Leer	Normal	Status	—	100	30	2 foes	•
Base	Focus Energy	Normal	Status	—	—	30	Self	—
9	Fury Swipes	Normal	Physical	18	80	15	Normal	•
13	Karate Chop	Fighting	Physical	50	100	25	Normal	•
17	Seismic Toss	Fighting	Physical	—	100	20	Normal	•
21	Screech	Normal	Status	—	85	40	Normal	•
25	Assurance	Dark	Physical	50	100	10	Normal	•
33	Swagger	Normal	Status	—	90	15	Normal	—
37	Cross Chop	Fighting	Physical	100	80	5	Normal	•
41	Thrash	Normal	Physical	90	100	20	1 Random	•
45	Punishment	Dark	Physical	—	100	5	Normal	•
49	Close Combat	Fighting	Physical	120	100	5	Normal	•

056
MANKEY

Primeape

FIGHTING

STATS
HP ●●
ATTACK ●●●
DEFENSE ●●
SP. ATTACK ●
SP. DEFENSE ●●
SPEED ●●●

● M/F have same form

● EVOLUTION PATH

Mankey → Lv28 → Primeape

● MAIN WAYS TO OBTAIN

PLATINUM	Route 225 (use the Poké Radar)
DIAMOND	Route 225 (use the Poké Radar)
PEARL	Route 225 (use the Poké Radar)
GBA	Catch in FireRed/LeafGreen and transfer through Pal Park

ABILITY ● Vital Spirit ● Anger Point

● LEVEL-UP AND LEARNED MOVES

Lv	Name	Type	Kind	Power	Acc	PP	Range	DA
Base	Fling	Dark	Physical	—	100	10	Normal	
Base	Scratch	Normal	Physical	40	100	35	Normal	•
Base	Low Kick	Fighting	Physical	—	100	25	Normal	•
Base	Leer	Normal	Status	—	100	30	2 foes	
Base	Focus Energy	Normal	Status	—	—	30	Self	—
9	Fury Swipes	Normal	Physical	18	80	15	Normal	•
13	Karate Chop	Fighting	Physical	50	100	25	Normal	•
17	Seismic Toss	Fighting	Physical	—	100	20	Normal	•
21	Screech	Normal	Status	—	85	40	Normal	
25	Assurance	Dark	Physical	50	100	10	Normal	•
28	Rage	Normal	Physical	20	100	20	Normal	•
35	Swagger	Normal	Status	—	90	15	Normal	
41	Cross Chop	Fighting	Physical	100	80	5	Normal	
47	Thrash	Normal	Physical	90	100	20	1 Random	
53	Punishment	Dark	Physical	—	100	5	Normal	
59	Close Combat	Fighting	Physical	120	100	5	Normal	

Growlithe

FIRE

STATS
HP ●●
ATTACK ●●
DEFENSE ●●
SP. ATTACK ●●
SP. DEFENSE ●●
SPEED ●●

● M/F have same form

● EVOLUTION PATH

Growlithe → Use Fire Stone → Arcanine

● MAIN WAYS TO OBTAIN

PLATINUM	Route 201 (after you get the National Pokédex, insert a Pokémon FireRed cartridge into the Nintendo DS's GBA cartridge slot)
DIAMOND	Route 201 (after you get the National Pokédex, insert a Pokémon FireRed cartridge into the Nintendo DS's GBA cartridge slot)
PEARL	Route 201 (after you get the National Pokédex, insert a Pokémon FireRed cartridge into the Nintendo DS's GBA cartridge slot)
GBA	Catch in FireRed and transfer through Pal Park

ABILITY ● Intimidate ● Flash Fire

● LEVEL-UP AND LEARNED MOVES

Lv	Name	Type	Kind	Power	Acc	PP	Range	DA
Base	Bite	Dark	Physical	60	100	25	Normal	•
Base	Roar	Normal	Status	—	100	20	Normal	
6	Ember	Fire	Special	40	100	25	Normal	
9	Leer	Normal	Status	—	100	30	2 foes	
14	Odor Sleuth	Normal	Status	—	—	40	Normal	
17	Helping Hand	Normal	Status	—	—	20	1 ally	
20	Flame Wheel	Fire	Physical	60	100	25	Normal	•
25	Reversal	Fighting	Physical	—	100	15	Normal	•
28	Fire Fang	Fire	Physical	65	95	15	Normal	•
31	Take Down	Normal	Physical	90	85	20	Normal	•
34	Flamethrower	Fire	Special	95	100	15	Normal	
39	Agility	Psychic	Status	—	—	30	Self	
42	Crunch	Dark	Physical	80	100	15	Normal	•
45	Heat Wave	Fire	Special	100	90	10	2 foes	
48	Flare Blitz	Fire	Physical	120	100	15	Normal	•

Arcanine

FIRE

STATS
HP ●●●
ATTACK ●●●
DEFENSE ●●
SP. ATTACK ●●●
SP. DEFENSE ●●
SPEED ●●●

● M/F have same form

● EVOLUTION PATH

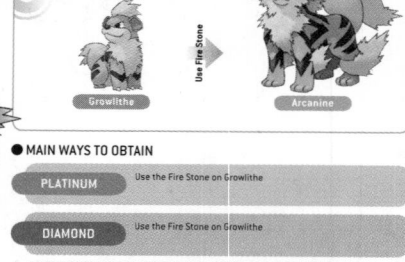

Growlithe → Use Fire Stone → Arcanine

● MAIN WAYS TO OBTAIN

PLATINUM	Use the Fire Stone on Growlithe
DIAMOND	Use the Fire Stone on Growlithe
PEARL	Use the Fire Stone on Growlithe
GBA	Catch and evolve in FireRed, and transfer through Pal Park

ABILITY ● Intimidate ● Flash Fire

● LEVEL-UP AND LEARNED MOVES

Lv	Name	Type	Kind	Power	Acc	PP	Range	DA
Base	Thunder Fang	Electric	Physical	65	95	15	Normal	•
Base	Bite	Dark	Physical	60	100	25	Normal	•
Base	Roar	Normal	Status	—	100	20	Normal	
Base	Fire Fang	Fire	Physical	65	95	15	Normal	•
Base	Odor Sleuth	Normal	Status	—	—	40	Normal	
39	ExtremeSpeed	Normal	Physical	80	100	5	Normal	•

Poliwag

WATER

STATS
HP ●●
ATTACK ●●
DEFENSE ●●
SP. ATTACK ●●
SP. DEFENSE ●●
SPEED ●●●

● M/F have same form

● EVOLUTION PATH

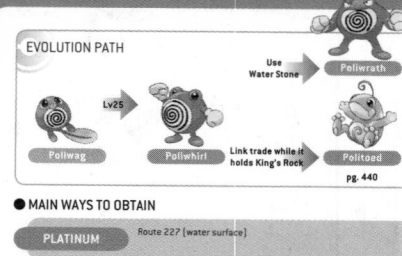

Poliwag → Lv25 → Poliwhirl → Use Water Stone → Poliwrath

Link trade while it holds King's Rock → Politoed
pg. 440

● MAIN WAYS TO OBTAIN

PLATINUM	Route 227 (water surface)
DIAMOND	Route 227 (water surface)
PEARL	Route 227 (water surface)
GBA	Catch in FireRed/LeafGreen and transfer through Pal Park

ABILITY ● Water Absorb ● Damp

● LEVEL-UP AND LEARNED MOVES

Lv	Name	Type	Kind	Power	Acc	PP	Range	DA
Base	Water Sport	Water	Status	—	—	15	All	
5	Bubble	Water	Special	20	100	30	2 foes	
8	Hypnosis	Psychic	Status	—	60	20	Normal	
11	Water Gun	Water	Special	40	100	25	Normal	
15	DoubleSlap	Normal	Physical	15	85	10	Normal	•
18	Rain Dance	Water	Status	—	—	5	All	
21	Body Slam	Normal	Physical	85	100	15	Normal	•
25	BubbleBeam	Water	Special	65	100	20	Normal	
28	Mud Shot	Ground	Special	55	95	15	Normal	
31	Belly Drum	Normal	Status	—	—	10	Self	
35	Wake-Up Slap	Fighting	Physical	60	100	10	Normal	•
38	Hydro Pump	Water	Special	120	80	5	Normal	
41	Mud Bomb	Ground	Special	65	85	10	Normal	

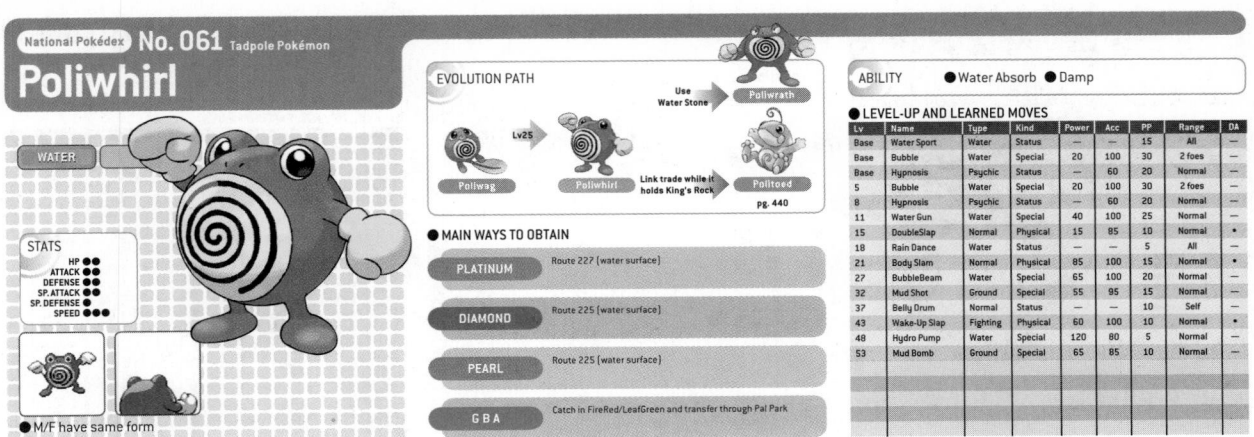

National Pokédex No. 061 — Poliwhirl

Tadpole Pokémon

WATER

STATS
- HP ●●
- ATTACK ●●
- DEFENSE ●●
- SP. ATTACK ●●
- SP. DEFENSE ●●
- SPEED ●●●

● M/F have same form

EVOLUTION PATH

Poliwag → Lv25 → Poliwhirl → Use Water Stone → Poliwrath
Poliwhirl → Link trade while it holds King's Rock → Politoed — pg. 440

● **MAIN WAYS TO OBTAIN**

PLATINUM	Route 227 (water surface)
DIAMOND	Route 225 (water surface)
PEARL	Route 225 (water surface)
G B A	Catch in FireRed/LeafGreen and transfer through Pal Park

ABILITY ● Water Absorb ● Damp

● **LEVEL-UP AND LEARNED MOVES**

Lv	Name	Type	Kind	Power	Acc	PP	Range	DA
Base	Water Sport	Water	Status	—	—	15	All	—
Base	Bubble	Water	Special	20	100	30	2 foes	—
Base	Hypnosis	Psychic	Status	—	60	20	Normal	—
5	Bubble	Water	Special	20	100	30	2 foes	—
8	Hypnosis	Psychic	Status	—	60	20	Normal	—
11	Water Gun	Water	Special	40	100	25	Normal	—
15	DoubleSlap	Normal	Physical	15	85	10	Normal	●
18	Rain Dance	Water	Status	—	—	5	All	—
21	Body Slam	Normal	Physical	85	100	15	Normal	●
27	BubbleBeam	Water	Special	65	100	20	Normal	—
32	Mud Shot	Ground	Special	55	95	15	Normal	—
37	Belly Drum	Normal	Status	—	—	10	Self	—
43	Wake-Up Slap	Fighting	Physical	60	100	10	Normal	●
48	Hydro Pump	Water	Special	120	80	5	Normal	—
53	Mud Bomb	Ground	Special	65	85	10	Normal	—

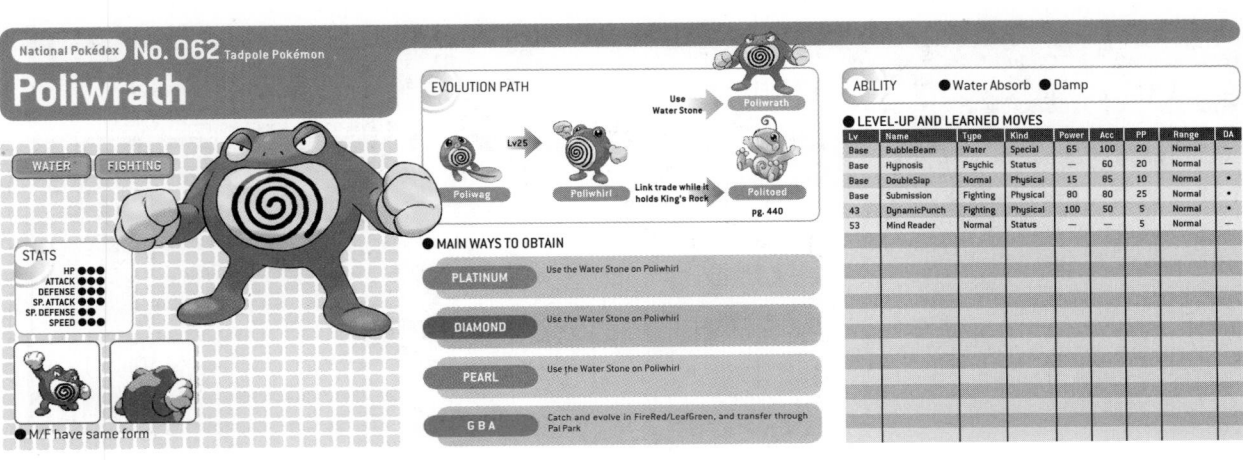

National Pokédex No. 062 — Poliwrath

Tadpole Pokémon

WATER   FIGHTING

STATS
- HP ●●●
- ATTACK ●●●●
- DEFENSE ●●●
- SP. ATTACK ●●
- SP. DEFENSE ●●●
- SPEED ●●●

● M/F have same form

EVOLUTION PATH

Poliwag → Lv25 → Poliwhirl → Use Water Stone → Poliwrath
Poliwhirl → Link trade while it holds King's Rock → Politoed — pg. 440

● **MAIN WAYS TO OBTAIN**

PLATINUM	Use the Water Stone on Poliwhirl
DIAMOND	Use the Water Stone on Poliwhirl
PEARL	Use the Water Stone on Poliwhirl
G B A	Catch and evolve in FireRed/LeafGreen, and transfer through Pal Park

ABILITY ● Water Absorb ● Damp

● **LEVEL-UP AND LEARNED MOVES**

Lv	Name	Type	Kind	Power	Acc	PP	Range	DA
Base	BubbleBeam	Water	Special	65	100	20	Normal	—
Base	Hypnosis	Psychic	Status	—	60	20	Normal	—
Base	DoubleSlap	Normal	Physical	15	85	10	Normal	●
Base	Submission	Fighting	Physical	80	80	25	Normal	●
43	DynamicPunch	Fighting	Physical	100	50	5	Normal	—
53	Mind Reader	Normal	Status	—	—	5	Normal	—

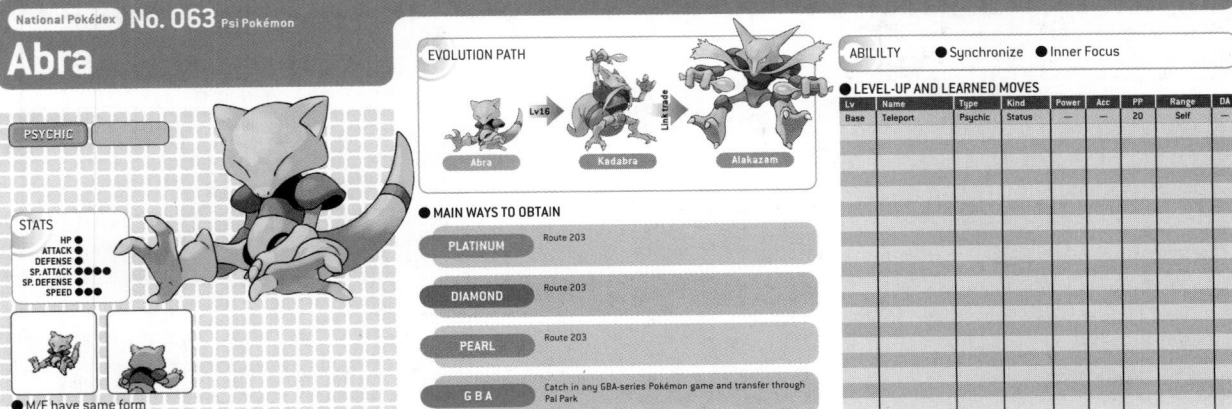

National Pokédex No. 063 — Abra

Psi Pokémon

PSYCHIC

STATS
- HP ●
- ATTACK ●
- DEFENSE ●
- SP. ATTACK ●●●
- SP. DEFENSE ●●●●
- SPEED ●●●

● M/F have same form

EVOLUTION PATH

Abra → Lv16 → Kadabra → Link trade → Alakazam

● **MAIN WAYS TO OBTAIN**

PLATINUM	Route 203
DIAMOND	Route 203
PEARL	Route 203
G B A	Catch in any GBA-series Pokémon game and transfer through Pal Park

ABILILTY ● Synchronize ● Inner Focus

● **LEVEL-UP AND LEARNED MOVES**

Lv	Name	Type	Kind	Power	Acc	PP	Range	DA
Base	Teleport	Psychic	Status	—	—	20	Self	—

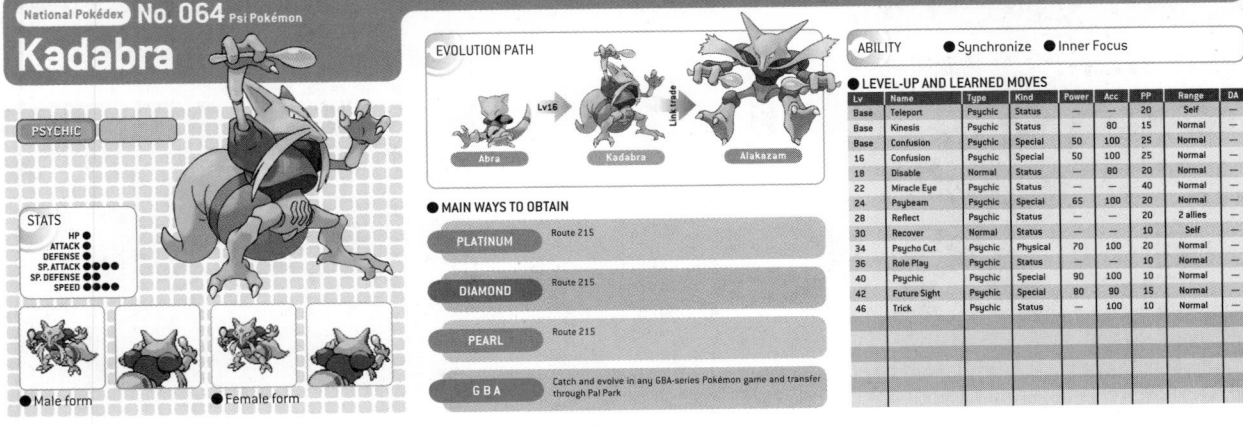

National Pokédex No. 064 — Kadabra

Psi Pokémon

PSYCHIC

STATS
- HP ●
- ATTACK ●
- DEFENSE ●
- SP. ATTACK ●●●●
- SP. DEFENSE ●●●
- SPEED ●●●●

● Male form   ● Female form

EVOLUTION PATH

Abra → Lv16 → Kadabra → Link trade → Alakazam

● **MAIN WAYS TO OBTAIN**

PLATINUM	Route 215
DIAMOND	Route 215
PEARL	Route 215
G B A	Catch and evolve in any GBA-series Pokémon game and transfer through Pal Park

ABILITY ● Synchronize ● Inner Focus

● **LEVEL-UP AND LEARNED MOVES**

Lv	Name	Type	Kind	Power	Acc	PP	Range	DA
Base	Teleport	Psychic	Status	—	—	20	Self	—
Base	Kinesis	Psychic	Status	—	80	15	Normal	—
Base	Confusion	Psychic	Special	50	100	25	Normal	—
16	Confusion	Psychic	Special	50	100	25	Normal	—
18	Disable	Normal	Status	—	80	20	Normal	—
22	Miracle Eye	Psychic	Status	—	—	40	Normal	—
24	Psybeam	Psychic	Special	65	100	20	Normal	—
28	Reflect	Psychic	Status	—	—	20	2 allies	—
30	Recover	Normal	Status	—	—	10	Self	—
34	Psycho Cut	Psychic	Physical	70	100	20	Normal	—
36	Role Play	Psychic	Status	—	—	10	Normal	—
40	Psychic	Psychic	Special	90	100	10	Normal	—
42	Future Sight	Psychic	Special	80	90	15	Normal	—
46	Trick	Psychic	Status	—	100	10	Normal	—

064
KADABRA

National Pokédex No. 065 Psi Pokémon

Alakazam

PSYCHIC

STATS
- HP ●●
- ATTACK ●●●
- DEFENSE ●●
- SP. ATTACK ●●●●●
- SP. DEFENSE ●●●●
- SPEED ●●●●●

● Male form   ● Female form

EVOLUTION PATH

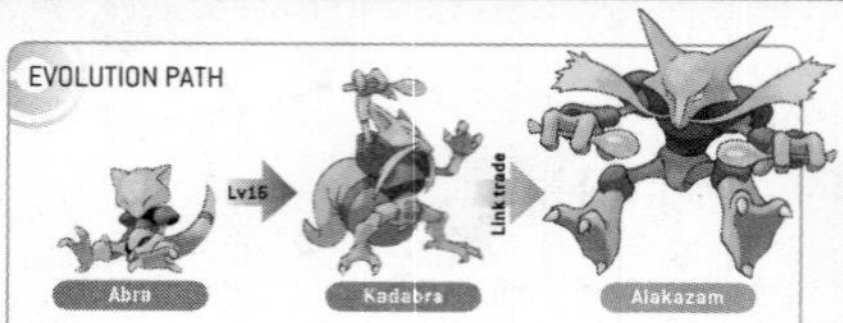

Abra → (Lv15) Kadabra → (Link trade) Alakazam

● MAIN WAYS TO OBTAIN

PLATINUM	Link trade Kadabra
DIAMOND	Link trade Kadabra
PEARL	Link trade Kadabra
GBA	Catch and evolve in any GBA-series Pokémon game and transfer through Pal Park

ABILITY ● Synchronize   ● Inner Focus

● LEVEL-UP AND LEARNED MOVES

Lv	Name	Type	Kind	Power	Acc	PP	Range	DA
Base	Teleport	Psychic	Status	—	—	20	Self	—
Base	Kinesis	Psychic	Status	—	80	15	Normal	—
Base	Confusion	Psychic	Special	50	100	25	Normal	—
16	Confusion	Psychic	Special	50	100	25	Normal	—
18	Disable	Normal	Status	—	80	20	Normal	—
22	Miracle Eye	Normal	Status	—	—	40	Normal	—
24	Psybeam	Psychic	Special	65	100	20	Normal	—
28	Reflect	Psychic	Status	—	—	20	2 allies	—
30	Recover	Normal	Status	—	—	10	Self	—
34	Psycho Cut	Psychic	Physical	70	100	20	Normal	—
36	Calm Mind	Psychic	Status	—	—	20	Self	—
40	Psychic	Psychic	Special	90	100	10	Normal	—
42	Future Sight	Psychic	Special	80	90	15	Normal	—
46	Trick	Psychic	Status	—	100	10	Normal	—

National Pokédex No. 066 Superpower Pokémon

Machop

FIGHTING

STATS
- HP ●●
- ATTACK ●●●
- DEFENSE ●
- SP. ATTACK ●
- SP. DEFENSE ●
- SPEED ●

● M/F have same form

EVOLUTION PATH

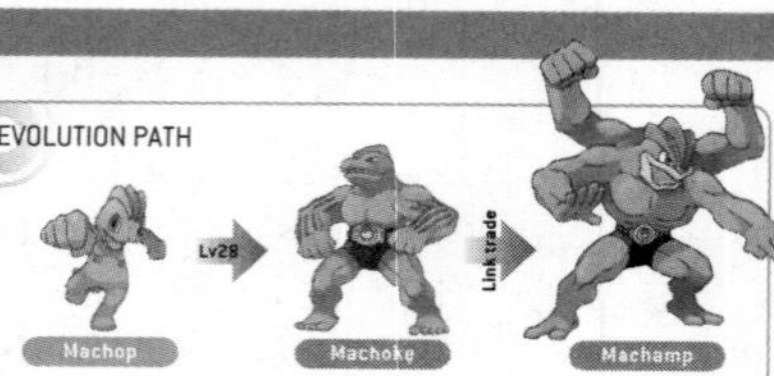

Machop → (Lv28) Machoke → (Link trade) Machamp

● MAIN WAYS TO OBTAIN

PLATINUM	Route 207
DIAMOND	Route 207
PEARL	Route 207
GBA	Catch in any GBA-series Pokémon game and transfer through Pal Park

ABILITY ● Guts   ● No Guard

● LEVEL-UP AND LEARNED MOVES

Lv	Name	Type	Kind	Power	Acc	PP	Range	DA
Base	Low Kick	Fighting	Physical	—	100	20	Normal	•
Base	Leer	Normal	Status	—	100	30	2 foes	•
?	Focus Energy	Normal	Status	—	—	30	Self	—
10	Karate Chop	Fighting	Physical	50	100	25	Normal	•
13	Foresight	Normal	Status	—	—	40	Normal	•
19	Seismic Toss	Fighting	Physical	—	100	20	Normal	•
22	Revenge	Fighting	Physical	60	100	10	Normal	•
25	Vital Throw	Fighting	Physical	70	—	10	Normal	•
31	Submission	Fighting	Physical	80	80	25	Normal	•
34	Wake-Up Slap	Fighting	Physical	60	100	10	Normal	•
37	Cross Chop	Fighting	Physical	100	80	5	Normal	•
43	Scary Face	Normal	Status	—	90	10	Normal	—
46	DynamicPunch	Fighting	Physical	100	50	5	Normal	•

National Pokédex No. 067 Superpower Pokémon

Machoke

FIGHTING

STATS
- HP ●●●
- ATTACK ●●●
- DEFENSE ●●●
- SP. ATTACK ●●
- SP. DEFENSE ●●
- SPEED ●●

● M/F have same form

EVOLUTION PATH

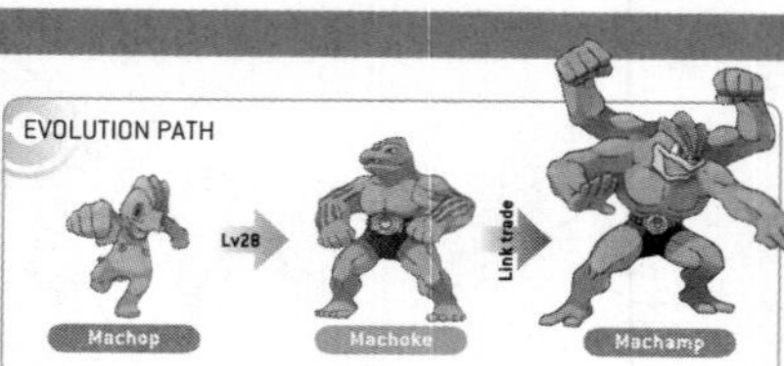

Machop → (Lv28) Machoke → (Link trade) Machamp

● MAIN WAYS TO OBTAIN

PLATINUM	Celestic Town side of Route 210
DIAMOND	Route 210
PEARL	Route 210
GBA	Catch and evolve in any GBA-series Pokémon game and transfer through Pal Park

ABILITY ● Guts   ● No Guard

● LEVEL-UP AND LEARNED MOVES

Lv	Name	Type	Kind	Power	Acc	PP	Range	DA
Base	Low Kick	Fighting	Physical	—	100	20	Normal	•
Base	Leer	Normal	Status	—	100	30	2 foes	•
Base	Focus Energy	Normal	Status	—	—	30	Self	—
?	Focus Energy	Normal	Status	—	—	30	Self	—
10	Karate Chop	Fighting	Physical	50	100	25	Normal	•
13	Foresight	Normal	Status	—	—	40	Normal	•
19	Seismic Toss	Fighting	Physical	—	100	20	Normal	•
22	Revenge	Fighting	Physical	60	100	10	Normal	•
25	Vital Throw	Fighting	Physical	70	—	10	Normal	•
32	Submission	Fighting	Physical	80	80	25	Normal	•
36	Wake-Up Slap	Fighting	Physical	60	100	10	Normal	•
40	Cross Chop	Fighting	Physical	100	80	5	Normal	•
44	Scary Face	Normal	Status	—	90	10	Normal	—
51	DynamicPunch	Fighting	Physical	100	50	5	Normal	•

National Pokédex No. 068 Superpower Pokémon

Machamp

FIGHTING

STATS
- HP ●●●
- ATTACK ●●●●
- DEFENSE ●●●
- SP. ATTACK ●●
- SP. DEFENSE ●●
- SPEED ●●

● M/F have same form

EVOLUTION PATH

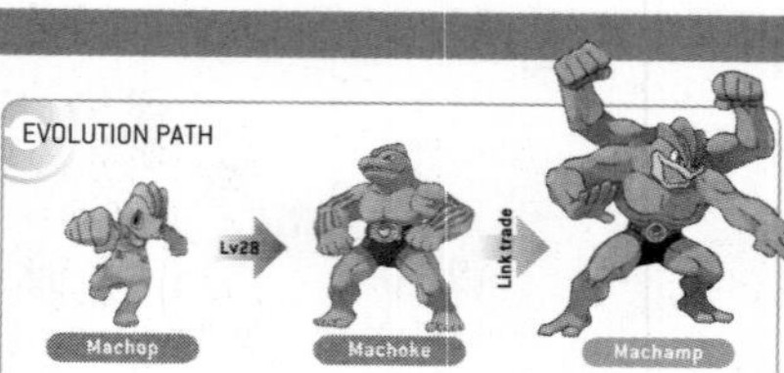

Machop → (Lv28) Machoke → (Link trade) Machamp

● MAIN WAYS TO OBTAIN

PLATINUM	Link trade Machoke
DIAMOND	Link trade Machoke
PEARL	Link trade Machoke
GBA	Catch and evolve in any GBA-series Pokémon game and transfer through Pal Park

ABILITY ● Guts   ● No Guard

● LEVEL-UP AND LEARNED MOVES

Lv	Name	Type	Kind	Power	Acc	PP	Range	DA
Base	Low Kick	Fighting	Physical	—	100	20	Normal	•
Base	Leer	Normal	Status	—	100	30	2 foes	•
Base	Focus Energy	Normal	Status	—	—	30	Self	—
?	Focus Energy	Normal	Status	—	—	30	Self	—
10	Karate Chop	Fighting	Physical	50	100	25	Normal	•
13	Foresight	Normal	Status	—	—	40	Normal	•
19	Seismic Toss	Fighting	Physical	—	100	20	Normal	•
22	Revenge	Fighting	Physical	60	100	10	Normal	•
25	Vital Throw	Fighting	Physical	70	—	10	Normal	•
32	Submission	Fighting	Physical	80	80	25	Normal	•
36	Wake-Up Slap	Fighting	Physical	60	100	10	Normal	•
40	Cross Chop	Fighting	Physical	100	80	5	Normal	•
44	Scary Face	Normal	Status	—	90	10	Normal	—
51	DynamicPunch	Fighting	Physical	100	50	5	Normal	•

National Pokédex No. 069 Flower Pokémon
Bellsprout

GRASS　POISON

STATS
- HP ●●
- ATTACK ●●●
- DEFENSE ●●
- SP. ATTACK ●●●
- SP. DEFENSE ●
- SPEED ●●

● M/F have same form

EVOLUTION PATH

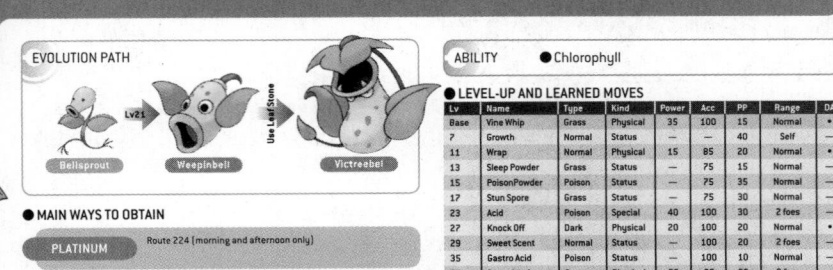

Bellsprout → (Lv21) Weepinbell → (Use Leaf Stone) Victreebel

● MAIN WAYS TO OBTAIN

PLATINUM	Route 224 (morning and afternoon only)
DIAMOND	Route 229
PEARL	Route 229
G B A	Catch in LeafGreen and transfer through Pal Park

ABILITY ● Chlorophyll

● LEVEL-UP AND LEARNED MOVES

Lv	Name	Type	Kind	Power	Acc	PP	Range	DA
Base	Vine Whip	Grass	Physical	35	100	15	Normal	●
7	Growth	Normal	Status	—	—	40	Self	●
11	Wrap	Normal	Physical	15	85	20	Normal	●
13	Sleep Powder	Grass	Status	—	75	15	Normal	—
15	PoisonPowder	Poison	Status	—	75	35	Normal	●
17	Stun Spore	Grass	Status	—	75	30	Normal	—
23	Acid	Poison	Special	40	100	30	2 foes	—
27	Knock Off	Dark	Physical	20	100	20	Normal	●
29	Sweet Scent	Normal	Status	—	100	20	2 foes	—
35	Gastro Acid	Poison	Status	—	100	10	Normal	—
39	Razor Leaf	Grass	Physical	55	95	25	2 foes	—
41	Slam	Normal	Physical	80	75	20	Normal	●
47	Wring Out	Normal	Special	—	100	5	Normal	●

National Pokédex No. 070 Flycatcher Pokémon
Weepinbell

GRASS　POISON

STATS
- HP ●●●
- ATTACK ●●●
- DEFENSE ●●
- SP. ATTACK ●●●
- SP. DEFENSE ●●
- SPEED ●●

● M/F have same form

EVOLUTION PATH

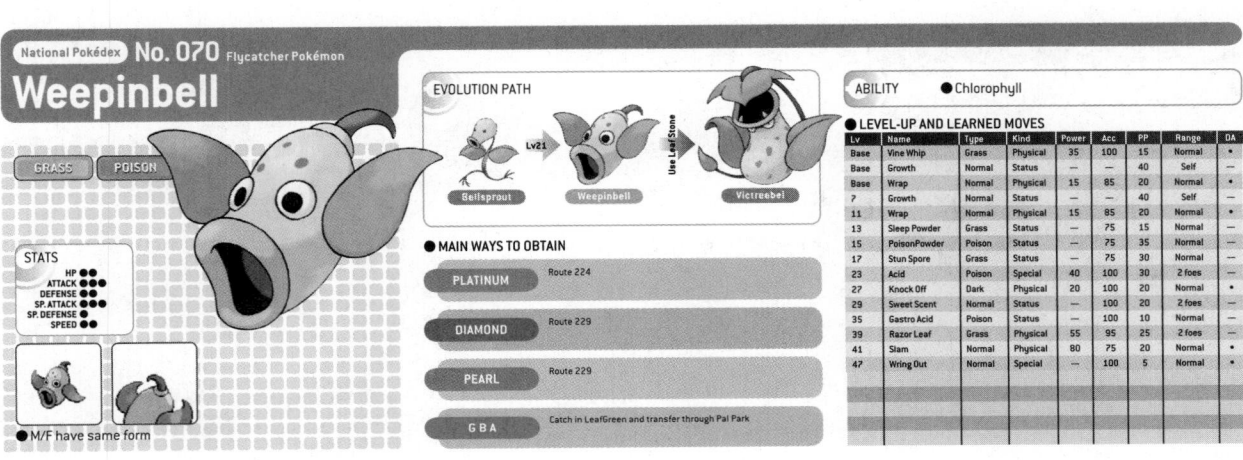

Bellsprout → (Lv21) Weepinbell → (Use Leaf Stone) Victreebel

● MAIN WAYS TO OBTAIN

PLATINUM	Route 224
DIAMOND	Route 229
PEARL	Route 229
G B A	Catch in LeafGreen and transfer through Pal Park

ABILITY ● Chlorophyll

● LEVEL-UP AND LEARNED MOVES

Lv	Name	Type	Kind	Power	Acc	PP	Range	DA
Base	Vine Whip	Grass	Physical	35	100	15	Normal	●
Base	Growth	Normal	Status	—	—	40	Self	●
Base	Wrap	Normal	Physical	15	85	20	Normal	●
7	Growth	Normal	Status	—	—	40	Self	●
11	Wrap	Normal	Physical	15	85	20	Normal	●
13	Sleep Powder	Grass	Status	—	75	15	Normal	—
15	PoisonPowder	Poison	Status	—	75	35	Normal	●
17	Stun Spore	Grass	Status	—	75	30	Normal	—
23	Acid	Poison	Special	40	100	30	2 foes	—
27	Knock Off	Dark	Physical	20	100	20	Normal	●
29	Sweet Scent	Normal	Status	—	100	20	2 foes	—
35	Gastro Acid	Poison	Status	—	100	10	Normal	—
39	Razor Leaf	Grass	Physical	55	95	25	2 foes	—
41	Slam	Normal	Physical	80	75	20	Normal	●
47	Wring Out	Normal	Special	—	100	5	Normal	●

National Pokédex No. 071 Flycatcher Pokémon
Victreebel

GRASS　POISON

STATS
- HP ●●●
- ATTACK ●●●●
- DEFENSE ●●●
- SP. ATTACK ●●●●
- SP. DEFENSE ●●●
- SPEED ●●●

● M/F have same form

EVOLUTION PATH

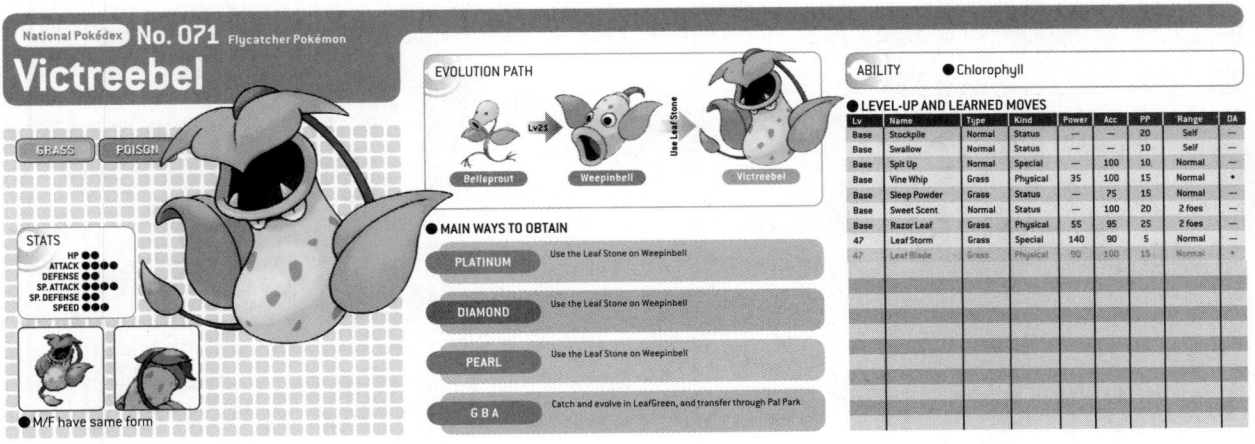

Bellsprout → (Lv21) Weepinbell → (Use Leaf Stone) Victreebel

● MAIN WAYS TO OBTAIN

PLATINUM	Use the Leaf Stone on Weepinbell
DIAMOND	Use the Leaf Stone on Weepinbell
PEARL	Use the Leaf Stone on Weepinbell
G B A	Catch and evolve in LeafGreen, and transfer through Pal Park

ABILITY ● Chlorophyll

● LEVEL-UP AND LEARNED MOVES

Lv	Name	Type	Kind	Power	Acc	PP	Range	DA
Base	Stockpile	Normal	Status	—	—	20	Self	●
Base	Swallow	Normal	Status	—	—	10	Self	●
Base	Spit Up	Normal	Special	—	100	10	Normal	●
Base	Vine Whip	Grass	Physical	35	100	15	Normal	●
Base	Sleep Powder	Grass	Status	—	75	15	Normal	—
Base	Sweet Scent	Normal	Status	—	100	30	2 foes	—
Base	Razor Leaf	Grass	Physical	55	95	25	2 foes	—
47	Leaf Storm	Grass	Special	140	90	5	Normal	—
47	Leaf Blade	Grass	Physical	90	100	15	Normal	●

National Pokédex No. 072 Jellyfish Pokémon
Tentacool

WATER　POISON

STATS
- HP ●
- ATTACK ●●
- DEFENSE ●●
- SP. ATTACK ●●
- SP. DEFENSE ●●●●
- SPEED ●●●

● M/F have same form

EVOLUTION PATH

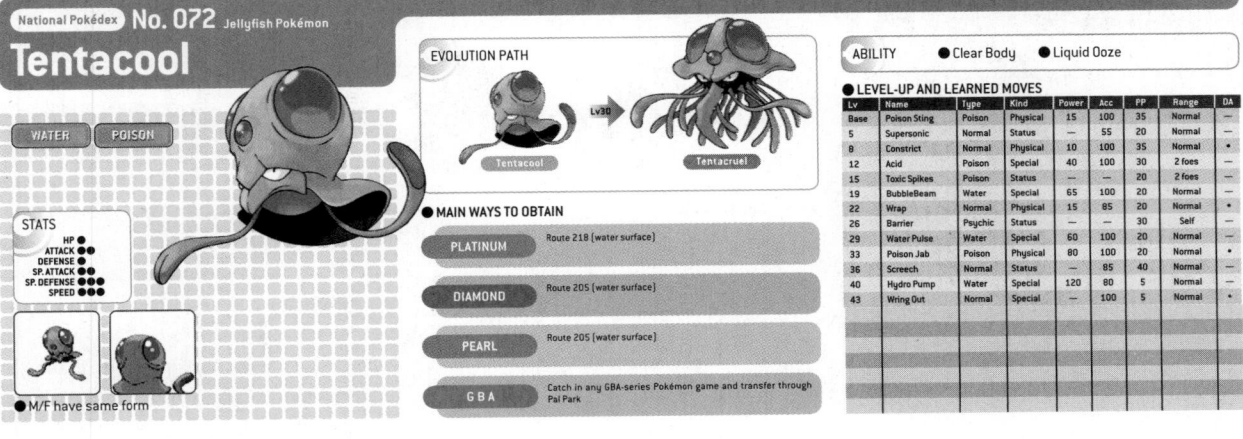

Tentacool → (Lv30) Tentacruel

● MAIN WAYS TO OBTAIN

PLATINUM	Route 218 (water surface)
DIAMOND	Route 205 (water surface)
PEARL	Route 205 (water surface)
G B A	Catch in any GBA-series Pokémon game and transfer through Pal Park

ABILITY ● Clear Body ● Liquid Ooze

● LEVEL-UP AND LEARNED MOVES

Lv	Name	Type	Kind	Power	Acc	PP	Range	DA
Base	Poison Sting	Poison	Physical	15	100	35	Normal	—
5	Supersonic	Normal	Status	—	55	20	Normal	●
8	Constrict	Normal	Physical	10	100	35	Normal	●
12	Acid	Poison	Special	40	100	30	2 foes	—
15	Toxic Spikes	Poison	Status	—	—	20	2 foes	—
19	BubbleBeam	Water	Special	65	100	20	Normal	—
22	Wrap	Normal	Physical	15	85	20	Normal	●
26	Barrier	Psychic	Status	—	—	30	Self	—
29	Water Pulse	Water	Special	60	100	20	Normal	—
33	Poison Jab	Poison	Physical	80	100	20	Normal	●
36	Screech	Normal	Status	—	85	40	Normal	—
40	Hydro Pump	Water	Special	120	80	5	Normal	—
43	Wring Out	Normal	Special	—	100	5	Normal	●

072
TENTACOOL

Tentacruel

National Pokédex No. 073 Jelyfish Pokémon

WATER POISON

STATS
HP ●●
ATTACK ●●●
DEFENSE ●●●
SP.ATTACK ●●●
SP.DEFENSE ●●●●●
SPEED ●●●●

● M/F have same form

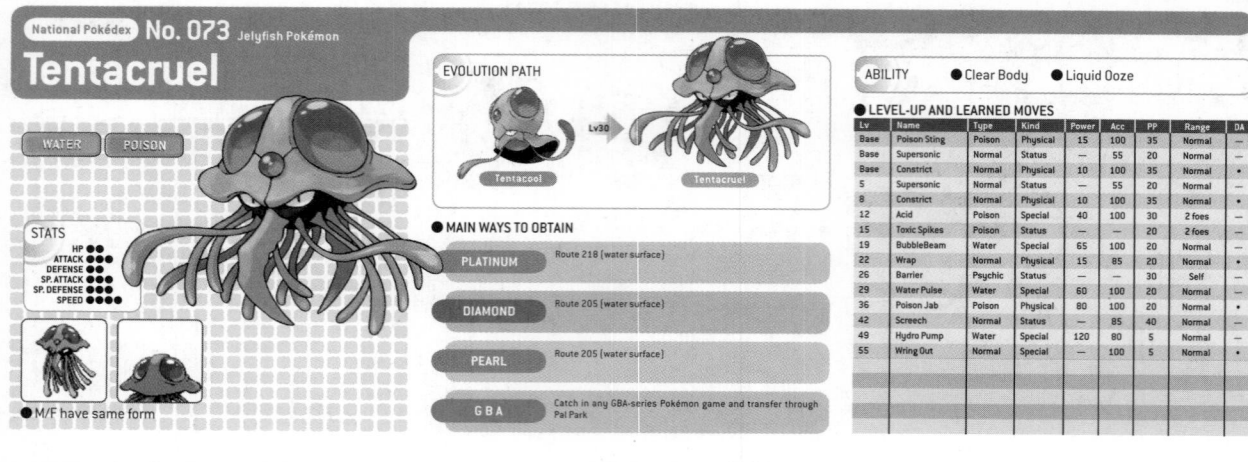

EVOLUTION PATH
Tentacool — Lv30 → Tentacruel

● MAIN WAYS TO OBTAIN

PLATINUM	Route 218 (water surface)
DIAMOND	Route 205 (water surface)
PEARL	Route 205 (water surface)
GBA	Catch in any GBA-series Pokémon game and transfer through Pal Park

ABILITY ● Clear Body ● Liquid Ooze

● LEVEL-UP AND LEARNED MOVES

Lv	Name	Type	Kind	Power	Acc	PP	Range	DA
Base	Poison Sting	Poison	Physical	15	100	35	Normal	—
Base	Supersonic	Normal	Status	—	55	20	Normal	—
Base	Constrict	Normal	Physical	10	100	35	Normal	•
5	Supersonic	Normal	Status	—	55	20	Normal	—
8	Constrict	Normal	Physical	10	100	35	Normal	•
12	Acid	Poison	Special	40	100	30	2 foes	—
15	Toxic Spikes	Poison	Status	—	—	20	2 foes	—
19	BubbleBeam	Water	Special	65	100	20	Normal	—
22	Wrap	Normal	Physical	15	85	20	Normal	•
26	Barrier	Psychic	Status	—	—	30	Self	—
29	Water Pulse	Water	Special	60	100	20	Normal	•
36	Poison Jab	Poison	Physical	80	100	20	Normal	•
42	Screech	Normal	Status	—	85	40	Normal	—
49	Hydro Pump	Water	Special	120	80	5	Normal	—
55	Wring Out	Normal	Special	—	100	5	Normal	—

Geodude

National Pokédex No. 074 Rock Pokémon

ROCK GROUND

STATS
HP ●
ATTACK ●●●
DEFENSE ●●●●
SP.ATTACK ●
SP.DEFENSE ●
SPEED ●

● M/F have same form

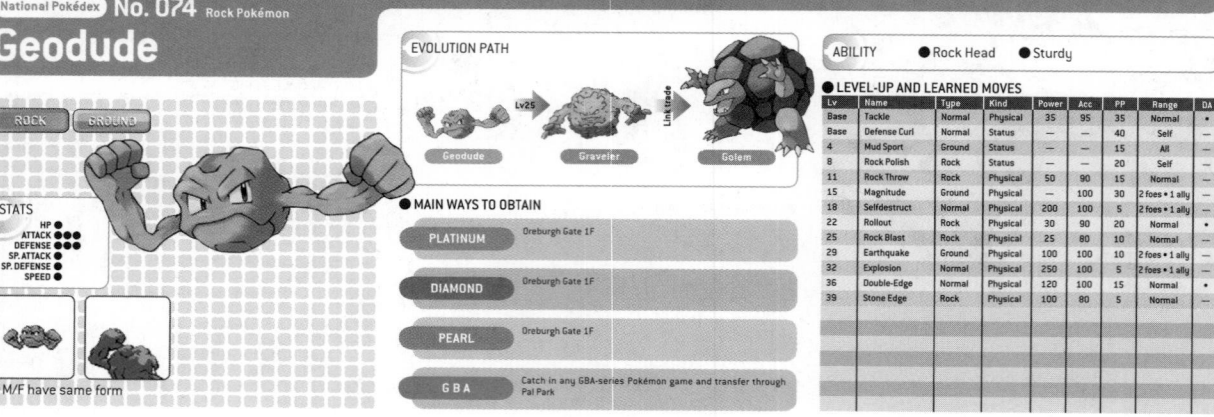

EVOLUTION PATH
Geodude — Lv25 → Graveler — Link trade → Golem

● MAIN WAYS TO OBTAIN

PLATINUM	Oreburgh Gate 1F
DIAMOND	Oreburgh Gate 1F
PEARL	Oreburgh Gate 1F
GBA	Catch in any GBA-series Pokémon game and transfer through Pal Park

ABILITY ● Rock Head ● Sturdy

● LEVEL-UP AND LEARNED MOVES

Lv	Name	Type	Kind	Power	Acc	PP	Range	DA
Base	Tackle	Normal	Physical	35	95	35	Normal	•
Base	Defense Curl	Normal	Status	—	—	40	Self	—
4	Mud Sport	Ground	Status	—	—	15	All	—
8	Rock Polish	Rock	Status	—	—	20	Self	—
11	Rock Throw	Rock	Physical	50	90	15	Normal	—
15	Magnitude	Ground	Physical	—	100	30	2 foes • 1 ally	—
18	Selfdestruct	Normal	Physical	200	100	5	2 foes • 1 ally	—
22	Rollout	Rock	Physical	30	90	20	Normal	•
25	Rock Blast	Rock	Physical	25	80	10	Normal	—
29	Earthquake	Ground	Physical	100	100	10	2 foes • 1 ally	—
32	Explosion	Normal	Physical	250	100	5	2 foes • 1 ally	—
36	Double-Edge	Normal	Physical	120	100	15	Normal	—
39	Stone Edge	Rock	Physical	100	80	5	Normal	—

Graveler

National Pokédex No. 075 Rock Pokémon

ROCK GROUND

STATS
HP ●●
ATTACK ●●●
DEFENSE ●●●
SP.ATTACK ●
SP.DEFENSE ●
SPEED ●

● M/F have same form

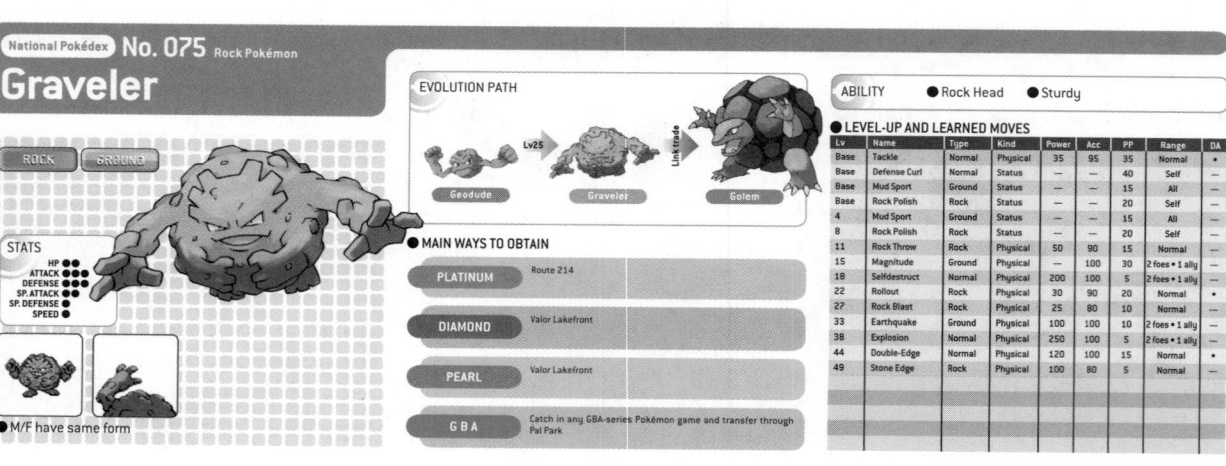

EVOLUTION PATH
Geodude — Lv25 → Graveler — Link trade → Golem

● MAIN WAYS TO OBTAIN

PLATINUM	Route 214
DIAMOND	Valor Lakefront
PEARL	Valor Lakefront
GBA	Catch in any GBA-series Pokémon game and transfer through Pal Park

ABILITY ● Rock Head ● Sturdy

● LEVEL-UP AND LEARNED MOVES

Lv	Name	Type	Kind	Power	Acc	PP	Range	DA
Base	Tackle	Normal	Physical	35	95	35	Normal	•
Base	Defense Curl	Normal	Status	—	—	40	Self	—
Base	Mud Sport	Ground	Status	—	—	15	All	—
Base	Rock Polish	Rock	Status	—	—	20	Self	—
4	Mud Sport	Ground	Status	—	—	15	All	—
8	Rock Polish	Rock	Status	—	—	20	Self	—
11	Rock Throw	Rock	Physical	50	90	15	Normal	—
15	Magnitude	Ground	Physical	—	100	30	2 foes • 1 ally	—
18	Selfdestruct	Normal	Physical	200	100	5	2 foes • 1 ally	—
22	Rollout	Rock	Physical	30	90	20	Normal	•
27	Rock Blast	Rock	Physical	25	80	10	Normal	—
33	Earthquake	Ground	Physical	100	100	10	2 foes • 1 ally	—
38	Explosion	Normal	Physical	250	100	5	2 foes • 1 ally	—
44	Double-Edge	Normal	Physical	120	100	15	Normal	•
49	Stone Edge	Rock	Physical	100	80	5	Normal	—

Golem

National Pokédex No. 076 Megaton Pokémon

ROCK GROUND

STATS
HP ●●
ATTACK ●●●●
DEFENSE ●●●●
SP.ATTACK ●●
SP.DEFENSE ●●
SPEED ●●

● M/F have same form

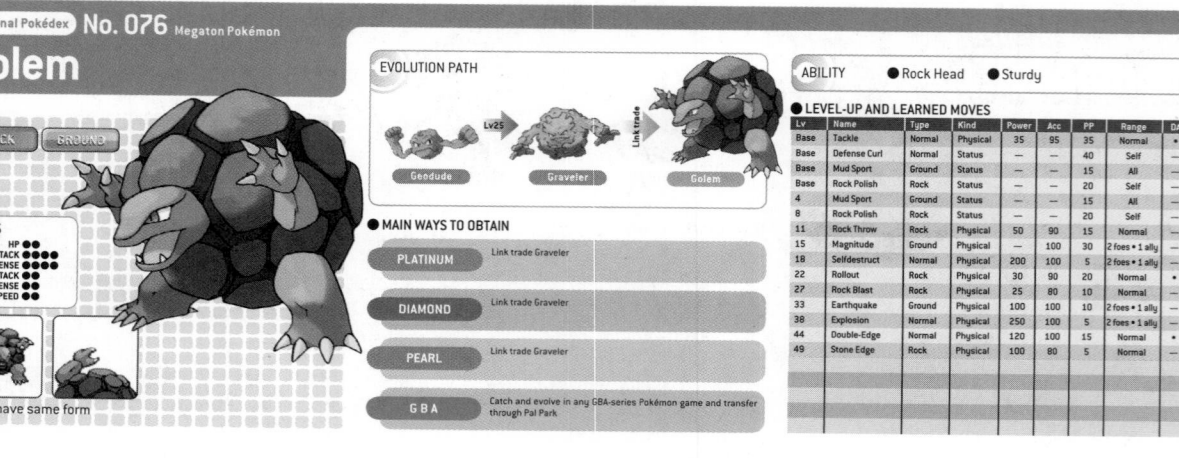

EVOLUTION PATH
Geodude — Lv25 → Graveler — Link trade → Golem

● MAIN WAYS TO OBTAIN

PLATINUM	Link trade Graveler
DIAMOND	Link trade Graveler
PEARL	Link trade Graveler
GBA	Catch and evolve in any GBA-series Pokémon game and transfer through Pal Park

ABILITY ● Rock Head ● Sturdy

● LEVEL-UP AND LEARNED MOVES

Lv	Name	Type	Kind	Power	Acc	PP	Range	DA
Base	Tackle	Normal	Physical	35	95	35	Normal	•
Base	Defense Curl	Normal	Status	—	—	40	Self	—
Base	Mud Sport	Ground	Status	—	—	15	All	—
Base	Rock Polish	Rock	Status	—	—	20	Self	—
4	Mud Sport	Ground	Status	—	—	15	All	—
8	Rock Polish	Rock	Status	—	—	20	Self	—
11	Rock Throw	Rock	Physical	50	90	15	Normal	—
15	Magnitude	Ground	Physical	—	100	30	2 foes • 1 ally	—
18	Selfdestruct	Normal	Physical	200	100	5	2 foes • 1 ally	—
22	Rollout	Rock	Physical	30	90	20	Normal	•
27	Rock Blast	Rock	Physical	25	80	10	Normal	—
33	Earthquake	Ground	Physical	100	100	10	2 foes • 1 ally	—
38	Explosion	Normal	Physical	250	100	5	2 foes • 1 ally	—
44	Double-Edge	Normal	Physical	120	100	15	Normal	—
49	Stone Edge	Rock	Physical	100	80	5	Normal	—

National Pokédex No. 077 Fire Horse Pokémon
Ponyta

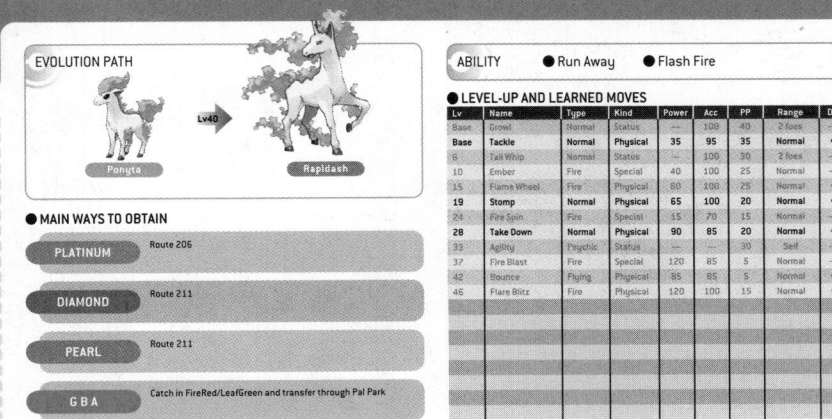

FIRE

STATS
HP ●●●
ATTACK ●●●●
DEFENSE ●●●
SP. ATTACK ●●●
SP. DEFENSE ●●●
SPEED ●●●●

● M/F have same form

● EVOLUTION PATH
Ponyta → Lv40 → Rapidash

● MAIN WAYS TO OBTAIN
PLATINUM	Route 206
DIAMOND	Route 211
PEARL	Route 211
G B A	Catch in FireRed/LeafGreen and transfer through Pal Park

ABILITY   ● Run Away   ● Flash Fire

● LEVEL-UP AND LEARNED MOVES
Lv	Name	Type	Kind	Power	Acc	PP	Range	DA
Base	Growl	Normal	Status	—	100	40	2 foes	—
Base	Tackle	Normal	Physical	35	95	35	Normal	●
5	Tail Whip	Normal	Status	—	100	30	2 foes	—
10	Ember	Fire	Special	40	100	25	Normal	—
15	Flame Wheel	Fire	Physical	60	100	25	Normal	●
19	Stomp	Normal	Physical	65	100	20	Normal	●
24	Fire Spin	Fire	Special	15	70	15	Normal	—
28	Take Down	Normal	Physical	90	85	20	Normal	●
33	Agility	Psychic	Status	—	—	30	Self	—
37	Fire Blast	Fire	Special	120	85	5	Normal	—
42	Bounce	Flying	Physical	85	85	5	Normal	●
46	Flare Blitz	Fire	Physical	120	100	15	Normal	●

National Pokédex No. 078 Fire Horse Pokémon
Rapidash

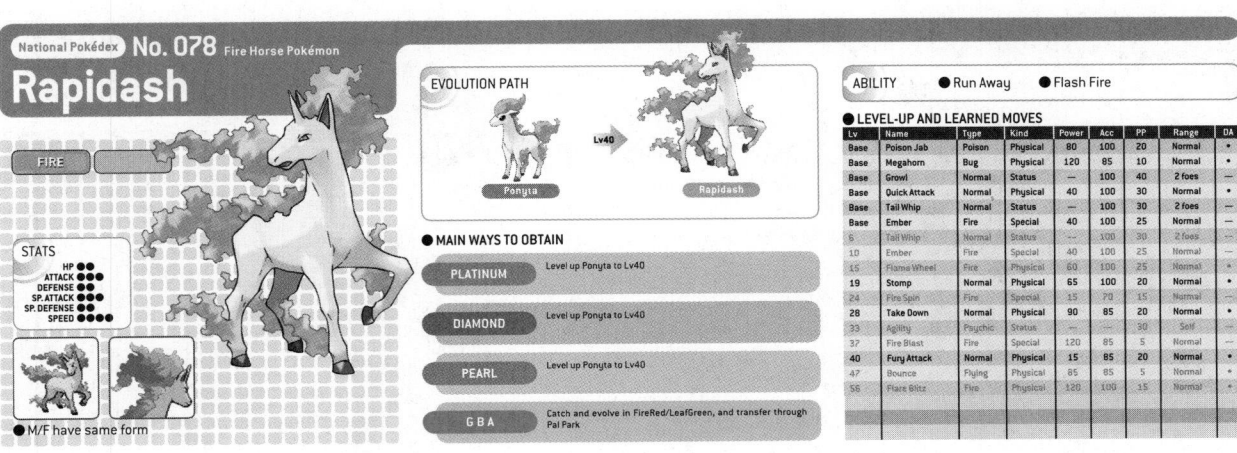

FIRE

STATS
HP ●●●
ATTACK ●●●●
DEFENSE ●●●
SP. ATTACK ●●●
SP. DEFENSE ●●●
SPEED ●●●●●

● M/F have same form

● EVOLUTION PATH
Ponyta → Lv40 → Rapidash

● MAIN WAYS TO OBTAIN
PLATINUM	Level up Ponyta to Lv40
DIAMOND	Level up Ponyta to Lv40
PEARL	Level up Ponyta to Lv40
G B A	Catch and evolve in FireRed/LeafGreen, and transfer through Pal Park

ABILITY   ● Run Away   ● Flash Fire

● LEVEL-UP AND LEARNED MOVES
Lv	Name	Type	Kind	Power	Acc	PP	Range	DA
Base	Poison Jab	Poison	Physical	80	100	20	Normal	●
Base	Megahorn	Bug	Physical	120	85	10	Normal	●
Base	Growl	Normal	Status	—	100	40	2 foes	—
Base	Quick Attack	Normal	Physical	40	100	30	Normal	●
Base	Tail Whip	Normal	Status	—	100	30	2 foes	—
Base	Ember	Fire	Special	40	100	25	Normal	—
5	Tail Whip	Normal	Status	—	100	30	2 foes	—
10	Ember	Fire	Special	40	100	25	Normal	—
15	Flame Wheel	Fire	Physical	60	100	25	Normal	●
19	Stomp	Normal	Physical	65	100	20	Normal	●
24	Fire Spin	Fire	Special	15	70	15	Normal	—
28	Take Down	Normal	Physical	90	85	20	Normal	●
33	Agility	Psychic	Status	—	—	30	Self	—
37	Fire Blast	Fire	Special	120	85	5	Normal	—
40	Fury Attack	Normal	Physical	15	85	20	Normal	●
47	Bounce	Flying	Physical	85	85	5	Normal	●
56	Flare Blitz	Fire	Physical	120	100	15	Normal	●

National Pokédex No. 079 Dopey Pokémon
Slowpoke

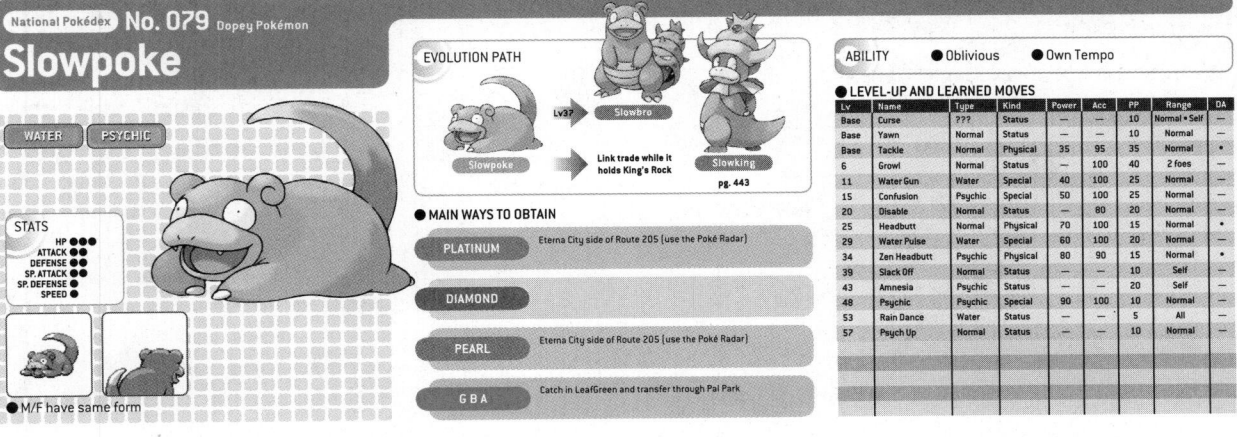

WATER   PSYCHIC

STATS
HP ●●●●
ATTACK ●●●
DEFENSE ●●●
SP. ATTACK ●●●
SP. DEFENSE ●●●
SPEED ●●

● M/F have same form

● EVOLUTION PATH
Slowpoke → Lv37 → Slowbro
Link trade while it holds King's Rock → Slowking
pg. 443

● MAIN WAYS TO OBTAIN
PLATINUM	Eterna City side of Route 205 (use the Poké Radar)
DIAMOND	
PEARL	Eterna City side of Route 205 (use the Poké Radar)
G B A	Catch in LeafGreen and transfer through Pal Park

ABILITY   ● Oblivious   ● Own Tempo

● LEVEL-UP AND LEARNED MOVES
Lv	Name	Type	Kind	Power	Acc	PP	Range	DA
Base	Curse	???	Status	—	—	10	Normal • Self	—
Base	Yawn	Normal	Status	—	—	10	Normal	—
Base	Tackle	Normal	Physical	35	95	35	Normal	●
6	Growl	Normal	Status	—	100	40	2 foes	—
11	Water Gun	Water	Special	40	100	25	Normal	—
15	Confusion	Psychic	Special	50	100	25	Normal	—
20	Disable	Normal	Status	—	80	20	Normal	—
25	Headbutt	Normal	Physical	70	100	15	Normal	●
29	Water Pulse	Water	Special	60	100	20	Normal	—
34	Zen Headbutt	Psychic	Physical	80	90	15	Normal	●
39	Slack Off	Normal	Status	—	—	10	Self	—
43	Amnesia	Psychic	Status	—	—	20	Self	—
48	Psychic	Psychic	Special	90	100	10	Normal	—
53	Rain Dance	Water	Status	—	—	5	All	—
57	Psych Up	Normal	Status	—	—	10	Normal	—

National Pokédex No. 080 Hermit Crab Pokémon
Slowbro

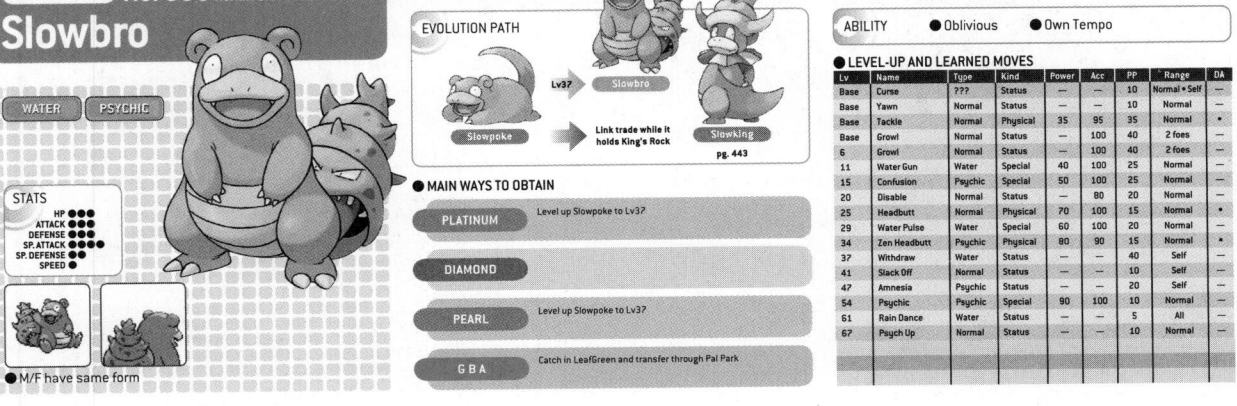

WATER   PSYCHIC

STATS
HP ●●●
ATTACK ●●●
DEFENSE ●●●●
SP. ATTACK ●●●
SP. DEFENSE ●●●
SPEED ●●●

● M/F have same form

● EVOLUTION PATH
Slowpoke → Lv37 → Slowbro
Link trade while it holds King's Rock → Slowking
pg. 443

● MAIN WAYS TO OBTAIN
PLATINUM	Level up Slowpoke to Lv37
DIAMOND	
PEARL	Level up Slowpoke to Lv37
G B A	Catch in LeafGreen and transfer through Pal Park

ABILITY   ● Oblivious   ● Own Tempo

● LEVEL-UP AND LEARNED MOVES
Lv	Name	Type	Kind	Power	Acc	PP	Range	DA
Base	Curse	???	Status	—	—	10	Normal • Self	—
Base	Yawn	Normal	Status	—	—	10	Normal	—
Base	Tackle	Normal	Physical	35	95	35	Normal	●
Base	Growl	Normal	Status	—	100	40	2 foes	—
6	Growl	Normal	Status	—	100	40	2 foes	—
11	Water Gun	Water	Special	40	100	25	Normal	—
15	Confusion	Psychic	Special	50	100	25	Normal	—
20	Disable	Normal	Status	—	80	20	Normal	—
25	Headbutt	Normal	Physical	70	100	15	Normal	●
29	Water Pulse	Water	Special	60	100	20	Normal	—
34	Zen Headbutt	Psychic	Physical	80	90	15	Normal	●
37	Withdraw	Water	Status	—	—	40	Self	—
41	Slack Off	Normal	Status	—	—	10	Self	—
47	Amnesia	Psychic	Status	—	—	20	Self	—
54	Psychic	Psychic	Special	90	100	10	Normal	—
61	Rain Dance	Water	Status	—	—	5	All	—
67	Psych Up	Normal	Status	—	—	10	Normal	—

National Pokédex No. 081 Magnet Pokémon
Magnemite

ELECTRIC STEEL

STATS
HP ●
ATTACK ●●
DEFENSE ●●
SP. ATTACK ●●●●
SP. DEFENSE ●●
SPEED ●●

● Gender unknown

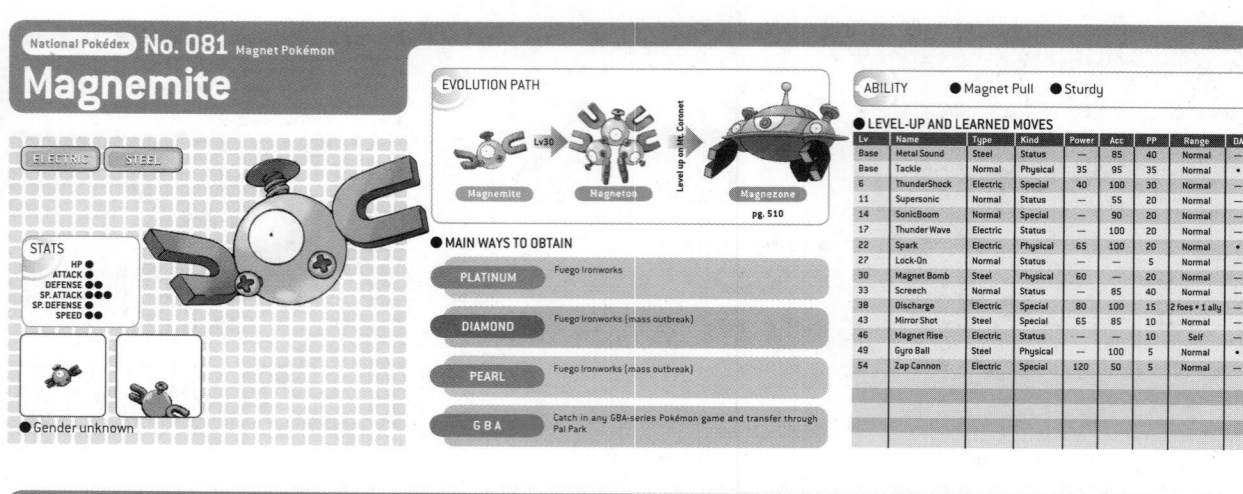

EVOLUTION PATH
Magnemite → Lv30 → Magneton → Level up on Mt. Coronet → Magnezone pg. 510

● MAIN WAYS TO OBTAIN

PLATINUM	Fuego Ironworks
DIAMOND	Fuego Ironworks (mass outbreak)
PEARL	Fuego Ironworks (mass outbreak)
G B A	Catch in any GBA-series Pokémon game and transfer through Pal Park

ABILITY ● Magnet Pull ● Sturdy

● LEVEL-UP AND LEARNED MOVES

Lv	Name	Type	Kind	Power	Acc	PP	Range	DA
Base	Metal Sound	Steel	Status	—	85	40	Normal	—
Base	Tackle	Normal	Physical	35	95	35	Normal	•
6	ThunderShock	Electric	Special	40	100	30	Normal	—
11	Supersonic	Normal	Status	—	55	20	Normal	—
14	SonicBoom	Normal	Special	—	90	20	Normal	—
17	Thunder Wave	Normal	Status	—	100	20	Normal	—
22	Spark	Electric	Physical	65	100	20	Normal	•
27	Lock-On	Normal	Status	—	—	5	Normal	—
30	Magnet Bomb	Steel	Physical	60	—	20	Normal	—
33	Screech	Normal	Status	—	85	40	Normal	—
38	Discharge	Electric	Special	80	100	15	2 foes • 1 ally	—
43	Mirror Shot	Steel	Special	65	85	10	Normal	—
46	Magnet Rise	Electric	Status	—	—	10	Self	—
49	Gyro Ball	Steel	Physical	—	100	5	Normal	•
54	Zap Cannon	Electric	Special	120	50	5	Normal	—

National Pokédex No. 082 Magnet Pokémon
Magneton

ELECTRIC STEEL

STATS
HP ●●
ATTACK ●●●
DEFENSE ●●●
SP. ATTACK ●●●●
SP. DEFENSE ●●●
SPEED ●●●

● Gender unknown

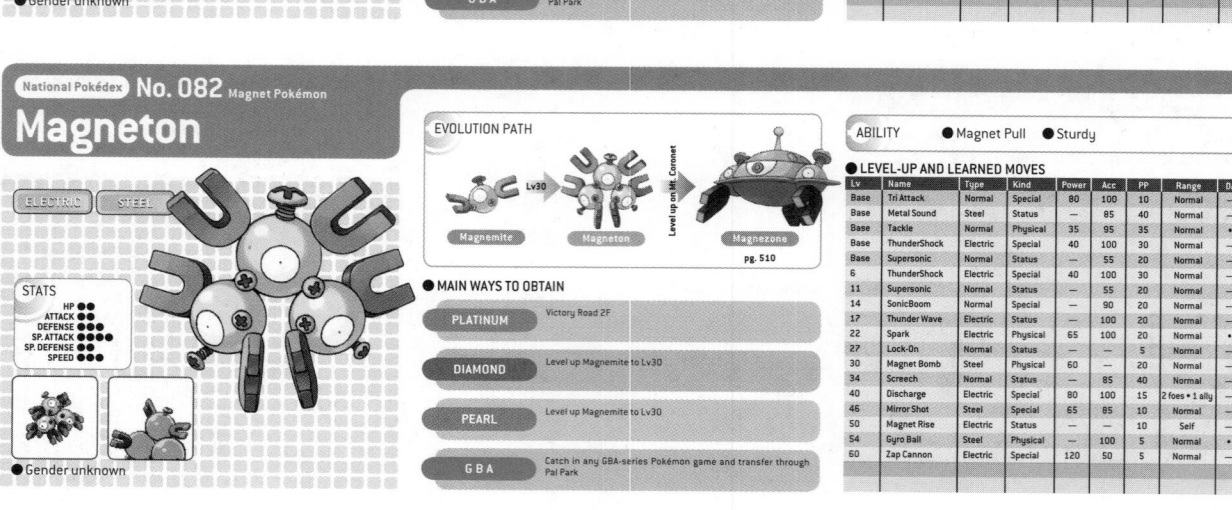

EVOLUTION PATH
Magnemite → Lv30 → Magneton → Level up on Mt. Coronet → Magnezone pg. 510

● MAIN WAYS TO OBTAIN

PLATINUM	Victory Road 2F
DIAMOND	Level up Magnemite to Lv30
PEARL	Level up Magnemite to Lv30
G B A	Catch in any GBA-series Pokémon game and transfer through Pal Park

ABILITY ● Magnet Pull ● Sturdy

● LEVEL-UP AND LEARNED MOVES

Lv	Name	Type	Kind	Power	Acc	PP	Range	DA
Base	Tri Attack	Normal	Special	80	100	10	Normal	—
Base	Metal Sound	Steel	Status	—	85	40	Normal	—
Base	Tackle	Normal	Physical	35	95	35	Normal	•
Base	ThunderShock	Electric	Special	40	100	30	Normal	—
Base	Supersonic	Normal	Status	—	55	20	Normal	—
6	ThunderShock	Electric	Special	40	100	30	Normal	—
11	Supersonic	Normal	Status	—	55	20	Normal	—
14	SonicBoom	Normal	Special	—	90	20	Normal	—
17	Thunder Wave	Electric	Status	—	100	20	Normal	—
22	Spark	Electric	Physical	65	100	20	Normal	•
27	Lock-On	Normal	Status	—	—	5	Normal	—
30	Magnet Bomb	Steel	Physical	60	—	20	Normal	—
34	Screech	Normal	Status	—	85	40	Normal	—
40	Discharge	Electric	Special	80	100	15	2 foes • 1 ally	—
46	Mirror Shot	Steel	Special	65	85	10	Normal	—
50	Magnet Rise	Electric	Status	—	—	10	Self	—
54	Gyro Ball	Steel	Physical	—	100	5	Normal	—
60	Zap Cannon	Electric	Special	120	50	5	Normal	—

National Pokédex No. 083 Wild Duck Pokémon
Farfetch'd

NORMAL FLYING

STATS
HP ●●
ATTACK ●●●
DEFENSE ●●
SP. ATTACK ●●
SP. DEFENSE ●●
SPEED ●●

● M/F have same form

EVOLUTION PATH
Does not evolve

● MAIN WAYS TO OBTAIN

PLATINUM	Route 221 (mass outbreak)
DIAMOND	Route 221 (mass outbreak)
PEARL	Route 221 (mass outbreak)
G B A	Acquire in FireRed/LeafGreen and transfer through Pal Park

ABILITY ● Keen Eye ● Inner Focus

● LEVEL-UP AND LEARNED MOVES

Lv	Name	Type	Kind	Power	Acc	PP	Range	DA
Base	Poison Jab	Poison	Physical	80	100	20	Normal	•
Base	Peck	Flying	Physical	35	100	35	Normal	•
Base	Sand-Attack	Ground	Status	—	100	15	Normal	—
Base	Leer	Normal	Status	—	100	30	2 foes	—
Base	Fury Cutter	Bug	Physical	10	95	20	Normal	•
7	Fury Attack	Normal	Physical	15	85	20	Normal	•
9	Knock Off	Dark	Physical	20	100	20	Normal	•
13	Aerial Ace	Flying	Physical	60	—	20	Normal	•
19	Slash	Normal	Physical	70	100	20	Normal	•
21	Air Cutter	Flying	Special	55	95	25	2 foes	—
25	Swords Dance	Normal	Status	—	—	30	Self	—
31	Agility	Psychic	Status	—	—	30	Self	—
33	Night Slash	Dark	Physical	70	100	15	Normal	•
37	Air Slash	Flying	Special	75	95	20	Normal	—
43	Feint	Normal	Physical	50	100	10	Normal	—
45	False Swipe	Normal	Physical	40	100	40	Normal	•

National Pokédex No. 084 Twin Bird Pokémon
Doduo

NORMAL FLYING

STATS
HP ●●
ATTACK ●●●
DEFENSE ●●
SP. ATTACK ●●
SP. DEFENSE ●●
SPEED ●●●

● Male form ● Female form

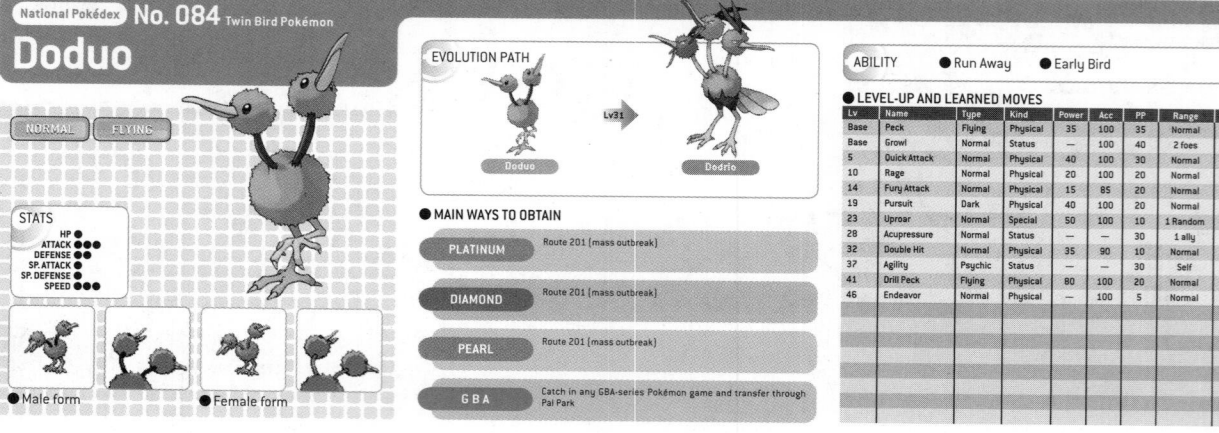

EVOLUTION PATH
Doduo → Lv31 → Dodrio

● MAIN WAYS TO OBTAIN

PLATINUM	Route 201 (mass outbreak)
DIAMOND	Route 201 (mass outbreak)
PEARL	Route 201 (mass outbreak)
G B A	Catch in any GBA-series Pokémon game and transfer through Pal Park

ABILITY ● Run Away ● Early Bird

● LEVEL-UP AND LEARNED MOVES

Lv	Name	Type	Kind	Power	Acc	PP	Range	DA
Base	Peck	Flying	Physical	35	100	35	Normal	•
Base	Growl	Normal	Status	—	100	40	2 foes	—
5	Quick Attack	Normal	Physical	40	100	30	Normal	•
10	Rage	Normal	Physical	20	100	20	Normal	•
14	Fury Attack	Normal	Physical	15	85	20	Normal	•
19	Pursuit	Dark	Physical	40	100	20	Normal	•
23	Uproar	Normal	Special	50	100	10	Normal	•
28	Acupressure	Normal	Status	—	—	30	1 ally	—
32	Double Hit	Normal	Physical	35	90	10	Normal	•
37	Agility	Psychic	Status	—	—	30	Self	—
41	Drill Peck	Flying	Physical	80	100	20	Normal	•
46	Endeavor	Normal	Physical	—	100	5	Normal	—

National Pokédex No. 085 Triple Bird Pokémon
Dodrio

NORMAL | FLYING

STATS
- HP ●●
- ATTACK ●●●●
- DEFENSE ●●●
- SP. ATTACK ●●
- SP. DEFENSE ●●
- SPEED ●●●●

● Male form   ● Female form

EVOLUTION PATH

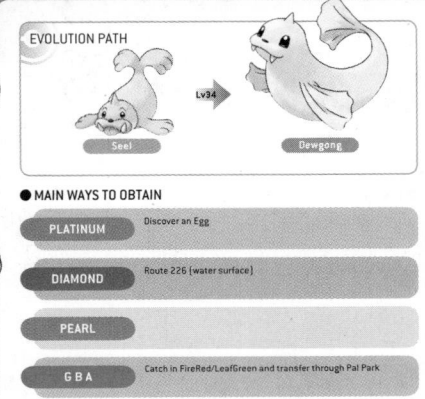

Doduo → Lv31 → Dodrio

● MAIN WAYS TO OBTAIN

PLATINUM	Level up Doduo to Lv31
DIAMOND	Level up Doduo to Lv31
PEARL	Level up Doduo to Lv31
G B A	Catch and evolve in any GBA-series Pokémon game and transfer through Pal Park

ABILITY ● Run Away ● Early Bird

● LEVEL-UP AND LEARNED MOVES

Lv	Name	Type	Kind	Power	Acc	PP	Range	DA
Base	Pluck	Flying	Physical	60	100	20	Normal	•
Base	Peck	Flying	Physical	35	100	35	Normal	•
Base	Growl	Normal	Status	—	100	40	2 foes	—
Base	Quick Attack	Normal	Physical	40	100	30	Normal	•
Base	Rage	Normal	Physical	20	100	30	Normal	•
5	Quick Attack	Normal	Physical	40	100	30	Normal	•
10	Rage	Normal	Physical	20	100	30	Normal	•
14	Fury Attack	Normal	Physical	15	85	20	Normal	•
19	Pursuit	Dark	Physical	40	100	20	Normal	•
23	Uproar	Normal	Special	50	100	10	1 Random	•
28	Acupressure	Normal	Status	—	—	30	1 ally	—
34	Tri Attack	Normal	Special	80	100	10	Normal	•
41	Agility	Psychic	Status	—	—	30	Self	—
47	Drill Peck	Flying	Physical	80	100	20	Normal	•
54	Endeavor	Normal	Physical	—	100	5	Normal	•

National Pokédex No. 086 Sea Lion Pokémon
Seel

WATER

STATS
- HP ●●
- ATTACK ●●
- DEFENSE ●●
- SP. ATTACK ●●
- SP. DEFENSE ●●
- SPEED ●●

● M/F have same form

EVOLUTION PATH

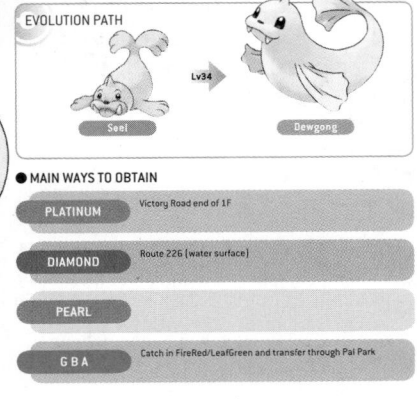

Seel → Lv34 → Dewgong

● MAIN WAYS TO OBTAIN

PLATINUM	Discover an Egg
DIAMOND	Route 226 (water surface)
PEARL	
G B A	Catch in FireRed/LeafGreen and transfer through Pal Park

ABILITY ● Thick Fat ● Hydration

● LEVEL-UP AND LEARNED MOVES

Lv	Name	Type	Kind	Power	Acc	PP	Range	DA
Base	Headbutt	Normal	Physical	70	100	15	Normal	•
3	Growl	Normal	Status	—	100	40	2 foes	—
7	Water Sport	Water	Status	—	—	15	All	—
11	Icy Wind	Ice	Special	55	95	15	2 foes	—
13	Encore	Normal	Status	—	100	5	Normal	—
17	Ice Shard	Ice	Physical	40	100	30	Normal	•
21	Rest	Psychic	Status	—	—	10	Self	—
23	Aqua Ring	Water	Status	—	—	20	Self	—
27	Aurora Beam	Ice	Special	65	100	20	Normal	•
31	Aqua Jet	Water	Physical	40	100	20	Normal	•
33	Brine	Water	Special	65	100	10	Normal	•
37	Take Down	Normal	Physical	90	85	20	Normal	•
41	Dive	Water	Physical	80	100	10	Normal	•
43	Aqua Tail	Water	Physical	90	90	10	Normal	•
47	Ice Beam	Ice	Special	95	100	10	Normal	•
51	Safeguard	Normal	Status	—	—	25	2 allies	—

National Pokédex No. 087 Sea Lion Pokémon
Dewgong

WATER | ICE

STATS
- HP ●●●
- ATTACK ●●●
- DEFENSE ●●●
- SP. ATTACK ●●●
- SP. DEFENSE ●●●●
- SPEED ●●●

● M/F have same form

EVOLUTION PATH

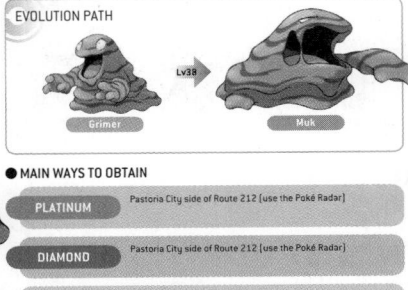

Seel → Lv34 → Dewgong

● MAIN WAYS TO OBTAIN

PLATINUM	Victory Road end of 1F
DIAMOND	Route 226 (water surface)
PEARL	
G B A	Catch in FireRed/LeafGreen and transfer through Pal Park

ABILITY ● Thick Fat ● Hydration

● LEVEL-UP AND LEARNED MOVES

Lv	Name	Type	Kind	Power	Acc	PP	Range	DA
Base	Headbutt	Normal	Physical	70	100	15	Normal	•
Base	Growl	Normal	Status	—	100	40	2 foes	—
Base	Signal Beam	Bug	Special	75	100	15	Normal	—
Base	Icy Wind	Ice	Special	55	95	15	2 foes	—
3	Growl	Normal	Status	—	100	40	2 foes	—
7	Signal Beam	Bug	Special	75	100	15	Normal	—
11	Icy Wind	Ice	Special	55	95	15	2 foes	—
13	Encore	Normal	Status	—	100	5	Normal	—
17	Ice Shard	Ice	Physical	40	100	30	Normal	•
21	Rest	Psychic	Status	—	—	10	Self	—
23	Aqua Ring	Water	Status	—	—	20	Self	—
27	Aurora Beam	Ice	Special	65	100	20	Normal	•
31	Aqua Jet	Water	Physical	40	100	20	Normal	•
33	Brine	Water	Special	65	100	10	Normal	•
34	Sheer Cold	Ice	Special	—	30	5	Normal	—
37	Take Down	Normal	Physical	90	85	20	Normal	•
41	Dive	Water	Physical	80	100	10	Normal	•
43	Aqua Tail	Water	Physical	90	90	10	Normal	•
47	Ice Beam	Ice	Special	95	100	10	Normal	•
51	Safeguard	Normal	Status	—	—	25	2 allies	—

National Pokédex No. 088 Sludge Pokémon
Grimer

POISON

STATS
- HP ●●●
- ATTACK ●●●
- DEFENSE ●●
- SP. ATTACK ●●
- SP. DEFENSE ●●
- SPEED ●

● M/F have same form

EVOLUTION PATH

Grimer → Lv38 → Muk

● MAIN WAYS TO OBTAIN

PLATINUM	Pastoria City side of Route 212 (use the Poké Radar)
DIAMOND	Pastoria City side of Route 212 (use the Poké Radar)
PEARL	Pastoria City side of Route 212 (use the Poké Radar)
G B A	Catch in any GBA-series Pokémon game and transfer through Pal Park

ABILITY ● Stench ● Sticky Hold

● LEVEL-UP AND LEARNED MOVES

Lv	Name	Type	Kind	Power	Acc	PP	Range	DA
Base	Poison Gas	Poison	Status	—	55	40	Normal	—
Base	Pound	Normal	Physical	40	100	35	Normal	•
4	Harden	Normal	Status	—	—	30	Self	—
7	Mud-Slap	Ground	Special	20	100	10	Normal	—
12	Disable	Normal	Status	—	80	20	Normal	—
17	Minimize	Normal	Status	—	—	20	Self	—
20	Sludge	Poison	Special	65	100	20	Normal	•
23	Mud Bomb	Ground	Special	65	85	10	Normal	—
28	Fling	Dark	Physical	—	100	10	Normal	•
33	Screech	Normal	Status	—	85	40	Normal	—
36	Sludge Bomb	Poison	Special	90	100	10	Normal	•
39	Acid Armor	Poison	Status	—	—	40	Self	—
44	Gunk Shot	Poison	Physical	120	70	5	Normal	•
49	Memento	Dark	Status	—	100	10	Normal	—

088
GRIMER

No. 089 Sludge Pokémon
Muk

POISON

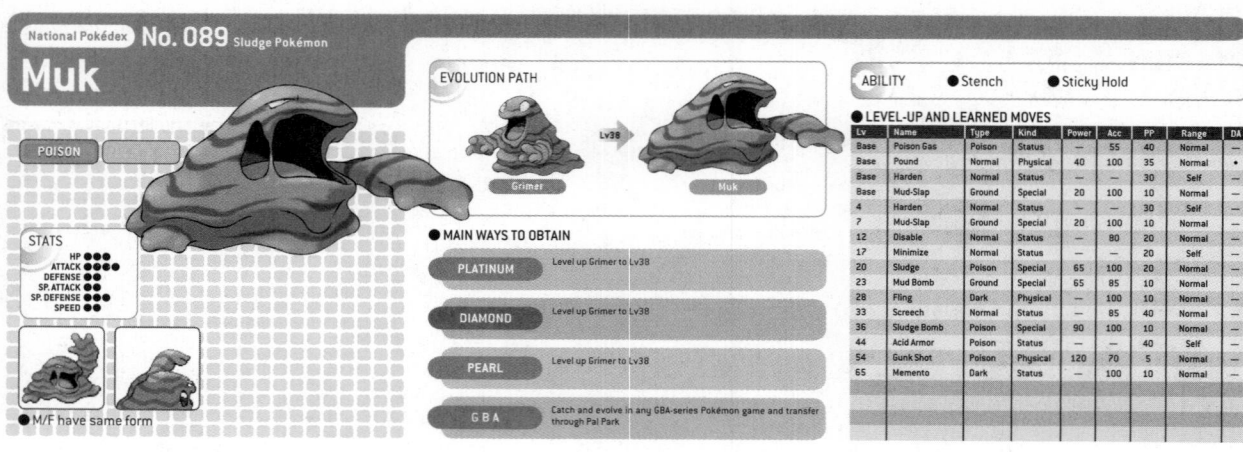

STATS
HP ●●●
ATTACK ●●●●
DEFENSE ●●
SP. ATTACK ●●
SP. DEFENSE ●●●
SPEED ●●●

● M/F have same form

EVOLUTION PATH
Grimer — Lv38 → Muk

● MAIN WAYS TO OBTAIN
PLATINUM	Level up Grimer to Lv38
DIAMOND	Level up Grimer to Lv38
PEARL	Level up Grimer to Lv38
G B A	Catch and evolve in any GBA-series Pokémon game and transfer through Pal Park

ABILITY ● Stench ● Sticky Hold

● LEVEL-UP AND LEARNED MOVES
Lv	Name	Type	Kind	Power	Acc	PP	Range	DA
Base	Poison Gas	Poison	Status	—	55	40	Normal	—
Base	Pound	Normal	Physical	40	100	35	Normal	●
Base	Harden	Normal	Status	—	—	30	Self	—
Base	Mud-Slap	Ground	Special	20	100	10	Normal	—
4	Harden	Normal	Status	—	—	30	Self	—
7	Mud-Slap	Ground	Special	20	100	10	Normal	—
12	Disable	Normal	Status	—	80	20	Normal	—
17	Minimize	Normal	Status	—	—	20	Self	—
20	Sludge	Poison	Special	65	100	20	Normal	—
23	Mud Bomb	Ground	Special	65	85	10	Normal	—
28	Fling	Dark	Physical	—	100	10	Normal	—
33	Screech	Normal	Status	—	85	40	Normal	—
36	Sludge Bomb	Poison	Special	90	100	10	Normal	—
44	Acid Armor	Poison	Status	—	—	40	Self	—
54	Gunk Shot	Poison	Physical	120	70	5	Normal	—
65	Memento	Dark	Status	—	100	10	Normal	—

No. 090 Bivalve Pokémon
Shellder

WATER

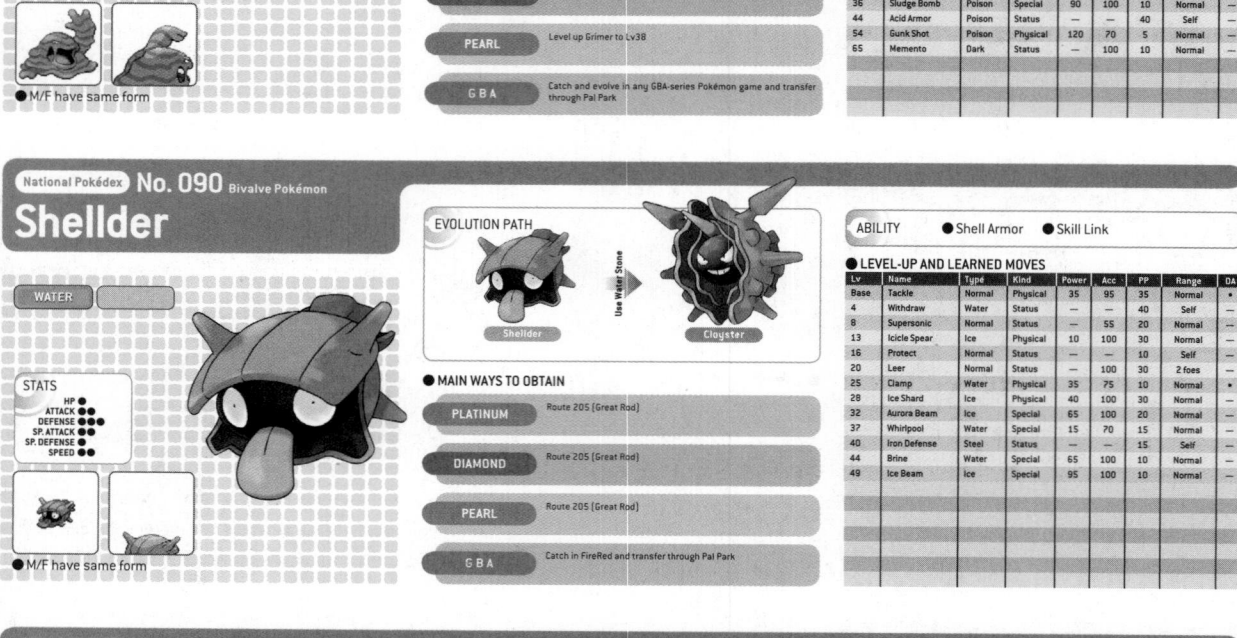

STATS
HP ●
ATTACK ●●●
DEFENSE ●●●●
SP. ATTACK ●●
SP. DEFENSE ●
SPEED ●●

● M/F have same form

EVOLUTION PATH
Shellder — Use Water Stone → Cloyster

● MAIN WAYS TO OBTAIN
PLATINUM	Route 205 (Great Rod)
DIAMOND	Route 205 (Great Rod)
PEARL	Route 205 (Great Rod)
G B A	Catch in FireRed and transfer through Pal Park

ABILITY ● Shell Armor ● Skill Link

● LEVEL-UP AND LEARNED MOVES
Lv	Name	Type	Kind	Power	Acc	PP	Range	DA
Base	Tackle	Normal	Physical	35	95	35	Normal	●
4	Withdraw	Water	Status	—	—	40	Self	—
8	Supersonic	Normal	Status	—	55	20	Normal	—
13	Icicle Spear	Ice	Physical	10	100	30	Normal	—
16	Protect	Normal	Status	—	—	10	Self	—
20	Leer	Normal	Status	—	100	30	2 foes	—
25	Clamp	Water	Physical	35	75	10	Normal	●
28	Ice Shard	Ice	Physical	40	100	30	Normal	—
32	Aurora Beam	Ice	Special	65	100	20	Normal	—
37	Whirlpool	Water	Special	15	70	15	Normal	—
40	Iron Defense	Steel	Status	—	—	15	Self	—
44	Brine	Water	Special	65	100	10	Normal	—
49	Ice Beam	Ice	Special	95	100	10	Normal	—

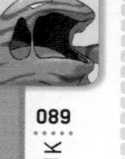

089
•••••
MUK

No. 091 Bivalve Pokémon
Cloyster

WATER ICE

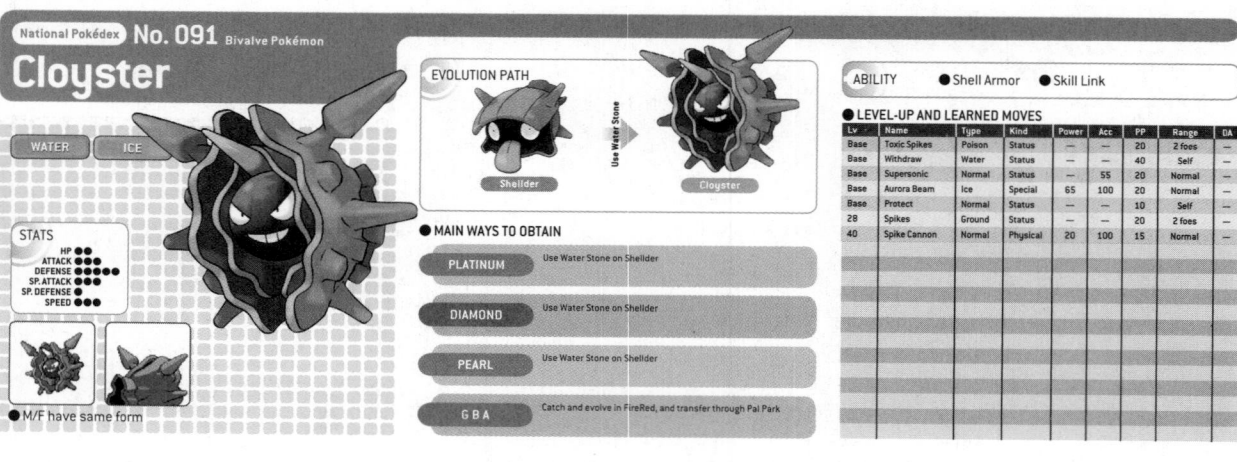

STATS
HP ●●
ATTACK ●●●
DEFENSE ●●●●●
SP. ATTACK ●●●
SP. DEFENSE ●
SPEED ●●●

● M/F have same form

EVOLUTION PATH
Shellder — Use Water Stone → Cloyster

● MAIN WAYS TO OBTAIN
PLATINUM	Use Water Stone on Shellder
DIAMOND	Use Water Stone on Shellder
PEARL	Use Water Stone on Shellder
G B A	Catch and evolve in FireRed, and transfer through Pal Park

ABILITY ● Shell Armor ● Skill Link

● LEVEL-UP AND LEARNED MOVES
Lv	Name	Type	Kind	Power	Acc	PP	Range	DA
Base	Toxic Spikes	Poison	Status	—	—	20	2 foes	—
Base	Withdraw	Water	Status	—	—	40	Self	—
Base	Supersonic	Normal	Status	—	55	20	Normal	—
Base	Aurora Beam	Ice	Special	65	100	20	Normal	—
Base	Protect	Normal	Status	—	—	10	Self	—
28	Spikes	Ground	Status	—	—	20	2 foes	—
40	Spike Cannon	Normal	Physical	20	100	15	Normal	—

No. 092 Gas Pokémon
Gastly

GHOST POISON

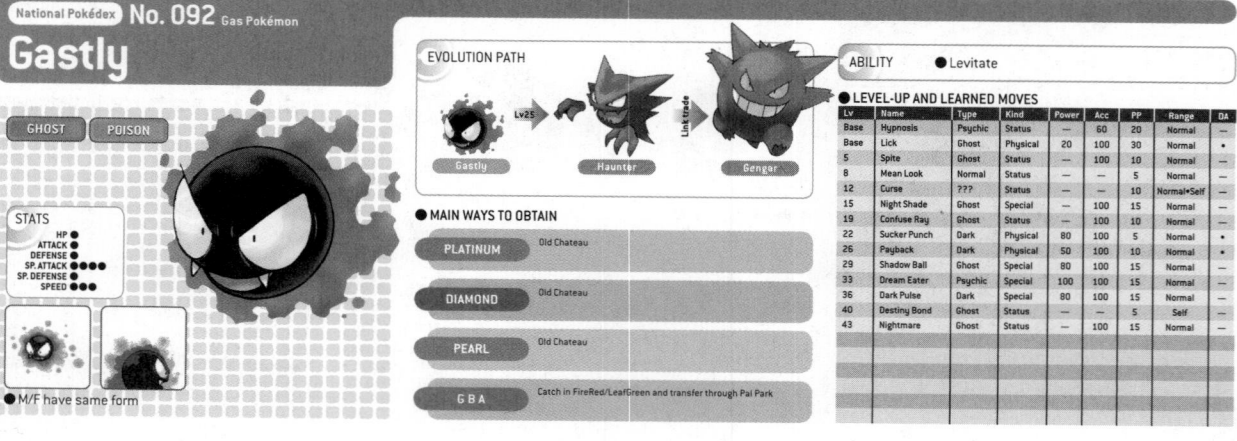

STATS
HP ●
ATTACK ●
DEFENSE ●
SP. ATTACK ●●●
SP. DEFENSE ●●●
SPEED ●●●●

● M/F have same form

EVOLUTION PATH
Gastly — Lv25 → Haunter — Link trade → Gengar

● MAIN WAYS TO OBTAIN
PLATINUM	Old Chateau
DIAMOND	Old Chateau
PEARL	Old Chateau
G B A	Catch in FireRed/LeafGreen and transfer through Pal Park

ABILITY ● Levitate

● LEVEL-UP AND LEARNED MOVES
Lv	Name	Type	Kind	Power	Acc	PP	Range	DA
Base	Hypnosis	Psychic	Status	—	60	20	Normal	—
Base	Lick	Ghost	Physical	20	100	30	Normal	●
5	Spite	Ghost	Status	—	100	10	Normal	—
8	Mean Look	Normal	Status	—	—	5	Normal	—
12	Curse	???	Status	—	—	10	Normal•Self	—
15	Night Shade	Ghost	Special	—	100	15	Normal	—
19	Confuse Ray	Ghost	Status	—	100	10	Normal	—
22	Sucker Punch	Dark	Physical	80	100	5	Normal	—
26	Payback	Dark	Physical	50	100	10	Normal	●
29	Shadow Ball	Ghost	Special	80	100	15	Normal	—
33	Dream Eater	Psychic	Special	100	100	15	Normal	—
36	Dark Pulse	Dark	Special	80	100	15	Normal	—
40	Destiny Bond	Ghost	Status	—	—	5	Self	—
43	Nightmare	Ghost	Status	—	100	15	Normal	—

National Pokédex No. 093 Gas Pokémon

Haunter

GHOST POISON

STATS
- HP ●●
- ATTACK ●●
- DEFENSE ●●
- SP. ATTACK ●●●
- SP. DEFENSE ●●
- SPEED ●●●

● M/F have same form

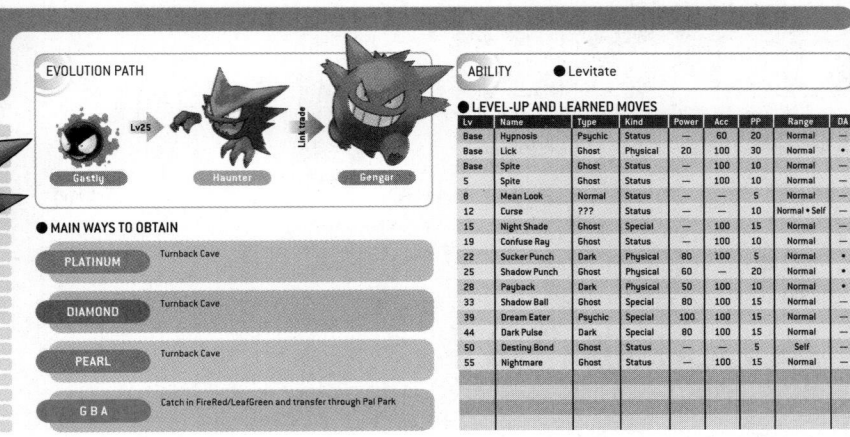

EVOLUTION PATH

Gastly → Lv25 → Haunter → Link trade → Gengar

ABILITY ● Levitate

MAIN WAYS TO OBTAIN

PLATINUM	Turnback Cave
DIAMOND	Turnback Cave
PEARL	Turnback Cave
G B A	Catch in FireRed/LeafGreen and transfer through Pal Park

● LEVEL-UP AND LEARNED MOVES

Lv	Name	Type	Kind	Power	Acc	PP	Range	DA
Base	Hypnosis	Psychic	Status	—	60	20	Normal	—
Base	Lick	Ghost	Physical	20	100	30	Normal	●
Base	Spite	Ghost	Status	—	100	10	Normal	—
5	Spite	Ghost	Status	—	100	10	Normal	—
8	Mean Look	Normal	Status	—	—	5	Normal	—
12	Curse	???	Status	—	—	10	Normal • Self	—
15	Night Shade	Ghost	Special	—	100	15	Normal	—
19	Confuse Ray	Ghost	Status	—	100	10	Normal	—
22	Sucker Punch	Dark	Physical	80	100	5	Normal	●
25	Shadow Punch	Ghost	Physical	60	—	20	Normal	●
28	Payback	Dark	Physical	50	100	10	Normal	●
33	Shadow Ball	Ghost	Special	80	100	15	Normal	—
39	Dream Eater	Psychic	Special	100	100	15	Normal	—
44	Dark Pulse	Dark	Special	80	100	15	Normal	—
50	Destiny Bond	Ghost	Status	—	—	5	Self	—
55	Nightmare	Ghost	Status	—	100	15	Normal	—

National Pokédex No. 094 Shadow Pokémon

Gengar

GHOST POISON

STATS
- HP ●●
- ATTACK ●●
- DEFENSE ●●
- SP. ATTACK ●●●●
- SP. DEFENSE ●●
- SPEED ●●●●

● M/F have same form

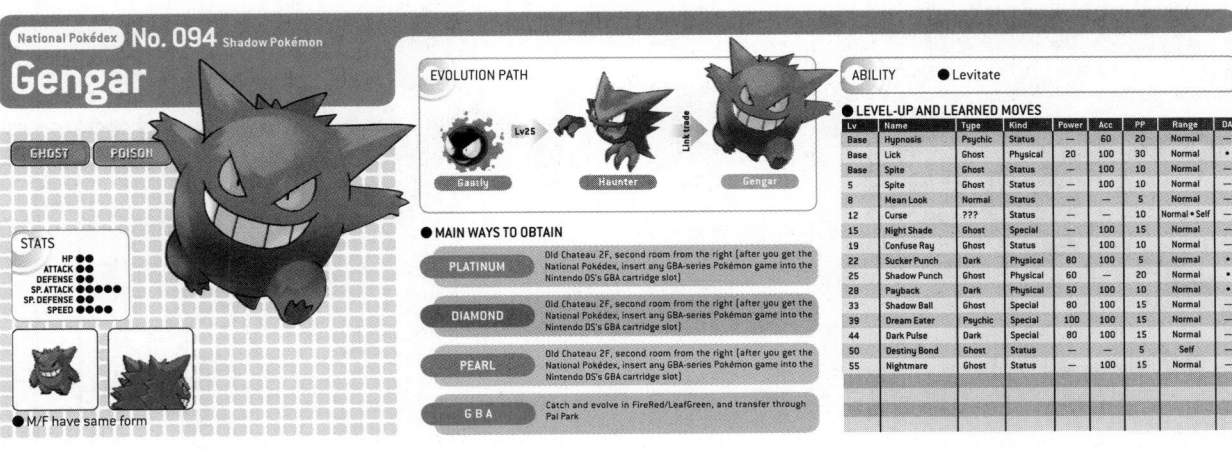

EVOLUTION PATH

Gastly → Lv25 → Haunter → Link trade → Gengar

ABILITY ● Levitate

MAIN WAYS TO OBTAIN

PLATINUM	Old Chateau 2F, second room from the right (after you get the National Pokédex, insert any GBA-series Pokémon game into the Nintendo DS's GBA cartridge slot)
DIAMOND	Old Chateau 2F, second room from the right (after you get the National Pokédex, insert any GBA-series Pokémon game into the Nintendo DS's GBA cartridge slot)
PEARL	Old Chateau 2F, second room from the right (after you get the National Pokédex, insert any GBA-series Pokémon game into the Nintendo DS's GBA cartridge slot)
G B A	Catch and evolve in FireRed/LeafGreen, and transfer through Pal Park

● LEVEL-UP AND LEARNED MOVES

Lv	Name	Type	Kind	Power	Acc	PP	Range	DA
Base	Hypnosis	Psychic	Status	—	60	20	Normal	—
Base	Lick	Ghost	Physical	20	100	30	Normal	●
Base	Spite	Ghost	Status	—	100	10	Normal	—
5	Spite	Ghost	Status	—	100	10	Normal	—
8	Mean Look	Normal	Status	—	—	5	Normal	—
12	Curse	???	Status	—	—	10	Normal • Self	—
15	Night Shade	Ghost	Special	—	100	15	Normal	—
19	Confuse Ray	Ghost	Status	—	100	10	Normal	—
22	Sucker Punch	Dark	Physical	80	100	5	Normal	●
25	Shadow Punch	Ghost	Physical	60	—	20	Normal	●
28	Payback	Dark	Physical	50	100	10	Normal	●
33	Shadow Ball	Ghost	Special	80	100	15	Normal	—
39	Dream Eater	Psychic	Special	100	100	15	Normal	—
44	Dark Pulse	Dark	Special	80	100	15	Normal	—
50	Destiny Bond	Ghost	Status	—	—	5	Self	—
55	Nightmare	Ghost	Status	—	100	15	Normal	—

National Pokédex No. 095 Rock Snake Pokémon

Onix

ROCK GROUND

STATS
- HP ●
- ATTACK ●●
- DEFENSE ●●●
- SP. ATTACK ●
- SP. DEFENSE ●
- SPEED ●●●

● M/F have same form

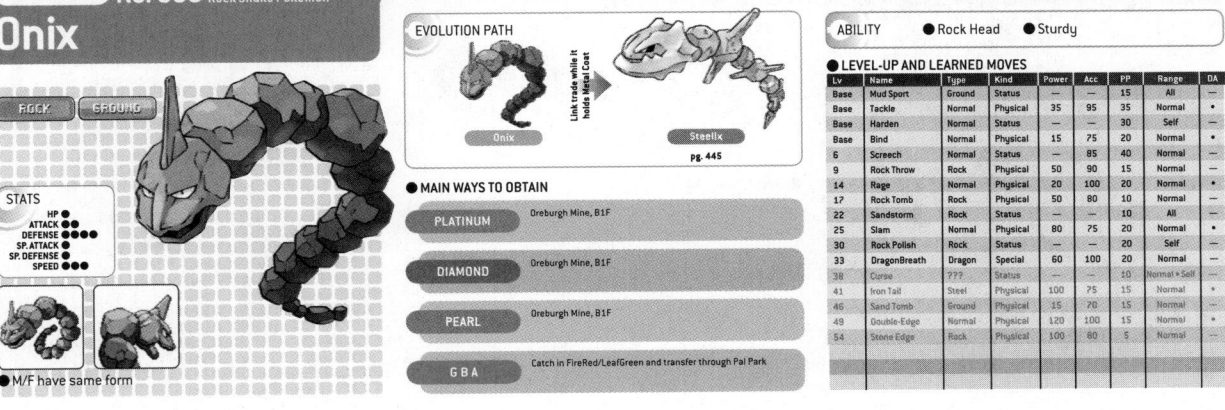

EVOLUTION PATH

Onix → Link trade while it holds Metal Coat → Steelix (pg. 445)

ABILITY ● Rock Head ● Sturdy

MAIN WAYS TO OBTAIN

PLATINUM	Oreburgh Mine, B1F
DIAMOND	Oreburgh Mine, B1F
PEARL	Oreburgh Mine, B1F
G B A	Catch in FireRed/LeafGreen and transfer through Pal Park

● LEVEL-UP AND LEARNED MOVES

Lv	Name	Type	Kind	Power	Acc	PP	Range	DA
Base	Mud Sport	Ground	Status	—	—	15	All	—
Base	Tackle	Normal	Physical	35	95	35	Normal	●
Base	Harden	Normal	Status	—	—	30	Self	—
Base	Bind	Normal	Physical	15	75	20	Normal	—
6	Screech	Normal	Status	—	85	40	Normal	—
9	Rock Throw	Rock	Physical	50	90	15	Normal	—
14	Rage	Normal	Physical	20	100	20	Normal	●
17	Rock Tomb	Rock	Physical	50	80	10	Normal	—
22	Sandstorm	Rock	Status	—	—	10	All	—
25	Slam	Normal	Physical	80	75	20	Normal	●
30	Rock Polish	Rock	Status	—	—	20	Self	—
33	DragonBreath	Dragon	Special	60	100	20	Normal	—
38	Curse	???	Status	—	—	10	Normal • Self	—
41	Iron Tail	Steel	Physical	100	75	15	Normal	—
46	Sand Tomb	Ground	Physical	15	70	15	Normal	—
49	Double-Edge	Normal	Physical	120	100	15	Normal	●
54	Stone Edge	Rock	Physical	100	80	5	Normal	—

National Pokédex No. 096 Hypnosis Pokémon

Drowzee

PSYCHIC

STATS
- HP ●●
- ATTACK ●●
- DEFENSE ●●
- SP. ATTACK ●●
- SP. DEFENSE ●●●
- SPEED ●●

● M/F have same form

EVOLUTION PATH

Drowzee → Lv26 → Hypno

ABILITY ● Insomnia ● Forewarn

MAIN WAYS TO OBTAIN

PLATINUM	Route 215 (mass outbreak)
DIAMOND	Route 215 (mass outbreak)
PEARL	Route 215 (mass outbreak)
G B A	Catch in FireRed/LeafGreen and transfer through Pal Park

● LEVEL-UP AND LEARNED MOVES

Lv	Name	Type	Kind	Power	Acc	PP	Range	DA
Base	Pound	Normal	Physical	40	100	35	Normal	●
Base	Hypnosis	Psychic	Status	—	60	20	Normal	—
7	Disable	Normal	Status	—	80	20	Normal	—
9	Confusion	Psychic	Special	50	100	25	Normal	—
15	Headbutt	Normal	Physical	70	100	15	Normal	●
18	Poison Gas	Poison	Status	—	55	40	Normal	—
21	Meditate	Psychic	Status	—	—	40	Self	—
26	Psybeam	Psychic	Special	65	100	20	Normal	—
29	Psych Up	Normal	Status	—	—	10	Normal	—
32	Headbutt	Normal	Physical	70	100	15	Normal	●
37	Swagger	Normal	Status	—	90	15	Normal	—
40	Psychic	Psychic	Special	90	100	10	Normal	—
43	Nasty Plot	Dark	Status	—	—	20	Self	—
50	Zen Headbutt	Psychic	Physical	80	90	15	Normal	●
53	Future Sight	Psychic	Special	80	90	15	Normal	—

National Pokédex No. 097 Hypnosis Pokémon

Hypno

PSYCHIC

STATS
HP ●●●
ATTACK ●●●
DEFENSE ●●●
SP. ATTACK ●●●
SP. DEFENSE ●●●
SPEED ●●

● Male form   ● Female form

EVOLUTION PATH

Drowzee → Lv26 → Hypno

● MAIN WAYS TO OBTAIN

PLATINUM	Level up Drowzee to Lv26
DIAMOND	Level up Drowzee to Lv26
PEARL	Level up Drowzee to Lv26
G B A	Catch in FireRed/LeafGreen and transfer through Pal Park

ABILITY   ● Insomnia   ● Forewarn

● LEVEL-UP AND LEARNED MOVES

Lv	Name	Type	Kind	Power	Acc	PP	Range	DA
Base	Nightmare	Ghost	Status	—	100	15	Normal	—
Base	Switcheroo	Dark	Status	—	100	10	Normal	—
Base	Pound	Normal	Physical	40	100	35	Normal	●
Base	Hypnosis	Psychic	Status	—	60	20	Normal	—
Base	Disable	Normal	Status	—	80	20	Normal	—
Base	Confusion	Psychic	Special	50	100	25	Normal	—
7	Disable	Normal	Status	—	80	20	Normal	—
9	Confusion	Psychic	Special	50	100	25	Normal	—
15	Headbutt	Normal	Physical	70	100	15	Normal	●
18	Poison Gas	Poison	Status	—	55	40	Normal	—
21	Meditate	Normal	Status	—	—	40	Self	—
28	Psybeam	Psychic	Special	65	100	20	Normal	—
33	Psych Up	Normal	Status	—	—	10	Normal	—
38	Headbutt	Normal	Physical	70	100	15	Normal	●
45	Swagger	Normal	Status	—	90	15	Normal	—
50	Psychic	Psychic	Special	90	100	10	Normal	—
55	Nasty Plot	Dark	Status	—	—	20	Self	—
64	Zen Headbutt	Psychic	Physical	80	90	15	Normal	●
69	Future Sight	Psychic	Special	80	90	15	Normal	—

National Pokédex No. 098 River Crab Pokémon

Krabby

WATER

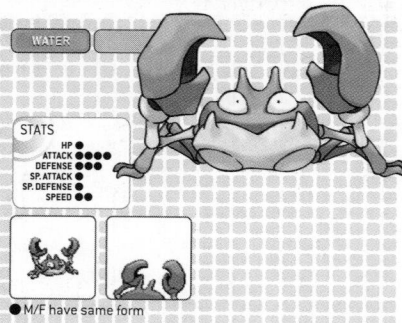

STATS
HP ●●
ATTACK ●●●●
DEFENSE ●●●●
SP. ATTACK ●
SP. DEFENSE ●●
SPEED ●●

● M/F have same form

EVOLUTION PATH

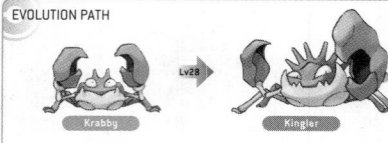

Krabby → Lv28 → Kingler

● MAIN WAYS TO OBTAIN

PLATINUM	Route 226 (mass outbreak)
DIAMOND	Route 226 (mass outbreak)
PEARL	Route 226 (mass outbreak)
G B A	Catch in FireRed/LeafGreen and transfer through Pal Park

ABILITY   ● Hyper Cutter   ● Shell Armor

● LEVEL-UP AND LEARNED MOVES

Lv	Name	Type	Kind	Power	Acc	PP	Range	DA
Base	Mud Sport	Ground	Status	—	—	15	All	—
Base	Bubble	Water	Special	20	100	30	2 foes	—
5	ViceGrip	Normal	Physical	55	100	30	Normal	—
9	Leer	Normal	Status	—	100	30	2 foes	—
11	Harden	Normal	Status	—	—	30	Self	—
15	BubbleBeam	Water	Special	65	100	20	Normal	—
19	Mud Shot	Ground	Special	55	95	15	Normal	—
21	Metal Claw	Steel	Physical	50	95	35	Normal	—
25	Stomp	Normal	Physical	65	100	20	Normal	—
29	Protect	Normal	Status	—	—	10	Self	—
31	Guillotine	Normal	Physical	—	30	5	Normal	—
35	Slam	Normal	Physical	80	75	20	Normal	—
39	Brine	Water	Special	65	100	10	Normal	—
41	Crabhammer	Water	Physical	90	85	10	Normal	—
45	Flail	Normal	Physical	—	100	15	Normal	—

National Pokédex No. 099 Pincer Pokémon

Kingler

WATER

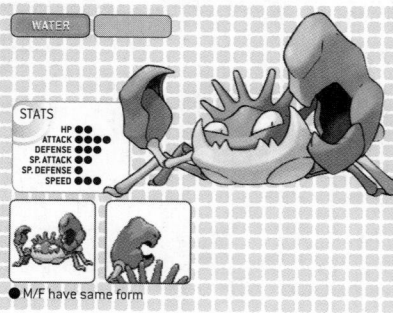

STATS
HP ●●●
ATTACK ●●●●
DEFENSE ●●●●
SP. ATTACK ●●
SP. DEFENSE ●●
SPEED ●●●

● M/F have same form

EVOLUTION PATH

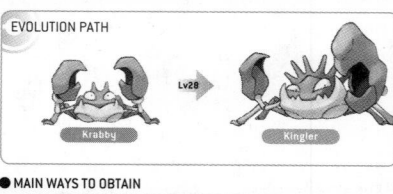

Krabby → Lv28 → Kingler

● MAIN WAYS TO OBTAIN

PLATINUM	Level up Krabby to Lv28
DIAMOND	Level up Krabby to Lv28
PEARL	Level up Krabby to Lv28
G B A	Catch and evolve in FireRed/LeafGreen, and transfer through Pal Park

ABILITY   ● Hyper Cutter   ● Shell Armor

● LEVEL-UP AND LEARNED MOVES

Lv	Name	Type	Kind	Power	Acc	PP	Range	DA
Base	Mud Sport	Ground	Status	—	—	15	All	—
Base	Bubble	Water	Special	20	100	30	2 foes	—
Base	ViceGrip	Normal	Physical	55	100	30	Normal	—
5	ViceGrip	Normal	Physical	55	100	30	Normal	—
9	Leer	Normal	Status	—	100	30	2 foes	—
11	Harden	Normal	Status	—	—	30	Self	—
15	BubbleBeam	Water	Special	65	100	20	Normal	—
19	Mud Shot	Ground	Special	55	95	15	Normal	—
21	Metal Claw	Steel	Physical	50	95	35	Normal	—
25	Stomp	Normal	Physical	65	100	20	Normal	—
32	Protect	Normal	Status	—	—	10	Self	—
37	Guillotine	Normal	Physical	—	30	5	Normal	—
44	Slam	Normal	Physical	80	75	20	Normal	—
51	Brine	Water	Special	65	100	10	Normal	—
56	Crabhammer	Water	Physical	90	85	10	Normal	—
63	Flail	Normal	Physical	—	100	15	Normal	—

National Pokédex No. 100 Ball Pokémon

Voltorb

ELECTRIC

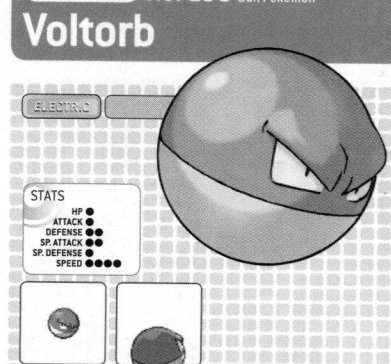

STATS
HP ●
ATTACK ●
DEFENSE ●●
SP. ATTACK ●●●
SP. DEFENSE ●●
SPEED ●●●●

● Gender unknown

EVOLUTION PATH

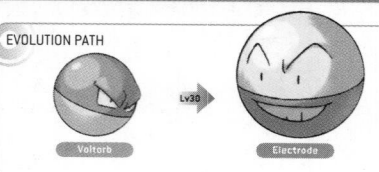

Voltorb → Lv30 → Electrode

● MAIN WAYS TO OBTAIN

PLATINUM	Route 218 (mass outbreak)
DIAMOND	Route 218 (mass outbreak)
PEARL	Route 218 (mass outbreak)
G B A	Catch in any GBA-series Pokémon game, and transfer through Pal Park

ABILITY   ● Soundproof   ● Static

● LEVEL-UP AND LEARNED MOVES

Lv	Name	Type	Kind	Power	Acc	PP	Range	DA
Base	Charge	Electric	Status	—	—	20	Self	—
5	Tackle	Normal	Physical	35	95	35	Normal	●
8	SonicBoom	Normal	Special	—	90	20	Normal	—
12	Spark	Electric	Physical	65	100	20	Normal	●
15	Rollout	Rock	Physical	30	90	20	Normal	●
19	Screech	Normal	Status	—	85	40	Normal	—
22	Light Screen	Psychic	Status	—	—	30	2 Allies	—
26	Charge Beam	Electric	Special	50	90	10	Normal	—
29	Selfdestruct	Normal	Physical	200	100	5	2 foes 1 Ally	—
33	Swift	Normal	Special	60	—	20	2 foes	—
36	Magnet Rise	Electric	Status	—	—	10	Self	—
40	Gyro Ball	Steel	Physical	—	100	5	Normal	—
43	Explosion	Normal	Physical	250	100	5	2 foes 1 Ally	—
47	Mirror Coat	Psychic	Special	—	100	20	Self	—

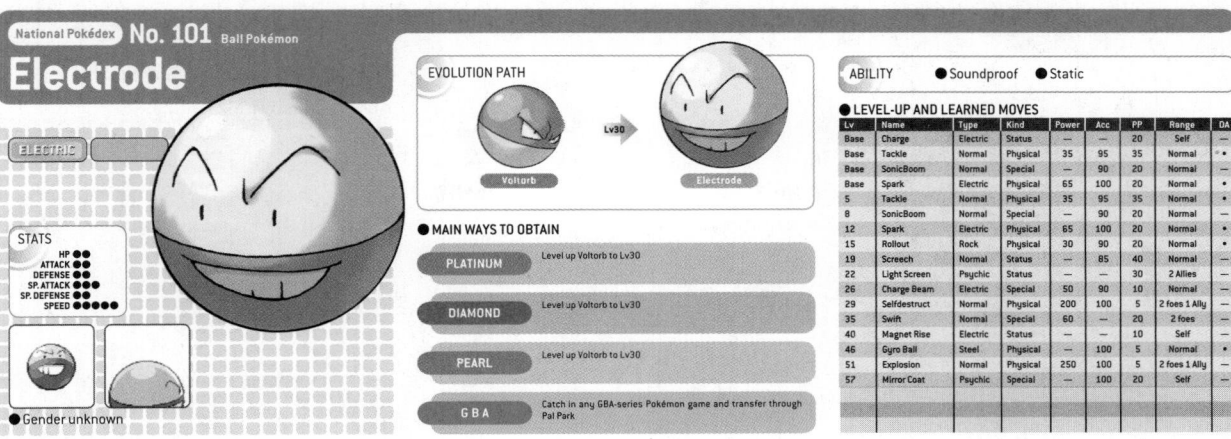

National Pokédex No. 101 Ball Pokémon
Electrode

ELECTRIC

STATS
HP ●●
ATTACK ●●
DEFENSE ●●
SP.ATTACK ●●●
SP.DEFENSE ●●●
SPEED ●●●●●

● Gender unknown

EVOLUTION PATH
Voltorb — Lv30 → Electrode

● MAIN WAYS TO OBTAIN

PLATINUM	Level up Voltorb to Lv30
DIAMOND	Level up Voltorb to Lv30
PEARL	Level up Voltorb to Lv30
GBA	Catch in any GBA-series Pokémon game and transfer through Pal Park

ABILITY ● Soundproof ● Static

● LEVEL-UP AND LEARNED MOVES

Lv	Name	Type	Kind	Power	Acc	PP	Range	DA
Base	Charge	Electric	Status	—	—	20	Self	
Base	Tackle	Normal	Physical	35	95	35	Normal	•
Base	SonicBoom	Normal	Special	—	90	20	Normal	
Base	Spark	Electric	Physical	65	100	20	Normal	•
5	Tackle	Normal	Physical	35	95	35	Normal	•
8	SonicBoom	Normal	Special	—	90	20	Normal	
12	Spark	Electric	Physical	65	100	20	Normal	•
15	Rollout	Rock	Physical	30	90	20	Normal	•
19	Screech	Normal	Status	—	85	40	Normal	•
22	Light Screen	Psychic	Status	—	—	30	2 Allies	
26	Charge Beam	Electric	Special	50	90	10	Normal	•
29	Selfdestruct	Normal	Physical	200	100	5	2 foes 1 Ally	
35	Swift	Normal	Special	60	—	20	2 foes	
40	Magnet Rise	Electric	Status	—	—	10	Self	
46	Gyro Ball	Steel	Physical	—	100	5	Normal	•
51	Explosion	Normal	Physical	250	100	5	2 foes 1 Ally	
57	Mirror Coat	Psychic	Special	—	100	20	Self	

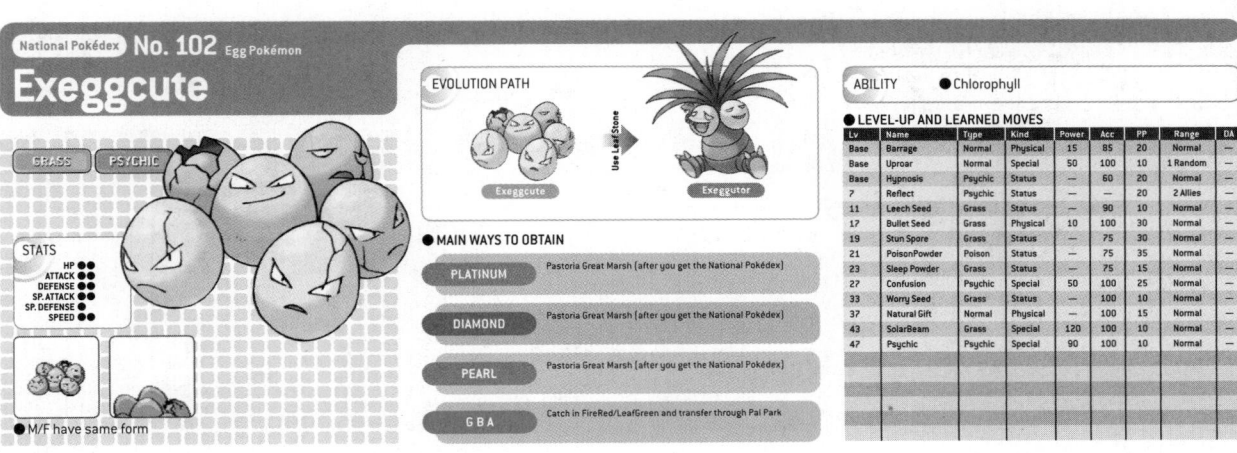

National Pokédex No. 102 Egg Pokémon
Exeggcute

GRASS PSYCHIC

STATS
HP ●●
ATTACK ●●
DEFENSE ●●●
SP.ATTACK ●●
SP.DEFENSE ●●
SPEED ●●

● M/F have same form

EVOLUTION PATH
Exeggcute — Use Leaf Stone → Exeggutor

● MAIN WAYS TO OBTAIN

PLATINUM	Pastoria Great Marsh (after you get the National Pokédex)
DIAMOND	Pastoria Great Marsh (after you get the National Pokédex)
PEARL	Pastoria Great Marsh (after you get the National Pokédex)
GBA	Catch in FireRed/LeafGreen and transfer through Pal Park

ABILITY ● Chlorophyll

● LEVEL-UP AND LEARNED MOVES

Lv	Name	Type	Kind	Power	Acc	PP	Range	DA
Base	Barrage	Normal	Physical	15	85	20	Normal	—
Base	Uproar	Normal	Special	50	100	10	1 Random	—
Base	Hypnosis	Psychic	Status	—	60	20	Normal	—
7	Reflect	Psychic	Status	—	—	20	2 Allies	—
11	Leech Seed	Grass	Status	—	90	10	Normal	—
17	Bullet Seed	Grass	Physical	10	100	30	Normal	—
19	Stun Spore	Grass	Status	—	75	30	Normal	—
21	PoisonPowder	Poison	Status	—	75	35	Normal	—
23	Sleep Powder	Grass	Status	—	75	15	Normal	—
27	Confusion	Psychic	Special	50	100	25	Normal	—
33	Worry Seed	Grass	Status	—	100	10	Normal	—
37	Natural Gift	Normal	Physical	—	100	15	Normal	—
43	SolarBeam	Grass	Special	120	100	10	Normal	—
47	Psychic	Psychic	Special	90	100	10	Normal	—

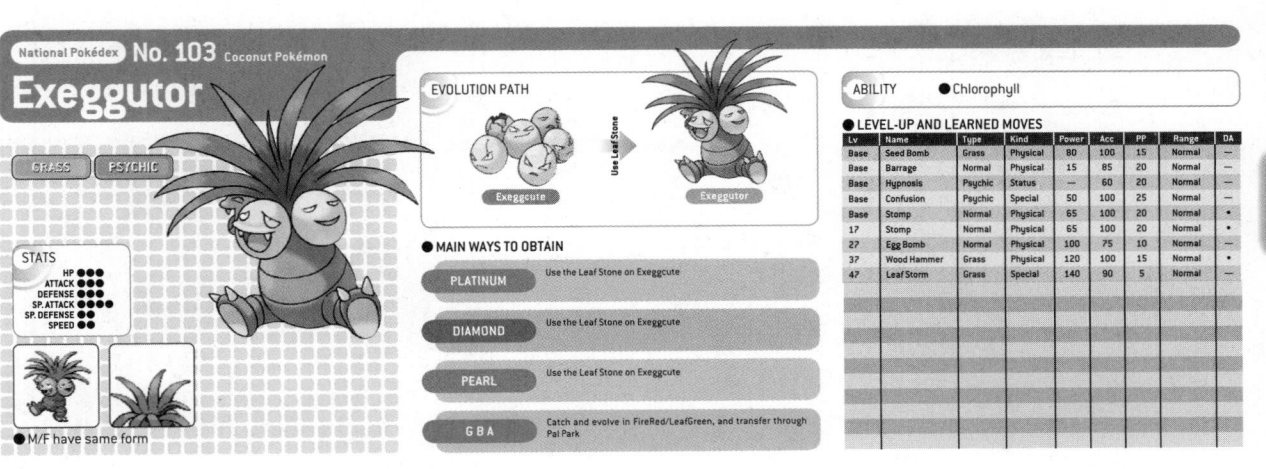

National Pokédex No. 103 Coconut Pokémon
Exeggutor

GRASS PSYCHIC

STATS
HP ●●●
ATTACK ●●●●
DEFENSE ●●●
SP.ATTACK ●●●●
SP.DEFENSE ●●●
SPEED ●●

● M/F have same form

EVOLUTION PATH
Exeggcute — Use Leaf Stone → Exeggutor

● MAIN WAYS TO OBTAIN

PLATINUM	Use the Leaf Stone on Exeggcute
DIAMOND	Use the Leaf Stone on Exeggcute
PEARL	Use the Leaf Stone on Exeggcute
GBA	Catch and evolve in FireRed/LeafGreen, and transfer through Pal Park

ABILITY ● Chlorophyll

● LEVEL-UP AND LEARNED MOVES

Lv	Name	Type	Kind	Power	Acc	PP	Range	DA
Base	Seed Bomb	Grass	Physical	80	100	15	Normal	—
Base	Barrage	Normal	Physical	15	85	20	Normal	—
Base	Hypnosis	Psychic	Status	—	60	20	Normal	—
Base	Confusion	Psychic	Special	50	100	25	Normal	—
Base	Stomp	Normal	Physical	65	100	20	Normal	•
17	Stomp	Normal	Physical	65	100	20	Normal	•
27	Egg Bomb	Normal	Physical	100	75	10	Normal	—
37	Wood Hammer	Grass	Physical	120	100	15	Normal	•
47	Leaf Storm	Grass	Special	140	90	5	Normal	—

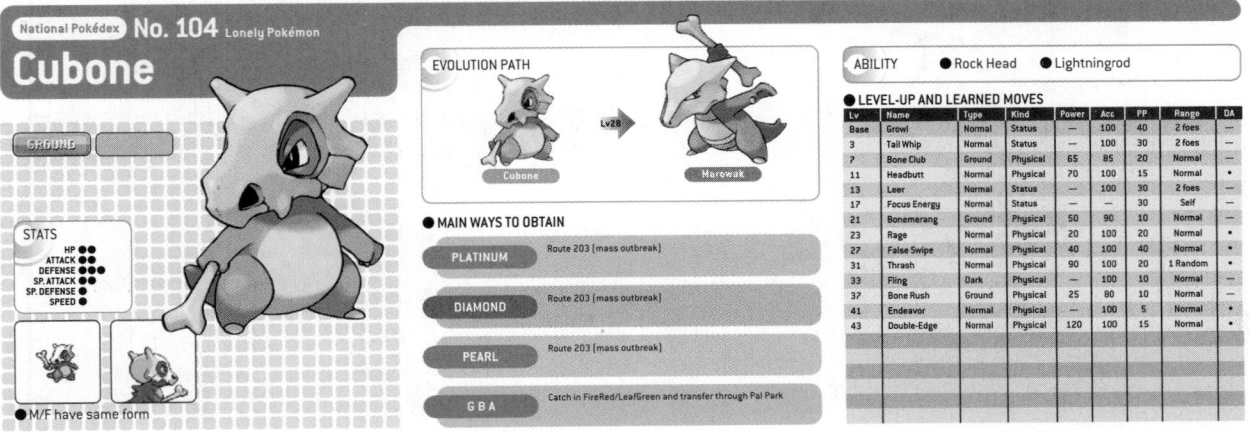

National Pokédex No. 104 Lonely Pokémon
Cubone

GROUND

STATS
HP ●●
ATTACK ●●●
DEFENSE ●●●
SP.ATTACK ●●
SP.DEFENSE ●●
SPEED ●●

● M/F have same form

EVOLUTION PATH
Cubone — Lv28 → Marowak

● MAIN WAYS TO OBTAIN

PLATINUM	Route 203 (mass outbreak)
DIAMOND	Route 203 (mass outbreak)
PEARL	Route 203 (mass outbreak)
GBA	Catch in FireRed/LeafGreen and transfer through Pal Park

ABILITY ● Rock Head ● Lightningrod

● LEVEL-UP AND LEARNED MOVES

Lv	Name	Type	Kind	Power	Acc	PP	Range	DA
Base	Growl	Normal	Status	—	100	40	2 foes	—
3	Tail Whip	Normal	Status	—	100	30	2 foes	—
7	Bone Club	Ground	Physical	65	85	20	Normal	—
11	Headbutt	Normal	Physical	70	100	15	Normal	•
13	Leer	Normal	Status	—	100	10	2 foes	—
17	Focus Energy	Normal	Status	—	—	30	Self	—
21	Bonemerang	Ground	Physical	50	90	10	Normal	—
23	Rage	Normal	Physical	20	100	20	Normal	—
27	False Swipe	Normal	Physical	40	100	40	Normal	—
31	Thrash	Normal	Physical	90	100	10	1 Random	—
33	Fling	Dark	Physical	—	100	10	Normal	—
37	Bone Rush	Ground	Physical	25	80	10	Normal	—
41	Endeavor	Normal	Physical	—	100	5	Normal	—
43	Double-Edge	Normal	Physical	120	100	15	Normal	•

National Pokédex No. 105 Bone Keeper Pokémon
Marowak

GROUND

STATS
HP ●●
ATTACK ●●●
DEFENSE ●●●
SP. ATTACK ●●
SP. DEFENSE ●●●
SPEED ●●

● M/F have same form

EVOLUTION PATH

Cubone → Lv28 → Marowak

● MAIN WAYS TO OBTAIN

PLATINUM	Level up Cubone for Lv28
DIAMOND	Level up Cubone for Lv28
PEARL	Level up Cubone for Lv28
G B A	Catch in FireRed/LeafGreen and transfer through Pal Park

ABILITY ● Rock Head ● Lightningrod

● LEVEL-UP AND LEARNED MOVES

Lv	Name	Type	Kind	Power	Acc	PP	Range	DA
Base	Growl	Normal	Status	—	100	40	2 foes	—
Base	Tail Whip	Normal	Status	—	100	30	2 foes	—
Base	Bone Club	Ground	Physical	65	85	20	Normal	—
Base	Headbutt	Normal	Physical	70	100	15	Normal	●
3	Tail Whip	Normal	Status	—	100	30	2 foes	—
7	Bone Club	Ground	Physical	65	85	20	Normal	—
11	Headbutt	Normal	Physical	70	100	15	Normal	●
13	Leer	Normal	Status	—	100	30	2 foes	—
17	Focus Energy	Normal	Status	—	—	30	Self	—
21	Bonemerang	Ground	Physical	50	90	10	Normal	—
23	Rage	Normal	Physical	20	100	20	Normal	●
27	False Swipe	Normal	Physical	40	100	40	Normal	●
33	Thrash	Normal	Physical	90	100	20	1 Random	●
37	Fling	Dark	Physical	—	100	10	Normal	●
43	Bone Rush	Ground	Physical	25	80	10	Normal	—
49	Endeavor	Normal	Physical	—	100	5	Normal	●
53	Double-Edge	Normal	Physical	120	100	15	Normal	●

National Pokédex No. 106 Kicking Pokémon
Hitmonlee

FIGHTING

STATS
HP ●●
ATTACK ●●●●
DEFENSE ●●
SP. ATTACK ●●
SP. DEFENSE ●●●
SPEED ●●●

● Male form

EVOLUTION PATH

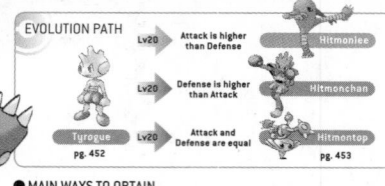

Tyrogue pg. 452
- Lv20 Attack is higher than Defense → Hitmonlee
- Lv20 Defense is higher than Attack → Hitmonchan
- Lv20 Attack and Defense are equal → Hitmontop pg. 453

● MAIN WAYS TO OBTAIN

PLATINUM	Make Tyrogue's Attack higher than its Defense and level it up to Lv20
DIAMOND	Make Tyrogue's Attack higher than its Defense and level it up to Lv21
PEARL	Make Tyrogue's Attack higher than its Defense and level it up to Lv22
G B A	Receive in FireRed/LeafGreen and transfer through Pal Park

ABILITY ● Limber ● Reckless

● LEVEL-UP AND LEARNED MOVES

Lv	Name	Type	Kind	Power	Acc	PP	Range	DA
Base	Revenge	Fighting	Physical	60	100	10	Normal	●
Base	Double Kick	Fighting	Physical	30	100	30	Normal	●
5	Meditate	Psychic	Status	—	—	40	Self	—
9	Rolling Kick	Fighting	Physical	60	85	15	Normal	●
13	Jump Kick	Fighting	Physical	85	95	25	Normal	●
17	Brick Break	Fighting	Physical	75	100	15	Normal	●
21	Focus Energy	Normal	Status	—	—	30	Self	—
25	Feint	Normal	Physical	50	100	10	Normal	—
29	Hi Jump Kick	Fighting	Physical	100	90	20	Normal	●
33	Mind Reader	Normal	Status	—	—	5	Normal	—
37	Foresight	Normal	Status	—	—	40	Normal	—
41	Blaze Kick	Fire	Physical	85	90	10	Normal	●
45	Endure	Normal	Status	—	—	10	Self	—
49	Mega Kick	Normal	Physical	120	75	5	Normal	●
53	Close Combat	Fighting	Physical	120	100	5	Normal	●
57	Reversal	Fighting	Physical	—	100	15	Normal	●

National Pokédex No. 107 Punching Pokémon
Hitmonchan

FIGHTING

STATS
HP ●●
ATTACK ●●●●
DEFENSE ●●●
SP. ATTACK ●●
SP. DEFENSE ●●●●
SPEED ●●●

● Male form

EVOLUTION PATH

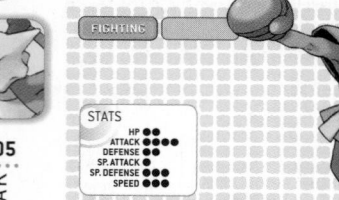

Tyrogue pg. 452
- Lv20 Attack is higher than Defense → Hitmonlee
- Lv20 Defense is higher than Attack → Hitmonchan
- Lv20 Attack and Defense are equal → Hitmontop pg. 453

● MAIN WAYS TO OBTAIN

PLATINUM	Make Tyrogue's Defense higher than its Attack and level it up to Lv20
DIAMOND	Make Tyrogue's Defense higher than its Attack and level it up to Lv20
PEARL	Make Tyrogue's Defense higher than its Attack and level it up to Lv20
G B A	Receive in FireRed/LeafGreen and transfer through Pal Park

ABILITY ● Keen Eye ● Iron Fist

● LEVEL-UP AND LEARNED MOVES

Lv	Name	Type	Kind	Power	Acc	PP	Range	DA
Base	Revenge	Fighting	Physical	60	100	10	Normal	●
Base	Comet Punch	Normal	Physical	18	85	15	Normal	●
6	Agility	Psychic	Status	—	—	30	Self	—
11	Pursuit	Dark	Physical	40	100	20	Normal	●
16	Mach Punch	Fighting	Physical	40	100	30	Normal	●
16	Bullet Punch	Steel	Physical	40	100	30	Normal	●
21	Feint	Normal	Physical	50	100	10	Normal	—
26	Vacuum Wave	Fighting	Special	40	100	30	Normal	—
31	ThunderPunch	Electric	Physical	75	100	15	Normal	●
31	Ice Punch	Ice	Physical	75	100	15	Normal	●
31	Fire Punch	Fire	Physical	75	100	15	Normal	●
36	Sky Uppercut	Fighting	Physical	85	90	15	Normal	●
41	Mega Punch	Normal	Physical	80	85	20	Normal	●
46	Detect	Fighting	Status	—	—	5	Self	—
51	Counter	Fighting	Physical	—	100	20	Self	●
56	Close Combat	Fighting	Physical	120	100	5	Normal	●

National Pokédex No. 108 Licking Pokémon
Lickitung

NORMAL

STATS
HP ●●●
ATTACK ●●
DEFENSE ●●●
SP. ATTACK ●●
SP. DEFENSE ●●
SPEED ●

● M/F have same form

EVOLUTION PATH

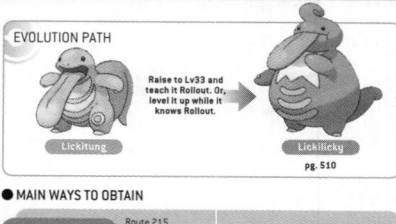

Lickitung → Raise to Lv33 and teach it Rollout. Or, level it up while it knows Rollout. → Lickilicky pg. 510

● MAIN WAYS TO OBTAIN

PLATINUM	Route 215
DIAMOND	Lake Valor (mass outbreak)
PEARL	Lake Valor (mass outbreak)
G B A	Acquire in FireRed/LeafGreen and transfer through Pal Park

ABILITY ● Own Tempo ● Oblivious

● LEVEL-UP AND LEARNED MOVES

Lv	Name	Type	Kind	Power	Acc	PP	Range	DA
Base	Lick	Ghost	Physical	20	100	30	Normal	●
5	Supersonic	Normal	Status	—	55	20	Normal	—
9	Defense Curl	Normal	Status	—	—	40	Self	—
13	Knock Off	Dark	Physical	20	100	20	Normal	●
17	Wrap	Normal	Physical	15	85	20	Normal	●
21	Stomp	Normal	Physical	65	100	20	Normal	●
25	Disable	Normal	Status	—	80	20	Normal	—
29	Slam	Normal	Physical	80	75	20	Normal	●
33	Rollout	Rock	Physical	30	90	20	Normal	●
37	Me First	Normal	Status	—	—	20	DoM	—
41	Refresh	Normal	Status	—	—	20	Self	—
45	Screech	Normal	Status	—	85	40	Normal	—
49	Power Whip	Grass	Physical	120	85	10	Normal	●
53	Wring Out	Normal	Special	—	100	5	Normal	●

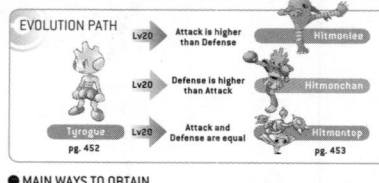

Koffing

POISON

STATS
HP
ATTACK
DEFENSE
SP. ATTACK
SP. DEFENSE
SPEED

● M/F have same form

EVOLUTION PATH

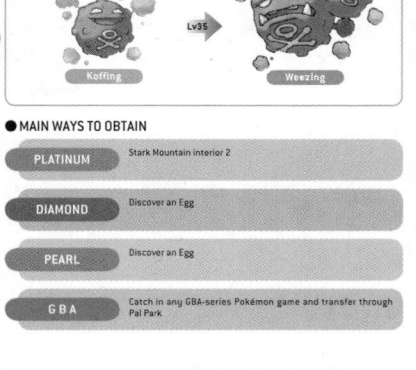

Koffing — Lv35 → Weezing

ABILITY   ● Levitate

● LEVEL-UP AND LEARNED MOVES

Lv	Name	Type	Kind	Power	Acc	PP	Range	DA
Base	Poison Gas	Poison	Status	—	55	40	Normal	—
Base	Tackle	Normal	Physical	35	95	35	Normal	•
6	Smog	Poison	Special	20	70	20	Normal	•
10	SmokeScreen	Normal	Status	—	100	20	Normal	—
15	Assurance	Dark	Physical	50	100	10	Normal	•
19	Selfdestruct	Normal	Physical	200	100	5	2 foes 1 Ally	—
24	Sludge	Poison	Special	65	100	20	Normal	•
28	Haze	Ice	Status	—	—	30	All	—
33	Gyro Ball	Steel	Physical	—	100	5	Normal	•
37	Explosion	Normal	Physical	250	100	5	2 foes 1 Ally	—
42	Sludge Bomb	Poison	Special	90	100	10	Normal	•
46	Destiny Bond	Ghost	Status	—	—	5	Self	—
51	Memento	Dark	Status	—	100	10	Normal	—

● MAIN WAYS TO OBTAIN

PLATINUM	Stark Mountain interior 2
DIAMOND	Discover an Egg
PEARL	Discover an Egg
GBA	Catch in any GBA-series Pokémon game and transfer through Pal Park

---

Weezing

POISON

STATS
HP
ATTACK
DEFENSE
SP. ATTACK
SP. DEFENSE
SPEED

● M/F have same form

EVOLUTION PATH

Koffing — Lv35 → Weezing

ABILITY   ● Levitate

● LEVEL-UP AND LEARNED MOVES

Lv	Name	Type	Kind	Power	Acc	PP	Range	DA
Base	Poison Gas	Poison	Status	—	55	40	Normal	—
Base	Tackle	Normal	Physical	35	95	35	Normal	•
Base	Smog	Poison	Special	20	70	20	Normal	•
Base	SmokeScreen	Normal	Status	—	100	20	Normal	—
6	Smog	Poison	Special	20	70	20	Normal	•
10	SmokeScreen	Normal	Status	—	100	20	Normal	—
15	Assurance	Dark	Physical	50	100	10	Normal	•
19	Selfdestruct	Normal	Physical	200	100	5	2 foes 1 Ally	—
24	Sludge	Poison	Special	65	100	20	Normal	•
28	Haze	Ice	Status	—	—	30	All	—
33	Double Hit	Normal	Physical	35	90	10	Normal	•
40	Explosion	Normal	Physical	250	100	5	2 foes 1 Ally	—
48	Sludge Bomb	Poison	Special	90	100	10	Normal	•
55	Destiny Bond	Ghost	Status	—	—	5	Self	—
63	Memento	Dark	Status	—	100	10	Normal	—

● MAIN WAYS TO OBTAIN

PLATINUM	Route 227
DIAMOND	Route 227
PEARL	Route 227
GBA	Catch and evolve in any GBA-series Pokémon game, and transfer through Pal Park

---

Rhyhorn

GROUND   ROCK

STATS
HP
ATTACK
DEFENSE
SP. ATTACK
SP. DEFENSE
SPEED

● Male form   ● Female form

EVOLUTION PATH

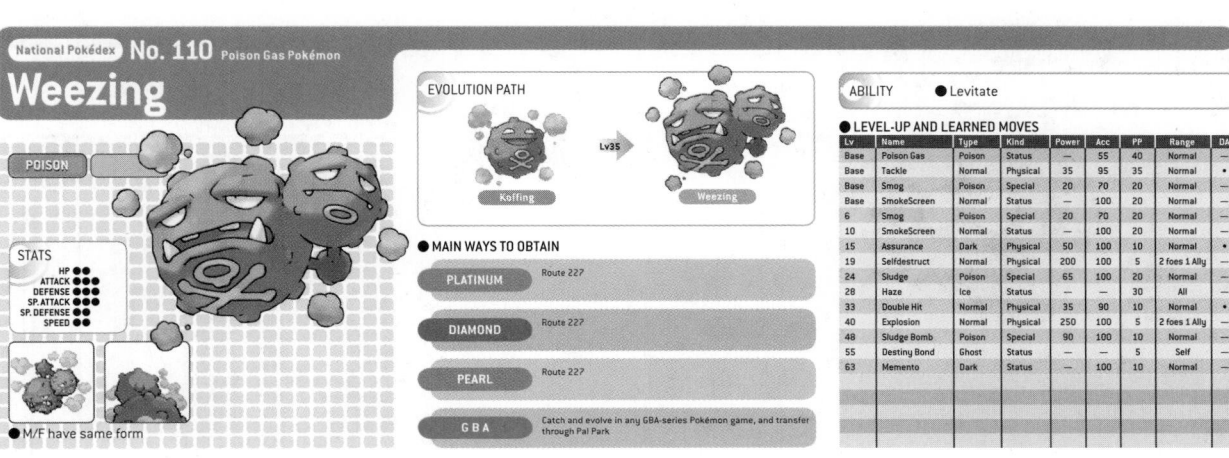

Rhyhorn — Lv42 → Rhydon — Link trade while it holds Protector → Rhyperior   pg. 511

ABILITY   ● Lightningrod   ● Rock Head

● LEVEL-UP AND LEARNED MOVES

Lv	Name	Type	Kind	Power	Acc	PP	Range	DA
Base	Horn Attack	Normal	Physical	65	100	25	Normal	•
Base	Tail Whip	Normal	Status	—	100	30	2 foes	—
9	Stomp	Normal	Physical	65	100	20	Normal	•
13	Fury Attack	Normal	Physical	15	85	20	Normal	•
21	Scary Face	Normal	Status	—	90	10	Normal	—
25	Rock Blast	Rock	Physical	25	80	10	Normal	•
33	Take Down	Normal	Physical	90	85	20	Normal	•
37	Horn Drill	Normal	Physical	—	30	5	Normal	•
45	Stone Edge	Rock	Physical	100	80	5	Normal	—
49	Earthquake	Ground	Physical	100	100	10	2 foes 1 Ally	•
57	Megahorn	Bug	Physical	120	85	10	Normal	•

● MAIN WAYS TO OBTAIN

PLATINUM	Route 214
DIAMOND	Route 227
PEARL	Route 227
GBA	Catch in any GBA-series Pokémon game and transfer through Pal Park

---

Rhydon

GROUND   ROCK

STATS
HP
ATTACK
DEFENSE
SP. ATTACK
SP. DEFENSE
SPEED

● Male form   ● Female form

EVOLUTION PATH

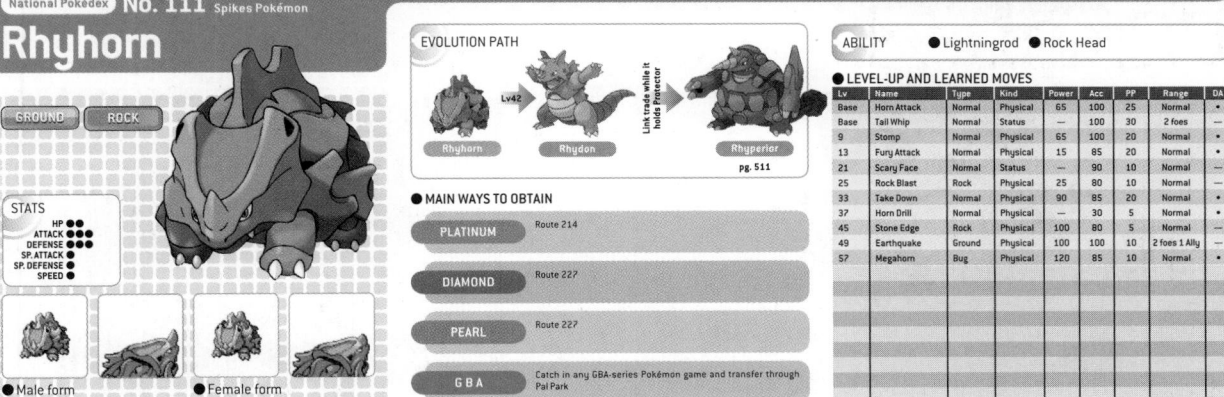

Rhyhorn — Lv42 → Rhydon — Link trade while it holds Protector → Rhyperior   pg. 511

ABILITY   ● Lightningrod   ● Rock Head

● LEVEL-UP AND LEARNED MOVES

Lv	Name	Type	Kind	Power	Acc	PP	Range	DA
Base	Horn Attack	Normal	Physical	65	100	25	Normal	•
Base	Tail Whip	Normal	Status	—	100	30	2 foes	—
Base	Stomp	Normal	Physical	65	100	20	Normal	•
Base	Fury Attack	Normal	Physical	15	85	20	Normal	•
9	Stomp	Normal	Physical	65	100	20	Normal	•
13	Fury Attack	Normal	Physical	15	85	20	Normal	•
21	Scary Face	Normal	Status	—	90	10	Normal	—
25	Rock Blast	Rock	Physical	25	80	10	Normal	•
33	Take Down	Normal	Physical	90	85	20	Normal	•
37	Horn Drill	Normal	Physical	—	30	5	Normal	•
42	Hammer Arm	Fighting	Physical	100	90	10	Normal	•
45	Stone Edge	Rock	Physical	100	80	5	Normal	—
49	Earthquake	Ground	Physical	100	100	10	2 foes 1 Ally	•
57	Megahorn	Bug	Physical	120	85	10	Normal	•

● MAIN WAYS TO OBTAIN

PLATINUM	Victory Road 1F
DIAMOND	Route 227
PEARL	Route 227
GBA	Catch and evolve in any GBA-series Pokémon game, and transfer through Pal Park

National Pokédex No. 113 Egg Pokémon
Chansey

NORMAL

STATS
HP ●●●●●
ATTACK ●
DEFENSE ●
SP. ATTACK ●●●
SP. DEFENSE ●●●
SPEED ●●

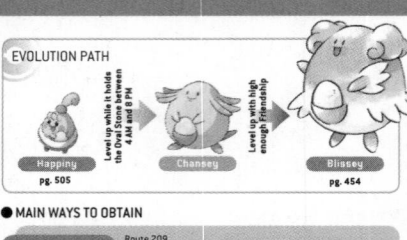

● Female form

EVOLUTION PATH

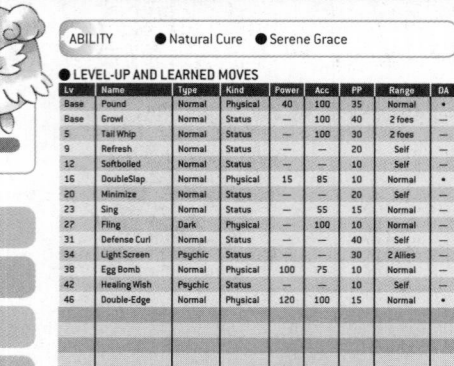

Happiny
pg. 505

Level up while it holds the Oval Stone between 4 AM and 8 PM

Chansey

Level up with high enough Friendship

Blissey
pg. 454

● MAIN WAYS TO OBTAIN
PLATINUM	Route 209
DIAMOND	Route 209
PEARL	Route 209
GBA	Catch in FireRed/LeafGreen and transfer through Pal Park

ABILITY ● Natural Cure ● Serene Grace

● LEVEL-UP AND LEARNED MOVES
Lv	Name	Type	Kind	Power	Acc	PP	Range	DA
Base	Pound	Normal	Physical	40	100	35	Normal	●
Base	Growl	Normal	Status	—	100	40	2 foes	●
5	Tail Whip	Normal	Status	—	100	30	2 foes	—
9	Refresh	Normal	Status	—	—	20	Self	—
12	Softboiled	Normal	Status	—	—	10	Self	—
16	DoubleSlap	Normal	Physical	15	85	10	Normal	●
20	Minimize	Normal	Status	—	—	20	Self	—
23	Sing	Normal	Status	—	55	15	Normal	—
27	Fling	Dark	Physical	—	100	10	Normal	●
31	Defense Curl	Normal	Status	—	—	40	Self	—
34	Light Screen	Psychic	Status	—	—	30	2 Allies	—
38	Egg Bomb	Normal	Physical	100	75	10	Normal	●
42	Healing Wish	Psychic	Status	—	—	10	Self	—
46	Double-Edge	Normal	Physical	120	100	15	Normal	●

National Pokédex No. 114 Vine Pokémon
Tangela

GRASS

STATS
HP ●●
ATTACK ●●●
DEFENSE ●●●●
SP. ATTACK ●●●
SP. DEFENSE ●●
SPEED ●●

● M/F have same form

EVOLUTION PATH

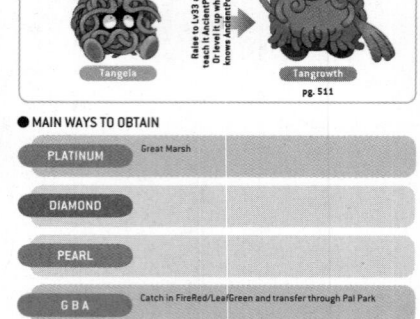

Tangela

Raise to Lv33 and teach it AncientPower. Or level up while it knows AncientPower.

Tangrowth
pg. 511

● MAIN WAYS TO OBTAIN
PLATINUM	Great Marsh
DIAMOND	
PEARL	
GBA	Catch in FireRed/LeafGreen and transfer through Pal Park

ABILITY ● Chlorophyll ● Leaf Guard

● LEVEL-UP AND LEARNED MOVES
Lv	Name	Type	Kind	Power	Acc	PP	Range	DA
Base	Ingrain	Grass	Status	—	—	20	Self	—
Base	Constrict	Normal	Physical	10	100	35	Normal	●
5	Sleep Powder	Grass	Status	—	75	15	Normal	—
8	Absorb	Grass	Special	20	100	25	Normal	—
12	Growth	Normal	Status	—	—	40	Self	—
15	PoisonPowder	Poison	Status	—	75	35	Normal	—
19	Vine Whip	Grass	Physical	35	100	15	Normal	●
22	Bind	Normal	Physical	15	75	20	Normal	●
26	Mega Drain	Grass	Special	40	100	15	Normal	—
29	Stun Spore	Grass	Status	—	75	30	Normal	—
33	AncientPower	Rock	Special	60	100	5	Normal	—
36	Knock Off	Dark	Physical	20	100	20	Normal	●
40	Natural Gift	Normal	Physical	—	100	15	Normal	—
43	Slam	Normal	Physical	80	75	20	Normal	●
47	Tickle	Normal	Status	—	100	20	Normal	—
50	Wring Out	Normal	Special	—	100	5	Normal	—
54	Power Whip	Grass	Physical	120	85	10	Normal	●

National Pokédex No. 115 Parent Pokémon
Kangaskhan

NORMAL

STATS
HP ●●●
ATTACK ●●●●
DEFENSE ●●●
SP. ATTACK ●●
SP. DEFENSE ●●●
SPEED ●●●

● Female form

EVOLUTION PATH

Does not evolve

● MAIN WAYS TO OBTAIN
PLATINUM	Pastoria Great Marsh (after you get the National Pokédex)
DIAMOND	Pastoria Great Marsh (after you get the National Pokédex)
PEARL	Pastoria Great Marsh (after you get the National Pokédex)
GBA	Catch in FireRed/LeafGreen and transfer through Pal Park

ABILITY ● Early Bird ● Scrappy

● LEVEL-UP AND LEARNED MOVES
Lv	Name	Type	Kind	Power	Acc	PP	Range	DA
Base	Comet Punch	Normal	Physical	18	85	15	Normal	●
Base	Leer	Normal	Status	—	100	30	2 foes	—
7	Fake Out	Normal	Physical	40	100	10	Normal	●
10	Tail Whip	Normal	Status	—	100	30	2 foes	—
13	Bite	Dark	Physical	60	100	25	Normal	●
19	Mega Punch	Normal	Physical	80	85	20	Normal	●
22	Rage	Normal	Physical	20	100	20	Normal	●
25	Dizzy Punch	Normal	Physical	70	100	10	Normal	●
31	Crunch	Dark	Physical	80	100	15	Normal	●
34	Endure	Normal	Status	—	—	10	Self	—
37	Outrage	Dragon	Physical	120	100	15	1 Random	●
43	Double Hit	Normal	Physical	35	90	10	Normal	●
46	Sucker Punch	Dark	Physical	80	100	5	Normal	●
49	Reversal	Fighting	Physical	—	100	15	Normal	●

National Pokédex No. 116 Dragon Pokémon
Horsea

WATER

STATS
HP ●●
ATTACK ●●
DEFENSE ●●
SP. ATTACK ●●●
SP. DEFENSE ●●
SPEED ●●

● M/F have same form

EVOLUTION PATH

Horsea

Lv32

Seadra

Link trade while it holds the Dragon Scale

Kingdra
pg. 451

● MAIN WAYS TO OBTAIN
PLATINUM	Route 226 (Good Rod)
DIAMOND	Route 226 (Good Rod)
PEARL	Route 226 (Good Rod)
GBA	Catch in any GBA-series Pokémon game and transfer through Pal Park

ABILITY ● Swift Swim ● Sniper

● LEVEL-UP AND LEARNED MOVES
Lv	Name	Type	Kind	Power	Acc	PP	Range	DA
Base	Bubble	Water	Special	20	100	30	2 foes	—
4	SmokeScreen	Normal	Status	—	100	20	Normal	—
8	Leer	Normal	Status	—	100	30	2 foes	—
11	Water Gun	Water	Special	40	100	25	Normal	—
14	Focus Energy	Normal	Status	—	—	30	Self	—
18	BubbleBeam	Water	Special	65	100	20	Normal	—
23	Agility	Psychic	Status	—	—	30	Self	—
26	Twister	Dragon	Special	40	100	20	2 foes	—
30	Brine	Water	Special	65	100	10	Normal	—
35	Hydro Pump	Water	Special	120	80	5	Normal	—
38	Dragon Dance	Dragon	Status	—	—	20	Self	—
42	Dragon Pulse	Dragon	Special	90	100	10	Normal	—

National Pokédex No. 117 Dragon Pokémon
Seadra

WATER

STATS
HP ●●
ATTACK ●●●
DEFENSE ●●●
SP. ATTACK ●●●
SP. DEFENSE ●●●
SPEED ●●●

● M/F have same form

EVOLUTION PATH

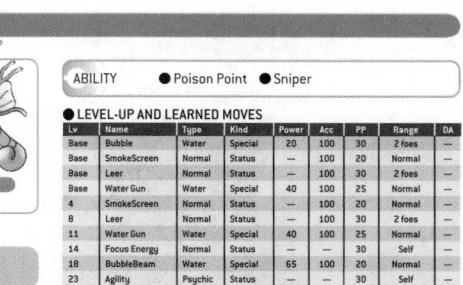

Horsea — Lv32 → Seadra — Link trade while it holds the Dragon Scale → Kingdra (pg. 451)

● MAIN WAYS TO OBTAIN

PLATINUM	Route 226 (Super Rod)
DIAMOND	Route 226 (Super Rod)
PEARL	Route 226 (Super Rod)
GBA	Catch and evolve in any GBA-series Pokémon game, and transfer through Pal Park

ABILITY ● Poison Point ● Sniper

● LEVEL-UP AND LEARNED MOVES

Lv	Name	Type	Kind	Power	Acc	PP	Range	DA
Base	Bubble	Water	Special	20	100	30	2 foes	
Base	SmokeScreen	Normal	Status	—	100	20	Normal	
Base	Leer	Normal	Status	—	100	30	2 foes	
Base	Water Gun	Water	Special	40	100	25	Normal	
4	SmokeScreen	Normal	Status	—	100	20	2 foes	
8	Leer	Normal	Status	—	100	30	2 foes	
11	Water Gun	Water	Special	40	100	25	Normal	
14	Focus Energy	Normal	Status	—	—	30	Self	
18	BubbleBeam	Water	Special	65	100	20	Normal	
23	Agility	Psychic	Status	—	—	30	Self	
26	Twister	Dragon	Special	40	100	20	2 foes	
30	Brine	Water	Special	65	100	10	Normal	
40	Hydro Pump	Water	Special	120	80	5	Normal	
48	Dragon Dance	Dragon	Status	—	—	20	Self	
57	Dragon Pulse	Dragon	Special	90	100	10	Normal	

National Pokédex No. 118 Goldfish Pokémon
Goldeen

WATER

STATS
HP ●●
ATTACK ●●
DEFENSE ●●
SP. ATTACK ●●
SP. DEFENSE ●●
SPEED ●●

● Male form ● Female form

EVOLUTION PATH

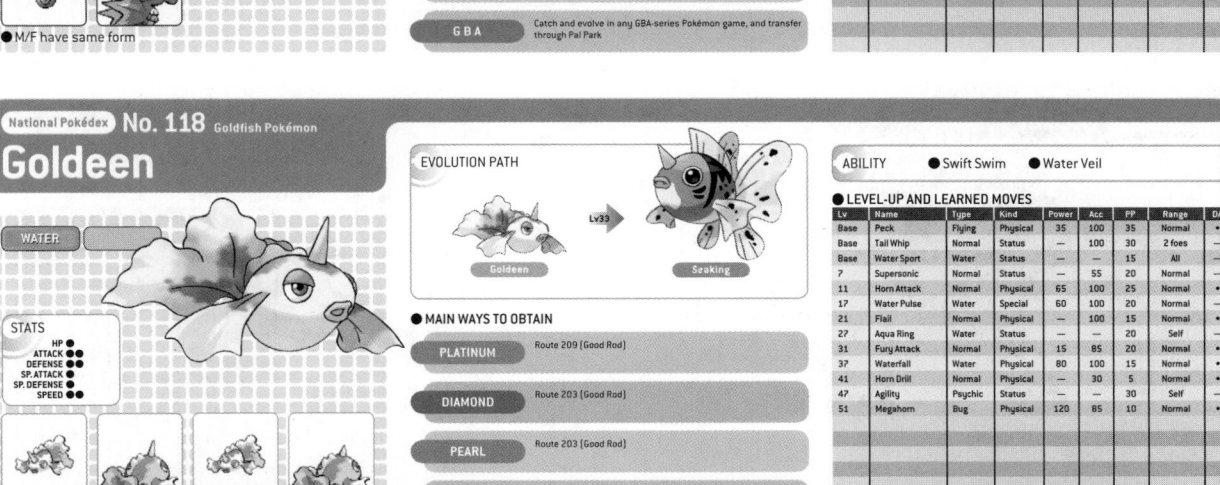

Goldeen — Lv33 → Seaking

● MAIN WAYS TO OBTAIN

PLATINUM	Route 209 (Good Rod)
DIAMOND	Route 203 (Good Rod)
PEARL	Route 203 (Good Rod)
GBA	Catch in any GBA-series Pokémon game and transfer through Pal Park

ABILITY ● Swift Swim ● Water Veil

● LEVEL-UP AND LEARNED MOVES

Lv	Name	Type	Kind	Power	Acc	PP	Range	DA
Base	Peck	Flying	Physical	35	100	35	Normal	•
Base	Tail Whip	Normal	Status	—	100	30	2 foes	—
Base	Water Sport	Water	Status	—	—	15	All	—
7	Supersonic	Normal	Status	—	55	20	Normal	—
11	Horn Attack	Normal	Physical	65	100	25	Normal	•
17	Water Pulse	Water	Special	60	100	20	Normal	—
21	Flail	Normal	Physical	—	100	15	Normal	•
27	Aqua Ring	Water	Status	—	—	20	Self	—
31	Fury Attack	Normal	Physical	15	85	20	Normal	•
37	Waterfall	Water	Physical	80	100	15	Normal	•
41	Horn Drill	Normal	Physical	—	30	5	Normal	•
47	Agility	Psychic	Status	—	—	30	Self	—
51	Megahorn	Bug	Physical	120	85	10	Normal	•

National Pokédex No. 119 Goldfish Pokémon
Seaking

WATER

STATS
HP ●●●
ATTACK ●●●
DEFENSE ●●
SP. ATTACK ●●
SP. DEFENSE ●●
SPEED ●●●

● Male form ● Female form

EVOLUTION PATH

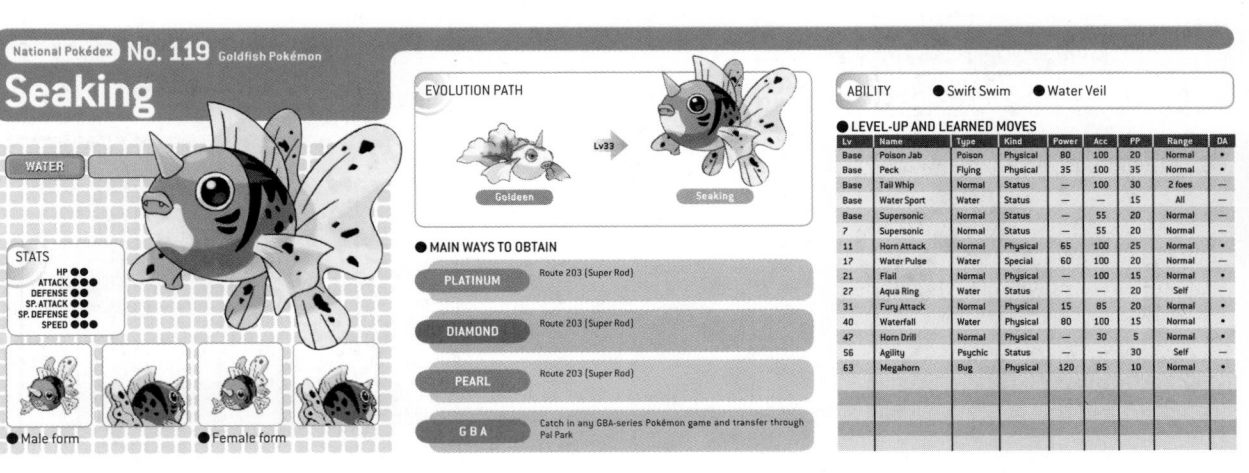

Goldeen — Lv33 → Seaking

● MAIN WAYS TO OBTAIN

PLATINUM	Route 203 (Super Rod)
DIAMOND	Route 203 (Super Rod)
PEARL	Route 203 (Super Rod)
GBA	Catch in any GBA-series Pokémon game and transfer through Pal Park

ABILITY ● Swift Swim ● Water Veil

● LEVEL-UP AND LEARNED MOVES

Lv	Name	Type	Kind	Power	Acc	PP	Range	DA
Base	Poison Jab	Poison	Physical	80	100	20	Normal	•
Base	Peck	Flying	Physical	35	100	35	Normal	•
Base	Tail Whip	Normal	Status	—	100	30	2 foes	—
Base	Water Sport	Water	Status	—	—	15	All	—
Base	Supersonic	Normal	Status	—	55	20	Normal	—
7	Supersonic	Normal	Status	—	55	20	Normal	—
11	Horn Attack	Normal	Physical	65	100	25	Normal	•
17	Water Pulse	Water	Special	60	100	20	Normal	—
21	Flail	Normal	Physical	—	100	15	Normal	•
27	Aqua Ring	Water	Status	—	—	20	Self	—
31	Fury Attack	Normal	Physical	15	85	20	Normal	•
40	Waterfall	Water	Physical	80	100	15	Normal	•
47	Horn Drill	Normal	Physical	—	30	5	Normal	•
56	Agility	Psychic	Status	—	—	30	Self	—
63	Megahorn	Bug	Physical	120	85	10	Normal	•

120 ••••• STARYU

National Pokédex No. 120 Star Shape Pokémon
Staryu

WATER

STATS
HP ●
ATTACK ●●
DEFENSE ●●
SP. ATTACK ●●
SP. DEFENSE ●●
SPEED ●●●

● Gender unknown

EVOLUTION PATH

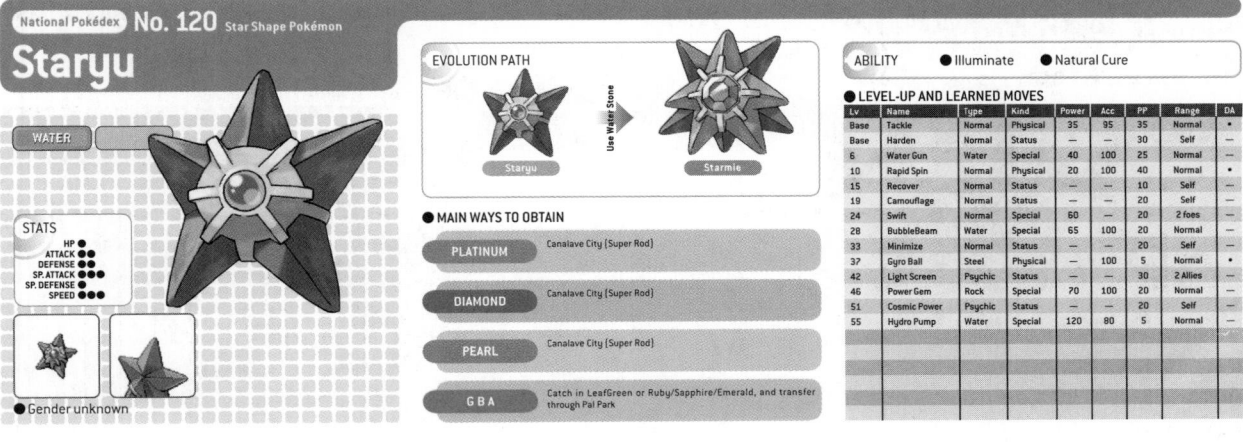

Staryu — Use Water Stone → Starmie

● MAIN WAYS TO OBTAIN

PLATINUM	Canalave City (Super Rod)
DIAMOND	Canalave City (Super Rod)
PEARL	Canalave City (Super Rod)
GBA	Catch in LeafGreen or Ruby/Sapphire/Emerald, and transfer through Pal Park

ABILITY ● Illuminate ● Natural Cure

● LEVEL-UP AND LEARNED MOVES

Lv	Name	Type	Kind	Power	Acc	PP	Range	DA
Base	Tackle	Normal	Physical	35	95	35	Normal	•
Base	Harden	Normal	Status	—	—	30	Self	—
6	Water Gun	Water	Special	40	100	25	Normal	—
10	Rapid Spin	Normal	Physical	20	100	40	Normal	•
15	Recover	Normal	Status	—	—	10	Self	—
19	Camouflage	Normal	Status	—	—	20	Self	—
24	Swift	Normal	Special	60	—	20	2 foes	—
28	BubbleBeam	Water	Special	65	100	20	Normal	—
33	Minimize	Normal	Status	—	—	20	Self	—
37	Gyro Ball	Steel	Physical	—	100	5	Normal	•
42	Light Screen	Psychic	Status	—	—	30	2 Allies	—
46	Power Gem	Rock	Special	70	100	20	Normal	—
51	Cosmic Power	Psychic	Status	—	—	20	Self	—
55	Hydro Pump	Water	Special	120	80	5	Normal	—

Starmie

National Pokédex No. 121 Mysterious Pokémon

WATER PSYCHIC

STATS
HP ●●
ATTACK ●●●
DEFENSE ●●●
SP. ATTACK ●●●●
SP. DEFENSE ●●●
SPEED ●●●●

● Gender unknown

EVOLUTION PATH

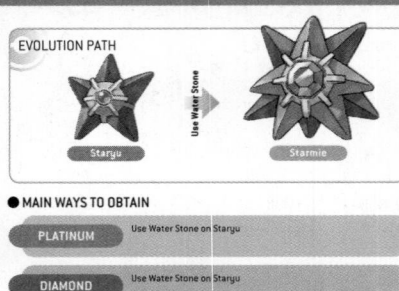

Staryu → Use Water Stone → Starmie

MAIN WAYS TO OBTAIN

PLATINUM	Use Water Stone on Staryu
DIAMOND	Use Water Stone on Staryu
PEARL	Use Water Stone on Staryu
GBA	Catch and evolve in LeafGreen or Ruby/Sapphire/Emerald, and transfer through Pal Park

ABILITY ● Illuminate ● Natural Cure

● LEVEL-UP AND LEARNED MOVES

Lv	Name	Type	Kind	Power	Acc	PP	Range	DA
Base	Water Gun	Water	Special	40	100	25	Normal	—
Base	Rapid Spin	Normal	Physical	20	100	40	Normal	•
Base	Recover	Normal	Status	—	—	10	Self	—
Base	Swift	Normal	Special	60	—	20	2 foes	—
28	Confuse Ray	Ghost	Status	—	100	10	Normal	—

Mr. Mime

National Pokédex No. 122 Barrier Pokémon

PSYCHIC

STATS
HP ●●
ATTACK ●●
DEFENSE ●●
SP. ATTACK ●●●●
SP. DEFENSE ●●●
SPEED ●●●

● M/F have same form

EVOLUTION PATH

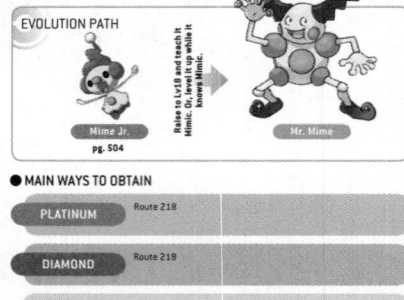

Mime Jr. (pg. 504) → Raise to Lv18 and teach it Mimic. Or, level it up while it knows Mimic. → Mr. Mime

MAIN WAYS TO OBTAIN

PLATINUM	Route 218
DIAMOND	Route 218
PEARL	
GBA	Acquire in FireRed/LeafGreen and transfer through Pal Park

ABILITY ● Soundproof ● Filter

● LEVEL-UP AND LEARNED MOVES

Lv	Name	Type	Kind	Power	Acc	PP	Range	DA
Base	Magical Leaf	Grass	Special	60	—	20	Normal	—
Base	Power Swap	Psychic	Status	—	—	10	Normal	—
Base	Guard Swap	Psychic	Status	—	—	10	Normal	—
Base	Barrier	Psychic	Status	—	—	30	Self	—
Base	Confusion	Psychic	Special	50	100	25	Normal	—
4	Copycat	Normal	Status	—	—	20	DoM	—
8	Meditate	Psychic	Status	—	—	40	Self	—
11	Encore	Normal	Status	—	100	5	Normal	—
15	DoubleSlap	Normal	Physical	15	85	10	Normal	•
18	Mimic	Normal	Status	—	—	10	Normal	—
22	Light Screen	Psychic	Status	—	—	30	2 Allies	—
22	Reflect	Psychic	Status	—	—	20	2 Allies	—
25	Psybeam	Psychic	Special	65	100	20	Normal	—
29	Substitute	Normal	Status	—	—	10	Self	—
32	Recycle	Normal	Status	—	—	10	Self	—
36	Trick	Psychic	Status	—	100	10	Normal	—
39	Psychic	Psychic	Special	90	100	10	Normal	—
43	Role Play	Psychic	Status	—	—	10	Normal	—
46	Baton Pass	Normal	Status	—	—	40	Self	—
50	Safeguard	Normal	Status	—	—	25	2 Allies	—

Scyther

National Pokédex No. 123 Mantis Pokémon

BUG FLYING

STATS
HP ●●●
ATTACK ●●●●
DEFENSE ●●●
SP. ATTACK ●●
SP. DEFENSE ●●●
SPEED ●●●●

● Male form   ● Female form

EVOLUTION PATH

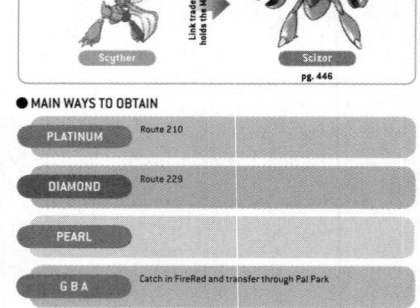

Scyther → Link trade while it holds the Metal Coat → Scizor (pg. 446)

MAIN WAYS TO OBTAIN

PLATINUM	Route 210
DIAMOND	Route 229
PEARL	
GBA	Catch in FireRed and transfer through Pal Park

ABILITY ● Swarm ● Technician

● LEVEL-UP AND LEARNED MOVES

Lv	Name	Type	Kind	Power	Acc	PP	Range	DA
Base	Vacuum Wave	Fighting	Special	40	100	30	Normal	—
Base	Quick Attack	Normal	Physical	40	100	30	Normal	•
Base	Leer	Normal	Status	—	100	30	2 foes	•
5	Focus Energy	Normal	Status	—	—	30	Self	—
9	Pursuit	Dark	Physical	40	100	20	Normal	•
13	False Swipe	Normal	Physical	40	100	40	Normal	•
17	Agility	Psychic	Status	—	—	30	Self	—
21	Wing Attack	Flying	Physical	60	100	35	Normal	•
25	Fury Cutter	Bug	Physical	10	95	20	Normal	•
29	Slash	Normal	Physical	70	100	20	Normal	•
33	Razor Wind	Normal	Special	80	100	10	2 foes	—
37	Double Team	Normal	Status	—	—	15	Self	—
41	X-Scissor	Bug	Physical	80	100	15	Normal	•
45	Night Slash	Dark	Physical	70	100	15	Normal	•
49	Double Hit	Normal	Physical	35	90	10	Normal	•
53	Air Slash	Flying	Special	75	95	20	Normal	—
57	Swords Dance	Normal	Status	—	—	30	Self	—
61	Feint	Normal	Physical	50	100	10	Normal	—

Jynx

National Pokédex No. 124 Human Shape Pokémon

ICE PSYCHIC

STATS
HP ●●
ATTACK ●●
DEFENSE ●●
SP. ATTACK ●●●●
SP. DEFENSE ●●●
SPEED ●●●

● Female form

EVOLUTION PATH

Smoochum (pg. 453) → Lv30 → Jynx

MAIN WAYS TO OBTAIN

PLATINUM	Snowpoint Temple B1F
DIAMOND	Level up Smoochum to Lv30
PEARL	Level up Smoochum to Lv30
GBA	Acquire in FireRed/LeafGreen and transfer through Pal Park

ABILITY ● Oblivious ● Forewarn

● LEVEL-UP AND LEARNED MOVES

Lv	Name	Type	Kind	Power	Acc	PP	Range	DA
Base	Pound	Normal	Physical	40	100	35	Normal	•
Base	Lick	Ghost	Physical	20	100	30	Normal	•
Base	Lovely Kiss	Normal	Status	—	75	10	Normal	—
Base	Powder Snow	Ice	Special	40	100	25	2 foes	—
5	Lick	Ghost	Physical	20	100	30	Normal	•
8	Lovely Kiss	Normal	Status	—	75	10	Normal	—
11	Powder Snow	Ice	Special	40	100	25	2 foes	—
15	DoubleSlap	Normal	Physical	15	85	10	Normal	•
18	Ice Punch	Ice	Physical	75	100	15	Normal	•
21	Mean Look	Normal	Status	—	—	5	Normal	—
25	Fake Tears	Dark	Status	—	100	20	Normal	—
28	Wake-Up Slap	Fighting	Physical	60	100	10	Normal	•
33	Avalanche	Ice	Physical	60	100	10	Normal	•
39	Body Slam	Normal	Physical	85	100	15	Normal	•
44	Wring Out	Normal	Special	—	100	5	Normal	•
49	Perish Song	Normal	Status	—	—	5	All	—
55	Blizzard	Ice	Special	120	70	5	2 foes	—

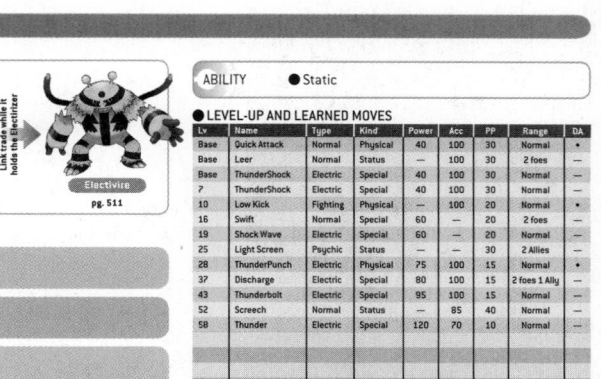

No. 125 Electric Pokémon — Electabuzz

Type: ELECTRIC

STATS: HP ●● / ATTACK ●●● / DEFENSE ●● / SP.ATTACK ●●● / SP.DEFENSE ●●● / SPEED ●●●●

● M/F have same form

ABILITY: ● Static

EVOLUTION PATH: Elekid (pg. 453) → Lv30 → Electabuzz → Link trade while it holds the Electirizer → Electivire (pg. 511)

MAIN WAYS TO OBTAIN:
- PLATINUM: Route 222
- DIAMOND: Level up Elekid to Lv30
- PEARL: Level up Elekid to Lv30
- GBA: Catch in FireRed and transfer through Pal Park

LEVEL-UP AND LEARNED MOVES

Lv	Name	Type	Kind	Power	Acc	PP	Range	DA
Base	Quick Attack	Normal	Physical	40	100	30	Normal	●
Base	Leer	Normal	Status	—	100	30	2 foes	—
Base	ThunderShock	Electric	Special	40	100	30	Normal	—
7	ThunderShock	Electric	Special	40	100	30	Normal	—
10	Low Kick	Fighting	Physical	—	100	20	Normal	●
16	Swift	Normal	Special	60	—	20	2 foes	—
19	Shock Wave	Electric	Special	60	—	20	Normal	—
25	Light Screen	Psychic	Status	—	—	30	2 Allies	—
28	ThunderPunch	Electric	Physical	75	100	15	Normal	●
37	Discharge	Electric	Special	80	100	15	2 foes 1 Ally	—
43	Thunderbolt	Electric	Special	95	100	15	Normal	—
52	Screech	Normal	Status	—	85	40	Normal	—
58	Thunder	Electric	Special	120	70	10	Normal	—

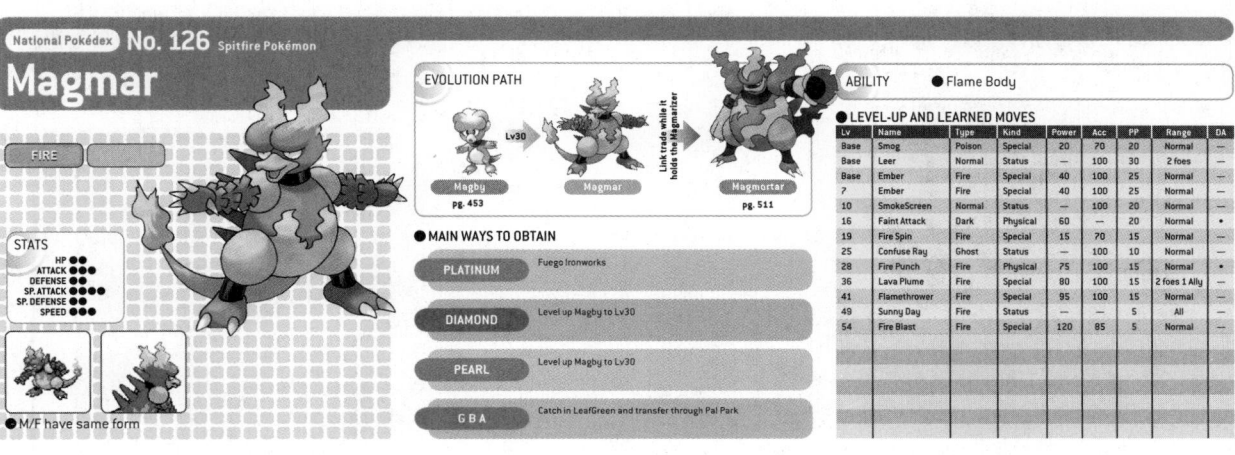

No. 126 Spitfire Pokémon — Magmar

Type: FIRE

STATS: HP ●● / ATTACK ●●● / DEFENSE ●● / SP.ATTACK ●●● / SP.DEFENSE ●● / SPEED ●●●

● M/F have same form

ABILITY: ● Flame Body

EVOLUTION PATH: Magby (pg. 453) → Lv30 → Magmar → Link trade while it holds the Magmarizer → Magmortar (pg. 511)

MAIN WAYS TO OBTAIN:
- PLATINUM: Fuego Ironworks
- DIAMOND: Level up Magby to Lv30
- PEARL: Level up Magby to Lv30
- GBA: Catch in LeafGreen and transfer through Pal Park

LEVEL-UP AND LEARNED MOVES

Lv	Name	Type	Kind	Power	Acc	PP	Range	DA
Base	Smog	Poison	Special	20	70	20	Normal	—
Base	Leer	Normal	Status	—	100	30	2 foes	—
Base	Ember	Fire	Special	40	100	25	Normal	—
7	Ember	Fire	Special	40	100	25	Normal	—
10	SmokeScreen	Normal	Status	—	100	20	Normal	—
16	Faint Attack	Dark	Physical	60	—	20	Normal	●
19	Fire Spin	Fire	Special	15	70	15	Normal	—
25	Confuse Ray	Ghost	Status	—	100	10	Normal	—
28	Fire Punch	Fire	Physical	75	100	15	Normal	●
36	Lava Plume	Fire	Special	80	100	15	2 foes 1 Ally	—
41	Flamethrower	Fire	Special	95	100	15	Normal	—
49	Sunny Day	Fire	Status	—	—	5	All	—
54	Fire Blast	Fire	Special	120	85	5	Normal	—

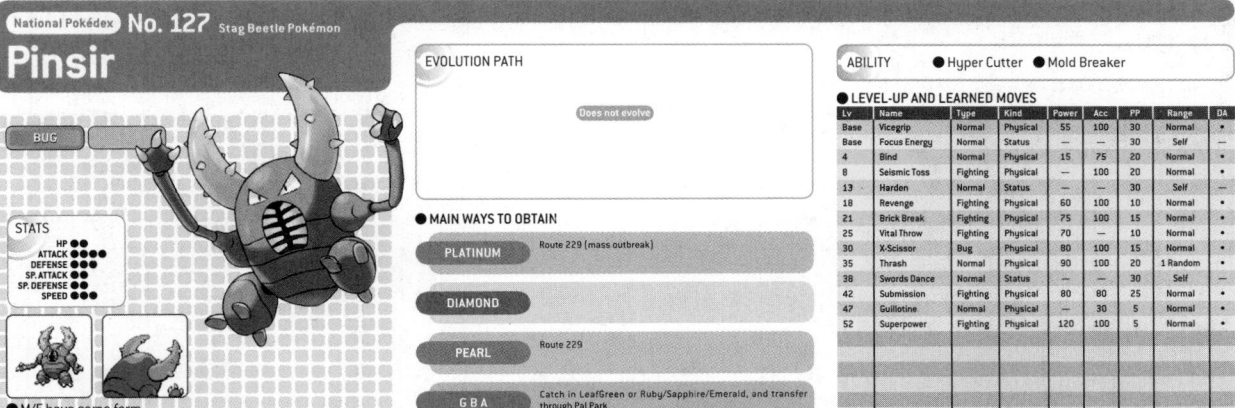

No. 127 Stag Beetle Pokémon — Pinsir

Type: BUG

STATS: HP ●● / ATTACK ●●●● / DEFENSE ●●● / SP.ATTACK ●● / SP.DEFENSE ●● / SPEED ●●●

● M/F have same form

ABILITY: ● Hyper Cutter ● Mold Breaker

EVOLUTION PATH: Does not evolve

MAIN WAYS TO OBTAIN:
- PLATINUM: Route 229 (mass outbreak)
- DIAMOND:
- PEARL: Route 229
- GBA: Catch in LeafGreen or Ruby/Sapphire/Emerald, and transfer through Pal Park

LEVEL-UP AND LEARNED MOVES

Lv	Name	Type	Kind	Power	Acc	PP	Range	DA
Base	Vicegrip	Normal	Physical	55	100	30	Normal	●
Base	Focus Energy	Normal	Status	—	—	30	Self	—
4	Bind	Normal	Physical	15	75	20	Normal	—
8	Seismic Toss	Fighting	Physical	—	100	20	Normal	—
13	Harden	Normal	Status	—	—	30	Self	—
18	Revenge	Fighting	Physical	60	100	10	Normal	—
21	Brick Break	Fighting	Physical	75	100	15	Normal	●
25	Vital Throw	Fighting	Physical	70	—	10	Normal	—
30	X-Scissor	Bug	Physical	80	100	15	Normal	●
35	Thrash	Normal	Physical	90	100	20	1 Random	●
38	Swords Dance	Normal	Status	—	—	30	Self	—
42	Submission	Fighting	Physical	80	80	25	Normal	●
47	Guillotine	Normal	Physical	—	30	5	Normal	—
52	Superpower	Fighting	Physical	120	100	5	Normal	●

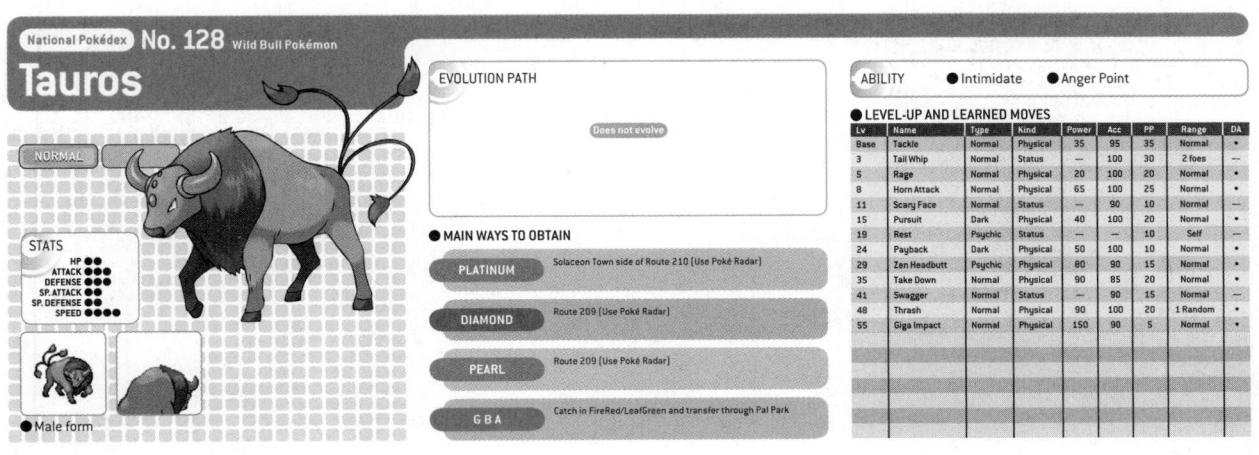

No. 128 Wild Bull Pokémon — Tauros

Type: NORMAL

STATS: HP ●● / ATTACK ●●● / DEFENSE ●●● / SP.ATTACK ●● / SP.DEFENSE ●●● / SPEED ●●●●

● Male form

ABILITY: ● Intimidate ● Anger Point

EVOLUTION PATH: Does not evolve

MAIN WAYS TO OBTAIN:
- PLATINUM: Solaceon Town side of Route 210 (Use Poké Radar)
- DIAMOND: Route 209 (Use Poké Radar)
- PEARL: Route 209 (Use Poké Radar)
- GBA: Catch in FireRed/LeafGreen and transfer through Pal Park

LEVEL-UP AND LEARNED MOVES

Lv	Name	Type	Kind	Power	Acc	PP	Range	DA
Base	Tackle	Normal	Physical	35	95	35	Normal	—
3	Tail Whip	Normal	Status	—	100	30	2 foes	—
5	Rage	Normal	Physical	20	100	20	Normal	—
8	Horn Attack	Normal	Physical	65	100	25	Normal	—
11	Scary Face	Normal	Status	—	90	10	Normal	—
15	Pursuit	Dark	Physical	40	100	20	Normal	—
19	Rest	Psychic	Status	—	—	10	Self	—
24	Payback	Dark	Physical	50	100	10	Normal	—
29	Zen Headbutt	Psychic	Physical	80	90	15	Normal	●
35	Take Down	Normal	Physical	90	85	20	Normal	●
41	Swagger	Normal	Status	—	90	15	Normal	—
48	Thrash	Normal	Physical	90	100	20	1 Random	●
55	Giga Impact	Normal	Physical	150	90	5	Normal	●

128 ***** TAUROS

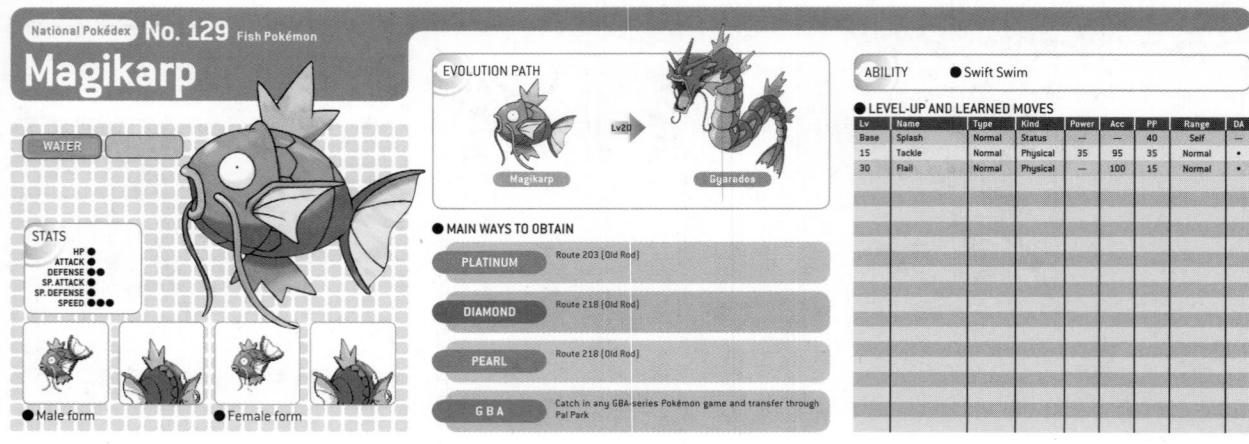

National Pokédex No. 129 Fish Pokémon
Magikarp

WATER

STATS
HP ●
ATTACK ●●
DEFENSE ●●
SP. ATTACK ●
SP. DEFENSE ●
SPEED ●●●

●Male form　●Female form

EVOLUTION PATH

Magikarp —Lv20→ Gyarados

● MAIN WAYS TO OBTAIN

PLATINUM	Route 203 (Old Rod)
DIAMOND	Route 218 (Old Rod)
PEARL	Route 218 (Old Rod)
GBA	Catch in any GBA-series Pokémon game and transfer through Pal Park

ABILITY　● Swift Swim

● LEVEL-UP AND LEARNED MOVES

Lv	Name	Type	Kind	Power	Acc	PP	Range	DA
Base	Splash	Normal	Status	—	—	40	Self	—
15	Tackle	Normal	Physical	35	95	35	Normal	●
30	Flail	Normal	Physical	—	100	15	Normal	●

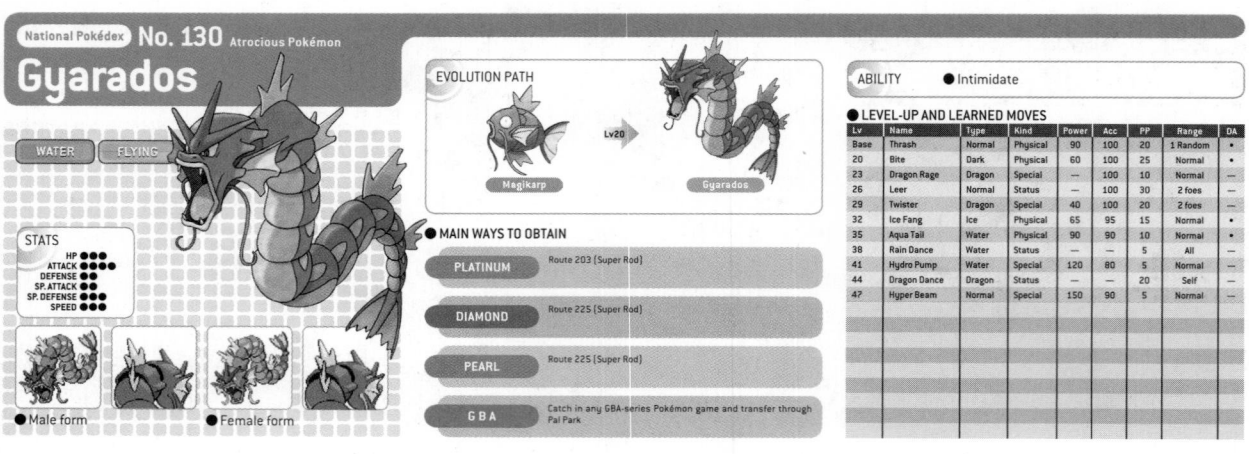

National Pokédex No. 130 Atrocious Pokémon
Gyarados

WATER　FLYING

STATS
HP ●●●
ATTACK ●●●●
DEFENSE ●●●
SP. ATTACK ●●●
SP. DEFENSE ●●●
SPEED ●●●

●Male form　●Female form

EVOLUTION PATH

Magikarp —Lv20→ Gyarados

● MAIN WAYS TO OBTAIN

PLATINUM	Route 203 (Super Rod)
DIAMOND	Route 225 (Super Rod)
PEARL	Route 225 (Super Rod)
GBA	Catch in any GBA-series Pokémon game and transfer through Pal Park

ABILITY　● Intimidate

● LEVEL-UP AND LEARNED MOVES

Lv	Name	Type	Kind	Power	Acc	PP	Range	DA
Base	Thrash	Normal	Physical	90	100	20	1 Random	●
20	Bite	Dark	Physical	60	100	25	Normal	●
23	Dragon Rage	Dragon	Special	—	100	10	Normal	—
26	Leer	Normal	Status	—	100	30	2 foes	—
29	Twister	Dragon	Special	40	100	20	2 foes	—
32	Ice Fang	Ice	Physical	65	95	15	Normal	●
35	Aqua Tail	Water	Physical	90	90	10	Normal	●
38	Rain Dance	Water	Status	—	—	5	All	—
41	Hydro Pump	Water	Special	120	80	5	Normal	—
44	Dragon Dance	Dragon	Status	—	—	20	Self	—
47	Hyper Beam	Normal	Special	150	90	5	Normal	—

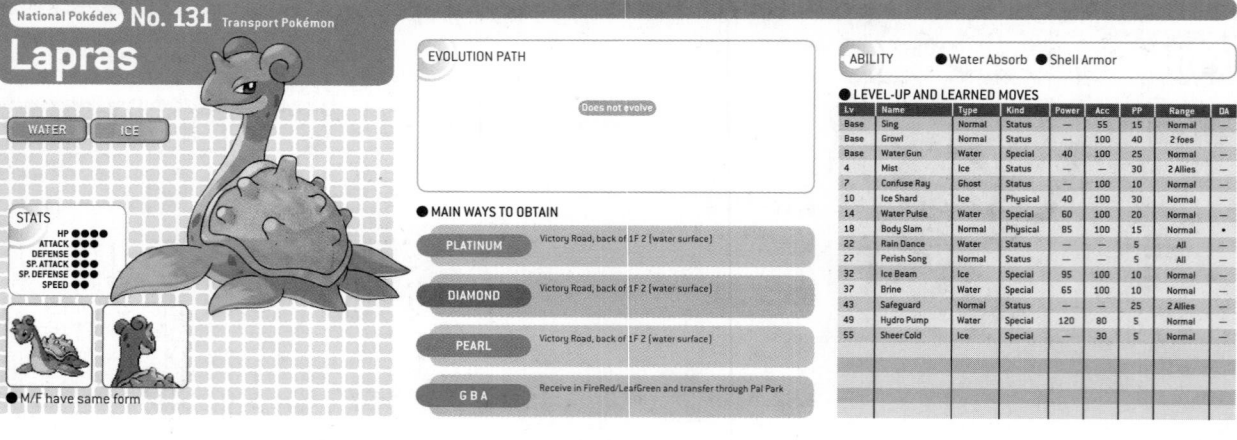

National Pokédex No. 131 Transport Pokémon
Lapras

WATER　ICE

STATS
HP ●●●●
ATTACK ●●●
DEFENSE ●●●
SP. ATTACK ●●●
SP. DEFENSE ●●●
SPEED ●●●

●M/F have same form

EVOLUTION PATH

Does not evolve

● MAIN WAYS TO OBTAIN

PLATINUM	Victory Road, back of 1F 2 (water surface)
DIAMOND	Victory Road, back of 1F 2 (water surface)
PEARL	Victory Road, back of 1F 2 (water surface)
GBA	Receive in FireRed/LeafGreen and transfer through Pal Park

ABILITY　● Water Absorb　● Shell Armor

● LEVEL-UP AND LEARNED MOVES

Lv	Name	Type	Kind	Power	Acc	PP	Range	DA
Base	Sing	Normal	Status	—	55	15	Normal	—
Base	Growl	Normal	Status	—	100	40	2 foes	—
Base	Water Gun	Water	Special	40	100	25	Normal	—
4	Mist	Ice	Status	—	—	30	2 Allies	—
7	Confuse Ray	Ghost	Status	—	100	10	Normal	—
10	Ice Shard	Ice	Physical	40	100	30	Normal	—
14	Water Pulse	Water	Special	60	100	20	Normal	—
18	Body Slam	Normal	Physical	85	100	15	Normal	●
22	Rain Dance	Water	Status	—	—	5	All	—
27	Perish Song	Normal	Status	—	—	5	All	—
32	Ice Beam	Ice	Special	95	100	10	Normal	—
37	Brine	Water	Special	65	100	10	Normal	—
43	Safeguard	Normal	Status	—	—	25	2 Allies	—
49	Hydro Pump	Water	Special	120	80	5	Normal	—
55	Sheer Cold	Ice	Special	—	30	5	Normal	—

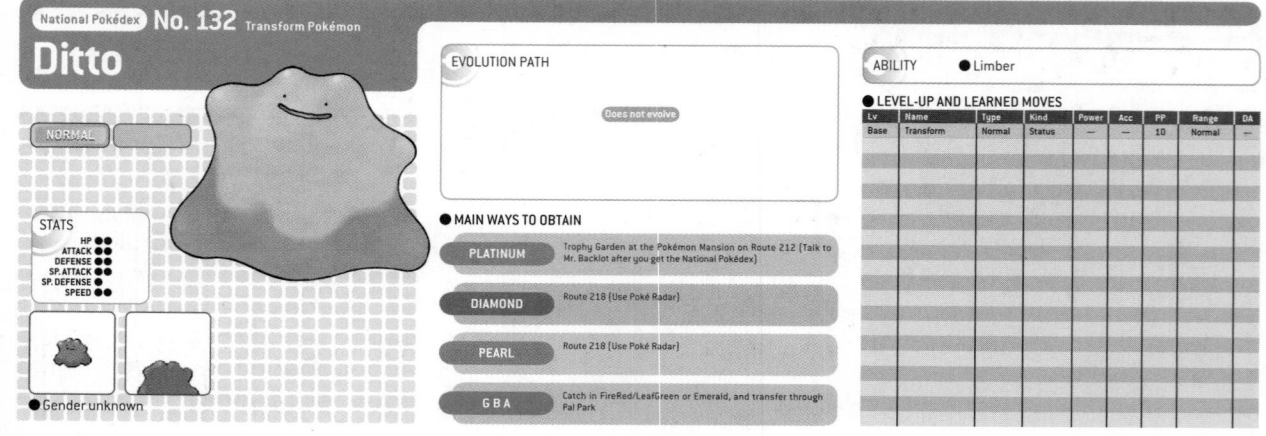

National Pokédex No. 132 Transform Pokémon
Ditto

NORMAL

STATS
HP ●●
ATTACK ●●
DEFENSE ●●
SP. ATTACK ●●
SP. DEFENSE ●●
SPEED ●●

●Gender unknown

EVOLUTION PATH

Does not evolve

● MAIN WAYS TO OBTAIN

PLATINUM	Trophy Garden at the Pokémon Mansion on Route 212 (Talk to Mr. Backlot after you get the National Pokédex)
DIAMOND	Route 218 (Use Poké Radar)
PEARL	Route 218 (Use Poké Radar)
GBA	Catch in FireRed/LeafGreen or Emerald, and transfer through Pal Park

ABILITY　● Limber

● LEVEL-UP AND LEARNED MOVES

Lv	Name	Type	Kind	Power	Acc	PP	Range	DA
Base	Transform	Normal	Status	—	—	10	Normal	—

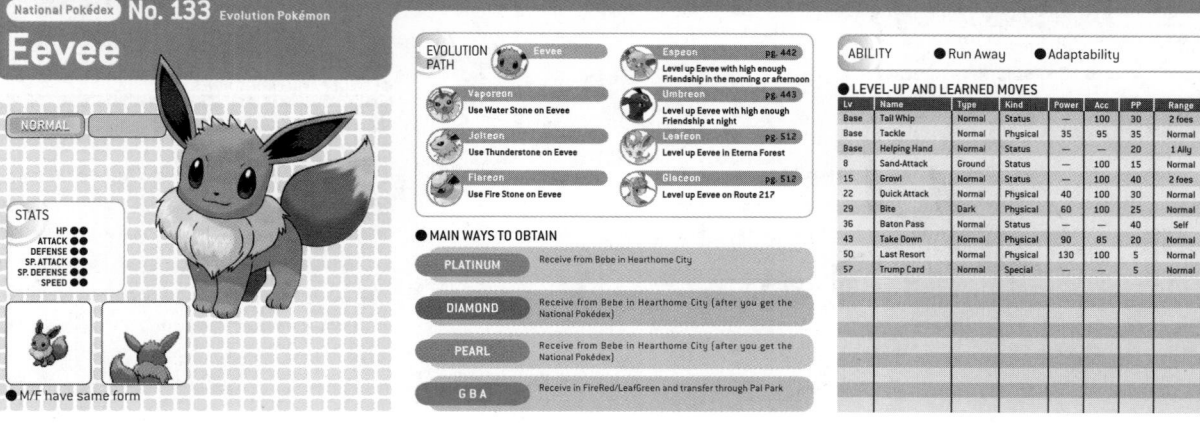

National Pokédex No. 133 — Eevee — Evolution Pokémon

NORMAL

STATS
HP
ATTACK
DEFENSE
SP. ATTACK
SP. DEFENSE
SPEED

● M/F have same form

EVOLUTION PATH

Eevee

Espeon — pg. 442 — Level up Eevee with high enough Friendship in the morning or afternoon

Vaporeon — Use Water Stone on Eevee

Umbreon — pg. 443 — Level up Eevee with high enough Friendship at night

Jolteon — Use Thunderstone on Eevee

Leafeon — pg. 512 — Level up Eevee in Eterna Forest

Flareon — Use Fire Stone on Eevee

Glaceon — pg. 512 — Level up Eevee on Route 217

● **MAIN WAYS TO OBTAIN**

PLATINUM	Receive from Bebe in Hearthome City
DIAMOND	Receive from Bebe in Hearthome City (after you get the National Pokédex)
PEARL	Receive from Bebe in Hearthome City (after you get the National Pokédex)
G B A	Receive in FireRed/LeafGreen and transfer through Pal Park

ABILITY ● Run Away ● Adaptability

● **LEVEL-UP AND LEARNED MOVES**

Lv	Name	Type	Kind	Power	Acc	PP	Range	DA
Base	Tail Whip	Normal	Status	—	100	30	2 foes	—
Base	Tackle	Normal	Physical	35	95	35	Normal	●
Base	Helping Hand	Normal	Status	—	—	20	1 Ally	●
8	Sand-Attack	Ground	Status	—	100	15	Normal	●
15	Growl	Normal	Status	—	100	40	2 foes	—
22	Quick Attack	Normal	Physical	40	100	30	Normal	●
29	Bite	Dark	Physical	60	100	25	Normal	●
36	Baton Pass	Normal	Status	—	—	40	Self	—
43	Take Down	Normal	Physical	90	85	20	Normal	●
50	Last Resort	Normal	Physical	130	100	5	Normal	●
57	Trump Card	Normal	Special	—	—	5	Normal	—

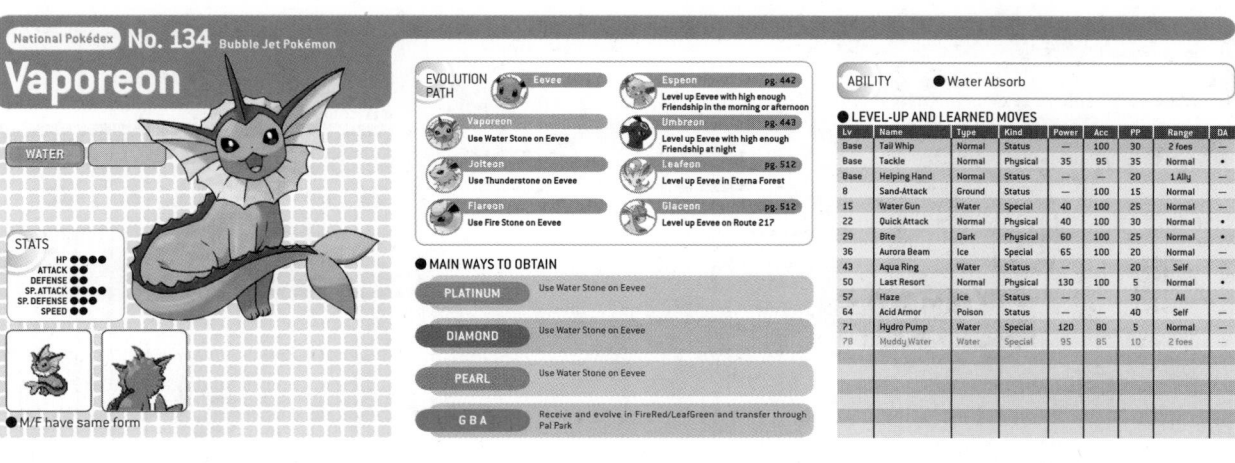

National Pokédex No. 134 — Vaporeon — Bubble Jet Pokémon

WATER

STATS
HP
ATTACK
DEFENSE
SP. ATTACK
SP. DEFENSE
SPEED

● M/F have same form

EVOLUTION PATH

Eevee

Espeon — pg. 442 — Level up Eevee with high enough Friendship in the morning or afternoon

Vaporeon — Use Water Stone on Eevee

Umbreon — pg. 443 — Level up Eevee with high enough Friendship at night

Jolteon — Use Thunderstone on Eevee

Leafeon — pg. 512 — Level up Eevee in Eterna Forest

Flareon — Use Fire Stone on Eevee

Glaceon — pg. 512 — Level up Eevee on Route 217

● **MAIN WAYS TO OBTAIN**

PLATINUM	Use Water Stone on Eevee
DIAMOND	Use Water Stone on Eevee
PEARL	Use Water Stone on Eevee
G B A	Receive and evolve in FireRed/LeafGreen and transfer through Pal Park

ABILITY ● Water Absorb

● **LEVEL-UP AND LEARNED MOVES**

Lv	Name	Type	Kind	Power	Acc	PP	Range	DA
Base	Tail Whip	Normal	Status	—	100	30	2 foes	—
Base	Tackle	Normal	Physical	35	95	35	Normal	●
Base	Helping Hand	Normal	Status	—	—	20	1 Ally	●
8	Sand-Attack	Ground	Status	—	100	15	Normal	●
15	Water Gun	Water	Special	40	100	25	Normal	●
22	Quick Attack	Normal	Physical	40	100	30	Normal	●
29	Bite	Dark	Physical	60	100	25	Normal	●
36	Aurora Beam	Ice	Special	65	100	20	Normal	●
43	Aqua Ring	Water	Status	—	—	20	Self	—
50	Last Resort	Normal	Physical	130	100	5	Normal	●
57	Haze	Ice	Status	—	—	30	All	—
64	Acid Armor	Poison	Status	—	—	40	Self	—
71	Hydro Pump	Water	Special	120	80	5	Normal	●
78	Muddy Water	Water	Special	95	85	10	2 foes	●

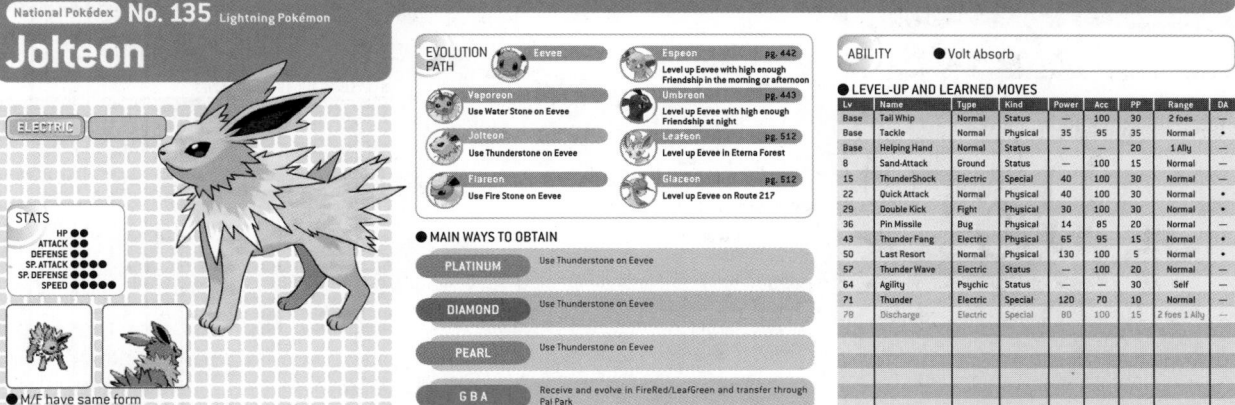

National Pokédex No. 135 — Jolteon — Lightning Pokémon

ELECTRIC

STATS
HP
ATTACK
DEFENSE
SP. ATTACK
SP. DEFENSE
SPEED

● M/F have same form

EVOLUTION PATH

Eevee

Espeon — pg. 442 — Level up Eevee with high enough Friendship in the morning or afternoon

Vaporeon — Use Water Stone on Eevee

Umbreon — pg. 443 — Level up Eevee with high enough Friendship at night

Jolteon — Use Thunderstone on Eevee

Leafeon — pg. 512 — Level up Eevee in Eterna Forest

Flareon — Use Fire Stone on Eevee

Glaceon — pg. 512 — Level up Eevee on Route 217

● **MAIN WAYS TO OBTAIN**

PLATINUM	Use Thunderstone on Eevee
DIAMOND	Use Thunderstone on Eevee
PEARL	Use Thunderstone on Eevee
G B A	Receive and evolve in FireRed/LeafGreen and transfer through Pal Park

ABILITY ● Volt Absorb

● **LEVEL-UP AND LEARNED MOVES**

Lv	Name	Type	Kind	Power	Acc	PP	Range	DA
Base	Tail Whip	Normal	Status	—	100	30	2 foes	—
Base	Tackle	Normal	Physical	35	95	35	Normal	●
Base	Helping Hand	Normal	Status	—	—	20	1 Ally	●
8	Sand-Attack	Ground	Status	—	100	15	Normal	●
15	ThunderShock	Electric	Special	40	100	30	Normal	●
22	Quick Attack	Normal	Physical	40	100	30	Normal	●
29	Double Kick	Fight	Physical	30	100	30	Normal	●
36	Pin Missile	Bug	Physical	14	85	20	Normal	●
43	Thunder Fang	Electric	Physical	65	95	15	Normal	●
50	Last Resort	Normal	Physical	130	100	5	Normal	●
57	Thunder Wave	Electric	Status	—	100	20	Normal	—
64	Agility	Psychic	Status	—	—	30	Self	—
71	Thunder	Electric	Special	120	70	10	Normal	●
78	Discharge	Electric	Special	80	100	15	2 foes 1 Ally	●

136

FLAREON

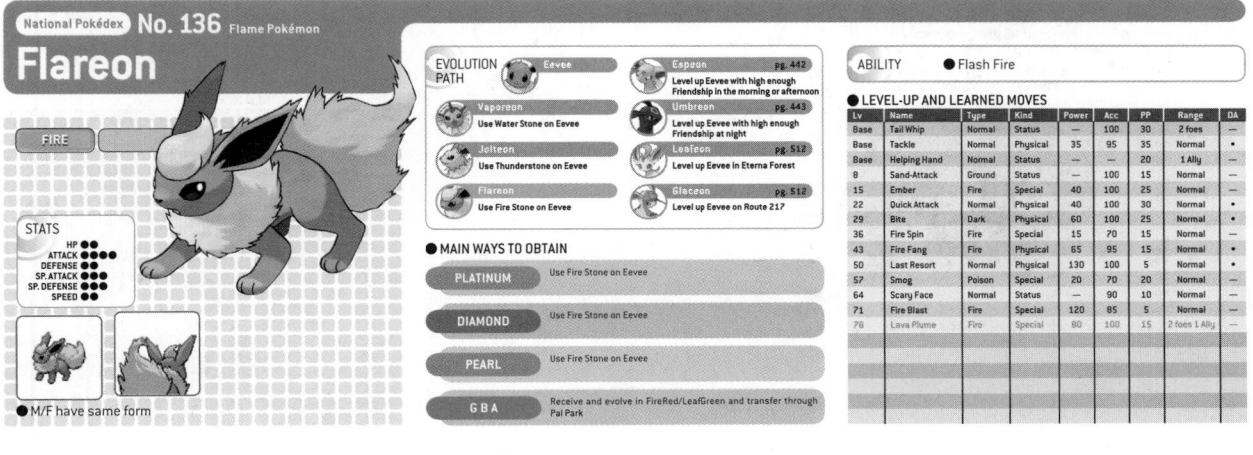

National Pokédex No. 136 — Flareon — Flame Pokémon

FIRE

STATS
HP
ATTACK
DEFENSE
SP. ATTACK
SP. DEFENSE
SPEED

● M/F have same form

EVOLUTION PATH

Eevee

Espeon — pg. 442 — Level up Eevee with high enough Friendship in the morning or afternoon

Vaporeon — Use Water Stone on Eevee

Umbreon — pg. 443 — Level up Eevee with high enough Friendship at night

Jolteon — Use Thunderstone on Eevee

Leafeon — pg. 512 — Level up Eevee in Eterna Forest

Flareon — Use Fire Stone on Eevee

Glaceon — pg. 512 — Level up Eevee on Route 217

● **MAIN WAYS TO OBTAIN**

PLATINUM	Use Fire Stone on Eevee
DIAMOND	Use Fire Stone on Eevee
PEARL	Use Fire Stone on Eevee
G B A	Receive and evolve in FireRed/LeafGreen and transfer through Pal Park

ABILITY ● Flash Fire

● **LEVEL-UP AND LEARNED MOVES**

Lv	Name	Type	Kind	Power	Acc	PP	Range	DA
Base	Tail Whip	Normal	Status	—	100	30	2 foes	—
Base	Tackle	Normal	Physical	35	95	35	Normal	●
Base	Helping Hand	Normal	Status	—	—	20	1 Ally	●
8	Sand-Attack	Ground	Status	—	100	15	Normal	●
15	Ember	Fire	Special	40	100	25	Normal	●
22	Quick Attack	Normal	Physical	40	100	30	Normal	●
29	Bite	Dark	Physical	60	100	25	Normal	●
36	Fire Spin	Fire	Special	15	70	15	Normal	●
43	Fire Fang	Fire	Physical	65	95	15	Normal	●
50	Last Resort	Normal	Physical	130	100	5	Normal	●
57	Smog	Poison	Special	20	70	20	Normal	●
64	Scary Face	Normal	Status	—	90	10	Normal	—
71	Fire Blast	Fire	Special	120	85	5	Normal	●
78	Lava Plume	Fire	Special	80	100	15	2 foes 1 Ally	●

Porygon

National Pokédex **No. 137** Virtual Pokémon

NORMAL

STATS
HP ●●
ATTACK ●●
DEFENSE ●●
SP. ATTACK ●●●
SP. DEFENSE ●●
SPEED ●●

● Gender unknown

EVOLUTION PATH

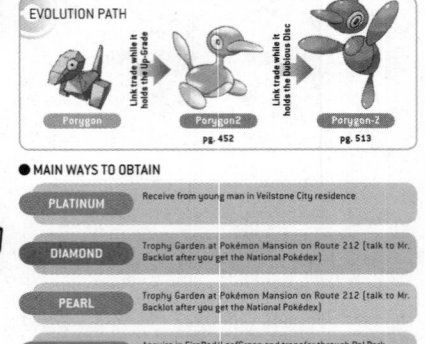

Porygon → (Link trade while it holds the Up-Grade) Porygon2 pg. 452 → (Link trade while it holds the Dubious Disc) Porygon-Z pg. 513

MAIN WAYS TO OBTAIN

PLATINUM	Receive from young man in Veilstone City residence
DIAMOND	Trophy Garden at Pokémon Mansion on Route 212 (talk to Mr. Backlot after you get the National Pokédex)
PEARL	Trophy Garden at Pokémon Mansion on Route 212 (talk to Mr. Backlot after you get the National Pokédex)
GBA	Acquire in FireRed/LeafGreen and transfer through Pal Park

ABILITY ● Trace ● Download

LEVEL-UP AND LEARNED MOVES

Lv	Name	Type	Kind	Power	Acc	PP	Range	DA
Base	Conversion 2	Normal	Status	—	—	30	Self	—
Base	Tackle	Normal	Physical	35	95	35	Normal	●
Base	Conversion	Normal	Status	—	—	30	Self	—
Base	Sharpen	Normal	Status	—	—	30	Self	—
7	Psybeam	Psychic	Special	65	100	20	Normal	—
12	Agility	Psychic	Status	—	—	30	Self	—
18	Recover	Normal	Status	—	—	10	Self	—
23	Magnet Rise	Electric	Status	—	—	10	Self	—
29	Signal Beam	Bug	Special	75	100	15	Normal	—
34	Recycle	Normal	Status	—	—	10	Self	—
40	Discharge	Electric	Special	80	100	15	2 foes 1 Ally	—
45	Lock-On	Normal	Status	—	—	5	Normal	—
51	Tri Attack	Normal	Special	80	100	10	Normal	—
56	Magic Coat	Psychic	Status	—	—	15	Self	—
62	Zap Cannon	Electric	Special	120	50	5	Normal	—

Omanyte

National Pokédex **No. 138** Spiral Pokémon

ROCK WATER

STATS
HP ●
ATTACK ●●
DEFENSE ●●●
SP. ATTACK ●●●
SP. DEFENSE ●●
SPEED ●

● M/F have same form

EVOLUTION PATH

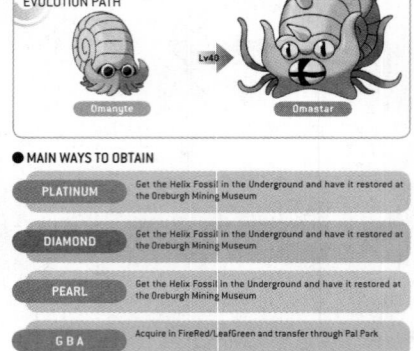

Omanyte → Lv40 → Omastar

MAIN WAYS TO OBTAIN

PLATINUM	Get the Helix Fossil in the Underground and have it restored at the Oreburgh Mining Museum
DIAMOND	Get the Helix Fossil in the Underground and have it restored at the Oreburgh Mining Museum
PEARL	Get the Helix Fossil in the Underground and have it restored at the Oreburgh Mining Museum
GBA	Acquire in FireRed/LeafGreen and transfer through Pal Park

ABILITY ● Swift Swim ● Shell Armor

LEVEL-UP AND LEARNED MOVES

Lv	Name	Type	Kind	Power	Acc	PP	Range	DA
Base	Constrict	Normal	Physical	10	100	40	Normal	●
Base	Withdraw	Water	Status	—	—	40	Self	—
7	Bite	Dark	Physical	60	100	25	Normal	●
10	Water Gun	Water	Special	40	100	25	Normal	—
16	Rollout	Rock	Physical	30	90	20	Normal	●
19	Leer	Normal	Status	—	100	30	2 foes	—
25	Mud Shot	Ground	Special	55	95	15	Normal	—
28	Brine	Water	Special	65	100	10	Normal	—
34	Protect	Normal	Status	—	—	10	Self	—
37	AncientPower	Rock	Special	60	100	5	Normal	—
43	Tickle	Normal	Status	—	100	20	Normal	—
46	Rock Blast	Rock	Physical	25	80	10	Normal	—
52	Hydro Pump	Water	Special	120	80	5	Normal	—

Omastar

National Pokédex **No. 139** Spiral Pokémon

ROCK WATER

STATS
HP ●●
ATTACK ●●
DEFENSE ●●●●
SP. ATTACK ●●●
SP. DEFENSE ●●
SPEED ●●

● M/F have same form

EVOLUTION PATH

Omanyte → Lv40 → Omastar

MAIN WAYS TO OBTAIN

PLATINUM	Level up Omanyte to Lv40
DIAMOND	Level up Omanyte to Lv40
PEARL	Level up Omanyte to Lv40
GBA	Catch and evolve in FireRed/LeafGreen, and transfer through Pal Park

ABILITY ● Swift Swim ● Shell Armor

LEVEL-UP AND LEARNED MOVES

Lv	Name	Type	Kind	Power	Acc	PP	Range	DA
Base	Constrict	Normal	Physical	10	100	40	Normal	●
Base	Withdraw	Water	Status	—	—	40	Self	—
Base	Bite	Dark	Physical	60	100	25	Normal	●
7	Bite	Dark	Physical	60	100	25	Normal	●
10	Water Gun	Water	Special	40	100	25	Normal	—
16	Rollout	Rock	Physical	30	90	20	Normal	●
19	Leer	Normal	Status	—	100	30	2 foes	—
25	Mud Shot	Ground	Special	55	95	15	Normal	—
28	Brine	Water	Special	65	100	10	Normal	—
34	Protect	Normal	Status	—	—	10	Self	—
37	AncientPower	Rock	Special	60	100	5	Normal	—
40	Spike Cannon	Normal	Physical	20	100	15	Normal	—
48	Tickle	Normal	Status	—	100	20	Normal	—
56	Rock Blast	Rock	Physical	25	80	10	Normal	—
67	Hydro Pump	Water	Special	120	80	5	Normal	—

Kabuto

National Pokédex **No. 140** Shellfish Pokémon

ROCK WATER

STATS
HP ●
ATTACK ●●●
DEFENSE ●●●
SP. ATTACK ●●
SP. DEFENSE ●●
SPEED ●●

● M/F have same form

EVOLUTION PATH

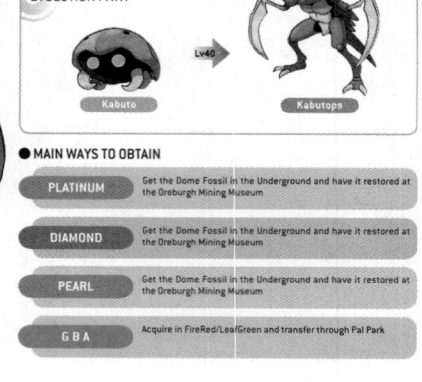

Kabuto → Lv40 → Kabutops

MAIN WAYS TO OBTAIN

PLATINUM	Get the Dome Fossil in the Underground and have it restored at the Oreburgh Mining Museum
DIAMOND	Get the Dome Fossil in the Underground and have it restored at the Oreburgh Mining Museum
PEARL	Get the Dome Fossil in the Underground and have it restored at the Oreburgh Mining Museum
GBA	Acquire in FireRed/LeafGreen and transfer through Pal Park

ABILITY ● Swift Swim ● Battle Armor

LEVEL-UP AND LEARNED MOVES

Lv	Name	Type	Kind	Power	Acc	PP	Range	DA
Base	Scratch	Normal	Physical	40	100	35	Normal	●
Base	Harden	Normal	Status	—	—	30	Self	—
6	Absorb	Grass	Special	20	100	25	Normal	—
11	Leer	Normal	Status	—	100	30	2 foes	—
16	Mud Shot	Ground	Special	55	95	15	Normal	—
21	Sand-Attack	Ground	Status	—	100	15	Normal	—
26	Endure	Normal	Status	—	—	10	Self	—
31	Aqua Jet	Water	Physical	40	100	20	Normal	●
36	Mega Drain	Grass	Special	40	100	15	Normal	—
41	Metal Sound	Steel	Status	—	85	40	Normal	—
46	AncientPower	Rock	Special	60	100	5	Normal	—
51	Wring Out	Normal	Special	—	100	5	Normal	—

Kabutops

National Pokédex No. 141 Shellfish Pokémon

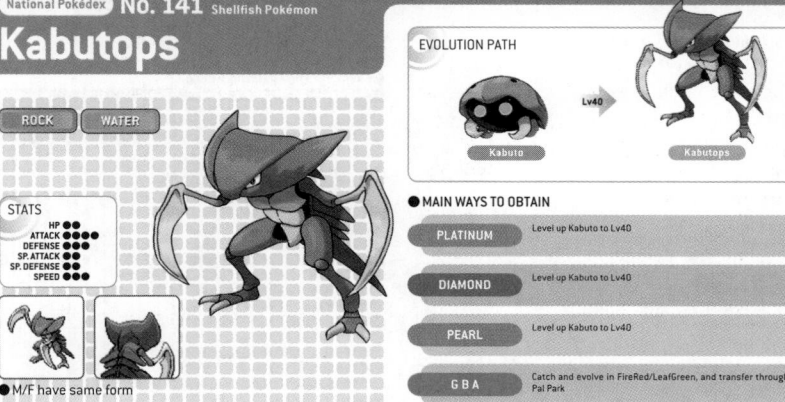

ROCK WATER

STATS
- HP ●●
- ATTACK ●●●●
- DEFENSE ●●●
- SP. ATTACK ●●
- SP. DEFENSE ●●
- SPEED ●●●

● M/F have same form

● EVOLUTION PATH

Kabuto → Lv40 → Kabutops

● MAIN WAYS TO OBTAIN

PLATINUM	Level up Kabuto to Lv40
DIAMOND	Level up Kabuto to Lv40
PEARL	Level up Kabuto to Lv40
G B A	Catch and evolve in FireRed/LeafGreen, and transfer through Pal Park

ABILITY ● Swift Swim ● Battle Armor

● LEVEL-UP AND LEARNED MOVES

Lv	Name	Type	Kind	Power	Acc	PP	Range	DA
Base	Feint	Normal	Physical	50	100	10	Normal	—
Base	Scratch	Normal	Physical	40	100	35	Normal	•
Base	Harden	Normal	Status	—	—	30	Self	•
Base	Absorb	Grass	Special	20	100	25	Normal	•
Base	Leer	Normal	Status	—	100	30	2 foes	—
6	Absorb	Grass	Special	20	100	25	Normal	•
11	Leer	Normal	Status	—	100	30	2 foes	•
16	Mud Shot	Ground	Special	55	95	15	Normal	•
21	Sand-Attack	Ground	Status	—	100	15	Normal	•
26	Endure	Normal	Status	—	—	10	Self	•
31	Aqua Jet	Water	Physical	40	100	20	Normal	•
36	Mega Drain	Grass	Special	40	100	15	Normal	•
40	Slash	Normal	Physical	70	100	20	Normal	•
45	Metal Sound	Steel	Status	—	85	40	Normal	•
54	AncientPower	Rock	Special	60	100	5	Normal	•
63	Wring Out	Normal	Special	—	100	5	Normal	•
72	Night Slash	Dark	Physical	70	100	15	Normal	•

Aerodactyl

National Pokédex No. 142 Fossil Pokémon

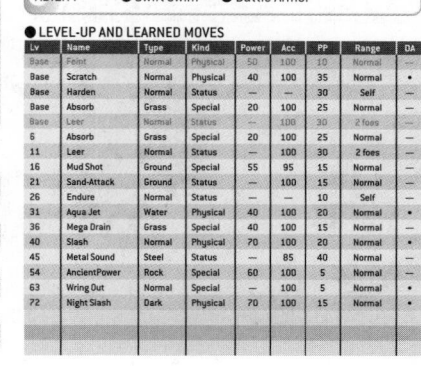

ROCK FLYING

STATS
- HP ●●●
- ATTACK ●●●●
- DEFENSE ●●●
- SP. ATTACK ●●
- SP. DEFENSE ●●●
- SPEED ●●●●●

● M/F have same form

● EVOLUTION PATH

Does not evolve

● MAIN WAYS TO OBTAIN

PLATINUM	Get the Old Amber in the Underground and have it restored at the Oreburgh Mining Museum
DIAMOND	Get the Old Amber in the Underground and have it restored at the Oreburgh Mining Museum
PEARL	Get the Old Amber in the Underground and have it restored at the Oreburgh Mining Museum
G B A	Acquire in FireRed/LeafGreen and transfer through Pal Park

ABILITY ● Rock Head ● Pressure

● LEVEL-UP AND LEARNED MOVES

Lv	Name	Type	Kind	Power	Acc	PP	Range	DA
Base	Ice Fang	Ice	Physical	65	95	15	Normal	•
Base	Fire Fang	Fire	Physical	65	95	15	Normal	•
Base	Thunder Fang	Electric	Physical	65	95	15	Normal	•
Base	Wing Attack	Flying	Physical	60	100	35	Normal	•
Base	Supersonic	Normal	Status	—	55	20	Normal	—
Base	Bite	Dark	Physical	60	100	25	Normal	•
Base	Scary Face	Normal	Status	—	90	10	Normal	—
9	Roar	Normal	Status	—	100	20	Normal	—
17	Agility	Psychic	Status	—	—	30	Self	—
25	AncientPower	Rock	Special	60	100	5	Normal	•
33	Crunch	Dark	Physical	80	100	15	Normal	•
41	Take Down	Normal	Physical	90	85	20	Normal	•
49	Iron Head	Steel	Physical	80	100	15	Normal	•
57	Hyper Beam	Normal	Special	150	90	5	Normal	•
65	Rock Slide	Rock	Physical	75	90	10	2 foes	•
73	Giga Impact	Normal	Physical	150	90	5	Normal	•

Snorlax

National Pokédex No. 143 Sleeping Pokémon

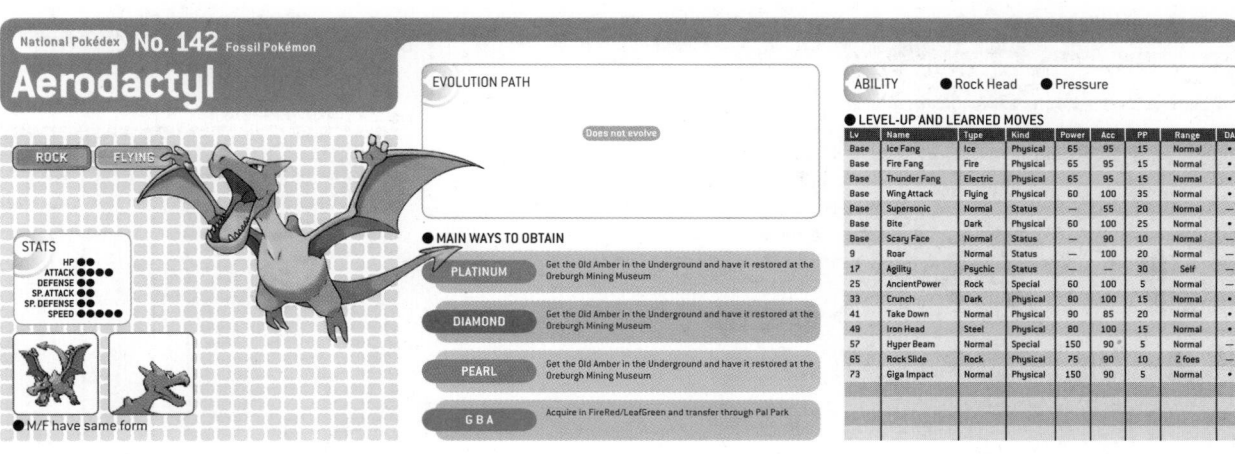

NORMAL

STATS
- HP ●●●●●
- ATTACK ●●●●
- DEFENSE ●●
- SP. ATTACK ●●
- SP. DEFENSE ●●●
- SPEED ●

● M/F have same form

● EVOLUTION PATH

Munchlax → Level up with high enough Friendship → Snorlax
pg. 506

● MAIN WAYS TO OBTAIN

PLATINUM	Level up Munchlax with high enough Friendship
DIAMOND	Level up Munchlax with high enough Friendship
PEARL	Level up Munchlax with high enough Friendship
G B A	Catch in FireRed/LeafGreen and transfer through Pal Park

ABILITY ● Immunity ● Thick Fat

● LEVEL-UP AND LEARNED MOVES

Lv	Name	Type	Kind	Power	Acc	PP	Range	DA
Base	Tackle	Normal	Physical	35	95	35	Normal	•
4	Defense Curl	Normal	Status	—	—	40	Self	•
9	Amnesia	Psychic	Status	—	—	20	Self	•
12	Lick	Ghost	Physical	20	100	30	Normal	•
17	Belly Drum	Normal	Status	—	—	10	Self	•
20	Yawn	Normal	Status	—	—	10	Normal	—
25	Rest	Psychic	Status	—	—	10	Self	•
28	Snore	Normal	Special	40	100	15	Normal	•
28	Sleep Talk	Normal	Status	—	—	10	Last move	—
33	Body Slam	Normal	Physical	85	100	15	Normal	•
36	Block	Normal	Status	—	—	5	Normal	•
41	Rollout	Rock	Physical	30	90	20	Normal	•
44	Crunch	Dark	Physical	80	100	15	Normal	•
49	Giga Impact	Normal	Physical	150	90	5	Normal	•

Articuno

National Pokédex No. 144 Freeze Pokémon

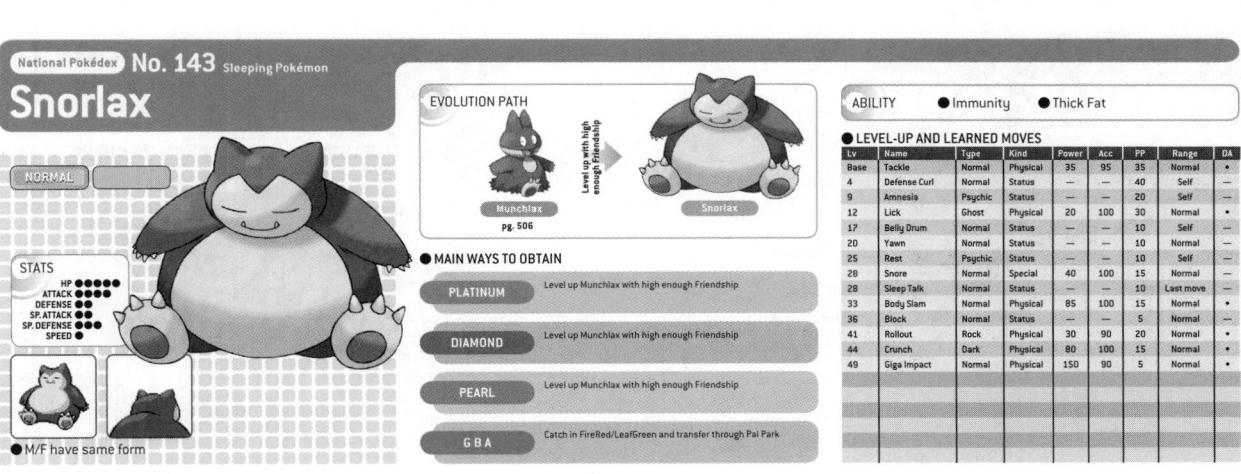

ICE FLYING

STATS
- HP ●●●
- ATTACK ●●●
- DEFENSE ●●●
- SP. ATTACK ●●●
- SP. DEFENSE ●●●●
- SPEED ●●●

● Gender unknown

● EVOLUTION PATH

Does not evolve

● MAIN WAYS TO OBTAIN

PLATINUM	Roams the Sinnoh region after you talk to Professor Oak in Eterna City after getting the National Pokédex
DIAMOND	
PEARL	
G B A	Catch in FireRed/LeafGreen and transfer through Pal Park

ABILITY ● Pressure

● LEVEL-UP AND LEARNED MOVES

Lv	Name	Type	Kind	Power	Acc	PP	Range	DA
Base	Gust	Flying	Special	40	100	35	Normal	—
Base	Powder Snow	Ice	Special	40	100	25	2 foes	—
8	Mist	Ice	Status	—	—	30	2 Allies	—
15	Ice Shard	Ice	Physical	40	100	30	Normal	—
22	Mind Reader	Normal	Status	—	—	5	Normal	—
29	AncientPower	Rock	Special	60	100	5	Normal	—
36	Agility	Psychic	Status	—	—	30	Self	—
43	Ice Beam	Ice	Special	95	100	10	Normal	—
50	Reflect	Psychic	Status	—	—	20	2 Allies	—
57	Roost	Flying	Status	—	—	10	Self	—
64	Tailwind	Flying	Status	—	—	30	2 Allies	—
71	Blizzard	Ice	Special	120	70	5	2 foes	—
78	Sheer Cold	Ice	Special	—	30	5	Normal	—
85	Hail	Ice	Status	—	—	10	All	—

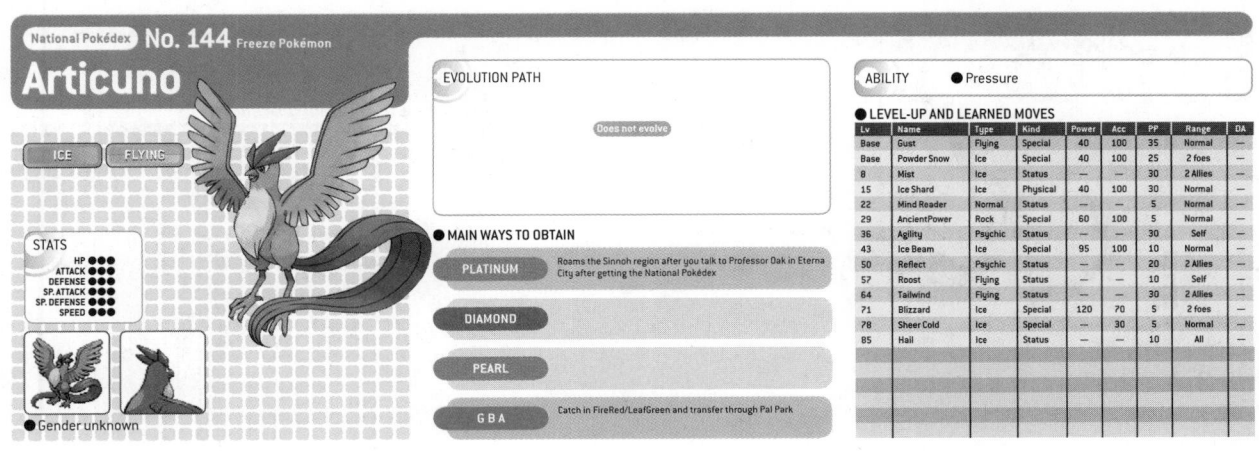

144 ARTICUNO

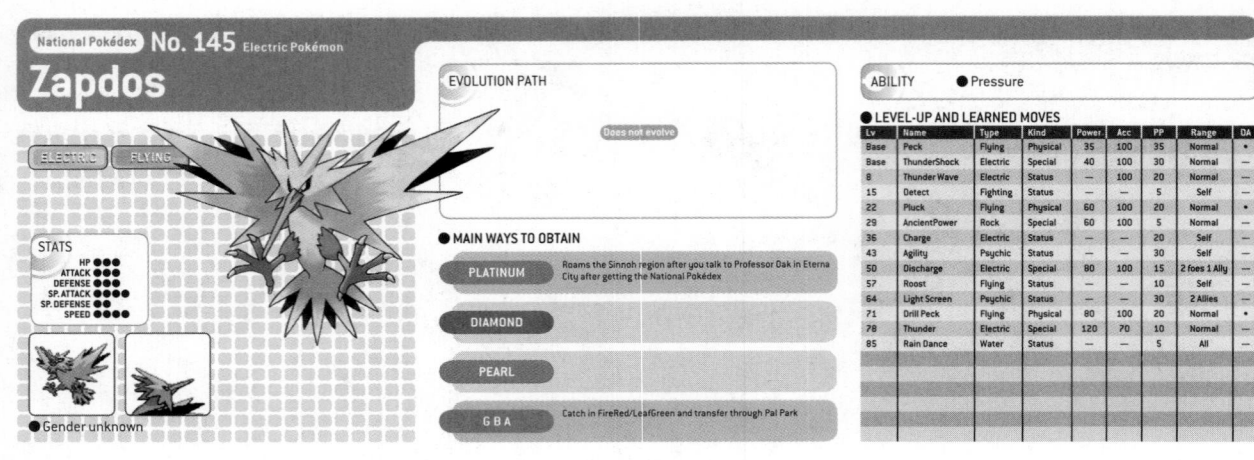

National Pokédex No. 145 Electric Pokémon
Zapdos

ELECTRIC FLYING

STATS
- HP ●●●
- ATTACK ●●●
- DEFENSE ●●●
- SP. ATTACK ●●●●
- SP. DEFENSE ●●●
- SPEED ●●●●

● Gender unknown

EVOLUTION PATH

Does not evolve

● MAIN WAYS TO OBTAIN

PLATINUM	Roams the Sinnoh region after you talk to Professor Oak in Eterna City after getting the National Pokédex
DIAMOND	
PEARL	
G B A	Catch in FireRed/LeafGreen and transfer through Pal Park

ABILITY ● Pressure

● LEVEL-UP AND LEARNED MOVES

Lv	Name	Type	Kind	Power	Acc	PP	Range	DA
Base	Peck	Flying	Physical	35	100	35	Normal	●
Base	ThunderShock	Electric	Special	40	100	30	Normal	—
8	Thunder Wave	Electric	Status	—	100	20	Normal	—
15	Detect	Fighting	Status	—	—	5	Self	—
22	Pluck	Flying	Physical	60	100	20	Normal	—
29	AncientPower	Rock	Special	60	100	5	Normal	—
36	Charge	Electric	Status	—	—	20	Self	—
43	Agility	Psychic	Status	—	—	30	Self	—
50	Discharge	Electric	Special	80	100	15	2 foes 1 Ally	—
57	Roost	Flying	Status	—	—	10	Self	—
64	Light Screen	Psychic	Status	—	—	30	2 Allies	—
71	Drill Peck	Flying	Physical	80	100	20	Normal	●
78	Thunder	Electric	Special	120	70	10	Normal	—
85	Rain Dance	Water	Status	—	—	5	All	—

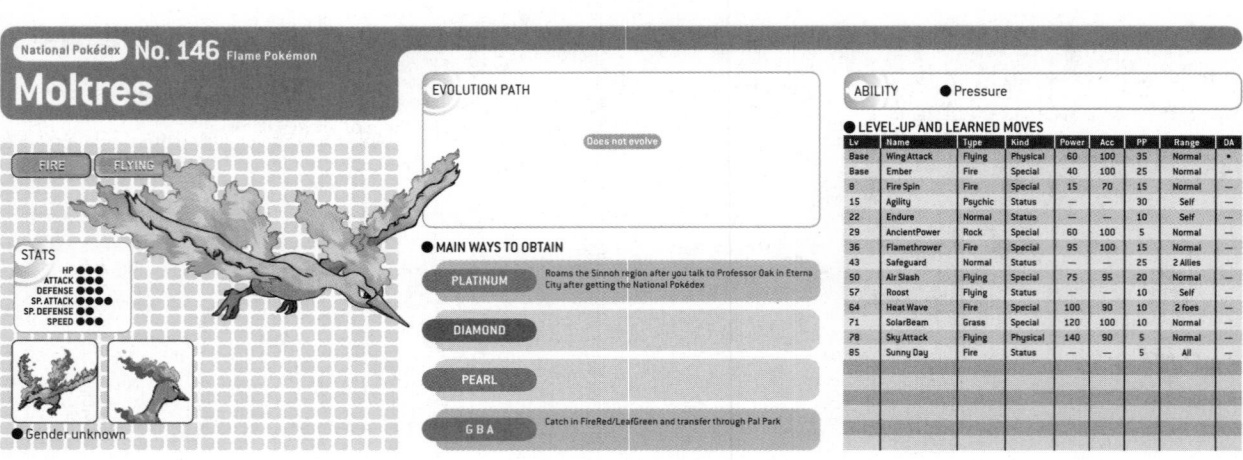

National Pokédex No. 146 Flame Pokémon
Moltres

FIRE FLYING

STATS
- HP ●●●●
- ATTACK ●●●
- DEFENSE ●●●
- SP. ATTACK ●●●●
- SP. DEFENSE ●●●
- SPEED ●●●

● Gender unknown

EVOLUTION PATH

Does not evolve

● MAIN WAYS TO OBTAIN

PLATINUM	Roams the Sinnoh region after you talk to Professor Oak in Eterna City after getting the National Pokédex
DIAMOND	
PEARL	
G B A	Catch in FireRed/LeafGreen and transfer through Pal Park

ABILITY ● Pressure

● LEVEL-UP AND LEARNED MOVES

Lv	Name	Type	Kind	Power	Acc	PP	Range	DA
Base	Wing Attack	Flying	Physical	60	100	35	Normal	●
Base	Ember	Fire	Special	40	100	25	Normal	—
8	Fire Spin	Fire	Special	15	70	15	Normal	—
15	Agility	Psychic	Status	—	—	30	Self	—
22	Endure	Normal	Status	—	—	10	Self	—
29	AncientPower	Rock	Special	60	100	5	Normal	—
36	Flamethrower	Fire	Special	95	100	15	Normal	—
43	Safeguard	Normal	Status	—	—	25	2 Allies	—
50	Air Slash	Flying	Special	75	95	20	Normal	—
57	Roost	Flying	Status	—	—	10	Self	—
64	Heat Wave	Fire	Special	100	90	10	2 foes	—
71	SolarBeam	Grass	Special	120	100	10	Normal	—
78	Sky Attack	Flying	Physical	140	90	5	Normal	—
85	Sunny Day	Fire	Status	—	—	5	All	—

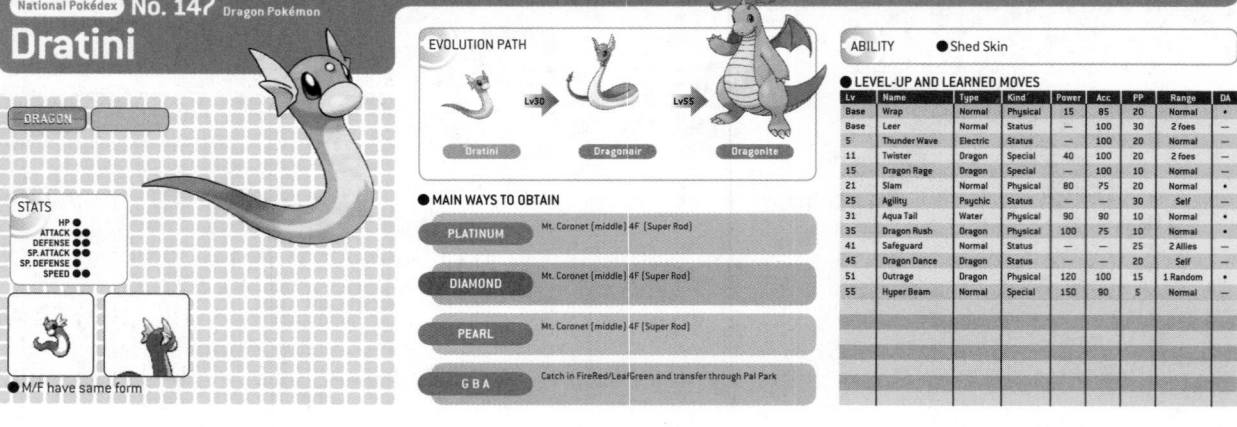

National Pokédex No. 147 Dragon Pokémon
Dratini

DRAGON

STATS
- HP ●
- ATTACK ●●
- DEFENSE ●●●
- SP. ATTACK ●●
- SP. DEFENSE ●●
- SPEED ●●

● M/F have same form

EVOLUTION PATH

Dratini → Lv30 → Dragonair → Lv55 → Dragonite

● MAIN WAYS TO OBTAIN

PLATINUM	Mt. Coronet (middle) 4F (Super Rod)
DIAMOND	Mt. Coronet (middle) 4F (Super Rod)
PEARL	Mt. Coronet (middle) 4F (Super Rod)
G B A	Catch in FireRed/LeafGreen and transfer through Pal Park

ABILITY ● Shed Skin

● LEVEL-UP AND LEARNED MOVES

Lv	Name	Type	Kind	Power	Acc	PP	Range	DA
Base	Wrap	Normal	Physical	15	85	20	Normal	●
Base	Leer	Normal	Status	—	100	30	2 foes	—
5	Thunder Wave	Electric	Status	—	100	20	Normal	—
11	Twister	Dragon	Special	40	100	20	2 foes	—
15	Dragon Rage	Dragon	Special	—	100	10	Normal	—
21	Slam	Normal	Physical	80	75	20	Normal	●
25	Agility	Psychic	Status	—	—	30	Self	—
31	Aqua Tail	Water	Physical	90	90	10	Normal	●
35	Dragon Rush	Dragon	Physical	100	75	10	Normal	●
41	Safeguard	Normal	Status	—	—	25	2 Allies	—
45	Dragon Dance	Dragon	Status	—	—	20	Self	—
51	Outrage	Dragon	Physical	120	100	5	1 Random	—
55	Hyper Beam	Normal	Special	150	90	5	Normal	—

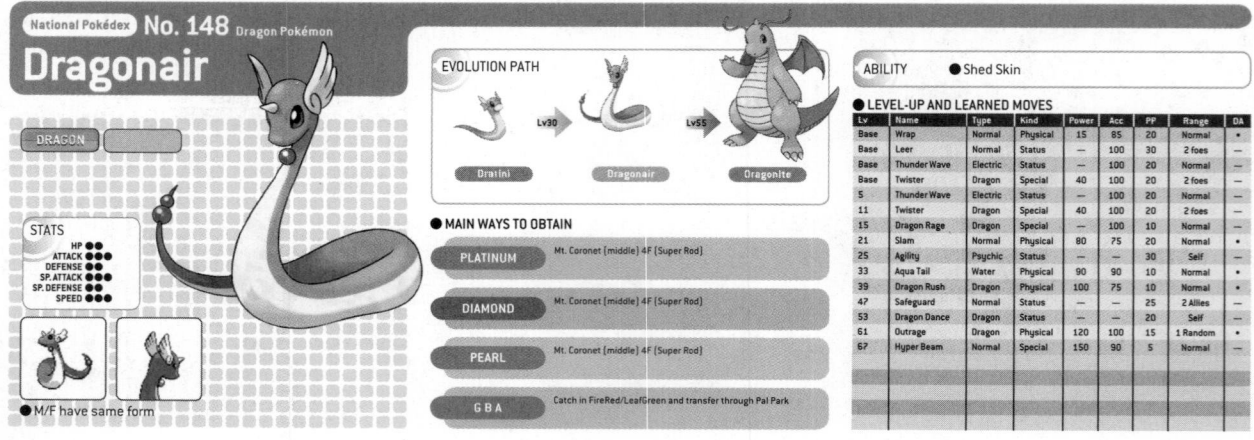

National Pokédex No. 148 Dragon Pokémon
Dragonair

DRAGON

STATS
- HP ●●●
- ATTACK ●●●
- DEFENSE ●●●
- SP. ATTACK ●●●
- SP. DEFENSE ●●●
- SPEED ●●●

● M/F have same form

EVOLUTION PATH

Dratini → Lv30 → Dragonair → Lv55 → Dragonite

● MAIN WAYS TO OBTAIN

PLATINUM	Mt. Coronet (middle) 4F (Super Rod)
DIAMOND	Mt. Coronet (middle) 4F (Super Rod)
PEARL	Mt. Coronet (middle) 4F (Super Rod)
G B A	Catch in FireRed/LeafGreen and transfer through Pal Park

ABILITY ● Shed Skin

● LEVEL-UP AND LEARNED MOVES

Lv	Name	Type	Kind	Power	Acc	PP	Range	DA
Base	Wrap	Normal	Physical	15	85	20	Normal	●
Base	Leer	Normal	Status	—	100	30	2 foes	—
Base	Thunder Wave	Electric	Status	—	100	20	Normal	—
Base	Twister	Dragon	Special	40	100	20	2 foes	—
5	Thunder Wave	Electric	Status	—	100	20	Normal	—
11	Twister	Dragon	Special	40	100	20	2 foes	—
15	Dragon Rage	Dragon	Special	—	100	10	Normal	—
21	Slam	Normal	Physical	80	75	20	Normal	●
25	Agility	Psychic	Status	—	—	30	Self	—
33	Aqua Tail	Water	Physical	90	90	10	Normal	●
39	Dragon Rush	Dragon	Physical	100	75	10	Normal	●
47	Safeguard	Normal	Status	—	—	25	2 Allies	—
53	Dragon Dance	Dragon	Status	—	—	20	Self	—
61	Outrage	Dragon	Physical	120	100	15	1 Random	—
67	Hyper Beam	Normal	Special	150	90	5	Normal	—

National Pokédex No. 149 Dragon Pokémon
Dragonite

DRAGON FLYING

STATS
HP
ATTACK
DEFENSE
SP. ATTACK
SP. DEFENSE
SPEED

● M/F have same form

EVOLUTION PATH

Dratini — Lv30 → Dragonair — Lv55 → Dragonite

● MAIN WAYS TO OBTAIN

PLATINUM	Level up Dragonair to Lv55
DIAMOND	Level up Dragonair to Lv55
PEARL	Level up Dragonair to Lv55
G B A	Catch and evolve in FireRed/LeafGreen, and transfer through Pal Park

ABILITY ● Inner Focus

● LEVEL-UP AND LEARNED MOVES

Lv	Name	Type	Kind	Power	Acc	PP	Range	DA
Base	Fire Punch	Fire	Physical	75	100	15	Normal	•
Base	ThunderPunch	Electric	Physical	75	100	15	Normal	•
Base	Roost	Flying	Status	—	—	10	Self	•
Base	Wrap	Normal	Physical	15	85	20	Normal	•
Base	Leer	Normal	Status	—	100	30	2 foes	—
Base	Thunder Wave	Electric	Status	—	100	20	Normal	—
Base	Twister	Dragon	Special	40	100	20	2 foes	—
5	Thunder Wave	Electric	Status	—	100	20	Normal	—
11	Twister	Dragon	Special	40	100	20	2 foes	—
15	Dragon Rage	Dragon	Special	—	100	10	Normal	—
21	Slam	Normal	Physical	80	75	20	Normal	—
25	Agility	Psychic	Status	—	—	30	Self	—
33	Aqua Tail	Water	Physical	90	90	10	Normal	—
39	Dragon Rush	Dragon	Physical	100	75	10	Normal	—
47	Safeguard	Normal	Status	—	—	25	2 Allies	—
53	Dragon Dance	Dragon	Status	—	—	20	Self	—
55	Wing Attack	Flying	Physical	60	100	35	Normal	—
64	Outrage	Dragon	Physical	120	100	15	1 Random	—
73	Hyper Beam	Normal	Special	150	90	5	Normal	—

National Pokédex No. 150 Genetic Pokémon
Mewtwo

PSYCHIC

STATS
HP
ATTACK
DEFENSE
SP. ATTACK
SP. DEFENSE
SPEED

● Gender unknown

EVOLUTION PATH

Does not evolve

● MAIN WAYS TO OBTAIN

PLATINUM	
DIAMOND	
PEARL	
G B A	Catch in FireRed/LeafGreen and transfer through Pal Park

ABILITY ● Pressure

● LEVEL-UP AND LEARNED MOVES

Lv	Name	Type	Kind	Power	Acc	PP	Range	DA
Base	Confusion	Psychic	Special	50	100	25	Normal	—
Base	Disable	Normal	Status	—	80	20	Normal	—
8	Barrier	Psychic	Status	—	—	30	Self	—
15	Swift	Normal	Special	60	—	20	2 foes	—
22	Future Sight	Psychic	Special	80	90	15	Normal	—
29	Psych Up	Normal	Status	—	—	10	Normal	—
36	Miracle Eye	Psychic	Status	—	—	40	Normal	—
43	Mist	Ice	Status	—	—	30	2 Allies	—
50	Psycho Cut	Psychic	Physical	70	100	20	Normal	—
57	Amnesia	Psychic	Status	—	—	20	Self	—
64	Power Swap	Psychic	Status	—	—	10	Normal	—
64	Guard Swap	Psychic	Status	—	—	10	Normal	—
71	Psychic	Psychic	Special	90	100	10	Normal	—
79	Me First	Normal	Status	—	—	20	DoM	—
86	Recover	Normal	Status	—	—	10	Self	—
93	Safeguard	Normal	Status	—	—	25	2 Allies	—
100	Aura Sphere	Fighting	Special	90	—	20	Normal	—

National Pokédex No. 151 New Species Pokémon
Mew

PSYCHIC

STATS
HP
ATTACK
DEFENSE
SP. ATTACK
SP. DEFENSE
SPEED

● Gender unknown

EVOLUTION PATH

Does not evolve

● MAIN WAYS TO OBTAIN

PLATINUM	After you've met the requirements and gotten Mew in trade from Hayley in My Pokémon Ranch, then transferred it to Pokémon Diamond/Pearl, transfer it again to Pokémon Platinum
DIAMOND	Meet the requirements and receive in trade from Hayley in My Pokémon Ranch
PEARL	Meet the requirements and receive in trade from Hayley in My Pokémon Ranch
G B A	Acquire in any of the GBA-series Pokémon games and transfer through Pal Park. Cannot be obtained through regular gameplay.

Only available through distribution at special events and not through regular gameplay. Check Pokémon.com for the latest news on how to catch this Pokémon.

ABILITY ● Synchronize

● LEVEL-UP AND LEARNED MOVES

Lv	Name	Type	Kind	Power	Acc	PP	Range	DA
Base	Pound	Normal	Physical	40	100	35	Normal	•
Base	Status	Normal	Status	—	—	10	Normal	—
10	Mega Punch	Normal	Physical	80	85	20	Normal	—
20	Metronome	Normal	Status	—	—	10	DoM	—
30	Psychic	Psychic	Special	90	100	10	Normal	—
40	Barrier	Psychic	Status	—	—	30	Self	—
50	AncientPower	Rock	Special	60	100	5	Normal	—
60	Amnesia	Psychic	Status	—	—	20	Self	—
70	Me First	Normal	Status	—	—	20	DoM	—
80	Baton Pass	Normal	Status	—	—	40	Self	—
90	Nasty Plot	Dark	Status	—	—	20	Self	—
100	Aura Sphere	Fighting	Special	90	—	20	Normal	—

National Pokédex No. 152 Leaf Pokémon
Chikorita

GRASS

STATS
HP
ATTACK
DEFENSE
SP. ATTACK
SP. DEFENSE
SPEED

● M/F have same form

EVOLUTION PATH

Chikorita — Lv16 → Bayleef — Lv32 → Meganium

● MAIN WAYS TO OBTAIN

PLATINUM	
DIAMOND	
PEARL	
G B A	Receive in Emerald and transfer through Pal Park

ABILITY ● Overgrow

● LEVEL-UP AND LEARNED MOVES

Lv	Name	Type	Kind	Power	Acc	PP	Range	DA
Base	Tackle	Normal	Physical	35	95	35	Normal	•
Base	Growl	Normal	Status	—	100	40	2 foes	—
6	Razor Leaf	Grass	Physical	55	95	25	2 foes	—
9	PoisonPowder	Poison	Status	—	75	35	Normal	—
12	Synthesis	Grass	Status	—	—	5	Self	—
17	Reflect	Psychic	Status	—	—	20	2 Allies	—
20	Magical Leaf	Grass	Special	60	—	20	Normal	—
23	Natural Gift	Normal	Physical	—	100	15	Normal	—
28	Sweet Scent	Normal	Status	—	100	20	2 foes	—
31	Light Screen	Psychic	Status	—	—	30	2 Allies	—
34	Body Slam	Normal	Physical	85	100	15	Normal	•
39	Safeguard	Normal	Status	—	—	25	2 Allies	—
42	Aromatherapy	Grass	Status	—	—	5	All	—
45	SolarBeam	Grass	Special	120	100	10	Normal	—

152
CHIKORITA

No. 153 Bayleef — Leaf Pokémon

National Pokédex No. 153

GRASS

STATS
- HP
- ATTACK
- DEFENSE
- SP. ATTACK
- SP. DEFENSE
- SPEED

● M/F have same form

EVOLUTION PATH

Chikorita —Lv16→ Bayleef —Lv32→ Meganium

● MAIN WAYS TO OBTAIN

PLATINUM

DIAMOND

PEARL

GBA — Receive and evolve in Emerald, and transfer through Pal Park

ABILITY ● Overgrow

● LEVEL-UP AND LEARNED MOVES

Lv	Name	Type	Kind	Power	Acc	PP	Range	DA
Base	Tackle	Normal	Physical	35	95	35	Normal	—
Base	Growl	Normal	Status	—	100	40	2 foes	—
Base	Razor Leaf	Grass	Physical	55	95	25	2 foes	—
Base	PoisonPowder	Poison	Status	—	75	35	Normal	—
6	Razor Leaf	Grass	Physical	55	95	25	2 foes	—
9	PoisonPowder	Poison	Status	—	75	35	Normal	—
12	Synthesis	Grass	Status	—	—	5	Self	—
18	Reflect	Psychic	Status	—	—	20	2 Allies	—
22	Magical Leaf	Grass	Special	60	—	20	Normal	—
26	Natural Gift	Normal	Physical	—	100	15	Normal	—
32	Sweet Scent	Normal	Status	—	100	20	2 foes	—
36	Light Screen	Psychic	Status	—	—	30	2 Allies	—
40	Body Slam	Normal	Physical	85	100	15	Normal	•
46	Safeguard	Normal	Status	—	—	25	2 Allies	—
50	Aromatherapy	Grass	Status	—	—	5	All	—
54	SolarBeam	Grass	Special	120	100	10	Normal	—

No. 154 Meganium — Herb Pokémon

National Pokédex No. 154

GRASS

STATS
- HP
- ATTACK
- DEFENSE
- SP. ATTACK
- SP. DEFENSE
- SPEED

● Male form ● Female form

EVOLUTION PATH

Chikorita —Lv16→ Bayleef —Lv32→ Meganium

● MAIN WAYS TO OBTAIN

PLATINUM

DIAMOND

PEARL

GBA — Receive and evolve in Emerald, and transfer through Pal Park

ABILITY ● Overgrow

● LEVEL-UP AND LEARNED MOVES

Lv	Name	Type	Kind	Power	Acc	PP	Range	DA
Base	Tackle	Normal	Physical	35	95	35	Normal	•
Base	Growl	Normal	Status	—	100	40	2 foes	—
Base	Razor Leaf	Grass	Physical	55	95	25	2 foes	—
Base	PoisonPowder	Poison	Status	—	75	35	Normal	—
6	Razor Leaf	Grass	Physical	55	95	25	2 foes	—
9	PoisonPowder	Poison	Status	—	75	35	Normal	—
12	Synthesis	Grass	Status	—	—	5	Self	—
18	Reflect	Psychic	Status	—	—	20	2 Allies	—
22	Magical Leaf	Grass	Special	60	—	20	Normal	—
26	Natural Gift	Normal	Physical	—	100	15	Normal	—
32	Petal Dance	Grass	Special	90	100	20	1 Random	•
34	Sweet Scent	Normal	Status	—	100	20	2 foes	—
40	Light Screen	Psychic	Status	—	—	30	2 Allies	—
46	Body Slam	Normal	Physical	85	100	15	Normal	•
54	Safeguard	Normal	Status	—	—	25	2 Allies	—
60	Aromatherapy	Grass	Status	—	—	5	All	—
66	SolarBeam	Grass	Special	120	100	10	Normal	—

No. 155 Cyndaquil — Fire Mouse Pokémon

National Pokédex No. 155

FIRE

STATS
- HP
- ATTACK
- DEFENSE
- SP. ATTACK
- SP. DEFENSE
- SPEED

● M/F have same form

EVOLUTION PATH

Cyndaquil —Lv14→ Quilava —Lv36→ Typhlosion

● MAIN WAYS TO OBTAIN

PLATINUM

DIAMOND

PEARL

GBA — Receive in Emerald and transfer through Pal Park

ABILITY ● Blaze

● LEVEL-UP AND LEARNED MOVES

Lv	Name	Type	Kind	Power	Acc	PP	Range	DA
Base	Tackle	Normal	Physical	35	95	35	Normal	•
Base	Leer	Normal	Status	—	100	30	2 foes	—
4	SmokeScreen	Normal	Status	—	100	20	Normal	—
10	Ember	Fire	Special	40	100	25	Normal	—
13	Quick Attack	Normal	Physical	40	100	30	Normal	•
19	Flame Wheel	Fire	Physical	60	100	25	Normal	•
22	Defense Curl	Normal	Status	—	—	40	Self	—
28	Swift	Normal	Special	60	—	20	2 foes	—
31	Lava Plume	Fire	Special	80	100	15	2 foes 1 Ally	—
37	Flamethrower	Fire	Special	95	100	15	Normal	—
40	Rollout	Rock	Physical	30	90	20	Normal	•
46	Double-Edge	Normal	Physical	120	100	15	Normal	•
49	Eruption	Fire	Special	150	100	5	2 foes	—

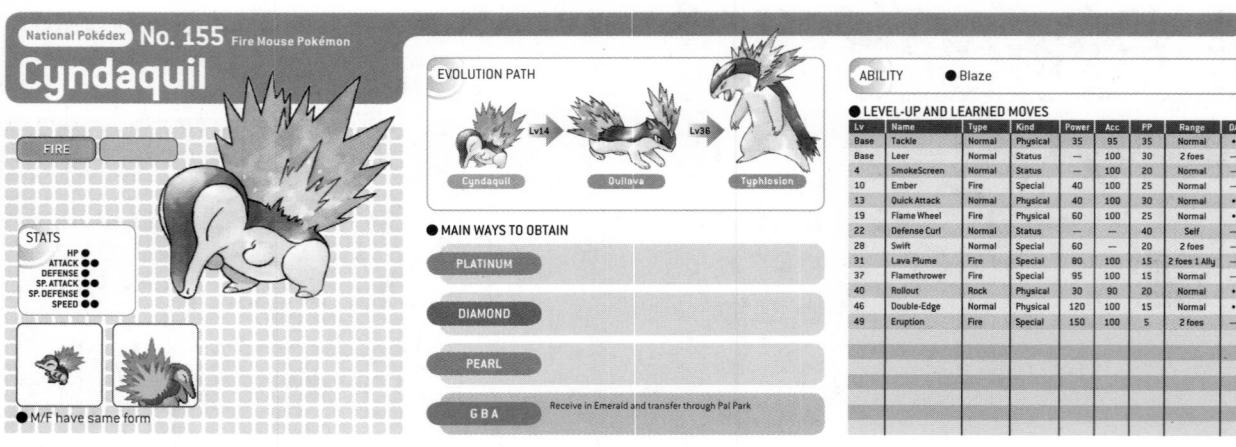

No. 156 Quilava — Volcano Pokémon

National Pokédex No. 156

FIRE

STATS
- HP
- ATTACK
- DEFENSE
- SP. ATTACK
- SP. DEFENSE
- SPEED

● M/F have same form

EVOLUTION PATH

Cyndaquil —Lv14→ Quilava —Lv36→ Typhlosion

● MAIN WAYS TO OBTAIN

PLATINUM

DIAMOND

PEARL

GBA — Receive and evolve in Emerald, and transfer through Pal Park

ABILITY ● Blaze

● LEVEL-UP AND LEARNED MOVES

Lv	Name	Type	Kind	Power	Acc	PP	Range	DA
Base	Tackle	Normal	Physical	35	95	35	Normal	•
Base	Leer	Normal	Status	—	100	30	2 foes	—
Base	SmokeScreen	Normal	Status	—	100	20	Normal	—
4	SmokeScreen	Normal	Status	—	100	20	Normal	—
10	Ember	Fire	Special	40	100	25	Normal	—
13	Quick Attack	Normal	Physical	40	100	30	Normal	•
20	Flame Wheel	Fire	Physical	60	100	25	Normal	•
24	Defense Curl	Normal	Status	—	—	40	Self	—
31	Swift	Normal	Special	60	—	20	2 foes	—
35	Lava Plume	Fire	Special	80	100	15	2 foes 1 Ally	—
42	Flamethrower	Fire	Special	95	100	15	Normal	—
46	Rollout	Rock	Physical	30	90	20	Normal	•
53	Double-Edge	Normal	Physical	120	100	15	Normal	•
57	Eruption	Fire	Special	150	100	5	2 foes	—

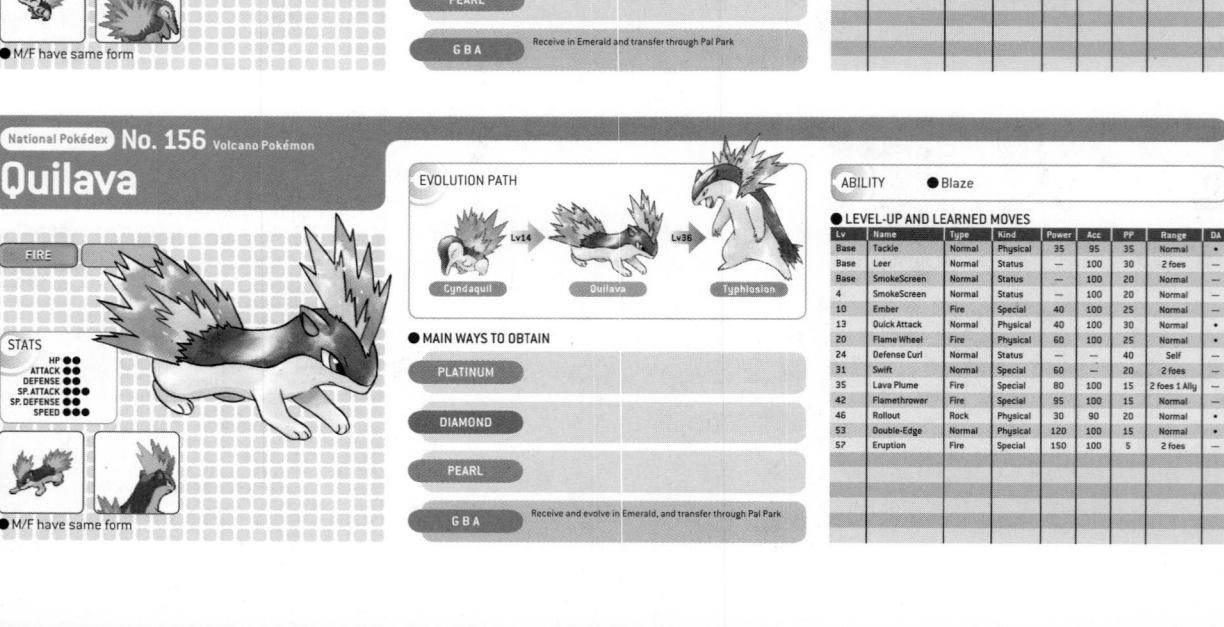

No. 157 Typhlosion

National Pokédex — Volcano Pokémon

FIRE

STATS
- HP ●●●
- ATTACK ●●●
- DEFENSE ●●●
- SP. ATTACK ●●●●
- SP. DEFENSE ●●●
- SPEED ●●●●

● M/F have same form

EVOLUTION PATH

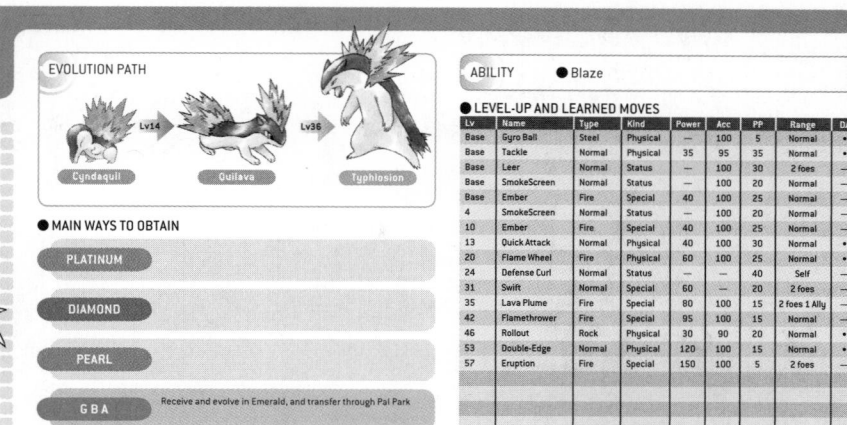

Cyndaquil → Lv14 → Quilava → Lv36 → Typhlosion

● MAIN WAYS TO OBTAIN
- PLATINUM
- DIAMOND
- PEARL
- G B A — Receive and evolve in Emerald, and transfer through Pal Park

ABILITY ● Blaze

● LEVEL-UP AND LEARNED MOVES

Lv	Name	Type	Kind	Power	Acc	PP	Range	DA
Base	Gyro Ball	Steel	Physical	—	100	5	Normal	—
Base	Tackle	Normal	Physical	35	95	35	Normal	•
Base	Leer	Normal	Status	—	100	30	2 foes	—
Base	SmokeScreen	Normal	Status	—	100	20	Normal	—
Base	Ember	Fire	Special	40	100	25	Normal	•
4	SmokeScreen	Normal	Status	—	100	20	Normal	—
10	Ember	Fire	Special	40	100	25	Normal	•
13	Quick Attack	Normal	Physical	40	100	30	Normal	•
20	Flame Wheel	Fire	Physical	60	100	25	Normal	•
24	Defense Curl	Normal	Status	—	—	40	Self	—
31	Swift	Normal	Special	60	—	20	2 foes	•
35	Lava Plume	Fire	Special	80	100	15	2 foes 1 Ally	•
42	Flamethrower	Fire	Special	95	100	15	Normal	•
46	Rollout	Rock	Physical	30	90	20	Normal	•
53	Double-Edge	Normal	Physical	120	100	15	Normal	•
57	Eruption	Fire	Special	150	100	5	2 foes	—

No. 158 Totodile

National Pokédex — Big Jaw Pokémon

WATER

STATS
- HP ●●
- ATTACK ●●
- DEFENSE ●●
- SP. ATTACK ●●
- SP. DEFENSE ●●
- SPEED ●●

● M/F have same form

EVOLUTION PATH

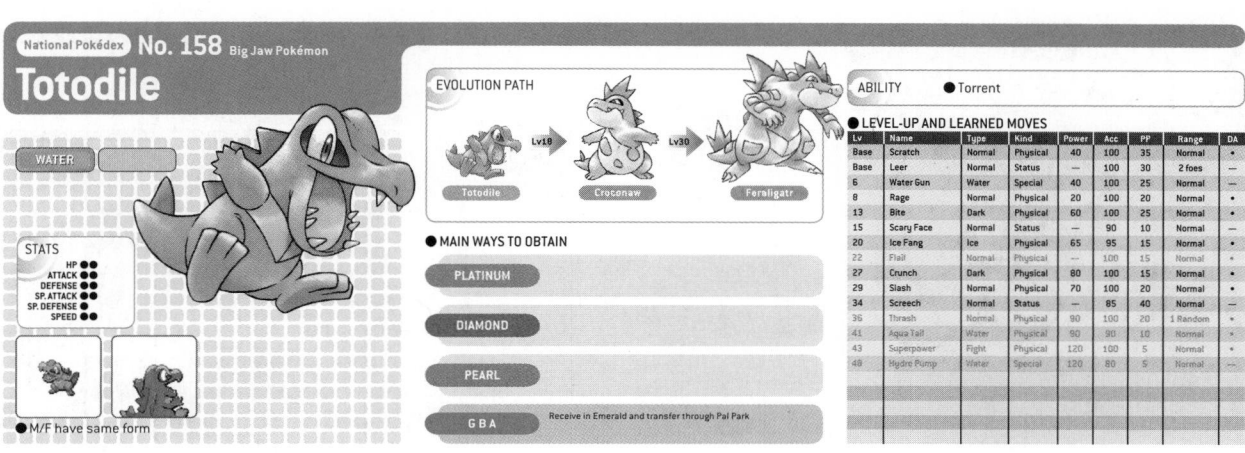

Totodile → Lv18 → Croconaw → Lv30 → Feraligatr

● MAIN WAYS TO OBTAIN
- PLATINUM
- DIAMOND
- PEARL
- G B A — Receive in Emerald and transfer through Pal Park

ABILITY ● Torrent

● LEVEL-UP AND LEARNED MOVES

Lv	Name	Type	Kind	Power	Acc	PP	Range	DA
Base	Scratch	Normal	Physical	40	100	35	Normal	•
Base	Leer	Normal	Status	—	100	30	2 foes	—
6	Water Gun	Water	Special	40	100	25	Normal	•
8	Rage	Normal	Physical	20	100	20	Normal	•
13	Bite	Dark	Physical	60	100	25	Normal	•
15	Scary Face	Normal	Status	—	90	10	Normal	—
20	Ice Fang	Ice	Physical	65	95	15	Normal	•
22	Flail	Normal	Physical	—	100	15	Normal	•
27	Crunch	Dark	Physical	80	100	15	Normal	•
29	Slash	Normal	Physical	70	100	20	Normal	•
34	Screech	Normal	Status	—	85	40	Normal	—
36	Thrash	Normal	Physical	90	100	20	1 Random	•
41	Aqua Tail	Water	Physical	90	90	10	Normal	•
43	Superpower	Fight	Physical	120	100	5	Normal	•
48	Hydro Pump	Water	Special	120	80	5	Normal	—

No. 159 Croconaw

National Pokédex — Big Jaw Pokémon

WATER

STATS
- HP ●●●
- ATTACK ●●●
- DEFENSE ●●●
- SP. ATTACK ●●
- SP. DEFENSE ●●
- SPEED ●●

● M/F have same form

EVOLUTION PATH

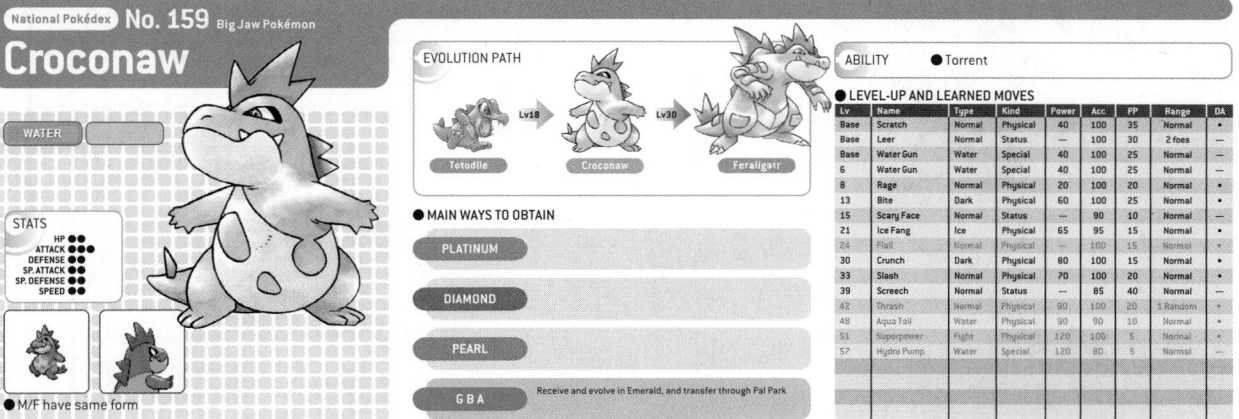

Totodile → Lv18 → Croconaw → Lv30 → Feraligatr

● MAIN WAYS TO OBTAIN
- PLATINUM
- DIAMOND
- PEARL
- G B A — Receive and evolve in Emerald, and transfer through Pal Park

ABILITY ● Torrent

● LEVEL-UP AND LEARNED MOVES

Lv	Name	Type	Kind	Power	Acc	PP	Range	DA
Base	Scratch	Normal	Physical	40	100	35	Normal	•
Base	Leer	Normal	Status	—	100	30	2 foes	—
Base	Water Gun	Water	Special	40	100	25	Normal	•
6	Water Gun	Water	Special	40	100	25	Normal	•
8	Rage	Normal	Physical	20	100	20	Normal	•
13	Bite	Dark	Physical	60	100	25	Normal	•
15	Scary Face	Normal	Status	—	90	10	Normal	—
21	Ice Fang	Ice	Physical	65	95	15	Normal	•
24	Flail	Normal	Physical	—	100	15	Normal	•
30	Crunch	Dark	Physical	80	100	15	Normal	•
33	Slash	Normal	Physical	70	100	20	Normal	•
39	Screech	Normal	Status	—	85	40	Normal	—
42	Thrash	Normal	Physical	90	100	20	1 Random	•
48	Aqua Tail	Water	Physical	90	90	10	Normal	•
51	Superpower	Fight	Physical	120	100	5	Normal	•
57	Hydro Pump	Water	Special	120	80	5	Normal	—

No. 160 Feraligatr

National Pokédex — Big Jaw Pokémon

WATER

STATS
- HP ●●●
- ATTACK ●●●
- DEFENSE ●●●
- SP. ATTACK ●●
- SP. DEFENSE ●●
- SPEED ●●●

● M/F have same form

EVOLUTION PATH

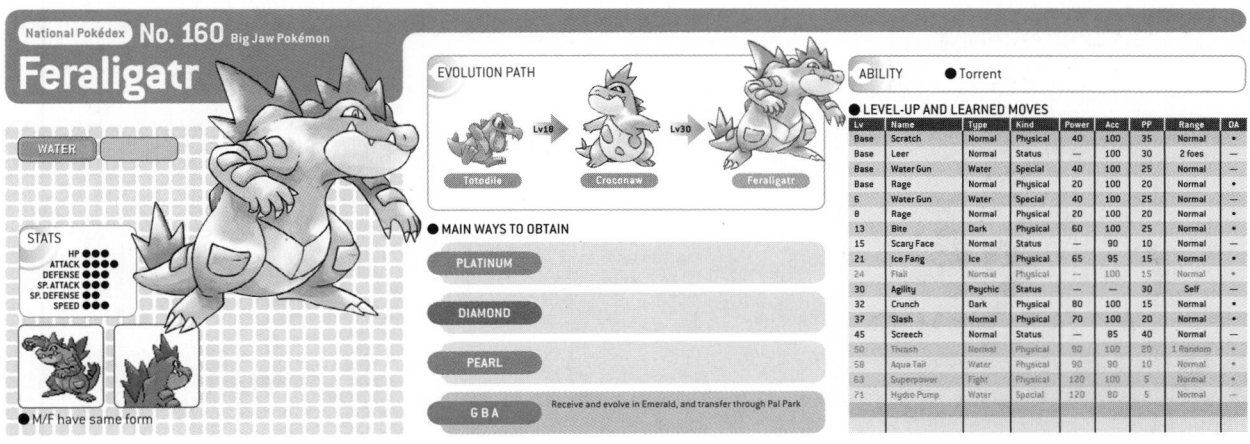

Totodile → Lv18 → Croconaw → Lv30 → Feraligatr

● MAIN WAYS TO OBTAIN
- PLATINUM
- DIAMOND
- PEARL
- G B A — Receive and evolve in Emerald, and transfer through Pal Park

ABILITY ● Torrent

● LEVEL-UP AND LEARNED MOVES

Lv	Name	Type	Kind	Power	Acc	PP	Range	DA
Base	Scratch	Normal	Physical	40	100	35	Normal	•
Base	Leer	Normal	Status	—	100	30	2 foes	—
Base	Water Gun	Water	Special	40	100	25	Normal	•
Base	Rage	Normal	Physical	20	100	20	Normal	•
6	Water Gun	Water	Special	40	100	25	Normal	•
8	Rage	Normal	Physical	20	100	20	Normal	•
13	Bite	Dark	Physical	60	100	25	Normal	•
15	Scary Face	Normal	Status	—	90	10	Normal	—
21	Ice Fang	Ice	Physical	65	95	15	Normal	•
24	Flail	Normal	Physical	—	100	15	Normal	•
30	Agility	Psychic	Status	—	—	30	Self	—
32	Crunch	Dark	Physical	80	100	15	Normal	•
37	Slash	Normal	Physical	70	100	20	Normal	•
45	Screech	Normal	Status	—	85	40	Normal	—
50	Thrash	Normal	Physical	90	100	20	1 Random	•
58	Aqua Tail	Water	Physical	90	90	10	Normal	•
63	Superpower	Fight	Physical	120	100	5	Normal	•
71	Hydro Pump	Water	Special	120	80	5	Normal	—

160 FERALIGATR

Sentret

National Pokédex No. 161 Scout Pokémon

NORMAL

● M/F have same form

STATS
- HP ●
- ATTACK ●●
- DEFENSE ●
- SP.ATTACK ●
- SP.DEFENSE ●
- SPEED ●

EVOLUTION PATH

Sentret → Lv15 → Furret

● MAIN WAYS TO OBTAIN

PLATINUM	Route 202 (use Poké Radar)
DIAMOND	Route 202 (use Poké Radar)
PEARL	Route 202 (use Poké Radar)
GBA	Catch in FireRed/LeafGreen and transfer through Pal Park

ABILITY ● Run Away ● Keen Eye

● LEVEL-UP AND LEARNED MOVES

Lv	Name	Type	Kind	Power	Acc	PP	Range	DA
Base	Scratch	Normal	Physical	40	100	35	Normal	●
Base	Foresight	Normal	Status	—	—	40	Normal	—
4	Defense Curl	Normal	Status	—	—	40	Self	—
7	Quick Attack	Normal	Physical	40	100	30	Normal	●
13	Fury Swipes	Normal	Physical	18	80	15	Normal	●
16	Helping Hand	Normal	Status	—	—	20	1 Ally	—
19	Follow Me	Normal	Status	—	—	20	Self	—
25	Slam	Normal	Physical	80	75	20	Normal	●
28	Rest	Psychic	Status	—	—	10	Self	—
31	Sucker Punch	Dark	Physical	80	100	5	Normal	●
36	Amnesia	Normal	Status	—	—	20	Self	—
39	Baton Pass	Normal	Status	—	—	40	Self	—
42	Me First	Normal	Status	—	—	20	Last move	—
47	Hyper Voice	Normal	Special	90	100	10	2 foes	—

Furret

National Pokédex No. 162 Long Body Pokémon

NORMAL

● M/F have same form

STATS
- HP ●●●
- ATTACK ●●●
- DEFENSE ●●
- SP.ATTACK ●●
- SP.DEFENSE ●●
- SPEED ●●●

EVOLUTION PATH

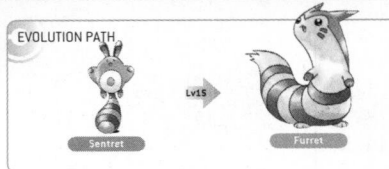

Sentret → Lv15 → Furret

● MAIN WAYS TO OBTAIN

PLATINUM	Level up Sentret to Lv15
DIAMOND	Level up Sentret to Lv15
PEARL	Level up Sentret to Lv15
GBA	Catch and evolve in FireRed/LeafGreen, and transfer through Pal Park

ABILITY ● Run Away ● Keen Eye

● LEVEL-UP AND LEARNED MOVES

Lv	Name	Type	Kind	Power	Acc	PP	Range	DA
Base	Scratch	Normal	Physical	40	100	35	Normal	●
Base	Foresight	Normal	Status	—	—	40	Normal	—
Base	Defense Curl	Normal	Status	—	—	40	Self	—
Base	Quick Attack	Normal	Physical	40	100	30	Normal	●
4	Defense Curl	Normal	Status	—	—	40	Self	—
7	Quick Attack	Normal	Physical	40	100	30	Normal	●
13	Fury Swipes	Normal	Physical	18	80	15	Normal	●
17	Helping Hand	Normal	Status	—	—	20	1 Ally	—
21	Follow Me	Normal	Status	—	—	20	Self	—
28	Slam	Normal	Physical	80	75	20	Normal	●
32	Rest	Psychic	Status	—	—	10	Self	—
36	Sucker Punch	Dark	Physical	80	100	5	Normal	●
42	Amnesia	Normal	Status	—	—	20	Self	—
46	Baton Pass	Normal	Status	—	—	40	Self	—
50	Me First	Normal	Status	—	—	20	Last move	—
56	Hyper Voice	Normal	Special	90	100	10	2 foes	—

Hoothoot

National Pokédex No. 163 Owl Pokémon

NORMAL FLYING

● M/F have same form

STATS
- HP ●●
- ATTACK ●
- DEFENSE ●
- SP.ATTACK ●
- SP.DEFENSE ●●
- SPEED ●●

EVOLUTION PATH

Hoothoot → Lv20 → Noctowl

● MAIN WAYS TO OBTAIN

PLATINUM	Eterna Forest (night only)
DIAMOND	Route 210
PEARL	Route 210
GBA	Catch in Emerald and transfer through Pal Park

ABILITY ● Insomnia ● Keen Eye

● LEVEL-UP AND LEARNED MOVES

Lv	Name	Type	Kind	Power	Acc	PP	Range	DA
Base	Tackle	Normal	Physical	35	95	35	Normal	●
Base	Growl	Normal	Status	—	100	40	2 foes	—
Base	Foresight	Normal	Status	—	—	40	Normal	—
5	Hypnosis	Psychic	Status	—	60	20	Normal	—
9	Peck	Flying	Physical	35	100	35	Normal	●
13	Uproar	Normal	Special	50	100	10	1 Random	—
17	Reflect	Psychic	Status	—	—	20	2 Allies	—
21	Confusion	Psychic	Special	50	100	25	Normal	—
25	Take Down	Normal	Physical	90	85	20	Normal	●
29	Air Slash	Flying	Special	75	95	20	Normal	—
33	Zen Headbutt	Psychic	Physical	80	90	15	Normal	●
37	Extrasensory	Psychic	Special	80	100	30	Normal	—
41	Psycho Shift	Psychic	Status	—	90	10	Normal	—
45	Roost	Flying	Status	—	—	10	Self	—
49	Dream Eater	Psychic	Special	100	100	15	Normal	—

Noctowl

National Pokédex No. 164 Owl Pokémon

NORMAL FLYING

● M/F have same form

STATS
- HP ●●●
- ATTACK ●
- DEFENSE ●●
- SP.ATTACK ●●●
- SP.DEFENSE ●●●
- SPEED ●●●

EVOLUTION PATH

Hoothoot → Lv20 → Noctowl

● MAIN WAYS TO OBTAIN

PLATINUM	Route 210 (night only)
DIAMOND	Route 210
PEARL	Route 210
GBA	Catch and evolve in Emerald, and transfer through Pal Park

ABILITY ● Insomnia ● Keen Eye

● LEVEL-UP AND LEARNED MOVES

Lv	Name	Type	Kind	Power	Acc	PP	Range	DA
Base	Sky Attack	Flying	Physical	140	90	5	Normal	—
Base	Tackle	Normal	Physical	35	95	35	Normal	●
Base	Growl	Normal	Status	—	100	40	2 foes	—
Base	Foresight	Normal	Status	—	—	40	Normal	—
Base	Hypnosis	Psychic	Status	—	60	20	Normal	—
5	Hypnosis	Psychic	Status	—	60	20	Normal	—
9	Peck	Flying	Physical	35	100	35	Normal	●
13	Uproar	Normal	Special	50	100	10	1 Random	—
17	Reflect	Psychic	Status	—	—	20	2 Allies	—
22	Confusion	Psychic	Special	50	100	25	Normal	—
27	Take Down	Normal	Physical	90	85	20	Normal	●
32	Air Slash	Flying	Special	75	95	20	Normal	—
37	Zen Headbutt	Psychic	Physical	80	90	15	Normal	●
42	Extrasensory	Psychic	Special	80	100	30	Normal	—
47	Psycho Shift	Psychic	Status	—	90	10	Normal	—
52	Roost	Flying	Status	—	—	10	Self	—
57	Dream Eater	Psychic	Special	100	100	15	Normal	—

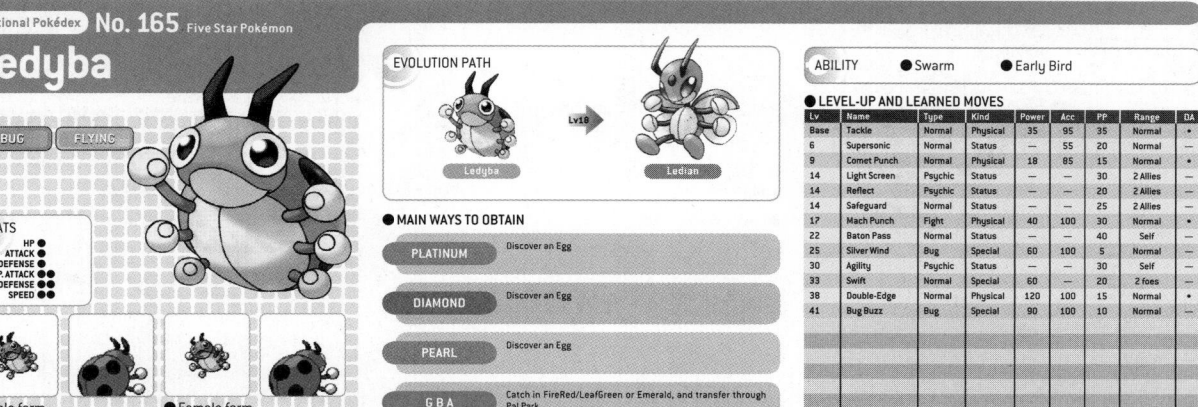

National Pokédex No. 165 — Five Star Pokémon
Ledyba

Types: BUG / FLYING

STATS: HP ●● / ATTACK ● / DEFENSE ● / SP. ATTACK ● / SP. DEFENSE ●● / SPEED ●●

● Male form ● Female form

EVOLUTION PATH

Ledyba → (Lv 18) → Ledian

● MAIN WAYS TO OBTAIN

PLATINUM	Discover an Egg
DIAMOND	Discover an Egg
PEARL	Discover an Egg
GBA	Catch in FireRed/LeafGreen or Emerald, and transfer through Pal Park

ABILITY ● Swarm ● Early Bird

● LEVEL-UP AND LEARNED MOVES

Lv	Name	Type	Kind	Power	Acc	PP	Range	DA
Base	Tackle	Normal	Physical	35	95	35	Normal	•
6	Supersonic	Normal	Status	—	55	20	Normal	—
9	Comet Punch	Normal	Physical	18	85	15	Normal	•
14	Light Screen	Psychic	Status	—	—	30	2 Allies	
14	Reflect	Psychic	Status	—	—	20	2 Allies	
14	Safeguard	Normal	Status	—	—	25	2 Allies	
17	Mach Punch	Fight	Physical	40	100	30	Normal	•
22	Baton Pass	Normal	Status	—	—	40	Self	
25	Silver Wind	Bug	Special	60	100	5	Normal	
30	Agility	Psychic	Status	—	—	30	Self	
33	Swift	Normal	Special	60	—	20	2 foes	
38	Double-Edge	Normal	Physical	120	100	15	Normal	•
41	Bug Buzz	Bug	Special	90	100	10	Normal	

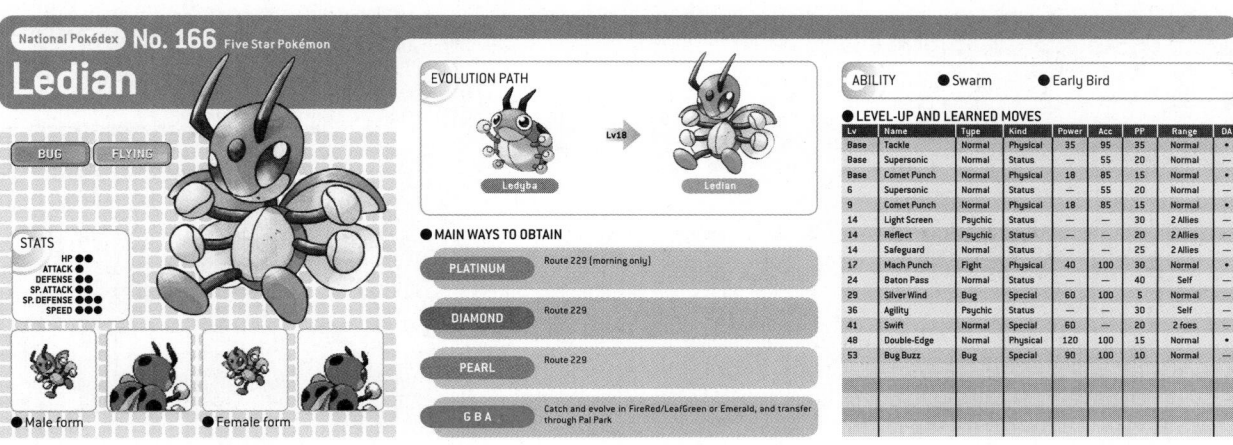

National Pokédex No. 166 — Five Star Pokémon
Ledian

Types: BUG / FLYING

STATS: HP ●● / ATTACK ●● / DEFENSE ● / SP. ATTACK ●● / SP. DEFENSE ●●● / SPEED ●●●

● Male form ● Female form

EVOLUTION PATH

Ledyba → (Lv 18) → Ledian

● MAIN WAYS TO OBTAIN

PLATINUM	Route 229 (morning only)
DIAMOND	Route 229
PEARL	Route 229
GBA	Catch and evolve in FireRed/LeafGreen or Emerald, and transfer through Pal Park

ABILITY ● Swarm ● Early Bird

● LEVEL-UP AND LEARNED MOVES

Lv	Name	Type	Kind	Power	Acc	PP	Range	DA
Base	Tackle	Normal	Physical	35	95	35	Normal	—
Base	Supersonic	Normal	Status	—	55	20	Normal	—
Base	Comet Punch	Normal	Physical	18	85	15	Normal	—
6	Supersonic	Normal	Status	—	55	20	Normal	—
9	Comet Punch	Normal	Physical	18	85	15	Normal	—
14	Light Screen	Psychic	Status	—	—	30	2 Allies	
14	Reflect	Psychic	Status	—	—	20	2 Allies	
14	Safeguard	Normal	Status	—	—	25	2 Allies	
17	Mach Punch	Fight	Physical	40	100	30	Normal	•
24	Baton Pass	Normal	Status	—	—	40	Self	
29	Silver Wind	Bug	Special	60	100	5	Normal	
36	Agility	Psychic	Status	—	—	30	Self	
41	Swift	Normal	Special	60	—	20	2 foes	
48	Double-Edge	Normal	Physical	120	100	15	Normal	•
53	Bug Buzz	Bug	Special	90	100	10	Normal	

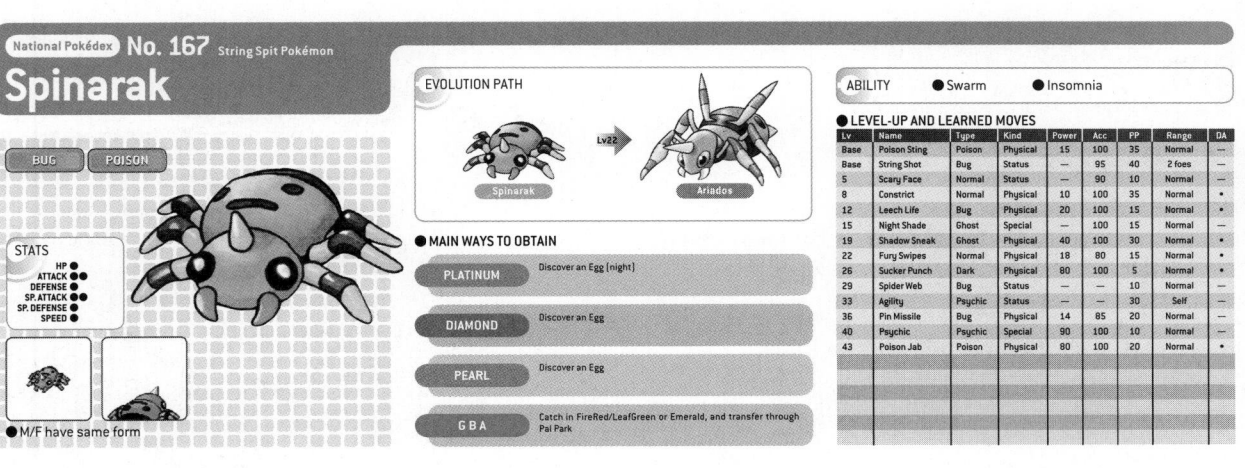

National Pokédex No. 167 — String Spit Pokémon
Spinarak

Types: BUG / POISON

STATS: HP ● / ATTACK ●● / DEFENSE ● / SP. ATTACK ● / SP. DEFENSE ● / SPEED ●

● M/F have same form

EVOLUTION PATH

Spinarak → (Lv 22) → Ariados

● MAIN WAYS TO OBTAIN

PLATINUM	Discover an Egg (night)
DIAMOND	Discover an Egg
PEARL	Discover an Egg
GBA	Catch in FireRed/LeafGreen or Emerald, and transfer through Pal Park

ABILITY ● Swarm ● Insomnia

● LEVEL-UP AND LEARNED MOVES

Lv	Name	Type	Kind	Power	Acc	PP	Range	DA
Base	Poison Sting	Poison	Physical	15	100	35	Normal	—
Base	String Shot	Bug	Status	—	95	40	2 foes	—
5	Scary Face	Normal	Status	—	90	10	Normal	—
8	Constrict	Normal	Physical	10	100	35	Normal	•
12	Leech Life	Bug	Physical	20	100	15	Normal	•
15	Night Shade	Ghost	Special	—	100	15	Normal	—
19	Shadow Sneak	Ghost	Physical	40	100	30	Normal	•
22	Fury Swipes	Normal	Physical	18	80	15	Normal	•
26	Sucker Punch	Dark	Physical	80	100	5	Normal	•
29	Spider Web	Bug	Status	—	—	10	Normal	—
33	Agility	Psychic	Status	—	—	30	Self	—
36	Pin Missile	Bug	Physical	14	85	20	Normal	•
40	Psychic	Psychic	Special	90	100	10	Normal	—
43	Poison Jab	Poison	Physical	80	100	20	Normal	•

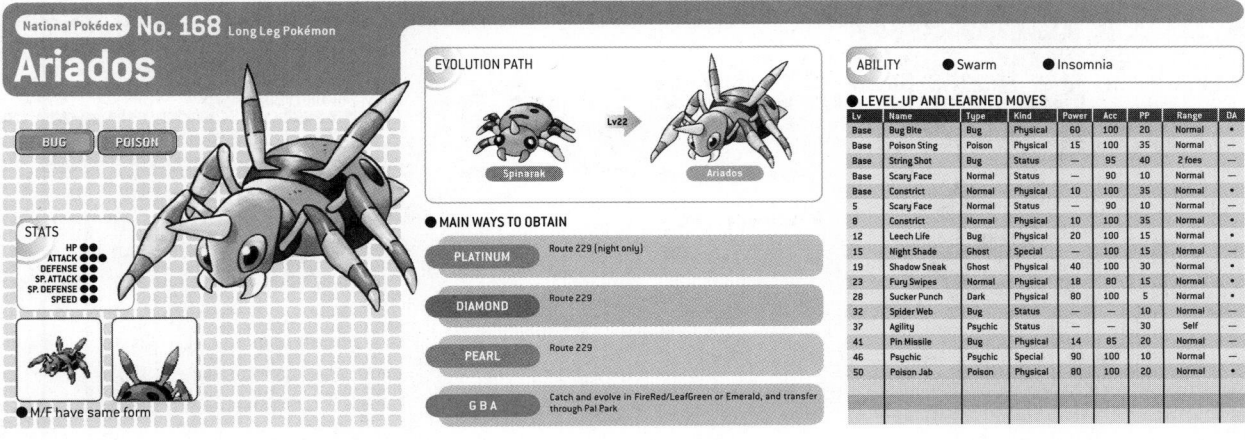

National Pokédex No. 168 — Long Leg Pokémon
Ariados

Types: BUG / POISON

STATS: HP ●● / ATTACK ●●● / DEFENSE ●● / SP. ATTACK ●● / SP. DEFENSE ●● / SPEED ●●

● M/F have same form

EVOLUTION PATH

Spinarak → (Lv 22) → Ariados

● MAIN WAYS TO OBTAIN

PLATINUM	Route 229 (night only)
DIAMOND	Route 229
PEARL	Route 229
GBA	Catch and evolve in FireRed/LeafGreen or Emerald, and transfer through Pal Park

ABILITY ● Swarm ● Insomnia

● LEVEL-UP AND LEARNED MOVES

Lv	Name	Type	Kind	Power	Acc	PP	Range	DA
Base	Bug Bite	Bug	Physical	60	100	20	Normal	•
Base	Poison Sting	Poison	Physical	15	100	35	Normal	—
Base	String Shot	Bug	Status	—	95	40	2 foes	—
Base	Scary Face	Normal	Status	—	90	10	Normal	—
Base	Constrict	Normal	Physical	10	100	35	Normal	•
5	Scary Face	Normal	Status	—	90	10	Normal	—
8	Constrict	Normal	Physical	10	100	35	Normal	•
12	Leech Life	Bug	Physical	20	100	15	Normal	•
15	Night Shade	Ghost	Special	—	100	15	Normal	—
19	Shadow Sneak	Ghost	Physical	40	100	30	Normal	•
23	Fury Swipes	Normal	Physical	18	80	15	Normal	•
28	Sucker Punch	Dark	Physical	80	100	5	Normal	•
32	Spider Web	Bug	Status	—	—	10	Normal	—
37	Agility	Psychic	Status	—	—	30	Self	—
41	Pin Missile	Bug	Physical	14	85	20	Normal	•
46	Psychic	Psychic	Special	90	100	10	Normal	—
50	Poison Jab	Poison	Physical	80	100	20	Normal	•

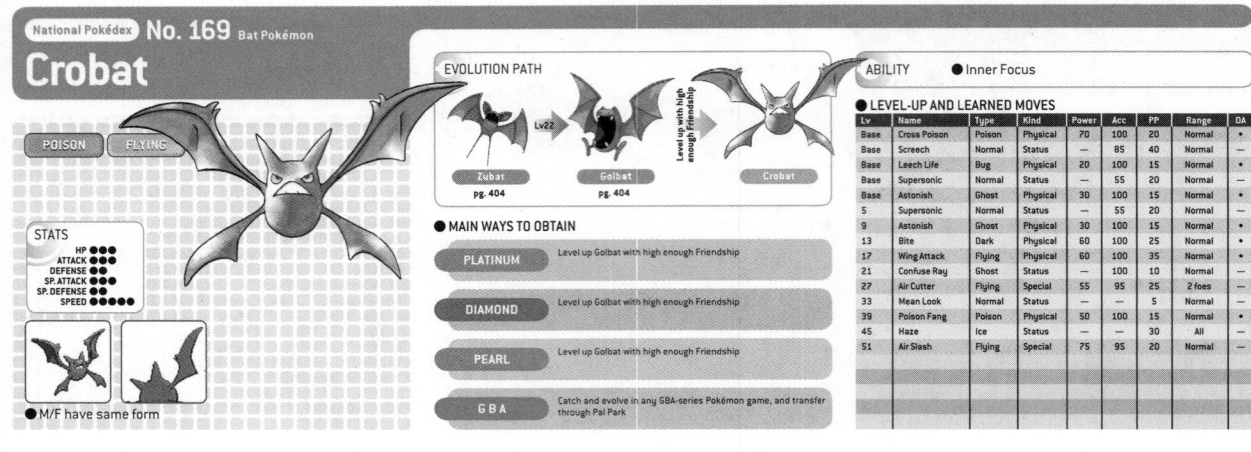

Crobat

POISON   FLYING

STATS
HP ●●●
ATTACK ●●●
DEFENSE ●●●
SP.ATTACK ●●●
SP.DEFENSE ●●●
SPEED ●●●●●

● M/F have same form

EVOLUTION PATH

Zubat pg. 404 → Lv22 → Golbat pg. 404 → Level up with high enough Friendship → Crobat

● MAIN WAYS TO OBTAIN

PLATINUM	Level up Golbat with high enough Friendship
DIAMOND	Level up Golbat with high enough Friendship
PEARL	Level up Golbat with high enough Friendship
G B A	Catch and evolve in any GBA-series Pokémon game, and transfer through Pal Park

ABILITY ● Inner Focus

● LEVEL-UP AND LEARNED MOVES

Lv	Name	Type	Kind	Power	Acc	PP	Range	DA
Base	Cross Poison	Poison	Physical	70	100	20	Normal	•
Base	Screech	Normal	Status	—	85	40	Normal	—
Base	Leech Life	Bug	Physical	20	100	15	Normal	—
Base	Supersonic	Normal	Status	—	55	20	Normal	—
Base	Astonish	Ghost	Physical	30	100	15	Normal	•
5	Supersonic	Normal	Status	—	55	20	Normal	—
9	Astonish	Ghost	Physical	30	100	15	Normal	•
13	Bite	Dark	Physical	60	100	25	Normal	•
17	Wing Attack	Flying	Physical	60	100	35	Normal	•
21	Confuse Ray	Ghost	Status	—	100	10	Normal	—
27	Air Cutter	Flying	Special	55	95	25	2 foes	—
33	Mean Look	Normal	Status	—	—	5	Normal	—
39	Poison Fang	Poison	Physical	50	100	15	Normal	•
45	Haze	Ice	Status	—	—	30	All	—
51	Air Slash	Flying	Special	75	95	20	Normal	—

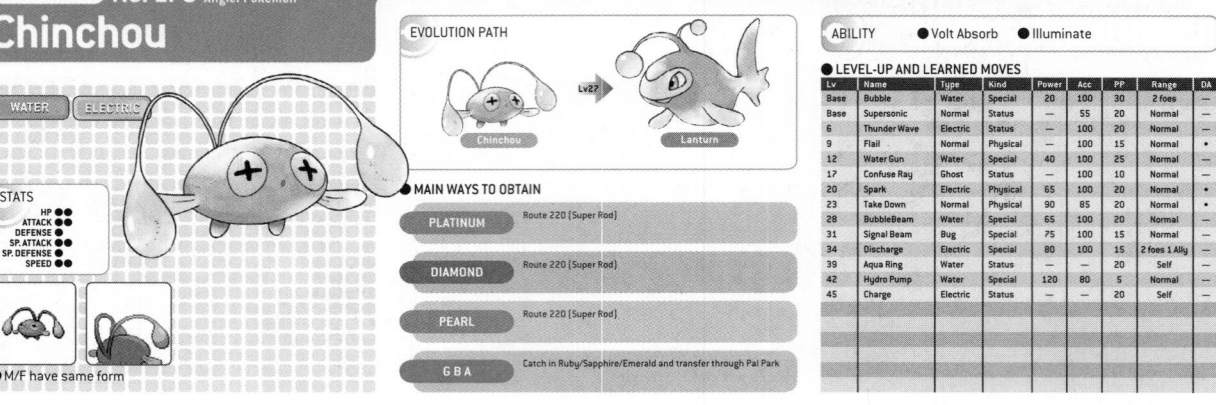

Chinchou

WATER   ELECTRIC

STATS
HP ●●
ATTACK ●
DEFENSE ●●
SP.ATTACK ●●
SP.DEFENSE ●●
SPEED ●●

● M/F have same form

EVOLUTION PATH

Chinchou → Lv27 → Lanturn

● MAIN WAYS TO OBTAIN

PLATINUM	Route 220 (Super Rod)
DIAMOND	Route 220 (Super Rod)
PEARL	Route 220 (Super Rod)
G B A	Catch in Ruby/Sapphire/Emerald and transfer through Pal Park

ABILITY ● Volt Absorb ● Illuminate

● LEVEL-UP AND LEARNED MOVES

Lv	Name	Type	Kind	Power	Acc	PP	Range	DA
Base	Bubble	Water	Special	20	100	30	2 foes	—
Base	Supersonic	Normal	Status	—	55	20	Normal	—
6	Thunder Wave	Electric	Status	—	100	20	Normal	—
9	Flail	Normal	Physical	—	100	15	Normal	•
12	Water Gun	Water	Special	40	100	25	Normal	—
17	Confuse Ray	Ghost	Status	—	100	10	Normal	—
20	Spark	Electric	Physical	65	100	20	Normal	•
23	Take Down	Normal	Physical	90	85	20	Normal	•
28	BubbleBeam	Water	Special	65	100	20	Normal	—
31	Signal Beam	Bug	Special	75	100	15	Normal	—
34	Discharge	Electric	Special	80	100	15	2 foes 1 Ally	—
39	Aqua Ring	Water	Status	—	—	20	Self	—
42	Hydro Pump	Water	Special	120	80	5	Normal	—
45	Charge	Electric	Status	—	—	20	Self	—

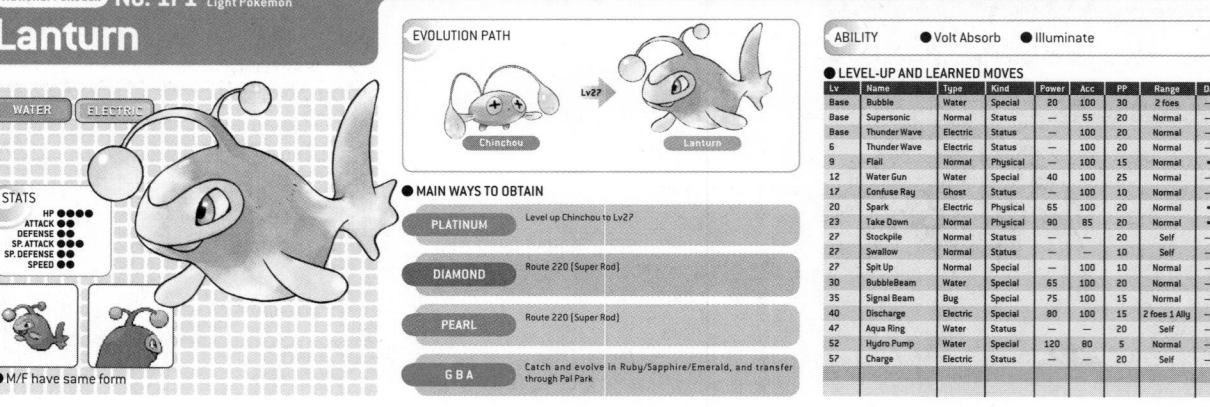

Lanturn

WATER   ELECTRIC

STATS
HP ●●●●
ATTACK ●●
DEFENSE ●●
SP.ATTACK ●●●
SP.DEFENSE ●●●
SPEED ●●

● M/F have same form

EVOLUTION PATH

Chinchou → Lv27 → Lanturn

● MAIN WAYS TO OBTAIN

PLATINUM	Level up Chinchou to Lv27
DIAMOND	Route 220 (Super Rod)
PEARL	Route 220 (Super Rod)
G B A	Catch and evolve in Ruby/Sapphire/Emerald, and transfer through Pal Park

ABILITY ● Volt Absorb ● Illuminate

● LEVEL-UP AND LEARNED MOVES

Lv	Name	Type	Kind	Power	Acc	PP	Range	DA
Base	Bubble	Water	Special	20	100	30	2 foes	—
Base	Supersonic	Normal	Status	—	55	20	Normal	—
Base	Thunder Wave	Electric	Status	—	100	20	Normal	—
6	Thunder Wave	Electric	Status	—	100	20	Normal	—
9	Flail	Normal	Physical	—	100	15	Normal	•
12	Water Gun	Water	Special	40	100	25	Normal	—
17	Confuse Ray	Ghost	Status	—	100	10	Normal	—
20	Spark	Electric	Physical	65	100	20	Normal	•
23	Take Down	Normal	Physical	90	85	20	Normal	•
27	Stockpile	Normal	Status	—	—	20	Self	—
27	Swallow	Normal	Status	—	—	10	Self	—
27	Spit Up	Normal	Special	—	100	10	Normal	—
30	BubbleBeam	Water	Special	65	100	20	Normal	—
35	Signal Beam	Bug	Special	75	100	15	Normal	—
40	Discharge	Electric	Special	80	100	15	2 foes 1 Ally	—
47	Aqua Ring	Water	Status	—	—	20	Self	—
52	Hydro Pump	Water	Special	120	80	5	Normal	—
57	Charge	Electric	Status	—	—	20	Self	—

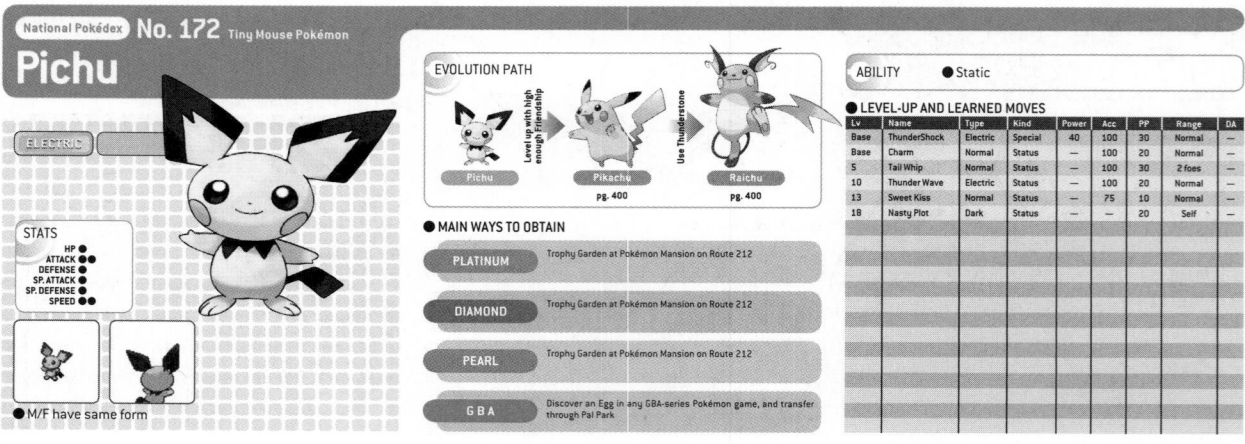

Pichu

ELECTRIC

STATS
HP ●
ATTACK ●
DEFENSE ●
SP.ATTACK ●
SP.DEFENSE ●
SPEED ●●

● M/F have same form

EVOLUTION PATH

Pichu → Level up with high enough Friendship → Pikachu pg. 400 → Use Thunderstone → Raichu pg. 400

● MAIN WAYS TO OBTAIN

PLATINUM	Trophy Garden at Pokémon Mansion on Route 212
DIAMOND	Trophy Garden at Pokémon Mansion on Route 212
PEARL	Trophy Garden at Pokémon Mansion on Route 212
G B A	Discover an Egg in any GBA-series Pokémon game, and transfer through Pal Park

ABILITY ● Static

● LEVEL-UP AND LEARNED MOVES

Lv	Name	Type	Kind	Power	Acc	PP	Range	DA
Base	ThunderShock	Electric	Special	40	100	30	Normal	—
Base	Charm	Normal	Status	—	100	20	Normal	—
5	Tail Whip	Normal	Status	—	100	30	2 foes	—
10	Thunder Wave	Electric	Status	—	100	20	Normal	—
13	Sweet Kiss	Normal	Status	—	75	10	Normal	—
18	Nasty Plot	Dark	Status	—	—	20	Self	—

National Pokédex No. 173 — Star Shape Pokémon

Cleffa

NORMAL

STATS
- HP ●●
- ATTACK ●●
- DEFENSE ●●
- SP. ATTACK ●●●
- SP. DEFENSE ●●●
- SPEED ●●

● M/F have same form

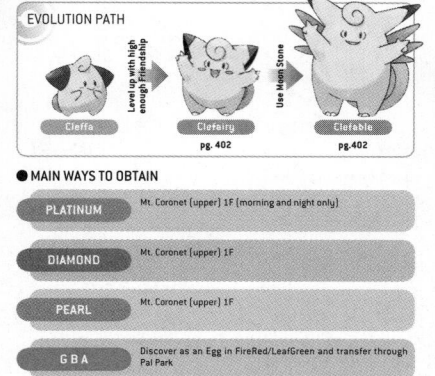

● EVOLUTION PATH

Cleffa → (Level up with high enough Friendship) → Clefairy (pg. 402) → (Use Moon Stone) → Clefable (pg. 402)

● MAIN WAYS TO OBTAIN

PLATINUM	Mt. Coronet (upper) 1F (morning and night only)
DIAMOND	Mt. Coronet (upper) 1F
PEARL	Mt. Coronet (upper) 1F
GBA	Discover as an Egg in FireRed/LeafGreen and transfer through Pal Park

ABILITY ● Cute Charm ● Magic Guard

● LEVEL-UP AND LEARNED MOVES

Lv	Name	Type	Kind	Power	Acc	PP	Range	DA
Base	Pound	Normal	Physical	40	100	35	Normal	●
Base	Charm	Normal	Status	—	100	20	Normal	—
4	Encore	Normal	Status	—	100	5	Normal	—
7	Sing	Normal	Status	—	55	15	Normal	—
10	Sweet Kiss	Normal	Status	—	75	10	Normal	—
13	Copycat	Normal	Status	—	—	20	Last move	—
16	Magical Leaf	Grass	Special	60	—	20	Normal	—

National Pokédex No. 174 — Balloon Pokémon

Igglybuff

NORMAL

STATS
- HP ●●●
- ATTACK ●
- DEFENSE ●
- SP. ATTACK ●
- SP. DEFENSE ●
- SPEED ●

● M/F have same form

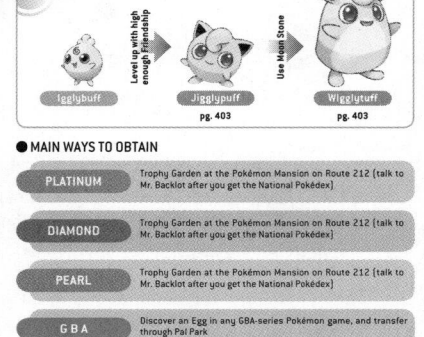

● EVOLUTION PATH

Igglybuff → (Level up with high enough Friendship) → Jigglypuff (pg. 403) → (Use Moon Stone) → Wigglytuff (pg. 403)

● MAIN WAYS TO OBTAIN

PLATINUM	Trophy Garden at the Pokémon Mansion on Route 212 (talk to Mr. Backlot after you get the National Pokédex)
DIAMOND	Trophy Garden at the Pokémon Mansion on Route 212 (talk to Mr. Backlot after you get the National Pokédex)
PEARL	Trophy Garden at the Pokémon Mansion on Route 212 (talk to Mr. Backlot after you get the National Pokédex)
GBA	Discover an Egg in any GBA-series Pokémon game, and transfer through Pal Park

ABILITY ● Cute Charm

● LEVEL-UP AND LEARNED MOVES

Lv	Name	Type	Kind	Power	Acc	PP	Range	DA
Base	Sing	Normal	Status	—	55	15	Normal	—
Base	Charm	Normal	Status	—	100	20	Normal	—
5	Defense Curl	Normal	Status	—	—	40	Self	—
9	Pound	Normal	Physical	40	100	35	Normal	●
13	Sweet Kiss	Normal	Status	—	75	10	Normal	—
17	Copycat	Normal	Status	—	—	20	Last move	—

National Pokédex No. 175 — Spike Ball Pokémon

Togepi

NORMAL

STATS
- HP ●
- ATTACK ●
- DEFENSE ●●●
- SP. ATTACK ●●●
- SP. DEFENSE ●●●
- SPEED ●

● M/F have same form

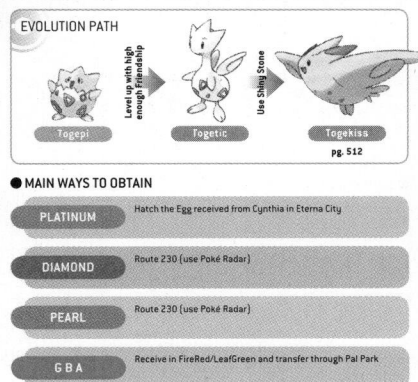

● EVOLUTION PATH

Togepi → (Level up with high enough Friendship) → Togetic → (Use Shiny Stone) → Togekiss (pg. 512)

● MAIN WAYS TO OBTAIN

PLATINUM	Hatch the Egg received from Cynthia in Eterna City
DIAMOND	Route 230 (use Poké Radar)
PEARL	Route 230 (use Poké Radar)
GBA	Receive in FireRed/LeafGreen and transfer through Pal Park

ABILITY ● Hustle ● Serene Grace

● LEVEL-UP AND LEARNED MOVES

Lv	Name	Type	Kind	Power	Acc	PP	Range	DA
Base	Growl	Normal	Status	—	100	40	2 foes	—
Base	Charm	Normal	Status	—	100	20	Normal	—
6	Metronome	Normal	Status	—	—	10	Last move	—
10	Sweet Kiss	Normal	Status	—	75	10	Normal	—
15	Yawn	Normal	Status	—	—	10	Normal	—
19	Encore	Normal	Status	—	100	5	Normal	—
24	Follow Me	Normal	Status	—	—	20	Self	—
28	Wish	Normal	Status	—	—	10	Self	—
33	AncientPower	Rock	Special	60	100	5	Normal	—
37	Safeguard	Normal	Status	—	—	25	2 Allies	—
42	Baton Pass	Normal	Status	—	—	40	Self	—
46	Double-Edge	Normal	Physical	120	100	15	Normal	●
51	Last Resort	Normal	Physical	130	100	5	Normal	—

National Pokédex No. 176 — Happiness Pokémon

Togetic

NORMAL FLYING

STATS
- HP ●●
- ATTACK ●●
- DEFENSE ●●●
- SP. ATTACK ●●●
- SP. DEFENSE ●●●
- SPEED ●●

● M/F have same form

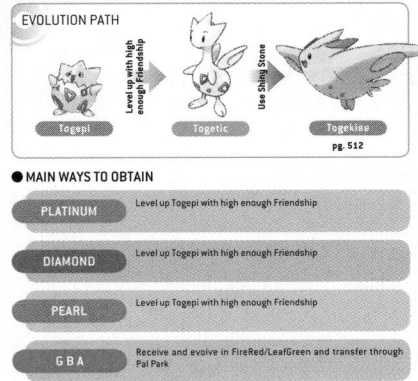

● EVOLUTION PATH

Togepi → (Level up with high enough Friendship) → Togetic → (Use Shiny Stone) → Togekiss (pg. 512)

● MAIN WAYS TO OBTAIN

PLATINUM	Level up Togepi with high enough Friendship
DIAMOND	Level up Togepi with high enough Friendship
PEARL	Level up Togepi with high enough Friendship
GBA	Receive and evolve in FireRed/LeafGreen and transfer through Pal Park

ABILITY ● Hustle ● Serene Grace

● LEVEL-UP AND LEARNED MOVES

Lv	Name	Type	Kind	Power	Acc	PP	Range	DA
Base	Magical Leaf	Grass	Special	60	—	20	Normal	—
Base	Growl	Normal	Status	—	100	40	2 foes	—
Base	Charm	Normal	Status	—	100	20	Normal	—
Base	Metronome	Normal	Status	—	—	10	Last move	—
Base	Sweet Kiss	Normal	Status	—	75	10	Normal	—
6	Metronome	Normal	Status	—	—	10	Last move	—
10	Sweet Kiss	Normal	Status	—	75	10	Normal	—
15	Yawn	Normal	Status	—	—	10	Normal	—
19	Encore	Normal	Status	—	100	5	Normal	—
24	Follow Me	Normal	Status	—	—	20	Self	—
28	Wish	Normal	Status	—	—	10	Self	—
33	AncientPower	Rock	Special	60	100	5	Normal	—
37	Safeguard	Normal	Status	—	—	25	2 Allies	—
42	Baton Pass	Normal	Status	—	—	40	Self	—
46	Double-Edge	Normal	Physical	120	100	15	Normal	●
51	Last Resort	Normal	Physical	130	100	5	Normal	—

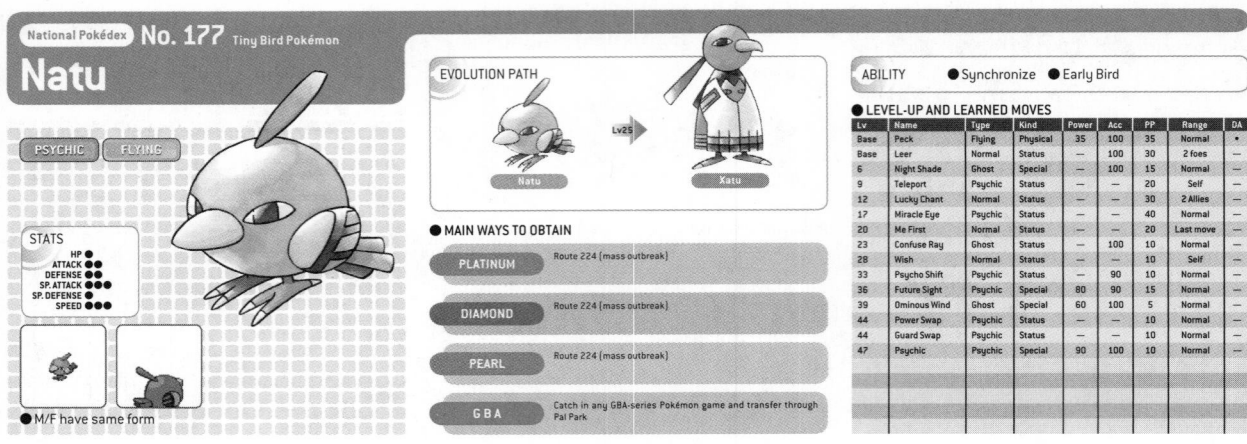

National Pokédex No. 177 — Natu

Tiny Bird Pokémon

Type: PSYCHIC / FLYING

STATS
HP ●
ATTACK ●●
DEFENSE ●●
SP. ATTACK ●●●
SP. DEFENSE ●●
SPEED ●●●

● M/F have same form

EVOLUTION PATH
Natu → Lv25 → Xatu

ABILITY
● Synchronize ● Early Bird

LEVEL-UP AND LEARNED MOVES

Lv	Name	Type	Kind	Power	Acc	PP	Range	DA
Base	Peck	Flying	Physical	35	100	35	Normal	●
Base	Leer	Normal	Status	—	100	30	2 foes	
6	Night Shade	Ghost	Special	—	100	15	Normal	—
9	Teleport	Psychic	Status	—	—	20	Self	—
12	Lucky Chant	Normal	Status	—	—	30	2 Allies	—
17	Miracle Eye	Psychic	Status	—	—	40	Normal	—
20	Me First	Normal	Status	—	—	20	Last move	—
23	Confuse Ray	Ghost	Status	—	100	10	Normal	—
28	Wish	Normal	Status	—	—	10	Self	—
33	Psycho Shift	Psychic	Status	—	90	10	Normal	—
36	Future Sight	Psychic	Special	80	90	15	Normal	—
39	Ominous Wind	Ghost	Special	60	100	5	Normal	—
44	Power Swap	Psychic	Status	—	—	10	Normal	—
44	Guard Swap	Psychic	Status	—	—	10	Normal	—
47	Psychic	Psychic	Special	90	100	10	Normal	—

MAIN WAYS TO OBTAIN
- PLATINUM: Route 224 (mass outbreak)
- DIAMOND: Route 224 (mass outbreak)
- PEARL: Route 224 (mass outbreak)
- GBA: Catch in any GBA-series Pokémon game and transfer through Pal Park

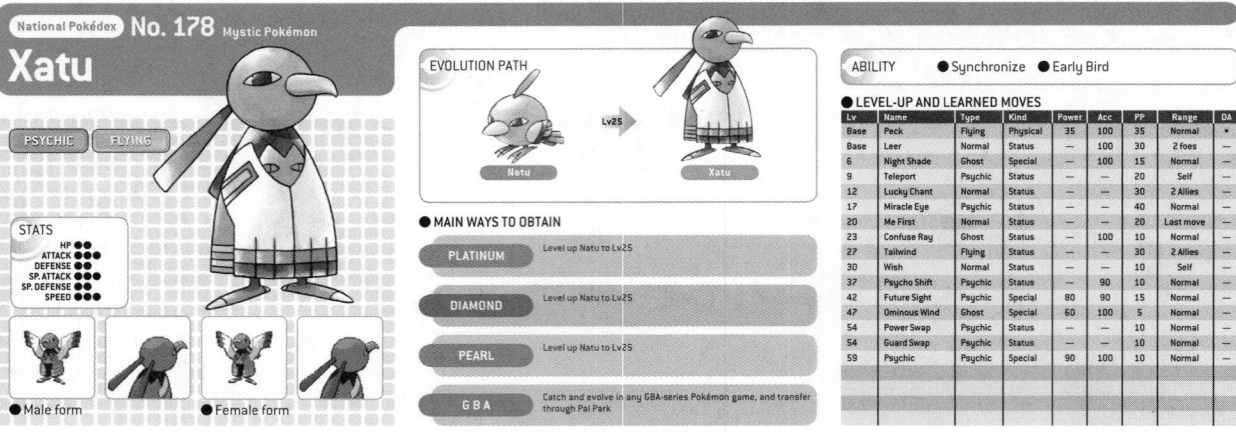

National Pokédex No. 178 — Xatu

Mystic Pokémon

Type: PSYCHIC / FLYING

STATS
HP ●●
ATTACK ●●●
DEFENSE ●●
SP. ATTACK ●●●
SP. DEFENSE ●●
SPEED ●●●

● Male form   ● Female form

EVOLUTION PATH
Natu → Lv25 → Xatu

ABILITY
● Synchronize ● Early Bird

LEVEL-UP AND LEARNED MOVES

Lv	Name	Type	Kind	Power	Acc	PP	Range	DA
Base	Peck	Flying	Physical	35	100	35	Normal	●
Base	Leer	Normal	Status	—	100	30	2 foes	
6	Night Shade	Ghost	Special	—	100	15	Normal	—
9	Teleport	Psychic	Status	—	—	20	Self	—
12	Lucky Chant	Normal	Status	—	—	30	2 Allies	—
17	Miracle Eye	Psychic	Status	—	—	40	Normal	—
20	Me First	Normal	Status	—	—	20	Last move	—
23	Confuse Ray	Ghost	Status	—	100	10	Normal	—
27	Tailwind	Flying	Status	—	—	30	2 Allies	—
30	Wish	Normal	Status	—	—	10	Self	—
37	Psycho Shift	Psychic	Status	—	90	10	Normal	—
42	Future Sight	Psychic	Special	80	90	15	Normal	—
47	Ominous Wind	Ghost	Special	60	100	5	Normal	—
54	Power Swap	Psychic	Status	—	—	10	Normal	—
54	Guard Swap	Psychic	Status	—	—	10	Normal	—
59	Psychic	Psychic	Special	90	100	10	Normal	—

MAIN WAYS TO OBTAIN
- PLATINUM: Level up Natu to Lv25
- DIAMOND: Level up Natu to Lv25
- PEARL: Level up Natu to Lv25
- GBA: Catch and evolve in any GBA-series Pokémon game, and transfer through Pal Park

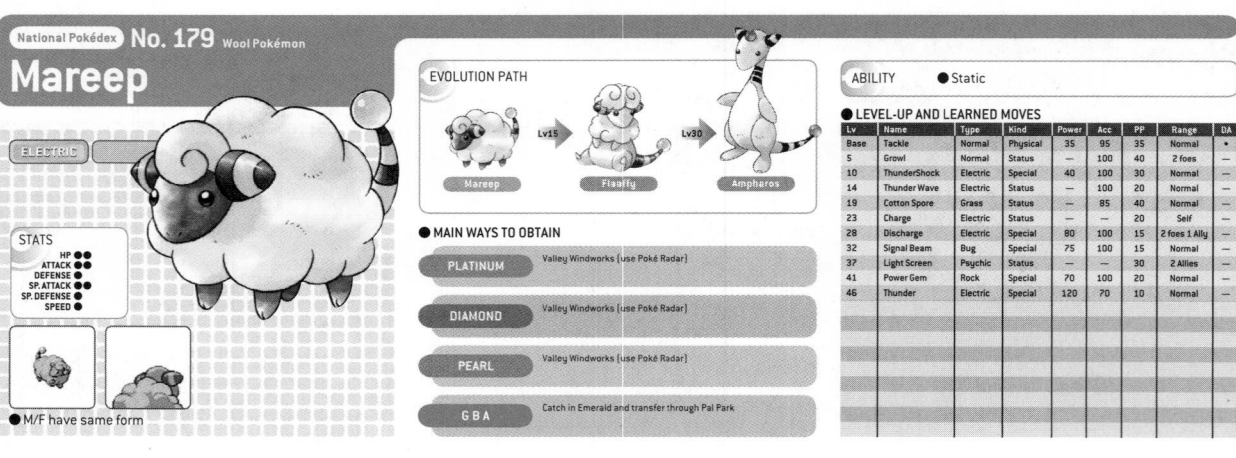

National Pokédex No. 179 — Mareep

Wool Pokémon

Type: ELECTRIC

STATS
HP ●●
ATTACK ●●
DEFENSE ●●
SP. ATTACK ●●
SP. DEFENSE ●
SPEED ●

● M/F have same form

EVOLUTION PATH
Mareep → Lv15 → Flaaffy → Lv30 → Ampharos

ABILITY
● Static

LEVEL-UP AND LEARNED MOVES

Lv	Name	Type	Kind	Power	Acc	PP	Range	DA
Base	Tackle	Normal	Physical	35	95	35	Normal	●
5	Growl	Normal	Status	—	100	40	2 foes	—
10	ThunderShock	Electric	Special	40	100	30	Normal	—
14	Thunder Wave	Electric	Status	—	100	20	Normal	—
19	Cotton Spore	Grass	Status	—	85	40	Normal	—
23	Charge	Electric	Status	—	—	20	Self	—
28	Discharge	Electric	Special	80	100	15	2 foes 1 Ally	—
32	Signal Beam	Bug	Special	75	100	15	Normal	—
37	Light Screen	Psychic	Status	—	—	30	2 Allies	—
41	Power Gem	Rock	Special	70	100	20	Normal	—
46	Thunder	Electric	Special	120	70	10	Normal	—

MAIN WAYS TO OBTAIN
- PLATINUM: Valley Windworks (use Poké Radar)
- DIAMOND: Valley Windworks (use Poké Radar)
- PEARL: Valley Windworks (use Poké Radar)
- GBA: Catch in Emerald and transfer through Pal Park

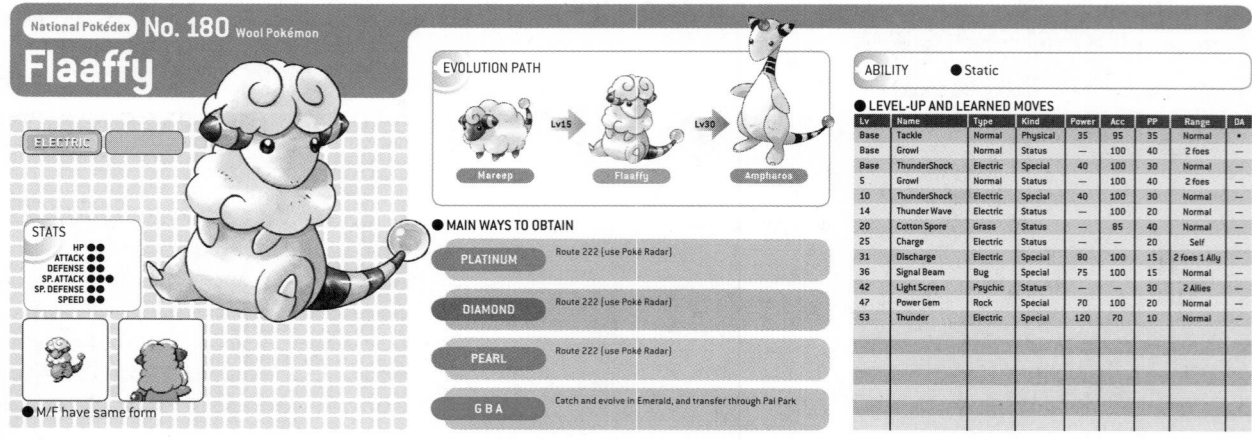

National Pokédex No. 180 — Flaaffy

Wool Pokémon

Type: ELECTRIC

STATS
HP ●●
ATTACK ●●
DEFENSE ●●
SP. ATTACK ●●●
SP. DEFENSE ●●
SPEED ●●

● M/F have same form

EVOLUTION PATH
Mareep → Lv15 → Flaaffy → Lv30 → Ampharos

ABILITY
● Static

LEVEL-UP AND LEARNED MOVES

Lv	Name	Type	Kind	Power	Acc	PP	Range	DA
Base	Tackle	Normal	Physical	35	95	35	Normal	●
Base	Growl	Normal	Status	—	100	40	2 foes	—
Base	ThunderShock	Electric	Special	40	100	30	Normal	—
5	Growl	Normal	Status	—	100	40	2 foes	—
10	ThunderShock	Electric	Special	40	100	30	Normal	—
14	Thunder Wave	Electric	Status	—	100	20	Normal	—
20	Cotton Spore	Grass	Status	—	85	40	Normal	—
25	Charge	Electric	Status	—	—	20	Self	—
31	Discharge	Electric	Special	80	100	15	2 foes 1 Ally	—
36	Signal Beam	Bug	Special	75	100	15	Normal	—
42	Light Screen	Psychic	Status	—	—	30	2 Allies	—
47	Power Gem	Rock	Special	70	100	20	Normal	—
53	Thunder	Electric	Special	120	70	10	Normal	—

MAIN WAYS TO OBTAIN
- PLATINUM: Route 222 (use Poké Radar)
- DIAMOND: Route 222 (use Poké Radar)
- PEARL: Route 222 (use Poké Radar)
- GBA: Catch and evolve in Emerald, and transfer through Pal Park

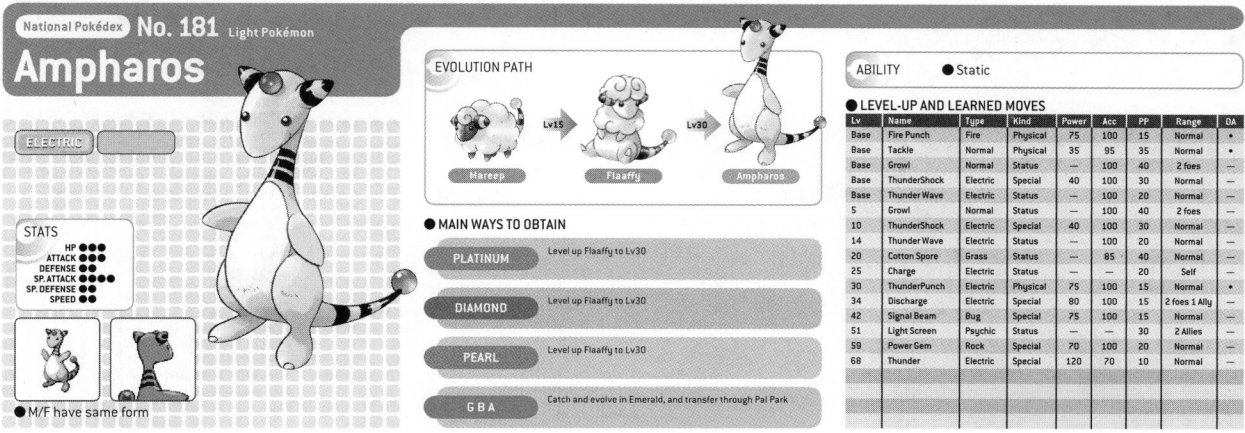

National Pokédex No. 181 — Ampharos — Light Pokémon

ELECTRIC

STATS
- HP ●●●
- ATTACK ●●●
- DEFENSE ●●●
- SP. ATTACK ●●●●
- SP. DEFENSE ●●●
- SPEED ●●

● M/F have same form

EVOLUTION PATH

Mareep → Lv15 → Flaaffy → Lv30 → Ampharos

MAIN WAYS TO OBTAIN

PLATINUM	Level up Flaaffy to Lv30
DIAMOND	Level up Flaaffy to Lv30
PEARL	Level up Flaaffy to Lv30
GBA	Catch and evolve in Emerald, and transfer through Pal Park

ABILITY ● Static

● **LEVEL-UP AND LEARNED MOVES**

Lv	Name	Type	Kind	Power	Acc	PP	Range	DA
Base	Fire Punch	Fire	Physical	75	100	15	Normal	●
Base	Tackle	Normal	Physical	35	95	35	Normal	●
Base	Growl	Normal	Status	—	100	40	2 foes	—
Base	ThunderShock	Electric	Special	40	100	30	Normal	—
Base	Thunder Wave	Electric	Status	—	100	20	Normal	—
5	Growl	Normal	Status	—	100	40	2 foes	—
10	ThunderShock	Electric	Special	40	100	30	Normal	—
14	Thunder Wave	Electric	Status	—	100	20	Normal	—
20	Cotton Spore	Grass	Status	—	85	40	Normal	—
25	Charge	Electric	Status	—	—	20	Self	—
30	ThunderPunch	Electric	Physical	75	100	15	Normal	●
34	Discharge	Electric	Special	80	100	15	2 foes 1 Ally	—
42	Signal Beam	Bug	Special	75	100	15	Normal	—
51	Light Screen	Psychic	Status	—	—	30	2 Allies	—
59	Power Gem	Rock	Special	70	100	20	Normal	—
68	Thunder	Electric	Special	120	70	10	Normal	—

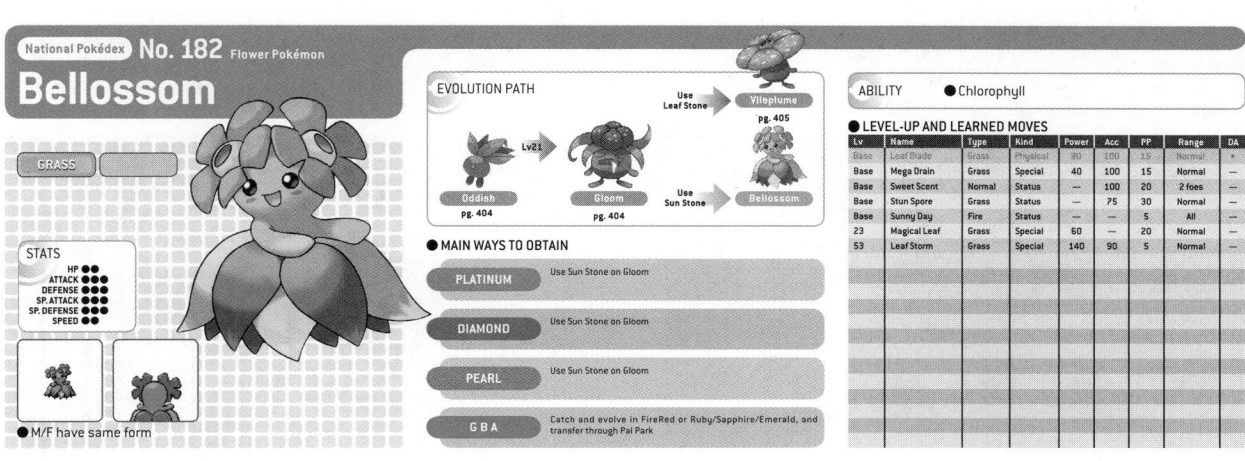

National Pokédex No. 182 — Bellossom — Flower Pokémon

GRASS

STATS
- HP ●●●
- ATTACK ●●
- DEFENSE ●●●
- SP. ATTACK ●●●
- SP. DEFENSE ●●●●
- SPEED ●●

● M/F have same form

EVOLUTION PATH

Oddish (pg. 404) → Lv21 → Gloom (pg. 404) → Use Leaf Stone → Vileplume (pg. 405)
Gloom → Use Sun Stone → Bellossom

MAIN WAYS TO OBTAIN

PLATINUM	Use Sun Stone on Gloom
DIAMOND	Use Sun Stone on Gloom
PEARL	Use Sun Stone on Gloom
GBA	Catch and evolve in FireRed or Ruby/Sapphire/Emerald, and transfer through Pal Park

ABILITY ● Chlorophyll

● **LEVEL-UP AND LEARNED MOVES**

Lv	Name	Type	Kind	Power	Acc	PP	Range	DA
Base	Leaf Blade	Grass	Physical	90	100	15	Normal	●
Base	Mega Drain	Grass	Special	40	100	15	Normal	—
Base	Sweet Scent	Normal	Status	—	100	20	2 foes	—
Base	Stun Spore	Grass	Status	—	75	30	Normal	—
Base	Sunny Day	Fire	Status	—	—	5	All	—
23	Magical Leaf	Grass	Special	60	—	20	Normal	—
53	Leaf Storm	Grass	Special	140	90	5	Normal	—

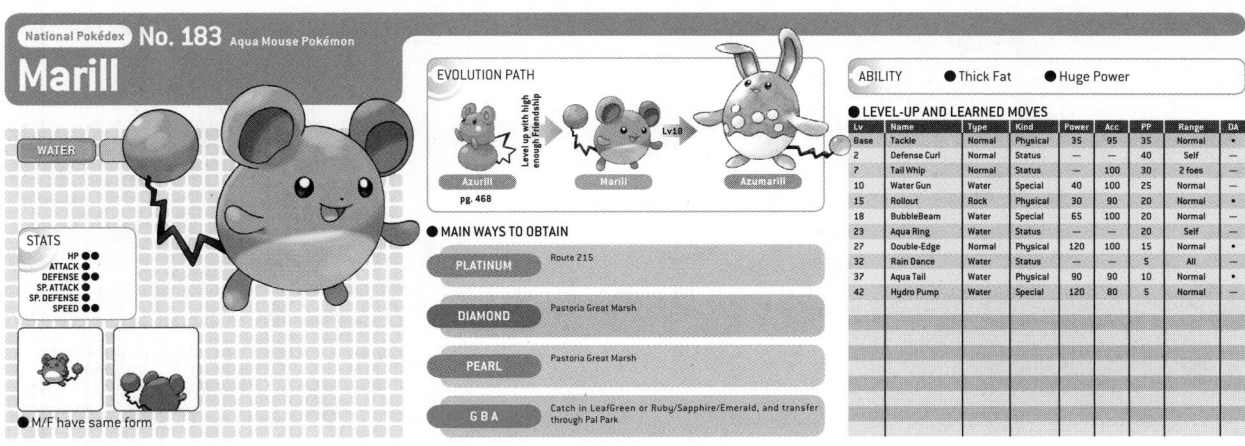

National Pokédex No. 183 — Marill — Aqua Mouse Pokémon

WATER

STATS
- HP ●●
- ATTACK ●●
- DEFENSE ●●
- SP. ATTACK ●●
- SP. DEFENSE ●●
- SPEED ●●

● M/F have same form

EVOLUTION PATH

Azurill (pg. 468) → Level up with high enough Friendship → Marill → Lv18 → Azumarill

MAIN WAYS TO OBTAIN

PLATINUM	Route 215
DIAMOND	Pastoria Great Marsh
PEARL	Pastoria Great Marsh
GBA	Catch in LeafGreen or Ruby/Sapphire/Emerald, and transfer through Pal Park

ABILITY ● Thick Fat ● Huge Power

● **LEVEL-UP AND LEARNED MOVES**

Lv	Name	Type	Kind	Power	Acc	PP	Range	DA
Base	Tackle	Normal	Physical	35	95	35	Normal	●
2	Defense Curl	Normal	Status	—	—	40	Self	—
7	Tail Whip	Normal	Status	—	100	30	2 foes	—
10	Water Gun	Water	Special	40	100	25	Normal	—
15	Rollout	Rock	Physical	30	90	20	Normal	●
18	BubbleBeam	Water	Special	65	100	20	Normal	—
23	Aqua Ring	Water	Status	—	—	20	Self	—
27	Double-Edge	Normal	Physical	120	100	15	Normal	●
32	Rain Dance	Water	Status	—	—	5	All	—
37	Aqua Tail	Water	Physical	90	90	10	Normal	●
42	Hydro Pump	Water	Special	120	80	5	Normal	—

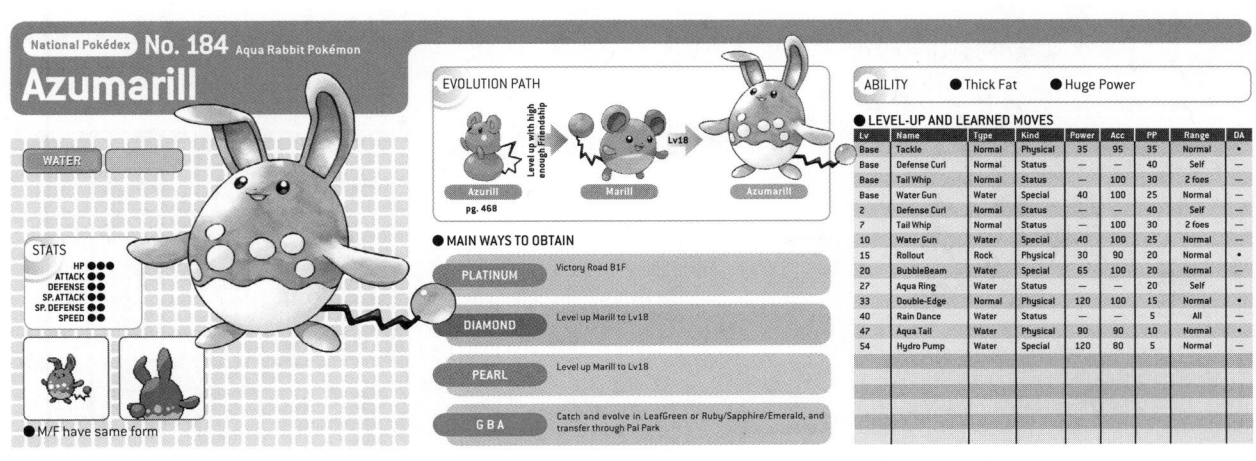

National Pokédex No. 184 — Azumarill — Aqua Rabbit Pokémon

WATER

STATS
- HP ●●●
- ATTACK ●●●
- DEFENSE ●●●
- SP. ATTACK ●●
- SP. DEFENSE ●●●
- SPEED ●●

● M/F have same form

EVOLUTION PATH

Azurill (pg. 468) → Level up with high enough Friendship → Marill → Lv18 → Azumarill

MAIN WAYS TO OBTAIN

PLATINUM	Victory Road B1F
DIAMOND	Level up Marill to Lv18
PEARL	Level up Marill to Lv18
GBA	Catch and evolve in LeafGreen or Ruby/Sapphire/Emerald, and transfer through Pal Park

ABILITY ● Thick Fat ● Huge Power

● **LEVEL-UP AND LEARNED MOVES**

Lv	Name	Type	Kind	Power	Acc	PP	Range	DA
Base	Tackle	Normal	Physical	35	95	35	Normal	●
Base	Defense Curl	Normal	Status	—	—	40	Self	—
Base	Tail Whip	Normal	Status	—	100	30	2 foes	—
Base	Water Gun	Water	Special	40	100	25	Normal	—
2	Defense Curl	Normal	Status	—	—	40	Self	—
7	Tail Whip	Normal	Status	—	100	30	2 foes	—
10	Water Gun	Water	Special	40	100	25	Normal	—
15	Rollout	Rock	Physical	30	90	20	Normal	●
20	BubbleBeam	Water	Special	65	100	20	Normal	—
27	Aqua Ring	Water	Status	—	—	20	Self	—
33	Double-Edge	Normal	Physical	120	100	15	Normal	●
40	Rain Dance	Water	Status	—	—	5	All	—
47	Aqua Tail	Water	Physical	90	90	10	Normal	●
54	Hydro Pump	Water	Special	120	80	5	Normal	—

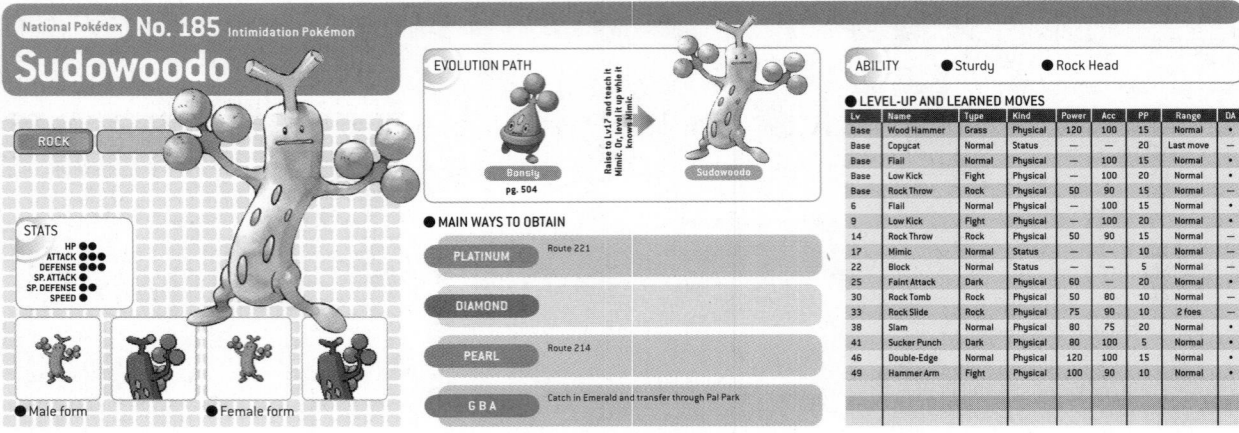

National Pokédex No. 185 · Intimidation Pokémon

Sudowoodo

ROCK

STATS
HP ●●
ATTACK ●●●
DEFENSE ●●●
SP. ATTACK ●●
SP. DEFENSE ●●
SPEED ●

● Male form   ● Female form

EVOLUTION PATH

Bonsly
pg. 504

Raise to Lv17 and teach it Mimic. Or, level it up while it knows Mimic.

Sudowoodo

● MAIN WAYS TO OBTAIN

PLATINUM	Route 221
DIAMOND	
PEARL	Route 214
GBA	Catch in Emerald and transfer through Pal Park

ABILITY ● Sturdy   ● Rock Head

● LEVEL-UP AND LEARNED MOVES

Lv	Name	Type	Kind	Power	Acc	PP	Range	DA
Base	Wood Hammer	Grass	Physical	120	100	15	Normal	●
Base	Copycat	Normal	Status	—	—	20	Last move	—
Base	Flail	Normal	Physical	—	100	15	Normal	●
Base	Low Kick	Fight	Physical	—	100	20	Normal	●
Base	Rock Throw	Rock	Physical	50	90	15	Normal	●
6	Flail	Normal	Physical	—	100	15	Normal	●
9	Low Kick	Fight	Physical	—	100	20	Normal	●
14	Rock Throw	Rock	Physical	50	90	15	Normal	●
17	Mimic	Normal	Status	—	—	10	Normal	—
22	Block	Normal	Status	—	—	5	Normal	—
25	Faint Attack	Dark	Physical	60	—	20	Normal	●
30	Rock Tomb	Rock	Physical	50	80	10	Normal	●
33	Rock Slide	Rock	Physical	75	90	10	2 foes	●
38	Slam	Normal	Physical	80	75	20	Normal	●
41	Sucker Punch	Dark	Physical	80	100	5	Normal	●
46	Double-Edge	Normal	Physical	120	100	15	Normal	●
49	Hammer Arm	Fight	Physical	100	90	10	Normal	●

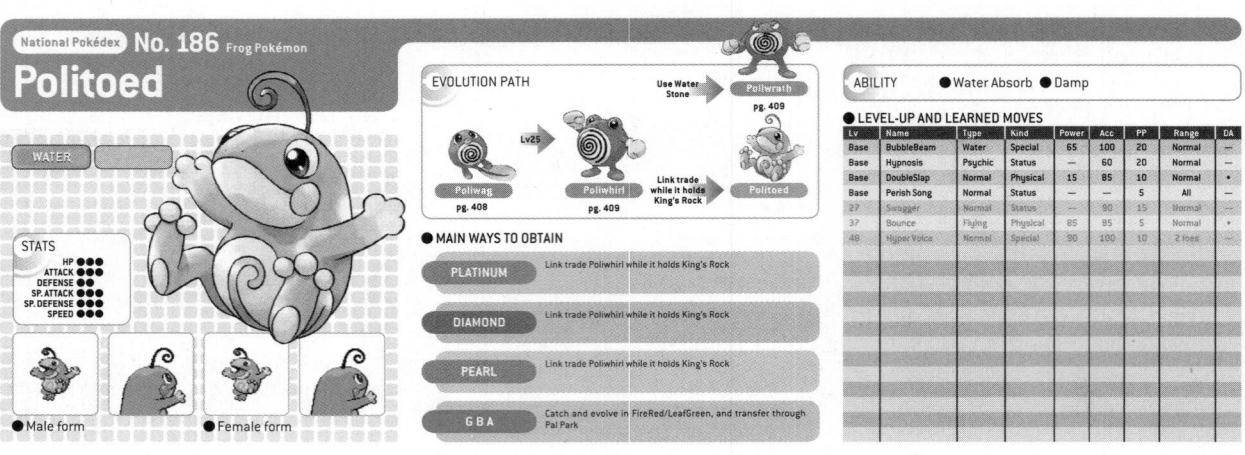

National Pokédex No. 186 · Frog Pokémon

Politoed

WATER

STATS
HP ●●●
ATTACK ●●●
DEFENSE ●●●
SP. ATTACK ●●●
SP. DEFENSE ●●●
SPEED ●●●

● Male form   ● Female form

EVOLUTION PATH

Poliwag
pg. 408

Lv25

Poliwhirl
pg. 409

Use Water Stone → Poliwrath
pg. 409

Link trade while it holds King's Rock → Politoed

● MAIN WAYS TO OBTAIN

PLATINUM	Link trade Poliwhirl while it holds King's Rock
DIAMOND	Link trade Poliwhirl while it holds King's Rock
PEARL	Link trade Poliwhirl while it holds King's Rock
GBA	Catch and evolve in FireRed/LeafGreen, and transfer through Pal Park

ABILITY ● Water Absorb   ● Damp

● LEVEL-UP AND LEARNED MOVES

Lv	Name	Type	Kind	Power	Acc	PP	Range	DA
Base	BubbleBeam	Water	Special	65	100	20	Normal	—
Base	Hypnosis	Psychic	Status	—	60	20	Normal	—
Base	DoubleSlap	Normal	Physical	15	85	10	Normal	●
Base	Perish Song	Normal	Status	—	—	5	All	—
27	Swagger	Normal	Status	—	90	15	Normal	—
37	Bounce	Flying	Physical	85	85	5	Normal	●
48	Hyper Voice	Normal	Special	90	100	10	2 foes	—

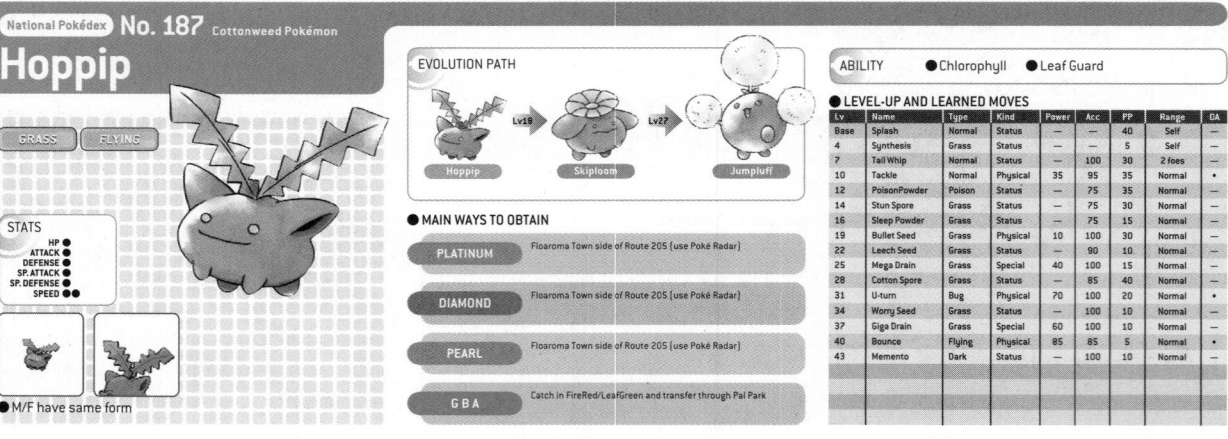

National Pokédex No. 187 · Cottonweed Pokémon

Hoppip

GRASS   FLYING

STATS
HP ●
ATTACK ●
DEFENSE ●
SP. ATTACK ●
SP. DEFENSE ●●
SPEED ●●

● M/F have same form

EVOLUTION PATH

Hoppip

Lv18

Skiploom

Lv27

Jumpluff

● MAIN WAYS TO OBTAIN

PLATINUM	Floaroma Town side of Route 205 (use Poké Radar)
DIAMOND	Floaroma Town side of Route 205 (use Poké Radar)
PEARL	Floaroma Town side of Route 205 (use Poké Radar)
GBA	Catch in FireRed/LeafGreen and transfer through Pal Park

ABILITY ● Chlorophyll   ● Leaf Guard

● LEVEL-UP AND LEARNED MOVES

Lv	Name	Type	Kind	Power	Acc	PP	Range	DA
Base	Splash	Normal	Status	—	—	40	Self	—
4	Synthesis	Grass	Status	—	—	5	Self	—
7	Tail Whip	Normal	Status	—	100	30	2 foes	—
10	Tackle	Normal	Physical	35	95	35	Normal	●
12	PoisonPowder	Poison	Status	—	75	35	Normal	—
14	Stun Spore	Grass	Status	—	75	30	Normal	—
16	Sleep Powder	Grass	Status	—	75	15	Normal	—
19	Bullet Seed	Grass	Physical	10	100	30	Normal	—
22	Leech Seed	Grass	Status	—	90	10	Normal	—
25	Mega Drain	Grass	Special	40	100	15	Normal	—
28	Cotton Spore	Grass	Status	—	85	40	Normal	—
31	U-turn	Bug	Physical	70	100	20	Normal	●
34	Worry Seed	Grass	Status	—	100	10	Normal	—
37	Giga Drain	Grass	Special	60	100	10	Normal	—
40	Bounce	Flying	Physical	85	85	5	Normal	●
43	Memento	Dark	Status	—	100	10	Normal	—

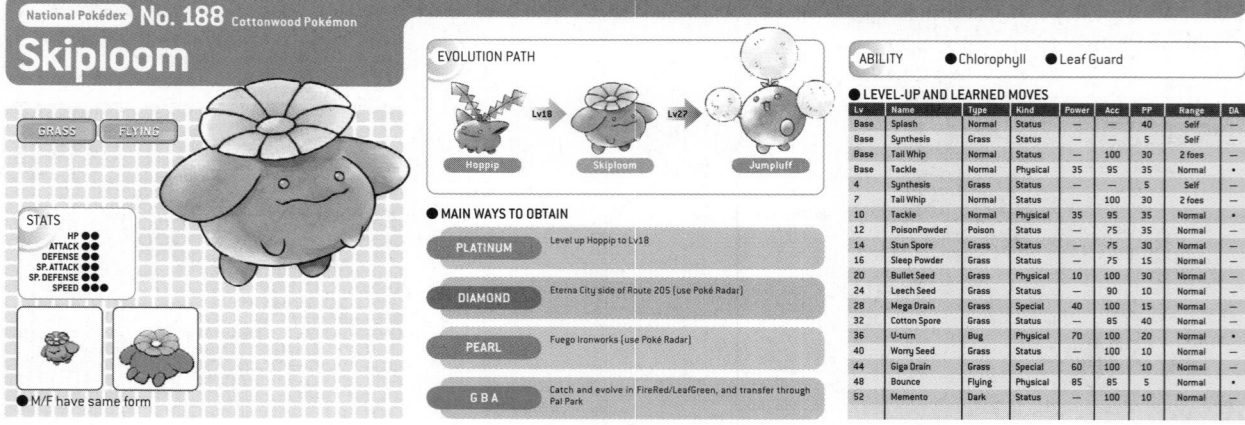

National Pokédex No. 188 · Cottonwood Pokémon

Skiploom

GRASS   FLYING

STATS
HP ●●
ATTACK ●●
DEFENSE ●●
SP. ATTACK ●●
SP. DEFENSE ●●●
SPEED ●●●

● M/F have same form

EVOLUTION PATH

Hoppip

Lv18

Skiploom

Lv27

Jumpluff

● MAIN WAYS TO OBTAIN

PLATINUM	Level up Hoppip to Lv18
DIAMOND	Eterna City side of Route 205 (use Poké Radar)
PEARL	Fuego Ironworks (use Poké Radar)
GBA	Catch and evolve in FireRed/LeafGreen, and transfer through Pal Park

ABILITY ● Chlorophyll   ● Leaf Guard

● LEVEL-UP AND LEARNED MOVES

Lv	Name	Type	Kind	Power	Acc	PP	Range	DA
Base	Splash	Normal	Status	—	—	40	Self	—
Base	Synthesis	Grass	Status	—	—	5	Self	—
Base	Tail Whip	Normal	Status	—	100	30	2 foes	—
Base	Tackle	Normal	Physical	35	95	35	Normal	●
4	Synthesis	Grass	Status	—	—	5	Self	—
7	Tail Whip	Normal	Status	—	100	30	2 foes	—
10	Tackle	Normal	Physical	35	95	35	Normal	●
12	PoisonPowder	Poison	Status	—	75	35	Normal	—
14	Stun Spore	Grass	Status	—	75	30	Normal	—
16	Sleep Powder	Grass	Status	—	75	15	Normal	—
20	Bullet Seed	Grass	Physical	10	100	30	Normal	—
24	Leech Seed	Grass	Status	—	90	10	Normal	—
28	Mega Drain	Grass	Special	40	100	15	Normal	—
32	Cotton Spore	Grass	Status	—	85	40	Normal	—
36	U-turn	Bug	Physical	70	100	20	Normal	●
40	Worry Seed	Grass	Status	—	100	10	Normal	—
44	Giga Drain	Grass	Special	60	100	10	Normal	—
48	Bounce	Flying	Physical	85	85	5	Normal	●
52	Memento	Dark	Status	—	100	10	Normal	—

National Pokédex No. 189 Cottonweed Pokémon
Jumpluff

GRASS | FLYING

STATS
HP ●●
ATTACK ●●
DEFENSE ●●
SP. ATTACK ●●
SP. DEFENSE ●●●
SPEED ●●●●

● M/F have same form

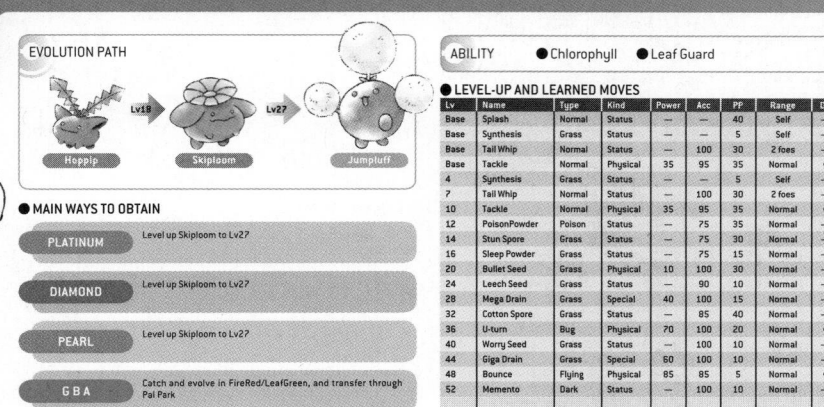

● EVOLUTION PATH

Hoppip — Lv18 → Skiploom — Lv27 → Jumpluff

● MAIN WAYS TO OBTAIN

PLATINUM	Level up Skiploom to Lv27
DIAMOND	Level up Skiploom to Lv27
PEARL	Level up Skiploom to Lv27
G B A	Catch and evolve in FireRed/LeafGreen, and transfer through Pal Park

ABILITY ● Chlorophyll ● Leaf Guard

● LEVEL-UP AND LEARNED MOVES

Lv	Name	Type	Kind	Power	Acc	PP	Range	DA
Base	Splash	Normal	Status	—	—	40	Self	—
Base	Synthesis	Grass	Status	—	—	5	Self	—
Base	Tail Whip	Normal	Status	—	100	30	2 foes	—
Base	Tackle	Normal	Physical	35	95	35	Normal	•
4	Synthesis	Grass	Status	—	—	5	Self	—
7	Tail Whip	Normal	Status	—	100	30	2 foes	—
10	Tackle	Normal	Physical	35	95	35	Normal	•
12	PoisonPowder	Poison	Status	—	75	35	Normal	—
14	Stun Spore	Grass	Status	—	75	30	Normal	—
16	Sleep Powder	Grass	Status	—	75	15	Normal	—
20	Bullet Seed	Grass	Physical	10	100	30	Normal	—
24	Leech Seed	Grass	Status	—	90	10	Normal	—
28	Mega Drain	Grass	Special	40	100	15	Normal	—
32	Cotton Spore	Grass	Status	—	85	40	Normal	—
36	U-turn	Bug	Physical	70	100	20	Normal	•
40	Worry Seed	Grass	Status	—	100	10	Normal	—
44	Giga Drain	Grass	Special	60	100	10	Normal	—
48	Bounce	Flying	Physical	85	85	5	Normal	•
52	Memento	Dark	Status	—	100	10	Normal	—

National Pokédex No. 190 Long Tail Pokémon
Aipom

NORMAL

STATS
HP ●●
ATTACK ●●●
DEFENSE ●●
SP. ATTACK ●●
SP. DEFENSE ●●
SPEED ●●●

● Male form ● Female form

● EVOLUTION PATH

Aipom → Ambipom pg. 501

Raise it to Lv32 and teach it Double Hit. Or, level it up while it knows Double Hit.

● MAIN WAYS TO OBTAIN

PLATINUM	Spread Honey on a Honey Tree
DIAMOND	Spread Honey on a Honey Tree
PEARL	Spread Honey on a Honey Tree
G B A	Catch in Emerald and transfer through Pal Park

ABILITY ● Run Away ● Pickup

● LEVEL-UP AND LEARNED MOVES

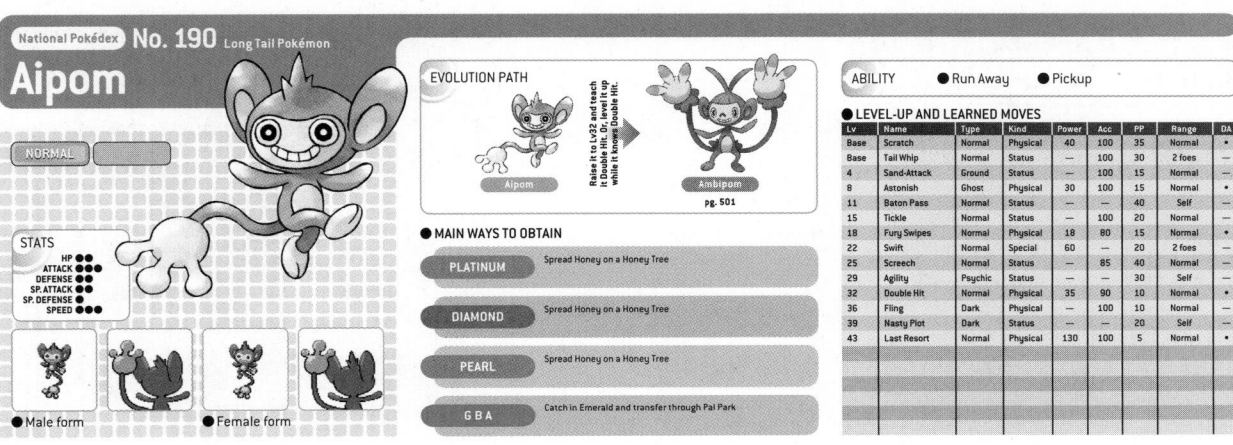

Lv	Name	Type	Kind	Power	Acc	PP	Range	DA
Base	Scratch	Normal	Physical	40	100	35	Normal	•
Base	Tail Whip	Normal	Status	—	100	30	2 foes	—
4	Sand-Attack	Ground	Status	—	100	15	Normal	—
8	Astonish	Ghost	Physical	30	100	15	Normal	•
11	Baton Pass	Normal	Status	—	—	40	Self	—
15	Tickle	Normal	Status	—	100	20	Normal	—
18	Fury Swipes	Normal	Physical	18	80	15	Normal	•
22	Swift	Normal	Special	60	—	20	2 foes	—
25	Screech	Normal	Status	—	85	40	Normal	—
29	Agility	Psychic	Status	—	—	30	Self	—
32	Double Hit	Normal	Physical	35	90	10	Normal	•
36	Fling	Dark	Physical	—	100	10	Normal	—
39	Nasty Plot	Dark	Status	—	—	20	Self	—
43	Last Resort	Normal	Physical	130	100	5	Normal	—

National Pokédex No. 191 Seed Pokémon
Sunkern

GRASS

STATS
HP ●
ATTACK ●
DEFENSE ●
SP. ATTACK ●
SP. DEFENSE ●
SPEED ●

● M/F have same form

● EVOLUTION PATH

Sunkern — Use Sun Stone → Sunflora

● MAIN WAYS TO OBTAIN

PLATINUM	Route 204 [use Poké Radar]
DIAMOND	Floaroma Town side of Route 204 [use Poké Radar]
PEARL	Floaroma Town side of Route 204 [use Poké Radar]
G B A	Catch in Emerald and transfer through Pal Park

ABILITY ● Chlorophyll ● Solar Power

● LEVEL-UP AND LEARNED MOVES

Lv	Name	Type	Kind	Power	Acc	PP	Range	DA
Base	Absorb	Grass	Special	20	100	25	Normal	—
Base	Growth	Normal	Status	—	—	40	Self	—
5	Mega Drain	Grass	Special	40	100	15	Normal	—
9	Ingrain	Grass	Status	—	—	20	Self	—
13	GrassWhistle	Grass	Status	—	55	15	Normal	—
17	Leech Seed	Grass	Status	—	90	10	Normal	—
21	Endeavor	Normal	Physical	—	100	5	Normal	•
25	Worry Seed	Grass	Status	—	100	10	Normal	—
29	Razor Leaf	Grass	Physical	55	95	25	2 foes	—
33	Synthesis	Grass	Status	—	—	5	Self	—
37	Sunny Day	Fire	Status	—	—	5	All	—
41	Giga Drain	Grass	Special	60	100	10	Normal	—
45	Seed Bomb	Grass	Physical	80	100	15	Normal	—

National Pokédex No. 192 Sun Pokémon
Sunflora

GRASS

STATS
HP ●●●
ATTACK ●●●
DEFENSE ●●●
SP. ATTACK ●●●●
SP. DEFENSE ●●●
SPEED ●

● M/F have same form

192
SUNFLORA

● EVOLUTION PATH

Sunkern — Use Sun Stone → Sunflora

● MAIN WAYS TO OBTAIN

PLATINUM	Use Sun Stone on Sunkern
DIAMOND	Use Sun Stone on Sunkern
PEARL	Use Sun Stone on Sunkern
G B A	Catch and evolve in Emerald, and transfer through Pal Park

ABILITY ● Chlorophyll ● Solar Power

● LEVEL-UP AND LEARNED MOVES

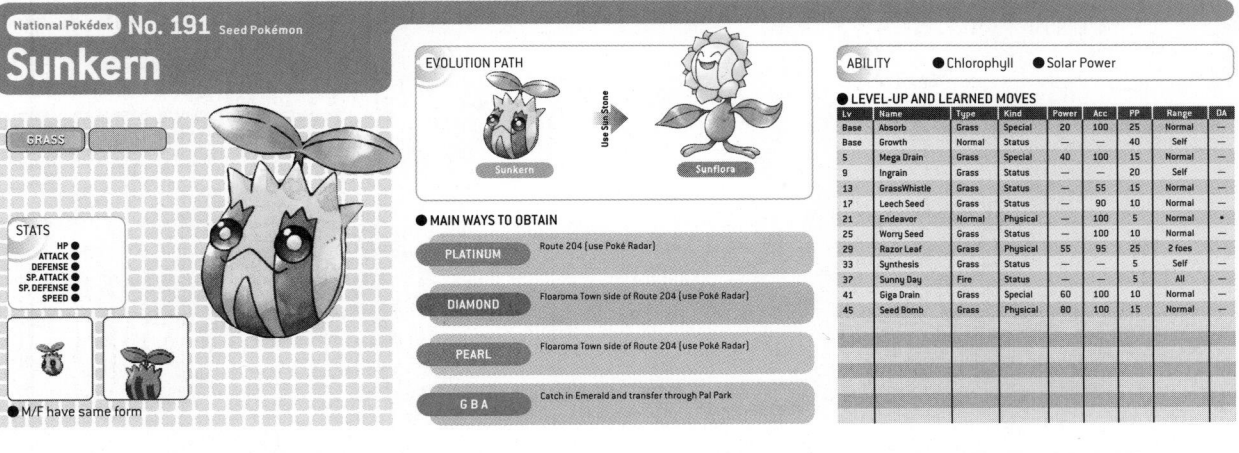

Lv	Name	Type	Kind	Power	Acc	PP	Range	DA
Base	Absorb	Grass	Special	20	100	25	Normal	—
Base	Pound	Normal	Physical	40	100	35	Normal	•
Base	Growth	Normal	Status	—	—	40	Self	—
5	Mega Drain	Grass	Special	40	100	15	Normal	—
9	Ingrain	Grass	Status	—	—	20	Self	—
13	GrassWhistle	Grass	Status	—	55	15	Normal	—
17	Leech Seed	Grass	Status	—	90	10	Normal	—
21	Bullet Seed	Grass	Physical	10	100	30	Normal	•
25	Worry Seed	Grass	Status	—	100	10	Normal	—
29	Razor Leaf	Grass	Physical	55	95	25	2 foes	—
33	Petal Dance	Grass	Special	90	100	10	1 Random	•
37	Sunny Day	Fire	Status	—	—	5	All	—
41	SolarBeam	Grass	Special	120	100	10	Normal	—
43	Leaf Storm	Grass	Special	140	90	5	Normal	—

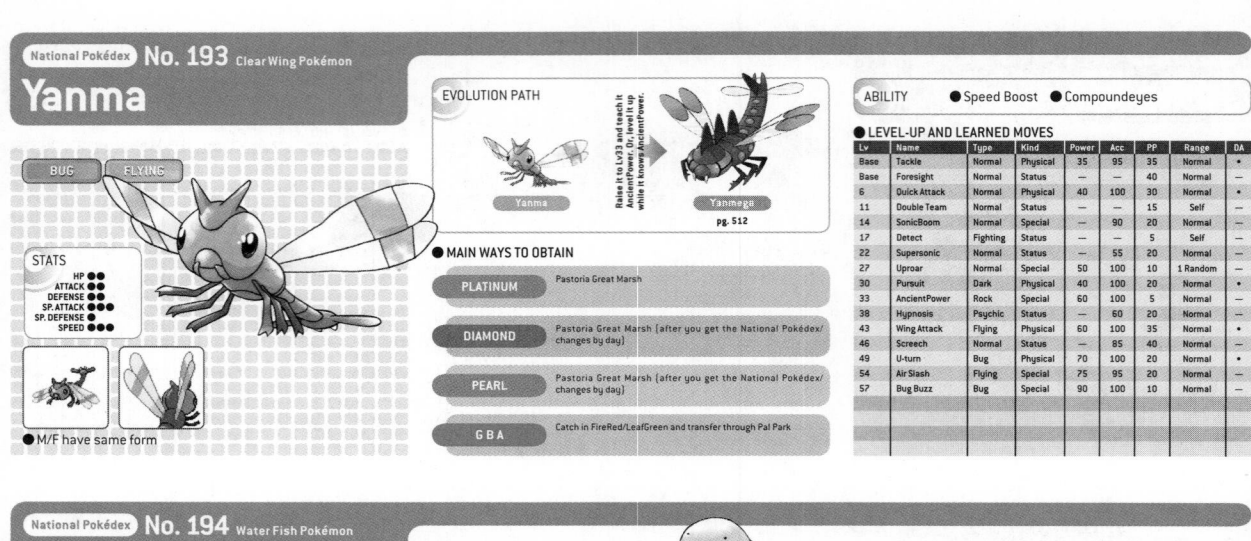

Yanma

BUG / FLYING

STATS
HP ●●
ATTACK ●●
DEFENSE ●●
SP.ATTACK ●●●
SP.DEFENSE ●●
SPEED ●●●

● M/F have same form

EVOLUTION PATH

Yanma → Raise it to Lv.33 and teach it AncientPower. Or, level it up while it knows AncientPower. → Yanmega pg. 512

● **MAIN WAYS TO OBTAIN**

PLATINUM	Pastoria Great Marsh
DIAMOND	Pastoria Great Marsh (after you get the National Pokédex/changes by day)
PEARL	Pastoria Great Marsh (after you get the National Pokédex/changes by day)
G B A	Catch in FireRed/LeafGreen and transfer through Pal Park

ABILITY ● Speed Boost ● Compoundeyes

● **LEVEL-UP AND LEARNED MOVES**

Lv	Name	Type	Kind	Power	Acc	PP	Range	DA
Base	Tackle	Normal	Physical	35	95	35	Normal	●
Base	Foresight	Normal	Status	—	—	40	Normal	—
6	Quick Attack	Normal	Physical	40	100	30	Normal	●
11	Double Team	Normal	Status	—	—	15	Self	—
14	SonicBoom	Normal	Special	—	90	20	Normal	—
17	Detect	Fighting	Status	—	—	5	Self	—
22	Supersonic	Normal	Status	—	55	20	Normal	—
27	Uproar	Normal	Special	50	100	10	1 Random	—
30	Pursuit	Dark	Physical	40	100	20	Normal	●
33	AncientPower	Rock	Special	60	100	5	Normal	—
38	Hypnosis	Psychic	Status	—	60	20	Normal	—
43	Wing Attack	Flying	Physical	60	100	35	Normal	—
46	Screech	Normal	Status	—	85	40	Normal	—
49	U-turn	Bug	Physical	70	100	20	Normal	—
54	Air Slash	Flying	Special	75	95	20	Normal	—
57	Bug Buzz	Bug	Special	90	100	10	Normal	—

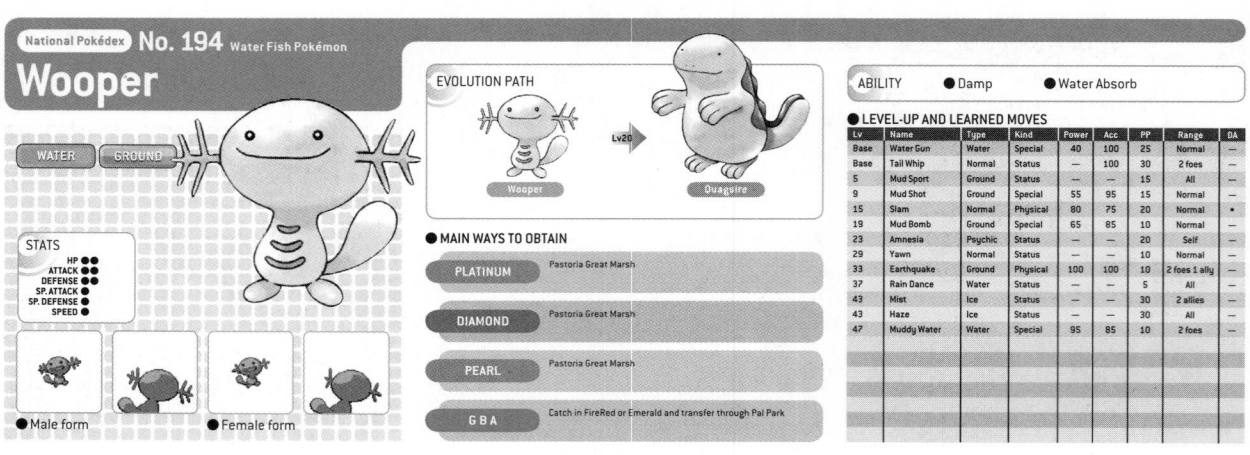

Wooper

WATER / GROUND

STATS
HP ●●
ATTACK ●●●
DEFENSE ●●
SP.ATTACK ●
SP.DEFENSE ●●
SPEED ●

● Male form   ● Female form

EVOLUTION PATH

Wooper — Lv20 → Quagsire

● **MAIN WAYS TO OBTAIN**

PLATINUM	Pastoria Great Marsh
DIAMOND	Pastoria Great Marsh
PEARL	Pastoria Great Marsh
G B A	Catch in FireRed or Emerald and transfer through Pal Park

ABILITY ● Damp ● Water Absorb

● **LEVEL-UP AND LEARNED MOVES**

Lv	Name	Type	Kind	Power	Acc	PP	Range	DA
Base	Water Gun	Water	Special	40	100	25	Normal	—
Base	Tail Whip	Normal	Status	—	100	30	2 foes	—
5	Mud Sport	Ground	Status	—	—	15	All	—
9	Mud Shot	Ground	Special	55	95	15	Normal	—
15	Slam	Normal	Physical	80	75	20	Normal	●
19	Mud Bomb	Ground	Special	65	85	10	Normal	—
23	Amnesia	Psychic	Status	—	—	20	Self	—
29	Yawn	Normal	Status	—	—	10	Normal	—
33	Earthquake	Ground	Physical	100	100	10	2 foes 1 ally	—
37	Rain Dance	Water	Status	—	—	5	All	—
43	Mist	Ice	Status	—	—	30	2 allies	—
43	Haze	Ice	Status	—	—	30	All	—
47	Muddy Water	Water	Special	95	85	10	2 foes	—

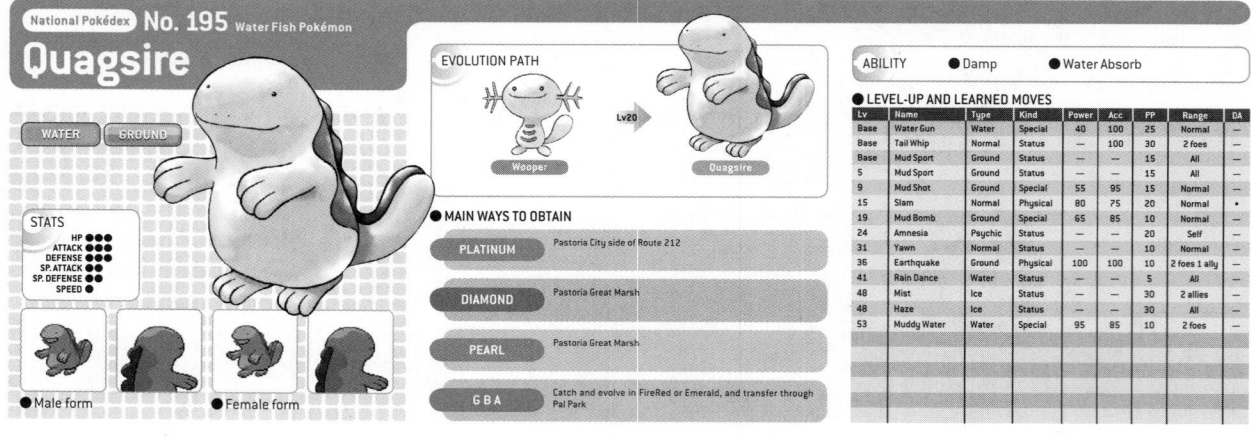

Quagsire

WATER / GROUND

STATS
HP ●●●
ATTACK ●●●
DEFENSE ●●●
SP.ATTACK ●●
SP.DEFENSE ●●
SPEED ●●

● Male form   ● Female form

EVOLUTION PATH

Wooper — Lv20 → Quagsire

● **MAIN WAYS TO OBTAIN**

PLATINUM	Pastoria City side of Route 212
DIAMOND	Pastoria Great Marsh
PEARL	Pastoria Great Marsh
G B A	Catch and evolve in FireRed or Emerald, and transfer through Pal Park

ABILITY ● Damp ● Water Absorb

● **LEVEL-UP AND LEARNED MOVES**

Lv	Name	Type	Kind	Power	Acc	PP	Range	DA
Base	Water Gun	Water	Special	40	100	25	Normal	—
Base	Tail Whip	Normal	Status	—	100	30	2 foes	—
Base	Mud Sport	Ground	Status	—	—	15	All	—
5	Mud Sport	Ground	Status	—	—	15	All	—
9	Mud Shot	Ground	Special	55	95	15	Normal	—
15	Slam	Normal	Physical	80	75	20	Normal	●
19	Mud Bomb	Ground	Special	65	85	10	Normal	—
24	Amnesia	Psychic	Status	—	—	20	Self	—
31	Yawn	Normal	Status	—	—	10	Normal	—
36	Earthquake	Ground	Physical	100	100	10	2 foes 1 ally	—
41	Rain Dance	Water	Status	—	—	5	All	—
48	Mist	Ice	Status	—	—	30	2 allies	—
48	Haze	Ice	Status	—	—	30	All	—
53	Muddy Water	Water	Special	95	85	10	2 foes	—

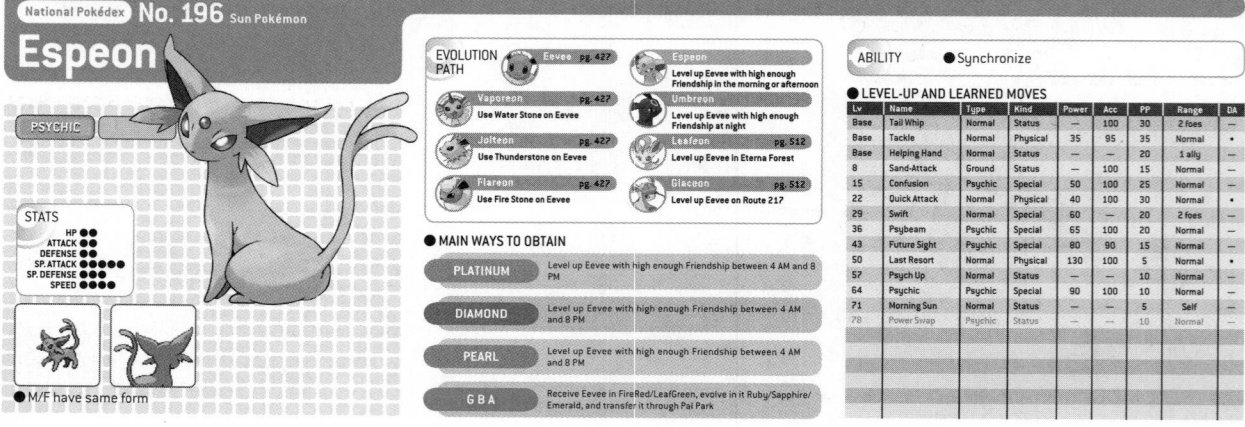

Espeon

PSYCHIC

STATS
HP ●●
ATTACK ●●
DEFENSE ●●
SP.ATTACK ●●●●
SP.DEFENSE ●●●
SPEED ●●●●

● M/F have same form

EVOLUTION PATH

Eevee pg. 427

Espeon — Level up Eevee with high enough Friendship in the morning or afternoon

Vaporeon pg. 427 — Use Water Stone on Eevee
Jolteon pg. 427 — Use Thunderstone on Eevee
Flareon pg. 427 — Use Fire Stone on Eevee
Umbreon — Level up Eevee with high enough Friendship at night
Leafeon pg. 512 — Level up Eevee in Eterna Forest
Glaceon pg. 512 — Level up Eevee on Route 217

● **MAIN WAYS TO OBTAIN**

PLATINUM	Level up Eevee with high enough Friendship between 4 AM and 8 PM
DIAMOND	Level up Eevee with high enough Friendship between 4 AM and 8 PM
PEARL	Level up Eevee with high enough Friendship between 4 AM and 8 PM
G B A	Receive Eevee in FireRed/LeafGreen, evolve in it Ruby/Sapphire/Emerald, and transfer it through Pal Park

ABILITY ● Synchronize

● **LEVEL-UP AND LEARNED MOVES**

Lv	Name	Type	Kind	Power	Acc	PP	Range	DA
Base	Tail Whip	Normal	Status	—	100	30	2 foes	—
Base	Tackle	Normal	Physical	35	95	35	Normal	—
Base	Helping Hand	Normal	Status	—	—	20	1 ally	—
8	Sand-Attack	Ground	Status	—	100	15	Normal	—
15	Confusion	Psychic	Special	50	100	25	Normal	—
22	Quick Attack	Normal	Physical	40	100	30	Normal	●
29	Swift	Normal	Special	60	—	20	2 foes	—
36	Psybeam	Psychic	Special	65	100	20	Normal	—
43	Future Sight	Psychic	Special	80	90	15	Normal	—
50	Last Resort	Normal	Physical	130	100	5	Normal	●
57	Psych Up	Normal	Status	—	—	10	Normal	—
64	Psychic	Psychic	Special	90	100	10	Normal	—
71	Morning Sun	Normal	Status	—	—	5	Self	—
78	Power Swap	Psychic	Status	—	—	10	Normal	—

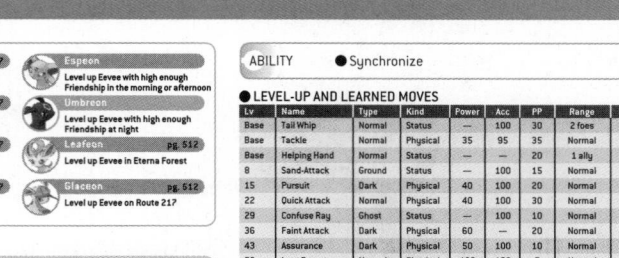

National Pokédex No. 197 — Moonlight Pokémon

Umbreon

DARK

STATS
- HP ●●●
- ATTACK ●●●
- DEFENSE ●●●●●
- SP. ATTACK ●●●
- SP. DEFENSE ●●●●●
- SPEED ●●●●

● M/F have same form

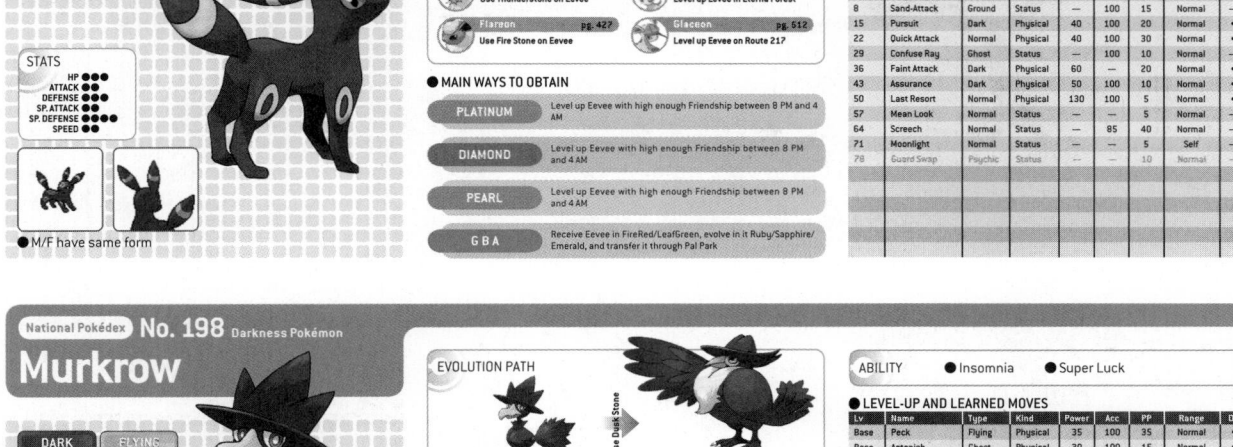

EVOLUTION PATH

Eevee pg. 427		
Vaporeon pg. 427 — Use Water Stone on Eevee	Espeon — Level up Eevee with high enough Friendship in the morning or afternoon	
Jolteon pg. 427 — Use Thunderstone on Eevee	Umbreon — Level up Eevee with high enough Friendship at night	
Flareon pg. 427 — Use Fire Stone on Eevee	Leafeon pg. 512 — Level up Eevee in Eterna Forest	
	Glaceon pg. 512 — Level up Eevee on Route 217	

● MAIN WAYS TO OBTAIN

PLATINUM	Level up Eevee with high enough Friendship between 8 PM and 4 AM
DIAMOND	Level up Eevee with high enough Friendship between 8 PM and 4 AM
PEARL	Level up Eevee with high enough Friendship between 8 PM and 4 AM
G B A	Receive Eevee in FireRed/LeafGreen, evolve in it Ruby/Sapphire/Emerald, and transfer it through Pal Park

ABILITY ● Synchronize

● LEVEL-UP AND LEARNED MOVES

Lv	Name	Type	Kind	Power	Acc	PP	Range	DA
Base	Tail Whip	Normal	Status	—	100	30	2 foes	
Base	Tackle	Normal	Physical	35	95	35	Normal	●
Base	Helping Hand	Normal	Status	—	—	20	1 ally	
8	Sand-Attack	Ground	Status	—	100	15	Normal	—
15	Pursuit	Dark	Physical	40	100	20	Normal	●
22	Quick Attack	Normal	Physical	40	100	30	Normal	●
29	Confuse Ray	Ghost	Status	—	100	10	Normal	—
36	Faint Attack	Dark	Physical	60	—	20	Normal	●
43	Assurance	Dark	Physical	50	100	10	Normal	●
50	Last Resort	Normal	Physical	130	100	5	Normal	●
57	Mean Look	Normal	Status	—	—	5	Normal	—
64	Screech	Normal	Status	—	85	40	Normal	—
71	Moonlight	Normal	Status	—	—	5	Self	—
78	Guard Swap	Psychic	Status	—	—	10	Normal	—

National Pokédex No. 198 — Darkness Pokémon

Murkrow

DARK **FLYING**

STATS
- HP ●●
- ATTACK ●●●
- DEFENSE ●●
- SP. ATTACK ●●●
- SP. DEFENSE ●●
- SPEED ●●●

● Male form   ● Female form

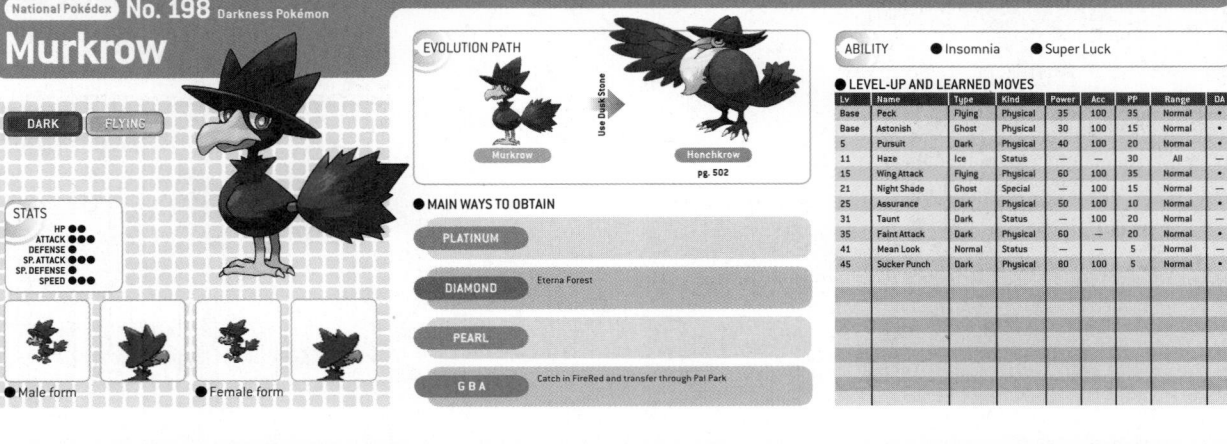

EVOLUTION PATH

Murkrow → (Use Dusk Stone) → Honchkrow pg. 502

● MAIN WAYS TO OBTAIN

PLATINUM	
DIAMOND	Eterna Forest
PEARL	
G B A	Catch in FireRed and transfer through Pal Park

ABILITY ● Insomnia ● Super Luck

● LEVEL-UP AND LEARNED MOVES

Lv	Name	Type	Kind	Power	Acc	PP	Range	DA
Base	Peck	Flying	Physical	35	100	35	Normal	●
Base	Astonish	Ghost	Physical	30	100	15	Normal	●
5	Pursuit	Dark	Physical	40	100	20	Normal	●
11	Haze	Ice	Status	—	—	30	All	—
15	Wing Attack	Flying	Physical	60	100	35	Normal	●
21	Night Shade	Ghost	Special	—	100	15	Normal	—
25	Assurance	Dark	Physical	50	100	10	Normal	●
31	Taunt	Dark	Status	—	100	20	Normal	—
35	Faint Attack	Dark	Physical	60	—	20	Normal	●
41	Mean Look	Normal	Status	—	—	5	Normal	—
45	Sucker Punch	Dark	Physical	80	100	5	Normal	●

National Pokédex No. 199 — Royal Pokémon

Slowking

WATER **PSYCHIC**

STATS
- HP ●●●
- ATTACK ●●●
- DEFENSE ●●●
- SP. ATTACK ●●●
- SP. DEFENSE ●●●●●
- SPEED ●●

● M/F have same form

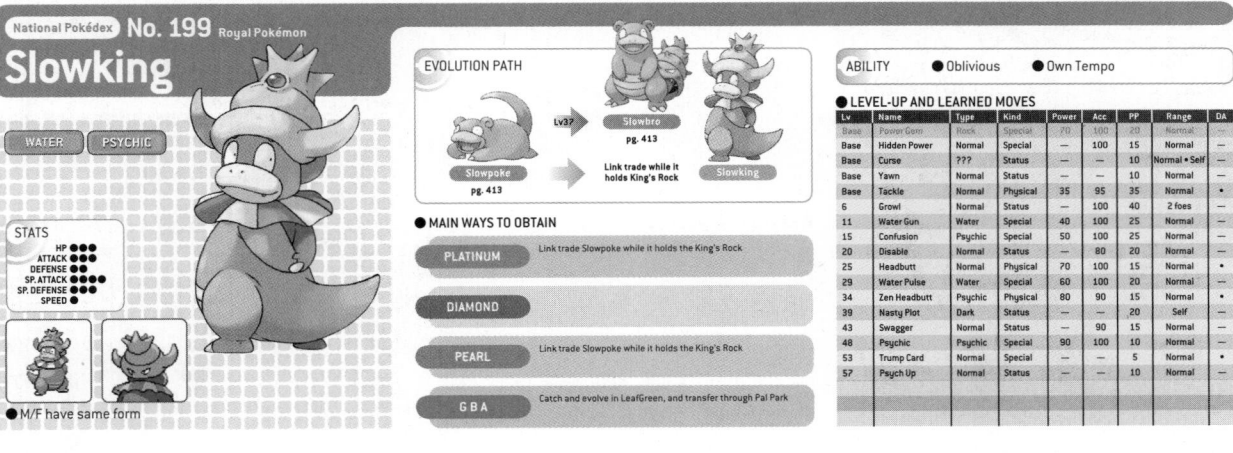

EVOLUTION PATH

Slowpoke pg. 413 → (Lv37) → Slowbro pg. 413
Slowpoke → (Link trade while it holds King's Rock) → Slowking

● MAIN WAYS TO OBTAIN

PLATINUM	Link trade Slowpoke while it holds the King's Rock
DIAMOND	
PEARL	Link trade Slowpoke while it holds the King's Rock
G B A	Catch and evolve in LeafGreen, and transfer through Pal Park

ABILITY ● Oblivious ● Own Tempo

● LEVEL-UP AND LEARNED MOVES

Lv	Name	Type	Kind	Power	Acc	PP	Range	DA
Base	Power Gem	Rock	Special	70	100	20	Normal	—
Base	Hidden Power	Normal	Special	—	100	15	Normal	—
Base	Curse	???	Status	—	—	10	Normal • Self	—
Base	Yawn	Normal	Status	—	—	10	Normal	—
Base	Tackle	Normal	Physical	35	95	35	Normal	●
6	Growl	Normal	Status	—	100	40	2 foes	—
11	Water Gun	Water	Special	40	100	25	Normal	—
15	Confusion	Psychic	Special	50	100	25	Normal	—
20	Disable	Normal	Status	—	80	20	Normal	—
25	Headbutt	Normal	Physical	70	100	15	Normal	●
29	Water Pulse	Water	Special	60	100	20	Normal	—
34	Zen Headbutt	Psychic	Physical	80	90	15	Normal	●
39	Nasty Plot	Dark	Status	—	—	20	Self	—
43	Swagger	Normal	Status	—	90	15	Normal	—
48	Psychic	Psychic	Special	90	100	10	Normal	—
53	Trump Card	Normal	Special	—	—	5	Normal	—
57	Psych Up	Normal	Status	—	—	10	Normal	—

National Pokédex No. 200 — Screech Pokémon

Misdreavus

GHOST

STATS
- HP ●●
- ATTACK ●●
- DEFENSE ●●
- SP. ATTACK ●●●
- SP. DEFENSE ●●●
- SPEED ●●●

● M/F have same form

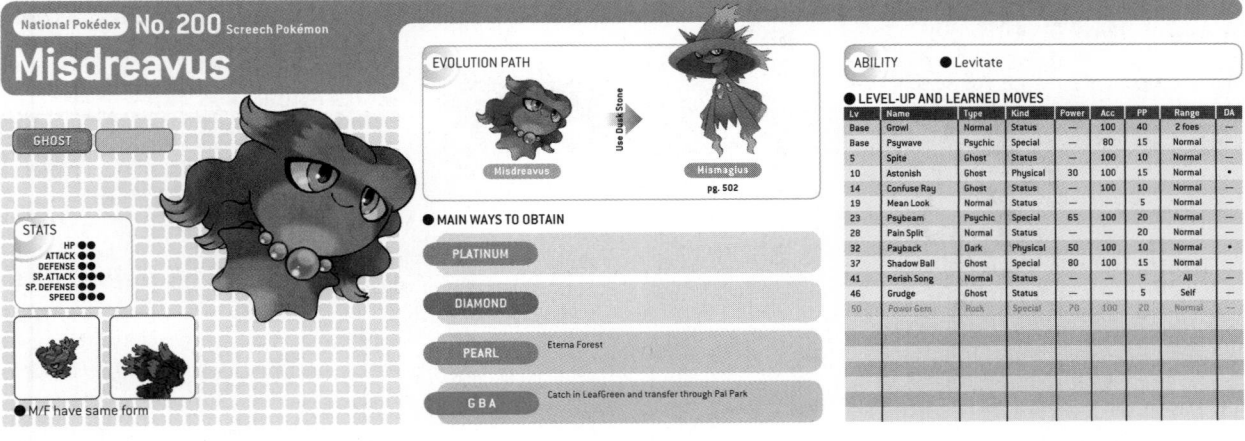

EVOLUTION PATH

Misdreavus → (Use Dusk Stone) → Mismagius pg. 502

● MAIN WAYS TO OBTAIN

PLATINUM	
DIAMOND	
PEARL	Eterna Forest
G B A	Catch in LeafGreen and transfer through Pal Park

ABILITY ● Levitate

● LEVEL-UP AND LEARNED MOVES

Lv	Name	Type	Kind	Power	Acc	PP	Range	DA
Base	Growl	Normal	Status	—	100	40	2 foes	—
Base	Psywave	Psychic	Special	—	80	15	Normal	—
5	Spite	Ghost	Status	—	100	10	Normal	—
10	Astonish	Ghost	Physical	30	100	15	Normal	●
14	Confuse Ray	Ghost	Status	—	100	10	Normal	—
19	Mean Look	Normal	Status	—	—	5	Normal	—
23	Psybeam	Psychic	Special	65	100	20	Normal	—
28	Pain Split	Normal	Status	—	—	20	Normal	—
32	Payback	Dark	Physical	50	100	10	Normal	●
37	Shadow Ball	Ghost	Special	80	100	15	Normal	—
41	Perish Song	Normal	Status	—	—	5	All	—
46	Grudge	Ghost	Status	—	—	5	Self	—
50	Power Gem	Rock	Special	70	100	20	Normal	—

 NATIONAL POKÉDEX

200
MISDREAVUS

National Pokédex No. 201 Symbol Pokémon
Unown

PSYCHIC

STATS
HP ●●
ATTACK ●●●
DEFENSE ●●
SP. ATTACK ●●●
SP. DEFENSE ●●
SPEED ●●

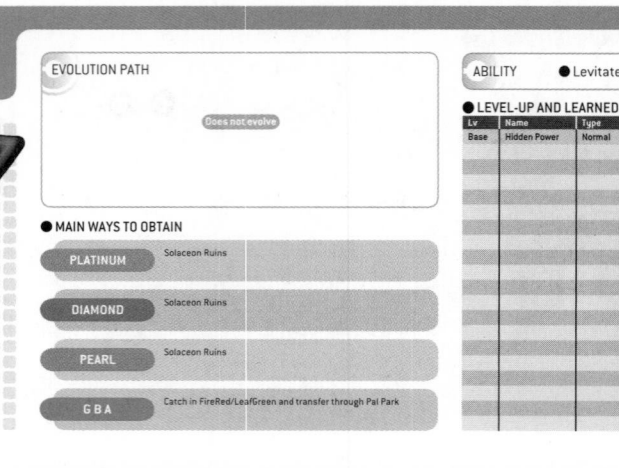

● Gender unknown

EVOLUTION PATH
Does not evolve

● MAIN WAYS TO OBTAIN

PLATINUM	Solaceon Ruins
DIAMOND	Solaceon Ruins
PEARL	Solaceon Ruins
G B A	Catch in FireRed/LeafGreen and transfer through Pal Park

ABILITY ● Levitate

● LEVEL-UP AND LEARNED MOVES

Lv	Name	Type	Kind	Power	Acc	PP	Range	DA
Base	Hidden Power	Normal	Special	—	100	15	Normal	—

National Pokédex No. 202 Patient Pokémon
Wobbuffet

PSYCHIC

STATS
HP ●●●●●
ATTACK ●●
DEFENSE ●●
SP. ATTACK ●●
SP. DEFENSE ●●
SPEED ●●

● Male form ● Female form

EVOLUTION PATH

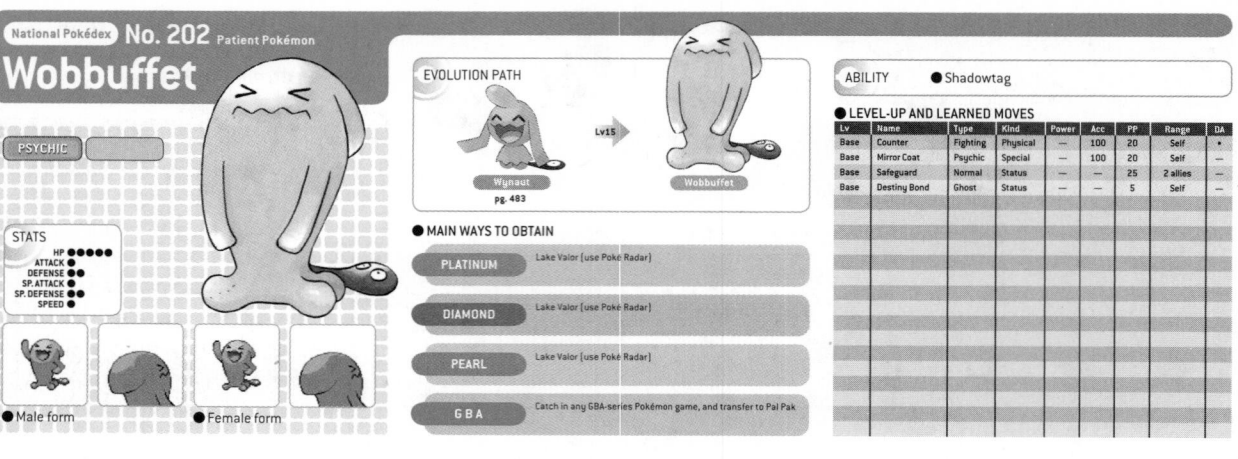

Wynaut → Lv15 → Wobbuffet
pg. 483

● MAIN WAYS TO OBTAIN

PLATINUM	Lake Valor [use Poke Radar]
DIAMOND	Lake Valor [use Poke Radar]
PEARL	Lake Valor [use Poke Radar]
G B A	Catch in any GBA-series Pokémon game, and transfer to Pal Pak

ABILITY ● Shadowtag

● LEVEL-UP AND LEARNED MOVES

Lv	Name	Type	Kind	Power	Acc	PP	Range	DA
Base	Counter	Fighting	Physical	—	100	20	Self	●
Base	Mirror Coat	Psychic	Special	—	100	20	Self	—
Base	Safeguard	Normal	Status	—	—	25	2 allies	—
Base	Destiny Bond	Ghost	Status	—	—	5	Self	—

National Pokédex No. 203 Long Neck Pokémon
Girafarig

NORMAL   PSYCHIC

STATS
HP ●●●
ATTACK ●●●
DEFENSE ●●●
SP. ATTACK ●●●
SP. DEFENSE ●●●
SPEED ●●●

● Male form ● Female form

EVOLUTION PATH
Does not evolve

● MAIN WAYS TO OBTAIN

PLATINUM	Valor Lakefront
DIAMOND	Route 214
PEARL	Route 214
G B A	Catch in Ruby/Sapphire/Emerald and transfer through Pal Park

ABILITY ● Inner Focus ● Early Bird

● LEVEL-UP AND LEARNED MOVES

Lv	Name	Type	Kind	Power	Acc	PP	Range	DA
Base	Power Swap	Psychic	Status	—	—	10	Normal	—
Base	Guard Swap	Psychic	Status	—	—	10	Normal	—
Base	Astonish	Ghost	Physical	30	100	15	Normal	●
Base	Tackle	Normal	Physical	35	95	35	Normal	●
Base	Growl	Normal	Status	—	100	40	2 foes	—
Base	Confusion	Psychic	Special	50	100	25	Normal	—
5	Odor Sleuth	Normal	Status	—	—	40	Normal	—
10	Stomp	Normal	Physical	65	100	20	Normal	●
14	Agility	Psychic	Status	—	—	30	Self	—
19	Psybeam	Psychic	Special	65	100	20	Normal	—
23	Baton Pass	Normal	Status	—	—	40	Self	—
28	Assurance	Dark	Physical	50	100	10	Normal	●
32	Double Hit	Normal	Physical	35	90	10	Normal	●
37	Psychic	Psychic	Special	90	100	10	Normal	—
41	Zen Headbutt	Psychic	Physical	80	90	15	Normal	●
46	Crunch	Dark	Physical	80	100	15	Normal	●

National Pokédex No. 204 Bagworm Pokémon
Pineco

BUG

STATS
HP ●●●
ATTACK ●●●
DEFENSE ●●●
SP. ATTACK ●●
SP. DEFENSE ●●●
SPEED ●

● M/F have same form

EVOLUTION PATH

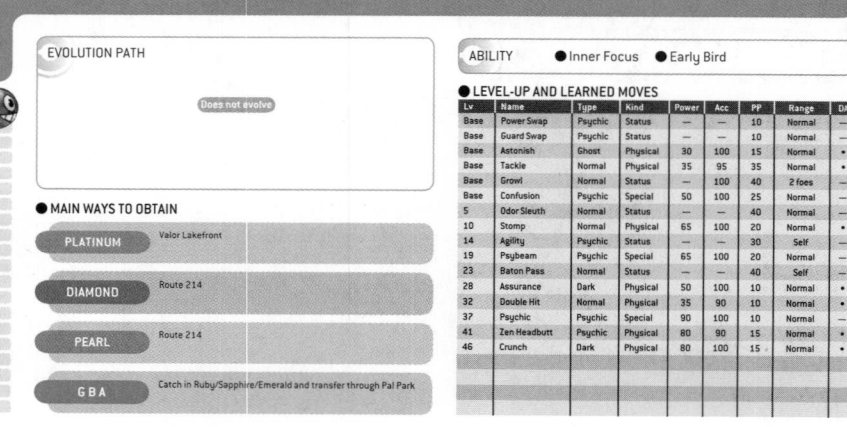

Pineco → Lv31 → Forretress

● MAIN WAYS TO OBTAIN

PLATINUM	Route 203 [after you get the National Pokédex, insert Pokémon Emerald into the Nintendo DS's GBA cartridge slot]
DIAMOND	Route 203 [after you get the National Pokédex, insert Pokémon Emerald into the Nintendo DS's GBA cartridge slot]
PEARL	Route 203 [after you get the National Pokédex, insert Pokémon Emerald into the Nintendo DS's GBA cartridge slot]
G B A	Catch in Emerald and transfer through Pal Park

ABILITY ● Sturdy

● LEVEL-UP AND LEARNED MOVES

Lv	Name	Type	Kind	Power	Acc	PP	Range	DA
Base	Tackle	Normal	Physical	35	95	35	Normal	●
Base	Protect	Normal	Status	—	—	10	Self	—
6	Selfdestruct	Normal	Physical	200	100	5	2 foes 1 ally	—
9	Bug Bite	Bug	Physical	60	100	20	Normal	●
12	Take Down	Normal	Physical	90	85	20	Normal	●
17	Rapid Spin	Normal	Physical	20	100	40	Normal	●
20	Bide	Normal	Physical	—	—	10	Self	●
23	Natural Gift	Normal	Physical	—	100	15	Normal	—
28	Spikes	Ground	Status	—	—	20	2 foes	—
31	Payback	Dark	Physical	50	100	10	Normal	●
34	Explosion	Normal	Physical	250	100	5	2 foes+1 ally	—
39	Iron Defense	Steel	Status	—	—	15	Self	—
42	Gyro Ball	Steel	Physical	—	100	5	Normal	●
45	Double-Edge	Normal	Physical	120	100	15	Normal	●

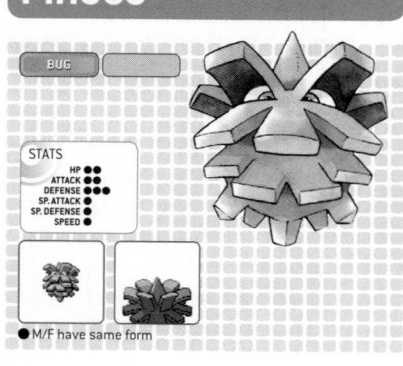

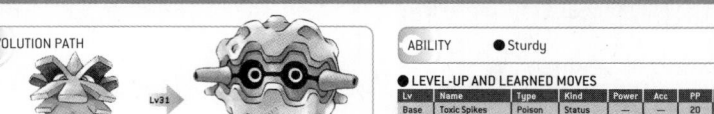

National Pokédex No. 205 — Bagworm Pokémon
Forretress

BUG · STEEL

STATS
- HP ●●●
- ATTACK ●●●●
- DEFENSE ●●●●●
- SP. ATTACK ●●●
- SP. DEFENSE ●●●
- SPEED ●●

● M/F have same form

EVOLUTION PATH

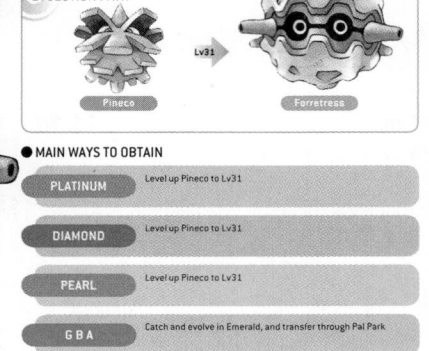

Pineco → Lv31 → Forretress

ABILITY ● Sturdy

MAIN WAYS TO OBTAIN

PLATINUM	Level up Pineco to Lv31
DIAMOND	Level up Pineco to Lv31
PEARL	Level up Pineco to Lv31
GBA	Catch and evolve in Emerald, and transfer through Pal Park

● LEVEL-UP AND LEARNED MOVES

Lv	Name	Type	Kind	Power	Acc	PP	Range	DA
Base	Toxic Spikes	Poison	Status	—	—	20	2 foes	—
Base	Tackle	Normal	Physical	35	95	35	Normal	●
Base	Protect	Normal	Status	—	—	10	Self	—
Base	Selfdestruct	Normal	Physical	200	100	5	2 foes 1 ally	—
Base	Bug Bite	Bug	Physical	60	100	20	Normal	●
6	Selfdestruct	Normal	Physical	200	100	5	2 foes 1 ally	—
9	Bug Bite	Bug	Physical	60	100	20	Normal	●
12	Take Down	Normal	Physical	90	85	20	Normal	●
17	Rapid Spin	Normal	Physical	20	100	40	Normal	●
20	Bide	Normal	Physical	—	—	10	Self	●
23	Natural Gift	Normal	Physical	—	100	15	Normal	—
28	Spikes	Ground	Status	—	—	20	2 foes	—
31	Mirror Shot	Steel	Special	65	85	10	Normal	●
33	Payback	Dark	Physical	50	100	10	Normal	●
38	Explosion	Normal	Physical	250	100	5	2 foes 1 ally	—
45	Iron Defense	Steel	Status	—	—	15	Self	—
50	Gyro Ball	Steel	Physical	—	100	5	Normal	●
55	Double-Edge	Normal	Physical	120	100	15	Normal	●
62	Magnet Rise	Electric	Status	—	—	10	Self	—
67	Zap Cannon	Electric	Special	120	50	5	Normal	●

National Pokédex No. 206 — Land Snake Pokémon
Dunsparce

NORMAL

STATS
- HP ●●●
- ATTACK ●●●
- DEFENSE ●●●
- SP. ATTACK ●●●
- SP. DEFENSE ●●●
- SPEED ●●

● M/F have same form

EVOLUTION PATH

Does not evolve

ABILITY ● Serene Grace ● Run Away

MAIN WAYS TO OBTAIN

PLATINUM	Route 208 (mass outbreak)
DIAMOND	Route 208 (mass outbreak)
PEARL	Route 208 (mass outbreak)
GBA	Catch in FireRed/LeafGreen and transfer through Pal Park

● LEVEL-UP AND LEARNED MOVES

Lv	Name	Type	Kind	Power	Acc	PP	Range	DA
Base	Rage	Normal	Physical	20	100	20	Normal	●
5	Defense Curl	Normal	Status	—	—	40	Self	—
9	Yawn	Normal	Status	—	—	10	Normal	—
13	Glare	Normal	Status	—	75	30	Normal	—
17	Rollout	Rock	Physical	30	90	20	Normal	●
21	Spite	Ghost	Status	—	100	10	Normal	—
25	Pursuit	Dark	Physical	40	100	20	Normal	●
29	Screech	Normal	Status	—	85	40	Normal	—
33	Roost	Flying	Status	—	—	10	Self	—
37	Take Down	Normal	Physical	90	85	20	Normal	●
41	AncientPower	Rock	Special	60	100	5	Normal	—
45	Dig	Ground	Physical	80	100	10	Normal	●
49	Endeavor	Normal	Physical	—	100	5	Normal	●
53	Flail	Normal	Physical	—	100	15	Normal	●

National Pokédex No. 207 — Flyscorpion Pokémon
Gligar

GROUND · FLYING

STATS
- HP ●●
- ATTACK ●●●
- DEFENSE ●●●
- SP. ATTACK ●●
- SP. DEFENSE ●●
- SPEED ●●●

● Male form   ● Female form

EVOLUTION PATH

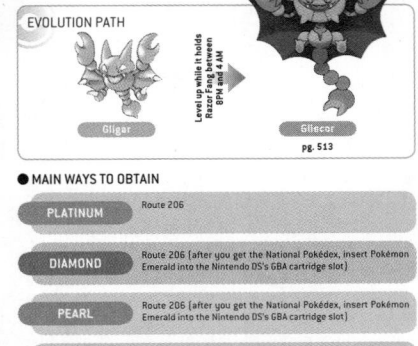

Gligar → Level up while it holds Razor Fang between 8PM and 4AM → Gliscor (pg. 513)

ABILITY ● Hyper Cutter ● Sand Veil

MAIN WAYS TO OBTAIN

PLATINUM	Route 206
DIAMOND	Route 206 (after you get the National Pokédex, insert Pokémon Emerald into the Nintendo DS's GBA cartridge slot)
PEARL	Route 206 (after you get the National Pokédex, insert Pokémon Emerald into the Nintendo DS's GBA cartridge slot)
GBA	Catch in Emerald and transfer through Pal Park

● LEVEL-UP AND LEARNED MOVES

Lv	Name	Type	Kind	Power	Acc	PP	Range	DA
Base	Poison Sting	Poison	Physical	15	100	35	Normal	—
5	Sand-Attack	Ground	Status	—	100	15	Normal	—
9	Harden	Normal	Status	—	—	30	Self	—
12	Knock Off	Dark	Physical	20	100	20	Normal	●
16	Quick Attack	Normal	Physical	40	100	30	Normal	●
20	Fury Cutter	Bug	Physical	10	95	20	Normal	●
23	Faint Attack	Dark	Physical	60	—	20	Normal	●
27	Screech	Normal	Status	—	85	40	Normal	—
31	Slash	Normal	Physical	70	100	20	Normal	●
34	Swords Dance	Normal	Status	—	—	30	Self	—
38	U-turn	Bug	Physical	70	100	20	Normal	●
42	X-Scissor	Bug	Physical	80	100	15	Normal	●
45	Guillotine	Normal	Physical	—	30	5	Normal	●

National Pokédex No. 208 — Iron Snake Pokémon
Steelix

STEEL · GROUND

STATS
- HP ●●
- ATTACK ●●●
- DEFENSE ●●●●●
- SP. ATTACK ●●
- SP. DEFENSE ●●
- SPEED ●●

● Male form   ● Female form

EVOLUTION PATH

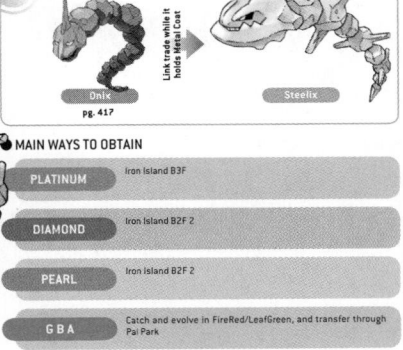

Onix (pg. 417) → Link trade while it holds Metal Coat → Steelix

ABILITY ● Rock Head ● Sturdy

MAIN WAYS TO OBTAIN

PLATINUM	Iron Island B3F
DIAMOND	Iron Island B2F 2
PEARL	Iron Island B2F 2
GBA	Catch and evolve in FireRed/LeafGreen, and transfer through Pal Park

● LEVEL-UP AND LEARNED MOVES

Lv	Name	Type	Kind	Power	Acc	PP	Range	DA
Base	Thunder Fang	Electric	Physical	65	95	15	Normal	●
Base	Ice Fang	Ice	Physical	65	95	15	Normal	●
Base	Fire Fang	Fire	Physical	65	95	15	Normal	●
Base	Mud Sport	Ground	Status	—	—	15	All	—
Base	Tackle	Normal	Physical	35	95	35	Normal	●
Base	Harden	Normal	Status	—	—	30	Self	—
Base	Bind	Normal	Physical	15	75	20	Normal	●
6	Screech	Normal	Status	—	85	40	Normal	—
9	Rock Throw	Rock	Physical	50	90	15	Normal	●
14	Rage	Normal	Physical	20	100	20	Normal	●
17	Rock Tomb	Rock	Physical	50	80	10	Normal	●
22	Sandstorm	Rock	Status	—	—	10	All	—
25	Slam	Normal	Physical	80	75	20	Normal	●
30	Rock Polish	Rock	Status	—	—	20	Self	—
33	DragonBreath	Dragon	Special	60	100	20	Normal	●
38	Curse	???	—	—	—	10	Normal · Self	—
41	Iron Tail	Steel	Physical	100	75	15	Normal	●
46	Crunch	Dark	Physical	80	100	15	Normal	●
49	Double-Edge	Normal	Physical	120	100	15	Normal	●
54	Stone Edge	Rock	Physical	100	80	5	Normal	●

208 STEELIX

National Pokédex No. 209 Fairy Pokémon
Snubbull

NORMAL

STATS
HP
ATTACK
DEFENSE
SP. ATTACK
SP. DEFENSE
SPEED

● M/F have same form

EVOLUTION PATH

Snubbull → Lv23 → Granbull

● ABILITY ● Intimidate ● Run Away

● LEVEL-UP AND LEARNED MOVES

Lv	Name	Type	Kind	Power	Acc	PP	Range	DA
Base	Ice Fang	Ice	Physical	65	95	15	Normal	●
Base	Fire Fang	Fire	Physical	65	95	15	Normal	●
Base	Thunder Fang	Electric	Physical	65	95	15	Normal	●
Base	Tackle	Normal	Physical	35	95	35	Normal	●
Base	Scary Face	Normal	Status	—	90	10	Normal	—
Base	Tail Whip	Normal	Status	—	100	30	2 foes	●
Base	Charm	Normal	Status	—	100	20	Normal	●
7	Bite	Dark	Physical	60	100	25	Normal	●
13	Lick	Ghost	Physical	20	100	30	Normal	●
19	Headbutt	Normal	Physical	70	100	15	Normal	●
25	Roar	Normal	Status	—	100	20	Normal	—
31	Rage	Normal	Physical	20	100	20	Normal	●
37	Take Down	Normal	Physical	90	85	20	Normal	●
43	Payback	Dark	Physical	50	100	10	Normal	●
49	Crunch	Dark	Physical	80	100	15	Normal	●

● MAIN WAYS TO OBTAIN

PLATINUM	Route 209 (mass outbreak)
DIAMOND	Route 209 (mass outbreak)
PEARL	Route 209 (mass outbreak)
GBA	Catch in Emerald and transfer through Pal Park

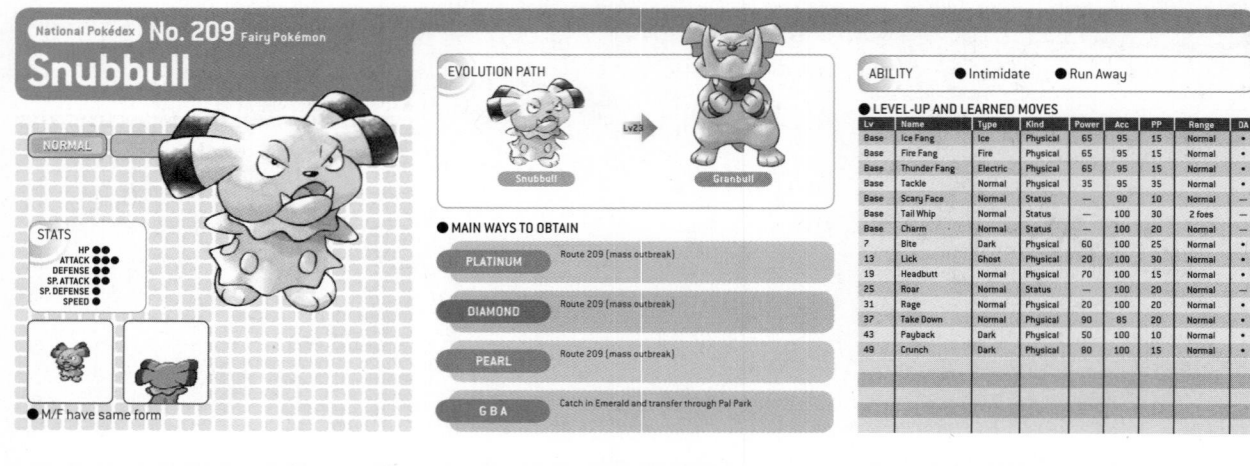

National Pokédex No. 210 Fairy Pokémon
Granbull

NORMAL

STATS
HP
ATTACK
DEFENSE
SP. ATTACK
SP. DEFENSE
SPEED

● M/F have same form

EVOLUTION PATH

Snubbull → Lv23 → Granbull

● ABILITY ● Intimidate ● Quick Feet

● LEVEL-UP AND LEARNED MOVES

Lv	Name	Type	Kind	Power	Acc	PP	Range	DA
Base	Ice Fang	Ice	Physical	65	95	15	Normal	●
Base	Fire Fang	Fire	Physical	65	95	15	Normal	●
Base	Thunder Fang	Electric	Physical	65	95	15	Normal	●
Base	Tackle	Normal	Physical	35	95	35	Normal	●
Base	Scary Face	Normal	Status	—	90	10	Normal	—
Base	Tail Whip	Normal	Status	—	100	30	2 foes	●
Base	Charm	Normal	Status	—	100	20	Normal	●
7	Bite	Dark	Physical	60	100	25	Normal	●
13	Lick	Ghost	Physical	20	100	30	Normal	●
19	Headbutt	Normal	Physical	70	100	15	Normal	●
27	Roar	Normal	Status	—	100	20	Normal	—
35	Rage	Normal	Physical	20	100	20	Normal	●
43	Take Down	Normal	Physical	90	85	20	Normal	●
51	Payback	Dark	Physical	50	100	10	Normal	●
59	Crunch	Dark	Physical	80	100	15	Normal	●

● MAIN WAYS TO OBTAIN

PLATINUM	Level up Snubbull to Lv23
DIAMOND	Level up Snubbull to Lv23
PEARL	Level up Snubbull to Lv23
GBA	Catch and evolve in Emerald, and transfer through Pal Park

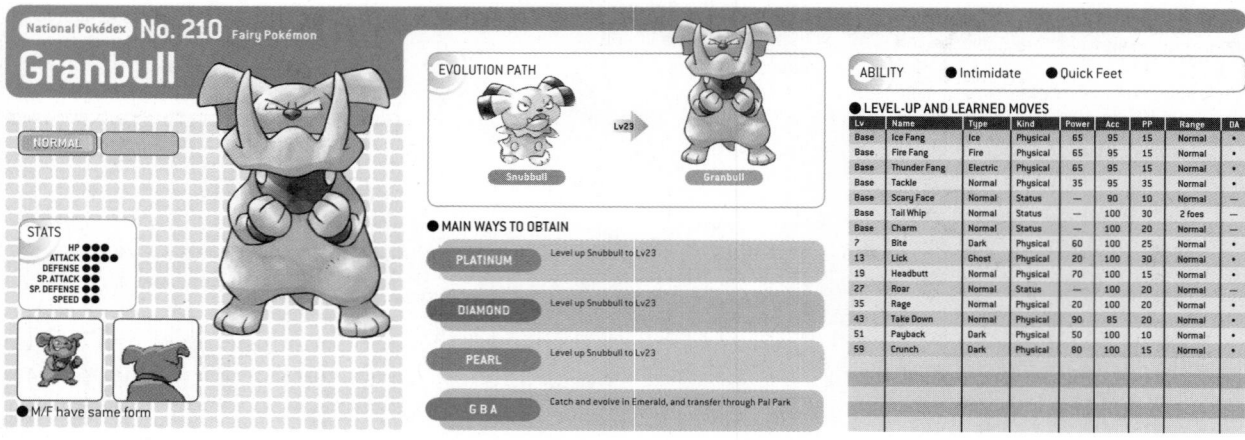

National Pokédex No. 211 Balloon Pokémon
Qwilfish

WATER POISON

STATS
HP
ATTACK
DEFENSE
SP. ATTACK
SP. DEFENSE
SPEED

● M/F have same form

EVOLUTION PATH

Does not evolve

● ABILITY ● Poison Point ● Swift Swim

● LEVEL-UP AND LEARNED MOVES

Lv	Name	Type	Kind	Power	Acc	PP	Range	DA
Base	Spikes	Ground	Status	—	—	20	2 foes	—
Base	Tackle	Normal	Physical	35	95	35	Normal	—
Base	Poison Sting	Poison	Physical	15	100	35	Normal	—
9	Harden	Normal	Status	—	—	30	Self	—
9	Minimize	Normal	Status	—	—	10	Self	—
13	Water Gun	Water	Special	40	100	25	Normal	—
17	Rollout	Rock	Physical	30	90	20	Normal	●
21	Toxic Spikes	Poison	Status	—	—	20	2 foes	—
25	Stockpile	Normal	Status	—	—	20	Self	—
25	Spit Up	Normal	Special	—	100	10	Normal	●
29	Revenge	Fighting	Physical	60	100	10	Normal	●
33	Brine	Water	Special	65	100	10	Normal	—
37	Pin Missile	Bug	Physical	14	85	20	Normal	●
41	Take Down	Normal	Physical	90	85	20	Normal	●
45	Aqua Tail	Water	Physical	90	90	10	Normal	●
49	Poison Jab	Poison	Physical	80	100	20	Normal	●
53	Destiny Bond	Ghost	Status	—	—	5	Self	—
57	Hydro Pump	Water	Special	120	80	5	Normal	—

● MAIN WAYS TO OBTAIN

PLATINUM	Iron Island exterior (Super Rod)
DIAMOND	Iron Island exterior (Super Rod)
PEARL	Iron Island exterior (Super Rod)
GBA	Catch in FireRed and transfer through Pal Park

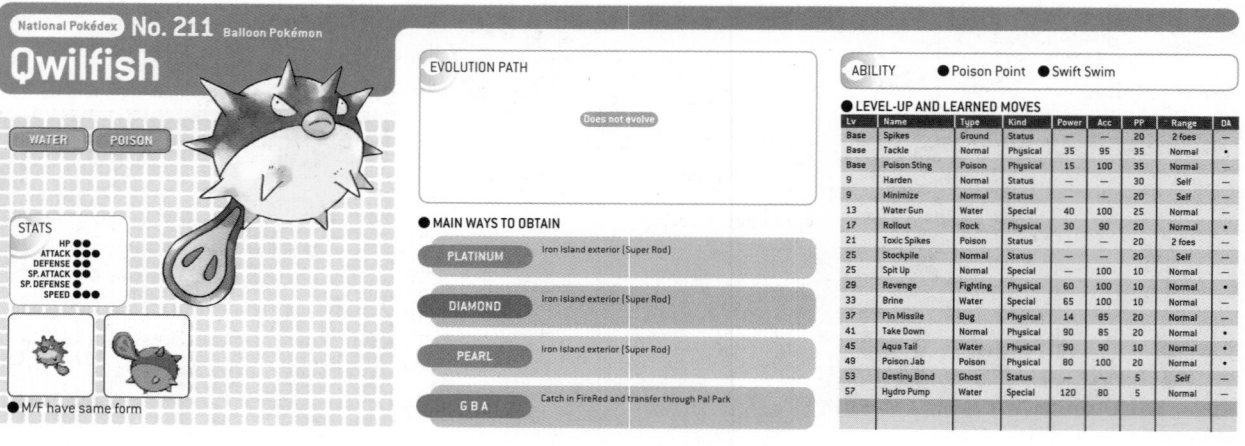

National Pokédex No. 212 Pincer Pokémon
Scizor

BUG STEEL

STATS
HP
ATTACK
DEFENSE
SP. ATTACK
SP. DEFENSE
SPEED

● Male form ● Female form

EVOLUTION PATH

Scyther (pg. 424) → Link trade while it holds Metal Coat → Scizor

● ABILITY ● Swarm ● Technician

● LEVEL-UP AND LEARNED MOVES

Lv	Name	Type	Kind	Power	Acc	PP	Range	DA
Base	Bullet Punch	Steel	Physical	40	100	30	Normal	●
Base	Quick Attack	Normal	Physical	40	100	30	Normal	●
Base	Leer	Normal	Status	—	100	30	2 foes	●
5	Focus Energy	Normal	Status	—	—	30	Self	—
9	Pursuit	Dark	Physical	40	100	20	Normal	●
13	False Swipe	Normal	Physical	40	100	40	Normal	●
17	Agility	Psychic	Status	—	—	30	Self	—
21	Metal Claw	Steel	Physical	50	95	35	Normal	●
25	Fury Cutter	Bug	Physical	10	95	20	Normal	●
29	Slash	Normal	Physical	70	100	20	Normal	●
33	Razor Wind	Normal	Special	80	100	10	2 foes	—
37	Iron Defense	Steel	Status	—	—	15	Self	—
41	X-Scissor	Bug	Physical	80	100	15	Normal	●
45	Night Slash	Dark	Physical	70	100	15	Normal	●
49	Double Hit	Normal	Physical	35	90	10	Normal	●
53	Iron Head	Steel	Physical	80	100	15	Normal	●
57	Swords Dance	Normal	Status	—	—	30	Self	—
61	Feint	Normal	Physical	50	100	10	Normal	●

● MAIN WAYS TO OBTAIN

PLATINUM	Link trade Scyther while it holds Metal Coat
DIAMOND	Link trade Scyther while it holds Metal Coat
PEARL	
GBA	Catch and evolve in FireRed, and transfer through Pal Park

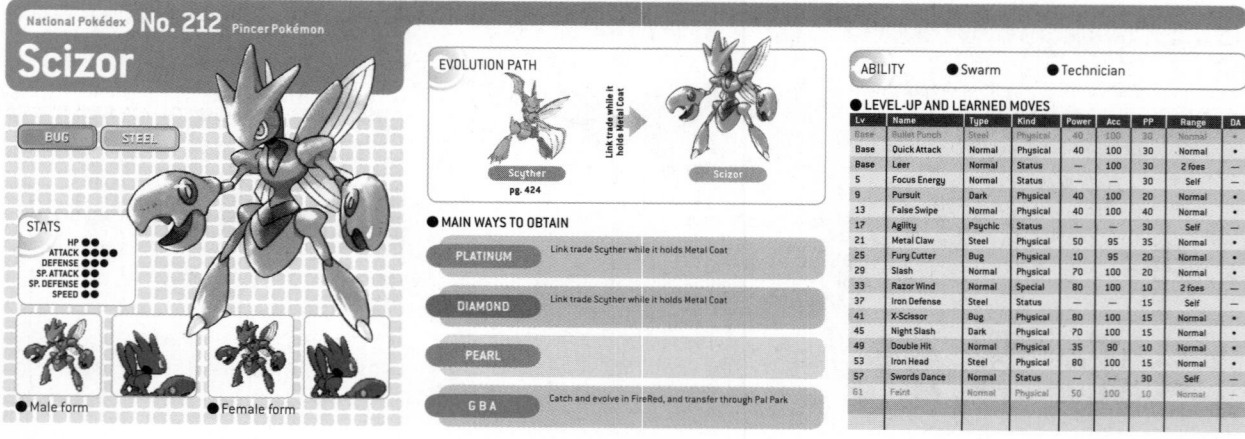

Shuckle

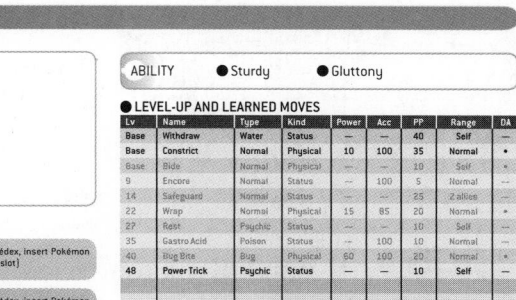

BUG | ROCK

STATS
- HP
- ATTACK
- DEFENSE
- SP. ATTACK
- SP. DEFENSE
- SPEED

● M/F have same form

EVOLUTION PATH

Does not evolve

MAIN WAYS TO OBTAIN

PLATINUM	Route 224 [after you get the National Pokédex, insert Pokémon Emerald in the Nintendo DS's GBA cartridge slot]
DIAMOND	Route 224 [after you get the National Pokédex, insert Pokémon Emerald in the Nintendo DS's GBA cartridge slot]
PEARL	Route 224 [after you get the National Pokédex, insert Pokémon Emerald in the Nintendo DS's GBA cartridge slot]
GBA	Catch in Emerald and transfer through Pal Park

ABILITY ● Sturdy ● Gluttony

● LEVEL-UP AND LEARNED MOVES

Lv	Name	Type	Kind	Power	Acc	PP	Range	DA
Base	Withdraw	Water	Status	—	—	40	Self	
Base	Constrict	Normal	Physical	10	100	35	Normal	•
Base	Bide	Normal	Physical	—	—	10	Self	
9	Encore	Normal	Status	—	100	5	Normal	
14	Safeguard	Normal	Status	—	—	25	2 allies	
22	Wrap	Normal	Physical	15	85	20	Normal	•
27	Rest	Psychic	Status	—	—	10	Self	
35	Gastro Acid	Poison	Status	—	100	10	Normal	•
40	Bug Bite	Bug	Physical	60	100	20	Normal	•
48	Power Trick	Psychic	Status	—	—	10	Self	

Heracross

BUG | Fighting-

STATS
- HP
- ATTACK
- DEFENSE
- SP. ATTACK
- SP. DEFENSE
- SPEED

● Male form   ● Female form

EVOLUTION PATH

Does not evolve

MAIN WAYS TO OBTAIN

PLATINUM	Spread Honey on a Honey Tree
DIAMOND	Spread Honey on a Honey Tree
PEARL	Spread Honey on a Honey Tree
GBA	Catch in any GBA-series Pokémon game, and transfer to Pal Pak

ABILITY ● Swarm ● Guts

● LEVEL-UP AND LEARNED MOVES

Lv	Name	Type	Kind	Power	Acc	PP	Range	DA
Base	Night Slash	Dark	Physical	70	100	15	Normal	•
Base	Tackle	Normal	Physical	35	95	35	Normal	•
Base	Leer	Normal	Status	—	100	30	2 foes	—
Base	Horn Attack	Normal	Physical	65	100	25	Normal	•
Base	Endure	Normal	Status	—	—	10	Self	—
7	Fury Attack	Normal	Physical	15	85	20	Normal	•
13	Aerial Ace	Flying	Physical	60	—	20	Normal	•
19	Brick Break	Fighting	Physical	75	100	15	Normal	•
25	Counter	Fighting	Physical	—	100	20	Self	•
31	Take Down	Normal	Physical	90	85	20	Normal	•
37	Close Combat	Fighting	Physical	120	100	5	Normal	•
43	Reversal	Fighting	Physical	—	100	15	Normal	•
49	Feint	Normal	Physical	50	100	10	Normal	•
55	Megahorn	Bug	Physical	120	85	10	Normal	•

Sneasel

DARK | ICE

STATS
- HP
- ATTACK
- DEFENSE
- SP. ATTACK
- SP. DEFENSE
- SPEED

● Male form   ● Female form

EVOLUTION PATH

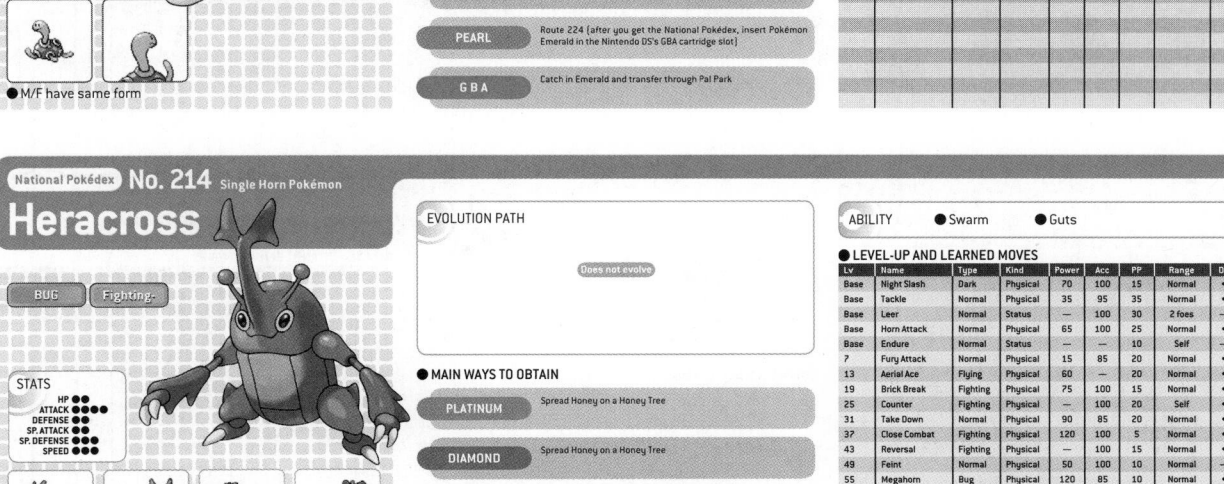

Sneasel → Level up while it holds the Razor Claw between 8 PM and 4 AM → Weavile pg. 510

MAIN WAYS TO OBTAIN

PLATINUM	Route 216
DIAMOND	Route 216
PEARL	Route 216
GBA	Catch in LeafGreen and transfer through Pal Park

ABILITY ● Inner Focus ● Keen Eye

● LEVEL-UP AND LEARNED MOVES

Lv	Name	Type	Kind	Power	Acc	PP	Range	DA
Base	Scratch	Normal	Physical	40	100	35	Normal	•
Base	Leer	Normal	Status	—	100	30	2 foes	•
Base	Taunt	Dark	Status	—	100	20	Normal	•
8	Quick Attack	Normal	Physical	40	100	30	Normal	•
10	Screech	Normal	Status	—	85	40	Normal	•
14	Faint Attack	Dark	Physical	60	—	20	Normal	•
21	Fury Swipes	Normal	Physical	18	80	15	Normal	•
24	Agility	Psychic	Status	—	—	30	Self	•
28	Icy Wind	Ice	Special	55	95	15	2 foes	•
35	Slash	Normal	Physical	70	100	20	Normal	•
38	Beat Up	Dark	Physical	10	100	10	Normal	•
42	Metal Claw	Steel	Physical	50	95	35	Normal	•
49	Ice Shard	Ice	Physical	40	100	30	Normal	•

Teddiursa

NORMAL

STATS
- HP
- ATTACK
- DEFENSE
- SP. ATTACK
- SP. DEFENSE
- SPEED

● M/F have same form

EVOLUTION PATH

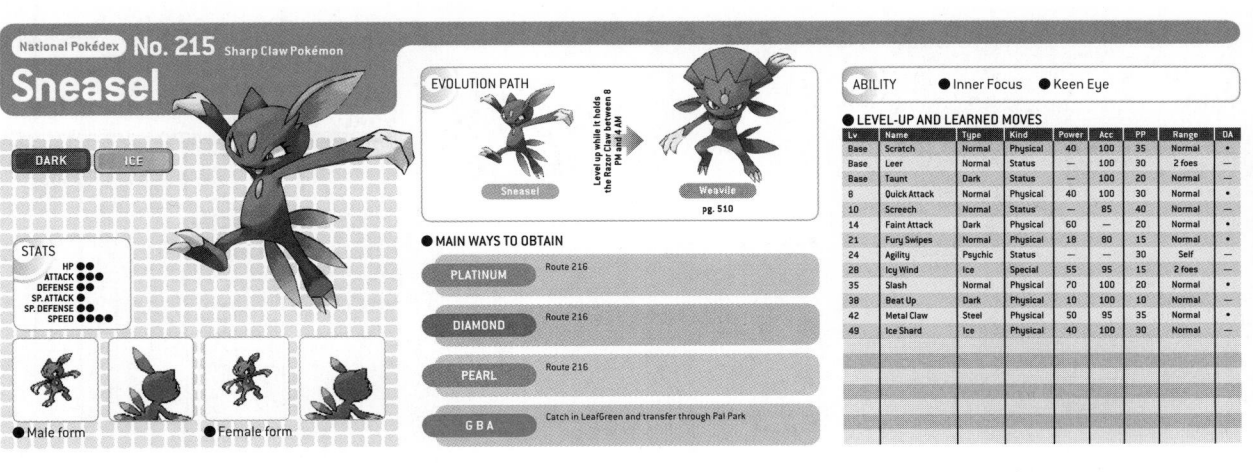

Teddiursa → Lv30 → Ursaring

MAIN WAYS TO OBTAIN

PLATINUM	Eterna City side of Route 211 [after you get the National Pokédex, insert Pokémon Emerald in the Nintendo DS's GBA cartridge slot]
DIAMOND	Route 211 [after you get the National Pokédex, insert Pokémon Emerald in the Nintendo DS's GBA cartridge slot]
PEARL	Route 211 [after you get the National Pokédex, insert Pokémon Emerald in the Nintendo DS's GBA cartridge slot]
GBA	Catch in Emerald and transfer through Pal Park

ABILITY ● Pickup ● Quick Feet

● LEVEL-UP AND LEARNED MOVES

Lv	Name	Type	Kind	Power	Acc	PP	Range	DA
Base	Covet	Normal	Physical	40	100	40	Normal	•
Base	Scratch	Normal	Physical	40	100	35	Normal	•
Base	Leer	Normal	Status	—	100	30	2 foes	•
Base	Lick	Ghost	Physical	20	100	30	Normal	•
Base	Fake Tears	Dark	Status	—	100	20	Normal	—
8	Fury Swipes	Normal	Physical	18	80	15	Normal	•
15	Faint Attack	Dark	Physical	60	—	20	Normal	•
22	Sweet Scent	Normal	Status	—	100	20	2 foes	—
29	Slash	Normal	Physical	70	100	20	Normal	•
36	Charm	Normal	Status	—	100	20	Normal	—
43	Rest	Psychic	Status	—	—	10	Self	—
43	Snore	Normal	Special	40	100	15	Normal	•
50	Thrash	Normal	Physical	90	100	20	1 Random	•
57	Fling	Dark	Physical	—	100	10	Normal	•

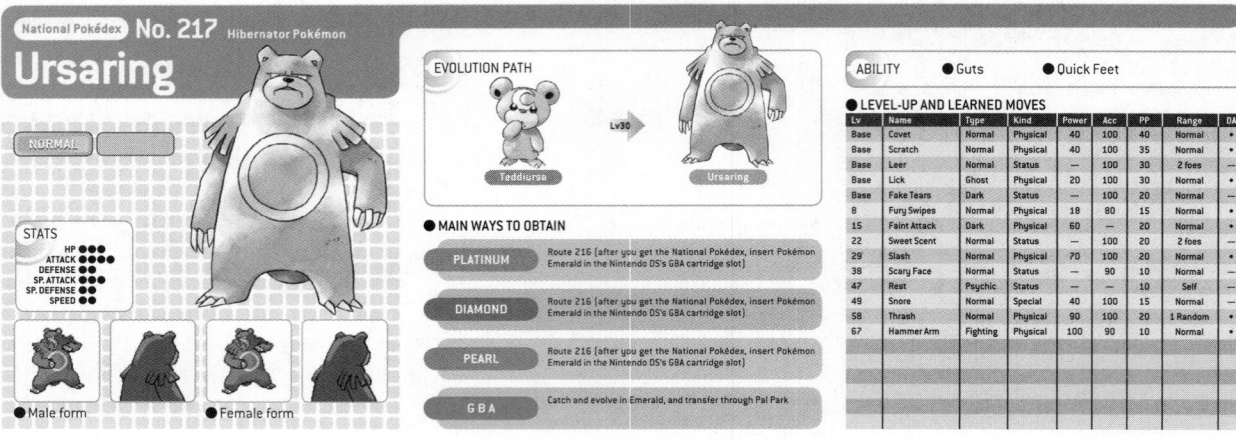

National Pokédex No. 217 Hibernator Pokémon
Ursaring

NORMAL

STATS
- HP ●●●●
- ATTACK ●●●●●
- DEFENSE ●●●
- SP. ATTACK ●●
- SP. DEFENSE ●●
- SPEED ●●

● Male form   ● Female form

EVOLUTION PATH
Teddiursa → (Lv30) → Ursaring

MAIN WAYS TO OBTAIN
PLATINUM	Route 216 (after you get the National Pokédex, insert Pokémon Emerald in the Nintendo DS's GBA cartridge slot)
DIAMOND	Route 216 (after you get the National Pokédex, insert Pokémon Emerald in the Nintendo DS's GBA cartridge slot)
PEARL	Route 216 (after you get the National Pokédex, insert Pokémon Emerald in the Nintendo DS's GBA cartridge slot)
GBA	Catch and evolve in Emerald, and transfer through Pal Park

ABILITY ● Guts   ● Quick Feet

● LEVEL-UP AND LEARNED MOVES
Lv	Name	Type	Kind	Power	Acc	PP	Range	DA
Base	Covet	Normal	Physical	40	100	40	Normal	•
Base	Scratch	Normal	Physical	40	100	35	Normal	•
Base	Leer	Normal	Status	—	100	30	2 foes	•
Base	Lick	Ghost	Physical	20	100	30	Normal	•
Base	Fake Tears	Dark	Status	—	100	20	Normal	—
8	Fury Swipes	Normal	Physical	18	80	15	Normal	•
15	Faint Attack	Dark	Physical	60	—	20	Normal	•
22	Sweet Scent	Normal	Status	—	100	20	2 foes	—
29	Slash	Normal	Physical	70	100	20	Normal	•
38	Scary Face	Normal	Status	—	90	10	Normal	—
47	Rest	Psychic	Status	—	—	10	Self	—
49	Snore	Normal	Special	40	100	15	Normal	—
58	Thrash	Normal	Physical	90	100	20	1 Random	—
67	Hammer Arm	Fighting	Physical	100	90	10	Normal	•

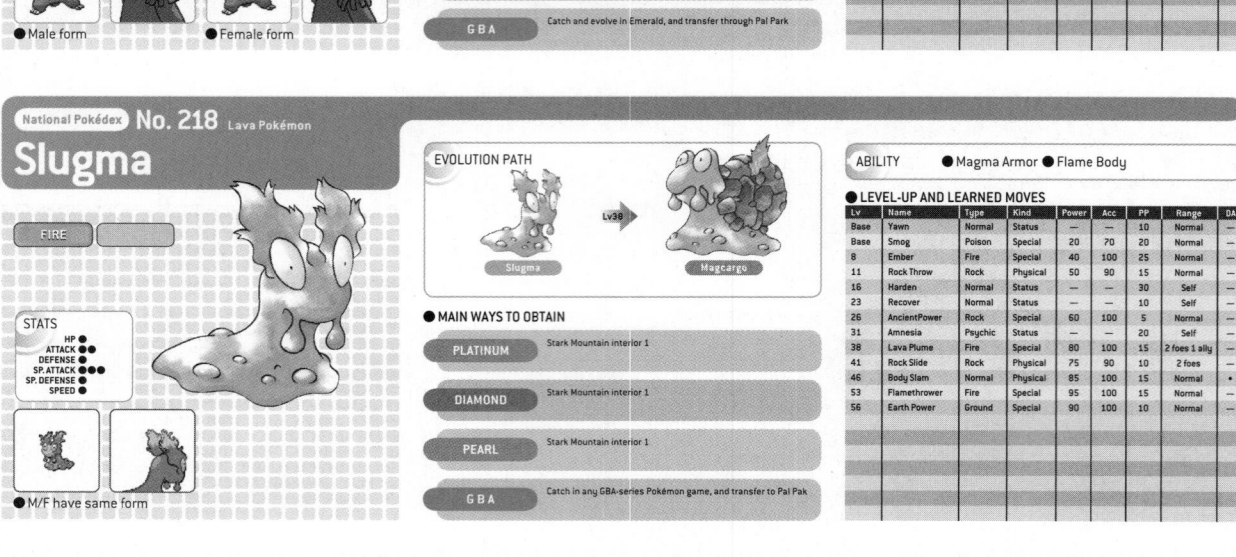

National Pokédex No. 218 Lava Pokémon
Slugma

FIRE

STATS
- HP ●
- ATTACK ●
- DEFENSE ●●
- SP. ATTACK ●●●
- SP. DEFENSE ●
- SPEED ●●

● M/F have same form

EVOLUTION PATH
Slugma → (Lv38) → Magcargo

MAIN WAYS TO OBTAIN
PLATINUM	Stark Mountain interior 1
DIAMOND	Stark Mountain interior 1
PEARL	Stark Mountain interior 1
GBA	Catch in any GBA-series Pokémon game, and transfer to Pal Pak

ABILITY ● Magma Armor   ● Flame Body

● LEVEL-UP AND LEARNED MOVES
Lv	Name	Type	Kind	Power	Acc	PP	Range	DA
Base	Yawn	Normal	Status	—	—	10	Normal	—
Base	Smog	Poison	Special	20	70	20	Normal	—
8	Ember	Fire	Special	40	100	25	Normal	—
11	Rock Throw	Rock	Physical	50	90	15	Normal	—
16	Harden	Normal	Status	—	—	30	Self	—
23	Recover	Normal	Status	—	—	10	Self	—
26	AncientPower	Rock	Special	60	100	5	Normal	—
31	Amnesia	Psychic	Status	—	—	20	Self	—
38	Lava Plume	Fire	Special	80	100	15	2 foes 1 ally	—
41	Rock Slide	Rock	Physical	75	90	10	2 foes	—
46	Body Slam	Normal	Physical	85	100	15	Normal	•
53	Flamethrower	Fire	Special	95	100	15	Normal	—
56	Earth Power	Ground	Special	90	100	10	Normal	—

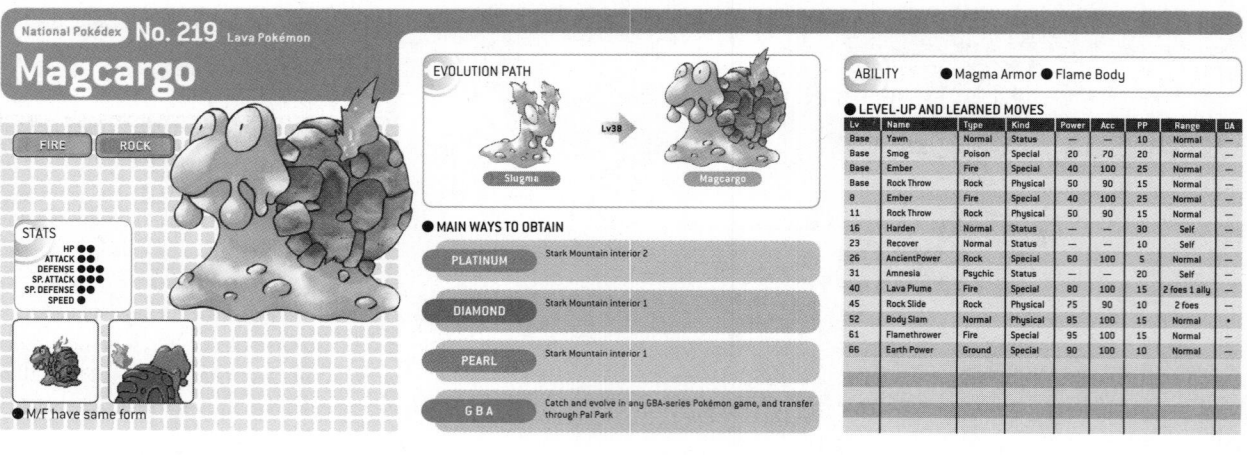

National Pokédex No. 219 Lava Pokémon
Magcargo

FIRE   ROCK

STATS
- HP ●●
- ATTACK ●●
- DEFENSE ●●●●●
- SP. ATTACK ●●●
- SP. DEFENSE ●●
- SPEED ●

● M/F have same form

EVOLUTION PATH
Slugma → (Lv38) → Magcargo

MAIN WAYS TO OBTAIN
PLATINUM	Stark Mountain interior 2
DIAMOND	Stark Mountain interior 1
PEARL	Stark Mountain interior 1
GBA	Catch and evolve in any GBA-series Pokémon game, and transfer through Pal Park

ABILITY ● Magma Armor   ● Flame Body

● LEVEL-UP AND LEARNED MOVES
Lv	Name	Type	Kind	Power	Acc	PP	Range	DA
Base	Yawn	Normal	Status	—	—	10	Normal	—
Base	Smog	Poison	Special	20	70	20	Normal	—
Base	Ember	Fire	Special	40	100	25	Normal	—
Base	Rock Throw	Rock	Physical	50	90	15	Normal	—
8	Ember	Fire	Special	40	100	25	Normal	—
11	Rock Throw	Rock	Physical	50	90	15	Normal	—
16	Harden	Normal	Status	—	—	30	Self	—
23	Recover	Normal	Status	—	—	10	Self	—
26	AncientPower	Rock	Special	60	100	5	Normal	—
31	Amnesia	Psychic	Status	—	—	20	Self	—
40	Lava Plume	Fire	Special	80	100	15	2 foes 1 ally	—
45	Rock Slide	Rock	Physical	75	90	10	2 foes	—
52	Body Slam	Normal	Physical	85	100	15	Normal	•
61	Flamethrower	Fire	Special	95	100	15	Normal	—
66	Earth Power	Ground	Special	90	100	10	Normal	—

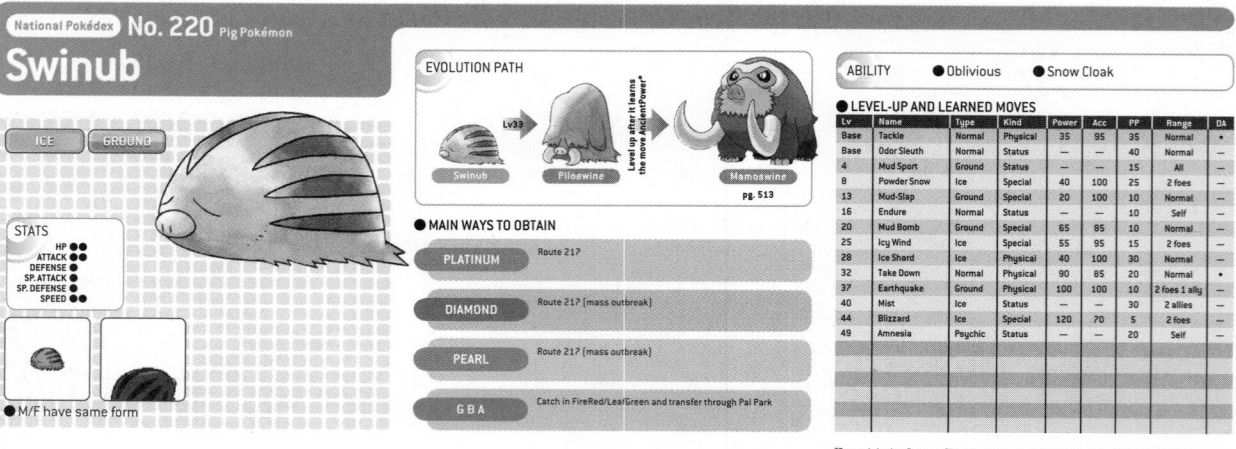

National Pokédex No. 220 Pig Pokémon
Swinub

ICE   GROUND

STATS
- HP ●●
- ATTACK ●●
- DEFENSE ●
- SP. ATTACK ●
- SP. DEFENSE ●
- SPEED ●●

● M/F have same form

EVOLUTION PATH
Swinub → (Lv33) → Piloswine → Level up after it learns the move AncientPower* → Mamoswine (pg. 513)

MAIN WAYS TO OBTAIN
PLATINUM	Route 217
DIAMOND	Route 217 (mass outbreak)
PEARL	Route 217 (mass outbreak)
GBA	Catch in FireRed/LeafGreen and transfer through Pal Park

ABILITY ● Oblivious   ● Snow Cloak

● LEVEL-UP AND LEARNED MOVES
Lv	Name	Type	Kind	Power	Acc	PP	Range	DA
Base	Tackle	Normal	Physical	35	95	35	Normal	•
Base	Odor Sleuth	Normal	Status	—	—	40	Normal	—
4	Mud Sport	Ground	Status	—	—	15	All	—
8	Powder Snow	Ice	Special	40	100	25	2 foes	—
13	Mud-Slap	Ground	Special	20	100	10	Normal	—
16	Endure	Normal	Status	—	—	10	Self	—
20	Mud Bomb	Ground	Special	65	85	10	Normal	—
25	Icy Wind	Ice	Special	55	95	15	2 foes	—
28	Ice Shard	Ice	Physical	40	100	30	Normal	—
32	Take Down	Normal	Physical	90	85	20	Normal	•
37	Earthquake	Ground	Physical	100	100	10	2 foes 1 ally	—
40	Mist	Ice	Status	—	—	30	2 allies	—
44	Blizzard	Ice	Special	120	70	5	2 foes	—
49	Amnesia	Psychic	Status	—	—	20	Self	—

*To teach AncientPower to Piloswine, give 1 Heart Scale to the move tutor in Pastoria City

National Pokédex No. 221 Swine Pokémon

Piloswine

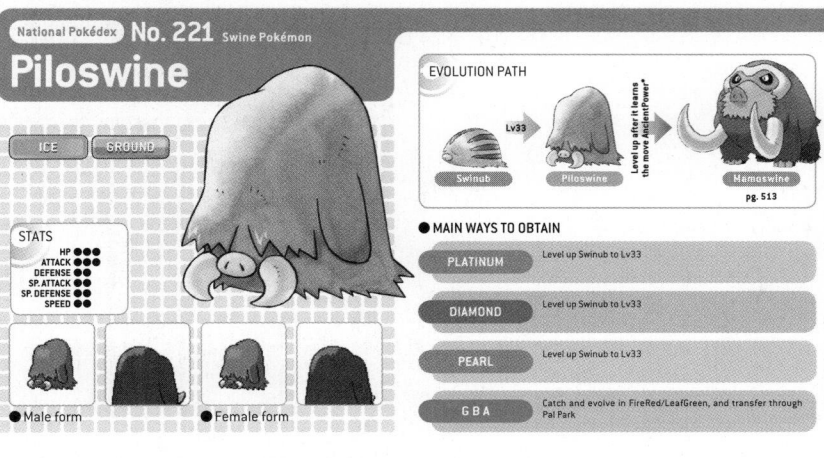

ICE · GROUND

STATS
- HP ●●●
- ATTACK ●●●
- DEFENSE ●●●
- SP. ATTACK ●●
- SP. DEFENSE ●●
- SPEED ●●

● Male form ● Female form

EVOLUTION PATH

Swinub → Lv33 → Piloswine → Level up after it learns the move AncientPower* → Mamoswine pg. 513

● MAIN WAYS TO OBTAIN

PLATINUM	Level up Swinub to Lv33
DIAMOND	Level up Swinub to Lv33
PEARL	Level up Swinub to Lv33
GBA	Catch and evolve in FireRed/LeafGreen, and transfer through Pal Park

ABILITY ● Oblivious ● Snow Cloak

● LEVEL-UP AND LEARNED MOVES

Lv	Name	Type	Kind	Power	Acc	PP	Range	DA
Base	AncientPower	Rock	Special	60	100	5	Normal	—
Base	Peck	Flying	Physical	35	100	—	Normal	●
Base	Odor Sleuth	Normal	Status	—	—	40	Normal	—
Base	Mud Sport	Ground	Status	—	—	15	All	—
Base	Powder Snow	Ice	Special	40	100	25	2 foes	—
4	Mud Sport	Ground	Status	—	—	15	All	—
8	Powder Snow	Ice	Special	40	100	25	2 foes	—
13	Mud-Slap	Ground	Special	20	100	10	Normal	—
16	Endure	Normal	Status	—	—	10	Self	—
20	Mud Bomb	Ground	Special	65	85	10	Normal	—
25	Icy Wind	Ice	Special	55	95	15	2 foes	—
28	Ice Fang	Ice	Physical	65	95	15	Normal	●
32	Take Down	Normal	Physical	90	85	20	Normal	●
33	Fury Attack	Normal	Physical	15	85	20	Normal	●
40	Earthquake	Ground	Physical	100	100	10	2 foes 1 ally	—
48	Mist	Ice	Status	—	—	30	2 allies	—
56	Blizzard	Ice	Special	120	70	5	2 foes	—
65	Amnesia	Psychic	Status	—	—	20	Self	—

*To teach AncientPower to Piloswine, give 1 Heart Scale to the move tutor in Pastoria City

---

National Pokédex No. 222 Coral Pokémon

Corsola

WATER · ROCK

STATS
- HP ●●
- ATTACK ●●
- DEFENSE ●●●
- SP. ATTACK ●●
- SP. DEFENSE ●●●
- SPEED ●●

● M/F have same form

EVOLUTION PATH

Does not evolve

● MAIN WAYS TO OBTAIN

PLATINUM	Route 230 (mass outbreak)
DIAMOND	Route 230 (mass outbreak)
PEARL	Route 230 (mass outbreak)
GBA	Catch in Ruby/Sapphire/Emerald and transfer through Pal Park

ABILITY ● Hustle ● Natural Cure

● LEVEL-UP AND LEARNED MOVES

Lv	Name	Type	Kind	Power	Acc	PP	Range	DA
Base	Tackle	Normal	Physical	35	95	35	Normal	●
4	Harden	Normal	Status	—	—	30	Self	—
8	Bubble	Water	Special	20	100	30	2 foes	—
13	Recover	Normal	Status	—	—	10	Self	—
16	Refresh	Normal	Status	—	—	20	Self	—
20	Rock Blast	Rock	Physical	25	90	10	Normal	—
25	BubbleBeam	Water	Special	65	100	20	Normal	—
28	Lucky Chant	Normal	Status	—	—	30	2 allies	—
32	AncientPower	Rock	Special	60	100	5	Normal	—
37	Aqua Ring	Water	Status	—	—	20	Self	—
40	Spike Cannon	Normal	Physical	20	100	15	Normal	—
44	Power Gem	Rock	Special	70	100	20	Normal	—
48	Mirror Coat	Psychic	Special	—	100	20	Self	—
53	Earth Power	Ground	Special	90	100	10	Normal	—

National Pokédex No. 223 Jet Pokémon

Remoraid

WATER

STATS
- HP ●●
- ATTACK ●●
- DEFENSE ●●
- SP. ATTACK ●●
- SP. DEFENSE ●●
- SPEED ●●

● M/F have same form

EVOLUTION PATH

Remoraid → Lv25 → Octillery

● MAIN WAYS TO OBTAIN

PLATINUM	Route 222 (Good Rod)
DIAMOND	Route 213 (Good Rod)
PEARL	Route 213 (Good Rod)
GBA	Catch in LeafGreen or Emerald and transfer through Pal Park

ABILITY ● Hustle ● Sniper

● LEVEL-UP AND LEARNED MOVES

Lv	Name	Type	Kind	Power	Acc	PP	Range	DA
Base	Water Gun	Water	Special	40	100	25	Normal	—
6	Lock-On	Normal	Status	—	—	5	Normal	—
10	Psybeam	Psychic	Special	65	100	20	Normal	—
14	Aurora Beam	Ice	Special	65	100	20	Normal	—
19	BubbleBeam	Water	Special	65	100	20	Normal	—
23	Focus Energy	Normal	Status	—	—	30	Self	—
27	Bullet Seed	Grass	Physical	10	100	30	Normal	—
32	Water Pulse	Water	Special	60	100	20	Normal	—
36	Signal Beam	Bug	Special	75	100	15	Normal	—
40	Ice Beam	Ice	Special	95	100	10	Normal	—
45	Hyper Beam	Normal	Special	150	90	5	Normal	—

National Pokédex No. 224 Jet Pokémon

Octillery

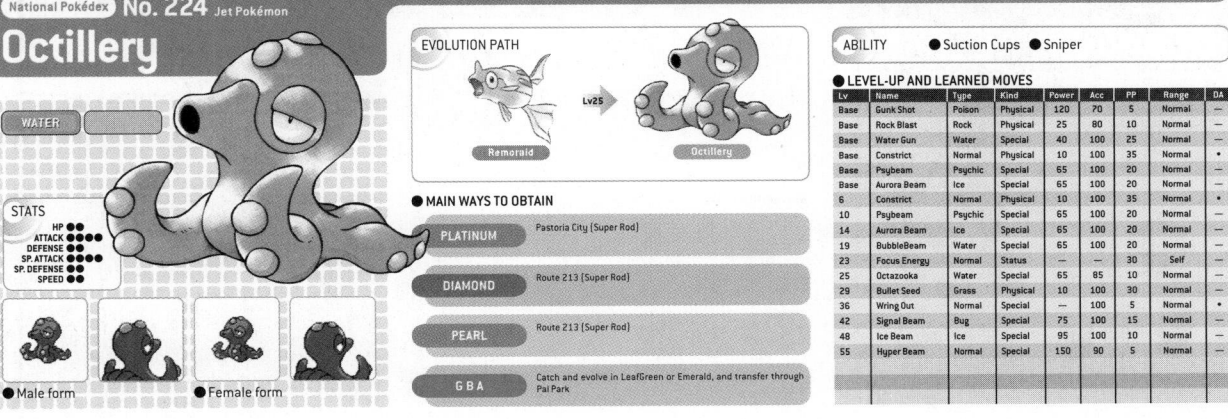

WATER

STATS
- HP ●●
- ATTACK ●●●
- DEFENSE ●●
- SP. ATTACK ●●●
- SP. DEFENSE ●●
- SPEED ●●

● Male form ● Female form

EVOLUTION PATH

Remoraid → Lv25 → Octillery

● MAIN WAYS TO OBTAIN

PLATINUM	Pastoria City (Super Rod)
DIAMOND	Route 213 (Super Rod)
PEARL	Route 213 (Super Rod)
GBA	Catch and evolve in LeafGreen or Emerald, and transfer through Pal Park

ABILITY ● Suction Cups ● Sniper

● LEVEL-UP AND LEARNED MOVES

Lv	Name	Type	Kind	Power	Acc	PP	Range	DA
Base	Gunk Shot	Poison	Physical	120	70	5	Normal	—
Base	Rock Blast	Rock	Physical	25	80	10	Normal	—
Base	Water Gun	Water	Special	40	100	25	Normal	—
Base	Constrict	Normal	Physical	10	100	35	Normal	●
Base	Psybeam	Psychic	Special	65	100	20	Normal	—
Base	Aurora Beam	Ice	Special	65	100	20	Normal	—
6	Constrict	Normal	Physical	10	100	35	Normal	●
10	Psybeam	Psychic	Special	65	100	20	Normal	—
14	Aurora Beam	Ice	Special	65	100	20	Normal	—
19	BubbleBeam	Water	Special	65	100	20	Normal	—
23	Focus Energy	Normal	Status	—	—	30	Self	—
25	Octazooka	Water	Special	65	85	10	Normal	—
29	Bullet Seed	Grass	Physical	10	100	30	Normal	—
36	Wring Out	Normal	Special	—	100	5	Normal	—
42	Signal Beam	Bug	Special	75	100	15	Normal	—
48	Ice Beam	Ice	Special	95	100	10	Normal	—
55	Hyper Beam	Normal	Special	150	90	5	Normal	—

National Pokédex No. 225 Delivery Pokémon
Delibird

ICE FLYING

STATS
HP ●●
ATTACK ●●
DEFENSE ●●
SP. ATTACK ●●
SP. DEFENSE ●●●
SPEED ●●●

● M/F have same form

EVOLUTION PATH

Does not evolve

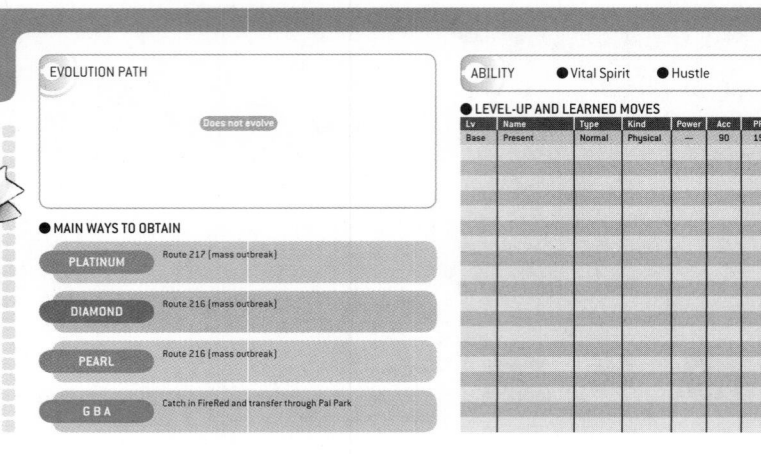

● **ABILITY** ● Vital Spirit ● Hustle

● **LEVEL-UP AND LEARNED MOVES**

Lv	Name	Type	Kind	Power	Acc	PP	Range	DA
Base	Present	Normal	Physical	—	90	15	Normal	

● **MAIN WAYS TO OBTAIN**

PLATINUM	Route 217 (mass outbreak)
DIAMOND	Route 216 (mass outbreak)
PEARL	Route 216 (mass outbreak)
GBA	Catch in FireRed and transfer through Pal Park

National Pokédex No. 226 Kite Pokémon
Mantine

WATER FLYING

STATS
HP ●●●
ATTACK ●●●
DEFENSE ●●●
SP. ATTACK ●●●
SP. DEFENSE ●●●●●
SPEED ●●●

● M/F have same form

EVOLUTION PATH

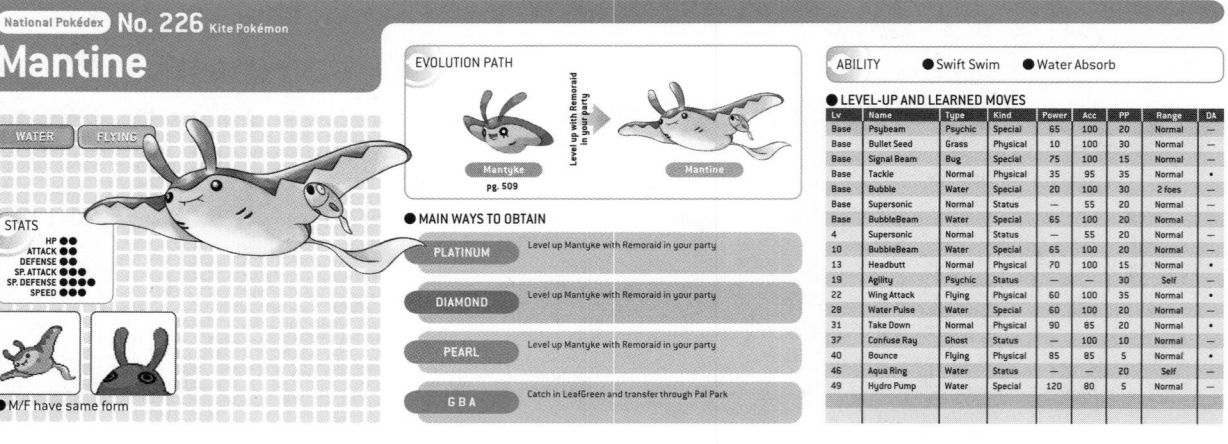

Mantyke
pg. 509

Level up with Remoraid in your party

Mantine

● **ABILITY** ● Swift Swim ● Water Absorb

● **LEVEL-UP AND LEARNED MOVES**

Lv	Name	Type	Kind	Power	Acc	PP	Range	DA
Base	Psybeam	Psychic	Special	65	100	20	Normal	—
Base	Bullet Seed	Grass	Physical	10	100	30	Normal	—
Base	Signal Beam	Bug	Special	75	100	15	Normal	—
Base	Tackle	Normal	Physical	35	95	35	Normal	●
Base	Bubble	Water	Special	20	100	30	2 foes	—
Base	Supersonic	Normal	Status	—	55	20	Normal	—
Base	BubbleBeam	Water	Special	65	100	20	Normal	—
4	Supersonic	Normal	Status	—	55	20	Normal	—
10	BubbleBeam	Water	Special	65	100	20	Normal	—
13	Headbutt	Normal	Physical	70	100	15	Normal	●
19	Agility	Psychic	Status	—	—	30	Self	—
22	Wing Attack	Flying	Physical	60	100	35	Normal	●
28	Water Pulse	Water	Special	60	100	20	Normal	—
31	Take Down	Normal	Physical	90	85	20	Normal	●
37	Confuse Ray	Ghost	Status	—	100	10	Normal	—
40	Bounce	Flying	Physical	85	85	5	Normal	●
46	Aqua Ring	Water	Status	—	—	20	Self	—
49	Hydro Pump	Water	Special	120	80	5	Normal	—

● **MAIN WAYS TO OBTAIN**

PLATINUM	Level up Mantyke with Remoraid in your party
DIAMOND	Level up Mantyke with Remoraid in your party
PEARL	Level up Mantyke with Remoraid in your party
GBA	Catch in LeafGreen and transfer through Pal Park

National Pokédex No. 227 Armor Bird Pokémon
Skarmory

STEEL FLYING

STATS
HP ●●●
ATTACK ●●●
DEFENSE ●●●●●
SP. ATTACK ●●
SP. DEFENSE ●●●
SPEED ●●●

● M/F have same form

EVOLUTION PATH

Does not evolve

● **ABILITY** ● Keen Eye ● Sturdy

● **LEVEL-UP AND LEARNED MOVES**

Lv	Name	Type	Kind	Power	Acc	PP	Range	DA
Base	Leer	Normal	Status	—	100	30	2 foes	—
Base	Peck	Flying	Physical	35	100	35	Normal	●
6	Sand-Attack	Ground	Status	—	100	15	Normal	—
9	Swift	Normal	Special	60	—	20	2 foes	—
12	Agility	Psychic	Status	—	—	30	Self	—
17	Fury Attack	Normal	Physical	15	85	20	Normal	●
20	Feint	Normal	Physical	50	100	10	Normal	—
23	Air Cutter	Flying	Special	55	95	25	2 foes	—
28	Spikes	Ground	Status	—	—	20	2 foes	—
31	Metal Sound	Steel	Status	—	85	40	Normal	—
34	Steel Wing	Steel	Physical	70	90	25	Normal	●
39	Air Slash	Flying	Special	75	95	20	Normal	—
42	Slash	Normal	Physical	70	100	20	Normal	●
45	Night Slash	Dark	Physical	70	100	15	Normal	●

● **MAIN WAYS TO OBTAIN**

PLATINUM	Route 227
DIAMOND	Route 227
PEARL	Route 227
GBA	Catch in FireRed or Ruby/Sapphire/Emerald, and transfer through Pal Park

---

National Pokédex No. 228 Dark Pokémon
Houndour

DARK FIRE

STATS
HP ●
ATTACK ●●
DEFENSE ●
SP. ATTACK ●●
SP. DEFENSE ●
SPEED ●●

● M/F have same form

EVOLUTION PATH

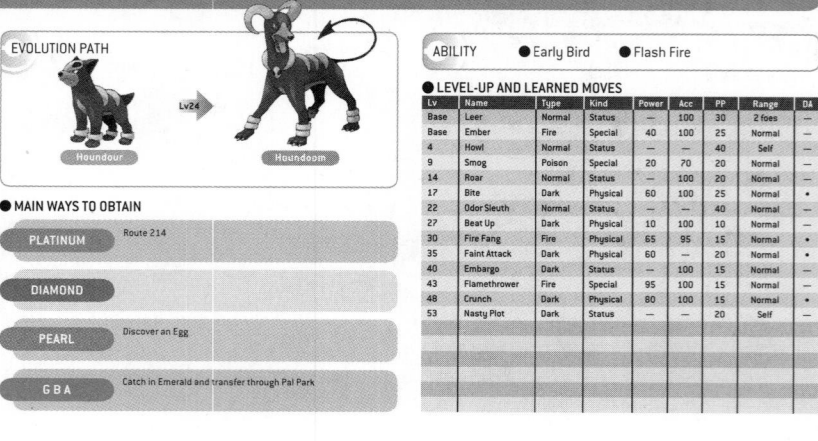

Houndour

Lv24

Houndoom

● **ABILITY** ● Early Bird ● Flash Fire

● **LEVEL-UP AND LEARNED MOVES**

Lv	Name	Type	Kind	Power	Acc	PP	Range	DA
Base	Leer	Normal	Status	—	100	30	2 foes	—
Base	Ember	Fire	Special	40	100	25	Normal	—
4	Howl	Normal	Status	—	—	40	Self	—
9	Smog	Poison	Special	20	70	20	Normal	—
14	Roar	Normal	Status	—	100	20	Normal	—
17	Bite	Dark	Physical	60	100	25	Normal	●
22	Odor Sleuth	Normal	Status	—	—	40	Normal	—
27	Beat Up	Dark	Physical	10	100	10	Normal	—
30	Fire Fang	Fire	Physical	65	95	15	Normal	●
35	Faint Attack	Dark	Physical	60	—	20	Normal	—
40	Embargo	Dark	Status	—	100	15	Normal	—
43	Flamethrower	Fire	Special	95	100	15	Normal	—
48	Crunch	Dark	Physical	80	100	15	Normal	●
53	Nasty Plot	Dark	Status	—	—	20	Self	—

● **MAIN WAYS TO OBTAIN**

PLATINUM	Route 214
DIAMOND	
PEARL	Discover an Egg
GBA	Catch in Emerald and transfer through Pal Park

National Pokédex No. 229 Dark Pokémon
Houndoom

DARK FIRE

STATS
HP ●●
ATTACK ●●●
DEFENSE ●●
SP. ATTACK ●●●●
SP. DEFENSE ●●●
SPEED ●●●

● Male form   ● Female form

EVOLUTION PATH

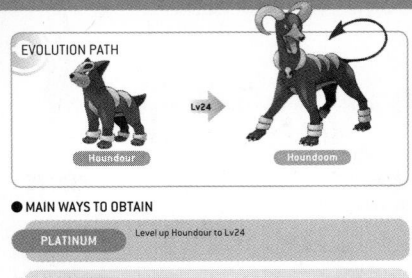

Houndour → Lv24 → Houndoom

● MAIN WAYS TO OBTAIN

PLATINUM	Level up Houndour to Lv24
DIAMOND	
PEARL	Route 214 (use Poké Radar)
GBA	Catch and evolve in Emerald, and transfer through Pal Park

ABILITY   ● Early Bird   ● Flash Fire

● LEVEL-UP AND LEARNED MOVES

Lv	Name	Type	Kind	Power	Acc	PP	Range	DA
Base	Thunder Fang	Electric	Physical	65	95	15	Normal	•
Base	Leer	Normal	Status	—	100	30	2 foes	—
Base	Ember	Fire	Special	40	100	25	Normal	—
Base	Howl	Normal	Status	—	—	40	Self	—
Base	Smog	Poison	Special	20	70	20	Normal	—
4	Howl	Normal	Status	—	—	40	Self	—
9	Smog	Poison	Special	20	70	20	Normal	—
14	Roar	Normal	Status	—	100	20	Normal	—
17	Bite	Dark	Physical	60	100	25	Normal	•
22	Odor Sleuth	Normal	Status	—	—	40	Normal	—
28	Beat Up	Dark	Physical	10	100	10	Normal	•
32	Fire Fang	Fire	Physical	65	95	15	Normal	•
38	Faint Attack	Dark	Physical	60	—	20	Normal	•
44	Embargo	Dark	Status	—	100	15	Normal	—
48	Flamethrower	Fire	Special	95	100	15	Normal	—
54	Crunch	Dark	Physical	80	100	15	Normal	•
60	Nasty Plot	Dark	Status	—	—	20	Self	—

National Pokédex No. 230 Dragon Pokémon
Kingdra

WATER DRAGON

STATS
HP ●●
ATTACK ●●●
DEFENSE ●●●
SP. ATTACK ●●●
SP. DEFENSE ●●●
SPEED ●●●

● M/F have same form

EVOLUTION PATH

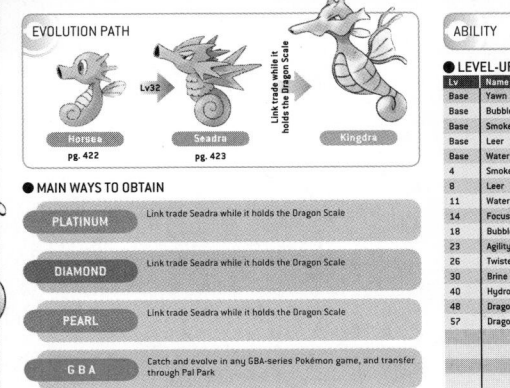

Horsea pg. 422 → Lv32 → Seadra pg. 423 → Link trade while it holds the Dragon Scale → Kingdra

● MAIN WAYS TO OBTAIN

PLATINUM	Link trade Seadra while it holds the Dragon Scale
DIAMOND	Link trade Seadra while it holds the Dragon Scale
PEARL	Link trade Seadra while it holds the Dragon Scale
GBA	Catch and evolve in any GBA-series Pokémon game, and transfer through Pal Park

ABILITY   ● Swift Swim   ● Sniper

● LEVEL-UP AND LEARNED MOVES

Lv	Name	Type	Kind	Power	Acc	PP	Range	DA
Base	Yawn	Normal	Status	—	—	10	Normal	—
Base	Bubble	Water	Special	20	100	30	2 foes	—
Base	SmokeScreen	Normal	Status	—	100	20	Normal	—
Base	Leer	Normal	Status	—	100	30	2 foes	—
Base	Water Gun	Water	Special	40	100	25	Normal	—
4	SmokeScreen	Normal	Status	—	100	20	Normal	—
8	Leer	Normal	Status	—	100	30	2 foes	—
11	Water Gun	Water	Special	40	100	25	Normal	—
14	Focus Energy	Normal	Status	—	—	30	Self	—
18	BubbleBeam	Water	Special	65	100	20	Normal	—
23	Agility	Psychic	Status	—	—	30	Self	—
26	Twister	Dragon	Special	40	100	20	2 foes	—
30	Brine	Water	Special	65	100	10	Normal	—
40	Hydro Pump	Water	Special	120	80	5	Normal	—
48	Dragon Dance	Dragon	Status	—	—	20	Self	—
57	Dragon Pulse	Dragon	Special	90	100	10	Normal	—

National Pokédex No. 231 Long Nose Pokémon
Phanpy

GROUND

STATS
HP ●●●
ATTACK ●●
DEFENSE ●●
SP. ATTACK ●●
SP. DEFENSE ●●
SPEED ●●

● M/F have same form

EVOLUTION PATH

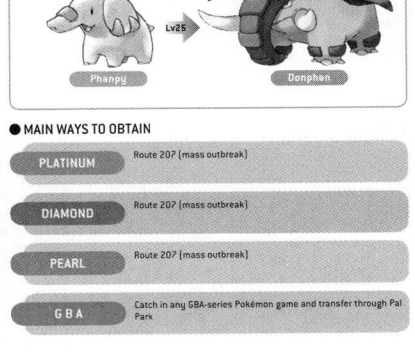

Phanpy → Lv25 → Donphan

● MAIN WAYS TO OBTAIN

PLATINUM	Route 207 (mass outbreak)
DIAMOND	Route 207 (mass outbreak)
PEARL	Route 207 (mass outbreak)
GBA	Catch in any GBA-series Pokémon game and transfer through Pal Park

ABILITY   ● Pickup

● LEVEL-UP AND LEARNED MOVES

Lv	Name	Type	Kind	Power	Acc	PP	Range	DA
Base	Odor Sleuth	Normal	Status	—	—	40	Normal	—
Base	Tackle	Normal	Physical	35	95	35	Normal	•
Base	Growl	Normal	Status	—	100	40	2 foes	—
Base	Defense Curl	Normal	Status	—	—	40	Self	—
6	Flail	Normal	Physical	—	100	15	Normal	•
10	Take Down	Normal	Physical	90	85	20	Normal	•
15	Rollout	Rock	Physical	30	90	20	Normal	•
19	Natural Gift	Normal	Physical	—	100	15	Normal	•
24	Slam	Normal	Physical	80	75	20	Normal	•
28	Endure	Normal	Status	—	—	10	Self	—
33	Charm	Normal	Status	—	100	20	Normal	—
37	Last Resort	Normal	Physical	130	100	5	Normal	•
42	Double-Edge	Normal	Physical	120	100	15	Normal	•

National Pokédex No. 232 Armor Pokémon
Donphan

GROUND

STATS
HP ●●●
ATTACK ●●●●
DEFENSE ●●●●
SP. ATTACK ●●
SP. DEFENSE ●●
SPEED ●●●

● Male form   ● Female form

EVOLUTION PATH

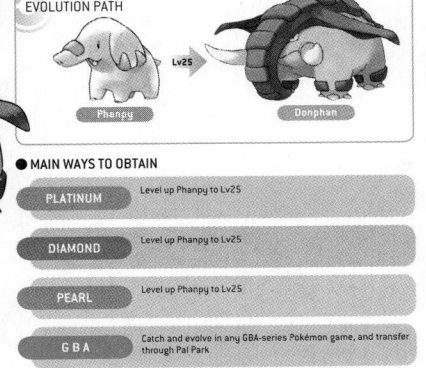

Phanpy → Lv25 → Donphan

● MAIN WAYS TO OBTAIN

PLATINUM	Level up Phanpy to Lv25
DIAMOND	Level up Phanpy to Lv25
PEARL	Level up Phanpy to Lv25
GBA	Catch and evolve in any GBA-series Pokémon game, and transfer through Pal Park

ABILITY   ● Sturdy

● LEVEL-UP AND LEARNED MOVES

Lv	Name	Type	Kind	Power	Acc	PP	Range	DA
Base	Fire Fang	Fire	Physical	65	95	15	Normal	•
Base	Thunder Fang	Electric	Physical	65	95	15	Normal	•
Base	Horn Attack	Normal	Physical	65	100	25	Normal	•
Base	Growl	Normal	Status	—	100	40	2 foes	—
Base	Defense Curl	Normal	Status	—	—	40	Self	—
Base	Flail	Normal	Physical	—	100	15	Normal	•
6	Rapid Spin	Normal	Physical	20	100	40	Normal	•
10	Knock Off	Dark	Physical	20	100	20	Normal	•
15	Rollout	Rock	Physical	30	90	20	Normal	•
19	Magnitude	Ground	Physical	—	100	30	2 foes + 1 ally	•
24	Slam	Normal	Physical	80	75	20	Normal	•
25	Fury Attack	Normal	Physical	15	85	20	Normal	•
31	Assurance	Dark	Physical	50	100	10	Normal	•
39	Scary Face	Normal	Status	—	90	10	Normal	—
46	Earthquake	Ground	Physical	100	100	10	2 foes + 1 ally	•
54	Giga Impact	Normal	Physical	150	90	5	Normal	•

National Pokédex No. 233 Virtual Pokémon
Porygon2

NORMAL

STATS
- HP ●●●
- ATTACK ●●●
- DEFENSE ●●●
- SP. ATTACK ●●●●
- SP. DEFENSE ●●●
- SPEED ●●

● Gender unkown

EVOLUTION PATH

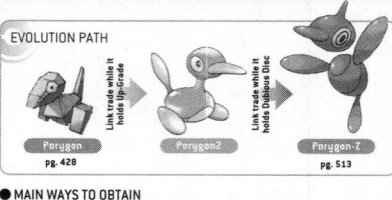

Porygon — Link trade while it holds Up-Grade → Porygon2 — Link trade while it holds Dubious Disc → Porygon-Z

Porygon pg. 428 · Porygon-Z pg. 513

● MAIN WAYS TO OBTAIN

PLATINUM	Link trade Porygon while it holds the Up-Grade
DIAMOND	Link trade Porygon while it holds the Up-Grade
PEARL	Link trade Porygon while it holds the Up-Grade
GBA	Acquire and evolve in FireRed/LeafGreen, and transfer through Pal Park

ABILITY ● Trace ● Download

● LEVEL-UP AND LEARNED MOVES

Lv	Name	Type	Kind	Power	Acc	PP	Range	DA
Base	Conversion 2	Normal	Status	—	—	30	Self	—
Base	Tackle	Normal	Physical	35	95	35	Normal	●
Base	Conversion	Normal	Status	—	—	30	Self	—
Base	Defense Curl	Normal	Status	—	—	40	Self	—
7	Psybeam	Psychic	Special	65	100	20	Normal	—
12	Agility	Psychic	Status	—	—	30	Self	—
18	Recover	Normal	Status	—	—	10	Self	—
23	Magnet Rise	Electric	Status	—	—	10	Self	—
29	Signal Beam	Bug	Special	75	100	15	Normal	—
34	Recycle	Normal	Status	—	—	10	Self	—
40	Discharge	Electric	Special	80	100	15	2 foes • 1 ally	—
45	Lock-On	Normal	Status	—	—	5	Normal	—
51	Tri Attack	Normal	Special	80	100	10	Normal	—
56	Magic Coat	Psychic	Status	—	—	15	Self	—
62	Zap Cannon	Electric	Special	120	50	5	Normal	—
67	Hyper Beam	Normal	Special	150	90	5	Normal	—

National Pokédex No. 234 Big Horn Pokémon
Stantler

NORMAL

STATS
- HP ●●
- ATTACK ●●●
- DEFENSE ●●
- SP. ATTACK ●●●
- SP. DEFENSE ●●
- SPEED ●●●

● M/F have same form

EVOLUTION PATH

Does not evolve

● MAIN WAYS TO OBTAIN

PLATINUM	Route 207 (use Poké Radar)
DIAMOND	
PEARL	Route 207 (use Poké Radar)
GBA	Catch in Emerald and transfer through Pal Park

ABILITY ● Intimidate ● Frisk

● LEVEL-UP AND LEARNED MOVES

Lv	Name	Type	Kind	Power	Acc	PP	Range	DA
Base	Tackle	Normal	Physical	35	95	35	Normal	●
3	Leer	Normal	Status	—	100	30	2 foes	—
7	Astonish	Ghost	Physical	30	100	15	Normal	●
10	Hypnosis	Psychic	Status	—	60	20	Normal	—
13	Stomp	Normal	Physical	65	100	20	Normal	●
16	Sand-Attack	Ground	Status	—	100	15	Normal	—
21	Take Down	Normal	Physical	90	85	20	Normal	●
23	Confuse Ray	Ghost	Status	—	100	10	Normal	—
27	Calm Mind	Psychic	Status	—	—	20	Self	—
33	Role Play	Psychic	Status	—	—	10	Normal	—
38	Zen Headbutt	Psychic	Physical	80	90	15	Normal	●
43	Imprison	Psychic	Status	—	—	10	Self	—
49	Captivate	Normal	Status	—	100	20	2 foes	—
53	Me First	Normal	Status	—	—	20	DoM	—

National Pokédex No. 235 Painter Pokémon
Smeargle

NORMAL

STATS
- HP ●●
- ATTACK ●
- DEFENSE ●
- SP. ATTACK ●
- SP. DEFENSE ●
- SPEED ●●●

● M/F have same form

EVOLUTION PATH

Does not evolve

● MAIN WAYS TO OBTAIN

PLATINUM	Route 208 (use Poké Radar)
DIAMOND	Hearthome City side of Route 212 (use Poké Radar)
PEARL	Hearthome City side of Route 212 (use Poké Radar)
GBA	Catch in Emerald and transfer through Pal Park

ABILITY ● Own Tempo ● Technician

● LEVEL-UP AND LEARNED MOVES

Lv	Name	Type	Kind	Power	Acc	PP	Range	DA
Base	Sketch	Normal	Status	—	—	1	Normal	—
11	Sketch	Normal	Status	—	—	1	Normal	—
21	Sketch	Normal	Status	—	—	1	Normal	—
31	Sketch	Normal	Status	—	—	1	Normal	—
41	Sketch	Normal	Status	—	—	1	Normal	—
51	Sketch	Normal	Status	—	—	1	Normal	—
61	Sketch	Normal	Status	—	—	1	Normal	—
71	Sketch	Normal	Status	—	—	1	Normal	—
81	Sketch	Normal	Status	—	—	1	Normal	—
91	Sketch	Normal	Status	—	—	1	Normal	—

National Pokédex No. 236 Scuffle Pokémon
Tyrogue

FIGHTING

STATS
- HP ●
- ATTACK ●
- DEFENSE ●
- SP. ATTACK ●
- SP. DEFENSE ●
- SPEED ●

● Male form

EVOLUTION PATH

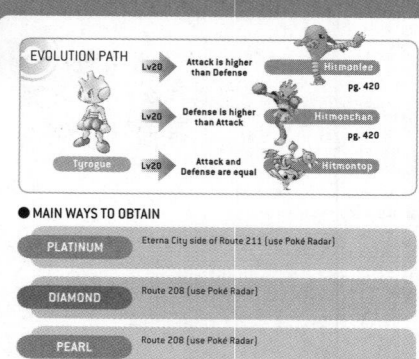

Tyrogue — Lv20 Attack is higher than Defense → Hitmonlee pg. 420
Tyrogue — Lv20 Defense is higher than Attack → Hitmonchan pg. 420
Tyrogue — Lv20 Attack and Defense are equal → Hitmontop

● MAIN WAYS TO OBTAIN

PLATINUM	Eterna City side of Route 211 (use Poké Radar)
DIAMOND	Route 208 (use Poké Radar)
PEARL	Route 208 (use Poké Radar)
GBA	Discover as an Egg in FireRed/LeafGreen and transfer through Pal Park

ABILITY ● Guts ● Steadfast

● LEVEL-UP AND LEARNED MOVES

Lv	Name	Type	Kind	Power	Acc	PP	Range	DA
Base	Tackle	Normal	Physical	35	95	35	Normal	●
Base	Helping Hand	Normal	Status	—	—	20	1 ally	—
Base	Fake Out	Normal	Physical	40	100	10	Normal	●
Base	Foresight	Normal	Status	—	—	40	Normal	—

Hitmontop

National Pokédex No. 237 Handstand Pokémon

FIGHTING

STATS
HP ●●
ATTACK ●●●
DEFENSE ●●●
SP.ATTACK ●
SP.DEFENSE ●●●
SPEED ●●●

● Male form

● EVOLUTION PATH

Tyrogue — Lv20 — Attack is higher than Defense → Hitmonlee pg. 420
Lv20 — Defense is higher than Attack → Hitmonchan pg. 420
Lv20 — Attack and Defense are equal → Hitmontop

● MAIN WAYS TO OBTAIN

PLATINUM	Make Tyrogue's Attack and Defense equal, and level it up to Lv20
DIAMOND	Make Tyrogue's Attack and Defense equal, and level it up to Lv20
PEARL	Make Tyrogue's Attack and Defense equal, and level it up to Lv20
GBA	Discover as an Egg and evolve in FireRed/LeafGreen, and transfer through Pal Park

ABILITY   ● Intimidate   ● Technician

● LEVEL-UP AND LEARNED MOVES

Lv	Name	Type	Kind	Power	Acc	PP	Range	DA
Base	Revenge	Fight	Physical	60	100	10	Normal	•
Base	Rolling Kick	Fight	Physical	60	85	15	Normal	•
6	Focus Energy	Normal	Status	—	—	30	Self	—
10	Pursuit	Dark	Physical	40	100	20	Normal	•
15	Quick Attack	Normal	Physical	40	100	30	Normal	•
19	Triple Kick	Fight	Physical	10	90	10	Normal	•
24	Rapid Spin	Normal	Physical	20	100	40	Normal	•
28	Counter	Fight	Physical	—	100	20	Self	—
33	Feint	Normal	Physical	50	100	10	Normal	•
37	Agility	Psychic	Status	—	—	30	Self	—
42	Gyro Ball	Steel	Physical	—	100	5	Normal	•
46	Detect	Fight	Status	—	—	5	Self	—
51	Close Combat	Fight	Physical	120	100	5	Normal	•
55	Endeavor	Normal	Physical	—	100	5	Normal	•

Smoochum

National Pokédex No. 238 Kiss Pokémon

ICE   PSYCHIC

STATS
HP ●
ATTACK ●
DEFENSE ●
SP.ATTACK ●●●
SP.DEFENSE ●●
SPEED ●●

● Female form

● EVOLUTION PATH

Smoochum — Lv30 → Jynx pg. 424

● MAIN WAYS TO OBTAIN

PLATINUM	Snowpoint Temple 1F
DIAMOND	Lake Acuity (mass outbreak)
PEARL	Lake Acuity (mass outbreak)
GBA	Discover as an Egg in FireRed/LeafGreen and transfer through Pal Park

ABILITY   ● Oblivious   ● Forewarn

● LEVEL-UP AND LEARNED MOVES

Lv	Name	Type	Kind	Power	Acc	PP	Range	DA
Base	Pound	Normal	Physical	40	100	35	Normal	•
5	Lick	Ghost	Physical	20	100	30	Normal	•
8	Sweet Kiss	Normal	Status	—	75	10	Normal	—
11	Powder Snow	Ice	Special	40	100	25	2 foes	•
15	Confusion	Psychic	Special	50	100	25	Normal	•
18	Sing	Normal	Status	—	55	15	Normal	—
21	Mean Look	Normal	Status	—	—	5	Normal	—
25	Fake Tears	Dark	Status	—	100	20	Normal	—
28	Lucky Chant	Normal	Status	—	—	30	2 allies	—
31	Avalanche	Ice	Physical	60	100	10	Normal	•
35	Psychic	Psychic	Special	90	100	10	Normal	—
38	Copycat	Normal	Status	—	—	20	DoM	—
41	Perish Song	Normal	Status	—	—	5	All	—
45	Blizzard	Ice	Special	120	70	5	2 foes	—

Elekid

National Pokédex No. 239 Electric Pokémon

ELECTRIC

STATS
HP ●●
ATTACK ●●
DEFENSE ●
SP.ATTACK ●●
SP.DEFENSE ●
SPEED ●●●

● M/F have same form

● EVOLUTION PATH

Elekid — Lv30 — Electabuzz pg. 425 — Link trade while it holds Electirizer — Electivire pg. 511

● MAIN WAYS TO OBTAIN

PLATINUM	Discover an Egg
DIAMOND	Valley Windworks (after you get the National Pokédex, insert Pokémon FireRed into the Nintendo DS's GBA cartridge slot)
PEARL	Valley Windworks (after you get the National Pokédex, insert Pokémon FireRed into the Nintendo DS's GBA cartridge slot)
GBA	Discover as an Egg in FireRed and transfer through Pal Park

ABILITY   ● Static

● LEVEL-UP AND LEARNED MOVES

Lv	Name	Type	Kind	Power	Acc	PP	Range	DA
Base	Quick Attack	Normal	Physical	40	100	30	Normal	•
Base	Leer	Normal	Status	—	100	30	2 foes	—
7	ThunderShock	Electric	Special	40	100	30	Normal	—
10	Low Kick	Fight	Physical	—	100	20	Normal	•
16	Swift	Normal	Special	60	—	20	2 foes	—
19	Shock Wave	Electric	Special	60	—	20	Normal	—
25	Light Screen	Psychic	Status	—	—	30	2 allies	—
28	ThunderPunch	Electric	Physical	75	100	15	Normal	•
34	Discharge	Electric	Special	80	100	15	2 foes • 1 ally	—
37	Thunderbolt	Electric	Special	95	100	15	Normal	—
43	Screech	Normal	Status	—	85	40	Normal	—
46	Thunder	Electric	Special	120	70	10	Normal	—

Magby

National Pokédex No. 240 Live Coal Pokémon

FIRE

STATS
HP ●
ATTACK ●●
DEFENSE ●
SP.ATTACK ●●●
SP.DEFENSE ●
SPEED ●●●

● M/F have same form

● EVOLUTION PATH

Magby — Lv30 — Magmar pg. 425 — Link trade while it holds Magmarizer — Magmortar pg. 511

● MAIN WAYS TO OBTAIN

PLATINUM	Discover an Egg
DIAMOND	Route 227 (after you get the National Pokédex, insert Pokémon LeafGreen into the Nintendo DS's GBA cartridge slot)
PEARL	Route 227 (after you get the National Pokédex, insert Pokémon LeafGreen into the Nintendo DS's GBA cartridge slot)
GBA	Discover as an Egg in LeafGreen and transfer through Pal Park

ABILITY   ● Flame Body

● LEVEL-UP AND LEARNED MOVES

Lv	Name	Type	Kind	Power	Acc	PP	Range	DA
Base	Smog	Poison	Special	20	70	20	Normal	—
Base	Leer	Normal	Status	—	100	30	2 foes	—
7	Ember	Fire	Special	40	100	25	Normal	—
10	SmokeScreen	Normal	Status	—	100	20	Normal	—
16	Faint Attack	Dark	Physical	60	—	20	Normal	•
19	Fire Spin	Fire	Special	15	70	15	Normal	—
25	Confuse Ray	Ghost	Status	—	100	10	Normal	—
28	Fire Punch	Fire	Physical	75	100	15	Normal	•
34	Lava Plume	Fire	Special	80	100	15	2 foes • 1 ally	—
37	Flamethrower	Fire	Special	95	100	15	Normal	—
43	Sunny Day	Fire	Status	—	—	5	All	—
46	Fire Blast	Fire	Special	120	85	5	Normal	—

240
★★★★★
MAGBY

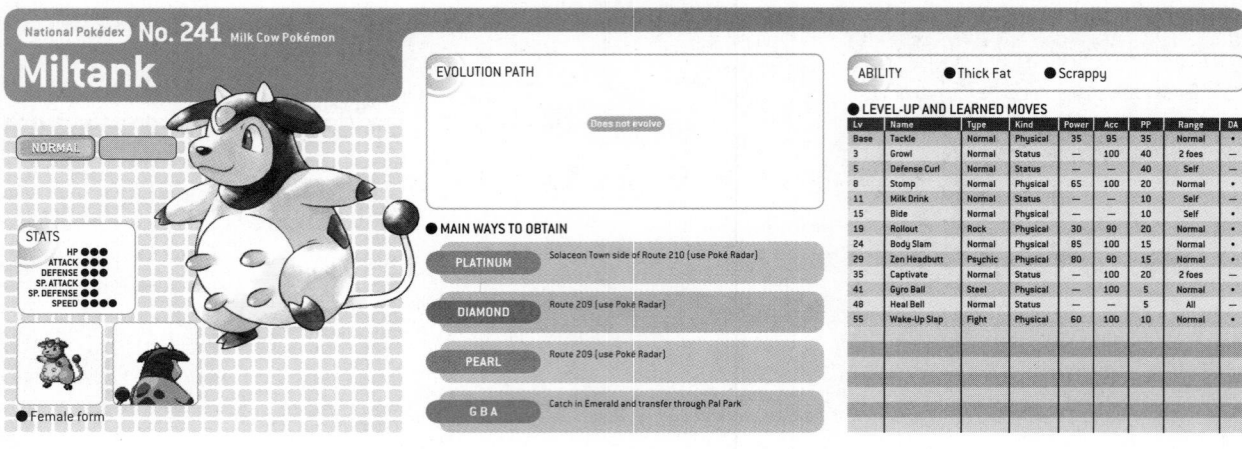

National Pokédex No. 241 Milk Cow Pokémon
Miltank

NORMAL

STATS
HP
ATTACK
DEFENSE
SP. ATTACK
SP. DEFENSE
SPEED

● Female form

EVOLUTION PATH

Does not evolve

ABILITY ● Thick Fat ● Scrappy

● LEVEL-UP AND LEARNED MOVES

Lv	Name	Type	Kind	Power	Acc	PP	Range	DA
Base	Tackle	Normal	Physical	35	95	35	Normal	•
3	Growl	Normal	Status	—	100	40	2 foes	—
5	Defense Curl	Normal	Status	—	—	40	Self	—
8	Stomp	Normal	Physical	65	100	20	Normal	•
11	Milk Drink	Normal	Status	—	—	10	Self	—
15	Bide	Normal	Physical	—	—	10	Self	—
19	Rollout	Rock	Physical	30	90	20	Normal	•
24	Body Slam	Normal	Physical	85	100	15	Normal	•
29	Zen Headbutt	Psychic	Physical	80	90	15	Normal	•
35	Captivate	Normal	Status	—	100	20	2 foes	—
41	Gyro Ball	Steel	Physical	—	100	5	Normal	•
48	Heal Bell	Normal	Status	—	—	5	All	—
55	Wake-Up Slap	Fight	Physical	60	100	10	Normal	•

● MAIN WAYS TO OBTAIN

PLATINUM	Solaceon Town side of Route 210 (use Poké Radar)
DIAMOND	Route 209 (use Poké Radar)
PEARL	Route 209 (use Poké Radar)
G B A	Catch in Emerald and transfer through Pal Park

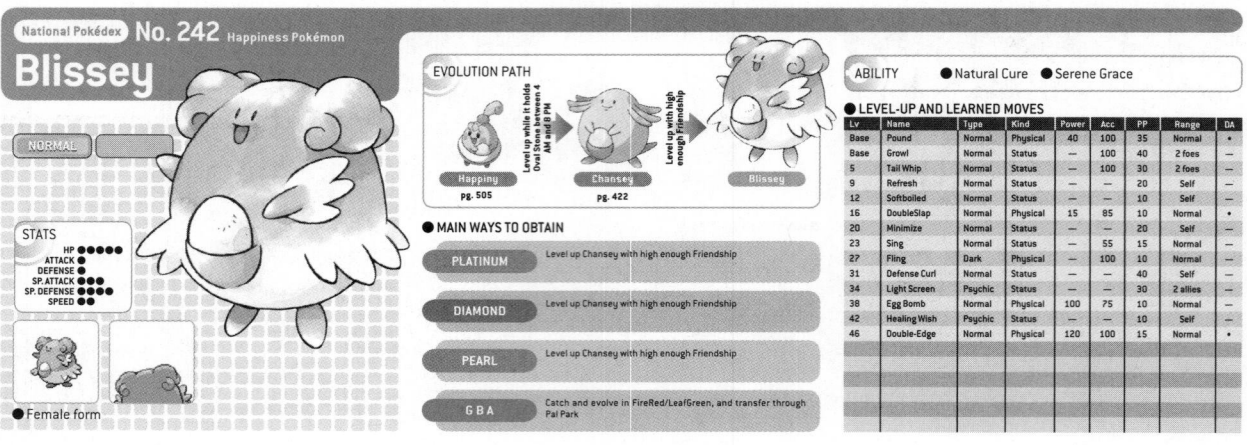

National Pokédex No. 242 Happiness Pokémon
Blissey

NORMAL

STATS
HP
ATTACK
DEFENSE
SP. ATTACK
SP. DEFENSE
SPEED

● Female form

EVOLUTION PATH

Happiny pg. 505 → *(Level up while it holds Oval Stone between 4 AM and 8 PM)* → Chansey pg. 422 → *(Level up with high enough Friendship)* → Blissey

ABILITY ● Natural Cure ● Serene Grace

● LEVEL-UP AND LEARNED MOVES

Lv	Name	Type	Kind	Power	Acc	PP	Range	DA
Base	Pound	Normal	Physical	40	100	35	Normal	•
Base	Growl	Normal	Status	—	100	40	2 foes	—
5	Tail Whip	Normal	Status	—	100	30	2 foes	—
9	Refresh	Normal	Status	—	—	20	Self	—
12	Softboiled	Normal	Status	—	—	10	Self	—
16	DoubleSlap	Normal	Physical	15	85	10	Normal	•
20	Minimize	Normal	Status	—	—	20	Self	—
23	Sing	Normal	Status	—	55	15	Normal	—
27	Fling	Dark	Physical	—	100	10	Normal	•
31	Defense Curl	Normal	Status	—	—	40	Self	—
34	Light Screen	Psychic	Status	—	—	30	2 allies	—
38	Egg Bomb	Normal	Physical	100	75	10	Normal	•
42	Healing Wish	Psychic	Status	—	—	10	Self	—
46	Double-Edge	Normal	Physical	120	100	15	Normal	•

● MAIN WAYS TO OBTAIN

PLATINUM	Level up Chansey with high enough Friendship
DIAMOND	Level up Chansey with high enough Friendship
PEARL	Level up Chansey with high enough Friendship
G B A	Catch and evolve in FireRed/LeafGreen, and transfer through Pal Park

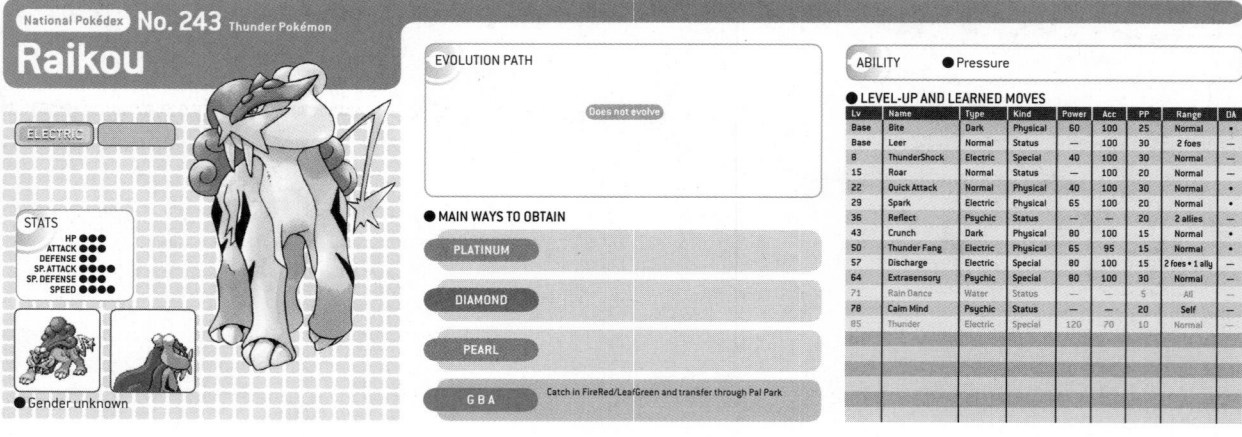

National Pokédex No. 243 Thunder Pokémon
Raikou

ELECTRIC

STATS
HP
ATTACK
DEFENSE
SP. ATTACK
SP. DEFENSE
SPEED

● Gender unknown

EVOLUTION PATH

Does not evolve

ABILITY ● Pressure

● LEVEL-UP AND LEARNED MOVES

Lv	Name	Type	Kind	Power	Acc	PP	Range	DA
Base	Bite	Dark	Physical	60	100	25	Normal	•
Base	Leer	Normal	Status	—	100	30	2 foes	—
8	ThunderShock	Electric	Special	40	100	30	Normal	—
15	Roar	Normal	Status	—	100	20	Normal	—
22	Quick Attack	Normal	Physical	40	100	30	Normal	•
29	Spark	Electric	Physical	65	100	20	Normal	•
36	Reflect	Psychic	Status	—	—	20	2 allies	—
43	Crunch	Dark	Physical	80	100	15	Normal	•
50	Thunder Fang	Electric	Physical	65	95	15	Normal	•
57	Discharge	Electric	Special	80	100	15	2 foes + 1 ally	—
64	Extrasensory	Psychic	Special	80	100	30	Normal	—
71	Rain Dance	Water	Status	—	—	5	All	—
78	Calm Mind	Psychic	Status	—	—	20	Self	—
85	Thunder	Electric	Special	120	70	10	Normal	—

● MAIN WAYS TO OBTAIN

PLATINUM	
DIAMOND	
PEARL	
G B A	Catch in FireRed/LeafGreen and transfer through Pal Park

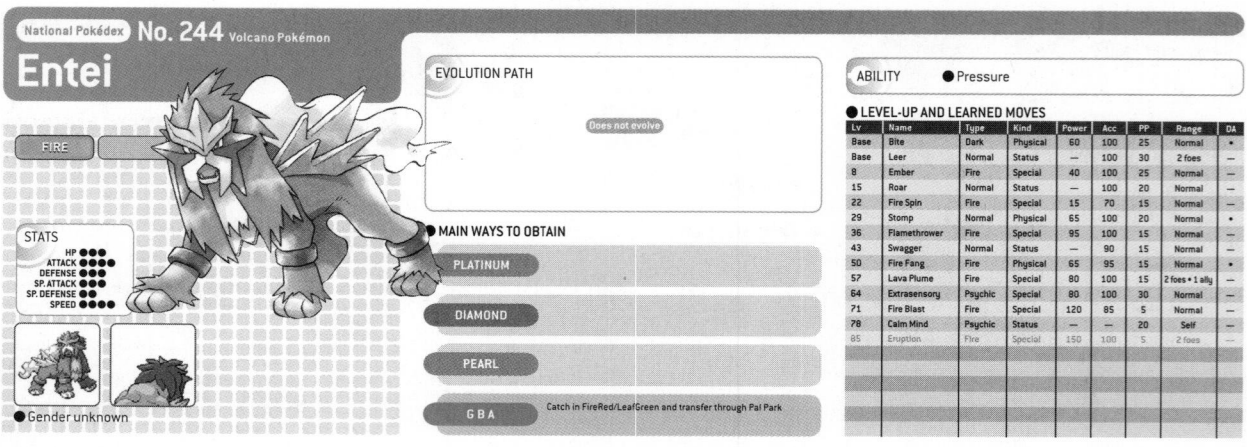

National Pokédex No. 244 Volcano Pokémon
Entei

FIRE

STATS
HP
ATTACK
DEFENSE
SP. ATTACK
SP. DEFENSE
SPEED

● Gender unknown

EVOLUTION PATH

Does not evolve

ABILITY ● Pressure

● LEVEL-UP AND LEARNED MOVES

Lv	Name	Type	Kind	Power	Acc	PP	Range	DA
Base	Bite	Dark	Physical	60	100	25	Normal	•
Base	Leer	Normal	Status	—	100	30	2 foes	—
8	Ember	Fire	Special	40	100	25	Normal	—
15	Roar	Normal	Status	—	100	20	Normal	—
22	Fire Spin	Fire	Special	15	70	15	Normal	—
29	Stomp	Normal	Physical	65	100	20	Normal	•
36	Flamethrower	Fire	Special	95	100	15	Normal	—
43	Swagger	Normal	Status	—	90	15	Normal	—
50	Fire Fang	Fire	Physical	65	95	15	Normal	•
57	Lava Plume	Fire	Special	80	100	15	2 foes + 1 ally	—
64	Extrasensory	Psychic	Special	80	100	30	Normal	—
71	Fire Blast	Fire	Special	120	85	5	Normal	—
78	Calm Mind	Psychic	Status	—	—	20	Self	—
85	Eruption	Fire	Special	150	100	5	2 foes	—

● MAIN WAYS TO OBTAIN

PLATINUM	
DIAMOND	
PEARL	
G B A	Catch in FireRed/LeafGreen and transfer through Pal Park

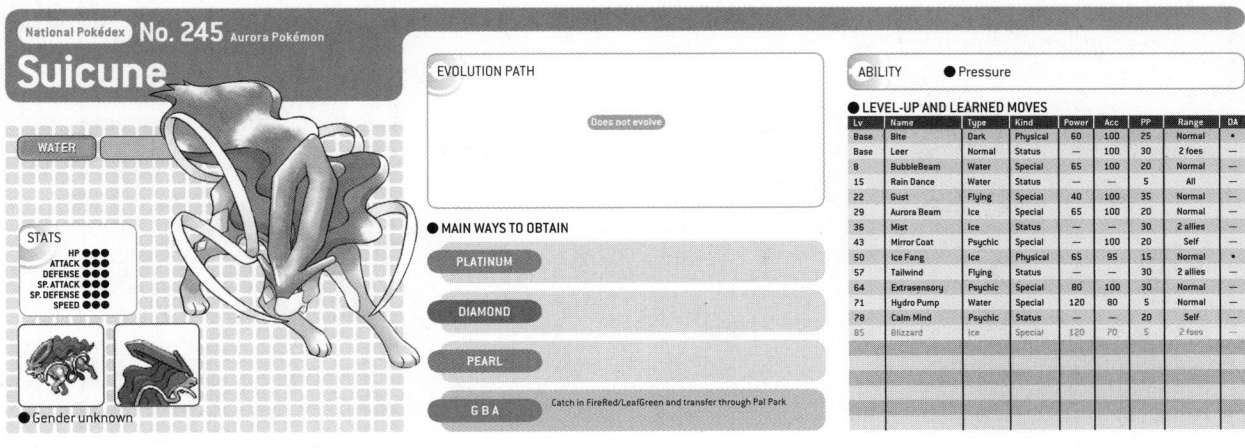

National Pokédex No. 245 Aurora Pokémon

Suicune

WATER

STATS
HP ●●●
ATTACK ●●●
DEFENSE ●●●●
SP. ATTACK ●●●
SP. DEFENSE ●●●●
SPEED ●●●

● Gender unknown

EVOLUTION PATH

Does not evolve

● MAIN WAYS TO OBTAIN

PLATINUM

DIAMOND

PEARL

GBA — Catch in FireRed/LeafGreen and transfer through Pal Park

ABILITY ● Pressure

● LEVEL-UP AND LEARNED MOVES

Lv	Name	Type	Kind	Power	Acc	PP	Range	DA
Base	Bite	Dark	Physical	60	100	25	Normal	●
Base	Leer	Normal	Status	—	100	30	2 foes	—
8	BubbleBeam	Water	Special	65	100	20	Normal	—
15	Rain Dance	Water	Status	—	—	5	All	—
22	Gust	Flying	Special	40	100	35	Normal	—
29	Aurora Beam	Ice	Special	65	100	20	Normal	—
36	Mist	Ice	Status	—	—	30	2 allies	—
43	Mirror Coat	Psychic	Special	—	100	20	Self	—
50	Ice Fang	Ice	Physical	65	95	15	Normal	●
57	Tailwind	Flying	Status	—	—	30	2 allies	—
64	Extrasensory	Psychic	Special	80	100	30	Normal	—
71	Hydro Pump	Water	Special	120	80	5	Normal	—
78	Calm Mind	Psychic	Status	—	—	20	Self	—
85	Blizzard	Ice	Special	120	70	5	2 foes	—

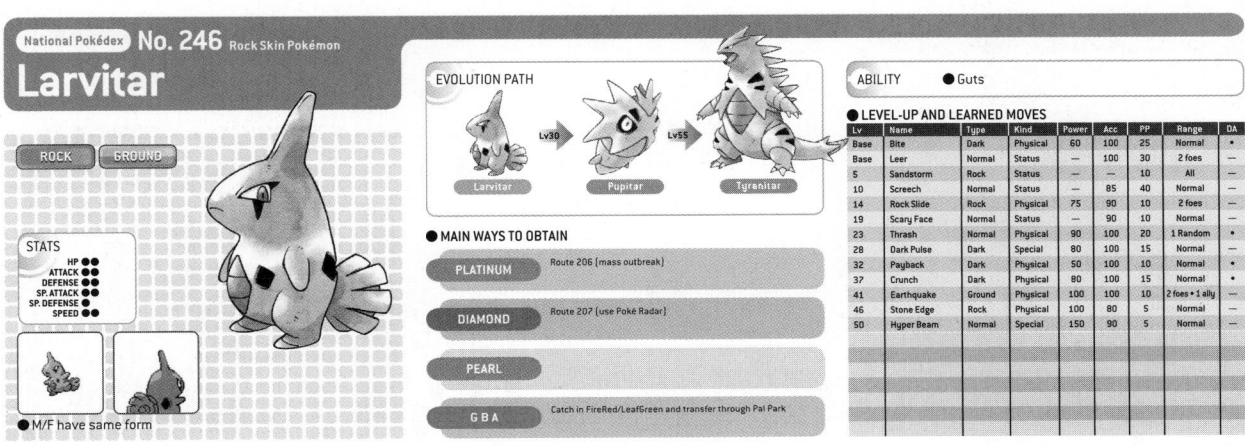

National Pokédex No. 246 Rock Skin Pokémon

Larvitar

ROCK GROUND

STATS
HP ●●
ATTACK ●●●
DEFENSE ●●
SP. ATTACK ●●
SP. DEFENSE ●●
SPEED ●●

● M/F have same form

EVOLUTION PATH

Larvitar — Lv30 → Pupitar — Lv55 → Tyranitar

● MAIN WAYS TO OBTAIN

PLATINUM — Route 206 (mass outbreak)

DIAMOND — Route 207 (use Poké Radar)

PEARL

GBA — Catch in FireRed/LeafGreen and transfer through Pal Park

ABILITY ● Guts

● LEVEL-UP AND LEARNED MOVES

Lv	Name	Type	Kind	Power	Acc	PP	Range	DA
Base	Bite	Dark	Physical	60	100	25	Normal	●
Base	Leer	Normal	Status	—	100	30	2 foes	—
5	Sandstorm	Rock	Status	—	—	10	All	—
10	Screech	Normal	Status	—	85	40	Normal	—
14	Rock Slide	Rock	Physical	75	90	10	2 foes	—
19	Scary Face	Normal	Status	—	90	10	Normal	—
23	Thrash	Normal	Physical	90	100	20	1 Random	●
28	Dark Pulse	Dark	Special	80	100	15	Normal	—
32	Payback	Dark	Physical	50	100	10	Normal	—
37	Crunch	Dark	Physical	80	100	15	Normal	●
41	Earthquake	Ground	Physical	100	100	10	2 foes • 1 ally	—
46	Stone Edge	Rock	Physical	100	80	5	Normal	—
50	Hyper Beam	Normal	Special	150	90	5	Normal	—

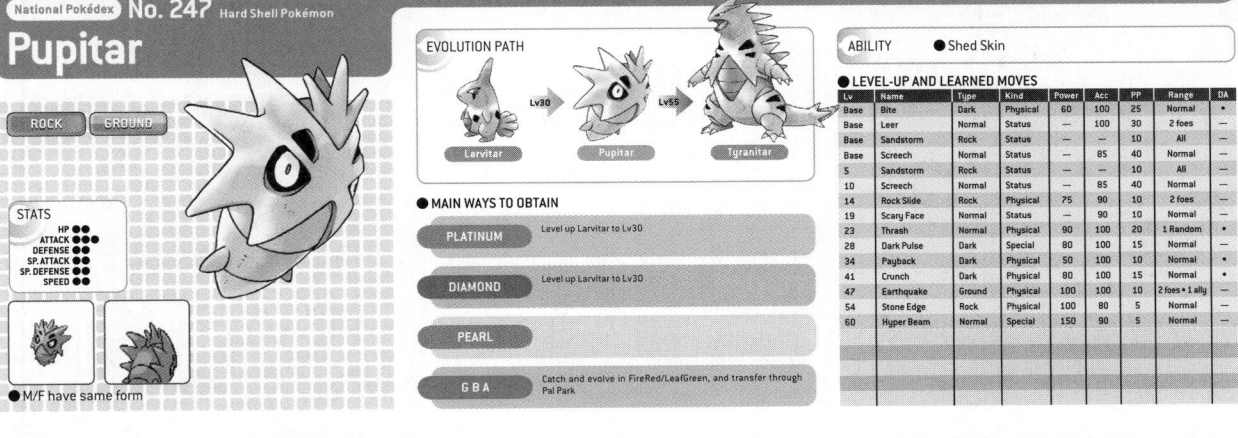

National Pokédex No. 247 Hard Shell Pokémon

Pupitar

ROCK GROUND

STATS
HP ●●●
ATTACK ●●●
DEFENSE ●●●
SP. ATTACK ●●
SP. DEFENSE ●●●
SPEED ●●●

● M/F have same form

EVOLUTION PATH

Larvitar — Lv30 → Pupitar — Lv55 → Tyranitar

● MAIN WAYS TO OBTAIN

PLATINUM — Level up Larvitar to Lv30

DIAMOND — Level up Larvitar to Lv30

PEARL

GBA — Catch and evolve in FireRed/LeafGreen, and transfer through Pal Park

ABILITY ● Shed Skin

● LEVEL-UP AND LEARNED MOVES

Lv	Name	Type	Kind	Power	Acc	PP	Range	DA
Base	Bite	Dark	Physical	60	100	25	Normal	●
Base	Leer	Normal	Status	—	100	30	2 foes	—
Base	Sandstorm	Rock	Status	—	—	10	All	—
Base	Screech	Normal	Status	—	85	40	Normal	—
5	Sandstorm	Rock	Status	—	—	10	All	—
10	Screech	Normal	Status	—	85	40	Normal	—
14	Rock Slide	Rock	Physical	75	90	10	2 foes	—
19	Scary Face	Normal	Status	—	90	10	Normal	—
23	Thrash	Normal	Physical	90	100	20	1 Random	●
28	Dark Pulse	Dark	Special	80	100	15	Normal	—
34	Payback	Dark	Physical	50	100	10	Normal	—
41	Crunch	Dark	Physical	80	100	15	Normal	●
47	Earthquake	Ground	Physical	100	100	10	2 foes • 1 ally	—
54	Stone Edge	Rock	Physical	100	80	5	Normal	—
60	Hyper Beam	Normal	Special	150	90	5	Normal	—

248
•••••
TYRANITAR

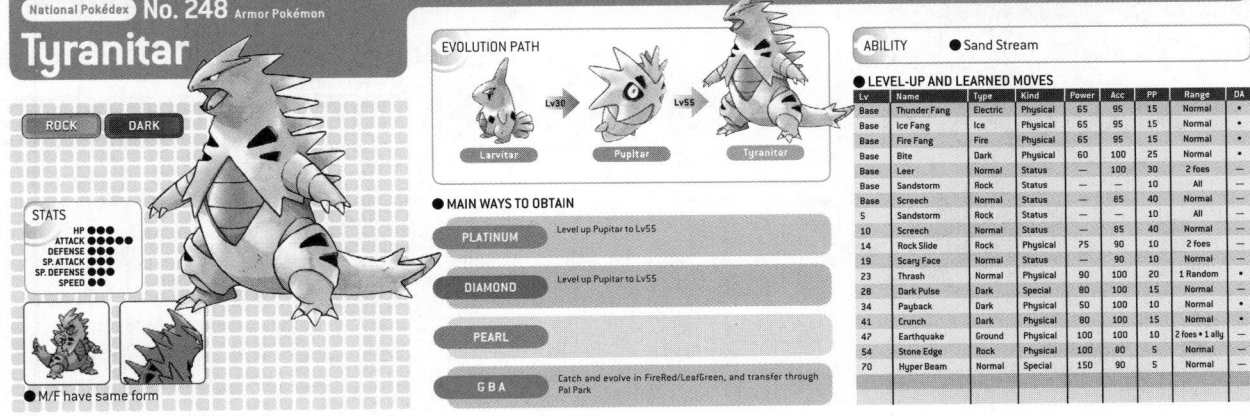

National Pokédex No. 248 Armor Pokémon

Tyranitar

ROCK DARK

STATS
HP ●●●
ATTACK ●●●●
DEFENSE ●●●
SP. ATTACK ●●●
SP. DEFENSE ●●●
SPEED ●●●

● M/F have same form

EVOLUTION PATH

Larvitar — Lv30 → Pupitar — Lv55 → Tyranitar

● MAIN WAYS TO OBTAIN

PLATINUM — Level up Pupitar to Lv55

DIAMOND — Level up Pupitar to Lv55

PEARL

GBA — Catch and evolve in FireRed/LeafGreen, and transfer through Pal Park

ABILITY ● Sand Stream

● LEVEL-UP AND LEARNED MOVES

Lv	Name	Type	Kind	Power	Acc	PP	Range	DA
Base	Thunder Fang	Electric	Physical	65	95	15	Normal	●
Base	Ice Fang	Ice	Physical	65	95	15	Normal	●
Base	Fire Fang	Fire	Physical	65	95	15	Normal	●
Base	Bite	Dark	Physical	60	100	25	Normal	●
Base	Leer	Normal	Status	—	100	30	2 foes	—
Base	Sandstorm	Rock	Status	—	—	10	All	—
Base	Screech	Normal	Status	—	85	40	Normal	—
5	Sandstorm	Rock	Status	—	—	10	All	—
10	Screech	Normal	Status	—	85	40	Normal	—
14	Rock Slide	Rock	Physical	75	90	10	2 foes	—
19	Scary Face	Normal	Status	—	90	10	Normal	—
23	Thrash	Normal	Physical	90	100	20	1 Random	●
28	Dark Pulse	Dark	Special	80	100	15	Normal	—
34	Payback	Dark	Physical	50	100	10	Normal	—
41	Crunch	Dark	Physical	80	100	15	Normal	●
47	Earthquake	Ground	Physical	100	100	10	2 foes • 1 ally	—
54	Stone Edge	Rock	Physical	100	80	5	Normal	—
70	Hyper Beam	Normal	Special	150	90	5	Normal	—

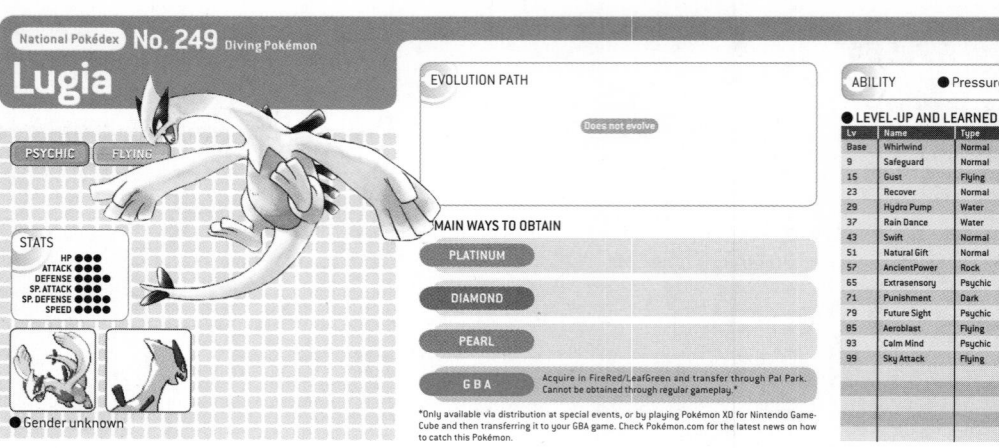

National Pokédex No. 249 Diving Pokémon

Lugia

PSYCHIC FLYING

STATS
- HP ●●●●
- ATTACK ●●●
- DEFENSE ●●●
- SP. ATTACK ●●●
- SP. DEFENSE ●●●●
- SPEED ●●●●

● Gender unknown

EVOLUTION PATH

Does not evolve

MAIN WAYS TO OBTAIN

PLATINUM

DIAMOND

PEARL

GBA — Acquire in FireRed/LeafGreen and transfer through Pal Park. Cannot be obtained through regular gameplay.*

*Only available via distribution at special events, or by playing Pokémon XD for Nintendo GameCube and then transferring it to your GBA game. Check Pokémon.com for the latest news on how to catch this Pokémon.

ABILITY ● Pressure

● LEVEL-UP AND LEARNED MOVES

Lv	Name	Type	Kind	Power	Acc	PP	Range	DA
Base	Whirlwind	Normal	Status	—	100	20	Normal	—
9	Safeguard	Normal	Status	—	—	25	2 allies	—
15	Gust	Flying	Special	40	100	35	Normal	—
23	Recover	Normal	Status	—	—	10	Self	—
29	Hydro Pump	Water	Special	120	80	5	Normal	—
37	Rain Dance	Water	Status	—	—	5	All	—
43	Swift	Normal	Special	60	—	20	2 foes	—
51	Natural Gift	Normal	Physical	—	100	15	Normal	—
57	AncientPower	Rock	Special	60	100	5	Normal	—
65	Extrasensory	Psychic	Special	80	100	30	Normal	—
71	Punishment	Dark	Physical	—	100	5	Normal	●
79	Future Sight	Psychic	Special	80	90	15	Normal	—
85	Aeroblast	Flying	Special	100	95	5	Normal	—
93	Calm Mind	Psychic	Status	—	—	20	Self	—
99	Sky Attack	Flying	Physical	140	90	5	Normal	—

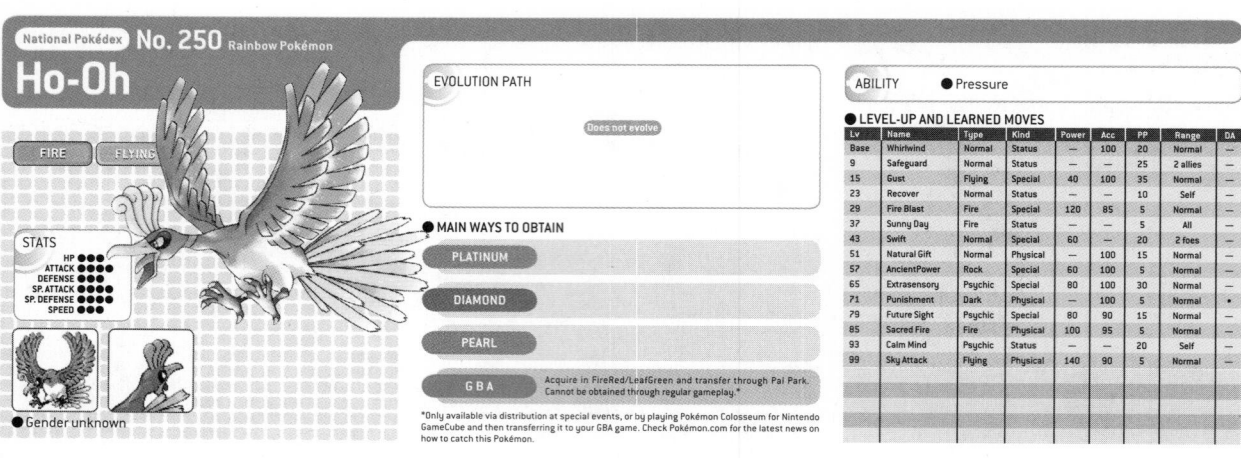

National Pokédex No. 250 Rainbow Pokémon

Ho-Oh

FIRE FLYING

STATS
- HP ●●●
- ATTACK ●●●
- DEFENSE ●●●
- SP. ATTACK ●●●
- SP. DEFENSE ●●●●
- SPEED ●●●

● Gender unknown

EVOLUTION PATH

Does not evolve

MAIN WAYS TO OBTAIN

PLATINUM

DIAMOND

PEARL

GBA — Acquire in FireRed/LeafGreen and transfer through Pal Park. Cannot be obtained through regular gameplay.*

*Only available via distribution at special events, or by playing Pokémon Colosseum for Nintendo GameCube and then transferring it to your GBA game. Check Pokémon.com for the latest news on how to catch this Pokémon.

ABILITY ● Pressure

● LEVEL-UP AND LEARNED MOVES

Lv	Name	Type	Kind	Power	Acc	PP	Range	DA
Base	Whirlwind	Normal	Status	—	100	20	Normal	—
9	Safeguard	Normal	Status	—	—	25	2 allies	—
15	Gust	Flying	Special	40	100	35	Normal	—
23	Recover	Normal	Status	—	—	10	Self	—
29	Fire Blast	Fire	Special	120	85	5	Normal	—
37	Sunny Day	Fire	Status	—	—	5	All	—
43	Swift	Normal	Special	60	—	20	2 foes	—
51	Natural Gift	Normal	Physical	—	100	15	Normal	—
57	AncientPower	Rock	Special	60	100	5	Normal	—
65	Extrasensory	Psychic	Special	80	100	30	Normal	—
71	Punishment	Dark	Physical	—	100	5	Normal	●
79	Future Sight	Psychic	Special	80	90	15	Normal	—
85	Sacred Fire	Fire	Physical	100	95	5	Normal	—
93	Calm Mind	Psychic	Status	—	—	20	Self	—
99	Sky Attack	Flying	Physical	140	90	5	Normal	—

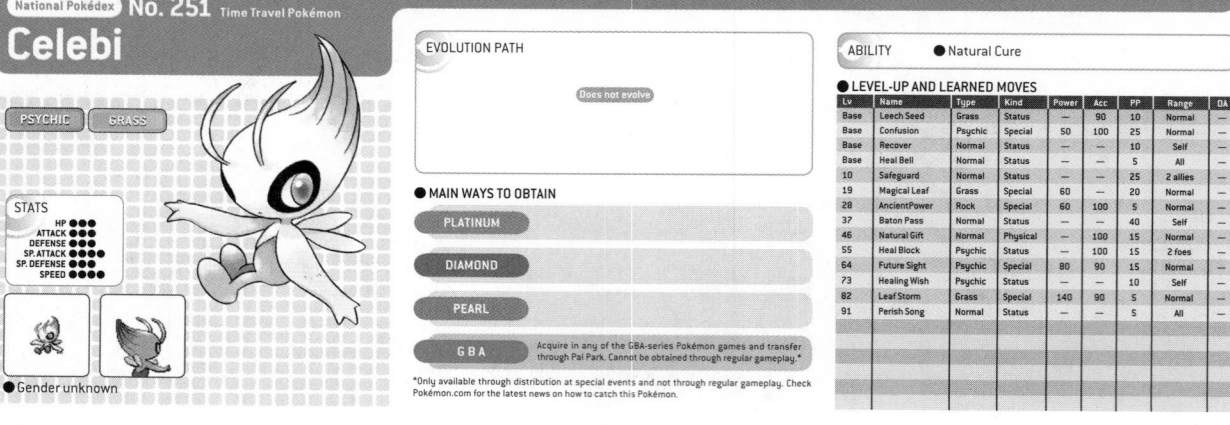

National Pokédex No. 251 Time Travel Pokémon

Celebi

PSYCHIC GRASS

STATS
- HP ●●●
- ATTACK ●●●
- DEFENSE ●●●
- SP. ATTACK ●●●
- SP. DEFENSE ●●●
- SPEED ●●●●

● Gender unknown

EVOLUTION PATH

Does not evolve

MAIN WAYS TO OBTAIN

PLATINUM

DIAMOND

PEARL

GBA — Acquire in any of the GBA-series Pokémon games and transfer through Pal Park. Cannot be obtained through regular gameplay.*

*Only available through distribution at special events and not through regular gameplay. Check Pokémon.com for the latest news on how to catch this Pokémon.

ABILITY ● Natural Cure

● LEVEL-UP AND LEARNED MOVES

Lv	Name	Type	Kind	Power	Acc	PP	Range	DA
Base	Leech Seed	Grass	Status	—	90	10	Normal	—
Base	Confusion	Psychic	Special	50	100	25	Normal	—
Base	Recover	Normal	Status	—	—	10	Self	—
Base	Heal Bell	Normal	Status	—	—	5	All	—
10	Safeguard	Normal	Status	—	—	25	2 allies	—
19	Magical Leaf	Grass	Special	60	—	20	Normal	—
28	AncientPower	Rock	Special	60	100	5	Normal	—
37	Baton Pass	Normal	Status	—	—	40	Self	—
46	Natural Gift	Normal	Physical	—	100	15	Normal	—
55	Heal Block	Psychic	Status	—	100	15	2 foes	—
64	Future Sight	Psychic	Special	80	90	15	Normal	—
73	Healing Wish	Psychic	Status	—	—	10	Self	—
82	Leaf Storm	Grass	Special	140	90	5	Normal	—
91	Perish Song	Normal	Status	—	—	5	All	—

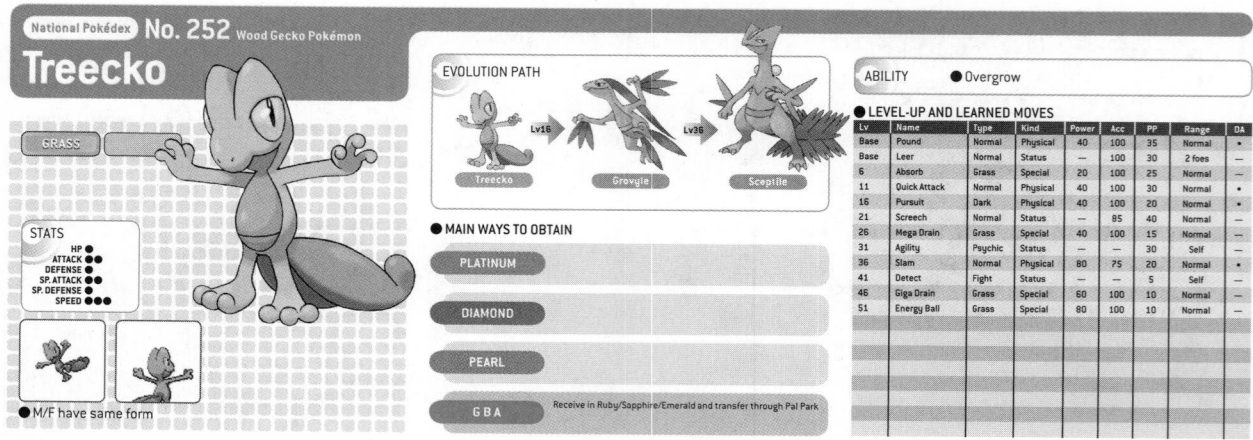

National Pokédex No. 252 Wood Gecko Pokémon

Treecko

GRASS

STATS
- HP ●●
- ATTACK ●●
- DEFENSE ●
- SP. ATTACK ●●
- SP. DEFENSE ●●
- SPEED ●●●

● M/F have same form

EVOLUTION PATH

Treecko → Lv16 → Grovyle → Lv36 → Sceptile

MAIN WAYS TO OBTAIN

PLATINUM

DIAMOND

PEARL

GBA — Receive in Ruby/Sapphire/Emerald and transfer through Pal Park

ABILITY ● Overgrow

● LEVEL-UP AND LEARNED MOVES

Lv	Name	Type	Kind	Power	Acc	PP	Range	DA
Base	Pound	Normal	Physical	40	100	35	Normal	●
Base	Leer	Normal	Status	—	100	30	2 foes	—
6	Absorb	Grass	Special	20	100	25	Normal	—
11	Quick Attack	Normal	Physical	40	100	30	Normal	●
16	Pursuit	Dark	Physical	40	100	20	Normal	●
21	Screech	Normal	Status	—	85	40	Normal	—
26	Mega Drain	Grass	Special	40	100	15	Normal	—
31	Agility	Psychic	Status	—	—	30	Self	—
36	Slam	Normal	Physical	80	75	20	Normal	●
41	Detect	Fight	Status	—	—	5	Self	—
46	Giga Drain	Grass	Special	60	100	10	Normal	—
51	Energy Ball	Grass	Special	80	100	10	Normal	—

No. 253 Wood Gecko Pokémon
Grovyle

GRASS

STATS
- HP ●●
- ATTACK ●●●
- DEFENSE ●●
- SP. ATTACK ●●●
- SP. DEFENSE ●●
- SPEED ●●●

● M/F have same form

EVOLUTION PATH

Treecko → Lv16 → Grovyle → Lv36 → Sceptile

● MAIN WAYS TO OBTAIN
- PLATINUM
- DIAMOND
- PEARL
- GBA — Receive and evolve in Ruby/Sapphire/Emerald, and transfer through Pal Park

ABILITY ● Overgrow

● LEVEL-UP AND LEARNED MOVES

Lv	Name	Type	Kind	Power	Acc	PP	Range	DA
Base	Pound	Normal	Physical	40	100	35	Normal	•
Base	Leer	Normal	Status	—	100	30	2 foes	
Base	Absorb	Grass	Special	20	100	25	Normal	
Base	Quick Attack	Normal	Physical	40	100	30	Normal	•
6	Absorb	Grass	Special	20	100	25	Normal	
11	Quick Attack	Normal	Physical	40	100	30	Normal	•
16	Fury Cutter	Bug	Physical	10	95	20	Normal	•
17	Pursuit	Dark	Physical	40	100	20	Normal	•
23	Screech	Normal	Status	—	85	40	Normal	
29	Leaf Blade	Grass	Physical	90	100	15	Normal	
35	Agility	Psychic	Status	—	—	30	Self	
41	Slam	Normal	Physical	80	75	20	Normal	
47	Detect	Fight	Status	—	—	5	Self	
53	False Swipe	Normal	Physical	40	100	40	Normal	
59	Leaf Storm	Grass	Special	140	90	5	Normal	

No. 254 Forest Pokémon
Sceptile

GRASS

STATS
- HP ●●
- ATTACK ●●●
- DEFENSE ●●
- SP. ATTACK ●●●
- SP. DEFENSE ●●●
- SPEED ●●●●

● M/F have same form

EVOLUTION PATH

Treecko → Lv16 → Grovyle → Lv36 → Sceptile

● MAIN WAYS TO OBTAIN
- PLATINUM
- DIAMOND
- PEARL
- GBA — Receive and evolve in Ruby/Sapphire/Emerald, and transfer through Pal Park

ABILITY ● Overgrow

● LEVEL-UP AND LEARNED MOVES

Lv	Name	Type	Kind	Power	Acc	PP	Range	DA
Base	Night Slash	Dark	Physical	70	100	15	Normal	•
Base	Pound	Normal	Physical	40	100	30	2 foes	—
Base	Leer	Normal	Status	—	100	30	2 foes	—
Base	Absorb	Grass	Special	20	100	25	Normal	—
Base	Quick Attack	Normal	Physical	40	100	30	Normal	—
6	Absorb	Grass	Special	20	100	25	Normal	—
11	Quick Attack	Normal	Physical	40	100	30	Normal	—
16	X-Scissor	Bug	Physical	80	100	15	Normal	•
17	Pursuit	Dark	Physical	40	100	20	Normal	•
23	Screech	Normal	Status	—	85	40	Normal	
29	Leaf Blade	Grass	Physical	90	100	15	Normal	
35	Agility	Psychic	Status	—	—	30	Self	
43	Slam	Normal	Physical	80	75	20	Normal	
51	Detect	Fight	Status	—	—	5	Self	
59	False Swipe	Normal	Physical	40	100	40	Normal	
67	Leaf Storm	Grass	Special	140	90	5	Normal	

No. 255 Chick Pokémon
Torchic

FIRE

STATS
- HP ●●
- ATTACK ●●
- DEFENSE ●●
- SP. ATTACK ●●●
- SP. DEFENSE ●●
- SPEED ●●

● Male form ● Female form

EVOLUTION PATH

Torchic → Lv16 → Combusken → Lv35 → Blaziken

● MAIN WAYS TO OBTAIN
- PLATINUM
- DIAMOND
- PEARL
- GBA — Receive in Ruby/Sapphire/Emerald and transfer through Pal Park

ABILITY ● Blaze

● LEVEL-UP AND LEARNED MOVES

Lv	Name	Type	Kind	Power	Acc	PP	Range	DA
Base	Scratch	Normal	Physical	40	100	35	Normal	•
Base	Growl	Normal	Status	—	100	40	2 foes	•
7	Focus Energy	Normal	Status	—	—	30	Self	
10	Ember	Fire	Special	40	100	25	Normal	•
16	Peck	Flying	Physical	35	100	35	Normal	•
19	Sand-Attack	Ground	Status	—	100	15	Normal	•
25	Fire Spin	Fire	Special	15	70	15	Normal	•
28	Quick Attack	Normal	Physical	40	100	30	Normal	•
34	Slash	Normal	Physical	70	100	20	Normal	•
37	Mirror Move	Flying	Status	—	—	20	DoM	
43	Flamethrower	Fire	Special	95	100	15	Normal	•

No. 256 Young Fowl Pokémon
Combusken

FIRE FIGHTING

STATS
- HP ●●●
- ATTACK ●●●
- DEFENSE ●●
- SP. ATTACK ●●●
- SP. DEFENSE ●●
- SPEED ●●

● Male form ● Female form

EVOLUTION PATH

Torchic → Lv16 → Combusken → Lv36 → Blaziken

● MAIN WAYS TO OBTAIN
- PLATINUM
- DIAMOND
- PEARL
- GBA — Receive and evolve in Ruby/Sapphire/Emerald, and transfer through Pal Park

ABILITY ● Blaze

● LEVEL-UP AND LEARNED MOVES

Lv	Name	Type	Kind	Power	Acc	PP	Range	DA
Base	Scratch	Normal	Physical	40	100	35	Normal	•
Base	Growl	Normal	Status	—	100	40	2 foes	•
Base	Focus Energy	Normal	Status	—	—	30	Self	
Base	Ember	Fire	Special	40	100	25	Normal	•
7	Focus Energy	Normal	Status	—	—	30	Self	
13	Ember	Fire	Special	40	100	25	Normal	•
16	Double Kick	Fight	Physical	30	100	30	Normal	•
17	Peck	Flying	Physical	35	100	35	Normal	•
21	Sand-Attack	Ground	Status	—	100	15	Normal	•
28	Bulk Up	Fight	Status	—	—	20	Self	
32	Quick Attack	Normal	Physical	40	100	30	Normal	•
39	Slash	Normal	Physical	70	100	20	Normal	•
43	Mirror Move	Flying	Status	—	—	20	DoM	
50	Sky Uppercut	Fight	Physical	85	90	15	Normal	•
54	Flare Blitz	Fire	Physical	120	100	15	Normal	•

National Pokédex No. 257 Blaze Pokémon
Blaziken

FIRE | Fighting

STATS
HP ●●●
ATTACK ●●●●
DEFENSE ●●
SP. ATTACK ●●
SP. DEFENSE ●●
SPEED ●●●

●Male form   ●Female form

EVOLUTION PATH
Torchic — Lv16 → Combusken — Lv36 → Blaziken

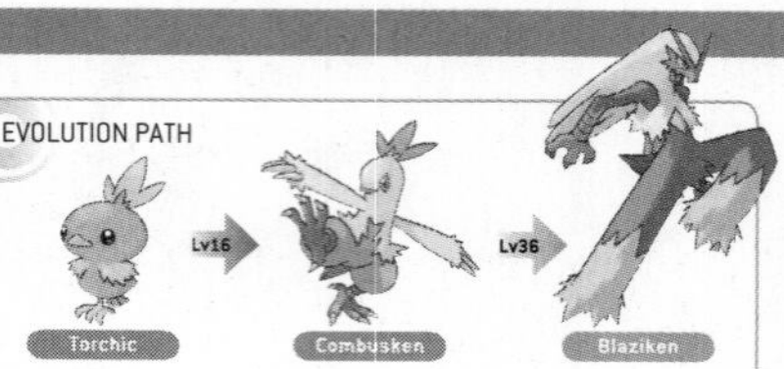

ABILITY   ●Blaze

● LEVEL-UP AND LEARNED MOVES
Lv	Name	Type	Kind	Power	Acc	PP	Range	DA
Base	Fire Punch	Fire	Physical	75	100	15	Normal	●
Base	Scratch	Normal	Physical	40	100	35	Normal	—
Base	Growl	Normal	Status	—	100	40	2 foes	—
Base	Focus Energy	Normal	Status	—	—	30	Self	—
Base	Ember	Fire	Special	40	100	25	Normal	—
?	Focus Energy	Normal	Status	—	—	30	Self	—
13	Ember	Fire	Special	40	100	25	Normal	—
16	Double Kick	Fighting	Physical	30	100	30	Normal	●
17	Peck	Flying	Physical	35	100	35	Normal	—
21	Sand-Attack	Ground	Status	—	100	15	Normal	—
28	Bulk Up	Fighting	Status	—	—	20	Self	—
32	Quick Attack	Normal	Physical	40	100	30	Normal	—
36	Blaze Kick	Fire	Physical	85	90	10	Normal	●
42	Slash	Normal	Physical	70	100	20	Normal	—
49	Brave Bird	Flying	Physical	120	100	15	Normal	●
59	Sky Uppercut	Fighting	Physical	85	90	15	Normal	—
66	Flare Blitz	Fire	Physical	120	100	15	Normal	●

● MAIN WAYS TO OBTAIN
PLATINUM
DIAMOND
PEARL
G B A   Receive and evolve in Ruby/Sapphire/Emerald, and transfer through Pal Park

---

National Pokédex No. 258 Mud Fish Pokémon
Mudkip

WATER

STATS
HP ●●●
ATTACK ●●●
DEFENSE ●●●
SP. ATTACK ●●
SP. DEFENSE ●●
SPEED ●●

●M/F have same form

EVOLUTION PATH
Mudkip — Lv16 → Marshtomp — Lv36 → Swampert

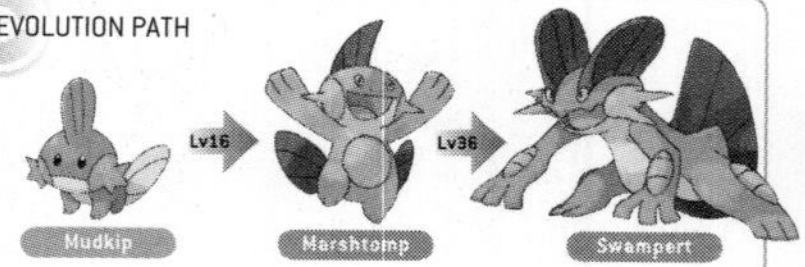

ABILITY   ●Torrent

● LEVEL-UP AND LEARNED MOVES
Lv	Name	Type	Kind	Power	Acc	PP	Range	DA
Base	Tackle	Normal	Physical	35	95	35	Normal	●
Base	Growl	Normal	Status	—	100	40	2 foes	—
6	Mud-Slap	Ground	Special	20	100	10	Normal	—
10	Water Gun	Water	Special	40	100	25	Normal	—
15	Bide	Normal	Physical	—	—	10	Self	●
19	Foresight	Normal	Status	—	—	40	Normal	—
24	Mud Sport	Ground	Status	—	—	15	All	—
28	Take Down	Normal	Physical	90	85	20	Normal	●
33	Whirlpool	Water	Special	15	70	15	Normal	—
37	Protect	Normal	Status	—	—	10	Self	—
42	Hydro Pump	Water	Special	120	80	5	Normal	—
46	Endeavor	Normal	Physical	—	100	5	Normal	—

● MAIN WAYS TO OBTAIN
PLATINUM
DIAMOND
PEARL
G B A   Receive in Ruby/Sapphire/Emerald and transfer through Pal Park

---

National Pokédex No. 259 Mud Fish Pokémon
Marshtomp

WATER | GROUND

STATS
HP ●●●
ATTACK ●●●
DEFENSE ●●●
SP. ATTACK ●●
SP. DEFENSE ●●
SPEED ●●●

●M/F have same form

EVOLUTION PATH
Mudkip — Lv16 → Marshtomp — Lv36 → Swampert

ABILITY   ●Torrent

● LEVEL-UP AND LEARNED MOVES
Lv	Name	Type	Kind	Power	Acc	PP	Range	DA
Base	Tackle	Normal	Physical	35	95	35	Normal	●
Base	Growl	Normal	Status	—	100	40	2 foes	—
Base	Mud-Slap	Ground	Special	20	100	10	Normal	—
Base	Water Gun	Water	Special	40	100	25	Normal	—
6	Mud-Slap	Ground	Special	20	100	10	Normal	—
10	Water Gun	Water	Special	40	100	25	Normal	—
15	Bide	Normal	Physical	—	—	10	Self	●
16	Mud Shot	Ground	Special	55	95	15	Normal	—
20	Foresight	Normal	Status	—	—	40	Normal	—
25	Mud Bomb	Ground	Special	65	85	10	Normal	—
31	Take Down	Normal	Physical	90	85	20	Normal	●
37	Muddy Water	Water	Special	95	85	10	2 foes	—
42	Protect	Normal	Status	—	—	10	Self	—
46	Earthquake	Ground	Physical	100	100	10	2 foes + 1 ally	●
53	Endeavor	Normal	Physical	—	100	5	Normal	—

● MAIN WAYS TO OBTAIN
PLATINUM
DIAMOND
PEARL
G B A   Receive and evolve in Ruby/Sapphire/Emerald, and transfer through Pal Park

---

National Pokédex No. 260 Mud Fish Pokémon
Swampert

WATER | GROUND

STATS
HP ●●●
ATTACK ●●●●
DEFENSE ●●●
SP. ATTACK ●●●
SP. DEFENSE ●●●
SPEED ●●

●M/F have same form

EVOLUTION PATH
Mudkip — Lv16 → Marshtomp — Lv36 → Swampert

ABILITY   ●Torrent

● LEVEL-UP AND LEARNED MOVES
Lv	Name	Type	Kind	Power	Acc	PP	Range	DA
Base	Tackle	Normal	Physical	3S	95	35	Normal	●
Base	Growl	Normal	Status	—	100	40	2 foes	—
Base	Mud-Slap	Ground	Special	20	100	10	Normal	—
Base	Water Gun	Water	Special	40	100	25	Normal	—
6	Mud-Slap	Ground	Special	20	100	10	Normal	—
10	Water Gun	Water	Special	40	100	25	Normal	—
15	Bide	Normal	Physical	—	—	10	Self	●
16	Mud Shot	Ground	Special	55	95	15	Normal	—
20	Foresight	Normal	Status	—	—	40	Normal	—
25	Mud Bomb	Ground	Special	65	85	10	Normal	—
31	Take Down	Normal	Physical	90	85	20	Normal	—
39	Muddy Water	Water	Special	95	85	10	2 foes	—
46	Protect	Normal	Status	—	—	10	Self	—
52	Earthquake	Ground	Physical	100	100	10	2 foes + 1 ally	—
61	Endeavor	Normal	Physical	—	100	5	Normal	—
69	Hammer Arm	Fighting	Physical	100	90	10	Normal	—

● MAIN WAYS TO OBTAIN
PLATINUM
DIAMOND
PEARL
G B A   Receive and evolve in Ruby/Sapphire/Emerald, and transfer through Pal Park

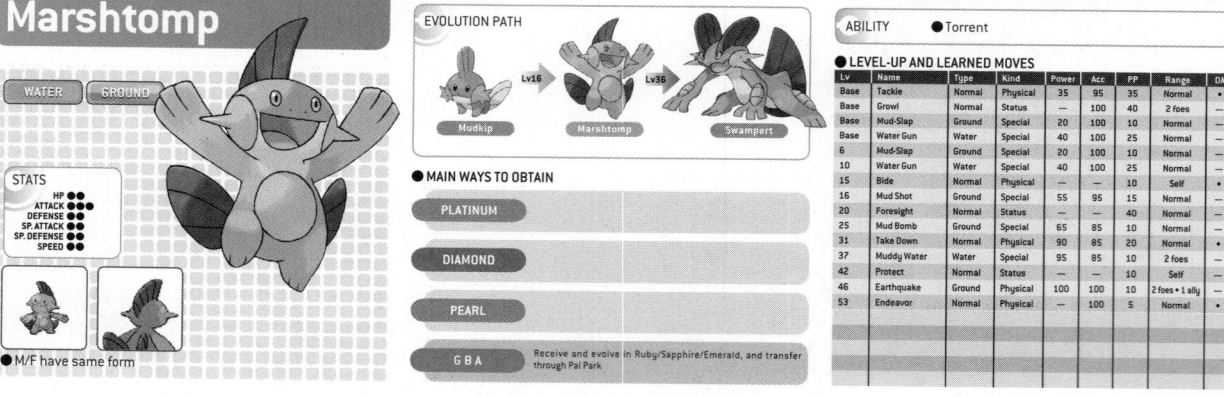
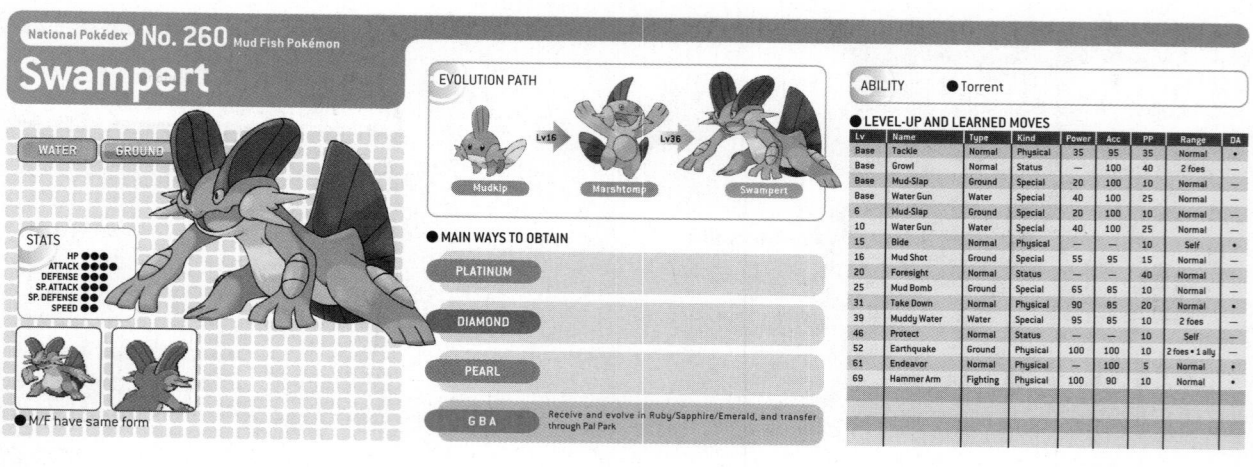

National Pokédex No. 261 Bite Pokémon
Poochyena

DARK

STATS
- HP ●
- ATTACK ● ●
- DEFENSE ● ●
- SP. ATTACK ● ●
- SP. DEFENSE ● ●
- SPEED ● ●

● M/F have same form

EVOLUTION PATH

Poochyena → Lv18 → Mightyena

● MAIN WAYS TO OBTAIN

PLATINUM	Route 214 (use Poké Radar)
DIAMOND	Discover an Egg
PEARL	
GBA	Catch in Ruby/Sapphire/Emerald and transfer through Pal Park

ABILITY
● Run Away ● Quick Feet

● LEVEL-UP AND LEARNED MOVES

Lv	Name	Type	Kind	Power	Acc	PP	Range	DA
Base	Tackle	Normal	Physical	35	95	35	Normal	—
5	Howl	Normal	Status	—	—	40	Self	—
9	Sand-Attack	Ground	Status	—	100	15	Normal	—
13	Bite	Dark	Physical	60	100	25	Normal	●
17	Odor Sleuth	Normal	Status	—	—	40	Normal	—
21	Roar	Normal	Status	—	100	20	Normal	—
25	Swagger	Normal	Status	—	90	15	Normal	—
29	Assurance	Dark	Physical	50	100	10	Normal	●
33	Scary Face	Normal	Status	—	90	10	Normal	—
37	Taunt	Dark	Status	—	100	20	Normal	—
41	Embargo	Dark	Status	—	100	15	Normal	—
45	Take Down	Normal	Physical	90	85	20	Normal	●
49	Sucker Punch	Dark	Physical	80	100	5	Normal	●
53	Crunch	Dark	Physical	80	100	15	Normal	●

National Pokédex No. 262 Bite Pokémon
Mightyena

DARK

STATS
- HP ● ● ●
- ATTACK ● ● ● ●
- DEFENSE ● ● ●
- SP. ATTACK ● ● ●
- SP. DEFENSE ● ● ●
- SPEED ● ● ●

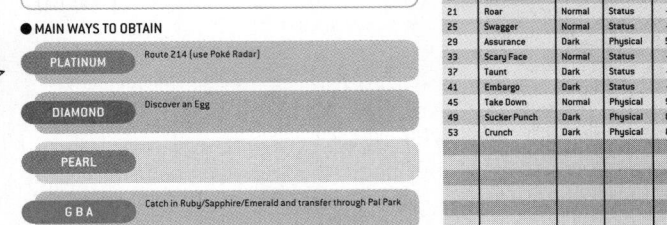

● M/F have same form

EVOLUTION PATH

Poochyena → Lv18 → Mightyena

● MAIN WAYS TO OBTAIN

PLATINUM	Level up Poochyena to Lv18
DIAMOND	Route 214 (use Poké Radar)
PEARL	
GBA	Catch and evolve in Ruby/Sapphire/Emerald, and transfer through Pal Park

ABILITY
● Intimidate ● Quick Feet

● LEVEL-UP AND LEARNED MOVES

Lv	Name	Type	Kind	Power	Acc	PP	Range	DA
Base	Tackle	Normal	Physical	35	95	35	Normal	—
Base	Howl	Normal	Status	—	—	40	Self	—
Base	Sand-Attack	Ground	Status	—	100	15	Normal	—
Base	Bite	Dark	Physical	60	100	25	Normal	●
5	Howl	Normal	Status	—	—	40	Self	—
9	Sand-Attack	Ground	Status	—	100	15	Normal	—
13	Bite	Dark	Physical	60	100	25	Normal	●
17	Odor Sleuth	Normal	Status	—	—	40	Normal	—
22	Roar	Normal	Status	—	100	20	Normal	—
27	Swagger	Normal	Status	—	90	15	Normal	—
32	Assurance	Dark	Physical	50	100	10	Normal	●
37	Scary Face	Normal	Status	—	90	10	Normal	—
42	Taunt	Dark	Status	—	100	20	Normal	—
47	Embargo	Dark	Status	—	100	15	Normal	—
52	Take Down	Normal	Physical	90	85	20	Normal	●
57	Thief	Dark	Physical	40	100	10	Normal	●
62	Sucker Punch	Dark	Physical	80	100	5	Normal	●

National Pokédex No. 263 TinyRaccoon Pokémon
Zigzagoon

NORMAL

STATS
- HP ●
- ATTACK ●
- DEFENSE ●
- SP. ATTACK ●
- SP. DEFENSE ●
- SPEED ● ●

● M/F have same form

EVOLUTION PATH

Zigzagoon → Lv20 → Linoone

● MAIN WAYS TO OBTAIN

PLATINUM	Route 202 (mass outbreak)
DIAMOND	Route 202 (mass outbreak)
PEARL	Route 202 (mass outbreak)
GBA	Catch in Ruby/Sapphire/Emerald and transfer through Pal Park

ABILITY
● Pickup ● Gluttony

● LEVEL-UP AND LEARNED MOVES

Lv	Name	Type	Kind	Power	Acc	PP	Range	DA
Base	Tackle	Normal	Physical	35	95	35	Normal	●
Base	Growl	Normal	Status	—	100	40	2 foes	—
5	Tail Whip	Normal	Status	—	100	30	2 foes	—
9	Headbutt	Normal	Physical	70	100	15	Normal	●
13	Sand-Attack	Ground	Status	—	100	15	Normal	—
17	Odor Sleuth	Normal	Status	—	—	40	Normal	—
21	Mud Sport	Ground	Status	—	—	15	All	—
25	Pin Missile	Bug	Physical	14	85	20	Normal	—
29	Covet	Normal	Physical	40	100	40	Normal	●
33	Flail	Normal	Physical	—	100	15	Normal	—
37	Rest	Psychic	Status	—	—	10	Self	—
41	Belly Drum	Normal	Status	—	—	10	Self	—
45	Fling	Dark	Physical	—	100	10	Normal	●

National Pokédex No. 264 Rushing Pokémon
Linoone

NORMAL

STATS
- HP ● ●
- ATTACK ● ● ●
- DEFENSE ● ● ●
- SP. ATTACK ● ● ●
- SP. DEFENSE ● ●
- SPEED ● ● ● ●

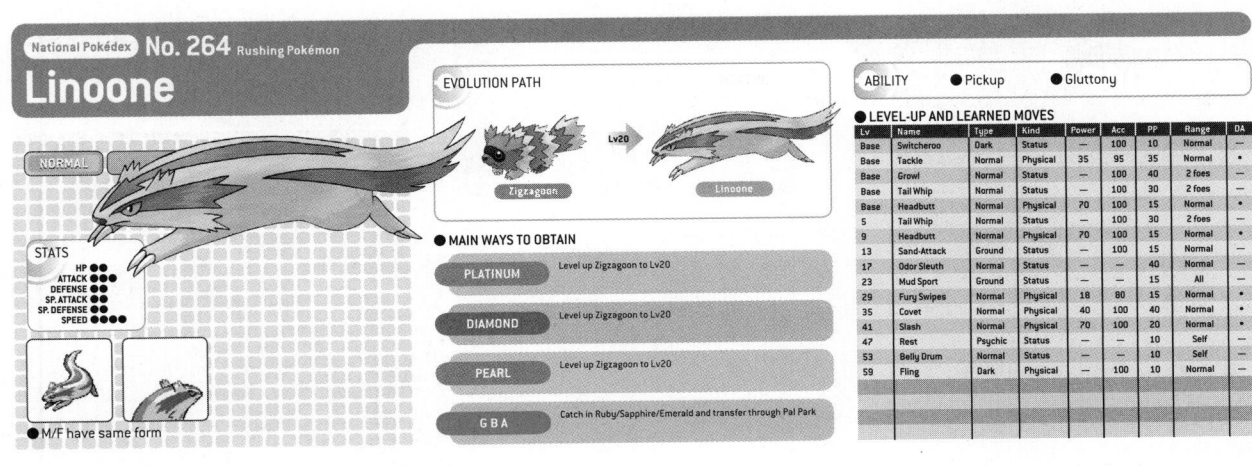

● M/F have same form

EVOLUTION PATH

Zigzagoon → Lv20 → Linoone

● MAIN WAYS TO OBTAIN

PLATINUM	Level up Zigzagoon to Lv20
DIAMOND	Level up Zigzagoon to Lv20
PEARL	Level up Zigzagoon to Lv20
GBA	Catch in Ruby/Sapphire/Emerald and transfer through Pal Park

ABILITY
● Pickup ● Gluttony

● LEVEL-UP AND LEARNED MOVES

Lv	Name	Type	Kind	Power	Acc	PP	Range	DA
Base	Switcheroo	Dark	Status	—	100	10	Normal	—
Base	Tackle	Normal	Physical	35	95	35	Normal	●
Base	Growl	Normal	Status	—	100	40	2 foes	—
Base	Tail Whip	Normal	Status	—	100	30	2 foes	—
Base	Headbutt	Normal	Physical	70	100	15	Normal	●
5	Tail Whip	Normal	Status	—	100	30	2 foes	—
9	Headbutt	Normal	Physical	70	100	15	Normal	●
13	Sand-Attack	Ground	Status	—	100	15	Normal	—
17	Odor Sleuth	Normal	Status	—	—	40	Normal	—
23	Mud Sport	Ground	Status	—	—	15	All	—
29	Fury Swipes	Normal	Physical	18	80	15	Normal	—
35	Covet	Normal	Physical	40	100	40	Normal	●
41	Slash	Normal	Physical	70	100	20	Normal	●
47	Rest	Psychic	Status	—	—	10	Self	—
53	Belly Drum	Normal	Status	—	—	10	Self	—
59	Fling	Dark	Physical	—	100	10	Normal	●

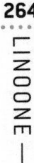

WURMPLE

Wurmple

BUG

STATS
HP ●●
ATTACK ●●
DEFENSE ●●
SP. ATTACK ●
SP. DEFENSE ●
SPEED ●

● M/F have same form

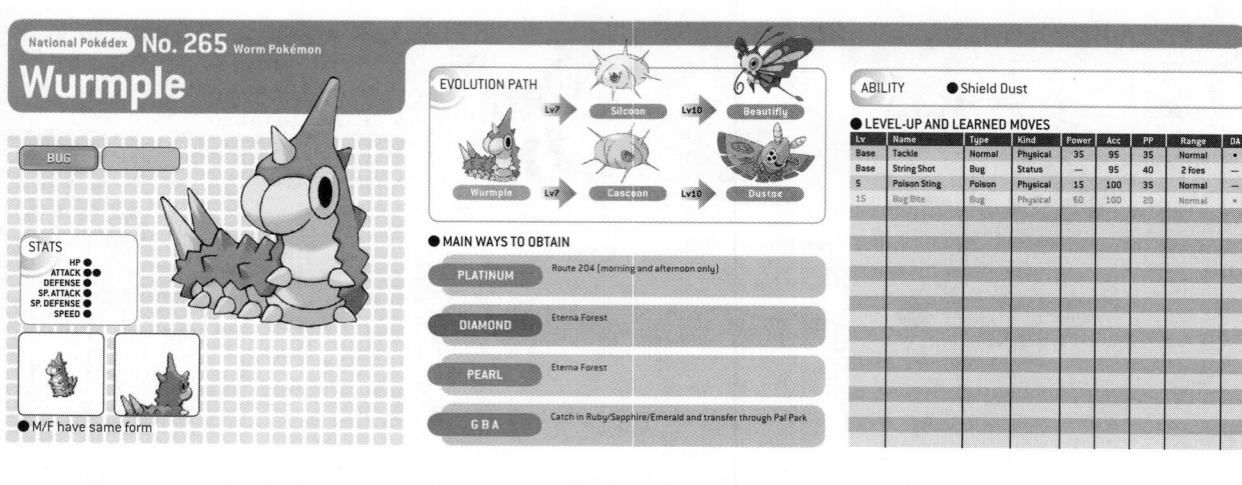

EVOLUTION PATH

Wurmple — Lv7 → Silcoon — Lv10 → Beautifly
Wurmple — Lv7 → Cascoon — Lv10 → Dustox

● **MAIN WAYS TO OBTAIN**

PLATINUM	Route 204 (morning and afternoon only)
DIAMOND	Eterna Forest
PEARL	Eterna Forest
G B A	Catch in Ruby/Sapphire/Emerald and transfer through Pal Park

ABILITY ● Shield Dust

● **LEVEL-UP AND LEARNED MOVES**

Lv	Name	Type	Kind	Power	Acc	PP	Range	DA
Base	Tackle	Normal	Physical	35	95	35	Normal	•
Base	String Shot	Bug	Status	—	95	40	2 foes	—
5	Poison Sting	Poison	Physical	15	100	35	Normal	—
15	Bug Bite	Bug	Physical	60	100	20	Normal	•

Silcoon

BUG

STATS
HP ●●
ATTACK ●
DEFENSE ●●
SP. ATTACK ●
SP. DEFENSE ●
SPEED ●

● M/F have same form

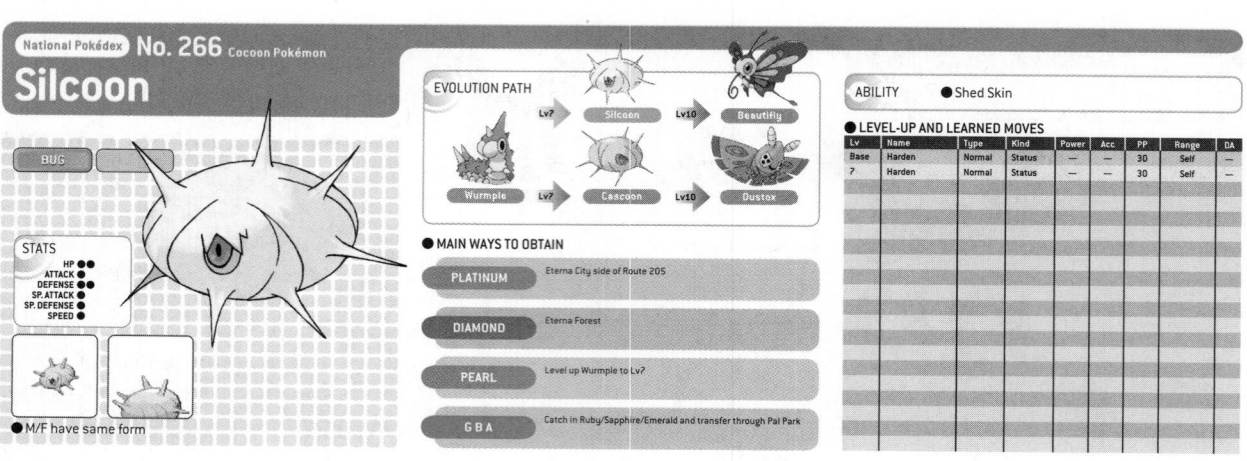

EVOLUTION PATH

Wurmple — Lv7 → Silcoon — Lv10 → Beautifly
Wurmple — Lv7 → Cascoon — Lv10 → Dustox

● **MAIN WAYS TO OBTAIN**

PLATINUM	Eterna City side of Route 205
DIAMOND	Eterna Forest
PEARL	Level up Wurmple to Lv7
G B A	Catch in Ruby/Sapphire/Emerald and transfer through Pal Park

ABILITY ● Shed Skin

● **LEVEL-UP AND LEARNED MOVES**

Lv	Name	Type	Kind	Power	Acc	PP	Range	DA
Base	Harden	Normal	Status	—	—	30	Self	—
7	Harden	Normal	Status	—	—	30	Self	—

Beautifly

BUG FLYING

STATS
HP ●●
ATTACK ●●●
DEFENSE ●●
SP. ATTACK ●●●
SP. DEFENSE ●●
SPEED ●●

● Male form   ● Female form

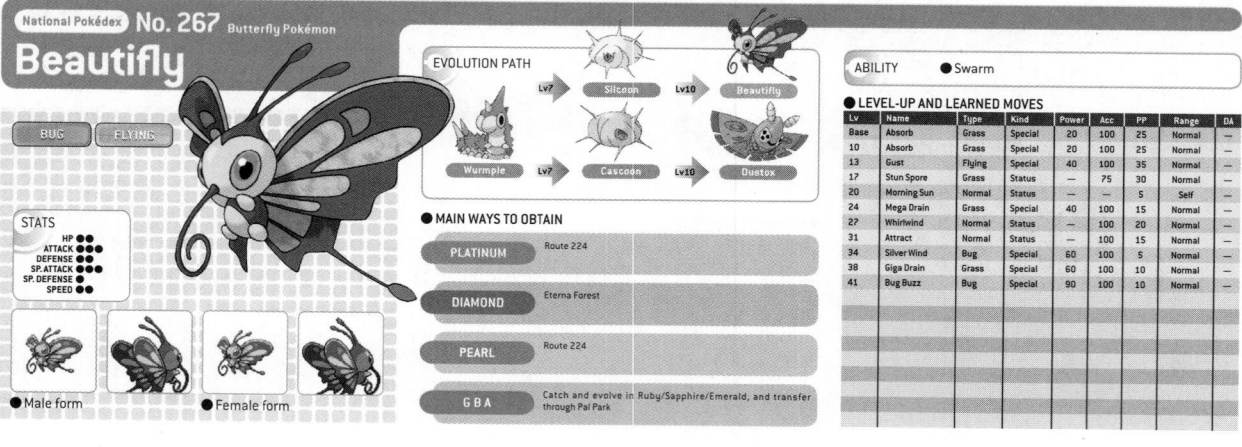

EVOLUTION PATH

Wurmple — Lv7 → Silcoon — Lv10 → Beautifly
Wurmple — Lv7 → Cascoon — Lv10 → Dustox

● **MAIN WAYS TO OBTAIN**

PLATINUM	Route 224
DIAMOND	Eterna Forest
PEARL	Route 224
G B A	Catch and evolve in Ruby/Sapphire/Emerald, and transfer through Pal Park

ABILITY ● Swarm

● **LEVEL-UP AND LEARNED MOVES**

Lv	Name	Type	Kind	Power	Acc	PP	Range	DA
Base	Absorb	Grass	Special	20	100	25	Normal	—
10	Absorb	Grass	Special	20	100	25	Normal	—
13	Gust	Flying	Special	40	100	35	Normal	—
17	Stun Spore	Grass	Status	—	75	30	Normal	—
20	Morning Sun	Normal	Status	—	—	5	Self	—
24	Mega Drain	Grass	Special	40	100	15	Normal	—
27	Whirlwind	Normal	Status	—	100	20	Normal	—
31	Attract	Normal	Status	—	100	15	Normal	—
34	Silver Wind	Bug	Special	60	100	5	Normal	—
38	Giga Drain	Grass	Special	60	100	10	Normal	—
41	Bug Buzz	Bug	Special	90	100	10	Normal	—

Cascoon

BUG

STATS
HP ●●
ATTACK ●
DEFENSE ●●
SP. ATTACK ●
SP. DEFENSE ●●
SPEED ●

● M/F have same form

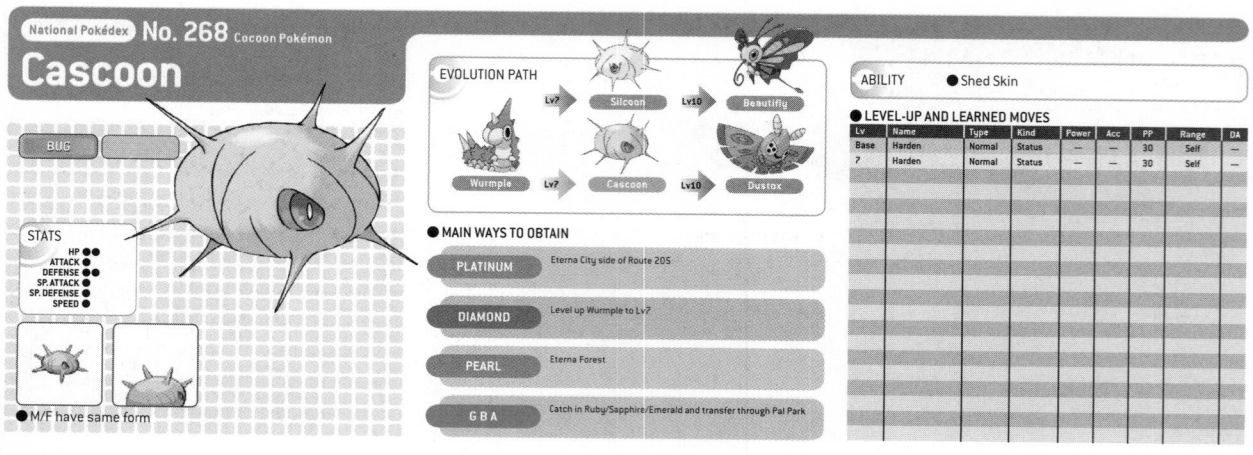

EVOLUTION PATH

Wurmple — Lv7 → Silcoon — Lv10 → Beautifly
Wurmple — Lv7 → Cascoon — Lv10 → Dustox

● **MAIN WAYS TO OBTAIN**

PLATINUM	Eterna City side of Route 205
DIAMOND	Level up Wurmple to Lv7
PEARL	Eterna Forest
G B A	Catch in Ruby/Sapphire/Emerald and transfer through Pal Park

ABILITY ● Shed Skin

● **LEVEL-UP AND LEARNED MOVES**

Lv	Name	Type	Kind	Power	Acc	PP	Range	DA
Base	Harden	Normal	Status	—	—	30	Self	—
7	Harden	Normal	Status	—	—	30	Self	—

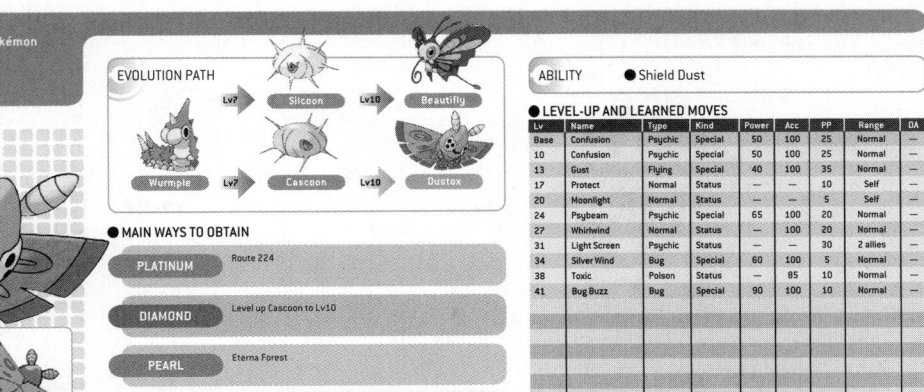

National Pokédex No. 269 — Poison Moth Pokémon

Dustox

BUG · POISON

STATS
- HP ●●
- ATTACK ●●
- DEFENSE ●●
- SP. ATTACK ●●
- SP. DEFENSE ●●
- SPEED ●●

● Male form ● Female form

EVOLUTION PATH

Wurmple → (Lv7) Silcoon → (Lv10) Beautifly
Wurmple → (Lv7) Cascoon → (Lv10) Dustox

MAIN WAYS TO OBTAIN

PLATINUM	Route 224
DIAMOND	Level up Cascoon to Lv10
PEARL	Eterna Forest
GBA	Catch and evolve in Ruby/Sapphire/Emerald, and transfer through Pal Park

ABILITY ● Shield Dust

LEVEL-UP AND LEARNED MOVES

Lv	Name	Type	Kind	Power	Acc	PP	Range	DA
Base	Confusion	Psychic	Special	50	100	25	Normal	—
10	Confusion	Psychic	Special	50	100	25	Normal	—
13	Gust	Flying	Special	40	100	35	Normal	—
17	Protect	Normal	Status	—	—	10	Self	—
20	Moonlight	Normal	Status	—	—	5	Self	—
24	Psybeam	Psychic	Special	65	100	20	Normal	—
27	Whirlwind	Normal	Status	—	100	20	Normal	—
31	Light Screen	Psychic	Status	—	—	30	2 allies	—
34	Silver Wind	Bug	Special	60	100	5	Normal	—
38	Toxic	Poison	Status	—	85	10	Normal	—
41	Bug Buzz	Bug	Special	90	100	10	Normal	—

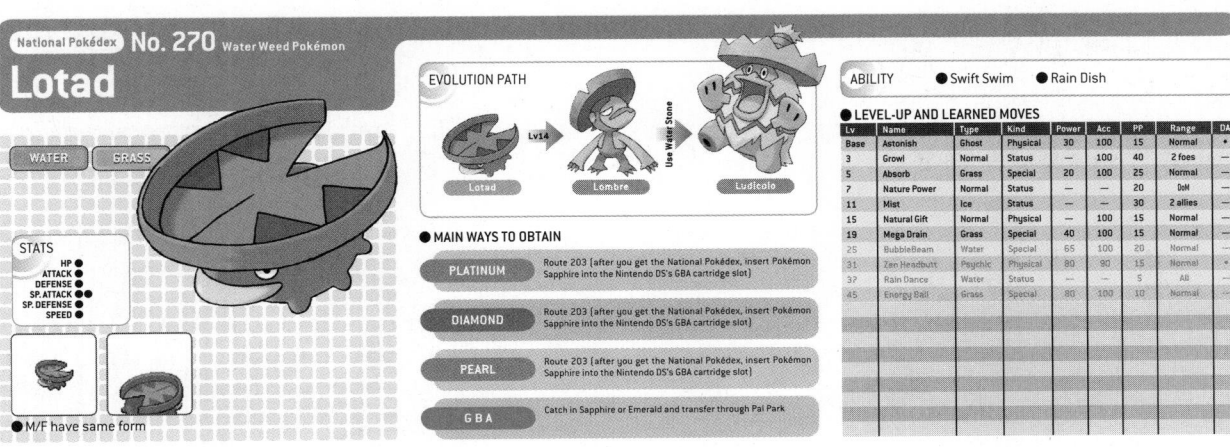

National Pokédex No. 270 — Water Weed Pokémon

Lotad

WATER · GRASS

STATS
- HP ●
- ATTACK ●
- DEFENSE ●●
- SP. ATTACK ●●
- SP. DEFENSE ●●
- SPEED ●

● M/F have same form

EVOLUTION PATH

Lotad → (Lv14) Lombre → (Use Water Stone) Ludicolo

MAIN WAYS TO OBTAIN

PLATINUM	Route 203 (after you get the National Pokédex, insert Pokémon Sapphire into the Nintendo DS's GBA cartridge slot)
DIAMOND	Route 203 (after you get the National Pokédex, insert Pokémon Sapphire into the Nintendo DS's GBA cartridge slot)
PEARL	Route 203 (after you get the National Pokédex, insert Pokémon Sapphire into the Nintendo DS's GBA cartridge slot)
GBA	Catch in Sapphire or Emerald and transfer through Pal Park

ABILITY ● Swift Swim ● Rain Dish

LEVEL-UP AND LEARNED MOVES

Lv	Name	Type	Kind	Power	Acc	PP	Range	DA
Base	Astonish	Ghost	Physical	30	100	15	Normal	●
3	Growl	Normal	Status	—	100	40	2 foes	—
5	Absorb	Grass	Special	20	100	25	Normal	—
7	Nature Power	Normal	Status	—	—	20	DoM	—
11	Mist	Ice	Status	—	—	30	2 allies	—
15	Natural Gift	Normal	Physical	—	100	15	Normal	—
19	Mega Drain	Grass	Special	40	100	15	Normal	—
25	BubbleBeam	Water	Special	65	100	20	Normal	—
31	Zen Headbutt	Psychic	Physical	80	90	15	Normal	●
37	Rain Dance	Water	Status	—	—	5	All	—
45	Energy Ball	Grass	Special	80	100	10	Normal	—

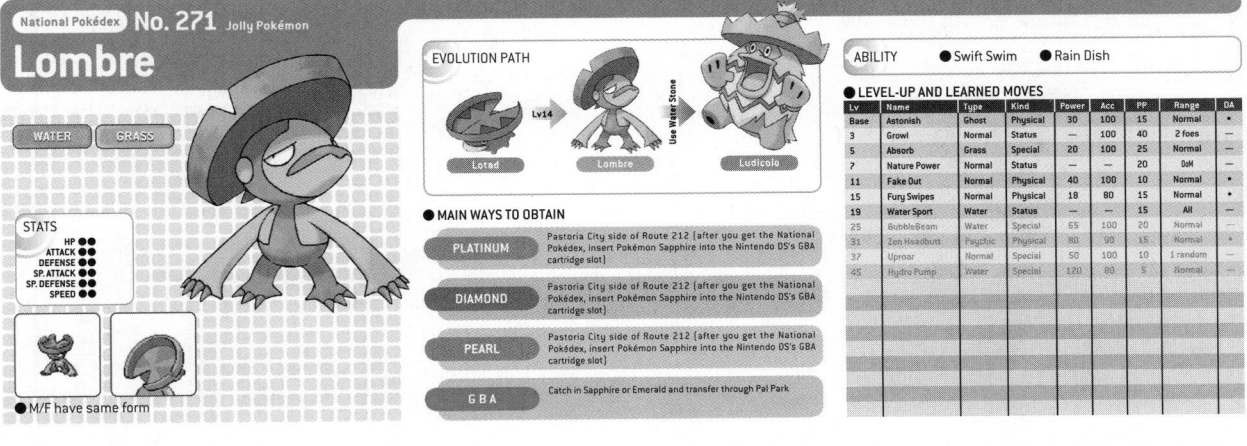

National Pokédex No. 271 — Jolly Pokémon

Lombre

WATER · GRASS

STATS
- HP ●●
- ATTACK ●●
- DEFENSE ●●●
- SP. ATTACK ●●●
- SP. DEFENSE ●●●
- SPEED ●●

● M/F have same form

EVOLUTION PATH

Lotad → (Lv14) Lombre → (Use Water Stone) Ludicolo

MAIN WAYS TO OBTAIN

PLATINUM	Pastoria City side of Route 212 (after you get the National Pokédex, insert Pokémon Sapphire into the Nintendo DS's GBA cartridge slot)
DIAMOND	Pastoria City side of Route 212 (after you get the National Pokédex, insert Pokémon Sapphire into the Nintendo DS's GBA cartridge slot)
PEARL	Pastoria City side of Route 212 (after you get the National Pokédex, insert Pokémon Sapphire into the Nintendo DS's GBA cartridge slot)
GBA	Catch in Sapphire or Emerald and transfer through Pal Park

ABILITY ● Swift Swim ● Rain Dish

LEVEL-UP AND LEARNED MOVES

Lv	Name	Type	Kind	Power	Acc	PP	Range	DA
Base	Astonish	Ghost	Physical	30	100	15	Normal	●
3	Growl	Normal	Status	—	100	40	2 foes	—
5	Absorb	Grass	Special	20	100	25	Normal	—
7	Nature Power	Normal	Status	—	—	20	DoM	—
11	Fake Out	Normal	Physical	40	100	10	Normal	●
15	Fury Swipes	Normal	Physical	18	80	15	Normal	—
19	Water Sport	Water	Status	—	—	15	All	—
25	BubbleBeam	Water	Special	65	100	20	Normal	—
31	Zen Headbutt	Psychic	Physical	80	90	15	Normal	●
37	Uproar	Normal	Special	50	100	10	1 random	—
45	Hydro Pump	Water	Special	120	80	5	Normal	—

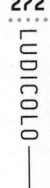

272
LUDICOLO

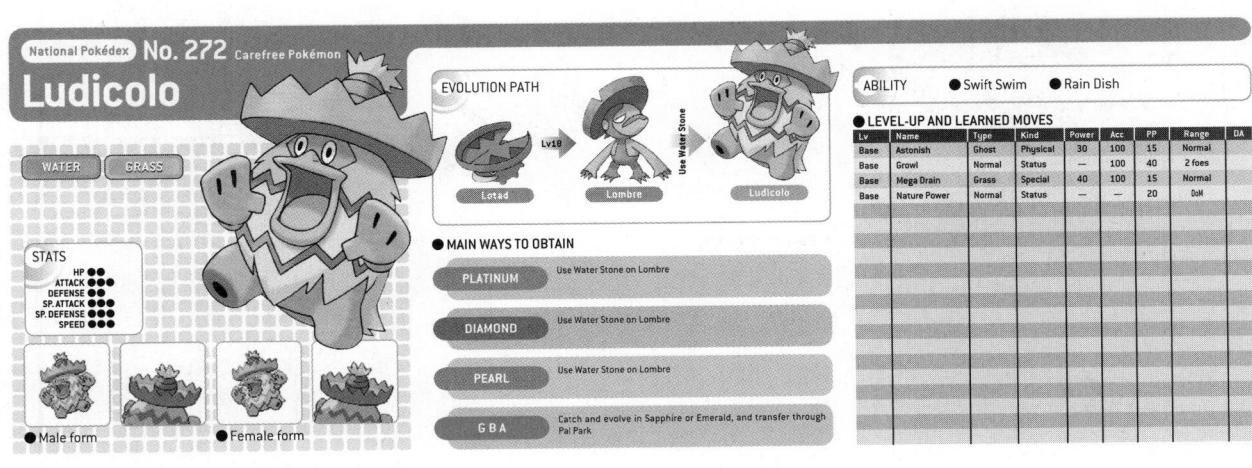

National Pokédex No. 272 — Carefree Pokémon

Ludicolo

WATER · GRASS

STATS
- HP ●●
- ATTACK ●●●
- DEFENSE ●●●
- SP. ATTACK ●●●
- SP. DEFENSE ●●●
- SPEED ●●

● Male form ● Female form

EVOLUTION PATH

Lotad → (Lv18) Lombre → (Use Water Stone) Ludicolo

MAIN WAYS TO OBTAIN

PLATINUM	Use Water Stone on Lombre
DIAMOND	Use Water Stone on Lombre
PEARL	Use Water Stone on Lombre
GBA	Catch and evolve in Sapphire or Emerald, and transfer through Pal Park

ABILITY ● Swift Swim ● Rain Dish

LEVEL-UP AND LEARNED MOVES

Lv	Name	Type	Kind	Power	Acc	PP	Range	DA
Base	Astonish	Ghost	Physical	30	100	15	Normal	—
Base	Growl	Normal	Status	—	100	40	2 foes	—
Base	Mega Drain	Grass	Special	40	100	15	Normal	—
Base	Nature Power	Normal	Status	—	—	20	DoM	—

No. 273 Acorn Pokémon
Seedot

GRASS

STATS
- HP ●●
- ATTACK ●●
- DEFENSE ●●
- SP.ATTACK ●●
- SP. DEFENSE ●●
- SPEED ●●

● M/F have same form

EVOLUTION PATH
Seedot → (Lv14) → Nuzleaf → (Use Leaf Stone) → Shiftry

ABILITY
● Chlorophyll ● Early Bird

LEVEL-UP AND LEARNED MOVES
Lv	Name	Type	Kind	Power	Acc	PP	Range	DA
Base	Bide	Normal	Physical	—	—	10	Self	●
3	Harden	Normal	Status	—	—	30	Self	—
7	Growth	Normal	Status	—	—	40	Self	—
13	Nature Power	Normal	Status	—	—	20	DoM	—
21	Synthesis	Grass	Status	—	—	5	Self	—
31	Sunny Day	Fire	Status	—	—	5	All	—
43	Explosion	Normal	Physical	250	100	5	2 foes + 1 ally	—

MAIN WAYS TO OBTAIN
- **PLATINUM** — Route 203 (after you get the National Pokédex, insert Pokémon Ruby into the Nintendo DS's GBA cartridge slot)
- **DIAMOND** — Route 203 (after you get the National Pokédex, insert Pokémon Ruby into the Nintendo DS's GBA cartridge slot)
- **PEARL** — Route 203 (after you get the National Pokédex, insert Pokémon Ruby into the Nintendo DS's GBA cartridge slot)
- **GBA** — Catch in Ruby or Emerald and transfer through Pal Park

No. 274 Wily Pokémon
Nuzleaf

GRASS DARK

STATS
- HP ●●
- ATTACK ●●
- DEFENSE ●●
- SP.ATTACK ●●
- SP. DEFENSE ●●
- SPEED ●●

● Male form ● Female form

EVOLUTION PATH
Seedot → (Lv14) → Nuzleaf → (Use Leaf Stone) → Shiftry 

ABILITY
● Chlorophyll ● Early Bird

LEVEL-UP AND LEARNED MOVES
Lv	Name	Type	Kind	Power	Acc	PP	Range	DA
Base	Razor Leaf	Grass	Physical	55	95	25	2 foes	—
Base	Pound	Normal	Physical	40	100	35	Normal	●
3	Harden	Normal	Status	—	—	30	Self	—
7	Growth	Normal	Status	—	—	40	Self	—
13	Nature Power	Normal	Status	—	—	20	DoM	—
19	Fake Out	Normal	Physical	40	100	10	Normal	●
25	Torment	Dark	Status	—	100	15	Normal	—
31	Faint Attack	Dark	Physical	60	—	20	Normal	—
37	Razor Wind	Normal	Special	80	100	10	2 foes	—
43	Swagger	Normal	Status	—	90	15	Normal	—
49	Extrasensory	Psychic	Special	80	100	30	Normal	—

MAIN WAYS TO OBTAIN
- **PLATINUM** — Solaceon Town side of Route 210 (after you get the National Pokédex, insert Pokémon Ruby into the Nintendo DS's GBA cartridge slot)
- **DIAMOND** — Solaceon Town side of Route 210 (after you get the National Pokédex, insert Pokémon Ruby into the Nintendo DS's GBA cartridge slot)
- **PEARL** — Solaceon Town side of Route 210 (after you get the National Pokédex, insert Pokémon Ruby into the Nintendo DS's GBA cartridge slot)
- **GBA** — Catch in Ruby or Emerald and transfer through Pal Park

No. 275 Wicked Pokémon
Shiftry

GRASS DARK

STATS
- HP ●●●
- ATTACK ●●●
- DEFENSE ●●
- SP.ATTACK ●●●
- SP. DEFENSE ●●
- SPEED ●●●

● Male form ● Female form

EVOLUTION PATH
Seedot → (Lv14) → Nuzleaf → (Use Leaf Stone) → Shiftry 

ABILITY
● Chlorophyll ● Early Bird

LEVEL-UP AND LEARNED MOVES
Lv	Name	Type	Kind	Power	Acc	PP	Range	DA
Base	Faint Attack	Dark	Physical	60	—	20	Normal	●
Base	Whirlwind	Normal	Status	—	100	20	Normal	—
Base	Nasty Plot	Dark	Status	—	—	20	Self	—
Base	Razor Leaf	Grass	Physical	55	95	25	2 foes	—
49	Leaf Storm	Grass	Special	140	90	5	Normal	—

MAIN WAYS TO OBTAIN
- **PLATINUM** — Use Leaf Stone on Nuzleaf
- **DIAMOND** — Use Leaf Stone on Nuzleaf
- **PEARL** — Use Leaf Stone on Nuzleaf
- **GBA** — Catch and evolve in Ruby or Emerald and transfer through Pal Park

No. 276 TinySwallow Pokémon
Taillow

NORMAL FLYING

STATS
- HP ●●
- ATTACK ●●
- DEFENSE ●
- SP.ATTACK ●
- SP. DEFENSE ●
- SPEED ●●●

● M/F have same form

EVOLUTION PATH
Taillow → (Lv22) → Swellow 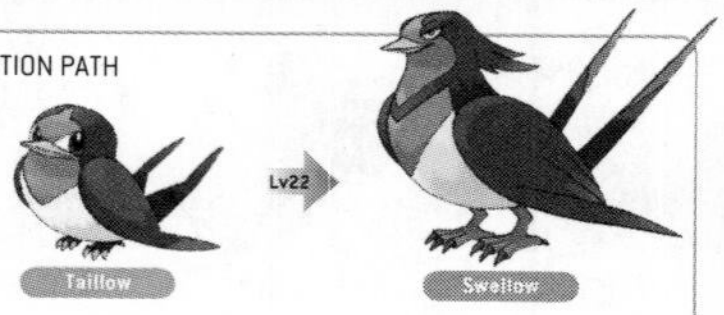

ABILITY
● Guts

LEVEL-UP AND LEARNED MOVES
Lv	Name	Type	Kind	Power	Acc	PP	Range	DA
Base	Peck	Flying	Physical	35	100	35	Normal	●
Base	Growl	Normal	Status	—	100	40	2 foes	●
4	Focus Energy	Normal	Status	—	—	30	Self	—
8	Quick Attack	Normal	Physical	40	100	30	Normal	●
13	Wing Attack	Flying	Physical	60	100	35	Normal	●
19	Double Team	Normal	Status	—	—	15	Self	—
26	Endeavor	Normal	Physical	—	100	5	Normal	●
34	Aerial Ace	Flying	Physical	60	—	20	Normal	●
43	Agility	Psychic	Status	—	—	30	Self	—
53	Air Slash	Flying	Special	75	95	20	Normal	—

MAIN WAYS TO OBTAIN
- **PLATINUM** — Discover an Egg
- **DIAMOND** — Discover an Egg
- **PEARL** — Discover an Egg
- **GBA** — Catch in Ruby/Sapphire/Emerald and transfer through Pal Park

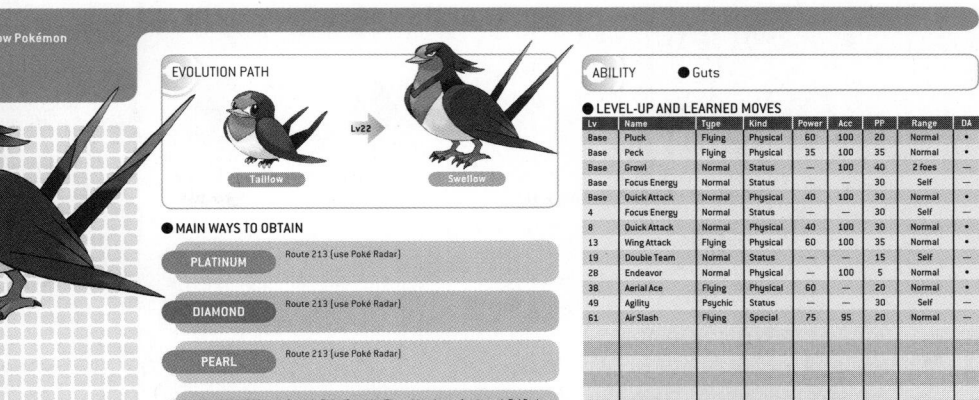

National Pokédex No. 277 Swallow Pokémon
Swellow

NORMAL | FLYING

STATS
- HP ●●
- ATTACK ●●●
- DEFENSE ●●
- SP.ATTACK ●
- SP.DEFENSE ●
- SPEED ●●●●

● M/F have same form

EVOLUTION PATH

Taillow —Lv22→ Swellow

MAIN WAYS TO OBTAIN

PLATINUM	Route 213 (use Poké Radar)
DIAMOND	Route 213 (use Poké Radar)
PEARL	Route 213 (use Poké Radar)
GBA	Catch in Ruby/Sapphire/Emerald and transfer through Pal Park

ABILITY ● Guts

● LEVEL-UP AND LEARNED MOVES

Lv	Name	Type	Kind	Power	Acc	PP	Range	DA
Base	Pluck	Flying	Physical	60	100	20	Normal	●
Base	Peck	Flying	Physical	35	100	35	Normal	●
Base	Growl	Normal	Status	—	100	40	2 foes	●
Base	Focus Energy	Normal	Status	—	—	30	Self	●
Base	Quick Attack	Normal	Physical	40	100	30	Normal	●
4	Focus Energy	Normal	Status	—	—	30	Self	
8	Quick Attack	Normal	Physical	40	100	30	Normal	
13	Wing Attack	Normal	Physical	60	100	35	Normal	
19	Double Team	Normal	Status	—	—	15	Self	
28	Endeavor	Normal	Physical	—	100	5	Normal	
38	Aerial Ace	Flying	Physical	60	—	20	Normal	
49	Agility	Psychic	Status	—	—	30	Self	
61	Air Slash	Flying	Special	75	95	20	Normal	

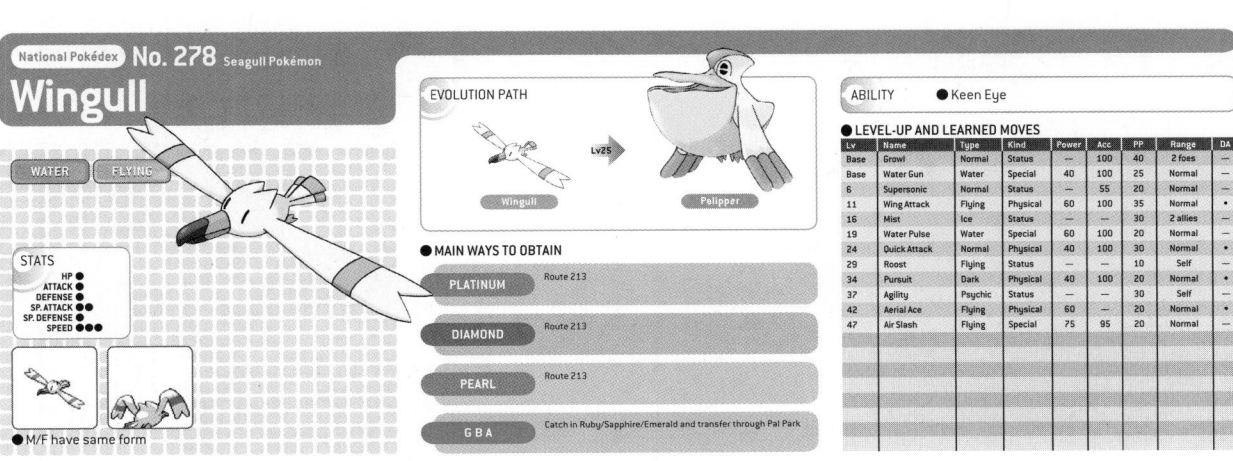

National Pokédex No. 278 Seagull Pokémon
Wingull

WATER | FLYING

STATS
- HP ●
- ATTACK ●
- DEFENSE ●
- SP.ATTACK ●
- SP.DEFENSE ●
- SPEED ●●●

● M/F have same form

EVOLUTION PATH

Wingull —Lv25→ Pelipper

MAIN WAYS TO OBTAIN

PLATINUM	Route 213
DIAMOND	Route 213
PEARL	Route 213
GBA	Catch in Ruby/Sapphire/Emerald and transfer through Pal Park

ABILITY ● Keen Eye

● LEVEL-UP AND LEARNED MOVES

Lv	Name	Type	Kind	Power	Acc	PP	Range	DA
Base	Growl	Normal	Status	—	100	40	2 foes	—
Base	Water Gun	Water	Special	40	100	25	Normal	—
6	Supersonic	Normal	Status	—	55	20	Normal	—
11	Wing Attack	Flying	Physical	60	100	35	Normal	●
16	Mist	Ice	Status	—	—	30	2 allies	—
19	Water Pulse	Water	Special	60	100	20	Normal	—
24	Quick Attack	Normal	Physical	40	100	30	Normal	—
29	Roost	Flying	Status	—	—	10	Self	—
34	Pursuit	Dark	Physical	40	100	20	Normal	—
37	Agility	Psychic	Status	—	—	30	Self	—
42	Aerial Ace	Flying	Physical	60	—	20	Normal	—
47	Air Slash	Flying	Special	75	95	20	Normal	—

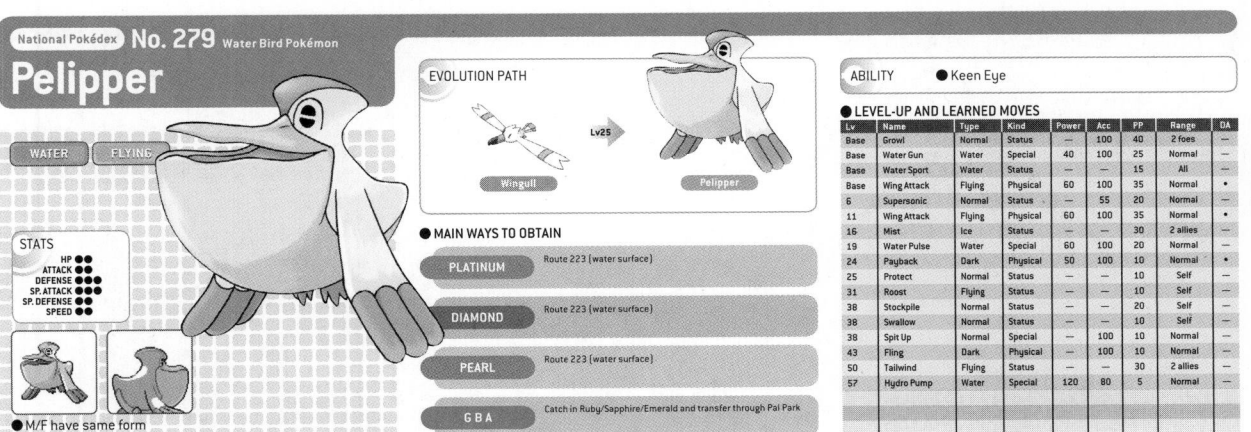

National Pokédex No. 279 Water Bird Pokémon
Pelipper

WATER | FLYING

STATS
- HP ●●
- ATTACK ●●
- DEFENSE ●●●
- SP.ATTACK ●●●
- SP.DEFENSE ●●
- SPEED ●●

● M/F have same form

EVOLUTION PATH

Wingull —Lv25→ Pelipper

MAIN WAYS TO OBTAIN

PLATINUM	Route 223 (water surface)
DIAMOND	Route 223 (water surface)
PEARL	Route 223 (water surface)
GBA	Catch in Ruby/Sapphire/Emerald and transfer through Pal Park

ABILITY ● Keen Eye

● LEVEL-UP AND LEARNED MOVES

Lv	Name	Type	Kind	Power	Acc	PP	Range	DA
Base	Growl	Normal	Status	—	100	40	2 foes	—
Base	Water Gun	Water	Special	40	100	25	Normal	—
Base	Water Sport	Water	Status	—	—	15	All	—
Base	Supersonic	Normal	Status	—	55	20	Normal	—
6	Supersonic	Normal	Status	—	55	20	Normal	—
11	Wing Attack	Flying	Physical	60	100	35	Normal	●
16	Mist	Ice	Status	—	—	30	2 allies	—
19	Water Pulse	Water	Special	60	100	20	Normal	—
24	Payback	Dark	Physical	50	100	10	Normal	—
25	Protect	Normal	Status	—	—	10	Self	—
31	Roost	Flying	Status	—	—	10	Self	—
38	Stockpile	Normal	Status	—	—	20	Self	—
38	Swallow	Normal	Status	—	—	10	Self	—
38	Spit Up	Normal	Special	—	100	10	Normal	—
43	Fling	Dark	Physical	—	100	10	Normal	—
50	Tailwind	Flying	Status	—	—	30	2 allies	—
57	Hydro Pump	Water	Special	120	80	5	Normal	—

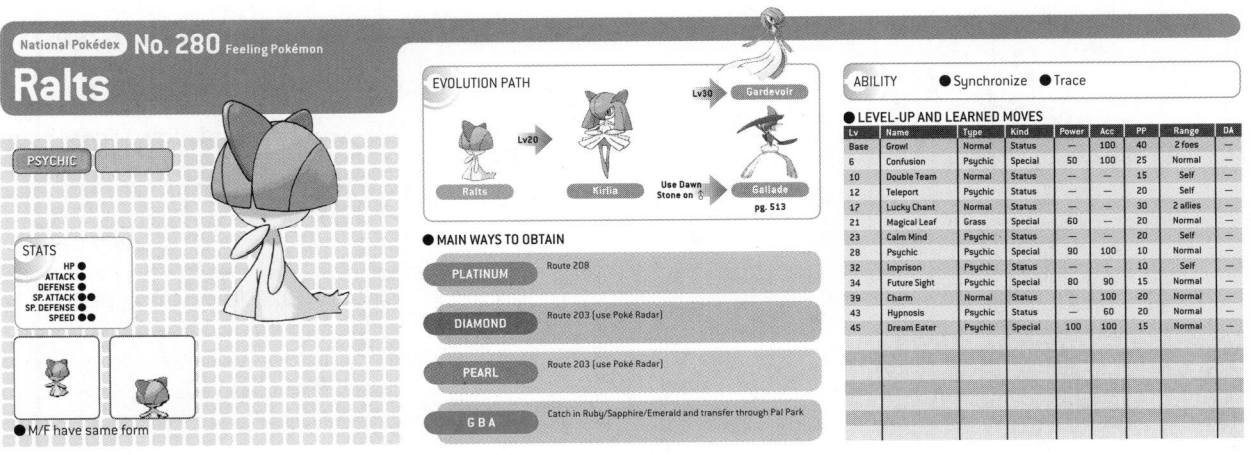

National Pokédex No. 280 Feeling Pokémon
Ralts

PSYCHIC

STATS
- HP ●
- ATTACK ●
- DEFENSE ●
- SP.ATTACK ●
- SP.DEFENSE ●●
- SPEED ●●

● M/F have same form

EVOLUTION PATH

Ralts —Lv20→ Kirlia —Lv30→ Gardevoir

Kirlia — Use Dawn Stone on ♂ → Gallade pg. 513

MAIN WAYS TO OBTAIN

PLATINUM	Route 208
DIAMOND	Route 203 (use Poké Radar)
PEARL	Route 203 (use Poké Radar)
GBA	Catch in Ruby/Sapphire/Emerald and transfer through Pal Park

ABILITY ● Synchronize ● Trace

● LEVEL-UP AND LEARNED MOVES

Lv	Name	Type	Kind	Power	Acc	PP	Range	DA
Base	Growl	Normal	Status	—	100	40	2 foes	—
6	Confusion	Psychic	Special	50	100	25	Normal	—
10	Double Team	Normal	Status	—	—	15	Self	—
12	Teleport	Psychic	Status	—	—	20	Self	—
17	Lucky Chant	Normal	Status	—	—	30	2 allies	—
21	Magical Leaf	Grass	Special	60	—	20	Normal	—
23	Calm Mind	Psychic	Status	—	—	20	Self	—
28	Psychic	Psychic	Special	90	100	10	Normal	—
32	Imprison	Psychic	Status	—	—	10	Self	—
34	Future Sight	Psychic	Special	80	90	15	Normal	—
39	Charm	Normal	Status	—	100	20	Normal	—
43	Hypnosis	Psychic	Status	—	60	20	Normal	—
45	Dream Eater	Psychic	Special	100	100	15	Normal	—

280
RALTS

No. 281 Emotion Pokémon

Kirlia

PSYCHIC

STATS
- HP ●
- ATTACK ●
- DEFENSE ●
- SP. ATTACK ●●
- SP. DEFENSE ●●
- SPEED ●●

● M/F have same form

EVOLUTION PATH

Ralts → (Lv20) Kirlia → (Lv30) Gardevoir / Use Dawn Stone on ♂ → Gallade
pg. 513

MAIN WAYS TO OBTAIN

PLATINUM	Hearthome City side of Route 212
DIAMOND	Route 203 (use Poké Radar)
PEARL	Route 203 (use Poké Radar)
GBA	Catch and evolve in Ruby/Sapphire/Emerald, and transfer through Pal Park

ABILITY ● Synchronize ● Trace

● LEVEL-UP AND LEARNED MOVES

Lv	Name	Type	Kind	Power	Acc	PP	Range	DA
Base	Growl	Normal	Status	—	100	40	2 foes	—
Base	Confusion	Psychic	Special	50	100	25	Normal	—
Base	Double Team	Normal	Status	—	—	15	Self	—
Base	Teleport	Psychic	Status	—	—	20	Self	—
6	Confusion	Psychic	Special	50	100	25	Normal	—
10	Double Team	Normal	Status	—	—	15	Self	—
12	Teleport	Psychic	Status	—	—	20	Self	—
17	Lucky Chant	Normal	Status	—	—	30	2 allies	—
22	Magical Leaf	Grass	Special	60	—	20	Normal	—
25	Calm Mind	Psychic	Status	—	—	20	Self	—
31	Psychic	Psychic	Special	90	100	10	Normal	—
36	Imprison	Psychic	Status	—	—	10	Self	—
39	Future Sight	Psychic	Special	80	90	15	Normal	—
45	Charm	Normal	Status	—	100	20	Normal	—
50	Hypnosis	Psychic	Status	—	60	20	Normal	—
53	Dream Eater	Psychic	Special	100	100	15	Normal	—

No. 282 Embrace Pokémon

Gardevoir

PSYCHIC

STATS
- HP ●●
- ATTACK ●●
- DEFENSE ●●
- SP. ATTACK ●●●●
- SP. DEFENSE ●●●
- SPEED ●●●

● M/F have same form

EVOLUTION PATH

Ralts → (Lv20) Kirlia → (Lv30) Gardevoir / Use Dawn Stone on ♂ → Gallade
pg. 513

MAIN WAYS TO OBTAIN

PLATINUM	Level up Kirlia to Lv30
DIAMOND	Level up Kirlia to Lv30
PEARL	Level up Kirlia to Lv30
GBA	Catch and evolve in Ruby/Sapphire/Emerald, and transfer through Pal Park

ABILITY ● Synchronize ● Trace

● LEVEL-UP AND LEARNED MOVES

Lv	Name	Type	Kind	Power	Acc	PP	Range	DA
Base	Healing Wish	Psychic	Status	—	—	10	Self	—
Base	Growl	Normal	Status	—	100	40	2 foes	—
Base	Confusion	Psychic	Special	50	100	25	Normal	—
Base	Double Team	Normal	Status	—	—	15	Self	—
Base	Teleport	Psychic	Status	—	—	20	Self	—
6	Confusion	Psychic	Special	50	100	25	Normal	—
10	Double Team	Normal	Status	—	—	15	Self	—
12	Teleport	Psychic	Status	—	—	20	Self	—
17	Wish	Normal	Status	—	—	10	Self	—
22	Magical Leaf	Grass	Special	60	—	20	Normal	—
25	Calm Mind	Psychic	Status	—	—	20	Self	—
33	Psychic	Psychic	Special	90	100	10	Normal	—
40	Imprison	Psychic	Status	—	—	10	Self	—
45	Future Sight	Psychic	Special	80	90	15	Normal	—
53	Captivate	Normal	Status	—	100	20	2 foes	—
60	Hypnosis	Psychic	Status	—	60	20	Normal	—
65	Dream Eater	Psychic	Special	100	100	15	Normal	—

No. 283 Pond Skater Pokémon

Surskit

BUG WATER

STATS
- HP ●
- ATTACK ●
- DEFENSE ●
- SP. ATTACK ●
- SP. DEFENSE ●●
- SPEED ●●

● M/F have same form

EVOLUTION PATH

Surskit → (Lv22) Masquerain

MAIN WAYS TO OBTAIN

PLATINUM	Route 229 (water surface)
DIAMOND	Lake Verity (mass outbreak)
PEARL	Lake Verity (mass outbreak)
GBA	Catch in Ruby/Sapphire and transfer through Pal Park

ABILITY ● Swift Swim

● LEVEL-UP AND LEARNED MOVES

Lv	Name	Type	Kind	Power	Acc	PP	Range	DA
Base	Bubble	Water	Special	20	100	30	2 foes	—
7	Quick Attack	Normal	Physical	40	100	30	Normal	●
13	Sweet Scent	Normal	Status	—	100	20	2 foes	—
19	Water Sport	Water	Status	—	—	15	All	—
25	BubbleBeam	Water	Special	65	100	20	Normal	—
31	Agility	Psychic	Status	—	—	30	Self	—
37	Mist	Ice	Status	—	—	30	2 allies	—
37	Haze	Ice	Status	—	—	30	All	—
43	Baton Pass	Normal	Status	—	—	40	Self	—

No. 284 Eyeball Pokémon

Masquerain

BUG FLYING

STATS
- HP ●●
- ATTACK ●●
- DEFENSE ●●
- SP. ATTACK ●●●
- SP. DEFENSE ●●
- SPEED ●●

● M/F have same form

EVOLUTION PATH

Surskit → (Lv22) Masquerain

MAIN WAYS TO OBTAIN

PLATINUM	Route 229 (water surface)
DIAMOND	Level up Surskit to Lv22
PEARL	Level up Surskit to Lv22
GBA	Catch and evolve in Ruby/Sapphire, and transfer through Pal Park

ABILITY ● Intimidate

● LEVEL-UP AND LEARNED MOVES

Lv	Name	Type	Kind	Power	Acc	PP	Range	DA
Base	Ominous Wind	Ghost	Special	60	100	5	Normal	—
Base	Bubble	Water	Special	20	100	30	2 foes	—
Base	Quick Attack	Normal	Physical	40	100	30	Normal	●
Base	Sweet Scent	Normal	Status	—	100	20	2 foes	—
Base	Water Sport	Water	Status	—	—	15	All	—
7	Quick Attack	Normal	Physical	40	100	30	Normal	●
13	Sweet Scent	Normal	Status	—	100	20	2 foes	—
19	Water Sport	Water	Status	—	—	15	All	—
22	Gust	Flying	Special	40	100	35	Normal	—
26	Scary Face	Normal	Status	—	90	10	Normal	—
33	Stun Spore	Grass	Status	—	75	30	Normal	—
40	Silver Wind	Bug	Special	60	100	5	Normal	—
47	Air Slash	Flying	Special	75	95	20	Normal	—
54	Whirlwind	Normal	Status	—	100	20	Normal	—
61	Bug Buzz	Bug	Special	90	100	10	Normal	—

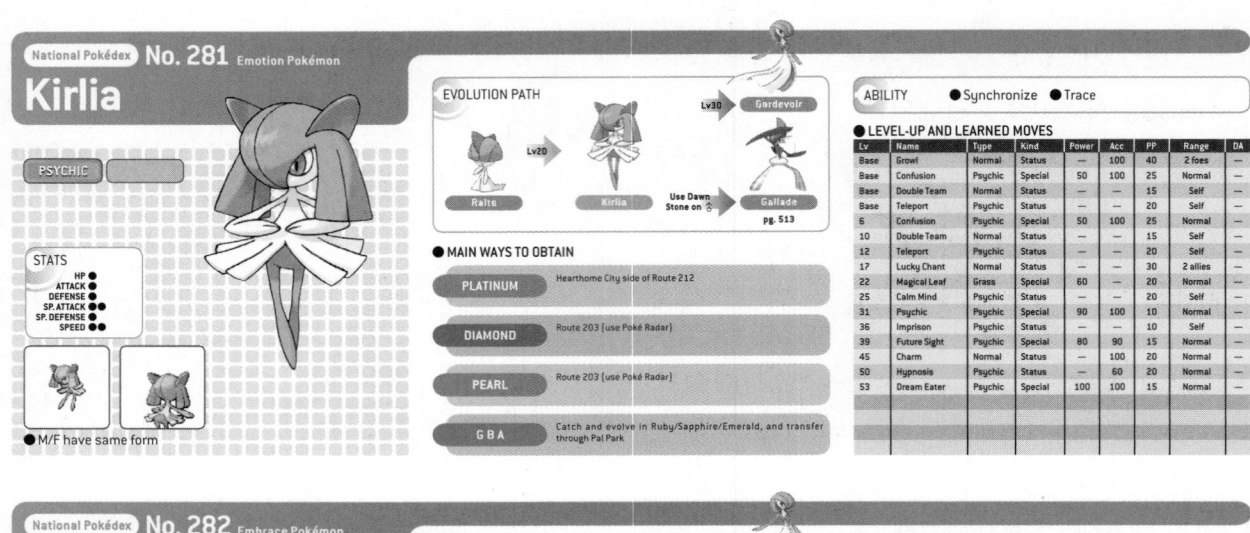
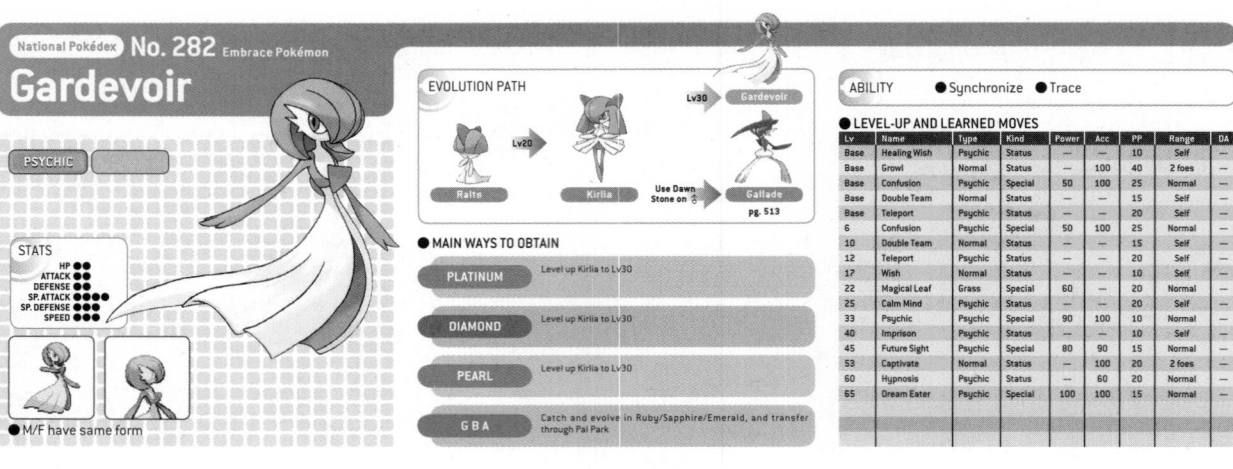
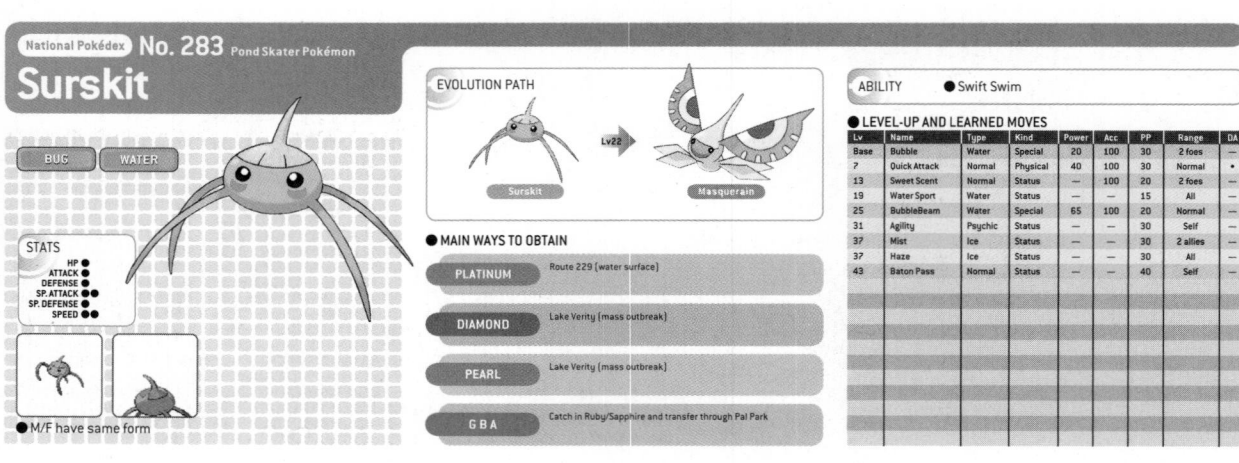
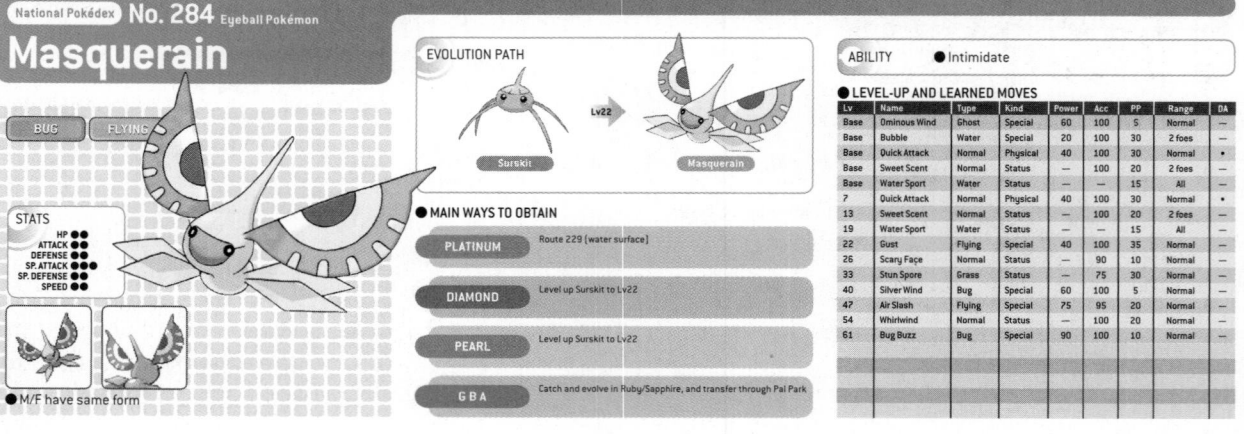

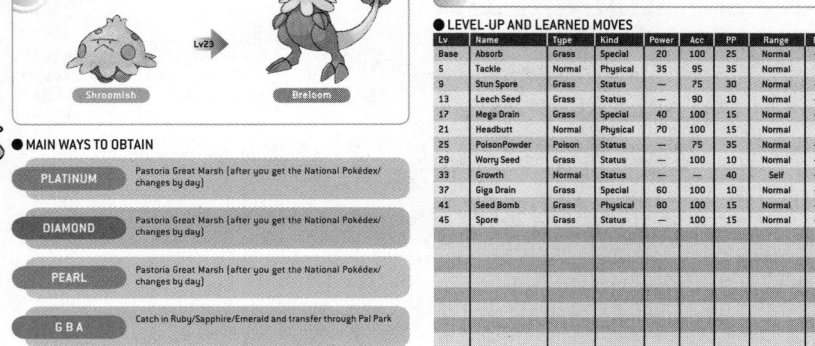

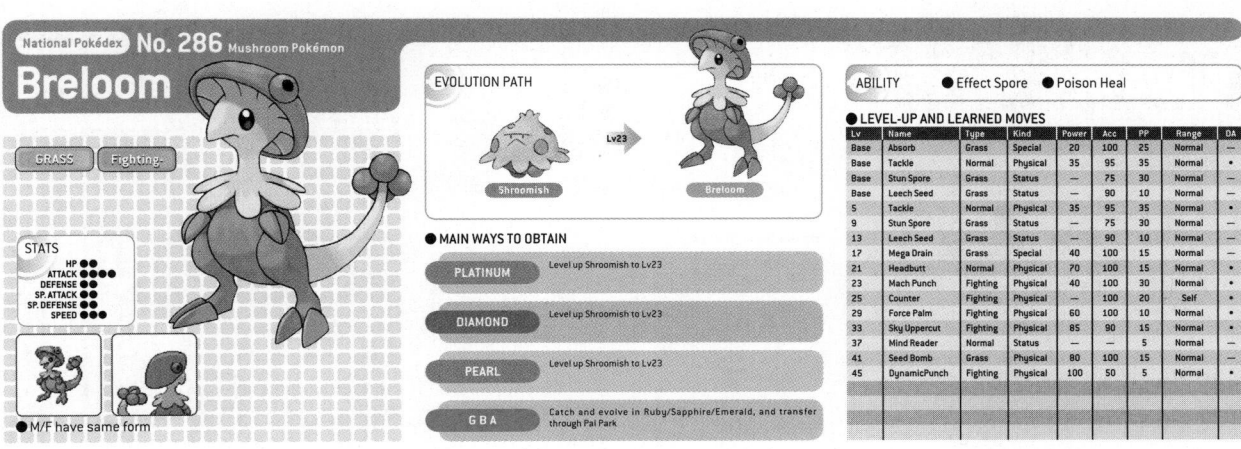

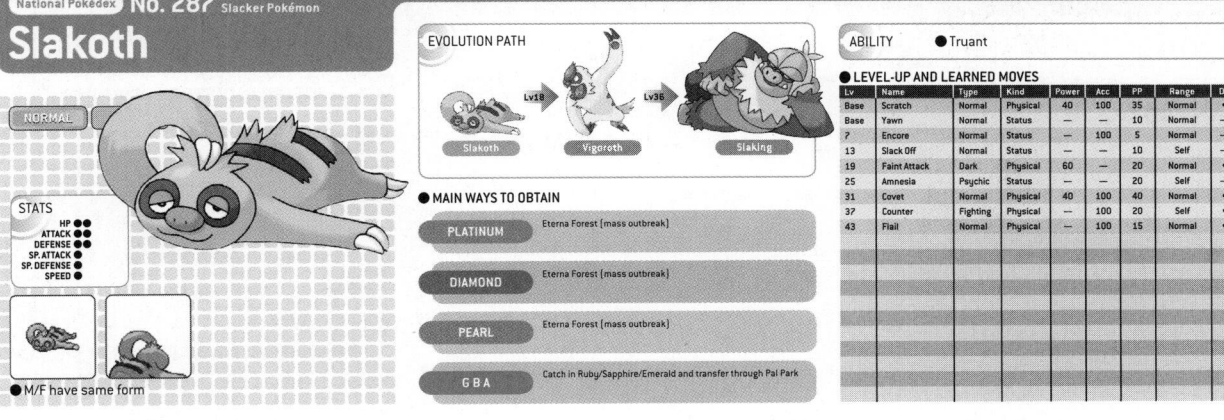

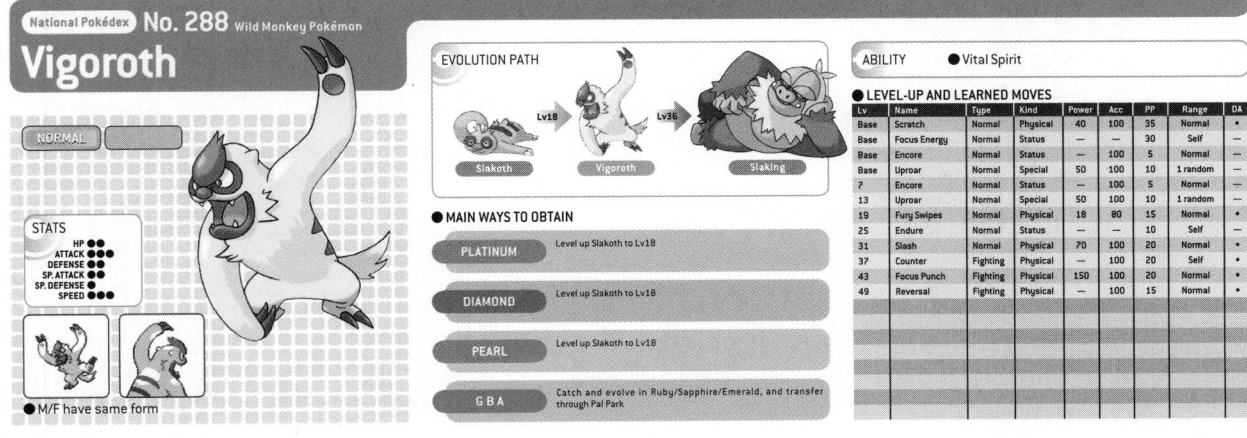

National Pokédex No. 289 Lazy Pokémon
Slaking

NORMAL

STATS
- HP ●●●●
- ATTACK ●●●●●
- DEFENSE ●●●
- SP. ATTACK ●●●
- SP. DEFENSE ●●●
- SPEED ●●●

● M/F have same form

EVOLUTION PATH
Slakoth → Lv18 → Vigoroth → Lv36 → Slaking

MAIN WAYS TO OBTAIN
PLATINUM	Level up Vigoroth to Lv36
DIAMOND	Level up Vigoroth to Lv36
PEARL	Level up Vigoroth to Lv36
G B A	Catch and evolve in Ruby/Sapphire/Emerald, and transfer through Pal Park

ABILITY ● Truant

● LEVEL-UP AND LEARNED MOVES
Lv	Name	Type	Kind	Power	Acc	PP	Range	DA
Base	Scratch	Normal	Physical	40	100	35	Normal	●
Base	Yawn	Normal	Status	—	—	10	Normal	—
Base	Encore	Normal	Status	—	100	5	Normal	—
Base	Slack Off	Normal	Status	—	—	10	Self	—
7	Encore	Normal	Status	—	100	5	Normal	—
13	Slack Off	Normal	Status	—	—	10	Self	—
19	Faint Attack	Dark	Physical	60	—	20	Normal	●
25	Amnesia	Psychic	Status	—	—	20	Self	—
31	Covet	Normal	Physical	40	100	40	Normal	●
36	Swagger	Normal	Status	—	90	15	Normal	—
37	Counter	Fighting	Physical	—	100	20	Self	●
43	Flail	Normal	Physical	—	100	15	Normal	●
49	Fling	Dark	Physical	—	100	10	Normal	●
55	Punishment	Dark	Physical	—	100	5	Normal	●
61	Hammer Arm	Fighting	Physical	100	90	10	Normal	●

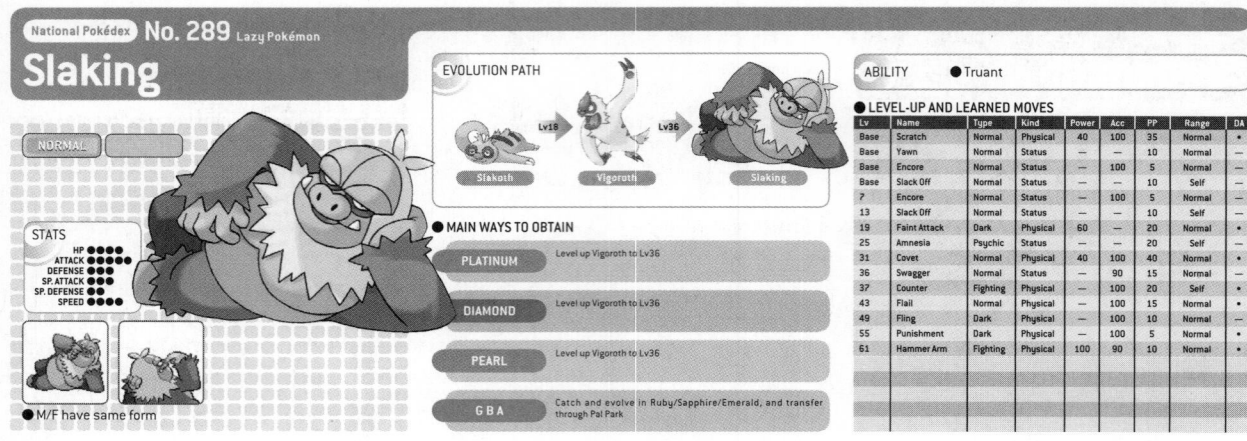

National Pokédex No. 290 Trainee Pokémon
Nincada

BUG GROUND

STATS
- HP ●
- ATTACK ●●
- DEFENSE ●●●
- SP. ATTACK ●
- SP. DEFENSE ●●
- SPEED ●●

● M/F have same form

EVOLUTION PATH
Nincada → Lv20 → Ninjask
Nincada → Lv20 → Shedinja (Have a Poké Ball and an empty slot in your party)

MAIN WAYS TO OBTAIN
PLATINUM	Eterna Forest (use Poké Radar)
DIAMOND	Eterna Forest (use Poké Radar)
PEARL	Eterna Forest (use Poké Radar)
G B A	Catch in Ruby/Sapphire/Emerald and transfer through Pal Park

ABILITY ● Compoundeyes

● LEVEL-UP AND LEARNED MOVES
Lv	Name	Type	Kind	Power	Acc	PP	Range	DA
Base	Scratch	Normal	Physical	40	100	35	Normal	●
Base	Harden	Normal	Status	—	—	30	Self	—
5	Leech Life	Bug	Physical	20	100	15	Normal	●
9	Sand-Attack	Ground	Status	—	100	15	Normal	—
14	Fury Swipes	Normal	Physical	18	80	15	Normal	●
19	Mind Reader	Normal	Status	—	—	5	Normal	—
25	False Swipe	Normal	Physical	40	100	40	Normal	●
31	Mud-Slap	Ground	Special	20	100	10	Normal	—
38	Metal Claw	Steel	Physical	50	95	35	Normal	●
45	Dig	Ground	Physical	80	100	10	Normal	●

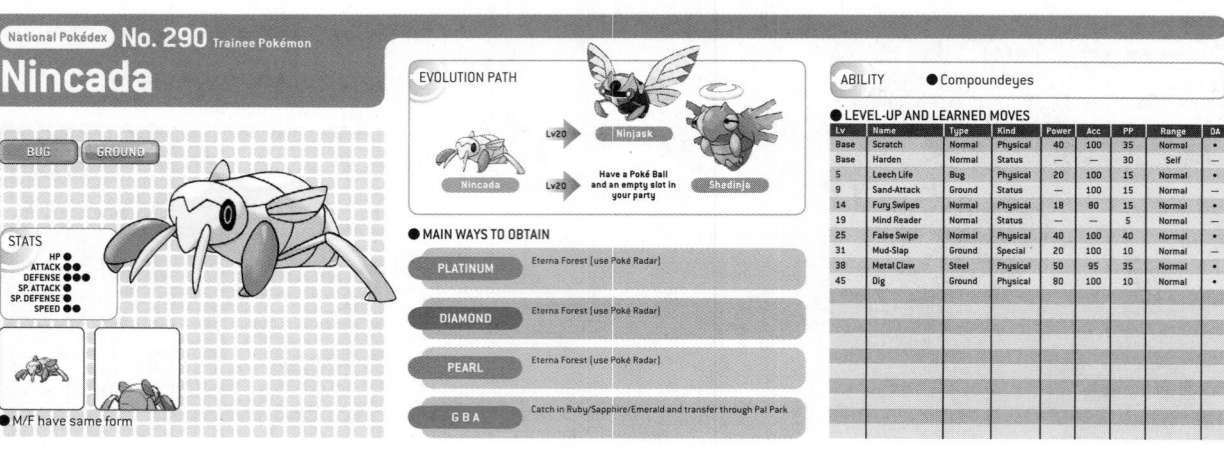

National Pokédex No. 291 Ninja Pokémon
Ninjask

BUG FLYING

STATS
- HP ●●●
- ATTACK ●●●
- DEFENSE ●●●
- SP. ATTACK ●●●
- SP. DEFENSE ●●●
- SPEED ●●●●●

● M/F have same form

EVOLUTION PATH
Nincada → Lv20 → Ninjask
Nincada → Lv20 → Shedinja (Have a Poké Ball and an empty slot in your party)

MAIN WAYS TO OBTAIN
PLATINUM	Level up Nincada to Lv20
DIAMOND	Level up Nincada to Lv20
PEARL	Level up Nincada to Lv20
G B A	Catch and evolve in Ruby/Sapphire/Emerald, and transfer through Pal Park

ABILITY ● Speed Boost

● LEVEL-UP AND LEARNED MOVES
Lv	Name	Type	Kind	Power	Acc	PP	Range	DA
Base	Bug Bite	Bug	Physical	60	100	20	Normal	●
Base	Scratch	Normal	Physical	40	100	35	Normal	●
Base	Harden	Normal	Status	—	—	30	Self	—
Base	Leech Life	Bug	Physical	20	100	15	Normal	●
Base	Sand-Attack	Ground	Status	—	100	15	Normal	—
5	Leech Life	Bug	Physical	20	100	15	Normal	●
9	Sand-Attack	Ground	Status	—	100	15	Normal	—
14	Fury Swipes	Normal	Physical	18	80	15	Normal	●
19	Mind Reader	Normal	Status	—	—	5	Normal	—
20	Double Team	Normal	Status	—	—	15	Self	—
20	Fury Cutter	Bug	Physical	10	95	20	Normal	●
20	Screech	Normal	Status	—	85	40	Normal	—
25	Swords Dance	Normal	Status	—	—	30	Self	—
31	Slash	Normal	Physical	70	100	20	Normal	●
38	Agility	Psychic	Status	—	—	30	Self	—
45	Baton Pass	Normal	Status	—	—	40	Self	—
52	X-Scissor	Bug	Physical	80	100	15	Normal	●

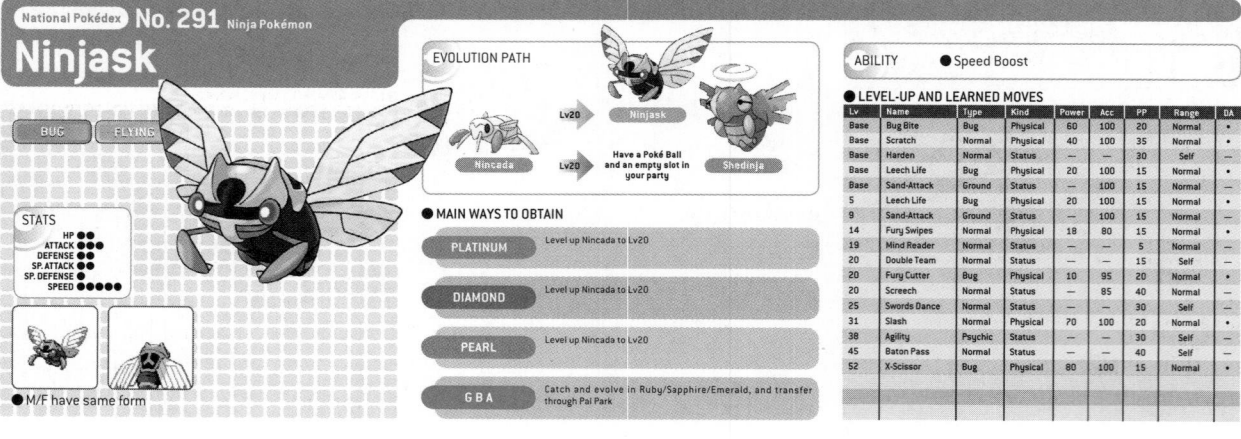

National Pokédex No. 292 Shed Pokémon
Shedinja

BUG GHOST

STATS
- HP ●
- ATTACK ●●●
- DEFENSE ●●●
- SP. ATTACK ●●●
- SP. DEFENSE ●●
- SPEED ●●

● Gender unkown

EVOLUTION PATH
Nincada → Lv20 → Ninjask
Nincada → Lv20 → Shedinja (Have a Poké Ball and an empty slot in your party)

MAIN WAYS TO OBTAIN
PLATINUM	Level up Nincada to Lv20 with an empty slot in your party
DIAMOND	Level up Nincada to Lv20 with an empty slot in your party
PEARL	Level up Nincada to Lv20 with an empty slot in your party
G B A	Catch and evolve in Ruby/Sapphire/Emerald, and transfer through Pal Park

ABILITY ● Wonder Guard

● LEVEL-UP AND LEARNED MOVES
Lv	Name	Type	Kind	Power	Acc	PP	Range	DA
Base	Scratch	Normal	Physical	40	100	35	Normal	●
Base	Harden	Normal	Status	—	—	30	Self	●
5	Leech Life	Bug	Physical	20	100	15	Normal	●
9	Sand-Attack	Ground	Status	—	100	15	Normal	—
14	Fury Swipes	Normal	Physical	18	80	15	Normal	●
19	Mind Reader	Normal	Status	—	—	5	Normal	—
25	Spite	Ghost	Status	—	100	10	Normal	—
31	Confuse Ray	Ghost	Status	—	100	10	Normal	—
38	Shadow Sneak	Ghost	Physical	40	100	30	Normal	●
45	Grudge	Ghost	Status	—	—	5	Self	—
52	Heal Block	Psychic	Status	—	100	15	2 foes	—
59	Shadow Ball	Ghost	Special	80	100	15	Normal	—

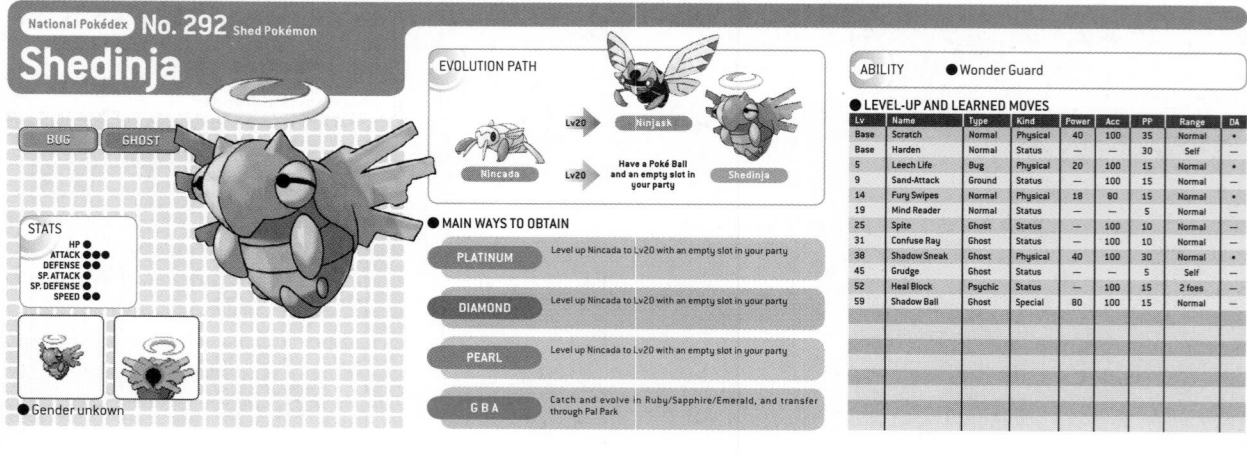

Whismur

National Pokédex No. 293 Whisper Pokémon

NORMAL

STATS
- HP ●●
- ATTACK ●●
- DEFENSE ●●
- SP. ATTACK ●●
- SP. DEFENSE ●
- SPEED ●

● M/F have same form

EVOLUTION PATH

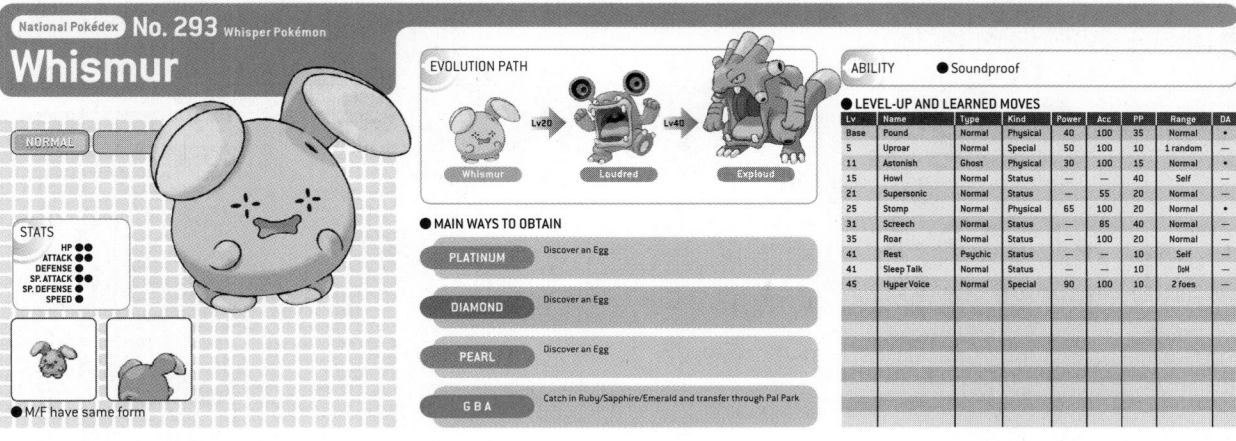

Whismur → Lv20 → Loudred → Lv40 → Exploud

MAIN WAYS TO OBTAIN

PLATINUM	Discover an Egg
DIAMOND	Discover an Egg
PEARL	Discover an Egg
G B A	Catch in Ruby/Sapphire/Emerald and transfer through Pal Park

ABILITY ● Soundproof

● LEVEL-UP AND LEARNED MOVES

Lv	Name	Type	Kind	Power	Acc	PP	Range	DA
Base	Pound	Normal	Physical	40	100	35	Normal	●
5	Uproar	Normal	Special	50	100	10	1 random	—
11	Astonish	Ghost	Physical	30	100	15	Normal	—
15	Howl	Normal	Status	—	—	40	Self	—
21	Supersonic	Normal	Status	—	55	20	Normal	—
25	Stomp	Normal	Physical	65	100	20	Normal	—
31	Screech	Normal	Status	—	85	40	Normal	—
35	Roar	Normal	Status	—	100	20	Normal	—
41	Rest	Psychic	Status	—	—	10	Self	—
41	Sleep Talk	Normal	Status	—	—	10	DaM	—
45	Hyper Voice	Normal	Special	90	100	10	2 foes	—

Loudred

National Pokédex No. 294 Big Voice Pokémon

NORMAL

STATS
- HP ●●
- ATTACK ●●●
- DEFENSE ●●
- SP. ATTACK ●●
- SP. DEFENSE ●●
- SPEED ●●

● M/F have same form

EVOLUTION PATH

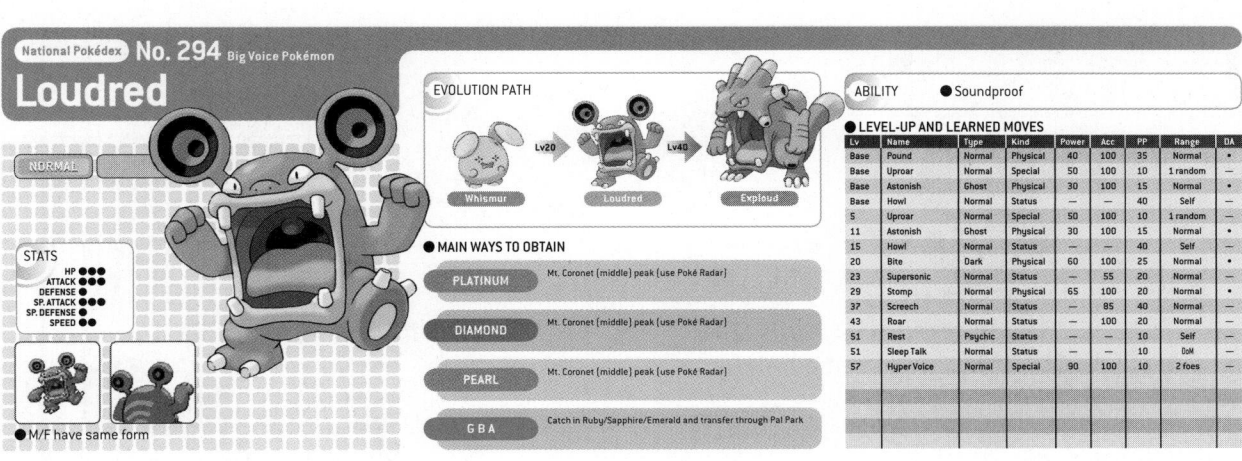

Whismur → Lv20 → Loudred → Lv40 → Exploud

MAIN WAYS TO OBTAIN

PLATINUM	Mt. Coronet (middle) peak (use Poké Radar)
DIAMOND	Mt. Coronet (middle) peak (use Poké Radar)
PEARL	Mt. Coronet (middle) peak (use Poké Radar)
G B A	Catch in Ruby/Sapphire/Emerald and transfer through Pal Park

ABILITY ● Soundproof

● LEVEL-UP AND LEARNED MOVES

Lv	Name	Type	Kind	Power	Acc	PP	Range	DA
Base	Pound	Normal	Physical	40	100	35	Normal	●
Base	Uproar	Normal	Special	50	100	10	1 random	—
Base	Astonish	Ghost	Physical	30	100	15	Normal	—
Base	Howl	Normal	Status	—	—	40	Self	—
5	Uproar	Normal	Special	50	100	10	1 random	—
11	Astonish	Ghost	Physical	30	100	15	Normal	—
15	Howl	Normal	Status	—	—	40	Self	—
20	Bite	Dark	Physical	60	100	25	Normal	—
23	Supersonic	Normal	Status	—	55	20	Normal	—
29	Stomp	Normal	Physical	65	100	20	Normal	—
37	Screech	Normal	Status	—	85	40	Normal	—
43	Roar	Normal	Status	—	100	20	Normal	—
51	Rest	Psychic	Status	—	—	10	Self	—
51	Sleep Talk	Normal	Status	—	—	10	DaM	—
57	Hyper Voice	Normal	Special	90	100	10	2 foes	—

Exploud

National Pokédex No. 295 Loud Noise Pokémon

NORMAL

STATS
- HP ●●●
- ATTACK ●●●
- DEFENSE ●●
- SP. ATTACK ●●●
- SP. DEFENSE ●●●
- SPEED ●●●

● M/F have same form

EVOLUTION PATH

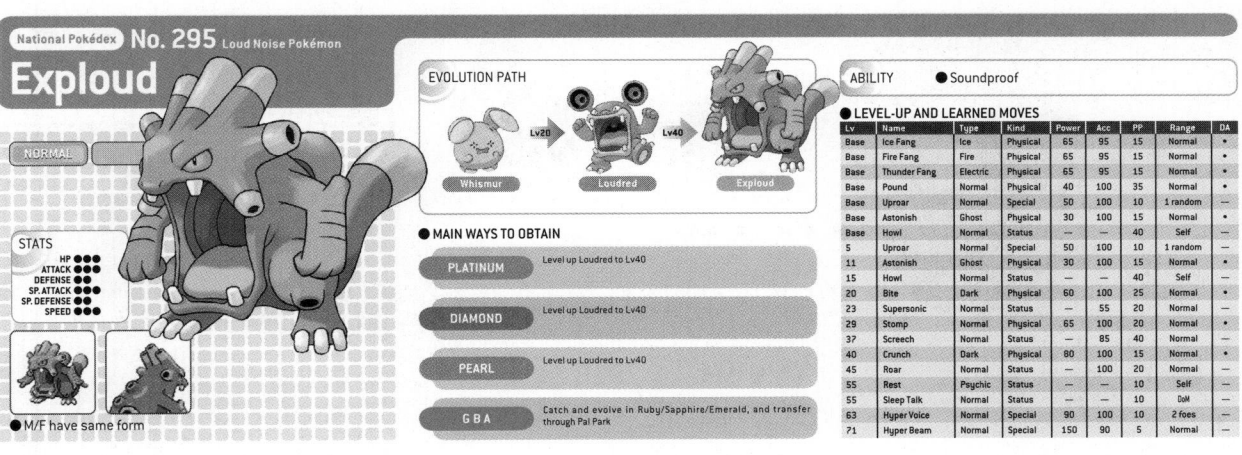

Whismur → Lv20 → Loudred → Lv40 → Exploud

MAIN WAYS TO OBTAIN

PLATINUM	Level up Loudred to Lv40
DIAMOND	Level up Loudred to Lv40
PEARL	Level up Loudred to Lv40
G B A	Catch and evolve in Ruby/Sapphire/Emerald, and transfer through Pal Park

ABILITY ● Soundproof

● LEVEL-UP AND LEARNED MOVES

Lv	Name	Type	Kind	Power	Acc	PP	Range	DA
Base	Ice Fang	Ice	Physical	65	95	15	Normal	●
Base	Fire Fang	Fire	Physical	65	95	15	Normal	●
Base	Thunder Fang	Electric	Physical	65	95	15	Normal	●
Base	Pound	Normal	Physical	40	100	35	Normal	●
Base	Uproar	Normal	Special	50	100	10	1 random	—
Base	Astonish	Ghost	Physical	30	100	15	Normal	—
Base	Howl	Normal	Status	—	—	40	Self	—
5	Uproar	Normal	Special	50	100	10	1 random	—
11	Astonish	Ghost	Physical	30	100	15	Normal	—
15	Howl	Normal	Status	—	—	40	Self	—
20	Bite	Dark	Physical	60	100	25	Normal	—
23	Supersonic	Normal	Status	—	55	20	Normal	—
29	Stomp	Normal	Physical	65	100	20	Normal	—
37	Screech	Normal	Status	—	85	40	Normal	—
40	Crunch	Dark	Physical	80	100	15	Normal	●
45	Roar	Normal	Status	—	100	20	Normal	—
55	Rest	Psychic	Status	—	—	10	Self	—
55	Sleep Talk	Normal	Status	—	—	10	DaM	—
63	Hyper Voice	Normal	Special	90	100	10	2 foes	—
71	Hyper Beam	Normal	Special	150	90	5	Normal	—

Makuhita

National Pokédex No. 296 Guts Pokémon

Fighting

STATS
- HP ●●
- ATTACK ●●
- DEFENSE ●
- SP. ATTACK ●
- SP. DEFENSE ●
- SPEED ●

● M/F have same form

EVOLUTION PATH

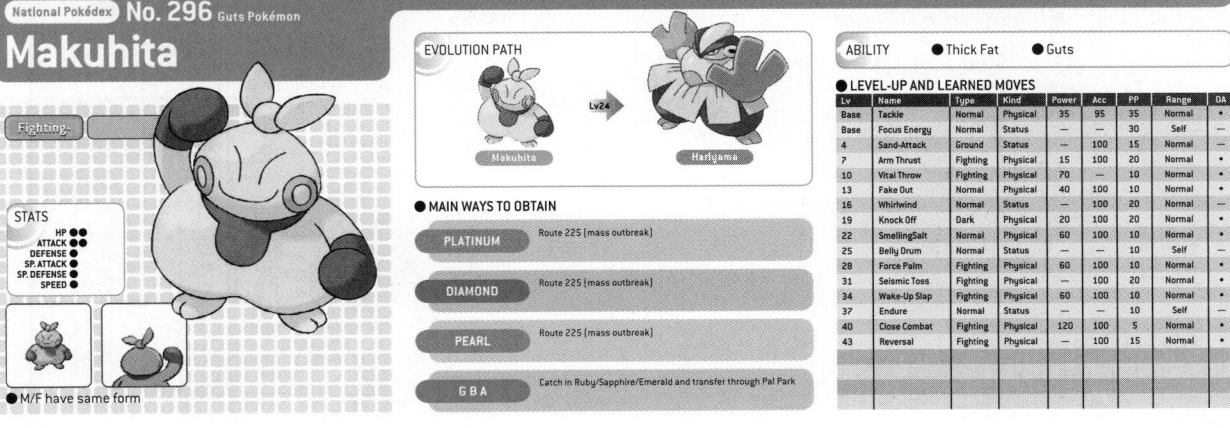

Makuhita → Lv24 → Hariyama

MAIN WAYS TO OBTAIN

PLATINUM	Route 225 (mass outbreak)
DIAMOND	Route 225 (mass outbreak)
PEARL	Route 225 (mass outbreak)
G B A	Catch in Ruby/Sapphire/Emerald and transfer through Pal Park

ABILITY ● Thick Fat ● Guts

● LEVEL-UP AND LEARNED MOVES

Lv	Name	Type	Kind	Power	Acc	PP	Range	DA
Base	Tackle	Normal	Physical	35	95	35	Normal	●
Base	Focus Energy	Normal	Status	—	—	30	Self	—
4	Sand-Attack	Ground	Status	—	100	15	Normal	—
7	Arm Thrust	Fighting	Physical	15	100	20	Normal	●
10	Vital Throw	Fighting	Physical	70	—	10	Normal	●
13	Fake Out	Normal	Physical	40	100	10	Normal	—
16	Whirlwind	Normal	Status	—	100	10	Normal	—
19	Knock Off	Dark	Physical	20	100	20	Normal	●
22	SmellingSalt	Normal	Physical	60	100	10	Normal	—
25	Belly Drum	Normal	Status	—	—	10	Self	—
28	Force Palm	Fighting	Physical	60	100	10	Normal	●
31	Seismic Toss	Fighting	Physical	—	100	20	Normal	—
34	Wake-Up Slap	Fighting	Physical	60	100	10	Normal	—
37	Endure	Normal	Status	—	—	10	Self	—
40	Close Combat	Fighting	Physical	120	100	5	Normal	●
43	Reversal	Fighting	Physical	—	100	15	Normal	●

296
MAKUHITA

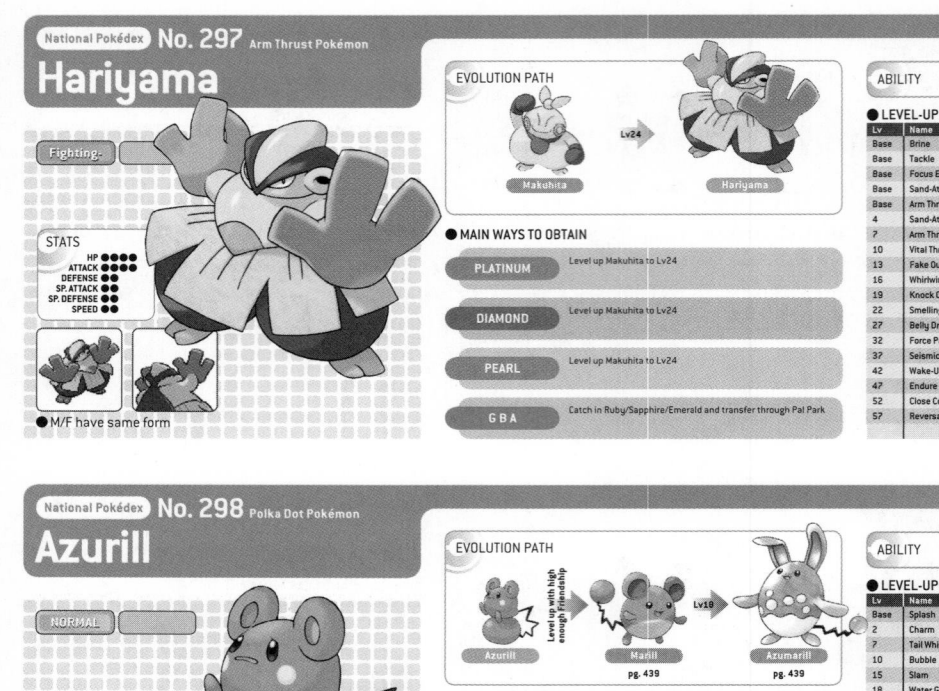

National Pokédex No. 297 Arm Thrust Pokémon

Hariyama

Fighting-

STATS
- HP ●●●●
- ATTACK ●●●●
- DEFENSE ●●
- SP. ATTACK ●
- SP. DEFENSE ●●
- SPEED ●●

● M/F have same form

EVOLUTION PATH

Makuhita → Lv24 → Hariyama

● MAIN WAYS TO OBTAIN

PLATINUM	Level up Makuhita to Lv24
DIAMOND	Level up Makuhita to Lv24
PEARL	Level up Makuhita to Lv24
GBA	Catch in Ruby/Sapphire/Emerald and transfer through Pal Park

ABILITY ● Thick Fat ● Guts

● LEVEL-UP AND LEARNED MOVES

Lv	Name	Type	Kind	Power	Acc	PP	Range	DA
Base	Brine	Water	Special	65	100	10	Normal	—
Base	Tackle	Normal	Physical	35	95	35	Normal	●
Base	Focus Energy	Normal	Status	—	—	30	Self	—
Base	Sand-Attack	Ground	Status	—	100	15	Normal	—
Base	Arm Thrust	Fighting	Physical	15	100	20	Normal	●
4	Sand-Attack	Ground	Status	—	100	15	Normal	—
7	Arm Thrust	Fighting	Physical	15	100	20	Normal	●
10	Vital Throw	Fighting	Physic!	70	—	10	Normal	●
13	Fake Out	Normal	Physical	40	100	10	Normal	●
16	Whirlwind	Normal	Status	—	100	20	Normal	—
19	Knock Off	Dark	Physical	20	100	20	Normal	●
22	SmellingSalt	Normal	Physical	60	100	10	Normal	●
27	Belly Drum	Normal	Status	—	—	10	Self	—
32	Force Palm	Fighting	Physical	60	100	10	Normal	●
37	Seismic Toss	Fighting	Physical	—	100	20	Normal	●
42	Wake-Up Slap	Fighting	Physical	60	100	10	Normal	●
47	Endure	Normal	Status	—	—	10	Self	—
52	Close Combat	Fighting	Physical	120	100	5	Normal	●
57	Reversal	Fighting	Physical	—	100	15	Normal	●

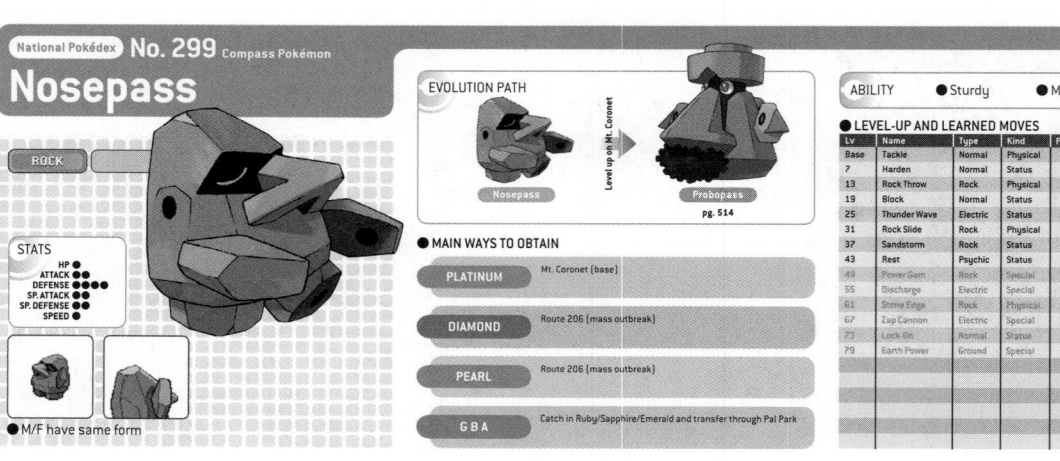

National Pokédex No. 298 Polka Dot Pokémon

Azurill

NORMAL

STATS
- HP ●●
- ATTACK ●●
- DEFENSE ●
- SP. ATTACK ●
- SP. DEFENSE ●
- SPEED ●

● M/F have same form

EVOLUTION PATH

Azurill → Level up with high enough Friendship → Marill pg. 439 → Lv18 → Azumarill pg. 439

● MAIN WAYS TO OBTAIN

PLATINUM	Trophy Garden in the Pokémon Mansion on Route 212 (talk to Mr. Backlot after you get the National Pokédex)
DIAMOND	Pastoria Great Marsh (changes by day)
PEARL	Pastoria Great Marsh (changes by day)
GBA	Discover as an Egg in LeafGreen or Ruby/Sapphire/Emerald, and transfer through Pal Park

ABILITY ● Thick Fat ● Huge Power

● LEVEL-UP AND LEARNED MOVES

Lv	Name	Type	Kind	Power	Acc	PP	Range	DA
Base	Splash	Normal	Status	—	—	40	Self	—
2	Charm	Normal	Status	—	100	20	Normal	—
7	Tail Whip	Normal	Status	—	100	30	2 foes	—
10	Bubble	Water	Special	20	100	30	2 foes	—
15	Slam	Normal	Physical	80	75	20	Normal	●
18	Water Gun	Water	Special	40	100	25	Normal	—

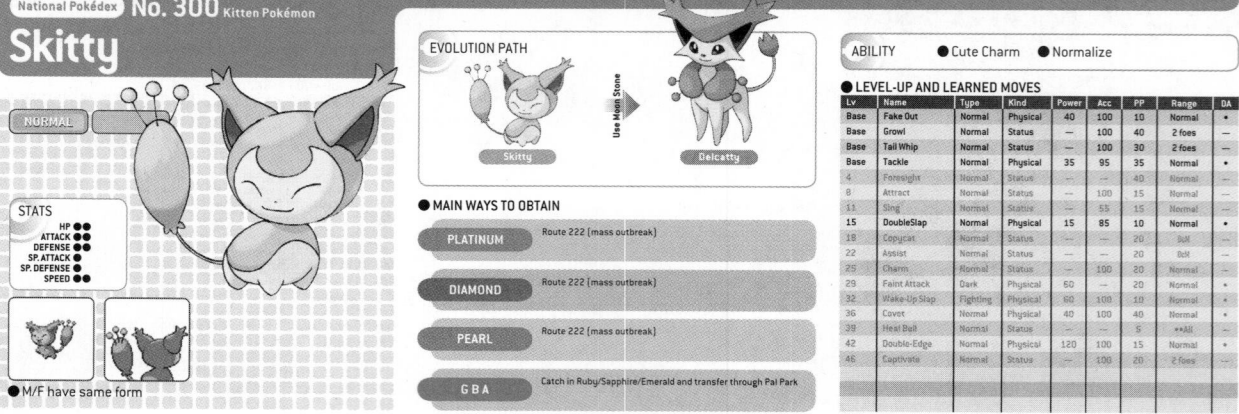

National Pokédex No. 299 Compass Pokémon

Nosepass

ROCK

STATS
- HP ●
- ATTACK ●●
- DEFENSE ●●●●
- SP. ATTACK ●●
- SP. DEFENSE ●●
- SPEED ●

● M/F have same form

EVOLUTION PATH

Nosepass → Level up on Mt. Coronet → Probopass pg. 514

● MAIN WAYS TO OBTAIN

PLATINUM	Mt. Coronet (base)
DIAMOND	Route 206 (mass outbreak)
PEARL	Route 206 (mass outbreak)
GBA	Catch in Ruby/Sapphire/Emerald and transfer through Pal Park

ABILITY ● Sturdy ● Magnet Pull

● LEVEL-UP AND LEARNED MOVES

Lv	Name	Type	Kind	Power	Acc	PP	Range	DA
Base	Tackle	Normal	Physical	35	95	35	Normal	●
7	Harden	Normal	Status	—	—	30	Self	—
13	Rock Throw	Rock	Physical	50	90	15	Normal	—
19	Block	Normal	Status	—	—	5	Normal	—
25	Thunder Wave	Electric	Status	—	100	20	Normal	—
31	Rock Slide	Rock	Physical	75	90	10	2 foes	—
37	Sandstorm	Rock	Status	—	—	10	All	—
43	Rest	Psychic	Status	—	—	10	Self	—
49	Power Gem	Rock	Special	70	100	20	Normal	—
55	Discharge	Electric	Special	80	100	15	2 foes 1 ally	—
61	Stone Edge	Rock	Physical	100	80	5	Normal	—
67	Zap Cannon	Electric	Special	120	50	5	Normal	—
73	Lock-On	Normal	Status	—	—	5	Normal	—
79	Earth Power	Ground	Special	90	100	10	Normal	—

National Pokédex No. 300 Kitten Pokémon

Skitty

NORMAL

STATS
- HP ●●
- ATTACK ●●
- DEFENSE ●
- SP. ATTACK ●
- SP. DEFENSE ●●
- SPEED ●●

● M/F have same form

EVOLUTION PATH

Skitty → Use Moon Stone → Delcatty

● MAIN WAYS TO OBTAIN

PLATINUM	Route 222 (mass outbreak)
DIAMOND	Route 222 (mass outbreak)
PEARL	Route 222 (mass outbreak)
GBA	Catch in Ruby/Sapphire/Emerald and transfer through Pal Park

ABILITY ● Cute Charm ● Normalize

● LEVEL-UP AND LEARNED MOVES

Lv	Name	Type	Kind	Power	Acc	PP	Range	DA
Base	Fake Out	Normal	Physical	40	100	10	Normal	●
Base	Growl	Normal	Status	—	100	40	2 foes	—
Base	Tail Whip	Normal	Status	—	100	30	2 foes	—
Base	Tackle	Normal	Physical	35	95	35	Normal	●
4	Foresight	Normal	Status	—	—	40	Normal	—
8	Attract	Normal	Status	—	100	15	Normal	—
11	Sing	Normal	Status	—	55	15	Normal	—
15	DoubleSlap	Normal	Physical	15	85	10	Normal	●
18	Copycat	Normal	Status	—	—	20	Self	—
22	Assist	Normal	Status	—	—	20	Self	—
25	Charm	Normal	Status	—	100	20	Normal	—
29	Faint Attack	Dark	Physical	60	—	20	Normal	—
32	Wake-Up Slap	Fighting	Physical	60	100	10	Normal	—
36	Covet	Normal	Physical	40	100	40	Normal	—
39	Heal Bell	Normal	Status	—	—	5	**All	—
42	Double-Edge	Normal	Physical	120	100	15	Normal	—
46	Captivate	Normal	Status	—	100	20	2 foes	—

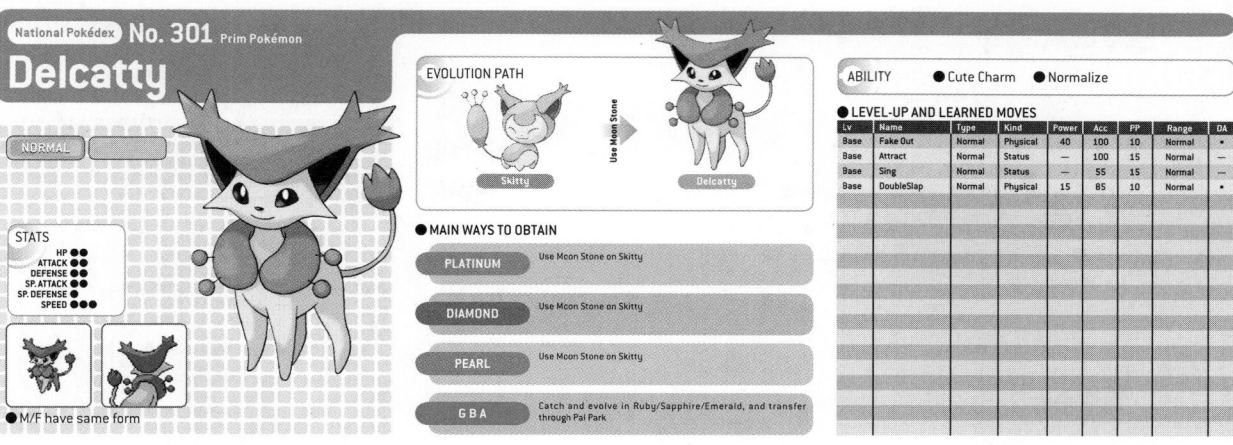

No. 301 Prim Pokémon

Delcatty

NORMAL

STATS
HP ●●
ATTACK ●●
DEFENSE ●
SP. ATTACK ●
SP. DEFENSE ●
SPEED ●●●

● M/F have same form

EVOLUTION PATH

Skitty → *Use Moon Stone* → Delcatty

● MAIN WAYS TO OBTAIN

PLATINUM	Use Moon Stone on Skitty
DIAMOND	Use Moon Stone on Skitty
PEARL	Use Moon Stone on Skitty
G B A	Catch and evolve in Ruby/Sapphire/Emerald, and transfer through Pal Park

ABILITY ● Cute Charm ● Normalize

● LEVEL-UP AND LEARNED MOVES

Lv	Name	Type	Kind	Power	Acc	PP	Range	DA
Base	Fake Out	Normal	Physical	40	100	10	Normal	●
Base	Attract	Normal	Status	—	100	15	Normal	—
Base	Sing	Normal	Status	—	55	15	Normal	—
Base	DoubleSlap	Normal	Physical	15	85	10	Normal	●

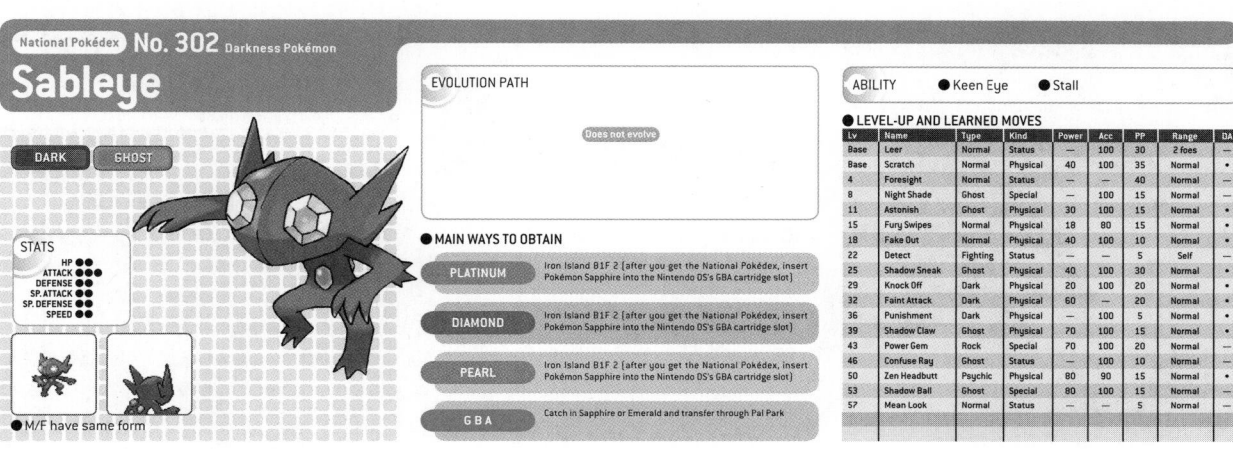

No. 302 Darkness Pokémon

Sableye

DARK | GHOST

STATS
HP ●
ATTACK ●●
DEFENSE ●●
SP. ATTACK ●●
SP. DEFENSE ●●
SPEED ●●

● M/F have same form

EVOLUTION PATH

Does not evolve

● MAIN WAYS TO OBTAIN

PLATINUM	Iron Island B1F 2 [after you get the National Pokédex, insert Pokémon Sapphire into the Nintendo DS's GBA cartridge slot]
DIAMOND	Iron Island B1F 2 [after you get the National Pokédex, insert Pokémon Sapphire into the Nintendo DS's GBA cartridge slot]
PEARL	Iron Island B1F 2 [after you get the National Pokédex, insert Pokémon Sapphire into the Nintendo DS's GBA cartridge slot]
G B A	Catch in Sapphire or Emerald and transfer through Pal Park

ABILITY ● Keen Eye ● Stall

● LEVEL-UP AND LEARNED MOVES

Lv	Name	Type	Kind	Power	Acc	PP	Range	DA
Base	Leer	Normal	Status	—	100	30	2 foes	—
Base	Scratch	Normal	Physical	40	100	35	Normal	●
4	Foresight	Normal	Status	—	—	40	Normal	—
8	Night Shade	Ghost	Special	—	100	15	Normal	—
11	Astonish	Ghost	Physical	30	100	15	Normal	●
15	Fury Swipes	Normal	Physical	18	80	15	Normal	●
18	Fake Out	Normal	Physical	40	100	10	Normal	●
22	Detect	Fighting	Status	—	—	5	Self	—
25	Shadow Sneak	Ghost	Physical	40	100	30	Normal	●
29	Knock Off	Dark	Physical	20	100	20	Normal	●
32	Faint Attack	Dark	Physical	60	—	20	Normal	●
36	Punishment	Dark	Physical	—	100	5	Normal	●
39	Shadow Claw	Ghost	Physical	70	100	15	Normal	●
43	Power Gem	Rock	Special	70	100	20	Normal	—
46	Confuse Ray	Ghost	Status	—	100	10	Normal	—
50	Zen Headbutt	Psychic	Physical	80	90	15	Normal	●
53	Shadow Ball	Ghost	Special	80	100	15	Normal	—
57	Mean Look	Normal	Status	—	—	5	Normal	—

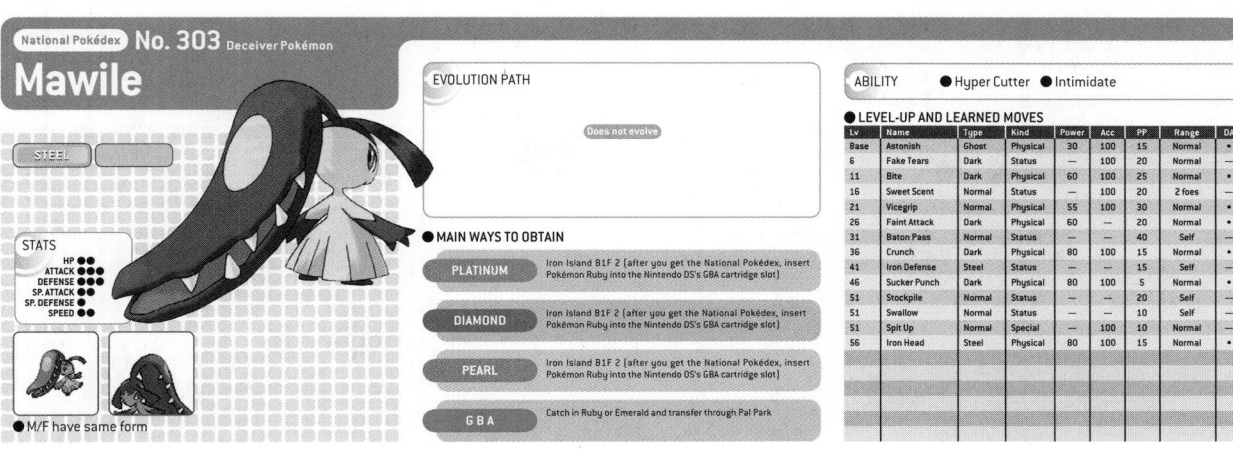

No. 303 Deceiver Pokémon

Mawile

STEEL

STATS
HP ●
ATTACK ●●●
DEFENSE ●●●
SP. ATTACK ●●
SP. DEFENSE ●●
SPEED ●●

● M/F have same form

EVOLUTION PATH

Does not evolve

● MAIN WAYS TO OBTAIN

PLATINUM	Iron Island B1F 2 [after you get the National Pokédex, insert Pokémon Ruby into the Nintendo DS's GBA cartridge slot]
DIAMOND	Iron Island B1F 2 [after you get the National Pokédex, insert Pokémon Ruby into the Nintendo DS's GBA cartridge slot]
PEARL	Iron Island B1F 2 [after you get the National Pokédex, insert Pokémon Ruby into the Nintendo DS's GBA cartridge slot]
G B A	Catch in Ruby or Emerald and transfer through Pal Park

ABILITY ● Hyper Cutter ● Intimidate

● LEVEL-UP AND LEARNED MOVES

Lv	Name	Type	Kind	Power	Acc	PP	Range	DA
Base	Astonish	Ghost	Physical	30	100	15	Normal	●
6	Fake Tears	Dark	Status	—	100	20	Normal	—
11	Bite	Dark	Physical	60	100	25	Normal	●
16	Sweet Scent	Normal	Status	—	100	20	2 foes	—
21	Vicegrip	Normal	Physical	55	100	30	Normal	●
26	Faint Attack	Dark	Physical	60	—	20	Normal	●
31	Baton Pass	Normal	Status	—	—	40	Self	—
36	Crunch	Dark	Physical	80	100	15	Normal	●
41	Iron Defense	Steel	Status	—	—	15	Self	—
46	Sucker Punch	Dark	Physical	80	100	5	Normal	●
51	Stockpile	Normal	Status	—	—	20	Self	—
51	Swallow	Normal	Status	—	—	10	Self	—
51	Spit Up	Normal	Special	—	100	10	Normal	—
56	Iron Head	Steel	Physical	80	100	15	Normal	●

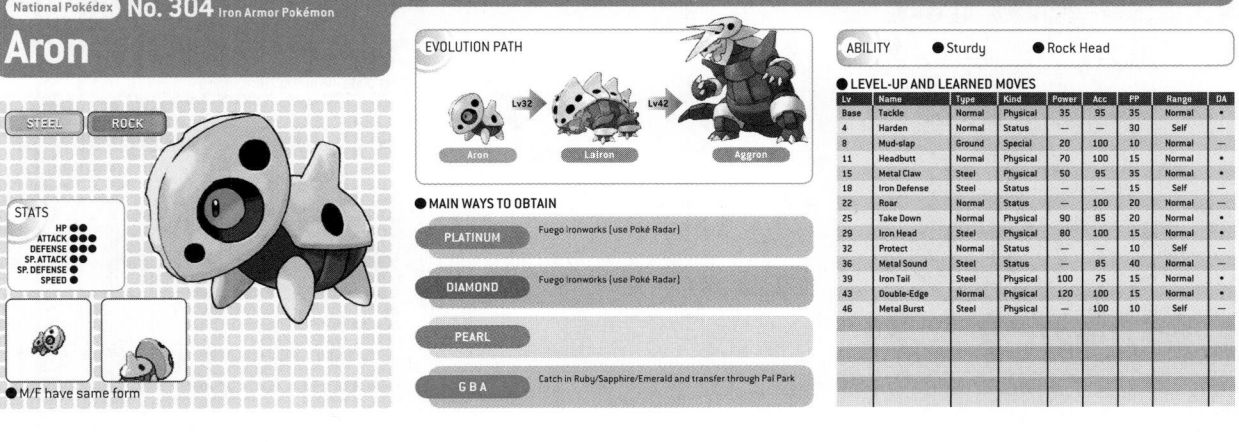

No. 304 Iron Armor Pokémon

Aron

STEEL | ROCK

STATS
HP ●●
ATTACK ●●
DEFENSE ●●●
SP. ATTACK ●
SP. DEFENSE ●
SPEED ●

● M/F have same form

EVOLUTION PATH

Aron → Lv32 → Lairon → Lv42 → Aggron

● MAIN WAYS TO OBTAIN

PLATINUM	Fuego Ironworks (use Poké Radar)
DIAMOND	Fuego Ironworks (use Poké Radar)
PEARL	
G B A	Catch in Ruby/Sapphire/Emerald and transfer through Pal Park

ABILITY ● Sturdy ● Rock Head

● LEVEL-UP AND LEARNED MOVES

Lv	Name	Type	Kind	Power	Acc	PP	Range	DA
Base	Tackle	Normal	Physical	35	95	35	Normal	●
4	Harden	Normal	Status	—	—	30	Self	—
8	Mud-slap	Ground	Special	20	100	10	Normal	—
11	Headbutt	Normal	Physical	70	100	15	Normal	●
15	Metal Claw	Steel	Physical	50	95	35	Normal	●
18	Iron Defense	Steel	Status	—	—	15	Self	—
22	Roar	Normal	Status	—	100	20	Normal	—
25	Take Down	Normal	Physical	90	85	20	Normal	●
29	Iron Head	Steel	Physical	80	100	15	Normal	●
32	Protect	Normal	Status	—	—	10	Self	—
36	Metal Sound	Steel	Status	—	85	40	Normal	—
39	Iron Tail	Steel	Physical	100	75	15	Normal	●
43	Double-Edge	Normal	Physical	120	100	15	Normal	●
46	Metal Burst	Steel	Physical	—	100	10	Self	—

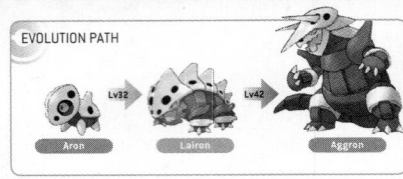

National Pokédex No. 305 Iron Armor Pokémon
Lairon

STEEL · ROCK

STATS
HP ●●
ATTACK ●●●
DEFENSE ●●●●
SP.ATTACK ●●
SP.DEFENSE ●●
SPEED ●●

● M/F have same form

EVOLUTION PATH
Aron → Lv32 → Lairon → Lv42 → Aggron

MAIN WAYS TO OBTAIN
PLATINUM — Level up Aron to Lv32
DIAMOND — Level up Aron to Lv32
PEARL —
GBA — Catch in Ruby/Sapphire/Emerald and transfer through Pal Park

ABILITY ● Sturdy ● Rock Head

● LEVEL-UP AND LEARNED MOVES

Lv	Name	Type	Kind	Power	Acc	PP	Range	DA
Base	Tackle	Normal	Physical	35	95	35	Normal	●
Base	Harden	Normal	Status	—	—	30	Self	—
Base	Mud-Slap	Ground	Special	20	100	10	Normal	●
Base	Headbutt	Normal	Physical	70	100	15	Normal	●
4	Harden	Normal	Status	—	—	30	Self	—
8	Mud-Slap	Ground	Special	20	100	10	Normal	●
11	Headbutt	Normal	Physical	70	100	15	Normal	●
15	Metal Claw	Steel	Physical	50	95	35	Normal	●
18	Iron Defense	Steel	Status	—	—	15	Self	—
22	Roar	Normal	Status	—	100	20	Normal	—
25	Take Down	Normal	Physical	90	85	20	Normal	●
29	Iron Head	Steel	Physical	80	100	15	Normal	●
34	Protect	Normal	Status	—	—	10	Self	—
40	Metal Sound	Steel	Status	—	85	40	Normal	—
45	Iron Tail	Steel	Physical	100	75	15	Normal	●
51	Double-Edge	Normal	Physical	120	100	15	Normal	●
56	Metal Burst	Steel	Physical	—	100	10	Self	—

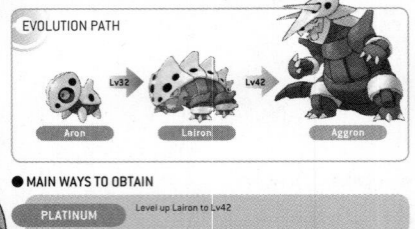

National Pokédex No. 306 Iron Armor Pokémon
Aggron

STEEL · ROCK

STATS
HP ●●
ATTACK ●●●●
DEFENSE ●●●●●
SP.ATTACK ●●
SP.DEFENSE ●●
SPEED ●●

● M/F have same form

EVOLUTION PATH
Aron → Lv32 → Lairon → Lv42 → Aggron

MAIN WAYS TO OBTAIN
PLATINUM — Level up Lairon to Lv42
DIAMOND — Level up Lairon to Lv42
PEARL —
GBA — Catch and evolve in Ruby/Sapphire/Emerald, and transfer through Pal Park

ABILITY ● Sturdy ● Rock Head

● LEVEL-UP AND LEARNED MOVES

Lv	Name	Type	Kind	Power	Acc	PP	Range	DA
Base	Tackle	Normal	Physical	35	95	35	Normal	●
Base	Harden	Normal	Status	—	—	30	Self	—
Base	Mud-Slap	Ground	Special	20	100	10	Normal	●
Base	Headbutt	Normal	Physical	70	100	15	Normal	●
4	Harden	Normal	Status	—	—	30	Self	—
8	Mud-Slap	Ground	Special	20	100	10	Normal	●
11	Headbutt	Normal	Physical	70	100	15	Normal	●
15	Metal Claw	Steel	Physical	50	95	35	Normal	●
18	Iron Defense	Steel	Status	—	—	15	Self	—
22	Roar	Normal	Status	—	100	20	Normal	—
25	Take Down	Normal	Physical	90	85	20	Normal	●
29	Iron Head	Steel	Physical	80	100	15	Normal	●
34	Protect	Normal	Status	—	—	10	Self	—
40	Metal Sound	Steel	Status	—	85	40	Normal	—
48	Iron Tail	Steel	Physical	100	75	15	Normal	●
57	Double-Edge	Normal	Physical	120	100	15	Normal	●
65	Metal Burst	Steel	Physical	—	100	10	Self	—

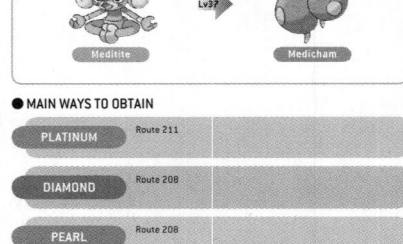

National Pokédex No. 307 Meditate Pokémon
Meditite

Fighting- · PSYCHIC

STATS
HP ●●
ATTACK ●●
DEFENSE ●●
SP.ATTACK ●●
SP.DEFENSE ●●
SPEED ●●

● Male form · ● Female form

EVOLUTION PATH
Meditite → Lv37 → Medicham

MAIN WAYS TO OBTAIN
PLATINUM — Route 211
DIAMOND — Route 208
PEARL — Route 208
GBA — Catch in Ruby/Sapphire and transfer through Pal Park

ABILITY ● Pure Power

● LEVEL-UP AND LEARNED MOVES

Lv	Name	Type	Kind	Power	Acc	PP	Range	DA
Base	Bide	Normal	Physical	—	—	10	Self	●
4	Meditate	Psychic	Status	—	—	40	Self	—
8	Confusion	Psychic	Special	50	100	25	Normal	—
11	Detect	Fighting	Status	—	—	5	Self	—
15	Hidden Power	Normal	Special	—	100	15	Normal	—
18	Mind Reader	Normal	Status	—	—	5	Normal	—
22	Feint	Normal	Physical	50	100	10	Normal	●
25	Calm Mind	Psychic	Status	—	—	20	Self	—
29	Force Palm	Fighting	Physical	60	100	10	Normal	●
32	Hi Jump Kick	Fighting	Physical	100	90	20	Normal	●
36	Psych Up	Normal	Status	—	—	10	Normal	—
39	Power Trick	Psychic	Status	—	—	10	Self	—
43	Reversal	Fighting	Physical	—	100	15	Normal	●
46	Recover	Normal	Status	—	—	10	Self	—

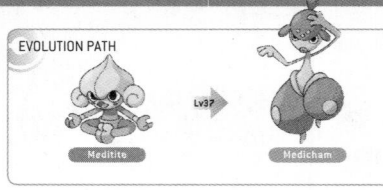

National Pokédex No. 308 Meditate Pokémon
Medicham

Fighting- · PSYCHIC

STATS
HP ●●
ATTACK ●●
DEFENSE ●●
SP.ATTACK ●●
SP.DEFENSE ●●●
SPEED ●●●

● Male form · ● Female form

EVOLUTION PATH
Meditite → Lv37 → Medicham

MAIN WAYS TO OBTAIN
PLATINUM — Mt. Coronet (middle) 2F
DIAMOND — Route 217
PEARL — Route 217
GBA — Catch in Ruby/Sapphire and transfer through Pal Park

ABILITY ● Pure Power

● LEVEL-UP AND LEARNED MOVES

Lv	Name	Type	Kind	Power	Acc	PP	Range	DA
Base	Fire Punch	Fire	Physical	75	100	15	Normal	●
Base	ThunderPunch	Electric	Physical	75	100	15	Normal	●
Base	Ice Punch	Ice	Physical	75	100	15	Normal	●
Base	Bide	Normal	Physical	—	—	10	Self	●
Base	Meditate	Psychic	Status	—	—	40	Self	—
Base	Confusion	Psychic	Special	50	100	25	Normal	—
Base	Detect	Fighting	Status	—	—	5	Self	—
4	Meditate	Psychic	Status	—	—	40	Self	—
8	Confusion	Psychic	Special	50	100	25	Normal	—
11	Detect	Fighting	Status	—	—	5	Self	—
15	Hidden Power	Normal	Special	—	100	15	Normal	—
18	Mind Reader	Normal	Status	—	—	5	Normal	—
22	Feint	Normal	Physical	50	100	10	Normal	●
25	Calm Mind	Psychic	Status	—	—	20	Self	—
29	Force Palm	Fighting	Physical	60	100	10	Normal	●
32	Hi Jump Kick	Fighting	Physical	100	90	20	Normal	●
36	Psych Up	Normal	Status	—	—	10	Normal	—
42	Power Trick	Psychic	Status	—	—	10	Self	—
49	Reversal	Fighting	Physical	—	100	15	Normal	●
55	Recover	Normal	Status	—	—	10	Self	—

NATIONAL POKÉDEX

National Pokédex No. 309 Lightning Pokémon
Electrike

ELECTRIC

STATS
HP
ATTACK
DEFENSE
SP.ATTACK
SP.DEFENSE
SPEED

● M/F have same form

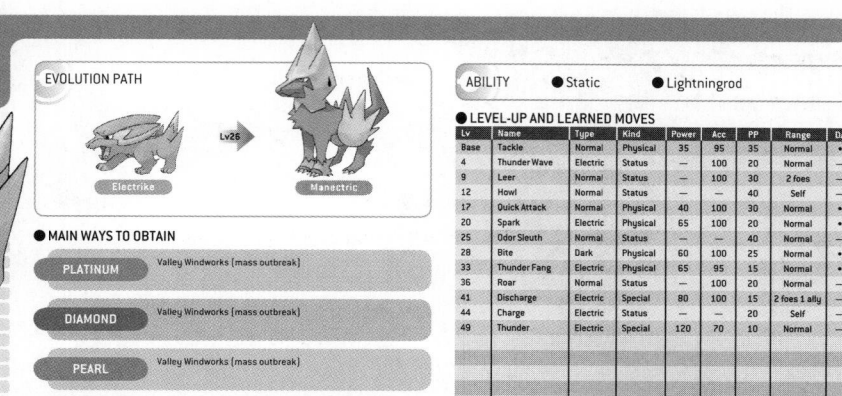

EVOLUTION PATH

Electrike — Lv26 → Manectric

● **MAIN WAYS TO OBTAIN**

PLATINUM	Valley Windworks (mass outbreak)
DIAMOND	Valley Windworks (mass outbreak)
PEARL	Valley Windworks (mass outbreak)
G B A	Catch in Ruby/Sapphire/Emerald and transfer through Pal Park

ABILITY ● Static   ● Lightningrod

● **LEVEL-UP AND LEARNED MOVES**

Lv	Name	Type	Kind	Power	Acc	PP	Range	DA
Base	Tackle	Normal	Physical	35	95	35	Normal	●
4	Thunder Wave	Electric	Status	—	100	20	Normal	●
9	Leer	Normal	Status	—	100	30	2 foes	●
12	Howl	Normal	Status	—	—	40	Self	●
17	Quick Attack	Normal	Physical	40	100	30	Normal	●
20	Spark	Electric	Physical	65	100	20	Normal	●
25	Odor Sleuth	Normal	Status	—	—	40	Normal	●
28	Bite	Dark	Physical	60	100	25	Normal	●
33	Thunder Fang	Electric	Physical	65	95	15	Normal	●
36	Roar	Normal	Status	—	100	20	Normal	●
41	Discharge	Electric	Special	80	100	15	2 foes	●
44	Charge	Electric	Status	—	—	20	Self	●
49	Thunder	Electric	Special	120	70	10	Normal	●

National Pokédex No. 310 Discharge Pokémon
Manectric

ELECTRIC

STATS
HP
ATTACK
DEFENSE
SP.ATTACK
SP.DEFENSE
SPEED

● M/F have same form

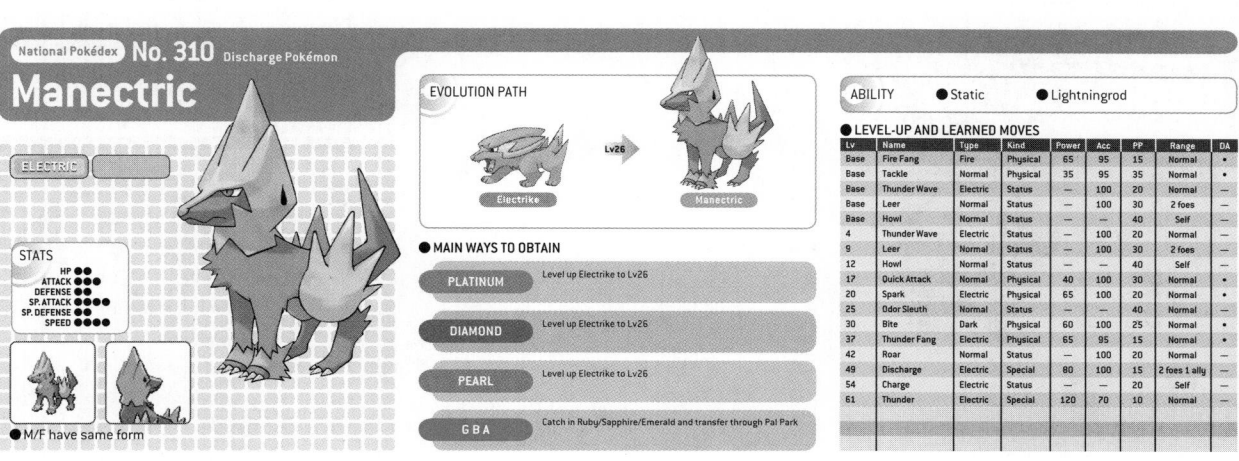

EVOLUTION PATH

Electrike — Lv26 → Manectric

● **MAIN WAYS TO OBTAIN**

PLATINUM	Level up Electrike to Lv26
DIAMOND	Level up Electrike to Lv26
PEARL	Level up Electrike to Lv26
G B A	Catch in Ruby/Sapphire/Emerald and transfer through Pal Park

ABILITY ● Static   ● Lightningrod

● **LEVEL-UP AND LEARNED MOVES**

Lv	Name	Type	Kind	Power	Acc	PP	Range	DA
Base	Fire Fang	Fire	Physical	65	95	15	Normal	●
Base	Tackle	Normal	Physical	35	95	35	Normal	●
Base	Thunder Wave	Electric	Status	—	100	20	Normal	—
Base	Leer	Normal	Status	—	100	30	2 foes	—
Base	Howl	Normal	Status	—	—	40	Self	—
4	Thunder Wave	Electric	Status	—	100	20	Normal	—
9	Leer	Normal	Status	—	100	30	2 foes	—
12	Howl	Normal	Status	—	—	40	Self	—
17	Quick Attack	Normal	Physical	40	100	30	Normal	—
20	Spark	Electric	Physical	65	100	20	Normal	—
25	Odor Sleuth	Normal	Status	—	—	40	Normal	—
30	Bite	Dark	Physical	60	100	25	Normal	—
37	Thunder Fang	Electric	Physical	65	95	15	Normal	—
42	Roar	Normal	Status	—	100	20	Normal	—
49	Discharge	Electric	Special	80	100	15	2 foes 1 ally	—
54	Charge	Electric	Status	—	—	20	Self	—
61	Thunder	Electric	Special	120	70	10	Normal	—

National Pokédex No. 311 Cheering Pokémon
Plusle

ELECTRIC

STATS
HP
ATTACK
DEFENSE
SP.ATTACK
SP.DEFENSE
SPEED

● M/F have same form

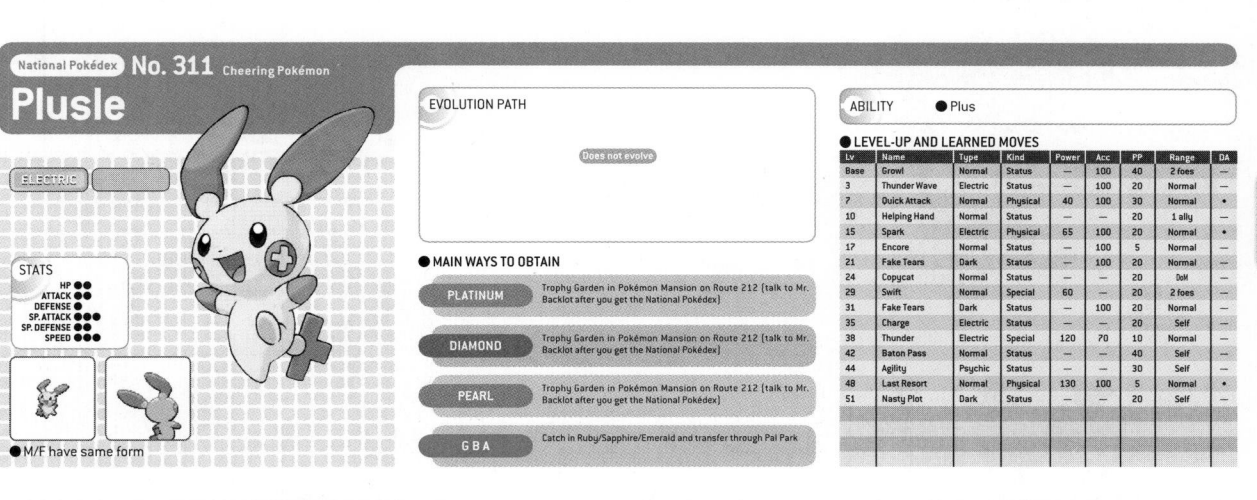

EVOLUTION PATH

Does not evolve

● **MAIN WAYS TO OBTAIN**

PLATINUM	Trophy Garden in Pokémon Mansion on Route 212 (talk to Mr. Backlot after you get the National Pokédex)
DIAMOND	Trophy Garden in Pokémon Mansion on Route 212 (talk to Mr. Backlot after you get the National Pokédex)
PEARL	Trophy Garden in Pokémon Mansion on Route 212 (talk to Mr. Backlot after you get the National Pokédex)
G B A	Catch in Ruby/Sapphire/Emerald and transfer through Pal Park

ABILITY ● Plus

● **LEVEL-UP AND LEARNED MOVES**

Lv	Name	Type	Kind	Power	Acc	PP	Range	DA
Base	Growl	Normal	Status	—	100	40	2 foes	—
3	Thunder Wave	Electric	Status	—	100	20	Normal	—
7	Quick Attack	Normal	Physical	40	100	30	Normal	—
10	Helping Hand	Normal	Status	—	—	20	1 ally	—
15	Spark	Electric	Physical	65	100	20	Normal	—
17	Encore	Normal	Status	—	100	5	Normal	—
21	Fake Tears	Dark	Status	—	100	20	Normal	—
24	Copycat	Normal	Status	—	—	20	DoM	—
29	Swift	Normal	Special	60	—	20	2 foes	—
31	Fake Tears	Dark	Status	—	100	20	Normal	—
35	Charge	Electric	Status	—	—	20	Self	—
38	Thunder	Electric	Special	120	70	10	Normal	—
42	Baton Pass	Normal	Status	—	—	40	Self	—
44	Agility	Psychic	Status	—	—	30	Self	—
48	Last Resort	Normal	Physical	130	100	5	Normal	●
51	Nasty Plot	Dark	Status	—	—	20	Self	—

National Pokédex No. 312 Cheering Pokémon
Minun

ELECTRIC

STATS
HP
ATTACK
DEFENSE
SP.ATTACK
SP.DEFENSE
SPEED

● M/F have same form

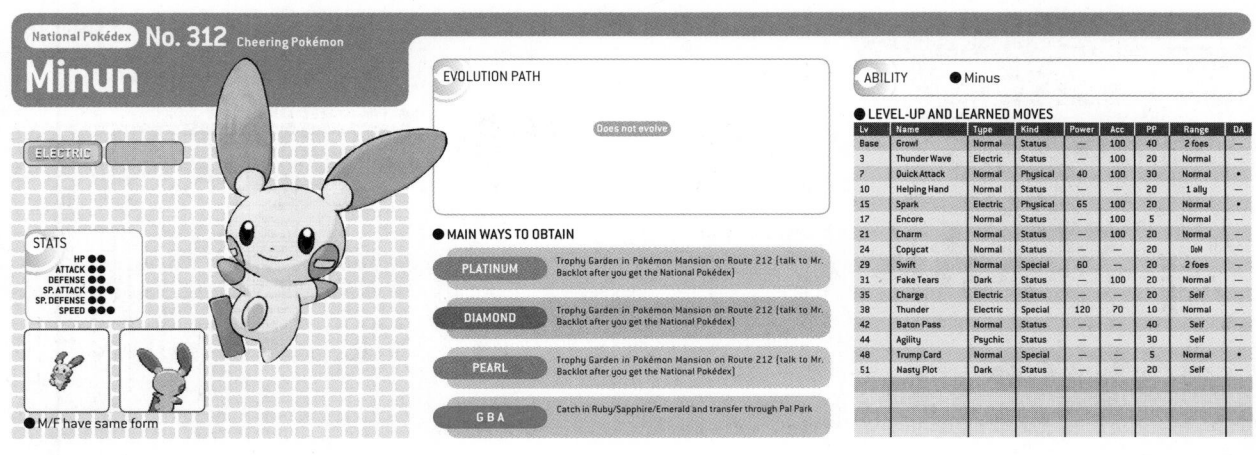

EVOLUTION PATH

Does not evolve

● **MAIN WAYS TO OBTAIN**

PLATINUM	Trophy Garden in Pokémon Mansion on Route 212 (talk to Mr. Backlot after you get the National Pokédex)
DIAMOND	Trophy Garden in Pokémon Mansion on Route 212 (talk to Mr. Backlot after you get the National Pokédex)
PEARL	Trophy Garden in Pokémon Mansion on Route 212 (talk to Mr. Backlot after you get the National Pokédex)
G B A	Catch in Ruby/Sapphire/Emerald and transfer through Pal Park

ABILITY ● Minus

● **LEVEL-UP AND LEARNED MOVES**

Lv	Name	Type	Kind	Power	Acc	PP	Range	DA
Base	Growl	Normal	Status	—	100	40	2 foes	—
3	Thunder Wave	Electric	Status	—	100	20	Normal	—
7	Quick Attack	Normal	Physical	40	100	30	Normal	—
10	Helping Hand	Normal	Status	—	—	20	1 ally	—
15	Spark	Electric	Physical	65	100	20	Normal	—
17	Encore	Normal	Status	—	100	5	Normal	—
21	Charm	Normal	Status	—	100	20	Normal	—
24	Copycat	Normal	Status	—	—	20	DoM	—
29	Swift	Normal	Special	60	—	20	2 foes	—
31	Fake Tears	Dark	Status	—	100	20	Normal	—
35	Charge	Electric	Status	—	—	20	Self	—
38	Thunder	Electric	Special	120	70	10	Normal	—
42	Baton Pass	Normal	Status	—	—	40	Self	—
44	Agility	Psychic	Status	—	—	30	Self	—
48	Trump Card	Normal	Special	—	—	5	Normal	—
51	Nasty Plot	Dark	Status	—	—	20	Self	—

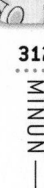

312
MINUN

National Pokédex No. 313 Firefly Pokémon
Volbeat

BUG

STATS
HP ●●●
ATTACK ●●●
DEFENSE ●●●
SP. ATTACK ●●●
SP. DEFENSE ●●●
SPEED ●●●

● Male form

EVOLUTION PATH

Does not evolve

● MAIN WAYS TO OBTAIN

PLATINUM	Route 229
DIAMOND	Route 229
PEARL	Route 229
GBA	Catch in Ruby/Sapphire/Emerald and transfer through Pal Park

ABILITY ● Illuminate ● Swarm

● LEVEL-UP AND LEARNED MOVES

Lv	Name	Type	Kind	Power	Acc	PP	Range	DA
Base	Flash	Normal	Status	—	100	20	Normal	—
Base	Tackle	Normal	Physical	35	95	35	Normal	●
5	Double Team	Normal	Status	—	—	15	Self	—
9	Confuse Ray	Ghost	Status	—	100	10	Normal	—
13	Moonlight	Normal	Status	—	—	5	Self	—
17	Quick Attack	Normal	Physical	40	100	30	Normal	●
21	Tail Glow	Bug	Status	—	—	20	Self	—
25	Signal Beam	Bug	Special	75	100	15	Normal	—
29	Protect	Normal	Status	—	—	10	Self	—
33	Helping Hand	Normal	Status	—	—	20	1 ally	—
37	Zen Headbutt	Psychic	Physical	80	90	15	Normal	●
41	Bug Buzz	Bug	Special	90	100	10	Normal	—
45	Double-Edge	Normal	Physical	120	100	15	Normal	●

National Pokédex No. 314 Firefly Pokémon
Illumise

BUG

STATS
HP ●●
ATTACK ●●
DEFENSE ●●
SP. ATTACK ●●●
SP. DEFENSE ●●●
SPEED ●●●

● Female form

EVOLUTION PATH

Does not evolve

● MAIN WAYS TO OBTAIN

PLATINUM	Route 229
DIAMOND	Route 229
PEARL	Route 229
GBA	Catch in Ruby/Sapphire/Emerald and transfer through Pal Park

ABILITY ● Oblivious ● Tinted Lens

● LEVEL-UP AND LEARNED MOVES

Lv	Name	Type	Kind	Power	Acc	PP	Range	DA
Base	Tackle	Normal	Physical	35	95	35	Normal	●
5	Sweet Scent	Normal	Status	—	100	20	2 foes	—
9	Charm	Normal	Status	—	100	20	Normal	—
13	Moonlight	Normal	Status	—	—	5	Self	—
17	Quick Attack	Normal	Physical	40	100	30	Normal	●
21	Wish	Normal	Status	—	—	10	Self	—
25	Encore	Normal	Status	—	100	5	Normal	—
29	Flatter	Dark	Status	—	100	15	Normal	—
33	Helping Hand	Normal	Status	—	—	20	1 ally	—
37	Zen Headbutt	Psychic	Physical	80	90	15	Normal	●
41	Bug Buzz	Bug	Special	90	100	10	Normal	—
45	Covet	Normal	Physical	40	100	40	Normal	—

National Pokédex No. 315 Thorn Pokémon
Roselia

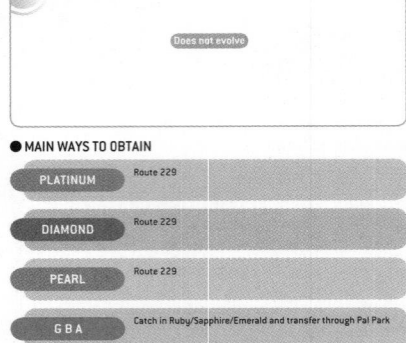

GRASS POISON

STATS
HP ●●
ATTACK ●●
DEFENSE ●●
SP. ATTACK ●●●●
SP. DEFENSE ●●●
SPEED ●●

● Male form   ● Female form

EVOLUTION PATH

Budew pg. 496 → (Level up with with enough friendship between 4 AM and 8 PM) → Roselia → (Use Shiny Stone) → Roserade pg. 496

● MAIN WAYS TO OBTAIN

PLATINUM	Route 208
DIAMOND	Route 212
PEARL	Route 212
GBA	Catch in Ruby/Sapphire and transfer through Pal Park

ABILITY ● Natural Cure ● Poison Point

● LEVEL-UP AND LEARNED MOVES

Lv	Name	Type	Kind	Power	Acc	PP	Range	DA
Base	Absorb	Grass	Special	20	100	25	Normal	—
4	Growth	Normal	Status	—	—	40	Self	—
7	Poison Sting	Poison	Physical	15	100	35	Normal	—
10	Stun Spore	Grass	Status	—	75	30	Normal	—
13	Mega Drain	Grass	Special	40	100	15	Normal	—
16	Leech Seed	Grass	Status	—	90	10	Normal	—
19	Magical Leaf	Grass	Special	60	—	20	Normal	—
22	GrassWhistle	Grass	Status	—	55	15	Normal	—
25	Giga Drain	Grass	Special	60	100	10	Normal	—
28	Toxic Spikes	Poison	Status	—	—	20	2 foes	—
31	Sweet Scent	Normal	Status	—	100	20	2 foes	—
34	Ingrain	Grass	Status	—	—	20	Self	—
37	Toxic	Poison	Status	—	85	10	Normal	—
40	Petal Dance	Grass	Special	90	100	20	1 random	●
43	Aromatherapy	Grass	Status	—	—	5	All	—
46	Synthesis	Grass	Status	—	—	5	Self	—

National Pokédex No. 316 Stomach Pokémon
Gulpin

POISON

STATS
HP ●●
ATTACK ●●
DEFENSE ●●●
SP. ATTACK ●●
SP. DEFENSE ●●
SPEED ●●

● Male form   ● Female form

EVOLUTION PATH

Gulpin → Lv26 → Swalot

● MAIN WAYS TO OBTAIN

PLATINUM	Pastoria Great Marsh [after you get the National Pokédex/ changes by day]
DIAMOND	Pastoria Great Marsh [after you get the National Pokédex/ changes by day]
PEARL	Pastoria Great Marsh [after you get the National Pokédex/ changes by day]
GBA	Catch in Ruby/Sapphire/Emerald and transfer through Pal Park

ABILITY ● Liquid Ooze ● Sticky Hold

● LEVEL-UP AND LEARNED MOVES

Lv	Name	Type	Kind	Power	Acc	PP	Range	DA
Base	Pound	Normal	Physical	40	100	35	Normal	●
6	Yawn	Normal	Status	—	—	10	Normal	—
9	Poison Gas	Poison	Status	—	55	40	Normal	—
14	Sludge	Poison	Special	65	100	20	Normal	—
17	Amnesia	Psychic	Status	—	—	20	Self	—
23	Encore	Normal	Status	—	100	5	Normal	—
28	Toxic	Poison	Status	—	85	10	Normal	—
34	Stockpile	Normal	Status	—	—	20	Self	—
34	Spit Up	Normal	Status	—	100	10	Normal	—
34	Swallow	Normal	Status	—	—	10	Self	—
39	Sludge Bomb	Poison	Special	90	100	10	Normal	—
44	Gastro Acid	Poison	Status	—	100	10	Normal	—
49	Wring Out	Normal	Special	—	100	5	Normal	●
54	Gunk Shot	Poison	Physical	120	70	5	Normal	—

Swalot

National Pokédex No. 317 Poison Bag Pokémon

POISON

STATS: HP, ATTACK, DEFENSE, SP.ATTACK, SP.DEFENSE, SPEED

●Male form ●Female form

EVOLUTION PATH: Gulpin → Lv26 → Swalot

ABILITY ●Liquid Ooze ●Steady Hold

MAIN WAYS TO OBTAIN
- PLATINUM: Level up Gulpin to Lv26
- DIAMOND: Level up Gulpin to Lv26
- PEARL: Level up Gulpin to Lv26
- GBA: Catch and evolve in Ruby/Sapphire/Emerald, and transfer through Pal Park

Lv	Name	Type	Kind	Power	Acc	PP	Range	DA
Base	Pound	Normal	Physical	40	100	35	Normal	●
Base	Yawn	Normal	Status	—	—	10	Normal	
Base	Poison Gas	Poison	Status	—	55	40	Normal	
Base	Sludge	Poison	Special	65	100	20	Normal	
6	Yawn	Normal	Status	—	—	10	Normal	
9	Poison Gas	Poison	Status	—	55	40	Normal	
14	Sludge	Poison	Special	65	100	20	Normal	
17	Amnesia	Psychic	Status	—	—	20	Self	
23	Encore	Normal	Status	—	100	5	Normal	
26	Body Slam	Normal	Physical	85	100	15	Normal	●
30	Toxic	Poison	Status	—	85	10	Normal	
38	Stockpile	Normal	Status	—	—	20	Self	
38	Spit Up	Normal	Special	—	100	10	Normal	
38	Swallow	Normal	Status	—	—	10	Self	
45	Sludge Bomb	Poison	Special	90	100	10	Normal	
52	Gastro Acid	Poison	Status	—	100	10	Normal	
55	Wring Out	Normal	Special	—	100	5	Normal	
66	Gunk Shot	Poison	Physical	120	70	5	Normal	

Carvanha

National Pokédex No. 318 Savage Pokémon

WATER DARK

●M/F have same form

EVOLUTION PATH: Carvanha → Lv30 → Sharpedo

ABILITY ●Rough Skin

MAIN WAYS TO OBTAIN
- PLATINUM: Pastoria Great Marsh (Super Rod)
- DIAMOND: Pastoria Great Marsh (Super Rod)
- PEARL: Pastoria Great Marsh (Super Rod)
- GBA: Catch in Ruby/Sapphire/Emerald and transfer through Pal Park

Lv	Name	Type	Kind	Power	Acc	PP	Range	DA
Base	Leer	Normal	Status	—	100	30	2 foes	
Base	Bite	Dark	Physical	60	100	25	Normal	●
6	Rage	Normal	Physical	20	100	20	Normal	
8	Focus Energy	Normal	Status	—	—	30	Self	
11	Scary Face	Normal	Status	—	90	10	Normal	
16	Ice Fang	Ice	Physical	65	95	15	Normal	●
18	Screech	Normal	Status	—	85	40	Normal	
21	Swagger	Normal	Status	—	90	15	Normal	
26	Assurance	Dark	Physical	50	100	10	Normal	
28	Crunch	Dark	Physical	80	100	15	Normal	●
31	Aqua Jet	Water	Physical	40	100	20	Normal	
36	Agility	Psychic	Status	—	—	30	Self	
38	Take Down	Normal	Physical	90	85	20	Normal	

Sharpedo

National Pokédex No. 319 Brutal Pokémon

WATER DARK

●M/F have same form

EVOLUTION PATH: Carvanha → Lv30 → Sharpedo

ABILITY ●Rough Skin

MAIN WAYS TO OBTAIN
- PLATINUM: Level up Carvanha to Lv30
- DIAMOND: Route 213 (Super Rod)
- PEARL: Route 213 (Super Rod)
- GBA: Catch in Ruby/Sapphire/Emerald and transfer through Pal Park

Lv	Name	Type	Kind	Power	Acc	PP	Range	DA
Base	Feint	Normal	Physical	50	100	10	Normal	
Base	Leer	Normal	Status	—	100	30	2 foes	
Base	Bite	Dark	Physical	60	100	25	Normal	●
Base	Rage	Normal	Physical	20	100	20	Normal	
Base	Focus Energy	Normal	Status	—	—	30	Self	
6	Rage	Normal	Physical	20	100	20	Normal	
8	Focus Energy	Normal	Status	—	—	30	Self	
11	Scary Face	Normal	Status	—	90	10	Normal	
16	Ice Fang	Ice	Physical	65	95	15	Normal	●
18	Screech	Normal	Status	—	85	40	Normal	
21	Swagger	Normal	Status	—	90	15	Normal	
26	Assurance	Dark	Physical	50	100	10	Normal	
28	Crunch	Dark	Physical	80	100	15	Normal	●
30	Slash	Normal	Physical	70	100	20	Normal	
34	Aqua Jet	Water	Physical	40	100	20	Normal	
40	Taunt	Dark	Status	—	100	20	Normal	
45	Agility	Psychic	Status	—	—	30	Self	
50	Skull Bash	Normal	Physical	100	100	15	Normal	
56	Night Slash	Dark	Physical	70	100	15	Normal	

Wailmer

National Pokédex No. 320 Ball Whale Pokémon

WATER

●M/F have same form

EVOLUTION PATH: Wailmer → Lv40 → Wailord

ABILITY ●Water Veil ●Oblivious

MAIN WAYS TO OBTAIN
- PLATINUM: Route 223 (Super Rod)
- DIAMOND: Route 223 (Super Rod)
- PEARL: Route 223 (Super Rod)
- GBA: Catch in Ruby/Sapphire/Emerald and transfer through Pal Park

Lv	Name	Type	Kind	Power	Acc	PP	Range	DA
Base	Splash	Normal	Status	—	—	40	Self	
4	Growl	Normal	Status	—	100	40	2 foes	
7	Water Gun	Water	Special	40	100	25	Normal	
11	Rollout	Rock	Physical	30	90	20	Normal	
14	Whirlpool	Water	Special	15	70	15	Normal	
17	Astonish	Ghost	Physical	30	100	15	Normal	
21	Water Pulse	Water	Special	60	100	20	Normal	
24	Mist	Ice	Status	—	—	30	2 allies	
27	Rest	Psychic	Status	—	—	10	Self	
31	Brine	Water	Special	65	100	10	Normal	
34	Water Spout	Water	Special	150	100	5	2 foes	
37	Amnesia	Psychic	Status	—	—	20	Self	
41	Dive	Water	Physical	80	100	10	Normal	
44	Bounce	Flying	Physical	85	85	5	Normal	
47	Hydro Pump	Water	Special	120	80	5	Normal	

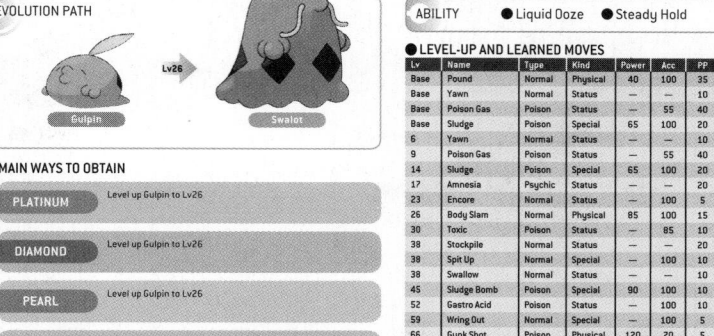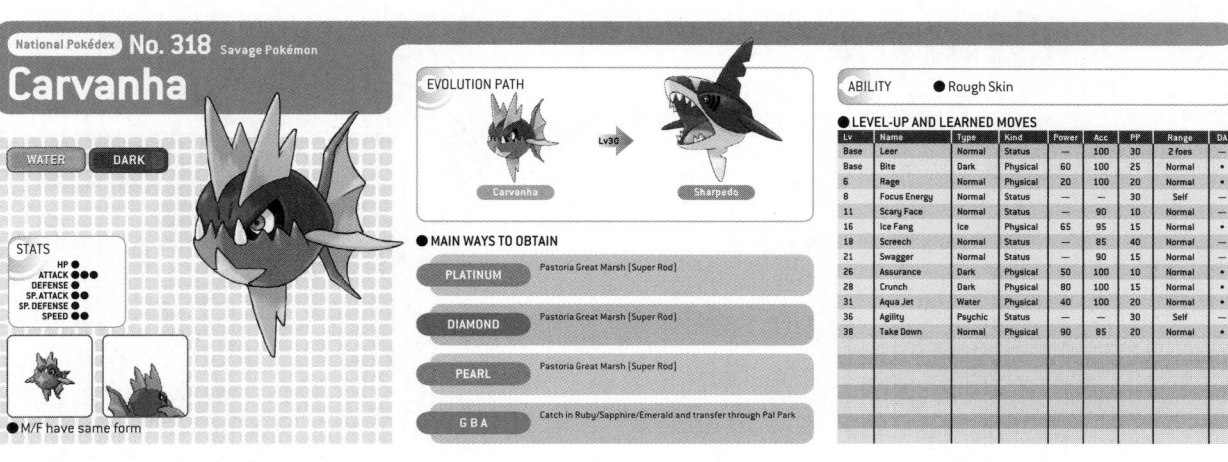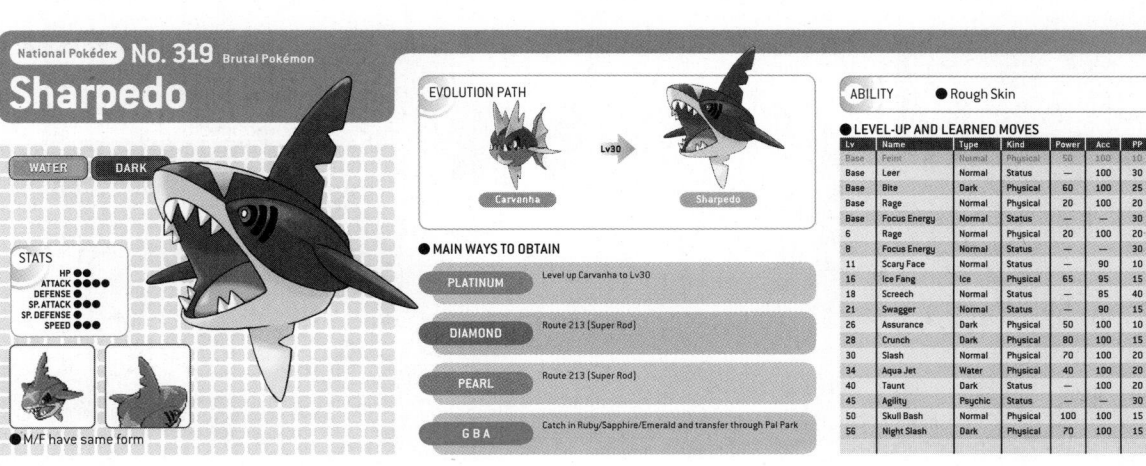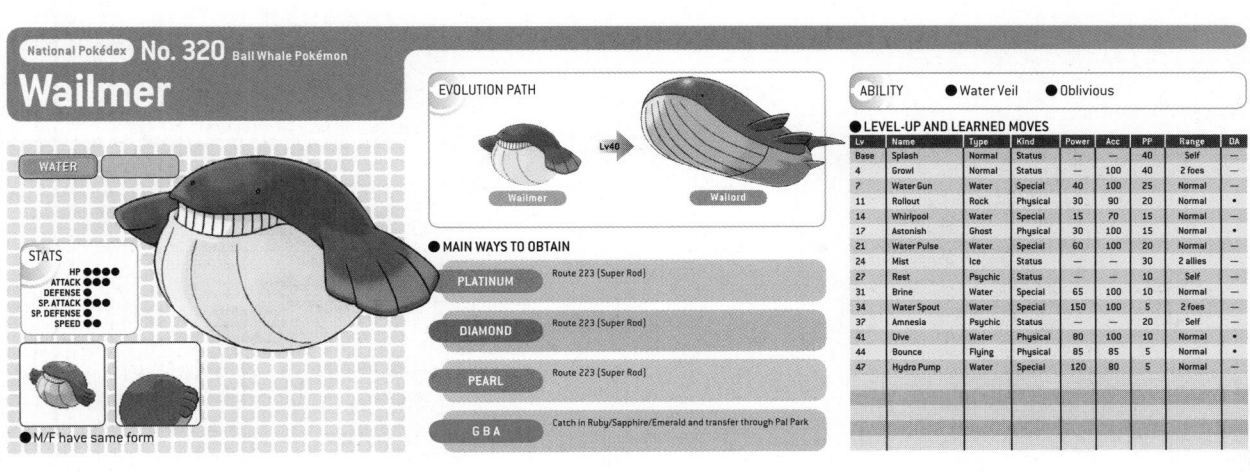

320 WAILMER

Wailord

National Pokédex No. 321 — Float Whale Pokémon

WATER

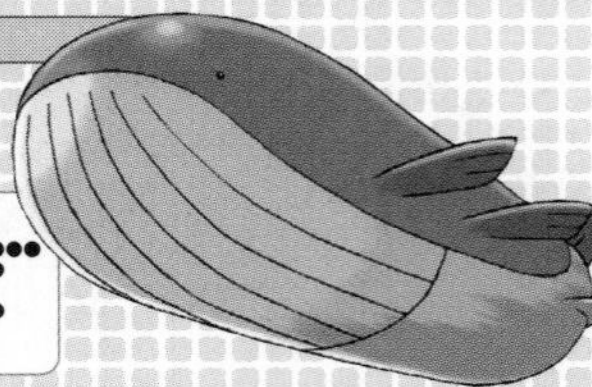

STATS
- HP ●●●●
- ATTACK ●●●
- DEFENSE ●●
- SP. ATTACK ●●●
- SP. DEFENSE ●●
- SPEED ●●

● M/F have same form

EVOLUTION PATH

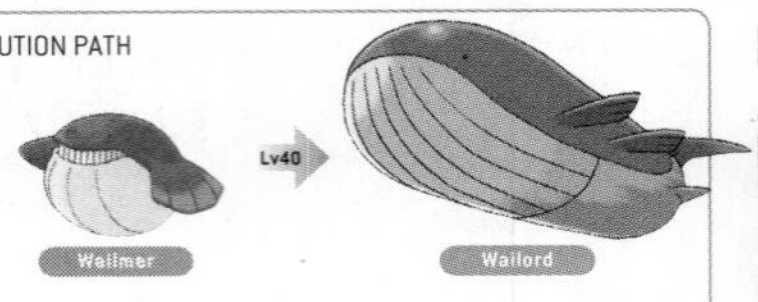

Wailmer → Lv40 → Wailord

MAIN WAYS TO OBTAIN

PLATINUM	Route 223 (Super Rod)
DIAMOND	Route 223 (Super Rod)
PEARL	Route 223 (Super Rod)
G B A	Catch in Ruby/Sapphire/Emerald and transfer through Pal Park

ABILITY ● Water Veil ● Oblivious

LEVEL-UP AND LEARNED MOVES

Lv	Name	Type	Kind	Power	Acc	PP	Range	DA
Base	Splash	Normal	Status	—		40	Self	—
Base	Growl	Normal	Status	—	100	40	2 foes	—
Base	Water Gun	Water	Special	40	100	25	Normal	—
Base	Rollout	Rock	Physical	30	90	20	Normal	•
4	Growl	Normal	Status	—	100	40	2 foes	—
7	Water Gun	Water	Special	40	100	25	Normal	—
11	Rollout	Rock	Physical	30	90	20	Normal	•
14	Whirlpool	Water	Special	15	70	15	Normal	—
17	Astonish	Ghost	Physical	30	100	15	Normal	•
21	Water Pulse	Water	Special	60	100	20	Normal	—
24	Mist	Ice	Status	—	—	30	2 allies	—
27	Rest	Psychic	Status	—	—	10	Self	—
31	Brine	Water	Special	65	100	10	Normal	—
34	Water Spout	Water	Special	150	100	5	2 foes	—
37	Amnesia	Psychic	Status	—	—	20	Self	—
46	Dive	Water	Physical	80	100	10	Normal	•
54	Bounce	Flying	Physical	85	85	5	Normal	—
62	Hydro Pump	Water	Special	120	80	5	Normal	—

Numel

National Pokédex No. 322 — Numb Pokémon

FIRE GROUND

STATS
- HP ●●
- ATTACK ●●
- DEFENSE ●●
- SP. ATTACK ●●
- SP. DEFENSE ●●
- SPEED ●

● Male form ● Female form

EVOLUTION PATH

Numel → Lv33 → Camerupt

MAIN WAYS TO OBTAIN

PLATINUM	Route 227
DIAMOND	Route 227
PEARL	Route 227
G B A	Catch in Ruby/Sapphire/Emerald and transfer through Pal Park

ABILITY ● Oblivious ● Simple

LEVEL-UP AND LEARNED MOVES

Lv	Name	Type	Kind	Power	Acc	PP	Range	DA
Base	Growl	Normal	Status	—	100	40	2 foes	—
Base	Tackle	Normal	Physical	35	95	35	Normal	•
5	Ember	Fire	Special	40	100	25	Normal	—
11	Magnitude	Ground	Physical	—	100	30	2 foes • 1 ally	—
15	Focus Energy	Normal	Status	—	—	30	Self	—
21	Take Down	Normal	Physical	90	85	20	Normal	•
25	Amnesia	Psychic	Status	—	—	20	Self	—
31	Lava Plume	Fire	Special	80	100	15	2 foes • 1 ally	—
35	Earth Power	Ground	Special	90	100	10	Normal	—
41	Earthquake	Ground	Physical	100	100	10	2 foes • 1 ally	—
45	Flamethrower	Fire	Special	95	100	15	Normal	—
51	Double-Edge	Normal	Physical	120	100	15	Normal	—

Camerupt

National Pokédex No. 323 — Eruption Pokémon

FIRE GROUND

STATS
- HP ●●●
- ATTACK ●●●
- DEFENSE ●●●
- SP. ATTACK ●●●●
- SP. DEFENSE ●●●
- SPEED ●●

● Male form ● Female form

EVOLUTION PATH

Numel → Lv33 → Camerupt

MAIN WAYS TO OBTAIN

PLATINUM	Route 227
DIAMOND	Route 227
PEARL	Route 227
G B A	Catch and evolve in Ruby/Sapphire/Emerald, and transfer through Pal Park

ABILITY ● Magma Armor ● Solid Rock

LEVEL-UP AND LEARNED MOVES

Lv	Name	Type	Kind	Power	Acc	PP	Range	DA
Base	Growl	Normal	Status	—	100	40	2 foes	—
Base	Tackle	Normal	Physical	35	95	35	Normal	•
Base	Ember	Fire	Special	40	100	25	Normal	—
Base	Magnitude	Ground	Physical	—	100	30	2 foes • 1 ally	—
5	Ember	Fire	Special	40	100	25	Normal	—
11	Magnitude	Ground	Physical	—	100	30	2 foes • 1 ally	—
15	Focus Energy	Normal	Status	—	—	30	Self	—
21	Take Down	Normal	Physical	90	85	20	Normal	•
25	Amnesia	Psychic	Status	—	—	20	Self	—
31	Lava Plume	Fire	Special	80	100	15	2 foes • 1 ally	—
33	Rock Slide	Rock	Physical	75	90	10	2 foes	—
39	Earth Power	Ground	Special	90	100	10	Normal	—
49	Earthquake	Ground	Physical	100	100	10	2 foes • 1 ally	—
57	Eruption	Fire	Special	150	100	5	2 foes	—
67	Fissure	Ground	Physical	—	30	5	Normal	—

Torkoal

National Pokédex No. 324 — Coal Pokémon

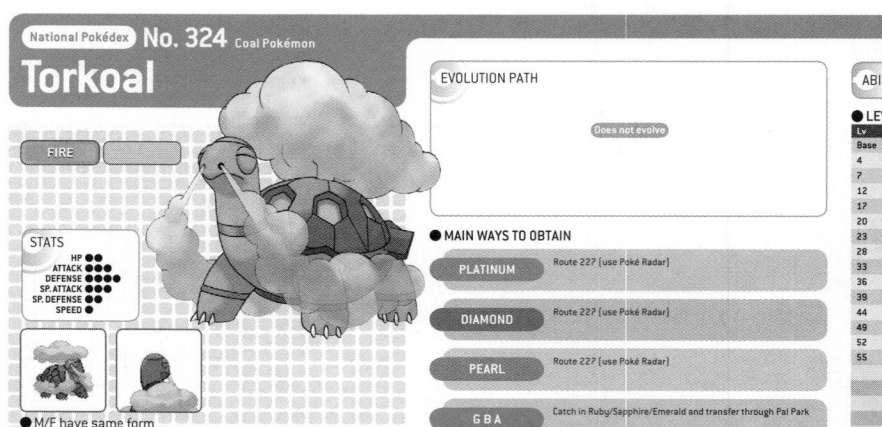

FIRE

STATS
- HP ●●
- ATTACK ●●●
- DEFENSE ●●●●●
- SP. ATTACK ●●●
- SP. DEFENSE ●●●
- SPEED ●●

● M/F have same form

EVOLUTION PATH

Does not evolve

MAIN WAYS TO OBTAIN

PLATINUM	Route 227 (use Poké Radar)
DIAMOND	Route 227 (use Poké Radar)
PEARL	Route 227 (use Poké Radar)
G B A	Catch in Ruby/Sapphire/Emerald and transfer through Pal Park

ABILITY ● White Smoke

LEVEL-UP AND LEARNED MOVES

Lv	Name	Type	Kind	Power	Acc	PP	Range	DA
Base	Ember	Fire	Special	40	100	25	Normal	—
4	Smog	Poison	Special	20	70	20	Normal	—
7	Withdraw	Water	Status	—	—	40	Self	—
12	Curse	???	Status	—	—	10	Normal • Self	—
17	Fire Spin	Fire	Special	15	70	15	Normal	—
20	SmokeScreen	Normal	Status	—	100	20	Normal	—
23	Rapid Spin	Normal	Physical	20	100	40	Normal	•
28	Flamethrower	Fire	Special	95	100	15	Normal	—
33	Body Slam	Normal	Physical	85	100	15	Normal	•
36	Protect	Normal	Status	—	—	10	Self	—
39	Lava Plume	Fire	Special	80	100	15	2 foes • 1 ally	—
44	Iron Defense	Steel	Status	—	—	15	Self	—
49	Amnesia	Psychic	Status	—	—	20	Self	—
52	Flail	Normal	Physical	—	100	15	Normal	•
55	Heat Wave	Fire	Special	100	90	10	2 foes	—

Spoink

National Pokédex **No. 325** Bounce Pokémon

PSYCHIC

STATS
- HP ●●
- ATTACK ●
- DEFENSE ●
- SP. ATTACK ●●●
- SP. DEFENSE ●●●
- SPEED ●●

● M/F have same form

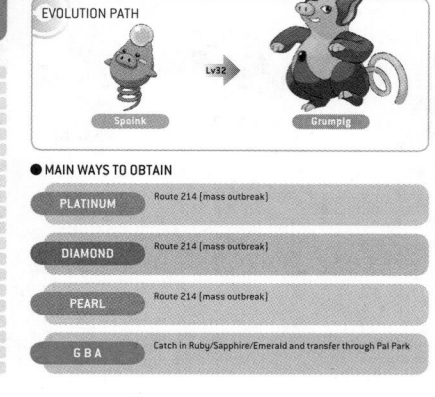

EVOLUTION PATH

Spoink → **Lv32** → Grumpig

● MAIN WAYS TO OBTAIN

PLATINUM	Route 214 (mass outbreak)
DIAMOND	Route 214 (mass outbreak)
PEARL	Route 214 (mass outbreak)
GBA	Catch in Ruby/Sapphire/Emerald and transfer through Pal Park

ABILITY ● Thick Fat ● Own Tempo

● LEVEL-UP AND LEARNED MOVES

Lv	Name	Type	Kind	Power	Acc	PP	Range	DA
Base	Splash	Normal	Status	—	—	40	Self	—
7	Psywave	Psychic	Special	—	80	15	Normal	—
10	Odor Sleuth	Normal	Status	—	—	40	Normal	—
14	Psybeam	Psychic	Special	65	100	20	Normal	—
15	Psych Up	Normal	Status	—	—	10	Normal	—
18	Confuse Ray	Ghost	Status	—	100	10	Normal	—
21	Magic Coat	Psychic	Status	—	—	15	Self	—
26	Zen Headbutt	Psychic	Physical	80	90	15	Normal	•
29	Rest	Psychic	Status	—	—	10	Self	—
29	Snore	Normal	Special	40	100	15	Normal	•
34	Payback	Dark	Physical	50	100	10	Normal	•
41	Psychic	Psychic	Special	90	100	10	Normal	—
46	Power Gem	Rock	Special	70	100	20	Normal	—
48	Bounce	Flying	Physical	85	85	5	Normal	•

Grumpig

National Pokédex **No. 326** Manipulate Pokémon

PSYCHIC

STATS
- HP ●●
- ATTACK ●●●
- DEFENSE ●●
- SP. ATTACK ●●●
- SP. DEFENSE ●●●●
- SPEED ●●●

● M/F have same form

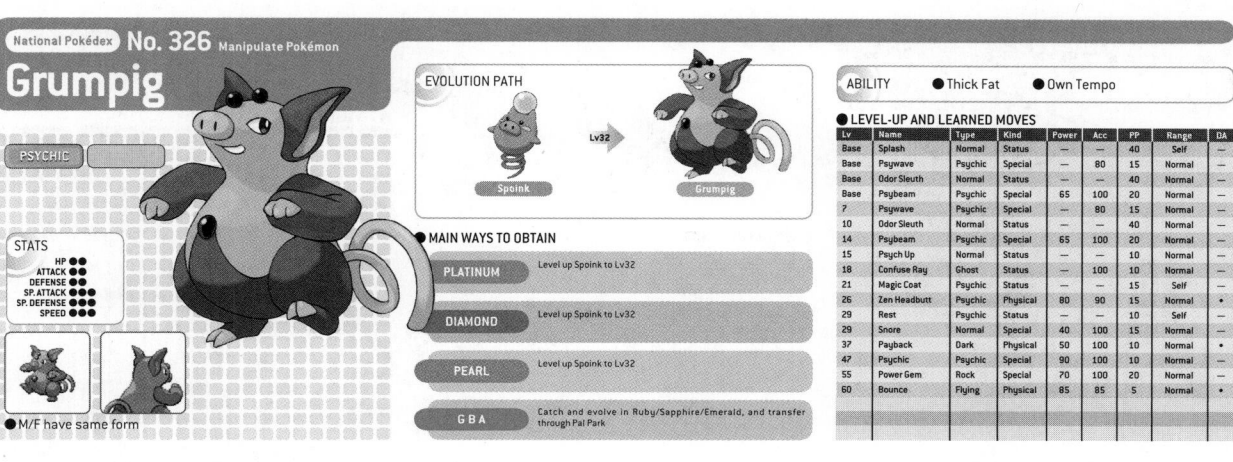

EVOLUTION PATH

Spoink → **Lv32** → Grumpig

● MAIN WAYS TO OBTAIN

PLATINUM	Level up Spoink to Lv32
DIAMOND	Level up Spoink to Lv32
PEARL	Level up Spoink to Lv32
GBA	Catch and evolve in Ruby/Sapphire/Emerald, and transfer through Pal Park

ABILITY ● Thick Fat ● Own Tempo

● LEVEL-UP AND LEARNED MOVES

Lv	Name	Type	Kind	Power	Acc	PP	Range	DA
Base	Splash	Normal	Status	—	—	40	Self	—
Base	Psywave	Psychic	Special	—	80	15	Normal	—
Base	Odor Sleuth	Normal	Status	—	—	40	Normal	—
Base	Psybeam	Psychic	Special	65	100	20	Normal	—
7	Psywave	Psychic	Special	—	80	15	Normal	—
10	Odor Sleuth	Normal	Status	—	—	40	Normal	—
14	Psybeam	Psychic	Special	65	100	20	Normal	—
15	Psych Up	Normal	Status	—	—	10	Normal	—
18	Confuse Ray	Ghost	Status	—	100	10	Normal	—
21	Magic Coat	Psychic	Status	—	—	15	Self	—
26	Zen Headbutt	Psychic	Physical	80	90	15	Normal	•
29	Rest	Psychic	Status	—	—	10	Self	—
29	Snore	Normal	Special	40	100	15	Normal	•
37	Payback	Dark	Physical	50	100	10	Normal	•
47	Psychic	Psychic	Special	90	100	10	Normal	—
55	Power Gem	Rock	Special	70	100	20	Normal	—
60	Bounce	Flying	Physical	85	85	5	Normal	—

Spinda

National Pokédex **No. 327** Spot Panda Pokémon

NORMAL

STATS
- HP ●●
- ATTACK ●●●
- DEFENSE ●●●
- SP. ATTACK ●●●
- SP. DEFENSE ●●●
- SPEED ●●●

● M/F have same form

EVOLUTION PATH

Does not evolve

● MAIN WAYS TO OBTAIN

PLATINUM	Route 227 (mass outbreak)
DIAMOND	Route 227 (mass outbreak)
PEARL	Route 227 (mass outbreak)
GBA	Catch in Ruby/Sapphire/Emerald and transfer through Pal Park

ABILITY ● Own Tempo ● Tangled Feet

● LEVEL-UP AND LEARNED MOVES

Lv	Name	Type	Kind	Power	Acc	PP	Range	DA
Base	Tackle	Normal	Physical	35	95	35	Normal	—
5	Uproar	Normal	Special	50	100	10	1 random	—
10	Copycat	Normal	Status	—	—	20	Self	—
14	Faint Attack	Dark	Physical	60	—	20	Normal	—
19	Psybeam	Psychic	Special	65	100	20	Normal	—
23	Hypnosis	Psychic	Status	—	60	20	Normal	—
28	Dizzy Punch	Normal	Physical	70	100	10	Normal	—
32	Sucker Punch	Dark	Physical	80	100	5	Normal	—
37	Teeter Dance	Normal	Status	—	100	20	2 foes • 1 ally	—
41	Psych Up	Normal	Status	—	—	10	Normal	—
46	Double-Edge	Normal	Physical	120	100	15	Normal	—
50	Flail	Normal	Physical	—	100	15	Normal	—
55	Thrash	Normal	Physical	90	100	20	1 random	—

Trapinch

National Pokédex **No. 328** Ant Pit Pokémon

GROUND

STATS
- HP ●
- ATTACK ●●●●
- DEFENSE ●●●
- SP. ATTACK ●
- SP. DEFENSE ●
- SPEED ●

● M/F have same form

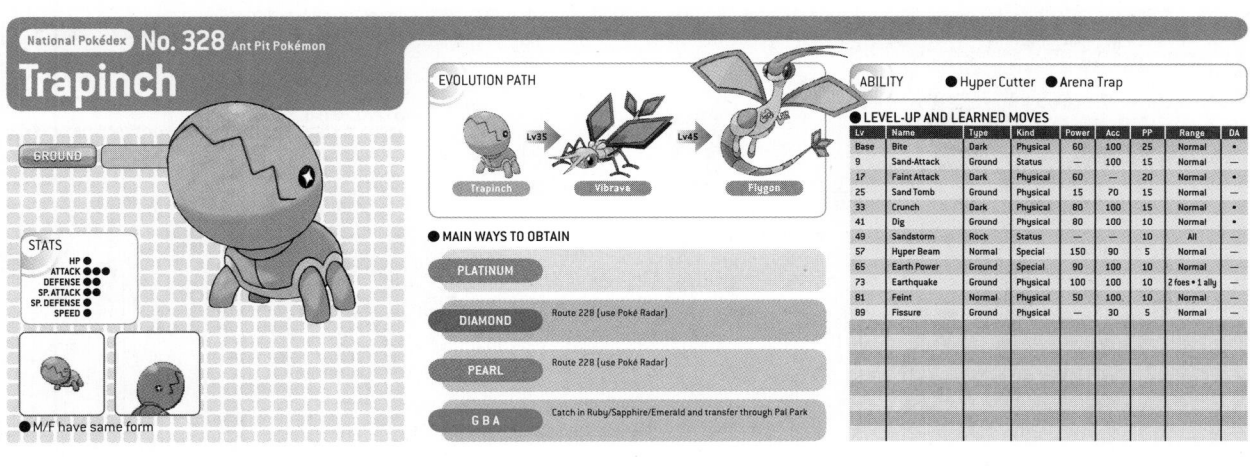

EVOLUTION PATH

Trapinch → **Lv35** → Vibrava → **Lv45** → Flygon

● MAIN WAYS TO OBTAIN

PLATINUM	
DIAMOND	Route 228 (use Poké Radar)
PEARL	Route 228 (use Poké Radar)
GBA	Catch in Ruby/Sapphire/Emerald and transfer through Pal Park

ABILITY ● Hyper Cutter ● Arena Trap

● LEVEL-UP AND LEARNED MOVES

Lv	Name	Type	Kind	Power	Acc	PP	Range	DA
Base	Bite	Dark	Physical	60	100	25	Normal	•
9	Sand-Attack	Ground	Status	—	100	15	Normal	—
17	Faint Attack	Dark	Physical	60	—	20	Normal	—
25	Sand Tomb	Ground	Physical	15	70	15	Normal	—
33	Crunch	Dark	Physical	80	100	15	Normal	—
41	Dig	Ground	Physical	80	100	10	Normal	—
49	Sandstorm	Rock	Status	—	—	10	All	—
57	Hyper Beam	Normal	Special	150	90	5	Normal	—
65	Earth Power	Ground	Special	90	100	10	Normal	—
73	Earthquake	Ground	Physical	100	100	10	2 foes • 1 ally	—
81	Feint	Normal	Physical	50	100	10	Normal	—
89	Fissure	Ground	Physical	—	30	5	Normal	—

No. 329 Vibration Pokémon
Vibrava

GROUND DRAGON

STATS
HP ●●
ATTACK ●●●
DEFENSE ●●
SP.ATTACK ●●●
SP.DEFENSE ●●
SPEED ●●●

● M/F have same form

EVOLUTION PATH
Trapinch → Lv35 → Vibrava → Lv45 → Flygon

ABILITY ● Levitate

● LEVEL-UP AND LEARNED MOVES

Lv	Name	Type	Kind	Power	Acc	PP	Range	DA
Base	SonicBoom	Normal	Special	—	90	20	Normal	—
Base	Sand-Attack	Ground	Status	—	100	15	Normal	—
Base	Faint Attack	Dark	Physical	60	—	20	Normal	•
Base	Sand Tomb	Ground	Physical	15	70	15	Normal	—
9	Sand-Attack	Ground	Status	—	100	15	Normal	—
17	Faint Attack	Dark	Physical	60	—	20	Normal	•
25	Sand Tomb	Ground	Physical	15	70	15	Normal	—
33	Supersonic	Normal	Status	—	55	20	Normal	—
35	DragonBreath	Dragon	Special	60	100	20	Normal	—
41	Screech	Normal	Status	—	85	40	Normal	—
49	Sandstorm	Rock	Status	—	—	10	All	—
57	Hyper Beam	Normal	Special	150	90	5	Normal	—

● MAIN WAYS TO OBTAIN

PLATINUM	
DIAMOND	Route 228 (use Poké Radar)
PEARL	Route 228 (use Poké Radar)
GBA	Catch and evolve in Ruby/Sapphire/Emerald, and transfer through Pal Park

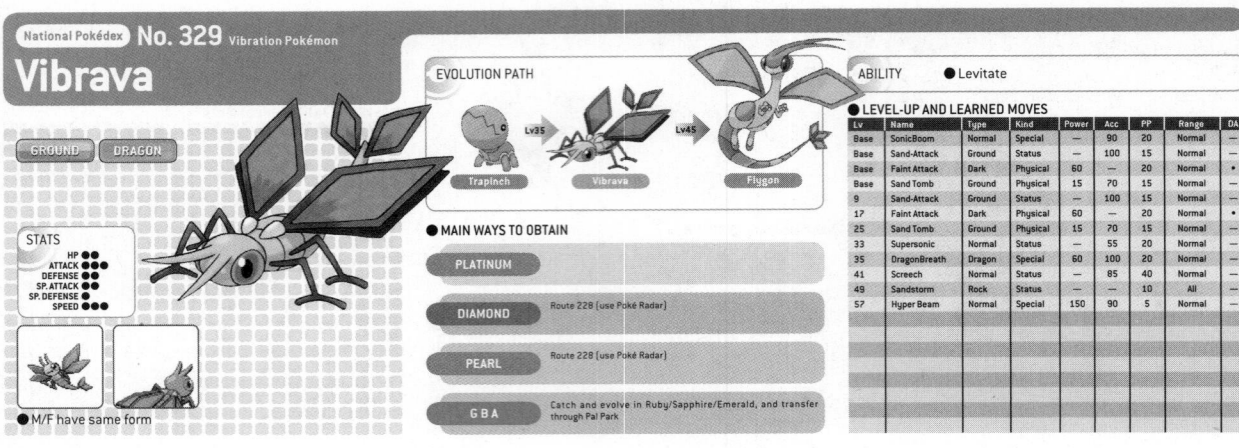

No. 330 Mystic Pokémon
Flygon

GROUND DRAGON

STATS
HP ●●●
ATTACK ●●●●
DEFENSE ●●●
SP.ATTACK ●●●
SP.DEFENSE ●●●
SPEED ●●●●

● M/F have same form

EVOLUTION PATH
Trapinch → Lv35 → Vibrava → Lv45 → Flygon

ABILITY ● Levitate

● LEVEL-UP AND LEARNED MOVES

Lv	Name	Type	Kind	Power	Acc	PP	Range	DA
Base	SonicBoom	Normal	Special	—	90	20	Normal	—
Base	Sand-Attack	Ground	Status	—	100	15	Normal	—
Base	Faint Attack	Dark	Physical	60	—	20	Normal	•
Base	Sand Tomb	Ground	Physical	15	70	15	Normal	—
9	Sand-Attack	Ground	Status	—	100	15	Normal	—
17	Faint Attack	Dark	Physical	60	—	20	Normal	•
25	Sand Tomb	Ground	Physical	15	70	15	Normal	—
33	Supersonic	Normal	Status	—	55	20	Normal	—
35	DragonBreath	Dragon	Special	60	100	20	Normal	—
41	Screech	Normal	Status	—	85	40	Normal	—
45	Dragon Claw	Dragon	Physical	80	100	15	Normal	•
49	Sandstorm	Rock	Status	—	—	10	All	—
57	Hyper Beam	Normal	Special	150	90	5	Normal	—

● MAIN WAYS TO OBTAIN

PLATINUM	
DIAMOND	Level up Vibrava to Lv45
PEARL	Level up Vibrava to Lv45
GBA	Catch and evolve in Ruby/Sapphire/Emerald, and transfer through Pal Park

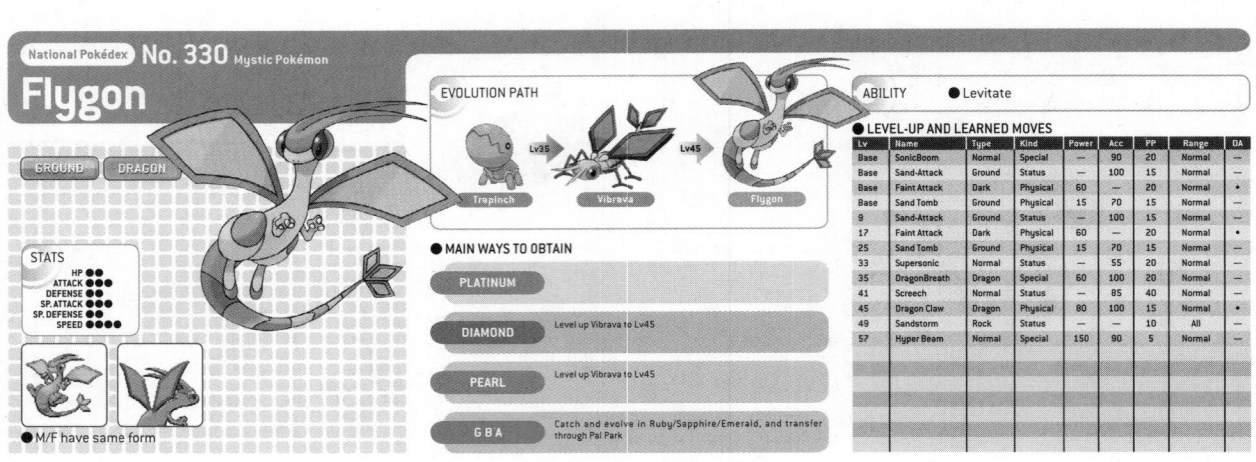

No. 331 Cactus Pokémon
Cacnea

GRASS

STATS
HP ●●●
ATTACK ●●●
DEFENSE ●●
SP.ATTACK ●●●
SP.DEFENSE ●●
SPEED ●

● M/F have same form

EVOLUTION PATH
Cacnea → Lv32 → Cacturne

ABILITY ● Sand Veil

● LEVEL-UP AND LEARNED MOVES

Lv	Name	Type	Kind	Power	Acc	PP	Range	DA
Base	Poison Sting	Poison	Physical	15	100	35	Normal	—
Base	Leer	Normal	Status	—	100	30	2 foes	—
5	Absorb	Grass	Special	20	100	25	Normal	—
9	Growth	Normal	Status	—	—	40	Self	—
13	Leech Seed	Grass	Status	—	90	10	Normal	—
17	Sand-Attack	Ground	Status	—	100	15	Normal	—
21	Pin Missile	Bug	Physical	14	85	20	Normal	—
25	Ingrain	Grass	Status	—	—	20	Self	—
29	Faint Attack	Dark	Physical	60	—	20	Normal	•
33	Spikes	Ground	Status	—	—	20	2 foes	—
37	Sucker Punch	Dark	Physical	80	100	5	Normal	•
41	Payback	Dark	Physical	50	100	10	Normal	•
45	Needle Arm	Grass	Physical	60	100	15	Normal	•
49	Cotton Spore	Grass	Status	—	85	40	Normal	—
53	Sandstorm	Rock	Status	—	—	10	All	—
57	Destiny Bond	Ghost	Status	—	—	5	Self	—

● MAIN WAYS TO OBTAIN

PLATINUM	Route 228
DIAMOND	Route 228
PEARL	Route 228
GBA	Catch in Ruby/Sapphire/Emerald and transfer through Pal Park

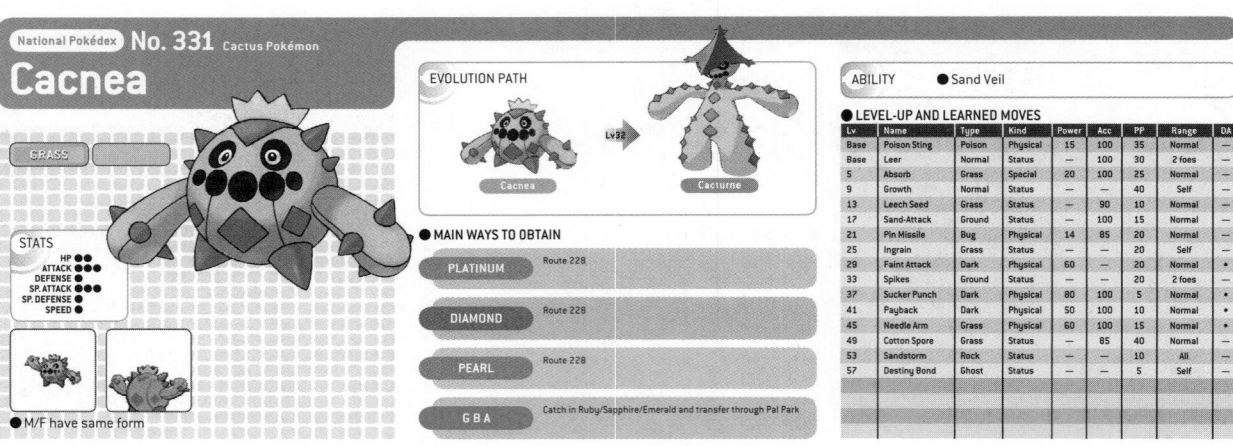

No. 332 Scarecrow Pokémon
Cacturne

GRASS DARK

STATS
HP ●●
ATTACK ●●●●
DEFENSE ●●●
SP.ATTACK ●●●
SP.DEFENSE ●●
SPEED ●●

● Male form   ● Female form

EVOLUTION PATH
Cacnea → Lv32 → Cacturne

ABILITY ● Sand Veil

● LEVEL-UP AND LEARNED MOVES

Lv	Name	Type	Kind	Power	Acc	PP	Range	DA
Base	Revenge	Fighting	Physical	60	100	10	Normal	•
Base	Poison Sting	Poison	Physical	15	100	35	Normal	—
Base	Leer	Normal	Status	—	100	30	2 foes	—
Base	Absorb	Grass	Special	20	100	25	Normal	—
Base	Growth	Normal	Status	—	—	40	Self	—
5	Absorb	Grass	Special	20	100	25	Normal	—
9	Growth	Normal	Status	—	—	40	Self	—
13	Leech Seed	Grass	Status	—	90	10	Normal	—
17	Sand-Attack	Ground	Status	—	100	15	Normal	—
21	Pin Missile	Bug	Physical	14	85	20	Normal	—
25	Ingrain	Grass	Status	—	—	20	Self	—
29	Faint Attack	Dark	Physical	60	—	20	Normal	•
35	Spikes	Ground	Status	—	—	20	2 foes	—
41	Sucker Punch	Dark	Physical	80	100	5	Normal	•
47	Payback	Dark	Physical	50	100	10	Normal	•
53	Needle Arm	Grass	Physical	60	100	15	Normal	•
59	Cotton Spore	Grass	Status	—	85	40	Normal	—
65	Sandstorm	Rock	Status	—	—	10	All	—
71	Destiny Bond	Ghost	Status	—	—	5	Self	—

● MAIN WAYS TO OBTAIN

PLATINUM	Route 228
DIAMOND	Route 228
PEARL	Route 228
GBA	Catch and evolve in Ruby/Sapphire/Emerald, and transfer through Pal Park

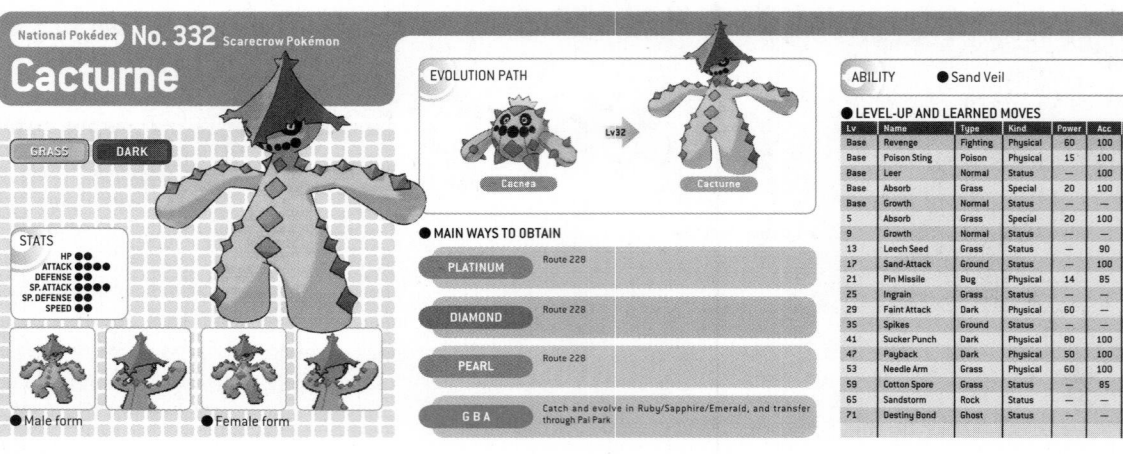

Swablu

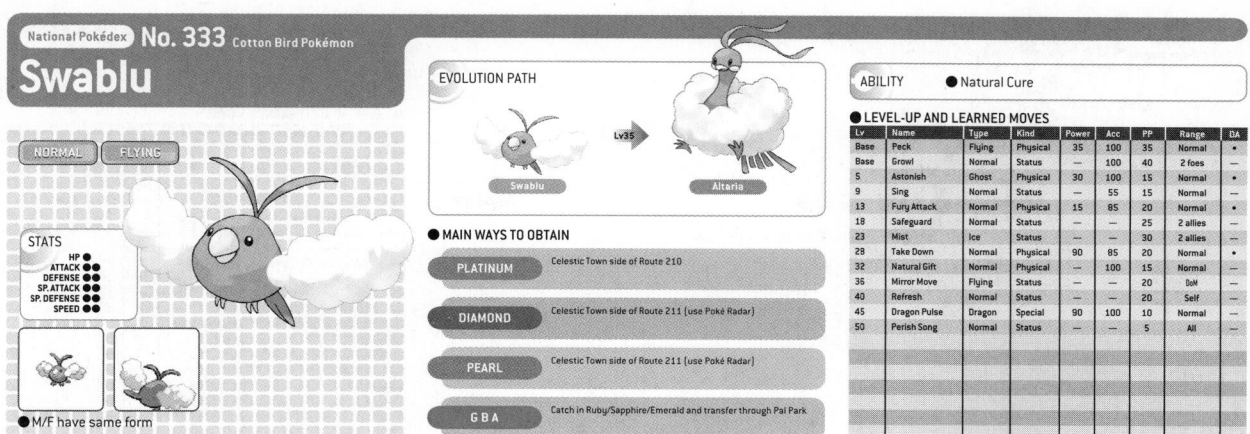

National Pokédex No. 333 Cotton Bird Pokémon

NORMAL FLYING

STATS
HP ●
ATTACK ●●
DEFENSE ●●
SP.ATTACK ●●
SP.DEFENSE ●●
SPEED ●●

● M/F have same form

EVOLUTION PATH
Swablu — Lv35 → Altaria

ABILITY ● Natural Cure

● **LEVEL-UP AND LEARNED MOVES**

Lv	Name	Type	Kind	Power	Acc	PP	Range	DA
Base	Peck	Flying	Physical	35	100	35	Normal	•
Base	Growl	Normal	Status	—	100	40	2 foes	•
5	Astonish	Ghost	Physical	30	100	15	Normal	•
9	Sing	Normal	Status	—	55	15	Normal	•
13	Fury Attack	Normal	Physical	15	85	20	Normal	•
18	Safeguard	Normal	Status	—	—	25	2 allies	•
23	Mist	Ice	Status	—	—	30	2 allies	•
28	Take Down	Normal	Physical	90	85	20	Normal	•
32	Natural Gift	Normal	Physical	—	100	15	Normal	•
36	Mirror Move	Flying	Status	—	—	20	DoM	•
40	Refresh	Normal	Status	—	—	20	Self	•
45	Dragon Pulse	Dragon	Special	90	100	10	Normal	•
50	Perish Song	Normal	Status	—	—	5	All	•

● **MAIN WAYS TO OBTAIN**

PLATINUM — Celestic Town side of Route 210

DIAMOND — Celestic Town side of Route 211 (use Poké Radar)

PEARL — Celestic Town side of Route 211 (use Poké Radar)

G B A — Catch in Ruby/Sapphire/Emerald and transfer through Pal Park

---

Altaria

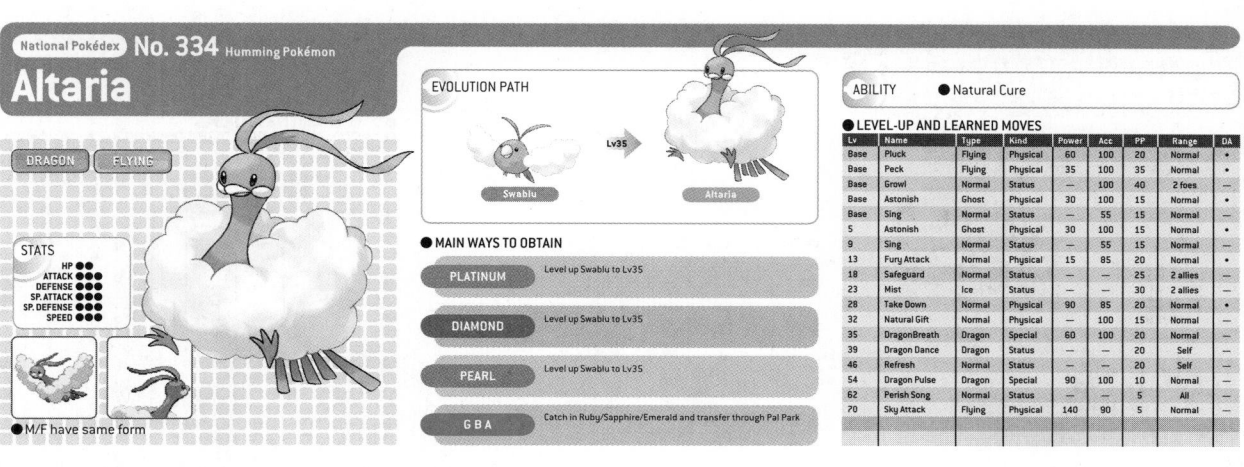

National Pokédex No. 334 Humming Pokémon

DRAGON FLYING

STATS
HP ●
ATTACK ●●●
DEFENSE ●●●
SP.ATTACK ●●●
SP.DEFENSE ●●●●
SPEED ●●●

● M/F have same form

EVOLUTION PATH
Swablu — Lv35 → Altaria

ABILITY ● Natural Cure

● **LEVEL-UP AND LEARNED MOVES**

Lv	Name	Type	Kind	Power	Acc	PP	Range	DA
Base	Pluck	Flying	Physical	60	100	20	Normal	•
Base	Peck	Flying	Physical	35	100	35	Normal	•
Base	Growl	Normal	Status	—	100	40	2 foes	—
Base	Astonish	Ghost	Physical	30	100	15	Normal	•
Base	Sing	Normal	Status	—	55	15	Normal	—
5	Astonish	Ghost	Physical	30	100	15	Normal	•
9	Sing	Normal	Status	—	55	15	Normal	•
13	Fury Attack	Normal	Physical	15	85	20	Normal	•
18	Safeguard	Normal	Status	—	—	25	2 allies	•
23	Mist	Ice	Status	—	—	30	2 allies	•
28	Take Down	Normal	Physical	90	85	20	Normal	•
32	Natural Gift	Normal	Physical	—	100	15	Normal	•
35	DragonBreath	Dragon	Special	60	100	20	Normal	•
39	Dragon Dance	Dragon	Status	—	—	20	Self	•
46	Refresh	Normal	Status	—	—	20	Self	•
54	Dragon Pulse	Dragon	Special	90	100	10	Normal	•
62	Perish Song	Normal	Status	—	—	5	All	•
70	Sky Attack	Flying	Physical	140	90	5	Normal	•

● **MAIN WAYS TO OBTAIN**

PLATINUM — Level up Swablu to Lv35

DIAMOND — Level up Swablu to Lv35

PEARL — Level up Swablu to Lv35

G B A — Catch in Ruby/Sapphire/Emerald and transfer through Pal Park

---

Zangoose

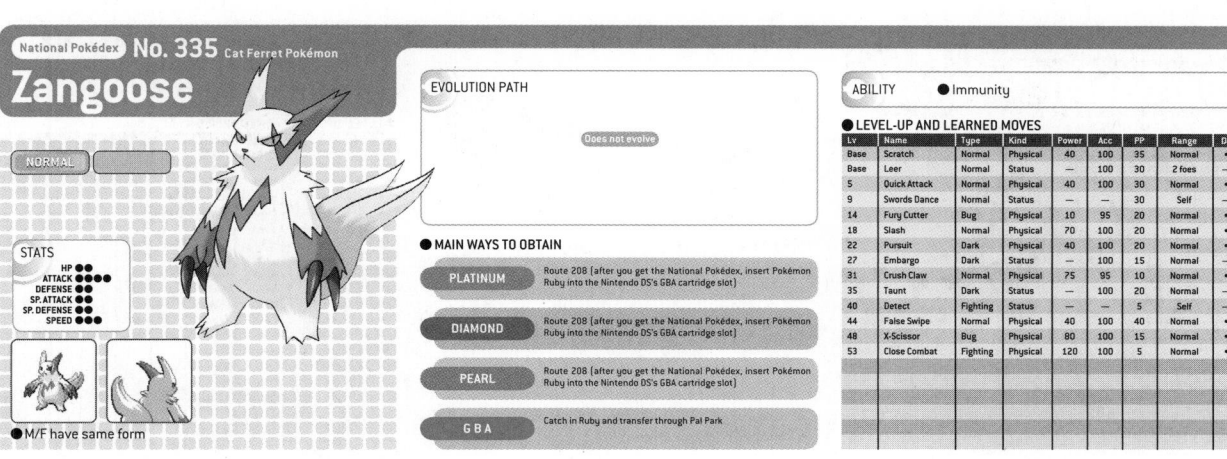

National Pokédex No. 335 Cat Ferret Pokémon

NORMAL

STATS
HP ●●
ATTACK ●●●●
DEFENSE ●●●
SP.ATTACK ●●
SP.DEFENSE ●●●
SPEED ●●●

● M/F have same form

EVOLUTION PATH
Does not evolve

ABILITY ● Immunity

● **LEVEL-UP AND LEARNED MOVES**

Lv	Name	Type	Kind	Power	Acc	PP	Range	DA
Base	Scratch	Normal	Physical	40	100	35	Normal	•
Base	Leer	Normal	Status	—	100	30	2 foes	—
5	Quick Attack	Normal	Physical	40	100	30	Normal	•
9	Swords Dance	Normal	Status	—	—	30	Self	•
14	Fury Cutter	Bug	Physical	10	95	20	Normal	•
18	Slash	Normal	Physical	70	100	20	Normal	•
22	Pursuit	Dark	Physical	40	100	20	Normal	•
27	Embargo	Dark	Status	—	100	15	Normal	•
31	Crush Claw	Normal	Physical	75	95	10	Normal	•
35	Taunt	Dark	Status	—	100	20	Normal	•
40	Detect	Fighting	Status	—	—	5	Self	•
44	False Swipe	Normal	Physical	40	100	40	Normal	•
48	X-Scissor	Bug	Physical	80	100	15	Normal	•
53	Close Combat	Fighting	Physical	120	100	5	Normal	•

● **MAIN WAYS TO OBTAIN**

PLATINUM — Route 208 (after you get the National Pokédex, insert Pokémon Ruby into the Nintendo DS's GBA cartridge slot)

DIAMOND — Route 208 (after you get the National Pokédex, insert Pokémon Ruby into the Nintendo DS's GBA cartridge slot)

PEARL — Route 208 (after you get the National Pokédex, insert Pokémon Ruby into the Nintendo DS's GBA cartridge slot)

G B A — Catch in Ruby and transfer through Pal Park

Seviper

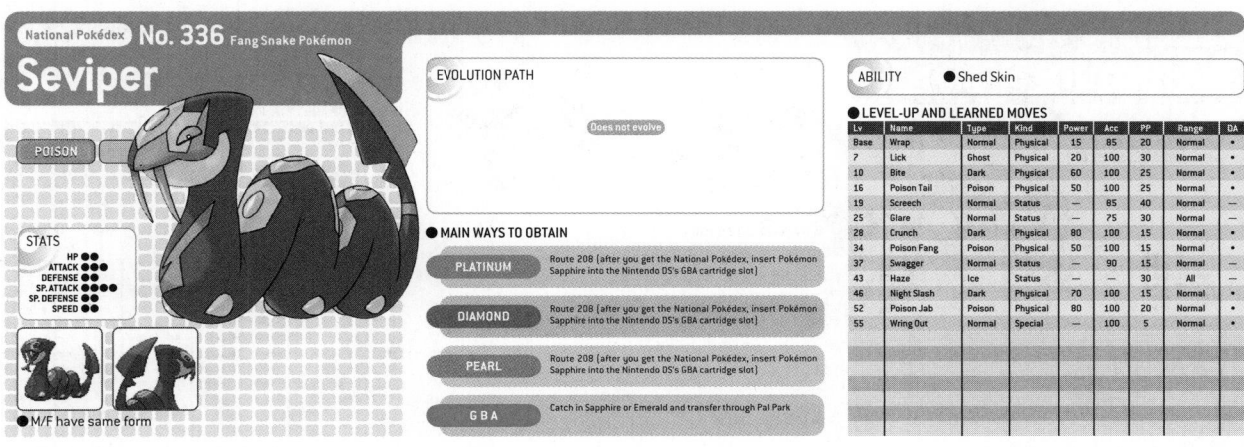

National Pokédex No. 336 Fang Snake Pokémon

POISON

STATS
HP ●●
ATTACK ●●●
DEFENSE ●●●
SP.ATTACK ●●●
SP.DEFENSE ●●●
SPEED ●●

● M/F have same form

EVOLUTION PATH
Does not evolve

ABILITY ● Shed Skin

● **LEVEL-UP AND LEARNED MOVES**

Lv	Name	Type	Kind	Power	Acc	PP	Range	DA
Base	Wrap	Normal	Physical	15	85	20	Normal	•
7	Lick	Ghost	Physical	20	100	30	Normal	•
10	Bite	Dark	Physical	60	100	25	Normal	•
16	Poison Tail	Poison	Physical	50	100	25	Normal	•
19	Screech	Normal	Status	—	85	40	Normal	•
25	Glare	Normal	Status	—	75	30	Normal	•
28	Crunch	Dark	Physical	80	100	15	Normal	•
34	Poison Fang	Poison	Physical	50	100	15	Normal	•
37	Swagger	Normal	Status	—	90	15	Normal	•
43	Haze	Ice	Status	—	—	30	All	•
46	Night Slash	Dark	Physical	70	100	15	Normal	•
52	Poison Jab	Poison	Physical	80	100	20	Normal	•
55	Wring Out	Normal	Special	—	100	5	Normal	•

● **MAIN WAYS TO OBTAIN**

PLATINUM — Route 208 (after you get the National Pokédex, insert Pokémon Sapphire into the Nintendo DS's GBA cartridge slot)

DIAMOND — Route 208 (after you get the National Pokédex, insert Pokémon Sapphire into the Nintendo DS's GBA cartridge slot)

PEARL — Route 208 (after you get the National Pokédex, insert Pokémon Sapphire into the Nintendo DS's GBA cartridge slot)

G B A — Catch in Sapphire or Emerald and transfer through Pal Park

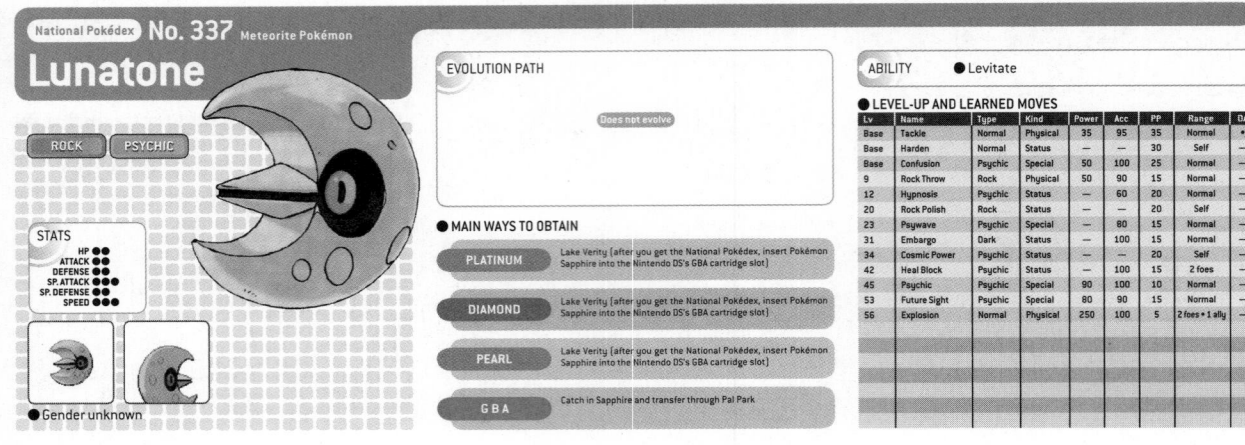

National Pokédex No. 337 Meteorite Pokémon
Lunatone

ROCK · PSYCHIC

STATS
- HP ●●
- ATTACK ●●
- DEFENSE ●●●
- SP. ATTACK ●●●●
- SP. DEFENSE ●●●
- SPEED ●●●

● Gender unknown

EVOLUTION PATH
Does not evolve

● MAIN WAYS TO OBTAIN
PLATINUM	Lake Verity (after you get the National Pokédex, insert Pokémon Sapphire into the Nintendo DS's GBA cartridge slot)
DIAMOND	Lake Verity (after you get the National Pokédex, insert Pokémon Sapphire into the Nintendo DS's GBA cartridge slot)
PEARL	Lake Verity (after you get the National Pokédex, insert Pokémon Sapphire into the Nintendo DS's GBA cartridge slot)
GBA	Catch in Sapphire and transfer through Pal Park

ABILITY ● Levitate

● LEVEL-UP AND LEARNED MOVES
Lv	Name	Type	Kind	Power	Acc	PP	Range	DA
Base	Tackle	Normal	Physical	35	95	35	Normal	●
Base	Harden	Normal	Status	—	—	30	Self	—
Base	Confusion	Psychic	Special	50	100	25	Normal	—
9	Rock Throw	Rock	Physical	50	90	15	Normal	—
12	Hypnosis	Psychic	Status	—	60	20	Normal	—
20	Rock Polish	Rock	Status	—	—	20	Self	—
23	Psywave	Psychic	Special	—	80	15	Normal	—
31	Embargo	Dark	Status	—	100	15	Normal	—
34	Cosmic Power	Psychic	Status	—	—	20	Self	—
42	Heal Block	Psychic	Status	—	100	15	2 foes	—
45	Psychic	Psychic	Special	90	100	10	Normal	—
53	Future Sight	Psychic	Special	80	90	15	Normal	—
56	Explosion	Normal	Physical	250	100	5	2 foes + 1 ally	—

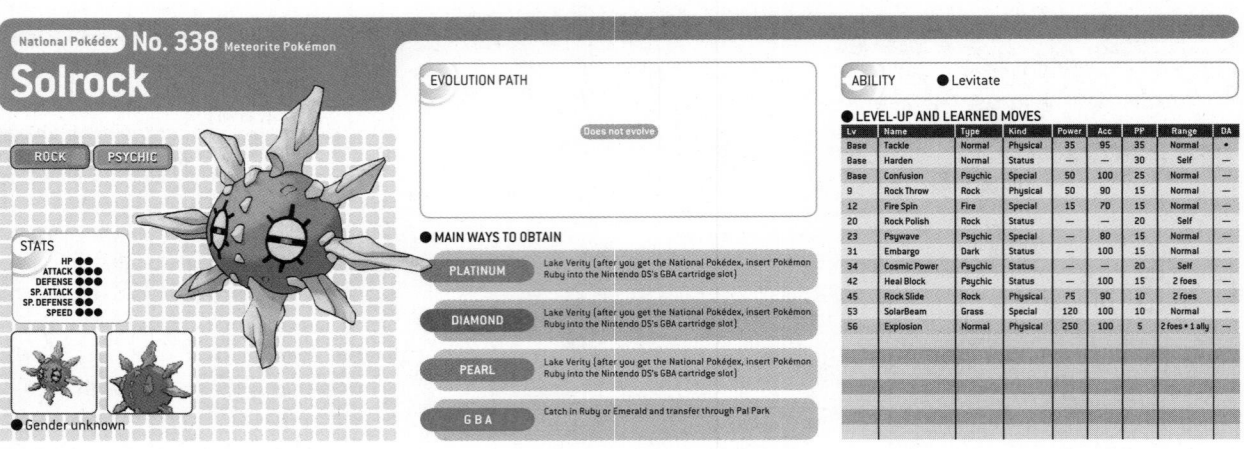

National Pokédex No. 338 Meteorite Pokémon
Solrock

ROCK · PSYCHIC

STATS
- HP ●●
- ATTACK ●●●●
- DEFENSE ●●●
- SP. ATTACK ●●●
- SP. DEFENSE ●●●
- SPEED ●●●

● Gender unknown

EVOLUTION PATH
Does not evolve

● MAIN WAYS TO OBTAIN
PLATINUM	Lake Verity (after you get the National Pokédex, insert Pokémon Ruby into the Nintendo DS's GBA cartridge slot)
DIAMOND	Lake Verity (after you get the National Pokédex, insert Pokémon Ruby into the Nintendo DS's GBA cartridge slot)
PEARL	Lake Verity (after you get the National Pokédex, insert Pokémon Ruby into the Nintendo DS's GBA cartridge slot)
GBA	Catch in Ruby or Emerald and transfer through Pal Park

ABILITY ● Levitate

● LEVEL-UP AND LEARNED MOVES
Lv	Name	Type	Kind	Power	Acc	PP	Range	DA
Base	Tackle	Normal	Physical	35	95	35	Normal	●
Base	Harden	Normal	Status	—	—	30	Self	—
Base	Confusion	Psychic	Special	50	100	25	Normal	—
9	Rock Throw	Rock	Physical	50	90	15	Normal	—
12	Fire Spin	Fire	Special	15	70	15	Normal	—
20	Rock Polish	Rock	Status	—	—	20	Self	—
23	Psywave	Psychic	Special	—	80	15	Normal	—
31	Embargo	Dark	Status	—	100	15	Normal	—
34	Cosmic Power	Psychic	Status	—	—	20	Self	—
42	Heal Block	Psychic	Status	—	100	15	2 foes	—
45	Rock Slide	Rock	Physical	75	90	10	2 foes	—
53	SolarBeam	Grass	Special	120	100	10	Normal	—
56	Explosion	Normal	Physical	250	100	5	2 foes + 1 ally	—

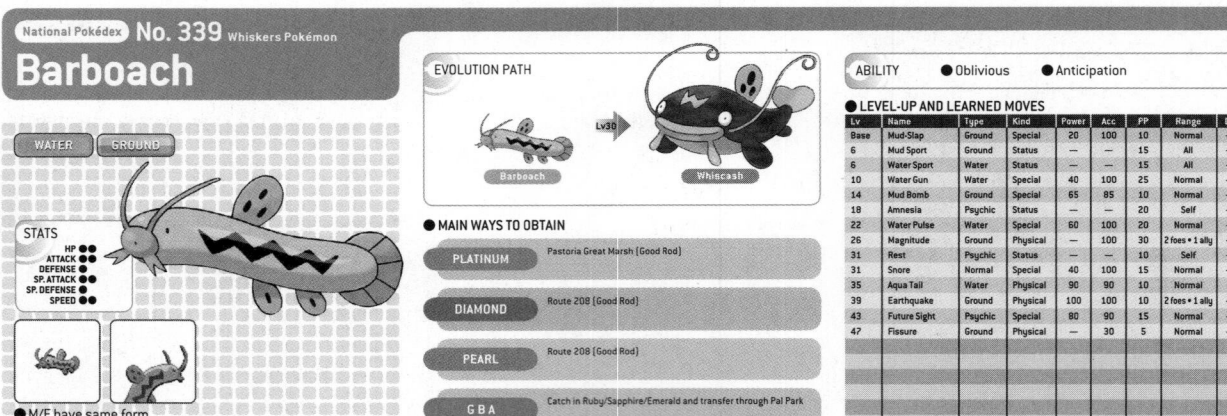

National Pokédex No. 339 Whiskers Pokémon
Barboach

WATER · GROUND

STATS
- HP ●●●
- ATTACK ●●
- DEFENSE ●●
- SP. ATTACK ●●
- SP. DEFENSE ●●
- SPEED ●●

● M/F have same form

EVOLUTION PATH
Barboach → Lv30 → Whiscash

● MAIN WAYS TO OBTAIN
PLATINUM	Pastoria Great Marsh (Good Rod)
DIAMOND	Route 208 (Good Rod)
PEARL	Route 208 (Good Rod)
GBA	Catch in Ruby/Sapphire/Emerald and transfer through Pal Park

ABILITY ● Oblivious ● Anticipation

● LEVEL-UP AND LEARNED MOVES
Lv	Name	Type	Kind	Power	Acc	PP	Range	DA
Base	Mud-Slap	Ground	Special	20	100	10	Normal	—
6	Mud Sport	Ground	Status	—	—	15	All	—
6	Water Sport	Water	Status	—	—	15	All	—
10	Water Gun	Water	Special	40	100	25	Normal	—
14	Mud Bomb	Ground	Special	65	85	10	Normal	—
18	Amnesia	Psychic	Status	—	—	20	Self	—
22	Water Pulse	Water	Special	60	100	20	Normal	—
26	Magnitude	Ground	Physical	—	100	30	2 foes + 1 ally	—
31	Rest	Psychic	Status	—	—	10	Self	—
31	Snore	Normal	Special	40	100	15	Normal	—
35	Aqua Tail	Water	Physical	90	90	10	Normal	●
39	Earthquake	Ground	Physical	100	100	10	2 foes + 1 ally	—
43	Future Sight	Psychic	Special	80	90	15	Normal	—
47	Fissure	Ground	Physical	—	30	5	Normal	—

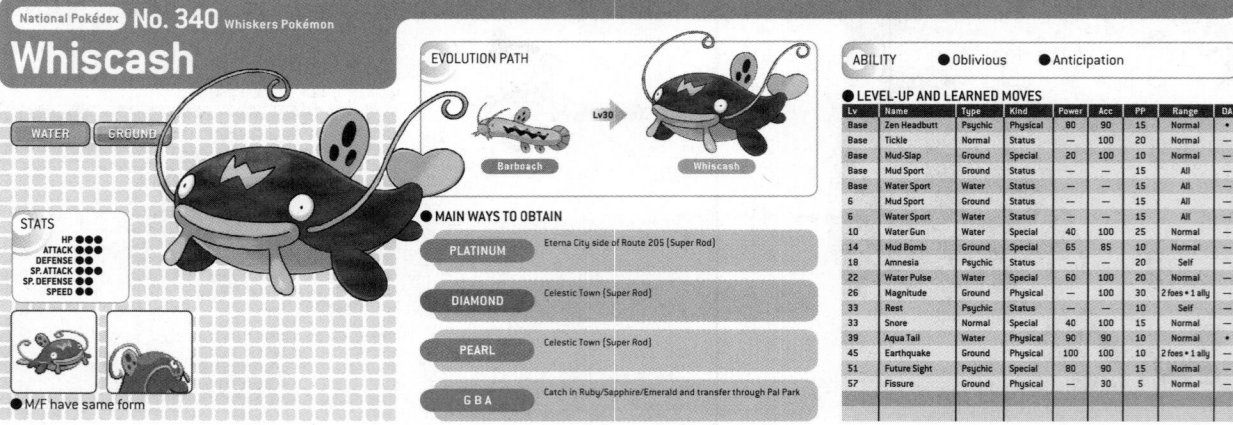

National Pokédex No. 340 Whiskers Pokémon
Whiscash

WATER · GROUND

STATS
- HP ●●●
- ATTACK ●●●
- DEFENSE ●●●
- SP. ATTACK ●●
- SP. DEFENSE ●●
- SPEED ●●

● M/F have same form

EVOLUTION PATH
Barboach → Lv30 → Whiscash

● MAIN WAYS TO OBTAIN
PLATINUM	Eterna City side of Route 205 (Super Rod)
DIAMOND	Celestic Town (Super Rod)
PEARL	Celestic Town (Super Rod)
GBA	Catch in Ruby/Sapphire/Emerald and transfer through Pal Park

ABILITY ● Oblivious ● Anticipation

● LEVEL-UP AND LEARNED MOVES
Lv	Name	Type	Kind	Power	Acc	PP	Range	DA
Base	Zen Headbutt	Psychic	Physical	80	90	15	Normal	●
Base	Tickle	Normal	Status	—	100	20	Normal	—
Base	Mud-Slap	Ground	Special	20	100	10	Normal	—
Base	Mud Sport	Ground	Status	—	—	15	All	—
Base	Water Sport	Water	Status	—	—	15	All	—
6	Mud Sport	Ground	Status	—	—	15	All	—
6	Water Sport	Water	Status	—	—	15	All	—
10	Water Gun	Water	Special	40	100	25	Normal	—
14	Mud Bomb	Ground	Special	65	85	10	Normal	—
18	Amnesia	Psychic	Status	—	—	20	Self	—
22	Water Pulse	Water	Special	60	100	20	Normal	—
26	Magnitude	Ground	Physical	—	100	30	2 foes + 1 ally	—
33	Rest	Psychic	Status	—	—	10	Self	—
33	Snore	Normal	Special	40	100	15	Normal	—
39	Aqua Tail	Water	Physical	90	90	10	Normal	—
45	Earthquake	Ground	Physical	100	100	10	2 foes + 1 ally	—
51	Future Sight	Psychic	Special	80	90	15	Normal	—
57	Fissure	Ground	Physical	—	30	5	Normal	—

National Pokédex No. 341 Ruffian Pokémon
Corphish

WATER

STATS
- HP ●
- ATTACK ●●●
- DEFENSE ●●●
- SP. ATTACK ●
- SP. DEFENSE ●●
- SPEED ●

● M/F have same form

EVOLUTION PATH

Corphish → Lv30 → Crawdaunt

● MAIN WAYS TO OBTAIN
PLATINUM	Celestic Town (Super Rod)
DIAMOND	Celestic Town (Super Rod)
PEARL	Celestic Town (Super Rod)
GBA	Catch in Ruby/Sapphire/Emerald and transfer through Pal Park

ABILITY ● Hyper Cutter ● Shell Armor

● LEVEL-UP AND LEARNED MOVES
Lv	Name	Type	Kind	Power	Acc	PP	Range	DA
Base	Bubble	Water	Special	20	100	30	2 foes	—
7	Harden	Normal	Status	—	—	30	Self	—
10	ViceGrip	Normal	Physical	55	100	30	Normal	●
13	Leer	Normal	Status	—	100	30	2 foes	—
20	BubbleBeam	Water	Special	65	100	20	Normal	—
23	Protect	Normal	Status	—	—	10	Self	—
26	Knock Off	Dark	Physical	20	100	20	Normal	●
32	Taunt	Dark	Status	—	100	20	Normal	—
35	Night Slash	Dark	Physical	70	100	15	Normal	●
38	Crabhammer	Water	Physical	90	85	10	Normal	●
44	Swords Dance	Normal	Status	—	—	30	Self	—
47	Crunch	Dark	Physical	80	100	15	Normal	●
53	Guillotine	Normal	Physical	—	30	5	Normal	—

National Pokédex No. 342 Rogue Pokémon
Crawdaunt

WATER DARK

STATS
- HP ●●
- ATTACK ●●●●
- DEFENSE ●●●
- SP. ATTACK ●●
- SP. DEFENSE ●●
- SPEED ●●

● M/F have same form

EVOLUTION PATH

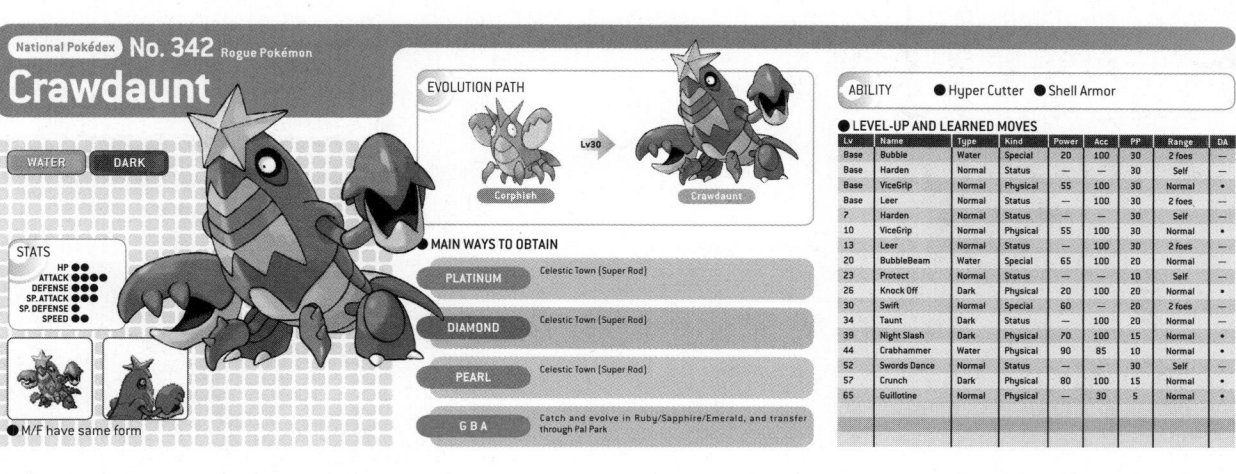

Corphish → Lv30 → Crawdaunt

● MAIN WAYS TO OBTAIN
PLATINUM	Celestic Town (Super Rod)
DIAMOND	Celestic Town (Super Rod)
PEARL	Celestic Town (Super Rod)
GBA	Catch and evolve in Ruby/Sapphire/Emerald, and transfer through Pal Park

ABILITY ● Hyper Cutter ● Shell Armor

● LEVEL-UP AND LEARNED MOVES
Lv	Name	Type	Kind	Power	Acc	PP	Range	DA
Base	Bubble	Water	Special	20	100	30	2 foes	—
Base	Harden	Normal	Status	—	—	30	Self	—
Base	ViceGrip	Normal	Physical	55	100	30	Normal	●
Base	Leer	Normal	Status	—	100	30	2 foes	—
7	Harden	Normal	Status	—	—	30	Self	—
10	ViceGrip	Normal	Physical	55	100	30	Normal	●
13	Leer	Normal	Status	—	100	30	2 foes	—
20	BubbleBeam	Water	Special	65	100	20	Normal	—
23	Protect	Normal	Status	—	—	10	Self	—
26	Knock Off	Dark	Physical	20	100	20	Normal	●
30	Swift	Normal	Special	60	—	20	2 foes	—
34	Taunt	Dark	Status	—	100	20	Normal	—
39	Night Slash	Dark	Physical	70	100	15	Normal	●
44	Crabhammer	Water	Physical	90	85	10	Normal	●
52	Swords Dance	Normal	Status	—	—	30	Self	—
57	Crunch	Dark	Physical	80	100	15	Normal	●
65	Guillotine	Normal	Physical	—	30	5	Normal	—

National Pokédex No. 343 Clay Doll Pokémon
Baltoy

GROUND PSYCHIC

STATS
- HP ●●
- ATTACK ●●
- DEFENSE ●●●
- SP. ATTACK ●●
- SP. DEFENSE ●●●
- SPEED ●●

● Gender unknown

EVOLUTION PATH

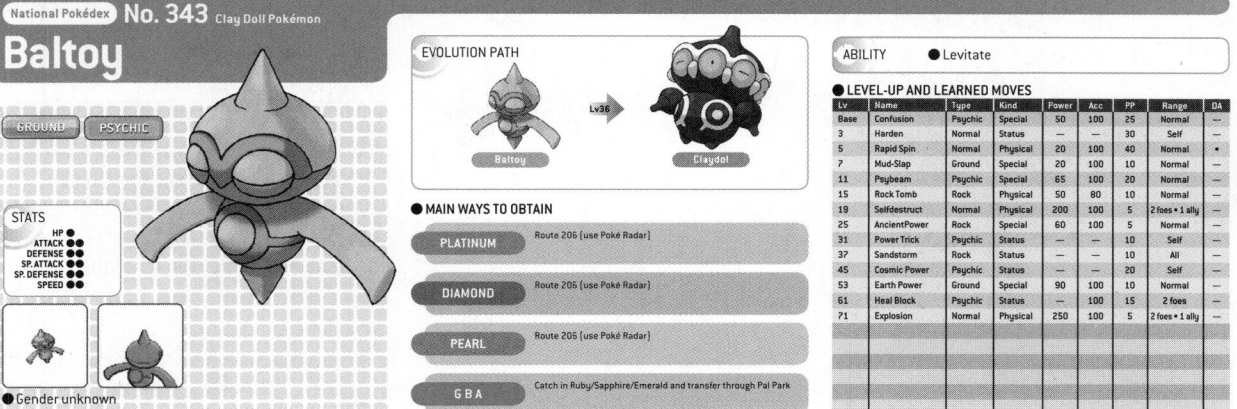

Baltoy → Lv36 → Claydol

● MAIN WAYS TO OBTAIN
PLATINUM	Route 206 (use Poké Radar)
DIAMOND	Route 206 (use Poké Radar)
PEARL	Route 206 (use Poké Radar)
GBA	Catch in Ruby/Sapphire/Emerald and transfer through Pal Park

ABILITY ● Levitate

● LEVEL-UP AND LEARNED MOVES
Lv	Name	Type	Kind	Power	Acc	PP	Range	DA
Base	Confusion	Psychic	Special	50	100	25	Normal	—
3	Harden	Normal	Status	—	—	30	Self	—
5	Rapid Spin	Normal	Physical	20	100	40	Normal	●
7	Mud-Slap	Ground	Special	20	100	10	Normal	—
11	Psybeam	Psychic	Special	65	100	20	Normal	—
15	Rock Tomb	Rock	Physical	50	80	10	Normal	—
19	Selfdestruct	Normal	Physical	200	100	5	2 foes + 1 ally	—
25	AncientPower	Rock	Special	60	100	5	Normal	—
31	Power Trick	Psychic	Status	—	—	10	Self	—
37	Sandstorm	Rock	Status	—	—	10	All	—
45	Cosmic Power	Psychic	Status	—	—	20	Self	—
53	Earth Power	Ground	Special	90	100	10	Normal	—
61	Heal Block	Psychic	Status	—	100	15	2 foes	—
71	Explosion	Normal	Physical	250	100	5	2 foes + 1 ally	—

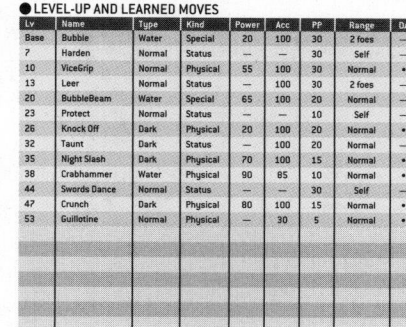

National Pokédex No. 344 Clay Doll Pokémon
Claydol

GROUND PSYCHIC

STATS
- HP ●●
- ATTACK ●●●
- DEFENSE ●●●●
- SP. ATTACK ●●●
- SP. DEFENSE ●●●●
- SPEED ●●●

● Gender unknown

EVOLUTION PATH

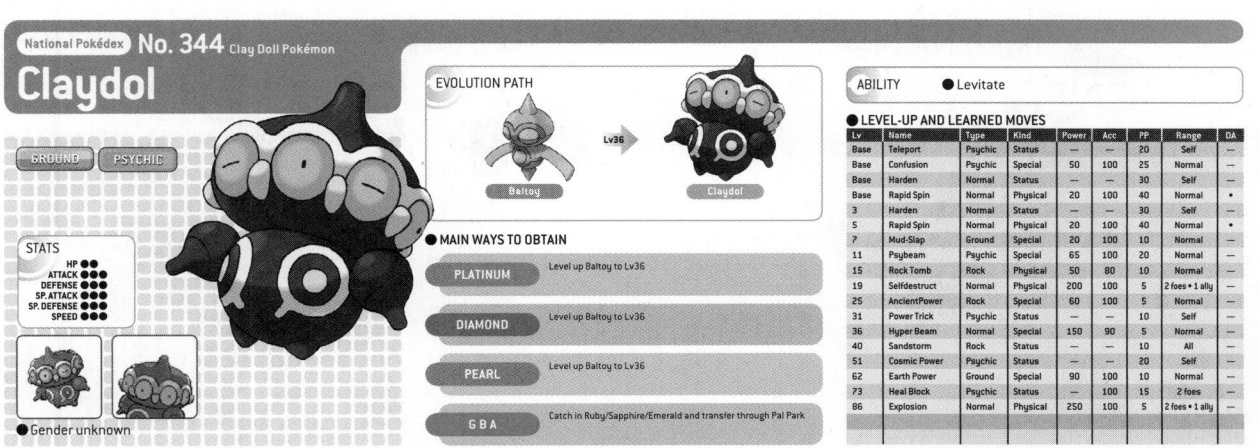

Baltoy → Lv36 → Claydol

● MAIN WAYS TO OBTAIN
PLATINUM	Level up Baltoy to Lv36
DIAMOND	Level up Baltoy to Lv36
PEARL	Level up Baltoy to Lv36
GBA	Catch in Ruby/Sapphire/Emerald and transfer through Pal Park

ABILITY ● Levitate

● LEVEL-UP AND LEARNED MOVES
Lv	Name	Type	Kind	Power	Acc	PP	Range	DA
Base	Teleport	Psychic	Status	—	—	20	Self	—
Base	Confusion	Psychic	Special	50	100	25	Normal	—
Base	Harden	Normal	Status	—	—	30	Self	—
Base	Rapid Spin	Normal	Physical	20	100	40	Normal	●
3	Harden	Normal	Status	—	—	30	Self	—
5	Rapid Spin	Normal	Physical	20	100	40	Normal	●
7	Mud-Slap	Ground	Special	20	100	10	Normal	—
11	Psybeam	Psychic	Special	65	100	20	Normal	—
15	Rock Tomb	Rock	Physical	50	80	10	Normal	—
19	Selfdestruct	Normal	Physical	200	100	5	2 foes + 1 ally	—
25	AncientPower	Rock	Special	60	100	5	Normal	—
31	Power Trick	Psychic	Status	—	—	10	Self	—
36	Hyper Beam	Normal	Special	150	90	5	Normal	—
40	Sandstorm	Rock	Status	—	—	10	All	—
51	Cosmic Power	Psychic	Status	—	—	20	Self	—
62	Earth Power	Ground	Special	90	100	10	Normal	—
73	Heal Block	Psychic	Status	—	100	15	2 foes	—
86	Explosion	Normal	Physical	250	100	5	2 foes + 1 ally	—

National Pokédex No. 345 Sea Lily Pokémon
Lileep

ROCK GRASS

STATS
HP ●●
ATTACK ●●●
DEFENSE ●●●
SP. ATTACK ●●●
SP. DEFENSE ●●●
SPEED ●

● M/F have same form

EVOLUTION PATH

Lileep —Lv40→ Cradily

● MAIN WAYS TO OBTAIN

PLATINUM	Get the Root Fossil in the Underground, and have it restored at the Oreburgh Mining Museum
DIAMOND	Get the Root Fossil in the Underground, and have it restored at the Oreburgh Mining Museum
PEARL	Get the Root Fossil in the Underground, and have it restored at the Oreburgh Mining Museum
G B A	Acquire in Ruby/Sapphire/Emerald and transfer through Pal Park

ABILITY ● Suction Cups

● LEVEL-UP AND LEARNED MOVES

Lv	Name	Type	Kind	Power	Acc	PP	Range	DA
Base	Astonish	Ghost	Physical	30	100	15	Normal	●
Base	Constrict	Normal	Physical	10	100	35	Normal	—
8	Acid	Poison	Special	40	100	30	2 foes	—
15	Ingrain	Grass	Status	—	—	20	Self	—
22	Confuse Ray	Ghost	Status	—	100	10	Normal	—
29	Amnesia	Psychic	Status	—	—	20	Self	—
36	Gastro Acid	Poison	Status	—	100	10	Normal	—
43	AncientPower	Rock	Special	60	100	5	Normal	—
50	Energy Ball	Grass	Special	80	100	10	Normal	—
57	Stockpile	Normal	Status	—	—	20	Self	—
57	Spit Up	Normal	Special	—	100	10	Normal	—
57	Swallow	Normal	Status	—	—	10	Self	—
64	Wring Out	Normal	Special	—	100	5	Normal	●

National Pokédex No. 346 Barnacle Pokémon
Cradily

ROCK GRASS

STATS
HP ●●●
ATTACK ●●●
DEFENSE ●●●
SP. ATTACK ●●●
SP. DEFENSE ●●●
SPEED ●●

● M/F have same form

EVOLUTION PATH

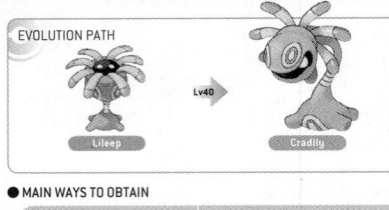

Lileep —Lv40→ Cradily

● MAIN WAYS TO OBTAIN

PLATINUM	Level up Lileep to Lv40
DIAMOND	Level up Lileep to Lv40
PEARL	Level up Lileep to Lv40
G B A	Acquire and evolve in Ruby/Sapphire/Emerald, and transfer through Pal Park

ABILITY ● Suction Cups

● LEVEL-UP AND LEARNED MOVES

Lv	Name	Type	Kind	Power	Acc	PP	Range	DA
Base	Astonish	Ghost	Physical	30	100	15	Normal	●
Base	Constrict	Normal	Physical	10	100	35	Normal	—
Base	Acid	Poison	Special	40	100	30	2 foes	—
Base	Ingrain	Grass	Status	—	—	20	Self	—
8	Acid	Poison	Special	40	100	30	2 foes	—
15	Ingrain	Grass	Status	—	—	20	Self	—
22	Confuse Ray	Ghost	Status	—	100	10	Normal	—
29	Amnesia	Psychic	Status	—	—	20	Self	—
36	AncientPower	Rock	Special	60	100	5	Normal	—
46	Gastro Acid	Poison	Status	—	100	10	Normal	—
56	Energy Ball	Grass	Special	80	100	10	Normal	—
66	Stockpile	Normal	Status	—	—	20	Self	—
66	Spit Up	Normal	Special	—	100	10	Normal	—
66	Swallow	Normal	Status	—	—	10	Self	—
76	Wring Out	Normal	Special	—	100	5	Normal	●

National Pokédex No. 347 Old Shrimp Pokémon
Anorith

ROCK BUG

STATS
HP ●
ATTACK ●●●
DEFENSE ●●●
SP. ATTACK ●●
SP. DEFENSE ●●
SPEED ●●

● M/F have same form

EVOLUTION PATH

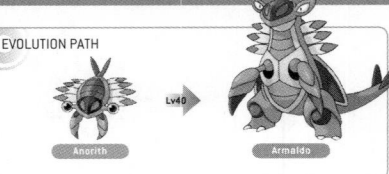

Anorith —Lv40→ Armaldo

● MAIN WAYS TO OBTAIN

PLATINUM	Get the Claw Fossil in the Underground, and have it restored at the Oreburgh Mining Museum
DIAMOND	Get the Claw Fossil in the Underground, and have it restored at the Oreburgh Mining Museum
PEARL	Get the Claw Fossil in the Underground, and have it restored at the Oreburgh Mining Museum
G B A	Acquire in Ruby/Sapphire/Emerald and transfer through Pal Park

ABILITY ● Battle Armor

● LEVEL-UP AND LEARNED MOVES

Lv	Name	Type	Kind	Power	Acc	PP	Range	DA
Base	Scratch	Normal	Physical	40	100	35	Normal	●
Base	Harden	Normal	Status	—	—	30	Self	—
7	Mud Sport	Ground	Status	—	—	15	All	—
13	Water Gun	Water	Special	40	100	25	Normal	—
19	Metal Claw	Steel	Physical	50	95	35	Normal	●
25	Protect	Normal	Status	—	—	10	Self	—
31	AncientPower	Rock	Special	60	100	5	Normal	—
37	Fury Cutter	Bug	Physical	10	95	20	Normal	●
43	Slash	Normal	Physical	70	100	20	Normal	●
49	Rock Blast	Rock	Physical	25	80	10	Normal	—
55	Crush Claw	Normal	Physical	75	95	10	Normal	●
61	X-Scissor	Bug	Physical	80	100	15	Normal	●

National Pokédex No. 348 Plate Pokémon
Armaldo

ROCK BUG

STATS
HP ●●●
ATTACK ●●●●
DEFENSE ●●●
SP. ATTACK ●●●
SP. DEFENSE ●●●
SPEED ●●

● M/F have same form

EVOLUTION PATH

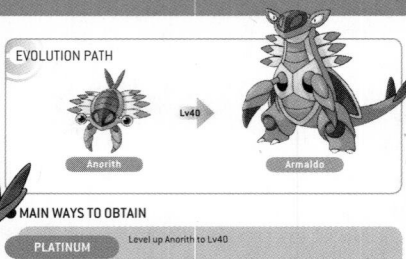

Anorith —Lv40→ Armaldo

● MAIN WAYS TO OBTAIN

PLATINUM	Level up Anorith to Lv40
DIAMOND	Level up Anorith to Lv40
PEARL	Level up Anorith to Lv40
G B A	Acquire and evolve in Ruby/Sapphire/Emerald, and transfer through Pal Park

ABILITY ● Battle Armor

● LEVEL-UP AND LEARNED MOVES

Lv	Name	Type	Kind	Power	Acc	PP	Range	DA
Base	Scratch	Normal	Physical	40	100	35	Normal	●
Base	Harden	Normal	Status	—	—	30	Self	—
Base	Mud Sport	Ground	Status	—	—	15	All	—
Base	Water Gun	Water	Special	40	100	25	Normal	—
7	Mud Sport	Ground	Status	—	—	15	All	—
13	Water Gun	Water	Special	40	100	25	Normal	—
19	Metal Claw	Steel	Physical	50	95	35	Normal	●
25	Protect	Normal	Status	—	—	10	Self	—
31	AncientPower	Rock	Special	60	100	5	Normal	—
37	Fury Cutter	Bug	Physical	10	95	20	Normal	●
46	Slash	Normal	Physical	70	100	20	Normal	●
55	Rock Blast	Rock	Physical	25	80	10	Normal	—
67	Crush Claw	Normal	Physical	75	95	10	Normal	●
73	X-Scissor	Bug	Physical	80	100	15	Normal	●

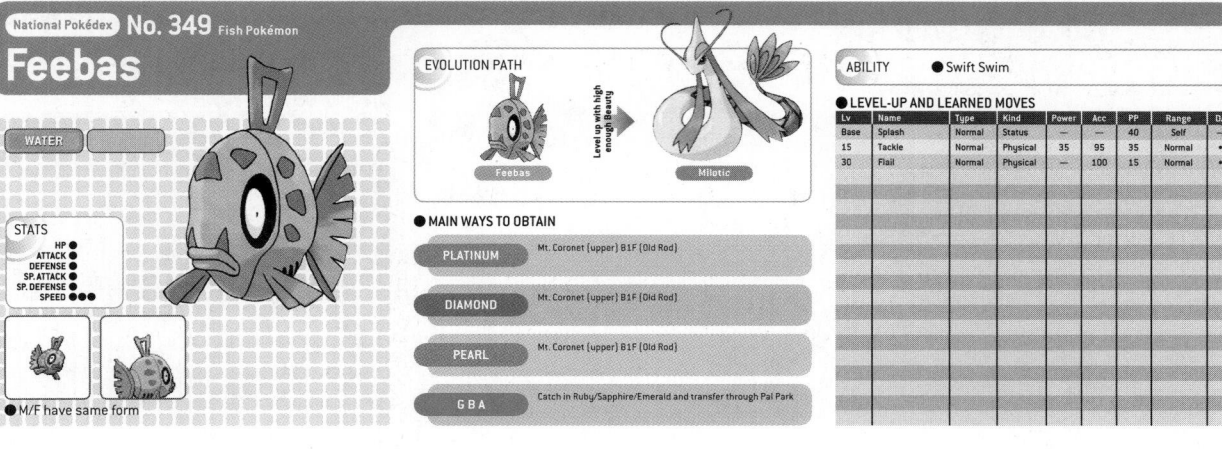

National Pokédex No. 349 Fish Pokémon
Feebas

WATER

STATS
- HP ●
- ATTACK ●
- DEFENSE ●
- SP. ATTACK ●
- SP. DEFENSE ●●
- SPEED ●●●

● M/F have same form

EVOLUTION PATH

Feebas → (Level up with high enough Beauty) → Milotic

● MAIN WAYS TO OBTAIN

PLATINUM	Mt. Coronet (upper) B1F (Old Rod)
DIAMOND	Mt. Coronet (upper) B1F (Old Rod)
PEARL	Mt. Coronet (upper) B1F (Old Rod)
G B A	Catch in Ruby/Sapphire/Emerald and transfer through Pal Park

ABILITY ● Swift Swim

● LEVEL-UP AND LEARNED MOVES

Lv	Name	Type	Kind	Power	Acc	PP	Range	DA
Base	Splash	Normal	Status	—	—	40	Self	
15	Tackle	Normal	Physical	35	95	35	Normal	●
30	Flail	Normal	Physical	—	100	15	Normal	●

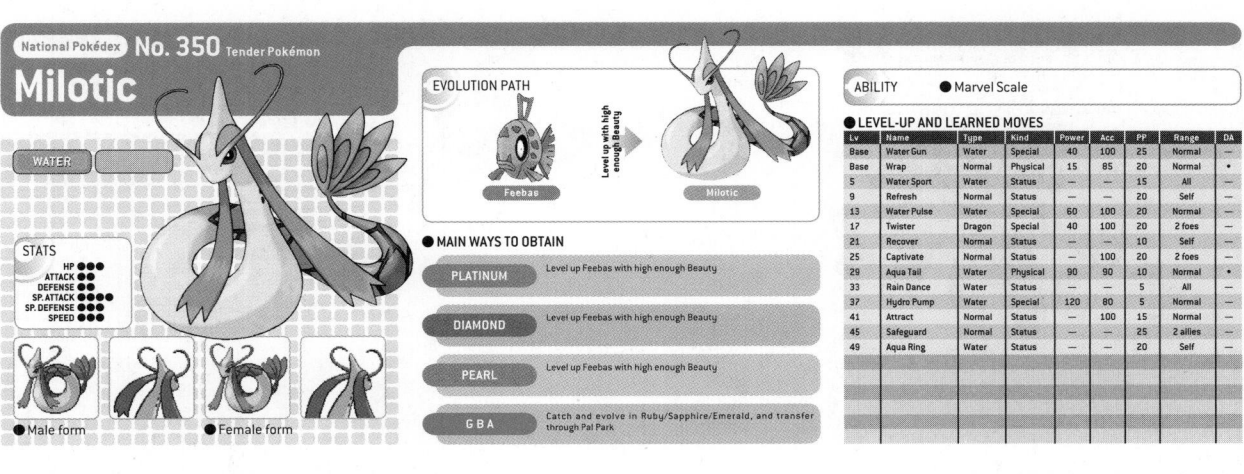

National Pokédex No. 350 Tender Pokémon
Milotic

WATER

STATS
- HP ●●●
- ATTACK ●●●
- DEFENSE ●●●
- SP. ATTACK ●●●●
- SP. DEFENSE ●●●●
- SPEED ●●●

● Male form　● Female form

EVOLUTION PATH

Feebas → (Level up with high enough Beauty) → Milotic

● MAIN WAYS TO OBTAIN

PLATINUM	Level up Feebas with high enough Beauty
DIAMOND	Level up Feebas with high enough Beauty
PEARL	Level up Feebas with high enough Beauty
G B A	Catch and evolve in Ruby/Sapphire/Emerald, and transfer through Pal Park

ABILITY ● Marvel Scale

● LEVEL-UP AND LEARNED MOVES

Lv	Name	Type	Kind	Power	Acc	PP	Range	DA
Base	Water Gun	Water	Special	40	100	25	Normal	
Base	Wrap	Normal	Physical	15	85	20	Normal	●
5	Water Sport	Water	Status	—	—	15	All	
9	Refresh	Normal	Status	—	—	20	Self	—
13	Water Pulse	Water	Special	60	100	20	Normal	—
17	Twister	Dragon	Special	40	100	20	2 foes	
21	Recover	Normal	Status	—	—	10	Self	—
25	Captivate	Normal	Status	—	100	20	2 foes	—
29	Aqua Tail	Water	Physical	90	90	10	Normal	●
33	Rain Dance	Water	Status	—	—	5	All	
37	Hydro Pump	Water	Special	120	80	5	Normal	—
41	Attract	Normal	Status	—	100	15	Normal	—
45	Safeguard	Normal	Status	—	—	25	2 allies	
49	Aqua Ring	Water	Status	—	—	20	Self	—

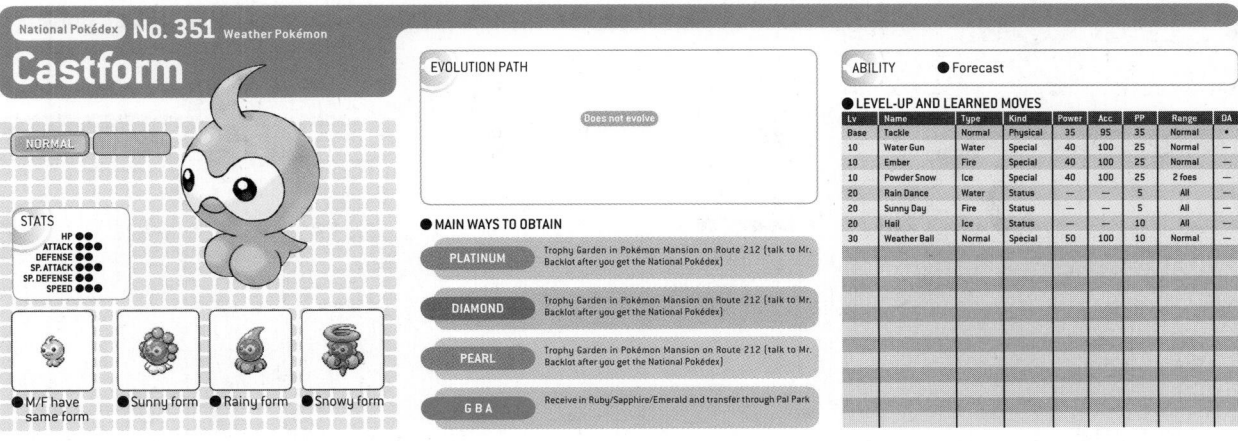

National Pokédex No. 351 Weather Pokémon
Castform

NORMAL

STATS
- HP ●●
- ATTACK ●●●
- DEFENSE ●●●
- SP. ATTACK ●●●
- SP. DEFENSE ●●●
- SPEED ●●●

● M/F have same form　● Sunny form　● Rainy form　● Snowy form

EVOLUTION PATH

Does not evolve

● MAIN WAYS TO OBTAIN

PLATINUM	Trophy Garden in Pokémon Mansion on Route 212 (talk to Mr. Backlot after you get the National Pokédex)
DIAMOND	Trophy Garden in Pokémon Mansion on Route 212 (talk to Mr. Backlot after you get the National Pokédex)
PEARL	Trophy Garden in Pokémon Mansion on Route 212 (talk to Mr. Backlot after you get the National Pokédex)
G B A	Receive in Ruby/Sapphire/Emerald and transfer through Pal Park

ABILITY ● Forecast

● LEVEL-UP AND LEARNED MOVES

Lv	Name	Type	Kind	Power	Acc	PP	Range	DA
Base	Tackle	Normal	Physical	35	95	35	Normal	●
10	Water Gun	Water	Special	40	100	25	Normal	
10	Ember	Fire	Special	40	100	25	Normal	
10	Powder Snow	Ice	Special	40	100	25	2 foes	
20	Rain Dance	Water	Status	—	—	5	All	
20	Sunny Day	Fire	Status	—	—	5	All	
20	Hail	Ice	Status	—	—	10	All	
30	Weather Ball	Normal	Special	50	100	10	Normal	

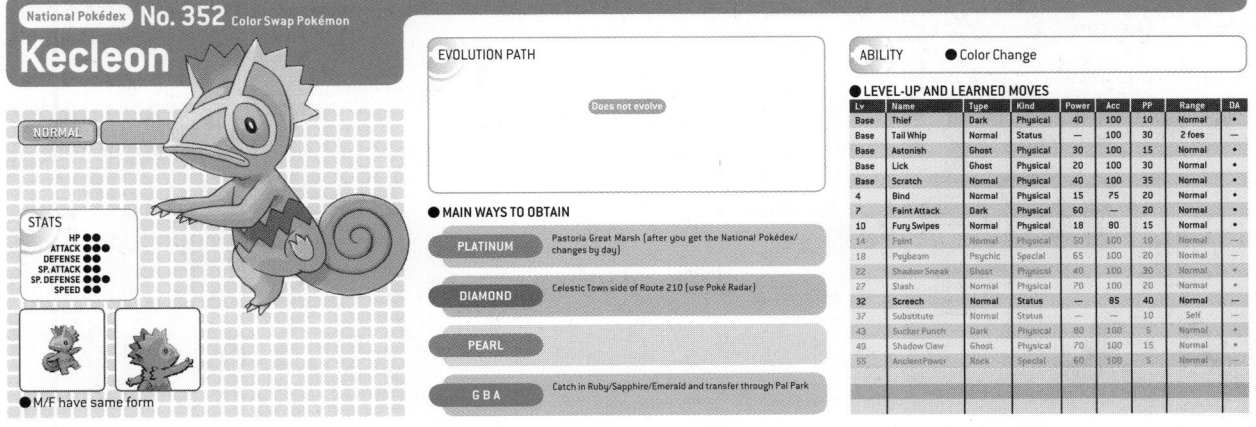

National Pokédex No. 352 Color Swap Pokémon
Kecleon

NORMAL

STATS
- HP ●●
- ATTACK ●●●
- DEFENSE ●●●
- SP. ATTACK ●●●
- SP. DEFENSE ●●●
- SPEED ●●

● M/F have same form

EVOLUTION PATH

Does not evolve

● MAIN WAYS TO OBTAIN

PLATINUM	Pastoria Great Marsh (after you get the National Pokédex/ changes by day)
DIAMOND	Celestic Town side of Route 210 (use Poké Radar)
PEARL	
G B A	Catch in Ruby/Sapphire/Emerald and transfer through Pal Park

ABILITY ● Color Change

● LEVEL-UP AND LEARNED MOVES

Lv	Name	Type	Kind	Power	Acc	PP	Range	DA
Base	Thief	Dark	Physical	40	100	10	Normal	●
Base	Tail Whip	Normal	Status	—	100	30	2 foes	—
Base	Astonish	Ghost	Physical	30	100	15	Normal	●
Base	Lick	Ghost	Physical	20	100	30	Normal	●
Base	Scratch	Normal	Physical	40	100	35	Normal	●
4	Bind	Normal	Physical	15	75	20	Normal	●
7	Faint Attack	Dark	Physical	60	—	20	Normal	●
10	Fury Swipes	Normal	Physical	18	80	15	Normal	●
14	Feint	Normal	Physical	50	100	10	Normal	—
18	Psybeam	Psychic	Special	65	100	20	Normal	—
22	Shadow Sneak	Ghost	Physical	40	100	30	Normal	●
27	Slash	Normal	Physical	70	100	20	Normal	●
32	Screech	Normal	Status	—	85	40	Normal	—
37	Substitute	Normal	Status	—	—	10	Self	—
43	Sucker Punch	Dark	Physical	80	100	5	Normal	●
49	Shadow Claw	Ghost	Physical	70	100	15	Normal	●
55	AncientPower	Rock	Special	60	100	5	Normal	—

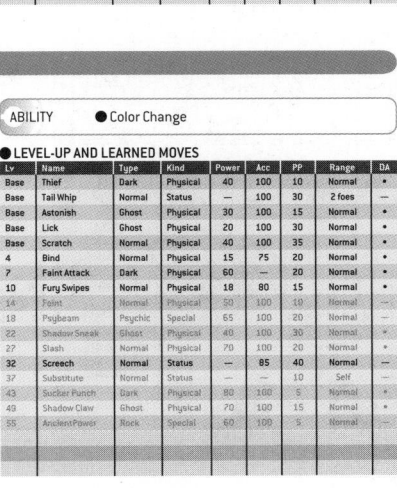

Shuppet

National Pokédex No. 353 Puppet Pokémon

GHOST

STATS
- HP ●
- ATTACK ●●●
- DEFENSE ●●
- SP. ATTACK ●●●
- SP. DEFENSE ●●
- SPEED ●●

● M/F have same form

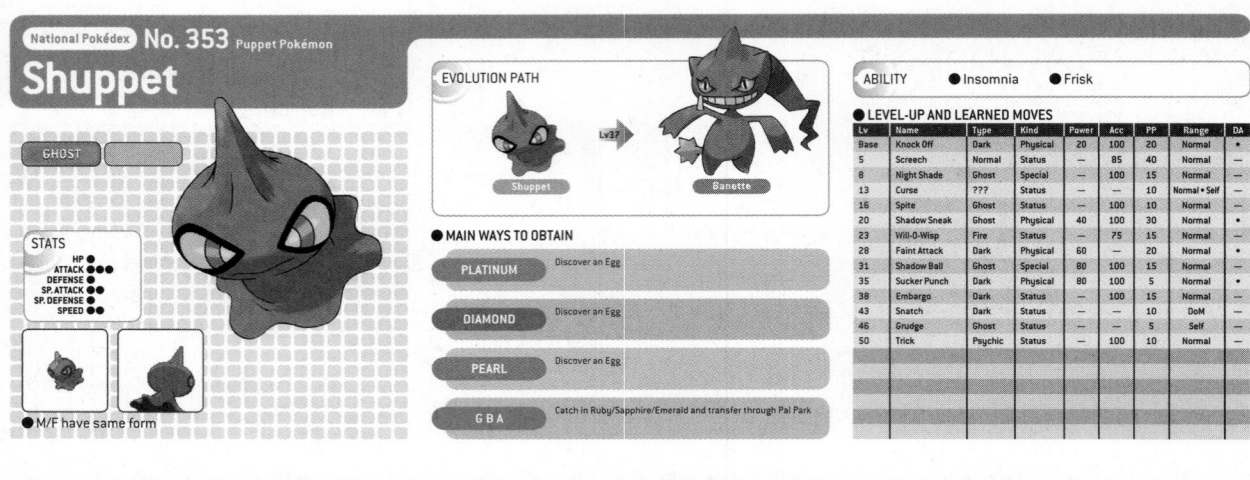

● EVOLUTION PATH

Shuppet — Lv37 → Banette

● MAIN WAYS TO OBTAIN

PLATINUM	Discover an Egg
DIAMOND	Discover an Egg
PEARL	Discover an Egg
GBA	Catch in Ruby/Sapphire/Emerald and transfer through Pal Park

ABILITY ● Insomnia ● Frisk

● LEVEL-UP AND LEARNED MOVES

Lv	Name	Type	Kind	Power	Acc	PP	Range	DA
Base	Knock Off	Dark	Physical	20	100	20	Normal	•
5	Screech	Normal	Status	—	85	40	Normal	
8	Night Shade	Ghost	Special	—	100	15	Normal	
13	Curse	???	Status	—	—	10	Normal • Self	
16	Spite	Ghost	Status	—	100	10	Normal	
20	Shadow Sneak	Ghost	Physical	40	100	30	Normal	
23	Will-O-Wisp	Fire	Status	—	75	15	Normal	
28	Faint Attack	Dark	Physical	60	—	20	Normal	
31	Shadow Ball	Ghost	Special	80	100	15	Normal	
35	Sucker Punch	Dark	Physical	80	100	5	Normal	
38	Embargo	Dark	Status	—	100	15	Normal	
43	Snatch	Dark	Status	—	—	10	DoM	
46	Grudge	Ghost	Status	—	—	5	Self	
50	Trick	Psychic	Status	—	100	10	Normal	

Banette

National Pokédex No. 354 Marionette Pokémon

GHOST

STATS
- HP ●
- ATTACK ●●●●
- DEFENSE ●●●
- SP. ATTACK ●●●
- SP. DEFENSE ●●●
- SPEED ●●●

● M/F have same form

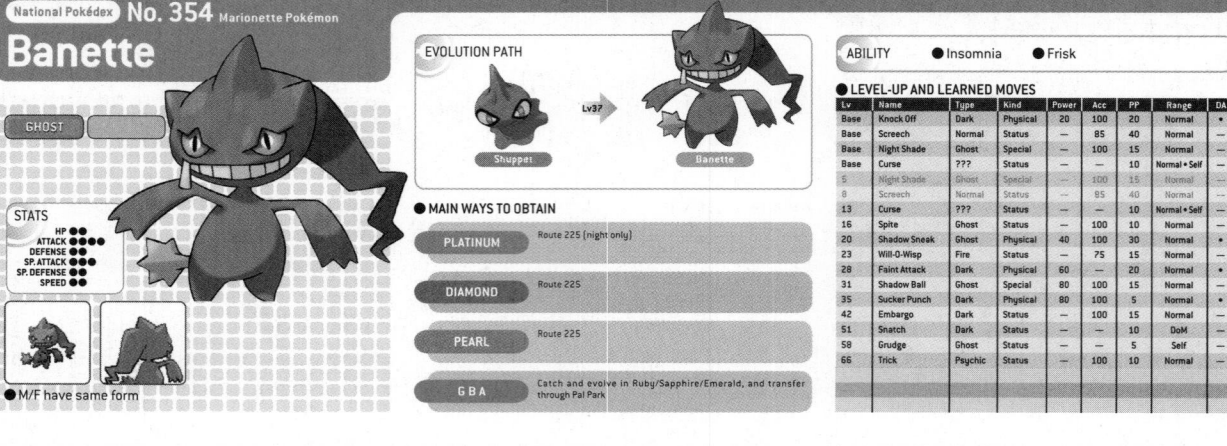

● EVOLUTION PATH

Shuppet — Lv37 → Banette

● MAIN WAYS TO OBTAIN

PLATINUM	Route 225 (night only)
DIAMOND	Route 225
PEARL	Route 225
GBA	Catch and evolve in Ruby/Sapphire/Emerald, and transfer through Pal Park

ABILITY ● Insomnia ● Frisk

● LEVEL-UP AND LEARNED MOVES

Lv	Name	Type	Kind	Power	Acc	PP	Range	DA
Base	Knock Off	Dark	Physical	20	100	20	Normal	•
Base	Screech	Normal	Status	—	85	40	Normal	
Base	Night Shade	Ghost	Special	—	100	15	Normal	
Base	Curse	???	Status	—	—	10	Normal • Self	
5	Night Shade	Ghost	Special	—	100	15	Normal	
8	Screech	Normal	Status	—	85	40	Normal	
13	Curse	???	Status	—	—	10	Normal • Self	
16	Spite	Ghost	Status	—	100	10	Normal	
20	Shadow Sneak	Ghost	Physical	40	100	30	Normal	
23	Will-O-Wisp	Fire	Status	—	75	15	Normal	
28	Faint Attack	Dark	Physical	60	—	20	Normal	
31	Shadow Ball	Ghost	Special	80	100	15	Normal	
35	Sucker Punch	Dark	Physical	80	100	5	Normal	
42	Embargo	Dark	Status	—	100	15	Normal	
51	Snatch	Dark	Status	—	—	10	DoM	
58	Grudge	Ghost	Status	—	—	5	Self	
66	Trick	Psychic	Status	—	100	10	Normal	

Duskull

National Pokédex No. 355 Requiem Pokémon

GHOST

STATS
- HP ●
- ATTACK ●●
- DEFENSE ●●●
- SP. ATTACK ●●
- SP. DEFENSE ●●●
- SPEED ●

● M/F have same form

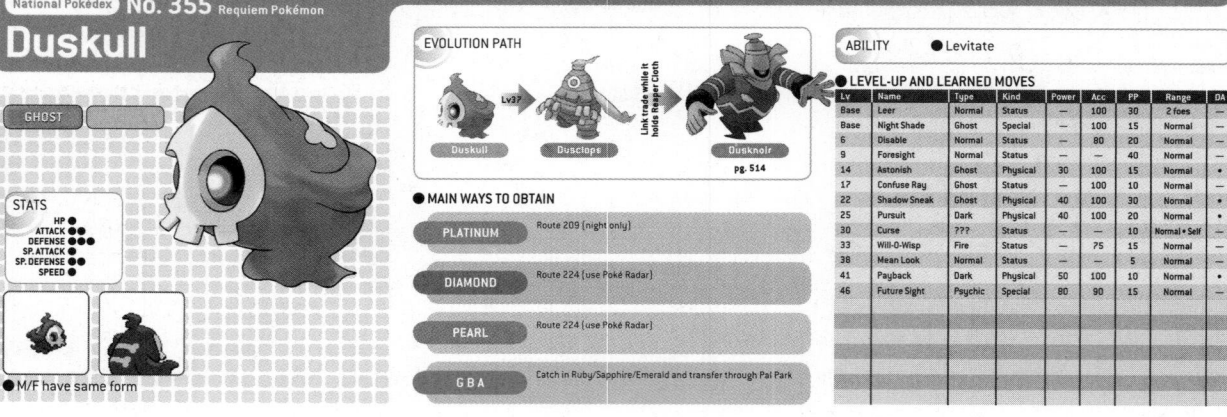

● EVOLUTION PATH

Duskull — Lv37 → Dusclops — Link trade while it holds Reaper Cloth → Dusknoir pg. 514

● MAIN WAYS TO OBTAIN

PLATINUM	Route 209 (night only)
DIAMOND	Route 224 (use Poké Radar)
PEARL	Route 224 (use Poké Radar)
GBA	Catch in Ruby/Sapphire/Emerald and transfer through Pal Park

ABILITY ● Levitate

● LEVEL-UP AND LEARNED MOVES

Lv	Name	Type	Kind	Power	Acc	PP	Range	DA
Base	Leer	Normal	Status	—	100	30	2 foes	—
Base	Night Shade	Ghost	Special	—	100	15	Normal	
6	Disable	Normal	Status	—	80	20	Normal	
9	Foresight	Normal	Status	—	—	40	Normal	
14	Astonish	Ghost	Physical	30	100	15	Normal	•
17	Confuse Ray	Ghost	Status	—	100	10	Normal	
22	Shadow Sneak	Ghost	Physical	40	100	30	Normal	•
25	Pursuit	Dark	Physical	40	100	20	Normal	
30	Curse	???	Status	—	—	10	Normal • Self	
33	Will-O-Wisp	Fire	Status	—	75	15	Normal	
38	Mean Look	Normal	Status	—	—	5	Normal	
41	Payback	Dark	Physical	50	100	10	Normal	
46	Future Sight	Psychic	Special	80	90	15	Normal	

Dusclops

National Pokédex No. 356 Beckon Pokémon

GHOST

STATS
- HP ●
- ATTACK ●●
- DEFENSE ●●●●
- SP. ATTACK ●●
- SP. DEFENSE ●●●●
- SPEED ●

● M/F have same form

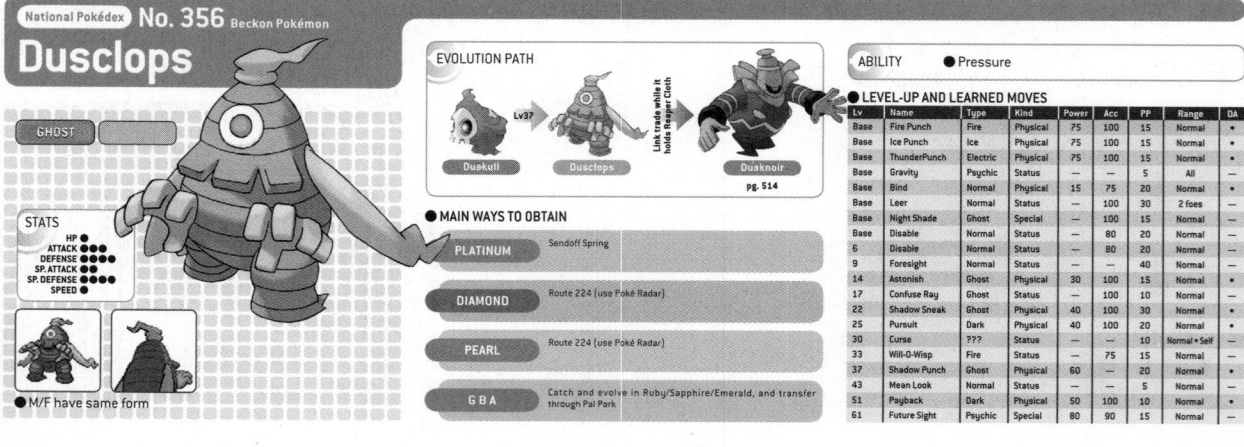

● EVOLUTION PATH

Duskull — Lv37 → Dusclops — Link trade while it holds Reaper Cloth → Dusknoir pg. 514

● MAIN WAYS TO OBTAIN

PLATINUM	Sendoff Spring
DIAMOND	Route 224 (use Poké Radar)
PEARL	Route 224 (use Poké Radar)
GBA	Catch and evolve in Ruby/Sapphire/Emerald, and transfer through Pal Park

ABILITY ● Pressure

● LEVEL-UP AND LEARNED MOVES

Lv	Name	Type	Kind	Power	Acc	PP	Range	DA
Base	Fire Punch	Fire	Physical	75	100	15	Normal	•
Base	Ice Punch	Ice	Physical	75	100	15	Normal	•
Base	ThunderPunch	Electric	Physical	75	100	15	Normal	•
Base	Gravity	Psychic	Status	—	—	5	All	—
Base	Bind	Normal	Physical	15	75	20	Normal	—
Base	Leer	Normal	Status	—	100	30	2 foes	—
Base	Night Shade	Ghost	Special	—	100	15	Normal	—
Base	Disable	Normal	Status	—	80	20	Normal	—
6	Disable	Normal	Status	—	80	20	Normal	—
9	Foresight	Normal	Status	—	—	40	Normal	—
14	Astonish	Ghost	Physical	30	100	15	Normal	•
17	Confuse Ray	Ghost	Status	—	100	10	Normal	—
22	Shadow Sneak	Ghost	Physical	40	100	30	Normal	•
25	Pursuit	Dark	Physical	40	100	20	Normal	—
30	Curse	???	Status	—	—	10	Normal • Self	
33	Will-O-Wisp	Fire	Status	—	75	15	Normal	—
37	Shadow Punch	Ghost	Physical	60	—	20	Normal	—
43	Mean Look	Normal	Status	—	—	5	Normal	—
51	Payback	Dark	Physical	50	100	10	Normal	—
61	Future Sight	Psychic	Special	80	90	15	Normal	—

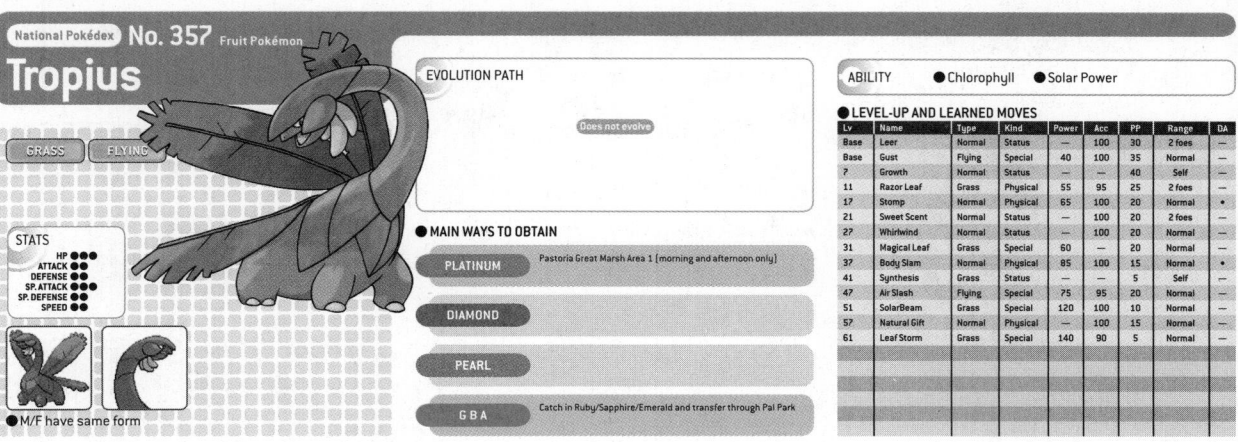

National Pokédex No. 357 Fruit Pokémon

Tropius

GRASS FLYING

STATS
HP ●●●
ATTACK ●●●
DEFENSE ●●●
SP. ATTACK ●●●
SP. DEFENSE ●●●
SPEED ●●

● M/F have same form

EVOLUTION PATH

Does not evolve

● **MAIN WAYS TO OBTAIN**

PLATINUM — Pastoria Great Marsh Area 1 (morning and afternoon only)

DIAMOND

PEARL

G B A — Catch in Ruby/Sapphire/Emerald and transfer through Pal Park

ABILITY ● Chlorophyll ● Solar Power

● **LEVEL-UP AND LEARNED MOVES**

Lv	Name	Type	Kind	Power	Acc	PP	Range	DA
Base	Leer	Normal	Status	—	100	30	2 foes	—
Base	Gust	Flying	Special	40	100	35	Normal	—
?	Growth	Normal	Status	—	—	40	Self	—
11	Razor Leaf	Grass	Physical	55	95	25	2 foes	—
17	Stomp	Normal	Physical	65	100	20	Normal	●
21	Sweet Scent	Normal	Status	—	100	20	2 foes	—
27	Whirlwind	Normal	Status	—	100	20	Normal	—
31	Magical Leaf	Grass	Special	60	—	20	Normal	—
37	Body Slam	Normal	Physical	85	100	15	Normal	●
41	Synthesis	Grass	Status	—	—	5	Self	—
47	Air Slash	Flying	Special	75	95	20	Normal	—
51	SolarBeam	Grass	Special	120	100	10	Normal	—
57	Natural Gift	Normal	Physical	—	100	15	Normal	—
61	Leaf Storm	Grass	Special	140	90	5	Normal	—

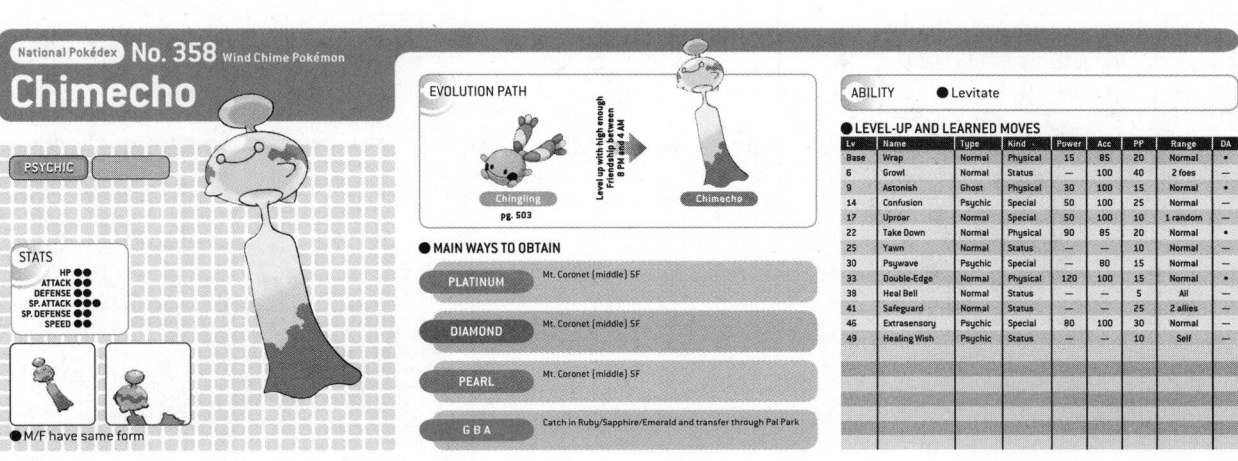

National Pokédex No. 358 Wind Chime Pokémon

Chimecho

PSYCHIC

STATS
HP ●●
ATTACK ●●
DEFENSE ●●●
SP. ATTACK ●●●
SP. DEFENSE ●●●
SPEED ●●

● M/F have same form

EVOLUTION PATH

Chingling → (Level up with high enough Friendship between 8 PM and 4 AM) → Chimecho
pg. 503

● **MAIN WAYS TO OBTAIN**

PLATINUM — Mt. Coronet (middle) 5F

DIAMOND — Mt. Coronet (middle) 5F

PEARL — Mt. Coronet (middle) 5F

G B A — Catch in Ruby/Sapphire/Emerald and transfer through Pal Park

ABILITY ● Levitate

● **LEVEL-UP AND LEARNED MOVES**

Lv	Name	Type	Kind	Power	Acc	PP	Range	DA
Base	Wrap	Normal	Physical	15	85	20	Normal	—
6	Growl	Normal	Status	—	100	40	2 foes	—
9	Astonish	Ghost	Physical	30	100	15	Normal	—
14	Confusion	Psychic	Special	50	100	25	Normal	—
17	Uproar	Normal	Special	50	100	10	1 random	—
22	Take Down	Normal	Physical	90	85	20	Normal	●
25	Yawn	Normal	Status	—	—	10	Normal	—
30	Psywave	Psychic	Special	—	80	15	Normal	—
33	Double-Edge	Normal	Physical	120	100	15	Normal	●
38	Heal Bell	Normal	Status	—	—	5	All	—
41	Safeguard	Normal	Status	—	—	25	2 allies	—
46	Extrasensory	Psychic	Special	80	100	30	Normal	—
49	Healing Wish	Psychic	Status	—	—	10	Self	—

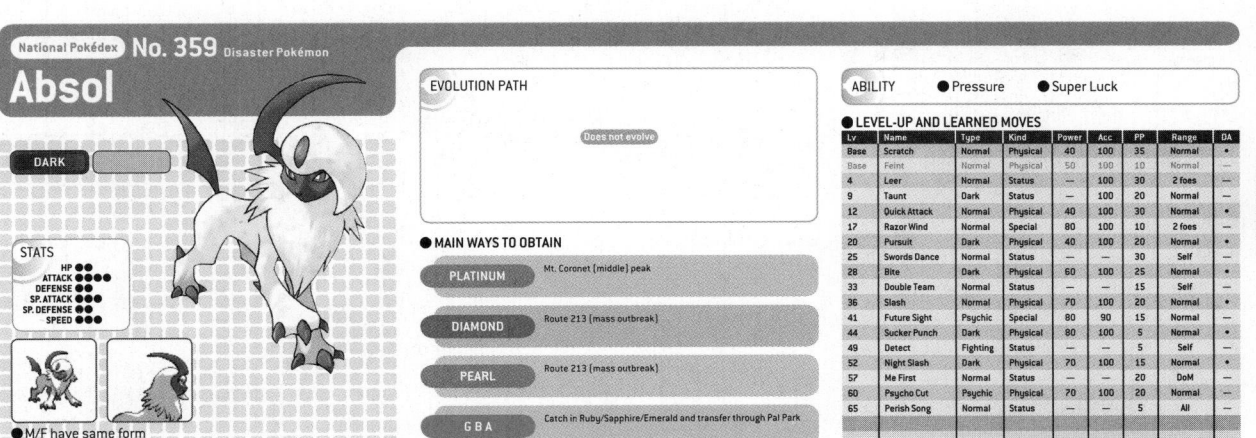

National Pokédex No. 359 Disaster Pokémon

Absol

DARK

STATS
HP ●●●
ATTACK ●●●●
DEFENSE ●●●
SP. ATTACK ●●●
SP. DEFENSE ●●●
SPEED ●●●

● M/F have same form

EVOLUTION PATH

Does not evolve

● **MAIN WAYS TO OBTAIN**

PLATINUM — Mt. Coronet (middle) peak

DIAMOND — Route 213 (mass outbreak)

PEARL — Route 213 (mass outbreak)

G B A — Catch in Ruby/Sapphire/Emerald and transfer through Pal Park

ABILITY ● Pressure ● Super Luck

● **LEVEL-UP AND LEARNED MOVES**

Lv	Name	Type	Kind	Power	Acc	PP	Range	DA
Base	Scratch	Normal	Physical	40	100	35	Normal	●
Base	Feint	Normal	Physical	50	100	10	Normal	—
4	Leer	Normal	Status	—	100	30	2 foes	—
9	Taunt	Dark	Status	—	100	20	Normal	—
12	Quick Attack	Normal	Physical	40	100	30	Normal	●
17	Razor Wind	Normal	Special	80	100	10	2 foes	—
20	Pursuit	Dark	Physical	40	100	20	Normal	●
25	Swords Dance	Normal	Status	—	—	30	Self	—
28	Bite	Dark	Physical	60	100	25	Normal	●
33	Double Team	Normal	Status	—	—	15	Self	—
36	Slash	Normal	Physical	70	100	20	Normal	●
41	Future Sight	Psychic	Special	80	90	15	Normal	—
44	Sucker Punch	Dark	Physical	80	100	5	Normal	●
49	Detect	Fighting	Status	—	—	5	Self	—
52	Night Slash	Dark	Physical	70	100	15	Normal	●
57	Me First	Normal	Status	—	—	20	DoM	—
60	Psycho Cut	Psychic	Physical	70	100	20	Normal	●
65	Perish Song	Normal	Status	—	—	5	All	—

360
WYNAUT

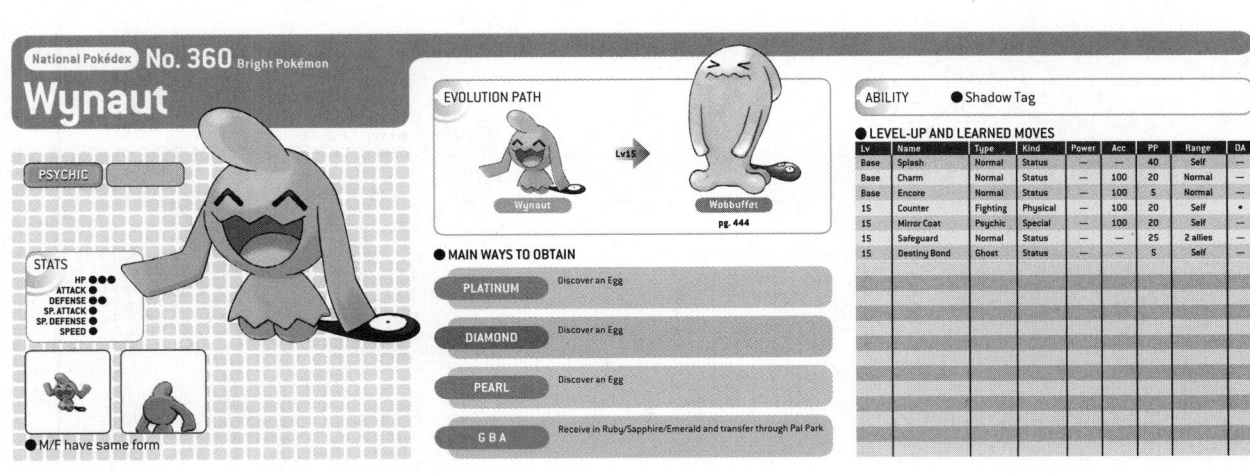

National Pokédex No. 360 Bright Pokémon

Wynaut

PSYCHIC

STATS
HP ●●●
ATTACK ●●
DEFENSE ●●
SP. ATTACK ●●
SP. DEFENSE ●●
SPEED ●

● M/F have same form

EVOLUTION PATH

Wynaut → (Lv15) → Wobbuffet
pg. 444

● **MAIN WAYS TO OBTAIN**

PLATINUM — Discover an Egg

DIAMOND — Discover an Egg

PEARL — Discover an Egg

G B A — Receive in Ruby/Sapphire/Emerald and transfer through Pal Park

ABILITY ● Shadow Tag

● **LEVEL-UP AND LEARNED MOVES**

Lv	Name	Type	Kind	Power	Acc	PP	Range	DA
Base	Splash	Normal	Status	—	—	40	Self	—
Base	Charm	Normal	Status	—	100	20	Normal	—
Base	Encore	Normal	Status	—	100	5	Normal	—
15	Counter	Fighting	Physical	—	100	20	Self	●
15	Mirror Coat	Psychic	Special	—	100	20	Self	—
15	Safeguard	Normal	Status	—	—	25	2 allies	—
15	Destiny Bond	Ghost	Status	—	—	5	Self	—

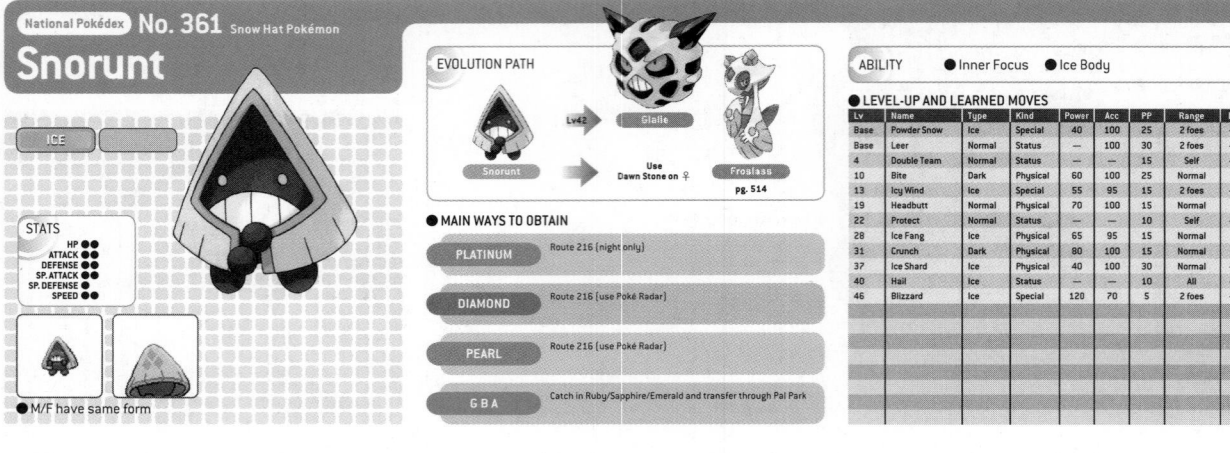

No. 361 Snow Hat Pokémon
Snorunt

ICE

STATS
- HP ●●
- ATTACK ●●
- DEFENSE ●●
- SP. ATTACK ●●
- SP. DEFENSE ●●
- SPEED ●●

● M/F have same form

EVOLUTION PATH

Snorunt → (Lv42) → Glalie

Snorunt → Use Dawn Stone on ♀ → Froslass pg. 514

ABILITY ● Inner Focus ● Ice Body

● **MAIN WAYS TO OBTAIN**

PLATINUM	Route 216 [night only]
DIAMOND	Route 216 [use Poké Radar]
PEARL	Route 216 [use Poké Radar]
GBA	Catch in Ruby/Sapphire/Emerald and transfer through Pal Park

● **LEVEL-UP AND LEARNED MOVES**

Lv	Name	Type	Kind	Power	Acc	PP	Range	DA
Base	Powder Snow	Ice	Special	40	100	25	2 foes	—
Base	Leer	Normal	Status	—	100	30	2 foes	—
4	Double Team	Normal	Status	—	—	15	Self	—
10	Bite	Dark	Physical	60	100	25	Normal	●
13	Icy Wind	Ice	Special	55	95	15	2 foes	—
19	Headbutt	Normal	Physical	70	100	15	Normal	●
22	Protect	Normal	Status	—	—	10	Self	—
28	Ice Fang	Ice	Physical	65	95	15	Normal	●
31	Crunch	Dark	Physical	80	100	15	Normal	●
37	Ice Shard	Ice	Physical	40	100	30	Normal	—
40	Hail	Ice	Status	—	—	10	All	—
46	Blizzard	Ice	Special	120	70	5	2 foes	—

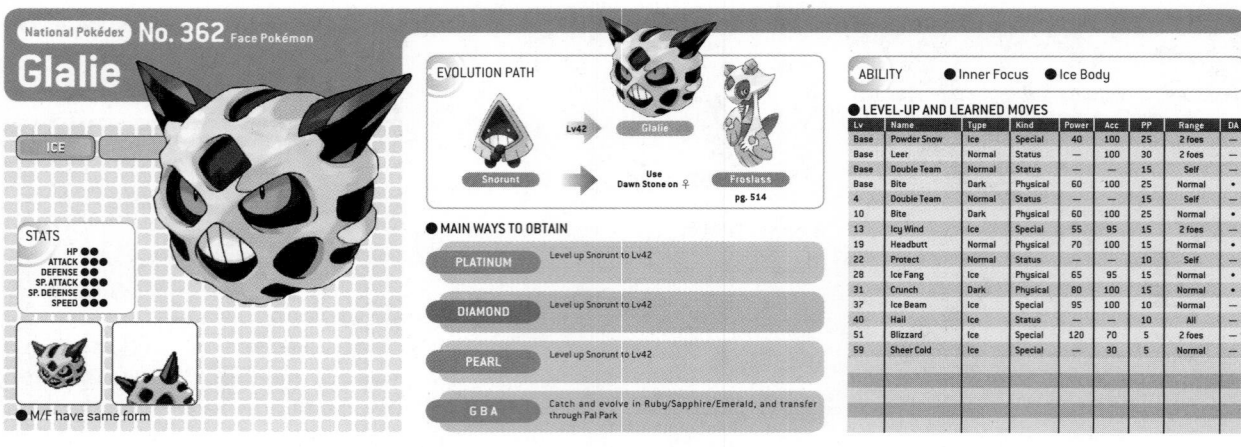

No. 362 Face Pokémon
Glalie

ICE

STATS
- HP ●●●
- ATTACK ●●●
- DEFENSE ●●●
- SP. ATTACK ●●●
- SP. DEFENSE ●●●
- SPEED ●●●

● M/F have same form

EVOLUTION PATH

Snorunt → (Lv42) → Glalie

Snorunt → Use Dawn Stone on ♀ → Froslass pg. 514

ABILITY ● Inner Focus ● Ice Body

● **MAIN WAYS TO OBTAIN**

PLATINUM	Level up Snorunt to Lv42
DIAMOND	Level up Snorunt to Lv42
PEARL	Level up Snorunt to Lv42
GBA	Catch and evolve in Ruby/Sapphire/Emerald, and transfer through Pal Park

● **LEVEL-UP AND LEARNED MOVES**

Lv	Name	Type	Kind	Power	Acc	PP	Range	DA
Base	Powder Snow	Ice	Special	40	100	25	2 foes	—
Base	Leer	Normal	Status	—	100	30	2 foes	—
Base	Double Team	Normal	Status	—	—	15	Self	—
Base	Bite	Dark	Physical	60	100	25	Normal	●
4	Double Team	Normal	Status	—	—	15	Self	—
10	Bite	Dark	Physical	60	100	25	Normal	●
13	Icy Wind	Ice	Special	55	95	15	2 foes	—
19	Headbutt	Normal	Physical	70	100	15	Normal	●
22	Protect	Normal	Status	—	—	10	Self	—
28	Ice Fang	Ice	Physical	65	95	15	Normal	●
31	Crunch	Dark	Physical	80	100	15	Normal	●
37	Ice Beam	Ice	Special	95	100	10	Normal	—
40	Hail	Ice	Status	—	—	10	All	—
51	Blizzard	Ice	Special	120	70	5	2 foes	—
59	Sheer Cold	Ice	Special	—	30	5	Normal	—

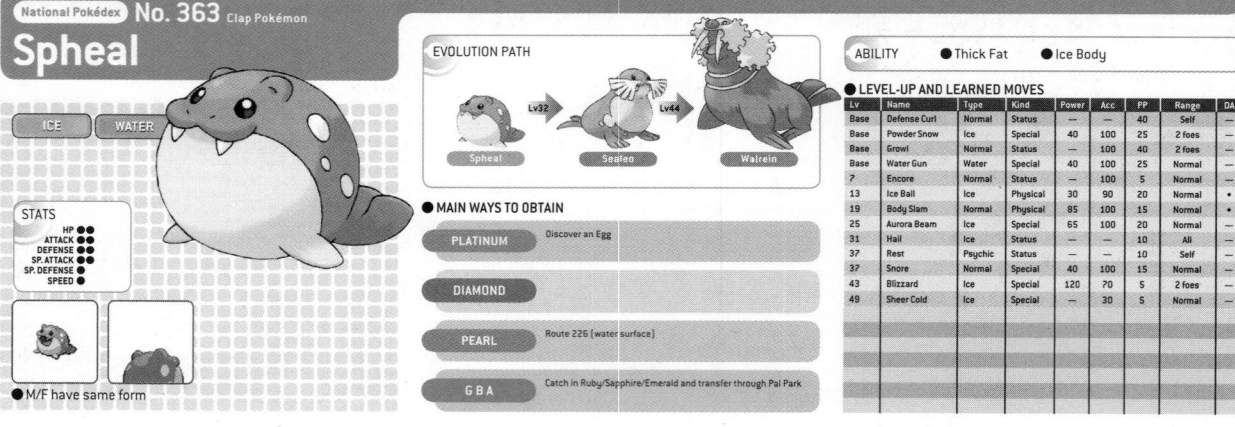

No. 363 Clap Pokémon
Spheal

ICE | WATER

STATS
- HP ●●
- ATTACK ●●
- DEFENSE ●●
- SP. ATTACK ●●
- SP. DEFENSE ●●
- SPEED ●

● M/F have same form

EVOLUTION PATH

Spheal → (Lv32) → Sealeo → (Lv44) → Walrein

ABILITY ● Thick Fat ● Ice Body

● **MAIN WAYS TO OBTAIN**

PLATINUM	Discover an Egg
DIAMOND	
PEARL	Route 226 [water surface]
GBA	Catch in Ruby/Sapphire/Emerald and transfer through Pal Park

● **LEVEL-UP AND LEARNED MOVES**

Lv	Name	Type	Kind	Power	Acc	PP	Range	DA
Base	Defense Curl	Normal	Status	—	—	40	Self	—
Base	Powder Snow	Ice	Special	40	100	25	2 foes	—
Base	Growl	Normal	Status	—	100	40	2 foes	—
Base	Water Gun	Water	Special	40	100	25	Normal	—
?	Encore	Normal	Status	—	100	5	Normal	—
13	Ice Ball	Ice	Physical	30	90	20	Normal	●
19	Body Slam	Normal	Physical	85	100	15	Normal	●
25	Aurora Beam	Ice	Special	65	100	20	Normal	—
31	Hail	Ice	Status	—	—	10	All	—
37	Rest	Psychic	Status	—	—	10	Self	—
37	Snore	Normal	Special	40	100	15	Normal	—
43	Blizzard	Ice	Special	120	70	5	2 foes	—
49	Sheer Cold	Ice	Special	—	30	5	Normal	—

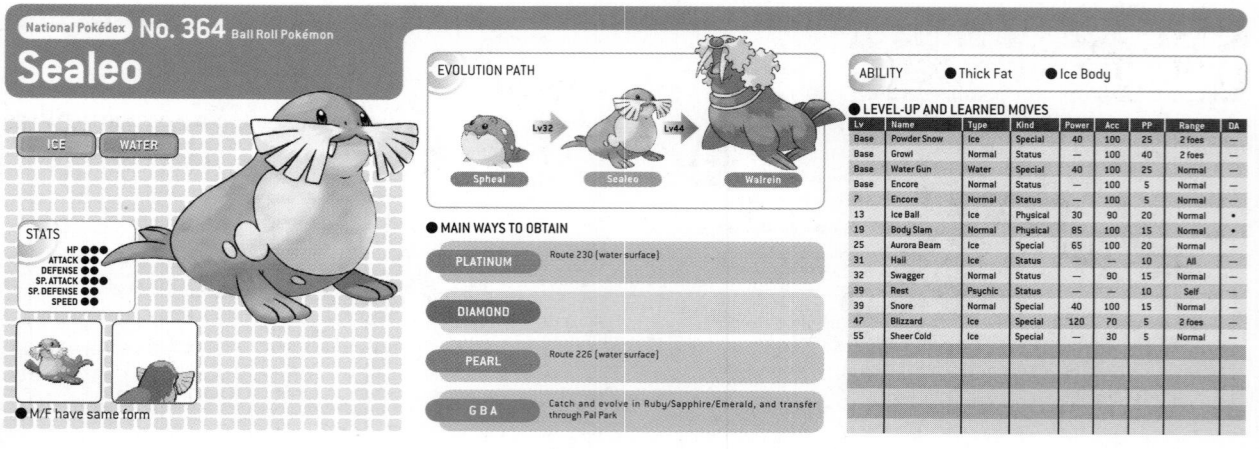

No. 364 Ball Roll Pokémon
Sealeo

ICE | WATER

STATS
- HP ●●●
- ATTACK ●●●
- DEFENSE ●●
- SP. ATTACK ●●
- SP. DEFENSE ●●
- SPEED ●●

● M/F have same form

EVOLUTION PATH

Spheal → (Lv32) → Sealeo → (Lv44) → Walrein

ABILITY ● Thick Fat ● Ice Body

● **MAIN WAYS TO OBTAIN**

PLATINUM	Route 230 [water surface]
DIAMOND	
PEARL	Route 226 [water surface]
GBA	Catch and evolve in Ruby/Sapphire/Emerald, and transfer through Pal Park

● **LEVEL-UP AND LEARNED MOVES**

Lv	Name	Type	Kind	Power	Acc	PP	Range	DA
Base	Powder Snow	Ice	Special	40	100	25	2 foes	—
Base	Growl	Normal	Status	—	100	40	2 foes	—
Base	Water Gun	Water	Special	40	100	25	Normal	—
Base	Encore	Normal	Status	—	100	5	Normal	—
?	Encore	Normal	Status	—	100	5	Normal	—
13	Ice Ball	Ice	Physical	30	90	20	Normal	●
19	Body Slam	Normal	Physical	85	100	15	Normal	●
25	Aurora Beam	Ice	Special	65	100	20	Normal	—
31	Hail	Ice	Status	—	—	10	All	—
32	Swagger	Normal	Status	—	90	15	Normal	—
39	Rest	Psychic	Status	—	—	10	Self	—
39	Snore	Normal	Special	40	100	15	Normal	—
47	Blizzard	Ice	Special	120	70	5	2 foes	—
55	Sheer Cold	Ice	Special	—	30	5	Normal	—

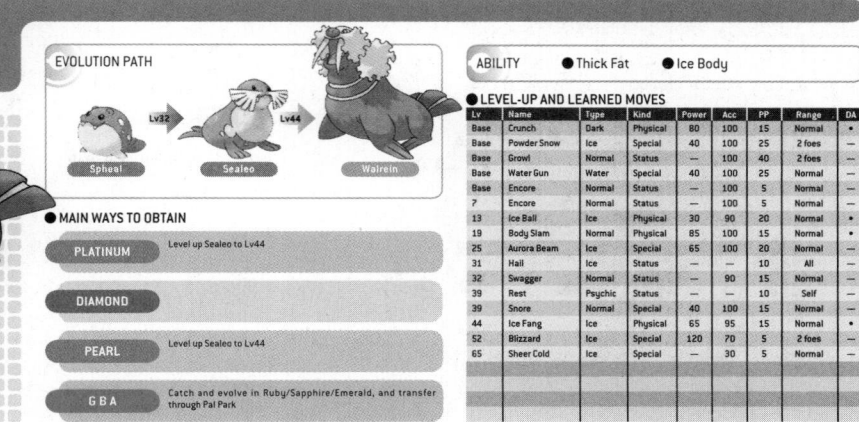

National Pokédex No. 365 Ice Break Pokémon
Walrein

ICE | WATER

STATS
HP ●●●
ATTACK ●●●
DEFENSE ●●●
SP. ATTACK ●●●
SP. DEFENSE ●●

● M/F have same form

EVOLUTION PATH

Spheal — Lv32 → Sealeo — Lv44 → Walrein

● MAIN WAYS TO OBTAIN

PLATINUM	Level up Sealeo to Lv44
DIAMOND	
PEARL	Level up Sealeo to Lv44
G B A	Catch and evolve in Ruby/Sapphire/Emerald, and transfer through Pal Park

ABILITY ● Thick Fat ● Ice Body

● LEVEL-UP AND LEARNED MOVES

Lv	Name	Type	Kind	Power	Acc	PP	Range	DA
Base	Crunch	Dark	Physical	80	100	15	Normal	●
Base	Powder Snow	Ice	Special	40	100	25	2 foes	—
Base	Growl	Normal	Status	—	100	40	2 foes	—
Base	Water Gun	Water	Special	40	100	25	Normal	—
Base	Encore	Normal	Status	—	100	5	Normal	—
7	Encore	Normal	Status	—	100	5	Normal	—
13	Ice Ball	Ice	Physical	30	90	20	Normal	●
19	Body Slam	Normal	Physical	85	100	15	Normal	●
25	Aurora Beam	Ice	Special	65	100	20	Normal	●
31	Hail	Ice	Status	—	—	10	All	—
32	Swagger	Normal	Status	—	90	15	Normal	—
39	Rest	Psychic	Status	—	—	10	Self	—
39	Snore	Normal	Special	40	100	15	Normal	●
44	Ice Fang	Ice	Physical	65	95	15	Normal	●
52	Blizzard	Ice	Special	120	70	5	2 foes	—
65	Sheer Cold	Ice	Special	—	30	5	Normal	—

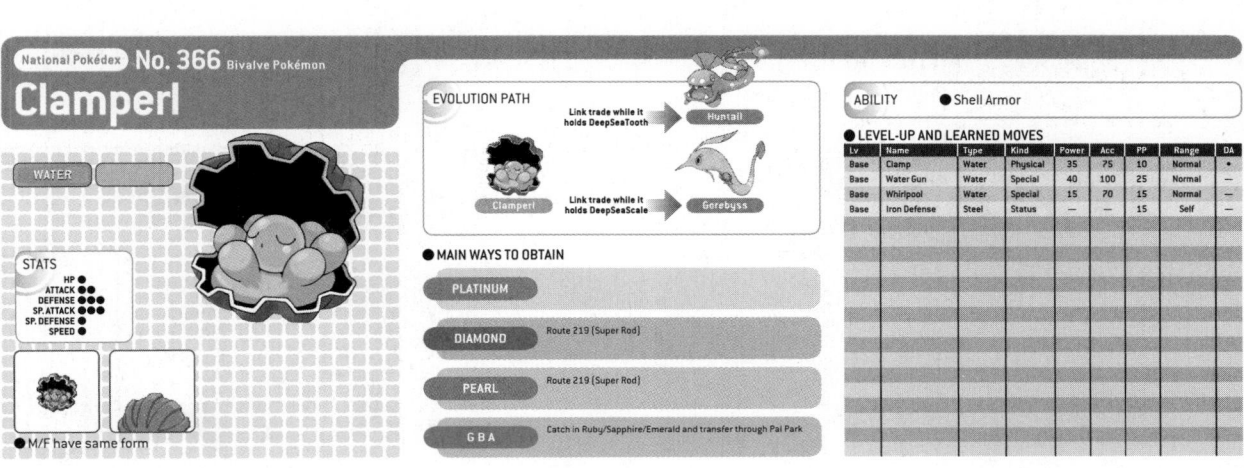

National Pokédex No. 366 Bivalve Pokémon
Clamperl

WATER

STATS
HP ●
ATTACK ●●●
DEFENSE ●●●
SP. ATTACK ●●●
SP. DEFENSE ●
SPEED ●

● M/F have same form

EVOLUTION PATH

Clamperl — Link trade while it holds DeepSeaTooth → Huntail
Clamperl — Link trade while it holds DeepSeaScale → Gorebyss

● MAIN WAYS TO OBTAIN

PLATINUM	
DIAMOND	Route 219 [Super Rod]
PEARL	Route 219 [Super Rod]
G B A	Catch in Ruby/Sapphire/Emerald and transfer through Pal Park

ABILITY ● Shell Armor

● LEVEL-UP AND LEARNED MOVES

Lv	Name	Type	Kind	Power	Acc	PP	Range	DA
Base	Clamp	Water	Physical	35	75	10	Normal	●
Base	Water Gun	Water	Special	40	100	25	Normal	—
Base	Whirlpool	Water	Special	15	70	15	Normal	—
Base	Iron Defense	Steel	Status	—	—	15	Self	—

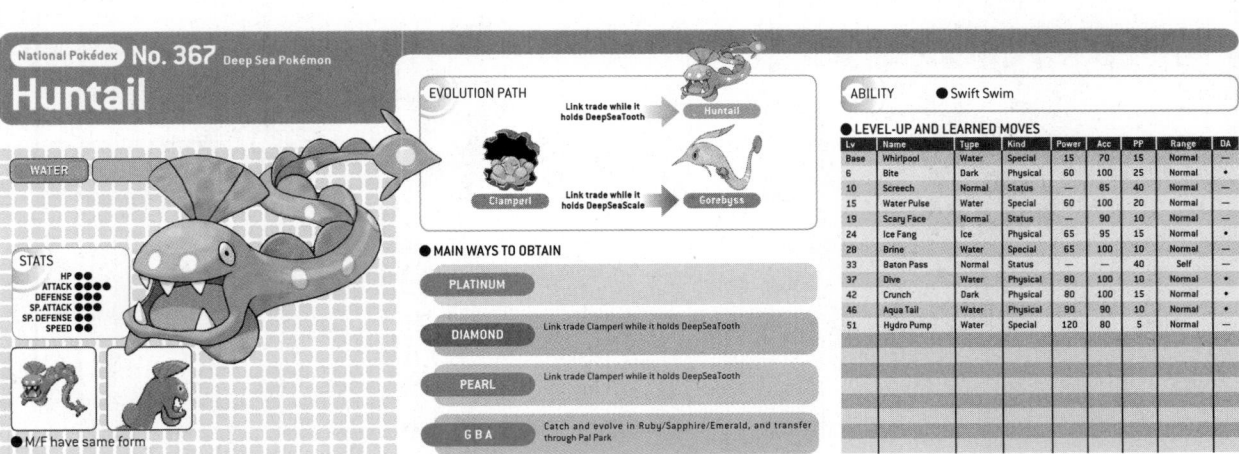

National Pokédex No. 367 Deep Sea Pokémon
Huntail

WATER

STATS
HP ●●
ATTACK ●●●
DEFENSE ●●●
SP. ATTACK ●●●
SP. DEFENSE ●●
SPEED ●●

● M/F have same form

EVOLUTION PATH

Clamperl — Link trade while it holds DeepSeaTooth → Huntail
Clamperl — Link trade while it holds DeepSeaScale → Gorebyss

● MAIN WAYS TO OBTAIN

PLATINUM	
DIAMOND	Link trade Clamperl while it holds DeepSeaTooth
PEARL	Link trade Clamperl while it holds DeepSeaTooth
G B A	Catch and evolve in Ruby/Sapphire/Emerald, and transfer through Pal Park

ABILITY ● Swift Swim

● LEVEL-UP AND LEARNED MOVES

Lv	Name	Type	Kind	Power	Acc	PP	Range	DA
Base	Whirlpool	Water	Special	15	70	15	Normal	—
6	Bite	Dark	Physical	60	100	25	Normal	●
10	Screech	Normal	Status	—	85	40	Normal	—
15	Water Pulse	Water	Special	60	100	20	Normal	—
19	Scary Face	Normal	Status	—	90	10	Normal	—
24	Ice Fang	Ice	Physical	65	95	15	Normal	●
28	Brine	Water	Special	65	100	10	Normal	—
33	Baton Pass	Normal	Status	—	—	40	Self	—
37	Dive	Water	Physical	80	100	10	Normal	●
42	Crunch	Dark	Physical	80	100	15	Normal	●
46	Aqua Tail	Water	Physical	90	90	10	Normal	●
51	Hydro Pump	Water	Special	120	80	5	Normal	—

368
GOREBYSS

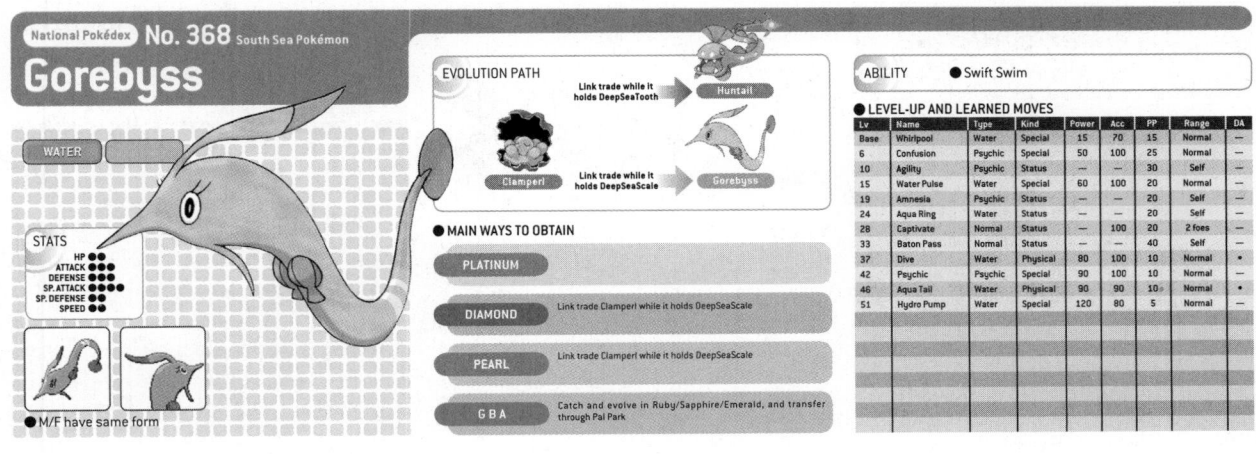

National Pokédex No. 368 South Sea Pokémon
Gorebyss

WATER

STATS
HP ●●
ATTACK ●●●
DEFENSE ●●●
SP. ATTACK ●●●
SP. DEFENSE ●●●
SPEED ●●●

● M/F have same form

EVOLUTION PATH

Clamperl — Link trade while it holds DeepSeaTooth → Huntail
Clamperl — Link trade while it holds DeepSeaScale → Gorebyss

● MAIN WAYS TO OBTAIN

PLATINUM	
DIAMOND	Link trade Clamperl while it holds DeepSeaScale
PEARL	Link trade Clamperl while it holds DeepSeaScale
G B A	Catch and evolve in Ruby/Sapphire/Emerald, and transfer through Pal Park

ABILITY ● Swift Swim

● LEVEL-UP AND LEARNED MOVES

Lv	Name	Type	Kind	Power	Acc	PP	Range	DA
Base	Whirlpool	Water	Special	15	70	15	Normal	—
6	Confusion	Psychic	Special	50	100	25	Normal	—
10	Agility	Psychic	Status	—	—	30	Self	—
15	Water Pulse	Water	Special	60	100	20	Normal	—
19	Amnesia	Psychic	Status	—	—	20	Self	—
24	Aqua Ring	Water	Status	—	—	20	Self	—
28	Captivate	Normal	Status	—	100	20	2 foes	—
33	Baton Pass	Normal	Status	—	—	40	Self	—
37	Dive	Water	Physical	80	100	10	Normal	●
42	Psychic	Psychic	Special	90	100	10	Normal	—
46	Aqua Tail	Water	Physical	90	90	10	Normal	●
51	Hydro Pump	Water	Special	120	80	5	Normal	—

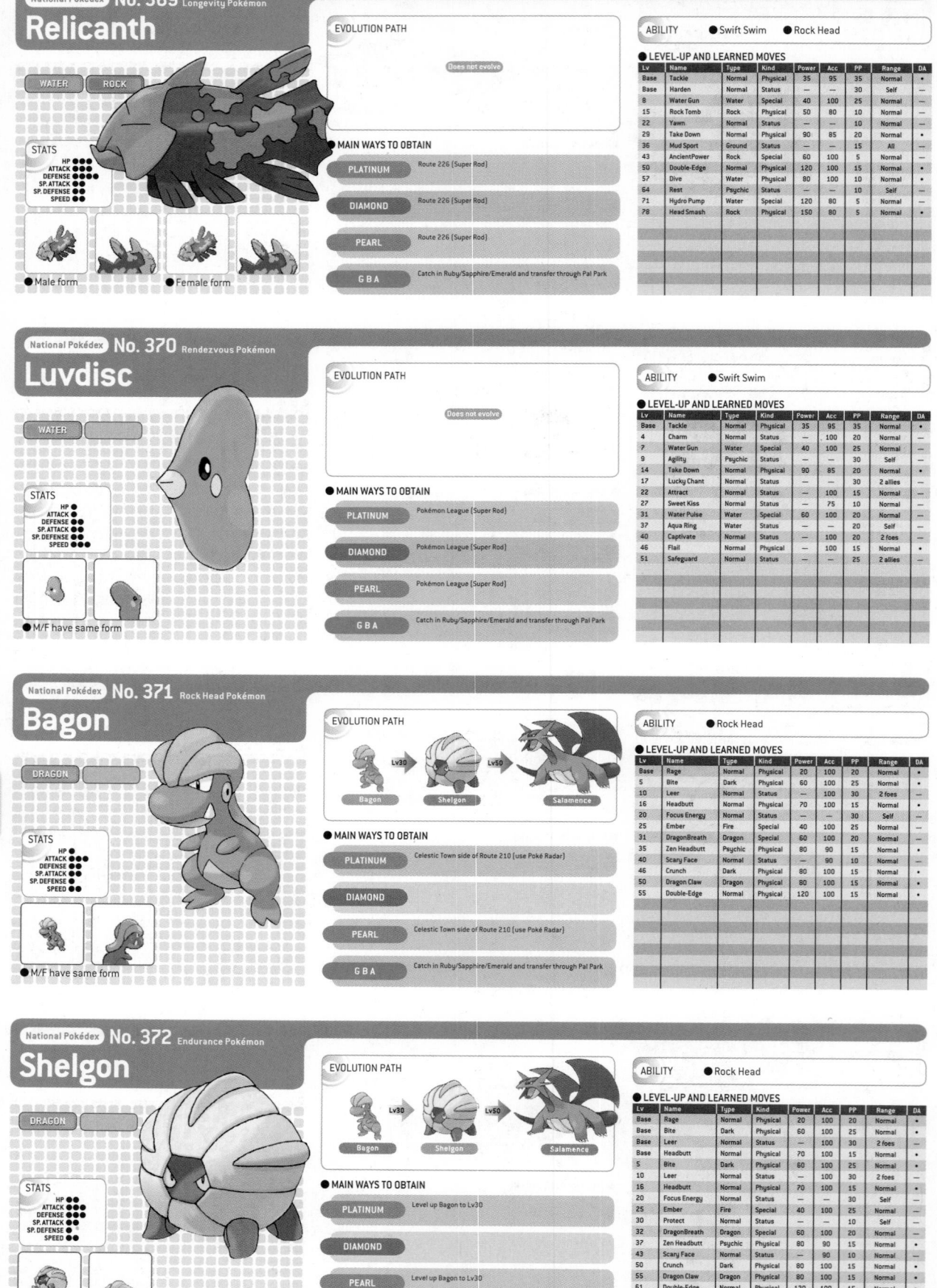

National Pokédex No. 369 Longevity Pokémon

Relicanth

WATER ROCK

STATS
- HP ●●●
- ATTACK ●●●
- DEFENSE ●●●●
- SP. ATTACK ●●
- SP. DEFENSE ●●●
- SPEED ●●

●Male form ●Female form

EVOLUTION PATH

Does not evolve

● MAIN WAYS TO OBTAIN

PLATINUM	Route 226 (Super Rod)
DIAMOND	Route 226 (Super Rod)
PEARL	Route 226 (Super Rod)
G B A	Catch in Ruby/Sapphire/Emerald and transfer through Pal Park

ABILITY ● Swift Swim ● Rock Head

● LEVEL-UP AND LEARNED MOVES

Lv	Name	Type	Kind	Power	Acc	PP	Range	DA
Base	Tackle	Normal	Physical	35	95	35	Normal	●
Base	Harden	Normal	Status	—	—	30	Self	—
8	Water Gun	Water	Special	40	100	25	Normal	—
15	Rock Tomb	Rock	Physical	50	80	10	Normal	—
22	Yawn	Normal	Status	—	—	10	Normal	—
29	Take Down	Normal	Physical	90	85	20	Normal	●
36	Mud Sport	Ground	Status	—	—	15	All	—
43	AncientPower	Rock	Special	60	100	5	Normal	●
50	Double-Edge	Normal	Physical	120	100	15	Normal	●
57	Dive	Water	Physical	80	100	10	Normal	●
64	Rest	Psychic	Status	—	—	10	Self	—
71	Hydro Pump	Water	Special	120	80	5	Normal	—
78	Head Smash	Rock	Physical	150	80	5	Normal	●

National Pokédex No. 370 Rendezvous Pokémon

Luvdisc

WATER

STATS
- HP ●
- ATTACK ●
- DEFENSE ●●
- SP. ATTACK ●●
- SP. DEFENSE ●●●
- SPEED ●●●

●M/F have same form

EVOLUTION PATH

Does not evolve

● MAIN WAYS TO OBTAIN

PLATINUM	Pokémon League (Super Rod)
DIAMOND	Pokémon League (Super Rod)
PEARL	Pokémon League (Super Rod)
G B A	Catch in Ruby/Sapphire/Emerald and transfer through Pal Park

ABILITY ● Swift Swim

● LEVEL-UP AND LEARNED MOVES

Lv	Name	Type	Kind	Power	Acc	PP	Range	DA
Base	Tackle	Normal	Physical	35	95	35	Normal	●
4	Charm	Normal	Status	—	100	20	Normal	—
7	Water Gun	Water	Special	40	100	25	Normal	—
9	Agility	Psychic	Status	—	—	30	Self	—
14	Take Down	Normal	Physical	90	85	20	Normal	●
17	Lucky Chant	Normal	Status	—	—	30	2 allies	—
22	Attract	Normal	Status	—	100	15	Normal	—
27	Sweet Kiss	Normal	Status	—	75	10	Normal	—
31	Water Pulse	Water	Special	60	100	20	Normal	—
37	Aqua Ring	Water	Status	—	—	20	Self	—
40	Captivate	Normal	Status	—	100	20	2 foes	—
46	Flail	Normal	Physical	—	100	15	Normal	●
51	Safeguard	Normal	Status	—	—	25	2 allies	—

National Pokédex No. 371 Rock Head Pokémon

Bagon

DRAGON

STATS
- HP ●●
- ATTACK ●●●
- DEFENSE ●●
- SP. ATTACK ●●
- SP. DEFENSE ●●
- SPEED ●●

●M/F have same form

EVOLUTION PATH

Bagon → Lv30 → Shelgon → Lv50 → Salamence

● MAIN WAYS TO OBTAIN

PLATINUM	Celestic Town side of Route 210 (use Poké Radar)
DIAMOND	
PEARL	Celestic Town side of Route 210 (use Poké Radar)
G B A	Catch in Ruby/Sapphire/Emerald and transfer through Pal Park

ABILITY ● Rock Head

● LEVEL-UP AND LEARNED MOVES

Lv	Name	Type	Kind	Power	Acc	PP	Range	DA
Base	Rage	Normal	Physical	20	100	20	Normal	●
5	Bite	Dark	Physical	60	100	25	Normal	●
10	Leer	Normal	Status	—	100	30	2 foes	—
16	Headbutt	Normal	Physical	70	100	15	Normal	●
20	Focus Energy	Normal	Status	—	—	30	Self	—
25	Ember	Fire	Special	40	100	25	Normal	—
31	DragonBreath	Dragon	Special	60	100	20	Normal	—
35	Zen Headbutt	Psychic	Physical	80	90	15	Normal	●
40	Scary Face	Normal	Status	—	90	10	Normal	—
46	Crunch	Dark	Physical	80	100	15	Normal	●
50	Dragon Claw	Dragon	Physical	80	100	15	Normal	●
55	Double-Edge	Normal	Physical	120	100	15	Normal	●

National Pokédex No. 372 Endurance Pokémon

Shelgon

DRAGON

STATS
- HP ●●
- ATTACK ●●●
- DEFENSE ●●●●
- SP. ATTACK ●●
- SP. DEFENSE ●●
- SPEED ●●

●M/F have same form

EVOLUTION PATH

Bagon → Lv30 → Shelgon → Lv50 → Salamence

● MAIN WAYS TO OBTAIN

PLATINUM	Level up Bagon to Lv30
DIAMOND	
PEARL	Level up Bagon to Lv30
G B A	Catch and evolve in Ruby/Sapphire/Emerald, and transfer through Pal Park

ABILITY ● Rock Head

● LEVEL-UP AND LEARNED MOVES

Lv	Name	Type	Kind	Power	Acc	PP	Range	DA
Base	Rage	Normal	Physical	20	100	20	Normal	●
Base	Bite	Dark	Physical	60	100	25	Normal	●
Base	Leer	Normal	Status	—	100	30	2 foes	—
Base	Headbutt	Normal	Physical	70	100	15	Normal	●
5	Bite	Dark	Physical	60	100	25	Normal	●
10	Leer	Normal	Status	—	100	30	2 foes	—
16	Headbutt	Normal	Physical	70	100	15	Normal	●
20	Focus Energy	Normal	Status	—	—	30	Self	—
25	Ember	Fire	Special	40	100	25	Normal	—
30	Protect	Normal	Status	—	—	10	Self	—
32	DragonBreath	Dragon	Special	60	100	20	Normal	—
37	Zen Headbutt	Psychic	Physical	80	90	15	Normal	●
43	Scary Face	Normal	Status	—	90	10	Normal	—
50	Crunch	Dark	Physical	80	100	15	Normal	●
55	Dragon Claw	Dragon	Physical	80	100	15	Normal	●
61	Double-Edge	Normal	Physical	120	100	15	Normal	●

National Pokédex No. 373 Dragon Pokémon
Salamence

DRAGON · FLYING

STATS
HP ●●●
ATTACK ●●●●
DEFENSE ●●●
SP. ATTACK ●●●
SP. DEFENSE ●●
SPEED ●●●

● M/F have same form

EVOLUTION PATH
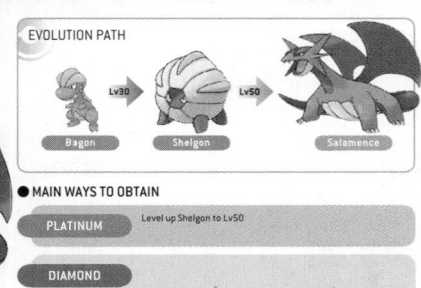
Bagon — Lv30 → Shelgon — Lv50 → Salamence

● MAIN WAYS TO OBTAIN
PLATINUM	Level up Shelgon to Lv50
DIAMOND	
PEARL	Level up Shelgon to Lv50
GBA	Catch and evolve in Ruby/Sapphire/Emerald, and transfer through Pal Park

ABILITY ● Intimidate

● LEVEL-UP AND LEARNED MOVES
Lv	Name	Type	Kind	Power	Acc	PP	Range	DA
Base	Fire Fang	Fire	Physical	65	95	15	Normal	●
Base	Thunder Fang	Electric	Physical	65	95	15	Normal	●
Base	Rage	Normal	Physical	20	100	20	Normal	●
Base	Bite	Dark	Physical	60	100	25	Normal	●
Base	Leer	Normal	Status	—	100	30	2 foes	—
Base	Headbutt	Normal	Physical	70	100	15	Normal	●
5	Bite	Dark	Physical	60	100	25	Normal	●
10	Leer	Normal	Status	—	100	30	2 foes	—
16	Headbutt	Normal	Physical	70	100	15	Normal	●
20	Focus Energy	Normal	Status	—	—	30	Self	—
25	Ember	Fire	Special	40	100	25	Normal	●
30	Protect	Normal	Status	—	—	10	Self	—
32	DragonBreath	Dragon	Special	60	100	20	Normal	●
37	Zen Headbutt	Psychic	Physical	80	90	15	Normal	●
43	Scary Face	Normal	Status	—	90	10	Normal	—
50	Fly	Flying	Physical	90	95	15	Normal	●
53	Crunch	Dark	Physical	80	100	15	Normal	●
61	Dragon Claw	Dragon	Physical	80	100	15	Normal	●
70	Double-Edge	Normal	Physical	120	100	15	Normal	●

National Pokédex No. 374 Iron Ball Pokémon
Beldum

STEEL · PSYCHIC

STATS
HP ●
ATTACK ●●
DEFENSE ●●●
SP. ATTACK ●●
SP. DEFENSE ●●
SPEED ●●

● Gender unknown

EVOLUTION PATH
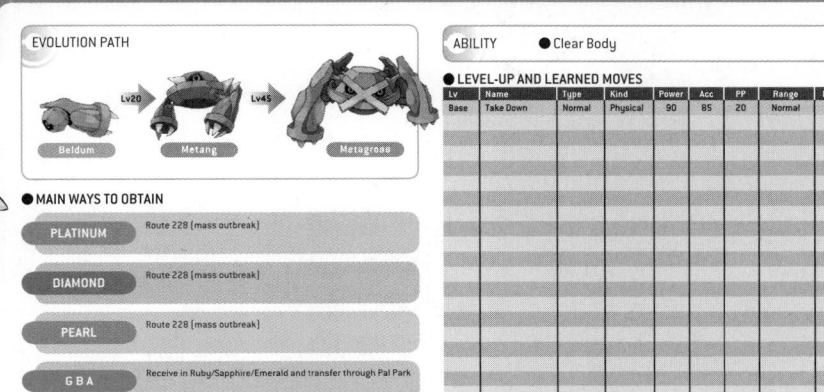
Beldum — Lv20 → Metang — Lv45 → Metagross

● MAIN WAYS TO OBTAIN
PLATINUM	Route 228 [mass outbreak]
DIAMOND	Route 228 [mass outbreak]
PEARL	Route 228 [mass outbreak]
GBA	Receive in Ruby/Sapphire/Emerald and transfer through Pal Park

ABILITY ● Clear Body

● LEVEL-UP AND LEARNED MOVES
Lv	Name	Type	Kind	Power	Acc	PP	Range	DA
Base	Take Down	Normal	Physical	90	85	20	Normal	●

National Pokédex No. 375 Iron Claw Pokémon
Metang

STEEL · PSYCHIC

STATS
HP ●●
ATTACK ●●●
DEFENSE ●●●
SP. ATTACK ●●
SP. DEFENSE ●●
SPEED ●●

● Gender unknown

EVOLUTION PATH
Beldum — Lv20 → Metang — Lv45 → Metagross

● MAIN WAYS TO OBTAIN
PLATINUM	Level up Beldum to Lv20
DIAMOND	Level up Beldum to Lv20
PEARL	Level up Beldum to Lv20
GBA	Receive and evolve in Ruby/Sapphire/Emerald, and transfer through Pal Park

ABILITY ● Clear Body

● LEVEL-UP AND LEARNED MOVES
Lv	Name	Type	Kind	Power	Acc	PP	Range	DA
Base	Magnet Rise	Electric	Status	—	—	10	Self	—
Base	Take Down	Normal	Physical	90	85	20	Normal	●
Base	Metal Claw	Steel	Physical	50	95	35	Normal	●
Base	Confusion	Psychic	Special	50	100	25	Normal	●
20	Metal Claw	Steel	Physical	50	95	35	Normal	●
20	Confusion	Psychic	Special	50	100	25	Normal	●
24	Scary Face	Normal	Status	—	90	10	Normal	—
28	Pursuit	Dark	Physical	40	100	20	Normal	●
32	Bullet Punch	Steel	Physical	40	100	30	Normal	●
36	Psychic	Psychic	Special	90	100	10	Normal	●
40	Iron Defense	Steel	Status	—	—	15	Self	—
44	Agility	Psychic	Status	—	—	30	Self	—
48	Meteor Mash	Steel	Physical	100	85	10	Normal	●
52	Zen Headbutt	Psychic	Physical	80	90	15	Normal	●
56	Hyper Beam	Normal	Special	150	90	5	Normal	●

National Pokédex No. 376 Iron Leg Pokémon
Metagross

STEEL · PSYCHIC

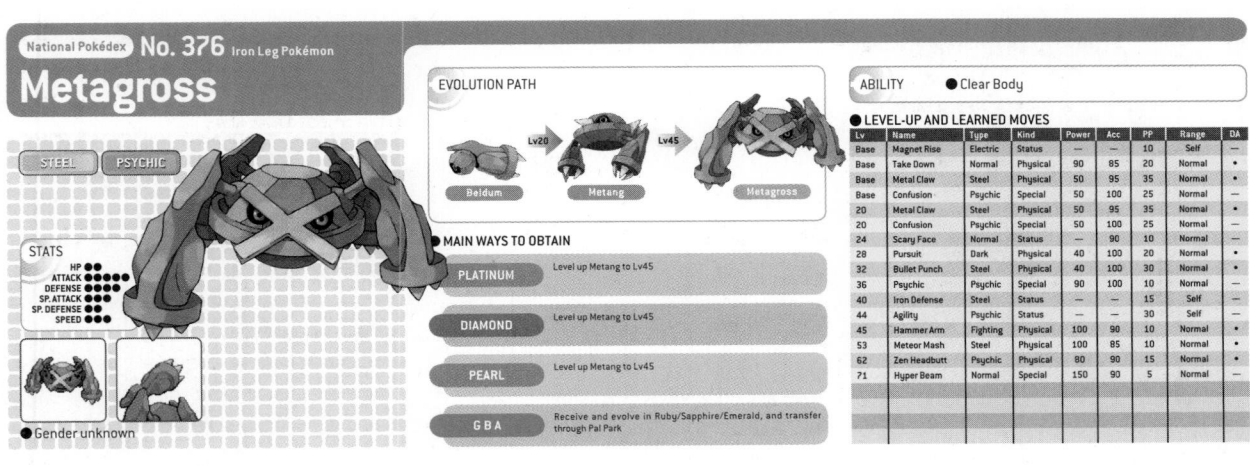

STATS
HP ●●
ATTACK ●●●●
DEFENSE ●●●●
SP. ATTACK ●●●
SP. DEFENSE ●●●
SPEED ●●●

● Gender unknown

EVOLUTION PATH
Beldum — Lv20 → Metang — Lv45 → Metagross

● MAIN WAYS TO OBTAIN
PLATINUM	Level up Metang to Lv45
DIAMOND	Level up Metang to Lv45
PEARL	Level up Metang to Lv45
GBA	Receive and evolve in Ruby/Sapphire/Emerald, and transfer through Pal Park

ABILITY ● Clear Body

● LEVEL-UP AND LEARNED MOVES
Lv	Name	Type	Kind	Power	Acc	PP	Range	DA
Base	Magnet Rise	Electric	Status	—	—	10	Self	—
Base	Take Down	Normal	Physical	90	85	20	Normal	●
Base	Metal Claw	Steel	Physical	50	95	35	Normal	●
Base	Confusion	Psychic	Special	50	100	25	Normal	●
20	Metal Claw	Steel	Physical	50	95	35	Normal	●
20	Confusion	Psychic	Special	50	100	25	Normal	●
24	Scary Face	Normal	Status	—	90	10	Normal	—
28	Pursuit	Dark	Physical	40	100	20	Normal	●
32	Bullet Punch	Steel	Physical	40	100	30	Normal	●
36	Psychic	Psychic	Special	90	100	10	Normal	●
40	Iron Defense	Steel	Status	—	—	15	Self	—
44	Agility	Psychic	Status	—	—	30	Self	—
45	Hammer Arm	Fighting	Physical	100	90	10	Normal	●
53	Meteor Mash	Steel	Physical	100	85	10	Normal	●
62	Zen Headbutt	Psychic	Physical	80	90	15	Normal	●
71	Hyper Beam	Normal	Special	150	90	5	Normal	●

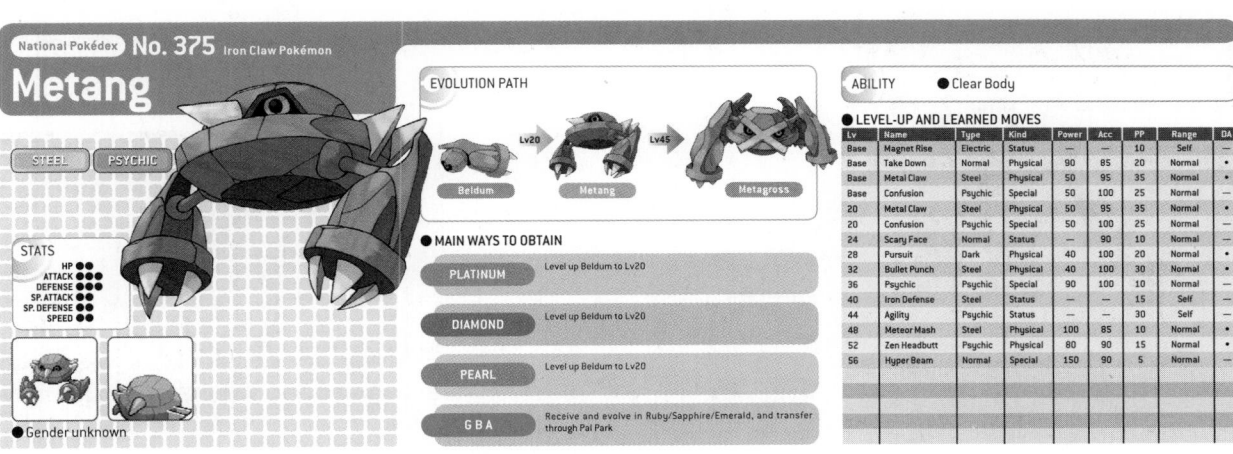

Regirock

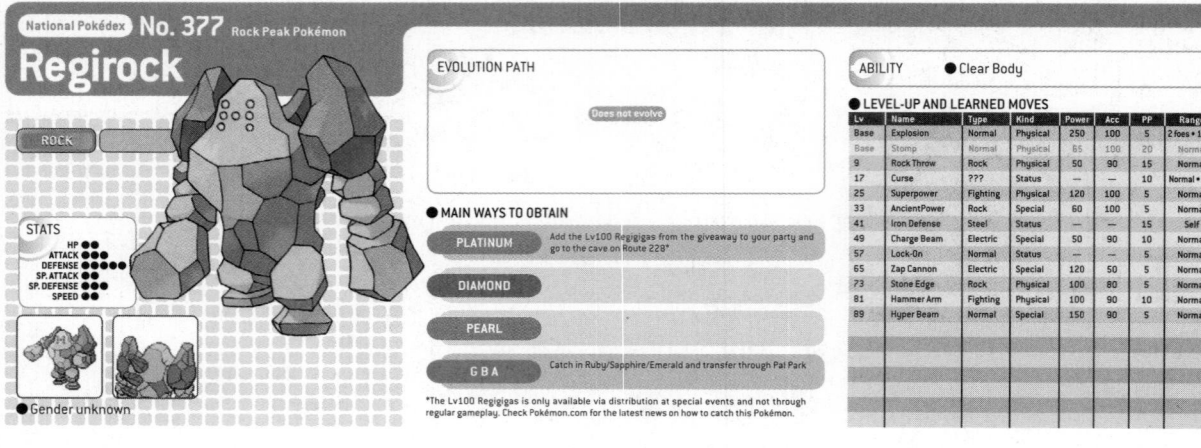

ROCK

STATS
HP ●●
ATTACK ●●●●
DEFENSE ●●●●●
SP. ATTACK ●●
SP. DEFENSE ●●●
SPEED ●●

● Gender unknown

EVOLUTION PATH
Does not evolve

MAIN WAYS TO OBTAIN
PLATINUM — Add the Lv100 Regigigas from the giveaway to your party and go to the cave on Route 228*

DIAMOND

PEARL

GBA — Catch in Ruby/Sapphire/Emerald and transfer through Pal Park

*The Lv100 Regigigas is only available via distribution at special events and not through regular gameplay. Check Pokémon.com for the latest news on how to catch this Pokémon.

ABILITY ● Clear Body

● LEVEL-UP AND LEARNED MOVES

Lv	Name	Type	Kind	Power	Acc	PP	Range	DA
Base	Explosion	Normal	Physical	250	100	5	2 foes + 1 ally	—
Base	Stomp	Normal	Physical	65	100	20	Normal	•
9	Rock Throw	Rock	Physical	50	90	15	Normal	—
17	Curse	???	Status	—	—	10	Normal + Self	—
25	Superpower	Fighting	Physical	120	100	5	Normal	•
33	AncientPower	Rock	Special	60	100	5	Normal	—
41	Iron Defense	Steel	Status	—	—	15	Self	—
49	Charge Beam	Electric	Special	50	90	10	Normal	—
57	Lock-On	Normal	Status	—	—	5	Normal	—
65	Zap Cannon	Electric	Special	120	50	5	Normal	—
73	Stone Edge	Rock	Physical	100	80	5	Normal	—
81	Hammer Arm	Fighting	Physical	100	90	10	Normal	•
89	Hyper Beam	Normal	Special	150	90	5	Normal	—

Regice

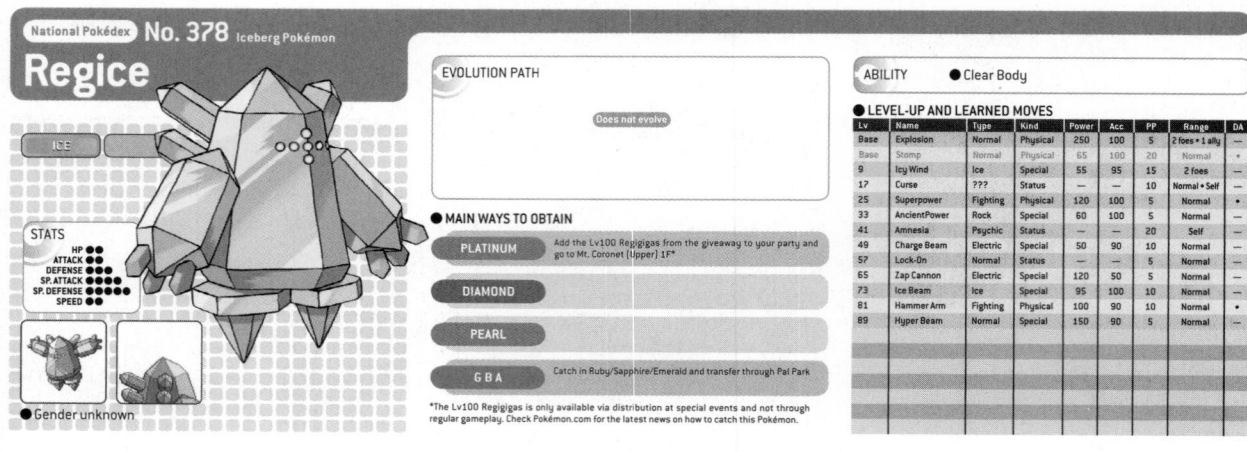

ICE

STATS
HP ●●
ATTACK ●●
DEFENSE ●●●●
SP. ATTACK ●●●●
SP. DEFENSE ●●●●●
SPEED ●●

● Gender unknown

EVOLUTION PATH
Does not evolve

MAIN WAYS TO OBTAIN
PLATINUM — Add the Lv100 Regigigas from the giveaway to your party and go to Mt. Coronet (Upper) 1F*

DIAMOND

PEARL

GBA — Catch in Ruby/Sapphire/Emerald and transfer through Pal Park

*The Lv100 Regigigas is only available via distribution at special events and not through regular gameplay. Check Pokémon.com for the latest news on how to catch this Pokémon.

ABILITY ● Clear Body

● LEVEL-UP AND LEARNED MOVES

Lv	Name	Type	Kind	Power	Acc	PP	Range	DA
Base	Explosion	Normal	Physical	250	100	5	2 foes + 1 ally	—
Base	Stomp	Normal	Physical	65	100	20	Normal	•
9	Icy Wind	Ice	Special	55	95	15	2 foes	—
17	Curse	???	Status	—	—	10	Normal + Self	—
25	Superpower	Fighting	Physical	120	100	5	Normal	•
33	AncientPower	Rock	Special	60	100	5	Normal	—
41	Amnesia	Psychic	Status	—	—	20	Self	—
49	Charge Beam	Electric	Special	50	90	10	Normal	—
57	Lock-On	Normal	Status	—	—	5	Normal	—
65	Zap Cannon	Electric	Special	120	50	5	Normal	—
73	Ice Beam	Ice	Special	95	100	10	Normal	—
81	Hammer Arm	Fighting	Physical	100	90	10	Normal	•
89	Hyper Beam	Normal	Special	150	90	5	Normal	—

Registeel

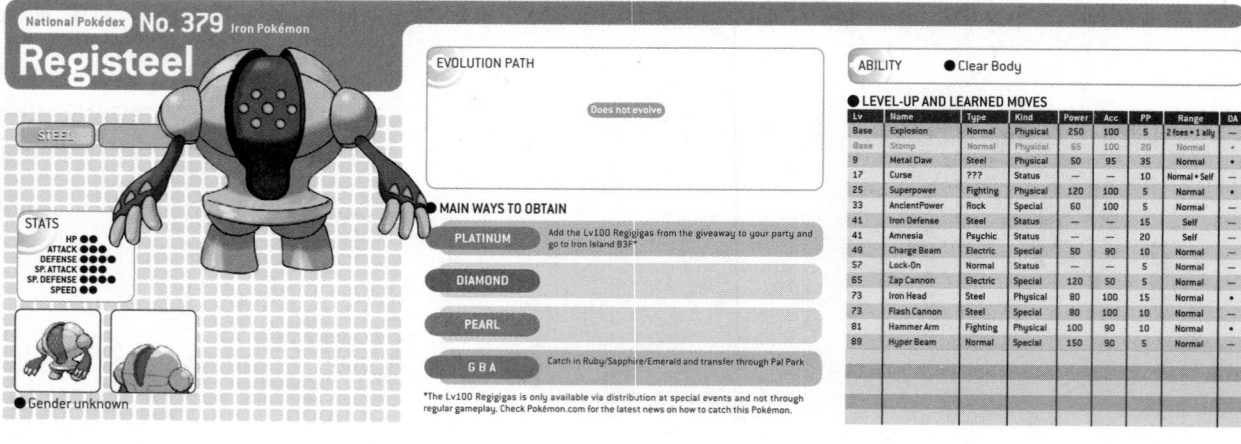

STEEL

STATS
HP ●●
ATTACK ●●
DEFENSE ●●●●●
SP. ATTACK ●●
SP. DEFENSE ●●●●●
SPEED ●●

● Gender unknown

EVOLUTION PATH
Does not evolve

MAIN WAYS TO OBTAIN
PLATINUM — Add the Lv100 Regigigas from the giveaway to your party and go to Iron Island B3F*

DIAMOND

PEARL

GBA — Catch in Ruby/Sapphire/Emerald and transfer through Pal Park

*The Lv100 Regigigas is only available via distribution at special events and not through regular gameplay. Check Pokémon.com for the latest news on how to catch this Pokémon.

ABILITY ● Clear Body

● LEVEL-UP AND LEARNED MOVES

Lv	Name	Type	Kind	Power	Acc	PP	Range	DA
Base	Explosion	Normal	Physical	250	100	5	2 foes + 1 ally	—
Base	Stomp	Normal	Physical	65	100	20	Normal	•
9	Metal Claw	Steel	Physical	50	95	35	Normal	•
17	Curse	???	Status	—	—	10	Normal + Self	—
25	Superpower	Fighting	Physical	120	100	5	Normal	•
33	AncientPower	Rock	Special	60	100	5	Normal	—
41	Iron Defense	Steel	Status	—	—	15	Self	—
41	Amnesia	Psychic	Status	—	—	20	Self	—
49	Charge Beam	Electric	Special	50	90	10	Normal	—
57	Lock-On	Normal	Status	—	—	5	Normal	—
65	Zap Cannon	Electric	Special	120	50	5	Normal	—
73	Iron Head	Steel	Physical	80	100	15	Normal	•
73	Flash Cannon	Steel	Special	80	100	10	Normal	—
81	Hammer Arm	Fighting	Physical	100	90	10	Normal	—
89	Hyper Beam	Normal	Special	150	90	5	Normal	—

Latias

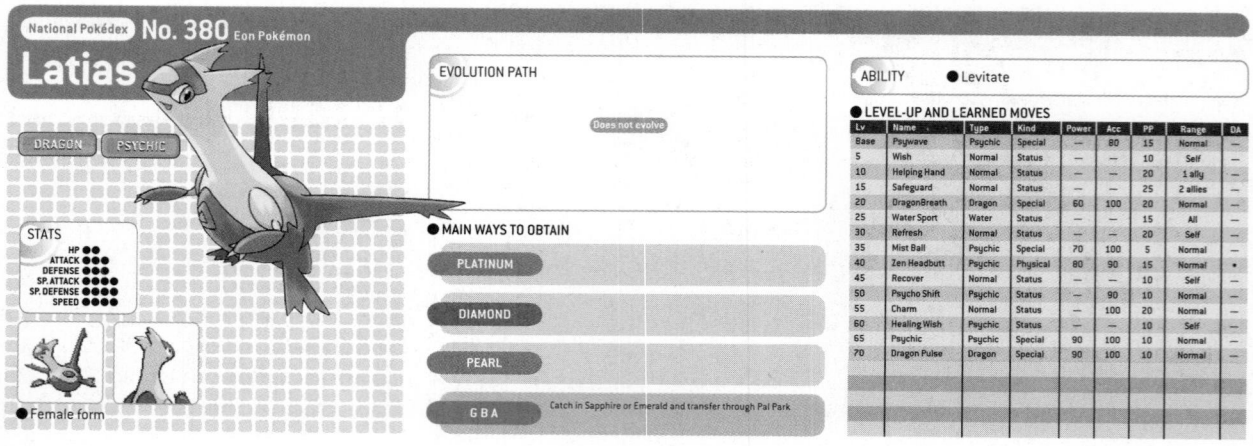

DRAGON PSYCHIC

STATS
HP ●●
ATTACK ●●
DEFENSE ●●●
SP. ATTACK ●●●●
SP. DEFENSE ●●●●●
SPEED ●●●●

● Female form

EVOLUTION PATH
Does not evolve

MAIN WAYS TO OBTAIN
PLATINUM

DIAMOND

PEARL

GBA — Catch in Sapphire or Emerald and transfer through Pal Park

ABILITY ● Levitate

● LEVEL-UP AND LEARNED MOVES

Lv	Name	Type	Kind	Power	Acc	PP	Range	DA
Base	Psywave	Psychic	Special	—	80	15	Normal	—
5	Wish	Normal	Status	—	—	10	Self	—
10	Helping Hand	Normal	Status	—	—	20	1 ally	—
15	Safeguard	Normal	Status	—	—	25	2 allies	—
20	DragonBreath	Dragon	Special	60	100	20	Normal	—
25	Water Sport	Water	Status	—	—	15	All	—
30	Refresh	Normal	Status	—	—	20	Self	—
35	Mist Ball	Psychic	Special	70	100	5	Normal	—
40	Zen Headbutt	Psychic	Physical	80	90	15	Normal	•
45	Recover	Normal	Status	—	—	10	Self	—
50	Psycho Shift	Psychic	Status	—	90	10	Normal	—
55	Charm	Normal	Status	—	100	20	Normal	—
60	Healing Wish	Psychic	Status	—	—	10	Self	—
65	Psychic	Psychic	Special	90	100	10	Normal	—
70	Dragon Pulse	Dragon	Special	90	100	10	Normal	—

National Pokédex No. 381 — Latios — Eon Pokémon

Type: DRAGON / PSYCHIC

EVOLUTION PATH

Does not evolve

STATS

- HP ●●●
- ATTACK ●●●
- DEFENSE ●●●
- SP. ATTACK ●●●●
- SP. DEFENSE ●●●●
- SPEED ●●●●

● Male form

ABILITY ● Levitate

● LEVEL-UP AND LEARNED MOVES

Lv	Name	Type	Kind	Power	Acc	PP	Range	DA
Base	Psywave	Psychic	Special	—	80	15	Normal	—
5	Heal Block	Psychic	Status	—	100	15	2 foes	—
10	Helping Hand	Normal	Status	—	—	20	1 ally	—
15	Safeguard	Normal	Status	—	—	25	2 allies	—
20	DragonBreath	Dragon	Special	60	100	20	Normal	—
25	Protect	Normal	Status	—	—	10	Self	—
30	Refresh	Normal	Status	—	—	20	Self	—
35	Luster Purge	Psychic	Special	70	100	5	Normal	—
40	Zen Headbutt	Psychic	Physical	80	90	15	Normal	●
45	Recover	Normal	Status	—	—	10	Self	—
50	Psycho Shift	Psychic	Status	—	90	10	Normal	—
55	Dragon Dance	Dragon	Status	—	—	20	Self	—
60	Memento	Dark	Status	—	100	10	Normal	—
65	Psychic	Psychic	Special	90	100	10	Normal	—
70	Dragon Pulse	Dragon	Special	90	100	10	Normal	—

● MAIN WAYS TO OBTAIN

- PLATINUM
- DIAMOND
- PEARL
- GBA — Catch in Ruby or Emerald and transfer through Pal Park

---

National Pokédex No. 382 — Kyogre — Sea Basin Pokémon

Type: WATER

EVOLUTION PATH

Does not evolve

STATS

- HP ●●●●
- ATTACK ●●●
- DEFENSE ●●●
- SP. ATTACK ●●●●
- SP. DEFENSE ●●●●
- SPEED ●●●

● Gender unknown

ABILITY ● Drizzle

● LEVEL-UP AND LEARNED MOVES

Lv	Name	Type	Kind	Power	Acc	PP	Range	DA
Base	Water Pulse	Water	Special	60	100	20	Normal	—
5	Scary Face	Normal	Status	—	90	10	Normal	—
15	AncientPower	Rock	Special	60	100	5	Normal	—
20	Body Slam	Normal	Physical	85	100	15	Normal	●
30	Calm Mind	Psychic	Status	—	—	20	Self	—
35	Ice Beam	Ice	Special	95	100	10	Normal	—
45	Hydro Pump	Water	Special	120	80	5	Normal	—
50	Rest	Psychic	Status	—	—	10	Self	—
60	Sheer Cold	Ice	Special	—	30	5	Normal	—
65	Double-Edge	Normal	Physical	120	100	15	Normal	●
75	Aqua Tail	Water	Physical	90	90	10	Normal	—
80	Water Spout	Water	Special	150	100	5	2 foes	—

● MAIN WAYS TO OBTAIN

- PLATINUM
- DIAMOND
- PEARL
- GBA — Catch in Sapphire or Emerald and transfer through Pal Park

---

National Pokédex No. 383 — Groudon — Continent Pokémon

Type: GROUND

EVOLUTION PATH

Does not evolve

STATS

- HP ●●●
- ATTACK ●●●●
- DEFENSE ●●●●
- SP. ATTACK ●●●
- SP. DEFENSE ●●●
- SPEED ●●●

● Gender unknown

ABILITY ● Drought

● LEVEL-UP AND LEARNED MOVES

Lv	Name	Type	Kind	Power	Acc	PP	Range	DA
Base	Mud Shot	Ground	Special	55	95	15	Normal	—
5	Scary Face	Normal	Status	—	90	10	Normal	—
15	AncientPower	Rock	Special	60	100	5	Normal	—
20	Slash	Normal	Physical	70	100	20	Normal	●
30	Bulk Up	Fighting	Status	—	—	20	Self	—
35	Earthquake	Ground	Physical	100	100	10	2 foes + 1 ally	—
45	Fire Blast	Fire	Special	120	85	5	Normal	—
50	Rest	Psychic	Status	—	—	10	Self	—
60	Fissure	Ground	Physical	—	30	5	Normal	—
65	SolarBeam	Grass	Special	120	100	10	Normal	—
75	Earth Power	Ground	Special	90	100	10	Normal	—
80	Eruption	Fire	Special	150	100	5	2 foes	—

● MAIN WAYS TO OBTAIN

- PLATINUM
- DIAMOND
- PEARL
- GBA — Catch in Ruby or Emerald and transfer through Pal Park

---

National Pokédex No. 384 — Rayquaza — Sky High Pokémon

Type: DRAGON / FLYING

EVOLUTION PATH

Does not evolve

STATS

- HP ●●●
- ATTACK ●●●●
- DEFENSE ●●●
- SP. ATTACK ●●●●
- SP. DEFENSE ●●●
- SPEED ●●●

● Gender unknown

ABILITY ● Air Lock

● LEVEL-UP AND LEARNED MOVES

Lv	Name	Type	Kind	Power	Acc	PP	Range	DA
Base	Twister	Dragon	Special	40	100	20	2 foes	—
5	Scary Face	Normal	Status	—	90	10	Normal	—
15	AncientPower	Rock	Special	60	100	5	Normal	—
20	Dragon Claw	Dragon	Physical	80	100	15	Normal	●
30	Dragon Dance	Dragon	Status	—	—	20	Self	—
35	Crunch	Dark	Physical	80	100	15	Normal	●
45	Fly	Flying	Physical	90	95	15	Normal	●
50	Rest	Psychic	Status	—	—	10	Self	—
60	ExtremeSpeed	Normal	Physical	80	100	5	Normal	●
65	Hyper Beam	Normal	Special	150	90	5	Normal	—
75	Dragon Pulse	Dragon	Special	90	100	10	Normal	—
80	Outrage	Dragon	Physical	120	100	15	1 random	●

● MAIN WAYS TO OBTAIN

- PLATINUM
- DIAMOND
- PEARL
- GBA — Catch in Ruby/Sapphire/Emerald and transfer through Pal Park

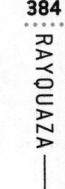

384 RAYQUAZA

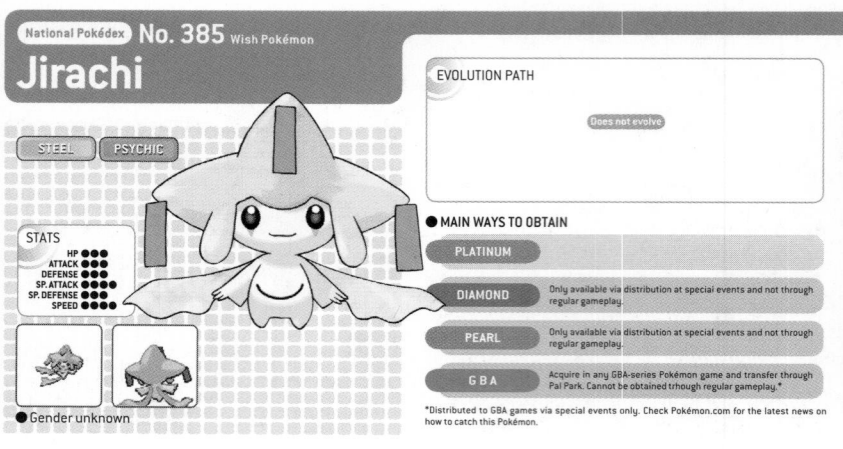

National Pokédex **No. 385** Wish Pokémon

Jirachi

STEEL   PSYCHIC

STATS
- HP
- ATTACK
- DEFENSE
- SP. ATTACK
- SP. DEFENSE
- SPEED

● Gender unknown

EVOLUTION PATH
Does not evolve

● MAIN WAYS TO OBTAIN
PLATINUM	
DIAMOND	Only available via distribution at special events and not through regular gameplay.
PEARL	Only available via distribution at special events and not through regular gameplay.
GBA	Acquire in any GBA-series Pokémon game and transfer through Pal Park. Cannot be obtained through regular gameplay.*

*Distributed to GBA games via special events only. Check Pokemon.com for the latest news on how to catch this Pokémon.

ABILITY   ● Serene Grace

● LEVEL-UP AND LEARNED MOVES
Lv	Name	Type	Kind	Power	Acc	PP	Range	DA
Base	Wish	Normal	Status	—	—	10	Self	—
Base	Confusion	Psychic	Special	50	100	25	Normal	—
5	Rest	Psychic	Status	—	—	10	Self	—
10	Swift	Normal	Special	60	—	20	2 foes	—
15	Helping Hand	Normal	Status	—	—	20	1 ally	—
20	Psychic	Psychic	Special	90	100	10	Normal	—
25	Refresh	Normal	Status	—	—	20	Self	—
30	Rest	Psychic	Status	—	—	10	Self	—
35	Zen Headbutt	Psychic	Physical	80	90	15	Normal	•
40	Double-Edge	Normal	Physical	120	100	15	Normal	—
45	Gravity	Psychic	Status	—	—	5	All	—
50	Healing Wish	Psychic	Status	—	—	10	Self	—
55	Future Sight	Psychic	Special	80	90	15	Normal	—
60	Cosmic Power	Psychic	Status	—	—	20	Self	—
65	Last Resort	Normal	Physical	130	100	5	Normal	•
70	Doom Desire	Steel	Special	120	85	5	Normal	—

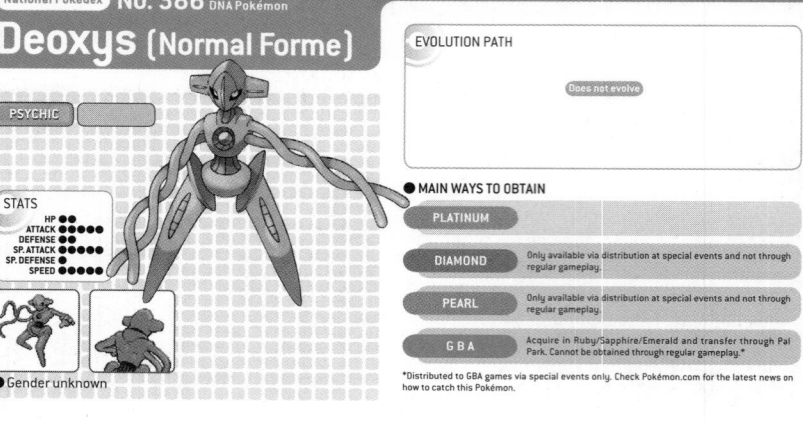

National Pokédex **No. 386** DNA Pokémon

Deoxys (Normal Forme)

PSYCHIC

STATS
- HP
- ATTACK
- DEFENSE
- SP. ATTACK
- SP. DEFENSE
- SPEED

● Gender unknown

EVOLUTION PATH
Does not evolve

● MAIN WAYS TO OBTAIN
PLATINUM	
DIAMOND	Only available via distribution at special events and not through regular gameplay.
PEARL	Only available via distribution at special events and not through regular gameplay.
GBA	Acquire in Ruby/Sapphire/Emerald and transfer through Pal Park. Cannot be obtained through regular gameplay.*

*Distributed to GBA games via special events only. Check Pokemon.com for the latest news on how to catch this Pokémon.

ABILITY   ● Pressure

● LEVEL-UP AND LEARNED MOVES
Lv	Name	Type	Kind	Power	Acc	PP	Range	DA
Base	Leer	Normal	Status	—	100	30	2 foes	—
Base	Wrap	Normal	Physical	15	85	20	Normal	•
9	Night Shade	Ghost	Special	—	100	15	Normal	—
17	Teleport	Psychic	Status	—	—	20	Self	—
25	Knock Off	Dark	Physical	20	100	20	Normal	•
33	Pursuit	Dark	Physical	40	100	20	Normal	•
41	Psychic	Psychic	Special	90	100	10	Normal	—
49	Snatch	Dark	Status	—	—	10	DoM	—
57	Psycho Shift	Psychic	Status	—	90	10	Normal	—
65	Zen Headbutt	Psychic	Physical	80	90	15	Normal	•
73	Cosmic Power	Psychic	Status	—	—	20	Self	—
81	Recover	Normal	Status	—	—	10	Self	—
89	Psycho Boost	Psychic	Special	140	90	5	Normal	—
97	Hyper Beam	Normal	Special	150	90	5	Normal	—

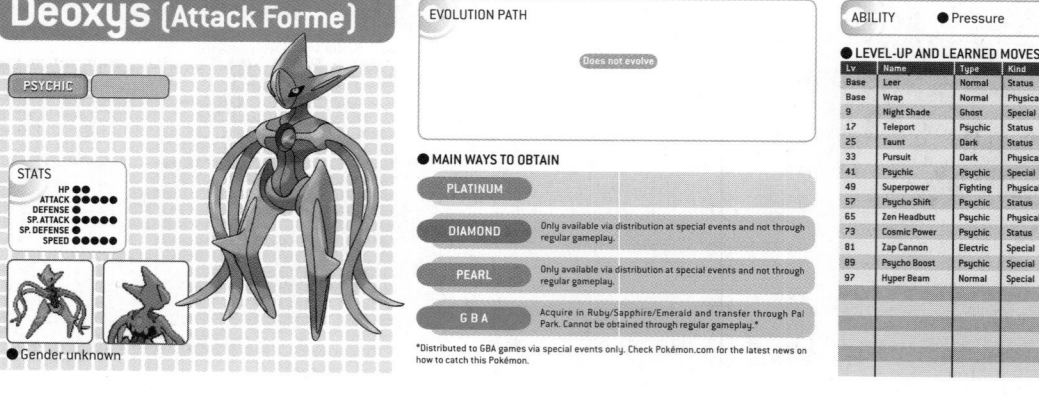

National Pokédex **No. 386** DNA Pokémon

Deoxys (Attack Forme)

PSYCHIC

STATS
- HP
- ATTACK
- DEFENSE
- SP. ATTACK
- SP. DEFENSE
- SPEED

● Gender unknown

EVOLUTION PATH
Does not evolve

● MAIN WAYS TO OBTAIN
PLATINUM	
DIAMOND	Only available via distribution at special events and not through regular gameplay.
PEARL	Only available via distribution at special events and not through regular gameplay.
GBA	Acquire in Ruby/Sapphire/Emerald and transfer through Pal Park. Cannot be obtained through regular gameplay.*

*Distributed to GBA games via special events only. Check Pokemon.com for the latest news on how to catch this Pokémon.

ABILITY   ● Pressure

● LEVEL-UP AND LEARNED MOVES
Lv	Name	Type	Kind	Power	Acc	PP	Range	DA
Base	Leer	Normal	Status	—	100	30	2 foes	—
Base	Wrap	Normal	Physical	15	85	20	Normal	•
9	Night Shade	Ghost	Special	—	100	15	Normal	—
17	Teleport	Psychic	Status	—	—	20	Self	—
25	Taunt	Dark	Status	—	100	20	Normal	—
33	Pursuit	Dark	Physical	40	100	20	Normal	•
41	Psychic	Psychic	Special	90	100	10	Normal	—
49	Superpower	Fighting	Physical	120	100	5	Normal	•
57	Psycho Shift	Psychic	Status	—	90	10	Normal	—
65	Zen Headbutt	Psychic	Physical	80	90	15	Normal	•
73	Cosmic Power	Psychic	Status	—	—	20	Self	—
81	Zap Cannon	Electric	Special	120	50	5	Normal	—
89	Psycho Boost	Psychic	Special	140	90	5	Normal	—
97	Hyper Beam	Normal	Special	150	90	5	Normal	—

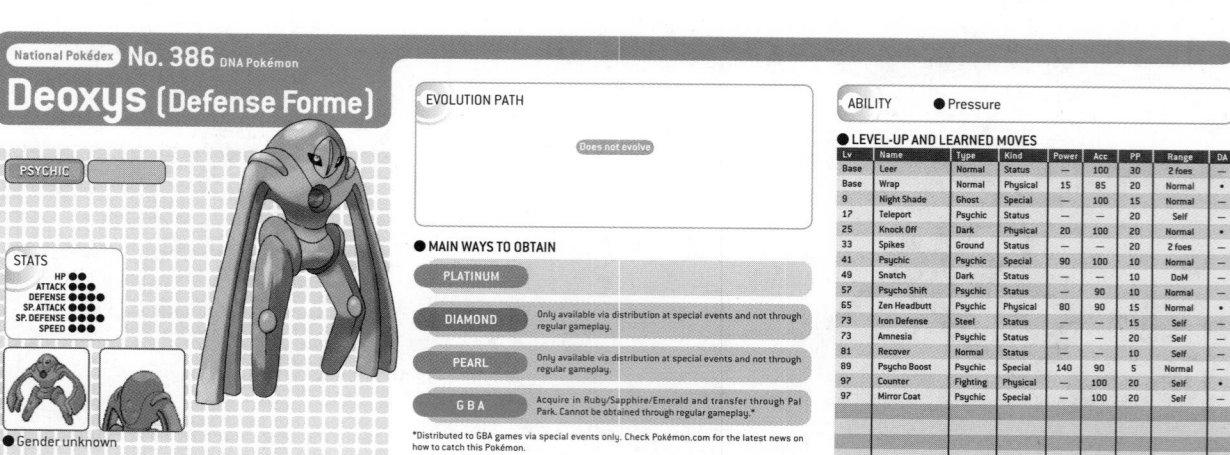

National Pokédex **No. 386** DNA Pokémon

Deoxys (Defense Forme)

PSYCHIC

STATS
- HP
- ATTACK
- DEFENSE
- SP. ATTACK
- SP. DEFENSE
- SPEED

● Gender unknown

EVOLUTION PATH
Does not evolve

● MAIN WAYS TO OBTAIN
PLATINUM	
DIAMOND	Only available via distribution at special events and not through regular gameplay.
PEARL	Only available via distribution at special events and not through regular gameplay.
GBA	Acquire in Ruby/Sapphire/Emerald and transfer through Pal Park. Cannot be obtained through regular gameplay.*

*Distributed to GBA games via special events only. Check Pokemon.com for the latest news on how to catch this Pokémon.

ABILITY   ● Pressure

● LEVEL-UP AND LEARNED MOVES
Lv	Name	Type	Kind	Power	Acc	PP	Range	DA
Base	Leer	Normal	Status	—	100	30	2 foes	—
Base	Wrap	Normal	Physical	15	85	20	Normal	•
9	Night Shade	Ghost	Special	—	100	15	Normal	—
17	Teleport	Psychic	Status	—	—	20	Self	—
25	Knock Off	Dark	Physical	20	100	20	Normal	•
33	Spikes	Ground	Status	—	—	20	2 foes	—
41	Psychic	Psychic	Special	90	100	10	Normal	—
49	Snatch	Dark	Status	—	—	10	DoM	—
57	Psycho Shift	Psychic	Status	—	90	10	Normal	—
65	Zen Headbutt	Psychic	Physical	80	90	15	Normal	•
73	Iron Defense	Steel	Status	—	—	15	Self	—
73	Amnesia	Psychic	Status	—	—	20	Self	—
81	Recover	Normal	Status	—	—	10	Self	—
89	Psycho Boost	Psychic	Special	140	90	5	Normal	—
97	Counter	Fighting	Physical	—	100	20	Self	—
97	Mirror Coat	Psychic	Special	—	100	20	Self	—

National Pokédex No. 386 DNA Pokémon
Deoxys (Speed Forme)

PSYCHIC

STATS
HP
ATTACK
DEFENSE
SP.ATTACK
SP.DEFENSE
SPEED

● Gender unknown

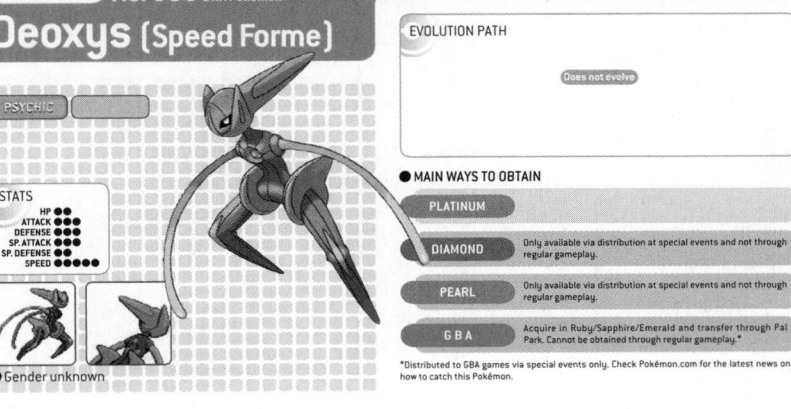

EVOLUTION PATH

Does not evolve

● **MAIN WAYS TO OBTAIN**

PLATINUM	
DIAMOND	Only available via distribution at special events and not through regular gameplay.
PEARL	Only available via distribution at special events and not through regular gameplay.
GBA	Acquire in Ruby/Sapphire/Emerald and transfer through Pal Park. Cannot be obtained through regular gameplay.*

*Distributed to GBA games via special events only. Check Pokémon.com for the latest news on how to catch this Pokémon.

ABILITY ● Pressure

● **LEVEL-UP AND LEARNED MOVES**

Lv	Name	Type	Kind	Power	Acc	PP	Range	DA
Base	Leer	Normal	Status	—	100	30	2 foes	
Base	Wrap	Normal	Physical	15	85	20	Normal	•
9	Night Shade	Ghost	Special	—	100	15	Normal	—
17	Double Team	Normal	Status	—	—	15	Self	
25	Knock Off	Dark	Physical	20	100	20	Normal	•
33	Pursuit	Dark	Physical	40	100	20	Normal	•
41	Psychic	Psychic	Special	90	100	10	Normal	•
49	Swift	Normal	Special	60	—	20	2 foes	
57	Psycho Shift	Psychic	Status	—	90	10	Normal	
65	Zen Headbutt	Psychic	Physical	80	90	15	Normal	•
73	Agility	Psychic	Status	—	—	30	Self	
81	Recover	Normal	Status	—	—	10	Self	
89	Psycho Boost	Psychic	Special	140	90	5	Normal	
97	ExtremeSpeed	Normal	Physical	80	100	5	Normal	

National Pokédex No. 387 Tiny Leaf Pokémon
Turtwig

GRASS

STATS
HP
ATTACK
DEFENSE
SP.ATTACK
SP.DEFENSE
SPEED

● M/F have same form

EVOLUTION PATH

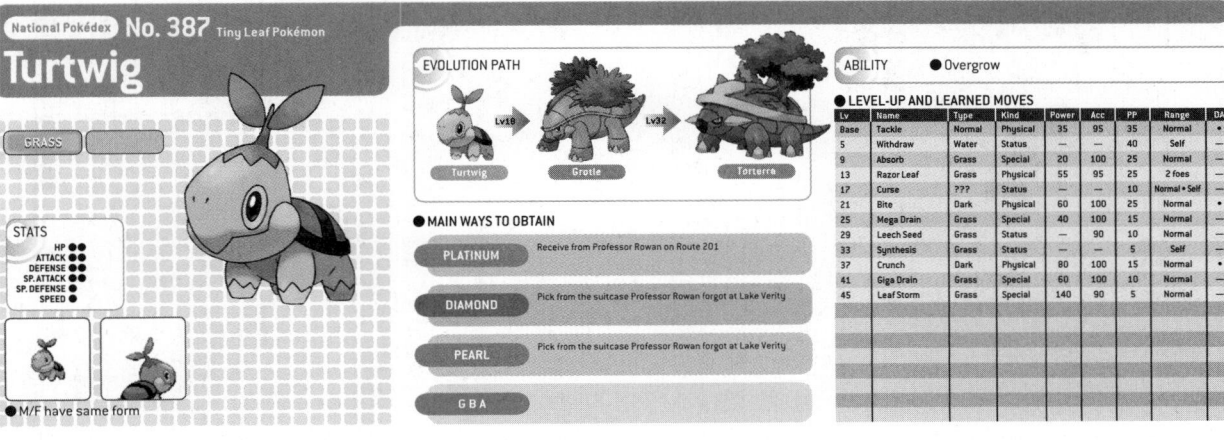

Turtwig → Lv18 → Grotle → Lv32 → Torterra

● **MAIN WAYS TO OBTAIN**

PLATINUM	Receive from Professor Rowan on Route 201
DIAMOND	Pick from the suitcase Professor Rowan forgot at Lake Verity
PEARL	Pick from the suitcase Professor Rowan forgot at Lake Verity
GBA	

ABILITY ● Overgrow

● **LEVEL-UP AND LEARNED MOVES**

Lv	Name	Type	Kind	Power	Acc	PP	Range	DA
Base	Tackle	Normal	Physical	35	95	35	Normal	—
5	Withdraw	Water	Status	—	—	40	Self	
9	Absorb	Grass	Special	20	100	25	Normal	
13	Razor Leaf	Grass	Physical	55	95	25	2 foes	
17	Curse	???	Status	—	—	10	Normal • Self	
21	Bite	Dark	Physical	60	100	25	Normal	•
25	Mega Drain	Grass	Special	40	100	15	Normal	
29	Leech Seed	Grass	Status	—	90	10	Normal	
33	Synthesis	Grass	Status	—	—	5	Self	
37	Crunch	Dark	Physical	80	100	15	Normal	
41	Giga Drain	Grass	Special	60	100	10	Normal	
45	Leaf Storm	Grass	Special	140	90	5	Normal	

National Pokédex No. 388 Grove Pokémon
Grotle

GRASS

STATS
HP
ATTACK
DEFENSE
SP.ATTACK
SP.DEFENSE
SPEED

● M/F have same form

EVOLUTION PATH

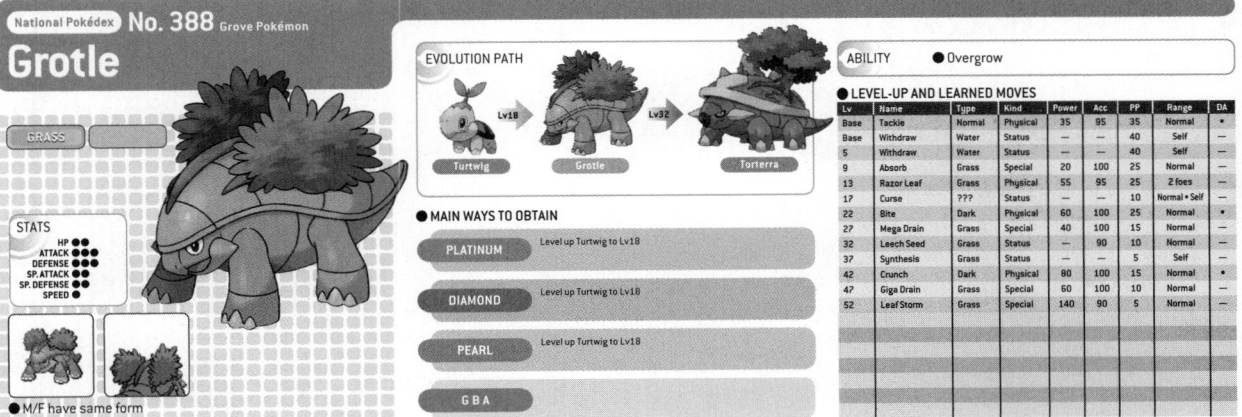

Turtwig → Lv18 → Grotle → Lv32 → Torterra

● **MAIN WAYS TO OBTAIN**

PLATINUM	Level up Turtwig to Lv18
DIAMOND	Level up Turtwig to Lv18
PEARL	Level up Turtwig to Lv18
GBA	

ABILITY ● Overgrow

● **LEVEL-UP AND LEARNED MOVES**

Lv	Name	Type	Kind	Power	Acc	PP	Range	DA
Base	Tackle	Normal	Physical	35	95	35	Normal	•
Base	Withdraw	Water	Status	—	—	40	Self	—
5	Withdraw	Water	Status	—	—	40	Self	—
9	Absorb	Grass	Special	20	100	25	Normal	—
13	Razor Leaf	Grass	Physical	55	95	25	2 foes	—
17	Curse	???	Status	—	—	10	Normal • Self	—
22	Bite	Dark	Physical	60	100	25	Normal	—
27	Mega Drain	Grass	Special	40	100	15	Normal	—
32	Leech Seed	Grass	Status	—	90	10	Normal	—
37	Synthesis	Grass	Status	—	—	5	Self	—
42	Crunch	Dark	Physical	80	100	15	Normal	—
47	Giga Drain	Grass	Special	60	100	10	Normal	—
52	Leaf Storm	Grass	Special	140	90	5	Normal	—

National Pokédex No. 389 Continent Pokémon
Torterra

GRASS GROUND

STATS
HP
ATTACK
DEFENSE
SP.ATTACK
SP.DEFENSE
SPEED

● M/F have same form

EVOLUTION PATH

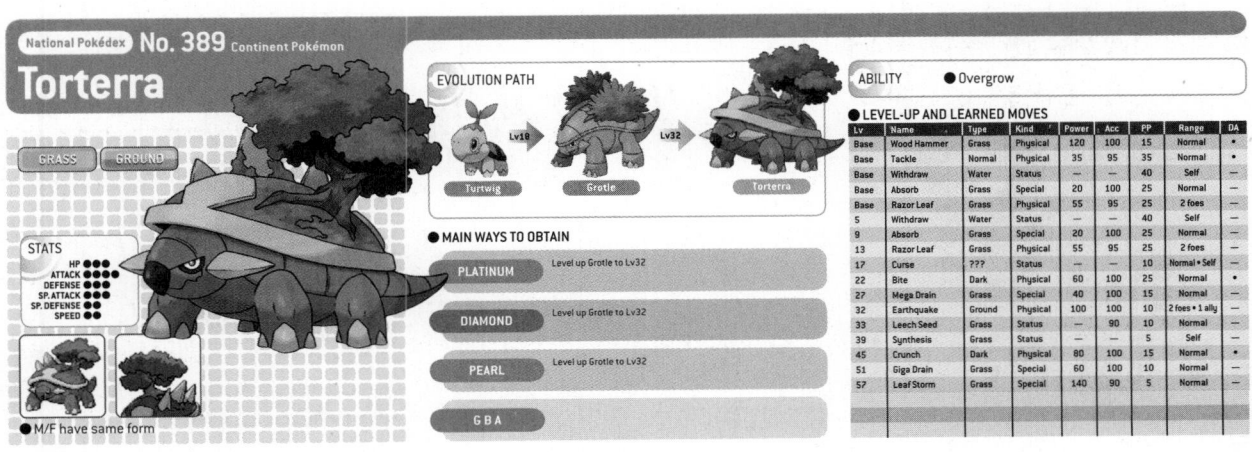

Turtwig → Lv18 → Grotle → Lv32 → Torterra

● **MAIN WAYS TO OBTAIN**

PLATINUM	Level up Grotle to Lv32
DIAMOND	Level up Grotle to Lv32
PEARL	Level up Grotle to Lv32
GBA	

ABILITY ● Overgrow

● **LEVEL-UP AND LEARNED MOVES**

Lv	Name	Type	Kind	Power	Acc	PP	Range	DA
Base	Wood Hammer	Grass	Physical	120	100	15	Normal	•
Base	Tackle	Normal	Physical	35	95	35	Normal	•
Base	Withdraw	Water	Status	—	—	40	Self	—
Base	Absorb	Grass	Special	20	100	25	Normal	—
Base	Razor Leaf	Grass	Physical	55	95	25	2 foes	—
5	Withdraw	Water	Status	—	—	40	Self	—
9	Absorb	Grass	Special	20	100	25	Normal	—
13	Razor Leaf	Grass	Physical	55	95	25	2 foes	—
17	Curse	???	Status	—	—	10	Normal • Self	—
22	Bite	Dark	Physical	60	100	25	Normal	—
27	Mega Drain	Grass	Special	40	100	15	Normal	—
32	Earthquake	Ground	Physical	100	100	10	2 foes • 1 ally	—
33	Leech Seed	Grass	Status	—	90	10	Normal	—
39	Synthesis	Grass	Status	—	—	5	Self	—
45	Crunch	Dark	Physical	80	100	15	Normal	—
51	Giga Drain	Grass	Special	60	100	10	Normal	—
57	Leaf Storm	Grass	Special	140	90	5	Normal	—

National Pokédex No. 390 Chimp Pokémon
Chimchar

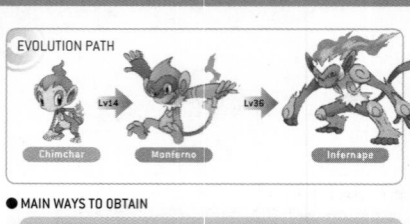

FIRE

STATS
- HP ●●
- ATTACK ●●●
- DEFENSE ●●
- SP. ATTACK ●●
- SP. DEFENSE ●●
- SPEED ●●

● M/F have same form

EVOLUTION PATH
Chimchar → Lv14 → Monferno → Lv36 → Infernape

MAIN WAYS TO OBTAIN
PLATINUM	Receive from Professor Rowan on Route 201
DIAMOND	Pick from the suitcase Professor Rowan forgot at Lake Verity
PEARL	Pick from the suitcase Professor Rowan forgot at Lake Verity
G B A	

ABILITY ● Blaze

LEVEL-UP AND LEARNED MOVES
Lv	Name	Type	Kind	Power	Acc	PP	Range	DA
Base	Scratch	Normal	Physical	40	100	35	Normal	●
Base	Leer	Normal	Status	—	100	30	2 foes	—
7	Ember	Fire	Special	40	100	25	Normal	—
9	Taunt	Dark	Status	—	100	20	Normal	—
15	Fury Swipes	Normal	Physical	18	80	15	Normal	●
17	Flame Wheel	Fire	Physical	60	100	25	Normal	●
23	Nasty Plot	Dark	Status	—	—	20	Self	—
25	Torment	Dark	Status	—	100	15	Normal	—
31	Facade	Normal	Physical	70	100	20	Normal	●
33	Fire Spin	Fire	Special	15	70	15	Normal	—
39	Slack Off	Normal	Status	—	—	10	Self	—
41	Flamethrower	Fire	Special	95	100	15	Normal	—

National Pokédex No. 391 Playful Pokémon
Monferno

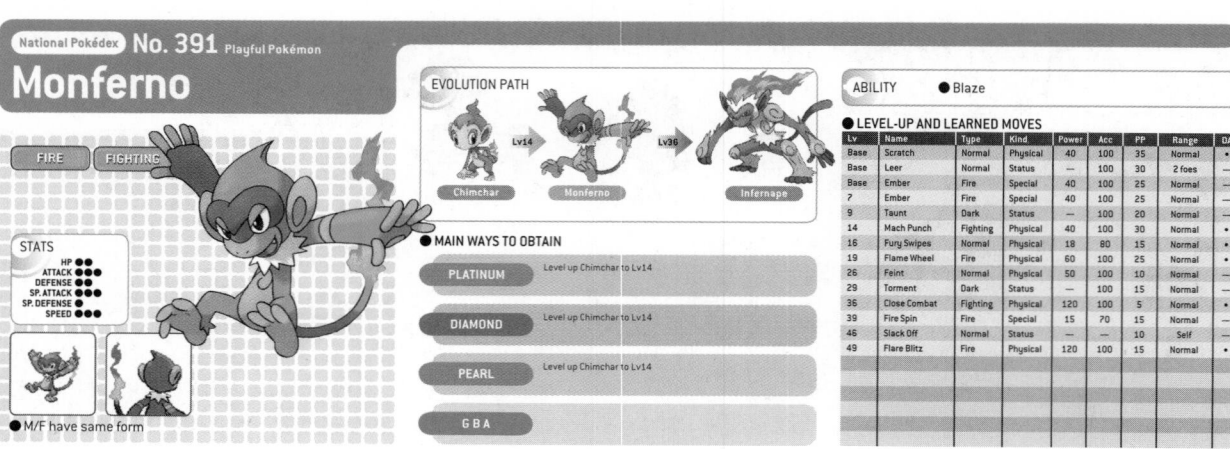

FIRE | FIGHTING

STATS
- HP ●●●
- ATTACK ●●●
- DEFENSE ●●
- SP. ATTACK ●●●
- SP. DEFENSE ●●
- SPEED ●●●

● M/F have same form

EVOLUTION PATH
Chimchar → Lv14 → Monferno → Lv36 → Infernape

MAIN WAYS TO OBTAIN
PLATINUM	Level up Chimchar to Lv14
DIAMOND	Level up Chimchar to Lv14
PEARL	Level up Chimchar to Lv14
G B A	

ABILITY ● Blaze

LEVEL-UP AND LEARNED MOVES
Lv	Name	Type	Kind	Power	Acc	PP	Range	DA
Base	Scratch	Normal	Physical	40	100	35	Normal	●
Base	Leer	Normal	Status	—	100	30	2 foes	—
Base	Ember	Fire	Special	40	100	25	Normal	—
7	Ember	Fire	Special	40	100	25	Normal	—
9	Taunt	Dark	Status	—	100	20	Normal	—
14	Mach Punch	Fighting	Physical	40	100	30	Normal	●
16	Fury Swipes	Normal	Physical	18	80	15	Normal	●
19	Flame Wheel	Fire	Physical	60	100	25	Normal	●
26	Feint	Normal	Physical	50	100	10	Normal	●
29	Torment	Dark	Status	—	100	15	Normal	—
36	Close Combat	Fighting	Physical	120	100	5	Normal	●
39	Fire Spin	Fire	Special	15	70	15	Normal	—
46	Slack Off	Normal	Status	—	—	10	Self	—
49	Flare Blitz	Fire	Physical	120	100	15	Normal	●

National Pokédex No. 392 Flame Pokémon
Infernape

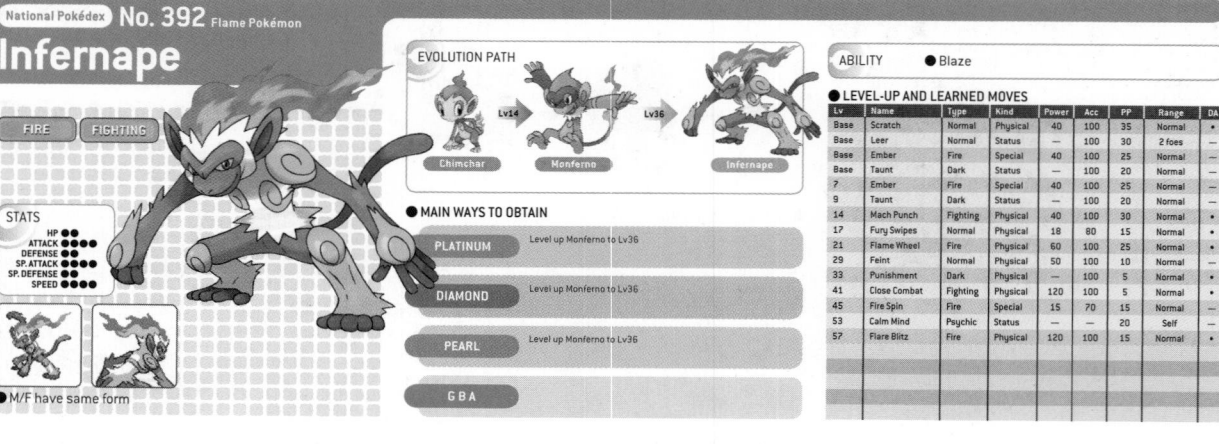

FIRE | FIGHTING

STATS
- HP ●●●
- ATTACK ●●●●
- DEFENSE ●●●
- SP. ATTACK ●●●●
- SP. DEFENSE ●●●
- SPEED ●●●●

● M/F have same form

EVOLUTION PATH
Chimchar → Lv14 → Monferno → Lv36 → Infernape

MAIN WAYS TO OBTAIN
PLATINUM	Level up Monferno to Lv36
DIAMOND	Level up Monferno to Lv36
PEARL	Level up Monferno to Lv36
G B A	

ABILITY ● Blaze

LEVEL-UP AND LEARNED MOVES
Lv	Name	Type	Kind	Power	Acc	PP	Range	DA
Base	Scratch	Normal	Physical	40	100	35	Normal	●
Base	Leer	Normal	Status	—	100	30	2 foes	—
Base	Ember	Fire	Special	40	100	25	Normal	—
Base	Taunt	Dark	Status	—	100	20	Normal	—
7	Ember	Fire	Special	40	100	25	Normal	—
9	Taunt	Dark	Status	—	100	20	Normal	—
14	Mach Punch	Fighting	Physical	40	100	30	Normal	●
17	Fury Swipes	Normal	Physical	18	80	15	Normal	●
21	Flame Wheel	Fire	Physical	60	100	25	Normal	●
29	Feint	Normal	Physical	50	100	10	Normal	●
33	Punishment	Dark	Physical	—	100	5	Normal	●
41	Close Combat	Fighting	Physical	120	100	5	Normal	●
45	Fire Spin	Fire	Special	15	70	15	Normal	—
53	Calm Mind	Psychic	Status	—	—	20	Self	—
57	Flare Blitz	Fire	Physical	120	100	15	Normal	●

National Pokédex No. 393 Penguin Pokémon
Piplup

WATER

STATS
- HP ●●●
- ATTACK ●●
- DEFENSE ●●
- SP. ATTACK ●●●
- SP. DEFENSE ●●
- SPEED ●●

● M/F have same form

EVOLUTION PATH
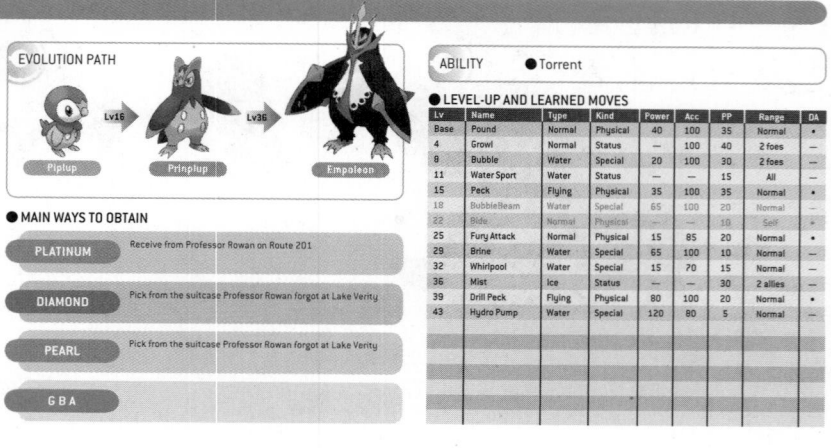
Piplup → Lv16 → Prinplup → Lv36 → Empoleon

MAIN WAYS TO OBTAIN
PLATINUM	Receive from Professor Rowan on Route 201
DIAMOND	Pick from the suitcase Professor Rowan forgot at Lake Verity
PEARL	Pick from the suitcase Professor Rowan forgot at Lake Verity
G B A	

ABILITY ● Torrent

LEVEL-UP AND LEARNED MOVES
Lv	Name	Type	Kind	Power	Acc	PP	Range	DA
Base	Pound	Normal	Physical	40	100	35	Normal	●
4	Growl	Normal	Status	—	100	40	2 foes	—
8	Bubble	Water	Special	20	100	30	2 foes	—
11	Water Sport	Water	Status	—	—	15	All	—
15	Peck	Flying	Physical	35	100	35	Normal	●
18	BubbleBeam	Water	Special	65	100	20	Normal	—
22	Bide	Normal	Physical	—	—	10	Self	—
25	Fury Attack	Normal	Physical	15	85	20	Normal	●
29	Brine	Water	Special	65	100	10	Normal	—
32	Whirlpool	Water	Special	15	70	15	Normal	—
36	Mist	Ice	Status	—	—	30	2 allies	—
39	Drill Peck	Flying	Physical	80	100	20	Normal	●
43	Hydro Pump	Water	Special	120	80	5	Normal	—

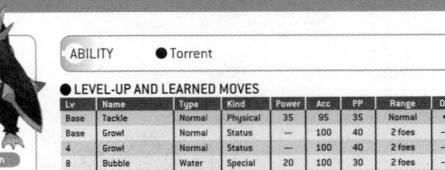

National Pokédex No. 394 Penguin Pokémon
Prinplup

WATER

STATS
- HP ••
- ATTACK ••
- DEFENSE ••
- SP. ATTACK •••
- SP. DEFENSE ••
- SPEED ••

● M/F have same form

EVOLUTION PATH

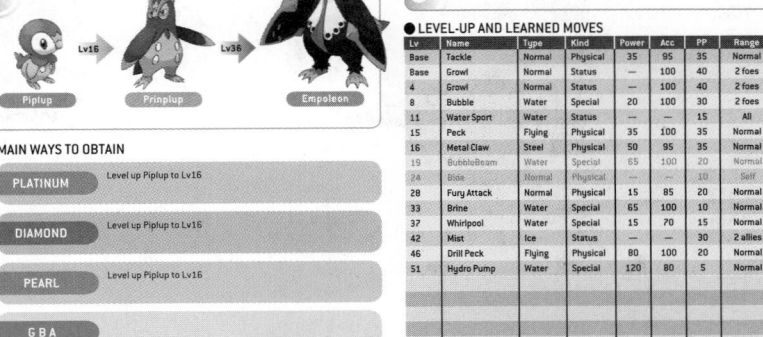

Piplup — Lv16 → Prinplup — Lv36 → Empoleon

● MAIN WAYS TO OBTAIN

PLATINUM	Level up Piplup to Lv16
DIAMOND	Level up Piplup to Lv16
PEARL	Level up Piplup to Lv16
GBA	

ABILITY   ● Torrent

● LEVEL-UP AND LEARNED MOVES

Lv	Name	Type	Kind	Power	Acc	PP	Range	DA
Base	Tackle	Normal	Physical	35	95	35	Normal	•
Base	Growl	Normal	Status	—	100	40	2 foes	—
4	Growl	Normal	Status	—	100	40	2 foes	—
8	Bubble	Water	Special	20	100	30	2 foes	—
11	Water Sport	Water	Status	—	—	15	All	—
15	Peck	Flying	Physical	35	100	35	Normal	•
16	Metal Claw	Steel	Physical	50	95	35	Normal	•
19	BubbleBeam	Water	Special	65	100	20	Normal	•
24	Bide	Normal	Physical	—	—	10	Self	•
28	Fury Attack	Normal	Physical	15	85	20	Normal	•
33	Brine	Water	Special	65	100	10	Normal	•
37	Whirlpool	Water	Special	15	70	15	Normal	•
42	Mist	Ice	Status	—	—	30	2 allies	—
46	Drill Peck	Flying	Physical	80	100	20	Normal	•
51	Hydro Pump	Water	Special	120	80	5	Normal	•

National Pokédex No. 395 Emperor Pokémon
Empoleon

WATER **STEEL**

STATS
- HP •••
- ATTACK •••
- DEFENSE •••
- SP. ATTACK ••••
- SP. DEFENSE •••
- SPEED •••

● M/F have same form

EVOLUTION PATH

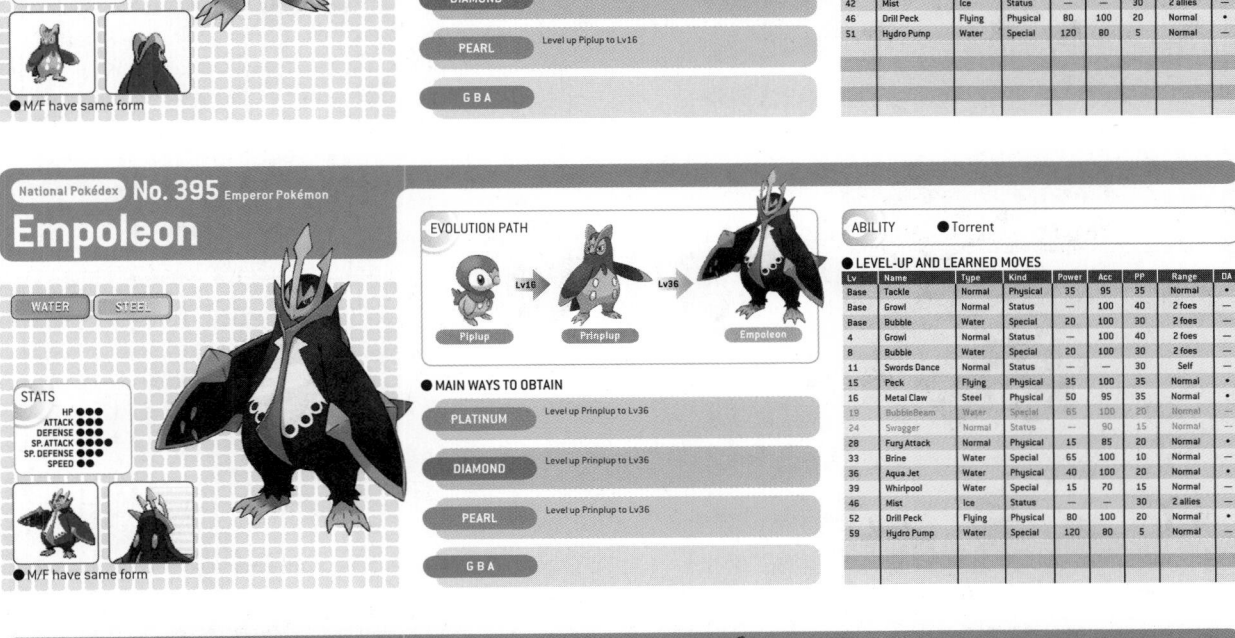

Piplup — Lv16 → Prinplup — Lv36 → Empoleon

● MAIN WAYS TO OBTAIN

PLATINUM	Level up Prinplup to Lv36
DIAMOND	Level up Prinplup to Lv36
PEARL	Level up Prinplup to Lv36
GBA	

ABILITY   ● Torrent

● LEVEL-UP AND LEARNED MOVES

Lv	Name	Type	Kind	Power	Acc	PP	Range	DA
Base	Tackle	Normal	Physical	35	95	35	Normal	—
Base	Growl	Normal	Status	—	100	40	2 foes	—
Base	Bubble	Water	Special	20	100	30	2 foes	—
4	Growl	Normal	Status	—	100	40	2 foes	—
8	Bubble	Water	Special	20	100	30	2 foes	—
11	Swords Dance	Normal	Status	—	—	30	Self	—
15	Peck	Flying	Physical	35	100	35	Normal	•
16	Metal Claw	Steel	Physical	50	95	35	Normal	•
19	BubbleBeam	Water	Special	65	100	20	Normal	•
24	Swagger	Normal	Status	—	90	15	Normal	—
28	Fury Attack	Normal	Physical	15	85	20	Normal	•
33	Brine	Water	Special	65	100	10	Normal	•
36	Aqua Jet	Water	Physical	40	100	20	Normal	•
39	Whirlpool	Water	Special	15	70	15	Normal	•
46	Mist	Ice	Status	—	—	30	2 allies	—
52	Drill Peck	Flying	Physical	80	100	20	Normal	•
59	Hydro Pump	Water	Special	120	80	5	Normal	•

National Pokédex No. 396 Starling Pokémon
Starly

NORMAL **FLYING**

STATS
- HP •
- ATTACK ••
- DEFENSE •
- SP. ATTACK •
- SP. DEFENSE •
- SPEED ••

● Male form   ● Female form

EVOLUTION PATH

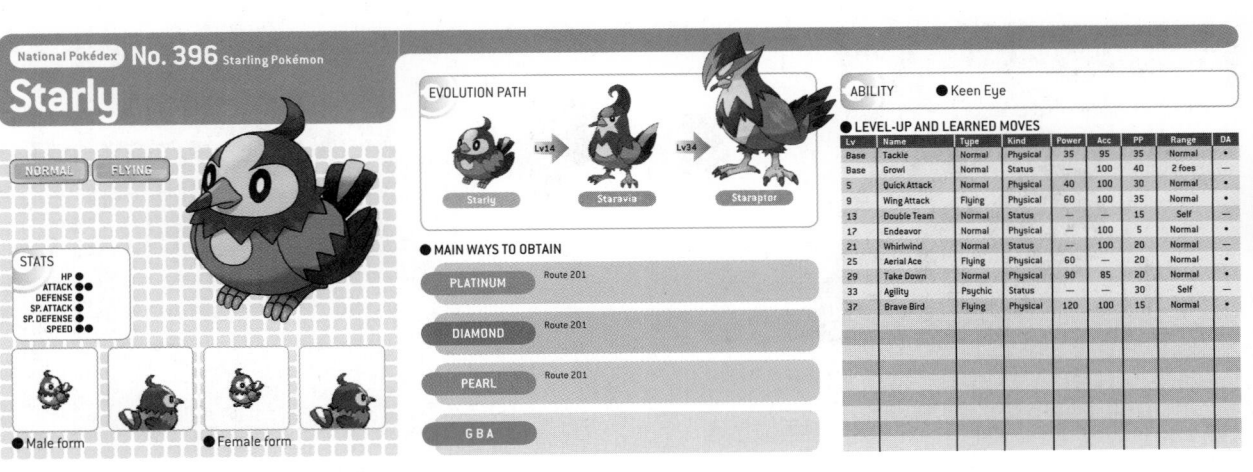

Starly — Lv14 → Staravia — Lv34 → Staraptor

● MAIN WAYS TO OBTAIN

PLATINUM	Route 201
DIAMOND	Route 201
PEARL	Route 201
GBA	

ABILITY   ● Keen Eye

● LEVEL-UP AND LEARNED MOVES

Lv	Name	Type	Kind	Power	Acc	PP	Range	DA
Base	Tackle	Normal	Physical	35	95	35	Normal	•
Base	Growl	Normal	Status	—	100	40	2 foes	—
5	Quick Attack	Normal	Physical	40	100	30	Normal	•
9	Wing Attack	Flying	Physical	60	100	35	Normal	•
13	Double Team	Normal	Status	—	—	15	Self	—
17	Endeavor	Normal	Physical	—	100	5	Normal	•
21	Whirlwind	Normal	Status	—	100	20	Normal	—
25	Aerial Ace	Flying	Physical	60	—	20	Normal	•
29	Take Down	Normal	Physical	90	85	20	Normal	•
33	Agility	Psychic	Status	—	—	30	Self	—
37	Brave Bird	Flying	Physical	120	100	15	Normal	•

National Pokédex No. 397 Starling Pokémon
Staravia

NORMAL **FLYING**

STATS
- HP ••
- ATTACK •••
- DEFENSE ••
- SP. ATTACK •
- SP. DEFENSE ••
- SPEED •••

● Male form   ● Female form

EVOLUTION PATH

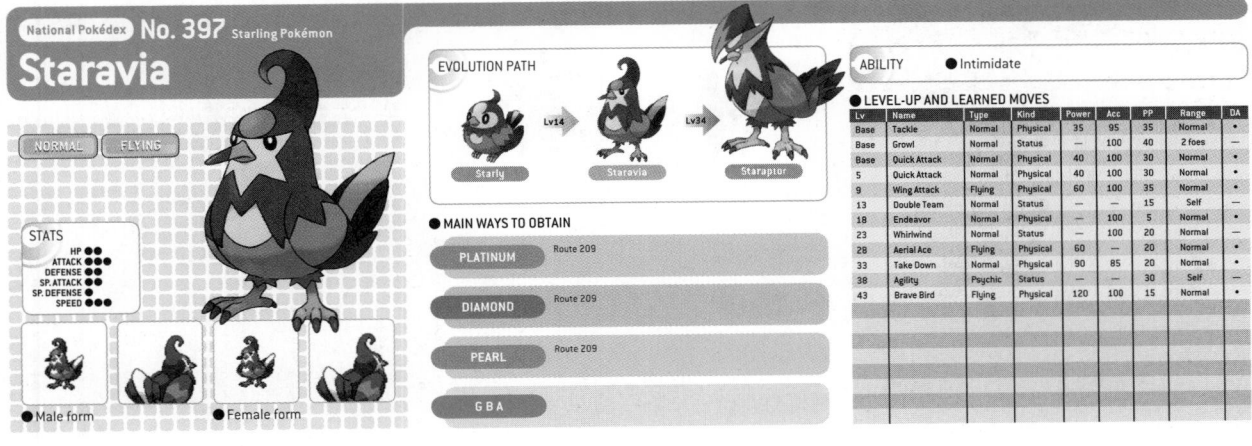

Starly — Lv14 → Staravia — Lv34 → Staraptor

● MAIN WAYS TO OBTAIN

PLATINUM	Route 209
DIAMOND	Route 209
PEARL	Route 209
GBA	

ABILITY   ● Intimidate

● LEVEL-UP AND LEARNED MOVES

Lv	Name	Type	Kind	Power	Acc	PP	Range	DA
Base	Tackle	Normal	Physical	35	95	35	Normal	•
Base	Growl	Normal	Status	—	100	40	2 foes	—
Base	Quick Attack	Normal	Physical	40	100	30	Normal	•
5	Quick Attack	Normal	Physical	40	100	30	Normal	•
9	Wing Attack	Flying	Physical	60	100	35	Normal	•
13	Double Team	Normal	Status	—	—	15	Self	—
18	Endeavor	Normal	Physical	—	100	5	Normal	•
23	Whirlwind	Normal	Status	—	100	20	Normal	—
28	Aerial Ace	Flying	Physical	60	—	20	Normal	•
33	Take Down	Normal	Physical	90	85	20	Normal	•
38	Agility	Psychic	Status	—	—	30	Self	—
43	Brave Bird	Flying	Physical	120	100	15	Normal	•

National Pokédex **No. 398** Predator Pokémon

Staraptor

NORMAL | FLYING

STATS
HP ●●●●
ATTACK ●●●●●
DEFENSE ●●●
SP. ATTACK ●●●
SP. DEFENSE ●●●
SPEED ●●●●

● Male form | ● Female form

EVOLUTION PATH

Starly → Lv14 → Staravia → Lv34 → Staraptor

● **MAIN WAYS TO OBTAIN**

PLATINUM	Level up Staravia to Lv34
DIAMOND	Level up Staravia to Lv34
PEARL	Level up Staravia to Lv34
G B A	

ABILITY ● Intimidate

● **LEVEL-UP AND LEARNED MOVES**

Lv	Name	Type	Kind	Power	Acc	PP	Range	DA
Base	Tackle	Normal	Physical	35	95	35	Normal	●
Base	Growl	Normal	Status	—	100	40	2 foes	—
Base	Quick Attack	Normal	Physical	40	100	30	Normal	●
Base	Wing Attack	Flying	Physical	60	100	35	Normal	●
5	Quick Attack	Normal	Physical	40	100	30	Normal	●
9	Wing Attack	Flying	Physical	60	100	35	Normal	●
13	Double Team	Normal	Status	—	—	15	Self	—
18	Endeavor	Normal	Physical	—	100	5	Normal	●
23	Whirlwind	Normal	Status	—	—	20	Normal	—
28	Aerial Ace	Flying	Physical	60	—	20	Normal	●
33	Take Down	Normal	Physical	90	85	20	Normal	●
34	Close Combat	Fighting	Physical	120	100	5	Normal	●
41	Agility	Psychic	Status	—	—	30	Self	—
49	Brave Bird	Flying	Physical	120	100	15	Normal	●

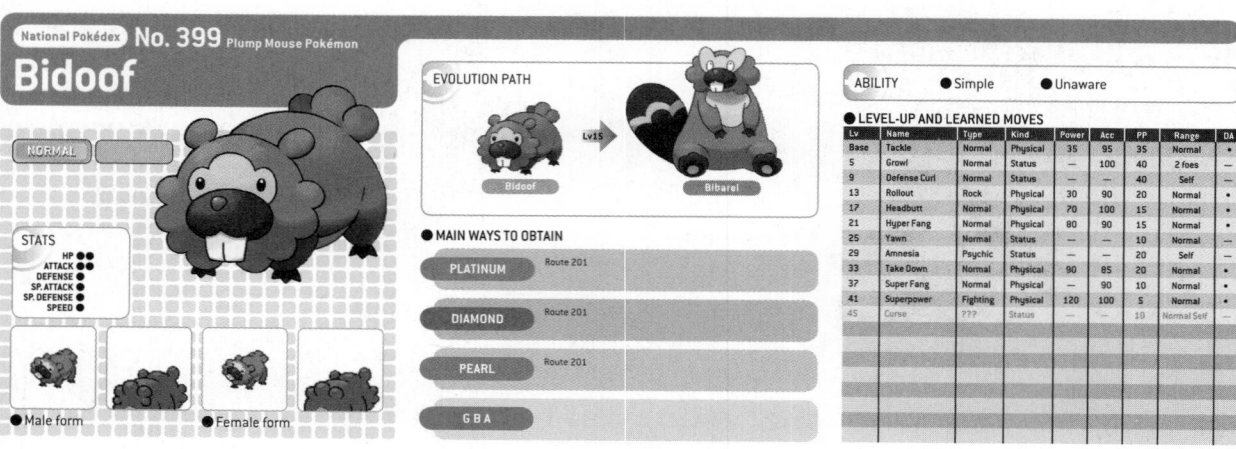

National Pokédex **No. 399** Plump Mouse Pokémon

Bidoof

NORMAL

STATS
HP ●●
ATTACK ●●
DEFENSE ●●
SP. ATTACK ●
SP. DEFENSE ●
SPEED ●

● Male form | ● Female form

EVOLUTION PATH

Bidoof → Lv15 → Bibarel

● **MAIN WAYS TO OBTAIN**

PLATINUM	Route 201
DIAMOND	Route 201
PEARL	Route 201
G B A	

ABILITY ● Simple ● Unaware

● **LEVEL-UP AND LEARNED MOVES**

Lv	Name	Type	Kind	Power	Acc	PP	Range	DA
Base	Tackle	Normal	Physical	35	95	35	Normal	●
5	Growl	Normal	Status	—	100	40	2 foes	—
9	Defense Curl	Normal	Status	—	—	40	Self	—
13	Rollout	Rock	Physical	30	90	20	Normal	●
17	Headbutt	Normal	Physical	70	100	15	Normal	●
21	Hyper Fang	Normal	Physical	80	90	15	Normal	●
25	Yawn	Normal	Status	—	—	10	Normal	●
29	Amnesia	Psychic	Status	—	—	20	Self	—
33	Take Down	Normal	Physical	90	85	20	Normal	●
37	Super Fang	Normal	Physical	—	90	10	Normal	●
41	Superpower	Fighting	Physical	120	100	5	Normal	●
45	Curse	???	Status	—	—	10	Normal Self	

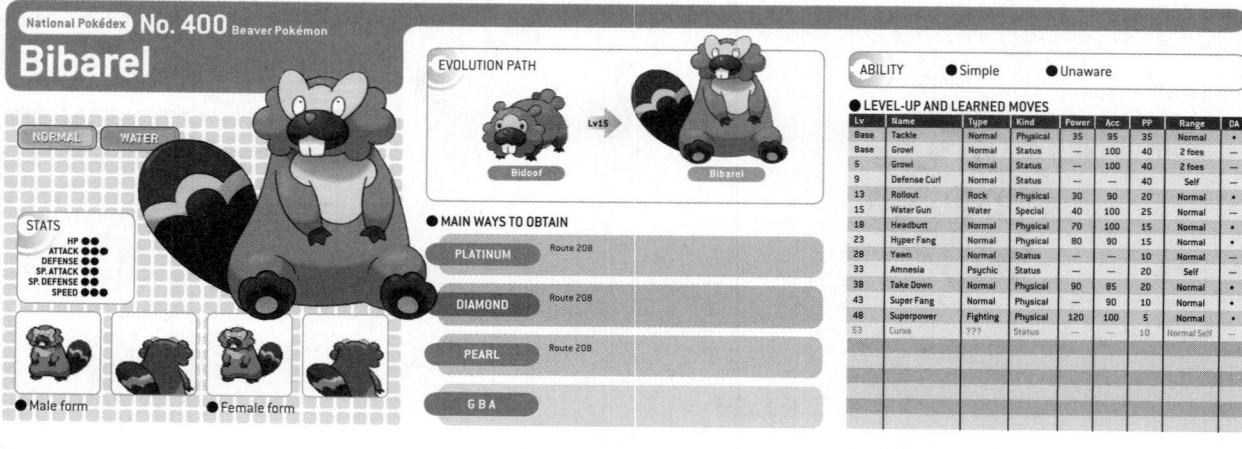

National Pokédex **No. 400** Beaver Pokémon

Bibarel

NORMAL | WATER

STATS
HP ●●●
ATTACK ●●●
DEFENSE ●●●
SP. ATTACK ●●
SP. DEFENSE ●●
SPEED ●●●

● Male form | ● Female form

EVOLUTION PATH

Bidoof → Lv15 → Bibarel

● **MAIN WAYS TO OBTAIN**

PLATINUM	Route 208
DIAMOND	Route 208
PEARL	Route 208
G B A	

ABILITY ● Simple ● Unaware

● **LEVEL-UP AND LEARNED MOVES**

Lv	Name	Type	Kind	Power	Acc	PP	Range	DA
Base	Tackle	Normal	Physical	35	95	35	Normal	●
Base	Growl	Normal	Status	—	100	40	2 foes	—
5	Growl	Normal	Status	—	100	40	2 foes	—
9	Defense Curl	Normal	Status	—	—	40	Self	—
13	Rollout	Rock	Physical	30	90	20	Normal	●
15	Water Gun	Water	Special	40	100	25	Normal	●
18	Headbutt	Normal	Physical	70	100	15	Normal	●
23	Hyper Fang	Normal	Physical	80	90	15	Normal	●
28	Yawn	Normal	Status	—	—	10	Normal	●
33	Amnesia	Psychic	Status	—	—	20	Self	—
38	Take Down	Normal	Physical	90	85	20	Normal	●
43	Super Fang	Normal	Physical	—	90	10	Normal	●
48	Superpower	Fighting	Physical	120	100	5	Normal	●
53	Curse	???	Status	—	—	10	Normal Self	

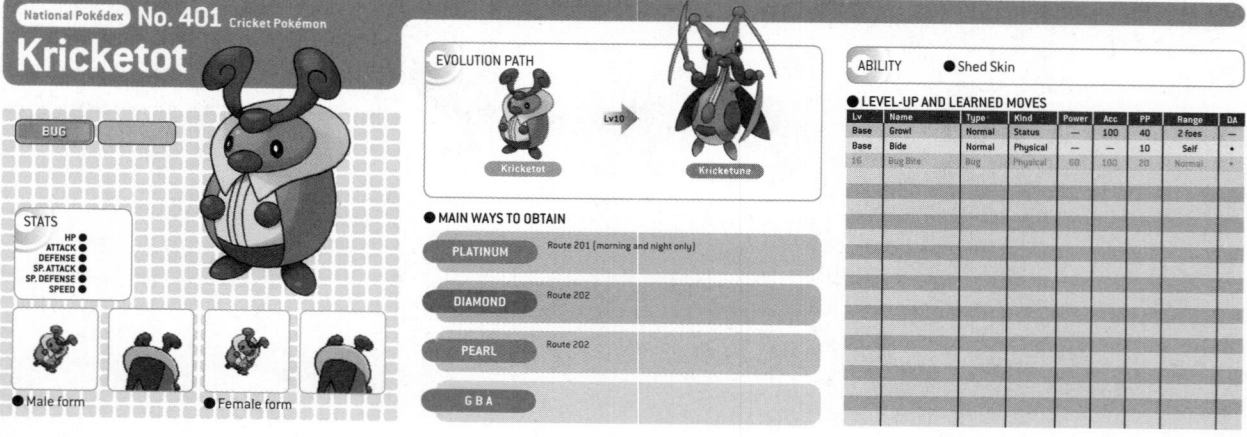

National Pokédex **No. 401** Cricket Pokémon

Kricketot

BUG

STATS
HP ●
ATTACK ●
DEFENSE ●
SP. ATTACK ●
SP. DEFENSE ●
SPEED ●

● Male form | ● Female form

EVOLUTION PATH

Kricketot → Lv10 → Kricketune

● **MAIN WAYS TO OBTAIN**

PLATINUM	Route 201 (morning and night only)
DIAMOND	Route 202
PEARL	Route 202
G B A	

ABILITY ● Shed Skin

● **LEVEL-UP AND LEARNED MOVES**

Lv	Name	Type	Kind	Power	Acc	PP	Range	DA
Base	Growl	Normal	Status	—	100	40	2 foes	—
Base	Bide	Normal	Physical	—	—	10	Self	—
16	Bug Bite	Bug	Physical	60	100	20	Normal	●

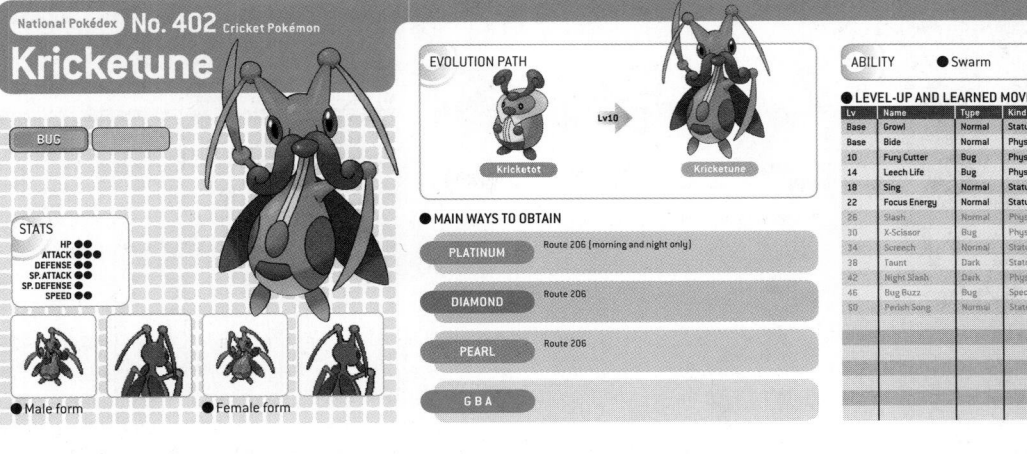

National Pokédex No. 402 Cricket Pokémon
Kricketune

BUG

STATS
- HP ●●
- ATTACK ●●●
- DEFENSE ●●
- SP. ATTACK ●●
- SP. DEFENSE ●●
- SPEED ●●

● Male form　　● Female form

EVOLUTION PATH
Kricketot → (Lv10) → Kricketune

● MAIN WAYS TO OBTAIN
PLATINUM	Route 206 (morning and night only)
DIAMOND	Route 206
PEARL	Route 206
G B A	

ABILITY　● Swarm

● LEVEL-UP AND LEARNED MOVES
Lv	Name	Type	Kind	Power	Acc	PP	Range	DA
Base	Growl	Normal	Status	—	100	40	2 foes	—
Base	Bide		Physical	—	—	10	Self	—
10	Fury Cutter	Bug	Physical	10	95	20	Normal	•
14	Leech Life	Bug	Physical	20	100	15	Normal	•
18	Sing	Normal	Status	—	55	15	Normal	—
22	Focus Energy	Normal	Status	—	—	30	Self	—
26	Slash	Normal	Physical	70	100	20	Normal	•
30	X-Scissor	Bug	Physical	80	100	15	Normal	•
34	Screech	Normal	Status	—	85	40	Normal	—
38	Taunt	Dark	Status	—	100	20	Normal	—
42	Night Slash	Dark	Physical	70	100	15	Normal	•
46	Bug Buzz	Bug	Special	90	100	10	Normal	—
50	Perish Song	Normal	Status	—	—	5	All	—

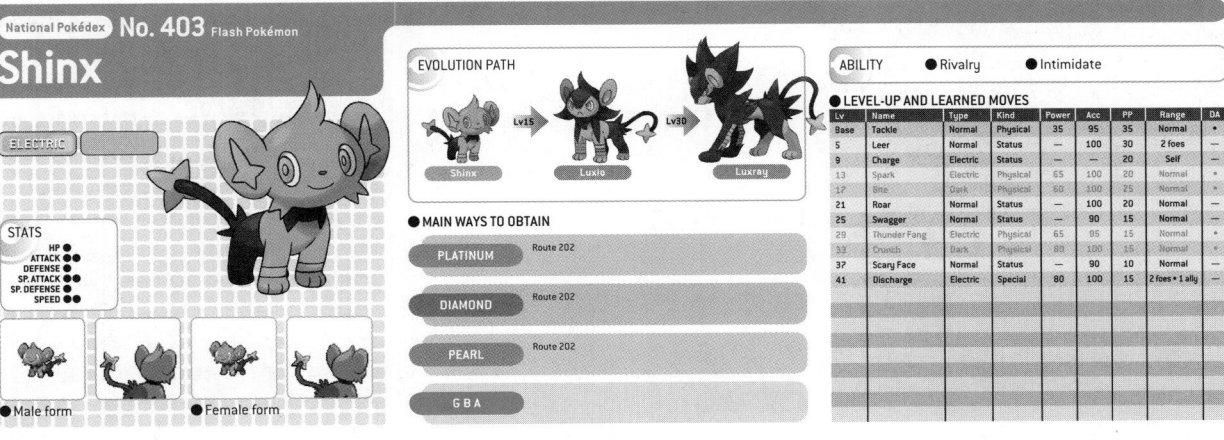

National Pokédex No. 403 Flash Pokémon
Shinx

ELECTRIC

STATS
- HP ●●
- ATTACK ●●
- DEFENSE ●●
- SP. ATTACK ●●
- SP. DEFENSE ●●
- SPEED ●●

● Male form　　● Female form

EVOLUTION PATH
Shinx → (Lv15) → Luxio → (Lv30) → Luxray

● MAIN WAYS TO OBTAIN
PLATINUM	Route 202
DIAMOND	Route 202
PEARL	Route 202
G B A	

ABILITY　● Rivalry　● Intimidate

● LEVEL-UP AND LEARNED MOVES
Lv	Name	Type	Kind	Power	Acc	PP	Range	DA
Base	Tackle	Normal	Physical	35	95	35	Normal	•
5	Leer	Normal	Status	—	100	30	2 foes	—
9	Charge	Electric	Status	—	—	20	Self	—
13	Spark	Electric	Physical	65	100	20	Normal	•
17	Bite	Dark	Physical	60	100	25	Normal	•
21	Roar	Normal	Status	—	100	20	Normal	—
25	Swagger	Normal	Status	—	90	15	Normal	—
29	Thunder Fang	Electric	Physical	65	95	15	Normal	•
33	Crunch	Dark	Physical	80	100	15	Normal	•
37	Scary Face	Normal	Status	—	90	10	Normal	—
41	Discharge	Electric	Special	80	100	15	2 foes • 1 ally	—

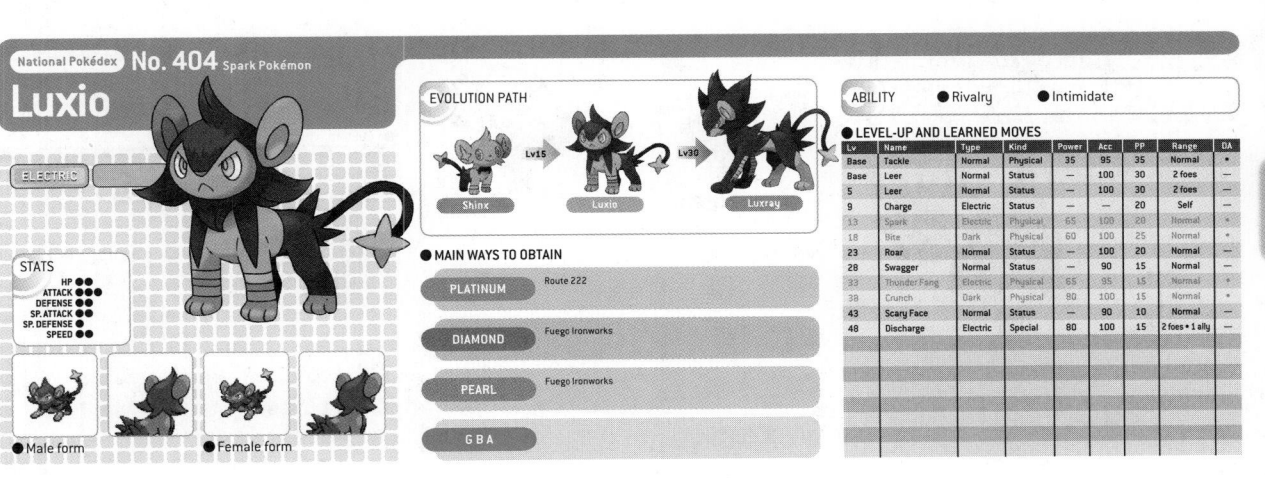

National Pokédex No. 404 Spark Pokémon
Luxio

ELECTRIC

STATS
- HP ●●
- ATTACK ●●●
- DEFENSE ●●
- SP. ATTACK ●●
- SP. DEFENSE ●●
- SPEED ●●

● Male form　　● Female form

EVOLUTION PATH
Shinx → (Lv15) → Luxio → (Lv30) → Luxray

● MAIN WAYS TO OBTAIN
PLATINUM	Route 222
DIAMOND	Fuego Ironworks
PEARL	Fuego Ironworks
G B A	

ABILITY　● Rivalry　● Intimidate

● LEVEL-UP AND LEARNED MOVES
Lv	Name	Type	Kind	Power	Acc	PP	Range	DA
Base	Tackle	Normal	Physical	35	95	35	Normal	•
Base	Leer	Normal	Status	—	100	30	2 foes	—
5	Leer	Normal	Status	—	100	30	2 foes	—
9	Charge	Electric	Status	—	—	20	Self	—
13	Spark	Electric	Physical	65	100	20	Normal	•
18	Bite	Dark	Physical	60	100	25	Normal	•
23	Roar	Normal	Status	—	100	20	Normal	—
28	Swagger	Normal	Status	—	90	15	Normal	—
33	Thunder Fang	Electric	Physical	65	95	15	Normal	•
38	Crunch	Dark	Physical	80	100	15	Normal	•
43	Scary Face	Normal	Status	—	90	10	Normal	—
48	Discharge	Electric	Special	80	100	15	2 foes • 1 ally	—

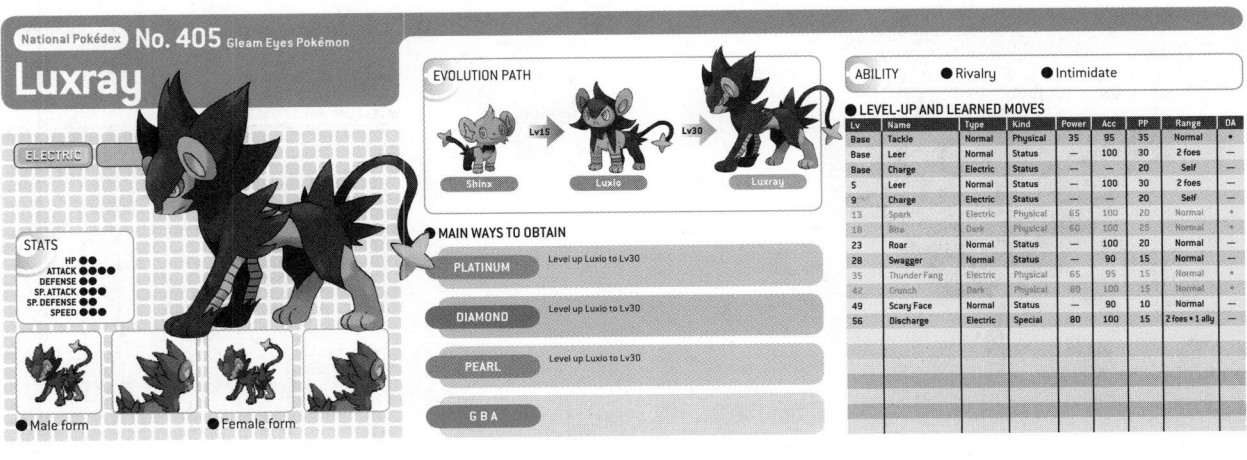

National Pokédex No. 405 Gleam Eyes Pokémon
Luxray

ELECTRIC

STATS
- HP ●●
- ATTACK ●●●●
- DEFENSE ●●●
- SP. ATTACK ●●●
- SP. DEFENSE ●●
- SPEED ●●●

● Male form　　● Female form

EVOLUTION PATH
Shinx → (Lv15) → Luxio → (Lv30) → Luxray

● MAIN WAYS TO OBTAIN
PLATINUM	Level up Luxio to Lv30
DIAMOND	Level up Luxio to Lv30
PEARL	Level up Luxio to Lv30
G B A	

ABILITY　● Rivalry　● Intimidate

● LEVEL-UP AND LEARNED MOVES
Lv	Name	Type	Kind	Power	Acc	PP	Range	DA
Base	Tackle	Normal	Physical	35	95	35	Normal	•
Base	Leer	Normal	Status	—	100	30	2 foes	—
Base	Charge	Electric	Status	—	—	20	Self	—
5	Leer	Normal	Status	—	100	30	2 foes	—
9	Charge	Electric	Status	—	—	20	Self	•
13	Spark	Electric	Physical	65	100	20	Normal	•
18	Bite	Dark	Physical	60	100	25	Normal	•
23	Roar	Normal	Status	—	100	20	Normal	—
28	Swagger	Normal	Status	—	90	15	Normal	—
35	Thunder Fang	Electric	Physical	65	95	15	Normal	•
42	Crunch	Dark	Physical	80	100	15	Normal	•
49	Scary Face	Normal	Status	—	90	10	Normal	—
56	Discharge	Electric	Special	80	100	15	2 foes • 1 ally	—

Budew

National Pokédex No. 406 Bud Pokémon

GRASS | POISON

STATS
- HP ●
- ATTACK ●
- DEFENSE ●
- SP. ATTACK ●●
- SP. DEFENSE ●●
- SPEED ●●

● M/F have same form

EVOLUTION PATH

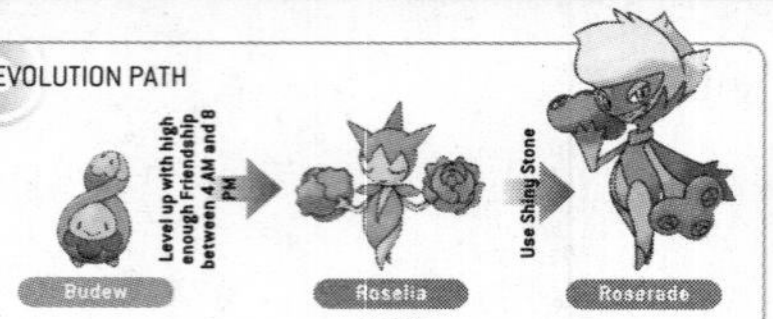

Budew → (Level up with high enough friendship between 4 AM and 8 PM) → Roselia pg. 472 → (Use Shiny Stone) → Roserade

● MAIN WAYS TO OBTAIN

PLATINUM	Route 204
DIAMOND	Route 204
PEARL	Route 204
G B A	

ABILITY   ● Natural Cure   ● Poison Point

● LEVEL-UP AND LEARNED MOVES

Lv	Name	Type	Kind	Power	Acc	PP	Range	DA
Base	Absorb	Grass	Special	20	100	25	Normal	—
4	Growth	Normal	Status	—	—	40	Self	—
7	Water Sport	Water	Status	—	—	15	All	—
10	Stun Spore	Grass	Status	—	75	30	Normal	—
13	Mega Drain	Grass	Special	40	100	15	Normal	—
16	Worry Seed	Grass	Status	—	100	10	Normal	—

Roserade

National Pokédex No. 407 Bouquet Pokémon

GRASS | POISON

STATS
- HP ●●
- ATTACK ●●●
- DEFENSE ●●
- SP. ATTACK ●●●●
- SP. DEFENSE ●●●
- SPEED ●●●

● Male form   ● Female form

EVOLUTION PATH

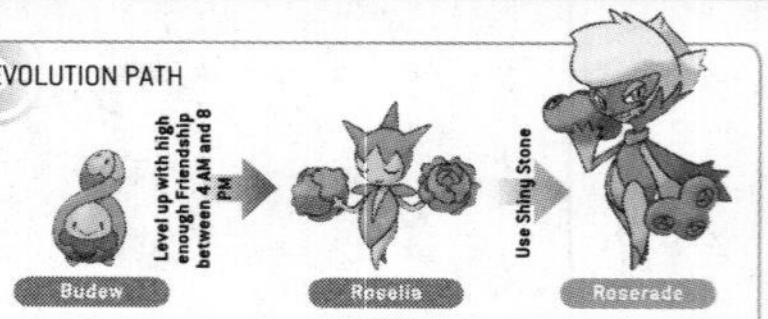

Budew → (Level up with high enough friendship between 4 AM and 8 PM) → Roselia pg. 472 → (Use Shiny Stone) → Roserade

● MAIN WAYS TO OBTAIN

PLATINUM	Use Shiny Stone on Roselia
DIAMOND	Use Shiny Stone on Roselia
PEARL	Use Shiny Stone on Roselia
G B A	

ABILITY   ● Natural Cure   ● Poison Point

● LEVEL-UP AND LEARNED MOVES

Lv	Name	Type	Kind	Power	Acc	PP	Range	DA
Base	Weather Ball	Normal	Special	50	100	10	Normal	—
Base	Poison Sting	Poison	Physical	15	100	35	Normal	—
Base	Mega Drain	Grass	Special	40	100	15	Normal	—
Base	Magical Leaf	Grass	Special	60	—	20	Normal	—
Base	Sweet Scent	Normal	Status	—	100	20	2 foes	—

Cranidos

National Pokédex No. 408 Head Butt Pokémon

ROCK

STATS
- HP ●●
- ATTACK ●●●●
- DEFENSE ●●●
- SP. ATTACK ●
- SP. DEFENSE ●●
- SPEED ●●

● M/F have same form

EVOLUTION PATH

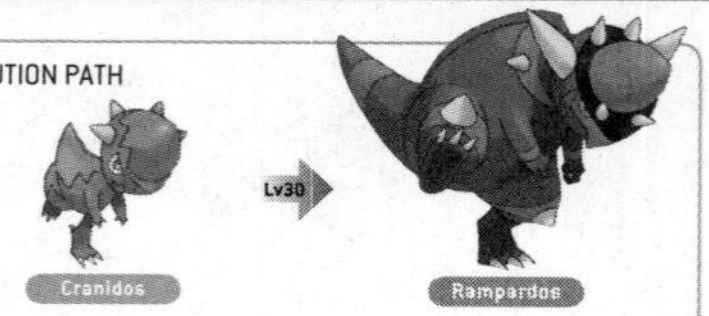

Cranidos → (Lv30) → Rampardos

● MAIN WAYS TO OBTAIN

PLATINUM	Get the Skull Fossil in the Underground, and have it restored at the Oreburgh Mining Museum
DIAMOND	Get the Skull Fossil in the Underground, and have it restored at the Oreburgh Mining Museum
PEARL	
G B A	

ABILITY   ● Mold Breaker

● LEVEL-UP AND LEARNED MOVES

Lv	Name	Type	Kind	Power	Acc	PP	Range	DA
Base	Headbutt	Normal	Physical	70	100	15	Normal	●
Base	Leer	Normal	Status	—	100	30	2 foes	●
6	Focus Energy	Normal	Status	—	—	30	Self	●
10	Pursuit	Dark	Physical	40	100	20	Normal	●
15	Take Down	Normal	Physical	90	85	20	Normal	●
19	Scary Face	Normal	Status	—	90	10	Normal	●
24	Assurance	Dark	Physical	50	100	10	Normal	●
28	AncientPower	Rock	Special	60	100	5	Normal	●
33	Zen Headbutt	Psychic	Physical	80	90	15	Normal	●
37	Screech	Normal	Status	—	85	40	Normal	●
43	Head Smash	Rock	Physical	150	80	5	Normal	●

Rampardos

National Pokédex No. 409 Head Butt Pokémon

ROCK

STATS
- HP ●●●
- ATTACK ●●●●●●
- DEFENSE ●●●
- SP. ATTACK ●●
- SP. DEFENSE ●●
- SPEED ●●

● M/F have same form

EVOLUTION PATH

Cranidos → (Lv30) → Rampardos

● MAIN WAYS TO OBTAIN

PLATINUM	Level up Cranidos to Lv30
DIAMOND	Level up Cranidos to Lv30
PEARL	
G B A	

ABILITY   ● Mold Breaker

● LEVEL-UP AND LEARNED MOVES

Lv	Name	Type	Kind	Power	Acc	PP	Range	DA
Base	Headbutt	Normal	Physical	70	100	15	Normal	●
Base	Leer	Normal	Status	—	100	30	2 foes	●
6	Focus Energy	Normal	Status	—	—	30	Self	—
10	Pursuit	Dark	Physical	40	100	20	Normal	—
15	Take Down	Normal	Physical	90	85	20	Normal	—
19	Scary Face	Normal	Status	—	90	10	Normal	—
24	Assurance	Dark	Physical	50	100	10	Normal	—
28	AncientPower	Rock	Special	60	100	5	Normal	—
30	Endeavor	Normal	Physical	—	100	5	Normal	—
36	Zen Headbutt	Psychic	Physical	80	90	15	Normal	—
43	Screech	Normal	Status	—	85	40	Normal	—
52	Head Smash	Rock	Physical	150	80	5	Normal	—

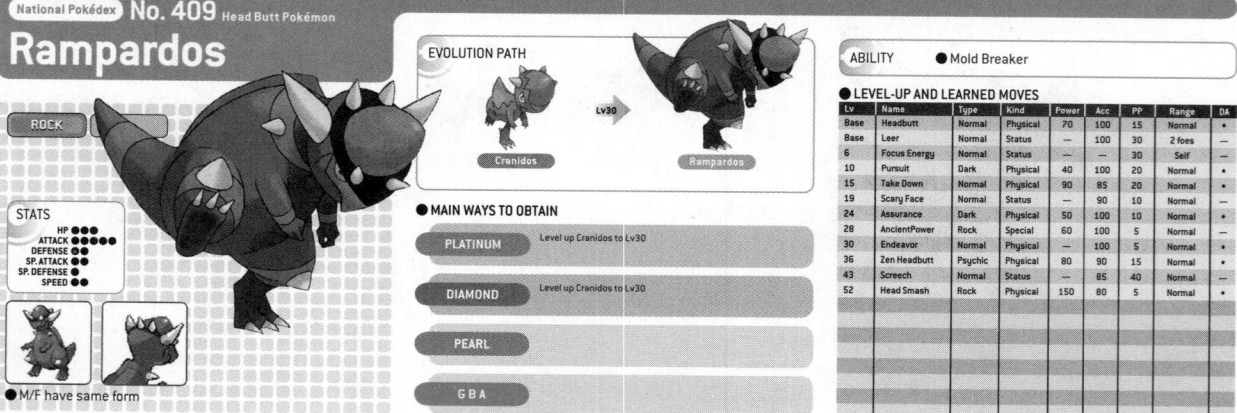

National Pokédex No. 410 Shield Pokémon
Shieldon

ROCK STEEL

STATS
- HP ●●
- ATTACK ●●●
- DEFENSE ●●●
- SP. ATTACK ●●
- SP. DEFENSE ●●●
- SPEED ●

● M/F have same form

EVOLUTION PATH

Shieldon → Lv30 → Bastiodon

● **MAIN WAYS TO OBTAIN**

PLATINUM	Get the Armor Fossil in the Underground, and have it restored at the Oreburgh Mining Museum
DIAMOND	
PEARL	Get the Armor Fossil in the Underground, and have it restored at the Oreburgh Mining Museum
G B A	

ABILITY ● Sturdy

● **LEVEL-UP AND LEARNED MOVES**

Lv	Name	Type	Kind	Power	Acc	PP	Range	DA
Base	Tackle	Normal	Physical	35	95	35	Normal	●
Base	Protect	Normal	Status	—	—	10	Self	
6	Taunt	Dark	Status	—	100	20	Normal	
10	Metal Sound	Steel	Status	—	85	40	Normal	
15	Take Down	Normal	Physical	90	85	20	Normal	●
19	Iron Defense	Steel	Status	—	—	15	Self	
24	Swagger	Normal	Status	—	90	15	Normal	
28	AncientPower	Rock	Special	60	100	5	Normal	
33	Endure	Normal	Status	—	—	10	Self	
37	Metal Burst	Steel	Physical	—	100	10	Self	
43	Iron Head	Steel	Physical	80	100	15	Normal	●

National Pokédex No. 411 Shield Pokémon
Bastiodon

ROCK STEEL

STATS
- HP ●●
- ATTACK ●●●
- DEFENSE ●●●●●
- SP. ATTACK ●●
- SP. DEFENSE ●●●●●
- SPEED ●

● M/F have same form

EVOLUTION PATH

Shieldon → Lv30 → Bastiodon

● **MAIN WAYS TO OBTAIN**

PLATINUM	Level up Shieldon to Lv30
DIAMOND	
PEARL	Level up Shieldon to Lv30
G B A	

ABILITY ● Sturdy

● **LEVEL-UP AND LEARNED MOVES**

Lv	Name	Type	Kind	Power	Acc	PP	Range	DA
Base	Tackle	Normal	Physical	35	95	35	Normal	●
Base	Protect	Normal	Status	—	—	10	Self	
Base	Taunt	Dark	Status	—	100	20	Normal	
Base	Metal Sound	Steel	Status	—	85	40	Normal	
6	Taunt	Dark	Status	—	100	20	Normal	
10	Metal Sound	Steel	Status	—	85	40	Normal	
15	Take Down	Normal	Physical	90	85	20	Normal	●
19	Iron Defense	Steel	Status	—	—	15	Self	
24	Swagger	Normal	Status	—	90	15	Normal	
28	AncientPower	Rock	Special	60	100	5	Normal	
30	Block	Normal	Status	—	—	5	Normal	
36	Endure	Normal	Status	—	—	10	Self	
43	Metal Burst	Steel	Physical	—	100	10	Self	
52	Iron Head	Steel	Physical	80	100	15	Normal	●

National Pokédex No. 412 Bagworm Pokémon
Burmy

BUG

Plant Cloak · Sandy Cloak · Trash Cloak

STATS
- HP ●
- ATTACK ●●
- DEFENSE ●●
- SP. ATTACK ●
- SP. DEFENSE ●●
- SPEED ●

● Plant Cloak ● Sandy Cloak ● Trash Cloak

EVOLUTION PATH

Burmy (Plant Cloak) → Lv20 → Wormadam (Plant Cloak)
Burmy (Sandy Cloak) → Lv20 → Wormadam (Sandy Cloak)
Burmy (Trash Cloak) → Lv20 → Wormadam (Trash Cloak)
Burmy ♂ → Lv20 → Mothim

● **MAIN WAYS TO OBTAIN**

PLATINUM	Spread Honey on a Honey Tree
DIAMOND	Spread Honey on a Honey Tree
PEARL	Spread Honey on a Honey Tree
G B A	

ABILITY ● Shed Skin

● **LEVEL-UP AND LEARNED MOVES**

Lv	Name	Type	Kind	Power	Acc	PP	Range	DA
Base	Protect	Normal	Status	—	—	10	Self	
10	Tackle	Normal	Physical	35	95	35	Normal	●
15	Bug Bite	Bug	Physical	60	100	20	Normal	●
20	Hidden Power	Normal	Special	—	100	15	Normal	

National Pokédex No. 413 Bagworm Pokémon
Wormadam (Plant Cloak)

BUG GRASS

STATS
- HP ●●
- ATTACK ●●●
- DEFENSE ●●●
- SP. ATTACK ●●●
- SP. DEFENSE ●●●●
- SPEED ●

● Female form

EVOLUTION PATH

Burmy (Plant Cloak) → Lv20 → Wormadam (Plant Cloak)
Burmy (Sandy Cloak) → Lv20 → Wormadam (Sandy Cloak)
Burmy (Trash Cloak) → Lv20 → Wormadam (Trash Cloak)
Burmy ♂ → Lv20 → Mothim

● **MAIN WAYS TO OBTAIN**

PLATINUM	Level up Burmy (Plant Cloak) ♀ to Lv20
DIAMOND	Level up Burmy (Plant Cloak) ♀ to Lv20
PEARL	Level up Burmy (Plant Cloak) ♀ to Lv20
G B A	

ABILITY ● Anticipation

● **LEVEL-UP AND LEARNED MOVES**

Lv	Name	Type	Kind	Power	Acc	PP	Range	DA
Base	Tackle	Normal	Physical	35	95	35	Normal	●
10	Protect	Normal	Status	—	—	10	Self	
15	Bug Bite	Bug	Physical	60	100	20	Normal	●
20	Hidden Power	Normal	Special	—	100	15	Normal	
23	Confusion	Psychic	Special	50	100	25	Normal	
26	Razor Leaf	Grass	Physical	55	95	25	2 foes	
29	Growth	Normal	Status	—	—	40	Self	
32	Psybeam	Psychic	Special	65	100	20	Normal	
35	Captivate	Normal	Status	—	100	20	2 foes	
38	Flail	Normal	Physical	—	100	15	Normal	●
41	Attract	Normal	Status	—	100	15	Normal	
44	Psychic	Psychic	Special	90	100	10	Normal	
47	Leaf Storm	Grass	Special	140	90	5	Normal	

413

WORMADAM (PLANT CLOAK)

Wormadam (Sandy Cloak)

National Pokédex No. 413 Bagworm Pokémon

BUG GROUND

STATS
- HP ●●
- ATTACK ●●●
- DEFENSE ●●●
- SP. ATTACK ●●
- SP. DEFENSE ●●
- SPEED ●

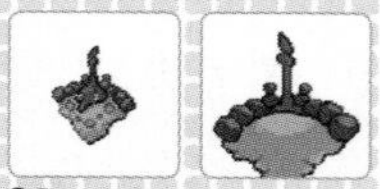

● Female form

EVOLUTION PATH

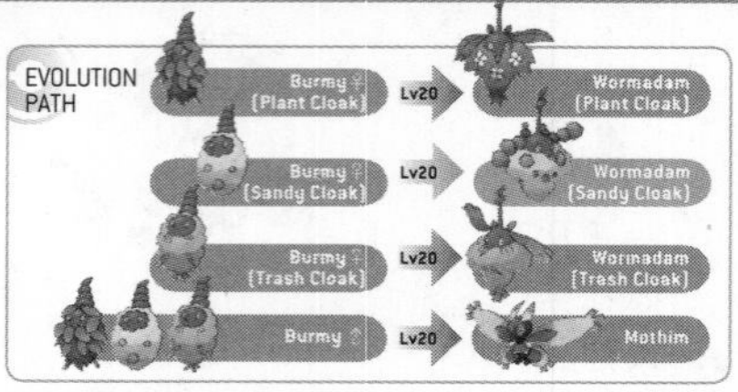

Burmy ♀ (Plant Cloak) — Lv20 → Wormadam (Plant Cloak)
Burmy (Sandy Cloak) — Lv20 → Wormadam (Sandy Cloak)
Burmy (Trash Cloak) — Lv20 → Wormadam (Trash Cloak)
Burmy ♂ — Lv20 → Mothim

● **MAIN WAYS TO OBTAIN**

PLATINUM	Level up Burmy (Sandy Cloak) ♀ to Lv20
DIAMOND	Level up Burmy (Sandy Cloak) ♀ to Lv20
PEARL	Level up Burmy (Sandy Cloak) ♀ to Lv20
GBA	

ABILITY ● Anticipation

● **LEVEL-UP AND LEARNED MOVES**

Lv	Name	Type	Kind	Power	Acc	PP	Range	DA
Base	Tackle	Normal	Physical	35	95	35	Normal	●
10	Protect	Normal	Status	—	—	10	Self	—
15	Bug Bite	Bug	Physical	60	100	20	Normal	●
20	Hidden Power	Normal	Special	—	100	15	Normal	—
23	Confusion	Psychic	Special	50	100	25	Normal	—
26	Rock Blast	Rock	Physical	25	80	10	Normal	—
29	Harden	Normal	Status	—	—	30	Self	—
32	Psybeam	Psychic	Special	65	100	20	Normal	—
35	Captivate	Normal	Status	—	100	20	2 foes	—
38	Flail	Normal	Physical	—	100	15	Normal	—
41	Attract	Normal	Status	—	100	15	Normal	—
44	Psychic	Psychic	Special	90	100	10	Normal	—
47	Fissure	Ground	Physical	—	30	5	Normal	—

Wormadam (Trash Cloak)

National Pokédex No. 413 Bagworm Pokémon

BUG STEEL

STATS
- HP ●●
- ATTACK ●●●
- DEFENSE ●●●●
- SP. ATTACK ●●●
- SP. DEFENSE ●●●
- SPEED ●

● Female form

EVOLUTION PATH

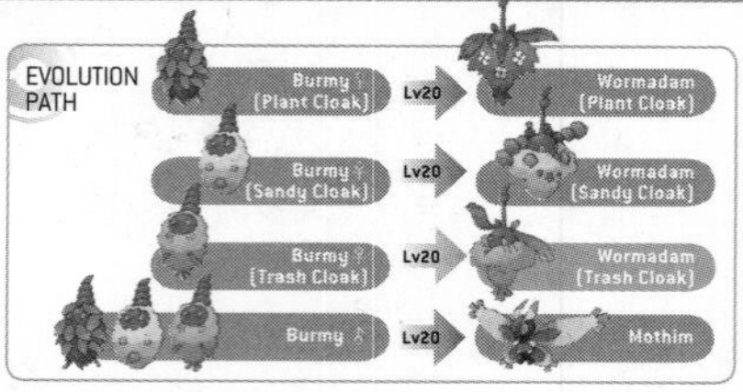

Burmy ♀ (Plant Cloak) — Lv20 → Wormadam (Plant Cloak)
Burmy (Sandy Cloak) — Lv20 → Wormadam (Sandy Cloak)
Burmy (Trash Cloak) — Lv20 → Wormadam (Trash Cloak)
Burmy ♂ — Lv20 → Mothim

● **MAIN WAYS TO OBTAIN**

PLATINUM	Level up Burmy (Trash Cloak) ♀ to Lv20
DIAMOND	Level up Burmy (Trash Cloak) ♀ to Lv20
PEARL	Level up Burmy (Trash Cloak) ♀ to Lv20
GBA	

ABILITY ● Anticipation

● **LEVEL-UP AND LEARNED MOVES**

Lv	Name	Type	Kind	Power	Acc	PP	Range	DA
Base	Tackle	Normal	Physical	35	95	35	Normal	●
10	Protect	Normal	Status	—	—	10	Self	—
15	Bug Bite	Bug	Physical	60	100	20	Normal	●
20	Hidden Power	Normal	Special	—	100	15	Normal	—
23	Confusion	Psychic	Special	50	100	25	Normal	—
26	Mirror Shot	Steel	Special	65	85	10	Normal	—
29	Metal Sound	Steel	Status	—	85	40	Normal	—
32	Psybeam	Psychic	Special	65	100	20	Normal	—
35	Captivate	Normal	Status	—	100	20	2 foes	—
38	Flail	Normal	Physical	—	100	15	Normal	—
41	Attract	Normal	Status	—	100	15	Normal	—
44	Psychic	Psychic	Special	90	100	10	Normal	—
47	Iron Head	Steel	Physical	80	100	15	Normal	●

Mothim

National Pokédex No. 414 Moth Pokémon

BUG FLYING

STATS
- HP ●●
- ATTACK ●●●
- DEFENSE ●●
- SP. ATTACK ●●●
- SP. DEFENSE ●●
- SPEED ●●

● Male form

EVOLUTION PATH

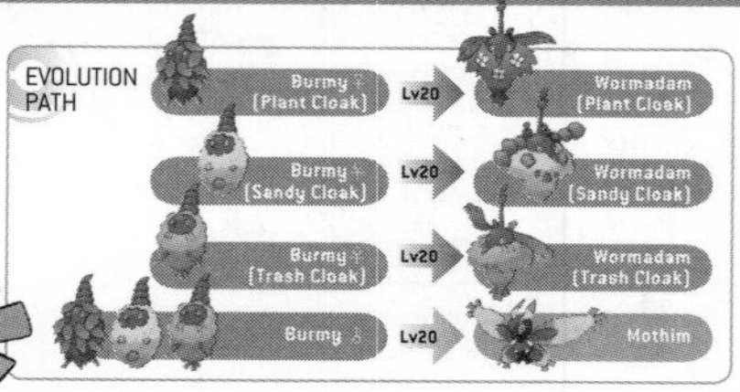

Burmy ♀ (Plant Cloak) — Lv20 → Wormadam (Plant Cloak)
Burmy (Sandy Cloak) — Lv20 → Wormadam (Sandy Cloak)
Burmy (Trash Cloak) — Lv20 → Wormadam (Trash Cloak)
Burmy ♂ — Lv20 → Mothim

● **MAIN WAYS TO OBTAIN**

PLATINUM	Level up Burmy ♂ to Lv20
DIAMOND	Level up Burmy ♂ to Lv20
PEARL	Level up Burmy ♂ to Lv20
GBA	

ABILITY ● Swarm

● **LEVEL-UP AND LEARNED MOVES**

Lv	Name	Type	Kind	Power	Acc	PP	Range	DA
Base	Tackle	Normal	Physical	35	95	35	Normal	●
10	Protect	Normal	Status	—	—	10	Self	—
15	Bug Bite	Bug	Physical	60	100	20	Normal	●
20	Hidden Power	Normal	Special	—	100	15	Normal	—
23	Confusion	Psychic	Special	50	100	25	Normal	—
26	Gust	Flying	Special	40	100	35	Normal	—
29	PoisonPowder	Poison	Status	—	75	35	Normal	—
32	Psybeam	Psychic	Special	65	100	20	Normal	—
35	Camouflage	Normal	Status	—	—	20	Self	—
38	Silver Wind	Bug	Special	60	100	5	Normal	—
41	Air Slash	Flying	Special	75	95	20	Normal	—
44	Psychic	Psychic	Special	90	100	10	Normal	—
47	Bug Buzz	Bug	Special	90	100	10	Normal	—

Combee

National Pokédex No. 415 Tiny Bee Pokémon

BUG FLYING

STATS
- HP ●
- ATTACK ●
- DEFENSE ●
- SP. ATTACK ●
- SP. DEFENSE ●
- SPEED ●●●

● Male form   ● Female form

EVOLUTION PATH

Combee ♀ — Lv21 → Vespiquen

● **MAIN WAYS TO OBTAIN**

PLATINUM	Spread Honey on a Honey Tree
DIAMOND	Spread Honey on a Honey Tree
PEARL	Spread Honey on a Honey Tree
GBA	

ABILITY ● Honey Gather

● **LEVEL-UP AND LEARNED MOVES**

Lv	Name	Type	Kind	Power	Acc	PP	Range	DA
Base	Sweet Scent	Normal	Status	—	100	20	2 foes	—
Base	Gust	Flying	Special	40	100	35	Normal	—
13	Bug Bite	Bug	Physical	60	100	20	Normal	●

413

WORMADAM (SANDY CLOAK)

National Pokédex No. 416 Beehive Pokémon

Vespiquen

BUG **FLYING**

STATS
- HP ●●
- ATTACK ●●●
- DEFENSE ●●●
- SP. ATTACK ●●●
- SP. DEFENSE ●●●
- SPEED ●●

● Female form

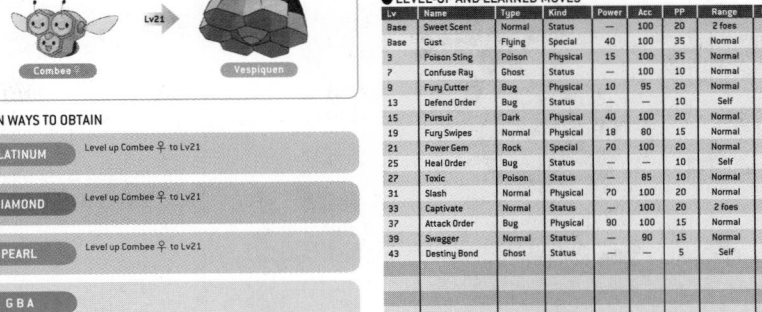

● EVOLUTION PATH

Combee ♀ → Lv21 → Vespiquen

● MAIN WAYS TO OBTAIN

PLATINUM	Level up Combee ♀ to Lv21
DIAMOND	Level up Combee ♀ to Lv21
PEARL	Level up Combee ♀ to Lv21
GBA	

● ABILITY ● Pressure

● LEVEL-UP AND LEARNED MOVES

Lv	Name	Type	Kind	Power	Acc	PP	Range	DA
Base	Sweet Scent	Normal	Status	—	100	20	2 foes	—
Base	Gust	Flying	Special	40	100	35	Normal	—
3	Poison Sting	Poison	Physical	15	100	35	Normal	—
7	Confuse Ray	Ghost	Status	—	100	10	Normal	—
9	Fury Cutter	Bug	Physical	10	95	20	Normal	●
13	Defend Order	Bug	Status	—	—	10	Self	—
15	Pursuit	Dark	Physical	40	100	20	Normal	—
19	Fury Swipes	Normal	Physical	18	80	15	Normal	—
21	Power Gem	Rock	Special	70	100	20	Normal	—
25	Heal Order	Bug	Status	—	—	10	Self	—
27	Toxic	Poison	Status	—	85	10	Normal	—
31	Slash	Normal	Physical	70	100	20	Normal	—
33	Captivate	Normal	Status	—	100	20	2 foes	—
37	Attack Order	Bug	Physical	90	100	15	Normal	—
39	Swagger	Normal	Status	—	90	15	Normal	—
43	Destiny Bond	Ghost	Status	—	—	5	Self	—

National Pokédex No. 417 Elesquirrel Pokémon

Pachirisu

ELECTRIC

STATS
- HP ●●
- ATTACK ●●
- DEFENSE ●●●
- SP. ATTACK ●●
- SP. DEFENSE ●●●
- SPEED ●●●

● Male form   ● Female form

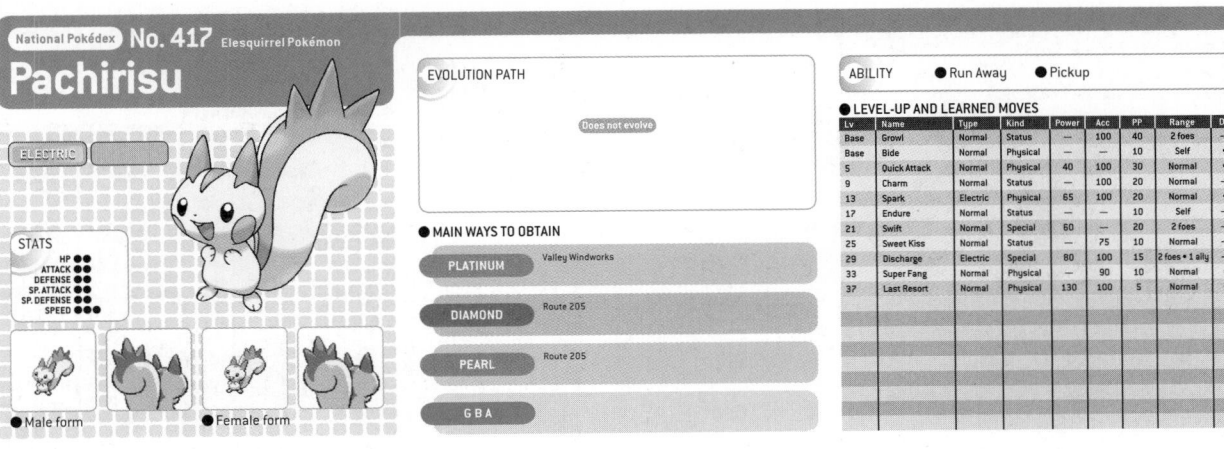

● EVOLUTION PATH

Does not evolve

● MAIN WAYS TO OBTAIN

PLATINUM	Valley Windworks
DIAMOND	Route 205
PEARL	Route 205
GBA	

● ABILITY ● Run Away ● Pickup

● LEVEL-UP AND LEARNED MOVES

Lv	Name	Type	Kind	Power	Acc	PP	Range	DA
Base	Growl	Normal	Status	—	100	40	2 foes	—
Base	Bide	Normal	Physical	—	—	10	Self	●
5	Quick Attack	Normal	Physical	40	100	30	Normal	—
9	Charm	Normal	Status	—	100	20	Normal	—
13	Spark	Electric	Physical	65	100	20	Normal	—
17	Endure	Normal	Status	—	—	10	Self	—
21	Swift	Normal	Special	60	—	20	2 foes	—
25	Sweet Kiss	Normal	Status	—	75	10	Normal	—
29	Discharge	Electric	Special	80	100	15	2 foes + 1 ally	—
33	Super Fang	Normal	Physical	—	90	10	Normal	—
37	Last Resort	Normal	Physical	130	100	5	Normal	●

National Pokédex No. 418 Sea Weasel Pokémon

Buizel

WATER

STATS
- HP ●●
- ATTACK ●●●
- DEFENSE ●●
- SP. ATTACK ●●
- SP. DEFENSE ●●
- SPEED ●●●

● Male form   ● Female form

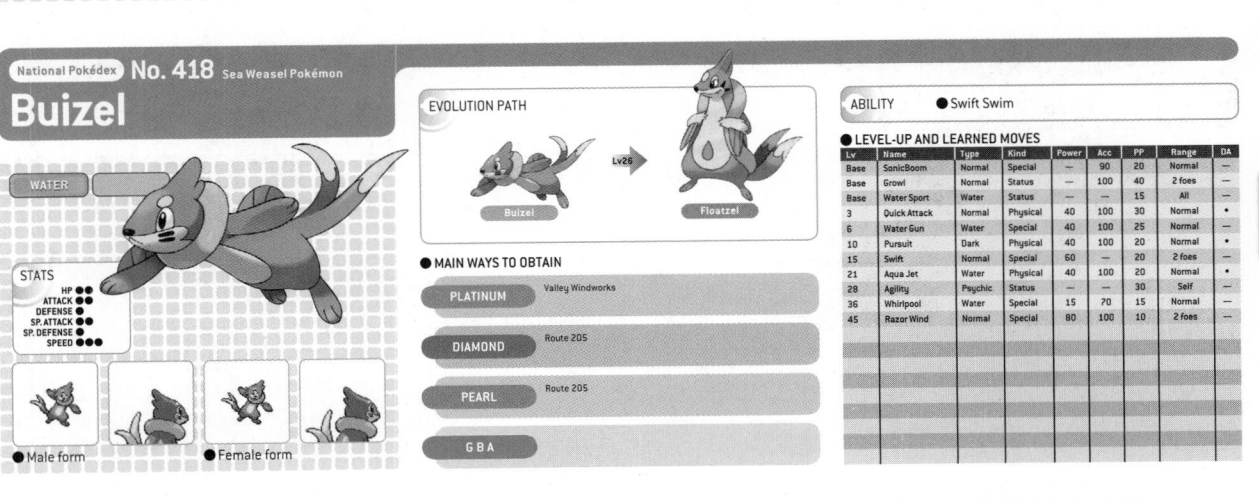

● EVOLUTION PATH

Buizel → Lv26 → Floatzel

● MAIN WAYS TO OBTAIN

PLATINUM	Valley Windworks
DIAMOND	Route 205
PEARL	Route 205
GBA	

● ABILITY ● Swift Swim

● LEVEL-UP AND LEARNED MOVES

Lv	Name	Type	Kind	Power	Acc	PP	Range	DA
Base	SonicBoom	Normal	Special	—	90	20	Normal	—
Base	Growl	Normal	Status	—	100	40	2 foes	—
Base	Water Sport	Water	Status	—	—	15	All	—
3	Quick Attack	Normal	Physical	40	100	30	Normal	●
6	Water Gun	Water	Special	40	100	25	Normal	●
10	Pursuit	Dark	Physical	40	100	20	Normal	—
15	Swift	Normal	Special	60	—	20	2 foes	—
21	Aqua Jet	Water	Physical	40	100	20	Normal	●
29	Agility	Psychic	Status	—	—	30	Self	—
36	Whirlpool	Water	Special	15	70	15	Normal	—
45	Razor Wind	Normal	Special	80	100	10	2 foes	—

National Pokédex No. 419 Sea Weasel Pokémon

Floatzel

WATER

STATS
- HP ●●●
- ATTACK ●●●
- DEFENSE ●●
- SP. ATTACK ●●●
- SP. DEFENSE ●●
- SPEED ●●●●

● Male form   ● Female form

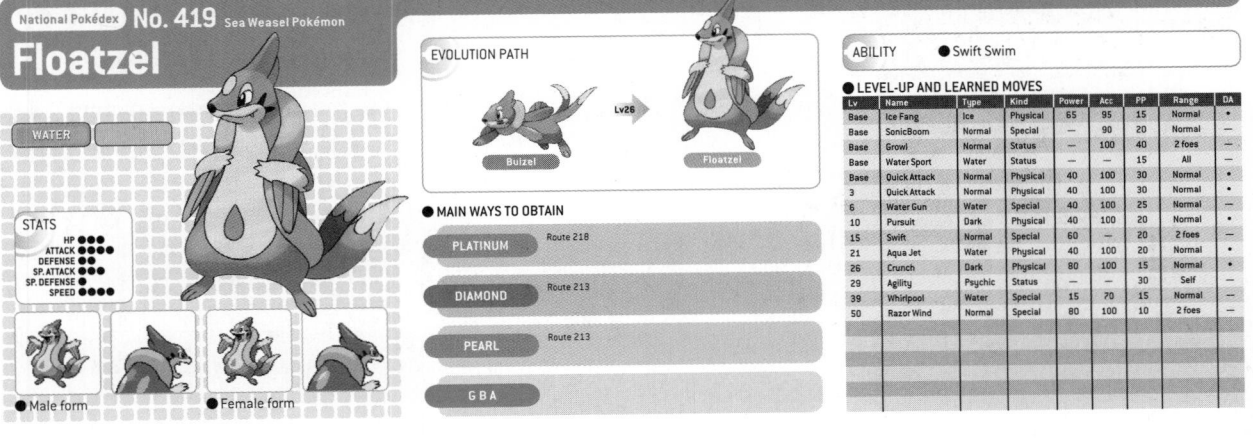

● EVOLUTION PATH

Buizel → Lv26 → Floatzel

● MAIN WAYS TO OBTAIN

PLATINUM	Route 218
DIAMOND	Route 213
PEARL	Route 213
GBA	

● ABILITY ● Swift Swim

● LEVEL-UP AND LEARNED MOVES

Lv	Name	Type	Kind	Power	Acc	PP	Range	DA
Base	Ice Fang	Ice	Physical	65	95	15	Normal	●
Base	SonicBoom	Normal	Special	—	90	20	Normal	—
Base	Growl	Normal	Status	—	100	40	2 foes	—
Base	Water Sport	Water	Status	—	—	15	All	—
Base	Quick Attack	Normal	Physical	40	100	30	Normal	●
3	Quick Attack	Normal	Physical	40	100	30	Normal	●
6	Water Gun	Water	Special	40	100	25	Normal	●
10	Pursuit	Dark	Physical	40	100	20	Normal	—
15	Swift	Normal	Special	60	—	20	2 foes	—
21	Aqua Jet	Water	Physical	40	100	20	Normal	●
26	Crunch	Dark	Physical	80	100	15	Normal	●
29	Agility	Psychic	Status	—	—	30	Self	—
39	Whirlpool	Water	Special	15	70	15	Normal	—
50	Razor Wind	Normal	Special	80	100	10	2 foes	—

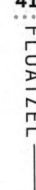

Cherubi

National Pokédex No. 420 Cherry Pokémon

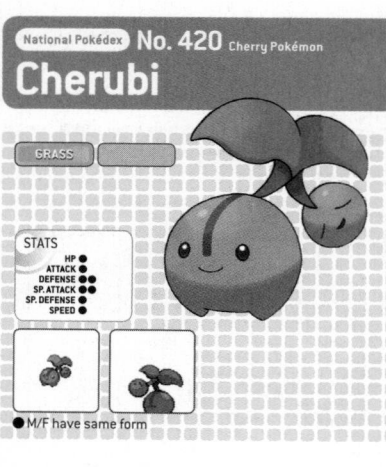

GRASS

STATS
- HP ●
- ATTACK ●●
- DEFENSE ●●
- SP. ATTACK ●●
- SP. DEFENSE ●●
- SPEED ●

● M/F have same form

EVOLUTION PATH

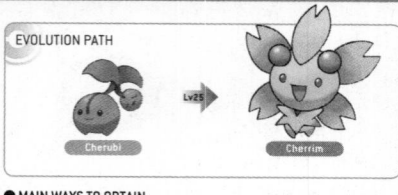

Cherubi → Lv25 → Cherrim

● **MAIN WAYS TO OBTAIN**

PLATINUM	Spread Honey on a Honey Tree
DIAMOND	Spread Honey on a Honey Tree
PEARL	Spread Honey on a Honey Tree
GBA	

ABILITY ● Chlorophyll

● **LEVEL-UP AND LEARNED MOVES**

Lv	Name	Type	Kind	Power	Acc	PP	Range	DA
Base	Tackle	Normal	Physical	35	95	35	Normal	●
7	Growth	Normal	Status	—	—	40	Self	
10	Leech Seed	Grass	Status	—	90	10	Normal	
13	Helping Hand	Normal	Status	—	—	20	1 ally	
19	Magical Leaf	Grass	Special	60	—	20	Normal	
22	Sunny Day	Fire	Status	—	—	5	All	
28	Worry Seed	Grass	Status	—	100	10	Normal	
31	Take Down	Normal	Physical	90	85	20	Normal	●
37	SolarBeam	Grass	Special	120	100	10	Normal	
40	Lucky Chant	Normal	Status	—	—	30	2 allies	

Cherrim

National Pokédex No. 421 Blossom Pokémon

GRASS

STATS
- HP ●●
- ATTACK ●●
- DEFENSE ●●
- SP. ATTACK ●●●
- SP. DEFENSE ●●●
- SPEED ●●●

Overcast form   Sunshine form

● Overcast form   ● Sunshine form

EVOLUTION PATH

Cherubi → Lv25 → Cherrim

● **MAIN WAYS TO OBTAIN**

PLATINUM	Level up Cherubi to Lv25
DIAMOND	Level up Cherubi to Lv25
PEARL	Level up Cherubi to Lv25
GBA	

ABILITY ● Flower Gift

● **LEVEL-UP AND LEARNED MOVES**

Lv	Name	Type	Kind	Power	Acc	PP	Range	DA
Base	Tackle	Normal	Physical	35	95	35	Normal	●
Base	Growth	Normal	Status	—	—	40	Self	
7	Growth	Normal	Status	—	—	40	Self	
10	Leech Seed	Grass	Status	—	90	10	Normal	
13	Helping Hand	Normal	Status	—	—	20	1 ally	
19	Magical Leaf	Grass	Special	60	—	20	Normal	
22	Sunny Day	Fire	Status	—	—	5	All	
25	Petal Dance	Grass	Special	90	100	20	1 random	●
30	Worry Seed	Grass	Status	—	100	10	Normal	
35	Take Down	Normal	Physical	90	85	20	Normal	●
43	SolarBeam	Grass	Special	120	100	10	Normal	
48	Lucky Chant	Normal	Status	—	—	30	2 allies	

Shellos

National Pokédex No. 422 Sea Slug Pokémon

WATER

STATS
- HP ●●●
- ATTACK ●●
- DEFENSE ●●
- SP. ATTACK ●●
- SP. DEFENSE ●●
- SPEED ●

West Sea   East Sea

● West Sea   ● East Sea

EVOLUTION PATH

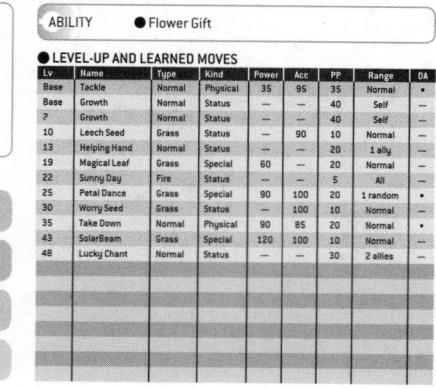

Shellos → Lv30 → Gastrodon

● **MAIN WAYS TO OBTAIN**

PLATINUM	Valley Windworks (West Sea)/Route 213 (East Sea)
DIAMOND	Route 205 (West Sea)/Route 213 (East Sea)
PEARL	Route 205 (West Sea)/Route 213 (East Sea)
GBA	

ABILITY ● Sticky Hold ● Storm Drain

● **LEVEL-UP AND LEARNED MOVES**

Lv	Name	Type	Kind	Power	Acc	PP	Range	DA
Base	Mud-Slap	Ground	Special	20	100	10	Normal	
2	Mud Sport	Ground	Status	—	—	15	All	
4	Harden	Normal	Status	—	—	30	Self	
7	Water Pulse	Water	Special	60	100	20	Normal	
11	Mud Bomb	Ground	Special	65	85	10	Normal	
16	Hidden Power	Normal	Special	—	100	15	Normal	
22	Rain Dance	Water	Status	—	—	5	All	
29	Body Slam	Normal	Physical	85	100	15	Normal	●
37	Muddy Water	Water	Special	95	85	10	2 foes	
46	Recover	Normal	Status	—	—	10	Self	

Gastrodon

National Pokédex No. 423 Sea Slug Pokémon

WATER   GROUND

STATS
- HP ●●●●
- ATTACK ●●●
- DEFENSE ●●
- SP. ATTACK ●●●
- SP. DEFENSE ●●●
- SPEED ●●

West Sea   East Sea

● West Sea   ● East Sea

EVOLUTION PATH

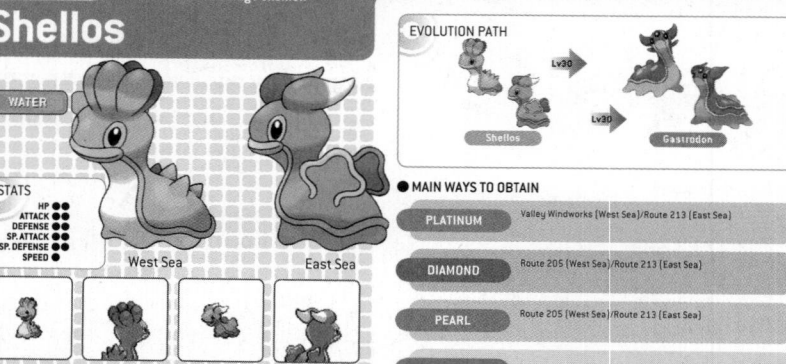

Shellos → Lv30 → Gastrodon

● **MAIN WAYS TO OBTAIN**

PLATINUM	Route 218 (West Sea)/Route 224 (East Sea)
DIAMOND	Route 218 (West Sea)/Route 222 (East Sea)
PEARL	Route 218 (West Sea)/Route 222 (East Sea)
GBA	

ABILITY ● Sticky Hold ● Storm Drain

● **LEVEL-UP AND LEARNED MOVES**

Lv	Name	Type	Kind	Power	Acc	PP	Range	DA
Base	Mud-Slap	Ground	Special	20	100	10	Normal	
Base	Mud Sport	Ground	Status	—	—	15	All	
Base	Harden	Normal	Status	—	—	30	Self	
Base	Water Pulse	Water	Special	60	100	20	Normal	
2	Mud Sport	Ground	Status	—	—	15	All	
4	Harden	Normal	Status	—	—	30	Self	
7	Water Pulse	Water	Special	60	100	20	Normal	
11	Mud Bomb	Ground	Special	65	85	10	Normal	
16	Hidden Power	Normal	Special	—	100	15	Normal	
22	Rain Dance	Water	Status	—	—	5	All	
29	Body Slam	Normal	Physical	85	100	15	Normal	●
41	Muddy Water	Water	Special	95	85	10	2 foes	
54	Recover	Normal	Status	—	—	10	Self	

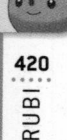

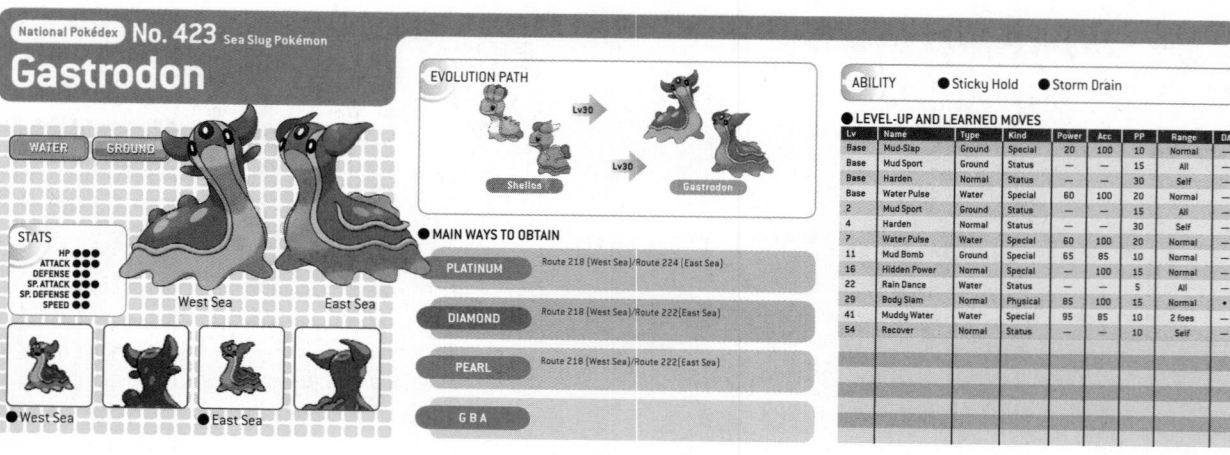

National Pokédex No. 424 Long Tail Pokémon

Ambipom

NORMAL

STATS
- HP ●●
- ATTACK ●●●
- DEFENSE ●●●
- SP. ATTACK ●●●
- SP. DEFENSE ●●●
- SPEED ●●●●

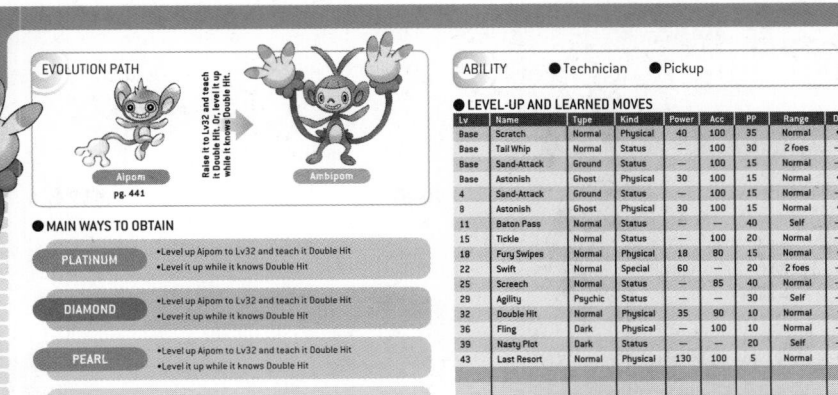

● Male form ● Female form

EVOLUTION PATH

Aipom → Ambipom

Raise it to Lv.32 and teach it Double Hit. Or, level it up while it knows Double Hit.

pg. 441

● MAIN WAYS TO OBTAIN

PLATINUM	• Level up Aipom to Lv.32 and teach it Double Hit • Level it up while it knows Double Hit
DIAMOND	• Level up Aipom to Lv.32 and teach it Double Hit • Level it up while it knows Double Hit
PEARL	• Level up Aipom to Lv.32 and teach it Double Hit • Level it up while it knows Double Hit
GBA	

ABILITY ● Technician ● Pickup

● LEVEL-UP AND LEARNED MOVES

Lv	Name	Type	Kind	Power	Acc	PP	Range	DA
Base	Scratch	Normal	Physical	40	100	35	Normal	●
Base	Tail Whip	Normal	Status	—	100	30	2 foes	—
Base	Sand-Attack	Ground	Status	—	100	15	Normal	—
Base	Astonish	Ghost	Physical	30	100	15	Normal	●
4	Sand-Attack	Ground	Status	—	100	15	Normal	●
8	Astonish	Ghost	Physical	30	100	15	Normal	●
11	Baton Pass	Normal	Status	—	—	40	Self	●
15	Tickle	Normal	Status	—	100	20	Normal	●
18	Fury Swipes	Normal	Physical	18	80	15	Normal	●
22	Swift	Normal	Special	60	—	20	2 foes	●
25	Screech	Normal	Status	—	85	40	Normal	●
29	Agility	Psychic	Status	—	—	30	Self	—
32	Double Hit	Normal	Physical	35	90	10	Normal	●
36	Fling	Dark	Physical	—	100	10	Normal	—
39	Nasty Plot	Dark	Status	—	—	20	Self	—
43	Last Resort	Normal	Physical	130	100	5	Normal	●

National Pokédex No. 425 Balloon Pokémon

Drifloon

GHOST FLYING

STATS
- HP ●●●
- ATTACK ●●
- DEFENSE ●
- SP. ATTACK ●●●
- SP. DEFENSE ●
- SPEED ●●●

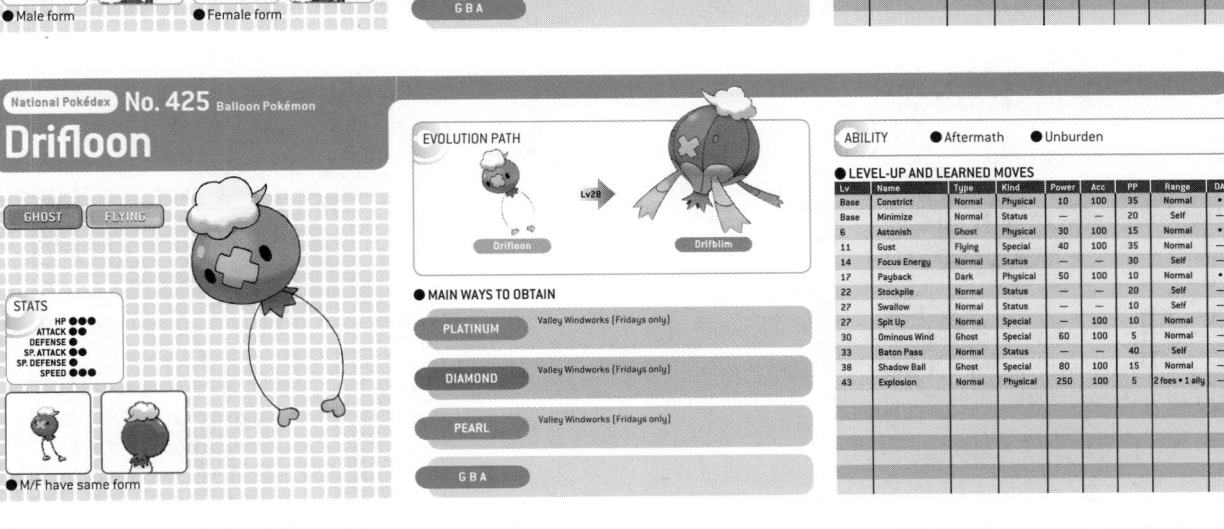

● M/F have same form

EVOLUTION PATH

Drifloon → Lv.28 → Drifblim

● MAIN WAYS TO OBTAIN

PLATINUM	Valley Windworks [Fridays only]
DIAMOND	Valley Windworks [Fridays only]
PEARL	Valley Windworks [Fridays only]
GBA	

ABILITY ● Aftermath ● Unburden

● LEVEL-UP AND LEARNED MOVES

Lv	Name	Type	Kind	Power	Acc	PP	Range	DA
Base	Constrict	Normal	Physical	10	100	35	Normal	●
Base	Minimize	Normal	Status	—	—	20	Self	—
6	Astonish	Ghost	Physical	30	100	15	Normal	●
11	Gust	Flying	Special	40	100	35	Normal	—
14	Focus Energy	Normal	Status	—	—	30	Self	—
17	Payback	Dark	Physical	50	100	10	Normal	●
22	Stockpile	Normal	Status	—	—	20	Self	—
27	Swallow	Normal	Status	—	—	10	Self	—
27	Spit Up	Normal	Special	—	100	10	Normal	—
30	Ominous Wind	Ghost	Special	60	100	5	Normal	—
33	Baton Pass	Normal	Status	—	—	40	Self	—
38	Shadow Ball	Ghost	Special	80	100	15	Normal	—
43	Explosion	Normal	Physical	250	100	5	2 foes • 1 ally	—

National Pokédex No. 426 Blimp Pokémon

Drifblim

GHOST FLYING

STATS
- HP ●●●●
- ATTACK ●●●
- DEFENSE ●
- SP. ATTACK ●●●
- SP. DEFENSE ●●●
- SPEED ●●●

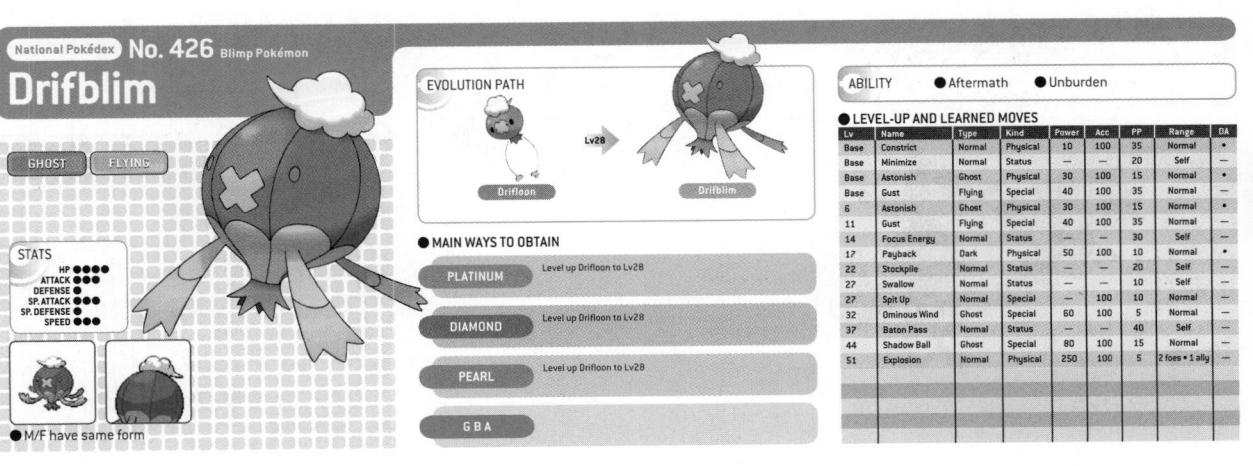

● M/F have same form

EVOLUTION PATH

Drifloon → Lv.28 → Drifblim

● MAIN WAYS TO OBTAIN

PLATINUM	Level up Drifloon to Lv.28
DIAMOND	Level up Drifloon to Lv.28
PEARL	Level up Drifloon to Lv.28
GBA	

ABILITY ● Aftermath ● Unburden

● LEVEL-UP AND LEARNED MOVES

Lv	Name	Type	Kind	Power	Acc	PP	Range	DA
Base	Constrict	Normal	Physical	10	100	35	Normal	●
Base	Minimize	Normal	Status	—	—	20	Self	—
Base	Astonish	Ghost	Physical	30	100	15	Normal	●
Base	Gust	Flying	Special	40	100	35	Normal	—
6	Astonish	Ghost	Physical	30	100	15	Normal	●
11	Gust	Flying	Special	40	100	35	Normal	—
14	Focus Energy	Normal	Status	—	—	30	Self	—
17	Payback	Dark	Physical	50	100	10	Normal	●
22	Stockpile	Normal	Status	—	—	20	Self	—
27	Swallow	Normal	Status	—	—	10	Self	—
27	Spit Up	Normal	Special	—	100	10	Normal	—
32	Ominous Wind	Ghost	Special	60	100	5	Normal	—
37	Baton Pass	Normal	Status	—	—	40	Self	—
44	Shadow Ball	Ghost	Special	80	100	15	Normal	—
51	Explosion	Normal	Physical	250	100	5	2 foes • 1 ally	—

National Pokédex No. 427 Rabbit Pokémon

Buneary

NORMAL

STATS
- HP ●●
- ATTACK ●●
- DEFENSE ●●
- SP. ATTACK ●●
- SP. DEFENSE ●●
- SPEED ●●●

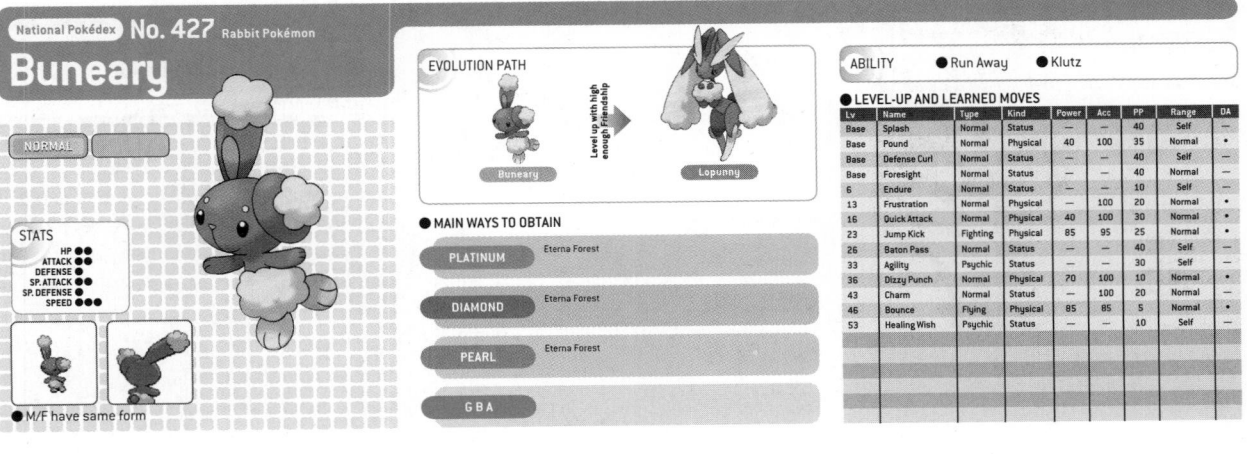

● M/F have same form

EVOLUTION PATH

Buneary → Level up with high enough Friendship → Lopunny

● MAIN WAYS TO OBTAIN

PLATINUM	Eterna Forest
DIAMOND	Eterna Forest
PEARL	Eterna Forest
GBA	

ABILITY ● Run Away ● Klutz

● LEVEL-UP AND LEARNED MOVES

Lv	Name	Type	Kind	Power	Acc	PP	Range	DA
Base	Splash	Normal	Status	—	—	40	Self	—
Base	Pound	Normal	Physical	40	100	35	Normal	●
Base	Defense Curl	Normal	Status	—	—	40	Self	—
Base	Foresight	Normal	Status	—	—	40	Normal	—
6	Endure	Normal	Status	—	—	10	Self	—
13	Frustration	Normal	Physical	—	100	20	Normal	●
16	Quick Attack	Normal	Physical	40	100	30	Normal	●
23	Jump Kick	Fighting	Physical	85	95	25	Normal	●
26	Baton Pass	Normal	Status	—	—	40	Self	—
33	Agility	Psychic	Status	—	—	30	Self	—
36	Dizzy Punch	Normal	Physical	70	100	10	Normal	●
43	Charm	Normal	Status	—	100	20	Normal	—
46	Bounce	Flying	Physical	85	85	5	Normal	●
53	Healing Wish	Psychic	Status	—	—	10	Self	—

427

BUNEARY

National Pokédex No. 428 Rabbit Pokémon

Lopunny

NORMAL

STATS
- HP ●●
- ATTACK ●●●
- DEFENSE ●●
- SP.ATTACK ●●
- SP. DEFENSE ●●●
- SPEED ●●●●

● M/F have same form

EVOLUTION PATH

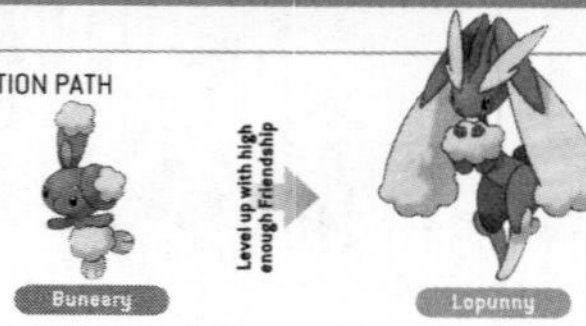

Buneary → *Level up with high enough Friendship* → Lopunny

● **MAIN WAYS TO OBTAIN**

PLATINUM	Level up Buneary with high enough Friendship
DIAMOND	Level up Buneary with high enough Friendship
PEARL	Level up Buneary with high enough Friendship
GBA	

ABILITY ● Cute Charm ● Klutz

● **LEVEL-UP AND LEARNED MOVES**

Lv	Name	Type	Kind	Power	Acc	PP	Range	DA
Base	Mirror Coat	Psychic	Special	—	100	20	Self	—
Base	Magic Coat	Psychic	Status	—	—	15	Self	—
Base	Splash	Normal	Status	—	—	40	Self	—
Base	Pound	Normal	Physical	40	100	35	Normal	●
Base	Defense Curl	Normal	Status	—	—	40	Self	—
Base	Foresight	Normal	Status	—	—	40	Normal	—
6	Endure	Normal	Status	—	—	10	Self	—
13	Return	Normal	Physical	—	100	20	Normal	●
16	Quick Attack	Normal	Physical	40	100	30	Normal	●
23	Jump Kick	Fighting	Physical	85	95	25	Normal	●
26	Baton Pass	Normal	Status	—	—	40	Self	—
33	Agility	Psychic	Status	—	—	30	Self	—
36	Dizzy Punch	Normal	Physical	70	100	10	Normal	●
43	Charm	Normal	Status	—	100	20	Normal	—
46	Bounce	Flying	Physical	85	85	5	Normal	●
53	Healing Wish	Psychic	Status	—	—	10	Self	—

National Pokédex No. 429 Magical Pokémon

Mismagius

GHOST

STATS
- HP ●●
- ATTACK ●●
- DEFENSE ●●●
- SP.ATTACK ●●●●
- SP. DEFENSE ●●●
- SPEED ●●●

● M/F have same form

EVOLUTION PATH

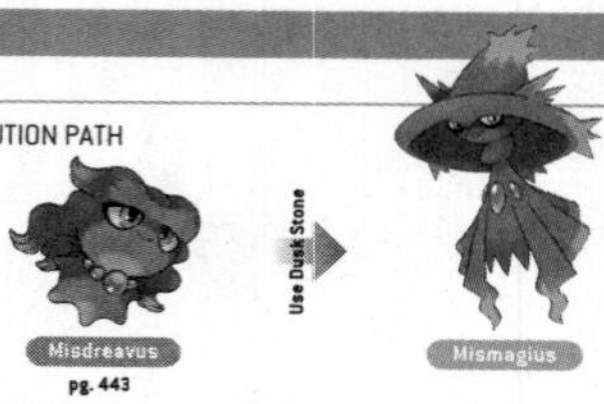

Misdreavus pg. 443 → *Use Dusk Stone* → Mismagius

● **MAIN WAYS TO OBTAIN**

PLATINUM	
DIAMOND	
PEARL	Use Dusk Stone on Misdreavus
GBA	

ABILITY ● Levitate

● **LEVEL-UP AND LEARNED MOVES**

Lv	Name	Type	Kind	Power	Acc	PP	Range	DA
Base	Lucky Chant	Normal	Status	—	—	30	2 allies	—
Base	Magical Leaf	Grass	Special	60	—	20	Normal	—
Base	Growl	Normal	Status	—	100	40	2 foes	—
Base	Psywave	Psychic	Special	—	80	15	Normal	—
Base	Spite	Ghost	Status	—	100	10	Normal	—
Base	Astonish	Ghost	Physical	30	100	15	Normal	●

National Pokédex No. 430 Big Boss Pokémon

Honchkrow

DARK FLYING

STATS
- HP ●●●
- ATTACK ●●●●
- DEFENSE ●●
- SP.ATTACK ●●●●
- SP. DEFENSE ●
- SPEED ●●●

● M/F have same form

EVOLUTION PATH

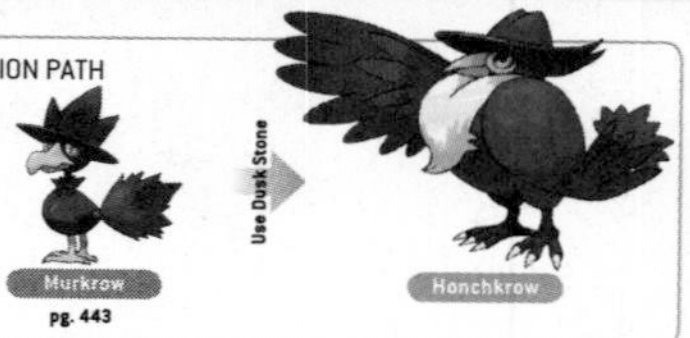

Murkrow pg. 443 → *Use Dusk Stone* → Honchkrow

● **MAIN WAYS TO OBTAIN**

PLATINUM	
DIAMOND	Use Dusk Stone on Murkrow
PEARL	
GBA	

ABILITY ● Insomnia ● Super Luck

● **LEVEL-UP AND LEARNED MOVES**

Lv	Name	Type	Kind	Power	Acc	PP	Range	DA
Base	Astonish	Ghost	Physical	30	100	15	Normal	●
Base	Pursuit	Dark	Physical	40	100	20	Normal	●
Base	Haze	Ice	Status	—	—	30	All	—
Base	Wing Attack	Flying	Physical	60	100	35	Normal	●
25	Swagger	Normal	Status	—	90	15	Normal	—
35	Nasty Plot	Dark	Status	—	—	20	Self	—
45	Night Slash	Dark	Physical	70	100	15	Normal	●
55	Dark Pulse	Dark	Special	80	100	15	Normal	—

National Pokédex No. 431 Catty Pokémon

Glameow

NORMAL

STATS
- HP ●
- ATTACK ●●
- DEFENSE ●●
- SP.ATTACK ●
- SP. DEFENSE ●●
- SPEED ●●●

● M/F have same form

EVOLUTION PATH

Glameow → *Lv38* → Purugly

● **MAIN WAYS TO OBTAIN**

PLATINUM	
DIAMOND	
PEARL	Route 218
GBA	

ABILITY ● Limber ● Own Tempo

● **LEVEL-UP AND LEARNED MOVES**

Lv	Name	Type	Kind	Power	Acc	PP	Range	DA
Base	Fake Out	Normal	Physical	40	100	10	Normal	●
5	Scratch	Normal	Physical	40	100	35	Normal	●
8	Growl	Normal	Status	—	100	40	2 foes	—
13	Hypnosis	Psychic	Status	—	60	20	Normal	—
17	Faint Attack	Dark	Physical	60	—	20	Normal	●
20	Fury Swipes	Normal	Physical	18	80	15	Normal	●
25	Charm	Normal	Status	—	100	20	Normal	—
29	Assist	Normal	Status	—	—	20	DoM	—
32	Captivate	Normal	Status	—	100	20	2 foes	—
37	Slash	Normal	Physical	70	100	20	Normal	●
41	Sucker Punch	Dark	Physical	80	100	5	Normal	●
45	Attract	Normal	Status	—	100	15	Normal	—

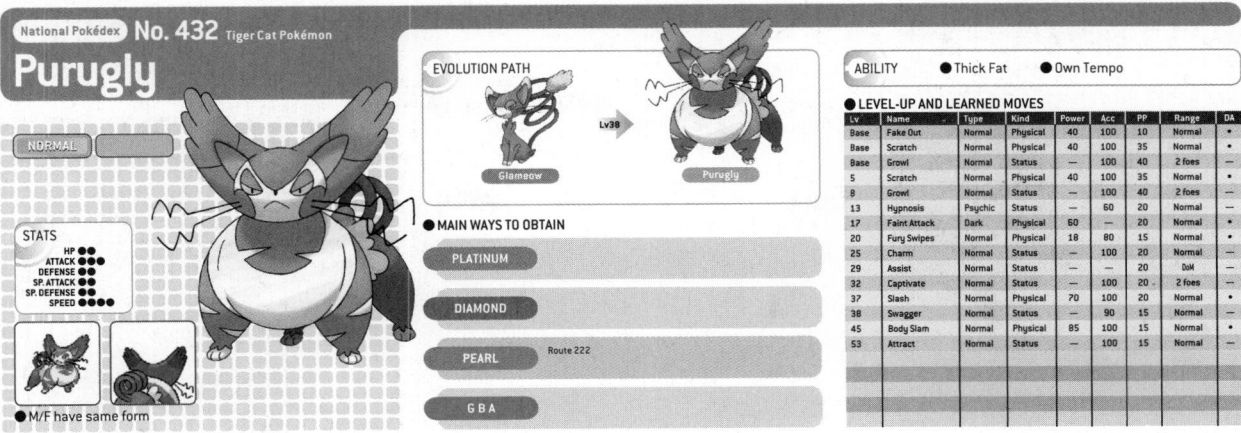

National Pokédex No. 432 · Tiger Cat Pokémon

Purugly

NORMAL

STATS
HP ●●
ATTACK ●●●
DEFENSE ●●●
SP.ATTACK ●●
SP.DEFENSE ●●
SPEED ●●●●

● M/F have same form

EVOLUTION PATH
Glameow → Lv38 → Purugly

MAIN WAYS TO OBTAIN
PLATINUM
DIAMOND
PEARL — Route 222
GBA

ABILITY
● Thick Fat   ● Own Tempo

LEVEL-UP AND LEARNED MOVES

Lv	Name	Type	Kind	Power	Acc	PP	Range	DA
Base	Fake Out	Normal	Physical	40	100	10	Normal	●
Base	Scratch	Normal	Physical	40	100	35	Normal	●
Base	Growl	Normal	Status	—	100	40	2 foes	—
5	Scratch	Normal	Physical	40	100	35	Normal	●
8	Growl	Normal	Status	—	100	40	2 foes	—
13	Hypnosis	Psychic	Status	—	60	20	Normal	—
17	Faint Attack	Dark	Physical	60	—	20	Normal	●
20	Fury Swipes	Normal	Physical	18	80	15	Normal	●
25	Charm	Normal	Status	—	100	20	Normal	—
29	Assist	Normal	Status	—	100	20	DoM	—
32	Captivate	Normal	Status	—	100	20	2 foes	—
37	Slash	Normal	Physical	70	100	20	Normal	●
38	Swagger	Normal	Status	—	90	15	Normal	—
45	Body Slam	Normal	Physical	85	100	15	Normal	●
53	Attract	Normal	Status	—	100	15	Normal	—

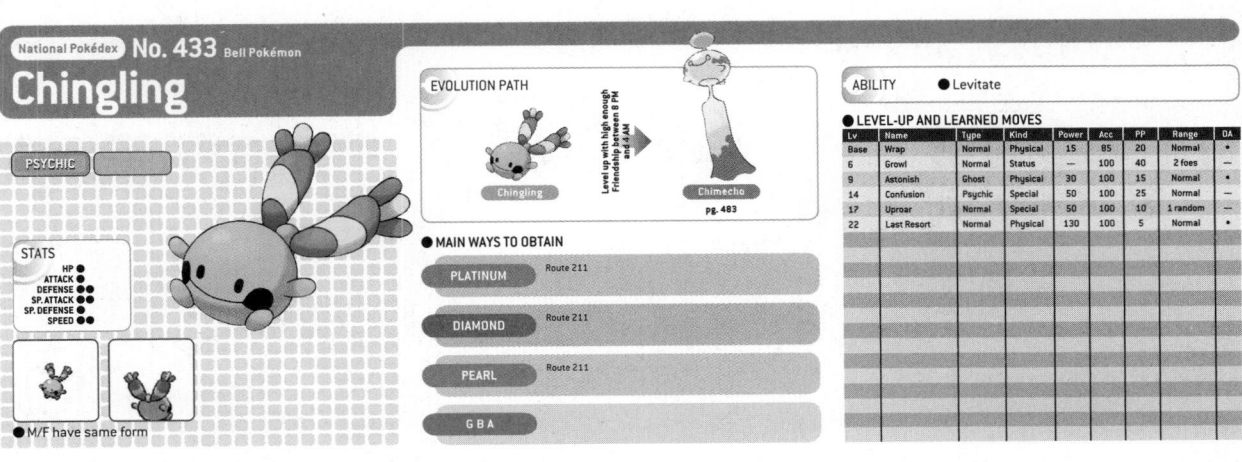

National Pokédex No. 433 · Bell Pokémon

Chingling

PSYCHIC

STATS
HP ●
ATTACK ●●
DEFENSE ●●
SP.ATTACK ●●
SP.DEFENSE ●●
SPEED ●●

● M/F have same form

EVOLUTION PATH
Chingling → Level up with high enough Friendship between 8 PM and 4 AM → Chimecho
pg. 483

MAIN WAYS TO OBTAIN
PLATINUM — Route 211
DIAMOND — Route 211
PEARL — Route 211
GBA

ABILITY
● Levitate

LEVEL-UP AND LEARNED MOVES

Lv	Name	Type	Kind	Power	Acc	PP	Range	DA
Base	Wrap	Normal	Physical	15	85	20	Normal	●
6	Growl	Normal	Status	—	100	40	2 foes	—
9	Astonish	Ghost	Physical	30	100	15	Normal	●
14	Confusion	Psychic	Special	50	100	25	Normal	—
17	Uproar	Normal	Special	50	100	10	1 random	—
22	Last Resort	Normal	Physical	130	100	5	Normal	●

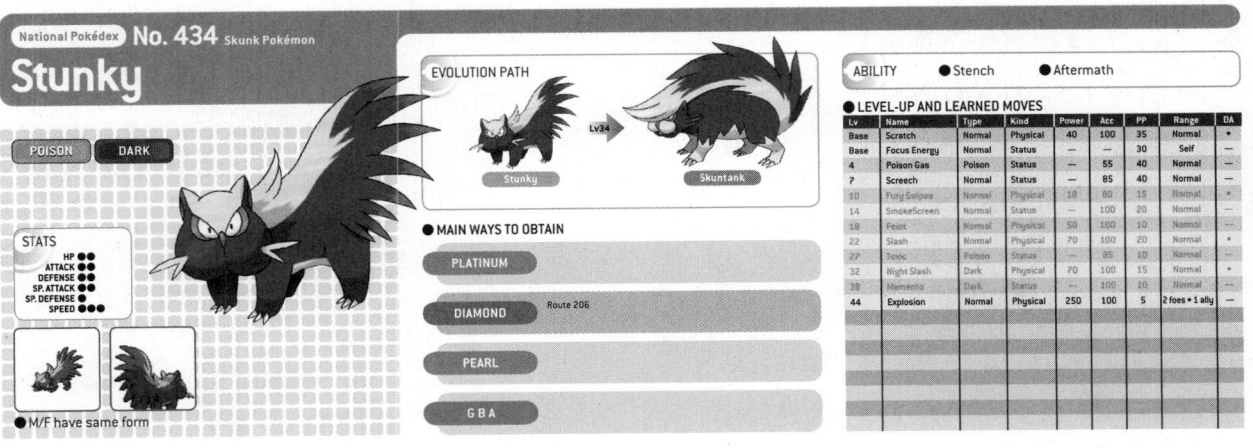

National Pokédex No. 434 · Skunk Pokémon

Stunky

POISON **DARK**

STATS
HP ●●
ATTACK ●●
DEFENSE ●●●
SP.ATTACK ●●
SP.DEFENSE ●●●
SPEED ●●●

● M/F have same form

EVOLUTION PATH
Stunky → Lv34 → Skuntank

MAIN WAYS TO OBTAIN
PLATINUM
DIAMOND — Route 206
PEARL
GBA

ABILITY
● Stench   ● Aftermath

LEVEL-UP AND LEARNED MOVES

Lv	Name	Type	Kind	Power	Acc	PP	Range	DA
Base	Scratch	Normal	Physical	40	100	35	Normal	●
Base	Focus Energy	Normal	Status	—	—	30	Self	—
4	Poison Gas	Poison	Status	—	55	40	Normal	—
7	Screech	Normal	Status	—	85	40	Normal	—
10	Fury Swipes	Normal	Physical	18	80	15	Normal	●
14	SmokeScreen	Normal	Status	—	100	20	Normal	—
18	Feint	Normal	Physical	50	100	10	Normal	—
22	Slash	Normal	Physical	70	100	20	Normal	●
27	Toxic	Poison	Status	—	85	10	Normal	—
32	Night Slash	Dark	Physical	70	100	15	Normal	●
38	Memento	Dark	Status	—	100	10	Normal	—
44	Explosion	Normal	Physical	250	100	5	2 foes + 1 ally	—

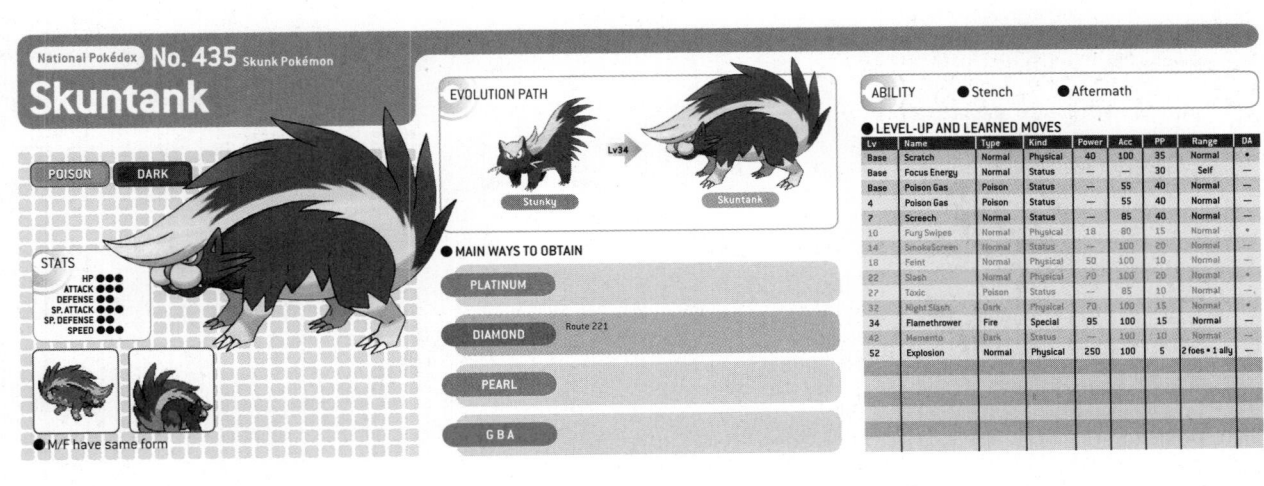

National Pokédex No. 435 · Skunk Pokémon

Skuntank

POISON **DARK**

STATS
HP ●●●
ATTACK ●●●
DEFENSE ●●●
SP.ATTACK ●●●
SP.DEFENSE ●●●
SPEED ●●●

● M/F have same form

EVOLUTION PATH
Stunky → Lv34 → Skuntank

MAIN WAYS TO OBTAIN
PLATINUM
DIAMOND — Route 221
PEARL
GBA

ABILITY
● Stench   ● Aftermath

LEVEL-UP AND LEARNED MOVES

Lv	Name	Type	Kind	Power	Acc	PP	Range	DA
Base	Scratch	Normal	Physical	40	100	35	Normal	●
Base	Focus Energy	Normal	Status	—	—	30	Self	—
Base	Poison Gas	Poison	Status	—	55	40	Normal	—
4	Poison Gas	Poison	Status	—	55	40	Normal	—
7	Screech	Normal	Status	—	85	40	Normal	—
10	Fury Swipes	Normal	Physical	18	80	15	Normal	●
14	SmokeScreen	Normal	Status	—	100	20	Normal	—
18	Feint	Normal	Physical	50	100	10	Normal	—
22	Slash	Normal	Physical	70	100	20	Normal	●
27	Toxic	Poison	Status	—	85	10	Normal	—
32	Night Slash	Dark	Physical	70	100	15	Normal	●
34	Flamethrower	Fire	Special	95	100	15	Normal	—
42	Memento	Dark	Status	—	100	10	Normal	—
52	Explosion	Normal	Physical	250	100	5	2 foes + 1 ally	—

435
SKUNTANK

National Pokédex No. 436 Bronze Pokémon

Bronzor

STEEL | PSYCHIC

STATS
HP ●●
ATTACK ●●
DEFENSE ●●●
SP. ATTACK ●●
SP. DEFENSE ●●●
SPEED ●

● Gender unknown

EVOLUTION PATH

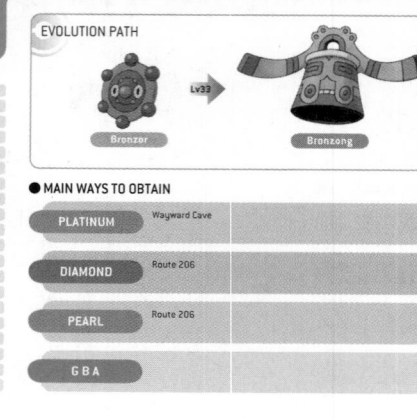

Bronzor —Lv33→ Bronzong

● MAIN WAYS TO OBTAIN

PLATINUM	Wayward Cave
DIAMOND	Route 206
PEARL	Route 206
G B A	

ABILITY ● Levitate ● Heatproof

● LEVEL-UP AND LEARNED MOVES

Lv	Name	Type	Kind	Power	Acc	PP	Range	DA
Base	Tackle	Normal	Physical	35	95	35	Normal	●
Base	Confusion	Psychic	Special	50	100	25	Normal	—
?	Hypnosis	Psychic	Status	—	60	20	Normal	—
12	Imprison	Psychic	Status	—	—	10	Self	—
14	Confuse Ray	Ghost	Status	—	100	10	Normal	—
19	Extrasensory	Psychic	Special	80	100	30	Normal	—
26	Iron Defense	Steel	Status	—	—	15	Self	—
30	Safeguard	Normal	Status	—	—	25	2 allies	—
35	Gyro Ball	Steel	Physical	—	100	5	Normal	●
37	Future Sight	Psychic	Special	80	90	15	Normal	—
41	Faint Attack	Dark	Physical	60	—	20	Normal	—
49	Payback	Dark	Physical	50	100	10	Normal	●
52	Heal Block	Psychic	Status	—	100	15	2 foes	—

National Pokédex No. 437 Bronze Bell Pokémon

Bronzong

STEEL | PSYCHIC

STATS
HP ●●
ATTACK ●●●
DEFENSE ●●●●
SP. ATTACK ●●●
SP. DEFENSE ●●●
SPEED ●

● Gender unknown

EVOLUTION PATH

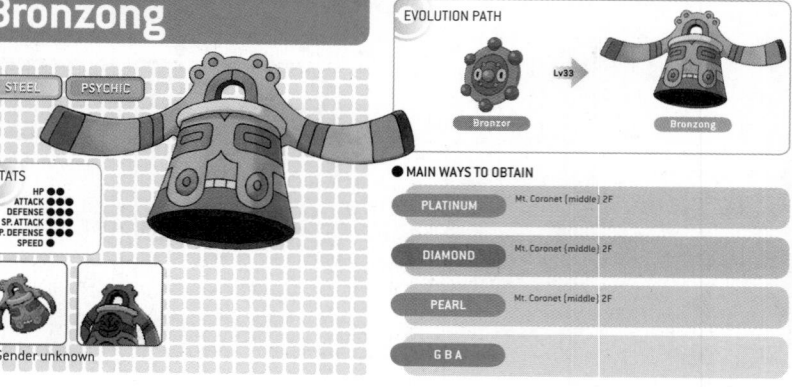

Bronzor —Lv33→ Bronzong

● MAIN WAYS TO OBTAIN

PLATINUM	Mt. Coronet (middle) 2F
DIAMOND	Mt. Coronet (middle) 2F
PEARL	Mt. Coronet (middle) 2F
G B A	

ABILITY ● Levitate ● Heatproof

● LEVEL-UP AND LEARNED MOVES

Lv	Name	Type	Kind	Power	Acc	PP	Range	DA
Base	Sunny Day	Fire	Status	—	—	5	All	—
Base	Rain Dance	Water	Status	—	—	5	All	—
Base	Tackle	Normal	Physical	35	95	35	Normal	●
Base	Confusion	Psychic	Special	50	100	25	Normal	—
Base	Hypnosis	Psychic	Status	—	60	20	Normal	—
Base	Imprison	Psychic	Status	—	—	10	Self	—
?	Hypnosis	Psychic	Status	—	60	20	Normal	—
12	Imprison	Psychic	Status	—	—	10	Self	—
14	Confuse Ray	Ghost	Status	—	100	10	Normal	—
19	Extrasensory	Psychic	Special	80	100	30	Normal	—
26	Iron Defense	Steel	Status	—	—	15	Self	—
30	Safeguard	Normal	Status	—	—	25	2 allies	—
33	Block	Normal	Status	—	—	5	Normal	—
38	Gyro Ball	Steel	Physical	—	100	5	Normal	●
43	Future Sight	Psychic	Special	80	90	15	Normal	—
50	Faint Attack	Dark	Physical	60	—	20	Normal	—
61	Payback	Dark	Physical	50	100	10	Normal	●
67	Heal Block	Psychic	Status	—	100	15	2 foes	—

National Pokédex No. 438 Bonsai Pokémon

Bonsly

ROCK

STATS
HP ●●●
ATTACK ●●●
DEFENSE ●●●
SP. ATTACK ●
SP. DEFENSE ●
SPEED ●

● M/F have same form

EVOLUTION PATH

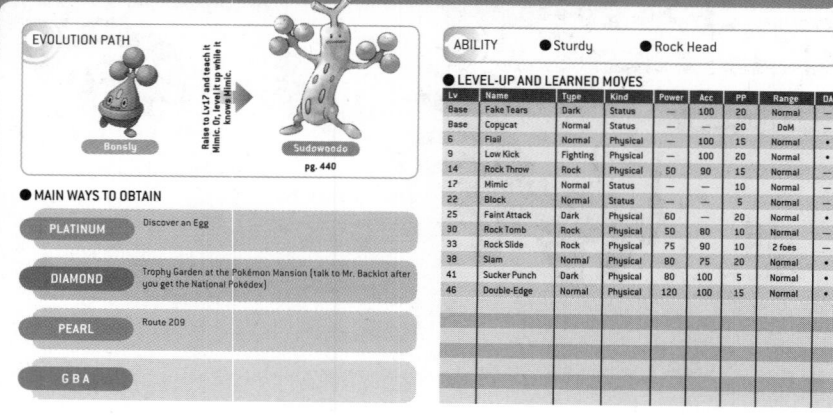

Bonsly —Raise to Lv17 and teach it Mimic. Or, level it up while it knows Mimic.→ Sudowoodo
pg. 440

● MAIN WAYS TO OBTAIN

PLATINUM	Discover an Egg
DIAMOND	Trophy Garden at the Pokémon Mansion (talk to Mr. Backlot after you get the National Pokédex)
PEARL	Route 209
G B A	

ABILITY ● Sturdy ● Rock Head

● LEVEL-UP AND LEARNED MOVES

Lv	Name	Type	Kind	Power	Acc	PP	Range	DA
Base	Fake Tears	Dark	Status	—	100	20	Normal	—
Base	Copycat	Normal	Status	—	—	20	DoM	—
6	Flail	Normal	Physical	—	100	15	Normal	●
9	Low Kick	Fighting	Physical	—	100	20	Normal	●
14	Rock Throw	Rock	Physical	50	90	15	Normal	—
17	Mimic	Normal	Status	—	—	10	Normal	—
22	Block	Normal	Status	—	—	5	Normal	—
25	Faint Attack	Dark	Physical	60	—	20	Normal	—
30	Rock Tomb	Rock	Physical	50	80	10	Normal	—
33	Rock Slide	Rock	Physical	75	90	10	2 foes	—
38	Slam	Normal	Physical	80	75	20	Normal	●
41	Sucker Punch	Dark	Physical	80	100	5	Normal	●
46	Double-Edge	Normal	Physical	120	100	15	Normal	●

National Pokédex No. 439 Mime Pokémon

Mime Jr.

PSYCHIC

STATS
HP ●
ATTACK ●
DEFENSE ●
SP. ATTACK ●●●
SP. DEFENSE ●●●
SPEED ●●

● M/F have same form

EVOLUTION PATH

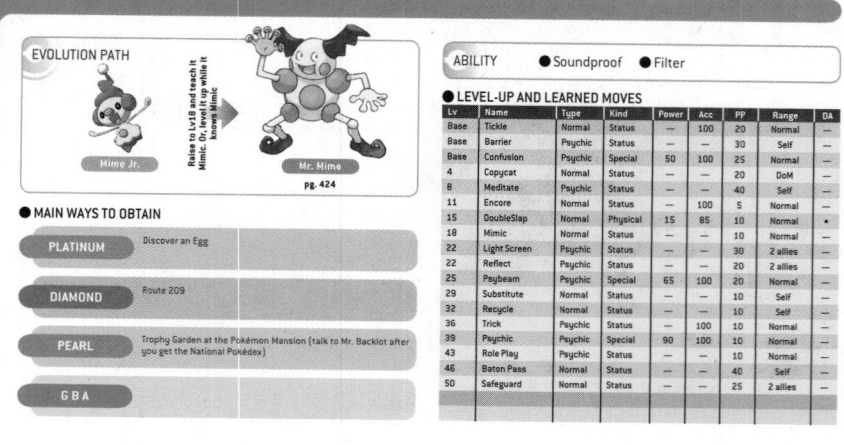

Mime Jr. —Raise to Lv18 and teach it Mimic. Or, level it up while it knows Mimic.→ Mr. Mime
pg. 424

● MAIN WAYS TO OBTAIN

PLATINUM	Discover an Egg
DIAMOND	Route 209
PEARL	Trophy Garden at the Pokémon Mansion (talk to Mr. Backlot after you get the National Pokédex)
G B A	

ABILITY ● Soundproof ● Filter

● LEVEL-UP AND LEARNED MOVES

Lv	Name	Type	Kind	Power	Acc	PP	Range	DA
Base	Tickle	Normal	Status	—	100	20	Normal	—
Base	Barrier	Psychic	Status	—	—	30	Self	—
Base	Confusion	Psychic	Special	50	100	25	Normal	—
4	Copycat	Normal	Status	—	—	20	DoM	—
8	Meditate	Psychic	Status	—	—	40	Self	—
11	Encore	Normal	Status	—	100	5	Normal	—
15	DoubleSlap	Normal	Physical	15	85	10	Normal	●
18	Mimic	Normal	Status	—	—	10	Normal	—
22	Light Screen	Psychic	Status	—	—	30	2 allies	—
22	Reflect	Psychic	Status	—	—	20	2 allies	—
25	Psybeam	Psychic	Special	65	100	20	Normal	—
29	Substitute	Normal	Status	—	—	10	Self	—
32	Recycle	Normal	Status	—	—	10	Self	—
36	Trick	Psychic	Status	—	100	10	Normal	—
39	Psychic	Psychic	Special	90	100	10	Normal	—
43	Role Play	Psychic	Status	—	—	10	Normal	—
46	Baton Pass	Normal	Status	—	—	40	Self	—
50	Safeguard	Normal	Status	—	—	25	2 allies	—

436
BRONZOR

National Pokédex No. 440 Playhouse Pokémon

Happiny

NORMAL

STATS
HP ●●●
ATTACK ●●
DEFENSE ●●
SP.ATTACK ●●
SP.DEFENSE ●●
SPEED ●●

● Female form

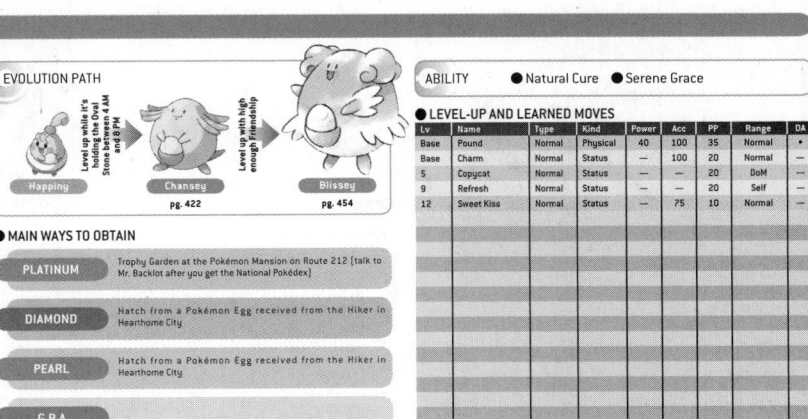

EVOLUTION PATH

Happiny → (Level up while it's holding the Oval Stone between 4 AM and 8 PM) → Chansey (pg. 422) → (Level up with high enough Friendship) → Blissey (pg. 454)

● **MAIN WAYS TO OBTAIN**

PLATINUM	Trophy Garden at the Pokémon Mansion on Route 212 (talk to Mr. Backlot after you get the National Pokédex)
DIAMOND	Hatch from a Pokémon Egg received from the Hiker in Hearthome City
PEARL	Hatch from a Pokémon Egg received from the Hiker in Hearthome City
G B A	

ABILITY ● Natural Cure ● Serene Grace

● **LEVEL-UP AND LEARNED MOVES**

Lv	Name	Type	Kind	Power	Acc	PP	Range	DA
Base	Pound	Normal	Physical	40	100	35	Normal	●
Base	Charm	Normal	Status	—	100	20	Normal	—
5	Copycat	Normal	Status	—	—	20	DoM	—
9	Refresh	Normal	Status	—	—	20	Self	—
12	Sweet Kiss	Normal	Status	—	75	10	Normal	—

National Pokédex No. 441 Music Note Pokémon

Chatot

NORMAL   FLYING

STATS
HP ●●
ATTACK ●●
DEFENSE ●●
SP.ATTACK ●●●
SP.DEFENSE ●●
SPEED ●●●

● M/F have same form

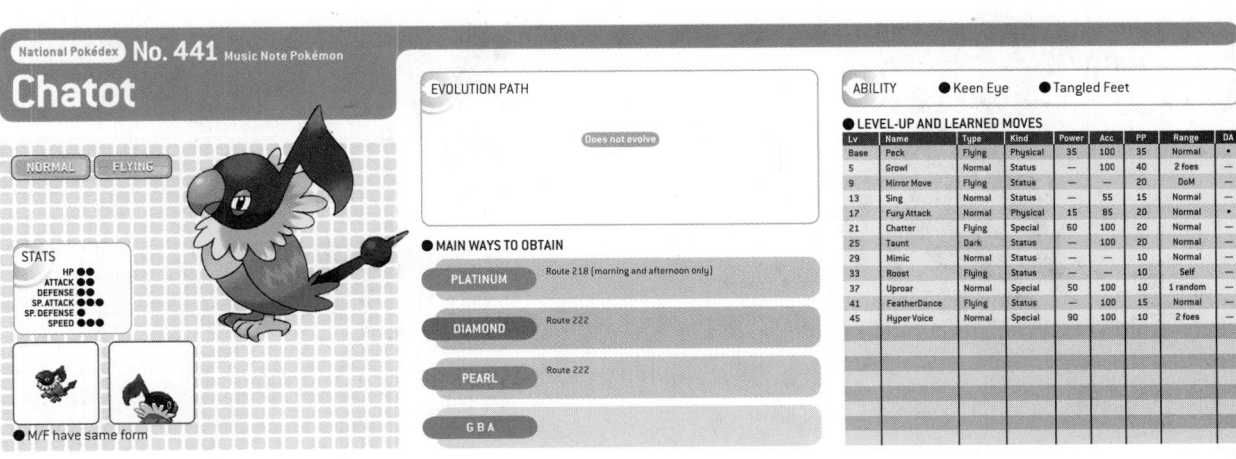

EVOLUTION PATH

Does not evolve

● **MAIN WAYS TO OBTAIN**

PLATINUM	Route 218 (morning and afternoon only)
DIAMOND	Route 222
PEARL	Route 222
G B A	

ABILITY ● Keen Eye ● Tangled Feet

● **LEVEL-UP AND LEARNED MOVES**

Lv	Name	Type	Kind	Power	Acc	PP	Range	DA
Base	Peck	Flying	Physical	35	100	35	Normal	●
5	Growl	Normal	Status	—	100	40	2 foes	—
9	Mirror Move	Flying	Status	—	—	20	DoM	—
13	Sing	Normal	Status	—	55	15	Normal	—
17	Fury Attack	Normal	Physical	15	85	20	Normal	●
21	Chatter	Flying	Special	60	100	20	Normal	—
25	Taunt	Dark	Status	—	100	20	Normal	—
29	Mimic	Normal	Status	—	—	10	Normal	—
33	Roost	Flying	Status	—	—	10	Self	—
37	Uproar	Normal	Special	50	100	10	1 random	—
41	FeatherDance	Flying	Status	—	100	15	Normal	—
45	Hyper Voice	Normal	Special	90	100	10	2 foes	—

National Pokédex No. 442 Forbidden Pokémon

Spiritomb

GHOST   DARK

STATS
HP ●●●
ATTACK ●●●
DEFENSE ●●●●
SP.ATTACK ●●●
SP.DEFENSE ●●●●
SPEED ●

● M/F have same form

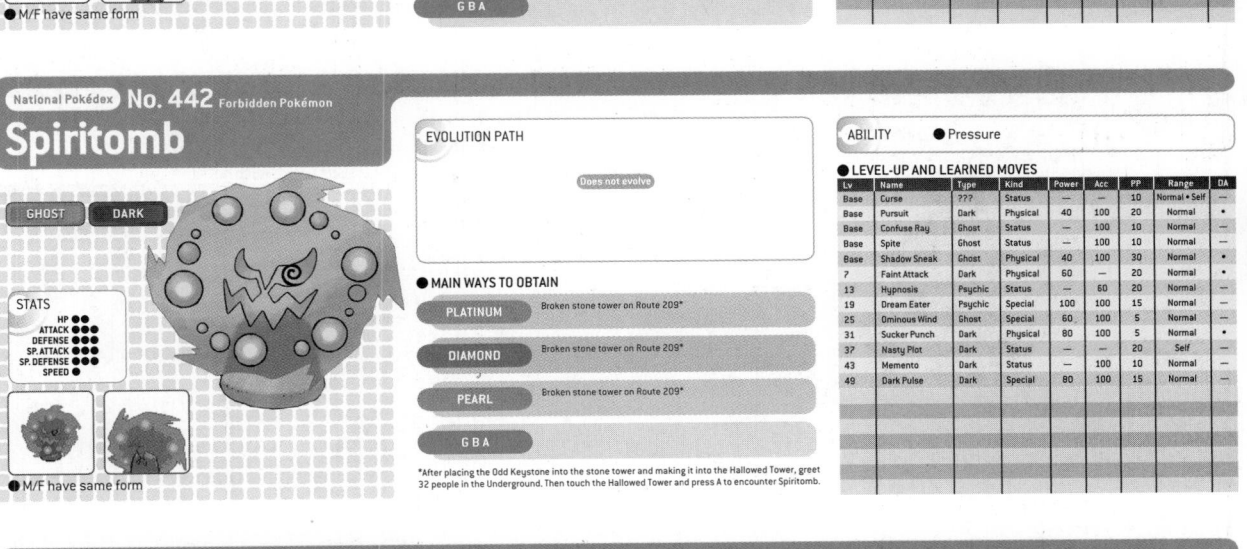

EVOLUTION PATH

Does not evolve

● **MAIN WAYS TO OBTAIN**

PLATINUM	Broken stone tower on Route 209*
DIAMOND	Broken stone tower on Route 209*
PEARL	Broken stone tower on Route 209*
G B A	

*After placing the Odd Keystone into the stone tower and making it into the Hallowed Tower, greet 32 people in the Underground. Then touch the Hallowed Tower and press A to encounter Spiritomb.

ABILITY ● Pressure

● **LEVEL-UP AND LEARNED MOVES**

Lv	Name	Type	Kind	Power	Acc	PP	Range	DA
Base	Curse	???	Status	—	—	10	Normal • Self	●
Base	Pursuit	Dark	Physical	40	100	20	Normal	●
Base	Confuse Ray	Ghost	Status	—	100	10	Normal	—
Base	Spite	Ghost	Status	—	100	10	Normal	—
Base	Shadow Sneak	Ghost	Physical	40	100	30	Normal	●
7	Faint Attack	Dark	Physical	60	—	20	Normal	●
13	Hypnosis	Psychic	Status	—	60	20	Normal	—
19	Dream Eater	Psychic	Special	100	100	15	Normal	—
25	Ominous Wind	Ghost	Special	60	100	5	Normal	—
31	Sucker Punch	Dark	Physical	80	100	5	Normal	●
37	Nasty Plot	Dark	Status	—	—	20	Self	—
43	Memento	Dark	Status	—	100	10	Normal	—
49	Dark Pulse	Dark	Special	80	100	15	Normal	—

National Pokédex No. 443 Land Shark Pokémon

Gible

DRAGON   GROUND

STATS
HP ●●●
ATTACK ●●●
DEFENSE ●●
SP.ATTACK ●●
SP.DEFENSE ●●
SPEED ●●

● Male form   ● Female form

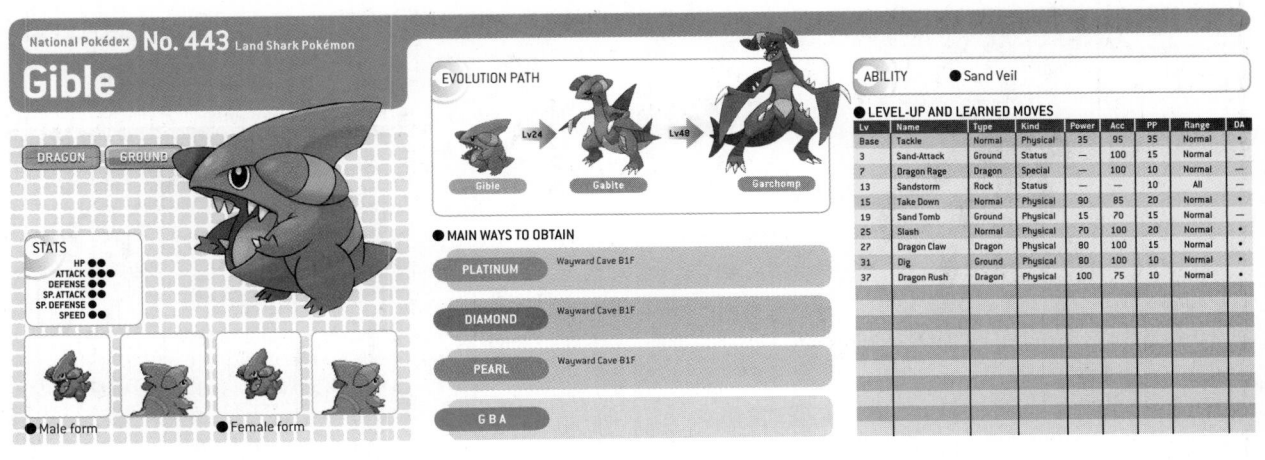

EVOLUTION PATH

Gible → Lv24 → Gabite → Lv49 → Garchomp

● **MAIN WAYS TO OBTAIN**

PLATINUM	Wayward Cave B1F
DIAMOND	Wayward Cave B1F
PEARL	Wayward Cave B1F
G B A	

ABILITY ● Sand Veil

● **LEVEL-UP AND LEARNED MOVES**

Lv	Name	Type	Kind	Power	Acc	PP	Range	DA
Base	Tackle	Normal	Physical	35	95	35	Normal	●
3	Sand-Attack	Ground	Status	—	100	15	Normal	—
7	Dragon Rage	Dragon	Special	—	100	10	Normal	—
13	Sandstorm	Rock	Status	—	—	10	All	—
15	Take Down	Normal	Physical	90	85	20	Normal	●
19	Sand Tomb	Ground	Physical	15	70	15	Normal	●
25	Slash	Normal	Physical	70	100	20	Normal	●
27	Dragon Claw	Dragon	Physical	80	100	15	Normal	●
31	Dig	Ground	Physical	80	100	10	Normal	●
37	Dragon Rush	Dragon	Physical	100	75	10	Normal	●

443
GIBLE

National Pokédex No. 444 Cave Pokémon
Gabite

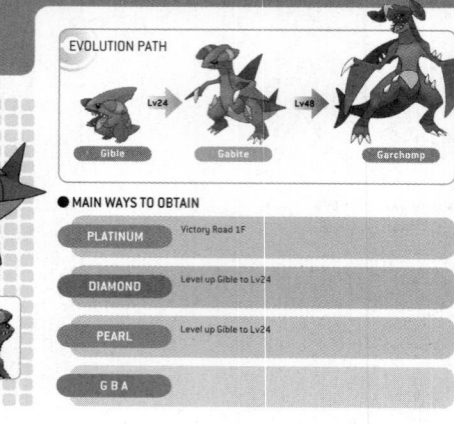

DRAGON GROUND

STATS
- HP ●●
- ATTACK ●●●
- DEFENSE ●●●
- SP.ATTACK ●●
- SP.DEFENSE ●●
- SPEED ●●●

● Male form   ● Female form

● EVOLUTION PATH
Gible → Lv24 → Gabite → Lv48 → Garchomp

● MAIN WAYS TO OBTAIN
PLATINUM	Victory Road 1F
DIAMOND	Level up Gible to Lv24
PEARL	Level up Gible to Lv24
G B A	

● ABILITY ● Sand Veil

● LEVEL-UP AND LEARNED MOVES
Lv	Name	Type	Kind	Power	Acc	PP	Range	DA
Base	Tackle	Normal	Physical	35	95	35	Normal	•
Base	Sand-Attack	Ground	Status	—	100	15	Normal	
3	Sand-Attack	Ground	Status	—	100	15	Normal	
7	Dragon Rage	Dragon	Special	—	100	10	Normal	
13	Sandstorm	Rock	Status	—	—	10	All	
15	Take Down	Normal	Physical	90	100	20	Normal	
19	Sand Tomb	Ground	Physical	15	70	15	Normal	
28	Slash	Normal	Physical	70	100	20	Normal	
33	Dragon Claw	Dragon	Physical	80	100	15	Normal	
40	Dig	Ground	Physical	80	100	10	Normal	
49	Dragon Rush	Dragon	Physical	100	75	10	Normal	

National Pokédex No. 445 Mach Pokémon
Garchomp

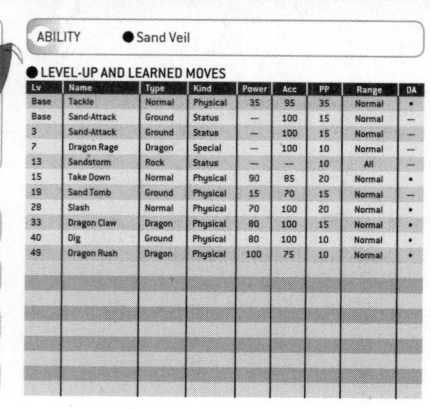

DRAGON GROUND

STATS
- HP ●●●
- ATTACK ●●●●
- DEFENSE ●●●
- SP.ATTACK ●●●
- SP.DEFENSE ●●●
- SPEED ●●●●

● Male form   ● Female form

● EVOLUTION PATH
Gible → Lv24 → Gabite → Lv48 → Garchomp

● MAIN WAYS TO OBTAIN
PLATINUM	Level up Gabite to Lv48
DIAMOND	Level up Gabite to Lv48
PEARL	Level up Gabite to Lv48
G B A	

● ABILITY ● Sand Veil

● LEVEL-UP AND LEARNED MOVES
Lv	Name	Type	Kind	Power	Acc	PP	Range	DA
Base	Fire Fang	Fire	Physical	65	95	15	Normal	•
Base	Tackle	Normal	Physical	35	95	35	Normal	
Base	Sand-Attack	Ground	Status	—	100	15	Normal	—
Base	Dragon Rage	Dragon	Special	—	100	10	Normal	—
Base	Sandstorm	Rock	Status	—	—	10	All	—
3	Sand-Attack	Ground	Status	—	100	15	Normal	
7	Dragon Rage	Dragon	Special	—	100	10	Normal	
13	Sandstorm	Rock	Status	—	—	10	All	
15	Take Down	Normal	Physical	90	85	20	Normal	•
19	Sand Tomb	Ground	Physical	15	70	15	Normal	
28	Slash	Normal	Physical	70	100	20	Normal	
33	Dragon Claw	Dragon	Physical	80	100	15	Normal	
40	Dig	Ground	Physical	80	100	10	Normal	
48	Crunch	Dark	Physical	80	100	15	Normal	
55	Dragon Rush	Dragon	Physical	100	75	10	Normal	

National Pokédex No. 446 Big Eater Pokémon
Munchlax

NORMAL

STATS
- HP ●●●●
- ATTACK ●●●
- DEFENSE ●●
- SP.ATTACK ●
- SP.DEFENSE ●●●
- SPEED ●

● M/F have same form

● EVOLUTION PATH
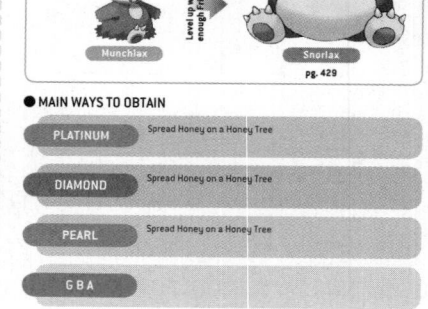
Munchlax → Level up with high enough Friendship → Snorlax pg. 429

● MAIN WAYS TO OBTAIN
PLATINUM	Spread Honey on a Honey Tree
DIAMOND	Spread Honey on a Honey Tree
PEARL	Spread Honey on a Honey Tree
G B A	

● ABILITY ● Pickup ● Thick Fat

● LEVEL-UP AND LEARNED MOVES
Lv	Name	Type	Kind	Power	Acc	PP	Range	DA
Base	Metronome	Normal	Status	—	—	10	DoM	
Base	Odor Sleuth	Normal	Status	—	—	40	Normal	
Base	Tackle	Normal	Physical	35	95	35	Normal	•
4	Defense Curl	Normal	Status	—	—	40	Self	•
9	Amnesia	Psychic	Status	—	—	20	Self	
12	Lick	Ghost	Physical	20	100	30	Normal	•
17	Recycle	Normal	Status	—	—	10	Self	
20	Screech	Normal	Status	—	85	40	Normal	
25	Stockpile	Normal	Status	—	—	20	Self	
28	Swallow	Normal	Status	—	—	10	Self	
33	Body Slam	Normal	Physical	85	100	15	Normal	•
36	Fling	Dark	Physical	—	100	10	Normal	
41	Rollout	Rock	Physical	30	90	20	Normal	•
44	Natural Gift	Normal	Physical	—	100	15	Normal	
49	Last Resort	Normal	Physical	130	100	5	Normal	

National Pokédex No. 447 Emanation Pokémon
Riolu

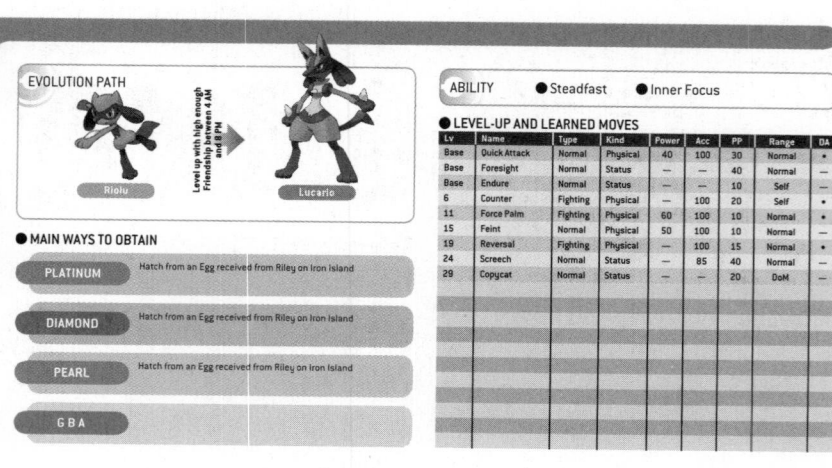

FIGHTING

STATS
- HP ●●
- ATTACK ●●●
- DEFENSE ●●
- SP.ATTACK ●●
- SP.DEFENSE ●●
- SPEED ●●

● M/F have same form

● EVOLUTION PATH
Riolu → Level up with high enough Friendship between 4 AM and 8 PM → Lucario

● MAIN WAYS TO OBTAIN
PLATINUM	Hatch from an Egg received from Riley on Iron Island
DIAMOND	Hatch from an Egg received from Riley on Iron Island
PEARL	Hatch from an Egg received from Riley on Iron Island
G B A	

● ABILITY ● Steadfast ● Inner Focus

● LEVEL-UP AND LEARNED MOVES
Lv	Name	Type	Kind	Power	Acc	PP	Range	DA
Base	Quick Attack	Normal	Physical	40	100	30	Normal	•
Base	Foresight	Normal	Status	—	—	40	Normal	
Base	Endure	Normal	Status	—	—	10	Self	
6	Counter	Fighting	Physical	—	100	20	Self	•
11	Force Palm	Fighting	Physical	60	100	10	Normal	
15	Feint	Normal	Physical	50	100	10	Normal	
19	Reversal	Fighting	Physical	—	100	15	Normal	•
24	Screech	Normal	Status	—	85	40	Normal	
29	Copycat	Normal	Status	—	—	20	DoM	

National Pokédex No. 448 Aura Pokémon
Lucario

FIGHTING | STEEL

STATS
- HP ●●●
- ATTACK ●●●●
- DEFENSE ●●●
- SP. ATTACK ●●●●
- SP. DEFENSE ●●●
- SPEED ●●●

● M/F have same form

EVOLUTION PATH

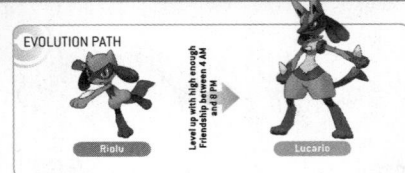

Riolu → (Level up with high enough Friendship between 4 AM and 8 PM) → Lucario

● MAIN WAYS TO OBTAIN

PLATINUM	Level up Riolu with high enough Friendship between 4 AM and 8 PM
DIAMOND	Level up Riolu with high enough Friendship between 4 AM and 8 PM
PEARL	Level up Riolu with high enough Friendship between 4 AM and 8 PM
GBA	

ABILITY ● Steadfast ● Inner Focus

● LEVEL-UP AND LEARNED MOVES

Lv	Name	Type	Kind	Power	Acc	PP	Range	DA
Base	Dark Pulse	Dark	Special	80	100	15	Normal	—
Base	Quick Attack	Normal	Physical	40	100	30	Normal	●
Base	Foresight	Normal	Status	—	—	40	Normal	●
Base	Detect	Fighting	Status	—	—	5	Self	●
Base	Metal Claw	Steel	Physical	50	95	35	Normal	●
6	Counter	Fighting	Physical	—	100	20	Self	●
11	Force Palm	Fighting	Physical	60	100	10	Normal	●
15	Feint	Normal	Physical	50	100	10	Normal	—
19	Bone Rush	Ground	Physical	25	80	10	Normal	●
24	Metal Sound	Steel	Status	—	85	40	Normal	—
29	Me First	Normal	Status	—	—	20	DoM	●
33	Swords Dance	Normal	Status	—	—	30	Self	—
37	Aura Sphere	Fighting	Special	90	—	20	Normal	—
42	Close Combat	Fighting	Physical	120	100	5	Normal	●
47	Dragon Pulse	Dragon	Special	90	100	10	Normal	—
51	ExtremeSpeed	Normal	Physical	80	100	5	Normal	●

National Pokédex No. 449 Hippo Pokémon
Hippopotas

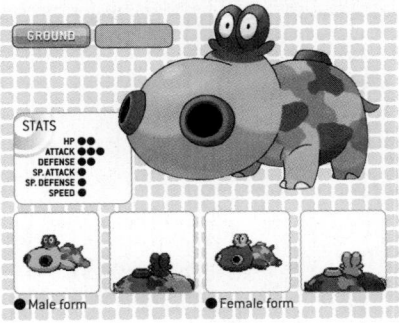

GROUND

STATS
- HP ●●
- ATTACK ●●●
- DEFENSE ●●●
- SP. ATTACK ●●
- SP. DEFENSE ●●
- SPEED ●●

● Male form ● Female form

EVOLUTION PATH

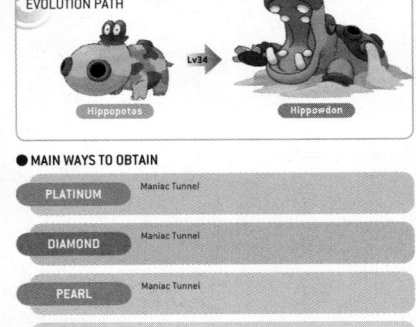

Hippopotas → (Lv34) → Hippowdon

● MAIN WAYS TO OBTAIN

PLATINUM	Maniac Tunnel
DIAMOND	Maniac Tunnel
PEARL	Maniac Tunnel
GBA	

ABILITY ● Sand Stream

● LEVEL-UP AND LEARNED MOVES

Lv	Name	Type	Kind	Power	Acc	PP	Range	DA
Base	Tackle	Normal	Physical	35	95	35	Normal	●
Base	Sand-Attack	Ground	Status	—	100	15	Normal	●
7	Bite	Dark	Physical	60	100	25	Normal	●
13	Yawn	Normal	Status	—	—	10	Normal	●
19	Take Down	Normal	Physical	90	85	20	Normal	●
25	Sand Tomb	Ground	Physical	15	70	15	Normal	●
31	Crunch	Dark	Physical	80	100	15	Normal	●
37	Earthquake	Ground	Physical	100	100	10	2 foes • 1 ally	●
44	Double-Edge	Normal	Physical	120	100	15	Normal	●
50	Fissure	Ground	Physical	—	30	5	Normal	—

National Pokédex No. 450 Heavyweight Pokémon
Hippowdon

GROUND

STATS
- HP ●●●
- ATTACK ●●●●
- DEFENSE ●●●●
- SP. ATTACK ●●
- SP. DEFENSE ●●
- SPEED ●●

● Male form ● Female form

EVOLUTION PATH

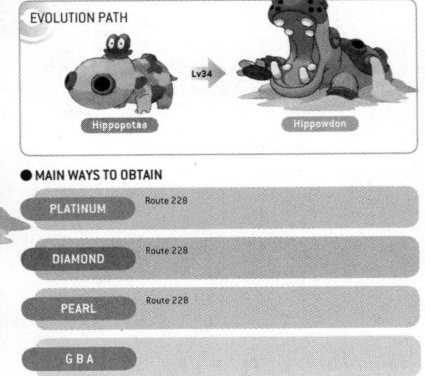

Hippopotas → (Lv34) → Hippowdon

● MAIN WAYS TO OBTAIN

PLATINUM	Route 228
DIAMOND	Route 228
PEARL	Route 228
GBA	

ABILITY ● Sand Stream

● LEVEL-UP AND LEARNED MOVES

Lv	Name	Type	Kind	Power	Acc	PP	Range	DA
Base	Ice Fang	Ice	Physical	65	95	15	Normal	●
Base	Fire Fang	Fire	Physical	65	95	15	Normal	●
Base	Thunder Fang	Electric	Physical	65	95	15	Normal	●
Base	Tackle	Normal	Physical	35	95	35	Normal	●
Base	Sand-Attack	Ground	Status	—	100	15	Normal	—
Base	Bite	Dark	Physical	60	100	25	Normal	●
Base	Yawn	Normal	Status	—	—	10	Normal	●
7	Bite	Dark	Physical	60	100	25	Normal	●
13	Yawn	Normal	Status	—	—	10	Normal	●
19	Take Down	Normal	Physical	90	85	20	Normal	●
25	Sand Tomb	Ground	Physical	15	70	15	Normal	●
31	Crunch	Dark	Physical	80	100	15	Normal	●
40	Earthquake	Ground	Physical	100	100	10	2 foes • 1 ally	●
50	Double-Edge	Normal	Physical	120	100	15	Normal	●
60	Fissure	Ground	Physical	—	30	5	Normal	—

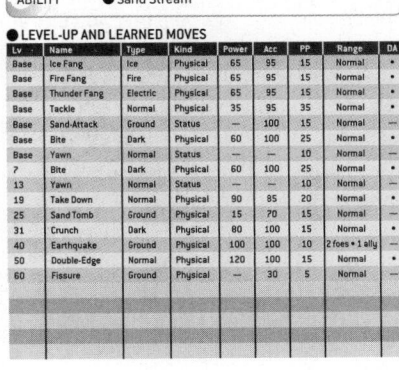

451
SKORUPI

National Pokédex No. 451 Scorpion Pokémon
Skorupi

POISON | BUG

STATS
- HP ●●
- ATTACK ●●
- DEFENSE ●●●
- SP. ATTACK ●
- SP. DEFENSE ●●
- SPEED ●●

● M/F have same form

EVOLUTION PATH

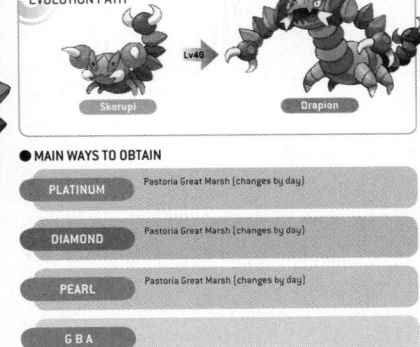

Skorupi → (Lv40) → Drapion

● MAIN WAYS TO OBTAIN

PLATINUM	Pastoria Great Marsh (changes by day)
DIAMOND	Pastoria Great Marsh (changes by day)
PEARL	Pastoria Great Marsh (changes by day)
GBA	

ABILITY ● Battle Armor ● Sniper

● LEVEL-UP AND LEARNED MOVES

Lv	Name	Type	Kind	Power	Acc	PP	Range	DA
Base	Bite	Dark	Physical	60	100	25	Normal	●
Base	Poison Sting	Poison	Physical	15	100	35	Normal	—
Base	Leer	Normal	Status	—	100	30	2 foes	—
6	Knock Off	Dark	Physical	20	100	20	Normal	●
12	Pin Missile	Bug	Physical	14	85	20	Normal	—
17	Acupressure	Normal	Status	—	—	30	1 ally	●
23	Scary Face	Normal	Status	—	90	10	Normal	—
28	Toxic Spikes	Poison	Status	—	—	20	2 foes	—
34	Bug Bite	Bug	Physical	60	100	20	Normal	●
39	Poison Fang	Poison	Physical	50	100	15	Normal	●
45	Crunch	Dark	Physical	80	100	15	Normal	●
50	Cross Poison	Poison	Physical	70	100	20	Normal	●

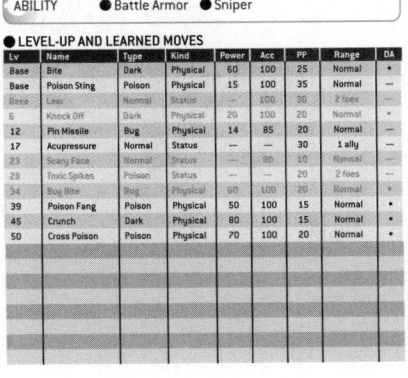

Drapion

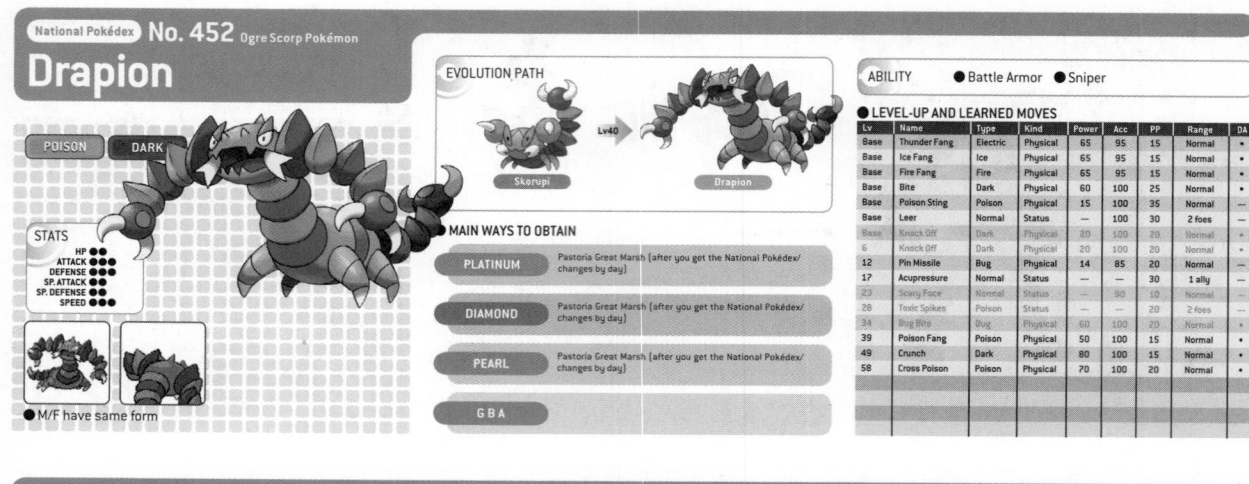

POISON | DARK

STATS
- HP ●●●
- ATTACK ●●●
- DEFENSE ●●●●
- SP.ATTACK ●●
- SP.DEFENSE ●●●
- SPEED ●●●

● M/F have same form

EVOLUTION PATH

Skorupi — Lv40 → Drapion

MAIN WAYS TO OBTAIN

PLATINUM	Pastoria Great Marsh (after you get the National Pokédex/ changes by day)
DIAMOND	Pastoria Great Marsh (after you get the National Pokédex/ changes by day)
PEARL	Pastoria Great Marsh (after you get the National Pokédex/ changes by day)
G B A	

ABILITY ● Battle Armor ● Sniper

● **LEVEL-UP AND LEARNED MOVES**

Lv	Name	Type	Kind	Power	Acc	PP	Range	DA
Base	Thunder Fang	Electric	Physical	65	95	15	Normal	●
Base	Ice Fang	Ice	Physical	65	95	15	Normal	●
Base	Fire Fang	Fire	Physical	65	95	15	Normal	●
Base	Bite	Dark	Physical	60	100	25	Normal	●
Base	Poison Sting	Poison	Physical	15	100	35	Normal	—
Base	Leer	Normal	Status	—	100	30	2 foes	—
Base	Knock Off	Dark	Physical	20	100	20	Normal	●
6	Knock Off	Dark	Physical	20	100	20	Normal	●
12	Pin Missile	Bug	Physical	14	85	20	Normal	—
17	Acupressure	Normal	Status	—	—	30	1 ally	—
23	Scary Face	Normal	Status	—	90	10	Normal	—
28	Toxic Spikes	Poison	Status	—	—	20	2 foes	—
34	Bug Bite	Bug	Physical	60	100	20	Normal	●
39	Poison Fang	Poison	Physical	50	100	15	Normal	●
49	Crunch	Dark	Physical	80	100	15	Normal	●
58	Cross Poison	Poison	Physical	70	100	20	Normal	●

Croagunk

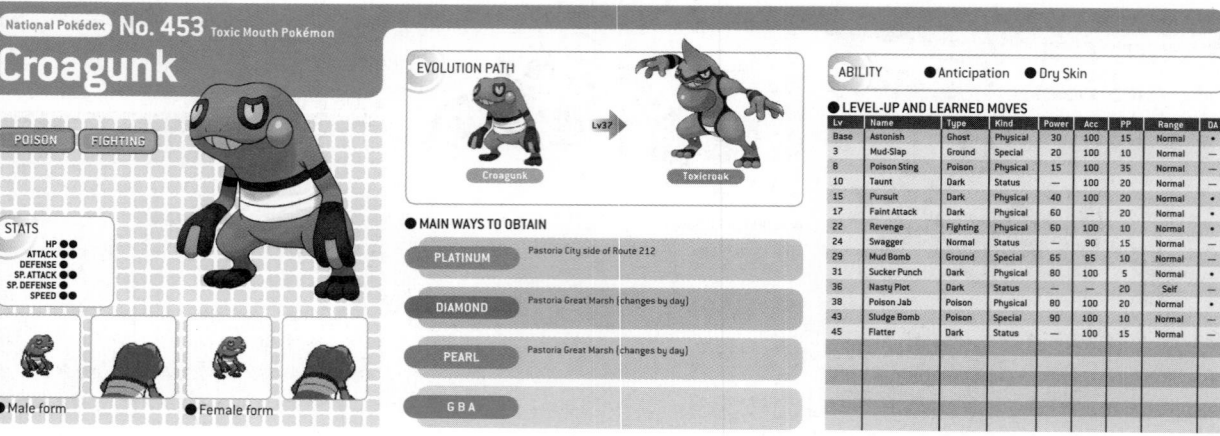

POISON | FIGHTING

STATS
- HP ●●
- ATTACK ●●
- DEFENSE ●
- SP.ATTACK ●●
- SP.DEFENSE ●●
- SPEED ●●

● Male form   ● Female form

EVOLUTION PATH

Croagunk — Lv37 → Toxicroak

MAIN WAYS TO OBTAIN

PLATINUM	Pastoria City side of Route 212
DIAMOND	Pastoria Great Marsh (changes by day)
PEARL	Pastoria Great Marsh (changes by day)
G B A	

ABILITY ● Anticipation ● Dry Skin

● **LEVEL-UP AND LEARNED MOVES**

Lv	Name	Type	Kind	Power	Acc	PP	Range	DA
Base	Astonish	Ghost	Physical	30	100	15	Normal	●
3	Mud-Slap	Ground	Special	20	100	10	Normal	—
8	Poison Sting	Poison	Physical	15	100	35	Normal	—
10	Taunt	Dark	Status	—	100	20	Normal	—
15	Pursuit	Dark	Physical	40	100	20	Normal	●
17	Faint Attack	Dark	Physical	60	—	20	Normal	●
22	Revenge	Fighting	Physical	60	100	10	Normal	●
24	Swagger	Normal	Status	—	90	15	Normal	—
29	Mud Bomb	Ground	Special	65	85	10	Normal	—
31	Sucker Punch	Dark	Physical	80	100	5	Normal	●
36	Nasty Plot	Dark	Status	—	—	20	Self	—
38	Poison Jab	Poison	Physical	80	100	20	Normal	●
43	Sludge Bomb	Poison	Special	90	100	10	Normal	—
45	Flatter	Dark	Status	—	100	15	Normal	—

Toxicroak

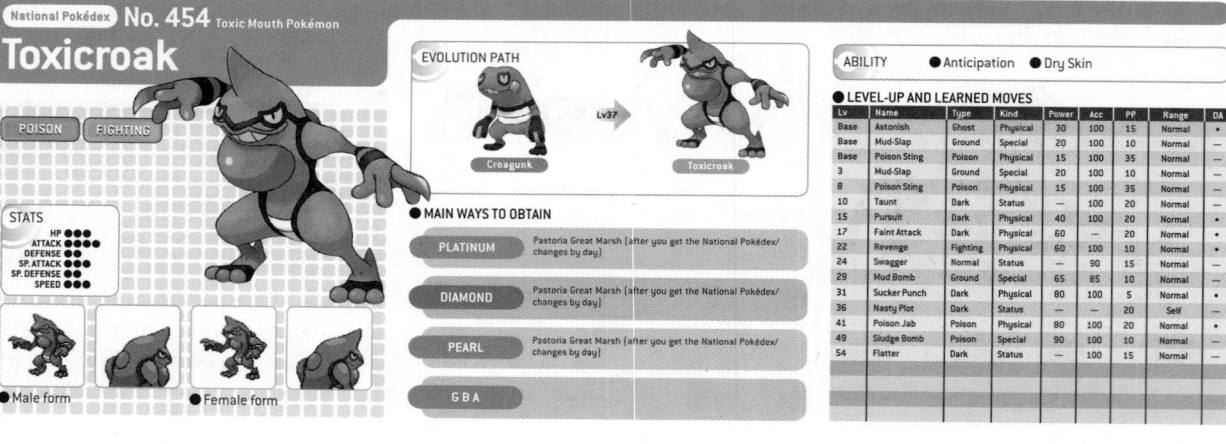

POISON | FIGHTING

STATS
- HP ●●●
- ATTACK ●●●
- DEFENSE ●●
- SP.ATTACK ●●●
- SP.DEFENSE ●●
- SPEED ●●●

● Male form   ● Female form

EVOLUTION PATH

Croagunk — Lv37 → Toxicroak

MAIN WAYS TO OBTAIN

PLATINUM	Pastoria Great Marsh (after you get the National Pokédex/ changes by day)
DIAMOND	Pastoria Great Marsh (after you get the National Pokédex/ changes by day)
PEARL	Pastoria Great Marsh (after you get the National Pokédex/ changes by day)
G B A	

ABILITY ● Anticipation ● Dry Skin

● **LEVEL-UP AND LEARNED MOVES**

Lv	Name	Type	Kind	Power	Acc	PP	Range	DA
Base	Astonish	Ghost	Physical	30	100	15	Normal	●
Base	Mud-Slap	Ground	Special	20	100	10	Normal	—
Base	Poison Sting	Poison	Physical	15	100	35	Normal	—
3	Mud-Slap	Ground	Special	20	100	10	Normal	—
8	Poison Sting	Poison	Physical	15	100	35	Normal	—
10	Taunt	Dark	Status	—	100	20	Normal	—
15	Pursuit	Dark	Physical	40	100	20	Normal	●
17	Faint Attack	Dark	Physical	60	—	20	Normal	●
22	Revenge	Fighting	Physical	60	100	10	Normal	●
24	Swagger	Normal	Status	—	90	15	Normal	—
29	Mud Bomb	Ground	Special	65	85	10	Normal	—
31	Sucker Punch	Dark	Physical	80	100	5	Normal	●
36	Nasty Plot	Dark	Status	—	—	20	Self	—
41	Poison Jab	Poison	Physical	80	100	20	Normal	●
49	Sludge Bomb	Poison	Special	90	100	10	Normal	—
54	Flatter	Dark	Status	—	100	15	Normal	—

Carnivine

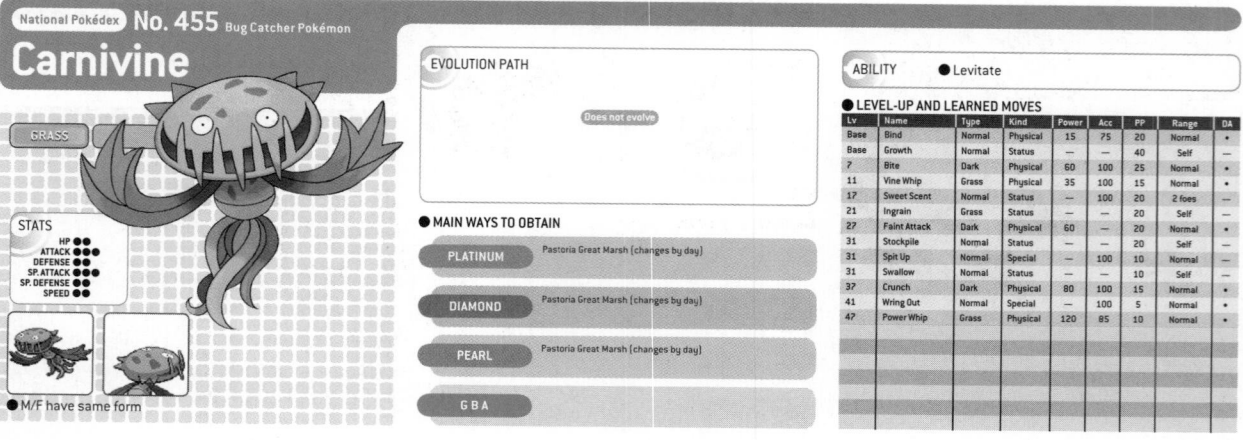

GRASS

STATS
- HP ●●●
- ATTACK ●●●
- DEFENSE ●●
- SP.ATTACK ●●●
- SP.DEFENSE ●●●
- SPEED ●●

● M/F have same form

EVOLUTION PATH

Does not evolve

MAIN WAYS TO OBTAIN

PLATINUM	Pastoria Great Marsh (changes by day)
DIAMOND	Pastoria Great Marsh (changes by day)
PEARL	Pastoria Great Marsh (changes by day)
G B A	

ABILITY ● Levitate

● **LEVEL-UP AND LEARNED MOVES**

Lv	Name	Type	Kind	Power	Acc	PP	Range	DA
Base	Bind	Normal	Physical	15	75	20	Normal	●
Base	Growth	Normal	Status	—	—	40	Self	—
7	Bite	Dark	Physical	60	100	25	Normal	●
11	Vine Whip	Grass	Physical	35	100	15	Normal	●
17	Sweet Scent	Normal	Status	—	100	20	2 foes	—
21	Ingrain	Grass	Status	—	—	20	Self	—
27	Faint Attack	Dark	Physical	60	—	20	Normal	●
31	Stockpile	Normal	Status	—	—	20	Self	—
31	Spit Up	Normal	Special	—	100	10	Normal	—
31	Swallow	Normal	Status	—	—	10	Self	—
37	Crunch	Dark	Physical	80	100	15	Normal	●
41	Wring Out	Normal	Special	—	100	5	Normal	●
47	Power Whip	Grass	Physical	120	85	10	Normal	●

NATIONAL POKÉDEX

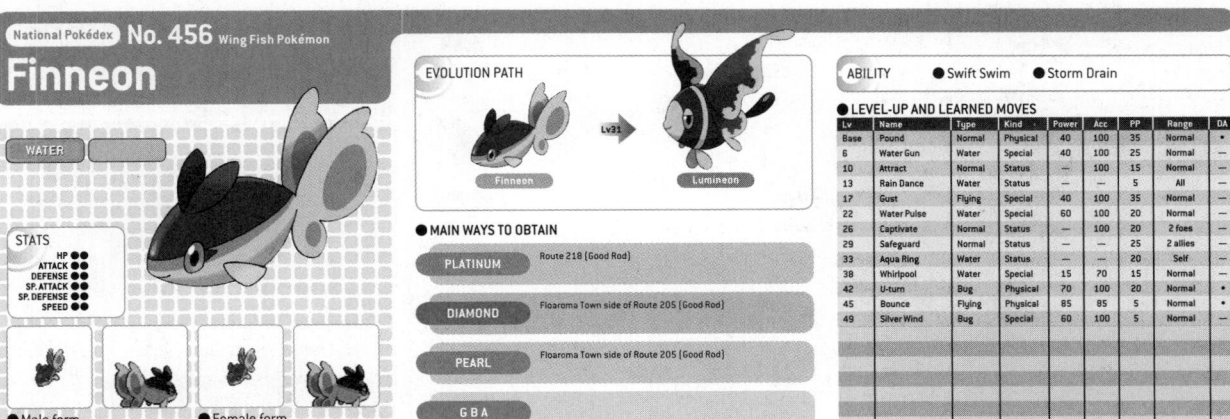

National Pokédex No. 456 Wing Fish Pokémon

Finneon

WATER

STATS
HP ●●
ATTACK ●●
DEFENSE ●●
SP. ATTACK ●●
SP. DEFENSE ●●
SPEED ●●

● Male form ● Female form

● EVOLUTION PATH

Finneon → Lv31 → Lumineon

● MAIN WAYS TO OBTAIN

PLATINUM	Route 218 (Good Rod)
DIAMOND	Floaroma Town side of Route 205 (Good Rod)
PEARL	Floaroma Town side of Route 205 (Good Rod)
G B A	

ABILITY ● Swift Swim ● Storm Drain

● LEVEL-UP AND LEARNED MOVES

Lv	Name	Type	Kind	Power	Acc	PP	Range	DA
Base	Pound	Normal	Physical	40	100	35	Normal	•
6	Water Gun	Water	Special	40	100	25	Normal	—
10	Attract	Normal	Status	—	100	15	Normal	—
13	Rain Dance	Water	Status	—	—	5	All	—
17	Gust	Flying	Special	40	100	35	Normal	—
22	Water Pulse	Water	Special	60	100	20	Normal	—
26	Captivate	Normal	Status	—	100	20	2 foes	—
29	Safeguard	Normal	Status	—	—	25	2 allies	—
33	Aqua Ring	Water	Status	—	—	20	Self	—
38	Whirlpool	Water	Special	15	70	15	Normal	—
42	U-turn	Bug	Physical	70	100	20	Normal	•
45	Bounce	Flying	Physical	85	85	5	Normal	•
49	Silver Wind	Bug	Special	60	100	5	Normal	—

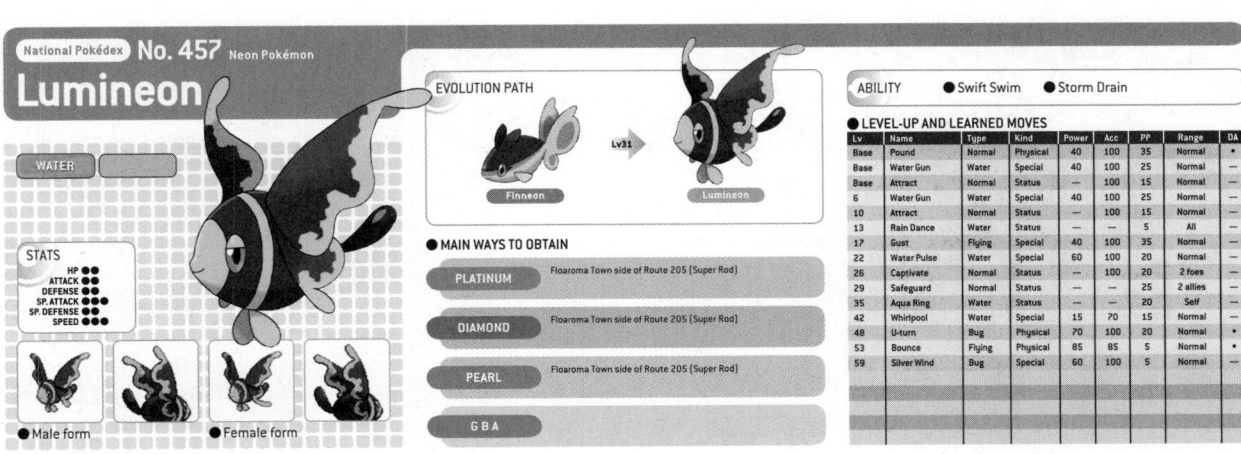

National Pokédex No. 457 Neon Pokémon

Lumineon

WATER

STATS
HP ●●
ATTACK ●●
DEFENSE ●●
SP. ATTACK ●●
SP. DEFENSE ●●
SPEED ●●●

● Male form ● Female form

● EVOLUTION PATH

Finneon → Lv31 → Lumineon

● MAIN WAYS TO OBTAIN

PLATINUM	Floaroma Town side of Route 205 (Super Rod)
DIAMOND	Floaroma Town side of Route 205 (Super Rod)
PEARL	Floaroma Town side of Route 205 (Super Rod)
G B A	

ABILITY ● Swift Swim ● Storm Drain

● LEVEL-UP AND LEARNED MOVES

Lv	Name	Type	Kind	Power	Acc	PP	Range	DA
Base	Pound	Normal	Physical	40	100	35	Normal	•
Base	Water Gun	Water	Special	40	100	25	Normal	—
Base	Attract	Normal	Status	—	100	15	Normal	—
6	Water Gun	Water	Special	40	100	25	Normal	—
10	Attract	Normal	Status	—	100	15	Normal	—
13	Rain Dance	Water	Status	—	—	5	All	—
17	Gust	Flying	Special	40	100	35	Normal	—
22	Water Pulse	Water	Special	60	100	20	Normal	—
26	Captivate	Normal	Status	—	100	20	2 foes	—
29	Safeguard	Normal	Status	—	—	25	2 allies	—
35	Aqua Ring	Water	Status	—	—	20	Self	—
42	Whirlpool	Water	Special	15	70	15	Normal	—
48	U-turn	Bug	Physical	70	100	20	Normal	•
53	Bounce	Flying	Physical	85	85	5	Normal	•
59	Silver Wind	Bug	Special	60	100	5	Normal	—

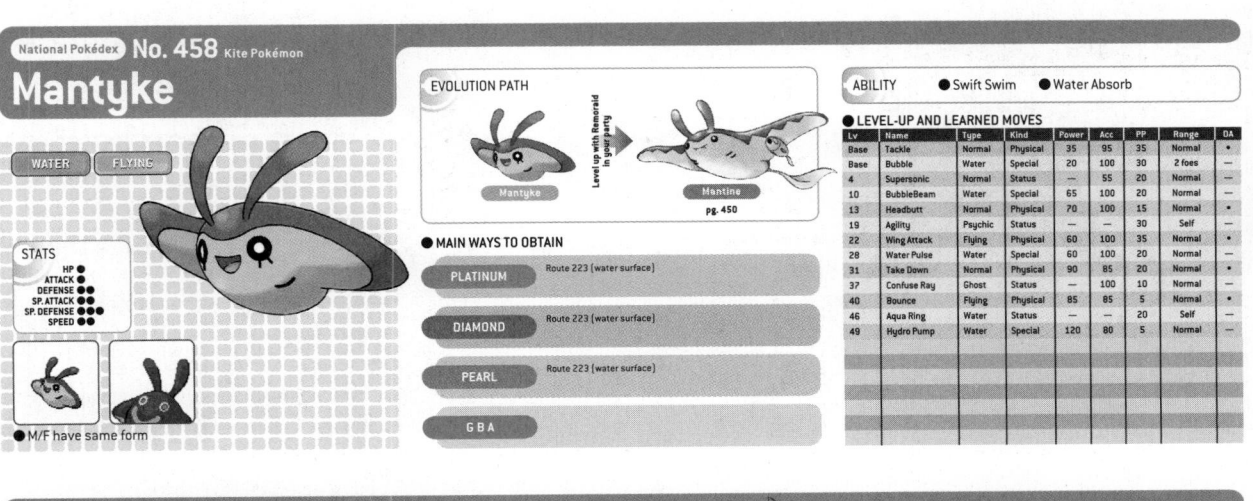

National Pokédex No. 458 Kite Pokémon

Mantyke

WATER FLYING

STATS
HP ●
ATTACK ●
DEFENSE ●●
SP. ATTACK ●●
SP. DEFENSE ●●●
SPEED ●●

● M/F have same form

● EVOLUTION PATH

Mantyke → Level up with Remoraid in your party → Mantine pg. 450

● MAIN WAYS TO OBTAIN

PLATINUM	Route 223 (water surface)
DIAMOND	Route 223 (water surface)
PEARL	Route 223 (water surface)
G B A	

ABILITY ● Swift Swim ● Water Absorb

● LEVEL-UP AND LEARNED MOVES

Lv	Name	Type	Kind	Power	Acc	PP	Range	DA
Base	Tackle	Normal	Physical	35	95	35	Normal	•
Base	Bubble	Water	Special	20	100	30	2 foes	—
4	Supersonic	Normal	Status	—	55	20	Normal	—
10	BubbleBeam	Water	Special	65	100	20	Normal	—
13	Headbutt	Normal	Physical	70	100	15	Normal	•
19	Agility	Psychic	Status	—	—	30	Self	—
22	Wing Attack	Flying	Physical	60	100	35	Normal	•
28	Water Pulse	Water	Special	60	100	20	Normal	—
31	Take Down	Normal	Physical	90	85	20	Normal	•
37	Confuse Ray	Ghost	Status	—	100	10	Normal	—
40	Bounce	Flying	Physical	85	85	5	Normal	•
46	Aqua Ring	Water	Status	—	—	20	Self	—
49	Hydro Pump	Water	Special	120	80	5	Normal	—

National Pokédex No. 459 Frost Tree Pokémon

Snover

GRASS ICE

STATS
HP ●●
ATTACK ●●●
DEFENSE ●●●
SP. ATTACK ●●●
SP. DEFENSE ●●
SPEED ●●

● Male form ● Female form

● EVOLUTION PATH

Snover → Lv40 → Abomasnow

● MAIN WAYS TO OBTAIN

PLATINUM	Route 216
DIAMOND	Route 216
PEARL	Route 216
G B A	

ABILITY ● Snow Warning

● LEVEL-UP AND LEARNED MOVES

Lv	Name	Type	Kind	Power	Acc	PP	Range	DA
Base	Powder Snow	Ice	Special	40	100	25	2 foes	—
Base	Leer	Normal	Status	—	100	30	2 foes	—
5	Razor Leaf	Grass	Physical	55	95	25	2 foes	—
9	Icy Wind	Ice	Special	55	95	15	2 foes	—
13	GrassWhistle	Grass	Status	—	55	15	Normal	—
17	Swagger	Normal	Status	—	90	15	Normal	—
21	Mist	Ice	Status	—	—	30	2 allies	—
26	Ice Shard	Ice	Physical	40	100	30	Normal	—
31	Ingrain	Grass	Status	—	—	20	Self	—
36	Wood Hammer	Grass	Physical	120	100	15	Normal	•
41	Blizzard	Ice	Special	120	70	5	2 foes	—
46	Sheer Cold	Ice	Special	—	30	5	Normal	—

459
SNOVER

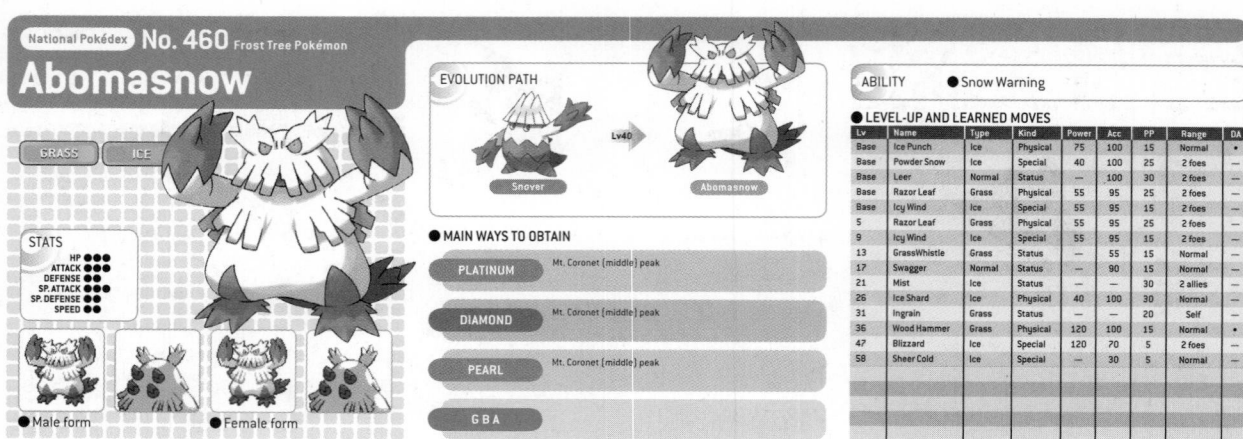

Abomasnow

National Pokédex **No. 460** Frost Tree Pokémon

GRASS · ICE

STATS — HP ●●●, ATTACK ●●●, DEFENSE ●●, SP.ATTACK ●●●, SP.DEFENSE ●●, SPEED ●●

● Male form ● Female form

EVOLUTION PATH: Snover → (Lv40) → Abomasnow

MAIN WAYS TO OBTAIN
- PLATINUM: Mt. Coronet [middle] peak
- DIAMOND: Mt. Coronet [middle] peak
- PEARL: Mt. Coronet [middle] peak
- G B A

ABILITY ● Snow Warning

LEVEL-UP AND LEARNED MOVES

Lv	Name	Type	Kind	Power	Acc	PP	Range	DA
Base	Ice Punch	Ice	Physical	75	100	15	Normal	●
Base	Powder Snow	Ice	Special	40	100	25	2 foes	
Base	Leer	Normal	Status	—	100	30	2 foes	
Base	Razor Leaf	Grass	Physical	55	95	25	2 foes	
Base	Icy Wind	Ice	Special	55	95	15	2 foes	
5	Razor Leaf	Grass	Physical	55	95	25	2 foes	
9	Icy Wind	Ice	Special	55	95	15	2 foes	
13	GrassWhistle	Grass	Status	—	55	15	Normal	
17	Swagger	Normal	Status	—	90	15	Normal	
21	Mist	Ice	Status	—	—	30	2 allies	
26	Ice Shard	Ice	Physical	40	100	30	Normal	
31	Ingrain	Grass	Status	—	—	20	Self	
36	Wood Hammer	Grass	Physical	120	100	15	Normal	
47	Blizzard	Ice	Special	120	70	5	2 foes	
58	Sheer Cold	Ice	Special	—	30	5	Normal	

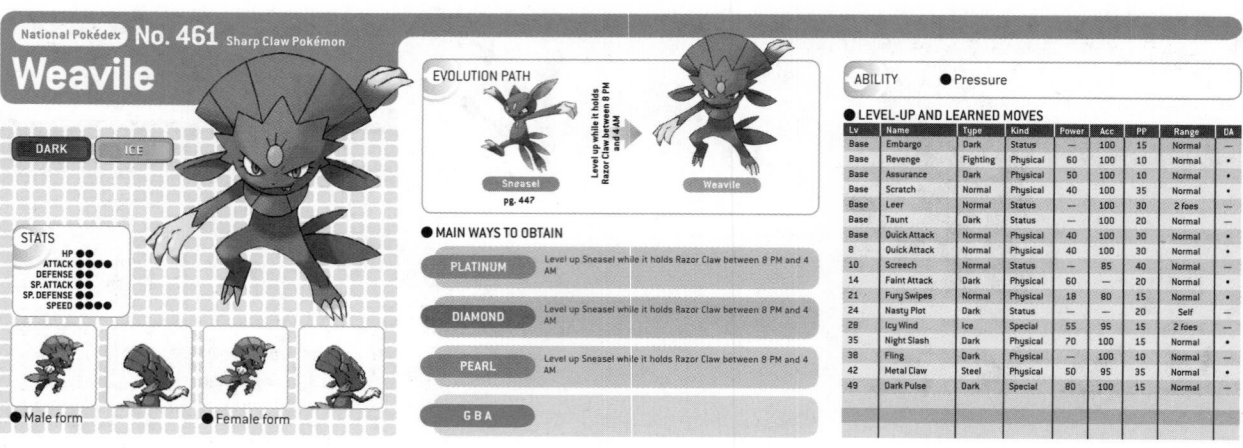

Weavile

National Pokédex **No. 461** Sharp Claw Pokémon

DARK · ICE

STATS — HP ●●, ATTACK ●●●●, DEFENSE ●●, SP.ATTACK ●●, SP.DEFENSE ●●, SPEED ●●●●

● Male form ● Female form

EVOLUTION PATH: Sneasel (pg. 447) → (Level up while it holds Razor Claw between 8 PM and 4 AM) → Weavile

MAIN WAYS TO OBTAIN
- PLATINUM: Level up Sneasel while it holds Razor Claw between 8 PM and 4 AM
- DIAMOND: Level up Sneasel while it holds Razor Claw between 8 PM and 4 AM
- PEARL: Level up Sneasel while it holds Razor Claw between 8 PM and 4 AM
- G B A

ABILITY ● Pressure

LEVEL-UP AND LEARNED MOVES

Lv	Name	Type	Kind	Power	Acc	PP	Range	DA
Base	Embargo	Dark	Status	—	100	15	Normal	●
Base	Revenge	Fighting	Physical	60	100	10	Normal	●
Base	Assurance	Dark	Physical	50	100	10	Normal	●
Base	Scratch	Normal	Physical	40	100	35	Normal	●
Base	Leer	Normal	Status	—	100	30	2 foes	●
Base	Taunt	Dark	Status	—	100	20	Normal	●
Base	Quick Attack	Normal	Physical	40	100	30	Normal	●
8	Quick Attack	Normal	Physical	40	100	30	Normal	
10	Screech	Normal	Status	—	85	40	Normal	
14	Faint Attack	Dark	Physical	60	—	20	Normal	
21	Fury Swipes	Normal	Physical	18	80	15	Normal	
24	Nasty Plot	Dark	Status	—	—	20	Self	
28	Icy Wind	Ice	Special	55	95	15	2 foes	
35	Night Slash	Dark	Physical	70	100	15	Normal	
38	Fling	Dark	Physical	—	100	10	Normal	
42	Metal Claw	Steel	Physical	50	95	35	Normal	
49	Dark Pulse	Dark	Special	80	100	15	Normal	

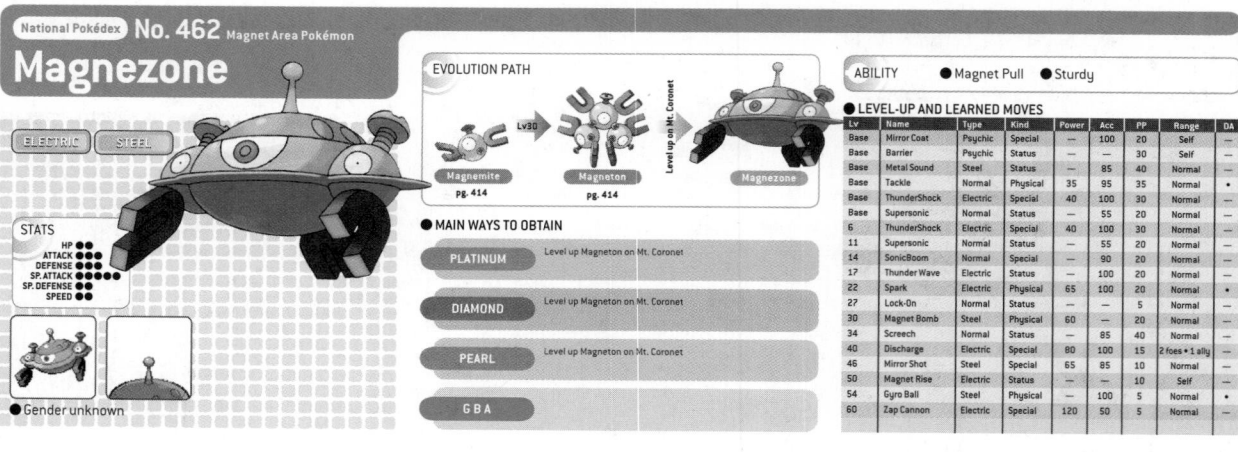

Magnezone

National Pokédex **No. 462** Magnet Area Pokémon

ELECTRIC · STEEL

STATS — HP ●●, ATTACK ●●●, DEFENSE ●●●, SP.ATTACK ●●●●, SP.DEFENSE ●●●, SPEED ●●

● Gender unknown

EVOLUTION PATH: Magnemite (pg. 414) → (Lv30) → Magneton (pg. 414) → (Level up on Mt. Coronet) → Magnezone

MAIN WAYS TO OBTAIN
- PLATINUM: Level up Magneton on Mt. Coronet
- DIAMOND: Level up Magneton on Mt. Coronet
- PEARL: Level up Magneton on Mt. Coronet
- G B A

ABILITY ● Magnet Pull ● Sturdy

LEVEL-UP AND LEARNED MOVES

Lv	Name	Type	Kind	Power	Acc	PP	Range	DA
Base	Mirror Coat	Psychic	Special	—	100	20	Self	—
Base	Barrier	Psychic	Status	—	—	30	Self	—
Base	Metal Sound	Steel	Status	—	85	40	Normal	—
Base	Tackle	Normal	Physical	35	95	35	Normal	●
Base	ThunderShock	Electric	Special	40	100	30	Normal	●
Base	Supersonic	Normal	Status	—	55	20	Normal	
6	ThunderShock	Electric	Special	40	100	30	Normal	
11	Supersonic	Normal	Status	—	55	20	Normal	
14	SonicBoom	Normal	Special	—	90	20	Normal	
17	Thunder Wave	Electric	Status	—	100	20	Normal	
22	Spark	Electric	Physical	65	100	20	Normal	
27	Lock-On	Normal	Status	—	—	5	Normal	
30	Magnet Bomb	Steel	Physical	60	—	20	Normal	
34	Screech	Normal	Status	—	85	40	Normal	
40	Discharge	Electric	Special	80	100	15	2 foes + 1 ally	
46	Mirror Shot	Steel	Special	65	85	10	Normal	
50	Magnet Rise	Electric	Status	—	—	10	Self	
54	Gyro Ball	Steel	Physical	—	100	5	Normal	
60	Zap Cannon	Electric	Special	120	50	5	Normal	

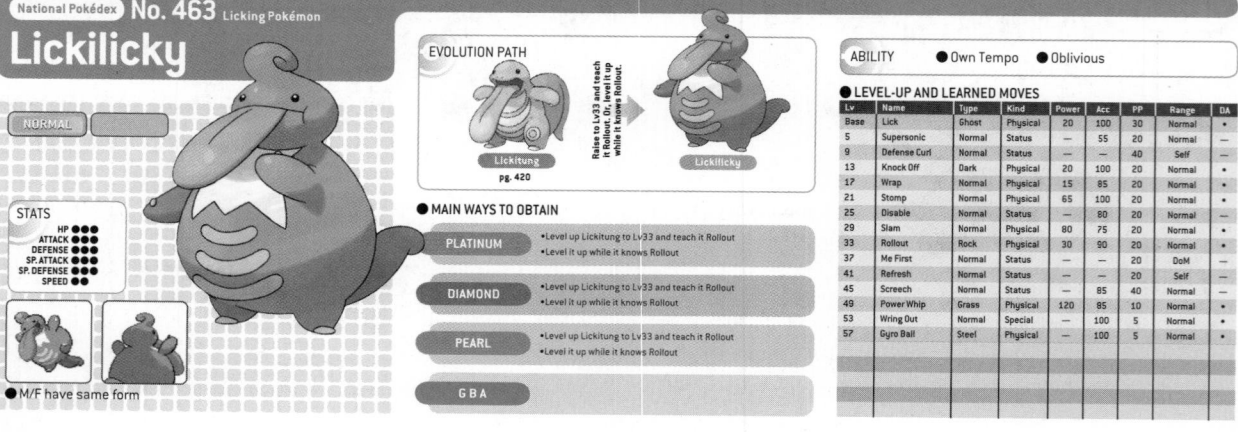

Lickilicky

National Pokédex **No. 463** Licking Pokémon

NORMAL

STATS — HP ●●●, ATTACK ●●●, DEFENSE ●●, SP.ATTACK ●●, SP.DEFENSE ●●●, SPEED ●●

● M/F have same form

EVOLUTION PATH: Lickitung (pg. 420) → (Raise to Lv33 and teach it Rollout. Or, level it up while it knows Rollout.) → Lickilicky

MAIN WAYS TO OBTAIN
- PLATINUM: • Level up Lickitung to Lv33 and teach it Rollout • Level it up while it knows Rollout
- DIAMOND: • Level up Lickitung to Lv33 and teach it Rollout • Level it up while it knows Rollout
- PEARL: • Level up Lickitung to Lv33 and teach it Rollout • Level it up while it knows Rollout
- G B A

ABILITY ● Own Tempo ● Oblivious

LEVEL-UP AND LEARNED MOVES

Lv	Name	Type	Kind	Power	Acc	PP	Range	DA
Base	Lick	Ghost	Physical	20	100	30	Normal	●
5	Supersonic	Normal	Status	—	55	20	Normal	—
9	Defense Curl	Normal	Status	—	—	40	Self	—
13	Knock Off	Dark	Physical	20	100	20	Normal	
17	Wrap	Normal	Physical	15	85	20	Normal	
21	Stomp	Normal	Physical	65	100	20	Normal	
25	Disable	Normal	Status	—	80	20	Normal	
29	Slam	Normal	Physical	80	75	20	Normal	
33	Rollout	Rock	Physical	30	90	20	Normal	
37	Me First	Normal	Status	—	—	20	DoM	
41	Refresh	Normal	Status	—	—	20	Self	
45	Screech	Normal	Status	—	85	40	Normal	
49	Power Whip	Grass	Physical	120	85	10	Normal	
53	Wring Out	Normal	Special	—	100	5	Normal	
57	Gyro Ball	Steel	Physical	—	100	5	Normal	

National Pokédex No. 464 Drill Pokémon
Rhyperior

GROUND | ROCK

STATS
HP ●●●
ATTACK ●●●●●
DEFENSE ●●●●
SP. ATTACK ●●
SP. DEFENSE ●●
SPEED ●●

● Male form   ● Female form

EVOLUTION PATH

Rhyhorn —Lv42→ Rhydon —(Link trade while it holds Protector)→ Rhyperior
Rhyhorn pg. 421   Rhydon pg. 421

MAIN WAYS TO OBTAIN

PLATINUM — Link trade Rhydon while it holds Protector
DIAMOND — Link trade Rhydon while it holds Protector
PEARL — Link trade Rhydon while it holds Protector
GBA —

ABILITY ● Lightningrod ● Solid Rock

LEVEL-UP AND LEARNED MOVES

Lv	Name	Type	Kind	Power	Acc	PP	Range	DA
Base	Poison Jab	Poison	Physical	80	100	20	Normal	•
Base	Horn Attack	Normal	Physical	65	100	25	Normal	•
Base	Tail Whip	Normal	Status	—	100	30	2 foes	—
Base	Stomp	Normal	Physical	65	100	20	Normal	•
Base	Fury Attack	Normal	Physical	15	85	20	Normal	•
9	Stomp	Normal	Physical	65	100	20	Normal	•
13	Fury Attack	Normal	Physical	15	85	20	Normal	•
21	Scary Face	Normal	Status	—	90	10	Normal	—
25	Rock Blast	Rock	Physical	25	80	10	Normal	•
33	Take Down	Normal	Physical	90	85	20	Normal	•
37	Horn Drill	Normal	Physical	—	30	5	Normal	•
42	Hammer Arm	Fighting	Physical	100	90	10	Normal	•
45	Stone Edge	Rock	Physical	100	80	5	Normal	•
49	Earthquake	Ground	Physical	100	100	10	2 foes • 1 ally	—
57	Megahorn	Bug	Physical	120	85	10	Normal	•
61	Rock Wrecker	Rock	Physical	150	90	5	Normal	—

National Pokédex No. 465 Vine Pokémon
Tangrowth

GRASS

STATS
HP ●●●
ATTACK ●●●●
DEFENSE ●●●
SP. ATTACK ●●●●
SP. DEFENSE ●●●
SPEED ●●

● Male form   ● Female form

EVOLUTION PATH

Tangela —(Raise to Lv33 and teach it AncientPower. Or, level it up while it knows AncientPower.)→ Tangrowth
Tangela pg. 422

MAIN WAYS TO OBTAIN

PLATINUM — • Level up Tangela to Lv33 and teach it the move AncientPower • Level it up while it knows AncientPower
DIAMOND — • Level up Tangela to Lv33 and teach it the move AncientPower • Level it up while it knows AncientPower
PEARL — • Level up Tangela to Lv33 and teach it the move AncientPower • Level it up while it knows AncientPower
GBA —

ABILITY ● Chlorophyll ● Leaf Guard

LEVEL-UP AND LEARNED MOVES

Lv	Name	Type	Kind	Power	Acc	PP	Range	DA
Base	Ingrain	Grass	Status	—	—	20	Self	•
Base	Constrict	Normal	Physical	10	100	35	Normal	•
5	Sleep Powder	Grass	Status	—	75	15	Normal	—
8	Absorb	Grass	Special	20	100	25	Normal	—
12	Growth	Normal	Status	—	—	40	Self	—
15	PoisonPowder	Poison	Status	—	75	35	Normal	—
19	Vine Whip	Grass	Physical	35	100	15	Normal	•
22	Bind	Normal	Physical	15	75	20	Normal	•
26	Mega Drain	Grass	Special	40	100	15	Normal	—
29	Stun Spore	Grass	Status	—	75	30	Normal	—
33	AncientPower	Rock	Special	60	100	5	Normal	—
36	Knock Off	Dark	Physical	20	100	20	Normal	•
40	Natural Gift	Normal	Physical	—	100	15	Normal	•
43	Slam	Normal	Physical	80	75	20	Normal	•
47	Tickle	Normal	Status	—	100	20	Normal	—
50	Wring Out	Normal	Special	—	100	5	Normal	•
54	Power Whip	Grass	Physical	120	85	10	Normal	•
57	Block	Normal	Status	—	—	5	Normal	—

National Pokédex No. 466 Thunderbolt Pokémon
Electivire

ELECTRIC

STATS
HP ●●●
ATTACK ●●●●●
DEFENSE ●●●
SP. ATTACK ●●●
SP. DEFENSE ●●●
SPEED ●●●

● M/F have same form

EVOLUTION PATH

Elekid —Lv30→ Electabuzz —(Link trade while it holds Electirizer)→ Electivire
Elekid pg. 453   Electabuzz pg. 425

MAIN WAYS TO OBTAIN

PLATINUM — Link trade Electabuzz while it holds Electirizer
DIAMOND — Link trade Electabuzz while it holds Electirizer
PEARL — Link trade Electabuzz while it holds Electirizer
GBA —

ABILITY ● Motor Drive

LEVEL-UP AND LEARNED MOVES

Lv	Name	Type	Kind	Power	Acc	PP	Range	DA
Base	Fire Punch	Fire	Physical	75	100	15	Normal	•
Base	Quick Attack	Normal	Physical	40	100	30	Normal	•
Base	Leer	Normal	Status	—	100	30	2 foes	—
Base	ThunderShock	Electric	Special	40	100	30	Normal	—
Base	Low Kick	Fighting	Physical	—	100	20	Normal	•
7	ThunderShock	Electric	Special	40	100	30	Normal	—
10	Low Kick	Fighting	Physical	—	100	20	Normal	•
16	Swift	Normal	Special	60	—	20	2 foes	—
19	Shock Wave	Electric	Special	60	—	20	Normal	—
25	Light Screen	Psychic	Status	—	—	30	2 allies	—
28	ThunderPunch	Electric	Physical	75	100	15	Normal	•
37	Discharge	Electric	Special	80	100	15	2 foes • 1 ally	—
43	Thunderbolt	Electric	Special	95	100	15	Normal	—
52	Screech	Normal	Status	—	85	40	Normal	—
58	Thunder	Electric	Special	120	70	10	Normal	—
67	Giga Impact	Normal	Physical	150	90	5	Normal	•

National Pokédex No. 467 Blast Pokémon
Magmortar

FIRE

STATS
HP ●●●
ATTACK ●●●
DEFENSE ●●●
SP. ATTACK ●●●●●
SP. DEFENSE ●●●●
SPEED ●●●

● M/F have same form

EVOLUTION PATH

Magby —Lv30→ Magmar —(Link trade while it holds Magmarizer)→ Magmortar
Magby pg. 453   Magmar pg. 425

MAIN WAYS TO OBTAIN

PLATINUM — Link trade Magmar while it holds Magmarizer
DIAMOND — Link trade Magmar while it holds Magmarizer
PEARL — Link trade Magmar while it holds Magmarizer
GBA —

ABILITY ● Flame Body

LEVEL-UP AND LEARNED MOVES

Lv	Name	Type	Kind	Power	Acc	PP	Range	DA
Base	ThunderPunch	Electric	Physical	75	100	15	Normal	•
Base	Smog	Poison	Special	20	70	20	Normal	•
Base	Leer	Normal	Status	—	100	30	2 foes	—
Base	Ember	Fire	Special	40	100	25	Normal	—
Base	SmokeScreen	Normal	Status	—	100	20	Normal	—
7	Ember	Fire	Special	40	100	25	Normal	—
10	SmokeScreen	Normal	Status	—	100	20	Normal	—
16	Faint Attack	Dark	Physical	60	—	20	Normal	•
19	Fire Spin	Fire	Special	15	70	15	Normal	—
25	Confuse Ray	Ghost	Status	—	100	10	Normal	—
28	Fire Punch	Fire	Physical	75	100	15	Normal	•
37	Lava Plume	Fire	Special	80	100	15	2 foes • 1 ally	—
43	Flamethrower	Fire	Special	95	100	15	Normal	—
52	Sunny Day	Fire	Status	—	—	5	All	—
58	Fire Blast	Fire	Special	120	85	5	Normal	—
67	Hyper Beam	Normal	Special	150	90	5	Normal	—

National Pokédex No. 468 Jubilee Pokémon
Togekiss

NORMAL FLYING

STATS
HP ●●●
ATTACK ●●
DEFENSE ●●
SP. ATTACK ●●●●●
SP. DEFENSE ●●●
SPEED ●●●

● M/F have same form

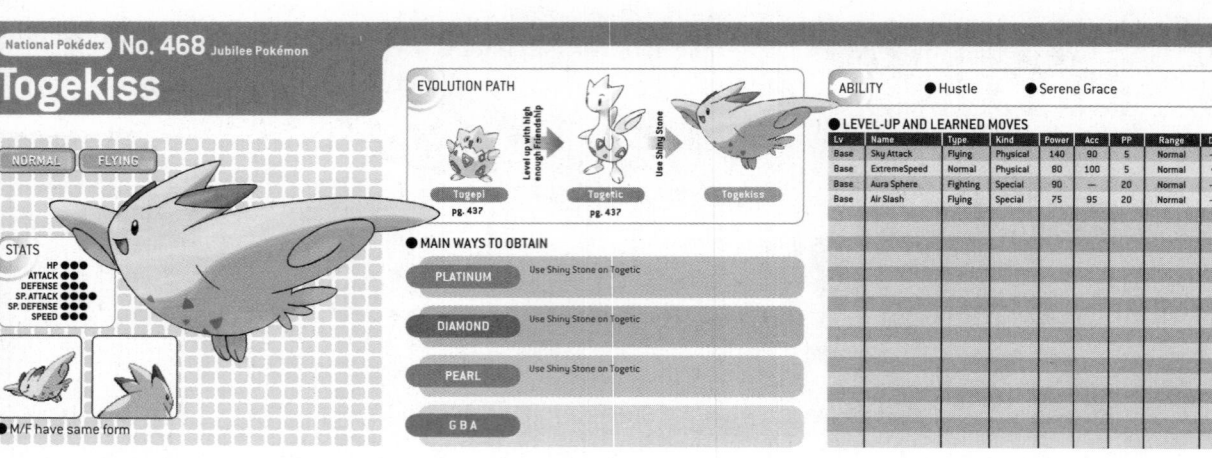

EVOLUTION PATH
Togepi → (Level up with high enough Friendship) → Togetic → (Using Shiny Stone) → Togekiss
pg. 437 .... pg. 437

● MAIN WAYS TO OBTAIN
PLATINUM	Use Shiny Stone on Togetic
DIAMOND	Use Shiny Stone on Togetic
PEARL	Use Shiny Stone on Togetic
GBA	

ABILITY ● Hustle ● Serene Grace

● LEVEL-UP AND LEARNED MOVES
Lv	Name	Type	Kind	Power	Acc	PP	Range	DA
Base	Sky Attack	Flying	Physical	140	90	5	Normal	—
Base	ExtremeSpeed	Normal	Physical	80	100	5	Normal	●
Base	Aura Sphere	Fighting	Special	90	—	20	Normal	—
Base	Air Slash	Flying	Special	75	95	20	Normal	—

National Pokédex No. 469 Ogre Darner Pokémon
Yanmega

BUG FLYING

STATS
HP ●●●
ATTACK ●●●●
DEFENSE ●●●
SP. ATTACK ●●●●
SP. DEFENSE ●●●
SPEED ●●●

● M/F have same form

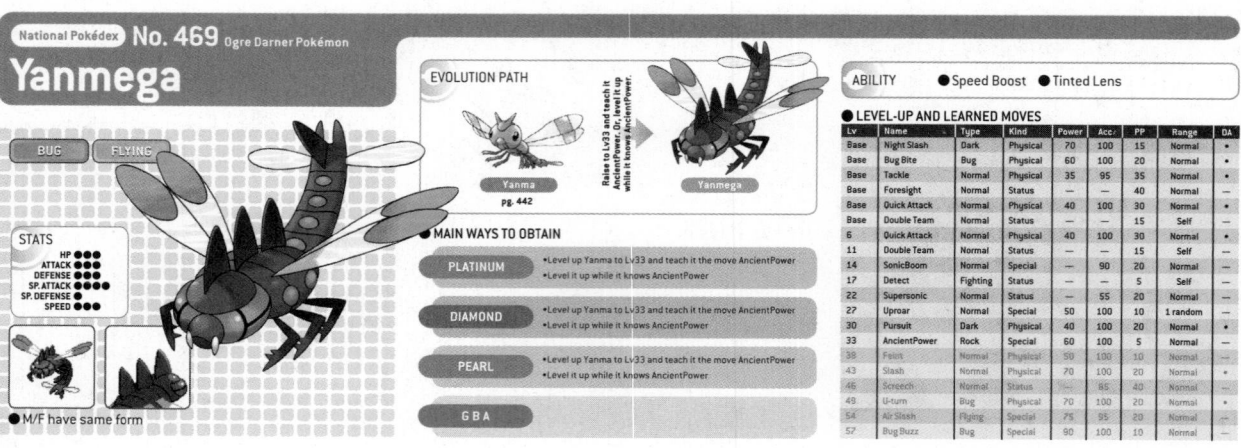

EVOLUTION PATH
Yanma → (Raise to Lv33 and teach it AncientPower. Or, level it up while it knows AncientPower.) → Yanmega
pg. 442

● MAIN WAYS TO OBTAIN
PLATINUM	• Level up Yanma to Lv33 and teach it the move AncientPower • Level it up while it knows AncientPower
DIAMOND	• Level up Yanma to Lv33 and teach it the move AncientPower • Level it up while it knows AncientPower
PEARL	• Level up Yanma to Lv33 and teach it the move AncientPower • Level it up while it knows AncientPower
GBA	

ABILITY ● Speed Boost ● Tinted Lens

● LEVEL-UP AND LEARNED MOVES
Lv	Name	Type	Kind	Power	Acc	PP	Range	DA
Base	Night Slash	Dark	Physical	70	100	15	Normal	●
Base	Bug Bite	Bug	Physical	60	100	20	Normal	●
Base	Tackle	Normal	Physical	35	95	35	Normal	●
Base	Foresight	Normal	Status	—	—	40	Normal	—
Base	Quick Attack	Normal	Physical	40	100	30	Normal	●
Base	Double Team	Normal	Status	—	—	15	Self	—
6	Quick Attack	Normal	Physical	40	100	30	Normal	●
11	Double Team	Normal	Status	—	—	15	Self	—
14	SonicBoom	Normal	Special	—	90	20	Normal	—
17	Detect	Fighting	Status	—	—	5	Self	—
22	Supersonic	Normal	Status	—	55	20	Normal	—
27	Uproar	Normal	Special	50	100	10	1 random	—
30	Pursuit	Dark	Physical	40	100	20	Normal	●
33	AncientPower	Rock	Special	60	100	5	Normal	—
38	Feint	Normal	Physical	50	100	10	Normal	●
43	Slash	Normal	Physical	70	100	20	Normal	●
46	Screech	Normal	Status	—	85	40	Normal	—
49	U-turn	Bug	Physical	70	100	20	Normal	—
54	Air Slash	Flying	Special	75	95	20	Normal	—
57	Bug Buzz	Bug	Special	90	100	10	Normal	—

National Pokédex No. 470 Verdant Pokémon
Leafeon

GRASS

STATS
HP ●●●
ATTACK ●●●●
DEFENSE ●●●●●
SP. ATTACK ●●●
SP. DEFENSE ●●
SPEED ●●●

● M/F have same form

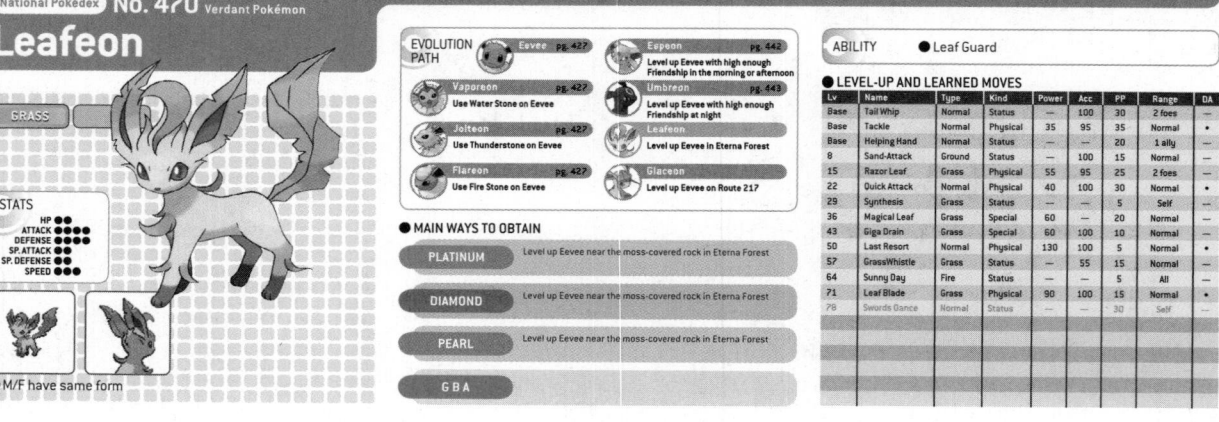

EVOLUTION PATH
Eevee pg. 427
- Espeon pg. 442 — Level up Eevee with high enough Friendship in the morning or afternoon
- Vaporeon pg. 427 — Use Water Stone on Eevee
- Umbreon pg. 443 — Level up Eevee with high enough Friendship at night
- Jolteon pg. 427 — Use Thunderstone on Eevee
- Leafeon — Level up Eevee in Eterna Forest
- Flareon pg. 427 — Use Fire Stone on Eevee
- Glaceon — Level up Eevee on Route 217

● MAIN WAYS TO OBTAIN
PLATINUM	Level up Eevee near the moss-covered rock in Eterna Forest
DIAMOND	Level up Eevee near the moss-covered rock in Eterna Forest
PEARL	Level up Eevee near the moss-covered rock in Eterna Forest
GBA	

ABILITY ● Leaf Guard

● LEVEL-UP AND LEARNED MOVES
Lv	Name	Type	Kind	Power	Acc	PP	Range	DA
Base	Tail Whip	Normal	Status	—	100	30	2 foes	—
Base	Tackle	Normal	Physical	35	95	35	Normal	●
Base	Helping Hand	Normal	Status	—	—	20	1 ally	—
8	Sand-Attack	Ground	Status	—	100	15	Normal	—
15	Razor Leaf	Grass	Physical	55	95	25	2 foes	—
22	Quick Attack	Normal	Physical	40	100	30	Normal	●
29	Synthesis	Grass	Status	—	—	5	Self	—
36	Magical Leaf	Grass	Special	60	—	20	Normal	—
43	Giga Drain	Grass	Special	60	100	10	Normal	—
50	Last Resort	Normal	Physical	130	100	5	Normal	●
57	GrassWhistle	Grass	Status	—	55	15	Normal	—
64	Sunny Day	Fire	Status	—	—	5	All	—
71	Leaf Blade	Grass	Physical	90	100	15	Normal	●
78	Swords Dance	Normal	Status	—	—	30	Self	—

National Pokédex No. 471 Fresh Snow Pokémon
Glaceon

ICE

STATS
HP ●●
ATTACK ●●●
DEFENSE ●●●●
SP. ATTACK ●●●●●
SP. DEFENSE ●●●●
SPEED ●●●

● M/F have same form

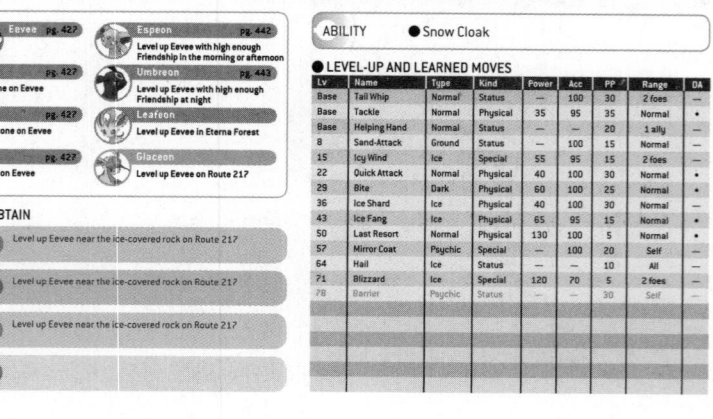

EVOLUTION PATH
Eevee pg. 427
- Espeon pg. 442 — Level up Eevee with high enough Friendship in the morning or afternoon
- Vaporeon pg. 427 — Use Water Stone on Eevee
- Umbreon pg. 443 — Level up Eevee with high enough Friendship at night
- Jolteon pg. 427 — Use Thunderstone on Eevee
- Leafeon — Level up Eevee in Eterna Forest
- Flareon pg. 427 — Use Fire Stone on Eevee
- Glaceon — Level up Eevee on Route 217

MAIN WAYS TO OBTAIN
PLATINUM	Level up Eevee near the ice-covered rock on Route 217
DIAMOND	Level up Eevee near the ice-covered rock on Route 217
PEARL	Level up Eevee near the ice-covered rock on Route 217
GBA	

ABILITY ● Snow Cloak

● LEVEL-UP AND LEARNED MOVES
Lv	Name	Type	Kind	Power	Acc	PP	Range	DA
Base	Tail Whip	Normal	Status	—	100	30	2 foes	—
Base	Tackle	Normal	Physical	35	95	35	Normal	●
Base	Helping Hand	Normal	Status	—	—	20	1 ally	—
8	Sand-Attack	Ground	Status	—	100	15	Normal	—
15	Icy Wind	Ice	Special	55	95	15	2 foes	—
22	Quick Attack	Normal	Physical	40	100	30	Normal	●
29	Bite	Dark	Physical	60	100	25	Normal	●
36	Ice Shard	Ice	Physical	40	100	30	Normal	●
43	Ice Fang	Ice	Physical	65	95	15	Normal	●
50	Last Resort	Normal	Physical	130	100	5	Normal	●
57	Mirror Coat	Psychic	Special	—	100	20	Self	—
64	Hail	Ice	Status	—	—	10	All	—
71	Blizzard	Ice	Special	120	70	5	2 foes	—
78	Barrier	Psychic	Status	—	—	30	Self	—

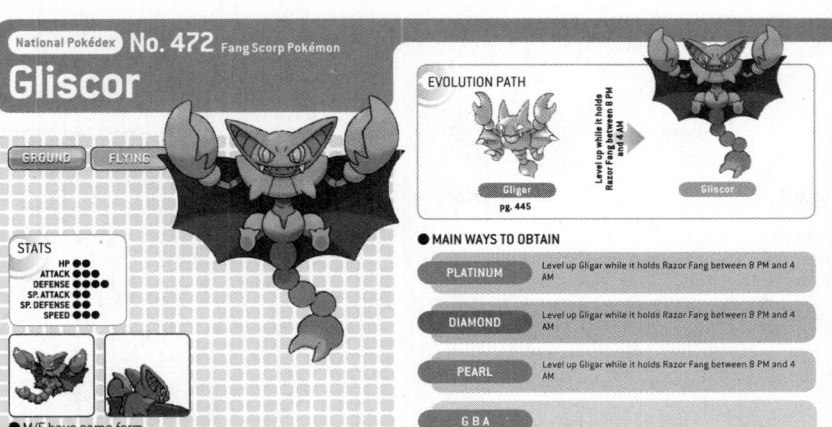
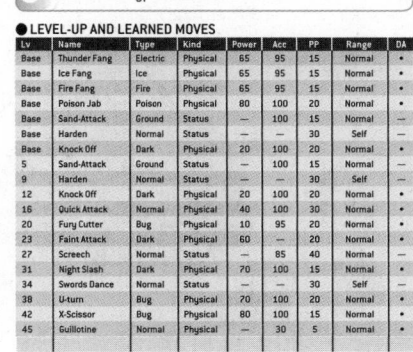

National Pokédex No. 472 Fang Scorp Pokémon
Gliscor

GROUND | FLYING

STATS
HP
ATTACK
DEFENSE
SP. ATTACK
SP. DEFENSE
SPEED

● M/F have same form

EVOLUTION PATH

Gligar pg. 445 → Level up while it holds Razor Fang between 8 PM and 4 AM → Gliscor

● MAIN WAYS TO OBTAIN

PLATINUM	Level up Gligar while it holds Razor Fang between 8 PM and 4 AM
DIAMOND	Level up Gligar while it holds Razor Fang between 8 PM and 4 AM
PEARL	Level up Gligar while it holds Razor Fang between 8 PM and 4 AM
GBA	

ABILITY ● Hyper Cutter ● Sand Veil

● LEVEL-UP AND LEARNED MOVES

Lv	Name	Type	Kind	Power	Acc	PP	Range	DA
Base	Thunder Fang	Electric	Physical	65	95	15	Normal	•
Base	Ice Fang	Ice	Physical	65	95	15	Normal	•
Base	Fire Fang	Fire	Physical	65	95	15	Normal	•
Base	Poison Jab	Poison	Physical	80	100	20	Normal	•
Base	Sand-Attack	Ground	Status	—	100	15	Normal	•
Base	Harden	Normal	Status	—	—	30	Self	—
Base	Knock Off	Dark	Physical	20	100	20	Normal	•
5	Sand-Attack	Ground	Status	—	100	15	Normal	•
9	Harden	Normal	Status	—	—	30	Self	—
12	Knock Off	Dark	Physical	20	100	20	Normal	•
16	Quick Attack	Normal	Physical	40	100	30	Normal	•
20	Fury Cutter	Bug	Physical	10	95	20	Normal	•
23	Faint Attack	Dark	Physical	60	—	20	Normal	•
27	Screech	Normal	Status	—	85	40	Normal	•
31	Night Slash	Dark	Physical	70	100	15	Normal	•
34	Swords Dance	Normal	Status	—	—	30	Self	—
38	U-turn	Bug	Physical	70	100	20	Normal	•
42	X-Scissor	Bug	Physical	80	100	15	Normal	•
45	Guillotine	Normal	Physical	—	30	5	Normal	—

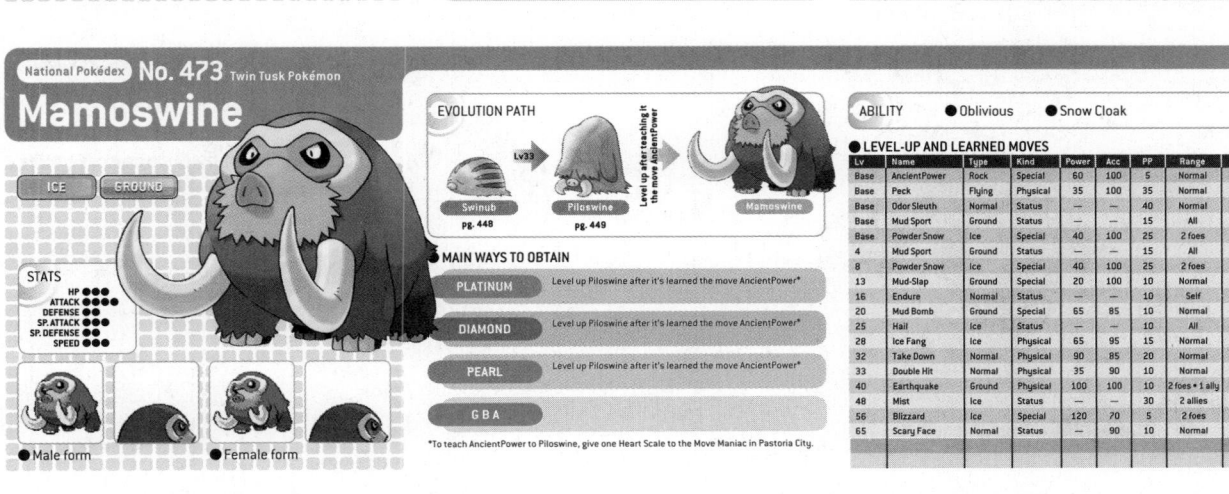

National Pokédex No. 473 Twin Tusk Pokémon
Mamoswine

ICE | GROUND

STATS
HP
ATTACK
DEFENSE
SP. ATTACK
SP. DEFENSE
SPEED

● Male form   ● Female form

EVOLUTION PATH

Swinub pg. 448 → Lv33 → Piloswine pg. 449 → Level up after teaching it the move AncientPower → Mamoswine

● MAIN WAYS TO OBTAIN

PLATINUM	Level up Piloswine after it's learned the move AncientPower*
DIAMOND	Level up Piloswine after it's learned the move AncientPower*
PEARL	Level up Piloswine after it's learned the move AncientPower*
GBA	

ABILITY ● Oblivious ● Snow Cloak

● LEVEL-UP AND LEARNED MOVES

Lv	Name	Type	Kind	Power	Acc	PP	Range	DA
Base	AncientPower	Rock	Special	60	100	5	Normal	—
Base	Peck	Flying	Physical	35	100	35	Normal	•
Base	Odor Sleuth	Normal	Status	—	—	40	Normal	—
Base	Mud Sport	Ground	Status	—	—	15	All	—
Base	Powder Snow	Ice	Special	40	100	25	2 foes	—
4	Mud Sport	Ground	Status	—	—	15	All	—
8	Powder Snow	Ice	Special	40	100	25	2 foes	—
13	Mud-Slap	Ground	Special	20	100	10	Normal	•
16	Endure	Normal	Status	—	—	10	Self	—
20	Mud Bomb	Ground	Special	65	85	10	Normal	•
25	Hail	Ice	Status	—	—	10	All	—
28	Ice Fang	Ice	Physical	65	95	15	Normal	•
32	Take Down	Normal	Physical	90	85	20	Normal	•
33	Double Hit	Normal	Physical	35	90	10	Normal	•
40	Earthquake	Ground	Physical	100	100	10	2 foes • 1 ally	•
48	Mist	Ice	Status	—	—	30	2 allies	—
56	Blizzard	Ice	Special	120	70	5	2 foes	—
65	Scary Face	Normal	Status	—	90	10	Normal	—

*To teach AncientPower to Piloswine, give one Heart Scale to the Move Maniac in Pastoria City.

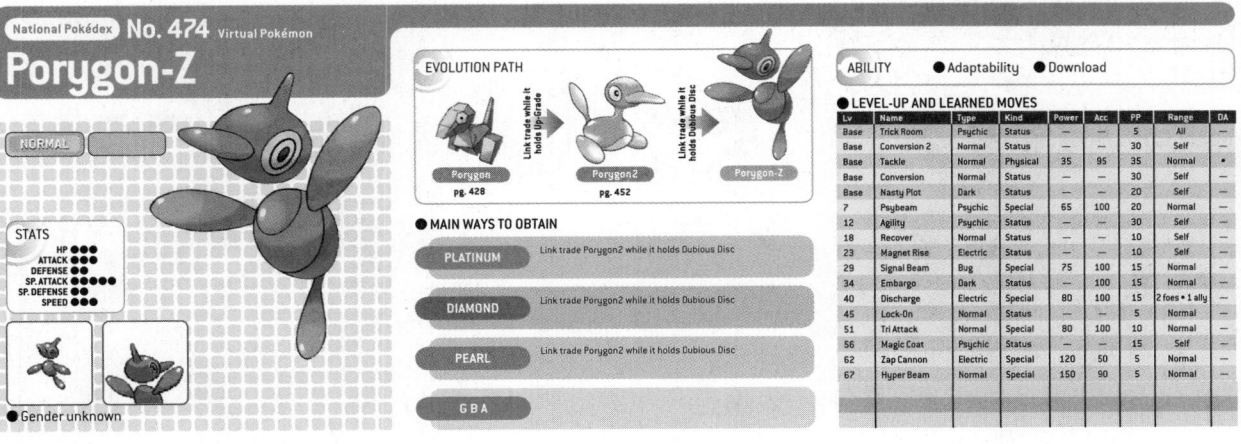

National Pokédex No. 474 Virtual Pokémon
Porygon-Z

NORMAL

STATS
HP
ATTACK
DEFENSE
SP. ATTACK
SP. DEFENSE
SPEED

● Gender unknown

EVOLUTION PATH

Porygon pg. 428 → Link trade while it holds Up-Grade → Porygon2 pg. 452 → Link trade while it holds Dubious Disc → Porygon-Z

● MAIN WAYS TO OBTAIN

PLATINUM	Link trade Porygon2 while it holds Dubious Disc
DIAMOND	Link trade Porygon2 while it holds Dubious Disc
PEARL	Link trade Porygon2 while it holds Dubious Disc
GBA	

ABILITY ● Adaptability ● Download

● LEVEL-UP AND LEARNED MOVES

Lv	Name	Type	Kind	Power	Acc	PP	Range	DA
Base	Trick Room	Psychic	Status	—	—	5	All	—
Base	Conversion 2	Normal	Status	—	—	30	Self	—
Base	Tackle	Normal	Physical	35	95	35	Normal	•
Base	Conversion	Normal	Status	—	—	30	Self	—
Base	Nasty Plot	Dark	Status	—	—	20	Self	—
7	Psybeam	Psychic	Special	65	100	20	Normal	•
12	Agility	Psychic	Status	—	—	30	Self	—
18	Recover	Normal	Status	—	—	10	Self	—
23	Magnet Rise	Electric	Status	—	—	10	Self	—
29	Signal Beam	Bug	Special	75	100	15	Normal	•
34	Embargo	Dark	Status	—	100	15	Normal	•
40	Discharge	Electric	Special	80	100	15	2 foes • 1 ally	•
45	Lock-On	Normal	Status	—	—	5	Normal	—
51	Tri Attack	Normal	Special	80	100	10	Normal	•
56	Magic Coat	Psychic	Status	—	—	15	Self	—
62	Zap Cannon	Electric	Special	120	50	5	Normal	•
67	Hyper Beam	Normal	Special	150	90	5	Normal	•

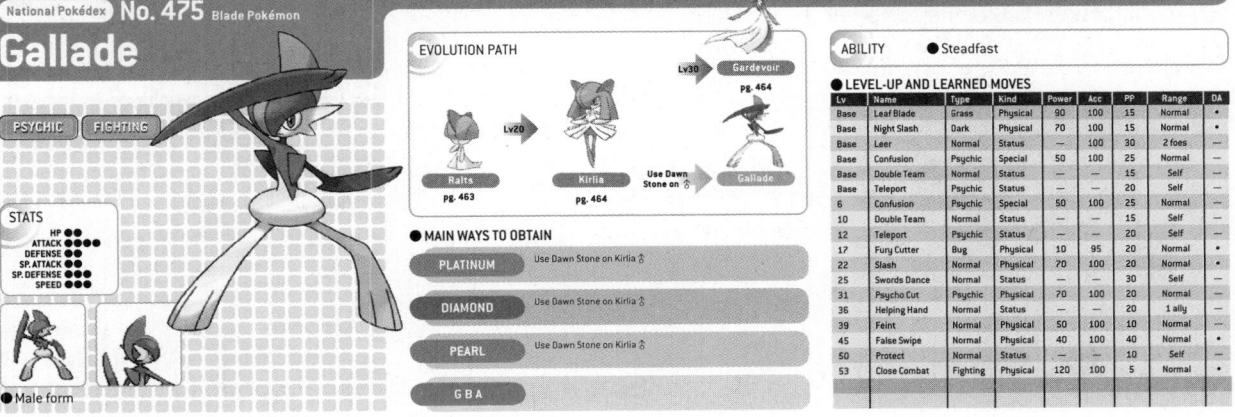

National Pokédex No. 475 Blade Pokémon
Gallade

PSYCHIC | FIGHTING

STATS
HP
ATTACK
DEFENSE
SP. ATTACK
SP. DEFENSE
SPEED

● Male form

EVOLUTION PATH

Ralts pg. 463 → Lv20 → Kirlia pg. 464 → Lv30 → Gardevoir pg. 464 / Use Dawn Stone on → Gallade

● MAIN WAYS TO OBTAIN

PLATINUM	Use Dawn Stone on Kirlia ♂
DIAMOND	Use Dawn Stone on Kirlia ♂
PEARL	Use Dawn Stone on Kirlia ♂
GBA	

ABILITY ● Steadfast

● LEVEL-UP AND LEARNED MOVES

Lv	Name	Type	Kind	Power	Acc	PP	Range	DA
Base	Leaf Blade	Grass	Physical	90	100	15	Normal	•
Base	Night Slash	Dark	Physical	70	100	15	Normal	•
Base	Leer	Normal	Status	—	100	30	2 foes	—
Base	Confusion	Psychic	Special	50	100	25	Normal	•
Base	Double Team	Normal	Status	—	—	15	Self	—
Base	Teleport	Psychic	Status	—	—	20	Self	—
6	Confusion	Psychic	Special	50	100	25	Normal	•
10	Double Team	Normal	Status	—	—	15	Self	—
12	Teleport	Psychic	Status	—	—	20	Self	—
17	Fury Cutter	Bug	Physical	10	95	20	Normal	•
22	Slash	Normal	Physical	70	100	20	Normal	•
25	Swords Dance	Normal	Status	—	—	30	Self	—
31	Psycho Cut	Psychic	Physical	70	100	20	Normal	•
36	Helping Hand	Normal	Status	—	—	20	1 ally	—
39	Feint	Normal	Physical	50	100	10	Normal	•
45	False Swipe	Normal	Physical	40	100	40	Normal	•
50	Protect	Normal	Status	—	—	10	Self	—
53	Close Combat	Fighting	Physical	120	100	5	Normal	•

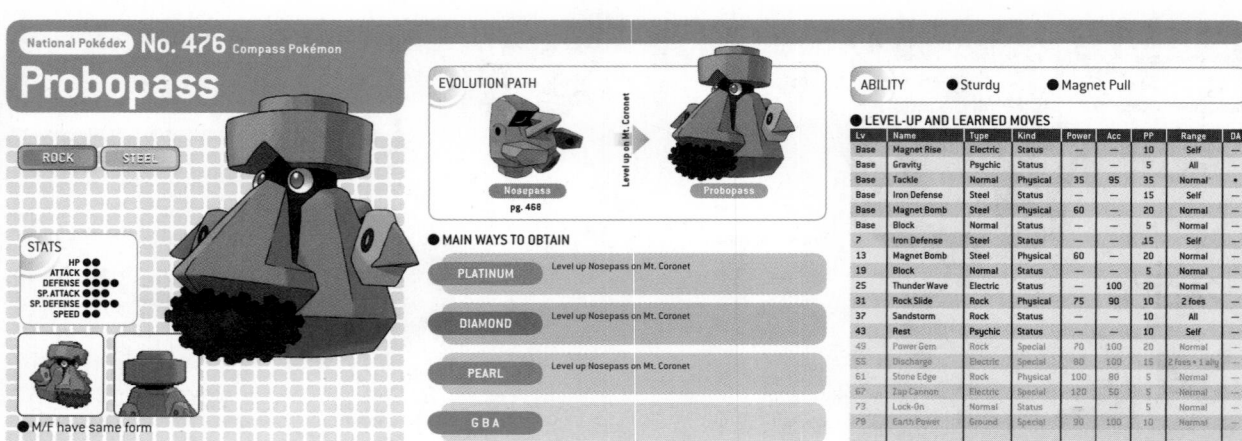

Probopass

National Pokédex No. 476 Compass Pokémon

ROCK STEEL

STATS
- HP ●●
- ATTACK ●●
- DEFENSE ●●●●●
- SP. ATTACK ●●●●
- SP. DEFENSE ●●●●
- SPEED ●●

● M/F have same form

EVOLUTION PATH

Nosepass → (Level up on Mt. Coronet) → Probopass
pg. 468

● MAIN WAYS TO OBTAIN

PLATINUM	Level up Nosepass on Mt. Coronet
DIAMOND	Level up Nosepass on Mt. Coronet
PEARL	Level up Nosepass on Mt. Coronet
G B A	

ABILITY ● Sturdy ● Magnet Pull

● LEVEL-UP AND LEARNED MOVES

Lv	Name	Type	Kind	Power	Acc	PP	Range	DA
Base	Magnet Rise	Electric	Status	—	—	10	Self	—
Base	Gravity	Psychic	Status	—	—	5	All	—
Base	Tackle	Normal	Physical	35	95	35	Normal	●
Base	Iron Defense	Steel	Status	—	—	15	Self	—
Base	Magnet Bomb	Steel	Physical	60	—	20	Normal	●
Base	Block	Normal	Status	—	—	5	Normal	—
7	Iron Defense	Steel	Status	—	—	15	Self	—
13	Magnet Bomb	Steel	Physical	60	—	20	Normal	●
19	Block	Normal	Status	—	—	5	Normal	—
25	Thunder Wave	Electric	Status	—	100	20	Normal	—
31	Rock Slide	Rock	Physical	75	90	10	2 foes	—
37	Sandstorm	Rock	Status	—	—	10	All	—
43	Rest	Psychic	Status	—	—	10	Self	—
49	Power Gem	Rock	Special	70	100	20	Normal	—
55	Discharge	Electric	Special	80	100	15	2 foes + 1 ally	—
61	Stone Edge	Rock	Physical	100	80	5	Normal	—
67	Zap Cannon	Electric	Special	120	50	5	Normal	—
73	Lock-On	Normal	Status	—	—	5	Normal	—
79	Earth Power	Ground	Special	90	100	10	Normal	—

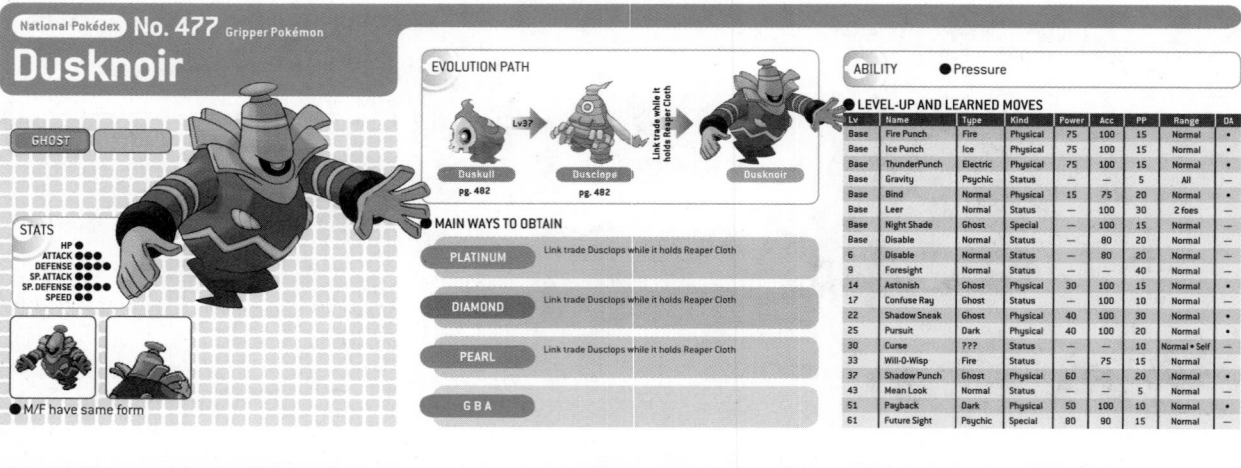

Dusknoir

National Pokédex No. 477 Gripper Pokémon

GHOST

STATS
- HP ●
- ATTACK ●●●
- DEFENSE ●●●●
- SP. ATTACK ●●●
- SP. DEFENSE ●●●●
- SPEED ●

● M/F have same form

EVOLUTION PATH

Duskull → Lv37 → Dusclops → (Link trade while it holds Reaper Cloth) → Dusknoir
pg. 482   pg. 482

● MAIN WAYS TO OBTAIN

PLATINUM	Link trade Dusclops while it holds Reaper Cloth
DIAMOND	Link trade Dusclops while it holds Reaper Cloth
PEARL	Link trade Dusclops while it holds Reaper Cloth
G B A	

ABILITY ● Pressure

● LEVEL-UP AND LEARNED MOVES

Lv	Name	Type	Kind	Power	Acc	PP	Range	DA
Base	Fire Punch	Fire	Physical	75	100	15	Normal	●
Base	Ice Punch	Ice	Physical	75	100	15	Normal	●
Base	ThunderPunch	Electric	Physical	75	100	15	Normal	●
Base	Gravity	Psychic	Status	—	—	5	All	—
Base	Bind	Normal	Physical	15	75	20	Normal	●
Base	Leer	Normal	Status	—	100	30	2 foes	—
Base	Night Shade	Ghost	Special	—	100	15	Normal	—
Base	Disable	Normal	Status	—	80	20	Normal	—
6	Disable	Normal	Status	—	80	20	Normal	—
9	Foresight	Normal	Status	—	—	40	Normal	—
14	Astonish	Ghost	Physical	30	100	15	Normal	●
17	Confuse Ray	Ghost	Status	—	100	10	Normal	—
22	Shadow Sneak	Ghost	Physical	40	100	30	Normal	●
25	Pursuit	Dark	Physical	40	100	20	Normal	●
30	Curse	???	Status	—	—	10	Normal • Self	—
33	Will-O-Wisp	Fire	Status	—	75	15	Normal	—
37	Shadow Punch	Ghost	Physical	60	—	20	Normal	●
43	Mean Look	Normal	Status	—	—	5	Normal	—
51	Payback	Dark	Physical	50	100	10	Normal	—
61	Future Sight	Psychic	Special	80	90	15	Normal	—

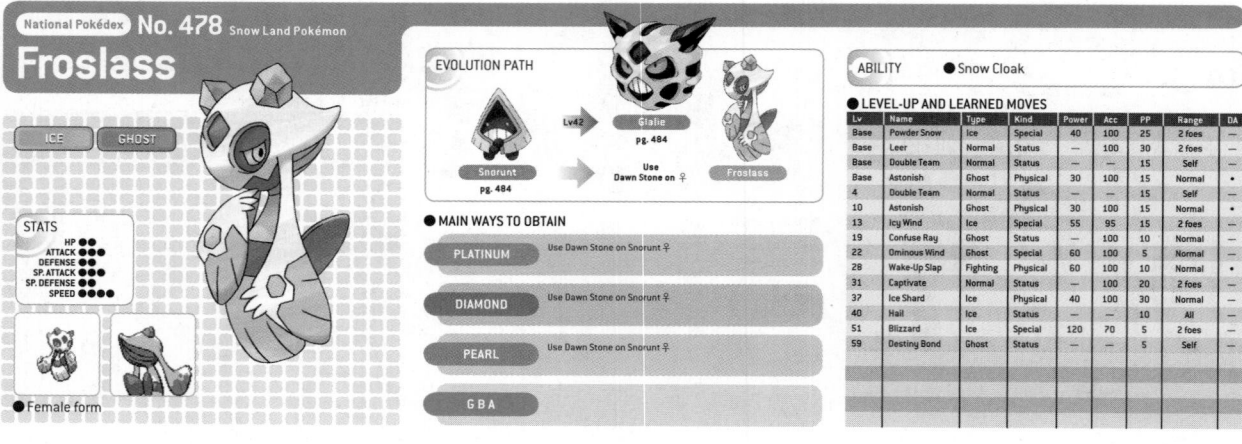

Froslass

National Pokédex No. 478 Snow Land Pokémon

ICE GHOST

STATS
- HP ●●●
- ATTACK ●●●
- DEFENSE ●●●
- SP. ATTACK ●●●
- SP. DEFENSE ●●●
- SPEED ●●●●

● Female form

EVOLUTION PATH

Snorunt → Lv42 → Glalie
pg. 484   pg. 484

Use Dawn Stone on ♀ → Froslass

● MAIN WAYS TO OBTAIN

PLATINUM	Use Dawn Stone on Snorunt ♀
DIAMOND	Use Dawn Stone on Snorunt ♀
PEARL	Use Dawn Stone on Snorunt ♀
G B A	

ABILITY ● Snow Cloak

● LEVEL-UP AND LEARNED MOVES

Lv	Name	Type	Kind	Power	Acc	PP	Range	DA
Base	Powder Snow	Ice	Special	40	100	25	2 foes	—
Base	Leer	Normal	Status	—	100	30	2 foes	—
Base	Double Team	Normal	Status	—	—	15	Self	—
Base	Astonish	Ghost	Physical	30	100	15	Normal	●
4	Double Team	Normal	Status	—	—	15	Self	—
10	Astonish	Ghost	Physical	30	100	15	Normal	●
13	Icy Wind	Ice	Special	55	95	15	2 foes	—
19	Confuse Ray	Ghost	Status	—	100	10	Normal	—
22	Ominous Wind	Ghost	Special	60	100	5	Normal	—
28	Wake-Up Slap	Fighting	Physical	60	100	10	Normal	—
31	Captivate	Normal	Status	—	100	20	2 foes	—
37	Ice Shard	Ice	Physical	40	100	30	Normal	—
40	Hail	Ice	Status	—	—	10	All	—
51	Blizzard	Ice	Special	120	70	5	2 foes	—
59	Destiny Bond	Ghost	Status	—	—	5	Self	—

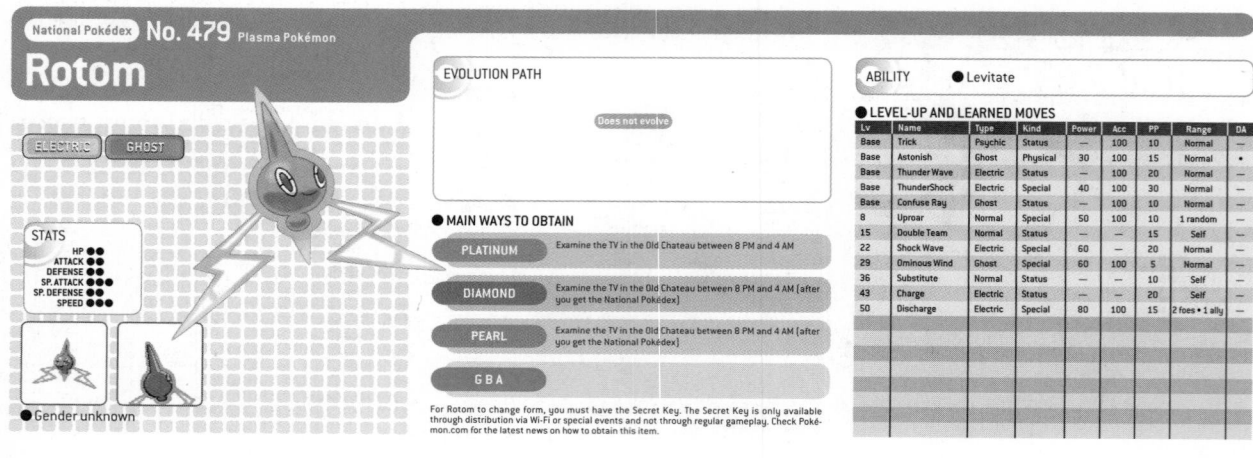

Rotom

National Pokédex No. 479 Plasma Pokémon

ELECTRIC GHOST

STATS
- HP ●●
- ATTACK ●●
- DEFENSE ●●●
- SP. ATTACK ●●●
- SP. DEFENSE ●●●
- SPEED ●●●

● Gender unknown

EVOLUTION PATH

Does not evolve

● MAIN WAYS TO OBTAIN

PLATINUM	Examine the TV in the Old Chateau between 8 PM and 4 AM
DIAMOND	Examine the TV in the Old Chateau between 8 PM and 4 AM (after you get the National Pokédex)
PEARL	Examine the TV in the Old Chateau between 8 PM and 4 AM (after you get the National Pokédex)
G B A	

ABILITY ● Levitate

● LEVEL-UP AND LEARNED MOVES

Lv	Name	Type	Kind	Power	Acc	PP	Range	DA
Base	Trick	Psychic	Status	—	100	10	Normal	—
Base	Astonish	Ghost	Physical	30	100	15	Normal	●
Base	Thunder Wave	Electric	Status	—	100	20	Normal	—
Base	ThunderShock	Electric	Special	40	100	30	Normal	—
Base	Confuse Ray	Ghost	Status	—	100	10	Normal	—
8	Uproar	Normal	Special	50	100	10	1 random	—
15	Double Team	Normal	Status	—	—	15	Self	—
22	Shock Wave	Electric	Special	60	—	20	Normal	—
29	Ominous Wind	Ghost	Special	60	100	5	Normal	—
36	Substitute	Normal	Status	—	—	10	Self	—
43	Charge	Electric	Status	—	—	20	Self	—
50	Discharge	Electric	Special	80	100	15	2 foes + 1 ally	—

For Rotom to change form, you must have the Secret Key. The Secret Key is only available through distribution via Wi-Fi or special events and not through regular gameplay. Check Poké-mon.com for the latest news on how to obtain this item.

Uxie

PSYCHIC

STATS
- HP ●●
- ATTACK ●●●
- DEFENSE ●●●●●
- SP. ATTACK ●●●
- SP. DEFENSE ●●●●●
- SPEED ●●●

● Gender unknown

● EVOLUTION PATH

Does not evolve

● MAIN WAYS TO OBTAIN

PLATINUM	Lake Acuity (after you've been to the Distortion World)
DIAMOND	Lake Acuity (after you've been to the Spear Pillar on Mt. Coronet)
PEARL	Lake Acuity (after you've been to the Spear Pillar on Mt. Coronet)
G B A	

● ABILITY ● Levitate

● LEVEL-UP AND LEARNED MOVES

Lv	Name	Type	Kind	Power	Acc	PP	Range	DA
Base	Rest	Psychic	Status	—	—	10	Self	—
Base	Confusion	Psychic	Special	50	100	25	Normal	
6	Imprison	Psychic	Status	—	—	10	Self	
16	Endure	Normal	Status	—	—	10	Self	
21	Swift	Normal	Special	60	—	20	2 foes	—
31	Yawn	Normal	Status	—	—	10	Normal	
36	Future Sight	Psychic	Special	80	90	15	Normal	
46	Amnesia	Psychic	Status	—	—	20	Self	
51	Extrasensory	Psychic	Special	80	100	30	Normal	●
61	Flail	Normal	Physical	—	100	15	Normal	
66	Natural Gift	Normal	Physical	—	100	15	Normal	
76	Memento	Dark	Status	—	100	10	Normal	

Mesprit

PSYCHIC

STATS
- HP ●●
- ATTACK ●●●
- DEFENSE ●●●
- SP. ATTACK ●●●
- SP. DEFENSE ●●●
- SPEED ●●●

● Gender unknown

● EVOLUTION PATH

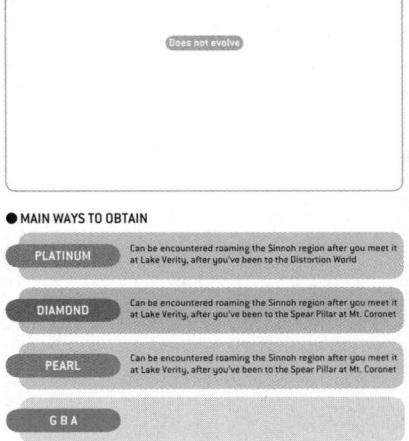

Does not evolve

● MAIN WAYS TO OBTAIN

PLATINUM	Can be encountered roaming the Sinnoh region after you meet it at Lake Verity, after you've been to the Distortion World
DIAMOND	Can be encountered roaming the Sinnoh region after you meet it at Lake Verity, after you've been to the Spear Pillar at Mt. Coronet
PEARL	Can be encountered roaming the Sinnoh region after you meet it at Lake Verity, after you've been to the Spear Pillar at Mt. Coronet
G B A	

● ABILITY ● Levitate

● LEVEL-UP AND LEARNED MOVES

Lv	Name	Type	Kind	Power	Acc	PP	Range	DA
Base	Rest	Psychic	Status	—	—	10	Self	—
Base	Confusion	Psychic	Special	50	100	25	Normal	
6	Imprison	Psychic	Status	—	—	10	Self	—
16	Protect	Normal	Status	—	—	10	Self	—
21	Swift	Normal	Special	60	—	20	2 foes	—
31	Lucky Chant	Normal	Status	—	—	30	2 allies	—
36	Future Sight	Psychic	Special	80	90	15	Normal	—
46	Charm	Normal	Status	—	100	20	Normal	—
51	Extrasensory	Psychic	Special	80	100	30	Normal	—
61	Copycat	Normal	Status	—	—	20	DoM	—
66	Natural Gift	Normal	Physical	—	100	15	Normal	—
76	Healing Wish	Psychic	Status	—	—	10	Self	—

Azelf

PSYCHIC

STATS
- HP ●●
- ATTACK ●●●●
- DEFENSE ●●
- SP. ATTACK ●●●●
- SP. DEFENSE ●●
- SPEED ●●●●●

● Gender unknown

● EVOLUTION PATH

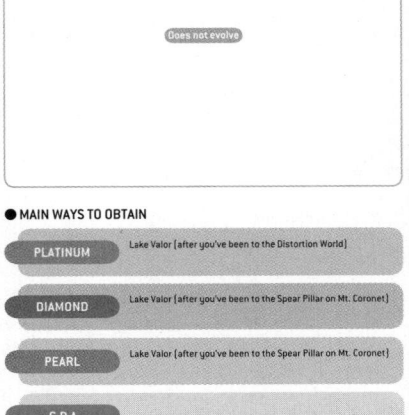

Does not evolve

● MAIN WAYS TO OBTAIN

PLATINUM	Lake Valor (after you've been to the Distortion World)
DIAMOND	Lake Valor (after you've been to the Spear Pillar on Mt. Coronet)
PEARL	Lake Valor (after you've been to the Spear Pillar on Mt. Coronet)
G B A	

● ABILITY ● Levitate

● LEVEL-UP AND LEARNED MOVES

Lv	Name	Type	Kind	Power	Acc	PP	Range	DA
Base	Rest	Psychic	Status	—	—	10	Self	—
Base	Confusion	Psychic	Special	50	100	25	Normal	—
6	Imprison	Psychic	Status	—	—	10	Self	—
16	Detect	Fighting	Status	—	—	5	Self	●
21	Swift	Normal	Special	60	—	20	2 foes	—
31	Uproar	Normal	Special	50	100	10	1 random	—
36	Future Sight	Psychic	Special	80	90	15	Normal	—
46	Nasty Plot	Dark	Status	—	—	20	Self	—
51	Extrasensory	Psychic	Special	80	100	30	Normal	—
61	Last Resort	Normal	Physical	130	100	5	Normal	●
66	Natural Gift	Normal	Physical	—	100	15	Normal	—
76	Explosion	Normal	Physical	250	100	5	2 foes + 1 ally	—

National Pokédex No. 483 Temporal Pokémon

Dialga

STEEL DRAGON

STATS
HP ●●●●
ATTACK ●●●●
DEFENSE ●●●●
SP. ATTACK ●●●●
SP. DEFENSE ●●●●
SPEED ●●●

● Gender unknown

EVOLUTION PATH

Does not evolve

MAIN WAYS TO OBTAIN

PLATINUM • Mt. Coronet (middle)
• Spear Pillar (post-Hall-of-Fame)

DIAMOND • Mt. Coronet (middle)
• Spear Pillar

PEARL

G B A

ABILITY ● Pressure

● LEVEL-UP AND LEARNED MOVES

Lv	Name	Type	Kind	Power	Acc	PP	Range	DA
Base	DragonBreath	Dragon	Special	60	100	20	Normal	—
Base	Scary Face	Normal	Status	—	90	10	Normal	—
10	Metal Claw	Steel	Physical	50	95	35	Normal	●
20	AncientPower	Rock	Special	60	100	5	Normal	—
30	Dragon Claw	Dragon	Physical	80	100	15	Normal	●
40	Roar Of Time	Dragon	Special	150	90	5	Normal	—
50	Heal Block	Psychic	Status	—	100	15	2 foes	—
60	Earth Power	Ground	Special	90	100	10	Normal	—
70	Slash	Normal	Physical	70	100	20	Normal	●
80	Flash Cannon	Steel	Special	80	100	10	Normal	—
90	Aura Sphere	Fighting	Special	90	—	20	Normal	—

National Pokédex No. 484 Spatial Pokémon

Palkia

WATER DRAGON

STATS
HP ●●●●
ATTACK ●●●●
DEFENSE ●●●●
SP. ATTACK ●●●●
SP. DEFENSE ●●●●
SPEED ●●●●

● Gender unknown

EVOLUTION PATH

Does not evolve

MAIN WAYS TO OBTAIN

PLATINUM • Mt. Coronet (middle)
• Spear Pillar (post-Hall-of-Fame)

DIAMOND

PEARL • Mt. Coronet (middle)
• Spear Pillar

G B A

ABILITY ● Pressure

● LEVEL-UP AND LEARNED MOVES

Lv	Name	Type	Kind	Power	Acc	PP	Range	DA
Base	DragonBreath	Dragon	Special	60	100	20	Normal	—
Base	Scary Face	Normal	Status	—	90	10	Normal	—
10	Water Pulse	Water	Special	60	100	20	Normal	—
20	AncientPower	Rock	Special	60	100	5	Normal	—
30	Dragon Claw	Dragon	Physical	80	100	15	Normal	—
40	Spacial Rend	Dragon	Special	100	95	5	Normal	—
50	Heal Block	Psychic	Status	—	100	15	2 foes	—
60	Earth Power	Ground	Special	90	100	10	Normal	—
70	Slash	Normal	Physical	70	100	20	Normal	●
80	Aqua Tail	Water	Physical	90	90	10	Normal	●
90	Aura Sphere	Fighting	Special	90	—	20	Normal	—

National Pokédex No. 485 Lava Dome Pokémon

Heatran

FIRE STEEL

STATS
HP ●●●
ATTACK ●●●●
DEFENSE ●●●●
SP. ATTACK ●●●●
SP. DEFENSE ●●●●
SPEED ●●●

● M/F have same form

EVOLUTION PATH

Does not evolve

MAIN WAYS TO OBTAIN

PLATINUM Stark Mountain interior 3 (after visiting Stark Mountain, talk to Buck in the Survival Area and enter the Battleground)

DIAMOND Stark Mountain interior 3 (after visiting Stark Mountain, talk to Buck in the Survival Area)

PEARL Stark Mountain interior 3 (after visiting Stark Mountain, talk to Buck in the Survival Area)

G B A

ABILITY ● Flash Fire

● LEVEL-UP AND LEARNED MOVES

Lv	Name	Type	Kind	Power	Acc	PP	Range	DA
Base	AncientPower	Rock	Special	60	100	5	Normal	—
9	Leer	Normal	Status	—	100	30	2 foes	—
17	Fire Fang	Fire	Physical	65	95	15	Normal	●
25	Metal Sound	Steel	Status	—	85	40	Normal	—
33	Crunch	Dark	Physical	80	100	15	Normal	●
41	Scary Face	Normal	Status	—	90	10	Normal	—
49	Lava Plume	Fire	Special	80	100	15	2 foes • 1 ally	—
57	Fire Spin	Fire	Special	15	70	15	Normal	—
65	Iron Head	Steel	Physical	80	100	15	Normal	—
73	Earth Power	Ground	Special	90	100	10	Normal	—
81	Heat Wave	Fire	Special	100	90	10	2 foes	—
88	Stone Edge	Rock	Physical	100	80	5	Normal	—
96	Magma Storm	Fire	Special	120	70	5	Normal	—

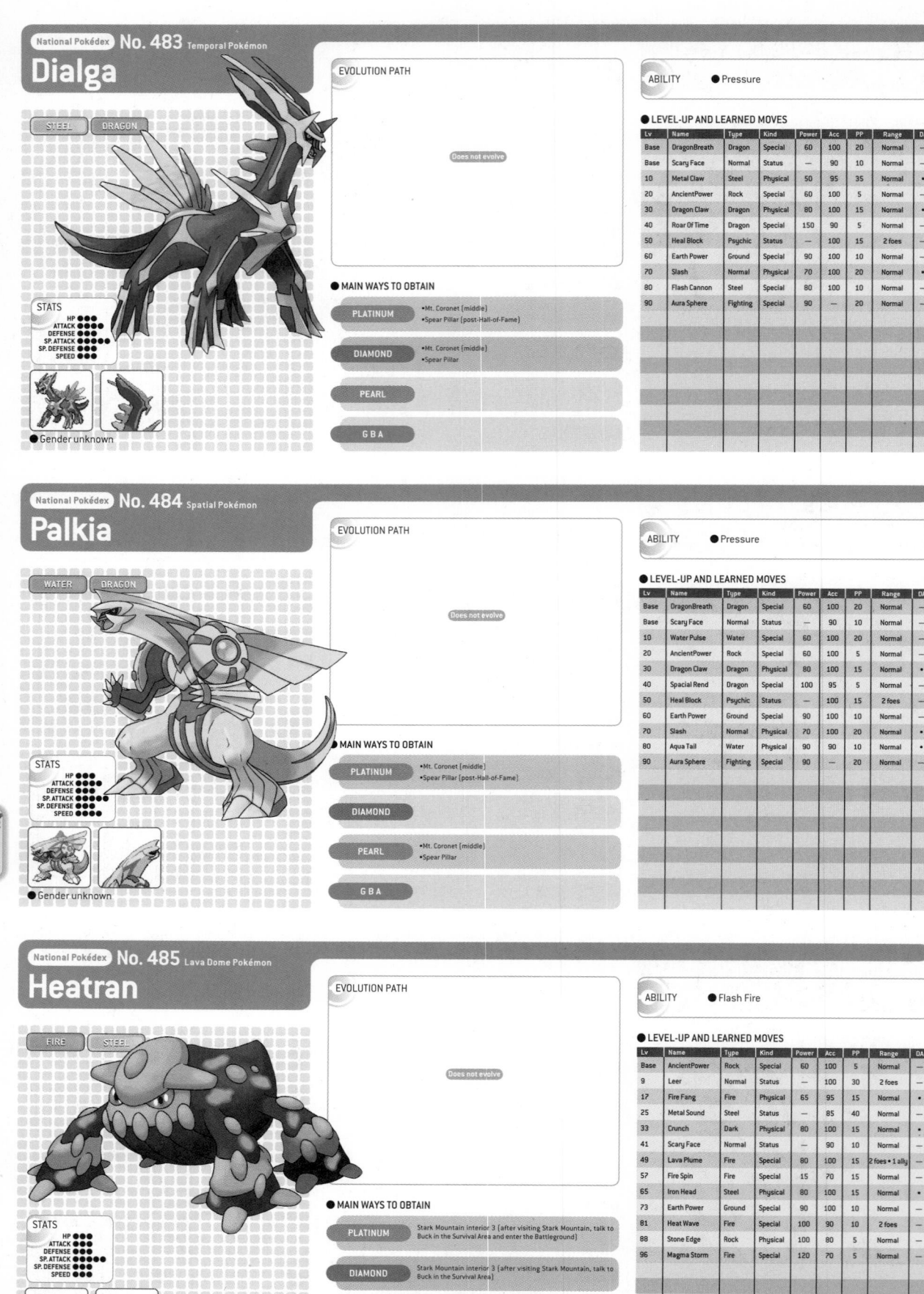

National Pokédex No. 486 Colossal Pokémon
Regigigas

NORMAL

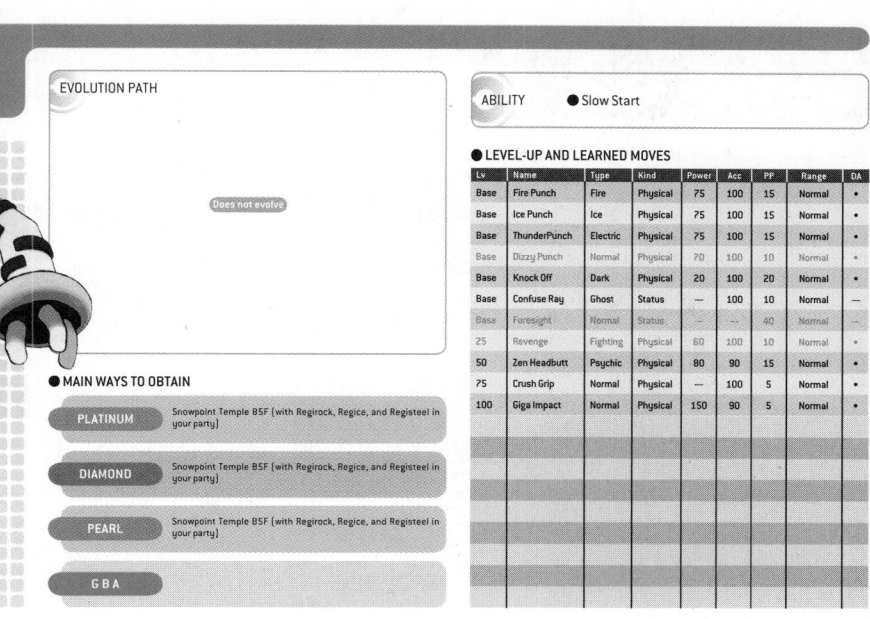

STATS
HP ●●●●
ATTACK ●●●●●
DEFENSE ●●●●
SP. ATTACK ●●●●
SP. DEFENSE ●●●●
SPEED ●●●●

● Gender unknown

EVOLUTION PATH
Does not evolve

● MAIN WAYS TO OBTAIN

PLATINUM	Snowpoint Temple B5F (with Regirock, Regice, and Registeel in your party)
DIAMOND	Snowpoint Temple B5F (with Regirock, Regice, and Registeel in your party)
PEARL	Snowpoint Temple B5F (with Regirock, Regice, and Registeel in your party)
G B A	

ABILITY ● Slow Start

● LEVEL-UP AND LEARNED MOVES

Lv	Name	Type	Kind	Power	Acc	PP	Range	DA
Base	Fire Punch	Fire	Physical	75	100	15	Normal	●
Base	Ice Punch	Ice	Physical	75	100	15	Normal	●
Base	ThunderPunch	Electric	Physical	75	100	15	Normal	●
Base	Dizzy Punch	Normal	Physical	70	100	10	Normal	●
Base	Knock Off	Dark	Physical	20	100	20	Normal	●
Base	Confuse Ray	Ghost	Status	—	100	10	Normal	—
Base	Foresight	Normal	Status	—	—	40	Normal	—
25	Revenge	Fighting	Physical	60	100	10	Normal	●
50	Zen Headbutt	Psychic	Physical	80	90	15	Normal	●
75	Crush Grip	Normal	Physical	—	100	5	Normal	●
100	Giga Impact	Normal	Physical	150	90	5	Normal	●

National Pokédex No. 487 Renegade Pokémon
Giratina (Altered Forme)

GHOST   DRAGON

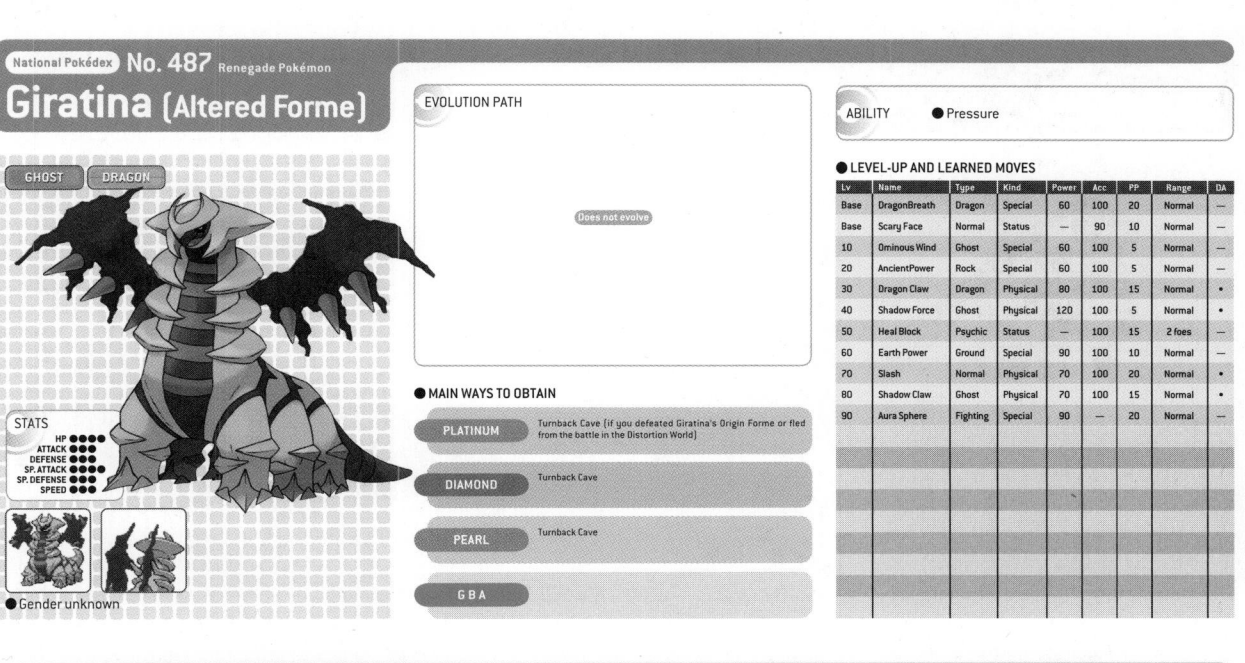

STATS
HP ●●●●
ATTACK ●●●●
DEFENSE ●●●●
SP. ATTACK ●●●●
SP. DEFENSE ●●●●
SPEED ●●●

● Gender unknown

EVOLUTION PATH
Does not evolve

● MAIN WAYS TO OBTAIN

PLATINUM	Turnback Cave (if you defeated Giratina's Origin Forme or fled from the battle in the Distortion World)
DIAMOND	Turnback Cave
PEARL	Turnback Cave
G B A	

ABILITY ● Pressure

● LEVEL-UP AND LEARNED MOVES

Lv	Name	Type	Kind	Power	Acc	PP	Range	DA
Base	DragonBreath	Dragon	Special	60	100	20	Normal	—
Base	Scary Face	Normal	Status	—	90	10	Normal	—
10	Ominous Wind	Ghost	Special	60	100	5	Normal	—
20	AncientPower	Rock	Special	60	100	5	Normal	—
30	Dragon Claw	Dragon	Physical	80	100	15	Normal	●
40	Shadow Force	Ghost	Physical	120	100	5	Normal	●
50	Heal Block	Psychic	Status	—	100	15	2 foes	—
60	Earth Power	Ground	Special	90	100	10	Normal	—
70	Slash	Normal	Physical	70	100	20	Normal	●
80	Shadow Claw	Ghost	Physical	70	100	15	Normal	●
90	Aura Sphere	Fighting	Special	90	—	20	Normal	—

487
●●●●●

National Pokédex No. 487 Renegade Pokémon
Giratina (Origin Forme)

GHOST   DRAGON

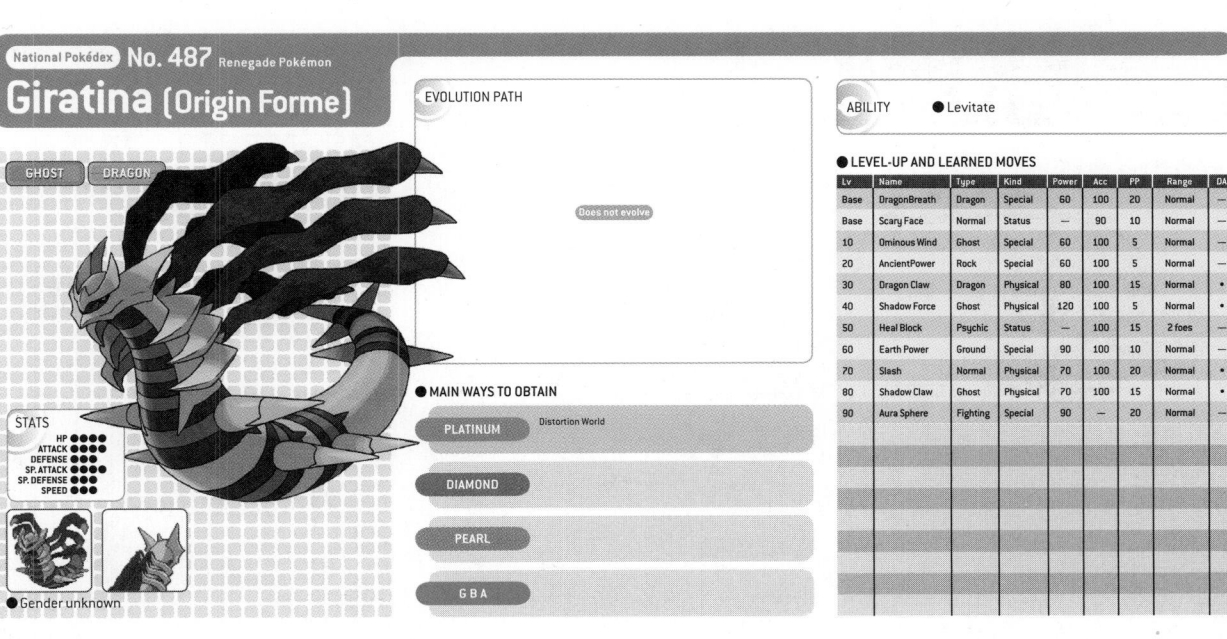

STATS
HP ●●●●
ATTACK ●●●●
DEFENSE ●●●
SP. ATTACK ●●●●
SP. DEFENSE ●●●
SPEED ●●●

● Gender unknown

EVOLUTION PATH
Does not evolve

● MAIN WAYS TO OBTAIN

PLATINUM	Distortion World
DIAMOND	
PEARL	
G B A	

ABILITY ● Levitate

● LEVEL-UP AND LEARNED MOVES

Lv	Name	Type	Kind	Power	Acc	PP	Range	DA
Base	DragonBreath	Dragon	Special	60	100	20	Normal	—
Base	Scary Face	Normal	Status	—	90	10	Normal	—
10	Ominous Wind	Ghost	Special	60	100	5	Normal	—
20	AncientPower	Rock	Special	60	100	5	Normal	—
30	Dragon Claw	Dragon	Physical	80	100	15	Normal	●
40	Shadow Force	Ghost	Physical	120	100	5	Normal	●
50	Heal Block	Psychic	Status	—	100	15	2 foes	—
60	Earth Power	Ground	Special	90	100	10	Normal	—
70	Slash	Normal	Physical	70	100	20	Normal	●
80	Shadow Claw	Ghost	Physical	70	100	15	Normal	●
90	Aura Sphere	Fighting	Special	90	—	20	Normal	—

National Pokédex No. 488 Lunar Pokémon
Cresselia

PSYCHIC

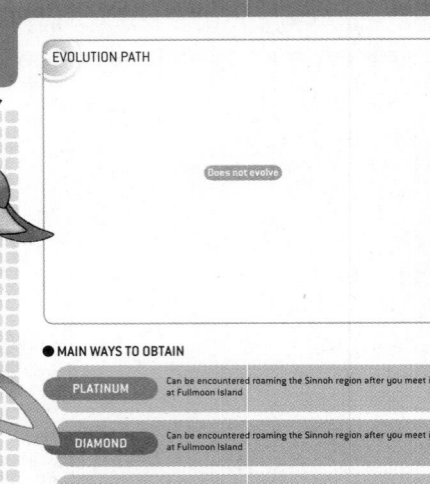

STATS
- HP ●●●●●
- ATTACK ●●●●
- DEFENSE ●●●●
- SP. ATTACK ●●●
- SP. DEFENSE ●●●●●
- SPEED ●●●

● Female form

EVOLUTION PATH
Does not evolve

● MAIN WAYS TO OBTAIN

PLATINUM	Can be encountered roaming the Sinnoh region after you meet it at Fullmoon Island
DIAMOND	Can be encountered roaming the Sinnoh region after you meet it at Fullmoon Island
PEARL	Can be encountered roaming the Sinnoh region after you meet it at Fullmoon Island
GBA	

ABILITY ● Levitate

● LEVEL-UP AND LEARNED MOVES

Lv	Name	Type	Kind	Power	Acc	PP	Range	DA
Base	Confusion	Psychic	Special	50	100	25	Normal	
Base	Double Team	Normal	Status	—	—	15	Self	
11	Safeguard	Normal	Status	—	—	25	2 allies	
20	Mist	Ice	Status	—	—	30	2 allies	
29	Aurora Beam	Ice	Special	65	100	20	Normal	
38	Future Sight	Psychic	Special	80	90	15	Normal	
47	Slash	Normal	Physical	70	100	20	Normal	●
57	Moonlight	Normal	Status	—	—	5	Self	
66	Psycho Cut	Psychic	Physical	70	100	20	Normal	
75	Psycho Shift	Psychic	Status	—	90	10	Normal	
84	Lunar Dance	Psychic	Status	—	—	10	Self	
93	Psychic	Psychic	Special	90	100	10	Normal	

National Pokédex No. 489 Sea Drifter Pokémon
Phione

WATER

STATS
- HP ●●
- ATTACK ●●●
- DEFENSE ●●●
- SP. ATTACK ●●●
- SP. DEFENSE ●●●
- SPEED ●●●

● Gender unknown

EVOLUTION PATH
Does not evolve

● MAIN WAYS TO OBTAIN

PLATINUM	
DIAMOND	Discover an Egg after leaving Manaphy and Ditto together at Pokémon Day Care*
PEARL	Discover an Egg after leaving Manaphy and Ditto together at Pokémon Day Care*
GBA	

*Complete the Special Missions in Pokémon Ranger or Pokémon Ranger: Shadows of Almia to receive a Manaphy Egg. Check Pokémon.com for information on obtaining these Missions or for more news on how to catch this Pokémon.

ABILITY ● Hydration

● LEVEL-UP AND LEARNED MOVES

Lv	Name	Type	Kind	Power	Acc	PP	Range	DA
Base	Bubble	Water	Special	20	100	30	2 foes	—
Base	Water Sport	Water	Status	—	—	15	All	—
9	Charm	Normal	Status	—	100	20	Normal	—
16	Supersonic	Normal	Status	—	55	20	Normal	—
24	BubbleBeam	Water	Special	65	100	20	Normal	—
31	Acid Armor	Poison	Status	—	—	40	Self	—
39	Whirlpool	Water	Special	15	70	15	Normal	—
46	Water Pulse	Water	Special	60	100	20	Normal	—
54	Aqua Ring	Water	Status	—	—	20	Self	—
61	Dive	Water	Physical	80	100	10	Normal	●
69	Rain Dance	Water	Status	—	—	5	All	—

National Pokédex No. 490 Seafaring Pokémon
Manaphy

WATER

STATS
- HP ●●●
- ATTACK ●●●
- DEFENSE ●●●
- SP. ATTACK ●●●
- SP. DEFENSE ●●●●
- SPEED ●●●●

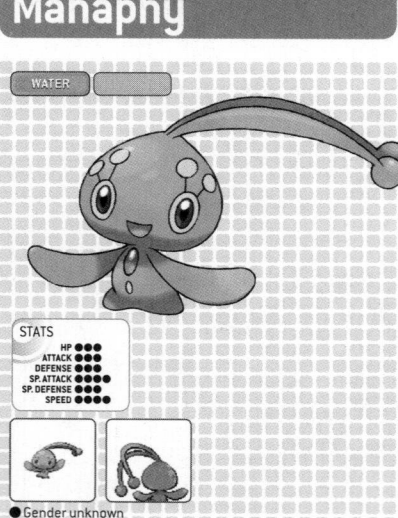

● Gender unknown

EVOLUTION PATH
Does not evolve

● MAIN WAYS TO OBTAIN

PLATINUM	
DIAMOND	Only available via distribution at special events and not through regular gameplay.*
PEARL	Only available via distribution at special events and not through regular gameplay.*
GBA	

*Complete the Special Missions in Pokémon Ranger or Pokémon Ranger: Shadows of Almia to receive a Manaphy Egg. Check Pokémon.com for news on obtaining these Missions or for more information on how to catch this Pokémon.

ABILITY ● Hydration

● LEVEL-UP AND LEARNED MOVES

Lv	Name	Type	Kind	Power	Acc	PP	Range	DA
Base	Tail Glow	Bug	Status	—	—	20	Self	—
Base	Bubble	Water	Special	20	100	30	2 foes	—
Base	Water Sport	Water	Status	—	—	15	All	—
9	Charm	Normal	Status	—	100	20	Normal	—
16	Supersonic	Normal	Status	—	55	20	Normal	—
24	BubbleBeam	Water	Special	65	100	20	Normal	—
31	Acid Armor	Poison	Status	—	—	40	Self	—
39	Whirlpool	Water	Special	15	70	15	Normal	—
46	Water Pulse	Water	Special	60	100	20	Normal	—
54	Aqua Ring	Water	Status	—	—	20	Self	—
61	Dive	Water	Physical	80	100	10	Normal	●
69	Rain Dance	Water	Status	—	—	5	All	—
76	Heart Swap	Psychic	Status	—	—	10	Normal	—

488

National Pokédex No. 491 Pitch-Black Pokémon
Darkrai

DARK

HEIGHT: **4'11"**
WEIGHT: **111.3 lbs.**
GENDER: **Unknown**
HELD ITEM: **None**

● Gender unknown

POKÉDEX — To protect itself, it afflicts those around it with nightmares. However, it means no harm.

EVOLUTION PATH

Does not evolve

● TM & HM MOVES

No.	Name	Type	Kind	Power	Acc	PP	Range	DA
TM01	Focus Punch	Fighting	Physical	150	100	20	Normal	—
TM04	Calm Mind	Psychic	Status	—	—	20	Self	—
TM06	Toxic	Poison	Status	—	85	10	Normal	—
TM10	Hidden Power	Normal	Special	—	100	15	Normal	—
TM11	Sunny Day	Fire	Status	—	—	5	All	—
TM12	Taunt	Dark	Status	—	100	20	Normal	—
TM13	Ice Beam	Ice	Special	95	100	10	Normal	—
TM14	Blizzard	Ice	Special	120	70	5	2 foes	—
TM15	Hyper Beam	Normal	Special	150	90	5	Normal	—
TM17	Protect	Normal	Status	—	—	10	Self	—
TM18	Rain Dance	Water	Status	—	—	5	All	—
TM21	Frustration	Normal	Physical	—	100	20	Normal	•
TM24	Thunderbolt	Electric	Special	95	100	15	Normal	—
TM25	Thunder	Electric	Special	120	70	10	Normal	—
TM27	Return	Normal	Physical	—	100	20	Normal	•
TM29	Psychic	Psychic	Special	90	100	10	Normal	—
TM30	Shadow Ball	Ghost	Special	80	100	15	Normal	—
TM31	Brick Break	Fighting	Physical	75	100	15	Normal	•
TM32	Double Team	Normal	Status	—	—	15	Self	—
TM34	Shock Wave	Electric	Special	60	—	20	Normal	—
TM36	Sludge Bomb	Poison	Special	90	100	10	Normal	—
TM39	Rock Tomb	Rock	Physical	50	80	10	Normal	•
TM40	Aerial Ace	Flying	Physical	60	—	20	Normal	•
TM41	Torment	Dark	Status	—	100	15	Normal	—
TM42	Facade	Normal	Physical	70	100	20	Normal	•
TM43	Secret Power	Normal	Physical	70	100	20	Normal	•
TM44	Rest	Psychic	Status	—	—	10	Self	—
TM46	Thief	Dark	Physical	40	100	10	Normal	•
TM49	Snatch	Dark	Status	—	—	10	DoM	
TM52	Focus Blast	Fighting	Special	120	70	5	Normal	—
TM56	Fling	Dark	Physical	—	100	10	Normal	•
TM57	Charge Beam	Electric	Special	50	90	10	Normal	—
TM58	Endure	Normal	Status	—	—	10	Self	—
TM60	Drain Punch	Fighting	Physical	60	100	5	Normal	•
TM61	Will-O-Wisp	Fire	Status	—	75	15	Normal	—
TM63	Embargo	Dark	Status	—	100	15	Normal	—
TM65	Shadow Claw	Ghost	Physical	70	100	15	Normal	•
TM66	Payback	Dark	Physical	50	100	10	Normal	•
TM68	Giga Impact	Normal	Physical	150	90	5	Normal	•
TM70	Flash	Normal	Status	—	100	20	Normal	—
TM73	Thunder Wave	Electric	Status	—	100	20	Normal	—
TM75	Swords Dance	Normal	Status	—	—	30	Self	—
TM77	Psych Up	Normal	Status	—	—	10	Normal	—
TM79	Dark Pulse	Dark	Special	80	100	15	Normal	—
TM80	Rock Slide	Rock	Physical	75	90	10	2 foes	•
TM81	X-Scissor	Bug	Physical	80	100	15	Normal	•
TM82	Sleep Talk	Normal	Status	—	—	10	DoM	
TM83	Natural Gift	Normal	Physical	—	100	15	Normal	•
TM84	Poison Jab	Poison	Physical	80	100	20	Normal	•
TM85	Dream Eater	Psychic	Special	100	100	15	Normal	—
TM87	Swagger	Normal	Status	—	90	15	Normal	—
TM90	Substitute	Normal	Status	—	—	10	Self	—
HM01	Cut	Normal	Physical	50	95	30	Normal	•
HM04	Strength	Normal	Physical	80	100	15	Normal	•
HM06	Rock Smash	Fighting	Physical	40	100	15	Normal	•
HM08	Rock Climb	Normal	Physical	90	85	20	Normal	•

● LEVEL-UP AND LEARNED MOVES

Lv	Name	Type	Kind	Power	Acc	PP	Range	DA
Base	Ominous Wind	Ghost	Special	60	100	5	Normal	—
Base	Disable	Normal	Status	—	80	20	Normal	—
11	Quick Attack	Normal	Physical	40	100	30	Normal	•
20	Hypnosis	Psychic	Status	—	60	20	Normal	—
29	Faint Attack	Dark	Physical	60	—	20	Normal	•
38	Nightmare	Ghost	Status	—	100	15	Normal	—
47	Double Team	Normal	Status	—	—	15	Self	—
57	Haze	Ice	Status	—	—	30	All	—
66	Dark Void	Dark	Status	—	80	10	2 foes	—
75	Nasty Plot	Dark	Status	—	—	20	Self	—
84	Dream Eater	Psychic	Special	100	100	15	Normal	—
93	Dark Pulse	Dark	Special	80	100	15	Normal	—

● MOVES TAUGHT IN EXCHANGE FOR COLORED SHARDS

Name	Type	Kind	Power	Acc	PP	Range	DA
Mud-Slap	Ground	Special	20	100	10	Normal	—
Icy Wind	Ice	Special	55	95	15	2 foes	—
Ominous Wind	Ghost	Special	60	100	5	Normal	—
Snore	Normal	Special	40	100	15	Normal	—
Spite	Ghost	Status	—	100	10	Normal	—
Last Resort	Normal	Physical	130	100	5	Normal	•
Trick	Psychic	Status	—	100	10	Normal	—
Knock Off	Dark	Physical	20	100	20	Normal	•
Sucker Punch	Dark	Physical	80	100	5	Normal	•
Swift	Normal	Special	60	—	20	2 foes	—

● MAIN WAYS TO OBTAIN

PLATINUM	
DIAMOND	Only available via distribution at special events and not through regular gameplay.*
PEARL	Only available via distribution at special events and not through regular gameplay.*
GBA	

*Complete the Special Mission in Pokémon Ranger: Shadows of Almia to capture a Darkrai. Check Pokemon.com for news on obtaining this Mission or for more information on how to catch this Pokémon.

ABILITY ● Bad Dreams

EGG GROUP No Egg discovered

STATS
HP ●●
ATTACK ●●●
DEFENSE ●●●
SP. ATTACK ●●●●●
SP. DEFENSE ●●●
SPEED ●●●●

National Pokédex No. 492 Gratitude Pokémon
Shaymin (Land Forme)

GRASS

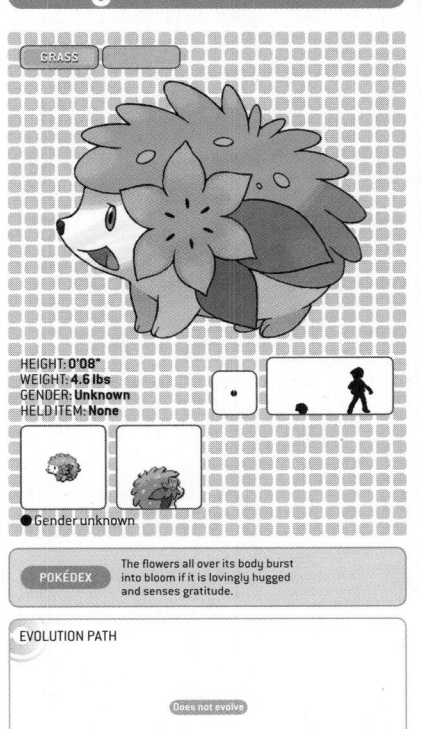

HEIGHT: **0'08"**
WEIGHT: **4.6 lbs**
GENDER: **Unknown**
HELD ITEM: **None**

● Gender unknown

POKÉDEX — The flowers all over its body burst into bloom if it is lovingly hugged and senses gratitude.

EVOLUTION PATH

Does not evolve

● TM & HM MOVES

No.	Name	Type	Kind	Power	Acc	PP	Range	DA
TM06	Toxic	Poison	Status	—	85	10	Normal	—
TM09	Bullet Seed	Grass	Physical	10	100	30	Normal	—
TM10	Hidden Power	Normal	Special	—	100	15	Normal	—
TM11	Sunny Day	Fire	Status	—	—	5	All	—
TM15	Hyper Beam	Normal	Special	150	90	5	Normal	—
TM17	Protect	Normal	Status	—	—	10	Self	—
TM19	Giga Drain	Grass	Special	60	100	10	Normal	—
TM20	Safeguard	Normal	Status	—	—	25	2 allies	—
TM21	Frustration	Normal	Physical	—	100	20	Normal	•
TM22	SolarBeam	Grass	Special	120	100	10	Normal	—
TM27	Return	Normal	Physical	—	100	20	Normal	•
TM29	Psychic	Psychic	Special	90	100	10	Normal	—
TM32	Double Team	Normal	Status	—	—	15	Self	—
TM42	Facade	Normal	Physical	70	100	20	Normal	•
TM43	Secret Power	Normal	Physical	70	100	20	Normal	•
TM44	Rest	Psychic	Status	—	—	10	Self	—
TM53	Energy Ball	Grass	Special	80	100	10	Normal	—
TM58	Endure	Normal	Status	—	—	10	Self	—
TM68	Giga Impact	Normal	Physical	150	90	5	Normal	•
TM70	Flash	Normal	Status	—	100	20	Normal	—
TM75	Swords Dance	Normal	Status	—	—	30	Self	—
TM77	Psych Up	Normal	Status	—	—	10	Normal	—
TM82	Sleep Talk	Normal	Status	—	—	10	DoM	
TM83	Natural Gift	Normal	Physical	—	100	15	Normal	•
TM86	Grass Knot	Grass	Special	—	100	20	Normal	•
TM87	Swagger	Normal	Status	—	90	15	Normal	—
TM90	Substitute	Normal	Status	—	—	10	Self	—

● LEVEL-UP AND LEARNED MOVES

Lv	Name	Type	Kind	Power	Acc	PP	Range	DA
Base	Growth	Normal	Status	—	—	40	Self	—
10	Magical Leaf	Grass	Special	60	—	20	Normal	—
19	Leech Seed	Grass	Status	—	90	10	Normal	—
28	Synthesis	Grass	Status	—	—	5	Self	—
37	Sweet Scent	Normal	Status	—	100	20	2 foes	•
46	Natural Gift	Normal	Physical	—	100	15	Normal	•
55	Worry Seed	Grass	Status	—	100	10	Normal	—
64	Aromatherapy	Grass	Status	—	—	5	All	—
73	Energy Ball	Grass	Special	80	100	10	Normal	—
82	Sweet Kiss	Normal	Status	—	75	10	Normal	—
91	Healing Wish	Psychic	Status	—	—	10	Self	—
100	Seed Flare	Grass	Special	120	85	5	Normal	—

● MOVES TAUGHT IN EXCHANGE FOR COLORED SHARDS

Name	Type	Kind	Power	Acc	PP	Range	DA
Mud-Slap	Ground	Special	20	100	10	Normal	—
Snore	Normal	Special	40	100	15	Normal	—
Endeavor	Normal	Physical	—	100	5	Normal	•
Synthesis	Grass	Status	—	—	5	Self	—
Zen Headbutt	Psychic	Physical	80	90	15	Normal	•
Earth Power	Ground	Special	90	100	10	Normal	—
Seed Bomb	Grass	Physical	80	100	15	Normal	•
Last Resort	Normal	Physical	130	100	5	Normal	•
Swift	Normal	Special	60	—	20	2 foes	—

● MAIN WAYS TO OBTAIN

PLATINUM	
DIAMOND	Only available via distribution at special events and not through regular gameplay.*
PEARL	Only available via distribution at special events and not through regular gameplay.*
GBA	

*Check Pokemon.com for the latest news on how to catch this Pokémon.

ABILITY ● Natural Cure

EGG GROUP No Egg discovered

STATS
HP ●●●
ATTACK ●●●
DEFENSE ●●●
SP. ATTACK ●●●●
SP. DEFENSE ●●●●
SPEED ●●●●

*Shaymin Forme Changes into its Sky Forme when you use the Gracidea obtained in Floaroma Town.
* It returns to its Land Forme between 8 PM and 4 AM (during which time you cannot use the Gracidea).
* It also returns to Land Forme when Frozen.

No. 492 Gratitude Pokémon

Shaymin (Sky Forme)

GRASS FLYING

HEIGHT: **1'04"**
WEIGHT: **11.5 lbs.**
GENDER: **Unknown**
HELD ITEM: **None**

● Gender unknown

POKÉDEX
The flowers all over its body burst into bloom if it is lovingly hugged and senses gratitude.

EVOLUTION PATH

Does not evolve

ABILITY ● Serene Grace

EGG GROUP No Egg discovered

● TM & HM MOVES

No.	Name	Type	Kind	Power	Acc	PP	Range	DA
TM06	Toxic	Poison	Status	—	85	10	Normal	—
TM09	Bullet Seed	Grass	Physical	10	100	30	Normal	—
TM10	Hidden Power	Normal	Special	—	100	15	Normal	—
TM11	Sunny Day	Fire	Status	—	—	5	All	—
TM15	Hyper Beam	Normal	Special	150	90	5	Normal	—
TM17	Protect	Normal	Status	—	—	10	Self	—
TM19	Giga Drain	Grass	Special	60	100	10	Normal	—
TM20	Safeguard	Normal	Status	—	—	25	2 allies	—
TM21	Frustration	Normal	Physical	—	100	20	Normal	•
TM22	SolarBeam	Grass	Special	120	100	10	Normal	—
TM27	Return	Normal	Physical	—	100	20	Normal	•
TM29	Psychic	Psychic	Special	90	100	10	Normal	—
TM32	Double Team	Normal	Status	—	—	15	Self	—
TM42	Facade	Normal	Physical	70	100	20	Normal	•
TM43	Secret Power	Normal	Physical	70	100	20	Normal	•
TM44	Rest	Psychic	Status	—	—	10	Self	—
TM53	Energy Ball	Grass	Special	80	100	10	Normal	—
TM58	Endure	Normal	Status	—	—	10	Self	—
TM68	Giga Impact	Normal	Physical	150	90	5	Normal	•
TM70	Flash	Normal	Status	—	100	20	Normal	—
TM75	Swords Dance	Normal	Status	—	—	30	Self	—
TM77	Psych Up	Normal	Status	—	—	10	Normal	—
TM82	Sleep Talk	Normal	Status	—	—	10	DoM	—
TM83	Natural Gift	Normal	Physical	—	100	15	Normal	—
TM86	Grass Knot	Grass	Special	—	100	20	Normal	•
TM87	Swagger	Normal	Status	—	90	15	Normal	—
TM90	Substitute	Normal	Status	—	—	10	Self	—

● LEVEL-UP AND LEARNED MOVES

Lv	Name	Type	Kind	Power	Acc	PP	Range	DA
Base	Growth	Normal	Status	—	—	40	Self	—
10	Magical Leaf	Grass	Special	60	—	20	Normal	—
19	Leech Seed	Grass	Status	—	90	10	Normal	—
28	Quick Attack	Normal	Physical	40	100	30	Normal	•
37	Sweet Scent	Normal	Status	—	100	20	2 foes	—
46	Natural Gift	Normal	Physical	—	100	15	Normal	—
55	Worry Seed	Grass	Status	—	100	10	Normal	—
64	Air Slash	Flying	Special	75	95	20	Normal	—
73	Energy Ball	Grass	Special	80	100	10	Normal	—
82	Sweet Kiss	Normal	Status	—	75	10	Normal	—
91	Leaf Storm	Grass	Special	140	90	5	Normal	—
100	Seed Flare	Grass	Special	120	85	5	Normal	—

● MOVES TAUGHT IN EXCHANGE FOR COLORED SHARDS

Name	Type	Kind	Power	Acc	PP	Range	DA
Mud-Slap	Ground	Special	20	100	10	Normal	—
Ominous Wind	Ghost	Special	60	100	5	Normal	—
Snore	Normal	Special	40	100	15	Normal	—
Air Cutter	Flying	Special	55	95	25	2 foes	—
Synthesis	Grass	Status	—	—	5	Self	—
Zen Headbutt	Psychic	Physical	80	90	15	Normal	•
Seed Bomb	Grass	Physical	80	100	15	Normal	—
Last Resort	Normal	Physical	130	100	5	Normal	•
Swift	Normal	Special	60	—	20	2 foes	—

● MAIN WAYS TO OBTAIN

PLATINUM

DIAMOND Only available via distribution at special events and not through regular gameplay.*

PEARL Only available via distribution at special events and not through regular gameplay.*

GBA

*Check Pokémon.com for the latest news on how to catch this Pokémon.

STATS
HP ●●●
ATTACK ●●●●
DEFENSE ●●
SP. ATTACK ●●●●
SP. DEFENSE ●●●
SPEED ●●●●

*Shaymin Forme Changes into its Sky Forme when you use the Gracidea obtained in Floaroma Town.
* It returns to its Land Forme between 8 PM and 4 AM (during which time you cannot use the Gracidea).
* It also returns to Land Forme when Frozen.

Adventure Data List

Move	Type	Kind	POW	Acc	PP	Range	DA	Effect
Absorb	Grass	Special	20	100	25	Normal		Restores HP equal to half of damage inflicted on target
Acid	Poison	Special	40	100	30	2 foes		10% chance of lowering target's Sp. Defense by 1. Has lower power in Double Battles
Acid Armor	Poison	Status	—	—	40	Self		Raises user's Defense by 2
Acupressure	Normal	Status	—	—	30	1 ally		Raises a random stat by 2
Aerial Ace	Flying	Physical	60	—	20	Normal	•	Always strikes target
Aeroblast	Flying	Special	100	95	5	Normal		High critical hit rate
Agility	Psychic	Status	—	—	30	Self		Raises user's Speed by 2
Air Cutter	Flying	Special	55	95	25	2 foes		High critical hit rate. Has weaker attack power in Double Battles
Air Slash	Flying	Special	75	95	20	Normal		30% chance of making target flinch (cannot use moves for that turn)
Amnesia	Psychic	Status	—	—	20	Self		Raises user's Sp. Defense by 2
AncientPower	Rock	Special	60	100	5	Normal		10% chance of lowering Attack, Defense, Speed, Sp. Attack, and Sp. Defense by 1
Aqua Jet	Water	Physical	40	100	20	Normal	•	Always attacks first (if both opponents use this move, the one with the higher Speed goes first)
Aqua Ring	Water	Status	—	—	20	Self		Restores HP gradually with every turn
Aqua Tail	Water	Physical	90	90	10	Normal	•	Regular attack
Arm Thrust	Fighting	Physical	15	100	20	Normal	•	Attacks 2-5 times in a row in one turn
Aromatherapy	Grass	Status	—	—	5	All allies		Heals status ailments for all ally Pokémon in your party
Assist	Normal	Status	—	—	20	Depends		Uses a random move from one of your Pokémon that isn't in battle
Assurance	Dark	Physical	50	100	10	Normal	•	Double damage if target has already taken damage that turn
Astonish	Ghost	Physical	30	100	15	Normal	•	30% chance of making target flinch (cannot use moves for that turn)
Attack Order	Bug	Physical	90	100	15	Normal		High critical hit rate
Attract	Normal	Status	—	100	15	Normal		50% chance of making target unable to attack. Only works if user and target are different genders
Aura Sphere	Fighting	Special	90	—	20	Normal		Always strikes target
Aurora Beam	Ice	Special	65	100	20	Normal		10% chance of lowering target's Attack by 1
Avalanche	Ice	Physical	60	100	10	Normal	•	Double damage if user has received damage from target that turn
Barrage	Normal	Physical	15	85	20	Normal		Attacks 2-5 times in a row in one turn
Barrier	Psychic	Status	—	—	30	Self		Raises user's Defense by 2
Baton Pass	Normal	Status	—	—	40	Self		Swaps out with an ally Pokémon, passing along any stat alterations
Beat Up	Dark	Physical	10	100	10	Normal		Attacks according to the number of Pokémon in your party, including user but not KO'ed Pokémon
Belly Drum	Normal	Status	—	—	10	Self		Halves user's HP, but raises its Attack to the maximum
Bide	Normal	Physical	—	—	10	Self	•	Counter-inflicts double the damage received in the 2 subsequent turns
Bind	Normal	Physical	15	75	20	Normal	•	Inflicts damage over 2-5 turns. Target cannot escape during that time
Bite	Dark	Physical	60	100	25	Normal	•	30% chance of making target flinch (cannot use moves for that turn)
Blast Burn	Fire	Special	150	90	5	Normal		Cannot act on following turn. If target is frozen, melts the ice
Blaze Kick	Fire	Physical	85	90	10	Normal	•	10% chance of burning target. If target is frozen, melts the ice. High critical hit rate.
Blizzard	Ice	Special	120	70	5	2 foes		10% chance of freezing target. Has less power in Double Battles
Block	Normal	Status	—	—	5	Normal		Makes target unable to escape. In a Trainer battle, the Trainer cannot switch Pokémon
Body Slam	Normal	Physical	85	100	15	Normal	•	30% chance of paralyzing target
Bone Club	Ground	Physical	65	85	20	Normal		10% chance of making target flinch (cannot use moves for that turn)
Bone Rush	Ground	Physical	25	80	10	Normal		Attacks 2-5 times in a row in one turn
Bonemerang	Ground	Physical	50	90	10	Normal		Attacks twice in a row in one turn
Bounce	Flying	Physical	85	85	5	Normal	•	Flies into the air on first turn, attacks on second. 30% chance of paralyzing target
Brave Bird	Flying	Physical	120	100	15	Normal	•	User takes 1/3 of the damage inflicted on target
Brick Break	Fighting	Physical	75	100	15	Normal	•	Not subject to the effects of Reflect. Breaks through Reflect and Light Screen
Brine	Water	Special	65	100	10	Normal		Double damage if target has less than half its HP
Bubble	Water	Special	20	100	30	2 foes		10% chance of lowering target's Speed. Weaker in Double Battles

Move	Type	Kind	POW	Acc	PP	Range	DA	Effect
BubbleBeam	Water	Special	65	100	20	Normal		10% chance of lowering target's Speed
Bug Bite	Bug	Physical	60	100	20	Normal	•	Hijacks the effects of any berry target is holding that has an effect in battle
Bug Buzz	Bug	Special	90	100	10	Normal		10% chance of lowering target's Sp. Defense by 1
Bulk Up	Fighting	Status	—	—	20	Self		Raises user's Attack and Defense by 1
Bullet Punch	Steel	Physical	40	100	30	Normal	•	Always strikes first (if both sides use this move, the one with the higher Speed goes first)
Bullet Seed	Grass	Physical	10	100	30	Normal		Attacks 2-5 times in a row in one turn
Calm Mind	Psychic	Status	—	—	20	Self		Raises user's Sp. Attack and Sp. Defense by 1
Camouflage	Normal	Status	—	—	20	Self		Changes user's type in accordance with the terrain. Tall grass/water puddle: Grass-type. Sandy ground/marsh: Ground-type. Rocky ground/cave: Rock-type. Water surface: Water-type. Snowy or icy ground: Ice-type. Floor: Normal-type.
Captivate	Normal	Status	—	100	20	2 foes		Lowers Sp. Attack by 2. Only works if user and target are opposite genders
Charge	Electric	Status	—	—	20	Self		Doubles attack power of Electric-type move used on following turn. Raises user's Sp. Defense by 1
Charge Beam	Electric	Special	50	90	10	Normal		70% chance of raising user's Sp. Attack by 1
Charm	Normal	Status	—	100	20	Normal		Lowers target's Attack by 1
Chatter	Flying	Special	60	100	20	Normal		May confuse target—likelihood depends on the volume of the sound you recorded (Chatot only)
Clamp	Water	Physical	35	75	10	Normal	•	Inflicts damage for 2-5 turns. Target cannot escape during that time
Close Combat	Fighting	Physical	120	100	5	Normal	•	Lowers user's Defense and Sp. Defense by 1
Comet Punch	Normal	Physical	18	85	15	Normal	•	Attacks 2-5 times in one turn
Confuse Ray	Ghost	Status	—	100	10	Normal		Confuses target
Confusion	Psychic	Special	50	100	25	Normal		10% chance of confusing target
Constrict	Normal	Physical	10	100	35	Normal	•	10% chance of lowering target's Speed by 1
Conversion	Normal	Status	—	—	30	Self		Changes user's type to that of one of its moves
Conversion 2	Normal	Status	—	—	30	Self		Changes user's type to one strong against the last move the target used
Copycat	Normal	Status	—	—	20	Depends		Uses the last move used
Cosmic Power	Psychic	Status	—	—	20	Self		Raises user's Defense and Sp. Defense by 1
Cotton Spore	Grass	Status	—	85	40	Normal		Lowers target's Speed by 2-5 levels
Counter	Fighting	Physical	—	100	20	Self	•	Counter-inflicts twice the damage received from a physical attack from target. Always strikes last
Covet	Normal	Physical	40	100	40	Normal	•	If user is not holding an item, steals target's item
Crabhammer	Water	Physical	90	85	10	Normal	•	High critical hit rate
Cross Chop	Fighting	Physical	100	80	5	Normal	•	High critical hit rate
Cross Poison	Poison	Physical	70	100	20	Normal	•	High critical hit rate. 10% chance of poisoning target
Crunch	Dark	Physical	80	100	15	Normal	•	20% chance of lowering target's Defense by 1
Crush Claw	Normal	Physical	75	95	10	Normal	•	50% chance of lowering target's Defense by 1
Crush Grip	Normal	Physical	—	100	5	Normal	•	Has higher attack power the more HP target has remaining (max 120)
Cut	Normal	Physical	50	95	30	Normal	•	Regular attack
Curse	???	Status	—	—	10	Normal •Self		Lowers user's Speed by 1 and raises its Attack and Defense by 1
Dark Pulse	Dark	Special	80	100	15	Normal		20% chance of making target flinch (cannot use moves for that turn)
Dark Void	Dark	Status	—	80	10	2 foes		Puts target to sleep
Defend Order	Bug	Status	—	—	10	Self		Raises user's Defense and Sp. Defense by 1
Defense Curl	Normal	Status	—	—	40	Self		Raises user's Defense by 1
Defog	Flying	Status	—	—	15	Normal		Lowers target's Evasion by 1. Nullifies the effects of target's Light Screen, Reflect, Safeguard, Mist, Spikes, or Toxic Spikes, and nullifies Fog weather
Destiny Bond	Ghost	Status	—	—	5	Self		After use, if user faints due to damage from target, target faints too
Detect	Fighting	Status	—	—	5	Self		Protects against move used by target on that turn. Chance of failure increases with each successive use
Dig	Ground	Physical	80	100	10	Normal	•	Burrows underground on first turn, and attacks on second
Disable	Normal	Status	—	80	20	Normal		Prevents target from using its last-used move for several turns

Move	Type	Kind	POW	Acc	PP	Range	DA	Effect
Discharge	Electric	Special	80	100	15	2 foes - 1 ally		30% chance of paralyzing target. Lower power in Double Battles
Dive	Water	Physical	80	100	10	Normal	•	Dives underwater on first turn, attacks on second
Dizzy Punch	Normal	Physical	70	100	10	Normal	•	20% chance of confusing target
Doom Desire	Steel	Special	120	85	5	Normal		Attacks target after 2 turns. Inflicts damage regardless of target's type
Double Hit	Normal	Physical	35	90	10	Normal	•	Attacks twice in a row in one turn
Double Kick	Fighting	Physical	30	100	30	Normal	•	Attacks twice in a row in one turn
Double Team	Normal	Status	—	—	15	Self		Raises user's Evasion by 1
Double-Edge	Normal	Physical	120	100	15	Normal	•	User takes damage equal to 1/3 of damage inflicted on target
DoubleSlap	Normal	Physical	15	85	10	Normal	•	Attacks successively 2-5 times
Draco Meteor	Dragon	Special	140	90	5	Normal		Lowers user's Sp. Attack by 2
Dream Eater	Psychic	Special	100	100	15	Normal		Only works when target is asleep. Restores HP equal to half the damage inflicted on target
Dragon Claw	Dragon	Physical	80	100	15	Normal	•	Regular attack
Dragon Dance	Dragon	Status	—	—	20	Self		Raises user's Attack and Speed by 1
Dragon Pulse	Dragon	Special	90	100	10	Normal		Regular attack
Dragon Rage	Dragon	Special	—	100	10	Normal		Deals a fixed 40 points of damage
Dragon Rush	Dragon	Physical	100	75	10	Normal	•	20% chance of making target flinch (cannot use moves for that turn)
DragonBreath	Dragon	Special	60	100	20	Normal		30% chance of paralyzing target
Drain Punch	Fighting	Physical	60	100	5	Normal	•	Restores HP equal to half the damage dealt to target
Drill Peck	Flying	Physical	80	100	20	Normal	•	Regular attack
DynamicPunch	Fighting	Physical	100	50	5	Normal	•	100% chance of confusing target
Earth Power	Ground	Special	90	100	10	Normal		10% chance of lowering target's Sp. Defense
Earthquake	Ground	Physical	100	100	10	2 foes 1 ally		Regular attack. Double damage if target is using Dig when hit. Has lower attack power in Double Battles.
Egg Bomb	Normal	Physical	100	75	10	Normal		Regular attack
Embargo	Dark	Status	—	100	15	Normal		Makes target unable to use items for 5 turns. Trainer cannot use items on that Pokémon either
Ember	Fire	Special	40	100	25	Normal		10% chance of burning target. If target is frozen, melts the ice
Encore	Normal	Status	—	100	5	Normal		Turns the target's last move back on itself. Works for 2-6 turns
Endeavor	Normal	Physical	—	100	5	Normal	•	Inflicts damage equal to target's HP minus user's HP
Endure	Normal	Status	—	—	10	Self		User is left with 1 HP even after a knock-out hit. Failure rate rises with each successive use
Energy Ball	Grass	Special	80	100	10	Normal		10% chance of lowering target's Sp. Defense by 1
Eruption	Fire	Special	150	100	5	2 foes		Lower power if user has low HP. If target is frozen, melts the ice. Lower power in Double Battles
Explosion	Normal	Physical	250	100	5	2 foes 1 ally		User faints after using. Deals damage as if target's Defense were halved. Has lower attack power in Double Battles
Extrasensory	Psychic	Special	80	100	30	Normal		10% chance of making target flinch (cannot use a move for this turn)
ExtremeSpeed	Normal	Physical	80	100	5	Normal	•	Always strikes first (if both sides use this move, the one with the higher Speed goes first)
Facade	Normal	Physical	70	100	20	Normal	•	Double damage if used when user is poisoned, paralyzed, or burned
Faint Attack	Dark	Physical	60	—	20	Normal	•	Always strikes target
Fake Out	Normal	Physical	40	100	10	Normal	•	Always strikes first. 100% chance of making target flinch. Only works on the turn that user is sent out
Fake Tears	Dark	Status	—	100	20	Normal		Lowers target's Sp. Defense by 2
False Swipe	Normal	Physical	40	100	40	Normal	•	Leaves target with 1 HP remaining even if the damage would have knocked it out
FeatherDance	Flying	Status	—	100	15	Normal		Lowers target's Attack by 2
Feint	Normal	Physical	50	100	10	Normal		Only hits targets using Protect or Detect, and eliminates those effects
Fire Blast	Fire	Special	120	85	5	Normal		10% chance of burning target. If target is frozen, melts the ice
Fire Fang	Fire	Physical	65	95	15	Normal	•	10% chance of burning target or making it flinch. If target is frozen, melts the ice
Fire Punch	Fire	Physical	75	100	15	Normal	•	10% chance of burning target. If target is frozen, melts the ice
Fire Spin	Fire	Special	15	70	15	Normal		Inflicts damage and prevents target from fleeing for 2-5 turns. If target is frozen, melts the ice
Fissure	Ground	Physical	—	30	5	Normal		One-hit KO. Does not strike if target's level is higher than user's. Has higher Accuracy the lower target's is

ADVENTURE DATA LIST

POKÉMON BATTLE MOVES

Move	Type	Kind	POW	Acc	PP	Range	DA	Effect
Flail	Normal	Physical	—	100	15	Normal	•	Deals greater damage to target the lower user's HP is
Flame Wheel	Fire	Physical	60	100	25	Normal	•	10% chance of burning target. If target is frozen, melts the ice. Can be used even if user is frozen. If so, melts the ice
Flamethrower	Fire	Special	95	100	15	Normal		10% chance of burning target. If target is frozen, melts the ice
Flare Blitz	Fire	Physical	120	100	15	Normal	•	User takes 1/3 of the damage inflicted. 10% chance of burning target. If target is frozen, melts the ice. Can be used even if user is frozen. In that case, melts the ice
Flash	Normal	Status	—	100	20	Normal		Lowers target's Accuracy by 1
Flash Cannon	Steel	Special	80	100	10	Normal		10% chance of lowering target's Sp. Attack by 1
Flatter	Dark	Status	—	100	15	Normal		Confuses target but raises its Sp. Attack by 1
Fling	Dark	Physical	—	100	10	Normal		Attacks by throwing user's held item at target. Power and effects depend on item thrown
Fly	Flying	Physical	90	95	15	Normal	•	Flies into the air on the first turn, attacks on the second
Focus Blast	Fighting	Special	120	70	5	Normal		10% chance of lowering target's Sp. Defense by 1
Focus Energy	Normal	Status	—	—	30	Self		Raises critical hit rate for subsequent move
Focus Punch	Fighting	Physical	150	100	20	Normal	•	Strikes last. Does not strike if target lands a hit before then
Follow Me	Normal	Status	—	—	20	Self		Draws all the target's attacks to user
Force Palm	Fighting	Physical	60	100	10	Normal	•	30% chance of paralyzing target
Foresight	Normal	Status	—	—	40	Normal		Hits target regardless of target's Evasion. Makes Ghost-type Pokémon vulnerable to Normal- and Fighting-type moves
Frenzy Plant	Grass	Special	150	90	5	Normal		Cannot act on following turn
Frustration	Normal	Physical	—	100	20	Normal	•	Power changes depending on user's Friendship. It's stronger the lower user's Friendship is
Fury Attack	Normal	Physical	15	85	20	Normal	•	Attacks 2-5 times in a row in one turn
Fury Cutter	Bug	Physical	10	95	20	Normal	•	Doubles in power every time it strikes (up to 5 times). Power returns to normal once it misses
Fury Swipes	Normal	Physical	18	80	15	Normal	•	Attacks 2-5 times in a row in one turn
Future Sight	Psychic	Special	80	90	15	Normal		Attacks target after 2 turns. Inflicts damage regardless of target's type
Gastro Acid	Poison	Status	—	100	10	Normal		Nullifies target's Ability
Giga Drain	Grass	Special	60	100	10	Normal		Restores HP equal to half the damage inflicted on target
Giga Impact	Normal	Physical	150	90	5	Normal	•	Cannot act on the following turn
Glare	Normal	Status	—	75	30	Normal		paralyzes target
Grass Knot	Grass	Special	—	100	20	Normal	•	Has higher attack power the heavier the target is
GrassWhistle	Grass	Status	—	55	15	Normal		Puts target to sleep
Gravity	Psychic	Status	—	—	5	All		Raises the Accuracy of all Pokémon in battle for 5 turns. Make Flying-type Pokémon and Pokémon with the Levitate Ability vulnerable to Ground-type moves. Cannot use Fly, Splash, Bounce, or Magnet Rise. (Will fall to earth as soon as they take flight.)
Growl	Normal	Status	—	100	40	2 foes		Lowers target's Attack by 1
Growth	Normal	Status	—	—	40	Self		Raises user's Sp. Attack by 1
Grudge	Ghost	Status	—	—	5	Self		If user faints from an enemy's move, that move's PP drops to 0
Guard Swap	Psychic	Status	—	—	10	Normal		Swaps Defense and Sp. Defense alterations between user and target
Guillotine	Normal	Physical	—	30	5	Normal	•	One-hit KO. Does not hit if target has a higher level than user. Has greater Accuracy the lower target's is
Gunk Shot	Poison	Physical	120	70	5	Normal		30% chance of poisoning target
Gust	Flying	Special	40	100	35	Normal		Regular attack. Double damage if target is using Fly or Bounce when it hits
Gyro Ball	Steel	Physical	—	100	5	Normal	•	Has higher attack power the more of a Speed advantage the target has over the user (max 150)
Hail	Ice	Status	—	—	10	All		Makes weather Hail for 5 turns, damaging all Pokémon except Ice-types every turn
Hammer Arm	Fighting	Physical	100	90	10	Normal	•	Raises user's Speed by 1
Harden	Normal	Status	—	—	30	Self		Raises user's Defense by 1
Haze	Ice	Status	—	—	30	All		Restores user's and target's stats to their unaltered state
Head Smash	Rock	Physical	150	80	5	Normal	•	User takes half the damage inflicted on target
Headbutt	Normal	Physical	70	100	15	Normal	•	30% chance of making target flinch (cannot use a move for that turn)
Heal Bell	Normal	Status	—	—	5	All allies		Heals status ailments for all ally Pokémon in your party
Heal Block	Psychic	Status	—	100	15	2 foes		Target cannot recover using moves for 5 turns

Move	Type	Kind	POW	Acc	PP	Range	DA	Effect
Heal Order	Bug	Status	—	—	10	Self		Restores half of max HP
Healing Wish	Psychic	Status	—	—	10	Self		Makes user faint, but completely heals the HP and status of the next Pokémon you send out
Heart Swap	Psychic	Status	—	—	10	Normal		Swaps all stat alterations between user and target
Heat Wave	Fire	Special	100	90	10	2 foes		10% chance of burning target. If target is frozen, melts the ice. Has lower power in Double Battles
Helping Hand	Normal	Status	—	—	20	1 ally		Strengthens ally's attack power by 1.5 times
Hi Jump Kick	Fighting	Physical	100	90	20	Normal	•	If attack misses, user takes 1/2 of the damage that would have been inflicted
Hidden Power	Normal	Special	—	100	15	Normal		Type and power change depending on the user
Horn Attack	Normal	Physical	65	100	25	Normal	•	Regular attack
Horn Drill	Normal	Physical	—	30	5	Normal	•	One-hit KO. Does not hit if target's level is higher than user's. Has higher Accuracy the lower target's is
Howl	Normal	Status	—	—	40	Self		Raises user's Attack by 1
Hydro Cannon	Water	Special	150	90	5	Normal		Cannot act on following turn
Hydro Pump	Water	Special	120	80	5	Normal		Regular attack
Hyper Beam	Normal	Special	150	90	5	Normal		Cannot act on following turn
Hyper Fang	Normal	Physical	80	90	15	Normal	•	10% chance of making target flinch (cannot use moves for that turn)
Hyper Voice	Normal	Special	90	100	10	2 foes		Regular attack. Has lower power in Double Battles
Hypnosis	Psychic	Status	—	60	20	Normal		Puts target to sleep
Ice Ball	Ice	Physical	30	90	20	Normal	•	Attacks in series for 5 turns, until it misses. Damage rises with each strike. Use Defense Curl first to double the damage
Ice Beam	Ice	Special	95	100	10	Normal		10% chance of freezing target
Ice Fang	Ice	Physical	65	95	15	Normal	•	10% chance of freezing target or making it flinch
Ice Punch	Ice	Physical	75	100	15	Normal	•	10% chance of freezing target
Ice Shard	Ice	Physical	40	100	30	Normal		Always strikes first (if both sides use this move, the one with the higher Speed goes first)
Icicle Spear	Ice	Physical	10	100	30	Normal		Attacks 2-5 times in a row in one turn
Icy Wind	Ice	Special	55	95	15	2 foes		100% chance of lowering target's Speed by 1. Has lower attack power in Double Battles
Imprison	Psychic	Status	—	—	10	Self		Makes target unable to use a move if user knows it too
Ingrain	Grass	Status	—	—	20	Self		Restores a little HP each turn. User cannot be switched out after using. Flying-type Pokémon and Pokémon with Levitate become vulnerable to Ground-type moves
Iron Defense	Steel	Status	—	—	15	Self		Raises user's Defense by 2
Iron Head	Steel	Physical	80	100	15	Normal	•	30% chance of making target flinch (cannot use moves for that turn)
Iron Tail	Steel	Physical	100	75	15	Normal	•	30% chance of lowering target's Defense by 1
Jump Kick	Fighting	Physical	85	95	25	Normal	•	If attack misses, user takes 1/2 of the damage that would have been inflicted
Karate Chop	Fighting	Physical	50	100	25	Normal	•	High critical hit rate
Kinesis	Psychic	Status	—	80	15	Normal		Lowers target's Accuracy by 1
Knock Off	Dark	Physical	20	100	20	Normal	•	Makes target as if it's not holding an item. The item is returned after battle
Last Resort	Normal	Physical	130	100	5	Normal	•	Fails if user has not used each of its other moves at least once
Lava Plume	Fire	Special	80	100	15	2 foes 1 ally		30% chance of burning target. If target is frozen, melts the ice. Lower power in Double Battles.
Leaf Blade	Grass	Physical	90	100	15	Normal	•	High critical hit rate
Leaf Storm	Grass	Special	140	90	5	Normal		Lowers user's Sp. Attack by 2
Leech Life	Bug	Physical	20	100	15	Normal	•	Restores HP equal to half the damage inflicted on target
Leer	Normal	Status	—	100	30	2 foes		Lowers target's Defense by 1
Lick	Ghost	Physical	20	100	30	Normal	•	30% chance of paralyzing target
Light Screen	Psychic	Status	—	—	30	2 allies		Halves damage from target's special moves for 5 turns. Effect serves out its full time even if user is switched out. Effect is lessened in Double Battles
Lock-On	Normal	Status	—	—	5	Normal		Guarantees that an attack on the next turn will hit
Lovely Kiss	Normal	Status	—	75	10	Normal		Puts target to sleep
Low Kick	Fighting	Physical	—	100	20	Normal	•	Has higher attack power the heavier the target is
Lucky Chant	Normal	Status	—	—	30	2 allies		Target cannot deliver critical hits for 5 turns
Lunar Dance	Psychic	Status	—	—	10	Self		Knocks out user, but completely restores the PP and status of the next Pokémon you send out

Move	Type	Kind	POW	Acc	PP	Range	DA	Effect
Mach Punch	Fighting	Physical	40	100	30	Normal	•	Always attacks first (if both opponents use this move, the one with the higher Speed goes first)
Magic Coat	Psychic	Status	—	—	15	Self		Reflects moves with effects like those of poison, paralyze, Sleep, confuse, and Leech Seed
Magical Leaf	Grass	Special	60	—	20	Normal		Always strikes target
Magma Storm	Fire	Special	120	70	5	Normal		Inflicts damage and prevents target from fleeing for 2-5 turns. If target is frozen, melts the ice
Magnet Bomb	Steel	Physical	60	—	20	Normal		Always strikes target
Magnet Rise	Electric	Status	—	—	10	Self		Nullifies Ground-type moves for 5 turns
Magnitude	Ground	Physical	—	100	30	2 foes 1 ally		Power shifts between 10, 30, 50, 70, 90, 110, and 150. Double damage against targets using Dig. Lower power in Double Battles.
Me First	Normal	Status	—	—	20	Depends		Raises the attack power of target's next move. Fails if it does not strike first
Mean Look	Normal	Status	—	—	5	Normal		Makes target unable to escape. If used in a Trainer battle, the Trainer cannot switch Pokémon
Meditate	Psychic	Status	—	—	40	Self		Raises user's Attack by 1
Mega Drain	Grass	Special	40	100	15	Normal		Recovers HP equal to half the damage inflicted on target
Mega Kick	Normal	Physical	120	75	5	Normal	•	Regular attack
Mega Punch	Normal	Physical	80	85	20	Normal	•	Regular attack
Megahorn	Bug	Physical	120	85	10	Normal	•	Regular attack
Memento	Dark	Status	—	100	10	Normal		User faints, but target's Attack and Sp. Attack are lowered by 2
Metal Burst	Steel	Physical	—	100	10	Self		Inflicts damage on target equal to 1.5 times the damage last received from target that turn
Metal Claw	Steel	Physical	50	95	35	Normal	•	10% chance of raising user's Attack by 1
Metal Sound	Steel	Status	—	85	40	Normal		Lowers target's Sp. Defense by 2
Meteor Mash	Steel	Physical	100	85	10	Normal	•	20% chance of raising user's Attack by 1
Metronome	Normal	Status	—	—	10	Depends		Uses one move randomly chosen from all possible moves
Milk Drink	Normal	Status	—	—	10	Self		Restores half of max HP
Mimic	Normal	Status	—	—	10	Normal		Turns into a copy of the last move used by target (move has 5 PP). Only lasts for duration of battle
Mind Reader	Normal	Status	—	—	5	Normal		The attack on the following turn will have perfect accuracy
Minimize	Normal	Status	—	—	20	Self		Raises user's Evasion by 1
Miracle Eye	Psychic	Status	—	—	40	Normal		Hits target regardless of target's Evasion. Makes Dark-type Pokémon vulnerable to Psychic-type attacks
Mirror Coat	Psychic	Special	—	100	20	Self		Returns two times the damage received from a special move from target. Always strikes last
Mirror Move	Flying	Status	—	—	20	Depends		Uses the same move that target just used on user
Mirror Shot	Steel	Special	65	85	10	Normal		30% chance of lowering target's Accuracy by 1
Mist	Ice	Status	—	—	30	2 allies		Protects against stat-lowering moves and side effects for 5 turns
Mist Ball	Psychic	Special	70	100	5	Normal		50% chance of lowering target's Sp. Attack
Moonlight	Normal	Status	—	—	5	Self		Restores HP. Effect changes based on the weather. Sunny weather: Restore 2/3 of HP. Normally restores 1/2 of HP Rainy/Sandstorm/Hail/Fog weather: restores 1/4 of HP
Morning Sun	Normal	Status	—	—	5	Self		Restores HP. Effect changes based on the weather. Sunny weather: Recovers 2/3 of HP. Normally recovers 1/2 of HP. Rainy/Sandstorm/Hail/Fog weather: Recovers 1/4 of HP.
Mud Bomb	Ground	Special	65	85	10	Normal		30% chance of lowering target's Accuracy by 1
Mud Shot	Ground	Special	55	95	15	Normal		100% chance of lowering target's Speed by 1
Mud Sport	Ground	Status	—	—	15	All		Halves the power of Electric-type moves as long as user is in play
Mud-Slap	Ground	Special	20	100	10	Normal		100% chance of lowering target's Accuracy by 1
Muddy Water	Water	Special	95	85	10	2 foes		30% chance of lowering target's Accuracy by 1. Has lower attack power in Double Battles
Nasty Plot	Dark	Status	—	—	20	Self		Raises user's Sp. Attack by 2
Natural Gift	Normal	Physical	—	100	15	Normal		Type and attack power change according to the berry held by user. Move uses up berry
Nature Power	Normal	Status	—	—	20	Depends		Move changes according to the terrain. Tall grass or water puddle: Seed Bomb. Sandy ground: Earthquake. Rocky area or cave: Rock Slide. Marsh: Mud Bomb. Water surface: Hydro Pump. Snowy ground: Blizzard. Icy ground: Ice Beam. Floor: Tri-Attack.

Move	Type	Kind	POW	Acc	PP	Range	DA	Effect
Needle Arm	Grass	Physical	60	100	15	Normal	•	30% chance of making target flinch (cannot use moves for that turn)
Night Shade	Ghost	Special	—	100	15	Normal		Inflicts fixed damage equal to user's level
Night Slash	Dark	Physical	70	100	15	Normal	•	High critical hit rate
Nightmare	Ghost	Status	—	100	15	Normal		Lowers target's HP by 1/4 of max every turn. Fails if target is not asleep
Octazooka	Water	Special	65	85	10	Normal		50% chance of lowering target's Accuracy by 1
Odor Sleuth	Normal	Status	—	—	40	Normal		Always hits, regardless of target's Evasion. Makes Ghost-type Pokémon vulnerable to Normal- and Fighting-type moves
Ominous Wind	Ghost	Special	60	100	5	Normal		10% chance of raising Attack, Defense, Speed, Sp. Attack, and Sp. Defense by 1
Outrage	Dragon	Physical	120	100	15	1 Random	•	Attacks successively for 2-3 turns. If attack is broken off, user becomes confused
Overheat	Fire	Special	140	90	5	Normal		Lowers user's Sp. Attack by 2. If target is frozen, melts the ice
Pain Split	Normal	Status	—	—	20	Normal		Averages user's HP and target's HP
Pay Day	Normal	Physical	40	100	20	Normal		Wins a lot of prize money at the end of battle (User's level X number of attacks X 5 Poké)
Payback	Dark	Physical	50	100	10	Normal	•	Double damage if user attacks after target
Peck	Flying	Physical	35	100	35	Normal	•	Regular attack
Perish Song	Normal	Status	—	—	5	All		All Pokémon in battle at the time of use will faint in 3 turns
Petal Dance	Grass	Special	90	100	20	1 Random	•	Attacks 2-3 turns in succession. If attack is cut off, user becomes Confused
Pin Missile	Bug	Physical	14	85	20	Normal		Attacks 2-5 times in a row in one turn
Pluck	Flying	Physical	60	100	20	Normal	•	Hijacks the effects of any berry held by target
Poison Fang	Poison	Physical	50	100	15	Normal	•	30% chance of badly poisoning target. Damage from being badly poisoned increases with every turn
Poison Gas	Poison	Status	—	55	40	Normal		Poisons target
Poison Jab	Poison	Physical	80	100	20	Normal	•	30% chance of poisoning target
Poison Sting	Poison	Physical	15	100	35	Normal	•	30% chance of poisoning target
Poison Tail	Poison	Physical	50	100	25	Normal	•	10% chance of poisoning target. High critical hit rate
PoisonPowder	Poison	Status	—	75	35	Normal		Poisons target
Pound	Normal	Physical	40	100	35	Normal	•	Regular attack
Powder Snow	Ice	Special	40	100	25	2 foes		10% chance of freezing target. Has lower attack power in Double Battles
Power Gem	Rock	Special	70	100	20	Normal		Regular attack
Power Swap	Psychic	Status	—	—	10	Normal		Swaps alterations to Attack and Sp. Attack between user and target
Power Trick	Psychic	Status	—	—	10	Self		Swaps Attack and Defense (does not swap stat alterations)
Power Whip	Grass	Physical	120	85	10	Normal	•	Regular attack
Present	Normal	Physical	—	90	15	Normal		Restores different amounts of HP: 40% chance of 40, 30% of 80, 10% of 120, and 20% of 1/4 max HP
Protect	Normal	Status	—	—	10	Self		Protects against move used by target on that turn. Chance of failure increases with each successive use
Psybeam	Psychic	Special	65	100	20	Normal		10% chance of confusing target
Psych Up	Normal	Status	—	—	10	Normal		Duplicates target's stat alterations on user
Psychic	Psychic	Special	90	100	10	Normal		10% chance of lowering target's Sp. Defense by 1
Psycho Boost	Psychic	Special	140	90	5	Normal		Lowers user's Sp. Attack by 2
Psycho Cut	Psychic	Physical	70	100	20	Normal		High critical hit rate
Psycho Shift	Psychic	Status	—	90	10	Normal		Transfers status ailments poison, badly poisoned, Sleep, paralysis, and burn to target, healing user
Psywave	Psychic	Special	—	80	15	Normal		Inflicts damage equal to user's level times a random number from 0.5 to 1.5
Punishment	Dark	Physical	—	100	5	Normal	•	Has higher attack power if target has elevated stats
Pursuit	Dark	Physical	40	100	20	Normal	•	Double damage against a target Pokémon that's switching out
Quick Attack	Normal	Physical	40	100	30	Normal	•	Always strikes first (if both sides use this move, the one with the higher Speed goes first)
Rage	Normal	Physical	20	100	20	Normal	•	Attack power rises as user takes hits from the target
Rain Dance	Water	Status	—	—	5	All		Makes weather Rainy for 5 turns, strengthening Water-type moves
Rapid Spin	Normal	Physical	20	100	40	Normal	•	Releases user from Bind, Wrap, Leech Seed, or Spikes
Razor Leaf	Grass	Physical	55	95	25	2 foes		High critical hit rate. Has lower power in Double Battles
Razor Wind	Normal	Special	80	100	10	2 foes		Builds power on first turn and attacks on second. High critical hit rate. Has lower attack power in Double Battles

Move	Type	Kind	POW	Acc	PP	Range	DA	Effect
Recover	Normal	Status	—	—	10	Self		Restores half of max HP
Recycle	Normal	Status	—	—	10	Self		Makes a used held item useable again
Reflect	Psychic	Status	—	—	20	2 allies		Halves damage from target's physical moves for 5 turns. Effects serve out their term even if user is switched out. Has weakened effects in Double Battles
Refresh	Normal	Status	—	—	20	Self		Heals poison, paralysis, and burn
Rest	Psychic	Status	—	—	10	Self		Completely restores HP and puts user to sleep for 2 turns
Return	Normal	Physical	—	100	20	Normal	•	Has higher attack power the higher the user's Friendship is
Revenge	Fighting	Physical	60	100	10	Normal	•	Double damage if user has sustained damage from target on that turn
Reversal	Fighting	Physical	—	100	15	Normal	•	Inflicts more damage on target the lower user's HP is
Roar	Normal	Status	—	100	20	Normal		Ends a battle with a wild Pokémon. In a Trainer battle, forces Trainer to switch Pokémon
Roar of Time	Dragon	Special	150	90	5	Normal		Cannot act on the following turn
Rock Blast	Rock	Physical	25	80	10	Normal		Attacks 2-5 times in one turn
Rock Climb	Normal	Physical	90	85	20	Normal	•	20% chance of confusing target
Rock Polish	Rock	Status	—	—	20	Self		Raises user's Speed by 2
Rock Slide	Rock	Physical	75	90	10	2 foes		30% chance of making target flinch (cannot use moves for that turn). Attack power is weaker in Double Battles
Rock Smash	Fighting	Physical	40	100	15	Normal		50% chance of lowering target's Defense by 1
Rock Throw	Rock	Physical	50	90	15	Normal		Regular attack
Rock Tomb	Rock	Physical	50	80	10	Normal		100% chance of lowering target's Speed by 1
Rock Wrecker	Rock	Physical	150	90	5	Normal		Cannot act on the following turn
Role Play	Psychic	Status	—	—	10	Normal		Copies target's Ability (cannot copy Wonder Guard)
Rolling Kick	Fighting	Physical	60	85	15	Normal	•	30% chance of making target flinch
Rollout	Rock	Physical	30	90	20	Normal	•	Attacks continuously for 5 turns until it misses. Inflicts greater damage with every successful hit. Double damage if used after Defense Curl
Roost	Flying	Status	—	—	10	Self		Restores half of max HP, but nullifies user's Flying type
Sacred Fire	Fire	Physical	100	95	5	Normal		50% chance of burning target. If target is frozen, melts the ice. Can be used even if user is frozen. In that case, melts the ice
Safeguard	Normal	Status	—	—	25	2 allies		Protects against status ailments for 5 turns. Effects last even if user is switched out
Sand Tomb	Ground	Physical	15	70	15	Normal		Inflicts damage over 2-5 turns. Target cannot escape during that time
Sand-Attack	Ground	Status	—	100	15	Normal		Lowers target's Accuracy by 1
Sandstorm	Rock	Status	—	—	10	All		Sandstorm weather for 5 turns. All Pokémon but Rock-, Steel-, and Ground-types take damage every turn
Scary Face	Normal	Status	—	90	10	Normal		Lowers target's Speed by 2
Scratch	Normal	Physical	40	100	35	Normal	•	Regular attack
Screech	Normal	Status	—	85	40	Normal		Lowers target's Defense by 2
Secret Power	Normal	Physical	70	100	20	Normal		Regular attack with 30% chance of one of the following side effects, depending on the terrain. Tall grass or water puddle: sleep. Sandy ground: lowers Accuracy by 1. Rocky ground or cave: flinch. Marsh: lowers Speed by 1. Water surface: lowers Attack by 1. Snowy or icy ground: freezes. Floor: paralyzes.
Seed Bomb	Grass	Physical	80	100	15	Normal		Regular attack
Seed Flare	Grass	Special	120	85	5	Normal		40% chance of lowering target's Sp. Defense by 2
Seismic Toss	Fighting	Physical	—	100	20	Normal	•	Deals fixed damage equal to user's level
Selfdestruct	Normal	Physical	200	100	5	2 foes 1 ally		User faints after using. Damages target as if its Defense were halved. Has lower attack power in Double Battles.
Shadow Ball	Ghost	Special	80	100	15	Normal		20% chance of lowering target's Sp. Defense by 1
Shadow Claw	Ghost	Physical	70	100	15	Normal	•	High critical hit rate
Shadow Force	Ghost	Physical	120	100	5	Normal	•	Makes user invisible on the first turn, attacks on the second. Strikes target even if it's using Protect or Detect
Shadow Punch	Ghost	Physical	60	—	20	Normal	•	Always strikes target
Shadow Sneak	Ghost	Physical	40	100	30	Normal	•	Always strikes first (if both sides use this move, the one with the higher Speed goes first)
Sharpen	Normal	Status	—	—	30	Self		Raises user's Attack by 1

Move	Type	Kind	POW	Acc	PP	Range	DA	Effect
Sheer Cold	Ice	Special	—	30	5	Normal		One-hit KO. Does not strike if target's level is higher than user's. Has higher Accuracy the lower target's is
Shock Wave	Electric	Special	60	—	20	Normal		Always strikes target
Signal Beam	Bug	Special	75	100	15	Normal		10% chance of confusing target
Silver Wind	Bug	Special	60	100	5	Normal		10% chance of raising Attack, Defense, Speed, Sp. Attack, and Sp. Defense
Sing	Normal	Status	—	55	15	Normal		Puts target to sleep
Sketch	Normal	Status	—	—	1	Normal		Copies the last move used by target. User forgets Sketch and learns the copied move
Skill Swap	Psychic	Status	—	—	10	Normal		Swaps Abilities between user and target (except for Wonder Guard)
Skull Bash	Normal	Physical	100	100	15	Normal	•	Powers up on the first turn and attacks on the second. On the first turn, raises user's Defense by 1
Sky Attack	Flying	Physical	140	90	5	Normal		Builds up power on the first turn and attacks on the second. 30% chance of making target flinch. High critical hit rate
Sky Uppercut	Fighting	Physical	85	90	15	Normal	•	Deals damage even to targets using Fly or Bounce
Slack Off	Normal	Status	—	—	10	Self		Restores 1/2 of max HP
Slam	Normal	Physical	80	75	20	Normal	•	Regular attack
Slash	Normal	Physical	70	100	20	Normal	•	High critical hit rate
Sleep Powder	Grass	Status	—	75	15	Normal		Puts target to sleep
Sleep Talk	Normal	Status	—	—	10	Depends		Only works when user is asleep. Uses one of user's moves, randomly selected
Sludge	Poison	Special	65	100	20	Normal		30% chance of poisoning target
Sludge Bomb	Poison	Special	90	100	10	Normal		30% chance of poisoning target
SmellingSalt	Normal	Physical	60	100	10	Normal	•	Double damage against paralyzed targets, but heals paralysis
Smog	Poison	Special	20	70	20	Normal		40% chance of poisoning target
SmokeScreen	Normal	Status	—	100	20	Normal		Lowers target's Accuracy by 1
Snatch	Dark	Status	—	—	10	Depends		Steals the effects of recovery or stat-altering moves used by target on that turn
Snore	Normal	Special	40	100	15	Normal		Only works when user is asleep. 30% chance of making target flinch
Softboiled	Normal	Status	—	—	10	Self		Restores half of max HP
SolarBeam	Grass	Special	120	100	10	Normal		Powers up on the first move, attacks on the second. Can attack without a power-up turn in Sunny weather. Attack power is halved in Rainy, Sandstorm, Hail, and Fog weather.
SonicBoom	Normal	Special	—	90	20	Normal		Deals a fixed 20 points of damage
Spacial Rend	Dragon	Special	100	95	5	Normal		High critical hit rate
Spark	Electric	Physical	65	100	20	Normal	•	30% chance of paralyzing target
Spider Web	Bug	Status	—	—	10	Normal		Makes target unable to escape. If used in a Trainer battle, the Trainer cannot switch Pokémon
Spike Cannon	Normal	Physical	20	100	15	Normal		Attacks 2-5 times in a row in one turn
Spikes	Ground	Status	—	—	20	2 foes		Damages target as it switches out. Power rises with each use, up to 3. No effect on Pokémon with Levitate Ability or Flying-types
Spit Up	Normal	Special	—	100	10	Normal		Damage increases the more times user used Stockpile. Does not work if user has not used Stockpile first. Stockpile returns elevated Defense and Sp. Defense to normal
Spite	Ghost	Status	—	100	10	Normal		Takes 4 points from the PP of the target's last move used
Splash	Normal	Status	—	—	40	Self		No effect
Spore	Grass	Status	—	100	15	Normal		Puts target to sleep
Stealth Rock	Rock	Status	—	—	20	2 foes		Target takes damage when sending out Pokémon. Damage is subject to type match-ups
Steel Wing	Steel	Physical	70	90	25	Normal	•	10% chance of raising user's Defense by 1
Stockpile	Normal	Status	—	—	20	Self		Raises user's Defense and Sp. Defense by 1. Can be used up to 3 times
Stomp	Normal	Physical	65	100	20	Normal	•	30% chance of making target flinch (cannot use moves for that turn). Double damage if target is using Minimize
Stone Edge	Rock	Physical	100	80	5	Normal		High critical hit rate
Strength	Normal	Physical	80	100	15	Normal	•	Regular attack
String Shot	Bug	Status	—	95	40	2 foes		Lowers target's Speed by 1
Struggle	Normal	Physical	50	—	1	Normal	•	Becomes available when all other moves are out of PP. User loses 1/4 of max HP. Inflicts damage regardless of type effects

Move	Type	Kind	POW	Acc	PP	Range	DA	Effect
Stun Spore	Grass	Status	—	75	30	Normal		Paralyzes target
Submission	Fighting	Physical	80	80	25	Normal	•	User takes damage equal to 1/4 that inflicted on target
Substitute	Normal	Status	—	—	10	Self		Uses 1/4 of max HP to create an offshoot of the user
Sucker Punch	Dark	Physical	80	100	5	Normal	•	Attacks first if target's chosen move is an attack move, and deals damage
Sunny Day	Fire	Status	—	—	5	All		Changes the weather to Sunny for 5 turns, strengthening Fire-type moves
Super Fang	Normal	Physical	—	90	10	Normal	•	Halves target's HP
Superpower	Fighting	Physical	120	100	5	Normal	•	Lowers user's Attack and Defense by 1
Supersonic	Normal	Status	—	55	20	Normal		Confuses target
Surf	Water	Special	95	100	15	2 foes 1 ally		Regular attack. Double damage against targets using Dive. Has lower power in Double Battles.
Swagger	Normal	Status	—	90	15	Normal		Confuses target but raises its Attack by 2
Swallow	Normal	Status	—	—	10	Self		Recovers more HP the more user used Stockpile. Does not work if user has not used Stockpile first. Stockpile restores elevated Defense and Sp. Defense to normal
Sweet Kiss	Normal	Status	—	75	10	Normal		Confuses target
Sweet Scent	Normal	Status	—	100	20	2 foes		Lowers target's Evasion by 1
Swift	Normal	Special	60	—	20	2 foes		Always strikes target. Has lower attack power in Double Battles
Switcheroo	Dark	Status	—	100	10	Normal		Swaps items between user and target
Swords Dance	Normal	Status	—	—	30	Self		Raises user's Attack by 2
Synthesis	Grass	Status	—	—	5	Self		Recovers HP. Effect changes based on the weather. Sunny weather: Recovers 2/3 of HP. Normally recovers 1/2 of HP. Rainy/Sandstorm/Hail/Fog weather: Restores 1/4 of HP.
Tackle	Normal	Physical	35	95	35	Normal	•	Regular attack
Tail Glow	Bug	Status	—	—	20	Self		Raises user's Sp. Attack by 2
Tail Whip	Normal	Status	—	100	30	2 foes		Lowers target's Defense by 1
Tailwind	Flying	Status	—	—	30	2 allies		Doubles user's and ally's Speed for 3 turns
Take Down	Normal	Physical	90	85	20	Normal	•	User takes damage equal to 1/4 of the damage inflicted on target
Taunt	Dark	Status	—	100	20	Normal		Prevents target from using anything other than attack moves for 2-4 turns
Teeter Dance	Normal	Status	—	100	20	2 foes •1 ally		Confuses target
Teleport	Psychic	Status	—	—	20	Self		Ends a battle with a wild Pokémon
Thief	Dark	Physical	40	100	10	Normal	•	If target has an item and user has none, user steals target's item
Thrash	Normal	Physical	90	100	20	1 Random	•	Attacks 2-3 times in series. If the effects are interrupted, user becomes confused
Thunder	Electric	Special	120	70	10	Normal		30% chance of paralyzing target. Always hits in Rainy weather. Has 50% accuracy in Sunny weather. Strikes targets that are using Fly or Bounce
Thunder Fang	Electric	Physical	65	95	15	Normal	•	10% chance of paralyzing target or making it flinch
Thunder Wave	Electric	Status	—	100	20	Normal		Paralyzes target
Thunderbolt	Electric	Special	95	100	15	Normal		10% chance of paralyzing target
ThunderPunch	Electric	Physical	75	100	15	Normal	•	10% chance of paralyzing target
ThunderShock	Electric	Special	40	100	30	Normal		10% chance of paralyzing target
Tickle	Normal	Status	—	100	20	Normal		Lowers target's Attack and Defense by 1
Torment	Dark	Status	—	100	15	Normal		Makes target unable to use the same move twice in a row
Toxic	Poison	Status	—	85	10	Normal		Badly poisons target. Damage from being badly poisoned increases with every turn
Toxic Spikes	Poison	Status	—	—	20	2 foes		If target sends out Pokémon, poisons target. Use Toxic Spikes twice to badly poison target. Ineffective against Poison-type Pokémon. Ineffective against Flying-type Pokémon and Pokémon with Levitate
Transform	Normal	Status	—	—	10	Normal		Transforms into target. User can use same moves and Ability as target. (All moves have PP of 5)
Tri Attack	Normal	Special	80	100	10	Normal		20% chance of inflicting paralysis, burn, or freeze
Trick	Psychic	Status	—	100	10	Normal		Swaps items between user and target
Trick Room	Psychic	Status	—	—	5	All		For 5 turns, the Pokémon with the lower Speed strikes first. First-strike moves still go first. If used again while still in effect, cancels the effect
Triple Kick	Fighting	Physical	10	90	10	Normal	•	Attacks 3 times in a row in one turn. Power rises from 10 to 20 to 30 as long as it continues to hit
Trump Card	Normal	Special	—	—	5	Normal	•	Always hits. Has higher attack power the lower its PP is
Twineedle	Bug	Physical	25	100	20	Normal		Attacks twice in a row in one turn. 20% chance of poisoning target

Move	Type	Kind	POW	Acc	PP	Range	DA	Effect
Twister	Dragon	Special	40	100	20	2 foes		20% chance of making target flinch (cannot use moves for that turn). Double damage to targets using Fly or Bounce. Has lower attack power in Double Battles
Uproar	Normal	Special	50	100	10	1 Random		User is in an uproar for 2-5 turns. During that time, neither Pokémon can fall asleep
U-turn	Bug	Physical	70	100	20	Normal	•	After attacking, user switches out with the next Pokémon in your party
Vacuum Wave	Fighting	Special	40	100	30	Normal		Always strikes first (if both sides use this move, the one with the higher Speed goes first)
ViceGrip	Normal	Physical	55	100	30	Normal	•	Regular attack
Vine Whip	Grass	Physical	35	100	15	Normal	•	Regular attack
Vital Throw	Fighting	Physical	70	—	10	Normal	•	Strikes last, but always hits
Volt Tackle	Electric	Physical	120	100	15	Normal	•	User takes 1/3 of the damage inflicted on target. 10% chance of paralyzing target
Wake-Up Slap	Fighting	Physical	60	100	10	Normal	•	Deals double damage against sleeping targets, but heals them from sleep
Water Gun	Water	Special	40	100	25	Normal		Regular attack
Water Pulse	Water	Special	60	100	20	Normal		20% chance of confusing target
Water Sport	Water	Status	—	—	15	All		Halves the power of Fire-type moves for as long as user is in play
Water Spout	Water	Special	150	100	5	2 foes		Has lower attack power if user's HP is low. Attack power is lower in Double Battles
Waterfall	Water	Physical	80	100	15	Normal	•	20% chance of making target flinch (cannot use moves for that turn)
Weather Ball	Normal	Special	50	100	10	Normal		Move type changes in special weather conditions. Sunny weather: Fire-type. Rainy weather: Water-type. Hail weather: Ice-type. Sandstorm weather: Rock-type.
Whirlpool	Water	Special	15	70	15	Normal		Inflicts damage over 2-5 turns. Target cannot flee during that time. Double damage if target is using Dive when attacked
Whirlwind	Normal	Status	—	100	20	Normal		Ends a battle with a wild Pokémon. In a Trainer battle, forces the Trainer to switch Pokémon
Will-O-Wisp	Fire	Status	—	75	15	Normal		Burns target
Wing Attack	Flying	Physical	60	100	35	Normal	•	Regular attack
Wish	Normal	Status	—	—	10	Self		Restores 1/2 of max HP at the end of the next turn. Works even if user is switched out
Withdraw	Water	Status	—	—	40	Self		Raises user's Defense by 1
Wood Hammer	Grass	Physical	120	100	15	Normal	•	User takes 1/3 of the damage inflicted on target
Worry Seed	Grass	Status	—	100	10	Normal		Changes target's Ability to Insomnia. Does not work against the Truant Ability
Wrap	Normal	Physical	15	85	20	Normal	•	Inflicts damage and prevents target from fleeing for 2-5 turns
Wring Out	Normal	Special	—	100	5	Normal	•	Has higher attack power the higher the target's remaining HP is (max attack power: 120)
X-Scissor	Bug	Physical	80	100	15	Normal	•	Regular attack
Yawn	Normal	Status	—	—	10	Normal		Puts target to sleep on the following turn. No effect if target switches out before then
Zap Cannon	Electric	Special	120	50	5	Normal		100% chance of paralyzing target
Zen Headbutt	Psychic	Physical	80	90	15	Normal	•	20% chance of making target flinch (cannot use moves for that turn)

Moves that have an effect on the field

Move	Field Effect
Cut	Cuts down narrow trees to clear the way
Defog	Blows away thick fog, improving visibility
Dig	Gets you out of caves, returns you to the last entrance you came in
Flash	Illuminates dark caves
Fly	Whisks you instantaneously to a town you've been to before
Milk Drink	Shares user's HP with other party Pokémon
Rock Climb	Lets you climb up or down rough rock faces
Rock Smash	Smashes rocks with cracks in them, clearing the way
Strength	Moves large rocks out of the way
Surf	Carries you over the water
Sweet Scent	When used in a place where wild Pokémon appear, triggers a wild Pokémon encounter
Teleport	Transports you to the last Pokémon Center you visited (cannot be used in locations like towns or caves)
Waterfall	Lets you climb up waterfalls

Moves taught by Move Tutors

Location	Move	Type	No. shards needed			
			Red Shards	Blue Shards	Yellow Shard	Green Shards
Route 212	Air Cutter	Flying	2	4	0	2
	Dive	Water	2	4	2	0
	Fire Punch	Fire	2	6	0	0
	Fury Cutter	Bug	0	8	0	0
	Ice Punch	Ice	2	6	0	0
	Icy Wind	Ice	0	6	0	2
	Knock Off	Dark	4	4	0	0
	Ominous Wind	Ghost	0	6	0	2
	Sucker Punch	Dark	0	6	2	0
	ThunderPunch	Electric	2	6	0	0
	Trick	Psychic	0	4	4	0
	Vacuum Wave	Fighting	2	4	0	2
	Zen Headbutt	Psychic	0	4	4	0
Snowpoint City	Helping Hand	Normal	0	0	6	2
	Last Resort	Normal	0	0	0	8
	Magnet Rise	Electric	0	2	4	2
	Snore	Normal	2	0	4	2
	Spite	Ghost	0	0	8	0
	Swift	Normal	0	2	2	4
	Synthesis	Grass	0	0	2	6
	Uproar	Normal	0	0	6	2
Survival Area	AncientPower	Rock	6	0	0	2
	Aqua Tail	Water	6	0	0	2
	Bounce	Flying	4	0	2	2
	Earth Power	Ground	6	0	0	2
	Endeavor	Normal	4	0	4	0
	Gastro Acid	Poison	4	0	2	2
	Gunk Shot	Poison	4	2	0	2
	Heat Wave	Fire	4	2	0	2
	Iron Defense	Steel	4	2	2	0
	Iron Head	Steel	6	0	2	0
	Mud-Slap	Ground	4	4	0	0
	Outrage	Dragon	6	0	2	0
	Rollout	Rock	4	2	0	2
	Seed Bomb	Grass	4	0	0	4
	Signal Beam	Bug	2	2	2	2
	Superpower	Fighting	8	0	0	0
	Twister	Dragon	6	0	0	2

TMs

No.	Move	How to Get	Value
1	Focus Punch	Oreburgh Gate B1F (after winning at Canalave Gym)/Pickup Ability	—
2	Dragon Claw	Mt. Coronet (upper) 1F (after visiting the Distortion World)	—
3	Water Pulse	Ravaged Path (after winning at Pastoria Gym)	—
4	Calm Mind	Trade in Battle Points at the Battle Frontier (48 BP)	—
5	Roar	Route 213 (after winning at Snowpoint Gym)	—
6	Toxic	Route 212/Trade in Battle Points at the Battle Frontier (32 BP)	—
7	Hail	Route 217	—
8	Bulk Up	Trade in Battle Points at the Battle Frontier (48 BP)	—
9	Bullet Seed	Route 204	—
10	Hidden Power	Prize at the Veilstone Game Corner (6,000 coins)	—
11	Sunny Day	Route 212	—
12	Taunt	Route 211	—
13	Ice Beam	Route 216 (after winning at Snowpoint Gym)/Prize at Veilstone Game Corner (10,000 Coins)	—
14	Blizzard	Lake Acuity/Veilstone Dept. Store 3F	5500P
15	Hyper Beam	Veilstone Dept. Store 3F	7500P
16	Light Screen	Veilstone Dept. Store 3F	2000P
17	Protect	Veilstone Dept. Store 3F	2000P
18	Rain Dance	Route 223	—
19	Giga Drain	Route 209 (after winning at Pastoria Gym)	—
20	Safeguard	Veilstone Dept. Store 3F	2000P
21	Frustration	Galactic Veilstone Bldg. 3F/Prize at Veilstone Game Corner (8,000 Coins)	—
22	SolarBeam	Veilstone Dept. Store 3F	3000P
23	Iron Tail	Iron Island B2F - 1	—
24	Thunderbolt	Valley Windworks (after winning at Pastoria Gym)/Prize at the Veilstone Game Corner (10,000 Coins)	—
25	Thunder	Lake Valor (after visiting the Distortion World)/Veilstone Dept. Store 3F	5500P
26	Earthquake	Wayward Cave 1F/Pickup Ability/Trade in Battle Points at the Battle Frontier (80 BP)	—
27	Return	Sandgem Town (get from Professor Rowan)/Lost Tower 4F/Prize at Veilstone Game Corner (8,000 Coins)	—
28	Dig	Ruin Maniac's cave	—
29	Psychic	Route 211 (after winning at Snowpoint Gym)/Prize at the Veilstone Game Corner (10,000 Coins)	—
30	Shadow Ball	Route 210 (after you get the Secret Potion)/Trade in Battle Points at the Battle Frontier (64 BP)	—
31	Brick Break	Oreburgh Gate B1F (after you get the Bicycle)/Trade in Battle Points at the Battle Frontier (40 BP)	—
32	Double Team	Wayward Cave 1F/Prize at the Veilstone Game Corner (4,000 Coins)	—
33	Reflect	Veilstone Dept. Store 3F	2000P
34	Shock Wave	Route 215	—
35	Flamethrower	Fuego Ironworks/Prize at Veilstone Game Corner (10,000 Coins)	—
36	Sludge Bomb	Galactic Veilstone Bldg. B2F/Trade in Battle Points at the Battle Frontier (80 BP)	—
37	Sandstorm	Route 228	—
38	Fire Blast	Lake Verity (second visit)/Veilstone Dept. Store 3F	5500P
39	Rock Tomb	Ravaged Path	—
40	Aerial Ace	Route 213/Trade in Battle Points at the Battle Frontier (40 BP)	—
41	Torment	Victory Road 1F	—
42	Facade	Young man in a residence in the Survival Area	—
43	Secret Power	Amity Square in Hearthome City (west Gate side)	—
44	Rest	Prize at the Veilstone Game corner (6,000 coins)/Pickup Ability	—
45	Attract	Amity Square in Hearthome City (west Gate side)/Trade in Battle Points at the Battle Frontier (32 BP)	—
46	Thief	Eterna City (after winning at Eterna Gym)	—
47	Steel Wing	Route 209	—
48	Skill Swap	Girl in a residence in Canalave City	—
49	Snatch	Galactic Veilstone Bldg. 1F	—
50	Overheat	Stark Mountain interior - 2	—
51	Roost	Route 210	—
52	Focus Blast	Veilstone Dept. Store 3F	5500P
53	Energy Ball	Route 226/Trade in Battle Points at the Battle Frontier (64 BP)	—
54	False Swipe	Veilstone Dept. Store 3F	2000P
55	Brine	Pastoria Gym Battle	—
56	Fling	Young man on Route 222	—
57	Charge Beam	Pastoria Gym Battle	—
58	Endure	Prize at Veilstone Game Corner (2,000 Coins)	—
59	Dragon Pulse	Victory Road B1F/Trade in 80 BP at the Battle Frontier	—
60	Drain Punch	Veilstone Gym Battle	—
61	Will-O-Wisp	Trade in 32 BP at the Battle Frontier	—
62	Silver Wind	Route 212	—
63	Embargo	Young man in Veilstone City	—
64	Explosion	Prize for getting a 10-win combo on the slots at the Veilstone Game Corner	—
65	Shadow Claw	Hearthome Gym Battle	—
66	Payback	Young man on Route 215	—
67	Recycle	Old lady on 2F of Eterna Condominiums in Eterna City	—
68	Giga Impact	Prize at Veilstone Game Corner (20,000 Coins)	—
69	Rock Polish	Mt. Coronet (upper) 1F (after winning at Canalave Gym)	—
70	Flash	Oreburgh Gate B1F (after winning at Oreburgh Gym)/Veilstone Dept. Store 3F	1000P
71	Stone Edge	Victory Road 2F/Trade in 80 BP at the Battle Frontier	—
72	Avalanche	Snowpoint Gym Battle	—
73	Thunder Wave	Trade in 32 BP at the Battle Frontier	—
74	Gyro Ball	Prize at Veilstone Game Corner (15,000 Coins)	—
75	Swords Dance	Prize at Veilstone Game Corner (4,000 Coins)	—
76	Stealth Rock	Oreburgh Gym Battle	—
77	Psych Up	Young man on Route 211 (Celestic Town side)	—
78	Captivate	Route 204 (after winning at Eterna Gym)	—
79	Dark Pulse	Victory Road 2F	—
80	Rock Slide	Mt. Coronet (middle) 2F	—
81	X-Scissor	Route 221/Trade in 64 BP at the Battle Frontier	—
82	Sleep Talk	Eterna Forest (after winning at Eterna Gym)	—
83	Natural Gift	Veilstone Dept. Store 3F	2000P
84	Poison Jab	Route 212 (after winning at Pastoria Gym)	—
85	Dream Eater	Valor Lakefront (After winning at Snowpoint City)	—
86	Grass Knot	Eterna Gym Battle	—
87	Swagger	Mr. Backlot's room at the Pokémon Mansion	—
88	Pluck	Girl in a residence in Floaroma Town	—
89	U-turn	Canalave City/Prize at Veilstone Game Corner (6,000 Coins)	—
90	Substitute	Old Chateau 2F, first room on the right/Prize at Veilstone Game Corner (2,000 Coins)	—
91	Flash Cannon	Canalave Gym Battle	—
92	Trick Room	Clown in cottage on Route 213	—

HMs

No.	Move	How to Get	Value
01	Cut	Receive from Cynthia in Eterna City	—
02	Fly	Get at the Galactic Warehouse in Veilstone City	—
03	Surf	Receive from elder at Celestic Town	—
04	Strength	Receive from Riley at Iron Island cave entrance	—
05	Defog	Get at Solaceon Ruins B4F 2	—
06	Rock Smash	Receive from young man at Oreburgh Gate	—
07	Waterfall	Receive from Jasmine at the Sunyshore City beach (after winning at Sunyshore Gym)	—
08	Rock Climb	Get on Route 217	—

Move	Category	Hearts	Effect
Absorb	Smart	♥	Heart +3 if 2 Pokémon in a row raise the Voltage
Acid	Smart	♥♥♥	Basic performance move
Acid Armor	Tough	—	Move doubles in value on the next turn
Acupressure	Cool	—	Move doubles in value on the next turn
Aerial Ace	Cool	♥♥	Heart +2 if performed first in the turn
Aeroblast	Cool	♥♥	Heart +3 if the previous Pokémon's performance achieved a Voltage of 5
Agility	Cool	♥♥	User goes first on the next turn
Air Cutter	Cool	♥♥♥	Basic performance move
Air Slash	Cool	♥♥	Heart +2 if performed first in the turn
Amnesia	Cute	—	Move doubles in value on the next turn
AncientPower	Tough	♥♥	Heart +2 if used last in the turn
Aqua Jet	Beauty	♥♥	User goes first on the next turn
Aqua Ring	Beauty	—	Hearts are added equal to the number of the Voltage of your chosen judge
Aqua Tail	Cute	♥♥♥	Basic performance move
Arm Thrust	Tough	♥♥	Can perform using the same move twice in a row
Aromatherapy	Smart	—	Hearts are added equal to the number of the Voltage of your chosen judge
Assist	Cute	♥♥	Next turn goes in a random order
Assurance	Beauty	♥♥	Double hearts if it was used last turn
Astonish	Smart	♥♥♥	Basic performance move
Attack Order	Smart	♥♥	Heart +2 if user's performance raises the judge's Voltage
Attract	Cute	♥♥	Voltage cannot be lowered on that same turn
Aura Sphere	Beauty	♥♥	Heart +2 if performed first in the turn
Aurora Beam	Beauty	♥♥	Heart +2 if performed first in the turn
Avalanche	Cool	♥♥	Double hearts if it was used last turn
Barrage	Tough	♥♥	Can perform using the same move twice in a row
Barrier	Cool	♥♥	Voltage cannot be raised on that same turn
Baton Pass	Cute	—	Has higher value the lower the Voltage is. If your chosen judge's Voltage is 0: Heart +4. 1: +3. 2: +2. 3: +1. 4: none.
Beat Up	Smart	♥♥	Can perform using the same move twice in a row
Belly Drum	Cute	—	Move doubles in value on the next turn
Bide	Tough	♥♥	Double hearts if it was used last turn
Bind	Tough	—	Value depends on when in the lineup it is performed. First: Heart +1. 2nd: +2. 3rd: +3. Last: +4.
Bite	Tough	♥♥♥	Basic performance move
Blast Burn	Beauty	♥♥	Heart +3 if the previous Pokémon's performance achieved a Voltage of 5
Blaze Kick	Beauty	♥♥	Heart +2 if performed first in the turn
Blizzard	Beauty	♥♥	Heart +2 if performed first in the turn
Block	Cute	♥♥	Voltage cannot be raised on that same turn
Body Slam	Tough	♥♥♥	Basic performance move
Bone Club	Tough	♥♥♥	Basic performance move
Bone Rush	Tough	♥♥	Can perform using the same move twice in a row
Bonemerang	Tough	♥♥	Can perform using the same move twice in a row
Bounce	Cute	♥	Heart +3 if your judge is not taken by other Pokémon
Brave Bird	Cute	♥♥	Heart +2 if used last in the turn
Brick Break	Cool	♥♥♥	Basic performance move
Brine	Smart	♥♥	Heart +2 if user's performance raises the judge's Voltage
Bubble	Cute	♥♥	User goes last on the next turn
BubbleBeam	Beauty	♥♥	User goes last on the next turn
Bug Bite	Tough	—	If the previous Pokémon generated a Voltage of 5, steals its bonus hearts
Bug Buzz	Cute	♥♥	Heart +2 if user's performance raises the judge's Voltage
Bulk Up	Beauty	—	Move doubles in value on the next turn

Move	Category	Hearts	Effect
Bullet Punch	Smart	♥♥	User goes first on the next turn
Bullet Seed	Cool	♥♥	Can perform using the same move twice in a row
Calm Mind	Smart	—	Move doubles in value on the next turn
Camouflage	Smart	♥♥	Voltage cannot be raised on that same turn
Captivate	Beauty	♥♥	Voltage cannot be lowered on that same turn
Charge	Smart	—	Move doubles in value on the next turn
Charge Beam	Beauty	♥♥	Heart +2 if performed first in the turn
Charm	Cute	♥♥	Voltage cannot be lowered on that same turn
Chatter	Smart	♥	Heart +3 if user has the lowest value in the turn
Clamp	Tough	♥♥♥	Basic performance move
Close Combat	Smart	♥♥	Heart +3 if the previously performing Pokémon earned a Voltage of 5
Comet Punch	Tough	♥♥	Can perform using the same move twice in a row
Confuse Ray	Smart	♥♥	Voltage is lowered by one notch for all judges
Confusion	Smart	♥♥♥	Basic performance move
Constrict	Tough	—	Value depends on when in the lineup it is performed. First: Heart +1. 2nd: +2. 3rd: +3. Last: +4.
Conversion	Beauty	♥	Heart +3 if user has the lowest value in the turn
Conversion 2	Beauty	♥	Heart +3 if user has the lowest value in the turn
Copycat	Cool	—	If the previous Pokémon generated a Voltage of 5, steals its bonus hearts
Cosmic Power	Cool	—	Move doubles in value on the next turn
Cotton Spore	Beauty	♥♥	User goes first on the next turn
Counter	Tough	♥♥	Double hearts if it was used last turn
Covet	Cute	—	If the previous Pokémon generated a Voltage of 5, steals its bonus hearts
Crabhammer	Tough	♥♥	Heart +2 if used last in the turn
Cross Chop	Cool	♥♥	Heart +2 if used last in the turn
Cross Poison	Cool	♥♥♥	Basic performance move
Crunch	Tough	♥♥	Heart +2 if used last in the turn
Crush Claw	Cool	♥♥♥	Basic performance move
Crush Grip	Tough	♥♥	Double hearts if it was used last turn
Curse	Tough	—	Value depends on when in the lineup it is performed. First: Heart +1. 2nd: +2. 3rd: +3. Last: +4.
Cut	Cool	♥♥♥	Basic performance move
Dark Pulse	Cool	♥♥	Heart +2 if used first in the turn
Dark Void	Smart	♥♥	Voltage cannot be lowered on that same turn
Defend Order	Smart	—	Move doubles in value on the next turn
Defense Curl	Cute	♥♥	Voltage cannot be raised on that same turn
Defog	Beauty	♥♥	Voltage cannot be raised on that same turn
Destiny Bond	Smart	—	Heart +15 if all Pokémon choose the same judge
Detect	Cool	—	Has higher value the lower the Voltage is. If your chosen judge's Voltage is 0: Heart +4. 1: +3. 2: +2. 3: +1. 4: none.
Dig	Smart	♥	Heart +3 if your judge is not taken by other Pokémon
Disable	Smart	♥♥	Voltage cannot be lowered on that same turn
Discharge	Cool	♥♥	Heart +2 if performed first in the turn
Dive	Beauty	♥	Heart +3 if your judge is not taken by other Pokémon
Dizzy Punch	Cool	—	Has higher value the lower the Voltage is. If your chosen judge's Voltage is 0: Heart +4. 1: +3. 2: +2. 3: +1. 4: none.
Doom Desire	Cool	♥♥	Heart +2 if performed first in the turn
Double Hit	Smart	♥♥	Can perform using the same move twice in a row
Double Kick	Cool	♥♥	Can perform using the same move twice in a row
Double Team	Cool	♥♥	User goes first on the next turn
Double-Edge	Tough	—	Heart +15 if all Pokémon choose the same judge
DoubleSlap	Tough	♥♥	Can perform using the same move twice in a row
Draco Meteor	Smart	♥♥	Heart +3 if the previous Pokémon's performance achieved a Voltage of 5

Move	Category	Hearts	Effect
Dragon Claw	Cool	♥♥	Heart +2 if performed first in the turn
Dragon Dance	Cool	—	Move doubles in value on the next turn
Dragon Pulse	Smart	♥♥	Heart +2 if user's performance raises the judge's Voltage
Dragon Rage	Cool	♥♥♥	Basic performance move
Dragon Rush	Cool	♥♥	Heart +2 if used last in the turn
DragonBreath	Cool	♥♥	Heart +2 if performed first in the turn
Drain Punch	Beauty	♥	Heart +3 if 2 Pokémon in a row raise the Voltage
Dream Eater	Smart	♥	Heart +3 if 2 Pokémon in a row raise the Voltage
Drill Peck	Cool	♥♥♥	Basic performance move
DynamicPunch	Cool	♥♥	Heart +2 if used last in the turn
Earth Power	Smart	♥♥	Heart +2 if used last in the turn
Earthquake	Tough	♥♥	Heart +2 if used last in the turn
Egg Bomb	Tough	♥♥♥	Basic performance move
Embargo	Cute	♥♥	Voltage cannot be raised on that same turn
Ember	Beauty	♥♥♥	Basic performance move
Encore	Cute	♥	Heart +3 if 2 Pokémon in a row raise the Voltage
Endeavor	Tough	♥♥	Double hearts if it was used last turn
Endure	Tough	♥♥	Voltage cannot be raised on that same turn
Energy Ball	Beauty	♥♥	Heart +2 if performed first in the turn
Eruption	Beauty	♥♥	Heart +2 if used last in the turn
Explosion	Beauty	—	Heart +15 if all 4 Pokémon choose the same judge
Extrasensory	Cool	♥♥	Heart +2 if performed first in the turn
ExtremeSpeed	Cool	♥♥	User goes first on the next turn
Facade	Cute	♥♥	Double hearts if it was used last turn
Faint Attack	Smart	♥♥	Heart +2 if used last in the turn
Fake Out	Cute	♥♥	Heart +2 if performed first in the turn
Fake Tears	Smart	♥♥	Voltage cannot be lowered on that same turn
False Swipe	Cool	—	Has higher value the lower the Voltage is. If your chosen judge's Voltage is 0: Heart +4. 1: +3. 2: +2. 3: +1. 4: none.
FeatherDance	Beauty	♥♥	Voltage cannot be lowered on that same turn
Feint	Beauty	—	Has higher value the lower the Voltage is. If your chosen judge's Voltage is 0: Heart +4. 1: +3. 2: +2. 3: +1. 4: none.
Fire Blast	Beauty	♥♥	Heart +2 if performed first in the turn
Fire Fang	Beauty	♥♥♥	Basic performance move
Fire Punch	Beauty	♥♥	Heart +2 if performed first in the turn
Fire Spin	Beauty	—	Value depends on when in the lineup it is performed. First: Heart +1. 2nd: +2. 3rd: +3. Last: +4.
Fissure	Tough	—	Heart +15 if all Pokémon choose the same judge
Flail	Cute	♥♥	Double hearts if it was used last turn
Flame Wheel	Beauty	♥♥	Can perform using the same move twice in a row
Flamethrower	Beauty	♥♥	Heart +2 if performed first in the turn
Flare Blitz	Smart	♥♥	Heart +3 if the previous Pokémon's performance achieved a Voltage of 5
Flash	Beauty	♥♥	Voltage is lowered by one notch for all judges
Flash Cannon	Smart	♥♥	Heart +2 if performed first in the turn
Flatter	Smart	♥♥	Voltage cannot be lowered on that same turn
Fling	Tough	♥	Heart +3 if user has the lowest value in the turn
Fly	Smart	♥	Heart +3 if your judge is not taken by other Pokémon
Focus Blast	Cool	♥♥	Heart +2 if performed first in the turn
Focus Energy	Cool	—	Move doubles in value on the next turn
Focus Punch	Tough	♥	Heart +3 if your judge is not taken by other Pokémon
Follow Me	Cute	♥♥	Next turn goes in a random order
Force Palm	Cool	♥♥	Heart +2 if used last in the turn

Move	Category	Hearts	Effect
Foresight	Smart	♥	Heart +3 if 2 Pokémon in a row raise the Voltage
Frenzy Plant	Cool	♥ ♥	Heart +3 if the previous Pokémon's performance achieved a Voltage of 5
Frustration	Cute	♥ ♥	Heart +2 if used last in the turn
Fury Attack	Cool	♥ ♥	Can perform using the same move twice in a row
Fury Cutter	Cool	♥ ♥	Can perform using the same move twice in a row
Fury Swipes	Tough	♥ ♥	Can perform using the same move twice in a row
Future Sight	Smart	♥ ♥	Heart +2 if performed first in the turn
Gastro Acid	Beauty	♥ ♥	Voltage cannot be raised on that same turn
Giga Drain	Smart	♥	Heart +3 if 2 Pokémon in a row raise the Voltage
Giga Impact	Beauty	♥ ♥	Heart +3 if the previous Pokémon's performance achieved a Voltage of 5
Glare	Tough	♥ ♥	Voltage cannot be lowered on that same turn
Grass Knot	Smart	♥ ♥	Heart +2 if user's performance raises the judge's Voltage
GrassWhistle	Smart	♥ ♥	Voltage cannot be lowered on that same turn
Gravity	Beauty	♥ ♥	Voltage cannot be raised on that same turn
Growl	Cute	♥ ♥	Voltage cannot be lowered on that same turn
Growth	Beauty	—	Move doubles in value on the next turn
Grudge	Tough	♥ ♥	Voltage is lowered by one notch for all judges
Guard Swap	Cute	—	Has higher value the lower the Voltage is. If your chosen judge's Voltage is 0: Heart +4. 1: +3. 2: +2. 3: +1. 4: none.
Guillotine	Cool	—	Heart +15 if all Pokémon choose the same judge
Gunk Shot	Cool	♥ ♥ ♥	Basic performance move
Gust	Smart	♥ ♥ ♥	Basic performance move
Gyro Ball	Beauty	♥ ♥	Double hearts if it was used last turn
Hail	Beauty	♥ ♥	Voltage cannot be raised on that same turn
Hammer Arm	Cool	♥ ♥	User goes last on the next turn
Harden	Tough	♥ ♥	Voltage cannot be raised on that same turn
Haze	Beauty	♥ ♥	Voltage cannot be raised on that same turn
Head Smash	Tough	♥ ♥	Heart +3 if the previous Pokémon's performance achieved a Voltage of 5
Headbutt	Tough	♥ ♥ ♥	Basic performance move
Heal Bell	Beauty	—	Hearts are added equal to the number of the Voltage of your chosen judge
Heal Block	Cute	♥ ♥	Voltage cannot be raised on that same turn
Heal Order	Smart	—	Hearts are added equal to the number of the Voltage of your chosen judge
Healing Wish	Cute	—	Hearts are added equal to the number of the Voltage of your chosen judge
Heart Swap	Cool	—	Has higher value the lower the Voltage is. If your chosen judge's Voltage is 0: Heart +4. 1: +3. 2: +2. 3: +1. 4: none.
Heat Wave	Beauty	♥ ♥	Heart +2 if performed first in the turn
Helping Hand	Smart	♥	Heart +3 if 2 Pokémon in a row raise the Voltage
Hi Jump Kick	Cool	♥ ♥ ♥	Basic performance move
Hidden Power	Smart	♥	Heart +3 if user has the lowest value in the turn
Horn Attack	Cool	♥ ♥ ♥	Basic performance move
Horn Drill	Cool	—	Heart +15 if all Pokémon choose the same judge
Howl	Cool	—	Move doubles in value on the next turn
Hydro Cannon	Beauty	♥ ♥	Heart +3 if the previous Pokémon's performance achieved a Voltage of 5
Hydro Pump	Beauty	♥ ♥	Heart +2 if performed first in the turn
Hyper Beam	Cool	♥ ♥	Heart +3 if the previous Pokémon's performance achieved a Voltage of 5
Hyper Fang	Cool	♥ ♥	Heart +2 if used last in the turn
Hyper Voice	Cool	♥ ♥ ♥	Basic performance move
Hypnosis	Smart	♥ ♥	Voltage cannot be lowered on that same turn
Ice Ball	Beauty	♥ ♥	Can use the same move twice in a row
Ice Beam	Beauty	♥ ♥	Heart +2 if performed first in the turn
Ice Fang	Cool	♥ ♥ ♥	Basic performance move

Move	Category	Hearts	Effect
Ice Punch	Beauty	♥♥	Heart +2 if performed first in the turn
Ice Shard	Beauty	♥♥	User goes first on the next turn
Icicle Spear	Beauty	♥♥	Can perform using the same move twice in a row
Icy Wind	Beauty	♥♥	User goes last on the next turn
Imprison	Smart	♥	Heart +3 if 2 Pokémon in a row raise the Voltage
Ingrain	Smart	—	Value depends on when in the lineup it is performed. First: Heart +1. 2nd: +2. 3rd: +3. Last: +4.
Iron Defense	Tough	♥♥	Voltage cannot be raised on that same turn
Iron Head	Tough	♥♥	Heart +2 if used last in the turn
Iron Tail	Cool	♥♥	Heart +2 if used last in the turn
Jump Kick	Cool	♥♥♥	Basic performance move
Karate Chop	Tough	♥♥♥	Basic performance move
Kinesis	Smart	—	Move doubles in value on the next turn
Knock Off	Smart	♥♥♥	Basic performance move
Last Resort	Cute	—	Value depends on when in the lineup it is performed. First: Heart +1. 2nd: +2. 3rd: +3. Last: +4.
Lava Plume	Tough	♥♥	Heart +2 if performed first in the turn
Leaf Blade	Cool	♥♥	Heart +2 if performed first in the turn
Leaf Storm	Cute	♥♥	Heart +3 if the previous Pokémon's performance achieved a Voltage of 5
Leech Life	Smart	♥	Heart +3 if 2 Pokémon in a row raise the Voltage
Leech Seed	Smart	—	Value depends on when in the lineup it is performed. First: Heart +1. 2nd: +2. 3rd: +3. Last: +4.
Leer	Cool	♥♥	Voltage cannot be lowered on that same turn
Lick	Tough	—	Has higher value the lower the Voltage is. If your chosen judge's Voltage is 0: Heart +4. 1: +3. 2: +2. 3: +1. 4: none.
Light Screen	Beauty	♥♥	Voltage cannot be raised on that same turn
Lock-On	Smart	♥	Heart +3 if 2 Pokémon in a row raise the Voltage
Lovely Kiss	Beauty	♥♥	Voltage cannot be lowered on that same turn
Low Kick	Tough	♥♥♥	Basic performance move
Lucky Chant	Cute	♥♥	Voltage cannot be raised on that same turn
Lunar Dance	Beauty	—	Hearts are added equal to the number of the Voltage of your chosen judge
Luster Purge	Smart	♥♥	Heart +3 if the previous Pokémon's performance achieved a Voltage of 5
Mach Punch	Cool	♥♥	User goes first on the next turn
Magic Coat	Beauty	♥♥	Double hearts if it was used last turn
Magical Leaf	Beauty	♥♥	Heart +2 if performed first in the turn
Magma Storm	Tough	♥♥	Can perform using the same move twice in a row
Magnet Bomb	Cool	♥♥♥	Basic performance move
Magnet Rise	Cute	♥♥	Voltage cannot be raised on that same turn
Magnitude	Tough	♥♥	Heart +2 if used last in the turn
Me First	Cute	♥♥	User goes first on the next turn
Mean Look	Beauty	♥♥	Voltage is lowered by one notch for all judges
Meditate	Beauty	—	Move doubles in value on the next turn
Mega Drain	Smart	♥	Heart +3 if 2 Pokémon in a row raise the Voltage
Mega Kick	Cool	♥♥	Heart +2 if used last in the turn
Mega Punch	Tough	♥♥	Heart +2 if used last in the turn
Megahorn	Cool	♥♥	Heart +2 if used last in the turn
Memento	Tough	—	Heart +15 if all Pokémon choose the same judge
Metal Burst	Beauty	♥♥	Double hearts if it was used last turn
Metal Claw	Cool	♥♥	Heart +2 if used last in the turn
Metal Sound	Smart	♥♥	Voltage is lowered by one notch for all judges
Meteor Mash	Cool	♥♥	Heart +2 if used last in the turn
Metronome	Cute	♥♥	Next turn goes in a random order
Milk Drink	Cute	—	Hearts are added equal to the number of the Voltage of your chosen judge

Move	Category	Hearts	Effect
Mimic	Cute	—	If the previous Pokémon generated a Voltage of 5, steals its bonus hearts
Mind Reader	Smart	♥	Heart +3 if 2 Pokémon in a row raise the Voltage
Minimize	Cute	♥ ♥	Voltage cannot be raised on that same turn
Miracle Eye	Cute	♥	Heart +3 if 2 Pokémon in a row raise the Voltage
Mirror Coat	Beauty	♥ ♥	Double hearts if it was used last turn
Mirror Move	Smart	♥ ♥	Double hearts if it was used last turn
Mirror Shot	Cute	♥ ♥	Heart +2 if performed first in the turn
Mist	Beauty	♥ ♥	Voltage cannot be raised on that same turn
Mist Ball	Smart	♥ ♥	Heart +3 if the previous Pokémon's performance achieved a Voltage of 5
Moonlight	Beauty	—	Hearts are added equal to the number of the Voltage of your chosen judge
Morning Sun	Beauty	—	Hearts are added equal to the number of the Voltage of your chosen judge
Mud Bomb	Smart	♥ ♥	Heart +2 if used last in the turn
Mud Shot	Tough	♥ ♥	User goes last on the next turn
Mud Sport	Cute	♥ ♥	Voltage cannot be raised on that same turn
Muddy Water	Tough	♥ ♥	Heart +2 if used last in the turn
Mud-Slap	Cute	♥ ♥ ♥	Basic performance move
Nasty Plot	Cute	—	Move doubles in value on the next turn
Natural Gift	Cool	♥ ♥	Heart +2 if used last in the turn
Nature Power	Beauty	♥ ♥	Next turn goes in a random order
Needle Arm	Smart	♥ ♥ ♥	Basic performance move
Night Shade	Smart	♥ ♥ ♥	Basic performance move
Night Slash	Beauty	♥ ♥ ♥	Basic performance move
Nightmare	Smart	♥ ♥	Voltage cannot be lowered on that same turn
Octazooka	Tough	♥ ♥	Heart +2 if user's performance raises the judge's Voltage
Odor Sleuth	Smart	♥	Heart +3 if 2 Pokémon in a row raise the Voltage
Ominous Wind	Smart	—	Move doubles in value on the next turn
Outrage	Cool	♥ ♥	Can perform using the same move twice in a row
Overheat	Beauty	♥ ♥	Heart +3 if the previous Pokémon's performance achieved a Voltage of 5
Pain Split	Smart	♥ ♥	Voltage is lowered by one notch for all judges
Pay Day	Smart	♥	Heart +3 if user has the lowest value in the turn
Payback	Cool	♥	Heart +3 if your judge is not taken by other Pokémon
Peck	Cool	♥ ♥ ♥	Basic performance move
Perish Song	Beauty	♥ ♥	Voltage is lowered by one notch for all judges
Petal Dance	Beauty	—	Value depends on when in the lineup it is performed. First: Heart +1. 2nd: +2. 3rd: +3. Last: +4.
Pin Missile	Cool	♥ ♥	Can perform using the same move twice in a row
Pluck	Cute	—	If the previous Pokémon generated a Voltage of 5, steals its bonus hearts
Poison Fang	Smart	♥ ♥	Heart +2 if user's performance raises the judge's Voltage
Poison Gas	Smart	♥ ♥ ♥	Basic performance move
Poison Jab	Smart	♥ ♥	Heart +2 if user's performance raises the judge's Voltage
Poison Sting	Smart	♥ ♥	Voltage cannot be lowered on that same turn
Poison Tail	Smart	♥ ♥	Heart +2 if user's performance raises the judge's Voltage
PoisonPowder	Smart	♥ ♥	Voltage cannot be lowered on that same turn
Pound	Tough	♥ ♥ ♥	Basic performance move
Powder Snow	Beauty	♥ ♥ ♥	Basic performance move
Power Gem	Beauty	♥ ♥ ♥	Basic performance move
Power Swap	Beauty	—	Has higher value the lower the Voltage is. If your chosen judge's Voltage is 0: Heart +4. 1: +3. 2: +2. 3: +1. 4: none.
Power Trick	Cool	—	Has higher value the lower the Voltage is. If your chosen judge's Voltage is 0: Heart +4. 1: +3. 2: +2. 3: +1. 4: none.
Power Whip	Beauty	♥ ♥ ♥	Basic performance move
Present	Cute	—	Has higher value the lower the Voltage is. If your chosen judge's Voltage is 0: Heart +4. 1: +3. 2: +2. 3: +1. 4: none.

Move	Category	Hearts	Effect
Protect	Cute	—	Has higher value the lower the Voltage is. If your chosen judge's Voltage is 0: Heart +4. 1: +3. 2: +2. 3: +1. 4: none.
Psybeam	Beauty	♥♥	Heart +2 if performed first in the turn
Psych Up	Smart	—	Move doubles in value on the next turn
Psychic	Smart	♥♥	Heart +2 if performed first in the turn
Psycho Boost	Smart	♥♥	Heart +3 if the previous Pokémon's performance achieved a Voltage of 5
Psycho Cut	Cool	♥♥	Heart +2 if performed first in the turn
Psycho Shift	Cool	—	Has higher value the lower the Voltage is. If your chosen judge's Voltage is 0: Heart +4. 1: +3. 2: +2. 3: +1. 4: none.
Psywave	Smart	♥♥♥	Basic performance move
Punishment	Smart	♥	Heart +3 if user has the lowest value in the turn
Pursuit	Smart	♥	Heart +3 if 2 Pokémon in a row raise the Voltage
Quick Attack	Cool	♥♥	User goes first on the next turn
Rage	Cool	—	Move doubles in value on the next turn
Rain Dance	Tough	♥♥	Voltage cannot be raised on that same turn
Rapid Spin	Cool	♥♥	Heart +2 if performed first in the turn
Razor Leaf	Cool	♥♥♥	Basic performance move
Razor Wind	Cool	♥	Heart +3 if your judge is not taken by other Pokémon
Recover	Smart	—	Hearts are added equal to the number of the Voltage of your chosen judge
Recycle	Smart	—	If the previous Pokémon generated a Voltage of 5, steals its bonus hearts
Reflect	Smart	♥♥	Voltage cannot be raised on that same turn
Refresh	Cute	—	Hearts are added equal to the number of the Voltage of your chosen judge
Rest	Cute	—	Hearts are added equal to the number of the Voltage of your chosen judge
Return	Cute	♥♥	Heart +2 if performed first in the turn
Revenge	Tough	♥♥	Double hearts if it was used last turn
Reversal	Cool	♥♥	Double hearts if it was used last turn
Roar	Cool	♥♥	Voltage cannot be lowered on that same turn
Roar of Time	Cool	♥♥	Heart +3 if the previous Pokémon's performance achieved a Voltage of 5
Rock Blast	Tough	♥♥	Can perform using the same move twice in a row
Rock Climb	Cool	♥♥	Heart +2 if used last in the turn
Rock Polish	Tough	♥♥	User goes first on the next turn
Rock Slide	Tough	♥♥♥	Basic performance move
Rock Smash	Tough	♥♥	Heart +2 if used last in the turn
Rock Throw	Tough	♥♥♥	Basic performance move
Rock Tomb	Smart	♥♥	User goes last on the next turn
Rock Wrecker	Tough	♥♥	Heart +3 if the previous Pokémon's performance achieved a Voltage of 5
Role Play	Cute	♥	Heart +3 if user has the lowest value in the turn
Rolling Kick	Cool	♥♥♥	Basic performance move
Rollout	Tough	♥♥	Can perform using the same move twice in a row
Roost	Cool	—	Hearts are added equal to the number of the Voltage of your chosen judge
Sacred Fire	Beauty	♥♥	Heart +3 if the previous Pokémon's performance achieved a Voltage of 5
Safeguard	Beauty	♥♥	Voltage cannot be raised on that same turn
Sand Tomb	Smart	—	Value depends on when in the lineup it is performed. First: Heart +1. 2nd: +2. 3rd: +3. Last: +4.
Sand-Attack	Cute	♥♥	Voltage cannot be lowered on that same turn
Sandstorm	Tough	♥♥	Voltage cannot be raised on that same turn
Scary Face	Tough	♥♥	User goes last on the next turn
Scratch	Tough	♥♥♥	Basic performance move
Screech	Smart	♥♥	Voltage is lowered by one notch for all judges
Secret Power	Smart	♥♥	Next turn goes in a random order
Seed Bomb	Smart	♥♥♥	Basic performance move
Seed Flare	Cool	♥♥	Heart +3 if the previous Pokémon's performance achieved a Voltage of 5

Move	Category	Hearts	Effect
Seismic Toss	Tough	♥♥♥	Basic performance move
Selfdestruct	Beauty	—	Heart +15 if all Pokémon choose the same judge
Shadow Ball	Smart	♥♥	Heart +2 if performed first in the turn
Shadow Claw	Cute	♥♥	Heart +2 if performed first in the turn
Shadow Force	Smart	♥♥	Heart +3 if the previous Pokémon's performance achieved a Voltage of 5
Shadow Punch	Smart	♥♥	Heart +2 if performed first in the turn
Shadow Sneak	Smart	♥♥	User goes first on the next turn
Sharpen	Cute	—	Move doubles in value on the next turn
Sheer Cold	Beauty	—	Heart +15 if all Pokémon choose the same judge
Shock Wave	Cool	♥♥	Heart +2 if performed first in the turn
Signal Beam	Beauty	♥♥	Heart +2 if user's performance raises the judge's Voltage
Silver Wind	Beauty	♥♥	Heart +2 if user's performance raises the judge's Voltage
Sing	Cute	♥♥	Voltage cannot be lowered on that same turn
Sketch	Smart	♥	Heart +3 if user has the lowest value in the turn
Skill Swap	Smart	—	If the previous Pokémon generated a Voltage of 5, steals its bonus hearts
Skull Bash	Tough	♥	Heart +3 if your judge is not taken by other Pokémon
Sky Attack	Cool	♥	Heart +3 if your judge is not taken by other Pokémon
Sky Uppercut	Cool	♥♥	Heart +2 if performed first in the turn
Slack Off	Cute	—	Hearts are added equal to the number of the Voltage of your chosen judge
Slam	Tough	♥♥♥	Basic performance move
Slash	Cool	♥♥♥	Basic performance move
Sleep Powder	Smart	♥♥	Voltage cannot be lowered on that same turn
Sleep Talk	Cute	♥♥♥	Basic performance move
Sludge	Tough	♥♥	Heart +2 if used last in the turn
Sludge Bomb	Tough	♥♥	Heart +2 if used last in the turn
SmellingSalt	Smart	—	Has higher value the lower the Voltage is. If your chosen judge's Voltage is 0: Heart +4. 1: +3. 2: +2. 3: +1. 4: none.
Smog	Tough	♥♥♥	Basic performance move
SmokeScreen	Smart	♥♥	Voltage is lowered by one notch for all judges
Snatch	Smart	—	If the previous Pokémon generated a Voltage of 5, steals its bonus hearts
Snore	Cute	♥♥♥	Basic performance move
Softboiled	Beauty	—	Hearts are added equal to the number of the Voltage of your chosen judge
SolarBeam	Cool	♥	Heart +3 if your judge is not taken by other Pokémon
SonicBoom	Cool	♥♥♥	Basic performance move
Spacial Rend	Tough	♥♥	Heart +2 if user's performance raises the judge's Voltage
Spark	Cool	♥♥♥	Basic performance move
Spider Web	Smart	♥♥	Voltage cannot be raised on that same turn
Spike Cannon	Cool	♥♥	Can perform using the same move twice in a row
Spikes	Smart	♥♥	Voltage cannot be raised on that same turn
Spit Up	Tough	♥♥	Heart +2 if used last in the turn
Spite	Tough	♥♥	Voltage cannot be lowered on that same turn
Splash	Cute	—	Has higher value the lower the Voltage is. If your chosen judge's Voltage is 0: Heart +4. 1: +3. 2: +2. 3: +1. 4: none.
Spore	Beauty	♥♥	Voltage is lowered by one notch for all judges
Stealth Rock	Cool	♥♥	Voltage cannot be raised on that same turn
Steel Wing	Cool	♥♥♥	Basic performance move
Stockpile	Tough	—	Move doubles in value on the next turn
Stomp	Tough	♥♥♥	Basic performance move
Stone Edge	Tough	♥♥	Heart +2 if user's performance raises the judge's Voltage
Strength	Tough	♥♥♥	Basic performance move
String Shot	Smart	♥♥	Voltage cannot be lowered on that same turn

Move	Category	Hearts	Effect
Stun Spore	Smart	♥♥	Voltage cannot be lowered on that same turn
Submission	Cool	♥♥♥	Basic performance move
Substitute	Smart	♥	Heart +3 if user has the lowest value in the turn
Sucker Punch	Smart	♥♥	User goes first on the next turn
Sunny Day	Beauty	♥♥	Voltage cannot be raised on that same turn
Super Fang	Tough	♥♥♥	Basic performance move
Superpower	Tough	♥♥	Heart +2 if used last in the turn
Supersonic	Smart	♥♥	Voltage cannot be lowered on that same turn
Surf	Beauty	♥♥	Heart +2 if performed first in the turn
Swagger	Cute	♥♥	Voltage cannot be lowered on that same turn
Swallow	Tough	—	Hearts are added equal to the number of the Voltage of your chosen judge
Sweet Kiss	Cute	♥♥	Voltage cannot be lowered on that same turn
Sweet Scent	Cute	♥♥	Voltage cannot be lowered on that same turn
Swift	Cool	♥♥	Heart +2 if performed first in the turn
Switcheroo	Cool	—	If the previous Pokémon generated a Voltage of 5, steals its bonus hearts
Swords Dance	Beauty	—	Move doubles in value on the next turn
Synthesis	Smart	—	Hearts are added equal to the number of the Voltage of your chosen judge
Tackle	Tough	♥♥♥	Basic performance move
Tail Glow	Beauty	—	Move doubles in value on the next turn
Tail Whip	Cute	♥♥	Voltage cannot be lowered on that same turn
Tailwind	Smart	♥♥	User goes first on the next turn
Take Down	Tough	♥♥♥	Basic performance move
Taunt	Smart	—	Has higher value the lower the Voltage is. If your chosen judge's Voltage is 0: Heart +4. 1: +3. 2: +2. 3: +1. 4: none.
Teeter Dance	Cute	♥♥	Next turn goes in a random order
Teleport	Cool	♥♥	User goes first on the next turn
Thief	Tough	—	If the previous Pokémon generated a Voltage of 5, steals its bonus hearts
Thrash	Tough	♥♥	Can use the same move twice in a row
Thunder	Cool	♥♥	Heart +2 if performed first in the turn
Thunder Fang	Smart	♥♥♥	Basic performance move
Thunder Wave	Cool	♥♥	Voltage cannot be lowered on that same turn
Thunderbolt	Cool	♥♥	Heart +2 if performed first in the turn
ThunderPunch	Cool	♥♥	Heart +2 if performed first in the turn
ThunderShock	Cool	♥♥♥	Basic performance move
Tickle	Cute	♥♥	Voltage cannot be lowered on that same turn
Torment	Tough	—	The lower the Voltage, the higher the value. If your chosen judge's Voltage is 0: Heart +4. 1: +3. 2: +2. 3: +1. 4: none.
Toxic	Smart	♥♥	Voltage cannot be lowered on that same turn
Toxic Spikes	Smart	♥♥	Voltage cannot be raised on that same turn
Transform	Smart	♥	Heart +3 if user has the lowest value in the turn
Tri Attack	Beauty	♥♥♥	Basic performance move
Trick	Smart	—	If the previous Pokémon generated a Voltage of 5, steals its bonus hearts
Trick Room	Cute	♥♥	Next turn goes in a random order
Triple Kick	Cool	♥♥	Can perform using the same move twice in a row
Trump Card	Cool	—	Value depends on when in the lineup it is performed. First: Heart +1. 2nd: +2. 3rd: +3. Last: +4.
Twineedle	Cool	♥♥	Can perform using the same move twice in a row
Twister	Cool	♥♥♥	Basic performance move
U-turn	Cute	—	Has higher value the lower the Voltage is. If your chosen judge's Voltage is 0: Heart +4. 1: +3. 2: +2. 3: +1. 4: none.
Uproar	Cute	♥♥	Voltage is lowered by one notch for all judges
Vacuum Wave	Smart	♥♥	User goes first on the next turn
Vicegrip	Tough	♥♥♥	Basic performance move

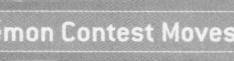
Move	Category	Hearts	Effect
Vine Whip	Cool	♥♥♥	Basic performance move
Vital Throw	Cool	♥♥	User goes last on the next turn
Volt Tackle	Cool	♥♥	Heart +3 if the previous Pokémon's performance achieved a Voltage of 5
Wake-Up Slap	Smart	—	Has higher value the lower the Voltage is. If your chosen judge's Voltage is 0: Heart +4. 1: +3. 2: +2. 3: +1. 4: none.
Water Gun	Cute	♥♥♥	Basic performance move
Water Pulse	Beauty	♥♥	Heart +2 if performed first in the turn
Water Sport	Cute	♥♥	Voltage cannot be raised on that same turn
Water Spout	Beauty	♥♥	Heart +3 if the previous Pokémon's performance achieved a Voltage of 5
Waterfall	Tough	♥♥♥	Basic performance move
Weather Ball	Smart	♥♥	Heart +2 if user's performance raises the judge's Voltage
Whirlpool	Beauty	—	Value depends on when in the lineup it is performed. First: Heart +1. 2nd: +2. 3rd: +3. Last: +4.
Whirlwind	Smart	—	Heart +15 if all Pokémon choose the same judge
Will-O-Wisp	Beauty	♥♥	Heart +2 if performed first in the turn
Wing Attack	Cool	♥♥♥	Basic performance move
Wish	Cute	—	Hearts are added equal to the number of the Voltage of your chosen judge
Withdraw	Cute	♥♥	Voltage cannot be raised on that same turn
Wood Hammer	Tough	♥♥	Heart +2 if used last in the turn
Worry Seed	Beauty	♥♥	Voltage cannot be lowered on that same turn
Wrap	Tough	—	Value depends on when in the lineup it is performed. First: Heart +1. 2nd: +2. 3rd: +3. Last: +4.
Wring Out	Smart	♥♥	Heart +3 if the previous Pokémon's performance achieved a Voltage of 5
X-Scissor	Beauty	♥♥	Heart +2 if performed first in the turn
Yawn	Cute	♥♥	Voltage cannot be lowered on that same turn
Zap Cannon	Cool	♥♥	Heart +2 if user's performance raises the judge's Voltage
Zen Headbutt	Beauty	♥♥	Heart +2 if used last in the turn

Pokémon Natures and Personalities

Pokémon Natures

Each individual Pokémon has its own particular Nature. Nature affects which stats will develop the most when the Pokémon levels up, and which flavors of Poffin the Pokémon will prefer.

Poffin Flavor	Spicy	Sour	Sweet	Dry	Bitter
Pokémon stats	Attack	Defense	Speed	Sp. Attack	Sp. Defense
Hardy					
Lonely	O	▼			
Brave	O		▼		
Adamant	O			▼	
Naughty	O				▼
Bold	▼	O			
Docile					
Relaxed		O	▼		
Impish		O		▼	
Lax		O			▼
Timid	▼		O		
Hasty		▼	O		
Serious					
Jolly			O	▼	
Naive			O		▼
Modest	▼			O	
Mild		▼		O	
Quiet			▼	O	
Bashful					
Rash				O	▼
Calm	▼				O
Gentle		▼			O
Sassy			▼		O
Careful				▼	O
Quirky					

O.....Stat that rises the most readily upon leveling up/Favorite flavor of Poffin
▼.....Stat that rises most slowly upon leveling up/Most disliked Poffin flavor

Pokémon personalities

In addition to having a Nature, each individual Pokémon has a personality. The personality affects which stat rises the most easily when the Pokémon levels up.

Most-developed stat	Personality
HP	Loves to eat
	Often dozes off
	Often scatters things
	Scatters things often
	Likes to relax

Most-developed stat	Personality
Attack	Proud of its power
	Likes to thrash about
	A little quick tempered
	Likes to fight
	Quick tempered

Most-developed stat	Personality
Defense	Sturdy body
	Capable of taking hits
	Highly persistent
	Good endurance
	Good perseverence

Most-developed stat	Personality
Speed	Likes to run
	Alert to sounds
	Impetuous and silly
	Somewhat of a clown
	Quick to flee

Most-developed stat	Personality
Sp. Attack	Highly curious
	Mischevious
	Thoroughly cunning
	Often lost in thought
	Very finicky

Most-developed stat	Personality
Sp. Defense	Strong willed
	Somewhat vain
	Strongly defiant
	Hates to lose
	Somewhat stubborn

Ability	Effect in Battle		Effect when held by party leader
Adaptability	Type match-up effects are pronounced when user's move is the same type as itself		
Aftermath	Knocks off 1/4 of foe's HP if foe's direct attack causes user to faint		
Air Lock	Makes all Pokémon in battle immune to weather effects		
Anger Point	Raises user's Attack to the maximum level when user is hit by a critical hit		
Anticipation	Lets you know if foe has super effective moves or one-hit KO moves		
Arena Trap	Prevents foe from fleeing or switching out. No effect against Flying Pokémon or Pokémon with Levitate.		Raises wild Pokémon encounter rate
Bad Dreams	Slightly lowers the HP of sleeping Pokémon every turn		
Battle Armor	Foe cannot score a critical hit		
Blaze	Raises the power of Fire-type moves by 50% when user's HP is below 1/3		
Chlorophyll	Raises Speed by 2 when in Sunny weather		
Clear Body	Protects against stat-lowering moves and Abilities		
Cloud Nine	All Pokémon in battle become immune to weather effects		
Color Change	Changes user into the type of the move that just hit it		
Compoundeyes	Raises Accuracy by 30%		Raises encounter rate with wild Pokémon holding items
Cute Charm	30% chance of charming a foe that hits user with a direct attack		Raises encounter rate of wild Pokémon of the opposite gender
Damp	Makes both sides unable to use Selfdestruct and Explosion. Nullifies the Aftermath Ability.		
Download	When user enters battle, raises Attack by 1 if foe's Defense is lower than its Sp. Defense, Sp. Attack by 1 if foe's Sp. Defense is lower than its Defense.		
Drizzle	Turns weather to Rainy when user enters battle		
Drought	Makes the weather Sunny when user enters battle		
Dry Skin	Restores HP when user is hit by a Water-type move. Restores HP every turn in Rainy weather. However, user receives increased damage from Fire-type moves. User takes damage every turn when in Sunny weather.		
Early Bird	User wakes quickly from sleep		
Effect Spore	30% chance of counter-inflicting poison, paralysis, or sleep when hit by a direct attack		
Filter	Minimizes the damage received from super effective moves		
Flame Body	30% chance of burning a foe that hits user with a direct attack		Facilitates hatching Eggs when in your party
Flash Fire	When user is hit by a Fire-type move, instead of taking damage, it powers up its Fire-type moves by 50%		
Flower Gift	Raises Attack and Sp. Defense of user and ally when in Sunny weather		
Forecast	Changes Castform's appearance and type according to the weather. Sunny weather: Fire-type. Rainy: Water-type. Hail: Ice-type.		
Forewarn	Lets you know one of foe's moves when user enters battle. Focuses on the move with the most power or damage.		
Frisk	Lets you know your foe's held item when user enters battle		
Gluttony	Makes user use its held berry sooner when it has low HP		
Guts	Attack rises by 50% when user has a status ailment		
Heatproof	Halves damage from Fire moves and from the burn status ailment		
Honey Gather	If user isn't holding an item, sometimes it will be holding Honey after battle (even if it didn't participate). Its chance of finding Honey increases with its level.		
Huge Power	Gives user high Attack (if Huge Power is nullified, Attack is halved)		
Hustle	Raises Attack by 50%, but lowers the Accuracy of user's physical moves by 20%		Raises encounter rate with high-level wild Pokémon

Ability	Effect in Battle	Effect when held by party leader
Hydration	Cures user's status ailments at the end of the turn when in Rainy weather	
Hyper Cutter	Attack cannot be lowered	
Ice Body	Gradually restores HP in Hail weather	
Illuminate	No effect	Raises wild Pokémon encounter rate
Immunity	User cannot be poisoned	
Inner Focus	Foe's moves cannot make user flinch as a side effect	
Insomnia	Pokémon cannot fall asleep	
Intimidate	Lowers foe's Attack by 1 when user enters battle	Lowers encounter rate of low-level wild Pokémon
Iron Fist	Increases the power of Ice Punch, Fire Punch, ThunderPunch, Mach Punch, Mega Punch, Comet Punch, Bullet Punch, and Sky Uppercut	
Keen Eye	Accuracy cannot be lowered	Lowers encounter rate with low-level wild Pokémon
Klutz	User's held items are ineffective	
Leaf Guard	Protects user from status ailments when in Sunny weather	
Levitate	Makes user immune to Ground-type moves	
Lightningrod	Draws all Electric-type moves to user	
Limber	Protects against paralysis	
Liquid Ooze	When foe uses an HP-draining move on user, damages foe instead	
Magic Guard	Except for direct attacks, user cannot take damage from the situations below: Abilities: Liquid Ooze, Aftermath, Rough Skin. Weather: Sandstorm, Hail. Status ailments: Poison, badly poisoned, burn, Bad Dream, Curse, Leech, Bind, Sand Tomb, Fire Spin, Wrap, Clamp, Magma Storm. Moves: Toxic Spikes, Stealth Rock, Spikes. Items: Black Sludge, Sticky Barb, Life Orb. Also recoil damage or move failure damage.	
Magma Armor	User cannot become frozen	Facilitates hatching Eggs when in your party
Magnet Pull	Prevents Steel-type Pokémon from fleeing or switching out	Raises encounter rate with wild Steel-type Pokémon
Marvel Scale	Raises Defense by 50% when user has a status ailment	
Minus	Raises Sp. Defense by 50% when a Pokémon with the Plus Abillity is in battle	
Mold Breaker	User can attack without being affected by foe's Ability. Does not work against Abilities that activate after the attack. For instance, user can score a critical hit against a foe with Battle Armor, but still takes damage from Rough Skin.	
Motor Drive	When user is hit by an Electric-type move, its Speed goes up 1 rather than it taking damage	
Natural Cure	Cures user's status ailments when user leaves the battle	
No Guard	Both sides' moves always strikes their targets	Raises wild Pokémon encounter rate
Normalize	All of user's moves become Normal-type	
Oblivious	User cannot be charmed/attracted	
Overgrow	Raises the power of Grass-type moves by 50% when user's HP is below 1/3	
Own Tempo	User cannot become confused	
Pickup	If user has no held item, it sometimes picks one up after battle (even if it didn't participate). It picks up different items depending on its level.	
Plus	Raises Sp. Attack by 50% if a Pokémon with the Minus Ability is in battle	
Poison Heal	Restores HP every turn when user is poisoned	
Poison Point	30% chance of counter-inflicting poison on a foe that hits user with a direct attack	
Pressure	When user is hit by a foe's move, depletes 1 PP from that move	Raises encounter rate with high-level wild Pokémon

Ability	Effect in Battle		Effect when held by party leader
Pure Power	Gives user high Attack (Attack is halved if Pure Power is nullified)		
Quick Feet	Raises Speed by 2 when user has a status ailment		Lowers wild Pokémon encounter rate
Rain Dish	Gradually restores HP in Rainy weather		
Reckless	Raises the power of moves with recoil damage, like Jump Kick and Hi Jump Kick		
Rivalry	Raises Attack when user and foe are same gender, lowers it when they're opposite genders.		
Rock Head	No recoil damage from moves like Takedown and Double-Edge		
Rough Skin	Slightly damages a foe that comes in for a direct attack		
Run Away	User can always escape from a battle (except Trainer battles)		
Sand Stream	Makes the weather Sandstorm when user enters battle		
Sand Veil	Raises Evasion when in Sandstorm weather		Lowers encounter rate with wild Pokémon in Sandstorm weather
Scrappy	Lets user hit Ghost-type Pokémon with Normal-type moves		
Serene Grace	Doubles chances of moves inflicting side effects		
Shadow Tag	Prevents foe from fleeing or switching out. No effect if both sides have Shadow Tag.		
Shed Skin	1/3 chance every turn of curing user's status ailments		
Shell Armor	Foe cannot score a critical hit		
Shield Dust	Protects user from the side effects of moves		
Simple	The effects of stat alterations become more powerful		
Skill Link	Lets moves that strike successively strike the maximum number of times		
Slow Start	Halves Attack and Speed for 5 turns after user enters battle		
Sniper	Moves that strike a critical hit deal a great amount of damage		
Snow Cloak	Raises Evasion when in Hail weather		Lowers wild Pokémon encounter rate when in Hail weather
Snow Warning	Makes the weather Hail when user enters battle		
Solar Power	In Sunny weather, raises Sp. Attack by 50% but lowers HP every turn		
Solid Rock	Minimizes the damage received from super-effective moves		
Soundproof	Protects user from the sound-based moves Snore, Heal Bell, Screech, Sing, Chatter, Metal Sound, GrassWhistle, Uproar, Supersonic, Growl, Hyper Voice, Roar, Perish Song, and Bug Buzz		
Speed Boost	Raises Speed by 1 every turn		
Stall	User's moves come last in the turn		
Static	30% of counter-inflicting paralysis on a foe that makes a direct attack		Raises encounter rate with wild Electric-type Pokémon
Steadfast	Raises Speed by 1 every time foe flinches		
Stench	No effect		Lowers wild Pokémon encounter rate
Sticky Hold	User's held item cannot be stolen by foe		Makes it easier to hook Pokémon when fishing
Storm Drain	Draws all Water-type moves to user		
Sturdy	Protects user against one-hit KO moves like Horn Drill and Sheer Cold		
Suction Cups	Nullifies moves like Whirlwind and Roar, which would make the foe switch out		Makes Pokémon easier to hook when fishing
Super Luck	Raises user's critical hit rate		
Swarm	Raises the power of Bug-type moves by 50% when user's HP is below 1/3		

Ability	Effect in Battle	Effect when held by party leader
Swift Swim	Doubles Speed in Rainy weather	
Synchronize	When user has poison, paralysis, or burn, inflicts the same ailment on foe	Raises encounter rate with wild Pokémon with the same Nature
Tangled Feet	Raises Evasion when user is confused	
Technician	Raises the power of moves with a power of less than 60 by 50%. Also has an effect when power is altered by moves and the like.	
Thick Fat	Halves damage from Fire- and Ice-type moves	
Tinted Lens	Nullifies the type disadvantage of user's "not very effective" moves. 1/2 damage turns into regular damage, 1/4 damage into 1/2.	
Torrent	Strengthens Water-type moves by 50% when user's HP is below 1/3	
Trace	Becomes the same Ability as that of foe. Cannot trace the Abilities Forecast or Trace.	
Truant	User can only use a move once every other turn	
Unaware	Protects against stat-changing moves by foe	
Unburden	Doubles speed if user loses its held item. Speed returns to normal if user takes another item. No effect if user starts out with no held item.	
Vital Spirit	User cannot fall asleep	Raises encounter rate with high-level wild Pokémon
Volt Absorb	When user is hit by an Electric-type move, it restores HP rather than taking damage	
Water Absorb	When user is hit by an Water-type move, it restores HP rather than taking damage	
Water Veil	User cannot be burned	
White Smoke	Protects against stat-lowering moves and Abilities	Lowers wild Pokémon encounter rate
Wonder Guard	Protects user against all moves except super effective ones	

ADVENTURE DATA LIST

POKÉMON ABILITIES

Item	Explanation	How to get	Value
Adamant Orb	Just for Dialga. Raises the power of Dragon- and Steel-type moves	Mt. Coronet (middle) 4F - 2	—
Air Mail	Mail with a colorful image of a mail transport printed on it	Jubilife City/Eterna City/Solaceon Town	50P
Amulet Coin	Hold to double your battle prize money (even if holder fights only once)	Amity Square at Hearthome City	
Antidote	Cures poison	Pokémart	100P
Armor Fossil	Pokémon fossil. Can be restored into Shieldon.	Unearth in the Underground (only if your Trainer ID is an even number)	—
Awakening	Cures sleep	Pokémart (after winning at Oreburgh Gym)	250P
Big Mushroom	Can be sold for 2,500P	Route 212/Route 226/Sometimes held by wild Paras	—
Big Pearl	Can be sold for 3,750P	Oreburgh Gate B1F/Old Chateau1F	—
Big Root	Hold to increase the amount of HP restored by HP-draining moves	Route 214	—
Black Belt	Raises the power of Fighting-type moves when held	Man in residence on Route 221	—
Black Flute	A glass flute. Lowers wild Pokémon encounter rate.	Mt. Coronet (middle) 2F (receive from Looker)	—
Black Sludge	Restores a Poison-type Pokémon's HP during battle when held. Conversely, lowers the HP of other types of Pokémon when held.	Sometimes held by wild Croagunk and Toxicroak	—
BlackGlasses	Raises the power of Dark-type moves when held	Talk to a young man in a Celestic Town residence between 10 AM and 8 PM	—
Bloom Mail	Mail printed with a pretty flower petal pattern	Veilstone Dept. Store 1F	50P
Blue Flute	A glass flute. Cures sleep.	Held by Pokémon transferred from *Pokémon Ruby, Sapphire, Emerald*	—
Blue Scarf	Hold for greater value in Beauty Contests	Scarf Guy in a Pastoria City residence	—
Blue Shard	Item needed to have moves taught on Route 212 and in Snowpoint City and the Survival Area	Unearth in the Underground/Galactic Eterna Bldg. 3F/ Great Marsh/Route 212/Fuego Ironworks/ Route 217	—
Bright Powder	Raises Evasion when held	Trade in Battle Points at the Battle Frontier (48BP)	—
Bubble Mail	Mail with a print of a blue, watery world	Veilstone Dept. Store 1F	50P
Burn Heal	Cures burn	Pokémart (after winning at Oreburgh Gym)	250P
Calcium	Raises Sp. Attack EVs	Veilstone Dept. Store 2F/Route 209/Fuego Ironworks	9800P
Carbos	Raises Speed EVs	Veilstone Dept. Store 2F/Route 220/Route 211	9800P
Charcoal	Raises power of Fire-type moves when held	Route 227	—
Choice Band	You can only use one move, but Attack is raised by 50%	Trade in Battle Points at the Battle Frontier (48BP)	—
Choice Scarf	You can only use one move, but Speed is raised by 50%	Trade in Battle Points at the Battle Frontier (48BP)	—
Choice Specs	You can only use one move, but Sp. Attack is raised by 50%	Talk to a young man in a Celestic Town residence between 4 AM and 10 AM	—
Claw Fossil	Pokémon fossil. Can be restored into Anorith.	Unearth in the Underground (after you get the National Pokédex)	—
Cleanse Tag	Lowers wild Pokémon encounter rate when held by party leader	Old lady on Lost Tower 5F (after winning at Hearthome Gym)	—
Damp Rock	Hold to increase the duration of Rainy weather	Unearth in the Underground	—
Damp Mulch	Spread to make the soil stay moist longer, and make berries mature more slowly	Berry Master's house on Route 208	200P
Dawn Stone	Evolves certain Pokémon	Mt. Coronet (middle)1F/Route 225/Pickup Ability	—
DeepSeaScale	Doubles Sp. Attack when held by Clamperl. Give to Clamperl and link trade to evolve it into Gorebyss.	Sometimes held by wild Relicanth and Chinchou	—
DeepSeaTooth	Doubles Sp. Defense when held by Clamperl. Link trade Clamperl while it holds to evolve it into Huntail.	Sometimes held by wild Carvanha	—
Destiny Knot	Can share charmed/attracted status with foe when held	Route 224	—
Dire Hit	Raises a Pokémon's critical hit rate	Veilstone Dept. Store 2F/Oreburgh City	650P
Dome Fossil	Pokémon fossil. Can be restored into Kabuto.	Unearth in the Underground (after you get the National Pokédex)	—
Draco Plate	Raises power of Dragon-type moves when held	Unearth in the Underground	—
Dragon Fang	Raises power of Dragon-type moves when held	Celestic Town/Sometimes held by wild Bagon	—
Dragon Scale	Link trade Seadra while it holds the Dragon Scale to evolve it into Kingdra	Sometimes held by wild Horsea, Seadra, Dratini, and Dragonair	—
Dread Plate	Raises the power of Dark-type moves when held	Left-hand room in Old Chateau 2F/Unearth in the Underground	—
Dubious Disc	Link trade Porygon2 while it holds Dubious Disc to evolve it into Porygon-Z	Galactic Veilstone Bldg. 1F/Route 225	—
Dusk Stone	Evolves certain Pokémon	Galactic Warehouse/End of Victory Road 1F - 2/Pickup Ability	—
Earth Plate	Raises the power of Ground-type moves when held	Oreburgh Gate B1F/Unearth in the Underground	—
Electirizer	Link trade Electabuzz while it holds Electirizer to evolve it into Electivire	Valley Windworks/Sometimes held by wild Electabuzz	—
Elixir	Restores 10 PP to all moves	Route 212/Iron Island B2F - 1/Pickup Ability	—
Energy Root	Restores 200 HP to a Pokémon. Very bitter.	Herbal medicine shop in Eterna City	800P

Item	Explanation	How to get	Value
EnergyPowder	Restores 50 HP to a Pokémon. Very bitter.	Herbal medicine shop in Eterna City	500P
Escape Rope	Returns you to the entrance of a cave or similar area	Pokémart (after winning at Oreburgh Gym)	550P
Ether	Restores 10 PP to a single move	Eterna Forest/Route 208/Pickup Ability	—
Everstone	Prevents Pokémon Evolution when held	Unearth in the Underground/Sometimes held by wild Geodude and Graveler	—
Exp. Share	Hold to collect Exp. even if user doesn't go into battle	Receive from Professor Rowan's assistant at Eterna City	—
Expert Belt	Raises the power of super-effective moves	Man in residence on Route 221	—
Fire Stone	Evolves certain Pokémon	Fuego Ironworks/Unearth in the Underground	—
Fist Plate	Raises the power of Fighting-type moves when held	Route 215/Unearth in the Underground	—
Flame Mail	Mail with a print of red-hot flames	Veilstone Dept. Store 1F	50P
Flame Orb	Inflicts burn status on user when held	Trade in Battle Points at the Battle Frontier (16BP)	—
Flame Plate	Raises the power of Fire-type moves when held	Unearth in the Underground	—
Fluffy Tail	Can always run away from a wild Pokémon encounter	Held by Pokémon transferred from *Pokémon Ruby, Sapphire, Emerald*	—
Focus Band	When held, sometimes leaves user with 1 HP if hit by a knock-out move	Trade in Battle Points at the Battle Frontier (48BP)	—
Focus Sash	When held, leaves user with 1 HP if hit by a knock-out move	Man in residence on Route 221/Trade in Battle Points at the Battle Frontier (48BP)	—
Fresh Water	Restores 50 HP to a Pokémon	Veilstone Dept. Store 5F	200P
Full Heal	Cures all status ailments	Pokémart (after winning at Pastoria Gym)	600P
Full Incense	When held, makes user strike last	Veilstone City	—
Full Restore	Completely heals a Pokémon's HP and status	Pokémart (after winning at Sunyshore Gym)	3000P
Gooey Mulch	Spread to increase the frequency at which fallen berries grow into new sprouts	Berry Master's house on Route 208	200P
Grass Mail	Mail with a print of fresh, green grass	Veilstone Dept. Store 1F	50P
Green Scarf	Hold to raise value in Smart Contests	Scarf Guy in a Pastoria City residence	—
Green Shard	Item needed to have moves taught on Route 212 and in Snowpoint City and the Survival Area	Unearth in the Underground/Eterna Forest/Route 212/Great Marsh/Fuego Ironworks/Galactic Veilstone Bldg.2F	—
Grip Claw	Lengthens the effective time of moves like Bind and Wrap	Wayward Cave B1F/Often held by wild Sneasel	—
Griseous Orb	Makes Giratina change to Origin Forme when held	Distortion World at the end of Turnback Cave	—
Growth Mulch	Spread to hasten the soil drying out but speed up berry maturation	Berry Master's house on Route 208	200P
Guard Spec.	For 5 turns, allies' stats cannot be lowered	Veilstone Dept. Store 2F/Route 205	700P
Hard Stone	Raises the power of Rock-type moves when held	Unearth in the Underground/cave on Route 228	—
Heal Powder	Cures all status ailments. Very bitter.	Herbal medicine shop in Eterna City	450P
Heart Mail	Mail with a big heart pattern printed on it	Hearthome City	50P
Heart Scale	Give to the move tutor in Pastoria City to have him teach one move	Unearth in the Underground/Job for Pokémon News Press at Solaceon Town	—
Heat Rock	Extends the duration of Sunny weather when held	Unearth in the Underground	—
Helix Fossil	Pokémon fossil. Can be restored into Omanyte.	Unearth in the Underground (after you get the National Pokédex)	—
Honey	Use to make wild Pokémon appear. Spread on Honey Trees.	Floaroma Meadow/Always held by wild Combee	100P
HP Up	Raises HP	Veilstone Dept. Store 2F/Route 215/Ravaged Path	9800P
Hyper Potion	Restores 200 HP to a Pokémon	Pokémart (after winning at Pastoria Gym)	1200P
Ice Heal	Heals Frozen status	Pokémart (after winning at Oreburgh Gym)	250P
Icicle Plate	Raises the power of Ice moves when held	Young man in residence on Route 217/Unearth in the Underground	—
Icy Rock	Lengthens the duration of Hail weather when held	Unearth in the Underground	—
Insect Plate	Raises the power of Bug-type moves when held	Unearth in the Underground	—
Iron	Raises Defense	Veilstone Dept. Store 2F/Route 212/Route 217	9800P
Iron Ball	When held, lowers user's Speed. Makes Flying Pokémon and Pokémon with Levitate vulnerable to Ground-type moves when held.	Stark Mountain interior - 2/Unearth in the Underground	—
Iron Plate	Raises the power of Steel-type moves when held	Unearth in the Underground	—
King's Rock	Hold to make an attacking foe flinch occasionally	Pickup Ability/Sometimes held by wild Poliwhirl	—
Lagging Tail	When held, makes user strike last	Route 226/Sometimes held by wild Slowpoke and Lickitung	—
Lava Cookie	Specialty of Lavaridge Town. Cures all status ailments.	Veilstone Dept. Store B1F	200P
Lax Incense	Raises Evasion when held	Route 225	—
Leaf Stone	Evolves certain Pokémon	Floaroma Meadow in Floaroma Town/Unearth in the Underground	—
Leftovers	Restores a bit of HP each turn when held	Back of Victory Road1F - 2/Always held by wild Munchlax	—
Lemonade	Restores 80 HP to a Pokémon	Veilstone Dept. Store 5F	350P

Item	Explanation	How to get	Value
Life Orb	When held, lowers user's HP with every attack, but raises power	Stark Mountain Exterior	—
Light Ball	Doubles Attack and Sp. Attack when held by Pikachu	Sometimes held by wild Pikachu	—
Light Clay	Lengthens the duration of Reflect and Light Screen	Mt. Coronet (upper) B1F/Unearth in the Underground	—
Luck Incense	When held, doubles your battle winnings if user goes into battle even once	Ravaged Path	—
Lucky Egg	Makes user receive slightly more Exp. when held	Sometimes held by wild Chansey	—
Lucky Punch	Raises critical hit rate when held by Chansey	Sometimes held by wild Happiny	—
Lustrous Orb	Just for Palkia. Raises the power of Dragon- and Water-type moves.	Mt. Coronet (middle) 4F - 2	—
Macho Brace	Halves Speed but raises stat EVs greatly	Show a male and a female Combee to the boy at a Pastoria City residence	—
Magmarizer	Link trade Magmar while it holds the Magmarizer to evolve it into Magmortar	Route 214/Sometimes held by wild Magmar	—
Magnet	Raises the power of Electric-type moves when held	Iron Island B2F - 2	—
Max Elixir	Restores all PP to all moves	Mt. Coronet (upper) B1F/Galactic Veilstone Bldg. 3F	—
Max Ether	Restores all PP to a single move	Wayward Cave B1F/Route 215	—
Max Potion	Completely restores a Pokémon's HP	Pokémart (after winning at Snowpoint Gym)	2500P
Max Repel	Prevents wild Pokémon encounters for 250 steps	Pokémart (after winning at Pastoria Gym)	700P
Max Revive	Revives a fainted Pokémon and restores all of its HP	Route 213/Galactic Veilstone Bldg.2F/Unearth in the Underground	—
Meadow Plate	Raises the power of Grass-type moves when held	Unearth in the Underground	—
Mental Herb	Makes charm/attraction go away on its own. Goes away after use.	Route 216	—
Metal Coat	Raises the power of Steel-type moves when held	Iron Island B3F - 2	—
Metal Powder	Doubles Defense when held by Ditto	Sometimes held by wild Ditto	—
Metronome	Raises power of a move used multiple times in a row	Prize at Veilstone Game Corner (1,000 Coins)/Sometimes held by wild Kricketot, Kricketune, and Chatot	—
Mind Plate	Raises power of Psychic moves when held	Solaceon Ruins B4F - 2/Unearth in the Underground	—
Miracle Seed	Raises the power of Grass-type moves when held	Floaroma Meadow in Floaroma Town/Sometimes held by wild Cherubi	—
Moomoo Milk	Restores 100 HP to a Pokémon	Cafe Cabin on Route 210	500P
Moon Stone	Evolves certain Pokémon	Unearth in the Underground/Sometimes held by wild Cleffa, Clefairy, and Lunatone	—
Muscle Band	Raises the power of physical moves when held	Trade in Battle Points at the Battle Frontier (48BP)	—
Mystic Water	Raises the power of Water-type moves when held	Pastoria City/Always held by wild Castform	—
NeverMeltIce	Raises the power of Ice-type moves when held	Mt. Coronet (upper)1F - 3/Sometimes held by wild Snover and Abomasnow	—
Nugget	Can be sold for 5,000P	Solaceon Ruins B4F - 2/Back of Victory Road 1F - 2/Route 229	—
Odd Incense	Raises the power of Psychic-type moves when held	Solaceon Town B4F - 2	—
Odd Keystone	A stone that fits into the broken stone tower on Route 209	Youth on Route 208/Dig in the Underground (after you get the National Pokédex)	—
Old Amber	Amber with DNA sealed inside. Can be restored into Aerodactyl.	Unearth in the Underground (after you get the National Pokédex)	—
Old Gateau	A hidden gem of Eterna City. Cures all status ailments.	Old Chateau 2F	—
Oval Stone	Level up Happiny while it holds the Oval Stone between 4 AM and 8 PM to evolve it into Chansey	Lost Tower2F/Often held by wild Happiny and Chansey	—
Parlyz Heal	Cures paralysis	Pokémart	200P
Pearl	Can be sold for 700P	Often held by wild Shellder	—
Pink Scarf	Hold to raise value in Cute Contests	Scarf Guy in a Pastoria City residence	—
Poison Sting	Raises the power of Poison-type moves when held	Route 206/sometimes held by wild Tentacool, Tentacruel, Qwilfish, Roselia, Budew, Skorupi, and Drapion	—
Poké Doll	Ensures that user can flee from a wild Pokémon encounter	Veilstone Dept. Store 1F/Galactic Veilstone Bldg. 2F	1000P
Potion	Restores 20 HP to a Pokémon	Pokémart	300P
Power Anklet	Lowers Speed but makes it easier to raise	Trade in Battle Points at the Battle Frontier (16BP)	—
Power Band	Lowers Speed but makes Sp. Defense easier to raise	Trade in Battle Points at the Battle Frontier (16BP)	—
Power Belt	Lowers Speed but makes Defense easier to raise	Trade in Battle Points at the Battle Frontier (16BP)	—
Power Bracer	Lowers Speed but makes Attack easier to raise	Trade in Battle Points at the Battle Frontier (16BP)	—
Power Herb	User can use moves with a power-up period instantly. Goes away after use.	Trade in Battle Points at the Battle Frontier (32BP)	—
Power Lens	Lowers Speed but makes Sp. Attack easier to raise	Trade in Battle Points at the Battle Frontier (16BP)	—
Power Weight	Lowers Speed but makes HP easier to raise	Trade in Battle Points at the Battle Frontier (16BP)	—

ADVENTURE DATA LIST

ITEMS

Item	Explanation	How to get	Value
PP Max	Raises max PP to the limit	Route 224	—
PP Up	Raises max PP by 1	Route 206/Solaceon Town/Route 213	—
Protector	Trade Rhydon while it holds Protector to evolve it into Rhyperior	Iron Island B1F - 1/Route 228	—
Protein	Raises Attack	Veilstone Dept. Store 2F/Route 221/Route 213	9800P
Pure Incense	Lowers wild Pokémon encounter rate when held by party leader	Route 221	—
Quick Claw	Hold to strike first occasionally	Young woman on Jubilife Apts. 1F in Jubilife City/Sometimes held by wild Sandshrew, Sandslash, Sneasel, Meowth, and Zangoose	—
Quick Powder	Raises Ditto's Speed when held	Often held by wild Ditto	—
Rare Bone	Can be sold for 5,000P	Unearth in the Underground/Turnback Cave	—
Rare Candy	Raises a Pokémon's level by 1.	Old Chateau 1F/Wayward Cave B1F/Pickup Ability	—
Razor Claw	Raises critical hit rate when held. Gligar and Sneasel evolve if they level up holding the Razor Claw between 8 PM and 4 AM.	Victory Road 1F/Route 224/Trade in Battle Points at the Battle Frontier (48BP)	—
Razor Fang	Hold to make an attacking foe flinch occasionally. Gligar evolves when it levels up holding the Razor Fang between 8 PM and 4 AM.	Route 225/Trade in Battle Points at the Battle Frontier (48BP)	—
Reaper Cloth	Link trade Dusclops while it holds the Reaper Cloth to evolve it into Dusknoir	Acuity Lakefront/Route 229/Turnback Cave	—
Red Flute	A glass flute. Cures charm/attraction.	Held by Pokémon transferred from Pokémon Ruby, Sapphire, Emerald	—
Red Scarf	Hold for greater value in Cool Contests	Scarf Guy in a Pastoria City residence	—
Red Shard	Item needed to have moves taught on Route 212 and in Snowpoint City and the Survival Area	Unearth in the Underground/Route 214/Great Marsh/Route 210/Fuego Ironworks/Iron Island B2F - 2	—
Repel	Prevents wild Pokémon encounters for 100 steps	Pokémart (after winning at Oreburgh Gym)	350P
Revival Herb	Revives a fainted Pokémon. Very bitter.	Herbal medicine shop in Eterna City	2800P
Revive	Revives a fainted Pokémon and restores half its HP	Pokémart (after winning at Hearthome Gym)/Unearth in the Underground	1500P
Rock Incense	Raises the power of Rock-type moves when held	Fuego Ironworks	—
Root Fossil	Pokémon fossil. Can be restored into Lileep.	Unearth in the Underground (after you get the National Pokédex)	—
Rose Incense	Raises the power of Grass-type moves when held	Route 212	—
Sacred Ash	Revives a fainted Pokémon and restores all of its HP	Get the Sacred Ash in Pokémon XD: Gale of Darkness for the GameCube, transfer it to a GBA Pokémon game, have a Pokémon hold it, and transfer that Pokémon through Pal Park	—
Scope Lens	Increases critical hit rate when held	Old lady in the Pokémart in the Fight Area	—
Sea Incense	Raises the power of Water-type moves when held	Route 204 (after winning at Pastoria Gym)	—
Sharp Beak	Raises the power of Flying-type moves when held	Sometimes held by wild Fearow and Doduo	—
Shed Shell	Hold to make sure the user can always switch out	Route 228/Sometimes held by wild Venomoth, Beautifly, and Dustox	—
Shell Bell	Restores 1/8 of damage inflicted when held	Young woman at Hearthome City Apts. 2F	—
Shiny Stone	Evolves certain Pokémon	Iron Island B3F - 1/Route 228/Pickup Ability	—
Shoal Salt	Salt found at the Shoal Cave	Held by Pokémon transferred from Pokémon Ruby, Sapphire, Emerald	—
Shoal Shell	Shell found at the Shoal Cave	Held by Pokémon transferred from Pokémon Ruby, Sapphire, Emerald	—
Silk Scarf	Raises the power of Normal-type moves when held	Prize at Veilstone Game Corner (1,000 Coins)	—
SilverPowder	Raises the power of Bug-type moves when held	Eterna Forest/Sometimes held by wild Masquerain	—
Skull Fossil	A Pokémon Fossil. Can be restored into Cranidos.	Unearth in the Underground (Only if your Trainer ID # is an odd number)	—
Sky Plate	Raises the power of Flying-type moves when held	Unearth in the Underground	—
Smoke Ball	When held, ensures user can always escape from a wild Pokémon	Route 210/Sometimes held by wild Koffing and Weezing	—
Smooth Rock	Extends the effects of Sandstorm weather	Unearth in the Underground	—
Snow Mail	Mail with a print of frigid snow	Snowpoint City	50P
Soda Pop	Restores 60 HP to a Pokémon	Veilstone Dept. Store 5F	300P
Soft Sand	Raises power of Ground-type moves when held	Mt. Coronet (upper) B1F/Sometimes held by wild Diglett and Dugtrio	—
Soothe Bell	When held, makes user more inclined to like you	Receive from Cheryl in Eterna Forest/Maid at Pokémon Mansion	—
Soul Dew	Raises Sp. Attack and Sp. Defense when held by Latios or Latias	Held by Pokémon transferred from Pokémon Ruby, Sapphire, Emerald	—
Space Mail	Mail with a print of majestic outer space	Veilstone Dept. Store 1F	50P
Spell Tag	Raises the power of Ghost-type moves when held	Old lady on Lost Tower 5F (after winning at Hearthome Gym)	—
Splash Plate	Raises the power of Water-type moves when held	Route 220/Unearth in the Underground	—
Spooky Plate	Raises power of Ghost-type moves when held	Amity Square at Hearthome City/Unearth in the Underground	—
Stable Mulch	Spread to lengthen berries' life span	Berry Master's house on Route 208	200P
Star Piece	Can be sold for 4,900P	Veilstone City/Unearth in the Underground	—
Stardust	Can be sold for 1,000P	Often held by wild Staryu	—
Steel Mail	Mail with a printed pattern of a cool machine	Sunyshore City	50P

Item	Explanation	How to get	Value
Stick	Raises critical hit rate when held by Farfetch'd	Sometimes held by wild Farfetch'd	—
Sticky Barb	Inflicts damage on user every turn when held. Sometimes sticks to and damages foe if touched.	Young man at Veilstone Dept. Store 5F/Sometimes held by wild Cacnea and Cacturne	—
Stone Plate	Raises the power of Rock-type moves when held	Unearth in the Underground	—
Sun Stone	Evolves certain Pokémon	Unearth in the Underground/Sometimes held by wild Solrock	—
Super Potion	Restores 50 HP to a Pokémon	Pokémart (after winning at Oreburgh Gym)	700P
Super Repel	Prevents wild Pokémon encounters for 200 steps	Pokémart (after winning at Hearthome Gym)	500P
Thick Club	Doubles Attack when held by Cubone or Marowak	Sometimes held by wild Cubone	—
Thunderstone	Evolves certain Pokémon	Sunyshore City/Unearth in the Underground	—
TinyMushroom	Can be sold for 250P	Often held by wild Paras	—
Toxic Orb	Badly poisons user when held in battle	Trade in Battle Points at the Battle Frontier (16BP)	—
Toxic Plate	Raises power of Poison-type moves when held	Unearth in the Underground	—
Tunnel Mail	Mail with a print of the dark world of mining	Oreburgh City	50P
TwistedSpoon	Raises the power of Psychic-type moves when held	Sometimes held by wild Abra and Kadabra	—
Up-Grade	Link trade Porygon while it holds Up-Grade to evolve it into Porygon2	Galactic Eterna Bldg.4F/Eterna City (receive from Professor Oak)	—
Water Stone	Evolves certain Pokémon	Route 213/Unearth in the Underground	—
Wave Incense	Raises the power of Water-type moves when held	Route 210	—
White Flute	A glass flute. Raises wild Pokémon encounter rate.	Give the Suite Key to the young woman at Valor Lakefront	—
White Herb	Returns lowered stats to normal. Goes away after you use it.	Trade in Battle Points at the Battle Frontier (32BP)/Pickup Ability	—
Wide Lens	Raises move Accuracy when held	Prize at Veilstone Game Corner (1,000 Coins)/Sometimes held by wild Yanma	—
Wise Glasses	Raises power of special moves when held	Talk to the young man in a Celestic Town residence between 8 PM and 4 AM	—
X Accuracy	Raises a Pokémon's Accuracy	Veilstone Dept. Store 2F/Route 218	950P
X Attack	Raises a Pokémon's Attack by 1	Veilstone Dept. Store 2F/Jubilife City	500P
X Defend	Raises a Pokémon's Defense by 1	Veilstone Dept. Store 2F/Route 203	550P
X Sp. Def	Raises a Pokémon's Sp. Defense by 1	Veilstone Dept. Store 2F/Route 205	350P
X Special	Raises a Pokémon's Sp. Attack by 1	Veilstone Dept. Store 2F/Galactic Eterna Bldg. 3F	350P
X Speed	Raises the Speed of a Pokémon by 1	Veilstone Dept. Store 2F/Galactic Eterna Bldg. 2F	350P
Yellow Flute	A glass flute. Cures confusion.	Held by Pokémon transferred from Ruby/Sapphire/Emerald	—
Yellow Scarf	Raises value in Tough Contests when held	Scarf Guy in a Pastoria City residence	—
Yellow Shard	Item needed to have moves taught on Route 212 and in Snowpoint City and the Survival Area	Unearth in the Underground/Oreburgh City/Route 213/Pastoria Great Marsh/Fuego Ironworks/Iron Island B1F - 1	—
Zap Plate	Raises the power of Electric-type moves when held	Unearth in the Underground	—
Zinc	Raises Sp. Defense	Veilstone Dept. Store 2F/Route 212/Route 210	9800P
Zoom Lens	Raises move Accuracy if user's move strikes after foe's move.	Prize at Veilstone Game Corner (1,000 Coins)	—

Key items

Item	Explanation	How to get	Value
Bicycle	A bike that lets you go really fast. Can switch gears.	Receive from bike shop employee in Eterna City	—
Coin Case	A case for coins. Can hold 50,000 coins.	Receive from a clown in a Veilstone City residence	—
Coupon 1	A ticket you can trade in for a Pokétch	Receive when you correctly answer a clown's question in Jubilife City	—
Coupon 2	A ticket you can trade in for a Pokétch	Receive when you correctly answer a clown's question in Jubilife City	—
Coupon 3	A ticket you can trade in for a Pokétch	Receive when you correctly answer a clown's question in Jubilife City	—
Explorer Kit	A bag containing the tools you need for exploring. Lets you go to the Underground.	Receive from the Underground Man in Eterna City	—
Fashion Case	A case for neatly storing your Accessories	Receive from a Jubilife TV employee in Jubilife City	—
Galactic Key	A cardkey for clearing the security in the Team Galactic base	Acquire at Galactic Veilstone Bldg. B2F	—
Good Rod	A nice new fishing rod. Use near the water to catch Pokémon.	Receive from fisherman on Route 209	—
Journal	The notebook recording your journey so far	Receive from your mom at Twinleaf Town	—
Lunar Wing	A wing that shines like the moon. It's said to have the power to chase off nightmares.	Acquire at Fullmoon Island	—
Old Charm	A charm given to you by Cynthia for you to deliver to the Celestic Town elder	Entrusted by Cynthia on Route 210	—
Old Rod	A shabby old fishing rod. Use near water to catch Pokémon.	Receive from a fisherman in Jubilife City	—
Pal Pad	A useful notepad that records friends and good times	Receive from Teala at the Oreburgh City Pokémon Wi-Fi Club	—
Parcel	Stuff received from your rival's mother for you to deliver to your rival	Entrusted by your rival's mother in Twinleaf Town	—
Poffin Case	A protective case to store the Poffins you've baked	Receive from the president of the Pokémon Fan Club in Hearthome City	—
Poké Radar	Lets you discover Pokémon hidden in the tall grass. Recharges as you walk.	Receive from Professor Rowan after you get the National Pokédex	—
Seal Case	A case for storing the Seals that go on Ball Capsules	Receive from young woman in a Solaceon Town residence	—
SecretPotion	Medicine to cure the headaches of the Psyduck on Route 210	Receive from Cynthia at Lake Valor	—
Sprayduck	A tool for spraying water. Use it on soil to grow berries.	Receive from Flower Shop employee in Floaroma Town	—
Suite Key	A key to a hotel suite at Valor Lakefront	Use the Dowsing Machine to find on Route 213	—
Super Rod	The latest and greatest in fishing rods. Use it near water to catch Pokémon.	Receive from fisherman in the Fight Area	—
Town Map	A handy map you can look at anytime. Also displays your own location.	Receive when you hand over the Parcel to your rival in Jubilife City	—
Vs. Recorder	Records battles with friends and at the Battle Frontier	Receive from Looker in Jubilife City	—
Vs. Seeker	Shows you Trainers that want to battle. Recharges as you walk.	Receive from Dawn/Lucas on Route 207	—
Works Key	Key that opens the Valley Windworks door	Acquire after defeating the Galactic Grunt in Floaroma Meadow	—

Poké Balls

Item	Explanation	How to get	Value
Poké Ball	An item for catching wild Pokémon	Pokémart	200P
Great Ball	A Ball with a better capture rate than the Poké Ball	Pokémart (after winning at Hearthome Gym)	600P
Ultra Ball	A Ball with a better capture rate than the Great Ball	Pokémart (after winning at Pastoria Gym)	1200P
Master Ball	A Ball that can successfully catch any wild Pokémon	Receive from Cyrus at the Galactic Veilstone Bldg. 4F in Veilstone City	—
Net Ball	A Ball with a high success rate against Bug- and Water-type Pokémon	Oreburgh City/Floaroma Town/Eterna City	1000P
Nest Ball	A Ball that does better against weaker Pokémon	Eterna City/Hearthome City/Solaceon Town	1000P
Repeat Ball	A Ball that does better against Pokémon you've caught before	Canalave City/Pokémon League	1000P
Timer Ball	A Ball that does better the more turns have elapsed in battle	Celestic Town/Snowpoint City/Canalave City	1000P
Luxury Ball	A Ball that endears you to the captured Pokémon	Sunyshore City/Pokémon League	1000P
Dusk Ball	A Ball that does better at night and in caves	Solaceon Town/Pastoria City/Celestic Town	1000P
Heal Ball	A gentle Ball that heals the captured Pokémon's HP and status	Jubilife City/Oreburgh City/Floaroma Town	300P
Quick Ball	A Ball that does better when thrown at the very beginning of battle	Pastoria City/Celestic Town/Snowpoint City	1000P
Dive Ball	A Ball that does better on Pokémon that live in the water	Job for Pokémon News Press at Solaceon Town/Route 223	—
Premier Ball	A rare Poké Ball made in commemoration of something	Receive when you buy 10 Poké Balls at once	—
Safari Ball	A special Ball for use exclusively in the Pastoria Great Marsh	Great Marsh (receive 30 for your 500P entry fee)	—

Items held by wild Pokémon

Some wild Pokémon hold items. Catching them will also net you the item at the same time. This is the only way to find some items, like Chansey's Lucky Egg or Pikachu's Light Ball.

Sinnoh No.	National No.	Pokémon	Always Holding	Often Holding	Sometimes Holding
	19	Rattata	—	—	Chilan Berry
	20	Raticate	—	—	Chilan Berry
	22	Fearow	—	—	Sharp Beak
104	25	Pikachu	—	Oran Berry	Light Ball
	27	Sandshrew	—	—	Quick Claw
	28	Sandslash	—	—	Quick Claw
100	35	Clefairy	—	Leppa Berry	Moon Stone
	37	Vulpix	Rawst Berry	—	—
	46	Paras	—	TinyMushroom	Big Mushroom
	49	Venomoth	—	—	Shed Shell
	50	Diglett	—	—	Soft Sand
	51	Dugtrio	—	—	Soft Sand
	52	Meowth	—	—	Quick Claw
	56	Mankey	—	—	Payapa Berry
	57	Primeape	—	—	Payapa Berry
	58	Growlithe	Rawst Berry	—	—
	61	Poliwhirl	—	—	King's Rock
20	63	Abra	—	—	TwistedSpoon
21	64	Kadabra	—	—	TwistedSpoon
136	72	Tentacool	—	—	Poison Sting
137	73	Tentacruel	—	—	Poison Sting
31	74	Geodude	—	—	Everstone
32	75	Graveler	—	—	Everstone
90	77	Ponyta	—	—	Shuca Berry
	79	Slowpoke	—	—	Lagging Tail
178	81	Magnemite	—	—	Metal Coat
179	82	Magneton	—	—	Metal Coat
	83	Farfetch'd	—	—	Stick
	84	Doduo	—	—	Sharp Beak
	88	Grimer	—	—	Nugget
	90	Shellder	—	Pearl	Big Pearl
	104	Cubone	—	—	Thick Club
161	108	Lickitung	—	—	Lagging Tail
	109	Koffing	—	—	Smoke Ball
	110	Weezing	—	—	Smoke Ball
97	113	Chansey	—	Oval Stone	Lucky Egg
	116	Horsea	—	—	Dragon Scale
	117	Seadra	—	—	Dragon Scale
	120	Staryu	—	Stardust	Star Piece
95	122	Mr. Mime	—	—	Leppa Berry
	124	Jynx	Aspear Berry	—	—

Sinnoh No.	National No.	Pokémon	Always Holding	Often Holding	Sometimes Holding
198	125	Electabuzz	—	—	Electirizer
201	126	Magmar	—	—	Magmarizer
	132	Ditto	—	Quick Powder	Metal Powder
	147	Dratini	—	—	Dragon Scale
	148	Dragonair	—	—	Dragon Scale
	161	Sentret	—	—	Oran Berry
	170	Chinchou	—	—	DeepSeaScale
103	172	Pichu	—	—	Oran Berry
99	173	Cleffa	—	Leppa Berry	Moon Stone
	191	Sunkern	—	—	Coba Berry
183	193	Yanma	—	—	Wide Lens
121	203	Girafarig	—	—	Persim Berry
35	208	Steelix	—	—	Metal Coat
	211	Qwilfish	—	—	Poison Sting
	213	Shuckle	Oran Berry	—	—
144	215	Sneasel	—	Grip Claw	Quick Claw
	222	Corsola	—	—	Hard Stone
	231	Phanpy	—	—	Passho Berry
	238	Smoochum	Aspear Berry	—	—
	241	Miltank	Moomoo Milk	—	—
	261	Poochyena	—	—	Pecha Berry
	263	Zigzagoon	—	—	Oran Berry
50	267	Beautifly	—	—	Shed Shell
52	269	Dustox	—	—	Shed Shell
	277	Swellow	—	—	Charti Berry
	284	Masquerain	—	—	SilverPowder
	285	Shroomish	—	—	Kebia Berry
	294	Loudred	—	—	Chesto Berry
155	299	Nosepass	—	—	Hard Stone
	300	Skitty	—	—	Leppa Berry
	303	Mawile	—	—	Occa Berry
	304	Aron	—	—	Hard Stone
26	315	Roselia	—	—	Poison Sting
	316	Gulpin	—	—	Big Pearl
	318	Carvanha	—	—	DeepSeaTooth
	322	Numel	Rawst Berry	—	—
	323	Camerupt	Rawst Berry	—	—
	325	Spoink	—	—	Tanga Berry
	327	Spinda	—	—	Chesto Berry
	331	Cacnea	—	—	Sticky Barb
	332	Cacturne	—	—	Sticky Barb
	335	Zangoose	—	—	Quick Claw
	337	Lunatone	—	—	Moon Stone
	338	Solrock	—	—	Sun Stone

Sinnoh No.	National No.	Pokémon	Always Holding	Often Holding	Sometimes Holding
	351	Castform	Mystic Water	—	—
	352	Kecleon	—	—	Persim Berry
	354	Banette	—	—	Spell Tag
189	355	Duskull	—	—	Kasib Berry
83	358	Chimecho	—	—	Colbur Berry
206	361	Snorunt	—	—	Babiri Berry
	369	Relicanth	—	—	DeepSeaScale
	370	Luvdisc	—	Heart Scale	—
	371	Bagon	—	—	Dragon Fang
	374	Beldum	—	—	Metal Coat
10	396	Starly	—	—	Yache Berry
11	397	Staravia	—	—	Yache Berry
14	400	Bibarel	—	Oran Berry	Sitrus Berry
15	401	Kricketot	—	—	Metronome
16	402	Kricketune	—	—	Metronome
25	406	Budew	—	—	Poison Sting
53	415	Combee	Honey	—	—
56	418	Buizel	—	—	Wacan Berry
57	419	Floatzel	—	—	Wacan Berry
58	420	Cherubi	—	—	Miracle Seed
67	427	Buneary	—	—	Chople Berry
82	433	Chingling	—	—	Colbur Berry
88	436	Bronzor	—	—	Metal Coat
89	437	Bronzong	—	—	Metal Coat
94	439	Mime Jr.	—	—	Leppa Berry
96	440	Happiny	—	Oval Stone	Lucky Punch
102	441	Chatot	—	—	Metronome
109	443	Gible	—		Haban Berry
110	444	Gabite	—	—	Haban Berry
112	446	Munchlax	Leftovers	—	—
127	451	Skorupi	—	—	Poison Sting
128	452	Drapion	—	—	Poison Sting
129	453	Croagunk	—	—	Black Sludge
130	454	Toxicroak	—	—	Black Sludge
134	456	Finneon	—	—	Rindo Berry
135	457	Lumineon	—	—	Rindo Berry
142	459	Snover	—	—	NeverMeltIce
143	460	Abomasnow	—	—	NeverMeltIce

ADVENTURE DATA LIST

ITEMS

Items gathered using the Pickup Ability

A Pokémon with the Pickup Ability will sometimes find an item after battle. It will find different items depending on its level. Keep a Pokémon with Pickup in your party—such as Aipom, Phanpy, Meowth, Munchlax, Zigzagoon, or Teddiursa—and sweep up the items.

Item	Level of Pokémon with Pickup									
	Low level	→	→	→	→	→	→	→	High level	Lv100
Potion	●									
Antidote	O	●								
Super Potion	O	O	●							
Great Ball	O	O	O	●						
Repel	O	O	O	O	●					
Escape Rope	O	O	O	O	O	●				
Full Heal	O	O	O	O	O	O	●			
Hyper Potion	▲	O	O	O	O	O	O	●		
Ultra Ball	▲	▲	O	O	O	O	O	O	●	
Revive		▲	▲	O	O	O	O	O	O	●
Rare Candy			▲	▲	O	O	O	O	O	O
Dusk Stone				▲	▲	O	O	O	O	O
Shiny Stone					▲	▲	O	O	O	O
Dawn Stone						▲	▲	O	O	O
Full Restore							▲	▲	O	O
Max Revive								▲	▲	O
PP Up									▲	▲
Max Elixir										▲
Nugget	▼	▼								
King's Rock		▼	▼							
Full Restore			▼	▼						
Ether				▼	▼					
White Herb					▼	▼				
TM44 Sleep						▼	▼			
Elixir							▼	▼		
TM01 Focus Punch								▼	▼	
Leftovers									▼	▼
TM26 Earthquake										▼

●.....Often finds O.....Sometimes finds ▲.....Rarely finds ▼.....Very rarely finds

ADVENTURE DATA LIST

ITEMS

Legendary Pokémon like Uxie, Azelf, and Mesprit are one-of-a-kind in the Sinnoh region. But don't sweat it if you accidentally defeat them in battle or flee from the battle. There are ways to get a rematch. Check off the Legendary Pokémon on this chart as you catch them.

National No.	Pokémon	Level	Location	Items needed	Pokédex	Conditions for meeting	
144	Articuno	60	Starts roving the Sinnoh routes and waterways after you talk to Professor Oak in Eterna City		National	Visit Professor Oak in an Eterna City residence after you've made it into the Hall of Fame and gotten your Pokédex upgraded to the National Pokédex	
145	Zapdos	60	Starts roving the Sinnoh routes and waterways after you talk to Professor Oak in Eterna City		National	Visit Professor Oak in an Eterna City residence after you've made it into the Hall of Fame and gotten your Pokédex upgraded to the National Pokédex	
146	Moltres	60	Starts roving the Sinnoh routes and waterways after you talk to Professor Oak in Eterna City		National	Visit Professor Oak in an Eterna City residence after you've made it into the Hall of Fame and gotten your Pokédex upgraded to the National Pokédex	
425	Drifloon	15	Valley Windworks		Sinnoh	Every Friday, once you've defeated Team Galactic Commander Mars at the Valley Windworks	
442	Spiritomb	25	Broken stone tower on Route 209	Odd Keystone	Sinnoh	After you've used the Odd Keystone on the broken stone tower on Route 209, greet 32 people in the Underground	
479	Rotom	20	TV in Old Chateau		Sinnoh	Examine the TV in the Old Chateau between 8 PM and 4 AM (you need HM Cut to enter the Old Chateau)	
480	Uxie	50	Acuity Cavern		Sinnoh	Talk to Professor Rowan at the Pokémon lab in Sandgem Town after battling Giratina in the Distortion World	
481	Mesprit	50	Starts roving the Sinnoh routes and waterways after you encounter it at Verity Cavern		Sinnoh	Talk to Professor Rowan at the Pokémon lab in Sandgem Town after battling Giratina in the Distortion World	
482	Azelf	50	Valor Cavern		Sinnoh	Talk to Professor Rowan at the Pokémon lab in Sandgem Town after battling Giratina in the Distortion World	
483	Dialga	70	Mt. Coronet (middle) • Spear Pillar	Adamant Orb	Sinnoh	Talk to the Celestic Town elder once you've made it into the Hall of Fame	
484	Palkia	70	Mt. Coronet (middle) • Spear Pillar	Lustrous Orb	Sinnoh	Talk to the Celestic Town elder once you've made it into the Hall of Fame	
485	Heatran	50	Stark Mountain interior - 3		National	Post-Hall-of-Fame, visit Stark Mountain, battle Team Galactic Commander Mars and Jupiter, and head to the interior - 3. Afterward, talk to Buck at the Survival Area and enter the Battle Spot.	
486	Regigigas*	1	Snowpoint Temple at Snowpoint City		National	With Regirock, Regice, and Registeel in your party, examine the Regigigas statue on B5F	
487	Giratina Origin Forme	47	Distortion World		Sinnoh	Visit the Distortion World during the course of the story	
	Giratina Altered Forme	47	Giratina's chamber at Turnback Cave		Sinnoh	Defeat Giratina Origin Forme in the Distortion World (do not catch)	
488	Cresselia	50	Starts roving the Sinnoh routes and waterways after you encounter it at Fullmoon Island		National	Visit sailor Eldritch's house post-Hall of Fame and talk to the young woman	

*You need to transfer Regirock, Regice, and Registeel from your Ruby/Sapphire/Emerald game to catch Regigigas. A Lv100 Regigigas is also sometimes available via special distribution events. Check Pokemon.com for more details.

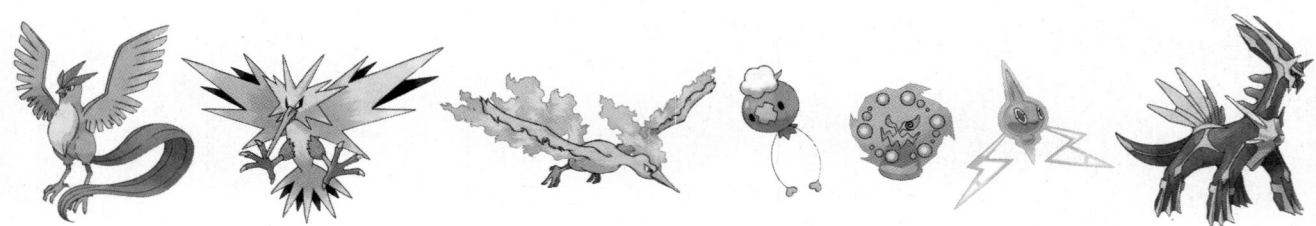

ADVENTURE DATA LIST

CONDITIONS FOR MEETING/REGENERATING POKÉMON

	Rematch	Conditions to regenerate if you defeat it in battle	Conditions to regenerate if you fled from battle	Conditions to regenerate if you lost the battle
	Y	Defeat the Elite Four and the Pokémon League Champion and get entered into the Hall of Fame. (Starts roaming when you talk to Professor Oak again. Continues regenerating until you catch it.)	Move to a different location	Start again from the Pokémon Center
		Defeat the Elite Four and the Pokémon League Champion, and get entered into the Hall of Fame. (Starts roaming when you talk to Professor Oak again. Keeps regenerating until you catch it.)	Move to a different location	Start again from the Pokémon Center
	Y	Defeat the Elite Four and the Pokémon League Champion, and get entered into the Hall of Fame. (Starts roaming when you talk to Professor Oak again. Keeps regenerating until you catch it.)	Move to a different location	Start again from the Pokémon Center
	Y	Fulfill the conditions for it to appear (you can catch it any number of times)	Meet the conditions to make it appear (can catch any number of times)	Start again from the Pokémon Center
	Y	Fulfill the conditions for it to appear (you can catch it any number of times)	Meet the conditions to make it appear (can catch any number of times)	Start again from the Pokémon Center
	Y	Fulfill the conditions for it to appear (you can catch it any number of times)	Meet the conditions to make it appear	Start again from the Pokémon Center
	Y	Defeat the Elite Four and the Pokémon League Champion, and get get entered into the Hall of Fame (Keeps regenerating until you catch it)	Defeat the Elite Four and the Pokémon League Champion, and get entered into the Hall of Fame (Keeps regenerating until you catch it)	Start again from the Pokémon Center
	Y	Defeat the Elite Four and the Pokémon League Champion, and get entered into the Hall of Fame (Starts roaming again from Verity Cavern. Keeps regenerating until you catch it)	Move to a different location	Start again from the Pokémon Center
	Y	Defeat the Elite Four and the Pokémon League Champion, and get entered into the Hall of Fame (Keeps regenerating until you catch it)	Defeat the Elite Four and the Pokémon League Champion, and get entered into the Hall of Fame (Keeps regenerating until you catch it)	Start again from the Pokémon Center
	Y	Defeat the Elite Four and the Pokémon League Champion, and get entered into the Hall of Fame (Keeps regenerating until you catch it)	Defeat the Elite Four and the Pokémon League Champion, and get entered into the Hall of Fame (Keeps regenerating until you catch it)	Start again from the Pokémon Center
	Y	Defeat the Elite Four and the Pokémon League Champion, and get entered into the Hall of Fame (Keeps regenerating until you catch it)	Defeat the Elite Four and the Pokémon League Champion, and get entered into the Hall of Fame (Keeps regenerating until you catch it)	Start again from the Pokémon Center
	Y	Defeat the Elite Four and the Pokémon League Champion, and get entered into the Hall of Fame (Keeps regenerating until you catch it)	Defeat the Elite Four and the Pokémon League Champion, and get entered into the Hall of Fame (Keeps regenerating until you catch it)	Start again from the Pokémon Center
	Y	Defeat the Elite Four and the Pokémon League Champion, and get entered into the Hall of Fame (Keeps regenerating until you catch it)	Defeat the Elite Four and the Pokémon League Champion, and get entered into the Hall of Fame (Keeps regenerating until you catch it)	Start again from the Pokémon Center
	N	Giratina Origin Forme does not regenerate; you encounter its Altered Forme at Turnback Cave after being entered into the Hall of Fame	Giratina Origin Forme does not regenerate; you encounter its Altered Forme at Turnback Cave after being entered into the Hall of Fame	Start again from the Pokémon Center
	Y	Defeat the Elite Four and the Pokémon League Champion, and get entered into the Hall of Fame (Keeps regenerating until you catch it)	Defeat the Elite Four and the Pokémon League Champion, and get entered into the Hall of Fame (Keeps regenerating until you catch it)	Start again from the Pokémon Center
	Y	Defeat the Elite Four and Pokémon League Champion, and get entered into the Hall of Fame	Move to a different location (Starts roaming again from Fullmoon Island. Keeps regenerating until you catch it)	Start again from the Pokémon Center

ADVENTURE DATA LIST

CONDITIONS FOR MEETING/REGENERATING POKÉMON

Value of Accessories for each theme

In the first judging portion of Pokémon Super Contest, you have to dress your Pokémon with Accessories that suit the given theme. The theme determines how much each Accessory is worth to your score. Choose items that match the theme to win lots of points.

Name	Theme					
	Shapely	Sharpness	The Created	The Natural	The Colored	The Solid
White Fluff	Average	Low	Low	High	Average	Average
Yellow Fluff	Average	Low	Low	High	High	Average
Pink Fluff	Average	Low	Low	High	High	Average
Brown Fluff	Average	Low	Low	High	High	Average
Black Fluff	Average	Low	Low	High	High	Average
Orange Fluff	Average	Low	Loe	High	High	Average
Round Pebble	High	Low	Average	Average	Average	High
Glitter Boulder	High	Low	Average	Average	Average	High
Snaggy Pebble	High	Low	Low	High	Low	High
Jagged Boulder	High	Low	Low	High	Low	High
Black Pebble	High	Low	Average	Average	High	High
Mini Pebble	High	Low	Average	Average	Average	High
Pink Scale	Average	Average	Low	High	High	High
Blue Scale	Average	High	Low	High	High	High
Green Scale	Average	Low	Low	High	High	High
Purple Scale	Average	High	Low	High	High	High
Big Scale	Average	High	Low	High	Average	High
Narrow Scale	Average	High	Low	High	Average	High
Blue Feather	Average	High	Low	High	High	Average
Red Feather	Average	High	Low	High	High	Average
Yellow Feather	Average	High	Low	High	High	Average
White Feather	Average	High	Low	High	High	Average
Black Moustache	Average	Average	High	Low	High	Average
White Moustache	Average	Average	High	Low	Average	Average
Black Beard	Average	High	High	Low	High	Average
White Beard	Average	High	High	Low	Average	Average
Small Leaf	Average	Average	Low	High	Average	Average
Big Leaf	High	Average	Low	High	Average	Average
Narrow Leaf	Average	High	Low	High	Average	Average
Shed Claw	High	High	Average	High	Low	High
Shed Horn	High	High	Average	High	Low	High
Thin Mushroom	Average	High	Average	High	Average	Average
Thick Mushroom	High	Average	Average	High	Average	Average
Stump	High	Average	Average	High	Low	High
Pretty Dewdrop	Average	Low	Low	High	Average	Low
Snow Crystal	Average	Average	Low	High	Average	Low
Sparks	Low	Low	Average	High	Average	Low
Shimmering Fire	Low	Low	Average	High	Average	Low
Mystic Fire	Low	Low	Average	High	Average	Low
Determination	Low	Average	Average	Average	Average	Low
Peculiar Spoon	High	Average	High	Low	Low	High
Puffy Smoke	Low	Low	Low	High	Average	Low
Poison Extract	Low	Low	Average	High	High	Low
Wealthy Coin	High	Low	High	Low	Average	High
Eerie Thing	Average	Low	Average	Average	High	Low
Spring	High	High	High	Low	Average	High
Seashell	High	Average	Low	High	Low	High
Humming Note	Low	Average	High	Average	Average	Average
Shiny Powder	Average	Low	High	Average	Average	Average
Glitter Powder	Average	Low	High	Average	Average	Average
Red Flower	High	Average	Low	High	High	Average
Pink Flower	High	Average	Low	High	High	Average
White Flower	High	Average	Low	High	Average	Average
Blue Flower	High	Average	Low	High	High	Average
Orange Flower	High	Average	Low	High	High	Average
Yellow Flower	High	Average	Low	High	High	Average
Googly Specs	High	Average	High	Low	Average	High
Black Specs	High	Average	High	Low	High	High
Gorgeous Specs	High	Average	High	Low	High	High
Sweet Candy	High	Average	High	Low	Average	High
Confetti	Average	Average	High	Low	High	Average
Colored Parasol	High	High	High	Low	High	High
Old Umbrella	High	High	High	Low	Average	High
Spotlight	High	Average	High	Low	Low	High
Cape	High	High	High	Low	High	Average
Standing Mike	High	High	High	Low	Average	High
Surfboard	High	High	High	Low	Average	High
Carpet	High	Low	High	Low	High	High
Retro Pipe	High	Average	High	Low	Average	High
Fluffy Bed	High	Low	High	Low	Average	Average
Mirror Ball	High	Low	High	Low	Average	High
Photo Board	High	Average	High	Low	Average	High
Pink Barrette	Average	Average	High	Low	High	Average
Red Barrette	Average	Average	High	Low	High	Average
Blue Barrette	Average	Average	High	Low	High	Average
Yellow Barrette	Average	Average	High	Low	High	Average
Green Barrette	Average	Aveerage	High	Low	High	Average
Pink Balloon	Average	Low	High	Low	High	Low
Red Balloon	Average	Low	High	Low	High	Low
Blue Balloon	Average	Low	High	Low	High	Low
Yellow Balloon	Average	Low	High	Low	High	Low
Green Balloon	Average	Low	High	Low	High	Low
Lace Headdress	High	High	High	Low	Low	Average
Top Hat	High	Average	High	Low	High	Average
Silk Veil	High	Average	High	Low	Average	Average
Heroic Headband	High	Average	High	Low	Average	Average
Professor Hat	High	High	High	Low	High	High
Flower Stage	High	Average	High	Low	Average	High
Gold Pedestal	High	Average	High	Low	High	High
Glass Stage	High	Average	High	Low	Average	High
Award Podium	High	Average	High	Low	Average	High
Cube Stage	High	Average	High	Low	Average	High
Turtwig Mask	High	Low	High	Low	Average	Average
Chimchar Mask	High	Low	High	Low	Average	Average
Piplup Mask	High	Low	High	Low	Average	Average
Big Tree	High	Average	Low	High	Average	High
Flag	High	High	High	Low	High	High
Crown	High	High	High	Low	Average	High
Tiara	High	High	High	Low	Average	High

The Brightness	The Guady	Flexibility	The Festive	The Intangible	Relaxation	Name
High	Average	High	Average	Average	Low	White Fluff
High	Average	High	Average	Average	Average	Yellow Fluff
Average	Average	High	Average	Average	Average	Pink Fluff
Average	Average	High	Average	Average	High	Brown Fluff
Low	Average	High	Average	Average	High	Black Fluff
Average	Average	High	Average	Average	Average	Orange Fluff
Average	High	Low	Average	Low	Average	Round Pebble
High	High	Low	High	Low	Low	Glitter Boulder
Average	Average	Low	Low	Low	Average	Snaggy Pebble
Average	Average	Low	Low	Low	High	Jagged Boulder
Low	High	Low	Average	Low	High	Black Pebble
Average	High	Low	Average	Low	Average	Mini Pebble
Average	High	Average	Average	Average	Average	Pink Scale
Average	High	Average	Average	Average	High	Blue Scale
Average	High	Average	Average	Average	Average	Green Scale
Average	High	Average	Average	Average	Average	Purple Scale
High	High	Average	Average	Average	Low	Big Scale
Low	High	Average	Average	Average	High	Narrow Scale
Average	High	Average	Average	Average	Average	Blue Feather
Average	High	Average	Average	Average	Average	Red Feather
High	High	Average	Average	Average	Average	Yellow Feather
High	High	Average	Average	Average	Low	White Feather
Low	High	High	Low	Average	High	Black Moustache
High	High	High	Low	Average	Low	White Moustache
Low	High	High	Low	Average	High	Black Beard
High	High	High	Low	Average	Low	White Beard
Average	Average	High	Low	Average	Average	Small Leaf
Average	Average	High	Low	Average	Average	Big Leaf
Average	Average	High	Low	Average	Average	Narrow Leaf
High	Average	Low	Average	Average	Low	Shed Claw
High	Average	Low	Average	Average	Low	Shed Horn
High	Average	Average	Average	Average	Low	Thin Mushroom
Average	Average	Average	Average	Average	Low	Thick Mushroom
Average	Average	Low	Low	Average	Average	Stump
Average	Average	High	High	High	Low	Pretty Dewdrop
High	Average	High	High	High	Low	Snow Crystal
High	Average	High	High	High	Average	Sparks
High	High	High	High	High	Average	Shimmering Fire
High	Average	High	High	High	Average	Mystic Fire
High	High	High	Average	High	Average	Determination
Average	Average	Average	Average	Low	Average	Peculiar Spoon
Average	Average	High	Low	High	Average	Puffy Smoke
Low	Low	High	Low	High	High	Poison Extract
Average	High	Low	High	Low	Low	Wealthy Coin
Low	Low	Low	Low	High	High	Eerie Thing
Average	High	High	Average	Average	Average	Spring
High	Average	Low	Average	Average	Average	Seashell
Average	High	High	High	High	Average	Humming Note
High	High	High	High	High	Low	Shiny Powder
High	High	High	High	High	Low	Glitter Powder
Average	Average	Average	Average	Average	Average	Red Flower
Average	Average	Average	Average	Average	Average	Pink Flower
High	Average	Average	Average	Average	Low	White Flower
Average	Average	Average	Average	Average	Average	Blue Flower
Average	Average	Average	Average	Average	Average	Orange Flower
High	Average	Average	Average	Average	Average	Yellow Flower
Average	Average	Low	Low	Average	High	Googly Specs
Low	High	Low	Low	Average	High	Black Specs
Low	High	Low	High	Average	Average	Gorgeous Specs
Average	High	Average	Average	Average	Average	Sweet Candy
Average	High	High	Average	High	Average	Confetti
High	High	Average	High	Average	Average	Colored Parasol
Average	Average	Average	Low	Average	High	Old Umbrella
High	High	Average	High	High	Low	Spotlight
Low	High	High	Average	Average	High	Cape
Average	High	Average	Average	Average	Average	Standing Mike
Average	High	Low	Average	Average	Average	Surfboard
Average	High	High	High	High	Average	Carpet
Average	Average	Low	Low	Low	Average	Retro Pipe
Average	High	High	Average	Average	Average	Fluffy Bed
High	High	Low	High	Average	Low	Mirror Ball
Average	High	Average	Average	High	Average	Photo Board
Average	High	Average	Average	Average	Average	Pink Barrette
Average	High	Average	Average	Average	Average	Red Barrette
Average	High	Average	Average	Average	Average	Blue Barrette
High	High	Average	Average	Average	Average	Yellow Barrette
Average	High	Average	Average	Average	Average	Green Barrette
Average	High	High	Average	High	Average	Pink Balloon
Average	High	High	Average	High	Average	Red Balloon
Average	High	High	Average	High	Average	Blue Balloon
High	High	High	Average	High	Average	Yellow Balloon
Average	High	High	Average	High	Average	Green Balloon
High	High	Average	High	Average	Average	Lace Headdress
Low	High	Average	High	Average	High	Top Hat
High	High	High	High	High	Low	Silk Veil
Average	High	High	Average	High	Average	Heroic Headband
Average	High	Average	Average	Average	Average	Professor Hat
Average	High	Low	High	Low	Average	Flower Stage
High	High	Low	High	Low	Low	Gold Pedestal
High	High	Low	High	Low	Average	Glass Stage
High	High	Low	Average	Low	Average	Award Podium
Average	High	Low	Average	Low	Average	Cube Stage
Average	High	Average	Average	Average	Average	Turtwig Mask
Average	High	Average	Average	Average	Average	Chimchar Mask
Average	High	Average	Average	Average	Average	Piplup Mask
Average	Average	Average	Average	Low	Average	Big Tree
Average	High	High	Average	High	Average	Flag
High	High	Average	High	Average	Low	Crown
High	High	Average	High	Average	Low	Tiara

ADVENTURE DATA LIST

VALUE OF ACCESSORIES FOR EACH THEME

Berries

	No.	Name	# Berries		Growing time to stage 1	Growing time to grow berries	Flavor and intensity					Sheen	
			Least	Most			Spicy	Dry	Sweet	Bitter	Sour		
	1	Cheri Berry	2	5	3 Hours	12 Hours	Average	—	—	—	—	◆◆◆◆	
	2	Chesto Berry	2	5	3 Hours	12 Hours	—	Average	—	—	—	◆◆◆◆	
	3	Pecha Berry	2	5	3 Hours	12 Hours	—	—	Average	—	—	◆◆◆◆	
	4	Rawst Berry	2	5	3 Hours	12 Hours	—	—	—	Average	—	◆◆◆◆	
	5	Aspear Berry	2	5	3 Hours	12 Hours	—	—	—	—	Average	◆◆◆◆	
	6	Leppa Berry	2	5	4 Hours	16 Hours	Average	—	Average	Average	Average	◆◆◆◆◆	
	7	Oran Berry	2	5	4 Hours	16 Hours	Average	Average	—	Average	Average	◆◆◆◆◆	
	8	Persim Berry	2	5	4 Hours	16 Hours	Average	Average	Average	—	Average	◆◆◆◆◆	
	9	Lum Berry	2	5	12 Hours	48 Hours	Average	Average	Average	Average	—	◆◆◆◆◆	
	10	Sitrus Berry	2	5	8 Hours	32 Hours	—	Average	Average	Average	Average	◆◆◆◆◆	
	11	Figy Berry	2	5	5 Hours	20 Hours	Average	—	—	—	—	◆◆◆◆	
	12	Wiki Berry	2	5	5 Hours	20 Hours	—	Average	—	—	—	◆◆◆◆	
	13	Mago Berry	2	5	5 Hours	20 Hours	—	—	Average	—	—	◆◆◆◆	
	14	Aguav Berry	2	5	5 Hours	20 Hours	—	—	—	Average	—	◆◆◆◆	
	15	Iapapa Berry	2	5	5 Hours	20 Hours	—	—	—	—	Average	◆◆◆◆	
	16	Razz Berry	2	10	2 Hours	8 Hours	Average	Average	—	—	—	◆◆◆◆◆	
	17	Bluk Berry	2	10	2 Hours	8 Hours	—	Average	Average	—	—	◆◆◆◆◆	
	18	Nanab Berry	2	10	2 Hours	8 Hours	—	—	Average	Average	—	◆◆◆◆◆	
	19	Wepear Berry	2	10	2 Hours	8 Hours	—	—	—	Average	Average	◆◆◆◆◆	
	20	Pinap Berry	2	10	2 Hours	8 Hours	Average	—	—	—	Average	◆◆◆◆◆	
	21	Pomeg Berry	2	5	8 Hours	32 Hours	Average	—	Average	Average	—	◆◆◆◆◆	
	22	Kelpsy Berry	2	5	8 Hours	32 Hours	—	Average	—	Average	Average	◆◆◆◆◆	
	23	Qualot Berry	2	5	8 Hours	32 Hours	Average	—	Average	—	Average	◆◆◆◆◆	
	24	Hondew Berry	2	5	8 Hours	32 Hours	Average	Average	—	Average	—	◆◆◆◆◆	
	25	Grepa Berry	2	5	8 Hours	32 Hours	—	Average	Average	—	Average	◆◆◆◆◆	
	26	Tamato Berry	2	5	8 Hours	32 Hours	Slightly intense	Average	—	—	—	◆◆◆◆	
	27	Cornn Berry	2	10	6 Hours	24 Hours	—	Slightly intense	Average	—	—	◆◆◆◆	
	28	Magost Berry	2	10	6 Hours	24 Hours	—	—	Slightly intense	Average	—	◆◆◆◆	
	29	Rabuta Berry	2	10	6 Hours	24 Hours	—	—	—	Slightly intense	Average	◆◆◆◆	
	30	Nomel Berry	2	10	6 Hours	24 Hours	Average	—	—	—	Slightly intense	◆◆◆◆	
	31	Spelon Berry	2	15	15 Hours	60 Hours	Intense	Average	—	—	—	◆◆◆	
	32	Pamtre Berry	2	15	15 Hours	60 Hours	—	Intense	Average	—	—	◆◆◆	
	33	Watmel Berry	2	15	15 Hours	60 Hours	—	—	Intense	Average	—	◆◆◆	
	34	Durin Berry	2	15	15 Hours	60 Hours	—	—	—	Intense	Average	◆◆◆	
	35	Belue Berry	2	15	15 Hours	60 Hours	Average	—	—	—	Intense	◆◆◆	
	36	Occa Berry	2	5	18 Hours	72 Hours	Average	—	Average	—	—	◆◆◆◆	
	37	Passho Berry	2	5	18 Hours	72 Hours	—	Average	—	Average	—	◆◆◆◆	
	38	Wacan Berry	2	5	18 Hours	72 Hours	—	—	Average	—	Average	◆◆◆◆	
	39	Rindo Berry	2	5	18 Hours	72 Hours	Average	—	—	Average	—	◆◆◆◆	
	40	Yache Berry	2	5	18 Hours	72 Hours	—	Average	—	—	Average	◆◆◆◆	
	41	Chople Berry	2	5	18 Hours	72 Hours	Average	—	—	Average	—	◆◆◆◆	
	42	Kebia Berry	2	5	18 Hours	72 Hours	—	Average	—	—	Average	◆◆◆◆	
	43	Shuca Berry	2	5	18 Hours	72 Hours	Average	—	Average	—	—	◆◆◆◆	
	44	Coba Berry	2	5	18 Hours	72 Hours	—	Average	—	Average	—	◆◆◆◆	
	45	Payapa Berry	2	5	18 Hours	72 Hours	—	—	Average	—	Average	◆◆◆◆	
	46	Tanga Berry	2	5	18 Hours	72 Hours	A bit intense	—	—	—	Average	◆◆◆	
	47	Charti Berry	2	5	18 Hours	72 Hours	Average	A bit intense	—	—	—	◆◆◆	
	48	Kasib Berry	2	5	18 Hours	72 Hours	—	Average	A bit intense	—	—	◆◆◆	
	49	Haban Berry	2	5	18 Hours	72 Hours	—	—	Average	A bit intense	—	◆◆◆	
	50	Colbur Berry	2	5	18 Hours	72 Hours	—	—	—	Average	A bit intense	◆◆◆	
	51	Babiri Berry	2	5	18 Hours	72 Hours	A bit intense	Average	—	—	—	◆◆◆	
	52	Chilan Berry	2	5	18 Hours	72 Hours	—	A bit intense	Average	—	—	◆◆◆	
	53	Liechi Berry	2	5	24 Hours	96 Hours	Intense	Average	Intense	—	—	◆◆◆	
	54	Ganlon Berry	2	5	24 Hours	96 Hours	—	Intense	Average	Intense	—	◆◆◆	
	55	Salac Berry	2	5	24 Hours	96 Hours	—	—	Intense	Average	Intense	◆◆◆	
	56	Petaya Berry	2	5	24 Hours	96 Hours	Intense	—	—	Intense	Average	◆◆◆	
	57	Apicot Berry	2	5	24 Hours	96 Hours	Average	Intense	—	—	Intense	◆◆◆	
	58	Lansat Berry	2	5	24 Hours	96 Hours	Intense	Average	Intense	Average	Intense	◆◆	
	59	Starf Berry	2	5	24 Hours	96 Hours	Intense	Average	Intense	Average	Intense	◆◆	
	60	Enigma Berry	2	5	24 Hours	96 Hours	Very intense	Average	—	—	—	◆	
	61	Micle Berry	2	5	24 Hours	96 Hours	—	Very intense	Average	—	—	◆	
	62	Custap Berry	2	5	24 Hours	96 Hours	—	—	Very intense	Average	—	◆	
	63	Jaboca Berry	2	5	24 Hours	96 Hours	—	—	—	Very intense	Average	◆	

◆ .... Pretty much no sheen
◆◆ .... Not much sheen
◆◆◆ .... A little sheen
◆◆◆◆ .... Sheen
◆◆◆◆◆ ...... A lot of sheen

Water absorbancy	Grows on routes	Effect	Main way to get	Name	No.
Fairly Strong	•	When held, enables user to cure paralysis on its own	Floaroma Town/Route 205/Floaroma Flower Shop	Cheri Berry	1
Fairly Strong	•	When held, enables user to cure sleep on its own	Route 205/Route 209/Floaroma Flower Shop	Chesto Berry	2
Fairly Strong	•	When held, enables user to cure poison on its own	Route 205/Route 215/Floaroma Flower Shop	Pecha Berry	3
Fairly Strong	•	When held, enables user to cure burn on its own	Route 206/Rotue 213/Floaroma Flower Shop	Rawst Berry	4
Fairly Strong	•	When held, enables user to cure freeze on its own	Route 210/Route 211/Floaroma Flower Shop	Aspear Berry	5
Fairly Strong	•	When held, enables user to restore 10 of its own PP when PP reaches 0	Route 209/Route 221/Berry Master on Route 208	Leppa Berry	6
Fairly Strong	•	When held, enables user to restore 10 of its own HP when HP dips under half	Floaroma Town/Route 205/Berry Master on Route 208	Oran Berry	7
Fairly Strong	•	When held, enables user to cure confusion on its own	Solaceon Town/Pastoria City/Berry Master on Route 208	Persim Berry	8
Fairly Weak	•	When held, enables user to cure its own status ailments	Route 212/Resort Area/Berry Master on Route 208	Lum Berry	9
Fairly Weak	•	When held, enables user to restore 1/4 of max HP on its own when its HP dips below half	Fuego Ironworks/Route 210/Berry Master on Route 208	Sitrus Berry	10
Average	•	When held, enables user to restore its own HP when HP dips under half. However, if user hates Spicy flavors, it can easily become confused.	Solaceon Town/Rotue 218/Berry Master on Route 208	Figy Berry	11
Average	•	When held, enables user to restore its own HP when HP dips under half. However, if user hates Dry flavors, it can easily become confused.	Route 215/Route 210/Berrry Master on Route 208	Wiki Berry	12
Average	•	When held, enables user to restore its own HP when HP dips under half. However, if user hates Sweet flavors, it can easily become confused.	Route 215/Route 221/Berry Master on Route 208	Mago Berry	13
Average	•	When held, enables user to restore its own HP when HP dips under half. However, if user hates Bitter flavors, it can easily become confused.	Route 213/Route 210/Berry Master on Route 208	Aguav Berry	14
Average	•	When held, enables user to restore its own HP when HP dips under half. However, if user hates Sour flavors, it can easily become confused.	Route 213/Route 211/Berry Master on Route 208	Iapapa Berry	15
Strong	•	Poffin ingredient	Route 206/Route 208/Berry Master on Route 208	Razz Berry	16
Strong	•	Poffin ingredient	Eterna Forest/Route 207/Berry Master on Route 208	Bluk Berry	17
Strong	•	Poffin ingredient	Solaceon Town/Route 208/Berry Master on Route 208	Nanab Berry	18
Strong	•	Poffin ingredient	Fuego Ironworks/Route 224/Berry Master on Route 208	Wepear Berry	19
Strong	•	Poffin ingredient	Route 208/Route 210/Berry Master on Route 208	Pinap Berry	20
Fairly Weak	•	Raises a Pokémon's Friendship slightly but lowers its HP EVs	Route 214/Fight Area/Berry Master on Route 208	Pomeg Berry	21
Fairly Weak	•	Raises a Pokémon's Friendship slightly but lowers its Attack EVs	Fuego Ironworks/Route 225/Berry Master on Route 208	Kelpsy Berry	22
Fairly Weak	•	Raises a Pokémon's Friendship slightly but lowers its Defense EVs	Route 222/Resort Area/Berry Master on Route 208	Qualot Berry	23
Fairly Weak	•	Raises a Pokémon's Friendship slightly but lowers its Sp. Attack EVs	Route 221/Fight Area/Berry Master on Route 208	Hondew Berry	24
Fairly Weak	•	Raises a Pokémon's Friendship slightly but lowers its Sp. Defense EVs	Route 2111/Resort Area/Berry Master on Route 208	Grepa Berry	25
Fairly Weak	•	Raises a Pokémon's Friendship slightly but lowers its Speed EVs	Route 212/Route 225/Berry Master on Route 208	Tamato Berry	26
Average	—	Poffin ingredient	Amity Square at Hearthome City (on walks and from man near the east gate)	Cornn Berry	27
Average	—	Poffin ingredient	Amity Square at Hearthome City (on walks and from man near the east gate)	Magost Berry	28
Average	—	Poffin ingredient	Amity Square at Hearthome City (on walks and from man near the east gate)	Rabuta Berry	29
Average	—	Poffin ingredient	Amity Square at Hearthome City (on walks and from man near the east gate)	Nomel Berry	30
Fairly Weak	—	Poffin ingredient	Amity Square at Hearthome City (on walks and from man near the east gate)	Spelon Berry	31
Fairly Weak	—	Poffin ingredient	Amity Square at Hearthome City (on walks and from man near the east gate)	Pamtre Berry	32
Fairly Weak	—	Poffin ingredient	Amity Square at Hearthome City (on walks and from man near the east gate)	Watmel Berry	33
Fairly Weak	—	Poffin ingredient	Amity Square at Hearthome City (on walks and from man near the east gate)	Durin Berry	34
Fairly Weak	—	Poffin ingredient	Amity Square at Hearthome City (on walks and from man near the east gate)	Belue Berry	35
Fairly Weak	—	Halves the damage from super effective Fire-type moves when held	Berry girl in Pastoria City/Sometimes held by wild Mawile	Occa Berry	36
Fairly Weak	—	Halves the damage from super effective Water-type moves when held	Berry girl in Pastoria City/Sometimes held by wild Phanpy	Passho Berry	37
Fairly Weak	—	Halves the damage from super effective Electric-type moves when held	Berry girl in Pastoria City/Sometimes held by wild Buizel and Floatzel	Wacan Berry	38
Fairly Weak	—	Halves the damage from super effective Grass-type moves when held	Berry girl in Pastoria City/Sometimes held by wild Finneon and Lumineon	Rindo Berry	39
Fairly Weak	—	Halves the damage from super effective Ice-type moves when held	Berry girl in Pastoria City/Sometimes held by wild Starly and Staravia	Yache Berry	40
Fairly Weak	—	Halves the damage from super effective Fighting-type moves when held	Berry girl in Pastoria City/Sometimes held by wild Buneary	Chople Berry	41
Fairly Weak	—	Halves the damage from super effective Poison-type moves when held	Berry girl in Pastoria City/Sometimes held by wild Shroomish	Kebia Berry	42
Fairly Weak	—	Halves the damage from super effective Ground-type moves when held	Berry girl in Pastoria City/Sometimes held by wild Ponyta	Shuca Berry	43
Fairly Weak	—	Halves the damage from super effective Flying-type moves when held	Berry girl in Pastoria City/Sometimes held by wild Sunkern	Coba Berry	44
Fairly Weak	—	Halves the damage from super effective Psychic-type moves when held	Berry girl in Pastoria City/Sometimes held by wild Mankey and Primeape	Payapa Berry	45
Fairly Weak	—	Halves the damage from super effective Bug-type moves when held	Berry girl in Pastoria City/Sometimes held by wild Spoink	Tanga Berry	46
Fairly Weak	—	Halves the damage from super effective Rock-type moves when held	Berry girl in Pastoria City/Sometimes held by wild Swellow	Charti Berry	47
Fairly Weak	—	Halves the damage from super effective Ghost-type moves when held	Berry girl in Pastoria City/Sometimes held by wild Duskull	Kasib Berry	48
Fairly Weak	—	Halves the damage from super effective Dragon-type moves when held	Berry girl in Pastoria City/Sometimes held by wild Gible and Gabite	Haban Berry	49
Fairly Weak	—	Halves the damage from super effective Dark-type moves when held	Berry girl in Pastoria City/Sometimes held by wild Chingling and Chimecho	Colbur Berry	50
Fairly Weak	—	Halves the damage from super effective Steel-type moves when held	Berry girl in Pastoria City/Sometimes held by wild Snorunt	Babiri Berry	51
Fairly Weak	—	Halves the damage from Normal-type moves when held	Berry girl in Pastoria City/Sometimes held by wild Rattata and Raticate	Chilan Berry	52
Weak	—	When held, allows user to raise its own Attack by 1 when its HP is low	Held by Pokémon transferred from *Pokémon Ruby, Sapphire, Emerald*	Liechi Berry	53
Weak	—	When held, allows user to raise its own Defense by 1 when its HP is low	Acquire the Mystery Gift in *Pokémon Battle Revolution*[1]	Ganlon Berry	54
Weak	—	When held, allows user to raise its own Speed by 1 when its HP is low	Acquire the Mystery Gift in *Pokémon Battle Revolution*[1]	Salac Berry	55
Weak	—	When held, allows user to raise its own Sp. Attack by 1 when its HP is low	Acquire the Mystery Gift in *Pokémon Battle Revolution*[1]	Petaya Berry	56
Weak	—	When held, allows user to raise its own Sp. Defense by 1 when its HP is low	Acquire the Mystery Gift in *Pokémon Battle Revolution*[1]	Apicot Berry	57
Weak	—	When held, allows user to raise its own critical hit rate by 1 when its HP is low	Held by Pokémon transferred from *Pokémon Emerald*	Lansat Berry	58
Weak	—	When held, allows user to raise any one of its own stats by 2	Held by Pokémon transferred from *Pokémon Emerald*	Starf Berry	59
Fairly Weak	—	When held, allows user to restore its own HP when damaged by a super effective move	Held by Pokémon transferred from *Pokémon Diamond or Pearl*[2]	Enigma Berry	60
Fairly Weak	—	When held, raises move Accuracy by 20% the turn after user's HP becomes low	Held by Pokémon transferred from *Pokémon Diamond or Pearl*[2]	Micle Berry	61
Fairly Weak	—	When held, lets user strike first the turn after user's HP becomes low	Held by Pokémon transferred from *Pokémon Diamond or Pearl*[2]	Custap Berry	62
Fairly Weak	—	When held, spreads damage to foe when user is hit by a physical attack	Held by Pokémon transferred from *Pokémon Diamond or Pearl*[2]	Jaboca Berry	63

*1 Get the Mystery Gift in *Pokémon Battle Revolution* and send it to *Pokémon Platinum*.

*2 May be held by Pokémon distributed via special events or selected retail locations. Check Pokémon.com for the latest news on how to acquire this berry.

ADVENTURE DATA LIST

BERRIES

Seals are items you can stick on your Ball Capsules to give them a style as wild as your own. The selection of Seals for sale at Sunyshore Market is different every day of the week. You can collect alphabet Seals by showing different Unown to the boy in a Solaceon Town residence.

🎴 Seals for sale on Monday

Item	Explanation	Location	Price
Heart Seal A	Emits a little pink heart	Sunyshore Market	50P
Star Seal B	Emits a burst of yellow stars	Sunyshore Market	50P
Line Seal C	A black line spans outward	Sunyshore Market	100P
Elec Seal B	Shoots green electricity upward	Sunyshore Market	100P
Fire Seal A	Emits a bit of orange flame	Sunyshore Market	50P
Party Seal D	Emits white confetti	Sunyshore Market	100P
Song Seal A	A green G clef shape	Sunyshore Market	50P

🎴 Seals for sale on Tuesday

Item	Explanation	Location	Price
Heart Seal B	Emits a big pink heart	Sunyshore Market	50P
Star Seal C	A few blue stars pop	Sunyshore Market	50P
Line Seal D	A blue line spans outward	Sunyshore Market	100P
Elec Seal C	Yellow electricity shoots downward	Sunyshore Market	100P
Fire Seal B	Emits a lot of orange flame	Sunyshore Market	50P
Flower Seal A	Pink petals flutter around	Sunyshore Market	50P
Song Seal B	A red quarter note shape	Sunyshore Market	50P

🎴 Seals for sale on Wednesday

Item	Explanation	Location	Price
Heart Seal C	Emits a little black heart	Sunyshore Market	50P
Star Seal D	A lot of blue stars pop	Sunyshore Market	50P
Smoke Seal A	White smoke rises	Sunyshore Market	100P
Elec Seal D	Green electricity shoots downward	Sunyshore Market	100P
Fire Seal C	Emits a little blue flame	Sunyshore Market	50P
Flower Seal B	Emits pink petals	Sunyshore Market	50P
Song Seal C	An orange quarter note shape	Sunyshore Market	50P

🎴 Seals for sale on Thursday

Item	Explanation	Location	Price
Heart Seal D	Emits a big black heart	Sunyshore Market	50P
Star Seal E	Color-changing stars pop	Sunyshore Market	100P
Smoke Seal B	Black smoke rises	Sunyshore Market	100P
Bubble Seal A	Emits a bit of blue bubbles	Sunyshore Market	50P
Fire Seal D	Emits a lot of blue flame	Sunyshore Market	50P
Flower Seal C	Purple petals flutter around	Sunyshore Market	50P
Song Seal D	A yellow eighth note shape	Sunyshore Market	50P

🎴 Seals for sale on Friday

Item	Explanation	Location	Price
Heart Seal E	A pink heart floats	Sunyshore Market	100P
Star Seal F	A lot of color-changing stars pop	Sunyshore Market	100P
Smoke Seal C	Emits white smoke	Sunyshore Market	100P
Bubble Seal B	Emits a lot of blue bubbles	Sunyshore Market	50P
Party Seal A	Emits red confetti	Sunyshore Market	50P
Flower Seal D	Emits purple petals	Sunyshore Market	50P
Song Seal E	A blue eighth note shape	Sunyshore Market	50P

🎴 Seals for sale on Saturday

Item	Explanation	Location	Price
Heart Seal F	A pink heart floats up	Sunyshore Market	100P
Line Seal A	A white line spreads outward	Sunyshore Market	100P
Smoke Seal D	Emits black smoke	Sunyshore Market	100P
Bubble Seal C	Emits a bit of pink bubbles	Sunyshore Market	50P
Party Seal B	Emits blue confetti	Sunyshore Market	50P
Flower Seal E	Yellow petals flutter around	Sunyshore Market	50P
Song Seal F	A yellow half-note shape	Sunyshore Market	50P

🎴 Seals for sale on Sunday

Item	Explanation	Location	Price
Star Seal A	A few yellow stars pop	Sunyshore Market	50P
Line Seal B	A red line spreads outward	Sunyshore Market	100P
Elec Seal A	Yellow electricity shoots upward	Sunyshore Market	100P
Bubble Seal D	Emits a lot of pink bubbles	Sunyshore Market	50P
Party Seal C	Emits yellow confetti	Sunyshore Market	100P
Flower Seal F	Emits yellow petals	Sunyshore Market	50P
Song Seal G	A deep blue long note shape	Sunyshore Market	50P

🎴 Alphabet seals

Item	Explanation	Location	Price
A Seal	Shape of the letter A	Show Unown A to the boy in a Solaceon Town residence	—
B Seal	Shape of the letter B	Show Unown B to the boy in a Solaceon Town residence	—
C Seal	Shape of the letter C	Show Unown C to the boy in a Solaceon Town residence	—
D Seal	Shape of the letter D	Show Unown D to the boy in a Solaceon Town residence	—
E Seal	Shape of the letter E	Show Unown E to the boy in a Solaceon Town residence	—
F Seal	Shape of the letter F	Show Unown F to the boy in a Solaceon Town residence	—
G Seal	Shape of the letter G	Show Unown G to the boy in a Solaceon Town residence	—
H Seal	Shape of the letter H	Show Unown H to the boy in a Solaceon Town residence	—
I Seal	Shape of the letter I	Show Unown I to the boy in a Solaceon Town residence	—
J Seal	Shape of the letter J	Show Unown J to the boy in a Solaceon Town residence	—
K Seal	Shape of the letter K	Show Unown K to the boy in a Solaceon Town residence	—
L Seal	Shape of the letter L	Show Unown L to the boy in a Solaceon Town residence	—
M Seal	Shape of the letter M	Show Unown M to the boy in a Solaceon Town residence	—
N Seal	Shape of the letter N	Show Unown N to the boy in a Solaceon Town residence	—
O Seal	Shape of the letter O	Show Unown O to the boy in a Solaceon Town residence	—
P Seal	Shape of the letter P	Show Unown P to the boy in a Solaceon Town residence	—
Q Seal	Shape of the letter Q	Show Unown Q to the boy in a Solaceon Town residence	—
R Seal	Shape of the letter R	Show Unown R to the boy in a Solaceon Town residence	—
S Seal	Shape of the letter S	Show Unown S to the boy in a Solaceon Town residence	—
T Seal	Shape of the letter T	Show Unown T to the boy in a Solaceon Town residence	—
U Seal	Shape of the letter U	Show Unown U to the boy in a Solaceon Town residence	—
V Seal	Shape of the letter V	Show Unown V to the boy in a Solaceon Town residence	—
W Seal	Shape of the letter W	Show Unown W to the boy in a Solaceon Town residence	—
X Seal	Shape of the letter X	Show Unown X to the boy in a Solaceon Town residence	—
Y Seal	Shape of the letter Y	Show Unown Y to the boy in a Solaceon Town residence	—
Z Seal	Shape of the letter Z	Show Unown Z to the boy in a Solaceon Town residence	—
Surprise Seal	Shape of an exclamation point	Show Unown ! to the boy in a Solaceon Town residence	—
Question Seal	Shape of a question mark	Show Unown ? to the boy in a Solaceon Town residence	—

Buried treasure in the Underground

There's all manner of treasure buried in the walls of the Sinnoh Underground. The kinds of items you can dig out will vary slightly based on whether your Trainer ID is an odd or even number. Also, some items are easier to find than others. Check the walls where you see something shining, and dig out your treasure.

Name	Rarity (before you get the National Pokédex)		Rarity (after you get the National Pokédex)		Spheres you can get in trade
	Odd Trainer ID	Even Trainer ID	Odd Trainer ID	Even Trainer ID	
Prism Sphere	○	○	○	○	—
Pale Sphere	○	○	○	○	—
Red Sphere	●	●	●	●	—
Blue Sphere	●	●	●	●	—
Green Sphere	●	●	●	●	—
Odd Keystone	×	×	▼	▼	50-60 Prism Sphere
Sun Stone	▼	▼	○	▼	25-35 Red Sphere
Star Piece	▼	▼	▲	▲	35-45 Pale Sphere
Moon Stone	▼	▼	▼	○	25-35 Pale Sphere
Hard Stone	▼	▼	○	○	25-35 Red Sphere
Thunderstone	▼	▼	○	▲	25-35 Prism Sphere
Everstone	▼	▼	○	○	25-35 Pale Sphere
Fire Stone	▼	▼	○	▲	25-35 Red Sphere
Water Stone	▼	▼	▲	○	25-35 Blue Sphere
Leaf Stone	▼	▼	▲	○	25-35 Green Sphere
Helix Fossil	×	×	○	▼	30-50 Blue Sphere
Dome Fossil	×	×	▼	○	30-50 Green Sphere
Claw Fossil	×	×	○	▼	30-50 Blue Sphere
Root Fossil	×	×	▼	○	30-50 Green Sphere
Old Amber	×	×	▲	▲	30-50 Prism Sphere
Rare Bone	▼	▼	▲	▲	25-35 Pale Sphere
Revive	▲	▲	▲	▲	5-10 Pale Sphere
Max Revive	▼	▼	▼	▼	40-50 Pale Sphere
Red Shard	○	○	○	○	20-25 Red Sphere
Blue Shard	○	○	○	○	20-25 Blue Sphere
Yellow Shard	○	○	○	○	20-25 Prism Sphere
Green Shard	○	○	○	○	20-25 Green Sphere
Heart Scale	○	○	○	○	5-10 Red Sphere
Armor Fossil	×	○	×	○	30-50 Blue Sphere
Skull Fossil	○	×	○	×	30-50 Green Sphere
Light Clay	▼	▼	▲	▼	40-50 Pale Sphere
Iron Ball	▼	▼	▼	▲	40-50 Prism Sphere
Icy Rock	▼	▼	○	▲	35-40 Pale Sphere
Smooth Rock	▼	▼	▲	○	35-40 Prism Sphere
Heat Rock	▼	▼	○	▲	40-50 Red Sphere
Damp Rock	▼	▼	▲	○	40-50 Blue Sphere
Flame Plate	▼	▼	▼	▼	70-80 Red Sphere
Splash Plate	▼	▼	▼	▼	70-80 Blue Sphere
Zap Plate	▼	▼	▼	▼	70-80 Prism Sphere
Meadow Plate	▼	▼	▼	▼	70-80 Green Sphere
Icicle Plate	▼	▼	▼	▼	70-80 Blue Sphere
Fist Plate	▼	▼	▼	▼	70-80 Prism Sphere
Toxic Plate	▼	▼	▼	▼	70-80 Pale Sphere
Earth Plate	▼	▼	▼	▼	70-80 Green Sphere
Sky Plate	▼	▼	▼	▼	70-80 Blue Sphere
Mind Plate	▼	▼	▼	▼	70-80 Pale Sphere
Insect Plate	▼	▼	▼	▼	70-80 Green Sphere
Stone Plate	▼	▼	▼	▼	70-80 Pale Sphere
Spooky Plate	▼	▼	▼	▼	70-80 Red Sphere
Draco Plate	▼	▼	▼	▼	70-80 Red Sphere
Dread Plate	▼	▼	▼	▼	70-80 Red Sphere
Iron Plate	▼	▼	▼	▼	70-80 Prism Sphere

●.....Common   ○.....Uncommon   ▲.....Very uncommon   ▼.....Extremely uncommon   ×.....Nonexistent

Underground traps

Traps can be set on the ground in the Underground. You can acquire traps in trade for Spheres from the trap traders in the Underground, and by collecting buried items there. If you tap the Touch Screen and see the floor sparkle, that usually means there's a trap there.

Trap	Explanation	How to clear	Main way to get
Move Trap ⬆	Moves you upward	—	Trade a 3-6 Blue Sphere in the Underground
Move Trap ➡	Moves you to the right	—	Trade a 3-6 Red Sphere in the Underground
Move Trap ⬇	Moves you downward	—	Trade a 3-6 Blue Sphere in the Underground
Move Trap ⬅	Moves you to the left	—	Trade a 3-6 Red Sphere in the Underground
Hurl Trap ⬆	Moves you far upward	—	Trade a 12-15 Blue Sphere in the Underground
Hurl Trap ➡	Moves you far to the right	—	Trade a 12-15 Red Sphere in the Underground
Hurl Trap ⬇	Moves you far downward	—	Trade a 12-15 Blue Sphere in the Underground
Hurl Trap ⬅	Moves you far to the left	—	Trade a 12-15 Red Sphere in the Underground
Hole Trap	Buries you and pins you to the spot	Press a button 10 times	Trade a 3-6 Prism Sphere in the Underground
Pit Trap	Buries you and pins you to the spot for a long time	Press a button 20 times	Trade a 12-15 Prism Sphere in the Underground
Reverse Trap	Moves you in the opposite direction from what you pressed on the D-pad	Take 20 steps	Trade a 10-12 Pale Sphere in the Underground
Confuse Trap	Moves you in random directions	Take 50 steps	Trade a 10-12 Pale Sphere in the Underground
Smoke Trap	Paralyzes you with a gust of smoke	Tap the smoke	Trade a 5-7 Red Sphere in the Underground
Big Smoke Trap	Paralyzes you with a huge gust of smoke	Tap the smoke	Trade a 12-16 Red Sphere in the Underground
Rock Trap	Drops cracked rocks, pinning you to the spot	Tap the rock	Trade a 3-6 Blue Sphere in the Underground
Rockfall Trap	Drops large cracked rocks, pinning you to the spot	Tap the large rocks	Trade a 8-15 Blue Sphere in the Underground
Foam Trap	Blows bubbles around, pinning you to the spot	Tap all the bubbles	Trade a 5-7 Blue Sphere in the Underground
Bubble Trap	Blows bubbles around, pinning you to the spot	Tap all the bubbles	Trade a 12-16 Blue Sphere in the Underground
Alert Trap 1	Displays "Hello! Nice to meet you!"	—	Trade a 5-9 Pale Sphere in the Underground
Alert Trap 2	Displays "Good-bye! I'm going back up!"	—	Trade a 5-9 Pale Sphere in the Underground
Alert Trap 3	Displays "Let's go to the Union Room!"	—	Trade a 5-9 Pale Sphere in the Underground
Alert Trap 4	Displays "Please come here!"	—	Trade a 5-9 Pale Sphere in the Underground
Leaf Trap	Leaves flutter around the screen, pinning you to the spot	Blow into the microphone	Trade a 15-19 Green Sphere in the Underground
Flower Trap	Petals flutter around the screen, pinning you to the spot	Blow into the microphone	Trade a 30-40 Green Sphere in the Underground
Ember Trap	Flame appears and pins you to the spot	Blow into the microphone	Trade a 5-9 Red Sphere in the Underground
Fire Trap	A hard-to-extinguish flame appears and pins you to the spot	Blow into the microphone	Trade a 20-30 Red Sphere in the Underground
Digger Drill	You can build a secret base in the wall in front of you	—	Trade a 15-20 Sphere in the Underground (random colors)

Pokémon Moves and Abilities alphabetical list

This alphabetical list of Pokémon moves compiles all the moves, as well as all of the Pokémon capable of learning each move. "TM" means the Pokémon needs a TM to learn the move; likewise, "HM" means it learns the move from an HM, "E" means it's an Egg move, "T" means it learns it from a Move Tutor, and "B" means base (the Pokémon comes pre-equipped with the move). The Abilities list gathers all the Abilities and the Pokémon that have them. On both lists, the entries for Deoxys, Wormadam, Rotom, Giratina, and Shaymin each distinguish between the Pokémon's different forms by including the first letter of the form or Forme in question.

Pokémon moves alphabetical list

Absorb		
43	Oddish	B
44	Gloom	B
114	Tangela	8
140	Kabuto	6
141	Kabutops	B,6
191	Sunkern	B
192	Sunflora	B
252	Treecko	6
253	Grovyle	B,6
254	Sceptile	B,6
267	Beautifly	B,10
270	Lotad	5
271	Lombre	5
285	Shroomish	B
286	Breloom	B
315	Roselia	B
331	Cacnea	5
332	Cacturne	B,5
387	Turtwig	9
388	Grotle	9
389	Torterra	B,9
406	Budew	B
465	Tangrowth	8

Acid		
23	Ekans	20
24	Arbok	20
43	Oddish	9
44	Gloom	B,9
69	Bellsprout	23
70	Weepinbell	23
72	Tentacool	12
73	Tentacruel	12
331	Cacnea	E
345	Lileep	8
346	Cradily	B,8

Acid Armor		
88	Grimer	39
89	Muk	44
134	Vaporeon	64
218	Slugma	E
316	Gulpin	E
489	Phione	31
490	Manaphy	31

Acupressure		
72	Tentacool	E
84	Doduo	28
85	Dodrio	28
213	Shuckle	E
451	Skorupi	17
452	Drapion	17

Aerial Ace		
4	Charmander	TM
5	Charmeleon	TM
6	Charizard	TM
12	Butterfree	TM
15	Beedrill	TM
16	Pidgey	TM
17	Pidgeotto	TM
18	Pidgeot	TM
21	Spearow	17,TM
22	Fearow	17,TM
27	Sandshrew	TM
28	Sandslash	TM
29	Nidoran♀	TM
30	Nidorina	TM
31	Nidoqueen	TM
41	Zubat	TM
42	Golbat	TM
46	Paras	TM
47	Parasect	TM
49	Venomoth	TM
50	Diglett	TM
51	Dugtrio	TM
52	Meowth	TM
53	Persian	TM
54	Psyduck	TM
55	Golduck	TM
56	Mankey	TM
57	Primeape	TM
58	Growlithe	TM
59	Arcanine	TM
83	Farfetch'd	13,TM
84	Doduo	TM
85	Dodrio	TM
104	Cubone	TM
105	Marowak	TM
115	Kangaskhan	TM
122	Mr. Mime	TM
123	Scyther	TM
137	Porygon	TM
141	Kabutops	TM
142	Aerodactyl	TM
144	Articuno	TM
145	Zapdos	TM
146	Moltres	TM
149	Dragonite	TM
150	Mewtwo	TM
151	Mew	TM
155	Cyndaquil	TM
156	Quilava	TM
157	Typhlosion	TM
158	Totodile	TM
159	Croconaw	TM
160	Feraligatr	TM
163	Hoothoot	TM
164	Noctowl	TM
165	Ledyba	TM
166	Ledian	TM
169	Crobat	TM
176	Togetic	TM
177	Natu	TM
178	Xatu	TM
187	Hoppip	TM
188	Skiploom	TM
189	Jumpluff	TM
190	Aipom	TM
193	Yanma	TM
198	Murkrow	TM
200	Misdreavus	TM
207	Gligar	TM
212	Scizor	TM
214	Heracross	13,TM
215	Sneasel	TM
216	Teddiursa	TM
217	Ursaring	TM
225	Delibird	TM
226	Mantine	TM
227	Skarmory	TM
233	Porygon2	TM
237	Hitmontop	TM
248	Tyranitar	TM
249	Lugia	TM
250	Ho-Oh	TM
251	Celebi	TM
252	Treecko	TM
253	Grovyle	TM
254	Sceptile	TM
255	Torchic	TM
256	Combusken	TM
257	Blaziken	TM
267	Beautifly	TM
269	Dustox	TM
275	Shiftry	TM
276	Taillow	34,TM
277	Swellow	38,TM
278	Wingull	42,TM
279	Pelipper	TM
284	Masquerain	TM
287	Slakoth	TM
288	Vigoroth	TM
289	Slaking	TM
290	Nincada	TM
291	Ninjask	TM
292	Shedinja	TM
302	Sableye	TM
304	Aron	TM
305	Lairon	TM
306	Aggron	TM
313	Volbeat	TM
314	Illumise	TM
330	Flygon	TM
333	Swablu	TM
334	Altaria	TM
335	Zangoose	TM
341	Corphish	TM
342	Crawdaunt	TM
347	Anorith	TM
348	Armaldo	TM
352	Kecleon	TM
357	Tropius	TM
359	Absol	TM
371	Bagon	TM
372	Shelgon	TM
373	Salamence	TM
375	Metang	TM
376	Metagross	TM
379	Registeel	TM
380	Latias	TM
381	Latios	TM
383	Groudon	TM
384	Rayquaza	TM
385	Jirachi	TM
386	Deoxys (N)	TM
386	Deoxys (A)	TM
386	Deoxys (D)	TM
386	Deoxys (S)	TM
390	Chimchar	TM
391	Monferno	TM
392	Infernape	TM
393	Piplup	TM
394	Prinplup	TM
395	Empoleon	TM
396	Starly	25,TM
397	Staravia	28,TM
398	Staraptor	28,TM
402	Kricketune	TM
414	Mothim	TM
416	Vespiquen	TM
424	Ambipom	TM
429	Mismagius	TM
430	Honchkrow	TM
431	Glameow	TM
432	Purugly	TM
441	Chatot	TM
443	Gible	TM
444	Gabite	TM
445	Garchomp	TM
451	Skorupi	TM
452	Drapion	TM
458	Mantyke	TM
461	Weavile	TM
465	Tangrowth	TM
468	Togekiss	TM
469	Yanmega	TM
470	Leafeon	TM
472	Gliscor	TM
474	Porygon-Z	TM
475	Gallade	TM
483	Dialga	TM
484	Palkia	TM
486	Regigigas	TM
487	Giratina (A)	TM
487	Giratina (O)	TM
491	Darkrai	TM

Aeroblast		
249	Lugia	85

Agility		
15	Beedrill	31
16	Pidgey	29
17	Pidgeotto	32
18	Pidgeot	32
21	Spearow	25
22	Fearow	29
25	Pikachu	34
48	Venonat	E
58	Growlithe	39
77	Ponyta	33
78	Rapidash	33
83	Farfetch'd	31
84	Doduo	37
85	Dodrio	41
107	Hitmonchan	6
116	Horsea	23
117	Seadra	23
118	Goldeen	47
119	Seaking	56
123	Scyther	17
135	Jolteon	64
137	Porygon	12
142	Aerodactyl	17
144	Articuno	36
145	Zapdos	43
146	Moltres	15
147	Dratini	25
148	Dragonair	25
149	Dragonite	25
160	Feraligatr	30
163	Hoothoot	E
165	Ledyba	30
166	Ledian	36
167	Spinarak	33
168	Ariados	37
170	Chinchou	E
190	Aipom	29,E
203	Girafarig	14
207	Gligar	E
212	Scizor	17
215	Sneasel	24
226	Mantine	19
227	Skarmory	12
230	Kingdra	23
233	Porygon2	12
237	Hitmontop	37
252	Treecko	31
253	Grovyle	35
254	Sceptile	35
255	Torchic	E
276	Taillow	43
277	Swellow	49
278	Wingull	37,E
283	Surskit	31
291	Ninjask	38
311	Plusle	44
312	Minun	44
318	Carvanha	36
319	Sharpedo	45
333	Swablu	E
368	Gorebyss	10
370	Luvdisc	9
375	Metang	44
376	Metagross	44
386	Deoxys (S)	73
393	Piplup	E
396	Starly	33
397	Staravia	38
398	Staraptor	41
418	Buizel	28
419	Floatzel	29
424	Ambipom	29
427	Buneary	33
428	Lopunny	33
441	Chatot	E
447	Riolu	E
451	Skorupi	E
456	Finneon	E
458	Mantyke	19
474	Porygon-Z	12

Air Cutter		
6	Charizard	T
12	Butterfree	T
15	Beedrill	T
16	Pidgey	T,E
17	Pidgeotto	T
18	Pidgeot	T
21	Spearow	T
22	Fearow	T
41	Zubat	25,T
42	Golbat	27,T
49	Venomoth	T
83	Farfetch'd	21,T
84	Doduo	T
85	Dodrio	T
142	Aerodactyl	T
144	Articuno	T
145	Zapdos	T
146	Moltres	T
149	Dragonite	T
151	Mew	T
163	Hoothoot	T
164	Noctowl	T
165	Ledyba	T
166	Ledian	T
169	Crobat	27,T
176	Togetic	T
177	Natu	T
178	Xatu	T
193	Yanma	T
198	Murkrow	T
226	Mantine	T
227	Skarmory	23,T
249	Lugia	T
250	Ho-Oh	T
267	Beautifly	T
269	Dustox	T
275	Shiftry	T
276	Taillow	T
277	Swellow	T
278	Wingull	T
279	Pelipper	T
284	Masquerain	T
291	Ninjask	T
313	Volbeat	T
314	Illumise	T
329	Vibrava	T
330	Flygon	T
333	Swablu	T
334	Altaria	T
357	Tropius	T
373	Salamence	T
396	Starly	T
397	Staravia	T
398	Staraptor	T
414	Mothim	T
415	Combee	T
416	Vespiquen	T
425	Drifloon	T
426	Drifblim	T
430	Honchkrow	T
441	Chatot	T
456	Finneon	T
457	Lumineon	T
458	Mantyke	T
468	Togekiss	T
469	Yanmega	T
487	Giratina (A)	T
487	Giratina (O)	T
492	Shaymin (S)	T

Air Slash		
6	Charizard	B
16	Pidgey	49,E
17	Pidgeotto	57
18	Pidgeot	62
41	Zubat	41
42	Golbat	51
83	Farfetch'd	37
123	Scyther	53
146	Moltres	50
163	Hoothoot	29
164	Noctowl	32
169	Crobat	51
193	Yanma	54
227	Skarmory	39
276	Taillow	53
277	Swellow	61
278	Wingull	47
284	Masquerain	47
357	Tropius	47
414	Mothim	41
468	Togekiss	B
469	Yanmega	54
479	Rotom (S)	*
492	Shaymin (S)	64

Amnesia		
1	Bulbasaur	E
32	Nidoran♂	E
52	Meowth	E
54	Psyduck	44
55	Golduck	50
79	Slowpoke	43
80	Slowbro	47
98	Krabby	E
108	Lickitung	E
114	Tangela	E
143	Snorlax	9
150	Mewtwo	57
151	Mew	60
161	Sentret	36
162	Furret	42
170	Chinchou	E
173	Cleffa	E
183	Marill	E
187	Hoppip	E
194	Wooper	23
195	Quagsire	24
203	Girafarig	E
218	Slugma	31
219	Magcargo	31
220	Swinub	49
221	Piloswine	65
222	Corsola	E
273	Seedot	E
287	Slakoth	25
289	Slaking	25
316	Gulpin	17
317	Swalot	17
320	Wailmer	37
321	Wailord	37
322	Numel	25
323	Camerupt	25
324	Torkoal	49
325	Spoink	E
339	Barboach	18
340	Whiscash	18
345	Lileep	29
346	Cradily	29
351	Castform	E
368	Gorebyss	19
369	Relicanth	E
378	Regice	41
379	Registeel	41
386	Deoxys (D)	73
387	Turtwig	E
399	Bidoof	29
400	Bibarel	33
422	Shellos	E
446	Munchlax	9
480	Uxie	46

AncientPower		
4	Charmander	E
50	Diglett	E
74	Geodude	T
75	Graveler	T
76	Golem	T
95	Onix	T
98	Krabby	T,E
99	Kingler	T
102	Exeggcute	T,E
103	Exeggutor	T
104	Cubone	E
111	Rhyhorn	T
112	Rhydon	T
114	Tangela	33,T
131	Lapras	T,E
138	Omanyte	37,T
139	Omastar	37,T
140	Kabuto	46,T
141	Kabutops	54,T
142	Aerodactyl	25,T
144	Articuno	29,T
145	Zapdos	29,T
146	Moltres	29,T
151	Mew	50,T
152	Chikorita	T,E
153	Bayleef	T
154	Meganium	T
158	Totodile	T,E
159	Croconaw	T
160	Feraligatr	T
175	Togepi	33,T
176	Togetic	33,T
193	Yanma	33,T
194	Wooper	T,E
195	Quagsire	T
206	Dunsparce	41,T,E
208	Steelix	T
213	Shuckle	T
218	Slugma	26,T
219	Magcargo	26,T
220	Swinub	T,E
221	Piloswine	B,T
222	Corsola	32,T
231	Phanpy	T,E
232	Donphan	T
246	Larvitar	T,E
247	Pupitar	T
248	Tyranitar	T
249	Lugia	57,T
250	Ho-Oh	57,T
251	Celebi	28,T
258	Mudkip	T,E
259	Marshtomp	T
260	Swampert	T
299	Nosepass	T
303	Mawile	T,E
304	Aron	T
305	Lairon	T
306	Aggron	T
318	Carvanha	T,E
319	Sharpedo	T
322	Numel	E
337	Lunatone	T
338	Solrock	T
341	Corphish	T,E
342	Crawdaunt	T
343	Baltoy	25,T
344	Claydol	25,T
345	Lileep	43,T
346	Cradily	36,T
347	Anorith	31,T
348	Armaldo	31,T
352	Kecleon	55,T
369	Relicanth	43,T
377	Regirock	33,T
378	Regice	33,T
379	Registeel	33,T
382	Kyogre	15,T
383	Groudon	15,T
384	Rayquaza	15,T
385	Jirachi	T
408	Cranidos	28,T
409	Rampardos	28,T
410	Shieldon	28,T
411	Bastiodon	28,T
422	Shellos	T
423	Gastrodon	T
436	Bronzor	T
437	Bronzong	T
464	Rhyperior	T
465	Tangrowth	33,T
468	Togekiss	T
469	Yanmega	33,T
473	Mamoswine	B,T
476	Probopass	T
483	Dialga	20,T
484	Palkia	20,T
485	Heatran	B,T
486	Regigigas	T
487	Giratina (A)	20,T
487	Giratina (O)	20,T
489	Phione	T
490	Manaphy	T

Aqua Jet		
7	Squirtle	E
55	Golduck	B
86	Seel	31
87	Dewgong	31
140	Kabuto	31
141	Kabutops	31
183	Marill	E
318	Carvanha	31
319	Sharpedo	34
395	Empoleon	36
418	Buizel	21
419	Floatzel	21

Aqua Ring		
7	Squirtle	E
86	Seel	23
87	Dewgong	23
118	Goldeen	27
119	Seaking	27
134	Vaporeon	43
170	Chinchou	39
171	Lanturn	47
183	Marill	23
184	Azumarill	27
222	Corsola	37,E
226	Mantine	46
278	Wingull	E
350	Milotic	49
366	Clamperl	E
368	Gorebyss	24
370	Luvdisc	37,E
393	Piplup	E
456	Finneon	33
457	Lumineon	35
458	Mantyke	46
489	Phione	46
490	Manaphy	54

Aqua Tail		
7	Squirtle	28,T
8	Wartortle	32,T
9	Blastoise	32,T

*Rotom learns one move when it changes form, which it forgets when it turns back into Rotom (p. 514).

23	Ekans	T
24	Arbok	T
31	Nidoqueen	T
34	Nidoking	T
54	Psyduck	T
55	Golduck	T
79	Slowpoke	T
80	Slowbro	T
86	Seel	43,T
87	Dewgong	43,T
108	Lickitung	T
111	Rhyhorn	T
112	Rhydon	T
115	Kangaskhan	T
118	Goldeen	T,E
119	Seaking	T
130	Gyarados	35,T
131	Lapras	T
134	Vaporeon	T
141	Kabutops	T
142	Aerodactyl	T
147	Dratini	31,T
148	Dragonair	33,T
149	Dragonite	33,T
150	Mewtwo	T
151	Mew	T
158	Totodile	41,T
159	Croconaw	48
160	Feraligatr	58,T
161	Sentret	T
162	Furret	T
171	Lanturn	T
183	Marill	37,T
184	Azumarill	47,T
194	Wooper	T
195	Quagsire	T
199	Slowking	T
206	Dunsparce	T
207	Gligar	T
208	Steelix	T
211	Qwilfish	45,T
226	Mantine	T
248	Tyranitar	T
249	Lugia	T
258	Mudkip	T
259	Marshtomp	T
260	Swampert	T
306	Aggron	T
336	Seviper	T
339	Barboach	35,T
340	Whiscash	39,T
348	Armaldo	T
350	Milotic	29,T
352	Kecleon	T
363	Spheal	T
364	Sealeo	T
365	Walrein	T
367	Huntail	46,T
368	Gorebyss	46,T
369	Relicanth	T,E
373	Salamence	T
382	Kyogre	75,T
384	Rayquaza	T
399	Bidoof	T,E
400	Bibarel	T
419	Floatzel	T
445	Garchomp	T
451	Skorupi	T
452	Drapion	T
456	Finneon	T,E
457	Lumineon	T
463	Lickilicky	T
464	Rhyperior	T
471	Glaceon	T
472	Gliscor	T
484	Palkia	80,T
487	Giratina (A)	T
487	Giratina (O)	T

Arm Thrust		
296	Makuhita	7
297	Hariyama	B,7

Aromatherapy		
45	Vileplume	B
46	Paras	38
47	Parasect	47
113	Chansey	E
152	Chikorita	42,E
153	Bayleef	50
154	Meganium	60
187	Hoppip	E
315	Roselia	43
420	Cherubi	E
440	Happiny	E
492	Shaymin (L)	64

Assist		
52	Meowth	E
96	Drowzee	E
161	Sentret	E
300	Skitty	22
327	Spinda	E
431	Glameow	29
432	Purugly	29

Assurance		
15	Beedrill	34
19	Rattata	25
20	Raticate	29
21	Spearow	29
22	Fearow	35
52	Meowth	41
53	Persian	49
56	Mankey	25
57	Primeape	25
109	Koffing	15
110	Weezing	15
142	Aerodactyl	E
197	Umbreon	43
198	Murkrow	25
203	Girafarig	28
227	Skarmory	E
232	Donphan	31
246	Larvitar	E
261	Poochyena	29
262	Mightyena	32
318	Carvanha	26
319	Sharpedo	26
336	Seviper	E
359	Absol	E
408	Cranidos	24
409	Rampardos	24
431	Glameow	E
461	Weavile	B

Astonish		
21	Spearow	E
41	Zubat	9
42	Golbat	B,9
50	Diglett	7,E
51	Dugtrio	7
92	Gastly	E
169	Crobat	B,9
190	Aipom	8
198	Murkrow	B
200	Misdreavus	10
203	Girafarig	B
206	Dunsparce	E
211	Qwilfish	E
234	Stantler	7
261	Poochyena	E
270	Lotad	B
271	Lombre	B
272	Ludicolo	B
293	Whismur	11
294	Loudred	B,11
295	Exploud	B,11
302	Sableye	11
303	Mawile	B
320	Wailmer	17
321	Wailord	17
333	Swablu	5
334	Altaria	B,5
345	Lileep	B
346	Cradily	B
352	Kecleon	B
353	Shuppet	E
355	Duskull	14
356	Dusclops	14
358	Chimecho	9
396	Starly	E
424	Ambipom	B,8
425	Drifloon	6
426	Drifblim	B,6
429	Mismagius	B
430	Honchkrow	B
433	Chingling	9
434	Stunky	E
453	Croagunk	B
454	Toxicroak	B
477	Dusknoir	14
478	Froslass	B,10
479	Rotom	B

Attack Order		
416	Vespiquen	37

Attract		
1	Bulbasaur	TM
2	Ivysaur	TM
3	Venusaur	TM
4	Charmander	TM
5	Charmeleon	TM
6	Charizard	TM
7	Squirtle	TM
8	Wartortle	TM
9	Blastoise	TM
12	Butterfree	TM
15	Beedrill	TM
16	Pidgey	TM
17	Pidgeotto	TM
18	Pidgeot	TM
19	Rattata	TM
20	Raticate	TM
21	Spearow	TM
22	Fearow	TM
23	Ekans	TM
24	Arbok	TM
25	Pikachu	TM
26	Raichu	TM
27	Sandshrew	TM
28	Sandslash	TM
29	Nidoran♀	TM
30	Nidorina	TM
31	Nidoqueen	TM
32	Nidoran♂	TM
33	Nidorino	TM
34	Nidoking	TM
35	Clefairy	TM
36	Clefable	TM
37	Vulpix	TM
38	Ninetales	TM
39	Jigglypuff	TM
40	Wigglytuff	TM
41	Zubat	TM
42	Golbat	TM
43	Oddish	TM
44	Gloom	TM
45	Vileplume	TM
46	Paras	TM
47	Parasect	TM
48	Venonat	TM
49	Venomoth	TM
50	Diglett	TM
51	Dugtrio	TM
52	Meowth	TM
53	Persian	TM
54	Psyduck	TM
55	Golduck	TM
56	Mankey	TM
57	Primeape	TM
58	Growlithe	TM
59	Arcanine	TM
60	Poliwag	TM
61	Poliwhirl	TM
62	Poliwrath	TM
63	Abra	TM
64	Kadabra	TM
65	Alakazam	TM
66	Machop	TM
67	Machoke	TM
68	Machamp	TM
69	Bellsprout	TM
70	Weepinbell	TM
71	Victreebel	TM
72	Tentacool	TM
73	Tentacruel	TM
74	Geodude	TM
75	Graveler	TM
76	Golem	TM
77	Ponyta	TM
78	Rapidash	TM
79	Slowpoke	TM
80	Slowbro	TM
83	Farfetch'd	TM
84	Doduo	TM
85	Dodrio	TM
86	Seel	TM
87	Dewgong	TM
88	Grimer	TM
89	Muk	TM
90	Shellder	TM
91	Cloyster	TM
92	Gastly	TM
93	Haunter	TM
94	Gengar	TM
95	Onix	TM
96	Drowzee	TM
97	Hypno	TM
98	Krabby	TM
99	Kingler	TM
102	Exeggcute	TM
103	Exeggutor	TM
104	Cubone	TM
105	Marowak	TM
106	Hitmonlee	TM
107	Hitmonchan	TM
108	Lickitung	TM
109	Koffing	TM
110	Weezing	TM
111	Rhyhorn	TM
112	Rhydon	TM
113	Chansey	TM
114	Tangela	TM
115	Kangaskhan	TM
116	Horsea	TM
117	Seadra	TM
118	Goldeen	TM
119	Seaking	TM
122	Mr. Mime	TM
123	Scyther	TM
124	Jynx	TM
125	Electabuzz	TM
126	Magmar	TM
127	Pinsir	TM
128	Tauros	TM
130	Gyarados	TM
131	Lapras	TM
133	Eevee	TM
134	Vaporeon	TM
135	Jolteon	TM
136	Flareon	TM
138	Omanyte	TM
139	Omastar	TM
140	Kabuto	TM
141	Kabutops	TM
142	Aerodactyl	TM
143	Snorlax	TM
147	Dratini	TM
148	Dragonair	TM
149	Dragonite	TM
151	Mew	TM
152	Chikorita	TM
153	Bayleef	TM
154	Meganium	TM
155	Cyndaquil	TM
156	Quilava	TM
157	Typhlosion	TM
158	Totodile	TM
159	Croconaw	TM
160	Feraligatr	TM
161	Sentret	TM
162	Furret	TM
163	Hoothoot	TM
164	Noctowl	TM
165	Ledyba	TM
166	Ledian	TM
167	Spinarak	TM
168	Ariados	TM
169	Crobat	TM
170	Chinchou	TM
171	Lanturn	TM
172	Pichu	TM
173	Cleffa	TM
174	Igglybuff	TM
175	Togepi	TM
176	Togetic	TM
177	Natu	TM
178	Xatu	TM
179	Mareep	TM
180	Flaaffy	TM
181	Ampharos	TM
182	Bellossom	TM
183	Marill	TM
184	Azumarill	TM
185	Sudowoodo	TM
186	Politoed	TM
187	Hoppip	TM
188	Skiploom	TM
189	Jumpluff	TM
190	Aipom	TM
191	Sunkern	TM
192	Sunflora	TM
193	Yanma	TM
194	Wooper	TM
195	Quagsire	TM
196	Espeon	TM
197	Umbreon	TM
198	Murkrow	TM
199	Slowking	TM
200	Misdreavus	TM
203	Girafarig	TM
204	Pineco	TM
205	Forretress	TM
206	Dunsparce	TM
207	Gligar	TM
208	Steelix	TM
209	Snubbull	TM
210	Granbull	TM
211	Qwilfish	TM
212	Scizor	TM
213	Shuckle	TM
214	Heracross	TM
215	Sneasel	TM
216	Teddiursa	TM
217	Ursaring	TM
218	Slugma	TM
219	Magcargo	TM
220	Swinub	TM
221	Piloswine	TM
222	Corsola	TM
223	Remoraid	TM
224	Octillery	TM
225	Delibird	TM
226	Mantine	TM
227	Skarmory	TM
228	Houndour	TM
229	Houndoom	TM
230	Kingdra	TM
231	Phanpy	TM
232	Donphan	TM
234	Stantler	TM
236	Tyrogue	TM
237	Hitmontop	TM
238	Smoochum	TM
239	Elekid	TM
240	Magby	TM
241	Miltank	TM
242	Blissey	TM
246	Larvitar	TM
247	Pupitar	TM
248	Tyranitar	TM
252	Treecko	TM
253	Grovyle	TM
254	Sceptile	TM
255	Torchic	TM
256	Combusken	TM
257	Blaziken	TM
258	Mudkip	TM
259	Marshtomp	TM
260	Swampert	TM
261	Poochyena	TM
262	Mightyena	TM
263	Zigzagoon	TM
264	Linoone	TM
267	Beautifly	31,TM
269	Dustox	TM
270	Lotad	TM
271	Lombre	TM
272	Ludicolo	TM
273	Seedot	TM
274	Nuzleaf	TM
275	Shiftry	TM
276	Taillow	TM
277	Swellow	TM
278	Wingull	TM
279	Pelipper	TM
280	Ralts	TM
281	Kirlia	TM
282	Gardevoir	TM
283	Surskit	TM
284	Masquerain	TM
285	Shroomish	TM
286	Breloom	TM
287	Slakoth	TM
288	Vigoroth	TM
289	Slaking	TM
291	Ninjask	TM
293	Whismur	TM
294	Loudred	TM
295	Exploud	TM
296	Makuhita	TM
297	Hariyama	TM
298	Azurill	TM
299	Nosepass	TM
300	Skitty	8,TM
301	Delcatty	B,TM
302	Sableye	TM
303	Mawile	TM
304	Aron	TM
305	Lairon	TM
306	Aggron	TM
307	Meditite	TM
308	Medicham	TM
309	Electrike	TM
310	Manectric	TM
311	Plusle	TM
312	Minun	TM
313	Volbeat	TM
314	Illumise	TM
315	Roselia	TM
316	Gulpin	TM
317	Swalot	TM
318	Carvanha	TM
319	Sharpedo	TM
320	Wailmer	TM
321	Wailord	TM
322	Numel	TM
323	Camerupt	TM
324	Torkoal	TM
325	Spoink	TM
326	Grumpig	TM
327	Spinda	TM
328	Trapinch	TM
329	Vibrava	TM
330	Flygon	TM
331	Cacnea	TM
332	Cacturne	TM
333	Swablu	TM
334	Altaria	TM
335	Zangoose	TM
336	Seviper	TM
339	Barboach	TM
340	Whiscash	TM
341	Corphish	TM
342	Crawdaunt	TM
345	Lileep	TM
346	Cradily	TM
347	Anorith	TM
348	Armaldo	TM
349	Feebas	TM
350	Milotic	41,TM
351	Castform	TM
352	Kecleon	TM
353	Shuppet	TM
354	Banette	TM
355	Duskull	TM
356	Dusclops	TM
357	Tropius	TM
358	Chimecho	TM
359	Absol	TM
361	Snorunt	TM
362	Glalie	TM
363	Spheal	TM
364	Sealeo	TM
365	Walrein	TM
366	Clamperl	TM
367	Huntail	TM
368	Gorebyss	TM
369	Relicanth	TM
370	Luvdisc	22,TM
371	Bagon	TM
372	Shelgon	TM
373	Salamence	TM
380	Latias	TM
381	Latios	TM
387	Turtwig	TM
388	Grotle	TM
389	Torterra	TM
390	Chimchar	TM
391	Monferno	TM
392	Infernape	TM
393	Piplup	TM
394	Prinplup	TM
395	Empoleon	TM
396	Starly	TM
397	Staravia	TM
398	Staraptor	TM
399	Bidoof	TM
400	Bibarel	TM
402	Kricketune	TM
403	Shinx	TM
404	Luxio	TM
405	Luxray	TM
406	Budew	TM
407	Roserade	TM
408	Cranidos	TM
409	Rampardos	TM
410	Shieldon	TM
411	Bastiodon	TM
413	Wormadam (P)	41,TM
413	Wormadam (S)	41,TM
413	Wormadam (T)	41,TM
414	Mothim	TM
416	Vespiquen	TM
417	Pachirisu	TM
418	Buizel	TM
419	Floatzel	TM
420	Cherubi	TM
421	Cherrim	TM
422	Shellos	TM
423	Gastrodon	TM
424	Ambipom	TM
425	Drifloon	TM
426	Drifblim	TM
427	Buneary	TM,E
428	Lopunny	TM
429	Mismagius	TM
430	Honchkrow	TM
431	Glameow	45,TM
432	Purugly	53,TM
433	Chingling	TM
434	Stunky	TM
435	Skuntank	TM
438	Bonsly	TM
439	Mime Jr.	TM
440	Happiny	TM
441	Chatot	TM
442	Spiritomb	TM
443	Gible	TM
444	Gabite	TM
445	Garchomp	TM
446	Munchlax	TM
447	Riolu	TM
448	Lucario	TM
449	Hippopotas	TM
450	Hippowdon	TM
451	Skorupi	TM
452	Drapion	TM
453	Croagunk	TM
454	Toxicroak	TM
455	Carnivine	TM
456	Finneon	10,TM
457	Lumineon	B,10,TM
458	Mantyke	TM
459	Snover	TM
460	Abomasnow	TM
461	Weavile	TM
463	Lickilicky	TM
464	Rhyperior	TM
465	Tangrowth	TM
466	Electivire	TM
467	Magmortar	TM
468	Togekiss	TM
469	Yanmega	TM
470	Leafeon	TM
471	Glaceon	TM
472	Gliscor	TM
473	Mamoswine	TM
475	Gallade	TM
476	Probopass	TM
477	Dusknoir	TM
478	Froslass	TM
485	Heatran	TM
488	Cresselia	TM

Aura Sphere		
150	Mewtwo	100
151	Mew	100
448	Lucario	37
468	Togekiss	B
483	Dialga	90
484	Palkia	90
487	Giratina (A)	90
487	Giratina (O)	90

Aurora Beam		
72	Tentacool	E
86	Seel	27
87	Dewgong	27
90	Shellder	32
91	Cloyster	B
116	Horsea	E
134	Vaporeon	36
138	Omanyte	E
140	Kabuto	E
223	Remoraid	14,E
224	Octillery	B,14
225	Delibird	E
245	Suicune	29
363	Spheal	25
364	Sealeo	25
365	Walrein	25
488	Cresselia	29

Avalanche		
9	Blastoise	TM
31	Nidoqueen	TM
34	Nidoking	TM
80	Slowbro	TM
87	Dewgong	TM
91	Cloyster	TM
112	Rhydon	TM
115	Kangaskhan	TM
121	Starmie	TM
124	Jynx	33,TM
130	Gyarados	TM
131	Lapras	TM
144	Articuno	TM
150	Mewtwo	TM
151	Mew	TM
160	Feraligatr	TM
199	Slowking	TM
215	Sneasel	TM
217	Ursaring	TM
221	Piloswine	TM
225	Delibird	TM
238	Smoochum	31,TM
242	Blissey	TM
245	Suicune	TM
248	Tyranitar	TM
249	Lugia	TM
260	Swampert	TM
295	Exploud	TM
306	Aggron	TM
319	Sharpedo	TM
320	Wailmer	TM
321	Wailord	TM
342	Crawdaunt	TM
350	Milotic	TM
351	Castform	TM
361	Snorunt	TM
362	Glalie	TM
365	Walrein	TM
378	Regice	TM
382	Kyogre	TM
384	Rayquaza	TM
386	Deoxys (N)	TM
386	Deoxys (A)	TM
386	Deoxys (D)	TM
386	Deoxys (S)	TM
395	Empoleon	TM

Avalanche continued		
409	Rampardos	TM
411	Bastiodon	TM
459	Snover	TM
460	Abomasnow	TM
461	Weavile	TM
464	Rhyperior	TM
471	Glaceon	TM
473	Mamoswine	TM
478	Froslass	TM
484	Palkia	TM
486	Regigigas	TM

Barrage		
102	Exeggcute	B
103	Exeggutor	B

Barrier		
63	Abra	E
72	Tentacool	26
73	Tentacruel	26
90	Shellder	E
96	Drowzee	E
122	Mr. Mime	B
150	Mewtwo	8
151	Mew	40
222	Corsola	E
239	Elekid	E
240	Magby	E
345	Lileep	E
366	Clamperl	E
439	Mime Jr.	B
462	Magnezone	B
471	Glaceon	78

Baton Pass		
48	Venonat	E
122	Mr. Mime	46
123	Scyther	E
133	Eevee	36
151	Mew	80
161	Sentret	39
162	Furret	46
165	Ledyba	22
166	Ledian	24
167	Spinarak	E
175	Togepi	42
176	Togetic	42
190	Aipom	11
203	Girafarig	23
207	Gligar	E
251	Celebi	37
255	Torchic	E
283	Surskit	43
291	Ninjask	45
300	Skitty	E
303	Mawile	31
307	Meditite	E
311	Plusle	42
312	Minun	42
313	Volbeat	E
314	Illumise	E
327	Spinda	E
359	Absol	E
367	Huntail	33
368	Gorebyss	33
418	Buizel	E
424	Ambipom	11
425	Drifloon	33
426	Drifblim	37
427	Buneary	26
428	Lopunny	26
439	Mime Jr.	46

Beat Up		
4	Charmander	E
23	Ekans	E
29	Nidoran♀	E
32	Nidoran♂	E
50	Diglett	E
56	Mankey	E
190	Aipom	E
203	Girafarig	E
215	Sneasel	38
228	Houndour	27,E
229	Houndoom	28

Belly Drum		
4	Charmander	E
60	Poliwag	31
61	Poliwhirl	37
79	Slowpoke	E
104	Cubone	E
108	Lickitung	E
143	Snorlax	17
173	Cleffa	E
183	Marill	E
263	Zigzagoon	41
264	Linoone	53
296	Makuhita	25
297	Hariyama	27

Bide		
165	Ledyba	E
172	Pichu	E
204	Pineco	20
205	Forretress	20
206	Dunsparce	E
213	Shuckle	B
214	Heracross	E
241	Miltank	15
258	Mudkip	15
259	Marshtomp	15
260	Swampert	15
273	Seedot	B
307	Meditite	B
308	Medicham	B
361	Snorunt	E
393	Piplup	22
394	Prinplup	24
401	Kricketot	B
402	Kricketune	B
417	Pachirisu	B

Bind		
95	Onix	B
114	Tangela	22
127	Pinsir	4
208	Steelix	B
352	Kecleon	4
356	Dusclops	B
455	Carnivine	B
465	Tangrowth	22
477	Dusknoir	B

Bite		
4	Charmander	E
7	Squirtle	16
8	Wartortle	16
9	Blastoise	16
19	Rattata	10,E
20	Raticate	10
23	Ekans	9
24	Arbok	B,9
29	Nidoran♀	21
30	Nidorina	23
41	Zubat	13
42	Golbat	13
52	Meowth	6
53	Persian	B,6
58	Growlithe	B
59	Arcanine	B
115	Kangaskhan	13
130	Gyarados	20
133	Eevee	29
134	Vaporeon	29
136	Flareon	29
138	Omanyte	7
139	Omastar	B,7
142	Aerodactyl	B
158	Totodile	13
159	Croconaw	13
160	Feraligatr	13
169	Crobat	13
206	Dunsparce	E
209	Snubbull	7
210	Granbull	7
215	Sneasel	E
220	Swinub	E
228	Houndour	17
229	Houndoom	17
234	Stantler	E
243	Raikou	B
244	Entei	B
245	Suicune	B
246	Larvitar	B
247	Pupitar	B
248	Tyranitar	B
258	Mudkip	E
261	Poochyena	13
262	Mightyena	B,13
294	Loudred	20
295	Exploud	20
303	Mawile	11
309	Electrike	28
310	Manectric	30
318	Carvanha	B
319	Sharpedo	B
328	Trapinch	B
336	Seviper	10
359	Absol	28
361	Snorunt	10
362	Glalie	B,10
367	Huntail	6
371	Bagon	5
372	Shelgon	B,5
373	Salamence	B,5
387	Turtwig	21
388	Grotle	22
389	Torterra	22
403	Shinx	17
404	Luxio	18
405	Luxray	18
417	Pachirisu	E
431	Glameow	E
447	Riolu	E
449	Hippopotas	7
450	Hippowdon	B,7
451	Skorupi	B
452	Drapion	B
455	Carnivine	7
471	Glaceon	29

Blast Burn		
6	Charizard	T
157	Typhlosion	T
257	Blaziken	T
392	Infernape	T

Blaze Kick		
106	Hitmonlee	41
257	Blaziken	36
390	Chimchar	E
447	Riolu	E

Blizzard		
7	Squirtle	TM
8	Wartortle	TM
9	Blastoise	TM
19	Rattata	TM
20	Raticate	TM
29	Nidoran♀	TM
30	Nidorina	TM
31	Nidoqueen	TM
32	Nidoran♂	TM
33	Nidorino	TM
34	Nidoking	TM
35	Clefairy	TM
36	Clefable	TM
39	Jigglypuff	TM
40	Wigglytuff	TM
54	Psyduck	TM
55	Golduck	TM
60	Poliwag	TM
61	Poliwhirl	TM
62	Poliwrath	TM
72	Tentacool	TM
73	Tentacruel	TM
79	Slowpoke	TM
80	Slowbro	TM
86	Seel	TM
87	Dewgong	TM
90	Shellder	TM
91	Cloyster	TM
98	Krabby	TM
99	Kingler	TM
104	Cubone	TM
105	Marowak	TM
108	Lickitung	TM
111	Rhyhorn	TM
112	Rhydon	TM
113	Chansey	TM
115	Kangaskhan	TM
116	Horsea	TM
117	Seadra	TM
118	Goldeen	TM
119	Seaking	TM
120	Staryu	TM
121	Starmie	TM
124	Jynx	55,TM
128	Tauros	TM
130	Gyarados	TM
131	Lapras	TM
134	Vaporeon	TM
137	Porygon	TM
138	Omanyte	TM
139	Omastar	TM
140	Kabuto	TM
141	Kabutops	TM
143	Snorlax	TM
144	Articuno	71,TM
147	Dratini	TM
148	Dragonair	TM
149	Dragonite	TM
150	Mewtwo	TM
151	Mew	TM
158	Totodile	TM
159	Croconaw	TM
160	Feraligatr	TM
162	Furret	TM
170	Chinchou	TM
171	Lanturn	TM
183	Marill	TM
184	Azumarill	TM
186	Politoed	TM
194	Wooper	TM
195	Quagsire	TM
199	Slowking	TM
206	Dunsparce	TM
211	Qwilfish	TM
215	Sneasel	TM
220	Swinub	44,TM
221	Piloswine	56,TM
222	Corsola	TM
223	Remoraid	TM
224	Octillery	TM
225	Delibird	TM
226	Mantine	TM
230	Kingdra	TM
233	Porygon2	TM
238	Smoochum	45,TM
241	Miltank	TM
242	Blissey	TM
245	Suicune	85,TM
248	Tyranitar	TM
249	Lugia	TM
258	Mudkip	TM
259	Marshtomp	TM
260	Swampert	TM
263	Zigzagoon	TM
264	Linoone	TM
270	Lotad	TM
271	Lombre	TM
272	Ludicolo	TM
278	Wingull	TM
279	Pelipper	TM
283	Surskit	TM
284	Masquerain	TM
287	Slakoth	TM
288	Vigoroth	TM
289	Slaking	TM
293	Whismur	TM
294	Loudred	TM
295	Exploud	TM
298	Azurill	TM
300	Skitty	TM
301	Delcatty	TM
306	Aggron	TM
318	Carvanha	TM
319	Sharpedo	TM
320	Wailmer	TM
321	Wailord	TM
335	Zangoose	TM
337	Lunatone	TM
339	Barboach	TM
340	Whiscash	TM
341	Corphish	TM
342	Crawdaunt	TM
349	Feebas	TM
350	Milotic	TM
351	Castform	TM
352	Kecleon	TM
355	Duskull	TM
356	Dusclops	TM
359	Absol	TM
361	Snorunt	46,TM
362	Glalie	51,TM
363	Spheal	43,TM
364	Sealeo	47,TM
365	Walrein	52,TM
366	Clamperl	TM
367	Huntail	TM
368	Gorebyss	TM
369	Relicanth	TM
370	Luvdisc	TM
378	Regice	TM
382	Kyogre	TM
384	Rayquaza	TM
393	Piplup	TM
394	Prinplup	TM
395	Empoleon	TM
399	Bidoof	TM
400	Bibarel	TM
408	Cranidos	TM
409	Rampardos	TM
410	Shieldon	TM
411	Bastiodon	TM
418	Buizel	TM
419	Floatzel	TM
422	Shellos	TM
423	Gastrodon	TM
428	Lopunny	TM
446	Munchlax	TM
456	Finneon	TM
457	Lumineon	TM
458	Mantyke	TM
459	Snover	41,TM
460	Abomasnow	47,TM
461	Weavile	TM
463	Lickilicky	TM
464	Rhyperior	TM
471	Glaceon	71,TM
473	Mamoswine	56,TM
474	Porygon-Z	TM
477	Dusknoir	TM
478	Froslass	51,TM
479	Rotom (F)	*
481	Mesprit	TM
483	Dialga	TM
484	Palkia	TM
489	Phione	TM
490	Manaphy	TM
491	Darkrai	TM

Block		
74	Geodude	E
79	Slowpoke	E
95	Onix	E
143	Snorlax	36
185	Sudowoodo	22
299	Nosepass	19,E
361	Snorunt	E
411	Bastiodon	30
437	Bronzong	33
438	Bonsly	22
465	Tangrowth	57
476	Probopass	B,19

Body Slam		
31	Nidoqueen	23
39	Jigglypuff	29
58	Growlithe	E
60	Poliwag	21
61	Poliwhirl	21
108	Lickitung	E
124	Jynx	39
131	Lapras	18
143	Snorlax	33
152	Chikorita	34
153	Bayleef	40
154	Meganium	46
179	Mareep	E
194	Wooper	E
218	Slugma	46
219	Magcargo	52
220	Swinub	E
231	Phanpy	E
241	Miltank	24
287	Slakoth	E
304	Aron	E
317	Swalot	26
320	Wailmer	E
322	Numel	E
324	Torkoal	33
336	Seviper	E
341	Corphish	E
357	Tropius	37
363	Spheal	19
364	Sealeo	19
365	Walrein	19
366	Clamperl	E
382	Kyogre	20
387	Turtwig	E
410	Shieldon	E
422	Shellos	29
423	Gastrodon	29
425	Drifloon	E
432	Purugly	45
443	Gible	E
446	Munchlax	33
449	Hippopotas	E

Bone Club		
104	Cubone	7
105	Marowak	B,7

Bone Rush		
104	Cubone	37
105	Marowak	43
448	Lucario	19

Bonemerang		
104	Cubone	21
105	Marowak	21

Bounce		
35	Clefairy	T
36	Clefable	T
39	Jigglypuff	T
40	Wigglytuff	T
77	Ponyta	42,T
78	Rapidash	47,T
106	Hitmonlee	T
116	Horsea	T
117	Seadra	T
118	Goldeen	T
119	Seaking	T
129	Magikarp	T
130	Gyarados	T
151	Mew	T
167	Spinarak	T
168	Ariados	T
170	Chinchou	T
171	Lanturn	T
174	Igglybuff	T
186	Politoed	37,T
187	Hoppip	40,T
188	Skiploom	48,T
189	Jumpluff	48,T
190	Aipom	T,E
211	Qwilfish	T
223	Remoraid	T
224	Octillery	T
225	Delibird	T
226	Mantine	40,T
230	Kingdra	T
232	Donphan	T
234	Stantler	T
255	Torchic	T
256	Combusken	T
257	Blaziken	T
275	Shiftry	T
318	Carvanha	T
319	Sharpedo	T
320	Wailmer	44,T
321	Wailord	54,T
325	Spoink	48,T
326	Grumpig	60,T
339	Barboach	T
340	Whiscash	T
359	Absol	T
367	Huntail	T
368	Gorebyss	T
369	Relicanth	T
370	Luvdisc	T
424	Ambipom	T
427	Buneary	46,T
428	Lopunny	46,T
453	Croagunk	T
454	Toxicroak	T
456	Finneon	45,T
457	Lumineon	53,T
458	Mantyke	40,T
489	Phione	T
490	Manaphy	T

Brave Bird		
16	Pidgey	E
41	Zubat	E
84	Doduo	E
227	Skarmory	E
257	Blaziken	49
276	Taillow	E
396	Starly	37
397	Staravia	43
398	Staraptor	49

Brick Break		
4	Charmander	TM
5	Charmeleon	TM
6	Charizard	TM
7	Squirtle	TM
8	Wartortle	TM
9	Blastoise	TM
15	Beedrill	TM
25	Pikachu	TM
26	Raichu	TM
27	Sandshrew	TM
28	Sandslash	TM
31	Nidoqueen	TM
34	Nidoking	TM
35	Clefairy	TM
36	Clefable	TM
39	Jigglypuff	TM
40	Wigglytuff	TM
46	Paras	TM
47	Parasect	TM
54	Psyduck	TM
55	Golduck	TM
56	Mankey	TM
57	Primeape	TM
61	Poliwhirl	TM
62	Poliwrath	TM
66	Machop	TM
67	Machoke	TM
68	Machamp	TM
74	Geodude	TM
75	Graveler	TM
76	Golem	TM
80	Slowbro	TM
89	Muk	TM
94	Gengar	TM
96	Drowzee	TM
97	Hypno	TM
98	Krabby	TM
99	Kingler	TM
104	Cubone	TM
105	Marowak	TM
106	Hitmonlee	17,TM
107	Hitmonchan	TM
108	Lickitung	TM
112	Rhydon	TM
113	Chansey	TM
115	Kangaskhan	TM
122	Mr. Mime	TM
123	Scyther	TM
124	Jynx	TM
125	Electabuzz	TM
126	Magmar	TM
127	Pinsir	21,TM
141	Kabutops	TM
143	Snorlax	TM
149	Dragonite	TM
150	Mewtwo	TM
151	Mew	TM
156	Quilava	TM
157	Typhlosion	TM
158	Totodile	TM
159	Croconaw	TM
160	Feraligatr	TM
161	Sentret	TM
162	Furret	TM
165	Ledyba	TM
166	Ledian	TM
176	Togetic	TM
180	Flaaffy	TM
181	Ampharos	TM
183	Marill	TM
184	Azumarill	TM
185	Sudowoodo	TM
186	Politoed	TM
190	Aipom	TM
195	Quagsire	TM
199	Slowking	TM
207	Gligar	TM
209	Snubbull	TM
210	Granbull	TM
212	Scizor	TM
214	Heracross	19,TM
215	Sneasel	TM
216	Teddiursa	TM
217	Ursaring	TM
225	Delibird	TM
236	Tyrogue	TM
237	Hitmontop	TM
239	Elekid	TM
240	Magby	TM
241	Miltank	TM
242	Blissey	TM
246	Larvitar	TM
247	Pupitar	TM
248	Tyranitar	TM
252	Treecko	TM
253	Grovyle	TM
254	Sceptile	TM
256	Combusken	TM
257	Blaziken	TM
259	Marshtomp	TM
260	Swampert	TM
271	Lombre	TM
272	Ludicolo	TM
274	Nuzleaf	TM
275	Shiftry	TM
286	Breloom	TM
287	Slakoth	TM
288	Vigoroth	TM
289	Slaking	TM
294	Loudred	TM
295	Exploud	TM
296	Makuhita	TM
297	Hariyama	TM
302	Sableye	TM
303	Mawile	TM
306	Aggron	TM
307	Meditite	TM
308	Medicham	TM
313	Volbeat	TM
314	Illumise	TM
326	Grumpig	TM
327	Spinda	TM
331	Cacnea	TM
332	Cacturne	TM
335	Zangoose	TM
341	Corphish	TM
342	Crawdaunt	TM
347	Anorith	TM
348	Armaldo	TM
352	Kecleon	TM
356	Dusclops	TM
371	Bagon	TM
372	Shelgon	TM
373	Salamence	TM
375	Metang	TM
376	Metagross	TM
377	Regirock	TM
378	Regice	TM
379	Registeel	TM
382	Kyogre	TM
383	Groudon	TM
384	Rayquaza	TM
386	Deoxys (N)	TM
386	Deoxys (A)	TM
386	Deoxys (D)	TM

*Rotom learns one move when it changes Form, which it forgets when it turns back into Rotom (p. 514).

386	Deoxys (S)	TM
390	Chimchar	TM
391	Monferno	TM
392	Infernape	TM
393	Piplup	TM
394	Prinplup	TM
395	Empoleon	TM
402	Kricketune	TM
409	Rampardos	TM
418	Buizel	TM
419	Floatzel	TM
424	Ambipom	TM
438	Bonsly	TM
439	Mime Jr.	TM
445	Garchomp	TM
446	Munchlax	TM
447	Riolu	TM
448	Lucario	TM
451	Skorupi	TM
452	Drapion	TM
453	Croagunk	TM
454	Toxicroak	TM
460	Abomasnow	TM
461	Weavile	TM
463	Lickilicky	TM
464	Rhyperior	TM
465	Tangrowth	TM
466	Electivire	TM
467	Magmortar	TM
468	Togekiss	TM
472	Gliscor	TM
475	Gallade	TM
477	Dusknoir	TM
483	Dialga	TM
484	Palkia	TM
486	Regigigas	TM
491	Darkrai	TM

Brine

7	Squirtle	TM
8	Wartortle	TM
9	Blastoise	TM
54	Psyduck	TM
55	Golduck	TM
72	Tentacool	TM
73	Tentacruel	TM
79	Slowpoke	TM
80	Slowbro	TM
86	Seel	33,TM
87	Dewgong	33,TM
90	Shellder	44,TM
91	Cloyster	TM
98	Krabby	39,TM
99	Kingler	51,TM
116	Horsea	30,TM
117	Seadra	30,TM
120	Staryu	TM
121	Starmie	TM
130	Gyarados	TM
131	Lapras	37,TM
134	Vaporeon	TM
138	Omanyte	28,TM
139	Omastar	28,TM
140	Kabuto	TM
141	Kabutops	TM
151	Mew	TM
170	Chinchou	TM
171	Lanturn	TM
199	Slowking	TM
211	Qwilfish	33,TM
222	Corsola	TM
223	Remoraid	TM
224	Octillery	TM
226	Mantine	TM
230	Kingdra	30,TM
245	Suicune	TM
249	Lugia	TM
278	Wingull	TM
279	Pelipper	TM
297	Hariyama	B,TM
318	Carvanha	TM
319	Sharpedo	TM
320	Wailmer	31,TM
321	Wailord	31,TM
363	Spheal	TM
364	Sealeo	TM
365	Walrein	TM
366	Clamperl	TM
367	Huntail	28,TM
368	Gorebyss	TM
369	Relicanth	TM
370	Luvdisc	TM
382	Kyogre	TM
393	Piplup	29,TM
394	Prinplup	33,TM
395	Empoleon	33,TM
418	Buizel	TM
419	Floatzel	TM
422	Shellos	TM
423	Gastrodon	TM
456	Finneon	TM
457	Lumineon	TM
484	Palkia	TM
489	Phione	TM
490	Manaphy	TM

Bubble

7	Squirtle	7
8	Wartortle	B,7
9	Blastoise	B,7
60	Poliwag	5
61	Poliwhirl	B,5
98	Krabby	B
99	Kingler	B
116	Horsea	B
117	Seadra	B
170	Chinchou	B
171	Lanturn	B
222	Corsola	8
226	Mantine	B
230	Kingdra	B
283	Surskit	B
284	Masquerain	B
298	Azurill	10
341	Corphish	B
342	Crawdaunt	B
393	Piplup	8
394	Prinplup	8
395	Empoleon	B,8
458	Mantyke	B
489	Phione	B
490	Manaphy	B

BubbleBeam

60	Poliwag	25,E
61	Poliwhirl	27
62	Poliwrath	B
72	Tentacool	19
73	Tentacruel	19
90	Shellder	E
98	Krabby	15
99	Kingler	15
116	Horsea	18
117	Seadra	18
120	Staryu	28
138	Omanyte	E
140	Kabuto	E
170	Chinchou	28
171	Lanturn	30
183	Marill	18
184	Azumarill	20
186	Politoed	B
211	Qwilfish	E
222	Corsola	25
223	Remoraid	19
224	Octillery	19
226	Mantine	B,10
230	Kingdra	18
245	Suicune	8
270	Lotad	25
271	Lombre	25
283	Surskit	25
341	Corphish	20
342	Crawdaunt	20
393	Piplup	18
394	Prinplup	19
395	Empoleon	19
458	Mantyke	10
489	Phione	24
490	Manaphy	24

Bug Bite

10	Caterpie	15
13	Weedle	15
46	Paras	E
48	Venonat	E
165	Ledyba	E
168	Ariados	B
204	Pineco	9
205	Forretress	B,9
213	Shuckle	40
265	Wurmple	15
283	Surskit	E
290	Nincada	E
291	Ninjask	B
401	Kricketot	16
412	Burmy	15
413	Wormadam (P)	15
413	Wormadam (S)	15
413	Wormadam (T)	15
414	Mothim	15
415	Combee	13
451	Skorupi	34
452	Drapion	34
469	Yanmega	B

Bug Buzz

12	Butterfree	40
49	Venomoth	59
123	Scyther	E
165	Ledyba	41,E
166	Ledian	53
193	Yanma	57
267	Beautifly	41
269	Dustox	41
284	Masquerain	61
290	Nincada	E
313	Volbeat	41,E
314	Illumise	41,E
402	Kricketune	46
414	Mothim	47
469	Yanmega	57

Bulk Up

56	Mankey	TM
57	Primeape	TM
62	Poliwrath	TM
66	Machop	TM
67	Machoke	TM
68	Machamp	TM
106	Hitmonlee	TM
107	Hitmonchan	TM
127	Pinsir	TM
150	Mewtwo	TM
151	Mew	TM
209	Snubbull	TM
210	Granbull	TM
214	Heracross	TM
216	Teddiursa	TM
217	Ursaring	TM
236	Tyrogue	TM
237	Hitmontop	TM
256	Combusken	28,TM
257	Blaziken	28,TM
286	Breloom	TM
287	Slakoth	TM
288	Vigoroth	TM
289	Slaking	TM
296	Makuhita	TM
297	Hariyama	TM
307	Meditite	TM
308	Medicham	TM
383	Groudon	30,TM
384	Rayquaza	TM
390	Chimchar	TM
391	Monferno	TM
392	Infernape	TM
418	Buizel	TM
419	Floatzel	TM
447	Riolu	TM
448	Lucario	TM
453	Croagunk	TM
454	Toxicroak	TM
475	Gallade	TM
483	Dialga	TM
484	Palkia	TM

Bullet Punch

66	Machop	E
107	Hitmonchan	16
212	Scizor	B
236	Tyrogue	E
296	Makuhita	E
307	Meditite	E
375	Metang	32
376	Metagross	32
447	Riolu	E
453	Croagunk	E

Bullet Seed

1	Bulbasaur	TM
2	Ivysaur	TM
3	Venusaur	TM
43	Oddish	TM
44	Gloom	TM
45	Vileplume	TM
46	Paras	TM
47	Parasect	TM
69	Bellsprout	TM
70	Weepinbell	TM
71	Victreebel	TM
102	Exeggcute	17,TM
103	Exeggutor	TM
114	Tangela	TM
151	Mew	TM
152	Chikorita	TM
153	Bayleef	TM
154	Meganium	TM
182	Bellossom	TM
187	Hoppip	19,TM
188	Skiploom	20,TM
189	Jumpluff	20,TM
191	Sunkern	TM
192	Sunflora	21,TM
223	Remoraid	27,TM
224	Octillery	29,TM
226	Mantine	B,TM
252	Treecko	TM
253	Grovyle	TM
254	Sceptile	TM
270	Lotad	TM
271	Lombre	TM
272	Ludicolo	TM
273	Seedot	TM
274	Nuzleaf	TM
275	Shiftry	TM
285	Shroomish	TM
286	Breloom	TM
315	Roselia	TM
316	Gulpin	TM
317	Swalot	TM
331	Cacnea	TM
332	Cacturne	TM
345	Lileep	TM
346	Cradily	TM
357	Tropius	TM
387	Turtwig	TM
388	Grotle	TM
389	Torterra	TM
406	Budew	TM
407	Roserade	TM
413	Wormadam (P)	TM
420	Cherubi	TM
421	Cherrim	TM
455	Carnivine	TM
459	Snover	TM
460	Abomasnow	TM
465	Tangrowth	TM
470	Leafeon	TM
492	Shaymin (L)	TM
492	Shaymin (S)	TM

Calm Mind

35	Clefairy	TM
36	Clefable	TM
38	Ninetales	TM
54	Psyduck	TM
55	Golduck	TM
63	Abra	TM
64	Kadabra	TM
65	Alakazam	36,TM
79	Slowpoke	TM
80	Slowbro	TM
96	Drowzee	TM
97	Hypno	TM
113	Chansey	TM
122	Mr. Mime	TM
124	Jynx	TM
150	Mewtwo	TM
151	Mew	TM
177	Natu	TM
178	Xatu	TM
185	Sudowoodo	TM
196	Espeon	TM
198	Murkrow	TM
199	Slowking	TM
200	Misdreavus	TM
203	Girafarig	TM
206	Dunsparce	TM
215	Sneasel	TM
222	Corsola	TM
234	Stantler	27,TM
238	Smoochum	TM
242	Blissey	TM
243	Raikou	78,TM
244	Entei	78,TM
245	Suicune	78,TM
249	Lugia	93,TM
250	Ho-Oh	93,TM
251	Celebi	TM
280	Ralts	23,TM
281	Kirlia	25,TM
282	Gardevoir	25,TM
300	Skitty	TM
301	Delcatty	TM
302	Sableye	TM
307	Meditite	25,TM
308	Medicham	25,TM
325	Spoink	TM
326	Grumpig	TM
327	Spinda	TM
337	Lunatone	TM
338	Solrock	TM
343	Baltoy	TM
344	Claydol	TM
353	Shuppet	TM
354	Banette	TM
355	Duskull	TM
356	Dusclops	TM
358	Chimecho	TM
359	Absol	TM
369	Relicanth	TM
380	Latias	TM
381	Latios	TM
382	Kyogre	30,TM
385	Jirachi	TM
386	Deoxys (N)	TM
386	Deoxys (A)	TM
386	Deoxys (D)	TM
386	Deoxys (S)	TM
392	Infernape	53,TM
425	Drifloon	TM
426	Drifblim	TM
429	Mismagius	TM
430	Honchkrow	TM
433	Chingling	TM
436	Bronzor	TM
437	Bronzong	TM
438	Bonsly	TM
439	Mime Jr.	TM
442	Spiritomb	TM
448	Lucario	TM
461	Weavile	TM
475	Gallade	TM
477	Dusknoir	TM
480	Uxie	TM
481	Mesprit	TM
482	Azelf	TM
487	Giratina (A)	TM
487	Giratina (O)	TM
488	Cresselia	TM
490	Manaphy	TM
491	Darkrai	TM

Camouflage

120	Staryu	19
414	Mothim	35

Captivate

1	Bulbasaur	TM
2	Ivysaur	TM
3	Venusaur	TM
4	Charmander	TM
5	Charmeleon	TM
6	Charizard	TM
7	Squirtle	TM
8	Wartortle	TM
9	Blastoise	TM
12	Butterfree	36,TM
15	Beedrill	TM
16	Pidgey	TM
17	Pidgeotto	TM
18	Pidgeot	TM
19	Rattata	TM
20	Raticate	TM
21	Spearow	TM
22	Fearow	TM
23	Ekans	TM
24	Arbok	TM
25	Pikachu	TM
26	Raichu	TM
27	Sandshrew	TM
28	Sandslash	TM
29	Nidoran♀	43,TM
30	Nidorina	50,TM
31	Nidoqueen	TM
32	Nidoran♂	43,TM
33	Nidorino	50,TM
34	Nidoking	TM
35	Clefairy	TM
36	Clefable	TM
37	Vulpix	37,TM
38	Ninetales	TM
39	Jigglypuff	TM
40	Wigglytuff	TM
41	Zubat	TM
42	Golbat	TM
43	Oddish	TM
44	Gloom	TM
45	Vileplume	TM
46	Paras	TM
47	Parasect	TM
48	Venonat	TM
49	Venomoth	TM
50	Diglett	TM
51	Dugtrio	TM
52	Meowth	46,TM
53	Persian	56,TM
54	Psyduck	TM
55	Golduck	TM
56	Mankey	TM
57	Primeape	TM
58	Growlithe	TM
59	Arcanine	TM
60	Poliwag	TM
61	Poliwhirl	TM
62	Poliwrath	TM
63	Abra	TM
64	Kadabra	TM
65	Alakazam	TM
66	Machop	TM
67	Machoke	TM
68	Machamp	TM
69	Bellsprout	TM
70	Weepinbell	TM
71	Victreebel	TM
72	Tentacool	TM
73	Tentacruel	TM
74	Geodude	TM
75	Graveler	TM
76	Golem	TM
77	Ponyta	TM
78	Rapidash	TM
79	Slowpoke	TM
80	Slowbro	TM
83	Farfetch'D	TM
84	Doduo	TM
85	Dodrio	TM
86	Seel	TM
87	Dewgong	TM
88	Grimer	TM
89	Muk	TM
90	Shellder	TM
91	Cloyster	TM
92	Gastly	TM
93	Haunter	TM
94	Gengar	TM
95	Onix	TM
96	Drowzee	TM
97	Hypno	TM
98	Krabby	TM
99	Kingler	TM
102	Exeggcute	TM
103	Exeggutor	TM
104	Cubone	TM
105	Marowak	TM
106	Hitmonlee	TM
107	Hitmonchan	TM
108	Lickitung	TM
109	Koffing	TM
110	Weezing	TM
111	Rhyhorn	TM
112	Rhydon	TM
113	Chansey	TM
114	Tangela	TM
115	Kangaskhan	TM
116	Horsea	TM
117	Seadra	TM
118	Goldeen	TM
119	Seaking	TM
122	Mr. Mime	TM
123	Scyther	TM
124	Jynx	TM
125	Electabuzz	TM
126	Magmar	TM
127	Pinsir	TM
128	Tauros	TM
130	Gyarados	TM
131	Lapras	TM
133	Eevee	TM
134	Vaporeon	TM
135	Jolteon	TM
136	Flareon	TM
138	Omanyte	TM
139	Omastar	TM
140	Kabuto	TM
141	Kabutops	TM
142	Aerodactyl	TM
143	Snorlax	TM
147	Dratini	TM
148	Dragonair	TM
149	Dragonite	TM
151	Mew	TM
152	Chikorita	TM
153	Bayleef	TM
154	Meganium	TM
155	Cyndaquil	TM
156	Quilava	TM
157	Typhlosion	TM
158	Totodile	TM
159	Croconaw	TM
160	Feraligatr	TM
161	Sentret	TM
162	Furret	TM
163	Hoothoot	TM
164	Noctowl	TM
165	Ledyba	TM
166	Ledian	TM
167	Spinarak	TM
168	Ariados	TM
169	Crobat	TM
170	Chinchou	TM
171	Lanturn	TM
172	Pichu	TM
173	Cleffa	TM
174	Igglybuff	TM
175	Togepi	TM
176	Togetic	TM
177	Natu	TM
178	Xatu	TM
179	Mareep	TM
180	Flaaffy	TM
181	Ampharos	TM
182	Bellossom	TM
183	Marill	TM
184	Azumarill	TM
185	Sudowoodo	TM
186	Politoed	TM
187	Hoppip	TM
188	Skiploom	TM
189	Jumpluff	TM
190	Aipom	TM
191	Sunkern	TM
192	Sunflora	TM
193	Yanma	TM
194	Wooper	TM
195	Quagsire	TM
196	Espeon	TM
197	Umbreon	TM
198	Murkrow	TM
199	Slowking	TM
200	Misdreavus	TM
203	Girafarig	TM
204	Pineco	TM
205	Forretress	TM
206	Dunsparce	TM
207	Gligar	TM
208	Steelix	TM
209	Snubbull	TM
210	Granbull	TM
211	Qwilfish	TM
212	Scizor	TM
213	Shuckle	TM
214	Heracross	TM
215	Sneasel	TM
216	Teddiursa	TM
217	Ursaring	TM
218	Slugma	TM
219	Magcargo	TM
220	Swinub	TM
221	Piloswine	TM
222	Corsola	TM
223	Remoraid	TM
224	Octillery	TM
225	Delibird	TM
226	Mantine	TM
227	Skarmory	TM
228	Houndour	TM
229	Houndoom	TM
230	Kingdra	TM
231	Phanpy	TM
232	Donphan	TM
234	Stantler	49,TM
236	Tyrogue	TM
237	Hitmontop	TM
238	Smoochum	TM
239	Elekid	TM
240	Magby	TM
241	Miltank	35,TM
242	Blissey	TM
246	Larvitar	TM
247	Pupitar	TM
248	Tyranitar	TM
252	Treecko	TM
253	Grovyle	TM
254	Sceptile	TM
255	Torchic	TM
256	Combusken	TM
257	Blaziken	TM
258	Mudkip	TM
259	Marshtomp	TM
260	Swampert	TM
261	Poochyena	TM
262	Mightyena	TM
263	Zigzagoon	TM
264	Linoone	TM
267	Beautifly	TM
269	Dustox	TM
270	Lotad	TM
271	Lombre	TM
272	Ludicolo	TM
273	Seedot	TM
274	Nuzleaf	TM
275	Shiftry	TM
276	Taillow	TM
277	Swellow	TM
278	Wingull	TM
279	Pelipper	TM
280	Ralts	TM
281	Kirlia	TM
282	Gardevoir	53,TM
283	Surskit	TM
284	Masquerain	TM
285	Shroomish	TM
286	Breloom	TM
287	Slakoth	TM
288	Vigoroth	TM
289	Slaking	TM
291	Ninjask	TM
293	Whismur	TM
294	Loudred	TM
295	Exploud	TM
296	Makuhita	TM

Captivate continued

297	Hariyama	TM
298	Azurill	TM
299	Nosepass	TM
300	Skitty	46,TM
301	Delcatty	TM
302	Sableye	TM
303	Mawile	TM
304	Aron	TM
305	Lairon	TM
306	Aggron	TM
307	Meditite	TM
308	Medicham	TM
309	Electrike	TM
310	Manectric	TM
311	Plusle	TM
312	Minun	TM
313	Volbeat	TM
314	Illumise	TM
315	Roselia	TM
316	Gulpin	TM
317	Swalot	TM
318	Carvanha	TM
319	Sharpedo	TM
320	Wailmer	TM
321	Wailord	TM
322	Numel	TM
323	Camerupt	TM
324	Torkoal	TM
325	Spoink	TM
326	Grumpig	TM
327	Spinda	TM
328	Trapinch	TM
329	Vibrava	TM
330	Flygon	TM
331	Cacnea	TM
332	Cacturne	TM
333	Swablu	TM
334	Altaria	TM
335	Zangoose	TM
336	Seviper	TM
339	Barboach	TM
340	Whiscash	TM
341	Corphish	TM
342	Crawdaunt	TM
345	Lileep	TM
346	Cradily	TM
347	Anorith	TM
348	Armaldo	TM
349	Feebas	TM
350	Milotic	25,TM
351	Castform	TM
352	Kecleon	TM
353	Shuppet	TM
354	Banette	TM
355	Duskull	TM
356	Dusclops	TM
357	Tropius	TM
358	Chimecho	TM
359	Absol	TM
361	Snorunt	TM
362	Glalie	TM
363	Spheal	TM
364	Sealeo	TM
365	Walrein	TM
366	Clamperl	TM
367	Huntail	TM
368	Gorebyss	28,TM
369	Relicanth	TM
370	Luvdisc	40,TM,E
371	Bagon	TM
372	Shelgon	TM
373	Salamence	TM
380	Latias	TM
381	Latios	TM
387	Turtwig	TM
388	Grotle	TM
389	Torterra	TM
390	Chimchar	TM
391	Monferno	TM
392	Infernape	TM
393	Piplup	TM
394	Prinplup	TM
395	Empoleon	TM
396	Starly	TM
397	Staravia	TM
398	Staraptor	TM
399	Bidoof	TM
400	Bibarel	TM
402	Kricketune	TM
403	Shinx	TM
404	Luxio	TM
405	Luxray	TM
406	Budew	TM
407	Roserade	TM
408	Cranidos	TM
409	Rampardos	TM
410	Shieldon	TM
411	Bastiodon	TM
413	Wormadam (P)	35,TM
413	Wormadam (S)	35,TM
413	Wormadam (T)	35,TM
414	Mothim	TM
416	Vespiquen	33,TM
417	Pachirisu	TM
418	Buizel	TM
419	Floatzel	TM
420	Cherubi	TM
421	Cherrim	TM
422	Shellos	TM
423	Gastrodon	TM
424	Ambipom	TM
425	Drifloon	TM
426	Drifblim	TM
427	Buneary	TM
428	Lopunny	TM
429	Mismagius	TM
430	Honchkrow	TM
431	Glameow	32,TM
432	Purugly	32,TM
433	Chingling	TM
434	Stunky	TM
435	Skuntank	TM
438	Bonsly	TM
439	Mime Jr.	TM
440	Happiny	TM
441	Chatot	TM
442	Spiritomb	TM
443	Gible	TM
444	Gabite	TM
445	Garchomp	TM
446	Munchlax	TM
447	Riolu	TM
448	Lucario	TM
449	Hippopotas	TM
450	Hippowdon	TM
451	Skorupi	TM
452	Drapion	TM
453	Croagunk	TM
454	Toxicroak	TM
455	Carnivine	TM
456	Finneon	26,TM
457	Lumineon	26,TM
458	Mantyke	TM
459	Snover	TM
460	Abomasnow	TM
461	Weavile	TM
463	Lickilicky	TM
464	Rhyperior	TM
465	Tangrowth	TM
466	Electivire	TM
467	Magmortar	TM
468	Togekiss	TM
469	Yanmega	TM
470	Leafeon	TM
471	Glaceon	TM
472	Gliscor	TM
473	Mamoswine	TM
475	Gallade	TM
476	Probopass	TM
477	Dusknoir	TM
478	Froslass	31,TM
485	Heatran	TM
488	Cresselia	TM

Charge

100	Voltorb	B
101	Electrode	B
145	Zapdos	36
170	Chinchou	45
171	Lanturn	57
172	Pichu	E
179	Mareep	23,E
180	Flaaffy	25
181	Ampharos	25
309	Electrike	44
310	Manectric	54
311	Plusle	35
312	Minun	35
403	Shinx	9
404	Luxio	9
405	Luxray	B,9
479	Rotom	43

Charge Beam

19	Rattata	TM
20	Raticate	TM
25	Pikachu	TM
26	Raichu	TM
35	Clefairy	TM
36	Clefable	TM
39	Jigglypuff	TM
40	Wigglytuff	TM
63	Abra	TM
64	Kadabra	TM
65	Alakazam	TM
81	Magnemite	TM
82	Magneton	TM
100	Voltorb	26,TM
101	Electrode	26,TM
113	Chansey	TM
122	Mr. Mime	TM
125	Electabuzz	TM
135	Jolteon	TM
137	Porygon	TM
145	Zapdos	TM
150	Mewtwo	TM
151	Mew	TM
161	Sentret	TM
162	Furret	TM
170	Chinchou	TM
171	Lanturn	TM
172	Pichu	TM
179	Mareep	TM
180	Flaaffy	TM
181	Ampharos	TM
200	Misdreavus	TM
203	Girafarig	TM
206	Dunsparce	TM
223	Remoraid	TM
224	Octillery	TM
233	Porygon2	TM
234	Stantler	TM
239	Elekid	TM
242	Blissey	TM
243	Raikou	TM
249	Lugia	TM
250	Ho-Oh	TM
251	Celebi	TM
263	Zigzagoon	TM
264	Linoone	TM
280	Ralts	TM
281	Kirlia	TM
282	Gardevoir	TM
300	Skitty	TM
301	Delcatty	TM
303	Mawile	TM
309	Electrike	TM
310	Manectric	TM
311	Plusle	TM
312	Minun	TM
313	Volbeat	TM
314	Illumise	TM
325	Spoink	TM
326	Grumpig	TM
337	Lunatone	TM
338	Solrock	TM
343	Baltoy	TM
344	Claydol	TM
352	Kecleon	TM
353	Shuppet	TM
354	Banette	TM
355	Duskull	TM
356	Dusclops	TM
358	Chimecho	TM
359	Absol	TM
377	Regirock	49,TM
378	Regice	49,TM
379	Registeel	49,TM
380	Latias	TM
381	Latios	TM
385	Jirachi	TM
386	Deoxys (N)	TM
386	Deoxys (A)	TM
386	Deoxys (D)	TM
386	Deoxys (S)	TM
399	Bidoof	TM
400	Bibarel	TM
403	Shinx	TM
404	Luxio	TM
405	Luxray	TM
417	Pachirisu	TM
425	Drifloon	TM
426	Drifblim	TM
427	Buneary	TM
428	Lopunny	TM
429	Mismagius	TM
433	Chingling	TM
436	Bronzor	TM
437	Bronzong	TM
439	Mime Jr.	TM
462	Magnezone	TM
466	Electivire	TM
474	Porygon-Z	TM
475	Gallade	TM
477	Dusknoir	TM
479	Rotom	TM
480	Uxie	TM
481	Mesprit	TM
482	Azelf	TM
487	Giratina (A)	TM
487	Giratina (O)	TM
488	Cresselia	TM
491	Darkrai	TM

Charm

1	Bulbasaur	E
29	Nidoran♀	E
43	Oddish	E
52	Meowth	E
77	Ponyta	E
133	Eevee	E
143	Snorlax	E
161	Sentret	E
172	Pichu	B
173	Cleffa	B
174	Igglybuff	B
175	Togepi	B
176	Togetic	B
209	Snubbull	B
210	Granbull	B
216	Teddiursa	36
231	Phanpy	33
263	Zigzagoon	E
280	Ralts	39
281	Kirlia	45
285	Shroomish	E
298	Azurill	2
300	Skitty	25
312	Minun	21
314	Illumise	9
360	Wynaut	B
370	Luvdisc	4
380	Latias	55
417	Pachirisu	9
427	Buneary	43
428	Lopunny	43
431	Glameow	25
432	Purugly	25
439	Mime Jr.	E
440	Happiny	B
446	Munchlax	E
456	Finneon	E
481	Mesprit	46
489	Phione	9
490	Manaphy	9

Chatter

441	Chatot	21

Clamp

90	Shellder	25
366	Clamperl	B

Close Combat

56	Mankey	49,E
57	Primeape	59
66	Machop	E
106	Hitmonlee	53
107	Hitmonchan	56
127	Pinsir	E
209	Snubbull	E
214	Heracross	37
216	Teddiursa	E
237	Hitmontop	51
296	Makuhita	40
297	Hariyama	52
335	Zangoose	53
391	Monferno	36
392	Infernape	41
398	Staraptor	34
448	Lucario	42
475	Gallade	53

Comet Punch

107	Hitmonchan	B
115	Kangaskhan	B
165	Ledyba	9
166	Ledian	B,9

Confuse Ray

37	Vulpix	17
38	Ninetales	B
41	Zubat	21
42	Golbat	21
54	Psyduck	E
72	Tentacool	E
92	Gastly	19
93	Haunter	19
94	Gengar	19
121	Starmie	28
122	Mr. Mime	E
126	Magmar	25
131	Lapras	7
140	Kabuto	E
169	Crobat	21
170	Chinchou	17
171	Lanturn	17
177	Natu	23
178	Xatu	23
197	Umbreon	29
198	Murkrow	E
200	Misdreavus	14
222	Corsola	E
226	Mantine	37
234	Stantler	23
240	Magby	25
280	Ralts	E
292	Shedinja	31
302	Sableye	46
313	Volbeat	9
325	Spoink	18
326	Grumpig	18
345	Lileep	22
346	Cradily	22
349	Feebas	E
353	Shuppet	E
355	Duskull	17
356	Dusclops	17
366	Clamperl	E
416	Vespiquen	7
436	Bronzor	14
437	Bronzong	14
439	Mime Jr.	E
442	Spiritomb	B
451	Skorupi	E
458	Mantyke	37
467	Magmortar	25
477	Dusknoir	17
478	Froslass	19
479	Rotom	B
486	Regigigas	B

Confusion

12	Butterfree	B,10
32	Nidoran♂	E
48	Venonat	11
49	Venomoth	11
54	Psyduck	18
55	Golduck	18
64	Kadabra	B,16
65	Alakazam	B,16
79	Slowpoke	15
80	Slowbro	15
96	Drowzee	9
97	Hypno	B,9
102	Exeggcute	27
103	Exeggutor	B
114	Tangela	E
122	Mr. Mime	B
150	Mewtwo	B
163	Hoothoot	21
164	Noctowl	22
187	Hoppip	E
196	Espeon	15
199	Slowking	15
203	Girafarig	B
238	Smoochum	15
251	Celebi	B
269	Dustox	B,10
280	Ralts	6
281	Kirlia	B,6
282	Gardevoir	B,6
307	Meditite	8
308	Medicham	B,8
337	Lunatone	B
338	Solrock	B
343	Baltoy	B
344	Claydol	B
358	Chimecho	14
368	Gorebyss	6
375	Metang	B,20
376	Metagross	B,20
385	Jirachi	B
413	Wormadam (P)	23
413	Wormadam (S)	23
413	Wormadam (T)	23
414	Mothim	23
433	Chingling	14
436	Bronzor	B
437	Bronzong	B
439	Mime Jr.	B
475	Gallade	B,6
480	Uxie	B
481	Mesprit	B
482	Azelf	B
488	Cresselia	B

Constrict

72	Tentacool	8
73	Tentacruel	B,8
114	Tangela	B
138	Omanyte	B
139	Omastar	B
167	Spinarak	8
168	Ariados	B,8
213	Shuckle	B
224	Octillery	B,6
345	Lileep	B
346	Cradily	B
425	Drifloon	B
426	Drifblim	B
465	Tangrowth	B

Conversion

137	Porygon	B
233	Porygon2	B
474	Porygon-Z	B

Conversion 2

137	Porygon	B
233	Porygon2	B
474	Porygon-Z	B

Copycat

122	Mr. Mime	4
173	Cleffa	13
174	Igglybuff	17
185	Sudowoodo	B
238	Smoochum	38
300	Skitty	18
311	Plusle	24
312	Minun	24
327	Spinda	10
438	Bonsly	B
439	Mime Jr.	4
440	Happiny	5
447	Riolu	29
481	Mesprit	61

Cosmic Power

35	Clefairy	25
120	Staryu	51
337	Lunatone	34
338	Solrock	34
343	Baltoy	45
344	Claydol	51
385	Jirachi	60
386	Deoxys (N)	73
386	Deoxys (A)	73

Cotton Spore

179	Mareep	19
180	Flaaffy	20
181	Ampharos	20
187	Hoppip	28
188	Skiploom	32
189	Jumpluff	32
315	Roselia	E
331	Cacnea	49
332	Cacturne	59
406	Budew	E

Counter

19	Rattata	E
27	Sandshrew	E
29	Nidoran♀	E
32	Nidoran♂	E
46	Paras	E
56	Mankey	E
66	Machop	E
107	Hitmonchan	51
111	Rhyhorn	E
113	Chansey	E
115	Kangaskhan	E
123	Scyther	E
152	Chikorita	E
190	Aipom	E
194	Wooper	E
202	Wobbuffet	B
204	Pineco	E
207	Gligar	E
214	Heracross	25
215	Sneasel	E
216	Teddiursa	E
228	Houndour	E
231	Phanpy	E
236	Tyrogue	E
237	Hitmontop	28
255	Torchic	E
258	Mudkip	E
286	Breloom	25
287	Slakoth	37
288	Vigoroth	37
289	Slaking	37
296	Makuhita	E
331	Cacnea	E
335	Zangoose	E
360	Wynaut	15
386	Deoxys (D)	97
390	Chimchar	E
422	Shellos	E
440	Happiny	E
447	Riolu	6
448	Lucario	6

Covet

56	Mankey	B
83	Farfetch'd	E
133	Eevee	E
155	Cyndaquil	E
161	Sentret	E
173	Cleffa	E
174	Igglybuff	E
190	Aipom	E
216	Teddiursa	B
217	Ursaring	B
261	Poochyena	E
263	Zigzagoon	29
264	Linoone	35
287	Slakoth	31
289	Slaking	31
300	Skitty	36
314	Illumise	45
417	Pachirisu	E

Crabhammer

98	Krabby	41
99	Kingler	56
341	Corphish	38
342	Crawdaunt	44

Cross Chop

54	Psyduck	E
56	Mankey	37
57	Primeape	41
66	Machop	37
67	Machoke	40
68	Machamp	40
216	Teddiursa	E
239	Elekid	E
240	Magby	E
296	Makuhita	E
447	Riolu	E
453	Croagunk	E

Cross Poison

46	Paras	E
47	Parasect	B
169	Crobat	B
207	Gligar	E
347	Anorith	E
451	Skorupi	50
452	Drapion	58

Crunch

4	Charmander	E
19	Rattata	22
20	Raticate	24
24	Arbok	22
29	Nidoran♀	37
30	Nidorina	43
58	Growlithe	42,E
111	Rhyhorn	E
115	Kangaskhan	31
142	Aerodactyl	33
143	Snorlax	44
158	Totodile	27,E
159	Croconaw	30
160	Feraligatr	32
203	Girafarig	46
208	Steelix	46
209	Snubbull	49,E
210	Granbull	59
216	Teddiursa	E
228	Houndour	48
229	Houndoom	54
243	Raikou	43
246	Larvitar	37
247	Pupitar	41
248	Tyranitar	41
252	Treecko	E
261	Poochyena	53
295	Exploud	40
303	Mawile	36
309	Electrike	E
318	Carvanha	28
319	Sharpedo	28
328	Trapinch	33
336	Seviper	28
341	Corphish	47
342	Crawdaunt	57
361	Snorunt	31
362	Glalie	31
365	Walrein	B
367	Huntail	42
371	Bagon	46
372	Shelgon	50
373	Salamence	53
384	Rayquaza	35
387	Turtwig	37
388	Grotle	42
389	Torterra	45
403	Shinx	33
404	Luxio	38
405	Luxray	42
408	Cranidos	E
419	Floatzel	26
434	Stunky	E
445	Garchomp	48
447	Riolu	E
449	Hippopotas	31

Pokémon moves and Abilities alphabetical list

450	Hippowdon	31
451	Skorupi	45
452	Drapion	49
455	Carnivine	37
485	Heatran	33

Crush Claw

27	Sandshrew	E
28	Sandslash	22
111	Rhyhorn	E
115	Kangaskhan	E
155	Cyndaquil	E
215	Sneasel	E
252	Treecko	E
255	Torchic	E
287	Slakoth	E
335	Zangoose	31
347	Anorith	55
348	Armaldo	67

Crush Grip

486	Regigigas	75

Curse

1	Bulbasaur	E
41	Zubat	E
79	Slowpoke	B
80	Slowbro	B
83	Farfetch'D	E
88	Grimer	E
92	Gastly	12
93	Haunter	12
94	Gengar	12
95	Onix	38
102	Exeggcute	E
108	Lickitung	E
109	Koffing	E
111	Rhyhorn	E
131	Lapras	E
133	Eevee	E
142	Aerodactyl	E
143	Snorlax	E
191	Sunkern	E
194	Wooper	E
199	Slowking	B
200	Misdreavus	E
206	Dunsparce	E
208	Steelix	38
218	Slugma	E
220	Swinub	E
227	Skarmory	E
241	Miltank	E
246	Larvitar	E
258	Mudkip	E
287	Slakoth	E
304	Aron	E
309	Electrike	E
316	Gulpin	E
320	Wailmer	E
324	Torkoal	12
335	Zangoose	E
353	Shuppet	13
354	Banette	B,13
355	Duskull	30
356	Dusclops	30
357	Tropius	E
358	Chimecho	E
359	Absol	E
363	Spheal	E
377	Regirock	17
378	Regice	17
379	Registeel	17
387	Turtwig	17
388	Grotle	17
389	Torterra	17
399	Bidoof	45
400	Bibarel	53
410	Shieldon	E
422	Shellos	E
433	Chingling	E
442	Spiritomb	B
446	Munchlax	E
449	Hippopotas	E
477	Dusknoir	30

Cut

1	Bulbasaur	HM
2	Ivysaur	HM
3	Venusaur	HM
4	Charmander	HM
5	Charmeleon	HM
6	Charizard	HM
15	Beedrill	HM
19	Rattata	HM
20	Raticate	HM
27	Sandshrew	HM
28	Sandslash	HM
29	Nidoran♀	HM
30	Nidorina	HM
31	Nidoqueen	HM
32	Nidoran♂	HM
33	Nidorino	HM
34	Nidoking	HM
43	Oddish	HM
44	Gloom	HM
45	Vileplume	HM
46	Paras	HM
47	Parasect	HM
50	Diglett	HM
51	Dugtrio	HM
52	Meowth	HM
53	Persian	HM
69	Bellsprout	HM
70	Weepinbell	HM
71	Victreebel	HM
72	Tentacool	HM
73	Tentacruel	HM
83	Farfetch'D	HM
98	Krabby	HM
99	Kingler	HM
108	Lickitung	HM
112	Rhydon	HM
114	Tangela	HM
115	Kangaskhan	HM
123	Scyther	HM
127	Pinsir	HM
141	Kabutops	HM
149	Dragonite	HM
151	Mew	HM
152	Chikorita	HM
153	Bayleef	HM
154	Meganium	HM
155	Cyndaquil	HM
156	Quilava	HM
157	Typhlosion	HM
158	Totodile	HM
159	Croconaw	HM
160	Feraligatr	HM
161	Sentret	HM
162	Furret	HM
182	Bellossom	HM
190	Aipom	HM
191	Sunkern	HM
192	Sunflora	HM
196	Espeon	HM
197	Umbreon	HM
207	Gligar	HM
208	Steelix	HM
212	Scizor	HM
214	Heracross	HM
215	Sneasel	HM
216	Teddiursa	HM
217	Ursaring	HM
227	Skarmory	HM
243	Raikou	HM
244	Entei	HM
245	Suicune	HM
248	Tyranitar	HM
251	Celebi	HM
252	Treecko	HM
253	Grovyle	HM
254	Sceptile	HM
255	Torchic	HM
256	Combusken	HM
257	Blaziken	HM
263	Zigzagoon	HM
264	Linoone	HM
274	Nuzleaf	HM
275	Shiftry	HM
286	Breloom	HM
287	Slakoth	HM
288	Vigoroth	HM
289	Slaking	HM
290	Nincada	HM
291	Ninjask	HM
292	Shedinja	HM
302	Sableye	HM
304	Aron	HM
305	Lairon	HM
306	Aggron	HM
315	Roselia	HM
331	Cacnea	HM
332	Cacturne	HM
341	Corphish	HM
342	Crawdaunt	HM
347	Anorith	HM
348	Armaldo	HM
352	Kecleon	HM
357	Tropius	HM
359	Absol	HM
371	Bagon	HM
372	Shelgon	HM
373	Salamence	HM
375	Metang	HM
376	Metagross	HM
380	Latias	HM
381	Latios	HM
383	Groudon	HM
386	Deoxys (N)	HM
386	Deoxys (A)	HM
386	Deoxys (D)	HM
386	Deoxys (S)	HM
387	Turtwig	HM
388	Grotle	HM
389	Torterra	HM
390	Chimchar	HM
391	Monferno	HM
392	Infernape	HM
393	Piplup	HM
394	Prinplup	HM
395	Empoleon	HM
399	Bidoof	HM
400	Bibarel	HM
402	Kricketune	HM
406	Budew	HM
407	Roserade	HM
409	Rampardos	HM
416	Vespiquen	HM
417	Pachirisu	HM
424	Ambipom	HM
425	Drifloon	HM
426	Drifblim	HM
427	Buneary	HM
428	Lopunny	HM
431	Glameow	HM
432	Purugly	HM
434	Stunky	HM
435	Skuntank	HM
443	Gible	HM
444	Gabite	HM
445	Garchomp	HM
451	Skorupi	HM
452	Drapion	HM
454	Toxicroak	HM
455	Carnivine	HM
461	Weavile	HM
463	Lickilicky	HM
464	Rhyperior	HM
465	Tangrowth	HM
472	Gliscor	HM
475	Gallade	HM
483	Dialga	HM
484	Palkia	HM
487	Giratina (A)	HM
487	Giratina (O)	HM
491	Darkrai	HM

Dark Pulse

23	Ekans	TM
24	Arbok	TM
37	Vulpix	TM
38	Ninetales	TM
52	Meowth	TM
53	Persian	TM
89	Muk	TM
92	Gastly	36,TM
93	Haunter	44,TM
94	Gengar	44,TM
109	Koffing	TM
110	Weezing	TM
130	Gyarados	TM
151	Mew	TM
169	Crobat	TM
197	Umbreon	TM
198	Murkrow	TM
200	Misdreavus	TM
207	Gligar	TM
208	Steelix	TM
215	Sneasel	TM
227	Skarmory	TM
228	Houndour	TM
229	Houndoom	TM
246	Larvitar	28,TM
247	Pupitar	28,TM
248	Tyranitar	28,TM
261	Poochyena	TM
262	Mightyena	TM
274	Nuzleaf	TM
275	Shiftry	TM
302	Sableye	TM
303	Mawile	TM
306	Aggron	TM
318	Carvanha	TM
319	Sharpedo	TM
331	Cacnea	TM
332	Cacturne	TM
336	Seviper	TM
342	Crawdaunt	TM
353	Shuppet	TM
354	Banette	TM
355	Duskull	TM
356	Dusclops	TM
359	Absol	TM
362	Glalie	TM
429	Mismagius	TM
430	Honchkrow	55,TM
434	Stunky	TM
435	Skuntank	TM
442	Spiritomb	49,TM
448	Lucario	B,TM
451	Skorupi	TM
452	Drapion	TM
453	Croagunk	TM
454	Toxicroak	TM
461	Weavile	49,TM
472	Gliscor	TM
474	Porygon-Z	TM
477	Dusknoir	TM
479	Rotom	TM
485	Heatran	TM
487	Giratina (A)	TM
487	Giratina (O)	TM
491	Darkrai	93,TM

Dark Void

491	Darkrai	66

Defend Order

416	Vespiquen	13

Defense Curl

27	Sandshrew	3
28	Sandslash	B,3
35	Clefairy	13
39	Jigglypuff	5
40	Wigglytuff	B
74	Geodude	B
75	Graveler	B
76	Golem	B
95	Onix	E
108	Lickitung	9
113	Chansey	31
143	Snorlax	4
155	Cyndaquil	22
156	Quilava	24
157	Typhlosion	24
161	Sentret	4
162	Furret	B,4
174	Igglybuff	5
183	Marill	2
184	Azumarill	B,2
185	Sudowoodo	E
206	Dunsparce	5
231	Phanpy	B
232	Donphan	B
233	Porygon2	B
241	Miltank	5
242	Blissey	31
320	Wailmer	E
322	Numel	E
363	Spheal	B
399	Bidoof	9,E
400	Bibarel	9
417	Pachirisu	E
427	Buneary	B
428	Lopunny	B
438	Bonsly	E
446	Munchlax	4
463	Lickilicky	9

Defog

6	Charizard	HM
12	Butterfree	HM
15	Beedrill	HM
16	Pidgey	HM
17	Pidgeotto	HM
18	Pidgeot	HM
21	Spearow	HM
22	Fearow	HM
41	Zubat	HM
42	Golbat	HM
49	Venomoth	HM
83	Farfetch'D	HM
123	Scyther	HM
142	Aerodactyl	HM
144	Articuno	HM
145	Zapdos	HM
146	Moltres	HM
149	Dragonite	HM
151	Mew	HM
163	Hoothoot	HM
164	Noctowl	HM
169	Crobat	HM
176	Togetic	HM
178	Xatu	HM
193	Yanma	HM
198	Murkrow	HM
207	Gligar	HM
212	Scizor	HM
225	Delibird	HM
226	Mantine	HM
227	Skarmory	HM
249	Lugia	HM
250	Ho-Oh	HM
267	Beautifly	HM
269	Dustox	HM
275	Shiftry	HM
276	Taillow	HM
277	Swellow	HM
278	Wingull	HM
279	Pelipper	HM
284	Masquerain	HM
291	Ninjask	HM
329	Vibrava	HM
330	Flygon	HM
357	Tropius	HM
373	Salamence	HM
380	Latias	HM
381	Latios	HM
393	Piplup	HM
394	Prinplup	HM
395	Empoleon	HM
396	Starly	HM
397	Staravia	HM
398	Staraptor	HM
414	Mothim	HM
416	Vespiquen	HM
425	Drifloon	HM
426	Drifblim	HM
430	Honchkrow	HM
434	Stunky	HM
435	Skuntank	HM
441	Chatot	HM
456	Finneon	HM
457	Lumineon	HM
468	Togekiss	HM
469	Yanmega	HM
472	Gliscor	HM
487	Giratina (A)	HM
487	Giratina (O)	HM

Destiny Bond

92	Gastly	40
93	Haunter	50
94	Gengar	50
109	Koffing	46,E
110	Weezing	55
200	Misdreavus	E
202	Wobbuffet	B
211	Qwilfish	53
280	Ralts	E
316	Gulpin	E
331	Cacnea	57
332	Cacturne	71
353	Shuppet	E
355	Duskull	E
360	Wynaut	15
416	Vespiquen	43
425	Drifloon	E
442	Spiritomb	E
478	Froslass	59

Detect

107	Hitmonchan	46
145	Zapdos	15
193	Yanma	17
237	Hitmontop	46
252	Treecko	41
253	Grovyle	47
254	Sceptile	51
296	Makuhita	E
302	Sableye	22
307	Meditite	11
308	Medicham	B,11
335	Zangoose	40
359	Absol	49
447	Riolu	E
448	Lucario	B
469	Yanmega	17
482	Azelf	16

Dig

4	Charmander	TM
5	Charmeleon	TM
6	Charizard	TM
7	Squirtle	TM
8	Wartortle	TM
9	Blastoise	TM
19	Rattata	TM
20	Raticate	TM
23	Ekans	TM
24	Arbok	TM
25	Pikachu	TM
26	Raichu	TM
27	Sandshrew	TM
28	Sandslash	TM
29	Nidoran♀	TM
30	Nidorina	TM
31	Nidoqueen	TM
32	Nidoran♂	TM
33	Nidorino	TM
34	Nidoking	TM
35	Clefairy	TM
36	Clefable	TM
37	Vulpix	TM
38	Ninetales	TM
39	Jigglypuff	TM
40	Wigglytuff	TM
46	Paras	TM
47	Parasect	TM
50	Diglett	18,TM
51	Dugtrio	18,TM
52	Meowth	TM
53	Persian	TM
54	Psyduck	TM
55	Golduck	TM
56	Mankey	TM
57	Primeape	TM
58	Growlithe	TM
59	Arcanine	TM
60	Poliwag	TM
61	Poliwhirl	TM
62	Poliwrath	TM
66	Machop	TM
67	Machoke	TM
68	Machamp	TM
74	Geodude	TM
75	Graveler	TM
76	Golem	TM
79	Slowpoke	TM
80	Slowbro	TM
88	Grimer	TM
89	Muk	TM
95	Onix	TM
98	Krabby	TM,E
99	Kingler	TM
104	Cubone	TM
105	Marowak	TM
108	Lickitung	TM
111	Rhyhorn	TM
112	Rhydon	TM
115	Kangaskhan	TM
127	Pinsir	TM
133	Eevee	TM
134	Vaporeon	TM
135	Jolteon	TM
136	Flareon	TM
140	Kabuto	TM,E
141	Kabutops	TM
151	Mew	TM
155	Cyndaquil	TM
156	Quilava	TM
157	Typhlosion	TM
158	Totodile	TM
159	Croconaw	TM
160	Feraligatr	TM
161	Sentret	TM
162	Furret	TM
165	Ledyba	TM
166	Ledian	TM
167	Spinarak	TM
168	Ariados	TM
173	Cleffa	TM
174	Igglybuff	TM
183	Marill	TM
184	Azumarill	TM
185	Sudowoodo	TM
186	Politoed	TM
190	Aipom	TM
194	Wooper	TM
195	Quagsire	TM
196	Espeon	TM
197	Umbreon	TM
199	Slowking	TM
204	Pineco	TM
205	Forretress	TM
206	Dunsparce	45,TM
207	Gligar	TM
208	Steelix	TM
209	Snubbull	TM
210	Granbull	TM
213	Shuckle	TM
214	Heracross	TM
215	Sneasel	TM
216	Teddiursa	TM
217	Ursaring	TM
220	Swinub	TM
221	Piloswine	TM
222	Corsola	TM
237	Hitmontop	TM
243	Raikou	TM
244	Entei	TM
245	Suicune	TM
246	Larvitar	TM
247	Pupitar	TM
248	Tyranitar	TM
252	Treecko	TM
253	Grovyle	TM
254	Sceptile	TM
255	Torchic	TM
256	Combusken	TM
257	Blaziken	TM
258	Mudkip	TM
259	Marshtomp	TM
260	Swampert	TM
261	Poochyena	TM
262	Mightyena	TM
263	Zigzagoon	TM
264	Linoone	TM
273	Seedot	TM
274	Nuzleaf	TM
275	Shiftry	TM
290	Nincada	45,TM
291	Ninjask	TM
292	Shedinja	TM
296	Makuhita	TM
297	Hariyama	TM
300	Skitty	TM
301	Delcatty	TM
302	Sableye	TM
304	Aron	TM
305	Lairon	TM
306	Aggron	TM
322	Numel	TM
323	Camerupt	TM
327	Spinda	TM
328	Trapinch	41,TM
329	Vibrava	TM
330	Flygon	TM
335	Zangoose	TM
336	Seviper	TM
341	Corphish	TM
342	Crawdaunt	TM
343	Baltoy	TM
344	Claydol	TM
347	Anorith	TM
348	Armaldo	TM
352	Kecleon	TM
377	Regirock	TM
383	Groudon	TM
390	Chimchar	TM
391	Monferno	TM
392	Infernape	TM
393	Piplup	TM
394	Prinplup	TM
395	Empoleon	TM
399	Bidoof	TM
400	Bibarel	TM
408	Cranidos	TM
409	Rampardos	TM
410	Shieldon	TM
411	Bastiodon	TM
413	Wormadam (S)	TM
417	Pachirisu	TM
418	Buizel	TM
419	Floatzel	TM
423	Gastrodon	TM
424	Ambipom	TM
427	Buneary	TM
428	Lopunny	TM
431	Glameow	TM
432	Purugly	TM
434	Stunky	TM
435	Skuntank	TM
438	Bonsly	TM
443	Gible	31,TM
444	Gabite	40,TM
445	Garchomp	40,TM
447	Riolu	TM
448	Lucario	TM
451	Skorupi	TM
452	Drapion	TM
453	Croagunk	TM
454	Toxicroak	TM
461	Weavile	TM
463	Lickilicky	TM
464	Rhyperior	TM
466	Electivire	TM
470	Leafeon	TM
471	Glaceon	TM
472	Gliscor	TM
473	Mamoswine	TM
485	Heatran	TM

Disable

23	Ekans	E
29	Nidoran♀	E
32	Nidoran♂	E
37	Vulpix	E
39	Jigglypuff	13
40	Wigglytuff	B
48	Venonat	B
49	Venomoth	B
54	Psyduck	14
55	Golduck	14
64	Kadabra	18
65	Alakazam	18
79	Slowpoke	20
80	Slowbro	20
86	Seel	E
88	Grimer	12
89	Muk	12
96	Drowzee	7

ADVENTURE DATA LIST
POKÉMON MOVES AND ABILITIES ALPHABETICAL LIST

Disable continued

97	Hypno	B,7
108	Lickitung	25
115	Kangaskhan	E
116	Horsea	E
150	Mewtwo	B
167	Spinarak	E
199	Slowking	20
234	Stantler	E
280	Ralts	E
327	Spinda	E
351	Castform	E
352	Kecleon	E
353	Shuppet	E
355	Duskull	6
356	Dusclops	B,6
358	Chimecho	E
361	Snorunt	E
425	Drifloon	E
433	Chingling	E
463	Lickilicky	25
477	Dusknoir	B,6
491	Darkrai	B

Discharge

25	Pikachu	37
81	Magnemite	38
82	Magneton	40
125	Electabuzz	37
135	Jolteon	78
137	Porygon	40
145	Zapdos	50
170	Chinchou	34
171	Lanturn	40
179	Mareep	28
180	Flaaffy	31
181	Ampharos	34
233	Porygon2	40
239	Elekid	34
243	Raikou	57
299	Nosepass	55
309	Electrike	41,E
310	Manectric	49
403	Shinx	41
404	Luxio	48
405	Luxray	56
417	Pachirisu	29
462	Magnezone	40
466	Electivire	37
474	Porygon-Z	40
476	Probopass	55
479	Rotom	50

Dive

7	Squirtle	T
8	Wartortle	T
9	Blastoise	T
54	Psyduck	T
55	Golduck	T
60	Poliwag	T
61	Poliwhirl	T
62	Poliwrath	T
72	Tentacool	T
73	Tentacruel	T
79	Slowpoke	T
80	Slowbro	T
86	Seel	41,T
87	Dewgong	41,T
90	Shellder	T
91	Cloyster	T
98	Krabby	T
99	Kingler	T
116	Horsea	T
117	Seadra	T
118	Goldeen	T
119	Seaking	T
120	Staryu	T
121	Starmie	T
130	Gyarados	T
131	Lapras	T
134	Vaporeon	T
138	Omanyte	T
139	Omastar	T
141	Kabutops	T
149	Dragonite	T
151	Mew	T
158	Totodile	T
159	Croconaw	T
160	Feraligatr	T
170	Chinchou	T
171	Lanturn	T
183	Marill	T
184	Azumarill	T
186	Politoed	T
194	Wooper	T
195	Quagsire	T
199	Slowking	T
211	Qwilfish	T
223	Remoraid	T
224	Octillery	T
226	Mantine	T
230	Kingdra	T
245	Suicune	T
249	Lugia	T
258	Mudkip	T
259	Marshtomp	T
260	Swampert	T
271	Lombre	T
272	Ludicolo	T
318	Carvanha	T
319	Sharpedo	T
320	Wailmer	41,T
321	Wailord	46,T
339	Barboach	T
340	Whiscash	T
342	Crawdaunt	T
349	Feebas	T
350	Milotic	T
363	Spheal	T
364	Sealeo	T
365	Walrein	T
366	Clamperl	T
367	Huntail	37,T
368	Gorebyss	37,T
369	Relicanth	57,T
370	Luvdisc	T
380	Latias	T
381	Latios	T
382	Kyogre	T
384	Rayquaza	T
393	Piplup	T
394	Prinplup	T
395	Empoleon	T
400	Bibarel	T
418	Buizel	T
419	Floatzel	T
422	Shellos	T
423	Gastrodon	T
456	Finneon	T
457	Lumineon	T
458	Mantyke	T
484	Palkia	T
489	Phione	61,T
490	Manaphy	61,T

Dizzy Punch

115	Kangaskhan	25
241	Miltank	E
327	Spinda	28
352	Kecleon	E
427	Buneary	36
428	Lopunny	36
486	Regigigas	B

Doom Desire

385	Jirachi	70

Double Hit

84	Doduo	32
110	Weezing	33
115	Kangaskhan	43
123	Scyther	49
190	Aipom	32
203	Girafarig	32
212	Scizor	49
215	Sneasel	E
335	Zangoose	E
393	Piplup	E
424	Ambipom	32
427	Buneary	E
473	Mamoswine	33

Double Kick

29	Nidoran♀	9
30	Nidorina	9
31	Nidoqueen	B
32	Nidoran♂	9
33	Nidorino	9
34	Nidoking	B
77	Ponyta	E
104	Cubone	E
106	Hitmonlee	B
135	Jolteon	29
155	Cyndaquil	E
194	Wooper	E
203	Girafarig	E
234	Stantler	E
252	Treecko	E
256	Combusken	16
257	Blaziken	16
335	Zangoose	E
390	Chimchar	E

Double Team

1	Bulbasaur	TM
2	Ivysaur	TM
3	Venusaur	TM
4	Charmander	TM
5	Charmeleon	TM
6	Charizard	TM
7	Squirtle	TM
8	Wartortle	TM
9	Blastoise	TM
12	Butterfree	TM
15	Beedrill	TM
16	Pidgey	TM
17	Pidgeotto	TM
18	Pidgeot	TM
19	Rattata	TM
20	Raticate	TM
21	Spearow	TM
22	Fearow	TM
23	Ekans	TM
24	Arbok	TM
25	Pikachu	18,TM
26	Raichu	TM
27	Sandshrew	TM
28	Sandslash	TM
29	Nidoran♀	TM
30	Nidorina	TM
31	Nidoqueen	TM
32	Nidoran♂	TM
33	Nidorino	TM
34	Nidoking	TM
35	Clefairy	TM
36	Clefable	TM
37	Vulpix	TM
38	Ninetales	TM
39	Jigglypuff	TM
40	Wigglytuff	TM
41	Zubat	TM
42	Golbat	TM
43	Oddish	TM
44	Gloom	TM
45	Vileplume	TM
46	Paras	TM
47	Parasect	TM
48	Venonat	TM
49	Venomoth	TM
50	Diglett	TM
51	Dugtrio	TM
52	Meowth	TM
53	Persian	TM
54	Psyduck	TM
55	Golduck	TM
56	Mankey	TM
57	Primeape	TM
58	Growlithe	TM
59	Arcanine	TM
60	Poliwag	TM
61	Poliwhirl	TM
62	Poliwrath	TM
63	Abra	TM
64	Kadabra	TM
65	Alakazam	TM
66	Machop	TM
67	Machoke	TM
68	Machamp	TM
69	Bellsprout	TM
70	Weepinbell	TM
71	Victreebel	TM
72	Tentacool	TM
73	Tentacruel	TM
74	Geodude	TM
75	Graveler	TM
76	Golem	TM
77	Ponyta	TM
78	Rapidash	TM
79	Slowpoke	TM
80	Slowbro	TM
81	Magnemite	TM
82	Magneton	TM
83	Farfetch'd	TM
84	Doduo	TM
85	Dodrio	TM
86	Seel	TM
87	Dewgong	TM
88	Grimer	TM
89	Muk	TM
90	Shellder	TM
91	Cloyster	TM
92	Gastly	TM
93	Haunter	TM
94	Gengar	TM
95	Onix	TM
96	Drowzee	TM
97	Hypno	TM
98	Krabby	TM
99	Kingler	TM
100	Voltorb	TM
101	Electrode	TM
102	Exeggcute	TM
103	Exeggutor	TM
104	Cubone	TM
105	Marowak	TM
106	Hitmonlee	TM
107	Hitmonchan	TM
108	Lickitung	TM
109	Koffing	TM
110	Weezing	TM
111	Rhyhorn	TM
112	Rhydon	TM
113	Chansey	TM
114	Tangela	TM
115	Kangaskhan	TM
116	Horsea	TM
117	Seadra	TM
118	Goldeen	TM
119	Seaking	TM
120	Staryu	TM
121	Starmie	TM
122	Mr. Mime	TM
123	Scyther	37,TM
124	Jynx	TM
125	Electabuzz	TM
126	Magmar	TM
127	Pinsir	TM
128	Tauros	TM
130	Gyarados	TM
131	Lapras	TM
133	Eevee	TM
134	Vaporeon	TM
135	Jolteon	TM
136	Flareon	TM
137	Porygon	TM
138	Omanyte	TM
139	Omastar	TM
140	Kabuto	TM
141	Kabutops	TM
142	Aerodactyl	TM
143	Snorlax	TM
144	Articuno	TM
145	Zapdos	TM
146	Moltres	TM
147	Dratini	TM
148	Dragonair	TM
149	Dragonite	TM
150	Mewtwo	TM
151	Mew	TM
152	Chikorita	TM
153	Bayleef	TM
154	Meganium	TM
155	Cyndaquil	TM
156	Quilava	TM
157	Typhlosion	TM
158	Totodile	TM
159	Croconaw	TM
160	Feraligatr	TM
161	Sentret	TM
162	Furret	TM
163	Hoothoot	TM
164	Noctowl	TM
165	Ledyba	TM
166	Ledian	TM
167	Spinarak	TM
168	Ariados	TM
169	Crobat	TM
170	Chinchou	TM
171	Lanturn	TM
172	Pichu	TM
173	Cleffa	TM
174	Igglybuff	TM
175	Togepi	TM
176	Togetic	TM
177	Natu	TM
178	Xatu	TM
179	Mareep	TM
180	Flaaffy	TM
181	Ampharos	TM
182	Bellossom	TM
183	Marill	TM
184	Azumarill	TM
185	Sudowoodo	TM
186	Politoed	TM
187	Hoppip	TM
188	Skiploom	TM
189	Jumpluff	TM
190	Aipom	TM
191	Sunkern	TM
192	Sunflora	TM
193	Yanma	11,TM
194	Wooper	TM
195	Quagsire	TM
196	Espeon	TM
197	Umbreon	TM
198	Murkrow	TM
199	Slowking	TM
200	Misdreavus	TM
203	Girafarig	TM
204	Pineco	TM
205	Forretress	TM
206	Dunsparce	TM
207	Gligar	TM
208	Steelix	TM
209	Snubbull	TM
210	Granbull	TM
211	Qwilfish	TM
212	Scizor	TM
213	Shuckle	TM
214	Heracross	TM
215	Sneasel	TM
216	Teddiursa	TM
217	Ursaring	TM
218	Slugma	TM
219	Magcargo	TM
220	Swinub	TM
221	Piloswine	TM
222	Corsola	TM
223	Remoraid	TM
224	Octillery	TM
225	Delibird	TM
226	Mantine	TM
227	Skarmory	TM
228	Houndour	TM
229	Houndoom	TM
230	Kingdra	TM
231	Phanpy	TM
232	Donphan	TM
233	Porygon2	TM
234	Stantler	TM
236	Tyrogue	TM
237	Hitmontop	TM
238	Smoochum	TM
239	Elekid	TM
240	Magby	TM
241	Miltank	TM
242	Blissey	TM
243	Raikou	TM
244	Entei	TM
245	Suicune	TM
246	Larvitar	TM
247	Pupitar	TM
248	Tyranitar	TM
249	Lugia	TM
250	Ho-Oh	TM
251	Celebi	TM
252	Treecko	TM
253	Grovyle	TM
254	Sceptile	TM
255	Torchic	TM
256	Combusken	TM
257	Blaziken	TM
258	Mudkip	TM
259	Marshtomp	TM
260	Swampert	TM
261	Poochyena	TM
262	Mightyena	TM
263	Zigzagoon	TM
264	Linoone	TM
267	Beautifly	TM
269	Dustox	TM
270	Lotad	TM
271	Lombre	TM
272	Ludicolo	TM
273	Seedot	TM
274	Nuzleaf	TM
275	Shiftry	TM
276	Taillow	19,TM
277	Swellow	19,TM
278	Wingull	TM
279	Pelipper	TM
280	Ralts	10,TM
281	Kirlia	B,10,TM
282	Gardevoir	B,10,TM
283	Surskit	TM
284	Masquerain	TM
285	Shroomish	TM
286	Breloom	TM
287	Slakoth	TM
288	Vigoroth	TM
289	Slaking	TM
290	Nincada	TM
291	Ninjask	20,TM
292	Shedinja	TM
293	Whismur	TM
294	Loudred	TM
295	Exploud	TM
296	Makuhita	TM
297	Hariyama	TM
298	Azurill	TM
299	Nosepass	TM
300	Skitty	TM
301	Delcatty	TM
302	Sableye	TM
303	Mawile	TM
304	Aron	TM
305	Lairon	TM
306	Aggron	TM
307	Meditite	TM
308	Medicham	TM
309	Electrike	TM
310	Manectric	TM
311	Plusle	TM
312	Minun	TM
313	Volbeat	5,TM
314	Illumise	TM
315	Roselia	TM
316	Gulpin	TM
317	Swalot	TM
318	Carvanha	TM
319	Sharpedo	TM
320	Wailmer	TM
321	Wailord	TM
322	Numel	TM
323	Camerupt	TM
324	Torkoal	TM
325	Spoink	TM
326	Grumpig	TM
327	Spinda	TM
328	Trapinch	TM
329	Vibrava	TM
330	Flygon	TM
331	Cacnea	TM
332	Cacturne	TM
333	Swablu	TM
334	Altaria	TM
335	Zangoose	TM
336	Seviper	TM
337	Lunatone	TM
338	Solrock	TM
339	Barboach	TM
340	Whiscash	TM
341	Corphish	TM
342	Crawdaunt	TM
343	Baltoy	TM
344	Claydol	TM
345	Lileep	TM
346	Cradily	TM
347	Anorith	TM
348	Armaldo	TM
349	Feebas	TM
350	Milotic	TM
351	Castform	TM
352	Kecleon	TM
353	Shuppet	TM
354	Banette	TM
355	Duskull	TM
356	Dusclops	TM
357	Tropius	TM
358	Chimecho	TM
359	Absol	33,TM
361	Snorunt	4,TM
362	Glalie	B,4,TM
363	Spheal	TM
364	Sealeo	TM
365	Walrein	TM
366	Clamperl	TM
367	Huntail	TM
368	Gorebyss	TM
369	Relicanth	TM
370	Luvdisc	TM
371	Bagon	TM
372	Shelgon	TM
373	Salamence	TM
375	Metang	TM
376	Metagross	TM
377	Regirock	TM
378	Regice	TM
379	Registeel	TM
380	Latias	TM
381	Latios	TM
382	Kyogre	TM
383	Groudon	TM
384	Rayquaza	TM
385	Jirachi	TM
386	Deoxys (N)	TM
386	Deoxys (A)	TM
386	Deoxys (D)	TM
386	Deoxys (S)	17,TM
387	Turtwig	TM
388	Grotle	TM
389	Torterra	TM
390	Chimchar	TM
391	Monferno	TM
392	Infernape	TM
393	Piplup	TM
394	Prinplup	TM
395	Empoleon	TM
396	Starly	13,TM
397	Staravia	13,TM
398	Staraptor	13,TM
399	Bidoof	TM
400	Bibarel	TM
402	Kricketune	TM
403	Shinx	TM
404	Luxio	TM
405	Luxray	TM
406	Budew	TM
407	Roserade	TM
408	Cranidos	TM
409	Rampardos	TM
410	Shieldon	TM
411	Bastiodon	TM
413	Wormadam (P)	TM
413	Wormadam (S)	TM
413	Wormadam (T)	TM
414	Mothim	TM
416	Vespiquen	TM
417	Pachirisu	TM
418	Buizel	TM
419	Floatzel	TM
420	Cherubi	TM
421	Cherrim	TM
422	Shellos	TM
423	Gastrodon	TM
424	Ambipom	TM
425	Drifloon	TM
426	Drifblim	TM
427	Buneary	TM
428	Lopunny	TM
429	Mismagius	TM
430	Honchkrow	TM
431	Glameow	TM
432	Purugly	TM
433	Chingling	TM
434	Stunky	TM
435	Skuntank	TM
436	Bronzor	TM
437	Bronzong	TM
438	Bonsly	TM
439	Mime Jr.	TM
440	Happiny	TM
441	Chatot	TM
442	Spiritomb	TM
443	Gible	TM
444	Gabite	TM
445	Garchomp	TM
446	Munchlax	TM
447	Riolu	TM
448	Lucario	TM
449	Hippopotas	TM
450	Hippowdon	TM
451	Skorupi	TM
452	Drapion	TM
453	Croagunk	TM
454	Toxicroak	TM
455	Carnivine	TM
456	Finneon	TM
457	Lumineon	TM
458	Mantyke	TM
459	Snover	TM
460	Abomasnow	TM
461	Weavile	TM
462	Magnezone	TM
463	Lickilicky	TM
464	Rhyperior	TM
465	Tangrowth	TM
466	Electivire	TM
467	Magmortar	TM
468	Togekiss	TM
469	Yanmega	B,11,TM
470	Leafeon	TM
471	Glaceon	TM
472	Gliscor	TM
473	Mamoswine	TM
474	Porygon-Z	TM
475	Gallade	B,10,TM
476	Probopass	TM
477	Dusknoir	TM
478	Froslass	B,4,TM
479	Rotom	15,TM
480	Uxie	TM
481	Mesprit	TM
482	Azelf	TM
483	Dialga	TM
484	Palkia	TM
485	Heatran	TM
486	Regigigas	TM
487	Giratina (A)	TM
487	Giratina (O)	TM
488	Cresselia	B,TM
489	Phione	TM
490	Manaphy	TM
491	Darkrai	47,TM
492	Shaymin (L)	TM
492	Shaymin (S)	TM

Double-Edge

1	Bulbasaur	27
2	Ivysaur	31
3	Venusaur	31
19	Rattata	31
20	Raticate	39
39	Jigglypuff	49
58	Growlithe	E
74	Geodude	36
75	Graveler	44
76	Golem	44
77	Ponyta	E
95	Onix	49
104	Cubone	43
105	Marowak	53
113	Chansey	46

Pokémon moves and Abilities alphabetical list

115	Kangaskhan	E
143	Snorlax	E
155	Cyndaquil	46,E
156	Quilava	53
157	Typhlosion	53
161	Sentret	E
165	Ledyba	38
166	Ledian	48
175	Togepi	46
176	Togetic	46
183	Marill	27
184	Azumarill	33
185	Sudowoodo	46
187	Hoppip	E
204	Pineco	45,E
205	Forretress	55
207	Gligar	E
208	Steelix	49
214	Heracross	E
216	Teddiursa	E
220	Swinub	E
231	Phanpy	42
241	Miltank	E
242	Blissey	46
258	Mudkip	E
299	Nosepass	E
300	Skitty	42
304	Aron	43
305	Lairon	51
306	Aggron	57
313	Volbeat	45
318	Carvanha	E
320	Wailmer	E
322	Numel	51
327	Spinda	46
358	Chimecho	33
359	Absol	E
369	Relicanth	50
371	Bagon	55
372	Shelgon	61
373	Salamence	70
382	Kyogre	65
385	Jirachi	40
387	Turtwig	E
396	Starly	E
399	Bidoof	E
408	Cranidos	E
410	Shieldon	E
434	Stunky	E
438	Bonsly	46
443	Gible	E
446	Munchlax	E
449	Hippopotas	44
450	Hippowdon	50
459	Snover	E

DoubleSlap		
35	Clefairy	10
36	Clefable	B
39	Jigglypuff	21
40	Wigglytuff	B
60	Poliwag	15
61	Poliwhirl	15
62	Poliwrath	B
113	Chansey	16
122	Mr. Mime	15
124	Jynx	15
172	Pichu	E
186	Politoed	B
190	Aipom	E
242	Blissey	16
300	Skitty	15
301	Delcatty	B
418	Buizel	E
439	Mime Jr.	15

Draco Meteor		
147	Dratini	T
148	Dragonair	T
149	Dragonite	T
230	Kingdra	T
329	Vibrava	T
330	Flygon	T
334	Altaria	T
371	Bagon	T
372	Shelgon	T
373	Salamence	T
380	Latias	T
381	Latios	T
384	Rayquaza	T
443	Gible	T
444	Gabite	T
445	Garchomp	T
483	Dialga	T
484	Palkia	T
487	Giratina (A)	T
487	Giratina (O)	T

Dragon Claw		
4	Charmander	TM
5	Charmeleon	TM
6	Charizard	B,TM
142	Aerodactyl	TM
149	Dragonite	TM
151	Mew	TM
158	Totodile	E
160	Feraligatr	TM
248	Tyranitar	TM
254	Sceptile	TM
306	Aggron	TM
330	Flygon	45,TM
334	Altaria	TM
371	Bagon	50,TM
372	Shelgon	55,TM
373	Salamence	61,TM
380	Latias	TM
381	Latios	TM
383	Groudon	TM
384	Rayquaza	20,TM
443	Gible	27,TM
444	Gabite	33,TM
445	Garchomp	33,TM
483	Dialga	30,TM
484	Palkia	30,TM
487	Giratina (A)	30,TM
487	Giratina (O)	30,TM

Dragon Dance		
4	Charmander	E
116	Horsea	38
117	Seadra	48
130	Gyarados	44
131	Lapras	E
147	Dratini	45,E
148	Dragonair	53
149	Dragonite	53
158	Totodile	E
230	Kingdra	48
246	Larvitar	E
334	Altaria	39
371	Bagon	E
381	Latios	55
384	Rayquaza	30

Dragon Pulse		
6	Charizard	TM
31	Nidoqueen	TM
34	Nidoking	TM
59	Arcanine	TM
95	Onix	TM
111	Rhyhorn	TM
112	Rhydon	TM
116	Horsea	42,TM
117	Seadra	57,TM
130	Gyarados	TM
131	Lapras	TM
142	Aerodactyl	TM
147	Dratini	TM
148	Dragonair	TM
149	Dragonite	TM
151	Mew	TM
160	Feraligatr	TM
208	Steelix	TM
230	Kingdra	57,TM
248	Tyranitar	TM
249	Lugia	TM
254	Sceptile	TM
306	Aggron	TM
329	Vibrava	TM
330	Flygon	TM
333	Swablu	45,TM
334	Altaria	54,TM
350	Milotic	TM
371	Bagon	TM
372	Shelgon	TM
373	Salamence	TM
380	Latias	70,TM
381	Latios	70,TM
383	Groudon	TM
384	Rayquaza	75,TM
408	Cranidos	TM
409	Rampardos	TM
443	Gible	TM
444	Gabite	TM
445	Garchomp	TM
448	Lucario	47,TM
464	Rhyperior	TM
483	Dialga	TM
484	Palkia	TM
485	Heatran	TM
487	Giratina (A)	TM
487	Giratina (O)	TM

Dragon Rage		
4	Charmander	16
5	Charmeleon	17
6	Charizard	17
116	Horsea	E
130	Gyarados	23
147	Dratini	15
148	Dragonair	15
149	Dragonite	15
371	Bagon	E
443	Gible	7
444	Gabite	7
445	Garchomp	B,7

Dragon Rush		
4	Charmander	E
111	Rhyhorn	E
147	Dratini	35,E
148	Dragonair	39
149	Dragonite	39
304	Aron	E
333	Swablu	E
371	Bagon	E
443	Gible	37
444	Gabite	49
445	Garchomp	55

DragonBreath		
95	Onix	33
116	Horsea	E
142	Aerodactyl	E
147	Dratini	E
208	Steelix	33
252	Treecko	E
329	Vibrava	35
330	Flygon	35
334	Altaria	35
349	Feebas	E
371	Bagon	31
372	Shelgon	32
373	Salamence	32
380	Latias	20
381	Latios	20
443	Gible	E
483	Dialga	B
484	Palkia	B
487	Giratina (A)	B
487	Giratina (O)	B

Drain Punch		
35	Clefairy	TM
36	Clefable	TM
39	Jigglypuff	TM
40	Wigglytuff	TM
44	Gloom	TM
45	Vileplume	TM
63	Abra	TM
64	Kadabra	TM
65	Alakazam	TM
80	Slowbro	TM
94	Gengar	TM
96	Drowzee	TM
97	Hypno	TM
107	Hitmonchan	TM
113	Chansey	TM
115	Kangaskhan	TM
122	Mr. Mime	TM
124	Jynx	TM
150	Mewtwo	TM
151	Mew	TM
165	Ledyba	TM
166	Ledian	TM
176	Togetic	TM
182	Bellossom	TM
199	Slowking	TM
242	Blissey	TM
252	Treecko	TM
253	Grovyle	TM
254	Sceptile	TM
271	Lombre	TM
272	Ludicolo	TM
286	Breloom	TM
307	Meditite	TM
308	Medicham	TM
326	Grumpig	TM
327	Spinda	TM
331	Cacnea	TM
332	Cacturne	TM
352	Kecleon	TM
377	Regirock	TM
385	Jirachi	TM
386	Deoxys (N)	TM
386	Deoxys (A)	TM
386	Deoxys (D)	TM
386	Deoxys (S)	TM
427	Buneary	TM
428	Lopunny	TM
439	Mime Jr.	TM
440	Happiny	TM
447	Riolu	TM
448	Lucario	TM
468	Togekiss	TM
475	Gallade	TM
486	Regigigas	TM
491	Darkrai	TM

Dream Eater		
12	Butterfree	TM
35	Clefairy	TM
36	Clefable	TM
38	Ninetales	TM
39	Jigglypuff	TM
40	Wigglytuff	TM
52	Meowth	TM
53	Persian	TM
63	Abra	TM
64	Kadabra	TM
65	Alakazam	TM
79	Slowpoke	TM
80	Slowbro	TM
92	Gastly	33,TM
93	Haunter	39,TM
94	Gengar	39,TM
96	Drowzee	TM
97	Hypno	TM
102	Exeggcute	TM
103	Exeggutor	TM
108	Lickitung	TM
113	Chansey	TM
121	Starmie	TM
122	Mr. Mime	TM
124	Jynx	TM
131	Lapras	TM
137	Porygon	TM
150	Mewtwo	TM
151	Mew	TM
163	Hoothoot	49,TM
164	Noctowl	57,TM
173	Cleffa	TM
174	Igglybuff	TM
175	Togepi	TM
176	Togetic	TM
177	Natu	TM
178	Xatu	TM
190	Aipom	TM
193	Yanma	TM
196	Espeon	TM
197	Umbreon	TM
198	Murkrow	TM
199	Slowking	TM
200	Misdreavus	TM
203	Girafarig	TM
206	Dunsparce	TM
215	Sneasel	TM
228	Houndour	TM
229	Houndoom	TM
233	Porygon2	TM
234	Stantler	TM
238	Smoochum	TM
242	Blissey	TM
249	Lugia	TM
250	Ho-Oh	TM
251	Celebi	TM
280	Ralts	45,TM
281	Kirlia	53,TM
282	Gardevoir	65,TM
292	Shedinja	TM
300	Skitty	TM
301	Delcatty	TM
302	Sableye	TM
307	Meditite	TM
308	Medicham	TM
316	Gulpin	TM,E
317	Swalot	TM
325	Spoink	TM
326	Grumpig	TM
327	Spinda	TM
333	Swablu	TM
334	Altaria	TM
337	Lunatone	TM
338	Solrock	TM
343	Baltoy	TM
344	Claydol	TM
353	Shuppet	TM
354	Banette	TM
355	Duskull	TM
356	Dusclops	TM
358	Chimecho	TM,E
359	Absol	TM
380	Latias	TM
381	Latios	TM
385	Jirachi	TM
386	Deoxys (N)	TM
386	Deoxys (A)	TM
386	Deoxys (D)	TM
386	Deoxys (S)	TM
413	Wormadam (P)	TM
413	Wormadam (S)	TM
413	Wormadam (T)	TM
414	Mothim	TM
424	Ambipom	TM
425	Drifloon	TM
426	Drifblim	TM
429	Mismagius	TM
430	Honchkrow	TM
431	Glameow	TM
432	Purugly	TM
433	Chingling	TM,E
436	Bronzor	TM
437	Bronzong	TM
439	Mime Jr.	TM
440	Happiny	TM
442	Spiritomb	19,TM
461	Weavile	TM
463	Lickilicky	TM
468	Togekiss	TM
469	Yanmega	TM
474	Porygon-Z	TM
475	Gallade	TM
477	Dusknoir	TM
478	Froslass	TM
479	Rotom	TM
480	Uxie	TM
481	Mesprit	TM
482	Azelf	TM
487	Giratina (A)	TM
487	Giratina (O)	TM
488	Cresselia	TM
491	Darkrai	84,TM

Drill Peck		
21	Spearow	37
22	Fearow	47
84	Doduo	41
85	Dodrio	47
145	Zapdos	71
177	Natu	E
198	Murkrow	E
227	Skarmory	E
393	Piplup	39
394	Prinplup	46
395	Empoleon	52

DynamicPunch		
62	Poliwrath	43
66	Machop	46
67	Machoke	51
68	Machamp	51
239	Elekid	E
240	Magby	E
286	Breloom	45
296	Makuhita	E
307	Meditite	E
331	Cacnea	E
453	Croagunk	E

Earth Power		
27	Sandshrew	T
28	Sandslash	T
31	Nidoqueen	43,T
34	Nidoking	43,T
50	Diglett	26,T
51	Dugtrio	28,T
74	Geodude	T
75	Graveler	T
76	Golem	T
95	Onix	T
104	Cubone	T
105	Marowak	T
111	Rhyhorn	T
112	Rhydon	T
138	Omanyte	T
139	Omastar	T
140	Kabuto	T
141	Kabutops	T
142	Aerodactyl	T
151	Mew	T
185	Sudowoodo	T
194	Wooper	T
195	Quagsire	T
207	Gligar	T
208	Steelix	T
213	Shuckle	T
218	Slugma	56,T
219	Magcargo	66,T
220	Swinub	T
221	Piloswine	T
222	Corsola	53,T
231	Phanpy	T
232	Donphan	T
246	Larvitar	T
247	Pupitar	T
248	Tyranitar	T
249	Lugia	T
250	Ho-Oh	T
251	Celebi	T
258	Mudkip	T
259	Marshtomp	T
260	Swampert	T
299	Nosepass	79,T
304	Aron	T
305	Lairon	T
306	Aggron	T
322	Numel	35,T
323	Camerupt	39,T
324	Torkoal	T
328	Trapinch	65,T
329	Vibrava	T
330	Flygon	T
337	Lunatone	T
338	Solrock	T
339	Barboach	T
340	Whiscash	T
343	Baltoy	53,T
344	Claydol	62,T
345	Lileep	T
346	Cradily	T
347	Anorith	T
348	Armaldo	T
369	Relicanth	T
377	Regirock	T
383	Groudon	75,T
384	Rayquaza	T
387	Turtwig	T
388	Grotle	T
389	Torterra	T
408	Cranidos	T
409	Rampardos	T
410	Shieldon	T
411	Bastiodon	T
413	Wormadam (S)	T
422	Shellos	T
423	Gastrodon	T
438	Bonsly	T
443	Gible	T
444	Gabite	T
445	Garchomp	T
449	Hippopotas	T
450	Hippowdon	T
464	Rhyperior	T
472	Gliscor	T
473	Mamoswine	T
476	Probopass	79,T
483	Dialga	60,T
484	Palkia	60,T
485	Heatran	73,T
486	Regigigas	T
487	Giratina (A)	60,T
487	Giratina (O)	60,T
492	Shaymin (L)	T

Earthquake		
3	Venusaur	TM
6	Charizard	TM
9	Blastoise	TM
23	Ekans	TM
24	Arbok	TM
27	Sandshrew	TM
28	Sandslash	TM
31	Nidoqueen	TM
34	Nidoking	TM
50	Diglett	37,TM
51	Dugtrio	45,TM
56	Mankey	TM
57	Primeape	TM
61	Poliwhirl	TM
62	Poliwrath	TM
66	Machop	TM
67	Machoke	TM
68	Machamp	TM
74	Geodude	29,TM
75	Graveler	33,TM
76	Golem	33,TM
79	Slowpoke	TM
80	Slowbro	TM
95	Onix	TM
104	Cubone	TM
105	Marowak	TM
106	Hitmonlee	TM
107	Hitmonchan	TM
108	Lickitung	TM
111	Rhyhorn	49,TM
112	Rhydon	49,TM
113	Chansey	TM
115	Kangaskhan	TM
127	Pinsir	TM
128	Tauros	TM
130	Gyarados	TM
142	Aerodactyl	TM
143	Snorlax	TM
149	Dragonite	TM
150	Mewtwo	TM
151	Mew	TM
154	Meganium	TM
157	Typhlosion	TM
160	Feraligatr	TM
185	Sudowoodo	TM
186	Politoed	TM
194	Wooper	33,TM
195	Quagsire	36,TM
199	Slowking	TM
203	Girafarig	TM
204	Pineco	TM
205	Forretress	TM
206	Dunsparce	TM
207	Gligar	TM
208	Steelix	TM
209	Snubbull	TM
210	Granbull	TM
213	Shuckle	TM
214	Heracross	TM
216	Teddiursa	TM
217	Ursaring	TM
219	Magcargo	TM
220	Swinub	37,TM
221	Piloswine	40,TM
222	Corsola	TM
226	Mantine	TM
231	Phanpy	TM
232	Donphan	46,TM
234	Stantler	TM
236	Tyrogue	TM
237	Hitmontop	TM
241	Miltank	TM
242	Blissey	TM
246	Larvitar	41,TM
247	Pupitar	47,TM
248	Tyranitar	47,TM
249	Lugia	TM
250	Ho-Oh	TM
254	Sceptile	TM
257	Blaziken	TM
259	Marshtomp	46,TM
260	Swampert	52,TM
288	Vigoroth	TM
289	Slaking	TM
294	Loudred	TM
295	Exploud	TM
296	Makuhita	TM
297	Hariyama	TM
299	Nosepass	TM
304	Aron	TM
305	Lairon	TM
306	Aggron	TM
317	Swalot	TM
319	Sharpedo	TM
320	Wailmer	TM
321	Wailord	TM
322	Numel	41,TM
323	Camerupt	49,TM
324	Torkoal	TM,E
328	Trapinch	73,TM
329	Vibrava	TM
330	Flygon	TM
334	Altaria	TM
336	Seviper	TM
337	Lunatone	TM
338	Solrock	TM
339	Barboach	39,TM
340	Whiscash	45,TM
343	Baltoy	TM
344	Claydol	TM
346	Cradily	TM
348	Armaldo	TM
356	Dusclops	TM
357	Tropius	TM
362	Glalie	TM
363	Spheal	TM
364	Sealeo	TM
365	Walrein	TM
369	Relicanth	TM
373	Salamence	TM
375	Metang	TM
376	Metagross	TM
377	Regirock	TM
378	Regice	TM
379	Registeel	TM
380	Latias	TM
381	Latios	TM
382	Kyogre	TM
383	Groudon	35,TM
384	Rayquaza	TM
389	Torterra	32,TM
392	Infernape	TM
395	Empoleon	TM
408	Cranidos	TM
409	Rampardos	TM
410	Shieldon	TM
411	Bastiodon	TM
413	Wormadam (S)	TM
423	Gastrodon	TM
436	Bronzor	TM
437	Bronzong	TM
443	Gible	TM
444	Gabite	TM
445	Garchomp	TM
446	Munchlax	TM
447	Riolu	TM
448	Lucario	TM

ADVENTURE DATA LIST
POKÉMON MOVES AND ABILITIES ALPHABETICAL LIST

Earthquake continued		
449	Hippopotas	37,TM
450	Hippowdon	40,TM
452	Drapion	TM
453	Croagunk	TM
454	Toxicroak	TM
458	Mantyke	TM
460	Abomasnow	TM
463	Lickilicky	TM
464	Rhyperior	49,TM
465	Tangrowth	TM
466	Electivire	TM
467	Magmortar	TM
472	Gliscor	TM
473	Mamoswine	40,TM
475	Gallade	TM
476	Probopass	TM
477	Dusknoir	TM
483	Dialga	TM
484	Palkia	TM
485	Heatran	TM
486	Regigigas	TM
487	Giratina (A)	TM
487	Giratina (O)	TM

Egg Bomb		
103	Exeggutor	27
113	Chansey	38
242	Blissey	38

Embargo		
53	Persian	TM
63	Abra	TM
64	Kadabra	TM
65	Alakazam	TM
92	Gastly	TM
93	Haunter	TM
94	Gengar	TM
150	Mewtwo	TM
151	Mew	TM
198	Murkrow	TM
200	Misdreavus	TM
215	Sneasel	TM
228	Houndour	40,TM
229	Houndoom	44,TM
261	Poochyena	41,TM
262	Mightyena	47,TM
274	Nuzleaf	TM
275	Shiftry	TM
302	Sableye	TM
303	Mawile	TM
332	Cacturne	TM
335	Zangoose	27,TM
337	Lunatone	31,TM
338	Solrock	31,TM
353	Shuppet	38,TM
354	Banette	42,TM
355	Duskull	TM
356	Dusclops	TM
425	Drifloon	TM
426	Drifblim	TM
429	Mismagius	TM
430	Honchkrow	TM
442	Spiritomb	TM
453	Croagunk	TM
454	Toxicroak	TM
461	Weavile	B,TM
474	Porygon-Z	34,TM
477	Dusknoir	TM
478	Froslass	TM
491	Darkrai	TM

Ember		
4	Charmander	7
5	Charmeleon	B,7
6	Charizard	B,7
37	Vulpix	B
38	Ninetales	B
58	Growlithe	6
77	Ponyta	10
78	Rapidash	B,10
126	Magmar	B,7
136	Flareon	15
146	Moltres	B
155	Cyndaquil	10
156	Quilava	10
157	Typhlosion	B,10
218	Slugma	8
219	Magcargo	B,8
228	Houndour	B
229	Houndoom	B
240	Magby	7
244	Entei	8
255	Torchic	10
256	Combusken	B,13
257	Blaziken	B,13
322	Numel	5
323	Camerupt	B,5
324	Torkoal	B
351	Castform	10
371	Bagon	25
372	Shelgon	25
373	Salamence	25
390	Chimchar	7
391	Monferno	B,7
392	Infernape	B,7
467	Magmortar	B,7

Encore		
35	Clefairy	4
63	Abra	E
66	Machop	E
69	Bellsprout	E
86	Seel	13,E
87	Dewgong	13
122	Mr. Mime	11
165	Ledyba	E
172	Pichu	E
173	Cleffa	4
175	Togepi	19
176	Togetic	19
187	Hoppip	E
191	Sunkern	E
194	Wooper	E
213	Shuckle	9
287	Slakoth	7
288	Vigoroth	B,7
289	Slaking	B,7
298	Azurill	E
311	Plusle	17
312	Minun	17
313	Volbeat	E
314	Illumise	25,E
316	Gulpin	23
317	Swalot	23
327	Spinda	E
360	Wynaut	B
363	Spheal	7
364	Sealeo	B,7
365	Walrein	B,7
390	Chimchar	E
427	Buneary	E
439	Mime Jr.	11
441	Chatot	E

Endeavor		
15	Beedrill	40,T
19	Rattata	34,T
20	Raticate	44,T
35	Clefairy	T
36	Clefable	T
39	Jigglypuff	T
40	Wigglytuff	T
56	Mankey	T
57	Primeape	T
60	Poliwag	E
84	Doduo	46,T,E
85	Dodrio	54,T
104	Cubone	41,T
105	Marowak	49,T
111	Rhyhorn	T
112	Rhydon	T
113	Chansey	T
114	Tangela	E
115	Kangaskhan	T,E
128	Tauros	T
151	Mew	T
173	Cleffa	T
174	Igglybuff	T
175	Togepi	T
176	Togetic	T
191	Sunkern	21,T
192	Sunflora	T
206	Dunsparce	49,T
220	Swinub	T
221	Piloswine	T
222	Corsola	T
231	Phanpy	T,E
232	Donphan	T
237	Hitmontop	55,T
242	Blissey	T
252	Treecko	T,E
253	Grovyle	T
254	Sceptile	T
258	Mudkip	46,T
259	Marshtomp	53,T
260	Swampert	61,T
276	Taillow	26,T
277	Swellow	28,T
293	Whismur	E
304	Aron	T,E
305	Lairon	T
306	Aggron	T
335	Zangoose	T
341	Corphish	T,E
342	Crawdaunt	T
390	Chimchar	T
391	Monferno	T
392	Infernape	T
396	Starly	17,T
397	Staravia	18,T
398	Staraptor	18,T
401	Kricketot	T
402	Kricketune	T
408	Cranidos	T
409	Rampardos	30,T
413	Wormadam (P)	T
413	Wormadam (S)	T
413	Wormadam (T)	T
415	Combee	T
416	Vespiquen	T
427	Buneary	T
428	Lopunny	T
440	Happiny	T
464	Rhyperior	T
468	Togekiss	T
473	Mamoswine	T
492	Shaymin (L)	T

Endure		
1	Bulbasaur	TM
2	Ivysaur	TM
3	Venusaur	TM
4	Charmander	TM
5	Charmeleon	TM
6	Charizard	TM
7	Squirtle	TM
8	Wartortle	TM
9	Blastoise	TM
12	Butterfree	TM
15	Beedrill	TM
16	Pidgey	TM
17	Pidgeotto	TM
18	Pidgeot	TM
19	Rattata	TM
20	Raticate	TM
21	Spearow	TM
22	Fearow	TM
23	Ekans	TM
24	Arbok	TM
25	Pikachu	TM
26	Raichu	TM
27	Sandshrew	TM
28	Sandslash	TM
29	Nidoran♀	TM
30	Nidorina	TM
31	Nidoqueen	TM
32	Nidoran♂	TM
33	Nidorino	TM
34	Nidoking	TM
35	Clefairy	TM
36	Clefable	TM
37	Vulpix	TM
38	Ninetales	TM
39	Jigglypuff	TM
40	Wigglytuff	TM
41	Zubat	TM
42	Golbat	TM
43	Oddish	TM
44	Gloom	TM
45	Vileplume	TM
46	Paras	TM
47	Parasect	TM
48	Venonat	TM
49	Venomoth	TM
50	Diglett	TM
51	Dugtrio	TM
52	Meowth	TM
53	Persian	TM
54	Psyduck	TM
55	Golduck	TM
56	Mankey	TM
57	Primeape	TM
58	Growlithe	TM
59	Arcanine	TM
60	Poliwag	TM
61	Poliwhirl	TM
62	Poliwrath	TM
63	Abra	TM
64	Kadabra	TM
65	Alakazam	TM
66	Machop	TM
67	Machoke	TM
68	Machamp	TM
69	Bellsprout	TM
70	Weepinbell	TM
71	Victreebel	TM
72	Tentacool	TM
73	Tentacruel	TM
74	Geodude	TM
75	Graveler	TM
76	Golem	TM
77	Ponyta	TM
78	Rapidash	TM
79	Slowpoke	TM
80	Slowbro	TM
81	Magnemite	TM
82	Magneton	TM
83	Farfetch'D	TM
84	Doduo	TM
85	Dodrio	TM
86	Seel	TM
87	Dewgong	TM
88	Grimer	TM
89	Muk	TM
90	Shellder	TM
91	Cloyster	TM
92	Gastly	TM
93	Haunter	TM
94	Gengar	TM
95	Onix	TM
96	Drowzee	TM
97	Hypno	TM
98	Krabby	TM
99	Kingler	TM
100	Voltorb	TM
101	Electrode	TM
102	Exeggcute	TM
103	Exeggutor	TM
104	Cubone	TM
105	Marowak	TM
106	Hitmonlee	45,TM
107	Hitmonchan	TM
108	Lickitung	TM
109	Koffing	TM
110	Weezing	TM
111	Rhyhorn	TM
112	Rhydon	TM
113	Chansey	TM
114	Tangela	TM
115	Kangaskhan	34,TM
116	Horsea	TM
117	Seadra	TM
118	Goldeen	TM
119	Seaking	TM
120	Staryu	TM
121	Starmie	TM
122	Mr. Mime	TM
123	Scyther	TM,E
124	Jynx	TM
125	Electabuzz	TM
126	Magmar	TM
127	Pinsir	TM
128	Tauros	TM
130	Gyarados	TM
131	Lapras	TM
133	Eevee	TM,E
134	Vaporeon	TM
135	Jolteon	TM
136	Flareon	TM
137	Porygon	TM
138	Omanyte	TM
139	Omastar	TM
140	Kabuto	26,TM
141	Kabutops	26,TM
142	Aerodactyl	TM
143	Snorlax	TM
144	Articuno	TM
145	Zapdos	TM
146	Moltres	22,TM
147	Dratini	TM
148	Dragonair	TM
149	Dragonite	TM
150	Mewtwo	TM
151	Mew	TM
152	Chikorita	TM
153	Bayleef	TM,E
154	Meganium	TM
155	Cyndaquil	TM
156	Quilava	TM
157	Typhlosion	TM
158	Totodile	TM
159	Croconaw	TM
160	Feraligatr	TM
161	Sentret	TM
162	Furret	TM
163	Hoothoot	TM
164	Noctowl	TM
165	Ledyba	TM
166	Ledian	TM
167	Spinarak	TM
168	Ariados	TM
169	Crobat	TM
170	Chinchou	TM
171	Lanturn	TM
172	Pichu	TM
173	Cleffa	TM
174	Igglybuff	TM
175	Togepi	TM
176	Togetic	TM
177	Natu	TM
178	Xatu	TM
179	Mareep	TM
180	Flaaffy	TM
181	Ampharos	TM
182	Bellossom	TM
183	Marill	TM
184	Azumarill	TM
185	Sudowoodo	TM
186	Politoed	TM
187	Hoppip	TM
188	Skiploom	TM
189	Jumpluff	TM
190	Aipom	TM
191	Sunkern	TM
192	Sunflora	TM
193	Yanma	TM
194	Wooper	TM
195	Quagsire	TM
196	Espeon	TM
197	Umbreon	TM
198	Murkrow	TM
199	Slowking	TM
200	Misdreavus	TM
203	Girafarig	TM
204	Pineco	TM
205	Forretress	TM
206	Dunsparce	TM
207	Gligar	TM
208	Steelix	TM
209	Snubbull	TM
210	Granbull	TM
211	Qwilfish	TM
212	Scizor	TM
213	Shuckle	TM
214	Heracross	B,TM
215	Sneasel	TM
216	Teddiursa	TM
217	Ursaring	TM
218	Slugma	TM
219	Magcargo	TM
220	Swinub	16,TM
221	Piloswine	16,TM
222	Corsola	TM
223	Remoraid	TM
224	Octillery	TM
225	Delibird	TM
226	Mantine	TM
227	Skarmory	TM
228	Houndour	TM
229	Houndoom	TM
230	Kingdra	TM
231	Phanpy	28,TM
232	Donphan	TM
233	Porygon2	TM
234	Stantler	TM
236	Tyrogue	TM
237	Hitmontop	TM
238	Smoochum	TM
239	Elekid	TM
240	Magby	TM
241	Miltank	TM,E
242	Blissey	TM
243	Raikou	TM
244	Entei	TM
245	Suicune	TM
246	Larvitar	TM
247	Pupitar	TM.
248	Tyranitar	TM
249	Lugia	TM
250	Ho-Oh	TM
251	Celebi	TM
252	Treecko	TM
253	Grovyle	TM
254	Sceptile	TM
255	Torchic	TM,E
256	Combusken	TM
257	Blaziken	TM
258	Mudkip	TM
259	Marshtomp	TM
260	Swampert	TM
261	Poochyena	TM
262	Mightyena	TM
263	Zigzagoon	TM
264	Linoone	TM
267	Beautifly	TM
269	Dustox	TM
270	Lotad	TM
271	Lombre	TM
272	Ludicolo	TM
273	Seedot	TM
274	Nuzleaf	TM
275	Shiftry	TM
276	Taillow	TM
277	Swellow	TM
278	Wingull	TM
279	Pelipper	TM
280	Ralts	TM
281	Kirlia	TM
282	Gardevoir	TM
283	Surskit	TM
284	Masquerain	TM
285	Shroomish	TM
286	Breloom	TM
287	Slakoth	TM
288	Vigoroth	25,TM
289	Slaking	TM
290	Nincada	TM,E
291	Ninjask	TM
292	Shedinja	TM
293	Whismur	TM
294	Loudred	TM
295	Exploud	TM
296	Makuhita	37,TM
297	Hariyama	47,TM
298	Azurill	TM
299	Nosepass	TM
300	Skitty	TM
301	Delcatty	TM
302	Sableye	TM
303	Mawile	TM
304	Aron	TM
305	Lairon	TM
306	Aggron	TM
307	Meditite	TM
308	Medicham	TM
309	Electrike	TM
310	Manectric	TM
311	Plusle	TM
312	Minun	TM
313	Volbeat	TM
314	Illumise	TM
315	Roselia	TM
316	Gulpin	TM
317	Swalot	TM
318	Carvanha	TM
319	Sharpedo	TM
320	Wailmer	TM
321	Wailord	TM
322	Numel	TM
323	Camerupt	TM
324	Torkoal	TM,E
325	Spoink	TM
326	Grumpig	TM
327	Spinda	TM
328	Trapinch	TM
329	Vibrava	TM
330	Flygon	TM
331	Cacnea	TM
332	Cacturne	TM
333	Swablu	TM
334	Altaria	TM
335	Zangoose	TM
336	Seviper	TM
337	Lunatone	TM
338	Solrock	TM
339	Barboach	TM
340	Whiscash	TM
341	Corphish	TM
342	Crawdaunt	TM
343	Baltoy	TM
344	Claydol	TM
345	Lileep	TM
346	Cradily	TM
347	Anorith	TM
348	Armaldo	TM
349	Feebas	TM
350	Milotic	TM
351	Castform	TM
352	Kecleon	TM
353	Shuppet	TM
354	Banette	TM
355	Duskull	TM
356	Dusclops	TM
357	Tropius	TM
358	Chimecho	TM
359	Absol	TM
361	Snorunt	TM
362	Glalie	TM
363	Spheal	TM
364	Sealeo	TM
365	Walrein	TM
366	Clamperl	TM
367	Huntail	TM
368	Gorebyss	TM
369	Relicanth	TM
370	Luvdisc	TM
371	Bagon	TM
372	Shelgon	TM
373	Salamence	TM
375	Metang	TM
376	Metagross	TM
377	Regirock	TM
378	Regice	TM
379	Registeel	TM
380	Latias	TM
381	Latios	TM
382	Kyogre	TM
383	Groudon	TM
384	Rayquaza	TM
385	Jirachi	TM
386	Deoxys (N)	TM
386	Deoxys (A)	TM
386	Deoxys (D)	TM
386	Deoxys (S)	TM
387	Turtwig	TM
388	Grotle	TM
389	Torterra	TM
390	Chimchar	TM
391	Monferno	TM
392	Infernape	TM
393	Piplup	TM
394	Prinplup	TM
395	Empoleon	TM
396	Starly	TM
397	Staravia	TM
398	Staraptor	TM
399	Bidoof	TM
400	Bibarel	TM
402	Kricketune	TM
403	Shinx	TM
404	Luxio	TM
405	Luxray	TM
406	Budew	TM
407	Roserade	TM
408	Cranidos	TM
409	Rampardos	TM
410	Shieldon	33,TM
411	Bastiodon	36,TM
413	Wormadam (P)	TM
413	Wormadam (S)	TM
413	Wormadam (T)	TM
414	Mothim	TM
416	Vespiquen	TM
417	Pachirisu	17,TM
418	Buizel	TM
419	Floatzel	TM
420	Cherubi	TM
421	Cherrim	TM
422	Shellos	TM
423	Gastrodon	TM
424	Ambipom	TM
425	Drifloon	TM
426	Drifblim	TM
427	Buneary	6,TM
428	Lopunny	6,TM
429	Mismagius	TM
430	Honchkrow	TM
431	Glameow	TM
432	Purugly	TM
433	Chingling	TM
434	Stunky	TM
435	Skuntank	TM
436	Bronzor	TM
437	Bronzong	TM
438	Bonsly	TM
439	Mime Jr.	TM
440	Happiny	TM
441	Chatot	TM
442	Spiritomb	TM
443	Gible	TM
444	Gabite	TM
445	Garchomp	TM
446	Munchlax	TM
447	Riolu	B,TM
448	Lucario	TM
449	Hippopotas	TM
450	Hippowdon	TM
451	Skorupi	TM
452	Drapion	TM
453	Croagunk	TM
454	Toxicroak	TM
455	Carnivine	TM
456	Finneon	TM
457	Lumineon	TM
458	Mantyke	TM
459	Snover	TM
460	Abomasnow	TM
461	Weavile	TM
462	Magnezone	TM
463	Lickilicky	TM
464	Rhyperior	TM
465	Tangrowth	TM
466	Electivire	TM
467	Magmortar	TM
468	Togekiss	TM
469	Yanmega	TM
470	Leafeon	TM
471	Glaceon	TM
472	Gliscor	TM
473	Mamoswine	16,TM
474	Porygon-Z	TM
475	Gallade	TM
476	Probopass	TM
477	Dusknoir	TM
478	Froslass	TM
479	Rotom	TM
480	Uxie	16,TM
481	Mesprit	TM
482	Azelf	TM
483	Dialga	TM
484	Palkia	TM
485	Heatran	TM

486	Regigigas	TM
487	Giratina (A)	TM
487	Giratina (O)	TM
488	Cresselia	TM
489	Phione	TM
490	Manaphy	TM
491	Darkrai	TM
492	Shaymin (L)	TM
492	Shaymin (S)	TM

Energy Ball		
1	Bulbasaur	TM
2	Ivysaur	TM
3	Venusaur	TM
12	Butterfree	TM
37	Vulpix	E
43	Oddish	TM
44	Gloom	TM
45	Vileplume	TM
46	Paras	TM
47	Parasect	TM
49	Venomoth	TM
63	Abra	TM
64	Kadabra	TM
65	Alakazam	TM
69	Bellsprout	TM
70	Weepinbell	TM
71	Victreebel	TM
92	Gastly	TM
93	Haunter	TM
94	Gengar	TM
102	Exeggcute	TM
103	Exeggutor	TM
114	Tangela	TM
122	Mr. Mime	TM
124	Jynx	TM
150	Mewtwo	TM
151	Mew	TM
152	Chikorita	TM
153	Bayleef	TM
154	Meganium	TM
182	Bellossom	TM
187	Hoppip	TM
188	Skiploom	TM
189	Jumpluff	TM
191	Sunkern	TM
192	Sunflora	TM
203	Girafarig	TM
224	Octillery	TM
234	Stantler	TM
251	Celebi	TM
252	Treecko	51,TM
253	Grovyle	TM
254	Sceptile	TM
267	Beautifly	TM
269	Dustox	TM
270	Lotad	45,TM
271	Lombre	TM
272	Ludicolo	TM
273	Seedot	TM
274	Nuzleaf	TM
275	Shiftry	TM
282	Gardevoir	TM
284	Masquerain	TM
285	Shroomish	TM
286	Breloom	TM
308	Medicham	TM
315	Roselia	TM
326	Grumpig	TM
331	Cacnea	TM
332	Cacturne	TM
345	Lileep	50,TM
346	Cradily	56,TM
351	Castform	TM
357	Tropius	TM
358	Chimecho	TM
380	Latias	TM
381	Latios	TM
384	Rayquaza	TM
385	Jirachi	TM
386	Deoxys (N)	TM
386	Deoxys (A)	TM
386	Deoxys (D)	TM
386	Deoxys (S)	TM
387	Turtwig	TM
388	Grotle	TM
389	Torterra	TM
406	Budew	TM
407	Roserade	TM
413	Wormadam (P)	TM
414	Mothim	TM
420	Cherubi	TM
421	Cherrim	TM
429	Mismagius	TM
455	Carnivine	TM
459	Snover	TM
460	Abomasnow	TM
465	Tangrowth	TM
470	Leafeon	TM

480	Uxie	TM
481	Mesprit	TM
482	Azelf	TM
487	Giratina (A)	TM
487	Giratina (O)	TM
488	Cresselia	TM
490	Manaphy	TM
492	Shaymin (L)	73,TM
492	Shaymin (S)	73,TM

Eruption		
155	Cyndaquil	49
156	Quilava	57
157	Typhlosion	57
244	Entei	85
323	Camerupt	57
324	Torkoal	E
383	Groudon	80

Explosion		
74	Geodude	32,TM
75	Graveler	38,TM
76	Golem	38,TM
81	Magnemite	TM
82	Magneton	TM
88	Grimer	TM,E
89	Muk	TM
90	Shellder	TM
91	Cloyster	TM
92	Gastly	TM,E
93	Haunter	TM
94	Gengar	TM
95	Onix	TM,E
100	Voltorb	43,TM
101	Electrode	51,TM
102	Exeggcute	TM
103	Exeggutor	TM
109	Koffing	37,TM
110	Weezing	40,TM
151	Mew	TM
185	Sudowoodo	TM
204	Pineco	34,TM
205	Forretress	38,TM
208	Steelix	TM
211	Qwilfish	TM
219	Magcargo	TM
222	Corsola	TM
273	Seedot	43,TM
274	Nuzleaf	TM
275	Shiftry	TM
299	Nosepass	TM,E
316	Gulpin	TM
317	Swalot	TM
323	Camerupt	TM
324	Torkoal	TM
337	Lunatone	56,TM
338	Solrock	56,TM
343	Baltoy	71,TM
344	Claydol	86,TM
362	Glalie	TM
375	Metang	TM
376	Metagross	TM
377	Regirock	B,TM
378	Regice	B,TM
379	Registeel	B,TM
425	Drifloon	43,TM
426	Drifblim	51,TM
434	Stunky	44,TM
435	Skuntank	52,TM
437	Bronzong	TM
438	Bonsly	TM
462	Magnezone	TM
463	Lickilicky	TM
476	Probopass	TM
482	Azelf	76,TM
485	Heatran	TM

Extrasensory		
37	Vulpix	44,E
163	Hoothoot	37
164	Noctowl	42
234	Stantler	E
243	Raikou	64
244	Entei	64
245	Suicune	64
249	Lugia	65
250	Ho-Oh	65
274	Nuzleaf	49
293	Whismur	E
325	Spoink	E
358	Chimecho	46
406	Budew	E
436	Bronzor	19
437	Bronzong	19
480	Uxie	51
481	Mesprit	51
482	Azelf	51

ExtremeSpeed		
59	Arcanine	39
384	Rayquaza	60
386	Deoxys (S)	97
448	Lucario	51
468	Togekiss	B

Facade		
1	Bulbasaur	TM
2	Ivysaur	TM
3	Venusaur	TM
4	Charmander	TM
5	Charmeleon	TM
6	Charizard	TM
7	Squirtle	TM
8	Wartortle	TM
9	Blastoise	TM
12	Butterfree	TM
15	Beedrill	TM
16	Pidgey	TM
17	Pidgeotto	TM
18	Pidgeot	TM
19	Rattata	TM
20	Raticate	TM
21	Spearow	TM
22	Fearow	TM
23	Ekans	TM
24	Arbok	TM
25	Pikachu	TM
26	Raichu	TM
27	Sandshrew	TM
28	Sandslash	TM
29	Nidoran♀	TM
30	Nidorina	TM
31	Nidoqueen	TM
32	Nidoran♂	TM
33	Nidorino	TM
34	Nidoking	TM
35	Clefairy	TM
36	Clefable	TM
37	Vulpix	TM
38	Ninetales	TM
39	Jigglypuff	TM
40	Wigglytuff	TM
41	Zubat	TM
42	Golbat	TM
43	Oddish	TM
44	Gloom	TM
45	Vileplume	TM
46	Paras	TM
47	Parasect	TM
48	Venonat	TM
49	Venomoth	TM
50	Diglett	TM
51	Dugtrio	TM
52	Meowth	TM
53	Persian	TM
54	Psyduck	TM
55	Golduck	TM
56	Mankey	TM
57	Primeape	TM
58	Growlithe	TM
59	Arcanine	TM
60	Poliwag	TM
61	Poliwhirl	TM
62	Poliwrath	TM
63	Abra	TM
64	Kadabra	TM
65	Alakazam	TM
66	Machop	TM
67	Machoke	TM
68	Machamp	TM
69	Bellsprout	TM
70	Weepinbell	TM
71	Victreebel	TM
72	Tentacool	TM
73	Tentacruel	TM
74	Geodude	TM
75	Graveler	TM
76	Golem	TM
77	Ponyta	TM
78	Rapidash	TM
79	Slowpoke	TM
80	Slowbro	TM
81	Magnemite	TM
82	Magneton	TM
83	Farfetch'd	TM
84	Doduo	TM
85	Dodrio	TM
86	Seel	TM
87	Dewgong	TM
88	Grimer	TM
89	Muk	TM
90	Shellder	TM
91	Cloyster	TM
92	Gastly	TM
93	Haunter	TM
94	Gengar	TM
95	Onix	TM
96	Drowzee	TM
97	Hypno	TM
98	Krabby	TM
99	Kingler	TM
100	Voltorb	TM
101	Electrode	TM
102	Exeggcute	TM
103	Exeggutor	TM
104	Cubone	TM
105	Marowak	TM
106	Hitmonlee	TM
107	Hitmonchan	TM
108	Lickitung	TM
109	Koffing	TM
110	Weezing	TM
111	Rhyhorn	TM
112	Rhydon	TM
113	Chansey	TM
114	Tangela	TM
115	Kangaskhan	TM
116	Horsea	TM
117	Seadra	TM
118	Goldeen	TM
119	Seaking	TM
120	Staryu	TM
121	Starmie	TM
122	Mr. Mime	TM
123	Scyther	TM
124	Jynx	TM
125	Electabuzz	TM
126	Magmar	TM
127	Pinsir	TM
128	Tauros	TM
130	Gyarados	TM
131	Lapras	TM
133	Eevee	TM
134	Vaporeon	TM
135	Jolteon	TM
136	Flareon	TM
137	Porygon	TM
138	Omanyte	TM
139	Omastar	TM
140	Kabuto	TM
141	Kabutops	TM
142	Aerodactyl	TM
143	Snorlax	TM
144	Articuno	TM
145	Zapdos	TM
146	Moltres	TM
147	Dratini	TM
148	Dragonair	TM
149	Dragonite	TM
150	Mewtwo	TM
151	Mew	TM
152	Chikorita	TM
153	Bayleef	TM
154	Meganium	TM
155	Cyndaquil	TM
156	Quilava	TM
157	Typhlosion	TM
158	Totodile	TM
159	Croconaw	TM
160	Feraligatr	TM
161	Sentret	TM
162	Furret	TM
163	Hoothoot	TM
164	Noctowl	TM
165	Ledyba	TM
166	Ledian	TM
167	Spinarak	TM
168	Ariados	TM
169	Crobat	TM
170	Chinchou	TM
171	Lanturn	TM
172	Pichu	TM
173	Cleffa	TM
174	Igglybuff	TM
175	Togepi	TM
176	Togetic	TM
177	Natu	TM
178	Xatu	TM
179	Mareep	TM
180	Flaaffy	TM
181	Ampharos	TM
182	Bellossom	TM
183	Marill	TM
184	Azumarill	TM
185	Sudowoodo	TM
186	Politoed	TM
187	Hoppip	TM
188	Skiploom	TM
189	Jumpluff	TM
190	Aipom	TM
191	Sunkern	TM
192	Sunflora	TM
193	Yanma	TM
194	Wooper	TM
195	Quagsire	TM
196	Espeon	TM
197	Umbreon	TM
198	Murkrow	TM
199	Slowking	TM
200	Misdreavus	TM
203	Girafarig	TM
204	Pineco	TM
205	Forretress	TM
206	Dunsparce	TM
207	Gligar	TM
208	Steelix	TM
209	Snubbull	TM
210	Granbull	TM
211	Qwilfish	TM
212	Scizor	TM
213	Shuckle	TM
214	Heracross	TM
215	Sneasel	TM
216	Teddiursa	TM
217	Ursaring	TM
218	Slugma	TM
219	Magcargo	TM
220	Swinub	TM
221	Piloswine	TM
222	Corsola	TM
223	Remoraid	TM
224	Octillery	TM
225	Delibird	TM
226	Mantine	TM
227	Skarmory	TM
228	Houndour	TM
229	Houndoom	TM
230	Kingdra	TM
231	Phanpy	TM
232	Donphan	TM
233	Porygon2	TM
234	Stantler	TM
236	Tyrogue	TM
237	Hitmontop	TM
238	Smoochum	TM
239	Elekid	TM
240	Magby	TM
241	Miltank	TM
242	Blissey	TM
243	Raikou	TM
244	Entei	TM
245	Suicune	TM
246	Larvitar	TM
247	Pupitar	TM
248	Tyranitar	TM
249	Lugia	TM
250	Ho-Oh	TM
251	Celebi	TM
252	Treecko	TM
253	Grovyle	TM
254	Sceptile	TM
255	Torchic	TM
256	Combusken	TM
257	Blaziken	TM
258	Mudkip	TM
259	Marshtomp	TM
260	Swampert	TM
261	Poochyena	TM
262	Mightyena	TM
263	Zigzagoon	TM
264	Linoone	TM
267	Beautifly	TM
269	Dustox	TM
270	Lotad	TM
271	Lombre	TM
272	Ludicolo	TM
273	Seedot	TM
274	Nuzleaf	TM
275	Shiftry	TM
276	Taillow	TM
277	Swellow	TM
278	Wingull	TM
279	Pelipper	TM
280	Ralts	TM
281	Kirlia	TM
282	Gardevoir	TM
283	Surskit	TM
284	Masquerain	TM
285	Shroomish	TM
286	Breloom	TM
287	Slakoth	TM
288	Vigoroth	TM
289	Slaking	TM
290	Nincada	TM
291	Ninjask	TM
292	Shedinja	TM
293	Whismur	TM
294	Loudred	TM
295	Exploud	TM
296	Makuhita	TM
297	Hariyama	TM
298	Azurill	TM
299	Nosepass	TM
300	Skitty	TM
301	Delcatty	TM
302	Sableye	TM
303	Mawile	TM
304	Aron	TM
305	Lairon	TM
306	Aggron	TM
307	Meditite	TM
308	Medicham	TM
309	Electrike	TM
310	Manectric	TM
311	Plusle	TM
312	Minun	TM
313	Volbeat	TM
314	Illumise	TM
315	Roselia	TM
316	Gulpin	TM
317	Swalot	TM
318	Carvanha	TM
319	Sharpedo	TM
320	Wailmer	TM
321	Wailord	TM
322	Numel	TM
323	Camerupt	TM
324	Torkoal	TM
325	Spoink	TM
326	Grumpig	TM
327	Spinda	TM
328	Trapinch	TM
329	Vibrava	TM
330	Flygon	TM
331	Cacnea	TM
332	Cacturne	TM
333	Swablu	TM
334	Altaria	TM
335	Zangoose	TM
336	Seviper	TM
337	Lunatone	TM
338	Solrock	TM
339	Barboach	TM
340	Whiscash	TM
341	Corphish	TM
342	Crawdaunt	TM
343	Baltoy	TM
344	Claydol	TM
345	Lileep	TM
346	Cradily	TM
347	Anorith	TM
348	Armaldo	TM
349	Feebas	TM
350	Milotic	TM
351	Castform	TM
352	Kecleon	TM
353	Shuppet	TM
354	Banette	TM
355	Duskull	TM
356	Dusclops	TM
357	Tropius	TM
358	Chimecho	TM
359	Absol	TM
361	Snorunt	TM
362	Glalie	TM
363	Spheal	TM
364	Sealeo	TM
365	Walrein	TM
366	Clamperl	TM
367	Huntail	TM
368	Gorebyss	TM
369	Relicanth	TM
370	Luvdisc	TM
371	Bagon	TM
372	Shelgon	TM
373	Salamence	TM
375	Metang	TM
376	Metagross	TM
377	Regirock	TM
378	Regice	TM
379	Registeel	TM
380	Latias	TM
381	Latios	TM
382	Kyogre	TM
383	Groudon	TM
384	Rayquaza	TM
385	Jirachi	TM
386	Deoxys (N)	TM
386	Deoxys (A)	TM
386	Deoxys (D)	TM
386	Deoxys (S)	TM
387	Turtwig	TM
388	Grotle	TM
389	Torterra	TM
390	Chimchar	31,TM
391	Monferno	TM
392	Infernape	TM
393	Piplup	TM
394	Prinplup	TM
395	Empoleon	TM
396	Starly	TM
397	Staravia	TM
398	Staraptor	TM
399	Bidoof	TM
400	Bibarel	TM
402	Kricketune	TM
403	Shinx	TM
404	Luxio	TM
405	Luxray	TM
406	Budew	TM
407	Roserade	TM
408	Cranidos	TM
409	Rampardos	TM
410	Shieldon	TM
411	Bastiodon	TM
413	Wormadam (P)	TM
413	Wormadam (S)	TM
413	Wormadam (T)	TM
414	Mothim	TM
416	Vespiquen	TM
417	Pachirisu	TM
418	Buizel	TM
419	Floatzel	TM
420	Cherubi	TM
421	Cherrim	TM
422	Shellos	TM
423	Gastrodon	TM
424	Ambipom	TM
425	Drifloon	TM
426	Drifblim	TM
427	Buneary	TM
428	Lopunny	TM
429	Mismagius	TM
430	Honchkrow	TM
431	Glameow	TM
432	Purugly	TM
433	Chingling	TM
434	Stunky	TM
435	Skuntank	TM
436	Bronzor	TM
437	Bronzong	TM
438	Bonsly	TM
439	Mime Jr.	TM
440	Happiny	TM
441	Chatot	TM
442	Spiritomb	TM
443	Gible	TM
444	Gabite	TM
445	Garchomp	TM
446	Munchlax	TM
447	Riolu	TM
448	Lucario	TM
449	Hippopotas	TM
450	Hippowdon	TM
451	Skorupi	TM
452	Drapion	TM
453	Croagunk	TM
454	Toxicroak	TM
455	Carnivine	TM
456	Finneon	TM
457	Lumineon	TM
458	Mantyke	TM
459	Snover	TM
460	Abomasnow	TM
461	Weavile	TM
462	Magnezone	TM
463	Lickilicky	TM
464	Rhyperior	TM
465	Tangrowth	TM
466	Electivire	TM
467	Magmortar	TM
468	Togekiss	TM
469	Yanmega	TM
470	Leafeon	TM
471	Glaceon	TM
472	Gliscor	TM
473	Mamoswine	TM
474	Porygon-Z	TM
475	Gallade	TM
476	Probopass	TM
477	Dusknoir	TM
478	Froslass	TM
479	Rotom	TM
480	Uxie	TM
481	Mesprit	TM
482	Azelf	TM
483	Dialga	TM
484	Palkia	TM
485	Heatran	TM
486	Regigigas	TM
487	Giratina (A)	TM
487	Giratina (O)	TM
488	Cresselia	TM
489	Phione	TM
490	Manaphy	TM
491	Darkrai	TM
492	Shaymin (L)	TM
492	Shaymin (S)	TM

Faint Attack		
16	Pidgey	E
21	Spearow	E
37	Vulpix	E

Faint Attack continued

41	Zubat	E
50	Diglett	E
52	Meowth	22
53	Persian	22
84	Doduo	E
126	Magmar	16
127	Pinsir	E
163	Hoothoot	E
174	Igglybuff	E
177	Natu	E
185	Sudowoodo	25
193	Yanma	E
197	Umbreon	36
198	Murkrow	35,E
207	Gligar	23
209	Snubbull	E
215	Sneasel	14
216	Teddiursa	15
217	Ursaring	15
228	Houndour	35
229	Houndoom	38
240	Magby	16
274	Nuzleaf	31
275	Shiftry	B
287	Slakoth	19
289	Slaking	19
290	Nincada	E
296	Makuhita	E
300	Skitty	29
302	Sableye	32
303	Mawile	26
327	Spinda	14
328	Trapinch	17
329	Vibrava	B,17
330	Flygon	B,17
331	Cacnea	29
332	Cacturne	29
352	Kecleon	7
353	Shuppet	28
354	Banette	28
355	Duskull	E
359	Absol	E
431	Glameow	17
432	Purugly	17
436	Bronzor	41
437	Bronzong	50
438	Bonsly	25
442	Spiritomb	7
451	Skorupi	E
453	Croagunk	17
454	Toxicroak	17
455	Carnivine	27
461	Weavile	14
467	Magmortar	16
472	Gliscor	23
491	Darkrai	29

Fake Out

7	Squirtle	E
52	Meowth	9
53	Persian	B,9
86	Seel	E
115	Kangaskhan	7
122	Mr. Mime	E
172	Pichu	E
190	Aipom	E
215	Sneasel	E
236	Tyrogue	B
238	Smoochum	E
271	Lombre	11
274	Nuzleaf	19
296	Makuhita	13
297	Hariyama	13
300	Skitty	B,E
301	Delcatty	B
302	Sableye	18
307	Meditite	E
327	Spinda	E
352	Kecleon	E
390	Chimchar	E
427	Buneary	E
431	Glameow	B
432	Purugly	B
439	Mime Jr.	E
453	Croagunk	E

Fake Tears

124	Jynx	25
133	Eevee	E
173	Cleffa	E
174	Igglybuff	E
216	Teddiursa	B,E
217	Ursaring	B
238	Smoochum	25
285	Shroomish	E
298	Azurill	E
300	Skitty	E
303	Mawile	6
311	Plusle	21,31
312	Minun	31
417	Pachirisu	E
427	Buneary	E
431	Glameow	E
438	Bonsly	B

False Swipe

15	Beedrill	TM
21	Spearow	E
46	Paras	TM,E
47	Parasect	TM
83	Farfetch'd	45,TM
98	Krabby	TM
99	Kingler	TM
104	Cubone	27,TM
105	Marowak	27,TM
123	Scyther	13,TM
127	Pinsir	TM,E
151	Mew	TM
207	Gligar	TM
212	Scizor	13,TM
214	Heracross	E
215	Sneasel	TM
253	Grovyle	53,TM
254	Sceptile	59,TM
273	Seedot	E
285	Shroomish	E
290	Nincada	25,TM
291	Ninjask	TM
292	Shedinja	TM
303	Mawile	E
335	Zangoose	44,TM
341	Corphish	TM
342	Crawdaunt	TM
347	Anorith	TM
348	Armaldo	TM
359	Absol	TM
402	Kricketune	TM
445	Garchomp	TM
451	Skorupi	TM
452	Drapion	TM
461	Weavile	TM
472	Gliscor	TM
475	Gallade	45,TM

FeatherDance

16	Pidgey	25
17	Pidgeotto	27
18	Pidgeot	27
83	Farfetch'd	E
163	Hoothoot	E
177	Natu	E
198	Murkrow	E
333	Swablu	E
396	Starly	E
441	Chatot	41

Feint

25	Pikachu	29
52	Meowth	54
53	Persian	68
83	Farfetch'd	43
106	Hitmonlee	25
107	Hitmonchan	21
123	Scyther	61
127	Pinsir	E
141	Kabutops	B
193	Yanma	E
207	Gligar	E
212	Scizor	61
214	Heracross	49
227	Skarmory	20
237	Hitmontop	33
255	Torchic	E
307	Meditite	22
308	Medicham	22
319	Sharpedo	B
328	Trapinch	81
352	Kecleon	14
359	Absol	B
391	Monferno	26
392	Infernape	29
434	Stunky	18
435	Skuntank	18
447	Riolu	15
448	Lucario	15
453	Croagunk	E
469	Yanmega	38
475	Gallade	39

Fire Blast

4	Charmander	TM
5	Charmeleon	TM
6	Charizard	TM
31	Nidoqueen	TM
34	Nidoking	TM
35	Clefairy	TM
36	Clefable	TM
37	Vulpix	47,TM
38	Ninetales	TM
39	Jigglypuff	TM
40	Wigglytuff	TM
58	Growlithe	TM
59	Arcanine	TM
66	Machop	TM
67	Machoke	TM
68	Machamp	TM
74	Geodude	TM
75	Graveler	TM
76	Golem	TM
77	Ponyta	37,TM
78	Rapidash	37,TM
79	Slowpoke	TM
80	Slowbro	TM
88	Grimer	TM
89	Muk	TM
104	Cubone	TM
105	Marowak	TM
108	Lickitung	TM
109	Koffing	TM
110	Weezing	TM
111	Rhyhorn	TM
112	Rhydon	TM
113	Chansey	TM
115	Kangaskhan	TM
126	Magmar	54,TM
128	Tauros	TM
130	Gyarados	TM
136	Flareon	71,TM
142	Aerodactyl	TM
143	Snorlax	TM
146	Moltres	TM
147	Dratini	TM
148	Dragonair	TM
149	Dragonite	TM
150	Mewtwo	TM
151	Mew	TM
155	Cyndaquil	TM
156	Quilava	TM
157	Typhlosion	TM
173	Cleffa	TM
174	Igglybuff	TM
175	Togepi	TM
176	Togetic	TM
199	Slowking	TM
206	Dunsparce	TM
209	Snubbull	TM
210	Granbull	TM
218	Slugma	TM
219	Magcargo	TM
223	Remoraid	TM
224	Octillery	TM
228	Houndour	TM
229	Houndoom	TM
240	Magby	46,TM
242	Blissey	TM
244	Entei	71,TM
248	Tyranitar	TM
250	Ho-Oh	29,TM
255	Torchic	TM
256	Combusken	TM
257	Blaziken	TM
287	Slakoth	TM
288	Vigoroth	TM
289	Slaking	TM
293	Whismur	TM
294	Loudred	TM
295	Exploud	TM
303	Mawile	TM
306	Aggron	TM
322	Numel	TM
323	Camerupt	TM
324	Torkoal	TM
330	Flygon	TM
334	Altaria	TM
335	Zangoose	TM
338	Solrock	TM
351	Castform	TM
352	Kecleon	TM
359	Absol	TM
371	Bagon	TM
372	Shelgon	TM
373	Salamence	TM
383	Groudon	45,TM
384	Rayquaza	TM
390	Chimchar	TM
391	Monferno	TM
392	Infernape	TM
408	Cranidos	TM
409	Rampardos	TM
410	Shieldon	TM
411	Bastiodon	TM
434	Stunky	TM
435	Skuntank	TM
440	Happiny	TM
443	Gible	TM
444	Gabite	TM
445	Garchomp	TM
446	Munchlax	TM
463	Lickilicky	TM
464	Rhyperior	TM
467	Magmortar	58,TM
468	Togekiss	TM
482	Azelf	TM
483	Dialga	TM
484	Palkia	TM
485	Heatran	TM

Fire Fang

4	Charmander	25
5	Charmeleon	28
6	Charizard	28
24	Arbok	B
58	Growlithe	28
59	Arcanine	B
111	Rhyhorn	E
136	Flareon	43
142	Aerodactyl	B
208	Steelix	B
209	Snubbull	B,E
210	Granbull	B
228	Houndour	30,E
229	Houndoom	32
232	Donphan	B
244	Entei	50
248	Tyranitar	B
261	Poochyena	E
295	Exploud	B
303	Mawile	E
309	Electrike	E
310	Manectric	B
371	Bagon	E
373	Salamence	B
403	Shinx	E
445	Garchomp	B
450	Hippowdon	B
452	Drapion	B
472	Gliscor	B
485	Heatran	17

Fire Punch

4	Charmander	T
5	Charmeleon	T
6	Charizard	T
31	Nidoqueen	T
34	Nidoking	T
35	Clefairy	T
36	Clefable	T
39	Jigglypuff	T
40	Wigglytuff	T
56	Mankey	T
57	Primeape	T
63	Abra	T,E
64	Kadabra	T
65	Alakazam	T
66	Machop	T,E
67	Machoke	T
68	Machamp	T
74	Geodude	T
75	Graveler	T
76	Golem	T
88	Grimer	T
89	Muk	T
92	Gastly	T,E
93	Haunter	T
94	Gengar	T
96	Drowzee	T,E
97	Hypno	T
104	Cubone	T
105	Marowak	T
107	Hitmonchan	31,T
108	Lickitung	T
112	Rhydon	T
113	Chansey	T
115	Kangaskhan	T
122	Mr. Mime	T
125	Electabuzz	T
126	Magmar	28,T
143	Snorlax	T
149	Dragonite	B,T
150	Mewtwo	T
151	Mew	T
157	Typhlosion	T
161	Sentret	T
162	Furret	T
180	Flaaffy	T
181	Ampharos	B,T
185	Sudowoodo	T
190	Aipom	T
209	Snubbull	T
210	Granbull	T
216	Teddiursa	T
217	Ursaring	T
239	Elekid	T,E
240	Magby	28,T
241	Miltank	T
242	Blissey	T
248	Tyranitar	T
256	Combusken	T
257	Blaziken	B,T
271	Lombre	T
272	Ludicolo	T
280	Ralts	T
281	Kirlia	T
282	Gardevoir	T
287	Slakoth	T
288	Vigoroth	T
289	Slaking	T
293	Whismur	T
294	Loudred	T
295	Exploud	T
296	Makuhita	T
297	Hariyama	T
299	Nosepass	T
302	Sableye	T
306	Aggron	T
307	Meditite	T,E
308	Medicham	B,T
316	Gulpin	T
317	Swalot	T
326	Grumpig	T
327	Spinda	T
330	Flygon	T
335	Zangoose	T
352	Kecleon	T
356	Dusclops	B,T
377	Regirock	T
383	Groudon	T
385	Jirachi	T
386	Deoxys (N)	T
390	Chimchar	T,E
391	Monferno	T
392	Infernape	T
408	Cranidos	T
409	Rampardos	T
424	Ambipom	T
427	Buneary	E
428	Lopunny	T
446	Munchlax	T
463	Lickilicky	T
464	Rhyperior	T
466	Electivire	B,T
467	Magmortar	28,T
475	Gallade	T
476	Probopass	T
477	Dusknoir	B,T
480	Uxie	T
481	Mesprit	T
482	Azelf	T
486	Regigigas	B,T

Fire Spin

4	Charmander	37
5	Charmeleon	43
6	Charizard	49
37	Vulpix	34
58	Growlithe	E
77	Ponyta	24
78	Rapidash	24
126	Magmar	19
136	Flareon	36
146	Moltres	8
228	Houndour	E
240	Magby	19
244	Entei	22
255	Torchic	25
324	Torkoal	17
338	Solrock	12
390	Chimchar	33
391	Monferno	39
392	Infernape	45
467	Magmortar	19
485	Heatran	57

Fissure

50	Diglett	40
51	Dugtrio	50
131	Lapras	E
143	Snorlax	E
220	Swinub	E
231	Phanpy	E
320	Wailmer	E
323	Camerupt	67
324	Torkoal	E
328	Trapinch	89
339	Barboach	47
340	Whiscash	57
363	Spheal	E
383	Groudon	60
410	Shieldon	E
413	Wormadam (S)	47
422	Shellos	E
449	Hippopotas	50
450	Hippowdon	60

Flail

7	Squirtle	E
27	Sandshrew	E
37	Vulpix	E
43	Oddish	E
46	Paras	E
52	Meowth	E
74	Geodude	E
83	Farfetch'd	E
84	Doduo	E
95	Onix	E
98	Krabby	45,E
99	Kingler	63
114	Tangela	E
116	Horsea	E
118	Goldeen	21
119	Seaking	21
127	Pinsir	E
129	Magikarp	30
133	Eevee	E
140	Kabuto	E
152	Chikorita	E
158	Totodile	22
159	Croconaw	24
160	Feraligatr	24
170	Chinchou	9,E
171	Lanturn	9
185	Sudowoodo	B,6
204	Pineco	E
206	Dunsparce	53
211	Qwilfish	E
214	Heracross	E
223	Remoraid	E
231	Phanpy	6
232	Donphan	B
263	Zigzagoon	33
270	Lotad	E
287	Slakoth	43
289	Slaking	43
324	Torkoal	52
327	Spinda	50
328	Trapinch	E
335	Zangoose	E
339	Barboach	E
349	Feebas	30
370	Luvdisc	46
393	Piplup	E
413	Wormadam (P)	38
413	Wormadam (S)	38
413	Wormadam (T)	38
417	Pachirisu	E
438	Bonsly	6
456	Finneon	E
480	Uxie	61

Flame Wheel

19	Rattata	E
58	Growlithe	20
77	Ponyta	15,E
78	Rapidash	15
155	Cyndaquil	19
156	Quilava	20
157	Typhlosion	20
390	Chimchar	17
391	Monferno	19
392	Infernape	21

Flamethrower

4	Charmander	34,TM
5	Charmeleon	39,TM
6	Charizard	42,TM
31	Nidoqueen	TM
34	Nidoking	TM
35	Clefairy	TM
36	Clefable	TM
37	Vulpix	24,TM
38	Ninetales	TM
39	Jigglypuff	TM
40	Wigglytuff	TM
58	Growlithe	34,TM
59	Arcanine	TM
66	Machop	TM
67	Machoke	TM
68	Machamp	TM
74	Geodude	TM
75	Graveler	TM
76	Golem	TM
77	Ponyta	TM
78	Rapidash	TM
79	Slowpoke	TM
80	Slowbro	TM
88	Grimer	TM
89	Muk	TM
104	Cubone	TM
105	Marowak	TM
108	Lickitung	TM
109	Koffing	TM
110	Weezing	TM
111	Rhyhorn	TM
112	Rhydon	TM
113	Chansey	TM
115	Kangaskhan	TM
126	Magmar	41,TM
128	Tauros	TM
130	Gyarados	TM
136	Flareon	TM
142	Aerodactyl	TM
143	Snorlax	TM
146	Moltres	36,TM
147	Dratini	TM
148	Dragonair	TM
149	Dragonite	TM
150	Mewtwo	TM
151	Mew	TM
155	Cyndaquil	37,TM
156	Quilava	42,TM
157	Typhlosion	42,TM
161	Sentret	TM
162	Furret	TM
173	Cleffa	TM
174	Igglybuff	TM
175	Togepi	TM
176	Togetic	TM
199	Slowking	TM
206	Dunsparce	TM
209	Snubbull	TM
210	Granbull	TM
218	Slugma	53,TM
219	Magcargo	61,TM
223	Remoraid	TM
224	Octillery	TM
228	Houndour	43,TM
229	Houndoom	48,TM
240	Magby	37,TM
242	Blissey	TM
244	Entei	36,TM
248	Tyranitar	TM
250	Ho-Oh	TM
255	Torchic	43,TM
256	Combusken	TM
257	Blaziken	TM
287	Slakoth	TM
288	Vigoroth	TM
289	Slaking	TM
293	Whismur	TM
294	Loudred	TM
295	Exploud	TM
303	Mawile	TM
306	Aggron	TM
309	Electrike	TM
310	Manectric	TM
322	Numel	45,TM
323	Camerupt	TM
324	Torkoal	28,TM
330	Flygon	TM
334	Altaria	TM
335	Zangoose	TM
336	Seviper	TM
338	Solrock	TM
351	Castform	TM
352	Kecleon	TM
359	Absol	TM
371	Bagon	TM
372	Shelgon	TM
373	Salamence	TM
383	Groudon	TM
384	Rayquaza	TM
390	Chimchar	41,TM
391	Monferno	TM
392	Infernape	TM
408	Cranidos	TM
409	Rampardos	TM
410	Shieldon	TM
411	Bastiodon	TM
434	Stunky	TM
435	Skuntank	34,TM
440	Happiny	TM
443	Gible	TM
444	Gabite	TM
445	Garchomp	TM
446	Munchlax	TM
463	Lickilicky	TM
464	Rhyperior	TM
466	Electivire	TM
467	Magmortar	43,TM
468	Togekiss	TM
482	Azelf	TM
483	Dialga	TM
484	Palkia	TM
485	Heatran	TM

Flare Blitz

4	Charmander	E
6	Charizard	66
37	Vulpix	E
58	Growlithe	48,E
77	Ponyta	46
78	Rapidash	56

155	Cyndaquil	E
240	Magby	E
256	Combusken	54
257	Blaziken	66
391	Monferno	49
392	Infernape	57

Flash

1	Bulbasaur	TM
2	Ivysaur	TM
3	Venusaur	TM
12	Butterfree	TM
15	Beedrill	TM
25	Pikachu	TM
26	Raichu	TM
35	Clefairy	TM
36	Clefable	TM
39	Jigglypuff	TM
40	Wigglytuff	TM
43	Oddish	TM
44	Gloom	TM
45	Vileplume	TM
46	Paras	TM
47	Parasect	TM
48	Venonat	TM
49	Venomoth	TM
52	Meowth	TM
53	Persian	TM
54	Psyduck	TM
55	Golduck	TM
63	Abra	TM
64	Kadabra	TM
65	Alakazam	TM
69	Bellsprout	TM
70	Weepinbell	TM
71	Victreebel	TM
79	Slowpoke	TM
80	Slowbro	TM
81	Magnemite	TM
82	Magneton	TM
96	Drowzee	TM
97	Hypno	TM
100	Voltorb	TM
101	Electrode	TM
102	Exeggcute	TM
103	Exeggutor	TM
109	Koffing	TM
110	Weezing	TM
113	Chansey	TM
114	Tangela	TM
120	Staryu	TM
121	Starmie	TM
122	Mr. Mime	TM
124	Jynx	TM
125	Electabuzz	TM
135	Jolteon	TM
137	Porygon	TM
145	Zapdos	TM
150	Mewtwo	TM
151	Mew	TM
152	Chikorita	TM
153	Bayleef	TM
154	Meganium	TM
165	Ledyba	TM
166	Ledian	TM
167	Spinarak	TM
168	Ariados	TM
170	Chinchou	TM
171	Lanturn	TM
172	Pichu	TM
173	Cleffa	TM
174	Igglybuff	TM
175	Togepi	TM
176	Togetic	TM
177	Natu	TM
178	Xatu	TM
179	Mareep	TM
180	Flaaffy	TM
181	Ampharos	TM
182	Bellossom	TM
187	Hoppip	TM
188	Skiploom	TM
189	Jumpluff	TM
191	Sunkern	TM
192	Sunflora	TM
193	Yanma	TM
194	Wooper	TM
195	Quagsire	TM
196	Espeon	TM
197	Umbreon	TM
199	Slowking	TM
200	Misdreavus	TM
203	Girafarig	TM
213	Shuckle	TM
227	Skarmory	TM
233	Porygon2	TM
234	Stantler	TM
238	Smoochum	TM
239	Elekid	TM
242	Blissey	TM
243	Raikou	TM
244	Entei	TM
249	Lugia	TM
250	Ho-Oh	TM
251	Celebi	TM
252	Treecko	TM
253	Grovyle	TM
254	Sceptile	TM
267	Beautifly	TM
269	Dustox	TM
270	Lotad	TM
271	Lombre	TM
272	Ludicolo	TM
273	Seedot	TM
274	Nuzleaf	TM
275	Shiftry	TM
280	Ralts	TM
281	Kirlia	TM
282	Gardevoir	TM
283	Surskit	TM
284	Masquerain	TM
285	Shroomish	TM
286	Breloom	TM
290	Nincada	TM
291	Ninjask	TM
292	Shedinja	TM
300	Skitty	TM
301	Delcatty	TM
302	Sableye	TM
307	Meditite	TM
308	Medicham	TM
309	Electrike	TM
310	Manectric	TM
311	Plusle	TM
312	Minun	TM
313	Volbeat	B,TM
314	Illumise	TM
315	Roselia	TM
325	Spoink	TM
326	Grumpig	TM
327	Spinda	TM
331	Cacnea	TM
332	Cacturne	TM
337	Lunatone	TM
338	Solrock	TM
343	Baltoy	TM
344	Claydol	TM
345	Lileep	TM
346	Cradily	TM
351	Castform	TM
352	Kecleon	TM
353	Shuppet	TM
354	Banette	TM
355	Duskull	TM
356	Dusclops	TM
357	Tropius	TM
358	Chimecho	TM
359	Absol	TM
361	Snorunt	TM
362	Glalie	TM
375	Metang	TM
376	Metagross	TM
380	Latias	TM
381	Latios	TM
385	Jirachi	TM
386	Deoxys (N)	TM
386	Deoxys (A)	TM
386	Deoxys (D)	TM
386	Deoxys (S)	TM
387	Turtwig	TM
388	Grotle	TM
389	Torterra	TM
402	Kricketune	TM
403	Shinx	TM
404	Luxio	TM
405	Luxray	TM
406	Budew	TM
407	Roserade	TM
413	Wormadam (P)	TM
413	Wormadam (S)	TM
413	Wormadam (T)	TM
414	Mothim	TM
416	Vespiquen	TM
417	Pachirisu	TM
420	Cherubi	TM
421	Cherrim	TM
423	Gastrodon	TM
425	Drifloon	TM
426	Drifblim	TM
429	Mismagius	TM
431	Glameow	TM
432	Purugly	TM
433	Chingling	TM
436	Bronzor	TM
437	Bronzong	TM
439	Mime Jr.	TM
440	Happiny	TM
442	Spiritomb	TM
451	Skorupi	TM
452	Drapion	TM
455	Carnivine	TM
456	Finneon	TM
457	Lumineon	TM
459	Snover	TM
460	Abomasnow	TM
462	Magnezone	TM
465	Tangrowth	TM
466	Electivire	TM
468	Togekiss	TM
469	Yanmega	TM
470	Leafeon	TM
474	Porygon-Z	TM
475	Gallade	TM
477	Dusknoir	TM
478	Froslass	TM
479	Rotom	TM
480	Uxie	TM
481	Mesprit	TM
482	Azelf	TM
483	Dialga	TM
488	Cresselia	TM
490	Manaphy	TM
491	Darkrai	TM
492	Shaymin (L)	TM
492	Shaymin (S)	TM

Flash Cannon

9	Blastoise	B,TM
81	Magnemite	TM
82	Magneton	TM
95	Onix	TM
116	Horsea	TM
117	Seadra	TM
120	Staryu	TM
121	Starmie	TM
151	Mew	TM
205	Forretress	TM
208	Steelix	TM
212	Scizor	TM
224	Octillery	TM
227	Skarmory	TM
230	Kingdra	TM
303	Mawile	TM
306	Aggron	TM
323	Camerupt	TM
348	Armaldo	TM
375	Metang	TM
376	Metagross	TM
378	Regice	TM
379	Registeel	73,TM
385	Jirachi	TM
386	Deoxys (N)	TM
386	Deoxys (A)	TM
386	Deoxys (D)	TM
386	Deoxys (S)	TM
395	Empoleon	TM
410	Shieldon	TM
411	Bastiodon	TM
413	Wormadam (T)	TM
436	Bronzor	TM
437	Bronzong	TM
448	Lucario	TM
462	Magnezone	TM
464	Rhyperior	TM
476	Probopass	TM
483	Dialga	80,TM
485	Heatran	TM

Flatter

29	Nidoran♀	33
30	Nidorina	38
32	Nidoran♂	33
33	Nidorino	38
96	Drowzee	E
179	Mareep	E
302	Sableye	E
314	Illumise	29
417	Pachirisu	E
453	Croagunk	45
454	Toxicroak	54

Fling

4	Charmander	TM
5	Charmeleon	TM
6	Charizard	TM
7	Squirtle	TM
8	Wartortle	TM
9	Blastoise	TM
25	Pikachu	TM
26	Raichu	TM
27	Sandshrew	TM
28	Sandslash	TM
31	Nidoqueen	TM
34	Nidoking	TM
35	Clefairy	TM
36	Clefable	TM
39	Jigglypuff	TM
40	Wigglytuff	TM
44	Gloom	TM
45	Vileplume	TM
54	Psyduck	TM
55	Golduck	TM
56	Mankey	TM
57	Primeape	B,TM
61	Poliwhirl	TM
62	Poliwrath	TM
63	Abra	TM
64	Kadabra	TM
65	Alakazam	TM
66	Machop	TM
67	Machoke	TM
68	Machamp	TM
74	Geodude	TM
75	Graveler	TM
76	Golem	TM
80	Slowbro	TM
86	Seel	TM
87	Dewgong	TM
88	Grimer	28,TM
89	Muk	28,TM
93	Haunter	TM
94	Gengar	TM
96	Drowzee	TM
97	Hypno	TM
98	Krabby	TM
99	Kingler	TM
104	Cubone	33,TM
105	Marowak	37,TM
106	Hitmonlee	TM
107	Hitmonchan	TM
108	Lickitung	TM
112	Rhydon	TM
113	Chansey	27,TM
115	Kangaskhan	TM
122	Mr. Mime	TM
124	Jynx	TM
125	Electabuzz	TM
126	Magmar	TM
127	Pinsir	TM
143	Snorlax	TM
149	Dragonite	TM
150	Mewtwo	TM
151	Mew	TM
157	Typhlosion	TM
158	Totodile	TM
159	Croconaw	TM
160	Feraligatr	TM
161	Sentret	TM
162	Furret	TM
165	Ledyba	TM
166	Ledian	TM
172	Pichu	TM
173	Cleffa	TM
174	Igglybuff	TM
175	Togepi	TM
176	Togetic	TM
180	Flaaffy	TM
181	Ampharos	TM
182	Bellossom	TM
183	Marill	TM
184	Azumarill	TM
185	Sudowoodo	TM
186	Politoed	TM
190	Aipom	36,TM
195	Quagsire	TM
199	Slowking	TM
207	Gligar	TM
209	Snubbull	TM
210	Granbull	TM
212	Scizor	TM
214	Heracross	TM
215	Sneasel	TM
216	Teddiursa	57,TM
217	Ursaring	TM
225	Delibird	TM
238	Smoochum	TM
239	Elekid	TM
240	Magby	TM
241	Miltank	TM
242	Blissey	27,TM
248	Tyranitar	TM
251	Celebi	TM
252	Treecko	TM
253	Grovyle	TM
254	Sceptile	TM
256	Combusken	TM
257	Blaziken	TM
259	Marshtomp	TM
260	Swampert	TM
263	Zigzagoon	45,TM
264	Linoone	59,TM
271	Lombre	TM
272	Ludicolo	TM
274	Nuzleaf	TM
275	Shiftry	TM
279	Pelipper	43,TM
280	Ralts	TM
281	Kirlia	TM
282	Gardevoir	TM
286	Breloom	TM
287	Slakoth	TM
288	Vigoroth	TM
289	Slaking	49,TM
293	Whismur	TM
294	Loudred	TM
295	Exploud	TM
296	Makuhita	TM
297	Hariyama	TM
302	Sableye	TM
303	Mawile	TM
306	Aggron	TM
307	Meditite	TM
308	Medicham	TM
311	Plusle	TM
312	Minun	TM
313	Volbeat	TM
314	Illumise	TM
326	Grumpig	TM
327	Spinda	TM
331	Cacnea	TM
332	Cacturne	TM
335	Zangoose	TM
341	Corphish	TM
342	Crawdaunt	TM
352	Kecleon	TM
354	Banette	TM
355	Duskull	TM
356	Dusclops	TM
377	Regirock	TM
378	Regice	TM
379	Registeel	TM
383	Groudon	TM
384	Rayquaza	TM
385	Jirachi	TM
386	Deoxys (N)	TM
386	Deoxys (A)	TM
386	Deoxys (D)	TM
386	Deoxys (S)	TM
390	Chimchar	TM
391	Monferno	TM
392	Infernape	TM
393	Piplup	TM
394	Prinplup	TM
395	Empoleon	TM
400	Bibarel	TM
408	Cranidos	TM
409	Rampardos	TM
416	Vespiquen	TM
417	Pachirisu	TM
424	Ambipom	36,TM
427	Buneary	TM
428	Lopunny	TM
439	Mime Jr.	TM
440	Happiny	TM
445	Garchomp	TM
446	Munchlax	36,TM
447	Riolu	TM
448	Lucario	TM
451	Skorupi	TM
452	Drapion	TM
453	Croagunk	TM
454	Toxicroak	TM
455	Carnivine	TM
460	Abomasnow	TM
461	Weavile	38,TM
463	Lickilicky	TM
464	Rhyperior	TM
465	Tangrowth	TM
466	Electivire	TM
467	Magmortar	TM
468	Togekiss	TM
472	Gliscor	TM
475	Gallade	TM
477	Dusknoir	TM
478	Froslass	TM
480	Uxie	TM
481	Mesprit	TM
482	Azelf	TM
484	Palkia	TM
486	Regigigas	TM
489	Phione	TM
490	Manaphy	TM
491	Darkrai	TM

Fly

6	Charizard	HM
16	Pidgey	HM
17	Pidgeotto	HM
18	Pidgeot	HM
21	Spearow	HM
22	Fearow	HM
41	Zubat	HM
42	Golbat	HM
83	Farfetch'd	HM
84	Doduo	HM
85	Dodrio	HM
142	Aerodactyl	HM
144	Articuno	HM
145	Zapdos	HM
146	Moltres	HM
149	Dragonite	HM
151	Mew	HM
163	Hoothoot	HM
164	Noctowl	HM
169	Crobat	HM
176	Togetic	HM
178	Xatu	HM
198	Murkrow	HM
225	Delibird	HM
227	Skarmory	HM
249	Lugia	HM
250	Ho-Oh	HM
276	Taillow	HM
277	Swellow	HM
278	Wingull	HM
279	Pelipper	HM
329	Vibrava	HM
330	Flygon	HM
333	Swablu	HM
334	Altaria	HM
357	Tropius	HM
373	Salamence	50,HM
380	Latias	HM
381	Latios	HM
384	Rayquaza	45,HM
396	Starly	HM
397	Staravia	HM
398	Staraptor	HM
426	Drifblim	HM
430	Honchkrow	HM
441	Chatot	HM
468	Togekiss	HM
487	Giratina (A)	HM
487	Giratina (O)	HM

Focus Blast

6	Charizard	TM
9	Blastoise	TM
26	Raichu	TM
28	Sandslash	TM
31	Nidoqueen	TM
34	Nidoking	TM
36	Clefable	TM
40	Wigglytuff	TM
55	Golduck	TM
56	Mankey	TM
57	Primeape	TM
62	Poliwrath	TM
65	Alakazam	TM
66	Machop	TM
67	Machoke	TM
68	Machamp	TM
76	Golem	TM
80	Slowbro	TM
89	Muk	TM
94	Gengar	TM
97	Hypno	TM
105	Marowak	TM
106	Hitmonlee	TM
107	Hitmonchan	TM
112	Rhydon	TM
115	Kangaskhan	TM
122	Mr. Mime	TM
124	Jynx	TM
125	Electabuzz	TM
126	Magmar	TM
127	Pinsir	TM
143	Snorlax	TM
149	Dragonite	TM
150	Mewtwo	TM
151	Mew	TM
157	Typhlosion	TM
160	Feraligatr	TM
162	Furret	TM
166	Ledian	TM
181	Ampharos	TM
184	Azumarill	TM
186	Politoed	TM
195	Quagsire	TM
199	Slowking	TM
210	Granbull	TM
214	Heracross	TM
217	Ursaring	TM
241	Miltank	TM
242	Blissey	TM
248	Tyranitar	TM
254	Sceptile	TM
256	Combusken	TM
257	Blaziken	TM
260	Swampert	TM
272	Ludicolo	TM
275	Shiftry	TM
282	Gardevoir	TM
286	Breloom	TM
288	Vigoroth	TM
289	Slaking	TM
295	Exploud	TM
296	Makuhita	TM
297	Hariyama	TM
303	Mawile	TM
306	Aggron	TM
307	Meditite	TM
308	Medicham	TM
326	Grumpig	TM
332	Cacturne	TM
335	Zangoose	TM
377	Regirock	TM
378	Regice	TM
379	Registeel	TM
383	Groudon	TM
384	Rayquaza	TM
386	Deoxys (N)	TM
386	Deoxys (A)	TM
386	Deoxys (D)	TM
386	Deoxys (S)	TM
391	Monferno	TM
392	Infernape	TM
409	Rampardos	TM
419	Floatzel	TM
428	Lopunny	TM
447	Riolu	TM
448	Lucario	TM
453	Croagunk	TM
454	Toxicroak	TM
460	Abomasnow	TM
461	Weavile	TM
463	Lickilicky	TM
464	Rhyperior	TM
465	Tangrowth	TM
466	Electivire	TM
467	Magmortar	TM
475	Gallade	TM
477	Dusknoir	TM
484	Palkia	TM
486	Regigigas	TM
491	Darkrai	TM

Focus Energy

15	Beedrill	13
19	Rattata	7
20	Raticate	B,7
29	Nidoran♀	E
32	Nidoran♂	7
33	Nidorino	7
34	Nidoking	B
56	Mankey	B
57	Primeape	B
66	Machop	7
67	Machoke	B,7
68	Machamp	B,7
104	Cubone	17
105	Marowak	17
106	Hitmonlee	21
115	Kangaskhan	E
116	Horsea	14
117	Seadra	14
123	Scyther	5
127	Pinsir	B
161	Sentret	E
212	Scizor	5
223	Remoraid	23
224	Octillery	23
230	Kingdra	14
231	Phanpy	E
237	Hitmontop	6
246	Larvitar	E
255	Torchic	7
256	Combusken	B,7
257	Blaziken	B,7
276	Taillow	4
277	Swellow	B,4
288	Vigoroth	B
296	Makuhita	B
297	Hariyama	B
318	Carvanha	8
319	Sharpedo	B,8
322	Numel	15
323	Camerupt	15
328	Trapinch	E
371	Bagon	20
372	Shelgon	20
373	Salamence	20
390	Chimchar	E
402	Kricketune	22
408	Cranidos	6
409	Rampardos	6
410	Shieldon	E
425	Drifloon	14
426	Drifblim	14
434	Stunky	B
435	Skuntank	B

Focus Punch

4	Charmander	TM
5	Charmeleon	TM
6	Charizard	TM
7	Squirtle	TM
8	Wartortle	TM
9	Blastoise	TM
25	Pikachu	TM
26	Raichu	TM
27	Sandshrew	TM
28	Sandslash	TM
31	Nidoqueen	TM
34	Nidoking	TM
35	Clefairy	TM
36	Clefable	TM
39	Jigglypuff	TM
40	Wigglytuff	TM
54	Psyduck	TM
55	Golduck	TM
56	Mankey	TM
57	Primeape	TM
61	Poliwhirl	TM
62	Poliwrath	TM
63	Abra	TM
64	Kadabra	TM
65	Alakazam	TM
66	Machop	TM
67	Machoke	TM
68	Machamp	TM
74	Geodude	TM
75	Graveler	TM
76	Golem	TM
80	Slowbro	TM
89	Muk	TM
94	Gengar	TM
96	Drowzee	TM
97	Hypno	TM
104	Cubone	TM
105	Marowak	TM
106	Hitmonlee	TM
107	Hitmonchan	TM
108	Lickitung	TM
112	Rhydon	TM
113	Chansey	TM
115	Kangaskhan	TM
122	Mr. Mime	TM
124	Jynx	TM
125	Electabuzz	TM
126	Magmar	TM
127	Pinsir	TM
143	Snorlax	TM
149	Dragonite	TM
150	Mewtwo	TM
151	Mew	TM
156	Quilava	TM
157	Typhlosion	TM
158	Totodile	TM
159	Croconaw	TM
160	Feraligatr	TM
161	Sentret	TM
162	Furret	TM
165	Ledyba	TM
166	Ledian	TM
176	Togetic	TM
180	Flaaffy	TM
181	Ampharos	TM
183	Marill	TM
184	Azumarill	TM
185	Sudowoodo	TM
186	Politoed	TM
190	Aipom	TM
195	Quagsire	TM
199	Slowking	TM
209	Snubbull	TM
210	Granbull	TM
214	Heracross	TM
215	Sneasel	TM
216	Teddiursa	TM
217	Ursaring	TM
225	Delibird	TM
239	Elekid	TM
240	Magby	TM
241	Miltank	TM
242	Blissey	TM
248	Tyranitar	TM
252	Treecko	TM
253	Grovyle	TM
254	Sceptile	TM
256	Combusken	TM
257	Blaziken	TM
260	Swampert	TM
272	Ludicolo	TM
286	Breloom	TM
287	Slakoth	TM
288	Vigoroth	43,TM
289	Slaking	TM
296	Makuhita	TM
297	Hariyama	TM
302	Sableye	TM
303	Mawile	TM
306	Aggron	TM
307	Meditite	TM
308	Medicham	TM
313	Volbeat	TM
314	Illumise	TM
326	Grumpig	TM
327	Spinda	TM
331	Cacnea	TM
332	Cacturne	TM
335	Zangoose	TM
352	Kecleon	TM
356	Dusclops	TM
377	Regirock	TM
378	Regice	TM
379	Registeel	TM
386	Deoxys (N)	TM
386	Deoxys (A)	TM
386	Deoxys (D)	TM
386	Deoxys (S)	TM
390	Chimchar	TM
391	Monferno	TM
392	Infernape	TM
400	Bibarel	TM
409	Rampardos	TM
418	Buizel	TM
419	Floatzel	TM
424	Ambipom	TM
427	Buneary	TM
428	Lopunny	TM
439	Mime Jr.	TM
446	Munchlax	TM
447	Riolu	TM
448	Lucario	TM
453	Croagunk	TM
454	Toxicroak	TM
460	Abomasnow	TM
461	Weavile	TM
463	Lickilicky	TM
464	Rhyperior	TM
466	Electivire	TM
467	Magmortar	TM
468	Togekiss	TM
475	Gallade	TM
477	Dusknoir	TM
484	Palkia	TM
486	Regigigas	TM
491	Darkrai	TM

Follow Me

35	Clefairy	16
161	Sentret	19
162	Furret	21
175	Togepi	24
176	Togetic	24

Force Palm

286	Breloom	29
296	Makuhita	28
297	Hariyama	32
307	Meditite	29
308	Medicham	29
447	Riolu	11
448	Lucario	11

Foresight

7	Squirtle	E
16	Pidgey	E
48	Venonat	B
49	Venomoth	B
54	Psyduck	E
56	Mankey	E
66	Machop	13
67	Machoke	13
68	Machamp	13
83	Farfetch'd	E
106	Hitmonlee	37
115	Kangaskhan	E
131	Lapras	E
142	Aerodactyl	E
155	Cyndaquil	E
161	Sentret	B
162	Furret	B
163	Hoothoot	B
164	Noctowl	B
175	Togepi	E
193	Yanma	B
203	Girafarig	E
215	Sneasel	E
236	Tyrogue	B
258	Mudkip	19
259	Marshtomp	20
260	Swampert	20
283	Surskit	E
296	Makuhita	E
300	Skitty	4
302	Sableye	4
307	Meditite	E
353	Shuppet	E
355	Duskull	9
356	Dusclops	9
396	Starly	E
427	Buneary	B
428	Lopunny	B
447	Riolu	B
448	Lucario	B
469	Yanmega	B
477	Dusknoir	9
486	Regigigas	B

Frenzy Plant

3	Venusaur	T
154	Meganium	T
254	Sceptile	T
389	Torterra	T

Frustration

1	Bulbasaur	TM
2	Ivysaur	TM
3	Venusaur	TM
4	Charmander	TM
5	Charmeleon	TM
6	Charizard	TM
7	Squirtle	TM
8	Wartortle	TM
9	Blastoise	TM
12	Butterfree	TM
15	Beedrill	TM
16	Pidgey	TM
17	Pidgeotto	TM
18	Pidgeot	TM
19	Rattata	TM
20	Raticate	TM
21	Spearow	TM
22	Fearow	TM
23	Ekans	TM
24	Arbok	TM
25	Pikachu	TM
26	Raichu	TM
27	Sandshrew	TM
28	Sandslash	TM
29	Nidoran♀	TM
30	Nidorina	TM
31	Nidoqueen	TM
32	Nidoran♂	TM
33	Nidorino	TM
34	Nidoking	TM
35	Clefairy	TM
36	Clefable	TM
37	Vulpix	TM
38	Ninetales	TM
39	Jigglypuff	TM
40	Wigglytuff	TM
41	Zubat	TM
42	Golbat	TM
43	Oddish	TM
44	Gloom	TM
45	Vileplume	TM
46	Paras	TM
47	Parasect	TM
48	Venonat	TM
49	Venomoth	TM
50	Diglett	TM
51	Dugtrio	TM
52	Meowth	TM
53	Persian	TM
54	Psyduck	TM
55	Golduck	TM
56	Mankey	TM
57	Primeape	TM
58	Growlithe	TM
59	Arcanine	TM
60	Poliwag	TM
61	Poliwhirl	TM
62	Poliwrath	TM
63	Abra	TM
64	Kadabra	TM
65	Alakazam	TM
66	Machop	TM
67	Machoke	TM
68	Machamp	TM
69	Bellsprout	TM
70	Weepinbell	TM
71	Victreebel	TM
72	Tentacool	TM
73	Tentacruel	TM
74	Geodude	TM
75	Graveler	TM
76	Golem	TM
77	Ponyta	TM
78	Rapidash	TM
79	Slowpoke	TM
80	Slowbro	TM
81	Magnemite	TM
82	Magneton	TM
83	Farfetch'd	TM
84	Doduo	TM
85	Dodrio	TM
86	Seel	TM
87	Dewgong	TM
88	Grimer	TM
89	Muk	TM
90	Shellder	TM
91	Cloyster	TM
92	Gastly	TM
93	Haunter	TM
94	Gengar	TM
95	Onix	TM
96	Drowzee	TM
97	Hypno	TM
98	Krabby	TM
99	Kingler	TM
100	Voltorb	TM
101	Electrode	TM
102	Exeggcute	TM
103	Exeggutor	TM
104	Cubone	TM
105	Marowak	TM
106	Hitmonlee	TM
107	Hitmonchan	TM
108	Lickitung	TM
109	Koffing	TM
110	Weezing	TM
111	Rhyhorn	TM
112	Rhydon	TM
113	Chansey	TM
114	Tangela	TM
115	Kangaskhan	TM
116	Horsea	TM
117	Seadra	TM
118	Goldeen	TM
119	Seaking	TM
120	Staryu	TM
121	Starmie	TM
122	Mr. Mime	TM
123	Scyther	TM
124	Jynx	TM
125	Electabuzz	TM
126	Magmar	TM
127	Pinsir	TM
128	Tauros	TM
130	Gyarados	TM
131	Lapras	TM
133	Eevee	TM
134	Vaporeon	TM
135	Jolteon	TM
136	Flareon	TM
137	Porygon	TM
138	Omanyte	TM
139	Omastar	TM
140	Kabuto	TM
141	Kabutops	TM
142	Aerodactyl	TM
143	Snorlax	TM
144	Articuno	TM
145	Zapdos	TM
146	Moltres	TM
147	Dratini	TM
148	Dragonair	TM
149	Dragonite	TM
150	Mewtwo	TM
151	Mew	TM
152	Chikorita	TM
153	Bayleef	TM
154	Meganium	TM
155	Cyndaquil	TM
156	Quilava	TM
157	Typhlosion	TM
158	Totodile	TM
159	Croconaw	TM
160	Feraligatr	TM
161	Sentret	TM
162	Furret	TM
163	Hoothoot	TM
164	Noctowl	TM
165	Ledyba	TM
166	Ledian	TM
167	Spinarak	TM
168	Ariados	TM
169	Crobat	TM
170	Chinchou	TM
171	Lanturn	TM
172	Pichu	TM
173	Cleffa	TM
174	Igglybuff	TM
175	Togepi	TM
176	Togetic	TM
177	Natu	TM
178	Xatu	TM
179	Mareep	TM
180	Flaaffy	TM
181	Ampharos	TM
182	Bellossom	TM
183	Marill	TM
184	Azumarill	TM
185	Sudowoodo	TM
186	Politoed	TM
187	Hoppip	TM
188	Skiploom	TM
189	Jumpluff	TM
190	Aipom	TM
191	Sunkern	TM
192	Sunflora	TM
193	Yanma	TM
194	Wooper	TM
195	Quagsire	TM
196	Espeon	TM
197	Umbreon	TM
198	Murkrow	TM
199	Slowking	TM
200	Misdreavus	TM
203	Girafarig	TM
204	Pineco	TM
205	Forretress	TM
206	Dunsparce	TM
207	Gligar	TM
208	Steelix	TM
209	Snubbull	TM
210	Granbull	TM
211	Qwilfish	TM
212	Scizor	TM
213	Shuckle	TM
214	Heracross	TM
215	Sneasel	TM
216	Teddiursa	TM
217	Ursaring	TM
218	Slugma	TM
219	Magcargo	TM
220	Swinub	TM
221	Piloswine	TM
222	Corsola	TM
223	Remoraid	TM
224	Octillery	TM
225	Delibird	TM
226	Mantine	TM
227	Skarmory	TM
228	Houndour	TM
229	Houndoom	TM
230	Kingdra	TM
231	Phanpy	TM
232	Donphan	TM
233	Porygon2	TM
234	Stantler	TM
236	Tyrogue	TM
237	Hitmontop	TM
238	Smoochum	TM
239	Elekid	TM
240	Magby	TM
241	Miltank	TM
242	Blissey	TM
243	Raikou	TM
244	Entei	TM
245	Suicune	TM
246	Larvitar	TM
247	Pupitar	TM
248	Tyranitar	TM
249	Lugia	TM
250	Ho-Oh	TM
251	Celebi	TM
252	Treecko	TM
253	Grovyle	TM
254	Sceptile	TM
255	Torchic	TM
256	Combusken	TM
257	Blaziken	TM
258	Mudkip	TM
259	Marshtomp	TM
260	Swampert	TM
261	Poochyena	TM
262	Mightyena	TM
263	Zigzagoon	TM
264	Linoone	TM
267	Beautifly	TM
269	Dustox	TM
270	Lotad	TM
271	Lombre	TM
272	Ludicolo	TM
273	Seedot	TM
274	Nuzleaf	TM
275	Shiftry	TM
276	Taillow	TM
277	Swellow	TM
278	Wingull	TM
279	Pelipper	TM
280	Ralts	TM
281	Kirlia	TM
282	Gardevoir	TM
283	Surskit	TM
284	Masquerain	TM
285	Shroomish	TM
286	Breloom	TM
287	Slakoth	TM
288	Vigoroth	TM
289	Slaking	TM
290	Nincada	TM
291	Ninjask	TM
292	Shedinja	TM
293	Whismur	TM
294	Loudred	TM
295	Exploud	TM
296	Makuhita	TM
297	Hariyama	TM
298	Azurill	TM
299	Nosepass	TM
300	Skitty	TM
301	Delcatty	TM
302	Sableye	TM
303	Mawile	TM
304	Aron	TM
305	Lairon	TM
306	Aggron	TM
307	Meditite	TM
308	Medicham	TM
309	Electrike	TM
310	Manectric	TM
311	Plusle	TM
312	Minun	TM
313	Volbeat	TM
314	Illumise	TM
315	Roselia	TM
316	Gulpin	TM
317	Swalot	TM
318	Carvanha	TM
319	Sharpedo	TM
320	Wailmer	TM
321	Wailord	TM
322	Numel	TM
323	Camerupt	TM
324	Torkoal	TM
325	Spoink	TM
326	Grumpig	TM
327	Spinda	TM
328	Trapinch	TM
329	Vibrava	TM
330	Flygon	TM
331	Cacnea	TM
332	Cacturne	TM
333	Swablu	TM
334	Altaria	TM
335	Zangoose	TM
336	Seviper	TM
337	Lunatone	TM
338	Solrock	TM
339	Barboach	TM
340	Whiscash	TM
341	Corphish	TM
342	Crawdaunt	TM
343	Baltoy	TM
344	Claydol	TM
345	Lileep	TM
346	Cradily	TM
347	Anorith	TM
348	Armaldo	TM
349	Feebas	TM
350	Milotic	TM
351	Castform	TM
352	Kecleon	TM
353	Shuppet	TM
354	Banette	TM
355	Duskull	TM
356	Dusclops	TM
357	Tropius	TM
358	Chimecho	TM
359	Absol	TM
361	Snorunt	TM
362	Glalie	TM
363	Spheal	TM
364	Sealeo	TM
365	Walrein	TM
366	Clamperl	TM
367	Huntail	TM
368	Gorebyss	TM
369	Relicanth	TM
370	Luvdisc	TM
371	Bagon	TM
372	Shelgon	TM
373	Salamence	TM
375	Metang	TM
376	Metagross	TM
377	Regirock	TM
378	Regice	TM
379	Registeel	TM
380	Latias	TM
381	Latios	TM
382	Kyogre	TM
383	Groudon	TM
384	Rayquaza	TM
385	Jirachi	TM
386	Deoxys (N)	TM
386	Deoxys (A)	TM
386	Deoxys (D)	TM
386	Deoxys (S)	TM
387	Turtwig	TM
388	Grotle	TM
389	Torterra	TM
390	Chimchar	TM
391	Monferno	TM
392	Infernape	TM
393	Piplup	TM
394	Prinplup	TM
395	Empoleon	TM
396	Starly	TM
397	Staravia	TM
398	Staraptor	TM
399	Bidoof	TM
400	Bibarel	TM
402	Kricketune	TM
403	Shinx	TM
404	Luxio	TM
405	Luxray	TM
406	Budew	TM
407	Roserade	TM
408	Cranidos	TM
409	Rampardos	TM
410	Shieldon	TM
411	Bastiodon	TM
413	Wormadam (P)	TM
413	Wormadam (S)	TM
413	Wormadam (T)	TM
414	Mothim	TM
416	Vespiquen	TM
417	Pachirisu	TM
418	Buizel	TM
419	Floatzel	TM
420	Cherubi	TM
421	Cherrim	TM
422	Shellos	TM
423	Gastrodon	TM
424	Ambipom	TM
425	Drifloon	TM
426	Drifblim	TM
427	Buneary	13,TM
428	Lopunny	TM
429	Mismagius	TM
430	Honchkrow	TM
431	Glameow	TM
432	Purugly	TM
433	Chingling	TM
434	Stunky	TM
435	Skuntank	TM
436	Bronzor	TM
437	Bronzong	TM
438	Bonsly	TM
439	Mime Jr.	TM
440	Happiny	TM
441	Chatot	TM
442	Spiritomb	TM
443	Gible	TM
444	Gabite	TM
445	Garchomp	TM
446	Munchlax	TM
447	Riolu	TM
448	Lucario	TM
449	Hippopotas	TM
450	Hippowdon	TM
451	Skorupi	TM
452	Drapion	TM
453	Croagunk	TM
454	Toxicroak	TM
455	Carnivine	TM
456	Finneon	TM
457	Lumineon	TM
458	Mantyke	TM
459	Snover	TM
460	Abomasnow	TM
461	Weavile	TM
462	Magnezone	TM
463	Lickilicky	TM
464	Rhyperior	TM
465	Tangrowth	TM
466	Electivire	TM
467	Magmortar	TM
468	Togekiss	TM
469	Yanmega	TM
470	Leafeon	TM
471	Glaceon	TM
472	Gliscor	TM
473	Mamoswine	TM
474	Porygon-Z	TM
475	Gallade	TM
476	Probopass	TM
477	Dusknoir	TM
478	Froslass	TM
479	Rotom	TM
480	Uxie	TM
481	Mesprit	TM
482	Azelf	TM
483	Dialga	TM
484	Palkia	TM
485	Heatran	TM
486	Regigigas	TM
487	Giratina (A)	TM
487	Giratina (O)	TM
488	Cresselia	TM

489	Phione	TM
490	Manaphy	TM
491	Darkrai	TM
492	Shaymin (L)	TM
492	Shaymin (S)	TM

Fury Attack		
15	Beedrill	B,10
21	Spearow	9
22	Fearow	B,9
32	Nidoran♂	19
33	Nidorino	20
78	Rapidash	40
83	Farfetch'd	7
84	Doduo	14
85	Dodrio	14
111	Rhyhorn	13
112	Rhydon	B,13
118	Goldeen	31
119	Seaking	31
127	Pinsir	E
214	Heracross	7
221	Piloswine	33
227	Skarmory	17
232	Donphan	25
333	Swablu	13
334	Altaria	13
393	Piplup	25
394	Prinplup	28
395	Empoleon	28
396	Starly	E
441	Chatot	17
464	Rhyperior	B,13

Fury Cutter		
1	Bulbasaur	T
2	Ivysaur	T
3	Venusaur	T
4	Charmander	T
5	Charmeleon	T
6	Charizard	T
15	Beedrill	T
27	Sandshrew	25,T
28	Sandslash	28,T
31	Nidoqueen	T
34	Nidoking	T
46	Paras	T
47	Parasect	T
55	Golduck	T
76	Golem	T
80	Slowbro	T
83	Farfetch'd	B,T
98	Krabby	T
99	Kingler	T
104	Cubone	T
105	Marowak	T
112	Rhydon	T
115	Kangaskhan	T
118	Goldeen	T
119	Seaking	T
123	Scyther	25,T
127	Pinsir	T
141	Kabutops	T
149	Dragonite	T
151	Mew	T
152	Chikorita	T
153	Bayleef	T
154	Meganium	T
156	Quilava	T
157	Typhlosion	T
159	Croconaw	T
160	Feraligatr	T
161	Sentret	T
162	Furret	T
190	Aipom	T
199	Slowking	T
207	Gligar	20,T
212	Scizor	25,T
214	Heracross	T
215	Sneasel	T
216	Teddiursa	T
217	Ursaring	T
227	Skarmory	T
248	Tyranitar	T
252	Treecko	T
253	Grovyle	16,T
254	Sceptile	T
256	Combusken	T
257	Blaziken	T
263	Zigzagoon	T
264	Linoone	T
274	Nuzleaf	T
275	Shiftry	T
286	Breloom	T
287	Slakoth	T
288	Vigoroth	T
289	Slaking	T
290	Nincada	T
291	Ninjask	20,T
292	Shedinja	T
302	Sableye	T
304	Aron	T
305	Lairon	T
306	Aggron	T
315	Roselia	T
318	Carvanha	T
319	Sharpedo	T
328	Trapinch	T,E
329	Vibrava	T
330	Flygon	T
331	Cacnea	T
332	Cacturne	T
335	Zangoose	14,T
336	Seviper	T
341	Corphish	T
342	Crawdaunt	T
347	Anorith	37,T
348	Armaldo	37,T
352	Kecleon	T
357	Tropius	T
359	Absol	T
365	Walrein	T
371	Bagon	T
372	Shelgon	T
373	Salamence	T
375	Metang	T
376	Metagross	T
380	Latias	T
381	Latios	T
383	Groudon	T
384	Rayquaza	T
395	Empoleon	T
399	Bidoof	T
400	Bibarel	T
402	Kricketune	10,T
403	Shinx	T
404	Luxio	T
405	Luxray	T
407	Roserade	T
416	Vespiquen	9,T
418	Buizel	E
424	Ambipom	T
428	Lopunny	T
431	Glameow	T
432	Purugly	T
434	Stunky	T
435	Skuntank	T
443	Gible	T
444	Gabite	T
445	Garchomp	T
447	Riolu	T
448	Lucario	T
451	Skorupi	T
452	Drapion	T
453	Croagunk	T
454	Toxicroak	T
455	Carnivine	T
461	Weavile	T
464	Rhyperior	T
470	Leafeon	T
472	Gliscor	20,T
473	Mamoswine	T
475	Gallade	17,T
483	Dialga	T
484	Palkia	T
487	Giratina (A)	T
487	Giratina (O)	T
488	Cresselia	T

Fury Swipes		
19	Rattata	E
27	Sandshrew	19
28	Sandslash	19
29	Nidoran♀	19
30	Nidorina	20
52	Meowth	14
53	Persian	14
54	Psyduck	27
55	Golduck	27
56	Mankey	9
57	Primeape	9
155	Cyndaquil	E
161	Sentret	13
162	Furret	13
167	Spinarak	22
168	Ariados	23
190	Aipom	18
215	Sneasel	21
216	Teddiursa	8
217	Ursaring	8
264	Linoone	29
271	Lombre	15
288	Vigoroth	19
290	Nincada	14
291	Ninjask	14
292	Shedinja	14
302	Sableye	15
335	Zangoose	E
352	Kecleon	10
390	Chimchar	15
391	Monferno	16
392	Infernape	17
399	Bidoof	E
416	Vespiquen	19
418	Buizel	E
424	Ambipom	18
431	Glameow	20
432	Purugly	20
434	Stunky	10
435	Skuntank	10
461	Weavile	21

Future Sight		
54	Psyduck	E
64	Kadabra	42
65	Alakazam	42
79	Slowpoke	E
96	Drowzee	53
97	Hypno	69
122	Mr. Mime	E
150	Mewtwo	22
175	Togepi	E
177	Natu	36
178	Xatu	42
183	Marill	E
196	Espeon	43
203	Girafarig	E
225	Delibird	E
249	Lugia	79
250	Ho-Oh	79
251	Celebi	64
280	Ralts	34
281	Kirlia	39
282	Gardevoir	45
325	Spoink	E
337	Lunatone	53
339	Barboach	43
340	Whiscash	51
351	Castform	E
355	Duskull	46
356	Dusclops	61
358	Chimecho	E
359	Absol	41
385	Jirachi	55
433	Chingling	E
436	Bronzor	37
437	Bronzong	43
439	Mime Jr.	E
477	Dusknoir	61
480	Uxie	36
481	Mesprit	36
482	Azelf	36
488	Cresselia	38

Gastro Acid		
23	Ekans	33,T
24	Arbok	42,T
43	Oddish	T
44	Gloom	T
45	Vileplume	T
69	Bellsprout	35,T
70	Weepinbell	35,T
71	Victreebel	T
151	Mew	T
182	Bellossom	T
213	Shuckle	35,T
316	Gulpin	44,T
317	Swalot	52,T
345	Lileep	36,T
346	Cradily	46,T
455	Carnivine	T

Giga Drain		
1	Bulbasaur	TM
2	Ivysaur	TM
3	Venusaur	TM
12	Butterfree	TM
15	Beedrill	TM
23	Ekans	TM
24	Arbok	TM
41	Zubat	TM
42	Golbat	TM
43	Oddish	37,TM
44	Gloom	47,TM
45	Vileplume	TM
46	Paras	33,TM
47	Parasect	39,TM
48	Venonat	TM,E
49	Venomoth	TM
69	Bellsprout	TM
70	Weepinbell	TM
71	Victreebel	TM
72	Tentacool	TM
73	Tentacruel	TM
88	Grimer	TM
89	Muk	TM
92	Gastly	TM
93	Haunter	TM
94	Gengar	TM
102	Exeggcute	TM
103	Exeggutor	TM
114	Tangela	TM
140	Kabuto	TM
141	Kabutops	TM
151	Mew	TM
152	Chikorita	TM
153	Bayleef	TM
154	Meganium	TM
165	Ledyba	TM
166	Ledian	TM
167	Spinarak	TM
168	Ariados	TM
169	Crobat	TM
177	Natu	TM
178	Xatu	TM
182	Bellossom	TM
187	Hoppip	37,TM
188	Skiploom	44,TM
189	Jumpluff	44,TM
191	Sunkern	41,TM
192	Sunflora	TM
193	Yanma	TM
204	Pineco	TM
205	Forretress	TM
249	Lugia	TM
250	Ho-Oh	TM
251	Celebi	TM
252	Treecko	46,TM
253	Grovyle	TM
254	Sceptile	TM
267	Beautifly	38,TM
269	Dustox	TM
270	Lotad	TM
271	Lombre	TM
272	Ludicolo	TM
273	Seedot	TM
274	Nuzleaf	TM
275	Shiftry	TM
283	Surskit	TM
284	Masquerain	TM
285	Shroomish	37,TM
286	Breloom	TM
290	Nincada	TM
291	Ninjask	TM
292	Shedinja	TM
313	Volbeat	TM
314	Illumise	TM
315	Roselia	25,TM
316	Gulpin	TM
317	Swalot	TM
328	Trapinch	TM
329	Vibrava	TM
330	Flygon	TM
331	Cacnea	TM
332	Cacturne	TM
335	Zangoose	TM
336	Seviper	TM
345	Lileep	TM
346	Cradily	TM
357	Tropius	TM
387	Turtwig	41,TM
388	Grotle	47,TM
389	Torterra	51,TM
406	Budew	TM
407	Roserade	TM
413	Wormadam (P)	TM
414	Mothim	TM
420	Cherubi	TM
421	Cherrim	TM
455	Carnivine	TM
459	Snover	TM
460	Abomasnow	TM
465	Tangrowth	TM
469	Yanmega	TM
470	Leafeon	43,TM
480	Uxie	TM
492	Shaymin (L)	TM
492	Shaymin (S)	TM

Giga Impact		
3	Venusaur	TM
6	Charizard	TM
9	Blastoise	TM
12	Butterfree	TM
15	Beedrill	TM
18	Pidgeot	TM
20	Raticate	TM
22	Fearow	TM
24	Arbok	TM
26	Raichu	TM
28	Sandslash	TM
31	Nidoqueen	TM
34	Nidoking	TM
36	Clefable	TM
38	Ninetales	TM
40	Wigglytuff	TM
42	Golbat	TM
45	Vileplume	TM
47	Parasect	TM
49	Venomoth	TM
51	Dugtrio	TM
53	Persian	TM
55	Golduck	TM
57	Primeape	TM
59	Arcanine	TM
62	Poliwrath	TM
65	Alakazam	TM
68	Machamp	TM
71	Victreebel	TM
73	Tentacruel	TM
76	Golem	TM
78	Rapidash	TM
80	Slowbro	TM
82	Magneton	TM
85	Dodrio	TM
87	Dewgong	TM
89	Muk	TM
91	Cloyster	TM
94	Gengar	TM
97	Hypno	TM
99	Kingler	TM
101	Electrode	TM
103	Exeggutor	TM
105	Marowak	TM
108	Lickitung	TM
110	Weezing	TM
112	Rhydon	TM
113	Chansey	TM
114	Tangela	TM
115	Kangaskhan	TM
117	Seadra	TM
119	Seaking	TM
121	Starmie	TM
122	Mr. Mime	TM
123	Scyther	TM
124	Jynx	TM
125	Electabuzz	TM
126	Magmar	TM
127	Pinsir	TM
128	Tauros	55,TM
130	Gyarados	TM
131	Lapras	TM
134	Vaporeon	TM
135	Jolteon	TM
136	Flareon	TM
137	Porygon	TM
139	Omastar	TM
141	Kabutops	TM
142	Aerodactyl	73,TM
143	Snorlax	49,TM
144	Articuno	TM
145	Zapdos	TM
146	Moltres	TM
149	Dragonite	TM
150	Mewtwo	TM
151	Mew	TM
154	Meganium	TM
157	Typhlosion	TM
160	Feraligatr	TM
162	Furret	TM
164	Noctowl	TM
166	Ledian	TM
168	Ariados	TM
169	Crobat	TM
171	Lanturn	TM
176	Togetic	TM
178	Xatu	TM
181	Ampharos	TM
182	Bellossom	TM
184	Azumarill	TM
186	Politoed	TM
189	Jumpluff	TM
192	Sunflora	TM
195	Quagsire	TM
196	Espeon	TM
197	Umbreon	TM
199	Slowking	TM
205	Forretress	TM
208	Steelix	TM
210	Granbull	TM
212	Scizor	TM
214	Heracross	TM
217	Ursaring	TM
219	Magcargo	TM
221	Piloswine	TM
224	Octillery	TM
226	Mantine	TM
229	Houndoom	TM
230	Kingdra	TM
232	Donphan	54,TM
233	Porygon2	TM
234	Stantler	TM
241	Miltank	TM
242	Blissey	TM
243	Raikou	TM
244	Entei	TM
245	Suicune	TM
248	Tyranitar	TM
249	Lugia	TM
250	Ho-Oh	TM
251	Celebi	TM
254	Sceptile	TM
257	Blaziken	TM
260	Swampert	TM
262	Mightyena	TM
264	Linoone	TM
267	Beautifly	TM
269	Dustox	TM
272	Ludicolo	TM
275	Shiftry	TM
277	Swellow	TM
279	Pelipper	TM
282	Gardevoir	TM
284	Masquerain	TM
286	Breloom	TM
289	Slaking	TM
291	Ninjask	TM
292	Shedinja	TM
295	Exploud	TM
297	Hariyama	TM
301	Delcatty	TM
303	Mawile	TM
306	Aggron	TM
308	Medicham	TM
310	Manectric	TM
317	Swalot	TM
319	Sharpedo	TM
321	Wailord	TM
323	Camerupt	TM
324	Torkoal	TM
326	Grumpig	TM
330	Flygon	TM
332	Cacturne	TM
334	Altaria	TM
337	Lunatone	TM
338	Solrock	TM
340	Whiscash	TM
342	Crawdaunt	TM
344	Claydol	TM
346	Cradily	TM
348	Armaldo	TM
350	Milotic	TM
354	Banette	TM
356	Dusclops	TM
357	Tropius	TM
359	Absol	TM
362	Glalie	TM
365	Walrein	TM
367	Huntail	TM
368	Gorebyss	TM
369	Relicanth	TM
373	Salamence	TM
376	Metagross	TM
377	Regirock	TM
378	Regice	TM
379	Registeel	TM
380	Latias	TM
381	Latios	TM
382	Kyogre	TM
383	Groudon	TM
384	Rayquaza	TM
385	Jirachi	TM
386	Deoxys (N)	TM
386	Deoxys (A)	TM
386	Deoxys (D)	TM
386	Deoxys (S)	TM
389	Torterra	TM
392	Infernape	TM
395	Empoleon	TM
398	Staraptor	TM
400	Bibarel	TM
402	Kricketune	TM
405	Luxray	TM
407	Roserade	TM
409	Rampardos	TM
411	Bastiodon	TM
413	Wormadam (P)	TM
413	Wormadam (S)	TM
413	Wormadam (T)	TM
414	Mothim	TM
416	Vespiquen	TM
419	Floatzel	TM
421	Cherrim	TM
423	Gastrodon	TM
424	Ambipom	TM
426	Drifblim	TM
428	Lopunny	TM
429	Mismagius	TM
430	Honchkrow	TM
432	Purugly	TM
435	Skuntank	TM
437	Bronzong	TM
442	Spiritomb	TM
445	Garchomp	TM
448	Lucario	TM
450	Hippowdon	TM
452	Drapion	TM
454	Toxicroak	TM
455	Carnivine	TM
457	Lumineon	TM
460	Abomasnow	TM
461	Weavile	TM
462	Magnezone	TM
463	Lickilicky	TM
464	Rhyperior	TM
465	Tangrowth	TM
466	Electivire	67,TM
467	Magmortar	TM
468	Togekiss	TM
469	Yanmega	TM
470	Leafeon	TM
471	Glaceon	TM
472	Gliscor	TM
473	Mamoswine	TM
474	Porygon-Z	TM
475	Gallade	TM
476	Probopass	TM
477	Dusknoir	TM
478	Froslass	TM
480	Uxie	TM
481	Mesprit	TM
482	Azelf	TM
483	Dialga	TM
484	Palkia	TM
485	Heatran	TM
486	Regigigas	100,TM
487	Giratina (A)	TM
487	Giratina (O)	TM
488	Cresselia	TM
490	Manaphy	TM
491	Darkrai	TM
492	Shaymin (L)	TM
492	Shaymin (S)	TM

Glare		
23	Ekans	12
24	Arbok	12
206	Dunsparce	13
336	Seviper	25

Grass Knot		
1	Bulbasaur	TM
2	Ivysaur	TM
3	Venusaur	TM
19	Rattata	TM
20	Raticate	TM
25	Pikachu	TM
26	Raichu	TM
35	Clefairy	TM
36	Clefable	TM
39	Jigglypuff	TM
40	Wigglytuff	TM
43	Oddish	TM
44	Gloom	TM
45	Vileplume	TM
46	Paras	TM
47	Parasect	TM
63	Abra	TM
64	Kadabra	TM
65	Alakazam	TM
69	Bellsprout	TM
70	Weepinbell	TM
71	Victreebel	TM
79	Slowpoke	TM
80	Slowbro	TM
96	Drowzee	TM
97	Hypno	TM
102	Exeggcute	TM
103	Exeggutor	TM
113	Chansey	TM
114	Tangela	TM
121	Starmie	TM
122	Mr. Mime	TM
124	Jynx	TM
150	Mewtwo	TM
151	Mew	TM
152	Chikorita	TM
153	Bayleef	TM
154	Meganium	TM
161	Sentret	TM
162	Furret	TM
172	Pichu	TM
173	Cleffa	TM
174	Igglybuff	TM
175	Togepi	TM
176	Togetic	TM
177	Natu	TM
178	Xatu	TM
182	Bellossom	TM
183	Marill	TM
184	Azumarill	TM
187	Hoppip	TM
188	Skiploom	TM

Grass Knot continued		
189	Jumpluff	TM
190	Aipom	TM
191	Sunkern	TM
192	Sunflora	TM
196	Espeon	TM
199	Slowking	TM
203	Girafarig	TM
238	Smoochum	TM
242	Blissey	TM
251	Celebi	TM
252	Treecko	TM
253	Grovyle	TM
254	Sceptile	TM
263	Zigzagoon	TM
264	Linoone	TM
270	Lotad	TM
271	Lombre	TM
272	Ludicolo	TM
273	Seedot	TM
274	Nuzleaf	TM
275	Shiftry	TM
280	Ralts	TM
281	Kirlia	TM
282	Gardevoir	TM
285	Shroomish	TM
286	Breloom	TM
300	Skitty	TM
301	Delcatty	TM
303	Mawile	TM
307	Meditite	TM
308	Medicham	TM
311	Plusle	TM
312	Minun	TM
315	Roselia	TM
325	Spoink	TM
326	Grumpig	TM
331	Cacnea	TM
332	Cacturne	TM
337	Lunatone	TM
338	Solrock	TM
343	Baltoy	TM
344	Claydol	TM
345	Lileep	TM
346	Cradily	TM
352	Kecleon	TM
357	Tropius	TM
358	Chimecho	TM
375	Metang	TM
376	Metagross	TM
380	Latias	TM
381	Latios	TM
385	Jirachi	TM
386	Deoxys (N)	TM
386	Deoxys (A)	TM
386	Deoxys (D)	TM
386	Deoxys (S)	TM
387	Turtwig	TM
388	Grotle	TM
389	Torterra	TM
390	Chimchar	TM
391	Monferno	TM
392	Infernape	TM
393	Piplup	TM
394	Prinplup	TM
395	Empoleon	TM
399	Bidoof	TM
400	Bibarel	TM
406	Budew	TM
407	Roserade	TM
413	Wormadam (P)	TM
417	Pachirisu	TM
420	Cherubi	TM
421	Cherrim	TM
424	Ambipom	TM
427	Buneary	TM
428	Lopunny	TM
433	Chingling	TM
436	Bronzor	TM
437	Bronzong	TM
439	Mime Jr.	TM
440	Happiny	TM
455	Carnivine	TM
459	Snover	TM
460	Abomasnow	TM
465	Tangrowth	TM
468	Togekiss	TM
470	Leafeon	TM
475	Gallade	TM
480	Uxie	TM
481	Mesprit	TM
482	Azelf	TM
488	Cresselia	TM
489	Phione	TM
490	Manaphy	TM
492	Shaymin (L)	TM
492	Shaymin (S)	TM

GrassWhistle		
1	Bulbasaur	E
152	Chikorita	E
191	Sunkern	13,E
192	Sunflora	13
252	Treecko	E
315	Roselia	22
331	Cacnea	E
420	Cherubi	E
459	Snover	13
460	Abomasnow	13
470	Leafeon	57

Gravity		
35	Clefairy	34
113	Chansey	E
174	Igglybuff	E
356	Dusclops	B
385	Jirachi	45
440	Happiny	E
476	Probopass	B
477	Dusknoir	B

Growl		
1	Bulbasaur	3
2	Ivysaur	B,3
3	Venusaur	B,3
4	Charmander	B
5	Charmeleon	B
6	Charizard	B
21	Spearow	B
22	Fearow	B
25	Pikachu	B
29	Nidoran♀	B
30	Nidorina	B
35	Clefairy	B
50	Diglett	4
51	Dugtrio	B,4
52	Meowth	B
53	Persian	B
77	Ponyta	B
78	Rapidash	B
79	Slowpoke	6
80	Slowbro	B,6
84	Doduo	B
85	Dodrio	B
86	Seel	3
87	Dewgong	B,3
104	Cubone	B
105	Marowak	B
113	Chansey	B
131	Lapras	B
133	Eevee	15
152	Chikorita	B
153	Bayleef	B
154	Meganium	B
163	Hoothoot	B
164	Noctowl	B
175	Togepi	B
176	Togetic	B
179	Mareep	5
180	Flaaffy	B,5
181	Ampharos	B,5
199	Slowking	6
200	Misdreavus	B
203	Girafarig	B
231	Phanpy	B
232	Donphan	B
241	Miltank	3
242	Blissey	B
255	Torchic	B
256	Combusken	B
257	Blaziken	B
258	Mudkip	B
259	Marshtomp	B
260	Swampert	B
263	Zigzagoon	B
264	Linoone	B
270	Lotad	3
271	Lombre	3
272	Ludicolo	B
276	Taillow	B
277	Swellow	B
278	Wingull	B
279	Pelipper	B
280	Ralts	B
281	Kirlia	B
282	Gardevoir	B
300	Skitty	B
311	Plusle	B
312	Minun	B
320	Wailmer	4
321	Wailord	B,4
322	Numel	B
323	Camerupt	B
333	Swablu	B
334	Altaria	B
358	Chimecho	6
363	Spheal	B
364	Sealeo	B
365	Walrein	B
393	Piplup	4
394	Prinplup	B,4
395	Empoleon	B,4
396	Starly	B
397	Staravia	B
398	Staraptor	B
399	Bidoof	5
400	Bibarel	B,5
401	Kricketot	B
402	Kricketune	B
417	Pachirisu	B
418	Buizel	B
419	Floatzel	B
429	Mismagius	B
431	Glameow	8
432	Purugly	B,8
433	Chingling	6
441	Chatot	5

Growth		
1	Bulbasaur	25
2	Ivysaur	28
3	Venusaur	28
46	Paras	27
47	Parasect	30
69	Bellsprout	7
70	Weepinbell	B,7
114	Tangela	12
191	Sunkern	B
192	Sunflora	B
273	Seedot	7
274	Nuzleaf	7
285	Shroomish	33
314	Illumise	E
315	Roselia	4
331	Cacnea	9
332	Cacturne	B,9
357	Tropius	7
387	Turtwig	E
406	Budew	4
413	Wormadam (P)	29
420	Cherubi	7
421	Cherrim	B,7
455	Carnivine	B
459	Snover	E
465	Tangrowth	12
492	Shaymin (L)	B
492	Shaymin (S)	B

Grudge		
37	Vulpix	41
92	Gastly	E
109	Koffing	E
200	Misdreavus	46
280	Ralts	E
292	Shedinja	45
353	Shuppet	46
354	Banette	58
355	Duskull	E
442	Spiritomb	E

Guard Swap		
63	Abra	E
122	Mr. Mime	B
150	Mewtwo	64
177	Natu	44
178	Xatu	54
197	Umbreon	78
203	Girafarig	B
307	Meditite	E

Guillotine		
98	Krabby	31
99	Kingler	37
127	Pinsir	47
207	Gligar	45
341	Corphish	53
342	Crawdaunt	65
472	Gliscor	45

Gunk Shot		
23	Ekans	41,T
24	Arbok	56,T
52	Meowth	T
53	Persian	T
56	Mankey	T
57	Primeape	T
88	Grimer	44,T
89	Muk	54,T
143	Snorlax	T
151	Mew	T
190	Aipom	T
216	Teddiursa	T
217	Ursaring	T
223	Remoraid	T
224	Octillery	B,T
225	Delibird	T
226	Mantine	T
231	Phanpy	T
232	Donphan	T
263	Zigzagoon	T
264	Linoone	T
279	Pelipper	T
287	Slakoth	T
288	Vigoroth	T
289	Slaking	T
316	Gulpin	54,T
317	Swalot	66,T
390	Chimchar	T
391	Monferno	T
392	Infernape	T
413	Wormadam (T)	T
417	Pachirisu	T
424	Ambipom	T
446	Munchlax	T
453	Croagunk	T
454	Toxicroak	T

Gust		
12	Butterfree	16
16	Pidgey	9
17	Pidgeotto	B,9
18	Pidgeot	B,9
41	Zubat	E
49	Venomoth	31
83	Farfetch'd	E
144	Articuno	B
245	Suicune	22
249	Lugia	15
250	Ho-Oh	15
267	Beautifly	13
269	Dustox	13
278	Wingull	E
284	Masquerain	22
290	Nincada	E
328	Trapinch	E
357	Tropius	B
414	Mothim	26
415	Combee	B
416	Vespiquen	B
425	Drifloon	11
426	Drifblim	B,11
456	Finneon	17
457	Lumineon	17

Gyro Ball		
7	Squirtle	TM
8	Wartortle	TM
9	Blastoise	TM
27	Sandshrew	33,TM
28	Sandslash	45,TM
39	Jigglypuff	33,TM
40	Wigglytuff	TM
74	Geodude	TM
75	Graveler	TM
76	Golem	TM
81	Magnemite	49,TM
82	Magneton	54,TM
95	Onix	TM
100	Voltorb	40,TM
101	Electrode	46,TM
109	Koffing	33,TM
110	Weezing	TM
120	Staryu	37,TM
121	Starmie	TM
138	Omanyte	TM
139	Omastar	TM
151	Mew	TM
157	Typhlosion	B,TM
204	Pineco	42,TM
205	Forretress	50,TM
206	Dunsparce	TM
208	Steelix	TM
211	Qwilfish	TM
213	Shuckle	TM
219	Magcargo	TM
232	Donphan	TM
237	Hitmontop	42,TM
241	Miltank	41,TM
324	Torkoal	TM
337	Lunatone	TM
338	Solrock	TM
343	Baltoy	TM
344	Claydol	TM
362	Glalie	TM
375	Metang	TM
376	Metagross	TM
384	Rayquaza	TM
413	Wormadam (T)	TM
425	Drifloon	TM
426	Drifblim	TM
436	Bronzor	35,TM
437	Bronzong	38,TM
462	Magnezone	54,TM
463	Lickilicky	57,TM

Hail		
7	Squirtle	TM
8	Wartortle	TM
9	Blastoise	TM
54	Psyduck	TM
55	Golduck	TM
60	Poliwag	TM
61	Poliwhirl	TM
62	Poliwrath	TM
72	Tentacool	TM
73	Tentacruel	TM
79	Slowpoke	TM
80	Slowbro	TM
86	Seel	TM
87	Dewgong	TM
90	Shellder	TM
91	Cloyster	TM
98	Krabby	TM
99	Kingler	TM
113	Chansey	TM
115	Kangaskhan	TM
116	Horsea	TM
117	Seadra	TM
118	Goldeen	TM
119	Seaking	TM
120	Staryu	TM
121	Starmie	TM
124	Jynx	TM
130	Gyarados	TM
131	Lapras	TM
134	Vaporeon	TM
138	Omanyte	TM
139	Omastar	TM
140	Kabuto	TM
141	Kabutops	TM
144	Articuno	85,TM
147	Dratini	TM
148	Dragonair	TM
149	Dragonite	TM
150	Mewtwo	TM
151	Mew	TM
158	Totodile	TM
159	Croconaw	TM
160	Feraligatr	TM
170	Chinchou	TM
171	Lanturn	TM
183	Marill	TM
184	Azumarill	TM
186	Politoed	TM
194	Wooper	TM
195	Quagsire	TM
199	Slowking	TM
211	Qwilfish	TM
215	Sneasel	TM
220	Swinub	TM
221	Piloswine	TM
222	Corsola	TM
225	Delibird	TM
226	Mantine	TM
230	Kingdra	TM
238	Smoochum	TM
242	Blissey	TM
245	Suicune	TM
249	Lugia	TM
258	Mudkip	TM
259	Marshtomp	TM
260	Swampert	TM
270	Lotad	TM
271	Lombre	TM
272	Ludicolo	TM
278	Wingull	TM
279	Pelipper	TM
298	Azurill	TM
318	Carvanha	TM
319	Sharpedo	TM
320	Wailmer	TM
321	Wailord	TM
339	Barboach	TM
340	Whiscash	TM
341	Corphish	TM
342	Crawdaunt	TM
349	Feebas	TM
350	Milotic	TM
351	Castform	20,TM
359	Absol	TM
361	Snorunt	40,TM
362	Glalie	40,TM
363	Spheal	31,TM
364	Sealeo	31,TM
365	Walrein	31,TM
366	Clamperl	TM
367	Huntail	TM
368	Gorebyss	TM
369	Relicanth	TM
370	Luvdisc	TM
378	Regice	TM
382	Kyogre	TM
393	Piplup	TM
394	Prinplup	TM
395	Empoleon	TM
418	Buizel	TM
419	Floatzel	TM
422	Shellos	TM
423	Gastrodon	TM
440	Happiny	TM
456	Finneon	TM
457	Lumineon	TM
458	Mantyke	TM
459	Snover	TM
460	Abomasnow	TM
461	Weavile	TM
471	Glaceon	64,TM
473	Mamoswine	25,TM
478	Froslass	40,TM
484	Palkia	TM
489	Phione	TM
490	Manaphy	TM

Hammer Arm		
74	Geodude	E
108	Lickitung	E
112	Rhydon	42
115	Kangaskhan	E
185	Sudowoodo	49
217	Ursaring	67
241	Miltank	E
260	Swampert	69
287	Slakoth	E
289	Slaking	61
376	Metagross	45
377	Regirock	81
378	Regice	81
379	Registeel	81
408	Cranidos	E
464	Rhyperior	42

Harden		
11	Metapod	B,7
14	Kakuna	B,7
88	Grimer	4
89	Muk	B,4
95	Onix	B
98	Krabby	11
99	Kingler	11
120	Staryu	B
127	Pinsir	13
140	Kabuto	B
141	Kabutops	B
185	Sudowoodo	E
207	Gligar	9
208	Steelix	B
211	Qwilfish	9
214	Heracross	E
218	Slugma	16
219	Magcargo	16
222	Corsola	4
266	Silcoon	B,7
268	Cascoon	B,7
273	Seedot	3
274	Nuzleaf	3
290	Nincada	B
291	Ninjask	B
292	Shedinja	B
299	Nosepass	7
304	Aron	4
305	Lairon	B,4
306	Aggron	B,4
337	Lunatone	B
338	Solrock	B
341	Corphish	7
342	Crawdaunt	B,7
343	Baltoy	3
344	Claydol	B,3
347	Anorith	B
348	Armaldo	B
369	Relicanth	B
413	Wormadam (S)	29
422	Shellos	B
423	Gastrodon	B,4
438	Bonsly	E
472	Gliscor	B,9

Haze		
7	Squirtle	E
23	Ekans	36
24	Arbok	48
41	Zubat	37
42	Golbat	45
60	Poliwag	E
72	Tentacool	E
84	Doduo	E
88	Grimer	E
92	Gastly	E
98	Krabby	E
109	Koffing	28
110	Weezing	28
118	Goldeen	E
134	Vaporeon	57
138	Omanyte	E
147	Dratini	E
169	Crobat	45
177	Natu	E
194	Wooper	43
195	Quagsire	48
198	Murkrow	11
211	Qwilfish	E
223	Remoraid	E
226	Mantine	E
283	Surskit	37
333	Swablu	E
336	Seviper	43
349	Feebas	E
425	Drifloon	E
430	Honchkrow	B
458	Mantyke	E
491	Darkrai	57

Head Smash		
369	Relicanth	78
408	Cranidos	43
409	Rampardos	52

Headbutt		
79	Slowpoke	25
80	Slowbro	25
86	Seel	B
87	Dewgong	B
96	Drowzee	15,32
97	Hypno	15,38
104	Cubone	11
105	Marowak	B,11
185	Sudowoodo	E
199	Slowking	25
206	Dunsparce	E
209	Snubbull	19
210	Granbull	19
226	Mantine	13
263	Zigzagoon	9
264	Linoone	B,9
285	Shroomish	21
286	Breloom	21
304	Aron	11
305	Lairon	B,11
306	Aggron	B,11
309	Electrike	E
357	Tropius	E
361	Snorunt	19
362	Glalie	19
371	Bagon	16
372	Shelgon	B,16
373	Salamence	B,16
399	Bidoof	17
400	Bibarel	18
408	Cranidos	B
409	Rampardos	B
410	Shieldon	E
418	Buizel	E
438	Bonsly	E
453	Croagunk	E
458	Mantyke	13

Heal Bell		
113	Chansey	E
209	Snubbull	E
241	Miltank	48
251	Celebi	B
300	Skitty	39
358	Chimecho	38
440	Happiny	E

Heal Block		
251	Celebi	55
292	Shedinja	52
337	Lunatone	42
338	Solrock	42
343	Baltoy	61
344	Claydol	73
381	Latios	5
436	Bronzor	52
437	Bronzong	67
483	Dialga	50
484	Palkia	50
487	Giratina (A)	50
487	Giratina (O)	50

Heal Order		
416	Vespiquen	25

Healing Wish		
35	Clefairy	46
113	Chansey	42
242	Blissey	42
251	Celebi	73
282	Gardevoir	B
358	Chimecho	49
380	Latias	60
385	Jirachi	50

427	Buneary	53
428	Lopunny	53
439	Mime Jr.	E
481	Mesprit	76
492	Shaymin (L)	91

Heart Swap		
490	Manaphy	76Hi

Heat Wave		
4	Charmander	T
5	Charmeleon	T
6	Charizard	59,T
16	Pidgey	T
17	Pidgeotto	T
18	Pidgeot	T
21	Spearow	T
22	Fearow	T
37	Vulpix	T,E
38	Ninetales	T
41	Zubat	T
42	Golbat	T
58	Growlithe	45,T,E
59	Arcanine	T
77	Ponyta	T
78	Rapidash	T
83	Farfetch'd	T
126	Magmar	T
136	Flareon	T
142	Aerodactyl	T
145	Zapdos	T
146	Moltres	64,T
149	Dragonite	T
151	Mew	T
155	Cyndaquil	T
156	Quilava	T
157	Typhlosion	T
163	Hoothoot	T
164	Noctowl	T
169	Crobat	T
176	Togetic	T
177	Natu	T
178	Xatu	T
198	Murkrow	T
218	Slugma	T,E
219	Magcargo	T
228	Houndour	T
229	Houndoom	T
240	Magby	T
244	Entei	T
250	Ho-Oh	T
255	Torchic	T
256	Combusken	T
257	Blaziken	T
276	Taillow	T
277	Swellow	T
322	Numel	T,E
323	Camerupt	T
324	Torkoal	55,T
329	Vibrava	T
330	Flygon	T
333	Swablu	T
334	Altaria	T
373	Salamence	T
390	Chimchar	T,E
391	Monferno	T
392	Infernape	T
396	Starly	T
397	Staravia	T
398	Staraptor	T
430	Honchkrow	T
441	Chatot	T
467	Magmortar	T
468	Togekiss	T
485	Heatran	81,T

Helping Hand		
25	Pikachu	T
26	Raichu	T
29	Nidoran♀	25,T
30	Nidorina	28,T
31	Nidoqueen	T
32	Nidoran♂	25,T
33	Nidorino	28,T
34	Nidoking	T
35	Clefairy	T
36	Clefable	T
39	Jigglypuff	T
40	Wigglytuff	T
56	Mankey	T
57	Primeape	T
58	Growlithe	17,T
59	Arcanine	T
60	Poliwag	T
61	Poliwhirl	T
62	Poliwrath	T
66	Machop	T
67	Machoke	T
68	Machamp	T
106	Hitmonlee	T
107	Hitmonchan	T
113	Chansey	T,E
115	Kangaskhan	T
122	Mr. Mime	T
124	Jynx	T
125	Electabuzz	T
126	Magmar	T
128	Tauros	T
133	Eevee	B,T
134	Vaporeon	B,T
135	Jolteon	B,T
136	Flareon	B,T
151	Mew	T
161	Sentret	16,T
162	Furret	17,T
172	Pichu	T
173	Cleffa	T
174	Igglybuff	T
183	Marill	T
184	Azumarill	T
185	Sudowoodo	T
186	Politoed	T
187	Hoppip	T,E
188	Skiploom	T
189	Jumpluff	T
191	Sunkern	T,E
192	Sunflora	T
196	Espeon	B,T
197	Umbreon	B,T
213	Shuckle	T,E
214	Heracross	T
226	Mantine	T
236	Tyrogue	B,T,E
237	Hitmontop	T
238	Smoochum	T
239	Elekid	T
240	Magby	T
241	Miltank	T,E
242	Blissey	T
251	Celebi	T
255	Torchic	T
256	Combusken	T
257	Blaziken	T
263	Zigzagoon	T,E
264	Linoone	T
280	Ralts	T
281	Kirlia	T
282	Gardevoir	T
285	Shroomish	T,E
286	Breloom	T
296	Makuhita	T,E
297	Hariyama	T
298	Azurill	T
300	Skitty	T,E
301	Delcatty	T
307	Meditite	T
308	Medicham	T
311	Plusle	10,T
312	Minun	10,T
313	Volbeat	33,T
314	Illumise	33,T
327	Spinda	T
337	Lunatone	T
338	Solrock	T
358	Chimecho	T
380	Latias	10,T
381	Latios	10,T
385	Jirachi	15,T
390	Chimchar	T,E
391	Monferno	T
392	Infernape	T
417	Pachirisu	T
420	Cherubi	13,T
421	Cherrim	13,T
427	Buneary	T
428	Lopunny	T
433	Chingling	T
438	Bonsly	T
439	Mime Jr.	T
440	Happiny	T,E
447	Riolu	T
448	Lucario	T
453	Croagunk	T
454	Toxicroak	T
458	Mantyke	T
466	Electivire	T
467	Magmortar	T
470	Leafeon	B,T
471	Glaceon	B,T
475	Gallade	36,T
480	Uxie	T
481	Mesprit	T
482	Azelf	T
488	Cresselia	T
489	Phione	T
490	Manaphy	T

Hi Jump Kick		
106	Hitmonlee	29
236	Tyrogue	E
307	Meditite	32
308	Medicham	32
447	Riolu	E

Hidden Power		
1	Bulbasaur	TM
2	Ivysaur	TM
3	Venusaur	TM
4	Charmander	TM
5	Charmeleon	TM
6	Charizard	TM
7	Squirtle	TM
8	Wartortle	TM
9	Blastoise	TM
12	Butterfree	TM
15	Beedrill	TM
16	Pidgey	TM
17	Pidgeotto	TM
18	Pidgeot	TM
19	Rattata	TM
20	Raticate	TM
21	Spearow	TM
22	Fearow	TM
23	Ekans	TM
24	Arbok	TM
25	Pikachu	TM
26	Raichu	TM
27	Sandshrew	TM
28	Sandslash	TM
29	Nidoran♀	TM
30	Nidorina	TM
31	Nidoqueen	TM
32	Nidoran♂	TM
33	Nidorino	TM
34	Nidoking	TM
35	Clefairy	TM
36	Clefable	TM
37	Vulpix	TM
38	Ninetales	TM
39	Jigglypuff	TM
40	Wigglytuff	TM
41	Zubat	TM
42	Golbat	TM
43	Oddish	TM
44	Gloom	TM
45	Vileplume	TM
46	Paras	TM
47	Parasect	TM
48	Venonat	TM
49	Venomoth	TM
50	Diglett	TM
51	Dugtrio	TM
52	Meowth	TM
53	Persian	TM
54	Psyduck	TM
55	Golduck	TM
56	Mankey	TM
57	Primeape	TM
58	Growlithe	TM
59	Arcanine	TM
60	Poliwag	TM
61	Poliwhirl	TM
62	Poliwrath	TM
63	Abra	TM
64	Kadabra	TM
65	Alakazam	TM
66	Machop	TM
67	Machoke	TM
68	Machamp	TM
69	Bellsprout	TM
70	Weepinbell	TM
71	Victreebel	TM
72	Tentacool	TM
73	Tentacruel	TM
74	Geodude	TM
75	Graveler	TM
76	Golem	TM
77	Ponyta	TM
78	Rapidash	TM
79	Slowpoke	TM
80	Slowbro	TM
81	Magnemite	TM
82	Magneton	TM
83	Farfetch'd	TM
84	Doduo	TM
85	Dodrio	TM
86	Seel	TM
87	Dewgong	TM
88	Grimer	TM
89	Muk	TM
90	Shellder	TM
91	Cloyster	TM
92	Gastly	TM
93	Haunter	TM
94	Gengar	TM
95	Onix	TM
96	Drowzee	TM
97	Hypno	TM
98	Krabby	TM
99	Kingler	TM
100	Voltorb	TM
101	Electrode	TM
102	Exeggcute	TM
103	Exeggutor	TM
104	Cubone	TM
105	Marowak	TM
106	Hitmonlee	TM
107	Hitmonchan	TM
108	Lickitung	TM
109	Koffing	TM
110	Weezing	TM
111	Rhyhorn	TM
112	Rhydon	TM
113	Chansey	TM
114	Tangela	TM
115	Kangaskhan	TM
116	Horsea	TM
117	Seadra	TM
118	Goldeen	TM
119	Seaking	TM
120	Staryu	TM
121	Starmie	TM
122	Mr. Mime	TM
123	Scyther	TM
124	Jynx	TM
125	Electabuzz	TM
126	Magmar	TM
127	Pinsir	TM
128	Tauros	TM
130	Gyarados	TM
131	Lapras	TM
133	Eevee	TM
134	Vaporeon	TM
135	Jolteon	TM
136	Flareon	TM
137	Porygon	TM
138	Omanyte	TM
139	Omastar	TM
140	Kabuto	TM
141	Kabutops	TM
142	Aerodactyl	TM
143	Snorlax	TM
144	Articuno	TM
145	Zapdos	TM
146	Moltres	TM
147	Dratini	TM
148	Dragonair	TM
149	Dragonite	TM
150	Mewtwo	TM
151	Mew	TM
152	Chikorita	TM
153	Bayleef	TM
154	Meganium	TM
155	Cyndaquil	TM
156	Quilava	TM
157	Typhlosion	TM
158	Totodile	TM
159	Croconaw	TM
160	Feraligatr	TM
161	Sentret	TM
162	Furret	TM
163	Hoothoot	TM
164	Noctowl	TM
165	Ledyba	TM
166	Ledian	TM
167	Spinarak	TM
168	Ariados	TM
169	Crobat	TM
170	Chinchou	TM
171	Lanturn	TM
172	Pichu	TM
173	Cleffa	TM
174	Igglybuff	TM
175	Togepi	TM
176	Togetic	TM
177	Natu	TM
178	Xatu	TM
179	Mareep	TM
180	Flaaffy	TM
181	Ampharos	TM
182	Bellossom	TM
183	Marill	TM
184	Azumarill	TM
185	Sudowoodo	TM
186	Politoed	TM
187	Hoppip	TM
188	Skiploom	TM
189	Jumpluff	TM
190	Aipom	TM
191	Sunkern	TM
192	Sunflora	TM
193	Yanma	TM
194	Wooper	TM
195	Quagsire	TM
196	Espeon	TM
197	Umbreon	TM
198	Murkrow	TM
199	Slowking	B,TM
200	Misdreavus	TM
201	Unown	B
203	Girafarig	TM
204	Pineco	TM
205	Forretress	TM
206	Dunsparce	TM
207	Gligar	TM
208	Steelix	TM
209	Snubbull	TM
210	Granbull	TM
211	Qwilfish	TM
212	Scizor	TM
213	Shuckle	TM
214	Heracross	TM
215	Sneasel	TM
216	Teddiursa	TM
217	Ursaring	TM
218	Slugma	TM
219	Magcargo	TM
220	Swinub	TM
221	Piloswine	TM
222	Corsola	TM
223	Remoraid	TM
224	Octillery	TM
225	Delibird	TM
226	Mantine	TM
227	Skarmory	TM
228	Houndour	TM
229	Houndoom	TM
230	Kingdra	TM
231	Phanpy	TM
232	Donphan	TM
233	Porygon2	TM
234	Stantler	TM
236	Tyrogue	TM
237	Hitmontop	TM
238	Smoochum	TM
239	Elekid	TM
240	Magby	TM
241	Miltank	TM
242	Blissey	TM
243	Raikou	TM
244	Entei	TM
245	Suicune	TM
246	Larvitar	TM
247	Pupitar	TM
248	Tyranitar	TM
249	Lugia	TM
250	Ho-Oh	TM
251	Celebi	TM
252	Treecko	TM
253	Grovyle	TM
254	Sceptile	TM
255	Torchic	TM
256	Combusken	TM
257	Blaziken	TM
258	Mudkip	TM
259	Marshtomp	TM
260	Swampert	TM
261	Poochyena	TM
262	Mightyena	TM
263	Zigzagoon	TM
264	Linoone	TM
267	Beautifly	TM
269	Dustox	TM
270	Lotad	TM
271	Lombre	TM
272	Ludicolo	TM
273	Seedot	TM
274	Nuzleaf	TM
275	Shiftry	TM
276	Taillow	TM
277	Swellow	TM
278	Wingull	TM
279	Pelipper	TM
280	Ralts	TM
281	Kirlia	TM
282	Gardevoir	TM
283	Surskit	TM
284	Masquerain	TM
285	Shroomish	TM
286	Breloom	TM
287	Slakoth	TM
288	Vigoroth	TM
289	Slaking	TM
290	Nincada	TM
291	Ninjask	TM
292	Shedinja	TM
293	Whismur	TM
294	Loudred	TM
295	Exploud	TM
296	Makuhita	TM
297	Hariyama	TM
298	Azurill	TM
299	Nosepass	TM
300	Skitty	TM
301	Delcatty	TM
302	Sableye	TM
303	Mawile	TM
304	Aron	TM
305	Lairon	TM
306	Aggron	TM
307	Meditite	15,TM
308	Medicham	15,TM
309	Electrike	TM
310	Manectric	TM
311	Plusle	TM
312	Minun	TM
313	Volbeat	TM
314	Illumise	TM
315	Roselia	TM
316	Gulpin	TM
317	Swalot	TM
318	Carvanha	TM
319	Sharpedo	TM
320	Wailmer	TM
321	Wailord	TM
322	Numel	TM
323	Camerupt	TM
324	Torkoal	TM
325	Spoink	TM
326	Grumpig	TM
327	Spinda	TM
328	Trapinch	TM
329	Vibrava	TM
330	Flygon	TM
331	Cacnea	TM
332	Cacturne	TM
333	Swablu	TM
334	Altaria	TM
335	Zangoose	TM
336	Seviper	TM
337	Lunatone	TM
338	Solrock	TM
339	Barboach	TM
340	Whiscash	TM
341	Corphish	TM
342	Crawdaunt	TM
343	Baltoy	TM
344	Claydol	TM
345	Lileep	TM
346	Cradily	TM
347	Anorith	TM
348	Armaldo	TM
349	Feebas	TM
350	Milotic	TM
351	Castform	TM
352	Kecleon	TM
353	Shuppet	TM
354	Banette	TM
355	Duskull	TM
356	Dusclops	TM
357	Tropius	TM
358	Chimecho	TM
359	Absol	TM
361	Snorunt	TM
362	Glalie	TM
363	Spheal	TM
364	Sealeo	TM
365	Walrein	TM
366	Clamperl	TM
367	Huntail	TM
368	Gorebyss	TM
369	Relicanth	TM
370	Luvdisc	TM
371	Bagon	TM
372	Shelgon	TM
373	Salamence	TM
375	Metang	TM
376	Metagross	TM
377	Regirock	TM
378	Regice	TM
379	Registeel	TM
380	Latias	TM
381	Latios	TM
382	Kyogre	TM
383	Groudon	TM
384	Rayquaza	TM
385	Jirachi	TM
386	Deoxys (N)	TM
386	Deoxys (A)	TM
386	Deoxys (D)	TM
386	Deoxys (S)	TM
387	Turtwig	TM
388	Grotle	TM
389	Torterra	TM
390	Chimchar	TM
391	Monferno	TM
392	Infernape	TM
393	Piplup	TM
394	Prinplup	TM
395	Empoleon	TM
396	Starly	TM
397	Staravia	TM
398	Staraptor	TM
399	Bidoof	TM
400	Bibarel	TM
402	Kricketune	TM
403	Shinx	TM
404	Luxio	TM
405	Luxray	TM
406	Budew	TM
407	Roserade	TM
408	Cranidos	TM
409	Rampardos	TM
410	Shieldon	TM
411	Bastiodon	TM
412	Burmy	20
413	Wormadam (P)	20,TM
413	Wormadam (S)	20,TM
413	Wormadam (T)	20,TM
414	Mothim	20,TM
416	Vespiquen	TM
417	Pachirisu	TM
418	Buizel	TM
419	Floatzel	TM
420	Cherubi	TM
421	Cherrim	TM
422	Shellos	16,TM
423	Gastrodon	16,TM
424	Ambipom	TM
425	Drifloon	TM
426	Drifblim	TM
427	Buneary	TM
428	Lopunny	TM
429	Mismagius	TM
430	Honchkrow	TM
431	Glameow	TM
432	Purugly	TM
433	Chingling	TM
434	Stunky	TM
435	Skuntank	TM
436	Bronzor	TM
437	Bronzong	TM
438	Bonsly	TM
439	Mime Jr.	TM
440	Happiny	TM
441	Chatot	TM
442	Spiritomb	TM
443	Gible	TM
444	Gabite	TM
445	Garchomp	TM
446	Munchlax	TM
447	Riolu	TM
448	Lucario	TM
449	Hippopotas	TM
450	Hippowdon	TM
451	Skorupi	TM
452	Drapion	TM
453	Croagunk	TM
454	Toxicroak	TM
455	Carnivine	TM
456	Finneon	TM
457	Lumineon	TM
458	Mantyke	TM
459	Snover	TM
460	Abomasnow	TM
461	Weavile	TM
462	Magnezone	TM
463	Lickilicky	TM
464	Rhyperior	TM
465	Tangrowth	TM
466	Electivire	TM
467	Magmortar	TM
468	Togekiss	TM
469	Yanmega	TM
470	Leafeon	TM
471	Glaceon	TM
472	Gliscor	TM
473	Mamoswine	TM
474	Porygon-Z	TM
475	Gallade	TM
476	Probopass	TM
477	Dusknoir	TM
478	Froslass	TM
479	Rotom	TM
480	Uxie	TM
481	Mesprit	TM
482	Azelf	TM
483	Dialga	TM
484	Palkia	TM
485	Heatran	TM
486	Regigigas	TM
487	Giratina (A)	TM
487	Giratina (O)	TM
488	Cresselia	TM
489	Phione	TM
490	Manaphy	TM
491	Darkrai	TM
492	Shaymin (L)	TM
492	Shaymin (S)	TM

Horn Attack		
32	Nidoran♂	21

Pokémon Moves and Abilities alphabetical list

Horn Attack continued

33	Nidorino	23
111	Rhyhorn	B
112	Rhydon	B
118	Goldeen	11
119	Seaking	11
128	Tauros	8
214	Heracross	B
232	Donphan	B
464	Rhyperior	B

Horn Drill

32	Nidoran♂	45
33	Nidorino	58
77	Ponyta	E
86	Seel	E
111	Rhyhorn	37
112	Rhydon	37
118	Goldeen	41
119	Seaking	47
131	Lapras	E
464	Rhyperior	37

Howl

37	Vulpix	E
58	Growlithe	E
155	Cyndaquil	E
228	Houndour	4
229	Houndoom	B,4
261	Poochyena	5
262	Mightyena	B,5
293	Whismur	15
294	Loudred	B,15
295	Exploud	B,15
309	Electrike	12
310	Manectric	B,12
322	Numel	E
403	Shinx	E

Hydro Cannon

9	Blastoise	T
160	Feraligatr	T
260	Swampert	T
395	Empoleon	T

Hydro Pump

7	Squirtle	40
8	Wartortle	48
9	Blastoise	60
54	Psyduck	48
55	Golduck	56
60	Poliwag	38
61	Poliwhirl	48
72	Tentacool	40
73	Tentacruel	49
116	Horsea	35
117	Seadra	40
118	Goldeen	E
120	Staryu	55
130	Gyarados	41
131	Lapras	49
134	Vaporeon	71
138	Omanyte	52
139	Omastar	67
158	Totodile	48,E
159	Croconaw	57
160	Feraligatr	71
170	Chinchou	42
171	Lanturn	52
183	Marill	42
184	Azumarill	54
211	Qwilfish	57
226	Mantine	49,E
230	Kingdra	40
245	Suicune	71
249	Lugia	29
258	Mudkip	42
271	Lombre	45
279	Pelipper	57
283	Surskit	E
318	Carvanha	E
320	Wailmer	47
321	Wailord	62
339	Barboach	E
350	Milotic	37
367	Huntail	51
368	Gorebyss	51
369	Relicanth	71
371	Bagon	E
382	Kyogre	45
393	Piplup	43,E
394	Prinplup	51
395	Empoleon	59
458	Mantyke	49,E
479	Rotom (W)	*

Hyper Beam

3	Venusaur	TM
6	Charizard	TM
9	Blastoise	TM
12	Butterfree	TM
15	Beedrill	TM
18	Pidgeot	TM
20	Raticate	TM
22	Fearow	TM
24	Arbok	TM
26	Raichu	TM
28	Sandslash	TM
31	Nidoqueen	TM
34	Nidoking	TM
36	Clefable	TM
38	Ninetales	TM
40	Wigglytuff	TM
42	Golbat	TM
45	Vileplume	TM
47	Parasect	TM
49	Venomoth	TM
51	Dugtrio	TM
53	Persian	TM
55	Golduck	TM
57	Primeape	TM
59	Arcanine	TM
62	Poliwrath	TM
65	Alakazam	TM
68	Machamp	TM
71	Victreebel	TM
73	Tentacruel	TM
76	Golem	TM
78	Rapidash	TM
80	Slowbro	TM
82	Magneton	TM
85	Dodrio	TM
87	Dewgong	TM
89	Muk	TM
91	Cloyster	TM
94	Gengar	TM
97	Hypno	TM
99	Kingler	TM
101	Electrode	TM
103	Exeggutor	TM
105	Marowak	TM
108	Lickitung	TM
110	Weezing	TM
112	Rhydon	TM
113	Chansey	TM
114	Tangela	TM
115	Kangaskhan	TM
117	Seadra	TM
119	Seaking	TM
121	Starmie	TM
122	Mr. Mime	TM
123	Scyther	TM
124	Jynx	TM
125	Electabuzz	TM
126	Magmar	TM
127	Pinsir	TM
128	Tauros	TM
130	Gyarados	47,TM
131	Lapras	TM
134	Vaporeon	TM
135	Jolteon	TM
136	Flareon	TM
137	Porygon	TM
139	Omastar	TM
141	Kabutops	TM
142	Aerodactyl	57,TM
143	Snorlax	TM
144	Articuno	TM
145	Zapdos	TM
146	Moltres	TM
147	Dratini	55,TM
148	Dragonair	67,TM
149	Dragonite	73,TM
150	Mewtwo	TM
151	Mew	TM
154	Meganium	TM
157	Typhlosion	TM
160	Feraligatr	TM
162	Furret	TM
164	Noctowl	TM
166	Ledian	TM
168	Ariados	TM
169	Crobat	TM
171	Lanturn	TM
176	Togetic	TM
178	Xatu	TM
181	Ampharos	TM
182	Bellossom	TM
184	Azumarill	TM
186	Politoed	TM
189	Jumpluff	TM
192	Sunflora	TM
195	Quagsire	TM
196	Espeon	TM
197	Umbreon	TM
199	Slowking	TM
205	Forretress	TM
208	Steelix	TM
210	Granbull	TM
212	Scizor	TM
214	Heracross	TM
217	Ursaring	TM
219	Magcargo	TM
221	Piloswine	TM
223	Remoraid	45,TM
224	Octillery	55,TM
226	Mantine	TM
229	Houndoom	TM
230	Kingdra	TM
232	Donphan	TM
233	Porygon2	67,TM
241	Miltank	TM
242	Blissey	TM
243	Raikou	TM
244	Entei	TM
245	Suicune	TM
246	Larvitar	50,TM
247	Pupitar	60,TM
248	Tyranitar	70,TM
249	Lugia	TM
250	Ho-Oh	TM
251	Celebi	TM
254	Sceptile	TM
257	Blaziken	TM
260	Swampert	TM
262	Mightyena	TM
264	Linoone	TM
267	Beautifly	TM
269	Dustox	TM
272	Ludicolo	TM
274	Nuzleaf	TM
275	Shiftry	TM
277	Swellow	TM
279	Pelipper	TM
282	Gardevoir	TM
284	Masquerain	TM
286	Breloom	TM
289	Slaking	TM
291	Ninjask	TM
292	Shedinja	TM
295	Exploud	71,TM
297	Hariyama	TM
301	Delcatty	TM
303	Mawile	TM
306	Aggron	TM
308	Medicham	TM
310	Manectric	TM
317	Swalot	TM
319	Sharpedo	TM
321	Wailord	TM
323	Camerupt	TM
324	Torkoal	TM
326	Grumpig	TM
328	Trapinch	57,TM
329	Vibrava	57,TM
330	Flygon	57,TM
332	Cacturne	TM
334	Altaria	TM
337	Lunatone	TM
338	Solrock	TM
340	Whiscash	TM
342	Crawdaunt	TM
344	Claydol	36,TM
346	Cradily	TM
348	Armaldo	TM
350	Milotic	TM
354	Banette	TM
356	Dusclops	TM
357	Tropius	TM
359	Absol	TM
362	Glalie	TM
365	Walrein	TM
367	Huntail	TM
368	Gorebyss	TM
369	Relicanth	TM
373	Salamence	TM
375	Metang	56,TM
376	Metagross	71,TM
377	Regirock	89,TM
378	Regice	89,TM
379	Registeel	89,TM
380	Latias	TM
381	Latios	TM
382	Kyogre	TM
383	Groudon	TM
384	Rayquaza	65,TM
385	Jirachi	TM
386	Deoxys (N)	97,TM
386	Deoxys (A)	97,TM
386	Deoxys (D)	TM
386	Deoxys (S)	TM
389	Torterra	TM
392	Infernape	TM
395	Empoleon	TM
398	Staraptor	TM
400	Bibarel	TM
402	Kricketune	TM
405	Luxray	TM
407	Roserade	TM
409	Rampardos	TM
411	Bastiodon	TM
413	Wormadam (P)	TM
413	Wormadam (S)	TM
413	Wormadam (T)	TM
414	Mothim	TM
416	Vespiquen	TM
419	Floatzel	TM
421	Cherrim	TM
423	Gastrodon	TM
424	Ambipom	TM
426	Drifblim	TM
428	Lopunny	TM
429	Mismagius	TM
430	Honchkrow	TM
432	Purugly	TM
435	Skuntank	TM
437	Bronzong	TM
442	Spiritomb	TM
445	Garchomp	TM
448	Lucario	TM
450	Hippowdon	TM
452	Drapion	TM
454	Toxicroak	TM
455	Carnivine	TM
457	Lumineon	TM
460	Abomasnow	TM
461	Weavile	TM
462	Magnezone	TM
463	Lickilicky	TM
464	Rhyperior	TM
465	Tangrowth	TM
466	Electivire	TM
467	Magmortar	67,TM
468	Togekiss	TM
469	Yanmega	TM
470	Leafeon	TM
471	Glaceon	TM
472	Gliscor	TM
473	Mamoswine	TM
474	Porygon-Z	67,TM
475	Gallade	TM
476	Probopass	TM
477	Dusknoir	TM
478	Froslass	TM
480	Uxie	TM
481	Mesprit	TM
482	Azelf	TM
483	Dialga	TM
484	Palkia	TM
485	Heatran	TM
486	Regigigas	TM
487	Giratina (A)	TM
487	Giratina (O)	TM
488	Cresselia	TM
490	Manaphy	TM
491	Darkrai	TM
492	Shaymin (L)	TM
492	Shaymin (S)	TM

Hyper Fang

19	Rattata	16
20	Raticate	16
399	Bidoof	21
400	Bibarel	23

Hyper Voice

39	Jigglypuff	45
161	Sentret	47
162	Furret	56
186	Politoed	48
293	Whismur	45
294	Loudred	57
295	Exploud	63
441	Chatot	45

Hypnosis

37	Vulpix	E
41	Zubat	E
52	Meowth	E
54	Psyduck	E
60	Poliwag	8
61	Poliwhirl	B,8
62	Poliwrath	B
77	Ponyta	E
92	Gastly	B
93	Haunter	B
94	Gengar	B
96	Drowzee	B
97	Hypno	B
102	Exeggcute	B
103	Exeggutor	B
122	Mr. Mime	E
163	Hoothoot	5
164	Noctowl	B,5
186	Politoed	B
193	Yanma	38
234	Stantler	10
280	Ralts	43
281	Kirlia	50
282	Gardevoir	60
327	Spinda	23
337	Lunatone	12
349	Feebas	E
358	Chimecho	E
425	Drifloon	E
431	Glameow	13
432	Purugly	13
433	Chingling	E
436	Bronzor	7
437	Bronzong	B,7
439	Mime Jr.	E
442	Spiritomb	13
491	Darkrai	20

Ice Ball

60	Poliwag	E
225	Delibird	E
258	Mudkip	E
363	Spheal	13
364	Sealeo	13
365	Walrein	13

Ice Beam

7	Squirtle	TM
8	Wartortle	TM
9	Blastoise	TM
19	Rattata	TM
20	Raticate	TM
29	Nidoran♀	TM
30	Nidorina	TM
31	Nidoqueen	TM
32	Nidoran♂	TM
33	Nidorino	TM
34	Nidoking	TM
35	Clefairy	TM
36	Clefable	TM
39	Jigglypuff	TM
40	Wigglytuff	TM
54	Psyduck	TM
55	Golduck	TM
60	Poliwag	TM
61	Poliwhirl	TM
62	Poliwrath	TM
72	Tentacool	TM
73	Tentacruel	TM
79	Slowpoke	TM
80	Slowbro	TM
86	Seel	47,TM
87	Dewgong	47,TM
90	Shellder	49,TM
91	Cloyster	TM
98	Krabby	TM
99	Kingler	TM
104	Cubone	TM
105	Marowak	TM
108	Lickitung	TM
111	Rhyhorn	TM
112	Rhydon	TM
113	Chansey	TM
115	Kangaskhan	TM
116	Horsea	TM
117	Seadra	TM
118	Goldeen	TM
119	Seaking	TM
120	Staryu	TM
121	Starmie	TM
124	Jynx	TM
128	Tauros	TM
130	Gyarados	TM
131	Lapras	32,TM
134	Vaporeon	TM
137	Porygon	TM
138	Omanyte	TM
139	Omastar	TM
140	Kabuto	TM
141	Kabutops	TM
143	Snorlax	TM
144	Articuno	43,TM
147	Dratini	TM
148	Dragonair	TM
149	Dragonite	TM
150	Mewtwo	TM
151	Mew	TM
158	Totodile	TM
159	Croconaw	TM
160	Feraligatr	TM
161	Sentret	TM
162	Furret	TM
170	Chinchou	TM
171	Lanturn	TM
183	Marill	TM
184	Azumarill	TM
186	Politoed	TM
194	Wooper	TM
195	Quagsire	TM
199	Slowking	TM
206	Dunsparce	TM
211	Qwilfish	TM
215	Sneasel	TM
220	Swinub	TM
221	Piloswine	TM
222	Corsola	TM
223	Remoraid	40,TM
224	Octillery	48,TM
225	Delibird	TM
226	Mantine	TM
230	Kingdra	TM
233	Porygon2	TM
238	Smoochum	TM
241	Miltank	TM
242	Blissey	TM
245	Suicune	TM
248	Tyranitar	TM
249	Lugia	TM
258	Mudkip	TM
259	Marshtomp	TM
260	Swampert	TM
263	Zigzagoon	TM
264	Linoone	TM
270	Lotad	TM
271	Lombre	TM
272	Ludicolo	TM
278	Wingull	TM
279	Pelipper	TM
283	Surskit	TM
284	Masquerain	TM
287	Slakoth	TM
288	Vigoroth	TM
289	Slaking	TM
293	Whismur	TM
294	Loudred	TM
295	Exploud	TM
298	Azurill	TM
300	Skitty	TM
301	Delcatty	TM
303	Mawile	TM
306	Aggron	TM
316	Gulpin	TM
317	Swalot	TM
318	Carvanha	TM
319	Sharpedo	TM
320	Wailmer	TM
321	Wailord	TM
333	Swablu	TM
334	Altaria	TM
335	Zangoose	TM
337	Lunatone	TM
339	Barboach	TM
340	Whiscash	TM
341	Corphish	TM
342	Crawdaunt	TM
343	Baltoy	TM
344	Claydol	TM
349	Feebas	TM
350	Milotic	TM
351	Castform	TM
352	Kecleon	TM
355	Duskull	TM
356	Dusclops	TM
359	Absol	TM
361	Snorunt	TM
362	Glalie	37,TM
363	Spheal	TM
364	Sealeo	TM
365	Walrein	TM
366	Clamperl	TM
367	Huntail	TM
368	Gorebyss	TM
369	Relicanth	TM
370	Luvdisc	TM
378	Regice	73,TM
380	Latias	TM
381	Latios	TM
382	Kyogre	35,TM
384	Rayquaza	TM
386	Deoxys (N)	TM
386	Deoxys (A)	TM
386	Deoxys (D)	TM
386	Deoxys (S)	TM
393	Piplup	TM
394	Prinplup	TM
395	Empoleon	TM
399	Bidoof	TM
400	Bibarel	TM
408	Cranidos	TM
409	Rampardos	TM
410	Shieldon	TM
411	Bastiodon	TM
418	Buizel	TM
419	Floatzel	TM
422	Shellos	TM
423	Gastrodon	TM
427	Buneary	TM
428	Lopunny	TM
446	Munchlax	TM
456	Finneon	TM
457	Lumineon	TM
458	Mantyke	TM
459	Snover	TM
460	Abomasnow	TM
461	Weavile	TM
463	Lickilicky	TM
464	Rhyperior	TM
471	Glaceon	TM
473	Mamoswine	TM
474	Porygon-Z	TM
477	Dusknoir	TM
478	Froslass	TM
481	Mesprit	TM
483	Dialga	TM
484	Palkia	TM
488	Cresselia	TM
489	Phione	TM
490	Manaphy	TM
491	Darkrai	TM

Ice Fang

24	Arbok	B
111	Rhyhorn	E
130	Gyarados	32
142	Aerodactyl	B
158	Totodile	20
159	Croconaw	21
160	Feraligatr	21
208	Steelix	B
209	Snubbull	B,E
210	Granbull	B
221	Piloswine	28
245	Suicune	50
248	Tyranitar	B
261	Poochyena	E
295	Exploud	B
303	Mawile	E
309	Electrike	E
318	Carvanha	16
319	Sharpedo	16
361	Snorunt	28
362	Glalie	28
365	Walrein	44
367	Huntail	24
403	Shinx	E
419	Floatzel	B
450	Hippowdon	B
452	Drapion	B
471	Glaceon	43
472	Gliscor	B
473	Mamoswine	28

Ice Punch

7	Squirtle	T
8	Wartortle	T
9	Blastoise	T
31	Nidoqueen	T
34	Nidoking	T
35	Clefairy	T
36	Clefable	T
39	Jigglypuff	T
40	Wigglytuff	T
54	Psyduck	T
55	Golduck	T
56	Mankey	T
57	Primeape	T
61	Poliwhirl	T
62	Poliwrath	T
63	Abra	T,E
64	Kadabra	T
65	Alakazam	T
66	Machop	T,E
67	Machoke	T
68	Machamp	T
80	Slowbro	T
88	Grimer	T
89	Muk	T
92	Gastly	T,E
93	Haunter	T
94	Gengar	T
96	Drowzee	T,E
97	Hypno	T
107	Hitmonchan	31,T
108	Lickitung	T
112	Rhydon	T
113	Chansey	T
115	Kangaskhan	T
122	Mr. Mime	T
124	Jynx	18,T
125	Electabuzz	T
143	Snorlax	T
149	Dragonite	T
150	Mewtwo	T
151	Mew	T
158	Totodile	T,E
159	Croconaw	T
160	Feraligatr	T

*Rotom learns one move when it changes Form, which it forgets when it turns back into Rotom (p. 514).

161	Sentret	T
162	Furret	T
165	Ledyba	T
166	Ledian	T
183	Marill	T
184	Azumarill	T
185	Sudowoodo	T
190	Aipom	T
194	Wooper	T
195	Quagsire	T
199	Slowking	T
209	Snubbull	T
210	Granbull	T
215	Sneasel	T,E
216	Teddiursa	T
217	Ursaring	T
225	Delibird	E
238	Smoochum	T,E
239	Elekid	T,E
241	Miltank	T
242	Blissey	T
248	Tyranitar	T
259	Marshtomp	T
260	Swampert	T
271	Lombre	T
272	Ludicolo	T
280	Ralts	T
281	Kirlia	T
282	Gardevoir	T
287	Slakoth	T
288	Vigoroth	T
289	Slaking	T
293	Whismur	T
294	Loudred	T
295	Exploud	T
296	Makuhita	T
297	Hariyama	T
299	Nosepass	T
302	Sableye	T
303	Mawile	T
306	Aggron	T
307	Meditite	T,E
308	Medicham	B,T
313	Volbeat	T
314	Illumise	T
316	Gulpin	T
317	Swalot	T
326	Grumpig	T
327	Spinda	T
335	Zangoose	T
352	Kecleon	T
356	Dusclops	B,T
375	Metang	T
376	Metagross	T
377	Regirock	T
378	Regice	T
379	Registeel	T
385	Jirachi	T
386	Deoxys (N)	T
418	Buizel	T
419	Floatzel	T
424	Ambipom	T
427	Buneary	E
428	Lopunny	T
446	Munchlax	T
447	Riolu	T
448	Lucario	T
453	Croagunk	T
454	Toxicroak	T
459	Snover	T
460	Abomasnow	B,T
461	Weavile	T
463	Lickilicky	T
464	Rhyperior	T
466	Electivire	T
475	Gallade	T
476	Probopass	T
477	Dusknoir	B,T
478	Froslass	T
480	Uxie	T
481	Mesprit	T
482	Azelf	T
486	Regigigas	B,T

Ice Shard

86	Seel	17
87	Dewgong	17
90	Shellder	28
131	Lapras	10
144	Articuno	15
215	Sneasel	49,E
220	Swinub	28
225	Delibird	E
231	Phanpy	E
361	Snorunt	37
459	Snover	26
460	Abomasnow	26
471	Glaceon	36
478	Froslass	37

Icicle Spear

86	Seel	E
90	Shellder	13,E
220	Swinub	E
222	Corsola	E

Icy Wind

7	Squirtle	T
8	Wartortle	T
9	Blastoise	T
19	Rattata	T
20	Raticate	T
31	Nidoqueen	T
34	Nidoking	T
35	Clefairy	T
36	Clefable	T
39	Jigglypuff	T
40	Wigglytuff	T
52	Meowth	T
53	Persian	T
54	Psyduck	T
55	Golduck	T
60	Poliwag	T
61	Poliwhirl	T
62	Poliwrath	T
72	Tentacool	T
73	Tentacruel	T
79	Slowpoke	T
80	Slowbro	T
86	Seel	11,T
87	Dewgong	B,11,T
90	Shellder	T
91	Cloyster	T
92	Gastly	T
93	Haunter	T
94	Gengar	T
98	Krabby	T
99	Kingler	T
104	Cubone	T
105	Marowak	T
108	Lickitung	T
111	Rhyhorn	T
112	Rhydon	T
113	Chansey	T
115	Kangaskhan	T
116	Horsea	T
117	Seadra	T
118	Goldeen	T
119	Seaking	T
120	Staryu	T
121	Starmie	T
124	Jynx	T
128	Tauros	T
130	Gyarados	T
131	Lapras	T
134	Vaporeon	T
137	Porygon	T
138	Omanyte	T
139	Omastar	T
140	Kabuto	T,E
141	Kabutops	T
143	Snorlax	T
144	Articuno	T
147	Dratini	T
148	Dragonair	T
149	Dragonite	T
150	Mewtwo	T
151	Mew	T
158	Totodile	T
159	Croconaw	T
160	Feraligatr	T
170	Chinchou	T
171	Lanturn	T
173	Cleffa	T
174	Igglybuff	T
183	Marill	T
184	Azumarill	T
186	Politoed	T
194	Wooper	T
195	Quagsire	T
198	Murkrow	T
199	Slowking	T
200	Misdreavus	T
211	Qwilfish	T
215	Sneasel	28,T
220	Swinub	25,T
221	Piloswine	25,T
222	Corsola	T
223	Remoraid	T
224	Octillery	T
225	Delibird	T
226	Mantine	T
227	Skarmory	T
230	Kingdra	T
233	Porygon2	T
238	Smoochum	T
241	Miltank	T
242	Blissey	T
245	Suicune	T
249	Lugia	T
258	Mudkip	T
259	Marshtomp	T
260	Swampert	T
263	Zigzagoon	T
264	Linoone	T
270	Lotad	T
271	Lombre	T
272	Ludicolo	T
275	Shiftry	T
278	Wingull	T
279	Pelipper	T
280	Ralts	T
281	Kirlia	T
282	Gardevoir	T
283	Surskit	T
284	Masquerain	T
287	Slakoth	T
288	Vigoroth	T
289	Slaking	T
293	Whismur	T
294	Loudred	T
295	Exploud	T
298	Azurill	T
300	Skitty	T
301	Delcatty	T
302	Sableye	T
303	Mawile	T
306	Aggron	T
318	Carvanha	T
319	Sharpedo	T
320	Wailmer	T
321	Wailord	T
325	Spoink	T
326	Grumpig	T
327	Spinda	T
335	Zangoose	T
339	Barboach	T
340	Whiscash	T
341	Corphish	T
342	Crawdaunt	T
349	Feebas	T
350	Milotic	T
351	Castform	T
352	Kecleon	T
353	Shuppet	T
354	Banette	T
355	Duskull	T
356	Dusclops	T
358	Chimecho	T
359	Absol	T
361	Snorunt	13,T
362	Glalie	13,T
363	Spheal	T
364	Sealeo	T
365	Walrein	T
366	Clamperl	T
367	Huntail	T
368	Gorebyss	T
369	Relicanth	T
370	Luvdisc	T
375	Metang	T
376	Metagross	T
378	Regice	9,T
380	Latias	T
381	Latios	T
382	Kyogre	T
384	Rayquaza	T
385	Jirachi	T
386	Deoxys (N)	T
393	Piplup	T
394	Prinplup	T
395	Empoleon	T
399	Bidoof	T
400	Bibarel	T
418	Buizel	T
419	Floatzel	T
422	Shellos	T
423	Gastrodon	T
425	Drifloon	T
426	Drifblim	T
429	Mismagius	T
433	Chingling	T
440	Happiny	T
442	Spiritomb	T
446	Munchlax	T
453	Croagunk	T
454	Toxicroak	T
456	Finneon	T
457	Lumineon	T
458	Mantyke	T
459	Snover	9,T
460	Abomasnow	B,9,T
461	Weavile	28,T
463	Lickilicky	T
464	Rhyperior	T
471	Glaceon	15,T
473	Mamoswine	T
474	Porygon-Z	T
477	Dusknoir	T
478	Froslass	13,T
486	Regigigas	T
487	Giratina (A)	T
487	Giratina (O)	T
488	Cresselia	T
489	Phione	T
490	Manaphy	T
491	Darkrai	T

Imprison

37	Vulpix	21
88	Grimer	E
200	Misdreavus	E
234	Stantler	43
280	Ralts	32
281	Kirlia	36
282	Gardevoir	40
353	Shuppet	E
355	Duskull	E
436	Bronzor	12
437	Bronzong	B,12
442	Spiritomb	E
480	Uxie	6
481	Mesprit	6
482	Azelf	6

Ingrain

1	Bulbasaur	E
43	Oddish	E
69	Bellsprout	E
102	Exeggcute	E
114	Tangela	B
152	Chikorita	E
191	Sunkern	9,E
192	Sunflora	9
222	Corsola	E
315	Roselia	34
331	Cacnea	25
332	Cacturne	25
345	Lileep	15
346	Cradily	B,15
455	Carnivine	21
459	Snover	31
460	Abomasnow	31
465	Tangrowth	B

Iron Defense

7	Squirtle	34,T
8	Wartortle	40,T
9	Blastoise	46,T
11	Metapod	T
14	Kakuna	T
80	Slowbro	T
81	Magnemite	T
82	Magneton	T
90	Shellder	40,T
91	Cloyster	T
98	Krabby	T
99	Kingler	T
104	Cubone	T
105	Marowak	T
122	Mr. Mime	T
127	Pinsir	T
138	Omanyte	T
139	Omastar	T
140	Kabuto	T
141	Kabutops	T
151	Mew	T
199	Slowking	T
204	Pineco	39,T
205	Forretress	45,T
212	Scizor	37,T
214	Heracross	T
218	Slugma	T
219	Magcargo	T
227	Skarmory	T
232	Donphan	T
246	Larvitar	E
247	Pupitar	T
266	Silcoon	T
268	Cascoon	T
299	Nosepass	T
303	Mawile	41,T
304	Aron	18,T
305	Lairon	18,T
306	Aggron	18,T
324	Torkoal	44,T
338	Solrock	T
341	Corphish	T
342	Crawdaunt	T
347	Anorith	T
348	Armaldo	T
366	Clamperl	B,T
372	Shelgon	T
374	Beldum	T
375	Metang	40,T
376	Metagross	40,T
377	Regirock	41
379	Registeel	41,T
385	Jirachi	T
386	Deoxys (D)	73,T
395	Empoleon	T
410	Shieldon	19,T
411	Bastiodon	19,T
413	Wormadam (T)	T
436	Bronzor	26
437	Bronzong	26
447	Riolu	T,E
448	Lucario	T
462	Magnezone	T
476	Probopass	B,7,T
483	Dialga	T
485	Heatran	T

Iron Head

59	Arcanine	T
76	Golem	T
95	Onix	T
104	Cubone	E
128	Tauros	T
130	Gyarados	T
131	Lapras	T
142	Aerodactyl	49,T
143	Snorlax	T
149	Dragonite	T
151	Mew	T
208	Steelix	T
212	Scizor	53,T
226	Mantine	T
230	Kingdra	T
241	Miltank	T
243	Raikou	T
244	Entei	T
245	Suicune	T
246	Larvitar	T,E
247	Pupitar	T
248	Tyranitar	T
249	Lugia	T
250	Ho-Oh	T
297	Hariyama	T
303	Mawile	56,T
304	Aron	29,T,E
305	Lairon	29,T
306	Aggron	29,T
321	Wailord	T
323	Camerupt	T
337	Lunatone	T
338	Solrock	T
350	Milotic	T
362	Glalie	T
365	Walrein	T
374	Beldum	T
375	Metang	T
376	Metagross	T
377	Regirock	T
378	Regice	T
379	Registeel	73,T
382	Kyogre	T
383	Groudon	T
384	Rayquaza	T
385	Jirachi	T
389	Torterra	T
408	Cranidos	T
409	Rampardos	T
410	Shieldon	43,T
411	Bastiodon	52,T
413	Wormadam (T)	47,T
437	Bronzong	T
443	Gible	T,E
444	Gabite	T
445	Garchomp	T
450	Hippowdon	T
462	Magnezone	T
464	Rhyperior	T
473	Mamoswine	T
476	Probopass	T
483	Dialga	T
485	Heatran	65,T
486	Regigigas	T
487	Giratina (A)	T
487	Giratina (O)	T

Iron Tail

4	Charmander	TM
5	Charmeleon	TM
6	Charizard	TM
7	Squirtle	TM
8	Wartortle	TM
9	Blastoise	TM
19	Rattata	TM
20	Raticate	TM
23	Ekans	TM
24	Arbok	TM
25	Pikachu	TM
26	Raichu	TM
27	Sandshrew	TM
28	Sandslash	TM
29	Nidoran♀	TM
30	Nidorina	TM
31	Nidoqueen	TM
32	Nidoran♂	TM
33	Nidorino	TM
34	Nidoking	TM
35	Clefairy	TM
36	Clefable	TM
37	Vulpix	TM
38	Ninetales	TM
52	Meowth	TM
53	Persian	TM
54	Psyduck	TM
55	Golduck	TM
56	Mankey	TM
57	Primeape	TM
58	Growlithe	TM
59	Arcanine	TM
63	Abra	TM
64	Kadabra	TM
65	Alakazam	TM
77	Ponyta	TM
78	Rapidash	TM
79	Slowpoke	TM
80	Slowbro	TM
83	Farfetch'd	TM
95	Onix	41,TM
104	Cubone	TM
105	Marowak	TM
108	Lickitung	TM
111	Rhyhorn	TM
112	Rhydon	TM
113	Chansey	TM
115	Kangaskhan	TM
125	Electabuzz	TM
126	Magmar	TM
128	Tauros	TM
131	Lapras	TM
133	Eevee	TM
134	Vaporeon	TM
135	Jolteon	TM
136	Flareon	TM
137	Porygon	TM
142	Aerodactyl	TM
147	Dratini	TM
148	Dragonair	TM
149	Dragonite	TM
150	Mewtwo	TM
151	Mew	TM
152	Chikorita	TM
153	Bayleef	TM
154	Meganium	TM
158	Totodile	TM
159	Croconaw	TM
160	Feraligatr	TM
161	Sentret	TM
162	Furret	TM
172	Pichu	TM
173	Cleffa	TM
179	Mareep	TM
180	Flaaffy	TM
181	Ampharos	TM
183	Marill	TM
184	Azumarill	TM
190	Aipom	TM
194	Wooper	TM
195	Quagsire	TM
196	Espeon	TM
197	Umbreon	TM
199	Slowking	TM
203	Girafarig	TM
206	Dunsparce	TM
207	Gligar	TM
208	Steelix	41,TM
210	Granbull	TM
215	Sneasel	TM
228	Houndour	TM
229	Houndoom	TM
231	Phanpy	TM
232	Donphan	TM
233	Porygon2	TM
234	Stantler	TM
240	Magby	TM
241	Miltank	TM
242	Blissey	TM
243	Raikou	TM
244	Entei	TM
245	Suicune	TM
248	Tyranitar	TM
249	Lugia	TM
252	Treecko	TM
253	Grovyle	TM
254	Sceptile	TM
258	Mudkip	TM
259	Marshtomp	TM
260	Swampert	TM
261	Poochyena	TM
262	Mightyena	TM
263	Zigzagoon	TM
264	Linoone	TM
286	Breloom	TM
298	Azurill	TM
300	Skitty	TM
301	Delcatty	TM
304	Aron	39,TM
305	Lairon	45,TM
306	Aggron	48,TM
309	Electrike	TM
310	Manectric	TM
311	Plusle	TM
312	Minun	TM
324	Torkoal	TM
325	Spoink	TM
326	Grumpig	TM
330	Flygon	TM
334	Altaria	TM
335	Zangoose	TM
336	Seviper	TM
348	Armaldo	TM
350	Milotic	TM
352	Kecleon	TM
359	Absol	TM
363	Spheal	TM
364	Sealeo	TM
365	Walrein	TM
373	Salamence	TM
383	Groudon	TM
384	Rayquaza	TM
387	Turtwig	TM
388	Grotle	TM
389	Torterra	TM
390	Chimchar	TM
391	Monferno	TM
392	Infernape	TM
399	Bidoof	TM
400	Bibarel	TM
403	Shinx	TM
404	Luxio	TM
405	Luxray	TM
408	Cranidos	TM
409	Rampardos	TM
410	Shieldon	TM
411	Bastiodon	TM
417	Pachirisu	TM
418	Buizel	TM
419	Floatzel	TM
424	Ambipom	TM
427	Buneary	TM
428	Lopunny	TM
431	Glameow	TM
432	Purugly	TM
434	Stunky	TM
435	Skuntank	TM
444	Gabite	TM
445	Garchomp	TM
447	Riolu	TM
448	Lucario	TM
449	Hippopotas	TM
450	Hippowdon	TM
451	Skorupi	TM
452	Drapion	TM
459	Snover	TM
460	Abomasnow	TM
461	Weavile	TM
463	Lickilicky	TM
464	Rhyperior	TM
466	Electivire	TM
467	Magmortar	TM
470	Leafeon	TM
471	Glaceon	TM
472	Gliscor	TM
474	Porygon-Z	TM
480	Uxie	TM
481	Mesprit	TM
482	Azelf	TM
483	Dialga	TM
487	Giratina (A)	TM
487	Giratina (O)	TM

Jump Kick

106	Hitmonlee	13
427	Buneary	23
428	Lopunny	23

Karate Chop

56	Mankey	13
57	Primeape	13
66	Machop	10
67	Machoke	10
68	Machamp	10
239	Elekid	E
240	Magby	E

Kinesis

64	Kadabra	B
65	Alakazam	B

Knock Off		
1	Bulbasaur	T
2	Ivysaur	T
3	Venusaur	T
15	Beedrill	T
25	Pikachu	T
26	Raichu	T
27	Sandshrew	T
28	Sandslash	T
35	Clefairy	T
36	Clefable	T
39	Jigglypuff	T
40	Wigglytuff	T
46	Paras	T
47	Parasect	T
52	Meowth	T
53	Persian	T
63	Abra	T,E
64	Kadabra	T
65	Alakazam	T
69	Bellsprout	27,T
70	Weepinbell	27,T
71	Victreebel	T
72	Tentacool	T,E
73	Tentacruel	T
83	Farfetch'd	9,T
84	Doduo	T
85	Dodrio	T
92	Gastly	T
93	Haunter	T
94	Gengar	T
98	Krabby	T,E
99	Kingler	T
104	Cubone	T
105	Marowak	T
106	Hitmonlee	T
108	Lickitung	13,T
114	Tangela	36,T
118	Goldeen	T
119	Seaking	T
123	Scyther	T
127	Pinsir	T
138	Omanyte	T,E
139	Omastar	T
140	Kabuto	T,E
141	Kabutops	T
151	Mew	T
161	Sentret	T
162	Furret	T
165	Ledyba	T,E
166	Ledian	T
183	Marill	T
184	Azumarill	T
190	Aipom	T
207	Gligar	12,T
212	Scizor	T
213	Shuckle	E
214	Heracross	T
215	Sneasel	T
231	Phanpy	T
232	Donphan	10,T
257	Blaziken	T
275	Shiftry	T
278	Wingull	T,E
279	Pelipper	T
296	Makuhita	19,T
297	Hariyama	19,T
298	Azurill	T
302	Sableye	29,T
303	Mawile	T
335	Zangoose	T
336	Seviper	T
341	Corphish	26,T,E
342	Crawdaunt	26,T
347	Anorith	T,E
348	Armaldo	T
352	Kecleon	T
353	Shuppet	B,T
354	Banette	B,T
358	Chimecho	T
359	Absol	T
386	Deoxys (N)	25,T
386	Deoxys (D)	25,T
386	Deoxys (S)	25,T
395	Empoleon	T
402	Kricketune	T
424	Ambipom	T
425	Drifloon	T
426	Drifblim	T
431	Glameow	T
432	Purugly	T
433	Chingling	T
451	Skorupi	6,T
452	Drapion	B,6,T
453	Croagunk	T
454	Toxicroak	T
455	Carnivine	T
461	Weavile	T
463	Lickilicky	13,T
465	Tangrowth	36,T
470	Leafeon	T
472	Gliscor	B,12,T
473	Mamoswine	T
475	Gallade	T
480	Uxie	T
481	Mesprit	T
482	Azelf	T
486	Regigigas	B
489	Phione	T
490	Manaphy	T
491	Darkrai	T

Last Resort		
19	Rattata	T,E
20	Raticate	T
35	Clefairy	T
36	Clefable	T
39	Jigglypuff	T
40	Wigglytuff	T
52	Meowth	T,E
53	Persian	T
83	Farfetch'd	T
113	Chansey	T
133	Eevee	50,T
134	Vaporeon	50,T
135	Jolteon	50,T
136	Flareon	50,T
137	Porygon	T
143	Snorlax	T
151	Mew	T
161	Sentret	T,E
162	Furret	T
173	Cleffa	T
174	Igglybuff	T,E
175	Togepi	51,T
176	Togetic	51,T
190	Aipom	43,T
196	Espeon	50,T
197	Umbreon	50,T
206	Dunsparce	T
209	Snubbull	T
210	Granbull	T
216	Teddiursa	T
217	Ursaring	T
231	Phanpy	37
233	Porygon2	T
234	Stantler	T
242	Blissey	T
251	Celebi	T
255	Torchic	T,E
256	Combusken	T
257	Blaziken	T
263	Zigzagoon	T
264	Linoone	T
300	Skitty	T,E
301	Delcatty	T
311	Plusle	48,T
312	Minun	T
327	Spinda	T
335	Zangoose	T
351	Castform	T
352	Kecleon	T
358	Chimecho	T
380	Latias	T
381	Latios	T
385	Jirachi	65,T
399	Bidoof	T
400	Bibarel	T
417	Pachirisu	37,T
424	Ambipom	43,T
427	Buneary	T
428	Lopunny	T
431	Glameow	T
432	Purugly	T
433	Chingling	22,T
440	Happiny	T,E
446	Munchlax	49,T
468	Togekiss	T
470	Leafeon	50,T
471	Glaceon	50,T
474	Porygon-Z	T
482	Azelf	61,T
489	Phione	T
490	Manaphy	T
491	Darkrai	T
492	Shaymin (L)	T
492	Shaymin (S)	T

Lava Plume		
126	Magmar	36
136	Flareon	78
155	Cyndaquil	31
156	Quilava	35
157	Typhlosion	35
218	Slugma	38
219	Magcargo	40
240	Magby	34
244	Entei	57
322	Numel	31
323	Camerupt	31
324	Torkoal	39
467	Magmortar	37
485	Heatran	49

Leaf Blade		
71	Victreebel	47
182	Bellossom	B
253	Grovyle	29
254	Sceptile	29
357	Tropius	E
470	Leafeon	71
475	Gallade	B

Leaf Storm		
1	Bulbasaur	E
71	Victreebel	47
102	Exeggcute	E
103	Exeggutor	47
114	Tangela	E
152	Chikorita	E
182	Bellossom	53
192	Sunflora	43
251	Celebi	82
252	Treecko	E
253	Grovyle	59
254	Sceptile	67
275	Shiftry	49
315	Roselia	E
357	Tropius	61,E
387	Turtwig	45
388	Grotle	52
389	Torterra	57
406	Budew	E
413	Wormadam (P)	47
479	Rotom (G)	*
492	Shaymin (S)	91

Leech Life		
41	Zubat	B
42	Golbat	B
46	Paras	11
47	Parasect	B,11
48	Venonat	17
49	Venomoth	17
69	Bellsprout	E
167	Spinarak	12
168	Ariados	12
169	Crobat	B
193	Yanma	E
290	Nincada	5
291	Ninjask	B,5
292	Shedinja	5
402	Kricketune	14

Leech Seed		
1	Bulbasaur	7
2	Ivysaur	B,7
3	Venusaur	B,7
102	Exeggcute	11
114	Tangela	E
152	Chikorita	E
187	Hoppip	22
188	Skiploom	24
189	Jumpluff	24
191	Sunkern	17,E
192	Sunflora	17
251	Celebi	B
252	Treecko	E
270	Lotad	E
273	Seedot	E
285	Shroomish	13
286	Breloom	B,13
315	Roselia	16
331	Cacnea	13
332	Cacturne	13
357	Tropius	E
387	Turtwig	29
388	Grotle	32
389	Torterra	33
420	Cherubi	10
421	Cherrim	10
455	Carnivine	E
459	Snover	E
492	Shaymin (L)	19
492	Shaymin (S)	19

Leer		
21	Spearow	5
22	Fearow	B,5
23	Ekans	B
24	Arbok	B
32	Nidoran♂	B
33	Nidorino	B
56	Mankey	B
57	Primeape	B
58	Growlithe	9
66	Machop	B
67	Machoke	B
68	Machamp	B
83	Farfetch'd	B
90	Shellder	20
98	Krabby	9
99	Kingler	9
104	Cubone	13
105	Marowak	13
115	Kangaskhan	B
116	Horsea	B
117	Seadra	B,8
123	Scyther	B
125	Electabuzz	B
126	Magmar	B
130	Gyarados	26
138	Omanyte	19
139	Omastar	19
140	Kabuto	11
141	Kabutops	B,11
147	Dratini	B
148	Dragonair	B
149	Dragonite	B
155	Cyndaquil	B
156	Quilava	B
157	Typhlosion	B
158	Totodile	B
159	Croconaw	B
160	Feraligatr	B
177	Natu	B
178	Xatu	B
212	Scizor	B
214	Heracross	B
215	Sneasel	B
216	Teddiursa	B
217	Ursaring	B
227	Skarmory	B
228	Houndour	B
229	Houndoom	B
230	Kingdra	B,8
234	Stantler	3
239	Elekid	B
240	Magby	B
243	Raikou	B
244	Entei	B
245	Suicune	B
246	Larvitar	B
247	Pupitar	B
248	Tyranitar	B
252	Treecko	B
253	Grovyle	B
254	Sceptile	B
261	Poochyena	E
302	Sableye	B
309	Electrike	9
310	Manectric	B,9
318	Carvanha	B
319	Sharpedo	B
331	Cacnea	B
332	Cacturne	B
335	Zangoose	B
341	Corphish	13
342	Crawdaunt	B,13
355	Duskull	B
356	Dusclops	B
357	Tropius	B
359	Absol	4
361	Snorunt	B
362	Glalie	B
371	Bagon	10
372	Shelgon	B,10
373	Salamence	B,10
386	Deoxys (N)	B
386	Deoxys (A)	B
386	Deoxys (D)	B
386	Deoxys (S)	B
390	Chimchar	B
391	Monferno	B
392	Infernape	B
403	Shinx	5
404	Luxio	B,5
405	Luxray	B,5
408	Cranidos	B,E
409	Rampardos	B
434	Stunky	E
451	Skorupi	B
452	Drapion	B
459	Snover	B
460	Abomasnow	B
461	Weavile	B
466	Electivire	B
467	Magmortar	B
475	Gallade	B
477	Dusknoir	B
478	Froslass	B
485	Heatran	9

Lick		
86	Seel	E
88	Grimer	E
92	Gastly	B
93	Haunter	B
94	Gengar	B
108	Lickitung	B
124	Jynx	B,5
143	Snorlax	12,E
209	Snubbull	13
210	Granbull	13
216	Teddiursa	B
217	Ursaring	B
238	Smoochum	5
336	Seviper	7
352	Kecleon	B
446	Munchlax	12,E
463	Lickilicky	B

Light Screen		
1	Bulbasaur	E
25	Pikachu	42,TM
26	Raichu	TM
35	Clefairy	40,TM
36	Clefable	TM
39	Jigglypuff	TM
40	Wigglytuff	TM
46	Paras	E
54	Psyduck	E
63	Abra	TM
64	Kadabra	TM
65	Alakazam	TM
66	Machop	E
79	Slowpoke	TM
80	Slowbro	TM
81	Magnemite	TM
82	Magneton	TM
96	Drowzee	TM
97	Hypno	TM
100	Voltorb	22,TM
101	Electrode	22,TM
102	Exeggcute	TM
103	Exeggutor	TM
113	Chansey	34,TM
120	Staryu	42,TM
121	Starmie	TM
122	Mr. Mime	22,TM
123	Scyther	E
124	Jynx	TM
125	Electabuzz	25,TM
135	Jolteon	TM
145	Zapdos	64,TM
147	Dratini	E
150	Mewtwo	TM
151	Mew	TM
152	Chikorita	31,TM
153	Bayleef	36,TM
154	Meganium	40,TM
165	Ledyba	14,TM
166	Ledian	14,TM
172	Pichu	TM
173	Cleffa	TM
174	Igglybuff	TM
175	Togepi	TM
176	Togetic	TM
177	Natu	TM
178	Xatu	TM
179	Mareep	37,TM
180	Flaaffy	42,TM
181	Ampharos	51,TM
183	Marill	E
191	Sunkern	TM
192	Sunflora	TM
196	Espeon	TM
199	Slowking	TM
203	Girafarig	TM
204	Pineco	TM
205	Forretress	TM
218	Slugma	TM
219	Magcargo	TM
220	Swinub	TM
221	Piloswine	TM
222	Corsola	TM
234	Stantler	TM
238	Smoochum	TM
239	Elekid	25,TM
242	Blissey	34,TM
243	Raikou	TM
249	Lugia	TM
250	Ho-Oh	TM
251	Celebi	TM
269	Dustox	31,TM
280	Ralts	TM
281	Kirlia	TM
282	Gardevoir	TM
307	Meditite	TM
308	Medicham	TM
309	Electrike	TM
310	Manectric	TM
311	Plusle	TM
312	Minun	TM
313	Volbeat	TM
314	Illumise	TM
325	Spoink	TM
326	Grumpig	TM
337	Lunatone	TM
338	Solrock	TM
343	Baltoy	TM
344	Claydol	TM
349	Feebas	E
358	Chimecho	TM
361	Snorunt	TM
362	Glalie	TM
375	Metang	TM
376	Metagross	TM
380	Latias	TM
381	Latios	TM
385	Jirachi	TM
386	Deoxys (N)	TM
386	Deoxys (A)	TM
386	Deoxys (D)	TM
386	Deoxys (S)	TM
387	Turtwig	TM
388	Grotle	TM
389	Torterra	TM
403	Shinx	TM
404	Luxio	TM
405	Luxray	TM
417	Pachirisu	TM
433	Chingling	TM
436	Bronzor	TM
437	Bronzong	TM
439	Mime Jr.	22,TM
440	Happiny	TM
459	Snover	TM
460	Abomasnow	TM
462	Magnezone	TM
466	Electivire	25,TM
468	Togekiss	TM
473	Mamoswine	TM
475	Gallade	TM
478	Froslass	TM
479	Rotom	TM
480	Uxie	TM
481	Mesprit	TM
482	Azelf	TM
488	Cresselia	TM
490	Manaphy	TM

Lock-On		
81	Magnemite	27
82	Magneton	27
137	Porygon	45
223	Remoraid	6
233	Porygon2	45
299	Nosepass	73
377	Regirock	57
378	Regice	57
379	Registeel	57
462	Magnezone	27
474	Porygon-Z	45
476	Probopass	73

Lovely Kiss		
124	Jynx	B,8

Low Kick		
56	Mankey	B
57	Primeape	B
66	Machop	B
67	Machoke	B
68	Machamp	B
125	Electabuzz	10
185	Sudowoodo	B,9
239	Elekid	10
331	Cacnea	E
427	Buneary	E
438	Bonsly	9
447	Riolu	E
466	Electivire	B,10

Lucky Chant		
35	Clefairy	28
43	Oddish	25
44	Gloom	29
102	Exeggcute	E
175	Togepi	E
177	Natu	12
178	Xatu	12
222	Corsola	28
238	Smoochum	28
280	Ralts	17
281	Kirlia	17
351	Castform	E
370	Luvdisc	17
420	Cherubi	40
421	Cherrim	48
429	Mismagius	B
481	Mesprit	31

Lunar Dance		
488	Cresselia	84

Luster Purge		
381	Latios	35

Mach Punch		
107	Hitmonchan	16
165	Ledyba	17
166	Ledian	17
236	Tyrogue	E
240	Magby	E
286	Breloom	23
391	Monferno	14
392	Infernape	14

Magic Coat		
137	Porygon	56
203	Girafarig	E
206	Dunsparce	E
233	Porygon2	56
325	Spoink	21
326	Grumpig	21
352	Kecleon	E
359	Absol	E
428	Lopunny	B
474	Porygon-Z	56

Magical Leaf		
1	Bulbasaur	E
69	Bellsprout	E
122	Mr. Mime	B
152	Chikorita	20
153	Bayleef	22
154	Meganium	22
173	Cleffa	16
176	Togetic	B
182	Bellossom	23
251	Celebi	19
252	Treecko	E
280	Ralts	21
281	Kirlia	22
282	Gardevoir	22
315	Roselia	19
331	Cacnea	E
357	Tropius	31
407	Roserade	B
420	Cherubi	19
421	Cherrim	19
429	Mismagius	B
455	Carnivine	E
459	Snover	E
470	Leafeon	36
492	Shaymin (L)	10
492	Shaymin (S)	10

Magma Storm		
485	Heatran	96

Magnet Bomb		
81	Magnemite	30
82	Magneton	30
462	Magnezone	30
476	Probopass	B,13

Magnet Rise		
25	Pikachu	T
26	Raichu	T
81	Magnemite	45,T
82	Magneton	50,T
100	Voltorb	36,T
101	Electrode	40,T
125	Electabuzz	T
135	Jolteon	T
137	Porygon	23
151	Mew	T
172	Pichu	T
179	Mareep	T
180	Flaaffy	T
181	Ampharos	T
205	Forretress	62,T
208	Steelix	T
233	Porygon2	23
239	Elekid	T
243	Raikou	T
299	Nosepass	T
303	Mawile	T
304	Aron	T
305	Lairon	T
306	Aggron	T
309	Electrike	T
310	Manectric	T
311	Plusle	T
312	Minun	T
375	Metang	B,T
376	Metagross	B,T
379	Registeel	T
403	Shinx	T
404	Luxio	T

405	Luxray	T
410	Shieldon	T
411	Bastiodon	T
413	Wormadam (T)	T
417	Pachirisu	T
447	Riolu	T
448	Lucario	T
462	Magnezone	50,T
466	Electivire	T
474	Porygon-Z	23
476	Probopass	B,T
483	Dialga	T

Magnitude

50	Diglett	12
51	Dugtrio	12
74	Geodude	15
75	Graveler	15
76	Golem	15
108	Lickitung	E
111	Rhyhorn	E
232	Donphan	19
299	Nosepass	E
322	Numel	11
323	Camerupt	B,11
339	Barboach	26
340	Whiscash	26
369	Relicanth	E

Me First

19	Rattata	E
79	Slowpoke	E
108	Lickitung	37
150	Mewtwo	79
151	Mew	70
161	Sentret	42
162	Furret	50
177	Natu	20
178	Xatu	20
234	Stantler	53
261	Poochyena	E
359	Absol	57,E
448	Lucario	29
453	Croagunk	E
463	Lickilicky	37

Mean Look

41	Zubat	29
42	Golbat	33
88	Grimer	E
92	Gastly	8
93	Haunter	8
94	Gengar	8
124	Jynx	21
169	Crobat	33
197	Umbreon	57
198	Murkrow	41
200	Misdreavus	19
238	Smoochum	21
280	Ralts	E
302	Sableye	57
355	Duskull	38
356	Dusclops	43
359	Absol	E
477	Dusknoir	43

Meditate

56	Mankey	E
66	Machop	E
96	Drowzee	21
97	Hypno	21
106	Hitmonlee	5
122	Mr. Mime	8
238	Smoochum	E
239	Elekid	E
307	Meditite	4
308	Medicham	B,4
439	Mime Jr.	8
453	Croagunk	E

Mega Drain

43	Oddish	21
44	Gloom	23
45	Vileplume	B
114	Tangela	26,E
140	Kabuto	36
141	Kabutops	36
182	Bellossom	B
187	Hoppip	25
188	Skiploom	28
189	Jumpluff	28
191	Sunkern	5
192	Sunflora	5
252	Treecko	26
267	Beautifly	24
270	Lotad	19
272	Ludicolo	B
285	Shroomish	17
286	Breloom	17
315	Roselia	13
387	Turtwig	25
388	Grotle	27
389	Torterra	27
406	Budew	13
407	Roserade	B
465	Tangrowth	26

Mega Kick

106	Hitmonlee	49

Mega Punch

74	Geodude	E
107	Hitmonchan	41
115	Kangaskhan	19
151	Mew	10
240	Magby	E

Megahorn

34	Nidoking	58
78	Rapidash	B
111	Rhyhorn	57
112	Rhydon	57
118	Goldeen	51
119	Seaking	63
214	Heracross	55
464	Rhyperior	57

Memento

88	Grimer	49
89	Muk	65
109	Koffing	51
110	Weezing	63
187	Hoppip	43
188	Skiploom	52
189	Jumpluff	52
200	Misdreavus	E
218	Slugma	E
280	Ralts	E
355	Duskull	E
381	Latios	60
422	Shellos	E
425	Drifloon	E
434	Stunky	38
435	Skuntank	42
442	Spiritomb	43
480	Uxie	76

Metal Burst

304	Aron	46
305	Lairon	56
306	Aggron	65
410	Shieldon	37
411	Bastiodon	43

Metal Claw

4	Charmander	E
27	Sandshrew	E
46	Paras	E
98	Krabby	21
99	Kingler	21
158	Totodile	E
207	Gligar	E
212	Scizor	21
215	Sneasel	42
216	Teddiursa	E
290	Nincada	38
304	Aron	15
305	Lairon	15
306	Aggron	15
335	Zangoose	E
341	Corphish	E
347	Anorith	19
348	Armaldo	19
375	Metang	B,20
376	Metagross	B,20
379	Registeel	9
394	Prinplup	16
395	Empoleon	16
443	Gible	E
448	Lucario	B
461	Weavile	42
483	Dialga	10

Metal Sound

81	Magnemite	B
82	Magneton	B
140	Kabuto	41
141	Kabutops	45
227	Skarmory	31
304	Aron	36
305	Lairon	40
306	Aggron	40
410	Shieldon	10
411	Bastiodon	B,10
413	Wormadam (T)	29
448	Lucario	24
462	Magnezone	B
485	Heatran	25

Meteor Mash

35	Clefairy	43
375	Metang	48
376	Metagross	53

Metronome

35	Clefairy	31
36	Clefable	B
113	Chansey	E
151	Mew	20
173	Cleffa	E
175	Togepi	6
176	Togetic	B,6
209	Snubbull	E
440	Happiny	E
446	Munchlax	B

Milk Drink

241	Miltank	11

Mimic

39	Jigglypuff	41
122	Mr. Mime	18,E
173	Cleffa	E
185	Sudowoodo	17
438	Bonsly	17
439	Mime Jr.	18,E
441	Chatot	29

Mind Reader

60	Poliwag	E
62	Poliwrath	53
106	Hitmonlee	33
144	Articuno	22
236	Tyrogue	E
283	Surskit	E
286	Breloom	37
290	Nincada	19
291	Ninjask	19
292	Shedinja	19
307	Meditite	18
308	Medicham	18
315	Roselia	E
406	Budew	E
447	Riolu	E

Minimize

35	Clefairy	19
36	Clefable	B
88	Grimer	17
89	Muk	17
113	Chansey	20
120	Staryu	33
211	Qwilfish	9
242	Blissey	20
425	Drifloon	B
426	Drifblim	B

Miracle Eye

64	Kadabra	22
65	Alakazam	22
150	Mewtwo	36
177	Natu	17
178	Xatu	17
238	Smoochum	E

Mirror Coat

7	Squirtle	E
72	Tentacool	E
100	Voltorb	47
101	Electrode	57
202	Wobbuffet	B
203	Girafarig	E
222	Corsola	48
226	Mantine	E
245	Suicune	43
258	Mudkip	E
325	Spoink	E
345	Lileep	E
349	Feebas	E
360	Wynaut	15
386	Deoxys (D)	97
422	Shellos	E
428	Lopunny	B
458	Mantyke	E
462	Magnezone	B
471	Glaceon	57

Mirror Move

16	Pidgey	45
17	Pidgeotto	52
18	Pidgeot	56
21	Spearow	21
22	Fearow	23
83	Farfetch'd	E
84	Doduo	E
163	Hoothoot	E
175	Togepi	E
198	Murkrow	E
255	Torchic	37
256	Combusken	43
276	Taillow	E
333	Swablu	36
441	Chatot	9

Mirror Shot

81	Magnemite	43
82	Magneton	46
205	Forretress	31
413	Wormadam (T)	26
462	Magnezone	46

Mist

7	Squirtle	E
60	Poliwag	E
131	Lapras	4
144	Articuno	8
147	Dratini	E
150	Mewtwo	43
170	Chinchou	E
194	Wooper	43
195	Quagsire	48
220	Swinub	40
221	Piloswine	48
222	Corsola	E
245	Suicune	36
270	Lotad	11
278	Wingull	16,E
279	Pelipper	16
283	Surskit	37
320	Wailmer	24
321	Wailord	24
333	Swablu	23
334	Altaria	23
349	Feebas	E
393	Piplup	36
394	Prinplup	42
395	Empoleon	46
459	Snover	21,E
460	Abomasnow	21
473	Mamoswine	48
488	Cresselia	20

Mist Ball

380	Latias	35

Moonlight

35	Clefairy	37
43	Oddish	33
44	Gloom	41
102	Exeggcute	E
197	Umbreon	71
269	Dustox	20
302	Sableye	E
313	Volbeat	13
314	Illumise	13
488	Cresselia	57

Morning Sun

48	Venonat	E
196	Espeon	71
267	Beautifly	20

Mud Bomb

23	Ekans	28
24	Arbok	34
50	Diglett	29,E
51	Dugtrio	33
54	Psyduck	E
60	Poliwag	41
61	Poliwhirl	53
88	Grimer	23
89	Muk	23
194	Wooper	19
195	Quagsire	19
220	Swinub	20
221	Piloswine	20
258	Mudkip	E
259	Marshtomp	25
260	Swampert	25
322	Numel	E
339	Barboach	14
340	Whiscash	14
422	Shellos	11
423	Gastrodon	11
453	Croagunk	29
454	Toxicroak	29
473	Mamoswine	20

Mud Shot

60	Poliwag	28,E
61	Poliwhirl	32
90	Shellder	E
98	Krabby	19
99	Kingler	19
138	Omanyte	25
139	Omastar	25
140	Kabuto	16,E
141	Kabutops	16
194	Wooper	9
195	Quagsire	9
220	Swinub	E
259	Marshtomp	16
260	Swampert	16
283	Surskit	E
383	Groudon	B

Mud Sport

7	Squirtle	E
74	Geodude	4
75	Graveler	B,4
76	Golem	B,4
79	Slowpoke	E
95	Onix	B
98	Krabby	B
99	Kingler	B
118	Goldeen	E
158	Totodile	E
194	Wooper	5,E
195	Quagsire	B,5
208	Steelix	B
220	Swinub	4
221	Piloswine	B,4
226	Mantine	E
252	Treecko	E
258	Mudkip	24
263	Zigzagoon	21
264	Linoone	23
339	Barboach	6
340	Whiscash	B,6
341	Corphish	E
347	Anorith	7
348	Armaldo	B,7
349	Feebas	E
366	Clamperl	E
369	Relicanth	36
370	Luvdisc	E
393	Piplup	E
422	Shellos	2
423	Gastrodon	B,2
458	Mantyke	E
473	Mamoswine	B,4

Muddy Water

7	Squirtle	E
134	Vaporeon	78
194	Wooper	47
195	Quagsire	53
259	Marshtomp	37
260	Swampert	39
422	Shellos	37
423	Gastrodon	41

Mud-Slap

1	Bulbasaur	T
2	Ivysaur	T
3	Venusaur	T
4	Charmander	T
5	Charmeleon	T
6	Charizard	T
7	Squirtle	T
8	Wartortle	T
9	Blastoise	T
16	Pidgey	T
17	Pidgeotto	T
18	Pidgeot	T
19	Rattata	T
20	Raticate	T
21	Spearow	T
22	Fearow	T
25	Pikachu	T
26	Raichu	T
27	Sandshrew	T
28	Sandslash	T
29	Nidoran♀	T
30	Nidorina	T
31	Nidoqueen	T
32	Nidoran♂	T
33	Nidorino	T
34	Nidoking	T
35	Clefairy	T
36	Clefable	T
39	Jigglypuff	T
40	Wigglytuff	T
50	Diglett	15,T
51	Dugtrio	15,T
52	Meowth	T
53	Persian	T
54	Psyduck	T
55	Golduck	T
56	Mankey	T
57	Primeape	T
58	Growlithe	T
59	Arcanine	T
61	Poliwhirl	T
62	Poliwrath	T
66	Machop	T
67	Machoke	T
68	Machamp	T
74	Geodude	T
75	Graveler	T
76	Golem	T
79	Slowpoke	T
80	Slowbro	T
83	Farfetch'd	T,E
84	Doduo	T
85	Dodrio	T
88	Grimer	7,T
89	Muk	B,7,T
95	Onix	T
98	Krabby	T
99	Kingler	T
104	Cubone	T
105	Marowak	T
106	Hitmonlee	T
107	Hitmonchan	T
108	Lickitung	T
111	Rhyhorn	T
112	Rhydon	T
113	Chansey	T
115	Kangaskhan	T
118	Goldeen	T,E
119	Seaking	T
122	Mr. Mime	T
124	Jynx	T
125	Electabuzz	T
126	Magmar	T
133	Eevee	T
134	Vaporeon	T
135	Jolteon	T
136	Flareon	T
140	Kabuto	T
141	Kabutops	T
143	Snorlax	T
144	Articuno	T
145	Zapdos	T
146	Moltres	T
149	Dragonite	T
150	Mewtwo	T
151	Mew	T
152	Chikorita	T
153	Bayleef	T
154	Meganium	T
155	Cyndaquil	T
156	Quilava	T
157	Typhlosion	T
158	Totodile	T
159	Croconaw	T
160	Feraligatr	T
161	Sentret	T
162	Furret	T
163	Hoothoot	T
164	Noctowl	T
172	Pichu	T
173	Cleffa	T
174	Igglybuff	T
175	Togepi	T
176	Togetic	T
183	Marill	T
184	Azumarill	T
185	Sudowoodo	T
186	Politoed	T
190	Aipom	T
194	Wooper	T
195	Quagsire	T
196	Espeon	T
197	Umbreon	T
198	Murkrow	T
199	Slowking	T
203	Girafarig	T
206	Dunsparce	T
208	Steelix	T
209	Snubbull	T
210	Granbull	T
213	Shuckle	T,E
215	Sneasel	T
216	Teddiursa	T
217	Ursaring	T
218	Slugma	T
219	Magcargo	T
220	Swinub	13,T
221	Piloswine	13,T
222	Corsola	T
223	Remoraid	T
224	Octillery	T
225	Delibird	T
226	Mantine	T
227	Skarmory	T
228	Houndour	T
229	Houndoom	T
231	Phanpy	T
232	Donphan	T
234	Stantler	T
236	Tyrogue	T
237	Hitmontop	T
238	Smoochum	T
239	Elekid	T
240	Magby	T
241	Miltank	T
242	Blissey	T
243	Raikou	T
244	Entei	T
245	Suicune	T
246	Larvitar	T
247	Pupitar	T
248	Tyranitar	T
249	Lugia	T
250	Ho-Oh	T
251	Celebi	T
252	Treecko	T
253	Grovyle	T
254	Sceptile	T
255	Torchic	T
256	Combusken	T
257	Blaziken	T
258	Mudkip	6,T
259	Marshtomp	B,6,T
260	Swampert	B,6,T
261	Poochyena	T
262	Mightyena	T
263	Zigzagoon	T,E
264	Linoone	T
271	Lombre	T
272	Ludicolo	T
274	Nuzleaf	T
275	Shiftry	T
276	Taillow	T
277	Swellow	T
278	Wingull	T
279	Pelipper	T
280	Ralts	T
281	Kirlia	T
282	Gardevoir	T
283	Surskit	T
284	Masquerain	T
286	Breloom	T
287	Slakoth	T
288	Vigoroth	T
289	Slaking	T
290	Nincada	31,T
291	Ninjask	T
292	Shedinja	T
293	Whismur	T
294	Loudred	T
295	Exploud	T
296	Makuhita	T
297	Hariyama	T
298	Azurill	T
299	Nosepass	T
300	Skitty	T
301	Delcatty	T
302	Sableye	T
303	Mawile	T
304	Aron	B,T
305	Lairon	B,8,T
306	Aggron	B,8,T
307	Meditite	T
308	Medicham	T
309	Electrike	T
310	Manectric	T
311	Plusle	T
312	Minun	T
313	Volbeat	T
314	Illumise	T
315	Roselia	T
316	Gulpin	T
317	Swalot	T
318	Carvanha	T
319	Sharpedo	T
322	Numel	T
323	Camerupt	T
324	Torkoal	T
326	Grumpig	T
327	Spinda	T
328	Trapinch	T
329	Vibrava	T
330	Flygon	T
331	Cacnea	T
332	Cacturne	T
333	Swablu	T
334	Altaria	T
335	Zangoose	T
336	Seviper	T
339	Barboach	B,T
340	Whiscash	B,T
341	Corphish	T
342	Crawdaunt	T
343	Baltoy	7,T
344	Claydol	7,T
345	Lileep	T
346	Cradily	T
347	Anorith	T
348	Armaldo	T
350	Milotic	T
352	Kecleon	T

Mud-Slap continued

354	Banette	T
356	Dusclops	T
357	Tropius	T
359	Absol	T
363	Spheal	T
364	Sealeo	T
365	Walrein	T
367	Huntail	T
368	Gorebyss	T
369	Relicanth	T,E
371	Bagon	T
372	Shelgon	T
373	Salamence	T
375	Metang	T
376	Metagross	T
377	Regirock	T
378	Regice	T
379	Registeel	T
380	Latias	T
381	Latios	T
382	Kyogre	T
383	Groudon	T
384	Rayquaza	T
385	Jirachi	T
386	Deoxys (N)	T
386	Deoxys (A)	T
386	Deoxys (D)	T
386	Deoxys (S)	T
387	Turtwig	T
388	Grotle	T
389	Torterra	T
390	Chimchar	T
391	Monferno	T
392	Infernape	T
393	Piplup	T,E
394	Prinplup	T
395	Empoleon	T
396	Starly	T
397	Staravia	T
398	Staraptor	T
399	Bidoof	T
400	Bibarel	T
401	Kricketot	T
402	Kricketune	T
403	Shinx	T
404	Luxio	T
405	Luxray	T
406	Budew	T
407	Roserade	T
408	Cranidos	T
409	Rampardos	T
410	Shieldon	T
411	Bastiodon	T
413	Wormadam (S)	T
414	Mothim	T
415	Combee	T
416	Vespiquen	T
417	Pachirisu	T
418	Buizel	T,E
419	Floatzel	T
422	Shellos	B,T
423	Gastrodon	B,T
424	Ambipom	T
425	Drifloon	T
426	Drifblim	T
427	Buneary	T
428	Lopunny	T
430	Honchkrow	T
431	Glameow	T
432	Purugly	T
434	Stunky	T
435	Skuntank	T
439	Mime Jr.	T
440	Happiny	T
441	Chatot	T
443	Gible	T
444	Gabite	T
445	Garchomp	T
446	Munchlax	T
447	Riolu	T
448	Lucario	T
449	Hippopotas	T
450	Hippowdon	T
451	Skorupi	T
452	Drapion	T
453	Croagunk	3,T
454	Toxicroak	B,3,T
455	Carnivine	T
458	Mantyke	T
459	Snover	T
460	Abomasnow	T
461	Weavile	T
463	Lickilicky	T
464	Rhyperior	T
465	Tangrowth	T
466	Electivire	T
467	Magmortar	T
468	Togekiss	T
469	Yanmega	T
470	Leafeon	T
471	Glaceon	T
472	Gliscor	T
473	Mamoswine	13,T
475	Gallade	T
476	Probopass	T
477	Dusknoir	T
478	Froslass	T
479	Rotom	T
480	Uxie	T
481	Mesprit	T
482	Azelf	T
483	Dialga	T
484	Palkia	T
485	Heatran	T
486	Regigigas	T
487	Giratina (A)	T
487	Giratina (O)	T
488	Cresselia	T
489	Phione	T
490	Manaphy	T
491	Darkrai	T
492	Shaymin (L)	T
492	Shaymin (S)	T

Nasty Plot

38	Ninetales	B
41	Zubat	E
52	Meowth	38
53	Persian	44
96	Drowzee	43,E
97	Hypno	55
151	Mew	90
172	Pichu	18
175	Togepi	E
190	Aipom	39
199	Slowking	39
228	Houndour	53,E
229	Houndoom	60
273	Seedot	E
275	Shiftry	B
302	Sableye	E
311	Plusle	51
312	Minun	51
352	Kecleon	E
390	Chimchar	23
424	Ambipom	39
430	Honchkrow	35
441	Chatot	E
442	Spiritomb	37
453	Croagunk	36
454	Toxicroak	36
461	Weavile	24
474	Porygon-Z	B
482	Azelf	46
491	Darkrai	75

Natural Gift

1	Bulbasaur	TM
2	Ivysaur	TM
3	Venusaur	TM
4	Charmander	TM
5	Charmeleon	TM
6	Charizard	TM
7	Squirtle	TM
8	Wartortle	TM
9	Blastoise	TM
12	Butterfree	TM
15	Beedrill	TM
16	Pidgey	TM
17	Pidgeotto	TM
18	Pidgeot	TM
19	Rattata	TM
20	Raticate	TM
21	Spearow	TM
22	Fearow	TM
23	Ekans	TM
24	Arbok	TM
25	Pikachu	TM
26	Raichu	TM
27	Sandshrew	TM
28	Sandslash	TM
29	Nidoran ♀	TM
30	Nidorina	TM
31	Nidoqueen	TM
32	Nidoran ♂	TM
33	Nidorino	TM
34	Nidoking	TM
35	Clefairy	TM
36	Clefable	TM
37	Vulpix	TM
38	Ninetales	TM
39	Jigglypuff	TM
40	Wigglytuff	TM
41	Zubat	TM
42	Golbat	TM
43	Oddish	29,TM
44	Gloom	35,TM
45	Vileplume	TM
46	Paras	TM
47	Parasect	TM
48	Venonat	TM
49	Venomoth	TM
50	Diglett	TM
51	Dugtrio	TM
52	Meowth	TM
53	Persian	TM
54	Psyduck	TM
55	Golduck	TM
56	Mankey	TM
57	Primeape	TM
58	Growlithe	TM
59	Arcanine	TM
60	Poliwag	TM
61	Poliwhirl	TM
62	Poliwrath	TM
63	Abra	TM
64	Kadabra	TM
65	Alakazam	TM
66	Machop	TM
67	Machoke	TM
68	Machamp	TM
69	Bellsprout	TM
70	Weepinbell	TM
71	Victreebel	TM
72	Tentacool	TM
73	Tentacruel	TM
74	Geodude	TM
75	Graveler	TM
76	Golem	TM
77	Ponyta	TM
78	Rapidash	TM
79	Slowpoke	TM
80	Slowbro	TM
81	Magnemite	TM
82	Magneton	TM
83	Farfetch'd	TM
84	Doduo	TM
85	Dodrio	TM
86	Seel	TM
87	Dewgong	TM
88	Grimer	TM
89	Muk	TM
90	Shellder	TM
91	Cloyster	TM
92	Gastly	TM
93	Haunter	TM
94	Gengar	TM
95	Onix	TM
96	Drowzee	TM
97	Hypno	TM
98	Krabby	TM
99	Kingler	TM
100	Voltorb	TM
101	Electrode	TM
102	Exeggcute	37,TM
103	Exeggutor	TM
104	Cubone	TM
105	Marowak	TM
106	Hitmonlee	TM
107	Hitmonchan	TM
108	Lickitung	TM
109	Koffing	TM
110	Weezing	TM
111	Rhyhorn	TM
112	Rhydon	TM
113	Chansey	TM
114	Tangela	40,TM
115	Kangaskhan	TM
116	Horsea	TM
117	Seadra	TM
118	Goldeen	TM
119	Seaking	TM
120	Staryu	TM
121	Starmie	TM
122	Mr. Mime	TM
123	Scyther	TM
124	Jynx	TM
125	Electabuzz	TM
126	Magmar	TM
127	Pinsir	TM
128	Tauros	TM
130	Gyarados	TM
131	Lapras	TM
133	Eevee	TM
134	Vaporeon	TM
135	Jolteon	TM
136	Flareon	TM
137	Porygon	TM
138	Omanyte	TM
139	Omastar	TM
140	Kabuto	TM
141	Kabutops	TM
142	Aerodactyl	TM
143	Snorlax	TM
144	Articuno	TM
145	Zapdos	TM
146	Moltres	TM
147	Dratini	TM
148	Dragonair	TM
149	Dragonite	TM
150	Mewtwo	TM
151	Mew	TM
152	Chikorita	23,TM
153	Bayleef	26,TM
154	Meganium	26,TM
155	Cyndaquil	TM
156	Quilava	TM
157	Typhlosion	TM
158	Totodile	TM
159	Croconaw	TM
160	Feraligatr	TM
161	Sentret	TM
162	Furret	TM
163	Hoothoot	TM
164	Noctowl	TM
165	Ledyba	TM
166	Ledian	TM
167	Spinarak	TM
168	Ariados	TM
169	Crobat	TM
170	Chinchou	TM
171	Lanturn	TM
172	Pichu	TM
173	Cleffa	TM
174	Igglybuff	TM
175	Togepi	TM
176	Togetic	TM
177	Natu	TM
178	Xatu	TM
179	Mareep	TM
180	Flaaffy	TM
181	Ampharos	TM
182	Bellossom	TM
183	Marill	TM
184	Azumarill	TM
185	Sudowoodo	TM
186	Politoed	TM
187	Hoppip	TM
188	Skiploom	TM
189	Jumpluff	TM
190	Aipom	TM
191	Sunkern	TM
192	Sunflora	TM
193	Yanma	TM
194	Wooper	TM
195	Quagsire	TM
196	Espeon	TM
197	Umbreon	TM
198	Murkrow	TM
199	Slowking	TM
200	Misdreavus	TM
203	Girafarig	TM
204	Pineco	23,TM
205	Forretress	23,TM
206	Dunsparce	TM
207	Gligar	TM
208	Steelix	TM
209	Snubbull	TM
210	Granbull	TM
211	Qwilfish	TM
212	Scizor	TM
213	Shuckle	TM
214	Heracross	TM
215	Sneasel	TM
216	Teddiursa	TM
217	Ursaring	TM
218	Slugma	TM
219	Magcargo	TM
220	Swinub	TM
221	Piloswine	TM
222	Corsola	TM
223	Remoraid	TM
224	Octillery	TM
225	Delibird	TM
226	Mantine	TM
227	Skarmory	TM
228	Houndour	TM
229	Houndoom	TM
230	Kingdra	TM
231	Phanpy	19,TM
232	Donphan	TM
233	Porygon2	TM
234	Stantler	TM
236	Tyrogue	TM
237	Hitmontop	TM
238	Smoochum	TM
239	Elekid	TM
240	Magby	TM
241	Miltank	TM
242	Blissey	TM
243	Raikou	TM
244	Entei	TM
245	Suicune	TM
246	Larvitar	TM
247	Pupitar	TM
248	Tyranitar	TM
249	Lugia	51,TM
250	Ho-Oh	51,TM
251	Celebi	46,TM
252	Treecko	TM
253	Grovyle	TM
254	Sceptile	TM
255	Torchic	TM
256	Combusken	TM
257	Blaziken	TM
258	Mudkip	TM
259	Marshtomp	TM
260	Swampert	TM
261	Poochyena	TM
262	Mightyena	TM
263	Zigzagoon	TM
264	Linoone	TM
267	Beautifly	TM
269	Dustox	TM
270	Lotad	15,TM
271	Lombre	TM
272	Ludicolo	TM
273	Seedot	TM
274	Nuzleaf	TM
275	Shiftry	TM
276	Taillow	TM
277	Swellow	TM
278	Wingull	TM
279	Pelipper	TM
280	Ralts	TM
281	Kirlia	TM
282	Gardevoir	TM
283	Surskit	TM
284	Masquerain	TM
285	Shroomish	TM
286	Breloom	TM
287	Slakoth	TM
288	Vigoroth	TM
289	Slaking	TM
290	Nincada	TM
291	Ninjask	TM
292	Shedinja	TM
293	Whismur	TM
294	Loudred	TM
295	Exploud	TM
296	Makuhita	TM
297	Hariyama	TM
298	Azurill	TM
299	Nosepass	TM
300	Skitty	TM
301	Delcatty	TM
302	Sableye	TM
303	Mawile	TM
304	Aron	TM
305	Lairon	TM
306	Aggron	TM
307	Meditite	TM
308	Medicham	TM
309	Electrike	TM
310	Manectric	TM
311	Plusle	TM
312	Minun	TM
313	Volbeat	TM
314	Illumise	TM
315	Roselia	TM
316	Gulpin	TM
317	Swalot	TM
318	Carvanha	TM
319	Sharpedo	TM
320	Wailmer	TM
321	Wailord	TM
322	Numel	TM
323	Camerupt	TM
324	Torkoal	TM
325	Spoink	TM
326	Grumpig	TM
327	Spinda	TM
328	Trapinch	TM
329	Vibrava	TM
330	Flygon	TM
331	Cacnea	TM
332	Cacturne	TM
333	Swablu	32,TM
334	Altaria	32,TM
335	Zangoose	TM
336	Seviper	TM
337	Lunatone	TM
338	Solrock	TM
339	Barboach	TM
340	Whiscash	TM
341	Corphish	TM
342	Crawdaunt	TM
343	Baltoy	TM
344	Claydol	TM
345	Lileep	TM
346	Cradily	TM
347	Anorith	TM
348	Armaldo	TM
349	Feebas	TM
350	Milotic	TM
351	Castform	TM
352	Kecleon	TM
353	Shuppet	TM
354	Banette	TM
355	Duskull	TM
356	Dusclops	TM
357	Tropius	57,TM
358	Chimecho	TM
359	Absol	TM
361	Snorunt	TM
362	Glalie	TM
363	Spheal	TM
364	Sealeo	TM
365	Walrein	TM
366	Clamperl	TM
367	Huntail	TM
368	Gorebyss	TM
369	Relicanth	TM
370	Luvdisc	TM
371	Bagon	TM
372	Shelgon	TM
373	Salamence	TM
375	Metang	TM
376	Metagross	TM
377	Regirock	TM
378	Regice	TM
379	Registeel	TM
380	Latias	TM
381	Latios	TM
382	Kyogre	TM
383	Groudon	TM
384	Rayquaza	TM
385	Jirachi	TM
386	Deoxys (N)	TM
386	Deoxys (A)	TM
386	Deoxys (D)	TM
386	Deoxys (S)	TM
387	Turtwig	TM
388	Grotle	TM
389	Torterra	TM
390	Chimchar	TM
391	Monferno	TM
392	Infernape	TM
393	Piplup	TM
394	Prinplup	TM
395	Empoleon	TM
396	Starly	TM
397	Staravia	TM
398	Staraptor	TM
399	Bidoof	TM
400	Bibarel	TM
402	Kricketune	TM
403	Shinx	TM
404	Luxio	TM
405	Luxray	TM
406	Budew	TM
407	Roserade	TM
408	Cranidos	TM
409	Rampardos	TM
410	Shieldon	TM
411	Bastiodon	TM
413	Wormadam (P)	TM
413	Wormadam (S)	TM
413	Wormadam (T)	TM
414	Mothim	TM
416	Vespiquen	TM
417	Pachirisu	TM
418	Buizel	TM
419	Floatzel	TM
420	Cherubi	TM
421	Cherrim	TM
422	Shellos	TM
423	Gastrodon	TM
424	Ambipom	TM
425	Drifloon	TM
426	Drifblim	TM
427	Buneary	TM
428	Lopunny	TM
429	Mismagius	TM
430	Honchkrow	TM
431	Glameow	TM
432	Purugly	TM
433	Chingling	TM
434	Stunky	TM
435	Skuntank	TM
436	Bronzor	TM
437	Bronzong	TM
438	Bonsly	TM
439	Mime Jr.	TM
440	Happiny	TM
441	Chatot	TM
442	Spiritomb	TM
443	Gible	TM
444	Gabite	TM
445	Garchomp	TM
446	Munchlax	44,TM
447	Riolu	TM
448	Lucario	TM
449	Hippopotas	TM
450	Hippowdon	TM
451	Skorupi	TM
452	Drapion	TM
453	Croagunk	TM
454	Toxicroak	TM
455	Carnivine	TM
456	Finneon	TM
457	Lumineon	TM
458	Mantyke	TM
459	Snover	TM
460	Abomasnow	TM
461	Weavile	TM
462	Magnezone	TM
463	Lickilicky	TM
464	Rhyperior	TM
465	Tangrowth	40,TM
466	Electivire	TM
467	Magmortar	TM
468	Togekiss	TM
469	Yanmega	TM
470	Leafeon	TM
471	Glaceon	TM
472	Gliscor	TM
473	Mamoswine	TM
474	Porygon-Z	TM
475	Gallade	TM
476	Probopass	TM
477	Dusknoir	TM
478	Froslass	TM
479	Rotom	TM
480	Uxie	66,TM
481	Mesprit	66,TM
482	Azelf	66,TM
483	Dialga	TM
484	Palkia	TM
485	Heatran	TM
486	Regigigas	TM
487	Giratina (A)	TM
487	Giratina (O)	TM
488	Cresselia	TM
489	Phione	TM
490	Manaphy	TM
491	Darkrai	TM
492	Shaymin (L)	46,TM
492	Shaymin (S)	46,TM

Nature Power

1	Bulbasaur	E
102	Exeggcute	E
114	Tangela	E
152	Chikorita	E
191	Sunkern	E
222	Corsola	E
270	Lotad	7
271	Lombre	7
272	Ludicolo	B
273	Seedot	13
274	Nuzleaf	13
357	Tropius	E
420	Cherubi	E

Needle Arm

331	Cacnea	45
332	Cacturne	53

Night Shade

92	Gastly	15
93	Haunter	15
94	Gengar	15
163	Hoothoot	E
167	Spinarak	15
168	Ariados	15
177	Natu	6
178	Xatu	6
198	Murkrow	21
302	Sableye	8
353	Shuppet	8
354	Banette	B,5
355	Duskull	B
356	Dusclops	B
386	Deoxys (N)	9
386	Deoxys (A)	9
386	Deoxys (D)	9
386	Deoxys (S)	9
441	Chatot	E
477	Dusknoir	B

Night Slash

27	Sandshrew	E
51	Dugtrio	B
52	Meowth	49
53	Persian	61
83	Farfetch'd	33,E
123	Scyther	45,E
141	Kabutops	72
207	Gligar	E
212	Scizor	45
214	Heracross	B

Pokémon moves and Abilities alphabetical list

216	Teddiursa	E
227	Skarmory	45
254	Sceptile	B
255	Torchic	E
287	Slakoth	E
290	Nincada	E
319	Sharpedo	56
335	Zangoose	E
336	Seviper	46,E
341	Corphish	35
342	Crawdaunt	39
359	Absol	52
402	Kricketune	42
430	Honchkrow	45
434	Stunky	32
435	Skuntank	32
451	Skorupi	E
461	Weavile	35
469	Yanmega	B
472	Gliscor	31
475	Gallade	B

Nightmare		
92	Gastly	43
93	Haunter	55
94	Gengar	55
97	Hypno	B
491	Darkrai	38

Octazooka		
116	Horsea	E
223	Remoraid	E
224	Octillery	25

Odor Sleuth		
52	Meowth	E
58	Growlithe	14
59	Arcanine	B
179	Mareep	E
203	Girafarig	5
220	Swinub	B
221	Piloswine	B
228	Houndour	22
229	Houndoom	22
231	Phanpy	B
261	Poochyena	17
262	Mightyena	17
263	Zigzagoon	17
264	Linoone	17
309	Electrike	25
310	Manectric	25
325	Spoink	10
326	Grumpig	B,10
399	Bidoof	E
418	Buizel	E
446	Munchlax	B
473	Mamoswine	B

Ominous Wind		
6	Charizard	T
12	Butterfree	T
15	Beedrill	T
16	Pidgey	T
17	Pidgeotto	T
18	Pidgeot	T
21	Spearow	T
22	Fearow	T
37	Vulpix	T
38	Ninetales	T
41	Zubat	T
42	Golbat	T
49	Venomoth	T
83	Farfetch'd	T
92	Gastly	T
93	Haunter	T
94	Gengar	T
123	Scyther	T
142	Aerodactyl	T
144	Articuno	T
145	Zapdos	T
146	Moltres	T
149	Dragonite	T
151	Mew	T
163	Hoothoot	T
164	Noctowl	T
165	Ledyba	T
166	Ledian	T
169	Crobat	T
176	Togetic	T
177	Natu	39,T
178	Xatu	47,T
193	Yanma	T
198	Murkrow	T
200	Misdreavus	T,E
212	Scizor	T
227	Skarmory	T
245	Suicune	T
249	Lugia	T
250	Ho-Oh	T
267	Beautifly	T
269	Dustox	T
275	Shiftry	T
276	Taillow	T
277	Swellow	T
278	Wingull	T
279	Pelipper	T
284	Masquerain	B,T
291	Ninjask	T
302	Sableye	T
313	Volbeat	T
314	Illumise	T
329	Vibrava	T
330	Flygon	T
333	Swablu	T
334	Altaria	T
351	Castform	T,E
353	Shuppet	T
354	Banette	T
355	Duskull	T,E
356	Dusclops	T
357	Tropius	T
373	Salamence	T
396	Starly	T
397	Staravia	T
398	Staraptor	T
414	Mothim	T
415	Combee	T
416	Vespiquen	T
425	Drifloon	30,T
426	Drifblim	32,T
429	Mismagius	T
430	Honchkrow	T
441	Chatot	T
442	Spiritomb	25,T
456	Finneon	T
457	Lumineon	T
468	Togekiss	T
469	Yanmega	T
477	Dusknoir	T
478	Froslass	22,T
479	Rotom	29,T
487	Giratina (A)	10,T
487	Giratina (O)	10,T
491	Darkrai	B,T
492	Shaymin (S)	T

Outrage		
3	Venusaur	T
4	Charmander	E
6	Charizard	T
9	Blastoise	T
31	Nidoqueen	T
34	Nidoking	T
56	Mankey	T
57	Primeape	T
105	Marowak	T
112	Rhydon	T
115	Kangaskhan	37,T
116	Horsea	T
117	Seadra	T
128	Tauros	T
130	Gyarados	T
131	Lapras	T
143	Snorlax	T
147	Dratini	51,T
148	Dragonair	61,T
149	Dragonite	64,T
151	Mew	T
154	Meganium	T
160	Feraligatr	T
181	Ampharos	T
230	Kingdra	T
246	Larvitar	E
248	Tyranitar	T
254	Sceptile	T
260	Swampert	T
295	Exploud	T
306	Aggron	T
329	Vibrava	T
330	Flygon	T
333	Swablu	T
334	Altaria	T
357	Tropius	T
371	Bagon	T
372	Shelgon	T
373	Salamence	T
380	Latias	T
381	Latios	T
384	Rayquaza	80,T
389	Torterra	T
409	Rampardos	T
411	Bastiodon	T
443	Gible	T,E
444	Gabite	T
445	Garchomp	T
460	Abomasnow	T
464	Rhyperior	T
483	Dialga	T
484	Palkia	T
487	Giratina (A)	T
487	Giratina (O)	T

Overheat		
4	Charmander	TM
5	Charmeleon	TM
6	Charizard	TM
37	Vulpix	TM
38	Ninetales	TM
56	Mankey	TM
57	Primeape	TM
58	Growlithe	TM
59	Arcanine	TM
77	Ponyta	TM
78	Rapidash	TM
126	Magmar	TM
136	Flareon	TM
146	Moltres	TM
151	Mew	TM
155	Cyndaquil	TM
156	Quilava	TM
157	Typhlosion	TM
209	Snubbull	TM
210	Granbull	TM
218	Slugma	TM
219	Magcargo	TM
228	Houndour	TM
229	Houndoom	TM
240	Magby	TM
244	Entei	TM
250	Ho-Oh	TM
255	Torchic	TM
256	Combusken	TM
257	Blaziken	TM
294	Loudred	TM
295	Exploud	TM
310	Manectric	TM
322	Numel	TM
323	Camerupt	TM
324	Torkoal	TM
338	Solrock	TM
383	Groudon	TM
384	Rayquaza	TM
390	Chimchar	TM
391	Monferno	TM
392	Infernape	TM
467	Magmortar	TM
479	Rotom (H)	*
483	Dialga	TM
485	Heatran	TM

Pain Split		
109	Koffing	E
200	Misdreavus	28
316	Gulpin	E
355	Duskull	E
442	Spiritomb	E

Pay Day		
52	Meowth	30

Payback		
15	Beedrill	TM
23	Ekans	TM
24	Arbok	TM
37	Vulpix	31,TM
38	Ninetales	TM
41	Zubat	TM
42	Golbat	TM
52	Meowth	TM
53	Persian	TM
56	Mankey	TM
57	Primeape	TM
62	Poliwrath	TM
66	Machop	TM
67	Machoke	TM
68	Machamp	TM
72	Tentacool	TM
73	Tentacruel	TM
85	Dodrio	TM
88	Grimer	TM
89	Muk	TM
90	Shellder	TM
91	Cloyster	TM
92	Gastly	26,TM
93	Haunter	28,TM
94	Gengar	28,TM
95	Onix	TM
109	Koffing	TM
110	Weezing	TM
111	Rhyhorn	TM
112	Rhydon	TM
122	Mr. Mime	TM
124	Jynx	TM
128	Tauros	24,TM
130	Gyarados	TM
142	Aerodactyl	TM
151	Mew	TM
169	Crobat	TM
186	Politoed	TM
190	Aipom	TM
197	Umbreon	TM
198	Murkrow	TM
200	Misdreavus	32,TM
204	Pineco	31,TM
205	Forretress	33,TM
207	Gligar	TM
208	Steelix	TM
209	Snubbull	43,TM
210	Granbull	51,TM
211	Qwilfish	TM
215	Sneasel	TM
216	Teddiursa	TM
217	Ursaring	TM
224	Octillery	TM
227	Skarmory	TM
228	Houndour	TM
229	Houndoom	TM
238	Smoochum	TM
246	Larvitar	32,TM
247	Pupitar	34,TM
248	Tyranitar	34,TM
261	Poochyena	TM
262	Mightyena	TM
274	Nuzleaf	TM
275	Shiftry	TM
279	Pelipper	24,TM
297	Hariyama	TM
300	Skitty	TM
301	Delcatty	TM
302	Sableye	TM
303	Mawile	TM
306	Aggron	TM
318	Carvanha	TM
319	Sharpedo	TM
325	Spoink	34,TM
326	Grumpig	37,TM
331	Cacnea	41,TM
332	Cacturne	47,TM
335	Zangoose	TM
336	Seviper	TM
341	Corphish	TM
342	Crawdaunt	TM
353	Shuppet	TM,E
354	Banette	TM
355	Duskull	41,TM
356	Dusclops	51,TM
359	Absol	TM
362	Glalie	TM
408	Cranidos	TM
409	Rampardos	TM
419	Floatzel	TM
424	Ambipom	TM
425	Drifloon	17,TM
426	Drifblim	17,TM
429	Mismagius	TM
430	Honchkrow	TM
431	Glameow	TM
432	Purugly	TM
434	Stunky	TM
435	Skuntank	TM
436	Bronzor	49,TM
437	Bronzong	61,TM
447	Riolu	TM
448	Lucario	TM
451	Skorupi	TM
452	Drapion	TM
453	Croagunk	TM
454	Toxicroak	TM
455	Carnivine	TM
456	Finneon	TM
457	Lumineon	TM
461	Weavile	TM
464	Rhyperior	TM
465	Tangrowth	TM
472	Gliscor	TM
477	Dusknoir	51,TM
478	Froslass	TM
482	Azelf	TM
485	Heatran	TM
487	Giratina (A)	TM
487	Giratina (O)	TM
491	Darkrai	TM

Peck		
21	Spearow	B
22	Fearow	B
32	Nidoran♂	B
33	Nidorino	B
34	Nidoking	B
83	Farfetch'd	B
84	Doduo	B
85	Dodrio	B
118	Goldeen	B
119	Seaking	B
145	Zapdos	B
163	Hoothoot	9
164	Noctowl	9
175	Togepi	E
177	Natu	B
178	Xatu	B
198	Murkrow	B
221	Piloswine	B
227	Skarmory	B
255	Torchic	16
256	Combusken	17
257	Blaziken	17
276	Taillow	B
277	Swellow	B
333	Swablu	B
334	Altaria	B
393	Piplup	15
394	Prinplup	15
395	Empoleon	15
441	Chatot	B
473	Mamoswine	B

Perish Song		
86	Seel	E
92	Gastly	E
104	Cubone	E
124	Jynx	49
131	Lapras	27
174	Igglybuff	E
183	Marill	E
186	Politoed	B
198	Murkrow	E
200	Misdreavus	41
238	Smoochum	41
251	Celebi	91
333	Swablu	50
334	Altaria	62
359	Absol	65
402	Kricketune	50

Petal Dance		
1	Bulbasaur	E
3	Venusaur	32
43	Oddish	41
44	Gloom	53
45	Vileplume	53
154	Meganium	32
192	Sunflora	33
315	Roselia	40
421	Cherrim	25

Pin Missile		
15	Beedrill	28
135	Jolteon	36
167	Spinarak	36
168	Ariados	41
204	Pineco	E
211	Qwilfish	37
263	Zigzagoon	25
315	Roselia	E
331	Cacnea	21
332	Cacturne	21
406	Budew	E
451	Skorupi	12
452	Drapion	12

Pluck		
16	Pidgey	TM
17	Pidgeotto	TM
18	Pidgeot	TM
19	Rattata	TM
20	Raticate	TM
21	Spearow	TM
22	Fearow	B,TM
41	Zubat	TM
42	Golbat	TM
83	Farfetch'd	TM
84	Doduo	TM
85	Dodrio	B,TM
144	Articuno	TM
145	Zapdos	22,TM
146	Moltres	TM
151	Mew	TM
163	Hoothoot	TM
164	Noctowl	TM
169	Crobat	TM
177	Natu	TM
178	Xatu	TM
198	Murkrow	TM
225	Delibird	TM
227	Skarmory	TM
250	Ho-Oh	TM
276	Taillow	TM
277	Swellow	B,TM
278	Wingull	TM
279	Pelipper	TM
333	Swablu	TM
334	Altaria	B,TM
393	Piplup	TM
394	Prinplup	TM
395	Empoleon	TM
396	Starly	TM
397	Staravia	TM
398	Staraptor	TM
399	Bidoof	TM
400	Bibarel	TM
430	Honchkrow	TM
441	Chatot	TM
468	Togekiss	TM

Poison Fang		
23	Ekans	E
29	Nidoran♀	45
30	Nidorina	58
41	Zubat	33
42	Golbat	39
48	Venonat	41
49	Venomoth	47
169	Crobat	39
261	Poochyena	E
303	Mawile	E
336	Seviper	34
451	Skorupi	39
452	Drapion	39

Poison Gas		
88	Grimer	B
89	Muk	B
96	Drowzee	18
97	Hypno	18
109	Koffing	B
110	Weezing	B
316	Gulpin	9
317	Swalot	B,9
434	Stunky	4
435	Skuntank	B,4

Poison Jab		
15	Beedrill	37,TM
23	Ekans	TM
24	Arbok	TM
27	Sandshrew	TM
28	Sandslash	TM
29	Nidoran♀	TM
30	Nidorina	TM
31	Nidoqueen	TM
32	Nidoran♂	37,TM
33	Nidorino	43,TM
34	Nidoking	TM
56	Mankey	TM
57	Primeape	TM
62	Poliwrath	TM
66	Machop	TM
67	Machoke	TM
68	Machamp	TM
72	Tentacool	33,TM
73	Tentacruel	36,TM
78	Rapidash	B,TM
83	Farfetch'd	B,TM
88	Grimer	TM
89	Muk	TM
91	Cloyster	TM
93	Haunter	TM
94	Gengar	TM
106	Hitmonlee	TM
111	Rhyhorn	TM
112	Rhydon	TM
118	Goldeen	TM
119	Seaking	B,TM
150	Mewtwo	TM
151	Mew	TM
167	Spinarak	43,TM,E
168	Ariados	50,TM
206	Dunsparce	TM
207	Gligar	TM
211	Qwilfish	49,TM,E
215	Sneasel	TM
232	Donphan	TM
256	Combusken	TM
257	Blaziken	TM
296	Makuhita	TM
297	Hariyama	TM
302	Sableye	TM
307	Meditite	TM
308	Medicham	TM
315	Roselia	TM
319	Sharpedo	TM
331	Cacnea	TM
332	Cacturne	TM
335	Zangoose	TM
336	Seviper	52,TM
386	Deoxys (N)	TM
386	Deoxys (A)	TM
386	Deoxys (D)	TM
386	Deoxys (S)	TM
391	Monferno	TM
392	Infernape	TM
407	Roserade	TM
435	Skuntank	TM
445	Garchomp	TM
447	Riolu	TM
448	Lucario	TM
451	Skorupi	TM
452	Drapion	TM
453	Croagunk	38,TM
454	Toxicroak	41,TM
461	Weavile	TM
464	Rhyperior	B,TM
465	Tangrowth	TM
472	Gliscor	B,TM
475	Gallade	TM
491	Darkrai	TM

Poison Sting		
13	Weedle	B
23	Ekans	4
24	Arbok	B,4
27	Sandshrew	9
28	Sandslash	9
29	Nidoran♀	13
30	Nidorina	13
31	Nidoqueen	B
32	Nidoran♂	13
33	Nidorino	13
34	Nidoking	B
72	Tentacool	B
73	Tentacruel	B
167	Spinarak	B
168	Ariados	B
207	Gligar	B
211	Qwilfish	B
265	Wurmple	5
315	Roselia	7
331	Cacnea	B
332	Cacturne	B
407	Roserade	B
416	Vespiquen	3
451	Skorupi	B
452	Drapion	B
453	Croagunk	B
454	Toxicroak	B,8

Poison Tail		
23	Ekans	E
336	Seviper	16

PoisonPowder		
1	Bulbasaur	13
2	Ivysaur	13
3	Venusaur	13
12	Butterfree	12
43	Oddish	13
44	Gloom	13
45	Vileplume	B
46	Paras	6
47	Parasect	B,6
48	Venonat	13
49	Venomoth	13
69	Bellsprout	15
70	Weepinbell	15
102	Exeggcute	21
114	Tangela	15
152	Chikorita	9
153	Bayleef	B,9
154	Meganium	B,9
187	Hoppip	12
188	Skiploom	12
189	Jumpluff	12
285	Shroomish	25
414	Mothim	29
465	Tangrowth	15

Pound		
35	Clefairy	B
39	Jigglypuff	9
88	Grimer	B
89	Muk	B
96	Drowzee	B
97	Hypno	B
113	Chansey	B
124	Jynx	B
151	Mew	B
173	Cleffa	B
174	Igglybuff	9
192	Sunflora	B
238	Smoochum	B
242	Blissey	B
252	Treecko	B
253	Grovyle	B
254	Sceptile	B
274	Nuzleaf	B
293	Whismur	B
294	Loudred	B
295	Exploud	B
316	Gulpin	B
317	Swalot	B
393	Piplup	B
427	Buneary	B
428	Lopunny	B

*Rotom learns one move when it changes Form, which it forgets when it turns back into Rotom (p. 514).

ADVENTURE DATA LIST
POKÉMON MOVES AND ABILITIES ALPHABETICAL LIST

Pound continued

440	Happiny	B
456	Finneon	B
457	Lumineon	B

Powder Snow

124	Jynx	B,11
144	Articuno	B
220	Swinub	B
221	Piloswine	B,B
238	Smoochum	11
351	Castform	10
361	Snorunt	B
362	Glalie	B
363	Spheal	B
364	Sealeo	B
365	Walrein	B
459	Snover	B
460	Abomasnow	B
473	Mamoswine	B,B
478	Froslass	B

Power Gem

53	Persian	32
120	Staryu	46
179	Mareep	41
180	Flaaffy	47
181	Ampharos	59
199	Slowking	B
200	Misdreavus	50
222	Corsola	44
299	Nosepass	49
302	Sableye	43
325	Spoink	46
326	Grumpig	55
416	Vespiquen	21
476	Probopass	49

Power Swap

122	Mr. Mime	B
150	Mewtwo	64
177	Natu	44
178	Xatu	54
196	Espeon	78
203	Girafarig	B
307	Meditite	E

Power Trick

63	Abra	E
213	Shuckle	48
307	Meditite	39
308	Medicham	42
343	Baltoy	31
344	Claydol	31

Power Whip

108	Lickitung	49
114	Tangela	54
455	Carnivine	47
463	Lickilicky	49
465	Tangrowth	54

Present

113	Chansey	E
172	Pichu	E
173	Cleffa	E
174	Igglybuff	E
175	Togepi	E
183	Marill	E
209	Snubbull	E
225	Delibird	B
241	Miltank	E
440	Happiny	E

Protect

1	Bulbasaur	TM
2	Ivysaur	TM
3	Venusaur	TM
4	Charmander	TM
5	Charmeleon	TM
6	Charizard	TM
7	Squirtle	22,TM
8	Wartortle	24,TM
9	Blastoise	24,TM
12	Butterfree	TM
15	Beedrill	TM
16	Pidgey	TM
17	Pidgeotto	TM
18	Pidgeot	TM
19	Rattata	TM
20	Raticate	TM
21	Spearow	TM
22	Fearow	TM
23	Ekans	TM
24	Arbok	TM
25	Pikachu	TM
26	Raichu	TM
27	Sandshrew	TM
28	Sandslash	TM
29	Nidoran♀	TM
30	Nidorina	TM
31	Nidoqueen	TM
32	Nidoran♂	TM
33	Nidorino	TM
34	Nidoking	TM
35	Clefairy	TM
36	Clefable	TM
37	Vulpix	TM
38	Ninetales	TM
39	Jigglypuff	TM
40	Wigglytuff	TM
41	Zubat	TM
42	Golbat	TM
43	Oddish	TM
44	Gloom	TM
45	Vileplume	TM
46	Paras	TM
47	Parasect	TM
48	Venonat	TM
49	Venomoth	TM
50	Diglett	TM
51	Dugtrio	TM
52	Meowth	TM
53	Persian	TM
54	Psyduck	TM
55	Golduck	TM
56	Mankey	TM
57	Primeape	TM
58	Growlithe	TM
59	Arcanine	TM
60	Poliwag	TM
61	Poliwhirl	TM
62	Poliwrath	TM
63	Abra	TM
64	Kadabra	TM
65	Alakazam	TM
66	Machop	TM
67	Machoke	TM
68	Machamp	TM
69	Bellsprout	TM
70	Weepinbell	TM
71	Victreebel	TM
72	Tentacool	TM
73	Tentacruel	TM
74	Geodude	TM
75	Graveler	TM
76	Golem	TM
77	Ponyta	TM
78	Rapidash	TM
79	Slowpoke	TM
80	Slowbro	TM
81	Magnemite	TM
82	Magneton	TM
83	Farfetch'd	TM
84	Doduo	TM
85	Dodrio	TM
86	Seel	TM
87	Dewgong	TM
88	Grimer	TM
89	Muk	TM
90	Shellder	16,TM
91	Cloyster	B,TM
92	Gastly	TM
93	Haunter	TM
94	Gengar	TM
95	Onix	TM
96	Drowzee	TM
97	Hypno	TM
98	Krabby	29,TM
99	Kingler	32,TM
100	Voltorb	TM
101	Electrode	TM
102	Exeggcute	TM
103	Exeggutor	TM
104	Cubone	TM
105	Marowak	TM
106	Hitmonlee	TM
107	Hitmonchan	TM
108	Lickitung	TM
109	Koffing	TM
110	Weezing	TM
111	Rhyhorn	TM
112	Rhydon	TM
113	Chansey	TM
114	Tangela	TM
115	Kangaskhan	TM
116	Horsea	TM
117	Seadra	TM
118	Goldeen	TM
119	Seaking	TM
120	Staryu	TM
121	Starmie	TM
122	Mr. Mime	TM
123	Scyther	TM
124	Jynx	TM
125	Electabuzz	TM
126	Magmar	TM
127	Pinsir	TM
128	Tauros	TM
130	Gyarados	TM
131	Lapras	TM
133	Eevee	TM
134	Vaporeon	TM
135	Jolteon	TM
136	Flareon	TM
137	Porygon	TM
138	Omanyte	34,TM
139	Omastar	34,TM
140	Kabuto	TM
141	Kabutops	TM
142	Aerodactyl	TM
143	Snorlax	TM
144	Articuno	TM
145	Zapdos	TM
146	Moltres	TM
147	Dratini	TM
148	Dragonair	TM
149	Dragonite	TM
150	Mewtwo	TM
151	Mew	TM
152	Chikorita	TM
153	Bayleef	TM
154	Meganium	TM
155	Cyndaquil	TM
156	Quilava	TM
157	Typhlosion	TM
158	Totodile	TM
159	Croconaw	TM
160	Feraligatr	TM
161	Sentret	TM
162	Furret	TM
163	Hoothoot	TM
164	Noctowl	TM
165	Ledyba	TM
166	Ledian	TM
167	Spinarak	TM
168	Ariados	TM
169	Crobat	TM
170	Chinchou	TM
171	Lanturn	TM
172	Pichu	TM
173	Cleffa	TM
174	Igglybuff	TM
175	Togepi	TM
176	Togetic	TM
177	Natu	TM
178	Xatu	TM
179	Mareep	TM
180	Flaaffy	TM
181	Ampharos	TM
182	Bellossom	TM
183	Marill	TM
184	Azumarill	TM
185	Sudowoodo	TM
186	Politoed	TM
187	Hoppip	TM
188	Skiploom	TM
189	Jumpluff	TM
190	Aipom	TM
191	Sunkern	TM
192	Sunflora	TM
193	Yanma	TM
194	Wooper	TM
195	Quagsire	TM
196	Espeon	TM
197	Umbreon	TM
198	Murkrow	TM
199	Slowking	TM
200	Misdreavus	TM
203	Girafarig	TM
204	Pineco	B,TM
205	Forretress	B,TM
206	Dunsparce	TM
207	Gligar	TM
208	Steelix	TM
209	Snubbull	TM
210	Granbull	TM
211	Qwilfish	TM
212	Scizor	TM
213	Shuckle	TM
214	Heracross	TM
215	Sneasel	TM
216	Teddiursa	TM
217	Ursaring	TM
218	Slugma	TM
219	Magcargo	TM
220	Swinub	TM
221	Piloswine	TM
222	Corsola	TM
223	Remoraid	TM
224	Octillery	TM
225	Delibird	TM
226	Mantine	TM
227	Skarmory	TM
228	Houndour	TM
229	Houndoom	TM
230	Kingdra	TM
231	Phanpy	TM
232	Donphan	TM
233	Porygon2	TM
234	Stantler	TM
236	Tyrogue	TM
237	Hitmontop	TM
238	Smoochum	TM
239	Elekid	TM
240	Magby	TM
241	Miltank	TM
242	Blissey	TM
243	Raikou	TM
244	Entei	TM
245	Suicune	TM
246	Larvitar	TM
247	Pupitar	TM
248	Tyranitar	TM
249	Lugia	TM
250	Ho-Oh	TM
251	Celebi	TM
252	Treecko	TM
253	Grovyle	TM
254	Sceptile	TM
255	Torchic	TM
256	Combusken	TM
257	Blaziken	TM
258	Mudkip	37,TM
259	Marshtomp	42,TM
260	Swampert	46,TM
261	Poochyena	TM
262	Mightyena	TM
263	Zigzagoon	TM
264	Linoone	TM
267	Beautifly	TM
269	Dustox	17,TM
270	Lotad	TM
271	Lombre	TM
272	Ludicolo	TM
273	Seedot	TM
274	Nuzleaf	TM
275	Shiftry	TM
276	Taillow	TM
277	Swellow	TM
278	Wingull	TM
279	Pelipper	25,TM
280	Ralts	TM
281	Kirlia	TM
282	Gardevoir	TM
283	Surskit	TM
284	Masquerain	TM
285	Shroomish	TM
286	Breloom	TM
287	Slakoth	TM
288	Vigoroth	TM
289	Slaking	TM
290	Nincada	TM
291	Ninjask	TM
292	Shedinja	TM
293	Whismur	TM
294	Loudred	TM
295	Exploud	TM
296	Makuhita	TM
297	Hariyama	TM
298	Azurill	TM
299	Nosepass	TM
300	Skitty	TM
301	Delcatty	TM
302	Sableye	TM
303	Mawile	TM
304	Aron	32,TM
305	Lairon	34,TM
306	Aggron	34,TM
307	Meditite	TM
308	Medicham	TM
309	Electrike	TM
310	Manectric	TM
311	Plusle	TM
312	Minun	TM
313	Volbeat	29,TM
314	Illumise	TM
315	Roselia	TM
316	Gulpin	TM
317	Swalot	TM
318	Carvanha	TM
319	Sharpedo	TM
320	Wailmer	TM
321	Wailord	TM
322	Numel	TM
323	Camerupt	TM
324	Torkoal	36,TM
325	Spoink	TM
326	Grumpig	TM
327	Spinda	TM
328	Trapinch	TM
329	Vibrava	TM
330	Flygon	TM
331	Cacnea	TM
332	Cacturne	TM
333	Swablu	TM
334	Altaria	TM
335	Zangoose	TM
336	Seviper	TM
337	Lunatone	TM
338	Solrock	TM
339	Barboach	TM
340	Whiscash	TM
341	Corphish	23,TM
342	Crawdaunt	23,TM
343	Baltoy	TM
344	Claydol	TM
345	Lileep	TM
346	Cradily	TM
347	Anorith	25,TM
348	Armaldo	25,TM
349	Feebas	TM
350	Milotic	TM
351	Castform	TM
352	Kecleon	TM
353	Shuppet	TM
354	Banette	TM
355	Duskull	TM
356	Dusclops	TM
357	Tropius	TM
358	Chimecho	TM
359	Absol	TM
361	Snorunt	22,TM
362	Glalie	22,TM
363	Spheal	TM
364	Sealeo	TM
365	Walrein	TM
366	Clamperl	TM
367	Huntail	TM
368	Gorebyss	TM
369	Relicanth	TM
370	Luvdisc	TM
371	Bagon	TM
372	Shelgon	30,TM
373	Salamence	30,TM
375	Metang	TM
376	Metagross	TM
377	Regirock	TM
378	Regice	TM
379	Registeel	TM
380	Latias	TM
381	Latios	25,TM
382	Kyogre	TM
383	Groudon	TM
384	Rayquaza	TM
385	Jirachi	TM
386	Deoxys (N)	TM
386	Deoxys (A)	TM
386	Deoxys (D)	TM
386	Deoxys (S)	TM
387	Turtwig	TM
388	Grotle	TM
389	Torterra	TM
390	Chimchar	TM
391	Monferno	TM
392	Infernape	TM
393	Piplup	TM
394	Prinplup	TM
395	Empoleon	TM
396	Starly	TM
397	Staravia	TM
398	Staraptor	TM
399	Bidoof	TM
400	Bibarel	TM
402	Kricketune	TM
403	Shinx	TM
404	Luxio	TM
405	Luxray	TM
406	Budew	TM
407	Roserade	TM
408	Cranidos	TM
409	Rampardos	TM
410	Shieldon	B,TM
411	Bastiodon	B,TM
412	Burmy	B
413	Wormadam (P)	10,TM
413	Wormadam (S)	10,TM
413	Wormadam (T)	10,TM
414	Mothim	10,TM
416	Vespiquen	TM
417	Pachirisu	TM
418	Buizel	TM
419	Floatzel	TM
420	Cherubi	TM
421	Cherrim	TM
422	Shellos	TM
423	Gastrodon	TM
424	Ambipom	TM
425	Drifloon	TM
426	Drifblim	TM
427	Buneary	TM
428	Lopunny	TM
429	Mismagius	TM
430	Honchkrow	TM
431	Glameow	TM
432	Purugly	TM
433	Chingling	TM
434	Stunky	TM
435	Skuntank	TM
436	Bronzor	TM
437	Bronzong	TM
438	Bonsly	TM
439	Mime Jr.	TM
440	Happiny	TM
441	Chatot	TM
442	Spiritomb	TM
443	Gible	TM
444	Gabite	TM
445	Garchomp	TM
446	Munchlax	TM
447	Riolu	TM
448	Lucario	TM
449	Hippopotas	TM
450	Hippowdon	TM
451	Skorupi	TM
452	Drapion	TM
453	Croagunk	TM
454	Toxicroak	TM
455	Carnivine	TM
456	Finneon	TM
457	Lumineon	TM
458	Mantyke	TM
459	Snover	TM
460	Abomasnow	TM
461	Weavile	TM
462	Magnezone	TM
463	Lickilicky	TM
464	Rhyperior	TM
465	Tangrowth	TM
466	Electivire	TM
467	Magmortar	TM
468	Togekiss	TM
469	Yanmega	TM
470	Leafeon	TM
471	Glaceon	TM
472	Gliscor	TM
473	Mamoswine	TM
474	Porygon-Z	TM
475	Gallade	50,TM
476	Probopass	TM
477	Dusknoir	TM
478	Froslass	TM
479	Rotom	TM
480	Uxie	TM
481	Mesprit	16,TM
482	Azelf	TM
483	Dialga	TM
484	Palkia	TM
485	Heatran	TM
487	Giratina (A)	TM
487	Giratina (O)	TM
488	Cresselia	TM
489	Phione	TM
490	Manaphy	TM
491	Darkrai	TM
492	Shaymin (L)	TM
492	Shaymin (S)	TM

Psybeam

12	Butterfree	24
46	Paras	E
48	Venonat	25
49	Venomoth	25
54	Psyduck	E
64	Kadabra	24
65	Alakazam	24
96	Drowzee	26
97	Hypno	28
109	Koffing	E
118	Goldeen	E
122	Mr. Mime	25
137	Porygon	7
165	Ledyba	E
167	Spinarak	E
170	Chinchou	E
196	Espeon	36
200	Misdreavus	23
203	Girafarig	19
223	Remoraid	10
224	Octillery	B,10
226	Mantine	B
233	Porygon2	7
269	Dustox	24
283	Surskit	E
325	Spoink	14
326	Grumpig	B,14
327	Spinda	19
343	Baltoy	11
344	Claydol	11
352	Kecleon	18
413	Wormadam (P)	32
413	Wormadam (S)	32
413	Wormadam (T)	32
414	Mothim	32
439	Mime Jr.	25
456	Finneon	E
474	Porygon-Z	7

Psych Up

12	Butterfree	TM
35	Clefairy	TM
36	Clefable	TM
37	Vulpix	TM,E
38	Ninetales	TM
39	Jigglypuff	TM
40	Wigglytuff	TM
52	Meowth	TM,E
53	Persian	TM
54	Psyduck	35,TM
55	Golduck	37,TM
63	Abra	TM
64	Kadabra	TM
65	Alakazam	TM
79	Slowpoke	57,TM
80	Slowbro	67,TM
81	Magnemite	TM
82	Magneton	TM
83	Farfetch'd	TM
92	Gastly	TM
93	Haunter	TM
94	Gengar	TM
95	Onix	TM
96	Drowzee	29,TM
97	Hypno	33,TM
102	Exeggcute	TM,E
103	Exeggutor	TM
108	Lickitung	TM
113	Chansey	TM
114	Tangela	TM
120	Staryu	TM
121	Starmie	TM
122	Mr. Mime	TM,E
124	Jynx	TM
137	Porygon	TM
150	Mewtwo	29,TM
151	Mew	TM
163	Hoothoot	TM
164	Noctowl	TM
173	Cleffa	TM
174	Igglybuff	TM
175	Togepi	TM,E
176	Togetic	TM
177	Natu	TM,E
178	Xatu	TM
185	Sudowoodo	TM
187	Hoppip	E
196	Espeon	57,TM
197	Umbreon	TM
198	Murkrow	TM
199	Slowking	57,TM
200	Misdreavus	TM,E
203	Girafarig	TM,E
206	Dunsparce	TM,E
208	Steelix	TM
215	Sneasel	TM
233	Porygon2	TM
234	Stantler	TM,E
238	Smoochum	TM,E
241	Miltank	TM,E
242	Blissey	TM
243	Raikou	TM
244	Entei	TM
245	Suicune	TM
249	Lugia	TM
250	Ho-Oh	TM
251	Celebi	TM
274	Nuzleaf	TM
275	Shiftry	TM
280	Ralts	TM
281	Kirlia	TM
282	Gardevoir	TM
283	Surskit	TM
284	Masquerain	TM
300	Skitty	TM,E
301	Delcatty	TM
302	Sableye	TM,E
303	Mawile	E
307	Meditite	36,TM
308	Medicham	36,TM
313	Volbeat	TM
314	Illumise	TM
315	Roselia	TM
325	Spoink	15,TM
326	Grumpig	15,TM
327	Spinda	41,TM
333	Swablu	TM
334	Altaria	TM
337	Lunatone	TM
338	Solrock	TM
343	Baltoy	TM
344	Claydol	TM
350	Milotic	TM
351	Castform	TM,E
352	Kecleon	TM

353	Shuppet	TM
354	Banette	TM
355	Duskull	TM
356	Dusclops	TM
358	Chimecho	TM
359	Absol	TM
368	Gorebyss	TM
369	Relicanth	TM
370	Luvdisc	TM
375	Metang	TM
376	Metagross	TM
377	Regirock	TM
378	Regice	TM
379	Registeel	TM
380	Latias	TM
381	Latios	TM
382	Kyogre	TM
383	Groudon	TM
384	Rayquaza	TM
385	Jirachi	TM
386	Deoxys (N)	TM
386	Deoxys (A)	TM
386	Deoxys (D)	TM
386	Deoxys (S)	TM
406	Budew	TM
407	Roserade	TM
413	Wormadam (P)	TM
413	Wormadam (S)	TM
413	Wormadam (T)	TM
414	Mothim	TM
425	Drifloon	TM
426	Drifblim	TM
429	Mismagius	TM
430	Honchkrow	TM
431	Glameow	TM
432	Purugly	TM
433	Chingling	TM
436	Bronzor	TM
437	Bronzong	TM
438	Bonsly	TM
439	Mime Jr.	TM,E
440	Happiny	TM
442	Spiritomb	TM
456	Finneon	TM
457	Lumineon	TM
461	Weavile	TM
462	Magnezone	TM
463	Lickilicky	TM
465	Tangrowth	TM
468	Togekiss	TM
469	Yanmega	TM
474	Porygon-Z	TM
475	Gallade	TM
477	Dusknoir	TM
478	Froslass	TM
479	Rotom	TM
480	Uxie	TM
481	Mesprit	TM
482	Azelf	TM
483	Dialga	TM
484	Palkia	TM
486	Regigigas	TM
487	Giratina (A)	TM
487	Giratina (O)	TM
488	Cresselia	TM
489	Phione	TM
490	Manaphy	TM
491	Darkrai	TM
492	Shaymin (L)	TM
492	Shaymin (S)	TM

Psychic

12	Butterfree	TM
35	Clefairy	TM
36	Clefable	TM
39	Jigglypuff	TM
40	Wigglytuff	TM
48	Venonat	47,TM
49	Venomoth	55,TM
54	Psyduck	TM,E
55	Golduck	TM
60	Poliwag	TM
61	Poliwhirl	TM
62	Poliwrath	TM
63	Abra	TM
64	Kadabra	40,TM
65	Alakazam	40,TM
79	Slowpoke	48,TM
80	Slowbro	54,TM
92	Gastly	TM
93	Haunter	TM
94	Gengar	TM
96	Drowzee	40,TM
97	Hypno	50,TM
102	Exeggcute	47,TM
103	Exeggutor	TM
113	Chansey	TM
120	Staryu	TM
121	Starmie	TM
122	Mr. Mime	39,TM
124	Jynx	TM
125	Electabuzz	TM
126	Magmar	TM
131	Lapras	TM
137	Porygon	TM
143	Snorlax	TM
150	Mewtwo	71,TM
151	Mew	30,TM
163	Hoothoot	TM
164	Noctowl	TM
167	Spinarak	40,TM
168	Ariados	46,TM
173	Cleffa	TM
174	Igglybuff	TM
175	Togepi	TM
176	Togetic	TM
177	Natu	47,TM
178	Xatu	59,TM
186	Politoed	TM
193	Yanma	TM
196	Espeon	64,TM
197	Umbreon	TM
198	Murkrow	TM
199	Slowking	48,TM
200	Misdreavus	TM
203	Girafarig	37,TM
222	Corsola	TM
223	Remoraid	TM
224	Octillery	TM
233	Porygon2	TM
234	Stantler	TM
238	Smoochum	35,TM
239	Elekid	TM
240	Magby	TM
242	Blissey	TM
249	Lugia	TM
250	Ho-Oh	TM
251	Celebi	TM
267	Beautifly	TM
269	Dustox	TM
280	Ralts	28,TM
281	Kirlia	31,TM
282	Gardevoir	33,TM
302	Sableye	TM
307	Meditite	TM
308	Medicham	TM
325	Spoink	41,TM
326	Grumpig	47,TM
327	Spinda	TM
337	Lunatone	45,TM
338	Solrock	TM
343	Baltoy	TM
344	Claydol	TM
353	Shuppet	TM
354	Banette	TM
355	Duskull	TM
356	Dusclops	TM
358	Chimecho	TM
368	Gorebyss	42,TM
375	Metang	36,TM
376	Metagross	36,TM
380	Latias	65,TM
381	Latios	65,TM
385	Jirachi	20,TM
386	Deoxys (N)	41,TM
386	Deoxys (A)	41,TM
386	Deoxys (D)	41,TM
386	Deoxys (S)	41,TM
413	Wormadam (P)	44,TM
413	Wormadam (S)	44,TM
413	Wormadam (T)	44,TM
414	Mothim	44,TM
425	Drifloon	TM
426	Drifblim	TM
429	Mismagius	TM
430	Honchkrow	TM
433	Chingling	TM
436	Bronzor	TM
437	Bronzong	TM
439	Mime Jr.	39,TM
440	Happiny	TM
442	Spiritomb	TM
446	Munchlax	TM
448	Lucario	TM
466	Electivire	TM
467	Magmortar	TM
468	Togekiss	TM
469	Yanmega	TM
474	Porygon-Z	TM
475	Gallade	TM
477	Dusknoir	TM
478	Froslass	TM
480	Uxie	TM
481	Mesprit	TM
482	Azelf	TM
487	Giratina (A)	TM
487	Giratina (O)	TM
488	Cresselia	93,TM
490	Manaphy	TM
491	Darkrai	TM
492	Shaymin (L)	TM
492	Shaymin (S)	TM

Psycho Boost

386	Deoxys (N)	89
386	Deoxys (A)	89
386	Deoxys (D)	89
386	Deoxys (S)	89

Psycho Cut

64	Kadabra	34
65	Alakazam	34
96	Drowzee	E
150	Mewtwo	50
307	Meditite	E
327	Spinda	E
359	Absol	60
475	Gallade	31
488	Cresselia	66

Psycho Shift

163	Hoothoot	41
164	Noctowl	47
175	Togepi	E
177	Natu	33
178	Xatu	37
198	Murkrow	E
380	Latias	50
381	Latios	50
386	Deoxys (N)	57
386	Deoxys (A)	57
386	Deoxys (D)	57
386	Deoxys (S)	57
488	Cresselia	75

Psywave

92	Gastly	E
109	Koffing	E
200	Misdreavus	B
325	Spoink	7
326	Grumpig	B,7
337	Lunatone	23
338	Solrock	23
358	Chimecho	30
380	Latias	B
381	Latios	B
429	Mismagius	B

Punishment

52	Meowth	E
56	Mankey	45
57	Primeape	53
215	Sneasel	E
228	Houndour	E
241	Miltank	E
249	Lugia	71
250	Ho-Oh	71
289	Slaking	55
302	Sableye	36
303	Mawile	E
359	Absol	E
392	Infernape	33
434	Stunky	E

Pursuit

15	Beedrill	22
16	Pidgey	E
19	Rattata	13
20	Raticate	13
21	Spearow	13
22	Fearow	13
23	Ekans	E
29	Nidoran♀	E
41	Zubat	E
46	Paras	E
50	Diglett	E
84	Doduo	19
85	Dodrio	19
107	Hitmonchan	11
123	Scyther	9
128	Tauros	15
142	Aerodactyl	E
143	Snorlax	E
161	Sentret	E
167	Spinarak	E
190	Aipom	E
193	Yanma	30,E
197	Umbreon	15
198	Murkrow	5
206	Dunsparce	25
212	Scizor	9
214	Heracross	E
215	Sneasel	E
227	Skarmory	E
228	Houndour	E
237	Hitmontop	10
246	Larvitar	E
252	Treecko	16
253	Grovyle	17
254	Sceptile	17
263	Zigzagoon	E
276	Taillow	E
278	Wingull	34
287	Slakoth	E
333	Swablu	E
335	Zangoose	22
353	Shuppet	E
355	Duskull	25
356	Dusclops	25
359	Absol	20
375	Metang	28
376	Metagross	28
386	Deoxys (N)	33
386	Deoxys (A)	33
386	Deoxys (S)	33
396	Starly	E
408	Cranidos	10
409	Rampardos	10
416	Vespiquen	15
418	Buizel	10
419	Floatzel	10
430	Honchkrow	B
434	Stunky	E
442	Spiritomb	B
446	Munchlax	E
451	Skorupi	E
453	Croagunk	15
454	Toxicroak	15
469	Yanmega	30
477	Dusknoir	25

Quick Attack

16	Pidgey	13
17	Pidgeotto	13
18	Pidgeot	B,13
19	Rattata	4
20	Raticate	B,4
21	Spearow	E
25	Pikachu	13
26	Raichu	B
37	Vulpix	11
38	Ninetales	B
41	Zubat	E
78	Rapidash	B
83	Farfetch'd	E
84	Doduo	5,E
85	Dodrio	B,5
123	Scyther	B
125	Electabuzz	B
127	Pinsir	E
133	Eevee	22
134	Vaporeon	22
135	Jolteon	22
136	Flareon	22
155	Cyndaquil	13,E
156	Quilava	13
157	Typhlosion	13
161	Sentret	7
162	Furret	B,7
177	Natu	E
193	Yanma	6
196	Espeon	22
197	Umbreon	22
207	Gligar	16
212	Scizor	B
215	Sneasel	8
225	Delibird	E
237	Hitmontop	15
239	Elekid	B
243	Raikou	22
252	Treecko	11
253	Grovyle	B,11
254	Sceptile	B,11
255	Torchic	28
256	Combusken	32
257	Blaziken	32
273	Seedot	E
276	Taillow	8
277	Swellow	B,8
278	Wingull	24
283	Surskit	7
284	Masquerain	B,7
309	Electrike	17
310	Manectric	17
311	Plusle	7
312	Minun	7
313	Volbeat	17
314	Illumise	17
328	Trapinch	E
335	Zangoose	5
359	Absol	12
396	Starly	5
397	Staravia	B,5
398	Staraptor	B,5
399	Bidoof	E
403	Shinx	E
417	Pachirisu	5
418	Buizel	3
419	Floatzel	B,3
427	Buneary	16
428	Lopunny	16
431	Glameow	E
447	Riolu	B
448	Lucario	B
461	Weavile	B,8
466	Electivire	B
469	Yanmega	B,6
470	Leafeon	22
471	Glaceon	22
472	Gliscor	16
491	Darkrai	11
492	Shaymin (S)	28

Rage

15	Beedrill	19
57	Primeape	28
84	Doduo	10
85	Dodrio	B,10
95	Onix	14
104	Cubone	23
105	Marowak	23
115	Kangaskhan	22
128	Tauros	5
158	Totodile	8
159	Croconaw	8
160	Feraligatr	B,8
206	Dunsparce	B
208	Steelix	14
209	Snubbull	31
210	Granbull	35
228	Houndour	E
276	Taillow	E
318	Carvanha	6
319	Sharpedo	B,6
333	Swablu	E
371	Bagon	B
372	Shelgon	B
373	Salamence	B

Rain Dance

7	Squirtle	37,TM
8	Wartortle	44,TM
9	Blastoise	53,TM
12	Butterfree	TM
16	Pidgey	TM
17	Pidgeotto	TM
18	Pidgeot	TM
19	Rattata	TM
20	Raticate	TM
21	Spearow	TM
22	Fearow	TM
23	Ekans	TM
24	Arbok	TM
25	Pikachu	TM
26	Raichu	TM
29	Nidoran♀	TM
30	Nidorina	TM
31	Nidoqueen	TM
32	Nidoran♂	TM
33	Nidorino	TM
34	Nidoking	TM
35	Clefairy	TM
36	Clefable	TM
39	Jigglypuff	TM
40	Wigglytuff	TM
41	Zubat	TM
42	Golbat	TM
52	Meowth	TM
53	Persian	TM
54	Psyduck	TM
55	Golduck	TM
56	Mankey	TM
57	Primeape	TM
60	Poliwag	18,TM
61	Poliwhirl	18,TM
62	Poliwrath	TM
63	Abra	TM
64	Kadabra	TM
65	Alakazam	TM
66	Machop	TM
67	Machoke	TM
68	Machamp	TM
72	Tentacool	TM
73	Tentacruel	TM
79	Slowpoke	53,TM
80	Slowbro	61,TM
81	Magnemite	TM
82	Magneton	TM
86	Seel	TM
87	Dewgong	TM
88	Grimer	TM
89	Muk	TM
90	Shellder	TM
91	Cloyster	TM
92	Gastly	TM
93	Haunter	TM
94	Gengar	TM
96	Drowzee	TM
97	Hypno	TM
98	Krabby	TM
99	Kingler	TM
100	Voltorb	TM
101	Electrode	TM
106	Hitmonlee	TM
107	Hitmonchan	TM
108	Lickitung	TM
109	Koffing	TM
110	Weezing	TM
111	Rhyhorn	TM
112	Rhydon	TM
113	Chansey	TM
115	Kangaskhan	TM
116	Horsea	TM
117	Seadra	TM
118	Goldeen	TM
119	Seaking	TM
120	Staryu	TM
121	Starmie	TM
122	Mr. Mime	TM
123	Scyther	TM
124	Jynx	TM
125	Electabuzz	TM
127	Pinsir	TM
128	Tauros	TM
130	Gyarados	38,TM
131	Lapras	22,TM
133	Eevee	TM
134	Vaporeon	TM
135	Jolteon	TM
136	Flareon	TM
137	Porygon	TM
138	Omanyte	TM
139	Omastar	TM
140	Kabuto	TM
141	Kabutops	TM
142	Aerodactyl	TM
143	Snorlax	TM
144	Articuno	TM
145	Zapdos	85,TM
146	Moltres	TM
147	Dratini	TM
148	Dragonair	TM
149	Dragonite	TM
150	Mewtwo	TM
151	Mew	TM
158	Totodile	TM
159	Croconaw	TM
160	Feraligatr	TM
161	Sentret	TM
162	Furret	TM
163	Hoothoot	TM
164	Noctowl	TM
169	Crobat	TM
170	Chinchou	TM
171	Lanturn	TM
172	Pichu	TM
173	Cleffa	TM
174	Igglybuff	TM
175	Togepi	TM
176	Togetic	TM
177	Natu	TM
178	Xatu	TM
179	Mareep	TM
180	Flaaffy	TM
181	Ampharos	TM
183	Marill	32,TM
184	Azumarill	40,TM
186	Politoed	TM
190	Aipom	TM
194	Wooper	37,TM
195	Quagsire	41,TM
196	Espeon	TM
197	Umbreon	TM
198	Murkrow	TM
199	Slowking	TM
200	Misdreavus	TM
203	Girafarig	TM
206	Dunsparce	TM
207	Gligar	TM
209	Snubbull	TM
210	Granbull	TM
211	Qwilfish	TM
212	Scizor	TM
214	Heracross	TM
215	Sneasel	TM
216	Teddiursa	TM
217	Ursaring	TM
220	Swinub	TM
221	Piloswine	TM
222	Corsola	TM
223	Remoraid	TM
224	Octillery	TM
225	Delibird	TM
226	Mantine	TM
230	Kingdra	TM
233	Porygon2	TM
234	Stantler	TM
236	Tyrogue	TM
237	Hitmontop	TM
238	Smoochum	TM
239	Elekid	TM
241	Miltank	TM
242	Blissey	TM
243	Raikou	71,TM
244	Entei	TM
245	Suicune	15,TM
246	Larvitar	TM
247	Pupitar	TM
248	Tyranitar	TM
249	Lugia	37,TM
250	Ho-Oh	TM
251	Celebi	TM
258	Mudkip	TM
259	Marshtomp	TM
260	Swampert	TM
261	Poochyena	TM
262	Mightyena	TM
263	Zigzagoon	TM
264	Linoone	TM
270	Lotad	37,TM
271	Lombre	TM
272	Ludicolo	TM
276	Taillow	TM
277	Swellow	TM
278	Wingull	TM
279	Pelipper	TM
280	Ralts	TM
281	Kirlia	TM
282	Gardevoir	TM
283	Surskit	TM
284	Masquerain	TM
287	Slakoth	TM
288	Vigoroth	TM
289	Slaking	TM
293	Whismur	TM
294	Loudred	TM
295	Exploud	TM
296	Makuhita	TM
297	Hariyama	TM
298	Azurill	TM
300	Skitty	TM
301	Delcatty	TM
302	Sableye	TM
303	Mawile	TM
304	Aron	TM
305	Lairon	TM
306	Aggron	TM
307	Meditite	TM
308	Medicham	TM
309	Electrike	TM
310	Manectric	TM
311	Plusle	TM
312	Minun	TM
313	Volbeat	TM
314	Illumise	TM
315	Roselia	TM
316	Gulpin	TM
317	Swalot	TM
318	Carvanha	TM
319	Sharpedo	TM
320	Wailmer	TM
321	Wailord	TM
325	Spoink	TM
326	Grumpig	TM
327	Spinda	TM
333	Swablu	TM
334	Altaria	TM
335	Zangoose	TM
336	Seviper	TM
337	Lunatone	TM
339	Barboach	TM
340	Whiscash	TM
341	Corphish	TM
342	Crawdaunt	TM
343	Baltoy	TM
344	Claydol	TM
349	Feebas	TM
350	Milotic	33,TM
351	Castform	20,TM
352	Kecleon	TM
353	Shuppet	TM
354	Banette	TM
355	Duskull	TM
356	Dusclops	TM
358	Chimecho	TM
359	Absol	TM
361	Snorunt	TM
362	Glalie	TM
363	Spheal	TM
364	Sealeo	TM
365	Walrein	TM
366	Clamperl	TM
367	Huntail	TM

Pokémon Moves and Abilities alphabetical list

Rain Dance continued

368	Gorebyss	TM
369	Relicanth	TM
370	Luvdisc	TM
371	Bagon	TM
372	Shelgon	TM
373	Salamence	TM
375	Metang	TM
376	Metagross	TM
378	Regice	TM
379	Registeel	TM
380	Latias	TM
381	Latios	TM
382	Kyogre	TM
384	Rayquaza	TM
385	Jirachi	TM
386	Deoxys (N)	TM
386	Deoxys (A)	TM
386	Deoxys (D)	TM
386	Deoxys (S)	TM
393	Piplup	TM
394	Prinplup	TM
395	Empoleon	TM
396	Starly	TM
397	Staravia	TM
398	Staraptor	TM
399	Bidoof	TM
400	Bibarel	TM
402	Kricketune	TM
403	Shinx	TM
404	Luxio	TM
405	Luxray	TM
406	Budew	TM
407	Roserade	TM
408	Cranidos	TM
409	Rampardos	TM
410	Shieldon	TM
411	Bastiodon	TM
413	Wormadam (P)	TM
413	Wormadam (S)	TM
413	Wormadam (T)	TM
414	Mothim	TM
416	Vespiquen	TM
417	Pachirisu	TM
418	Buizel	TM
419	Floatzel	TM
422	Shellos	22,TM
423	Gastrodon	22,TM
424	Ambipom	TM
425	Drifloon	TM
426	Drifblim	TM
427	Buneary	TM
428	Lopunny	TM
429	Mismagius	TM
430	Honchkrow	TM
431	Glameow	TM
432	Purugly	TM
433	Chingling	TM
434	Stunky	TM
435	Skuntank	TM
436	Bronzor	TM
437	Bronzong	TM
439	Mime Jr.	TM
440	Happiny	TM
441	Chatot	TM
442	Spiritomb	TM
443	Gible	TM
444	Gabite	TM
445	Garchomp	TM
446	Munchlax	TM
447	Riolu	TM
448	Lucario	TM
451	Skorupi	TM
452	Drapion	TM
453	Croagunk	TM
454	Toxicroak	TM
456	Finneon	13,TM
457	Lumineon	13,TM
458	Mantyke	TM
459	Snover	TM
460	Abomasnow	TM
461	Weavile	TM
462	Magnezone	TM
463	Lickilicky	TM
464	Rhyperior	TM
466	Electivire	TM
468	Togekiss	TM
470	Leafeon	TM
471	Glaceon	TM
472	Gliscor	TM
473	Mamoswine	TM
474	Porygon-Z	TM
475	Gallade	TM
477	Dusknoir	TM
478	Froslass	TM
479	Rotom	TM
480	Uxie	TM
481	Mesprit	TM
482	Azelf	TM
483	Dialga	TM
484	Palkia	TM
486	Regigigas	TM
487	Giratina (A)	TM
487	Giratina (O)	TM
488	Cresselia	TM
489	Phione	69,TM
490	Manaphy	69,TM
491	Darkrai	TM

Rapid Spin

7	Squirtle	19
8	Wartortle	20
9	Blastoise	20
27	Sandshrew	13,E
28	Sandslash	13
72	Tentacool	E
90	Shellder	E
120	Staryu	10
121	Starmie	B
140	Kabuto	E
204	Pineco	17
205	Forretress	17
225	Delibird	E
232	Donphan	6
236	Tyrogue	E
237	Hitmontop	24
324	Torkoal	23
343	Baltoy	5
344	Claydol	B,5
347	Anorith	E

Razor Leaf

1	Bulbasaur	19
2	Ivysaur	20
3	Venusaur	20
43	Oddish	E
69	Bellsprout	39
70	Weepinbell	39
71	Victreebel	B
152	Chikorita	6
153	Bayleef	B,6
154	Meganium	B,6
191	Sunkern	29
192	Sunflora	29
270	Lotad	E
274	Nuzleaf	B
275	Shiftry	B
315	Roselia	E
357	Tropius	11
387	Turtwig	13
388	Grotle	13
389	Torterra	B,13
406	Budew	E
413	Wormadam (P)	26
420	Cherubi	E
455	Carnivine	E
459	Snover	5
460	Abomasnow	B,5
470	Leafeon	15

Razor Wind

123	Scyther	33,E
207	Gligar	E
212	Scizor	33
273	Seedot	E
274	Nuzleaf	37
335	Zangoose	E
357	Tropius	E
359	Absol	17
418	Buizel	45
419	Floatzel	50

Recover

64	Kadabra	30
65	Alakazam	30
120	Staryu	15
121	Starmie	B
137	Porygon	18
150	Mewtwo	86
218	Slugma	23
219	Magcargo	23
222	Corsola	13
233	Porygon2	18
249	Lugia	23
250	Ho-Oh	23
251	Celebi	B
302	Sableye	E
307	Meditite	46
308	Medicham	55
345	Lileep	E
350	Milotic	21
380	Latias	45
381	Latios	45
386	Deoxys (N)	81
386	Deoxys (D)	81
386	Deoxys (S)	81
422	Shellos	46
423	Gastrodon	54
433	Chingling	E
474	Porygon-Z	18

Recycle

35	Clefairy	TM
36	Clefable	TM
39	Jigglypuff	TM
40	Wigglytuff	TM
63	Abra	TM
64	Kadabra	TM
65	Alakazam	TM
79	Slowpoke	TM
80	Slowbro	TM
81	Magnemite	TM
82	Magneton	TM
96	Drowzee	TM
97	Hypno	TM
113	Chansey	TM
120	Staryu	TM
121	Starmie	TM
122	Mr. Mime	32,TM
124	Jynx	TM
137	Porygon	34,TM
143	Snorlax	TM
150	Mewtwo	TM
151	Mew	TM
163	Hoothoot	TM
164	Noctowl	TM
173	Cleffa	TM
174	Igglybuff	TM
199	Slowking	TM
203	Girafarig	TM
225	Delibird	TM
233	Porygon2	34,TM
238	Smoochum	TM
242	Blissey	TM
280	Ralts	TM
281	Kirlia	TM
282	Gardevoir	TM
307	Meditite	TM
308	Medicham	TM
325	Spoink	TM
326	Grumpig	TM
327	Spinda	TM
337	Lunatone	TM
338	Solrock	TM
343	Baltoy	TM
344	Claydol	TM
352	Kecleon	TM
358	Chimecho	TM
385	Jirachi	TM
386	Deoxys (N)	TM
386	Deoxys (A)	TM
386	Deoxys (D)	TM
386	Deoxys (S)	TM
425	Drifloon	TM
426	Drifblim	TM
433	Chingling	TM
436	Bronzor	TM
437	Bronzong	TM
439	Mime Jr.	32,TM
440	Happiny	TM
446	Munchlax	17,TM
462	Magnezone	TM
474	Porygon-Z	TM
475	Gallade	TM
480	Uxie	TM
481	Mesprit	TM
482	Azelf	TM
488	Cresselia	TM

Reflect

35	Clefairy	TM
36	Clefable	TM
39	Jigglypuff	TM
40	Wigglytuff	TM
63	Abra	TM
64	Kadabra	28,TM
65	Alakazam	28,TM
69	Bellsprout	E
81	Magnemite	TM
82	Magneton	TM
96	Drowzee	TM
97	Hypno	TM
102	Exeggcute	7,TM,E
103	Exeggutor	TM
114	Tangela	TM,E
120	Staryu	TM
121	Starmie	TM
122	Mr. Mime	22,TM
124	Jynx	TM
144	Articuno	50,TM
150	Mewtwo	TM
151	Mew	TM
152	Chikorita	17,TM
153	Bayleef	18,TM
154	Meganium	18,TM
163	Hoothoot	17,TM
164	Noctowl	17,TM
165	Ledyba	14,TM
166	Ledian	14,TM
173	Cleffa	TM
174	Igglybuff	TM
175	Togepi	TM
176	Togetic	TM
177	Natu	TM
178	Xatu	TM
179	Mareep	E
187	Hoppip	E
196	Espeon	TM
203	Girafarig	TM
204	Pineco	TM,E
205	Forretress	TM
209	Snubbull	E
215	Sneasel	E
218	Slugma	TM
219	Magcargo	TM
220	Swinub	TM
221	Piloswine	TM
222	Corsola	TM
234	Stantler	TM
238	Smoochum	TM
243	Raikou	36,TM
244	Entei	TM
245	Suicune	TM
249	Lugia	TM
250	Ho-Oh	TM
251	Celebi	TM
280	Ralts	TM
281	Kirlia	TM
282	Gardevoir	TM
307	Meditite	TM
308	Medicham	TM
325	Spoink	TM
326	Grumpig	TM
337	Lunatone	TM
338	Solrock	TM
343	Baltoy	TM
344	Claydol	TM
358	Chimecho	TM
375	Metang	TM
376	Metagross	TM
380	Latias	TM
381	Latios	TM
385	Jirachi	TM
386	Deoxys (N)	TM
386	Deoxys (A)	TM
386	Deoxys (D)	TM
386	Deoxys (S)	TM
387	Turtwig	TM
388	Grotle	TM
389	Torterra	TM
433	Chingling	TM
436	Bronzor	TM
437	Bronzong	TM
439	Mime Jr.	22,TM
462	Magnezone	TM
465	Tangrowth	TM
468	Togekiss	TM
473	Mamoswine	TM
475	Gallade	TM
479	Rotom	TM
480	Uxie	TM
481	Mesprit	TM
482	Azelf	TM
488	Cresselia	TM
490	Manaphy	TM

Refresh

7	Squirtle	E
54	Psyduck	E
60	Poliwag	E
108	Lickitung	41
113	Chansey	9
131	Lapras	E
177	Natu	E
183	Marill	E
222	Corsola	16
242	Blissey	9
258	Mudkip	E
276	Taillow	E
298	Azurill	E
333	Swablu	40
334	Altaria	46
350	Milotic	9
366	Clamperl	E
380	Latias	30
381	Latios	30
385	Jirachi	25
440	Happiny	9
463	Lickilicky	41

Rest

1	Bulbasaur	TM
2	Ivysaur	TM
3	Venusaur	TM
4	Charmander	TM
5	Charmeleon	TM
6	Charizard	TM
7	Squirtle	TM
8	Wartortle	TM
9	Blastoise	TM
12	Butterfree	TM
15	Beedrill	TM
16	Pidgey	TM
17	Pidgeotto	TM
18	Pidgeot	TM
19	Rattata	TM
20	Raticate	TM
21	Spearow	TM
22	Fearow	TM
23	Ekans	TM
24	Arbok	TM
25	Pikachu	TM
26	Raichu	TM
27	Sandshrew	TM
28	Sandslash	TM
29	Nidoran♀	TM
30	Nidorina	TM
31	Nidoqueen	TM
32	Nidoran♂	TM
33	Nidorino	TM
34	Nidoking	TM
35	Clefairy	TM
36	Clefable	TM
37	Vulpix	TM
38	Ninetales	TM
39	Jigglypuff	25,TM
40	Wigglytuff	TM
41	Zubat	TM
42	Golbat	TM
43	Oddish	TM
44	Gloom	TM
45	Vileplume	TM
46	Paras	TM
47	Parasect	TM
48	Venonat	TM
49	Venomoth	TM
50	Diglett	TM
51	Dugtrio	TM
52	Meowth	TM
53	Persian	TM
54	Psyduck	TM
55	Golduck	TM
56	Mankey	TM
57	Primeape	TM
58	Growlithe	TM
59	Arcanine	TM
60	Poliwag	TM
61	Poliwhirl	TM
62	Poliwrath	TM
63	Abra	TM
64	Kadabra	TM
65	Alakazam	TM
66	Machop	TM
67	Machoke	TM
68	Machamp	TM
69	Bellsprout	TM
70	Weepinbell	TM
71	Victreebel	TM
72	Tentacool	TM
73	Tentacruel	TM
74	Geodude	TM
75	Graveler	TM
76	Golem	TM
77	Ponyta	TM
78	Rapidash	TM
79	Slowpoke	TM
80	Slowbro	TM
81	Magnemite	TM
82	Magneton	TM
83	Farfetch'd	TM
84	Doduo	TM
85	Dodrio	TM
86	Seel	21,TM
87	Dewgong	21,TM
88	Grimer	TM
89	Muk	TM
90	Shellder	TM
91	Cloyster	TM
92	Gastly	TM
93	Haunter	TM
94	Gengar	TM
95	Onix	TM
96	Drowzee	TM
97	Hypno	TM
98	Krabby	TM
99	Kingler	TM
100	Voltorb	TM
101	Electrode	TM
102	Exeggcute	TM
103	Exeggutor	TM
104	Cubone	TM
105	Marowak	TM
106	Hitmonlee	TM
107	Hitmonchan	TM
108	Lickitung	TM
109	Koffing	TM
110	Weezing	TM
111	Rhyhorn	TM
112	Rhydon	TM
113	Chansey	TM
114	Tangela	TM
115	Kangaskhan	TM
116	Horsea	TM
117	Seadra	TM
118	Goldeen	TM
119	Seaking	TM
120	Staryu	TM
121	Starmie	TM
122	Mr. Mime	TM
123	Scyther	TM
124	Jynx	TM
125	Electabuzz	TM
126	Magmar	TM
127	Pinsir	TM
128	Tauros	19,TM
130	Gyarados	TM
131	Lapras	TM
133	Eevee	TM
134	Vaporeon	TM
135	Jolteon	TM
136	Flareon	TM
137	Porygon	TM
138	Omanyte	TM
139	Omastar	TM
140	Kabuto	TM
141	Kabutops	TM
142	Aerodactyl	TM
143	Snorlax	25,TM
144	Articuno	TM
145	Zapdos	TM
146	Moltres	TM
147	Dratini	TM
148	Dragonair	TM
149	Dragonite	TM
150	Mewtwo	TM
151	Mew	TM
152	Chikorita	TM
153	Bayleef	TM
154	Meganium	TM
155	Cyndaquil	TM
156	Quilava	TM
157	Typhlosion	TM
158	Totodile	TM
159	Croconaw	TM
160	Feraligatr	TM
161	Sentret	28,TM
162	Furret	32,TM
163	Hoothoot	TM
164	Noctowl	TM
165	Ledyba	TM
166	Ledian	TM
167	Spinarak	TM
168	Ariados	TM
169	Crobat	TM
170	Chinchou	TM
171	Lanturn	TM
172	Pichu	TM
173	Cleffa	TM
174	Igglybuff	TM
175	Togepi	TM
176	Togetic	TM
177	Natu	TM
178	Xatu	TM
179	Mareep	TM
180	Flaaffy	TM
181	Ampharos	TM
182	Bellossom	TM
183	Marill	TM
184	Azumarill	TM
185	Sudowoodo	TM
186	Politoed	TM
187	Hoppip	TM
188	Skiploom	TM
189	Jumpluff	TM
190	Aipom	TM
191	Sunkern	TM
192	Sunflora	TM
193	Yanma	TM
194	Wooper	TM
195	Quagsire	TM
196	Espeon	TM
197	Umbreon	TM
198	Murkrow	TM
199	Slowking	TM
200	Misdreavus	TM
203	Girafarig	TM
204	Pineco	TM
205	Forretress	TM
206	Dunsparce	TM
207	Gligar	TM
208	Steelix	TM
209	Snubbull	TM
210	Granbull	TM
211	Qwilfish	TM
212	Scizor	TM
213	Shuckle	27,TM
214	Heracross	TM
215	Sneasel	TM
216	Teddiursa	43,TM
217	Ursaring	47,TM
218	Slugma	TM
219	Magcargo	TM
220	Swinub	TM
221	Piloswine	TM
222	Corsola	TM
223	Remoraid	TM
224	Octillery	TM
225	Delibird	TM
226	Mantine	TM
227	Skarmory	TM
228	Houndour	TM
229	Houndoom	TM
230	Kingdra	TM
231	Phanpy	TM
232	Donphan	TM
233	Porygon2	TM
234	Stantler	TM
236	Tyrogue	TM
237	Hitmontop	TM
238	Smoochum	TM
239	Elekid	TM
240	Magby	TM
241	Miltank	TM
242	Blissey	TM
243	Raikou	TM
244	Entei	TM
245	Suicune	TM
246	Larvitar	TM
247	Pupitar	TM
248	Tyranitar	TM
249	Lugia	TM
250	Ho-Oh	TM
251	Celebi	TM
252	Treecko	TM
253	Grovyle	TM
254	Sceptile	TM
255	Torchic	TM
256	Combusken	TM
257	Blaziken	TM
258	Mudkip	TM
259	Marshtomp	TM
260	Swampert	TM
261	Poochyena	TM
262	Mightyena	TM
263	Zigzagoon	37,TM
264	Linoone	47,TM
267	Beautifly	TM
269	Dustox	TM
270	Lotad	TM
271	Lombre	TM
272	Ludicolo	TM
273	Seedot	TM
274	Nuzleaf	TM
275	Shiftry	TM
276	Taillow	TM
277	Swellow	TM
278	Wingull	TM
279	Pelipper	TM
280	Ralts	TM
281	Kirlia	TM
282	Gardevoir	TM
283	Surskit	TM
284	Masquerain	TM
285	Shroomish	TM
286	Breloom	TM
287	Slakoth	TM
288	Vigoroth	TM
289	Slaking	TM
290	Nincada	TM
291	Ninjask	TM
292	Shedinja	TM
293	Whismur	41,TM
294	Loudred	51,TM
295	Exploud	55,TM
296	Makuhita	TM
297	Hariyama	TM
298	Azurill	TM
299	Nosepass	43,TM
300	Skitty	TM
301	Delcatty	TM
302	Sableye	TM
303	Mawile	TM
304	Aron	TM
305	Lairon	TM
306	Aggron	TM
307	Meditite	TM
308	Medicham	TM
309	Electrike	TM
310	Manectric	TM
311	Plusle	TM
312	Minun	TM
313	Volbeat	TM
314	Illumise	TM

Pokémon moves and Abilities alphabetical list

315	Roselia	TM
316	Gulpin	TM
317	Swalot	TM
318	Carvanha	TM
319	Sharpedo	TM
320	Wailmer	27,TM
321	Wailord	27,TM
322	Numel	TM
323	Camerupt	TM
324	Torkoal	TM
325	Spoink	29,TM
326	Grumpig	29,TM
327	Spinda	TM
328	Trapinch	TM
329	Vibrava	TM
330	Flygon	TM
331	Cacnea	TM
332	Cacturne	TM
333	Swablu	TM
334	Altaria	TM
335	Zangoose	TM
336	Seviper	TM
337	Lunatone	TM
338	Solrock	TM
339	Barboach	31,TM
340	Whiscash	33,TM
341	Corphish	TM
342	Crawdaunt	TM
343	Baltoy	TM
344	Claydol	TM
345	Lileep	TM
346	Cradily	TM
347	Anorith	TM
348	Armaldo	TM
349	Feebas	TM
350	Milotic	TM
351	Castform	TM
352	Kecleon	TM
353	Shuppet	TM
354	Banette	TM
355	Duskull	TM
356	Dusclops	TM
357	Tropius	TM
358	Chimecho	TM
359	Absol	TM
361	Snorunt	TM
362	Glalie	TM
363	Spheal	37,TM
364	Sealeo	39,TM
365	Walrein	39,TM
366	Clamperl	TM
367	Huntail	TM
368	Gorebyss	TM
369	Relicanth	64,TM
370	Luvdisc	TM
371	Bagon	TM
372	Shelgon	TM
373	Salamence	TM
375	Metang	TM
376	Metagross	TM
377	Regirock	TM
378	Regice	TM
379	Registeel	TM
380	Latias	TM
381	Latios	TM
382	Kyogre	50,TM
383	Groudon	50,TM
384	Rayquaza	50,TM
385	Jirachi	5,30,TM
386	Deoxys (N)	TM
386	Deoxys (A)	TM
386	Deoxys (D)	TM
386	Deoxys (S)	TM
387	Turtwig	TM
388	Grotle	TM
389	Torterra	TM
390	Chimchar	TM
391	Monferno	TM
392	Infernape	TM
393	Piplup	TM
394	Prinplup	TM
395	Empoleon	TM
396	Starly	TM
397	Staravia	TM
398	Staraptor	TM
399	Bidoof	TM
400	Bibarel	TM
402	Kricketune	TM
403	Shinx	TM
404	Luxio	TM
405	Luxray	TM
406	Budew	TM
407	Roserade	TM
408	Cranidos	TM
409	Rampardos	TM
410	Shieldon	TM
411	Bastiodon	TM
413	Wormadam (P)	TM
413	Wormadam (S)	TM
413	Wormadam (T)	TM
414	Mothim	TM
416	Vespiquen	TM
417	Pachirisu	TM
418	Buizel	TM
419	Floatzel	TM
420	Cherubi	TM
421	Cherrim	TM
422	Shellos	TM
423	Gastrodon	TM
424	Ambipom	TM
425	Drifloon	TM
426	Drifblim	TM
427	Buneary	TM
428	Lopunny	TM
429	Mismagius	TM
430	Honchkrow	TM
431	Glameow	TM
432	Purugly	TM
433	Chingling	TM
434	Stunky	TM
435	Skuntank	TM
436	Bronzor	TM
437	Bronzong	TM
438	Bonsly	TM
439	Mime Jr.	TM
440	Happiny	TM
441	Chatot	TM
442	Spiritomb	TM
443	Gible	TM
444	Gabite	TM
445	Garchomp	TM
446	Munchlax	TM
447	Riolu	TM
448	Lucario	TM
449	Hippopotas	TM
450	Hippowdon	TM
451	Skorupi	TM
452	Drapion	TM
453	Croagunk	TM
454	Toxicroak	TM
455	Carnivine	TM
456	Finneon	TM
457	Lumineon	TM
458	Mantyke	TM
459	Snover	TM
460	Abomasnow	TM
461	Weavile	TM
462	Magnezone	TM
463	Lickilicky	TM
464	Rhyperior	TM
465	Tangrowth	TM
466	Electivire	TM
467	Magmortar	TM
468	Togekiss	TM
469	Yanmega	TM
470	Leafeon	TM
471	Glaceon	TM
472	Gliscor	TM
473	Mamoswine	TM
474	Porygon-Z	TM
475	Gallade	TM
476	Probopass	43,TM
477	Dusknoir	TM
478	Froslass	TM
479	Rotom	TM
480	Uxie	B,TM
481	Mesprit	B,TM
482	Azelf	B,TM
483	Dialga	TM
484	Palkia	TM
485	Heatran	TM
487	Giratina (A)	TM
487	Giratina (O)	TM
488	Cresselia	TM
489	Phione	TM
490	Manaphy	TM
491	Darkrai	TM
492	Shaymin (L)	TM
492	Shaymin (S)	TM

Return		
1	Bulbasaur	TM
2	Ivysaur	TM
3	Venusaur	TM
4	Charmander	TM
5	Charmeleon	TM
6	Charizard	TM
7	Squirtle	TM
8	Wartortle	TM
9	Blastoise	TM
12	Butterfree	TM
15	Beedrill	TM
16	Pidgey	TM
17	Pidgeotto	TM
18	Pidgeot	TM
19	Rattata	TM
20	Raticate	TM
21	Spearow	TM
22	Fearow	TM
23	Ekans	TM
24	Arbok	TM
25	Pikachu	TM
26	Raichu	TM
27	Sandshrew	TM
28	Sandslash	TM
29	Nidoran♀	TM
30	Nidorina	TM
31	Nidoqueen	TM
32	Nidoran♂	TM
33	Nidorino	TM
34	Nidoking	TM
35	Clefairy	TM
36	Clefable	TM
37	Vulpix	TM
38	Ninetales	TM
39	Jigglypuff	TM
40	Wigglytuff	TM
41	Zubat	TM
42	Golbat	TM
43	Oddish	TM
44	Gloom	TM
45	Vileplume	TM
46	Paras	TM
47	Parasect	TM
48	Venonat	TM
49	Venomoth	TM
50	Diglett	TM
51	Dugtrio	TM
52	Meowth	TM
53	Persian	TM
54	Psyduck	TM
55	Golduck	TM
56	Mankey	TM
57	Primeape	TM
58	Growlithe	TM
59	Arcanine	TM
60	Poliwag	TM
61	Poliwhirl	TM
62	Poliwrath	TM
63	Abra	TM
64	Kadabra	TM
65	Alakazam	TM
66	Machop	TM
67	Machoke	TM
68	Machamp	TM
69	Bellsprout	TM
70	Weepinbell	TM
71	Victreebel	TM
72	Tentacool	TM
73	Tentacruel	TM
74	Geodude	TM
75	Graveler	TM
76	Golem	TM
77	Ponyta	TM
78	Rapidash	TM
79	Slowpoke	TM
80	Slowbro	TM
81	Magnemite	TM
82	Magneton	TM
83	Farfetch'd	TM
84	Doduo	TM
85	Dodrio	TM
86	Seel	TM
87	Dewgong	TM
88	Grimer	TM
89	Muk	TM
90	Shellder	TM
91	Cloyster	TM
92	Gastly	TM
93	Haunter	TM
94	Gengar	TM
95	Onix	TM
96	Drowzee	TM
97	Hypno	TM
98	Krabby	TM
99	Kingler	TM
100	Voltorb	TM
101	Electrode	TM
102	Exeggcute	TM
103	Exeggutor	TM
104	Cubone	TM
105	Marowak	TM
106	Hitmonlee	TM
107	Hitmonchan	TM
108	Lickitung	TM
109	Koffing	TM
110	Weezing	TM
111	Rhyhorn	TM
112	Rhydon	TM
113	Chansey	TM
114	Tangela	TM
115	Kangaskhan	TM
116	Horsea	TM
117	Seadra	TM
118	Goldeen	TM
119	Seaking	TM
120	Staryu	TM
121	Starmie	TM
122	Mr. Mime	TM
123	Scyther	TM
124	Jynx	TM
125	Electabuzz	TM
126	Magmar	TM
127	Pinsir	TM
128	Tauros	TM
130	Gyarados	TM
131	Lapras	TM
133	Eevee	TM
134	Vaporeon	TM
135	Jolteon	TM
136	Flareon	TM
137	Porygon	TM
138	Omanyte	TM
139	Omastar	TM
140	Kabuto	TM
141	Kabutops	TM
142	Aerodactyl	TM
143	Snorlax	TM
144	Articuno	TM
145	Zapdos	TM
146	Moltres	TM
147	Dratini	TM
148	Dragonair	TM
149	Dragonite	TM
150	Mewtwo	TM
151	Mew	TM
152	Chikorita	TM
153	Bayleef	TM
154	Meganium	TM
155	Cyndaquil	TM
156	Quilava	TM
157	Typhlosion	TM
158	Totodile	TM
159	Croconaw	TM
160	Feraligatr	TM
161	Sentret	TM
162	Furret	TM
163	Hoothoot	TM
164	Noctowl	TM
165	Ledyba	TM
166	Ledian	TM
167	Spinarak	TM
168	Ariados	TM
169	Crobat	TM
170	Chinchou	TM
171	Lanturn	TM
172	Pichu	TM
173	Cleffa	TM
174	Igglybuff	TM
175	Togepi	TM
176	Togetic	TM
177	Natu	TM
178	Xatu	TM
179	Mareep	TM
180	Flaaffy	TM
181	Ampharos	TM
182	Bellossom	TM
183	Marill	TM
184	Azumarill	TM
185	Sudowoodo	TM
186	Politoed	TM
187	Hoppip	TM
188	Skiploom	TM
189	Jumpluff	TM
190	Aipom	TM
191	Sunkern	TM
192	Sunflora	TM
193	Yanma	TM
194	Wooper	TM
195	Quagsire	TM
196	Espeon	TM
197	Umbreon	TM
198	Murkrow	TM
199	Slowking	TM
200	Misdreavus	TM
203	Girafarig	TM
204	Pineco	TM
205	Forretress	TM
206	Dunsparce	TM
207	Gligar	TM
208	Steelix	TM
209	Snubbull	TM
210	Granbull	TM
211	Qwilfish	TM
212	Scizor	TM
213	Shuckle	TM
214	Heracross	TM
215	Sneasel	TM
216	Teddiursa	TM
217	Ursaring	TM
218	Slugma	TM
219	Magcargo	TM
220	Swinub	TM
221	Piloswine	TM
222	Corsola	TM
223	Remoraid	TM
224	Octillery	TM
225	Delibird	TM
226	Mantine	TM
227	Skarmory	TM
228	Houndour	TM
229	Houndoom	TM
230	Kingdra	TM
231	Phanpy	TM
232	Donphan	TM
233	Porygon2	TM
234	Stantler	TM
236	Tyrogue	TM
237	Hitmontop	TM
238	Smoochum	TM
239	Elekid	TM
240	Magby	TM
241	Miltank	TM
242	Blissey	TM
243	Raikou	TM
244	Entei	TM
245	Suicune	TM
246	Larvitar	TM
247	Pupitar	TM
248	Tyranitar	TM
249	Lugia	TM
250	Ho-Oh	TM
251	Celebi	TM
252	Treecko	TM
253	Grovyle	TM
254	Sceptile	TM
255	Torchic	TM
256	Combusken	TM
257	Blaziken	TM
258	Mudkip	TM
259	Marshtomp	TM
260	Swampert	TM
261	Poochyena	TM
262	Mightyena	TM
263	Zigzagoon	TM
264	Linoone	TM
267	Beautifly	TM
269	Dustox	TM
270	Lotad	TM
271	Lombre	TM
272	Ludicolo	TM
273	Seedot	TM
274	Nuzleaf	TM
275	Shiftry	TM
276	Taillow	TM
277	Swellow	TM
278	Wingull	TM
279	Pelipper	TM
280	Ralts	TM
281	Kirlia	TM
282	Gardevoir	TM
283	Surskit	TM
284	Masquerain	TM
285	Shroomish	TM
286	Breloom	TM
287	Slakoth	TM
288	Vigoroth	TM
289	Slaking	TM
290	Nincada	TM
291	Ninjask	TM
292	Shedinja	TM
293	Whismur	TM
294	Loudred	TM
295	Exploud	TM
296	Makuhita	TM
297	Hariyama	TM
298	Azurill	TM
299	Nosepass	TM
300	Skitty	TM
301	Delcatty	TM
302	Sableye	TM
303	Mawile	TM
304	Aron	TM
305	Lairon	TM
306	Aggron	TM
307	Meditite	TM
308	Medicham	TM
309	Electrike	TM
310	Manectric	TM
311	Plusle	TM
312	Minun	TM
313	Volbeat	TM
314	Illumise	TM
315	Roselia	TM
316	Gulpin	TM
317	Swalot	TM
318	Carvanha	TM
319	Sharpedo	TM
320	Wailmer	TM
321	Wailord	TM
322	Numel	TM
323	Camerupt	TM
324	Torkoal	TM
325	Spoink	TM
326	Grumpig	TM
327	Spinda	TM
328	Trapinch	TM
329	Vibrava	TM
330	Flygon	TM
331	Cacnea	TM
332	Cacturne	TM
333	Swablu	TM
334	Altaria	TM
335	Zangoose	TM
336	Seviper	TM
337	Lunatone	TM
338	Solrock	TM
339	Barboach	TM
340	Whiscash	TM
341	Corphish	TM
342	Crawdaunt	TM
343	Baltoy	TM
344	Claydol	TM
345	Lileep	TM
346	Cradily	TM
347	Anorith	TM
348	Armaldo	TM
349	Feebas	TM
350	Milotic	TM
351	Castform	TM
352	Kecleon	TM
353	Shuppet	TM
354	Banette	TM
355	Duskull	TM
356	Dusclops	TM
357	Tropius	TM
358	Chimecho	TM
359	Absol	TM
361	Snorunt	TM
362	Glalie	TM
363	Spheal	TM
364	Sealeo	TM
365	Walrein	TM
366	Clamperl	TM
367	Huntail	TM
368	Gorebyss	TM
369	Relicanth	TM
370	Luvdisc	TM
371	Bagon	TM
372	Shelgon	TM
373	Salamence	TM
375	Metang	TM
376	Metagross	TM
377	Regirock	TM
378	Regice	TM
379	Registeel	TM
380	Latias	TM
381	Latios	TM
382	Kyogre	TM
383	Groudon	TM
384	Rayquaza	TM
385	Jirachi	TM
386	Deoxys (N)	TM
386	Deoxys (A)	TM
386	Deoxys (D)	TM
386	Deoxys (S)	TM
387	Turtwig	TM
388	Grotle	TM
389	Torterra	TM
390	Chimchar	TM
391	Monferno	TM
392	Infernape	TM
393	Piplup	TM
394	Prinplup	TM
395	Empoleon	TM
396	Starly	TM
397	Staravia	TM
398	Staraptor	TM
399	Bidoof	TM
400	Bibarel	TM
402	Kricketune	TM
403	Shinx	TM
404	Luxio	TM
405	Luxray	TM
406	Budew	TM
407	Roserade	TM
408	Cranidos	TM
409	Rampardos	TM
410	Shieldon	TM
411	Bastiodon	TM
413	Wormadam (P)	TM
413	Wormadam (S)	TM
413	Wormadam (T)	TM
414	Mothim	TM
416	Vespiquen	TM
417	Pachirisu	TM
418	Buizel	TM
419	Floatzel	TM
420	Cherubi	TM
421	Cherrim	TM
422	Shellos	TM
423	Gastrodon	TM
424	Ambipom	TM
425	Drifloon	TM
426	Drifblim	TM
427	Buneary	TM
428	Lopunny	13,TM
429	Mismagius	TM
430	Honchkrow	TM
431	Glameow	TM
432	Purugly	TM
433	Chingling	TM
434	Stunky	TM
435	Skuntank	TM
436	Bronzor	TM
437	Bronzong	TM
438	Bonsly	TM
439	Mime Jr.	TM
440	Happiny	TM
441	Chatot	TM
442	Spiritomb	TM
443	Gible	TM
444	Gabite	TM
445	Garchomp	TM
446	Munchlax	TM
447	Riolu	TM
448	Lucario	TM
449	Hippopotas	TM
450	Hippowdon	TM
451	Skorupi	TM
452	Drapion	TM
453	Croagunk	TM
454	Toxicroak	TM
455	Carnivine	TM
456	Finneon	TM
457	Lumineon	TM
458	Mantyke	TM
459	Snover	TM
460	Abomasnow	TM
461	Weavile	TM
462	Magnezone	TM
463	Lickilicky	TM
464	Rhyperior	TM
465	Tangrowth	TM
466	Electivire	TM
467	Magmortar	TM
468	Togekiss	TM
469	Yanmega	TM
470	Leafeon	TM
471	Glaceon	TM
472	Gliscor	TM
473	Mamoswine	TM
474	Porygon-Z	TM
475	Gallade	TM
476	Probopass	TM
477	Dusknoir	TM
478	Froslass	TM
479	Rotom	TM
480	Uxie	TM
481	Mesprit	TM
482	Azelf	TM
483	Dialga	TM
484	Palkia	TM
485	Heatran	TM
486	Regigigas	TM
487	Giratina (A)	TM
487	Giratina (O)	TM
488	Cresselia	TM
489	Phione	TM
490	Manaphy	TM
491	Darkrai	TM
492	Shaymin (L)	TM
492	Shaymin (S)	TM

Revenge		
56	Mankey	E
66	Machop	22
67	Machoke	22
68	Machamp	22
106	Hitmonlee	B
107	Hitmonchan	B
127	Pinsir	18
204	Pineco	E
211	Qwilfish	29
214	Heracross	E
237	Hitmontop	B
296	Makuhita	E
332	Cacturne	B
453	Croagunk	22
454	Toxicroak	22
461	Weavile	B
486	Regigigas	25

Reversal		
19	Rattata	E
56	Mankey	E
58	Growlithe	25
106	Hitmonlee	57
111	Rhyhorn	E
115	Kangaskhan	49
123	Scyther	E
155	Cyndaquil	E
161	Sentret	E

ADVENTURE DATA LIST
POKÉMON MOVES AND ABILITIES ALPHABETICAL LIST

Pokémon Moves and Abilities alphabetical list

Reversal continued

172	Pichu	E
193	Yanma	E
214	Heracross	43
228	Houndour	E
241	Miltank	E
255	Torchic	E
288	Vigoroth	49
296	Makuhita	43
297	Hariyama	57
307	Meditite	43
308	Medicham	49
447	Riolu	19

Roar

3	Venusaur	TM
6	Charizard	TM
9	Blastoise	TM
20	Raticate	TM
31	Nidoqueen	TM
34	Nidoking	TM
37	Vulpix	7,TM
38	Ninetales	TM
53	Persian	TM
58	Growlithe	B,TM
59	Arcanine	B,TM
76	Golem	TM
95	Onix	TM
111	Rhyhorn	TM
112	Rhydon	TM
115	Kangaskhan	TM
130	Gyarados	TM
131	Lapras	TM
134	Vaporeon	TM
135	Jolteon	TM
136	Flareon	TM
142	Aerodactyl	9,TM
144	Articuno	TM
145	Zapdos	TM
146	Moltres	TM
149	Dragonite	TM
151	Mew	TM
156	Quilava	TM
157	Typhlosion	TM
159	Croconaw	TM
160	Feraligatr	TM
208	Steelix	TM
209	Snubbull	25,TM
210	Granbull	27,TM
216	Teddiursa	TM
217	Ursaring	TM
220	Swinub	TM
221	Piloswine	TM
227	Skarmory	TM
228	Houndour	14,TM
229	Houndoom	14,TM
231	Phanpy	TM
232	Donphan	TM
234	Stantler	TM
243	Raikou	15,TM
244	Entei	15,TM
245	Suicune	TM
248	Tyranitar	TM
249	Lugia	TM
250	Ho-Oh	TM
254	Sceptile	TM
257	Blaziken	TM
260	Swampert	TM
261	Poochyena	21,TM
262	Mightyena	22,TM
264	Linoone	TM
288	Vigoroth	TM
289	Slaking	TM
293	Whismur	35,TM
294	Loudred	43,TM
295	Exploud	45,TM
304	Aron	22,TM
305	Lairon	22,TM
306	Aggron	22,TM
309	Electrike	36,TM
310	Manectric	42,TM
319	Sharpedo	TM
320	Wailmer	TM
321	Wailord	TM
323	Camerupt	TM
334	Altaria	TM
335	Zangoose	TM,E
357	Tropius	TM
364	Sealeo	TM
365	Walrein	TM
371	Bagon	TM
372	Shelgon	TM
373	Salamence	TM
380	Latias	TM
381	Latios	TM
382	Kyogre	TM
383	Groudon	TM
384	Rayquaza	TM
389	Torterra	TM
392	Infernape	TM
395	Empoleon	TM
403	Shinx	21,TM
404	Luxio	23,TM
405	Luxray	23,TM
408	Cranidos	TM
409	Rampardos	TM
410	Shieldon	TM
411	Bastiodon	TM
419	Floatzel	TM
432	Purugly	TM
434	Stunky	TM
435	Skuntank	TM
443	Gible	TM
444	Gabite	TM
445	Garchomp	TM
447	Riolu	TM
448	Lucario	TM
449	Hippopotas	TM
450	Hippowdon	TM
452	Drapion	TM
464	Rhyperior	TM
470	Leafeon	TM
471	Glaceon	TM
473	Mamoswine	TM
483	Dialga	TM
484	Palkia	TM
485	Heatran	TM
487	Giratina (A)	TM
487	Giratina (O)	TM

Roar of Time

483	Dialga	40

Rock Blast

74	Geodude	25
75	Graveler	27
76	Golem	27
95	Onix	E
111	Rhyhorn	25
112	Rhydon	25
138	Omanyte	46
139	Omastar	56
222	Corsola	20
223	Remoraid	E
224	Octillery	B
347	Anorith	49
348	Armaldo	55
410	Shieldon	E
413	Wormadam (S)	26
464	Rhyperior	25

Rock Climb

3	Venusaur	HM
9	Blastoise	HM
27	Sandshrew	HM
28	Sandslash	HM
31	Nidoqueen	HM
34	Nidoking	HM
55	Golduck	HM
56	Mankey	HM
57	Primeape	HM
59	Arcanine	HM
62	Poliwrath	HM
66	Machop	HM
67	Machoke	HM
68	Machamp	HM
74	Geodude	HM
75	Graveler	HM
76	Golem	HM
95	Onix	HM
104	Cubone	HM
105	Marowak	HM
106	Hitmonlee	HM
107	Hitmonchan	HM
108	Lickitung	HM
111	Rhyhorn	HM
112	Rhydon	HM
113	Chansey	HM
115	Kangaskhan	HM
125	Electabuzz	HM
126	Magmar	HM
127	Pinsir	HM
128	Tauros	HM
139	Omastar	HM
141	Kabutops	HM
143	Snorlax	HM
150	Mewtwo	HM
151	Mew	HM
154	Meganium	HM
157	Typhlosion	HM
160	Feraligatr	HM
181	Ampharos	HM
208	Steelix	HM
210	Granbull	HM
217	Ursaring	HM
242	Blissey	HM
243	Raikou	HM
244	Entei	HM
245	Suicune	HM
248	Tyranitar	HM
254	Sceptile	HM
257	Blaziken	HM
260	Swampert	HM
272	Ludicolo	HM
288	Vigoroth	HM
289	Slaking	HM
295	Exploud	HM
296	Makuhita	HM
297	Hariyama	HM
306	Aggron	HM
335	Zangoose	HM
377	Regirock	HM
378	Regice	HM
379	Registeel	HM
383	Groudon	HM
387	Turtwig	HM
388	Grotle	HM
389	Torterra	HM
390	Chimchar	HM
391	Monferno	HM
392	Infernape	HM
395	Empoleon	HM
400	Bibarel	HM
408	Cranidos	HM
409	Rampardos	HM
443	Gible	HM
444	Gabite	HM
445	Garchomp	HM
446	Munchlax	HM
448	Lucario	HM
452	Drapion	HM
453	Croagunk	HM
454	Toxicroak	HM
460	Abomasnow	HM
463	Lickilicky	HM
464	Rhyperior	HM
466	Electivire	HM
467	Magmortar	HM
473	Mamoswine	HM
485	Heatran	HM
486	Regigigas	HM
487	Giratina (A)	HM
487	Giratina (O)	HM
491	Darkrai	HM

Rock Polish

74	Geodude	8,TM
75	Graveler	B,8,TM
76	Golem	B,8,TM
95	Onix	30,TM
111	Rhyhorn	TM
112	Rhydon	TM
138	Omanyte	TM
139	Omastar	TM
140	Kabuto	TM
141	Kabutops	TM
142	Aerodactyl	TM
151	Mew	TM
185	Sudowoodo	TM
205	Forretress	TM
207	Gligar	TM
208	Steelix	30,TM
213	Shuckle	TM
219	Magcargo	TM
222	Corsola	TM
232	Donphan	TM
246	Larvitar	TM
247	Pupitar	TM
248	Tyranitar	TM
299	Nosepass	TM
304	Aron	TM
305	Lairon	TM
306	Aggron	TM
323	Camerupt	TM
337	Lunatone	20,TM
338	Solrock	20,TM
343	Baltoy	TM
344	Claydol	TM
345	Lileep	TM
346	Cradily	TM
347	Anorith	TM
348	Armaldo	TM
369	Relicanth	TM
375	Metang	TM
376	Metagross	TM
377	Regirock	TM
378	Regice	TM
379	Registeel	TM
383	Groudon	TM
389	Torterra	TM
408	Cranidos	TM
409	Rampardos	TM
410	Shieldon	TM
411	Bastiodon	TM
436	Bronzor	TM
437	Bronzong	TM
438	Bonsly	TM
464	Rhyperior	TM
472	Gliscor	TM
476	Probopass	TM
486	Regigigas	TM

Rock Slide

4	Charmander	TM,E
5	Charmeleon	TM
6	Charizard	TM
9	Blastoise	TM
23	Ekans	TM
24	Arbok	TM
27	Sandshrew	TM,E
28	Sandslash	TM
31	Nidoqueen	TM
34	Nidoking	TM
50	Diglett	TM,E
51	Dugtrio	TM
56	Mankey	TM,E
57	Primeape	TM
62	Poliwrath	TM
66	Machop	TM,E
67	Machoke	TM
68	Machamp	TM
74	Geodude	TM,E
75	Graveler	TM
76	Golem	TM
88	Grimer	TM
89	Muk	TM
95	Onix	TM,E
98	Krabby	TM
99	Kingler	TM
104	Cubone	TM,E
105	Marowak	TM
106	Hitmonlee	TM
107	Hitmonchan	TM
108	Lickitung	TM
111	Rhyhorn	TM,E
112	Rhydon	TM
113	Chansey	TM
115	Kangaskhan	TM
127	Pinsir	TM
128	Tauros	TM
138	Omanyte	TM,E
139	Omastar	TM
140	Kabuto	TM
141	Kabutops	TM
142	Aerodactyl	65,TM
143	Snorlax	TM
149	Dragonite	TM
150	Mewtwo	TM
151	Mew	TM
157	Typhlosion	TM
158	Totodile	TM,E
159	Croconaw	TM
160	Feraligatr	TM
185	Sudowoodo	33,TM
195	Quagsire	TM
204	Pineco	TM
205	Forretress	TM
206	Dunsparce	TM,E
207	Gligar	TM
208	Steelix	TM
210	Granbull	TM
213	Shuckle	TM
214	Heracross	TM
216	Teddiursa	TM
217	Ursaring	TM
218	Slugma	41,TM
219	Magcargo	45,TM
220	Swinub	TM,E
221	Piloswine	TM
222	Corsola	TM,E
226	Mantine	TM,E
227	Skarmory	TM
231	Phanpy	TM
232	Donphan	TM
236	Tyrogue	TM
237	Hitmontop	TM
241	Miltank	TM
242	Blissey	TM
246	Larvitar	14,TM
247	Pupitar	14,TM
248	Tyranitar	14,TM
252	Treecko	TM
253	Grovyle	TM
254	Sceptile	TM
255	Torchic	TM,E
256	Combusken	TM
257	Blaziken	TM
258	Mudkip	TM
259	Marshtomp	TM
260	Swampert	TM
274	Nuzleaf	TM
275	Shiftry	TM
286	Breloom	TM
287	Slakoth	TM
288	Vigoroth	TM
289	Slaking	TM
294	Loudred	TM
295	Exploud	TM
296	Makuhita	TM
297	Hariyama	TM
299	Nosepass	31,TM
303	Mawile	TM
304	Aron	TM
305	Lairon	TM
306	Aggron	TM
307	Meditite	TM
308	Medicham	TM
322	Numel	TM
323	Camerupt	33,TM
324	Torkoal	TM
327	Spinda	TM,E
328	Trapinch	TM
329	Vibrava	TM
330	Flygon	TM
335	Zangoose	TM
337	Lunatone	TM
338	Solrock	45,TM
340	Whiscash	TM
341	Corphish	TM
342	Crawdaunt	TM
343	Baltoy	TM
344	Claydol	TM
345	Lileep	TM,E
346	Cradily	TM
347	Anorith	TM,E
348	Armaldo	TM
352	Kecleon	TM
356	Dusclops	TM
359	Absol	TM
363	Spheal	TM,E
364	Sealeo	TM
365	Walrein	TM
369	Relicanth	TM,E
371	Bagon	TM
372	Shelgon	TM
373	Salamence	TM
375	Metang	TM
376	Metagross	TM
377	Regirock	TM
378	Regice	TM
379	Registeel	TM
382	Kyogre	TM
383	Groudon	TM
384	Rayquaza	TM
386	Deoxys (N)	TM
386	Deoxys (A)	TM
386	Deoxys (D)	TM
386	Deoxys (S)	TM
389	Torterra	TM
391	Monferno	TM
392	Infernape	TM
395	Empoleon	TM
408	Cranidos	TM
409	Rampardos	TM
410	Shieldon	TM
411	Bastiodon	TM
423	Gastrodon	TM
436	Bronzor	TM
437	Bronzong	TM
438	Bonsly	33,TM
443	Gible	TM
444	Gabite	TM
445	Garchomp	TM
446	Munchlax	TM
447	Riolu	TM
448	Lucario	TM
449	Hippopotas	TM
450	Hippowdon	TM
452	Drapion	TM
453	Croagunk	TM
454	Toxicroak	TM
458	Mantyke	E
460	Abomasnow	TM
463	Lickilicky	TM
464	Rhyperior	TM
465	Tangrowth	TM
466	Electivire	TM
467	Magmortar	TM
472	Gliscor	TM
473	Mamoswine	TM
475	Gallade	TM
476	Probopass	31,TM
477	Dusknoir	TM
483	Dialga	TM
484	Palkia	TM
485	Heatran	TM
486	Regigigas	TM
491	Darkrai	TM

Rock Smash

1	Bulbasaur	HM
2	Ivysaur	HM
3	Venusaur	HM
4	Charmander	HM
5	Charmeleon	HM
6	Charizard	HM
7	Squirtle	HM
8	Wartortle	HM
9	Blastoise	HM
15	Beedrill	HM
19	Rattata	HM
20	Raticate	HM
25	Pikachu	HM
26	Raichu	HM
27	Sandshrew	HM
28	Sandslash	HM
29	Nidoran♀	HM
30	Nidorina	HM
31	Nidoqueen	HM
32	Nidoran♂	HM
33	Nidorino	HM
34	Nidoking	HM
35	Clefairy	HM
36	Clefable	HM
46	Paras	HM
47	Parasect	HM
50	Diglett	HM
51	Dugtrio	HM
54	Psyduck	HM
55	Golduck	HM
56	Mankey	HM
57	Primeape	HM
58	Growlithe	HM
59	Arcanine	HM
61	Poliwhirl	HM
62	Poliwrath	HM
66	Machop	HM
67	Machoke	HM
68	Machamp	HM
74	Geodude	HM
75	Graveler	HM
76	Golem	HM
80	Slowbro	HM
89	Muk	HM
94	Gengar	HM
95	Onix	HM
98	Krabby	HM
99	Kingler	HM
104	Cubone	HM
105	Marowak	HM
106	Hitmonlee	HM
107	Hitmonchan	HM
108	Lickitung	HM
111	Rhyhorn	HM
112	Rhydon	HM
113	Chansey	HM
114	Tangela	HM
115	Kangaskhan	HM
123	Scyther	HM
125	Electabuzz	HM
126	Magmar	HM
127	Pinsir	HM
128	Tauros	HM
130	Gyarados	HM
131	Lapras	HM
134	Vaporeon	HM
135	Jolteon	HM
136	Flareon	HM
138	Omanyte	HM
139	Omastar	HM
140	Kabuto	HM
141	Kabutops	HM
142	Aerodactyl	HM
143	Snorlax	HM
144	Articuno	HM
145	Zapdos	HM
146	Moltres	HM
149	Dragonite	HM
150	Mewtwo	HM
151	Mew	HM
153	Bayleef	HM
154	Meganium	HM
156	Quilava	HM
157	Typhlosion	HM
159	Croconaw	HM
160	Feraligatr	HM
162	Furret	HM
166	Ledian	HM
175	Togepi	HM
176	Togetic	HM
180	Flaaffy	HM
181	Ampharos	HM
183	Marill	HM
184	Azumarill	HM
185	Sudowoodo	HM
186	Politoed	HM
190	Aipom	HM
194	Wooper	HM
195	Quagsire	HM
199	Slowking	HM
203	Girafarig	HM
204	Pineco	HM
205	Forretress	HM
206	Dunsparce	HM
207	Gligar	HM
208	Steelix	HM
209	Snubbull	HM
210	Granbull	HM
212	Scizor	HM
213	Shuckle	HM
214	Heracross	HM
215	Sneasel	HM
216	Teddiursa	HM
217	Ursaring	HM
218	Slugma	HM
219	Magcargo	HM
220	Swinub	HM
221	Piloswine	HM
222	Corsola	HM
227	Skarmory	HM
228	Houndour	HM
229	Houndoom	HM
231	Phanpy	HM
232	Donphan	HM
236	Tyrogue	HM
237	Hitmontop	HM
239	Elekid	HM
240	Magby	HM
241	Miltank	HM
242	Blissey	HM
243	Raikou	HM
244	Entei	HM
245	Suicune	HM
246	Larvitar	HM
247	Pupitar	HM
248	Tyranitar	HM
249	Lugia	HM
250	Ho-Oh	HM
252	Treecko	HM
253	Grovyle	HM
254	Sceptile	HM
255	Torchic	HM
256	Combusken	HM
257	Blaziken	HM
258	Mudkip	HM
259	Marshtomp	HM
260	Swampert	HM
261	Poochyena	HM
262	Mightyena	HM
263	Zigzagoon	HM
264	Linoone	HM
271	Lombre	HM
272	Ludicolo	HM
273	Seedot	HM
274	Nuzleaf	HM
275	Shiftry	HM
286	Breloom	HM
287	Slakoth	HM
288	Vigoroth	HM
289	Slaking	HM
294	Loudred	HM
295	Exploud	HM
296	Makuhita	HM
297	Hariyama	HM
299	Nosepass	HM
301	Delcatty	HM
302	Sableye	HM
303	Mawile	HM
304	Aron	HM
305	Lairon	HM
306	Aggron	HM
307	Meditite	HM
308	Medicham	HM
316	Gulpin	HM
317	Swalot	HM
319	Sharpedo	HM
320	Wailmer	HM
321	Wailord	HM
322	Numel	HM
323	Camerupt	HM
324	Torkoal	HM
327	Spinda	HM
328	Trapinch	HM
329	Vibrava	HM
330	Flygon	HM
334	Altaria	HM
335	Zangoose	HM
336	Seviper	HM
340	Whiscash	HM
341	Corphish	HM
342	Crawdaunt	HM
344	Claydol	HM
346	Cradily	HM
347	Anorith	HM
348	Armaldo	HM
352	Kecleon	HM
356	Dusclops	HM
357	Tropius	HM
359	Absol	HM
363	Spheal	HM
364	Sealeo	HM
365	Walrein	HM
369	Relicanth	HM

POKÉMON MOVES AND ABILITIES ALPHABETICAL LIST — ADVENTURE DATA LIST
594

Pokémon moves and Abilities alphabetical list

371	Bagon	HM
372	Shelgon	HM
373	Salamence	HM
375	Metang	HM
376	Metagross	HM
377	Regirock	HM
378	Regice	HM
379	Registeel	HM
382	Kyogre	HM
383	Groudon	HM
384	Rayquaza	HM
386	Deoxys (N)	HM
386	Deoxys (A)	HM
386	Deoxys (D)	HM
386	Deoxys (S)	HM
387	Turtwig	HM
388	Grotle	HM
389	Torterra	HM
390	Chimchar	HM
391	Monferno	HM
392	Infernape	HM
394	Prinplup	HM
395	Empoleon	HM
399	Bidoof	HM
400	Bibarel	HM
402	Kricketune	HM
408	Cranidos	HM
409	Rampardos	HM
410	Shieldon	HM
411	Bastiodon	HM
418	Buizel	HM
419	Floatzel	HM
423	Gastrodon	HM
424	Ambipom	HM
427	Buneary	HM
428	Lopunny	HM
434	Stunky	HM
435	Skuntank	HM
437	Bronzong	HM
443	Gible	HM
444	Gabite	HM
445	Garchomp	HM
446	Munchlax	HM
447	Riolu	HM
448	Lucario	HM
449	Hippopotas	HM
450	Hippowdon	HM
451	Skorupi	HM
452	Drapion	HM
453	Croagunk	HM
454	Toxicroak	HM
460	Abomasnow	HM
461	Weavile	HM
463	Lickilicky	HM
464	Rhyperior	HM
465	Tangrowth	HM
466	Electivire	HM
467	Magmortar	HM
468	Togekiss	HM
470	Leafeon	HM
471	Glaceon	HM
472	Gliscor	HM
473	Mamoswine	HM
475	Gallade	HM
476	Probopass	HM
477	Dusknoir	HM
483	Dialga	HM
484	Palkia	HM
485	Heatran	HM
486	Regigigas	HM
487	Giratina (A)	HM
487	Giratina (O)	HM
491	Darkrai	HM

Rock Throw

74	Geodude	11
75	Graveler	11
76	Golem	11
95	Onix	9
185	Sudowoodo	B,14
208	Steelix	9
218	Slugma	11
219	Magcargo	B,11
299	Nosepass	13
337	Lunatone	9
338	Solrock	9
377	Regirock	9
438	Bonsly	14

Rock Tomb

4	Charmander	TM
5	Charmeleon	TM
6	Charizard	TM
7	Squirtle	TM
8	Wartortle	TM
9	Blastoise	TM
23	Ekans	TM
24	Arbok	TM
27	Sandshrew	TM
28	Sandslash	TM
31	Nidoqueen	TM
34	Nidoking	TM
50	Diglett	TM
51	Dugtrio	TM
56	Mankey	TM
57	Primeape	TM
62	Poliwrath	TM
66	Machop	TM
67	Machoke	TM
68	Machamp	TM
74	Geodude	TM
75	Graveler	TM
76	Golem	TM
88	Grimer	TM
89	Muk	TM
95	Onix	17,TM
98	Krabby	TM
99	Kingler	TM
104	Cubone	TM
105	Marowak	TM
106	Hitmonlee	TM
107	Hitmonchan	TM
108	Lickitung	TM
111	Rhyhorn	TM
112	Rhydon	TM
113	Chansey	TM
115	Kangaskhan	TM
127	Pinsir	TM
128	Tauros	TM
138	Omanyte	TM
139	Omastar	TM
140	Kabuto	TM
141	Kabutops	TM
142	Aerodactyl	TM
143	Snorlax	TM
149	Dragonite	TM
150	Mewtwo	TM
151	Mew	TM
157	Typhlosion	TM
158	Totodile	TM
159	Croconaw	TM
160	Feraligatr	TM
185	Sudowoodo	30,TM
195	Quagsire	TM
204	Pineco	TM
205	Forretress	TM
206	Dunsparce	TM
207	Gligar	TM
208	Steelix	17,TM
210	Granbull	TM
213	Shuckle	TM
214	Heracross	TM
216	Teddiursa	TM
217	Ursaring	TM
218	Slugma	TM
219	Magcargo	TM
220	Swinub	TM
221	Piloswine	TM
222	Corsola	TM
226	Mantine	TM
227	Skarmory	TM
231	Phanpy	TM
232	Donphan	TM
241	Miltank	TM
242	Blissey	TM
246	Larvitar	TM
247	Pupitar	TM
248	Tyranitar	TM
252	Treecko	TM
253	Grovyle	TM
254	Sceptile	TM
255	Torchic	TM
256	Combusken	TM
257	Blaziken	TM
258	Mudkip	TM
259	Marshtomp	TM
260	Swampert	TM
274	Nuzleaf	TM
275	Shiftry	TM
286	Breloom	TM
287	Slakoth	TM
288	Vigoroth	TM
289	Slaking	TM
294	Loudred	TM
295	Exploud	TM
296	Makuhita	TM
297	Hariyama	TM
299	Nosepass	TM
302	Sableye	TM
303	Mawile	TM
304	Aron	TM
305	Lairon	TM
306	Aggron	TM
307	Meditite	TM
308	Medicham	TM
319	Sharpedo	TM
320	Wailmer	TM
321	Wailord	TM
322	Numel	TM
323	Camerupt	TM
324	Torkoal	TM
327	Spinda	TM
328	Trapinch	TM
329	Vibrava	TM
330	Flygon	TM
335	Zangoose	TM
337	Lunatone	TM
338	Solrock	TM
339	Barboach	TM
340	Whiscash	TM
341	Corphish	TM
342	Crawdaunt	TM
343	Baltoy	15,TM
344	Claydol	15,TM
345	Lileep	TM
346	Cradily	TM
347	Anorith	TM
348	Armaldo	TM
352	Kecleon	TM
356	Dusclops	TM
359	Absol	TM
363	Spheal	TM
364	Sealeo	TM
365	Walrein	TM
367	Huntail	TM
369	Relicanth	15,TM
371	Bagon	TM
372	Shelgon	TM
373	Salamence	TM
375	Metang	TM
376	Metagross	TM
377	Regirock	TM
378	Regice	TM
379	Registeel	TM
382	Kyogre	TM
383	Groudon	TM
384	Rayquaza	TM
386	Deoxys (N)	TM
386	Deoxys (A)	TM
386	Deoxys (D)	TM
386	Deoxys (S)	TM
389	Torterra	TM
391	Monferno	TM
392	Infernape	TM
393	Piplup	TM
394	Prinplup	TM
395	Empoleon	TM
408	Cranidos	TM
409	Rampardos	TM
410	Shieldon	TM
411	Bastiodon	TM
413	Wormadam (S)	TM
418	Buizel	TM
419	Floatzel	TM
423	Gastrodon	TM
436	Bronzor	TM
437	Bronzong	TM
438	Bonsly	30,TM
442	Spiritomb	TM
443	Gible	TM
444	Gabite	TM
445	Garchomp	TM
446	Munchlax	TM
447	Riolu	TM
448	Lucario	TM
449	Hippopotas	TM
450	Hippowdon	TM
451	Skorupi	TM
452	Drapion	TM
453	Croagunk	TM
454	Toxicroak	TM
460	Abomasnow	TM
463	Lickilicky	TM
464	Rhyperior	TM
465	Tangrowth	TM
466	Electivire	TM
467	Magmortar	TM
472	Gliscor	TM
473	Mamoswine	TM
475	Gallade	TM
476	Probopass	TM
477	Dusknoir	TM
483	Dialga	TM
484	Palkia	TM
485	Heatran	TM
486	Regigigas	TM
491	Darkrai	TM

Rock Wrecker

464	Rhyperior	61

Role Play

64	Kadabra	36
96	Drowzee	E
122	Mr. Mime	43
234	Stantler	33
327	Spinda	E
439	Mime Jr.	43

Rolling Kick

66	Machop	E
106	Hitmonlee	9
237	Hitmontop	B
239	Elekid	E

Rollout

7	Squirtle	T
8	Wartortle	T
9	Blastoise	T
25	Pikachu	T
26	Raichu	T
27	Sandshrew	21,T
28	Sandslash	21,T
35	Clefairy	T
36	Clefable	T
39	Jigglypuff	17,T
40	Wigglytuff	T
74	Geodude	22,T
75	Graveler	22,T
76	Golem	22,T
81	Magnemite	T
82	Magneton	T
95	Onix	T,E
100	Voltorb	15,T
101	Electrode	15,T
102	Exeggcute	T
103	Exeggutor	T
108	Lickitung	33,T
109	Koffing	T
110	Weezing	T
111	Rhyhorn	T
112	Rhydon	T
113	Chansey	T
120	Staryu	T
121	Starmie	T
138	Omanyte	16,T
139	Omastar	16,T
140	Kabuto	T
141	Kabutops	T
143	Snorlax	41,T
151	Mew	T
155	Cyndaquil	40,T
156	Quilava	46,T
157	Typhlosion	46,T
161	Sentret	T
162	Furret	T
165	Ledyba	T
166	Ledian	T
172	Pichu	T
173	Cleffa	T
174	Igglybuff	T
175	Togepi	T
176	Togetic	T
183	Marill	15,T
184	Azumarill	15,T
185	Sudowoodo	T,E
194	Wooper	T
195	Quagsire	T
204	Pineco	T
205	Forretress	T
206	Dunsparce	17,T
208	Steelix	T
211	Qwilfish	17,T
213	Shuckle	T
216	Teddiursa	T
217	Ursaring	T
218	Slugma	T
219	Magcargo	T
222	Corsola	T
225	Delibird	T
231	Phanpy	15,T
232	Donphan	15,T
237	Hitmontop	T
241	Miltank	19,T
242	Blissey	T
258	Mudkip	T
259	Marshtomp	T
260	Swampert	T
263	Zigzagoon	T
264	Linoone	T
273	Seedot	T
274	Nuzleaf	T
275	Shiftry	T
293	Whismur	T
294	Loudred	T
295	Exploud	T
298	Azurill	T
299	Nosepass	T,E
300	Skitty	T
301	Delcatty	T
304	Aron	T
305	Lairon	T
306	Aggron	T
311	Plusle	T
312	Minun	T
316	Gulpin	T
317	Swalot	T
320	Wailmer	11,T
321	Wailord	B,11,T
322	Numel	T,E
323	Camerupt	T
324	Torkoal	T
327	Spinda	T
335	Zangoose	T
337	Lunatone	T
338	Solrock	T
352	Kecleon	T
358	Chimecho	T
361	Snorunt	T,E
362	Glalie	T
363	Spheal	T
364	Sealeo	T
365	Walrein	T
372	Shelgon	T
373	Salamence	T
375	Metang	T
376	Metagross	T
377	Regirock	T
378	Regice	T
379	Registeel	T
383	Groudon	T
390	Chimchar	T
391	Monferno	T
392	Infernape	T
399	Bidoof	13,T,E
400	Bibarel	13,T
413	Wormadam (S)	T
417	Pachirisu	T,E
420	Cherubi	T
421	Cherrim	T
425	Drifloon	T
426	Drifblim	T
432	Purugly	T
433	Chingling	T
436	Bronzor	T
437	Bronzong	T
438	Bonsly	T,E
440	Happiny	T
446	Munchlax	41,T
462	Magnezone	T
463	Lickilicky	33,T
464	Rhyperior	T
468	Togekiss	T
476	Probopass	T
478	Froslass	T

Roost

6	Charizard	TM
12	Butterfree	TM
15	Beedrill	TM
16	Pidgey	37,TM
17	Pidgeotto	42,TM
18	Pidgeot	44,TM
21	Spearow	33,TM
22	Fearow	41,TM
41	Zubat	TM
42	Golbat	TM
49	Venomoth	TM
83	Farfetch'd	TM
84	Doduo	TM
85	Dodrio	TM
123	Scyther	TM
142	Aerodactyl	TM
144	Articuno	57,TM
145	Zapdos	57,TM
146	Moltres	57,TM
149	Dragonite	B,TM
151	Mew	TM
163	Hoothoot	45,TM
164	Noctowl	52,TM
165	Ledyba	TM
166	Ledian	TM
169	Crobat	TM
176	Togetic	TM
177	Natu	TM
178	Xatu	TM
193	Yanma	TM
198	Murkrow	TM
206	Dunsparce	33,TM
207	Gligar	TM
212	Scizor	TM
227	Skarmory	TM
249	Lugia	TM
250	Ho-Oh	TM
267	Beautifly	TM
269	Dustox	TM
276	Taillow	TM
277	Swellow	TM
278	Wingull	29,TM
279	Pelipper	31,TM
284	Masquerain	TM
291	Ninjask	TM
313	Volbeat	TM
314	Illumise	TM
329	Vibrava	TM
330	Flygon	TM
333	Swablu	TM
334	Altaria	TM
357	Tropius	TM
373	Salamence	TM
380	Latias	TM
381	Latios	TM
396	Starly	TM
397	Staravia	TM
398	Staraptor	TM
414	Mothim	TM
416	Vespiquen	TM
430	Honchkrow	TM
441	Chatot	33,TM
468	Togekiss	TM
469	Yanmega	TM
472	Gliscor	TM

Sacred Fire

250	Ho-Oh	85

Safeguard

1	Bulbasaur	E
12	Butterfree	34,TM
27	Sandshrew	E
35	Clefairy	TM
36	Clefable	TM
37	Vulpix	27,TM
38	Ninetales	B,TM
39	Jigglypuff	TM
40	Wigglytuff	TM
58	Growlithe	E
63	Abra	TM
64	Kadabra	TM
65	Alakazam	TM
72	Tentacool	E
79	Slowpoke	TM,E
80	Slowbro	TM
86	Seel	51,TM
87	Dewgong	51,TM
96	Drowzee	TM
97	Hypno	TM
113	Chansey	TM
115	Kangaskhan	E
122	Mr. Mime	50,TM
123	Scyther	E
131	Lapras	43,TM
146	Moltres	43,TM
147	Dratini	41,TM
148	Dragonair	47,TM
149	Dragonite	47,TM
150	Mewtwo	93,TM
151	Mew	TM
152	Chikorita	39,TM
153	Bayleef	46,TM
154	Meganium	54,TM
165	Ledyba	14,TM
166	Ledian	14,TM
173	Cleffa	TM
174	Igglybuff	TM
175	Togepi	37,TM
176	Togetic	37,TM
179	Mareep	E
182	Bellossom	TM
191	Sunkern	TM
192	Sunflora	TM
194	Wooper	E
199	Slowking	TM
202	Wobbuffet	B
213	Shuckle	14,TM
222	Corsola	TM
242	Blissey	TM
249	Lugia	9,TM
250	Ho-Oh	9,TM
251	Celebi	10,TM
252	Treecko	TM
253	Grovyle	TM
254	Sceptile	TM
267	Beautifly	TM
280	Ralts	TM
281	Kirlia	TM
282	Gardevoir	TM
285	Shroomish	TM
286	Breloom	TM
300	Skitty	TM
301	Delcatty	TM
327	Spinda	TM
333	Swablu	18,TM
334	Altaria	18,TM
337	Lunatone	TM
338	Solrock	TM
343	Baltoy	TM
344	Claydol	TM
350	Milotic	45,TM
357	Tropius	TM
358	Chimecho	41,TM
360	Wynaut	15
361	Snorunt	TM
362	Glalie	TM
368	Gorebyss	TM
369	Relicanth	TM
370	Luvdisc	51,TM
377	Regirock	TM
378	Regice	TM
379	Registeel	TM
380	Latias	15,TM
381	Latios	15,TM
382	Kyogre	TM
383	Groudon	TM
385	Jirachi	TM
386	Deoxys (N)	TM
386	Deoxys (A)	TM
386	Deoxys (D)	TM
386	Deoxys (S)	TM
387	Turtwig	TM
388	Grotle	TM
389	Torterra	TM
413	Wormadam (P)	TM
413	Wormadam (S)	TM
413	Wormadam (T)	TM
414	Mothim	TM
420	Cherubi	TM
421	Cherrim	TM
433	Chingling	TM
436	Bronzor	30,TM
437	Bronzong	30,TM
439	Mime Jr.	50,TM
440	Happiny	TM
456	Finneon	29,TM
457	Lumineon	29,TM
459	Snover	TM
460	Abomasnow	TM
468	Togekiss	TM
475	Gallade	TM
478	Froslass	TM
480	Uxie	TM
481	Mesprit	TM
482	Azelf	TM
483	Dialga	TM
484	Palkia	TM
486	Regigigas	TM
487	Giratina (A)	TM
487	Giratina (O)	TM
488	Cresselia	11,TM
489	Phione	TM
490	Manaphy	TM
492	Shaymin (L)	TM
492	Shaymin (S)	TM

Sand Tomb

27	Sandshrew	27
28	Sandslash	33
51	Dugtrio	26
95	Onix	46
185	Sudowoodo	E
204	Pineco	E
207	Gligar	E
213	Shuckle	E
328	Trapinch	25
329	Vibrava	B,25
330	Flygon	B,25
387	Turtwig	E
438	Bonsly	E
443	Gible	19,E
444	Gabite	19
445	Garchomp	19
449	Hippopotas	25,E
450	Hippowdon	25

Sand-Attack

16	Pidgey	5
17	Pidgeotto	B,5
18	Pidgeot	B,5
27	Sandshrew	7
28	Sandslash	B,7
50	Diglett	B
51	Dugtrio	B
83	Farfetch'd	B
133	Eevee	8
134	Vaporeon	8
135	Jolteon	8
136	Flareon	8
140	Kabuto	21
141	Kabutops	21
179	Mareep	E
190	Aipom	4
196	Espeon	8
197	Umbreon	8
207	Gligar	5
227	Skarmory	6
234	Stantler	16
255	Torchic	19
256	Combusken	21
257	Blaziken	21
261	Poochyena	9
262	Mightyena	B,9
263	Zigzagoon	13
264	Linoone	13

ADVENTURE DATA LIST
POKÉMON MOVES AND ABILITIES ALPHABETICAL LIST —

Sand-Attack continued

290	Nincada	9
291	Ninjask	B,9
292	Shedinja	9
296	Makuhita	4
297	Hariyama	B,4
328	Trapinch	9
329	Vibrava	B,9
330	Flygon	B,9
331	Cacnea	17
332	Cacturne	17
347	Anorith	E
396	Starly	E
424	Ambipom	B,4
431	Glameow	E
443	Gible	3
444	Gabite	B,3
445	Garchomp	B,3
449	Hippopotas	B
450	Hippowdon	B
451	Skorupi	E
470	Leafeon	8
471	Glaceon	8
472	Gliscor	B,5

Sandstorm

27	Sandshrew	37,TM
28	Sandslash	52,TM
31	Nidoqueen	TM
34	Nidoking	TM
50	Diglett	TM
51	Dugtrio	TM
74	Geodude	TM
75	Graveler	TM
76	Golem	TM
95	Onix	22,TM
104	Cubone	TM
105	Marowak	TM
108	Lickitung	TM
111	Rhyhorn	TM
112	Rhydon	TM
113	Chansey	TM
115	Kangaskhan	TM
128	Tauros	TM
130	Gyarados	TM
138	Omanyte	TM
139	Omastar	TM
140	Kabuto	TM
141	Kabutops	TM
142	Aerodactyl	TM
143	Snorlax	TM
144	Articuno	TM
145	Zapdos	TM
146	Moltres	TM
149	Dragonite	TM
150	Mewtwo	TM
151	Mew	TM
185	Sudowoodo	TM
194	Wooper	TM
195	Quagsire	TM
204	Pineco	TM
205	Forretress	TM
207	Gligar	TM
208	Steelix	22,TM
212	Scizor	TM
213	Shuckle	TM
219	Magcargo	TM
220	Swinub	TM
221	Piloswine	TM
222	Corsola	TM
227	Skarmory	TM
231	Phanpy	TM
232	Donphan	TM
237	Hitmontop	TM
241	Miltank	TM
242	Blissey	TM
243	Raikou	TM
244	Entei	TM
245	Suicune	TM
246	Larvitar	5,TM
247	Pupitar	B,5,TM
248	Tyranitar	B,5,TM
249	Lugia	TM
250	Ho-Oh	TM
251	Celebi	TM
290	Nincada	TM
291	Ninjask	TM
292	Shedinja	TM
299	Nosepass	37,TM
303	Mawile	TM
304	Aron	TM
305	Lairon	TM
306	Aggron	TM
322	Numel	TM
323	Camerupt	TM
328	Trapinch	49,TM
329	Vibrava	49,TM
330	Flygon	49,TM
331	Cacnea	53,TM
332	Cacturne	65,TM
337	Lunatone	TM
338	Solrock	TM
339	Barboach	TM
340	Whiscash	TM
343	Baltoy	37,TM
344	Claydol	40,TM
345	Lileep	TM
346	Cradily	TM
347	Anorith	TM
348	Armaldo	TM
351	Castform	TM
359	Absol	TM
369	Relicanth	TM
375	Metang	TM
376	Metagross	TM
377	Regirock	TM
379	Registeel	TM
380	Latias	TM
381	Latios	TM
383	Groudon	TM
384	Rayquaza	TM
385	Jirachi	TM
389	Torterra	TM
408	Cranidos	TM
409	Rampardos	TM
410	Shieldon	TM
411	Bastiodon	TM
413	Wormadam (S)	TM
423	Gastrodon	TM
436	Bronzor	TM
437	Bronzong	TM
438	Bonsly	TM
443	Gible	13,TM
444	Gabite	13,TM
445	Garchomp	B,13,TM
446	Munchlax	TM
449	Hippopotas	TM
450	Hippowdon	TM
463	Lickilicky	TM
464	Rhyperior	TM
472	Gliscor	TM
473	Mamoswine	TM
476	Probopass	37,TM
480	Uxie	TM
481	Mesprit	TM
482	Azelf	TM
483	Dialga	TM
484	Palkia	TM

Scary Face

4	Charmander	19
5	Charmeleon	21
6	Charizard	21
20	Raticate	20
21	Spearow	E
23	Ekans	E
66	Machop	43
67	Machoke	44
68	Machamp	44
111	Rhyhorn	21
112	Rhydon	21
128	Tauros	11
136	Flareon	64
142	Aerodactyl	B
158	Totodile	15
159	Croconaw	15
160	Feraligatr	15
167	Spinarak	5
168	Ariados	B,5
209	Snubbull	B
210	Granbull	B
217	Ursaring	38
232	Donphan	39
246	Larvitar	19
247	Pupitar	19
248	Tyranitar	19
261	Poochyena	33
262	Mightyena	37
284	Masquerain	26
318	Carvanha	11
319	Sharpedo	11
322	Numel	E
336	Seviper	E
367	Huntail	19
371	Bagon	40
372	Shelgon	43
373	Salamence	43
375	Metang	24
376	Metagross	24
382	Kyogre	5
383	Groudon	5
384	Rayquaza	5
403	Shinx	37
404	Luxio	43
405	Luxray	49
408	Cranidos	19
409	Rampardos	19
410	Shieldon	E
434	Stunky	E
443	Gible	E
451	Skorupi	23
452	Drapion	23
464	Rhyperior	21
473	Mamoswine	65
483	Dialga	B
484	Palkia	B
485	Heatran	41
487	Giratina (A)	B
487	Giratina (O)	B

Scratch

4	Charmander	B
5	Charmeleon	B
6	Charizard	B
27	Sandshrew	B
28	Sandslash	B
29	Nidoran♀	B
30	Nidorina	B
31	Nidoqueen	B
46	Paras	B
47	Parasect	B
50	Diglett	B
51	Dugtrio	B
52	Meowth	B
53	Persian	B
54	Psyduck	B
55	Golduck	B
56	Mankey	B
57	Primeape	B
140	Kabuto	B
141	Kabutops	B
158	Totodile	B
159	Croconaw	B
160	Feraligatr	B
161	Sentret	B
162	Furret	B
190	Aipom	B
215	Sneasel	B
216	Teddiursa	B
217	Ursaring	B
255	Torchic	B
256	Combusken	B
257	Blaziken	B
287	Slakoth	B
288	Vigoroth	B
289	Slaking	B
290	Nincada	B
291	Ninjask	B
292	Shedinja	B
302	Sableye	B
335	Zangoose	B
347	Anorith	B
348	Armaldo	B
352	Kecleon	B
359	Absol	B
390	Chimchar	B
391	Monferno	B
392	Infernape	B
424	Ambipom	B
431	Glameow	5
432	Purugly	B,5
434	Stunky	B
435	Skuntank	B
461	Weavile	B

Screech

19	Rattata	E
23	Ekans	17
24	Arbok	17
42	Golbat	B
46	Paras	E
48	Venonat	E
50	Diglett	E
52	Meowth	17
53	Persian	17
54	Psyduck	31
55	Golduck	31
56	Mankey	21
57	Primeape	21
72	Tentacool	36
73	Tentacruel	42
81	Magnemite	33
82	Magneton	34
88	Grimer	33
89	Muk	33
90	Shellder	E
95	Onix	6
100	Voltorb	19
101	Electrode	19
104	Cubone	E
108	Lickitung	45
109	Koffing	E
125	Electabuzz	52
140	Kabuto	E
158	Totodile	34
159	Croconaw	39
160	Feraligatr	45
165	Ledyba	E
169	Crobat	B
170	Chinchou	E
179	Mareep	E
190	Aipom	25,E
193	Yanma	46
197	Umbreon	64
198	Murkrow	E
200	Misdreavus	E
206	Dunsparce	29
207	Gligar	27
208	Steelix	6
215	Sneasel	10
222	Corsola	E
223	Remoraid	E
239	Elekid	43
240	Magby	E
246	Larvitar	10
247	Pupitar	B,10
248	Tyranitar	B,10
252	Treecko	21
253	Grovyle	23
254	Sceptile	23
291	Ninjask	20
293	Whismur	31
294	Loudred	37
295	Exploud	37
304	Aron	E
318	Carvanha	18
319	Sharpedo	18
329	Vibrava	41
330	Flygon	41
336	Seviper	19
347	Anorith	E
352	Kecleon	32
353	Shuppet	5
354	Banette	B,8
367	Huntail	10
402	Kricketune	34
408	Cranidos	37
409	Rampardos	43
410	Shieldon	E
424	Ambipom	25
434	Stunky	7
435	Skuntank	7
446	Munchlax	20
447	Riolu	24
451	Skorupi	E
461	Weavile	10
462	Magnezone	34
463	Lickilicky	45
466	Electivire	52
469	Yanmega	46
472	Gliscor	27

Secret Power

1	Bulbasaur	TM
2	Ivysaur	TM
3	Venusaur	TM
4	Charmander	TM
5	Charmeleon	TM
6	Charizard	TM
7	Squirtle	TM
8	Wartortle	TM
9	Blastoise	TM
12	Butterfree	TM
15	Beedrill	TM
16	Pidgey	TM
17	Pidgeotto	TM
18	Pidgeot	TM
19	Rattata	TM
20	Raticate	TM
21	Spearow	TM
22	Fearow	TM
23	Ekans	TM
24	Arbok	TM
25	Pikachu	TM
26	Raichu	TM
27	Sandshrew	TM
28	Sandslash	TM
29	Nidoran♀	TM
30	Nidorina	TM
31	Nidoqueen	TM
32	Nidoran♂	TM
33	Nidorino	TM
34	Nidoking	TM
35	Clefairy	TM
36	Clefable	TM
37	Vulpix	TM
38	Ninetales	TM
39	Jigglypuff	TM
40	Wigglytuff	TM
41	Zubat	TM
42	Golbat	TM
43	Oddish	TM
44	Gloom	TM
45	Vileplume	TM
46	Paras	TM
47	Parasect	TM
48	Venonat	TM
49	Venomoth	TM
50	Diglett	TM
51	Dugtrio	TM
52	Meowth	TM
53	Persian	TM
54	Psyduck	TM
55	Golduck	TM
56	Mankey	TM
57	Primeape	TM
58	Growlithe	TM
59	Arcanine	TM
60	Poliwag	TM
61	Poliwhirl	TM
62	Poliwrath	TM
63	Abra	TM
64	Kadabra	TM
65	Alakazam	TM
66	Machop	TM
67	Machoke	TM
68	Machamp	TM
69	Bellsprout	TM
70	Weepinbell	TM
71	Victreebel	TM
72	Tentacool	TM
73	Tentacruel	TM
74	Geodude	TM
75	Graveler	TM
76	Golem	TM
77	Ponyta	TM
78	Rapidash	TM
79	Slowpoke	TM
80	Slowbro	TM
81	Magnemite	TM
82	Magneton	TM
83	Farfetch'd	TM
84	Doduo	TM
85	Dodrio	TM
86	Seel	TM
87	Dewgong	TM
88	Grimer	TM
89	Muk	TM
90	Shellder	TM
91	Cloyster	TM
92	Gastly	TM
93	Haunter	TM
94	Gengar	TM
95	Onix	TM
96	Drowzee	TM
97	Hypno	TM
98	Krabby	TM
99	Kingler	TM
100	Voltorb	TM
101	Electrode	TM
102	Exeggcute	TM
103	Exeggutor	TM
104	Cubone	TM
105	Marowak	TM
106	Hitmonlee	TM
107	Hitmonchan	TM
108	Lickitung	TM
109	Koffing	TM
110	Weezing	TM
111	Rhyhorn	TM
112	Rhydon	TM
113	Chansey	TM
114	Tangela	TM
115	Kangaskhan	TM
116	Horsea	TM
117	Seadra	TM
118	Goldeen	TM
119	Seaking	TM
120	Staryu	TM
121	Starmie	TM
122	Mr. Mime	TM
123	Scyther	TM
124	Jynx	TM
125	Electabuzz	TM
126	Magmar	TM
127	Pinsir	TM
128	Tauros	TM
130	Gyarados	TM
131	Lapras	TM
133	Eevee	TM
134	Vaporeon	TM
135	Jolteon	TM
136	Flareon	TM
137	Porygon	TM
138	Omanyte	TM
139	Omastar	TM
140	Kabuto	TM
141	Kabutops	TM
142	Aerodactyl	TM
143	Snorlax	TM
144	Articuno	TM
145	Zapdos	TM
146	Moltres	TM
147	Dratini	TM
148	Dragonair	TM
149	Dragonite	TM
150	Mewtwo	TM
151	Mew	TM
152	Chikorita	TM
153	Bayleef	TM
154	Meganium	TM
155	Cyndaquil	TM
156	Quilava	TM
157	Typhlosion	TM
158	Totodile	TM
159	Croconaw	TM
160	Feraligatr	TM
161	Sentret	TM
162	Furret	TM
163	Hoothoot	TM
164	Noctowl	TM
165	Ledyba	TM
166	Ledian	TM
167	Spinarak	TM
168	Ariados	TM
169	Crobat	TM
170	Chinchou	TM
171	Lanturn	TM
172	Pichu	TM
173	Cleffa	TM
174	Igglybuff	TM
175	Togepi	TM
176	Togetic	TM
177	Natu	TM
178	Xatu	TM
179	Mareep	TM
180	Flaaffy	TM
181	Ampharos	TM
182	Bellossom	TM
183	Marill	TM
184	Azumarill	TM
185	Sudowoodo	TM
186	Politoed	TM
187	Hoppip	TM
188	Skiploom	TM
189	Jumpluff	TM
190	Aipom	TM
191	Sunkern	TM
192	Sunflora	TM
193	Yanma	TM
194	Wooper	TM
195	Quagsire	TM
196	Espeon	TM
197	Umbreon	TM
198	Murkrow	TM
199	Slowking	TM
200	Misdreavus	TM
203	Girafarig	TM
204	Pineco	TM
205	Forretress	TM
206	Dunsparce	TM
207	Gligar	TM
208	Steelix	TM
209	Snubbull	TM
210	Granbull	TM
211	Qwilfish	TM
212	Scizor	TM
213	Shuckle	TM
214	Heracross	TM
215	Sneasel	TM
216	Teddiursa	TM
217	Ursaring	TM
218	Slugma	TM
219	Magcargo	TM
220	Swinub	TM
221	Piloswine	TM
222	Corsola	TM
223	Remoraid	TM
224	Octillery	TM
225	Delibird	TM
226	Mantine	TM
227	Skarmory	TM
228	Houndour	TM
229	Houndoom	TM
230	Kingdra	TM
231	Phanpy	TM
232	Donphan	TM
233	Porygon2	TM
234	Stantler	TM
236	Tyrogue	TM
237	Hitmontop	TM
238	Smoochum	TM
239	Elekid	TM
240	Magby	TM
241	Miltank	TM
242	Blissey	TM
243	Raikou	TM
244	Entei	TM
245	Suicune	TM
246	Larvitar	TM
247	Pupitar	TM
248	Tyranitar	TM
249	Lugia	TM
250	Ho-Oh	TM
251	Celebi	TM
252	Treecko	TM
253	Grovyle	TM
254	Sceptile	TM
255	Torchic	TM
256	Combusken	TM
257	Blaziken	TM
258	Mudkip	TM
259	Marshtomp	TM
260	Swampert	TM
261	Poochyena	TM
262	Mightyena	TM
263	Zigzagoon	TM
264	Linoone	TM
267	Beautifly	TM
269	Dustox	TM
270	Lotad	TM
271	Lombre	TM
272	Ludicolo	TM
273	Seedot	TM
274	Nuzleaf	TM
275	Shiftry	TM
276	Taillow	TM
277	Swellow	TM
278	Wingull	TM
279	Pelipper	TM
280	Ralts	TM
281	Kirlia	TM
282	Gardevoir	TM
283	Surskit	TM
284	Masquerain	TM
285	Shroomish	TM
286	Breloom	TM
287	Slakoth	TM
288	Vigoroth	TM
289	Slaking	TM
290	Nincada	TM
291	Ninjask	TM
292	Shedinja	TM
293	Whismur	TM
294	Loudred	TM
295	Exploud	TM
296	Makuhita	TM
297	Hariyama	TM
298	Azurill	TM
299	Nosepass	TM
300	Skitty	TM
301	Delcatty	TM
302	Sableye	TM
303	Mawile	TM
304	Aron	TM
305	Lairon	TM
306	Aggron	TM
307	Meditite	TM
308	Medicham	TM
309	Electrike	TM
310	Manectric	TM
311	Plusle	TM
312	Minun	TM
313	Volbeat	TM
314	Illumise	TM
315	Roselia	TM
316	Gulpin	TM
317	Swalot	TM
318	Carvanha	TM
319	Sharpedo	TM
320	Wailmer	TM
321	Wailord	TM
322	Numel	TM
323	Camerupt	TM
324	Torkoal	TM
325	Spoink	TM
326	Grumpig	TM
327	Spinda	TM
328	Trapinch	TM
329	Vibrava	TM
330	Flygon	TM
331	Cacnea	TM
332	Cacturne	TM
333	Swablu	TM
334	Altaria	TM
335	Zangoose	TM
336	Seviper	TM
337	Lunatone	TM
338	Solrock	TM
339	Barboach	TM
340	Whiscash	TM
341	Corphish	TM
342	Crawdaunt	TM
343	Baltoy	TM
344	Claydol	TM
345	Lileep	TM
346	Cradily	TM
347	Anorith	TM
348	Armaldo	TM
349	Feebas	TM
350	Milotic	TM
351	Castform	TM
352	Kecleon	TM

353	Shuppet	TM
354	Banette	TM
355	Duskull	TM
356	Dusclops	TM
357	Tropius	TM
358	Chimecho	TM
359	Absol	TM
361	Snorunt	TM
362	Glalie	TM
363	Spheal	TM
364	Sealeo	TM
365	Walrein	TM
366	Clamperl	TM
367	Huntail	TM
368	Gorebyss	TM
369	Relicanth	TM
370	Luvdisc	TM
371	Bagon	TM
372	Shelgon	TM
373	Salamence	TM
375	Metang	TM
376	Metagross	TM
377	Regirock	TM
378	Regice	TM
379	Registeel	TM
380	Latias	TM
381	Latios	TM
382	Kyogre	TM
383	Groudon	TM
384	Rayquaza	TM
385	Jirachi	TM
386	Deoxys (N)	TM
386	Deoxys (A)	TM
386	Deoxys (D)	TM
386	Deoxys (S)	TM
387	Turtwig	TM
388	Grotle	TM
389	Torterra	TM
390	Chimchar	TM
391	Monferno	TM
392	Infernape	TM
393	Piplup	TM
394	Prinplup	TM
395	Empoleon	TM
396	Starly	TM
397	Staravia	TM
398	Staraptor	TM
399	Bidoof	TM
400	Bibarel	TM
402	Kricketune	TM
403	Shinx	TM
404	Luxio	TM
405	Luxray	TM
406	Budew	TM
407	Roserade	TM
408	Cranidos	TM
409	Rampardos	TM
410	Shieldon	TM
411	Bastiodon	TM
413	Wormadam (P)	TM
413	Wormadam (S)	TM
413	Wormadam (T)	TM
414	Mothim	TM
416	Vespiquen	TM
417	Pachirisu	TM
418	Buizel	TM
419	Floatzel	TM
420	Cherubi	TM
421	Cherrim	TM
422	Shellos	TM
423	Gastrodon	TM
424	Ambipom	TM
425	Drifloon	TM
426	Drifblim	TM
427	Buneary	TM
428	Lopunny	TM
429	Mismagius	TM
430	Honchkrow	TM
431	Glameow	TM
432	Purugly	TM
433	Chingling	TM
434	Stunky	TM
435	Skuntank	TM
436	Bronzor	TM
437	Bronzong	TM
438	Bonsly	TM
439	Mime Jr.	TM
440	Happiny	TM
441	Chatot	TM
442	Spiritomb	TM
443	Gible	TM
444	Gabite	TM
445	Garchomp	TM
446	Munchlax	TM
447	Riolu	TM
448	Lucario	TM
449	Hippopotas	TM
450	Hippowdon	TM
451	Skorupi	TM
452	Drapion	TM
453	Croagunk	TM
454	Toxicroak	TM
455	Carnivine	TM
456	Finneon	TM
457	Lumineon	TM
458	Mantyke	TM
459	Snover	TM
460	Abomasnow	TM
461	Weavile	TM
462	Magnezone	TM
463	Lickilicky	TM
464	Rhyperior	TM
465	Tangrowth	TM
466	Electivire	TM
467	Magmortar	TM
468	Togekiss	TM
469	Yanmega	TM
470	Leafeon	TM
471	Glaceon	TM
472	Gliscor	TM
473	Mamoswine	TM
474	Porygon-Z	TM
475	Gallade	TM
476	Probopass	TM
477	Dusknoir	TM
478	Froslass	TM
479	Rotom	TM
480	Uxie	TM
481	Mesprit	TM
482	Azelf	TM
483	Dialga	TM
484	Palkia	TM
485	Heatran	TM
486	Regigigas	TM
487	Giratina (A)	TM
487	Giratina (O)	TM
488	Cresselia	TM
489	Phione	TM
490	Manaphy	TM
491	Darkrai	TM
492	Shaymin (L)	TM
492	Shaymin (S)	TM

Seed Bomb		
1	Bulbasaur	37,T
2	Ivysaur	T
3	Venusaur	T
23	Ekans	T
24	Arbok	T
43	Oddish	T
44	Gloom	T
45	Vileplume	T
46	Paras	T
47	Parasect	T
52	Meowth	T
53	Persian	T
56	Mankey	T
57	Primeape	T
69	Bellsprout	T
70	Weepinbell	T
71	Victreebel	T
102	Exeggcute	T
103	Exeggutor	B,T
114	Tangela	T
143	Snorlax	T
151	Mew	T
152	Chikorita	T
153	Bayleef	T
154	Meganium	T
182	Bellossom	T
187	Hoppip	T
188	Skiploom	T
189	Jumpluff	T
190	Aipom	T
191	Sunkern	45,T
192	Sunflora	T
216	Teddiursa	T
217	Ursaring	T
223	Remoraid	T
224	Octillery	T
225	Delibird	T
226	Mantine	T
231	Phanpy	T
232	Donphan	T
251	Celebi	T
252	Treecko	T
253	Grovyle	T
254	Sceptile	T
263	Zigzagoon	T
264	Linoone	T
270	Lotad	T
271	Lombre	T
272	Ludicolo	T
273	Seedot	T
274	Nuzleaf	T
275	Shiftry	T
279	Pelipper	T
285	Shroomish	41,T,E
286	Breloom	41,T
315	Roselia	T
316	Gulpin	T
317	Swalot	T
331	Cacnea	T,E
332	Cacturne	T
345	Lileep	T
346	Cradily	T
387	Turtwig	T,E
388	Grotle	T
389	Torterra	T
406	Budew	T
407	Roserade	T
413	Wormadam (P)	T
417	Pachirisu	T
420	Cherubi	T
421	Cherrim	T
424	Ambipom	T
446	Munchlax	T
455	Carnivine	T
459	Snover	T,E
460	Abomasnow	T
465	Tangrowth	T
470	Leafeon	T
492	Shaymin (L)	T
492	Shaymin (S)	T

Seed Flare		
492	Shaymin (L)	100
492	Shaymin (S)	100

Seismic Toss		
56	Mankey	17
57	Primeape	17
66	Machop	19
67	Machoke	19
68	Machamp	19
127	Pinsir	8
216	Teddiursa	E
241	Miltank	E
296	Makuhita	31
297	Hariyama	37

Selfdestruct		
74	Geodude	18
75	Graveler	18
76	Golem	18
100	Voltorb	29
101	Electrode	29
109	Koffing	19
110	Weezing	19
185	Sudowoodo	E
204	Pineco	6
205	Forretress	B,6
343	Baltoy	19
344	Claydol	19
438	Bonsly	E

Shadow Ball		
12	Butterfree	TM
19	Rattata	TM
20	Raticate	TM
31	Nidoqueen	TM
34	Nidoking	TM
35	Clefairy	TM
36	Clefable	TM
39	Jigglypuff	TM
40	Wigglytuff	TM
41	Zubat	TM
42	Golbat	TM
52	Meowth	TM
53	Persian	TM
63	Abra	TM
64	Kadabra	TM
65	Alakazam	TM
79	Slowpoke	TM
80	Slowbro	TM
88	Grimer	TM
89	Muk	TM
92	Gastly	29,TM
93	Haunter	33,TM
94	Gengar	33,TM
96	Drowzee	TM
97	Hypno	TM
108	Lickitung	TM
109	Koffing	TM
110	Weezing	TM
113	Chansey	TM
115	Kangaskhan	TM
122	Mr. Mime	TM
124	Jynx	TM
133	Eevee	TM
134	Vaporeon	TM
135	Jolteon	TM
136	Flareon	TM
137	Porygon	TM
143	Snorlax	TM
150	Mewtwo	TM
151	Mew	TM
161	Sentret	TM
162	Furret	TM
163	Hoothoot	TM
164	Noctowl	TM
169	Crobat	TM
173	Cleffa	TM
174	Igglybuff	TM
175	Togepi	TM
176	Togetic	TM
177	Natu	TM
178	Xatu	TM
190	Aipom	TM
193	Yanma	TM
196	Espeon	TM
197	Umbreon	TM
198	Murkrow	TM
199	Slowking	TM
200	Misdreavus	37,TM
203	Girafarig	TM
206	Dunsparce	TM
209	Snubbull	TM
210	Granbull	TM
211	Qwilfish	TM
215	Sneasel	TM
222	Corsola	TM
228	Houndour	TM
229	Houndoom	TM
233	Porygon2	TM
234	Stantler	TM
238	Smoochum	TM
241	Miltank	TM
242	Blissey	TM
243	Raikou	TM
244	Entei	TM
245	Suicune	TM
249	Lugia	TM
250	Ho-Oh	TM
251	Celebi	TM
261	Poochyena	TM
262	Mightyena	TM
263	Zigzagoon	TM
264	Linoone	TM
267	Beautifly	TM
269	Dustox	TM
273	Seedot	TM
274	Nuzleaf	TM
275	Shiftry	TM
280	Ralts	TM
281	Kirlia	TM
282	Gardevoir	TM
283	Surskit	TM
284	Masquerain	TM
287	Slakoth	TM
288	Vigoroth	TM
289	Slaking	TM
290	Nincada	TM
291	Ninjask	TM
292	Shedinja	59,TM
293	Whismur	TM
294	Loudred	TM
295	Exploud	TM
300	Skitty	TM
301	Delcatty	TM
302	Sableye	53,TM
303	Mawile	TM
307	Meditite	TM
308	Medicham	TM
313	Volbeat	TM
314	Illumise	TM
315	Roselia	TM
316	Gulpin	TM
317	Swalot	TM
325	Spoink	TM
326	Grumpig	TM
327	Spinda	TM
335	Zangoose	TM
337	Lunatone	TM
338	Solrock	TM
343	Baltoy	TM
344	Claydol	TM
351	Castform	TM
352	Kecleon	TM
353	Shuppet	31,TM
354	Banette	31,TM
355	Duskull	TM
356	Dusclops	TM
358	Chimecho	TM
359	Absol	TM
361	Snorunt	TM
362	Glalie	TM
368	Gorebyss	TM
375	Metang	TM
376	Metagross	TM
380	Latias	TM
381	Latios	TM
385	Jirachi	TM
386	Deoxys (N)	TM
386	Deoxys (A)	TM
386	Deoxys (D)	TM
386	Deoxys (S)	TM
399	Bidoof	TM
400	Bibarel	TM
406	Budew	TM
407	Roserade	TM
413	Wormadam (P)	TM
413	Wormadam (S)	TM
413	Wormadam (T)	TM
414	Mothim	TM
424	Ambipom	TM
425	Drifloon	38,TM
426	Drifblim	44,TM
427	Buneary	TM
428	Lopunny	TM
429	Mismagius	TM
430	Honchkrow	TM
431	Glameow	TM
432	Purugly	TM
433	Chingling	TM
434	Stunky	TM
435	Skuntank	TM
436	Bronzor	TM
437	Bronzong	TM
439	Mime Jr.	TM
440	Happiny	TM
442	Spiritomb	TM
446	Munchlax	TM
448	Lucario	TM
451	Skorupi	TM
452	Drapion	TM
453	Croagunk	TM
454	Toxicroak	TM
459	Snover	TM
460	Abomasnow	TM
461	Weavile	TM
463	Lickilicky	TM
468	Togekiss	TM
469	Yanmega	TM
470	Leafeon	TM
471	Glaceon	TM
474	Porygon-Z	TM
475	Gallade	TM
477	Dusknoir	TM
478	Froslass	TM
479	Rotom	TM
480	Uxie	TM
481	Mesprit	TM
482	Azelf	TM
487	Giratina (A)	TM
487	Giratina (O)	TM
488	Cresselia	TM
490	Manaphy	TM
491	Darkrai	TM

Shadow Claw		
4	Charmander	TM
5	Charmeleon	TM
6	Charizard	B,TM
27	Sandshrew	TM
28	Sandslash	TM
29	Nidoran♀	TM
30	Nidorina	TM
31	Nidoqueen	TM
32	Nidoran♂	TM
33	Nidorino	TM
34	Nidoking	TM
50	Diglett	TM
51	Dugtrio	TM
52	Meowth	TM
53	Persian	TM
54	Psyduck	TM
55	Golduck	TM
93	Haunter	TM
94	Gengar	TM
112	Rhydon	TM
115	Kangaskhan	TM
151	Mew	TM
157	Typhlosion	TM
158	Totodile	TM
159	Croconaw	TM
160	Feraligatr	TM
161	Sentret	TM
162	Furret	TM
190	Aipom	TM
214	Heracross	TM
215	Sneasel	TM
216	Teddiursa	TM
217	Ursaring	TM
248	Tyranitar	TM
255	Torchic	TM
256	Combusken	TM
257	Blaziken	TM
264	Linoone	TM
287	Slakoth	TM
288	Vigoroth	TM
289	Slaking	TM
292	Shedinja	TM
302	Sableye	39,TM
304	Aron	TM
305	Lairon	TM
306	Aggron	TM
335	Zangoose	TM
352	Kecleon	49,TM
354	Banette	TM
359	Absol	TM
371	Bagon	TM,E
372	Shelgon	TM
373	Salamence	TM
379	Registeel	TM
380	Latias	TM
381	Latios	TM
383	Groudon	TM
384	Rayquaza	TM
390	Chimchar	TM
391	Monferno	TM
392	Infernape	TM
394	Prinplup	TM
395	Empoleon	TM
424	Ambipom	TM
431	Glameow	TM
432	Purugly	TM
434	Stunky	TM
435	Skuntank	TM
443	Gible	TM
444	Gabite	TM
445	Garchomp	TM
447	Riolu	TM
448	Lucario	TM
461	Weavile	TM
464	Rhyperior	TM
483	Dialga	TM
484	Palkia	TM
487	Giratina (A)	80,TM
487	Giratina (O)	80,TM
491	Darkrai	TM

Shadow Force		
487	Giratina (A)	40
487	Giratina (O)	40

Shadow Punch		
88	Grimer	E
93	Haunter	25
94	Gengar	25
356	Dusclops	37
477	Dusknoir	37

Shadow Sneak		
88	Grimer	E
167	Spinarak	19
168	Ariados	19
200	Misdreavus	E
280	Ralts	E
292	Shedinja	38
302	Sableye	25
352	Kecleon	22
353	Shuppet	20,E
354	Banette	20
355	Duskull	22
356	Dusclops	22
442	Spiritomb	B,E
477	Dusknoir	22

Sharpen		
137	Porygon	B

Sheer Cold		
87	Dewgong	34
131	Lapras	55
144	Articuno	78
362	Glalie	59
363	Spheal	49
364	Sealeo	55
365	Walrein	65
382	Kyogre	60
459	Snover	46
460	Abomasnow	58

Shock Wave		
19	Rattata	TM
20	Raticate	TM
25	Pikachu	TM
26	Raichu	TM
29	Nidoran♀	TM
30	Nidorina	TM
31	Nidoqueen	TM
32	Nidoran♂	TM
33	Nidorino	TM
34	Nidoking	TM
35	Clefairy	TM
36	Clefable	TM
39	Jigglypuff	TM
40	Wigglytuff	TM
52	Meowth	TM
53	Persian	TM
63	Abra	TM
64	Kadabra	TM
65	Alakazam	TM
81	Magnemite	TM
82	Magneton	TM
88	Grimer	TM
89	Muk	TM
100	Voltorb	TM
101	Electrode	TM
108	Lickitung	TM
109	Koffing	TM
110	Weezing	TM
111	Rhyhorn	TM
112	Rhydon	TM
113	Chansey	TM
114	Tangela	TM
115	Kangaskhan	TM
122	Mr. Mime	TM
125	Electabuzz	19,TM
128	Tauros	TM
131	Lapras	TM
135	Jolteon	TM
137	Porygon	TM
143	Snorlax	TM
145	Zapdos	TM
147	Dratini	TM
148	Dragonair	TM
149	Dragonite	TM
150	Mewtwo	TM
151	Mew	TM
161	Sentret	TM
162	Furret	TM
170	Chinchou	TM
171	Lanturn	TM
172	Pichu	TM
173	Cleffa	TM
174	Igglybuff	TM
175	Togepi	TM
176	Togetic	TM
179	Mareep	TM
180	Flaaffy	TM
181	Ampharos	TM
190	Aipom	TM
200	Misdreavus	TM
203	Girafarig	TM
206	Dunsparce	TM
209	Snubbull	TM
210	Granbull	TM
211	Qwilfish	TM
233	Porygon2	TM
234	Stantler	TM
239	Elekid	19,TM
241	Miltank	TM
242	Blissey	TM
243	Raikou	TM
248	Tyranitar	TM
249	Lugia	TM
250	Ho-Oh	TM
251	Celebi	TM
263	Zigzagoon	TM
264	Linoone	TM
278	Wingull	TM
279	Pelipper	TM
280	Ralts	TM
281	Kirlia	TM
282	Gardevoir	TM
287	Slakoth	TM
288	Vigoroth	TM
289	Slaking	TM
293	Whismur	TM
294	Loudred	TM
295	Exploud	TM
299	Nosepass	TM
300	Skitty	TM
301	Delcatty	TM
302	Sableye	TM
304	Aron	TM
305	Lairon	TM
306	Aggron	TM
309	Electrike	TM
310	Manectric	TM
311	Plusle	TM
312	Minun	TM
313	Volbeat	TM
314	Illumise	TM
316	Gulpin	TM
317	Swalot	TM
325	Spoink	TM
326	Grumpig	TM
327	Spinda	TM
335	Zangoose	TM
351	Castform	TM
352	Kecleon	TM
353	Shuppet	TM
354	Banette	TM
358	Chimecho	TM
359	Absol	TM
377	Regirock	TM
378	Regice	TM
379	Registeel	TM
380	Latias	TM
381	Latios	TM

Shock Wave continued

382	Kyogre	TM
383	Groudon	TM
384	Rayquaza	TM
385	Jirachi	TM
386	Deoxys (N)	TM
386	Deoxys (A)	TM
386	Deoxys (D)	TM
386	Deoxys (S)	TM
399	Bidoof	TM
400	Bibarel	TM
403	Shinx	TM
404	Luxio	TM
405	Luxray	TM
408	Cranidos	TM
409	Rampardos	TM
410	Shieldon	TM
411	Bastiodon	TM
417	Pachirisu	TM
424	Ambipom	TM
425	Drifloon	TM
426	Drifblim	TM
427	Buneary	TM
428	Lopunny	TM
429	Mismagius	TM
431	Glameow	TM
432	Purugly	TM
433	Chingling	TM
439	Mime Jr.	TM
440	Happiny	TM
442	Spiritomb	TM
446	Munchlax	TM
462	Magnezone	TM
463	Lickilicky	TM
464	Rhyperior	TM
465	Tangrowth	TM
466	Electivire	19,TM
468	Togekiss	TM
474	Porygon-Z	TM
475	Gallade	TM
476	Probopass	TM
478	Froslass	TM
479	Rotom	22,TM
480	Uxie	TM
481	Mesprit	TM
482	Azelf	TM
483	Dialga	TM
484	Palkia	TM
486	Regigigas	TM
487	Giratina (A)	TM
487	Giratina (O)	TM
491	Darkrai	TM

Signal Beam

9	Blastoise	T
12	Butterfree	T
25	Pikachu	T
26	Raichu	T
35	Clefairy	T
36	Clefable	T
48	Venonat	35,T,E
49	Venomoth	37,T
54	Psyduck	T
55	Golduck	T
63	Abra	T
64	Kadabra	T
65	Alakazam	T
79	Slowpoke	T
80	Slowbro	T
81	Magnemite	T
82	Magneton	T
86	Seel	T,E
87	Dewgong	B,7,T
91	Cloyster	T
96	Drowzee	T
97	Hypno	T
100	Voltorb	T
101	Electrode	T
116	Horsea	T,E
117	Seadra	T
120	Staryu	T
121	Starmie	T
122	Mr. Mime	T
124	Jynx	T
125	Electabuzz	T
131	Lapras	T
134	Vaporeon	T
135	Jolteon	T
137	Porygon	29,T
144	Articuno	T
145	Zapdos	T
150	Mewtwo	T
151	Mew	T
167	Spinarak	T,E
168	Ariados	T
170	Chinchou	31,T
171	Lanturn	35,T
172	Pichu	T
173	Cleffa	T
175	Togepi	T
176	Togetic	T
177	Natu	T
178	Xatu	T
179	Mareep	32,T
180	Flaaffy	36,T
181	Ampharos	42,T
193	Yanma	T,E
196	Espeon	T
199	Slowking	T
203	Girafarig	T
205	Forretress	T
211	Qwilfish	T,E
223	Remoraid	36,T
224	Octillery	42,T
225	Delibird	T
226	Mantine	B,T
230	Kingdra	T
233	Porygon2	29,T
234	Stantler	T
238	Smoochum	T
239	Elekid	T
243	Raikou	T
245	Suicune	T
249	Lugia	T
250	Ho-Oh	T
251	Celebi	T
267	Beautifly	T
269	Dustox	T
280	Ralts	T
281	Kirlia	T
282	Gardevoir	T
283	Surskit	T,E
284	Masquerain	T
302	Sableye	T
307	Meditite	T
308	Medicham	T
309	Electrike	T
310	Manectric	T
311	Plusle	T
312	Minun	T
313	Volbeat	25,T
325	Spoink	T
326	Grumpig	T
337	Lunatone	T
338	Solrock	T
343	Baltoy	T
344	Claydol	T
358	Chimecho	T
362	Glalie	T
363	Spheal	T,E
364	Sealeo	T
365	Walrein	T
368	Gorebyss	T
375	Metang	T
376	Metagross	T
378	Regice	T
382	Kyogre	T
385	Jirachi	T
386	Deoxys (N)	T
386	Deoxys (A)	T
386	Deoxys (D)	T
386	Deoxys (S)	T
393	Piplup	T
394	Prinplup	T
395	Empoleon	T
403	Shinx	T
404	Luxio	T
405	Luxray	T
413	Wormadam (P)	T
413	Wormadam (S)	T
413	Wormadam (T)	T
414	Mothim	T
416	Vespiquen	T
433	Chingling	T
436	Bronzor	T
437	Bronzong	T
439	Mime Jr.	T
458	Mantyke	E
462	Magnezone	T
466	Electivire	T
468	Togekiss	T
469	Yanmega	T
471	Glaceon	T
474	Porygon-Z	29,T
475	Gallade	T
478	Froslass	T
479	Rotom	T
480	Uxie	T
481	Mesprit	T
482	Azelf	T
488	Cresselia	T
489	Phione	T
490	Manaphy	T

Silver Wind

12	Butterfree	28,TM
15	Beedrill	TM
49	Venomoth	B,TM
123	Scyther	TM,E
151	Mew	TM
163	Hoothoot	TM
164	Noctowl	TM
165	Ledyba	25,TM,E
166	Ledian	29,TM
176	Togetic	TM
177	Natu	TM
178	Xatu	TM
187	Hoppip	TM
188	Skiploom	TM
189	Jumpluff	TM
193	Yanma	TM,E
212	Scizor	TM
251	Celebi	TM
267	Beautifly	34,TM
269	Dustox	34,TM
275	Shiftry	TM
284	Masquerain	40,TM
290	Nincada	E
291	Ninjask	TM
313	Volbeat	TM,E
314	Illumise	TM,E
329	Vibrava	TM
330	Flygon	TM
357	Tropius	TM
402	Kricketune	TM
414	Mothim	38,TM
416	Vespiquen	TM
425	Drifloon	TM
426	Drifblim	TM
442	Spiritomb	TM
456	Finneon	49,TM
457	Lumineon	59,TM
468	Togekiss	TM
469	Yanmega	TM
487	Giratina (A)	TM
487	Giratina (O)	TM

Sing

35	Clefairy	7
36	Clefable	B
39	Jigglypuff	B
40	Wigglytuff	B
113	Chansey	23
131	Lapras	B
173	Cleffa	7
174	Igglybuff	B
238	Smoochum	18
242	Blissey	23
298	Azurill	E
300	Skitty	11
301	Delcatty	B
311	Plusle	E
312	Minun	E
333	Swablu	9
334	Altaria	B,9
402	Kricketune	18
441	Chatot	13

Sketch

235	Smeargle	B
235	Smeargle	11
235	Smeargle	21
235	Smeargle	31
235	Smeargle	41
235	Smeargle	51
235	Smeargle	61
235	Smeargle	71
235	Smeargle	81
235	Smeargle	91

Skill Swap

12	Butterfree	TM
48	Venonat	TM
49	Venomoth	TM
63	Abra	TM
64	Kadabra	TM
65	Alakazam	TM
79	Slowpoke	TM
80	Slowbro	TM
92	Gastly	TM
93	Haunter	TM
94	Gengar	TM
96	Drowzee	TM
97	Hypno	TM
102	Exeggcute	TM
103	Exeggutor	TM
113	Chansey	TM
121	Starmie	TM
122	Mr. Mime	TM
124	Jynx	TM
150	Mewtwo	TM
151	Mew	TM
177	Natu	TM
178	Xatu	TM
196	Espeon	TM
199	Slowking	TM
200	Misdreavus	TM
203	Girafarig	TM
234	Stantler	TM
238	Smoochum	TM
242	Blissey	TM
249	Lugia	TM
251	Celebi	TM
280	Ralts	TM
281	Kirlia	TM
282	Gardevoir	TM
325	Spoink	TM
326	Grumpig	TM
327	Spinda	TM
337	Lunatone	TM
338	Solrock	TM
343	Baltoy	TM
344	Claydol	TM
352	Kecleon	TM
353	Shuppet	TM
354	Banette	TM
355	Duskull	TM
356	Dusclops	TM
358	Chimecho	TM
385	Jirachi	TM
386	Deoxys (N)	TM
386	Deoxys (A)	TM
386	Deoxys (D)	TM
386	Deoxys (S)	TM
413	Wormadam (P)	TM
413	Wormadam (S)	TM
413	Wormadam (T)	TM
414	Mothim	TM
425	Drifloon	TM
426	Drifblim	TM
429	Mismagius	TM
433	Chingling	TM
436	Bronzor	TM
437	Bronzong	TM
439	Mime Jr.	TM
475	Gallade	TM
477	Dusknoir	TM
480	Uxie	TM
481	Mesprit	TM
482	Azelf	TM
488	Cresselia	TM
490	Manaphy	TM

Skull Bash

1	Bulbasaur	E
7	Squirtle	31
8	Wartortle	36
9	Blastoise	39
104	Cubone	E
319	Sharpedo	50
369	Relicanth	E

Sky Attack

21	Spearow	E
146	Moltres	78
163	Hoothoot	E
164	Noctowl	B
198	Murkrow	E
227	Skarmory	E
249	Lugia	99
250	Ho-Oh	99
276	Taillow	E
334	Altaria	70
468	Togekiss	B

Sky Uppercut

107	Hitmonchan	36
256	Combusken	50
257	Blaziken	59
286	Breloom	33
427	Buneary	E
447	Riolu	E

Slack Off

79	Slowpoke	39
80	Slowbro	41
287	Slakoth	13
289	Slaking	B,13
390	Chimchar	39
391	Monferno	46
449	Hippopotas	E

Slam

23	Ekans	E
25	Pikachu	21
69	Bellsprout	41
70	Weepinbell	41
86	Seel	E
95	Onix	25
98	Krabby	35,E
99	Kingler	44
108	Lickitung	29
114	Tangela	43
138	Omanyte	E
147	Dratini	21
148	Dragonair	21
149	Dragonite	21
161	Sentret	25
162	Furret	28
185	Sudowoodo	38
190	Aipom	E
194	Wooper	15
195	Quagsire	15
208	Steelix	25
226	Mantine	E
231	Phanpy	24
232	Donphan	24
252	Treecko	36
253	Grovyle	41
254	Sceptile	43
298	Azurill	15,E
357	Tropius	E
408	Cranidos	E
438	Bonsly	38
455	Carnivine	E
458	Mantyke	E
463	Lickilicky	29
465	Tangrowth	43

Slash

4	Charmander	28
5	Charmeleon	32
6	Charizard	32
27	Sandshrew	31
28	Sandslash	40
46	Paras	22
47	Parasect	22
50	Diglett	34
51	Dugtrio	40
52	Meowth	33
53	Persian	37
83	Farfetch'd	19
123	Scyther	29
141	Kabutops	40
158	Totodile	29
159	Croconaw	33
160	Feraligatr	37
161	Sentret	E
207	Gligar	31
212	Scizor	29
215	Sneasel	35
216	Teddiursa	29
217	Ursaring	29
227	Skarmory	42
255	Torchic	34
256	Combusken	39
257	Blaziken	42
264	Linoone	41
287	Slakoth	E
288	Vigoroth	31
291	Ninjask	31
319	Sharpedo	30
335	Zangoose	18
347	Anorith	43
348	Armaldo	46
352	Kecleon	27
359	Absol	36
383	Groudon	20
402	Kricketune	26
416	Vespiquen	31
418	Buizel	E
431	Glameow	37
432	Purugly	37
434	Stunky	22
435	Skuntank	22
443	Gible	25
444	Gabite	28
445	Garchomp	28
451	Skorupi	E
469	Yanmega	43
475	Gallade	22
483	Dialga	70
484	Palkia	70
487	Giratina (A)	70
487	Giratina (O)	70
488	Cresselia	47

Sleep Powder

1	Bulbasaur	13
2	Ivysaur	13
3	Venusaur	13
12	Butterfree	12
43	Oddish	17
44	Gloom	17
48	Venonat	29
49	Venomoth	29
69	Bellsprout	13
70	Weepinbell	13
71	Victreebel	B
102	Exeggcute	23
114	Tangela	5
187	Hoppip	16
188	Skiploom	16
189	Jumpluff	16
315	Roselia	E
406	Budew	E
455	Carnivine	E
465	Tangrowth	5

Sleep Talk

1	Bulbasaur	TM
2	Ivysaur	TM
3	Venusaur	TM
4	Charmander	TM
5	Charmeleon	TM
6	Charizard	TM
7	Squirtle	TM
8	Wartortle	TM
9	Blastoise	TM
12	Butterfree	TM
15	Beedrill	TM
16	Pidgey	TM
17	Pidgeotto	TM
18	Pidgeot	TM
19	Rattata	TM
20	Raticate	TM
21	Spearow	TM
22	Fearow	TM
23	Ekans	TM
24	Arbok	TM
25	Pikachu	TM
26	Raichu	TM
27	Sandshrew	TM
28	Sandslash	TM
29	Nidoran♀	TM
30	Nidorina	TM
31	Nidoqueen	TM
32	Nidoran♂	TM
33	Nidorino	TM
34	Nidoking	TM
35	Clefairy	TM
36	Clefable	TM
37	Vulpix	TM
38	Ninetales	TM
39	Jigglypuff	TM
40	Wigglytuff	TM
41	Zubat	TM
42	Golbat	TM
43	Oddish	TM
44	Gloom	TM
45	Vileplume	TM
46	Paras	TM
47	Parasect	TM
48	Venonat	TM
49	Venomoth	TM
50	Diglett	TM
51	Dugtrio	TM
52	Meowth	TM
53	Persian	TM
54	Psyduck	TM
55	Golduck	TM
56	Mankey	TM
57	Primeape	TM
58	Growlithe	TM
59	Arcanine	TM
60	Poliwag	TM
61	Poliwhirl	TM
62	Poliwrath	TM
63	Abra	TM
64	Kadabra	TM
65	Alakazam	TM
66	Machop	TM
67	Machoke	TM
68	Machamp	TM
69	Bellsprout	TM
70	Weepinbell	TM
71	Victreebel	TM
72	Tentacool	TM
73	Tentacruel	TM
74	Geodude	TM
75	Graveler	TM
76	Golem	TM
77	Ponyta	TM
78	Rapidash	TM
79	Slowpoke	TM,E
80	Slowbro	TM
81	Magnemite	TM
82	Magneton	TM
83	Farfetch'd	TM
84	Doduo	TM
85	Dodrio	TM
86	Seel	TM
87	Dewgong	TM
88	Grimer	TM
89	Muk	TM
90	Shellder	TM
91	Cloyster	TM
92	Gastly	TM
93	Haunter	TM
94	Gengar	TM
95	Onix	TM
96	Drowzee	TM
97	Hypno	TM
98	Krabby	TM
99	Kingler	TM
100	Voltorb	TM
101	Electrode	TM
102	Exeggcute	TM
103	Exeggutor	TM
104	Cubone	TM
105	Marowak	TM
106	Hitmonlee	TM
107	Hitmonchan	TM
108	Lickitung	TM,E
109	Koffing	TM
110	Weezing	TM
111	Rhyhorn	TM
112	Rhydon	TM
113	Chansey	TM
114	Tangela	TM
115	Kangaskhan	TM
116	Horsea	TM
117	Seadra	TM
118	Goldeen	TM,E
119	Seaking	TM
120	Staryu	TM
121	Starmie	TM
122	Mr. Mime	TM
123	Scyther	TM
124	Jynx	TM
125	Electabuzz	TM
126	Magmar	TM
127	Pinsir	TM
128	Tauros	TM
130	Gyarados	TM
131	Lapras	TM,E
133	Eevee	TM
134	Vaporeon	TM
135	Jolteon	TM
136	Flareon	TM
137	Porygon	TM
138	Omanyte	TM
139	Omastar	TM
140	Kabuto	TM
141	Kabutops	TM
142	Aerodactyl	TM
143	Snorlax	28,TM
144	Articuno	TM
145	Zapdos	TM
146	Moltres	TM
147	Dratini	TM
148	Dragonair	TM
149	Dragonite	TM
150	Mewtwo	TM
151	Mew	TM
152	Chikorita	TM
153	Bayleef	TM
154	Meganium	TM
155	Cyndaquil	TM
156	Quilava	TM
157	Typhlosion	TM
158	Totodile	TM
159	Croconaw	TM
160	Feraligatr	TM
161	Sentret	TM
162	Furret	TM
163	Hoothoot	TM
164	Noctowl	TM
165	Ledyba	TM
166	Ledian	TM
167	Spinarak	TM
168	Ariados	TM
169	Crobat	TM
170	Chinchou	TM
171	Lanturn	TM
172	Pichu	TM
173	Cleffa	TM
174	Igglybuff	TM
175	Togepi	TM
176	Togetic	TM
177	Natu	TM
178	Xatu	TM
179	Mareep	TM
180	Flaaffy	TM
181	Ampharos	TM
182	Bellossom	TM
183	Marill	TM
184	Azumarill	TM
185	Sudowoodo	TM
186	Politoed	TM
187	Hoppip	TM
188	Skiploom	TM
189	Jumpluff	TM
190	Aipom	TM
191	Sunkern	TM
192	Sunflora	TM
193	Yanma	TM
194	Wooper	TM
195	Quagsire	TM
196	Espeon	TM
197	Umbreon	TM
198	Murkrow	TM
199	Slowking	TM

200	Misdreavus	TM
203	Girafarig	TM
204	Pineco	TM
205	Forretress	TM
206	Dunsparce	TM
207	Gligar	TM
208	Steelix	TM
209	Snubbull	TM
210	Granbull	TM
211	Qwilfish	TM
212	Scizor	TM
213	Shuckle	TM
214	Heracross	TM
215	Sneasel	TM
216	Teddiursa	TM,E
217	Ursaring	TM
218	Slugma	TM
219	Magcargo	TM
220	Swinub	TM
221	Piloswine	TM
222	Corsola	TM
223	Remoraid	TM
224	Octillery	TM
225	Delibird	TM
226	Mantine	TM
227	Skarmory	TM
228	Houndour	TM
229	Houndoom	TM
230	Kingdra	TM
231	Phanpy	TM
232	Donphan	TM
233	Porygon2	TM
234	Stantler	TM
236	Tyrogue	TM
237	Hitmontop	TM
238	Smoochum	TM
239	Elekid	TM
240	Magby	TM
241	Miltank	TM,E
242	Blissey	TM
243	Raikou	TM
244	Entei	TM
245	Suicune	TM
246	Larvitar	TM
247	Pupitar	TM
248	Tyranitar	TM
249	Lugia	TM
250	Ho-Oh	TM
251	Celebi	TM
252	Treecko	TM
253	Grovyle	TM
254	Sceptile	TM
255	Torchic	TM
256	Combusken	TM
257	Blaziken	TM
258	Mudkip	TM
259	Marshtomp	TM
260	Swampert	TM
261	Poochyena	TM
262	Mightyena	TM
263	Zigzagoon	TM
264	Linoone	TM
267	Beautifly	TM
269	Dustox	TM
270	Lotad	TM
271	Lombre	TM
272	Ludicolo	TM
273	Seedot	TM
274	Nuzleaf	TM
275	Shiftry	TM
276	Taillow	TM
277	Swellow	TM
278	Wingull	TM
279	Pelipper	TM
280	Ralts	TM
281	Kirlia	TM
282	Gardevoir	TM
283	Surskit	TM
284	Masquerain	TM
285	Shroomish	TM
286	Breloom	TM
287	Slakoth	TM,E
288	Vigoroth	TM
289	Slaking	TM
290	Nincada	TM
291	Ninjask	TM
292	Shedinja	TM
293	Whismur	41,TM
294	Loudred	51,TM
295	Exploud	55,TM
296	Makuhita	TM
297	Hariyama	TM
298	Azurill	TM
299	Nosepass	TM
300	Skitty	TM
301	Delcatty	TM
302	Sableye	TM
303	Mawile	TM
304	Aron	TM
305	Lairon	TM
306	Aggron	TM
307	Meditite	TM
308	Medicham	TM
309	Electrike	TM
310	Manectric	TM
311	Plusle	TM
312	Minun	TM
313	Volbeat	TM
314	Illumise	TM
315	Roselia	TM
316	Gulpin	TM
317	Swalot	TM
318	Carvanha	TM
319	Sharpedo	TM
320	Wailmer	TM,E
321	Wailord	TM
322	Numel	TM
323	Camerupt	TM
324	Torkoal	TM,E
325	Spoink	TM
326	Grumpig	TM
327	Spinda	TM
328	Trapinch	TM
329	Vibrava	TM
330	Flygon	TM
331	Cacnea	TM
332	Cacturne	TM
333	Swablu	TM
334	Altaria	TM
335	Zangoose	TM
336	Seviper	TM
337	Lunatone	TM
338	Solrock	TM
339	Barboach	TM
340	Whiscash	TM
341	Corphish	TM
342	Crawdaunt	TM
343	Baltoy	TM
344	Claydol	TM
345	Lileep	TM
346	Cradily	TM
347	Anorith	TM
348	Armaldo	TM
349	Feebas	TM
350	Milotic	TM
351	Castform	TM
352	Kecleon	TM
353	Shuppet	TM
354	Banette	TM
355	Duskull	TM
356	Dusclops	TM
357	Tropius	TM
358	Chimecho	TM
359	Absol	TM
361	Snorunt	TM
362	Glalie	TM
363	Spheal	TM
364	Sealeo	TM
365	Walrein	TM
366	Clamperl	TM
367	Huntail	TM
368	Gorebyss	TM
369	Relicanth	TM,E
370	Luvdisc	TM
371	Bagon	TM
372	Shelgon	TM
373	Salamence	TM
375	Metang	TM
376	Metagross	TM
377	Regirock	TM
378	Regice	TM
379	Registeel	TM
380	Latias	TM
381	Latios	TM
382	Kyogre	TM
383	Groudon	TM
384	Rayquaza	TM
385	Jirachi	TM
386	Deoxys (N)	TM
386	Deoxys (A)	TM
386	Deoxys (D)	TM
386	Deoxys (S)	TM
387	Turtwig	TM
388	Grotle	TM
389	Torterra	TM
390	Chimchar	TM
391	Monferno	TM
392	Infernape	TM
393	Piplup	TM
394	Prinplup	TM
395	Empoleon	TM
396	Starly	TM
397	Staravia	TM
398	Staraptor	TM
399	Bidoof	TM
400	Bibarel	TM
402	Kricketune	TM
403	Shinx	TM
404	Luxio	TM
405	Luxray	TM
406	Budew	TM
407	Roserade	TM
408	Cranidos	TM
409	Rampardos	TM
410	Shieldon	TM
411	Bastiodon	TM
413	Wormadam (P)	TM
413	Wormadam (S)	TM
413	Wormadam (T)	TM
414	Mothim	TM
416	Vespiquen	TM
417	Pachirisu	TM
418	Buizel	TM
419	Floatzel	TM
420	Cherubi	TM
421	Cherrim	TM
422	Shellos	TM
423	Gastrodon	TM
424	Ambipom	TM
425	Drifloon	TM
426	Drifblim	TM
427	Buneary	TM
428	Lopunny	TM
429	Mismagius	TM
430	Honchkrow	TM
431	Glameow	TM
432	Purugly	TM
433	Chingling	TM
434	Stunky	TM
435	Skuntank	TM
436	Bronzor	TM
437	Bronzong	TM
438	Bonsly	TM
439	Mime Jr.	TM
440	Happiny	TM
441	Chatot	TM
442	Spiritomb	TM
443	Gible	TM
444	Gabite	TM
445	Garchomp	TM
446	Munchlax	TM
447	Riolu	TM
448	Lucario	TM
449	Hippopotas	TM
450	Hippowdon	TM
451	Skorupi	TM
452	Drapion	TM
453	Croagunk	TM
454	Toxicroak	TM
455	Carnivine	TM
456	Finneon	TM
457	Lumineon	TM
458	Mantyke	TM
459	Snover	TM
460	Abomasnow	TM
461	Weavile	TM
462	Magnezone	TM
463	Lickilicky	TM
464	Rhyperior	TM
465	Tangrowth	TM
466	Electivire	TM
467	Magmortar	TM
468	Togekiss	TM
469	Yanmega	TM
470	Leafeon	TM
471	Glaceon	TM
472	Gliscor	TM
473	Mamoswine	TM
474	Porygon-Z	TM
475	Gallade	TM
476	Probopass	TM
477	Dusknoir	TM
478	Froslass	TM
479	Rotom	TM
480	Uxie	TM
481	Mesprit	TM
482	Azelf	TM
483	Dialga	TM
484	Palkia	TM
485	Heatran	TM
486	Regigigas	TM
487	Giratina (A)	TM
487	Giratina (O)	TM
488	Cresselia	TM
489	Phione	TM
490	Manaphy	TM
491	Darkrai	TM
492	Shaymin (L)	TM
492	Shaymin (S)	T

Sludge		
88	Grimer	20
89	Muk	20
109	Koffing	24
110	Weezing	24
316	Gulpin	14
317	Swalot	B,14

Sludge Bomb		
1	Bulbasaur	TM
2	Ivysaur	TM
3	Venusaur	TM
15	Beedrill	TM
23	Ekans	TM
24	Arbok	TM
29	Nidoran♀	TM
30	Nidorina	TM
31	Nidoqueen	TM
32	Nidoran♂	TM
33	Nidorino	TM
34	Nidoking	TM
41	Zubat	TM
42	Golbat	TM
43	Oddish	TM
44	Gloom	TM
45	Vileplume	TM
46	Paras	TM
47	Parasect	TM
48	Venonat	TM
49	Venomoth	TM
50	Diglett	TM
51	Dugtrio	TM
69	Bellsprout	TM
70	Weepinbell	TM
71	Victreebel	TM
72	Tentacool	TM
73	Tentacruel	TM
88	Grimer	36,TM
89	Muk	36,TM
92	Gastly	TM
93	Haunter	TM
94	Gengar	TM
102	Exeggcute	TM
103	Exeggutor	TM
109	Koffing	42,TM
110	Weezing	48,TM
114	Tangela	TM
151	Mew	TM
167	Spinarak	TM
168	Ariados	TM
169	Crobat	TM
182	Bellossom	TM
191	Sunkern	TM
192	Sunflora	TM
194	Wooper	TM
195	Quagsire	TM
207	Gligar	TM
209	Snubbull	TM
210	Granbull	TM
211	Qwilfish	TM
213	Shuckle	TM
224	Octillery	TM
228	Houndour	TM
229	Houndoom	TM
269	Dustox	TM
285	Shroomish	TM
286	Breloom	TM
303	Mawile	TM
315	Roselia	TM
316	Gulpin	39,TM
317	Swalot	45,TM
324	Torkoal	TM
336	Seviper	TM
341	Corphish	TM
342	Crawdaunt	TM
345	Lileep	TM
346	Cradily	TM
375	Metang	TM
376	Metagross	TM
406	Budew	TM
407	Roserade	TM
416	Vespiquen	TM
423	Gastrodon	TM
434	Stunky	TM
435	Skuntank	TM
451	Skorupi	TM
452	Drapion	TM
453	Croagunk	43,TM
454	Toxicroak	49,TM
455	Carnivine	TM
465	Tangrowth	TM
472	Gliscor	TM
491	Darkrai	TM

SmellingSalt		
56	Mankey	E
66	Machop	E
108	Lickitung	E
209	Snubbull	E
255	Torchic	E
293	Whismur	E
296	Makuhita	22
297	Hariyama	22
304	Aron	E
327	Spinda	E
331	Cacnea	E
453	Croagunk	E

Smog		
109	Koffing	6
110	Weezing	B,6
126	Magmar	B
136	Flareon	57
218	Slugma	B
219	Magcargo	B
228	Houndour	9
229	Houndoom	B,9
240	Magby	B
316	Gulpin	E
324	Torkoal	4
434	Stunky	E
467	Magmortar	B

SmokeScreen		
4	Charmander	10
5	Charmeleon	10
6	Charizard	B,10
109	Koffing	10
110	Weezing	B,10
116	Horsea	4
117	Seadra	B,4
126	Magmar	10
155	Cyndaquil	4
156	Quilava	B,4
157	Typhlosion	B,4
218	Slugma	E
230	Kingdra	B,4
240	Magby	10
293	Whismur	E
324	Torkoal	20
434	Stunky	14
435	Skuntank	14
442	Spiritomb	E
467	Magmortar	B,10

Snatch		
23	Ekans	TM
24	Arbok	TM
35	Clefairy	TM
36	Clefable	TM
39	Jigglypuff	TM
40	Wigglytuff	TM
41	Zubat	TM
42	Golbat	TM
52	Meowth	TM
53	Persian	TM
63	Abra	TM
64	Kadabra	TM
65	Alakazam	TM
92	Gastly	TM
93	Haunter	TM
94	Gengar	TM
96	Drowzee	TM
97	Hypno	TM
113	Chansey	TM
122	Mr. Mime	TM
150	Mewtwo	TM
151	Mew	TM
169	Crobat	TM
190	Aipom	TM
197	Umbreon	TM
198	Murkrow	TM
200	Misdreavus	TM
215	Sneasel	TM
228	Houndour	TM
229	Houndoom	TM
242	Blissey	TM
261	Poochyena	TM
262	Mightyena	TM
280	Ralts	TM
281	Kirlia	TM
282	Gardevoir	TM
285	Shroomish	TM
286	Breloom	TM
302	Sableye	TM
316	Gulpin	TM
317	Swalot	TM
325	Spoink	TM
326	Grumpig	TM
327	Spinda	TM
336	Seviper	TM
352	Kecleon	TM
353	Shuppet	43,TM
354	Banette	51,TM
355	Duskull	TM
356	Dusclops	TM
358	Chimecho	TM
359	Absol	TM
367	Huntail	TM
386	Deoxys (N)	49,TM
386	Deoxys (A)	TM
386	Deoxys (D)	49,TM
386	Deoxys (S)	TM
424	Ambipom	TM
429	Mismagius	TM
430	Honchkrow	TM
431	Glameow	TM
432	Purugly	TM
433	Chingling	TM
434	Stunky	TM
435	Skuntank	TM
439	Mime Jr.	TM
442	Spiritomb	TM
453	Croagunk	TM
454	Toxicroak	TM
461	Weavile	TM
475	Gallade	TM
477	Dusknoir	TM
478	Froslass	TM
479	Rotom	TM
491	Darkrai	TM

Snore		
1	Bulbasaur	T
2	Ivysaur	T
3	Venusaur	T
4	Charmander	T
5	Charmeleon	T
6	Charizard	T
7	Squirtle	T
8	Wartortle	T
9	Blastoise	T
10	Caterpie	T
12	Butterfree	T
15	Beedrill	T
16	Pidgey	T
17	Pidgeotto	T
18	Pidgeot	T
19	Rattata	T
20	Raticate	T
21	Spearow	T
22	Fearow	T
23	Ekans	T
24	Arbok	T
25	Pikachu	T
26	Raichu	T
27	Sandshrew	T
28	Sandslash	T
29	Nidoran♀	T
30	Nidorina	T
31	Nidoqueen	T
32	Nidoran♂	T
33	Nidorino	T
34	Nidoking	T
35	Clefairy	T
36	Clefable	T
37	Vulpix	T
38	Ninetales	T
39	Jigglypuff	T
40	Wigglytuff	T
41	Zubat	T
42	Golbat	T
43	Oddish	T
44	Gloom	T
45	Vileplume	T
46	Paras	T
47	Parasect	T
48	Venonat	T
49	Venomoth	T
50	Diglett	T
51	Dugtrio	T
52	Meowth	T
53	Persian	T
54	Psyduck	T
55	Golduck	T
58	Growlithe	T
59	Arcanine	T
60	Poliwag	T
61	Poliwhirl	T
62	Poliwrath	T
63	Abra	T
64	Kadabra	T
65	Alakazam	T
66	Machop	T
67	Machoke	T
68	Machamp	T
69	Bellsprout	T
70	Weepinbell	T
71	Victreebel	T
72	Tentacool	T
73	Tentacruel	T
74	Geodude	T
75	Graveler	T
76	Golem	T
77	Ponyta	T
78	Rapidash	T
79	Slowpoke	T,E
80	Slowbro	T
81	Magnemite	T
82	Magneton	T
83	Farfetch'd	T
84	Doduo	T
85	Dodrio	T
86	Seel	T
87	Dewgong	T
88	Grimer	T
89	Muk	T
90	Shellder	T
91	Cloyster	T
92	Gastly	T
93	Haunter	T
94	Gengar	T
95	Onix	T
98	Krabby	T
99	Kingler	T
100	Voltorb	T
101	Electrode	T
102	Exeggcute	T
103	Exeggutor	T
104	Cubone	T
105	Marowak	T
106	Hitmonlee	T
107	Hitmonchan	T
108	Lickitung	T,E
109	Koffing	T
110	Weezing	T
111	Rhyhorn	T
112	Rhydon	T
113	Chansey	T
114	Tangela	T
115	Kangaskhan	T
116	Horsea	T
117	Seadra	T
118	Goldeen	T
119	Seaking	T
120	Staryu	T
121	Starmie	T
122	Mr. Mime	T
123	Scyther	T
124	Jynx	T
125	Electabuzz	T
126	Magmar	T
127	Pinsir	T
128	Tauros	T
130	Gyarados	T
131	Lapras	T
133	Eevee	T
134	Vaporeon	T
135	Jolteon	T
136	Flareon	T
137	Porygon	T
138	Omanyte	T
139	Omastar	T
140	Kabuto	T
141	Kabutops	T
142	Aerodactyl	T
143	Snorlax	28,T
144	Articuno	T
145	Zapdos	T
146	Moltres	T
147	Dratini	T
148	Dragonair	T
149	Dragonite	T
150	Mewtwo	T
151	Mew	T
152	Chikorita	T
153	Bayleef	T
154	Meganium	T
155	Cyndaquil	T
156	Quilava	T
157	Typhlosion	T
158	Totodile	T
159	Croconaw	T
160	Feraligatr	T
161	Sentret	T
162	Furret	T
165	Ledyba	T
166	Ledian	T
169	Crobat	T
170	Chinchou	T
171	Lanturn	T
172	Pichu	T
173	Cleffa	T
174	Igglybuff	T
175	Togepi	T
176	Togetic	T
177	Natu	T
178	Xatu	T
179	Mareep	T
180	Flaaffy	T
181	Ampharos	T
182	Bellossom	T
183	Marill	T
184	Azumarill	T
185	Sudowoodo	T
186	Politoed	T
187	Hoppip	T
188	Skiploom	T
189	Jumpluff	T
190	Aipom	T
191	Sunkern	T
192	Sunflora	T
193	Yanma	T
194	Wooper	T
195	Quagsire	T

Snore continued

196	Espeon	T
197	Umbreon	T
199	Slowking	T
200	Misdreavus	T
203	Girafarig	T
204	Pineco	T
205	Forretress	T
206	Dunsparce	T,E
207	Gligar	T
208	Steelix	T
209	Snubbull	T,E
210	Granbull	T
211	Qwilfish	T
212	Scizor	T
213	Shuckle	T
214	Heracross	T
215	Sneasel	T
216	Teddiursa	43,T
217	Ursaring	49,T
218	Slugma	T
219	Magcargo	T
220	Swinub	T
221	Piloswine	T
222	Corsola	T
223	Remoraid	T,E
224	Octillery	T
226	Mantine	T
227	Skarmory	T
228	Houndour	T
229	Houndoom	T
230	Kingdra	T
231	Phanpy	T,E
232	Donphan	T
233	Porygon2	T
234	Stantler	T
236	Tyrogue	T
237	Hitmontop	T
238	Smoochum	T
239	Elekid	T
240	Magby	T
241	Miltank	T
242	Blissey	T
243	Raikou	T
244	Entei	T
245	Suicune	T
246	Larvitar	T
247	Pupitar	T
248	Tyranitar	T
249	Lugia	T
250	Ho-Oh	T
251	Celebi	T
252	Treecko	T
253	Grovyle	T
254	Sceptile	T
255	Torchic	T
256	Combusken	T
257	Blaziken	T
258	Mudkip	T
259	Marshtomp	T
260	Swampert	T
261	Poochyena	T
262	Mightyena	T
263	Zigzagoon	T
264	Linoone	T
265	Wurmple	T
267	Beautifly	T
269	Dustox	T
270	Lotad	T
271	Lombre	T
272	Ludicolo	T
273	Seedot	T
274	Nuzleaf	T
275	Shiftry	T
276	Taillow	T
277	Swellow	T
278	Wingull	T
279	Pelipper	T
280	Ralts	T
281	Kirlia	T
282	Gardevoir	T
283	Surskit	T
284	Masquerain	T
285	Shroomish	T
286	Breloom	T
287	Slakoth	T,E
289	Slaking	T
290	Nincada	T
291	Ninjask	T
292	Shedinja	T
293	Whismur	T,E
294	Loudred	T
295	Exploud	T
296	Makuhita	T
297	Hariyama	T
298	Azurill	T
299	Nosepass	T
300	Skitty	T
301	Delcatty	T
302	Sableye	T
303	Mawile	T
304	Aron	T
305	Lairon	T
306	Aggron	T
307	Meditite	T
308	Medicham	T
309	Electrike	T
310	Manectric	T
311	Plusle	T
312	Minun	T
313	Volbeat	T
314	Illumise	T
315	Roselia	T
316	Gulpin	T
317	Swalot	T
318	Carvanha	T
319	Sharpedo	T
320	Wailmer	T,E
321	Wailord	T
322	Numel	T
323	Camerupt	T
324	Torkoal	T
325	Spoink	29,T
326	Grumpig	29,T
327	Spinda	T
328	Trapinch	T
329	Vibrava	T
330	Flygon	T
331	Cacnea	T
332	Cacturne	T
333	Swablu	T
334	Altaria	T
335	Zangoose	T
336	Seviper	T
337	Lunatone	T
338	Solrock	T
339	Barboach	31,T
340	Whiscash	33,T
341	Corphish	T
342	Crawdaunt	T
343	Baltoy	T
344	Claydol	T
345	Lileep	T
346	Cradily	T
347	Anorith	T
348	Armaldo	T
349	Feebas	T
350	Milotic	T
351	Castform	T
352	Kecleon	T
355	Duskull	T
356	Dusclops	T
357	Tropius	T
358	Chimecho	T
359	Absol	T
361	Snorunt	T
362	Glalie	T
363	Spheal	37,T
364	Sealeo	39,T
365	Walrein	39,T
366	Clamperl	T
367	Huntail	T
368	Gorebyss	T
369	Relicanth	T,E
370	Luvdisc	T
371	Bagon	T
372	Shelgon	T
373	Salamence	T
375	Metang	T
376	Metagross	T
377	Regirock	T
378	Regice	T
379	Registeel	T
380	Latias	T
381	Latios	T
382	Kyogre	T
383	Groudon	T
384	Rayquaza	T
385	Jirachi	T
386	Deoxys (N)	T
386	Deoxys (A)	T
386	Deoxys (D)	T
386	Deoxys (S)	T
387	Turtwig	T
388	Grotle	T
389	Torterra	T
390	Chimchar	T
391	Monferno	T
392	Infernape	T
393	Piplup	T,E
394	Prinplup	T
395	Empoleon	T
396	Starly	T
397	Staravia	T
398	Staraptor	T
399	Bidoof	T
400	Bibarel	T
401	Kricketot	T
402	Kricketune	T
403	Shinx	T
404	Luxio	T
405	Luxray	T
406	Budew	T
407	Roserade	T
408	Cranidos	T
409	Rampardos	T
410	Shieldon	T
411	Bastiodon	T
412	Burmy	T
413	Wormadam (P)	T
413	Wormadam (S)	T
413	Wormadam (T)	T
414	Mothim	T
415	Combee	T
416	Vespiquen	T
417	Pachirisu	T
418	Buizel	T
419	Floatzel	T
420	Cherubi	T
421	Cherrim	T
422	Shellos	T
423	Gastrodon	T
424	Ambipom	T
425	Drifloon	T
426	Drifblim	T
427	Buneary	T
428	Lopunny	T
429	Mismagius	T
431	Glameow	T
432	Purugly	T
433	Chingling	T
434	Stunky	T
435	Skuntank	T
436	Bronzor	T
437	Bronzong	T
438	Bonsly	T
439	Mime Jr.	T
440	Happiny	T
441	Chatot	T
442	Spiritomb	T
443	Gible	T
444	Gabite	T
445	Garchomp	T
446	Munchlax	T
447	Riolu	T
448	Lucario	T
449	Hippopotas	T
450	Hippowdon	T
451	Skorupi	T
452	Drapion	T
453	Croagunk	T
454	Toxicroak	T
455	Carnivine	T
456	Finneon	T
457	Lumineon	T
458	Mantyke	T
459	Snover	T
460	Abomasnow	T
461	Weavile	T
462	Magnezone	T
463	Lickilicky	T
464	Rhyperior	T
465	Tangrowth	T
466	Electivire	T
467	Magmortar	T
468	Togekiss	T
469	Yanmega	T
470	Leafeon	T
471	Glaceon	T
472	Gliscor	T
473	Mamoswine	T
474	Porygon-Z	T
475	Gallade	T
476	Probopass	T
477	Dusknoir	T
478	Froslass	T
479	Rotom	T
480	Uxie	T
481	Mesprit	T
482	Azelf	T
483	Dialga	T
484	Palkia	T
485	Heatran	T
486	Regigigas	T
487	Giratina (A)	T
487	Giratina (O)	T
488	Cresselia	T
489	Phione	T
490	Manaphy	T
491	Darkrai	T
492	Shaymin (L)	T
492	Shaymin (S)	T

Softboiled

113	Chansey	12
242	Blissey	12

SolarBeam

1	Bulbasaur	TM
2	Ivysaur	44,TM
3	Venusaur	53,TM
6	Charizard	TM
12	Butterfree	TM
15	Beedrill	TM
35	Clefairy	TM
36	Clefable	TM
38	Ninetales	TM
39	Jigglypuff	TM
40	Wigglytuff	TM
43	Oddish	TM
44	Gloom	TM
45	Vileplume	65,TM
46	Paras	TM
47	Parasect	TM
48	Venonat	TM
49	Venomoth	TM
59	Arcanine	TM
69	Bellsprout	TM
70	Weepinbell	TM
71	Victreebel	TM
77	Ponyta	TM
78	Rapidash	TM
102	Exeggcute	43,TM
103	Exeggutor	TM
108	Lickitung	TM
113	Chansey	TM
114	Tangela	TM
115	Kangaskhan	TM
122	Mr. Mime	TM
128	Tauros	TM
137	Porygon	TM
143	Snorlax	TM
146	Moltres	71,TM
150	Mewtwo	TM
151	Mew	TM
152	Chikorita	45,TM
153	Bayleef	54,TM
154	Meganium	66,TM
157	Typhlosion	TM
161	Sentret	TM
162	Furret	TM
165	Ledyba	TM
166	Ledian	TM
167	Spinarak	TM
168	Ariados	TM
173	Cleffa	TM
174	Igglybuff	TM
175	Togepi	TM
176	Togetic	TM
177	Natu	TM
178	Xatu	TM
182	Bellossom	TM
187	Hoppip	TM
188	Skiploom	TM
189	Jumpluff	TM
190	Aipom	TM
191	Sunkern	TM
192	Sunflora	41,TM
193	Yanma	TM
204	Pineco	TM
205	Forretress	TM
206	Dunsparce	TM
209	Snubbull	TM
210	Granbull	TM
219	Magcargo	TM
228	Houndour	TM
229	Houndoom	TM
233	Porygon2	TM
234	Stantler	TM
241	Miltank	TM
242	Blissey	TM
244	Entei	TM
250	Ho-Oh	TM
251	Celebi	TM
252	Treecko	TM
253	Grovyle	TM
254	Sceptile	TM
257	Blaziken	TM
267	Beautifly	TM
269	Dustox	TM
270	Lotad	TM
271	Lombre	TM
272	Ludicolo	TM
273	Seedot	TM
274	Nuzleaf	TM
275	Shiftry	TM
283	Surskit	TM
284	Masquerain	TM
285	Shroomish	TM
286	Breloom	TM
287	Slakoth	TM
288	Vigoroth	TM
289	Slaking	TM
290	Nincada	TM
291	Ninjask	TM
292	Shedinja	TM
293	Whismur	TM
294	Loudred	TM
295	Exploud	TM
300	Skitty	TM
301	Delcatty	TM
303	Mawile	TM
306	Aggron	TM
313	Volbeat	TM
314	Illumise	TM
315	Roselia	TM
316	Gulpin	TM
317	Swalot	TM
323	Camerupt	TM
324	Torkoal	TM
328	Trapinch	TM
329	Vibrava	TM
330	Flygon	TM
331	Cacnea	TM
332	Cacturne	TM
333	Swablu	TM
334	Altaria	TM
335	Zangoose	TM
338	Solrock	53,TM
343	Baltoy	TM
344	Claydol	TM
345	Lileep	TM
346	Cradily	TM
351	Castform	TM
352	Kecleon	TM
357	Tropius	51,TM
380	Latias	TM
381	Latios	TM
383	Groudon	65,TM
384	Rayquaza	TM
386	Deoxys (N)	TM
386	Deoxys (A)	TM
386	Deoxys (D)	TM
386	Deoxys (S)	TM
387	Turtwig	TM
388	Grotle	TM
389	Torterra	TM
392	Infernape	TM
406	Budew	TM
407	Roserade	TM
413	Wormadam (P)	TM
414	Mothim	TM
420	Cherubi	37,TM
421	Cherrim	43,TM
424	Ambipom	TM
427	Buneary	TM
428	Lopunny	TM
436	Bronzor	TM
437	Bronzong	TM
439	Mime Jr.	TM
440	Happiny	TM
446	Munchlax	TM
455	Carnivine	TM
459	Snover	TM
460	Abomasnow	TM
463	Lickilicky	TM
465	Tangrowth	TM
467	Magmortar	TM
468	Togekiss	TM
469	Yanmega	TM
470	Leafeon	TM
474	Porygon-Z	TM
480	Uxie	TM
485	Heatran	TM
488	Cresselia	TM
492	Shaymin (L)	TM
492	Shaymin (S)	TM

SonicBoom

81	Magnemite	14
82	Magneton	14
100	Voltorb	8
101	Electrode	B,8
167	Spinarak	E
193	Yanma	14
329	Vibrava	B
330	Flygon	B
418	Buizel	B
419	Floatzel	B
462	Magnezone	14
469	Yanmega	14

Spacial Rend

484	Palkia	40

Spark

81	Magnemite	22
82	Magneton	22
100	Voltorb	12
101	Electrode	B,12
170	Chinchou	20
171	Lanturn	20
243	Raikou	29
309	Electrike	20
310	Manectric	20
311	Plusle	15
312	Minun	15
339	Barboach	E
403	Shinx	13
404	Luxio	13
405	Luxray	13
417	Pachirisu	13
462	Magnezone	22

Spider Web

167	Spinarak	29
168	Ariados	32

Spike Cannon

91	Cloyster	40
139	Omastar	40
222	Corsola	40

Spikes

91	Cloyster	28
138	Omanyte	E
204	Pineco	28
205	Forretress	28
211	Qwilfish	B
227	Skarmory	28
315	Roselia	E
331	Cacnea	33
332	Cacturne	35
361	Snorunt	E
386	Deoxys (D)	33
406	Budew	E

Spit Up

23	Ekans	25
24	Arbok	28
71	Victreebel	B
88	Grimer	E
171	Lanturn	27
194	Wooper	E
211	Qwilfish	25
218	Slugma	E
279	Pelipper	38
303	Mawile	51
316	Gulpin	34
317	Swalot	38
336	Seviper	E
345	Lileep	57
346	Cradily	66
363	Spheal	E
422	Shellos	E
425	Drifloon	27
426	Drifblim	27
449	Hippopotas	E
455	Carnivine	31

Spite

23	Ekans	T,E
24	Arbok	T
37	Vulpix	T,E
38	Ninetales	T
52	Meowth	T,E
53	Persian	T
56	Mankey	T
57	Primeape	T
92	Gastly	5,T
93	Haunter	B,5,T
94	Gengar	B,5,T
109	Koffing	T,E
110	Weezing	T
111	Rhyhorn	T
112	Rhydon	T
115	Kangaskhan	T
128	Tauros	T
130	Gyarados	T
151	Mew	T
158	Totodile	T
159	Croconaw	T
160	Feraligatr	T
190	Aipom	T,E
197	Umbreon	T
198	Murkrow	T
200	Misdreavus	5,T,E
206	Dunsparce	21,T
215	Sneasel	T,E
228	Houndour	T,E
229	Houndoom	T
234	Stantler	T,E
246	Larvitar	T
247	Pupitar	T
248	Tyranitar	T
261	Poochyena	T
262	Mightyena	T
273	Seedot	T
274	Nuzleaf	T
275	Shiftry	T
290	Nincada	T
291	Ninjask	T
292	Shedinja	25,T
302	Sableye	T
304	Aron	T
305	Lairon	T
306	Aggron	T
318	Carvanha	T
319	Sharpedo	T
331	Cacnea	T
332	Cacturne	T
341	Corphish	T
342	Crawdaunt	T
353	Shuppet	16,T
354	Banette	16,T
355	Duskull	T
356	Dusclops	T
359	Absol	T
361	Snorunt	T
362	Glalie	T
408	Cranidos	T
409	Rampardos	T
424	Ambipom	T
425	Drifloon	T
426	Drifblim	T
429	Mismagius	B,T
430	Honchkrow	T
442	Spiritomb	B,T
453	Croagunk	T
454	Toxicroak	T
461	Weavile	T
464	Rhyperior	T
477	Dusknoir	T
478	Froslass	T
479	Rotom	T
487	Giratina (A)	T
487	Giratina (O)	T
491	Darkrai	T

Splash

60	Poliwag	E
116	Horsea	E
129	Magikarp	B
173	Cleffa	E
187	Hoppip	B
188	Skiploom	B
189	Jumpluff	B
225	Delibird	E
226	Mantine	E
298	Azurill	B
320	Wailmer	B
321	Wailord	B
325	Spoink	B
326	Grumpig	B
349	Feebas	B
360	Wynaut	B
370	Luvdisc	E
427	Buneary	B
428	Lopunny	B
456	Finneon	E
458	Mantyke	E

Spore

46	Paras	17
47	Parasect	17
285	Shroomish	45

Stealth Rock

27	Sandshrew	TM
28	Sandslash	TM
31	Nidoqueen	TM
34	Nidoking	TM
35	Clefairy	TM
36	Clefable	TM
39	Jigglypuff	TM
40	Wigglytuff	TM
50	Diglett	TM
51	Dugtrio	TM
74	Geodude	TM
75	Graveler	TM
76	Golem	TM
95	Onix	TM
104	Cubone	TM
105	Marowak	TM
111	Rhyhorn	TM
112	Rhydon	TM
113	Chansey	TM
127	Pinsir	TM
138	Omanyte	TM
139	Omastar	TM
140	Kabuto	TM
141	Kabutops	TM
142	Aerodactyl	TM
151	Mew	TM
185	Sudowoodo	TM
204	Pineco	TM
205	Forretress	TM
206	Dunsparce	TM
207	Gligar	TM
208	Steelix	TM
213	Shuckle	TM
219	Magcargo	TM
220	Swinub	TM

221	Piloswine	TM
222	Corsola	TM
227	Skarmory	TM
231	Phanpy	TM
232	Donphan	TM
241	Miltank	TM
242	Blissey	TM
246	Larvitar	TM
247	Pupitar	TM
248	Tyranitar	TM
251	Celebi	TM
259	Marshtomp	TM
260	Swampert	TM
299	Nosepass	TM
304	Aron	TM
305	Lairon	TM
306	Aggron	TM
322	Numel	TM
323	Camerupt	TM
324	Torkoal	TM
337	Lunatone	TM
338	Solrock	TM
343	Baltoy	TM
344	Claydol	TM
345	Lileep	TM
346	Cradily	TM
347	Anorith	TM
348	Armaldo	TM
352	Kecleon	TM
369	Relicanth	TM
375	Metang	TM
376	Metagross	TM
377	Regirock	TM
379	Registeel	TM
383	Groudon	TM
385	Jirachi	TM
386	Deoxys (N)	TM
386	Deoxys (A)	TM
386	Deoxys (D)	TM
386	Deoxys (S)	TM
387	Turtwig	TM
388	Grotle	TM
389	Torterra	TM
390	Chimchar	TM
391	Monferno	TM
392	Infernape	TM
393	Piplup	TM
394	Prinplup	TM
395	Empoleon	TM
399	Bidoof	TM
400	Bibarel	TM
408	Cranidos	TM
409	Rampardos	TM
410	Shieldon	TM
411	Bastiodon	TM
413	Wormadam (T)	TM
436	Bronzor	TM
437	Bronzong	TM
438	Bonsly	TM
443	Gible	TM
444	Gabite	TM
445	Garchomp	TM
449	Hippopotas	TM
450	Hippowdon	TM
464	Rhyperior	TM
472	Gliscor	TM
473	Mamoswine	TM
476	Probopass	TM
480	Uxie	TM
481	Mesprit	TM
482	Azelf	TM
483	Dialga	TM
485	Heatran	TM

Steel Wing

6	Charizard	TM
16	Pidgey	TM,E
17	Pidgeotto	TM
18	Pidgeot	TM
21	Spearow	TM
22	Fearow	TM
41	Zubat	TM
42	Golbat	TM
83	Farfetch'd	TM,E
84	Doduo	TM
85	Dodrio	TM
123	Scyther	TM
142	Aerodactyl	TM,E
144	Articuno	TM
145	Zapdos	TM
146	Moltres	TM
149	Dragonite	TM
151	Mew	TM
163	Hoothoot	TM
164	Noctowl	TM
169	Crobat	TM
176	Togetic	TM
177	Natu	TM,E
178	Xatu	TM

193	Yanma	TM
198	Murkrow	TM
207	Gligar	TM
212	Scizor	TM
227	Skarmory	34,TM
249	Lugia	TM
250	Ho-Oh	TM
276	Taillow	TM
277	Swellow	TM
278	Wingull	TM
279	Pelipper	TM
329	Vibrava	TM
330	Flygon	TM
333	Swablu	TM
334	Altaria	TM
357	Tropius	TM
373	Salamence	TM
380	Latias	TM
381	Latios	TM
395	Empoleon	TM
396	Starly	TM
397	Staravia	TM
398	Staraptor	TM
430	Honchkrow	TM
441	Chatot	TM
468	Togekiss	TM
469	Yanmega	TM
472	Gliscor	TM
487	Giratina (A)	TM
487	Giratina (O)	TM

Stockpile

23	Ekans	25
24	Arbok	28
71	Victreebel	B
88	Grimer	E
171	Lanturn	27
194	Wooper	E
211	Qwilfish	25
218	Slugma	E
279	Pelipper	38
303	Mawile	51
316	Gulpin	34
317	Swalot	38
336	Seviper	E
345	Lileep	57
346	Cradily	66
363	Spheal	E
422	Shellos	E
425	Drifloon	22
426	Drifblim	22
446	Munchlax	25
449	Hippopotas	E
455	Carnivine	31

Stomp

77	Ponyta	19
78	Rapidash	19
79	Slowpoke	E
98	Krabby	25
99	Kingler	25
103	Exeggutor	B,17
108	Lickitung	21
111	Rhyhorn	9
112	Rhydon	B,9
115	Kangaskhan	E
203	Girafarig	10
234	Stantler	13
241	Miltank	8
244	Entei	29
246	Larvitar	E
258	Mudkip	E
293	Whismur	25
294	Loudred	29
295	Exploud	29
304	Aron	E
322	Numel	E
357	Tropius	17
377	Regirock	B
378	Regice	B
379	Registeel	B
408	Cranidos	E
459	Snover	E
463	Lickilicky	21
464	Rhyperior	B,9

Stone Edge

28	Sandslash	TM
31	Nidoqueen	TM
34	Nidoking	TM
51	Dugtrio	TM
57	Primeape	TM
68	Machamp	TM
74	Geodude	39,TM
75	Graveler	49,TM
76	Golem	49,TM
95	Onix	54,TM
105	Marowak	TM
106	Hitmonlee	TM
107	Hitmonchan	TM
111	Rhyhorn	45,TM
112	Rhydon	45,TM
127	Pinsir	TM
128	Tauros	TM
130	Gyarados	TM
139	Omastar	TM
141	Kabutops	TM
142	Aerodactyl	TM
149	Dragonite	TM
150	Mewtwo	TM
151	Mew	TM
185	Sudowoodo	TM
195	Quagsire	TM
207	Gligar	TM
208	Steelix	54,TM
210	Granbull	TM
213	Shuckle	TM
214	Heracross	TM
217	Ursaring	TM
219	Magcargo	TM
221	Piloswine	TM
222	Corsola	TM
232	Donphan	TM
237	Hitmontop	TM
244	Entei	TM
246	Larvitar	46,TM
247	Pupitar	54,TM
248	Tyranitar	54,TM
257	Blaziken	TM
260	Swampert	TM
286	Breloom	TM
297	Hariyama	TM
299	Nosepass	61,TM
305	Lairon	TM
306	Aggron	TM
323	Camerupt	TM
324	Torkoal	TM
330	Flygon	TM
337	Lunatone	TM
338	Solrock	TM
340	Whiscash	TM
344	Claydol	TM
346	Cradily	TM
348	Armaldo	TM
359	Absol	TM
369	Relicanth	TM
373	Salamence	TM
377	Regirock	73,TM
383	Groudon	TM
384	Rayquaza	TM
389	Torterra	TM
392	Infernape	TM
408	Cranidos	TM
409	Rampardos	TM
410	Shieldon	TM
411	Bastiodon	TM
423	Gastrodon	TM
443	Gible	TM
444	Gabite	TM
445	Garchomp	TM
448	Lucario	TM
450	Hippowdon	TM
454	Toxicroak	TM
464	Rhyperior	45,TM
472	Gliscor	TM
473	Mamoswine	TM
475	Gallade	TM
476	Probopass	61,TM
483	Dialga	TM
484	Palkia	TM
485	Heatran	88,TM
486	Regigigas	TM
487	Giratina (A)	TM
487	Giratina (O)	TM

Strength

1	Bulbasaur	HM
2	Ivysaur	HM
3	Venusaur	HM
4	Charmander	HM
5	Charmeleon	HM
6	Charizard	HM
7	Squirtle	HM
8	Wartortle	HM
9	Blastoise	HM
20	Raticate	HM
23	Ekans	HM
24	Arbok	HM
25	Pikachu	HM
26	Raichu	HM
27	Sandshrew	HM
28	Sandslash	HM
29	Nidoran ♀	HM
30	Nidorina	HM
31	Nidoqueen	HM
32	Nidoran ♂	HM
33	Nidorino	HM
34	Nidoking	HM
35	Clefairy	HM
36	Clefable	HM
39	Jigglypuff	HM
40	Wigglytuff	HM
54	Psyduck	HM
55	Golduck	HM
56	Mankey	HM
57	Primeape	HM
58	Growlithe	HM
59	Arcanine	HM
61	Poliwhirl	HM
62	Poliwrath	HM
66	Machop	HM
67	Machoke	HM
68	Machamp	HM
74	Geodude	HM
75	Graveler	HM
76	Golem	HM
77	Ponyta	HM
78	Rapidash	HM
79	Slowpoke	HM
80	Slowbro	HM
88	Grimer	HM
89	Muk	HM
94	Gengar	HM
95	Onix	HM
98	Krabby	HM
99	Kingler	HM
102	Exeggcute	HM
103	Exeggutor	HM
104	Cubone	HM
105	Marowak	HM
106	Hitmonlee	HM
107	Hitmonchan	HM
108	Lickitung	HM
111	Rhyhorn	HM
112	Rhydon	HM
113	Chansey	HM
115	Kangaskhan	HM
125	Electabuzz	HM
126	Magmar	HM
127	Pinsir	HM
128	Tauros	HM
130	Gyarados	HM
131	Lapras	HM
134	Vaporeon	HM
135	Jolteon	HM
136	Flareon	HM
142	Aerodactyl	HM
143	Snorlax	HM
149	Dragonite	HM
150	Mewtwo	HM
151	Mew	HM
153	Bayleef	HM
154	Meganium	HM
156	Quilava	HM
157	Typhlosion	HM
159	Croconaw	HM
160	Feraligatr	HM
162	Furret	HM
166	Ledian	HM
180	Flaaffy	HM
181	Ampharos	HM
183	Marill	HM
184	Azumarill	HM
185	Sudowoodo	HM
186	Politoed	HM
190	Aipom	HM
195	Quagsire	HM
199	Slowking	HM
203	Girafarig	HM
204	Pineco	HM
205	Forretress	HM
206	Dunsparce	HM
207	Gligar	HM
208	Steelix	HM
209	Snubbull	HM
210	Granbull	HM
212	Scizor	HM
213	Shuckle	HM
214	Heracross	HM
215	Sneasel	HM
216	Teddiursa	HM
217	Ursaring	HM
219	Magcargo	HM
220	Swinub	HM
221	Piloswine	HM
222	Corsola	HM
229	Houndoom	HM
231	Phanpy	HM
232	Donphan	HM
236	Tyrogue	HM
237	Hitmontop	HM
241	Miltank	HM
242	Blissey	HM
243	Raikou	HM
244	Entei	HM
248	Tyranitar	HM
249	Lugia	HM
250	Ho-Oh	HM
252	Treecko	HM
253	Grovyle	HM
254	Sceptile	HM
255	Torchic	HM
256	Combusken	HM
257	Blaziken	HM
258	Mudkip	HM
259	Marshtomp	HM
260	Swampert	HM
262	Mightyena	HM
264	Linoone	HM
271	Lombre	HM
272	Ludicolo	HM
274	Nuzleaf	HM
275	Shiftry	HM
286	Breloom	HM
287	Slakoth	HM
288	Vigoroth	HM
289	Slaking	HM
294	Loudred	HM
295	Exploud	HM
296	Makuhita	HM
297	Hariyama	HM
299	Nosepass	HM
301	Delcatty	HM
303	Mawile	HM
304	Aron	HM
305	Lairon	HM
306	Aggron	HM
307	Meditite	HM
308	Medicham	HM
309	Electrike	HM
310	Manectric	HM
316	Gulpin	HM
317	Swalot	HM
319	Sharpedo	HM
320	Wailmer	HM
321	Wailord	HM
322	Numel	HM
323	Camerupt	HM
324	Torkoal	HM
327	Spinda	HM
328	Trapinch	HM
329	Vibrava	HM
330	Flygon	HM
332	Cacturne	HM
335	Zangoose	HM
336	Seviper	HM
340	Whiscash	HM
341	Corphish	HM
342	Crawdaunt	HM
344	Claydol	HM
346	Cradily	HM
348	Armaldo	HM
352	Kecleon	HM
356	Dusclops	HM
357	Tropius	HM
359	Absol	HM
363	Spheal	HM
364	Sealeo	HM
365	Walrein	HM
371	Bagon	HM
372	Shelgon	HM
373	Salamence	HM
375	Metang	HM
376	Metagross	HM
377	Regirock	HM
378	Regice	HM
379	Registeel	HM
382	Kyogre	HM
383	Groudon	HM
384	Rayquaza	HM
386	Deoxys (N)	HM
386	Deoxys (A)	HM
386	Deoxys (D)	HM
386	Deoxys (S)	HM
387	Turtwig	HM
388	Grotle	HM
389	Torterra	HM
390	Chimchar	HM
391	Monferno	HM
392	Infernape	HM
394	Prinplup	HM
395	Empoleon	HM
400	Bibarel	HM
402	Kricketune	HM
403	Shinx	HM
404	Luxio	HM
405	Luxray	HM
408	Cranidos	HM
409	Rampardos	HM
410	Shieldon	HM
411	Bastiodon	HM
418	Buizel	HM
419	Floatzel	HM
423	Gastrodon	HM
424	Ambipom	HM
428	Lopunny	HM
435	Skuntank	HM
437	Bronzong	HM
443	Gible	HM
444	Gabite	HM
445	Garchomp	HM
446	Munchlax	HM
447	Riolu	HM
448	Lucario	HM
449	Hippopotas	HM
450	Hippowdon	HM
451	Skorupi	HM
452	Drapion	HM
453	Croagunk	HM
454	Toxicroak	HM
460	Abomasnow	HM
461	Weavile	HM
463	Lickilicky	HM
464	Rhyperior	HM
465	Tangrowth	HM
466	Electivire	HM
467	Magmortar	HM
470	Leafeon	HM
471	Glaceon	HM
472	Gliscor	HM
473	Mamoswine	HM
475	Gallade	HM
476	Probopass	HM
477	Dusknoir	HM
483	Dialga	HM
484	Palkia	HM
485	Heatran	HM
486	Regigigas	HM
487	Giratina (A)	HM
487	Giratina (O)	HM
491	Darkrai	HM

String Shot

10	Caterpie	B
13	Weedle	B
167	Spinarak	B
168	Ariados	B
265	Wurmple	B

Stun Spore

12	Butterfree	12
43	Oddish	15
44	Gloom	15
45	Vileplume	B
46	Paras	6
47	Parasect	B,6
48	Venonat	23
49	Venomoth	23
69	Bellsprout	17
70	Weepinbell	17
102	Exeggcute	19
114	Tangela	29
182	Bellossom	B
187	Hoppip	14
188	Skiploom	14
189	Jumpluff	14
267	Beautifly	17
284	Masquerain	33
285	Shroomish	9
286	Breloom	B,9
315	Roselia	10
406	Budew	10
455	Carnivine	E
465	Tangrowth	29

Submission

62	Poliwrath	B
66	Machop	31
67	Machoke	32
68	Machamp	32
127	Pinsir	42

Substitute

1	Bulbasaur	TM
2	Ivysaur	TM
3	Venusaur	TM
4	Charmander	TM
5	Charmeleon	TM
6	Charizard	TM
7	Squirtle	TM
8	Wartortle	TM
9	Blastoise	TM
12	Butterfree	TM
15	Beedrill	TM
16	Pidgey	TM
17	Pidgeotto	TM
18	Pidgeot	TM
19	Rattata	TM
20	Raticate	TM
21	Spearow	TM
22	Fearow	TM
23	Ekans	TM
24	Arbok	TM
25	Pikachu	TM
26	Raichu	TM
27	Sandshrew	TM
28	Sandslash	TM
29	Nidoran ♀	TM
30	Nidorina	TM
31	Nidoqueen	TM
32	Nidoran ♂	TM
33	Nidorino	TM
34	Nidoking	TM
35	Clefairy	TM
36	Clefable	TM
37	Vulpix	TM
38	Ninetales	TM
39	Jigglypuff	TM
40	Wigglytuff	TM
41	Zubat	TM
42	Golbat	TM
43	Oddish	TM
44	Gloom	TM
45	Vileplume	TM
46	Paras	TM
47	Parasect	TM
48	Venonat	TM
49	Venomoth	TM
50	Diglett	TM
51	Dugtrio	TM
52	Meowth	TM
53	Persian	TM
54	Psyduck	TM
55	Golduck	TM
56	Mankey	TM
57	Primeape	TM
58	Growlithe	TM
59	Arcanine	TM
60	Poliwag	TM
61	Poliwhirl	TM
62	Poliwrath	TM
63	Abra	TM
64	Kadabra	TM
65	Alakazam	TM
66	Machop	TM
67	Machoke	TM
68	Machamp	TM
69	Bellsprout	TM
70	Weepinbell	TM
71	Victreebel	TM
72	Tentacool	TM
73	Tentacruel	TM
74	Geodude	TM
75	Graveler	TM
76	Golem	TM
77	Ponyta	TM
78	Rapidash	TM
79	Slowpoke	TM
80	Slowbro	TM
81	Magnemite	TM
82	Magneton	TM
83	Farfetch'd	TM
84	Doduo	TM
85	Dodrio	TM
86	Seel	TM
87	Dewgong	TM
88	Grimer	TM
89	Muk	TM
90	Shellder	TM
91	Cloyster	TM
92	Gastly	TM
93	Haunter	TM
94	Gengar	TM
95	Onix	TM
96	Drowzee	TM
97	Hypno	TM
98	Krabby	TM
99	Kingler	TM
100	Voltorb	TM
101	Electrode	TM
102	Exeggcute	TM
103	Exeggutor	TM
104	Cubone	TM
105	Marowak	TM
106	Hitmonlee	TM
107	Hitmonchan	TM
108	Lickitung	TM,E
109	Koffing	TM
110	Weezing	TM
111	Rhyhorn	TM
112	Rhydon	TM
113	Chansey	TM,E
114	Tangela	TM
115	Kangaskhan	TM,E
116	Horsea	TM
117	Seadra	TM
118	Goldeen	TM
119	Seaking	TM
120	Staryu	TM
121	Starmie	TM
122	Mr. Mime	29,TM
123	Scyther	TM
124	Jynx	TM
125	Electabuzz	TM

Substitute continued

No.	Pokémon		No.	Pokémon		No.	Pokémon		No.	Pokémon	
126	Magmar	TM	228	Houndour	TM	331	Cacnea	TM	430	Honchkrow	TM
127	Pinsir	TM	229	Houndoom	TM	332	Cacturne	TM	431	Glameow	TM
128	Tauros	TM	230	Kingdra	TM	333	Swablu	TM	432	Purugly	TM
130	Gyarados	TM	231	Phanpy	TM	334	Altaria	TM	433	Chingling	TM
131	Lapras	TM,E	232	Donphan	TM	335	Zangoose	TM	434	Stunky	TM
133	Eevee	TM	233	Porygon2	TM	336	Seviper	TM	435	Skuntank	TM
134	Vaporeon	TM	234	Stantler	TM	337	Lunatone	TM	436	Bronzor	TM
135	Jolteon	TM	236	Tyrogue	TM	338	Solrock	TM	437	Bronzong	TM
136	Flareon	TM	237	Hitmontop	TM	339	Barboach	TM	438	Bonsly	TM
137	Porygon	TM	238	Smoochum	TM	340	Whiscash	TM	439	Mime Jr.	29,TM
138	Omanyte	TM	239	Elekid	TM	341	Corphish	TM	440	Happiny	TM,E
139	Omastar	TM	240	Magby	TM	342	Crawdaunt	TM	441	Chatot	TM
140	Kabuto	TM	241	Miltank	TM	343	Baltoy	TM	442	Spiritomb	TM
141	Kabutops	TM	242	Blissey	TM	344	Claydol	TM	443	Gible	TM
142	Aerodactyl	TM	243	Raikou	TM	345	Lileep	TM	444	Gabite	TM
143	Snorlax	TM,E	244	Entei	TM	346	Cradily	TM	445	Garchomp	TM
144	Articuno	TM	245	Suicune	TM	347	Anorith	TM	446	Munchlax	TM,E
145	Zapdos	TM	246	Larvitar	TM	348	Armaldo	TM	447	Riolu	TM
146	Moltres	TM	247	Pupitar	TM	349	Feebas	TM	448	Lucario	TM
147	Dratini	TM	248	Tyranitar	TM	350	Milotic	TM	449	Hippopotas	TM
148	Dragonair	TM	249	Lugia	TM	351	Castform	TM	450	Hippowdon	TM
149	Dragonite	TM	250	Ho-Oh	TM	352	Kecleon	37,TM	451	Skorupi	TM
150	Mewtwo	TM	251	Celebi	TM	353	Shuppet	TM	452	Drapion	TM
151	Mew	TM	252	Treecko	TM	354	Banette	TM	453	Croagunk	TM
152	Chikorita	TM	253	Grovyle	TM	355	Duskull	TM	454	Toxicroak	TM
153	Bayleef	TM	254	Sceptile	TM	356	Dusclops	TM	455	Carnivine	TM
154	Meganium	TM	255	Torchic	TM	357	Tropius	TM	456	Finneon	TM
155	Cyndaquil	TM	256	Combusken	TM	358	Chimecho	TM	457	Lumineon	TM
156	Quilava	TM	257	Blaziken	TM	359	Absol	TM,E	458	Mantyke	TM
157	Typhlosion	TM	258	Mudkip	TM	361	Snorunt	TM	459	Snover	TM
158	Totodile	TM	259	Marshtomp	TM	362	Glalie	TM	460	Abomasnow	TM
159	Croconaw	TM	260	Swampert	TM	363	Spheal	TM	461	Weavile	TM
160	Feraligatr	TM	261	Poochyena	TM	364	Sealeo	TM	462	Magnezone	TM
161	Sentret	TM,E	262	Mightyena	TM	365	Walrein	TM	463	Lickilicky	TM
162	Furret	TM	263	Zigzagoon	TM,E	366	Clamperl	TM	464	Rhyperior	TM
163	Hoothoot	TM	264	Linoone	TM	367	Huntail	TM	465	Tangrowth	TM
164	Noctowl	TM	267	Beautifly	TM	368	Gorebyss	TM	466	Electivire	TM
165	Ledyba	TM	269	Dustox	TM	369	Relicanth	TM	467	Magmortar	TM
166	Ledian	TM	270	Lotad	TM	370	Luvdisc	TM	468	Togekiss	TM
167	Spinarak	TM	271	Lombre	TM	371	Bagon	TM	469	Yanmega	TM
168	Ariados	TM	272	Ludicolo	TM	372	Shelgon	TM	470	Leafeon	TM
169	Crobat	TM	273	Seedot	TM	373	Salamence	TM	471	Glaceon	TM
170	Chinchou	TM	274	Nuzleaf	TM	375	Metang	TM	472	Gliscor	TM
171	Lanturn	TM	275	Shiftry	TM	376	Metagross	TM	473	Mamoswine	TM
172	Pichu	TM	276	Taillow	TM	377	Regirock	TM	474	Porygon-Z	TM
173	Cleffa	TM,E	277	Swellow	TM	378	Regice	TM	475	Gallade	TM
174	Igglybuff	TM	278	Wingull	TM	379	Registeel	TM	476	Probopass	TM
175	Togepi	TM,E	279	Pelipper	TM	380	Latias	TM	477	Dusknoir	TM
176	Togetic	TM	280	Ralts	TM	381	Latios	TM	478	Froslass	TM
177	Natu	TM	281	Kirlia	TM	382	Kyogre	TM	479	Rotom	36,TM
178	Xatu	TM	282	Gardevoir	TM	383	Groudon	TM	480	Uxie	TM
179	Mareep	TM	283	Surskit	TM	384	Rayquaza	TM	481	Mesprit	TM
180	Flaaffy	TM	284	Masquerain	TM	385	Jirachi	TM	482	Azelf	TM
181	Ampharos	TM	285	Shroomish	TM	386	Deoxys (N)	TM	483	Dialga	TM
182	Bellossom	TM	286	Breloom	TM	386	Deoxys (A)	TM	484	Palkia	TM
183	Marill	TM,E	287	Slakoth	TM	386	Deoxys (D)	TM	485	Heatran	TM
184	Azumarill	TM	288	Vigoroth	TM	386	Deoxys (S)	TM	486	Regigigas	TM
185	Sudowoodo	TM	289	Slaking	TM	387	Turtwig	TM	487	Giratina (A)	TM
186	Politoed	TM	290	Nincada	TM	388	Grotle	TM	487	Giratina (O)	TM
187	Hoppip	TM	291	Ninjask	TM	389	Torterra	TM	488	Cresselia	TM
188	Skiploom	TM	292	Shedinja	TM	390	Chimchar	TM	489	Phione	TM
189	Jumpluff	TM	293	Whismur	TM	391	Monferno	TM	490	Manaphy	TM
190	Aipom	TM	294	Loudred	TM	392	Infernape	TM	491	Darkrai	TM
191	Sunkern	TM	295	Exploud	TM	393	Piplup	TM	492	Shaymin (L)	TM
192	Sunflora	TM	296	Makuhita	TM	394	Prinplup	TM	492	Shaymin (S)	TM
193	Yanma	TM	297	Hariyama	TM	395	Empoleon	TM			
194	Wooper	TM	298	Azurill	TM	396	Starly	TM			
195	Quagsire	TM	299	Nosepass	TM	397	Staravia	TM			
196	Espeon	TM	300	Skitty	TM,E	398	Staraptor	TM			
197	Umbreon	TM	301	Delcatty	TM	399	Bidoof	TM			
198	Murkrow	TM	302	Sableye	TM	400	Bibarel	TM			
199	Slowking	TM	303	Mawile	TM	402	Kricketune	TM			
200	Misdreavus	TM	304	Aron	TM	403	Shinx	TM			
203	Girafarig	TM	305	Lairon	TM	404	Luxio	TM			
204	Pineco	TM	306	Aggron	TM	405	Luxray	TM			
205	Forretress	TM	307	Meditite	TM	406	Budew	TM			
206	Dunsparce	TM	308	Medicham	TM	407	Roserade	TM			
207	Gligar	TM	309	Electrike	TM	408	Cranidos	TM			
208	Steelix	TM	310	Manectric	TM	409	Rampardos	TM			
209	Snubbull	TM	311	Plusle	TM,E	410	Shieldon	TM			
210	Granbull	TM	312	Minun	TM,E	411	Bastiodon	TM			
211	Qwilfish	TM	313	Volbeat	TM	413	Wormadam (P)	TM			
212	Scizor	TM	314	Illumise	TM	413	Wormadam (S)	TM			
213	Shuckle	TM	315	Roselia	TM	413	Wormadam (T)	TM			
214	Heracross	TM	316	Gulpin	TM	414	Mothim	TM			
215	Sneasel	TM	317	Swalot	TM	416	Vespiquen	TM			
216	Teddiursa	TM	318	Carvanha	TM	417	Pachirisu	TM			
217	Ursaring	TM	319	Sharpedo	TM	418	Buizel	TM			
218	Slugma	TM	320	Wailmer	TM	419	Floatzel	TM			
219	Magcargo	TM	321	Wailord	TM	420	Cherubi	TM			
220	Swinub	TM	322	Numel	TM	421	Cherrim	TM			
221	Piloswine	TM	323	Camerupt	TM	422	Shellos	TM			
222	Corsola	TM	324	Torkoal	TM	423	Gastrodon	TM			
223	Remoraid	TM	325	Spoink	TM,E	424	Ambipom	TM			
224	Octillery	TM	326	Grumpig	TM	425	Drifloon	TM			
225	Delibird	TM	327	Spinda	TM	426	Drifblim	TM			
226	Mantine	TM	328	Trapinch	TM	427	Buneary	TM			
227	Skarmory	TM	329	Vibrava	TM	428	Lopunny	TM			
			330	Flygon	TM	429	Mismagius	TM			

Sucker Punch

No.	Pokémon		No.	Pokémon	
19	Rattata	19,T	200	Misdreavus	T,E
20	Raticate	19,T	203	Girafarig	T
32	Nidoran♂	T,E	222	Corsola	T
33	Nidorino	T	228	Houndour	T
34	Nidoking	T	229	Houndoom	T
50	Diglett	23,T	234	Stantler	T
51	Dugtrio	23,T	237	Hitmontop	T
69	Bellsprout	T	251	Celebi	T
70	Weepinbell	T	261	Poochyena	49,T,E
71	Victreebel	T	262	Mightyena	62,T
74	Geodude	T	275	Shiftry	T
75	Graveler	T	287	Slakoth	T
76	Golem	T	288	Vigoroth	T
92	Gastly	22,T	289	Slaking	T
93	Haunter	22,T	292	Shedinja	T
94	Gengar	22,T	300	Skitty	T,E
100	Voltorb	T	301	Delcatty	T
101	Electrode	T	302	Sableye	T
106	Hitmonlee	T	303	Mawile	46,T,E
115	Kangaskhan	46,T	327	Spinda	32,T
151	Mew	T	331	Cacnea	37,T
161	Sentret	31,T	332	Cacturne	41,T
162	Furret	36,T	336	Seviper	T
167	Spinarak	26,T	352	Kecleon	43,T
168	Ariados	28,T	353	Shuppet	35,T
170	Chinchou	T	354	Banette	35,T
171	Lanturn	T	355	Duskull	T
177	Natu	T,E	356	Dusclops	T
178	Xatu	T	359	Absol	44,T,E
185	Sudowoodo	41,T	367	Huntail	T
197	Umbreon	T	380	Latias	T
198	Murkrow	45,T	413	Wormadam (P)	T
			413	Wormadam (S)	T
			413	Wormadam (T)	T
			425	Drifloon	T
			426	Drifblim	T
			429	Mismagius	T
			430	Honchkrow	T
			431	Glameow	41,T
			432	Purugly	T
			434	Stunky	T
			435	Skuntank	T
			438	Bonsly	41,T
			442	Spiritomb	31,T
			453	Croagunk	31,T
			454	Toxicroak	31,T
			477	Dusknoir	T
			478	Froslass	T
			479	Rotom	T
			491	Darkrai	T

Sunny Day

No.	Pokémon		No.	Pokémon		No.	Pokémon	
1	Bulbasaur		59	Arcanine	TM	203	Girafarig	TM
2	Ivysaur	TM	63	Abra	TM	204	Pineco	TM
3	Venusaur	TM	64	Kadabra	TM	205	Forretress	TM
4	Charmander	TM	65	Alakazam	TM	206	Dunsparce	TM
5	Charmeleon	TM	66	Machop	TM	207	Gligar	TM
6	Charizard	TM	67	Machoke	TM	208	Steelix	TM
12	Butterfree	TM	68	Machamp	TM	209	Snubbull	TM
15	Beedrill	TM	69	Bellsprout	TM	210	Granbull	TM
16	Pidgey	TM	70	Weepinbell	TM	212	Scizor	TM
17	Pidgeotto	TM	71	Victreebel	TM	213	Shuckle	TM
18	Pidgeot	TM	74	Geodude	TM	214	Heracross	TM
20	Rattata	TM	75	Graveler	TM	215	Sneasel	TM
21	Spearow	TM	76	Golem	TM	216	Teddiursa	TM
22	Fearow	TM	77	Ponyta	TM	217	Ursaring	TM
23	Ekans	TM	78	Rapidash	TM	218	Slugma	TM
24	Arbok	TM	79	Slowpoke	TM	219	Magcargo	TM
27	Sandshrew	TM	80	Slowbro	TM	222	Corsola	TM
28	Sandslash	TM	81	Magnemite	TM	223	Remoraid	TM
29	Nidoran♀	TM	82	Magneton	TM	224	Octillery	TM
30	Nidorina	TM	83	Farfetch'd	TM	227	Skarmory	TM
31	Nidoqueen	TM	84	Doduo	TM	228	Houndour	TM
32	Nidoran♂	TM	85	Dodrio	TM	229	Houndoom	TM
33	Nidorino	TM	88	Grimer	TM	231	Phanpy	TM
34	Nidoking	TM	89	Muk	TM	232	Donphan	TM
35	Clefairy	TM	92	Gastly	TM	233	Porygon2	TM
36	Clefable	TM	93	Haunter	TM	234	Stantler	TM
37	Vulpix	TM	94	Gengar	TM	236	Tyrogue	TM
38	Ninetales	TM	95	Onix	TM	237	Hitmontop	TM
39	Jigglypuff	TM	96	Drowzee	TM	240	Magby	43,TM
40	Wigglytuff	TM	97	Hypno	TM	241	Miltank	TM
41	Zubat	TM	102	Exeggcute	TM	242	Blissey	TM
42	Golbat	TM	103	Exeggutor	TM	243	Raikou	TM
43	Oddish	TM	104	Cubone	TM	244	Entei	TM
44	Gloom	TM	105	Marowak	TM	245	Suicune	TM
45	Vileplume	TM	106	Hitmonlee	TM	246	Larvitar	TM
46	Paras	TM	107	Hitmonchan	TM	247	Pupitar	TM
47	Parasect	TM	108	Lickitung	TM	248	Tyranitar	TM
48	Venonat	TM	109	Koffing	TM	249	Lugia	TM
49	Venomoth	TM	110	Weezing	TM	250	Ho-Oh	37,TM
50	Diglett	TM	111	Rhyhorn	TM	251	Celebi	TM
51	Dugtrio	TM	112	Rhydon	TM	252	Treecko	TM
52	Meowth	TM	113	Chansey	TM	253	Grovyle	TM
53	Persian	TM	114	Tangela	TM	254	Sceptile	TM
54	Mankey	TM	115	Kangaskhan	TM	255	Torchic	TM
56	Primeape	TM	122	Mr. Mime	TM	256	Combusken	TM
58	Growlithe	TM	123	Scyther	TM	257	Blaziken	TM
			126	Magmar	49,TM	261	Poochyena	TM
			127	Pinsir	TM	262	Mightyena	TM
			128	Tauros	TM	263	Zigzagoon	TM
			133	Eevee	TM	264	Linoone	TM
			134	Vaporeon	TM	267	Beautifly	TM
			135	Jolteon	TM	269	Dustox	TM
			136	Flareon	TM	270	Lotad	TM
			137	Porygon	TM	271	Lombre	TM
			142	Aerodactyl	TM	272	Ludicolo	TM
			143	Snorlax	TM	273	Seedot	31,TM
			144	Articuno	TM	274	Nuzleaf	TM
			145	Zapdos	TM	275	Shiftry	TM
			146	Moltres	85,TM	276	Taillow	TM
			147	Dratini	TM	277	Swellow	TM
			148	Dragonair	TM	280	Ralts	TM
			149	Dragonite	TM	281	Kirlia	TM
			150	Mewtwo	TM	282	Gardevoir	TM
			151	Mew	TM	283	Surskit	TM
			152	Chikorita	TM	284	Masquerain	TM
			153	Bayleef	TM	285	Shroomish	TM
			154	Meganium	TM	286	Breloom	TM
			155	Cyndaquil	TM	287	Slakoth	TM
			156	Quilava	TM	288	Vigoroth	TM
			157	Typhlosion	TM	289	Slaking	TM
			161	Sentret	TM	290	Nincada	TM
			162	Furret	TM	291	Ninjask	TM
			163	Hoothoot	TM	292	Shedinja	TM
			164	Noctowl	TM	293	Whismur	TM
			165	Ledyba	TM	294	Loudred	TM
			166	Ledian	TM	295	Exploud	TM
			167	Spinarak	TM	296	Makuhita	TM
			168	Ariados	TM	297	Hariyama	TM
			169	Crobat	TM	299	Nosepass	TM
			173	Cleffa	TM	300	Skitty	TM
			174	Igglybuff	TM	301	Delcatty	TM
			175	Togepi	TM	302	Sableye	TM
			176	Togetic	TM	303	Mawile	TM
			177	Natu	TM	304	Aron	TM
			178	Xatu	TM	305	Lairon	TM
			182	Bellossom	B,TM	306	Aggron	TM
			185	Sudowoodo	TM	307	Meditite	TM
			187	Hoppip	TM	308	Medicham	TM
			188	Skiploom	TM	313	Volbeat	TM
			189	Jumpluff	TM	314	Illumise	TM
			190	Aipom	TM	315	Roselia	TM
			191	Sunkern	37,TM	316	Gulpin	TM
			192	Sunflora	37,TM	317	Swalot	TM
			193	Yanma	TM	322	Numel	TM
			196	Espeon	TM	323	Camerupt	TM
			197	Umbreon	TM	324	Torkoal	TM
			198	Murkrow	TM	325	Spoink	TM
			199	Slowking	TM	326	Grumpig	TM
			200	Misdreavus	TM	327	Spinda	TM

328	Trapinch	TM
329	Vibrava	TM
330	Flygon	TM
331	Cacnea	TM
332	Cacturne	TM
333	Swablu	TM
334	Altaria	TM
335	Zangoose	TM
336	Seviper	TM
338	Solrock	TM
343	Baltoy	TM
344	Claydol	TM
345	Lileep	TM
346	Cradily	TM
347	Anorith	TM
348	Armaldo	TM
351	Castform	20,TM
352	Kecleon	TM
353	Shuppet	TM
354	Banette	TM
355	Duskull	TM
356	Dusclops	TM
357	Tropius	TM
358	Chimecho	TM
359	Absol	TM
371	Bagon	TM
372	Shelgon	TM
373	Salamence	TM
375	Metang	TM
376	Metagross	TM
377	Regirock	TM
379	Registeel	TM
380	Latias	TM
381	Latios	TM
383	Groudon	TM
384	Rayquaza	TM
385	Jirachi	TM
386	Deoxys (N)	TM
386	Deoxys (A)	TM
386	Deoxys (D)	TM
386	Deoxys (S)	TM
387	Turtwig	TM
388	Grotle	TM
389	Torterra	TM
390	Chimchar	TM
391	Monferno	TM
392	Infernape	TM
396	Starly	TM
397	Staravia	TM
398	Staraptor	TM
399	Bidoof	TM
400	Bibarel	TM
402	Kricketune	TM
406	Budew	TM
407	Roserade	TM
408	Cranidos	TM
409	Rampardos	TM
410	Shieldon	TM
411	Bastiodon	TM
413	Wormadam (P)	TM
413	Wormadam (S)	TM
413	Wormadam (T)	TM
414	Mothim	TM
416	Vespiquen	TM
420	Cherubi	22,TM
421	Cherrim	22,TM
424	Ambipom	TM
425	Drifloon	TM
426	Drifblim	TM
427	Buneary	TM
428	Lopunny	TM
429	Mismagius	TM
430	Honchkrow	TM
431	Glameow	TM
432	Purugly	TM
433	Chingling	TM
434	Stunky	TM
435	Skuntank	TM
436	Bronzor	TM
437	Bronzong	B,TM
438	Bonsly	TM
439	Mime Jr.	TM
440	Happiny	TM
441	Chatot	TM
442	Spiritomb	TM
443	Gible	TM
444	Gabite	TM
445	Garchomp	TM
446	Munchlax	TM
447	Riolu	TM
448	Lucario	TM
449	Hippopotas	TM
450	Hippowdon	TM
451	Skorupi	TM
452	Drapion	TM
453	Croagunk	TM
454	Toxicroak	TM
455	Carnivine	TM
461	Weavile	TM
462	Magnezone	TM
463	Lickilicky	TM
464	Rhyperior	TM
465	Tangrowth	TM
467	Magmortar	52,TM
468	Togekiss	TM
469	Yanmega	TM
470	Leafeon	64,TM
471	Glaceon	TM
472	Gliscor	TM
474	Porygon-Z	TM
475	Gallade	TM
476	Probopass	TM
477	Dusknoir	TM
479	Rotom	TM
480	Uxie	TM
481	Mesprit	TM
482	Azelf	TM
483	Dialga	TM
484	Palkia	TM
485	Heatran	TM
486	Regigigas	TM
487	Giratina (A)	TM
487	Giratina (O)	TM
488	Cresselia	TM
491	Darkrai	TM
492	Shaymin (L)	TM
492	Shaymin (S)	TM

Super Fang		
19	Rattata	28
20	Raticate	34
399	Bidoof	37
400	Bibarel	43
417	Pachirisu	33

Superpower		
31	Nidoqueen	58,T
34	Nidoking	T
66	Machop	T
67	Machoke	T
68	Machamp	T
74	Geodude	T
75	Graveler	T
76	Golem	T
98	Krabby	T
99	Kingler	T
106	Hitmonlee	T
111	Rhyhorn	T
112	Rhydon	T
127	Pinsir	52,T
136	Flareon	T
141	Kabutops	T
143	Snorlax	T
149	Dragonite	T
151	Mew	T
158	Totodile	43,T
159	Croconaw	51,T
160	Feraligatr	63,T
183	Marill	T,E
184	Azumarill	T
209	Snubbull	T
210	Granbull	T
212	Scizor	T
216	Teddiursa	T
217	Ursaring	T
220	Swinub	T
221	Piloswine	T
231	Phanpy	T
232	Donphan	T
246	Larvitar	T
247	Pupitar	T
248	Tyranitar	T
257	Blaziken	T
258	Mudkip	T
259	Marshtomp	T
260	Swampert	T
286	Breloom	T
296	Makuhita	T
297	Hariyama	T
304	Aron	T
305	Lairon	T
306	Aggron	T
332	Cacturne	T
341	Corphish	T,E
342	Crawdaunt	T
348	Armaldo	T
359	Absol	T
377	Regirock	25,T
378	Regice	25,T
379	Registeel	25,T
386	Deoxys (A)	49,T
387	Turtwig	T,E
388	Grotle	T
389	Torterra	T
399	Bidoof	41,T
400	Bibarel	48,T
405	Luxray	T
408	Cranidos	T
409	Rampardos	T
430	Honchkrow	T
446	Munchlax	T
449	Hippopotas	T
450	Hippowdon	T
464	Rhyperior	T
473	Mamoswine	T
486	Regigigas	T

Supersonic		
12	Butterfree	18
29	Nidoran♀	E
32	Nidoran♂	E
41	Zubat	5
42	Golbat	B,5
48	Venonat	5
49	Venomoth	B,5
72	Tentacool	5
73	Tentacruel	B,5
81	Magnemite	11
82	Magneton	B,11
84	Doduo	E
90	Shellder	8
91	Cloyster	B
108	Lickitung	5
118	Goldeen	7
119	Seaking	B,7
138	Omanyte	E
142	Aerodactyl	B
147	Dratini	E
163	Hoothoot	E
165	Ledyba	6
166	Ledian	B,6
169	Crobat	B,5
170	Chinchou	B
171	Lanturn	B
183	Marill	E
193	Yanma	22
211	Qwilfish	E
223	Remoraid	E
226	Mantine	B,4
276	Taillow	E
278	Wingull	6
279	Pelipper	6
293	Whismur	21
294	Loudred	23
295	Exploud	23
329	Vibrava	33
330	Flygon	33
366	Clamperl	E
370	Luvdisc	E
393	Piplup	E
441	Chatot	E
458	Mantyke	4
462	Magnezone	B,11
463	Lickilicky	5
469	Yanmega	22
489	Phione	16
490	Manaphy	16

Surf		
7	Squirtle	HM
8	Wartortle	HM
9	Blastoise	HM
31	Nidoqueen	HM
34	Nidoking	HM
54	Psyduck	HM
55	Golduck	HM
60	Poliwag	HM
61	Poliwhirl	HM
62	Poliwrath	HM
72	Tentacool	HM
73	Tentacruel	HM
79	Slowpoke	HM
80	Slowbro	HM
86	Seel	HM
87	Dewgong	HM
90	Shellder	HM
91	Cloyster	HM
98	Krabby	HM
99	Kingler	HM
108	Lickitung	HM
112	Rhydon	HM
115	Kangaskhan	HM
116	Horsea	HM
117	Seadra	HM
118	Goldeen	HM
119	Seaking	HM
120	Staryu	HM
121	Starmie	HM
128	Tauros	HM
130	Gyarados	HM
131	Lapras	HM
134	Vaporeon	HM
138	Omanyte	HM
139	Omastar	HM
140	Kabuto	HM
141	Kabutops	HM
143	Snorlax	HM
147	Dratini	HM
148	Dragonair	HM
149	Dragonite	HM
151	Mew	HM
158	Totodile	HM
159	Croconaw	HM
160	Feraligatr	HM
161	Sentret	HM
162	Furret	HM
170	Chinchou	HM
171	Lanturn	HM
183	Marill	HM
184	Azumarill	HM
186	Politoed	HM
194	Wooper	HM
195	Quagsire	HM
199	Slowking	HM
211	Qwilfish	HM
215	Sneasel	HM
222	Corsola	HM
223	Remoraid	HM
224	Octillery	HM
226	Mantine	HM
230	Kingdra	HM
241	Miltank	HM
245	Suicune	HM
248	Tyranitar	HM
249	Lugia	HM
258	Mudkip	HM
259	Marshtomp	HM
260	Swampert	HM
263	Zigzagoon	HM
264	Linoone	HM
270	Lotad	HM
271	Lombre	HM
272	Ludicolo	HM
279	Pelipper	HM
295	Exploud	HM
296	Makuhita	HM
297	Hariyama	HM
298	Azurill	HM
306	Aggron	HM
318	Carvanha	HM
319	Sharpedo	HM
320	Wailmer	HM
321	Wailord	HM
339	Barboach	HM
340	Whiscash	HM
341	Corphish	HM
342	Crawdaunt	HM
349	Feebas	HM
350	Milotic	HM
363	Spheal	HM
364	Sealeo	HM
365	Walrein	HM
366	Clamperl	HM
367	Huntail	HM
368	Gorebyss	HM
369	Relicanth	HM
370	Luvdisc	HM
380	Latias	HM
381	Latios	HM
382	Kyogre	HM
384	Rayquaza	HM
393	Piplup	HM
394	Prinplup	HM
395	Empoleon	HM
400	Bibarel	HM
409	Rampardos	HM
418	Buizel	HM
419	Floatzel	HM
422	Shellos	HM
423	Gastrodon	HM
445	Garchomp	HM
446	Munchlax	HM
456	Finneon	HM
457	Lumineon	HM
458	Mantyke	HM
461	Weavile	HM
463	Lickilicky	HM
464	Rhyperior	HM
484	Palkia	HM
489	Phione	HM
490	Manaphy	HM

Swagger		
1	Bulbasaur	TM
2	Ivysaur	TM
3	Venusaur	TM
4	Charmander	TM
5	Charmeleon	TM
6	Charizard	TM
7	Squirtle	TM
8	Wartortle	TM
9	Blastoise	TM
12	Butterfree	TM
15	Beedrill	TM
16	Pidgey	TM
17	Pidgeotto	TM
18	Pidgeot	TM
19	Rattata	TM,E
20	Raticate	TM
21	Spearow	TM
22	Fearow	TM
23	Ekans	TM
24	Arbok	TM
25	Pikachu	TM
26	Raichu	TM
27	Sandshrew	TM
28	Sandslash	TM
29	Nidoran♀	TM
30	Nidorina	TM
31	Nidoqueen	TM
32	Nidoran♂	TM
33	Nidorino	TM
34	Nidoking	TM
35	Clefairy	TM
36	Clefable	TM
37	Vulpix	TM
38	Ninetales	TM
39	Jigglypuff	TM
40	Wigglytuff	TM
41	Zubat	TM
42	Golbat	TM
43	Oddish	TM
44	Gloom	TM
45	Vileplume	TM
46	Paras	TM
47	Parasect	TM
48	Venonat	TM
49	Venomoth	TM
50	Diglett	TM
51	Dugtrio	TM
52	Meowth	TM
53	Persian	TM
54	Psyduck	TM
55	Golduck	TM
56	Mankey	33,TM
57	Primeape	35,TM
58	Growlithe	TM
59	Arcanine	TM
60	Poliwag	TM
61	Poliwhirl	TM
62	Poliwrath	TM
63	Abra	TM
64	Kadabra	TM
65	Alakazam	TM
66	Machop	TM
67	Machoke	TM
68	Machamp	TM
69	Bellsprout	TM
70	Weepinbell	TM
71	Victreebel	TM
72	Tentacool	TM
73	Tentacruel	TM
74	Geodude	TM
75	Graveler	TM
76	Golem	TM
77	Ponyta	TM
78	Rapidash	TM
79	Slowpoke	TM
80	Slowbro	TM
81	Magnemite	TM
82	Magneton	TM
83	Farfetch'd	TM
84	Doduo	TM
85	Dodrio	TM
86	Seel	TM
87	Dewgong	TM
88	Grimer	TM
89	Muk	TM
90	Shellder	TM
91	Cloyster	TM
92	Gastly	TM
93	Haunter	TM
94	Gengar	TM
95	Onix	TM
96	Drowzee	37,TM
97	Hypno	45,TM
98	Krabby	TM
99	Kingler	TM
100	Voltorb	TM
101	Electrode	TM
102	Exeggcute	TM
103	Exeggutor	TM
104	Cubone	TM
105	Marowak	TM
106	Hitmonlee	TM
107	Hitmonchan	TM
108	Lickitung	TM
109	Koffing	TM
110	Weezing	TM
111	Rhyhorn	TM
112	Rhydon	TM
113	Chansey	TM
114	Tangela	TM
115	Kangaskhan	TM
116	Horsea	TM
117	Seadra	TM
118	Goldeen	TM
119	Seaking	TM
120	Staryu	TM
121	Starmie	TM
122	Mr. Mime	TM
123	Scyther	TM
124	Jynx	TM
125	Electabuzz	TM
126	Magmar	TM
127	Pinsir	TM
128	Tauros	41,TM
130	Gyarados	TM
131	Lapras	TM
133	Eevee	TM
134	Vaporeon	TM
135	Jolteon	TM
136	Flareon	TM
137	Porygon	TM
138	Omanyte	TM
139	Omastar	TM
140	Kabuto	TM
141	Kabutops	TM
142	Aerodactyl	TM
143	Snorlax	TM
144	Articuno	TM
145	Zapdos	TM
146	Moltres	TM
147	Dratini	TM
148	Dragonair	TM
149	Dragonite	TM
150	Mewtwo	TM
151	Mew	TM
152	Chikorita	TM
153	Bayleef	TM
154	Meganium	TM
155	Cyndaquil	TM
156	Quilava	TM
157	Typhlosion	TM
158	Totodile	TM
159	Croconaw	TM
160	Feraligatr	TM
161	Sentret	TM
162	Furret	TM
163	Hoothoot	TM
164	Noctowl	TM
165	Ledyba	TM
166	Ledian	TM
167	Spinarak	TM
168	Ariados	TM
169	Crobat	TM
170	Chinchou	TM
171	Lanturn	TM
172	Pichu	TM
173	Cleffa	TM
174	Igglybuff	TM
175	Togepi	TM
176	Togetic	TM
177	Natu	TM
178	Xatu	TM
179	Mareep	TM
180	Flaaffy	TM
181	Ampharos	TM
182	Bellossom	TM
183	Marill	TM
184	Azumarill	TM
185	Sudowoodo	TM
186	Politoed	27,TM
187	Hoppip	TM
188	Skiploom	TM
189	Jumpluff	TM
190	Aipom	TM
191	Sunkern	TM
192	Sunflora	TM
193	Yanma	TM
194	Wooper	TM
195	Quagsire	TM
196	Espeon	TM
197	Umbreon	TM
198	Murkrow	TM
199	Slowking	43,TM
200	Misdreavus	TM
203	Girafarig	TM
204	Pineco	TM
205	Forretress	TM
206	Dunsparce	TM
207	Gligar	TM
208	Steelix	TM
209	Snubbull	TM
210	Granbull	TM
211	Qwilfish	TM
212	Scizor	TM
213	Shuckle	TM
214	Heracross	TM
215	Sneasel	TM
216	Teddiursa	TM
217	Ursaring	TM
218	Slugma	TM
219	Magcargo	TM
220	Swinub	TM
221	Piloswine	TM
222	Corsola	TM
223	Remoraid	TM
224	Octillery	TM
225	Delibird	TM
226	Mantine	TM
227	Skarmory	TM
228	Houndour	TM
229	Houndoom	TM
230	Kingdra	TM
231	Phanpy	TM
232	Donphan	TM
233	Porygon2	TM
234	Stantler	TM,E
236	Tyrogue	TM
237	Hitmontop	TM
238	Smoochum	TM
239	Elekid	TM
240	Magby	TM
241	Miltank	TM
242	Blissey	TM
243	Raikou	TM
244	Entei	43,TM
245	Suicune	TM
246	Larvitar	TM
247	Pupitar	TM
248	Tyranitar	TM
249	Lugia	TM
250	Ho-Oh	TM
251	Celebi	TM
252	Treecko	TM
253	Grovyle	TM
254	Sceptile	TM
255	Torchic	TM,E
256	Combusken	TM
257	Blaziken	TM
258	Mudkip	TM
259	Marshtomp	TM
260	Swampert	TM
261	Poochyena	25,TM
262	Mightyena	27,TM
263	Zigzagoon	TM
264	Linoone	TM
267	Beautifly	TM
269	Dustox	TM
270	Lotad	TM
271	Lombre	TM
272	Ludicolo	TM
273	Seedot	TM
274	Nuzleaf	43,TM
275	Shiftry	TM
276	Taillow	TM
277	Swellow	TM
278	Wingull	TM
279	Pelipper	TM
280	Ralts	TM
281	Kirlia	TM
282	Gardevoir	TM
283	Surskit	TM
284	Masquerain	TM
285	Shroomish	TM,E
286	Breloom	TM
287	Slakoth	TM
288	Vigoroth	TM
289	Slaking	36,TM
290	Nincada	TM
291	Ninjask	TM
292	Shedinja	TM
293	Whismur	TM,E
294	Loudred	TM
295	Exploud	TM
296	Makuhita	TM
297	Hariyama	TM
298	Azurill	TM
299	Nosepass	TM
300	Skitty	TM
301	Delcatty	TM
302	Sableye	TM
303	Mawile	TM
304	Aron	TM
305	Lairon	TM
306	Aggron	TM
307	Meditite	TM
308	Medicham	TM
309	Electrike	TM
310	Manectric	TM
311	Plusle	TM
312	Minun	TM
313	Volbeat	TM
314	Illumise	TM
315	Roselia	TM
316	Gulpin	TM
317	Swalot	TM
318	Carvanha	21,TM
319	Sharpedo	21,TM
320	Wailmer	TM,E
321	Wailord	TM
322	Numel	TM

Swagger continued		
323	Camerupt	TM
324	Torkoal	TM
325	Spoink	TM
326	Grumpig	TM
327	Spinda	TM
328	Trapinch	TM
329	Vibrava	TM
330	Flygon	TM
331	Cacnea	TM
332	Cacturne	TM
333	Swablu	TM
334	Altaria	TM
335	Zangoose	TM
336	Seviper	37,TM
337	Lunatone	TM
338	Solrock	TM
339	Barboach	TM
340	Whiscash	TM
341	Corphish	TM
342	Crawdaunt	TM
343	Baltoy	TM
344	Claydol	TM
345	Lileep	TM
346	Cradily	TM
347	Anorith	TM
348	Armaldo	TM
349	Feebas	TM
350	Milotic	TM
351	Castform	TM
352	Kecleon	TM
353	Shuppet	TM
354	Banette	TM
355	Duskull	TM
356	Dusclops	TM
357	Tropius	TM
358	Chimecho	TM
359	Absol	TM
361	Snorunt	TM
362	Glalie	TM
363	Spheal	TM
364	Sealeo	32,TM
365	Walrein	32,TM
366	Clamperl	TM
367	Huntail	TM
368	Gorebyss	TM
369	Relicanth	TM
370	Luvdisc	TM
371	Bagon	TM
372	Shelgon	TM
373	Salamence	TM
375	Metang	TM
376	Metagross	TM
377	Regirock	TM
378	Regice	TM
379	Registeel	TM
380	Latias	TM
381	Latios	TM
382	Kyogre	TM
383	Groudon	TM
384	Rayquaza	TM
385	Jirachi	TM
386	Deoxys (N)	TM
386	Deoxys (A)	TM
386	Deoxys (D)	TM
386	Deoxys (S)	TM
387	Turtwig	TM
388	Grotle	TM
389	Torterra	TM
390	Chimchar	TM
391	Monferno	TM
392	Infernape	TM
393	Piplup	TM
394	Prinplup	TM
395	Empoleon	24,TM
396	Starly	TM
397	Staravia	TM
398	Staraptor	TM
399	Bidoof	TM
400	Bibarel	TM
402	Kricketune	TM
403	Shinx	25,TM
404	Luxio	28,TM
405	Luxray	28,TM
406	Budew	TM
407	Roserade	TM
408	Cranidos	TM
409	Rampardos	TM
410	Shieldon	24,TM
411	Bastiodon	24,TM
413	Wormadam (P)	TM
413	Wormadam (S)	TM
413	Wormadam (T)	TM
414	Mothim	TM
416	Vespiquen	39,TM
417	Pachirisu	TM
418	Buizel	TM
419	Floatzel	TM
420	Cherubi	TM
421	Cherrim	TM
422	Shellos	TM
423	Gastrodon	TM
424	Ambipom	TM
425	Drifloon	TM
426	Drifblim	TM
427	Buneary	TM
428	Lopunny	TM
429	Mismagius	TM
430	Honchkrow	25,TM
431	Glameow	TM
432	Purugly	38,TM
433	Chingling	TM
434	Stunky	TM
435	Skuntank	TM
436	Bronzor	TM
437	Bronzong	TM
438	Bonsly	TM
439	Mime Jr.	TM
440	Happiny	TM
441	Chatot	TM
442	Spiritomb	TM
443	Gible	TM
444	Gabite	TM
445	Garchomp	TM
446	Munchlax	TM
447	Riolu	TM
448	Lucario	TM
449	Hippopotas	TM
450	Hippowdon	TM
451	Skorupi	TM
452	Drapion	TM
453	Croagunk	24,TM
454	Toxicroak	24,TM
455	Carnivine	TM
456	Finneon	TM
457	Lumineon	TM
458	Mantyke	TM
459	Snover	17,TM
460	Abomasnow	17,TM
461	Weavile	TM
462	Magnezone	TM
463	Lickilicky	TM
464	Rhyperior	TM
465	Tangrowth	TM
466	Electivire	TM
467	Magmortar	TM
468	Togekiss	TM
469	Yanmega	TM
470	Leafeon	TM
471	Glaceon	TM
472	Gliscor	TM
473	Mamoswine	TM
474	Porygon-Z	TM
475	Gallade	TM
476	Probopass	TM
477	Dusknoir	TM
478	Froslass	TM
479	Rotom	TM
480	Uxie	TM
481	Mesprit	TM
482	Azelf	TM
483	Dialga	TM
484	Palkia	TM
485	Heatran	TM
486	Regigigas	TM
487	Giratina (A)	TM
487	Giratina (O)	TM
488	Cresselia	TM
489	Phione	TM
490	Manaphy	TM
491	Darkrai	TM
492	Shaymin (L)	TM
492	Shaymin (S)	TM

Swallow		
23	Ekans	25
24	Arbok	28
71	Victreebel	B
88	Grimer	E
171	Lanturn	27
194	Wooper	E
218	Slugma	E
279	Pelipper	38
303	Mawile	51
316	Gulpin	34
317	Swalot	38
336	Seviper	E
345	Lileep	57
346	Cradily	66
363	Spheal	E
422	Shellos	E
425	Drifloon	27
426	Drifblim	27
446	Munchlax	28
449	Hippopotas	E
455	Carnivine	31

Sweet Kiss		
172	Pichu	13
173	Cleffa	10
174	Igglybuff	13
175	Togepi	10
176	Togetic	B,10
238	Smoochum	8
311	Plusle	E
312	Minun	E
370	Luvdisc	27
417	Pachirisu	25
427	Buneary	E
440	Happiny	12
456	Finneon	E
492	Shaymin (L)	82
492	Shaymin (S)	82

Sweet Scent		
1	Bulbasaur	21
2	Ivysaur	23
3	Venusaur	23
43	Oddish	5
44	Gloom	B,5
46	Paras	E
69	Bellsprout	29
70	Weepinbell	29
71	Victreebel	B
152	Chikorita	28
153	Bayleef	32
154	Meganium	34
182	Bellossom	B
191	Sunkern	E
213	Shuckle	E
216	Teddiursa	22
217	Ursaring	22
270	Lotad	E
283	Surskit	13
284	Masquerain	B,13
303	Mawile	16
314	Illumise	5
315	Roselia	31
357	Tropius	21
407	Roserade	B
415	Combee	B
416	Vespiquen	B
420	Cherubi	E
455	Carnivine	17
492	Shaymin (L)	37
492	Shaymin (S)	37

Swift		
4	Charmander	T
5	Charmeleon	T
6	Charizard	T
12	Butterfree	T
15	Beedrill	T
16	Pidgey	T
17	Pidgeotto	T
18	Pidgeot	T
19	Rattata	T
20	Raticate	T
21	Spearow	T
22	Fearow	T
25	Pikachu	T
26	Raichu	T
27	Sandshrew	15,T
28	Sandslash	15,T
37	Vulpix	T
38	Ninetales	T
41	Zubat	T
42	Golbat	T
48	Venonat	T
49	Venomoth	T
52	Meowth	T
53	Persian	T
54	Psyduck	T
55	Golduck	T
56	Mankey	T
57	Primeape	T
58	Growlithe	T
59	Arcanine	T
77	Ponyta	T
78	Rapidash	T
79	Slowpoke	T
80	Slowbro	T
81	Magnemite	T
82	Magneton	T
83	Farfetch'd	T
84	Doduo	T
85	Dodrio	T
90	Shellder	T
91	Cloyster	T
100	Voltorb	33,T
101	Electrode	35,T
106	Hitmonlee	T
107	Hitmonchan	T
116	Horsea	T
117	Seadra	T
118	Goldeen	T
119	Seaking	T
120	Staryu	24,T
121	Starmie	B,T
123	Scyther	T
125	Electabuzz	16,T
133	Eevee	T
134	Vaporeon	T
135	Jolteon	T
136	Flareon	T
137	Porygon	T
142	Aerodactyl	T
144	Articuno	T
145	Zapdos	T
146	Moltres	T
147	Dratini	T
148	Dragonair	T
149	Dragonite	T
150	Mewtwo	15,T
151	Mew	T
155	Cyndaquil	28,T
156	Quilava	31,T
157	Typhlosion	31,T
161	Sentret	T
162	Furret	T
163	Hoothoot	T
164	Noctowl	T
165	Ledyba	33,T
166	Ledian	41,T
169	Crobat	T
172	Pichu	T
175	Togepi	T
176	Togetic	T
177	Natu	T
178	Xatu	T
179	Mareep	T
180	Flaaffy	T
181	Ampharos	T
183	Marill	T
184	Azumarill	T
190	Aipom	22,T
193	Yanma	T
196	Espeon	29,T
197	Umbreon	T
198	Murkrow	T
199	Slowking	T
200	Misdreavus	T
203	Girafarig	T
204	Pineco	E
207	Gligar	T
211	Qwilfish	T
212	Scizor	T
215	Sneasel	T
216	Teddiursa	T
217	Ursaring	T
223	Remoraid	T
224	Octillery	T
225	Delibird	T
226	Mantine	T
227	Skarmory	9,T
228	Houndour	T
229	Houndoom	T
230	Kingdra	T
233	Porygon2	T
234	Stantler	T
236	Tyrogue	T
237	Hitmontop	T
239	Elekid	16,T
243	Raikou	T
244	Entei	T
245	Suicune	T
249	Lugia	43,T
250	Ho-Oh	43,T
251	Celebi	T
252	Treecko	T
253	Grovyle	T
254	Sceptile	T
255	Torchic	T
256	Combusken	T
257	Blaziken	T
263	Zigzagoon	T
264	Linoone	T
267	Beautifly	T
269	Dustox	T
274	Nuzleaf	T
275	Shiftry	T
276	Taillow	T
277	Swellow	T
278	Wingull	T
279	Pelipper	T
280	Ralts	T
281	Kirlia	T
282	Gardevoir	T
283	Surskit	T
284	Masquerain	T
291	Ninjask	T
298	Azurill	T
300	Skitty	T
301	Delcatty	T
307	Meditite	T
308	Medicham	T
309	Electrike	T,E
310	Manectric	T
311	Plusle	29,T
312	Minun	29,T
313	Volbeat	T
314	Illumise	T
315	Roselia	T
318	Carvanha	T
319	Sharpedo	T
325	Spoink	T
326	Grumpig	T
327	Spinda	T
329	Vibrava	T
330	Flygon	T
333	Swablu	T
334	Altaria	T
335	Zangoose	T
336	Seviper	T
337	Lunatone	T
338	Solrock	T
342	Crawdaunt	30,T
349	Feebas	T
350	Milotic	T
351	Castform	T
352	Kecleon	T
359	Absol	T
367	Huntail	T
368	Gorebyss	T
370	Luvdisc	T
373	Salamence	T
375	Metang	T
376	Metagross	T
380	Latias	T
381	Latios	T
382	Kyogre	T
383	Groudon	T
384	Rayquaza	T
385	Jirachi	10,T
386	Deoxys (N)	T
386	Deoxys (S)	49,T
390	Chimchar	T
391	Monferno	T
392	Infernape	T
396	Starly	T
397	Staravia	T
398	Staraptor	T
399	Bidoof	T
400	Bibarel	T
403	Shinx	T
404	Luxio	T
405	Luxray	T
406	Budew	T
407	Roserade	T
414	Mothim	T
415	Combee	T
416	Vespiquen	T
417	Pachirisu	21,T
418	Buizel	15,T
419	Floatzel	15,T
424	Ambipom	22,T
425	Drifloon	T
426	Drifblim	T
427	Buneary	T
428	Lopunny	T
429	Mismagius	T
430	Honchkrow	T
431	Glameow	T
432	Purugly	T
433	Chingling	T
434	Stunky	T
435	Skuntank	T
441	Chatot	T
443	Gible	T
444	Gabite	T
445	Garchomp	T
447	Riolu	T
448	Lucario	T
456	Finneon	T
457	Lumineon	T
458	Mantyke	T
461	Weavile	T
462	Magnezone	T
466	Electivire	16,T
468	Togekiss	T
469	Yanmega	T
470	Leafeon	T
471	Glaceon	T
472	Gliscor	T
474	Porygon-Z	T
475	Gallade	T
479	Rotom	T
480	Uxie	21,T
481	Mesprit	21,T
482	Azelf	21,T
483	Dialga	T
484	Palkia	T
487	Giratina (A)	T
487	Giratina (O)	T
488	Cresselia	T
489	Phione	T
490	Manaphy	T
491	Darkrai	T
492	Shaymin (L)	T
492	Shaymin (S)	T

Switcheroo		
53	Persian	B
97	Hypno	B
264	Linoone	B
427	Buneary	E

Swords Dance		
1	Bulbasaur	TM
2	Ivysaur	TM
3	Venusaur	TM
4	Charmander	TM,E
5	Charmeleon	TM
6	Charizard	TM
15	Beedrill	TM
20	Raticate	B,TM
27	Sandshrew	TM,E
28	Sandslash	TM
43	Oddish	TM,E
44	Gloom	TM
45	Vileplume	TM
46	Paras	TM
47	Parasect	TM
69	Bellsprout	TM,E
70	Weepinbell	TM
71	Victreebel	TM
72	Tentacool	TM
73	Tentacruel	TM
83	Farfetch'd	25,TM
98	Krabby	TM,E
99	Kingler	TM
102	Exeggcute	TM
103	Exeggutor	TM
104	Cubone	TM,E
105	Marowak	TM
108	Lickitung	TM
111	Rhyhorn	TM,E
112	Rhydon	TM
114	Tangela	TM
123	Scyther	57,TM
127	Pinsir	38,TM
141	Kabutops	TM
151	Mew	TM
152	Chikorita	TM
153	Bayleef	TM
154	Meganium	TM
158	Totodile	TM
159	Croconaw	TM
160	Feraligatr	TM
165	Ledyba	TM
166	Ledian	TM
182	Bellossom	TM
187	Hoppip	TM
188	Skiploom	TM
189	Jumpluff	TM
191	Sunkern	TM
192	Sunflora	TM
207	Gligar	34,TM
212	Scizor	57,TM
214	Heracross	TM
215	Sneasel	TM
216	Teddiursa	TM
217	Ursaring	TM
227	Skarmory	TM
251	Celebi	TM
252	Treecko	TM
253	Grovyle	TM
254	Sceptile	TM
255	Torchic	TM
256	Combusken	TM
257	Blaziken	TM
270	Lotad	TM
271	Lombre	TM
272	Ludicolo	TM
273	Seedot	TM
274	Nuzleaf	TM
275	Shiftry	TM
285	Shroomish	TM
286	Breloom	TM
291	Ninjask	25,TM
303	Mawile	TM,E
315	Roselia	TM
331	Cacnea	TM
332	Cacturne	TM
335	Zangoose	9,TM
341	Corphish	44,TM
342	Crawdaunt	52,TM
345	Lileep	TM
346	Cradily	TM
347	Anorith	TM,E
348	Armaldo	TM
357	Tropius	TM
359	Absol	25,TM
383	Groudon	TM
384	Rayquaza	TM
387	Turtwig	TM
388	Grotle	TM
389	Torterra	TM
390	Chimchar	TM
391	Monferno	TM
392	Infernape	TM
395	Empoleon	11,TM
402	Kricketune	TM
406	Budew	TM
407	Roserade	TM
408	Cranidos	TM
409	Rampardos	TM
420	Cherubi	TM
421	Cherrim	TM
445	Garchomp	TM
447	Riolu	TM
448	Lucario	33,TM
451	Skorupi	TM
452	Drapion	TM
454	Toxicroak	TM
455	Carnivine	TM
459	Snover	TM
460	Abomasnow	TM
461	Weavile	TM
463	Lickilicky	TM
464	Rhyperior	TM
465	Tangrowth	TM
470	Leafeon	78,TM
472	Gliscor	34,TM
475	Gallade	25,TM
491	Darkrai	TM
492	Shaymin (L)	TM
492	Shaymin (S)	TM

Synthesis		
1	Bulbasaur	33,T
2	Ivysaur	39,T
3	Venusaur	45,T
43	Oddish	T,E
44	Gloom	T
45	Vileplume	T
46	Paras	T
47	Parasect	T
69	Bellsprout	T,E
70	Weepinbell	T
71	Victreebel	T
102	Exeggcute	T,E
103	Exeggutor	T
114	Tangela	T
151	Mew	T
152	Chikorita	12,T
153	Bayleef	12,T
154	Meganium	12,T
182	Bellossom	T
187	Hoppip	4,T
188	Skiploom	B,4,T
189	Jumpluff	B,4,T
191	Sunkern	33,T
192	Sunflora	T
251	Celebi	T
252	Treecko	T,E
253	Grovyle	T
254	Sceptile	T
270	Lotad	T,E
271	Lombre	T
272	Ludicolo	T
273	Seedot	21,T
274	Nuzleaf	T
275	Shiftry	T
285	Shroomish	T
286	Breloom	T
315	Roselia	46,T,E
331	Cacnea	T
332	Cacturne	T
345	Lileep	T
346	Cradily	T
357	Tropius	41,T,E
387	Turtwig	33,T
388	Grotle	37,T
389	Torterra	39,T
406	Budew	T,E
407	Roserade	T
413	Wormadam (P)	T
420	Cherubi	T
421	Cherrim	T
455	Carnivine	T,E
459	Snover	T
460	Abomasnow	T
465	Tangrowth	T
470	Leafeon	29,T
492	Shaymin (L)	28,T
492	Shaymin (S)	T

Tackle		
1	Bulbasaur	B
2	Ivysaur	B
3	Venusaur	B

7	Squirtle	B
8	Wartortle	B
9	Blastoise	B
10	Caterpie	B
16	Pidgey	B
17	Pidgeotto	B
18	Pidgeot	B
19	Rattata	B
20	Raticate	B
48	Venonat	B
49	Venomoth	B
74	Geodude	B
75	Graveler	B
76	Golem	B
77	Ponyta	B
79	Slowpoke	B
80	Slowbro	B
81	Magnemite	B
82	Magneton	B
90	Shellder	B
95	Onix	B
100	Voltorb	5
101	Electrode	B,5
109	Koffing	B
110	Weezing	B
120	Staryu	B
128	Tauros	B
129	Magikarp	15
133	Eevee	B
134	Vaporeon	B
135	Jolteon	B
136	Flareon	B
137	Porygon	B
143	Snorlax	B
152	Chikorita	B
153	Bayleef	B
154	Meganium	B
155	Cyndaquil	B
156	Quilava	B
157	Typhlosion	B
163	Hoothoot	B
164	Noctowl	B
165	Ledyba	B
166	Ledian	B
179	Mareep	B
180	Flaaffy	B
181	Ampharos	B
183	Marill	B
184	Azumarill	B
187	Hoppip	10
188	Skiploom	B,10
189	Jumpluff	B,10
193	Yanma	B
196	Espeon	B
197	Umbreon	B
199	Slowking	B
203	Girafarig	B
204	Pineco	B
205	Forretress	B
208	Steelix	B
209	Snubbull	B
210	Granbull	B
211	Qwilfish	B
214	Heracross	B
220	Swinub	B
222	Corsola	B
226	Mantine	B
231	Phanpy	B
233	Porygon2	B
234	Stantler	B
236	Tyrogue	B
241	Miltank	B
258	Mudkip	B
259	Marshtomp	B
260	Swampert	B
261	Poochyena	B
262	Mightyena	B
263	Zigzagoon	B
264	Linoone	B
265	Wurmple	B
285	Shroomish	5
286	Breloom	B,5
296	Makuhita	B
297	Hariyama	B
299	Nosepass	B
300	Skitty	B
304	Aron	B
305	Lairon	B
306	Aggron	B
309	Electrike	B
310	Manectric	B
313	Volbeat	B
314	Illumise	B
322	Numel	B
323	Camerupt	B
327	Spinda	B
337	Lunatone	B
338	Solrock	B
349	Feebas	15
351	Castform	B
369	Relicanth	B
370	Luvdisc	B
387	Turtwig	B
388	Grotle	B
389	Torterra	B
394	Prinplup	B
395	Empoleon	B
396	Starly	B
397	Staravia	B
398	Staraptor	B
399	Bidoof	B
400	Bibarel	B
403	Shinx	B
404	Luxio	B
405	Luxray	B
410	Shieldon	B
411	Bastiodon	B
412	Burmy	10
413	Wormadam (P)	B
413	Wormadam (S)	B
413	Wormadam (T)	B
414	Mothim	B
420	Cherubi	B
421	Cherrim	B
436	Bronzor	B
437	Bronzong	B
443	Gible	B
444	Gabite	B
445	Garchomp	B
446	Munchlax	B
449	Hippopotas	B
450	Hippowdon	B
458	Mantyke	B
462	Magnezone	B
469	Yanmega	B
470	Leafeon	B
471	Glaceon	B
474	Porygon-Z	B
476	Probopass	B

Tail Glow

313	Volbeat	21
490	Manaphy	B

Tail Whip

7	Squirtle	4
8	Wartortle	B,4
9	Blastoise	B,4
19	Rattata	B
20	Raticate	B
25	Pikachu	5
26	Raichu	B
29	Nidoran♀	7
30	Nidorina	7
31	Nidoqueen	B
37	Vulpix	4
54	Psyduck	5
55	Golduck	B,5
77	Ponyta	6
78	Rapidash	B,6
104	Cubone	3
105	Marowak	B,3
111	Rhyhorn	B
112	Rhydon	B
113	Chansey	5
115	Kangaskhan	10
118	Goldeen	B
119	Seaking	B
128	Tauros	3
133	Eevee	B
134	Vaporeon	B
135	Jolteon	B
136	Flareon	B
172	Pichu	5
183	Marill	7
184	Azumarill	B,7
187	Hoppip	7
188	Skiploom	B,7
189	Jumpluff	B,7
190	Aipom	B
194	Wooper	B
195	Quagsire	B
196	Espeon	B
197	Umbreon	B
209	Snubbull	B
210	Granbull	B
242	Blissey	5
263	Zigzagoon	5
264	Linoone	B,5
298	Azurill	7
300	Skitty	B
352	Kecleon	B
424	Ambipom	B
431	Glameow	E
464	Rhyperior	B
470	Leafeon	B
471	Glaceon	B

Tailwind

12	Butterfree	30
16	Pidgey	41
17	Pidgeotto	47
18	Pidgeot	50
144	Articuno	64
178	Xatu	27
245	Suicune	57
279	Pelipper	50

Take Down

1	Bulbasaur	15
2	Ivysaur	15
3	Venusaur	15
29	Nidoran♀	E
32	Nidoran♂	E
58	Growlithe	31
77	Ponyta	28
78	Rapidash	28
86	Seel	37
87	Dewgong	37
90	Shellder	E
111	Rhyhorn	33
112	Rhydon	33
128	Tauros	35
133	Eevee	43
142	Aerodactyl	41
163	Hoothoot	25
164	Noctowl	27
170	Chinchou	23
171	Lanturn	23
179	Mareep	E
203	Girafarig	E
204	Pineco	12
205	Forretress	12
206	Dunsparce	37
209	Snubbull	37
210	Granbull	43
211	Qwilfish	41
214	Heracross	31
216	Teddiursa	E
220	Swinub	32,E
221	Piloswine	32
226	Mantine	31
231	Phanpy	10
234	Stantler	21
258	Mudkip	28
259	Marshtomp	31
260	Swampert	31
261	Poochyena	45
262	Mightyena	52
273	Seedot	E
293	Whismur	E
304	Aron	25
305	Lairon	25
306	Aggron	25
318	Carvanha	38
322	Numel	21
323	Camerupt	21
333	Swablu	28
334	Altaria	28
339	Barboach	E
358	Chimecho	22
369	Relicanth	29
370	Luvdisc	14
374	Beldum	B
375	Metang	B
376	Metagross	B
396	Starly	29
397	Staravia	33
398	Staraptor	33
399	Bidoof	33
400	Bibarel	38
403	Shinx	E
408	Cranidos	15
409	Rampardos	15
410	Shieldon	15
411	Bastiodon	15
420	Cherubi	31
421	Cherrim	35
443	Gible	15
444	Gabite	15
445	Garchomp	15
449	Hippopotas	19
450	Hippowdon	19
458	Mantyke	31
464	Rhyperior	33
473	Mamoswine	32

Taunt

19	Rattata	TM
20	Raticate	TM
31	Nidoqueen	TM
34	Nidoking	TM
41	Zubat	TM
42	Golbat	TM
52	Meowth	25,TM
53	Persian	25,TM
56	Mankey	TM
57	Primeape	TM
63	Abra	TM
64	Kadabra	TM
65	Alakazam	TM
85	Dodrio	TM
88	Grimer	TM
89	Muk	TM
92	Gastly	TM
93	Haunter	TM
94	Gengar	TM
95	Onix	TM
96	Drowzee	TM
97	Hypno	TM
100	Voltorb	TM
101	Electrode	TM
109	Koffing	TM
110	Weezing	TM
122	Mr. Mime	TM
124	Jynx	TM
130	Gyarados	TM
142	Aerodactyl	TM
150	Mewtwo	TM
151	Mew	TM
169	Crobat	TM
185	Sudowoodo	TM
190	Aipom	TM
197	Umbreon	TM
198	Murkrow	31,TM
200	Misdreavus	TM
207	Gligar	TM
208	Steelix	TM
209	Snubbull	TM
210	Granbull	TM
211	Qwilfish	TM
215	Sneasel	B,TM
216	Teddiursa	TM
217	Ursaring	TM
227	Skarmory	TM
228	Houndour	TM
229	Houndoom	TM
246	Larvitar	TM
247	Pupitar	TM
248	Tyranitar	TM
261	Poochyena	37,TM
262	Mightyena	42,TM
280	Ralts	TM
281	Kirlia	TM
282	Gardevoir	TM
288	Vigoroth	TM
289	Slaking	TM
294	Loudred	TM
295	Exploud	TM
299	Nosepass	TM
302	Sableye	TM
303	Mawile	TM
306	Aggron	TM
318	Carvanha	TM
319	Sharpedo	40,TM
325	Spoink	TM
326	Grumpig	TM
335	Zangoose	35,TM
336	Seviper	TM
341	Corphish	32,TM
342	Crawdaunt	34,TM
353	Shuppet	TM
354	Banette	TM
355	Duskull	TM
356	Dusclops	TM
358	Chimecho	TM
359	Absol	9,TM
362	Glalie	TM
386	Deoxys (N)	TM
386	Deoxys (A)	25,TM
386	Deoxys (D)	TM
386	Deoxys (S)	TM
390	Chimchar	9,TM
391	Monferno	9,TM
392	Infernape	B,9,TM
399	Bidoof	TM
400	Bibarel	TM
402	Kricketune	38
410	Shieldon	6,TM
411	Bastiodon	B,6,TM
419	Floatzel	TM
424	Ambipom	TM
429	Mismagius	TM
430	Honchkrow	TM
431	Glameow	TM
432	Purugly	TM
433	Chingling	TM
434	Stunky	TM
435	Skuntank	TM
439	Mime Jr.	TM
441	Chatot	25,TM
442	Spiritomb	TM
451	Skorupi	TM
452	Drapion	TM
453	Croagunk	10,TM
454	Toxicroak	10,TM
461	Weavile	B,TM
466	Electivire	TM
467	Magmortar	TM
472	Gliscor	TM
475	Gallade	TM
476	Probopass	TM
477	Dusknoir	TM
478	Froslass	TM
482	Azelf	TM
485	Heatran	TM
491	Darkrai	TM

Teeter Dance

122	Mr. Mime	E
327	Spinda	37
331	Cacnea	E
439	Mime Jr.	E

Teleport

63	Abra	B
64	Kadabra	B
65	Alakazam	B
177	Natu	9
178	Xatu	9
280	Ralts	12
281	Kirlia	B,12
282	Gardevoir	B,12
344	Claydol	B
386	Deoxys (N)	17
386	Deoxys (A)	17
386	Deoxys (D)	17
475	Gallade	B,12

Thief

12	Butterfree	TM
15	Beedrill	TM
16	Pidgey	TM
17	Pidgeotto	TM
18	Pidgeot	TM
19	Rattata	TM
20	Raticate	TM
21	Spearow	TM
22	Fearow	TM
23	Ekans	TM
24	Arbok	TM
26	Raichu	TM
27	Sandshrew	TM
28	Sandslash	TM
29	Nidoran♀	TM
30	Nidorina	TM
31	Nidoqueen	TM
32	Nidoran♂	TM
33	Nidorino	TM
34	Nidoking	TM
41	Zubat	TM
42	Golbat	TM
46	Paras	TM
47	Parasect	TM
48	Venonat	TM
49	Venomoth	TM
50	Diglett	TM
51	Dugtrio	TM
52	Meowth	TM
53	Persian	TM
56	Mankey	TM
57	Primeape	TM
58	Growlithe	TM
59	Arcanine	TM
60	Poliwag	TM
61	Poliwhirl	TM
62	Poliwrath	TM
63	Abra	TM
64	Kadabra	TM
65	Alakazam	TM
66	Machop	TM
67	Machoke	TM
68	Machamp	TM
69	Bellsprout	TM
70	Weepinbell	TM
71	Victreebel	TM
72	Tentacool	TM
73	Tentacruel	TM
83	Farfetch'd	TM
84	Doduo	TM
85	Dodrio	TM
86	Seel	TM
87	Dewgong	TM
88	Grimer	TM
89	Muk	TM
92	Gastly	TM
93	Haunter	TM
94	Gengar	TM
96	Drowzee	TM
97	Hypno	TM
98	Krabby	TM
99	Kingler	TM
100	Voltorb	TM
101	Electrode	TM
102	Exeggcute	TM
103	Exeggutor	TM
104	Cubone	TM
105	Marowak	TM
106	Hitmonlee	TM
107	Hitmonchan	TM
108	Lickitung	TM
109	Koffing	TM
110	Weezing	TM
111	Rhyhorn	TM
112	Rhydon	TM
114	Tangela	TM
115	Kangaskhan	TM
122	Mr. Mime	TM
123	Scyther	TM
124	Jynx	TM
125	Electabuzz	TM
126	Magmar	TM
127	Pinsir	TM
137	Porygon	TM
138	Omanyte	TM
139	Omastar	TM
140	Kabuto	TM
141	Kabutops	TM
142	Aerodactyl	TM
151	Mew	TM
161	Sentret	TM
162	Furret	TM
163	Hoothoot	TM
164	Noctowl	TM
165	Ledyba	TM
166	Ledian	TM
167	Spinarak	TM
168	Ariados	TM
169	Crobat	TM
177	Natu	TM
178	Xatu	TM
185	Sudowoodo	TM
186	Politoed	TM
190	Aipom	TM
193	Yanma	TM
198	Murkrow	TM
200	Misdreavus	TM
203	Girafarig	TM
206	Dunsparce	TM
207	Gligar	TM
209	Snubbull	TM
210	Granbull	TM
212	Scizor	TM
214	Heracross	TM
215	Sneasel	TM
216	Teddiursa	TM
217	Ursaring	TM
223	Remoraid	TM
224	Octillery	TM
225	Delibird	TM
227	Skarmory	TM
228	Houndour	TM
229	Houndoom	TM
233	Porygon2	TM
234	Stantler	TM
236	Tyrogue	TM
237	Hitmontop	TM
238	Smoochum	TM
239	Elekid	TM
240	Magby	TM
261	Poochyena	TM
262	Mightyena	57,TM
263	Zigzagoon	TM
264	Linoone	TM
267	Beautifly	TM
269	Dustox	TM
270	Lotad	TM
271	Lombre	TM
272	Ludicolo	TM
274	Nuzleaf	TM
275	Shiftry	TM
276	Taillow	TM
277	Swellow	TM
278	Wingull	TM
279	Pelipper	TM
280	Ralts	TM
281	Kirlia	TM
282	Gardevoir	TM
283	Surskit	TM
284	Masquerain	TM
291	Ninjask	TM
292	Shedinja	TM
302	Sableye	TM
309	Electrike	TM
310	Manectric	TM
313	Volbeat	TM
314	Illumise	TM
318	Carvanha	TM
319	Sharpedo	TM
325	Spoink	TM
326	Grumpig	TM
327	Spinda	TM
333	Swablu	TM
334	Altaria	TM
335	Zangoose	TM
336	Seviper	TM
351	Castform	TM
352	Kecleon	B,TM
353	Shuppet	TM
354	Banette	TM
355	Duskull	TM
356	Dusclops	TM
359	Absol	TM
396	Starly	TM
397	Staravia	TM
398	Staraptor	TM
399	Bidoof	TM
400	Bibarel	TM
403	Shinx	TM
404	Luxio	TM
405	Luxray	TM
408	Cranidos	TM
409	Rampardos	TM
413	Wormadam (P)	TM
413	Wormadam (S)	TM
413	Wormadam (T)	TM
414	Mothim	TM
416	Vespiquen	TM
424	Ambipom	TM
425	Drifloon	TM
426	Drifblim	TM
429	Mismagius	TM
430	Honchkrow	TM
431	Glameow	TM
432	Purugly	TM
434	Stunky	TM
435	Skuntank	TM
438	Bonsly	TM
439	Mime Jr.	TM
441	Chatot	TM
442	Spiritomb	TM
451	Skorupi	TM
452	Drapion	TM
453	Croagunk	TM
454	Toxicroak	TM
455	Carnivine	TM
461	Weavile	TM
463	Lickilicky	TM
464	Rhyperior	TM
465	Tangrowth	TM
466	Electivire	TM
467	Magmortar	TM
469	Yanmega	TM
472	Gliscor	TM
474	Porygon-Z	TM
475	Gallade	TM
477	Dusknoir	TM
479	Rotom	TM
491	Darkrai	TM

Thrash

34	Nidoking	23
56	Mankey	41
57	Primeape	47
58	Growlithe	E
77	Ponyta	E
104	Cubone	31
105	Marowak	33
127	Pinsir	35
128	Tauros	48
130	Gyarados	B
155	Cyndaquil	E
158	Totodile	36,E
159	Croconaw	42
160	Feraligatr	50
216	Teddiursa	50
217	Ursaring	58
234	Stantler	E
246	Larvitar	23
247	Pupitar	23
248	Tyranitar	23
318	Carvanha	E
320	Wailmer	E
327	Spinda	55
339	Barboach	E
371	Bagon	E
387	Turtwig	E
408	Cranidos	E
443	Gible	E

Thunder

19	Rattata	TM
20	Raticate	TM
25	Pikachu	45,TM
26	Raichu	TM
29	Nidoran♀	TM
30	Nidorina	TM
31	Nidoqueen	TM
32	Nidoran♂	TM
33	Nidorino	TM
34	Nidoking	TM
35	Clefairy	TM
36	Clefable	TM

Pokémon Moves and Abilities alphabetical list

Thunder continued

39	Jigglypuff	TM
40	Wigglytuff	TM
52	Meowth	TM
53	Persian	TM
56	Mankey	TM
57	Primeape	TM
81	Magnemite	TM
82	Magneton	TM
88	Grimer	TM
89	Muk	TM
94	Gengar	TM
100	Voltorb	TM
101	Electrode	TM
108	Lickitung	TM
109	Koffing	TM
110	Weezing	TM
111	Rhyhorn	TM
112	Rhydon	TM
113	Chansey	TM
115	Kangaskhan	TM
120	Staryu	TM
121	Starmie	TM
122	Mr. Mime	TM
125	Electabuzz	58,TM
128	Tauros	TM
130	Gyarados	TM
131	Lapras	TM
135	Jolteon	71,TM
137	Porygon	TM
143	Snorlax	TM
145	Zapdos	78,TM
147	Dratini	TM
148	Dragonair	TM
149	Dragonite	TM
150	Mewtwo	TM
151	Mew	TM
162	Furret	TM
170	Chinchou	TM
171	Lanturn	TM
172	Pichu	TM
179	Mareep	46,TM
180	Flaaffy	53,TM
181	Ampharos	68,TM
190	Aipom	TM
200	Misdreavus	TM
203	Girafarig	TM
206	Dunsparce	TM
209	Snubbull	TM
210	Granbull	TM
233	Porygon2	TM
234	Stantler	TM
239	Elekid	46,TM
241	Miltank	TM
242	Blissey	TM
243	Raikou	85,TM
248	Tyranitar	TM
249	Lugia	TM
250	Ho-Oh	TM
263	Zigzagoon	TM
264	Linoone	TM
287	Slakoth	TM
288	Vigoroth	TM
289	Slaking	TM
299	Nosepass	TM
300	Skitty	TM
301	Delcatty	TM
306	Aggron	TM
309	Electrike	49,TM
310	Manectric	61,TM
311	Plusle	38,TM
312	Minun	38,TM
313	Volbeat	TM
314	Illumise	TM
335	Zangoose	TM
351	Castform	TM
352	Kecleon	TM
353	Shuppet	TM
354	Banette	TM
359	Absol	TM
377	Regirock	TM
378	Regice	TM
379	Registeel	TM
380	Latias	TM
381	Latios	TM
382	Kyogre	TM
383	Groudon	TM
384	Rayquaza	TM
385	Jirachi	TM
386	Deoxys (N)	TM
386	Deoxys (A)	TM
386	Deoxys (D)	TM
386	Deoxys (S)	TM
399	Bidoof	TM
400	Bibarel	TM
403	Shinx	TM
404	Luxio	TM
405	Luxray	TM
408	Cranidos	TM
409	Rampardos	TM
410	Shieldon	TM
411	Bastiodon	TM
417	Pachirisu	TM
424	Ambipom	TM
425	Drifloon	TM
426	Drifblim	TM
428	Lopunny	TM
429	Mismagius	TM
431	Glameow	TM
432	Purugly	TM
439	Mime Jr.	TM
446	Munchlax	TM
462	Magnezone	TM
463	Lickilicky	TM
464	Rhyperior	TM
466	Electivire	58,TM
474	Porygon-Z	TM
476	Probopass	TM
478	Froslass	TM
479	Rotom	TM
480	Uxie	TM
481	Mesprit	TM
482	Azelf	TM
483	Dialga	TM
484	Palkia	TM
486	Regigigas	TM
487	Giratina (A)	TM
487	Giratina (O)	TM
491	Darkrai	TM

Thunder Fang

24	Arbok	B
59	Arcanine	B
111	Rhyhorn	E
135	Jolteon	43
142	Aerodactyl	B
208	Steelix	B
209	Snubbull	B,E
210	Granbull	B
228	Houndour	E
229	Houndoom	B
232	Donphan	B
243	Raikou	50
248	Tyranitar	B
261	Poochyena	E
295	Exploud	B
303	Mawile	E
309	Electrike	33,E
310	Manectric	37
373	Salamence	B
403	Shinx	29,E
404	Luxio	33
405	Luxray	35
450	Hippowdon	B
452	Drapion	B
472	Gliscor	B

Thunder Wave

19	Rattata	TM
20	Raticate	TM
25	Pikachu	10,TM
26	Raichu	TM
35	Clefairy	TM
36	Clefable	TM
39	Jigglypuff	TM
40	Wigglytuff	TM
63	Abra	TM
64	Kadabra	TM
65	Alakazam	TM
79	Slowpoke	TM
80	Slowbro	TM
81	Magnemite	17,TM
82	Magneton	17,TM
96	Drowzee	TM
97	Hypno	TM
100	Voltorb	TM
101	Electrode	TM
113	Chansey	TM
120	Staryu	TM
121	Starmie	TM
122	Mr. Mime	TM
125	Electabuzz	TM
130	Gyarados	TM
135	Jolteon	57,TM
137	Porygon	TM
145	Zapdos	8,TM
147	Dratini	5,TM
148	Dragonair	B,5,TM
149	Dragonite	B,5,TM
150	Mewtwo	TM
151	Mew	TM
170	Chinchou	6,TM
171	Lanturn	B,6,TM
172	Pichu	10,TM
173	Cleffa	TM
174	Igglybuff	TM
175	Togepi	TM
176	Togetic	TM
177	Natu	TM
178	Xatu	TM
179	Mareep	14,TM
180	Flaaffy	14,TM
181	Ampharos	B,14,TM
190	Aipom	TM
198	Murkrow	TM
199	Slowking	TM
200	Misdreavus	TM
203	Girafarig	TM
206	Dunsparce	TM
209	Snubbull	TM
210	Granbull	TM
211	Qwilfish	TM
223	Remoraid	TM,E
224	Octillery	TM
233	Porygon2	TM
234	Stantler	TM
239	Elekid	TM
241	Miltank	TM
242	Blissey	TM
243	Raikou	TM
248	Tyranitar	TM
249	Lugia	TM
250	Ho-Oh	TM
251	Celebi	TM
263	Zigzagoon	TM
264	Linoone	TM
280	Ralts	TM
281	Kirlia	TM
282	Gardevoir	TM
299	Nosepass	25,TM
300	Skitty	TM
301	Delcatty	TM
306	Aggron	TM
309	Electrike	4,TM
310	Manectric	B,4,TM
311	Plusle	3,TM
312	Minun	3,TM
313	Volbeat	TM
314	Illumise	TM
325	Spoink	TM
326	Grumpig	TM
351	Castform	TM
352	Kecleon	TM
353	Shuppet	TM
354	Banette	TM
358	Chimecho	TM
359	Absol	TM
377	Regirock	TM
378	Regice	TM
379	Registeel	TM
380	Latias	TM
381	Latios	TM
382	Kyogre	TM
383	Groudon	TM
384	Rayquaza	TM
385	Jirachi	TM
386	Deoxys (N)	TM
386	Deoxys (A)	TM
386	Deoxys (D)	TM
386	Deoxys (S)	TM
399	Bidoof	TM
400	Bibarel	TM
403	Shinx	TM
404	Luxio	TM
405	Luxray	TM
417	Pachirisu	TM
424	Ambipom	TM
425	Drifloon	TM
426	Drifblim	TM
427	Buneary	TM
428	Lopunny	TM
429	Mismagius	TM
430	Honchkrow	TM
433	Chingling	TM
439	Mime Jr.	TM
440	Happiny	TM
462	Magnezone	17,TM
466	Electivire	TM
468	Togekiss	TM
474	Porygon-Z	TM
475	Gallade	TM
476	Probopass	25,TM
478	Froslass	TM
479	Rotom	B,TM
480	Uxie	TM
481	Mesprit	TM
482	Azelf	TM
483	Dialga	TM
484	Palkia	TM
486	Regigigas	TM
487	Giratina (A)	TM
487	Giratina (O)	TM
488	Cresselia	TM
491	Darkrai	TM

Thunderbolt

19	Rattata	TM
20	Raticate	TM
25	Pikachu	26,TM
26	Raichu	B,TM
29	Nidoran♀	TM
30	Nidorina	TM
31	Nidoqueen	TM
32	Nidoran♂	TM
33	Nidorino	TM
34	Nidoking	TM
35	Clefairy	TM
36	Clefable	TM
39	Jigglypuff	TM
40	Wigglytuff	TM
52	Meowth	TM
53	Persian	TM
56	Mankey	TM
57	Primeape	TM
81	Magnemite	TM
82	Magneton	TM
88	Grimer	TM
89	Muk	TM
92	Gastly	TM
93	Haunter	TM
94	Gengar	TM
100	Voltorb	TM
101	Electrode	TM
108	Lickitung	TM
109	Koffing	TM
110	Weezing	TM
111	Rhyhorn	TM
112	Rhydon	TM
113	Chansey	TM
115	Kangaskhan	TM
120	Staryu	TM
121	Starmie	TM
122	Mr. Mime	TM
125	Electabuzz	43,TM
128	Tauros	TM
130	Gyarados	TM
131	Lapras	TM
135	Jolteon	TM
137	Porygon	TM
143	Snorlax	TM
145	Zapdos	TM
147	Dratini	TM
148	Dragonair	TM
149	Dragonite	TM
150	Mewtwo	TM
151	Mew	TM
161	Sentret	TM
162	Furret	TM
170	Chinchou	TM
171	Lanturn	TM
172	Pichu	TM
179	Mareep	TM
180	Flaaffy	TM
181	Ampharos	TM
190	Aipom	TM
200	Misdreavus	TM
203	Girafarig	TM
206	Dunsparce	TM
209	Snubbull	TM
210	Granbull	TM
233	Porygon2	TM
234	Stantler	TM
239	Elekid	37,TM
241	Miltank	TM
242	Blissey	TM
243	Raikou	TM
248	Tyranitar	TM
249	Lugia	TM
250	Ho-Oh	TM
263	Zigzagoon	TM
264	Linoone	TM
280	Ralts	TM
281	Kirlia	TM
282	Gardevoir	TM
287	Slakoth	TM
288	Vigoroth	TM
289	Slaking	TM
299	Nosepass	TM
300	Skitty	TM
301	Delcatty	TM
306	Aggron	TM
309	Electrike	TM
310	Manectric	TM
311	Plusle	TM
312	Minun	TM
313	Volbeat	TM
314	Illumise	TM
335	Zangoose	TM
351	Castform	TM
352	Kecleon	TM
353	Shuppet	TM
354	Banette	TM
359	Absol	TM
377	Regirock	TM
378	Regice	TM
379	Registeel	TM
380	Latias	TM
381	Latios	TM
382	Kyogre	TM
383	Groudon	TM
384	Rayquaza	TM
385	Jirachi	TM
386	Deoxys (N)	TM
386	Deoxys (A)	TM
386	Deoxys (D)	TM
386	Deoxys (S)	TM
399	Bidoof	TM
400	Bibarel	TM
403	Shinx	TM
404	Luxio	TM
405	Luxray	TM
408	Cranidos	TM
409	Rampardos	TM
410	Shieldon	TM
411	Bastiodon	TM
417	Pachirisu	TM
424	Ambipom	TM
425	Drifloon	TM
426	Drifblim	TM
427	Buneary	TM
428	Lopunny	TM
429	Mismagius	TM
431	Glameow	TM
432	Purugly	TM
439	Mime Jr.	TM
446	Munchlax	TM
462	Magnezone	TM
463	Lickilicky	TM
464	Rhyperior	TM
466	Electivire	43,TM
467	Magmortar	TM
474	Porygon-Z	TM
475	Gallade	TM
476	Probopass	TM
478	Froslass	TM
479	Rotom	TM
480	Uxie	TM
481	Mesprit	TM
482	Azelf	TM
483	Dialga	TM
484	Palkia	TM
486	Regigigas	TM
487	Giratina (A)	TM
487	Giratina (O)	TM
491	Darkrai	TM

ThunderPunch

4	Charmander	T
5	Charmeleon	T
6	Charizard	T
25	Pikachu	T
26	Raichu	T
31	Nidoqueen	T
34	Nidoking	T
35	Clefairy	T
36	Clefable	T
39	Jigglypuff	T
40	Wigglytuff	T
56	Mankey	T
57	Primeape	T
63	Abra	T,E
64	Kadabra	T
65	Alakazam	T
66	Machop	T,E
67	Machoke	T
68	Machamp	T
74	Geodude	T
75	Graveler	T
76	Golem	T
88	Grimer	T
89	Muk	T
92	Gastly	T,E
93	Haunter	T
94	Gengar	T
96	Drowzee	T,E
97	Hypno	T
104	Cubone	T
105	Marowak	T
107	Hitmonchan	31,T
108	Lickitung	T
112	Rhydon	T
113	Chansey	T
115	Kangaskhan	T
122	Mr. Mime	T
125	Electabuzz	28,T
126	Magmar	T
143	Snorlax	T
149	Dragonite	B,T
150	Mewtwo	T
151	Mew	T
157	Typhlosion	T
161	Sentret	T
162	Furret	T
165	Ledyba	T
166	Ledian	T
172	Pichu	E
180	Flaaffy	T
181	Ampharos	30,T
185	Sudowoodo	T
190	Aipom	T
209	Snubbull	T
210	Granbull	T
216	Teddiursa	T
217	Ursaring	T
239	Elekid	28,T
240	Magby	T,E
241	Miltank	T
242	Blissey	T
248	Tyranitar	T
252	Treecko	T
253	Grovyle	T
254	Sceptile	T
256	Combusken	T
257	Blaziken	T
271	Lombre	T
272	Ludicolo	T
280	Ralts	T
281	Kirlia	T
282	Gardevoir	T
286	Breloom	T
287	Slakoth	T
288	Vigoroth	T
289	Slaking	T
293	Whismur	T
294	Loudred	T
295	Exploud	T
296	Makuhita	T
297	Hariyama	T
299	Nosepass	T
302	Sableye	T
303	Mawile	T
306	Aggron	T
307	Meditite	T,E
308	Medicham	B,T
311	Plusle	T
312	Minun	T
313	Volbeat	T
314	Illumise	T
316	Gulpin	T
317	Swalot	T
326	Grumpig	T
327	Spinda	T
330	Flygon	T
331	Cacnea	T
332	Cacturne	T
335	Zangoose	T
352	Kecleon	T
356	Dusclops	B,T
375	Metang	T
376	Metagross	T
377	Regirock	T
378	Regice	T
379	Registeel	T
383	Groudon	T
385	Jirachi	T
386	Deoxys (N)	T
390	Chimchar	T,E
391	Monferno	T
392	Infernape	T
408	Cranidos	T
409	Rampardos	T
417	Pachirisu	T
424	Ambipom	T
427	Buneary	E
428	Lopunny	T
446	Munchlax	T
447	Riolu	T
448	Lucario	T
453	Croagunk	T
454	Toxicroak	T
463	Lickilicky	T
464	Rhyperior	T
466	Electivire	28,T
467	Magmortar	B,T
475	Gallade	T
476	Probopass	T
477	Dusknoir	B,T
480	Uxie	T
481	Mesprit	T
482	Azelf	T
486	Regigigas	B,T

ThunderShock

25	Pikachu	B
26	Raichu	B
81	Magnemite	6
82	Magneton	B,6
125	Electabuzz	B,7
135	Jolteon	15
145	Zapdos	B
172	Pichu	B
179	Mareep	10
180	Flaaffy	B,10
181	Ampharos	B,10
239	Elekid	7
243	Raikou	8
462	Magnezone	B,6
466	Electivire	B,7
479	Rotom	B

Tickle

43	Oddish	E
69	Bellsprout	E
98	Krabby	E
114	Tangela	47
131	Lapras	E
133	Eevee	E
138	Omanyte	43
139	Omastar	48
172	Pichu	E
190	Aipom	15
263	Zigzagoon	E
270	Lotad	E
298	Azurill	E
300	Skitty	E
303	Mawile	E
320	Wailmer	E
340	Whiscash	B
345	Lileep	E
349	Feebas	E
387	Turtwig	E
420	Cherubi	E
424	Ambipom	15
439	Mime Jr.	B
456	Finneon	E
465	Tangrowth	47

Torment

23	Ekans	TM
24	Arbok	TM
31	Nidoqueen	TM
34	Nidoking	TM
41	Zubat	TM
42	Golbat	TM
52	Meowth	TM
53	Persian	TM
63	Abra	TM
64	Kadabra	TM
65	Alakazam	TM
85	Dodrio	TM
88	Grimer	TM
89	Muk	TM
91	Cloyster	TM
92	Gastly	TM
93	Haunter	TM
94	Gengar	TM
95	Onix	TM
96	Drowzee	TM
97	Hypno	TM
100	Voltorb	TM
101	Electrode	TM
109	Koffing	TM
110	Weezing	TM
122	Mr. Mime	TM
124	Jynx	TM
130	Gyarados	TM
142	Aerodactyl	TM
150	Mewtwo	TM
151	Mew	TM
169	Crobat	TM
185	Sudowoodo	TM
197	Umbreon	TM
198	Murkrow	TM
200	Misdreavus	TM
207	Gligar	TM
208	Steelix	TM
209	Snubbull	TM
210	Granbull	TM
215	Sneasel	TM
216	Teddiursa	TM
217	Ursaring	TM
227	Skarmory	TM
228	Houndour	TM
229	Houndoom	TM
246	Larvitar	TM
247	Pupitar	TM
248	Tyranitar	TM
261	Poochyena	TM
262	Mightyena	TM
274	Nuzleaf	25,TM
275	Shiftry	TM
280	Ralts	TM
281	Kirlia	TM
282	Gardevoir	TM
294	Loudred	TM
295	Exploud	TM
299	Nosepass	TM
302	Sableye	TM
303	Mawile	TM
318	Carvanha	TM
319	Sharpedo	TM
325	Spoink	TM
326	Grumpig	TM

Pokémon moves and Abilities alphabetical list

353	Shuppet	TM
354	Banette	TM
355	Duskull	TM
356	Dusclops	TM
358	Chimecho	TM
359	Absol	TM
362	Glalie	TM
386	Deoxys (N)	TM
386	Deoxys (A)	TM
386	Deoxys (D)	TM
386	Deoxys (S)	TM
390	Chimchar	25,TM
391	Monferno	29,TM
392	Infernape	TM
410	Shieldon	TM
411	Bastiodon	TM
419	Floatzel	TM
429	Mismagius	TM
430	Honchkrow	TM
431	Glameow	TM
432	Purugly	TM
433	Chingling	TM
434	Stunky	TM
435	Skuntank	TM
439	Mime Jr.	TM
441	Chatot	TM
442	Spiritomb	TM
451	Skorupi	TM
452	Drapion	TM
453	Croagunk	TM
454	Toxicroak	TM
461	Weavile	TM
466	Electivire	TM
467	Magmortar	TM
472	Gliscor	TM
475	Gallade	TM
476	Probopass	TM
477	Dusknoir	TM
478	Froslass	TM
482	Azelf	TM
485	Heatran	TM
491	Darkrai	TM

Toxic		
1	Bulbasaur	TM
2	Ivysaur	TM
3	Venusaur	TM
4	Charmander	TM
5	Charmeleon	TM
6	Charizard	TM
7	Squirtle	TM
8	Wartortle	TM
9	Blastoise	TM
12	Butterfree	TM
15	Beedrill	TM
16	Pidgey	TM
17	Pidgeotto	TM
18	Pidgeot	TM
19	Rattata	TM
20	Raticate	TM
21	Spearow	TM
22	Fearow	TM
23	Ekans	TM
24	Arbok	TM
25	Pikachu	TM
26	Raichu	TM
27	Sandshrew	TM
28	Sandslash	TM
29	Nidoran♀	TM
30	Nidorina	TM
31	Nidoqueen	TM
32	Nidoran♂	TM
33	Nidorino	TM
34	Nidoking	TM
35	Clefairy	TM
36	Clefable	TM
37	Vulpix	TM
38	Ninetales	TM
39	Jigglypuff	TM
40	Wigglytuff	TM
41	Zubat	TM
42	Golbat	TM
43	Oddish	TM
44	Gloom	TM
45	Vileplume	TM
46	Paras	TM
47	Parasect	TM
48	Venonat	TM
49	Venomoth	TM
50	Diglett	TM
51	Dugtrio	TM
52	Meowth	TM
53	Persian	TM
54	Psyduck	TM
55	Golduck	TM
56	Mankey	TM
57	Primeape	TM
58	Growlithe	TM
59	Arcanine	TM
60	Poliwag	TM
61	Poliwhirl	TM
62	Poliwrath	TM
63	Abra	TM
64	Kadabra	TM
65	Alakazam	TM
66	Machop	TM
67	Machoke	TM
68	Machamp	TM
69	Bellsprout	TM
70	Weepinbell	TM
71	Victreebel	TM
72	Tentacool	TM
73	Tentacruel	TM
74	Geodude	TM
75	Graveler	TM
76	Golem	TM
77	Ponyta	TM
78	Rapidash	TM
79	Slowpoke	TM
80	Slowbro	TM
81	Magnemite	TM
82	Magneton	TM
83	Farfetch'd	TM
84	Doduo	TM
85	Dodrio	TM
86	Seel	TM
87	Dewgong	TM
88	Grimer	TM
89	Muk	TM
90	Shellder	TM
91	Cloyster	TM
92	Gastly	TM
93	Haunter	TM
94	Gengar	TM
95	Onix	TM
96	Drowzee	TM
97	Hypno	TM
98	Krabby	TM
99	Kingler	TM
100	Voltorb	TM
101	Electrode	TM
102	Exeggcute	TM
103	Exeggutor	TM
104	Cubone	TM
105	Marowak	TM
106	Hitmonlee	TM
107	Hitmonchan	TM
108	Lickitung	TM
109	Koffing	TM
110	Weezing	TM
111	Rhyhorn	TM
112	Rhydon	TM
113	Chansey	TM
114	Tangela	TM
115	Kangaskhan	TM
116	Horsea	TM
117	Seadra	TM
118	Goldeen	TM
119	Seaking	TM
120	Staryu	TM
121	Starmie	TM
122	Mr. Mime	TM
123	Scyther	TM
124	Jynx	TM
125	Electabuzz	TM
126	Magmar	TM
127	Pinsir	TM
128	Tauros	TM
130	Gyarados	TM
131	Lapras	TM
133	Eevee	TM
134	Vaporeon	TM
135	Jolteon	TM
136	Flareon	TM
137	Porygon	TM
138	Omanyte	TM
139	Omastar	TM
140	Kabuto	TM
141	Kabutops	TM
142	Aerodactyl	TM
143	Snorlax	TM
144	Articuno	TM
145	Zapdos	TM
146	Moltres	TM
147	Dratini	TM
148	Dragonair	TM
149	Dragonite	TM
150	Mewtwo	TM
151	Mew	TM
152	Chikorita	TM
153	Bayleef	TM
154	Meganium	TM
155	Cyndaquil	TM
156	Quilava	TM
157	Typhlosion	TM
158	Totodile	TM
159	Croconaw	TM
160	Feraligatr	TM
161	Sentret	TM
162	Furret	TM
163	Hoothoot	TM
164	Noctowl	TM
165	Ledyba	TM
166	Ledian	TM
167	Spinarak	TM
168	Ariados	TM
169	Crobat	TM
170	Chinchou	TM
171	Lanturn	TM
172	Pichu	TM
173	Cleffa	TM
174	Igglybuff	TM
175	Togepi	TM
176	Togetic	TM
177	Natu	TM
178	Xatu	TM
179	Mareep	TM
180	Flaaffy	TM
181	Ampharos	TM
182	Bellossom	TM
183	Marill	TM
184	Azumarill	TM
185	Sudowoodo	TM
186	Politoed	TM
187	Hoppip	TM
188	Skiploom	TM
189	Jumpluff	TM
190	Aipom	TM
191	Sunkern	TM
192	Sunflora	TM
193	Yanma	TM
194	Wooper	TM
195	Quagsire	TM
196	Espeon	TM
197	Umbreon	TM
198	Murkrow	TM
199	Slowking	TM
200	Misdreavus	TM
203	Girafarig	TM
204	Pineco	TM
205	Forretress	TM
206	Dunsparce	TM
207	Gligar	TM
208	Steelix	TM
209	Snubbull	TM
210	Granbull	TM
211	Qwilfish	TM
212	Scizor	TM
213	Shuckle	TM
214	Heracross	TM
215	Sneasel	TM
216	Teddiursa	TM
217	Ursaring	TM
218	Slugma	TM
219	Magcargo	TM
220	Swinub	TM
221	Piloswine	TM
222	Corsola	TM
223	Remoraid	TM
224	Octillery	TM
225	Delibird	TM
226	Mantine	TM
227	Skarmory	TM
228	Houndour	TM
229	Houndoom	TM
230	Kingdra	TM
231	Phanpy	TM
232	Donphan	TM
233	Porygon2	TM
234	Stantler	TM
236	Tyrogue	TM
237	Hitmontop	TM
238	Smoochum	TM
239	Elekid	TM
240	Magby	TM
241	Miltank	TM
242	Blissey	TM
243	Raikou	TM
244	Entei	TM
245	Suicune	TM
246	Larvitar	TM
247	Pupitar	TM
248	Tyranitar	TM
249	Lugia	TM
250	Ho-Oh	TM
251	Celebi	TM
252	Treecko	TM
253	Grovyle	TM
254	Sceptile	TM
255	Torchic	TM
256	Combusken	TM
257	Blaziken	TM
258	Mudkip	TM
259	Marshtomp	TM
260	Swampert	TM
261	Poochyena	TM
262	Mightyena	TM
263	Zigzagoon	TM
264	Linoone	TM
267	Beautifly	TM
269	Dustox	38,TM
270	Lotad	TM
271	Lombre	TM
272	Ludicolo	TM
273	Seedot	TM
274	Nuzleaf	TM
275	Shiftry	TM
276	Taillow	TM
277	Swellow	TM
278	Wingull	TM
279	Pelipper	TM
280	Ralts	TM
281	Kirlia	TM
282	Gardevoir	TM
283	Surskit	TM
284	Masquerain	TM
285	Shroomish	TM
286	Breloom	TM
287	Slakoth	TM
288	Vigoroth	TM
289	Slaking	TM
290	Nincada	TM
291	Ninjask	TM
292	Shedinja	TM
293	Whismur	TM
294	Loudred	TM
295	Exploud	TM
296	Makuhita	TM
297	Hariyama	TM
298	Azurill	TM
299	Nosepass	TM
300	Skitty	TM
301	Delcatty	TM
302	Sableye	TM
303	Mawile	TM
304	Aron	TM
305	Lairon	TM
306	Aggron	TM
307	Meditite	TM
308	Medicham	TM
309	Electrike	TM
310	Manectric	TM
311	Plusle	TM
312	Minun	TM
313	Volbeat	TM
314	Illumise	TM
315	Roselia	37,TM
316	Gulpin	28,TM
317	Swalot	30,TM
318	Carvanha	TM
319	Sharpedo	TM
320	Wailmer	TM
321	Wailord	TM
322	Numel	TM
323	Camerupt	TM
324	Torkoal	TM
325	Spoink	TM
326	Grumpig	TM
327	Spinda	TM
328	Trapinch	TM
329	Vibrava	TM
330	Flygon	TM
331	Cacnea	TM
332	Cacturne	TM
333	Swablu	TM
334	Altaria	TM
335	Zangoose	TM
336	Seviper	TM
337	Lunatone	TM
338	Solrock	TM
339	Barboach	TM
340	Whiscash	TM
341	Corphish	TM
342	Crawdaunt	TM
343	Baltoy	TM
344	Claydol	TM
345	Lileep	TM
346	Cradily	TM
347	Anorith	TM
348	Armaldo	TM
349	Feebas	TM
350	Milotic	TM
351	Castform	TM
352	Kecleon	TM
353	Shuppet	TM
354	Banette	TM
355	Duskull	TM
356	Dusclops	TM
357	Tropius	TM
358	Chimecho	TM
359	Absol	TM
361	Snorunt	TM
362	Glalie	TM
363	Spheal	TM
364	Sealeo	TM
365	Walrein	TM
366	Clamperl	TM
367	Huntail	TM
368	Gorebyss	TM
369	Relicanth	TM
370	Luvdisc	TM
371	Bagon	TM
372	Shelgon	TM
373	Salamence	TM
375	Metang	TM
376	Metagross	TM
377	Regirock	TM
378	Regice	TM
379	Registeel	TM
380	Latias	TM
381	Latios	TM
382	Kyogre	TM
383	Groudon	TM
384	Rayquaza	TM
385	Jirachi	TM
386	Deoxys (N)	TM
386	Deoxys (A)	TM
386	Deoxys (D)	TM
386	Deoxys (S)	TM
387	Turtwig	TM
388	Grotle	TM
389	Torterra	TM
390	Chimchar	TM
391	Monferno	TM
392	Infernape	TM
393	Piplup	TM
394	Prinplup	TM
395	Empoleon	TM
396	Starly	TM
397	Staravia	TM
398	Staraptor	TM
399	Bidoof	TM
400	Bibarel	TM
402	Kricketune	TM
403	Shinx	TM
404	Luxio	TM
405	Luxray	TM
406	Budew	TM
407	Roserade	TM
408	Cranidos	TM
409	Rampardos	TM
410	Shieldon	TM
411	Bastiodon	TM
413	Wormadam (P)	TM
413	Wormadam (S)	TM
413	Wormadam (T)	TM
414	Mothim	TM
416	Vespiquen	27,TM
417	Pachirisu	TM
418	Buizel	TM
419	Floatzel	TM
420	Cherubi	TM
421	Cherrim	TM
422	Shellos	TM
423	Gastrodon	TM
424	Ambipom	TM
425	Drifloon	TM
426	Drifblim	TM
427	Buneary	TM
428	Lopunny	TM
429	Mismagius	TM
430	Honchkrow	TM
431	Glameow	TM
432	Purugly	TM
433	Chingling	TM
434	Stunky	27,TM
435	Skuntank	27,TM
436	Bronzor	TM
437	Bronzong	TM
438	Bonsly	TM
439	Mime Jr.	TM
440	Happiny	TM
441	Chatot	TM
442	Spiritomb	TM
443	Gible	TM
444	Gabite	TM
445	Garchomp	TM
446	Munchlax	TM
447	Riolu	TM
448	Lucario	TM
449	Hippopotas	TM
450	Hippowdon	TM
451	Skorupi	TM
452	Drapion	TM
453	Croagunk	TM
454	Toxicroak	TM
455	Carnivine	TM
456	Finneon	TM
457	Lumineon	TM
458	Mantyke	TM
459	Snover	TM
460	Abomasnow	TM
461	Weavile	TM
462	Magnezone	TM
463	Lickilicky	TM
464	Rhyperior	TM
465	Tangrowth	TM
466	Electivire	TM
467	Magmortar	TM
468	Togekiss	TM
469	Yanmega	TM
470	Leafeon	TM
471	Glaceon	TM
472	Gliscor	TM
473	Mamoswine	TM
474	Porygon-Z	TM
475	Gallade	TM
476	Probopass	TM
477	Dusknoir	TM
478	Froslass	TM
479	Rotom	TM
480	Uxie	TM
481	Mesprit	TM
482	Azelf	TM
483	Dialga	TM
484	Palkia	TM
485	Heatran	TM
486	Regigigas	TM
487	Giratina (A)	TM
487	Giratina (O)	TM
488	Cresselia	TM
489	Phione	TM
490	Manaphy	TM
491	Darkrai	TM
492	Shaymin (L)	TM
492	Shaymin (S)	TM

Toxic Spikes		
15	Beedrill	25
29	Nidoran♀	31
30	Nidorina	35
32	Nidoran♂	31
33	Nidorino	35
48	Venonat	E
72	Tentacool	15
73	Tentacruel	15
91	Cloyster	B
138	Omanyte	E
167	Spinarak	E
204	Pineco	E
205	Forretress	B
211	Qwilfish	21
315	Roselia	28
451	Skorupi	28
452	Drapion	28

Transform		
132	Ditto	B
151	Mew	B

Tri Attack		
21	Spearow	E
51	Dugtrio	B
82	Magneton	B
85	Dodrio	34
137	Porygon	51
233	Porygon2	51
474	Porygon-Z	51

Trick		
35	Clefairy	T
36	Clefable	T
63	Abra	T
64	Kadabra	46,T
65	Alakazam	46,T
79	Slowpoke	T
80	Slowbro	T
92	Gastly	T
93	Haunter	T
94	Gengar	T
96	Drowzee	T
97	Hypno	T
121	Starmie	T
122	Mr. Mime	36,T,E
124	Jynx	T
137	Porygon	T
150	Mewtwo	T
151	Mew	T
161	Sentret	E
173	Cleffa	T
175	Togepi	T
176	Togetic	T
177	Natu	T
178	Xatu	T
196	Espeon	T
199	Slowking	T
200	Misdreavus	T
203	Girafarig	T
233	Porygon2	T
238	Smoochum	T
249	Lugia	T
251	Celebi	T
263	Zigzagoon	T,E
264	Linoone	T
280	Ralts	T
281	Kirlia	T
282	Gardevoir	T
292	Shedinja	T
302	Sableye	T
307	Meditite	T
308	Medicham	T
313	Volbeat	E
325	Spoink	T,E
326	Grumpig	T
327	Spinda	E
343	Baltoy	T
344	Claydol	T
352	Kecleon	T,E
353	Shuppet	50,T
354	Banette	66,T
355	Duskull	T
356	Dusclops	T
358	Chimecho	T
375	Metang	T
376	Metagross	T
380	Latias	T
381	Latios	T
385	Jirachi	T
386	Deoxys (N)	T
386	Deoxys (A)	T
386	Deoxys (D)	T
386	Deoxys (S)	T
425	Drifloon	T
426	Drifblim	T
429	Mismagius	T
433	Chingling	T
436	Bronzor	T
437	Bronzong	T
439	Mime Jr.	36,T,E
442	Spiritomb	T
468	Togekiss	T
474	Porygon-Z	T
475	Gallade	T
477	Dusknoir	T
478	Froslass	T
479	Rotom	B,T
480	Uxie	T
481	Mesprit	T
482	Azelf	T
488	Cresselia	T
491	Darkrai	T

Trick Room		
63	Abra	TM
64	Kadabra	TM
65	Alakazam	TM
79	Slowpoke	TM
80	Slowbro	TM
92	Gastly	TM
93	Haunter	TM
94	Gengar	TM
96	Drowzee	TM
97	Hypno	TM
102	Exeggcute	TM
103	Exeggutor	TM
121	Starmie	TM
122	Mr. Mime	TM
124	Jynx	TM
137	Porygon	TM
150	Mewtwo	TM
151	Mew	TM
177	Natu	TM
178	Xatu	TM
196	Espeon	TM
199	Slowking	TM
200	Misdreavus	TM
203	Girafarig	TM
233	Porygon2	TM
234	Stantler	TM
238	Smoochum	TM
251	Celebi	TM
280	Ralts	TM
281	Kirlia	TM
282	Gardevoir	TM
325	Spoink	TM
326	Grumpig	TM
327	Spinda	TM
337	Lunatone	TM
338	Solrock	TM
343	Baltoy	TM
344	Claydol	TM
352	Kecleon	TM
353	Shuppet	TM
354	Banette	TM
355	Duskull	TM
356	Dusclops	TM
358	Chimecho	TM
385	Jirachi	TM
386	Deoxys (N)	TM
386	Deoxys (A)	TM
386	Deoxys (D)	TM
386	Deoxys (S)	TM
429	Mismagius	TM

ADVENTURE DATA LIST
POKÉMON MOVES AND ABILITIES ALPHABETICAL LIST

Trick Room continued		
433	Chingling	TM
436	Bronzor	TM
437	Bronzong	TM
439	Mime Jr.	TM
474	Porygon-Z	B,TM
475	Gallade	TM
477	Dusknoir	TM
480	Uxie	TM
481	Mesprit	TM
482	Azelf	TM
483	Dialga	TM
484	Palkia	TM
488	Cresselia	TM

Triple Kick		
237	Hitmontop	19

Trump Card		
133	Eevee	57
199	Slowking	53
206	Dunsparce	E
312	Minun	48

Twineedle		
15	Beedrill	16

Twister		
6	Charizard	T
12	Butterfree	T
16	Pidgey	21,T
17	Pidgeotto	22,T
18	Pidgeot	22,T
21	Spearow	T
22	Fearow	T
41	Zubat	T
42	Golbat	T
49	Venomoth	T
83	Farfetch'd	T
95	Onix	T
116	Horsea	26,T
117	Seadra	26,T
120	Staryu	T
121	Starmie	T
130	Gyarados	29,T
142	Aerodactyl	T
144	Articuno	T
145	Zapdos	T
146	Moltres	T
147	Dratini	11,T
148	Dragonair	B,11,T
149	Dragonite	B,11,T
151	Mew	T
163	Hoothoot	T
164	Noctowl	T
169	Crobat	T
176	Togetic	T
177	Natu	T
178	Xatu	T
198	Murkrow	T
208	Steelix	T
226	Mantine	E
227	Skarmory	T
230	Kingdra	26,T
237	Hitmontop	T
249	Lugia	T
250	Ho-Oh	T
267	Beautifly	T
269	Dustox	T
275	Shiftry	T
276	Taillow	T
277	Swellow	T
278	Wingull	T,E
279	Pelipper	T
284	Masquerain	T
329	Vibrava	T
330	Flygon	T
333	Swablu	T
334	Altaria	T
350	Milotic	17,T
357	Tropius	T
371	Bagon	T,E
372	Shelgon	T
373	Salamence	T
380	Latias	T
381	Latios	T
384	Rayquaza	B,T
396	Starly	T
397	Staravia	T
398	Staraptor	T
414	Mothim	T
430	Honchkrow	T
441	Chatot	T
443	Gible	T,E
444	Gabite	T
445	Garchomp	T
456	Finneon	T
457	Lumineon	T
458	Mantyke	E
468	Togekiss	T
483	Dialga	T
484	Palkia	T
487	Giratina (A)	T
487	Giratina (O)	T

Uproar		
16	Pidgey	T,E
17	Pidgeotto	T
18	Pidgeot	T
19	Rattata	E
21	Spearow	E
31	Nidoqueen	T
34	Nidoking	T
41	Zubat	T
42	Golbat	T
50	Diglett	E
52	Meowth	T
53	Persian	T
56	Mankey	T
57	Primeape	T
83	Farfetch'd	T
84	Doduo	23,T
85	Dodrio	23,T
92	Gastly	T
93	Haunter	T
94	Gengar	T
102	Exeggcute	B,T
104	Cubone	T
105	Marowak	T
109	Koffing	T
110	Weezing	T
111	Rhyhorn	T
112	Rhydon	T
115	Kangaskhan	T
128	Tauros	T
130	Gyarados	T
151	Mew	T
158	Totodile	T
159	Croconaw	T
160	Feraligatr	T
161	Sentret	T
162	Furret	T
163	Hoothoot	13,T
164	Noctowl	13,T
165	Ledyba	T
166	Ledian	T
169	Crobat	T
172	Pichu	T
173	Cleffa	T
174	Igglybuff	T
175	Togepi	T
182	Bellossom	T
190	Aipom	T
191	Sunkern	T
192	Sunflora	T
193	Yanma	27,T
198	Murkrow	T
200	Misdreavus	T
203	Girafarig	T
217	Ursaring	T
228	Houndour	T
229	Houndoom	T
234	Stantler	T
236	Tyrogue	T
238	Smoochum	T
239	Elekid	T
240	Magby	T
246	Larvitar	T
247	Pupitar	T
248	Tyranitar	T
251	Celebi	T
258	Mudkip	E
261	Poochyena	T
262	Mightyena	T
270	Lotad	T
271	Lombre	37,T
272	Ludicolo	T
278	Wingull	T
279	Pelipper	T
288	Vigoroth	B,13,T
291	Ninjask	T
293	Whismur	5,T
294	Loudred	B,5,T
295	Exploud	B,5,T
298	Azurill	T
300	Skitty	E
304	Aron	T
305	Lairon	T
306	Aggron	T
309	Electrike	E
311	Plusle	T
312	Minun	T
318	Carvanha	T
319	Sharpedo	T
327	Spinda	5,T
333	Swablu	T
334	Altaria	T
358	Chimecho	17,T
382	Kyogre	T
383	Groudon	T
384	Rayquaza	T
385	Jirachi	T
390	Chimchar	T
401	Kricketot	T
402	Kricketune	T
406	Budew	T
408	Cranidos	T
409	Rampardos	T
413	Wormadam (P)	T
413	Wormadam (S)	T
413	Wormadam (T)	T
417	Pachirisu	T
424	Ambipom	T
427	Buneary	T
428	Lopunny	T
429	Mismagius	T
430	Honchkrow	T
433	Chingling	17,T
438	Bonsly	T
439	Mime Jr.	T
440	Happiny	T
441	Chatot	37,T
442	Spiritomb	T
446	Munchlax	T
464	Rhyperior	T
469	Yanmega	27,T
474	Porygon-Z	T
479	Rotom	B,T
482	Azelf	31,T
485	Heatran	T
489	Phione	T
490	Manaphy	T

U-turn		
12	Butterfree	TM
15	Beedrill	TM
16	Pidgey	TM
17	Pidgeotto	TM
18	Pidgeot	TM
19	Rattata	TM
20	Raticate	TM
21	Spearow	TM
22	Fearow	TM
41	Zubat	TM
42	Golbat	TM
49	Venomoth	TM
52	Meowth	TM
53	Persian	TM
56	Mankey	TM
57	Primeape	TM
83	Farfetch'd	TM
123	Scyther	TM
144	Articuno	TM
145	Zapdos	TM
146	Moltres	TM
151	Mew	TM
161	Sentret	TM
162	Furret	TM
165	Ledyba	TM
166	Ledian	TM
169	Crobat	TM
177	Natu	TM
178	Xatu	TM
187	Hoppip	31,TM
188	Skiploom	36,TM
189	Jumpluff	36,TM
190	Aipom	TM
193	Yanma	49,TM
207	Gligar	38,TM
212	Scizor	TM
251	Celebi	TM
267	Beautifly	TM
269	Dustox	TM
276	Taillow	TM
277	Swellow	TM
278	Wingull	TM
279	Pelipper	TM
284	Masquerain	TM
291	Ninjask	TM
313	Volbeat	TM
314	Illumise	TM
329	Vibrava	TM
330	Flygon	TM
385	Jirachi	TM
390	Chimchar	TM
391	Monferno	TM
392	Infernape	TM
396	Starly	TM
397	Staravia	TM
398	Staraptor	TM
414	Mothim	TM
416	Vespiquen	TM
417	Pachirisu	TM
424	Ambipom	TM
431	Glameow	TM
432	Purugly	TM
441	Chatot	TM
456	Finneon	42,TM
457	Lumineon	48,TM
469	Yanmega	49,TM
472	Gliscor	38,TM
480	Uxie	TM
481	Mesprit	TM
482	Azelf	TM
489	Phione	TM
490	Manaphy	TM

Vacuum Wave		
56	Mankey	T
57	Primeape	T
62	Poliwrath	T
66	Machop	T
67	Machoke	T
68	Machamp	T
106	Hitmonlee	T
107	Hitmonchan	26,T
123	Scyther	B
151	Mew	T
214	Heracross	T
236	Tyrogue	T,E
237	Hitmontop	T
256	Combusken	T
257	Blaziken	T
286	Breloom	T
296	Makuhita	T
297	Hariyama	T
307	Meditite	T
308	Medicham	T
390	Chimchar	T
391	Monferno	T
392	Infernape	T
447	Riolu	T,E
448	Lucario	T
453	Croagunk	T,E
454	Toxicroak	T
475	Gallade	T

ViceGrip		
98	Krabby	5
99	Kingler	B,5
127	Pinsir	B
303	Mawile	21
341	Corphish	10
342	Crawdaunt	B,10

Vine Whip		
1	Bulbasaur	9
2	Ivysaur	9
3	Venusaur	B,9
69	Bellsprout	B
70	Weepinbell	B
71	Victreebel	B
114	Tangela	19
152	Chikorita	E
455	Carnivine	11
465	Tangrowth	19

Vital Throw		
66	Machop	25
67	Machoke	25
68	Machamp	25
127	Pinsir	25
296	Makuhita	10
297	Hariyama	10

Volt Tackle		
172	Pichu	E*

Wake-Up Slap		
35	Clefairy	22
39	Jigglypuff	37
60	Poliwag	35
61	Poliwhirl	43
66	Machop	34
67	Machoke	36
68	Machamp	36
122	Mr. Mime	E
124	Jynx	28
241	Miltank	55
285	Shroomish	E
296	Makuhita	34,E
297	Hariyama	42
300	Skitty	32
439	Mime Jr.	E
453	Croagunk	E
478	Froslass	28

Water Gun		
7	Squirtle	13
8	Wartortle	13
9	Blastoise	13
54	Psyduck	9
55	Golduck	B,9
60	Poliwag	11
61	Poliwhirl	11
79	Slowpoke	11
80	Slowbro	11
116	Horsea	11
117	Seadra	B,11
120	Staryu	6
121	Starmie	B
131	Lapras	B
134	Vaporeon	15
138	Omanyte	10
139	Omastar	10
158	Totodile	6
159	Croconaw	B,6
160	Feraligatr	B,6
170	Chinchou	12
171	Lanturn	12
183	Marill	10
184	Azumarill	B,10
194	Wooper	B
195	Quagsire	B
199	Slowking	11
211	Qwilfish	13
223	Remoraid	B
224	Octillery	B
230	Kingdra	B,11
258	Mudkip	10
259	Marshtomp	B,10
260	Swampert	B,10
270	Lotad	E
278	Wingull	B
279	Pelipper	B
298	Azurill	18
320	Wailmer	7
321	Wailord	B,7
339	Barboach	10
340	Whiscash	10
347	Anorith	13
348	Armaldo	B,13
350	Milotic	B
351	Castform	10
363	Spheal	B
364	Sealeo	B
365	Walrein	B
366	Clamperl	B
369	Relicanth	8
370	Luvdisc	7
400	Bibarel	15
418	Buizel	6
419	Floatzel	6
456	Finneon	6
457	Lumineon	B,6

Water Pulse		
7	Squirtle	25,TM
8	Wartortle	28,TM
9	Blastoise	28,TM
29	Nidoran♀	TM
30	Nidorina	TM
31	Nidoqueen	TM
32	Nidoran♂	TM
33	Nidorino	TM
34	Nidoking	TM
35	Clefairy	TM
36	Clefable	TM
39	Jigglypuff	TM
40	Wigglytuff	TM
52	Meowth	TM
53	Persian	TM
54	Psyduck	22,TM
55	Golduck	22,TM
60	Poliwag	TM
61	Poliwhirl	TM
62	Poliwrath	TM
72	Tentacool	29,TM
73	Tentacruel	29,TM
79	Slowpoke	29,TM
80	Slowbro	29,TM
86	Seel	TM
87	Dewgong	TM
90	Shellder	TM
91	Cloyster	TM
98	Krabby	TM
99	Kingler	TM
108	Lickitung	TM
113	Chansey	TM
115	Kangaskhan	TM
116	Horsea	TM
117	Seadra	TM
118	Goldeen	17,TM
119	Seaking	17,TM
120	Staryu	TM
121	Starmie	TM
124	Jynx	TM
128	Tauros	TM
130	Gyarados	TM
131	Lapras	14,TM
134	Vaporeon	TM
138	Omanyte	TM
139	Omastar	TM
140	Kabuto	TM
141	Kabutops	TM
143	Snorlax	TM
144	Articuno	TM
147	Dratini	TM
148	Dragonair	TM
149	Dragonite	TM
150	Mewtwo	TM
151	Mew	TM
158	Totodile	TM
159	Croconaw	TM
160	Feraligatr	TM
161	Sentret	TM
162	Furret	TM
170	Chinchou	TM
171	Lanturn	TM
173	Cleffa	TM
174	Igglybuff	TM
175	Togepi	TM
176	Togetic	TM
183	Marill	TM
184	Azumarill	TM
186	Politoed	TM
190	Aipom	TM
194	Wooper	TM
195	Quagsire	TM
199	Slowking	29,TM
206	Dunsparce	TM
209	Snubbull	TM
210	Granbull	TM
211	Qwilfish	TM
222	Corsola	TM
223	Remoraid	32,TM
224	Octillery	TM
225	Delibird	TM
226	Mantine	28,TM
230	Kingdra	TM
238	Smoochum	TM
241	Miltank	TM
242	Blissey	TM
245	Suicune	TM
248	Tyranitar	TM
249	Lugia	TM
251	Celebi	TM
258	Mudkip	TM
259	Marshtomp	TM
260	Swampert	TM
263	Zigzagoon	TM
264	Linoone	TM
270	Lotad	TM
271	Lombre	TM
272	Ludicolo	TM
278	Wingull	19,TM
279	Pelipper	19,TM
283	Surskit	TM
284	Masquerain	TM
287	Slakoth	TM
288	Vigoroth	TM
289	Slaking	TM
293	Whismur	TM
294	Loudred	TM
295	Exploud	TM
298	Azurill	TM
300	Skitty	TM
301	Delcatty	TM
302	Sableye	TM
304	Aron	TM
305	Lairon	TM
306	Aggron	TM
313	Volbeat	TM
314	Illumise	TM
316	Gulpin	TM
317	Swalot	TM
318	Carvanha	TM
319	Sharpedo	TM
320	Wailmer	21,TM
321	Wailord	21,TM
327	Spinda	TM
335	Zangoose	TM
339	Barboach	22,TM
340	Whiscash	22,TM
341	Corphish	TM
342	Crawdaunt	TM
347	Anorith	TM
348	Armaldo	TM
349	Feebas	TM
350	Milotic	13,TM
351	Castform	TM
352	Kecleon	TM
359	Absol	TM
361	Snorunt	TM
362	Glalie	TM
363	Spheal	TM
364	Sealeo	TM
365	Walrein	TM
366	Clamperl	TM
367	Huntail	15,TM
368	Gorebyss	15,TM
369	Relicanth	TM
370	Luvdisc	31,TM
380	Latias	TM
381	Latios	TM
382	Kyogre	B,TM
384	Rayquaza	TM
385	Jirachi	TM
386	Deoxys (N)	TM
386	Deoxys (A)	TM
386	Deoxys (D)	TM
386	Deoxys (S)	TM
393	Piplup	TM
394	Prinplup	TM
395	Empoleon	TM
400	Bibarel	TM
418	Buizel	TM
419	Floatzel	TM
422	Shellos	7,TM
423	Gastrodon	B,7,TM
424	Ambipom	TM
427	Buneary	TM
428	Lopunny	TM
431	Glameow	TM
432	Purugly	TM
440	Happiny	TM
442	Spiritomb	TM
446	Munchlax	TM
448	Lucario	TM
449	Hippopotas	TM
450	Hippowdon	TM
456	Finneon	22,TM
457	Lumineon	22,TM
458	Mantyke	28,TM
459	Snover	TM
460	Abomasnow	TM
463	Lickilicky	TM
468	Togekiss	TM
471	Glaceon	TM
478	Froslass	TM
480	Uxie	TM
481	Mesprit	TM
482	Azelf	TM
484	Palkia	10,TM
489	Phione	46,TM
490	Manaphy	46,TM

Water Sport		
54	Psyduck	B
55	Golduck	B
60	Poliwag	B,E
61	Poliwhirl	B
86	Seel	7
118	Goldeen	B
119	Seaking	B
158	Totodile	E
226	Mantine	E
271	Lombre	19
278	Wingull	E
279	Pelipper	B
283	Surskit	19
284	Masquerain	B,19
339	Barboach	6
340	Whiscash	B,6
350	Milotic	5
363	Spheal	E
369	Relicanth	E
370	Luvdisc	E
380	Latias	25
393	Piplup	11
394	Prinplup	11
399	Bidoof	E
406	Budew	7
418	Buizel	B
419	Floatzel	B
458	Mantyke	E
489	Phione	B
490	Manaphy	B

Water Spout		
320	Wailmer	34
321	Wailord	34
382	Kyogre	80

Waterfall		
7	Squirtle	HM
8	Wartortle	HM
9	Blastoise	HM
54	Psyduck	HM
55	Golduck	HM
60	Poliwag	HM
61	Poliwhirl	HM
62	Poliwrath	HM
72	Tentacool	HM
73	Tentacruel	HM
86	Seel	HM
87	Dewgong	HM
116	Horsea	HM
117	Seadra	HM
118	Goldeen	37,HM
119	Seaking	40,HM
120	Staryu	HM
121	Starmie	HM

Pokémon moves and Abilities alphabetical list

130	Gyarados	HM
131	Lapras	HM
134	Vaporeon	HM
138	Omanyte	HM
139	Omastar	HM
140	Kabuto	HM
141	Kabutops	HM
147	Dratini	HM
148	Dragonair	HM
149	Dragonite	HM
151	Mew	HM
158	Totodile	HM
159	Croconaw	HM
160	Feraligatr	HM
170	Chinchou	HM
171	Lanturn	HM
183	Marill	HM
184	Azumarill	HM
186	Politoed	HM
194	Wooper	HM
195	Quagsire	HM
211	Qwilfish	HM
223	Remoraid	HM
224	Octillery	HM
226	Mantine	HM
230	Kingdra	HM
245	Suicune	HM
249	Lugia	HM
258	Mudkip	HM
259	Marshtomp	HM
260	Swampert	HM
271	Lombre	HM
272	Ludicolo	HM
298	Azurill	HM
318	Carvanha	HM
319	Sharpedo	HM
320	Wailmer	HM
321	Wailord	HM
339	Barboach	HM
340	Whiscash	HM
341	Corphish	HM
342	Crawdaunt	HM
349	Feebas	HM
350	Milotic	HM
363	Spheal	HM
364	Sealeo	HM
365	Walrein	HM
366	Clamperl	HM
367	Huntail	HM
368	Gorebyss	HM
369	Relicanth	HM
370	Luvdisc	HM
380	Latias	HM
381	Latios	HM
382	Kyogre	HM
384	Rayquaza	HM
393	Piplup	HM
394	Prinplup	HM
395	Empoleon	HM
400	Bibarel	HM
418	Buizel	HM
419	Floatzel	HM
423	Gastrodon	HM
456	Finneon	HM
457	Lumineon	HM
458	Mantyke	HM
489	Phione	HM
490	Manaphy	HM

Weather Ball		
351	Castform	30
407	Roserade	B

Whirlpool		
90	Shellder	37
131	Lapras	E
170	Chinchou	E
258	Mudkip	33,E
320	Wailmer	14
321	Wailord	14
339	Barboach	E
366	Clamperl	B
367	Huntail	B
368	Gorebyss	B
393	Piplup	32
394	Prinplup	37
395	Empoleon	39
418	Buizel	36
419	Floatzel	39
456	Finneon	38
457	Lumineon	42
489	Phione	39
490	Manaphy	39

Whirlwind		
12	Butterfree	22
16	Pidgey	17
17	Pidgeotto	17
18	Pidgeot	17

21	Spearow	E
41	Zubat	E
142	Aerodactyl	E
143	Snorlax	E
163	Hoothoot	E
193	Yanma	E
198	Murkrow	E
227	Skarmory	E
249	Lugia	B
250	Ho-Oh	B
267	Beautifly	27
269	Dustox	27
275	Shiftry	B
276	Taillow	E
284	Masquerain	54
296	Makuhita	16
297	Hariyama	16
357	Tropius	27
396	Starly	21
397	Staravia	23
398	Staraptor	23
408	Cranidos	E
446	Munchlax	E
451	Skorupi	E

Will-O-Wisp		
4	Charmander	TM
5	Charmeleon	TM
6	Charizard	TM
37	Vulpix	14,TM
38	Ninetales	TM
58	Growlithe	TM
59	Arcanine	TM
77	Ponyta	TM
78	Rapidash	TM
92	Gastly	TM,E
93	Haunter	TM
94	Gengar	TM
109	Koffing	TM,E
110	Weezing	TM
126	Magmar	TM
136	Flareon	TM
146	Moltres	TM
150	Mewtwo	TM
151	Mew	TM
155	Cyndaquil	TM
156	Quilava	TM
157	Typhlosion	TM
200	Misdreavus	TM
218	Slugma	TM
219	Magcargo	TM
228	Houndour	TM,E
229	Houndoom	TM
240	Magby	TM
244	Entei	TM
250	Ho-Oh	TM
255	Torchic	TM
256	Combusken	TM
257	Blaziken	TM
280	Ralts	E
292	Shedinja	TM
302	Sableye	TM
322	Numel	TM
323	Camerupt	TM
324	Torkoal	TM
338	Solrock	TM
353	Shuppet	23,TM
354	Banette	23,TM
355	Duskull	33,TM
356	Dusclops	33,TM
359	Absol	TM
390	Chimchar	TM
391	Monferno	TM
392	Infernape	TM
425	Drifloon	TM
426	Drifblim	TM
429	Mismagius	TM
442	Spiritomb	TM
467	Magmortar	TM
477	Dusknoir	33,TM
479	Rotom	TM
485	Heatran	TM
487	Giratina (A)	TM
487	Giratina (O)	TM
491	Darkrai	TM

Wing Attack		
6	Charizard	36
16	Pidgey	33
17	Pidgeotto	37
18	Pidgeot	38
41	Zubat	17
42	Golbat	17
123	Scyther	21
142	Aerodactyl	B
146	Moltres	B
149	Dragonite	55
163	Hoothoot	E
169	Crobat	17

193	Yanma	43
198	Murkrow	15,E
207	Gligar	E
226	Mantine	22
276	Taillow	13
277	Swellow	13
278	Wingull	11
279	Pelipper	B,11
396	Starly	9
397	Staravia	9
398	Staraptor	B,9
430	Honchkrow	B
458	Mantyke	22

Wish		
133	Eevee	E
172	Pichu	E
173	Cleffa	E
174	Igglybuff	E
175	Togepi	28
176	Togetic	28
177	Natu	28
178	Xatu	30
203	Girafarig	E
238	Smoochum	E
282	Gardevoir	17
300	Skitty	E
311	Plusle	E
312	Minun	E
314	Illumise	21
327	Spinda	E
358	Chimecho	E
380	Latias	5
385	Jirachi	B
433	Chingling	E

Withdraw		
7	Squirtle	10
8	Wartortle	10
9	Blastoise	B,10
80	Slowbro	37
90	Shellder	4
91	Cloyster	B
138	Omanyte	B
139	Omastar	B
213	Shuckle	B
324	Torkoal	7
387	Turtwig	5
388	Grotle	B,5
389	Torterra	B,5

Wood Hammer		
103	Exeggcutor	37
185	Sudowoodo	B
389	Torterra	B
459	Snover	36
460	Abomasnow	36

Worry Seed		
1	Bulbasaur	31
2	Ivysaur	36
3	Venusaur	39
69	Bellsprout	E
102	Exeggcute	33
187	Hoppip	34,E
188	Skiploom	40
189	Jumpluff	40
191	Sunkern	25
192	Sunflora	25
252	Treecko	E
273	Seedot	E
285	Shroomish	29,E
387	Turtwig	E
406	Budew	16
420	Cherubi	28
421	Cherrim	30
455	Carnivine	E
492	Shaymin (L)	55
492	Shaymin (S)	55

Wrap		
23	Ekans	B
24	Arbok	B
69	Bellsprout	11
70	Weepinbell	B,11
72	Tentacool	22
73	Tentacruel	22
108	Lickitung	17
147	Dratini	B
148	Dragonair	B
149	Dragonite	B
213	Shuckle	22
336	Seviper	B
350	Milotic	B
358	Chimecho	B
386	Deoxys (N)	B
386	Deoxys (A)	B
386	Deoxys (D)	B
386	Deoxys (S)	B

433	Chingling	B
463	Lickilicky	17

Wring Out		
69	Bellsprout	47
70	Weepinbell	47
72	Tentacool	43
73	Tentacruel	55
108	Lickitung	53
114	Tangela	50
124	Jynx	44
138	Omanyte	E
140	Kabuto	55
141	Kabutops	63
152	Chikorita	E
224	Octillery	36
316	Gulpin	49
317	Swalot	59
336	Seviper	55
345	Lileep	64,E
346	Cradily	76
455	Carnivine	41
463	Lickilicky	53
465	Tangrowth	50

X-Scissor		
15	Beedrill	TM
27	Sandshrew	TM
28	Sandslash	TM
46	Paras	43,TM
47	Parasect	55,TM
98	Krabby	TM
99	Kingler	TM
123	Scyther	41,TM
127	Pinsir	30,TM
141	Kabutops	TM
151	Mew	TM
169	Crobat	TM
207	Gligar	42,TM
212	Scizor	41,TM
215	Sneasel	TM
227	Skarmory	TM
253	Grovyle	TM
254	Sceptile	16,TM
275	Shiftry	TM
290	Nincada	TM
291	Ninjask	52,TM
292	Shedinja	TM
335	Zangoose	48,TM
336	Seviper	TM
341	Corphish	TM
342	Crawdaunt	TM
347	Anorith	61,TM
348	Armaldo	73,TM
359	Absol	TM
402	Kricketune	30,TM
416	Vespiquen	TM
451	Skorupi	TM
452	Drapion	TM
453	Croagunk	TM
454	Toxicroak	TM
461	Weavile	TM
470	Leafeon	TM
472	Gliscor	42,TM
475	Gallade	TM
491	Darkrai	TM

Yawn		
7	Squirtle	E
54	Psyduck	E
79	Slowpoke	B
80	Slowbro	B
133	Eevee	E
143	Snorlax	20
175	Togepi	15
176	Togetic	15
194	Wooper	29
195	Quagsire	31
199	Slowking	B
206	Dunsparce	9
216	Teddiursa	E
218	Slugma	B
219	Magcargo	B
230	Kingdra	B
261	Poochyena	E
287	Slakoth	B
289	Slaking	B
316	Gulpin	6
317	Swalot	B,6
322	Numel	E
324	Torkoal	E
358	Chimecho	25
363	Spheal	E
369	Relicanth	22
393	Piplup	E
399	Bidoof	25
400	Bibarel	28
422	Shellos	E
449	Hippopotas	13

450	Hippowdon	B,13
480	Uxie	31

Zap Cannon		
81	Magnemite	54
82	Magneton	60
137	Porygon	62
205	Forretress	67
233	Porygon2	62
299	Nosepass	67
377	Regirock	65
378	Regice	65
379	Registeel	65
386	Deoxys (A)	81
462	Magnezone	60
474	Porygon-Z	62
476	Probopass	67

Zen Headbutt		
7	Squirtle	T
8	Wartortle	T
9	Blastoise	T
19	Rattata	T
20	Raticate	T
35	Clefairy	T
36	Clefable	T
37	Vulpix	T
38	Ninetales	T
41	Zubat	T,E
42	Golbat	T
48	Venonat	37,T
49	Venomoth	41,T
54	Psyduck	40,T
55	Golduck	44,T
63	Abra	T
64	Kadabra	T
65	Alakazam	T
79	Slowpoke	34,T,E
80	Slowbro	34,T
96	Drowzee	50,T
97	Hypno	64,T
103	Exeggutor	T
108	Lickitung	T
113	Chansey	T
122	Mr. Mime	T
124	Jynx	T
128	Tauros	29,T
131	Lapras	T
137	Porygon	T
143	Snorlax	T
150	Mewtwo	T
151	Mew	T
163	Hoothoot	33,T
164	Noctowl	37,T
169	Crobat	T
173	Cleffa	T
175	Togepi	T
176	Togetic	T
177	Natu	T,E
178	Xatu	T
196	Espeon	T
199	Slowking	34,T
203	Girafarig	41,T
206	Dunsparce	T
233	Porygon2	T
234	Stantler	38,T,E
238	Smoochum	T
241	Miltank	29,T
242	Blissey	T
249	Lugia	T
250	Ho-Oh	T
251	Celebi	T
270	Lotad	31,T
271	Lombre	31,T
272	Ludicolo	T
280	Ralts	T
281	Kirlia	T
282	Gardevoir	T
293	Whismur	T
294	Loudred	T
295	Exploud	T
300	Skitty	T,E
301	Delcatty	T
302	Sableye	50,T
307	Meditite	T
308	Medicham	T
313	Volbeat	37,T
314	Illumise	37,T
318	Carvanha	T
319	Sharpedo	T
325	Spoink	26,T,E
326	Grumpig	26,T
327	Spinda	T
337	Lunatone	T
338	Solrock	T
340	Whiscash	B,T
343	Baltoy	T
344	Claydol	T
358	Chimecho	T
359	Absol	T,E
371	Bagon	35,T
372	Shelgon	37,T
373	Salamence	37,T
374	Beldum	T
375	Metang	52,T
376	Metagross	62,T
380	Latias	40,T
381	Latios	40,T
385	Jirachi	35,T
386	Deoxys (N)	65,T
386	Deoxys (A)	65,T
386	Deoxys (D)	65,T
386	Deoxys (S)	65,T
408	Cranidos	33,T
409	Rampardos	36,T
433	Chingling	T
437	Bronzong	T
440	Happiny	T
446	Munchlax	T,E
447	Riolu	T
448	Lucario	T
463	Lickilicky	T
468	Togekiss	T
474	Porygon-Z	T
475	Gallade	T
480	Uxie	T
481	Mesprit	T
482	Azelf	T
486	Regigigas	50,T
488	Cresselia	T
492	Shaymin (L)	T
492	Shaymin (S)	T

ADVENTURE DATA LIST
POKÉMON MOVES AND ABILITIES ALPHABETICAL LIST

Pokémon Abilities alphabetical list

Adaptability
133 Eevee
474 Porygon-Z

Aftermath
425 Drifloon
426 Drifblim
434 Stunky
435 Skuntank

Air Lock
384 Rayquaza

Anger Point
56 Mankey
57 Primeape
128 Tauros

Anticipation
339 Barboach
340 Whiscash
413 Wormadam (P)
413 Wormadam (S)
413 Wormadam (T)
453 Croagunk
454 Toxicroak

Arena Trap
50 Diglett
51 Dugtrio
328 Trapinch

Bad Dreams
491 Darkrai

Battle Armor
140 Kabuto
141 Kabutops
347 Anorith
348 Armaldo
451 Skorupi
452 Drapion

Blaze
4 Charmander
5 Charmeleon
6 Charizard
155 Cyndaquil
156 Quilava
157 Typhlosion
255 Torchic
256 Combusken
257 Blaziken
390 Chimchar
391 Monferno
392 Infernape

Chlorophyll
43 Oddish
44 Gloom
45 Vileplume
69 Bellsprout
70 Weepinbell
71 Victreebel
102 Exeggcute
103 Exeggutor
114 Tangela
182 Bellossom
187 Hoppip
188 Skiploom
189 Jumpluff
191 Sunkern

192 Sunflora
273 Seedot
274 Nuzleaf
275 Shiftry
357 Tropius
420 Cherubi
465 Tangrowth

Clear Body
72 Tentacool
73 Tentacruel
374 Beldum
375 Metang
376 Metagross
377 Regirock
378 Regice
379 Registeel

Cloud Nine
54 Psyduck
55 Golduck

Color Change
352 Kecleon

Compoundeyes
12 Butterfree
48 Venonat
193 Yanma
290 Nincada

Cute Charm
35 Clefairy
36 Clefable
39 Jigglypuff
40 Wigglytuff
173 Cleffa
174 Igglybuff
300 Skitty
301 Delcatty
428 Lopunny

Damp
54 Psyduck
55 Golduck
60 Poliwag
61 Poliwhirl
62 Poliwrath
186 Politoed
194 Wooper
195 Quagsire

Download
137 Porygon
233 Porygon2
474 Porygon-Z

Drizzle
382 Kyogre

Drought
383 Groudon

Dry Skin
46 Paras
47 Parasect
453 Croagunk
454 Toxicroak

Early Bird
84 Doduo
85 Dodrio

115 Kangaskhan
165 Ledyba
166 Ledian
177 Natu
178 Xatu
203 Girafarig
228 Houndour
229 Houndoom
273 Seedot
274 Nuzleaf
275 Shiftry

Effect Spore
46 Paras
47 Parasect
285 Shroomish
286 Breloom

Filter
122 Mr. Mime
439 Mime Jr.

Flame Body
126 Magmar
218 Slugma
219 Magcargo
240 Magby
467 Magmortar

Flash Fire
37 Vulpix
38 Ninetales
58 Growlithe
59 Arcanine
77 Ponyta
78 Rapidash
136 Flareon
228 Houndour
229 Houndoom
485 Heatran

Flower Gift
421 Cherrim

Forecast
351 Castform

Forewarn
96 Drowzee
97 Hypno
124 Jynx
238 Smoochum

Frisk
234 Stantler
353 Shuppet
354 Banette

Gluttony
213 Shuckle
263 Zigzagoon
264 Linoone

Guts
19 Rattata
20 Raticate
63 Abra
64 Kadabra
65 Alakazam
83 Farfetch'd
149 Dragonite
169 Crobat
203 Girafarig
215 Sneasel

246 Larvitar
276 Taillow
277 Swellow
296 Makuhita
297 Hariyama

Heatproof
436 Bronzor
437 Bronzong

Honey Gather
415 Combee

Huge Power
183 Marill
184 Azumarill
298 Azurill

Hustle
175 Togepi
176 Togetic
222 Corsola
223 Remoraid
225 Delibird
468 Togekiss

Hydration
86 Seel
87 Dewgong
489 Phione
490 Manaphy

Hyper Cutter
98 Krabby
99 Kingler
127 Pinsir
207 Gligar
303 Mawile
328 Trapinch
341 Corphish
342 Crawdaunt
472 Gliscor

Ice Body
361 Snorunt
362 Glalie
363 Spheal
364 Sealeo
365 Walrein

Illuminate
120 Staryu
121 Starmie
170 Chinchou
171 Lanturn
313 Volbeat

Immunity
143 Snorlax
335 Zangoose

Inner Focus
41 Zubat
42 Golbat
63 Abra
64 Kadabra
65 Alakazam
83 Farfetch'd
149 Dragonite
169 Crobat
203 Girafarig
215 Sneasel

361 Snorunt
362 Glalie
447 Riolu
448 Lucario

Insomnia
96 Drowzee
97 Hypno
163 Hoothoot
164 Noctowl
167 Spinarak
168 Ariados
198 Murkrow
353 Shuppet
354 Banette
430 Honchkrow

Intimidate
23 Ekans
24 Arbok
58 Growlithe
59 Arcanine
128 Tauros
130 Gyarados
209 Snubbull
210 Granbull
234 Stantler
237 Hitmontop
262 Mightyena
284 Masquerain
303 Mawile
373 Salamence
397 Staravia
398 Staraptor
403 Shinx
404 Luxio
405 Luxray

Iron Fist
107 Hitmonchan

Keen Eye
16 Pidgey
17 Pidgeotto
18 Pidgeot
21 Spearow
22 Fearow
83 Farfetch'd
107 Hitmonchan
161 Sentret
162 Furret
163 Hoothoot
164 Noctowl
215 Sneasel
227 Skarmory
278 Wingull
279 Pelipper
302 Sableye
396 Starly
441 Chatot

Klutz
427 Buneary
428 Lopunny

Leaf Guard
114 Tangela
187 Hoppip
188 Skiploom
189 Jumpluff
465 Tangrowth
470 Leafeon

Levitate
92 Gastly
93 Haunter
94 Gengar
109 Koffing
110 Weezing
200 Misdreavus
201 Unown
329 Vibrava
330 Flygon
337 Lunatone
338 Solrock
343 Baltoy
344 Claydol
355 Duskull
358 Chimecho
380 Latias
381 Latios
429 Mismagius
433 Chingling
436 Bronzor
437 Bronzong
455 Carnivine
479 Rotom
480 Uxie
481 Mesprit
482 Azelf
488 Cresselia
487 Giratina (O)

Lightningrod
104 Cubone
105 Marowak
111 Rhyhorn
112 Rhydon
309 Electrike
310 Manectric
464 Rhyperior

Limber
53 Persian
106 Hitmonlee
132 Ditto
431 Glameow

Liquid Ooze
72 Tentacool
73 Tentacruel
316 Gulpin
317 Swalot

Magic Guard
35 Clefairy
36 Clefable
173 Cleffa

Magma Armor
218 Slugma
219 Magcargo
323 Camerupt

Magnet Pull
81 Magnemite
82 Magneton
299 Nosepass
462 Magnezone
476 Probopass

Marvel Scale
350 Milotic

Minus
312 Minun

Mold Breaker
127 Pinsir
408 Cranidos
409 Rampardos

Motor Drive
466 Electivire

Natural Cure
113 Chansey
120 Staryu
121 Starmie
222 Corsola
242 Blissey
251 Celebi
315 Roselia
333 Swablu
334 Altaria
406 Budew
407 Roserade
440 Happiny
492 Shaymin (L)

No Guard
66 Machop
67 Machoke
68 Machamp

Normalize
300 Skitty
301 Delcatty

Oblivious
79 Slowpoke
80 Slowbro
108 Lickitung
124 Jynx
199 Slowking
220 Swinub
221 Piloswine
238 Smoochum
314 Illumise
320 Wailmer
321 Wailord
322 Numel
339 Barboach
340 Whiscash
463 Lickilicky
473 Mamoswine

Overgrow
1 Bulbasaur
2 Ivysaur
3 Venusaur
152 Chikorita
153 Bayleef
154 Meganium
252 Treecko
253 Grovyle
254 Sceptile
387 Turtwig
388 Grotle
389 Torterra

Own Tempo
79 Slowpoke
80 Slowbro
108 Lickitung

199 Slowking
235 Smeargle
325 Spoink
326 Grumpig
327 Spinda
431 Glameow
432 Purugly
463 Lickilicky

Pickup
52 Meowth
190 Aipom
216 Teddiursa
231 Phanpy
263 Zigzagoon
264 Linoone
417 Pachirisu
424 Ambipom
446 Munchlax

Plus
311 Plusle

Poison Heal
285 Shroomish
286 Breloom

Poison Point
29 Nidoran ♀
30 Nidorina
31 Nidoqueen
32 Nidoran ♂
33 Nidorino
34 Nidoking
117 Seadra
211 Qwilfish
315 Roselia
406 Budew
407 Roserade

Pressure
142 Aerodactyl
144 Articuno
145 Zapdos
146 Moltres
150 Mewtwo
243 Raikou
244 Entei
245 Suicune
249 Lugia
250 Ho-Oh
356 Dusclops
359 Absol
386 Deoxys (N)
386 Deoxys (A)
386 Deoxys (D)
386 Deoxys (S)
416 Vespiquen
442 Spiritomb
461 Weavile
477 Dusknoir
483 Dialga
484 Palkia
487 Giratina (A)

Pure Power
307 Meditite
308 Medicham

Quick Feet
210 Granbull
216 Teddiursa
217 Ursaring
261 Poochyena
262 Mightyena

Rain Dish
270 Lotad
271 Lombre
272 Ludicolo

Reckless
106 Hitmonlee

Rivalry
29 Nidoran ♀
30 Nidorina
31 Nidoqueen
32 Nidoran ♂
33 Nidorino
34 Nidoking
403 Shinx
404 Luxio
405 Luxray

Rock Head
74 Geodude
75 Graveler
76 Golem
95 Onix
104 Cubone
105 Marowak
111 Rhyhorn
112 Rhydon
142 Aerodactyl
185 Sudowoodo
208 Steelix
304 Aron
305 Lairon
306 Aggron
369 Relicanth
371 Bagon
372 Shelgon
438 Bonsly

Rough Skin
318 Carvanha
319 Sharpedo

Run Away
19 Rattata
20 Raticate
77 Ponyta
78 Rapidash
84 Doduo
85 Dodrio
133 Eevee
161 Sentret
162 Furret
190 Aipom
206 Dunsparce
209 Snubbull
261 Poochyena
417 Pachirisu
427 Buneary

Sand Stream
248 Tyranitar
449 Hippopotas
450 Hippowdon

Sand Veil
27 Sandshrew
28 Sandslash
50 Diglett
51 Dugtrio
207 Gligar
331 Cacnea
332 Cacturne
443 Gible
444 Gabite

445 Garchomp
472 Gliscor

Scrappy
115 Kangaskhan
241 Miltank

Serene Grace
113 Chansey
175 Togepi
176 Togetic
206 Dunsparce
242 Blissey
385 Jirachi
440 Happiny
468 Togekiss
492 Shaymin (S)

Shadow Tag
202 Wobbuffet
360 Wynaut

Shed Skin
11 Metapod
14 Kakuna
23 Ekans
24 Arbok
147 Dratini
148 Dragonair
247 Pupitar
266 Silcoon
268 Cascoon
336 Seviper
401 Kricketot
412 Burmy

Shell Armor
90 Shellder
91 Cloyster
98 Krabby
99 Kingler
131 Lapras
138 Omanyte
139 Omastar
341 Corphish
342 Crawdaunt
366 Clamperl

Shield Dust
10 Caterpie
13 Weedle
49 Venomoth
265 Wurmple
269 Dustox

Simple
322 Numel
399 Bidoof
400 Bibarel

Skill Link
90 Shellder
91 Cloyster

Slow Start
486 Regigigas

Sniper
116 Horsea
117 Seadra
223 Remoraid
224 Octillery
230 Kingdra
451 Skorupi
452 Drapion

Snow Cloak
220 Swinub
221 Piloswine
471 Glaceon
473 Mamoswine
478 Froslass

Snow Warning
459 Snover
460 Abomasnow

Solar Power
191 Sunkern
192 Sunflora
357 Tropius

Solid Rock
323 Camerupt
464 Rhyperior

Soundproof
100 Voltorb
101 Electrode
122 Mr. Mime
293 Whismur
294 Loudred
295 Exploud
439 Mime Jr.

Speed Boost
193 Yanma
291 Ninjask
469 Yanmega

Stall
302 Sableye

Static
25 Pikachu
26 Raichu
100 Voltorb
101 Electrode
125 Electabuzz
172 Pichu
179 Mareep
180 Flaaffy
181 Ampharos
239 Elekid
309 Electrike
310 Manectric

Steadfast
236 Tyrogue
447 Riolu
448 Lucario
475 Gallade

Stench
88 Grimer
89 Muk
434 Stunky
435 Skuntank

Sticky Hold
88 Grimer
89 Muk
316 Gulpin
317 Swalot
422 Shellos
423 Gastrodon

Storm Drain
422 Shellos
423 Gastrodon
456 Finneon

457 Lumineon

Sturdy
74 Geodude
75 Graveler
76 Golem
81 Magnemite
82 Magneton
95 Onix
185 Sudowoodo
204 Pineco
205 Forretress
208 Steelix
213 Shuckle
227 Skarmory
232 Donphan
299 Nosepass
304 Aron
305 Lairon
306 Aggron
410 Shieldon
411 Bastiodon
438 Bonsly
462 Magnezone
476 Probopass

Suction Cups
224 Octillery
345 Lileep
346 Cradily

Super Luck
198 Murkrow
359 Absol
430 Honchkrow

Swarm
15 Beedrill
123 Scyther
165 Ledyba
166 Ledian
167 Spinarak
168 Ariados
212 Scizor
214 Heracross
267 Beautifly
313 Volbeat
402 Kricketune
414 Mothim

Swift Swim
116 Horsea
118 Goldeen
119 Seaking
129 Magikarp
138 Omanyte
139 Omastar
140 Kabuto
141 Kabutops
211 Qwilfish
226 Mantine
230 Kingdra
270 Lotad
271 Lombre
272 Ludicolo
283 Surskit
349 Feebas
367 Huntail
368 Gorebyss
369 Relicanth
370 Luvdisc
418 Buizel
419 Floatzel
456 Finneon
457 Lumineon

458 Mantyke

Synchronize
63 Abra
64 Kadabra
65 Alakazam
151 Mew
177 Natu
178 Xatu
196 Espeon
197 Umbreon
280 Ralts
281 Kirlia
282 Gardevoir

Tangled Feet
16 Pidgey
17 Pidgeotto
18 Pidgeot
327 Spinda
441 Chatot

Technician
52 Meowth
53 Persian
123 Scyther
212 Scizor
235 Smeargle
237 Hitmontop
424 Ambipom

Thick Fat
86 Seel
87 Dewgong
143 Snorlax
183 Marill
184 Azumarill
241 Miltank
296 Makuhita
297 Hariyama
298 Azurill
325 Spoink
326 Grumpig
363 Spheal
364 Sealeo
365 Walrein
432 Purugly
446 Munchlax

Tinted Lens
48 Venonat
49 Venomoth
314 Illumise
469 Yanmega

Torrent
7 Squirtle
8 Wartortle
9 Blastoise
158 Totodile
159 Croconaw
160 Feraligatr
258 Mudkip
259 Marshtomp
260 Swampert
393 Piplup
394 Prinplup
395 Empoleon

Trace
137 Porygon
233 Porygon2
280 Ralts
281 Kirlia
282 Gardevoir

Truant
287 Slakoth
289 Slaking

Unaware
399 Bidoof
400 Bibarel

Unburden
425 Drifloon
426 Drifblim

Vital Spirit
56 Mankey
57 Primeape
225 Delibird
288 Vigoroth

Volt Absorb
135 Jolteon
170 Chinchou
171 Lanturn

Water Absorb
60 Poliwag
61 Poliwhirl
62 Poliwrath
131 Lapras
134 Vaporeon
186 Politoed
194 Wooper
195 Quagsire
226 Mantine
458 Mantyke

Water Veil
118 Goldeen
119 Seaking
320 Wailmer
321 Wailord

White Smoke
324 Torkoal

Wonder Guard
292 Shedinja

ADVENTURE DATA LIST

POKÉMON MOVES AND ABILITIES ALPHABETICAL LIST

This chart compiles the weaknesses of all 492 Pokémon in the *Pokémon Platinum* National Pokédex. Check here for a quick reference to effective moves against whichever foe you're facing.

Pokémon	Type		Ability		Type of move weakness						Type of ineffective moves		
Abomasnow	GRS	ICE	Snow Warning		FIR ◆	FGT	PSN	FLY	BUG	RCK	STL		
Abra	PSY		Synchronize	Inner Focus	BUG	GHO	DRK						
Absol	DRK		Pressure	Super Luck	FGT	BUG					PSY		
Aerodactyl	RCK	FLY	Rock Head	Pressure	WTR	ELC	ICE	RCK	STL		GRD		
Aggron	STL	RCK	Sturdy	Rock Head	FGT ◆	GRD ◆	WTR				PSN		
Aipom	NRM		Run Away	Pickup	FGT						GHO		
Alakazam	PSY		Synchronize	Inner Focus	BUG	GHO	DRK						
Altaria	NRM	FLY	Natural Cure		ELC ◆	ICE	RCK				GRD	GHO	
Ambipom	NRM		Technician	Pickup	FGT						GHO		
Ampharos	ELC		Static		GRD								
Anorith	RCK	BUG	Battle Armor		WTR	RCK	STL						
Arbok	PSN		Intimidate	Shed Skin	GRD	PSY							
Arcanine	FIR		Intimidate	Flash Fire	WTR	GRD	RCK				FIR*2		RCK
Ariados	BUG	PSN	Swarm	Insomnia	FIR	FLY	PSY	RCK					
Armaldo	RCK	BUG	Battle Armor		WTR	RCK	STL						
Aron	STL	RCK	Sturdy	Rock Head	FGT ◆	GRD ◆	WTR				PSN		
Articuno	ICE	FLY	Pressure		RCK ◆	FIR	ELC	STL			GRD		
Azelf	PSY		Levitate		BUG	GHO	DRK				GRD*1		BUG
Azumarill	WTR		Thick Fat	Huge Power	GRS	ELC							
Azurill	NRM		Thick Fat	Huge Power	FGT						GHO		
Bagon	RCK	STL	Sturdy		FGT	GRD	WTR				PSN		
Baltoy	GRD	PSY	Levitate		GRS	WTR	ICE	BUG	GHO	DRK	ELC	GRD*1	
Banette	GHO		Insomnia	Frisk	GHO	DRK					NRM	FGT	
Barboach	WTR	GRD	Oblivious	Anticipation	GRS ◆						ELC		
Bastiodon	RCK	STL	Sturdy		FGT ◆	GRD ◆	WTR				PSN		
Bayleef	GRS		Overgrow		FIR	ICE	PSN	FLY	BUG				
Beautifly	FLY		Swarm		RCK	FIR ◆	ELC	ICE	FLY		GRD		
Beedrill	BUG	PSN	Swarm		FIR	FLY	PSY	RCK					
Beldum	GRS		Flower Gift		FIR	ICE	PSN	FLY	BUG				
Bellossom	GRS		Chlorophyll		FIR	ICE	PSN	FLY	BUG				
Bellsprout	GRS	PSN	Chlorophyll		FIR	ICE	FLY	PSY					
Bibarel	NRM	WTR	Simple	Unaware	GRS	ELC	FGT				GHO		
Bidoof	NRM		Simple	Unaware	FGT						GHO		
Blastoise	WTR		Torrent		GRS	ELC							
Blaziken	FIR	FGT	Blaze		WTR	GRD	FLY	PSY					
Blissey	NRM		Natural Cure	Serene Grace	FGT						GHO		
Bonsly	RCK		Sturdy	Rock Head	GRS	WTR	FGT	GRD	STL				
Breloom	GRS	FGT	Effect Spore	Poison Heal	FLY ◆	FIR	ICE	PSN	PSY				
Bronzong	STL	PSY	Levitate	Heatproof	FIR	GRD*3				PSN			
Bronzor	STL	PSY	Levitate	Heatproof	FIR	GRD*3				PSN			
Budew	GRS	PSN	Natural Cure	Poison Point	FIR	ICE	FLY	PSY					
Buizel	WTR		Swift Swim		GRS	ELC							
Bulbasaur	GRS	PSN	Overgrow		FIR	ICE	FLY	PSY					
Buneary	NRM		Run Away	Klutz	FGT						GHO		
Burmy	BUG		Shed Skin		FIR	FLY	RCK						
Butterfree	BUG	FLY	Compoundeyes		RCK ◆	FIR	ELC	ICE	FLY		GRD		
Cacnea	GRS		Sand Veil		FIR	ICE	PSN	FLY	BUG				
Cacturne	GRS	DRK	Sand Veil		BUG ◆	FIR	ICE	FGT	PSN	FLY	PSY		
Camerupt	FIR	GRD	Magma Armor	Solid Rock	WTR ◆	GRD					ELC		
Carnivine	GRS		Levitate		FIR	ICE	PSN	FLY	BUG		GRD*1		
Carvanha	WTR	DRK	Rough Skin		GRS	ELC	FGT	BUG			PSY		
Cascoon	BUG		Shed Skin		FIR	FLY	RCK						
Castform	NRM		Forecast		FGT						GHO		
Caterpie	BUG		Shield Dust		FIR	FLY	RCK						
Celebi	PSY	GRS	Natural Cure		BUG ◆	FIR	ICE	PSN	FLY	GHO	DRK		

◆ ..... Deals 4x damage.
*1 May not deal damage, depending on Ability effects. *2 May deal damage, depending on that Pokémon's Ability. *3 May not deal damage, depending on that Pokémon's Ability.

Pokémon	Type		Ability		Type of move weakness						Type of ineffective moves		
Chansey	NRM		Natural Cure	Serene Grace	FGT						GHO		
Charizard	FIR	FLY	Blaze		RCK ◆	WTR	ELC				GRD		
Charmander	FIR		Blaze		WTR	GRD	RCK						
Charmeleon	FIR		Blaze		WTR	GRD	RCK						
Chatot	NRM	FLY	Keen Eye	Tangled Feet	ELC	ICE	RCK				GRD	GHO	
Cherrim	GRS		Chlorophyll		FIR	ICE	PSN	FLY	BUG				
Cherubi	GRS		Overgrow		FIR	ICE	PSN	FLY	BUG				
Chikorita	FGT	PSY	Pure Power		FLY	GHO							
Chimchar	FIR		Blaze		WTR	GRD	RCK						
Chimecho	PSY		Natural Cure		ICE	RCK	DRG				GRD	GRD*1	
Chinchou	WTR	ELC	Levitate		BUG	GHO	DRK				GRD*1	ELC*2	FLY
Chingling	PSY		Levitate		BUG	GHO	DRK				GRD*1		
Clamperl	WTR		Shell Armor		GRS	ELC							
Claydol	GRD	PSY	Levitate		GRS	WTR	ICE	BUG	GHO	DRK	ELC	GRD*1	
Clefable	NRM		Cute Charm	Magic Guard	FGT						GHO		
Clefairy	NRM		Cute Charm	Magic Guard	FGT						GHO		
Cleffa	NRM		Cute Charm	Magic Guard	FGT						GHO		
Cloyster	WTR	ICE	Shell Armor	Skill Link	GRS	ELC	FGT	RCK					
Combee	BUG	FLY	Honey Gather		RCK ◆	FIR	ELC	ICE	FLY		GRD		
Combusken	FIR	FGT	Blaze		WTR	GRD	FLY	PSY					
Corphish	WTR		Hyper Cutter	Shell Armor	GRS	ELC							
Corsola	WTR	RCK	Hustle	Natural Cure	GRS ◆	ELC	FGT	GRD					
Cradily	RCK	GRS	Suction Cups		ICE	FGT	BUG	STL					
Cranidos	RCK		Mold Breaker		GRS	WTR	FGT	GRD	STL				
Crawdaunt	WTR	DRK	Hyper Cutter	Shell Armor	GRS	ELC	FGT	BUG			PSY		
Cresselia	PSY		Levitate		BUG	GHO	DRK				GRD*1		
Croagunk	PSN	FGT	Anticipation	Dry Skin	PSY ◆	GRD	FLY				WTR*2		
Crobat	PSN	FLY	Inner Focus		ELC	ICE	PSY	RCK			GRD		
Croconaw	WTR		Torrent		GRS	ELC							
Cubone	GRD		Rock Head	Lightningrod	GRS	WTR	ICE				ELC		
Cyndaquil	FIR		Blaze		WTR	GRD	RCK						
Darkrai	DRK		Bad Dreams		BUG	FIR	ICE	FGT	PSN	FLY	PSY		
Delcatty	NRM		Cute Charm	Normalize	FGT						GHO		
Delibird	DRK	FIR	Early Bird	Flash Fire	WTR ◆	FGT	GRD	RCK			PSY	FIR*2	
Deoxys	PSY		Pressure		RCK	FIR	ELC	ICE	FLY		GRD		
Dewgong	WTR	ICE	Thick Fat	Hydration	GRS	ELC	FGT	RCK					
Dialga	GRD		Sand Veil	Arena Trap	GRS	WTR	ICE				ELC		
Diglett	PSY		Pressure		BUG	GHO	DRK						
Ditto	NRM		Limber		FGT						GHO		
Dodrio	NRM	FLY	Run Away	Early Bird	ELC	ICE	RCK				GRD	GHO	
Doduo	NRM	FLY	Run Away	Early Bird	ELC	ICE	RCK				GRD	GHO	
Donphan	GRD		Sturdy		GRS	WTR	ICE				ELC		
Dragonair	DRG		Shed Skin		ICE	DRG							
Dragonite	DRG	FLY	Inner Focus		ICE ◆	RCK	DRG				GRD		
Drapion	PSN	DRK	Battle Armor	Sniper	GRD						PSY		
Dratini	DRG		Shed Skin		ICE	DRG							
Drifblim	GHO	FLY	Aftermath	Unburden	ELC	ICE	RCK	GHO	DRK		NRM	FGT	GRD
Drifloon	GHO	FLY	Aftermath	Unburden	ELC	ICE	RCK	GHO	DRK		NRM	FGT	GRD
Drowzee	PSY		Insomnia	Forewarn	BUG	GHO	DRK						
Dugtrio	WTR		Swift Swim	Sniper	GRS	ELC							
Dunsparce	NRM		Serene Grace	Run Away	FGT						GHO		
Dusclops	GHO		Pressure		GHO	DRK					NRM	FGT	
Dusknoir	GHO		Pressure		GHO	DRK					NRM	FGT	
Duskull	GHO		Levitate		GHO	DRK					NRM	FGT	GRD*1
Dustox	BUG	PSN	Shield Dust		FIR	FLY	PSY	RCK					
Eevee	NRM		Run Away	Adaptability	FGT						GHO		
Ekans	PSN		Intimidate	Shed Skin	GRD	PSY							
Electabuzz	ELC		Static		GRD								

ADVENTURE DATA LIST

POKÉMON WEAKNESSES QUICK REFERENCE

Pokémon	Type		Ability		Type of move weakness						Type of ineffective moves		
Electivire	ELC		Motor Drive		GRD						ELC*1		ELC
Electrike	ELC		Static	Lightningrod	GRD								
Electrode	ELC		Soundproof	Static	GRD								
Elekid	ELC		Static		GRD								
Empoleon	WTR	STL	Torrent		ELC	FGT	GRD				PSN		
Entei	FIR		Pressure		WTR	GRD	RCK						
Espeon	PSY		Synchronize		BUG	GHO	DRK						
Exeggcute	WTR	FLY	Swift Swim	Water Absorb	ELC ◆	RCK					GRD	WTR*2	
Exeggutor	GRS	PSY	Chlorophyll		BUG ◆	FIR	ICE	PSN	FLY	GHO	DRK		
Exploud	NRM		Soundproof		FGT						GHO		
Farfetch'd	NRM	FLY	Keen Eye	Inner Focus	ELC	ICE	RCK				GRD	GHO	
Fearow	NRM	FLY	Keen Eye		ELC	ICE	RCK				GRD	GHO	
Feebas	WTR		Swift Swim		GRS	ELC							
Feraligatr	WTR		Torrent		GRS	ELC							
Finneon	WTR		Swift Swim	Storm Drain	GRS	ELC							
Flaaffy	ELC		Static		GRD								
Flareon	FIR		Flash Fire		WTR	GRD	RCK				FIR*1		
Floatzel	WTR		Swift Swim		GRS	ELC							
Flygon	GRD	DRG	Levitate		ICE ◆	DRG					ELC	GRD*1	
Forretress	BUG	STL	Sturdy		FIR ◆						PSN		
Froslass	ICE	GHO	Snow Cloak		FIR	RCK	GHO	DRK	STL		NRM	FGT	
Furret	NRM		Run Away	Keen Eye	FGT						GHO		
Gabite	DRG	GRD	Sand Veil		ICE ◆	DRG					ELC		
Gallade	FGT		Steadfast		FLY	GHO							
Garchomp	DRG	GRD	Sand Veil		ICE ◆	DRG					ELC		
Gardevoir	PSY		Synchronize	Trace	BUG	GHO	DRK						
Gastly	GHO	PSN	Levitate		PSY	GHO	DRK				NRM	FGT	GRD*1
Gastrodon	WTR	GRD	Sticky Hold	Storm Drain	GRS ◆						ELC		
Gengar	GHO	PSN	Levitate		PSY	GHO	DRK				NRM	FGT	GRD*1
Geodude	RCK	GRD	Rock Head	Sturdy	GRS ◆	WTR ◆	ICE	FGT	GRD	STL	ELC		
Gible	DRG	GRD	Sand Veil		ICE ◆	DRG					ELC		
Girafarig	NRM	PSY	Inner Focus	Early Bird	BUG	DRK					GHO		
Giratina [Altered Forme]	GHO	DRG	Pressure		ICE	GHO	DRG	DRK			NRM	FGT	
Giratina [Origin Forme]	GHO	DRG	Levitate		ICE	GHO	DRG	DRK			NRM	FGT	GRD*1
Glaceon	ICE		Snow Cloak		FIR	FGT	RCK	STL					
Glalie	ICE		Inner Focus	Ice Body	FIR	FGT	RCK	STL					
Glameow	NRM		Limber	Own Tempo	FGT						GHO		
Gligar	GRD	FLY	Hyper Cutter	Sand Veil	ICE ◆	WTR					ELC	GRD	
Gliscor	GRD	FLY	Hyper Cutter	Sand Veil	ICE ◆	WTR					ELC	GRD	
Gloom	GRS	PSN	Chlorophyll		FIR	ICE	FLY	PSY					
Golbat	PSN	FLY	Inner Focus		ELC	ICE	PSY	RCK			GRD		
Goldeen	WTR		Swift Swim	Water Veil	GRS	ELC							
Golduck	WTR		Damp	Cloud Nine	GRS	ELC							
Golem	RCK	GRD	Rock Head	Sturdy	GRS ◆	WTR ◆	ICE	FGT	GRD	STL	ELC		
Gorebyss	WTR		Swift Swim		GRS	ELC							
Granbull	NRM		Intimidate	Quick Feet	FGT						GHO		
Graveler	RCK	GRD	Rock Head	Sturdy	GRS ◆	WTR ◆	ICE	FGT	GRD	STL	ELC		
Grimer	PSN		Stench	Sticky Hold	GRD	PSY							
Grotle	GRS		Overgrow		FIR	ICE	PSN	FLY	BUG				
Groudon	GRD		Drought		GRS	WTR	ICE				ELC		
Grovyle	GRS		Overgrow		FIR	ICE	PSN	FLY	BUG				
Growlithe	FIR		Intimidate	Flash Fire	WTR	GRD	RCK				FIR*2		BUG
Grumpig	PSY		Thick Fat	Own Tempo	BUG	GHO	DRK						
Gulpin	PSN		Liquid Ooze	Sticky Hold	GRD	PSY							
Gyarados	WTR	FLY	Intimidate		ELC ◆	RCK					GRD		
Happiny	NRM		Natural Cure	Serene Grace	FGT						GHO		
Hariyama	FGT		Thick Fat	Guts	FLY	PSY							
Haunter	GHO	PSN	Levitate		PSY	GHO	DRK				NRM	FGT	GRD*1

◆ ..... Deals 4x damage.
*1 May not deal damage, depending on Ability effects. *2 May deal damage, depending on that Pokémon's Ability. *3 May not deal damage, depending on that Pokémon's Ability.

Pokémon	Type		Ability		Type of move weakness						Type of ineffective moves		
Heatran	FIR	STL	Flash Fire		GRD◆	WTR	FGT				PSN	FIR*1	
Heracross	BUG	FGT	Swarm	Guts	FLY◆	FIR	PSY						
Hippopotas	GRD		Sand Stream		GRS	WTR	ICE				ELC		
Hippowdon	GRD		Sand Stream		GRS	WTR	ICE				ELC		
Hitmonchan	FGT		Keen Eye	Iron Fist	FLY	PSY							
Hitmonlee	FGT		Limber	Reckless	FLY	PSY							
Hitmontop	FGT		Intimidate	Technician	FLY	PSY							
Ho-Oh	FIR	FLY	Pressure		RCK◆	WTR	ELC				GRD		
Honchkrow	DRK	FLY	Insomnia	Super Luck	ELC	ICE	RCK				GRD	PSY	
Hoothoot	NRM	FLY	Insomnia	Keen Eye	ELC	ICE	RCK				GRD	GHO	
Hoppip	GRS	FLY	Chlorophyll	Leaf Guard	ICE◆	FIR	PSN	FLY	RCK		GRD		
Horsea	DRG		Rock Head		ICE	DRG							
Houndoom	DRK	FIR	Early Bird	Flash Fire	WTR	FGT	GRD	RCK			PSY	FIR*2	
Houndour	DRK	FIR	Early Bird	Flash Fire							PSY	FIR*2	
Huntail	WTR		Swift Swim		GRS	ELC							
Hypno	PSY		Insomnia	Forewarn	BUG	GHO	DRK						
Igglybuff	NRM		Cute Charm		FGT						GHO		
Illumise	BUG		Oblivious	Tinted Lens	FIR	FLY	RCK						
Infernape	FIR	FGT	Blaze		WTR	GRD	FLY	PSY					
Ivysaur	GRS	PSN	Overgrow		FIR	ICE	FLY	PSY					
Jigglypuff	NRM		Cute Charm		FGT						GHO		
Jirachi	STL	PSY	Serene Grace		FIR	GRD					PSN		
Jolteon	ELC		Volt Absorb		GRD						ELC*1		GRD
Jumpluff	GRS	FLY	Chlorophyll	Leaf Guard	ICE◆	FIR	PSN	FLY	RCK		GRD		
Jynx	ICE	PSY	Oblivious	Forewarn	FIR	BUG	RCK	GHO	DRK	STL			
Kabuto	RCK	WTR	Swift Swim	Battle Armor	GRS◆	ELC	FGT	GRD					
Kabutops	RCK	WTR	Swift Swim	Battle Armor	GRS◆	ELC	FGT	GRD					
Kadabra	PSY		Synchronize	Inner Focus	BUG	GHO	DRK						
Kakuna	BUG	PSN	Shed Skin		FIR	FLY	PSY	RCK					
Kangaskhan	NRM		Early Bird	Scrappy	FGT						GHO		
Kecleon	NRM		Color Change		FGT						GHO		
Kingdra	WTR	DRG	Swift Swim	Sniper	DRG								
Kingler	WTR		Hyper Cutter	Shell Armor	GRS	ELC							
Kirlia	PSY		Synchronize	Trace	BUG	GHO	DRK						
Koffing	PSN		Levitate		PSY						GRD*1		
Krabby	WTR		Hyper Cutter	Shell Armor	GRS	ELC							
Kricketot	BUG		Shed Skin		FIR	FLY	RCK						
Kricketune	BUG		Swarm		FIR	FLY	RCK						
Kyogre	WTR		Drizzle		GRS	ELC							
Lairon	STL	RCK	Sturdy	Rock Head	FGT◆	GRD◆	WTR				PSN		
Lanturn	WTR	ELC	Volt Absorb	Illuminate	GRS	GRD					ELC*2		
Lapras	WTR	ICE	Water Absorb	Shell Armor	GRS	ELC	FGT	RCK			WTR*2		
Larvitar	RCK	GRD	Guts		GRS◆	WTR◆	ICE	FGT	GRD	STL	ELC		
Latias	DRG	PSY	Levitate		ICE	BUG	GHO	DRG	DRK		GRD*1		
Latios	DRG	PSY	Levitate		ICE	BUG	GHO	DRG	DRK		GRD*1		
Leafeon	GRS		Leaf Guard		FIR	ICE	PSN	FLY	BUG				
Ledian	BUG	FLY	Swarm	Early Bird	RCK◆	FIR	ELC	ICE	FLY		GRD		
Ledyba	BUG	FLY	Swarm	Early Bird	RCK◆	FIR	ELC	ICE	FLY		GRD		
Lickilicky	NRM		Own Tempo	Oblivious	FGT						GHO		
Lickitung	NRM		Own Tempo	Oblivious	FGT						GHO		
Lileep	RCK	GRS	Suction Cups		ICE	FGT	BUG	STL					
Linoone	NRM		Pickup	Gluttony	FGT						GHO		
Lombre	WTR	GRS	Swift Swim	Rain Dish	PSN	FLY	BUG						
Lopunny	NRM		Cute Charm	Klutz	FGT						GHO		
Lotad	WTR	GRS	Swift Swim	Rain Dish	PSN	FLY	BUG						
Loudred	NRM		Soundproof		FGT						GHO		
Lucario	FGT	STL	Steadfast	Inner Focus	FIR	FGT	GRD				PSN		
Ludicolo	WTR	GRS	Swift Swim	Rain Dish	PSN	FLY	BUG						

Pokémon	Type		Ability		Type of move weakness						Type of ineffective moves		
Lugia	PSY	FLY	Pressure		ELC	ICE	RCK	GHO	DRK		GRD		
Lumineon	WTR		Swift Swim	Storm Drain	GRS	ELC							
Lunatone	RCK	PSY	Levitate		GRS	WTR	BUG	GHO	DRK	STL	GRD*1		
Luvdisc	WTR		Swift Swim		GRS	ELC							
Luxio	ELC		Rivalry	Intimidate	GRD								
Luxray	ELC		Rivalry	Intimidate	GRD								
Machamp	FGT		Guts	No Guard	FLY	PSY							
Machoke	FGT		Guts	No Guard	FLY	PSY							
Machop	FGT		Guts	No Guard	FLY	PSY							
Magby	FIR		Flame Body		WTR	GRD	RCK						
Magcargo	FIR	RCK	Magma Armor	Flame Body	WTR ◆	GRD ◆	FGT	RCK					
Magikarp	WTR		Swift Swim		GRS	ELC							
Magmar	FIR		Flame Body		WTR	GRD	RCK						
Magmortar	FIR		Flame Body		WTR	GRD	RCK						
Magnemite	ELC	STL	Magnet Pull	Sturdy	GRD ◆	FIR	FGT				PSN		
Magneton	ELC	STL	Magnet Pull	Sturdy	GRD ◆	FIR	FGT				PSN		
Magnezone	ELC	STL	Magnet Pull	Sturdy	GRD ◆	FIR	FGT				PSN		
Makuhita	FGT		Thick Fat	Guts	FLY	PSY							
Mamoswine	ICE	GRD	Oblivious	Snow Cloak	GRS	FIR	WTR	FGT	STL		ELC		
Manaphy	WTR		Hydration		GRS	ELC							
Manectric	ELC		Static	Lightningrod	GRD								
Mankey	FGT		Vital Spirit	Anger Point	FLY	PSY							
Mantine	WTR	FLY	Swift Swim	Water Absorb	ELC ◆	RCK					GRD	WTR*2	
Mantyke	STL	PSY	Clear Body		FIR ◆	GRD					PSN		
Mareep	ELC		Static		GRD								
Marill	WTR		Thick Fat	Huge Power	GRS	ELC							
Marowak	GRD		Rock Head	Lightningrod	GRS	WTR	ICE				ELC		
Marshtomp	WTR	GRD	Torrent		GRS ◆						ELC		
Masquerain	BUG	FLY	Intimidate		RCK ◆	FIR	ELC	ICE	FLY		GRD		
Mawile	STL		Hyper Cutter	Intimidate	FIR	FGT	GRD				PSN		
Medicham	WTR	ELC	Volt Absorb	Illuminate	GRS	GRD					ELC*2		PSY
Meditite	FGT	PSY	Pure Power		FLY	GHO							
Meganium	GRS		Overgrow		FIR	ICE	PSN	FLY	BUG				
Meowth	NRM		Pickup	Technician	FGT						GHO		
Mesprit	PSY		Levitate		BUG	GHO	DRK				GRD*1		PSY
Metagross	STL	PSY	Clear Body		FIR	GRD					PSN		
Metang	STL	PSY	Clear Body		FIR	GRD					PSN		
Metapod	BUG		Shed Skin		FIR	FLY	RCK						
Mew	PSY		Synchronize		BUG	GHO	DRK						
Mewtwo	PSY		Pressure		BUG	GHO	DRK						
Mightyena	DRK		Intimidate	Quick Feet	FGT	BUG					PSY		
Milotic	WTR		Marvel Scale		GRS	ELC							
Miltank	NRM		Thick Fat	Scrappy	FGT						GHO		
Mime Jr.	PSY		Soundproof	Filter	BUG	GHO	DRK						
Minun	ELC		Minus		GRD								
Misdreavus	GHO		Levitate		GHO	DRK					NRM	FGT	GRD*1
Mismagius	GHO		Levitate		GHO	DRK					NRM	FGT	GRD*1
Moltres	FIR	FLY	Pressure		RCK ◆	WTR	ELC				GRD		
Monferno	FIR	FGT	Blaze		WTR	GRD	FLY	PSY					
Mothim	FLY		Swarm		RCK	FIR ◆	ELC	ICE	FLY		GRD		
Mr. Mime	PSY		Soundproof	Filter	BUG	GHO	DRK						
Mudkip	WTR		Torrent		GRS	ELC							
Muk	PSN		Stench	Sticky Hold	GRD	PSY							
Munchlax	NRM		Pickup	Thick Fat	FGT						GHO		
Murkrow	DRK	FLY	Insomnia	Super Luck	ELC	ICE	RCK				GRD	PSY	
Natu	PSY	FLY	Synchronize	Early Bird	ELC	ICE	RCK	GHO	DRK		GRD		
Nidoking	PSN	GRD	Poison Point	Rivalry	WTR	ICE	GRD	PSY			ELC		
Nidoqueen	PSN	GRD	Poison Point	Rivalry	WTR	ICE	GRD	PSY			ELC		

◆ . . . . . Deals 4x damage.
*1 May not deal damage, depending on Ability effects. *2 May deal damage, depending on that Pokémon's Ability. *3 May not deal damage, depending on that Pokémon's Ability.

ADVENTURE DATA LIST — POKÉMON WEAKNESSES QUICK REFERENCE

Pokémon	Type		Ability		Type of move weakness						Type of ineffective moves	
Nidoran ♀	PSN		Poison Point	Rivalry	GRD	PSY						
Nidoran ♂	PSN		Poison Point	Rivalry	GRD	PSY						
Nidorina	PSN		Poison Point	Rivalry	GRD	PSY						
Nidorino	PSN		Poison Point	Rivalry	GRD	PSY						
Nincada	BUG	RCK	Sturdy	Gluttony	WTR	RCK	STL					
Ninetales	FIR		Flash Fire		WTR	GRD	RCK				FIR*1	
Ninjask	WTR		Hustle	Sniper	GRS ◆	ELC						
Noctowl	NRM	FLY	Insomnia	Keen Eye	ELC	ICE	RCK				GRD	GHO
Nosepass	RCK		Sturdy	Magnet Pull	GRS	WTR	FGT	GRD	STL			
Numel	FIR	GRD	Oblivious	Simple	WTR ◆	GRD					ELC	
Nuzleaf	GRS	DRK	Chlorophyll	Early Bird	BUG ◆	FIR	ICE	FGT	PSN	FLY	PSY	
Octillery	WTR		Suction Cups	Sniper	GRS	ELC						
Oddish	GRS	PSN	Chlorophyll		FIR	ICE	FLY	PSY				
Omanyte	RCK	WTR	Swift Swim	Shell Armor	GRS ◆	ELC	FGT	GRD				
Omastar	RCK	WTR	Swift Swim	Shell Armor	GRS ◆	ELC	FGT	GRD				
Onix	RCK	GRD	Rock Head	Sturdy	GRS ◆	WTR ◆	ICE	FGT	GRD	STL	ELC	
Pachirisu	ELC		Run Away	Pickup	GRD							
Palkia	WTR	DRG	Pressure		DRG							
Paras	BUG	GRS	Effect Spore	Dry Skin	FIR ◆	FLY ◆	ICE	PSN	BUG	RCK	WTR*2	
Parasect	BUG	GRS	Effect Spore	Dry Skin	FIR ◆	FLY ◆	ICE	PSN	BUG	RCK	WTR*2	
Pelipper	WTR	FLY	Keen Eye		ELC ◆	RCK					GRD	
Persian	NRM		Limber	Technician	FGT						GHO	
Phanpy	GRD		Pickup		GRS	WTR	ICE				ELC	
Phione	WTR		Hydration		GRS	ELC						
Pichu	ELC		Static		GRD							
Pidgeot	NRM	FLY	Keen Eye	Tangled Feet	ELC	ICE	RCK				GRD	GHO
Pidgeotto	NRM	FLY	Keen Eye	Tangled Feet	ELC	ICE	RCK				GRD	GHO
Pidgey	NRM	FLY	Keen Eye	Tangled Feet	ELC	ICE	RCK				GRD	GHO
Pikachu	ELC		Static		GRD							
Piloswine	ICE	GRD	Oblivious	Snow Cloak	GRS	FIR	WTR	FGT	STL		ELC	
Pineco	BUG		Sturdy		FIR	FLY	RCK					
Pinsir	BUG		Hyper Cutter	Mold Breaker	FIR	FLY	RCK					
Piplup	WTR		Torrent		GRS	ELC						
Plusle	ELC		Plus		GRD							
Politoed	WTR		Water Absorb	Damp	GRS	ELC					WTR*2	
Poliwag	WTR		Water Absorb	Damp	GRS	ELC					WTR*2	
Poliwhirl	WTR		Water Absorb	Damp	GRS	ELC					WTR*2	
Poliwrath	WTR	FGT	Water Absorb	Damp	GRS	ELC	FLY	PSY			WTR*2	
Ponyta	FIR		Run Away	Flash Fire	WTR	GRD	RCK				FIR*2	
Poochyena	DRK		Run Away	Quick Feet	FGT	BUG					PSY	
Porygon	NRM		Trace	Download	FGT						GHO	
Porygon2	NRM		Trace	Download	FGT						GHO	
Porygon-Z	NRM		Adaptability	Download	FGT						GHO	
Primeape	FGT		Vital Spirit	Anger Point	FLY	PSY						
Prinplup	WTR		Torrent		GRS	ELC						
Probopass	GRD		Sand Veil	Arena Trap	GRS ◆	WTR ◆	ICE				ELC	
Psyduck	WTR		Damp	Cloud Nine	GRS	ELC						
Pupitar	RCK	GRD	Shed Skin		GRS ◆	WTR ◆	ICE	FGT	GRD	STL	ELC	
Purugly	NRM		Thick Fat	Own Tempo	FGT						GHO	
Quagsire	WTR	GRD	Damp	Water Absorb	GRS ◆						ELC	WTR*2
Quilava	FIR		Blaze		WTR	GRD	RCK					
Qwilfish	WTR	PSN	Poison Point	Swift Swim	ELC	GRD	PSY					
Raichu	ELC		Static		GRD							
Raikou	ELC		Pressure		GRD							
Ralts	PSY		Synchronize	Trace	BUG	GHO	DRK					
Rampardos	RCK		Mold Breaker		GRS	WTR	FGT	GRD	STL			
Rapidash	FIR		Run Away	Flash Fire	WTR	GRD	RCK				FIR*2	FIR
Raticate	NRM		Run Away	Guts	FGT						GHO	

Pokémon	Type		Ability		Type of move weakness						Type of ineffective moves		
Rattata	NRM		Run Away	Guts	FGT						GHO		
Rayquaza	DRG	FLY	Air Lock		ICE ◆	RCK	DRG				GRD		
Regice	ICE		Clear Body		FIR	FGT	RCK	STL					
Regigigas	NRM		Slow Start		FGT						GHO		
Regirock	RCK		Clear Body		GRS	WTR	FGT	GRD	STL				
Registeel	STL		Clear Body		FIR	FGT	GRD				PSN		
Relicanth	WTR	RCK	Swift Swim	Rock Head	GRS	ELC	FGT	GRD					
Remoraid	ICE	FLY	Vital Spirit	Hustle	RCK	FIR	ELC	STL			GRD		
Rhydon	GRD	RCK	Lightningrod	Rock Head	GRS ◆	WTR ◆	ICE	FGT	GRD	STL	ELC		
Rhyhorn	GRD	RCK	Lightningrod	Rock Head	GRS ◆	WTR ◆	ICE	FGT	GRD	STL	ELC		
Rhyperior	GRD	RCK	Lightningrod	Solid Rock	GRS ◆	WTR ◆	ICE	FGT	GRD	STL	ELC		
Riolu	FGT		Steadfast	Inner Focus	FLY	PSY							
Roselia	GRS	PSN	Natural Cure	Poison Point	FIR	ICE	FLY	PSY					
Roserade	GRS	PSN	Natural Cure	Poison Point	FIR	ICE	FLY	PSY					
Rotom	ELC	GHO	Levitate		GHO	DRK					NRM	FGT	GRD*1
Sableye	DRK	GHO	Keen Eye	Stall							NRM	FGT	PSY
Salamence	DRG	FLY	Intimidate		ICE ◆	RCK	DRG				GRD		
Sandshrew	GRD		Sand Veil		GRS	WTR	ICE				ELC		
Sandslash	GRD		Sand Veil		GRS	WTR	ICE				ELC		
Sceptile	GRS		Overgrow		FIR	ICE	PSN	FLY	BUG				
Scizor	BUG	STL	Swarm	Technician	FIR ◆						PSN		
Scyther	BUG	FLY	Swarm	Technician	RCK ◆	FIR	ELC	ICE	FLY		GRD		
Seadra	WTR		Poison Point	Sniper	GRS	ELC							
Seaking	WTR		Swift Swim	Water Veil	GRS	ELC							
Sealeo	ICE	WTR	Thick Fat	Ice Body	GRS	ELC	FGT	RCK					
Seedot	ICE	WTR	Thick Fat	Ice Body	GRS	ELC	FGT	RCK					
Seel	WTR		Thick Fat	Hydration	GRS	ELC							
Sentret	NRM		Run Away	Keen Eye	FGT						GHO		
Seviper	PSN		Shed Skin		GRD	PSY							
Sharpedo	WTR	DRK	Rough Skin		GRS	ELC	FGT	BUG			PSY		
Shaymin [Land Forme]	GRS		Natural Cure		FIR	ICE	PSN	FLY	BUG				
Shaymin [Sky Forme]	GRS	FLY	Serene Grace		ICE ◆	FIR	PSN	FLY	RCK		GRD		
Shedinja	BUG	GHO	Wonder Guard		FIR	FLY	RCK	GHO	DRK		*4		
Shelgon	DRG		Rock Head		ICE	DRG							
Shellder	WTR		Shell Armor	Skill Link	GRS	ELC							
Shellos	WTR		Sticky Hold	Storm Drain	GRS	ELC							
Shieldon	GRS		Chlorophyll	Early Bird	FIR ◆	ICE ◆	PSN	FLY	BUG				
Shiftry	RCK	STL	Sturdy	Magnet Pull	FGT ◆	GRD	WTR				PSN		
Shinx	ELC		Rivalry	Intimidate	GRD								
Shroomish	GRS		Effect Spore	Poison Heal	FIR	ICE	PSN	FLY	BUG				
Shuckle	STL	DRG	Pressure		FGT	GRD					PSN		
Shuppet	GHO		Insomnia	Frisk	GHO	DRK					NRM	FGT	
Silcoon	BUG		Shed Skin		FIR	FLY	RCK						
Skarmory	STL	FLY	Keen Eye	Sturdy	FIR	ELC					PSN	GRD	
Skiploom	GRS	FLY	Chlorophyll	Leaf Guard	ICE ◆	FIR	PSN	FLY	RCK		GRD		
Skitty	NRM		Cute Charm	Normalize	FGT						GHO		
Skorupi	PSN	BUG	Battle Armor	Sniper	FIR	FLY	PSY	RCK					
Skuntank	PSN	DRK	Stench	Aftermath	GRD						PSY		
Slaking	NRM		Truant		FGT						GHO		
Slakoth	NRM		Truant		FGT						GHO		
Slowbro	WTR	PSY	Oblivious	Own Tempo	GRS	ELC	BUG	GHO	DRK				
Slowking	WTR	PSY	Oblivious	Own Tempo	GRS	ELC	BUG	GHO	DRK				
Slowpoke	WTR	PSY	Oblivious	Own Tempo	GRS	ELC	BUG	GHO	DRK				
Slugma	FIR		Magma Armor	Flame Body	WTR	GRD	RCK						
Smeargle	NRM		Own Tempo	Technician	FGT						GHO		
Smoochum	ICE	PSY	Oblivious	Forewarn	FIR	BUG	RCK	GHO	DRK	STL			
Sneasel	DRK	ICE	Inner Focus	Keen Eye	FGT ◆	FIR	BUG	RCK	STL		PSY		
Snorlax	NRM		Immunity	Thick Fat	FGT						GHO		

◆ ..... Deals 4x damage.
*1 May not deal damage, depending on Ability effects. *2 May deal damage, depending on that Pokémon's Ability. *3 May not deal damage, depending on that Pokémon's Ability. *4 All types except for Fire, Flying, Rock, Ghost, and Dark.

Pokémon	Type		Ability		Type of move weakness							Type of ineffective moves		
Snorunt	ICE		Inner Focus	Ice Body	FIR	FGT	RCK	STL						
Snover	GRS	ICE	Snow Warning		FIR ◆	FGT	PSN	FLY	BUG	RCK	STL			
Snubbull	NRM		Intimidate	Run Away	FGT							GHO		
Solrock	RCK	PSY	Levitate		GRS	WTR	BUG	GHO	DRK	STL		GRD*1		
Spearow	NRM	FLY	Keen Eye		ELC	ICE	RCK					GRD	GHO	
Spheal	GRS	PSY	Chlorophyll		BUG	FIR	ICE	PSN	FLY	GHO	DRK			
Spinarak	BUG	PSN	Swarm	Insomnia	FIR	FLY	PSY	RCK						
Spinda	NRM		Own Tempo	Tangled Feet	FGT							GHO		
Spiritomb	GHO	DRK	Pressure									NRM	FGT	PSY
Spoink	PSY		Thick Fat	Own Tempo	BUG	GHO	DRK							
Squirtle	WTR		Torrent		GRS	ELC								
Stantler	NRM		Intimidate	Frisk	FGT							GHO		
Staraptor	NRM	FLY	Intimidate		ELC	ICE	RCK					GRD	GHO	
Staravia	NRM	FLY	Intimidate		ELC	ICE	RCK					GRD	GHO	
Starly	NRM	FLY	Keen Eye		ELC	ICE	RCK					GRD	GHO	
Starmie	WTR	PSY	Illuminate	Natural Cure	GRS	ELC	BUG	GHO	DRK					
Staryu	WTR		Illuminate	Natural Cure	GRS	ELC								
Steelix	STL	GRD	Rock Head	Sturdy	FIR	WTR	FGT	GRD				ELC	PSN	
Stunky	PSN	DRK	Stench	Aftermath	GRD							PSY		
Sudowoodo	RCK		Sturdy	Rock Head	GRS	WTR	FGT	GRD	STL					
Suicune	WTR		Pressure		GRS	ELC								
Sunflora	GRS		Chlorophyll	Solar Power	FIR	ICE	PSN	FLY	BUG					
Sunkern	GRS		Chlorophyll	Solar Power	FIR	ICE	PSN	FLY	BUG					
Surskit	BUG	WTR	Swift Swim		ELC	FLY	RCK							
Swablu	BUG	GRD	Compoundeyes		FIR	WTR	ICE	FLY				ELC		
Swalot	PSN		Liquid Ooze	Sticky Hold	GRD	PSY								
Swampert	WTR	GRD	Torrent		GRS ◆							ELC		
Swellow	NRM	FLY	Guts		ELC	ICE	RCK					GRD	GHO	
Swinub	ICE	GRD	Oblivious	Snow Cloak	GRS	FIR	WTR	FGT	STL			ELC		
Taillow	NRM	FLY	Guts		ELC	ICE	RCK					GRD	GHO	
Tangela	GRS		Chlorophyll	Leaf Guard	FIR	ICE	PSN	FLY	BUG					
Tangrowth	GRS		Chlorophyll	Leaf Guard	FIR	ICE	PSN	FLY	BUG					
Tauros	NRM		Intimidate	Anger Point	FGT							GHO		
Teddiursa	NRM		Pickup	Quick Feet	FGT							GHO		
Tentacool	WTR	PSN	Clear Body	Liquid Ooze	ELC	GRD	PSY							
Tentacruel	WTR	PSN	Clear Body	Liquid Ooze	ELC	GRD	PSY							
Togekiss	NRM	FLY	Hustle	Serene Grace	ELC	ICE	RCK					GRD	GHO	
Togepi	NRM		Hustle	Serene Grace	FGT							GHO		
Togetic	NRM	FLY	Hustle	Serene Grace	ELC	ICE	RCK					GRD	GHO	
Torchic	FIR		Blaze		WTR	GRD	RCK							
Torkoal	FIR		White Smoke		WTR	GRD	RCK							
Torterra	GRS	GRD	Overgrow		ICE ◆	FIR	FLY	BUG				ELC		
Totodile	WTR		Torrent		GRS	ELC								
Toxicroak	PSN	FGT	Anticipation	Dry Skin	PSY ◆	GRD	FLY					WTR*2		
Trapinch	GRD		Hyper Cutter	Arena Trap	GRS	WTR	ICE					ELC		
Treecko	GRS		Overgrow		FIR	ICE	PSN	FLY	BUG					
Tropius	GRS	FLY	Chlorophyll	Solar Power	ICE ◆	FIR	PSN	FLY	RCK			GRD		
Turtwig	GRS		Overgrow		FIR	ICE	PSN	FLY	BUG					
Typhlosion	FIR		Blaze		WTR	GRD	RCK							
Tyranitar	RCK	DRK	Sand Stream		FGT ◆	GRS	WTR	GRD	BUG	STL		PSY		
Tyrogue	FGT		Guts	Steadfast	FLY	PSY								
Umbreon	DRK		Synchronize		FGT	BUG						PSY		
Unown	PSY		Levitate		BUG	GHO	DRK					GRD*1		NRM
Ursaring	NRM		Guts	Quick Feet	FGT							GHO		
Uxie	PSY		Levitate		BUG	GHO	DRK					GRD*1		
Vaporeon	WTR		Water Absorb		GRS	ELC						WTR*1		
Venomoth	BUG	PSN	Shield Dust	Tinted Lens	FIR	FLY	PSY	RCK						
Venonat	BUG	PSN	Compoundeyes	Tinted Lens	FIR	FLY	PSY	RCK						

Pokémon weaknesses quick reference

Pokémon	Type		Ability		Type of move weakness						Type of ineffective moves	
Venusaur	GRS	PSN	Overgrow		FIR	ICE	FLY	PSY				
Vespiquen	BUG	FLY	Pressure		RCK ◆	FIR	ELC	ICE	FLY		GRD	
Vibrava	GRD	DRG	Levitate		ICE	DRG					ELC	GRD*1
Victreebel	GRS	PSN	Chlorophyll		FIR	ICE	FLY	PSY				
Vigoroth	NRM		Vital Spirit		FGT						GHO	
Vileplume	GRS	PSN	Chlorophyll		FIR	ICE	FLY	PSY				
Volbeat	BUG		Illuminate	Swarm	FIR	FLY	RCK					
Voltorb	ELC		Soundproof	Static	GRD							
Vulpix	FIR		Flash Fire		WTR	GRD	RCK				FIR*1	
Wailmer	WTR		Water Veil	Oblivious	GRS	ELC						
Wailord	WTR		Water Veil	Oblivious	GRS	ELC						
Walrein	ICE	WTR	Thick Fat	Ice Body	GRS	ELC	FGT	RCK				
Wartortle	WTR		Torrent		GRS	ELC						
Weavile	DRK	ICE	Pressure		FGT ◆	FIR	BUG	RCK	STL		PSY	
Weedle	BUG	PSN	Shield Dust		FIR	FLY	PSY	RCK				
Weepinbell	GRS	PSN	Chlorophyll		FIR	ICE	FLY	PSY				
Weezing	PSN		Levitate		PSY						GRD*1	
Whiscash	WTR	GRD	Oblivious	Anticipation	GRS ◆						ELC	
Whismur	NRM		Soundproof		FGT						GHO	
Wigglytuff	NRM		Cute Charm		FGT						GHO	
Wingull	WTR	FLY	Keen Eye		ELC ◆	RCK					GRD	
Wobbuffet	PSY		Shadow Tag		BUG	GHO	DRK					
Wooper	WTR	GRD	Damp	Water Absorb	GRS ◆						ELC	WTR*2
Wormadam [Plant Cloak]	BUG	GRS	Anticipation		FIR ◆	FLY ◆	ICE	PSN	BUG	RCK		
Wormadam [Sandy Cloak]	BUG	GRD	Anticipation		FIR	WTR	ICE	FLY			ELC	
Wormadam [Trash Cloak]	BUG	STL	Anticipation		FIR ◆						PSN	
Wurmple	BUG		Shield Dust		FIR	FLY	RCK					
Wynaut	PSY		Shadow Tag		BUG	GHO	DRK					
Xatu	PSY	FLY	Synchronize	Early Bird	ELC	ICE	RCK	GHO	DRK		GRD	
Yanma	BUG	FLY	Speed Boost	Compoundeyes	RCK ◆	FIR	ELC	ICE	FLY		GRD	
Yanmega	BUG	FLY	Speed Boost	Tinted Lens	RCK ◆	FIR	ELC	ICE	FLY		GRD	
Zangoose	NRM		Immunity		FGT						GHO	
Zapdos	ELC	FLY	Pressure		ICE	RCK					GRD	
Zigzagoon	NRM		Pickup	Gluttony	FGT						GHO	
Zubat	PSN	FLY	Inner Focus		ELC	ICE	PSY	RCK			GRD	

◆ ..... Deals 4x damage.
*1 May not deal damage, depending on Ability effects. *2 May deal damage, depending on that Pokémon's Ability. *3 May not deal damage, depending on that Pokémon's Ability.

Types can count in two ways: when attacking, check the move type, and when receiving an attack, check the defending Pokémon type. The interplay between these two types can have a major effect on the amount of damage that's dealt or received.

Type of defending Pokémon / **Type of attacking Pokémon's move**

	NRM	FIR	WTR	GRS	ELC	ICE	FGT	PSN	GRD	FLY	PSY	BUG	RCK	GHO	DRG	DRK	STL
NRM													△	X			△
FIR		△	△	◉		◉						◉	△		△		◉
WTR		◉	△	△					◉				◉		△		
GRS		△	◉	△				△	◉	△		△	◉		△		△
ELC			◉	△	△				X	◉					△		
ICE		△	△	◉		△			◉	◉					◉		△
FGT	◉					◉		△		△	△	△	◉	X		◉	◉
PSN				◉				△	△				△	△			X
GRD		◉		△	◉			◉		X		△	◉				◉
FLY				◉	△		◉					◉	△				△
PSY							◉	◉			△					X	△
BUG		△		◉			△	△		△	◉			△		◉	△
RCK		◉				◉	△		△	◉		◉					△
GHO	X										◉			◉		△	△
DRG															◉		△
DRK							△				◉			◉		△	△
STL		△	△		△	◉							◉				△

Legend

Symbol	Meaning	Multiplier
◉	....."It's super effective!"	**x2**
△	....."It's not very effective!"	**x0.5**
X	....."It has no effect."	**x0**
Blank	..... Normal damage	**x1**

*.....Fire-type Pokémon cannot be burned. • Grass-type Pokémon are immune to Leech Seed. • Ice-type Pokémon cannot be frozen, and take no damage from Hail weather. • Poison-type Pokémon cannot be poisoned or badly poisoned, even when switching in with Toxic Spikes in play. They nullify the Toxic Spikes (unless they are also Flying-type or have the Levitate Ability). • Ground-type Pokémon are immune to Thunder Wave and to damage from Sandstorm weather. • Flying Pokémon cannot be damaged by Spikes when switching in, or poisoned or badly poisoned by Toxic Spikes when switching in. • Rock-type Pokémon are immune to damage from Sandstorm weather. • Steel-type Pokémon are immune to damage from Sandstorm weather.

ADVENTURE DATA LIST

ALPHABETICAL POKÉDEX

Abomasnow	510	Chimecho	483	Feebas	481	Infernape	492
Abra	409	Chinchou	436	Feraligatr	433	Ivysaur	394
Absol	483	Chingling	503	Finneon	509	Jigglypuff	403
Aerodactyl	429	Clamperl	485	Flaaffy	438	Jirachi	490
Aggron	470	Claydol	479	Flareon	427	Jolteon	427
Aipom	441	Clefable	402	Floatzel	499	Jumpluff	441
Alakazam	410	Clefairy	402	Flygon	476	Jynx	424
Altaria	477	Cleffa	437	Forretress	445	Kabuto	428
Ambipom	501	Cloyster	416	Froslass	514	Kabutops	429
Ampharos	439	Combee	498	Furret	434	Kadabra	409
Anorith	480	Combusken	457	Gabite	506	Kakuna	397
Arbok	399	Corphish	479	Gallade	513	Kangaskhan	422
Arcanine	408	Corsola	449	Garchomp	506	Kecleon	481
Ariados	435	Cradily	480	Gardevoir	464	Kingdra	451
Armaldo	480	Cranidos	496	Gastly	416	Kingler	418
Aron	469	Crawdaunt	479	Gastrodon	500	Kirlia	464
Articuno	429	Cresselia	518	Gengar	417	Koffing	421
Azelf	515	Croagunk	508	Geodude	412	Krabby	418
Azumarill	439	Crobat	436	Gible	505	Kricketot	494
Azurill	468	Croconaw	433	Girafarig	444	Kricketune	495
Bagon	486	Cubone	419	Giratina (Altered Forme)	517	Kyogre	489
Baltoy	479	Cyndaquil	432	Giratina (Origin Forme)	517	Lairon	470
Banette	482	Darkrai	519	Glaceon	512	Lanturn	436
Barboach	478	Delcatty	469	Glalie	484	Lapras	426
Bastiodon	497	Delibird	450	Glameow	502	Larvitar	455
Bayleef	432	Deoxys (A)	490	Gligar	445	Latias	488
Beautifly	460	Deoxys (D)	490	Gliscor	513	Latios	489
Beedrill	397	Deoxys (N)	490	Gloom	404	Leafeon	512
Beldum	487	Deoxys (S)	491	Golbat	404	Ledian	435
Bellossom	439	Dewgong	415	Goldeen	423	Ledyba	435
Bellsprout	411	Dialga	516	Golduck	407	Lickilicky	510
Bibarel	494	Diglett	406	Golem	412	Lickitung	420
Bidoof	494	Ditto	426	Gorebyss	485	Lileep	480
Blastoise	396	Dodrio	415	Granbull	446	Linoone	459
Blaziken	458	Doduo	414	Graveler	412	Lombre	461
Blissey	454	Donphan	451	Grimer	415	Lopunny	502
Bonsly	504	Dragonair	430	Grotle	491	Lotad	461
Breloom	465	Dragonite	431	Groudon	489	Loudred	467
Bronzong	504	Drapion	508	Grovyle	457	Lucario	507
Bronzor	504	Dratini	430	Growlithe	408	Ludicolo	461
Budew	496	Drifblim	501	Grumpig	475	Lugia	456
Buizel	499	Drifloon	501	Gulpin	472	Lumineon	509
Bulbasaur	394	Drowzee	417	Gyarados	426	Lunatone	478
Buneary	501	Dugtrio	406	Happiny	505	Luvdisc	486
Burmy	497	Dunsparce	445	Hariyama	468	Luxio	495
Butterfree	396	Dusclops	482	Haunter	417	Luxray	495
Cacnea	476	Dusknoir	514	Heatran	516	Machamp	410
Cacturne	476	Duskull	482	Heracross	447	Machoke	410
Camerupt	474	Dustox	461	Hippopotas	507	Machop	410
Carnivine	508	Eevee	427	Hippowdon	507	Magby	453
Carvanha	473	Ekans	399	Hitmonchan	420	Magcargo	448
Cascoon	460	Electabuzz	425	Hitmonlee	420	Magikarp	426
Castform	481	Electivire	511	Hitmontop	453	Magmar	425
Caterpie	396	Electrike	471	Honchkrow	502	Magmortar	511
Celebi	456	Electrode	419	Ho-Oh	456	Magnemite	414
Chansey	422	Elekid	453	Hoothoot	434	Magneton	414
Charizard	395	Empoleon	493	Hoppip	440	Magnezone	510
Charmander	394	Entei	454	Horsea	422	Makuhita	467
Charmeleon	395	Espeon	442	Houndoom	451	Mamoswine	513
Chatot	505	Exeggcute	419	Houndour	450	Manaphy	518
Cherrim	500	Exeggutor	419	Huntail	485	Manectric	471
Cherubi	500	Exploud	467	Hypno	418	Mankey	407
Chikorita	431	Farfetch'd	414	Igglybuff	437	Mantine	450
Chimchar	492	Fearow	399	Illumise	472	Mantyke	509

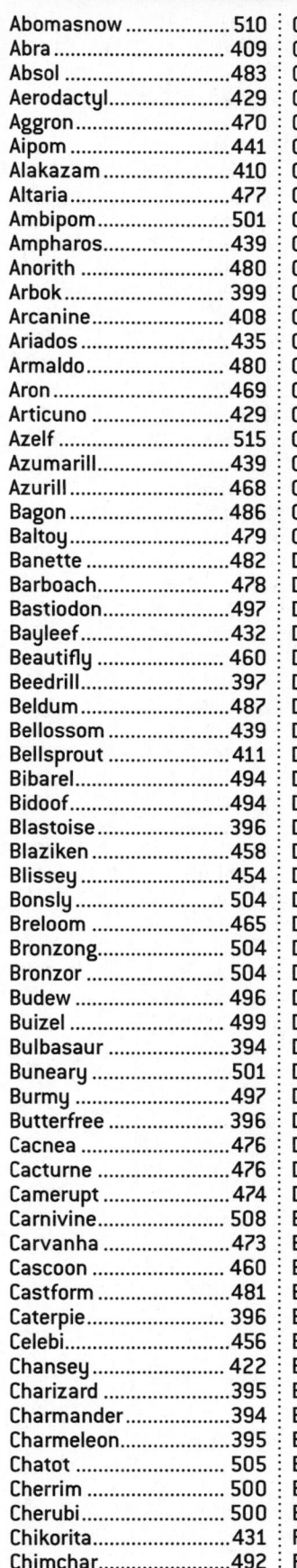

ADVENTURE DATA LIST